a LANGE medical book

CURRENT

Diagnosis & Treatment in
INFECTIOUS DISEASES

Editors

Walter R. Wilson, MD
Professor of Medicine
Mayo Medical School
Consultant
Mayo Clinic, Rochester

Merle A. Sande, MD
Professor and Chairman
The Clarence M. and Ruth N. Birrer
Presidential Endowed Chair in Internal Medicine
Department of Internal Medicine
University of Utah, Salt Lake City

Associate Editors

W. Lawrence Drew, MD, PhD
Professor, Laboratory Medicine and Medicine
Director, Viral Diagnostic Laboratory
Chief, Infectious Diseases
Mt. Zion Medical Center
University of California, San Francisco

David A. Relman, MD
Associate Professor of Medicine, Microbiology &
Immunology
Departments of Medicine, Microbiology &
Immunology
Stanford University School of Medicine
Physician, Veterans Affairs Palo Alto Health Care
System

Nancy K. Henry, PhD, MD
Associate Professor of Pediatrics
Mayo Graduate School of Medicine
Chair, Division of Pediatric Infectious Diseases
Department of Pediatric and Adolescent Medicine
Mayo Clinic, Rochester

James M. Steckelberg, MD
Professor of Medicine
Mayo Medical School
Chair, Division of Infectious Diseases
Mayo Clinic and Foundation, Rochester

Julie Louise Gerberding, MD, MPH
Associate Professor of Medicine
San Francisco General Hospital
University of California, San Francisco

Lange Medical Books/McGraw-Hill
Medical Publishing Division

New York Chicago San Francisco Lisbon London Madrid Mexico City Milan New Delhi
San Juan Seoul Singapore Sydney Toronto

McGraw-Hill

A Division of The **McGraw·Hill** *Companies*

Current Diagnosis & Treatment in Infectious Diseases

Copyright © 2001 by The McGraw-Hill Companies, Inc. All rights reserved. Printed in the United States of America. Except as permitted under the United States Copyright Act of 1976, no part of this publication may be reproduced or distributed in any form or by any means, or stored in a data base or retrieval system, without the prior written permission of the publisher.

1 2 3 4 5 6 7 8 9 0   DOWDOW   0 9 8 7 6 5 4 3 2 1

ISBN: 0-8385-1494-4 (domestic)
ISBN: 0-07-118185-3 (international)
ISSN: 1535-1971

Notice

This book was set in Times Roman by Pine Tree Composition.
The editors were Shelley Reinhardt, Isabel Nogueira, and Peter J. Boyle.
The production supervisor was Richard Ruzycka.
The art manager was Charissa Baker.
The illustrators were Laura Pardi Duprey and Teshin Associates.
The index was prepared by Katherine Pitcoff.

R.R. Donnelley and Sons, Inc. was printer and binder.

This book is printed on acid-free paper.

Contents

I. BASIC PRINCIPLES

II. CLINICAL SYNDROMES

III. SPECIAL PATIENT POPULATIONS

IV. VIRAL INFECTIONS

VIII. MISCELLANEOUS INFECTIONS

Authors

Andrew D. Badley, MD, FRCPC
Assistant Professor of Medicine, Division of Infectious Diseases, Ottawa Hospital; Clinician Scientist, Ottawa Hospital Research Institute, Ottawa, Ontario, Canada
Internet: abadley@ottawahospital.on.ca
Sepsis Syndrome; Cestodes

Michael Bell, MD
Post-Doctoral Fellow, Division of Infectious Diseases, Department of Internal Medicine, University of California, San Francisco; Assistant Hospital Epidemiologist, San Francisco General Hospital
Internet: zzb8@cdc.gov
Legionella

Elie F. Berbari, MD
Fellow, Division of Infectious Diseases, Mayo Clinic, Rochester
Internet: berbari.elie@mayo.edu
Brucella, Francisella, Pasteurella, Yersinia, and HACEK

Karen C. Bloch, MD, MPH
Assistant Professor, Departments of Internal Medicine (Division of Infectious Diseases) and Preventive Medicine, Vanderbilt University School of Medicine, Nashville
Internet: kbloch@stthomas.org
Staphylococci

Julie Brahmer, MD
Instructor, Department of Oncology, The Johns Hopkins University School of Medicine, Baltimore
Internet: brahmju@jhmi.edu
Fever of Unknown Origin; Tuberculosis; Other Mycobacteria

James J. Chamberlain, MD
Former Chief Medical Resident, Department of Internal Medicine, University of Utah, Salt Lake City; Medalia Medical Group, North Everett Internal Medicine, Everett, Washington
Internet: jimchammd@yahoo.com
Cryptococcus; Pneumocystis Carinii

Sandra V. Chaparro, MD
Postdoctoral Fellow, Division of Infectious Diseases, Stanford University
Internet: sandra@molepi.stanford.edu
Borrelia & Leptospira Species

William P. Ciesla, Jr., MD
Assistant Professor of Research, Division of Geographic and International Medicine, University of Virginia School of Medicine, Charlottesville
Internet: wpc6n@virginia.edu
Infectious Diarrhea

Franklin R. Cockerill, III, MD
Professor, Laboratory Medicine and Pathology and Medicine, Mayo Medical School; Director of Bacteriology and Chairman, Clinical Microbiology and Consultant, Infectious Diseases and Internal Medicine, Mayo Clinic, Rochester
Internet: cockerill.franklin@mayo.edu
Laboratory Diagnosis; Laboratory Diagnosis: Diagnosis of Bacterial, Fungal, & Parasitic Infections; Enteritis Caused by Escherichia coli & Shigella & Salmonella Species; Vibrio & Campylobacter

Lisa Danzig, MD
Assistant Clinical Professor of Medicine, University of California, San Francisco; Director, Clinical Development, Chiron Corporation, Emeryville, California
Internet: lisa_danzig@chiron.com
Influenza

David H. Dockrell, MD, MRCPI
Instructor in Medicine, Mayo Graduate School of Medicine; Fellow in Infectious Diseases, Mayo Clinic, Rochester
Internet: d.h.dockrell@sheffield.ac.uk
Patients With Neutropenia & Fever; Pseudomonas Aeruginosa

W. Lawrence Drew, MD, PhD
Professor, Laboratory Medicine and Medicine Director; Viral Diagnostic Laboratory, University of California, San Francisco; Chief, Infectious Diseases, University of California, San Francisco/ Mt. Zion Medical Center, University of California, San Francisco
Internet: lawrencedrew@clinlab.ucsfmedctr.org
Laboratory Diagnosis; Enteroviruses; Rhinoviruses; Adenoviruses; Herpesviruses; Other Gastrointestinal Viruses; Hepatitis; HIV & Other Retroviruses; Poxviruses; Parvoviruses; Viral Infection of the Central Nervous System; Miscellaneous Systemic Viral Syndromes; Papovaviruses

Marlene L. Durand, MD
Assistant Professor of Medicine, Harvard Medical School; Director, Infectious Disease Service, Massachusetts Eye & Ear Infirmary; and Assistant Physician, Massachusetts General Hospital, Boston
Internet: marlene_durand@meei.harvard.edu
Infections of the Eye & Orbit

Paul B. Eckburg, MD
Fellow in Infectious Diseases, Stanford University School of Medicine
Internet: paul_eckburg@hotmail.com
Hepatobiliary Infections

Randall S. Edson, MD, FACP
Associate Professor and Infectious Disease Consultant, Mayo Medical School, Rochester
Internet: edson.randall@mayo.edu
Skin & Soft-Tissue Infections

Christopher R. Fox, MD
Clinical Fellow, Division of Endocrinology and Metabolism, University of Virginia, Charlottesville
Internet: crf2f@virginia.edu
Candida Species; Pathogenic Amebas

Keiji Fukuda, MD, MPH
Chief, Epidemiology Section, Influenza Branch, Centers for Disease Control and Prevention, Atlanta
Internet: kfukuda@cdc.gov
Influenza

Julie Louise Gerberding, MD, MPH
Associate Professor of Medicine (Infectious Diseases), San Francisco General Hospital, University of California, San Francisco
Infection Prevention in Healthcare Settings; Patients With AIDS

Donald L. Granger, MD
Professor of Internal Medicine, Division of Infectious Diseases, University of Utah School of Medicine, Salt Lake City
Internet: dgranger@hsc.utah.edu
Basic Principles of Host Defense; Cryptococcus

Richard L. Guerrant, MD
Professor, Department of Internal Medicine and Head, Division of Geographic Medicine, University of Virginia School of Medicine, Charlottesville
Internet: rlg9a@virginia.edu
Infectious Diarrhea

DeVon C. Hale, MD
Professor of Medicine and Pathology; Director of International Travel Clinic, University of Utah School of Medicine, Salt Lake City
Internet: devon.hale@hsc.utah.edu
Cryptosporidium, Cyclospora, & Isospora Species & Microsporidia; Giardia; Infections in Travelers

Nancy K. Henry, PhD, MD
Associate Professor of Pediatrics, Mayo Graduate School of Medicine; Chair, Division of Pediatric Infectious Diseases, Department of Pediatric and Adolescent Medicine, Mayo Clinic, Rochester
Internet: henry.nancy@mayo.edu
Laboratory Diagnosis; Upper Respiratory Tract Infections; Sexually Transmitted Diseases; Urinary Tract Infections; Parainfluenza Virus; Respiratory Syncytial Virus; Measles; Mumps; Rubella; Rotavirus

Harry R. Hill, MD
Professor of Pathology, Pediatrics, and Medicine, University of Utah School of Medicine, Salt Lake City
Internet: harry.hill@path.med.utah.edu
Patients With Recurrent Infections and Leukocyte Abnormalities

Yenjean Syn Hwang, MD
Department of Medicine, Alta Bates Medical Center, Berkeley
Internet: yshwang@pol.net
Obstetric & Gynecologic Infections; Other Mycobacteria

Michael R. Keating, MD
Assistant Professor of Medicine and Consultant, Infectious Diseases and Internal Medicine, Mayo Clinic, Rochester
Internet: keating.michael@mayo.edu
Aspergillus, Pseudallescheria, & Agents of Mucormycosis; Fusarium, Penicillium, Paracoccidioides, & Agents of Chromomycosis

Timothy R. La Pine, MD
Adjunct Clinical Assistant Professor, Department of Pathology, Division of Clinical Immunology, University of Utah Medical Center, Salt Lake City
Patients With Recurrent Infections and Leukocyte Abnormalities

Linda L. Lewis, MD
Attending Physician, Division of Pediatric Infectious Diseases, Walter Reed Army Medical Center, Washington, D.C.; Medical Officer, Division of Antiviral Drug Products, Center for Drug Evaluation and Research, U.S. Food and Drug Administration, Rockville, Maryland
Internet: lewisl@cder.fda.gov
Patients With Neutropenia & Fever

Peter K. Lindenauer, MD, MSc
Assistant Professor of Medicine, Tufts University School of Medicine, Boston; Associate Medical Director, Division of Healthcare Quality, Baystate Medical Center, Springfield, Massachusetts
Internet: peter.lindenauer@bhs.org
Fever & Rash

Fred A. Lopez, MD
Assistant Professor and Vice Chair, Department of Medicine, Louisiana State University Health Sciences Center; Associate Director of Medicine (Hospital Center), Medical Center of Louisiana, New Orleans
Internet: alopez1@lsuhsc.edu
Treponema Pallidum

Jeffery S. Loutit, MB, ChB
Clinical Director, Intrabiotics Pharmaceuticals, Mountain View, California
Internet: jloutit@intrabiotics.com
Intra-Abdominal Infections; Gram-Positive Aerobic Bacilli; Coxiella, Ehrlichia, & Rickettsia; Bartonella

Jeffrey N. Martin, MD, MPH
Assistant Professor, Epidemiology, Biostatistics, and Medicine, University of California, San Francisco
Internet: martin@psg.ucsf.edu
Streptococcus Pneumoniae

Zell A. McGee, MD
Professor of Medicine and Pathology, and Director, Center for Infectious Diseases, University of Utah School of Medicine, Salt Lake City
Internet: zell.mcgee@hsc.utah.edu
Infections of the Central Nervous System

Caroline K. Milne, MD
General Medicine Fellow, Division of General Medicine, University of Pennsylvania School of Medicine, Philadelphia
Internet: milnec@mail.med.upenn.edu
Coccidioides; Infections in Travelers

Jose G. Montoya, MD
Assistant Professor of Medicine, Department of Medicine and Division of Infectious Diseases and Geographic Medicine, Stanford University School of Medicine; Attending Physician, Stanford University Medical Center; Adjunct Associate Staff Scientist, Department of Immunology and Infectious Diseases, Palo Alto Medical Foundation Research Institute, California
Internet: gilberto@leland.stanford.edu
Hepatobiliary Infections; Borrelia & Leptospira Species; Mycoplasma & Ureaplasma; Chlamydia; Toxoplasma Gondii

Cathryn L. Murphy, RN, MPH, PhD, CIC
Senior Policy Analyst, Infection Control, New South Wales Department of Health, Sydney, Australia
Internet: cmurp@doh.health.nsw.gov.au
Infection Prevention in Healthcare Settings

Douglas R. Osmon, MD
Assistant Professor of Medicine, and Consultant in Infectious Diseases, Division of Infectious Diseases, Mayo Clinic, Mayo Foundation, Rochester
Internet: osmon.douglas@mayo.edu
Osteomyelitis, Infectious Arthritis & Prosthetic-Joint Infection

Robin Patel, MD, FRCP
Associate Professor of Medicine and Associate Professor of Microbiology and Laboratory Medicine and Pathology, Mayo Medical School; Consultant, Division of Infectious Diseases, Department of Internal Medicine, and Consultant, Division of Clinical Microbiology, Department of Laboratory Medicine and Pathology; Director, Molecular Microbiology Laboratory, Mayo Clinic, Rochester
Internet: patel.robin@mayo.edu
Infections in Transplant Recipients; Enterococci; Other Gram-Positive Cocci

David H. Persing, MD, PhD
Vice President, Corixa Corporation; Medical Director, Infectious Disease Research Institute, Seattle
Internet: persing@corixa.com
Malaria & Babesia

Gary W. Procop, MD, MS
Section Head, Clinical Microbiology, Cleveland Clinic Foundation
Internet: procopg@ccf.org
Enteritis Caused by Escherichia coli & Shigella & Salmonella Species; Vibrio & Campylobacter; Malaria & Babesia

David A. Relman, MD
Associate Professor of Medicine, Microbiology & Immunology, Departments of Medicine, Microbiology & Immunology, Stanford University School of Medicine; Physician, Veterans Affairs Palo Alto Health Care System, Palo Alto, California
Internet: relman@cmgm.stanford.edu
Basic Principles of Microbial Virulence; Gram-Positive Aerobic Bacilli; Neisseria Gonorrhoeae & Neisseria Meningitidis; Actinomycetes; Treponema Pallidum; Dermatophytes; Leishmania & Trypanosoma; Zoonotic Infections

Susan A. Resnik, RN, Grad Dip (IC), CIC (Syd)
Director, New South Wales Infection Control Resource Center, Australia
Internet: resniksu@sesahs.nsw.gov.au
Infection Prevention in Healthcare Settings

Kristen Ries, MD
Professor of Medicine; Director of AIDS Clinical Services, University of Utah School of Medicine, Salt Lake City
Internet: kristen.ries@hsc.utah.edu
Pneumocystis Carinii

Joseph W. St. Geme, III, MD
Associate Professor of Pediatrics and Molecular Microbiology, Washington University School of Medicine; Attending Physician, St. Louis Children's Hospital, St. Louis
Internet: stgeme@borcim.wustl.edu
Haemophilus, Bordetella, & Branhamella Species

Merle A. Sande, MD
Professor and Chairman, The Clarence M. and Ruth N. Birrer Presidential Endowed Chair in Internal Medicine, Department of Internal Medicine, University of Utah, Salt Lake City
Internet: merle.sande@med.utah.edu
Introduction; Fever of Unknown Origin; Fever & Rash; Obstetric & Gynecologic Infections; Patients With AIDS; Tuberculosis; Other Mycobacteria; Coccidioides; Candida Species; Pathogenic Amebas

Javeed Siddiqui, MD, MPH
Fellow, Division of Infectious Diseases, University of California, Davis Medical Center, Sacramento
Internet: jsmdmph@yahoo.com
Helicobacter Pylori

Stephanie B. Silas, MD
Rheumatology Fellow, Department of Internal Medicine, University of Utah Health Sciences Center, Salt Lake City
Internet: stephanie.silas@hsc.utah.edu
Cryptosporidium, Cyclospora, & Isospora Species & Microsporidia; Giardia

D. Scott Smith, MD, SM, DTM&T
Clinical Instructor (VCF), Stanford Medical School, Stanford, California; Chief, Infectious Disease and Geographic Medicine, Kaiser Permanente Hospital, Redwood City, California
Internet: darvin.s.smith@kp.org
Neisseria Gonorrhoeae & Neisseria Meningitidis; Dermatophytes; Leishmania & Trypanosoma; Zoonotic Infections

Jay V. Solnick, MD, PhD
Assistant Professor, Department of Internal Medicine, Division of Infectious & Immunologic Diseases, University of California, Davis Medical Center, Sacramento
Internet: jvsolnick@ucdavis.edu
Helicobacter Pylori

Gregory M. Sonnen, MD, FAAP
Clinical Instructor in Pediatrics, University of Texas Southwestern Medical Center; Staff Physician, Children's Medical Center; Staff Physician, Baylor University Medical Center, Dallas
Internet: gregso@baylordallas.edu
Parainfluenza Virus; Respiratory Syncytial Virus; Measles; Mumps; Rubella; Rotavirus

James M. Steckelberg, MD
Professor of Medicine, Mayo Medical School; Chair, Division of Infectious Diseases, Mayo Clinic and Foundation, Rochester
Infective Endocarditis; Osteomyelitis, Infectious Arthritis & Prosthetic-Joint Infection; Sepsis Syndrome; Important Anaerobes; Nematodes; Cestodes; Trematodes; Ectoparasitic Infestations & Arthropod Stings & Bites

Dennis L. Stevens, MD, PhD
Professor of Medicine, University of Washington School of Medicine, Seattle; Chief, Infectious Diseases Section, Veterans Affairs Medical Center, Boise
Internet: dlsteven@primenet.com
Streptococcus Pyogenes

Zelalem Temesgen, MD
Assistant Professor of Medicine, Mayo Medical School; Consultant, Division of Infectious Diseases, and Director, HIV Clinic, Mayo Clinic, Rochester
Internet: temesgen.zelalem@mayo.edu
Histoplasma Capsulatum; Blastomyces Dermatitidis; Sporothrix Schenckii

Phyllis C. Tien, MD, SM
Assistant Professor of Medicine, University of California, San Francisco
Internet: ptien@medicine.ucsf.edu
Actinomycetes; Bartonella

Jorge S. Villacian, MD
Consultant Physician, Communicable Disease Centre, Tan Tock Seng Hospital, Singapore
Internet: j_villacian@notes.ttsh.gov.sg
Important Anaerobes

Abinash Virk, MD, DTMH
Consultant, Infectious Diseases, Mayo Clinic, Rochester
Internet: virka@mayo.edu
Upper Respiratory Tract Infections; Tracheobronchitis & Lower Respiratory Tract Infections

Mark P. Wilhelm, MD, FACP
Assistant Professor of Medicine, Mayo Medical School; Consultant in Infectious Diseases, Mayo Clinic, Rochester
Internet: wilhelm.mark@mayo.edu
Skin & Soft-Tissue Infections

John W. Wilson, MD
Senior Associate Consultant, Instructor of Medicine, Division of Infectious Diseases, Department of Internal Medicine, Mayo Clinic, Rochester
Internet: wilson.john@mayo.edu
Sexually Transmitted Diseases

Walter R. Wilson, MD
Professor of Medicine, Mayo Medical School; Consultant, Mayo Clinic, Rochester
General Principles of Antimicrobial Therapy; Tracheobronchitis & Lower Respiratory Tract Infections; Infective Endocarditis; Urinary Tract Infections; Pseudomonas Aeruginosa; Brucella, Francisella, Pasteurella, Yersinia, and HACEK; Nematodes; Cestodes; Trematodes; Ectoparasitic Infestations & Arthropod Stings & Bites

Dani-Margot Zavasky, MD
Fellow, Department of Infectious Diseases, University of Utah, Salt Lake City
Internet: dani-margot@nyc.rr.com
Patients With AIDS

Preface

Current Diagnosis & Treatment in Infectious Diseases is a "one-stop" source of essential, clinically oriented information on infectious diseases for students, house officers, practitioners, and other health care providers in both hospital and ambulatory settings. *CDTID* covers all infectious disease topics of concern to primary care physicians, infectious disease specialists, and other specialists who provide preventative, diagnostic, or therapeutic care for patients with infectious diseases. It stresses the practical features of clinical diagnosis and patient management.

OUTSTANDING FEATURES

- Incorporates current advances up to time of publication
- Practical information on clinical presentation, physical findings, laboratory diagnosis, treatment, and prevention of the vast array of infectious diseases that infect humans
- Concise, readable format facilitates efficient use in any practice setting
- Emphasis on diagnosis, treatment, and prevention
- Current recommendations for drug dosages for adults and children
- Up-to-date coverage of HIV infection and highly active antiretroviral therapy (HAART)
- More than 300 boxes summarize key diagnostic and treatment information
- Coverage of antibiotic use and misuse
- Discussion of significant new and reemerging infectious diseases
- Overviews of basic principles of host defense, microbial virulence, hospital infection control, and lab tests
- Useful evaluation, testing, and decision-making tools and criteria

INTENDED AUDIENCE

House officers and medical students will find concise, clinically oriented descriptions of diagnosis and treatment of use daily in the care of patients and for preparation for rounds and clinical conferences.

Internists, family physicians, pediatricians, and other specialists who provide generalist care, as well as infectious disease specialists, will appreciate *CDTID* as a quick reference and review text.

Physicians in other specialties, surgeons, and dentists may use the book as a basic reference on infectious diseases.

Nurses, nurse practitioners, physicians' assistants, and other health care workers will welcome *CDTID* as a useful reference for all aspects of care of patients with infectious diseases.

ACKNOWLEDGMENTS

We wish to thank our contributing authors for their time and hard work involved in preparing this text. We wish to thank the editors of McGraw-Hill and their staff for their valuable assistance and support. We welcome comments and recommendations for future editions in writing or via electronic mail. The editors' and authors' institutional addresses are given in the preceding listing of Authors.

Walter R. Wilson, MD
Merle A. Sande, MD

Rochester, Minnesota and Salt Lake City, Utah
April 2001

Introduction

Merle A. Sande, MD

As a leading cause of death worldwide, infectious diseases have hardly been conquered or controlled. In fact, one might consider the 1990s as an era of reawakening, when new and reemerging infectious diseases were recognized as a major worldwide health problem. The continued explosion of cases of infections caused by the human immunodeficiency virus has now produced negative population growth and major disruption in the societies of many African countries, where more than 35% of young adults are infected and more than 25% of children are orphans. By the end of the millennium, the virus had infected more than 50 million people; it now ranks with childhood diarrheal diseases, pneumonia, malaria, and tuberculosis as a leading cause of death. While highly active antiretroviral therapy (HAART) has been astonishingly effective in treating the disease, the necessary drugs are available to only a small percentage of infected populations, and transmission of the virus continues unabated in many regions of the world.

The ability of modern technology to control infectious diseases has been found lacking. Antibiotics, which were developed within the last 60 years, resulted in the cure of many previously lethal infections, rightfully earning the name "wonder drugs." However, only several years into the "antibiotic age," pathogenic staphylococci were found to have the ability to produce enzymes (penicillinases) that destroyed penicillin, thus rendering the drug useless against these strains. The future quickly became clear to microbiologists and infectious disease clinicians studying bacterial genetics; the methods used to impede the organism's ambition to multiply and grow will eventually be defeated by the power of natural selection through the rapid emergence of resistant mutations. The more antibiotic pressure that has been applied, the more rapidly these subpopulations of drug-resistant pathogenic organisms have emerged. Public health-minded clinicians and scientists have issued warnings that overuse and misuse of these "wonder drugs" will eventually render them useless. These warnings have gone largely unheeded.

As we enter the next century, the possibility is quite real that these organisms have won and that we will return, in a sense, to the preantibiotic era. It will

remain for our children or grandchildren to try to answer the question: Why did this generation of health providers not take better care of the future? It will be incomprehensible to them that we allowed antibiotics to be used in animal feed, to be used to treat colds and bronchitis due to viruses, and to be given to inpatients and outpatients without careful diagnostic evaluation. Will future generations eventually blame societal need to be "cost-effective" and the emergence of so-called managed care? Will they blame the pharmaceutical industry, whose need to make a profit led to misleading advertising, often directed at patients themselves? Will they blame physicians who did not learn microbiology and never bothered to consider the public health implications of their prescribing practices? Or will they blame our governmental agencies (the FDA, CDC, EPA, or NIH), whose job was to protect the public's health and make available scientific information that would dictate public policy but who did not do this? Will they blame patients themselves, who, because of misperceptions of the value and effectiveness of antibiotics, insisted on having their physicians prescribe them? Whatever future generations conclude about us, the facts are obvious: we continue to misuse and abuse antibiotics, one of the most important advances in human history, with little attempt to change.

The impact of antibiotic resistance is especially felt in hospitals, where infections caused by resistant organisms are increasing dramatically and have the potential to destroy gains enjoyed in other medical disciplines, such as organ transplantation, prosthetic devices, artificial organs, indwelling pacemakers, and neonatal and adult intensive care. Future medical advances will be determined to a large extent by the ability to prevent and successfully treat the nosocomial infections caused by antibiotic-resistant pathogens. The great irony is that the same areas of medicine where these latest dramatic advances are happening are also those where the most dramatic changes in microbes have taken place. Physicians involved in caring for transplant recipients, cancer patients, and patients requiring intensive care are entirely free to prescribe any and all antibiotics they want *without* consulting infectious disease specialists. There seems to be a puritanical obsession at work in medicine whereby narcotics, which relieve a patient's pain, are considered controlled substances that require a prescribing physician to fill out duplicate and triplicate forms, whereas any physician is free to prescribe any antibiotic, whether indicated or not.

Another great human accomplishment during the last century was the worldwide elimination of smallpox though vaccination. It was an example of warring nations actually cooperating for the common good. In the early 1970s, the majority of the world stopped vaccinating against smallpox. Only two vials of the virus were thought to be preserved and the two "superpowers" had agreed to destroy those vials in 1999, to rid the world forever of this deadly virus. It therefore came as a horrible shock, in 1998, to find out from Russian scientists that they had "weaponized" the smallpox virus and readied it for use against the West, along with anthrax spores, *Yersinia pestis,* and other organisms. The human potential for destructive acts seems limitless.

Other infectious diseases have also slipped back into our society. Our attempts to control mosquitoes were initially successful, and federally funded programs reduced the *Aedes aegypti* and *Anopheles* species to the point where the arthropod-borne encephalitis viruses almost disappeared.

Malaria, once the scourge of the southern United States and Central America, was nearly eliminated. However, while these mosquitoes became resistant to DDT, apathy dominated the governments' response, and funding was cut. The mosquitoes have returned en masse, as have dengue, yellow fever, diseases induced by the various encephalitis viruses, and malaria. Finally, cholera, which had disappeared from the Western Hemisphere for decades, reappeared in Peru in the early 1990s and spread throughout Central and South America, wherever poor sanitation and poverty dominate the domestic scene. Within several years, over a million cases and thousands of deaths were reported, another reminder of the fragile control we have on infectious diseases.

When the public health infrastructure of our cities is allowed to deteriorate, microbial pathogens are ready and willing to take advantage of our citizens. In New York City in the late 1980s, funding for the tu-berculosis program, among many others, was reduced and case follow-up was discontinued; the follow-up rate for patients discharged from hospitals with a diagnosis of active tuberculosis was approximately 10%. Partly because of poor patient compliance with therapy, multiple-drug-resistant tuberculosis emerged and began to spread to other parts of the country. Many people, especially AIDS patients, died before the epidemic was finally controlled, when directly observed therapy was widely embraced and implemented. Similarly, when immunization slackened in Eastern Europe after the fall of communism, diphtheria reappeared, and more than 50,000 cases per year were reported in the early 1990s.

Our record of dealing with infectious diseases has been a checkered one, with some fantastic successes followed by dramatic mistakes and failures. It now seems clear that the virtual sea of microorganisms with which we must share this planet must be treated with care and understanding. We must learn to live in harmony with our normal flora and protect it from factors that breed resistance. We need to understand better the public health implications of unwise interventions such as mass use of antibiotics for the purpose of stimulating animal growth, or prophylaxis to prevent otitis media, or routine antibiotic treatment of respiratory tract infections caused by viruses.

One might be justified in greeting these challenges with an air of optimism. The requisite tools and insight necessary to predict, blunt, or suppress microbial virulence are at hand. The molecular language spoken between microbe and host cell is increasingly well described. So far, we know that the host-pathogen relationship is a two-way, intricate affair with features of codependence.

This textbook of infectious diseases is aimed at the student, house officer, or other trainee and at the practicing healthcare provider, with the hope of teaching these principles while providing a source of information that will help in the recognition, diagnosis, treatment, and prevention of these many emerging and reemerging infections. The book's format is one we hope allows easy access to the pertinent information that will facilitate the decision-making process and become a useful reference as we fight these current and future battles.

Section I.
Basic Principles

Basic Principles of Host Defense

2

Donald L. Granger, MD

Higher animals have evolved many host defense mechanisms that ensure the relatively long-term survival of individuals despite their coexistence with countless microorganisms. Healthy people are at equilibrium with the microbial world; their internal soma, rich in nutrients, remains free of replicating microorganisms. Disease can be viewed as progression away from this equilibrium, in which microorganisms invade the body from the environment and replicate, causing inflammation and destruction of the tissues, as well as depletion of the host's nutrients. Unchecked, the rapid expansion of the microbial population leads to the death of the host.

A similar but distinct scenario is that the internal environment contains a variety of viruses, bacteria, fungi, protozoa, and microscopic metazoa, which are acquired throughout life. Again, these organisms achieve equilibrium with the mammalian host. Under these conditions they do not replicate, nor do they produce toxins. Instead, they exist in a dormant or latent state, which is infection without disease. Disease is a progression away from the equilibrium. When the balance is disturbed, microbial replication begins; host nutrients are then consumed by the proliferating population of microorganisms. This process leads to disease and ultimately death unless microbial replication is blocked.

To maintain equilibrium with the microbial world—that is, to maintain a state of health—host-protective mechanisms must fulfill distinct functions. In a broad sense, the functions come in two forms.

The first form includes the antimicrobial defense mechanisms that have evolved throughout the vertebrate species. Specifically, this first form is composed of a variety of mechanisms to prevent invasion of sterile tissues from contiguous body sites that are teeming with microbial flora. These mechanisms involve the actions of specialized cells—phagocytes and lymphocytes. For example, the upper respiratory tract is colonized with large numbers of bacteria, yet further down into the respiratory tract, below the vocal cords and into the lungs, few or no bacteria are found. Those bacteria that do gain access to the lung

are rapidly destroyed. In another example, microbes may gain entrance to sterile body sites when an open injury introduces bacteria into the skin, subcutaneous tissue, muscle, or bone. This is countered by mechanisms in which the injured tissue is walled off to prevent spread and is invaded by phagocytic cells that envelop and kill bacteria. This is bactericidal activity. Yet another example involves specialized microorganisms that have evolved into successful parasites and that gain ready access to sterile sites in the host. They may be highly resistant to host-killing mechanisms. Under these conditions, equilibrium between parasite and host is reached by establishing microbiostasis in the tissues. In this way, living microbes may remain dormant or latent within host tissues for years, or even decades. This scenario implies microbiostatic host-defense mechanisms. For example, the human tubercle bacillus (*Mycobacterium tuberculosis*) is inhaled into the lung. In the immunocompetent host, immunity is acquired, microbial replication ceases, and the mycobacteria become dormant, especially (but not exclusively) in the lung apices.

A second way to thwart infectious disease is through a set of uniquely human prevention schemes that have resulted from brain development and intelligence. Our understanding of infectious disease transmission has led to effective prevention methods, such as the addition of chlorine to the water supply and modern sewage treatment. Knowledge of immunology has led to vaccine strategies that have achieved results such as the elimination of smallpox from the human population. Understanding microbial physiology and metabolism led to the discovery of antibiotics for treating heretofore lethal infections.

This chapter deals exclusively with the first category of anti-infection mechanisms. These mechanisms can be subdivided into two broad categories: (1) innate or natural host defenses and (2) adaptive immune responses. There are distinct mechanisms characteristic of each of these two, but there is overlap as well. Some innate responses use mechanisms that, when analyzed at the cellular and molecular levels, were previously thought to reside exclusively as part of the adaptive immune response. Conversely, acquired immunity may lead to microbicidal mechanisms, which are not immunologically (antigen) specific and probably exist as an evolutionary blend of the innate and adaptive host defenses.

INNATE HOST DEFENSES

DEFENSE MECHANISMS AT THE PHYSIOLOGIC LEVEL

Numerous physiologic factors influence susceptibility to infection. Prime examples of these factors are discussed in the sections that follow.

Normal Microbial Flora

Body surfaces in continuity with the environment typically support a complex but characteristic set of numerous microbial species (Table 2–1). This group of microorganisms is called the normal flora and includes microorganisms that inhabit the integument, upper respiratory tract, gastrointestinal tract, and urogenital tract. More than 200 different bacterial species occupy the human colon as normal flora. The normal flora fill these body sites to the exclusion of other species. Thus, the presence of the normal flora provides a protective function. A relatively virulent species such as the fungus *Candida albicans* cannot occupy the vagina unless the normal flora are eliminated, for example, by use of broad-spectrum antibacterial agents used to treat urinary tract infections. Sometimes virulent microorganisms colonize a body site and coexist along with the normal flora. For example, *Streptococcus pneumoniae* is often found in the oropharynx of healthy individuals. Colonization is a critical requirement for the pathogenesis of bacterial pneumonia caused by this pathogen. At some point microaspiration events introduce *S pneumoniae* into the lower respiratory tract. Then virulence mechanisms prevent the killing of these microorganisms by innate host defense mechanisms. This leads to microbial replication in a nutrient-rich environment that is devoid of competing microbial species, and bacterial pneumonia results.

What determines which species predominate as the normal flora at a particular site? Although this is a complex process, the phenomenon of attachment to host cells is an important requisite. Particular microbial species express structures on their surface that bind to receptors on host epithelial cells. For example, strains of viridans streptococci adhere (by special attachments) to pharyngeal epithelial cells and are able to flourish and exist as the predominant species in the oropharynx.

Anatomic & Physiologic Factors

The normal human anatomy provides numerous examples of anatomic barriers that prevent microbial replication and invasion. This is best illustrated when a breach in these barriers occurs and infection follows. The skin is a highly efficient barrier that prevents bacteria and fungi from entering into the subcutaneous tissue. In burn victims this barrier is lost. Without aggressive countermeasures, individuals with extensive burns succumb to overwhelming bacteremia because enormous numbers of bacteria invade the damaged tissue and thereby gain access to the circulatory system.

Physiologic mechanisms provide similar functions that prevent microbial invasion. Secretions contain antimicrobial molecules. For example, lysozyme in tears dissolves the cell walls of particular gram-positive bacteria. Salivary secretions contain bactericidal proteins. Smooth muscle peristaltic movements prevent the overgrowth of bacteria in the small intestine by creating a continuous flow, which has a cleansing effect; hydrochloric acid in the stomach kills numerous bacterial cells that enter upon swallowing. The respiratory tract contains a mucociliary carpet that is

Table 2–1. Normal flora occupy niches of the human host.[1]

Site	Examples of Predominant Microorganisms at These Sites	Conditions of Invasion	Disease Potential
Skin	*Staphylococcus epidermidis*	Insertion of plastic catheter into blood vessel	Low
Oropharynx	Viridans streptococci	Periodontal procedures	Usually low but may be high (endocarditis)
GI tract (colon primarily)	*Escherichia coli*	Mucositis	Usually low
GU tract	*Haemophilus vaginalis*	Rarely occurs	None
Mouth	Anaerobes	Gingivitis	May be high
Nose	*Staphylococcus aureus*	Breaks in skin	High

[1]GI, Gastrointestinal; GU, genitourinary.

under constant motion outward, which helps remove inhaled bacteria from the respiratory epithelium.

Similar to a breach in an anatomical barrier, when physiologic processes malfunction, disease is usually the result. For example, autoimmune diseases that destroy the salivary glands lead to severe problems with dental caries and gingivitis, which are caused by overgrowth of oral bacteria. Periodontal disease and loss of permanent teeth follow. This is in part because the saliva normally contains antibacterial and antifungal compounds.

Host Nutritional Status

The nutritional status of the host ranks as a critical factor for both innate and acquired resistance to infection. Protein-calorie malnutrition in children is associated with severe measles (rubeola virus). Historical observations point to reactivation of dormant tubercle bacilli during acute food shortage in populations with a high prevalence of this pathogen. Pyogenic bacterial infections and periodontal disease are additional examples. The original description of *Pneumocystis carinii* as a human pathogen was based on observations of pulmonary disease in starving European infants during and after World War II. Experimental research shows that starvation impairs phagocytes and cell-mediated immunity (CMI) before its effects on antibody production are observed.

Hormonal Influences

Glucocorticoids exert profound effects on host resistance to infection. In severe bacteremia, physiologic cortisol secretion improves chances of survival. Yet it is well known that pharmacologic dosages of glucocorticoids depress the inflammatory response and increase susceptibility to primary infection as well as reactivation of latent infection. Pregnancy, as it progresses into the third trimester, results in immunosuppression, primarily of CMI. This leads to increased susceptibility to certain infections such as the food-borne infection listeriosis.

Aging

Aging affects many aspects of innate defenses. Consequently, pneumonia, urinary tract infections, cholecystitis, diverticulitis, and bacteremia caused by pyogenic bacteria are increased. The aged are more likely to reactivate latent organisms such as Herpes zoster virus and *Mycobacterium tuberculosis,* which suggests decreased CMI. Aged individuals have reduced ability to mount immunoglobulin (Ig) synthesis against polysaccharide antigens.

The Acute-Phase Response

The acute-phase response is a phylogenetically primitive, pleiotropic collection of responses designed by evolution to inhibit microbial replication and enhance acquired immune responses. The acute-phase response is triggered by invasion of microorganisms. Its complex, multiorgan involvement is fundamental for the inflammatory response characterized by swelling, pain, redness, heat, and loss of function. With the evolution of specific adaptive immune responses in vertebrates, the acute-phase response was preserved and is used as an activator of T and B lymphocytes.

Signal molecules that emanate from bacteria and other microorganisms (eg, endotoxin, muramyl dipeptide from the peptidoglycan of cell walls, glucans, mannans, and microbial toxins) bind to receptors on mononuclear phagocytes (MNPs) and endothelial cells [the reticuloendothelial system (RES)]. Secretion of a major proinflammatory cytokine, interleukin-1 (IL-1), and possibly others induces a pleiotropic response that involves a variety of different organs and functions (Table 2–2). The acute-phase response also leads to induction of specific immune responses, namely antibody synthesis by B cells and CMI, which are controlled by T cells. In a practical sense, measurements of the acute-phase response in blood samples are used in diagnosis of infections and other inflammatory diseases. Phenomena affected by IL-1, namely fever, increased erythrocyte sedimentation rate, high white blood cell count, and muscle wasting are important clues to the presence of infection, autoimmune inflammatory diseases, and neoplastic diseases that involve lymphoreticular cells.

INNATE DEFENSE MECHANISMS AT THE CELLULAR LEVEL

Ever-present cells and molecules (constitutive mechanisms) form an on-the-spot defensive line against microbial invasion. Compromise of this innate multifaceted system results in predictable serious infections, usually with invading species of the microflora. Thus, the importance of constitutive nonspecific defense mechanisms is revealed. Phagocytes and natural killer (NK) cells are discussed as examples of innate cellular defenses.

Phagocytes

Two types of cells can be considered "professional phagocytes" or cells that consume microbes. These are the polymorphonuclear leukocytes (called neutrophils, or granulocytes) and the MNPs (monocytes and macrophages). These cells emanate from bone marrow precursors and enter the circulation to perform their antimicrobial functions. Lack of either of these cell lineages is incompatible with life.

Neutrophils live for 1–4 days after entering the circulation. Continued neutrophil production is essential for survival. Neutrophils are an important regulator of homeostasis between the body, which harbors sterile enclaves, and the microbial world. Neutrophils deal with pyogenic bacteria and fungi. Neutrophils possess tightly regulated microbicidal systems that

Table 2–2. The acute-phase response.[1]

Organ or Cell Type	Effect Produced	Action Used in Antimicrobial Defense
Hypothalamus	Fever via prostaglandin synthesis	Postulated effect is inhibitory to microbial replication
Brain	Somnolence, release of endorphins	Sleep with muscle rest may be adaptive response
Pituitary gland	ACTH, TSH release	Adrenocorticosteroids adapt body to stress
Autonomic nervous system	Neurotransmitter release	Cardiovascular and pulmonary adaptation to inflammation
Liver	Decreased albumin synthesis; increased synthesis of acute-phase proteins (fibrinogen, complement proteins, amyloid A protein, ceruloplasmin, C-reactive protein, LPS-binding protein, proteinase inhibitors, fibronectin, haptoglobin	Generalized metabolic adaptation to infection; nonspecific opsonins; mollify effects of tissue destruction caused by inflammation
Skeletal muscle	Proteolysis—release of free amino acids to the circulatory system	Substrates for protein synthesis by cells of immune system
Fibroblasts	Proliferation; collagen synthesis	Wound healing
Endothelial cells	Activation; cytokine secretion; adhesion; molecule expression	Participate in leukocyte flux to inflamed sites
Bone marrow	Increased release, production, and activation of neutrophils	Effector cells in pyogenic infections
Lymphocytes	Cytokine secretion; blastogenesis; initiate specific, antigen-driven immune responses	Adaptive antimicrobial immune responses

[1] Abbreviations: ACTH, adrenocorticotropic hormone; TSH, thyroid-stimulating hormone; LPS, lipopolysaccharide.

are activated within seconds after encountering microorganisms. In healthy individuals, neutrophils are constantly at work destroying small numbers of microbes that enter the body by various routes. Severe neutropenia (< 500 cells/μL of blood) leads to overwhelming bacteremia from enteric bacilli. Neutrophils are constitutively bactericidal to a high degree for gram-positive and gram-negative cocci and enteric bacilli. To maintain this constitutive defense, neutrophils have special functional properties, to be discussed below. A defect in any one of these important functions invariably leads to a life-threatening infection. However, neutrophils have less or little activity against facultative or obligate intracellular pathogens such as mycobacteria, dimorphic fungi, and protozoans. The human immune system has evolved other mechanisms for dealing with these pathogens.

MNPs leave the bone marrow as blood monocytes. They mature into macrophages in the periphery. Stationed throughout all organs of the body, they compose the RES. The RES of the sinusoids of the liver and spleen provides an important clearance mechanism to remove a variety of microbes from the circulation. Thus, the spleen serves as a highly efficient, specialized RES site for removal of virulent bacteria. These bacteria avoid clearance in other RES sites, such as the lung or liver, because they possess virulence factors that have extraordinary antiphagocytic properties, such as particular serotypes of exo-

polysaccharide capsules. Individuals with no spleen may succumb to high-grade infection caused by bacteria that possess antiphagocytic capsules. The alveolar spaces of the lung are inhabited by macrophages, which form a first-line defense of the lung. These cells phagocytize and kill inhaled viruses, bacteria, and fungi. Macrophages and macrophage-like cells (eg, dendritic cells) contribute to the adaptive immune response. Macrophages, which function in concert with T lymphocytes, are responsible for CMI defense against intracellular pathogens. Macrophages process and present antigen to lymphocytes and receive "activating" signals during the immune response. These signals enable the macrophages to control the replication of intracellular microorganisms; they are also capable of killing these microorganisms (see below). Some of the functions listed in Table 2–3 for neutrophils are also relevant for MNPs.

To kill bacteria and fungi, phagocytes must make physical contact with them. This involves a coordinated sequence of regulated events: (1) production, (2) release into the circulation, (3) attraction to a site of infection, (4) adherence onto and translocation through (diapedesis) adjacent capillary walls, (5) chemotaxis, (6) attachment to and phagocytosis of the microbe, (7) activation of killing mechanisms, and (8) digestion of dead microorganisms (see Table 2–3). These events are depicted in Figure 2–1. Genetic or acquired conditions that interfere with one or more of these steps are associated with increased

Table 2–3. Neutrophil functions required for homeostasis.

Stage	Function	Site	Required for	Correlates of Pathophysiology
1	Production	Bone marrow	Ready and constant supply of new cells	Neutropenia leads to life-threatening pyogenic infections
2	Release	Bone marrow, circulation	Increased cell numbers during active infections	Neutropenia leads to life-threatening pyogenic infections
3	Chemokinesis	Focus of infected tissue	Homing to sites of infection	Chemokines attract specific host defense cells to infected foci
4	Margination and Spreading	Endothelium adjacent to tissue infection	Attachment to endothelial cells	Phagocyte surface receptors engage endothelial cell surface proteins to promote adherence
5	Chemotaxis	Infected tissue	Tracking microbes	Concentration gradients of particular host ($C5_a$) and microbial products attract phagocytes
6	Phagocytosis	Phagocyte-microbe interaction	Engulfment of microorganisms	Opsonins are molecules that bind microbes to phagocytes and initiate engulfment
7	Microbicidal activity	Phagolysosome of phagocyte	Killing	Genetic defects result in decreased resistance to infections
8	Digestion	Vacuolar system of phagocyte	Eliminate microbial products	Lysosomal enzyme systems

propensity to develop pyogenic infections caused by microorganisms which are usually constituents of the normal flora.

A. Phagocyte Production (Stage 1). Phagocytes are produced in the bone marrow (see Figure 2–1A). Neutrophils are produced in bone marrow from precursor stem cells under the mitotic and differentiation influence of several low-molecular-weight proteins called colony-stimulating factors (CSF). CSF for granulocytes (neutrophils) (granulocyte CSF), monocytes/macrophages (macrophage CSF), phagocytes (granulocyte-macrophage CSF), and multiple cell types (IL-3) are secreted by endothelial cells, fibroblasts, and cells of the immune system. A large number of granulocytes are produced each day (~ 10^{11} cells). Granulocytes are short-lived cells; once they enter the tissues their half-life is only 6–8 h. There may be as many as 10^{10}–10^{11} granulocytes/ml of abscess fluid. Thus, the turnover of these cells is high, and, when production is inhibited, by anticancer drugs, for example, neutropenia may become severe and lead to invasive bacterial and fungal infections.

B. Phagocyte Release (Stage 2). Phagocytes are released into the circulation (see Figure 2–1B). IL-1, a cytokine product from macrophages, signals release of neutrophils from the marrow. The circulating neutrophil population increases the peripheral white blood cell count, a hallmark of acute infection. Neutrophils that normally adhere to the vascular endothelium form the marginated pool. Certain chronic stimuli (eg, drugs, hypoxia, stress, and exercise) cause demargination with increased white blood cell counts.

C. Chemokinesis (Stage 3). Phagocytes are guided to sites of infection by chemical signals called chemokines. Sentinel tissue macrophages and migrating immune cells, in response to invading microbes, secrete proteins called chemokines. Numerous distinct molecules have been identified—some are the ligands for specific receptors on different leukocytes, and some control the types of leukocytes that infiltrate inflammatory foci. The chemokines exert their effect by facilitating adherence of particular cell types to endothelium adjacent to an inflammatory site.

D. Margination, Spreading, and Diapedesis (Stage 4). For phagocytes to enter foci of infection, they must adhere to adjacent capillaries and migrate out of the bloodstream into the tissues. This is a multistep, tightly regulated process. The initial adherence step is mediated by surface molecules called selectins that bind neutrophil (L-selectin) to the endothelial cell (E-selectin) as well as to platelets (P-selectin). At this stage leukocytes roll along the endothelium in the direction of blood flow (Figure 2–1C). Tight adherence with leukocyte flattening is mediated by receptors (β-integrins) that bind to intercellular adhesion molecules called ICAMs that are expressed on endothelial cells. This interaction is controlled by regulation of these surface molecules through inflammatory mediators that diffuse from an infected site. Cytokines and arachidonic acid metabolites up-regulate β-integrin (on neutrophils) and ICAM-1 (on endothelial cells) expression. Specialized adhesion molecules localized at endothelial cell junctions (platelet/endothelial cell adhesion molecules) guide neutrophil motility between endothelial cells into infected tissue by a process called diapedesis (Figure 2–1D).

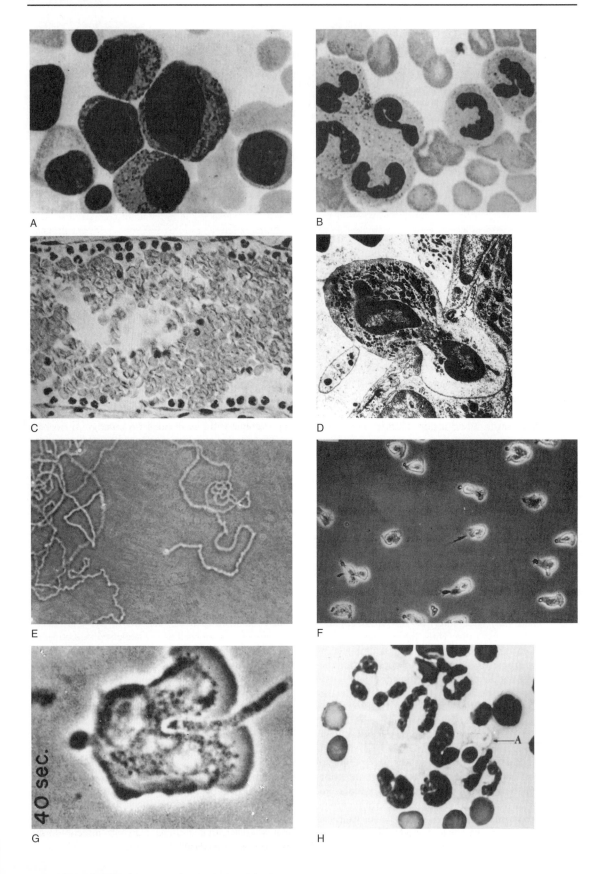

E. Chemotaxis (Stage 5). Phagocytes seek pathogens by attraction to gradients of microbial products and signals generated by the host inflammatory response. Motility of neutrophils increases in response to environmental signals called chemotaxins, which include cytokines [IL-6, IL-8, granulocyte macrophage CSF, tumor necrosis factor α (TNFα), interferon-γ (IFN-γ)], leukotrienes, and chemical products from microorganisms themselves (eg, microbial oligopeptides such as formylmethionine-leucine-phenylalanine). When no concentration gradient is present, increased motility is random [chemokinesis (Figure 2–1E)]; however, in the presence of even weak gradients, neutrophil motility becomes directed toward an increased concentration of stimulus [chemotaxis (Figure 2–1F)]. The interaction between chemotaxins, their high-affinity receptors on the neutrophil surface, and cytoplasmic cytoskeletal events, which propel the cell forward, are not entirely worked out. However, it is important that phagocyte motility depends on a substrate upon which the phagocytes crawl. These cells cannot swim. Thus it becomes clear that whenever bacteria gain access to nutrient-rich fluid-filled spaces (eg, cerebrospinal, pleural, peritoneal, pericardial, or synovial fluid), phagocyte defenses are put at considerable disadvantage. Neutrophils must make physical contact with the bacteria they kill. In a fluid-filled space (eg, massive ascites), this contact depends on random collisions between bacterial and phagocytic cells. Indeed, in the preantibiotic era, pyogenic infections of fluid-filled spaces were frequently fatal. Because bacteremia is often a precursor to meningitis, pericarditis, peritonitis, or septic arthritis, one major function of the RES is to clear bacteria from the bloodstream, which thereby prevents seeding of fluid-filled spaces. Bacteria that most often cause these infections are notoriously difficult to clear from the bloodstream because they possess antiphagocytic factors, most often capsules (*S pneumoniae, Streptococcus pyo-*

genes, Neisseria meningitidis, and *Haemophilus influenzae*).

F. Phagocytosis (Stage 6). Phagocytosis is required to kill invading microorganisms. Phagocytosis is a two-step process: (1) attachment of the particle to the phagocyte occurs and (2) the phagocyte extends lamellipodia circumferentially around the particle to enclose it within a phagocytic vacuole called the phagosome (Figure 2–1G). As noted above, opsonic proteins (Igs and complement proteins) coat microorganisms and, by engaging their receptors on the surface of phagocytes, they mediate attachment. These receptor-ligand interactions also induce intracellular events, which activate the engulfment process. Engulfment itself is a highly energy-dependent process and is powered by an ATP-dependent cytoskeletal polymerization-depolymerization of actin microfilaments. Nonopsonic phagocytosis may occur for some microorganisms. Molecules on the surfaces of both target and phagocyte interact with oligosaccharide moieties, which mediate attachment and activate the engulfment "motor" of the phagocyte.

Another aspect of phagocytosis involves interaction between the phagocyte and the surrounding tissue substrate (ie, the surface on which the phagocyte is crawling). This involves specialized serum molecules (extracellular matrix proteins) such as fibronectin, laminin, and vitronectin. These proteins do not interact with microorganisms directly. However, facilitation of interaction between phagocyte and substrate by these molecules leads to substantial enhancement of phagocytosis.

G. Microbicidal Activity (Stage 7). There are numerous phagocyte microbicidal mechanisms (Figure 2–1H). As microorganisms are internalized within phagosomes, microbicidal functions are initiated. Two general categories of killing mechanisms are recognized. These are the oxygen-dependent and -independent mechanisms. Oxygen-dependent killing is by the oxidative burst, sometimes called the respira-

Figure 2–1. The life of a neutrophil (~ 4 days). (A) Neutrophils are produced in the bone marrow from progenitor cells called myeloblasts. Here a group (4) of myeloblasts, which are heavily laden with granules, are seen amidst some red cell precursors (stage 1). (B) Mature and less mature (band forms) neutrophils seen in the bloodstream. The white blood cell count is elevated in response to a bacterial infection (stage 2). (C) Having been attracted to this focus of infection through the action of chemokines (stage 3), neutrophils are adherent (marginated) to the endothelium of a small blood vessel adjacent to an inflamed appendix (stage 4). (D) Diapedesis of a neutrophil as the cell leaves the circulation by crawling between endothelial cells from upper left to lower right (stage 4). (E) Random neutrophil mobility. These are neutrophils (bright dot at end of tracks) crawling on soft agar. As they crawl they leave tracks in the agar that can be visualized by the phase contrast microscope (stage 5, undirected motility). (F) Chemotaxis of neutrophils in vitro. A concentration gradient of a chemotactic stimulus is established by injecting the stimulus from a port on the right. The neutrophils sense the gradient, assume a polarized shape, and begin crawling along the substrate (a plastic petri dish) toward the greater concentration (stage 5, directed motility). (G) This neutrophil is phagocytizing a rod-shaped bacterium (stage 6). The cell is polarized and is extending its lamellipodia around the bacillus from its ruffled leading aspect. Photo taken 40 s after attachment of bacterium to phagocyte. (H) Neutrophils showing fungicidal activity (stage 7). The phagocytic vacuole labeled "A" contains two *C albicans* cells. The top yeast of the pair is disintegrating and fails to take up the stain (stage 8). The neutrophils are undergoing a "respiratory burst" used to kill the yeast cells (stage 7).

tory burst. There are multiple oxygen-independent mechanisms that are mediated by microbicidal proteins that are delivered into the phagosome by degranulation. Degranulation occurs when specific cytoplasmic granules in the neutrophil fuse with the phagocytic vacuole and discharge their contents on particles sequestered therein. A phagosome that has undergone this process is called a phagolysosome. The phagolysosomal membrane contains a proton pump that acidifies the compartment. The low pH (~ pH 4.5) is an ideal environment for many enzymes, acid proteases, defensins, cationic proteins, and other proteins (bactericidal permeability-increasing protein, azuricidin, indolicin, and bactenectins) that kill and digest (stage 8; see Figure 2–1H) bacteria.

The oxidative burst is based on a unique enzyme system, which in the resting cell is inactive. This enzyme is the NADPH/oxygen oxidoreductase of neutrophils and MNPs. The NADPH oxidase is activated upon stimulation induced by phagocytosis of a microorganism. Oxygen is reduced to superoxide with NADPH serving as the electron donor. There is abrupt, large-scale oxygen consumption by the enzymatic reaction—the respiratory or oxidative burst. Of the numerous biochemical events that ensue, the most important is the generation of several microbicidal products. All are formed ultimately from superoxide itself, the proximal enzymatic product. Hydrogen peroxide, singlet oxygen, and hydroxyl radical—all highly efficient microbicidal agents—are generated from superoxide. Hydrogen peroxide and chloride form hypochlorite and, ultimately, chloramines, through catalysis by myeloperoxidase. Thus the neutrophil relies on an arsenal of chemical weaponry to kill microorganisms. In the test tube, several million neutrophils undergoing the respiratory burst kill 10 million *Escherichia coli* within minutes; the same process occurs in the body, but only if neutrophils can phagocytose their targets and if substrates for the respiratory burst are available. It is evident that these highly reactive and toxic oxygen reduction products may destroy host cells along with invading microbes. Consequently, systems have evolved in mammals for protection of the surrounding host tissues at sites of inflammation. Catalase, superoxide dismutase, and glutathione peroxidase/glutathione reductase are detoxifying enzymes whose mechanisms scavenge oxygen intermediates. Other small organic molecules function as nonenzymatic scavengers. Neutrophil oxidative metabolism is extremely important for the maintenance of homeostasis in humans. Rare mutations that ablate NADPH oxidase activity lead to serious, frequent and invariably fatal pyogenic infections in children. Recent advancements have led to strategies that can augment other defenses and thereby prevent serious infections in these children.

Oxygen-independent microbicidal mechanisms compose a heterogeneous group. The most important are the microbicidal peptides and proteins that are re-

leased after bacteria are ingested during phagolysosomal fusion. An extensively studied example is the defensin family of molecules. By assembling into hydrophobic structures, which form pores through which bacterial components are lost, defensins lead to perturbation of bacterial membranes. This culminates in death of the bacterial cell.

Natural Killer Cells

NK cells are non-B, non-T lymphocytes that circulate in blood and function in constitutive host defense by identifying and destroying cells infected with viruses. Equipped with specialized proteins and enzymes packaged within intracellular granules, NK cells lyse virus-infected host cells and thereby interfere with viral replication. NK cells can bind yeast cells and destroy them. NK cells are an important source of cytokines, chemical messenger molecules that regulate the immune response. In rapidly developing infections, NK cell-derived IFN-γ (one of the most important cytokines) activates macrophages to a microbicidal state.

DEFENSE MECHANISMS AT THE LEVEL OF PROTEIN MOLECULES

The complement proteins, designated collectively as C′, constitute a complex system of plasma zymogens that operate as part of innate host-defenses (the alternate pathway) and with antibodies, in adaptive immunity (the classical pathway). Although composed of different proteins, the complement system bears a striking analogy to the blood clotting system.

Complement proteins are produced primarily in the liver by hepatocytes. MNPs also synthesize and secrete all of the complement proteins, but the bulk of production depends on the liver.

The initial step of the alternative pathway is always active, but it occurs at a very low level. When bound to a microbial surface product, such as the lipopolysaccharide polymer from the cell wall of gram-negative bacteria, limited proteolysis proceeds stepwise until C3 is cleaved to C3b and C3a. C3b is a short-lived protein. It forms a covalent thioester bond near its formation site, namely on the surface of a bacterial cell. MNPs and polymorphonuclear phagocytes express a family of distinct C3 receptors. Ligand-receptor binding anchors the bacterial cell to the phagocyte. This attachment event initiates phagocytosis. In animal models, depletion of C′ proteins with cobra venom factor renders the host highly susceptible to infection with encapsulated bacteria such as *S pneumoniae*. Thus, the main function of the complement system is to generate opsonins, primarily C3b, molecules that increase the efficiency of phagocytosis.

Further in the complement cascade, C5 is cleaved into large C5b and small C5a proteolytic fragments.

C5a diffuses from the site of inflammation, which sets up a concentration gradient that directs phagocyte emigration by chemotaxis.

Still later in the cascade a complex forms composed of C7, C8, and C9—the membrane attack complex (MAC). The MAC inserts itself into the outer lipid bilayers of gram-negative bacteria-forming pores visible by electron microscopy; this drastic perturbation leads to bacteriolysis. Bacteriolysis effected by the MAC is thus a mechanism for killing bacteria by fluid phase components—a phagocyte is not directly involved. However, bacteriolysis has limitations. First, gram-negative bacteria spawn mutants that are resistant to the lysing capability of the MAC. Second, gram-positive bacteria, mycobacteria, and fungi are naturally resistant to the MAC. Although protozoa may be killed by the MAC, CMI is the main defense mechanism against these pathogens.

The complement system performs three important host-defense functions: (1) it generates C3b, a major opsonic component that promotes phagocytosis; (2) it generates C5a, a chemotaxin that directs phagocyte motility toward an inflammatory stimulus; and (3) it kills some gram-negative bacteria through the MAC.

Humans with complement deficiencies, although uncommon, have been identified. These individuals exhibit characteristic susceptibilities to infection, such as disseminated infection with *Neisseria meningitidis* and *N gonorrhoeae*.

ADAPTIVE IMMUNE RESPONSES

There are two general categories of adaptive immune responses. The first comprises the synthesis of specific Ig proteins (antibodies) by specialized lymphocytes called plasma cells. This is called humoral immunity. The second type of response, CMI, involves direct or indirect attack on microorganisms mediated by lymphocytes and other accessory cells (eg, macrophages). Both humoral immunity and CMI are characterized by two important features. First, the responses are directed toward specific biochemical moieties on microorganisms, called antigens. Second, the responses impart a "memory" in the host. This means that subsequent exposures to specific antigens are met with a much enhanced immune response.

HUMORAL IMMUNITY

Production of Antibodies

Antibodies are complex glycoproteins called Igs, which bind specifically to moieties called antigens. After an antigen is bound by an antibody, a variety of cellular and molecular mechanisms come into play. These mechanisms, which function to protect the host from microbial invaders, are discussed in the sections that follow. In conjunction with the complement system, antibodies are the main effector molecules of humoral immunity. Antibodies are used to inhibit or destroy foreign cells. In the circulation and on mucosal surfaces, antibodies help define acquired resistance to particular pathogens. The mechanistic bases for antibody-mediated resistance are varied and complex. It is necessary for the antibody alone to bind the antigen. Even this is not sufficient in all cases because additional mechanisms may be required to kill microorganisms (eg, participation by a phagocyte). Examples of antibody effector mechanisms include the following: (1) complement activation that leads to bacteriolysis; (2) opsonophagocytic function, in which antibodies attach microorganisms to phagocytes, which then kill the microorganisms; (3) antibody-dependent cellular cytotoxicity (ADCC), an antibody bridge between an effector cell (eg, lymphocyte or monocyte) and target cell (eg, virus-infected somatic cell) that activates a killing mechanism, whereby the target cell is destroyed; and (4) neutralization, whereby the antibody binds to a microbial toxin or virus, which renders it unable to bind to its receptor through stearic hindrance.

Two critical functions are encoded in the structure of the antibody molecule. The N-terminal end (variable or V region) of the molecule defines the antigen recognition site. There are many possible different amino acid sequences that lead to different antigen-binding specificities. The carboxy-terminal portion determines one of nine classes and subclasses of Ig isotypes. Each isotype carries a distinct functional attribute suited for various biologic tasks, such as complement fixation, opsonization, or distribution into certain body sites and surfaces. B lymphocytes produce antibodies that express surface-bound Igs of a single specificity. When these antigen receptors are engaged by specific ligands, B cells proliferate and differentiate into plasma cells. These cells then begin to secrete Ig molecules that are specific for the target antigen.

Immunoglobulin Structure

All Igs share the same basic molecular structure. This structure consists of two identical peptide heterodimers linked by disulfide bridges. Each heterodimer consists of a heavy chain (C_H) and a light chain (C_L) (Figure 2–2).

The antigen-binding site is in the Fab portion. Three hypervariable regions containing 10–12 amino acids with markedly viable sequences occupy the V_K and V_H domains. The quaternary structure of the C_L and C_H in this region determines antigen specificity. Because each Ig molecule has two heavy and two light chains, antibodies are bivalent for antigen binding. The portion of the antigen recognized is called

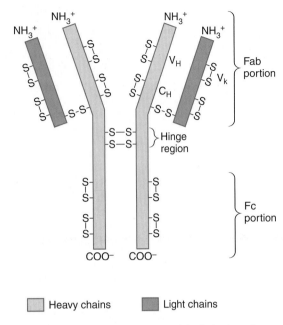

Figure 2–2. Protein structure of the Ig basic unit.

the epitope. The complementary Fab-binding site is called the paratope.

A constant region of the C_H is the product of distinct genes. This region defines the "class" of Igs. A hinge region determines flexibility of the molecule related to biological function. The Fc portion is critical for biological function, such as complement activation, the ability to bind to phagocyte receptors, and the ability to cross anatomic barriers such as placental membranes.

Immunoglobulins in Humans

Five Ig classes defined by their C_H type are present in humans (Table 2–4). There are four IgG and two IgA subclasses. There are two classes of C_Ls (κ and λ). Each B lymphocyte produces only one class of C_L.

A. Immunoglobulin M. During the primary immune response, IgM antibodies are the first to be produced. The pentameric structure endows IgM with 10 antigen-binding sites. This assists in complement activation and aggregation of antigen and microbes. Antigen affinity for IgM is usually less than for IgG. Measurement of IgM antibody specificity and concentration is useful in diagnosis because its presence correlates with primary, active infection.

B. Immunoglobulin D. IgD is expressed on the surface of B cells and functions as antigen receptor. Membrane anchoring is a function of the extended hinge region of IgD molecules.

C. Immunoglobulin G. IgG is the most abundant Ig, making up ~ 75% of the total. It crosses the placenta and hence provides protection to the newborn during the first 6 months of life. It is present in the lower respiratory tract and in exudative secretions. There are four subclasses (IgG_1, IgG_2, IgG_3, and IgG_4), which are determined by the constant regions of their heavy chains. Each bears distinct biologic activities. IgG_1 and IgG_3 fix complement well. IgG_3, but not IgG_2 and IgG_4, binds and activates leukocyte Fc receptors. IgG_2 is produced against the polysaccharide determinants of bacterial capsules. IgG_4 may compete with IgE for antigen and thereby alter immediate-type hypersensitivity reactions.

D. Immunoglobulin A. There are two subclasses of IgA—IgA_1 and IgA_2. IgA is produced in gut lymphoid tissue and is dimeric. It is transported from submucosa to the gut lumen. This is mediated by a special secretory component, expressed as an integral membrane protein on the basolateral surface of gastrointestinal epithelial cells. This secretory component is a receptor for dimeric IgA and initiates endocytosis, transcytoplasmic transport, and release of IgA dimers into the intestinal lumen. This process occurs at other mucosal sites in the respiratory and urogenital tracts, as well as in nasal secretions, tears, saliva, and colostrum. IgA interferes with attachment of microorganisms to mucosal surfaces. It neutralizes

Table 2–4. Human immunoglobulin (Ig) classes.

Characteristic	IgG Monomer	IgA Dimer	IgM Pentamer	IgD Monomer	IgE Monomer
Molecular weight	<150,000>	<400,000>	<900,000>	<180,000>	<190,000>
Serum concentration (mg/dl)	600–1600	60–330	45–150	Trace	Trace
Half-life (days)	23	6	5	3	2
Complement activation	2+	0	4+	0	0
Opsonic activity[1]	4+	2+	0	0	0
Reaginic activity	0	0	0	0	4+
Acts as B-cell receptor[†]	+	±	4+	4+	±

[†]Grading from 0 = no effect to 4+ = marked effect.

ingested toxins, and it may promote phagocytosis by leukocytes emigrating into mucosal epithelium.

E. Immunoglobulin E. Although only trace amounts are present in the circulation, IgE predominates on the surface of mast cells and basophils through noncovalent high-affinity receptor binding of its Fc portion. Immediate-type hypersensitivity or reaginic responses occur when antigen binds to cell surface IgE. Degranulation with release of histamine, eicosanoids, and peptide mediators of inflammation from mast cells may lead to urticaria, laryngeal and intestinal wall edema, and anaphylactic shock. The evolution of reaginic responses was driven by the necessity for a host-defense mechanism against invasion of tissues, especially epithelial surfaces, by helminths and ectoparasites. Monocytes, eosinophils, and platelets may cooperate with IgE in ADCC reactions against certain trematodes.

B Cells

Generation of an effective humoral immune response is vested in progenitor cells located in the bone marrow, which undergo differentiation to become mature B cells in the spleen and lymph nodes. Activation of mature B cells into antibody-producing plasma cells is a complex, highly regulated process. Regulation occurs through the expression of B-cell surface receptor molecules, which alter cell function upon binding ligand. Important B-cell receptors and their functions are shown in Table 2–5.

Antigen binding to its specific receptor on B cells leads to the formation of the B-cell receptor complex. When formed, the complex lowers the threshold for B-cell activation. Intracellular signal transduction through protein phosphorylation by Src kinases activates membrane phospholipase $C_\gamma 2$. Inositol triphosphate and diacylglycerol are formed. Intracellular calcium is mobilized and protein kinase C is activated. Transcription of cellular genes is induced by regulating cell division, differentiation, and Ig synthesis. However, these events are usually not sufficient for high-level antibody production. T cells, which recognize processed antigen-derived peptide in association with complementary major histocompatibility complex (MHC) class-II determinants, physically aggregate with B cells and promote B-cell activation. This is called T-cell helper function. This is the main pathway for antibody production against protein antigens.

Certain polymeric antigens, especially bacterial polysaccharides bearing repetitive monosaccharide units, can activate B cells without T cells. This type of T-cell–independent antibody response may relate to cross-linking B-cell receptor complexes (and hence more efficient signal transduction) by long strands to linear polysaccharide antigen molecules. T-cell–independent antibody responses tend to produce low-affinity IgM and IgG_2 isotypes in relatively low levels. Furthermore, memory B-cell formation is inefficient. Thus, bacterial polysaccharide vaccines may not be particularly immunogenic. By coupling a bacterial polysaccharide to a protein component (eg, tetanus toxoid) a T-cell–dependent B-cell response is induced, and memory cells become more abundant. Recently, lymphocytes not ordinarily classified as T or B cells, which bear the CD1 surface marker, were shown to help process polysaccharide antigens covalently attached to lipid moieties. This pathway of antigen presentation, which is not restricted by MHC, could prove useful for future development of polysaccharide vaccines.

Antibody Diversity

Antibody diversity is explained by rearrangements of DNA sequences within unique regions of Ig genes. Antibodies produced during a primary antibody response after an encounter with a new antigen are IgM in isotype. They appear 5–10 days after exposure to antigen, and their antigen affinity is relatively low. On reexposure to antigen, secondary antibody responses result in rapid production (1–3 days) of higher-affinity, higher-titer IgG, IgA, or IgE isotypes. Memory B cells formed during a primary response mediate the more efficient secondary response with the help of T cells. Switching of isotypes from IgM to IgG, for example, is controlled by T cells and the cytokines they secrete to communicate with B cells. Isotype switching and affinity maturation and epitope diversity of Igs are the result of four distinct molecular processes:

1. Multiple segments within the hypervariable region of the DNA encoding light and heavy chains (V_L and V_H; Figure 2–2) undergo recombination.

2. The segments are rejoined inexactly.

3. The quaternary association between V_H and V_L protein products leads to unique antigen-binding sites. These events lead to an enormous repertoire of

Table 2–5. B-cell receptors and their functions.[1]

Receptor Molecules	Function
B-cell receptor complex (IgM, IgD, CD19, CD21)	Antigen-specific receptor; triggers cell activation and endocytosis of bound antigen
MHC II, B7, CD72, ICAM	Major histocompatibility complex class II molecule. Presents antigenic peptide to complementary T-cell receptor. Engage T-cell receptors to promote T-cell–dependent B-cell activation.
Cytokine receptors	Transduce signals required for proliferation, activation, and differentiation
CD32 Fc low-affinity receptor	Down-regulates immunoglobulin production

[1]Abbreviations: Ig, immunoglobulin; MHC, major histocompatibility complex; ICAM, intercellular adhesion molecule.

B cells bearing different antigen receptor specificities. These specificities are directed against those portions of antigen molecules called epitopes.

4. A nonrecombinatorial mechanism involving somatic point mutations in the V_H and V_L regions leads to idiotype diversity. This mechanism is believed to account for maturation, when repeated administration of antigen results in antibody production with incrementally increased affinity for the eliciting epitope.

Immunoglobulin Fc Receptors

Antibodies function in host defense in conjunction with other proteins (eg, complement components) and cells (eg, phagocytes). Antigen bound to the Fab portions is connected to functional components by the Ig Fc portion. Thus, the specificity of Fc ligands interacting with Fc receptors on other immune cells determines the character of immune responses mediated by antibodies. Families of Fc receptors and their functional activities are shown in Table 2–6.

Function of Antibody-Mediated Host Defense

Through specific binding of antigen and Fc portion receptor-ligand interaction, antibodies facilitate destruction of microbes and neutralize toxins. They may act at a distance from their cell of origin, and their soluble properties allow for dispersion throughout the body in the circulation and lymph. The utility of Igs in host defense is multifactorial. However, the overriding feature is their functional capability for attaching microorganisms to phagocytes and lymphocytes bearing microbicidal mechanisms. The following sections summarize antibody-directed immune mechanisms.

A. Activation of Complement Proteins. The C_H2 (IgG) and C_H3 (IgM) domains (see Figure 2–2) of antibody Fc regions activate complement by binding to microbes and then interacting with multiple sites on C1q, the first component of the complement cascade (classical complement pathway). Activation of complement on microbial surfaces leads to bacteriolysis in some instances or, more commonly, to phagocytosis. Gram-negative bacteria are susceptible to bacteriolysis as are some protozoans. But gram-positive bacteria, fungi, and viruses cannot be lysed. Furthermore, gram-negative bacilli resistant to complement-mediated lysis (serum resistance) can be selected for during natural infection. Opsonophagocytic antibodies important for the resolution of infection have been identified during infection with *S pyogenes*, *S pneumoniae*, *H influenzae*, *N meningitidis*, and *Staphylococcus aureus*.

B. Promotion of Phagocytosis. The three classes of IgG Fc receptors mediate phagocytosis of IgG-coated particles. IgG_2 and IgG_3 subclasses are generally required. Mucosal phagocytes, namely macrophages and neutrophils, bearing IgA Fc receptors facilitate engulfment of microorganisms. Fc receptors alone are usually sufficient for phagocytosis of most bacteria and fungi; however, removal of encapsulated bacteria may require Fc and C3 receptors functioning in concert. In experimental *S pneumoniae* bacteremia caused by highly virulent strains, clearance of bacteria from the circulation failed when animals were depleted of complement proteins, even when anticapsular IgG antibody was present.

C. Antibody-Dependent Cellular Cytotoxicity. ADCC is a mechanism by which leukocytes destroy somatic cells infected with microorganisms. Antibody-coated microorganisms or parasitized host cells can be killed when Fc receptors on leukocytes are engaged. This reaction occurs without phagocytosis, but depends on contact between effector and target cells. Nonphagocytic immune cells (eg, NK cells) lyse antibody-coated virus-infected host cells through IgG RIII receptors. In this reaction, NK cells exocytose cytotoxin protein molecules called perforins onto target

Table 2–6. Classification of Fc receptors.[1]

Fc Receptor Type	Cell types bearing receptors	Function
IgG Fc receptors		
RI (CD64) (high affinity)	Monocytes, neutrophils	Phagocytosis; degranulation; ADCC
RII (CD32) (low affinity)	Monocytes, neutrophils, eosinophils, B cells, platelets	Phagocytosis, degranulation; ADCC; respiratory burst; scavenge immune complexes; inhibits Ig synthesis
RIII (low affinity)	Macrophages, neutrophils, NK cells	Phagocytosis; ADCC; cytokine secretion
IgA Fc receptors	Macrophages, neutrophils	Phagocytosis, respiratory burst
IgE Fc receptors		
RI (high affinity)	Mast cells, basophils	Degranulation, leukotriene and cytokine production
RII (low affinity)	Eosinophils, B cells, T cells, macrophages, platelets	Antigen uptake; phagocytosis; ADCC

[1]Abbreviations: Ig, immunoglobulin; ADCC, antibody-dependent cellular cytotoxicity; NK, natural killer cell; R, receptor.

cells. Perforins assemble in the target cell membrane-forming pores similar to the MAC of complement. Rapid lysis ensues. Macrophages and neutrophils participate in ADCC reactions. IgE-coated metazoans such as parasitic helminths are destroyed by eosinophils bearing Fc receptor II molecules. Eosinophils exocytose a cytotoxic molecule, called major basic protein, onto the parasite surface on engagement and cross-linking of these Fc receptors.

D. Neutralization of Microbial Toxins. Microbial toxin neutralization is a striking example of protection mediated by antibodies. Lethal toxins produced by *Clostridium* spp. (eg, botulinum toxin and tetanus toxin) and by *Corynebacterium diphtheriae* (diphtheria toxin) are efficiently detoxified by specific IgG. Antibodies bind to toxin molecules and, through stearic hindrance, block their receptor-mediated uptake by susceptible cells. The antitoxin effect of antibodies is the basis for some of the most successful immunization practices in medicine.

Endotoxins are the lipopolysaccharide polymers that form part of the structure of the outer membrane of gram-negative bacteria. Their biologic effects are myriad, but they include the induction of lethal collapse of the circulatory system. Much effort has been made to produce protective antibodies against endotoxins for administration to patients in shock. Despite broad reactivity and monoclonal antibody technology, this strategy has not yet led to significant advances for the treatment of endotoxemia.

E. Neutralization of Viruses. IgM, IgG, and IgA antibodies bind to specific epitopes on virions and block virus access to host cells. The effective prevention of polio, smallpox, hepatitis A and B, and rabies by immunization is based on this principle. Other viruses, most notably herpes viruses and human immunodeficiency virus (HIV)-1, spread from cell to cell and hence evade neutralizing antibody. One exception may be the intracellular neutralization of viruses within mucosal epithelial cells as polymeric IgA is transported through these cells.

F. Blockage of Microbial Adhesion. Pathogenic microorganisms entering the body via mucosal surfaces first attach to epithelial cells by receptor-ligand binding. Specific IgA directed at these determinants may block adherence and hence abort microbial invasion.

G. Agglutination of Microorganisms into Large Aggregates. Polyvalent IgM, IgG, and IgA can cross-link microbes forming large aggregates. In the respiratory tract, the mucociliary clearance mechanism may then facilitate removal of these aggregates before invasion can occur.

CELL-MEDIATED IMMUNITY

CMI refers to an immune response against organisms (usually facultative or obligate intracellular mi-

croorganisms) in which antibody has a subordinate or no role. CMI was first demonstrated experimentally as an immune response that occurred in passively immunized animals transfused with cells (lymphocytes) but not with specific Igs. Such strict division between cell-mediated and humoral immune responses is oversimplified because specific Igs and antigen-antibody complexes interact to both enhance and inhibit CMI reactions.

CMI involves signal transmission between cells participating in the response. Intercellular signaling is accomplished in two ways: (1) by cell-cell interaction involving surface molecules on the interacting cells and (2) via chemical messenger molecules called cytokines. These mechanisms operate both in innate immune responses and in antigen-specific CMI. Intercellular signaling mechanisms are then used to activate cytotoxic effector cells for microbiostatic and microbicidal functions. Cell signaling and activation are discussed individually in the next section.

Cell-Cell Interactions

A. Major Histocompatibility Complex Molecules. MHC molecules compose a group of polymorphic integral membrane proteins encoded by segments of clustered genetic loci. These molecules participate in binding antigenic peptides for T-cell recognition. Two structurally distinct types of MHC molecules exist. MHC class I molecules are involved in classic immune responses to virus-infected cells, foreign tissue grafts, and tumors. There are ~ 70 different alleles composing three separate subclasses of MHC class I genes. MHC class I molecules express peptides synthesized within the host cell (eg, a protein encoded by a viral gene) and transported from endoplasmic reticulum via the Golgi apparatus to the cell surface. β_2-Microglobulin and calnexin are required to stabilize MHC class I complexes. MHC class I antigens are presented as nonapeptides, and class I can be presented by all nucleated cells.

MHC class II molecules express antigens only on "professional" antigen-presenting cells (APCs), such as MNPs (macrophages) and related cells, dendritic cells throughout the body and Langerhans cells in the skin, and some B lymphocytes. MHC class II antigens are presented as 12- to 24-amino-acid peptides that are endocytosed from the environment and are expressed on the cell surface, having made their way through the endosomal/liposomal pathway.

B. T Lymphocytes. T cells interact directly with APCs. This cell-cell interaction drives specific immune responses by inducing clonal expansion of antigen-specific T cells. This expansion in turn results in secretion of signaling molecules, called cytokines. Cytokines direct the activities of additional immune response cells. Thus, the response to a specific antigen is vastly amplified. T cells bear receptors that bind to peptide antigen-MHC molecule complexes on antigen-presenting cells. Antigen-presenting cells bearing MHC class I antigens bind to T cells expressing the CD8[+] T-cell receptor surface marker. MHC class II antigens bind to CD4[+] T cells. This means that class I and II antigens stimulate separate populations of T cells. This separation directs the immune response toward different mechanisms adapted to deal with different antigenic challenges. CD4[+] T cells function as cytokine secretors, and they help B cells produce Igs. CD8[+] T cells become efficient cytotoxic cells, capable of lysing cells infected with viruses. Both CD4[+] and CD8[+] T cells bear the CD3 cell surface marker. The CD3 molecule transduces an up-regulating intracellular signal on binding to MHC class I or II antigens with CD8 or CD4 receptors, respectively. Mice with null mutations of the CD4 gene lack T-cell helper function; mice with null mutations of the CD8 gene lack cytotoxic T-cell function.

T-cell activation is maximized by coaggregation of the T-cell receptor with CD4 or CD8 bound to an MHC molecule-antigen complex on the APC. Other costimulatory molecules participate in T-cell activation, such as the CD28 T-cell marker bound to the B7/BB1 family of molecules on APCs. Upon aggregation and binding of these molecules between T cells and APCs, a complex cascade of intracellular events ensues. These events lead to T-cell differentiation and T-cell replication with clonal expansion. The latter is mediated by the T-cell growth factor, IL-2, which is secreted upon T-cell activation. The immunosuppressant antibiotic cyclosporin A inhibits IL-2 secretion by T cells by blocking the intracellular calcium-dependent functions in the complex cascade during T-cell activation.

Microbial superantigens activate T cells. Particular microbial toxins (ie, staphylococcal enterotoxin, toxic shock syndrome toxin, and streptococcal pyrogenic exotoxin A) are presented as MHC class II antigens, but they bind nonspecifically to the T-cell receptor. Up to 10% of T cells may be activated. This leads to widespread cytokine secretion and the systemic toxicity of a generalized cell-mediated immune response. Particular MHC class II genotypes and the T-cell receptor β-chain genotypes are more prone to these reactions.

Memory T cells help mediate secondary cell-mediated immune responses. These T cells bear the CD29 surface marker. Memory T cells show enhanced secretion of particular cytokines, and they mediate rapidly developing cytotoxicity responses.

Lymphocyte adhesion molecules mediate trafficking and homing of T cells to particular body sites. Some T cells home to mucosal sites where they are strategically stationed to participate with APCs upon entry of foreign antigens into the tissues.

Cytokines

Cytokines function as chemical messengers, sending signals from one immune cell to another. Cytokines are glycoprotein molecules secreted by lymphocytes. These molecules were originally called lymphokines. As their identities and cells of origin were defined, the term lymphokine was replaced by cytokine to include signal molecules elaborated during CMI whose cells of origin included other cell types (eg, macrophages, endothelial cells, and fibroblasts). As cytokines became characterized molecularly through cloning, sequencing, and expression techniques, they were assigned numbers and designated as interleukins (Table 2–7). However, some cytokines retained their original names, based primarily on their immunologic activities (eg, IFNs, TNFs, and CSFs). During CMI, cytokines act locally, infiltrating tissue sites of inflammatory cells. However, they may exert systemic effects when released into the circulation. This occurs during widespread infection and certain toxemias (eg, in response to superantigens as noted above).

Cytokines act to amplify or attenuate the immune response coordinately. Their action is not antigen specific, but their secretion is often driven by antigen-specific reactions. Certain microbial products (eg, lipopolysaccharide of gram-negative bacilli) directly stimulate cytokine secretion (eg, TNF and IL-1).

Table 2–7. General classification of cytokines.[1]

Class	Designation	Examples	Function
Interleukins	IL	IL-1, IL-2, IL-12	Cell signaling
Interferons	IFN	IFN-α, IFN-β, IFN-γ	Cell signaling; block viral replication
Monokines	TNF	TNF-α	Cell signaling; induce apoptosis
Colony-stimulating factors	CSF	M-CSF, GM-CSF, G-CSF	Hematopoietic growth and differentiation
Chemokines	CK	MCP-1, MIP-1α, RANTES	Attract immune response cells
Growth factors	GF	NGF, EGF	Tissue repair

[1]Abbreviations: TNF, tumor necrosis factor; IL, interleukin; IFN, interferon; CSF, colony-stimulating factor; CK, chemokine; GF, growth factor; M, macrophage monocyte; GM, granulocyte/monocyte; G, granulocyte; MCP, macrophage chemotactic peptide; MIP, macrophage inflammatory protein; RANTES, regulated activation normal T-cell–expressed/secreted; NGF, nerve growth factor; EGF, epithelial growth factor.

Cytokines regulate clonal expansion for both T and B lymphocytes. They mediate recruitment of immune cells to sites of inflammation. They activate effector cells (eg, macrophages) to microbicidal states. Some cytokines deactivate cells to prevent local tissue damage after the destruction of invading microbes. Cytokines interact with specific receptors on the cells they signal. The receptors act as transducers and relay signals into the cells, leading to additional secretions, replication, cell cycle arrest, and activation for microbicidal activities.

Cytokines secreted by MNPs are called monokines. Monokines help initiate CMI as macrophages phagocytose microbes and present their antigens to T cells. Two important cytokines come almost exclusively from T cells (hence they are lymphokines)— IL-2 and IFN-γ. IL-2 leads to many effects including replication of T cells activated by specific antigen. IFN-γ is the main lymphokine for activation of effector cells (macrophages) to destroy or inhibit pathogens. T cells respond with lymphokine secretion only if the T-cell receptor is engaged with specific antigen presented in context with MHC class I or class II molecules. An exception is the stimulation by superantigens. This is in contrast to monokine secretion, which occurs in response to a wide variety of stimuli. NK cells are also a source of IFN-γ during primary infection, before T-cell activation.

CD4$^+$ T cells change the profile of cytokines they secrete, and this directs the cell-mediated immune response toward activities suited best for defense against particular pathogenic agents. In the mouse during infection with intracellular pathogens, CD4$^+$ T cells secrete IL-2 and IFN-γ. This leads to macrophage activation and arrest of microbial intracellular replication by unknown mechanisms (T_H1 response). The monokine, IL-12, directs CD4$^+$ T cells into a T_H1 phenotype. During systemic helminth infections

CD4$^+$ T cells secrete IL-4, IL-5, IL-6, IL-9, IL-10, and IL-13. This profile leads to expansion of B-cell clones for production of Igs, including IgE (so-called T_H2 response). IgE participates in release of products from basophils, mast cells, and eosinophils that mediate cytotoxicity for multicellular animals that invade tissue usually via the intestinal tract. IL-10 directs CD4$^+$ T cells into a T_H2 phenotype.

Transforming growth factor-β, IL-4, and IL-10 down-regulate CMI to intracellular pathogens. Mice lacking a functional transforming growth factor-β gene die after birth with massive infiltration of lymphocytes and macrophages in their vital organs.

Other roles for cytokines include (1) control of hematopoiesis, (2) T-cell maturation and proliferation, (3) B-cell differentiation, and (4) T-cell suppressor function. Cytokines also regulate innate immune responses such as fever (IL-1) and the acute-phase response (IL-6, IL-1, and TNF). Cytokines released systemically cause shock (TNF) during septicemia.

Activation of Effector Cells

Effector cells of the cell-mediated immune response are microbiostatic and microbicidal for intracellular pathogens. These cells are cytotoxic T-cells, NK cells, and macrophages. Effector cells mediate and cytokines modulate antimicrobial activity during cell-mediated immune responses. Effector cells participating in CMI along with the functions they perform are listed in Table 2–8.

A. Cytotoxic T Cells. Cytotoxic T lymphocytes (CTLs) kill somatic cells that are infected with microbial pathogens. These T cells express CD8 and mediate antigen-specific, class I MHC-restricted cytolytic activity. Recall that class I recognition occurs for antigens synthesized within the host cell. This occurs during the replication cycle of viruses. CTLs are ideally suited for destroying virus-infected cells. Re-

Table 2–8. Effector cells for cell-mediated immunity.[1]

Class of Pathogens	Example	Effector Cells	Cytokines	CMI response
Bacteria	Mycobacterium tuberculosis	MNP CD4$^+$ CD8$^+$	IFN-γ TNF	T_H1
Fungi	Cryptococcus neoformans	CD4$^+$ NK CD8$^+$ MNP	IFN-γ	T_H1
Protozoa	Leishmania major	CD4$^+$ MNP	TNF IL-12 IFN-γ	T_H1
Metazoa	Schistosoma mansoni	CD4$^+$ MNP	IFN-γ	T_H1
Viruses	Cytomegalovirus	CD8*	IFN-γ	T_H1

[1]Abbreviations: CMI, cell-mediated immunity; MNP, mononuclear phagocytes; CD4$^+$, CD4$^+$ T cells; CD8$^+$, cytotoxic T cells; NK, natural killer cells; T_H1, type 1 helper cells.

lease of immature, unassembled virus components upon host-cell lysis blocks efficient viral replication. CTLs may lyse cells infected with bacteria. This thwarts the strategy of some facultative intracellular pathogens, whose survival in the host may depend on evasion of the immune system by sequestration within an intracellular niche. Differentiation of CTLs to the cytotoxic state is regulated by cytokines. Of those involved, IL-2 is most important. The biochemical mechanisms of cytolysis involve a Ca^{2+}-dependent assembly of a protein present in CTL granules, called perforin. The protein is assembled into a cylinderlike structure that is inserted into the plasma membrane of the antigen-bearing target cell. Serine proteases within CTL granules, called granzymes, enter the target cell through perforin pores. The enzymes then become catalytically active and participate in target cell destruction.

B. Natural Killer Cells. NK cells participate in CMI by acting as effector cells and cytokine-secreting cells. NK cells are CD158[+] lymphocytes that lack the T-cell receptor. They lyse certain neoplastic cells and virus-infected cells by a recognition mechanism that does not involve antigen-MHC restriction. These cells are active against virus-infected host cells, in particular the human herpes viruses. NK cells also function as an important source of IFN-γ early during bacterial infections before CD4 cell activation. Their large granules contain granzymes and perforin monomeres, such as CTLs.

C. Mononuclear Phagocytes. MNPs include circulating monocytes and tissue macrophages. They play two key roles in the cell-mediated immune response, as APCs and as cytotoxic effector cells. Their latter role is discussed here. Activated MNPs are recruited from a pool of precursor cells in the bone marrow. These phagocytes are released into the circulation and adhere to capillaries adjacent to infected tissue by a process involving intracellular adhesion molecules. Chemokines specific for MNPs participate to attract these cells. MNPs migrate between capillary endothelial cells and crawl toward microorganisms by chemotaxis. Chemotactic molecules from the host and infecting microbes act as stimuli, setting up a concentration gradient sensed by MNPs.

In the inflammatory milieu, MNPs are exposed to activating cytokines, primarily IFN-γ and TNF. Macrophages phagocytize microorganisms via a variety of receptor interactions involving IgG, IgA, and complement components, as well as via lipopolysaccharide and carbohydrate ligands present on bacteria, protozoa, fungi, and virus outer envelopes. Lysosomal granules within MNPs fuse with phagocytic vacuoles forming phagolysosomes. Granule components,

Table 2–9. Roles of mononuclear phagocytes in host defense.[1]

Category	Functions and Mediators
Fever	IL-6, TNF-α, IL-1 secretion
Inflammation	Prostaglandins Complement components Clotting factors
Lymphocyte activation	Antigen processing Antigen presentation IL-1 secretion
Tissue damage	Acid hydrolases C3a, TNF, H_2O_2
Tissue repair	Elastase Collagenase hyaluronidase Fibroblast-stimulating factor Angiogenesis
Microbicidal	Oxygen intermediates (eg, superoxide) Nitrogen intermediates (eg, nitric oxide) Cationic proteins Acid hydrolases and proteases
Directing CMI	IL-10 → T_H2 response IL-12 → T_H1 response

[1]Abbreviations: IL, interleukin; TNF, tumor necrosis factor; CMI, cell-mediated immunity; T_H1, type 1 helper T cell.

including proteases, lysozyme, and microbicidal proteins, are released as the phagolysosome is acidified.

Activated MNPs inhibit and kill phagocytized microorganisms by a variety of mechanisms involving reactive-oxygen and reactive-nitrogen (from nitric oxide) intermediates, microbicidal proteins, liposomal proteases, and as-yet-unknown biochemical mechanisms. Activated MNPs play an important host defense role in combating a wide variety of bacteria, protozoans, fungi, and metazoans that have adapted virulence mechanisms for intracellular survival. Activated MNPs are critical for granuloma formation. They become epithelioid cells occupying the centers of granulomas. Granulomas are the histopathologic hallmark of the cell-mediated immune response against intracellular pathogens such as tubercle bacilli. T_H1 response cytokines are required for granuloma formation. Activated MNPs may also mediate destruction of these same pathogens through a contact-dependent mechanism not requiring phagocytosis. Activated MNPs may also participate in cell-mediated immune responses through more efficient antigen presentation to T cells as well as through the production of cytokines that enhance T-cell–dependent killing mechanisms. Table 2–9 lists some examples of activated MNP-dependent host defenses against microbial pathogens.

REFERENCES

Joklik WK, et al (editors): *Zinsser Microbiology,* 20th ed. Appleton & Lange, 1992.

Mandell GL, Bennett JE, Dolin R: *Principles and Practice of Infectious Diseases,* 5th ed. Churchill Livingstone, 2000.

Mims C, et al: *Mims' Pathogenesis of Infectious Disease,* 4th ed. Academic Press, 1995.

Paul WE (editor): *Fundamental Immunology.* Lippincott-Raven, 1999.

Roitt I, Brostoff J, Male D: *Immunology,* 5th ed. Mosby, 1998.

3 Basic Principles of Microbial Virulence

David A. Relman, MD

Among the vast diversity of microscopic life on this planet, only a small subset is believed to be capable of infecting the human body and causing disease. For example, only 7 of the 38–40 extant bacterial divisions on the earth contain members that are recognized pathogens in humans. The features that distinguish this subset of microbes (bacteria, fungi, parasites, and viruses) from all others have been revealed in increasing detail over the past few decades through the development of methods in microbial genetic manipulation, host cell imaging, structural biology, and, more recently, genomics. The findings indicate adaptation and coevolution of host and pathogen. Common themes are apparent among the strategies and mechanisms used by some microbes in their behavior as pathogens; these themes are the focus of this chapter. From an evolutionary perspective, pathogenicity appears to have "arisen" on multiple occasions, among diverse putative microbial ancestors. The commonality of themes and strategies that we witness today in extant pathogens probably reflects convergent evolutionary processes, operating in part over long periods of time, as host and pathogen adapt and counteradapt. Pathogenic capabilities are also acquired over much shorter time periods through mechanisms of horizontal genetic exchange. A comparison of a pathogen and closely related nonpathogen often identifies only small discrete differences between the two, sometimes in the form of a single contiguous chromosomal segment, a plasmid, or a gene.

The intimate dynamic between human host and microbe is easily disrupted by changes in either participant, especially when strong selective pressures are brought to bear on the microbe, whose capabilities for adaptation are enormous. This is the concept behind the "emergence" of newly recognized infectious diseases, an issue that has received a great deal of attention over the past decade. Emergence occurs either when a microbe gains new relevant genetic traits (discussed in the next section) or when the host or environment provides new opportunities and niches that enhance microbial access to or survival within a host. Some of these opportunities can be appreciated from an understanding of normal host defenses to infection (see Chapter 2), as in the loss of humoral or cellular immunity (eg, from cytotoxic chemotherapy or malnutrition), or normal anatomic barriers (eg, from trauma). Others arise from human behavior at the individual (eg, sexual) or societal (eg, from war or migration) level. A better understanding of this dynamic might lead to more enlightened therapeutic and preventive strategies against infectious disease.

MICROORGANISMS AS PATHOGENS

The last few decades of experimental investigation in microbial pathogenesis have taught us that virulence is a polygenic attribute of certain microorganisms that chose to persist or multiply within privileged anatomic niches of a host. A pathogen is a microbe that causes damage to a host as part of its (the pathogen's) strategy for multiplication within the host or for transmission to or from a host. Some microbes routinely cause disease (damage) within a given host and are called primary pathogens; other microbes cause disease only when normal host defenses are impaired, and these are called opportunistic pathogens. The difference between these two types of pathogens is related to the particular skills of the first group in either finding a privileged anatomic niche within the host as a site for multiplication or competing with the normal endogenous microflora for a crowded niche (eg, mucosal surface or skin). Virulence is a measure of the frequency with which a microbe causes disease in a specific host, the severity of the resulting disease, the efficiency with which the organism is transmitted to or from a host, or a combination of these factors.

The mechanisms and strategies adopted by pathogens that result in disease are often encoded by genes that are clustered together in a pathogen's genome. The examination of genome structure in many bacterial pathogens reveals so-called pathogenicity islands, 10- to 200-kilobase segments of DNA with as many as tens to hundreds of genes that often have a significantly different guanine-plus-cytosine nucleotide composition from the rest of the genome. This difference in island nucleotide composition is believed to reflect its origin in a distantly related microorganism. Pathogenicity islands are usually flanked by direct repeats of DNA or transfer RNA genes, suggesting that they may have been transduced into the bacterium and into specific sites of the bacterial genome by a bacteriophage. Remnant plasmid mobilization genes suggest that in some cases the island may have existed as an extrachromosomal element at some time in the distant past (tens to hundreds of millions of years ago). Most islands contain genes that encode specialized secretion systems, adhesins, or toxins that are necessary for disease causation. It is not uncommon for bacterial pathogens to contain multiple islands; for example, *Salmonella* serovar Typhimurium has one island, SPI1, whose gene products are required for bacterial entry into host cells, and another island, SPI2, whose products mediate survival and replication inside a phagosomal vacuole within host cells.

Given this evidence for large-scale genetic exchange and the presence of clusters of specialized genes within pathogens, it should not be surprising to find frequent horizontal transmission of virulence-associated genes among contemporaneous microbes, on a shorter time scale. This form of horizontal transmission is mediated by bacteriophages, plasmids, and transposable elements such as transposons. The number of plasmid- and phage-associated virulence genes is substantial; a partial list is provided in Table 3–1. The clinical significance of these transmission events should not be underestimated. Outbreaks of diphtheria may result from corynephage infection of nontoxigenic *Corynebacterium diphtheriae* strains within hosts and the conversion of these strains to toxin producers after phage delivery of the diphtheria toxin gene (see Chapter 51). The same type of event appears to be responsible for the dissemination of Shiga-like toxin genes among otherwise harmless *Escherichia coli* serotypes and the subsequent creation of enterohemorrhagic strains. Furthermore, recent data indicate that fluoroquinolone exposure may boost Shiga-like toxin production by these phage-infected strains through phage regulatory pathways and, therefore, may be detrimental to the host.

All microbial pathogens follow the same steps in causing disease. After entry into a susceptible host, they find a specialized niche for attachment and subsequent colonization. To multiply and successfully colonize, they must confront and counter host defenses. Toxins and other secreted products often play a role in this effort, as well as in the effort to find an appropriate anatomic niche in this and other hosts. Transmissibility and transmission are a trait and process less well understood, except in those circumstances that involve a mechanical or biological vector. Pathogens, like other microbes, constantly sense their changing environment and regulate their behavior accordingly. The regulation of virulence-associated traits is complex and well integrated into systems used to regulate other microbial characteristics. Despite the universal nature of these steps, each pathogen displays a unique set of mechanisms, products, and responses that defines its pathogenic signature. Two members of the poxvirus family, smallpox virus and molluscum contagiosum virus, cause radically distinct clinical syndromes (skin lesions with and without a fulminant systemic inflammatory response, respectively). Although they share 103 genes, molluscum contagiosum virus and smallpox virus possess 59 and 83 genes, respectively, that the other does not contain; these virus-specific genes are predicted to encode proteins that subvert host innate immune defenses in a contrasting manner.

Table 3–1. Examples of virulence factors encoded on mobile genetic elements

Location	Virulence Factor	Organism
Encoded on plasmids	Tetanus toxin	*Clostridium tetani*
	Capsule	*Bacillus anthracis*
	Lethal and edema toxins	*B anthracis*
	Type III secretion system and secreted toxins/effectors	*Yersinia pseudotuberculosis*
	Secreted invasion factors	*Shigella flexneri*
	Heat-labile and heat-stable enterotoxins	Enterotoxigenic *Escherichia coli*
	Exfoliative toxin	*Staphylococcus aureus*
Encoded on bacteriophages	SopE (type III secreted effector)	*Salmonella* serovar Typhimurium
	Cholera toxin (CTX)	*Vibrio cholerae*
	Tcp pilus (CTX phage receptor)	*V cholerae*
	Diphtheria toxin	*Corynebacterium diphtheriae*
	Shiga-like toxin	Enterohemorrhagic *E coli*
	Botulinum toxin	*Clostridium botulinum*
	Erythrogenic toxin	*Streptococcus pyogenes*

REGULATION OF VIRULENCE

Precisely timed and measured responses characterize the expression of microbial virulence attributes. Timing and measurement are critical to a successful pathogenic strategy, owing to the highly changing environments faced by microbial pathogens and the energy costs associated with expression of virulence, as well as the complex set of host defenses designed to recognize and neutralize pathogens. For these reasons, pathogens recognize multiple environmental cues, use diverse regulatory mechanisms and systems, and integrate these cues and systems in a well-tuned network. A regulon is a group of physically unlinked genes that respond in a coordinated fashion to a given stimulus. Common features of microbial virulence-associated regulatory schemes are apparent.

Some of the most important environmental signals recognized by pathogens are extracellular iron concentration, temperature, osmolarity, oxygen and CO_2 partial pressures, specific signaling factors secreted by themselves, and contact with a host cell surface. Extracellular iron concentration, for example, tells pathogens when they have arrived within an animal host, since the latter expends great efforts to sequester and keep this critical element from microorganisms at mucosal surfaces. Pathogens and other microbes use a wide variety of sensing systems to read these signals and transduce the information into an appropriate response. Iron is recognized in some bacteria by intracellular iron-binding proteins that regulate the expression of iron acquisition proteins and receptors (eg, transferrin-binding proteins), as well as a number of bacterial toxins (eg, diphtheria and Shiga toxins) at the level of transcription. Other sensing systems that transcriptionally regulate virulence genes include the AraC class of transcriptional activators (eg, *V cholerae* ToxT), alternative RNA polymerase sigma factors, histonelike proteins, quorum-sensing systems whereby bacterial population density and growth phase are recognized in a species-specific manner, and the two-component sensor-response regulator family.

The two-component family is one of the most well-studied bacterial virulence-associated regulatory systems. Each of these systems comprises a sensor protein that spans the cytoplasmic membrane and a cytoplasmic response regulator protein with which it interacts, usually by means of high-energy phosphate transfer. Phosphorylation induces activation of the response regulator, thereby allowing it to bind DNA promoter sequences and control gene expression. It is not surprising that the genomes of pathogens whose lifestyles require adaptation to multiple diverse environments contain a large number of such systems (eg, *E coli*, > 40), whereas those pathogens that face a restricted number of environments contain few (eg, *Helicobacter pylori*, only 5). With closer examination, variations on this theme become apparent. *Vibrio* spp., for example, express a protein in the cytoplasmic membrane, ToxR, that acts as both sensor (of osmolarity) and response regulator (of porin expression) (Figure 3–1). This protein is expressed by most marine vibrios. For *Vibrio cholerae*, the expansion of its preferred environments to include the human intestinal tract has brought with it the means to acquire cholera toxin genes (via a bacteriophage) and to acquire an intestinal attachment organelle that also serves as the toxin phage receptor (also via a phage), and this expansion placed both of these virulence attributes under the control of ToxR.

Regulation of virulence genes also takes place at the level of genome structure. Amplification of gene copy number enables up-regulation of gene product expression. Gene rearrangements are responsible for antigenic variation in such diverse pathogens as *Neisseria gonorrhoeae* (see Chapter 52), *Borrelia recurrentis* (see Chapter 65), and *Trypanosoma brucei* (see Chapter 85). Changes in DNA or RNA conformation can also effect modulation of gene expression.

ADHERENCE & COLONIZATION

Attachment to host substrates is an early and critical step for most pathogens. Those organisms that remain outside a host cell often rely on redundant and complementary attachment systems to ensure continued colonization of the host. In some cases, the expression of an attachment factor (ie, adhesin) alone confers on a microbe the ability to cause disease. In many other cases, adhesins and their cognate host receptors determine host species specificity for the pathogen, as well as tissue or organ tropism, and cell specificity. For many of the reasons described above, adhesin expression is regulated. The dominant adhesin for *Bordetella pertussis* is the 220-kDa protein filamentous hemagglutinin. Because filamentous hemagglutinin is the most abundant secreted protein for this organism, consuming a considerable proportion of the cell's resources for expression, it is important for *B pertussis* to make this protein only when it is needed. Thus, it is placed under the control of a two-component system.

Microbial adherence is critical for microbe-microbe interactions and the formation of biofilms. Bacteria such as *Staphylococcus* spp. secrete a polysaccharide slime substance that enables them to colonize foreign material and exclude antimicrobial agents. Surfaces of foreign and natural acellular material in the human body provide a substrate for microbial community development. On the tooth surface, for example, a diverse but well-ordered community of bacteria form a biofilm that begins on a layer of host proline-rich proteins and relies on many different binding interactions between bacterial receptors and ligands. The streptococci and *Actinomyces* spp. are among the "early colonizers," whose presence is nec-

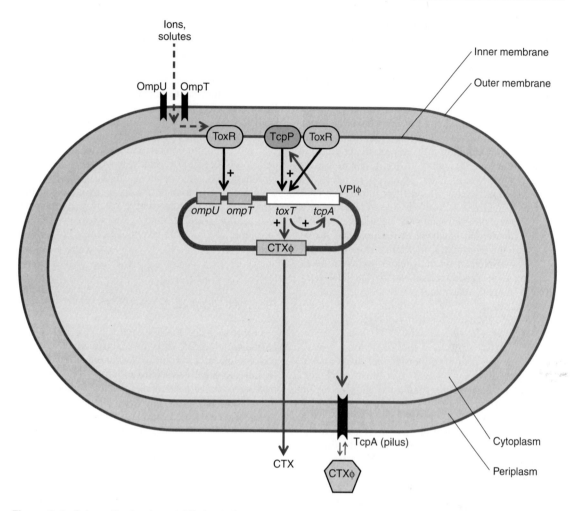

Figure 3–1. Schematic drawing of *Vibrio cholerae,* its chromosomally integrated prophages, and the regulation of cholera toxin (CTX) expression. ToxR is a transmembrane protein that activates expression of chromosomal genes encoding the porins OmpU and OmpT under certain osmotic conditions. In collaboration with the transmembrane protein TcpP, it also regulates expression of the transcriptional activator ToxT, which in turn is responsible for cholera toxin expression, and the pilin subunit TcpA expression. ToxT and TcpA are encoded by the integrated VPIϕ prophage, and CTX by the CTXϕ prophage. The CTXϕ phage uses the TcpA pilus as a receptor for entry into *V cholerae.*

essary before "late colonizers" such as *Porphyromonas gingivalis* and treponemes can attach.

Complex multimeric structures are critical for the attachment of many microbial pathogens. The hairlike bacterial appendage known as a pilus (or fimbria) is a well-characterized example. Pili are composed of structural subunits arranged in a helical fashion, extending out from the bacterial surface. They are flexible and are often capped by adhesin proteins that provide diverse binding specificities. Pili mediate lectinlike interactions with host cells and are also recognized by protein receptors. Regulated expression and assembly of pili are highly orchestrated and involve clusters of cotranscribed genes organized as an operon. Because pilin proteins are often

antigenic, their expression and structure are variable. A class of protozoa shares a different sort of attachment organelle, known as the apical complex. This polar structure found on *Toxoplasma* spp., *Cryptosporidium* spp., and other "apicomplexans" controls host cell attachment through an active mechanism and secretes factors necessary for entry of the protozoan into host cells in some cases.

Pathogens often co-opt host attachment proteins and host receptors for their own adherence-related purposes. A wide variety of pathogens coat themselves with host extracellular matrix proteins such as fibronectin in order to bind to extracellular matrix receptors such as integrins. In this way, extracellular matrix proteins act as a molecular bridge between microbe and host cell. Rhinoviruses bind to intercellular adhesion molecule-1, a critical host cell attachment receptor, and HIV binds to CD4 and chemokine receptors on lymphocytes and macrophages, which are critical for antigen recognition and chemotactic responses, respectively.

The particular selection of ligand-receptor combinations by any given microbe dictates the subsequent course of events. These events include induction of up-regulated binding affinity, microbial internalization, and host cell intoxication. In a dramatic example, enteropathogenic *E coli* (and other bacterial pathogens) inject their own receptor into a host cell, using a specialized ("type" III) secretion system, where the receptor subsequently becomes activated by phosphorylation, localized to the host cell membrane and then promotes formation of an unusual host cell cytoskeletal rearrangement, culminating in formation of a "pedestal" on which the bacterium forms an intimate attachment.

TOXINS

Host cell intoxication is one of the oldest-known mechanisms associated with microbial virulence. Toxins block host cellular defenses, elicit or create microbial nutrients, break down anatomic barriers, and facilitate microbial transmission. In some extreme cases, virulence can be entirely ascribed to the action of a secreted toxin; examples include diphtheria and tetanus. In these cases, antitoxin immunity is sufficient for protection against disease. But most infectious diseases and pathogenic strategies are not that simple. Microbial toxins exist in many forms and with many different activities. Some are intrinsic to the microbial cell wall, such as the lipopolysaccharide (or endotoxin) of gram-negative bacteria, while other toxins are secreted (exotoxins), either nonspecifically from the cell or through specialized secretion systems, such as the type III and type IV systems, directly into a host cell. Exotoxins of the first type usually facilitate their own entry into a host cell by means of a binding subunit that may take advantage of host cell internalization pathways. In a manner and for reasons similar to those described for adhesins, toxin expression is often tightly regulated.

Microbial toxins can be classified on the basis of shared mechanisms of action. The nature of the host cell receptor or molecular target, the mechanism of activation, or the intracellular trafficking of a microbial toxin may determine its specificity of effect. One of the most well-known families of microbial exotoxins is the group of bacterial ADP-ribosylating toxins, which includes diphtheria toxin, cholera toxin, pertussis toxin, *E coli* heat-labile enterotoxin, and *Pseudomonas* exotoxin A. Each catalyzes the transfer and covalent binding of ADP-ribose from NAD to a target protein. The different targets explain the diverse biological outcomes of these toxins. Sometimes, the explanation for difference in effect lies elsewhere. Tetanus and botulinum toxins are zinc metalloproteases that enter motor neurons at the neuromuscular junction. They cleave the same group of proteins within neurotransmitter-containing vesicles. But the clearly distinct neurological results of this action, flaccid and spastic paralysis, can be explained by differential intracellular trafficking of these two toxins: botulinum toxin remains in the terminal neuron at the neuromuscular junction where excitatory neurotransmitters are normally released, while tetanus toxin is transported in a retrograde fashion across the interneuron synapse where inhibitory neurotransmitters are normally released. Other families of microbial toxins include pore-forming hemolysins, secreted adenylate cyclase toxins, RNA glycosidases, and superantigens.

ENTRY INTO & LIFE WITHIN HOST CELLS

For viruses and more specialized bacterial and eukaryotic pathogens, entry into a host cell is an essential feature of their survival or replication strategy within the host. Intracellular entry can be either a passive or active process on the part of either participant. Although most microbes that routinely enter host cells find the intracellular compartment a favored site for replication, this is not always the case; some may be simply passing through on their way to deeper portions of a tissue or the bloodstream (eg, *Neisseria meningitidis* and the Whipple's disease bacillus *Tropheryma whippelii*) or may remain inside a cell in a nonreplicating state. Only those agents that replicate inside a host cell or exist primarily within host cells rather than outside them are properly defined as intracellular pathogens. The inside of a host cell offers a number of significant features for a microbe. First, there may be essential nutrients, macromolecular synthetic machinery, and sources of energy. Organisms that can replicate only when inside a host cell (eg, viruses or *Coxiella burnetii*) are obligate intracellular pathogens, while those that can replicate both inside and outside (eg, *Salmonella* serovar Typhimurium) are facultative intracellular pathogens. Second, the intracellular compartment offers protection from a variety of extracellular microbicidal factors. Third, it may provide a ready means for dissemination. Pathogens (eg, *Salmonella* spp. or HIV) that persist or grow within leukocytes may be carried to distant sites within the host by these cells. For *Legionella* spp., the internal compartment of a free-living amoeba provides a protected niche in external freshwater environments. Encystment of the amoebae allows persistence of the two symbionts under environmental conditions that are unfavorable for growth.

Intracellular pathogens take advantage of many naturally occurring internalization pathways in professional phagocytic cells, as well as creating their own opportunities and pathways in nonprofessional phagocytes. Leukocyte integrin receptors mediate host cell-cell contact, communication, and development; they also mediate internalization or attachment of complement-coated microbes, as well as those that express their own integrin ligand (eg, *B pertussis* filamentous hemagglutinin). Entry through this route does not necessarily trigger an oxidative burst; ie, microorganisms can survive this process. Fc receptors on phagocytes offer another route for entry, but they target the subsequent phagocytic compartment for fusion with lysosomes. Most intracellular pathogens seek to avoid this event. For example, the highly successful intracellular pathogen *Toxoplasma gondii*, if forced to bind to Fc receptors, will die within a host cell.

Entry into nonprofessional phagocytes is usually either induced by the pathogen or forced by the pathogen through an active process. These entry processes require actin polymerization in most cases. Induced entry involves manipulation of the host cell actin cytoskeleton, through a zipperlike mechanism. Host cell receptors that are coupled to the host cell cytoskeleton, such as dystroglycan, E-cadherin, and integrins, provide internalization pathways of this sort for microbes (*Mycobacterium leprae* and arenaviruses, *Listeria monocytogenes,* and *Yersinia* spp., respectively), even though the usual role for these receptors may involve cell adhesion. On the other hand, induced entry is sometimes a more dramatic event, when microbes elicit membrane ruffling to become internalized. *Shigella* and *Salmonella* spp. both secrete proteins into nonprofessional host cells that cause this type of event (a trigger mechanism) through interactions between these effector proteins (eg, *Salmonella* SopE) and host low-molecular-weight GTP-binding proteins of the Rho family. Active, forced entry is described for the apicomplexan parasites, which rely on their own actin-based contractile skeleton and attachment proteins localized near the apical complex to pull the host membrane around them.

Intracellular pathogens choose different sorts of anatomic compartments for themselves, once inside (Table 3–2). To a large degree they create or modify these compartments by selecting entry receptors and then by secreting a variety of factors. All pathogens are encompassed by a vacuolar membrane immediately upon entry. Some remain within this vacuole and allow it to mature through the endocytic pathway and fuse with lysosomes. *Coxiella burnetti* requires the acidic environment of a phagolysosome for completion of its lifecycle. Others block phagosomal development and modify intravacuolar conditions to suit their needs. *Legionella pneumophila,* for example, recruits mitochondria and other organelles so that they surround the vacuole. Finally, some pathogens destroy the vacuolar membrane quickly and escape into the host cell cytoplasm. *L monocytogenes* illus-

Table 3–2. The preferred intracellular niches for some microbial pathogens.

Intracellular Niche		Examples
Host cell vacuole	Fully acidified?	
	No	*Toxoplasma gondii*
	No	*Mycobacterium tuberculosis*
	Slowly	*Salmonella* serovar Typhimurium
	Yes	*Coxiella burnetti*
	No	*Legionella pneumophila*
	Yes	*Leishmania mexicana*
Host cell cytoplasm		*Listeria monocytogenes*
		Shigella flexneri
		Rickettsia prowazekii
		Trypanosoma cruzi

trates this last strategy. Listeriolysin-O lyses the vacuole membrane and is required for bacterial virulence. Once in the cytoplasm, *L monocytogenes* induces actin polymerization at one bacterial pole and is thereby pushed through the cytoplasm at the end of a comet tail-like structure (see Chapter 51). The bacterium moves from the inside of one cell to the inside of an adjacent cell through protrusions of host cell membrane and subsequent engulfment by the next cell. *Shigella* and *Rickettsia* spp. and vaccinia virus also induce the same kind of actin-based movement within host cell cytoplasm.

MANIPULATION OR AVOIDANCE OF THE HOST IMMUNE RESPONSE

Coevolution and adaptation of host with pathogen are well illustrated by the extensive efforts of pathogens to evade, subvert, or co-opt the wide array of host immune defenses. These efforts include the establishment of latency, antigenic variation (described above), inhibition of antigen processing or presentation, inhibition of phagocytosis or oxidative burst, inhibition or stimulation of cytokine responses, anticomplement strategies, induction or inhibition of apoptosis, and inhibition of lymphocyte homing (Table 3–3). Viruses provide many examples, although they are by no means the exclusive operators of these mechanisms. Apoptosis (programmed cell death) is a common host cell antivirus defense mechanism. Some viruses, such as papillomaviruses and adenoviruses, prevent host cell apoptosis by expressing proteins that bind to the host cell cycle control proteins p53 and Rb. It makes sense that papillomavirus would want to promote the growth of its host cell, the squamous cell of the skin, since this cell is terminally differentiated and poorly able to replicate.

Table 3–3. Strategies used by pathogens to subvert normal host defenses.[1]

Mechanism	Example (Pathogen, Virulence factor)[2]
Induction of host cell apoptosis	• *Shigella* spp. IpaB • *Salmonella* spp. SipB • *Yersinia* spp. YopJ
Prevent host cell death or promote growth	• Papillomavirus E6, E7 • Adenovirus E1B • Herpesvirus Bcl-2 homologs • KSHV IL-8R homolog • CMV gpUL40 (up-regulates HLA-E)
Interfere with host cell signaling	• *Yersinia* spp. YopH (tyrosine phosphatase)
Interfere with antigen presentation	• *Mycobacterium tuberculosis* • Adenovirus E3 • CMV US11, US6
Protect host cell from oxidative stress	• *Molluscum contagiosum* virus MC066L selenoprotein
Interfere with cytokine responses	• Poxvirus soluble IL-1R • KSHV IL-6 homolog • EBV IL-10 homolog • Cowpox TNF receptor homolog
Interfere with immunoglobulin or complement	• *Neisseria* spp. IgA protease • HSV gC (blocks complement activation) • *Yersinia* YadA
Disrupt lymphocyte homing	• *Bordetella pertussis* pertussis toxin

[1]Adapted from McFadden G: Even viruses can learn to cope with stress. Science 1998;279:40–41.
[2]If known. Abbreviations: KSHV, Kaposi's sarcoma herpesvirus; CMV, cytomegalovirus; EBV, Epstein-Barr virus; HSV, herpes simplex virus; TNF, tumor necrosis factor; IL, interleukin; HLA, human leukocyte antigen.

Epstein-Barr virus and other herpesviruses express homologs of Bcl-2, a human antiapoptotic protein, whereas molluscum contagiosum virus and herpesviruses produce proteins with death effector domains that interfere with Fas- and tumor necrosis factor receptor-1–associated apoptotic signaling pathways. In contrast, a number of bacterial pathogens induce apoptosis as a means of eliminating host defense cells (eg, activated macrophages).

Disruption or co-optation of cytokine-mediated host responses is also a common pathogen counterdefensive strategy. Kaposi's sarcoma herpesvirus (human herpesvirus 8) encodes homologs of the human chemoattractant cytokines macrophage inflammatory protein-1α and RANTES that are biologically active. They are angiogenic and also compete with other ligands for their cognate chemokine receptors. Kaposi's sarcoma herpesvirus produces a version of interleukin-6 that signals through the same proinflammatory pathways as does the human homolog. Finally, Kaposi's sarcoma herpesvirus expresses a G-protein–coupled receptor that is homologous to the human interleukin-8 receptor. It stimulates constitutive host cell proliferation. Poxviruses encode a soluble form of the human interleukin-1 receptor. Deliberate disruption of the viral gene in animal models of poxvirus infection causes more fulminant disease. It is believed that this soluble receptor downregulates the effects of host interleukin-1, which is elicited by the virus and which would otherwise kill the host before the virus has had adequate time for replication.

TRANSMISSION & LIFE OUTSIDE THE MAMMALIAN HOST

Transmission of pathogens is essential to their ultimate survival. Some rely on arthropod (biological) or mechanical vectors; this is especially true of pathogens that reside in nonhuman animal reservoirs (zoonotic agents; see Chapter 90). Adaptation to and recognition of vector niches are increasingly well understood for these microbes. The agent of Lyme disease, *Borrelia burgdorferi,* for example, expresses certain outer surface proteins only when it is in the tick and expresses others only when it is in a human. Other pathogens rely on human disease symptoms such as cough and diarrhea for transmission. Any pathogen that spends significant time in an external inanimate environment must find a strategy for surviving harsh conditions. Sporulation or encystation is one strategy. Another is incorporation within the integument or internal structures of another life form; for example, *V cholerae* attaches to algae and copepods during the periods that it spends in brackish estuarine aquatic environments. The bridging of the environmental sciences with medical microbiology will be an important step in further elucidating this poorly understood phase in the life of microbial pathogens.

REFERENCES

Cotter PA, Miller JF: *In vivo* and *ex vivo* regulation of bacterial virulence gene expression. Curr Opin Microbiol 1998;1:17.

Finlay BB, Falkow S: Common themes in microbial pathogenicity revisited. Microbiol Mol Biol Rev 1997;61(2):136.

Groisman EA, Ochman H: Pathogenicity islands: bacterial evolution in quantum leaps. Cell 1996;87:791.

Guiney DG: Regulation of bacterial virulence gene expression by the host environment. J Clin Invest 1997;99:565.

Hueck CJ: Type III protein secretion systems in bacterial pathogens of animals and plants. Microbiol Mol Biol Rev 1998;62:379.

Hultgren SJ, et al: Pilus and nonpilus bacterial adhesins: assembly and function in cell recognition. Cell 1993;73(5):887.

Marrack P, Kappler J: Subversion of the immune system by pathogens. Cell 1994;76:323.

Miao EA, Miller SI: Bacteriophages in the evolution of pathogen-host interactions. Proc Natl Acad Sci USA 1999;96:9452.

Wilson M, Seymour R, Henderson B: Bacterial perturbation of cytokine networks. Infect Immun 1998;66:2401.

4

General Principles of Antimicrobial Therapy

Walter R. Wilson, MD

Anti-infective agents such as inorganic salts, myrrh, and acidic solutions have been used topically for centuries. For several hundred years, European and Arabic physicians noted that the administration of heavy metals such as arsenic, mercury, or bismuth was effective against syphilis and other infections. The modern era of antimicrobial chemotherapy began in the 1930s with the introduction of sulfonamides and gathered momentum in the 1940s with the discovery of penicillin and streptomycin. Currently, antimicrobial agents are among the most widely used classes of drugs. Worldwide expenditures for antimicrobial agents exceed $20 billion annually, and antimicrobial agents represent 20–40% of drugs administered to hospitalized patients. Although the choice of a single agent or a combination of agents should be individualized for each patient, certain general principles of therapy should guide the selection of specific drugs. The following factors are important in determining appropriate antimicrobial therapy for patients with bacterial or fungal infections. The drugs of choice for the treatment of infections are discussed in the chapters on specific infections. Antimicrobial therapies for mycobacterial, fungal, parasitic, and viral infections are discussed in their respective chapters.

ETIOLOGIC AGENT & SUSCEPTIBILITY TESTING

The identification and antimicrobial susceptibility of an etiological agent(s) are the most important factors in determining the choice of antimicrobial therapy. When a microorganism is identified and its susceptibilities are known, specific antimicrobial therapy may be administered. In general, the agent selected should be bactericidal, have a narrow spectrum, be well tolerated, and be cost effective. However, in many instances, empiric therapy must be instituted before such information is known. For empiric therapy, the choice of a single drug or a combination of drugs should be based on the suspected site of infection and knowledge of which microorganisms are likely to cause infection in a specific site.

For example, the bacteria that most likely cause community-acquired pneumonia are *Streptococcus pneumoniae, Haemophilus influenzae, Branhamella catarrhalis, Mycoplasma pneumoniae,* or *Chlamydia* spp.; acute pyelonephritis is usually caused by *Escherichia coli* or other *Enterobacteriaceae,* a soft-tissue infection is usually caused by *Streptococcus pyogenes* or *Staphylococcus aureus;* and otitis media is usually caused by *S pneumoniae, H influenzae,* or *B catarrhalis.*

Most infections may be treated with a single antimicrobial agent. However, in either specific or empiric therapy, it may be necessary to administer a combination of drugs. Synergistic combinations of drugs may be necessary to treat certain infections such as some central nervous system infections or prosthetic valve endocarditis or to treat serious infections caused by enterococci. In other infections, synergistic combinations may be advantageous for the therapy of infections caused by a resistant microorganism or for infections involving a site where antimicrobial penetration is reduced, such as endocarditis, osteomyelitis, or meningitis (Table 4–1). Combination therapy may be necessary for the treatment of polymicrobial infections such as intra-abdominal or pelvic infections. In febrile neutropenic patients or other immunocompromised hosts, combination therapy for empiric or specific treatment may be preferable to single-drug therapy.

Appropriate cultures should be obtained before starting antimicrobial therapy. An exception to this rule is a patient with acute bacterial meningitis. In these patients, blood cultures should be obtained and antimicrobial agents administered, and spinal fluid cultures may be obtained as soon as possible after onset of therapy (see Chapter 7).

A Gram stain of an appropriate specimen is the most useful and cost-effective method for rapid diagnosis. Immunologic methods for antigen detection, polymerase chain reaction, and DNA probes are described in Chapter 6. Antimicrobial susceptibility tests should be performed using disk diffusion, agar dilution, E-testing, or other standard methodology on most bacterial pathogens, and antimicrobial therapy adjusted as necessary according to the results.

Table 4–1. Penetration of antimicrobial agents into the cerebrospinal fluid.

Therapeutic concentration with or without inflammation
  Metronidazole
  Rifampin
  Chloramphenicol
  Sulfonamides
  Trimethoprim
Therapeutic concentration with inflammation
  Penicillin
  Ampicillin[1]
  Ticarcillin[1]
  Piperacillin[1]
  Mezlocillin
  Nafcillin
  Oxacillin
  Ceftriaxone
  Ceftizoxime
  Cefotaxime
  Ceftazidime
  Cefepime
  Cefuroxime
  Aztreonam
  Imipenem
  Meropenem
  Fluoroquinolones[2]
  Vancomycin
  Flucytosine
  Fluconazole
Nontherapeutic concentration with or without inflammation
  Aminoglycosides
  Cefoperazone
  Clindamycin
  First-generation cephalosporins
  Second-generation cephalosporins[3]
  Ketoconazole
  Itraconazole[4]
  Amphotericin preparations[4]
  Macrolides

[1]Penetration of beta-lactamase inhibitors, sulbactam, clavulanate, and tazobactam may not achieve therapeutic concentrations.
[2]Fluoroquinolones that achieve therapeutic concentrations are ciprofloxacin, ofloxacin, levofloxacin, gatifloxacin, and moxifloxacin.
[3]Cefuroxime achieves therapeutic concentrations.
[4]Achieves therapeutic concentration for treatment of *Cryptococcus neoformans*.

DOSAGE & ROUTE OF ADMINISTRATION

Once the decision is made to initiate antimicrobial therapy, the next choice is between oral and parenteral administration, with the later either intravenous or intramuscular. The oral administration is appropriate for mild to moderately severe infections in patients with a normally functioning gastrointestinal tract. Some antimicrobial agents, such as vancomycin, quinupristin-dalfopristin, and aminoglycosides, are not absorbed after oral administration. They must be administered parenterally. Others, like fluoroquinolones and trimethoprim-sulfamethoxazole, have excellent bioavailability after oral administration and may be administered orally even in patients with serious infections.

The mechanism of bacterial killing by antimicrobial agents affects decisions regarding the amount of drug administered, the frequency, and the route of administration (Table 4–2). There are two major mechanisms of bactericidal activity by antimicrobial agents (Table 4–3). The first is characterized by saturation of the rate of killing by concentrations of antibiotic at or near the minimum inhibitory concentration (MIC) of the microorganism. Accordingly, increasing the concentration of drug in serum does not result in an increased rate or magnitude of bacterial killing. With these drugs, the duration of time of drug concentration in serum or tissue that exceeds the MIC is the major determinant of bacterial killing. This time-dependent killing is observed with beta-lactams, vancomycin, macrolides, and clindamycin. This phenomenon should be considered when selecting optimal dosing of these antimicrobial agents. Failure to do so may result in administration of unnecessarily high or frequent dosages. With this mechanism of killing, the dosage of an antimicrobial agent should be adjusted so that the concentration in serum exceeds the MIC for 40–50% of the dosing interval. However, in bacterial meningitis, infective endocarditis, or other infections in sites with diminished antibiotic penetration, the administration of higher dosages of antimicrobial agents, often at more frequent intervals, may be necessary to ensure an adequate concentration of drug at the site of infection.

The second major mechanism of bactericidal activity is characterized by concentration-dependent killing. The higher the concentration of drug in serum or tissue, the greater the rate and magnitude of killing. This mechanism of killing occurs with aminoglycosides and fluoroquinolones. Additionally, these two drugs and others that inhibit bacterial protein synthe-

Table 4–2. Major mechanism of killing by antimicrobial agents.

Bacterial or fungal cell wall synthesis
  Penicillins
  Cephalosporins
  Vancomycin
  Carbapenems—imipenem, meropenem
  Monobactams
Cell membrane effect
  Azoles-ketoconazole, fluconazole, itraconazole
Inhibit protein synthesis
  Aminoglycosides—30S ribosome
  Tetracyclines—30S ribosome
  Macrolides, clindamycin, chloramphenicol—50S ribosome
  Rifampin—DNA-dependent RNA polymerase
  Fluoroquinolones—DNA gyrase, topoisomerase IV
  Quinupristin-dalfopristin—50S ribosome
  Oxazolidinones-linezolid—blocks initiation complex ribosomal protein synthesis
  Metronidazole—altered DNA
  Flucytosine—inhibit DNA synthesis
Folic acid synthesis
  Trimethoprim-sulfamethoxazole

Table 4–3. Mechanism of bactericidal activity.

Time above MIC
β-Lactams
Vancomycin
Clindamycin
Macrolides
Concentration dependent
Aminoglycosides
Fluoroquinolones
Metronidazole

sis, such as macrolides, rifampin, and tetracyclines, induce a prolonged post-antibiotic effect on gram-negative bacilli. In contrast, beta-lactams produce minimal or no postantibiotic effect. The phenomenon of concentration-dependent killing supports the concept of single daily dosing for this class of drugs, such as with aminoglycosides and some fluoroquinolones.

Other factors that influence the dosing of antimicrobial agents include the patient's age, renal and hepatic function, and immune status (see next section). Some antimicrobial agents require dosing adjustments in patients with abnormal renal function, and others do not (Table 4–4).

UNDERLYING HOST FACTORS

The underlying conditions of the host, such as history of drug allergy or intolerance, age, renal and hepatic function, and immunosuppression, are major factors which influence the selection of therapy, dosing, efficacy, and safety of antimicrobial agents.

Drug Allergy, Adverse Events, & Drug Interactions

The first factor to be considered in the choice of therapy is a history of adverse drug reactions or al-

Table 4–4. Antimicrobial agents that do not require dosage adjustments in patients with renal failure.

Cephalosporins
Cefoperazone
Ceftriaxone
Macrolides
Erythromycin
Clarithromycin
Azithromycin
Teracyclines
Doxycycline
Minocycline
Fluoroquinolones
Trovafloxacin
Grepafloxacin
Others
Clindamycin
Metronidazole
Chloramphenicol
Rifampin

lergy (Table 4–5). Failure to do so may result in serious or fatal consequences. Additionally, one should review carefully other medications administered concomitantly. Numerous drug interactions with antimicrobial agents have been reported. These may result in decreased absorption of orally administered antimicrobial agents or may result in or potentiate serious drug toxicity resulting from the concomitant drug, the antimicrobial agent, or both. The potential drug interactions are so numerous and newly described interactions are reported so frequently that it is difficult, if not impossible, for the practicing physician to be aware of all of these interactions. Computer software programs are available to identify potential drug interactions. It is important for the patient and the care team, which includes the physician, nursing staff, and pharmacist, to provide accurate and complete information regarding a history of drug allergy, intolerance, or concomitant medications before antimicrobial agents are prescribed.

Age

Patient age, especially at the extremes of lifespan, is a major factor that influences appropriate antimicrobial therapy. Elderly patients may have a normal serum creatinine, but creatinine clearance decreases with age. Antimicrobial agents that are renally excreted may require reduction in dosages in elderly patients, including those with a normal serum creatinine. Failure to recognize this factor may result in accumulation of toxic concentrations of antimicrobial agents in serum that may produce serious consequences, including central nervous system manifestations such as seizures or coma, nephrotoxicity, hepatotoxicity, or ototoxicity. Similarly, renal function is diminished in neonates. Dosages of antimicrobial agents that are excreted by the kidneys should be altered.

Hepatic function is underdeveloped in neonates. Chloramphenicol is metabolized in the liver. High serum concentrations of unconjugated chloramphenicol may occur in neonates, resulting in severe toxicity, such as shock and cardiovascular collapse (gray-baby syndrome). Chloramphenicol should not be administered to neonates. Sulfonamides compete with bilirubin for binding sites on serum albumin and, when administered to neonates, increase the concentrations of unbound bilirubin in serum, which may result in kernicterus. Consequently, sulfa drugs should not be administered to neonates.

Tetracyclines readily pass the placental barrier and bind to bone and teeth of neonates and children; therefore, the use of tetracyclines should be avoided in this age group. Fluoroquinolones cause arthropathy and cartilage damage in puppies and have not yet been approved for use in children. Fluoroquinolone use should be avoided, if possible, in children who are <15 years of age.

Table 4–5. Toxicities of antimicrobial agents.

Antimicrobial Agent(s)	More Common	Less Common
Penicillins and cephalosporins	Hypersensitivity; gastrointestinal; diarrhea; disulfiram with Methyltetrathiazole side chain (cefamandole, cefoperazone, cefotetan)	Bone marrow suppression; nephrotoxicity; hypoprothrombinemia with methyltetrathiazole side chain; hepatotoxocity with β-lactamase inhibitors
Carbapenems and monobactams	Nausea, metallic taste with imipenem; seizures with imipenem	Hypersensitivity with aztreonam
Fluoroquinolones	Gastrointestinal; phototoxicity with lomefloxacin, sparfloxacin	Hypersensitivity; cartilage damage (young patients); central nervous system; QT interval prolongation—sparfloxacin; Achilles tendon rupture; hepatic-trovafloxacin
Macrolides	Gastrointestinal; thrombophlebitis—erythromycin	Hypersensitivity; transient hearing loss—erythromycin
Trimethoprim-sulfamethoxazole	Hypersensitivity	Gastrointestinal; Stevens-Johnson syndrome
Aminoglycosides	Nephrotoxicity	CN[1]-VII; neuromuscular blockade
Vancomycin	Red man syndrome—histamine mediated	CN[1]-VIII; neuromuscular blockade
Clindamycin	Diarrhea	Hypersensitivity, gastrointestinal—nausea, vomiting
Metronidazole	Gastrointestinal—nausea, vomiting, metallic taste	
Tetracyclines	Phototoxicity; impaired bone growth and teeth discoloration in pediatric patients; skin, mucous membranes Discoloration with prolonged minocycline use	Gastrointestinal; hypersensitivity; hepatitis; dizziness with minocycline; lupus phenomena; pseudotumor cerebri
Rifampin	Orange secretions	Hypersensitivity; hepatic, bone marrow suppression
Quinupristin-dalfopristin	Muscle pain	Hypersensitivity; hepatitis
Oxazolidinones; linezolid	Gastrointestinal, headache	Bone marrow suppression; hypersensitivity
Chloramphenicol	Bone marrow suppression	Aplastic anemia; gray baby syndrome; neurotoxicity; gastrointestinal; hypersensitivity
Amphotericin compounds; amphotericin B; deoxycholate	Infusion-fever, nausea, vomiting, headache, hypotension, hypertension, flushing, myalgias, nephrotoxicity	Hepatic; anemia; neurotoxicity
Lipid complex;	Hypokalemia, hypomagnesemia	Infusion related; nephrotoxicity, anemia
Cholesterol sulfate	Infusion related; hypokalemia, hypomagnesemia	Nephrotoxicity, anemia
Liposomal	Hypokalemia, hypomagnesemia	Nephrotoxicity; infusion-related anemia
Flucytosine	Gastrointestinal	Bone marrow suppression; hepatotoxicity; hypersensitivity
Azole Ketoconazole	Gastrointestinal; hypersensitivity; gynecomastia; decreased libido; impotence	Hepatotoxicity; decreased synthesis of cortisol; hypertension with prolonged use; alopecia
Fluconazole	Headache; hypersensitivity	Gastrointestinal; hepatotoxicity; alopecia
Itraconazole	Headache; dizziness; hypersensitivity	Gastrointestinal; hepatotoxicity; gynecomastia; impotence; hypertension with prolonged use

[1]CN, cranial nerve.

Other Underlying Conditions

Patients with peripheral vascular disease or shock may not adequately absorb drugs administered intramuscularly. Sulfonamides, nitrofurantoin, or chloramphenicol may cause hemolysis in patients with glucose-6-phosphate dehydrogenase deficiency. Sulfonamides may cause hemolysis in patients with hemoglobinopathies, such as hemoglobin Zurich or hemoglobin H.

Antimicrobial agents must be chosen carefully for administration to pregnant or nursing mothers. Virtually all antimicrobial agents cross the placental barrier to some degree. Macrolides and beta-lactam drugs with the possible exception of ticarcillin, which may cause teratogenic effects in rodents, may be administered safely to pregnant females. Tetracycline use should be avoided in pregnant women as mentioned above. In addition, the administration of tetracycline intravenously has been associated with acute fatty necrosis of the liver in pregnant women. Streptomycin may cause vestibular or ototoxic damage to the fetus.

Most antimicrobial agents administered to women may be detected in the breast milk of nursing mothers, although their concentrations in breast milk are usually low. Sulfonamide and fluoroquinolone use should be avoided, if possible, in nursing mothers. Tetracyclines may be administered to nursing mothers. Tetracyclines are excreted in breast milk, but tetracycline forms an insoluble chelate with calcium in breast milk, which is not absorbed by the nursing child.

The underlying renal and hepatic function must be considered in the choice of antimicrobial agent. The effect of impaired renal function in elderly patients is described above. Tetracyclines (except doxycycline and possibly minocycline) should not be administered to patients with impaired renal function, because the elevated concentrations in serum that result may produce worsening of uremia because of their anti-anabolic effect. Additionally, the elevated serum concentration of tetracycline may result in hepatotoxicity. Antimicrobial agents which are metabolized or excreted primarily by the liver include rifampin, macrolides, clindamycin, metronidazole, some beta-lactams (eg, ceftriaxone and cefoperazone), nitrofurantoin, and some fluoroquinolones (eg, trovafloxacin). The dosages of these drugs do not require adjustment in patients with renal dysfunction but should be reduced in patients with hepatic failure, and some (eg, trovafloxacin and tetracycline) should be avoided or used with extreme caution.

The immunocompromised condition of the patient is a major factor that influences the selection of antimicrobial agents. Combinations of agents may be preferable, at least as initial therapy (see Chapters 23, 24, and 25 on AIDS, febrile neutropenic patients, and organ transplant recipients, respectively).

MONITORING THE RESPONSE TO ANTIMICROBIAL THERAPY

The most important factor in determining the response of patients to antimicrobial therapy is the clinical assessment. Measurement of concentrations in serum may help guide subsequent dosage adjustment in patients who are receiving vancomycin or an aminoglycoside or other agents in the presence of impairment of renal or hepatic functions. The major value in measuring concentrations in serum is to avoid toxicity from excessively high concentrations. After the onset of antimicrobial therapy, repeating cultures such as from blood, urine, or spinal fluid may be useful in selected patients. The determination of serum bactericidal titers is of minimal if any value in assessing the efficacy of therapy, and this test should not be performed routinely.

REFERENCES

Wilhelm MP (editor): Symposium on antimicrobial agents. Mayo Clin Proc 1997;73:994.

Wilhelm MP (editor): Symposium on antimicrobial agents. Mayo Clin Proc 1998;74:78.

Wilhelm MP (editor): Symposium on antimicrobial agents. Mayo Clin Proc 1999;75:86.

Wilhelm MP (editor): Symposium on antimicrobial agents. Mayo Clin Proc 2000;76: In press.

Infection Prevention in Healthcare Settings

5

Cathryn Louise Murphy, RN, PhD, CIC, Susan A Resnik, RN, Dip IC, CIC (Syd), &
Julie Louise Gerberding, MD, MPH

In 1958, the American Hospital Association first recommended that United States hospitals have formal programs to monitor and prevent infections. Early hospital infection control programs dealt primarily with the management and control of staphylococcal outbreaks in nurseries and among surgical patients, and these efforts emphasized teaching the principles of asepsis to clinical staff, monitoring cases of infection, and providing advice on the reprocessing of used equipment and instruments. Since that time, hospital epidemiology has grown in breadth and scope and is recognized as an important component of healthcare quality promotion. In recent years, changes in the healthcare delivery system and increased utilization of non-hospital-based healthcare services have created conditions conducive to the acquisition and spread of infections in long-term care facilities, outpatient clinics, dialysis centers, and the home care environment. Hence, the domain of infection control programs has expanded beyond the hospital to include these settings. The primary goals of a modern infection control program now include the following:

- preventing acquisition and spread of pathogens in healthcare settings, especially among high-risk populations;
- preventing emergence and spread of antimicrobial-agent-resistant pathogens;
- monitoring, analyzing, reporting, and responding to endemic healthcare-associated infections;
- recognizing and controlling outbreaks of infections and related adverse events;
- evaluating and modifying specific clinical procedures and equipment to promote patient safety;
- protecting healthcare workers through immunization programs, recommendations for use of protective apparel, and patient placement and isolation systems;
- preventing transmission of blood-borne pathogens among patients and their healthcare providers.

Principal stakeholders who have been responsible for developing clinical guidelines and supporting the development of programs to achieve these goals include the Centers for Disease Control and Prevention (CDC), the Association for Professionals in Infection Control and Epidemiology, and the Society for Healthcare Epidemiology of America.

This chapter provides healthcare providers with basic information that will enable them to prevent additional transmission of infectious agents in the healthcare setting and to respond appropriately in the event of inadvertent exposure to infectious agents prevalent in the health care environment.

ROLE OF THE INFECTION CONTROL PRACTITIONER

In the United States, early studies demonstrated that an effective infection control program with at least one trained infection control practitioner per 250 occupied hospital beds led to lower infection rates than programs with a lower ratio of expert infection control staff to patients. Most infection control practitioners are nurses, although in some settings physicians, epidemiologists, microbiologists, medical technologists, or specific administrators may coordinate the infection control program. Ideally, the infection control practitioner has experience and knowledge in adult education techniques, epidemiology, patient isolation strategies, and basic patient care. In addition, knowledge of antimicrobial agents, infectious diseases, microbiology, and basic principles of asepsis, sterilization, and disinfection is essential. The infection control practitioner often consults with other staff members on these issues and regularly assesses patient outcomes to evaluate the effectiveness of infection control recommendations. Additionally, the practitioner intervenes when data or direct observation suggests that variation from recommended practice is jeopardizing patient safety, recovery, or well being.

The specific functions performed by the infection

control practitioner vary according to the type and size of the facility as well as the acuity of the patient population. However, regardless of these factors, the practitioner usually is responsible for implementing and evaluating effective prevention and control activities. Additionally, the infection control practitioner ensures that staffers are aware of relevant regulatory and legislative mandates and are equipped to comply with them.

The principal goals for infection control and prevention programs in extended-care and nonhospital settings are identical to those for acute-care settings. These goals are to protect patients, healthcare workers, and visitors and to do so in a manner that is timely, evidence based, and cost effective. Surveillance, development of local policies, intervention to prevent infections, and provision of education and training to the staff provide mechanisms for these goals to be met.

ROLE OF THE HEALTHCARE EPIDEMIOLOGIST

Ideally, the infection control practitioner works in collaboration with a healthcare epidemiologist. Typically, the epidemiologist is a physician trained in infectious diseases, internal medicine, or pediatrics who has special skills or experience in utilizing the basic tools of epidemiologic investigation. This individual usually is employed by the facility or serves as a paid consultant to the facility's infection control service.

The epidemiologist complements the infection control practitioner by providing additional clinical insight into specific problems. In addition, the epidemiologist is often better able to persuade administration and fellow clinicians to support and comply with the recommendations and directives of the infection control program. In some facilities, including nonhospital settings, the size of facility, available resources, or both may dictate the level of involvement of consultants—outside experts in infectious diseases, infection control, and epidemiology—in coordination of the infection control program.

THE INFECTION CONTROL COMMITTEE

In hospitals, the infection control practitioner and the epidemiologist usually interact with a hospital-

based infection control committee (ICC). The ICC includes members with specific areas of expertise and interest, including hospital administration, infectious diseases, surgery, microbiology, pharmacy, occupational health, reprocessing, and other related fields. A primary function of the ICC is to develop and implement infection control policies and procedures. The multidisciplinary nature of the ICC ensures that the specific interests and needs of individual clinical and administrative units within the hospital are represented and addressed in infection control decisions and recommendations. Increasingly, nonhospital facilities also rely on multidisciplinary committees to oversee the infection control program.

INFECTION CONTROL POLICIES & PROCEDURES

ICCs routinely develop local policy positions that address specific clinical issues. These policy positions are often available in a locally focused infection control manual, a useful document that usually includes relevant state or federal standards and regulations. The following sections summarize basic infection control recommendations for common clinical issues. Clinicians should seek additional detail from the infection control manual within their respective facilities. Assisting other staff to comply with appropriate accreditation and regulatory requirements is a key role of the infection control program staff.

The Joint Commission on Accreditation of Healthcare Organizations (JCAHO) stipulates that the goal of hospital infection control is to identify and reduce the risk of infection acquisition and transmission among patients and healthcare providers. Hospitals participating in the JCAHO accreditation process must demonstrate their efforts to achieve this goal. These efforts involve compliance with six specific infection control standards. The standards address staffing and management systems, monitoring and reporting of infections, intervention in outbreaks, and other preventive actions. The JCAHO also accredits infection control components of ambulatory and long-term-care facilities as well as pathology and clinical laboratory services.

The Health Care Financing Administration (HCFA) is a federal agency that, in addition to providing healthcare insurance, surveys and certifies nonhospital healthcare facilities. Facilities surveyed by HCFA are expected to comply with predetermined infection control standards. Similarly, the National Committee for Quality Assurance administers an accreditation program and combines the results with data from a set of standardized performance measures to provide information to healthcare purchasers and consumers on comparative performance of managed-healthcare plans. Finally, several state and federal agencies promulgate regulatory directives that have direct implications for infection control programs. Generally, the infection control team ensures that staffers understand and comply with such requirements.

INFECTION MONITORING & PREVENTION

One of the most important activities of the infection control team is to monitor healthcare-associated infections and related events within the facility. Routine monitoring potentially provides valuable data that can be used to establish the endemic infection or event rate, identify the need for targeted prevention interventions, and assess the effectiveness of specific interventions. The quality and usefulness of data are improved if the system uses methods that are standardized and based on sound epidemiological principles. If a facility intends to compare its data with those collected by others, it is critical that the data be collected in a standard manner and that adjustment be made for relevant intrinsic (eg, severity of illness) and extrinsic (eg, use of central venous catheters) risk factors in the patient population.

The CDC's National Nosocomial Infections Surveillance (NNIS) system is a comprehensive system for standardized monitoring of healthcare-associated infections. By 2000, more than 300 hospitals were contributing data to the NNIS system about surgical-site infections, central venous catheter infections, ventilator-associated pneumonia, and other serious infections among intensive care patients. These data are used to develop risk-adjusted benchmarks that are widely disseminated and that serve as a reference for comparing and monitoring infection rates in comparable hospitals.

The NNIS system recently identified significant reductions of reported infection rates over the past decade. The reasons for these improvements are not entirely known, but activities characterizing hospitals that have reported improvements are presented in Figure 5–1. This model, which is based on the continuous-quality-improvement paradigm, involves initial measurement of infection rates, using standardized case definitions. The second stage involves comparison of data with an aggregate data set such as the benchmarks periodically published by CDC. In the next stage, the comparative data are interpreted locally to identify needed targeted interventions. Multidisciplinary teams of local experts and stakeholders are assembled to help develop and implement these interventions. Finally, follow-up progress is measured and disseminated to local stakeholders to motivate and document ongoing improvements. By default, completion of this final stage actually initiates

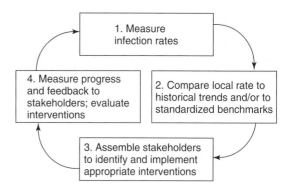

Figure 5–1. Activities characterizing hospitals that have reported significant reductions of infection rates over the past decade.

the first stage of the next continuous-quality-improvement cycle.

Similar strategies have been successful in improving use of antimicrobial agents and limiting resistance to them in some intensive care units. A national system for standardized monitoring of occupational exposures and infections among healthcare personnel (CDC's National Surveillance System for Healthcare Workers) is in the early stages of development. As interest in patient safety and reporting of adverse events increases, it is likely that similar systems for monitoring and motivating improvements will be adopted in other healthcare settings to address infectious diseases and other patient safety issues.

PATIENT ISOLATION

CDC currently advocates a two-tiered approach for infection control and isolation systems. The first tier includes "standard precautions." Standard precautions are precautions recommended for the delivery of care to all patients regardless of their diagnosis or presumed infection status. Standard precautions apply to the following:

- blood;
- all body substances, secretions, and excretions except sweat, regardless of whether they exhibit visible blood;
- nonintact skin;
- mucous membranes.

Standard precautions are designed to limit healthcare exposure to blood or other body substances and include elements such as routine hand hygiene and use of appropriate protective apparel, eg, masks, eye protection, and gloves when needed to prevent direct contact.

The second tier in the infection control and isolation system recommended by CDC encompasses "transmission-based precautions," which are specifically designed for the management of patients known or suspected to be infected with pathogens whose transmission can be limited by the adoption of additional precautions beyond those included as standard precautions. The three defined types of transmission-based precautions are the following:

- airborne-organism precautions, for organisms transmitted by airborne or aerosol routes (eg, agents of tuberculosis or varicella);
- droplet precautions, for organisms transmitted in droplets from airway secretions (eg, *Neiserria meningitidis*);
- contact precautions, for organisms transmitted from person to person via hands, fomites, or environmental sources (eg, vancomycin-resistant enterococci).

The essential components of each individual type of precaution are summarized in Table 5–1.

PREVENTING ANTIMICROBIAL-AGENT-RESISTANT INFECTIONS

The expanding use of broad-spectrum agents in more severely ill patients (eg, critically ill patients in intensive care) and those housed in settings with a high potential for person-to-person transmission (eg, long-term-care facilities) has resulted in emergence and spread of multidrug-resistant pathogens. By 2000, at least 70% of hospital-acquired pathogens were resistant to one or more antimicrobial agents commonly used for treatment. These resistant pathogens adversely affect the outcome of care for many patients and add to the expense of treatment.

Antimicrobial-agent-resistant pathogens emerge and spread through several convergent mechanisms. First, pathogens develop or acquire the genetic traits responsible for resistance. Then they are introduced into healthcare settings via patients, visitors, or healthcare personnel or via contaminated materials. Antimicrobial therapy selects for strains that express the resistance mechanism, which in turn increases their capacity to spread to other patients or personnel.

Previous studies have demonstrated a relationship between the emergence of resistant organisms and inappropriate or extended use of antimicrobial agents, noncompliance with hand hygiene and other infection

control precautions, and indiscriminate use in food animals of products containing antimicrobial agents.

Clinicians can act to prevent the emergence and spread of multidrug-resistant infections in all healthcare settings. Professional societies, healthcare organizations, healthcare purchasers, and federal agencies have mounted efforts to promote judicious antimicrobial use. CDC has developed a series of 12-step programs to prevent infections in various patient settings. These programs emphasize four key strategies: infection prevention (eg, through immunization and decreased use of invasive devices in other procedures); effective pathogen-directed antimicrobial treatment to eradicate infection when present; judicious antimicrobial use; and prevention of person-to-person spread (eg, through effective hand hygiene and patient isolation practices) (Table 5–2). Effective strategies for improving antimicrobial-agent prescription practices are outlined in Table 5–3. Of these, providing individual clinicians or groups with feedback on prescription practices and real-time decision support via computerized pharmaceutical-ordering systems holds the most promise for effecting meaningful improvements.

HAND HYGIENE

Hand hygiene is a critical component of programs to prevent transmission of healthcare-associated infections. When hands or other skin surfaces are contaminated with blood or other body substances, they should be cleaned as soon as practicable. The requirements for hand hygiene apply regardless of whether gloves are worn.

There are three key methods for healthcare personnel to maintain hand hygiene: hand washing, hand antisepsis, and surgical scrubbing. The appropriate method depends on the degree of soiling of the hands, the available equipment and supplies, the nature of the intended work that will be undertaken immediately following hand hygiene, and the susceptibility of the patient with whom the healthcare provider will be in contact.

Hand washing typically involves the use of running water and plain soap to remove soil and transient skin flora. Hand antisepsis is preferred when contact with pathogens is highly likely and when patients are highly susceptible to infection. Removal or destruction of transient flora occurs when personnel perform hand antisepsis using an antimicrobial soap or hand rub. Some commonly used agents for hand antisepsis include products that contain alcohols (eg, *n*-propanol, isopropanol, and ethanol in appropriate concentrations), chlorhexidine gluconate, iodine or

Table 5–1. Summary of the essential elements of recommended isolation precautions.[1]

Element	Standard Precautions	Airborne Precautions	Droplet Precautions	Contact Precautions
Hand washing	Before and after patient contact, regardless of glove use.	As for standard precautions	As for standard precautions	Should be performed using antimicrobial or antiseptic immediately after removal of gloves.
Gloves	To prevent contact with blood and body fluids, mucous membranes, and contaminated equipment.	As for standard precautions	As for standard precautions	Gloves should be worn on entry to patient room and removed before leaving the room.
Masks, eye protection, face shield	To protect against potential splashes/sprays of blood/body fluids.	If susceptible persons must enter the room of a patient with measles or varicella, respiratory protection should be worn; respiratory protection should be worn if patient has infectious pulmonary tuberculosis.	Masks should be worn as for standard precautions and when within 3 ft of patient.	As for standard precautions
Gown	To prevent soiling of clothing; gown material dependent on expected activity and risk of contamination.	As for standard precautions	As for standard precautions	Worn if clothing likely to have contact with environmental surfaces or items or if patient drainage or discharge likely to contaminate clothing.
Patient care equipment, & patient transport	Protective apparel should be worn when handling contaminated equipment; reprocessing should be appropriate for the intended use of the item.	Patient transport should be minimized; droplet nuclei dispersal can be limited by patient wearing a surgical mask during movement.	Patient transport should be minimized; droplet dispersal can be limited by patient wearing a surgical mask during movement.	Equipment should be cleaned or reprocessed between patient use; preferably, equipment should be dedicated for use only by the one patient if possible.
Control of the environment	Cleanliness of the environment should include all surfaces and patient care equipment.	As for standard precautions	As for standard precautions	Equipment and patient care items should be dedicated for single patient use; shared equipment must be cleaned and disinfected before use on another patient.
Linen	Gloves should be worn and careful handling should be used to limit contact with soiled linen and transmission of pathogens in the environment.	As for standard precautions	As for standard precautions	As for standard precautions
Occupational health, blood-borne pathogens	Sharps and needles should be handled, used, and disposed in a manner that limits the risk of occupational exposure.	As for standard precautions	As for standard precautions	As for standard precautions
Patient placement	Private room may be required if soiling of the environment or poor personal hygiene is likely.	Door must be closed; optimally patient requires negative-pressure room, 6–12 changes an hour, external discharge of air, or HEPA filtration before recirculation; if no private room is available, cohort with similar patient.	Private room or if no private room is available cohort with similar patient; a 3-ft zone should separate the patient and other patients or visitors.	Private room preferable or cohorting with similarly infected patient; where private rooms or cohorting are impractical consideration of transmission of pathogens should be undertaken.

[1]Source: Garner JS: *Guideline for isolation precautions in hospitals. Part I. Evolution of isolation practices, Hospital Infection Control Practices Advisory Committee. Am J Infect Control*

Table 5–2. Twelve steps to prevent antimicrobial resistance in hospitalized adults.

Prevent infection
1. Vaccinate.
   Get influenza vaccine.
   Give influenza/*S pneumoniae* vaccine to at-risk patients before discharge.
2. Get the catheters out.
   Use catheters/invasive devices only when essential.
   Use proper insertion/catheter care protocols.
   Remove catheters/invasive devices when no longer essential.

Diagnose and treat infection
3. Target the pathogen.
   Diagnose infection.
   Diagnose the pathogen.
   Diagnose antimicrobial susceptibility.
4. Access the experts.
   Optimize regimen, dose, route, and duration.
   Monitor response.
   Adjust treatment when needed.

Use antimicrobials wisely
5. Practice antimicrobial control.
   Support your local antimicrobial control programs.
6. Use local data.
   Customize antibiograms by:
   Infection site
   Healthcare setting/unit
   Patient population
   Duration of hospitalization
7. Know when to "say no to vanco." (vancomycin)
   Know the MRSA epidemiology in your hospital.
   Fever and an IV are not routine indications for vancomycin treatment.
   MRSA may be sensitive to other antimicrobial agents.
8. Don't treat contaminants.
   Use proper antisepsis for blood cultures.
   Don't routinely culture catheter tips.
   Don't routinely culture through lines.
9. Don't treat colonization.
   Treat pneumonia, not the endotracheal tube.
   Treat urinary tract infection, not the Foley catheter.
   Treat bacteremia, not the catheter tip.
   Treat the bone infection, not the skin flora.
10. Quit when you are ahead.
   Stop antimicrobials . . .
   When infection is not diagnosed
   When infection is unlikely
   When cultures are negative

Prevent transmission.
11. Isolate the pathogen.
   Use standard infection control precautions.
   Contain infectious body fluids by using . . .
   Airborne/droplet/contact precautions
   Cohorting
   When in doubt, use common sense.
12. Break the chain of contagion.
   Keep your hands clean.
   Contain your contagion.
   Keep your hands clean.
   Stay home when you are sick.
   Set an example!

MRSA, methicillin-resistant *Staphylococcus aureus;* IV, intravenous line.

Table 5–3. Effective strategies to promote judicious antimicrobial use.

Prescriber education
Formulary restrictions
   Prior approval to start/continue
Standardized antimicrobial order forms
Drug utilization evaluation
Pharmacy substitution or switch (eg, IV to oral)
Performance feedback
   On-line ordering/decision support

iodophors, *para*-chloro-*meta*-xylenol, and triclosan. The optimal duration of either hand washing or hand antisepsis is not clearly defined, but most experts suggest that hand washing for 15–30 s is sufficient. Manufacturers' instructions should be followed for determining the duration of hand contact with antiseptics.

The most aggressive form of hand hygiene is the surgical scrub. The surgical scrub is undertaken to remove or destroy transient flora and to reduce the resident flora so that surgical wounds will not be contaminated even if gloves are torn. If an antimicrobial soap or detergent is used, personnel should use a brush and an action that involves friction for a minimum of 2 min. Care must be taken to include nail beds, wrists, and all surfaces of the hand.

Clinician compliance with hand hygiene recommendations is universally poor. Accordingly, hand hygiene should be encouraged whenever there is any doubt about the need to do so. Hand-washing facilities should be easily accessible and supplied with clean, running water and either soap or an antiseptic hand-washing agent. When clean, running water is inaccessible, waterless antiseptic agents such as alcohol-based hand rubs or foam products may provide acceptable alternatives.

ASEPSIS

Asepsis refers to the absence of microorganisms that are capable of causing disease. Healthcare workers routinely use the following methods to provide healthcare aseptically:

- cutaneous antisepsis—skin antisepsis designed to inactivate as much of the skin flora as possible;
- cleaning—the removal of soil and organic matter through a physical or mechanical action involving the use of water and a cleaning agent;
- decontamination—a nonspecific term for removal of pathogenic microorganisms from objects or equipment;

- disinfection—the elimination of pathogenic microorganisms, excluding spores, from inanimate objects and environmental surfaces through thermal or chemical means;
- sterilization—the complete destruction of all pathogenic microorganisms including spores through chemical or physical means.

Clinicians should first use an antiseptic solution to prepare a patient's skin for insertion of invasive devices or for other invasive procedures that breach the skin. The goals are to prevent translocation of flora into the wound and egress of flora from adjacent tissue into the wound. When a maximum and immediate antiseptic effect of relatively short duration is required, alcohols are preferred. When a more prolonged duration of antiseptic activity is relevant (eg, during intravenous-catheter insertion), a product containing 2% aqueous chlorhexidine may be superior to plain alcohols or povidone-iodine. For preoperative surgical cutaneous disinfection, an alcohol-based preparation of iodine or povidone-iodine solution is preferred.

The intended use of an item or piece of equipment and manufacturer's instructions dictate its appropriate method of reprocessing, ie, whether cleaning, disinfection, or sterilization is in order. Intact skin provides an effective barrier to most microorganisms; thus, items touching only intact skin require only routine cleaning unless contaminated by blood or other body fluids. Instruments or equipment coming into contact with mucous membranes or nonsterile tissue (other than intact skin) must, before use, be cleaned and then disinfected with a suitable disinfectant. Those instruments or pieces of equipment used to enter or capable of entering tissue that would be sterile under normal circumstances or to enter the vascular system of a patient must be thoroughly cleaned and then sterilized before use.

Proper cleaning to remove organic debris is essential before any disinfection or sterilization procedure. Relevant manufacturer's instructions for equipment, instruments, disinfectants, sterilants, sterilizers, and processors should be followed during reprocessing. Sterilized items should be handled and stored in a manner that ensures the integrity of packing material and prevents contamination of contents from any source. If an item is suspected of being nonsterile or its sterility cannot be guaranteed, the item should not be used.

OCCUPATIONAL HEALTH ISSUES

A core component of any healthcare infection control program is a system that ensures that clinical and nonclinical healthcare personnel can perform their work in an environment where the risk of acquiring or transmitting infection is as low as possible. Provision of education, training, personal protective gear, safety equipment, appropriate patient placement, and protection through immunization or vaccination are strategies routinely used to minimize the risk of transmission of infectious disease from or to healthcare personnel. In 1998, CDC developed a new guideline for infection prevention in healthcare personnel (see Bolyard 1998). This guideline outlines the requirements for an effective occupational health program in healthcare settings and provides specific recommendations for prevention and management of occupational infectious diseases.

INFECTIOUS CONDITIONS OF CONCERN

BLOOD-BORNE PATHOGENS

Blood-borne pathogens are an important concern in healthcare settings. Most attention has been focused on hepatitis B virus (HBV), hepatitis C virus (HCV), and HIV, but any infectious pathogen in the blood can probably be transmitted under some circumstances. HBV is the most highly transmissible of these agents, but vaccination programs have dramatically reduced the proportion of healthcare personnel at risk. For HIV, the best estimate of the average risk associated with punctures by a needle or similar "sharp" contaminated with blood from an HIV-infected patient is still approximately 0.32%. Risk is highest when the exposure involves blood from a patient with preterminal AIDS, the injury is deep, or it is inflicted by a visibly blood-contaminated device that has been used in an artery or vein. Fewer data are available to determine the HCV transmission risk, but current data suggest that approximately 1.9% of HCV-contaminated-needle injuries result in infection.

CDC's standard precautions (above) include measures to prevent exposure to blood and other body fluids, which will in turn prevent transmission of blood-borne occupational infections. The single most important prevention strategy is to eliminate or at least prevent, to the extent technologically possible, injuries caused by needles and other sharps. Reducing the number of needle punctures and injections used for patient treatment is an important and sometimes overlooked component of this effort. Proper training and supervision are also important. Facilities that use trained phlebotomists or other skilled staff to obtain blood samples and insert catheters are often rewarded with fewer injuries and exposures. Technologic improvements in the design of needles and related devices also contribute to safety efforts, provided that their implementation is accompanied by comprehensive training in their safe use and disposal.

Management of an occupational exposure to blood or another body fluid should include the following:

- immediate first aid—cleaning the wound or nonintact skin with soap and water and rinsing exposed mucous membranes with clean water or sterile eye irrigant if available;
- reporting the incident to the relevant supervisor or manager;
- medically assessing the type of exposure and whether indicated postexposure care was provided, including prophylaxis for HBV, HIV, and tetanus;
- documenting the exposure circumstances and characteristics in a confidential medical record;
- collecting a blood specimen from the exposed person to document hepatitis B immune status (if not known) and baseline HIV and HCV serostatus;
- evaluating the status of the source patient's bloodborne infection (eg, by testing for HbsAg, HCV antibody, or HIV antibody with appropriate consent) if exposure circumstances suggest a risk of transmission of blood-borne pathogens;
- follow-up testing for implicated viruses for at least 6 months to identify new infections, if the source patient was infected with that virus and the exposure posed a risk for transmission.

Detailed guidelines for postexposure care, including HBV, HCV, and HIV prophylaxis, have been prepared by CDC and are periodically updated. These documents can be found on the World Wide Web at http://www.cdc.gov/ncidod/hip/Guide/guide.htm.

TUBERCULOSIS

Tuberculosis infection can be acquired and transmitted in healthcare settings. Patients, healthcare personnel, and even visitors have been sources of spread to others. Outbreaks of drug-resistant infection in New York City in the early 1990s, with high attack rates observed among exposed healthcare and prison personnel, illustrate the tremendous morbidity this infection can still cause. Employee health programs in settings where exposure to tuberculosis can reasonably be expected are now charged with the responsibility for conducting surveillance (skin testing) and postexposure follow-up. Current CDC guidelines for preventing tuberculosis transmission in healthcare facilities can be found at http://www.cdc.gov/ncidod/hip/Guide/tb_excerpt.htm.

Tuberculosis prevention in healthcare settings relies first and foremost on prompt recognition and iso-lation of suspected cases. Precautions against airborne infectious agents include appropriate air containment, filtration, and exchange to prevent tuberculosis transmission. Appropriate respiratory protection may provide an additional measure of safety, but it cannot substitute for proper ventilation. Patients suspected of having tuberculosis should be placed in a room that meets the precautionary specifications for such airborne pathogens, including monitored negative air pressure in relation to the surrounding area, 6–12 air changes per hour, and appropriate discharge of air outdoors or monitored high-efficiency filtration of room air before the air is circulated to other areas in the hospital.

If these steps are not feasible in the short run, then patients should at least be advised to don a surgical mask to reduce dissemination of droplets that may desiccate to form infectious aerosols. Healthcare personnel and others sharing air with patients who are known or suspected to have active tuberculosis should use a properly fitted respirator (eg, the N95 respirator—a half-mask filtering face piece respirator rated at least 95% efficient by the National Institute for Occupational Safety and Health [see National Institute for Occupational Safety and Health 1987]). High-risk procedures, eg, bronchoscopy and other cough-inducing procedures, should be performed in isolation rooms with suitable ventilation, by personnel using appropriate respiratory protection.

CDC recommends periodic tuberculin skin tests (TST) for healthcare workers who have the potential for exposure to *Mycobacterium tuberculosis.* Results are used in the clinical management of healthcare workers and in the assessment of the adequacy of infection control measures in healthcare facilities. CDC recommends that the periodicity of routine TSTs be based on an assessment of the risk of transmission of *M tuberculosis* in that particular setting. This includes a profile of TB in the community, the number of infectious TB patients admitted to the area or ward, or the estimated number of infectious TB patients to whom healthcare workers in an occupational group may be exposed, and the results of analysis of healthcare workers' TST conversions, where applicable, and possible person-to person transmission of *M tuberculosis.* Epidemiologic investigations to evaluate the possibility of nosocomial transmission should be conducted when TST conversions are noted. Finally, TST programs should be evaluated periodically to ensure that healthcare workers who should be included are being tested at the appropriate intervals.

VACCINE-PREVENTABLE DISEASES

The CDC's Advisory Committee on Immunization Practices (ACIP) strongly recommends that healthcare personnel with direct patient contact be immunized against HBV, influenza, measles, mumps, and rubella. Depending on the nature of their work, susceptibility, and risk, individual staff may benefit from immunization against hepatitis A virus, meningococcal disease, pertussis, typhoid, and smallpox. Specific recommendations regarding preimmunization screening, dose schedule, indications, precautions, contraindications, and other considerations are contained in the relevant CDC guideline, which is based on the recommendations of the U.S. Public Health Service's Advisory Committee on Immunization Practices that is available at http://www.cdc.gov/epo/mmwr/preview/mmwrhtml/00050577.htm.

Personnel performing work that involves contact with blood or other body fluids containing blood are at greatest risk of acquiring occupational HBV infection. This group should routinely be vaccinated against HBV. Persons vaccinated due to occupational risk do not require prevaccination serologic screening although serologic testing should be undertaken 1–2 months postvaccination to establish and record the serologic response.

Influenza is also gaining appreciation as an important occupational infection. Healthcare personnel are at risk for acquiring and transmitting this pathogen across the entire spectrum of care delivery sites. Despite widespread recognition that immunization of healthcare personnel saves time lost from work, money, and probably lives, most healthcare personnel still do not receive the yearly vaccination. With the growing concern about another global influenza pandemic, emergence of new influenza strains, and advent of new antiviral treatments, influenza detection and prevention are growing components of infection prevention in healthcare settings.

The U.S. Public Health Service's Advisory Committee on Immunization Practices recommends that all healthcare personnel should be immune to varicella. Accordingly, it is prudent to ensure that all healthcare workers are screened for varicella immunity within 2 weeks of commencing duties. Healthcare personnel are considered immune if they have either a positive history of varicella-zoster virus (VZV) infection or proof of varicella immunization. Cases of nosocomial transmission of VZV have been reported, and patients, visitors, and staff have been implicated as sources of infection. Healthcare worker exposure to VZV is considered to have occurred when a susceptible healthcare worker not wearing respiratory protection enters a confined space occupied by a person with active varicella or zoster. A person is also infectious in the 48 h before the appearance of varicella, and contact during this time may also lead to infection in susceptible persons. Airborne precautions should be used in the care of patients with varicella or zoster. Following exposure, healthcare personnel should be assessed and a decision made regarding administration of varicellazoster immune globulin (VZIG). Exposed susceptible healthcare workers should cease work for 8–21 days. Healthcare personnel with varicella are considered fit for duty when they are well enough to return and only when all lesions have dried and crusted, which is most often after 5 days.

NEW & EMERGING AGENTS

Infectious diseases continue to emerge, threatening the health and well being of both patients and healthcare providers. Legionnaires' disease, Lyme disease, AIDS, and the development of drug-resistant strains of tuberculosis, certain pneumonias, and *Staphylococcus aureus* demonstrate the seriousness of emergent infectious diseases. Vigilant compliance with recommended infection control measures and judicious prescribing and dispensing of antimicrobial agents offer two opportunities for healthcare workers to limit the emergence of further infectious disease. Timely identification and reporting of cases of notifiable disease assists in the accurate estimation of the magnitude of the infectious disease problem and in the development of additional preventative and treatment measures.

REFERENCES

Arias KM: *Infection Control Tool Kit Series: Assessing and Developing an Infection Control Program in the Acute Care Setting.* Association for Professionals in Infection Control and Epidemiology Inc., 2000.

Beltrami EM et al: Risk and management of blood-borne infections in health care workers. Clin Microbiol Rev 2000;13:385.

Bolyard EA et al: Guideline for infection control in healthcare personnel, 1998. Hospital Infection Control Practices Advisory Committee. Infect Control Hosp Epidemiol 1998;19:407. Erratum. Infect Control Hosp Epidemiol 1998;19:493.

Cardo DM et al: A case-control study of HIV seroconversion in health care workers after percutaneous exposure. Centers for Disease Control and Prevention Needlestick Surveillance Group. N Engl J Med 1997;337:1485.

Centers for Disease Control and Prevention: Monitoring hospital-acquired infections to promote patient safety–United States, 1990–1999. Morb Mortal Wkly Rep 2000;49:149.

Centers for Disease Control and Prevention: Immunization of health-care workers. Morb Mortal Wkly Rep 1997;46(RR–18).

Fridkin SK et al: Surveillance of antimicrobial use and antimicrobial resistance in United States hospitals: project ICARE phase 2. Project Intensive Care Antimicrobial Resistance Epidemiology (ICARE) hospitals. Clin Infect Dis 1999;29:245.

Friedman C et al: Requirements for infrastructure and essential activities of infection control and epidemiology in out-of-hospital settings: a consensus panel report. Association for Professionals in Infection Control and Epidemiology and Society for Healthcare Epidemiology of America. Infect Control Hosp Epidemiol 1999;20:695.

Graham M: Frequency and duration of handwashing in an intensive care unit. Am J Infect Control 1990;18:77.

Haley RW et al: The efficacy of infection surveillance and control programs in preventing nosocomial infections in US hospitals. Am J Epidemiol 1985;121:182.

Jennings J, Manian F (editors): *APIC Handbook of Infection Control.* Association for Professionals in Infection Control and Epidemiology, 1999.

Larson EL: APIC guideline for handwashing and hand antisepsis in health care settings. Am J Infect Control 1995;23:251.

Maki DG, Ringer M, Alvarado CJ: Prospective randomised trial of povidone-iodine, alcohol, and chlorhexidine for prevention of infection associated with central venous and arterial catheters. Lancet 1991;338:339.

National Center for Infectious Diseases: *Preventing Emerging Infectious Diseases: A Strategy for the 21st Century.* Centers for Disease Control and Prevention, 1998.

National Institute for Occupational Safety and Health: *NIOSH Respirator Decision Logic. DHHS publication (NIOSH)87-108.* U.S. Public Health Service, 1987.

Scheckler WE et al: Requirements for infrastructure and essential activities of infection control and epidemiology in hospitals: a consensus panel report. Society for Healthcare Epidemiology of America. Infect Control Hosp Epidemiol 1998;19:114.

Weber DJ, Rutala WA: Varicella immunization of health care workers. In Panlilio AL, Cardo DM: *Bailliere's Clinical Infectious Diseases: International Practice and Research: Prevention Strategies for Health Care Workers.* Bailliere Tindall, 1999.

Laboratory Diagnosis 6

W. Lawrence Drew, MD, PhD, Franklin R. Cockerill, III, MD, & Nancy K. Henry, PhD, MD

Throughout the world, bacteria and viruses are among the most commonly encountered microbial pathogens in humans. Dimorphic fungi (ie, *Histoplasma capsulatum, Blastomyces dermatitidis, Coccidioides immitis, Sporothrix schenckii,* and *Paracoccidioidomyces brasiliensis*) and most parasites are generally limited to certain geographic areas. Immunocompromised patients are susceptible to common bacterial, viral, and parasitic pathogens that cause disease in normal hosts and to unusual bacterial, viral, fungal, and parasitic pathogens that infrequently cause disease in normal hosts. These latter organisms are opportunists and, owing to humoral or cell-mediated immune dysfunction within the host, may produce life-threatening disease.

Other organisms may cause disease in patients as the result of anatomical-barrier disruption. Endotracheal intubation may permit colonization of the oropharynx with nosocomial pathogens. These include gram-negative bacteria, especially members of the family *Enterobacteriaceae* (eg, *Escherichia coli, Klebsiella* spp., *Enterobacter* spp., *Proteus* spp., and *Serratia* spp), *Pseudomonas* spp., *Stenotrophomonas maltophilia,* or *Burkholderia cepacia;* or gram-positive bacteria, especially methicillin-resistant staphylococci (methicillin-resistant *Staphylococcus aureus* and methicillin-resistant coagulase-negative staphylococci) and vancomycin-resistant *Enterococcus* spp. (VRE) and yeasts. Any of these nosocomial pathogens may colonize the upper respiratory tract and spread to the lower respiratory tract, secondary to endotracheal intubation. VRE may also colonize the lower gastrointestinal tract and be spread from one patient to another by fecal contamination. Mucositis, as the result of total body irradiation and/or chemotherapy, may be associated with septicemia caused by oral flora, especially *Streptococcus* spp. of the viridans group and *Candida* spp. Intravascular catheters may become infected with cutaneous flora or nosocomial pathogens. These organisms include *Staphylococcus* spp., *Streptococcus* spp., and *Corynebacterium* spp., including *Corynebacterium jeikeium,* the same nosocomial gram-positive and gram-negative bacteria described previously, and yeasts. All of these organisms may be introduced into the bloodstream directly if intravenous fluids or medications are injected through an infected catheter port. Alterna-

tively, these organisms may first colonize a proximal port and over time ascend to the catheter tip.

Neutropenia secondary to chemotherapeutic agents is frequently associated with bacteremia. Enteric gram-negative bacteria, notably members of the family *Enterobacteriaceae, Pseudomonas* spp., and the gram-positive organisms *Staphylococcus* spp. or *Enterococcus* spp., account for the majority of these bacteremias. Disseminated fungal infections caused by *Candida* spp. or *Aspergillus* spp. may also occur.

Because of the wide variety of microorganisms (bacteria, fungi, viruses, and parasites) that can cause infections in immunocompromised patients, in some instances, test-ordering protocols may be useful to assure that appropriate specimen processing and analyses are performed. This is especially important for specimens that are obtained by using relatively invasive procedures. For example, a standard battery of microbiology tests should be considered for all specimens obtained by bronchoalveolar lavage or transbronchoscopic, transthorascopic, or open-lung biopsies from immunocompromised patients. For all patients (normal or immunocompromised), the development of disease management strategies for commonly encountered infections may result in more consistent and appropriate use of laboratory tests.

Diagnosis of Bacterial, Fungal, & Parasitic Infections

Franklin R. Cockerill, III, MD, & Nancy K. Henry, PhD, MD

Tables 6–1, 6–2, and 6–3 summarize currently available recommended test methods for the detection of bacterial, fungal, and parasitic pathogens from human specimens. Methods for detection of viral pathogens are discussed later in this chapter. For completeness, the tables include pathogens common to both normal and immunocompromised hosts. Selected specimen collection procedures are shown in Table 6–4. However, this important step in the diag-

Table 6–1. Recommended rapid direct tests for detecting bacteria, fungi, or parasites in human specimens.

Specimen	Stains	Immunologic Tests[1]	Organism(s) Detected
Blood		LA, CIE, COA, FA	*Haemophilus influenzae, Neisseria meningitidis, Streptococcus agalactiae* (group B streptococcus), *Streptococcus pneumoniae*
			Cryptococcus neoformans
	Acridine orange	LA	*Histoplasma capsulatum*
		RIA, EIA	Generally all bacteria but may be especially useful for detecting organisms present at < 10^4 colony forming units (CFU)/ml or organisms that do not stain well with the Gram-stain method, eg, *Bartonella henselae* (agent of cat scratch disease, bacillary angiomatosis, and peliosis hepatis)
	Wright's, Giemsa, or Dark-field examination		*Borrelia recurrentis* (agent of relapsing fever) or other spirochetes
	Giemsa or Diff-Quik (buffy coat)		*Ehrlichia* spp.
	Dark field		*Leptospira* spp.
	Acid-fast or auramine-rhodamine		*Mycobacteria* spp. (occasionally positive when the quantity of organisms is high as may occur with severe immunodeficiency)
	Wright's or Giemsa (thick and and thin smears)		*Plasmodium* spp. (agents of malaria), *Trypanosoma* spp., *Theileria* spp., *Babesia microti*)
	H & E		Microfilariae (*Wuchereria bancrofti, Brugia malayi, Loa loa*)
Cerebrospinal fluid	Gram	LA, CIE, COA, FA	Generally all bacteria, although typical morphologies may not be present in cerebrospinal fluid
			Haemophilus influenzae, Neisseria meningitidis, Streptococcus agalactiae, Streptococcus pneumoniae
		LA	*Cryptococcus neoformans*
	Acid-fast or auramine rhodamine		*Mycobacteria* spp.
	Modified acid-fast		*Nocardia* spp., *Rhodococcus* spp.[2]
	India ink		*Cryptococcus neoformans*
	Giemsa		*Trypanosoma* spp., *Toxoplasma gondii*
	Wet mount phase (contrast), trichrome		*Naegleria fowleri* (agent of primary amebic meningoencephalitis), *Acanthamoeba* spp., *Balamuthia mandrillaris* (agents of chronic granulomatous amebic encephalitis)
	Modified trichrome, acid-fast, Giemsa, calcofluor white, methenamine silver		Microsporidia (*Encephalitozoan* spp.)
Brain tissue	Gram		Generally all bacteria
	Acid-fast or auramine-rhodamine		*Mycobacteria* spp.
	Modified acid-fast		*Nocardia* spp., *Rhodococcus* spp.[2]
	H & E		*Naegleria fowleri* (agent of primary amebic encephalitis), *Taenia solium* (agent of cysticercosis)
Bone marrow	Gram		*Brucella* spp., *Salmonella typhi*
	Acid-fast or auramine rhodamine		*Mycobacteria* spp.
	H & E		*Coxiella burnetii*[3] (agent of Q fever) (organisms are not visualized but perivascular or ring granulomas may be seen, which are characteristic)

Specimen	Stain or method	Test	Organisms
Sterile body fluids other than blood, cerebrospinal fluid, or urine; sterile tissues; exudates or pus	Methenamine silver Giemsa		*Histoplasma capsulatum, Cryptococcus neoformans*, other fungi *Trypanosoma* spp., *Leishmania* spp.
	Gram		Generally all bacteria
	Acid-fast or auramine-rhodamine		*Mycobacteria* spp.
	Modified acid-fast		*Nocardia* spp., *Rhodococcus* spp.[2]
	Warthin-Starry		*Bartonella* spp., *Borrelia* spp.
	Methenamine silver		*Histoplasma capsulatum, Blastomyces dermatitidis, Coccidioides immitis, Sporothrix schenckii*, other fungi
	Giemsa		*Trypanosoma* spp., *Leishmania* spp., *Toxoplasma gondii*
	H & E		Trematodes (*Schistosoma* spp, *Fasciola* spp., *Clonorchis sinensis, Paragonimus westermani*)
	Wet mount		*Echinococcus* spp. (especially lung, liver), *Trichinella spiralis* (muscle)
	Wet mount, trichrome		*Entamoeba histolytica* (especially liver)
	Modified acid-fast		*Cryptosporidium parvum* (especially liver, spleen)
	Acid-fast, Giemsa, modified trichrome, methenamine silver, calcofluor white		Microsporidia (especially muscle, kidney)
	H & E	FA	*Taenia solium* (cysticerci), *Onchocercus volvulus* (nodules), *Trypanosoma cruzi* *Borrelia burgdorferi, Rickettsia* spp.
Eye fluid, tissue	Gram		Generally all bacteria
	Acid-fast or auramine-rhodamine		*Mycobacteria* spp.
	Modified acid-fast	EIA, FA	*Rhodococcus* spp.,[2] *Nocardia* spp.
	Trichrome, Giemsa, calcofluor white		*Chlamydia trachomatis*
	Giemsa		*Acanthamoeba* spp.
	H & E		*Toxoplasma gondii*
	Acid-fast, Giemsa, modified trichrome, methenamine silver, calcofluor white		*Loa loa* Microsporidia

(continued)

Table 6–1. Recommended rapid direct tests for detecting bacteria, fungi, or parasites in human specimens. *(continued)*

Specimen	Stains	Immunologic Tests[1]	Organism(s) Detected
Upper respiratory tract secretions		FA COA, LA, FA	*Bordetella pertussis* *Streptococcus pyogenes* (group A streptococcus)
Lower respiratory tract secretions including bronchial alveolar lavage (BAL), transtracheal or transbronchoscopic aspirates and lung tissue (transbronchoscopic biopsy or open-lung biopsy)	Gram		Generally all bacteria
	Acid-fast or auramine-rhodamine		*Mycobacteria* spp.
	Modified acid-fast		*Nocardia* spp., *Rhodococcus* spp.[2]
		FA	*Legionella* spp. (see also urine, below for *Legionella pneumophila, Pneumocystis carinii*)
	Methenamine silver, calcofluor white		*Pneumocystis carinii, Histoplasma capsulatum, Blastomyces dermatitidis, Coccidioides immitis, Sporothrix schenckii, Paracoccidioides brasiliensis,* and other fungi
	Wet mount		*Ascaris lumbricoides, Strongyloides stercoralis, Paragonimus westermani, Echinococcus granulosa,* and occasionally other parasites including hookworms
	Acid-fast, Giemsa, modified trichrome, methenamine silver, calcofluor white		Microsporidia
	Giemsa Modified acid-fast		*Toxoplasma gondii* *Cryptosporidium parvum*
Urethral exudate (male)	Gram	EIA EIA, FA	*Neisseria gonorrhoeae* *Chlamydia trachomatis*
Cervical or vaginal exudate		EIA EIA, FA EIA, LA	*Neisseria gonorrhoeae* *Chlamydia trachomatis* *Trichomonas vaginalis*
	Wet mount, Giemsa		*Trichomonas vaginalis*
Stomach[4]	Gram; Warthin-Starry or Giemsa (tissue)		*Helicobacter pylori*[4]

Specimen	Stain/method	Test[1]	Organism/comment
Small-bowel or colon tissue	Periodic acid Schiff		*Tropheryma whippelii* (agent of Whipple's disease)
	Acid-fast or auramine-rhodamine		*Mycobacterium* spp.
	H & E		A large variety of protozoa or helminths [nematodes, cestodes (tapeworms), or trematodes] may be identified.
Feces	Wet mount		*Campylobacter jejuni*
	Methylene blue		Evaluation for leukocytes associated with invasive bacterial diarrhea
		EIA [O157 antigen and/or Shiga-like toxin (verocytotoxin)]	*Escherichia coli* O157:H7
		EIA	*Helicobacter pylori*
		EIA, LA	*Clostridium difficile*
		EIA, FA	*Giardia lamblia, Cryptosporidium parvum, Entamoeba histolytica*
	Direct exam for ova and parasites—wet mount and fixed stains (trichrome or iron-hematoxylin)		Permits identification of a large variety of protozoa and helminths [nematodes, cestodes (tapeworms), or trematodes]
	Anal swab		Pinworm
Genital chancre or chancroid lesion (male or female)	Gram		Donovan bodies (associated with *Calymmatobacterium granulomatis*, agent of granuloma inguinale)
	Dark-field examination		*Trepenoma pallidum* (agent of syphilis)
Urine	Gram		Generally all bacteria (observation of ≥2 bacteria per oil immersion field (×1000) in a Gram-stained smear of a drop of unconcentrated urine indicates ~ 10^5 bacteria/ml)
	Acid-fast or auramine-rhodamine		*Mycobacteria* spp.
		EIA	*Chlamydia trachomatis* (males only)
		EIA, RIA	*Legionella pneumophila, Histoplasma capsulatum*
		LA	*Cryptococcus neoformans*
	Dark-field		*Leptospira* spp.
	Wet mount		*Schistosoma haematobium*

[1]LA, Latex agglutination; CIE, counterimmunoelectrophoresis; COA, coagglutination; FA, fluorescent antibody; RIA, radioimmunoassay; H & E, hematoxylin and eosin.
[2]*Rhodococcus* spp. may not stain by the modified acid-fast method.
[3]*Coxiella burnetti* is a rickettsia-like bacterium.
[4]*Helicobacter pylori* can be detected by the rapid urease test on tissue from a stomach biopsy or by the urea breath test.

Table 6–2. Recommended culture methods for detecting bacteria, fungi, and parasites in human specimens.

Specimen	Media[1]	Bacteria

Blood	Broth based systems (manual or automated)
	Effective broths that are most commonly used include tryptic or trypticase soy broth with ~0.025% SPS; one bottle is vented (aerobic), and the second is unvented (anaerobic); manual or automated systems are incubated 5–7 d, or longer if fastidious organisms are anticipated.
	Lysis centrifugation
	Blood is added to a test tube containing saponin, a chemcal which lyses white and red blood cells. The contents are centrifuged and the sediment is cultured to:
	
	  BA and CBA
	  MB7H10, MB7H11, and a BACTEC bottle containing 13A media
	  CBA and TSB-RS
	
	  BRA
	  BCYE
	  BHI, SD, IM
	
	  SD overlaid with olive oil
	  Other
	    FL, EH
	    BSK-H
		Generally all commonly encountered aerobic, facultatively anaerobic, and obligately anaerobic bacteria and many yeasts (*Candida* spp.) can be isolated with broth-based blood culture systems; some fastidious organisms may require prolonged incubation, eg, HACEK[2] bacteria, which most frequently cause endocarditis.
		
		Most aerobic and facultatively anaerobic bacteria (including *Rhodococcus* spp.)
		Mycobacteria spp., *Nocardia* spp.
		
		Bartonella spp. (agents of cat scratch disease, bacillary angiomatosis and peliosis hepatis)
		Brucella spp.
		Legionella spp., *Francisella* spp., *Nocardia* spp., *Brucella* spp.
		Histoplasma capsulatum, *Blastomyces dermatitidis*, *Coccidioides immitis*, *Sporothrix schenckii*, *Paracoccidioides brasiliensis*, *Aspergillus* spp., and other fungi including dermatophytes (cyclohexamide-containing media may inhibit the growth of *Cryptococcus neoformans* and *Aspergillus fumigatus*)
		Malassezia furfur
		
		Leptospira spp.
		Borrelia burgdorferi

Cerebrospinal fluid	BA, CBA, TGB(A) (specimen should be concentrated) BSK-H LJ, MB7H10, MB7H11, BACTEC 13A BCYE BRA BHI, SD, IM Non-nutrient agar with overlay of bacteria (eg, *E coli*)	Most aerobic and facultatively anaerobic bacteria *Borrelia burgdorferi* *Mycobacterium* spp., *Nocardia* spp. *Nocardia* spp. *Brucella* spp. Fungi, especially *Blastomyces dermatitidis*, *Cryptococcus neoformans*, *Coccidioides immitis* *Acanthamoeba* spp. (agents of chronic granulomatous amebic encephalitis) and *Naegleria* spp. (agents of primary amebic meningoencephalitis)
Bone marrow	BRA BA, CBA, TGB(A) LJ, MB710, MB7H11, BACTEC 13A BCYE BHI, SD, IM	*Brucella* spp. *Salmonella* spp. *Mycobacteria* spp., *Nocardia* spp. *Nocardia* spp. Fungi, especially *Histoplasma capsulatum*

Specimen	Media	Organisms

Brain tissue	BA, CBA, TGB
	Abscess
	  Aerobic media: BA, CBA, TGB(A), and EMB or MAC
	  Anaerobic media: TGB(An)
	BHI, SD, IM
	Non-nutrient agar with overlay of bacteria (eg, *E coli*)
		Most aerobic and facultative anaerobic bacteria
		Aerobic and facultatively anaerobic
		
		Obligately anaerobic bacteria
		Fungi, especially *Aspergillus* spp., *Blastomyces dermatitidis*, *Coccidioides immitis*
		Acanthamoeba spp., *Naegleria* spp.

Sterile body fluids other than blood, cerebrospinal fluid, or urine; sterile tissues	BA, CBA CBA or TSB-RS LJ, MB7H10, MB7H11, BACTEC 13A BCYE BSK-H (skin or, rarely, blood and cerebrospinal fluid) BHI, SD, IM	Most aerobic and facultatively anaerobic bacteria *Bartonella* spp. *Mycobacteria* spp.,[3] *Nocardia* spp. *Nocardia* spp. *Borrelia burgdorferi* Fungi
Exudate or pus	BA, CBA, EMB or MAC, CNA, TGB(A) CBA or TSB-RS LJ, MB7H10, MB7H11, BACTEC 13A BCYE BHI, SD, IM	Most aerobic and facultatively anaerobic bacteria. *Bartonella* spp. *Mycobacteria* spp., *Nocardia* spp. *Nocardia* spp. Fungi
Eye fluid, tissue	BA, CBA, EMB or MAC, CNA, TGB(A) LJ, MB7H10, MB7H11, BACTEC 13A BCYE BHI, SD, IM Non-nutrient agar with overlay of bacteria (eg, *E coli*) McCoy cell culture	Most aerobic and facultatively anaerobic bacteria *Mycobacteria* spp., *Nocardia* spp. *Nocardia* spp. Fungi *Acanthamoeba* spp. *Chlamydia trachomatis*
Upper respiratory	BG or RIA BA BA and TA or CTA and LA BHI, SD, IM	*Bordetella pertussis* *Streptococcus pyogenes* *Corynebacterium diphtheria* Fungi, especially *Histoplasma capsulatum* from oral pharyngeal ulcers
Lower respiratory tract secretions (including BAL, transtracheal or transbronchoscopic aspirates) and lung tissue (transbronchoscopic biopsy or open-lung biopsy)	BA, CBA, EMB, or MAC, CNA; consider BC for cystic fibrosis patients BCYE	Most aerobic and facultatively anaerobic bacteria *Legionella* spp, *Nocardia* spp.
	LJ, MB7H10, MB7H11, BACTEC 13A BHI, SD, IM	*Mycobacteria* spp., *Nocardia* spp. *Histoplasma capsulatum*, *Blastomyces dermatitidis*, *Paracoccidioides brasiliensis*, *Coccidioides immitis*, *Cryptococcus neoformans*, *Aspergillus* spp., and other fungi
Urethral exudate, cervical or vaginal exudate	CBA, TM	*Neisseria gonorrhoeae*
	McCoy cell culture SP4 glucose broth and agar	*Chlamydia trachomatis* *Mycoplasma hominis*

(continued)

Table 6–2. Recommended culture methods for detecting bacteria, fungi, and parasites in human specimens. *(continued)*

Specimen	Media	Bacteria
Urine	BA and EMB or MAC FL, EH LJ, MB7H10, MB7H11, BACTEC 13A BYCE BHI, SD, IM	Most aerobic and facultatively anaerobic bacteria *Leptospira* spp. *Mycobacteria* spp., *Nocardia* spp. *Nocardia* spp. Fungi, especially *Blastomyces dermatitidis*
Gastric tissue	HA	*Helicobacter pylori*
Small- or large-bowel tissue	MB7H11, BACTEC 13A	*Mycobacterium* spp.
Feces	BA, EMB or MAC, HE, XLD and/or SS, SB or GNB TCBS CIN SMAC CA MB7H11	*Salmonella* spp., *Shigella* spp. *Vibrio cholerae* *Yersinia enterocolitica* E coli O157:H7 Campylobacter jejuni *Mycobacteria* spp., especially *M tuberculosis* and *M avium-intracellulare* (should only be performed on acid-fast positive specimens)
Intravascular catheters Ports (swabs)	Plate and incubate as per exudate or pus described above	Most aerobic and facultatively anaerobic bacteria and yeasts; if *Malassezia furfur* infection suspected, overlay SD with olive oil
Blood cultures	See blood cultures above; simultaneous peripheral blood cultures should be obtained	Most aerobic and facultatively anaerobic bacteria and yeasts; if *Malassezia furfur* infection suspected, overlay SD with olive oil
Catheter tip cultures	CBA	Most aerobic and facultative anaerobic bacteria; ≥15 CFU [colony forming units considered significant, (Maki criteria)] and yeasts
Surveillance cultures Upper respiratory tract (throat swabs or sputum) and gastrointestinal tract (rectal swab)	BA, EMB or MAC, BHIB	Most aerobic and facultatively anaerobic bacteria and yeasts
Vancomycin-resistant enterococci screen (rectal swab or feces)	ES	Vancomycin-resistant *Enterococcus* spp.
Urine	BA; EMB or MAC	Most aerobic and facultatively anaerobic bacteria.

1 BA, blood agar; BC, *Burkholderia cepacia* agar; BCYE, buffered charcoal yeast extract agar; BG, Bordet-Gengou agar; BHI, brain heart infusion agar; BHIB, brain heart infusion broth; BRA, *Brucella* agar; BSK-H, Barbour-Stoenner-Kelly agar; CA, *Campylobacter* agar (types Skirrow, CVA [*Campylobacter*-cefoperazone-vancomycin-amphotericin), CCDA [blood-free charcoal cefoperazone deoxycholate agar or CSM (charcoal-based selective medium]); CBA, chocolate blood agar; CIN, cefsulodin-irgasan-novobiocin agar; CNA, colistin nalidixic acid agar; CTA, cysteine tellurite agar; EH, Ellinghausen's agar; EMB, eosin-methylene blue agar; ES, enterococcosel agar; FL, Fletcher's agar; GNB, gram-negative broth; HA, *Helicobacter pylori* agar; HE, Hektoen enteric agar; IM, inhibitory mold agar; LA, Loefflers agar; LJ, Lowenstein-Jensen agar; MAC, MacConenkey agar; MB7H11, Middlebrook 7H11 agar; MB7H10 Middlebrook 7H10 agar; RA, Regan-Lowe agar; SD, Sabouraud's dextrose agar; SMAC, sorbitol MacConenkey agar; SPS, sodium polyanethol sulfonate; SB, Sellenite broth; SS, *Salmonella-Shigella* agar; TA, Tindale's agar; TCBS, thiosulfate-citrate-bile salts-sucrose agar; TGB, thioglycollate broth; TGB(A), thioglycol-late broth used for aerobic isolation, containing rabbit serum; TGB (An), thioglycollate broth with vitamin K, and rabbit serum used for anaerobic isolation; TM, Thayer-Martin agar; TSB-RS, tryptic soy agar with defibrinated rabbit serum; XLD, xylose-lysine-deoxycholate agar.

2 The HACEK group includes the following bacteria: *Haemophilus aphrophilus/paraphrophilus, Actinobacillus actinomycetemcomitans, Cardiobacterium hominis, Eikenella corrodens,* and *Kingella* spp.

3 Also incubate separate plates at 30°C if *M marinum, M ulcerans, M chelonae,* or *M haemophilum* is possible.

Table 6–3. Serologic methods currently available for detecting antibodies to bacterial, fungal, or parasitic pathogens

Organism	Technique[1]
Bacteria	
Brucella spp.[2]	TA, EIA
Francisella tularensis	EIA
Helicobacter pylori	EIA
Legionella spp.	IFA, EIA
Leptospira spp.	IHA
Bartonella henselae (agent of cat scratch disease, bacillary angiomatosis, and peliosis hepatis)	IFA, EIA
Borrelia burgdorferi (agent of Lyme disease)	EIA, IB
Chlamydia trachomatis, Chlamydia pneumoniae, Chlamydia psittaci	CF, IFA, EIA
Mycoplasma pneumoniae	CF, IFA, EIA
Treponema pallidum (agent of syphilis)	Nonspecific treponemal tests: RPR, VDRL
	Specific treponemal tests: IFA, FTA-ABS, IgG, IgM; MH; MHA-TP
	EIA
Ehrlichia spp. [*E. chafeensis* and the agent of Human Granulocytic Ehrlichiosis (HGE)]	EIA
Rickettsia spp. (*R rickettsia, R typhi*)	IFA, CF, EIA
Coxiella burnetii	IFA, CF
Streptococcus pyogenes (group A streptococci) (anti-streptolysin O and anti-DNase B)	N
Fungi	
Aspergillus fumigatus, Aspergillus niger, Aspergillus flavus	ID
Blastomyces dermatitidis	CF
Candida albicans	ID
Coccidioides immitis	CF, ID
Histoplasma capsulatum	CF, ID
Sporothrix schenckii	A
Parasites	
Echinococcus granulosa	EIA, IB
Entamoeba histolyticum	EIA
Taenia solium (cysticercosis)	EIA
Toxoplasma gondii	EIA, FA

[1]A, agglutination; CF, complement fixation; EIA, enzyme immunoassay; FTA-ABS, fluorescent treponemal antibody absorbed; IB, immunoblot; ID, immunodiffusion; IFA, indirect flurorescent antibody; IHA, indirect hemagglutination; MH, microhemagglutination; MHA-TP, microhemagglutinin assay for *T pallidum;* N, neutralization; RPR, rapid plasma reagin; TA, tube agglutination; VDRL, Venereal Disease Research Laboratory
[2]Not all test profiles may include *Brucella canis.*

nostic-testing process cannot be overstated. An adequate amount of specimen (using sterile techniques when appropriate) should be placed in the appropriate transport device, and the specimen should be transported to the laboratory under appropriate environmental conditions and within a reasonable period. Because a large number of transport devices are available, consultation with the laboratory personnel is important, especially when unusual bacteria are considered. Comprehensive reviews of the specifics of specimen collection, transport, and storage are described elsewhere. As a general point, specimens requiring strictly anaerobic conditions for viability must be sent in appropriate anaerobic transport devices. Depending on the volume, most other specimens can be sent in either a swab transport device (the swab is immersed in nutrient broth) or a sterile container. Some studies have demonstrated the utility of blood culture bottles for transporting as well as culturing sterile body fluids, especially peritoneal fluid.

RAPID, DIRECT TEST METHODS & CULTURE-BASED METHODS

Direct, rapid diagnostic-test methods if available should be used in addition to conventional culturing techniques for diagnosing bacterial or fungal infections in critically ill patients. Most parasitic infections can be diagnosed by direct staining methods, and these tests should be performed emergently, especially if life-threatening infections like malaria are suspected. Rapid diagnostic tests are provided in Table 6–1, and culture-based diagnostic tests, which require longer time periods to complete, are presented in Table 6–2.

Blood

Both direct and culture-based techniques may be useful for identifying common and uncommon bacterial, fungal, and parasitic pathogens in blood. Some of the specialized testing methods shown in Tables 6–1 and 6–2 are generally available only at reference laboratories. If the clinician feels strongly that one of

Table 6–4. Selected specimen considerations for bacterial, fungal, and parasitic agents.

Specimen Source	Considerations
Throat, nasopharyngeal, nasal secretions	Nasopharyngeal aspirates are superior to swabs for culturing *Bordetella pertussis;* swabs are adequate for the detection of *S pyogenes;* nasal swabs are recommended for detecting carriers of methicillin-resistant *Staphylococcus aureus.*
Respiratory secretions	Sputa may be induced with nebulized saline in patients who cannot spontaneously produce sputa; spontaneously produced specimens should be screened by microscopy for suitability for bacterial culture.
Eye	Secretions are obtained by swab from the palpebral conjunctiva; NOTE: eye scrapings should be obtained by an ophthalmologist or other trained person and plated directly at bedside if possible.
Blood	For adults, 20–30 ml of blood are collected per phlebotomy (ie, one set of blood cultures), and 10 ml are placed in each blood culture receptacle; at least one 10-ml aliquot should be cultured anaerobically; three blood culture sets collected over a 24-h period are adequate for diagnosing ~99% of bacteremias; peripheral blood smears and malaria thick and thin smears should be performed at the bedside.
Sterile body fluids other than blood and urine	Disinfect site if collection obtained percutaneously by aspiration; sterile fluids (pleural, peritoneal, pericardial, and joint) are best transported to the laboratory in an anaerobic transport system; some studies have demonstrated the utility of blood culture media for recovery of organisms from these sources.
Abscess	Tissue or fluid is superior to a swab specimen; swabs are especially inadequate for anaerobic bacterial culture; use an anaerobic transport system for sending specimen to the laboratory.
Tissue	A Stomacher may be useful to homogenize the samples for culture.
Urine	A spontaneously voided midstream urine sample is collected after proper cleansing of the genitalia; catheterized specimens or suprapubic specimens may be preferred in some instances where midstream collection is not possible or is impractical.
Rectal swabs and stool specimens	Rectal swabs may be used to survey patients for vancomycin-resistant enterococci; spontaneously passed stool samples are preferred for bacterial cultures; spontaneously passed or purged stool samples may be used for ova and parasite (O&P) examinations; a series of three specimens collected on separate days is recommended for O&P examination; collection kits with stool preservatives are required for O&P evaluation if there is significant delay between the time the stool is passed and the time it is evaluated in the laboratory; however, freshly passed specimens are mandatory for the recovery of motile trophozoites; pinworm exams may be performed with an adhesive (scotch tape or a paddle kit) that is applied to the perianal area.

these tests is useful, an aliquot of the specimen should be sent to a reference laboratory. Direct test methods for the detection of bacterial or fungal pathogens in blood are limited in the number of different bacteria that they can detect and are less sensitive than culture methods. Bacterial-antigen tests for commonly encountered encapsulated organisms (*Haemophilus influenzae* type b, *Neisseria meningitidis,* or *Streptococcus pneumoniae*) are easy to perform and available in most laboratories. A latex agglutination procedure can be used to detect the yeast *Cryptococcus neoformans.*

Blood cultures should be obtained from all patients in whom sepsis is considered. The standard blood culture set for adults consists of 20–30 ml of blood equally distributed between two or among three culture receptacles. Blood volume for pediatric patients is less and is dependent on patient weight. When 20 ml of blood is drawn, the standard practice is to culture 10 ml in an aerobic atmosphere and 10 ml in an anaerobic atmosphere. If 30 ml of blood is drawn, the same practice is followed except that the additional 10 ml is cultured under aerobic conditions. In patients with suspected endocarditis or endovascular infections, conditions in which bacteremia is continuous, two or three separate blood cultures collected at various intervals over a 24-h period are sufficient. For other types of bacteremia, 99% will be detected by three separate blood cultures collected at various intervals over a 24-h period. Most conventional broth-based blood culture systems also have the ability to detect candidemias. Specialized broth or procedures (see lysis centrifugation below) may be required to detect fastidious bacteria and dimorphic fungi, especially *Histoplasma capsulatum.*

Recently some authorities have questioned whether anaerobic blood cultures should be performed routinely in all patients, especially those in whom anaerobic bacteremia is unlikely. However, it has recently been demonstrated that anaerobic blood cultures may recover some facultatively anaerobic bacteria (eg, *Enterococcus* spp. and viridans streptococci) more efficiently than aerobic blood cultures. The lysis centrifugation method is a specialized blood culture method which is useful for recovering common as well as many unusual bacterial pathogens and fungi. In this system, blood is inoculated into a test tube containing saponin, a chemical that lyses erythrocytes and leukocytes, thereby releasing intracellular bacteria. The tube is centrifuged, and the sediment is inoculated onto solid agar plates or into broth. *Mycobacterium* spp., especially *Mycobacterium avium-intracellulare,* occasionally produce bacteremias in severely immunocompromised patients. The inoculation of the sediment from a lysis centrifugation blood culture tube onto specialized mycobacteria agar or into BACTEC 13A broth bottles is useful for recovering mycobacteria. Controversy exists as to whether blood cultures can be obtained from intravascular lines. Several investigators have shown that such a practice results in the isolation of more contaminating microorganisms than if blood is obtained from peripheral veins. Whenever possible, blood for culturing should be obtained from peripheral veins; however, this recommendation must be considered in the context of the clinical situation of the patients. For example, phlebotomy via peripheral veins may be risky in severely thrombocytopenic bone marrow transplant patients.

Parasitemias caused by malarial or filarial organisms are diagnosed with thick and thin blood smears. Thick smears permit screening for malaria parasites, and speciation is possible by careful evaluation of thin smears. When parasitemias are suspected, the laboratory director should be notified so that proper processing and careful evaluation of blood specimens are undertaken. In some cases, referral of specimens to reference laboratories may be beneficial.

Other Sterile Body Fluids or Tissues

Direct antigen testing for *H influenzae* type b, *N meningitidis, S pneumoniae,* group B streptococci, *E coli,* and *C neoformans* can be performed on cerebrospinal fluid (CSF) or urine. Direct antigen testing for *Legionella pneumophila* and *H capsulatum* can be performed on urine. For staining and culturing methods, CSF or joint, peritoneal, or pleural fluids should be concentrated by filtering or centrifugation. In contrast, Gram stains of urine should be performed on unconcentrated specimens. The presence of ≥2 bacteria per oil immersion field (×1000) in a Gram-stained smear of a drop of unconcentrated urine should represent ~ 10^5 colony forming units of bacteria/ml of urine. Other rapid screening tests for bacteriuria are commercially available. These tests, which detect either bacteria or leukocytes by direct or indirect methods, are generally no more accurate than the Gram stain method and may be more costly.

Cultures of bone marrow specimens may be particularly valuable for diagnosing *Salmonella typhi* (the agent of typhoid fever), *Brucella* spp., disseminated mycobacteria infections (*M avium-intracellulare*) or *H capsulatum* and can be processed by using the lysis centrifugation method. Granulomas surrounding small vessels in a bone marrow biopsy (ring granulomas) are associated with *Coxiella burnetti* (agent of Q fever) infection. Bone marrow specimens may be positive by staining methods in patients with disseminated infection caused by a variety of organisms, including *H capsulatum, M avium-intracellulare, Trypanosoma* spp. or *Leishmania* spp.

Respiratory Tract Specimens

All spontaneously produced sputa that are submitted for general bacteria culture should be screened for the presence of squamous epithelial cells. It has been demonstrated that expectorated sputum samples having > 25 squamous epithelial cells per low-power microscopic field are unacceptable for bacterial culture, because these samples likely are contaminated by oropharyngeal secretions. Common community-acquired respiratory bacterial pathogens include *S pneumoniae, Streptococcus pyogenes* (Lancefield group A β-hemolytic streptococci), *Klebsiella pneumoniae, S aureus, Legionella* spp., *Chlamydia pneumoniae,* and *Mycoplasma pneumoniae.* Gram-negative bacilli, especially *Enterobacteriaceae* and *Pseudomonas* spp., and VRE and staphylococci may cause nosocomial respiratory infection. *Pseudomonas aeruginosa* and *B cepacia* are frequently associated with pulmonary infection in patients with cystic fibrosis. All of the above bacteria, with the exception of *C pneumoniae* and *M pneumoniae,* are easily diagnosed by culture-based methods. Indirect serologic methods are the best methods for diagnosing the latter two pathogens.

Although *Legionella* spp., *Mycobacteria* spp., and *Nocardia* spp. can cause pulmonary disease in normal hosts, they may be a more frequent cause of pulmonary disease in immunocompromised hosts. *Legionella* spp. can be diagnosed by direct examination of pulmonary secretions or alveolar tissue, with a fluorescent antibody technique. Alternatively, acute infection with the most frequently encountered *Legionella* spp., *L pneumophila,* can be diagnosed by screening for antigen in the urine. *Legionella* antigenuria can persist for months after acute infection, a factor that may limit the usefulness of this direct test for diagnosing subsequent *L pneumophila* infections. Microorganisms that stain poorly by the Gram stain method and that appear to branch or are beaded in appearance should be suspect for *Nocardia* spp. These organisms frequently stain acid-fast by a modified acid-fast staining method. This method uses less intense decolorizing agents than those used for conventional acid-fast staining of mycobacteria. *Nocardia* spp. grow more slowly than other bacteria, but can be recovered on standard bacteriologic media. *Nocardia* spp. also grow well on media used for isolating fungi and mycobacteria and on media used to isolate *Legionella* spp. (buffered charcoal yeast extract). A recently described opportunist gram-positive bacillus, *Rhodococcus equi,* also may cause pulmonary infection in immunocompromised patients and, like *Nocardia* spp., may branch and stain acid-fast by a modified acid-fast staining method.

The dimorphic fungal pathogens (yeast and hyphal forms) *H capsulatum, Blastomyces dermatitidis, Coccidioides immitis* and *Paracoccidioides brasiliensis* and the monomorphic fungus (yeast form only) *C neoformans* may cause pulmonary or disseminated disease in both normal and immunocompromised hosts. The dimorphic fungal pathogen *Sporothrix schenckii* rarely produces respiratory disease and more frequently presents as cutaneous disease in normal hosts. Monomorphic fungi (hyphal form only) such as *Aspergillus* spp. generally cause respiratory or disseminated infection in immunocompromised hosts. *Pneumocystis carinii* has recently been reclassified as a fungus. It is an opportunistic fungal pathogen that causes disease only in immunocompromised hosts, especially patients coinfected with human immunodeficiency virus (HIV). All fungal pathogens, with the exception of *P carinii,* can be cultured from pulmonary secretions. Diagnosis of *P carinii* requires direct examination of pulmonary secretions or tissue. Some fungal infections can also be diagnosed by indirect serologic methods; additionally, *H capsulatum* antigen and *C neoformans* antigen can be detected in urine and in the serum in disseminated disease.

In certain areas of the world where helminths (*Ascaris lumbricoides, Strongyloides stercoralis, Paragonimus westermani,* and *Echinococcus granulosa*) are endemic, pulmonary infection with these parasites may occur. Disseminated infection with *S stercoralis,* including respiratory infection, may occur in immunocompromised hosts. *Toxoplasma gondii* may cause pulmonary disease in immunocompromised hosts. Direct examination of wet preps of pulmonary secretions may be useful to identify helminths; direct examination of tissue, culture, and indirect serologic methods are useful for diagnosing *T gondii.*

Feces

Enteric infections caused by *Salmonella* spp., *Shigella* spp., *Yersinia enterocolitica,* pathogenic *E coli,* and *Campylobacter* spp. are increasing in frequency in the United States. These infections are diagnosed by culture of feces, although direct detection of antigens by enzyme-linked immunoassays are sometimes useful for *Salmonella* spp. and *E coli* O157:H7. At present, Whipple's disease caused by the bacterium *Tropheryma whippelii* can be definitively diagnosed by evaluating small-bowel tissue for the presence of nucleic acid that is unique to this organism. Traditionally, periodic acid Schiff staining has been used to demonstrate the organism in tissue (see subsequent discussion).

Occasionally, in severely immunocompromised patients, acid-fast staining and culture may be useful for diagnosing enteric infection caused by *Mycobacterium tuberculosis* or *M avium-intracellulare.* However, cultures for mycobacteria should be performed only on stools with positive acid-fast stains. If mycobacteria are recovered from feces, disseminated disease is frequently present.

Enteric parasitic infections are diagnosed by direct examination of fresh or preserved stools; however, direct immunoassays may be useful for some parasitic organisms (*Giardia lamblia* and *Cryptosporidium parvum*). Extraintestinal parasitic infections may require other methods, including culture for diagnosis. Not shown in Table 6–2 are culture methods for *Trypanosoma* spp., *Leishmania* spp., *T gondii,* and *Entamoeba histolytica.* These specialized tests are available only at a few reference laboratories in North America. Culture methods for *Acanthamoeba* spp. and *Naegleria* spp. are included in Table 6–1. These methods are easy to perform and especially useful for diagnosing these parasitic infections in patients with corneal infections, which can occur with contact lens use.

Considerable attention has focused recently on newly discovered parasites that are opportunists in immunocompromised patients. These include species of four genera of coccidia (*Isospora, Sarcocystis, Cryptosporidium,* and *Cyclospora*) and species of five genera of microsporidia (*Enterocytozoon, Septata, Nosema, Encephalitozoon,* and *Pleistophora*). Infections caused by the coccidia or microsporidia have been reported in immunosuppressed patients, notably those patients coinfected with human immunodeficiency virus. Intestinal disease has been demonstrated to occur with all coccidia genera, *Enterocytozoon* spp., and *Septata* spp. Extraintestinal disease has been reported with *Sarcocystis* spp., *Cryptosporidium* spp., *Septata* spp., *Encephalitozoon* spp., *Nosema* spp., and *Pleistophora* spp. As previously mentioned, *T gondii* and the helminth *S stercoralis* can cause severe disseminated disease in immunocompromised hosts.

Intravascular Catheters

Patients who have indwelling central intravascular catheters for prolonged periods are susceptible to infection. If other sources for infection are ruled out, then infection related to the intravascular catheter must be considered. Diagnosing intravascular-catheter–associated infection can be challenging for the clinician, considering that a definitive diagnosis cannot be achieved unless the catheter is removed and a culture of the tip yields potentially pathogenic bacterium in sufficient quantity (ie, >15 colony forming units of bacteria). If there is evidence for a catheter tunnel infection (subcutaneous infection around the catheter), swabs of the affected area or pus if present should be stained and cultured for bacteria, mycobacteria, and fungi. Occasionally, the fungus *Malassezia furfur* can infect intravascular catheters and the blood in patients receiving intralipid infusions. Special culture techniques are required to isolate this organism (see Table 6–2).

Surveillance Cultures

In certain instances, surveillance cultures for bacteria and fungi may be useful. Patients who are immunocompromised, receiving broad-spectrum antimicrobial agents, or both may be surveyed for drug resistant bacteria or fungi. As part of infection control programs, institutionalized patients may be surveyed for VRE or methicillin-resistant *S aureus* carriage. In both of these examples, cultures of the upper airway, feces, or both may be useful to screen for carriage of these potential pathogens.

SEROLOGIC TEST METHODS

Indirect serologic methods may be useful for diagnosing infections caused by certain bacteria, fungi, and parasites and in some cases may be the only means by which a diagnosis is achieved. To diagnose infections by *Rickettsia* spp., for which alternative diagnostic test methods are limited (attempts at culturing these organisms should be avoided owing to their high infectivity), these tests may be the only means by which a diagnosis is established. Table 6–3 shows the serologic test methods currently available at most reference laboratories. Of note, these methods detect immunoglobulin G (IgG) antibody, IgM antibody, or both to specific bacteria pathogens and for the most part require that the infection has existed in a patient for a finite period so that detectable levels of antibody exist. For IgG analyses, a fourfold increase between baseline and convalescent antibody titers may be required to confirm infection. Because the demonstration of a fourfold rise in antibodies may require > 4 weeks, the diagnostic utility of IgG analyses may be limited, especially in the acute disease phase. However, in some situations, baseline IgG antibody levels may exceed a critical threshold, which is considered diagnostic for infection. Except for the last example, indirect serological methods cannot be considered as rapid diagnostic tests and therefore may be of limited utility. These tests may also be of limited value in patients who lack a humoral response, especially bone marrow transplant recipients.

MOLECULAR TEST METHODS

Molecular test methods, including nucleic acid-probing and -sequencing techniques, allow for the detection of pathogens directly from human specimens. Molecular test methods and nucleic acid amplification techniques, which are frequently available at most reference laboratories are shown in Table 6–5. These methods are potentially useful for fastidious or slowly growing organisms like *Legionella* spp., *Bartonella* spp., *Mycobacterium* spp., *Borrelia burgdorferi*, and dimorphic fungi. The bacterial agent of Whipple's disease, *T whippelii*, has never been recovered on culture and presently can be diagnosed only by nucleic acid testing methods. Quantities of parasites in blood or tissue might be sufficiently low (eg, *T gondii* or *Babesia microtii*) that direct examination does not provide a diagnosis. In these cases, molecular diagnostic tests may also be useful. It must be emphasized that some studies, particularly those that have evaluated molecular identification methods for group A streptococci and mycobacteria, have demonstrated that these methods, including those that use nucleic acid amplification techniques, are less sensitive than culture. Therefore, if the results for molecular test methods such as these are negative, other diagnostic test methods including culture techniques should be considered.

SUSCEPTIBILITY TESTING OF BACTERIAL & FUNGAL ISOLATES TO ANTIMICROBIAL AGENTS

The National Committee for Clinical Laboratory Standards (NCCLS) provides published guidelines for conventional susceptibility test methods for commonly encountered bacterial organisms that grow aerobically or anaerobically and for yeasts. For bacteria that are not easily cultured (eg, *Bartonella* spp., *Ehrlichia* spp., or *T whippelii*), antimicrobial susceptibility testing is currently not possible. Tentative NCCLS guidelines exist for mycobacteria. No standards exist for parasites. Antimicrobial susceptibility methods include disk diffusion, broth dilution, and agar dilution. For disk diffusion, the inhibition of growth of an organism on solid media is assessed around a paper disk from which an antimicrobial agent diffuses. The greater the zone of inhibition of bacterial growth, the more effective the antimicrobial agent. In the broth dilution procedure, the effect of a known concentration of antimicrobial agent dispersed along with the organism in liquid media is assessed. No growth of the organism (the broth remains clear) indicates that the organism is inhibited at the concentration of antimicrobial agent tested. For agar dilution, a known amount of antimicrobial agent is dispersed in solid medium, and its effect on growth of organisms that are spot inoculated onto the surface of the medium is assessed. No visible growth of the organism means that it is inhibited by the specific concentration of antimicrobial agent that is present in the solid medium.

Table 6–5. Molecular test methods currently available for direct detection of bacteria in human specimens.

Organism	Test Method	Commercial Kits
Streptococcus pyogenes	Specific ribosomal RNA (rRNA) sequences unique to *S pyogenes* are detected with a chemiluminescent single-stranded DNA probe.	Gen-Probe Group A *Streptococcus* Direct Test (Gen-Probe, Inc., San Diego, CA)
Mycobacterium tuberculosis	Transcription-mediated replication and hybridization protection assay to detect rRNA	Amplified MTB Direct Test (Gen-Probe)
	DNA probing of a conserved region of the 16S rRNA gene amplified by PCR	Roche Amplicor MTB PCR Test (Roche Molecular Systems, Branchburg, NJ)
	DNA probing of an insertion sequence unique to *M tuberculosis* (IS6110) amplified by PCR	
Neisseria gonorrhoeae	DNA probing of the *opa* gene amplified by the ligase chain reaction (LCR)	Abbott LCx Probe System (Abbott Laboratories, Abbott Park, IL)
Chlamydia trachomatis	DNA probing of a conserved region of a cryptic plasmid amplified by the LCR	
Borrelia burgdorferi (agent of Lyme disease)	DNA probing of the outer surface protein A gene—*ospA* amplified by PCR	
Bordetella pertussis	DNA probing of an insertion sequence amplified by PCR	
Bartonella henselae (agent of cat scratch disease, bacillary angiomatosis, and peliosis hepatis) *Bartonella quintana* (agent of trench fever)	DNA probing of 16S rRNA, or the citrate synthase gene (*gltA*)	
Tropheryma whippelii (agent of Whipple's disease)	DNA probing of a conserved region of the 16S rRNA gene amplified by PCR	
Ehrlichia spp. [agent of human granulocytic ehrlichiosis (HGE)]	DNA probing of a conserved region of the 16S rRNA genes of *E equi* and *E phagocytophila* (which are closely related to the agent for HGE) amplified by PCR	
Ehrlichia chafeensis	DNA probing of a conserved region of the 16S rRNA gene amplified by PCR	
Toxoplasma gondii	DNA probing of a portion of the B1 gene amplified by PCR	
Babesia microti	DNA probing of a conserved region of the nuclear small subunit RNA (SSrDNA) amplified by PCR	

Interpretation of the results for each of these methods may differ with the antimicrobial agent and organism tested, and guidelines for such are provided by the NCCLS. These interpretations are provided as the following categories: resistant, susceptible, or intermediately susceptible. If an organism is identified as resistant to a particular antimicrobial agent, that agent should not be used in the clinical setting.

Diagnosis of Viral Infections

W. Lawrence Drew, MD, PhD

It is becoming increasingly important for the practitioner to perform viral diagnostic studies because prognostic, epidemiologic, and therapeutic considerations may be greatly influenced by knowledge of the specific virus causing a given illness. Even if no therapy is available, the establishment of a definite diagnosis of viral infection is often beneficial in (1) epidemiologic monitoring, (2) educating physicians and patients, (3) defining the disease process, and (4) evaluating therapeutic implications, both positive and negative. Moreover, identification of a virus as the cause of a patient's illness may be cost effective, because expensive diagnostic procedures and antibiotic therapy may be avoided or discontinued.

The virology laboratory can confirm the suspected diagnosis by cytologic examination of clinical specimens; attempting to isolate the virus; detecting the presence of viral antigens, or nucleic acids or evaluating the patient's immune response to the virus (serology).

CYTOLOGY

The simplest technique for viral diagnosis is cytologic examination of specimens for the presence of characteristic viral inclusions, but this approach is insensitive and applicable to only a few viruses, especially herpes viruses. These intracellular structures may represent aggregates of virus within an infected cell or may be abnormal accumulations of cellular material resulting from the virus-induced metabolic disruption. Papanicolaou (Pap) smears may show these inclusions in single cells or in large syncytia (aggregates of cells containing more than one nucleus), as in a patient with herpes simplex infection of the cervix. Cytology can be used to detect infections with herpes simplex virus, varicella-zoster virus, cytomegalovirus, human papillomavirus, and adenoviruses. Rabies infection may also be detected by finding Negri bodies (rabies virus inclusions) in brain tissue.

CULTURE-BASED METHODS

The historical "gold standard" of viral diagnosis is recovery of the agent in tissue culture, embryonated eggs, or experimental animals. Embryonated eggs are still used for the growth of virus for some vaccines but have been replaced by cell cultures for routine virus isolation in clinical laboratories. Likewise, the use of experimental animals rarely occurs in most clinical laboratories. Just as multiple media are used in bacteriology, several different types of tissue culture cells (eg, monkey kidney, human fetal lung, human amnion, or human cancer cells) are inoculated with each viral specimen.

Most clinically significant viruses can be recovered in at least one of these cell cultures, but several clinically important viruses are not isolated in these cells. For example, specimens submitted for the identification of viruses such as human immunodeficiency virus, coxsackie A virus, and rubella virus require, respectively, cocultivation with normal human peripheral blood mononuclear cells, inoculation of suckling mice, and the use of specialized cell cultures, which are not generally available. Therefore infections caused by these and several other viruses are most frequently diagnosed serologically or by detection of virus-specific antigens or nucleic acids.

Detection of the growth of a virus is by observation of changes in the cell culture monolayer [cytopathic effect (CPE)]. Characteristic CPEs include changes in cell morphology, cell lysis, vacuolation, syncytia formation, and presence of inclusion bodies. Inclusion bodies are histologic changes in cells caused by the presence of viral components or changes in cell structures. With experience a technologist can distinguish CPE characteristics of the major virus groups. The observation of which cell culture exhibits CPEs and the rapidity of viral growth can be used for the presumptive identification of many clinically important viruses. This approach for identifying viruses is similar to bacterial identification based on growth and morphology of colonies on selective, differential media. Some viruses do not readily cause CPEs in cell lines typically used in clinical virology laboratories. However, some of these can be detected by other techniques, such as (1) erythrocyte hemadsorption onto cells infected with paramyxoviruses or mumps virus or (2) interference with the replication of other viruses (eg, picornaviruses cannot replicate in cells previously infected with rubella virus; this is known as heterologous interference).

In contrast with the intrinsic delay of antibody studies, the results of viral culture can be surprisingly rapid. Almost 50% of all viral isolates can be reported within 3 to 4 days of culture, with herpes simplex virus and influenza A virus usually detected within 1 to 3 days (Table 6–6).

The selection of the appropriate specimen for viral culture is complicated because several different

Table 6–6. Average detection time for commonly isolated viruses.

Virus	Average Detection Time in Days
Herpes simplex	1.8
Influenza A	3.8
Enteroviruses (echovirus, coxsackie-viruses A and B)	4.2
Cytomegalovirus	5.8
Respiratory syncytial virus	6.1
Varicella-zoster virus	6.1
Adenoviruses	6.4
Parainfluenzaviruses 1 and 3	6.4
overall average	4.1

viruses may cause the same clinical disease (Table 6–7). For example, several types of specimens should be submitted from patients with viral meningitis to enhance the recovery of the possible etiologic agents: CSF (enteroviruses, mumps virus, and herpes simplex virus), throat swabs and washings (enteroviruses), and stool or rectal swabs (enteroviruses). Also, serum should be collected as an acute-phase specimen in case subsequent serologic tests are indicated (eg, acute and convalescent sera for mumps virus or arbovirus infections). Many considerations, however, allow the physician to select the most appropriate specimens (Table 6–8). For example, during the summer, when enteroviral meningitis is prevalent, CSF, throat, and stool specimens should be submitted. On the other hand, the development of encephalitis in children after being bitten by mosquitos in wooded areas endemic for California encephalitis virus suggests that a serum specimen for antibody testing would be preferred. Central nervous system disease after parotitis would suggest collection of CSF and urine for the isolation of mumps virus. The specimens that should be collected for other viruses are summarized in Table 6–7.

Timing of Specimen Collection

Proper timing of specimen collection is essential for adequate recovery of viruses. Specimens should be collected early in the acute phase of infection. Studies with respiratory viruses indicate that the mean duration of viral shedding may be only 3–7 days. Also, herpes simplex virus and varicella-zoster virus may not be recovered from lesions beyond 5 days after onset. Isolation of an enterovirus from the CSF may be possible for only 2–3 days after onset of the central nervous system manifestations.

Transport to Laboratory

The shorter the interval between collection of a specimen and its delivery to the laboratory, the greater is the potential for isolating an agent. When feasible, all specimens other than blood, feces, urine, and tissue, which need special processing, should be inoculated directly onto cell cultures at the patient's bedside (Table 6–9). These should then be transported to the laboratory promptly.

For specimens that cannot be inoculated onto cell cultures immediately, several types of transport media have been used. It is generally believed that protein (serum, albumin, or gelatin) incorporated into a transport medium enhances survival of viruses.

Improper storage of specimens before processing can also adversely affect viral recovery. Significant losses in infective titer occur with enveloped viruses (eg, herpes simplex virus, varicella-zoster virus, or influenza virus) after specimens have been frozen and then thawed. This is not observed with nonenveloped viruses (eg, adenoviruses or enteroviruses). Therefore, when it is impossible to process a specimen immediately, it should be refrigerated *but not frozen* and packed in shaved ice for delivery to the laboratory if delays in transit are anticipated. Storage of specimens for the recovery of viruses at 4°C is far superior to storage at ambient temperature.

Interpretation of Culture Results

In general the detection of any virus in host tissues, CSF, blood, or vesicular fluid can be considered highly significant. Recovery of viruses other than cytomegalovirus in urine may be diagnostic of significant infection. For example, both mumps virus and adenovirus type 11 (associated with acute hemorrhagic cystitis) may be recovered in urine and indicate acute infection. However, the presence of cytomegalovirus in urine is difficult to interpret because this may reflect asymptomatic virus replication long after infection or indicate a significant active infection in the patient. In the newborn, viruria (isolation of virus in urine) in the first 3 weeks of life establishes a diagnosis of congenital cytomegalovirus infection, whereas the onset of viral excretion after 3–4 weeks of life reflects intrapartum or postpartum infection. Diagnosis of acquired cytomegalovirus in older patients usually requires a combination of findings, including positive cultures, illness compatible with cytomegalovirus disease, reasonable exclusion of other potential etiologic agents, and support by specific serologic or histologic data.

The significance of viruses isolated in upper respiratory tract, vaginal, or fecal specimens varies greatly. At one extreme, isolates such as measles, mumps, influenza, parainfluenza, and respiratory syncytial virus are significant because asymptomatic carriage and prolonged shedding of these viruses are unusual. Conversely, other viruses can be shed continually or intermittently without symptoms for periods ranging from several weeks (enteroviruses in feces) to many months or years (herpes simplex virus or cytomegalovirus in the oropharynx and genital

Table 6–7. Appropriate specimens for viral isolation.[1]

Syndromes and Probable Viral Agents	Throat/ Nasopharynx	Stool	CSF	Urine	Other
Respiratory syndrome	++++				
Adenoviruses[2]					
Influenza virus[2]					
Parainfluenza virus[2]					
Respiratory syncytial virus[2]					
Rhinoviruses					+++ nasal
Enteroviruses					
Dermatologic and mucous membrane disease	+				++++
Vesicular					
Enterovirus (hand, foot, mouth syndrome)	++	+++			+++ (vesicle fluid or scraping)
Herpes simplex[2]					
Varicella-zoster[2]	++				
Exanthematous	++				
Enterovirus		+++			
Measles[3]					
Rubella[3]					
Meningoencephalitis	++		+++		
Arboviruses					
Enteroviruses[6]		++++			
Herpes simplex[6]					
Lymphocytic choriomeningitis[3]					
Mumps virus					
Gastrointestinal		++			
Adenoviruses[4]					
Rotavirus[5]					
Congenital and perinatal	++	+	++		++
Cytomegalovirus				+++	Blood
Enteroviruses					
Herpes simplex virus					Vesicle fluid, blood
Eye syndrome					++++
Adenoviruses	++				Conjunctival swab or scraping
Herpes simplex virus					
Varicella-zoster virus					
Cytomegalovirus infection				+	++++ blood
Myocarditis, pericarditis	++	++++			+ Pericardial fluid
Coxsackie B					

[1]Specimens indicated beside the disease categories should be obtained in all instances; others should be obtained if the specific virus is suspected.
[2]Direct fluorescent antibody studies are available.
[3]Best diagnosed serologically.
[4]Best diagnosed by EM because the adenoviruses responsible for gastroenteritis are not culturable by standard techniques.
[5]Best diagnosed by antigen detection or EM.
[6]Best diagnosed by PCR of CSF.
[7]Best diagnosed by antigenemia, PCR, hybrid capture.

tract; adenoviruses in the oropharynx and intestinal tract). Herpes simplex virus, cytomegalovirus, varicella zoster virus, and Epstein-Barr virus may remain latent for long periods and then become reactivated in response to a variety of stressful stimuli, including other infectious agents. In this setting their detection may not be significant, may merely represent a secondary problem complicating the primary infection (eg, herpes simplex virus "cold sores" in patients with bacterial sepsis), or may be associated with significant disease, especially in the immunocompromised patient.

Based on the epidemiology of adenovirus infec-
tions and observed serologic responses, the simultaneous isolation of these viruses from throat and feces is significantly associated with febrile respiratory disease. Isolation of viruses from the throat alone is less frequently associated with disease, and isolates from feces alone are probably nondiagnostic in a patient with respiratory disease.

Enteroviruses are generally found in infants and children, particularly during the late summer and early autumn. A knowledge of the relative frequency of virus shedding among various age groups in a particular locale is extremely helpful in assessing the significance of results of throat or stool cultures. For

Table 6–8. Specimen collection considerations for viral agents.

Specimen Source	Considerations[1]
Throat, nasopharyngeal swab and aspirate	Nasopharyngeal aspirates are superior to swabs; throat swabs are probably adequate for enteroviruses, adenoviruses, and HSV; nasopharyngeal specimens are preferred for respiratory syncytial virus and most other respiratory viruses; nasal specimens are best choice for rhinoviruses.
Rectal swabs and stool specimens	In suspected enteroviral disease (aseptic meningitis, myopericarditis, hand-foot-and-mouth disease), positive cultures from rectal cultures support but do not prove that enteroviruses are cause of disease; stool specimens are more productive than rectal swabs; fecal specimens from patients with viral gastroenteritis show nonculturable agents such as rotaviruses or adenoviruses.
Urine	Used for CMV, mumps, and adenoviruses; in mumps-related central nervous system disease, virus can be isolated from urine even when specimens from other sites are negative.
Dermal lesions	Fluid and cells from vesicles are superior to specimens from ulcers or crusts for both cultures and antigen stains.
Cerebrospinal fluid (and other sterile fluids)	Can be inoculated directly into tissue culture.
Eye	Secretions are obtained by swab from the palpebral conjunctiva; NOTE: eye scrapings should be obtained by an ophthalmologist or other trained person.
Blood serum for HBgAg	Leukocytes are collected by centrifugation to obtain buffy coat layer or by Ficoll-Hypaque separation; anticoagulated blood or a clot can be used for isolation of arboviruses; Plasma for HIV, HCV, HBV by PCR bDNA.
Tissue	Lung intestine, liver is used for CMV, influenza virus, and adenoviruses; brain is used for HSV.

[1]HSV, Herpes simplex virus; CMV, cytomegalovirus.

example, the peak prevalence of enteroviruses in the stools of toddlers during the late summer may range from 5% in temperate zones to > 20% in subtropical climates. Even in temperate areas, rates may approach 30% in infants during periods of enterovirus activity. Shedding of enterovirus in the throat usually occurs for 1–2 weeks, whereas fecal shedding may last 4–16 weeks. Thus, in a clinically compatible illness, isolation of an enterovirus from the throat supports a stronger temporal relationship to the disease than does an isolate from only the feces.

Herpes simplex virus is unusual in a fecal culture. In such cases it usually represents either severe disseminated infection or local infection of the perianal

Table 6–9. Summary of procedures for obtaining and transporting specimens for viral studies.

Specimen	Procedures
General	Obtain specimens as early in the patients[1] illness as possible; inoculate tissue cultures at patient's bedside if possible.
Throat	Use swabs in transport medium.
Nasopharynx	Obtain a nasopharyngeal swab in transport medium or a nasal wash specimen with a bulb syringe and buffered saline.
Stool	Obtain as for bacteriologic culture; if a specimen cannot be passed, a rectal swab of feces may be obtained.
Cerebrospinal fluid	Obtain 1 ml as for bacteriologic culture.
Urine	Obtain as for bacteriologic culture.
Skin or mucosal scraping	Obtain with swab in transport medium.
Biopsy material	Use sterile technique and submit in a sterile container (urine culture container).
Blood for culture	Submit ≥3 ml of heparinized blood.
Blood for serologic studies	Submit at least 5 ml of clotted whole blood (red-top vacutainer tube; in certain viral syndromes (lower respiratory) an acute-phase specimen should be submitted; if a virus is not isolated, a convalescent specimen should be obtained ≥7 days after the acute specimen; certain viral illnesses (rubella, rubeola, hepatitis, arbovirus, and encephalitis) are diagnosed most readily by serologic studies.
Transportation	Transport specimens as rapidly as possible, using a messenger service; specimens should be stored and transported at refrigerator temperature (4°C); do not freeze.

areas. Detection of herpes simplex virus in the upper respiratory tract may mean nothing other than nonspecific reactivation of virus caused by fever unless typical vesicles or ulcers are also present. Because of the fever-related phenomenon, isolation of herpes simplex virus in the throat or mucocutaneous lesions of patients with encephalitis cannot be interpreted as causing the central nervous system disease. Currently the definitive way to establish a diagnosis of herpes simplex encephalitis is by direct demonstration of the virus in a brain biopsy or by polymerase chain reaction (PCR) on CSF. In neonates, however, isolation of the virus from any site should raise the possibility of severe infection.

Isolation of adenoviruses, herpes simplex virus, varicella-zoster virus, and some enteroviruses from the cornea and conjunctiva in patients with inflammatory disease at these sites usually establishes the etiology of the infection.

DETECTION OF VIRAL ANTIGENS

Antibodies can be used as sensitive tools to detect, identify, and quantitate the presence of viral antigen in clinical specimens or cell culture. Monoclonal or polyclonal antibodies prepared in animals may be used. Viral antigens on the cell surface, within the cell, or released from infected cells can be detected by IF, EIA, RIA, and latex agglutination (LA). IF detects and locates cell-associated antigens, whereas RIA or different variations of enzyme-linked immunosorbent assay (ELISA) are used to detect and quantitate soluble antigens. LA is a rapid, easy assay for antigen; viruses or viral antigens in a sample cause the clumping of latex particles coated with specific antibody.

Virus-infected tissue or cell cultures can be detected by IF or EIA. By attaching a fluorescent signal to an antiviral antibody, and reacting it with the sample, viral antigen can be detected; this is called direct IF. A modification of this technique is the use of unlabeled antiviral antibodies and then a second antibody with a fluorescent label that will bind to IgM or IgG antibodies. EIA uses a second antibody conjugated to an enzyme, such as horseradish peroxidase or alkaline phosphatase, which releases a chromophore to mark the presence of antigen.

Direct IF assay is especially useful for (1) respiratory viruses (eg, respiratory syncytial virus or influenza A), (2) varicella-zoster virus and herpes simplex virus antigen in lung and visceral biopsies, and (3) cytomegalovirus in leukocytes from blood or CSF.

Soluble antigen can be quantitated by ELISA, RIA, and LA. The basis for these procedures is the separation and quantitation of antibody-bound and free antigen. Many of the ELISA and RIA techniques use an antibody immobilized to a solid support to capture soluble antigen and a labeled antibody to detect captured antigen.

Influenza, parainfluenza, and togaviruses produce a glycoprotein that binds erythrocytes. This property allows detection of free virus produced in cell culture by agglutination of erythrocytes, a process termed hemagglutination. The infected cells also adsorb erythrocytes to the surface by a process referred to as hemadsorption.

Detection and assay of characteristic enzymes can identify and quantitate specific viruses. For example, reverse transcriptase in cell culture is used as an indicator of infection by retroviruses.

SEROLOGIC TEST METHODS

Serology can be used to determine whether an infection is primary or a reinfection and if acute or chronic. The first antibodies to be produced by the immune system are directed against antigens on the virion or infected cell surfaces and are best detected by, eg, IF. Later in the infection, when cells have been lysed by the infecting virus or the cellular immune response, antibodies are directed against the cytoplasmic viral proteins and enzymes and can be detected by, eg, complement fixation. Seroconversion is characterized by a change from negative to positive antibody between serum taken during the acute phase of disease and that taken $\geq$ 2–3 weeks later; it is the best serologic marker of recent infection. A fourfold or greater rise in antibody titer in paired sera may also be significant but fluctuations in antibody titer do occur naturally. Detection of virus-specific IgM is theoretically associated with recent infection, but technical difficulty in measuring specific IgM responses may lead to false-positive and false-negative results.

For many viruses, culture or antigen detection is the best diagnostic test. However, certain viruses (eg, HIV, hepatitis A and B viruses, rubella virus, Epstein-Barr virus, measles virus, coronaviruses, and togaviruses) are difficult to isolate in cell culture, and infections are diagnosed most easily by serologic techniques. When a virologic workup is planned for a patient, it is generally useful to obtain $\geq$ 2–3 ml of serum during the acute phase of disease and store it at –20°C. This may become valuable, particularly if virus detection subsequently fails or if the significance of an isolate is uncertain. In these instances a convalescent-phase serum specimen may be requested 2–3 weeks later, and both the acute and convalescent sera may then be tested against appropriate viral antigens. In general, if a virus is isolated, the antibody titers need not be measured to confirm infection; for example, if a patient has aseptic meningitis and an enterovirus is recovered from the throat, that agent is probably responsible for the illness. Similarly, if influenza virus is recovered from the throat of a patient who has clinical influenza, no serologic confirmation of the etiology is necessary.

Complement fixation is a standard but technically difficult serologic test. The serum is first reacted with the suspected viral antigen and complement, and the residual complement is assayed by lysis of indicator antibody-coated erythrocytes. If the complement is used in the first reaction and is therefore not available for the second reaction, it indicates the presence of antibody to the suspected virus. Antibodies measured by this system generally develop slightly later in the course of an illness than those measured by other techniques. This delayed response is useful for documenting seroconversion when the initial serum specimen is collected late in the clinical course. Members of some virus groups (eg, enteroviruses) do not possess group-specific antigen and must be tested individually.

The neutralization test is essentially a protection test. When a virus is incubated with homologous type-specific antibody, the virus is rendered incapable of producing infection in an indicator cell culture system. A neutralization antibody response is virus type specific, with titers rising rapidly and persisting for long periods.

The hemagglutination inhibition test can be performed with a variety of viruses that can selectively agglutinate erythrocytes of various animal species (eg, chicken, guinea pig, or human). The hemagglutination capacity of a virus is inhibited by specific immune or convalescent sera. Hemagglutination-inhibiting antibody develops rapidly after the onset of symptoms, plateaus, declines slowly, and may last indefinitely at low levels. This test is useful for both the detection of acute viral infection and the determination of immunity.

For the indirect fluorescent antibody test, virus-infected cells are placed in prepared wells on microscope slides and then fixed in cold acetone and dried. Patient serum is applied and, after incubation, anti-human globulin conjugated with fluorescein is added. If fluorescence is observed, it indicates the presence of specific antiviral antibody.

Interpretation of Serologic Results

Virus-specific IgM antibody usually rises during the first 2–3 weeks of infection and persists for several weeks to months. Thus an elevated titer of specific IgM antibody suggests a recent primary infection, which may be further supported by demonstrating a fall in IgM antibody in subsequent sera. Detection of specific IgM has been used with success in the diagnosis of infections caused by cytomegalovirus and rubella virus and is currently the procedure of choice to establish a recent or acute infection from hepatitis A or B.

Several limitations of interpretation must be remembered. It is now recognized that IgM-specific antibody responses are not always restricted to primary infections. Reactivation or reinfection may result in IgM responses, particularly in herpes virus infection. In addition, patients may continue to produce IgM-specific antibody to rubella virus or cytomegalovirus for many months after a primary infection. Heterotypic IgM responses may also occur. For example, antibody responses to cytomegalovirus may develop in Epstein-Barr virus infections and vice versa. Other pitfalls include falsely low or negative IgM titers caused by competition from high-titer IgG antibody for antigen-binding sites and false-positive reactions resulting from rheumatoid factor. Both types of errors appear to occur most frequently in solid-phase assays with IF.

The serologic diagnosis of most viral infections is based on demonstration of a seroconversion or a rise (fourfold or greater) of IgG antibody. However, significant antibody titer rises may result from cross-reactions to related antigens; for example, an antibody rise to parainfluenza virus may actually result from infection with mumps virus. Furthermore, seroconversions may not be seen with some patient populations (eg, infants and immunocompromised patients) or when the initial serum is collected late in the course of disease.

A serum specimen can also be used for screening an infant's blood for certain antibodies of the IgG class. Antibodies to *Toxoplasma* spp., rubella virus, cytomegalovirus, and herpes simplex virus (known as the "TORCH" screen) may be measured to determine possible congenital infection with these agents. However, the value of these tests must be understood. They are useful in excluding a possible infection but not in proving an etiology. For example, if rubella antibody is absent, an infant almost certainly does not have congenital rubella infection. To diagnose active rubella infection in such a baby, viral cultures are required. Screening of blood supplies for cytomegalovirus antibody is used to eliminate transmission of antibody-positive blood to seronegative babies and other immunocompromised patients.

Serologic Panels

Selection of several antigens for testing with paired sera in cases in which a virus is suspected can usually be made based on clinical syndrome, the known local epidemiology of particular viruses, and the patient's age. This has led to the concept of serologic batteries of panels. Some examples of possible panels are included in Table 6–10.

Antigens from mumps, western equine encephalitis, eastern equine encephalitis, St. Louis encephalitis, and California encephalitis viruses—and perhaps lymphocytic choriomeningitis virus, Epstein-Barr virus, and HIV—may be included in a panel of tests for central nervous system diseases. Although herpes simplex antigen is sometimes included in such a panel, a rise in antibody titer is not sufficient to diagnose herpes encephalitis. Many viral central nervous

Table 6–10. Serological panels.

Clinical Syndrome	Panels
Myocarditis/pericarditis	Group B coxsackievirus types 1–5, influenzaviruses A and B, cytomegalovirus
Hepatitis	Hepatitis viruses
Exanthem	Rubella virus, measles virus, varicella-zoster virus
Central nervous system infections	Western and eastern equine encephalitis virus, California encephalitis virus, St. Louis encephalitis virus, lymphocytic choriomeningitis virus, measles virus, Epstein-Barr virus, rabies virus
Heterophile-negative mononucleosis syndromes	Epstein-Barr virus, cytomegalovirus, human immunodeficiency virus
Respiratory infections	Influenza viruses A and B; respiratory syncytial virus; parainfluenza virus types 1, 2, and 3; adenoviruses

system illnesses, especially aseptic meningitis, are caused by the enteroviruses; however, the many serotypes and the cumbersome serologic methods necessary for their diagnosis usually make it impractical to include them in a panel. When one or two enteroviruses have been shown to be epidemic in an area in one summer, one can pick up some additional cases by performing neutralization tests on paired sera by using only those specific enteroviruses that are endemic in the community.

The viral antigen panel for testing respiratory syndromes might include influenza A and B; respiratory syncytial virus; parainfluenza types 1, 2, and 3; and adenoviruses.

To test for viral causes of exanthems, the panel would include measles and rubella. If the disease is vesicular, herpes simplex virus and varicella-zoster virus should be included, although the herpes viruses are best diagnosed by culture or antigen detection.

Antigens from group B coxsackie virus types 1–5 and perhaps influenza A and B viruses could make up the panel for myocarditis and pericarditis. Although numerous viruses have been implicated in inflammatory diseases of the heart and its covering membranes, the group B coxsackieviruses are believed to account for almost one half of the cases. Unfortunately, much of the clinical illness is expressed late in the infection, at the time when standard methods of virus detection are likely to fail and it is too late to demonstrate seroconversion or significant antibody titer rises.

MOLECULAR TEST METHODS

In recent years a variety of assays have been developed to detect viral nucleic acid—either DNA or RNA. The best known of these is PCR, an amplification technique that allows the detection and selective replication of a targeted portion of the genome. The technique uses special DNA polymerases that initiate replication in either the 3' or 5' direction. The specificity is provided by primers that recognize a pair of unique sites on the genome so that the DNA between them can be replicated by repetitive cycling of the test conditions. Because each newly synthesized fragment can serve as the template for its own replication, the amount of DNA doubles with each cycle. The amplification power of PCR offers a solution for the sensitivity problems inherent in the direct application of probes. Although the nucleic acid segment amplified by PCR can be seen directly on a gel, the greatest sensitivity and specificity are achieved when probe hybridization is carried out after PCR. A probe is a fragment of DNA that has been cloned or otherwise recovered from a genomic or plasmid source. In some cases the probe is synthesized as a single chain of nucleotides (oligonucleotide probe) from known sequence data. The probes are labeled with a radioisotope or other marker and used in hybridization reactions either to detect the homologous sequences in unknown specimens or in gel electrophoresis.

The diagnostic use of DNA probes is to detect or identify microorganisms by hybridization of the probe to homologous sequences in DNA extracted from the entire organism. A number of probes have been developed that will quickly and reliably identify organisms that have already been isolated in culture. The application of probes for detection of infectious agents directly in clinical specimens such as blood, urine and sputum is more difficult.

Recently, the branched DNA (bDNA) a rapid assay for direct quantification of viral nucleic acid has been developed for hepatitis B, hepatitis C, and HIV infections. Because the bDNA assay measures viral nucleic acids at physiological levels by boosting the reporter signal, rather than by amplifying target sequences, it is not subject to the errors inherent in the amplification steps of PCR-based methods. Inherently quantitative and amenable to routine use in a clinical setting, the bDNA assay may be useful in the management of patients with chronic viral diseases. Recent studies have illustrated the potential clinical utility of the bDNA assay in determining the prognosis and in therapeutic monitoring of infection. Additional nucleic acid tests include hybrid capture and nucleic acid sequence-based amplification.

REFERENCES

Diagnosis of Bacterial, Fungal, & Parasitic Infections

Bryant JK, Strand CL: Reliability of blood cultures collected from intravascular catheter versus venipuncture. Am J Clin Pathol 1987;88:113.

Cockerill FR III et al: Analysis of 281,797 consecutive blood cultures over an eight-year period: trends in microorganisms isolated and the value of anaerobic culture of blood. Clin Infect Dis 197;24:403.

Current WL, Garcia LS: Cryptosporidiosis. Clin Microbiol Rev 1991;4:325.

Dalovisio JR et al: Comparison of the amplified *Mycobacterium tuberculosis* (MTB) Direct Test, Amplicor MTB PCR, and IS6110-PCR for detection of MTB in respiratory specimens. Clin Infect Dis 1996;23:1099.

Douard MC et al: Quantitative blood cultures for diagnosis and management of catheter-related sepsis in pediatric hematology and oncology patients. Intensive Care Med 1991;17:30.

Entemadi HA et al: Isolation of *Brucella* spp. from clinical specimens. J Clin Microbiol 1984;20:586.

Felices FJ et al: Use of the central venous pressure catheter to obtain blood cultures. Crit Care Med 1979;7:78.

Havlik JA et al: A prospective evaluation of *Mycobacterium avium-complex* colonization of the respiratory and gastrointestinal tracts of persons with human immunodeficiency virus infection. J Infect Dis 1993;168:1045.

Hay JE et al: Clinical comparison of Isolator, Septi-Chek, nonvented tryptic soy broth, and direct agar plating combined with thioglycollate broth for diagnosing spontaneous bacterial peritonitis. J Clin Microbiol 1996;34:34.

Kaditis A et al: Yield of positive blood cultures in pediatric oncology patients by a new method of blood culture collection. Pediatr Infect Dis J 1996;15:615.

Kiehn TE, Commarato R: Comparative recoveries of *Mycobacterium avium–M. intracellulare* from Isolator lysis-centrifugation and BACTEC 13A blood culture systems. J Clin Microbiol 1988;26:760.

Kohler RB, Winn WC Jr, Wheat LJ: Onset and duration of urinary antigen excretion in Legionnaires' disease. J Clin Microbiol 1984;20:605.

Maki DG, Weiss CE, Sarafin HW: A semiquantitative culture method for identifying intravenous catheter-related infection. N Engl J Med 1977;296:1305.

Miller JM: *Specimen Management in Clinical Microbiology.* American Society for Microbiology Press, 1999.

Mosca R et al: The benefits of Isolator cultures in the management of suspected catheter sepsis. Surgery 1987;718.

Murray PR, Washington JA: Microscopic and bacteriologic analysis of sputum. Mayo Clin Proc 1975;50:339.

National Committee for Clinical Laboratory Standards: *Performance Standards for Antimicrobial Susceptibility Testing—Ninth Informational Supplement; Approved Standard 100-59.* National Committee for Clinical Laboratory Standards, 1999.

National Committee for Clinical Microbiology Standards: *Antimycobacterial Susceptibility Testing: Publication No. NCCLS M24-P.* National Committee for Clinical Laboratory Standards, 1990.

National Committee for Clinical Microbiology Standards: *Reference Method for Broth Antifungal Susceptibility Testing of Yeasts: Approved Standard M27-A. Publication No. NCCLS M27-A.* National Committee for Clinical Laboratory Standards, 1997.

Ortega Y et al: Cyclospora species: a new protozoan pathogen of humans. N Engl J Med 1993;328:1308.

Paya CV, Roberts GD, Cockerill FR III: Laboratory diagnosis of disseminated histoplasmosis—clinical importance of the lysis-centrifugation blood culture technique. Mayo Clinic Proc 1987;62:480.

Pokorski SJ et al: Comparison of Gen-Probe Group A Streptococcus Direct Test with culture for diagnosing streptococcal pharyngitis. J Clin Microbiol 1994;32:1440.

Sharp SE: Routine anaerobic blood cultures: still appropriate today? Clin Microbiol Newslett 1991;13:179.

Tonnesen A, Peuler M, Lockwood WR: Cultures of blood drawn by catheters vs venipunctures. J Am Med Assoc 1976;235:1877.

Vallenas C et al: Efficacy of bone marrow, blood, stool, and duodenal content cultures for bacteriologic confirmation of typhoid fever in children. Pediatr Infect Dis 1985;4:496.

Voigtz J, Delsol G, Fabre J: Liver and bone marrow granulomas in Q fever. Gastroenterology 1983;84:887.

Washington JA II: Blood cultures: principles and techniques. Mayo Clin Proc 1975;50:91.

Washington JA II: Collection, transport, and processing of blood cultures. Clinics Lab Med 1994;14:59.

Weber R et al: Human microsporidial infections. Clin Microbiol Rev 1994;7:426.

Diagnosis of Viral Infections

Tang Y-W, Procop GW, Persing DH: Molecular diagnostics of infectious diseases. Clin Chem 1997;43:2021.

Section II.
Clinical Syndromes

Infections of the Central Nervous System 7

Zell A. McGee, MD*

The signs and symptoms of infections of the central nervous system (CNS) are not specific to each type of infection (eg, brain abscess or meningitis), but certain clusters of signs and symptoms can limit the range of CNS infectious diseases that must be considered. The following elements of a patient's history, signs, and symptoms may indicate or accompany meningeal or parenchymal CNS infections, especially if one or more occur in the same patient: fever; headache; nausea and vomiting; confusion, obtundation, or uncharacteristic behavior; stiff neck; or focal neurologic dysfunction.

When these signs and symptoms follow those of infection of the upper or lower respiratory tract, the cluster suggests the transition of the respiratory tract infection to bacteremia or viremia and then its progression to meningitis or another type of CNS infection.

ACUTE BACTERIAL MENINGITIS

General Considerations

More than most other infectious diseases, acute bacterial meningitis threatens the life, personality, and functional ability of a patient. The disease may be obvious or quite subtle in its initial presentation. Empiric therapy usually relies on a one-step (or monosynaptic) thought process (disease → antimicrobial agent) that is not optimal for managing most infectious diseases. Optimal recognition and management of acute bacterial meningitis use a progressive, three-step (or polysynaptic) thought process that is also effective for managing most other infectious diseases (Table 7–1).

*The author is grateful to J. Richard Baringer, MD, Professor of Neurology, University of Utah School of Medicine, for his careful review of this chapter, his constructive suggestions, and the several sections he wrote on subjects that represent special areas of his expertise.

1. DISEASE (DIAGNOSIS)

The key findings in meningitis are the presence of fever, headache, stiff neck, nausea and vomiting, and, often, variable states of confusion. Note that neck stiffness, although usually present, is often overlooked. Although a stiff neck is *not* required to make the diagnosis of meningitis, its presence demands immediate pursuit of the diagnosis of meningitis.

Perhaps the most helpful indication that the diagnosis of meningitis should be considered seriously enough to warrant the performance of a spinal tap (if a thorough examination yields no signs of an intracranial mass or increased intracranial pressure) is the transition of a sore throat or other upper respiratory tract irritation to nausea and vomiting. Whereas most patients who actually have meningitis have fever and headache, the pattern of evolution of meningitis, especially meningococcal meningitis, is from sore throat to tachypnea (perhaps a sign of early meningococcemia with disseminated intravascular coagulation) and then to nausea and vomiting as the meningococcemia seeds the cerebrospinal fluid (CSF) space and establishes meningitis with cerebral edema.

The constellation of headache, fever, nausea, vomiting, or a combination of these symptoms should immediately prompt the consideration of meningitis, especially in the context of previous disease or irritation of the upper respiratory tract (eg, sinusitis, otitis media, or pharyngitis). Often patients with meningitis will complain of ocular pain or an increase in headache when turning their eyes from side to side. Although this sign is not specific for meningitis, its presence should prompt suspicion of the disease.

Although the accuracy of the clinical examination in the diagnosis of meningitis is limited by the paucity of prospective data, Attia et al (1999) have evaluated the clinical findings in meningitis and cite the 97% sensitivity and 60% specificity of the jolt test of Uchihara and Tsukagoshi (1991) in diagnosing meningitis. The jolt test, accentuation of headache by rapid movement of the head from side to side, ap-

Table 7–1. Polysynaptic thought process for managing infectious diseases.

Diagnosis/Disease	→	Most Likely Organism	→	Best Antimicrobial[1]
eg, Meningitis		*Consider:* a. Patient's personal risk factors b. Community risk factors (what's going around) c. Physical examination d. Laboratory: (Gram stain) cultures and imaging studies		*Consider:* a. Which antimicrobial is likely to be active against the most likely organism? b. Which antimicrobial is delivered to the site of the infection? c. Which antimicrobial has a bactericidal mode of action? d. Which antimicrobial avoids the patient's special vulnerabilities (eg, allergy, myasthenia gravis, young age)?

[1]In known or suspected meningitis, the antimicrobial therapy should be initiated as soon as possible, ideally within 30 min after strongly suspecting or confirming the diagnosis.

pears to have potential usefulness, but more widespread systematic evaluation is needed before incorporation of the test into routine practice can be recommended.

In a febrile patient with a history of previous upper respiratory tract irritation, vomiting should elicit concern about meningitis rather than being considered a sign of gastroenteritis or "the flu."

Note that almost all patients with bacterial meningitis give a history of upper respiratory tract irritation that can be interpreted as pharyngitis. However, health care personnel should consider the context of such complaints, and, if there is fever > 101 °F, nausea or vomiting, headache, confusion, or any signs of neurologic irritation, meningitis should be strongly suspected. The author has seen patients who suffered permanent neurologic damage because their meningitis was not recognized and health care personnel, using an algorithm for pharyngitis, gave oral antimicrobial therapy, which is inappropriate for meningitis.

Although patients often do not complain spontaneously of neck stiffness, they frequently will admit to the symptom if questioned. Detecting neck stiffness is best done by cupping the patients occiput in the examiner's hands, gently turning the head from side to side, which usually causes little discomfort, and then gently flexing the neck while observing the patient's face for signs of pain and feeling for sudden resistance as the neck is flexed. Modest degrees of meningeal irritation are usually evident with this procedure. Whereas the traditional Kernig and Brudzinski signs may be present in acute meningitis, in the author's experience they are present much less often than is neck stiffness and are less sensitive in the detection of minor degrees of meningeal irritation than is testing for neck stiffness as described above.

Once the diagnosis of meningitis has been seriously considered and care has been taken to assure that there are no signs of an intracranial mass (eg, no papilledema or focal neurologic abnormalities), a lumbar puncture should be performed.

2. PREDICTION OF THE MOST LIKELY CAUSATIVE ORGANISM

Acute meningitis is most often caused by bacteria that have capsules (eg, *Neisseria meningitidis, Haemophilus influenzae,* and *Streptococcus pneumoniae*). These organisms are passed from person to person by droplet spread or mucosa-to-mucosa spread during close contact. Although some yeasts (eg, *Cryptococcus neoformans*) cause acute meningitis in patients with ostensibly normal immunity, they cause meningitis more often in patients whose cell-mediated immunity is compromised (eg, by lymphoma, AIDS, steroids, or other forms of iatrogenic immunosuppression), and yeast infections must be sought in such patients.

Empiric therapy entailing the choice of broad-spectrum antibiotics instead of organism-specific therapy is suboptimal for acute meningitis, because such therapy is at danger of being less active and less effective than therapy specifically targeted for the most likely organism. Therefore, optimal therapy entails predicting the most likely organism to be causing the meningitis and then administering the therapy that is optimal for that organism. Usually one can correctly deduce the most likely organism to be causing the meningitis by considering four kinds of information regarding the patient: (1) personal risk factors, (2) community risk factors, (3) physical examination, and (4) laboratory and imaging studies (see Tables 7–1 through 7–4).

Personal Risk Factors

The bacterial pathogen most likely to cause meningitis varies with the site of acquisition and the age of the patient (Table 7–2). Patients who are asplenic or alcoholic or who have preexisting ear or paranasal sinus infections are at greater risk of having infections with *S pneumoniae*.

Among patients who have conditions that allow access of stool to CSF, for instance, a pilonidal sinus or *Strongyloides stercoralis* infestation, *Escherichia coli* is often the most likely organism to be causing their meningitis.

In some cases, the most likely organism may be predicted by the nature of prior antimicrobial therapy. Certain broad-spectrum, oral antimicrobial agents such as ciprofloxacin or cefixime may predispose a patient to bacterial meningitis, apparently by eradicating normal nasopharyngeal flora and allowing overgrowth of meningitis-causing bacteria, especially *S pneumoniae,* which is less susceptible to these antibiotics than are normal flora. A substantial number of patients have developed fatal pneumococcal sepsis and meningitis while being treated with such antibiotics (Lee et al, 1991; Ottolini et al, 1991). Ironically, most of the antibiotics were prescribed for upper respiratory tract infections, bronchitis, and otitis media, which may not benefit from antimicrobial therapy (Gonzales et al, 1997; Nyquist et al, 1998).

The microorganism causing the antecedent respiratory tract or other type of infection is the likely cause of meningitis in many patients. Patients with enteroviral meningitis have sometimes had recent contact with children or others with diarrhea. A recent episode of genital herpes should prompt consideration of a herpetic etiology of the meningitis.

Community Risk Factors

Cases of meningococcal disease may occur in epidemics or clusters, and state or local health departments may be helpful in predicting the most likely organism from such epidemiologic data.

Similarly, clusters of meningitis caused by *Listeria monocytogenes* have occurred in conjunction with the ingestion of raw and cooked meat, poultry, and, especially, unpasteurized dairy products such as cheese that have entered the commercial food supply contaminated with *L monocytogenes*.

Physical Examination

Several physical signs, considered in light of the patient's age, can be extremely helpful in correctly predicting the infecting organism (Table 7–3). If there are no physical signs suggesting the most likely organism, the organism can be predicted on the basis of the locale of acquisition of the meningitis and the patient's age as described above (see Table 7–2).

Laboratory/Imaging Studies

The laboratory findings in the CSF can also be helpful in either predicting or determining with certainty the most likely organism or type of organism to be causing the meningitis (Table 7–4).

Chest x-rays showing pneumonia in conjunction with meningitis suggest that the cause of the pneumonia may be the same as that of the meningitis; this association has been observed with *N meningitidis* and *S pneumoniae* infections. If the pneumonia in conjunction with meningitis is cavitary, organisms that cause cavitary pneumonia such as *Staphylococcus aureus* or *Pseudomonas aeruginosa* should be suspected.

Table 7–2. Value of locale of acquisition and age to predict the most likely organism to be causing the meningitis.[1]

Locale	Age Group	Most Likely Organism(s)
Community-acquired meningitis	< 1 mo (neonatal)	Group *B* streptococci Some *S pneumoniae* *L monocytogenes*
	1–23 mo (infants)	*S pneumoniae* *N meningitidis* Some group B streptococci *H influenzae*
	2–18 y	*N meningitidis* *S pneumoniae* Some *H influenzae*
	19–59 y	*S pneumoniae* *N meningitidis* Some *H influenzae*
	>60 y	*S pneumoniae* Some *L monocytogenes*
Hospital-acquired or trauma-related meningitis	Any age	<10 d post-trauma: *S pneumoniae,* *H influenzae* (patient's flora) >10 d post-trauma: *K pneumoniae,* *P aeruginosa, E coli,* other hospital flora

[1]Most of the data are from Schuchat et al. (N Engl J Med 1997;337:970), who did not include in their surveillance *E coli* or other enteric pathogens among infants <1 mo of age.

Table 7–3. Value of physical examination in predicting the most likely organism to be causing meningitis.

Physical Sign	Most Likely Organism
Otitis media	*S pneumoniae*
Sacral pilonidal sinus	Stool flora, probably *E coli*
Petechiae (depends on age)	Young adults, *N meningitidis* Children, *H influenzae*
Purpura fulminans	*N meningitidis*
Ecthyma gangrenosum	*P aeruginosa* > candida > other fungi, other gram-negative bacilli

Table 7–4. Value of CSF findings in predicting the most
likely cause of meningitis.

Type of Meningitis	Leukocyte Cell Type	Glucose	Stain	Other Tests
Bacterial meningitis	Polys	< 50% of blood	Gram	Culture PCR for some
Tuberculous meningitis	Lymphocytes[1]	< 50% of blood	Ziehl-Nielsen	Culture PCR[2]
Fungal meningitis	Lymphocytes	Low	India ink[3]	Culture Antigen[4] Antibody[5]
Viral meningitis	Lymphocytes[6]	Normal[7]		CSF culture PCR Stool culture
Carcinomatous meningitis	Lymphocytes, tumor cells	Very low	Cytologic exam	

[1]PMN cells may be present early in disease.
[2]Limited availability of test.
[3]For cryptococci; relatively insensitive.
[4]For cryptococcus.
[5]For coccidioides.
[6]PMN cells may predominate in first 24 h.
[7]May be low in mumps.

3. DESIGN OF OPTIMAL THERAPY FOR THE PARTICULAR PATIENT

It is important to initiate therapy as promptly as possible. In general, it is preferable to begin therapy after CSF and blood cultures have been obtained, but before the results of the laboratory examinations are available. Therefore, the hypothesis about the most likely organism should be used to initiate therapy, then the hypothesis should be tested by examining the CSF with nonspecific tests such as the leukocyte count and differential and CSF protein and glucose concentrations, all of which can be helpful in indicating groups of causative agents (see Table 7–4). A more sensitive and specific identification of the most likely organism often can then be obtained by performing a Gram stain on CSF subjected to cytospin slide centrifugation and culture and, if the Gram stain is negative, also testing the CSF for evidence of cryptococcal antigen and tuberculous infection, using polymerase chain reaction (PCR) or culture. Microscopic detection of the organism causing meningitis is more effective if the CSF is first subjected to cytospin slide centrifugation, which substantially increases the sensitivity of the Gram-staining endeavor (Shanholtzer et al, 1982). Rapid bacterial antigen tests were once used to attempt identification of the causative microorganism if prior antimicrobial therapy made it undetectable. However, bacterial antigen tests were found to be of "no detectable clinical benefit" in diagnostic and therapeutic decision-making (Perkins et al, 1995), and many laboratories no longer perform these tests.

If pneumococcal meningitis is likely (see Table 7–2), a premium should be put on culturing the organism from blood or CSF so that knowledge of its penicillin susceptibility can help facilitate design of an optimal treatment regimen. If specific tests such as PCR analysis of the CSF point to an organism different from the one originally hypothesized, the therapy can be changed to another specific therapy (such a change will seldom be necessary).

Whereas the foregoing considerations represent the optimal approach to acute bacterial meningitis, one must remember that tuberculous, cryptococcal, and occasionally coccidioidal meningitis also may have an acute onset and may produce clinical findings indistinguishable from those in acute bacterial meningitis.

Differential Diagnosis

Note that vomiting, although a common symptom of gastrointestinal disease, occurs frequently in meningitis. Meningitis is likely to be much more threatening to the life and function of the individual than is gastrointestinal disease, so one should not assume that vomiting in the febrile patient represents gastroenteritis.

A patient with meningococcal sepsis may have a normal or low total peripheral leukocyte count, but there is often an increased proportion of "bands" or immature polymorphonuclear leukocytes in the peripheral blood. In patients who have such laboratory findings in conjunction with other signs or symptoms of sepsis, strongly consider initiating parenteral therapy for sepsis, using antimicrobial agents appropriate for the most likely causative microorganism.

Syphilitic meningitis develops more often during the secondary or tertiary stages of the disease, generally at a slower pace than meningitis caused by other microorganisms, and presents with seizures in ~ 18% of patients with this disease. Thus, in patients with signs and symptoms suggestive of meningitis, especially seizures, syphilitic meningitis should be considered as part of the differential diagnosis, and appropriate serologic tests for syphilis should be performed on the serum and CSF.

Cautions Prior to Lumbar Puncture

It is very important to establish whether the patient with signs and symptoms of acute meningitis has papilledema, which is rare in acute meningitis without complications such as a mass lesion. A thorough examination should also be performed to detect any lateralizing findings (eg, hemiparesis or hemianopic field defect) or localizing findings (eg, aphasia), which might suggest the presence of some other process such as a brain abscess, subdural empyema, or cerebral infarction with mass effect. The presence of papilledema, localizing signs, or lateralizing signs mandates an imaging study before the performance of a lumbar puncture. A lumbar puncture performed in the presence of a mass lesion, particularly one that displaces intracranial structures, can result in a herniation syndrome and possibly death. However, antimicrobial therapy for the meningitis should be initiated before the patient is sent for the imaging study, as noted below.

In many emergency rooms, it is common practice to obtain a computed tomography (CT) scan for patients who have signs and symptoms suggestive of meningitis, before a diagnostic lumbar puncture is performed or antimicrobial therapy is instituted. Most authorities agree that any delay involved in obtaining such imaging studies could result in a significant hazard to the patient with meningitis if antibiotic treatment has not already been instituted. Bacteria multiply rapidly in the sheltered environment of the subarachnoid space, and the delays that are commonly encountered in obtaining imaging studies create a significant additional hazard to the patient. Therefore, if imaging studies are indicated (see previous paragraph), the patient should be stabilized, and optimal parenteral antibiotic therapy should be begun before such imaging studies are obtained. However, Baker et al (1994), after a systematic study of the efficacy of routine head CT scans prior to lumbar puncture in the emergency department concluded, "Routine use of CT scans in the absence of localizing signs prior to lumbar puncture in the emergency department is not indicated."

In some instances it may be necessary to perform a lumbar puncture without CT or magnetic resonance imaging (MRI) to establish the diagnosis of meningitis in order to permit initiation of prompt, optimal, specific antibiotic treatment. For instance, if a patient with signs of meningitis (but with no suggestion of papilledema or lateralizing or focal neurological deficits) is cared for in a setting where imaging studies are not available, eg, a rural office or clinic, it may be necessary to perform a lumbar puncture to establish the diagnosis of meningitis and institute optimal parenteral therapy. In such a situation, if the patient is to be transferred to a tertiary facility, the parenteral antimicrobial therapy should be continued and part of the CSF, as well as blood cultures obtained before therapy, should be transported with the patient. In addition, in the midst of a community-wide epidemic of meningococcal meningitis or when the patient has signs of meningococcal sepsis (eg, petechiae or purpura fulminans) with meningitis, it is probably safe to do a lumbar puncture without antecedent CT or MRI imaging if there are no signs of an intracranial mass.

Once treatment of meningitis has commenced and the patient has been stabilized, it is the practice of some experts to image the brain at some time during the course of therapy because of the frequency of associated pathologic processes. These associated processes include paranasal or mastoid sinusitis, subdural empyemas or effusions, basilar skull fractures, intracerebral abscesses or infarctions, and hydrocephalus, many of which may require neurosurgical intervention. Other experts reserve CT or MRI scans for patients with signs of a mass lesion, patients who remain febrile for > 5 days after initiation of optimal antimicrobial therapy, patients who have altered consciousness, or patients who were initially infected with bacteria such as *S pneumoniae* that are especially likely to cause sinusitis or loculated pus that requires drainage.

Optimally, for the diagnosis and therapy of most patients with known or suspected meningitis, the steps in Table 7–5 should be taken, but, if the presence of even questionable findings of papilledema, lateralizing signs, or localizing signs raises concerns over a possible mass lesion, or, if there is worsening headache or a diminishing level of consciousness, imaging studies should be considered as follows:

A. Immediately Available CT Scan. If a CT scan can immediately be performed, obtain a CT scan and proceed to a lumbar puncture if no mass lesion is present, and follow the remainder of the steps in Table 7–5.

B. CT Not Readily Available. If a CT scan is not readily available or a significant delay is anticipated, most experts recommend that blood cultures be obtained immediately and antibiotic treatment optimal for the most likely organism (see Tables 7–2 and 7–3) be instituted before the CT or other imaging study and before a lumbar puncture (see Treatment section below). The prior institution of antibiotic therapy will only minimally decrease the diagnostic sensitivity of CSF cultures and may still allow detection and identification of the causative microorganism by stains or PCR. The initial emergency therapy can be changed if findings of stains, cultures, or PCR

Table 7–5. Management of the patient with obvious meningitis.

If the patient has obvious meningitis (fever, stiff neck, and confusion or coma), set an ideal goal of allowing yourself 30 min to have an IV infusing the best antibiotic for the most likely organism to be causing the meningitis.

Suggested Use of the 30 Min

10 min to confirm the diagnosis and get history (eg, drug allergy, previous meningitis, recent sinusitis or trauma) and assure that there is no papilledema and that there are no focal neurological deficits that might suggest a mass lesion (such findings indicate that a spinal tap may result in a herniation syndrome)

5 min to start an IV and draw blood cultures

10 min to do a spinal tap (if no signs of a mass lesion are present)

Do not examine the CSF yet.

5 min to start an intravenous antibiotic appropriate for the most likely organism as judged by the patient's age and other risk factors (see Tables 7–2 to 7–4 and 7–6).

Now Examine the Spinal Fluid

Change antibiotics if necessary; it rarely will be necessary if guidelines for predicting the most likely organism (see Tables 7–2 and 7–3) are followed in conjunction with picking the best antimicrobial agent for the most likely organism (see Table 7–6).

on the CSF so indicate. A change in therapy will seldom be necessary. Especially in pneumococcal meningitis, with increasing resistance of pneumococci to beta-lactam antibiotics, it is helpful to culture the organism rather than simply detecting it with stains or PCR, because the viable organisms are necessary for determining the penicillin susceptibility of the infecting pneumococcus, which is information that may be important in designing an optimal antipneumococcal antimicrobial regimen.

Patients with known or suspected meningitis should not be sent out on oral antibiotics, but should be admitted to the hospital and treated with parenteral antimicrobial agents that are optimal for the most likely organism.

Treatment

To put the imperative for speed in initiating therapy into more concrete terms, some experts have suggested a goal of allowing no more than 30 min from the time of clinical diagnosis to starting an IV infusion of the best antibiotic for the most likely organism to be causing the meningitis. A suggested use of the 30 min appears in Table 7–5 and assumes that the above-mentioned precautions and procedures regarding signs of a mass lesion will be observed.

Intravenous antimicrobial agents are the optimal types of therapy for acute bacterial meningitis. Specific, optimal antimicrobial agents for the therapy of acute meningitis that is known or suspected to be caused by particular organisms are reviewed in Table 7–6. The antimicrobial agent chosen should meet a number of criteria, which are listed under "Best Antimicrobial" in Table 7–1. As noted, the antimicrobial

agent chosen should avoid the patient's special vulnerabilities. For example, if possible, the patient should not be given an antibiotic to which he or she is allergic; patients with myasthenia gravis, which causes intrinsic neuromuscular blockade, should not be given aminoglycosides, which may induce further neuromuscular blockade; and, if possible, patients with hemolytic anemias such as sickle cell disease should not be given chloramphenicol, which diminishes erythrocyte production.

Complications

It may be difficult to separate the complications of the bacteremia and septicemia that are associated with the meningitis from the complications of the meningitis per se. The complications of the septicemia include coagulation disorders such as disseminated intravascular coagulation (manifested in meningococcemia as a petechial rash and "purpura fulminans" or in some cases as hemorrhagic adrenal necrosis—"Waterhouse-Friderichsen syndrome"), myocarditis with congestive heart failure, shock, and prolonged fever. The more frequent complications of the meningitis per se result from the inflammatory reaction, including tumor necrosis factor-alpha (TNF-α) induction, which may cause damage to cranial nerves with resulting ophthalmoplegias, deafness, and blindness. Seizures or hydrocephalus may occur as early or late complications. In meningitis caused by *H influenzae* in children, some of these complications appear to occur less frequently if dexamethasone is administered in conjunction with antimicrobial agents to diminish the production of TNF-α (see Table 7–6). No comparable information is available for meningitis in adults or for meningitis caused by other bacteria.

Prognosis

Although the mortality rate for bacterial meningitis varies with the specific etiologic agent and the clinical circumstances, especially the age of the host, with early diagnosis and prompt, targeted (not broad-spectrum) antimicrobial therapy, the mortality rates for meningococcal and *H influenzae* meningitis are generally < 10% and 5%, respectively. Pneumococcal meningitis has a worse prognosis, with mortality rates of ~ 20%; in addition, neurologic complications, such as hydrocephalus, subdural empyema, seizures, and cranial nerve palsies, occur more frequently in meningitis caused by *S pneumoniae*.

Prevention & Control

A first line of defense against meningitis is the induction of anticapsular antibodies by means of vaccines or natural exposure. Timely administration of *H influenzae* type b (Hib) conjugate vaccine has dramatically reduced the frequency of *H influenzae* meningitis in the United States; however, in some

Table 7–6. Best antimicrobial regimens for specific most likely organisms.

Organism	Regimen[1,2]
N meningitidis	• Adults: Penicillin G,[3] 4 million U by volutrol over 30 min every 4 h • Children older than 28 d: Penicillin G,[3] 50,000 U/kg IV every 6 h • Children 7 d or younger: Penicillin G,[3] 50,000 U/kg IV every 12 h • Penicillin-allergic patients: Chloramphenicol • Some experts add dexamethasone (as described below for Hib) Penicillin may cure the meningitis but fail to eradicate the nasal carrier state of the patient. To prevent postdischarge transmission of meningococci from the patient to siblings or other contacts, eradicate the carrier state of the patient with rifampin before discharge.[4] **For children older than 1 m of age, give rifampin, 10 mg/kg (maximum dose, 600 mg) PO every 12 h for a total of 4 doses in 2 d. For children ≤ 28 d old, the dosage is 5 mg/kg PO every 12 h for a total of 4 doses in 2 d. For teenagers or adults, the dosage is 600 mg PO every 12 h for a total of 4 doses in 2 d.**
Group B streptococci	• Adults: ampicillin, 2.0 g IV every 4 h + cefotaxime, 2.0 g IV every 6 h • Neonates: ampicillin, 50 mg/kg IV every 12 h + cefotaxime, 50 mg/kg IV every 12 h With either regimen, repeat CSF exam/culture 24–36 h after start of therapy.
S pneumoniae (pneumococcus)	• Adults and children older than 1 m: If the pneumococcus is *known* to be susceptible to penicillin (MIC ≤ 0.1 µg/ml), use penicillin as above; otherwise, begin therapy with vancomycin, 15 mg/kg IV every 6 h **PLUS** either[5]: Cefotaxime, 50–75 mg/kg IV every 6 h (8–28 d > old) **OR** Ceftriaxone, 100 mg/kg IV at diagnosis, 12 h, then per day thereafter (>28 d old) **OR** (Adults) ceftriaxone, 2 g IV every 12 h Adjust the regimen when the susceptibility of the pneumococcus has been quantitated (eg, if the patient is responding well and the pneumococcus is susceptible to the cephalosporin, discontinue vancomycin). Some experts add dexamethasone (as described below for Hib).
Hib	There are three major components of therapy: 1. Antibiotics: • Adults: Cefotaxime, 2 g IV every 4–6 h • Children >28 d old: Ceftriaxone, 100 mg/kg IV per day • (8–28 days old) Cefotaxime, 50 mg/kg IV every 8 h[6] Ampicillin can be used for therapy of Hib meningitis only if the infecting strain is demostrated *not* to produce β-lactamase 2. Inhibition of TNF-α production: Data from studies in children with *H influenzae* meningitis indicate that an inhibitor of TNF-α production, dexamethasone, 0.4 mg/kg IV every 12 h for 2 d of antibiotic therapy, reduces the neurologic sequelae of meningitis (Lebel et al, 1988). There are no completely comparable data in adults or in meningitis caused by other pathogens, but, if there were *no* possible contraindication, such as a history of TB, many experts woiuld use dexamethasone in meningococcal, pneumococcal, and other bacterial meningitides in which the inflammatory reaction seems to be more deleterious than helpful to the patient. 3. Eradicate carrier state of treated patients with rifampin prior to discharge[4]: **For children older than 1 mo, give rifampin, 20 mg/kg (maximum dose, 600 mg) PO daily × 4 d. For adults or teenagers, each dose is 600 mg. Some experts forego this therapy if the patient was treated with cefotaxime or ceftriaxone, either of which eradicates nasal carriage of Hib.**
L monocytogenes	• Adults: Ampicillin, 2 g IV every 4 h (some experts add gentamicin, 2 mg/kg loading dose, then 1.7 mg/kg every 8 h)[7] • Children >28 d old: Ampicillin, 50 mg/kg per 6 h + gentamicin, 2.5 mg/kg IV per 8 h • Neonates: Ampicillin, 50 mg/kg IV per 12 h + gentamicin, 2.5 mg/kg IV per 18–24 h
S aureus	• Adults: Nafcillin or oxacillin (2 g IV every 4 h) **OR** Vancomycin (1.0 g IV every 6–12 h) plus rifampin, 600 mg PO per day • Children >28 d old: nafcillin or oxacillin (37 mg/kg IV per 6 h) or vancomycin (40–60 mg/kg IV divided every 6 h). • Neonates: Nafcillin or oxacillin (25 mg/kg IV per 12 h).
Gram-negative bacill	(*not H influenzae*)
Klebsiella spp., *E coli,* etc *Pseudomonas, Enterobacter,* and *Acinetobacter* species	• Adults: Ceftazidime, 2.0 g IV every 8 h, PLUS gentamicin, 2 mg/kg IV loading dose, 1.7 mg/kg every 8 h thereafter • Children: Seek pediatric infectious disease consultation Often develop resistance to cephalosporins during therapy; therefore, susceptibility testing should be done on each successive isolate,[8] and *if* cephalosporin resistance arises, some experts treat older children, teenagers, and adults with systemic plus intraventricular aminoglycosides, as follows (an infectious disease consultation is recommended): Give intraventricular gentamicin, 0.03 mg/ml of CSF volume (the total volume of the CSF can be estimated with reasonable accuracy by the neuroradiologist)

(continued)

Table 7–6. Best antimicrobial regimens for specific most likely organisms. (continued)

Organism	Regimen[1,2]
	OR Intraventricular amikacin, 0.1 mg/ml CSF volume **PLUS** Standard intravenous therapy with the same aminoglycoside

[1]Most of these therapeutic recommendations are from *The Sanford Guide to Antimicrobial Therapy 2000* (Gilbert et al. 2000), the American Academy of Pediatrics *Red Book,* or both. For therapy of children whose age or weight does not conform to the guidelines here, the reader is advised to refer to *The Sanford Guide to Antimicribial Therapy 2000* [Tables 1 (3)–1 (5) and 16] and the pediatric *Red Book.*

[2]Use half normal saline or saline for IV diluent fluid; D_5/water administration may result in cerebral edema or hyponatremic seizures if inappropriate antidiuretic hormone secretion accompanies the meningitis, as is often the case.

[3]Avoid bolus injection of penicillin, which may precipitate seizures or cause respiratory arrest.

[4]Chemoprophylaxis regimens to protect individuals exposed to an index patient with invasive disease cause by *N meningitidis* or Hib or to eradicate the carrier state in a treated patient are shown in boldface.

[5]Recent studies in children suggest that meropenem, 1 g IV every 8 h, can substitute for the vancomycin/cephalosporin regimen (see Odio et al, 1999). Many experts add dexamethasone to the antimicrobial regimen to decrease TNF-α production and help prevent nerve damage that may result in blindness, deafness, or both.

[6]A recent, prospective, randomized, multicenter trial showed meropenem to equal cefotaxime in efficacy and safety in meningitis of children (Odio et al, 1999). Further, in that study both drugs were administered without vancomycin. The *S pneumoniae* isolates with decreased susceptibility to penicillin or cefotaxime were susceptible to meropenem.

[7]Others prefer to treat *adults* with sulfamethoxazole-trimethoprim, 15–20 mg/kg, trimethoprim equivalent, in equally divided doses given every 6–8 h. Sulfamethoxazole-trimethoprim is contraindicated in infants <2 mo of age.

[8]Some clinical microbiology laboratories save the first isolate from an infected site, and when the same microorganism is subsequently isolated from that site, report the first set of susceptibility data. This pratice may result in failure to detect the transition of an initially cephalosporin-susceptible isolate to a cephalosporin-resistant isolate during cephalosporin therapy. Thus, susceptibility testing should be done on each successive isolate in meningitis caused by *Pseudomonas, Enterobacter,* or *Acinetobacter* spp., if the patient is treated with a cephalosporin.

states, less than half of the eligible children have been immunized.

By reducing pneumococcal bacteremia, a pneumococcal vaccine theoretically should decrease the frequency of pneumococcal meningitis, and the limited immunogenicity of some of the pneumococcal serotype polysaccharides in children < 2 years old has recently been circumvented by conjugating the polysaccharides to a diphtheria protein. The resulting, currently available, 7-valent pneumococcal vaccine has been shown to prevent pneumococcal carriage and invasive pneumococcal infections, including meningitis, in children < 2 years old.

A 23-valent pneumococcal vaccine is recommended for all patients aged ≥ 65 and for nursing home residents, as well as for immunocompromised and other high-risk patients. Anatomic or functional asplenia is an absolute indication for the vaccine, and the vaccine should be given, if possible, at least 2 weeks before splenectomy. The vaccine is also recommended 2 weeks before beginning any immunosuppressive treatment.

The conjugate pneumococcal vaccine is indicated for the active immunization of infants and toddlers against invasive disease caused by pneumococci of the capsular types represented in the vaccine. The routine schedule is vaccination at 2, 4, 6, and 12–15 months of age. This vaccine is not for use in adults.

A quadrivalent meningococcal vaccine (including groups A, C, Y, and W135) is available. If there is an epidemic or cluster of cases in a closed population, such as that of a college campus or group home, or for individuals traveling to countries where meningococcal disease is epidemic, the use of the meningococcal vaccine should be considered. The quadrivalent vaccine is recommended for use in epidemics of meningococcal disease caused by strains of any group whose capsular type is represented in the vaccine. Help in determining the need for a vaccine administration program and in planning such a program should be sought from the appropriate state health department or from the Centers for Disease Control [telephone (404) 639-2215].

Protection of Contacts in Cases of Meningitis

A. Meningococcal Meningitis. Individuals who have had prolonged close contact with a meningococcal meningitis patient, especially those who have had mucosa-to-mucosa contact with such a patient, are at risk of becoming newly colonized with meningococci either from the patient or from the same source as the patient. It is newly colonized individuals, lacking serum anti-meningococcal antibodies, that are at greatest risk of developing meningococcemia or meningitis. The purpose of chemoprophylaxis is to eradicate the newly acquired meningococci and their progeny before they cross the nasopharyngeal epithelium and enter the bloodstream.

The physician managing a patient with meningococcal meningitis should notify local public health authorities about the case and work out a strategy for announcing promptly and proactively who does need and who does not need chemoprophylaxis.

Meningococcal vaccine should not be used instead of rifampin chemoprophylaxis for individuals at risk, because the response to meningococcal vaccine is not rapid enough to meet the immediate need of protecting the contacts of patients with meningococcal meningitis. Such at-risk individuals should be given chemoprophylaxis with rifampin.

Chemoprophylaxis should be given to close contacts of the patient (eg, family members, girlfriends or boyfriends, or others who may have had direct contact with the index patient's oral secretions). Chemoprophylaxis is not recommended for casual contacts, such as individuals with no history of direct exposure to the index patient's oral secretions (eg, school- or workmates). Those medical personnel who have had mucosa-to-mucosa contact with victims of meningococcal disease (eg, through mouth-to-mouth resuscitation, intubation, or suctioning before antibiotic therapy is begun) appear to be at risk and should receive chemoprophylaxis. Other medical personnel appear to be at minimal risk, but most experts would offer them chemoprophylaxis if they were exposed to a case.

The chemoprophylaxis regimens for protecting individuals exposed to a case of invasive disease caused by *N meningitidis* or Hib are the same as those used to eradicate the carrier state of the index patient prior to discharge from the hospital (see boldfaced text under the respective organisms in Table 7–6). The rifampin powder in the proper dosage can be made into a liquid formulation or incorporated into other vehicles such as applesauce for young children.

B. *H influenzae* Meningitis. The recommendation for chemoprophylaxis for contacts of cases of Hib meningitis is as follows: "In those households with at least one contact younger than 48 months whose immunization status against Hib is incomplete, rifampin prophylaxis is recommended for all household contacts, irrespective of age" (*1997 Red Book,* p. 223). See Table 7–6 for the recommended rifampin prophylaxis for protection of individuals exposed to a case of invasive Hib disease.

Because penicillins and some cephalosporins—antimicrobial agents often used to treat meningococcal or *H influenzae* meningitis—do not penetrate human cells well, meningococci and *H influenzae* organisms may remain safely inside cells of the nasopharyngeal mucosa of a patient cured of meningitis and emerge later to cause meningitis in the patient's siblings. Therefore, depending on the type of therapy of a patient with meningitis, the patient may need to be given chemoprophylaxis-like antimicrobial therapy to eradicate his or her carrier state before discharge. Such predischarge therapy is recommended for patients with either meningococcal or *H influenzae* meningitis and, for children older than 1 month, should consist of rifampin given essentially as indicated for chemoprophylaxis of contacts and detailed

in Table 7–6. Some experts do not give such therapy if the cephalosporin used for treatment of the meningitis was cefotaxime or ceftriaxone, either of which appears to eradicate nasopharyngeal foci.

ASEPTIC MENINGITIS SYNDROME

Essentials of Diagnosis

- Signs and symptoms suggestive of the aseptic meningitis syndrome include fever, headache, nausea, and vomiting.
- CSF pleocytosis is present.
- Gram's stains as well as routine bacterial and fungal cultures are negative.

Some patients who present with the signs and symptoms of meningitis have CSF pleocytosis, but they also have negative Gram stains and routine bacterial cultures of the CSF, and they have no other evidence (such as positive blood cultures) to indicate the etiology of the meningeal inflammation. In considering the management of such patients, it is helpful to designate them as having the aseptic meningitis syndrome rather than "viral meningitis" because some of these patients have proven to have infectious processes that require antimicrobial therapy (Table 7–7), which is not indicated for most cases of viral meningitis.

Diagnosis and management of the aseptic meningitis syndrome and optimal care of the patient is made more difficult if a patient with the aseptic meningitis syndrome is casually diagnosed as having viral meningitis, with a resulting cessation of attempts to make an etiologic diagnosis or to determine the cause of the meningeal inflammation.

Table 7–7. Some antimicrobial-requiring causes of the aseptic meningitis syndrome.[1]

Amebic meningitis
Brain abscess
Contiguous sinusitis, otitis
Epidural abscess
Fungal meningitis
HIV meningitis
HSV2 aseptic meningitis
Infectious endocarditis
Lyme disease
Mollaret's meningitis[1]
Syphilitic meningitis
Tuberculous meningitis
Vertebral osteomyelitis (occasionally)

[1]Although herpes simplex virus has been associated with some cases of Mollaret's meningitis (Tang et al, 2000), there are insufficient data to warrant recommendations for antiviral therapy at this time.

General Considerations

Although viral infection is the most frequent cause of aseptic meningitis syndrome, there are many antimicrobial-requiring causes of the syndrome (see Table 7–7). Arthropod-borne viruses (arboviruses) cause disease more often in late summer and early fall; enterovirus disease follows a similar seasonal pattern, with echoviruses and coxsackieviruses predominating. Mumps virus meningitis occurs more often in late winter and early spring. Meningitis due to herpes simplex virus may occur at any time, often in association with a first episode of genital herpes infection.

Clinical Findings

In general, patients with aseptic meningitis syndrome are alert and complain of severe headache, primarily when they turn their eyes to one side or the other or flex their necks. They often seek a dark, quiet room. They rarely become confused or obtunded; so, if confusion or obtundation is evident, bacterial meningitis becomes much more likely. Nevertheless, patients in the early stages of bacterial meningitis can look exactly like those with the aseptic meningitis syndrome.

To determine the cause of the aseptic meningitis syndrome in a particular patient, it is helpful to consider three characteristics of the patient's illness: (1) the pace of development of the illness, (2) the presence or absence of focal or lateralizing neurologic findings, and (3) the presence or absence of confusion.

1. The Pace of Development of the Illness— Depending on the underlying disease and the specific causative microorganism, the development of signs and symptoms of meningeal inflammation may be relatively slow (taking weeks to months) or rather rapid (taking hours to days). Tuberculous and fungal meningitis, as well as syphilitic meningitis and meningeal inflammation caused by bacterial endocarditis, generally develop at a slower pace, whereas pyogenic bacterial meningitis and viral meningitis develop more rapidly (over hours to days). Tuberculous meningitis and fungal meningitis are most expeditiously diagnosed if consultation with a microbiology laboratory is sought, so that optimal media and genetic probing techniques can be used to test the CSF. Similarly, the most incisive serologic tests for syphilis should be used in consultation with an immunology laboratory if syphilis appears to be a likely etiologic agent. Syphilitic meningitis develops more often during the secondary or tertiary stages of the disease and presents with seizures in ~ 18% of patients. Thus, in patients with signs and symptoms suggestive of meningitis, especially seizures, syphilitic meningitis should be considered as part of the differential diagnosis, and appropriate serologic tests for syphilis should be performed on the serum and CSF.

2. The Presence or Absence of Focal or Lateralizing Neurologic and Other Findings— Whereas acute bacterial meningitis may cause cranial nerve abnormalities such as deafness or ophthalmoplegias, viral meningitis seldom causes such neurologic dysfunction. Similarly, brain abscesses, even if they have not ruptured into the subarachnoid space, may cause CSF pleocytosis in the absence of detectable bacteria in the CSF. Brain abscesses are more likely than bacterial or viral meningitis to cause focal neurological findings such as hemiparesis or aphasia. Spinal epidural abscesses, which may cause fever, CSF pleocytosis, and focal neurologic deficits, are usually accompanied by pain and percussion tenderness over the spine. With both brain abscesses and spinal epidural abscesses, CT scans with enhancement or MRI scans may be required to determine the cause of the culture-negative meningeal inflammation.

3. The Presence or Absence of Confusion— In general, patients with aseptic meningitis syndrome as a result of viral meningitis are alert; therefore, if confusion or obtundation is evident, a bacterial etiology or some other nonviral etiology of the meningeal inflammation is more likely.

A. Signs and Symptoms. Signs and symptoms suggestive of the aseptic meningitis syndrome depend on its underlying etiology, but often include fever, headache, nausea, vomiting, and neck stiffness.

B. Laboratory Findings. CSF pleocytosis is present. Gram stain and routine cultures are negative. The CSF glucose, protein, leukocyte count, and differential can be helpful in determining the cause of the syndrome (see Table 7–4).

C. Imaging. A number of the antimicrobial-requiring causes of aseptic meningitis syndrome require imaging studies to identify the lesion for diagnosis, optimal antimicrobial therapy, and, if indicated, surgical drainage. Whereas the CSF in true viral aseptic meningitis has a lymphocytic pleocytosis, abscesslike processes, including contiguous sinusitis, often have predominantly polymorphonuclear leukocyte pleocytosis of the CSF. Thus, the presence of the aseptic meningitis syndrome plus clinical signs suggesting the presence of a mass lesion, especially if there is polymorphonuclear pleocytosis of the CSF, should prompt imaging studies of the areas likely to be involved. A CT scan may suffice if acute intracranial hemorrhage is a possibility or if the patient cannot remain motionless in an MRI scanner; otherwise, MRI scans are the preferred imaging modality. Brain abscesses may not be visualized on CT scans unless contrast enhancement is used (Figure 7–1). Thus, contrast enhancement should be used with CT scans that are performed because a brain abscess is in the differential diagnosis. If a brain abscess is a possibility, a CT scan should not be considered to be completed unless it was done with contrast enhancement.

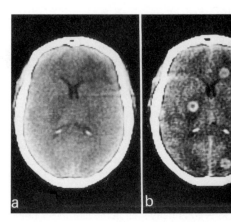

Figure 7–1. Effect of the use of contrast enhancement with CT scans on detection of brain abscesses. Two CT scan images made in the same plane within the head, ~ 30 min apart. (*a*) CT scan without contrast enhancement; (*b*) CT scan at the same level but with contrast enhancement, showing six areas of brain abscess or cerebritis not demonstrated in a. Reprinted by permission from the *Southern Medical Journal* 75:1261, 1982.

Table 7–9. Pharmaceutical products that may cause meningitis.

Category	Drug	Reference
Antibiotics	Trimethoprim-sulfamethoxazole[1]	Joffe et al, 1989
	Ciprofloxacin	Asperilla & Smego, 1989
Immuno-suppressives	OKT-3 monoclonal antibody[2]	CDC, 1986; Martin et al, 1988
Anticonvulsants	Carbamazepine	Simon et al, 1990
Nonsteroidal anti-inflammatory drugs	Ibuprofen Naproxen	Jensen et al, 1987 Sylvia et al, 1988
	Tolmentin	Ruppert & Barth 1981
	Sulindac	Ballas & Danta 1982

[1]Beware in AIDS patients receiving trimethoprim-sulfamethoxazole prophylaxis—this meningitis might be mistaken for cryptococcal or other meningitis.
[2]Might be mistaken for cryptococcal meningitis.

Differential Diagnosis

There are a substantial number of causes of aseptic meningitis syndrome, which can be life-threatening if not treated appropriately, sometimes with antimicrobial agents (see Table 7–7). The antimicrobial-requiring causes of aseptic meningitis syndrome should be excluded before embarking on an extensive workup of the non-antimicrobial-requiring causes (Table 7–8).

Some antibiotics and other pharmaceutical products can induce aseptic meningitis syndrome (Table 7–9). Whereas infectious causes of the meningitis should be excluded first, the drugs that cause meningitis are usually not critical, and substitutions of drugs that do not cause meningitis can easily be made. In a patient with meningitis who is having seizures, treatment with phenytoin usually suffices when intravenous administration is necessary; carbamazepine may be used when oral administration is possible, keeping in mind that it rarely may produce an aseptic meningitis syndrome.

To avoid inducing drug-related meningitis, avoid

Table 7–8. Some non-antimicrobial-requiring causes of the aseptic meningitis syndrome.

Chemical meningitis
Cyst-related meningitis
Drug-induced meningitis (eg, ibuprofen, sulfa-trimethoprim)
Leptospiral meningitis
Mollaret's, lupus-, sarcoid-, and Behçet-associated meningitis
Neoplastic meningitis
Viral meningitis (most)

antimicrobial treatment of respiratory tract infections (eg, sinusitis and pneumonia) with oral antibiotics that do not have optimal activity against pneumococci and other streptococci. A substantial number of patients have acquired fatal pneumococcal sepsis and meningitis while taking such antibiotics. For instance, life-threatening pneumococcal and other streptococcal infections, including meningitis, have complicated therapy with the following oral antimicrobial agents: ciprofloxacin (Lee et al, 1991; Righter, 1990) and cefixime (Ottolini et al, 1991).

Complications

The complications of aseptic meningitis syndrome depend on its etiology. If caused by a pharmaceutical product such as ibuprofen, cessation of the inciting drug usually results in disappearance of the meningitis without complications. On the other hand, aseptic meningitis syndrome resulting from a brain abscess may be fatal if the brain abscess is not identified and treated properly, so that it is allowed to rupture into the CSF space.

Treatment

As with bacterial meningitis, the antimicrobial therapy should be specifically targeted toward the most likely organism to cause the aseptic meningitis syndrome. For instance, the most likely organism to cause an epidural abscess is *S aureus,* whereas multiple brain abscesses associated with endocarditis are likely to be caused by the same organism that is infecting the heart valves.

In some patients, the best therapy for aseptic meningitis syndrome may be stopping a drug that is causing the meningitis. For instance, in a patient with AIDS who develops aseptic meningitis syndrome while receiving sulfa-trimethoprim prophylaxis against *Pneumocystis carinii* infections, it would be reasonable, after excluding infectious causes of the aseptic meningitis syndrome, to change the prophylaxis from sulfa-trimethoprim, which can cause an aseptic meningitis syndrome (see Table 7–9), to pentamidine for *Pneumocystis* prophylaxis. Antiviral therapy is not indicated for most cases of viral meningitis.

Prognosis

The prognosis of aseptic meningitis syndrome is the same as that of its underlying cause. For instance, neoplastic meningitis as the cause of aseptic meningitis syndrome has a dire prognosis, whereas drug-induced aseptic meningitis syndrome and virus-caused aseptic meningitis syndrome have an excellent prognosis.

Prevention & Control

Aseptic meningitis syndrome has such diverse causes that there is no single means of prevention and control. For instance, syphilis-related aseptic meningitis syndrome might be prevented by the use of condoms, and Lyme disease-related aseptic meningitis syndrome might be prevented by using an insect repellent that protects against the *Ixodes* tick vector.

INFECTIOUS DISORDERS WITH DEMENTIA AS A DOMINANT FEATURE

Essentials of Diagnosis

- If caused by infection, the progression of dementia is over weeks to months rather than years.
- Frontal lobe abscesses may produce dementia without lateralizing or localizing signs.
- Creutzfeldt-Jakob disease should be considered in middle-aged patients with dementia that progresses over a few weeks.

Most dementing processes with infectious causes progress subacutely, that is, over weeks to months rather than over a course of years. A more slowly progressive course may be seen occasionally with communicating hydrocephalus, as a result of prior meningeal infection and interference with reabsorption of CSF. The dementia of tertiary syphilis may also progress over a very long time course.

Frontal Lobe Infections

Infections localized to the frontal lobes of the brain can present as dementias with few other manifestations. For example, a brain abscess in the frontal lobes may fail to produce lateralizing or localizing signs that would be obvious if the abscess were located elsewhere in the brain. Progressive multifocal leukoencephalopathy (PML) (see Chapter 45), even though a disease predominantly affecting the white matter can be present in the frontal lobes and produce dementia prior to the appearance of focal deficits. Although previously encountered as a rare complication of lymphoma or Hodgkin's disease, PML is now most often seen as a complication of AIDS. Dementia in AIDS is commonly seen in the late stages of the process, where it appears to be a direct result of the viral infection. The dementia is characterized by slowness of thought, apathy, and inability to perform consecutive tasks. Loss of motor functions with ataxia and spasticity are seen as the disease progresses. Dementia becomes increasingly frequent as AIDS progresses, with 50–75% of patients affected in the terminal course of the disease.

Creutzfeldt-Jakob Disease

In middle-aged patients with dementia progressing over a few weeks, one must consider the possibility of Creutzfeldt-Jakob disease, which appears to be a prion disease (Ferrer et al, 2000). The dementia in these patients often presents abruptly and worsens perceptibly every few days to weekly, evolving into a state of mutism within 2–5 months. Myoclonic jerking of limb and trunk muscles often accompanies the process, and the patients often startle easily. The electroencephalogram is always abnormal and sometimes may show a characteristic periodic burst-suppression pattern. The CSF is usually normal. An unusual protein has recently been described in the CSF of Creutzfeldt-Jakob patients, but its presence is not sufficiently specific to serve as a diagnostic test. Recently a few cases of Creutzfeldt-Jakob disease have been described in which MRI has demonstrated increased signal in the anterior striatum.

Although Creutzfeldt-Jakob disease, as it is seen sporadically, is not due to an infection, it is thought to result from a mutation in the prion protein gene with production of abnormal isoforms of normal prion proteins; these abnormal prion proteins, if transmitted into another human host, are infectious and, after prolonged incubation, cause the same disease in the recipient. Examples have been the occurrence of the disease in recipients of corneal transplants, dura mater grafts, and human-derived pituitary growth hormone after incubation periods of many months to many years. A variant form of the disease has recently appeared in Great Britain in young individuals, perhaps related to ingestion of beef from animals afflicted by "mad cow disease," another disorder related to infectious prions.

INFECTIONS PRESENTING AS STROKE SYNDROMES

Essentials of Diagnosis

- History: known or recently acquired valvular heart disease *plus* prior infectious processes (eg, staphylococcal sepsis), genitourinary or dental procedures, or intravenous drug use; presence of indwelling intravenous catheters; immunocompromised host predisposed to fungal infections.
- Antecedent signs of infection: fever and chills, heart murmurs.
- Signs of systemic embolism: ocular (Roth spots and other hemorrhages); skin or mucosal (petechiae, Osler's nodes); renal (hematuria); splenic (abdominal pain).
- Laboratory studies: imaging of brain, CSF analysis, cardiac echo studies, blood cultures.

Infections as a cause of stroke are uncommon but must be considered in young individuals, in patients with valvular or congenital cardiac disease, or in immunocompromised hosts. Stroke in young individuals is less often due to atherosclerosis or hypertension and more often related to thrombosis or endocarditis complicating congenital or acquired valvular heart disease as a result of intravenous drug use, right-to-left cardiac shunts, or combinations of the above.

Bacterial Endocarditis

Bacterial endocarditis must always be considered in at-risk individuals, particularly if there is intravenous drug use or if the patients have recently undergone oral or genitourinary surgery or have a prosthetic cardiac valve (see Chapter 11). Embolic infarctions of brain in these individuals, although dominantly in the middle cerebral distribution, can occur in any vascular distribution and are often multiple, frequently in the distal territories of the cerebral vessels, and most frequently encountered when the causative organism is *S aureus.* The formation of mycotic aneurysms at the site of embolism is not uncommon, and may occur late in the course of the condition. Rupture of the mycotic aneurysm with subarachnoid hemorrhage is uncommon, but, when it occurs, is frequently fatal. The management of these problems, if caused by infective endocarditis, requires prolonged intravenous optimal antibiotic therapy and often repair or replacement of damaged cardiac valves.

Clues to the presence of subacute bacterial endocarditis include known previous congenital or rheumatic heart disease or rheumatic fever and the development of anorexia, backaches, myalgia, or signs of emboli in the spleen, kidney, eyes, or skin.

The foregoing signs may all be easily overlooked if attention is devoted exclusively to the neurological phenomena. Repeated blood cultures may be required to identify the causative organism; identification and determination of the organism's susceptibility to antibiotics is of critical importance in determining the nature and duration of treatment with intravenous antibiotics.

Fungal Infections

Immunocompromised hosts, particularly if neutropenic or diabetic, are susceptible to fungal diseases and, of these, *Candida, Aspergillus,* and *Mucor* species have a predilection for invading the walls of cerebral blood vessels, resulting in stroke syndromes. The source for *Aspergillus* infection of cerebral vessels is often in the respiratory tract (see Chapter 75). *Candida* infection with involvement of cerebral vessels is seen in association with prolonged use of intravenous lines and in intravenous drug users (see Chapter 73). *Mucor* infections are characteristically seen in diabetic patients with frequent episodes of acidosis (see Chapter 75). Branches of the internal carotid artery, cranial nerves III through VI, and orbital tissues are often involved.

Other Meningeal Infections

Stroke syndromes may be seen in a variety of meningeal infections as a result of the involvement in the inflammatory exudate of penetrating vessels at the base of the brain. Often such vascular involvement is seen relatively late in the course of a meningeal infection and is related perhaps to the duration and intensity of the inflammatory process. It is also seen in acute bacterial meningitides caused by pneumococci (see Chapter 47) or *H influenzae* (see Chapter 56), in subacute meningitides caused by tuberculosis or fungal infections, and in low-grade chronic meningeal infections such as those caused by syphilis (see Chapter 64). It is rarely observed in viral meningitides but can be seen in the aftermath of herpes zoster (see Chapter 33) when it affects the trigeminal nerves, presumably resulting from a zoster infection of adjacent cranial vessels.

INFECTIONS PRESENTING AS SPINAL CORD SYNDROMES

Essentials of Diagnosis

- Antecedent fever or peripheral bacterial infection.
- Development of back pain and tenderness, often with radicular pain.
- Development of paraparesis with involvement of the bladder.

Infections, along with tumors, can cause acutely or subacutely developing spinal cord deficits, frequently in the form of a paraparesis with lower-extremity weakness, paralysis of bladder function, and sensory deficits below a segmental spinal level.

Epidural Abscess

Epidural abscess is the most urgent infectious process causing a cord deficit. This infection usually originates in lung, skin, or elsewhere and spreads hematogenously to the epidural space, where the abscess typically causes radicular back pain, percussion tenderness over the spine, and a rapidly evolving loss of motor and sensory functions. Whereas S aureus is the most frequent causative organism (see Chapter 46), aerobic and anaerobic streptococci, gram-negative bacilli, and a wide spectrum of other bacterial and fungal organisms have been shown to cause epidural abscesses. Thus, a premium should be put on obtaining pus from the abscess for culture and determination of the antimicrobial susceptibility of the causative organism. Until that information is available, initial therapy should be an intravenous penicillinase-resistant synthetic penicillin such as oxacillin or nafcillin in conjunction with rifampin. However, if there is a likelihood of a methicillin-resistant S aureus (MRSA) strain in the patient (eg, recent hospitalization in a unit with prevalent MRSA), vancomycin should be included in initial therapy and discontinued if the S aureus proves susceptible to oxacillin or nafcillin, which should then be the drugs of choice, in conjunction with rifampin.

Epidural abscess must always be considered in patients with back pain and rapidly evolving signs of cord compression. The presence of an obvious primary infection, with recent bacteremia (eg, recent incision and drainage of an abscess and/or fever) may be helpful in pointing to the diagnosis (and to the most likely organism), but these antecedent signs may be absent. Intravenous drug abuse is an increasingly frequent cause of epidural abscess.

The most frequent process mimicking an epidural abscess is cord compression from metastatic tumor. The diagnosis of these conditions is most easily made or excluded by a sagittal-screening MRI scan, which shows (for epidural abscess) a diffuse or multiloculated collection of pyogenic material compressing the cord over several segments, most often in the mid thoracic region; as the next most likely location, in the lumbar spine; and also, but least likely, the cervical spine. Rapid surgical intervention is necessary in most cases and certainly in all cases in which the neurological deficit is progressing.

Genital Herpes

Genital infection with herpes simplex virus (usually type 2) occasionally causes meningitis resulting in paraparesis, a dysfunction at the sensory level or a dysfunction in the bowel, the bladder, or both (see

Chapter 33). A similar picture may occasionally be observed with segmental varicella-zoster infection. Whether these syndromes are caused by direct viral invasion of the spinal cord or an autoimmune-mediated myelopathy is unknown. A variety of viral illnesses such as mumps or chicken pox or vaccination procedures can cause a transverse myelitis, presumably by an immunologic reaction to CNS tissue triggered by the foreign antigen. The inciting agent in the majority of cases of acute transverse myelitis remains unknown. A chronic progressive myelopathy with ataxia, lightning-like pains, and later spastic weakness formerly was seen in tabes dorsalis but is rarely seen now. In contrast, HIV infection commonly causes a vacuolar myelopathy initially affecting the posterior columns; it presents with slowly progressive ataxia and culminates in a spastic paraparesis (see Chapter 23).

INFECTIOUS DISORDERS WITH FOCAL DISTURBANCES AS A DOMINANT FEATURE

Essentials of Diagnosis

- History: fever, headache, chills, sweats, malaise; focal neurological deficits—acute or subacute; infections in paranasal sinuses, mastoid, or elsewhere; intravenous drug use.
- Signs: Fever, leukocytosis; heart murmur; focal neurological deficits.
- Laboratory studies: MRI imaging; lumbar puncture, if not contraindicated by papilledema or presence of a mass lesion on MRI scanning; blood cultures, where appropriate.

The presence of fever, headache, focal neurological deficits, alterations of mental status, seizures, or some combination of these features suggests both focal disturbance of brain parenchyma and meningeal irritation. The range of conditions that can produce these disorders is large. Among the noninfectious causes, one must consider cerebrovascular disorders and primary or metastatic cancer as leading possibilities. In approaching such problems, it is important to try to determine the precise tempo of progression of the problem (ie, did the symptoms appear and become maximal in seconds to minutes, over a few hours, or over days?). Apoplectic onset or a seizure suggests an embolic process, whereas the development of a deficit over minutes to hours is more consistent with thrombosis or hemorrhage. Slower developing deficits suggest the growth of a mass lesion or sequential vascular insults which become additive.

Bacterial Endocarditis

The neurological complications of bacterial endocarditis are multiple, but the most frequent are those due to multiple emboli with infarction of the brain. Although larger emboli can cause obvious strokelike syndromes (most often in middle cerebral artery distribution), multiple smaller emboli may produce complex confusion states admixed with lesser degrees of focal disturbance. Brain abscesses, although infrequent in endocarditis, are usually associated with S aureus endocarditis and, if present in endocarditis, are usually small. They usually resolve with antimicrobial therapy alone. The formation of mycotic aneurysms at the site of embolism is not uncommon and may occur late in the course of the condition. As noted above, rupture of such aneurysms may be fatal.

One must be alert to the possibility of bacterial endocarditis in any patient with known congenital or acquired alteration of the heart valves, particularly if there has been recent oral or urogenital surgery or intravenous drug use. The traditional signs and symptoms of subacute bacterial endocarditis include asthenia, arthralgias, myalgia, anorexia, heart murmurs, splenomegaly, Roth spots, clubbing, fever, and sweats. Most such cases were caused, in the preantibiotic days, by oral streptococci, which have intrinsically low virulence, infecting heart valves damaged by rheumatic fever and causing small vegetations. However, such cases are now less prevalent and, with increasing intravenous drug use, S aureus, which can infect normal heart valves, is an increasingly prevalent cause of endocarditis. S aureus causes "acute" endocarditis with large vegetations, which embolize to cause metastatic abscesses, Osler's nodes, and, a much more toxic appearance than is typical of subacute endocarditis. The metastatic abscesses in staphylococcal endocarditis often occur in the brain and other parts of the CNS, so that the first presentation of endocarditis is often (20–40%) with stroke or another neurologic problem. The signs of endocarditis may all be easily overlooked, and the cause of the neurologic dysfunction missed if attention is devoted exclusively to the neurological phenomena. Thus, fever in the patient with neurologic findings should prompt a search for signs and symptoms of endocarditis, outlined above. The diagnostic criteria have recently been codified by Durack et al (1994). Once endocarditis is suspected, the most sensitive and specific diagnostic study is the transesophageal echocardiogram (ECHO). Repeated blood cultures may be required to identify the causative organism, but identification of the infecting microorganism and quantitative determination of its susceptibility to antibiotics are of critical importance in determining the nature and duration of treatment with intravenous antibiotics.

Herpes Simplex Virus-Induced Encephalitis

Encephalitides caused by viral infection of the brain frequently result in acutely or subacutely developing syndromes that combine headache, fever, alterations of mental status, seizures, and focal deficits. The most frequent cause of sporadic viral encephalitis is herpes simplex virus (HSV). The process in neonates is most frequently due to HSV type 2 (HSV2) resulting from maternal genital infection that was present at the time of birth. In children or adults, the encephalitic process is almost always caused by type 1 HSV (HSV1). Whether the brain infection results from exogenously acquired virus or from virus resident in cranial sensory ganglia or in the brain has not been determined.

In children or adults, the process usually takes place over a few hours to days. Initially the patient may exhibit behavioral changes or loss of memory or occasionally may complain of unusual olfactory or gustatory sensations. If present, these are valuable hints that herpes encephalitis should be considered. These symptoms may be followed by the development of headache, fever, focal deficits (hemiparesis or aphasia), and progressive disturbance of consciousness. Signs of meningeal irritation (stiff neck or vomiting) are often lacking. The diagnosis is most easily established by an MRI scan combined with typical CSF changes. The MRI scan is more sensitive than a CT scan for detecting HSV1 encephalitis; CT scans often appear normal during the first several days of the illness (when therapy is likely to have the greatest impact). Abnormalities on an MRI scan typically consist of contrast-enhancing lesions (bright on T-2–weighted images) in the medial temporal lobe and inferior frontal lobe, often extending medially and upwards into the putamen. Occasionally a seemingly separate area of disease is present in the cingulate gyrus.

The lesions are often associated with cerebral edema, and they are often bilateral, though rarely symmetrical. In our experience the lesions of HSV may be mimicked by cerebrovascular lesions in the temporal lobe or by the lesions associated with mitochondrial encephalopathies. The CSF is abnormal with a lymphocytic pleocytosis and moderately elevated protein concentration. The presence or absence of erythrocytes in the CSF is not of diagnostic help. Use of the HSV1 PCR to detect the presence of HSV genomes in CSF is generally very sensitive and highly specific, and this method has generally supplanted brain biopsy for diagnosis. The test may be falsely negative on the first day or two of the illness and after the second week. Tests for HSV antibody in the CSF are rarely positive early in the disease; cultures for HSV are almost always negative. The electroencephalogram may point to the presence of a temporal lobe abnormality; however, it is not highly specific for HSV infection. Nonetheless, a normal electroencephalogram weighs against a diagnosis of HSV encephalitis.

Treatment with intravenous acyclovir should be instituted as soon as the diagnosis is suspected, because delay in treatment is associated with a poorer outcome. With early, specific therapy, the mortality and morbidity are substantially reduced, and there is little risk from the drug except in patients with renal failure.

Arbovirus-Induced Encephalitis

A variety of arthropod-borne viruses (togaviruses) cause encephalitis, often in localized outbreaks associated with summertime increases in mosquito populations. The treatment of these encephalitides requires excellent supportive care until the patients improve on their own; there are no currently available specific antiviral compounds that are effective against arboviruses.

Brain Abscesses

A variety of bacterial infections must be considered in producing the brain abscess symptom complex. Brain abscesses commonly cause seizures, focal deficits, and, as they enlarge, progressive obtundation. Although many patients with brain abscesses have no evident primary source of infection, it is imperative to search carefully for a primary focus in the paranasal or mastoid sinuses with contiguous spread to the brain. These sites may yield the organism(s) causing the brain abscess. Additionally, metastatic (or "hematogenous") abscesses, ones seeded via the bloodstream, can arise from infection in skin or lung, by IV drug use, in association with endocarditis, or in association with dental procedures.

Brain abscesses are usually recognized by contrast-enhanced CT or MRI scans. The importance of performing CT or MRI scans with contrast enhancement when testing for brain abscesses is demonstrated in Figure 7–1. Brain abscesses may be confused with brain tumors but are usually more spherical with thinner walls; gas, if present, is a valuable diagnostic feature indicating their bacterial etiology. Brain abscesses are often associated with marked degrees of cerebral edema.

Management of patients who have brain abscesses usually involves a combination of surgery for diagnosis and drainage or excision, antibiotic therapy, and treatment of cerebral edema. The bacterial flora causing brain abscesses are highly variable and are often composed of mixed aerobic and anaerobic bacteria. Staphylococci, anaerobic streptococci, and *Bacteroides* species predominate, but gram-negative bacilli may also be found in brain abscesses. Initial treatment should include a penicillinase-resistant penicillin such as nafcillin or oxacillin to treat a staphylococcal component, a third-generation cephalosporin for gram-negative organisms, and metronidazole for anaerobic streptococci and *Bacteroides* species. Some authors include an anti-*Pseudomonas* drug if the abscess complicates chronic otitis.

Stereotaxic surgical aspiration is advisable to establish bacteriologic diagnosis and is often useful to decompress large abscesses or abscesses that block or threaten to rupture into the ventricular system. Repeated aspirations may be necessary to control a mass effect. Abscesses tend to enlarge by extending toward the ventricular system, and they pose a risk for rupture into the ventricles with an often fatal outcome. Thus, drainage efforts must be especially vigorous with abscesses enlarging toward the ventricular surfaces. Extirpation of abscesses should be considered when they are solitary, well encapsulated, and surgically accessible. Surgical extirpation should be considered for posterior fossa abscesses because of their propensity to compress the brainstem and to obstruct the ventricular system.

Management of the cerebral edema that accompanies brain abscesses should include dexamethasone administered intravenously. Mannitol may be used, especially as a temporizing measure prior to surgical drainage. Note that the cessation of steroid therapy, used to diminish cerebral edema, may allow an increase in the inflammatory component of the abscess, with a resulting increase in the degree of enhancement of the abscess wall on contrast-enhanced CT scans. This phenomenon may unnecessarily raise alarm that the abscess is not yielding to therapy; but this conclusion may be erroneous in the face of steroid withdrawal.

Subdural Empyemas

Abscesses in the subdural space (subdural empyemas) are often associated with frontal, sphenoid, or ethmoid sinus infection. For reasons that are not understood, these empyemas are seen almost exclusively in males. Because the subdural space is continuous over the entire surface of the brain and between the hemispheres, large amounts of pus can be contained within it, causing widespread irritation and edema of the underlying brain. The organisms responsible are similar to those in brain abscesses, with aerobic streptococci, anaerobic streptococci, *S aureus*, and *Bacteroides* species predominating. In addition, *S pneumoniae* and *H influenzae* may cause these empyemas. Often there is associated meningitis if organisms and/or cells spread through the arachnoid into the subarachnoid space. In addition, involvement of cortical veins and venous sinuses in the inflammatory process and possibly with associated thrombosis can be seen.

Seizures are common. Because the CSF is usually abnormal and under raised pressure in these cases, the hazard of a spinal tap often outweighs the potential value of the information that can be gained. The diagnosis is most readily established by MRI or CT scan with contrast enhancement. The treatment consists of prompt surgical drainage through bilateral or multiple burr holes or by means of formal craniotomy. Provisional antibiotic choices can then be modified on the basis of Gram staining and culture of the aspirated pus.

Cerebral Venous Sinus Infections

Infections of the cerebral venous sinuses can be seen in association with any of the above purulent infections (meningitis, brain abscess, or subdural empyema) or as a consequence of mastoid or sinus infection. Usually the venous sinus involved is contiguous to an infected structure such as an infected sinus. The lateral venous sinuses thus may be involved when there is mastoid or ear infection, and cavernous sinus thrombosis may be associated with ethmoid or sphenoid sinus infection or with facial cellulitis. With extension of infective thrombus into cortical veins, seizures and cortical venous infarction are common. Infections of the cavernous sinus may produce proptosis and chemosis of the eye and palsies of the third, fourth, and sixth cranial nerves because these nerves traverse the cavernous sinus. This constellation of signs is also seen in diabetics with nasal or sinus infection caused by *Mucor* or *Rhizopus* fungal species. Involvement of the superior sagittal sinus frequently produces cortical vein thrombosis with seizures and may result in infection of the upper convexities of the brain with consequent leg paralysis.

The diagnosis of thrombosis of these venous structures is best made by MRI scanning, which can demonstrate the presence or absence of flow voids, clotted blood, engorgement of these structures, or some combination of these findings. The diagnostic certainty can be further enhanced by the use of magnetic resonance venography.

Treatment consists of antibiotics as for the treatment of brain abscesses or for other specific causative microorganisms that may be identified. Consideration should be given to administration of anticoagulants to inhibit the propagation of clots within the venous sinuses. However, the use of anticoagulants must be weighed against the possibility of worsening the process by hemorrhage, accompanying venous occlusion and infarction of brain.

Fungal Infections

Fungi may cause focal disease in the brain with a constellation of signs and symptoms similar to those considered above. Fungal infections are most often encountered in hosts with compromised cell-mediated and other types of immunity. They are thus seen more often in patients with AIDS, lymphoma, Hodgkin's disease, leukemia, or advanced diabetes or in patients receiving cytotoxic or immunosuppressive regimens. Cryptococcal infection usually presents as severe meningitis and should be considered in the differential of acute bacterial meningitides discussed earlier. Infection caused by *Mucor* or *Rhizopus* species occurs most frequently in diabetics with multiple episodes of acidosis. The infection may spread from the oropharynx or paranasal sinuses into the skull base, involving the orbit, cranial nerves two through six, and the cavernous sinus as well as the carotid artery. The clinical picture of a red or proptotic eye with third or sixth nerve paralysis in a diabetic should prompt aggressive biopsy and culture of affected tissues as well as culturing of the nasopharynx and sinuses for *Mucor* or *Rhizopus* species. Optimal management requires a combination of surgical debridement and therapy with high-dose amphotericin B or lipid-formulated amphotericin B.

The most frequent fungi associated with parenchymal infection of brain are *Aspergillus* and *Candida* species. These infections are seen most frequently in immunocompromised hosts, particularly in those with neutropenia. *Aspergillus* infections usually have their origins in pulmonary or sinus infections whereas *Candida* infections are often seen in patients with indwelling intravenous lines, in intravenous drug users, or in patients who have previously been treated with corticosteroids or broad-spectrum antibiotics.

These organisms, especially *Aspergillus* and *Mucor* or *Rhizopus* species, share a predilection for invading the walls of cerebral blood vessels with resulting thrombosis of the blood vessel. Thus, in addition to causing cerebral abscesses and meningitis, they often produce strokelike events as a result of thrombi forming in inflamed vessels. Treatment of these fungal infections is with high-dose amphotericin B or lipid-formulated amphotericin B. Therapy for *Candida* infection is amphotericin B or lipid-formulated amphotericin B with or without 5-fluorocytosine, depending on the patient's underlying disease and the species of the *Candida* strain (some strains of certain species of *Candida*, such as *parapsilosis*, are exquisitely susceptible to the synergism of amphotericin B with 5-fluorocytosine).

Toxoplasmosis

Toxoplasmosis in the CNS presents most commonly with multifocal lesions, causing focal deficits, seizures, and impairment of cognitive functions over a period of days to weeks. Before the advent of AIDS, CNS toxoplasmosis was encountered only rarely, and then usually in the setting of Hodgkin's disease, lymphoma, or other states of severe immunosuppression. It has become a frequent complication in AIDS patients and should be immediately considered in the AIDS patient who develops multifocal neurologic deficits over a period of a few days to weeks.

The disease is often easily visualized by contrast-enhanced CT or (preferably) MRI scans, most often appearing as multicentric solid or ringlike enhancing lesions in the brain; the appearances are often quite characteristic but can be mimicked by cerebral lymphoma, also an AIDS-associated condition. A negative immunoglobulin G antibody test for *Toxoplasma gondii* makes the diagnosis unlikely. If the immunoglobulin G antibody test is positive, some experts advocate a therapeutic trial of sulfadiazine pyrimethamine, and folinic acid, in association with monitoring the clinical course as well as the size of the cerebral lesions on MRI scan. If there is no response in 10–14 days or if there is deterioration, a brain biopsy to examine other diagnostic possibilities should be strongly considered.

INFECTIOUS DISORDERS INVOLVING CRANIAL NERVES

Essentials of Diagnosis
- History: antecedent meningeal infection; infections of paranasal sinuses or skull base.
- Signs: cranial nerve deficits, especially nerves two, four, five, six, and seven.
- Laboratory: evidence of meningeal infection in CSF studies; MRI imaging of skull base and paranasal sinuses showing signs of an inflammatory process.

Involvement of the cranial nerves by infectious processes is usually the result of infection in the subarachnoid space at the base of the brain or in structures at the base near or through which cranial nerves course (eg, the cavernous sinus, as discussed previously). In the differential diagnosis, one must be aware that cranial nerves are also commonly involved by neoplastic processes, by inflammatory processes of other types (eg, sarcoidosis), or by vasculitic diseases, especially those affecting medium and small size vessels (eg, giant cell arteritis, polyarteritis nodosa, and diabetes mellitus).

Involvement of cranial nerves three, four, and six and the first division of five can be seen together because they traverse the cavernous sinus. Thus infections or infective thrombosis in the cavernous sinus can involve these nerves together.

Any meningeal infection, particularly if prolonged, can involve the cranial nerves at the base of the brain, so that palsies, particularly of the third, sixth, seventh, and eighth cranial nerves, can be seen in the course of pyogenic meningitis of any type or in more slowly evolving meningitides caused by tuberculosis, fungal infections, syphilis, or Lyme disease. Lyme disease seems to have a particular affinity for the seventh nerve; unilateral or bilateral facial paralysis is commonly seen. Involvement of the fifth nerve can be seen from reactivation of varicella-zoster virus in the trigeminal ganglion producing the well-known shingles eruption in one or more divisions of the nerve. Involvement of the intracranial portion of the carotid artery may occur in the course of ophthalmic zoster with thrombosis of the vessel and a middle cerebral distribution stroke. In contrast, reactivation of HSV in the same ganglion usually results only in the production of fever blisters on the lip.

The common Bell's palsy involving the facial nerve is tenuously associated with herpes simplex infections, prompting some authorities to recommend treatment of such cases with acyclovir. Involvement of the facial nerve by varicella results in the Ramsey-Hunt syndrome, with the appearance of vesicles in the ear. The facial nerve is susceptible to a variety of infections; in addition to those mentioned above, it is vulnerable to bacterial infections in the petrous apex. It, along with the eighth nerve, can be involved in *Pseudomonas* infections of the ear in diabetics (malignant external otitis).

INFECTIOUS DISORDERS WITH DYSPHAGIA & DYSARTHRIA AS DOMINANT FEATURES

Involvement of cranial nerves nine through twelve is less frequent in meningeal infections, perhaps because their dysfunctions are less obvious, and they are less carefully examined. Involvement of their nuclei in the brainstem is, however, common in polio, leading to severe dysphagia, dysarthria, and respiratory difficulties. Thus, polio must be considered in unvaccinated individuals who have traveled abroad.

Botulism & Pseudobotulism
Although botulism is a disorder of the neuromuscular junction rather than peripheral nerves, patients with botulism commonly present with dry mouth, dysarthria, dysphagia, diplopia, and impaired ocular accommodation. Rapid recognition of this disease is important. Prompt administration of antitoxin along with ventilatory support is essential in the management of botulism. In addition, recognition of the disease should prompt an intensive search for contaminated foodstuffs, which are most often the cause of the condition in adults. Victims who have only early symptoms may be recognized only because they were identified as sharing certain foodstuffs with individuals who have clear-cut disease.

A cluster of signs and symptoms similar to those in botulism may occur after ingestion of any part of the plant, Jimson weed (*Datura stramonium*); the syndrome may mimic botulism in patients who present with dysphagia; dilated, fixed pupils; and dry mouth (pseudobotulism), which is often accompanied by visual or auditory hallucinations. The *Datura* plant contains the anticholinergics atropine and scopo-lamine, which are highly concentrated in the seeds and can cause serious illness or death. Teenagers seeking mind-altering experiences sometimes experiment with *Datura,* only to die, probably from the cardiotoxic principle in the plant. They usually present with the pseudobotulism syndrome (fixed, dilated pupils and dry mouth), which is distinguishable from true botulism primarily by the history of contact with the *Datura* plant or its seeds and by the hallucinations, which are not a feature of true botulism. If the cardiovascular system is stable, the patients usually improve over time without therapy, other than emptying the stomach, using activated charcoal, or both; however, if the patients manifest profound toxicity, including bradycardia or tachycardia, the use of the antidote physostigmine should be considered.

Datura poisoning might also suggest rabies to the initial observer, if the hallucinations are mistaken for encephalopathy and if the dysphagia is mistaken for hydrophobia.

Rabies

Rabies should also be considered in the differential diagnosis of patients presenting with dysphagia and dysarthria, with or without hydrophobia and laryngeal spasms. Rabies must be considered in any patient who has traveled to third-world countries and who has had any contact with potentially infected animals. Skunks, raccoons, and bats are the main animal reservoirs of rabies in the United States.

Treatment with human immune globulin and diploid cell-derived vaccine is very effective for individuals exposed to or bitten by rabid animals, but it is ineffective once neurological symptoms have developed. It is important for persons in close contact with the victims, whose body fluids may be infectious or for others who have had contact with the same or other infected animals to receive postexposure prophylaxis. A detailed review of the indications and procedures for postexposure prophylaxis has been provided by the Centers for Disease Control and Prevention (CDC/MMWR, 1999).

REFERENCES

Asperilla MO, Smego RA Jr: Eosinophilic meningitis associated with ciprofloxacin. Am J Med 1989;87:589.

Attia J et al: Does this adult patient have acute meningitis? JAMA 1999;282:175.

Ballas ZK, Donta ST: Sulindac-induced aseptic meningitis. Arch Intern Med 1982;142:165.

Baker ND et al: The efficacy of routine head computed tomography (CT scan) prior to lumbar puncture in the emergency department. J Emerg Med 1994;12:597.

Boisseau FG: Physiological pyretology; or, a treatise on fevers: according to the principles of the new medical doctrine. Carey & Lea, 1832, p.67.

Carpenter RR, Petersdorf RG: The clinical spectrum of bacterial meningitis. Am J Med 1962;33:262.

Centers for Disease Control and Prevention: Aseptic meningitis among kidney transplant recipients receiving a newly marketed murine monoclonal antibody preparation. MMWR 1986;35:551.

Centers for Disease Control and Prevention: Epidemiologic notes and reports: Jimson weed poisoning—Texas, New York, and California, 1994. MMWR 1995;44:41 (updated May 24, 1999); or http://www.cdc.gov/epo/mmwr/preview//mmwrhtml/00035694.htm

Centers for Disease Control and Prevention: Human rabies prevention—United States, 1999: recommendations of the Advisory Committee on Immunization Practices (ACIP). MMWR(Suppl RR-1) 1999;48:1.

Committee on Infectious Diseases: Group B streptococcal infections. In Peter G, ed.: *1997 Red Book: Report of the Committee on Infectious Diseases,* 24th ed. American Academy of Pediatrics, 1997.

Committee on Infectious Diseases: Pneumococcal infections. In Peter G: *1997 Red Book: Report of the Committee on Infectious Diseases,* 24th ed. American Academy of Pediatrics, 1997, p. 410.

Committee on Infectious Diseases: *Haemophilus influenzae* infections. In Peter G, ed.: *1997 Red Book: Report of the Committee on Infectious Diseases,* 24th ed. American Academy of Pediatrics, 1997, p. 220.

Committee on Infectious Diseases: Meningococcal infections. In Peter G, ed.: *1997 Red Book: Report of the Committee on Infectious Diseases,* 24th ed. American Academy of Pediatrics, 1997, p. 357.

Doyle PW, Gibson G, Dohnan CL: Herpes zoster ophthalmicus with contralateral hemiplegia: identification of cause. Ann Neurol 1983;14:84.

Durack DT, Lukes AS, Bright DK, and the Duke Endocarditis Service: New criteria for diagnosis of infective endocarditis: utilization of specific echocardiographic findings. Am J Med 1994;96:200.

Ferrer et al: Prion protein deposition and abnormal synaptic protein expression in the cerebellum in Creutzfeldt-Jacob disease. Neuroscience 2000;97:715.

Gellin BG et al: Epidural abscess. In Scheld WM et al: *Infections of the Central Nervous System,* 2nd ed. Lippincott-Raven, 1997, p. 507.

Gilbert DN, Moellering RC Jr, Sande MA: *The Sanford Guide to Antimicrobial Therapy, 2000,* 30th ed. Antimicrobial Therapy, Inc., 2000.

Gilroy N et al: Trimethoprim-induced aseptic meningitis and uveitis, Lancet 1997;350:112.

Gonzales R, Steiner JF, Sande MA: Antibiotic prescribing for adults with colds, upper respiratory tract infections, and bronchitis by ambulatory care physicians. JAMA 1997;278(11):901.

Hsiao K, Prusiner SB: Inherited human prion diseases. Neurology 1990;40:1820.

Jensen S et al: Ibuprofen-induced meningitis in a male with systemic lupus erythematosus. Acta Med Scand 1987;221:509.

Joffe AM: Trimethoprim-sulfamethoxazole-associated aseptic meningitis: case reports and review of the literature. Am J Med 1989;87:332.

Koskiniemi M et al: Herpes encephalitis is a disease of middle aged and elderly people: polymerase chain reaction for detection of herpes simplex virus in the CSF of 516 patients with encephalitis. J Neurol Neurosurg Psychiat 1996;60:174.

Lebel NM et al: Dexamethasone therapy for bacterial meningitis: results of two double-blind, placebo-controlled trials. N Engl J Med 1988;319:964.

Lee BL et al: Infectious complications with respiratory pathogens despite ciprofloxacin therapy. N Engl J Med 1991;325:520.

Lemer PI: Neurological manifestations of infective endocarditis. In Aminoff MJ: *Neurology and General Medicine,* 2nd ed. Churchill Livingstone, 1995, p. 97.

Levy RM, Bredesen DE, Rosenblum ML: Neurological manifestations of the acquired immunodeficiency syndrome (AIDS): experience at U.C.S.F. and review of the literature. J Neurosurg 1986;62:475.

Martin MA et al: Nosocomial aseptic meningitis associated with administration of OKT3. JAMA 1988;259:2002.

McArthur JC, Harrison MJG: Cerebral infections in AIDS: neurosyphilis. Infect Med 1997;14:60, 65.

Navia BA, Price RW: The acquired immunodeficiency syndrome dementia complex as the presenting or sole manifestation of human immunodeficiency virus infection. Arch Neurol 1987;44:65.

Nyquist AC et al. Antibiotic prescribing for children with colds, upper respiratory tract infections, and bronchitis. JAMA 1998;279:875.

Odio CM et al: Prospective, randomized, investigator-blinded study of the efficacy and safety of meropenem vs. cefotaxime therapy in bacterial meningitis in children. Pediatr Infect Dis J 1999;18:581.

Ottolini MG et al: Pneumococcal bacteremia during oral treatment with cefixime for otitis media. Pediatr Infect Dis J 1991;10:467.

Perkins MD, Mirrett S, Reller LB: Rapid bacterial antigen detection is not clinically useful. J Clin Microbiol 1995;33:1486.

Quagliarello VJ, Scheld WM: Treatment of bacterial meningitis. N Engl J Med 1997;336:708.

Righter J: Pneumococcal meningitis during intravenous ciprofloxicin therapy. Am J Med 1990;88:548.

Roos R et al: The clinical characteristics of transmissible-Creutzfeldt-Jakob disease. Brain 1973;96:1.

Ruppert GB, Barth WF: Tolmentin-induced aseptic meningitis. JAMA 1981;245:67.

Simon LT, Hsu B, Adornato BT: Carbamazepine-induced aseptic meningitis. Ann Intern Med 1990;112:627.

Stanholtzer CJ, Schaper PJ, Peterson LR: Concentrated Gram stain smears prepared with a cytospin centrifuge. J Clin Microbiol 1982;16:1052.

Sylvia LM, Forlenza SW, Brocavich JM: Aseptic meningitis associated with naproxen. Drug Intell Clin Pharm 1988;22:399.

Tang Y-W et al: Analysis of candidate-host immunogenetic determinants in herpes simplex virus-associated Mollaret's meningitis. Clin Infect Dis 2000;30:176.

Tang Y-W, Hibbs JR, Tau KR, Qian Q, Skarhus HA, Smith TF, and Pershing DH: Effective use of polymerase chain reaction for diagnosis of central nervous system infections. Clin Infect Dis 1999;29:803.

Uchihara T, Tsukagoshi H: Jolt accentuation of headache: the most sensitive sign of CSF pleocytosis. Headache 1991;31:167.

Whitley RJ: Rabies. *In* Scheld WM, Whitley RJ, Durack DT, editors. *Infections of the Central Nervous System.* 2nd ed. Lippincott-Raven, 1997; p. 181.

Whitley RJ, Alford CA, Hirsch MS et al:. Vidarabine versus acyclovir therapy in herpes simplex encephalitis. N Engl J Med 1986;314:144.

Wiley CA, Schrier RD, Nelson JA, Lampert PW, Oldstone MBA: Cellular localization of the AIDS retrovirus infection within the brains of acquired immune deficiency patients. Proc Natl Acad Sci USA 1986;83:7089.

Will RG, Ironside JW, Zeidler M, Cousens SN, Estibeiro K, Alperovitch A, Poser S, Pocchiari M, Hofman A, Smith PG: A new variant of Creutzfeldt-Jakob disease in the U.K. Lancet 1996;347:921.

Infections of the Eye & Orbit

8

Marlene L. Durand, MD

EYELID INFECTIONS

Essentials of Diagnosis
- Generalized or localized erythema of lids.
- No change in visual acuity.
- No limitation in extraocular movements.

General Considerations
The eyelids contain meibomian glands (Figure 8–1) that secrete sebum, an oily substance that helps lubricate and protect the corneal surface. Inflammation of these glands may produce a localized swelling in the lid (hordeolum and chalazion) or redness and irritation of the lid margins (blepharitis).

HORDEOLUM

A hordeolum is an acute infection of a sebaceous gland of the upper or lower lid characterized by a red, painful swelling. The swelling may be within the lid (internal hordeolum) or at the lid margin (external hordeolum or stye). The usual cause is *Staphylococcus aureus*. Treatment is with warm compresses and topical erythromycin or bacitracin ointment (see Box 8–1).

CHALAZION

A chalazion is a firm, nontender, chronic mass within the lid. It is a sterile granulomatous reaction to either an internal hordeolum or to inspissated sebum within a meibomian gland. It is best seen on the inner surface of the lid, where the overlying conjunctiva may be reddened. Treatment is with either excision or with intralesional injection of steroids.

BLEPHARITIS

Blepharitis is an inflammation of the lid margins. It is usually bilateral and chronic and is caused by

---

Key Terms
Chemosis: edema of the conjunctiva
Endophthalmitis: infection of the vitreous
Epiphora: excessive tearing
Follicles: foci of lymphoid hyperplasia seen on the inner surface of the lids in viral or chlamydial conjunctivitis
Hypopyon: layer of white blood cells in the anterior chamber
Keratitis: infection of the cornea
Limbus: junction of the cornea and sclera
Meibomian glands: sebaceous glands of the lids
Uveitis: inflammation of the choroid, ciliary body, or iris; retinitis is often included in this term

---

dysfunction of the meibomian glands. Superinfection with *S aureus* seems to play a role. There is often associated rosacea or seborrheic dermatitis. The lid margins are red and irritated, often with skin scales clinging to the eyelashes. Symptoms are burning and itching of the lids. Treatment includes daily gentle lid scrubs with a baby shampoo to remove scales and application of topical bacitracin ointment at night. Tetracycline therapy may help if there is associated rosacea.

PRESEPTAL CELLULITIS

Preseptal cellulitis, sometimes called periorbital cellulitis, is an infection of the skin of the lids, anterior to the tarsal plate or "septum" (Figure 8–2). It is more common in children than in adults. The patient has tender, swollen, red lids but no eye pain, no change in vision or limitation of ocular movement, and no proptosis. Preseptal cellulitis must be distinguished from orbital cellulitis (see below). Common causes include *S aureus*, (group A) *Streptococcus pyogenes*, *Streptococcus pneumoniae*, and *Haemophilus influenzae*. Treatment should be with oral or intravenous (IV) antibiotics directed against these pathogens (eg, cefuroxime). Parenteral antibiotics are usually used in children as initial therapy, because some children with preseptal cellulitis are also bacteremic.

Upper lid

Meibomian glands

Lower lid

Figure 8–1. The meibomian glands of the eyelids. (Adapted from Last RJ: *Eugene Wolff's Anatomy of the Eye and Orbit*. W.B. Saunders, 1976.)

THE TEAR FILM

The tear film lubricates and nourishes the corneal surface and helps to focus light. It is composed of three layers. The outer lipid layer, produced by the meibomian glands, helps prevent evaporation of the middle aqueous layer. Chronic meibomitis, as occurs in chronic blepharitis, may decrease this lipid layer, allowing excessive evaporation of the aqueous layer, corneal dryness, and subsequent corneal defects. The middle aqueous layer is the largest layer and is produced by the lacrimal gland. The inner layer is composed of mucin produced by goblet cells in the conjunctiva. Destruction of these goblet cells, as occurs in Stevens-Johnson syndrome, leads to severe dryness and corneal damage.

LACRIMAL SYSTEM INFECTIONS

Essentials of Diagnosis
- Epiphora (excessive tearing).
- No change in visual acuity.
- Dacryocystitis: swelling and redness below the medial canthus (nasal side of the orbit).
- Canaliculitis: "pouting puncta".
- Dacryoadenitis: swelling and redness in the orbit above and lateral to the orbit of the eye.

General Considerations
The lacrimal system produces and drains the aqueous middle layer of the tear film. Tears are produced

---

BOX 8–1

Typical Microbiology and Suggested Empiric Antibiotic Therapy for Infections of the Ocular Adnexa (Lid, Lacrimal System, and Orbital Soft Tissue)

Condition	Common Organisms	Empiric Therapy[1]
Lid Infections • Hordeolum • Blepharitis • Preseptal cellulitis	• *Staphylococcus aureus* • *S aureus* • *S aureus*, group A streptococci, *Streptococcus pneumoniae*, *Haemophilus influenzae*	• Topical bacitracin or erythromycin • Same • Cefuroxime (orally or IV) (clarithromycin or clindamycin + ciprofloxacin)
Lacrimal System Infections • Dacryocystitis • Dacryoadenitis (acute) • Canaliculitis	• *S aureus*, *S pneumoniae*, *H influenzae* • Same • *Actinomyces israelii*	• Ampicillin-sulbactam or cefuroxime IV • Same • Irrigate with penicillin
Orbital Infections • Orbital cellulitis or abscess	• *S aureus*, group A streptococci, *H influenzae*, anaerobes	• Nafcillin + ceftriaxone or (vancomycin + metronidazole + ciprofloxacin)

[1]Suggestions for empiric therapy in patients who are highly penicillin allergic are given in parentheses. Note that ciprofloxacin is not approved for use in children. Treatment for some of these conditions requires prompt surgical drainage (see text).

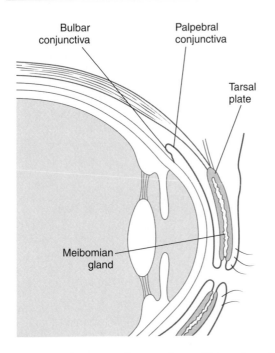

Figure 8–2. Schematic diagram of a sagittal section of the eyelids and anterior eye. The tarsal plate or septum is the connective tissue "skeleton" of the lids.

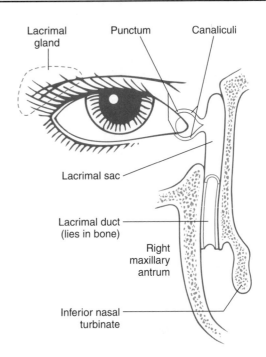

Figure 8–3. The lacrimal system. (Adapted from Barza M & Baum J: Ocular infections. Med Clin N Am 1983;67: 131.)

by the lacrimal gland, located in the upper outer portion of the globe. They flow medially across the surface of the eye and drain via canaliculi into the lacrimal sac and the nose (Figure 8–3).

DACRYOCYSTITIS

Acute dacryocystitis is the most common infection of the lacrimal system, and results from obstruction of the lacrimal sac and subsequent infection. Patients present with a unilateral acute, red, painful swelling near the bridge of the nose, just below the medial canthus. There is often a history of chronic epiphora (excessive tearing). The most common pathogens are *S aureus,* streptococci including *S pneumoniae,* and *H influenzae.* Treatment is with systemic antibiotics (eg, cefuroxime); incision and drainage may be necessary.

CANALICULITIS

Infection of the canaliculi causes epiphora, and "pouting puncta" are seen on examination. *Actinomyces israelii* is the most common pathogen, and applying pressure near the punctum causes the "sulfur granules" characteristic of this organism to be ex-

pressed. Treatment includes expressing this material and irrigating through the punctum with penicillin.

DACRYOADENITIS

Dacryoadenitis, or infection of the lacrimal gland, is rare. Acute dacryoadenitis causes redness and swelling in the upper outer portion of the orbit. Viral causes include Epstein-Barr virus, mumps, and adenovirus; bacterial causes include *S aureus, Streptococcus pneumoniae,* and *H influenzae.* Chronic enlargement of the gland may be caused by tuberculosis or syphilis, but tumors or autoimmune disorders (including sarcoidosis) are more likely causes and should be excluded first.

ORBITAL INFECTIONS

Essentials of Diagnosis

- Marked swelling, erythema, tenderness of lids.
- Proptosis (may be apparent only when measured).
- Pain with extraocular movements.

- Limitation of extraocular movements (except with early orbital cellulitis).
- Fever and leukocytosis.
- Concurrent sinusitis is common.

General Considerations

The bony orbit (eye socket) is shaped like a cone placed horizontally in the skull, point inwards. The medial wall is formed by the paper-thin lateral wall of the ethmoidal sinus, the "lamina papyracea" bone. Because this barrier is so thin, infection in the ethmoidal sinus may spread into the orbit (see Figure 8–4). Hence, ethmoidal sinusitis is the most common cause of orbital infections.

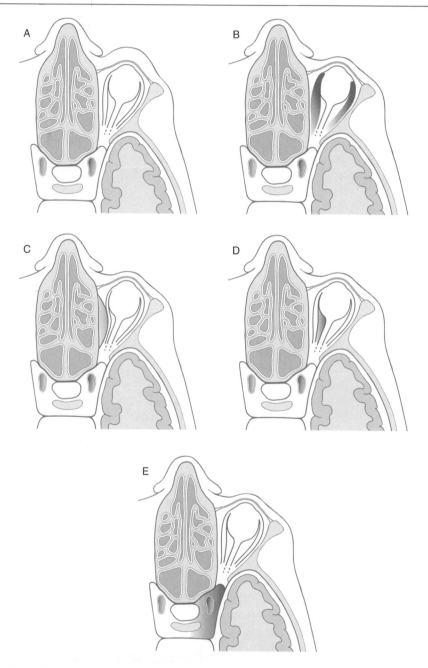

Figure 8–4. Schematic diagram of the five main categories of orbital infection. A, preseptal cellulitis; B, orbital cellulitis; C, subperiosteal abscess; D, orbital abscess; E, cavernous sinus thrombosis. (Adapted from Chandler JR, Langenbrunner DJ, Stevens FR: The pathogenesis of orbital complications in acute sinusitis. Laryngoscope 1970;80:1414.)

ORBITAL CELLULITIS

Orbital cellulitis is an infection of the orbital soft tissue contents, and usually results from sinusitis. The onset is acute, with symptoms often developing within 24 h. The patient complains of unilateral eye pain and lid swelling. It is more common in children than in adults. Fever and leukocytosis are common. The lids are red, tender, and edematous, and they may be swollen shut. There is chemosis (edema) and injection of the conjunctiva. There is proptosis, but this may not be noted until measured by an ophthalmologist. Visual acuity may be decreased, and there is pain with eye movement. With progression of the infection, there is limitation of extraocular movement. The characteristic findings on computed tomography (CT) are proptosis and stranding in the orbital fat. Evidence of sinusitis on the same side is often seen. Pathogens include *S aureus, Streptococcus pneumoniae,* anaerobes, and *H influenzae,* although the frequency of *H influenzae* infections has markedly decreased since the 1985 introduction of the *H influenzae* type b vaccine. Treatment includes IV antibiotics (eg, ampicillin-sulbactam or nafcillin plus ceftriaxone) and drainage of any sinus pus. Patients should be closely monitored by both an otolaryngologist and an ophthalmologist. Progression of symptoms despite IV antibiotics should be evaluated by a repeat CT to exclude a drainable orbital abscess.

ORBITAL ABSCESS

An orbital abscess is a collection of pus within the orbit. This is most often found in the medial or superior part of the orbit because infection usually begins in the ethmoid or frontal sinus. There is marked limitation of eye movement, and the eye usually looks "down and out" (away from the site of the abscess). Other signs and symptoms are similar to those of orbital cellulitis. On CT scan, a low-density collection within the orbit is seen. Treatment requires immediate drainage of the abscess and IV antibiotics directed against *S aureus,* streptococci, anaerobes, and *H influenzae* (eg, nafcillin plus ceftriaxone or ampicillin-sulbactam).

SUBPERIOSTEAL ABSCESS

A subperiosteal abscess is a collection of pus between the bony wall and periosteum of the orbit. Because this is usually an extension of infection from the ethmoidal sinuses, the medial wall is most often involved. It is difficult to distinguish a subperiosteal abscess from an orbital abscess on clinical grounds; both produce fever, leukocytosis, lid swelling, redness, warmth, tenderness, chemosis, decreased vision, and marked limitation of extraocular movement. As with orbital abscess, the eye is usually nearly fixed in position looking "down and out." On CT scan, a subperiosteal collection is seen. The bacteriology and treatment are the same as for orbital abscess: immediate surgical drainage plus IV antibiotics (eg, nafcillin plus ceftriaxone).

CAVERNOUS SINUS THROMBOSIS

Cavernous sinus thrombosis is a life-threatening complication of orbital infection and results from bacteria gaining access (via venous drainage of the orbit) to the cavernous sinus. It represents extension of the orbital infection (cellulitis or abscess) backwards. Because the cavernous sinus is a venous plexus that crosses the midline, inflammation in this region produces bilateral signs. Hence, bilateral signs of orbital cellulitis with systemic toxicity are very worrisome for cavernous sinus thrombophlebitis. The patient should be cared for in the intensive care unit; any drainable pus (eg, an orbital abscess or purulent sinusitis) should be drained, and nafcillin plus ceftriaxone should be given in meningeal doses (eg, in adults, 2 g of nafcillin every 4 h and 2 g of ceftriaxone every 12 h in patients with normal renal function).

CONJUNCTIVITIS

Essentials of Diagnosis
- Diffuse erythema (conjunctival injection).
- Discharge (watery or purulent).
- Eye discomfort but not pain (except in epidemic keratoconjunctivitis and in hyperacute conjunctivitis).
- No change in visual acuity.
- No change in pupillary reactivity.
- No limitation in extraocular movements.
- Conjunctival papillae or follicles may be seen.

General Considerations
Conjunctivitis is the most common type of eye infection. It is characterized by an inflamed conjunctiva, with injection and exudate. The conjunctiva is the mucous membrane that lines the inner surface of the lids (palpebral conjunctiva) and the surface of the sclera (bulbar conjunctiva) (see Figure 8–2). It does not cover the cornea, but abuts the corneal epithelium at the limbus (corneal-scleral border).

In general, patients with conjunctivitis complain of discomfort or pruritus, but they do not have deep eye pain unless the cornea is also involved (eg, epidemic keratoconjunctivitis or gonococcal disease). Any patient with a red eye and eye pain should see an ophthalmologist immediately, so that more serious eye conditions can be excluded (eg, acute glaucoma, uveitis, or endophthalmitis). Conjunctivitis may be classified by the speed with which symptoms develop: hyperacute, acute, and chronic (Table 8–1).

HYPERACUTE CONJUNCTIVITIS

Hyperacute conjunctivitis is a medical emergency because it may progress to corneal perforation and visual loss. It is nearly always caused by *Neisseria gonorrhoeae;* the remaining cases are caused by *N meningitidis.* It affects neonates and sexually active adults. Patients have copious purulent discharge (which reaccumulates within seconds to minutes of wiping clean), marked chemosis, injection, and mild lid swelling. Bilateral involvement and preauricular adenopathy may occur. The cornea is involved in about two-thirds of patients, causing true eye pain. Without prompt treatment, perforation of the cornea may occur.

The diagnosis of hyperacute conjunctivitis is made by clinical appearance and finding the gram-negative diplococci ("kissing kidney beans") characteristic of *Neisseria* spp. on the Gram stain of the exudate.

Treatment for gonococcal disease consists of a single 1-g IV or intramuscular injection of ceftriaxone. In highly penicillin-allergic patients, oral ciprofloxacin (500 mg) can be used, although efficacy data are lacking. Saline irrigation or ciprofloxacin eyedrops may be given to clear the exudate. Patients and their sexual partners should be screened for other sexually transmitted diseases and treated for possible coexistent infection by *Chlamydia* spp.

Meningococcal conjunctivitis is followed by systemic illness in 20% of patients. Blood cultures should be obtained and patients should be examined for signs of meningitis. Treatment is with ceftriaxone (2 g IV once or twice daily) or high-dose IV penicillin.

ACUTE CONJUNCTIVITIS

Acute conjunctivitis may be bacterial or viral; viral is more common. Distinguishing features are given in Table 8–1. In bacterial conjunctivitis, the discharge is purulent; in viral, it is usually watery. In bacterial conjunctivitis, papillae give the inner surface of the lids a velvety appearance. In viral conjunctivitis, fol-

Table 8–1. Clinical clues in the differential diagnosis of conjunctivitis.

Type	Discharge	Follicles	Papillae	Preauricular Adenopathy	Corneal Involvement	Organism	Comments
I. Hyperacute	Copious, purulent	−	+	+/−	+	*Neisseria gonorrhoeae*	Rarely, *N meningitidis*
II. Acute viral EKC[1]	Watery	+	−	+	+	Adenovirus 8	Highly contagious
Pharyngoconjunctival fever	Watery	+	−	+	−	Adenovirus 3	Pharyngitis common
III. Acute bacterial	Purulent	−	+	−	−	*Staphylococcus aureus,* *Streptococcus pneumoniae,* *Haemophilus influenzae,* group A streptococcus, *Haemophilus aegyptius* (tropics)	
IV. Chronic A. Bacterial	Minimal, purulent	−	+	−	−/+	*S aureus,* *Moraxella lacunata*	Associated with chronic blepharitis
B. Chlamydial 1. Inclusion conjunctivitis	Minimal	+ (lower lid)	−	+	−	Serotypes D–K	Sexually transmitted
2. Trachoma	Minimal	+ (upper lid)	−	+	+	Serotypes A–C	Fomite transmitted; Africa, Middle East, India

[1]EKC, Epidemic keratoconjunctivitis.

licles (larger than papillae) give the inner surface of the lids a pebbly appearance. Preauricular adenopathy is typical of viral conjunctivitis.

1. ACUTE VIRAL CONJUNCTIVITIS

Most cases of acute viral conjunctivitis are caused by adenovirus. Pharyngoconjunctival fever is caused by adenovirus types 3 and 7. Sore throat and fever accompany the conjunctivitis. It is easily spread from person to person; transmission in poorly chlorinated swimming pools has been reported.

Epidemic keratoconjunctivitis is usually caused by adenovirus type 8, although other serotypes have been noted. It is highly contagious and may survive on fomites (eg, doorknobs) for ≤ 2 mo. It has been associated with epidemics arising in ophthalmologists' offices where there has been inadequate disinfection. The name implies involvement of the cornea ("kerato"), and indeed corneal involvement is common, causing eye pain and photophobia. Treatment is supportive, and patients should stay home from work or school for 2 wk. Symptoms may persist for 6 wk.

Acute hemorrhagic conjunctivitis is caused by enterovirus type 70 and coxsackievirus A24 and is characterized by conjunctival hemorrhages and a 5- to 7-d course.

2. ACUTE BACTERIAL CONJUNCTIVITIS

The most common bacteria involved in acute bacterial conjunctivitis are *S aureus, Streptococcus pneumoniae, H influenzae* (especially in children), and *Moraxella catarrhalis. Haemophilus aegyptius* has caused epidemic conjunctivitis in tropical countries and may be part of Brazilian purpuric fever.

Culture of the exudate is usually not required, but should be done in any patient who fails to respond to therapy. Symptoms are self-limited and will last 7–10 d if untreated or 3–5 d if treated. Topical preparations are listed in Table 8–2; bacitracin, erythromycin, or bacitracin/polymyxin ointments are reasonable choices for empiric therapy.

CHRONIC CONJUNCTIVITIS

Chronic conjunctivitis is either follicular or nonfollicular. Nonfollicular conjunctivitis is often associated with chronic blepharitis, and *S aureus* or *M lacunata* may be cultured. Rarely, anaerobes have caused chronic conjunctivitis, and patients have responded to amoxicillin plus metronidazole.

Chronic follicular conjunctivitis is nearly always caused by *Chlamydia trachomatis.* There are two syndromes, depending on the serotype: trachoma (serotypes A–C), and inclusion conjunctivitis (sero-

Table 8–2. Some commercially available antibiotic eyedrops and ointments.

Antibiotic[1]	Trade Name[2]	Concentration
Bacitracin (o)	AK-TRACIN	500 U/g
Ciprofloxacin (s)	Ciloxan	0.3%
Ofloxacin (s)	Ocuflox	0.3%
Erythromycin (o)	–	0.5%
Gentamicin (o, s)	Genoptic	0.3%
Tobramycin (o, s)	Tobrex	0.3%
Sulfacetamide (o)	Cetamide	10.0%
Sulfacetamide (s)	Ocu-Sul-10, 15, 30	10%, 15%, 30%
Sulfisoxazole (s)	Gantrisin	4.0%
Tetracycline (o, s)	Achromycin	1.0%
Combinations		
Bacitracin, polymyxin (o)	Polysporin	—
Neomycin, polymyxin, plus bacitracin (o) or gramicidin (s)	Neosporin	—
Trimethoprim, polymyxin (s)	Polytrim	—

[1]o, Ointment available; s, solution available.
[2]The trade name list is not all-inclusive. Many of these antibiotics are also available as generic preparations.

types D–K). Diagnosis for either is by isolation of *C trachomatis* on tissue culture, demonstration of chlamydial antigen by enzyme immunoassay or fluorescent monoclonal antibody stain (eg, MicroTrak, Chlamydiazyme), or nucleic acid hybridization (Gen-Probe). Giemsa staining, an older technique, is less sensitive.

1. TRACHOMA

Trachoma is a potentially blinding disease because repeated infections lead to scarring of the cornea and corneal vascularization. It is the most common infectious cause of blindness in the world and is prevalent in parts of Africa, the Middle East, and northern India. Follicles are seen inside the upper lid. Transmission occurs by flies, fomites, or person-to-person contact. Treatment with tetracycline for 3–6 wk or azithromycin is effective, but reinfection is difficult to prevent in endemic areas. Hand washing significantly reduces the frequency of infection.

2. INCLUSION CONJUNCTIVITIS

Inclusion conjunctivitis occurs in ~ 1 in 300 sexually active adults with genital chlamydial infection. It is a chronic bilateral conjunctivitis with minimal discharge. Follicles are seen inside the lower lids. Unlike trachoma, corneal scarring does not occur. Treatment is with doxycycline, 100 mg orally 2 times/d (or erythromycin 500 mg orally 4 times/d) for 2 wk; sexual partners should also be examined and treated for chlamydial disease.

Inclusion conjunctivitis also occurs in neonates exposed to the infected mother during birth. Because neonates lack conjunctival lymphoid tissue, however, no follicles are seen. Treatment is with oral erythromycin (50 mg/kg/d) for 10–14 d.

KERATITIS (CORNEAL ULCER)

Essentials of Diagnosis
- Red, painful eye.
- Decreased vision.
- Photophobia.
- No fever or leukocytosis.

General Considerations

The cornea is only 0.5–1.0 mm thick, but it and the overlying tear film account for 75% of the refractive power of the eye. It has no blood vessels, but has many nerve fibers (hence corneal abrasions are painful). Its barrier to infection is a 5-cell-layer-thick epithelium that is contiguous with the conjunctiva. Microbes may infect this epithelium (epithelial keratitis), the corneal stroma or interstitium (interstitial keratitis), or both (ulcerative keratitis).

BACTERIAL KERATITIS

In the United States, ~ 30,000 cases of bacterial corneal ulcers are treated annually. Bacteria usually cause a craterlike ulcer when they infect the cornea (ulcerative keratitis). The patient complains of a red, painful eye; the redness is more intense near the limbus. A flashlight alone may show the defect in the cornea and a focal opacity. There may be a sterile hy-popyon (layer of leukocytes in the anterior chamber) (see Figure 8–5).

A major risk factor for ulcerative keratitis is contact lens wear. Most bacteria (except gonococci) cannot penetrate an intact corneal epithelium. Contact lenses can cause breaks in this epithelium. Soft contact lenses worn overnight carry an especially high risk of keratitis: > 10- to 15-fold the risk with daily-wear lenses. Other risk factors for keratitis include corneal abrasions, previous corneal graft, dry eyes, neurotrophic keratitis (absence of normal sensation), and exposure keratitis (eg, in comatose patients in the intensive care unit).

Patients with keratitis must be promptly evaluated by an ophthalmologist. For identification of the bacteria involved, the ophthalmologist will view the cornea with the slit lamp, carefully scrape the ulcer with a Kimura spatula, and directly plate the scrapings onto agar; a swab of the ulcer should be placed in broth.

Although coagulase-negative staphylococci are the most common organisms isolated from corneal ulcers, they may be surface colonizers rather than pathogens. Pathogens include *S aureus, Streptococcus pneumoniae,* viridans streptococci, and *Pseudomonas aeruginosa. P aeruginosa* is the most common pathogen in patients who wear contact lenses.

Empiric treatment is begun with a topical quinolone (eg, 0.3% ciprofloxacin or ofloxacin solution) or with cefazolin (50 mg/ml) plus fortified gentamicin or tobramycin (14 mg/ml) eyedrops. Of note, most eyedrops used to treat keratitis must be made up by the hospital pharmacy (the quinolones are exceptions). These are listed in Table 8–3. Antibiotic drops can be tailored to specific therapy when culture results are known. Drops must be given every hour. Patients with advanced ulcers require hospitalization, as drops should be given around the clock. IV antibiotics are needed only for extension into the sclera or for impending perforation.

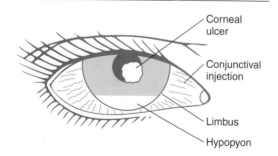

Figure 8–5. Typical bacterial corneal ulcer with sterile hypopyon. The patient has a red eye owing to conjunctival injection. The corneal ulcer appears white.

Table 8–3. Fortified antibiotic eyedrops for treating bacterial keratitis. Except as noted, these are not available commercially.

Antibiotic	Concentration[1]
Amikacin	20 mg/ml
Cefazolin	33, 50, or 133 mg/ml
Chloramphenicol[2]	5 mg/ml
Clindamycin	20 mg/ml
Ciprofloxacin (Ciloxan)[2]	3 mg/ml
Gentamicin	14 mg/ml
Ofloxacin (Ocuflox)[2]	3 mg/ml
Penicillin G	100,000 units/ml
Sulfacetamide[2]	10%, 15%, 30%
Ticarcillin	6 mg/ml
Tobramycin	14 mg/ml
Vancomycin	14 or 25 mg/ml

[1]Concentrations may be expressed as milligrams per milliliter or percent (10 mg/ml = 1%).
[2]These are available commercially. All others must be made up by a hospital pharmacy.

INTERSTITIAL KERATITIS

In interstitial keratitis, the interstitium or stroma of the cornea is involved rather than the surface. On examination, there is no craterlike ulcer, but rather a haze within the cornea. Vision is decreased, and there may be photophobia, but there is usually no pain. Syphilis, Lyme disease, and mycobacteria (tuberculosis, atypical mycobacteria, and leprosy) are the most common bacterial causes; herpes infections are the most common viral causes.

VIRAL KERATITIS

1. HERPES SIMPLEX KERATITIS

Herpes simplex virus is the most common cause of keratitis in the United States, causing 500,000 cases per year. Most cases are from reactivation of latent infection, acquired during an earlier subclinical primary ocular or orofacial infection. Herpes simplex virus type 1 is the cause of most ocular infections in adults, whereas type 2 is the major cause in neonates.

The hallmark of herpes keratitis is a dendritic (branching) defect of the epithelium. The deeper corneal stroma is not initially involved. Diagnosis may be confirmed by viral culture. Treatment includes débridement of the involved epithelium and frequent eyedrops with a topical antiviral such as trifluridine (Viroptic).

One-third of patients have recurrent episodes within 2 y. Each recurrence carries a greater risk of stromal involvement, which may lead to permanent corneal scarring. Although topical steroids should never be used in the epithelial disease, they are helpful in treating stromal keratitis. Oral acyclovir suppressive therapy (400 mg twice a day) decreases recurrences of both epithelial and stromal disease.

2. HERPES ZOSTER KERATITIS

Herpes zoster keratitis occurs in two-thirds of patients with herpes zoster ophthalmicus, the involvement of the ophthalmic division of the trigeminal nerve seen in ~ 10% of cases of zoster. An epithelial keratitis occurs at the time of the rash and consists of punctate or dendritic lesions. Treatment is with oral acyclovir (800 mg 5 times/d) or valacyclovir (1 g orally 3 times/d) for 10 d (doses assume normal renal function). Stromal keratitis may follow by several weeks. This is thought to be immune mediated and is treated with topical steroids.

PARASITIC KERATITIS

1. ACANTHAMOEBA KERATITIS

Acanthamoeba is an amoeba that lives in fresh water. It is a rare cause of keratitis, but is the most common cause of parasitic keratitis in the United States. Nearly all cases occur in contact lens wearers. Acanthamoeba may contaminate contact lens cases or lenses rinsed with water or homemade lens solutions. Acanthamoeba keratitis is characterized by pain out of proportion to clinical findings and a ring corneal infiltrate. Symptoms may be chronic, with relentless progression, while the patient is mistakenly treated for presumed herpes keratitis.

Diagnosis may be difficult. A calcofluor white stain of corneal scrapings may show the cysts. For culture, corneal scrapings should be transported in Page's saline, then plated on a nonnutrient agar overlain with a lawn of *Escherichia coli.* The organisms usually grow in 48 h and may be seen by viewing the agar plate under a light microscope.

Treatment is also difficult, and must be continued for weeks to months to prevent recrudescence of disease. The preferred drug is a swimming pool cleaner, the disinfectant Baquacil (polyhexamethylene biguanide). This is applied topically around the clock. Brolene (propamidine 0.1%) has also been used with success; it is available in England but not in the United States.

2. ONCHOCERCIASIS

Onchocerciasis is caused by a filarial parasite, *Onchocerca volvulus,* that is transmitted by *Simulium* blackflies. The flies breed in fast-moving streams in savannahs and rain forests in Africa, and hence the disease is called "river blindness." The worms (microfilariae) infect 20 million Africans and cause 290,000 cases of blindness. Microfilariae that invade the cornea and anterior chamber of the eye cause keratitis and uveitis. Treatment is with ivermectin. A major control program is underway in West Africa.

FUNGAL KERATITIS

Fungal infections of the cornea cause < 2% of corneal ulcers in this country, but are very difficult to treat. Infections caused by molds are more common in the southern United States, especially in agricultural workers. On examination, one sees a gray, plaquelike infiltrate with feathery edges and satellite lesions. *Fusarium* and *Aspergillus* spp. are the most common molds cultured. Treatment is with topical natamycin or amphotericin.

ENDOPHTHALMITIS

Essentials of Diagnosis
- Eye discomfort.
- Decreased vision.
- Hypopyon.
- Hazy or no view of retina.
- No fever or leukocytosis.

General Considerations

Endophthalmitis means infection within the eye and specifically the vitreous (see Figure 8–6). The vitreous is a gel-like substance that fills the posterior segment of the eye (volume ~ 6 ml). It is present at birth and becomes liquified with age. It is not reformed once removed, but may be replaced by saline, oil, etc.

Endophthalmitis is a medical emergency as it may quickly lead to blindness in the involved eye. Patients complain of eye discomfort (some have no pain) and a rapid decrease of vision. Patients feel otherwise well, are afebrile, and usually have a normal leukocyte count. On examination, the eye is injected and a hypopyon may be apparent. The view of the retina is hazy or obscured by the intraocular inflammation.

There are four major predisposing factors for endophthalmitis: cataract surgery, the presence of a filtering bleb for glaucoma, penetrating eye trauma, and bacteremia.

POSTCATARACT ENDOPHTHALMITIS

Endophthalmitis after cataract surgery is the most common type of endophthalmitis. It occurs as a complication of only 0.1–0.2% of cataract surgeries, but this is a large number because there are 2 million cataract surgeries performed annually in the United States. Onset of symptoms usually occurs 2–7 d after surgery, although it may occur later. Cultures of the vitreous are positive in ~ 70% of cases. The major pathogens are coagulase-negative staphylococci (70% of culture-positive cases). *S aureus* and streptococci each cause ~ 10%, whereas Gram-negative bacilli cause only 6% of cases.

BLEB-RELATED ENDOPHTHALMITIS

Patients with severe glaucoma may need a permanent "filtering bleb" created to reduce intraocular pressure. A bleb is a tunnel from the anterior chamber through the sclera, through which excess aqueous humor can leak. Endophthalmitis may occur abruptly months to years after surgery and is usually fulminant. The major pathogens are streptococci (including pneumococci), *M catarrhalis,* and *H influenzae.* The visual outcome is usually poor.

POST-TRAUMATIC ENDOPHTHALMITIS

Endophthalmitis develops in ~ 5% of patients who have penetrating eye injuries. The major pathogens are coagulase-negative staphylococci and *Bacillus cereus.* Bacillus produces a fulminant infection, and the eye is frequently lost. All penetrating eye trauma patients therefore should be given prophylactic antibiotics (eg, vancomycin plus ceftazidime) to prevent this complication.

ENDOGENOUS ENDOPHTHALMITIS

Endogenous endophthalmitis means that bacteria (or fungi) have seeded the eye from the bloodstream. Endocarditis is the major risk factor, but cases have occurred in patients with urinary tract/kidney infections, abdominal abscesses, cellulitis, and meningitis and even after upper gastrointestinal endoscopy. *S aureus* and streptococci account for ~ 50% of cases. Patients should be treated with intravitreal as well as IV antibiotics.

Candidemia is associated with intraocular infection in 5–30% of cases. Most intraocular infections produce chorioretinitis rather than vitreal infection, but endophthalmitis does occasionally occur. Vitrectomy with injection of intraocular amphotericin (10 μg) is indicated, along with prolonged therapy with

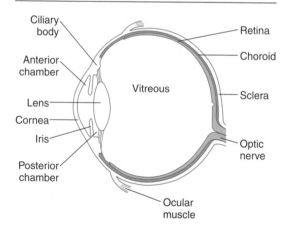

Figure 8–6. Eye anatomy. Endophthalmitis is an infection involving the vitreous. Uveitis is an inflammation of the uvea, which is made up of the choroid, ciliary body, and iris.

fluconazole (assuming normal renal function, 400 mg orally every day if the *Candida* species is sensitive).

Diagnosis

For diagnosis of endophthalmitis, an ophthalmologist will either use a syringe to aspirate and culture a sample of vitreous (a bedside procedure) or perform a vitrectomy in the operating room. A vitrectomy uses a cutting instrument (vitrector) to remove most of the vitreous, which is simultaneously replaced by saline. The dilute vitreous washings are filtered, and the filter paper is cut up and plated on agar.

Treatment

All patients should have antibiotics injected into the vitreous as soon as the vitreous sample is taken (Box 8–2). All patients should receive intravitreal vancomycin (1 mg in 0.1 ml) plus either amikacin (0.4 mg in 0.1 ml) or ceftazidime (2.25 mg in 0.1 ml). Amikacin is chosen because it has the least amount of retinal toxicity of the aminoglycosides, although a rare complication of any intravitreal aminoglycoside is macular infarction and loss of vision.

The role of systemic antibiotics in treating endophthalmitis is controversial. Some antibiotics, such as aminoglycosides, do not penetrate the blood-eye barrier well and do not achieve therapeutic levels in the vitreous. Vancomycin, quinolones, penicillins, third-generation cephalosporins (especially ceftazidime), and fluconazole are among the antimicrobials that can achieve therapeutic levels in inflamed eyes. A recent multicenter randomized trial (the Endophthalmi-

tis Vitrectomy Study) concluded that systemic antibiotics did not affect outcome in postcataract endophthalmitis, although the study was criticized because the antibiotics used (ceftazidime and amikacin) have poor activity against coagulase-negative staphylococci, the major pathogens. Vancomycin plus ceftazidime is the standard empiric IV antibiotic therapy to treat endophthalmitis.

The need for a vitrectomy to "debride" the vitreous (vs a vitreous aspirate only) is also controversial. In the Endophthalmitis Vitrectomy Study of postcataract endophthalmitis, patients who presented with severe loss of vision (light perception only) had a better visual outcome with vitrectomy than with vitreous aspirate. This difference was not apparent for patients who presented with a milder loss of vision. There were potentially confounding factors, however (patients in the vitreous aspirate group could have a subsequent vitrectomy and still be counted in the aspirate group).

A reasonable approach to the treatment of endophthalmitis would be intravitreal antibiotics for all patients with endophthalmitis, plus vitrectomy for any patient who presents with poor vision, fulminant eye symptoms and signs, or non-postcataract endophthalmitis. Intravitreal steroid (dexamethasone, 400 µg) may also be helpful. We favor using IV antibiotics for the initial 48 h until culture results are known. Therapy may be stopped then if the eye is improving and cultures are negative or reveal coagulase-negative staphylococci. For more virulent organisms, we favor 5–10 d of systemic therapy. Repeat

---

BOX 8–2

Typical Microbiology and Suggested Empiric Antibiotic Therapy for Bacterial Endophthalmitis

Type of Endophthalmitis	Common Organisms	Empiric Antibiotic Therapy[1]
Post cataract	• Coagulase-negative staphylococci (70%) • *Staphylococcus aureus* (10%) • Streptococci (10%)	Intravitreal vancomycin + either amikacin or ceftazidime PLUS IV vancomycin + ceftazidime or cipro-floxacin
Bleb-related	• Viridans streptococci • *Streptococcus pneumoniae* • *Haemophilus influenzae*	Same
Post-traumatic	• *Bacillus cereus* • Coagulase-negative staphylococci	Same
Endogenous	• *S aureus* • Streptococci • *Escherichia coli*	Same

[1]The need for systemic antibiotics in treating post cataract endophthalmitis is controversial (see text).

intraocular injections of vancomycin or ceftazidime (depending on the organism) may be helpful after the first 48 h, because antibiotic levels in the vitreous fall 24–48 h after injection.

UVEITIS & RETINITIS

Essentials of Diagnosis

- Uveitis and retinitis nearly always cause a decrease in vision.
- Anterior uveitis is usually painful.
- Posterior uveitis and retinitis are usually painless.
- In anterior uveitis, the conjunctiva is often injected (red) near the limbus.

General Considerations

The eye is made up of three coats: (1) the outer coat is composed of sclera plus cornea; (2) the middle coat is composed of the uvea (choroid, ciliary body, and iris); and (3) the inner coat is composed of the retina (see Figure 8–6). Uveitis is an inflammation of the middle, vascular layer. The term usually includes retinitis as well, because the retina is often involved when there is inflammation of the underlying choroid (a part of the uvea). Uveitis affects 1.2 million people and causes 10% of all blindness in the United States.

ANTERIOR UVEITIS

In anterior uveitis, the iris (iritis) or iris plus ciliary body (iridocyclitis) is involved. The patient has eye pain, photophobia, a red eye, and usually decreased vision. A slit lamp examination shows cells in the anterior chamber; some may coalesce on the back of the cornea ("kps" or keratic precipitates).

Of all anterior uveitis cases, ~ 10% have a known infectious etiology (eg, herpes simplex or zoster, syphilis, Lyme disease, or mycobacteria). The eye findings will regress when the underlying disease is treated. The remaining ~ 90% of cases are idiopathic or autoimmune (eg, ankylosing spondylitis, Reiter's disease, or systemic lupus erythematosus).

POSTERIOR UVEITIS

Unlike anterior uveitis, posterior uveitis usually produces no pain. The main symptom is gradual visual loss. Both choroid and overlying retina are usually involved (chorioretinitis).

1. TOXOPLASMA

Toxoplasma is the leading cause of posterior uveitis in normal hosts (see chapter 81, "Toxoplasma"). It usually represents reactivation of latent toxoplasma infection. On viewing the retina, new large yellow-white lesions are seen near old black scars. The vitreous often has inflammatory cells, so the view of the retina may be hazy—a "headlight in the fog" appearance. Diagnosis is by clinical appearance. Serology is helpful only if negative (usually excluding the diagnosis), because 50–70% of the general population is seropositive. Treatment is with pyrimethamine (with folinic acid "rescue"), sulfadiazine, and clindamycin. Corticosteroids are also used if there are lesions that threaten the macula.

2. CANDIDA SPECIES

Although *Candida* spp. may cause endophthalmitis, they more typically cause chorioretinitis, with fluffy white lesions seen on funduscopic examination. Treatment is with oral fluconazole (400 mg orally every day) if the *Candida* species is sensitive.

3. SYPHILIS

Syphilis may cause almost any retinal appearance, but typically produces a "salt and pepper" retina. Diagnosis is by clinical appearance and serology. Serology must include a fluorescent treponemal antibody test, because ocular syphilis may occur in tertiary syphilis when the nonspecific tests (eg, rapid plasma reagin test or Venereal Disease Research Laboratory test) are often negative. Ocular syphilis may also result from congenital infection. Any patient with ocular syphilis should have a lumbar puncture (to exclude neurosyphilis), as well as a test for human immunodeficiency virus [HIV (there is a higher incidence of ocular syphilis in patients with this viral infection)]. Treatment consists of high-dose IV penicillin (4 million U every 4 h, assuming normal renal function).

4. TUBERCULOSIS

Tuberculosis, like syphilis, may cause either an anterior or posterior uveitis. In posterior uveitis, the typical appearance is of bilateral multifocal choroid nodules. Treatment is the same as for other forms of extrapulmonary tuberculosis.

5. CYTOMEGALOVIRUS

Cytomegalovirus (CMV) is the most common cause of retinitis. Cytomegaloviral retinitis usually occurs in immunosuppressed patients and, until recently, occurred in 20–40% of patients with AIDS. The incidence is now much lower, owing to highly active antiretroviral therapy. The typical appearance is of retinal hemorrhages (red) and exudates (white), giving the retina a "brush-fire" appearance. Unlike toxoplasmosis, CMV does not usually cause inflammation in the vitreous, so the view of the retina is clear. Diagnosis is by clinical appearance of the retina. Serology is helpful only if negative, although patients with advanced AIDS may have falsely negative serologies. Treatment is with ganciclovir or foscarnet. Systemic therapy is favored because direct ganciclovir intraocular injections or implants treat the ocular disease but do not treat the systemic CMV disease. In patients with AIDS, life-long maintenance therapy has been required to prevent recrudescent retinitis. Recently, however, a study of seven patients on potent combination antiretroviral therapy (and with very low HIV viral loads) reported no recrudescence of retinitis when observed for 9–12 mo after maintenance CMV therapy was stopped.

REFERENCES

Eyelid Infections

Bajart AM: Lid inflammations. In Albert DM, Jakobiec FA: *Principles and Practice of Ophthalmology.* Philadelphia, WB Saunders, 1994. (An excellent chapter in a major textbook of ophthalmology.)

Donahue SP, Schwartz G: Preseptal and orbital cellulitis in childhood. Ophthalmology 1998;105:1902.

Jackson K, Baker SR: Periorbital cellulitis. Head Neck Surg 1987;9:227. (A retrospective review of 98 cases of preseptal cellulitis and 39 cases of orbital cellulitis)

Lacrimal System Infections

Lavrich JB, Nelson LB: Disorders of the lacrimal system apparatus. Pediatr Ophthalmol 1993;40:767.

Orbital Infections

Barone SR, Aiuto LT: Periorbital and orbital cellulitis in the *Haemophilus influenzae* vaccine era. J Pediatr Ophthalmol Strabismus 1997;34:293. (A review of 134 cases: *H influenzae* type b was no longer a significant pathogen. Sinusitis was present in 96% of children with orbital cellulitis.)

Chandler JR, Langenbrunner DJ, Stevens ER: The pathogenesis of orbital complications in acute sinusitis. Laryngoscope 1970;80:1414. (The classic paper on the topic.)

Lessner A, Stern GA: Preseptal and orbital cellulitis. Infect Dis Clin North Am 1992;6:933.

Conjunctivitis

Gigliotti F et al: Etiology of acute conjunctivitis in children. J Pediatr 1981;98:531.

Wan WL et al: The clinical characteristics and course of adult gonococcal conjunctivitis. Am J Ophthalmol 1986;102:575.

Keratitis

Durand M, Adamis A, Baker AS: Infections of the eyelid, lacrimal system, conjunctiva, and cornea. In Remington JS, Swartz MN: *Current Clinical Topics in Infectious Diseases,* vol. 16. Blackwell Science, 1996.

McLeod SD et al: The importance of initial management in the treatment of severe infectious corneal ulcers. Ophthalmology 1995;102:1943. (A retrospective review of 62 patients with corneal ulcers requiring hospitalization. Patients who received inadequate outpatient or inpatient therapy had a higher risk of requiring corneal transplant than those in whom initial therapy was appropriate ([73% vs 20%, respectively].)

O'Brien TP et al: Efficacy of ofloxacin vs cefazolin and tobramycin in the therapy of bacterial keratitis. Arch Ophthalmol 1995;113:1257. (A multicenter trial of 140 patients with culture-positive bacterial keratitis found no difference in efficacy between these two regimens.)

Endophthalmitis

Ciulla TA et al: Blebitis, early endophthalmitis, and late endophthalmitis after glaucoma-filtering surgery. Ophthalmology 1997;104:986.

Duch-Samper AM et al: Endophthalmitis following open-globe injuries. Curr Opin Ophthalmol 1998;9:59.

Endophthalmitis Vitrectomy Study Group: Results of the Endophthalmitis Vitrectomy Study: a randomized trial of immediate vitrectomy and of intravenous antibiotics for the treatment of postoperative bacterial endophthalmitis. *Arch Ophthalmol* 1995;113:1479. (A multicentered trial involving 420 patients. For shortcomings of the study, see Letters to Editor: Arch Ophthalmol 1996;114:1025.)

Okada AA, Johnson RP, Liles WC, et al: Endogenous bacterial endophthalmitis: report of a ten-year retrospective study. Ophthalmology 1994;101:832.

Uveitis & Retinitis

Forrester JV: Uveitis: pathogenesis. Lancet 1991;338:1498.

Holland GN: Acquired immunodeficiency syndrome and ophthalmology: the first decade. Am J Ophthalmol 1992;114:86.

Opremcak EM: *Uveitis: A Clinical Manual for Ocular Inflammation.* Springer-Verlag, 1995.

Rosenbaum JT: Uveitis: an internist's view. Arch Intern Med 1989;149:1173.

Tural C et al: Long-lasting remission of cytomegalovirus retinitis without maintenance therapy in human immunodeficiency virus-infected patients. J Infect Dis 1998;177:1080.

Upper Respiratory Tract Infections

Abinash Virk, MD, & Nancy K. Henry, PhD, MD

THE COMMON COLD

Essentials of Diagnosis

- Acute rhinorrhea, sneezing, sore throat, burning eyes, cough, malaise, headache, anosmia.
- Usually there is no or low-grade fever in adults, higher fever in infants and children.
- Examination may demonstrate serous nasal discharge, conjunctival and/or pharyngeal congestion, and rhonchi.
- Diagnosis is made clinically, can be confirmed by serology or nasopharyngeal viral cultures in selected cases.
- Imaging is helpful if bacterial superinfective complications suspected (ie, sinusitis).

General Considerations

A "cold" is a self-limited viral infection of the upper respiratory tract presenting with a coryzal syndrome. It is the most common cause for physician visits and absenteeism in school and industry. Infection rates increase sharply during the fall through spring months with peak activity being in the winter. During these months, adults and children have an average of 2–4 and 6–8 colds per year, respectively.

Rhinoviruses are the most common cause of colds, accounting for one third of all colds (Box 9–1). Parainfluenza 1–4 viruses, coronaviruses, influenza types A and B, adenovirus, respiratory syncytial virus (RSV), and their numerous serotypes also are predominant viruses that induce colds. These viruses share a common property of frequent antigenic variation and evasion from the host humoral defense mechanisms, thereby permitting their persistent survival in the community. Other viruses can present with coldlike symptoms during the prodromal period, but their primary syndrome may be localized to another organ system(s).

Transmission is via aerosol, droplet, or direct contact with infected saliva or fomite from an infected person. The rate of infection increases in families with school-age children and in overcrowded and poorly ventilated living spaces. Cigarette smokers are more likely to develop severe disease as compared with nonsmokers.

Once the virus enters the cell, replication and subsequent shedding of the virus occur. The cytopathic effect of the virus on the epithelium varies depending on the virus, being relatively mild in rhinovirus and more marked with influenza virus infection. There is an acute inflammatory response, increased vascular permeability, tissue edema, mucus production, and serum transudation, resulting in the typical cold symptoms of rhinorrhea, nasal obstruction, and cough. After the initial neutrophilic response, there is immunoglobulin M (IgM), IgG antibody, and cytokine production such as interferon, tumor necrosis factor-α, interleukin 8, interleukin 6, and others. Cytolytic T-cell response is more marked and significant in the immune response against influenza viruses than rhinoviruses. Antibody neutralization is the predominant immune mechanism for the latter. Production of antibodies coincides with the cessation of viral replication and waning of the inflammatory response and symptoms. This period may vary depending on the infecting virus. Viral shedding may occur for a few days to weeks.

Clinical Findings

A. Signs and Symptoms. Onset of symptoms is between 24 and 72 h after the infectious contact. Symptoms include malaise, rapid progression to serous nasal discharge and obstruction, sneezing, throat irritation, and cough. There may be nasal intonation of voice with nasal obstruction or hoarseness with laryngeal involvement, or both. Patients may complain of burning of the eyes. Fever usually is low-grade or absent in adults but can be much higher in infants and children. Loss of smell and taste occurs as a result of nasal mucosal edema and obstruction. Overall, the symptoms can last for 1–2 wk.

Associated clinical findings can suggest a specific viral diagnosis; for example, the presence of conjunctivitis suggests an adenoviral upper respiratory infection; myalgias and lower respiratory symptoms such as pneumonia or bronchiolitis may suggest an influenza or RSV infection. Mild disease suggests rhinovirus or coronaviruses. Symptoms of complications such as sinusitis, otitis media, or lower respiratory tract infection may be present. Patients with previous hyperactive airways or asthma can develop exacerbations.

The patient usually appears tired, with thin serous nasal discharge, mild tenderness over the sinuses, and mildly suffused conjunctiva without frank conjunctivitis, and the skin over the nostrils may be red from recurrent blowing of the nose. Pharyngeal erythema without any exudates or lymphadenopathy may be present. Lung examination may reveal evidence of bronchitis or bronchiolitis.

B. Laboratory Findings. Most colds are diagnosed clinically and do not need any further investigations. Mild leukocytosis or leukopenia with or without thrombocytopenia may be noted. Serologies and viral cultures can make a specific viral diagnosis; however, this should be attempted only in selected cases. Rapid RSV or influenza type A antigen detection enzyme immunoassays are very sensitive for nasopharyngeal specimens. Influenza, parainfluenza, adenovirus, cytomegalovirus (CMV), and other viruses can be isolated on cell line cultures. Serologies are available for influenza, parainfluenza, RSV, adenovirus, CMV, and Epstein-Barr virus (EBV). The serologic test is considered positive for active infection if an IgM is present during acute infection or a fourfold rise in IgG in paired sera is detected. Patients with equivocal histories for colds versus group A streptococcal (GAS) pharyngitis should have a rapid antigen detection test (RADT) and bacterial cultures for group A streptococcus.

C. Imaging. No imaging is recommended for uncomplicated colds. However if bacterial or viral complications such as sinusitis or pneumonia are suspected, then appropriate radiographs should be done. A computed-tomography (CT) scan study in patients with a common cold shows frequent involvement of the sinuses.

Differential Diagnosis

A common dilemma is clinically differentiating the common cold from GAS pharyngitis and prodromal symptoms related to systemic syndromes caused by other viruses such as measles, chickenpox, EBV, or CMV. The presence of high fever, chills, severe pharyngeal congestion with exudate, and tender lymphadenopathy is more likely to suggest GAS pharyngitis. An RADT and bacterial culture may be able to confirm this. An exposure history to chickenpox or other viral disease may be a helpful clue to the correct diagnosis. A diagnosis of allergies is evident with rapid resolution and no recurrences in the absence of exposure.

Complications

A complication of the common cold is viral or bacterial sinusitis. A common cold CT scan study by Gwaltney et al (1994) showed that sinus involvement occurs in > 60% of patients with a cold, with 79% of these resolving spontaneously in 2 wk without antibiotics. However, bacterial superinfections of the sinuses, middle ear, or both are potential complications. Viral pneumonia or worsening of bronchospastic airway disease is seen, particularly in children or immunocompromised hosts.

Treatment

The old idiom of "prevention is better than cure" is certainly true for the treatment of the common cold. Multiple different viruses, their many serotypes, and rapid mutations pose a considerable challenge in the development of one vaccine or drug for cold prevention or treatment. Symptomatic support is the only therapy because no effective antiviral therapy is available.

Treatment is directed to rhinorrhea, nasal obstruction, sore throat, and cough. Sneezing, rhinorrhea, and nasal blockage improve markedly with topical or systemic decongestants that decrease edema by vasoconstriction. Topical decongestants such as phenylephrine (0.5% or 0.25%) or ephedrine (1%) nasal spray or drops should be used for a short period. Rebound congestion particularly with use of decongestant sprays beyond 3–4 d can occur. Systemic decongestants include pseudoephedrine hydrochloride, ephedrine, phenylephrine hydrochloride, propylhexedrine hydrochloride, phenylpropanolamine hydrochloride, xylometazoline hydrochloride, oxymetazoline hydrochloride, naphazoline hydrochloride, and tramazoline hydrochloride. Decongestant side effects include tachycardia, elevated blood pressure, fatigue, and dizziness. These should be used cautiously in patients with hypertension and dysrhythmias.

Nasal anticholinergics are effective in inhibiting the parasympathetic activation that contributes to rhinorrhea. Ipratropium bromide nasal spray reduces rhinorrhea and sneezing in the first 3 d of the cold.

Antitussives such as codeine, dextromethorphan, hydrocodone bitartrate, and diphenhydramine hydrochloride suppress the cough reflex in the medullary cough center. Analgesics can be used to improve the myalgias, headache, and sore throat that accompany the common cold. Antihistaminics have no role in the treatment of common cold. The majority of the above mentioned drugs are available over the counter in combination with antihistaminics, analgesics, or antitussives.

Nonspecific measures such as warm saline gargles are encouraged. The role of vitamin C in the common cold is controversial. Studies with dosages of 1–30 g/d demonstrate a 5–29% decrease in severity and duration of symptoms. However, these studies had significant variations for conclusive evidence. Similarly, despite numerous studies of the role of zinc in the management of cold, zinc's role is still controversial and needs further confirmation. Antibiotics have no role in colds unless patients have evidence of bacterial superinfection of the upper respiratory tract.

Prevention & Control

Handwashing is key in the prevention of common colds. Minimizing aerosol or droplet transmission with tissues or covering the mouth should be taught to children and adults. Experimental therapies with interferon-α2 and leukocyte A interferon show some role in the prevention of cold. Producing vaccines for these viruses is difficult because of their numerous serotypes. However, active vaccination can be used for influenza types A and B along with the prophylactic use of amantadine or rimantadine.

PHARYNGITIS

Essentials of Diagnosis

- Pharyngeal discomfort or pain, pain on swallowing (odynophagia).
- Associated symptoms such as myalgia, fever, rhinorrhea, and lymphadenopathy depend on the etiologic agent.
- Pharyngeal erythema with or without exudate or lymphadenopathy.
- Leukocytosis, GAS RADT, and bacterial culture or other serologies may provide the definitive microbiologic diagnosis.

General Considerations

Pharyngitis is an acute infection of the pharyngeal mucosa caused by a variety of pathogenic microorganisms, the majority of which are viral (Box 9–2). A minority of pharyngitis episodes are bacterial and, of those, group A streptococcus is the most common cause. Viral pharyngitis is caused by respiratory viruses such as rhinoviruses, coronaviruses, adenoviruses, influenza, and EBV. Bacteria causing pharyngitis include group A and non-group A streptococci, *Corynebacterium diphtheria*, *Corynebacterium pseudodiphtherium*, *Neisseria gonorrhoeae*,

---

BOX 9–2

Microbiology of Pharyngitis

	Children	Adults
More Frequent	• *Streptococcus pyogenes* (GAS) • Adenovirus • Rhinovirus • Enterovirus • Influenza a/b • Parainfluenza virus • Respiratory syncytial virus • Coxsackievirus (herpangina)	• *S pyogenes* (GAS) • Adenovirus • Rhinovirus • Enterovirus • Epstein-Barr virus • *Mycoplasma pneumoniae* • *Chlamydia pneumoniae* • Influenza a/b • Cytomegalovirus
Less Frequent	• *Arcanobacterium hemolyticum* • Non-group A streptococci • *Yersinia enterocolitica* • Herpes simplex virus • *Fusarium tularensis*	• HIV • Herpes simplex virus • Anaerobic pharyngitis • Non-group A streptococci • *Yersinia enterocolitica* • *Neisseria gonorrhoeae* • *F tularensis*

Yersinia enterocolitica, Arcanobacterium hemolyticum, and anaerobic bacterial species. Persons infected with the human immunodeficiency virus (HIV) may present with an HIV-induced exudative pharyngitis during the acute retroviral syndrome or with *Candida*-induced pharyngitis. The etiology of pharyngitis remains obscure in 40% of cases. Most pharyngitis occurs as result of respiratory or contact transmission; few cases are foodborne. Outbreaks are common in winter or in crowded living situations, especially in families with children who serve as reservoirs by acquiring infections in daycare centers or school.

Clinical Findings

A. Signs and Symptoms. The severity of the pharyngitis may vary from mild to life threatening depending on the etiologic agent. Symptoms of mild pharyngitis are irritation or sore throat. With increasing severity there may be severe pain that increases on swallowing or talking, plus cervical lymphadenopathy with or without fever. Pharyngitis can be life threatening with inflammatory edema of pharyngeal walls and extension to the larynx leading to respiratory distress.

An erythematous pharynx with or without exudates or cervical lymphadenopathy is the common finding on examination. Because it impacts therapeutic decision-making, it is important to attempt clinical differentiation between viral and bacterial pharyngitis. However, this may be difficult. Associated clinical signs and symptoms provide diagnostic clues to formulate a differential diagnosis. Mild pharyngeal symptoms with rhinorrhea usually suggest a viral etiology. Pharyngeal exudates suggest streptococcal pharyngitis, HIV, or EBV. Presence of vesicles and ulcers is seen with herpes simplex and coxsackievirus. Coxsackievirus-related vesicles often occur on the hard palate. Adenoviral pharyngitis is associated with conjunctival congestion. EBV, HIV, *A hemolyticum,* and streptococcal toxic shock can present with pharyngitis and a generalized rash. Pharyngitis with elevated transaminases, splenomegaly, and atypical lymphocytosis is the typical manifestation of EBV-induced infectious mononucleosis. Aseptic meningitis along with pharyngitis should suggest an acute HIV or enteroviral syndrome. Systemic viral infections with CMV, measles, and rubella, among others, can present with acute pharyngitis.

Sore throat with cough and signs of pneumonia may suggest influenza, *Chlamydia pneumoniae* or *Mycoplasma pneumoniae.* Diphtherial pharyngitis is associated with a grayish pseudomembrane.

GAS (*Streptococcus pyogenes*) pharyngitis frequently presents with fever of > 38.3 °C, chills, sudden-onset sore throat, painful and difficult swallowing, and tender cervical lymph nodes. Lymphadenopathy is more likely to be anterior and tender in GAS pharyngitis, unlike viral pharyngitis, which is more likely to be generalized and nontender. Exudate with intense pharyngeal and tonsillar pillars erythema is seen. Occasionally patients, especially children, present with systemic symptoms of nausea, vomiting, and headache. Symptoms of non-group A, such as group C or G, streptococcal pharyngitis are very similar to GAS and clinically indistinguishable. These symptoms and signs are nonspecific for GAS pharyngitis. However, absence of fever or presence of other symptoms such as rhinorrhea, cough, oral ulcers, and viral exanthema strongly suggests a viral rather than a GAS pharyngitis.

B. Laboratory Findings. Laboratory values may not be of considerable help. Testing for GAS should be done in all patients in whom GAS pharyngitis cannot be confidently excluded on clinical grounds. Diagnosis of GAS pharyngitis can be made by RADT, which has a sensitivity of 80–95% and specificity of 95%. Use of RADT significantly increases the number of patients receiving appropriate antibiotic treatment. Because of its relatively lower sensitivity, a negative test should be confirmed with a throat culture. Throat cultures taken from the tonsillar fossae and posterior pharyngeal wall are 90–95% sensitive for the diagnosis of GAS pharyngitis. Follow-up cultures are not generally recommended except in patients with histories of acute rheumatic fever or poststreptococcal glomerulonephritis or in outbreaks. Asymptomatic contacts of the patient do not need to be screened unless there is an outbreak or the patient has a history of acute rheumatic fever.

Special culture media for *N gonorrhoeae* or *C diphtheria* should be specifically requested when these bacteria are suspected. Serologic testing can establish the diagnosis of EBV, HIV, CMV, influenza, *M pneumoniae,* and *C pneumoniae.* During acute HIV retroviral syndrome, HIV RNA polymerase chain reaction, or HIV culture can help make a diagnosis because HIV serology may be negative.

C. Imaging. A lateral neck x-ray should be done if the patient has associated symptoms of stridor or respiratory compromise, to rule out laryngeal obstruction.

Differential Diagnosis

In children, Kawasaki's syndrome can present with a clinical picture similar to an infectious pharyngitis. Noninfectious causes of pharyngitis include chemotherapy-induced mucositis, drug reactions, agranulocytosis, or connective-tissue disorders.

Complications

Local complications of bacterial pharyngitis include peritonsillar or retropharyngeal abscesses or *Fusobacterium necrophorum* jugular vein thrombophlebitis and its embolic complications (Lemeire's syndrome). In the United States, appropriate and timely antibiotics have decreased nonsuppurative complications of *S pyogenes* such as rheumatic heart disease or poststreptococcal glomerulonephritis. *C diphtheria* pharyngitis may become complicated by acute upper-airway obstruction, myocarditis, or neuritis. Viral pharyngitis may be complicated by secondary bacterial infection of the sinuses or lower respiratory tract.

Treatment

In patients with a clinical picture consistent with GAS pharyngitis, empirical therapy should be started to prevent suppurative and nonsuppurative complications, to decrease infectivity and transmissibility, and to induce clinical improvement of symptoms (Box 9–3). Patients with a high index of suspicion for GAS pharyngitis but negative or pending RADT/culture results can be given empirical antibiotics until the results are available. An alternative approach is to withhold antibiotics until the culture is positive for *S pyogenes.* Delaying therapy against GAS does not increase the incidence of rheumatic heart disease or recurrences with the same strain of *S pyogenes.* Following the latter course will decrease inappropriate antibiotic use and control the increase in antibiotic resistance.

Antibiotic selection is based on efficacy, ease of administration, cost, compliance, and spectrum of the antibiotic. The treatment of choice is penicillin V or amoxicillin for 10 d to treat and eradicate carriage. Intramuscular benzathine penicillin G may be given in patients unlikely to complete a 10-d course.

Shorter courses are not recommended until more definitive studies are available. Erythromycin or other macrolides (such as clarithromycin or azithromycin), or oral cephalosporins are the recommended alternatives for bacterial pharyngitis in patients who are allergic to penicillin. Absence of penicillin-resistant GAS and limited (5%) resistance to erythromycin make it imperative to choose a cheaper alternative to the newer more expensive antibiotics. In some patients with recurrent GAS pharyngitis, penicillin is unable to eradicate nasopharyngeal carriage. In such patients, rifampin, clindamycin, or amoxicillin/clavulanate use may decrease colonization. Patients with negative throat RADT/cultures should have antibiotics discontinued.

Pharyngitis caused by anaerobic bacteria may respond to penicillins, amoxicillin/clavulanate, or clindamycin. *A hemolyticum* is susceptible to erythromycin. *Yersinia* pharyngitis requires treatment with a third-generation cephalosporin, an aminoglycoside or trimethoprim-sulfamethoxazole (TMP-SMX). Effective therapies for gonococcal pharyngitis include ceftriaxone, cefixime, or fluoroquinolones such as norfloxacin, ofloxacin, or ciprofloxacin. Treatment of choice for *Mycoplasma* pharyngitis is either doxycycline or macrolides. Doxycycline is contraindicated in children < 8 y old because it causes discoloration of teeth.

Symptomatic oropharyngeal herpes simplex ulcers, particularly in an immunocompromised host,

BOX 9–3

Empiric Therapy of Acute Bacterial Pharyngitis

	Children	Adults
First Choice	• Oral penicillin, 50,000 U/kg/d divided every 12–8 h for 10 d • Amoxicillin 40 mg/kg/d divided q8h for 10 d	• Oral penicillin, 200,000–250,000 U/kg/d divided OR • Penicillin V, 500 mg every 8–12 h for 10 d • Amoxicillin, 500 mg every 8 h for 10 d
Second Choice	• Erythromycin, 40 mg/kg/d divided into 1 dose every 6 h for 10 d	• Erythromycin, 500 mg every 6 h for 10 d
Penicillin Allergic	• Erythromycin, 40 mg/kg/d divided every 6 h for 10 d • Clarithromycin, 15 mg/kg/d divided into 1 dose per 12 h for 10 d • Azithromycin, 12 mg/kg/d for 5 d (not to exceed 500 mg) • Oral cephalosporin	• Erythromycin, 500 mg every 6 h for 10 d • Clarithromycin, 250 mg every 12 h for 10 d • Azithromycin, 500 mg on Day 1, then 250 mg per day for 4 d • Oral cephalosporin

should be treated with acyclovir for 7–10 d. Influenza type A pharyngitis can be treated with amantadine or rimantadine or the neuraminidase inhibitors if the patient presents within 48–72 h of onset of symptoms. HIV acute retroviral syndrome should be considered for treatment with combination antiretroviral therapy.

General measures for symptomatic relief include fluids, warm saline gargles, and nonsteroidal anti-inflammatory drugs. Aspirin should be avoided in children with viral infections, particularly varicella-zoster virus infection, to prevent Reye's syndrome. Patients that appear toxic or patients with suppurative complications should be hospitalized for parenteral or surgical management.

Prognosis

Uncomplicated pharyngitis results in no sequelae. Prognosis of GAS pharyngitis complicated by rheumatic heart disease or poststreptococcal glomerulonephritis is good with penicillin prophylaxis in rheumatic heart disease and spontaneous remission in poststreptococcal glomerulonephritis. Suppurative complications have minimal long-term adverse effects.

Prevention & Control

Active immunization plays a role in prevention with regard to diphtheria and influenza types A and B (Box 9–4). Tonsillectomy is recommended in selected patients. Penicillin prophylaxis is required in patients at risk for recurrent rheumatic fever.

BOX 9–4

Control of Pharyngitis

Prophylactic Measures	• Active immunization for influenza a/b and diphtheria • Amantadine for influenza post-exposure prophylaxis • Tonsillectomy in recurrent pharyngitis in select children • Good hand washing, especially if there is an infected person in the family • Treatment of sexual partner in gonorrheal pharyngitis • Acyclovir for recurrent herpes simplex virus pharyngitis • Penicillin prophylaxis (oral or parenteral) for patients with rheumatic heart disease

ACUTE LARYNGITIS

Essentials of Diagnosis

- Hoarseness or loss of voice (aphonia).
- Associated symptoms of rhinitis, pharyngitis, or cough.
- Children tend to develop airway obstruction.
- On direct examination, the larynx is hyperemic and edematous, with or without ulcerations.
- Mostly viral, occasionally bacterial.
- Persistent hoarseness lasting > 10 d should prompt laryngoscopy to exclude other etiologies.

General Considerations

Laryngitis is the infection of the larynx that results in an inflammatory reaction and consequential symptoms and signs. Common cold viruses such as rhinovirus, influenza virus, adenoviruses, RSV, or parainfluenza viruses may cause acute laryngitis. It usually presents in winter as part of an upper respiratory tract infectious syndrome. Bacterial laryngitis is less common and is caused mainly by *S pyogenes* or *Moraxella catarrhalis*. Rarely laryngitis may be caused by *Mycobacterium tuberculosis,* syphilis, or fungi such as *Histoplasma capsulatum, Blastomyces dermatiditis,* or *Candida albicans.*

Clinical Findings

A. Signs and Symptoms. Hoarseness, aphonia, and symptoms of associated upper respiratory tract infection such as rhinitis or pharyngitis may accompany acute laryngitis. Respiratory obstruction may occur particularly in children. Direct examination when done shows the larynx to be hyperemic and edematous, with or without ulcerations. An exudate or membrane may be seen in diphtheria, streptococcal, or EBV laryngitis.

B. Imaging. Lateral x-ray of the neck may be helpful to exclude acute bacterial epiglottitis or bacterial tracheitis. If symptoms of hoarseness persist beyond 2 wk, patients should be evaluated by direct visualization of the larynx by laryngoscopy.

Differential Diagnosis

Voice abuse is the most frequent noninfectious cause of hoarseness. Differential diagnosis includes tumors, paralysis of the vocal cords, chemical irritants, or gastroesophageal reflux. Patients with laryngitis must also be differentiated from those with acute epiglottitis or bacterial tracheitis, which usually present with more systemic symptoms.

Complications

Respiratory obstruction in children is the most serious complication.

Treatment

Because the majority of laryngeal infections are viral, therapy is mostly supportive with voice rest, warm saline gargles, and increased humidity. If specific microbiologic diagnosis is made with positive microbiologic cultures, then therapy should be directed at the organism isolated.

Prognosis

Long-term prognosis is excellent with no residual symptoms.

Prevention & Control

Preventive measures for laryngitis are similar to those for common cold and pharyngitis.

ACUTE LARYNGOTRACHEOBRONCHITIS (CROUP)

Essentials of Diagnosis

- Most often in children ages 6 mo to 6 y, peak is at 2 y.
- Fever, hoarseness of voice followed by paroxysms of nonproductive, brassy cough that ends with a characteristic inspiratory stridor.
- The child appears anxious and has tachypnea, inspiratory stridor, retraction of intercostal muscles, and associated rhonchi or wheezing.
- Anterior-posterior x-ray view of the neck shows the subglottic obstruction.
- Microbiologic diagnosis can be established by serology, viral or bacterial cultures from the pharynx, or rapid antigen detection enzyme immunosorbent assays such as for RSV or influenza type A.

General Considerations

Acute laryngotracheobronchitis (LTB) or croup is subglottic inflammation and edema caused by a viral or bacterial infection of the larynx, trachea, and bronchi (Box 9–5). Croup is the most common cause of upper respiratory tract obstruction in children between the ages of 6 mo and 6 y, with the peak occurrence at 2 y old. It is caused mostly by viruses, primarily parainfluenza virus types I and II, although others, such as influenza type A or B, RSV, and adenovirus are also implicated. Occasionally *M pneumoniae* can cause LTB.

Clinical Findings

A. Signs and Symptoms. Most children have hoarseness of voice and a brassy cough with an associated inspiratory or even an expiratory stridor. Fever,

BOX 9–5		
Microbiology of Croup		
	Children	Adults
More Frequent	• Parainfluenza virus types 1 and 2 • Influenza A or B • Respiratory syncytial virus	• Herpes simplex virus • Influenza A or B
Less Frequent	• Adenovirus • Rhinovirus • Enterovirus • *Mycoplasma pneumoniae* • *Staphylococcus aureus* • *Haemophilus influenzae* • Measles virus	• *S aureus* • *H influenzae* • Fungal—*Candida, Aspergillus* spp.

rhinorrhea, sore throat, and cough usually precede this. Symptoms may vary in intensity and last ~ 3–4 d if mild. Patients appear apprehensive and tend to lean forward. The child may have tachypnea and might be using accessory respiratory muscles. Inspiratory or expiratory stridor is prominent. Pulmonary examination may reveal rhonchi, crepitations, or wheezing. Breath sounds may be diminished if upper airway obstruction is severe and air entry is greatly decreased.

B. Laboratory Findings. The white blood cell count may be normal or mildly elevated. Noninvasive pulse oximetry to monitor the oxygen saturation is recommended. Arterial blood gas assessment shows hypoxemia and/or hypercapnia, depending on the severity of the disease.

C. Imaging. Lateral neck x-rays show overdistended hypopharynx, subglottic narrowing that is wider on expiration than inspiration, thickened vocal cords, and a normal epiglottis. Anterior-posterior views of the neck show edematous subglottic walls converging to create a characteristic "steeple sign" (Figure 9–1). There may also be diffuse narrowing of the trachea and bronchi (Figure 9–2).

Differential Diagnosis

Acute epiglottitis is a major differential diagnosis to be considered when a child presents with these symptoms. Radiographs of the neck can easily help differentiate the two conditions. Other causes of similar symptoms include foreign-body aspiration, which can be determined by history, x-rays, or endoscopic evaluation. Membranous croup or bacterial tracheitis should also be considered if the child presents with a

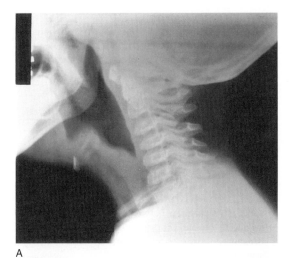

A

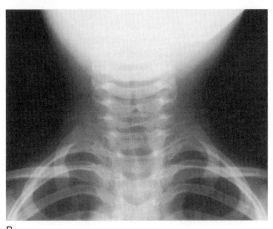

B

Figure 9–1. Lateral (A) and anterior-posterior (B) views of the neck of this 9-mo-old baby with 3 d of symptoms of upper respiratory infection show a normal appearing epiglottis and subglottic narrowing of the trachea consistent with LTB.

clinical picture similar to croup but appears more toxic and has subglottic narrowing on radiographs of the neck.

Complications

Severe croup, as may occur with influenza type A, may require tracheotomy or intubation in ≤ 13% of patients and have an associated mortality of 0–2.7%. A small percentage of children with prolonged intubation or severe disease may develop subglottic stenosis. A few follow-up studies have shown an increase in hyperactive airways in children with a history of croup.

Treatment

Antibiotics are not routinely recommended for the

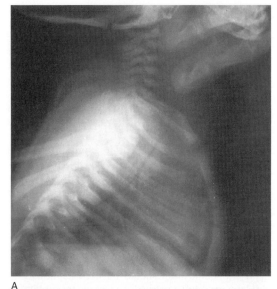

A

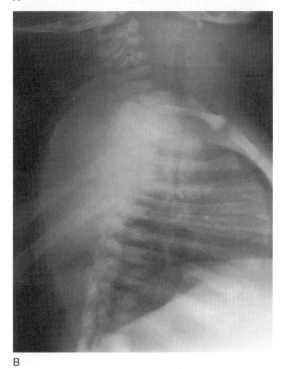

B

Figure 9–2. Lateral chest x-ray views of a 2-mo-old infant with LTB show diffuse narrowing of the trachea and bronchi (A) and normal caliber trachea noted a few weeks later with resolution of infection (B).

treatment of croup unless the patient has symptoms or cultures suggestive of bacterial etiology (Box 9–6). Cool air humidification and supportive care are essential to keep the child calm, to prevent further tachypnea and distress. Respiratory rate is the best predictor of hypoxemia. Noninvasive pulse oximetry or arterial blood gas testing for PaO_2 or $PaCO_2$ should aid in assessment of the patient's condition and response to therapy. Noninvasive monitoring is preferred to prevent further anxiety in the child.

Nebulized racemic epinephrine is important in the therapy for croup because the α and β agonists decrease edema and relieve obstruction by vasoconstriction. Racemic epinephrine nebulization is well tolerated, even by the younger children, and may decrease the need for intubation. Children receiving racemic epinephrine should be observed for relapse because epinephrine has a short half-life and rebound vasodilatation and edema can occur. Racemic epinephrine nebulization should be used cautiously in children with left ventricular outflow tract obstruction such as tetralogy of Fallot or idiopathic hypertrophic subaortic stenosis. In severe croup, corticosteroids (eg, dexamethasone) decrease subglottic edema, the number of racemic epinephrine treatments, and intubations.

Some children will fail medical management and require intubation. Intubation should be done in fully equipped units and preferably via the nasotracheal route. Extubation is usually attempted in ~ 5–7 d if extubation criteria are met. Extubation criteria include decreased secretions, decreased leakage around the endotracheal tube (which indicates decreased edema), and an alert child. Failure to extubate should prompt further endoscopic evaluation.

Prognosis

Croup is mostly a self-limited disease with complete uncomplicated resolution. As mentioned above, some children may develop hyperactive airways or become predisposed to recurrent croup. A few may develop subglottic stenosis caused by severe disease or prolonged intubation.

Prevention & Control

Good handwashing and cleanliness can help decrease transmission from an infected patient, particularly at daycare centers or even in the home environment.

ACUTE EPIGLOTTITIS

Essentials of Diagnosis

- Occurs in children between 2 and 6 y , can occur in adults although it presents with less severity.
- Irritable, febrile, sore throat; odynophagia, dysphonia, and dyspnea.
- Sits forward drooling, toxic appearing, tachypneic
- Examination of the larynx should not be attempted. Direct examination should be performed only by a trained person and in a unit where immediate intubation or tracheotomy can be performed.
- Direct laryngoscopic examination reveals a "cherry red" edematous epiglottis.
- Polymorphonuclear leukocytosis is common. Blood and epiglottis cultures are often positive for *Haemophilus influenzae* type b, *Staphylococcus aureus,* or other bacteria.

General Considerations

Acute epiglottitis is a true respiratory emergency. An epiglottic infection leads to acute inflammation and edema of the epiglottis and can cause upper airway obstruction. Acute epiglottitis can occur at any age, however it is more common in children between 2–6 y and most often occurs in the winter and spring. Unlike croup, which is predominantly a viral disease, acute epiglottitis is a bacterial disease caused mainly by *H influenzae* type b, *S aureus,* or streptococcal species (Box 9–7). *H influenzae* type b was the most common organism isolated from children with acute

---

BOX 9–6

Empiric Therapy of Croup

- Cool air humidification, keep child calm
- Racemic epinephrine 2.25%, 0.05 cc/kg nebulized in 3 cc saline (max = 0.5 cc). Doses may be repeated every 1–4 h
- For severe croup: dexamethasone 0.3–0.6 mg/kg IM in a single dose or repeated every 6 h for 2–4 doses (max = 10 mg)

BOX 9–7

Microbiology of Acute Epiglottitis

More Frequent	• *Haemophilus influenzae* type b • *Staphylococcus aureus* • *Streptococcus pneumoniae* • *Streptococcus pyogenes*
Less Frequent	• Non-group A streptococci

epiglottitis, but widespread use of the *H influenzae* type b vaccine has dramatically decreased the incidence of *H influenzae* type b acute epiglottitis.

Clinical Findings

A. Signs and Symptoms. The child presents with a short (6- to 12-h) rapidly progressive febrile illness, sore throat, pain on swallowing, and shortness of breath. There is usually no antecedent history of a viral infection. Adults have a similar clinical presentation with sore throat being a predominant symptom.

The patient looks anxious, appears toxic, and assumes a forward-leaning, neck-extended posture. Drooling of oral secretions and muffled voice are the sine qua non. The child has marked tachypnea and may have an inspiratory stridor from the supraglottic mucosa prolapsing into the glottis. Lung auscultation may reveal crepitations or bronchial breath sounds if there is associated pneumonia.

B. Laboratory Findings. The white blood cell count is elevated with a polymorphonuclear reaction. The blood and epiglottis cultures are frequently positive. Bacteremia occurs in almost all of the children with *H influenzae* type b acute epiglottitis. Serum latex agglutination tests against *H influenzae* type b may be helpful in making a rapid microbiologic diagnosis in patients from whom cultures were not obtained before starting antibiotics.

C. Imaging. Caution must be exercised in sending these patients for tests or x-rays without adequate supervision and to avoid a delay in intubation. Radiographs of the neck show an enlarged edematous epiglottis with a normal subglottic space. Some x-rays may be negative or show subglottic obstruction, and the diagnosis may be obscured. (Figure 9–3). Chest x-rays may show evidence of pneumonia. Laryngoscopic evaluation should be carried out by trained personnel in a controlled setting such as an operating room or unit equipped for immediate intubation.

Differential Diagnosis

Croup or acute LTB presents with a clinical picture similar to that of acute epiglottitis. Croup has slower-onset, viral prodromal symptoms, a nontoxic appearing child, and absence of drooling. Anterior-posterior x-rays of the neck confirm the diagnosis. Other conditions that have a similar presentation include angioedema, foreign-body aspiration, and retropharyngeal or peritonsillar abscesses. Angioedema and foreign-body aspiration are suspected based on history and imaging or endoscopic evaluation. Radiographs or laryngoscopic evaluation identifies retropharyngeal or peritonsillar abscesses.

Complications

Mortality associated with untreated obstructive acute epiglottitis is ~80%. Respiratory failure from upper-airway obstruction is the most common com-

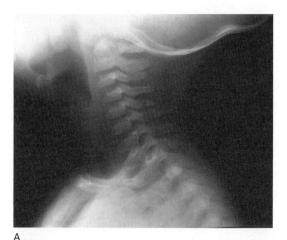

A

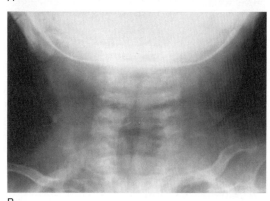

B

Figure 9–3. Lateral (A) and anterior-posterior (B) views of the neck of this 3-y-old child reveal marked swelling of the epiglottis and the aryepiglottic folds characteristic of epiglottitis. Cultures of the epiglottis and blood grew *H influenzae* type B.

plication. Occasionally patients will develop pulmonary edema along with the respiratory distress.

Treatment

Acute epiglottitis is a medical emergency. Once acute epiglottitis is suspected, the child should be kept in an upright position and be accompanied at all times by personnel trained in advanced cardiopulmonary life support. Diagnosis should be expeditiously established clinically or radiographically. Laryngoscopic examination should be attempted only in a unit equipped for immediate intubation and only by experienced personnel. Maintenance of a patent airway is of foremost importance in the care of a patient with acute epiglottitis. Patients with impending respiratory failure who cannot be intubated may require an emergency subglottic tracheotomy. All pediatric patients with acute epiglottitis should be intubated preferably via a nasotracheal or an uncuffed endotracheal tube. Observation alone is not recommended in pediatric patients because of high associated mortality. Management of adult patients depends on the severity of clinical symptoms and signs of upper-airway obstruction.

Blood and epiglottic cultures should be obtained once the airway is secured. Patients should be started on parenteral antibiotics that are active against *H influenzae* type b, *S aureus,* and streptococci (Box 9–8). Because of the high degree of β-lactamase–mediated resistance in *H influenzae* type b, third-generation cephalosporins such as ceftriaxone or cefotaxime or a β-lactam/β-lactamase inhibitor combination antibiotic such as ampicillin/sulbactam should be started. Patients with acute epiglottitis usually improve within 12–48 h with appropriate antibiotics, and these should be continued orally or parenterally for 7–10 d. The average period of intubation is ~ 2 d, and direct visualization is the most effective way to determine time of extubation.

Prognosis

Expeditious diagnosis, immediate management of upper-airway obstruction, and institution of antibiotics decreases morbidity and mortality related to acute epiglottitis. Full recovery without sequelae is expected in such patients.

Prevention & Control

H influenzae type b polysaccharide vaccination can further decrease the incidence of acute epiglottitis (Box 9–9). However, patients can still be suscepti-

---

BOX 9–9

Control of Acute Epiglottitis

Prophylactic Measures	• Patient and household contact
	• Children < 4 y of age: rifampin, 20 mg/kg/d in a single dose, for 4 d
	• Adults: rifampin, 600 mg/d for 4 d

---

ble to non–type-b *H influenzae* and other bacterial etiologies of epiglottitis.

The secondary attack rate of *H influenzae* type b among all household contacts, especially in children < 4 y old, can be decreased by a prophylactic 4-d course of rifampin (20 mg/kg/d in a single daily dose). Rifampin prophylaxis should be given to the patient and all household contacts regardless of previous immunization status, to prevent carriage state.

OTITIS MEDIA

Essentials of Diagnosis

• Commonest cause of office visits in children between 6 mo and 2 y.
• Irritability, fever, earache, discharge from the ear, occasional vertigo.
• On otoscopic examination, the tympanic mem-

BOX 9–8

Empiric Therapy of Acute Epiglottitis

	Children	Adults
First Choice	• Cefotaxime, 150–200 mg/kg/d IV divided every 6–8 h • Ceftriaxone, 80–100 mg/kg/d IV every 24 h	• Cefotaxime, 1–2 g IV every 6–8 h • Ceftriaxone, 2 g IV every 24 h
Second Choice	• Ampicillin/sulbactam, 100–200 mg ampicillin/kg/d IV divided every 6 h	• Ampicillin/sulbactam, 1.5–3.0 g IV every 6 h
Penicillin Allergic	• Cefotaxime, 150 mg/kg/d IV divided every 6–8 h • Ceftriaxone, 80–100 mg/kg/d IV every 24 h • Chloramphenicol, 50–75 mg/kg/d IV divided every 6 h	• Cefotaxime, 1–2 g IV every 6–8 h • Ceftriaxone, 2 g IV every 24 h • Chloramphenicol, 50–100 mg/kg/d IV divided every 6 h

brane is erythematous and has decreased mobility on pneumatic otoscopy, which demonstrates the presence of middle ear fluid.

- There may be diminished hearing.
- Laboratory values may show leukocytosis. Cultures of the ear are not routinely recommended.

General Considerations

Acute otitis media (AOM) is the middle ear inflammation that results in collection of fluid in the middle ear and associated local and systemic symptoms.

AOM is the most common reason for physician office visits for children under age 15 y. Children < 3 y and those at the age of school entry (5–6 y) are most vulnerable to AOM. Predisposing and recurrence factors for AOM include daycare attendance, particularly at large (> 6 children per room) centers, a sibling with AOM, parental smoking, and drinking from a bottle while lying flat on the back. Boys, Native Americans, and Alaskans have a higher incidence of AOM. A small percentage of children have an identifiable risk factor for recurrences such as congenital orofacial deformities and congenital or acquired immunodeficiencies such as HIV/AIDS. Recurrences occur in normal children with no apparent anatomic defects. A large percentage of AOM is viral, which may explain recurrences.

The most common bacterial organism responsible for otitis media is *Streptococcus pneumoniae*, which accounts for ~ 30–40% (Box 9–10) of cases. Cultures from the middle ear in various studies have demonstrated *S pneumoniae*, nontypable strains of *H influenzae* (21%), *M catarrhalis* (12%), *S aureus*, GAS (2–6%), and other less common gram-negative organisms including *Pseudomonas aeruginosa*. Penicillin-resistant *S pneumoniae* (PRSP) is increasing in the community and contributes to recalcitrant cases of AOM. PRSP is common in children < 6 y old, children who have received recent antibiotics, children with previous AOM, and children attending group daycare. Gram-negative organisms should be considered in neonates with AOM. Rare causes include *M pneumoniae,* which has a classic bullous le-

sion on the tympanic membrane, and *Chlamydia trachomatis* may be seen in very young infants. Occasionally mycobacterial or diphtheria middle-ear infections can occur.

Clinical Findings

A. Signs and Symptoms. Young infants or children may present with crying, irritability, anorexia, lethargy, or a history of pulling at the affected ear. Earache with or without associated drainage from the ear is the most common symptom in older children and adults. They may be febrile and occasionally present with vertigo, tinnitus, or decreased hearing.

Otoscopic examination reveals an erythematous tympanic membrane. The tympanic membrane may be bulging, retracted, or perforated and occasionally exuding purulent drainage from the perforation. Fluid in the middle ear is demonstrated by air-fluid levels, bulging, and decreased mobility of the tympanic membrane demonstrated by pneumatic otoscopy. Pneumatic otoscopy should be attempted in all children unless it is too painful. Other otologic techniques such as tympanometry and acoustic reflectometry can help assess the amount of fluid in the middle ear. Audiologic evaluation is necessary in children with hearing loss.

B. Laboratory Findings. Laboratory values are not helpful in the management of AOM. There may be polymorphonuclear leukocytosis. Routine middle ear cultures via tympanocentesis are not recommended unless the patient is toxic, has recurrent infections, or is not responding to empirical therapy. Swab cultures from the external auditory canal (EAC) do not accurately reflect the organism causing AOM because the EAC cannot be adequately decontaminated. Nasopharyngeal cultures are not specific in identifying the causative bacteria in AOM.

C. Imaging. Imaging is not of considerable help in otitis media. CT scans of the head should be done if mastoiditis or other complications are suspected.

Differential Diagnosis

Noninfectious causes of AOM, such as Wegener's granulomatosis, must be considered in a patient with recurrent and nonresponding disease. A foreign body in the EAC can present with earache and minimal erythema of the tympanic membrane. History and otoscopic visualization should identify a foreign body. A viral infection, fever, or crying or earwax removal can also cause a red tympanic membrane.

Complications

Chronic otitis media, effusion, mastoiditis, and intracranial extension may result from recurrent otitis media and persistent middle ear effusion. In the preantibiotic era, mastoiditis and intracranial extension occurred in ~ 20% and 2.5%, respectively, of AOM patients. Now that the use of antibiotics is common,

BOX 9–10

Microbiology of Acute Otitis Media	
More Frequent	• *Streptococcus pneumoniae* • *Haemophilus influenzae* non-typeable • *Moraxella catarrhalis*
Less Frequent	• *S aureus* • Group A streptococci • *Pseudomonas aeruginosa*

these rates have decreased to 2.8% and 0.13%, respectively. Contiguous spread to the cranial fossae, temporal or petrous bone, or sigmoid or lateral sinuses results in suppurative complications. Conductive hearing loss because of chronic otitis media and effusion can potentially impair language development and academic functioning of the child.

Treatment

A large number of AOM cases are viral in nature with or without bacterial superinfection. Approximately 30% of AOM cases are bacterial. Studies have also demonstrated spontaneous resolution in 16% of *S pneumoniae* infections, 50% of *H influenzae* infections, and ~ 80% of *M catarrhalis* AOM, particularly in children older than 2 y. Because of concerns regarding suppurative complications, parental expectation, and perhaps convenience, antibiotic therapy has become the norm for most AOM treatment (Box 9–11). Numerous studies have now demonstrated that antibiotics benefit defervescence and otalgia, decrease suppurative complications, and improve tympanic membrane healing, but they have no significant benefit in long-term outcomes such as recurrence rates or chronic middle ear effusion. These studies and the recent increase in multi–drug-resistant organisms that have no or minimally efficacious treatment

have brought this practice of judicious antibiotics use for AOM into question.

The approach to patients with AOM should be individualized. A delayed antibiotic approach can be considered in children older than 2 y with no immunodeficiency, no craniofacial anatomic abnormalities, intact tympanic membrane, and no previous AOM. The child should be scheduled for a follow-up visit. If a follow-up visit is not possible, an antibiotic can be started at the initial evaluation. The initial empirical antibiotic regimen should be active against the common organisms. Despite the emergence of resistance in these bacteria, amoxicillin is still the preferred and effective initial antibiotic of choice. In children with a history of antibiotic use in the preceding month, the initial antibiotic is still amoxicillin but given at a higher dose.

Antibiotics effective in the treatment of AOM include amoxicillin/clavulanate, cephalosporins such as cefaclor, cefixime, cefprozil, cefuroxime, cefpodoxime, loracarbef, or macrolides such as erythromycin, azithromycin, or clarithromycin, TMP-SMX, and erythromycin/sulfisoxazole (Pediazole). The newer expensive antibiotics do not have a significant benefit as first-line agents when compared with their cheaper counterparts (eg, amoxicillin and TMP-SMX). In patients with penicillin allergy, cephalosporins, mac-

BOX 9–11

Empiric Therapy of Acute Otitis Media

	Chidren	Adults
First Choice	• Amoxicillin, 40 mg/kg/d orally divided every 8 h • Erythromycin/sulfisoxazole, 50 mg erythromycin/kg/d and 150 mg sulfisoxazole/kg/d divided every 6 h (max 2 g of erythromycin and 6 g of sulfisoxazole)	• Amoxicillin, 250–500 mg orally every 8 h
Second Choice	• Amoxicillin/clavulanate, 40 mg/kg/d divided every 8 h • Cefpodoxime for > 6 months–12 y, 10 mg/kg/d divided every 12 h	• Amoxicillin/clavulanate, 250–500 mg every 8 h or 825 mg every 12 h • Cefpodoxime 100–400 mg every 12 h
Penicillin Allergic	• Trimethoprim/sulfamethoxazole, 8 mg TMP/kg/d divided every 12 h • Erythromycin stearate, 40 mg/kg divided every 6 h	• Trimethoprim/sulfamethoxazole double-strength 1 orally every 12 h • Erythromycin stearate, 250–500 mg every 6 h
Prophylaxis	• Amoxicillin, 20 mg/kg/d × 3–6 mo • Sulfisoxazole, 50 mg/kg/d × 3–6 months	

rolides, or TMP-SMX can be prescribed. Cephalosporins should be avoided in patients with histories of anaphylactic reaction to penicillin. Studies report mean clinical cure rates of 85–94% with amoxicillin.

Most patients start responding in 48–72 h. Causes for slower response or recurrence with lower-dose amoxicillin therapy include resistant organisms such as intermediate- or high-grade PRSP or β-lactamase–producing *H influenzae* or *M catarrhalis,* suppurative complications, or noncompliance. Treatment failure is defined as lack of improvement in fever, ear pain, and persistent tympanic congestion, bulging, or otorrhea. It is important not to mistake a persistent middle ear effusion without signs of active infection as treatment failure. Treatment failure may be early (3 d) or late (10–25 d). If a child requires further treatment, high-dose (80 mg/kg/d) amoxicillin, a cephalosporin, amoxicillin/clavulanate, or a macrolide (either azithromycin or clarithromycin) may be prescribed. The choice of retreatment antibiotic depends on the risk of PRSP in the patient. Higher-dose amoxicillin or amoxicillin/clavulanate is still efficacious against intermediate-penicillin-susceptible *S pneumoniae.* Cefaclor and cefprozil are not good alternatives as second-line therapy because of their lower efficacy against nonsusceptible *S pneumoniae* and *H influenzae.* Because of the lack of activity against PRSP, clarithromycin, azithromycin, TMP/SMX, cefixime, ceftibuten, and loracarbef are recommended only as second-line antibiotics for patients at low risk for PRSP AOM.

Patients suspected of having PRSP AOM who fail high-dose amoxicillin should be considered for tympanocentesis for culture and susceptibilities. If empiric therapy is decided, the antimicrobial therapy should be effective against the β-lactamase–producing *H influenza* and *M catarrhalis* in addition to being active against PRSP. Options include oral cefuroxime axetil, cefpodoxime or clindamycin, or parenteral cefotaxime, ceftriaxone or vancomycin. In children receiving clindamycin for PRSP, the addition of a β-lactamase–stable cephalosporin may be required to cover for β-lactamase–producing *H influenzae.* One parenteral dose of ceftriaxone 50 mg/kg/d is approved for AOM caused by susceptible *S pneumoniae.* However, ceftriaxone given daily for 3 d is likely to be more efficacious for AOM failing the first-line antimicrobial-agent therapy. Parenteral therapy is usually needed only for patients with severe AOM or those failing their second regimen. Middle ear aspirates should be sent for culture and susceptibilities to guide therapy in children failing second-line therapy. These patients should be reevaluated in 2 wk to ascertain that no suppurative complications have developed. A severely ill child failing initial therapy should be considered for admission and treatment with parenteral vancomycin and a third-generation cephalosporin, such as cefotaxime or ceftriaxone. A thorough evaluation for complications should also be conducted.

Symptomatic treatment is primarily pain control with analgesics such as acetaminophen or nonsteroidal anti-inflammatory drugs. On occasion, myringotomy (incision of the tympanic membrane) may be required to relieve the middle ear pressure. In most studies, myringotomy did not improve outcome even when combined with antibiotics. Antihistaminics and decongestants have equal efficacy as a placebo in AOM, and they are not recommended.

Treatment of recurrent otitis media includes prevention of recurrent attacks, a second course of antibiotics with broader antibacterial spectrum as mentioned above or specific treatment depending on middle ear cultures. Secondary antibiotic prophylaxis, surgical drainage or adenoidectomy, and active immunization are some of the measures used to prevent AOM. Children with three new episodes in 6 mo or four episodes in 1 y should be considered for antibiotic prophylaxis with amoxicillin or erythromycin/sulfisoxazole. Antibiotic prophylaxis decreases recurrences ≤ 44%. The patient should be regularly evaluated for middle ear effusion. Middle ear effusion is seen in ~ 50% of children with AOM and usually resolves in 3 mo in the majority of patients. Persistent middle ear effusion or otitis media with effusion (OME) beyond 3–4 mo requires further management. Children with OME should have an audiologic test to detect any hearing loss. Patients with OME with normal hearing should be retreated with a 2- to 3-wk course of an antibiotic. If the effusion resolves, then a prophylactic antibiotic course of 3 mo may be of benefit to prevent recurrences. Children with OME and conductive hearing loss should be evaluated by an otorhinolaryngologist for surgical drainage procedures such as myringotomy and tympanostomy tubes (tubes placed in the tympanic membrane for permanent drainage).

Prognosis

Recurrent AOM or OME may impair hearing, language development, and learning capabilities of the patient. The prognosis is worsened in patients with intracranial extension of infection. Uncomplicated AOM resolves without significant sequelae.

Prevention & Control

Currently available 23 polyvalent pneumococcal polysaccharide vaccine produces poor immunologic responses in children < 2 y old but can be used for children > 2 y. The Advisory Committee on Immunization Practices advises that this vaccine be given to children with higher likelihoods of pneumococcal infections such as HIV-positive, asplenic, or sickle cell anemia patients. Conjugated pneumococcal vaccine is available and is more efficacious in children < 2 y old and may contribute to lowering the incidence of pneumococcal otitis media.

OTITIS EXTERNA

Essentials of Diagnosis

- Infection and inflammation of the external auditory canal causing pain and itching, similar to infections of the skin and soft tissue.
- *S aureus* or group A *Streptococcus* often causes acute localized otitis externa, similar to furunculosis.
- Main symptoms are localized pain and itching.
- "Swimmer's ear" or acute diffuse otitis externa is often caused by *P aeruginosa* or by *Aspergillus* spp.
- Chronic otitis externa results from persistent drainage caused by chronic suppurative otitis media. This may present as chronic itching.
- "Malignant" otitis externa is a severe necrotizing *P aeruginosa* infection of the external auditory canal and adjacent tissues. Severe pain, tenderness, and other signs of complications may be present.

General Considerations

Inflammation of the EAC is particularly symptomatic because of the limited space for expansion of edematous tissue in the narrow external auditory canal.

Clinical Findings

A. Signs and Symptoms. Infection of the EAC is divided into four different categories (Box 9–12):

1. Acute localized otitis externa is the most common form of otitis externa. It is similar to staphylococcal infections of the skin and hair follicles. Because of limited area for expansion, inflammation and edema of the EAC wall cause intense pain and tenderness. The canal has local erythema, heat, and tenderness over the tragus. There may be associated preauricular lymphadenopathy.

2. Acute diffuse otitis externa or "swimmer's ear"

is caused mainly by gram-negative organisms, particularly *P aeruginosa*. It occurs in hot, humid climates or may be associated with contaminated hot-tub baths. Fungal organisms such as *Aspergillus* spp. may also cause symptoms of pain and itching in the ear. The canal is erythematous, edematous, and, in some severe cases, hemorrhagic.

3. Chronic otitis externa is a complication of persistent chronic otitis media and resultant drainage into the EAC leading to chronic irritation. Itching of the EAC is the main symptom.

4. "Malignant" or invasive otitis externa is a severe, necrotizing infection of the EAC with invasion into the surrounding tissues including blood vessels, cartilage, and bone. *P aeruginosa* is the most frequently isolated organism. Immunocompromised hosts, elderly, and particularly diabetics are predisposed to this disease

B. Laboratory Findings. Laboratory findings are not helpful in the diagnosis and management of otitis externa. The white blood cell count and sedimentation rate may be elevated in malignant otitis externa. Cultures from the EAC or involved tissue in malignant otitis externa are frequently positive for *P aeruginosa* or other bacteria.

C. Imaging. Imaging is not required for otitis externa but CT or magnetic resonance imaging of the head delineates the extent of damage in malignant otitis externa and its complications. This could potentially aid in the further management of this condition.

Complications

Complications develop by local invasion such as temporal bone osteomyelitis, septic thrombophlebitis of the sigmoid or lateral sinus or jugular bulb, cranial nerve palsies, meningitis, or brain abscess.

Treatment

Gentle cleaning is recommended for most otitis externa. Local heat, topical antibiotic solutions such as neomycin, polymyxin, or ofloxacin, or systemic antibiotics, or some combination of these are effective in the treatment of acute otitis externa (Box 9–13). Irrigation with hypertonic (3%) saline and cleansing with alcohol and acetic acid mixed 1:1 are recommended for acute diffuse otitis externa, whether it is bacterial or fungal. Fungal otitis externa may also be amenable to treatment with *m*-cresyl acetate. Topical antibiotics combined with steroids are sometimes used for 1–2 d to decrease edema. Severe infections may require systemic antibiotics with activity against *P aeruginosa*. Malignant otitis externa may be treated with parenteral antipseudomonal antibiotics such as ceftazidime or penicillins with antipseudomonal activity such as piperacillin with aminoglycoside or oral antipseudomonal antibiotics such as the fluoroquinolones. Topical antipseudomonal antibiotics, such as neomycin, polymyxin, or ofloxacin, are used for 4–6 wk.

BOX 9–12		
Microbiology of Otitis Externa		
More Frequent	• *Staphylococcus aureus* • Group A *Streptococcus* • *Pseudomonas aeruginosa* (swimmer's ear) • *Aspergillus*	
Less Frequent	• *Pseudomonas aeruginosa* (malignant otitis externa)	

BOX 9–13

Empiric Therapy of Otitis Externa

	Children	Adults
First Choice	Hypertonic (3%) saline plus alcohol:acetic acid (1:1)	Same
Second Choice	Topical neomycin, polymyxin, or quinolone	Same
Penicillin Allergic	Topical neomycin, polymyxin, or quinolone	Same

ACUTE & CHRONIC SINUSITIS

Essentials of Diagnosis

- Fever, facial pain or pressure, headache, purulent nasal or postnasal discharge (PND), cough.
- Tenderness over the sinuses, PND, other signs of complications may be seen such as meningismus or periorbital cellulitis.
- Leukocytosis in some cases, sinus or blood cul-

tures may be positive for *S pneumoniae, H influenzae,* or other bacteria.
- CT scan is a very sensitive method of detecting sinusitis.

General Considerations

Inflammation of the pseudostratified epithelium of the sinuses may occur as a result of an infection, allergy, toxin, or an autoimmune disorder. The paranasal sinuses (maxillary, ethmoid, frontal, and sphenoid) are sterile under normal conditions. Any one or all of them may become infected resulting in inflammation and edema of the pseudostratified epithelium that leads to an increase in tenacious secretions and the symptoms of acute sinusitis. The maxillary sinus is most commonly involved because its ostium is located at the highest part of the medial wall of the sinus. This leads to inadequate drainage and pooling of excess secretions, increased tenacity of secretions, and a drop in oxygen tension creating a more favorable environment for bacterial growth. Acute sinusitis occurs in all ages.

Infectious sinusitis may be bacterial, fungal, or viral. A large percent of acute sinusitis results from viral infection of the sinuses with or without bacterial superinfection. The latter is more symptomatic and patients are more likely to present to the physician. Episodes of sinusitis that occur all year round may be associated with allergies, polyps, or swimming.

The microbiology of acute bacterial sinusitis is sim-

BOX 9–14

Microbiology of Sinusitis

	Community-Acquired Acute Sinusitis	Chronic Sinusitis	Sinusitis in HIV-Positive Patients	Nosocomial Sinusitis
More Frequent	• *Streptococcus pneumoniae* • *Haemophilus influenzae* • *Moraxella catarrhalis* • Viruses—rhinovirus, adenovirus, influenza virus, cytomegalovirus	• Anaerobes such as *Peptostreptococcus* spp, *Prevotella* spp, *Fusobacterium* spp • *Staphylococcus aureus* • *Pseudomonas aeruginosa* • *Streptococcus pneumoniae*	• *Staphylococcus* species • *P aeruginosa* • Viridans streptococcal • *S pneumoniae* • Gram-negative bacilli	• Gram-negative bacilli, eg, *P aeruginosa*, *Klebsiella* spp; *Proteus* spp; *Enterobacter* spp; and others • *S aureus*
Less Frequent	• *S aureus* • Alpha- and beta-hemolytic *Streptococcus* • Gram-negative bacilli—*P aeruginosa* • Fungi—*Aspergillus, Mucor* spp.	• Fungi—*Aspergillus* spp. • *H influenzae* • *M catarrhalis*	• *Mycobacterium avium* complex • Cytomegalovirus • *H influenzae* • *Aspergillus* spp.	• *H influenzae* • *M catarrhalis*

ilar to that of otitis media (Box 9–14). *S pneumoniae* and *H influenzae* account for > 50% of the sinusitis cases. Other pathogenic bacteria include *M catarrhalis,* α- and β-hemolytic streptococci, *S aureus, C pneumoniae,* anaerobic bacteria, and occasionally gram-negative bacteria such as the Enterobacteriaceae or *P aeruginosa.* The β-lactamase–producing *H influenzae* and *M catarrhalis* and intermediate or PRSP have proportionally increased in the microbiology of sinusitis and have important implications for management of sinusitis. Anaerobic bacteria, such as *Peptostreptococcus, Fusobacterium,* or *Prevotella* species, are implicated in ~ 8–10% of cases of acute sinusitis. These are usually polymicrobial and result from contiguous spread from the roots of the teeth.

Patients with craniofacial fractures have a higher incidence of sinusitis. *P aeruginosa* is a frequent cause of sinusitis in HIV-positive and in cystic fibrosis patients and must be considered in a patient who fails empirical antibiotic therapy that does not include antipseudomonal activity. *S aureus* is slightly more common in frontal or sphenoidal sinusitis. Fungi such as *Aspergillus* spp., Zygomycetes (*Mucor* spp.), and *Pseudallescheria* spp., among others, can occur in normal hosts or in immunocompromised hosts. *Aspergillus* sinusitis may occur in normal hosts or present as an allergic syndrome. Zygomycetes infection is more common in people with diabetes (particularly during acidosis), neutropenic patients, and patients on deferoxamine treatment. Viruses such as rhinovirus, influenza virus, adenovirus, coronavirus, and occasionally CMV, among others, account for sinusitis that presents with the primary rhinitis or upper respiratory tract infection syndrome. Coinfections of viruses and bacteria have a higher rate of prolonged duration of symptoms. Recurrent sinusitis may occur as a result of allergies, enlarged adenoids (especially in children), anatomic obstruction such as septal deviation, polyps, tumors, or craniofacial abnormalities, congenital primary or acquired immunodeficiency syndromes, or coexisting disease such as cystic fibrosis, asthma, or gastroesophageal reflux disease.

Chronic sinusitis, infection of the paranasal sinuses for 3 mo or more, may occur in patients with persistently impaired sinus drainage, immunodeficiency, or inadequately treated previous sinusitis episodes. The microbiology of chronic sinusitis is difficult to interpret with previous antibiotic use. However, chronic sinusitis is more often polymicrobial in etiology. There is a higher incidence of *S aureus;* anaerobes such as *Peptostreptococcus, Fusobacterium,* or *Prevotella* species (25–80%); gram-negative bacilli, such as *P aeruginosa;* and fungi in chronic sinusitis as compared with acute bacterial sinusitis.

Clinical Findings

A. Signs and Symptoms. The symptoms may vary with the severity, cause of the infection and presence of complications. Acute uncomplicated bacterial sinusitis presents with high fever, facial pain, headache, and nasal discharge predominantly. Nasal discharge or PND is purulent and may have a foul smell. Cough secondary to the PND may be present. A more common presentation is sinusitis associated with a viral upper respiratory tract infection. The course is usually milder and presents with "flulike" symptoms such as myalgias, rhinorrhea, and sore throat.

The symptoms of sinusitis may last longer than a viral syndrome and ~ 60% of these patients will have positive sinus cultures. Headache is common and may be frontal, temporal, vertex, or retro-orbital depending on the sinus involved. Sphenoidal sinusitis predominantly causes a vertex headache. Eustachian tube blockage caused by local edema and nasopharyngeal secretions may cause the sensation of "blocked ears." Patients may give a history of a predisposing condition such as sneezing or nasal itching with allergies. History of recurrent sinusitis or sinopulmonary disease, arthritis, and other organ disorders is important to identify immunodeficiencies and noninfectious etiologic diagnosis. Chronic sinusitis symptoms are occasional headaches, fatigue, irritability, low-grade temperature, facial pressure, and PND.

In acute uncomplicated bacterial sinusitis, there is severe tenderness overlying the affected sinuses. There may be swelling, erythema, and induration of the overlying area. Cloudy, yellow-to-green purulent drainage is noted. Intranasal examination should be conducted to attempt identifying the site of purulent discharge. Percussion examination of teeth should be done in patients with unilateral sinusitis or with a history of dental pain. Patients may have signs resulting from complications of sinusitis such as erythema, edema, and proptosis in orbital cellulitis. Purulent discharge and elevated temperature may be the only signs of acute sinusitis. Transillumination of the maxillary sinuses may demonstrate the presence of fluid.

B. Laboratory Findings. Acute sinusitis is usually associated with leukocytosis of > 10,000 cells/mm^3. The sedimentation rate may be elevated. Cultures obtained by sinus puncture are regarded as the standard for an accurate microbiologic diagnosis and yield bacteria in ~ 60% of cases. Bacterial growth of > 10^5 colony-forming units (CFU)/mL suggests an etiologic role of those specific bacteria whereas growth of < 10^5 CFU/mL may represent contamination. Sinus puncture is recommended in patients who are severely ill; have intracranial or orbital complications, compromised immune systems, nosocomial sinusitis; or are not responding to standard empirical therapy. Newer endoscopic methods of collection of secretions are technically more difficult than puncture, especially from the maxillary antrum because of the location of its ostium. Endoscopic cultures obtained from the middle meatus may be contaminated with nasal secretions. In comparison with sinus puncture cultures, endoscopic cultures have a sensitivity of 65% and specificity of 40%, but this increases when evaluated specifically for *S pneumoniae, H influenzae,* and *M catarrhalis.*

C. Imaging. Standard radiography is useful for evaluating frontal and maxillary sinusitis with an anterior-posterior and Waters' view. Ethmoid sinuses are poorly seen on plain x-rays and difficult to interpret. Although standard radiography is less sensitive than CT, it may still be helpful in acute disease or determining bony erosion. The presence of air-fluid levels, opacification, and mucosal thickening is suggestive of acute disease. The coronal CT scan is a very sensitive imaging technique for sinus disease and is the imaging method of choice for accurate assessment. Findings on CT scan may include typical air-fluid levels that have a good correlation with acute bacterial sinusitis. Other findings such as membrane thickening, presence of polyps, and anatomic variations predisposing to or complicating sinusitis may help in defining the disease. Magnetic resonance imaging of the sinuses is also very sensitive in identifying mucosal disease. Both CT and magnetic resonance imaging are sensitive in detecting a fungus ball in the sinuses. Intracranial complications will require evaluation of the head with CT, especially if there are focal neurologic findings, or lumbar puncture for cell count, chemistry, and culture, and susceptibilities in a patient presenting with meningitis.

Differential Diagnosis

Patients with noninfectious sinusitis such as that related to Wegener's granulomatosis, tumors, or allergic rhinitis may present with signs and symptoms similar to those of infectious sinusitis.

Complications

The proximity of the orbits to the sinuses accounts for orbital complications. Orbital complications include periocular edema, orbital cellulitis, abscess, and further extension into the cavernous sinus leading to cavernous sinus thrombosis. Infection of the bone by direct spread or septic thrombophlebitis may occur. Frontal bone osteomyelitis and subperiosteal abscess cause a swelling and doughy feeling of the frontal bone called Pott's puffy tumor. Intracranial extension results in meningitis or epidural, subdural, or brain abscess. The incidence of these complications has declined, but they present as medical emergencies and require immediate attention. Cough or bronchitis from aspiration of postnasal drainage into the respiratory tract may also occur.

Treatment

Therapy of acute bacterial sinusitis includes symptomatic care along with an appropriate antibiotic regimen (Box 9–15). It may be helpful to stratify patients by the severity of symptoms. Patients who present with complicated sinusitis with evidence of intracranial or orbital extension should be hospitalized, undergo immediate appropriate diagnostic tests, and start on a parenteral empirical antibiotic regimen. Therapy should be guided by diagnostic sinus fluid aspiration. The recommended empirical antibiotic regimen in complicated sinusitis should include vancomycin, which is active against intermediate and highly PRSP, and a high-dose, third-generation cephalosporin (ie, cefotaxime or ceftriaxone) with activity against other usual pathogens. Empirical therapy should continue until culture and susceptibility results from sinus aspiration are available. Surgical consultations should be sought for possible drainage procedures. The increasing incidence of intermediate and highly PRSP and β-lactamase–producing organisms has led to a decrease in the efficacy of amoxicillin for sinusitis.

Current recommendations for empirical antimicrobial therapy for acute uncomplicated bacterial sinusitis include amoxicillin/clavulanate or oral cephalosporins such as cefuroxime for 10 d. Other efficacious antibiotics include cefprozil, cefaclor, loracarbef, or cefpodoxime. TMP-SMX achieved 95% cure rates in older sinusitis studies; however, it is less effective against GAS and *S pneumoniae.*

Alternative antibiotics include macrolides such as clarithromycin (15 mg/kg/d for children, 500 mg every 12 h in adults) or azithromycin. Erythromycin has poor activity against *H influenzae* and is not recommended. Newer fluoroquinolones, such as levofloxacin or gatifloxacin (not approved for use in children and adolescents < 18 y old), have good activity against PRSP and are approved for use in adults with upper respiratory tract infections. TMP-SMX, cephalosporins or macrolides could be used for penicillin allergic patients. Odontogenic sinusitis treatment should include anaerobic coverage with either a β-lactam/β-lactamase inhibitor combination or the alternative regimen should include clindamycin or metronidazole. Fungal sinusitis requires aggressive surgical debridement along with parenteral or oral antifungal therapy.

Supportive measures for symptomatic relief may be considered. Decongestants provide symptomatic improvement by decreasing the nasal edema and obstruction. Oral decongestants are preferred over topical ones to avoid rebound vasodilatation. Steroid inhalers are not recommended unless the patient has significant allergy history and symptoms. Most symptoms will resolve in 7–10 d. Indiscriminate use of antibiotics is strongly discouraged to prevent the emergence of resistant strains of bacteria, particularly if the symptoms are consistent with a viral upper respiratory tract infection.

Persistent symptoms after an appropriate course of treatment may result from retained secretions, resistant or unusual organisms, presence of allergies, or possible immunodeficiency. Recurrent bacterial sinusitis should prompt further evaluation of the paranasal anatomy; immunoglobulin levels; neutrophil function analysis; HIV serology; sinus aspira-

BOX 9-15

Empiric Therapy of Acute Bacterial Sinusitis

	Children	Adults
First Choice	• Amoxicillin/clavulanate, 40 mg amoxicillin/kg/d orally divided every 8 h for 10 d • Erythromycin/sulfisoxazole, 50 mg erythromycin/kg/d and 150 mg sulfisoxazole/kg/d divided every 6 h (max 2 g of erythromycin and 6 g sulfisoxazole) • Cefuroxime-axetil, 30 mg/kg/d	• Amoxicillin/clavulanate, 500 mg orally every 8 h for 10 d • Cefuroxime-axetil, 250 mg orally every 12 h
Second Choice	• Cefpodoxime for > 6 months– 12 years, 10 mg/kg/d divided every 12 h • Azithromycin, 12 mg/kg/d for 5 d • Clarithromycin, 15 mg/kg/d divided every 12 h for 10 d	• Cefpodoxime, 100–400 mg every 12 h • Azithromycin, 500 mg first day, then 250 mg every 24 h for 4 d • Clarithromycin, 500 mg orally twice daily for 10 d • Levofloxacin, 500 mg once daily for 10 d
Penicillin Allergic	• Trimethoprim/sulfamethoxa- zole 8 mg TMP/kg/d divided every 12 h • Erythromycin/sulfisoxazole, 50 mg erythromycin/kg/d and 150 mg sulfisoxazole/kg/d divided every 6 h (max 2 g of erythromycin and 6 g sulfisoxazole) • Azithromycin or clarithromy- cin (see above dosing)	• Trimethoprim/sulfamethoxazole, double-strength 1 orally every 12 h • Azithromycin, 500 mg first day, then 250 mg every 24 h for 4 d • Clarithromycin, 500 mg every 12 h • Levofloxacin, 500 mg every 24 h • Clindamycin, 450 mg every 8 h

tion; and cultures for aerobic and anaerobic bacteria, fungi, and mycobacteria. Sinus aspiration and lavage or other drainage procedures may be more efficacious in relieving symptoms in these patients. Sinus aspirate should be sent for aerobic and anaerobic bacterial, mycobacterial and fungal culture, and susceptibilities. Patients with chronic sinusitis may require retreatment with a second course of broad-spectrum antibiotics to include antimicrobial activity against *S aureus* and anaerobes. This could be achieved with amoxicillin/clavulanate or combination therapy of a cephalosporin with clindamycin or metronidazole given for 4–6 wk. Occasionally antipseudomonal therapy may need to be added particularly in patients with cystic fibrosis, patients who are hospitalized, or patients who are HIV positive. Acute or chronic sinusitis exacerbations should be treated similarly to acute sinusitis.

Prognosis

Most community-acquired bacterial sinusitis episodes respond well to antimicrobial therapy. Complicated sinusitis or sinusitis in an immunocompromised host may require aggressive treatment including surgery. Such patients may continue to have recurrences and the attendant morbidity. Mortality in sinusitis is related mostly to complications such as meningitis.

BOX 9-16

Control of Acute Bacterial Sinusitis

Prophylactic Measures	• Good hand washing • Simple measures such as covering your mouth while sneezing

Prevention & Control

Proper hygiene measures such as handwashing can reduce the incidence of acute sinusitis by decreasing transmission of infectious particles between persons (Box 9–16). Simple actions like covering the mouth with a handkerchief or tissue when sneezing or coughing can prevent aerosol or droplet transmission. Active immunization with pneumococcal polysaccharide vaccine or influenza vaccine may further decrease the incidence of these infections.

REFERENCES

Adderson EE: Preventing otitis media: medical approaches. Pediatr Ann 1998;27:101.

Barnett ED, Klein JO: The problem of resistant bacteria for the management of acute otitis media. Pediatr Clin North Am 1995;42:509.

Berman S: Otitis media in children. N Engl J Med 1995;332:1560.

Bisno AL et al: Diagnosis and management of group A streptococcal pharyngitis: a practice guideline. Clin Infect Dis 1997;25:574.

Brook I: Microbiology and management of sinusitis. J Otolaryngol 1996;25:249.

Byington CL: The diagnosis and management of otitis media with effusion. Pediatr Ann 1998;27:96.

Carroll K, Reimer L: Microbiology and laboratory diagnosis of upper respiratory tract infections. Clin Infect Dis 1996;23:442.

Chartrand SA, Pong A: Acute otitis media in the 1990's: the impact of antibiotic resistance. Pediatr Ann 1998; 27:86.

Church JA: Immunologic evaluation of the child with recurrent otitis media. Ear, Nose Throat J 1997;76:31.

Clement PA et al: Management of rhinosinusitis in children: consensus meeting, Brussels, Belgium, September 13, 1996. Arch Otolaryngol, Head Neck Surg 1998;124:31.

Conrad DA: Should acute otitis media ever be treated with antibiotics? Pediatr Ann 1998;27:66.

Cressman WR, Myer CM III: Diagnosis and management of croup and epiglottitis. Pediatr Clin North Am. 1994;41:265.

Diaz I, Bamberger DM: Acute sinusitis. Semin Respir Infect 1995;10:14.

Dowell SF et al: Acute otitis media: Management and surveillance in an era of pneumococcal resistance—a report from the Drug-Resistant Streptococcus Pneumoniae Therapeutic Group. Pediatr Infect Dis J 1999;18:1.

Engel JP: Viral upper respiratory infections. Semin Respir Infect 1995;10:3.

Farr BM, Hayden FG, Gwaltney JM Jr: Zinc gluconate lozenges for treating the common cold. (Letter; comment). Ann Intern Med 1997;126:739.

Fergie JE, Purcell K: The role of inflammatory mediators and anti-inflammatory drugs in otitis media. Pediatr Ann 1998;27:76.

Gwaltney JM Jr: Acute community-acquired sinusitis. Clin Infect Dis 1996;23:1209.

Gwaltney JM Jr et al: Rhinovirus infections in an industrial population. I. The occurrence of illness. N Engl J Med 1966;275:1261.

Gwaltney JM Jr: Acute laryngitis. In Mandell GL et al: *Mandell, Douglas, and Bennett's Principles and Practice of Infectious Diseases,* 4th ed. Churchill Livingstone, 1995.

Gwaltney, JM Jr: Sinusitis. In Mandell GL et al: *Mandell, Douglas, and Bennett's Principles and Practice of Infectious Diseases,* 4th ed. Churchill Livingstone, 1995.

Gwaltney JM Jr et al: Computed tomographic study of the common cold. N Engl J Med 1994;330:25.

Hall CB: Acute laryngo-tracheobronchitis (croup). In Mandell GL et al: *Mandell, Douglas, and Bennett's Principles and Practice of Infectious Diseases,* 4th ed. Churchill Livingstone, 1995.

Hemila, H: Does vitamin C alleviate the symptoms of the common cold? A review of current evidence. Scand J Infect Dis 1994;26:1.

Hilding, DA: Literature review: the common cold. Ear, Nose Throat J 1994;73:639.

Isaacson G: Sinusitis in childhood. Pediatr Clin North Am 1996;43:1297.

Jackson JL, Peterson C, Lesho E: A metaanalysis of zinc salts lozenges and the common cold. Arch Intern Med 1997;157:2373.

Kaliner MA et al: Sinusitis: bench to bedside. Current findings, future directions. J Allergy Clin Immunol 1997;99: S829.

Klassen TP: Recent advances in the treatment of bronchiolitis and laryngitis. Pediatr Clin North Am 1997;44: 249.

Klein JO: Otitis externa, otitis media, mastoiditis. In Mandell GL et al: *Mandell, Douglas, and Bennett's Principles and Practice of Infectious Diseases,* 4th ed. Churchill Livingstone, 1995.

Luks D, Anderson MR: Antihistamines and the common cold. A review and critique of the literature. J Gen Intern Med 1996;11:240.

Newton DA: Sinusitis in children and adolescents. Prim Care 1996;23:701.

Nissen AJ, Bui H: Complications of chronic otitis media. Ear, Nose Throat J 1996;75:284.

Sandler NA, Johns FR, Braun TW: Advances in the management of acute and chronic sinusitis. J Oral Maxillofac Surg 1996;54:1005.

Schroeder LL, Knapp JF: Recognition and emergency management of infectious causes of upper airway obstruction in children. Semin Respir Infect 1995;10:21.

Skolnik N: Croup. J Fam Pract 1993;37:165.

Slavin RG: Nasal polyps and sinusitis. J Am Med Assoc 1997;278:1849.

Smith MBH, Feldman W: Over-the-counter cold medications. A critical review of clinical trials between 1950 and 1991. J Am Med Assoc 1993;269(17):2258.

Swanson JA, Hoecker JL: Concise review for primary-care physicians: otitis media in young children. Mayo Clin Proc 1996;71:179.

Tracheobronchitis & Lower Respiratory Tract Infections

Abinash Virk, MD, & Walter R. Wilson, MD

ACUTE BRONCHITIS

Essentials of Diagnosis
- Acute inflammation of the tracheobronchial tree.
- Occurs more often in adults than in children.
- Most often caused by viruses; occurs most frequently in winter.
- Cough and low-grade fever are prominent symptoms; auscultation of lungs reveals rhonchi and/or wheezes.
- Diagnosis is on clinical basis; laboratory investigations and chest radiography are usually not helpful.
- Most patients require only symptomatic treatment; patients with chronic cardiopulmonary disease may require aggressive care including hospitalization, oxygen therapy, and occasionally mechanical ventilation.

General Considerations
Acute bronchitis is a common inflammatory condition of the tracheobronchial tree that results in many physician visits worldwide. By definition the inflammation is limited to the trachea and large and medium-sized bronchi, with absence of infection of the alveoli or lower respiratory tract.

Community-acquired respiratory viruses, such as respiratory syncytial virus (RSV), rhinovirus, coronavirus, adenovirus, influenza viruses, and parainfluenza viruses, are the most common causes of acute bronchitis (Box 10–1). Occasionally, herpes viruses and, more rarely, measles virus cause acute bronchitis. Less often, nonviral etiologies are implicated, such as *Mycoplasma pneumoniae, Chlamydia pneumoniae,* and, more rarely, *Bordetella pertussis.* Sputum cultures from patients with acute bronchitis may be positive for *Streptococcus pneumoniae* or *Haemophilus influenzae;* however, the role of these organisms in pathogenesis is unclear and may represent oral or upper respiratory tract colonization with no etiologic role. A small proportion of acute-bron-

chitis cases may be caused by noninfectious injury to the bronchial epithelium, eg, by exposure to pollution or other toxic substances.

Infection of the tracheobronchial epithelium results in various degrees of epithelial injury (depending on the infecting organism), which in turn results in a local acute polymorphonuclear (PMN) inflammatory response, edema, and hyperemia of the mucous lining. The mucous and serous glands of the bronchial lining secrete abundant mucus during this inflammation. Normally, ciliated epithelium of the bronchi aid in the upward passage of mucus, thereby preventing infection of the bronchioles and alveoli. This protective mechanism may not occur in infants or patients with other comorbid conditions such as chronic obstructive pulmonary disease. Smoking or exposure to air pollutants can increase the severity of attack.

Clinical Findings
A. Signs and Symptoms. Cough is the most prominent symptom of acute bronchitis. Cough is accompanied by mucoid expectoration, which may or may not be discolored and usually is worse in the morning. Fever is not a prominent symptom. If present, it is usually low grade. Some patients may complain of substernal discomfort with coughing and associated wheezing. Physical examination usually reveals a patient who is not in obvious respiratory distress. Respiratory distress is more likely to occur among patients with a history of smoking, multiple previous episodes or in those with comorbid diseases such as chronic cardiopulmonary diseases. On auscultation of the lungs, rhonchi or wheezes—particularly on expiration—are most often heard. These findings result from congested bronchial walls and partial obstruction caused by luminal mucus. Inspiratory or expiratory coarse crepitations may be heard. Complete occlusion of a bronchus by a mucus plug may result in absence of breath sounds in the area of atelectasis. Most acute bronchitis episodes are self-limited and resolve in 1–2 weeks.

B. Laboratory Findings. Diagnosis is based on clinical symptomatology. Laboratory investigations are not helpful. Complete blood counts are likely to be normal or include mildly elevated leukocyte

BOX 10–1

Microbiology of Acute Bronchitis

	Children	Adults
More Frequent	• Respiratory syncytial virus • Adenovirus • Rhinovirus • Parainfluenza virus • Enterovirus • Influenza A/B	• Influenza A/B • Adenovirus • Rhinovirus • Parainfluenza virus • Respiratory syncytial virus • Enterovirus
Less Frequent	• *Streptococcus pneumoniae* • *Haemophilus influenzae* • *Chlamydia pneumoniae* • *Mycoplasma pneumoniae* • *Bordetella pertussis*	• *Streptococcus pneumoniae* • *Haemophilus influenzae* • *Mycoplasma pneumoniae* • *Chlamydia pneumoniae* • *Bordetella pertussis*

counts. Sputum cultures usually do not accurately reflect the etiology of acute bronchitis. A sputum Gram stain may show many mononuclear or polymorphonuclear cells in viral or bacterial infections, respectively. Rapid diagnostic antigen detection by enzymatic immunoassay for RSV and influenza may be useful in selected patients. Serological studies that detect the acute-phase immunoglobulin M (IgM) response to viruses, *Mycoplasma* spp., or *C pneumoniae* may be useful diagnostically, but these are expensive tests and are usually not necessary. In the acute phase, IgG is not helpful unless a fourfold increase or decrease in titer can be demonstrated in paired sera. However, these tests require serum samples that are obtained several weeks apart, and therefore not practical.

C. Imaging. Chest radiographs do not demonstrate specific abnormalities in acute bronchitis. However, because there are many causes of cough, chest radiographs may help exclude other causes.

Differential Diagnosis

Cough is a common symptom of a number of cardiopulmonary diseases. Diagnosis of acute bronchitis should be made after appropriate evaluation and exclusion of other causes of cough. New onset of cough caused by pneumonia, presence of a foreign body, toxic-fume injury, drug side effects such as angiotensin-converting enzyme inhibitors, endobron-

chial malignancy, or congestive heart failure may be mistaken initially for acute bronchitis. Tuberculosis should be excluded in cases with chronic cough, particularly in patients with high-risk profiles, including immigrants, intravenous drug abusers, homeless populations, and those with previous tuberculosis exposure or immunocompromised status.

Complications

Most episodes of acute bronchitis resolve spontaneously. However, patients with underlying chronic cardiopulmonary diseases, such as chronic obstructive lung disease (COPD), congestive heart failure, or severe immunosuppression, may develop respiratory compromise that requires hospitalization and, in severe cases, mechanical ventilation. Cough in otherwise healthy persons may persist for 6–8 weeks because of increased airway reactivity.

Treatment

Because acute bronchitis is most often a viral infection, the majority of the episodes of community-acquired acute bronchitis require only symptomatic therapy and do not need antibiotic therapy. Nonetheless, studies have shown that 66% of patients with acute bronchitis are prescribed antibiotics for this self-limited disease. Antibiotic therapy for acute bronchitis should be reserved only for select patients, including the elderly, those with underlying cardiopulmonary disease and persistent cough (lasting > 7–10 days), or immunocompromised patients. The choice of antibiotics in such patients should be directed against *S pneumoniae, H influenzae, Mycoplasma* spp., or *C pneumoniae*. Antibiotics that can be administered on an outpatient basis and adequately cover these organisms include newer-generation macrolides such as clarithromycin, azithromycin, and doxycycline or a fluoroquinolone such as levofloxacin, administered for a 7- to 10-day course (Box 10–2). Hospitalized patients with acute bronchitis warrant antimicrobial therapy more often than do ambulatory patients. The choice of empiric antimicrobial therapy is the same for outpatients and inpatients.

Symptomatic therapy includes cough suppressants, adequate hydration, and antipyretics as necessary. Occasionally, patients may require β-adrenergic bronchodilators such as albuterol inhalers for bronchospasm associated with acute bronchitis.

Prognosis

Prognosis for patients with acute bronchitis is excellent. Morbidity and mortality are higher among patients with an underlying comorbid condition.

Prevention

Hand washing is an important measure in preventing the acquisition of viruses that cause viral lower respiratory tract infections (LRTIs) (Box 10–3). Care

BOX 10–2

Empiric Therapy of Acute Bronchitis[1]

	Children	Adults
First Choice	• No antibiotics • Fluids	• No antibiotics • Fluids and symptomatic therapy
Second Choice	• Erythromycin, 20–40 mg/kg/d orally, divided every 8 h for 10 d OR • Azithromycin, 12 mg/kg/d orally for 5 d (not to exceed 500 mg) OR • Clarithromycin, 7.5 mg/kg/d orally, divided every 12 h OR • Amoxicillin/clavulanate, 45 mg/kg/d orally, divided every 8 h OR • Trimethoprim/sulfamethoxazole, 8 mg/kg/d orally, divided every 12 h OR • Cefpodoxime, 10 mg/d orally, divided every 12 h or other second- or third-generation oral cephalosporin in equivalent doses for 10 d	• Azithromycin, 500 mg orally on day 1, then 250 mg per day for 4 d OR • Clarithromycin, 500 mg orally every 12 h for 10 d OR • Doxycycline, 100 mg every 12 h for 10–14 d OR • Levofloxacin, 500 mg IV or orally every 24 h for 10–14 d, or another fluoroquinolone with enhanced activity against *Streptococcus pneumoniae* in equivalent dosages OR • Trimethoprim/sulfamethoxazole, 1 DS tablet orally every 12 h OR • Amoxicillin/clavulanate, 500 mg orally every 8 h OR • Cefpodoxime, 200 mg orally every 12 h or another second- or third-generation oral cephalosporin in equivalent doses
Penicillin Allergic	• Erythromycin, 20–40 mg/kg/d orally, divided every 8 h for 10 d OR • Azithromycin, 12 mg/kg/d orally for 5 d (not to exceed 500 mg) OR • Clarithromycin, 7.5 mg/kg/d orally divided every 12 h for 10 d OR • Trimethoprim/sulfamethoxazole, 8 mg/kg/d orally, divided every 12 h	• Azithromycin, 500 mg on day 1, and then 250 mg/d for 4 d OR • Erythromycin, 500 mg per 6 h for 10 d OR • Clarithromycin, 500 mg every 12 h for 10 d OR • Levofloxacin, 500 mg orally every 24 h for 10–14 d, or another fluoroquinolone with enhanced activity against *Streptococcus pneumoniae* in equivalent dosages OR • Doxycycline, 100 mg orally every 12 h for 10–14 d OR • Trimethoprim/sulfamethoxazole, 1 DS tablet orally every 12 h

[1]Doses provided here for patients with normal renal function. DS, double-strength.

must also be taken in handling fomites from a person who is ill. Annual administration of influenza A/B vaccine is important for the prevention of influenza virus infection. Amantadine or rimantadine should be administered to exposed nonimmunized individuals. Active immunization with 23 polyvalent pneumococcal vaccine should be administered to high-risk patients. Droplet isolation for hospitalized patients, especially for infants and children, with *Mycoplasma,* influenza, RSV, and parainfluenza infections is recommended.

CHRONIC BRONCHITIS & ACUTE EXACERBATIONS

Essentials of Diagnosis

- Productive cough present for 3 months during 2 consecutive years.
- Exacerbations may be viral or bacterial; bacteria associated with chronic bronchitis with acute exacerbations (AECB) include *Haemophilus* spp., *S pneumoniae,* and *M catarrhalis.*
- Affects 10–25% of the adult population.
- Chronic cough productive of mucoid sputum, dyspnea, and signs of cor pulmonale in severe cases.
- Acute exacerbations are manifested by increases in volume and changes in the character of sputum production with or without fever; often accompanied by increased dyspnea and fatigue.
- Symptomatic therapy and a course of antimicrobial therapy are often required for acute exacerbations.

General Considerations

Chronic bronchitis is defined as chronic productive cough present for ≥ 3 months during 2 consecutive

years. Chronic bronchitis and acute exacerbations are clinical syndromes associated with COPD. COPD is characterized by obstruction to airflow in the distal airways. Pulmonary-function tests, especially forced expiratory volume at 1 s, are used to assess the severity and prognosis of the disease.

The essential pathological change in chronic bronchitis is the alteration of the epithelial lining of the bronchi. Initially, because of cigarette smoking, dust, or other chemical irritants, attacks of acute bronchitis occur. The initial airway changes include acute inflammatory PMN cell infiltration, hyperemia, edema, and increases in mucous and serous gland secretion that lead to mucus production. Over time and with repeated attacks of bronchitis, loss of the serous glands and hypertrophy of mucous secreting glands occur. The increase in tenacious secretions and ongoing destruction of the ciliated epithelium of the bronchi lead to inability to clear the bronchial lumen and further retention of mucus. The retained secretions encourage bacterial growth, which may result in repeated attacks of infection and inflammation.

The role of bacterial infection in chronic bronchitis and exacerbation is unclear. Bacteria do not seem to cause the initial bronchitis; however, they may play a role in acute exacerbations (Box 10–4). Randomized, placebo-controlled studies evaluating the role of antibiotic therapy and of bacteria in acute exacerbations show improved outcomes with antibiotic therapy, which suggests a causal relationship of the bacteria with AECB. Pathogenic bacteria may be recovered from normally sterile bronchi in the majority of patients with chronic bronchitis or during exacerbations. Chronic pathologic changes in the bronchi occur as cycles of recurrent bronchitis continue and are worsened by persistent exposure to noxious agents such as cigarette smoking or air pollutants. Ciliated epithelium disappears; goblet cells, which are normally not present, appear, resulting in partial obstruction of bronchi and atelectasis or consolidation distal to the obstructed lumen. Pathologically, severity of disease is measured by the Reid index, which is the ratio of the submucous layer (layer containing the mucous glands) to the thickness of the bronchial wall. The normal Reid index is 0.3; in chronic bronchitis the index is higher. In the later stages of the disease, the bronchial wall may become atrophic and thin.

Sputum may be chronically colonized with *Haemophilus* spp., *S pneumoniae,* or *M catarrhalis* in more than half of these patients. Bacteria such as *Staphylococcus aureus* or gram-negative bacilli occur less frequently. AECB may be precipitated by a viral infection. Viruses account for 25–50% of the acute exacerbations. These are usually the seasonal community-acquired viruses, such as influenza, parainfluenza, adenovirus, or RSV. Other microorganisms such as *M pneumoniae* or *C pneumoniae* are infrequent causes of infection.

Clinical Findings

A. Signs and Symptoms. Persistent cough is a hallmark of chronic bronchitis. Coughing spells can be triggered by conversation or laughing. Patients clear their throats frequently. On most days cough is productive of mucoid sputum. Expectoration of sputum is greater in the morning and during winter. Sputum is usually mucoid, clear to yellow in color, and green or purulent with an AECB. Patients often complain of postnasal drip. The voice may be raspy from chronic cough and cigarette smoking.

Patients have accompanying symptoms and signs of COPD. In some patients, chronic bronchitis predominates, whereas others have symptoms of emphysema alone or a combination of both. Patients with chronic bronchitis develop severe functional, bronchitis-mediated structural damage to bronchioles and alveoli and have minimal compensatory mechanisms or increase in lung capacity. Spasm and stenosis of the bronchioles lead to difficulty in inspiration, hyperinflation, reduced inspiratory flow, and reduced oxygen tension in the alveoli. Patients with these changes that result in chronic reduced oxygenation, cyanosis, and severe dyspnea are referred to as the "blue bloaters." Patients complain of dyspnea, lethargy, and somnolence. Daily cough is accompanied by copious amounts of sputum. On physical examination, clubbing of the extremities and cyanosis are common. Rhonchi, coarse crepitations, and wheezing may be heard on chest auscultation. Eventually, chronic hypoxemia and respiratory acidosis lead to increased pulmonary vascular resistance and pulmonary artery hypertension, which may result in right-heart failure or cor pulmonale. On physical examination, cor pulmonale results in peripheral edema, jugular venous engorgement, and hepatomegaly.

Patients with primarily emphysema, as opposed to those with primarily bronchitis, lose alveolar elasticity, which results in increased lung capacity, slowing of alveolar gas movement, and diminished oxygen exchange. Compensatory mechanisms lead to an increase in the respiratory rate to maintain normal oxygen and carbon dioxide exchange. As a result, these patients are described as "pink puffers," who are dyspneic but not cyanotic. Eventually, with progressive destruction of the alveoli, this compensatory mechanism fails. These patients are characteristically thin and barrel-chested, and they have hypertrophied accessory respiratory muscles. Expiration is prolonged and may be through pursed lips. Percussion of the chest is hyperresonant. Auscultation reveals diminished breath sounds, prolonged expiration, and often wheezing. Cor pulmonale is relatively uncommon in these patients but occurs in terminal stages.

B. Laboratory Findings. Blood test findings are often normal during chronic bronchitis. There may be mild leukocytosis with a left shift during an AECB, but most patients will not develop leukocytosis. Arterial blood gases are important in evaluating and managing patients during an AECB. Blood cultures are usually negative.

C. Imaging. Chest radiographs may show evidence of COPD with hyperinflated lungs, but findings are nonspecific. Chest radiography should be performed in AECB to exclude pneumonia, pneumothorax, and significant atelectasis caused by a mucus plug or a mass. Chest radiographs should be compared with previous images.

Differential Diagnosis

Congestive heart failure or acute myocardial infarction can be mistaken for AECB. An electrocardiogram, cardiac enzymes, and echocardiography can help to exclude cardiac causes of symptoms. Pulmonary malignancy should be considered in smokers. Other conditions that may present in a manner similar to chronic bronchitis are chronic aspiration or recurrent asthma attacks. In younger patients, cystic fibrosis, epithelial ciliary defect, immunoglobulin deficiency (IgA or subclasses of IgG), or defects in neutrophil function should be considered in the differential diagnosis.

Complications

Repeated attacks of chronic bronchitis can lead to right-heart failure or cor pulmonale. In acute cases, patients with minimal pulmonary reserve may develop respiratory failure that requires mechanical ventilation. Mechanical ventilation is required for 20–60% of hospitalized patients with AECB.

Treatment

Management of chronic bronchitis can be divided into two broad categories—symptomatic and antimicrobial therapy.

A. Symptomatic Therapy. Symptomatic therapy is directed toward smoking cessation measures and management of airway secretions and bronchospasm. Smoking cessation decreases the continual irritation of the epithelial lining, thereby decreasing mucus production within weeks of stopping.

Airway management includes clearance of secretions and use of bronchodilators. Secretions may be tenacious and difficult to clear. A good cough is the best mechanism for clearing secretions. Mobilization of secretions can be increased by the use of bronchodilators followed by chest physiotherapy and postural drainage. Mucolytics and cough suppressants are not recommended. Mucolytics can be irritants and can increase sputum production.

Inhaled-bronchodilator therapy with β-adrenergic or anticholinergic agents, either alone or in combination, is useful in patients with chronic bronchitis, particularly during acute exacerbations. Aerosol nebulization can be used to administer bronchodilators such as albuterol and ipratropium bromide. Patients with acute exacerbations may require supplemental oxygen. However, excessive oxygen may cause hypercarbia by overriding the hypoxic ventilatory drive. Therefore, if oxygen is used, levels of partial arterial O_2 (PaO_2) and partial arterial CO_2 ($PaCO_2$) should be carefully monitored.

Parenteral corticosteroids have been shown to improve pulmonary-function tests more rapidly than placebos among patients with acute exacerbations.

B. Antimicrobial Therapy. Antibiotic therapy in patients with chronic bronchitis is appropriate during acute exacerbations or occasionally as prophylaxis against acute exacerbations (Box 10–5). Risk assessment may help with the choice of antibiotics and route of administration. A patient stratification by risk factors and history has been suggested for empiric antibiotic management of acute exacerbations. In patients with no previous pulmonary problems and recent onset of acute bronchitis, who are otherwise healthy, no antibiotics are recommended. For patients with a short history of symptoms, infrequent exacerbations, and normal pulmonary function tests, empiric therapy with oral doxycycline, amoxicillin, a macrolide, or trimethoprim/sulfamethoxazole is recommended. For older patients with longer histories of COPD, multiple previous exacerbations (> 4/year), and impaired lung function tests, empiric therapy with a cephalosporin, fluoroquinolone, or amoxicillin/clavulanate is recommended. Choice of empiric antibiotic therapy for hospitalized patients or patients with comorbid conditions, severe impairment of lung function tests, or frequent previous exacerbations should include a fluoroquinolone, parenteral third-generation cephalosporin, or amoxicillin/clavulanate. It is important to consider regional antimicrobial resistance patterns and the possibility of colonization when selecting antibiotic therapy. Empiric therapy should be directed against *S pneumoniae, H influenzae,* and *M catarrhalis*. Penicillin resistance among *S pneumoniae* strains is increasing, with geographic variations in the percentage of resistance. Worldwide, penicillin resistance among *S pneumoniae* strains ranges from 20%

to > 60%. Most cases of penicillin-resistant *S pneumoniae* ACEB may be treated adequately with high-dose penicillin, a new fluoroquinolone such as levofloxacin or gatifloxacin, or a third-generation cephalosporin. β-Lactamase–mediated resistance to amoxicillin among *H influenzae* isolates is ~ 30–40%; intrinsic non-β-lactamase–mediated resistance among nontypable strains of *H influenzae* to penicillin and amoxicillin is > 20% worldwide. Similarly, > 90% of strains of *M catarrhalis* demonstrate β-lactamase–mediated resistance. Treatment with a second- or third-generation cephalosporin, amoxicillin/clavulanate, trimethoprim/famethoxazole, a macrolide such as clarithromycin or azithromycin, or a new fluoroquinolone is optimal. Owing to resistance to macrolides among *H influenzae,* higher failure rates may be observed. Antimicrobial therapy should be modified depending on the patient's sputum culture and susceptibility results. Antibiotics are usually continued for 7–10 days.

Patients with progressive disease and repeated hospitalizations are more prone to colonization with nosocomial gram-negative bacilli instead of or in addition to the usual oropharyngeal bacteria. It is prudent to choose empiric antibiotics to cover these organisms in such circumstances. Use of a fluoroquinolone such as levofloxacin or gatifloxacin is appropriate until sputum culture and susceptibility data can help guide further modification.

Administration of prophylactic antibiotics in patients with chronic bronchitis is usually not recommended unless a high-risk patient has > 4 exacerbations/year. Options include monthly rotation of antibiotics, daily antibiotic therapy during winter, or antibiotics started as soon as there is a change in pulmonary symptoms or onset of an upper respiratory infection. The use of prophylactic antibiotics should be individualized for each patient, based on factors such as the development of antimicrobial resistance, cost, and side effects. Patients on chronic antibiotic therapy are likely to become colonized with resistant bacteria that reduce therapeutic options for subsequent oral antibiotic therapy.

Prognosis

Advanced age (> 65 years), presence of other underlying diseases such as cardiac disease, multiple previous episodes of AECB, especially those requiring steroids, and severity of underlying COPD are poor prognostic factors. The mortality of hospitalized patients with AECB is ~ 10–30%.

Prevention

Smoking cessation is the most important factor in prevention of AECB (Box 10–6). Patients should be immunized with influenza vaccine and the 23 polyvalent pneumococcal vaccine.

BOX 10-5

Empiric Therapy of Acute Exacerbation of Chronic Bronchitis[1]

	Children	Adults
First Choice	• Amoxicillin/clavulanate, 45 mg/kg/d orally, divided every 8 h OR • Cefpodoxime, 10 mg/d orally divided every 12 h or other second- or third-generation oral cephalosporins in equivalent doses for 10 d OR • Trimethoprim/sulfamethoxazole, 8 mg/kg/d orally divided every 12 h	• Levofloxacin, 500 mg IV or orally every 24 h for 10–14 d or another fluoroquinolone with enhanced activity against *Streptococcus pneumoniae* in equivalent dosages OR • Amoxicillin/clavulanate, 500 mg orally every 8 h OR • Cefpodoxime, 200 mg orally every 12 h or other second- or third-generation oral cephalosporins in equivalent doses for 10 d OR • Trimethoprim/sulfamethoxazole 1 DS tablet orally every 12 h OR • Doxycycline, 100 mg orally or IV every 12 h for 10–14 d
Second Choice	• Azithromycin, 12 mg/kg/d orally for 5 d (not to exceed 500 mg) OR • Clarithromycin, 7.5 mg/kg/d orally divided every 12 h OR • Erythromycin, 20–40 mg/kg/d orally divided every 8 h for 10 d	• Azithromycin, 500 mg orally or IV on day 1, then 250 mg every day for 4 d OR • Clarithromycin, 500 mg orally every 12 h for 10 d OR • Erythromycin, 500 mg orally every 6 h for 10 d
Penicillin Allergic	• Azithromycin, 12 mg/kg/d orally for 5 d (not to exceed 500 mg) OR • Clarithromycin, 7.5 mg/kg/d orally, divided every 12 h for 10 d OR • Erythromycin, 20–40 mg/kg/d orally or IV divided every 8 h for 10 d OR • Trimethoprim/sulfamethoxazole, 8 mg/kg/d orally divided every 12 h	• Azithromycin, 500 mg orally or IV on day 1, then 250 mg every day for 4 d OR • Erythromycin, 500 mg every 6 h orally or IV for 10 d OR • Clarithromycin, 250 mg orally every 12 h for 10 d OR • Levofloxacin, 500 mg orally or IV every 24 h for 10–14 d OR • Doxycycline, 100 mg orally every 12 h for 10–14 d

[1]Doses provided here are for patients with normal renal function. DS, double-strength.

BOX 10–6

Control of Acute Exacerbation of Chronic Bronchitis

Prophylactic Measures	• Smoking cessation • Active immunization with influenza and the 23 polyvalent pneumococcal vaccine in high-risk patients • Amantadine or rimantadine for influenza postexposure prophylaxis • Droplet isolation for hospitalized patients with *Mycoplasma* infection, influenza, RSV infection, and parainfluenza

BOX 10–7

Microbiology of Acute Bronchiolitis

	Children	Adults[1]
More Frequent	• Respiratory syncytial virus (RSV) • Parainfluenza virus • Rhinovirus • Adenovirus • Influenza A/B virus • Enterovirus	• Influenza A/B virus • Parainfluenza virus • Adenovirus • RSV
Less Frequent	• *Mycoplasma pneumoniae*	

[1]Uncommon in adults.

BRONCHIOLITIS

Essentials of Diagnosis

- Inflammation of bronchioles.
- More common in younger children < 2 years of age, usually those 2–6 months of age.
- Symptoms of a viral upper respiratory tract infection followed by cough, tachypnea, and wheezing.
- Chest radiographs show diffuse hyperinflation, patchy perihilar infiltrates, peribronchial cuffing.
- Supportive care, bronchodilatation, and occasional ventilatory support required.

General Considerations

Bronchiolitis is defined as inflammation of the bronchioles as a response to injury because of infections, vasculitis, chemical exposure such as that from cigarette smoking, or transplant-associated airway injury. Infectious bronchiolitis is mainly a disease of infants and young children. Of infants < 1 year of age, ~ 1–6% will develop viral bronchiolitis. Viruses are the most common infectious causes of bronchiolitis (Box 10–7). These include RSV, parainfluenza virus types 1 and 3, influenza virus types A and B, adenovirus, rhinovirus, and enteroviruses. RSV is the most common cause, accounting for 45–75% of all bronchiolitis among infants, followed by parainfluenza virus. RSV is the most common cause of nosocomial bronchiolitis. Bronchiolitis has seasonal distribution with highest incidence in the winter, when RSV activity increases. Parainfluenza infections occur during the fall and spring. Risk factors for severe bronchiolitis and possible hospitalization include male sex (male:female = 1.5:1), prematurity, overcrowding, comorbidities such as congenital heart disease or chronic lung disease such as bronchopulmonary dysplasia, and lack of breast-feeding.

Acute bronchiolar inflammation occurs. Peribronchial mononuclear inflammation and resultant edema of the submucosa and adventitia may develop, resulting in bronchiolar epithelial necrosis. These changes may result in partial or complete bronchiolar obstruction and distal atelectasis, especially in infants. Positive pressure during expiration increases the degree of obstruction in the bronchioles. Inflammation and bronchospasm may be the result of virus-specific IgE, leukotriene C4, or other inflammatory mediators.

Clinical Findings

A. Signs and Symptoms. Prodromal symptoms include rhinorrhea, low-grade fever, and irritability. Increasing cough, lethargy, and anorexia follow the prodromal symptoms. As the disease progresses, the infant becomes dyspneic, has an audible wheeze, and is in obvious respiratory distress. Tachycardia and tachypnea with chest wall retractions and flaring of the nasal alae may be present. Diffuse fine crepitations and expiratory wheezes are heard on auscultation. In severe progressive disease, auscultatory findings may be minimal owing to obstruction. Other findings on examination include manifestations of the infecting virus or pathogen such as otitis media (10–30% of children) or diarrhea. The symptoms usually last for 3–7 days, with improvement occurring in the first 3–4 days and overall clinical resolution taking 1–2 weeks.

B. Laboratory Findings. Complete blood count is usually normal in mild infections, but leukocytosis with a left shift may be present in severe cases. Hypoxemia and hypercarbia may occur with a severe progressive infection. A specific viral diagnosis may be established with viral cultures or by rapid diagnostic procedures such as the enzyme immunoassay (EIA) for RSV or influenza virus on respiratory secretions—obtained either by nasopharyngeal swab or wash or from an endotracheal sample if the child is intubated. Although bacterial cultures may be positive for *S pneumoniae, H influenzae,* or other bacteria, secondary bacterial infection is infrequent. Serologic studies are helpful if an IgM antibody is positive or a fourfold increase or decrease in titers is detected. In general, serologic tests are of minimal value and should not be performed on a routine basis.

C. Imaging. Radiographic findings in bronchiolitis may not correlate with the clinical severity of the disease. On a chest radiograph, bronchiolitis appears as hyperinflation of the lungs, with decreased costophrenic angles and depressed diaphragms (Figure 10–1A and 1B). Prominent bronchovascular markings radiating from the hila appear as perihilar infiltrates with prominent peribronchial cuffing. Areas of atelectasis or consolidation may be seen. Occasionally, an associated pneumonic infiltrate may be present.

Differential Diagnosis

The differential diagnosis of bronchiolitis includes asthma or aspiration. The diagnosis is more likely to be bronchiolitis if wheezing occurs at < 1 year of age, RSV is detected, and there is no prior history of wheezing or family history of atopy. Other conditions that may simulate bronchiolitis include cystic fibrosis, lymphoid interstitial pneumonia as seen in HIV/AIDS patients, and congestive heart failure in very young infants.

Complications

Immediate complications include apneic spells, dehydration, hypoxia, and respiratory failure. Apnea occurs more frequently among premature or very young infants. Dehydration results from diarrhea, anorexia, or repeated coughing spells that cause vomiting. Mucus plugging, atelectasis, pneumonia, and ventilation-perfusion mismatch may cause respiratory failure. Immunocompromised children or those with comorbidities such as chronic pulmonary or cardiac disease or prematurity are more likely to develop a severe infection that requires ventilatory support.

Late complications include an increased tendency to develop recurrent hyperactive airways. This may occur in as many as two-thirds of the patients and persist ≤ 2–7 years after the episode, but this tendency gradually resolves. The risk of this late complication is less in children with mild disease that does not require hospitalization.

Treatment

Therapy of bronchiolitis is based on the severity of disease (Box 10–8). In mild cases, outpatient man-

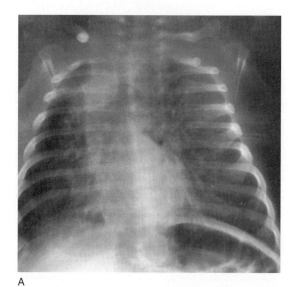

A

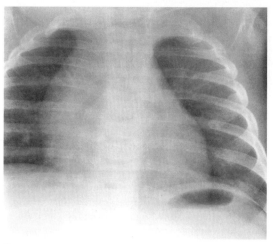

B

Figure 10–1. Respiratory syncytial virus (RSV) bronchiolitis and pneumonitis. A. Chest radiograph shows patchy perihilar infiltrates, overinflated lungs, and atelactasis in the right upper lobe. The radiograph depicts the airway distribution of the RSV infection. Consolidation, pleural effusion, and hilar adenopathy are rare. B. Follow-up chest radiograph taken 3 months later shows complete resolution of the infiltrates.

agement can be initiated with adequate hydration, feeding, and close follow-up. Children should be hospitalized if there is a history of underlying disease or prematurity; they are < 3 months of age; or they have pulse oximetry of < 93% on room air, apnea, severe dehydration, or signs of severe respiratory distress.

The cornerstone of inpatient management of bronchiolitis is the judicious use of oxygen and supportive care, including hydration and feeding. Oxygen satu-

BOX 10–8

Empiric Therapy of Acute Bronchiolitis[1]

	Children	Adults
First Choice	• No antibiotics • Fluids • Bronchodilators	• No antibiotics • Fluids and symptomatic therapy
Second Choice	• Aerosolized ribavirin, 20 mg/mL aerosolized over 12–18 h every day × 3 d, maximum 7 d [6 g in 300 mL sterile water (20 mg/mL)] given by small-particle generator for 12–20 h for 1–7 d No role for antibiotics unless secondary infection. In that case: • Cefotaxime, 50 mg/kg/dose IV every 8 h or other second-, third-, or fourth-generation cephalosporins in equivalent doses OR • Azithromycin, 12 mg/kg/d orally for 5 d (not to exceed 500 mg)	• Aerosolized ribavirin, 20 mg/mL over 12–18 h every day × 3 d, maximum 7 d [6 g in 300 mL of sterile water (20 mg/mL)] given by small-particle generator for 12–20 h for 1–7 d No role for antibiotics unless secondary infection. In that case: • Cefotaxime, 1 g IV every 8 h or other second-, third-, or fourth-generation cephalosporin in equivalent doses OR • Azithromycin, 500 mg orally on day 1, then 250 mg every day for 4 d OR • Erythromycin, 500 mg orally every 6 h for 10 d OR • Clarithromycin, 500 mg orally every 12 h for 10 d
Penicillin Allergic	• Azithromycin, 12 mg/kg/d orally or IV for 5 d (not to exceed 500 mg)	• Azithromycin, clarithromycin, or erythromycin, in dosages as above

[1]Doses provided here are for patients with normal renal function

ration should be maintained above 95%. Some high-risk infants will require mechanical ventilation.

The use of bronchodilators in bronchiolitis is controversial. Some studies show a benefit; others do not. Numerous studies have shown no benefit from corticosteroid therapy.

There is considerable debate regarding the use of aerosolized ribavirin for patients with RSV bronchiolitis. Ribavirin inhibits viral protein synthesis and is active in vitro against RSV. Initial studies that compared ribavirin with a placebo indicated significant improvement in oxygenation and decreased length of hospitalization in patients treated with aerosolized ribavirin. However, recent studies comparing ribavirin with a placebo did not show the same benefits for ribavirin therapy and, in fact, indicated that ribavirin therapy may prolong hospitalization. Accordingly, because of lack of clear benefit, high cost, and difficult delivery systems, the American Academy of Pediatrics recommends use of ribavirin only for a select population and at the discretion of the physician caring for the child with RSV bronchiolitis. Aerosolized ribavirin may be considered for high-risk pa-

tients such as those with a chronic underlying disease (pulmonary or cardiac), those in a severe immunocompromised state (organ transplant patients or patients with AIDS), those with severe RSV disease either with or without the need for mechanical ventilation, and those born prematurely at < 37 weeks gestational age or for infants < 6 weeks old.

Prognosis

Overall, the prognosis of patients with bronchiolitis is good. The prognosis is worse in an immunocompromised host or in children with chronic cardiopulmonary diseases. Mortality among hospitalized infants with RSV bronchiolitis ranges from 0.5% to 1.5%.

Prevention

Children, especially those with high-risk factors, should avoid contact with individuals with respiratory infections (Box 10–9). The American Academy of Pediatrics recommends the use of RSV immunoglobulin prophylactic therapy (RSV-IGIV) for patients at high risk for severe RSV disease. These

BOX 10-9

Control of Acute Bronchiolitis

Prophylactic Measures	• Avoid contact with ill persons • Respiratory syncytial virus (RSV) immunoglobulin, 750 mg/kg/mo during the RSV season (October to April) should be considered for select high-risk infants and children, including premature infants (gestational age < 28 wk or 29–32 wk, who are < 1 y or 6 mo of age, respectively), infants with bronchopulmonary dysplasia, or those who are severely immunocompromised • Droplet isolation for hospitalized patients with RSV infection, influenza, parainfluenza, and *Mycoplasma* infection

include premature infants (infants with a gestational age < 28 weeks or between 29 and 32 weeks may benefit from RSV-IGIV therapy until 12 months or 6 months of age, respectively), children with bronchopulmonary dysplasia who are < 24 months postnatal age and are currently using oxygen or have used oxygen within in the last 6 months, or severely immunocompromised children. RSV-IGIV has been shown to decrease RSV-related hospitalizations by 41–63%. RSV-IGIV is given monthly at the onset of the RSV season between October and April. RSV-IGIV is not approved or recommended for children with cyanotic heart disease because of possible higher mortality associated with RSV-IGIV prophylactic use in these patients. A new humanized RSV monoclonal antibody, palivizumab, is being studied as prophylaxis for high-risk patients. Palivizumab was effective in reducing the incidence of RSV hospitalization from 10.6% in the placebo group to 4.8% in the palivizumab group (a 55% decrease in RSV hospitalizations) and decreasing intensive-care unit admissions. The Food and Drug Administration has approved palivizumab for preventive use in patients at high risk of severe RSV infections.

Hospitalized patients with bronchiolitis should be placed in contact isolation to prevent nosocomial spread of the virus.

PNEUMONIA

Essentials of Diagnosis

- Affects any age group.
- Productive or nonproductive cough, fever, dyspnea, pleuritic chest pain.
- On examination, patient may have hyper or hypothermia, tachypnea, crepitations, rhonchi, and evidence of consolidation; some patients present with signs of septic shock.
- Laboratory findings usually include leukocytosis with an increase in neutrophilic response; hypoxemia, azotemia, and acidosis occur in severe cases; when positive, blood cultures are diagnostic of a specific microbiologic etiology; Gram stain of a good sputum specimen can be helpful diagnostically.
- Chest radiography demonstrates patchy, segmental lobar or multilobar consolidation or other patterns; false-negative chest radiographs can occur.

General Considerations

Entry of a pathogen into the lower respiratory tract induces a host inflammatory response that results in a fibrino-cellular exudate and consolidation of alveoli and smaller airways. This process is referred to as pneumonia. Patients present with symptoms and signs of an acute infection with associated radiographic findings. Pneumonia may be classified by microbiologic etiology, community versus hospital or nursing home setting, severity of onset (acute or chronic), or histologic appearance.

A. Epidemiology. In the United States, ~ 3 million individuals develop pneumonia annually. Pneumonia accounts for 10 million physician visits, 600,000 hospital admissions, and 45,000 deaths annually in the United States. The annual frequency of pneumonia varies by age, host factors, and season. It is more common in the winter and increases during influenza A season in the community. LRTIs are infrequent in infants < 6 months of age but increase in the second year of life. Overall, annual rates of pneumonia are highest in children 0–4 years of age. The rate increases during the childbearing years in parents who are exposed to children and in persons > 65 years old.

Certain host factors predispose patients to LRTIs. These include extremes of age; underlying diseases such as congestive heart failure, chronic renal disease, diabetes mellitus, chronic obstructive pulmonary disease, malnutrition, alcoholism, malignancy, cystic fibrosis or tracheobronchial obstruction; and institutionalization. Cerebrovascular diseases, dementia, and seizure disorders are also associated with an increased risk for LRTI. Risk factors for pediatric pneumonia include attendance at a day-care center, low birth weight, low maternal age, absence of breast-feeding, or a previous history of pneumonia or wheezing.

B. Microbiology. Pneumonia may be bacterial, viral, mycobacterial, or fungal. Certain host factors and exposures predispose patients to specific types of pneumonia.

1. Community-acquired pneumonia. Community-acquired pneumonia (CAP) is defined as pneumonia acquired in the patient's home or in a nonhospital environment such as a nursing home (Box 10–10). In general, viruses are the most common cause of LRTI.

Neonates are at an increased risk of CAP caused by gram-positive cocci, particularly group B streptococcal or staphylococcal pneumonia. There is also a predisposition to gram-negative bacillary pneumonia in this population. The risk for *S aureus* or gram-negative bacilli decreases with age. In children > 1 month old, viruses such as RSV, adenovirus, and influenza viruses play an important role in LRTI. Bacterial causes of pneumonia in children include *S pneumoniae, H influenzae,* and, occasionally, group A streptococci. The latter may complicate primary varicella infection. *M pneumoniae* is an important etiology of CAP, especially in school-aged children.

Among adults, no pathogen is identified in 33–47% of patients with CAP. *S pneumoniae* (30%) is the most common bacterial cause of CAP. Elderly patients, HIV-infected patients, and immunosuppressed, asplenic patients with immunoglobulin deficiencies or chronic cardiovascular, pulmonary (COPD, chronic bronchitis), or renal diseases are particularly predisposed to pneumococcal pneumonia. CAPs by encapsulated organisms like *S pneumoniae, H influenzae,* and *Neisseria meningitidis* are more common among patients with sickle cell disease, AIDS, asplenia, and immunoglobulin deficiencies.

C pneumoniae is the second most common cause of CAP requiring hospitalization. *H influenzae* type B or nontypable *H influenzae* is a common cause of CAP. *M pneumoniae, M catarrhalis,* and *L pneumophila* are other bacterial etiologies of CAP. Occasionally, *S aureus, Chlamydia psittaci, Coxiella burnetii* (the agent of Q fever), anaerobes, or aerobic gram-negative bacilli are the etiologic agents for CAP. Legionnaires' disease is caused by various *Legionella* spp., *L pneumophila* being the most common. *Legionella* spp. probably account for 2–6% of all hospitalized cases of CAP. They are associated with exposure to contaminated air-conditioning cooling towers or other contaminated water sources. *S aureus* pneumonia usually results from bacteremic spread to the lung and is often associated with endocarditis.

S pneumoniae, H influenzae, or *M catarrhalis* often causes pneumonia among patients with chronic

BOX 10–10

Microbiology of Community-Acquired Pneumonia

	Children	Adults
More Frequent	• Respiratory syncytial virus • Adenovirus • Enterovirus • Influenza A/B virus • Parainfluenza virus • *Streptococcus pneumoniae* • *Haemophilus influenzae* • *Chlamydia pneumoniae* • *Mycoplasma pneumoniae*	• Influenza A/B virus • *S pneumoniae* • *H influenzae* • *Moraxella catarrhalis* • *M pneumoniae* • *C pneumoniae* • *L pneumophila*
Less Frequent	• *Legionella pneumophila* • *Staphylococcus aureus* • Anaerobes	• *Streptococcus pyogenes* • *Staphylococcus aureus* • Anaerobes • *Pseudomonas aeruginosa* • *Mycobacterium tuberculosis* • *Coxiella burnetii* • *Coccidioides immitis* • *Cryptococcus neoformans* • *Histoplasma capsulatum*

pulmonary disease (COPD, chronic bronchitis). Nursing home residents are predisposed to pneumonia caused by *S pneumoniae,* gram-negative bacilli, influenza virus, RSV, and *S aureus.* Patients with structural pulmonary disease (cystic fibrosis or bronchiectasis) are commonly colonized and infected with gram-negative bacilli such as *P aeruginosa, Stenotrophomonas maltophilia,* or *Ralstonia (Burkholderia) cepacia* (Box 10–11). Alcohol use is also associated with pneumonia and colonization with aerobic gram-negative organisms such as *Klebsiella pneumoniae;* however, *S pneumoniae* is the most common cause of CAP among alcoholics. Children and adults with recurrent sinopulmonary infections should be suspected of having specific congenital or acquired conditions, such as abnormal leukocyte function, mucociliary defect (Kartagener syndrome), or immunoglobulin deficiencies.

Influenza virus accounts for 7–8% of all CAP, whereas community viruses such as RSV, cytomegalovirus (CMV), adenovirus, and others such as hantavirus are seen in specific epidemiologic settings. RSV pneumonia is more common in young infants, particularly those with cardiopulmonary diseases, or in patients with severe immunosuppression, as in bone marrow transplantation. CMV pneumonia is most often associated with patients with bone marrow transplantation, solid organ transplantation, or, occasionally, AIDS. Seasonal variation such as the predilection of RSV and influenza viruses for winter may help differentiate the etiology. Influenza pneumonia has a higher incidence of secondary infection with *S pneumoniae* or *S aureus.*

HIV-infected patients have predisposition for pneumonia caused by unusual pathogens such as *Pneumocystis carinii, Rhodococcus equi,* or fungi such as *Histoplasma capsulatum* or *Cryptococcus neoformans. Mycobacterium tuberculosis* causes CAP and should be considered among HIV-infected patients, homeless populations, intravenous drug abusers, immigrants, and institutionalized and nursing home patients.

Specific exposures provide clues to the microbiologic agent, such as *Coccidioides immitis* pneumonia in the southwest United States. Histoplasmosis is associated with exposure to bird droppings or bats. Psittacosis, caused by *C psittaci,* occurs after exposure to birds. Exposure to parturient cats or other animals is an epidemiological risk for *C burnetii* pneumonia. Hunting and skinning of rabbits, deer, or other wild animals are associated with *F tularensis* pneumonia. Recent or remote travel to Southeast Asia is associated with *Pseudomonas pseudomallei* pneumonia.

2. Nosocomial and aspiration pneumonia. Nosocomially acquired pneumonia (NAP) is pneumonia that occurs 48 h after hospitalization. Nosocomial pneumonia most often occurs in an intensive-care unit setting, especially among mechanically ventilated patients or patients at risk of aspiration. NAP is a leading cause of morbidity and mortality among patients with nosocomial infections, with an estimated annual incidence of 300,000 cases. Mortality from NAP is higher among patients with bacteremic pneumonia or pneumonia caused by resistant microorganisms. The microbiology of NAP is different from CAP (Box 10–12). The etiology of NAP varies geographically and by patient risk factors, du-

BOX 10–11

Microbiology of Infections in Patients with Cystic Fibrosis

	Children	Adults
More Frequent	• Influenza A/B virus • *Streptococcus pneumoniae* • *Haemophilus influenzae* • *Moraxella catarrhalis* • *Staphylococcus aureus* • *Klebsiella pneumoniae* • *Pseudomonas aeruginosa* • *Enterobacter* species • *Serratia marcescens*	• *P aeruginosa* • *Acinetobacter* species • *Enterobacter* species • *Ralstonia (Burkholderia)* cepacia • *Stenotrophomonas maltophilia* • *Achromobacter (Alcaligenes) xylosoxidans* • *K pneumoniae* • *S pneumoniae* • *H influenzae* • *S aureus*
Less Frequent	• *Mycobacteria avium intracellulare* • *Aspergillus* species	• *M avium intracellulare* • *Aspergillus* species • Influenza A/B virus

BOX 10-12

Microbiology of Nosocomial Pneumonia

	Children	Adults
More Frequent	• Respiratory syncytial virus • Influenza A/B virus • *Streptococcus pneumoniae* • *Haemophilus influenzae* • *Staphylococcus aureus* • *Klebsiella pneumoniae* • *Pseudomonas aeruginosa* • *Enterobacter* species • *Serratia marcescens*	• *S pneumoniae* • *H influenzae* • *S aureus* • Anaerobes • *P aeruginosa* • *Acinetobacter* species • *Enterobacter* species • *Stenotrophomonas maltophilia* • *Serratia marcescens* • *K pneumoniae*
Less Frequent	• *Legionella pneumophila* • Anaerobes • *Aspergillus* species	• *L pneumophila* • *Mycobacterium tuberculosis* • Influenza A/B virus • *Aspergillus* species

ration of stay in the hospital, and severity of pneumonia. Patient risk factors include advanced age (> 70 years); coexisting diseases such as diabetes, renal, or pulmonary disease; malnutrition; and impaired consciousness. Violations of infection-control practices, such as lack of hand washing or the use of contaminated devices, also increases the risk of NAP. Additional important risk factors for NAP are procedures that increase the risk of microaspirations. These include mechanical ventilation, nasogastric intubation, particularly when a patient is supine, sinusitis associated with nasogastric or nasotracheal tubes, use of sedatives, and use of H-2 blockers that increase the pH of the stomach acid, which results in gastric colonization with gram-negative bacilli. Certain surgical procedures, such as thoracic, abdominal, or head and neck surgery, predispose patients to NAP. Patients with minimal or no risk factors are likely to develop NAP with nonpseudomonal enteric gram-negative bacilli such as *K pneumoniae, Escherichia coli, Enterobacter* spp., *Serratia* spp. or with *S pneumoniae* or *S aureus*. However, with increased host risk factors, invasive procedures, severity of pneumonia, or prolonged duration of hospitalization, the microbial flora change toward *P aeruginosa* and other more virulent multi-drug-resistant gram-negative bacilli. Gram-negative bacilli such as *Klebsiella* spp., *P aeruginosa, Acinetobacter* spp., *Enterobacter* spp., and *S aureus* (methicillin-susceptible or methicillin-resistant) are the predominant microorganisms that cause NAP. Microaspiration of oropharyngeal secretions containing these bacteria results in the development of pneumonia. NAP is occasionally caused by

Legionella spp., influenza A and B, RSV, and, rarely, *Aspergillus* spp. or by nosocomial spread of *M tuberculosis.*

Aspiration pneumonia is predominantly caused by the oral flora, including aerobes and anaerobes such as *Peptostreptococcus* spp., *Prevotella* spp,. and *Bacteroides* spp., that form a large percentage of the microorganisms found in the mouth. Aspiration pneumonia must be considered among patients with seizures, neurological disease that impairs swallowing, altered mentation, vomiting, gastroesophageal reflux disease, and periodontal disease.

C. Pathogenesis. Pathogenesis of pneumonia depends on the interplay of host defense mechanisms and microbial factors. The normal defense systems of the respiratory tract play an important role in preventing LRTIs. These include anatomic barriers, humoral and cell-mediated immunity, and phagocytic function. Disruption of any of these mechanisms predisposes patients to respiratory tract infection. The first step in pneumonia pathogenesis is colonization of the upper respiratory tract mucosa with a microorganism capable of causing pneumonia. The nasal mucociliary barrier efficiently filters out particles by expulsion or by swallowing. Swallowing of saliva, local complement activity, local humoral immunity (IgA), and competition between normal oral flora and pathogens inhibit oropharyngeal colonization. Local IgA, adherence receptors, or fibronectin excretion normally prevents colonization of bacteria. Bacteria overcome these initial barriers because of large inoculum or virulence factors. The glottis and cough reflex help clear bacteria that reach the mucociliary lining of the tracheobronchial tree. The mucus overlying the ciliated columnar epithelial cells traps the bacteria, and the movement of the cilia pushes this mucus upward toward the glottis, to be either coughed up or swallowed. Humoral and cell-mediated immunity help clear the bacteria that reach the terminal airways and alveoli. Alveolar macrophages are the first line of defense in terminal airways and alveoli. The alveolar macrophages exhibit phagocytic function and induce chemotactic substances such as complement components, interleukin-1 (IL-1), IL-6, IL-8, IL-10, IL-12, and tumor necrosis factor (TNF). These mediate a local monocytic and neutrophilic influx. IL-8 is considered the most important chemokine that induces this neutrophilic response in the infected lung. In animal models, a neutralization of the IL-8 murine homolog macrophage inflammatory protein 2 resulted in decreased numbers of PMN cells, increased bacterial counts, and a higher incidence of bacteremia and dissemination. TNF-α is critical in orchestrating cytokines and chemotaxis. Circulating immunoglobulins and complement are incorporated into an inflammatory response. The pathologic appearance of the lung during this leukocytic influx into the alveoli is referred to as gray hepatization of the lung. The alveoli are filled with fluid containing the pathogenic bacteria, leukocytes, and macrophages. Subsequently, a slow resolution of the pneumonic process occurs.

Mechanical factors that impair cough and epiglottic reflexes predispose patients to aspiration. These include an impaired gag reflex that may be caused by neurologic disease, seizures, gastroesophageal reflux disease, anesthesia, or mental retardation.

Clinical Findings

A. Signs and Symptoms. Clinical presentation depends on the microbiologic agent and host factors such as age, immune status, exposures (geographic, animal, or sexual), and other comorbid conditions. Studies have confirmed that microbiologic differentiation by clinical criteria alone is extremely difficult. Some historical associations may suggest a microbiologic agent but cannot be relied on entirely for therapeutic decisions. A detailed history of exposures, travel, hobbies, and past medical history is helpful in suggesting a microbiologic etiology. Severity and presentation of CAP range from mild to life-threatening. Although the symptoms vary, most patients with CAP present with fever, chills, cough, dyspnea, and occasionally chest pain. Cough is the most common presenting symptom of CAP. Cough may be dry, productive, and associated with hemoptysis. Sputum is mucopurulent in bacterial pneumonias; classically, rusty-colored sputum is associated with pneumococcal pneumonia, whereas sputum may be like currant jelly (dark red mucoid) with *K pneumoniae* infection. When associated with a lung abscess, pneumonia may result in foul-smelling sputum that is indicative of the anaerobic or polymicrobial flora.

Lack of temperature elevation and confusion may occur in elderly patients. Patients with pneumococcal pneumonia typically develop sudden shaking, chills, fever, and mucopurulent, blood-tinged sputum, and they often have pleuritic chest pain. Gastrointestinal symptoms such as diarrhea may occur in pneumonia caused by *Chlamydia* or *Legionella* spp. A dry cough, an earache, aural discharge, and occasionally the presence of altered mental status may suggest pneumonia caused by *M pneumoniae*. Headache is common in patients with *Legionella* pneumonia. Patients with *Chlamydia* pneumonia may have a protracted upper respiratory infection with laryngitis that resembles a viral infection.

On examination, patients with a mild infection may not have acute distress, whereas patients with severe pneumonia often have severe respiratory distress and may appear toxic. The most common signs of pneumonia are tachycardia (heart rate > 100/min) and tachypnea. Temperature is commonly elevated but does not have a specific pattern. Pulse-temperature dissociation may be noted in viral, *Legionella*, mycoplasmal, or chlamydial pneumonia. To decrease pleuritic pain, splinting of the involved side may be noted. Pulmonary auscultation reveals crepitations and rhonchi. Signs of consolidation, such as dullness to percussion, increased vocal fremitus, bronchial breath sounds, and egophony, may be present. Signs of lobar consolidation are more likely in bacterial pneumonia. A pleural effusion may be detected. Use of accessory respiratory muscles, cyanosis, confusion, and severe tachypnea indicates severe respiratory distress. Hypotension and circulatory collapse occur in severe cases.

Assessment of the severity of infection and need for hospitalization must be done for all patients. Certain clinical signs predict higher morbidity and mortality. These include respiration rate > 30 breaths/min, diastolic blood pressure ≤ 60 mm Hg or a systolic blood pressure ≤ 90 mm Hg, temperature ≥ 38.3 °C, extrapulmonary complications (such as the presence of septic arthritis or meningitis), confusion and altered mental status, requirement for vasopressors for > 4 h, need for mechanical ventilation, decreased urine output to < 20 mL/h or total urine output < 80 mL in 4 h (except in patients with chronic renal disease), or acute renal failure. Occasionally, physical signs may suggest specific etiology such as bullous myringitis, central nervous system symptoms, or erythema multiforme in *M pneumoniae* infection; erythema nodosum is associated with *C pneumoniae, M tuberculosis,* or fungal infections. Physical findings among patients with *Mycoplasma, P carinii,* or viral pneumonia may be minimal despite significant changes on the chest radiographs. Pulmonary histoplasmosis may be associated with oral ulcers and is frequent among patients with AIDS.

B. Laboratory Findings. Complete blood counts reveal leukocytosis or leukopenia. Thrombocytopenia and evidence of disseminated intravascular coagulation may be present in severe pneumonia. HIV testing should be offered to patients with HIV risk factors. The selection of diagnostic tests is determined by the clinical severity of infection. Minimal laboratory investigation is necessary with mild disease. In critically ill patients, more extensive testing is necessary and includes, but is not limited to, serum chemistries, arterial blood gases, liver and renal function tests, and serum lactate. Poor prognosis is associated with leukocyte counts $< 4 \times 10^9/L$ or $30 \times 10^9/L$ or an absolute neutrophil count $< 1 \times 10^9/L$, $PaO_2 < 60$ mm Hg or $PaCO_2 > 50$ mm Hg at room air, hematocrit < 30 or hemoglobin < 9 g/dL, evidence of disseminated intravascular coagulation, and elevated creatinine > 1.2 mg/dL.

Gram stain examination and culture of sputum should be done in most outpatients and in all hospitalized patients. Sputum Gram stain provides a rapid and inexpensive method for a microbiologic diagnosis and aids in the selection of an appropriate management of pneumonia. A satisfactory sputum specimen is one that has < 10 epithelial cells and > 25 neutrophils in a low power ($\times$ 100) field. Sputum specimens that do not meet these strict criteria should be rejected for culture and the Gram stain results disregarded. For optimum sputum collection, patients must be alert and able to follow instructions. They should first rinse their mouths with water to decrease the oropharyngeal contamination and then collect expectorated material from a deep cough. Induced sputum is a more appropriate sample in patients unable to expectorate. Sputum induction is done with hypertonic saline aerosol. This method is useful for the diagnosis of *P carinii* pneumonia, *M tuberculosis,* or fungal disease.

Interpretation of the Gram stain of a sputum sample is dependent on knowledge of the normal flora of the mouth. Normal mouth flora includes abundant aerobic and anaerobic bacteria. Asymptomatic patients frequently harbor potentially pathogenic bacteria such as *S pneumoniae, H influenzae, S aureus,* and *N meningitidis* in the oropharynx. In healthy persons, $\le 9\%$ are colonized with *S pneumoniae,* and the carrier rate is higher in persons with preschool-aged children. Colonization with *S aureus* and gram-negative bacilli increases after 2 weeks of hospitalization and is frequent among nursing home residents and patients with chronic illnesses such as alcoholism, diabetes, or malignancies. Oropharyngeal colonization by gram-negative organisms increases the likelihood of a gram-negative bacillary pneumonia. However, isolation of gram-negative bacilli from sputum does not always implicate these organisms as the etiologic agent. Similarly, although *Candida* spp. are frequently recovered from sputa of normal individuals or from patients in intensive-care units, it rarely if ever causes LRTI.

Direct examination of the sputum is done by a Gram stain, by special stains such as acid fast (AFB) or KOH stain, or by immunofluorescence. Predominance of an organism on the sputum Gram stain examination sometimes identifies the causative agent. Abundant pathogenic bacteria with a characteristic morphology, such as the small lancet-shaped gram-positive diplococci of *S pneumoniae,* gram-negative coccobacillary forms of *H influenzae,* or gram-negative cocci of *M catarrhalis,* help in making the diagnosis. Polymicrobial bacteria suggest anaerobic gram-negative bacillary or aspiration pneumonia. Using an adequate sputum specimen, the sensitivity and specificity of the Gram stain approaches 50–60% and $> 80\%$ respectively, especially for *S pneumoniae.* Special stains must be performed on specimens to identify organisms not ordinarily seen on the Gram stain. *P carinii* is identified by using either methenamine silver staining or fluorescent Calcofluor stain. Mycobacteria are visualized with AFB, Kinyoun stain, or fluorescent auramine rhodamine stain. Modified AFB is required for the detection of *Nocardia* spp. Direct fluorescent antibody stains may detect *Legionella* spp.; KOH preparations may be necessary to identify fungi such as *Histoplasma, Blastomyces,* or *Coccidioides.*

Sputum cultures are not as sensitive or specific as Gram stains and are likely to be nondiagnostic in 50% of instances despite a highly suggestive Gram stain. In bacteremic pneumococcal pneumonia, only 40–50% of cases have a positive sputum culture for *S pneumoniae.* The recovery of some microorganisms from sputum culture usually implies their definitive role in pneumonia, and they do not usually represent contamination. These organisms include *L pneumophila, M tuberculosis, H capsulatum, Coccidioides immitis, Cryptococcus neoformans, Blastomyces* spp., *C burnetii, Nocardia* spp., *Francisella tularensis,* and *Yersinia pestis.* Anaerobic cultures of sputum are of no value owing to oropharyngeal contamination. *M pneumoniae* isolation from sputum cultures is technically difficult, and it may take ≤ 30 days to grow the microorganism.

Direct immunofluorescence assay (DFA) and EIA of sputum are useful in rapid diagnosis. DFA can detect *Legionella* spp. in respiratory secretions from 25% to 75% of patients with pneumonia caused by this organism. The sensitivity of the DFA varies with the antibody used, pathogenic species, and expertise of the personnel performing the test. Throat or nasopharyngeal swabs are the preferred specimens for DFA and cultures in suspected viral or *Chlamydia* pneumonia. DFA for *C trachomatis* has a sensitivity of 90%. Antigen detection tests for influenza A and B, parainfluenza, and RSV viruses have a sensitivity of 80%. DFA for RSV is more sensitive than cultures.

Blood cultures should be obtained from all hospitalized patients with pneumonia. Bacteremia occurs in 20–30% of patients with pneumococcal pneumonia. Positive blood cultures have a high specificity in providing a definitive diagnosis. Blood cultures are particularly useful in chronically ill, immunocompromised patients and in patients with a history of alcoholism or malignancies. Positive cultures from other infected body fluids such as pleural, joint, or cerebrospinal fluid also may be diagnostic.

Thoracentesis should be performed in patients with a pleural effusion who are not responding to appropriate antibiotics, or in seriously ill patients who are suspected of having empyema. Small pleural effusions should be considered for aspiration if fever persists for > 3 days on appropriate antimicrobial therapy. Pleural effusions occur more frequently in infections caused by group A streptococci, gram-negative bacilli, anaerobes, *S aureus,* or *S pneumoniae.* Pleural fluid should be promptly analyzed for pH, glucose, protein, and lactate dehydrogenase (LDH) and should be Gram stained and cultured for bacteria, mycobacteria, and fungi.

Serologies are not helpful in rapid etiologic diagnosis of pneumonia. They may be important in hospitalized patients with undiagnosed pneumonia, in which serology may be the only practical way to diagnose infections such as hantavirus or Q fever. Serologic tests are available for *Chlamydia* spp., *Legionella* spp., *Mycoplasma* spp., *C burnetii,* leptospirosis, and viruses such as influenza A and B, parainfluenza, RSV, adenovirus, hantavirus, CMV, herpesvirus, and varicella virus. Serologies may be useful for the diagnosis of histoplasmosis, coccidioidomycosis, blastomycosis, and cryptococcal pneumonia. Serologic diagnosis must be confirmed with an appropriate clinical picture and a positive IgM or a fourfold increase or decrease in the IgG titer in paired sera. A negative serology does not exclude the presumptive diagnosis. Delay in diagnosis and cost are the major disadvantages of serologic testing. Serologies are not practical or cost-effective in outpatient pneumonia.

Antigen detection by EIA, counterimmunoelectrophoresis, bacterial antigen test, or radioimmunoassay may be used to detect *S pneumoniae, H influenzae,* or *L pneumophila.* Urine, pleural fluid, or cerebrospinal fluid may be used to detect pneumococcal antigens. Pneumococcal antigen detection has the highest yield in sputum and persists for an extended period of time after an acute infection. Rapid EIA detection of RSV, influenza virus, or parainfluenza viruses has a sensitivity of > 80% and is useful in clinical practice. EIA detection of *L pneumophila* serogroup I antigen in urine may provide a rapid diagnosis. EIA has a 70–80% sensitivity and a specificity of > 95%, but the test currently detects only serogroup I. *Legionella* antigenuria persists for a considerable length of time after the initial infection. The presence of cold agglutinins in serum is insensitive (sensitivity of 30–60%) and nonspecific for the diagnosis of *M pneumoniae* infection.

Patients with unexplained pulmonary infiltrates who fail empiric therapy, have a fulminant clinical course, are immunocompromised, or are mechanically ventilated should be considered for fiber optic bronchoscopic examination and quantitative bronchoalveolar lavage (BAL) or sample collection with the protected specimen brush (PSB). Bronchoscopic aspiration with PSB has a sensitivity of 70–97% and a specificity of 95–100% in the diagnosis of bacterial pneumonia. Gram staining of the bronchoscopic specimen is important in early presumptive diagnosis and, when positive, predicts growth of > 10^3 organisms/mL. A BAL specimen is considered diagnostic if it has 10^3–10^5 cfu/mL growth of bacteria, especially if the Gram stain shows > 25 neutrophils and < 1% squamous cells. The diagnostic yield may be slightly less than with PSB. BAL is particularly helpful in the diagnosis of *P carinii* pneumonia (sensitivity of > 95%). Detection of CMV and *M tuberculosis* increases with BAL. Antibiotic use or a history of pulmonary diseases such as chronic bronchitis or cystic fibrosis decreases the diagnostic yield from bronchoscopic specimens.

Occasionally, fine-needle lung aspiration, transbronchial biopsy, or open-lung biopsy may be necessary for diagnosis. The risk of bleeding and pneumothorax (~ 20%) and variable diagnostic yields have decreased the utility of fine-needle lung aspiration. The diagnostic yield of a transbronchial biopsy is low. Thoracoscopic evaluation of the pleura and underlying lung is useful for the diagnosis of *M tuberculosis* infection, particularly when done in conjunction with a pleural biopsy. Finally, open-lung biopsy may be necessary when other procedures fail to yield a diagnosis. Open-lung biopsy is important in severely ill, immunocompromised patients or in patients not responding to empiric therapy. The diagnostic yield varies from 60% to 100%. The tissue should be examined for histopathology, Gram stained for bacteria, stained for acid fast bacilli, fungi, and *Legionella* spp., and cultured for these organisms. The lung tissue can also be subjected to molecular analysis by DNA probes or polymerase chain reaction techniques for rapid diagnoses of bacteria including mycobacteria, *C pneumoniae, Legionella* spp., or viruses. Open-lung biopsy alone may be useful for the diagnosis of noninfectious conditions such as malignancy, hemorrhage, vasculitis, bronchiolitis obliterans, drug-induced pulmonary injury, and others.

C. Imaging. Although chest radiographs alone cannot make a definitive diagnosis, they are essential in the evaluation of pneumonia (Figures 10–2 through 10–6). In general, chest radiographs can help characterize pneumonia as probably of bacterial origin, atypical, or complicated and help to assess the severity and extent of disease. Consolidation of one or more lobes with or without pleural effusion or cavitation suggests a bacterial pneumonia. Multilobar in-

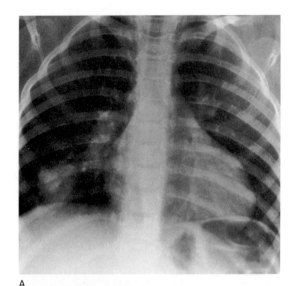

A

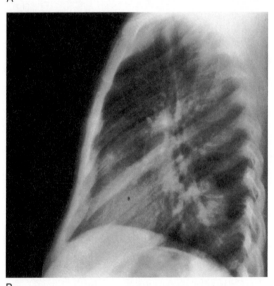

B

Figure 10–2. Round pneumonia. Round opacification is seen in the posterior right lower lobe with indistinct margins seen on (A) the posterior-anterior and (B) the lateral-view chest radiographs. Round pneumonia is mostly caused by *S pneumoniae* and is usually seen in children < 8 years of age.

volvement, rapidly increasing infiltrates, or the presence of cavities in CAP is an indicator of higher morbidity and mortality. Staphylococcal pneumonia results in multiple patchy infiltrates, which may cavitate and result in air-fluid levels from hematogenous spread, although occasionally gram-negative bacillary lung infections may present with similar findings. Cavitary pulmonary infiltrates may represent tuberculosis, particularly in the appropriate clini-

cal setting such as the homeless population, immigrant population, or HIV-infected patients. Cavitation in the dependent area of the lung, such as the superior segment of the right lower lobe or posterior segments of the upper lobe, suggests aspiration pneumonia. Less commonly, chronic aspiration can result in bilateral infiltrates.

Diffuse bilateral interstitial infiltrates are seen in pneumonias caused by *P carinii or Legionella* spp. and in viral, *Mycoplasma,* or *Chlamydia* pneumonia. These are usually present without a pleural effusion.

Differential Diagnosis

A large number of diseases and clinical syndromes can mimic pneumonia. These conditions include pulmonary manifestations of systemic vasculitis, hypersensitivity pneumonitis, bronchiolitis obliterans with organizing pneumonia, drug reactions, alveolar hemorrhage, chronic eosinophilic pneumonia, and pulmonary alveolar proteinosis. Malignancies or lymphoproliferative disorders can mimic CAP.

Distinguishing an infectious from a noninfectious etiology for pulmonary infiltrates may be difficult. The clues that suggest a noninfectious cause are an insidious onset, nonproductive cough, a relatively less toxic-appearing patient, a normal or only mildly elevated leukocyte count, and a lack of response to broad-spectrum-antibiotic therapy. The presence of extrapulmonary manifestations such as arthralgias or arthritis, rash, and multiorgan involvement in the absence of sepsis suggests a noninfectious process such as vasculitis.

An immune response to inhaled antigens results in pulmonary infiltration with lymphocytes, plasma cells, eosinophils, and neutrophils, with the development of sarcoidlike granulomas in the airways and pulmonary parenchyma, called hypersensitivity pneumonitis. Establishing a compatible exposure history, usually to farm animals or plants, suggests the diagnosis of hypersensitivity pneumonitis. Specific examples include thermophilic *Actinomyces* infection (eg, farmer's lung), fungi (maltworker's lung), or avian protein antigens (pigeon breeder's lung). Symptoms of hypersensitivity pneumonitis usually resolve within 24–48 h after removal of the offending antigen. Chest radiographic features and high-resolution chest computed tomography (CT) reveal bilateral mixed interstitial and alveolar infiltrates with some fibrosis in chronic cases. Of patients with chronic eosinophilic pneumonia, 60–80% present with radiographic findings of peripheral infiltrates with central clearing. Transbronchial biopsy and presence of eosinophilia, often > 40% in BAL fluid, establish the diagnosis. Bronchiolitis obliterans-organizing pneumonia is suspected in patients presenting with a clinical picture similar to CAP that does not respond to antimicrobial therapy. Chest radiographs demonstrate multifocal segmental or lobar alveolar infiltrates with air bronchograms in 60–80% of patients. There may

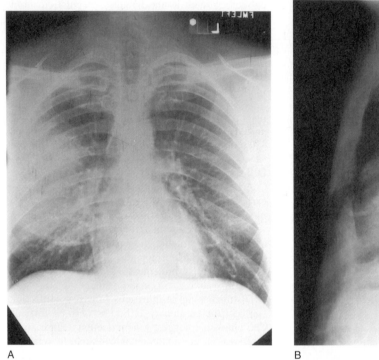

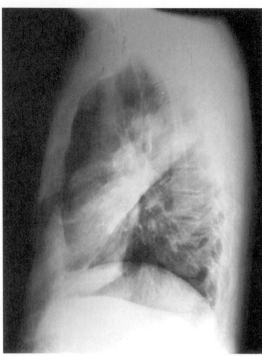

A   B

Figure 10–3. Pneumococcal pneumonia. (A) Posterior-anterior and (B) lateral views show opacification of the anterior and posterior segments of the right upper and middle lobes. Right lower lobe is not involved.

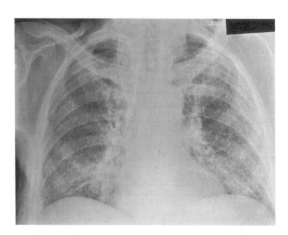

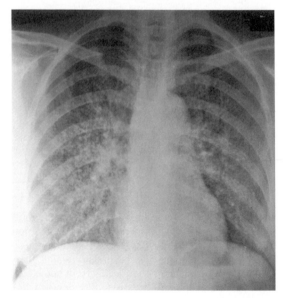

Figure 10–4. Blastomycosis in an immunocompromised host. Diffuse nodular interstitial pulmonary infiltrates. Open-lung biopsy confirmed granulomatous pneumonia with budding yeast forms and subsequent positive cultures for *Blastomyces dermatitidis.*

Figure 10–5. Miliary tuberculosis. Diffuse reticular-nodular bilateral pulmonary infiltrates.

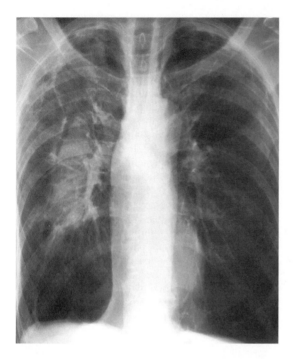

Figure 10–6. Aspergilloma. Large elongated cavitary mass in the right mid lung with central opacification and a crescent of lucency superiorly.

be a peripheral predilection for pulmonary infiltrates similar to chronic eosinophilic pneumonia; 20–30% of patients have reticulonodular infiltrates. Although open-lung biopsy is considered the most effective test for the diagnosis of bronchiolitis obliterans-organizing pneumonia, occasionally transbronchial biopsy may establish the diagnosis. Drug-induced acute pneumonitis caused by nitrofurantoin, amiodarone, methotrexate, and other drugs should be considered in the differential diagnosis of CAP that does not respond to antimicrobial therapy. Systemic vasculitis may affect the lung, either primarily or as part of multiorgan involvement. Wegener's granulomatosis and Churg-Strauss syndrome are granulomatous forms of vasculitis that have a striking affinity for lung manifestations. Pulmonary cavitation and severe extrapulmonary symptoms such as upper-airway, renal, or ocular symptoms suggest Wegener's granulomatosis. Although serum antineutrophil cytoplasmic antibody (ANCA), especially c-ANCA (diffuse granular cytoplasmic staining pattern), has a reported sensitivity of > 90% in patients with Wegener's granulomatosis, biopsies of involved organs are essential to confirm the diagnosis. Diagnosis of alveolar hemorrhage is supported by anemia and bronchoscopic evidence of blood-tinged BAL fluid with hemosiderin-laden macrophages.

Other conditions that simulate CAP include pulmonary embolism, which may present with cough, fever, and chest pain. Clinical history, physical findings such as calf tenderness, and the rapidity of onset of symptoms should suggest pulmonary embolism.

Complications

Pleural effusion and empyema are potential complications and may cause failure to respond to appropriate therapy. Lung abscess is another suppurative complication that can occur among patients, particularly after aspiration or in the presence of a pulmonary structural problem such as a malignancy. Patients can develop respiratory failure with or without septic shock and subsequent death. Respiratory failure and shock are more likely to occur in elderly, diabetic, alcoholic, or immunocompromised patients. Preexisting pulmonary disease is a risk factor for respiratory failure and ventilatory support. Young infants with RSV pneumonia can develop hyperactive airway disease later in childhood. Occasionally, *P carinii* pneumonia is associated with spontaneous pneumothorax.

Treatment

Severity of illness and risk factor assessment is essential in evaluating a patient for outpatient therapy compared with hospitalization. The presence of coexisting illnesses, immunosuppression, respiratory rate of > 30/min, hypotension, multilobar involvement, hypoxemia, acidosis, electrolyte abnormalities, leukopenia (leukocytes < 4.0/mm^3) or leukocytosis (leukocytes > 20/mm^3) are indices of severe pneumonia that warrant hospitalization. This assessment should be conducted expeditiously, because these patients can progress rapidly to circulatory collapse and respiratory distress necessitating mechanical ventilation. They should receive immediate antimicrobial therapy, because delay in onset of antimicrobial therapy may increase morbidity and mortality. Patients with some but not all of the poor prognostic signs may also warrant admission to a hospital, but not necessarily to an intensive-care unit. Patients without any underlying comorbidity and with normal or mildly abnormal physical findings represent low-risk individuals who may be treated with antimicrobial therapy as outpatients.

In addition to risk factors and objective findings, such factors as patient compliance and competence and the presence of a caregiver at home should be considered in making the decision for outpatient versus inpatient care. Patients with minimal or no home support may warrant hospitalization until outpatient support can be organized.

The choice of empiric antimicrobial therapy depends on the severity of disease, host factors, likely microorganism(s), epidemiological factors, and local antimicrobial resistance patterns. For instance, patients with a history of structural lung disease (cystic fibrosis, bronchiectasis) or nursing home residents require therapy with an antipseudomonal antibiotic (ceftazidime, cefepime, or antipseudomonal penicillin, or a carbapenem or fluoroquinolone). Aztreonam and a fluoroquinolone with or without an aminoglycoside are antibiotic options for β-lactam–allergic patients with gram-negative bacilli or NAP.

A. Community-acquired pneumonia. (See Boxes 10–13 A–C.)

1. Outpatient therapy. For outpatient empiric therapy of CAP, a macrolide such as clarithromycin or azithromycin, a newer fluoroquinolone with enhanced activity against *S pneumoniae* such as levofloxacin or gatifloxacin, or a tetracycline such as doxycycline is appropriate for pneumococci, *H influenzae,* and atypical organisms. Oral amoxicillin, a second-generation oral cephalosporin, or a macrolide is appropriate for outpatient treatment of CAP caused by penicillin-susceptible *S pneumoniae*. Amoxicillin or a fluoroquinolone such as levofloxacin or gatifloxacin is adequate for most mild outpatient CAP caused by *S pneumoniae* with intermediate resistance. Oral cephalosporins do not have adequate bactericidal activity to treat CAP caused by intermediate resistant *S pneumoniae* appropriately. Also, owing to multidrug resistance among these isolates, a macrolide, trimethoprim/sulfamethoxazole, or clindamycin may not be effective therapy. In vitro macrolide resistance among *S pneumoniae* isolates is ~ 10–25%. Therefore, these antibiotics should be used cautiously in patients with suspected *S pneumoniae* pneumonia. Outpatient treatment options for patients with high-level penicillin-resistant *S pneumoniae* pneumonia (PRSP) are limited. A new fluoroquinolone such as levofloxacin or gatifloxacin may be appropriate therapy. Ciprofloxacin has marginal activity against penicillin-susceptible *S pneumoniae*. Because multidrug resistance increases among penicillin-resistant pneumococci, susceptibilities to fluoroquinolones, macrolides, and other agents should be determined. Because penicillin resistance in pneumococci is caused by decreased affinity to altered penicillin-binding protein, β-lactam/β-lactamase inhibitor antibiotics such as amoxicillin/clavu-

---

BOX 10–13A

Empiric Outpatient Antimicrobial Therapy of Community-Acquired Pneumonia

	Children	Adults
First Choice	• Amoxicillin/clavulanate 45 mg/kg/d orally divided every 8 h for 10 days **OR** • Azithromycin 12 mg/kg/d orally or IV for 5 days (not to exceed 500 mg)	• A fluoroquinolone with enhanced activity against *S pneumoniae* such as levofloxacin 500 mg orally every 24 hours or another fluoroquinolone in equivalent dosages **OR** • Azithromycin 500 mg orally on day 1, then 250 mg orally every day for 4 days
Second Choice	• Cefpodoxime, 10 mg/d every 12 hours for 10 days or other oral second- or third-generation cephalosporin in equivalent dosages **OR** • Azithromycin 12 mg/kg/d orally for 5 days (not to exceed 500 mg) **OR** • Erythromycin 20–40 mg/kg/d orally divided every 8 h for 10 days **OR** • Clarithromycin 7.5 mg/kg orally every 12 h	• Cefpodoxime 200 mg orally every 12 hours or other oral cephalosporin such as cefdinir, cefproxil, or cefuroxime in equivalent dosages **OR** • Clarithromycin 500 mg every 12 h for 10 d **OR** • Erythromycin 500 mg orally every 6 h for 10 days **OR** • Doxycycline 100 mg orally every 12 h for 10–14 days **OR** • Amoxicillin/clavulanate 875/125 mg orally every 12 h for 10–14 d
Penicillin Allergic	• Azithromycin, erythromycin, or clarithromycin in doses given above	• A fluoroquinolone with enhanced activity against *S pneumoniae* such as levofloxacin 500 mg orally every 24 h or another fluoroquinolone in equivalent dosages **OR** • Erythromycin, clarithromycin, or azithromycin in doses given above **OR** • Doxycycline in doses given above

Note: Doses provided are for persons with normal renal function.

BOX 10–13B

Empiric Antimicrobial Therapy of Community-Acquired Pneumonia Requiring Hospitalization (Non-ICU)

	Children	Adults
First Choice	• Cefotaxime 50 mg/kg IV every 8 hours or ceftriaxone 50–75 mg/kg/d IV every 24 h **PLUS** a macrolide such as azithromycin, 12 mg/kg/d orally or IV for 5 days (not to exceed 500 mg)	• A fluroquinolone with enhanced activity against S pneumoniae such as levofloxacin 500 mg orally or IV every 24 hours or another fluoroquinolone in equivalent dosages **OR** • Cefotaxime 1 g IV every 8 hours or ceftriaxone 1 g every 24 h **PLUS** a macrolide such as azithromycin 500 mg IV or orally on day 1, then 250 mg every day for 4 d
Second Choice	• Ampicillin/sulbactam 200–300 mg/kg/d IV divided every 4 h **OR** Piperacillin/tazobactam (> 6 mo of age) 300–400 mg piperacillin component/kg/d; and for infants < 6 mo of age 150–300 mg piperacillin component/kg/d IV divided every 6–8 h **PLUS** azithromycin 12 mg/kg/d orally or IV for 5 days (not to exceed 500 mg)	• Ampicillin/sulbactam 3.0 gm every 6 h or piperacillin/tazobactam 3.375 gm IV every 6 hours **PLUS** a macrolide such as azithromycin 500 mg IV or orally on day 1, then 250 mg every day for 4 d
Penicillin Allergic	• Azithromycin 12 mg/kg/d orally or IV for 5 d (not to exceed 500 mg) **OR** • Erythromycin 20–40 mg/kg/d IV or orally divided every 8 h for 10 d **OR** • Clarithromycin 7.5 mg/kg IV or orally every 12 h	• A fluoroquinolone with enhanced activity against S pneumoniae such as levofloxacin 500 mg orally or IV every 24 h or another fluoroquinolone in equivalent dosages **WITH OR WITHOUT** clindamycin 900 mg IV every 8 h **OR** • A macrolide such as azithromycin 500 mg orally or IV on day 1, then 250 mg per day for 4 d

Note: Doses provided are for persons with normal renal function.

lanate are no more effective than penicillin against these microorganisms. Patients with additional risk factors such as advanced age or comorbidities and suspected penicillin-resistant pneumococcal pneumonia should be considered for hospitalization for parenteral antimicrobial therapy.

Doxycycline is appropriate therapy for younger (17- to 40-year-old) individuals with pneumonia because of the likelihood of *M pneumonia* infection.

2. Inpatient therapy. Severity of illness at presentation and host factors, including age, comorbidities, and drug allergies, help determine the empiric antimicrobial therapy for a hospitalized patient with CAP. A third-generation cephalosporin (eg, cefotaxime or ceftriaxone) with or without a macrolide is appropriate as the initial therapy for hospitalized patients with moderate illness not requiring admission into the intensive-care unit. Alternative antimicrobial therapies for such patients include a second-generation cephalosporin such as cefuroxime, a macrolide

alone (eg, clarithromycin or azithromycin), or a newer fluoroquinolone with activity against *S pneumoniae* (eg, levofloxacin or gatifloxacin). Fluoroquinolones are not approved for use in children < 18 years of age. Patients with serious CAP requiring management in an intensive-care unit require a broader-spectrum initial empiric antibiotic regimen with activity against PRSP, *P aeruginosa, S aureus,* or members of the *Enterobacteriaceae.* Empiric antimicrobial therapy should include a third- or fourth-generation cephalosporin or an extended-spectrum β–lactam/β-lactamase inhibitor combination such as piperacillin/tazobactam or ticarcillin/clavulanate, with a fluoroquinolone or macrolide.

Broad spectrum empirical antimicrobial therapy of severe CAP should also include therapy against atypical organisms such as *Legionella.* Co-administration of a macrolide or a fluoroquinolone together with a β-lactam antibiotic (a third- or fourth-generation cephalosporin such as cefotaxime, ceftriaxone, or cefepime;

BOX 10-13C

Empiric Antimicrobial Therapy of Community-Acquired Pneumonia Requiring Intensive Care Unit

	Children	Adults
First Choice	• Cefotaxime 50 mg/kg IV every 8 hours or ceftriaxone 50–75 mg/kg/d IV every 24 h **PLUS** a macrolide such as azithromycin 12 mg/kg/d orally or IV for 5 d (not to exceed 500 mg)	• Cefotaxime 1 g IV every 8 h or ceftriaxone 1 g every 24 h **PLUS** • A fluoroquinolone with enhanced activity against *S pneumoniae* such as levofloxacin 500 mg orally or IV every 24 h or another fluoroquinolone in equivalent doses **OR** a macrolide such as azithromycin 500 mg IV or orally on day 1, then 250 mg every day for 4 d, or erythromycin 500 mg IV every 6 h
Second Choice	• Ampicillin/sulbactam 200–300 mg/kg/d IV divided every 4 h **OR** piperacillin/tazobactam (> 6 mo of age) 300–400 mg piperacillin component/kg/d; and for infants < 6 mo of age 150–300 mg piperacillin component/kg/day IV divided every 6–8 h **PLUS** azithromycin 12 mg/kg/d IV for 5 d (not to exceed 500 mg)	• Ampicillin/sulbactam 3.0 g IV every 6 h **OR** piperacillin/tazobactam 3.375 g IV every 6 h **PLUS** • A fluoroquinolone with enhanced activity against *S pneumoniae*, such as levofloxacin 500 mg orally or IV every 24 h or another fluoroquinolone in equivalent doses **OR** a macrolide such as azithromycin 500 mg IV or orally on day 1, then 250 mg every day for 4 d, or erythromycin 500 mg IV every 6 h
Penicillin Allergic	• Azithromycin 12 mg/kg/d IV for 5 d (not to exceed 500 mg) **OR** • Erythromycin 20–40 mg/kg/d IV divided every 8 h for 10 d	• A fluoroquinolone with enhanced activity against *S pneumoniae*, such as levofloxacin 500 mg orally or IV every 24 h or another fluoroquinolone in equivalent doses **WITH OR WITHOUT** clindamycin 900 mg IV every 8 h **OR** • A macrolide such as azithromycin 500 mg IV on day 1, then 250 mg every day for 4 d

Note: Doses provided here are for persons with normal renal function.

or piperacillin/tazobactam) has been shown to decrease mortality in patients with severe CAP. Monotherapy with either a macrolide or a fluoroquinolone are not recommended in such patients. Patients with severe CAP with underlying chronic structural lung disease, frequent hospitalizations, or history of long-term care facility stay, the use of antimicrobials with antipseudomonal activity (such as cefepime, ceftazidime, or a fluoroquinolone with enhanced activity against *S pneumoniae* and *P aeruginosa* such as levofloxacin or gatifloxacin) is recommended.

Empiric antibiotic therapy may be modified once identification of a specific microorganism(s) and its susceptibilities is available. Parenteral penicillin G is the drug of choice for in-patient penicillin-susceptible pneumococcal pneumonia. Studies demonstrate that *S pneumoniae* strains that are penicillin-susceptible and intermediately penicillin-resistant (minimal inhibitory concentration < 2 μg/mL) may be treated

with a penicillin or a third-generation cephalosporin such as ceftriaxone or cefotaxime. Penicillin-resistant pneumococcal pneumonia may be successfully treated with high-dose penicillin or a third-generation cephalosporin, vancomycin, a fluoroquinolone such as levofloxacin or gatifloxacin, or a carbapenem such as imipenem/cilastin or meropenem.

A second- or third-generation cephalosporin; β-lactam/β-lactamase inhibitor antibiotics such as amoxicillin/clavulanate, ampicillin/sulbactam, and piperacillin/tazobactam; carbapenems such as imipenem or meropenem; macrolides such as azithromycin; and fluoroquinolones are effective therapy for CAP caused by *H influenzae* or *M catarrhalis*.

C pneumoniae, *M pneumoniae*, and *Legionella* pneumonia respond to therapy with a tetracycline, macrolide, or fluoroquinolone. Rifampin is active in vitro against *L pneumophila* and may be used as adjunctive therapy for severe *Legionella* pneumonia.

Parenteral therapy with either a fluoroquinolone or high-dose erythromycin is recommended for moderate to severe *Legionella* pneumonia. Azithromycin and clarithromycin are more active in vitro than erythromycin against *L pneumophila*. Treatment failures have been reported with erythromycin. Oral therapy with azithromycin or clarithromycin or with a fluoroquinolone such as ciprofloxacin, ofloxacin, or levofloxacin may be considered for mild to moderate infection. There is no evidence to suggest that the addition of rifampin or erythromycin to fluoroquinolone therapy is more effective than a fluoroquinolone used alone. Therapy is usually continued for 3 weeks for *Legionella* pneumonia.

Parenterally administered antibiotics should be switched to oral therapy once the patient has demonstrated clinical response, is hemodynamically stable, is able to tolerate medications administered orally, and has no evidence of malabsorption. The switch from parenteral to oral antibiotics also depends on the availability of an oral equivalent of the parenteral drug being administered.

Most patients defervesce and show improvement of cough, tachycardia, and tachypnea within 3–5 days of onset of effective antimicrobial therapy. Patients with bacteremic pneumococcal pneumonia or with *Legionella* pneumonia usually take longer to improve (6–7 days). The optimum duration of antimicrobial therapy for CAP has not been studied in controlled clinical trials. Most studies have administered antimicrobial therapy for 10–14 days. Studies have demonstrated that a 5-day course of azithromycin is effective for outpatient CAP.

B. Nosocomial and aspiration pneumonia.
Early and appropriate empiric antimicrobial therapy may reduce the mortality of NAP (Box 10–14). Guidelines for empiric antimicrobial therapy for NAP developed by the American Thoracic Society recommend the use of antibiotics depending upon risk factors and severity of disease. For patients with no underlying risk factors who develop mild to moderate NAP early or late during hospitalization or for patients with severe early onset NAP, the guidelines recommend that therapy should be directed against nonpseudomonal enteric gram-negative bacilli, *S pneumoniae, H influenzae*, or methicillin-susceptible *S aureus*. Appropriate empiric antibiotic therapy for these patients includes a third- (cefotaxime or ceftriaxone) or fourth-generation (cefepime) cephalosporin, a β-lactam/β-lactamase inhibitor combination, or a fluoroquinolone. Patients with multiple risk factors, such as mechanical ventilation, coexisting underlying disease, or impaired consciousness, who develop moderate or severe NAP should receive empiric antimicrobial therapy directed against *P aeruginosa, Acinetobacter* spp., *Enterobacter* spp., *K pneumoniae*, and *S aureus*. These bacteria are more likely to be multidrug resistant and require broader-spectrum initial empiric antimicrobial therapy. Empiric antimi-

crobial therapy for such patients should include an antipseudomonal cephalosporin such as ceftazidime or cefepime or an extended-spectrum antipseudomonal β-lactam/β-lactamase inhibitor combination such as piperacillin/tazobactam or ticarcillin/clavulanate, or a carbapenem such as imipenem or meropenem. For patients with β-lactam allergy, aztreonam may be used as an alternative antipseudomonal drug. Because aztreonam is not active against gram-positive cocci, clindamycin or vancomycin should be added if such coverage is required. An aminoglycoside or ciprofloxacin should be added to β-lactam therapy for patients with serious NAP, particularly when *P aeruginosa* is suspected or documented. Patients with suspected methicillin-resistant *S aureus* require the addition of vancomycin therapy. Patients with suspected or witnessed aspiration should receive therapy active against anaerobic microorganisms such as clindamycin, metronidazole, a β-lactam/β-lactamase inhibitor combination, or a carbapenem. Antimicrobial therapy may be modified once blood or tracheal culture and susceptibility results are available. Duration of antimicrobial therapy for NAP depends on severity, etiology, and response to antimicrobial therapy. Response to therapy is guided by defeversence, respiratory status, sputum production, gas exchange, and leukocyte counts. For patients with mild to moderate NAP, a 7- to 10-day course of antibiotics may be enough, whereas patients with severe NAP or NAP caused by *P aeruginosa* or other resistant gram-negative bacilli may require a longer course of therapy. Patients with slow or no response to appropriate antimicrobial therapy should undergo further diagnostic investigations for other infectious or noninfectious processes such as an empyema, cholecystitis, sinusitis, or catheter-associated infections. Patients with progressive pulmonary deterioration despite appropriate therapy may require bronchoscopy with PSB or BAL cultures.

C. Infections in patients with cystic fibrosis.
Patients with cystic fibrosis (CF) who are early in their disease process are more likely to be colonized with *H influenzae, S pneumoniae*, or *S aureus*. Appropriate empiric antimicrobial therapy for CF patients early in this disease includes a second-, third-, or fourth-generation cephalosporin, trimethoprim/sulfamethoxazole, or a macrolide (Box 10–15). As CF progresses, patients become colonized with more virulent and resistant gram-negative bacilli such as *P aeruginosa, Ralstonia (Burkholderia) cepacia, S maltophilia, Achromobacter (Alcaligenes) xylosoxidans*, and *Enterobacter* spp. Empiric antimicrobial therapy for patients with progressive disease should include an antipseudomonal cephalosporin such as ceftazidime, cefepime, an antipseudomonal β-lactam/β-lactamase combination piperacillin/tazobactam, or a carbapenem. Owing to the severity of disease, repeated courses of antibiotics, frequent colonization with resistant microorganisms, and the pres-

BOX 10-14

Empiric Antimicrobial Therapy of Nosocomially Acquired Pneumonia[1]

	Children	Adults
First Choice	*No risk factors and mild to moderate NAP:* • Cefotaxime, 50 mg/kg/dose IV every 8 h OR • Ceftriaxone, 50–75 mg/kg/d IV every 24 h OR • Other third- or fourth-generation parenteral cephalosporin *Severe NAP or with risk factors:* • Cefepime, 50 mg/kg IV every 12 h, or ceftazidime, 30–50 mg/kg IV every 8 h (maximum, 6 g/d) PLUS • Gentamicin, 2.5–3.5 mg/kg/dose IV every 8 h	*No risk factors and mild to moderate NAP:* • Cefotaxime, 1 g IV every 8 h OR • Ceftriaxone, 1 g every 24 h OR • Other third- or fourth-generation parenteral cephalosporin in equivalent dosages OR • Ciprofloxacin, 500 mg orally every 12 h or another fluoroquinolone with activity against *Pseudomonas aeruginosa,* such as levofloxacin in equivalent doses. *Severe NAP or with risk factors:* • Cefepime, 2 g IV every 12 h, or ceftazidime, 2 g IV every 8 h PLUS EITHER • Gentamicin 3–6 mg/kg/d IV divided every 8 h or single daily dosing of 4–9 mg/kg/d every 24 h OR • Ciprofloxacin, 500 mg orally every 12 h or other fluoroquinolones with activity against *P aeruginosa* such as levofloxacin in equivalent doses
Second Choice	• Piperacillin/tazobactam, ages 6 months and older, 300–400 mg of piperacillin component/kg/d IV, divide every 6–8 h, and for infants < 6 mo old, 150–300 mg piperacillin component/kg/d IV, divide every 6–8 h or imipenem, 15–25 mg/kg/dose every 6 h in patients older than 3 mo or meropenem in equivalent dosages PLUS • Gentamicin, 2.5–3.5 mg/kg/dose IV every 8 h	• Piperacillin/tazobactam, 4.5 g IV every 4 h, or imipenem, 500 mg IV every 6 h or meropenem in equivalent dosages PLUS EITHER • Gentamicin, 3–6 mg/kg/d IV every 8 h or single daily dosing of 4–9 mg/kg/d OR • Ciprofloxacin, 500 mg orally or IV every 12 h or other fluoroquinolones with activity against *P aeruginosa* such as levofloxacin in equivalent doses OR • Azithromycin, 500 mg IV every 24 h or clarithromycin, 500 mg orally every 12 h for suspected nosocomial *Legionella* disease
Penicillin Allergic	• Aztreonam, 30 mg/kg IV every 6–8 h maximum dose, 120 mg/kg/d PLUS • Clindamycin, 20–40 mg/kg/d IV, divided every 6–8 h	• Aztreonam, 1–2 g IV every 8 h PLUS • Clindamycin, 900 mg IV every 8 h OR • Ciprofloxacin, 500 mg orally or IV every 12 h or other fluoroquinolone with activity against *P aeruginosa* such as levofloxacin in equivalent doses

[1]Doses provided here are for patients with normal renal function. NAP, nosocomially acquired pneumonia.

BOX 10–15

Empiric Antimicrobial Therapy of Infections in Patients with Cystic Fibrosis[1]

	Children	Adults
First Choice	*Early mild disease:* • Cefotaxime, 50 mg/kg dose IV every 8 h OR • Ceftriaxone, 50–75 mg/kg/d IV every 24 h OR • Other second- third-, or fourth-generation parenteral cephalosporin OR • Oxacillin, 100–200 mg/kg divided every 6 h IV (maximum, 12 g/d) or other antistaphylococcal penicillin in equivalent doses *Advanced CF:* • Ceftazidime, 30–50 mg/kg IV every 8 h (maximum, 6 g/d) OR • Cefepime, 50 mg/kg IV every 12 h; PLUS • Gentamicin, 6–15 mg/kg/d IV divided every 8 h, peak gentamicin levels of 7–10 µg/mL and trough of 1–2 µg/mL, or tobramycin, 6–7.5 mg/kg/d IV divided equally every 8 h	*Early mild disease:* • Cefotaxime, 1 g IV every 8 h OR • Ceftriaxone, 1 g IV every 24 h OR • Other second-, third-, or fourth-generation parenteral cephalosporin *Advanced CF:* • Ceftazidime, 2 g IV every 8 h, or cefepime, 2 g IV every 12 h PLUS • Gentamicin, 6–15 mg/kg/d IV divided every 8 h, with peak gentamicin levels of 7–10 µg/mL and trough of 1–2 µg/mL, or tobramycin, 3 mg/kg/dose IV every 8 h, or ciprofloxacin, 500 mg orally or IV every 12 h or other fluoroquinolone with activity against *P seudomonas aeruginosa* such as levofloxacin in equivalent doses
Second Choice	• Piperacillin/tazobactam, 6 mo and older, 300–400 mg piperacillin component/kg/d IV divided every 6–8 h, and, for infants less than 6 months old, 150–300 mg piperacillin component/kg/d IV, divide every 6–8 h, OR imipenem, 15–25 mg/kg/dose every 6 h in patients older than 3 mo, or meropenem in equivalent dosages PLUS • Gentamicin, 2.5–3.5 mg/kg/dose IV every 8 h, or tobramycin as mentioned above	• Piperacillin/tazobactam, 4.5 g IV every 4 h, or imipenem, 500 mg IV every 6 h or meropenem in equivalent dosages PLUS • Gentamicin, 3–6 mg/kg/d IV divided every 8 h or single daily dosing of 4–9 mg/kg/d every 24 h, or tobramycin, 3 mg/kg/dose IV every 8 h, or ciprofloxacin, 500 mg orally or IV every 12 h or another fluoroquinolone with activity against *P aeruginosa* such as levofloxacin in equivalent doses
Peni-cillin Allergic	EITHER • Aztreonam, 30 mg/kg IV every 6–8 h, (maximum dose, 120 mg/kg/d), or ciprofloxacin, 15–30 mg/kg/d divided every 12 h IV or orally, (maximum, 1.5 g/d) or another fluoroquinolone with activity against *P aeruginosa* such as levofloxacin in equivalent doses PLUS • Vancomycin, 40 mg/kg/d IV every 6 h	EITHER • Aztreonam, 1–2 g IV every 8 h, or ciprofloxacin, 500 mg orally or IV every 12 h or another fluoroquinolone with activity against *P aeruginosa* such as levofloxacin in equivalent doses PLUS • Vancomycin, 15 mg/kg IV every 12 h

[1]Doses provided here are for patients with normal renal function.

ence of tenacious secretions, the use of combination therapy with an aminoglycoside together with an agent listed above is recommended. Because CF patients have an increased clearance of drugs, higher dosages of most antimicrobial agents are required. Aerosolized tobramycin has been approved for use as suppressive therapy in CF. Use of aerosolized tobramycin has been shown to improve pulmonary function, decrease *P aeruginosa* bacterial density in sputum, decrease hospitalizations, and reduce the use of other antipseudomonal drugs. It may be considered for bacterial suppression in patients who are > 6 years of age, have a forced expiratory volume in 1 s of ≥ 25% and ≤75% predicted, are colonized with *P aeruginosa,* and are able to comply with the recommended regimen. Such therapy may not be effective if the *P aeruginosa* or other gram-negative bacilli are resistant to tobramycin. Preservative-free 300-mg tobramycin is delivered by using a PARI LC PLUS nebulizer with a De Vilbiss PulmoAide compressor with doses administered 12 h apart for 28 days and then suspended or discontinued for 28 days. The average sputum concentration of tobramycin 10 min after an inhalation dose of 300 mg is 1237 µg/g (range, 35–7414 µg/g). The efficacy of aerosolized tobramycin as adjunctive therapy for CF exacerbations is unknown. Although fluoroquinolones are not approved by the Food and Drug Administration for persons < 18 years of age, their use in CF patients may be warranted because of drug resistance, where a fluoroquinolone may be the only alternative.

D. Follow-up. Radiologic clearance of pulmonary infiltrates takes ~ 4 weeks in immunocompetent patients and may be considerably slower for elderly patients or patients with comorbidities. Resolution of *L pneumophila* pulmonary infiltrates occurs in ~ 55% of patients by 12 weeks. Accordingly, chest radiographic findings should not be used to determine duration of antimicrobial therapy. However, a follow-up chest radiograph should be obtained in 6–8 weeks after completion of antimicrobial therapy to document clearance and to identify an underlying process such as malignancy or, in children, a foreign body or congenital malformation.

Prognosis

Pneumonia is associated with an average mortality rate of 14% in hospitalized patients and an estimated mortality of < 1% in nonhospitalized patients. Mortality from pneumococcal pneumonia among patients > 60 years of age varies from 5% to 25% and is ~ 20% in bacteremic pneumococcal pneumonia. It is the sixth most common cause of death in the United States. Risk factors for increased mortality include extremes of age and underlying diseases such as malignancy, diabetes, chronic lung disease, chronic renal failure, alcoholism, immunosuppression, congestive heart failure, and neurological disease. Previous episodes of pneumonia contribute to higher mortality. Gram-negative bacilli, *S aureus,* or polymicrobial pneumonia, as in aspiration or postobstructive pneumonia, are associated with a higher mortality. Asplenia and severe malnutrition are also associated with a high mortality.

Prevention

A. Community-Acquired Pneumonia. Immunization with the influenza A/B, 23 polyvalent pneumococcal, and *H influenzae* type B vaccines decreases the incidence of infections caused by these microorganisms (Box 10–16). Susceptible populations, such as the elderly (> 65 years of age) or those with comorbid conditions such as diabetes, immunocompromise, sickle cell disease, or asplenia, should be routinely immunized with influenza A/B and pneumococcal vaccines. *H influenzae* type B vaccine is recommended for infants and individuals of any age with sickle cell disease or asplenia.

The pneumococcal vaccine has an efficacy of > 60% in preventing bacteremic pneumococcal infection caused by vaccine strain bacteria and reduction of severity in immunocompetent patients, but this rate declines with advancing age and immunosuppression. Pneumococcal vaccine is repeated once in 6 years for asplenic patients and for patients > 65 years old who received their initial dose before the age of 65 years.

Appropriate identification and decontamination of water sources may prevent *Legionella* pneumonia. Control measures include hyperchlorination of water supplies and decontamination of air-conditioning cooling units.

B. Nosocomial Pneumonia. The Centers for Disease Control's Hospital Infection Control Practices Advisory Committee (HICPAC) has published guidelines for the prevention of NAP (Box 10–17). To prevent aspiration, elevation of the head end of the bed at a 30°–45° angle is recommended unless

---

BOX 10–16

Control of Community-Acquired Pneumonia

Prophylactic Measures	• Smoking cessation • Active immunization for influenza A/B for all persons > 50 y of age • Amantadine or rimantadine for influenza postexposure prophylaxis • Active immunization with 23 polyvalent pneumococcal vaccine • Treatment of water-cooling towers to prevent sources of *Legionella pneumophila*

BOX 10–17

Control of Nosocomially Acquired Pneumonia

Prophylactic Measures	• Active immunization for influenza A/B • Amantadine or rimantadine for influenza postexposure prophylaxis • Active immunization with 23 polyvalent pneumococcal vaccine • Elevation of the head end of the bed for patients with nasogastric tubes or mechanical ventilation • Handwashing • Aggressive pulmonary toilet • Appropriate sterilization and handling of devices and respiratory equipment

BOX 10–18

Control of Infections in Patients with Cystic Fibrosis

Prophylactic Measures	• Active immunization for influenza A/B • Amantadine or rimantadine for influenza postexposure prophylaxis • Active immunization with 23 polyvalent pneumococcal vaccine • Aggressive pulmonary toilet • Appropriate sterilization and handling of devices and respiratory equipment

contraindicated. Aspiration of gastric contents may be decreased by verifying the proper placement of enteral tubes, regular assessment of intestinal motility, and use of the appropriate volume and rate of oral or enteral feeding. Improved pulmonary toilet in postoperative patients may be accomplished by the use of frequent suctioning, incentive spirometry, and non-cough-suppressant analgesia. In addition, HICPAC recommended strict infection control surveillance measures, universal infection precautions for select patients, and the use of appropriate sterilization, disinfection, and handling of all devices and equipment used for respiratory therapy and mechanical ventilation. HICPAC strongly recommended hand washing after contact with mucous membranes or respiratory secretions, regardless of whether gloves were worn. Studies have shown that changing the ventilatory circuit every 24 h increases the risk of NAP when compared with ventilatory circuits that are changed every 48 h. In addition to these measures, use of cytokines such as filgrastim and sargramostim in neutropenic patients may decrease chemotherapy-related neutropenia. Selective decontamination of the digestive tract has not been proven to decrease the incidence of nosocomial pneumonia and is not recommended.

C. Infections in CF Patients. Patients with CF (Box 10–18) should receive pneumococcal and influenza vaccines regularly. Avoiding contact with persons with a respiratory illness may prevent acquisition of new viral infections and subsequent exacerbations. Prompt and aggressive treatment of the initial *P aeruginosa* infection may delay but not completely prevent colonization. Despite multiple courses of appropriate antibiotics and pulmonary toilet, chronic colonization and recurrent infections with

P aeruginosa or other multidrug-resistant bacteria are inevitable in CF patients. There are some data to suggest that the use of rhDNase is associated with lower rates of pulmonary exacerbations and improved forced expiratory volume.

PARAPNEUMONIC EFFUSION & PLEURAL EMPYEMA

Essentials of Diagnosis

• Collection of effusion or pus in the pleural space.
• Persistent fever, chills, chest pain, and dyspnea.
• Examination reveals dullness, increased vocal fremitus, and decreased breath sounds.
• Chest radiographic or CT scan evidence of fluid collection in the pleural space.
• Pleural empyema fluid usually has pH < 7.0, LDH > 1000 IU/L, glucose < 40 mg/dL, leukocyte count > 50,000/mm^3, and positive Gram stain or culture.
• Mainstay of treatment is drainage of pus followed by antimicrobial therapy for 2–4 weeks.

General Considerations

A parapneumonic effusion is defined as a pleural effusion that occurs secondary to a pulmonary infection. An empyema is defined as a collection of pus in a normally sterile body cavity, such as between the visceral and parietal pleurae. Empyema usually results from contiguous spread of an infection from the lung or other neighboring sites.

The pleural space is a sterile space, which normally contains a scant amount of fluid, between the visceral and parietal pleurae. The pleural space is a relatively immunodeficient space, because it does not contain a high number of phagocytes and lacks opsonins and complements.

Microorganisms enter the pleural space either by contiguous spread from an infected lung, perforated esophagus, mediastinum, or subdiaphragmatic structures or by direct entry as a result of trauma, thoracic surgery, or thoracentesis. The most common cause of a parapneumonic effusion or empyema is an underlying pneumonia. Less often, infection may spread from a retropharyngeal, retroperitoneal, vertebral, or paravertebral source. Once bacteria enter the pleural space, an inflammatory response results in migration of PMN leukocytes and induction of cytokines such as TNF. Because of the relative inefficiency of the defense mechanisms in the pleural space, the bacteria multiply rapidly. This leads to a fibrinopurulent effusion with increased chemotaxis of PMN leukocytes, increased inflammatory response, fibrin deposition, and loculations. With increasing bacterial growth, accumulation and lysis of inflammatory cells, the fluid pH, and glucose levels decrease, and LDH increases. This may be followed by fibroblast proliferation and scar formation.

The response to adjacent infection may result in either a parapneumonic effusion or an empyema. Parapneumonic effusions are classified by size and laboratory parameters. Small (< 10-mm-thick effusion on a decubitus radiograph) or larger effusions that have glucose > 40 mg/dL, pH > 7.00, and LDH < 1000 IU/L and that are culture-negative are considered parapneumonic effusions. These effusions usually respond to antibiotic therapy and require no surgical intervention. Empyema is defined by positive Gram stain or cultures, glucose < 40 mg/dL, pH < 7.00, and multiloculated collections of pus.

The microbiology of empyema depends on the source of infection and host factors (Box 10–19). Because an empyema usually is a complication of pneumonia, *S pneumoniae, S aureus,* and streptococci are the most common organisms isolated. *S aureus* is a common cause of empyema, particularly in children < 6 months of age or in postsurgical or trauma patients, and it occasionally occurs in association with hemothorax. Overall, *S aureus* accounts for 29–35% of all cases of pediatric empyema. In older children, *S pneumoniae, S aureus,* and *H influenzae* most often cause empyema. Aerobic gram-negative bacilli may cause empyema in alcoholics or after thoracic surgery or trauma not confined to alcoholics. Postsurgical or traumatic empyema may also be caused by *S aureus,* a polymicrobial infection, or, rarely, by *Aspergillus* spp. Polymicrobial empyema may result from aspiration pneumonia, lung abscess, or perforation of the esophagus or stomach. Anaerobic empyema is uncommon in young children < 6 years of age. An empyema can develop as an extension of a subdiaphragmatic abscess. Less common etiologies of empyema include *M tuberculosis, C neoformans, C immitis,* rupture of an echinococcal cyst, or an *Entamoeba histolytica* liver abscess that ruptures into the pleural cavity. Rarely,

BOX 10–19

Microbiology of Empyema

	Children	Adults
More Frequent	• *Staphylococcus aureus* • *Streptococcus pneumoniae* • *Haemophilus influenzae* • *Streptococcus pyogenes*	• *S aureus* • *S pneumoniae* • *S pyogenes* • *H influenzae* • Anaerobes
Less Frequent	• *Mycobacterium tuberculosis* • Anaerobes	• *Pseudomonas aeruginosa* • *M tuberculosis* • *Coccidioides immitis* • *Coxiella burnetii*

an empyema may erode and drain spontaneously through the chest wall. This condition is called empyema necessitatis and is typically associated with *Actinomyces, Nocardia* spp., or *M tuberculosis.*

Clinical Findings

A. Signs and Symptoms. Patient presentation depends on the underlying disease and organism. Symptoms usually resemble those of pneumonia. Fever, chills, cough, and chest pain are common. Persistent fever or leukocytosis and diaphoresis in a patient with pneumonia who is receiving appropriate antimicrobial therapy may be suggestive of an empyema. In chronic cases, patients develop low-grade fever, night sweats, and weight loss. On physical examination, dullness to percussion and increased vocal fremitus over the area of effusion or empyema are usually present. Auscultation of the corresponding area demonstrates decreased breath sounds; egophony or bronchophony is heard above the effusion.

B. Laboratory Findings. Leukocytosis with a left shift is common. Anemia is present in chronic empyema. Hypoxemia, azotemia, acidosis, and disseminated intravascular coagulation may occur in severely and acutely ill patients. Thoracentesis may show cloudy or grossly purulent fluid. The empyema fluid has a pH < 7.0, glucose < 40 mg/dL, LDH > 1000 IU/L, and leukocyte count > $50,000 \times 10^9$. High pleural fluid protein or specific gravity is not helpful in the diagnosis of empyema. Detection of amylase in the fluid suggests an esophageal rupture. Chylous effusion is characterized by the presence of high triglycerides and pH in pleural fluid that appears cloudy or milky after centrifugation. Gram stain, AFB, modified AFB for *Nocardia* spp., KOH, and direct fluorescent microscopy for *L pneumophila* or smears for parasites should be performed. Overall, 18–30% of empyemas are sterile. The yield of positive bacterial cultures decreases with the administration of antimicrobial therapy or because of bacterial cell lysis in the acidic medium of the pus. Pleural tuberculosis usually results in an effusion; however, occasionally a purulent tuberculous empyema may occur. In the former, a positive AFB smear of pleural fluid is unlikely, whereas many AFB are typically present on stain in patients with tubercular empyema. Stains and cultures are more likely to be positive for mycobacteria when performed on pleural biopsy specimens than on pleural fluid. A positive tuberculin skin test in patients with pleural effusion or empyema suggests a mycobacterial etiology. Molecular methods of diagnoses such as polymerase chain reaction are currently under investigation.

C. Imaging. A posterior-anterior and lateral chest radiograph is useful for the detection of pleural effusion or empyema (Figure 10–7). A decubitus chest roentgenogram may detect ≥5 mL of pleural fluid. Approximately 200 mL of fluid produces a concave obliteration of the costophrenic angle in an upright radiograph. Larger effusions may cause complete opacification of the hemithorax with a contralateral shift of the mediastinum and trachea. An empyema is typically a loculated, homogenous opacity with sharp margins. The fluid appears as an opaque density in the chest radiograph. A decubitus film helps to identify a free-flowing or a loculated fluid collection. Ultrasonography or CT scan may be required to differentiate this density from a solid parenchymal mass or to detect small fluid collections in patients in whom a decubitus radiograph is difficult to obtain. Ultrasonography has a 92% accuracy in correctly identifying a solid mass or a fluid collection. This accuracy increases to 98% when used in conjunction with chest radiographs. Ultrasonography may be superior to CT scan in visualizing septations within a complicated parapneumonic effusion, particularly in children. A CT scan is the optimal method to differentiate a loculated fluid collection from parenchymal consolidation or peripheral lung abscesses, particularly when the opacity has an atypical location. The characteristic CT appearance of an empyema is a lenticular shape, enclosed within enhancing thickened pleurae (the "split-pleura" sign), which forms an obtuse angle with the chest wall and causes displacement of vessels and bronchi around the fluid collection.

Differential Diagnosis

Noninfectious causes of pleural effusion must be differentiated for accurate therapy and response. Exudative effusions may result from congestive heart failure, malignancies, collagen vascular diseases, thoracic duct tears, or pancreatitis. Malignant effusion is often hemorrhagic and may be differentiated by cytological evaluation of the pleural fluid.

Complications

In children, empyema may result in pneumatoceles, pneumothorax, or scoliosis as a result of scar-

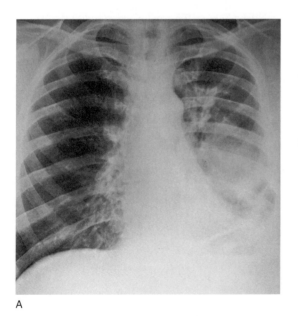

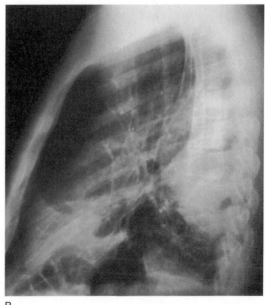

A   B

Figure 10–7. Empyema. Large, homogenous broad-based density against the left posterior chest wall. There are left lower lobe infiltrates as well. A. Posterior-anterior view. B. Lateral view.

ring. Other complications result from the local spread of infection to surrounding structures such as the lung, pericardium, and myocardium. Some patients develop a severe, overwhelming infection that results in multisystem organ failure and death. Empyema-associated mortality is low and varies from 1% to 19%. Mortality increases with age > 50 years, immunosuppression, comorbidities, and NAP.

Treatment

Gross appearance, biochemical composition, and the radiographic appearance of the fluid guide the management of an infected effusion. The goals of treatment include appropriate antimicrobial therapy, removal of infected fluid, and re-expansion of the underlying lung.

Empiric antimicrobial therapy depends on the putative etiology of parapneumonic effusion or empyema (Box 10–20). When it is the result of CAP, empiric antimicrobial therapy should be directed against *S pneumoniae,* and the use of a third-generation cephalosporin is appropriate. A specific antimicrobial agent may be administered for known pathogens recovered from the sputum, blood, or pleural fluid. Broad-spectrum antimicrobial therapy is indicated if the empyema is thought to be caused by a ruptured lung abscess, postobstructive pneumonia from an endobronchial lesion, postoperative complication, trauma, or a nosocomial infection. In such situations, therapy should include a drug or combination of drugs with activity against gram-negative bacilli, gram-positive cocci, and anaerobes. Duration of antimicrobial therapy is usually 4–6 weeks.

Parapneumonic effusions with pH > 7.20 should be treated with antimicrobial therapy and drainage. Parapneumonic effusions with pH between 7.0 and 7.20 and elevated LDH may require repeated thoracentesis or chest tube drainage, together with antimicrobial therapy. Chest tube drainage, open drainage, or decortication is required for adequate therapy of empyema.

BOX 10–20

Empiric Therapy of Empyema[1]

	Children	Adults
First Choice	• Ampicillin/sulbactam, 200–300 mg/kg/d IV divided every 4 h OR • Cefotaxime, 150–300 mg/d every 8 h or ceftriaxone, 50–75 mg/kg/d IV every 24 h PLUS clindamycin, 25–40 mg/d divided every 8 h or metronidazole, 15–35 mg/kg/d divided every 8 h OR • Cefepime, 2–4 g/d divided every 12 h PLUS clindamycin, 25–40 mg/d divided every 8 h, or metronidazole, 15–35 mg/kg/d divided every 8 h • Total duration of antibiotics should be 4–6 weeks	• Cefotaxime, 1 g IV every 8 h or ceftriaxone, 1 g IV every 24 h PLUS clindamycin, 900 mg IV every 8 h, or metronidazole, 500 mg IV every 6 h OR • Cefepime, 1 g IV every 12 h PLUS clindamycin, 900 mg IV every 8 h or metronidazole 500 mg IV every 6 h OR • Ampicillin/sulbactam, 3.0 g IV every 6 h OR • Piperacillin/tazobactam, 3.375 g IV every 6 h • Total duration of antibiotics should be 4–6 wk
Second Choice	• Imipenem, 15–25 mg/kg/dose every 6 h in patients older than 3 mo, or meropenem in equivalent dosages	• Imipenem, 500 mg IV every 8 h, or meropenem in equivalent dosages
Penicillin Allergic	• Vancomycin, 10 mg/kg/dose IV every 6 h PLUS aztreonam, 30 mg/kg IV every 6–8 h; maximum dose, 120 mg/kg/d, plus clindamycin, 20–40 mg/kg/d IV, divided every 6–8 h, or metronidazole, 15–35 mg/kg/d divided every 8 h	• Vancomycin, 15 mg/kg/dose IV every 12 h, or aztreonam, 1–2 g IV every 8 h, plus clindamycin, 900 mg IV every 8 h, or metronidazole, 500 mg IV every 6 h

[1]Doses provided here are for persons with normal renal function

Prognosis

The prognosis is extremely good, with cure rates of > 90% for uncomplicated parapneumonic effusions when treated with an appropriate antimicrobial agent and with drainage as necessary. Patients with loculated pleural effusions or leukocyte counts of < 6400 are associated with treatment failure if not managed with nonsurgical measures. With the advent of surgical and nonsurgical intervention techniques and the vast majority of antimicrobial agents, mortality from empyema is low, ranging from 4% to 10%. Mortality varies with the causative organisms, such as *Aspergillus* species, underlying risk factors such as malignancy or other comorbid conditions, older age, and delay in appropriate therapy. Chronic empyema with a thick pleural wall requires a surgical approach. These types of empyema may take months to resolve and are more likely to result in treatment failures.

Prevention

Early administration of effective antimicrobial therapy for LRTIs and early recognition and drainage of infected parapneumonic effusions are most important for the prevention of empyema (Box 10–21). Careful closure and inspection of the bronchial stump after pneumonectomy may prevent empyema that results from a postoperative bronchopleural fistula.

LUNG ABSCESS

Essentials of Diagnosis

- Infection resulting in destruction of lung parenchyma and formation of a cavity with an air-fluid level.
- Polymicrobial, mostly anaerobic microorganisms; often related to aspiration; symptoms: fevers, chills, cough, fatigue, weight loss.

BOX 10–21

Control of Empyema

Prophylactic Measures	• Aspiration precautions for high-risk patients such as those with neurological diseases, gastroesophageal reflux disease, or achalasia • Adequate pulmonary toilet among patients with chronic lung diseases • Regular dental visits for good dental hygiene

---

- Appears radiographically as a cavity with air-fluid levels, with or without surrounding infiltrate.
- Prolonged course of appropriate antimicrobial therapy is necessary, with or without surgical intervention.

General Considerations

Lung abscess is defined as an acute or chronic suppurative infection of the lung parenchyma caused by a single microorganism or multiple microorganisms, predominantly oral anaerobes, that results in destruction of the lung tissue and eventual cavity formation. Lung abscesses are classified as primary or secondary, depending on the pathogenesis and host factors. Primary lung abscesses occur because of aspiration or as the result of an infection of the lung caused by virulent organisms. Lung abscesses may be caused by microorganisms that cavitate, such as *Nocardia* spp., *M tuberculosis, S aureus,* or *S pyogenes.* Primary lung abscesses occur more frequently than secondary abscesses. Secondary lung abscesses are those that occur as a result of a remote primary infection with bacteremic spread to the lung or as an extension from a subphrenic abscess. Secondary infections may also include bacterial superinfection after a pulmonary infarct or as a complication of an underlying process, such as an endobronchial lesion or bronchiectasis.

Aspiration of infectious material is the most common cause of lung abscesses. Oropharyngeal fluid containing multiple aerobic and anaerobic microorganisms is aspirated and carried to the most dependent portions of the lung, which are usually the right upper lobe or the superior segment of the right lower lobe. However, other parts of the lung may be involved. After the initial localized pneumonitis, there is bacterial proliferation, extensive inflammation, necrosis, and destruction of the lung tissue. This destruction may erode into a bronchiole or bronchus, leading to expectoration and partial emptying of the cavity, which creates an air-fluid level. The lung abscess may involve the pleural space by rupture or direct extension.

The microbiology of lung abscesses varies by the cause (Box 10–22). Because aspiration is the most common cause, it results in a polymicrobial infection that includes gram-negative bacilli, gram-positive cocci, and anaerobes. Anaerobes encountered in lung abscesses are oral anaerobic gram-negative bacilli and gram-positive cocci or bacilli. Anaerobes that are commonly isolated include *Prevotella* spp., *Bacteroides* spp., *Fusobacterium* spp., *Peptostreptococcus* spp., *Clostridium* spp., and, rarely, *Actinomyces* spp. Aerobic gram-negative bacilli such as *K pneumoniae, Enterobacter* spp., or *P aeruginosa,* along with anaerobes, predominate among nursing home residents with NAP, alcoholics, and trauma patients. Patients with lung abscesses tend to have poor oral hygiene and dental and gingival disease. Lung ab-

BOX 10–22

Microbiology of Lung Abscess

	Children	Adults
More Frequent	• Staphylococcus aureus • Group A β-hemolytic streptococci • Streptococcus pneumoniae • Haemophilus influenzae • Prevotella species • Bacteroides species • Fusobacterium species	• Prevotella species • Bacteroides species • Fusobacterium species • S aureus • Group A β-hemolytic streptococci • Klebsiella pneumoniae • Pseudomonas aeruginosa • Proteus species • H influenzae
Less Frequent	• Gram-negative bacilli (neonates) • Mycobacterium tuberculosis • Nocardia species • Coccidioides immitis • Histoplasmosis	• M tuberculosis • Nocardia species • Coccidioides immitis • Histoplasmosis • Rhodococcus equi • Salmonella species • Legionella pneumophila

scesses occur less commonly in edentulous patients. Lung abscess may develop from a metastatic infection as seen with *Fusobacterium necrophorum* septicemia or thrombophlebitis complicating an anaerobic pharyngitis (Vincent's angina, Lemierre's syndrome).

A process similar to lung abscess is a severe non-localized necrotizing pneumonia caused by anaerobic or aerobic bacteria, involving one or more lobes, that presents as severe pneumonia and multiple small cavities. Anaerobic bacteria and *S aureus* are the most common causes of necrotizing pneumonia. Other microorganisms that may cause necrotizing pneumonia include *S pyogenes,* gram-negative bacilli such as *Proteus* spp., or, rarely, *Legionella* spp. *S aureus* is the most common cause of bacteremic spread to the lungs that results in multiple lung abscesses.

Fungi may also cause lung abscesses and include *Aspergillus* spp., *C immitis, B dermatitidis,* and *H*

capsulatum. Unusual causes of lung abscess include *Rhodococcus equi* and nontyphi strains of *Salmonella* spp.

Lung abscesses may result from direct extension of an intra-abdominal process. Examples of this include the direct extension of an amebic liver abscess or subphrenic abscesses.

The microbiology of lung abscess in children differs from that of adults. The most common cause of lung abscess in children is *S aureus,* followed by *S pyogenes, H influenzae,* and *S pneumoniae.* Abscesses in children may be polymicrobial and include anaerobes. In neonates, lung abscesses are usually caused by gram-negative bacilli.

Clinical Findings

A. Signs and Symptoms. Patients with lung abscess present with symptoms of pneumonia, including cough producing copious amounts of foul-smelling expectoration. The symptoms may persist despite antibiotic therapy. Patients may have a history of weight loss, fatigue, and a chronic illness lasting weeks to months before diagnosis. In such patients, it is important to elicit a history of either gastroesophageal reflux, vomiting, or aspiration related to a period of unconsciousness.

Examination often reveals a chronically ill-appearing patient with poor dental hygiene, signs of neurologic disorder with an impaired gag reflex, and putrid-smelling expectorated sputum. Clubbing of the fingers may be present. Pulmonary examination is similar to that of patients with pneumonia. Breath sounds overlying the cavity may be bronchial in character, with an intense, high-pitched tone called "amphoric breathing." However, if the cavity is completely filled, breath sounds may be faint or absent. There may be signs of consolidation with dullness to percussion, increased vocal and tactile fremitus, and bronchial breath sounds. A pleural effusion may be present. Signs of an underlying condition may be present, such as spider naevi, palmar erythema, and splenomegaly suggestive of hepatic cirrhosis.

B. Laboratory Findings. The diagnosis of lung abscess is based on the clinical appearance and radiographic findings. The sputum Gram stain is not specific and usually demonstrates mixed oral flora. Routine sputum cultures and anaerobic cultures of sputum are not helpful in diagnosis. The most reliable cultures are those obtained by percutaneous image-guided transthoracic aspiration or by PSB lavage and aspiration. Fungal and mycobacterial stains and cultures should be done in patients with an unusual presentation or who are in an immunocompromised status. In patients suspected of having an amebic lung abscess, cysts and trophozoites of *E histolytica* may be seen in a wet mount of the sputum. Serological tests are not helpful.

C. Imaging. On chest radiographs, a lung abscess appears as a cavitary infiltrate with or without

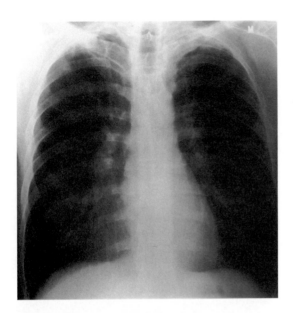

Figure 10–8. Cavitary coccidioidomycosis. Thin-walled cavities in the right upper lobe with adjacent pleural thickening and infiltrative process in a frequent traveler to the southwest United States. Sputum culture was positive for *Coccidioides immitis.*

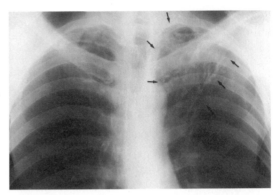

Figure 10–9. Cavitary blastomycosis. Left upper lung cavitary lesion.

an air-fluid level (Figures 10–8, 10–9, and 10–10). There may be multiple cavities with air-fluid levels as seen with *S aureus* hematogenous lung abscesses. Severe necrotizing pneumonia presents as extensive parenchymal infiltrates with multiple small cavities. Lung abscesses caused by *H capsulatum* are likely to appear as small nodules with cavities. CT may delineate lung abscess more clearly than a chest radiograph. CT helps differentiate a lung abscess from an empyema and may identify pleural involvement and an underlying lung mass. Extension of the CT scan into the abdomen may identify an intra-abdominal cause. Periodic CT scans may be used to assess response to therapy or development of complications such as empyema.

Differential Diagnosis

Wegener's granulomatosis, bronchogenic carcinoma, or a metastatic malignancy may cause cavitary lung infiltrates. Echinococcal cysts, *Paragonimus westermani* infection, emphysematous bullae, or a pulmonary infarct may be mistaken for a lung abscess. Occasionally, an empyema may be difficult to differentiate from a lung abscess in chest radiographs.

Complications

Complications of lung abscess primarily result from direct extension of infection into neighboring structures. Pleura-based lung abscesses may extend into the pleural cavity and result in an empyema, which occurs in about one-third of patients with a lung abscess. Bronchopleural fistula with resultant pyopneumothorax may occur. Some abscesses that are in close proximity to a large pulmonary vessel may erode into the vessel and cause massive or fatal hemorrhage. Systemic dissemination of infection to other locations, such as the brain, may occur.

Treatment

The principles of treatment for a lung abscess are the same as for abscesses elsewhere in the body—effective antimicrobial therapy and drainage.

Initial empiric antibiotic therapy should be directed against polymicrobial oropharyngeal flora, especially anaerobes (Box 10–23). This may be achieved with either a combination of a parenteral penicillin or a third-generation cephalosporin with clindamycin or metronidazole; or a β-lactam/β-lactamase inhibitor combination such as piperacillin/tazobactam or ampicillin/sulbactam. Alcoholics, nursing home residents, or patients with a nosocomially acquired lung abscess should receive therapy with a third- or fourth-generation cephalosporin with antipseudomonal activity, such as ceftazidime or cefepime, together with clindamycin or metronidazole; or a β-lactam/β-lactamase inhibitor combination or a carbapenem (imipenem or meropenem); or a fluoroquinolone such as levofloxacin or ciprofloxacin together with clindamycin or metronidazole. The duration of antibiotic therapy is usually 4–6 weeks, with reassessment at intervals for complications or lack of response. Clinical improvement is usually apparent within 1–2 weeks; however, there is a delay of ≤ 8–12 weeks before resolution of the cavity occurs on chest radiograph or CT scan.

Medical therapy is effective in 80–90% of patients with a lung abscess < 5 cm in diameter. The majority of lung abscesses spontaneously drain into a

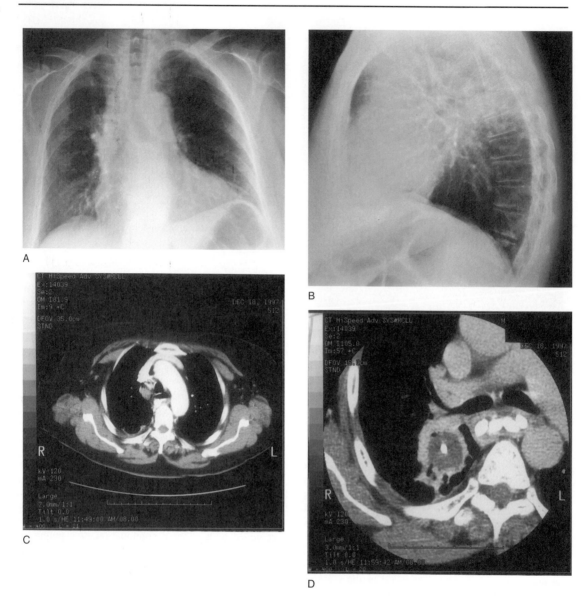

Figure 10–10. A and B. Chest radiograph of a patient with widened mediastinum and a right lower lobe cavitary infiltrate that is not clearly seen on the lateral view. C. CT of the chest shows the dilated esophagus in the posterior mediastinum, caused by achalasia in this patient. D. Magnified view of the CT shows the right lower lobe cavity caused by aspiration resulting from the achalasia.

bronchus. Postural drainage is strongly encouraged, and this may be improved with chest physiotherapy. Patients who do not respond to medical therapy or those with enlarging cavity size, ongoing sepsis, or associated empyema require drainage. Drainage of the lung abscess can be performed with transthoracic radiographic guidance or with open surgical drainage. Open surgical drainage is required in < 15% of patients. Indications for surgery include extent and severity of disease, underlying malignancy, large-volume hemoptysis, bronchopleural fistula with empyema, and inaccessibility of transthoracic drainage of the abscess.

Prognosis

The prognosis of patients with lung abscesses depends on severity of disease, underlying host factors, and promptness of treatment. Poor prognostic indicators include a large cavity, multiple abscesses, abscesses caused by *S aureus, P aeruginosa,* or *K pneu-*

BOX 10–23

Empiric Therapy of Lung Abscess[1]

	Children	Adults
First Choice	• Ampicillin/sulbactam, 200–300 mg/kg/d IV divided every 4 h OR • Cefotaxime, 150–300 mg/d every 8 h or ceftriaxone, 50–75 mg/kg/d IV every 24 h PLUS clindamycin, 25–40 mg/d divided every 8 h or metronidazole, 15–35 mg/kg/d divided every 8 h OR • Cefepime, 2–4 g/d divided every 12 h PLUS clindamycin, 25–40 mg/d divided every 8 h, or metronidazole, 15–35 mg/kg/d divided every 8 h • Total duration of antimicrobial therapy 4–6 wk	• Cefotaxime, 1 g IV every 8 h OR • Ceftriaxone, 1 g IV every 24 h PLUS clindamycin, 900 mg IV every 8 h or metronidazole, 500 mg IV every 6 h OR • Cefepime, 1 g IV every 12 h PLUS clindamycin, 900 mg IV every 8 h or metronidazole, 500 mg IV every 6 h OR • Ampicillin/sulbactam, 3.0 g IV every 6 h OR • Piperacillin/tazobactam, 3.375 g IV every 6 h • Total duration of antimicrobial therapy 4–6 wk
Second Choice	• Imipenem, 15–25 mg/kg/dose every 6 h in patients older than 3 mo, or meropenem in equivalent dosages	• Imipenem, 500 mg IV every 8 h, or meropenem in equivalent dosages
Penicillin Allergic	• Vancomycin, 10 mg/kg/dose IV every 6 h PLUS aztreonam, 30 mg/kg IV every 6–8 h; maximum dose, 12 mg/kg/d PLUS clindamycin, 20–40 mg/kg/d IV, divided every 6–8 h, or metronidazole, 15–35 mg/kg/d divided every 8 h	• Vancomycin, 15 mg/kg/dose IV every 12 h PLUS aztreonam, 1–2 g IV every 8 h PLUS clindamycin, 900 mg IV every 8 h, or metronidazole, 500 mg oral or IV every 6 h

[1]Doses provided here are for patients with normal renal function

moniae, necrotizing pneumonia, and underlying host factors such as an immunocompromised status, including that caused by HIV infection, extremes of age, and malignancy. Overall, mortality from lung abscess is ~ 15%, and it increases to 25% with the presence of necrotizing pneumonia.

Prevention

It is important to identify patients susceptible to aspiration and to institute aspiration precautions promptly in these patients (Box 10–24). Lung abscess should be suspected in patients with a slow response or progression of infection despite appropriate therapy for CAP.

BOX 10–24

Control of Lung Abscess

Prophylactic Measures	• Aspiration precautions for high-risk patients such as those with neurological diseases, gastroesophageal reflux disease, or achalasia • Adequate pulmonary toilet among patients with chronic lung diseases • Regular dental visits for good dental hygiene • Avoid alcohol abuse

REFERENCES

Anonymous: Palivizumab, a humanized respiratory syncytial virus monoclonal antibody, reduces hospitalization from respiratory syncytial virus infection in high-risk infants. The IMpact-RSV Study Group. Pediatrics 1998;102:531.

Auble TE, Yealy DM, Fine MJ: Assessing prognosis and selecting an initial site of care for adults with community-acquired pneumonia. Infect Dis Clin North Am 1998;12:741.

Bernstein JM: Treatment of community-acquired pneumonia—IDSA guidelines. Chest 1999;115:9S.

Bowton DL: Nosocomial pneumonia in the ICU—year 2000 and beyond. Chest 1999;115:28S.

Bruckheimer E et al: Primary lung abscess in infancy. Pediatr Pulmonol 1995;19:188.

Campbell PW III, Saiman L. Use of aerosolized antibiotics in patients with cystic fibrosis. Chest 1999;116(3):775.

Davis B, Systrom DM: Lung abscess: pathogenesis, diagnosis and treatment. Curr Clin Top Infect Dis 1998;18:252.

Donowitz G, Mandell GL: Acute pneumonia. In *Mandell, Douglas and Bennett's Principles and Practice of Infectious Diseases,* 4th ed. Churchill Livingstone Inc, pages, 619–637 1995.

Ernst A et al: Lung abscess complicating *Legionella micdadei* pneumonia in an adult liver transplant recipient: case report and review. Transplantation 1998;65:130.

Fine MJ et al: Processes and outcomes of care for patients with community-acquired pneumonia: results from the Pneumonia Patient Outcomes Research Team (PORT) cohort study. Arch Intern Med 1999;159:970.

Furman AC, Jacobs J, Sepkowitz KA: Lung abscess in patients with AIDS. Clin Infect Dis 1996;22:81.

Gilbert D, Moellering R, Sande M: *The Sanford Guide to Antimicrobial Therapy,* 29th ed. Antimicrobial Therapy Inc, 1999.

Gwaltney JM Jr: Acute bronchitis. In *Mandell, Douglas and Bennett's Principles and Practice of Infectious Diseases,* 4th ed. Churchill Livingstone Inc, pages 606–608 1995.

Heyland DK et al: The attributable morbidity and mortality of ventilator-associated pneumonia in the critically ill patient. The Canadian Critical Trials Group. Am J Respir Crit Care Med 1999;159:1249.

Hirshberg B et al: Factors predicting mortality of patients with lung abscess. Chest 1999;115:746.

Jones RN et al: A 1994–95 survey of *Haemophilus influenzae* susceptibility to ten orally administered agents. A 187 clinical laboratory center sample in the United States. Diagn Microbiol Infect Dis 1997;27:75.

Klassen TP: Determining the benefit of bronchodilators in bronchiolitis. When is there enough benefit to warrant adoption into clinical practice? (Editorial.) Arch Pediatr Adolesc Med 1996;150:1120.

Klassen TP: Recent advances in the treatment of bronchiolitis and laryngitis. Pediatr Clin North Am 1997;44: 249.

Klassen TP et al: Dexamethasone in salbutamol-treated inpatients with acute bronchiolitis: a randomized, controlled trial. J Pediatr 1997;130:191.

Klein JS, Schultz S, Heffner JE: Interventional radiology of the chest: image-guided percutaneous drainage of pleural effusions, lung abscess, and pneumothorax. Am J Roentgenol 1995;164:581.

Kollef MH: The prevention of ventilator-associated pneumonia. N Engl J Med 1999;340:627.

Lee RB: Radiologic evaluation and intervention for empyema thoracis. Chest Surg Clin North Am 1996;6: 439.

Levy BT, Graber MA: Respiratory syncytial virus infection in infants and young children. J Fam Pract 1997;45:473.

Light RW: A new classification of parapneumonic effusions and empyema. (Editorial.) Chest 1995;108:299.

Maffessanti M, Bortolotto P, Grotto M: Imaging of pleural diseases. Monaldi Arch Chest Dis 1996;51:138.

Marfin AA et al: Risk factors for adverse outcome in persons with pneumococcal pneumonia. Chest 1995; 107:457.

Marrie TJ: Community-acquired pneumonia: epidemiology, etiology, treatment. Infect Dis Clin North Am 1998; 12:723.

McEachern R, Campbell GD Jr.: Hospital-acquired pneumonia: epidemiology, etiology, and treatment. Infect Dis Clin North Am 1998;12:761.

Meissner HC et al: Immunoprophylaxis with palivizumab, a humanized respiratory syncytial virus monoclonal antibody, for prevention of respiratory syncytial virus infection in high risk infants: a consensus opinion. Pediatr Infect Dis J 1999;18:223.

Menon K, Sutcliffe T, Klassen TP: A randomized trial comparing the efficacy of epinephrine with salbutamol in the treatment of acute bronchiolitis. J Pediatr 1995;126: 1004.

Niroumand M, Grossman RF: Airway infection. Infect Dis Clin North Am 1998;12:671.

O'Brien JD, Ettinger NA: Nephrobronchial fistula and lung abscess resulting from nephrolithiasis and pyelonephritis. Chest 1995;108:1166.

Patz EF Jr, Goodman PC, Erasmus JJ: Percutaneous drainage of pleural collections. J Thorac Imaging 1998; 13:83.

Redding GJ, Braun S, Mayock D: Impact of respiratory syncytial virus immune globulin in 1996–1997: a local controlled comparison. Arch Pediatr Adolesc Med 1999;153:503.

Ridha AG et al: Lung abscess due to nontyphoid *Salmonella* in an immunocompromised host. Case report with review of the literature. Acta Clin Belg 1996;51:175.

Ruiz-Gonzalez A et al: Is *Streptococcus pneumoniae* the leading cause of pneumonia of unknown etiology? A microbiologic study of lung aspirates in consecutive patients with community-acquired pneumonia. Am J Med 1999;106:385.

Sanders CC et al: Detection of extended-spectrum-beta-lactamase-producing members of the family *Enterobacteriaceae* with Vitek ESBL test. J Clin Microbiol 1996; 34:2997.

Silen ML, Naunheim KS: Thoracoscopic approach to the management of empyema thoracis. Indications and results. Chest Surg Clin North Am 1996;6:491.

Thurer RJ: Decortication in thoracic empyema. Indications and surgical technique. Chest Surg Clin North Am 1996;6:461.

Wandstrat TL: Respiratory syncytial virus immune globulin intravenous. Ann Pharmacother 1997;31:83.

Washington JA: A multicenter study of the antimicrobial susceptibility of community-acquired lower respiratory tract pathogens in the United States, 1992–1994. The Alexander Project. Diagn Microbiol Infect Dis 1996;25:183.

Wendt CH, Hertz MI: Respiratory syncytial virus and parainfluenza virus infections in the immunocompromised host. Semin Respir Infect 1995;10:224.

Wu MH et al: Surgical treatment of pediatric lung abscess. Pediatr Surg Int 1997;12:293.

Infective Endocarditis

James M. Steckelberg, MD, & Walter R. Wilson, MD

Essentials of Diagnosis
- Persistent bacteremia with typical microorganisms: for native valves, viridans group streptococci, *Streptococcus bovis,* HACEK group microorganisms, or community-acquired *Staphylococcus aureus* or enterococci in the absence of a primary focus.
- Bacteremia, typically continuous in the absence of antimicrobial therapy.
- Evidence of endocardial involvement: a new regurgitant murmur or echocardiographic demonstration of valvular vegetations, prosthetic valve dehiscence, or perforation.
- Supporting findings: predisposing cardiac risk factors or intravenous drug use, vascular phenomena such as emboli, immune-mediated phenomena such as glomerulonephritis.

General Considerations
The term "infective endocarditis" refers to infection involving the endocardial surfaces of the heart. Typically, valvular surfaces are affected together with adjacent areas subject to trauma or shear forces from turbulent blood flow. Endocarditis has been recognized as a distinct clinical entity for well over 100 years but continues to be an important diagnostic and therapeutic challenge for clinicians in the modern era.

In studies in geographically defined populations, endocarditis occurs at a frequency of 4–5 cases/100,000 person years. Endocarditis occurs ninefold more frequently among people ≥ 65 years old than among younger persons. The incidence rate is two- to threefold higher in men than in women at all ages. Cardiac abnormalities associated with turbulent blood flow increase the risk of endocarditis (Table 11–1). Although the association between dental infection or procedures and infective endocarditis has been recognized since the 1930s, only a minority of cases have a clearly implicated dental procedure. Intravenous drug abuse may be associated with endocarditis which most often affects the tricuspid valve but may cause infection of the aortic or mitral valve as well. Endocarditis associated with intravenous drug abuse is most often caused by *S aureus,* gram-negative bacilli (including *Pseudomonas* spp.), or *Candida.*

Unlike most other bacterial infections, untreated endocarditis is uniformly fatal, typically within weeks to months. Accurate diagnosis and prompt therapy are therefore paramount.

Clinical Findings
The clinical manifestations of endocarditis are highly varied (Table 11–2). Patients may experience a prolonged, insidious onset of flulike symptoms over weeks to months, especially if partially treated with oral antibiotics empirically or for an erroneous diagnosis of minor infection. Other patients present with a more abrupt, devastating onset of flagrant sepsis with rapid cardiac valvular destruction and cardiac decompensation, typically with *S aureus* infection.

A. Signs and Symptoms. Most patients with endocarditis have daily fever. Other nonspecific symptoms include rigors; night sweats; malaise; anorexia; muscular, joint, or back pain; and weight loss. Physical examination may reveal evidence of preexisting (Table 11–1) or new cardiac abnormalities, including murmurs or congestive heart failure. Splenomegaly is present in a minority of patients. Osler nodes are painful nodules, typically on the pulps of the toes or fingers. Janeway lesions are painless erythematous macules characteristically on the soles of the feet or palms. Roth spots are hemorrhagic retinal or conjunctival lesions with central pallor.

Osler nodes, Janeway lesions, and Roth spots, if found, are highly suggestive of infective endocarditis but will be absent in 80–90% of cases.

B. Laboratory Findings. Blood cultures should always be obtained promptly when endocarditis is suspected, before antimicrobial therapy is begun. For most microorganisms that cause endocarditis (Box 11–1), bacteremia is continuous, and ≥ 90% of the first two sets of blood cultures obtained will be positive in the absence of recent antimicrobial therapy. Occasionally, endocarditis is caused by fastidious organisms (such as the HACEK group of oral gram-negative microorganisms or nutritionally variant viridans streptococci), which require longer periods of incubation of blood cultures or special culture techniques for optimal growth. Alerting the microbiology laboratory to the suspicion of endocarditis will aid in optimizing culture techniques.

Table 11–1. Cardiac conditions associated with endocarditis.[1]

Endocarditis prophylaxis recommended
  High-risk category:
    Prosthetic cardiac valves, including bioprosthetic and
      homograft valves
    Previous bacterial endocarditis
    Complex cyanotic congenital heart disease (eg, single
      ventricle states, transposition of the great arteries,
      tetralogy of Fallot)
    Surgically constructed systemic pulmonary shunts or
      conduits
  Moderate-risk category:
    Most other congenital cardiac malformations (other than
      above and below)
    Acquired valvar dysfunction (eg, rheumatic heart
      disease)
    Hypertrophic cardiomyopathy
    Mitral valve prolapse with valvar regurgitation, thickened
      leaflets, or both

Endocarditis prophylaxis not recommended
  Negligible-risk category (no greater risk than the general
    population):
    Isolated secundum atrial septal defect
    Surgical repair of atrial septal defect, ventricular septal
      defect, or patent ductus arteriosus (without residua
      beyond 6 mo)
    Previous coronary artery bypass graft surgery
    Mitral valve prolapse without valvar regurgitation
    Physiologic, functional, or innocent heart murmurs
    Previous Kawasaki disease without valvar dysfunction
    Previous rheumatic fever without valvar dysfunction
    Cardiac pacemakers (intravascular and epicardial) and
      implanted defibrillators

[1]*Source:* JAMA 1997; 277:1794–1801.

In established endocarditis, anemia and an elevated sedimentation rate are present in the majority but not all patients. The leukocyte count typically is normal or mildly elevated despite the presence of ongoing bacteremia, except in fulminant *S aureus* infection, in which leukocytosis is the rule. Polyclonal hypergammaglobulinemia, hypocomplementemia, and false-positive rheumatoid factor, Lyme serology, or syphilis serology may be found and reflect ongoing immunologic activation. Microhematuria or elevated creatinine and urinary sediment findings suggesting glomerulonephritis may be seen in advanced, late infection. Glomerulonephritis is caused by the deposi-

Table 11–2. Common clinical findings in infective
endocarditis.

History of cardiac risk factors or IVDA
Fever, malaise, night sweats
New regurgitant murmur, heart failure
Less commonly, Janeway lesions, Osler nodes, Roth spots
Persistently positive blood cultures for typical organisms are
  the hallmark of endocarditis
Vegetations seen by echocardiography—transesophageal
  more sensitive than transthoracic
Anemia, elevated ESR are common but nonspecific
WBC usually normal or mildly elevated

tion of circulating immune complexes on kidney basement membranes.

C. Imaging. Echocardiography demonstrates cardiac valvular vegetations in from < 60–95% of patients. Transesophageal echocardiography, while more invasive, is more sensitive for detecting valvular vegetations or perforations (especially in patients with prosthetic valves) as well as intracardiac complications of endocarditis such as myocardial abscesses. Although echocardiographic examination is frequently helpful, the absence of vegetations as seen by echocardiography does not completely exclude a diagnosis of infective endocarditis. Among patients with right-sided cardiac involvement, chest x-ray may show multiple, migratory pulmonary infiltrates resulting from septic pulmonary emboli.

Differential Diagnosis

The differential diagnosis of infective endocarditis is broad and includes many diseases discussed in Chapter 18. In addition to many infectious etiologies, rheumatologic conditions such as systemic lupus erythematosus or vasculitides and malignancies are the main categories to be considered. Numerous noninfectious processes may cause marantic (noninfectious) cardiac valvular vegetations or false-positive echocardiographic studies (Table 11–3).

Complications

Intracardiac Complications. Cardiac valvular destruction with resulting valvular insufficiency and cardiac failure is the most common intracardiac complication of infective endocarditis. Valvular dysfunction can occur from perforation of a valve leaflet, destruction of supporting apparatus such as an infected ruptured mitral chordae, or dehiscence of a prosthetic valve. Alternatively, large, bulky vegetations may occasionally result in valve outflow obstruction mimicking valvular stenosis.

Perivalvular extension of infection with abscess formation is associated more commonly with *S aureus* infections, infections of the aortic valve, and infections of prosthetic valves. Perivalvular extension may be clinically silent or manifested by conduction delays, persistent bacteremia or fever on appropriate therapy, fistulous tracts between cardiac chambers or the pericardial space, or prosthetic valve dehiscence. As noted above, transesophageal echocardiography is more accurate (positive predictive value, 87%; negative predictive value, 89%) than transthoracic echocardiography for the detection of perivalvular abscesses. The development of new atrioventricular block on electrocardiography has 88% specificity for abscess but poor sensitivity (45%).

Extracardiac Complications. Arterial emboli occur in 20–40% of patients with infective endocarditis. Symptomatic emboli occur most frequently in the central nervous system; other sites include abdominal viscera (especially the spleen), kidneys, pe-

BOX 11–1

Microbiology of Infective Endocarditis

	Native Valves	Prosthetic Valves
More Frequent	• Viridans group streptococci • S aureus (most common organism in IVDU) • Enterococci	• Coagulase-negative staphylococci (especially in the first 2 months postoperatively) • Viridans group streptococci • S aureus • Enterococci
Less Frequent	• HACEK group organisms[a] • S bovis • Coagulase-negative staphylococci	• Fungi (especially *Candida*) • Corynebacteria, diphtheroids • *Enterobacteriaceae*

[a]*Hemophilus aphrophilus* and related species, *Actinobacillus actinomycetemcomitans, Cardiobacterium hominis, Eikenella corrodens,* and *Kingella* spp.

ripheral arteries, coronary arteries, and (in right-sided endocarditis) the pulmonary arteries. About half of the embolic events occur before diagnosis. Endocarditis therefore should be considered in the differential diagnosis of every patient who presents with fever and an embolic event, such as a stroke. Overall, the incidence of emboli falls from 13 events/1000 patient days during the first week of effective antimicrobial therapy to < 1.2 events/1000 patient days after 2 weeks of antimicrobial therapy.

The relationship between vegetation size, as measured by echocardiography, and embolic events is complex. Not all studies have distinguished between an association with past embolic events (due in part to a longer course of illness associated with larger vegetations) and the ability to predict future embolic events. Some studies have suggested that large vegetations (> 1 cm), especially in the mitral position, are associated with higher embolic risk. In one study, vegetations were predictive of future embolic events only in patients with viridans group streptococcal infection and not in patients with other microorganisms. Staphylococcal infections had the highest incidence of embolic events, irrespective of vegetations.

Mycotic (infectious) aneurysms occur in 1–5% of patients with endocarditis, most commonly at bifurcation points in the central nervous system, although aortic, visceral, and peripheral arterial mycotic aneurysms also occur. Mycotic aneurysms may be caused by any of the microorganisms that cause endocarditis; the term "mycotic" in this context does not imply a fungal etiology. Clinically, the presentation of mycotic aneurysms in patients with endocarditis is highly variable.

In some patients, a sudden, catastrophic intracranial hemorrhage without premonitory symptoms is the first indication of an aneurysm. In others, severe, localized headache or neurological symptoms such as evidence of a mass lesion, altered sensorium, or focal deficits such as hemianopsia or cranial neuropathy may indicate an embolus preceding an aneurysm or a premonitory aneurysmal leak. Patients suspected of an intracranial mycotic aneurysm should undergo contrast-enhanced computerized tomographic scanning or magnetic resonance angiography. In selected cases or when surgical intervention is planned, four-vessel cerebral angiography is indicated.

Treatment of mycotic aneurysms is complex; more than half of intracerebral aneurysms resolve or decrease in size with antimicrobial therapy, whereas in other patients enlargement, rupture, or the formation of new aneurysms occurs. The decision to intervene surgically should be individualized and depends on the number of aneurysms, their location and course, as well as patient risk factors for surgery.

Abscess formation distant from the heart may complicate endocarditis as a consequence of the sus-

Table 11–3. Causes of noninfective vegetative endocarditis.[1]

Associated with neoplasia:
  Atrial myxoma
  Marantic endocarditis (adenocarcinoma)
  Neoplastic disease (lymphoma, rhabdomyosarcoma)
  Carcinoid
Associated with autoimmune diseases:
  Rheumatic heart disease
  Systemic lupus erythematosus (Libmann-Sacks endocarditis)
  Antiphospholipid syndrome
  Polyarteritis nodosa
  Behçet's disease
Postvalvular surgery:
  Thrombus
  Stitch after surgery
  Other postvalvular surgery changes
Miscellaneous
  Eosinophilic heart disease
  Ruptured mitral chordae
  Myxomatous degeneration

[1]*Source:* Berbari & Steckelberg, Mayo Clin Proc 1997; 72: 532–42.

tained and sometimes prolonged bacteremia. Identification of this complication is especially important, since a persistent metastatic focus of infection may cause relapse of the endocarditis or require an altered treatment regimen. Persistence of fever or intermittent bacteremia despite appropriate antimicrobial therapy, localized pain or tenderness, or laboratory abnormalities referable to the involved organ (such as abnormal liver function tests) provides clues to the diagnosis. Abscesses occur most frequently in the spleen, liver, brain, or disk spaces. Bacteremic seeding of muscle or single or multiple joint spaces may also be seen, most often associated with *S aureus* endocarditis.

Renal failure, once commonly seen in end-stage infective endocarditis, is now rarely seen. Microhematuria or red cell casts may be present in the urine. Renal failure may occur due to glomerulonephritis associated with endocarditis, renal infarcts due to emboli, or as complications of drug therapy. Renal failure due to immune complex deposition in glomeruli associated with infective endocarditis typically improves with the institution of appropriate antimicrobial therapy.

Treatment

Effective medical treatment of infective endocarditis requires identification and susceptibility testing of the responsible microorganism; sustained bactericidal antimicrobial therapy singly or in combination, usually in high concentrations, based on the susceptibility of the microorganism (Tables 11–4 through 11–9); identification and treatment of complications, including abscesses and complications of drug therapy; identification and eradication of the original source of infection (such as a dental abscess) if possible; and patient education about future endocarditis antimicrobial prophylaxis (Tables 11–1, 11–10 through 11–13).

Surgical intervention is necessary in about a third of patients with endocarditis and is lifesaving in some situations. The most common indication for valve replacement or valve repair surgery is congestive heart failure or hemodynamic instability due to valvular dysfunction that is unresponsive to medical therapy. In this setting, immediate surgery is indicated; a delay to complete a longer course of antimicrobial therapy may increase surgical mortality. Other accepted indications for surgery include sustained, per-

Table 11–4. Suggested regimens for therapy of native valve endocarditis due to penicillin-susceptible viridans streptococci and *Streptococcus bovis* (minimum inhibitory concentration ≤0.1 µg/mL).[1]

Antibiotic	Dosage and Route	Duration, wk	Comments
Aqueous crystalline penicillin G sodium or Ceftriaxone sodium	12–18 million U/24 h IV either continuously or in six equally divided doses 2 g once daily IV or IM[2]	4 4	Preferred in most patients older than 65 y and in those with impairment of the eighth nerve or renal function
Aqueous crystalline pencillin G sodium With gentamicin sulfate[3]	12–18 million U/24 h IV either continuously or in six equally divided doses 1 mg/kg IM or IV every 8 h	2 2	When obtained 1 h after a 20–30 min IV infusion or IM injection, serum concentration of gentamicin of approximately 3 µg/mL is desirable; trough concentration should be <1 µg/mL
Vancomycin hydrochloride[4]	30 mg/kg per 24 h IV in two equally divided doses, not to exceed 2 g/24 h unless serum levels are monitored	4	Vancomycin therapy is recommended for patients allergic to β-lactams (see text); peak serum concentrations of vancomycin should be obtained 1 h after completion of the infusion and should be in the range of 30–45 µg/mL for twice-daily dosing

[1]Dosages recommended are for patients with normal renal function. For nutritionally variant streptococci, see Table 11–6. IV indicates intravenous; IM, intramuscular.

[2]Patients should be informed that IM injection of ceftriaxone is painful.

[3]Dosing of gentamicin on a mg/kg basis will produce higher serum concentrations in obese patients than in lean patients. Therefore, in obese patients, dosing should be based on ideal body weight. (Ideal body weight for men is 50 kg + 2.3 kg per inch over 5 feet, and ideal body weight for women is 45.5 kg + 2.3 kg per inch over 5 feet.) Relative contraindications to the use of gentamicin are age >65 y, renal impairment, or impairment of the eighth nerve. Other potentially nephrotoxic agents (eg, nonsteroidal anti-inflammatory drugs) should be used cautiously in patients receiving gentamicin.

[4]Vancomycin dosage should be reduced in patients with impaired renal function. Vancomycin given on a mg/kg basis will produce higher serum concentrations in obese patients than in lean patients. Therefore, in obese patients, dosing should be based on ideal body weight. Each dose of vancomycin should be infused over at least 1 h to reduce the risk of the histamine-release "red man" syndrome.

Reprinted from JAMA 1995; 274:1706–1713.

Table 11–5. Therapy for native valve endocarditis due to strains of viridans streptococci and *Streptococcus bovis* relatively resistant to penciillin G (minimum inhibitory concentration >0.1 μg/mL and <0.5 μg/mL).[1]

Antibiotic	Dosage and Route	Duration, wk	Comments
Aqueous crystalline penicillin G sodium	18 million U/24 h IV either continuously or in six equally divided doses	4	Cefazolin or other first-generation cephalosporins may be substituted for penicillin in patients whose penicillin hypersensitivity is not of the immediate type
With gentamicin sulfate[2]	1 mg/kg IM or IV every 8 h	2	
Vancomycin hydrochloride[3]	30 mg/kg per 24 h IV in two equally divided doses, not to exceed 2 g/24 h unless serum levels are monitored	4	Vancomycin therapy is recommended for patients allergic to β-lactams

[1]Dosages recommended are for patients with normal renal function. IV indicates intravenous; IM, intramuscular.
[2]For specific dosing adjustment and issues concerning gentamicin (obese patients, relative contraindications), see Table 11–4 footnotes.
[3]For specific dosing adjustment and issues concerning vancomycin (obese patients, length of infusion), see Table 11–4 footnotes. Reprinted from JAMA 1995; 274:1706–1713.

sistent bacteremia despite appropriate antimicrobial therapy, especially in the setting of resistant microorganisms (eg, fungi) or myocardial abscess, and relapse with highly resistant microorganisms. Some patients with multiple emboli despite effective antimicrobial therapy may benefit from surgery.

Echocardiographic appearance per se of vegetations should not be used as the sole criterion for surgical intervention. Patients at risk of emboli from valvular vegetations demonstrable on echocardiography may be considered candidates for surgical intervention if emboli continue to occur after 2 weeks of effective antimicrobial therapy, or in those patients with large mobile vegetations located on the anterior leaflet of the mitral valve. However, generalizations should not be made regarding surgical intervention in these patients, and the decision for cardiac surgery to prevent systemic embolization should be individualized for each patient.

Prognosis

As noted above, untreated infective endocarditis is uniformly fatal. The prognosis with accurate diagnosis and treatment is highly variable, depending on the

Table 11–6. Standard therapy for endocarditis due to enterococci.[1]

Antibiotic	Dosage and Route	Duration, wk	Comments
Aqueous crystalline penicillin G sodium	18–30 million U/24 h IV either continuously or in six equally divided doses	4–6	
With gentamicin sulfate[2]	1 mg/kg IM or IV every 8 h	4–6	4-wk therapy recommended for patients with symptoms <3 mo in duration; 6-wk therapy recommended for patients with >3 mo in duration
Ampicillin sodium	12 g/24 h IV either continuously or in six equally divided doses	4–6	
With gentamicin sulfate[3]	1 mg/kg IM or IV every 8 h	4–6	
Vancomycin hydrochloride[2,3]	30 mg/kg per 24 h IV in two equally divided doses, not to exceed 2 g/24 h unless serum levels are monitored	4–6	Vancomycin therapy is recommended for patients allergic to β-lactams; cephalosporins are not acceptable alternatives for patients allergic to penicillin
With gentamicin sulfate[2]	1 mg/kg IM or IV every 8 h	4–6	

[1]All enterococci causing endocarditis must be tested for antimicrobial susceptibility in order to select optimal therapy (see text). This table is for endocarditis due to gentamicin- or vancomycin-susceptible enterococci, viridans streptococci with a minimum inhibitory concentration of >0.5 μg/mL, nutritionally variant viridans streptococci, or prosthetic valve endocarditis caused by viridans streptococci or *Streptococcus bovis*. Antibiotic dosages are for patients with normal renal function. IV indicates intravenous; IM, intramuscular.
[2]For specific dosing adjustment and issues concerning gentamicin (obese patients, relative contraindications), see Table 11–4 footnotes.
[3]For specific dosing adjustment and issues concerning vancomycin (obese patients, length of infusion), see Table 11–4 footnotes. Reprinted from JAMA 1995; 274:1706–1713.

Table 11–7. Therapy for endocarditis due to staphylococcus in the absence of prosthetic material.[1]

Antibiotic	Dosage and Route	Duration	Comments
Methicillin-Susceptible Staphylococci			
Regimens for non–β-lactam-allergic patients			
Naficillin sodium or oxacillin sodium	2 g IV every 4 h	4–6 wk	Benefit of additional aminoglycosides has not been established
With optional addition of gentamicin sulfate[2]	1 mg/kg IM or IV every 8 h	3–5 d	
Regimens for β-lactam-allergic patients			
Cefazolin (or other first-generation cephalosporins in equivalent dosages)	2 g IV every 8 h	4–6 wk	Cephalosporins should be avoided in patients with immediate-type hypersensitivity to penicillin
With optional addition of gentamicin[2]	1 mg/kg IM or IV every 8 h	3–6 d	
Vancomycin hydrochloride[3]	30 mg/kg per 24 h IV in two equally divided doses, not to exceed 2 g/24 h unless serum levels are monitored	4–6 wk	Recommended for patients allergic to pencillin
Methicillin-Resistant Staphylococci			
Vancomycin hydrochloride[3]	30 mg/kg per 24 h IV in two equally divided doses, not to exceed 2 g/24 h unless serum levels are monitored	4–6 wk	

[1]For treatment of endocarditis due to penicillin-susceptible staphylococci (minimum inhibitory concentration ≤0.1 μg/mL), aqueous crystalline penicillin G sodium (Table 1, first regimen) can be used for 4 to 6 wk instead of nafcillin or oxacillin. Shorter antibiotic courses have been effective in some drug addicts with right-sided endocarditis due to *Staphylococcus aureus* (see text). See text for comments on use of rifampin. IV indicates intravenous; IM, intramuscular.
[2]For specific dosing adjustment and issues concerning gentamicin (obese patients, relative contraindications), see Table 11–4 footnotes.
[3]For specific dosing adjustment and issues concerning vancomycin (obese patients, length of infusion), see Table 11–4 footnotes. Reprinted from JAMA 1995; 274:1706–1713.

Table 11–8. Treatment of staphylococcal endocarditis in the presence of a prosthetic valve or other prosthetic material.[1]

Antibiotic	Dosage and Route	Duration, wk	Comments
Regimen for Methicillin-Resistant Staphylococci			
Vancomycin hydrochloride[2]	30 mg/kg per 24 h IV in 2 or 4 equally divided doses, not to exceed 2 g/24 h unless serum levels are monitored	≥6	
With rifampin[3]	300 mg orally every 8 h	≥6	Rifampin increases the amount of warfarin sodium required for antithrombotic therapy.
And with gentamicin sulfate[4,5]	1.0 mg/kg IM or IV every 8 h	2	
Regimen for Methicillin-Susceptible Staphylococci			
Nafcillin sodium or oxacillin sodium	2 g IV every 4 h	≥6	First-generation cephalosporins or vancomycin should be used in patients allergic to β-lactam.
With rifampin[3]	300 mg orally every 8 h	≥6	Cephalosporins should be avoided in patients with immediate-type hypersensitivity to penicillin or with methicillin-resistant staphylococci.
And with gentamicin sulfate[4,5]	1.0 mg/kg IM or IV every 8 h	2	

[1]Dosages recommended are for patients with normal renal function. IV indicates intravenous; IM, intramuscular.
[2]For specific dosing adjustment and issues concerning vancomycin (obese patients, length of infusion), see Table 11–4 footnotes.
[3]Rifampin plays a unique role in the eradication of staphylococcal infection involving prosthetic material (see text); combination therapy is essential to prevent emergence of rifampin resistance.
[4]For specific dosing adjustment and issues concerning gentamicin (obese patients, relative contraindications), see Table 11–4 footnotes.
[5]Use during initial 2 wk.
Reprinted from JAMA 1995; 274:1706–1713.

Table 11–9. Therapy for endocarditis due to HACEK microorganisms (*Haemophilus parainfluenzae, Haemophilus aphrophilus, Actinobacillus actinomycetemcomitans, Cardiobacterium hominis, Eikenella corrodens,* and *Kingella kingae*).[1]

Antibiotic	Dosage and Route	Duration, wk	Comments
Ceftriaxone sodium[2]	2 g once daily IV or IM[2]	4	Cefotaxime sodium or other third-generation cephalosporins may be substituted
Ampicillin sodium[3]	12 g/24 h IV either continuously or in 6 equally divided doses	4	
With gentamicin sulfate[4]	1 mg/kg IM or IV every 8 h	4	

[1]Antibiotic dosages are for patients with normal renal function. IV indicates intravenous; IM, intramuscular.
[2]Patients should be informed that IM injection of ceftriaxone is painful. For patients unable to tolerate β-lactam therapy, consult text.
[3]Ampicillin should not be used if laboratory tests show β-lactamase production.
[4]For specific dosing adjustment and issues concerning gentamicin (obese patients, relative contraindications), see Table 11–4 footnotes.
Reprinted from JAMA 1995; 274:1706–1713.

Table 11–10. Dental procedures and endocarditis prophylaxis.[1]

Endocarditis prophylaxis recommended[2]
　Dental extractions
　Periodontal procedures including surgery, scaling and root planning, probing, and recall maintenance
　Dental implant placement and reimplantation of avulsed teeth
　Endodontic (root canal) instrumentation or surgery only beyond the apex
　Subgingival placement of antibiotic fibers or strips
　Initial placement of orthodontic bands but not brackets
　Intraligamentary local anesthetic injections
　Prophylactic cleaning of teeth or implants where bleeding is anticipated

Endocarditis prophylaxis not recommended
　Restorative dentistry[3] (operative and prosthodontic) with or without retraction cord[4]
　Local anesthetic injections (nonintraligamentary)
　Intracanal endodontic treatment; post-placement and buildup
　Placement of rubber dams
　Postoperative suture removal
　Placement of removable prosthodontic or orthodontic appliances
Taking of oral impressions
Fluoride treatments
Taking of oral radiographs
Orthodontic appliance adjustment
Shedding of primary teeth

[1]*Source:* JAMA 1997; 277:1794–1801.
[2]Prophylaxis is recommended for patients with high- and moderate-risk cardiac conditions.
[3]This includes restoration of decayed teeth (filling cavities) and replacement of missing teeth.
[4]Clinical judgment may indicate antibiotic use in selected circumstances that may create significant bleeding.

Table 11–11. Other procedures and endocarditis prophylaxis.[1]

Endocarditis prophylaxis recommended
　Respiratory tract
　　Tonsillectomy, adenoidectomy, or both
　　Surgical operations that involve respiratory mucosa
　　Bronchoscopy with a rigid bronchoscope
　Gastrointestinal tract[2]
　　Sclerotherapy for esophageal varices
　　Esophageal stricture dilation
　　Endoscopic retrograde cholangiography with biliary obstruction
　　Biliary tract surgery
　　Surgical operations that involve intestinal mucosa
　Genitourinary tract
　　Prostatic surgery
　　Cytoscopy
　　Urethral dilation

Endocarditis prophylaxis not recommended
　Respiratory tract
　　Endotracheal intubation
　　Bronchoscopy with a flexible bronchoscope, with or without biopsy[3]
　　Tympanostomy tube insertion
　Gastrointestinal tract
　　Transesophageal echocardiography[3]
　　Endoscopy with or without gastrointestinal biopsy
　Genitourinary tract
　　Vaginal hysterectomy[3]
　　Vaginal delivery[3]
　　Cesarean section
　　In uninfected tissue:
　　　Urethral catheterization
　　　Uterine dilatation and curettage
　　　Therapeutic abortion
　　　Sterilization procedures
　　　Insertion or removal of intrauterine devices
　Other
　　Cardiac catheterization, including balloon angioplasty
　　Implanted cardiac pacemakers, implanted defibrillators, and coronary stents
　　Incision or biopsy of surgically scrubbed skin
　　Circumcision

[1]Reprinted with permission from JAMA 1997; 277:1794–1801.
[2]Prophylaxis is recommended for high-risk patients; it is optional for medium-risk patients.
[3]Prophylaxis is optional for high-risk patients.

Table 11–12. Prophylactic regimens for dental, oral, respiratory tract, or esophageal procedures.[1]

Situation	Agent[2]	Regimen
Standard general prophylaxis	Amoxicillin	Adults: 2.0 g; children: 50 mg/kg orally 1 h before procedure
Unable to take oral medications	Ampicillin	Adults: 2.0 g IM or IV; children: 50 mg/kg IM or IV within 30 min before procedure
Allergic to penicillin	Clindamycin or cephalexin[3]	Adults: 600 mg; children: 20 mg/kg orally 1 h before procedure
	Cefadroxil	Adults: 2.0 g; children: 50 mg/kg orally 1 h before procedure
	Azithromycin or clarithromycin	Adults: 500 mg; children: 15 mg/kg orally 1 h before procedure
Allergic to penicillin and unable to take oral medications	Clindamycin	Adults: 600 mg; children: 20 mg/kg IV within 30 min before procedure
	Cefazolin[3]	Adults: 1.0 g; children: 25 mg/kg IM or IV within 30 min before procedure

[1]Reprinted with permission from JAMA 1997; 277:1794–1801. Abbreviations: IM, intramuscularly; IV, intravenously.
[2]Total children's dose should not exceed adult dose.
[3]Cephalosporins should not be used in individuals with immediate-type hypersensitivity reaction (urticaria, angiodema, or anaphylaxis) to penicillins.

microorganism, the degree of valvular destruction before antimicrobial treatment, and whether prosthetic material is involved. In uncomplicated *viridans* group streptococcal infection of a native valve, outcome is frequently excellent, including prompt response of fever and systemic symptoms to antimicrobial therapy and cure rates exceeding 98% with approved regimens in patients who survive to complete therapy. In contrast, mortality in prosthetic valve infection with staphylococci, gram-negative bacilli, or fungi remains in the range of ≥ 25–50%, despite aggressive medical and surgical therapy.

Even after cure of infective endocarditis, subsequent need for valve replacement because of valvular insufficiency is not uncommon, especially in the setting of aortic valve infection. Persons who have had infective endocarditis are at ≥ 100-fold increased risk of recurrent infection, compared with the general population.

Prevention

Patients with known cardiac risk factors for infective endocarditis should have regular professional dental care and practice good oral hygiene. The

Table 11–13. Prophylactic regimens for genitourinary/gastrointestinal (excluding esophageal) procedures.[1]

Situation	Agent[2]	Regimen[3]
High-risk patients	Ampicillin plus gentamicin	Adults: ampicillin, 2.0 g IM or IV, plus gentamcin, 1.5 mg/kg (not to exceed 120 mg) within 30 min of starting procedure; 6 h later, ampicillin, 1 g IM/IV, or amoxicillin, 1 g orally. Children: ampicillin, 50 mg/kg IM or IV (not to exceed 2.0 g) plus gentamicin 1.5 mg/kg within 30 min of starting the procedure; 6 h later, ampicillin, 25 mg/kg IM/IV, or amoxicillin, 25 mg/kg orally
High-risk patients allergic to ampicillin/amoxicillin	Vancomycin plus gentamicin	Adults: vancomycin, 1.0 g IV over 1–2 h, plus gentamicin, 1.5 mg/kg IV/IM (not to exceed 120 mg); complete injection/infusion within 30 min of starting procedure. Children: vancomycin, 20 mg/kg IV over 1–2 h, plus gentamicin, 1.5 mg/kg IV/IM; complete injection/infusion within 30 min of starting procedure
Moderate-risk patients	Amoxicillin or ampicillin	Adults: amoxicillin, 2.0 g orally 1 h before procedure, or ampicillin, 2.0 g IM/IV within 30 min of starting procedure. Children: amoxicillin, 50 mg/kg orally 1 h before procedure, or ampicillin, 50 mg/kg IM/IV within 30 min of starting procedure
Moderate-risk patients allergic to ampicillin/amoxicillin	Vancomycin	Adults: vancomycin, 1.0 g IV over 1–2 h, complete infusion within 30 min of starting procedure. Children: vancomycin, 20 mg/kg IV over 1–2 h; complete infusion within 30 min of starting procedure.

[1]*Source:* JAMA 1997; 277:1794–1801.
[2]Total children's dose should not exceed adult dose.
[3]No second dose of vancomycin or gentamicin is recommended. Abbreviations: IM, intramuscularly; IV, intravenously.

American Heart Association recommends specific antimicrobial prophylaxis for patients who have cardiac abnormalities associated with increased risk of endocarditis and who are undergoing certain invasive procedures associated with a risk of transient bacteremia caused by microorganisms commonly causing endocarditis (Tables 11–1,11–10 through 11–13).

REFERENCES

Dajani AS et al: Prevention of bacterial endocarditis. Recommendations by the American Heart Association. J Am Med Assoc 1997;277:1794.

Patel R, Steckelberg JM: Infections of the heart. In Murphy JG (editor): *Mayo Clinic Cardiology Review,* Futura Publishing Co, 1997.

Wilson WR et al: Antibiotic treatment of adults with infective endocarditis due to streptococci, enterococci, staphylococci, and HACEK microorganisms. J Am Med Assoc 1995;274:1706.

Wilson WR, Steckelberg JM (editors): Infective endocarditis. Infect Dis Clin North Am 1993;7.

12 Intra-abdominal Infections

Jeffery Loutit, MB, ChB

The term intra-abdominal infection encompasses many inflammatory processes of the peritoneum and/or an intra-abdominal organs. Therefore, patients may present with a clinical syndrome ranging from peritonitis to a localized abscess. Most cases of intra-abdominal infection are secondary to changes in the structure and function of the bowel wall that allow passage of aerobic gram-negative organisms and anaerobes into the intra-abdominal cavity. Bacterial pathogens appear to predominate. In this chapter, primary, secondary, and tertiary peritonitis and other intra-abdominal infections such as liver, splenic, and pancreatic abscesses are discussed. In addition, cholecystitis, appendicitis, and necrotizing pancreatitis are reviewed.

Abdominal pain is a common feature of intra-abdominal infection. In evaluation of the patient with abdominal pain, three distinct patterns can be described: acute, chronic intermittent, and chronic intractable abdominal pain. Temporal features, quality, location, exacerbating/relieving factors, and, of course, physical examination are paramount in the diagnosis of patients with abdominal pain.

ABDOMINAL PAIN

Abdominal pain is a common presenting complaint. To delineate the source of a patient's pain, the practitioner must be familiar with the neurologic innervation of the visceral organs. There are three levels of neurons that connect the abdominal organs with the cerebral cortex. The first-order neurons link receptors on the abdominal organs to the spinal cord; therefore, stimuli such as stretch, distention, or contraction of a hollow viscus will cause visceral pain. The second-order neurons in the dorsal horn of the spinal cord link the spinal cord and the brain stem; their fibers travel through the contralateral spinothalamic tract. The third-order neurons link the brain stem with the higher brain centers.

Visceral pain is often very poorly localized and vague. The neuronal fibers that carry painful stimuli to the central nervous system are relatively few and travel with the sympathetic nervous system. In addition, a relatively small number of fibers modify the stimulation of a majority of the second-order neurons. This is likely to be a cause of the imprecise localization of these stimuli, as well as a partial explanation for the observation that visceral pain is accompanied by a variety of autonomic responses, such as changes in muscle tone, pulse, blood pressure, and skin temperature. The gut itself begins to develop during embryologic development, as a midline structure; therefore, it has bilateral and symmetric innervation. Consequently, most visceral pain is felt as midline pain. In some areas of the gut, such as the ascending and descending colon, and in the biliary tree, nerve fibers from one side predominate over those from the other. Patients with pain that originates from these structures have a lateralized sensation that is appropriate to the predominant side of innervation. Other areas of pain localization in the abdominal wall also follow embryologic development. Nerves from foregut structures enter into the spinal cord at T/5–T/9 and cause pain in the epigastric region, usually between the xiphoid process and umbilicus. Nerves of the mid gut structure enter into the spinal cord from T/8–T/11 and L/1, and pain is perceived in the periumbilical area. Nerves of the hindgut structure enter into the spinal cord from T/11 through L/1 and cause pain between the umbilicus and the pubic bone.

Somatic pain occurs when intra-abdominal conditions cause stimulation of the somatic or abdominal wall nerves rather than visceral nerves; therefore, the characteristics of the painful sensation become more like those expected from the skin. Referred pain is felt as a deep ache that is perceived near the surface of the body and is accompanied by skin hyperalgesia and increased muscle tone.

CLINICAL SYNDROMES

PERITONITIS

1. SPONTANEOUS BACTERIAL PERITONITIS

Essentials of Diagnosis
- Presence of ascites.
- Fever in ~ 80% of cases.
- No symptoms or signs in 30% of patients at presentation.
- Abdominal tenderness in only 50% of patients.
- Ascitic fluid with > 250 neutrophils/mm^3.
- Ascitic fluid with > 10,000 neutrophils/ mm^3 and yielding > one microorganism by culture, suggests secondary peritonitis.

General Considerations
The peritoneum consists of a single layer of mesothelial cells that line the peritoneal cavity. The peritoneal cavity typically contains < 50 mL of clear sterile fluid with < 3000 cells/mm^3, composed of 50% macrophages and 40% lymphocytes.

A. Epidemiology. Primary peritonitis or spontaneous bacterial peritonitis (SBP) refers to peritonitis that arises without an obvious explanation, which is seen almost exclusively in patients with ascites, usually secondary to hepatic dysfunction or, less commonly, to nephrotic syndrome. It is thought that opsonic activity of the peritoneal fluid is decreased in the setting of ascites and that lymphatic clearance mechanisms are also impaired. The mechanism by which the peritoneal fluid becomes infected is unclear, with bacteremia and translocation across the bowel wall postulated as possible mechanisms.

Primary peritonitis may also be seen in children without ascites, usually girls < 10 years of age. The source of the infection is usually unknown, and the infecting organism in this group of patients is usually *Streptococcus pneumoniae* or group A streptococcus. Gram-negative aerobic bacilli are rarely implicated. The presence of the above organisms would suggest that the peritoneum is seeded via a hematogenous route. For unknown reasons, the incidence of primary peritonitis in young girls has decreased markedly over the past several decades.

SBP has also been noted in patients with systemic lupus erythematosus and lupus nephritis, without obvious ascites. Many of those patients are receiving corticosteroid therapy at the time of diagnosis, and the most common etiologic agents in this group of patients are gram-positive cocci such as S *pneumoniae* and group B streptococcus.

In the adult population, as mentioned above, most SBP is secondary to advanced chronic liver disease and ascites. The exact prevalence of SBP is unknown, but it occurs in ~ 8–27% of patients with cirrhosis and ascites. The mortality of SBP in this population is ~ 50% or higher in many studies.

B. Microbiology. The organisms isolated from ascitic fluid from adults in the setting of SBP are *Escherichia coli* in 50% of patients and *S pneumoniae* and other streptococcal species in 15–20% of cases (Box 12–1). *Klebsiella* spp. and anaerobes are isolated in ~ 10% and 5% of SBP cases, respectively. Bacteremia is documented in ~ 50% of SBP cases when the infection is caused by a single aerobic species, whereas in cases involving anaerobes, multiple organisms are usually involved, and documented bacteremia is rare. Within the ascitic fluid, organisms are able to proliferate because of impaired local host defense mechanisms and decreased bactericidal activity.

Clinical Findings
A. Signs and Symptoms. The clinical presentation of SBP is variable. On one hand, patients may be asymptomatic or complain of only mild, diffuse nonspecific abdominal pain. On the other hand, the process may produce signs of acute peritonitis. Fever is the most common sign, but may be absent in ~ 20% of cases. Approximately one-third of patients may be free of all signs and symptoms characteristic of intra-abdominal infection, and only 50% of patients will have abdominal tenderness on examination.

B. Laboratory Findings. The key to the diagnosis of SBP is a high index of suspicion in a patient with ascites, especially in those with an otherwise unexplained deterioration in hepatic or renal function; one should have a low threshold for performing paracentesis. The ascitic fluid should be cultured for bacteria, and a leukocyte count should be determined. A Gram stain of the fluid should also be performed, despite the fact that it often (60–80% of attempts) fails to reveal

---

BOX 12–1

Microbiology of Spontaneous Bacterial Peritonitis

	Children	Adults
More Frequent	• *Streptococcus pneumoniae* • Group A streptococcus	• *Escherichia coli* • *Streptococcus pneumoniae*
Less Frequent	• *Escherichia coli*	• *Klebsiella* spp. • Anaerobes

organisms. If the stain reveals organisms of a single morphologic type, then SBP should be suspected. If multiple bacterial types are observed, then secondary peritonitis is more likely, in which case a further search for the cause of the peritonitis should be performed. The polymorphonuclear (PMN) leukocyte count of the ascitic fluid is thought to be the best marker of SBP. PMN leukocyte counts of > 250 cells/mm^3 suggest a diagnosis of SBP, and counts > 500 cells/mm^3 should mandate antimicrobial therapy.

There are three variant forms of SBP ("typical" SBP, culture-negative neutrocytic ascites, and bacterascites), each of which is defined by the combination of PMN leukocyte count and bacterial culture results (Table 12–1). The clinical prognoses of SBP and culture-negative neutrophilic ascites are indistinguishable, and they should be managed identically; however, bacterascites is often self-limited, and patients can be managed by repeating the paracentesis after 48 h and with careful observation. An ascitic fluid with > 10,000 PMN leukocytes/mm^3 or the presence of multiple bacterial species, anaerobes, or fungal organisms should point the physician towards a diagnosis of secondary peritonitis.

Differential Diagnosis

The diagnosis of primary peritonitis is one of inclusion and exclusion. Patients who develop primary peritonitis usually do so in the setting of ascites, and other intra-abdominal infections must be excluded. CT scanning has greatly enhanced the ability to detect other intra-abdominal sources of peritonitis.

Prognosis

The mortality rate of spontaneous bacterial peritonitis in cirrhotic adults is high, with some studies reporting rates as high as 95%. The high mortality is mainly due to the accompanying end-stage cirrhosis, and more recent studies have reported mortality rates between 57% and 70%.

Treatment

SBP should be treated with broad antimicrobial coverage until culture results are available. Third-generation cephalosporins, such as cefotaxime, are recommended, but many other agents, such as β-lactam/β-lactamase inhibitor combinations or carbapen-

---

BOX 12–2

Empiric Therapy of Spontaneous Bacterial Peritonitis

	Children	Adults
First Choice	• As per adults with modified doses	• Ceftriaxone, 1–2 g/d OR • Cefotaxime, 1 g/ every 8 h
Second Choice		• Ampicillin-sulbactam, 3 g IV every 6 h OR • Ticarcillin-clavulanate, 3.1 g IV every 4–6 h OR • Piperacillin-tazobactam, 4.5 g IV every 8 h OR • Imipenem-cilastatin, 500 mg IV every 6 h OR • Clindamycin, 600 mg IV every 8 h plus ciprofloxacin, 400 mg IV every 12 h
Penicillin Allergic		• Clindamycin/ciprofloxacin (as above)

---

ems, are also effective (Box 12–2). If SBP develops during hospitalization, consideration should be given to antipseudomonal coverage by using an aminoglycoside plus an antipseudomonal penicillin or cephalosporin. Intravenous antimicrobial agents should be given for 10–14 days. More recent data indicate that 5 days of therapy may be sufficient in those patients who are clinically well and in whom the ascitic fluid is culture negative and the PMN leukocyte count is < 250 cells/mm^3, after this period of therapy.

Prevention

Recurrences of SBP occur in > 50% of patients within 6 mo of the initial episode; therefore, prophylaxis is recommended (Box 12–3). Agents such as norfloxacin (400 mg/d) or trimethoprim-sulfamethoxazole (one double-strength tablet/d) are effective. These antimicrobial agents have been shown to decrease significantly the incidence of primary

---

Table 12–1. Forms of spontaneous bacterial peritonitis.

	Ascitic Fluid PMNs	Cultures
"Typical" spontaneous bacterial peritonitis	> 250 cells/mm^3	Positive
Culture-negative neutrocytic ascites	> 500 cells/mm^3	Negative
Monomicrobial nonneutrocytic bacterascites	< 250 cells/mm^3	Positive

BOX 12-3

Prevention of Spontaneous
Bacterial Peritonitis

Preventive Measures	• Norfloxacin, 400 mg/d • Trimethoprim-sulfamethoxazole (1 double-strength tablet/d)
Isolation Precautions	• None

BOX 12-4

Microbiology of Secondary/Tertiary
Bacterial Peritonitis

	Children	Adults
More Frequent	• As per adults	• *Bacteroides fragilis* • *Peptostreptococcus* spp. • *Clostridium* spp. • *Bilophila wadsworthia* • *Escherichia coli* • *Proteus* spp. • *Klebsiella* spp. • *Streptococcus* spp.
Less Frequent		• *Pseudomonas aeruginosa* • *Enterococcus* spp. • *Candida* spp.

peritonitis, but they have not been shown to improve survival.

2. SECONDARY PERITONITIS

Essentials of Diagnosis
• Spillage of gastrointestinal or genitourinary organisms into the peritoneal space.
• Severe abdominal pain, nausea, vomiting, fevers, chills, avoiding movement with hips/knees flexed.
• Abdominal tenderness, involuntary guarding, rebound tenderness, high temperature, tachycardia, hypotension, sepsis, hypovolemic shock.
• Elevated peripheral leukocyte count.

General Considerations
A. Epidemiology. Secondary peritonitis occurs when there is gross soilage of the peritoneal space by contents (and organisms) from the gastrointestinal or genitourinary tracts. Appendicitis, diverticulitis, cholecystitis, and perforation of a peptic ulcer are settings in which this may take place. Postsurgical anastomotic leak is also a common cause of secondary peritonitis and intra-abdominal abscess. Secondary peritonitis can produce either a generalized peritoneal reaction or a localized abscess. Abscesses are usually restricted to the site of the perforation, and therefore are often pericholecystic, periappendiceal, or peridiverticular. They are also commonly restricted to peritoneal recesses such as the subdiaphragmatic or subhepatic regions.
B. Microbiology. Most cases of secondary peritonitis are polymicrobial (Box 12–4). The specific organisms that are involved reflect the segment of bowel or other hollow organ that perforates. The stomach contains few organisms because of low pH. In the proximal small bowel, the density of organisms increases and, in addition to α-hemolytic streptococci and lactobacilli, some *Enterobacteriaceae* and anaerobes are present. In the large bowel, anaerobic organisms predominate (1000–5000:1 aerobe), in particular, the *Bacteroides fragilis* group, other *Bacteroides* spp., *Bilophila wadsworthia*, *Peptostreptococcus* spp. and *Clostridium* spp. In one study of perforated appendicitis in which careful anaerobic

techniques were used, 9.4 anaerobes were isolated per patient. *B fragilis* is consistently the anaerobe isolated most often; *B wadsworthia,* a newly characterized gram-negative anaerobe, was the fourth most common anaerobe isolated from a study of patients with a perforated or gangrenous appendix.

The aerobic organisms present in the large bowel usually include *E coli, Proteus* spp., and *Klebsiella* spp., along with various *Streptococcus* and *Enterococcus* spp. But the microflora can be altered by previous antimicrobial therapy or by the underlying illness. For example, the loss of gastric acidity allows colonization of the stomach by oral flora, aerobes, and anaerobes. In severely ill hospitalized patients who receive antimicrobial agents, organisms such as *Pseudomonas* and *Enterobacter* spp., as well as multidrug-resistant *Enterococcus* and *Candida* spp., may proliferate; they will therefore contribute to any peritoneal infection that occurs while a patient is in a hospital. This is often referred to as tertiary peritonitis, ie, peritonitis in patients with impaired host defenses and multiple organ dysfunction, and it is often a nosocomial event.

The role of *Enterococcus* spp. in secondary peritonitis is unclear. Most intra-abdominal abscesses can be cured without antimicrobial agents that have specific activity against the *Enterococcus* spp. However, in the case of pure growth of these organisms from an infected intra-abdominal source, most experts would recommend an antibiotic regimen that includes enterococcal coverage, as well as coverage against the other typical aerobic and anaerobic organisms.
C. Pathogenesis. Generalized peritonitis may occur as a result of appendicitis, diverticulitis, penetrating abdominal wounds, blunt trauma to the abdomen, perforation of the gastrointestinal tract (eg,

perforated peptic ulcer or neoplasm), or rupture of an intra-abdominal abscess. The prognosis is poorest in a patient with appendicitis or a perforated peptic ulcer, and best with postoperative peritonitis.

Weinstein and coworkers demonstrated the sequence of events after contamination of the peritoneum with fecal flora. They showed that *E coli* is responsible for sepsis and for the mortality of early peritonitis, whereas *B fragilis,* in conjunction with *E coli,* is responsible for the late abscess formation. Synergy between anaerobes and facultative aerobic organisms has long been recognized as a key pathogenic feature in these mixed infections. After initial peritoneal contamination, bacteria encounter host defenses in the form of lymphatic clearance, phagocytosis, and sequestration by fibrin. The lymphatic clearance mechanism is usually very efficient, but the presence of necrotic debris facilitates the development of peritonitis or abscess formation. Local resident macrophages are the predominant host defense cells initially, but, if bacterial proliferation continues, PMN leukocytes become more numerous. The systemic and abdominal manifestations of peritonitis are mediated by cytokines such as tumor necrosis factor-α (TNF-α), interleukin-1 (IL-1), IL-6, interferon-α, and others. These cytokines are produced by macrophages and other host cells in response to bacteria or bacterial products such as lipopolysaccharide.

Clinical Findings

The purpose of the clinical evaluation should be to delineate whether urgent or semiurgent surgical intervention is indicated. History and physical examination are paramount in that decision-making process.

A. Signs and Symptoms. Pain, nausea, vomiting, altered bowel habits, and fever or chills are often present in patients with peritonitis. As mentioned previously, owing to the innervation of the abdomen, pain from an intra-abdominal viscus infection is usually midline and poorly localized. Localized pain that is exacerbated by movement is more characteristic of an irritated parietal peritoneum that stimulates the somatic nerve system. The actual presentation will vary depending on the location, extent, and maturity of the inflammatory process. Patients with diffuse peritonitis will often present with hypovolemic shock, whereas those with a chronic localized abscess often present with minimal vital-sign abnormalities and pain that may not be well localized. This is especially true if the parietal peritoneum is not a component of the wall of the abscess. Therefore, physical findings will also be variable. Patients with peritonitis typically avoid movement and may have their hips and knees flexed. Abdominal exam may reveal tenderness to percussion and/or palpation. Involuntary spasm of the abdominal wall elicited by palpation is indicative of an inflamed parietal peritoneum.

B. Laboratory Findings. As part of the evaluation of a patient with a suspected intra-abdominal in-

fection, a leukocyte count, urine analysis, and blood cultures should be performed.

C. Imaging. An upright chest x-ray or left lateral decubitus radiograph may reveal free air (Figure 12–1) in ≥ 70% of patients with a perforated gastric or duodenal ulcer, but will rarely reveal free air with other types of perforated viscus. Radiologic evaluation of patients with suspected peritonitis or localized abscess has become invaluable. In addition, computed-tomography (CT) or ultrasound-guided aspiration or drainage of a suspected intra-abdominal abscess has become standard practice in the evaluation and management of patients. Ultrasonography is usually less costly than CT; ultrasonography is also usually portable, it is noninvasive, and it may be obtained rapidly. It is very useful in the evaluation of gallbladder and biliary tract disease and is also useful for evaluating the pelvis in a female patient with signs of pelvic infection, in whom the pelvic and rectal examinations have not identified the cause. The weaknesses of ultrasonography include operator dependency and limitations imposed by bowel gas and fat in the abdominal wall and omentum. CT with intravenous, oral, and rectal contrast is the most definitive radiographic test (Figure 12–2). Its strengths include provision of a relatively complete picture of intraperitoneal and retroperitoneal anatomy, thereby revealing small or deep fluid collections and abscesses. CT can also detect and localize causes of bowel obstruction and detect free air trapped within the bowel wall better than any other method. Its drawbacks include the needs for ionizing radiation, intravenous contrast, and patient cooperation and its lack of portability.

Differential Diagnosis

The differential diagnosis of patients with symp-

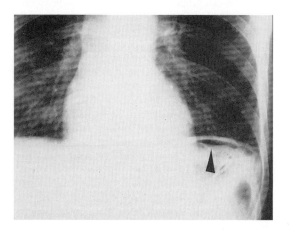

Figure 12–1. Abdominal radiograph of air under the left diaphragm secondary to perforation of a duodenal ulcer. (Reproduced with permission from Finegold and Wilson [1996].)

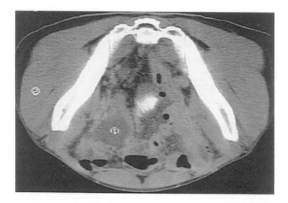

Figure 12–2. CT scan of the pelvis, showing an abscess in the right lower quadrant. (Reproduced with permission from Finegold and Wilson [1996].)

toms and signs of peritonitis includes pneumonia, sickle cell crisis, herpes zoster, diabetic ketoacidosis, porphyria, familial Mediterranean fever, lead poisoning, uremia, and systemic lupus erythematosus.

Prognosis

Survival in a patient with secondary peritonitis depends on many factors including age, comorbid conditions, duration of peritoneal contamination, and the primary intra-abdominal process and bacteria involved. Mortality ranges from 3.5% in those with early infection caused by penetrating abdominal trauma to > 60% in established intra-abdominal infections and secondary organ failure. Outcome has been mainly linked to host factors as predicted by the acute physiologic and chronic health evaluation (APACHE2) scores rather than type and source of infection.

Treatment

A. General Management. Based on the history, physical examination and initial laboratory data, patients with secondary peritonitis can usually be placed in one of two categories: those who should and those who should not undergo surgery in the next few hours. Those patients who do not undergo surgery should be observed and evaluated closely. Patients with ascites should have paracentesis performed and a PMN leukocyte count, along with bacterial cultures, obtained. The decision as to the most appropriate radiographic procedure is then made. Evaluation of each patient must be individualized and should be based on the patient's specific presentation. There is no concise set of infallible guidelines regarding when to order a test and which test or tests to order for any given patient. The decision must be made as to the immediacy of investigation and intra-abdominal exploration or observation.

Surgical intervention is the mainstay of therapy for some patients and must be performed promptly for peritonitis that is secondary to bowel perforation or penetrating trauma. The underlying pathology should be corrected, necrotic tissue debrided, and further peritoneal seeding by microorganisms prevented. The duration of antimicrobial therapy after surgery is usually 5–7 d, depending on the severity of the infection, clinical response, and normalization of the leukocyte count. Although treatment of enterococcal or *Candida* infections is controversial, the identification of either type of organism in the blood or as a pure culture within an intra-abdominal site is an indication for specific antimicrobial therapy, in addition to surgery. The surgical approach to management of secondary peritonitis includes: (1) bowel decompression, (2) closure of any traumatic perforation and/or resection of diseased perforated viscus, and (3) drainage of any purulent collections to reduce the bacterial load and reduce levels of pro-inflammatory cytokines. Intraoperative peritoneal lavage with saline is standard procedure during laparotomy for peritonitis, but only limited data are available to support the practice of continuous postoperative peritoneal lavage.

Percutaneous drainage via interventional radiology has increasingly become an acceptable alternative to surgery in many patients. A safe drainage route must first be identified. Once this is accomplished, most patients in whom a drain is placed will show resolution of abscess radiographically and resolution of their symptoms within 48–72 h. Persistent fever or leukocytosis is an indication for repeat imaging to assess possible incomplete drainage. Published success rates with percutaneous abscess drainage range from 80% to 90%. Drainage of more complex abscesses, ie, loculated, large, and less well-organized abscesses, has been less successful. One group reported a 45% success rate for percutaneous drainage of complex abscesses vs 82% for simple abscesses. The complication rate was also higher in the group of patients with complex abscesses (21% vs 5%).

B. Antimicrobial Therapy. The selection of an antimicrobial regimen is made empirically, based on the likely pathogens that are present in the bowel at the site of peritoneal seeding. Clinical trials have not definitively established the superiority of one antimicrobial regimen over another, but it is clear that, in patients with polymicrobial infection, both anaerobic and aerobic organisms must be covered. Antimicrobial agents must penetrate the site of infection, in concentrations that are sufficient to overcome the effects of high bacterial density, metabolic inactivity, and slow growth rates. Low pH, low redox potential, necrotic tissue, and bacterial products may also interfere with the therapeutic efficacy of certain antimicrobial agents. Early clinical trials established the combination of ampicillin, clindamycin, and an aminoglycoside as a gold standard regimen, despite the relative inactivity of the last group of agents at an acid pH.

Aminoglycosides are frequently under-dosed because of concerns of nephrotoxicity or underestimation of the expanded volume of distribution in critically ill patients with intra-abdominal sepsis. Once-daily aminoglycoside therapy obviates these dosing problems, but limited data are available concerning the use of this dosing regimen in these patients. Substitution of a third-generation cephalosporin for ampicillin and aminoglycoside is also effective in the treatment of severe intra-abdominal infections. Concerns about the emergence of drug resistance have limited the use of these agents somewhat. Selection of *Enterobacteriaceae* with stably derepressed β-lactamase production is sometimes seen after use of third-generation cephalosporins, and widespread use within an intensive care unit will often hasten the selection of these organisms. Traditionally, combination therapy has been the mainstay of treatment, but, in some settings, single antibiotics with broad-spectrum activity may be appropriate. β-Lactam/β-lactamase inhibitor combination agents such as ampicillin-sulbactam, ticarcillin-clavulanate, piperacillin-tazobactam, cephamycins such as cefoxitin and cefotetan, and the carbapenems, imipenem-cilastatin, and meropenem have all been shown to be as effective as traditional combination therapy. The choice of empiric antimicrobial agents should be dictated by the severity of illness and whether the infection was acquired in a community or hospital environment. Recommendations for empiric therapy of infections of mild to moderate severity acquired in a community setting include ampicillin-sulbactam, cefoxitin, cefotetan, and ticarcillin-clavulanate (Box 12–5). Recommendations for the treatment of severe infections or those acquired in a hospital environment include clindamycin or metronidazole plus a third-generation cephalosporin, ciprofloxacin, or an aminoglycoside, aztreonam plus clindamycin, or imipenem-cilastatin, meropenem, or piperacillin-tazobactam alone (Box 12–6).

3. TERTIARY PERITONITIS

Tertiary or nosocomial peritonitis is accompanied by the usual clinical signs of peritonitis, often with signs of sepsis, and occurs after treatment for secondary peritonitis. Organisms may gain access to the peritoneal cavity after intra-operative contamination or after selection by antibiotic therapy from an initial polymicrobial peritoneal inoculum or by translocation of bowel flora.

The organisms involved in tertiary peritonitis are usually those of low pathogenicity, such as *Candida* spp., enterococci, and coagulase-negative staphylococci. In addition, *Pseudomonas aeruginosa* is isolated in a significant portion of cases of tertiary peritonitis, owing to the selective pressure of broad-spectrum antimicrobial agents.

4. PERITONITIS COMPLICATING PERITONEAL DIALYSIS

Continuous ambulatory peritoneal dialysis (CAPD) was developed in the late 1970s, and this procedure creates a special predisposition for the development of peritonitis. The overall incidence of peritonitis is 1.3–1.4 episodes/CAPD patient per year. Organisms

---

BOX 12–5

Empiric Therapy of Community-Acquired Secondary Bacterial Peritonitis of Mild to Moderate Severity

	Children	Adults
First Choice	• As per adults, but avoid fluoroquinolones	• Ampicillin-sulbactam, 3 g IV every 6 h • Ticarcillin-clavulanate, 3.1 g IV every 4–6 h • Cefoxitin, 2 g IV every 4–6 h • Cefotetan, 2 g IV every 12 h • Clindamycin, 600 mg IV every 8 h PLUS ciprofloxacin, 400 mg IV every 12 h
Second Choice		
Penicillin Allergic		• Clindamycin/ciprofloxacin

BOX 12-6

Empiric Therapy of Severe or Hospital-Acquired Secondary Bacterial Peritonitis

	Children	Adults
First Choice	• As per adults but avoid fluoroquinolones	• Piperacillin-tazobactam, 4.5 g every 8 h • Imipenem-cilastatin, 500 mg every 6 h • Meropenem, 1 g IV every 6 h • Clindamycin, 600 mg IV every 6 h plus aztreonam, 2 g IV every 8 h • Antianaerobe[1] plus ciprofloxacin, 400 mg IV every 12 h • Antianaerobe[1] plus aminoglycoside[2] • Antianaerobe[1] plus third-generation[3] cephalosporin
Second Choice		
Penicillin Allergic		• Antianaerobe[1] plus ciprofloxacin • Antianaerobe[1] plus aminoglycoside[2] • Clindamycin plus aztreonam

[1]Clindamycin, 600 mg every 6 h, or metronidazole, 500 mg every 8 h.
[2]Gentamicin or tobramycin, 7 mg/kg every 24 h.
[3]Cefotaxime, ceftazidime, ceftizoxime, 1 g every 8 h, or cefepime, 2 g every 12 h, or ceftriaxone, 1–2 g every 24 h.

gain access to the peritoneal cavity in several ways. Most common is an organism traveling down the inside or the outside of the catheter, which can occur from a break in sterile technique or infection of the local exit site. Less common is seeding of the peritoneum through contaminated dialysate or bacteremia. Microbial factors that contribute to this disease include the ability of an organism to grow in dialysis fluids and the ability to produce an extracellular slime layer or biofilm. In most patients with CAPD peritonitis, there is a single pathogen. Gram-positive cocci are the cause in 60–70% of cases; 20–30% of cases are secondary to gram-negative bacilli. Coagulase-negative staphylococci are the single most common pathogen, followed by *Staphylococcus aureus* and *Streptococcus* spp. Among the gram-negative organisms, most of the *Enterobacteriaceae* have been associated with CAPD peritonitis, and no single species predominates. Fungi have become increasingly important. *Candida* spp. account for 80–90% of fungal cases, but *Aspergillus, Mucor,* and *Rhizopus* spp. have all been reported. *Mycobacterium* spp. are isolated in < 3% of CAPD peritonitis cases.

Clinical features of CAPD peritonitis include signs and symptoms of peritoneal irritation, cloudy dialysate fluid with a leukocyte count of > 100/mm^3, and a positive fluid culture. Any two of these criteria may be sufficient to establish the diagnosis. Laboratory evaluation of the dialysate is critical. The percentage of PMN leukocytes in the dialysate fluid is usually > 50% in affected patients.

The use of intraperitoneal antibiotics as therapy for CAPD peritonitis has allowed most patients to be treated on an ambulatory basis. Antimicrobial agents that have been used with success include third-generation cephalosporins and glycopeptides such as vancomycin. Initial therapy should include coverage of gram-negative and gram-positive organisms while the culture results are awaited. Therapy is usually continued for 10–14 days, but may be extended if disease is severe or response is slow.

INTRAPERITONEAL ABSCESS

Essentials of Diagnosis

• Previous bowel perforation.
• History of recent intra-abdominal surgery, particularly pancreatic, biliary tract, colon, and stomach surgery.
• Present with either abdominal pain with fever or constitutional symptoms such as fever, nausea, or vomiting.
• Peripheral blood leukocyte count always elevated.
• CT scan is procedure of choice.
• Ultrasound and nuclear medicine scans are alternatives.

General Considerations

Intra-abdominal abscesses form because of one of two processes: (1) diffuse peritonitis in which pus collects in dependent areas such as the pelvis, paracolic gutters, and subphrenic areas and (2) spread of infection from a local inflammatory process. A common example of the latter is an appendiceal or diverticular abscess after rupture of the appendix or diverticulum and localization of the inflammatory process.

A. Epidemiology. Almost half of all intraperitoneal abscesses occur in the right lower quadrant, after rupture of the appendix. Postoperative anastomotic disruption is also a common cause of abscess formation, with ≥ 80% of all intra-abdominal abscesses falling into this category in some reports. Pancreas, biliary tract, colon, and stomach are the operative sites that are most likely to lead to postoperative abscess.

B. Microbiology. The organisms found within an intra-abdominal abscess reflect the site of perforation. The microbiology of intraperitoneal abscess is similar to that of secondary and tertiary peritonitis (Box 12–4). Whereas a large number of bacterial species may contaminate the peritoneal cavity, only a few go on to cause abscess formation. Studies have shown that the capsular polysaccharide complex of B fragilis subspecies fragilis is the primary virulence determinant for abscess formation, but that a mixture of aerobic and anaerobic organisms must be present.

C. Pathogenesis. After the initial peritoneal soiling, many of the bacteria are cleared by the diaphragmatic lymphatic system. Peritoneal macrophages and mesothelial cells elaborate proinflammatory mediators with resultant hyperemia, exudation of protein-rich fluid containing fibrinogen, and massive influx of phagocytic cells. The fibrin deposition helps to sequester bacteria, localize the inflammation, and subsequently decrease the incidence of bacteremia and mortality. However, by walling off the organisms, the fibrin may also help to protect the organisms from the normal host clearance mechanisms.

Within an abscess, factors such as hypoxia, low pH, hyperosmolarity, and bacterial synergy impair host defenses and promote microbial persistence. A mature abscess consists of a central core of necrotic debris, dead cells, and bacteria; a surrounding ring of neutrophils and macrophages; and a peripheral ring of smooth muscle cells and fibroblasts within a collagen capsule.

1. SUBPHRENIC ABSCESS

A subphrenic abscess can result from four different processes. Over one half of these abscesses develop after surgery involving the duodenum or stomach, biliary tract, or appendix, and 20–40% develop after rupture of a hollow viscus, such as a perforated peptic ulcer or acute appendicitis. A smaller number of subphrenic abscesses develop after penetrating trauma, and < 5% occur without any obvious precipitating factor.

Clinical Findings

A. Signs and Symptoms. Abdominal pain and tenderness in the right or left upper quadrants in conjunction with weight loss are common features of patients with subphrenic abscesses. They may present as an acute febrile illness with abdominal pain or as an insidious, chronic process. Patients may present with hiccups, jaundice, shoulder pain, chest pain, cough, dyspnea, tachypnea, or a pleural effusion. The chronic syndrome is seen more commonly in those patients who have previously received antimicrobial agents. Patients with the chronic presentation will often complain of intermittent fever, weight loss, anemia, and other nonspecific constitutional symptoms. Subphrenic abscess should always be considered in any patient presenting with fever of unknown origin, especially if the patient has had abdominal surgery within the previous few months.

B. Laboratory Findings. The pleural effusion is usually transudative in nature. A peripheral blood leukocytosis is almost always present.

C. Imaging. Radiographic techniques such as CT scan and ultrasonogram are the best approaches for establishing the diagnosis. Plain radiographs often show a pleural effusion, decreased diaphragmatic movement in conjunction with an elevated hemidiaphragm, and concomitant lower-lobe pneumonia or atelectasis. An upright chest x-ray may reveal wide separation of the upper margin of the gastric air bubble and the diaphragm.

Treatment

The primary treatment of a subphrenic abscess is drainage, either via a percutaneous approach or an open laparotomy. Antimicrobial therapy is aimed at the likely spectrum of organisms associated with the presumed pathogenic mechanism and may be modified after the receipt of culture results. Caution should be used when assessing culture results from patients who have already been receiving antimicrobial therapy.

2. DIVERTICULAR ABSCESS

Diverticulitis and diverticular abscess occur in the setting of pre-existing colonic diverticula. The latter are mucosal outpouchings located at points of maximal weakness in the colonic wall, and they typically develop in the left colon with increasing patient age. When fecaliths become impacted in diverticula, an inflammatory process ensues, sometimes leading to erosion and perforation of the colonic wall. The spectrum and severity of acute diverticulitis and diverticular abscess vary in relation to the extent of involvement of the colonic wall and the extent of inflammation. Stage

1 lesions consist of microabscesses in the colonic wall and peridiverticular inflammation. Stage 2 lesions are small, well-defined macroabscesses contained within the mesentery and epiploic appendages of the colon. Patients with well-defined macroabscesses that are associated with diverticular perforation have stage 3 disease. Patients with generalized peritonitis resulting from a perforated diverticular abscess or from gross fecal soilage have stage 4 disease. CT has been useful in diagnosing and staging this disease.

The treatment of diverticulitis should be based on the severity of disease. A traditional approach for stage 1 or 2 disease has been conservative medical management with bowel rest, low-residue diet, and antimicrobial therapy (Boxes 12–5 and 12–6). Operative intervention, if it becomes necessary, may involve one-, two-, or three-stage resection procedures. Catheter drainage techniques may safely eliminate the need for surgery in some patients or may reduce the complexity of the required surgical procedure. Clinical studies report a 71–88% success rate for preoperative percutaneous drainage and subsequent primary anastomosis in selected patients. There are limitations to the use of percutaneous drainage. For example, if anastomotic dehiscence is suspected, open surgical drainage and repair are preferred. The presence of multiple loculations, excessive cellular debris, high fluid viscosity, or an inadequate drainage route may also prevent successful percutaneous drainage. The percutaneous catheter should remain in place until clinical evidence of infection has resolved and the drainage from the catheter ceases.

3. VISCERAL ABSCESSES

Liver Abscess

Essentials of Diagnosis.
- 15–30% are cryptogenic.
- Most common cause is biliary tract disease.
- Portal vein bacteremia accounts for 12–15%.
- Patients present with fever, chills, weight loss.
- Abdominal discomfort is uncommon, but 60% will have liver tenderness.
- Peripheral blood leukocytosis is present.
- Alkaline phosphatase serum levels are elevated.
- CT scan is the diagnostic test of choice.

General Considerations
A. Epidemiology. The incidence of pyogenic liver abscess is 0.005% for all hospital admissions. Biliary tract disease, such as ascending cholangitis secondary to obstruction from stones, stricture, or malignancy, is the most common associated factor. Bacteremia, via the portal vein or less commonly the hepatic artery, is the cause of hepatic abscess in 12–15% of cases, and 15–30% of cases are considered cryptogenic.

B. Microbiology. Pyogenic liver abscesses principally contain enteric bacteria, such as *E coli* or *Proteus, Klebsiella,* or *Enterobacter* spp. (Box 12–7). Approximately two-thirds of these abscesses are polymicrobial, with one-third involving anaerobic organisms. *S aureus,* seen in 30% of cases, is a more common etiologic agent in children and in patients with bacteremia. Streptococci are seen in 7% of cases. Blood cultures are positive in 30–50% of patients with pyogenic liver abscess. *Entamoeba histolytica* accounts for only 10% of all liver abscesses.

Clinical Findings
A. Signs and Symptoms. Fever is the most common symptom and is present in nearly 90% of patients with hepatic abscess. Chills and weight loss occur in about half of cases. The abdominal features are often less pronounced, and many patients will present with fever of unknown origin, without abdominal symptoms. Two-thirds of patients will have an enlarged tender liver; care should be taken in trying to identify an area of point tenderness. Pyogenic hepatic abscess must be differentiated from amebic liver abscess. Patients will often have a history of travel or of significant diarrhea.

B. Laboratory Findings. Peripheral blood leukocytosis is present in most cases. Serum alkaline phosphatase levels are elevated in almost all patients, but elevated bilirubin levels are infrequent.

The identification of *E histolytica* trophozoites or cysts in the stool can be helpful, but stool examinations are negative in most patients. If there is concern about the possibility of amebic liver abscess, then serologic testing should be performed with an enzyme-linked immunosorbent assay.

C. Imaging. CT is the most accurate diagnostic technique and yields positive results in ≥ 95% of confirmed cases. Ultrasound is helpful in ≥ 80% of confirmed cases. A plain x-ray may provide an initial clue to the diagnosis by revealing an elevated right hemidiaphragm, a right pleural effusion, or an air fluid level within the abscess itself. An amebic ab-

BOX 12-7

Microbiology of Liver Abscess		
	Children	Adults
More Frequent	• As per adult AND • *Staphylococcus aureus*	• *Escherichia coli* • *Proteus* spp. • *Klebsiella* spp. • *Enterobacter* spp. • Streptococci
Less Frequent		• *Entamoeba histolytica*

scess is more likely to be solitary and confined to the right lobe of the liver.

Differential Diagnosis

The infectious differential diagnosis of pyogenic liver abscess includes amoebic abscess and hydatid cyst.

Prognosis

The prognosis of pyogenic liver abscess depends on the rapidity with which the diagnosis is made and treatment started. Recent studies have shown very high cure rates, in the 80–100% range. The advent of percutaneous drainage has significantly affected treatment, because open surgical drainage is no longer necessary in every patient.

Treatment. Some small pyogenic liver abscesses respond to antibiotic treatment alone, but most experts advocate drainage of any such abscess. Percutaneous drainage is now the initial procedure of choice and is accompanied by success rates of ≥ 89%. Surgical drainage is reserved for cases that fail to respond to the percutaneous approach. Antibiotics should be administered intravenously with broad coverage of enteric organisms such as anaerobes, *Enterobacteriaceae,* and streptococci, until the specific agents have been identified. Empiric therapy for pyogenic liver abscess is the same as that for peritonitis (see Box 12–5). Amebic liver abscess is treated with metronidazole, 750 mg three times per day for 5–10 days, plus a luminal agent such as diloxanide furoate, 500 mg three times per day for 10 days.

Pancreatic Abscess

Essentials of Diagnosis
- Most occur as a complication of pancreatitis.
- 30–50% are polymicrobial.
- Abdominal pain radiating to the back; vomiting.
- Elevated amylase (80–90% of cases).

General Considerations

A. Epidemiology. Most pancreatic abscesses occur after an episode of pancreatitis, which most commonly develops as a result of alcoholism, gallstones, or surgical trauma. Pancreatic abscess may also develop after a secondary infection of an established pancreatic pseudocyst. The spectrum of severity ranges from unapparent to fulminant. Two relatively distinct patterns can be distinguished. In the first, the patient recovers from an episode of pancreatitis, but 1–5 wk later develops fever, chills, leukocytosis, and abdominal pain. These patients usually have a well-defined abscess, as revealed by CT scan. The other group of patients is those who never recover from an episode of pancreatitis and continue to appear ill, with hemodynamic instability and fever. A CT scan is usually performed earlier in the course of disease than in the first group, and

hence the infected tissues, as seen on CT scan, have not yet liquefied, and necrosis is seen without evidence of an abscess. Lesser sac abscesses also occur after pancreatitis. These involve an extensive collection of necrotic tissue and pus in the retrogastric area and in the region behind the gastrocolic ligament.

B. Microbiology. Organisms contained within pancreatic and lesser sac abscesses are predominantly *E coli, Enterococcus* spp., and other enteric organisms (Box 12–4). Anaerobic organisms are less common than in other types of intra-abdominal abscesses. Nonenteric organisms including *Staphylococcus* spp., *Pseudomonas* spp., and, less often, *Candida* spp. may also be involved.

Clinical Findings. The diagnosis of pancreatic abscess can be difficult, because patients may present with indolent disease or may be clinically indistinguishable from patients with a noninfected pancreatic inflammatory mass.

A. Signs and Symptoms. Pancreatic abscess should be suspected in any patient with pancreatitis and persistent fever and ileus or if clinical deterioration occurs < 4 wk after initial improvement. The classic presentation includes nausea, vomiting, abdominal pain, and abdominal tenderness on examination. A mass may be palpable.

B. Laboratory Findings. Peripheral blood leukocytosis is usually present. Pancreatic amylase levels are elevated in < 50% of cases; however, liver function tests are often abnormal.

C. Imaging. The abdominal CT scan is the key to diagnosis, and percutaneous aspiration is often the most effective method of diagnosis. Chest radiographs commonly show an elevated hemidiaphragm, atelectasis, and a pleural effusion. Ultrasound is useful in defining a pancreatic mass, but cannot reliably distinguish between a pseudocyst and an abscess.

Differential Diagnosis. The differential diagnosis of pancreatic and lesser sac infections includes other visceral infections such as hepatic abscess, cholecystitis/cholangitis, and other intra-abdominal infections such as subphrenic abscesses.

Prognosis. The mortality rate in untreated pancreatic abscesses is very high. Survival is dependent on early surgical drainage. Complications include erosion of the infections from the pancreas into major blood vessels with subsequent intra-abdominal hemorrhage. The abscess can also spread retroperitoneally, and fistulas may develop with the transverse colon, stomach, and duodenum.

Treatment. Pancreatic abscesses are highly lethal (Boxes 12–5 and 12–6); without drainage, the mortality is 100%. Surgical drainage is considered mandatory. Although percutaneous drainage may be helpful for diagnosis and for treatment of well-circumscribed infected pancreatic pseudocysts, it has been less successful in the treatment of true pancreatic abscesses than with other types of intra-abdominal abscess. Removal of necrotic debris, in addition to abscess cavity drainage, seems to be very important in decreasing morbidity. Broad-spectrum antimicrobial agents should be chosen that are directed against aerobic enteric gram-negative rods and anaerobic organisms. Therapy should be revised on the basis of cultures of the abscess material or blood, especially if *Pseudomonas* or *Candida* spp. are present.

Splenic Abscess

Splenic abscesses are uncommon but appear to be increasing in incidence. Of all splenic abscesses, ~ 25% have no obvious source. The others are usually documented to be the result of bacteremia or septic embolization; infected splenic infarcts; or contiguous spread. Fevers (92%), chills, and left upper quadrant abdominal pain (39%) are the most common symptoms seen with this entity. Diaphragmatic, pleuropulmonary symptoms may predominate if the upper pole of the spleen is involved, whereas peritoneal symptoms may predominate if the lower pole of the spleen is infected. Causative organisms include *S aureus, Streptococcus* spp., *Salmonella* spp., and enteric bacteria. Mixed infections are common, and anaerobes such as *Bacteroides* spp. are often cultured. Fungi, such as *Candida* spp., are important causes of splenic abscess in immunocompromised hosts but rarely occur in immunocompetent hosts. CT is the most useful radiographic procedure. Antimicrobial therapy is mandatory. Although splenectomy has been regarded as the treatment of choice, percutaneous drainage has been increasingly used with significant success. Percutaneous drainage should be considered when the abscess is unilocular, when the patient has significant risks for a standard surgical approach, and when a safe drainage window is present.

APPENDICITIS

Clinical Findings

Appendicitis most commonly manifests as right lower quadrant abdominal pain accompanied by nausea and vomiting. Upon examination there is usually tenderness in the right lower quadrant, along with low-grade temperature. Initially, voluntary guarding may be present, followed by rebound tenderness and abdominal rigidity. Variations in the anatomic location of the appendix may result in variations in the location of pain and physical findings. For example, a retrocecal appendix may present as principally flank pain and tenderness, and a pelvic appendix may present with suprapubic pain. The findings of appendicitis are often nonspecific, and many patients are admitted and found to have another diagnosis.

The organisms associated with appendicitis are found in the normal colonic flora, such as *B fragilis, P melaninogenica, B wadsworthia,* anaerobic gram-positive cocci, and *Enterobacteriaceae.*

Differential Diagnosis

The differential diagnosis of patients presenting with suspected appendicitis includes mesenteric lymphadenitis, rubeola, and infectious mononucleosis.

Treatment

Therapy for appendicitis is surgical removal and drainage of any abscess that may be present. Antibiotics need only be started before surgery if it is felt that the appendix has been perforated.

CAECITIS (TYPHLITIS)

Caecitis is inflammation of the cecum that occurs in immunocompromised patients such as those with HIV infection and severe neutropenia. Pathologically, the bowel wall is edematous with marked thickening. The luminal surface has discrete areas of ulceration, which may coalesce. The actual pathogenesis of this entity is unclear, but it is thought that bacteria opportunistically invade ulcerations in the bowel during periods of neutropenia. The organisms proliferate and cause local destruction by the production of exotoxins.

Clinical Findings

Patients with caecitis may present with signs and symptoms similar to those of acute appendicitis with fever, abdominal pain, rebound tenderness in the right lower quadrant, and diarrhea.

Plain radiographs and CT scans are useful in delineating and identifying this entity.

Treatment

Mortality rate is high and, although management is controversial, antimicrobial therapy, as outlined in Boxes 12–5 and 12–6, together with surgical resection of necrotic bowel, is generally recommended.

ACUTE CHOLECYSTITIS

Clinical Findings

Of patients with acute cholecystitis, 90% have gallstones affecting the cystic duct. The initial clinical manifestations of obstruction of the cystic duct may be only epigastric pain, nausea, and vomiting. The duct obstruction may be transient, but if it persists, findings of acute cholecystitis may evolve. Most patients will report pain in the right upper quadrant and may have signs of peritoneal inflammation on examination. The gallbladder is palpable in 30–40% of cases, and most patients will have significant fever. Most patients will resolve their symptoms within 1–4 days. A patient presenting with repeated chills, fever, and jaundice or hypotension is likely to have suppurative cholangitis as a consequence of the common duct obstruction.

Laboratory data usually show an elevated leukocyte count. In addition, ~ 50% of patients will have a markedly elevated bilirubin level, 40% will have a marked elevation in their AST levels, and 25% will have an increased serum alkaline phosphatase. Organisms causing cholecystitis include enteric gramnegative bacilli and enterococci plus anaerobic organisms such as *Bacteroides* sp. (Box 12–4).

Acute gangrenous cholecystitis is seen most commonly in elderly diabetic males. Systemic symptoms are more severe, and the classic radiographic picture of the abdomen reveals gas within the gallbladder, a gas fluid level within the lumen of the gallbladder, and gas in a ring along the contours of the gallbladder wall.

Complications

Complications include perforation in 10–15% of cases. These patients are readily recognizable because they present with acute symptoms and signs of diffuse peritonitis.

Differential Diagnosis

The differential diagnosis of acute cholecystitis includes myocardial infarction, perforating ulcer, rightlower-lobe pneumonia, intestinal obstruction, hepatitis, peri-hepatitis, and acute disease involving the right kidney.

Treatment

Antibiotics to treat acute obstructive cholecystitis include those outlined in Boxes 12–5 and 12–6. Coverage should be directed at the organisms already discussed (Box 12–4), although anaerobes play a lesser role in acute cholecystitis. Immediate surgery should be performed for gangrenous cholecystitis, perforation, or suspected peri-cholecystic abscess. The timing of surgery for patients with uncomplicated acute cholecystitis is controversial.

CHOLANGITIS

Cholangitis is defined as various degrees of inflammation, infection, or both involving the hepatic and common bile duct.

Clinical Findings

Patients with cholangitis usually have a history compatible with prior gallbladder disease and present acutely with high fever, chills, and diffusive pain and tenderness over the liver. Jaundice is usually prominent, and in many cases shock and other findings of gram-negative bacteremia may be present. Eightyfive percent of patients fulfill the classic triad of fever, chills, and jaundice.

Laboratory findings include marked leukocytosis with increase in immature forms, serum bilirubin concentration of > 4 mg/dL, and serum alkaline phosphatase levels significantly higher than those encountered in acute cholecystitis. In contrast to uncomplicated cholecystitis, bacteremia is seen in 50% of patients with cholangitis, of which *E coli, Klebsiella* spp., *B fragilis,* and *E faecalis* are the most frequently isolated organisms.

Ultrasound and nuclear medicine scanning are the most useful imaging studies in the setting of acute cholangitis.

Complications

Complications of bacteremia and shock occur more commonly in patients with obstructive cholangitis. Perforation of the gallbladder can occur leading to hepatic abscess, peritonitis, or a peri-cholecystic abscess.

Differential Diagnosis

The differential diagnosis of patients with cholangitis includes acute cholecystitis, perforating ulcer, pancreatitis, intestinal obstruction, right lower lobe pneumonia, acute disease involving the right kidney, and bacteremic shock related to another focus of infection.

Treatment

Prompt antimicrobial therapy is mandatory with choices as outlined in Boxes 12–5 and 12–6. Prompt operative intervention with decompression of the common duct is mandatory in most cases of cholangitis. In those patients who do undergo surgery, operative cholangiography should be performed.

REFERENCES

Bennion RS et al: The bacteriology of gangrenous and perforated appendicitis-revisited. Ann Surg 1990;211:165.

Bhuva M et al: Spontaneous bacterial peritonitis: an update on evaluation, management, and prevention. Am J Med 1994;97:169.

Finegold SM, Wilson SE: Intra-abdominal infections and abscesses. In Mandell GL, Lorber B: *Atlas of Infectious Diseases,* Vol VII. Churchill Livingstone, 1996.

Levison MA: Percutaneous versus open operative drainage of intraabdominal abscesses. Infect Dis Clin North Am 1992;6:525.

McClean KL et al: Intraabdominal infections: a review. Clin Infect Dis 1994;19:100.

Onderdonk AB et al: The capsular polysaccharide of *Bacteroides fragilis* as a virulence factor: comparison of the pathogenic potential of encapsulated and unencapsulated strains. J Infect Dis 1977;136:82.

Pitcher WD, Musher DM: Critical importance of early diagnosis and treatment of intra-abdominal infection. Arch Surg 1982;117:328.

Skin & Soft-Tissue Infections

13

Mark P. Wilhelm, MD, FACP, & Randall S. Edson, MD, FACP

General Considerations

Skin and soft-tissue infections range in severity from self-limited localized inflammation to rapidly progressive, life- and limb-threatening necrosis with severe systemic toxicity. The clinician must be alert to clinical symptoms and signs that help to distinguish between an inflammatory process that is likely to respond to antimicrobial therapy alone and one that is rapidly progressing and requires prompt surgical intervention. We address the following clinical entities: primary pyodermas (localized bacterial infections involving the skin and/or its appendages), necrotizing soft-tissue infections, infections associated with human or animal bites, and diabetic foot infections.

When evaluating a patient with soft-tissue infection, it is important to define the host (eg, immune status, integrity of integument, etc), obtain a detailed patient history, and examine the patient with careful attention to local features. For example, a patient with impaired cell-mediated immunity, due either to exogenous factors (eg, corticosteroid therapy) or an underlying immunosuppressive disease process (eg, late-stage HIV infection or hematologic malignancy), may be susceptible to infection from opportunistic microorganisms (eg, *Cryptococcus neoformans,* nontuberculous mycobacteria, and filamentous fungi), causing cellulitis which may be difficult to distinguish from typical staphylococcal or streptococcal cellulitis.

Historical features to be carefully investigated include symptoms of systemic toxicity (eg, fever, chills, or prostration), the rate of progression of the inflammatory process, the presence or absence of significant pain in the involved area, recent environmental exposures, the occurrence of a precipitating event (eg, a puncture injury or animal bite), and the presence of an associated underlying disease. Necrotizing infections occur most commonly in association with advanced age or underlying comorbidity (eg, peripheral vascular disease, diabetes mellitus, alcoholism, malignancy, organ failure, or immunosuppressive therapy).

The presence or absence of fever and other signs of systemic toxicity (eg, hypotension, confusion, or oliguria) should be noted during physical examination. A careful examination of the involved area should include an assessment of the presence of erythema, induration, lymphangitis, crepitus, tenderness, duskiness (evidence of ischemia), and bullae, as well as the presence and characteristics of any drainage. The presence of gas in soft tissues is not a pathognomonic sign for the presence of anaerobic bacteria; more common causes of gas include mechanical trauma and infection with aerobic/facultative gram-negative bacilli such as *Escherichia coli.* Because the disease may progress rapidly, frequent reassessment and monitoring are essential.

Soft-tissue infection syndromes are best understood and defined by considering the specific anatomic structures involved and the microbial etiology. Figure 13–1 provides an overview of the anatomy of soft tissue that should help facilitate understanding of specific clinical syndromes.

THE PYODERMAS

IMPETIGO

Essentials of Diagnosis
- A vesiculopustular or crusted superficial skin infection usually caused by *Streptococcus pyogenes* and/or *Staphylococcus aureus.*
- Absence of pain and constitutional symptoms
- Healing occurs without scarring.

General Considerations

Impetigo is generally considered a disease of early childhood, although it is occasionally seen in the elderly and in immunocompromised patients of all ages. Impetigo is more common in warmer climates and is typically caused by group A streptococci (GAS) (ie, *S pyogenes*). *S aureus* may also cause impetigo, occasionally in combination with GAS (Box 13–1). A bullous form of impetigo, which occurs in newborn and very young children, is caused by *S aureus* of phage group II.

Clinical Findings

Impetigo is a very superficial bacterial skin infection that begins with the formation of vesicles and

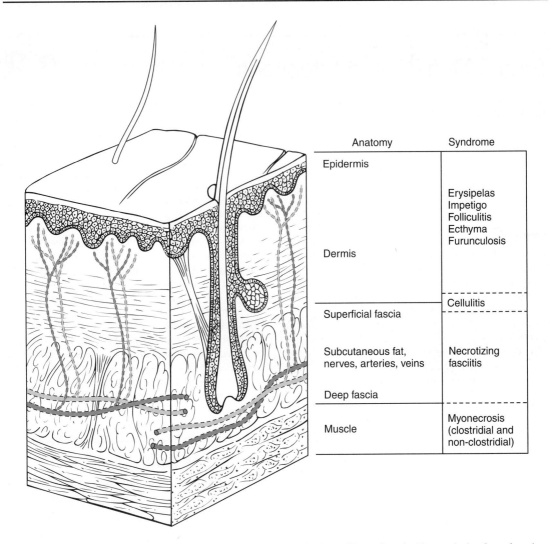

Anatomy	Syndrome
Epidermis	Erysipelas Impetigo Folliculitis Ecthyma Furunculosis
Dermis	
Superficial fascia	Cellulitis
Subcutaneous fat, nerves, arteries, veins	Necrotizing fasciitis
Deep fascia	
Muscle	Myonecrosis (clostridial and non-clostridial)

Figure 13–1. Anatomic and clinical classification of soft-tissue infections. (Reproduced with permission from American College of Chest Physicians.)

pustules in the epidermis beneath the stratum corneum. These lesions eventually rupture and release a honey-colored liquid, which forms a yellowish-brown crust. Impetigo typically develops on the face or on the extremities in areas that have sustained minor trauma. Pruritus is common—scratching of lesions can result in the spread of infection to previously uninvolved sites. The infection remains superficial and generally does not result in ulceration or scarring. Fever or other constitutional symptoms are absent or minimal.

Differential Diagnosis

Clinical entities that may be confused with impetigo include contact dermatitis, herpes simplex virus infection, and insect bites.

Complications

Occasionally, infections caused by nephritogenic strains of GAS can result in poststreptococcal glomerulonephritis. Mentioned in treatment section.

Treatment

Although impetigo may resolve spontaneously without anti-infective therapy, treatment is generally recommended for more rapid resolution of established lesions, deterring the formation of new lesions, preventing evolution to cellulitis, and possibly preventing the development of post-streptococcal glomerulonephritis, which occasionally follows infection caused by nephritogenic GAS strains (Box 13–2). Treatment options include a 10-day course of oral dicloxacillin sodium, a first-generation cepha-

BOX 13-1

Microbiology of Nonnecrotizing Soft-Tissue Infections

Syndrome	More Frequent	Less Frequent
Impetigo	S pyogenes, S aureus	
Erysipelas	S pyogenes	S aureus
Ecthyma	S aureus, S pyogenes	P aeruginosa
Cellulitis	S pyogenes, S aureus	H influenzae, P multocida, Enterobacteriaceae, Aeromonas spp.
Cutaneous abscess	S aureus	
Furuncle	S aureus	
Carbuncle	S aureus	
Folliculitis	S aureus	P aeruginosa

losporin (eg, cephalexin), clindamycin, or topical mupirocin. It has not been established conclusively that antibacterial therapy is effective in reducing the incidence of nephritis.

ERYSIPELAS

Essentials of Diagnosis

- Edematous, red, indurated, spreading lesion.
- Sharply demarcated, advancing, elevated margin.
- Occurs most commonly on the face.
- Pain, fever, and systemic toxicity are common.

General Considerations

Erysipelas is distinguished from cellulitis in that it involves the more superficial layers of the skin and cutaneous lymphatics and is more sharply demarcated; cellulitis tends to extend more deeply into subcutaneous tissues. It most commonly occurs on the face or extremities and is almost always caused by GAS. Rarely, other β-hemolytic streptococci or even S aureus may cause erysipelas. Organisms generally gain access through a break in the skin. Erysipelas tends to recur in an area of previous infection, partic-

ularly in patients with lymphedema or venous insufficiency. Facial erysipelas occasionally occurs after a streptococcal upper respiratory tract infection.

Clinical Findings

This lesion typically begins as a red spot, often at the nasolabial groove. Inflammation spreads, resulting in a tender, warm, glistening, red, edematous, and indurated area of skin. Vesicles or bullae are sometimes encountered on the surface, and there may be oozing of serous fluid. There is typically a distinct demarcation between involved and normal skin, and the area of inflammation is raised above the level of the surrounding skin. Desquamation of involved skin often occurs several days after the onset of symptoms. Skin necrosis does not occur, and healing is complete without scar formation. Associated symptoms include pain, malaise, fever, and chills. Occasionally, marked systemic toxicity is encountered.

Differential Diagnosis

The differential diagnosis of erysipelas includes cellulitis, contact dermatitis, thermal injury, and noninfectious inflammatory lesions such as the malar rash of systemic lupus erythematosus.

Treatment

In most cases of erysipelas, therapy is initiated with a parenteral agent active against β-hemolytic streptococci such as penicillin G or cefazolin (see Box 13–2). After clinical improvement is documented, therapy may be switched to an oral agent (eg, penicillin V or cephalexin). Parenteral therapy may not be necessary in mild cases with minimal systemic toxicity. Hot packs applied locally and aspirin are generally administered for symptomatic relief.

Prognosis

Skin necrosis does not occur in cases of erysipelas, and healing is generally complete without scar formation. However, involvement of superficial lymphatics may result in recurrence of erysipelas in the same area.

ECTHYMA

Essentials of Diagnosis

- Punched-out ulcers appearing beneath adherent crusts.
- Typically occur on lower extremities.

General Considerations

Ecthyma represents a deeper form of impetigo that begins as a vesicle and progresses to a punched-out ulcer that is surrounded by a violaceous border and covered by an adherent crust. It is most often caused by GAS, which either produce de novo lesions or in-

BOX 13–2

Empiric Therapy of Nonnecrotizing Soft-Tissue Infections

Syndrome	Treatment[1]	Penicillin Allergic
Impetigo	• Dicloxacillin, 250–500 mg four times daily, OR cephalexin, 250–500 mg four times daily, OR topical mupirocin	• Clindamycin, 150–300 mg four times daily OR erythromycin, 250–500 mg four times daily, or topical mupirocin
Erysipelas	• Parenteral: nafcillin, 2 g every 4–6 h, OR cefazolin, 1 g every 8h • Oral: dicloxacillin, 500 mg four times daily OR cephalexin, 500 mg four times daily	• Parenteral: clindamycin, 600–900 mg every 8 h, OR vancomycin, 15 mg/kg every 12 h • Oral: clindamycin, 300 mg q.i.d.
Ecthyma	• Dicloxacillin, 500 mg every 6 h, OR cephalexin, 500 mg every 6 h • For ecthyma gangrenosum caused by *P aeruginosa:* piperacillin 3–4 g IV every 4–6 h + gentamicin or tobramycin, 1.5 mg/kg every 8 h OR ceftazidime, 1–2 gm IV every 8 h +/– gentamicin or tobramycin	• Clindamycin, 150–300 mg four times daily • Ciprofloxacin, 400 mg IV or 750 mg orally every 12 h
Cellulitis	• Parenteral: nafcillin, 1–2 g every 4–6 h, OR cefazolin, 1 g every 8 h • Oral: dicloxacillin, 500 mg four times daily OR cephalexin, 500 mg four times daily	• Parenteral: clindamycin, 600–900 mg every 8 h, OR vancomycin, 15 mg/kg every 12 h • Oral: clindamycin, 150–300 mg four times daily
Cutaneous abscess	• Parenteral: nafcillin, 1–2 g every 4–6 h, OR cefazolin, 1 g every 8 h • Oral: dicloxacillin, 250–500 mg four times daily OR cephalexin, 250–500 mg four times daily	• Parenteral: clindamycin, 600–900 mg every 8 h, OR vancomycin, 15 mg/kg every 12 h • Oral: clindamycin, 150–300 mg four times daily
Furuncle	• Antimicrobial therapy generally not indicated; if associated cellulitis: dicloxacillin, 250–500 mg four times daily OR cephalexin, 250–500 mg four times daily	• Clindamycin, 150–300 mg four times daily
Carbuncle	• Parenteral: nafcillin, 1–2 g every 4–6 h OR cefazolin, 1 g every 8 h • Oral: dicloxacillin, 500 mg dour times daily OR cephalexin, 500 mg four times daily	• IV: clindamycin, 600–900 mg every 8 h, OR vancomycin, 15 mg/kg every 12 h • Oral: clindamycin, 300 mg four times daily
Folliculitis	• Antimicrobial therapy generally not indicated	

[1]Suggested dosages are for patients with normal renal function; quinolone antibacterial agents should be avoided in children and adolescents < 18 years old; pediatric dosages can be found in the *Pocket Book of Pediatric Antimicrobial Therapy,* 13th ed. Williams & Wilkins, 1998.

fect preexisting skin lesions such as insect bites, eczema, or excoriations. Lesions with a similar clinical appearance may be encountered with bacteremia caused by *Pseudomonas aeruginosa* (ecthyma gangrenosum).

Clinical Findings

Ecthyma typically occurs as a single erythematous ulceration or multiple erythematous ulcerations with overlying crusts on the lower extremities, especially in areas of minor trauma. Because of the deeper level of infection, ecthyma—unlike impetigo—often heals with scarring.

Treatment

The approach to treatment of ecthyma is the same

as for impetigo. Beyond removal of crusts and debris with warm compresses, surgery is generally not indicated. Ecthyma caused by *P aeruginosa* requires parenteral antipseudomonal therapy and occasionally débridement (see Box 13–2).

CELLULITIS

Essentials of Diagnosis

- Diffuse spreading infection of skin and subcutaneous tissue.
- Inflammatory lesion is hot, red, with diffuse or vague margins.
- Systemic toxicity is variable.

General Considerations

Cellulitis is a superficial infection of skin and subcutaneous tissues characterized by erythema, induration, and tenderness. Local trauma or underlying skin lesions are common predisposing conditions. Because inflammation from an episode of cellulitis, erysipelas, or lymphangitis can result in obstruction of lymphatic drainage, initial episodes are associated in many cases with an increased predisposition to develop recurrent infections involving the same area. Most cases are caused by either *S pyogenes* or *S aureus.* Mixed streptococcal and staphylococcal infection may also occur. Less common bacterial etiologies include groups B, C, and G streptococci, *Haemophilus influenzae* (in children), *Streptococcus pneumoniae, Pasteurella multocida* (cat or dog bites), enteric bacilli (*Enterobacteriaceae*), anaerobic bacteria, *Legionella* spp., *P aeruginosa, Helicobacter cinaedi* (immunocompromised patients), *Aeromonas hydrophila* (freshwater exposure), and *Vibrio vulnificus* (seawater exposure). *Erysipelothrix rhusiopathiae* is the etiologic agent of erysipeloid, which is a violaceous cellulitis of the hands occurring in persons handling raw fish, meat, or poultry. Nonbacterial causes of cellulitis, such as *Cryptococcus neoformans,* filamentous fungi, and nontuberculous mycobacteria, should be considered in unusual cases, particularly with immunocompromised patients.

Clinical Findings

A. Signs and Symptoms. Cellulitis typically presents with erythema, warmth, swelling, and local pain and tenderness. In contrast to erysipelas, the margins of the inflammatory erythematous lesion are neither elevated nor sharply demarcated from surrounding uninvolved tissue. The involved area is often quite extensive and may progress rapidly, particularly in patients with chronic dependent edema. Lymphangitis with regional lymphadenopathy is common. Although it is presumed that cellulitis often begins at the site of a break in the skin, this is often not clinically apparent. Systemic features of cellulitis vary considerably, ranging from the complete absence of systemic illness to severe systemic toxicity. Fever, chills, and malaise accompany most cases of significant bacterial cellulitis.

B. Laboratory Findings. Blood cultures should be obtained in most cases of cellulitis, before the initiation of empiric antimicrobial therapy. Although the culturing of a punch biopsy specimen or leading-edge aspirate has often been advocated, positive cultures occur in only ~ 20% of cases. This diagnostic approach is usually not necessary and is in practice rarely pursued in cases of uncomplicated bacterial cellulitis. However, material for culture should be obtained by aspiration, or biopsy should be considered in unusual cases, particularly in cases of necrotizing infection and in immunocompromised patients, who may develop soft-tissue infections that are caused by unusual pathogens.

C. Imaging. Most cases of simple bacterial cellulitis do not require radiologic investigations. Plain radiographs may disclose the presence of foreign bodies, adjacent bony involvement, or gas in soft tissues.

Differential Diagnosis

The differential diagnosis of cellulitis includes a wide variety of infectious and noninfectious inflammatory lesions, including erysipelas, erysipeloid, thermal injury, infiltrative malignancies, angioedema, neutrophilic dermatosis (Sweet's syndrome), erythema chronicum migrans, and cutaneous herpes zoster.

Complications

Although many instances of limited cellulitis resolve without treatment, cellulitis can cause serious disease by spreading rapidly via lymph vessels and the bloodstream. Patients who have undergone saphenous venectomy for myocardial revascularization may develop recurrent acute cellulitis in the involved limb, often with associated lymphangitis. These episodes are generally caused by non-group A β-hemolytic streptococci and commonly occur in association with tinea pedis, which may serve as a nidus for streptococcal colonization. Episodes tend to recur over many months or even years. Treatment of the dermatophytic fungal infection may abolish recurrent cellulitis episodes. Recurrent streptococcal cellulitis also occurs in patients with lymphedema of a limb, which may be caused by mastectomy, radiation therapy, radical pelvic surgery, or neoplastic involvement of lymph nodes. Although most cases of cellulitis resolve without suppurative complications, localized inflammation may occasionally evolve into a subcutaneous abscess that requires drainage.

Treatment

Uncomplicated bacterial cellulitis is most commonly caused by β-hemolytic streptococci or *S aureus.* Because the clinical features of streptococcal, staphylococcal, or combined infections are usually similar, in most cases therapy is directed against both streptococci and staphylococci without confirmation of the etiology. If the infection is mild, an oral agent such as dicloxacillin or a first-generation cephalosporin (eg, cephalexin) may be selected (see Box 13–2). Either a semisynthetic penicillin (eg, nafcillin or oxacillin) or a first-generation cephalosporin (eg, cefazolin) would be an appropriate first-line parenteral agent for mild cellulitis of undetermined etiology. Penicillin remains the drug of choice for streptococcal cellulitis, such as with recurrent cellulitis in a limb after saphenous venectomy.

Prognosis

The prognosis of most cases of simple bacterial cellulitis is good with appropriate antimicrobial therapy. Scarring is generally not encountered, and suppurative complications occur in a minority of cases. Episodes of cellulitis may heal with the development of lymphedema, thereby potentially predisposing the patient to recurrent episodes in the same location.

Prevention

Treatment of tinea and management of edema in involved limbs with appropriate mechanical measures such as support hose may lessen the risk for the development of bacterial cellulitis.

CUTANEOUS ABSCESSES

Essentials of Diagnosis

- A fluctuant, erythematous, tender, cutaneous nodule.
- Associated purulent drainage may occur.
- Features of systemic illness are variably present.

General Considerations

Cutaneous abscesses most commonly evolve by local extension of a primary epidermal/dermal infection. Although localized suppuration occurs, host defenses prevent systemic spread of the infection. Thus, cutaneous abscesses tend to be superficial, single, and well localized, and are not associated with systemic toxicity. A subcutaneous abscess may also arise through trauma, such as from puncture injuries. Abscesses may occur by hematogenous seeding of cutaneous/subcutaneous tissue, as is occasionally seen in the setting of S aureus bacteremia. Cutaneous abscesses may occur in any location, although they most commonly involve the head, neck, extremities, and perineal region. Cutaneous abscesses usually contain organisms that reflect the flora of the overlying skin or adjacent mucous membrane. Abscesses on the trunk or extremities are commonly caused by S aureus or streptococci.

Clinical Findings

Cutaneous abscesses are recognized clinically as tender, painful, erythematous nodules that become fluctuant. There may be evidence of surrounding inflammation or an overlying pustule.

Complications

Complications of cutaneous abscesses include bacteremia and spread of infection into adjacent structures, including bone or joints.

Treatment

Most cutaneous abscesses require incision and drainage when demonstrable fluctuance is present. If only a tender nodule is encountered, needle aspiration may be performed, followed by incision and drainage if pus is recovered. Because of the potential for extension to the cavernous sinus, lesions on the nose or lips should generally not be incised or otherwise manipulated. If the lesion is effectively drained surgically, antibiotic therapy may not be necessary. Antibiotic therapy is generally reserved for high-risk patients with impaired host defenses or for patients in whom there is evidence of bloodstream invasion or extension of infection to adjacent tissues (see Box 13–2). Because drainage of subcutaneous abscesses may cause transient bacteremia, antibiotic prophylaxis should be given for patients with underlying cardiac valvular disease. Empiric adjunctive antibiotic therapy should be based on the most likely bacterial pathogen(s). In most cases, a first-generation oral cephalosporin or an antistaphylococcal penicillin would be an appropriate agent. Definitive treatment can subsequently be selected based on culture and susceptibility data.

FURUNCLES AND CARBUNCLES

Clinical Findings

Furuncles present as tender, firm, erythematous nodules that become fluctuant. They develop from folliculitis, spreading to the subcutaneous layers of the skin. Furuncles occur in moist areas of skin that contain hair follicles and are subject to friction (eg, neck, axillae, buttocks, and face). An inflammatory nodule becomes fluctuant with subsequent spontaneous drainage of pus. Predisposing conditions include diabetes mellitus, corticosteroid therapy, and use of injected drugs.

A carbuncle is a more extensive, multiloculated subcutaneous lesion that occurs most commonly at the nape of the neck. It often drains along hair follicles from deep, septate pockets of suppuration; multiple sinus tracts are frequently present. Carbuncles tend to occur in areas covered by thick inelastic subcutaneous tissue such as the nape of the neck, back, or thighs; they are generally quite painful.

Both furuncles and carbuncles are almost always

caused by *S aureus*. Although systemic manifestations are not encountered with furuncles, fever and other systemic symptoms are frequently seen with carbuncles. Patients with recurrent furunculosis should be evaluated for the possibility of nasal carriage of *S aureus*.

Complications

Manipulation of furuncles on the upper lip or near the nasolabial groove should be avoided, because it may result in cavernous sinus thrombosis. Staphylococcal bacteremia may be encountered with large, inflamed lesions, possibly resulting in metastatic abscesses.

Treatment

For minor furuncles, moist heat should provide adequate therapy. Topical or systemic anti-infective therapy is generally not indicated. Larger furuncles and carbuncles require incision and drainage as well as oral or, occasionally, parenteral antistaphylococcal therapy.

FOLLICULITIS

Clinical Findings

Folliculitis is a bacterial infection that involves the ostium of a hair follicle, typically on the face, buttocks, or the extensor surface of an extremity. The lesions consist of small, tender erythematous papules or pustules that eventually drain, become crusted, and spontaneously heal. Lesions in different stages of evolution are often present simultaneously. Most cases of folliculitis are caused by *S aureus,* although folliculitis caused by *P aeruginosa* may be encountered in the setting of contaminated swimming pools or hot tubs. Healing occurs spontaneously in most cases, either by drainage or regression. Scarring is distinctly uncommon.

Treatment

Anti-infective therapy is generally not indicated. Local heat may provide symptomatic benefit.

NECROTIZING SOFT-TISSUE INFECTIONS

Essentials of Diagnosis

- Usually rapidly progressive infections with evidence of soft-tissue necrosis.
- Marked systemic toxicity generally but not invariably present.
- Multisystem organ failure may occur.

- Involved area generally painful.
- Variable microbiology—monomicrobial (eg, GAS, *Clostridium* spp.) vs polymicrobial.

General Considerations

Necrotizing soft-tissue infections are characterized by rapidly progressive inflammation and necrosis variably involving skin, subcutaneous fat, fascia, and occasionally muscle. Many classification schemes have been proposed for necrotizing soft-tissue infections, but they are often inconsistent and imprecise. In many cases, a variety of terms have been given to closely related or essentially identical processes. Furthermore, the classifications have been difficult to apply clinically and have resulted in considerable confusion in clinical practice. In approaching this group of infections, emphasis should be placed on differentiating necrotizing infections, which require prompt surgical intervention, from non-necrotizing infections, which usually do not.

Early clinical signs of a necrotizing infection include the presence of bullae, edema that extends beyond the area of erythema, focal cutaneous ecchymosis/ischemia, crepitus, cutaneous anesthesia, and the absence of lymphangitis. Early in the course of a necrotizing infection, patients complain of severe pain, usually out of proportion to the physical findings. Although skin changes are usually present, cutaneous evidence of necrotizing fasciitis may be absent. The most clinically important distinctions to be made in defining necrotizing soft-tissue infection syndromes are the tissues/structures involved and the microbial etiology.

Most necrotizing soft-tissue infections are polymicrobial, although there are two important exceptions: clostridial myonecrosis and type-2 necrotizing fasciitis caused by invasive GAS. All necrotizing soft-tissue infections should be cultured and require prompt surgical débridement and parenteral antimicrobial therapy (Boxes 13–3 and 13–4).

Ultrasonography is helpful in evaluating the possibility of complicating abscess formation and for providing imaging capability at the bedside in emergency situations. Although computed tomography scans provide considerable information about the extent of infection, magnetic resonance imaging provides the greatest resolution and level of detail in the definition of complex soft-tissue infection syndromes. In cases of suspected deep and/or necrotizing infections that are not clinically obvious, magnetic resonance imaging scans may provide substantial diagnostic benefit. However, pursuing imaging studies should not delay life-saving surgical intervention, which is also the most definitive mode of diagnosis. Detection of a significantly elevated serum creatine kinase level suggests involvement of muscle in the disease process.

The key to a successful outcome in the treatment of necrotizing soft-tissue infections is early diagnosis

BOX 13-3

Microbiology of Necrotizing Soft-Tissue Infections

Syndrome	Usual Microbiology
Clostridial myonecrosis (gas gangrene)	• *Clostridium* spp. (*C perfringens*, occasionally *C septicum*, or others)
Type-1 (polymicrobial) necrotizing fasciitis	• Mixed aerobes and anaerobes
Type-2 (streptococcal) necrotizing fasciitis	• *S pyogenes*
Progressive bacterial synergistic gangrene	• Microaerophilic streptococci Plus *S aureus* (or occasionally *Proteus* spp.)
Clostridial anaerobic cellulitis	• *C perfringens*
Nonclostridial anaerobic cellutitis	• Mixed aerobes and anaerobes

and treatment. Early findings of necrotizing infections may appear similar to nonoperative cellulitis; therefore, correct early diagnosis requires a high index of suspicion and an awareness of specific clinical findings that suggest a necrotizing infection.

Classification problems notwithstanding, several relatively well-defined necrotizing soft-tissue infection syndromes regularly encountered in the medical literature are discussed in the following sections.

CLOSTRIDIAL MYONECROSIS (GAS GANGRENE)

General Considerations

Clostridial myonecrosis (gas gangrene), usually caused by *Clostridium perfringens,* is an extremely serious, rapidly progressive infection that poses imminent risk to limb and life. It typically occurs in settings characterized by the presence of contaminated, devitalized tissue. Predisposing conditions include traumatic injuries such as compound fractures, penetrating wounds (eg, combat-induced wounds), surgical wounds after enteric surgery, and limb injuries in the setting of advanced arterial insufficiency.

Clinical Findings

There is rapid destruction of muscle and usually severe systemic toxicity. Prompt débridement of all nonviable tissue, often leading to amputation, is essential for cure. At surgery, involved muscle is typically pale and edematous and does not contract when probed.

A variant syndrome, referred to as spontaneous nontraumatic gas gangrene, occurs in the absence of trauma in patients with underlying diseases such as colon cancer, leukemia, or diabetes mellitus. It is commonly caused by *Clostridium septicum* and is thought to occur via hematogenous seeding.

The onset of gas gangrene is sudden, with severe pain, hypotension, and systemic toxicity. The affected limb becomes edematous; the surrounding skin is pale; a blood-tinged, serous discharge may be noted; and the surrounding tissue finally becomes dusky with fluid-filled bullae. In addition, gas may be palpable in the tissues.

Complications

Severe tissue destruction is generally encountered with gas gangrene, which may lead to loss of limb or death.

Treatment

When *Clostridium* spp. have been demonstrated or are highly suspected, high-dose penicillin G is generally considered the drug of choice (see Box 13–4). Although some studies have shown increasing resistance of clostridia to penicillin, almost all strains of *C perfringens* remain susceptible. Metronidazole, imipenem, clindamycin, and ampicillin/sulbactam or piperacillin/tazobactam are possible alternatives. It should be noted that clindamycin is relatively inactive in vitro against some strains of *Clostridia* spp. The combination of penicillin and clindamycin is often used in the setting of clostridial myonecrosis, largely based on experimental evidence in animals.

Although it is reasonable to use adjunctive hyperbaric oxygen therapy when available, under no circumstances should débridement be delayed to facilitate transport to a facility with hyperbaric oxygen facilities. Prompt surgical débridement should be performed, with removal of all devitalized tissue.

Prognosis

Prompt recognition and adequate débridement of devitalized tissues are essential to minimize tissue loss. More proximal amputation may sometimes be necessary if initial débridement is inadequate.

Prevention

Meticulous care of contaminated traumatic wounds, including thorough débridement of devitalized tissue and foreign material, is essential to lessen the likelihood of the development of gas gangrene.

BOX 13–4

Empiric Therapy of Necrotizing Soft-Tissue Infections

Syndrome	Treatment[1]	Penicillin Allergic
Clostridial anaerobic cellulitis	• Penicillin G, 24 million U IV every 24 h by continuous infusion	• Metronidazole, 500 mg IV every 6 h, **OR** clindamycin 900 mg IV q8h
Type 1 (polymicrobial) necrotizing fasciitis	• Piperacillin/tazobactam, 3.375 g IV every 6 h; **OR** imipenem, 500 mg IV every 6 h; **OR** ceftriaxone, 1–2 g IV once daily + metronidazole, 500 mg IV every 6 h	• Vancomycin, 15 mg/kg every 12 h + ciprofloxacin, 400 mg IV every 12 h + metronidazole, 500 mg IV every 6 h
Type 2 (streptococcal) necrotizing fasciitis	• Penicillin G, 24 million U IV every 24 h by continuous infusion + clindamycin, 900 mg IV every 8 h (+/– IVIG[2])	• Clindamycin, 900 mg IV every 8 h (+/– IVIG[2])
Progressive bacterial synergistic gangrene	• Piperacillin/tazobactam 3.375 g IV every 6 h	• Clindamycin, 900 mg IV every 8 h +/– ciprofloxacin, 400 mg IV every 12 h **OR** vancomycin, 15 mg/kg IV every 12 h +/– ciprofloxacin, 400 mg IV every 12 h
Clostridial myonecrosis (gas gangrene)	• Penicillin G, 24 million U IV every 24 h by continuous infusion (+/– clindamycin, 900 mg IV every 8 h)	• Metronidazole, 500 mg IV every 6 h
Nonclostridial anaerobic cellulitis	• Piperacillin/tazobactam, 3.375 g IV every 6 h, **OR** imipenem, 500 mg IV every 6 h, **OR** ceftriaxone, 1–2 g IV once daily + metronidazole, 500 mg IV every 6 h	• Vancomycin, 15 mg/kg every 12 h + ciprofloxacin, 400 mg IV every 12 h + metronidazole, 500 mg IV every 6 h

[1]Suggested dosages are for patients with normal renal function; quinolone antibacterial agents should be avoided in children or adolescents < 18 years of age; pediatric dosages can be found in the *Pocket Book of Pediatric Antimicrobial Therapy*, 13th ed. Williams & Wilkins, 1998.
[2]IVIG, Intravenous immunoglobin

NECROTIZING FASCIITIS

General Considerations

Necrotizing fasciitis is an infectious process that progressively destroys the subcutaneous fascia and fat with relative sparing of underlying muscle. Although it may affect any part of the body, including the abdominal wall and perineum, necrotizing fasciitis occurs most commonly on the extremities.

Clinical Findings

Early findings of necrotizing fasciitis may resemble cellulitis. However, the process spreads rapidly and is usually associated with severe pain and significant systemic toxicity. Edema may extend beyond the area of cutaneous inflammation. Infection spreads rapidly along fascial planes and through venous and lymphatic channels. Although there is often evidence of cutaneous necrosis, necrotizing fasciitis may occur with relatively intact overlying skin, particularly with an early presentation. Patchy cutaneous anesthesia, gangrene, or both may occur as a result of extensive undermining of subcutaneous tissue, which contains vascular structures and nerves. Patients generally appear "toxic," and hypotension and multiorgan failure often develop. The diagnosis is usually readily confirmed at surgery by the finding of gray necrotic fascia without frank pus and by easy dissection and undermining of the wound. Histopathologic findings include fascial necrosis, thrombosis of small arteries and veins, and the presence of microorganisms on Gram stains.

Based on microbial etiology, necrotizing fasciitis syndromes are classified into two types. Type-1 necrotizing fasciitis is a polymicrobial infectious process in which at least one anaerobic species (usually *Bac-*

teroides or *Peptostreptococcus* spp., or both) is isolated in combination with one or more facultative species, such as gram-negative bacilli of the *Enterobacteriaceae* family or streptococci (but not GAS). Fournier's gangrene represents a form of polymicrobial necrotizing fasciitis involving the male genitalia, typically occurring in diabetic patients. Synergistic necrotizing cellulitis represents essentially the same process as type-1 necrotizing fasciitis, although it often involves muscle. Type-2 necrotizing fasciitis, occasionally referred to as hemolytic streptococcal gangrene, is caused by invasive GAS, which may rarely be present in combination with another organism such as *S aureus*. There has been a marked increase in the reported incidence of invasive GAS infection over recent years. It often begins at the site of minor trauma. Although it typically occurs in the elderly and in patients with underlying medical conditions, it has also been encountered in otherwise healthy young patients. Varicella infection has also been shown to be a risk factor for the development of invasive *S pyogenes* infections. Although muscle involvement can occur, soft tissue gas is not seen. This type of necrotizing fasciitis is often seen in association with the streptococcal toxic shock syndrome. The use of nonsteroidal anti-inflammatory agents may adversely affect the clinical outcome, and there is a significant risk of nosocomial or domestic transmission.

Differential Diagnosis

The differential diagnosis of necrotizing fasciitis includes cellulitis, clostridial myonecrosis, myositis, and anaerobic and other necrotizing forms of cellulitis.

Complications

Complications of necrotizing fasciitis include compartment syndromes, progressive limb necrosis leading to amputation, bacteremia, multiorgan failure, and death.

Treatment

In all instances where drainage is present, aerobic and anaerobic cultures and a Gram stain should be performed. Initial anti-infective therapy may then be based on the results of the Gram stain morphology (see Box 13–4). When only streptococci are seen on Gram stain in the setting of a necrotizing infectious process, then high-dose penicillin G should be administered. It has been suggested, from limited experimental data and anecdotal clinical experience, that clindamycin should be administered in addition to penicillin in cases of invasive infection caused by *S pyogenes,* because of the theoretical ability of clindamycin to interfere with streptococcal toxin production. There is also anecdotal evidence supporting the use of intravenous gammaglobulin in cases of streptococcal necrotizing fasciitis. No controlled data are available to clearly define the potential additive benefit of this costly adjunctive therapeutic modality, however.

When the Gram stain reveals several bacterial morphologies, broad-spectrum antibacterial therapy should be directed at gram-positive and gram-negative anaerobic and aerobic/facultative organisms. Polymicrobial Gram stain findings may be encountered in many of the polymicrobial syndromes described above, including type-1 necrotizing fasciitis, progressive synergistic gangrene, and nonclostridial anaerobic cellulitis. Reasonable initial therapeutic regimens, pending definitive culture and susceptibility data, include (1) a third-generation cephalosporin (eg, cefotaxime or ceftriaxone) in combination with metronidazole or clindamycin; (2) ampicillin, gentamicin, and clindamycin or metronidazole; (3) piperacillin/tazobactam monotherapy; or (4) imipenem monotherapy.

Prognosis

The prognosis of necrotizing fasciitis largely depends on early recognition, prompt institution of antimicrobial therapy, and early complete débridement of all devitalized tissue.

PROGRESSIVE BACTERIAL SYNERGISTIC GANGRENE

This soft-tissue infection syndrome, also known as Meleney's synergistic gangrene, typically results from infection at the site of an abdominal surgical incision, around an enterostomy, in association with an abdominal fistula exit site, or in association with a chronic lower-extremity ulcer. As the term synergistic implies, this infection typically has a polymicrobial etiology and most commonly involves anaerobic or microaerophilic streptococci with *S aureus* or occasionally facultative gram-negative bacilli such as *Proteus* spp.

Progressive bacterial synergistic gangrene begins as a localized area of swelling, erythema, and tenderness that becomes ulcerated and gradually enlarges. Fever is usually minimal or absent. The ulcer is characteristically encircled by gangrenous skin with surrounding violaceous skin.

ANAEROBIC CELLULITIS

Clostridial anaerobic cellulitis describes an infection, usually caused by *C perfringens,* that typically involves devitalized subcutaneous tissues that result from a contaminated or inadequately débrided traumatic or surgical wound. Nonclostridial anaerobic cellulitis is clinically similar to clostridial anaerobic cellulitis but is caused by non–spore-forming anaerobic bacteria (eg, *Bacteroides* spp., peptostreptococci, and peptococci) often in conjunction with facultative organisms such as *Enterobacteriaceae,* streptococci, or staphylococci. Gram stains and cultures of exudate aspirated from the lesion will typically suggest the polymicrobial nature of this process.

Gas formation is evident in skin and subcutaneous tissue on examination and radiographically, and thin, malodorous drainage may emanate from the wound. There is no appreciable involvement of deeper structures such as fascia or muscle. The onset is generally gradual, and there is usually mild local pain and systemic toxicity, allowing clinical differentiation from the more fulminant clostridial myonecrosis.

INFECTIONS ASSOCIATED WITH HUMAN OR ANIMAL BITES

Essentials of Diagnosis

- Acute soft-tissue infection occurring at the site of a bite injury.
- May involve deeper structures such as joint space, tenosynovium, or bone.
- Etiology often polymicrobial—*P multocida* commonly seen with dog bite or cat bite infections.

General Considerations

Human and animal bite wounds account for ~ 1% of emergency room visits. Half of all Americans at some time during their lives are bitten by a cat or dog. These wounds can be clinically quite deceptive, because what initially appears to be a minor wound may involve the subjacent joint space or bone, resulting in serious complications. Box 13–5 summarizes the most common causes of each type of infection.

A. Dog Bites. Dog bites account for ~ 80% of animal bite wounds; 15–20% of these wounds become infected. The risk of infection is increased in the presence of associated crush or puncture injuries

and involvement of the hand. Organisms generally encountered are found in the oral flora of dogs: *P multocida, S aureus,* streptococci, and occasionally *Capnocytophaga canimorsus, Eikenella corrodens,* other gram-negative bacilli, and anaerobes.

B. Cat Bites. Cats have slender and extremely sharp teeth that typically cause a puncture-type injury with potential involvement of bone or joint. The overall rate of wound infection after cat bites is > 50%, with a proportionate increase in the incidence of associated septic arthritis and osteomyelitis. *P multocida* is the most frequently isolated pathogen, occurring in > 50% of cases. Other organisms, similar to those associated with dog bite injuries, may also be recovered.

C. Human Bites. Human bites tend to be more serious and more prone to infection than animal bites, in part because of the typical mechanisms of injury (eg, clenched fist and occlusional injuries). Clenched-fist injuries typically involve trauma to the metacarpophalangeal joints, and thus are at high risk for complications such as deep soft-tissue infections, septic arthritis, and osteomyelitis. Potential pathogens include *S aureus, H influenzae, E corrodens,* and anaerobic bacteria, including strains that produce β-lactamases.

Treatment

Wounds should be irrigated with saline and may require débridement and surgical repair depending on the severity of the injury. The risk for rabies infection should be assessed carefully and appropriate prophylaxis given, if indicated. Tetanus prophylaxis should also be addressed. If a wound is brought to clinical attention > 24 h after injury or if there are already signs of infection, it should be left open. If a patient presents with an infected wound, cultures for aerobic and anaerobic bacteria should be obtained. Radiography should be pursued if an underlying fracture is suspected. In general, relatively trivial bite wounds may not require antibiotic therapy, although it may be prudent to administer a short (3- to 5-day) course of a prophylactic oral antibiotic (eg, amoxicillin/clavulanate) in the setting of a more significant bite injury (especially for cat bite injuries) (Box 13–6). For an infected wound requiring hospitalization, ampicillin/sulbactam would be a reasonable initial empiric therapeutic choice.

BOX 13–5

Microbiology of Bite-Associated Infections

Type of Bite	Usual Microbiology
Dog	• Streptococci, *S aureus, Eikenella corrodens, Pasteurella multocida, Capnocytophaga canimorsus,* anaerobes
Cat	• *P multocida,* streptococci, anaerobes
Human	• *S aureus, E corrodens, H influenzae,* anaerobes

DIABETIC FOOT INFECTIONS

Essentials of Diagnosis

- Acute, subacute, or chronic soft-tissue infection of diabetic feet, often with associated ulceration.

BOX 13-6

Empiric Therapy of Bite-Associated Infections

Type of Bite	Treatment[1]	Penicillin Allergic[2]
Dog	• Oral: amoxicillin/clavulanate, 500 mg three times daily • Parenteral: ampicillin/sulbactam, 3 g every 6 h	• Oral: Levofloxacin 500 mg once daily **OR** gatifloxacin 400 mg once daily **PLUS** Clindamycin 300 mg every 6 h **OR** metronidazole 500 mg every 6 h
Cat	• Oral: amoxicillin/clavulanate, 500 mg three times daily • Parenteral: ampicillin/sulbactam, 3 g every 6 h	• Parenteral: levofloxacin 500 mg IV once daily **OR** gatifloxacin 400 mg IV once daily **PLUS** Clindamycin 900 mg IV every 8 h **OR** metronidazole 500 mg IV every 6 h
Human	• Oral: amoxicillin/clavulanate, 500 mg three times daily • Parenteral: ampicillin/sulbactam, 3 g every 6 h	

[1]Suggested dosages are for patients with normal renal function; quinolone antibacterial agents should be avoided in children and adolescents < 18 years of age; pediatric dosages can be found in the *Pocket Book of Pediatric Antimicrobial Therapy*, 13th ed. Williams & Wilkins, 1998.
[2]No alternatives have been clearly established for penicillin allergic patients.

- Commonly occurs in the setting of associated neuropathy and arterial insufficiency.
- Fever and other systemic symptoms may or may not be present.
- Need to exclude underlying osteomyelitis.
- Mild, non–limb-threatening infections usually caused by *S aureus* or β-hemolytic streptococci.
- Severe limb-threatening infections usually have a polymicrobial etiology.

General Considerations

Foot infections are a serious complication of diabetes mellitus and result in more days of hospitalization than any other complication. Diabetic foot infections account for > 50% of all nontraumatic amputations. Underlying pathogenic factors include sensory peripheral neuropathy, macro- and microangiopathy, and systemic factors. Diminished sensation places the patient at risk for skin trauma and subsequent ulceration.

Infections typically start with a break in the skin, followed by penetration of bacteria into the skin and subcutaneous tissue (Box 13–7). This leads initially to a localized cellulitis that may spread to deeper structures including the deep fascia, tendon, joint space, or bone. Penetration by a foreign body is often asymptomatic and may lead to deep infection with limited involvement of superficial structures. Repetitive minor trauma caused by ill-fitting shoes may also lead to skin breakdown with subsequent infection. Hyperglycemia has been shown to result in polymorphonuclear cell dysfunction, which may contribute to the development and progression of infection. Diabetic foot ulcer is not a common problem in pediatric diabetes.

A. Mild Non–Limb-Threatening Infections. Mild non–limb-threatening infections tend to be superficial, presenting with mild cellulitis and minimal systemic toxicity. They may be associated with an ulcer that, if present, does not traverse all layers of the skin. There is no subjacent bone or joint involvement and the involved limb generally has reasonably good arterial blood supply. These infections are monomicrobial in half the cases and are generally caused by *S aureus* or aerobic streptococci. Gram-negative bacilli and anaerobic bacteria are infrequently isolated.

BOX 13-7

Microbiology of Diabetic Soft-Tissue Foot Infections

Type	Usual Microbiology
Mild non–limb-threatening infections	• *S aureus*, beta-hemolytic streptococci
Severe limb-threatening infections	• *S aureus*, streptococci, enterococci, *Enterobacteriaceae*, anaerobes, coagulase-negative staphylococci

B. Severe Limb-Threatening Infections.
Limb-threatening diabetic foot infections are usually polymicrobial and involve both anaerobic and aerobic bacteria, including *S aureus*, β-hemolytic streptococci (often group B), *Enterobacteriaceae*, *Clostridium* spp., and *Bacteroides* spp. Although coagulase-negative staphylococci, enterococci, and *Corynebacterium* spp. are occasionally recovered in culture and may be pathogenic, the possibility of contamination or colonization should be considered, particularly when isolated from a superficial swab.

Clinical Findings

Limb-threatening diabetic foot infections typically occur in the setting of significant limb ischemia and often with associated gangrene. The cellulitis is more extensive, and full-thickness skin ulcers are often present. There may be infection of contiguous bone and/or joint space. When fever is present, it is often seen in association with extensive soft-tissue infection, deep abscesses, bacteremia, or hematogenously seeded metastatic infection.

Diagnostic evaluation involves detailed definition of the extent of disease and the potential for wound healing. The vascular status of the involved limb should be documented by physical examination, noninvasive laboratory studies including transcutaneous oximetry, and angiography in selected cases. The possibility of concomitant subjacent osteomyelitis should be considered in all cases. Visualization of bone or the ability to "probe to bone" in infected diabetic foot ulcers has been shown to strongly correlate with the presence of underlying osteomyelitis.

All available radiographic diagnostic modalities, including plain radiographs, computed tomography scans, and technetium and radioactive leukocyte scans, have limited sensitivity and/or specificity for the definitive diagnosis of osteomyelitis. Magnetic resonance imaging is a valuable diagnostic tool for the detection of osteomyelitis in feet of diabetic patients and may be superior to radionuclide imaging.

Complications

Complications of diabetic foot infections include persistence of infection, osteomyelitis, septic arthritis, progressive infection necessitating amputation, and systemic infection with severe toxicity.

Treatment

Selection of antimicrobial therapy (Box 13–8) depends to a large extent on the nature and severity of infection. In cases of mild non–limb-threatening cellulitis without evidence of tissue necrosis and in the absence of a foul odor, therapy may be directed at gram-positive cocci (ie, *S aureus*) with a first-generation cephalosporin such as cefazolin. In select cases, oral therapy with an agent such as dicloxacillin or cephalexin may be appropriate. More severe infections, particularly those with associated tissue necrosis, generally require broader-spectrum therapy. Possibilities include piperacillin/tazobactam, imipenem or meropenem, or combination therapy such as cefepime with clindamycin or metronidazole. Therapy should be guided by culture and susceptibility data if appropriate specimens are available for culture. Duration of antimicrobial therapy depends on specific clinical circumstances. Cases of mild cellulitis are generally treated for 7–10 days.

More severe soft-tissue infection may require 2–3 weeks of therapy. If osteomyelitis is present and

---

BOX 13–8

Empiric Therapy of Diabetic Soft-Tissue Foot Infections

Type	Treatment[1]	Penicillin Allergic
Mild non–limb-threatening infections	• Oral: cephalexin 500 mg four times daily; **OR** amoxicillin/clavulanate, 500 mg three times daily • Parenteral: cefazolin, 1 g every 8 h, **OR** ampicillin/sulbactam, 1.5–3 g IV every 6 h	• Oral: clindamycin, 300 mg four times daily • Parenteral: clindamycin, 600–900 mg every 8 h, **OR** vancomycin, 15 mg/kg every 12 h
Severe limb-threatening infections	• Piperacillin/tazobactam, 3.375–4.5 g IV every 6 h, **OR** cefepime, 1–2 g IV every 12 h + metronidazole, 500 mg IV every 6 h, **OR** meropenem. 1 g IV every 8 h	• Clindamycin, 900 mg IV every 8 h + ciprofloxacin, 400 mg IV every 12 h, **OR** vancomycin, 15 mg/kg IV every 12 h + ciprofloxacin, 400 mg IV every 12 h + metronidazole, 500 mg IV every 6 h

[1]Suggested dosages are for patients with normal renal function; quinolone antibacterial agents should be avoided in children and adolescents < 18 years of age; pediatric dosages can be found in the *Pocket Book of Pediatric Antimicrobial Therapy*, 13th ed. Williams & Wilkins, 1998.

complete surgical resection of diseased bone is not performed, a minimum of 4 weeks of parenteral therapy is usually indicated. Surgical removal of devitalized tissue and drainage of pus are important components of therapy. If osteomyelitis is present, the surgical approach should be dictated by the extent of bone involvement and the vascular status of the limb. Revascularization should be pursued in ischemic limbs to facilitate healing, if technically feasible.

Considerable controversy exists concerning the surgical approach to diabetic foot infections and the extent of débridement required for treatment of infected bone. Limited ablative surgery to remove infected bone, such as with toe amputation or ray resection, often allows for a shortened course of antibiotic therapy, a shorter hospital stay, a greater likelihood of cure, and an earlier return to normal living. In cases of severe underlying arterial occlusive disease that is not amenable to surgical repair or in the presence of significant tissue necrosis, more proximal amputation may be necessary.

Prognosis

The outcome of the treatment of diabetic foot infections is to a great extent related to the underlying vascular and neurologic status of the limb. In infections involving relatively well-perfused limbs, amputation is less likely to be necessary for ultimate cure. In general, severe infection in severely ischemic limbs requires amputation.

Prevention

Preventive measures that may lessen the incidence of diabetic foot infections include meticulous foot care, the use of properly fitting footwear, early treatment of mild infections, and optimizing blood flow to ischemic feet through revascularization procedures, if possible.

REFERENCES

Bisno AL, Stevens DL: Streptococcal infections of skin and soft tissues. N Engl J Med 1996;334:240.

Davies HD et al: Invasive group A streptococcal infections in Ontario, Canada. N Engl J Med 1996;335:547.

Eriksson B et al: Erysipelas: clinical and bacteriologic spectrum and serological aspects. Clin Infect Dis 1996;23:1091.

Frykberg RG, Veves A: Diabetic foot infections. Diabetes/Metab Rev 1996;12:255.

Green RJ, Dafoe DC, Raffin TA: Necrotizing fasciitis. Chest 1996;110:219.

Griego RD et al: Dog, cat, and human bites. J Am Acad Dermatol 1995;33:1019.

Lewis RT: Necrotizing soft-tissue infections. Infect Dis Clin N Am 1992;6:693.

Osteomyelitis, Infectious Arthritis & Prosthetic-Joint Infection

14

Douglas R. Osmon, MD & James M. Steckelberg, MD

OSTEOMYELITIS

Essentials of Diagnosis

- Localized pain and tenderness of the involved bone is common.
- Purulent drainage from a sinus tract may or may not be present.
- Systemic symptoms and signs (eg, fever and chills) are often absent, particularly in chronic osteomyelitis.
- The erythrocyte sedimentation rate may be elevated.
- Plain radiographs may be negative. Computed tomography (CT) and magnetic resonance imaging (MRI) examinations are sensitive and specific tests for the presence of osteomyelitis but are expensive.
- Biopsy of the involved bone for pathologic examination and culture is diagnostic.

General Considerations

A. Pathogenesis. Osteomyelitis is an inflammatory disease of bone due to infection by a variety of different microorganisms (Figure 14–1). Normal bone is very resistant to infection unless there has been antecedent trauma or a foreign body is present. Certain organisms such as *Staphylococcus aureus* preferentially cause osteomyelitis because the organisms bind to bone through the expression of receptors for fibronectin, laminin, collagen, or bone sialoglycoprotein and because *S aureus* is a frequent colonizer of the skin and anterior nares. Osteomyelitis occurs by several mechanisms, including hematogenous seeding caused by bacteremia from a focus of infection elsewhere in the body, contiguous spread from adjacent soft-tissue or joint infection, or direct inoculation of microorganisms into the bone during penetrating trauma or surgery.

Hematogenous Osteomyelitis. Hematogenous osteomyelitis occurs most often in children and the elderly. In children it usually occurs in the metaphyses of the femur, tibia, and humerus because the blood supply to these bones is derived from small capillary branches of the nutrient artery, which have few phagocytic cells and are prone to vascular obstruction from minor trauma. Once the blood supply is diminished, small areas of bone necrosis develop that are susceptible to hematogenous seeding. These areas of infected avascular bone become sequestra. In children < 1 y of age, the infection can spread to the epiphysis and joint space through capillaries that cross the growth plate. In children > 1 y of age, the infection is confined to the metaphysis, with resulting lateral extension of the infection through the Haversian and Volkmann canal system, rupture of the cortex, and subperiosteal abscess formation. The exception to this rule is the development of osteomyelitis in metaphyses that are intracapsular, such as the proximal femur, humerus, and radius.

Hematogenous osteomyelitis in adults is much less common than in children and most often involves two adjacent vertebrae and the intervertebral disc space (vertebral osteomyelitis). Hematogenous seeding occurs through the arterial and venous blood supply (retrograde flow through Batson's venous plexus) with the former thought to be more common. Common sources of a bacteremia that predisposes to vertebral osteomyelitis include infections of intravenous-access devices, pneumonia, and urinary tract infection.

Contiguous-focus osteomyelitis. Contiguous-focus osteomyelitis is much more common in adults than in children and is often seen in persons > 50 y of age. Contiguous-focus osteomyelitis occurs secondarily to spread of infection from adjacent soft tissue or joints or is caused by direct inoculation of microorganisms during trauma or surgery. Concomitant infection of orthopedic fixation devices is often present. Vascular insufficiency such as that seen in patients with longstanding diabetes mellitus often leads to recurrent soft-tissue infections and subsequent contiguous-focus osteomyelitis of the underlying bones.

B. Classification Schemes. Waldvogel has classified osteomyelitis as being of hematogenous origin or due to a contiguous focus of infection. Con-

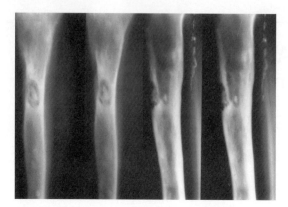

Figure 14–1. Chronic osteomyelitis of the tibia due to *S aureus*, illustrating sequestrum formation.

tiguous-focus osteomyelitis is further subdivided into osteomyelitis with or without vascular insufficiency. In addition, either type of osteomyelitis can be acute or chronic in its presentation. Acute infection is defined as a recently diagnosed bone infection of < 10-d duration, whereas chronic infection represents relapse of osteomyelitis at the same site or disease of > 10-d duration. Vertebral osteomyelitis can be acute or chronic and, depending on the pathogenesis of the infection, can be hematogenous in origin or caused by a contiguous focus of infection. Contiguous-focus osteomyelitis often occurs secondarily to a wound infection after surgery.

Cierney and Mader have proposed an alternative classification scheme (Table 14–1). This classification system is based on bone anatomy and the physiologic status of the host. This system is very useful in comparing medical and surgical treatment strategies in clinical trials. Examples of stage 1 disease include hematogenous osteomyelitis and infected intramedullary rods. Osteomyelitis of the surface of a bone at the base of a soft-tissue infection would be an example of stage 2 osteomyelitis. Osteomyelitis involving the full thickness of the bone, with or without cortical sequestration that can be débrided without endangering the stability of the bone, constitutes stage-3 disease. Osteomyelitis that involves the entire extent of bone and usually requires segmental resection to achieve adequate débridement (a débridement that often compromises the stability of the bone) is stage-4 osteomyelitis.

C. Microbiology and Epidemiology. The optimal selection of antimicrobial agents for the treatment of osteomyelitis depends on the definitive identification of the microorganism(s) causing infection and knowledge of its antimicrobial susceptibilities. Antimicrobial therapy should usually be withheld until all cultures from the involved tissue have been obtained.

Skin and serologic testing for unusual organisms such as mycobacteria and fungi should be done only if these infections are suspected clinically. Serologic tests to detect cell wall components of *S aureus*, such as teichoic acid, are not clinically helpful. Sinus tract swab cultures are not accurate in predicting polymicrobial infection but may be helpful if *S aureus* is the only pathogen isolated.

For culture, as much tissue and purulence as possible should be obtained at the time of bone biopsy and/or surgical débridement. All specimens should be sent immediately to the microbiology laboratory. Tissue specimens should be sent to both the pathology laboratory and the microbiology laboratory. Anaerobic cultures require anaerobic transport media.

The microbiologist should perform a Gram stain on all specimens. Stains for fungi or acid-fast bacilli may also be useful in selected cases. Cultures for aerobic and anaerobic bacteria should be routinely obtained. When the history, physical examination, or intraoperative findings suggest an unusual infection, special culturing techniques for organisms such as fungi, mycobacteria, *Mycoplasma* spp., *Brucella* spp., or other organisms may be required. Failure to obtain specimens for these cultures at the time of initial débridement may result in unnecessary procedures to

Table 14–1. Cierny and Mader staging system of osteomyelitis.[1]

Anatomic type
    Stage 1: medullary osteomyelitis
    Stage 2: superficial osteomyelitis
    Stage 3: localized osteomyelitis
    Stage 4: diffuse osteomyelitis
Physiologic Class
    A Host: Normal host
    B Host:
        Systemic compromise (Bs)
        Local compromise (Bi)
        Systemic and local compromise (Bis)
    C Host: Treatment worse than the disease.
Systemic or local factors that affect immune surveillance, metabolism, and local vascularity
    Systemic (Bs)
        Malnutrition
        Renal, hepatic failure
        Diabetes mellitus
        Chronic hypoxia
        Immune disease
        Malignancy
        Extremes of age
        Immunosuppression
    Local (Bi)
        Chronic lymphedema
        Major vessel compromise
        Small vessel disease
        Vasculitis
        Venous stasis
        Extensive scarring
        Radiation fibrosis
        Neuropathy
        Tobacco abuse

[1]Source: Mader et al 1996.

obtain further culture material or ultimately treatment failure despite adequate débridement.

The pathologist, although primarily looking for the presence or absence of inflammation, may also find evidence of a specific type of inflammation, such as granulomas, that provide a clue to the etiology of the infection. In this circumstance, it is useful to perform additional tissue stains for fungi and mycobacteria.

Once the microorganism responsible for the infection has been identified, antimicrobial susceptibility tests should be performed. A minimal inhibitory concentration (MIC) obtained by broth or agar dilution is the best guide to therapy. When only disc diffusion (Kirby-Bauer disc sensitivities) results are available, drugs with intermediate or resistant results should not be used. Some investigators also advocate performing a serum bactericidal titer. This test quantitates the bactericidal activity of the patient's serum. It is the dilution of patient's serum that shows $\geq 99.9\%$ killing of the organism in vitro. However, these tests are difficult to reproduce within and among laboratories, and their use is not advocated.

Hematogenous Osteomyelitis. *S aureus* is the most common cause of hematogenous osteomyelitis in children and adults (Box 14–1). Hematogenous osteomyelitis caused by beta-hemolytic streptococci and aerobic gram-negative bacilli is much less common. Some patient groups are predisposed to hematogenous infection due to certain organisms: neonates (*Enterobacteriaceae,* group B streptococci), patients with sickle cell disease (*Salmonella* spp., *S aureus*), and injection drug users (*Pseudomonas aeruginosa, S aureus*). *Haemophilus influenzae* causes infection in infants and children, but the incidence of invasive disease caused by *H influenzae* is decreasing owing to the *H influenzae* type b-conjugated vaccine that is now routinely administered to children. Anaerobic and polymicrobial infections are uncommon.

Vertebral Osteomyelitis. *S aureus* is the most common cause of vertebral osteomyelitis. Aerobic gram-negative bacilli cause $\leq 30\%$ of infections, particularly those associated with hematogenous seeding from a urinary tract infection. *P aeruginosa* and *S aureus* infections are common among injection drug users. Coagulase-negative staphylococci, *S aureus,* and aerobic gram-negative bacilli are common causes of vertebral osteomyelitis after spine surgery with or without spinal hardware implantation. Polymicrobial infection is uncommon. Candidal infection may occur after candidemia, due to infections of intravascular devices.

Contiguous-Focus Osteomyelitis. This infection is often polymicrobial, particularly in the setting of osteomyelitis of the phalanges or metatarsals in patients with diabetes mellitus or vascular insufficiency or in osteomyelitis of the long bones after a contaminated open fracture. *S aureus,* beta-hemolytic streptococci, enterococci, aerobic gram-negative bacilli, and anaerobes can all be pathogens. If soil contamination is present, *Clostridium* spp., *Bacillus* spp., *Stenotrophomonas maltophilia, Nocardia* spp., and rarely various mycobacteria and fungi may cause infection. If orthopedic fixation devices become infected, then monomicrobial infection due to *S aureus* or coagulase-negative staphylococci is more common. *Pasteurella multocida* osteomyelitis often complicates cat bites, and *P aeruginosa* is a common cause of osteomyelitis of the foot after puncture injuries by nails or other sharp objects. Normal oral flora and *Actinomyces* spp. cause mandibular or skull osteomyelitis after periodontal infection.

BOX 14–1

Microorganisms Isolated from Patients with Bacterial Osteomyelitis[1]

Microorganisms	Common Clinical Association
Staphylococcus aureus	Most frequent cause of all types of ostemyelitis
Coagulase-negative staphylococci	Common if orthopedic fixation devices are present
Streptococci	Diabetes mellitus, bite injuries
Enterobacteriaceae	Nosocomial infection or contaminated open fractures
Pseudomonas aeruginosa	Injection drug users and osteomyelitis of the foot after puncture injuries
Anaerobic bacteria	Osteomyelitis of the foot in patients with diabetes mellitus or after human and animal bites
Salmonella spp. or *Streptococcus pneumoniae, S aureus*	Sickle cell disease
Pasteurella multocida or *Eikenella corrodens*	Bite injuries

[1]Adapted from Lew & Waldvogel 1997.

Clinical Findings

A. Hematogenous osteomyelitis.

1. Signs and symptoms. Children most often present with severe bone pain, limitation of motion of the extremity, and fever and chills of several days to 3 wk in duration, although, in ≤ 40% of cases, vague symptoms of 1- to 2-mo duration occur. On examination, there may be soft-tissue swelling, erythema, and tenderness of the involved area. Neonates often have no fever and present with only a decreased range of motion of the involved limb and localized tenderness and swelling. The presence of a joint effusion is also common in neonates.

2. Laboratory findings. An elevated leukocyte count, erythrocyte sedimentation rate, and C-reactive protein are common, but the lack of any one or all of these laboratory abnormalities does not exclude the diagnosis of osteomyelitis. Blood cultures should be obtained and are positive in ≤ 50% of cases. Aspiration of associated soft tissue or subperiosteal abscesses or biopsy of involved bone is diagnostic. Arthrocentesis should be performed if a joint effusion is present.

3. Imaging. Plain radiographs may be negative early in the disease. Soft-tissue swelling and subperiosteal elevation are the earliest abnormalities and may not be seen for several weeks. Before lytic lesions appear, 30–50% of the bone must be destroyed, and typically these lesions do not appear for 2–6 wk after the onset of the illness. Sclerotic changes occur later and, when seen in association with periosteal new-bone formation, suggest chronicity of the infection.

Radionuclide scanning may be helpful early in the course of the disease, but the usefulness of this test is often limited by its lack of specificity. CT scans and MRI are better able to distinguish soft-tissue infection from osteomyelitis, are more sensitive than plain radiographs, and allow better identification of optimal areas for needle aspiration or biopsy.

B. Vertebral osteomyelitis.

1. Signs and symptoms. Patients are often > 50 y of age, except injection drug users, and usually present with back pain of several-months duration. The pain is often described as a continuous dull ache that is exacerbated by movement, cough, or straining. If neurologic complications (30%) are present secondary to nerve root or spinal cord compression from epidural extension of the infection, these symptoms may dominate the clinical picture. On physical examination, a draining sinus or wound is usually not present unless the infection is secondary to recent surgery. Fever is present in 20–50% of patients. Paraspinal muscle spasm and percussion tenderness of the spine are often present. The lumbar spine is most commonly involved, followed by the thoracic and cervical regions.

2. Laboratory findings. An elevated leukocyte count is often present. The erythrocyte sedimentation rate is elevated in ≤ 95% of patients. Blood cultures are positive in 25–50% of cases, and positive blood cultures negate the need for routine biopsy of the involved vertebra and intervertebral disc space. Needle biopsy of the involved intervertebral disc, vertebra, or associated epidural abscess is the diagnostic procedure of choice. In ≤ 25% of cases, the cultures from the initial needle biopsy may be negative. A second needle biopsy, an open biopsy, or both should then be performed.

3. Imaging. Plain radiographs of the spine often do not show characteristic vertebral endplate destruction, particularly in patients with a short duration of symptoms or other underlying vertebral pathology such as severe osteoarthritis. However, nonspecific abnormalities (ie, loss of disk height) on plain radiographs will be detected in the majority of cases. Gallium scans are more sensitive and specific than three-phase technetium (^{99}Tc) bone scans or indium-labeled leukocyte scans for the diagnosis of vertebral osteomyelitis. MRI, however, is the most sensitive and diagnostic imaging technique and, in addition, provides the best anatomic detail. Gallium scans should be used when spinal hardware is present that degrades the MRI images.

C. Contiguous-focus osteomyelitis.

1. Signs and symptoms. The patient usually presents with localized bone pain and/or drainage from a wound or sinus tract, of several-months duration. Fever and constitutional symptoms are uncommon. Overlying cellulitis may be present. A pathologic fracture may be present if extensive disease is present.

2. Laboratory findings. The leukocyte and the erythrocyte sedimentation rates are often normal. Blood cultures are usually negative. A bone biopsy is diagnostic and is usually obtained at the time of surgical débridement.

3. Imaging. Because the time from onset of infection to diagnosis of osteomyelitis is often delayed with contiguous focus osteomyelitis, plain radiographs, including tomography, often show abnormalities consistent with osteomyelitis. In the proper clinical setting, such as the presence of a draining sinus tract, plain radiography may be all that is required. In some circumstances, however, there are other pathologic processes present that mimic osteomyelitis (ie, neuropathic bone disease in patients with peripheral neuropathy), or there are partially healed fractures or orthopedic fixation devices in place that limit the usefulness of plain radiography. If the clinical situation warrants additional radiologic procedures to confirm the diagnosis of osteomyelitis or to help identify the optimal surgical therapy for the patient, MRI is the diagnostic test of choice. If orthopedic hardware is present that interferes with MRI examination, then the combination of a three-phase (^{99}Tc) technetium bone scan and indium-labeled leukocyte scan can be performed.

Differential Diagnosis

Acute hematogenous osteomyelitis in children must be distinguished from soft-tissue infection, infectious arthritis, and certain malignancies such as Ewing's sarcoma. Vertebral osteomyelitis should be distinguished from the multitude of disease entities that can cause acute to subacute onset of back pain in adults, including osteoarthritis, metastatic malignancy, and compression fractures. If recent surgery has been performed, it is often difficult to distinguish postoperative pain and radiographic changes from those secondary to infection. Contiguous-focus osteomyelitis must be distinguished from chronic soft-tissue infection and rarely malignancy. Contiguous-focus osteomyelitis of the feet in patients with diabetes mellitus must be distinguished from neuropathic bone disease.

Complications

Failure of medical and surgical therapy of osteomyelitis invariably leads to a relapse of infection. If treatment is delayed, osteomyelitis can progress from superficial to diffuse disease or from Cierney/Mader stage 1 or 2 to stage 3 or 4 and thus become much more difficult to eradicate. In severe cases, amputation may be required for control of infection. In addition, acute hematogenous osteomyelitis in children can spread to adjacent joints and cause infectious arthritis. Vertebral osteomyelitis in adults if untreated can cause neurologic sequelae including paralysis either through extension to the epidural space or spinal column instability. Rare complications of longstanding osteomyelitis include amyloidosis, squamous cell carcinoma at the site of chronic sinus tract or primary bone malignancies such as osteogenic sarcoma.

Treatment

The treatment of osteomyelitis depends on the goals of therapy and requires a multidisciplinary team of physicians, which may include the orthopedist, neurosurgeon, oral surgeon, plastic surgeon, vascular surgeon, invasive radiologist, and infectious disease specialist. If eradication of infection is the goal, then, in most circumstances, extensive débridement and resection of dead and infected bone are required, in conjunction with appropriate dead-space and soft-tissue management, rigid fixation of fractures, local antimicrobial therapy with antibiotic-impregnated polymethylmethacrylate beads, and prolonged systemic antimicrobial therapy directed at the causative organisms. In addition, modification of any physiologic factors (see Table 14–1) that may promote treatment failure, such as cessation of smoking, enhancement of the local blood supply in the area of the infection, and improved control of diabetes mellitus, should be accomplished. Often, delayed reconstructive orthopedic techniques such as bone grafting

and distraction osteogenesis (Ilizarov technique) are also necessary.

Exceptions to the absolute requirement for extensive débridement to arrest osteomyelitis include acute hematogenous osteomyelitis of the long bones in children and vertebral osteomyelitis in adults. The duration of therapy is usually 3–4 wk in children and 4–6 wk in adults. In children, after 7–10 d of intravenous antimicrobial therapy, the last 2–3 wk of therapy are often administered orally. Indications for surgery for acute osteomyelitis include failure to make a specific microbiologic diagnosis with less invasive techniques, involvement of the femoral head, neurologic complications, the presence of sequestra, and failure to improve while on appropriate antimicrobial therapy. In addition, the consequences of aggressive surgical and medical treatment for chronic osteomyelitis may in selected cases be worse than the consequences of the disease itself, and local wound care with or without oral antimicrobial suppressive therapy may be an option in these situations.

There are no large randomized studies to help guide the clinician in the antimicrobial therapy of osteomyelitis. Although several clinical trials have been performed, their interpretation is limited by their small sample size, differences in inclusion and exclusion criteria, definition of treatment failure, failure to stratify patients by the type and severity of osteomyelitis present, and a short duration of follow-up. The overall failure rate among the 154 evaluable patients in these studies was 22%.

Most experts administer 4–6 wk of intravenous antimicrobial therapy after surgical débridement for the treatment of chronic osteomyelitis. This therapy can be completed as an outpatient in the majority of cases. Data from animal models of osteomyelitis suggest that the addition of rifampin to beta-lactams or vancomycin for osteomyelitis caused by *S aureus* may be beneficial, but confirmation in clinical trials is needed before this practice can be routinely recommended.

The choice of a specific antibiotic depends on the antimicrobial activity, pharmacokinetics, tissue penetration, and potential toxicities of the antimicrobial agents under consideration. Integration of this knowledge with information about drug allergies, current medications, concurrent remote infection, and hepatic and renal insufficiency allows for selection of the optimal antimicrobial agent and dosage. For antimicrobial agents that have potential toxicities at concentrations close to therapeutic concentrations, such as aminoglycosides or vancomycin, the dosage and frequency of administration are guided by measurement of their concentration in serum. Although the cost of an antimicrobial agent is an important consideration, it is secondary to the safety and efficacy of the antibiotic. Suggested antimicrobial agents for specific pathogens that cause osteomyelitis are shown in Box 14–2.

BOX 14–2

Antibiotic Therapy for Chronic Osteomyelitis in Adults

Microorganisms	Antibiotic Therapy[1]	Alternative Therapy[1]
Staphylococcus aureus Methicillin sensitive	• Nafcillin sodium or oxacillin sodium, 1.5–2.0 g IV every 4 h for 4–6 wk. **OR** • Cefazolin (or other first-generation cephalosporins in equivalent dosages) 1 g IV every 8 h for 4–6 wk (cephalosporins should be avoided in patients with immediate-type hypersensitivity to penicillin)	• Vancomycin,[2] 30 mg/kg IV in 2 equally divided doses, not to exceed 2 g/24 h unless serum levels are monitored for 4–6 wk
Methicillin resistant	• Vancomycin,[2] 30 mg/kg IV in 2 equally divided doses, not to exceed 2 g/24 h unless serum levels are monitored for 4–6 wk	• Consult infectious diseases specialist
Penicillin-sensitive streptococci or pneumococci (MIC, < 0.1 µg/mL)	• Aqueous crystalline penicillin G, 20 × 10⁶ U/24 h IV either continuously or in six equally divided doses for 4–6 wk **OR** • Ceftriaxone, 2 g IV or IM for 4–6 wk[2]	• Vancomycin,[2] 30 mg/kg IV in 2 equally divided doses, not to exceed 2 g/24 h unless serum levels are monitored for 4–6 wk (vancomycin therapy is recommended for patients allergic to beta-lactams (immediate-type hypersensitivity)
Enterococci or streptococci with an MIC > 0.5 µg/mL or nutritionally variant streptococci (All enterococci causing osteomyelitis must be tested for antimicrobial susceptibility to select optimal therapy.)	• Cefazolin (or other first-generation cephalosporins in equivalent dosages), 1 g IV every 8 h for 4–6 wk (cephalosporins should be avoided in patients with immediate-type hypersensitivity to penicillin) • Aqueous crystalline penicillin G, 20 × 10⁶ U/24 h IV, either continuously or in six equally divided doses for 4–6 wk, **OR** • Ampicillin sodium, 12 g/24 h IV either continuously or in six equally divided doses (The addition of gentamicin sulfate,[3] 1 mg/kg IV or IM every 8 h for 1–2 wk is optional)	• Vancomycin,[2] 30 mg/kg IV in 2 equally divided doses, not to exceed 2 g/24 h unless serum levels are monitored for 4–6 wk (The addition of gentamicin sulfate,[3] 1 mg/kg IV or IM every 8 h for 1–2 wk is optional)
Enterobacteriaceae (based on in vitro susceptibility)	• Ceftriaxone, 2 g IV every day for 4–6 wk[2]	
Pseudomonas aeruginosa or **Enterobacter** spp.	• Most effective single drug or combination of drugs IV for 4–6 wk	• Ciprofloxacin, 500–750 mg orally every day for 4–6 wk

[1]Dosages recommended are for patients with normal renal function. IV, intravenous; IM, intramuscular.

[2]Vancomycin therapy is recommended for patients allergic to beta-lactams (immediate-type hypersensitivity); serum concentration of vancomycin should be obtained prior to and 1 h after completion of the infusion and should be in the range of 20–40 µg/mL for a peak and 5–10 µg/ml for a trough for twice-daily dosing. Vancomycin should be infused over at least 1 h to reduce the risk of the "red man" syndrome.

[3]Serum concentration of gentamicin should be obtained prior to and 30 min after completion of the infusion and should be in the range of 3–4 µg/mL for a peak and 0.5–1 µg/mL for a trough for synergistic therapy for enterococci. Relative contraindications to the use of gentamicin are age > 65 y, renal impairment, or impairment of the eighth cranial nerve. Other potentially nephrotoxic agents should be used cautiously in patients receiving gentamicin.

For osteomyelitis caused by susceptible aerobic gram-negative bacilli, some practitioners use initial oral antimicrobial therapy with fluoroquinolones such as ciprofloxacin or levofloxacin or completion of antimicrobial therapy with oral agents after intravenous therapy. Hyperbaric oxygen therapy for chronic osteomyelitis remains controversial.

Prognosis

Despite state-of-the-art medical and surgical therapy for osteomyelitis, relapse of infection occurs. Relapse is more common in cases of chronic osteomyelitis than acute osteomyelitis and can occur in ≤ 25–30% of cases. Relapse of infection is most often caused by suboptimal surgical débridement rather than a failure of antimicrobial therapy. Therefore, it is probably best not to think in terms of a cure for osteomyelitis but prolonged arrest of the disease process.

Prevention

Specific strategies to prevent osteomyelitis depend on the type of osteomyelitis. Decreasing the incidence of infections that predispose to transient or sustained bacteremia will prevent hematogenous osteomyelitis. Therefore, efforts to reduce the incidence of community- and nosocomially acquired infections such as pneumonia, urinary tract infections and soft-tissue infections through vaccination, infection control measures, and early treatment of established infection will prevent hematogenous osteomyelitis. The incidence of contiguous-focus osteomyelitis can be reduced through efforts such as improved foot care in patients with diabetes mellitus and infection control efforts to reduce the incidence of surgical-site infections after orthopedic and neurosurgical procedures.

INFECTIOUS ARTHRITIS

Essentials of Diagnosis

- Monoarticular arthritis of the knee, hip, or shoulder is most typical, but involvement of any joint can occur.
- Risk factors include systemic immune defects, a history of prior joint trauma or arthritis, or both.
- Fever and infection elsewhere in the body are common.
- Arthrocentesis commonly reveals a synovial-fluid leukocyte count of > 100,000/μl with a predominance of polymorphonuclear leukocytes.
- Gout and pseudogout must be excluded.

General Considerations

Infectious arthritis is an inflammatory disease of a joint (Figure 14–2). It is usually caused by hematogenous seeding of the joint. Synovial tissue has a rich vascular supply and no basement membrane and therefore is at increased risk of hematogenous infection should bacteremia occur, owing to a focus of infection elsewhere.

A. Epidemiology. An estimated 20,000 cases, or 7.8 cases per 100,000 person years, of infectious arthritis occurred in the United States in 1993, of which 56% were male and 45% were ≥ 65 y of age. Host factors that have been associated with an increased risk of acquiring infectious arthritis include systemic immune defects, as seen in patients with rheumatoid arthritis, diabetes mellitus, and malignancy and local abnormalities of host defenses owing to the presence of prior joint damage, which predisposes the joint to hematogenous infection. In addition, factors that increase the risk of bacteremia, such as intravenous drug use and chronic skin infection, or that allow direct inoculation of microorganisms, such as therapeutic arthrocentesis, predispose to infection.

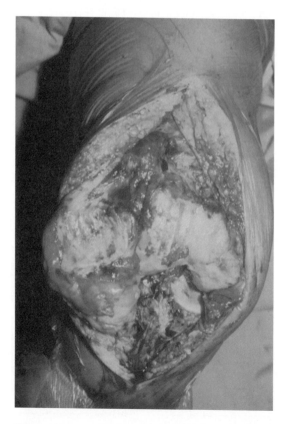

Figure 14–2. Intraoperative photograph of infectious arthritis of the knee due to *S aureus,* revealing severe joint destruction. Reprinted from: Armstrong D, Cohen J (eds), *Infectious Diseases.* Mosby-Year Book, 1999.

Disseminated gonococcal infection is more common among sexually active menstruating women.

B. Microbiology. A multitude of microorganisms can cause infectious arthritis, although bacteria cause the majority of cases in children and adults. Fungi, mycobacteria, *Borrelia burgdorferi,* and viruses, as well as other microorganisms, also cause infectious arthritis and are discussed in their specific chapters. Group B streptococci and gonococci cause ≤ 95% of community-acquired infections in neonates. In children, *S aureus, H influenzae,* and streptococci are the major pathogens. The frequency of disease caused by *H influenzae* is decreasing, owing to the use of the *H influenzae* b conjugate vaccine.

In persons 15–40 y of age, 94% of infectious arthritis cases are due to *Neisseria gonorrhoeae.* The most common pathogens among adults are shown in Box 14–3. Infection in patients with rheumatoid arthritis or polyarticular infectious arthritis is caused by *S aureus* in ≤ 90% of patients. Infectious arthritis caused by gram-negative bacilli is more common in the elderly and patients with other comorbid illnesses. Enterococcal or anaerobic infection is uncommon. *P aeruginosa* and *S aureus* are common pathogens among injection drug users. *Mycoplasma* spp. cause infection in patients who are hypogammaglobulinemic.

C. Pathogenesis. *S aureus* is the most common cause of joint infection, in part because of its ability to bind to sialoprotein, a glycoprotein found in joints. Direct inoculation of microorganisms caused by trauma, arthrotomy, arthroscopy, or arthrocentesis also occurs. Infection caused by contiguous soft-tissue infection or periarticular osteomyelitis is rare. The presence of bacteria in the synovial tissue results in an influx of polymorphonuclear leukocytes that release enzymes, which destroy the ground substance of the articular surface, erode the cartilage, and eventually narrow the joint space.

BOX 14–3

Microbiology of Infectious Arthritis in Adults[1,2]

Microorganisms	Percentage
S aureus	66
Streptococci[3]	20
H influenzae	1
Aerobic gram-negative bacilli	10
Polymicrobial and miscellaneous	1
Unknown	–

[1]Source: Adopted from Roberts & Mock 1996.
[2]Excluding *Neisseria gonorrhoeae.*
[3]Includes beta-hemolytic streptococci, viridans group streptococci, and *Streptococcus pneumoniae.*

Clinical Findings

A. Signs and Symptoms. Acute onset of an inflammatory arthritis of a weight-bearing joint over hours to days is typical. A chronic disease process is more common with infectious arthritis caused by mycobacteria or fungi. The knee, hip, and shoulder are the most commonly involved joints in adults. Infection of the hip or the knee is most common in children. Sacroiliac or sternoclavicular joint infection is common among injection drug users. Polyarticular infection occurs in ~ 10% of patients and is more common among patients with rheumatoid arthritis. Fever is often present but is mild.

Physical examination usually reveals a large effusion and a marked decrease in range of motion of the joint, although these findings may be minimal or absent in patients with rheumatoid arthritis. Tenosynovitis, a macular, vesicular, pustular or petechial rash, and polyarticular involvement are commonly seen with disseminated gonococcal infection, whereas monoarticular involvement without rash or tenosynovial involvement is common in later stages of the disease.

B. Laboratory Findings. The erythrocyte sedimentation rate and leukocyte count are elevated in the majority of cases. The diagnostic procedure of choice is an arthrocentesis. Synovial fluid is often purulent, and the leukocyte count is usually > 50,000/mm^3 and often > 100,000/mm^3, with > 75% polymorphonuclear leukocytes. Unfortunately these findings can also be seen in patients with rheumatoid arthritis and crystal deposition arthritis. A low glucose is common but is not specific for infection. The Gram stain will be positive in 35–65% of patients. Synovial fluid should be cultured for both aerobes and anaerobes and other organisms depending on the clinical circumstances. All synovial fluid from adults should be examined for uric acid and calcium pyrophosphate dihydrate crystals. The role of the powlymerase chain reaction in detecting bacterial pathogens remains to be defined although the technique seems a promising tool for the detection of infectious arthritis due to *B burgdorferi.* Synovial tissue cultures are indicated only for chronic infectious arthritis when mycobacterial or fungal arthritis is suspected. Blood cultures are positive in ≤ 30% of all patients and more often in patients with polyarticular involvement. In disseminated gonococcal disease, the blood cultures and/or cultures from the urethra, cervix, rectum, or pharynx are positive whereas synovial fluid cultures are negative. In monoarticular gonococcal arthritis, the synovial fluid cultures are usually positive, and the blood cultures negative.

C. Imaging. Periarticular soft-tissue swelling is the most common abnormality seen on plain radiography. Joint space narrowing from cartilage destruction occurs later. It is often difficult to distinguish infection from inflammatory arthritis by using radiographic methods in the setting of rheumatoid arthritis, but the development of a rapid destructive arthritis in one or two joints suggests infection. CT scans and MRI are more useful than radionuclide studies in identifying concomitant periarticular osteomyelitis. Sacroiliac or sternoclavicular joint disease can be evaluated with all three modalities.

Differential Diagnosis

In adults, the differential of patients with an acute onset of fever, chills, and an inflammatory arthritis of one or more joints revolves around infectious arthritis, gout, pseudogout, rheumatic fever, reactive arthritis, and rheumatic illnesses such as rheumatoid and psoriatic arthritis. In children, as stated previously, concomitant osteomyelitis is common and must be excluded. In addition, a painful hip and fever in a child should raise the possibility of acute transient synovitis of the hip.

Treatment

The principles in the management of infectious arthritis include drainage of the purulent synovial fluid, débridement of any concomitant periarticular osteomyelitis, and the administration of appropriate parenteral antimicrobial therapy. Experimental models of infectious arthritis suggest that early drainage and antimicrobial therapy prevent cartilage destruction. Local antimicrobial as opposed to systemic therapy is unnecessary. Joint immobilization and elevation are useful for symptomatic relief of pain early in the course of the disease, but early active range-of-motion therapy is beneficial for ultimate functional outcome.

The optimal method of drainage of an infected joint remains controversial, in part because no well-controlled randomized trials exist to guide therapy. Most children, except patients with infectious arthritis of the hip, and patients with gonococcal infection do not require repeated joint aspirations or arthrotomy. Historically, most adults with infectious arthritis have been managed with repeated joint aspirations, not surgical débridement. Arthrotomy has been reserved for cases in which there is failure to improve within 7 d of conservative therapy, inability to adequately drain the infected joint by aspiration either due to location (hip and shoulder) or loculations of purulence within the joint, and longstanding infectious arthritis. The exact role of arthroscopy remains unknown but is an attractive option for the initial therapy of infectious arthritis because of the minimal morbidity of the procedure and its improved ability to adequately drain purulent material from the joint compared with joint aspiration. Randomized trials are urgently needed to evaluate all of these modalities.

The principles of antimicrobial therapy, as well as the drugs of choice and their dosages for specific pathogens that cause infectious arthritis in adults, are the same as for osteomyelitis (Box 14–2). Most experts, however, recommend 2–4 wk of parenteral antimicrobial therapy for nongonococcal infectious arthritis instead of the usual 4–6 wk recommended for osteomyelitis. Oral antimicrobial therapy with an effective agent with excellent bioavailability, such as ciprofloxacin or cotrimoxazole, is also acceptable particularly if the patient has rapidly improved on intravenous therapy.

Up-to-date treatment guidelines for gonococcal arthritis can be obtained from the CDC but currently include 7–10 d of ceftriaxone (1 g IV daily) or intravenous penicillin (10 million U daily administered continuously or in divided doses) depending on in vitro susceptibility testing. If the patients improve substantially within 72 h, oral antimicrobial therapy with cefixime, ciprofloxacin, or amoxicillin, depending on in vitro susceptibility testing, can be substituted for intravenous therapy. As discussed previously children that are improving can usually be switched to oral antimicrobial therapy within 7–10 d. Compliance with therapy must be assured.

Prognosis

Patients with infectious arthritis have an estimated case fatality rate of 9%, but, in patients with polyarticular infectious arthritis and rheumatoid arthritis, it is $\leq 56\%$. Of patients who survive, $\leq 42\%$ will have a permanent loss of joint function. Predictors of morbidity and mortality include older age, the presence of rheumatoid arthritis, infection in the hip or shoulder, > 1-wk duration of symptoms before treatment, involvement of more than four joints, persistently positive cultures after 7 d of appropriate therapy, and the presence of bacteremia.

Prevention

Infectious arthritis can be prevented in certain patient populations through promotion of efforts by state and national officials to eradicate injection drug use, decrease the incidence of animal bites and nosocomial infections, and promote improved foot care in patients with diabetes mellitus. The routine use of *H influenzae* b conjugate vaccine in children has been shown to decrease the incidence of infectious arthritis caused by this microorganism.

PROSTHETIC-JOINT INFECTION

Essentials of Diagnosis

- Prosthetic-joint infection is most common in the first 2 y after prosthesis implantation.
- Clinical presentation can be one of either an acute infectious arthritis or chronic pain due to prosthesis failure without constitutional symptoms.
- A draining sinus is present in 30–40% of patients.

- Multiple positive cultures either from preoperative joint aspirations or intraoperatively obtained tissue are diagnostic.

General Considerations

A. Epidemiology. The overall rate of prosthetic-joint infection among the ~ 430,000 total hip and knee arthroplasties is highest in the first 6 mo postsurgery and declines thereafter. At the Mayo Clinic, the postoperative incidence rates of total hip and knee arthroplasty during the first year, second year, and after 2 y are ~ 6.5, 3.2, and 1.4 per 1000 joint years, respectively.

Most prosthetic-joint infections occur in immunocompetent hosts. The primary factors predisposing to infection appear to be local abnormalities of host defenses caused by the presence of the foreign body itself. Well-known risk factors for prosthetic-joint infection include prior joint surgery, perioperative wound complications, and rheumatoid arthritis. Other less-well-documented risk factors include diabetes mellitus, the use of steroids, obesity, extreme age, joint dislocation, poor nutrition, distant infection, psoriasis, hemophilia, sickle cell hemoglobinopathy, joint implantation for malignancy, prior infectious arthritis, and the presence of a hinged knee prosthesis.

B. Microbiology. The microbiology of prosthetic-joint infection in a large case series is detailed in Box 14–4. A common characteristic among the microorganisms that cause prosthetic-joint infection is their ability to adhere to foreign materials.

C. Pathogenesis. The majority of prosthetic-joint infections are acquired in the operating room either through direct inoculation during prosthesis implantation or as a result of airborne contamination of the wound. Hematogenous seeding during a bacteremia or through direct contiguous spread from an adjacent focus of infection also occurs but is much less common.

Clinical Findings

A. Signs and Symptoms. Patients may present with a range of clinical signs and symptoms varying from a syndrome of acute infectious arthritis to a syndrome of chronic pain without constitutional symptoms, which is difficult to distinguish from aseptic loosening of the prosthesis. On physical examination, limitation of the range of motion of the joint is present, and a draining sinus tract is present in 30–40% of patients. Virulent organisms such as *S aureus* or pyogenic beta-hemolytic streptococci more often cause the acute infectious arthritis syndrome, while infection with less virulent microorganisms such as coagulase-negative staphylococci often follows a more chronic course.

B. Laboratory Findings. As for all bone and joint infections, an elevated leukocyte count, erythrocyte sedimentation rate, or C-reactive protein is often present but is not sufficient to definitively make the diagnosis of prosthetic-joint infection. Multiple positive cultures from either a preoperative joint aspiration or an intraoperatively obtained tissue are diagnostic for prosthetic-joint infection. Blood cultures should be obtained if fever is present. In addition the presence of acute inflammation on a frozen section of periprosthetic tissue is an accurate way to identify infection intraoperatively at the time of revision surgery prior to the culture results. Because of the importance of making a microbiologic diagnosis antimicrobial therapy should usually be withheld until all aspirates have been obtained and/or the surgeon has obtained intraoperative cultures from the joint. If antimicrobial therapy has already been started, when possible it should be stopped for 10-14 d before any diagnostic procedure to avoid false-negative culture results. As much fluid for culture as possible should be obtained at the time of diagnostic joint aspiration.

C. Imaging. Plain radiographs, arthrograms, and radionuclide imaging are often useful in diagnosing prosthetic-joint infection (Figure 14–3). Abnormalities that can be seen on plain radiography include loosening of the prosthesis, lucency at the bone-cement interface, and periostitis or other evidence of osteomyelitis. An arthrogram can confirm the presence of a loose prosthesis and often allows for simultaneous aspiration of the joint for culture. The combination of a three-phase ^{99}Tc bone scan and an indium-labeled leukocyte scan is the most sensitive

---

BOX 14–4

Microbiology of 1033 Definite Prosthetic-Joint Infections (PJI) Seen at Mayo Clinic between 1969 and 1991

Microorganisms	Number (%) of PJI
Coagulase-negative staphylococci	254 (25)
S aureus	240 (23)
Polymicrobial	147 (14)
Gram-negative bacilli	114 (11)
Streptococci[1]	79 (8)
Unknown[2]	83 (8)
Anaerobes	62 (6)
Enterococci	29 (3)
Other microorganisms	25 (2)
Total	1033 (100)

[1]Includes beta-hemolytic streptococci and viridans group streptococci.
[2]Includes cases in which there was no growth on routine bacterial cultures, routine bacterial cultures were not obtained, or microbiologic information was not available.

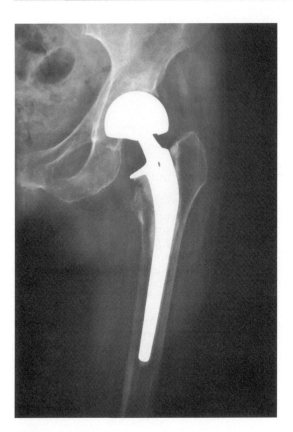

Figure 14–3. Plain radiograph of an infected total hip arthoplasty, illustrating lucency at the bone-cement interface of the femoral component.

and specific radionuclide test for the presence of prosthetic-joint infection.

Differential Diagnosis

When an acute infection occurs or if a draining sinus tract is present, the diagnosis of prosthetic-joint infection is clear. If only chronic pain is present then infection must be distinguished from aseptic loosening.

Complications

Failure of diagnosis and treatment of prosthetic joint infection may lead to chronic pain, loosening and failure of the prosthesis, loss of limb function, and rarely amputation. Squamous cell carcinoma may rarely complicate a draining sinus tract.

Treatment & Prognosis

A number of medical and surgical approaches have been described for the treatment of prosthetic-joint infection; however, there are no controlled trials to guide the clinician on which one may be best for the individual patient. The goal of treatment is a pain-free functional joint. Eradication of infection is the

most direct method to achieve this goal but may not be possible in certain instances. Basic treatment options include chronic suppressive antimicrobial therapy, surgical débridement with retention of the prosthesis, resection arthroplasty, arthrodesis, amputation, and one- or two-stage reimplantation.

Long-term eradication of infection can be achieved in between 85% and 95% of cases by removal of the infected prosthesis with or without subsequent staged reimplantation of another prosthesis, followed by 4–6 wk of intravenous antimicrobial therapy directed at the pathogens causing infection. The best functional results occur when another prosthesis can be reimplanted. Specific antimicrobial regimens are similar to those shown in Box 14–2.

If removal of the prosthesis is not feasible, then 4- to 6-wk intravenous antimicrobial therapy is administered after débridement of the prosthesis. This treatment option has been successful in between 50% and 70% percent of patients when the débridement has occurred within 1 mo of prosthesis implantation or within several days of the onset of an acute infection. Overall, however, this technique has a success rate of only 20–30%.

Occasionally chronic suppressive antibiotics may be used. Proposed criteria for the selection of appropriate candidates for chronic antimicrobial suppression include the following: (1) removal of the prosthesis is not feasible; (2) the microorganism is of low virulence and is highly susceptible to orally administered antimicrobial agents; (3) there are no signs of systemic infection; (4) the patient is compliant and tolerant of the antimicrobial agent; and (5) the prosthesis is not already loose.

Prevention

A. Perioperative Infection. The preponderance of evidence in multiple clinical trials favors the use of antimicrobial prophylaxis at the time of joint placement compared with no prophylaxis. Prophylactic antimicrobial agents should be directed against the common organisms that cause postoperative wound infection. Because staphylococci and streptococci are the most common organisms to cause these infections, agents directed against these pathogens, such as penicillinase-resistant penicillins and first-generation cephalosporins, are often used. Recent studies also suggest that antibiotic-impregnated cement may be effective in the prophylaxis of deep wound infection after total joint replacement. Further studies with longer follow-up periods are needed before this practice can be endorsed. The utility of laminar airflow devices in preventing prosthetic-joint infection remains controversial.

B. Hematogenous Infection. The majority of hematogenous infections are caused by *S aureus,* coagulase-negative staphylococci, and beta-hemolytic streptococci, presumably from a skin source. Urinary tract and respiratory tract infections have also been implicated as sources of infection. It seems prudent to aggressively diagnose and treat systemic infections in patients with a prosthetic joint, to prevent hematogenous seeding of the prosthesis. Optimal antimicrobial therapy for these infections will depend on the source of infection, in vitro susceptibility of the organism causing infection, and the patient's history of antibiotic allergies.

Antimicrobial prophylaxis is controversial for patients with a prosthetic joint who undergo a dental procedure or invasive procedures such as endoscopy and cystoscopy. Guidelines for this practice have recently been published.

REFERENCES

Carragee EJ: Pyogenic vertebral osteomyelitis. J Bone J Surg 1997;79:874. (Most recent review from surgical perspective.)

Fitzgerald RH et al: Advisory statement: antibiotic prophylaxis for dental patients with total joint replacements. American Dental Association–American Academy of Orthopedic Surgeons. J Am Dent Assoc 1997;128:1004.

Haas DW, McAndrew MP: Bacterial osteomyelitis in adults: evolving considerations in diagnosis and treatment. Am J Med 1996;101:550. (Excellent review of antimicrobial therapy.)

Lew DP, Waldvogel FA: Osteomyelitis. N Engl J Med 1997;336:999. (Most recent review.)

Mader JT, Oritz M, Calhoun JH: Update on the diagnosis and management of osteomyelitis. Clin Podiatr Med Surg 1996;4:701. (Review from surgical perspective.)

Nolan RL, Chapman SW: Osteomyelitis and diabetic foot infections. In Reese RE, Betts RF, eds: *A Practical Approach to Infectious Diseases,* 4th ed. Little, Brown, 1996. (Concise review from infectious diseases experts.)

Roberts NJ, Mock DJ: Joint infections. In Reese RE, Betts RF, eds: *A Practical Approach to Infectious Diseases,* 4th ed. Little, Brown, 1996. (Concise review from infectious diseases experts.)

Smith JW, Piercy EA: Infectious arthritis. Clin Infect Dis 1995;20:225.(Excellent review.)

Steckelberg JM, Osmon DR: Prosthetic joint infection. In Bisno AL, Waldvogel FA, eds: *Infections Associated with Indwelling Medical Devices,* 2nd ed. Am Soc Microbiol, 1994. (Concise review.)

Sexually Transmitted Diseases

15

John W. Wilson, MD & Nancy K. Henry, PhD, MD

URETHRITIS

Essentials of Diagnosis

- Mucopurulent or purulent urethral discharge and dysuria.
- Gram stain of urethral discharge shows > five leukocytes per high-power field.
- Positive leukocyte esterase test on first-void urine.
- Presence of gram-negative diplococci on stain or culture does not exclude other coinfecting pathogens.

General Considerations

Urethritis is the most common sexually transmitted disease (STD) syndrome recognized in men and is frequently seen in women with coinciding cervicitis. Cases can be of two types, gonococcal urethritis and nongonococcal urethritis (NGU), based on the presence or absence of *Neiserria gonorrhoeae*. The two forms are not mutually exclusive. Coinfection with *N gonorrhoeae* and *Chlamydia trachomatis* or *Ureaplasma urealyticum* occurs in 15–25% of heterosexual men with urethritis. NGU that occurs soon after curative therapy for gonorrhea is called postgonococcal urethritis (PGU).

The Centers for Disease Control and Prevention estimates that NGU is 2.5-fold more prevalent than gonococcal urethritis in the United States and much of the developed world. However, gonococcal urethritis accounts for up to 80% of acute urethritis cases in certain underdeveloped regions of the world. Among people of higher socioeconomic status and college students, NGU is more common. In urban STD clinics, gonococcal urethritis is more common.

Etiology

Box 15–1 lists causative organisms associated with various forms of urethritis. Noninfectious causes exist but should be considered only after infectious pathogens are excluded.

A. Gonococcal Urethritis. *N gonorrhoeae* is a gram-negative intracellular coccus that characteristically grows in pairs (diplococci). Two points deserve special mention. First, over the last 25 years, the prevalence of penicillin- and tetracycline-resistant gonococci has been increasing worldwide, requiring alternative treatment strategies. Second, *N gonorrhoeae* may not be limited to urethritis. Patients may present with coinfection of the cervix, rectum, or pharynx or have symptoms of disseminated infection.

B. Nongonococcal Urethritis. *C trachomatis* is the most common pathogen of NGU. It is isolated in 30–50% of patients with NGU. *U urealyticum* is found in 20–25% of cases. The other infectious causes of NGU account for 1–5% of cases and include *Trichomonas vaginalis,* herpes simplex virus (HSV), *Mycoplasma genitalium,* and *Candida* spp. The causes for the remaining 20–30% of NGU cases remain unclear.

C trachomatis is an obligate intracellular parasite. It causes > 4 million infections each year. However, a recent multicenter study reported a declining percentage of NGU cases caused by *C trachomatis,* < 25% in some centers. This may reflect the increasing use of faster diagnostic tests, enabling an earlier diagnosis and treatment. The result is a decrease in the reinfection rate and spread of disease.

The role of *U urealyticum* is less clear in NGU. *U urealyticum* may be found in the urethra of many asymptomatic sexually active men and is a common commensal organism in the genital tract of sexually active women. Nevertheless, *U urealyticum* is believed to have a pathogenic role. There is an increased prevalence and concentration of the organism in the urethra of men with NGU compared with those without NGU. Men with NGU and *U urealyticum* isolated from the urethra respond better to antimicrobial agents with antiureaplasma activity than to those without antiureaplasma activity.

The importance of *T vaginalis* as a cause of urethritis has been controversial. A recent study showed the organism to be present in 17% of patients with nonchlamydial NGU in one U.S. series, indicating a more epidemiological association between *T vaginalis* and NGU than previously thought. Furthermore, a favorable symptomatic response of men with trichomonad-positive NGU to metronidazole has been demonstrated.

There has been compelling evidence that *M genitalium* is another cause for urethritis. It is more

<table>
<tr><td colspan="2">

BOX 15-1

Cause of Urethritis
</td></tr>
</table>

Type	Organism/Cause
Infectious	
Gonococcal	• *Neisseria gonorrhoeae*
Nongonococcal	• *Chlamydia trachomatis* • *Ureaplasma urealyticum* • *Trichomonas vaginalis* • Herpes simplex virus • *Mycoplasma genitalium* • *Candida* spp.
Noninfectious	• Systemic disease Wegener's granulomatosis Stevens-Johnson's syndrome • Chemical Alcohol (dysuria) Spermicides (used by sexual partner) • Renal stones & crystals • Urethral trauma with instrumentation • Indwelling catheters

prevalent in homosexual men and in individuals with persistent and recurrent NGU. Detection is more for epidemiological interest because recurrent urethritis is usually treated with agents that are active against *M genitalium.*

HSV is an uncommon cause of urethritis. When it occurs, it is usually in the setting of primary genital herpes infection. Urethral involvement is less common in recurrent disease.

Clinical Findings

A. Signs and Symptoms. See Table 15–1 for a comparison of the clinical findings associated with gonococcal urethritis and NGU. Distinguishing between them may be difficult. The incubation period for gonococcal urethritis is 2–7 days, after which an acute onset of purulent urethral discharge and dysuria

usually develops. Of males with gonococcal urethritis, 5–10% are asymptomatic or have symptoms that are ignored.

The incubation of *C trachomatis* urethritis is longer, between 7 and 21 days. Symptoms of NGU tend to arise less abruptly, and the urethral discharge is less profuse and more mucoid in appearance. Dysuria may be present without urethral discharge. Urinary frequency, hematuria, and urgency are infrequent with either infection.

Trichomonas urethritis in men is often asymptomatic, making detection difficult. Acute symptomatic trichomoniasis in men usually presents with signs and symptoms similar to chlamydial urethritis. Purulent urethritis and prostatitis are unusual.

In HSV urethritis, dysuria is usually more severe, and the urethral discharge may be diffuse and mucoid. There may be regional lymphadenopathy and constitutional symptoms present with primary HSV urethritis. Genital lesions are not always present.

B. Laboratory Findings.

Examination of the Urethral Discharge. The diagnosis of urethritis can be made microscopically based on the presence of five or more leukocytes per high-power field in a sample of urethral exudate. The leukocyte esterase test is an alternative screening test for urethritis that can be used on first voided urine samples. It is nonspecific and has a sensitivity of 80%.

The diagnosis of gonococcal urethritis can be made on a stained slide of male urethral exudate if gram-negative diplococci are seen. This finding is present in >95% of symptomatic men with gonococcal urethritis. The presence of gram-negative diplococci, however, does not rule out the possibility of coinfection with NGU organisms.

Detection of *N gonorrhoeae.* If the urethral Gram stain is negative for gonococci, a culture should be done. *N gonorrhoeae* is a fastidious organism requiring a selective growth medium in a CO_2-rich environment. Selective growth media include Thayer-Martin, Martin-Lewis, and New York City media.

Nonculture or rapid diagnostic tests for gonococcal infection include Gonozyme, the Gen-Probe Pace 2 and the ligase chain reaction (LCR). Gonozyme is an enzyme immunoassay that can detect gonococcal

Table 15–1. Clinical comparison between gonococcal and nongonococcal urethritis.

Clinical Finding	Gonorrhea	NGU
Onset of symptoms	Classically abrupt 75% men develop symptoms within 4 days; 80–90% men develop symptoms within 2 weeks	Less acute onset Approximately 50% men develop symptoms within 4 days
Frankly purulent urethral discharge	75%	11–33%
Mucopurulent discharge	25%	50%
Completely clear discharge	4%	10–50%
Dysuria	73–88%	53–75%

antigens within the urethra, cervix, and urine. The Gen-Probe Pace 2 uses nonisotopic probes to detect ribosomal RNA. LCR utilizes a DNA amplification technique to detect trace amounts of organism-specific nucleic acid sequences from urethral and endocervical swab specimens and urine samples.

Detection of *C trachomatis.* Cell culture is considered the gold standard for chlamydial testing. It has a sensitivity of 75–80% and a specificity approaching 100%. The addition of an enzyme immunoassay to culture increases the sensitivity to 95%. Cultures are expensive and may require 3–7 days for results.

Nonculture rapid diagnostic tests, including the direct fluorescence antibody (DFA) test, enzyme-linked immunoassay (EIA) test, and DNA probe tests, provide a more prompt diagnosis than culture with roughly an equivalent specificity. The sensitivity is 70–90%. The Gen-Probe Pace 2 and LCR assays detect rRNA and DNA sequences, respectively, of both *N gonorrhoeae* and *C trachomatis.* The sensitivity is higher than that of cell cultures without compromise in specificity.

Detection of Other Pathogens. Identification of *U urealyticum* requires culture. Because *U urealyticum* can be isolated in men without urethritis, a positive culture for *U urealyticum* does not necessarily identify the cause of the urethritis.

The gold standard for diagnosing trichomoniasis is isolating the protozoa in culture. A more rapid and less expensive method is the direct microscopic wet mount examination of urethral discharge. The accuracy of the exam is based on identifying motile protozoa with characteristic morphology. The wet mount exam is routinely used to evaluate women for vaginal trichomoniasis (50–70% sensitive) but is less sensitive with urethral discharge from infected men.

Differential Diagnosis

Noninfectious causes of urethritis should be considered only after infectious pathogens are excluded. Urethritis caused by Wegener's granulomatosis may be suggested by the findings of upper- or lower-respiratory-tract disease, mucosal ulcerations, cartilaginous destruction, and glomerulonephritis. Stevens-Johnson's syndrome may produce a urethritis associated with characteristic skin and mucosal lesions with systemic toxicity. Prior exposure to certain drugs (eg, sulfonamides, nonsteroidal anti-inflammatory drugs, and phenytoin) is typical. Urethral trauma from instrumentation and indwelling urinary catheters is a frequent cause of urethritis in hospitalized patients. Urethral irritation from renal stones, spermicides, and alcohol can also occur.

Complications

Disseminated gonorrhea, which occurs in 0.5% of untreated cases of gonococcal infection, presents with fever, arthritis or tenosynovitis, and a skin rash.

The rash may be scattered pustular lesions or hemorrhagic necrotic blisters on extensor surfaces of the extremities. Reiter's syndrome is a human leukocyte antigen B27-associated spondyloarthropathy that can follow a genitourinary infection with *C trachomatis.* It is characterized by urethritis, asymmetric oligoarthritis, conjunctivitis, and skin and mucous membrane lesions. Reiter's syndrome can also follow bacterial gastroenteritis caused by *Salmonella, Shigella, Yersinia,* and *Campylobacter* spp. Epididymitis and urethral strictures secondary to urethritis are rare with treatment. A small proportion of patients may develop conjunctivitis caused by either *N gonorrhoeae* or *C trachomatis.* This is most likely a result of autoinoculation with these organisms from a genital source.

Treatment

A. Gonococcal Urethritis. In 1976, penicillin-resistant gonococci were identified and found to have acquired plasmids encoding for the production of beta-lactamase. Approximately 15% of all gonococci in the United States are now penicillin resistant. In some urban areas, the incidence is as high as 60–75%. In 1985, tetracycline-resistant gonococci were identified and also found to have plasmid-encoded resistance. Tetracycline-resistant gonococci are responsible for up to 15% of gonococcal infections along the eastern coast of the United States. *N gonorrhoeae* with chromosomal mutations conferring penicillin and tetracycline resistance has also been identified. Because of the increasing frequency of penicillin- and tetracycline-resistant gonococci, the penicillins and tetracyclines are no longer recommended by the Centers for Disease Control and Prevention for treatment. Quinolone-resistant gonococci have been identified but are rare in the United States and have not altered current treatment recommendations.

Gonococcal urethritis can be successfully treated with a number of single-dose regimens (Box 15–2). Intramuscular ceftriaxone cures nearly 100% of genital infections and is effective for the treatment of gonococcal infection at all sites. Ceftriaxone is also active against incubating syphilis. Oral cefixime is nearly as active against *N gonorrhoeae* and is less expensive.

For the beta-lactam–allergic patient, oral ciprofloxacin or ofloxacin is highly effective. Both are less expensive and better tolerated than ceftriaxone but are contraindicated in pregnancy and for patients under age 18. Patients with disseminated gonococcal infection should be hospitalized for intravenous therapy.

Many patients who experience symptomatic relief after a single-dose treatment for gonococcal urethritis develop a prompt recurrence or persistence of milder symptoms. This syndrome is called postgonococcal urethritis (PGU) and is the result of dual infection of the urethra with *N gonorrhoeae* and organisms of NGU. *N gonorrhoeae* is eradicated by a single dose

BOX 15-2

Treatment of Infectious Urethritis and/or Cervicitis

Syndrome/Microorganism	First-Line Therapy	Alternative Therapy
Empiric therapy (treat for both *N gonorrhoeae* and *C trachomatis*)	• Combination therapy for both organisms (see below)	
Gonococcal urethritis (*N gonorrhoeae*)	• Ceftriaxone, 125 mg IM ×1 • Ciprofloxacin, 500 mg orally × 1[1] • Ofloxacin, 400 mg orally × 1 • Cefixime, 400 mg orally × 1	• Spectinomycin, 2 g IM × 1[2] • Ceftizoxime, 250–500 mg IM × 1[3] • Cefuroxime axetil, 1 g orally × 1[3]
Nongonococcal urethritis (*C trachomatis* or *U urealyticum*)	Doxycycline, 100 mg orally twice daily × 7 d[4] • Azithromycin, 1 g orally x 1	• Erythromycin base, 500 mg orally four times daily × 7 d • Erythromycin ethylsuccinate, 800 mg orally four times daily × 7 d • Ofloxacin, 300 mg orally twice daily × 7 d • Amoxicillin, 500 mg orally twice daily × 7 d
Recurrent/Persistent Urethritis	• Ensure patient is compliant with therapy • Evaluate for possible reexposure to untreated infected sexual partner • Wet mount +/− culture for *T vaginalis*	• Retreat • Retreat • Metronidazole, 2 g orally × 1[5] plus erythromycin base, 500 mg orally four times daily × 7 d OR • Erythromycin ethylsuccinate, 800 mg orally four times daily × 7 d

[1]The fluoroquinolones should not be used during pregnancy or in patients under age 18.
[2]Spectinomycin, once widely used for the treatment of gonorrhea, has the disadvantages of higher cost, requirement for injection, and lack of sustained high-serum bactericidal levels.
[3]Ceftizoxime and cefuroxime are well tolerated but less active.
[4]Doxycycline should not be used during pregnancy.
[5]Metronidazole should not be given during the first trimester of pregnancy. Metronidazole may cause a disulfiramlike reaction with alcohol.

of the aforementioned cephalosporins and quinolones, but the organisms responsible for NGU are often spared. PGU should be suspected if signs, symptoms, or laboratory evidence of urethritis is found 4–7 days after a single-dose treatment for gonococcal urethritis. Unless chlamydial infection has been specifically ruled out through testing, all patients treated for gonococcal infections should also be treated for chlamydial infection.

B. Nongonococcal Urethritis. Empiric therapy is directed against the two most common pathogens, *C trachomatis* and *U urealyticum*. Oral doxycycline has been the traditional drug of choice for NGU. It is highly effective against *C trachomatis* and moderately effective against *U urealyticum*, and it is inexpensive. Azithromycin is a first-line drug that can be administered as a single oral dose. This offers a significant advantage of increased patient compliance, but is more expensive than doxycycline. For acute nongonococcal urethritis in men, single-dose oral azithromycin is as effective as the standard 7-day therapy with doxycycline. Alternative choices include ofloxacin and erythromycin. Ofloxacin remains the only single drug recommended for treatment of both gonococcal and chlamydial infections. Tetracycline/doxycycline-resistant *U urealyticum* exists and is the basis for treating patients with erythromycin who fail standard therapy.

Patients with recurrent or persistent symptoms should be retreated with the initial regimen if noncompliance is suspected; otherwise a wet mount and culture for *T vaginalis* can be done. Treatment of *Trichomonas*-caused urethritis with a single oral dose of metronidazole is usually sufficient.

Prognosis

In early gonococcal infections, a single course of the appropriate antimicrobial agent is almost always curative. Recurrent disease is more common in NGU; however, patients failing therapy need to be questioned about drug compliance and the possibility of re-exposure to an infected partner. Complications are rare when infectious urethritis is treated early. To prevent reinfection and the spread of disease, patients should avoid sexual contact for 7 days after a single-dose treatment or during a 7-day treatment regimen. Sexual contact should also be avoided until infected partners have been adequately treated.

CERVICITIS

Essentials of Diagnosis

- Characterized by purulent or mucopurulent endocervical discharge.
- Gram stain of cervical discharge shows > 10 leukocytes per high-power field.
- Most common in adolescent females.
- Commonly presents without symptoms.
- Abdominal pain and adnexal tenderness may signify pelvic inflammatory disease.

General Considerations

Cervicitis is the most common STD syndrome in women and is caused primarily by *N gonorrhoeae, C trachomatis,* HSV, and human papillomavirus (HPV). It represents an inflammation of the columnar and subepithelium of the endocervix and can involve any contiguous columnar epithelium that lies exposed on the ectocervix. In adolescent girls, the transition zone is frequently everted over part of the ectocervix, thereby increasing the amount of susceptible columnar tissue exposed to a pathogen. This biological circumstance, combined with an increased number of sexual partners without barrier methods of contraception, places adolescent girls at highest risk for cervicitis from an STD pathogen. Interestingly, oral contraceptives cause cervical eversion (ectropion) and may increase the risk of chlamydial infection but have not been shown to increase gonococcal infection.

Even though most of these organisms also cause male urethritis, there is a strong gender bias for infection in women. Male-to-female transmission of infection is more common than female to male.

Clinical Findings

Infectious cervicitis has often been referred to as the "silent partner" of male urethritis. The lack of well-recognized symptoms and signs of cervical in-flammation has largely impeded clinical recognition of sexually transmitted cervical infections.

A. Signs and Symptoms. Acute gonococcal cervicitis is characterized by a purulent cervical discharge and cervical edema. Nonspecific symptoms include increased vaginal discharge in approximately one-third of patients, increased menses, dysmenorrhea, dyspareunia, and dysuria. As many as 50 percent of women with gonococcal cervicitis also have gonococcal infection of the urethra, which may explain the urinary-tract symptoms reported by many female patients. Approximately 50% of women with uncomplicated gonococcal cervicitis are asymptomatic and may remain culture positive for 3–6 months after the initial infection.

C trachomatis typically causes a mucopurulent cervicitis, but nonspecific abdominal pain and spotting with intercourse may occur. Cervical abnormalities are often subtle, and only one-third of women note a vaginal discharge that originates from the inflamed cervix. On examination, 20–70% of infected women will have a completely normal appearing cervix.

HSV cervicitis usually presents with a more mucoid, less commonly mucopurulent cervical discharge. Affected patients may complain of lower abdominal pain. The cervix usually appears friable with occasional frank ulcers or necrosis. External genital lesions are usually absent. Inguinal adenopathy is unusual unless accompanied by external genital lesions.

B. Laboratory Findings. The presence of cervicitis can be established by a variety of diagnostic procedures, including Gram stain of the endocervical mucus, cervical cytology, colposcopy, and cervical biopsy. The microscopic presence of 10 leukocytes per high-power field supports the diagnosis of mucopurulent cervicitis. Gram-negative intracellular diplococci on a stain of cervical discharge can suggest, but not diagnose, gonococcal cervicitis. Because the presence of commensal *Neisseria* spp. and morphologically similar organisms such as *Haemophilus* spp. decreases the specificity of cervical-discharge Gram stains, a positive stain should be confirmed with a positive culture for *N gonorrhoeae.* The same culture and rapid nonculture diagnostic tests described for urethritis can be used to identify *N gonorrhoeae* and *C trachomatis* in cervical specimens.

The diagnosis of HSV cervicitis can be made cytologically by observing multinucleated giant cells, often with intranuclear inclusions. The diagnosis can be confirmed by isolating the virus in culture or by immunofluorescent staining. Viral isolation will permit the differentiation of HSV-1 from HSV-2. This has prognostic significance because HSV-1 is less likely than HSV-2 to cause recurrent genital herpes.

Differential Diagnosis

Symptoms of dysuria, vaginal discharge, and abdominal pain are not specific for cervicitis. Vulvovaginitis, pelvic inflammatory disease (PID), urethritis, and cystitis may produce a similar clinical picture. A speculum exam and urinalysis are indicated to rule out vaginitis, urethritis, and cystitis. Erythema around the cervical os can indicate infection or merely represent cervical ectropion.

Complications

There are four categories of complications from cervical infections: (*a*) ascending intraluminal spread of infection producing endometritis, salpingitis, PID, ectopic pregnancies, and infertility; (*b*) ascending infection during pregnancy, producing premature rupture of the membranes, premature birth, low birth weight, spontaneous abortion, and intrauterine death; (*c*) initiation or promotion of cervical neoplasia; and (*d*) perinatal infections acquired during delivery through an infected birth canal, including ophthalmia neonatorum/inclusion conjunctivitis and neonatal herpes.

Gonococcal and chlamydial infections are the most common causes of PID, ectopic pregnancy, and impaired fertility in women. If not adequately treated, 20–40% of women infected with *C trachomatis* and 10–40% of women infected with *N gonorrhoeae* develop PID. At least 25% of women with PID during their reproductive years develop a related complication, including infertility, ectopic pregnancy, and chronic pelvic pain.

Treatment

The treatment options for gonococcal and chlamydial cervicitis are the same as those described for infectious urethritis (Box 15–2). The treatment program should always include activity against both *C trachomatis* and *N gonorrhoeae*. The tetracyclines, including doxycycline, and the quinolones are contraindicated during pregnancy. For pregnant patients, erythromycin (base or ethylsuccinate) or amoxicillin is recommended for anti-Chlamydia therapy. Treatments for HSV and HPV are described later.

Prognosis

Early treatment of cervicitis is quite effective, usually with prompt resolution of symptoms. As with their male counterparts, women with recurrent disease need to be questioned regarding treatment compliance and reexposure. Asymptomatic disease remains a significant problem. Therefore, screening women is a major element in *Chlamydia* prevention. The recommendations for *Chlamydia* screening in women are listed in Table 15–2. To prevent reinfection and the spread of disease, the same measures should be taken as described for urethritis.

Table 15–2. Recommendations for chlamydia screening in women.

Sexually active adolescents (under age 20).

Women aged 20–24 who inconsistently use barrier methods of contraception, who have a new sex partner, or who have had more than one sex partner, within the past 3 months.

Women older than age 24 who inconsistently use barrier methods of contraception and have a new partner, or have had more than one sex partner, within the past 3 months.

Pregnant women in their third trimester.

Women undergoing an abortion.

Women with mucopurulent cervicitis on pelvic exam, regardless of symptoms

VULVOVAGINITIS

Essentials of Diagnosis

- Clinical clues include vaginal discharge, vulvar pruritus, and dyspareunia.
- Microscopic exam with a cover slip can reveal motile trichomonads and clue cells.
- Potassium hydroxide (KOH) preparation enables identification of *Candida* spp. as yeast or pseudohyphae.
- Positive whiff test in trichomoniasis and bacterial vaginosis (BV).
- Vaginal fluid pH is > 4.5 in trichomoniasis and BV.

General Considerations

The three most common types of vaginal infections in adult women are vulvovaginal candidiasis (20–25%), BV (30–45%), and trichomoniasis (15–20%). Other less common pathogen-related causes include ulcerative vaginitis attributed to *Staphylococcus aureus* toxins in women with toxic shock syndrome, clindamycin-responsive desquamative inflammatory vaginitis, group A streptococcal vaginitis, and idiopathic vulvovaginal ulceration associated with HIV infection.

A. Vulvovaginal Candidiasis. An estimated 75% of women experience at least one episode of vulvovaginal candidiasis during their lifetime, and 40–50% will have two or more episodes. Recurrent vulvovaginal candidiasis is defined as four or more episodes of infection per year and occurs in < 5% of healthy women. The role of vulvovaginal candidiasis as an STD is controversial. *Candida* spp. are among the normal vaginal flora, and vulvovaginal candidiasis can occur in women who have never engaged in sexual activity. Nonsexual predisposing risk factors for the development of vulvovaginal candidiasis include the use of broad-spectrum antibacterial agents, oral contraceptives, corticosteroids, pregnancy, diabetes mellitus, and a decrease in cell-mediated immunity. There is, however, an increase in the frequency of vulvovaginal candidiasis at the time most women begin regular sexual activity. Penile colonization with *Candida* spp. is fourfold more prevalent among male sexual partners of infected women than among other men of the same population. The most common pathogens for vulvovaginal candidiasis include *C albicans* (accounts for 80–90% of cases), *C glabrata* (10%), and *C tropicalis* (5%).

B. Bacterial Vaginosis. BV is the most common cause of infectious vaginitis. It signifies a change in the normal vaginal flora characterized by the replacement of hydrogen peroxide-producing lactobacilli with high concentrations of anaerobic bacteria (eg, *Bacteroides* spp., *Mobiluncus* spp., and *Peptostreptococcus* spp.), *Gardnerella vaginalis,* and *Mycoplasma hominis.* The cause of this microbial alteration is not fully understood. Most of these organisms are normally found in low numbers within the healthy vagina. The role of *G. vaginalis* as a pathogen remains unclear, but it may interact synergistically with vaginal anaerobes to produce disease. Sexual transmission of organisms associated with BV has been demonstrated; however transmission alone is not sufficient to cause disease. Additional risk factors for the development of BV include menstruation, poor hygiene, intrauterine devices, and previous pregnancies.

C. Trichomoniasis. *T vaginalis* is a common sexually transmitted pathogen and, unlike *Candida* spp., is closely linked epidemiologically to other STDs. *T vaginalis* can be identified in 30–40% of the male sexual partners of infected women. Risk factors associated with the acquisition of *T vaginalis* include sexual activity, pregnancy, and menopause. During menses, blood raises the vaginal pH, which is more suitable for trichomonad replication.

Clinical Findings

Table 15–3 summarizes the clinical and microscopic findings associated with vaginitis.

A. Vulvovaginal Candidiasis. Patients with vulvovaginal candidiasis often report intense perivaginal itching or burning sensations. The vaginal discharge classically has a thick white "cottage cheese" texture that is odorless and adherent to the vaginal walls. If external vaginitis is present, dysuria may be the major complaint. Labial erythema and edema, linear perineal fissures or excoriations, and pustulopapular perineal dermatitis often develop.

A normal vaginal pH (4–4.5) and the microscopic finding of budding yeasts or pseudohyphae on a slide of vaginal discharge with 10% KOH can make the diagnosis. If the KOH is negative and clinical suspicion for candidiasis is high, a culture for *Candida* spp. can be performed.

B. Bacterial Vaginosis. Affected women usually complain of a slightly increased malodorous vaginal discharge that is gray-white in color, thin, and homogenous. Pruritus and vulvar inflammation are notably absent. Many women with BV are asymptomatic.

The pH of the vaginal fluid is elevated above 4.5 (usually in the range of 4.7–5.5). A characteristic "fishy" odor is produced when the vaginal fluid is mixed with 10% KOH. This is called a positive "whiff test" and is the result of volatilization of aromatic amines at an alkaline pH. A wet mount or a

Table 15–3. Clinical features of vaginitis.[1]

	Normal	Vulvovaginal Candidiasis	Trichomoniasis	Bacterial Vaginosis
Symptoms	None	Pruritus Soreness Dyspareunia	Soreness Dyspareunia Often asymptomatic	Often asymptomatic Occasional abdominal pain
Discharge				
Amount	Variable	Scant/moderate	Profuse	Moderate
Color	Clear/white	White	Green-yellow	White/gray
Consistency	Nonhomogenous floccular	Clumped, adherent	Homogenous, frothy	Homogenous adherent
Vaginal fluid pH	4.0–4.5	4.0–4.5	5.0–6.0	>4.5
Amine test (fish odor)	None	None	Usually positive	Positive
Microscopy				
Saline	PMN:EC ratio <1 Lactobacilli predominate	PMN:EC <1 Pseudohyphae (~40%)	PMN:EC >1 Motile trichomonads PMNs predominate	PMN:EC <1 Clue cells Coccobacilli
10% KOH	Negative	Pseudohyphae (~70%)	Negative	Negative

[1]PMN, Polymorphonuclear leukocytes; EC, vaginal epithelial cells.

Gram stain of the vaginal fluid shows vaginal epithelial cells covered with coccobacilli. These characteristic epithelial cells are called "clue cells." Established diagnostic criteria for BV require three of the following four signs: (1) presence of clue cells, (2) homogenous noninflammatory discharge adherent to vaginal walls, (3) vaginal fluid pH > 4.5, and (4) positive whiff test.

C. Trichomoniasis. Trichomoniasis generally produces copious amounts of a thin, frothy, green-yellow or gray, malodorous vaginal discharge. Infected women may also complain of vaginal soreness and dyspareunia. However, a large proportion of women carrying trichomonads are asymptomatic.

On examination, the vaginal and exocervical epithelium may have an edematous and erythematous appearance with increased vascularity and petechiae formation. This is often referred to as the "strawberry cervix" of trichomoniasis. The vaginal pH is usually >5.0. The vaginal discharge contains many leukocytes and may elicit an odor when 10% KOH is added (positive whiff test). Confirmation of trichomoniasis is made when motile, pear-shaped trichomonads are seen on the wet mount; however, this occurs in only 50–70% of cases. In patients with an elevated vaginal pH, increased number of leukocytes, and an absence of motile trichomonads or clue cells on the wet mount, a culture for *T vaginalis* can be done to confirm the diagnosis.

Differential Diagnosis

Toxic shock syndrome with *S aureus* can produce vaginitis along with characteristic symptoms of fever, rash, hypotension, multiorgan abnormalities, and often a polymucositis. Desquamative inflammatory vaginitis may produce prominent cell exfoliation and purulent vaginal discharge with an elevated pH. Patients may respond to clindamycin or corticosteroids.

Noninfectious causes of vaginitis must be distinguished from infectious ones. Atrophic vaginitis commonly affects postmenopausal women and is the result of decreased estrogen levels. There is thinning of the vaginal epithelium, reduced lubrication, an increase in vaginal pH, and an overgrowth of nonacidophilic coliforms. Symptoms include vaginal soreness, dyspareunia, postcoital burning, and occasional vaginal spotting. Treatment consists of topical vaginal estrogen. Other noninfectious causes include chemicals or irritants (eg, spermicides, topical antimycotic drugs, minipads, or topical fluorouracil), contact dermatitis, and collagen vascular disease.

Complications

PID, plasma cell endometriosis, and posthysterectomy vaginal-cuff cellulitis are the major complications of BV (see Chapter 22). In pregnant women, BV is associated with preterm labor, premature rupture of the membranes, chorioamnionitis, and postcesarean and postpartum endometritis. Asymptomatic

high-risk pregnant women (eg, prior preterm delivery) should be screened for BV early in the second trimester. Trichomoniasis also may be associated with premature rupture of the membranes and preterm delivery.

Treatment

A. Vulvovaginal Candidiasis. Vulvovaginal candidiasis can be successfully treated with topical antifungal agents in > 80% of cases (Box 15–3). There are a variety of topical agents, including butoconazole, clotrimazole, miconazole, nystatin, tioconazole, and terconazole. They are applied intravaginally for 1, 3, or 7 days. Fluconazole is the only oral azole to be approved by the FDA for vulvovaginal candidiasis; however, oral ketoconazole is also effective. Non-*albicans* species are less susceptible to fluconazole and may require alternative agents. Treatment of male sexual partners is not necessary unless balanitis is present.

The optimal treatment for recurrent vulvovaginal candidiasis is not yet established. The initial treatment of recurrent vulvovaginal candidiasis is usually the same as for an acute episode. The duration, however, may be extended to 10–14 days, followed by a lower-dose maintenance regimen for 6 months. It is unclear whether the pathogenesis of recurrent infections involves the persistence of risk factors, repeated sexual transmission, an immunologic deficit, or a treatment failure. Treatment failure is not uncommon with *C glabrata.*

B. Bacterial Vaginosis. Metronidazole is quite active against vaginal anaerobic bacteria while its hydroxy-metabolite is moderately active against *G vaginalis.* Although the 7-day regimen has a slightly higher cure rate (> 90%), patient compliance may be greater with the single, higher-dose format. Clindamycin is an alternative oral treatment. Effective topical formulations include 2% clindamycin vaginal cream and 0.75% metronidazole vaginal gel. Routine treatment of male sexual partners has not been shown to improve cure rates. Symptomatic women in the first trimester of pregnancy should use oral clindamycin.

If BV is discovered during screening of asymptomatic pregnant women, treatment should be given at the beginning of the second trimester with metronidazole or clindamycin. If treatment must be given during the first trimester, clindamycin is recommended. Although there is concern for the effects of metronidazole to the unborn fetus, evidence of definitive teratogenicity remains unclear and is considered minimal after the first trimester. The treatment of high-risk pregnant women may reduce preterm delivery.

C. Trichomoniasis. The treatment of choice for trichomoniasis is metronidazole. Similar cure rates are obtained with the 7-day regimen (cure rate 85–90%) compared with the single, higher-dose for-

BOX 15–3

Treatment of Infectious Vaginitis

Syndrome/Microorganism	First Choice	Alternative Choice
Vulvovaginal Candidiasis	Intravaginal agents[1]: • Butoconazole, 2% cream 5 g[a] intravaginally for 3 days • Clotrimazole, 1% cream 5 g intravaginally for 7–14 days[2,3] • Clotrimazole, 100-mg vaginal tablet for 7 days,[2] or two 100-mg tablets for 3 days,[2] or 500-mg vaginal tablet in a single application • Miconazole, 2% cream 5 g intravaginally for 7 days[2,3] • Miconazole, 200-mg vaginal suppository for 3 days[2] or 100-mg suppository for 7 days[2] • Nystatin, 100,000 U vaginal tablet, one tablet for 7–14 days • Tioconazole, 6.5% ointment 5 g in a single application[2,3] • Terconazole, 0.4% cream 5 g intravaginally for 7 days[2] or 0.8% cream 5 g for 3 days[2] • Terconazole, 80 mg vaginal suppository for 3 days[2] Oral agents: • Fluconazole, 150-mg oral tablet once	Systemic agents • Fluconazole, 150-mg oral tablet once • Ketoconazole, 200 mg orally for 5–7 days or 400 mg orally for 3 days • Itraconazole, 400 mg orally once, then 200 mg orally for 2 more days
Bacterial Vaginosis	• Metronidazole, 500 mg orally twice daily for 7 days • Clindamycin cream, 2% 5 g intravaginally for 7 days • Metronidazole gel, 0.75% 5 g twice daily for 7 days	• Metronidazole, 2 g orally once • Clindamycin 300 mg orally twice daily for 7 days
Trichomoniasis	• Metronidazole, 2 g orally once	• Metronidazole 500 mg twice daily for 7 days

[1]Topical azole regimens should be used to treat pregnant women. Many experts recommend treating for 7 days during pregnancy.
[2]Available over the counter.
[3]These creams and suppositories are oil based and may weaken latex condoms and diaphragms.

mat (82–88%). Male sexual partners of infected women should also be treated. Pregnant patients can be treated with metronidazole after the first trimester.

Prognosis

Although not usually considered as a life-threatening disease, the symptoms of vaginitis can be severe and recurrent disease problematic. Screening during pregnancy can help lower BV and *Trichomonas*-associated maternal and neonatal complications.

GENITAL ULCER DISEASE

Essentials of Diagnosis

- Syphilis: Average incubation period 21 days, painless ulcer (chancre), nontender, nonfluctuant adenopathy.
- Chancroid: Incubation period 2–7 days, painful ulcers, fluctuant adenopathy.
- Genital herpes: Incubation period 2–7 days, multiple vesicles, painful ulcers, can be recurrent.
- Lymphogranuloma venereum (LGV): Variable incubation period, characteristic "groove sign," fluctuant buboes can rupture.
- Donovanosis: Variable incubation period, painless ulcers, scar formation.

General Considerations

Genital ulcer disease involves a disruption of the skin and mucous membranes of the genitalia and often is the presenting complaint of a sexually acquired infection. *Treponema pallidum* is the spirochete responsible for all stages of syphilis. It is the second most common cause of genital ulcer disease in both underdeveloped and developed countries, although it is more common in the latter. *Haemophilus ducreyi*, a gram-negative bacillus, is the organism responsible for chancroid. The disease is most prevalent in Africa and developing countries; however, a number of outbreaks have occurred in New Orleans and other large cities along the Gulf Coast. Genital herpes is the most common cause of genital ulcer disease in North America and Europe. It is an incurable and recurrent disease affecting an estimated 5 million–20 million Americans. Of all first-episode genital herpes lesions, 85% are produced by HSV-2 and the remaining 15% by HSV-1 (see Chapter 33). Recurrent infections are much more common with HSV-2. Sexual transmission of HSV can occur during asymptomatic periods. LGV is a chlamydial infection caused by the highly invasive L1, L2, and L3 serovars of *C trachomatis*. LGV is endemic in Africa, India, Southeast Asia, South America, and the Caribbean. Donovanosis is an ulcerative disease caused by the gram-negative bacillus *Calymmatobacterium granulomatosis*. Other names for this disorder include granuloma inguinale, granuloma venereum, granuloma donovani, chronic venereal sore, and granuloma inguinale tropicum. Although rare in the United States, donovanosis is a common cause of genital ulceration in southeastern India, New Guinea, the Caribbean, and parts of South America.

Clinical Findings

Table 15–4 summarizes the clinical findings associated with genital ulcer disease.

A. Signs and Symptoms.

Primary Syphilis. After an incubation period of ~21 days (range 3–90 days), a painless ulcer appears at the site of inoculation. This ulcer is called a chancre and is the hallmark of primary syphilis. Typically a solitary chancre exists, but multiple chancres may be present in HIV patients. The base of the chancre is usually clean and the borders smooth. The most common locations include the glans penis, frenulum, and penile shaft in men and the labia, vagina, and cervix in women. Extragenital locations for chancres include the perianal region (especially in homosexual men), oral mucosa, and pharynx. Unilateral or bilateral adenopathy usually develops after the chancre. The adenopathy is firm, nontender, and never fluctuant.

Chancroid. After a short incubation period of 2–7 days, one to three (or more) painful ulcers appear in the genital region. The ulcer base is typically necrotic and purulent with ragged undermined borders. The lesion is not indurated and has historically been called the "soft chancre." Painful inguinal lymphadenopathy is much more common in men (> 50%) than in women. It is usually unilateral but occasionally can be bilateral. The lymph nodes can enlarge and become fluctuant. Although the findings of a painful ulcer and tender inguinal adenopathy are suggestive of chancroid, the addition of suppurative adenopathy is almost pathognomonic.

Genital Herpes. Genital herpes also has a short incubation period of ~2–7 days. The characteristic lesions are multiple vesicles on an erythematous base. In women, these lesions frequently involve the labia minora and majora, cervix, and occasionally the vagina. In men, the glans and shaft of the penis are common sites. Homosexual men may manifest herpetic lesions over the perianal area. Several days after the appearance of the vesicles, they rupture, creating shallow, intensely painful ulcers that subsequently become crusted. Urethritis may occasionally develop.

Primary genital herpes is the initial infection by HSV in a patient without anti-HSV antibodies. It may be preceded by constitutional symptoms of low-grade fever, chills, headache, malaise, and myalgia. These symptoms are likely related to a transient viremia and usually subside after 1 week. More localized symptoms then develop, including genital pain, itching,

Table 15–4. Clinical features of genital ulcer disease.

	Syphilis	Chancroid	Genital Herpes	Lymphogranuloma Venereum	Donovanosis
Incubation period	Avg. 21 d Range 3–90 d	2–7 d Range 1–35 d	2–7 d	Avg. 10–14 d Range 3 d–3 wk	Variable
Number of lesions	Usually single, occasionally multiple	1–3; may be multiple	Multiple; may coalesce	Usually single	Single or multiple
Border	Sharply demarcated	Erythematous and undermined	Erythematous	Variable	Rolled and elevated
Base	Red, smooth; shiny or crusty	Yellow, gray; rough	Red, smooth	Variable	Red, rough; may be friable, beefy granulations
Induration	Firm	Rare, soft	None	None	Firm
Pain	Painless; pain may occur with secondary infection	Common	Common	Variable	Rare
Lymph nodes	Unilateral to bilateral; nontender, firm	Usually unilateral; may suppurate	Usually bilateral; firm and tender	Unilateral or bilateral; firm tender, later indolent, may suppurate	Pseudoadenopathy, inguinal swelling
Constitutional symptoms	Rare	Rare	Common in primary disease	Frequent	Rare

dysuria, and tender adenopathy. Localized paresthesia may develop in the outbreak site 24–48 h before the appearance of the vesicles. The skin lesions of primary genital herpes generally last 2–3 weeks. Nonprimary, first-episode genital herpes refers to patients previously infected with HSV, who have developed antibodies to HSV. The symptoms are usually milder, and the disease course shorter than in primary genital herpes. Systemic symptoms are generally absent. Recurrent genital herpes is a local disease without systemic symptoms and has a significantly milder presentation and shorter course than primary or nonprimary, first-episode genital herpes. These lesions generally resolve in 1 week.

Lymphogranuloma Venereum. Clinically, there are distinct stages of LGV. The first stage is marked by the formation of a primary genital skin or mucosal lesion in the form of a papule or herpetiform ulcer. It usually develops between 3 days and 3 weeks (up to 6 months) after exposure. It is painless and transient, and it heals rapidly without scarring. It is often unnoticed. The second stage is characterized by enlarged painful lymphadenopathy, which is unilateral in two-thirds of cases. This often is the presenting complaint of LGV and usually develops 2–6 weeks after exposure. Enlargement of nodes above and below the inguinal ligament produces the characteristic "groove sign." It is pathognomonic for LGV and occurs in approximately one-third of cases. Lymph nodes may become fluctuant (buboes) and can spontaneously rupture, forming loculated abscesses, fistulas, or sinus tracts. Approximately one-third of inguinal buboes become fluctuant and rupture, whereas the other two-thirds involute over time to form a hard inguinal mass without suppuration.

Systemic symptoms may include fever, chills, myalgia, and arthralgia.

Donovanosis. After a variable incubation period of 3–180 days, a small painless papule or nodule forms. It later erodes to form a beefy red, granulomatous ulcer. There are clinical variants of donovanosis classified by the appearance of the primary lesion: (1) ulcerative and ulcerogranulomatous, (2) hypertrophic or verrucous, (3) necrotic, and (4) sclerotic or cicatricial. Multiple lesions may coalesce to form large painless ulcers. Eventual healing occurs with scar formation. Classic buboes are absent in donovanosis.

B. Laboratory Findings.

Primary Syphilis. An immediate diagnosis of primary syphilis can be made by identifying the corkscrew appearance of *T pallidum* on dark-field microscopy. A negative result on dark-field microscopy does not rule out primary syphilis. Nontreponemal serologic tests such as VDRL (Venereal Disease Research Laboratory) and RPR (Rapid Plasma Reagin) have a sensitivity in primary syphilis of 59–87% and can be falsely nonreactive. Nontreponemal titers usually correlate with disease activity and should become nonreactive after treatment. Specific treponemal tests such the FTA-ABS (Fluorescent Treponemal Antibody Absorption Test) and the MHA-TP (Microhemagglutination—*Treponema pallidum*) are more specific serologic tests and usually remain positive indefinitely. Nontreponemal and treponemal tests should be interpreted together.

Chancroid. Because of the technical difficulty and specialized media required by *H ducreyi* for growth in the laboratory, the diagnosis of chancroid is made more frequently on clinical grounds. Culture media containing supplemented agar and vancomycin in a CO_2-enriched atmosphere can successfully be used to grow *H ducreyi*. If confirmation by culture is not possible, then a clinical diagnosis of chancroid should be made and treatment begun only after genital herpes and primary syphilis have been excluded.

Genital Herpes. A Tzank smear of tissue scraped from a herpetic lesion can reveal the characteristic multinucleated giant cells of HSV infection. Viral culture has been the standard and most specific test for genital herpes, but requires 1–3 days for a result. Rapid nonculture techniques such as immunofluorescent staining and the enzyme-linked immunosorbent assay have become more widely used but are more expensive.

Lymphogranuloma Venereum. The isolation of *C trachomatis* from an inguinal lymph node aspirate is the most definitive test for the diagnosis of LGV. However, the recovery of *Chlamydia* spp. by this method is < 30%. Serologic testing is an alternative diagnostic method.

Donovanosis. The diagnosis of donovanosis is usually made clinically based on the history and exam findings on a patient with recent sexual contact in an endemic part of the world. The diagnosis can be confirmed by demonstration of the typical intracellular "Donovan Bodies" in a Giemsa or Wright's stain of crushed tissue smears or biopsy specimens. Routine culturing and serologic tests are not widely available.

Differential Diagnosis

Any genital ulcer pathogen can produce a "textbook picture" of another pathogen. A complete patient history (including travel), examination for other lesions or adenopathy, and laboratory testing are essential for an accurate diagnosis. Acute ulcers restricted to the genital area in sexually active patients strongly suggest a sexually transmitted pathogen or possibly trauma secondary to coitus. Ulcers involving both the genital and nongenital areas suggest a noninfectious process such as Behçet's disease, dermatitis herpetiformis, erythema multiforme or Stevens-Johnson syndrome, pemphigus, pemphigoid, fixed drug eruption, contact dermatitis, or squamous cell carcinoma. Fellatio can result in the simultaneous presentation of oral and genital lesions, such as HSV and syphilis. In tropical endemic regions, additional considerations include filariasis, cutaneous leishmaniasis, amebiasis, and schistosomiasis.

Complications

All genital ulcers are prone to secondary bacterial infections with a variety of genital bacteria. Additionally, edema of the foreskin in uncircumcised men may produce phimosis. Without treatment, chancres of primary syphilis and lesions of genital herpes heal spontaneously. Patients with syphilis progress into the secondary stage, whereas those with genital herpes may later experience recurrence of their lesions. The ulcers of chancroid and LGV continue to grow slowly by local extension and can produce further tissue and organ damage. LGV may further lead to perianal abscesses and rectovaginal, rectovesical, and anal fistulas and strictures. Lymphatic obstruction and edema may occur. Rectal LGV is associated with an increased incidence of rectal cancer. Complications of donovanosis scarring include urethral, vaginal, and anal strictures and lymphedema of the external genitalia.

Treatment

Primary Syphilis. Penicillin remains the treatment of choice for any stage of syphilis (Box 15–4). For early syphilis (primary, secondary, and latent syphilis of < 1 year's duration), a single intramuscular dose of benzathine penicillin G is recommended. Some authorities, however, recommend giving two or three doses 1 week apart, especially in the immunocompromised patient. For the penicillin-allergic patient, doxycycline or tetracycline may be used. Patients intolerant to the tetracyclines can use erythromycin or intramuscular ceftriaxone, although treatment failures and lack of clinical experience, respectively, have limited their use. Because *T pallidum* has been isolated in the cerebrospinal fluid in patients with only a chancre, a lumbar puncture with cerebral spinal fluid exam should be performed in primary or secondary syphilis if there are signs or symptoms of neurologic involvement (ophthalmic and/or auditory symptoms or cranial nerve palsies) or treatment failures.

Chancroid. A single dose of intramuscular ceftriaxone or oral azithromycin or 7 days of erythromycin are recommended first-line treatments. Some HIV-positive patients require a more prolonged therapy than the single-dose formats. For these patients, the 7-day erythromycin regimen is preferred. Alternative therapies include amoxicillin/clavulanic acid or ciprofloxacin. Fluctuant adenopathy may require needle aspiration or drainage. Symptomatic improvement should occur within days, but complete healing of ulcers may require up to 1 month.

Genital Herpes. Uncomplicated genital herpes will heal spontaneously. Treatment is available to decrease viral shedding and shorten the duration of disease. For first-episode genital herpes, oral acyclovir, valacyclovir, or famciclovir is recommended for 10 days. For recurrent disease, any one of these regimens can be given for an additional 5 days. For immunocompromised patients, including HIV-positive patients, acyclovir should be given until clinical resolution. Suppressive therapy is recommended for patients with severe and frequent recurrent episodes of genital herpes. Acyclovir can be given for up to a year, after which a 1- or 2-month "drug-free" interval is recommended to assess recurrence rate. Valacyclovir or famciclovir can be used as an alternative agent for suppressive therapy.

Lymphogranuloma Venereum. The treatment of choice for LGV has been doxycycline or tetracycline. Alternative agents include erythromycin and sulfisoxazole. Fluctuant lymph nodes should be drained by needle aspiration to prevent rupture and sinus tract formation.

Donovanosis. There has been no general consensus regarding the optimal treatment of donovanosis because of the lack of controlled studies. Recommended oral treatments include doxycycline, tetracycline, or trimethoprim-sulfamethoxazole for at least 3 weeks or until visible healing has occurred. Alternative oral agents include ciprofloxacin and erythromycin base. The addition of an aminoglycoside should be considered if the lesions do not respond within the first few days of therapy.

Prognosis

The individual and societal impact of genital-ulcer disease depends on timely recognition and treatment of disease. Acknowledging the frequency of coinfecting pathogens and the increased risk of HIV transmission maximizes the potential for individual cure and regional containment.

OTHER SEXUALLY TRANSMITTED DISEASES

SKIN & MUCOUS MEMBRANE DISEASES

1. HUMAN PAPILLOMAVIRUS

There are > 70 different HPV genotypes based on differences within the DNA structure. HPV types 6 and 11 cause condyloma acuminatum (anogenital warts), the most common viral STD in the United States, which is rarely associated with cervical dysplasia. HPV types 16, 18, 31, 33, and 35 cause cervical infection, which is present in ~20% of reproductive-age women in the United States. Cervical infection is the most common source of squamous cell abnormalities on Pap smears and has a direct oncogenic association with cervical cancer.

Diagnosis is usually based on visual identification of genital warts, cytologic examination of scraped cervical cells, or cervical biopsy. Treatment options for genital warts include podofilox 0.5% solution, cryotherapy, podophyllin resin 10–25%, trichloroacetic acid or bichloracetic acid 80–90%, intralesional interferon, laser surgery, and surgical removal. Treatment of cervical HPV infection should be con-

ducted through an expert to exclude high-grade squamous intraepithelial lesions.

2. MOLLUSCUM CONTAGIOSUM

Molluscum contagiosum is a benign disease caused by a virus of the Poxviridae family. It is spread by close human contact, including sexual contact. There are classically 2- to 10-mm domed-shaped papules, often with a central depression (umbilication). They may occur anywhere on the body except the palms and are often grouped. In HIV infected patients, the infection is often generalized with skin lesions appearing on the face and upper body. The diagnosis is usually made clinically but can be confirmed with histopathologic examination. Local treatment includes curettage or cryotherapy. There is no systemic therapy available.

PELVIC INFLAMMATORY DISEASE

PID includes endometriosis, salpingitis, tuboovarian abscess, and pelvic peritonitis. When PID develops as a complication of cervicitis, *N gonorrhoeae* and *C trachomatis* are the pathogens primarily responsible. Symptoms of PID include abnormal cervical or vaginal discharge, abdominal pain, and fever. On exam there may be cervical motion and adnexal and lower abdominal tenderness. It is important to diagnose and treat PID as early as possible. For patients requiring hospitalization, intravenous cefoxitin or cefotetan plus doxycycline (IV or oral) can be given (Box 15–5). Alternatively, intravenous clindamycin plus gentamicin can be given, followed by oral doxycycline. Outpatient treatments include oral ofloxacin plus metronidazole or ceftriaxone (or cefoxitin and oral probenecid) plus oral doxycycline. Duration of intravenous treatment is dependent on the severity of the clinical presentation.

EPIDIDYMITIS

In men under age 35, the most common pathogens are *N gonorrhoeae* and *C trachomatis*. Homosexual men may have enteric pathogens from rectal intercourse. Unilateral testicular pain and tenderness are common. There is usually palpable swelling of the epididymis. The evaluation and diagnostic tests are the same as those for urethritis. Treatment regimens include ceftriaxone plus doxycycline or ofloxacin (Box 15–5).

PROCTITIS

Proctitis acquired through receptive anal intercourse can be caused by *N gonorrhoeae, C tra-*

BOX 15–4

Treatment of Genital Ulcer Disease

Syndrome/Microorganism	First Choice	Alternative Choice
Primary Syphilis	• Benzathine penicillin G, 2.4 million units once	• Doxycycline, 100 mg orally twice daily for 2 weeks[1] • Tetracycline, 500 mg orally four times daily for 2 weeks[1] • Erythromycin, 500 mg orally four times daily for 2 weeks[2] • Ceftriaxone, 250 mg IV daily or 1 g IV every other day for 8–10 days[1,2]
Chancroid	• Ceftriaxone, 250 mg IM once • Azithromycin, 1 g orally once • Erythromycin, 500 mg orally four times daily for 7 days	• Ciprofloxacin, 500 mg orally twice daily for 3 days[3] • Amoxicillin/clavulanic acid 500 mg/125 mg orally three times daily for 7 days
Genital Herpes First episode	• Acyclovir, 200 mg orally five times daily or 400 mg orally three times daily for 10 days[4] • Valacyclovir, 1 g orally twice daily for 10 days • Famciclovir, 250 mg orally three times daily for 10 days	• Any of the first line agents
Recurrent disease	• Acyclovir, 200 mg orally five times daily or 400 mg orally three times daily or 800 mg orally twice daily for 5 days • Valacyclovir, 500 mg orally twice daily for 5 days • Famciclovir, 125 mg orally twice daily for 5 days	• Any of the first line agents
Suppressive therapy	• Acyclovir, 400 mg orally twice daily for year(s)	• Valacyclovir 500 mg orally daily • Famciclovir 250 mg orally twice daily • Famciclovir, 500 mg orally twice daily
HIV/immunosuppressed patients	• Acyclovir, 400 mg orally three to five times daily until clinical resolution	• Valacyclovir[5]

Severe disease	• Acyclovir, 5–10 mg/kg IV every 8 h for 5–7 days	• Erythromycin, 500 mg orally four times daily for 21 days
Lymphogranuloma Venereum	• Doxycycline, 100 mg orally twice daily for 21 days • Tetracycline, 500 mg orally four times daily for 21 days	• Azithromycin, 1 g orally weekly for 3 weeks • Sulfisoxazole, 500 mg orally four times daily for 21 days
Donovanosis	• Trimethoprim–sulfamethoxazole, DS orally twice daily for a minimum of 3 weeks • Doxycycline, 100 mg orally twice daily for a minimum of 3 weeks • Tetracycline, 500 mg orally four times daily for a minimum of 3 weeks[1]	• Ciprofloxacin, 750 mg orally twice daily for 21 days • Erythromycin, 500 mg orally four times daily for 21 days

[1]The tetracyclines should not be used during pregnancy.
[2]Treatment failures reported with oral erythromycin and ceftriaxone.
[3]The fluoroquinolones should not be used during pregnancy or in patients under age 18.
[4]Current data suggest no increased risk for major birth defects after acyclovir treatment. Indications for acyclovir use during pregnancy include first episode of genital herpes and life threatening maternal infection (eg, encephalitis, disseminated disease, pneumonia, and hepatitis). There is insufficient data regarding the safety of valacyclovir and famciclovir during pregnancy.
[5]In immunocompromised patients, valacyclovir in doses of 8 g per day has been associated with a syndrome resembling hemolytic uremic syndrome or thrombotic thrombocytopenic purpura. However, in the doses recommended for treatment of genital herpes, valacyclovir is probably safe for use in immunocompromised patients.

BOX 15–5

Treatment of other Sexually Transmitted Diseases

Syndrome/Microorganism	First Choice	Alternate Choice
Pelvic Inflammatory Disease	Parenteral Regimen[1] • Cefoxitin, 2 g IV every 6 h or cefotetan, 2 g IV every 12 h **PLUS** doxycycline, 100 mg IV or orally every 12 h Oral Regimen • Ofloxacin, 400 mg orally twice daily for 14 days **PLUS** metronidazole, 500 mg orally twice daily for 14 days	Parenteral Regimen[2] • Clindamycin, 900 mg IV every 8 h **PLUS** gentamcin, 2 mg/kg IV loading dose followed by 1.5 mg/kg IV every 8 hours[3,4] Oral/Combined Regimen • Ceftriaxone, 250 mg IM once or cefoxitin, 2 g IM with probenecid 1 g orally once **PLUS** doxycycline 100 mg orally twice daily for 14 days
Epididymitis	• Ceftriaxone, 250 mg IM once **PLUS** doxycycline, 100 mg orally twice daily for 10 days	• Ofloxacin, 300 mg orally twice daily for 10 days
Proctitis	• Ceftriaxone, 125 mg IM once **PLUS** doxycycline 100 mg orally twice daily for 10 days	

[1]Parenteral regimens should be continued for at least 24 hours after clinical improvement; doxycycline should be continued for 14 days.
[2]Additional alternative parenteral regimens include ofloxacin plus metronidazole; ampicillin/sulbactam plus doxycycline; ciprofloxacin plus doxycycline plus metronidazole.
[3]Single daily dosing of gentamicin may be substituted.
[4]Parenteral therapy with clindamycin and gentamicin should be followed by oral doxycycline or oral clindamycin if tubo-ovarian abscess is present, to complete 14 days of therapy.

chomatis (including LGV serovars), *T pallidum* (syphilis), and HSV. Treatment includes ceftriaxone plus doxycycline (Box 15–5).

Prevention

STDs collectively rank as one of the most common groups of diseases throughout the world. There are ~150 million–300 million curable cases of STDs per year with 5 million–12 million cases in North America alone. The most significant global problem in STD management today is not one of treatment, but one of prevention. No single STD can be regarded as an isolated problem. The presence of an STD identifies high-risk behavior through which multiple infections, including HIV, can occur. The primary-care physician has a significant opportunity to not only rapidly diagnose and treat STDs, but also to reduce the risks of reinfection to the patient and spread of disease within a community.

STD prevention begins with the identification of high-risk patients by taking a sexual history. A risk factor assessment includes the patient's age during the first sexual encounter and first STD, number of previous STDs, number of partners, risk assessment of those partners, type of contraception used (if any), and future plans for sexual activity. Once the risk factors are identified, the educational process can begin.

Patient education is the most significant preventative measure against STDs. The goal is to educate patients about methods and behaviors that can reduce the potential for STD transmission. Male condoms, when used correctly, are the most effective method in preventing infections transmitted between mucosal surfaces and transmission of HIV disease. Condoms do not cover all exposed skin areas and may be less effective in preventing infections transmitted through skin-to-skin contact. Female condoms also serve as an effective mechanical barrier to prevent the transmission of infection. Diaphragms do offer protection against gonococcal and chlamydial cervicitis and trichomoniasis; however, they should not be assumed to protect against HIV infection. Vaginal spermicides may reduce the risk of gonococcal and chlamydial infections, but they offer minimal to no protection against HIV infection. Although nonbarrier contraceptive measures such as hormonal supplements, surgical sterilization, and hysterectomy prevent pregnancy, they offer no protection against HIV or other STDs.

Sexual contacts of infected patients must be evaluated. Partner identification enables the treatment of persons who may be infected but are asymptomatic.

Not only will early diagnosis and treatment prevent the serious, long-term complications of STDs, but it will also help reduce the spread of disease within a community.

As stated earlier, all patients with an STD should be evaluated for other STDs. The presence of one pathogen doesn't eliminate the possibility of other coinfecting pathogens or an earlier untreated infection with a different pathogen. The physician must balance a high index of suspicion with screening programs to diagnose STDs as early as possible and to break the chain of STD transmission.

REFERENCES

Urethritis

Heath CB, Heath JM: *Chlamydia trachomatis* infection update. Am Fam Physician 1995;52:1455.

Kreiger JN: Trichomoniasis in men: old issues and new data. Sex Transmit Dis 1995;22:83.

Lind I: Antimicrobial resistance in *Neisseria gonorrhoeae*. Clin Infect Dis 1997;24(Suppl 1):S93.

Schmid GP, Fontanarosa PB: Evolving strategies for management of the nongonococcal urethritis syndromes. J Am Med Assoc 1995;274:577.

Stamm WE et al: Azithromycin for empirical treatment of the nongonococcal urethritis syndrome in men. J Am Med Assoc 1995;274:545.

Weber JT, Johnson RE: New treatments for *Chlamydia trachomatis* genital infection. Clin Infect Dis 1995; 20(Suppl 1):S66.

Cervicitis

Centers for Disease Control and Prevention: 1998 guidelines for treatment of sexually transmitted diseases. Morbid Mortal Wkly Rep 1997;47:49.

Majeroni BA: Chlamydial cervicitis: complications and new treatment options. Am Fam Physician 1994;49:1825.

Miller KE: Women's health: sexually transmitted diseases. Prim Care Clin Off Pract 1997;24:179. (Women's health. Sexually transmitted diseases.)

Zenilman JM: Gonorrhea: clinical and public health issues. Hosp Pract 1993:29.(Review.)

Vulvovaginitis

Centers for Disease Control and Prevention: 1998 Guidelines for treatment of sexually transmitted diseases. Morbid Mortal Wkly Rep 1997;47:70.

Holmes KK: Lower genital tract infections in women. In Holmes KK et al: *Sexually Transmitted Diseases,* 3rd ed. McGraw-Hill, 1999.

Joesoef MR, Schmed GP: Bacterial vaginosis: review of treatment options and potential clinical indications for therapy. Clin Infect Dis 1995;20(Suppl 1):S72.

Reef SE et al: Treatment options for vulvovaginal candidiasis, 1993. Clin Infect Dis 1995;20(Suppl 1):S80.

Sobel JD: Vaginitis. N Engl J Med 1997;337:1899. (Review article.)

Genital Ulcer Disease

Centers for Disease Control and Prevention: 1998 Guidelines for treatment of sexually transmitted diseases. Morbid Mortal Wkly Rep 1997;47:18.

Mroczkowski TF, Martin DH: Genital ulcer disease. Dermatol Clin. 1994;12:753.

Ballard RC: Genital ulcer adenopathy syndrome. In Holmes KK et al: *Sexually Transmitted Diseases,* 3rd ed. McGraw-Hill, 1999.

Schulte JM, Schmid GP: Recommendations for treatment of chancroid, 1993. Clin Infect Dis 1995;20 (Suppl 1):S39.

Other Sexually Transmitted Diseases

Centers for Disease Control and Prevention: 1998 Guidelines for treatment of sexually transmitted diseases. Morbid Mortal Wkly Rep 1997;47.

Morrison EA: Natural history of cervical infection with human papillomavirus. Clin Infect Dis 1994;18:172.

Stone KM: Human papillomavirus infection and genital warts: update on epidemiology and treatment. Clin Infect Dis 1995;20(Suppl 1):S91.

Prevention

Borgatta L: Sexually transmitted diseases. Ann NY Acad Sci 1994;736:102.

Centers for Disease Control and Prevention: 1998 Guidelines for treatment of sexually transmitted diseases. Morbid Mortal Wkly Rep 1997;47:79.

Miller KE: Sexually transmitted diseases. Women's Health 1997;24:179.

Sciarra JJ: Sexually transmitted diseases: global importance. Int J Gynecol Obstet 1997;58:107.

Urinary Tract Infections

Walter R. Wilson, MD & Nancy K. Henry, PhD, MD

COMMUNITY-ACQUIRED URINARY TRACT INFECTIONS

Essentials of Diagnosis

Acute Cystitis-Urethritis.
- Women and girls older than 2 years.
- Acute onset dysuria, increased frequency urination.
- Pyuria ≥ 5–10 erythrocytes/high-power field of centrifuged urine or positive leukocyte esterase test.
- Positive urine culture (1000–100,000 colony forming units/mL) for *Escherichia coli,* other *Enterobacteriaceae,* enterococci, or *Staphylococcus saprophyticus.*

Acute Pyelonephritis.
- Fever, chills, flank pain.
- Pyuria.
- Positive urine Gram stain for gram-negative bacilli.
- Positive urine culture (≥ 100,000 colony forming units) or blood culture with gram-negative bacilli.

Acute Prostatitis (subjects older than age 35).
- Fever, chills, dysuria, increased frequency of urination, low back or pelvic pain.
- Pyuria.
- Positive urine culture for gram-negative bacilli or enterococci.

Chronic Prostatitis.
- Middle-aged to elderly men.
- Chronic intermittent dysuria, increased frequency of urination, pelvic pain.
- Enlarged prostate.
- Positive culture of prostatic secretions or voided urine after massage for gram-negative bacilli or enterococci. The number of colony forming units of bacteria should be 10-fold greater than the number in urine obtained before prostatic massage.

General Considerations

Infections involving the urinary tract are among the most common infectious diseases. Bacteriuria is defined as bacteria present in the urine. Bacteriuria may be asymptomatic or may be present in association with acute or chronic infection of the kidney, bladder, prostate, or urethra. Acute cystitis-urethritis is a syndrome consisting of dysuria, urgency, and increased frequency of urination with or without upper tract infection. Acute pyelonephritis is an infection of the kidneys and is described as a syndrome of fever and flank pain with or without dysuria. The term acute prostatitis describes a syndrome of fever, perineal and low-back pain, dysuria, urgency, and increased frequency of urination. Chronic urinary tract infection (UTI) refers to persistence or frequent reinfection of the kidney, bladder, or prostate.

A. Epidemiology.

1. Children. During infancy, the frequency of bacteriuria is 1–2% and is more common in boys during the first 3 months; thereafter, it is more common in girls. Lack of circumcision increases the risk of UTI in infant males. Among preschool children, bacteriuria is more common in females than in males, and, when present in males, bacteriuria is usually associated with congenital abnormalities. The prevalence of bacteriuria among school girls is 1–2%, and ≥ 5% have bacteriuria before finishing high school. Of these girls, ~ 3% develop symptomatic UTI. School girls with bacteriuria are at greater risk of developing bacteriuria in adulthood. Bacteriuria is rare among school boys, and, when present, it is associated with structural abnormalities.

2. Adults. Prevalence of bacteriuria in nonpregnant females is 1–3%. At least 10–25% of females develop symptomatic UTI during their lifetimes. The risk of subsequent UTIs is greater than the risk of the initial UTI. The prevalence of bacteriuria among adult men is low (< 0.1%) and is associated with anatomic abnormalities, such as obstruction.

3. Pregnancy. Pregnant women are at increased risk of bacteriuria, and the prevalence ranges from 4–7%. Beginning as early as the seventh week of gestation, dilatation of the uterus and renal pelvis occurs, and the bladder tone decreases, which may result in urinary stasis in the bladder. The majority of pregnant women with bacteriuria have bacteriuria detected at the first prenatal visit. Of pregnant women with bacteriuria, ~ 25% develop their infection during pregnancy.

Bacteriuria during pregnancy increases the risk of pyelonephritis during the latter stages of pregnancy. If untreated, ~ 20–40% of patients with bacteriuria early in pregnancy develop acute pyelonephritis later in pregnancy. Of pregnant women without bacteriuria early in gestation, < 1% develop acute pyelonephritis, which emphasizes the importance of early detection and treatment. Acute pyelonephritis is associated with premature delivery in 20–50% of patients. The eradication of bacteriuria probably reduces the frequency of prematurity and low birth weight. The association of bacteriuria and hypertension in pregnancy is not clear.

4. Elderly. Among individuals older than 65 years, ≥ 10% of men and 20% of women have bacteriuria. Risk factors include prostatic hypertrophy in males, bladder prolapse in females, soiling of the peritoneum, neurogenic bladder, and the use of a chronic indwelling urinary catheter.

B. Microbiology. *E coli* is the most common cause of acute uncomplicated community-acquired UTI, accounting for ~ 95% of cases. In recurrent infections, especially in association with structural abnormalities, the relative frequency increases for infection caused by other microorganisms, such as *Proteus* species, *Klebsiella* species, *Enterobacter* species, and enterococci. Nosocomial acquisition, especially in association with urinary catheterization, is often caused by *E coli, Pseudomonas* species, or other gram-negative nosocomial microorganisms (see section on "Nosocomially Acquired Infection" later in this chapter). Urea-splitting microorganisms, such as *Proteus* species, are associated with calculus formation. *S saprophyticus* accounts for 5–15% of acute cystitis in young sexually active females. Type 2 adenovirus may cause acute hemorrhagic cystitis in children and is more common in young boys than in girls.

C. Pathogenesis.
1. Routes of infection. Bacteria may cause UTIs by three possible routes: ascending, hematogenous, or lymphatic. Of these, the ascending route, especially in women, is probably the most common. Uropathogenic microorganisms colonize the vaginal introitus and periurethral area where they may ascend through the urethra, enter the bladder, multiply, and ascend the ureters to the renal pelvis and parenchyma. Urethral massage, sexual intercourse, or other factors enhance entry of microorganisms into the female urethra. In the male urethra, the mechanism of ascending infection is less understood than in females. Hematogenous infection of the kidney occurs uncommonly in gram-negative bacteremia, although gram-negative bacteremia originating from the urinary tract is one of the most common sources of bacteremia. *S aureus* bacteremia may cause intrarenal or perinephric abscess. Lymphatic spread of infection to the urinary tract is thought to be uncommon.

2. Microbial factors. Although virtually any microorganism is capable of causing UTI, *E coli* is responsible for the majority of infections (Box 16–1). Uropathogenic strains of *E coli* are selected from the fecal flora by the presence of virulence factors that enhance colonization of vaginal and periurethral cells, attachment to uroepithelium, and invasion of

---

BOX 16–1

Microbiology of Community-Acquired Urinary Tract Infection

Dysuria–Pyuria Syndrome in Females		
	Children	Adults
More Frequent	• *Escherichia coli*	• *E coli* • *Staphylococcus saprophyticus* (young, sexually active patients)
Less Frequent	• Other *Enterobacteriaceae* • Enterococci • *Streptococcus agalactiae*	• Other *Enterobacteriaceae* • Enterococci
Other Community–Acquired Infection		
	Children	Adults
More Frequent	• *E coli*	• *E coli*
Less Frequent	• Other *Enterobacteriaceae* • Enterococci	• Other *Enterobacteriaceae* • Enterococci

tissue. These factors include adhesions, resistance to serum bactericidal activity and phagocytosis, presence of a high amount of K antigen, and hemolysin production. Of these, adhesion is the most important property of uropathogenic *E coli.*

Fimbriae are the major type of surface adhesions of uropathogenic *E coli.* A number of specific, morphologic and functional *E coli* fimbriae have been identified. The two most important of these are P fimbriae and type 1 fimbriae. *E coli* expressing P fimbriae attach to globoseries, glycolipid receptors in the kidney, and are the strains most associated with acute pyelonephritis. These receptors are distributed throughout the urinary tract but are most prevalent in the kidney. The attachment of these strains is not inhibited by mannose, and the strains are referred to as mannose resistant. Type 1-fimbriaed *E coli* bind to mannose-containing receptors in the urinary tract and are more likely to cause cystitis than pyelonephritis. Attachment of these strains is inhibited in the presence of mannose, and these strains are referred to as mannose susceptible. Type 1 fimbriae increase the susceptibility of *E coli* to phagocytosis, but uropathogenic *E coli* fail to express type I fimbriae in renal parenchyma. Polymorphonuclear leukocytes lack a receptor for P fimbriae, which inhibits the phagocytosis of these strains. Nonfimbriated uropathogenic *E coli* bacteria express a variety of adhesions that bind to uroepithelium.

Proteus mirabilis and *Klebsiella* species also express fimbriae, which are responsible for attachment. *S saprophyticus* adheres more readily to uroepithelial cells than does *Staphylococcus epidermidis* or *S aureus.* The production of urease by *Proteus* species and other microorganisms increases the potential of these microorganisms to cause pyelonephritis. Bacterial K-antigen inhibits phagocytosis. Most uropathogenic bacterial strains produce hemolysins, which facilitate tissue invasion and enhance renal cell damage.

3. Host factors. Many host factors increase susceptibility to UTI. The most common of these is obstruction of normal urinary flow, resulting in stasis. This may occur as the result of extrarenal obstruction from congenital abnormalities, malignancies, calculi, vesicoureteral reflux, prostatic hypertrophy, neurogenic bladder, pregnancy, or other conditions.

Vesicoureteral reflux caused by congenital abnormalities or neurogenic bladder is highly associated with UTI. Reflux results in a residual pool of urine in the bladder after voiding which, when infected, predisposes to upper tract infection and renal scarring. Incomplete bladder emptying from any cause, such as prostatic hypertrophy, similarly results in residual urine in the bladder, which increases susceptibility to UTI.

Urinary tract instrumentation is another common cause of UTI. A single catheterization of the bladder results in bacteriuria in 0.1–1% of patients. Virtually all patients with a chronic indwelling urinary catheter develop UTI.

In sexually active women, the use of a diaphragm with spermicidal jelly increases the susceptibility to UTI. Spermicide may cause pH changes that increase colonization of the vagina with uropathogens. Diabetics are more susceptible to infection in general, including UTI. The presence of glucose in the urine enhances bacterial growth.

A variety of factors protect the host from UTI. With the exception of the urethral mucosa, the normal urinary tract is resistant to colonization by bacteria and rapidly clears most microorganisms that gain access to the bladder. High or low urine osmolality, high urea concentration, and low urinary pH inhibit the growth of microorganisms. Tamn-Horsfall protein secreted by cells in the ascending loop of Henle contains mannose, which binds type 1-fimbriated *E coli.* Mannose-bound strains prevent microorganisms from binding to uroepithelial cells, and the complexes are flushed from the urinary tract during micturition. Prostatic secretions contain zinc, which inhibits growth of bacteria in urine.

Clinical Findings

A. Signs and symptoms. Many patients with bacteriuria, especially older patients, are asymptomatic. Among neonates and children < 2 years of age, symptoms may be nonspecific and include fever, vomiting, irritability, and failure to thrive. Children older than 2 years usually develop increased frequency of urination and dysuria; with acute pyelonephritis, nausea, vomiting, fever, chills, and flank and abdominal pain may occur.

1. Acute cystitis-urethritis. Adult women with acute cystitis-urethritis typically have acute onset of dysuria, urgency, and increased frequency of urination. Fever is usually not present in uncomplicated cystitis-urethritis. Physical examination in women with cystitis-urethritis may reveal suprapubic tenderness.

2. Acute pyelonephritis. Adults with acute pyelonephritis present with fever, chills, and flank or back pain. On physical examination, flank tenderness is common.

3. Acute prostatitis. Men with acute prostatitis complain of fever, chills, and perineal and low-back pain together with dysuria and increased frequency of urination. The prostate is exquisitely tender in men with acute prostatitis. Physical examinations of the prostate in acute prostatitis should be avoided because of severe pain and the risk of inducing bacteremia.

4. Chronic prostatitis. Men with chronic prostatitis describe chronic intermittent episodes of dysuria and increased frequency of urination. On physical examination, the prostate is often enlarged, and tenderness may be present but is often absent.

B. Laboratory findings.

1. Urinalysis and Gram stain. A urinalysis should be performed in all patients suspected of having a UTI. The large majority of patients with symptomatic UTI have pyuria, described as 5–10 leukocytes/high-power field of centrifuged urinary sediment. A dipstick leukocyte esterase test is a rapid screening test and has a high sensitivity and specificity for detection of pyuria. Leukocyte casts are commonly present in patients with pyelonephritis. Microscopic or gross hematuria may occur in patients with cystitis-urethritis.

The presence on Gram stain of ≥ 1 bacterium/high-power field, performed on a midstream clean-catch urine specimen, correlates with $\geq 10^5$ bacteria/mL of uncentrifuged urine. Automated screening tests for detection of bacteria are available to rapidly screen large numbers of specimens.

2. Quantitative urine culture and antimicrobial susceptibility tests. A quantitative urine culture with antimicrobial susceptibility tests is not necessary in most women with urethritis-cystitis. Urine culture and susceptibility studies should be performed in women who relapse after short-course antimicrobial therapy or in those with frequent recurrence of UTI. A quantitative urine culture and antimicrobial susceptibility tests should be performed in all patients that are suspected of having pyelonephritis. Patients with symptomatic UTIs typically have $\geq 10^5$ bacteria/mL of midstream clean-catch urine. However, ≥ 40–50% of females with acute cystitis-urethritis have $< 10^5$ bacteria/mL of urine, and infection may be present with counts as low as ≥ 1000 bacteria/mL. The presence of < 1000 bacteria/mL of urine suggests a diagnosis other than UTI. Females with acute cystitis-urethritis and sterile pyuria should be suspected of having urethritis caused by *Chlamydia trachomatis* or *Neisseria gonorrhoeae*.

3. Blood cultures. Blood cultures are frequently positive in patients with acute pyelonephritis and should be obtained in all patients in whom this diagnosis is suspected.

C. Laboratory diagnosis of prostatitis.

1. Acute prostatitis. Acute prostatitis is most often caused by *E coli* or another member of the family *Enterobacteriaceae*. Expressed prostatic secretions contain polymorphonuclear leukocytes, and microorganisms are usually present on Gram stain and may be recovered from culture. However, prostatic massage should be avoided in these patients because the prostate is exquisitely tender to palpation, and massage may result in bacteremia. The clinical presentation of acute prostatitis is highly suggestive of the diagnosis, and the microorganism may be recovered from cultures of midstream urine. Antimicrobial susceptibility tests should be performed.

2. Chronic prostatitis. Of chronic prostatitis cases, $\geq 80\%$ are caused by *E coli;* the remaining cases are caused by *Klebsiella*, enterococci, *Enter-*obacter spp., and *P mirabilis*. Because bacteria in the urethra may contaminate prostatic secretions, the diagnosis requires simultaneous sequential quantitative cultures of four specimens: (1) urethral urine, (2) midstream urine, (3) prostatic secretions expressed by massage, and (4) voided urine after massage. Diagnosis is made by comparing the results of quantitative cultures. The diagnosis is suggested when the number of bacteria in the prostatic massage secretions exceeds those in specimens number 1 and 2 by ≥ 10-fold. If no prostatic secretion fluid is obtained, the postmassage urine quantitative culture should exceed cultures from specimens 1 and 2 by ≥ 10-fold. Antimicrobial susceptibility tests should be performed.

D. Imaging. Imaging studies should be performed in adult patients with complicated UTIs, such as those with urolithiasis or pyelonephritis, and in patients of any age in whom structural abnormalities are suspected. A plain abdominal roentgenogram may detect urolithiasis, a mass, or an abnormal gas pattern, all of which are suggestive of abscess. Previously, excretory urography or intravenous pyelography (IVP) was the most commonly used imaging technique. However, administration of the contrast material used in IVP may cause an allergic reaction or exacerbate renal insufficiency. Ultrasound imaging and computed tomographic (CT) scans are more sensitive than IVP for detection of renal pathology, and administration of contrast material is not necessary with ultrasonography. Compared with IVP, contrast-enhanced CT scans provide better parenchymal delineation but are less optimal to delineate the collecting system than is IVP. Ultrasonography is useful to detect urinary tract obstruction, and small calculi may be detected by spiral CT scans. Perinephric abscess, renal abscess, and emphysematous pyelonephritis may be diagnosed adequately by ultrasonography or CT scans. The detection of papillary necrosis requires contrast-enhanced urography (IVP) or CT scans.

Ultrasonography and voiding cystoureterography are recommended in patients suspected of having reflux disease. Radionuclide-voiding cystography may also detect reflux disease.

Differential Diagnosis

The acute cystitis-urethritis syndrome in women must be differentiated from herpes simplex infection, *C trachomatis* infection, and vaginitis. A pelvic examination should be performed to detect genital herpes simplex virus infection. *C trachomatis* infection has a more gradual onset of dysuria and should be suspected in sexually active women with a recent new sexual partner. Hematuria is usually absent in *Chlamydia* infection. A diagnosis of *Chlamydia* infection is confirmed by rapid diagnostic techniques using commercially available kits. Vaginitis is a common cause of dysuria, but patients usually complain of external dysuria, which begins shortly after the onset of micturition and results from urine contact with inflamed vaginal labia. Pyuria and hematuria are usually absent in vaginitis. The presence of gross or microhematuria may occur in association with genitourinary-tract neoplasms, urolithiasis, or structural abnormalities of the genitourinary tract system. Patients at opposite extremes of age groups may not present with symptoms that are typical of UTI. In children < 2 years of age, failure to thrive, vomiting, and fever may be the major manifestations. Elderly patients with pyelonephritis may present with fever, hypotension, and sepsis syndrome without symptoms of a urinary tract infection. Among elderly patients with gram-negative bacteremia without an obvious source, a UTI should be considered.

Complications

Uncommon or rare complications of UTI include acute papillary necrosis, perinephric or intrarenal abscess, emphysematous pyelonephritis, or xanthogranulomatous pyelonephritis. When present, acute papillary necrosis is most common in diabetic dehydrated patients with pyelonephritis and is characterized by diminished renal function and sloughing of renal papilla. The most common predisposing factors for perinephric abscess are renal stones and diabetes mellitus, and perinephric abscess usually occurs as the result of obstruction or, less commonly, bacteremia. The infecting organisms for perinephric abscess are usually gram-negative bacilli or *S aureus,* if the cause is bacteremia. Polymicrobial infection is present in ~ 25% of cases of perinephric abscess. Intrarenal abscess usually occurs as the result of *S aureus* bacteremia. Perinephric or intrarenal abscess should be considered in patients with pyelonephritis who have been ill for ≥ 2 weeks and in those who have a slow response or no response to effective antimicrobial therapy. Emphysematous pyelonephritis is a rare complication of pyelonephritis and most often occurs in elderly diabetics. This condition should be suspected in patients with rapidly progressive infections with sepsis syndrome that respond poorly to antimicrobial therapy. Xanthogranulomatous pyelonephritis is a rare form of chronic renal infection with massive enlargement of the kidney, in which the renal parenchyma is replaced by inflammatory granulomatous tissue, which is characterized by lipid-laden foamy macrophages. Renal calculus formation and obstruction are common. *P mirabilis* is occasionally recovered from urine culture.

Antimicrobial Therapy

A. Acute uncomplicated cystitis-urethritis in women.

1. Single-dose therapy. Single-dose antimicrobial therapy results in cure rates ranging from 65–100%, depending on the antimicrobial agent administered. High cure rates of 85–95% may be achieved after therapy with a fluoroquinolone, such as ciprofloxacin, ofloxacin, or levofloxacin, or with trimethoprim-sulfamethoxazole. β-Lactam therapy is less effective, possibly because of persistence of microorganisms in the periurethral and perirectal area or because of resistance of microorganisms to β-lactams. The advantages of single-dose therapy are high compliance and reduced adverse effects. The disadvantages include higher failure rates than longer courses of therapy, and the higher failure rates may be the result of undetected upper-tract infection that is inadequately treated with single-dose therapy. Patients who fail single-dose therapy with trimethoprim-sulfamethoxazole or a fluoroquinolone should be evaluated for possible upper-tract infection. Women with postcoital cystitis-urethritis are good candidates for single-dose therapy.

2. Three-day therapy. Numerous studies have demonstrated that 3 days of antimicrobial therapy are as effective as 7–10 days of therapy, and 3-day therapy should be considered as standard therapy. Trimethoprim-sulfamethoxazole or a fluoroquinolone should be considered as the agent of choice for 3-day therapy. With a susceptible microorganism, 3 days of β-lactam therapy results in cure rates similar to those after treatment with trimethoprim-sulfamethoxazole or a fluoroquinolone. However, therapy with ampicillin or amoxicillin may be less effective than a second- or third-generation oral cephalosporin because of the relatively high frequency of ampicillin-resistant *E coli* in community-acquired UTIs. Sexually active females with the gradual onset of symptoms or recent change in a sexual partner should be considered to have *C trachomatis* infection and should be treated as shown in Box 16–2.

There are currently insufficient data to recommend shorter-course therapy (single-dose or 3-day treatment) in men or children with UTIs. These patients are at higher risk of structural abnormalities or upper tract infection, and therapy should be administered for 7–10 days. Follow-up urine cultures should be obtained 1–2 weeks after completion of treatment to detect relapses or persistence.

B. Acute pyelonephritis. Patients with severe infections, such as those with nausea, vomiting, and hypotension, should be hospitalized. Others with mild to moderate infection may be treated as outpatients, provided that they are compliant and are able to tolerate oral antimicrobial therapy. Antimicrobial therapy is initially empiric and should be modified appropriately based on the results of cultures and susceptibilities. Effective therapy results in defervescence of fever and other symptoms, usually within 48 h after onset of treatment. Failure to respond may be the result of resistant microorganisms or the presence of perinephric or intrarenal abscess or persistence of infection in polycystic renal disease. Antimicrobial therapy of pyelonephritis should be administered for 14 days. Patients with acute pyelonephritis should

BOX 16-2

Empiric Antimicrobial Therapy of Urinary Tract Infections

Condition	First Choice	Second Choice
Women and girls, ≥2 years of age, with acute uncomplicated cystitis and/or urethritis	• TMP/SMX, 1 double strength OR TMP, 8–12 mg/kg, plus SMX, 40–60 mg/kg twice daily for 3 d OR • In patients 15 years of age or older, a fluoroquinolone[1] for 3 d	• Amoxicillin or amoxicillin/clavulanate, 500 mg or 45 mg/kg of amoxicillin three times daily for 3 d OR • An oral cephalosporin[1] for 3 d OR • TMP/SMX, 1 double-strength, single dose[2] OR • A fluoroquinolone[1] single dose[2]
Women with risk factors for sexually transmitted diseases	• Doxycycline, 100 mg twice daily for 7 d	• Azithromycin, 1 g single dose
Adults not hospitalized with acute pyelonephritis	• Fluoroquinolone[1] orally for 14 d	• Amoxicillin/clavulanate, 500 mg orally for 14 d OR • Second- or third-generation oral cephalosporin[1] for 14 d
Children or hospitalized adults with acute pyelonephritis	• Ampicillin, 1 g IV[3] or 25–50 mg/kg every 4 h OR • Ampicillin, 25–50 mg/kg every 6 h plus gentamicin or tobramycin, 5 mg/kg/d in divided or single daily dose for 14 d OR • A third-generation cephalosporin[1] IV[3] for 14 d OR • In patients 15 years of age or older, a fluoroquinolone[1] IV[3] or orally for 14 d	• Ticarcillin/clavulanate, 3.1 g or 50–75 mg/kg of ticarcillin component every 6 h OR • Piperacillin/tazobactam, 3.375 g IV[3] every 6 h for 14 d or 80 mg/kg every 8 h or piperacilllin component OR • Aztreonam, 1 g IV[3] every 8 h for 14 d or 30 mg/kg every 6–8 h
Asymptomatic bacteriuria Children Pregnancy Adults, elderly Caused by urinary tract instrumentation	• Treat with regimen for symptomatic cystitis-urethritis for 7 d • Amoxicillin (dosage above) or oral cephalosporin,[1] or TMP/SMX (dosage above) or TMP, 100 mg orally twice daily, or nitrofurantoin, 100 mg orally twice daily for 7 days. Discontinue sulfa 2 wk before delivery. Avoid fluoroquinolone or tetracycline use. • No treatment necessary • Choice of therapy depends on results of culture and antimicrobial sensitivity. Treat for 3 d	

BOX 16–2 (continued)

Condition	First Choice	Second Choice
Acute prostatitis Less than 35 years of age	• Fluoroquinolone[1] for 7 d	• Ceftriaxone, 125 mg IM single dose, or other FDA-approved cephalosporin[1] plus either doxycycline, 100 mg orally twice daily for 7 d or azithromycin, 1 g orally as a single dose
Older than 35 years of age	• Fluoroquinolone[1] or TMP/SMX, 1 DS orally twice daily for 4 wks	
Chronic prostatitis	• Fluoroquinolone[1] or TMP/SMX, 1 DS twice daily orally for 1–3 mo	
Urinary catheter associated	• Aminoglycoside plus one of the following: a fluoroquinolone, a third-generation cephalosporin, piperacillin/tazobactam, or aztreonam for 7–14 d.[4] Dosages are as above.	

[1]Dosage of fluoroquinolone or oral or parenteral cephalosporin depends upon specific drug selected for use.
[2]Single dose therapy not recommended for children 15 years of age or younger.
[3]Intravenous therapy may be changed to oral therapy with TMP/SMX or amoxicillin, amoxicillin/clavulanate, a cephalosporin, or a fluoroquinolone (see footnote 1) after initial satisfactory response and when culture results are available.
[4]Multiply resistant microorganisms are common; antimicrobial therapy may be adjusted based on results of susceptibility tests.

have an ultrasound examination to exclude obstruction or stones. A follow-up urine culture should be obtained 1–2 weeks after completion of therapy. In hospitalized patients, parenteral therapy may be changed to orally administered therapy when patients improve and are able to tolerate oral therapy.

C. Asymptomatic bacteriuria. Children should be treated with antimicrobial therapy as described for those with symptomatic infection, as shown in Box 16–2. Aside from pregnant women, adults, especially the elderly, do not benefit from antimicrobial therapy.

D. Pregnancy. The rationale for antimicrobial therapy in these patients is described above. The goal of treatment is to maintain sterile urine throughout pregnancy. The antimicrobial regimens are shown in Box 16–2. Single-dose therapy has not been adequately studied in these patients. Three-day therapy may be as effective as seven-day treatment but there are relatively few published studies with three-day treatment of asymptomatic bacteriuria in pregnant women. Follow-up urine cultures should be obtained 1–2 weeks after completion of therapy and at monthly intervals throughout the duration of pregnancy. If bacteriuria recurs, the patient should be retreated, and, if multiple relapses occur, suppressive therapy should be administered throughout gestation, and radiologic evaluation may be performed after delivery.

E. Asymptomatic bacteriuria after urinary tract instrumentation. The majority of patients with previously sterile urine who have persistent bacteriuria after instrumentation or removal of a urinary catheter should receive 3 days of antimicrobial therapy. The selection of therapy should be based on the results of culture and susceptibility tests.

F. Relapsing UTI. Relapse usually occurs within 1–2 weeks after completion of therapy and is most often associated with upper tract infection, structural abnormalities including stones, or chronic prostatitis. Bacteriologic eradication in patients with obstruction or calculi depends on surgical correction of obstruction or removal of stones. The treatment of relapsing chronic prostatitis is discussed below. Patients with upper tract infection who relapse after short-course therapy should be retreated for ≥ 2 weeks. A 6-week course of therapy should be administered to those patients that relapse after a 2-week course. Some women will continue to experience relapse with no obvious cause or despite surgical correction of structural abnormalities. If relapse occurs after a 6-week course, in selected patients who have continuous symptoms of UTI, a treatment course of 6–12 months should be considered. Patients selected for long-term therapy include children, adults with continuous symptoms, or adults at high risk of progressive renal damage or those patients with obstructions that are not amenable to surgery. Asymptomatic adults with bacteriuria without obstruction should not receive long-term therapy.

G. Reinfection. Women with infrequent reinfection (≤ 2–3 times/year) should be treated with short-course antimicrobial therapy as if each UTI were a new, discrete episode. Single-dose self-administered therapy taken after sexual intercourse is usually effective to decrease the frequency of UTI related to sexual activity. In some women with frequent lower-tract reinfection, no precipitating event is apparent. In these patients with symptomatic, frequent reinfection, long-term antimicrobial therapy is warranted. If reinfection occurs during treatment, urine culture and sensitivity should be obtained, and the prophylactic regimen should be changed based on the results.

H. Prostatitis.

1. Acute prostatitis. Antimicrobial therapy of acute prostatitis in young men (< 35 years of age) should include agents that are effective against *N gonorrhoeae* and *C trachomatis* (Box 16–2). Patients older than 35 years usually have infection caused by members of the *Enterobacteriaceae*. Studies suggest that the relapse rate or development of chronic prostatitis may be higher in patients with acute prostatitis who are treated for < 4 weeks with antimicrobial therapy. Prostatic abscess usually requires drainage; cure with antimicrobial therapy alone is uncommon.

2. Chronic prostatitis. The selection of an antimicrobial agent should be based on culture and sensitivity results. Cure is difficult to achieve, and relapses are common. Therapy with trimethoprim-sulfamethoxazole or a fluoroquinolone results in higher drug concentrations in prostate tissue and superior cure rates compared with therapy with a β-lactam. The presence of prostatic calcification or stones is associated with a high failure rate. Chronic suppressive therapy, usually with trimethoprim-sulfamethoxazole or a fluoroquinolone or trimethoprim alone, may control symptoms of chronic bacterial prostatitis in patients who relapse after 1–3 months of antimicrobial therapy. Transurethral resection of the prostate, together with antimicrobial therapy, may be necessary to cure patients with chronic prostatitis and an enlarged prostate with or without calcifications, who remain symptomatic despite antimicrobial therapy.

I. Perinephric or intrarenal abscess. Patients with perinephric or intrarenal abscess usually require open drainage or ultrasound or CT-guided drainage. Patients with polycystic renal disease who fail to respond to antimicrobial therapy may require aspiration or surgical drainage of infected cysts. Patients with emphysematous pyelonephritis should undergo immediate nephrectomy because of the high mortality in patients treated with medical therapy alone. Patients with xanthogranulomatous pyelonephritis require nephrectomy.

Prognosis

A. Children. Children without obstruction or vesicoureteral reflux have an excellent prognosis. Uncorrected obstruction with infection may result in severe progressive renal disease. Reflux, together with infection, is associated with development of progressive renal scarring and, if untreated, may progress to arterial hypertension and end-stage renal disease. Eradication of bacteriuria may reduce the severity of reflux. Mild to moderate reflux may disappear spontaneously in older children over time, probably as a result of maturation of the vesicoureteral junction. Surgery may be necessary to correct severe persistent reflux disease.

B. Adults. Prognosis of the large majority of adults with UTIs is excellent. Many women with UTIs had UTIs as children. A female who develops a UTI is more likely to develop subsequent infections than a woman who has had no prior UTI.

When associated with obstruction, infection may lead to progressive renal damage and failure. Recurrent infection in the absence of obstruction rarely, if ever, leads to progressive renal disease or arterial hypertension.

Prevention

Postcoital lower UTIs in females may usually be prevented by administration of a single dose of an antimicrobial agent after sexual intercourse (see above). Long-term prophylaxis should be considered for patients who have had frequent symptomatic relapses or recurrences of infection and are at risk of developing progressive renal damage, such as young children with vesicoureteral reflux or patients with obstruction or stones. For long-term prophylaxis, it is not usually necessary to administer the same dosage of an antimicrobial agent that has been used to treat symptomatic infection. For example, nightly administration of one single-strength trimethoprim-sulfamethoxazole or a lower dosage of a fluoroquinolone may suffice. Urine culture and antimicrobial sensitivity should be obtained periodically in patients who receive long-term prophylaxis, to monitor for development of resistance and persistence of bacteriuria. A change of antimicrobial therapy may be necessary in these patients.

NOSOCOMIALLY ACQUIRED URINARY TRACT INFECTIONS

Essentials of Diagnosis
- Majority asymptomatic.
- Fever, chills, possible suprapubic or flank pain.
- Positive urine or blood culture for gram-negative

bacilli; number of bacteria usually ≥ 100,000 colony forming units/mL of urine.

Urinary tract infection is the most common noso-comially acquired infection, accounting for ≥ 40% of all nosocomial infections. Of nosocomial UTIs, ≥ 80% are related to the use of a urethral catheter. The remaining cases are associated with other urinary tract instrumentations or surgery.

Catheter-associated UTI is one of the most common infections in acute care facilities and is the most common infection in chronic care settings. Before the development of closed catheter systems, the onset of bacteriuria in open draining systems occurred within 4 days after insertion of the catheter. With the closed-catheter system, the onset of bacteriuria is delayed to ≥ 30 days after insertion. All patients with a chronic indwelling urinary catheter will eventually develop bacteriuria.

Epidemiology and Microbiology

The duration of catheterization is the most important risk factor for the development of bacteriuria. The duration may be classified as short term (< 30 days) or long term (> 30 days).

Of patients with short-term catheterization, 15–30% will develop bacteriuria. *E coli* is the most common microorganism associated with short-term catheterization, accounting for ~ 25–30% of cases (Box 16–3). Other common microorganisms include *P aeruginosa, Klebsiella* spp., *Proteus* spp., and *S epidermidis*. Most cases of bacteriuria associated with short-term catheterization are caused by a single microorganism.

All patients with an indwelling urinary catheter for > 30 days will develop bacteriuria. New episodes of bacteriuria caused by different microorganisms occur commonly. In addition, some microorganisms may persist for weeks, months, or years. Polymicrobial bacteriuria occurs in ≥ 95% of patients with long-term catheterization. *Providencia stuartii* is one of the most common microorganisms that cause bacteri-uria in patients with long-term catheterization and may persist for months and years.

Pathogenesis

In patients with a urinary catheter, microorganisms may enter the bladder through at least three mecha-nisms: (1) At the time of catheter insertion, (2) through the lumen of the catheter, or (3) along the catheter-urethral interface.

The insertion of the urinary catheter through the urethra may transport microorganisms located within the periurethral area into the bladder. The insertion results in bacteriuria in from < 1% in young healthy individuals to > 20% in elderly or hospitalized pa-tients. Microorganisms may enter the drainage bag, multiply, persist in the film of urine within the bag and tubing, ascend the lumen of the tubing, and enter

BOX 16–3	
Microbiology of Nosocomially Acquired Urinary Tract Infection in Children or Adults	
Catheter–Associated Short-Term (<30-d) Catheterization	
More Frequent Less Frequent	• *Escherichia coli* • Other *Enterobacteriaceae* • *Pseudomonas* spp. • *Staphylococcus epidermidis*
Catheter–Associated Long-Term (> 30 days) Catheterization	
More frequent Less frequent	• *Providencia stuartii* • *Pseudomonas* spp. • *Escherichia coli* • Other *Enterobacteriaceae* • *Staphylococcus epidermidis*

the bladder. The closed drainage system reduces the risk of intraluminal entry of microorganisms into the bladder. The most likely mechanism for the entry of microorganisms into the bladder is along the catheter-ureteral interface. Microorganisms in the periurethral area enter the space between the catheter and the urethral mucosa and ascend into the bladder. This route probably accounts for 80% of episodes of bacteriuric females and 30% of those bacteriurias that occur in males.

Once bacteria enter the urinary bladder, they mul-tiply and maintain themselves primarily through the production of a biofilm, which covers and secures bacteria on the mucosal or catheter surface where they are protected from natural host defenses or from the activity of antimicrobial agents. Microorganisms may ascend the ureters to the kidneys. The presence of chronic bacteriuria in association with an in-dwelling urinary catheter may result in the formation of urolithiasis or acute and chronic infection includ-ing pyelonephritis. Risk factors that predispose to bacteriuria in patients with indwelling urinary cathe-ters include the duration of catheterization, diabetes mellitus, female sex, and errors in catheter care.

Clinical Findings

A. Signs and symptoms. The majority of pa-tients with short-term catheterization and bacteriuria are asymptomatic. However, 25–30% of these will develop signs of UTI with fever, suprapubic pain, or flank pain. Men are more likely to develop bacteri-uria than women. Bacteremia usually caused by *E* *coli* occurs in < 5% of patients with short-term catheterization. Patients with long-term catheterization may develop symptoms of UTI similar to those of patients with short-term catheterization.

B. Laboratory findings. The diagnosis of bacteriuria is made by performing quantitative urine cultures on a specimen obtained by using aseptic techniques from the urinary bag. In most instances, quantitative culture yields > 100,000 colonies of bacteria/mL of urine.

Differential Diagnosis

Among patients with indwelling urinary catheters who develop fever and signs of infection, the urinary tract should be considered the most likely source of bacteremia. However, many patients with a chronic indwelling urinary catheter are at risk of bacteremia from other sources such as decubitus ulcer, aspiration pneumonia, intra-abdominal infections, and other conditions that are common in chronically ill, elderly patients.

Complications

In addition, these patients may develop complications associated with catheter obstruction, stone formation, renal failure, or chronic pyelonephritis. Like patients with short-term catheterization, bacteremia may occur and is usually caused by *E coli* but also may be caused by *P stuartii* or other members of the *Enterobacteriaceae.*

Obstruction is the result of catheter plugging caused by a matrix composed of protein, bacteria, glycocalyx, and crystals. *P mirabilis* is the most common microorganism that causes catheter obstruction and stone formation in patients with long-term catheterization. Chronic pyelonephritis is related to the duration of catheterization. Chronic renal failure may occur, resulting from a combination of factors that includes chronic pyelonephritis, stone formation, and catheter obstruction.

Therapy

The use of antimicrobial therapy may delay the onset but does not prevent bacteriuria in patients with an indwelling urinary catheter. Moreover, long-term administration of antimicrobial agents to these patients results in selection of resistant microorganisms in the urine. Asymptomatic bacteriuria in patients with an indwelling urinary catheter should not be treated with antimicrobial therapy. For most patients, if bacteriuria persists after removal of the catheter, short-term (3-day) antimicrobial therapy is recommended (Box 16–2). Patients who develop symptoms of infection that are associated with an indwelling urinary catheter should receive 7–10 days of antimicrobial therapy with specific activity in vitro against microorganisms recovered from blood or urine cultures.

Asymptomatic candiduria develops frequently in patients with long-term catheterization, especially among patients who have received antimicrobial therapy. Some patients may develop complications of candiduria, which include catheter obstruction, fungus ball formation, or invasion of the bladder wall or kidney parenchyma. In asymptomatic patients, removal of the catheter usually results in the disappearance of candiduria. For patients who develop complications, change of an obstructed urinary catheter, cystoscopic removal of a fungus ball, bladder irrigation with amphotericin B, or systemic therapy with orally or parenterally administered anti-*Candida* therapy may be necessary.

Prognosis

The prognosis for bacteriuria in patients with short-term catheterization is excellent after removal of the catheter. The frequency of bacteremia originating from the urinary tract in patients with short-term catheterization is < 5%, and the mortality related to bacteremia from nosocomial bacteriuria in these patients is < 15%. Most deaths are related to severe underlying disease.

In patients with long-term urinary catheters, bacteriuria will persist for as long as the catheter is in place and may persist even after catheter removal, despite administration of antimicrobial therapy. The urinary tract is the source of the majority of febrile episodes of bacteremia in patients with long-term urinary catheters. The mortality during febrile periods that originate from a urinary source in patients with long-term catheters is 60-fold that of afebrile patients with chronic indwelling urinary catheters.

Prevention

Prevention of bacteriuria may be considered as follows: avoidance of long-term urinary catheterization, prevention of bacteriuria once a urinary catheter is inserted, prevention of complications of bacteriuria, and prevention of patient-to-patient transmission.

A. Avoidance of urinary catheterization. Methods such as biofeedback, patient training for bladder-emptying techniques, and the use of special clothing, including adult diapers, may be effective in selected patients. Condom catheters have been used in men and probably reduce the risk of bacteriuria. Intermittent self or assisted catheterization delays the onset of bacteriuria and may reduce the frequency of bacteremia, febrile episodes, stone formation, and renal disease. Suprapubic catheterization may reduce the incidence of bacteriuria and ureteral strictures.

B. Prevention of bacteriuria. Once a urinary catheter is inserted, the major methods for prevention of bacteriuria are to maintain a closed catheter system and to remove the catheter as soon as possible. Irrigation of the catheter and bladder with antimicrobial agents has not been effective in preventing bacteriuria. The use of silver- or antibiotic-coated or -impregnated urinary catheters has been investigated.

Conflicting results have been published, and more data are necessary to assess the efficacy of silver-coated urinary catheters in reducing the risk of bacteriuria. Antimicrobial agents should not be administered to patients with long-term catheterization, to prevent bacteriuria. Bacteriuria will occur despite antimicrobial therapy. Microorganisms will emerge that are resistant, and therapy is expensive. Methanamine is an antibacterial agent that forms formaldehyde in acidic urine and may be useful to reduce bacteriuria in patients with intermittent catheterization.

C. Prevention of complications. Blood and urine cultures should be obtained during febrile episodes, and antimicrobial therapy should be administered. Antimicrobial therapy should not be administered as prophylaxis for febrile episodes to patients with bacteriuria.

D. Prevention of patient-to-patient transfer. Nosocomial microorganisms reside on the skin and in the periurethral area of patients with indwelling urinary catheters. Patient-to-patient transmission may occur as the result of contamination of the hands of medical personnel who may then transmit these microorganisms to patients. Good hand-washing techniques and wound and skin precautions should be observed in patients with chronic urinary catheters. Education regarding good catheter hygiene and care of the closed catheter system is important for patients, family, and health care personnel. Outbreaks of multiresistant nosocomial catheter-associated urinary tract infections may occur. Hospital infection control should have adequate surveillance mechanisms in place and procedures to control and eradicate outbreaks, should they occur.

REFERENCES

Johnson J, Stamm W: Diagnosis and treatment of acute urinary tract infection. Infect Dis Clin North Am 1987;1:773.

Sobel JD, Kaye D: Urinary Tract Infections. In Mandel et al: *Principles and Practices of Infectious Diseases,* 4th ed. Churchill Livingstone, 1995.

Warren JW: Nosocomial urinary tract infections. In Mandel et al: *Principles and Practices of Infectious Diseases,* 4th ed. Churchill Livingstone, 1995.

Sepsis Syndrome

17

Andrew D. Badley, MD & James M. Steckelberg, MD

Essentials of Diagnosis

- Sepsis should be suspected in patients who present with any combination of fevers, hypotension, altered mental status, or evidence of tissue hypoperfusion.
- The diagnosis requires Systemic Inflammatory Response Syndrome (SIRS), documented infection as the presumed cause of SIRS, and absence of alternative causes of SIRS.
- In a patient who is critically ill with SIRS, the etiology is often not immediately apparent; therefore a careful history and physical exam are required to determine the most likely specific cause.

General Considerations

The Greek origins of the term sepsis refer to the process of putrefaction and decay. Historically, it has come to mean the presence of pathogenic microorganisms or their biologically active products in the host. It is the presence of biologically active products that causes the inflammatory response leading to such clinical sequelae as fever and hypotension. If the inflammatory response proceeds unchecked, it may ultimately lead to organ dysfunction, multiorgan failure, and death.

Recently, the term Systemic Inflammatory Response Syndrome (SIRS) has been introduced. This term refers to a specific host systemic response that may be elicited by a variety of clinical events, including infection, burns, pancreatitis, ischemia, trauma, hemorrhage, immune-mediated tissue injury, and exogenous stimuli. SIRS resulting from infection is called sepsis. Furthermore, sepsis that leads to altered tissue perfusion of vital organs (resulting in one or more of oliguria, hypoxemia, elevated lactate, or altered mentation) is called sepsis syndrome. Sepsis and sepsis syndrome are distinguished from infection, which is inflammation in response to invasion of a normally sterile site by microorganisms, and bacteremia, which is the presence of bacteria in the blood (Figure 17–1). When faced with a patient with SIRS, the objective is to define, if possible, its etiology, and, if SIRS is caused by infection, to administer appropriate antibiotics and supportive care guided by the patient's history and physical examination (Table 17–1).

A. Epidemiology. Data from the Centers for Disease Control indicate that the incidence of sepsis increased from 73.6 cases/100,000 person years in 1979 to 175.9 cases/100,000 person years in 1987, when sepsis became the 13th leading cause of death. Several factors may contribute to the increasing incidence of sepsis: (1) increased incidence and survival of persons predisposed to sepsis, such as persons infected with HIV, patients with cancer, the elderly, and those who have had organ transplants; (2) increased use of medical prostheses such as intravascular catheters and indwelling urinary catheters; and (3) widespread (and, at times, inappropriate) use of antimicrobial agents that predispose toward the selection of virulent or multiply resistant pathogens.

B. Pathogenesis. The leading microbial cause of sepsis and septic shock is infections with gram-negative bacteria that initiate a cascade of events leading to SIRS. Bacteria may be in the bloodstream only transiently; therefore, sepsis and septic shock are not always associated with bacteremia. An integral component of the gram-negative–bacterial cell wall, lipopolysaccharide (LPS), is responsible for initiating a cascade that results in cytokine release and the early physiologic changes associated with septic shock (Figure 17–2). LPS within the circulatory system may form a complex with either bactericidal permeability-increasing protein or with LPS-binding protein. Complexes of bactericidal permeability-increasing protein–LPS are fated for destruction, whereas LPS-binding protein–LPS complexes bind with their receptor, CD14. Once bound by LPS-binding protein–LPS complex, CD14 initiates an intracytoplasmic signaling cascade that ultimately results in the translocation of nuclear factor kappa B (NF-κB) into the nucleus. NF-κB is a transcription factor that, once present in the nucleus, initiates the transcription of numerous cytokines including tumor necrosis factor (TNF)-α, interleukin (IL)-1, IL-2, IL-6, IL-8, platelet activating factor, and interferon-γ. These and other potential mediators including nitrous oxide, intracellular adhesion molecules, prostaglandins, and leukotrienes have been directly or indirectly implicated in the pathogenesis of septic shock (Box 17–1).

The sepsis syndrome may also occur after infections with gram-positive bacteria, viruses, protozoa, rickettsia, and helminths (none of which contain LPS). In these situations, alternate pathways of cytokine induction are invoked. Components of gram-

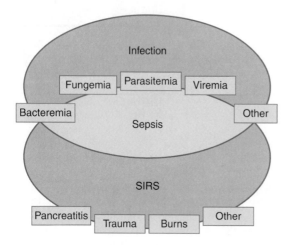

Figure 17–1. Interrelationship between infection, sepsis, and the systemic inflammatory response syndrome (Reproduced with permission, from JAMA 1995;273:155).

Table 17–1. Clues to the diagnosis of sepsis.

Epidemiology
- Any patient may develop sepsis.
- Patients with impaired immune systems are at higher risk.
- Alterations in local defenses (such as breaks in the skin, burns) place patients at risk.

Clinical
- Signs and symptoms of infection
- Impaired hemodynamics and tissue perfusion consistent with the Systemic Inflammatory Response Syndrome (SIRS):
- Hyperthermia (>38°C) or hypothermia (< 36°C)
- Tachypnea (respiratory rate > 20 breaths/min)
- Hypotension (systolic blood pressure < 90 mmHg, or drop of > 40 mmHg from baseline)

Laboratory
- Leukocytosis (> 12 × 109 cells/L) or leukopenia (< 4 × 109 cells/L)
- Left shift in leukocyte differential (> 10% band forms)
- Changes that reflect decreased tissue perfusion: elevated lactate dehydrogenase, evidence of organ hypoperfusion (elevated creatinine, rising transaminases, thrombocytopenia, hypoxemia)
- Changes associated with the site of underlying infection (decreased pO2 in a patient with pneumonia, etc.)

positive bacteria including peptidoglycan and teichoic acids can directly activate the alternate pathway of the complement cascade. Once activated, the complement cascade induces lymphocyte proliferation and activation, as well as phagocyte activation, which generates the production of inflammatory cytokines. Gram-positive–bacterial components can also directly induce cytokine production; both peptidoglycan and lipoteichoic acid can induce IL-1 release from monocytes and macrophages, and lipoteichoic acid can additionally induce TNF-α and IL-6 release. Other bacterial proteins are also capable of causing cytokine production. Gram-positive enterotoxins and exotoxins can directly cause the release of IL-1, IL-6, and TNF-α. Furthermore, staphylococcal toxic shock syndrome toxin-1 is a more potent stimulus of IL-1 release than is LPS.

Regardless of the organism responsible for inducing sepsis, a common final pathway characterized by the release of proinflammatory mediators is activated, resulting in fever, hypotension, decreased organ perfusion, and other potential complications (see below).

Clinical Findings

The clinical findings associated with sepsis syndrome may be related either to the pathophysiology of SIRS or to the infection that is the underlying cause of sepsis syndrome. The clinical findings associated with SIRS are similar regardless of the mechanism responsible for inducing the inflammatory cascade. Infections that are commonly associated with sepsis syndrome in a normal host include pneumonia, meningitis, upper urinary tract infections, cellulitis, and intra-abdominal catastrophes (perforated viscus,

diverticular abscess, etc). A careful history may identify an infection(s) for which a patient is at increased risk.

A. Signs and Symptoms. The signs and symptoms of sepsis syndrome are varied and may reflect in part the underlying infection that is the cause of the inflammatory response. A patient with sepsis may have few complaints or may complain of fevers, chills, pain, rash, or dyspnea. The focus of the physical examination should be to identify the source and severity of the underlying infection, as well as any associated complications. Essentials of the physical examination of a patient with suspected sepsis syndrome include the following:

- Vital signs should include temperature, respiratory rate, and blood pressure.
- Medical appliances such as intravenous lines and urinary catheters should be examined to determine whether these sites represent a potential portal of entry for infectious agents.
- The head and neck should be examined, looking for nuchal rigidity, conjunctival petechiae, and Roth spots.
- The oropharynx should be examined, looking for thrush (suggesting an underlying immunosuppressive state including chronic illness, HIV infection, malignancy, or chronic steroid use), quinsy, periodontal abscess, or evidence of herpes simplex infection.
- Examination of the skin may provide important

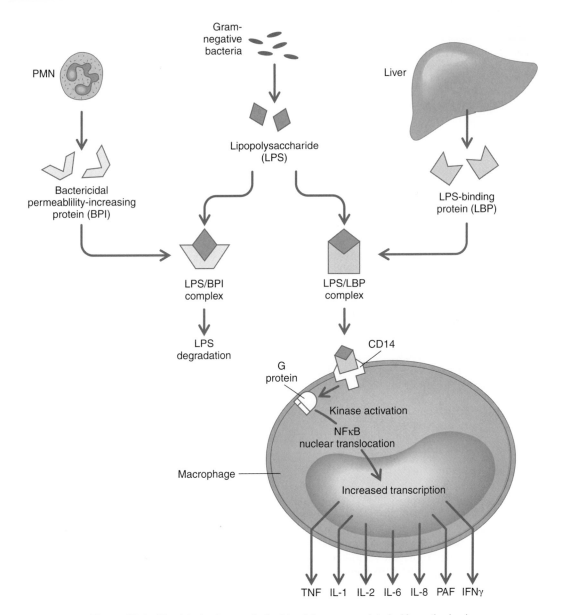

Figure 17–2. Physiologic changes in the bloodstream associated with septic shock.

diagnostic clues such as rashes of disseminated meningococcemia or ecthyma gangrenosum (seen with disseminated *Pseudomonas* infection) are important diagnostic clues. In addition, petechiae associated with disseminated intravascular coagulation may be present, as well as Janeway lesions and Osler's nodes. Last, signs of cellulitis or necrotizing fasciitis are an obvious clue to the cause of sepsis syndrome.

* The pulmonary system should be examined, focusing on signs of pneumonitis: impaired oxygenation, pulmonary consolidation, and empyema.

Because patients with sepsis syndrome often develop adult respiratory distress syndrome (ARDS), it may be difficult to differentiate the pulmonary findings of pneumonia form those of ARDS.

* The cardiac examination will frequently be abnormal, owing to the compensatory changes associated with sepsis. Although uncommon, infective endocarditis may uncommonly lead to sepsis syndrome; therefore the finding of a new or changing murmur (especially a regurgitant one) is important. In addition, patients with sepsis syn-

BOX 17–1

Cytokines Implicated in the Pathology of Sepsis Syndrome.

Cytokine	Source	Dominant Physiologic Effects
TNF-α	Macrophages	Vasodilation, hypotension, induces fever, induces production of acute-phase reactant proteins by liver
TNF-β	T-helper cells, NK cells	Similar effects to TNF-α
IL-1	Macrophages, endothelium	Vasodilation, induces fever
PAF	Neutrophils, endothelium	Causes microvascular leak, negative inotropic effects, causes platelet aggregation
IL-6	T cells, B cells	B-cell differentiation
IL-8	Endothelium, monocytes	Chemotaxis
IL-2	T cells	Decreases arterial pressure, cardiac ejection fraction
Interferon-γ	T lymphocytes	Acts on hypothalamus to produce fever
Leukotrienes	Metabolite of arachidonic acid	Increases vascular permeability and vasoconstriction, decreases coronary blood flow, increases pulmonary vascular resistance
Thromboxane A$_2$	Metabolite of arachidonic acid	Platelet aggregation, neutrophil aggregation, increased vascular permeability
Prostaglandin E$_2$	Metabolite of arachidonic acid	Promotes catabolism, acts on hypothalamus to cause fever

drome will frequently be hypotensive; therefore a careful cardiac examination is needed to differentiate cardiogenic shock (with elevated jugular venous pressure, gallop rhythms, and evidence of right and/or left-sided congestive failure) from noncardiogenic shock caused by sepsis, which is initially a hyperdynamic, high-cardiac-output state.

• Examination of the abdomen focuses on tenderness, guarding, or absence of bowel sounds, suggestive of an intra-abdominal event such as perforation of a hollow viscus. In addition, it should be noted whether a patient has had a prior splenectomy, which is associated with an increased risk for certain infections.

• Examination of kidneys seeks flank tenderness or increased size (by palpation, or by ballottement).

• Thorough pelvic and rectal examinations are necessary for all septic patients, to look for evidence of rectal or perirectal abscess, pelvic inflammatory disease, and prostatitis.

B. Laboratory Findings. Laboratory findings associated with sepsis syndrome may reflect decreased organ perfusion or may reflect the underlying infection. Frequently leukocytosis or leukopenia is present. In addition, anemia may be seen, which may be dilutional (after fluid resuscitation efforts) or associated with underlying chronic disease. Thrombocytopenia may accompany the development of disseminated intravascular coagulation, or reactive thrombocythemia may occur. Hypoxemia may be seen with pneumonitis or in response to the development of ARDS. If hypercarbia is seen in association with hypoxia, impending ventilatory failure may be present. Rising creatinine (with rising urea), elevations in lactose dehydrogenase (LDH), or rising transaminases are signs of decreased organ perfusion and are suggestive of sepsis syndrome.

For most patients with sepsis syndrome, initial laboratory screening should include the following: complete blood count, urinalysis, coagulation profile, glucose, blood urea nitrogen, creatinine, electrolytes, liver enzymes, bilirubin, lactose dehydrogenase, amylase, lipase, arterial blood gas, chest X-ray, and electrocardiogram. In addition, if meningitis is suspected, screening should also include cerebrospinal fluid testing for glucose, protein, cell count, culture, and rapid bacterial antigen testing. Microbiologic testing should be dictated by the clinical presentation, but in most patients, urine, sputum, and blood should be cultured for bacteria.

In selected patients, Swan Ganz catheters may be used to assess cardiac output, systemic vascular resistance, and pulmonary capillary wedge pressure. In early shock due to SIRS, cardiac output will be increased, systemic vascular resistance will be normal or low, pulmonary capillary wedge pressures will be normal or low, and venous oxygen saturation will be increased. These indices are of value in differentiating hypotension due to cardiogenic, hypovolemic, toxin mediated, or neurogenic causes, as well as assessing the adequacy of volume resuscitation.

C. Imaging. There are no imaging procedures that are specific for sepsis syndrome; however, carefully selected radiographic evaluations may aid in establishing the underlying infection. Every patient should have a chest X-ray performed, and, based on the clinical presentation, CT scanning or ultrasonography of the chest or abdomen may be appropriate.

Differential Diagnosis

A patient with sepsis syndrome will have characteristic findings suggestive of SIRS; however, at the time of presentation, it may not be readily apparent that the etiology of SIRS is infection. Therefore all potential etiologies for SIRS must be considered in the differential diagnosis. The presence of burns, trauma, and some exogenous stimuli may be readily apparent, although at times it may be difficult to determine whether these conditions are complicated by infection.

Clues to the potential presence of pancreatitis include an antecedent history of alcohol ingestion or of biliary colic. Not having such a history, however, does not exclude pancreatitis as a potential etiology of SIRS; therefore serum lipase and amylase determinations should be considered on all patients with SIRS. The diagnosis of ischemia (eg, ischemic bowel) as a potential precipitant of SIRS is often more difficult to establish, although signs and symptoms referable to the ischemic organ should provide clinical clues. In establishing the etiology of SIRS, the value of a careful history and physical exam cannot be overstated.

Virtually any focus of infection with virtually any organism can lead to the development of sepsis syndrome. Most commonly, the infectious agents responsible for causing sepsis syndrome in the community are bacteria, and the most common infections are community-acquired pneumonia, upper urinary tract infections, meningitis, and cellulitis. In hospitalized patients, line-associated bacteremia, aspiration pneumonia, ventilator-associated pneumonia, wound infections, and abscesses are typical causes of sepsis syndrome.

Complications

The clinical findings related to sepsis syndrome are a reflection of the pervasive nature of the inflammatory mediators of sepsis. Virtually every organ system is affected in sepsis syndrome, although the degree of involvement of each organ varies widely between patients. Just as the effects of sepsis syndrome are present in virtually every organ system so are potential complications.

A. Central Nervous System. Toxic metabolic encephalopathy is associated with sepsis syndrome and is a consequence of several factors including cerebral hypoperfusion, medications, hypoxia, the biologically active products of the infective agent, and inflammatory mediators of sepsis. Encephalopathy may progress to coma, seizures, cerebral edema, and potentially death. In addition, in patients who are critically ill for prolonged periods, a distal sensory/motor polyneuropathy of unknown etiology, called critical illness polyneuropathy, may develop. Last, cerebral hemorrhage, or infarction may occur as a result of the coagulation abnormalities associated with sepsis syndrome.

B. Pulmonary System. The lungs may be affected in sepsis in several ways. They may be the primary site of infection giving rise to sepsis (ie, pneumonia) or may be subject to the forces of increased left-ventricular end diastolic pressure characteristic of a failing left ventricle. The development of hypoxia and hypocarbia may reflect the development of capillary leakage, leading to impaired gas exchange and consequent hyperventilation characteristic of ARDS. Abnormalities of oxygenation and ventilation can become refractory to mechanical ventilation and lead to death.

C. Cardiovascular System. The early cardiovascular response to the release of circulating inflammatory cytokines is characterized by normal or increased cardiac output with low systemic vascular resistance and a loss of vascular responsiveness to sympathetic agents (such as epinephrine). Later, myocardial dysfunction and a decrease in the ejection fraction of the left ventricle may occur as a result of a putative myocardial depressant factor. The compensatory increase in heart rate is an attempt to maintain tissue perfusion by increasing cardiac output; failure to compensate appropriately may be indicative of a poor prognosis. Myocardial workload, in an attempt to compensate for the falling tissue perfusion, may increase markedly in sepsis syndrome; if the myocardium is unable to maintain adequate perfusion, cardiac ischemia may occur, leading to arrhythmias, myocardial infarctions, and death.

D. Gastrointestinal System. Normal gut motility and permeability may be altered in sepsis as a result of the effects of endotoxin and cytokines, resulting in the altered absorption of oral medications and bacterial overgrowth. Gastrointestinal complications of sepsis syndrome include bacterial overgrowth, which increases risk for developing nosocomial pneumonia, and functional obstructions such as toxic megacolon caused by impaired motility.

E. Renal and Hepatic Systems. The renal and hepatic systems commonly show evidence of dysfunction due to hypoperfusion and capillary leakage, although the use of medications including aminoglycosides, acetaminophen, and others may also contribute to organ injury. Elevations in levels of transaminases and hyperbilirubinemia are common and are associated with a poor prognosis. Rarely, liver injury may progress to ischemic hepatitis. Prerenal azotemia secondary to hypoperfusion is the most common form of renal dysfunction in sepsis syndrome, but other intrinsic renal disorders including acute glomerulonephritis and interstitial nephritis may occur.

F. Hematologic System. The hematologic system may be altered in sepsis syndrome, notably through the development of disseminated intravascular coagulation and impaired bone marrow synthesis of cellular precursors. Anemia, leukopenia, and thrombocytopenia may be due in part to failure of production of marrow precursors. Anemia may be corrected by transfusion, but leukopenia may impair host defenses, and thrombocytopenia may lead to bleeding, thereby aggravating hypotension, anemia, and tissue hypoperfusion.

G. Musculoskeletal System. Skeletal muscle dysfunction may be a consequence of the effects of endotoxin and hypoperfusion (also a consequence of the release of inflammatory mediators). Muscle injury may be reflected by rising creatinine kinase levels. Prolonged muscle dysfunction may lead to wasting and the development of critical illness myopathy.

H. Endocrine System. The physiologic stresses associated with sepsis may unmask occult endocrine deficiency states or, more rarely, may induce adrenal hemorrhage resulting in Addison's disease. The euthyroid sick syndrome is characterized by impaired conversion of T4 to T3 and by abnormal production of thyroid-binding globulin. This results in abnormal measurements of T4 and T3 with normal or decreased levels of thyroid-stimulating hormone.

Treatment

The aims of treatment for patients with sepsis syndrome are threefold:

- Elimination of the infectious agent(s) responsible for inducing sepsis.
- Supportive care based in the intensive care unit aimed at normalizing oxygenation, ventilation, blood pressure, and tissue perfusion.
- Therapies intended to interrupt inflammatory mediators of sepsis.

A. Elimination of Infectious Agent(s). Eliminating infectious agents often consists of administering empiric antibiotics together with appropriate surgical drainage or débridement. The complete medical history and physical examination, in addition to the clinical scenario, are used to generate a microbiologic differential diagnosis and guide selection of empiric antibiotic therapy. Host factors that may predispose patients to certain infections are shown in Box 17–2. In a critically ill patient with sepsis syndrome, several possible microbial etiologies commonly exist. Therefore broad-spectrum empiric antibiotic therapies are used until further microbiologic data are available, which might indicate that a more specific antimicrobial regimen is appropriate. Once available, culture data and sensitivity profiles should be used to narrow the spectrum of antibiotics (often to only one agent). The choice of initial antibiotics is based on the likelihood of specific microorganisms for the given clinical scenario (Box 17–3), and the choice of subsequent antibiotics is guided by the results of microbiology testing.

B. Supportive Care. Supportive care should be based in the intensive care unit and is aimed at normalizing oxygenation, ventilation, blood pressure, and tissue perfusion. The principal means of achieving this goal is aggressive fluid resuscitation, along with possible adjunctive therapy with pressors.

C. Experimental Therapies. Experimental therapies for sepsis are aimed at interrupting the inflammatory cascade that is common (SIRS caused by diverse stimuli). To date, no such therapies have become part of the standard practice of the medical management of the sepsis syndrome, but numerous strategies in various phases of development exist (Box 17–4).

Current knowledge concerning the pathogenesis of sepsis continues to increase. To date, > 30 mediators have been implicated; consequently, strategies aimed at blocking one mediator are not likely to be successful in reversing the process. Furthermore, clinical trials of sepsis therapies have enrolled patients with a variety of predisposing factors, in whom sepsis has been induced by a variety of agents. It is therefore possible that one therapy may be of benefit in a certain subgroup of patients (ie, cancer patients with pneumococcal sepsis), but this effect would not be detected in such trials. Future studies aimed at defined populations with similar etiologies for sepsis are underway.

Prognosis

The proportion of patients with sepsis who develop septic shock varies between 20% and 40%. Despite increased understanding of its pathogenesis and advances in supportive care, the crude mortality rate of septic shock remains between 50% and 80%.

Prevention & Control

Because sepsis syndrome is not one infection, there is no one thing that can be done to prevent its development. In general, early recognition of infection and appropriate therapy may help to prevent the development of the "sepsis cascade." For individuals

BOX 17–2

Common Microbial Etiologies of Sepsis.

Host Factor	Likely Pathogens
Normal host	*Streptococcus pneumoniae, Haemophilus influenzae, Neisseria meningitidis, Staphylococcus aureus*
Interrupted integument	*Staphylococcus* species, *Streptococcus pyogenes, Enterobacteriaceae, Pseudomonas aeruginosa*
Abnormal urinary tract	*Escherichia coli, Enterobacteriaceae*
Alcoholism	*Klebsiella* species, *Streptococcus pneumoniae*
Cirrhosis	Gram-negative rods; *Vibrio, Yersinia, Salmonella* species
Asplenia	*Streptococcus pneumoniae, Haemophilus influenzae, Neisseria meningitidis, Capnocytophagia canimorsus*
Diabetes	*Escherichia coli, Pseudomonas* species, mucormycosis
Hypogammaglobulinemia	*Streptococcus pneumoniae, Neisseria meningitidis, Escherichia coli, Haemophilus influenzae*
Burns	*Staphylococcus aureus, Pseudomonas aeruginosa*, nosocomial gram-negative bacteria
Cystic fibrosis	Multiresistant *Pseudomonas* and *Burkholderia* species
AIDS	*Pneumocystis carinii, Pseudomonas* species (pneumonia), *Mycobacterium avium intracellulare* complex, cytomegalovirus
Solid organ translant	Gram-negative bacteria, cytomegalovirus
Intravascular devices	*Staphylococcus aureus*, coagulase-negative *Staphylococcus* species
Chronic steroid use	*Streptococcus pneumoniae, Haemophilus influenzae*
Neonates	Group B *Streptococcus, Listeria monocytogenes, Streptococcus pneumoniae, Haemophilus influenzae*
Posoperative patients	*Staphylococcus aureus, Enterobacteriaceae*, nosocomial gram-negative bacteria
Elderly	*Streptococcus pneumoniae, Haemophilus influenzae, Staphylococcus aureus, Enterobacteriaceae, Listeria monocytogenes*

in the community, appropriate vaccinations, including pneumococcal vaccination for patients with chronic obstructive pulmonary disease, may help to decrease the incidence of infections and perhaps of sepsis syndrome. For hospitalized patients, several measures may decrease the incidence of sepsis syndrome: (1) appropriate use of prophylactic perioperative antibiotics, (2) restriction of the use of medical appliances (such as intravenous lines) to only those patients with definite indications, and (3) strict adherence to infection control procedures (to decrease the rate of spread of infection among other patients), including adherence to hand washing policies by hospital staff. In addition, for patients who are at special risk for the development of infections, such as transplant recipients, compliance with prophylactic antibiotics (such as trimethoprim-sulfamethoxazole) is also effective in reducing the incidence of infections and therefore the incidence of sepsis syndrome.

BOX 17-3

Empiric Therapies for Clinical Presentations Underlying Sepsis Syndrome.

Suspected Source	Empiric Therapy
Community-acquired pneumonia	Third-generation cephalosporin[1] + erythromycin[2] (or clarithromycin OR azithromycin) OR doxycycline[3]
Nosocomial aspiration pneumonia	Third-generation cephalosporin[1] +/− clindamycin[4]
Nosocomial pneumonia	Ceftazidime[5] OR cefepime[6] OR imipenem/meropenem[7] OR antipseudo-monal penicillin[8]
Cellulitis	Cefazolin[9] OR penicillinase-resistant penicillin[10]; vancomycin if methicillin-resistant staphylococcus aureus (MRSA) suspected
Upper urinary tract infection	Third-generation cephalosporin[1] OR ampicillin[11] + aminoglycoside[12]
Meningitis	Cefotaxime[13] OR ceftriaxone[14] PLUS Vancomycin in areas with penicillin-resistant pneumococci; Infant < 3 mo, ampicillin[11] and aminoglycoside[12]
Intra-abdominal sepsis (eg, perforated viscus)	Ampicillin[11] OR third-generation cephalosporin[1] and aminoglycoside[12] and metronidazole[15] OR ampicillin/sulbactam[16] OR ticarcillin/clavulanate[17] OR piperacillin/tazobactam[18] OR imipenem/meropenem[7]
Fever in neutropenic host	Ceftazidime[5] OR cefepime[6] OR imipenem/meropenem[7]
Septic arthritis	Cefazolin[9] OR penicillinase-resistant penicillin;[10] vancomycin if MRSA possible Infant, penicillinase-resistant penicillin[10] + third-generation cephalosporin[1]
Diabetic foot ulcer	Third-generation cephalosporin[1] and clindamycin[4] OR piperacillin/tazobactam[18] OR ticarcillin/clavulanate[17] OR imipenem/meropenem[5]
Pelvic inflammatory disease	Cefoxitin[19] or cefotetan[20] PLUS doxycycline[3] or clindamycin[4] Alternately, third-generation cephalosporin[1] plus metronidazole[15]
Biliary sepsis (eg, cholangitis)	Ampicillin[11] and aminoglycoside[12] and metronidazole[15] OR piperacillin/tazobactam[18] OR ampicillin/sulbactam[16] OR ticarcillin/clavulanate[17] OR imipenem/meropenem[5]
Unknown	Vancomycin + aminoglycoside[12] + piperacillin/tazobactam[8] OR imipenem/meropenem[5]

[1]Cefotaxime, 1–2 g IV every 8 h (pediatric 150 mg/kg IV divided every 8 h) or ceftriaxone 1–2 g IV every 24 h (pediatric 50 mg/kg IV once daily).
[2]Erythromycin, 1 g IV every 6 h (pediatric 40 mg/kg IV divided every 6 h).
[3]Doxycycline, 100 mg IV/PO every 12 h (pediatric 5 mg/kg PO divided every 12 h).
[4]Clindamycin, 600–900 mg IV every 8 h (pediatric 20 mg/kg IV divided every 8 h).
[5]Ceftazidime, 1–2 g IV every 8 h (pediatric 150 mg/kg IV divided every 8 h).
[6]Cefepime, 1–2 g IV every 12 h (pediatric 50 mg/kg IV every 8 h).
[7]Imipenem, 500 mg IV every 6 h (pediatric 50 mg/kg IV divided every 6 h); meropenem, 1 g IV every 8 h (pediatric 40 mg/kg IV divided every 8 h).
[8]Ticarcillin, 3 g IV every 6 h (pediatric 100 mg/kg IV every 8 h) or piperacillin, 3 g IV every 6 h (pediatric 300 mg/kg IV divided every 6 h).
[9]Cefazolin, 1 g IV every 8 h (pediatric 80 mg/kg IV divided every 8 h).
[10]Nafcillin, 1 g IV every 4 h (pediatric 150 mg/kg IV divided every 6 h) or oxacillin, 1 g IV every 4 h (pediatric 150 mg/kg IV divided every 6 h).
[11]Ampicillin, 1 g IV every 6 h (pediatric 150 mg/kg divided every 6 h).
[12]Gentamicin, 1.3 mg/kg IV every 8 h (pediatric 7.5 mg/kg divided every 8 h) or tobramicin, 1.3 mg/kg IV every 8 h (pediatric 5 mg/kg divided every 8 h)
[13]Cefotaxime, 2 g IV every 4 h (pediatric 200 mg/kg IV divided every 6 h).
[14]Ceftriaxone, 2 g IV every 12 h (pediatric 100 mg/kg IV divided every 12 h).
[15]Metronidazole, 500 mg IV every 6 h (pediatric 30 mg/kg IV divided every 12 h).
[16]Ampicillin/sulbactam, 3.0 g every 6 h (pediatric 150 mg/kg IV divided every 6 h, not for use below 12 years old).
[17]Ticarcillin/clavulanate, 3.1 g IV every 6 h (pediatric same dose, not for use below 12 years old).
[18]Piperacillin/tazobactam, 3.375 g IV every 6 h (pediatric dosage not established).
[19]Cefoxitin, 1–2 g IV every 8 h (pediatric 80 mg/kg IV divided every 6 h).
[20]Cefotetan, 2 g IV every 12 h (pediatric dose not established).

BOX 17-4

Potential Therapies for Interrupting the Inflammatory Mediators of Sepsis

Therapy	Status
Glucocorticoids	No benefit
Antiendotoxin monoclonal antibodies	No consistent benefits, ? decreased mortality in patients with gram-negative sepsis
IL-1 receptor antagonists	No benefit
Platelet-activating factor antagonists	No benefit
Bradykinin antagonists	No benefit
Nonsteroidal anti-inflammatory agents	No benefit
Anti-TNF antibodies	No survival benefit
TNF receptor fusion proteins	No survival benefit
NO synthetase blockade	Under investigation
Cell wall adhesion molecular blockade	Under investigation
Anti-intercellular adhesion molecule antibodies	Under investigation
Recombinant bactericidal/permeability increasing protein	No data in humans
IL-10	No data in humans
Anti-LPS binding protein antibodies	No data in humans
Anti-IL-6 antibodies	No data in humans
Lipid A competitive antagonists	No data in humans
Hemofiltration/plasma exchange	No data in humans

REFERENCES

Bone RC: The sepsis syndrome. Definition and general approach to management. Clin Chest Med 1996;17:175.

Bone RC, Sibbald WJ, Sprung CL: The ACCP-SCCM consensus conference on sepsis and organ failure. Chest 1992;101:1481.

Livingstone DH, Mosenthal AC, Deitch EA: Sepsis and multiple organ dysfunction syndrome: a clinical mechanistic overview. New Horizons 1995;3:257.

Lynn WA, Cohen J: Adjunctive therapy for septic shock: a review of experimental approaches. Clin Infect Dis 1995;20:143.

Fever of Unknown Origin

Julie Brahmer, MD & Merle A. Sande, MD

Essentials of Diagnosis

- Fever is defined as a core body temperature above 38.3 °C.
- Objective documentation of a fever is important in determining whether a patient is actually febrile.
- A thorough history and physical examination are necessary in order to focus diagnostic studies.
- Routine tests include chest x-ray, blood culture, chemistries, and a complete blood count.
- Knowing the most common causes of a fever of unknown origin (FUO) in each special population helps focus the diagnostic strategy.

General Considerations

Fever is defined as a core body temperature above the normal daily variation. Normal body temperature is 37–38 °C and varies by as much as 0.6 °C throughout the day. The core temperature, measured orally or rectally, is usually lowest in the morning and highest between 4:00 and 6:00 PM.

Several endogenous and exogenous pyrogens can cause fever. Exogenous pyrogens, such as toxins, products of microbes, and microbes themselves, cause release of endogenous pyrogens called cytokines, including interleukin-1, interferon, tumor necrosis factor, interleukin-6, and interleukin-11.

Most of these cytokines are produced by macrophages in the reaction to exogenous pyrogens. These cytokines cause the hypothalamus to increase prostaglandin synthesis, which is thought to cause an upward shift of the normal core temperature set point (Figure 18–1).

Definitions of FUO

The classic definition of FUO is a fever of >3 weeks' duration that is >38.3 °C on several occasions, the cause of which is not discovered after 1 week of evaluation in a hospital. This definition was a functional one because it eliminated acute causes of fevers, including acute viral infections, and, in > 90% of cases, the cause of the fever could be found. However, under current insurance guidelines and with newer technology available, a 1-week hospital stay is neither feasible nor practical. Therefore an updated

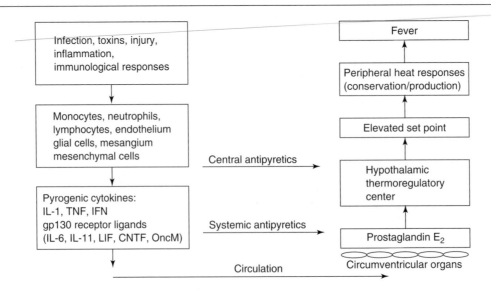

Figure 18–1. Scheme for the pathogenesis of fever. IL, Interleukin; TNF, tumor necrosis factor; IFN, interferon; LIF, leukemia inhibitory factor; CNTF, ciliary neurotropic factor; OncM, oncostatin M.

version of the classic FUO definition has been proposed that defines it as documented fevers > 38.3 °C for > 3 weeks' duration, when the source of the fever is not discovered during either 3 days of hospital investigation or 3 outpatient visits.

Additional definitions of FUO exist for different population subgroups, including HIV-positive patients, neutropenic patients (< 500 polymorphoneutrophils/mm^3), the elderly, hospitalized patients, and pediatric patients. These definitions help the clinician direct the investigation to discover the most likely cause of the fever.

FUO in HIV-infected patients is defined as a fever ≥ 38.3°C for 4 weeks' duration in outpatients or > 3 days in inpatients whose HIV infection has been previously documented. In neutropenic patients, FUO is defined as a fever ≥ 38.3 °C for 3 days with negative cultures after 2 days. In the elderly, the definition of FUOs is similar to the classic definition, except that the patients are elderly. In hospitalized patients, nosocomial FUO is defined as a fever > 38.3 °C lasting 3 days, which was not present or incubating on admission and produces negative cultures after 2 days. Definite criteria for FUOs in children have not been established, but, according to Gartner, the best definition is a fever occurring for ≥ 8 days for which the history, physical examination, and laboratory data fail to reveal a cause (Tables 18–1, 18–2, and 18–3).

Clinical Findings

To diagnose the cause of an FUO, the clinician should first document the presence of fever and its characteristics. Are there fevers, and how high do they get? Sometimes the presence of fever is only subjective (the patient feels warm but his or her temperature is normal). Although the fever pattern is rarely helpful in establishing a diagnosis, a history of periodic fever spikes suggests malaria, lymphoma, or cyclic neutropenia. Lymphoma (non-Hodgkin's and Hodgkin's) can present with the classic Pel-Ebstein fever, which is characterized by intermittent febrile periods lasting for days followed by days to weeks of afebrile periods. A reversal of the normal late-afternoon fever spike, that is, the presence of a morning fever spike, suggests tuberculosis, disseminated *Salmonella* infection, and polyarteritis nodosum. Two fever spikes may occur in a 24-h period with tuberculosis or malaria. Periodic fevers (those that last for days to weeks and then abate or occur at regular intervals) in children include cyclic neutropenia, familial Mediterranean fever, and a syndrome of fever, pharyngitis, and aphthous stomatitis.

The history and physical examination are extremely important for the diagnosis of an FUO because they enable the physician to focus the diagnostic studies. The history should include family history, ethnic background, travel history, and animal exposures. The history and physical examination should

Table 18–1. Historic clues to fever of unknown origin.[1]

Medication or toxic substances
- Drug fever
- Fume fever

Tick exposure
- Relapsing fever
- Rocky Mountain spotted fever
- Lyme disease

Animal contact
- Psittacosis
- Leptospirosis
- Brucellosis
- Toxoplasmosis
- Cat-scratch disease
- Q fever
- Rat-bite fever

Myalgias
- Trichinosis
- Subacute bacterial endocarditis
- Polyarteritis nodosa
- Rheumatoid arthritis
- Familial Mediterranean fever
- Polymyositis

Headache
- Relapsing fever
- Rat-bite fever
- Chronic meningitis/encephalitis
- Malaria
- Brucellosis
- CNS neoplasms
- Rocky Mountain spotted fever

Mental confusion
- Sarcoid meningitis
- Tuberculosis meningitis
- Cryptococcal meningitis
- Carcinomatous meningitis
- CNS neoplasms
- Brucellosis
- Typhoid fever
- HIV

Cardiovascular accident
- Subacute bacterial endocarditis
- Takayasu's arteritis
- Polyarteritis nodosa
- Rocky Mountain spotted fever

Nonproductive cough
- Tuberculosis
- Q fever
- Psittacosis
- Typhoid fever
- Pulmonary neoplasms
- Rocky Mountain spotted fever
- Acute rheumatic fever

Vision disorders or eye pain
- Temporal arteritis (emboli)
- Subacute bacterial endocarditis
- Relapsing fever
- Brain abscess
- Takayasu's arteritis

Fatigue
- Carcinomas
- Lymphomas
- Cytomegalovirus mononucleosis
- Typhoid fever
- Systemic lupus erythematosus
- Rheumatoid arthritis
- Toxoplasmosis

Abdominal pain
- Polyarteritis nodosa
- Abscesses
- Familial Mediterranean fever
- Porphyria
- Relapsing fever
- Cholecystitis

Back pain
- Brucellosis
- Subacute bacterial endocarditis

Neck pain
- Subacute thryoiditis
- Adult Still's disease
- Temporal arteritis (angle of jaw)
- Relapsing mastoiditis
- Septic jugular phlebitis

[1]Source: Cunha BA: Fever of unknown origin (FUO). In Gorbach SL, Bartlett, JB, Blacklow NR: *Infectious Diseases,* 2nd ed. Philadelphia, WB Saunders, 1996.

Table 18–2. Physical clues to fever of unknown origin.[1]

Skin hyperpigmentation
Whipple's disease
Hypersensitivity vasculitis
Addison's disease

Band keratopathy
Adult Still's disease

Dry eyes
Rheumatoid arthritis
Systemic lupus erythematosus
Sjögren's syndrome

Watery eyes
Polyarteritis nodosa

Epistaxis
Relapsing fever
Psittacosis

Conjunctivitis
Tuberculosis
Cat-scratch fever
Systemic lupus erythematosus

Conjunctival suffusion
Leptospirosis
Relapsing fever
Rocky Mountain spotted fever

Subconjunctival hemorrhage
Subacute bacterial endocarditis
Trichinosis

Uveitis
Tuberculosis
Adult Still's diease
Sarcoidosis
Systemic lupus erythematosus

Lymphadenopathy
Lymphomas
Cat-scratch fever
Tuberculosis
Lymphogranuloma venereum
Epstein-Barr virus mononucleosis
Cytomegalovirus
Toxoplasmosis
HIV
Adult Still's disease
Brucellosis

Lymphadenopathy (continued)
Whipple's disease
Pseudolymphoma
Kikuchi's disease
Mycobacterium avium complex

Sternal tenderness
Metastatic carcinoma
Pre-leukemias

Heart murmur
Subacute bacterial endocarditis

Hepatomegaly
Hepatoma
Relapsing fever
Lymphomas
Metastatic carcinoma
Alcoholic liver disease
Granulomatous hepatitis
Q fever
Typhoid fever
Mycobacterium avium complex

Splenomegaly
Leukemia
Lymphomas
Tuberculosis
Brucellosis
Subacute bacterial endocarditis
Cytomegalovirus
Epstein-Barr virus mononucleosis
Rheumatoid arthritis
Sarcoidosis
Psittacosis
Relapsing fever
Alcoholic liver disease
Typhoid fever
Rocky Mountain spotted fever
Kikuchi's disease
Mycobacterium avium complex

Trapezius tenderness
Subdiaphragmatic abscess

Thigh tenderness
Brucellosis
Polymyositis
Polymyositis rheumatica
Pyolnepositis

Relative bradycardia
Typhoid fever
Malaria
Leptospirosis
Psittacosis
Central fever
Drug fever

Splenic tenderness
Subacute bacterial endocarditis
Brucellosis
Salmonella

Epididymo-orchitis
Tuberculosis
Lymphoma
Brucellosis
Leptospirosis
Polyarteritis nodosa
Epstein-Barr virus mononucleosis

Spinal tenderness
Subacute vertebral osteomyelitis
Subacute bacterial endocarditis
Brucellosis
Typhoid fever

Arthritis/joint pain
Familial Mediterranean fever
Pseudogout
Rat-bite fever
Rheumatoid arthritis
Systemic lupus erythematosus
Lyme disease
Brucellosis
Hyper IgD syndrome

Calf tenderness
Rocky Mountain spotted fever
Polymyositis

Thrombophlebitis
Psittacosis

Abdominal tenderness
Cholecystitis

[1]Source: Cunha BA: Fever of unknown origin (FUO). In Gorbach SL, Bartlett JB, Blacklow NR: Infectious Diseases, 2nd ed. Philadelphia, WB Saunders, 1996.

be repeated periodically if no cause of the FUO is discovered during the first evaluation. It is also important to discontinue as many medications (prescription and over-the-counter) as the patient can tolerate since drug fevers are common.

Laboratory tests and evaluation should be focused by the history and physical examination and should not be used randomly. Serial blood cultures (three blood cultures over a 48-h period) should be drawn to detect a bacterial, fungal, or mycobacterial infectious cause

(Table 18–3). A history of exposures to animals might warrant specific serological studies, for example, brucellosis. A history of travel to endemic areas might dictate the need for a malaria smear. The Mantoux test with a purified protein derivative should be done in all patients, since tuberculosis is a common cause of FUOs even without a history of exposure.

However, if the clinical suspicion of tuberculosis is high (as for HIV-positive patients), a negative purified protein derivative does not rule out tuberculosis

Table 18–3. Laboratory clues to fever of unknown origin.[1]

Monocytosis
Tuberculosis
Polyarteritis nodosa
Cytomegalovirus
Sarcoidosis
Brucellosis
Subacute bacterial endo-
  carditis
Systemic lupus erythe-
  matosus
Lymphomas
Carcinomas
Reginal enteritis
Myeloproliferative
  diseases

Eosinophilia
Trichinosis
Lymphomas
Drug fever
Addison's disease
Polyarteritis nodosa
Hypersensitivity vasculitis
Hypernephroma
Myeloproliferative
  diseases

Leukopenia
Miliary tuberculosis
Brucellosis
Systemic lupus
  erythematosus
Lymphomas
Pre-leukemias
Typhoid fever
Kikuchi's disease

Basophilia
Carcinomas
Lymphomas
Pre-leukemias
Myeloproliferative
  diseases

Lymphocytosis
Tuberculosis
Epstein-Barr virus
  mononucleosis
Cytomegalovirus
Toxoplasmosis
Non-Hodgkin's lymphoma
Pertussis

Lymphocytopenia
HIV
Whipple's disease
Tuberculosis
Systemic lupus
  erythematosus
Sarcoidosis

Atypical Lymphocytosis
Epstein-Barr virus
  mononucleosis
Cytomegalovirus
Brucellosis
Toxoplasmosis
Drug fever

Thrombocytosis
Myeloproliferative
  diseases
Tuberculosis
Carcinomas
Lymphomas
Sarcoidosis
Vasculitis
Temporal arteritis
Subacute osteomyelitis
Hypernephroma

Thrombocytopenia
Leukemias
Lymphomas
Myeloproliferative
  diseases
Relapsing fever

Epstein-Barr virus
Drug fever
Vasculitis
Systemic lupus erythe-
  matosus
HIV

Rheumatoid factor
Subacute bacterial endo-
  carditis
Chronic active hepatitis
Rheumatoid arthritis
Malaria
Hypersensitivity vasculitis

ESR (> 100 mm/h)
Adult Still's disease
Temporal arteritis
Hypernephroma
Subacute bacterial
  endocarditis
Drug fever
Carcinomas
Lymphomas
Myeloproliferative
  diseases
Abscesses
Subacute osteomyelitis
Polymyositis
Hyper IgD syndrome

**Elevated alkaline
phosphatase**
Hepatoma
Miliary tuberculosis
Lymphomas
Epstein-Barr virus
  mononucleosis
Cytomegalovirus
Adult Still's disease
Subacute thyroiditis
Temporal arteritis
Hypernephroma

Polyarteritis nodosa
Liver metastases
Granulomatous hepatitis
Mycobacterium avium
  complex

**Increased serum
transaminases**
Epstein-Barr virus
  mononucleosis
Cytomegalovirus
Q fever
Psittacosis
Drug fever
Leptospirosis
Toxoplasmosis
Brucellosis
Relapsing fever
Kikuchi's disease
Idiopathic granulomatosis
Alcoholic hepatitis

**Abnormal renal-function
tests**
Subacute bacterial
  endocarditis
Renal tuberculosis
Polyarteritis nodosa
Fabry's disease
Leptospirosis
Brucellosis
Lymphomas
Systemic lupus
  erythematosus
Hypernephroma
HIV
Malakoplakia

[1]*Source:* Cunha BA: Fever of unknown origin (FUO). In Gorbach SL, Bartlett JB, Blacklow NR: *Infectious Diseases,* 2nd ed. Philadelphia, WB Saunders, 1996.

as a cause of FUO, and appropriate biopsies and cultures are indicated. A screening chest x-ray should be obtained to rule out lung diseases.

In general, noninvasive testing should be performed first. If the cause of an FUO is not discovered by these tests, then invasive testing may be necessary to establish a diagnosis. Invasive testing may include computed tomography scans, bone marrow biopsies, liver biopsies, and, rarely, abdominal laporotomy. Advanced scanning technology has significantly diminished the role for abdominal laparotomy.

Differential Diagnosis

The differential diagnosis for FUO is broad. It is therefore best to categorize the potential causes into disease processes and then consider their likelihood within different subgroups of patients. The most

common causes of classic FUOs (in nonhospitalized, ambulatory patients who do not fit into other subgroups) include infections, neoplasms, hypersensitivity, and autoimmune diseases (Table 18–4). In HIV-positive patients, the major causes of fever of unknown origin are infections such as tuberculosis, atypical mycobacterium such as *Mycobacterium avium* complex, and fungal infections. In contrast, the major causes of FUOs in elderly patients are malignancy and collagen vascular disorders, followed by occult infections.

In children, FUOs are rare. It is important to remember that normal mean temperatures increase with age until the child is 18 months old, after which they decrease. Therefore a temperature of 38.3 °C is normal in an 18-month-old child. Infectious diseases account for 45% of all FUOs in children, and half of

Table 18–4. Diseases causing fever of unknown origin.[1]

	Common	Uncommon	Rare
Malignancy	Lymphoma Metastases to liver/CNS Hypernephromas	Hepatomas Pancreatic carcinoma Preleukemias	Atrial myxomas CNS tumors Myelodysplastic diseases
Infections	Extrapulmonary tuberculosis (Renal TB, TB meningitis, Miliary TB) Intraabdominal abscesses (subdiaphragmatic abscesses: Periappendiceal Pericolonic Hepatic) Pelvic abscesses Subacute bacterial endocarditis *Mycobacterium avium* complex (AIDS) Permanently placed central IV line	Colon carcinoma Cytomegalovirus Toxoplasmosis *Salmonella* enteric fevers Intra/perinephric abscesses Dental abscesses HIV Cryptococcosis	Small brain abcesses Chronic sinusitis Subacute vertebral osteomyelitis Chronic subacute vertebral osteomyelitis *Listeria* *Yersinia* Brucellosis Relapsing fever Rat-bite fever Chronic Q fever Cat-scratch fever Epstein-Barr virus (elderly) Malaria Leptospirosis Blastomycosis Histoplasmosis Coccidioidomycosis Infected aortic aneurysms Infected vascular graft Rocky Mountain spotted fever Lyme disease Leishmaniasis Trypanosomiasis Trichinosis Prosthetic device Relapsing mastoiditis Septic jugular phlebitis
Rheumatologic	Still's disease (adult juvenile rheumatoid arthritis) Temporal arteritis (elderly)	Periarteritis nodosa Rheumatoid arthritis (elderly) Systemic lupus erythematosus	Vasculitis (eg, Takayasu's arteritis, hypersensitive vasculitis) Felty's syndrome Pseudogout Acute rheumatic fever Sjögren's syndrome Behçet's disease Familial Mediterranean fever
Miscellaneous causes	Drug fever Cirrhosis Alcoholic hepatitis	Granulomatous hepatitis Pulmonary emboli (multiple, recurrent)	Regional enteritis Whipple's disease Fabry's disease Hyperthyroidism Hyperparathyroidism Pheochromocytomas Addison's disease Subacute thyroiditis Cyclic neutropenias Polymyositis Wegener's granulomatosis Occult hematomas Weber-Christian disease Sarcoidosis (eg, basilar meningitis, hepatic granulomas) Hypothalamic dysfunction Habitual hyperthermia Factitious fever Giant hepatic hemangiomas Mesenteric fibromatosis Pseudolymphomas Idiopathic granulomatosis Kikuchi's disease Malakoplakia Hyper IgD syndrome

[1]*Source:* Cunha BA: Fever of unknown origin (FUO). In Gorbach SL, Bartlett JB, Blacklow NR: *Infectious Diseases,* 2nd ed. Philadelphia, WB Saunders, 1996.

Table 18–5. Most common causes of fevers of unknown origin.[1]

Category	Classic	Neutropenic	Elderly	HIV	Nosocomial	Pediatric
Definition	Not in other categories— fever ≥ 3 weeks	ANC < 500	Classic only in patients	HIV-positive patients	Hospitalized and not infected on admission	Fevers ≥ 8 days in < 18-year-old patients
Duration of investigation	3 Days as inpatient or 3 outpatient visits	3 Days as inpatient	Same as classic FUO	3 Days as inpatient or 4 wks as outpatient	3 Days	Not defined
Most common causes	Infection Malignancy Collagen-vascular diseases Drugs	Fungal infection Perianal infection Bacterial infection Drugs Underlying disease	Malignancy Infection Collagen-vascular diseases Drugs	Infections (MAC, TB, & fungal) Lymphoma Drugs	Infections (bacterial or fungal) Drugs	Infection Collagen-vascular diseases Malignancy Drugs

Abbreviations: ANC, absolute neutrophil count; HIV, human immunodeficiency virus; FUO, fever of unknown origin; MAC, *Mycobacterium avium* complex; TB, tuberculosis.

[1]*Source:* Mandell GL (ed): *Mandell, Douglas, and Bennett's Principles and Practice of Infectious Disease,* Churchill Livingstone, 1995.

these are respiratory tract infections. Of FUOs in children, ~ 13% are caused by connective tissue diseases, and ~ 6% are caused by neoplasia.

By knowing the frequency of the different diagnoses in each subgroup of patients, the clinician can narrow the search for the cause of the fever (Table 18–5). If these investigations are done properly, in > 90% of patients the causes of an FUO will be diagnosed.

A. HIV-Positive Patients. In HIV-positive patients with an FUO, other specialized testing should be performed. The differential diagnosis for HIV-related FUOs consists of mainly infectious causes such as tuberculosis, *Mycobacterium avium* complex, and disseminated fungal infections. Neoplasms such as lymphomas also cause FUOs in AIDS patients. Tuberculosis is a common cause, especially if the CD4 count is high. If the CD4 count is significantly decreased (< 100), atypical mycobacteria, mainly *Mycobacterium avium,* are the most common *Mycobacterium* species causing fever. Therefore work-ups of FUOs in AIDS patients should focus on those diagnoses.

Blood cultures should be done for bacteria, fungi, and mycobacteria. A serum cryptococcal antigen should also be ordered, because cryptococcal disease is also common in AIDS patients. Stool cultures should be obtained only if the patient has diarrhea. A chest x-ray should be obtained. A routine screening chest computed tomography scan to look for adenopathy may be useful, since *M avium* complex can cause isolated hilar and mediastinal adenopathy not seen on chest x-rays. Bone marrow biopsy and liver biopsy should be considered early in the evaluation if the above tests are negative. Of HIV patients with FUOs, 86% will have a diagnosis established.

B. Elderly Patients. In elderly patients, the dif-

ferential diagnosis of FUOs varies slightly from the classical differential. Neoplasms such as lymphoma or malignancies metastatic to the liver are the most common causes. Collagen vascular diseases, especially temporal arteritis, are also more frequent in the elderly. The classic presentation of jaw claudication and vision loss for giant cell arteritis may be absent in the elderly. Occult infections, especially abdominal infections or prostatitis in elderly males, can cause FUOs because the classical physical findings may be absent and the leukocyte count normal. Tuberculosis is also a significant cause of FUOs in the elderly. Other diseases such as sarcoidosis, lupus, Still's disease, and factitious fevers are more common in younger patients.

Because of the increased incidence of temporal arteritis, a temporal artery biopsy should be considered as a diagnostic test along with the other routine studies. Because of the increased incidence of occult abdominal abscesses, a computed tomography scan of the abdomen should be part of the evaluation. If, after a thorough investigation, no explanation for the fever is found, the patient may be monitored closely, weekly to biweekly, as an outpatient.

Treatment

Empiric drug trials should be used with extreme caution and should not take the place of a thorough investigation for the cause of the FUO, especially if an infection is suspected. If malignancy is strongly suspected, a trial of naproxen can be tried. If investigations for an FUO in an HIV-positive patient are not successful in finding the cause, an empiric trial of antimycobacterial therapy may be useful. However, empiric treatment has not been evaluated scientifically. Neutropenic patients are the only group in which empiric broad-spectrum antibiotics should be started (see Chapter 26). Empiric therapy for neutropenic patients classically includes ceftazidime and an aminoglycoside; however, this may vary depending on gram-negative bacterial antibiotic susceptibilities in each hospital. Vancomycin can be added if a gram-positive infection is suspected or if the patient has persistent fevers. If fevers persist in this setting, antifungal agents should be added to the antibiotic regimen. Empiric antibiotic therapy should be started only after appropriate cultures have been done.

REFERENCES

Bissuel F et al: Fever of unknown origin in HIV-infected patients: a critical analysis of a retrospective series of 57 cases. J Intern Med 1994;236:529.

Cunha BA: Fever of unknown origin. Infect Dis Clin North Am 1996;10:111.

Cunha BA: Fever of unknown origin in the elderly. Geriatrics 1982;37:30.

Engels E et al: Usefulness of bone marrow examination in the evaluation of unexplained fevers in patients infected with human immunodeficiency virus. Clin Infect Dis 1995;21:427.

Gartnew JC: Fever of unknown origin. Adv Pediatr Infect Dis 1992;7:1.

Gleckman RA, Esposito AL: Fever of unknown origin in the elderly: diagnosis and treatment. Geriatrics 1986;41:45.

Konecny P, Davidson R: Pyrexia of unknown origin in the 1990s: time to redefine. Br J Hosp Med 1996;56:21.

Long SS (editor): *Principles and Practice of Pediatric Infectious Diseases,* Churchill Livingstone, 1997.

Mandell GL (editor): *Mandell, Douglas, and Bennett's Principles and Practice of Infectious Diseases,* 4th ed. Churchill Livingstone, 1995.

Petersdorf RG, Beeson PB: Fever of unexplained origin: report on 100 cases. Medicine 1961;40:1.

Fever & Rash

Peter K. Lindenauer, MD MSc, & Merle A. Sande, MD

Essentials of Diagnosis

- The combination of fever and rash is not a specific finding and can be seen in a variety of infectious and noninfectious disorders. Adverse reactions to drugs are the most common noninfectious cause of fever and rash.
- Because of the life-threatening nature of many of the illnesses causing fever and rash, a thorough, yet rapid, evaluation is required.
- Rule out treatable but immediately life-threatening causes of fever and rash early on.
- Diagnosis is best made by a thorough history and a proper classification of the rash. Laboratory testing is useful and specific for some diseases but of limited value for many others.
- An empiric approach to therapy is warranted when patients appear ill and a definitive diagnosis has not been made.
- Isolation is often warranted for patients with fever and rash when meningococcemia or varicella is being considered, as these illnesses can be transmitted by respiratory droplets.

General Considerations

The combination of fever and rash is a dramatic finding and can often reflect a life-threatening illness. Because of the variety of infectious and noninfectious disease processes that can present in this manner, an organized and thoughtful approach to patients with this syndrome is essential (Table 19–1).

More than for many other clinical problems, the history obtained from patients with fever and rash is critical in establishing an accurate diagnosis and embarking on effective treatment. Essential historical elements to review include the following: drug and dietary history, human and animal contacts (including a detailed sexual history), occupational exposures, travel, and immunizations. Reviewing the patient's prior medical history is vital as is a review of prior adverse drug reactions. Both the season and geographic location should be factored into the differential diagnosis. Special populations to consider include hospitalized patients as well as the immunosuppressed, especially those with HIV infection. Finally, a careful review of the time course and distribution of the rash can provide extremely valuable diagnostic clues.

PATIENT HISTORY

Drug Use

Patients should be asked about all drug use: both prescription and over the counter, traditional and alternative, licit and illicit in the preceding weeks. Prescription drugs are common causes of fever and rash, and almost any drug may lead to this syndrome (Figure 19–1). Mechanisms underlying the development of adverse drug reactions can be either immunologically or nonimmunologically mediated, but in many instances the pathogenesis is not understood. Hospitalized patients who often begin treatment with multiple medications over a short time period are an extremely susceptible group. Because of the variety of mechanisms underlying the development of such adverse reactions, the cutaneous manifestations range from simple maculopapular to petechial or desquamating.

Frequently implicated medications include penicillins, sulfonamides, phenytoin, allopurinol, barbiturates, and occasionally nonsteroidal anti-inflammatory agents. Serum sickness is a multisystem illness that presents with fever, rash, arthritis, and glomerulonephritis and results from the deposition of circulating immune complexes throughout the body. It can be caused by exposure to sera but more commonly is induced by medications such as the ones listed above. Vasculitis syndromes can be caused by medications as well as by infections and malignancies. Photosensitivity is a property of certain drugs including tetracyclines, thiazide diuretics, and selected NSAIDS; as such, sun exposure should be reviewed. Because the preceding comments are, for the most part, equally applicable to over-the-counter as well as alternative medicines, use of both is important to document.

Illicit drug use, and injection drug use in particular, exposes the user to a range of bacterial and viral pathogens. Fever and rash in an injection drug user should raise the immediate possibility of infective endocarditis or acute hepatitis B infection. Moreover, because skin and soft tissue infections are common in this patient population, they are at higher risk of developing toxic shock and toxic streptococcal syndromes.

Diet

Diet is occasionally found to be the cause of fever

Table 19–1. Diagnostic approach to fever and rash.

- Obtain a thorough history, reviewing all drugs and medications used in the preceding weeks, travel, contacts with sick children and adults, exposure to pets, wild animals or insects, sexual history, prior immunizations, past medical history paying particular attention to rheumatic diseases, valvular heart disease or immunosuppression, and onset and distribution of the rash and associated symptoms.
- On physical examination, note the overall severity of the patient's illness, the form and distribution of the rash, and the presence of any associated physical findings.
- Rashes should be grouped as (*a*) macular and maculopapular, (*b*) vesicular and vesiculobullous, or (*c*) petechial, purpuric, and pustular. Each of these categroies has a fairly unique differential diagnosis.
- Petechial, purpuric, and pustular lesions **that** can be aspirated should be gram stained and sent for culture. Vesicular and vesiculobullous lesions should be unroofed, scraped, and examined for the presence of multinucleated giant cells or inclusion bodies. Punch biopsy is a useful method for diagnosing both infectious and noninfectious disorders and should be considered whenever Rocky Mountain Spotted Fever is suspected or whenever a diagnosis is in doubt. Aerobic and anaerobic blood cultures **should be obtained for all patients.**
- **In the acute setting,** serologic studies are of limited usefulness for most of the disorders **that** cause fever and rash.
- Polymerase chain reaction-based assays are rapidly emerging as the diagnostic tests of choice for a number of infections **that** cause fever and rash, but their use is limited by availability.

and rash. Food allergies to such substances as eggs, nuts, chocolate, and shellfish can cause both immediate, immunoglobulin E-mediated reactions and delayed hypersensitivity. The ingestion of undercooked pork or beef can result in trichinosis that may present with rash. Raw seafood and shellfish have been associated with vibrio vulnificus infections in patients with underlying liver disease. Typhoid fever is commonly associated with rash and is frequently seen in patients returning from the developing world where it is transmitted by the fecal oral route.

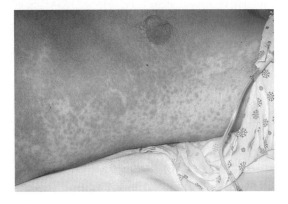

Figure 19–1. Drug-induced rash.

Contacts

Contacts with sick individuals or with animals are important modes of transmission for many of the diseases that can cause fever and rash (Box 19–1). Viral illnesses are commonly transmitted this way, especially the classic childhood exanthems varicella zoster, rubella, measles, "fifth disease" (erythema infections resulting from parvovirus B-19), along with mononucleosis and cytomegalovirus. Bacterial infections, notably streptococcal and meningococcal, are usually associated with contact with an afflicted individual. Sexual contact is a mode of transmission of hepatitis B and is the source of gonococcal, chlamydial, and syphilis infection. Acute HIV infection obtained sexually or through injection drug use often presents with fever, pharyngitis, and generalized rash.

Insect and Animal Exposure

Insect and animal contacts are another important source of exposure to microbial pathogens that cause fever and rash in the setting of severe illness. Ticks are the vectors for Rocky Mountain Spotted Fever and Lyme disease; however, in only one-half of patients with Rocky Mountain Spotted Fever and one-third of patients with Lyme disease is a history of tick exposure obtainable. Capnocytophagia is an infection strongly associated with dog and cat bites in patients who are immunosuppressed, usually in the setting of splenectomy. Contact with livestock or contaminated water should raise the possibility of leptospirosis, whereas tularemia is seen in patients exposed to infected wild rabbits.

Travel

Travel to endemic regions is usually described in cases of coccidioidomycosis and in viral hemorrhagic fever and scrub typhus. Malaria may present in travelers returning from an endemic area, and severe *Plasmodium falciparum* infections should be considered for those with petechial rashes accompanied by hemolysis, thrombocytopenia, and acute renal failure.

Occupational Exposure

Occupational exposures should not be overlooked. Florists and gardeners are prone to sporotrichosis as a result of their extensive contact with soil and vegetation. Erysipelothrix, or fishmonger's cellulitis, is an unusual cause of fever and rash seen in patients with occupational or recreational fish contact.

Prior Medical History

The prior medical history is the source of much valuable information when the clinician is confronted with a patient with fever and rash. Those with a history of valvular heart disease are at high risk for infective endocarditis. Immunosuppression from steroids, chemotherapy, or HIV is an important risk fac-

BOX 19–1

Microbiology of Fever and Rash[1]

	Children	Adults
More Frequent	• Varicella • Enteroviruses • Epstein-Barr virus • Parvovirus B-19 • Group A sterptococci[4] • Sepsis • Other viruses	• Sepsis[2] • Infective endocarditis[3] • Varicella zoster • *Neisseria meningitidis*
Less Frequent	• *Neisseria meningitidis* • *Borellia burgdorferi* • Measles • *Rickettsia rickettsii*	• *Rickettsia rickettsii* • *Borellia burgdorferi* • *T pallidum* • *Plasmodium falciparum* • Disseminated fungal disease • *Salmonella typhi* • Dengue

[1]Many of the causes of fever and rash discussed in this chapter are not infectious in origin.
[2]Bacterial sepsis from *S pneumonia,* enteric gram negatives, and *Pseudomonas aeruginosa.*
[3]Infective endocarditis most commonly caused by viridans streptococci. Parenteral drug users and hospitalized patients with vascular catheters are at high risk of *Staphylococcus aureus* endocarditis.
[4]Scarlet fever in association with group A streptococcal pharyngitis.

tor for the development of many of the infections previously discussed. Patients with a prior history of rheumatologic diseases or inflammatory bowel disease are often subject to flares that can include fever and rash as part of the presentation.

SEASON & GEOGRAPHIC SETTING

Season and geographic setting are important factors influencing the diagnosis in patients with fever and rash. Rocky Mountain spotted fever is a disease of late spring to early fall, coinciding with increased exposure to the tick vectors *Dermacentor variabilis* or *Dermacentor andersoni.* Like Rocky Mountain spotted fever, Lyme disease occurs most commonly in the spring and summer months following contact with the infected tick nymph *Ixodes dammini* or *Ixodes pacificus.* Outbreaks of the exanthems caused by enteroviruses occur in warmer months, whereas streptococcal and meningococcal disease occurs in late winter and early spring. Lyme disease cases cluster into three distinct geographic regions: the Northeast, the Upper Midwest, and the Far West. However, Rocky Mountain spotted fever has been reported in all states with the exception of Hawaii and Vermont, although its highest prevalence centers in the eastern and southern plains regions.

SPECIAL POPULATIONS

HOSPITALIZED & IMMUNOSUPPRESSED PATIENTS

Hospitalized patients are a special population and should be separately considered. As previously discussed, their high exposure to antibiotics and other new medications makes drug reaction a common cause of fever and rash. Neutropenic and immunosuppressed patients are at high risk of bacterial infection with *Pseudomonas aeruginosa, Clostridium* spp., and alpha hemolytic streptococci. Disseminated candidiasis, *Aspergillus,* and herpesvirus infections are common complications of neutropenia. Patients receiving broad-spectrum antibiotics or parenteral nutrition are at heightened risk of developing systemic candidiasis. Finally, indwelling catheters, shunts, prosthetic valves, and pacemakers place patients at risk of endovascular infections from recurrent transient bacteremic episodes.

HIV-INFECTED PATIENTS

Acute HIV infection may present with fever, rash, headache, pharyngitis, and aseptic meningitis. Dermatologic problems are common in this population and include eosinophilic folliculitis, papular dermatitis, and psoriasis. Pyoderma furunculosis and folliculitis can complicate HIV disease. Cutaneous manifestations of systemic infections may occur, and cutaneous infections may occur in severe forms. Varicella zoster and herpes simplex lesions are common and sometimes severe in HIV-infected patients. All disseminated fungal infections may involve the skin, and mycobacterial infection can present this way as well. Bacillary angiomatosis caused by *Bartonella* species is increasingly recognized as an important source of systemic illness (fever, hepatosplenomegaly, lymphadenopathy) accompanied by friable papules or nodules.

Clinical Findings

A. Signs and Symptoms.

Appearance. The appearance and distribution of the rash often provides valuable clues toward a diagnosis, and associated physical findings are characteristic of many of the entities described here.

The skin has a limited repertoire of responses to infections and immunologic challenges. Rashes can generally be divided into the following groups: (1) macular and maculopapular; (2) vesicular or bullous; and (3) pustular, petechial, or purpuric. Although this classification scheme can help limit the differential diagnosis, it must be understood that these distinctions are not absolute. Not only do many processes present with a similar rash, but each disease or process can produce more than one type of rash (Table 19–2). Moreover, exanthems may change over the course of several hours or several days. Rocky Mountain spotted fever, which initially appears as an erythematous maculopapular eruption, often evolves into a petechial rash.

1. Macular rashes. A macular or maculopapular rash is the most common exanthem caused by the nonherpetic viruses such as enteroviruses (Figure 19–2), rubella, rubeola, and parvovirus B-19. Nevertheless, many serious infections can present this way including Rocky Mountain spotted fever, meningococcemia, disseminated gonococcal infection, typhoid fever, and *Pseudomonas* sepsis. Lyme disease is associated with a characteristic rash termed erythema migrans, which is observed in > 60% of patients. Erythema migrans typically begins as a small red papule arising anywhere between 1 and 30 days after tick exposure and gradually expands to a ring of erythema with central clearing. Any site may be affected, but the axilla, groin, and thigh are most common. Some patients develop similar appearing secondary lesions at distant sites.

2. Toxic shock syndrome is characterized by a diffuse erythroderma (large macules) likened to a severe sunburn. The dermatologic findings are typically accompanied by fever, hypotension, and diffuse arthralgias and myalgias. Group A streptococci,

Table 19–2. Diagnosis of fever and rash based on rash appearance

Rash Category	Type	Cause
Macular/ Maculopapular	Bacterial	Scarlet fever, *Pseudomonas* sepsis, secondary syphilis, toxic shock syndrome, Lyme disease, *Chlamydia*, leptospirosis
	Viral	Measles, rubella, enteroviruses, parvovirus B-19, mononucleosis, cytomegalovirus, hepatitis B, roseola, human immunodeficiency virus
	Rickettsial	Rocky Mountain spotted fever (early), murine and scrub typhus
	Fungal	Disseminated candidiasis, coccidioidomycosis, histoplasmosis, blastomycosis, sporotrichosis
	Other	Drug reactions, serum sickness, erythema multiforme, systemic lupus erythematosus, dermatomyositis, Behçet's disease, Reiter's syndrome, inflammatory bowel disease
Vesicles	Bacterial	Staphylococcal scalded skin syndrome, *Pseudomonas* sepsis, bullous impetigo
	Viral	Herpes simplex, Varicella-zoster, eczema herpeticum, hand-foot and mouth disease
	Rickettsial	Ricketsial pox
	Other	Drug reactions, *Mycoplasma pneumonia*, Stevens-Johnson syndrome, inflammatory bowel disease, pemphigus, pemphigoid
Petechiae, Purpura, or Pustules	Bacterial	Meningococcemia, sepsis with disseminated intravascular coagulation, gonococcemia, *Pseudomonas sepsis*, staphylococcal sepsis, infective endocarditis, listeriosis
	Viral	Viral hemorrhagic fevers, enteroviruses
	Rickettsial	Rocky Mountain spotted fever, epidemic typhus
	Other	Drug reactions, Henoch-Schönlein purpura, thrombotic thrombocytopenic purpura

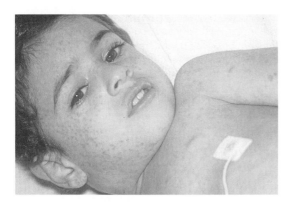

Figure 19–2. Enterovirus.

which elaborate exotoxin, are capable of causing a similar syndrome, sometimes referred to as "toxic strep syndrome." While the skin is the portal of entry of most cases of toxic shock, in only a minority of cases can the actual source be identified. Although tampon use during menses was initially described in the majority of patients, this now accounts for less than half of the 300 or so annual reported cases. Whereas the skin infections resulting in toxic shock syndrome are often minor, those associated with toxic streptococcal infections are often severe. Myositis and necrotizing fasciitis are common sequelae of these infections, and this virulence is reflected in a case fatality rate for toxic streptococcal infections that is some fivefold higher than that seen in toxic shock. Secondary syphilis occurs some 6–8 weeks after healing of the chancre seen in primary syphilis, although some patients may progress to secondary syphilis while a chancre remains present. The lesions are erythematous and macular or maculopapular, are symmetrically distributed, and often involve the palms and soles (Figure 19–3). The rash is frequently accompanied by constitutional symptoms and lymphadenopathy. Drugs often produce maculopapular exanthems that are "cherry-red" in appearance. The "target lesions" of erythema multiforme and the "slapped cheeks" of parvovirus B-19 are both examples of maculopapular lesions distinctive enough to be almost pathognomonic.

3. Vesicular rashes. Vesicular lesions are caused by a number of viruses including varicella-zoster, herpes simplex, vaccinia, and the enteroviruses. The staphylococcal scalded skin syndrome is characterized by large bullae that rupture, leaving behind beefy red areas of denuded skin. *Pseudomonas* septicemia can be associated with vesicles that rapidly become hemorrhagic or with the centrally necrotic lesions of ecthyma gangrenosum. Stevens-Johnson syndrome causes vesicular lesions of both the skin and mucosa. Ulcerative colitis and Crohn's disease can cause vesicular lesions that progress to chronic ulceration and may have prominent mucosal involvement.

4. Petechial, purpuric, or pustular rashes. Petechial, purpuric, or pustular skin lesions often indicate life threatening illness. The identification of such a rash should call immediate attention to the treatable bacterial or rickettsial infections that may be responsible for its appearance. Most prominent among these illnesses are meningococcemia, Rocky Mountain spotted fever (Figure 19–4), infective endocarditis, or sepsis with associated disseminated intravascular coagulation. Disseminated gonococcal infection produces a less severe illness often associated with migratory polyarthritis and tenosynovitis (Figure 19–5). Atypical measles can produce a petechial rash that may mimic that seen in Rocky Mountain spotted fever and is seen in that cohort of patients previously vaccinated with a killed measles vaccine. Occasionally, enteroviral infections can produce petechial lesions, and other viruses including dengue and Epstein-Barr virus may do so as well. Many noninfectious causes of fever and rash present with petechial lesions, the most important of which are systemic lupus erythematosus, Henoch-Schönlein purpura, thrombotic thrombocytopenic purpura, and many of the vasculitides.

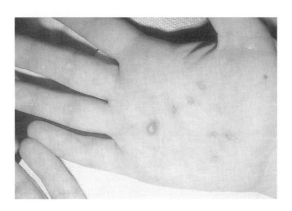

Figure 19–3. Palmar lesions of secondary syphilis.

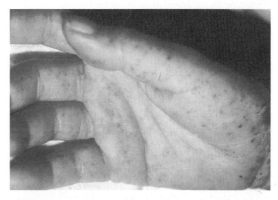

Figure 19–4. Rocky Mountain spotted fever.

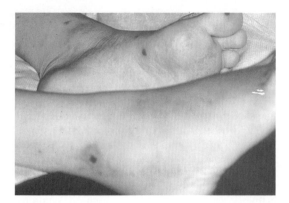

Figure 19–5. Pustular lesion of disseminated gonococcal infection.

Distribution. The distribution of the rash may also aid in diagnosis. A macular or petechial rash involving the palms or soles should suggest Rocky Mountain spotted fever, meningococcemia, infective endocarditis, *Mycoplasma* infection, scarlet fever, or bacteremia. The lesions of secondary syphilis, atypical measles, Kawasaki's disease, and many drug exanthems may present similarly. Maculopapular rashes caused by viruses usually spare the palms and soles, whereas these sites may be involved in vesicular exanthems caused by herpesvirus and certain coxsackie virus strains. Exanthems with a tendency to involve the extremities preferentially include gonococcemia, Henoch-Schönlein purpura, dermatomyositis, and sporotrichosis. The "rose spots" of typhoid fever and the maculopapular lesions of *Pseudomonas* sepsis are usually confined to the trunk. Scarlet fever begins on the face and neck and spreads to the trunk and extremities within 36 hours. Rubeola usually begins behind the ears and spreads throughout the body within the first day.

B. Laboratory Findings. As a general rule, diagnostic procedures that are likely to yield immediate results should be carried out on any lesion. Pustular, purpuric, or petechial lesions should be aspirated or scraped and the fluid obtained examined microscopically and cultured. Many patients with meningococcemia can be diagnosed by this simple procedure, which will demonstrate gram-negative biscuit-shaped cocci. Vesicular lesions should be unroofed, and the contents should be examined microscopically using a Wright or Giemsa stain to look for multinucleated giant cells or inclusion bodies characteristic of herpes virus infection (Tzanck test).

Needle aspiration can be used to diagnose group A streptococcal infections in patients with necrotizing fasciitis and should be considered as a means of diagnosing pseudomonal sepsis in immunosuppressed patients with maculopapular rashes. These techniques can provide immediate diagnosis long before a blood culture has had sufficient time to yield an organism. Punch biopsy can be used to identify fungal and mycobacterial disease involving the skin and is diagnostic of vasculitis and erythema multiforme. Immunofluorescent antibody staining is useful in skin biopsy specimens of patients with suspected Rocky Mountain spotted fever and is also used to diagnose systemic lupus erythematosus and pemphigus vulgaris.

In cases where genitourinary, articular, or neurologic symptoms coexist with rash, urethral and cervical swabbing and culturing is mandatory as is arthrocentesis and examination of the cerebrospinal fluid. Blood cultures should be routinely performed in all patients since bacteremia is an especially common cause of fever and rash.

Serologic testing is limited in its usefulness in the acute setting but can be important for confirming a diagnosis and for disease reporting purposes. For example, serologic tests for Lyme disease, especially early in the course of disease, are hampered by an unacceptably high false negative rate and the diagnosis of Lyme disease is largely a clinical one. Polymerase chain reaction–based assays are emerging as an accurate method for diagnosing many of the diseases discussed in this chapter, but today, their limited availability and relatively high cost makes them a poor choice for the typical patient with fever and rash.

C. Imaging. A chest radiograph is a useful adjunct in the evaluation of patients with fever and rash since it can be used to detect pulmonary infiltrates or hilar adenopathy. Other imaging tests cannot be recommended on a routine basis.

Differential Diagnosis

Because the differential diagnosis of fever and rash is so broad and because of the urgency involved in a small number of cases, it is useful to divide the disorders into the following categories: immediately life-threatening, treatable infectious, nontreatable infectious, and noninfectious causes (Table 19–3).

Associated physical findings are seen in many of the disorders that cause fever and rash, and their recognition is helpful in limiting one's differential diagnosis. Enathems are mucous membrane eruptions, and many of the processes that involve the skin can involve the mucous membrane as well. Koplik's spots are diagnostic of rubeola and are found on the buccal mucosa opposite the second molar (Figure 19–6). They are blue-gray specks on a red base resembling a grain of sand. "Strawberry tongue" is characteristic of Kawasaki's disease, toxic shock syndrome, or scarlet fever. Palatal petechia is observed in 50% of patients with infectious mononucleosis and is also seen in infective endocarditis. Ulcerative mucosal lesions are observed in hand-foot and mouth disease, Behçet's syndrome, Reiter's syndrome, inflammatory bowel disease, and the Stevens-Johnson syndrome.

Table 19–3. Differential diagnosis of fever and rash.

Category	Possible Causes
Immediately Life-threatening	• Meningococcemia • Rocky Mountain spotted fever • Bacterial or candidal sepsis syndromes • Infective endocarditis • Toxic shock syndrome • Toxic streptococcal syndromes • Staphylococcal scalded skin syndrome • Stevens-Johnson syndrome
Treatable Infectious	• Disseminated gonococcal infection • Syphilis • Lyme disease • Epidemic typhus • Rat-bite fever • *Mycoplasma* • Human ehrlichioses • Trichinosis • *Vibrio vulnificus* • Toxoplasmosis • *Varicella zoster* • Herpes simplex • Acute HIV • Disseminated fungal infections
Nontreatable Infectious	• Enteroviral infections • Classic childhood exanthems • Hepatitis B • Epstein-Barr virus • Cytomegalovirus • Dengue • Viral hemorrhagic fevers
Noninfectious	• Adverse drug reactions • Rheumatologic disorders [systemic lupus erythematosus, dermatomyositis, Behçet's disease, Reiter's syndrome, Still's disease, vasculitis (various forms)] • Serum sickness • Thrombotic thrombocytopenic purpura • Henoch-Schönlein purpura • Inflammatory bowel disease • Pemphigus, pemphigoid

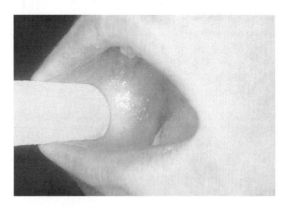

Figure 19–6. Koplik's spots of measles.

Complications

Complications relate to the specific pathogen responsible for the syndrome of fever and rash, and no complications are common to the group. Patients with meningococcemia are at risk for the development of the sepsis syndrome, disseminated intravascular coagulation, or death unless appropriate antibiotics are promptly begun. Rocky Mountain spotted fever is a multisystem disease that can cause encephalitis in approximately one quarter of cases. Infective endocarditis, if left untreated, rapidly progresses and is associated with valve destruction and incompetence as well as complications from septic emboli, such as stroke. Toxic shock syndrome is associated with profound hypotension, and it is this aspect of the illness that results in the vast majority of its complications. The complications from toxic epidermal necrolysis and staphylococcal scalded skin syndrome relate primarily to the degree of epidermal necrosis and include metabolic derangement and severe immunosuppression.

Treatment

Treatment of fever and rash may be specific (as in the case of a recognized bacterial infection presenting in a classic fashion), empiric (as for the toxic appearing patient with petechial skin lesions), or supportive (as in most viral infections). A general approach to patients with fever and rash depending on whether the illness was nosocomially acquired or in a community is found in Box 19–2. While this can provide a useful starting place, the clinician is strongly encouraged to tailor decisions regarding the need for, and type of, antibiotic therapy only after a careful review of the factors discussed earlier in this chapter.

Prognosis

Mortality in patients with fever and rash is closely tied to the organism or process responsible for the syndrome and to the timeliness of recognizing and instituting appropriate therapy.

Meningitis and other neurologic changes may be observed in meningococcemia, Rocky Mountain spotted fever, staphylococcal bacteremia leptospirosis, Kawasaki's disease, toxic shock syndrome, Lyme disease, and as part of the aseptic meningitis seen in acute HIV and enteroviral infections. Lymphadenopathy is prominent in mononucleosis, syphilis, sarcoidosis, and drug hypersensitivity. Cervical adenopathy is seen in streptococcal pharyngitis in the setting of scarlet fever and with rubella. The finding of a heart murmur should raise the possibility of infective endocarditis even if findings such as Osler nodes, Janeway lesions, or splinter hemorrhages are absent. Fever and rash associated with pneumonia is seen in *Mycoplasma* infection, atypical measles, Rocky Mountain spotted fever, coccidioidomycosis, or sepsis associated with staphylococcal or pseudomonal pneumonia.

BOX 19–2

Empiric Therapy of Fever and Rash[1,2]

	Community Acquired	Hospital Acquired[3]
First Choice	Ceftriaxone 2 g IV every 24 h **PLUS** doxycycline[4] 100 mg IV every 12 h	Ceftazidime 2 g IV every 8 h **PLUS** APAG **PLUS** vancomycin 1 g IV every 12 h
Second Choice	Chloramphenicol 100 mg/kg/d IV divided every 6 h	Piperacillin **PLUS** APAG **PLUS** vancomycin 1 g IV every 12 h
Penicillin Allergic	Ciprofloxacin[5] 500 mg IV every 12 h **PLUS** doxycycline 100 mg IV every 12 h	Ciprofloxacin 500 mg IV every 12 h **PLUS** APAG **PLUS** vancomycin 1 g IV every 12 h

[1]Because of the diverse causes of fever and rash, it is of limited value to suggest empiric antibiotic therapy in a blanket way.
[2]In immunocompromised patients, *Varicella zoster* infections should be treated aggressively with intravenous acyclovir.
[3]Hospitalized patients and those with immunosuppression are at higher risk of developing pseudomonal sepsis syndromes and disseminated staphyloccal infections and should have antibiotic coverage extended with a third-generation cephalosporin with activity against *Pseudomonas* spp., or an extended spectrum penicillin (piperacillin, ticarcillin) and an aminoglycoside, as well as vancomycin. However, antibiotics themselves may cause fever and rash, and discontinuation of drugs may be the treatment of choice. APAG, Antipseudomonal aminoglycoside. Dosing of gentamicin and tobramycin is 5 mg/kg every 24 h or 1.5 mg/kg every 12 h.
[4]Patients with a history compatible with Rocky Mountain spotted fever should be treated empirically with doxycycline because the laboratory diagnosis of this infection cannot be relied on.
[5]Ciprofloxacin should not be used in children.

Prevention and Control

Isolation is useful to reduce the risk of spread of meningococcemia and varicella zoster. Care in the avoidance of tick exposure is the only method of preventing Rocky Mountain spotted fever and Lyme disease. The practice of safe sex can eliminate the possibility of obtaining syphilis or gonococcal infections.

REFERENCES

Lindenauer PK, Sande MA: Fever and rash. In Stein JH: *Internal Medicine,* Mosby, 1998.

Meyers SA, Sexton DJ: Dermatologic manifestations of arthropod-borne diseases. Infect Dis Clin North Am 1994;8(3):689.

McCauliffe DP, Sontheimer RD: Dermatologic manifestations of rheumatic disorders. Primary Care 1993;20(4):925.

Walker DH: Rocky mountain spotted fever: a seasonal alert, Clin Infect Dis 1995;20:1111.

Weber DJ, Cohen MS: The acutely ill patient with fever and rash. In Mandell GL, Douglas RG, Bennett JE: *Principles and Practice of Infectious Disease,* 4th ed. Churchill Livingstone, 1995.

Infectious Diarrhea

20

William P. Ciesla, Jr., MD, & Richard L. Guerrant, MD

Essentials of Diagnosis

- Key signs and symptoms include increased frequency of stools and/or the presence of unformed or watery stools, grossly bloody stool, tenesmus, abdominal cramping or pain, fever, nausea and vomiting, and volume depletion.
- Most enteric pathogens are acquired by the fecal-oral route with food or water. Other risk factors include antibiotic use, travel to the developing world, AIDS, and institutional care.
- Infectious diarrhea is classified as inflammatory or noninflammatory based on the underlying pathophysiology; cases are distinguished clinically by the history and the presence or absence of fecal leukocytes or lactoferrin.
- Once the stool has been examined for fecal leukocytes or lactoferrin, additional laboratory workup should be individualized for each patient based on the available data.
- In the United States, inflammatory infectious diarrhea is caused chiefly by *Shigella, Salmonella,* and *Campylobacter* spp.; noninflammatory diarrhea has numerous viral, bacterial, and protozoal causes.
- Grossly bloody diarrhea is often secondary to enterohemorrhagic *Escherichia coli* (EHEC).
- Antibiotic-associated diarrhea and colitis are often caused by *Clostridium difficile.*

General Considerations

Diarrheal illnesses caused by bacterial, protozoal, or viral pathogens remain a major cause of morbidity and mortality throughout the world. In developing countries, poor sanitation and substandard living conditions create an environment in which diarrheal pathogens exact a terrible toll, especially among children. In the industrialized world, infectious diarrhea remains a common problem among all age groups. Moreover, epidemiologic events such as the AIDS epidemic, the globalization of the food supply, and emergence of new pathogens are increasingly factors in diarrheal illnesses. Chlorine-resistant *Cryptosporidium parvum* now threatens our drinking water, *Cyclospora cayetanensis* and EHEC menace our food supply, and toxigenic *C difficile* increasingly is a problem in hospitalized and institutionalized patients. Given the ubiquitous nature of infectious diarrhea, it is imperative that primary care physicians and infectious disease specialists have a firm understanding of the diagnosis and treatment of these diverse and potentially devastating illnesses.

A. Epidemiology. The magnitude of the morbidity and mortality related to infectious diarrhea is staggering. Overall, diarrheal illnesses are the second leading cause of death after cardiovascular diseases and the leading cause of death among children. In the developing world, the diarrheal attack rate can be as high as 6–12 episodes per child per year and an estimated 3–4 million children below the age of 5 years will die each year as a result of complications related to diarrhea (> 9,000 deaths per day). These regions continue to experience pandemics secondary to diarrheal pathogens, as witnessed for example, by the extension of the seventh cholera pandemic to South America in the early 1990s. The impact of infectious diarrhea on health of those infected reaches far beyond the acute symptoms. Repeated or chronic diarrheal illnesses are increasingly recognized as major contributors to malnutrition worldwide, potentially leading to impaired intellectual development, growth retardation, and increased susceptibility to other infectious pathogens.

In industrialized countries, a century of achievements in public health and sanitation have markedly diminished the widespread carnage of diarrheal pathogens common in the developing world. Nevertheless, infectious diarrhea remains a significant problem, one that appears to be increasing with the emergence of new epidemiologic factors and pathogens. Every year in the United States, there are an estimated 25 million cases and 5,000–10,000 deaths caused by infectious diarrhea. As elsewhere in the world, children experience the highest incidence of diarrhea; between 2.0 and 3.2 illnesses per child per year (up to 5.0 illnesses per child per year for children in day care). However, adults and especially the elderly are not spared. The elderly population especially is at risk for the more serious sequelae of infectious diarrhea, and most of the mortality related to gastroenteritis in adults occurs in this group.

A number of different epidemiologic factors are important to consider when approaching a patient who may have diarrhea caused by an infectious agent. Contaminated food or water ingestion, recent travel, antibiotic use, HIV positivity or AIDS, and institutional or day care all are important clues to identify the patient who may be at increased risk for developing infectious diarrhea.

Contaminated Food. The acquisition of diarrheal pathogens through the food supply is a major problem both in the developing world and in the United States, where 400–600 documented food-borne outbreaks and millions of cases are estimated to occur each year. A number of foods and pathogens have been associated with food-borne diarrheal illnesses: raw or poorly cooked shellfish (*Vibrio parahemolyticus,* Norwalk virus), chicken (*Campylobacter jejuni;* see Chapter 57), eggs (*Salmonella enteriditis;* see Chapter 53), chocolate milk (*Listeria monocytogenes;* see Chapter 51), reheated fried rice (*Bacillus cereus;* see Chapter 51), and undercooked beef, unpasteurized apple cider, lettuce, and alfalfa sprouts (EHEC; see Chapter 53). The mode of food contamination is varied; an infected food handler with poor hygiene, untreated human or animal waste used as fertilizer, unclean water used to wash or prepare food, and animal feces mixing with meat products during or after slaughter all have been implicated. In addition, evolving social and economic factors are emerging to further facilitate the spread of food-borne pathogens in the United States. First, over one-third of the produce now consumed in the United States is imported, often from developing regions with varied agricultural practices and abundant exotic pathogens. This threat manifested itself recently in several outbreaks associated with imported Guatemalan raspberries contaminated with the parasite *Cyclospora* sp. Second, an increasing proportion of meals are now prepared outside the home (eg, in restaurants), exposing large numbers of people to common source outbreaks related to, for example, an infected food handler or contaminated foodstuffs. Finally, the intentional contamination of the food supply by diarrheal pathogens has emerged as a form of biological terrorism. One incident in the United States involved > 700 cases of *Salmonella* gastroenteritis related to the intentional contamination of restaurant salad bars with *Salmonella typhimurium.* This criminal act was committed by a religious commune in an apparent attempt to influence voter turnout for a local election.

Contaminated Water. Drinking water, often contaminated by human or animal fecal waste, is a common mode of acquisition of diarrheal pathogens in the developing world and when natural disasters disrupt the normal sanitation infrastructure in industrialized countries. In addition, many lakes, rivers, and streams contain myriad organisms such as *Giardia lamblia* and EHEC. Hikers and swimmers are at risk when they drink unfiltered water from these sources. In the past, municipal water supplies in the United States were generally considered free from diarrheal

pathogens because of modern chlorination and filtering procedures. This notion was challenged in 1993 when a large water-borne outbreak of infectious diarrhea in Milwaukee was caused by the parasite *Cryptosporidium parvum.* This outbreak affected > 400,000 people despite the use of standard purification procedures; further outbreaks have occurred despite even more stringent filtration standards.

HIV and AIDS. HIV-positive and AIDS patients are at significant risk for diarrheal illnesses. More than 30 million patients are believed to be infected with HIV worldwide, and it has been estimated that 50–90% of these patients will develop a significant diarrheal illness at some point, especially as the CD4 count drops below 200. Depending on the pathogen involved, these patients can develop debilitating chronic diarrhea with few therapeutic options. Infectious agents and drug side effects are the two major causes of diarrhea in this population.

Hospitalization or Institutional Care. Hospitalization or institutional care is another important and often overlooked risk factor. In the United States, 1–2% of all hospitalized patients will develop an episode of nosocomial diarrhea, leading to volume and electrolyte losses as well as predisposing the patient to other nosocomial infections. Large populations of compromised patients, frequent antibiotic use, and *C difficile* spores in the hospital environment all contribute to the risk in this population. Children in day care are also at increased risk, given the poor personal hygiene and clustering of large numbers of children together in this setting. Outbreaks are often caused by organisms such as *Shigella* or *Giardia* spp. that require a small infectious dose and are readily spread from child to child by direct contact.

Antibiotic use places patients at risk for the development of antibiotic-associated diarrhea, especially in the hospital setting. The onset of diarrhea usually occurs while the antibiotic is being administered, but onset can be delayed for several weeks after the antibiotic has been stopped. Virtually all antibiotics have been implicated as a cause; clindamycin has the highest risk with 10–20% of patients who receive antibiotics developing antibiotic-associated diarrhea, but penicillins and cephalosporins are the most important culprits given their widespread use. *C difficile* infection accounts for ~20% of all antibiotic-associated diarrhea and virtually all cases of pseudomembranous colitis secondary to antibiotic use. The etiology of the remaining cases of antibiotic-associated diarrhea remains unknown.

Travel to Developing Countries. Travel from an industrialized country to the developing world places large numbers of people at risk for the acquisition of infectious diarrhea. An estimated 8 million Americans travel to developing regions each year, and up to 50% will develop diarrhea during their stay. Although these illnesses are rarely life-threatening, they have a significant impact on the tourist industry and on business travelers. Traveler's diarrhea has also been a major problem in military deployments, leading to the incapacitation of large numbers of soldiers. Early in operation Desert Storm during the Gulf War in 1990, for example, the attack rate for infectious diarrhea among American soldiers in Saudi Arabia was as high as 10%/week.

Clinical Findings

Documenting a careful and directed history is absolutely critical when approaching the patient who may have infectious diarrhea. Clues in the history are very helpful in assessing the severity of the patient's illness, narrowing the differential diagnosis of potential pathogens, and choosing an appropriate therapeutic course.

A. Signs and Symptoms. Diarrhea is defined as > 250 g of stool per 24 h, but such a measurement is rarely made clinically. A more practical definition is an increase in stools to ≥ 2–3 liquid stools per day, an increased frequency of stools compared with the patient's normal pattern or the presence of liquid stools. In infants, the number of diaper changes may help discern if a diarrheal illness is present.

In general, two different clinical syndromes are described in patients with infectious diarrhea, each with its own set of causative organisms. Noninflammatory diarrhea occurs with pathogens that act primarily in the small intestine to induce fluid secretion by various mechanisms and produce minimal, if any, intestinal inflammation. These patients usually present with voluminous watery diarrhea, nausea and vomiting, abdominal cramps, and minimal or low-grade fevers. The second syndrome, inflammatory diarrhea, is typically seen with pathogens that induce inflammation in the colon via invasion or cytotoxins. These patients present with fever, diarrhea with smaller volumes of stool (often < 1 L), blood or mucus in the stool (dysentery), tenesmus, and lower quadrant cramping. A history of grossly bloody stools should suggest EHEC infection, now the major infectious cause of bloody diarrhea in the United States. The duration of the diarrhea should be determined, because this information is also helpful in narrowing the differential.

Whether inflammatory or noninflammatory, diarrhea may be acute (lasting < 2 weeks) or persistent (lasting > 2 weeks); some refer to diarrhea lasting > 1 month as "chronic." Acute diarrhea is usually caused by infectious agents (viruses and bacteria), the ingestion of preformed bacterial toxins, or drugs. Persistent diarrhea is more often caused by parasitic pathogens or noninfectious causes.

The hydration status of the patient should be assessed by asking about orthostatic symptoms (dizziness or lightheadedness upon standing), decreased urine output, increased thirst, and the ability of the patient to take oral fluids. For viral infections and certain types of bacterial food poisoning, prominent nausea and vomiting may be a clue to the diagnosis.

High-grade fever is more common with pathogens that invade or disrupt the colonic epithelium, leading to intestinal inflammation. Mild abdominal cramping or pain is often present. More severe abdominal pain, localized to the right lower quadrant and mimicking acute appendicitis, can be seen with *Yersinia enterocolitica* and *C jejuni* infections.

The patient should be asked about similar illnesses in family members or close contacts, suggesting a common source outbreak related to a specific pathogen. The clinician must also be aware of any potential outbreaks that may be occurring in the community and always be alert to potential clustering of similar cases, which may point to an unrecognized outbreak. A careful history of recent food ingestion, including any deviations from the normal diet, should be obtained. HIV risk factors or a history of HIV positivity or AIDS is important, as is a sexual history for anal intercourse-related sexually transmitted diseases (STDs) (proctitis caused by gonorrhea, syphilis, herpes, or *Chlamydia* infection).

The key to examining the patient with diarrhea is to assess the hydration status and determine if there has been significant volume loss. Supine and standing blood pressure and pulse rates should be determined to assess for orthostatic hypotension. Supine hypotension and resting tachycardia can indicate life-threatening hypovolemia and the need for aggressive fluid resuscitation. The mucous membranes should be assessed for moisture and the skin for tenting. In infants, lethargy, dry mucous membranes, flat fontanelles, sunken eyes, poor capillary refill, and poor skin turgor may all be clues of significant hypovolemia.

The abdominal exam usually is unrevealing in most cases of infectious diarrhea. There may be diffuse, mild tenderness and hyperactive bowel sounds, but usually no rebound or guarding. However, severe cases of *C difficile* may result in peritoneal signs and *Y enterocolitica* and *C jejuni* can mimic an acute appendicitis as mentioned. A rectal examination and stool guaiac test should be performed to look for occult blood. A fresh stool sample should be obtained in a specimen cup for gross examination to give an objective assessment of the patient's complaints. The appearance of the stool—watery, mucoid, or grossly bloody—can be very helpful in narrowing the differential diagnosis and focusing the laboratory examination.

B. Laboratory Findings. The lab evaluation of suspected infectious diarrhea should begin with testing of the stool for the presence of fecal leukocytes. The stool normally does not contain fecal leukocytes, and if present, they are considered a marker for colonic inflammation secondary to both infectious and noninfectious causes. This test can be performed easily at the bedside using a stool smear stained with methylene blue or it can be done by the microbiology lab in most hospitals. Because the neutrophils will degenerate with time, the sample should be examined as soon as possible. In most series, the sensitivity of the fecal leukocyte test for various inflammatory pathogens (*Salmonella, Shigella,* and *Campylobacter* spp.) detected by stool culture varies from 45% to 95% depending on the pathogen (most sensitive for *Shigella* spp.).

Another, more stable marker for the presence of intestinal inflammation is lactoferrin. Lactoferrin is an iron-binding glycoprotein released from neutrophil secondary granules; its presence in stool is indicative of colon inflammation. False positives are known to occur in breast-fed infants, so fecal lactoferrin should be used with caution in this population. In one study, fecal lactoferrin, detected using a commercially available latex agglutination assay, was 83–93% sensitive and 61–100% specific for patients with *Salmonella, Campylobacter,* or *Shigella* spp. detected by stool culture. Lactoferrin tests have the advantage of being sensitive in cases in which the pathogen can lyse the fecal leukocytes as a result of cytotoxic toxins (*C difficile*), via adherence mechanisms (*Entamoeba histolytica*) or if the stool sample is not examined immediately.

Testing for fecal leukocytes or lactoferrin is advocated as a way to help identify infections by diarrheal pathogens that result in intestinal inflammation, because the patients may benefit from antimicrobial therapy and tend to have more severe sequelae. The clinical presentation can provide clues to identify these patients, but there can be considerable overlap in symptoms between the inflammatory and noninflammatory syndromes. The presence of fecal leukocytes or lactoferrin provides information in addition to the history to decide whether a stool culture and antibiotic therapy are indicated. The limitations of using fecal leukocyte or lactoferrin testing for this purpose are obvious from looking at their respective sensitivities and specificities. However, as long as the clinician recognizes these limitations and interprets the results in the context of the clinical setting, fecal leukocyte or lactoferrin tests should remain important tools in approaching the patient with infectious diarrhea.

Stool cultures should be considered for all patients suspected of having inflammatory diarrhea based on the clinical and epidemiologic history, a positive fecal leukocyte or lactoferrin test, or both. In the United States, the most common infectious causes of inflammatory enteritis are *C jejuni, Salmonella* spp., and *Shigella* spp. Most laboratories will automatically culture for these organisms if stool is sent for routine bacterial culture. Stool culture for other bacterial pathogens often will require special media or handling. In these cases, communication with the microbiology laboratory about the clinically suspected pathogens is very helpful to ensure that the specimens are cultured properly. Patients with grossly bloody diarrhea or a suggestive epidemiologic history should have their stool cultured for EHEC O157:H7.

However, an increasing portion of EHEC infections are now caused by non-O157 serotypes (≤ 50%), so if EHEC is suspected, non-O157 serotypes must be considered. A commercially available enzyme immunoassay can now identify the presence of Shiga bacillus toxin in *E coli* isolates or in the stool. It is sensitive, specific, and often will remain positive after the stool culture becomes negative.

For hospitalized patients, the use of routine bacterial stool cultures and parasite examinations should be governed by the "3-day rule" for bacterial cultures and the "4-day rule" for parasite exams recently advocated by the College of American Pathologists. These rules are based on several studies showing that the yield of such tests is extremely low in patients who develop diarrhea after being hospitalized for > 3–4 days and such tests are not cost effective. The pathogens that are detected by these tests are uncommonly acquired in the hospital setting in the United States. However, the application of these rules should be flexible and allow for those cases where, after careful clinical consideration, potential pathogens likely to be detected by these tests are still in the differential irrespective of the length of hospitalization.

If the diarrhea persists for > 7 days or if the history raises the possibility of a parasitic infection, then the stool should be examined by the appropriate studies. Helpful tests include the classic ova and parasite exam, the funnel gauze test for *Strongyloides* spp., direct fluorescence staining for *Giardia* and *Cryptosporidium* spp., modified acid fast stain of the stool for *Cryptosporidium* or *Cyclospora* spp., or trichrome staining for microsporidia. The ova and parasite (O+P) exam involves concentrating the stool specimen and then preparing a smear to look for parasite cysts or trophozoites and intestinal helminths. Among the diarrheal pathogens that can be detected by the O+P smear are *E histolytica* and *G lamblia.* Unfortunately, the O+P exam can have a low yield, so consideration should be given to using one of the pathogen-specific tests noted above.

A history of recent antibiotic use or hospitalization in a patient with diarrhea should raise the concern of *C difficile,* and the stool should be tested for the presence of *C difficile* toxins. The gold standard assay is the stool-cytotoxin test, looking at the ability of toxin B to induce cytopathic effects in cultured cells. It is 94–100% sensitive and 99% specific. Several new immunoassays are now available that are cheaper and faster than the stool-cytotoxin assay, but also less sensitive and specific. Several stool samples should be tested over sequential days before completely excluding *C difficile* infection.

In addition to stool studies, patients with severe diarrhea, fever, abdominal pain, or volume loss should have serum chemistries, including sodium, potassium, chloride, blood urea nitrogen, and creatinine, and have a complete blood count checked.

C. Imaging. Radiographic studies are usually

not helpful or indicated in the evaluation of infectious diarrhea except in specific cases. Severe *C difficile* colitis may lead to toxic megacolon and the associated risks of intestinal perforation. Patients with *C difficile* colitis who exhibit severe abdominal pain, peritoneal signs, and a decreasing output of diarrhea should be monitored for this potentially devastating complication with serial abdominal x-rays.

Direct imaging such as sigmoidoscopy, colonoscopy, or esophagogastroduodenoscopy can play a role in cases of chronic diarrhea in which the diagnosis remains unclear despite use of appropriate studies. Esophagogastroduodenoscopy with duodenal aspiration or biopsy can be used to detect *G lamblia.* Sigmoidoscopy or colonoscopy may show mucosal changes like erythema, ulcers, or pseudomembrane formation (*C difficile*). Biopsy may reveal adherent bacteria (enteroaggregrative *E coli*), viral inclusions (cytomegalovirus colitis) or pathology consistent with noninfectious diseases.

Differential Diagnosis

The most important question in managing the patient with suspected infectious diarrhea is to decide who will benefit from a directed laboratory evaluation and specific antimicrobial therapy. For most cases of noninflammatory diarrhea, the illness will be self-limited and require only supportive care. In these cases, extensive laboratory evaluation will be of no benefit except from an epidemiologic standpoint and will waste considerable health care resources. As a general rule, patients with a duration of illness longer than 2 days, high fever, systemic toxicity, bloody stools, fecal leukocytes or lactoferrin, severe volume depletion or abdominal pain, and those who are immunocompromised (ie, with immunosuppressive chemotherapy after organ transplant or with AIDS) should have a more extensive evaluation initiated at presentation. Other patients can be followed for resolution of their illness and evaluated only if one of the above criteria develops or as part of a public health investigation.

Figure 20–1 outlines a general approach to the patient with infectious diarrhea, using the history and the presence or absence of fecal leukocytes or lactoferrin to classify the diarrhea as noninflammatory or inflammatory. Unfortunately, there are no prospective studies that validate this algorithm by showing a decrease in morbidity or mortality. However, keeping in mind the limitations of fecal leukocytes or lactoferrin as previously discussed, it is useful to begin to formulate the differential diagnosis and to guide therapy. Box 20–1 lists the common pathogens causing inflammatory and noninflammatory diarrhea, bloody diarrhea, and diarrhea in AIDS patients and in travelers to developing countries. In the following section, we discuss some of the more common pathogens, briefly outlining general epidemiologic, clinical, and diagnostic information that will be useful in narrowing the differential diagnosis. The reader is referred

to the specific chapters elsewhere in this book for more detailed and complete information about the potential pathogens. Finally, in considering the differential diagnosis in a patient with diarrhea, the clinician must always remember noninfectious causes and obtain a careful history of medication use, enteral feedings, and symptoms suggestive of inflammatory bowel disease, endocrinopathies, ischemic colitis, or malabsorption.

A. Inflammatory Diarrhea [positive fecal white blood cells and or fever].

Bacterial Species. *C jejuni* (Chapter 57) is probably the major cause of community-acquired inflammatory enteritis in the United States, causing an estimated 2 million cases each year. The organism is transmitted via poorly cooked chicken and contaminated milk or water or on unwashed cooking utensils. The infection usually results in an acute enteritis with watery or bloody stools, fever, and abdominal pain that usually resolves within 1 week. The diagnosis is made by isolating the organism by stool culture.

Salmonella (Chapter 53) gastroenteritis is another major cause of inflammatory diarrhea acquired via contaminated food, milk, or water. Within 48 h of ingestion, most patients will develop fever, watery diarrhea, and abdominal cramping that resolves within 10 days. The stool contains moderate numbers of fecal leukocytes, and the diagnosis is made by stool culture. *S enteriditidis* (associated with undercooked eggs) and *S typhimurium* are the most common *Salmonella* isolates implicated in the United States. A small percentage of patients with enteric fever syndromes from *Salmonella typhi* or *Salmonella paratyphi,* characterized by fever and abdominal pain, may present with constipation, diarrhea, or both, early in the course. Bacteremia and subsequent metastatic foci of infection are serious complications that can occur with *Salmonella* gastroenteritis and enteric fever.

Shigella (Chapter 53) species should be suspected in patients who present with acute diarrhea combined with fever and blood or mucus in the stool. As compared with *Salmonella* or *Campylobacter* spp., transmission occurs more often via direct patient-to-patient spread. In the United States, *Shigella* infection affects mainly children and is especially important in the day care setting. *Shigella sonnei* accounts for 60–80% of cases in the United States and less commonly causes bloody stools. *Shigella flexerni* is most common in the developing world and is more frequently associated with grossly bloody stools. Other pathogenic species include *Shigella dysenteriae* and *Shigella boydii.* Patients usually complain of fever and watery diarrhea early in the course. Later, the stool volume may decrease and tenesmus with bloody stools (40% of cases) may develop. The duration usually is ≤ 5 days, but occasionally can last weeks. The stool classically has sheets of fecal leukocytes, and the diagnosis is confirmed by stool culture.

Several *E coli* species (Chapter 53) can lead to diar-

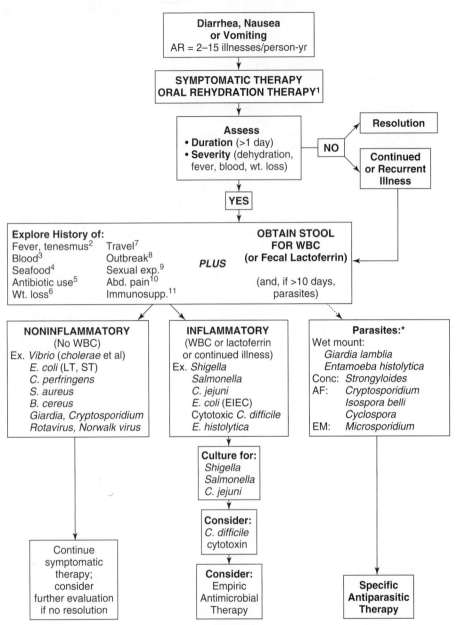

1. ORS can be prepared by adding 3.5g NaCl, 2.5g NaHCO3 (or 2.9g Na citrate), 1.5g KCl and 20g glucose or glucose polymer (ex. 40g sucrose or 4 tablespoons sugar or 50–60g cereal flour such as rice, maize, sorghum, millet, wheat or potato) per liter (1.05qt.) of clean water. This makes approximately Na 90, K 20, Cl 80, HCO3 30, glucose 111 mmol/L.
If prepared solutions or packets are not available, a substitute ORS can be made as follows: one half level teaspoon table salt, one half level teaspoon baking soda, 2 to 4 level teaspoons table sugar mixed in one liter of clean water to which one could add 1 cup orange juice or 2 bananas for potassium. The oral rehydration solution should be alternated with free water *ad libitum*.

2. Fever or tenesmus suggest an inflammatory proctocolitis.

3. Bloody diarrhea should prompt culture on Sorbitol-MacConkey agar for enterohemorrhagic (Shiga-like-toxin-producing) *E. coli* O157 and testing for the presence of shiga toxin in *E. coli* isolates or in stool (non-O157 serotypes). Amebiasis (in which leukocytes are destroyed by the parasite) should also be considered.

4. Ingestion of inadequately cooked seafood should prompt consideration of infections with Vibrio or Norwalk-like viruses.

5. Antibiotics should be stopped if possible and cytotoxigenic *C. difficile* considered. Antibiotics may also predispose to other infections such as salmonellosis.

6. Persistence (>10 days) with weight loss sould prompt consideration of giardiasis, cryptosporidiosis or *cyclospora* infection.*

* While many stool examinations for ova and parasites are often of low yield, specific requests for Giardia and *Cryptosporidium* ELISA (in patients with >10d or diarrhea) and acid fast stain for *Cryptosporidium, Isospora* or *Cyclospora* are worth considering. While these agents cause diarrhea in normal and immunocompromised patients, the latter may also have treatable microsporidial infection seen on modified trichrome stain.

7. Travel to tropical areas increases the chance of developing enterotoxigenic *E. coli*, as well as viral (Norwalk-like or rotaviral), parasitic (*Giardia, Entamoeba, Strongyloides, Crytoporidium, Cyclospora*), and, if fecal leukocytes are present, invasive bacterial infections as noted in the algorithm.

8. Outbreaks should prompt consideration of *S. aureus, B. cereus,* anisakiasis (incubation period <6 hours), *C perfringens,* ETEC, Vibrio, Salmonella, Campylobacter, Shigella, or EIEC infection. Consider saving *E. coli* for LT, ST, invasiveness, adherence testing, serotyping, and stool for rotavirus, and stool plus paired sera for Norwalk-like virus or toxin testing.

9. Sigmoidoscopy in symptomatic homosexual men should distinguish proctitis in the distal 15cm only (caused by herpesvirus, gonococcal, chlamydial, or syphilitic infection) from colitis (Campylobacter, Shigella, *C. difficile,* or chlamydial [LGV serotypes] infections) or noninflammatory diarrhea (due to giardiasis).

10. If unexplained abdominal pain and fever persist or suggest an appendicitis-like syndrome, culture for *Y. enterocolitica* with cold enrichment.

11. In immunocompromised hosts, a wide range of viral (cytomegalovirus, herpes simplex virus, coxsackievirus, rotavirus), bacterial (Salmonella, *M. avium-intracellulare*), and parasitic (Cryptosporidium, Isospora, Strongyloides, Entamoeba, and Giardia) agents should be considered.

12. Some inflammatory, colonic pathogens, such as, cytotoxigenic *C. difficile* or *Entamoeba histolytica* may destroy fecal leukocyte morphology, so a reliable leukocyte marker such as fecal lactoferrin may provide a better screening test.

Figure 20–1. General approach to the patient with infectious diarrhea. (Reprinted, with permission, from Guerrant R, Bobak D: Bacterial and protozoal gastroenteritis. N Engl J Med 1991;325:327.)

BOX 20–1

Microbiology of Infectious Diarrhea

Organisms	Inflammatory Diarrhea	Noninflammatory Diarrhea	Grossly Bloody Diarrhea	Diarrhea in HIV/AIDS Patients	Traveler's Diarrhea
	Bacteria • *Campylobacter jejuni* • *Shigella* spp. • *Salmonella* spp. • Enterohemorrhagic *E coli*[1] • *Clostridium difficile* • *Vibrio parahaemolyticus*[2] • *Listeria monocytogenes* • *Yersinia enterocolitica* • Enteroinvasive *E coli* • Enteroaggregative *E coli* **Viruses** • Cytomegalovirus **Protozoa** • *Entamoeba histolytica*	**Bacteria** • *Staphylococcus aureus* • *Bacillus cereus* • *Clostridium perfringens* • Enterotoxigenic *E coli* • *Vibrio cholerae* • *Mycobacterium avium*-complex • *Aeromonas hydrophila* • *Plesiomonas shigelloides* **Viruses** • Rotavirus • Enteric adenovirus • Caliciviruses • Norwalk virus • Cytomegalovirus **Protozoa** • *Cryptosporidium parvum* • *Giardia lamblia* • *Cyclospora cayetanensis* • *Isospora belli* • *Microsporidia* spp.	**Bacteria** • Enterohemorrhagic *E coli* • *Shigella* spp. • *Campylobacter jejuni* **Protozoa** • *Entamoeba histolytica*	**Bacteria** • *Campylobacter jejuni* • *Shigella* spp. • *Salmonella* spp. • *Clostridium difficile* • Enteroaggregative *E coli* • *Mycobacterium avium*-complex **Viruses** • Cytomegalovirus • Enteric adenovirus • Caliciviruses • HIV enteropathy **Protozoa** • *Cryptosporidium parvum* • *Isospora belli* • *Cyclospora cayetanensis* • *Microsporidia* spp.	**Major cause** • Enterotoxigenic *E coli* **Less common** • *Campylobacter jejuni* • *Shigella* spp. • *Salmonella* spp. • Rotavirus • Norwalk virus • *Vibrio parahaemolyticus* • *Entamoeba histolytica* • *Giardia lamblia* • *Cryptosporidium parvum* • *Cyclospora cayetanensis*

[1] As noted in the text, cases can have no fever or fecal leukocytes.
[2] May also cause a noninflammatory syndrome.

rhea. EHEC are Shiga toxin-producing *E coli* that are an emerging diarrheal pathogen. The intestines of cattle appear to be the major reservoir of the organism. Infection is associated with the ingestion of contaminated meats, vegetables, and water. The meat, especially ground beef, is contaminated by feces with slaughter. Vegetables and water are contaminated by cattle waste used as fertilizer or present in runoff. After an incubation period of 3–4 days, patients develop cramping, abdominal pain, and diarrhea. The stool may then become bloody over several days. Interestingly, EHEC infection may have no associated fever or fecal leukocytes or lactoferrin. Thus, acute bloody diarrhea with no fecal leukocytes or fever should not exclude the consideration of EHEC, which is now the major infectious cause of grossly bloody diarrhea in the United States. Of those infected, ≤ 6% may develop hemolytic uremic syndrome (HUS) 2–14 days after disease onset. The diagnosis is confirmed by isolating *E coli* O157:H7 by culture or via the demonstration of Shiga toxin from *E coli* isolates or in the stool (non-O157 serotypes). Enteroinvasive *E coli* strains cause diarrhea via invasion and induction of an inflammatory reaction in the intestine. Enteroinvasive *E coli* strains cause a disease similar to that caused by *Shigella* spp. and are rare in the United States. Enteroaggregative *E coli* is a recently described pathogen that can cause a persistent, mildly inflammatory diarrhea and malnutrition among people in the developing world and in patients with AIDS in the United States.

C difficile (Chapter 53) is a major cause of antibiotic-associated and nosocomial diarrhea. The disease normally occurs in the hospital setting, but community-acquired cases are being increasingly recognized. The organism overgrows the colon when the normal flora is altered by antibiotics, certain chemotherapeutic agents, or after abdominal surgery. Two protein toxins, toxins A and B, are released into the colon and lead to the development of diarrhea. The disease ranges from asymptomatic carriage to mild diarrhea to more severe forms of colitis with or without pseudomembrane formation. Pseudomembranes are mucosal plaques comprised of neutrophils and cellular debris, reflecting the inflammatory nature of the toxins. The most severe forms can lead to toxic megacolon and colonic perforation. The diagnosis is made by detecting the toxins in the stool via the methods discussed previously.

V parahaemolyticus and other *Vibrio* species (Chapter 57) are the major causes of seafood-related diarrhea in the United States, Japan, and the developing world. In the United States, the disease is most common along the Atlantic and Gulf coasts. The consumption of improperly cooked crab and shrimp meat and exposure to contaminated seawater (including the use of seawater to clean cooking utensils on cruise ships) are the main vehicles for disease transmission. In the United States, acute self-limited outbreaks are the rule, with explosive watery diarrhea and cramp-

ing abdominal pain developing within 24 h after exposure and lasting for up to several days. The organism will not grow on routine stool cultures; the diagnosis requires that the organism be isolated on thiosulfate citrate bile salts sucrose agar.

Parasites. *E histolytica* (Chapter 81) is a major protozoan cause of invasive diarrhea, especially in the developing world. It is typically found in lower socioeconomic areas with poor sanitation, in institutionalized patients, and in immigrants from endemic areas. The intestinal disease caused by *E histolytica* includes asymptomatic infection, noninvasive diarrhea, acute rectocolitis (dysentery), and fulminant colitis with the risk of toxic megacolon and colonic perforation. Amebic colitis is usually associated with heme-positive stools, but fecal leukocytes can be absent owing to the ability of the pathogen to lyse human polymorphonuclear neutrophil leukocytes. Male patients are at greater risk for developing amebic liver abscesses. The diagnosis is made by identifying the parasite in the stool, by commercially available antigen detection assays, or by serology.

Viruses. Cytomegalovirus (Chapter 33) is an important cause of inflammatory diarrhea in compromised patients, especially those with AIDS. AIDS patients with cytomegalovirus enteritis present with watery diarrhea and can develop hematochezia and fever. On endoscopy, the mucosa may show plaquelike pseudomembranes, erosions, or ulcers, and biopsy should reveal the characteristic intranuclear inclusions.

B. Noninflammatory Diarrhea (Watery Diarrhea with No Fecal Leukocytes).

Bacteria. Enterotoxigenic *E coli* strains (Chapter 53) producing heat-labile enterotoxin (LT) or heat-stable enterotoxin (ST) toxins are a major cause of diarrhea in the developing world and among travelers. Transmission occurs via contaminated food or water. After an incubation period of 1–2 days, the patient develops watery diarrhea (3–10 unformed stools per day) and cramps. The symptoms usually resolve over several days or < 1–2 days if treated early with effective antimicrobial agents. An unfortunate minority will have disease that lasts longer than 1 week. Fever and bloody stools are uncommon.

Vibrio cholerae (Chapter 57) is a well characterized diarrheal pathogen that has caused seven major pandemics since the 1800s. The seventh pandemic spread to Latin America in the early 1990s, and cases have been imported into the United States. The organism is ingested with contaminated food or water, and the infection that results ranges from asymptomatic to the full-blown cholera syndrome with voluminous watery diarrhea. Severe cases can rapidly progress to hypovolemic shock and death in < 12 h. Fever or abdominal pain is usually absent. The stool is often described as similar to rice water in appearance and is rarely bloody. Diagnosis is made clinically and confirmed by culturing the organism from the stool.

Mycobacterium avium complex (Chapter 62) is a common cause of diarrhea in patients with advanced HIV infection. Disseminated *M avium* complex presents with fever, sweats, weight loss, and, in 40% of cases, watery diarrhea. Diagnosis is made by isolating *M avium* complex from the stool and blood.

Protozoa. *G lamblia* (Chapter 84) causes prolonged diarrhea in both immunocompetent and compromised patients. The incubation period is 1–2 weeks after exposure to contaminated water or direct contact with an infected patient. The infection may be asymptomatic or loose, and foul-smelling stools can develop, often associated with cramping, flatulence, nausea, and cramps. The symptoms may persist for weeks to months if untreated. The diagnosis is confirmed by identifying the trophozoites or cysts in the stool or duodenal aspirates or by detecting *Giardia* antigens in the stool via a commercially available enzyme-linked immunosorbent assay.

Cryptosporidium parvum (Chapter 83) is another highly infectious protozoa that is endemic throughout much of the world, including the United States. The organism is spread via contaminated water and direct patient contact. After an incubation period of 1 week, immunocompetent hosts develop diarrhea, cramps, and weight loss lasting for days to weeks before resolving. Low-grade fever occurs in 50% of infected individuals. In AIDS patients, the organism can cause a severe chronic diarrhea and biliary tract infections. The diagnosis is made by identifying the cysts by a modified acid-fast stain of the stool (often missed on routine O+P) or via a commercially available fluorescence antibody stain.

Cyclospora cayetanensis (Chapter 83) is an emerging protozoal cause of diarrhea associated with contaminated drinking water or foods (raspberries and lettuce). Unlike *Cryptosporidium* spp., the life cycle of *C cayetanesis* requires a maturation phase outside the host and is thus less likely to be spread directly by person to person contact. In immunocompetent patients, after an incubation period of 1 week, a self-limited illness with watery diarrhea, cramps, and prominent fatigue ensues. It is a rare cause of diarrhea in AIDS patients in the United States, likely owing to the widespread use of trimethoprim-sulfamethoxazole (TMP-SMX) prophylaxis in these patients. It is, however, a common cause of diarrhea in this population elsewhere in the world. The diagnosis is made by identification of the organism on a modified acid-fast stain of the stool (not identified on routine O+P) or by detecting the oocytes in the stool by fluorescence microscopy (the autofluorescent oocysts without special staining).

Isospora belli (Chapter 83) is endemic in tropical countries, and infection is associated with travel or residence in these regions. Like *C cayetenesis*, it causes self-limited infections in normal hosts and chronic diarrhea in AIDS patients except in the United States, where it is uncommon probably owing to TMP-SMX use. It is diagnosed by modified acid-fast staining of stool to detect the cysts.

Microsporidia infections (Chapter 83) caused by *Enterocytozoon bieneusi* and *Septata intestinalis* are endemic in the United States and worldwide. Infection is commonly encountered in patients with advanced AIDS and causes a prolonged watery diarrhea with frequent relapses. The cysts are not identified by acid-fast stains, but rather require a modified trichrome stain of the stool or small-bowel biopsy.

Viral. Rotaviruses (Chapter 37) are a major cause of gastroenteritis worldwide and are estimated to be responsible for 10–20% of all diarrhea-related deaths. In the United States, millions of infections occur annually leading to > 100,000 pediatric admissions and 200 deaths. The peak incidence of disease is in the 6- to 24-month-old age group, and virtually all children have been infected by age 3. Adults remain susceptible to infection, but tend to have milder symptoms. Spread of the virus appears to be by the fecal-oral route and, for unknown reasons, the infection occurs mainly in the winter months. The disease is characterized by mild fever, watery diarrhea, nausea, and vomiting over 2–5 days. Immunodeficient children and adults are predisposed to developing chronic rotavirus infections with diarrhea that can last for months. The diagnosis is confirmed by rotavirus antigen enzyme-linked immunosorbent assay of the stool or by a less sensitive, more rapid latex agglutination test.

Caliciviruses (Chapter 38), including Norwalk or Norwalk-like viruses, are very common causes of viral gastroenteritis that are spread via the fecal-oral route. Outbreaks have occurred in relation to the consumption of contaminated water, food, or shellfish. Most outbreaks are characterized by an incubation period of 1–2 days, a duration of illness of 1–3 days, prominent vomiting, and a negative stool workup. Watery diarrhea with 4–8 stools/24 h is common, and low-grade fever occurs in 50% of cases. The secondary attack rate in affected households can be very high. Diagnosis is based on clinical features and a lack of identifiable pathogens on laboratory workup. Serologies can be helpful to confirm the diagnosis retrospectively.

Complications

Volume depletion and electrolyte abnormalities remain the most serious sequelae of diarrheal illnesses worldwide. It is especially a problem in the very young and the elderly, owing to a lack of ready access to fluids for rehydration or to underlying diseases that may limit the ability of elderly people to cope with the volume changes. In some diseases, such as cholera, the volume loss may be massive, and the patient can progress to hypovolemic shock within 24 h. Electrolyte losses in the stool are also common with diarrhea, potentially leading to hypokalemia and metabolic acidosis. Profound hypoglycemia, leading to lethargy, coma, and seizures, can occur rarely with severe cholera, especially in children.

Malnutrition is being increasingly recognized as a major complication of repeated or chronic diarrheal illnesses in the developing world. There is growing evidence that children with such infections exhibit growth retardation and possibly cognitive dysfunction compared with matched controls. If future studies confirm this relationship, then malnutrition may well emerge as the most devastating long-term sequela of infectious diarrhea.

Nosocomial infections are increased in hospitalized patients with preceding or ongoing episodes of nosocomial diarrhea. In one study, patients with nosocomial diarrhea had a 10-fold higher risk of nosocomial urinary tract infections as compared with matched controls without diarrhea.

Hemolytic uremic syndrome (HUS) is another complication of enteric pathogens, most notably EHEC. Patients with HUS typically present with renal failure, microangiopathic hemolytic anemia, and thrombocytopenia 2–14 days after the onset of the diarrhea. In prior outbreaks, 6% of infected patients with *E coli* O157:H7 developed HUS, 50% of whom required dialysis and had mortality as high as 1.2% (> 250 deaths per year in the United States). The risk of developing HUS after EHEC infection appears to be increased with the use of antimotility drugs, and these agents are contraindicated in suspected cases. Antimicrobial therapy may increase the risk of HUS as well, but this remains controversial.

Guillain-Barré syndrome, an acute demyelinating polyneuropathy, is another potential complication of enteric infections, especially after *C jejuni* infection. Of patients with Guillain–Barré, 20–40% had a documented *C jejuni* infection in the prior several weeks. Patients usually present with ascending motor weakness and may require mechanical ventilation for respiratory muscle involvement. The mechanism of how this infection may trigger this immune-mediated syndrome remains unknown.

Postinfectious arthritis has been described several weeks after an invasive diarrheal illness with *Campylobacter, Shigella, Salmonella,* or *Yersinia* spp., especially in patients with a human leukocyte antigen-B27 phenotype.

Treatment

As with the diagnostic approach, optimal therapy for a given diarrheal illness should be guided by a number of different factors. The age and health of the patient; volume status; ability to take oral fluids; presence of fever, blood, leukocytes, or lactoferrin in the stool; and suspected pathogen all need to be considered. For example, an adult in the United States with < 1 day of noninflammatory diarrhea can be treated with oral fluids and monitored. A child with voluminous diarrhea in a cholera-endemic region and significant volume loss will require more aggressive fluid resuscitation and antimicrobial therapy. Finally, a child with bloody diarrhea after consumption of an undercooked hamburger will require the consideration of different sequelae and treatment concerns than those in the first two cases. Given the huge range of presentations, sequelae, and therapies available with the various diarrheal pathogens, it is important to emphasize that therapy must be tailored to each patient based on the available clinical and laboratory data.

A. Volume and Electrolyte Replacement. The most important aspect to current diarrheal therapy is to maintain adequate hydration and electrolyte balance during the acute episode. This usually can be accomplished safely with oral rehydration therapy, which should be used in all patients except those unable to take oral glucose-electrolyte solutions or who have massive diarrhea that may require aggressive intravenous hydration to treat life-threatening hypovolemia. Ideally, oral rehydration solutions should contain 3.5 g of sodium chloride, 2.5 g of sodium bicarbonate, 1.5 g of potassium chloride, and 20 g of glucose per liter of water, alternated with free water ad libitum. Such solutions are commercially available in packets that are easily prepared by mixing with water. If commercial preparations are not available, a substitute oral rehydration solution can be made by adding 1/2 teaspoon table salt, 1/2 teaspoon baking soda, and 2–4 tablespoons of sugar per liter of clean water. Two bananas or 1 cup of orange juice is used to provide potassium. Instead of glucose, 40–60 g of cereal flour (rice) can be added to a liter of water and boiled with the other ingredients. Patients should drink as much fluid as their thirst dictates. If intravenous therapy is needed, a normotonic fluid such as normal saline or lactated Ringer's solution should be given with potassium supplementation as guided by the serum chemistries. The volume status should be monitored closely by observing the vital signs, respiratory status, and urine output, and the infusion rate adjusted as needed. The patient should be switched to oral rehydration solution as soon as feasible.

B. Antimicrobial Agents. In certain bacterial and protozoal infections, antimicrobial agents decrease symptom duration and fecal shedding, especially if started early in the disease. However, they have potential adverse effects, including increased cost, risk of inducing or selecting for resistant organisms, antibiotic-associated diarrhea, increased *Candida* infections, and a possible increased risk of HUS with EHEC infections. The challenge for clinicians is to decide which patients with diarrhea will benefit from starting antimicrobial therapy before the results of stool studies are available.

Antibacterial therapy should be considered in all patients with diarrhea in whom certain pathogens are suspected, because antibiotics in these cases can decrease the duration of symptoms and prevent serious sequelae. Which organisms should be covered in an individual patient will depend on the available clinical and epidemiologic data. In general, patients with suspected *Shigella, Campylobacter,* or severe *C diffi-*

cile infection, traveler's diarrhea, or *V cholerae* infection should be started on empiric therapy once the diagnosis is entertained, because the antimicrobial agents will influence the course of the illness. For *Shigella* and *Campylobacter* spp., antimicrobial therapy has been shown to decrease the duration of the diarrhea. Fecal excretion of these organisms is also decreased with antibiotic therapy and in settings where the potential for spread is present; for example, day care is another indication for therapy.

For nontyphoidal *Salmonella* gastroenteritis, antibiotic therapy may decrease the duration of illness, but paradoxically may prolong fecal excretion of the organism or predispose to systemic invasion. Antimicrobial therapy for *Salmonella* gastroenteritis should be considered for those patients who may be at increased risk for bacteremic dissemination, including the very young, the elderly, or immunocompromised patients, and for those with an enteric fever syndrome. Otherwise, nontyphoidal *Salmonella* gastroenteritis is generally self-limited and antimicrobial agents are best avoided. As mentioned, antibiotic therapy is not currently recommended for suspected or confirmed EHEC infections, especially in children. To date, studies are contradictory on whether the incidence of HUS is decreased or increased in patients who had received antibiotics, and further studies are needed to clarify this issue.

C difficile infections should be treated initially by stopping the antimicrobial therapy. If the symptoms persist or if the patient is severely ill and has underlying medical conditions, then specific therapy should be started. Although antibiotic therapy is generally not indicated in noninflammatory diarrhea, antimicrobial agents can shorten the duration of the symptoms and attenuate the volume loss in patients with cholera or traveler's diarrhea. Boxes 20–2 and 20–3 list the suggested therapies (for adults and children) that should be started once the respective pathogens are suspected.

The issue of antimicrobial resistance must be considered when choosing antibiotic therapy for enteric pathogens. For example, *Shigella* and *Salmonella* spp. are increasingly resistant to ampicillin and TMP-SMX, whereas *Campylobacter* resistance to fluoroquinolones is emerging (especially in Thailand). Stool cultures are therefore not only valuable to confirm suspected bacterial pathogens, but also to supply susceptibility patterns for a given isolate. Knowledge of the local resistance patterns, adequate culture specimens before antibiotic use, and monitoring of the patient's clinical response are all required to ensure that the correct antimicrobial therapy has been given.

Specific antiparasitic therapy is currently available for patients with confirmed or suspected *G lamblia, E histolytica, I belli,* and *C cayentanensis* infections. No specific therapy has proven consistently effective against *Cryptosporidium* spp. in AIDS patients; paromomycin has had limited success. In general, resistance has not been a problem with the protozoal

pathogens, but relapses can occur with pathogens like *Giardia* spp.

Traveler's diarrhea, most commonly caused by enterotoxigenic *E coli,* can be reduced from a duration of 3–5 days to 2 days or less with effective antimicrobial therapy. TMP-SMX and ciprofloxacin hydrochloride are the two most commonly used antibiotics, but resistance to TMP-SMX is now fairly widespread. As with other forms of diarrhea, oral rehydration is critical and should be initiated as soon as the illness begins regardless of the use of antimicrobial agents. Antimotility agents can be used once effective antimicrobial agents have been initiated, especially in patients with dysentery symptoms or bloody stools.

C. Antimotility Agents. These agents, such as the opiates loperamide hydrochloride or diphenoxylate, can help make the patient more comfortable, especially for cases of noninflammatory diarrhea. Antimotility agents can also be helpful in patients with dysentery symptoms or inflammatory diarrhea when these agents are administered after the appropriate antimicrobial agents have been started. Such agents are contraindicated in suspected EHEC infections, because they have been associated with an increased incidence of HUS in children, and in inflammatory diarrhea if specific antimicrobial therapy has not been started.

Prognosis

With adequate volume replacement, good supportive care, and antimicrobial therapy if indicated, the prognosis of infectious diarrhea is excellent with minimal morbidity and mortality. As with many illnesses, the morbidity and mortality are concentrated in the very young and the elderly. In the United States, the mortality now associated with infectious diarrhea is significantly < 1.0%. There are exceptions such as EHEC infections, which had an associated mortality of 1.2% in most studies related to the development of hemolytic uremic syndrome. Oral rehydration therapy and improvements in sanitation have begun to have an impact on mortality in the developing world. Nevertheless, considerable work remains to reduce the levels of mortality in these regions to that of the developed world. The biggest improvements likely will come with changes in economic and social conditions rather than from any further improvements in medical therapy.

Prevention & Control

Because most diarrheal pathogens are spread via the fecal-oral route, their acquisition can be prevented by maintaining good personal hygiene. This includes frequent handwashing after toilet use and especially during food preparation. The value of good hygiene by food handlers and cooks to avoid the spread of food-borne pathogens can not be overstated. Diapers of children with diarrhea should be disposed of as soon as possible with minimal contam-

BOX 20-2

Empiric Antimicrobial Therapy for Infectious Diarrhea in Adults

Organism	First Choice	Second Choice
Campylobacter Shigella, or *Salmonella* spp.[1]	• Ciprofloxacin, 500 mg, orally twice a day × 3–5 d[2,3]	*Salmonella/Shigella* spp. • Ceftriaxone, IM/IV 1 gm IM/IV daily × 3 days **OR** • TMP-SMX DS orally twice a day × 3 days[4,5] *Campylobacter* spp. • Azithromycin, 500 mg orally twice a day × 3 d **OR** • Erythromycin, 500 mg orally twice a day × 5 d
Clostridium difficile	• Metronidazole, 250–500 mg orally or IV four times a day × 7–14 d[6]	• Vancomycin, 125 mg orally four times a day for 7–14 d[7]
Vibrio cholerae	• Tetracycline, 500 mg orally four times a day × 3 d **OR** • Doxycycline, 300 mg orally × 1 dose	• Tetracycline-resistant strains: • Ciprofloxacin, 1 g orally × 1 dose **OR** • Erythromycin, 250 mg orally four times a day × 3 d
Traveler's diarrhea	• Ciprofloxacin, 500 mg orally twice a day × 1–3 days	• TMP-SMX DS orally twice a day × 3 d
Giardia lamblia	• Metronidazole, 250 mg orally three times a day × 7 d[6]	• Furazolidine, 100 mg orally four times a day × 7–10 d **OR** • Paromomycin, 500 mg orally three times a day × 7 d
Entamoeba histolytica (patients with acute colitis)	• Metronidazole, 750 mg orally three times a day × 10 d[6] followed by iodoquinol, 650 mg orally three times a day × 20 d **OR** paromomycin, 500 mg orally three times a day × 7 d	• Tinidazole, 600 mg orally three times a day × 5 d followed by either iodoquinol 650 mg orally three times a day × 20 d **OR** paromomycin, 500 mg orally three times a day × 7d
Cyclospora cayetanensis	• TMP-SMX DS orally twice a day × 7–10 d	• None
Isospora belli	• TMP-SMX DS orally twice a day × 10 d	• Pyrimethamine, 75 mg orally four times a day × 3 wk

[1]Antimicrobials for *Salmonella* gastroenteritis: use in patients at risk for bacteremic dissemination, with severe disease, or with an enteric fever syndrome.
[2]Resistance to fluoroquinolones increasing worldwide.
[3]Currently, fluoroquinolones are not recommended for patients below the age of 17.
[4]TMP-SMX, trimethoprim–sulfamethoxazole; DS, double-strength.
[5]Resistance increasing; need to check local patterns and isolate sensitivity.
[6]Use with caution in pregnant females.
[7]Use in patients who are intolerant to or have failed metronidazole therapy given concerns about selecting for resistant enterococci.
[8]Resistance common worldwide, except certain areas of Mexico.

BOX 20-3

Empiric Antimicrobial Therapy for Infectious Diarrhea in Children

Organism	First Choice	Second Choice
Campylobacter, Shigella, or *Samonella* spp.[1]	*Shigella/Salmonella* spp. • Ceftriaxone 50–75 mg/kg IM/IV a day • TMP 5 mg/kg and SMX 25 mg/kg orally twice a day × 5 d[2,3] *Campylobacter* spp. • Erythromycin, 12.5 mg/kg (max 500 mg) orally four times a day × 5–7 d	*Shigella/Salmonella* spp. • Ampicillin, 20 mg/kg (max 500 mg) orally four times a day × 5 d[3]
Clostridium difficile	• Metronidazole, 5–7 mg/kg (max 500 mg) orally three times a day × 7–14 d[4]	• Vancomycin, 5–10 mg/kg (125 mg) orally four times a day for 7–14 d[5]
Vibrio cholerae	• Tetracycline, 10 mg/kg (max 250 mg) orally twice a day × 3 d[6] OR • Doxycycline, 6 mg/kg (max 300 mg) orally × 1 dose[6]	• TMP-SMX, 5 mg/kg 25 mg/kg × 3 d[2] OR • Erythromycin, 12.5 mg/kg (max 500 mg) orally four times a day × 3 d
Traveler's diarrhea	• TMP 5 mg/kg and SMX 25 mg/kg orally twice a day × 3 d[2,7]	• Rehydration therapy alone
Giardia lamblia	• Metronidazole, 5 mg/kg (max 250 mg) orally three times a day × 5 d[4]	• Furazolidine, 2 mg/kg (max 100 mg) orally four times a day × 7–10 d
Entamoeba histolytica (patients with acute colitis)	• Metronidazole, 15 mg/kg (max 750 mg) orally three times a day × 10 d[4] followed by iodoquinol, 10 mg/kg (max 650 mg) orally three times a day × 20 d OR • Paromomycin, 10 mg/kg (max 500 mg) orally three times a day × 7 d	• Tinidazole, 50 mg/kg (max 2 g) orally daily × 3 d followed by either iodoquinol or paromomycin
Cyclospora cayetanensis	• TMP 5 mg/kg and SMX 25 mg/kg orally twice a day × 3–7 d[2]	
Isospora belli	• TMP 5 mg/kg and SMX 25 mg/kg orally twice a day × 10	

[1]Antimicrobials for *Salmonella* gastroenteritis: use in patients at risk for bacteremic dissemination, with severe disease or with an enteric fever syndrome.
[2]TMP-SMX = trimethoprim - sulfamethoxazole; DS = double-strength. Dosage - 5 mg/kg TMP, 25 mg/kg SMX per dose.
[3]Resistance increasing, need to check local patterns and isolate sensitivity.
[4]Use with caution in pregnant females.
[5]Use in patients who are intolerant to or have failed metronidazole therapy given concerns about selecting for resistant enterococci.
[6]Avoid in children less than 9 Y.O.; however, in severe cholera, benefits may outweigh the risks.
[7]Resistance common worldwide, except certain areas of Mexico.

ination of the living environment. Human sewage should be removed from living areas, and farm animals should be kept separate from human dwellings. Nosocomial diarrhea can be reduced by using antibiotics judiciously, by avoiding broad-spectrum antibiotics if possible, and by careful handwashing, which may potentially reduce the spread of *C difficile* spores within the hospital environment.

Because food and water are common vectors for pathogens, these areas should be given special attention. Drinking water, water used to clean food, or water that is used in cooking should be filtered and chlorinated. If there is any concern about water safety or if unpurified water is taken from lakes or rivers, then it should be boiled for several minutes before consumption. When swimming in lakes or rivers, people should take care not to ingest the water. Sea water is often contaminated with *Vibrio* species, and caution should be exercised when using this water for cooking or washing or when swimming.

All fruits and vegetables should be washed thoroughly with clean (boiled, filtered, or treated) water before consumption, especially given the quantity of produce now imported into the United States. Untreated human or animal waste should not be used to fertilize fruits and vegetables. All meats and seafood should be cooked adequately. Chicken and ground beef should be cooked until the red or pink is gone. Only pasteurized dairy products and juices should be consumed. A recent outbreak of EHEC was associated with drinking unpasteurized apple cider made with apples contaminated, after falling to the ground, by cattle feces.

The prevention of traveler's diarrhea begins with the avoidance of potentially contaminated food or water and with the maintenance of good personal hygiene. All drinking water should be boiled, or carbonated beverages should be consumed. Ice cubes should be avoided, unless made with boiled water. Food should be well cooked, and unpeeled fruits and food from salad bars and street vendors should be avoided.

These measures can reduce, but not eliminate, the risk of acquiring traveler's diarrhea and are difficult to strictly adhere to. Bismuth subsalicylate tablets taken 4 times a day for up to 3 weeks and antibiotic prophylaxis with fluoroquinolones are effective in preventing many cases of traveler's diarrhea. However, given the cost, the risk of contributing to resistance, drug side effects, and the fact that a short course of antimicrobial agents can significantly ameliorate traveler's diarrhea if it occurs, such prophylaxis is not currently recommended by most experts.

Vaccines are a promising area for the prevention of infectious diarrhea, but the effectiveness and scope of the currently available vaccines are limited. At present, vaccines are available for *V cholerae,* typhoid fever, and rotavirus. The current parenteral cholera vaccine is not very effective and not recommended for use. Newer oral cholera vaccines based on the toxin B-subunit or inactivated whole cells are more effective, and the immunity is of longer duration. However, neither is currently licensed in the United States. The older parenteral typhoid vaccine was only 70% effective and had frequent side effects. A newer parenteral vaccine based on the capsular polysaccharide Vi-antigen is now available in the United States. It is also 70% protective, but requires only 1 dose and has fewer side effects. An oral, live-attenuated typhoid vaccine is available, requiring 1 capsule every other day for 4 doses and having an efficacy similar to that of the other two vaccines. The recently approved oral rotavirus vaccine covers serotypes 1–4 and is given to infants at 2, 4, and 6 months of age. In several international trials, the vaccine decreased the incidence of gastroenteritis by 50%, severe disease by 75%, and hospitalization for dehydration by almost 100%. Fever was the most common side effect, especially in the first week after the administration, but overall the vaccine was very safe. More recent data, however, have shown an increased risk of intussusception in infants vaccinated in the prio 1–2 weeks. Vaccination in infants is no longer recommended.

REFERENCES

Choi SW et al: To culture or not to culture: fecal lactoferrin screening for inflammatory bacterial diarrhea. J Clin Microbiol 1996;34:928.

Dupont H et al: Guidelines on acute infectious diarrhea in adults. Am J Gastroenterol 1997;92:1962.

Griffin P: *Escherichia coli* O157:H7 and other enterohemorrhagic *E coli.* In Blaser M et al: *Infections of the Gastrointestinal Tract.* Raven, 1995.

Guerrant R: Lessons from diarrheal illnesses: demography to molecular pharmacology. J Infect Dis 1994;169:1206.

Guerrant R, Bobak D: Bacterial and protozoal gastroenteritis. N Engl J Med 1991;325:327.

Gueirent RL,0 von Gilder T, et al: Practice guidelines for the management of infectious diarrhea. Clin Infect Dis 2001; 32:331.

Fekety R: Guidelines for the diagnosis and management of *Clostridium difficile*-associated diarrhea and colitis. Am J Gastroenterol 1997;92:739.

Hines J, Nachamkin I: Effective use of the clinical microbiology laboratory for diagnosing diarrheal diseases. Clin Infect Dis 1996;23:1292.

Mackenzie W et al: A massive outbreak in Milwaukee of *Cryptosporidium* infection transmitted through the public water supply. N Engl J Med 1994;331:161.

Hepatobiliary Infections

21

Paul B. Eckburg, MD & Jose G. Montoya, MD

Essentials of Diagnosis

- History of household or sexual contact with individuals with hepatitis, travel or residence in endemic areas, human immunodeficiency virus (HIV) risk factors or established acquired immunodeficiency syndrome (AIDS), blood transfusion, needle stick injury, hepatotoxic medication or alcohol use, intravenous (IV) drug use, biliary colic or known gallstones, recurrent cholangitis, or liver transplant.
- Fever, nausea, vomiting, aversion to smoking, tender hepatomegaly, or right-upper-quadrant pain.
- Hepatocellular damage (elevated aminotransferases) or cholestasis (elevated bilirubin and alkaline phosphatase) on hepatic biochemical testing.
- Positive serologies for hepatitis viruses or *Entamoeba histolytica,* or positive blood culture for enteric bacteria.
- Inflamed gallbladder, dilated intra- or extrahepatic ducts, or intrahepatic lesion on hepatobiliary imaging.
- Liver biopsy histopathology with nonspecific hepatocellular necrosis or granulomas.

General Considerations

A large number of infectious organisms can cause liver or biliary tract abnormalities, either by direct invasion or by the effects of systemic infection and sepsis (Table 21–1). There is a wide range of clinical presentations in hepatobiliary infections, depending on the specific organism, the host response, and the immune status of the host. Clinical syndromes may feature abnormal hepatic biochemical tests, focal hepatic lesions, granulomatous disease, or obstructive jaundice. A thorough history, physical exam, and biochemical liver test panel are usually sufficient for making a diagnosis of the type of hepatobiliary disease in ≥ 80% of cases. However, symptoms, signs, and liver test abnormalities are often not specific enough to make an accurate diagnosis without the aid of cultures or serologies, hepatobiliary imaging, or liver biopsy.

A. History and physical exam. The history should elicit a detailed sexual, occupational-exposure, IV drug use, and blood transfusion record (eg, assess HIV and hepatitis risk factors), as well as travel to endemic areas, alcohol use, current medications, diet (eg, risk of hepatitis A), and history of cholelithiasis. Symptoms are often nonspecific (eg, prodromal fatigue and malaise in acute hepatitis) and rarely helpful in establishing the cause of hepatobiliary disease. Some clinical syndromes may be asymptomatic (eg, chronic hepatitis B), whereas others may have a fulminant course (eg, acute hepatitis B).

The clinical exam is also nonspecific, with fever, hepatomegaly, and right-upper-quadrant abdominal pain and tenderness being common in a variety of hepatobiliary infections. The abdominal exam may be unremarkable, as in some cases of chronic hepatitis and granulomatous hepatitis. Clues to the diagnosis can be obtained by finding extrahepatic manifestations of disease. For example, urticaria may be seen in early hepatitis B, and porphyria cutanea tarda may be associated with hepatitis C. Autoimmune phenomena such as thyroiditis and inflammatory bowel disease (IBS) may be seen with autoimmune hepatitis or sclerosing cholangitis. Glomerulonephritis may be seen in either hepatitis B or C infection.

B. Diagnostic methods for evaluation of hepatobiliary infection.

1. Laboratory studies. Abnormal hepatic biochemical tests may be the first evidence of liver disease. Elevated serum aminotransferase levels are sensitive indicators of hepatocellular injury. Alanine aminotransferase is located in the hepatocyte cytosol and is more specific for liver disease. Aspartate aminotransferase is located in both the cytosol and mitochondria and is also found in other organs such as the brain, kidneys, blood cells, and skeletal muscle. The degree of aminotransferase elevation does not seem to correlate with the severity of liver injury and is of little prognostic value. However, the magnitude of the elevation may help in differentiating the cause of liver injury. For example, markedly elevated levels are seen in ischemic injury, damage from toxins (eg, acetaminophen), viral hepatitis, and occasionally acute common bile duct obstruction.

Elevated alkaline phosphatase level is helpful in diagnosing biliary tract disease in the context of other abnormal hepatic tests, but it is not helpful in differentiating the site of damage within the biliary system. For example, elevated alkaline phosphatase is common in obstruction or disease of the extrahepatic bil-

Table 21–1. Systemic infectious diseases with associated hepatobiliary abnormalities.

Bacterial
Gram-negative sepsis
Pneumococcal pneumonia
Listeriosis
Toxic shock syndrome
Legionnaires' disease
Brucellosis
Fitz-Hugh-Curtis syndrome
Salmonellosis
Nocardiosis
Syphilis
Lyme disease
Leptospirosis
Psittacosis
Tuberculosis
Hansen's disease (Leprosy)
Tularemia
Rickettsial
Q fever
Rocky Mountain spotted fever
Viral
Cytomegalovirus
Infectious mononucleosis
Adenovirus
Fungal
Histoplasmosis
Coccidiodomycosis
Candidiasis
Invasive aspergillosis
Parasitic
Schistosomiasis
Toxoplasmosis
Hydatid cyst disease
Visceral larva migrans
Fascioliasis

Table 21–2. Diagnostic imaging of choice in hepatobiliary infections.

Suspected Disease	Diagnostic Imaging of Choice[1]
Cholelithiasis and cholecystitis	Abdominal ultrasonography
Choledocholithiasis and cholangitis	Direct cholangiography (ERCP preferred over PTC)
Extrahepatic biliary obstruction of unclear etiology	Abdominal CT
Liver abscess	Abdominal CT
Acute hepatitis	No role for diagnostic imaging

[1]Abbreviations: ERCP, endoscopic retrograde cholangiopancreatography; PTC, percutaneous transhepatic cholangiography; CT, computed tomography

iary tree (eg, acute cholangitis caused by choledocholithiasis), the main hepatic ducts (eg, in sclerosing cholangitis), interlobular ducts (eg, granulomatous hepatitis), and canalicular membranes (eg, with rifampin therapy). Serum γ-glutamyl transpeptidase can be used to confirm a hepatic origin of an elevated alkaline phosphatase, but it otherwise lacks specificity for hepatic dysfunction.

Hyperbilirubinemia is of little prognostic value in acute biliary obstruction, but its level can be correlated with mortality in chronic liver diseases. High levels of total bilirubin can be seen in acute cholangitis, sclerosing cholangitis, and certain systemic infections involving the liver, such as septic shock and leptospirosis. Most other hepatic infections are associated with only mild elevations in bilirubin (< 5 mg/dL). Almost all infections of the hepatobiliary system feature > 50% direct bilirubin as part of the total bilirubin level.

2. Imaging. See Table 21–2.

a. Ultrasonography. Ultrasonography is the preferred method for diagnostic imaging of the right upper quadrant when gallbladder disease is suspected. It is relatively inexpensive, noninvasive, and may be performed at the patient's bedside. Gallstones, gallbladder wall thickening, and localized tenderness over the gallbladder (sonographic Murphy's sign) correlate highly with the presence of acute cholecystitis. Cystic duct calculi may be more difficult to visualize, and the overlying duodenum may prevent visualization of choledocholithiasis (75% sensitivity vs 95% sensitivity in detecting cholelithiasis).

b. Abdominal computed tomography (CT). Abdominal CT is less reliable than ultrasound in detecting gallbladder wall abnormalities or gallstones, and it has sensitivity similar to that of ultrasound in detecting choledocholithiasis (75%). However, CT is the preferred test in detecting other causes of posthepatic biliary obstruction, because it has better visualization of the retroperitoneum and lymph nodes and can simultaneously visualize the liver, biliary tree, and pancreas. CT is also the test of choice in evaluating for liver abscesses, and it can identify air and calcifications within intrahepatic lesions (eg, echinococcal cysts).

c. Direct cholangiography. Direct cholangiography, with injection of contrast into the biliary tree, is used when there is strong suspicion of choledocholithiasis (eg, in acute cholangitis). This can be performed by either percutaneous transhepatic cholangiography (PTC) or by endoscopic retrograde cholangiopancreatography (ERCP). It is superior to both ultrasonography and CT in detecting common bile duct stones, and offers the potential for therapeutic intervention in removing the stones. ERCP has the advantage over PTC in being able to perform a papillotomy or placing a common bile duct stent if needed for stone extraction.

d. Hepatobiliary scintigraphy. Hepatobiliary scintigraphy (eg, dimethyl iminodiacetic acid scan) uses a radiolabel such as ^{99m}Tc to visualize the path of biliary excretion. This test may be used to evaluate for cystic duct obstruction (eg, in acute cholecystitis) if ultrasonography is negative.

e. Magnetic resonance cholangiography. Magnetic resonance cholangiography is emerging as an alternative to ERCP for imaging the biliary tree. The test is noninvasive and does not require contrast material. However, if choledocholithiasis is detected, the stone cannot be removed during the procedure as with ERCP.

3. **Liver biopsy.** Percutaneous liver biopsy is indicated when imaging studies reveal a space-occupying lesion and an infectious or neoplastic etiology is suspected but not yet established. It is also useful in staging disease and determining the severity of hepatocellular damage in chronic viral hepatitis (often used to assess the need for and predict response to antiviral therapy). Liver biopsy can be used to diagnose infiltrative processes such as granulomatous hepatitis (eg, in patients with fever of unknown origin). In patients with a focal hepatic lesion, liver biopsy should be performed under ultrasound or CT guidance.

INFECTIONS OF THE LIVER

ACUTE VIRAL HEPATITIS

Essentials of Diagnosis

- Prodrome of malaise, nausea, vomiting, and low-grade fever.
- Possible tender hepatomegaly, jaundice, dark urine, and acholic stools.
- Marked elevation in aminotransferase levels.
- Presence of serum antigen or antibody to a specific hepatitis virus.

General Considerations

Acute viral hepatitis is caused by five agents, the hepatitis A, B, C, D, and E viruses. Acute viral hepatitis may also be part of other systemic viral illnesses, such as infectious mononucleosis and cytomegalovirus (CMV) infection. Several recently discovered viruses (hepatitis F, GB-C, and G viruses) are currently being further characterized. In the United States, ~ 40% of cases of acute viral hepatitis are caused by hepatitis B virus (HBV), 30% by hepatitis A virus (HAV), 20% by hepatitis C virus (HCV), 2% by hepatitis D virus (HDV), and 1% by hepatitis E virus (HEV) (the remaining cases are of unclear etiology). All five viruses can cause acute hepatitis, which is clinically similar to other causes of hepatitis, eg, drug-induced or ischemic hepatitis, and can only be distinguished by specific viral serologies. Only HBV, HCV, and HDV can cause chronic infection. Each of these viruses is discussed briefly; for details on the hepatitis viruses, see Chapter 39.

HAV is a single-stranded RNA-containing picornavirus that causes sporadic outbreaks and epidemics of acute hepatitis. It does not cause chronic hepatitis. Its major route of transmission is fecal-oral spread, which is enhanced by crowding and poor hygiene.

Common-source outbreaks may involve contaminated water and food (eg, shellfish). Household contacts are at highest risk for infection (~ 25% of cases), followed by participants in daycare centers (15% of cases), travelers to endemic areas (5%), homosexual men (4%), and IV drug users (2%). Transfusion-associated HAV is extremely rare. Viremia occurs during the incubation period (2–6 weeks), and fecal excretion of HAV may occur for ≤ 2 weeks before clinical illness. Replication and shedding of the virus therefore may occur although the subject is asymptomatic, which suggests that this process is noncytopathic to the liver. Liver injury is mediated by the host immune response, primarily involving cytotoxic T cells and natural killer cells.

HBV is a hepadnavirus that has a partially double-stranded DNA genome, an inner core protein (hepatitis B core antigen), and outer surface antigen [hepatitis B surface antigen (HB$_s$Ag)]. It infects > 400 million people worldwide, although it is more prevalent in Southeast Asia, China, and Africa. In the United Sates, most HBV infection results from sexual exposure (≤ 60%), IV drug use (10–15%), and rarely occupational exposure; ≤ 30% have an unknown source of infection. In endemic countries, maternal-neonatal vertical transmission and horizontal spread among children is quite common. Like HAV, HBV does not kill hepatocytes. Liver injury occurs from the host's immune attack against the virus, including a specific cytotoxic T cell response against hepatitis B core antigen (presented on the surface of infected hepatocytes). The immature immune systems of neonates are unable to clear the virus, and > 90% of infected neonates become chronic asymptomatic carriers. Only 1–5% of immunocompetent adults remain chronically infected, however acute infection may feature severe hepatocellular injury and symptomatic illness. Fulminant hepatitis occurs in < 1% of cases.

HDV (or delta agent) is a blood-borne defective RNA virus that causes hepatitis only in association with HBV. Like HBV, prevalence rates vary from region to region, although it is endemic in the Mediterranean, Russia, Middle East, and the Amazon basin of South America. Percutaneous spread is the major route of transmission. The pathogenesis of HDV infection is not fully understood. Both acute HDV coinfection with HBV and HDV superinfection in HB$_s$Ag carriers have been well-described. In superinfection, acute disease is more severe, and chronic hepatitis with rapid progression to cirrhosis is more common.

HCV is a single-stranded RNA virus related to the flaviviruses. It is the most common cause of post-transfusion hepatitis worldwide. Six genotypes have been identified to date, each with varying disease severity and treatment response. The most common genotypes in the United States and Europe are 1a and 1b; the latter is associated with more advanced disease and suboptimal treatment response. Prevalences of HCV seropositivity are 1–2% in the United States and 4–6% in parts of Africa and the Middle East. HCV is primarily transmitted in contaminated blood and less effectively through other body fluids. Risk factors for infection include IV drug use (≤ 50% of cases), hemodialysis, tattooing, and blood and IV immunoglobulin (Ig) transfusion. Perinatal and sexual transmissions are relatively rare. The exact mechanism of hepatic injury remains undefined, but cytotoxic T cells directed against viral epitopes are likely involved. High rates of viral mutations into quasispecies allow the virus to evade immune surveillance, leading to chronic infection in > 80% of cases.

HEV is a caliciviruslike RNA virus involved in waterborne outbreaks of acute hepatitis. Like HAV, it causes a self-limited hepatitis spread via the fecal-oral route and does not result in a chronic carrier state. HEV causes epidemic and endemic disease in India, Southeast Asia, parts of Africa, and Mexico, and it should be suspected in travelers to these areas with acute hepatitis. Pathogenesis of liver damage by HEV is poorly understood, but may involve both direct viral and immune-mediated effects.

Clinical Findings

A. Signs and symptoms. The clinical presentation is variable, from asymptomatic (eg, majority of acute hepatitis C) to fulminant (eg, acute hepatitis E in pregnancy). The five types of viral hepatitis cannot be distinguished based on clinical findings alone (Table 21–3). During the incubation period, patients may have malaise, myalgias, arthralgias, anorexia, nausea, vomiting, and aversion to smoking. Low-grade fevers and abdominal pain may be experienced during this prodrome phase. An icteric phase that features jaundice and transient worsening of prodromal symptoms may follow, with subsequent gradual improvement during convalescence. On examination, tender hepatomegaly may be present in over half of cases; however splenomegaly is uncommon. Immune complexes may develop in acute hepatitis B, leading to a preicteric serum sickness-like syndrome with

glomerulonephritis, polyarthritis, urticaria, and systemic vasculitis in < 10% of cases. Extrahepatic syndromes have also been associated with acute hepatitis C, including cryoglobulinemia, membranoproliferative glomerulonephritis, porphyria cutanea tarda, and Mooren corneal ulcers.

B. Laboratory findings. Aminotransferase levels are typically > 300 U/L and often > 1000–2000 U/L. Elevated aminotransferases may be discovered on routine testing in asymptomatic patients. Moderately elevated bilirubin and alkaline phosphatase levels occur during the icteric phase and may persist after normalization of the aminotransferases. Leukocytosis is uncommon; however, a relative leukopenia may be seen. Urinalysis may reveal a mild proteinuria and bilirubinuria during the icteric phase.

Serology for the specific viral antibodies and antigens is key to making the correct diagnosis (see Chapter 39). In acute hepatitis A, HAV IgM is the most important diagnostic test. This antibody appears early in the disease, peaks within the first week of illness, and disappears in 3–6 months (HAV IgG may persist for years).

In hepatitis B, HB_sAg is the first serum marker to appear. It is detectable before evidence of abnormal biochemical tests and persists throughout acute (and chronic) hepatitis. Hepatitis B surface antibody rises after the clearance of HB_sAg, leaving a window of seronegativity to the surface protein (between the disappearance of HB_sAg and the appearance of hepatitis B surface antibody). The appearance of hepatitis B surface antibody signals noninfectivity and protection from recurrence and is the only positive marker in those vaccinated for HBV. Hepatitis B core antibody may be used to diagnose HBV infection because IgM rises shortly after the appearance of HB_sAg and will be present before hepatitis B surface antibody appears. Hepatitis B core IgG rises later and persists whether recovery or chronic hepatitis B develops; it is not a protective antibody. Of note, hepatitis B core antigen does not appear in the serum. HB_eAg and HBV DNA are more specific markers for infectivity and ongoing replication, and they appear only in

Table 21–3. Clinical characteristics of acute viral hepatitis.[1]

Characteristic	HAV	HBV	HCV	HDV	HEV
Incubation (mean days)	30	60–90	50	60–90	40
Severity	Mild	Moderate to severe	Moderate	Moderate to severe	Mild
Fulminant	<1% (higher if underlying chronic HBV or liver disease)	1%	<1%	10–15%	1% (10–20% in pregnancy)
Diagnostic serology	HAV Ab (IgM)	HBsAg and HBcAb (IgM)	HCV Ab and HCV RNA	HDV Ab and HBcAB (IgM in coinfection, IgG in superinfection)	HEV Ab (IgM)
Progression to chronicity	None	90% neonates, 1–5% adults	80%	Nearly 100% if superinfection of chronic HBV	None

[1]Abbreviations: HAV, hepatitis A virus; HBV, hepatitis B virus; HCV, hepatitis C virus; HDV, hepatitis D virus; HEV, hepatitis E virus; IgM, immunoglobulin M; HBsAg, hepatitis B surface antigen; HBcAg, hepatitis B core antigen antibody; Ab, antibody.

HB$_s$Ag-positive sera. HBV polymerase chain reaction is now available and has been used to assess the response of chronic hepatitis to antiviral therapy; however, its role has not been fully established. Coinfection with HDV is suggested by a positive HDV antibody or HDV RNA.

In hepatitis C, HCV antibody can be detected by enzyme-linked immunosorbent assay; however, this test has suboptimal sensitivity and 50% specificity. If a false-negative or -positive test is suspected, recombinant immunoblot assay for HCV antibody may be used to confirm the diagnosis. Serum HCV RNA can be detected by polymerase chain reaction; a positive result indicates infectivity. Polymerase chain reaction should be used only if recombinant immunoblot assay for antibodies is indeterminate or when assessing response to antiviral treatment. Similarly, HEV antibody and RNA are present in acute hepatitis E.

Differential Diagnosis

Acute hepatitis may be clinically similar in such systemic infections as infectious mononucleosis, CMV, herpes simplex virus, leptospirosis, secondary syphilis, brucellosis, and Q fever. Right-upper-quadrant pain, jaundice, and markedly elevated transaminases may also occur in drug-induced hepatotoxicity or ischemic liver damage (eg, "shock liver" in sepsis). Fever, jaundice, and abnormal hepatic biochemical tests may be seen in autoimmune hepatitis and cholangitis. The prodromal phase of acute viral hepatitis is nonspecific and may resemble influenza virus infection.

Treatment

Only supportive and symptomatic treatment is available. No specific antiviral agents have been shown to be useful in this syndrome, and there is no benefit of corticosteroid therapy. Patients should avoid hepatotoxic medications, alcohol, and narcotic agents. Those with fulminant hepatitis should be hospitalized for intensive monitoring and correction of coagulopathy. Limited studies in the treatment of acute hepatitis C with interferon-α (IFN-α) suggest a reduction in the risk of chronic hepatitis; however, this should be considered experimental at this time. This approach is impractical for HBV because > 95% of infected adults have self-limited hepatitis.

Prevention

Hand washing, needle precautions, and protected intercourse are important in preventing disease. Continued screening of blood donors and blood products may further reduce the frequency of blood-borne infections. Vaccines and immune globulin are available for the prevention and postexposure prophylaxis of HAV and HBV infection. HAV vaccination is recommended for those planning travel to endemic areas, and is available as Havrix (1.0 mL intramuscularly) or Vaqta (0.5 mL intramuscularly). HAV Ig is indicated for all close contacts (ie, household contacts) of known HAV-infected individuals, given as a 0.02 mL/kg intramuscular injection within the incubation period. HBV vaccine (Recombivax-HB or Engerix-B) is now universally recommended for all infants and high-risk adults, and is given in a series of three injections, at 0, 1, and 6 months. HDV is also best prevented by this vaccine. Postexposure prophylaxis with HBV Ig should be administered as early as possible after sexual, mucous membrane, or perinatal exposure (0.06 mL/kg intramuscularly), followed by the vaccination series. There is no effective vaccine for HCV.

Prognosis

Patients with acute viral hepatitis usually recover within 3–16 weeks of clinical illness. It is not uncommon for abnormal hepatic biochemical tests to persist longer. Overall mortality is < 1%. HAV and HEV do not have chronic carrier states, although HAV infection may persist up to 1 year with the potential for relapses before complete recovery. HEV infection during pregnancy is associated with a higher mortality. HBV infection is associated with a higher mortality if there is an associated HDV infection, and superinfection of HDV invariably leads to chronic infection. Chronic hepatitis B occurs in ≤ 90% of infected infants and 1–5% of adults. Chronic HCV infection occurs in 80% of all cases, with ≤ 30% progressing to cirrhosis.

CHRONIC VIRAL HEPATITIS

Essentials of Diagnosis

- Possible malaise, fatigue, weakness, and elevated aminotransferase levels.
- Persistent serum HB$_s$Ag or HCV antibodies for ≥ 6 months.
- Liver biopsy histopathology with characteristic hepatocellular necrosis and fibrosis.

General Considerations

Chronic viral hepatitis is currently the leading indication for liver transplantation and is the main cause of cirrhosis and hepatocellular carcinoma in the world. It is defined as persistently elevated aminotransferase levels with characteristic histopathologic changes for ≥ 6 months duration. Of the hepatitis viruses, only HBV, HCV, and HDV can cause chronic hepatitis.

Chronic hepatitis B features persistent HB$_s$Ag for > 6 months. It affects > 400 million people worldwide. The disease is highly endemic in Southeast Asia, the Pacific islands, Africa, and the Middle East, and ≤ 15% of these populations are chronically infected. Of infected neonates, ≥ 90% later develop chronic hepatitis B, in contrast to 1–5% of adults. The pathogenesis underlying the rates of chronic infection in different age groups is largely unknown. However, in children it likely involves immune tolerance, in allowing viral replication to proceed without a destructive cytotoxic T-cell response. The natural history of disease is variable. Some patients spontaneously enter a phase of immune clearance, with a decrease of HB_eAg and HBV DNA and appearance of HB_eAb. The course may fluctuate with recurrent flares or sustained remission.

Unlike HBV, HCV infection does not involve integration into the host genome (there is no DNA intermediate in its life cycle). Persistence of the virus results from a high mutation rate during replication, with production of quasispecies and avoidance of the host immune response. Of acute HCV cases, 80% develop chronic disease.

Clinical Findings

A. Signs and symptoms. The different forms of chronic hepatitis cannot be distinguished by clinical presentation. Patients may be asymptomatic with incidental abnormal hepatic serum tests, or they may present with end-stage liver disease with cirrhosis and portal hypertension. Malaise and weakness are common symptoms.

B. Laboratory findings. Hepatic biochemical tests usually reveal mildly elevated aminotransferases (2- to 20-fold), hyperbilirubinemia, elevated prothrombin time, and hypoalbuminemia. Chronic hepatitis B is distinguished by persistent serum HB_sAg, HB_eAg, and HBV DNA levels (Table 21–4), in conjunction with characteristic histopathologic findings on liver biopsy. Remission or response to treatment may be suggested by loss of HB_eAg and DNA levels despite persistent HB_sAg. Chronic HCV is diagnosed by persistent HCV antibodies and positive serum HCV RNA with concurrent histopathologic changes on biopsy. Of note, false-positive HCV antibodies can occur in autoimmune hepatitis, which can clinically present like chronic hepatitis C.

C. Biopsy. Liver biopsy is used to assess disease activity and is recommended before institution of treatment to determine disease severity and predict response to treatment. Histopathology of chronic hepatitis features nonspecific diffuse inflammation (T-cell infiltration) and hepatocyte necrosis. Chronic hepatitis C may be associated with periportal lymphoid aggregates, steatosis, and bile duct damage.

Treatment

Despite similarities in clinical and histopathologic characteristics, chronic viral hepatitis caused by HBV or HCV responds differently to therapy. IFN-α is the only effective treatment for both hepatitis C and B.

IFN-α induces the clearance of HBV by enhancing the host immune response. Of chronic hepatitis B cases, ~ 33% enter remission (negative HB_eAg) after a 4- to 6-month course of IFN. This therapy is indicated only when the patient has persistent elevations in aminotransferases, HB_eAg, and HBV DNA. Patients with normal aminotransferase levels respond poorly to IFN therapy (eg, Asian patients who acquired the disease in childhood). Liver biopsy is recommended before treatment to assess severity of fibrosis and cellular injury. IFN-α is administered over a 4- to 6-month course (Box 21–1). Patients with concomitant chronic HDV require higher and longer doses of IFN (9 million units thrice weekly for 12 months), which leads to a sustained response in only 15–25% of cases. In addition to IFN-α, long-term suppressive therapy with nucleoside analogs (eg, lamivudine) may prove to be beneficial in achieving sustained inhibition of HBV replication. Lamivudine is approved for treatment of chronic HBV with evidence of active replication (administered 100 mg orally daily for 1 year). However, long-term treatment may lead to the emergence of resistant mutant virus.

IFN-α is also recommended for patients with chronic HCV (Box 21–1). Therapy lasting 6 months may lead to remission of disease in 50% but a sustained response in only 10–25%. Long-term response is unlikely if HCV RNA is still detectable after 3 months of therapy. Ribavirin may prove to have long-term benefit when used initially in combination with IFN. Early studies showed that higher rates of remission are possible when ribavirin is used in combination with IFN-α. This has been confirmed in a recent double-blind, placebo-controlled trial from Sweden, show-

Table 21–4. Interpretation of serologic patterns in chronic viral hepatitis.[1]

HB_sAg	HB_cAb (IgG)	HB_eAg	HB_eAb	HBV DNA	HDV Ab	HCV Ab (IgG)	HCV RNA	Interpretation
+	+	+	−	+	−	−	−	Chronic HBV with high infectivity
+	+	−	+	+	−	−	−	Chronic HBV with low infectivity
−	+	−	+	−	−	−	−	Low-level HBV carrier (remote infection or response to treatment)
−	−	−	−	−	−	+	+	Chronic HCV
+	+	−	+	+	+	−	−	Superinfection of HDV on chronic HBV
−	+	−	−	−	−	+	+	Chronic HCV and distant acute HBV
−	−	−	−	−	−	+	−	False-positive HCV antibody or recovery after acute HCV

[1]Abbreviations: HB_sAg, hepatitis B surface antigen; HB_cAb, hepatitis B core antibody; HB_eAg, hepatis B_e antigen; HB_eAb, hepatis B_e antibody; HBV, hepatitis B virus; HDV Ab, hepatitis D virus antibody; HCV Ab, hepatitis C virus antibody; HCV, hepatitis C virus.

BOX 21–1

Use of Interferon-α in the Treatment of Chronic Hepatitis B and C[1]

	Chronic Hepatitis B	Chronic Hepatitis C[4]
Adults	5 million U SC daily, **OR** 10 million U SC three times weekly **OR** 30–35 million U SC weekly, for 16 weeks[2]	3 million U SC or IM three times weekly for 12 mos (interferon-α2a) or 18–24 mos (interferon-α2b)[2,3]
Children	5–6 million units/m^2/d IM or SC three times weekly for 3–6 mos	3 million U/m^2 SC three times weekly for 6 mos

[1]Abbreviations, SC, subcutaneously; IM, intramuscularly.
[2]A 50% dose reduction is recommended in patients who do not tolerate the initial dose.
[3]If there is no response after 12–16 weeks, discontinuation should be considered.
[4]In combination with ribavirin (600 mg orally twice a day if >75 kg weight, or 400 mg orally in the morning with 600 mg orally in the evening if ≤75 kg in weight).

ing that more patients have a sustained virologic response at 1 year after 24 weeks of therapy with combination IFN and ribavirin than IFN therapy alone. Combination of IFN and ribavirin is the therapy of choice for chronic HCV. A sustained virologic response rate of 40% is seen in patients treated with this combination for 48 weeks. This response rate is higher in patients with non-1 genotype or a low HCV viral load.

Prognosis

The exact frequency of progression of chronic hepatitis B to cirrhosis is unknown, but likely occurs in 10–50% of cases. HB$_s$Ag carriers have a 200-fold–higher relative risk of developing hepatocellular carcinoma than noncarriers. Chronic hepatitis C progresses to cirrhosis in 20–30% of cases, and the risk of developing hepatocellular carcinoma is higher than in HBV infection, occurring a mean of 30 years after initial HCV infection. Chronic hepatitis C has a better long-term response to IFN if HCV genotype 2 or 3 is present. In contrast, < 10% of HCV genotype 1 cases (80% of cases in the United States) respond to IFN.

GRANULOMATOUS HEPATITIS

Essentials of Diagnosis

- Fever and nonspecific liver test abnormalities.
- Constitutional symptoms or asymptomatic.
- Characteristic granulomas on liver biopsy histopathology.

General Considerations

Granulomas develop in the liver when the reticuloendothelial system is exposed to certain foreign antigens. They usually reflect a systemic disease process, whether being infectious or noninfectious in etiology. Granulomas are nodular infiltrates of epithelioid cells, which are transformed macrophages. The stimuli for such a transformation may include undegraded foreign matter (eg, mycobacterial products) or inflammatory mediators released by sensitized T cells. Triggered macrophages release interleukin-1 and other pyrogens that account for the fevers seen in this disease.

Infectious diseases are the most common cause of granulomatous hepatitis (Table 21–5), of which tuberculosis is the most common. The diagnosis of tuberculous granulomas is difficult, because *Mycobacterium tuberculosis* can cause either noncaseating or caseating hepatic granulomas, and the organism is demonstrated on staining or culture in < 50% of cases. Fungi are another common cause, with histoplasmosis being the most common fungal etiology of granulomatous hepatitis in the United States.

Clinical Findings

Fever is common, and granulomatous hepatitis may present as a fever of unknown origin. Clinical presentation varies from nonspecific hepatic biochemical abnormalities in asymptomatic individuals to vague abdominal pain, weight loss, and night sweats. Laboratory abnormalities are also nonspecific, however elevated alkaline phosphatase levels are common, and aminotransferase and erythrocyte sedimentation rate levels are variably elevated. Liver biopsy is essential for diagnosis to demonstrate the characteristic granulomas. This must be supplemented with specific stains (eg, acid-fast stains and silver staining), cultures (eg, for bacteria, fungi, and mycobacteria), and serum serologies (eg, for viral causes and Q fever) to diagnose the specific cause. Imaging is not helpful in the workup of granulomatous hepatitis.

Table 21–5. Systemic infections that can cause granulomatous hepatitis.

Bacterial
Tuberculosis
Atypical mycobacterial disease
Lepromatous leprosy
Brucellosis
Listeriosis
Bartonellosis
Secondary or tertiary syphilis
Tularemia
Rickettsial
Q fever
Viral
Cytomegalovirus infection
Infectious mononucleosis
Fungal
Histoplasmosis
Coccidioidomycosis
Candidiasis
Cryptococcosis
Parasitic
Schistosomiasis
Visceral larva migrans
Fascioliasis
Toxoplasmosis

Differential Diagnosis

This syndrome may be indistinguishable from hepatic granulomas caused by noninfectious diseases. Sarcoidosis and hypersensitivity drug reactions (eg, allopurinol, sulfonamides, and quinidine) are the most common, followed by chronic granulomatous disease of childhood, Hodgkin's disease, and other lymphomas. Of note, the cause remains unknown in ≤ 50% of cases in some series.

Treatment

Treatment of infectious causes of granulomatous hepatitis is directed toward the specific cause. Granulomas seem to resolve as the systemic infection clears. Corticosteroids have been shown to be efficacious in some cases of idiopathic granulomatous hepatitis. However, some experts recommend an empiric trial of two-drug antituberculous therapy before steroid administration, given the frequency of false-negative cultures for tuberculosis and the potential for disseminated tuberculosis with steroid therapy. Treatment response should be monitored by clinical parameters and repeat biopsy at 6–12 months.

HEPATIC ABSCESS

1. PYOGENIC LIVER ABSCESS

Essentials of Diagnosis

- Right upper quadrant abdominal pain.
- Fever, chills, and leukocytosis.
- Tender hepatomegaly.

- Intrahepatic lesion on hepatic imaging.
- Possible indolent course, with malaise and poorly localized abdominal pain.

General Considerations

Despite frequent exposure of the liver to bacteria in both the portal and systemic circulatory systems, the development of pyogenic liver abscesses is rather rare. The extensive network of reticuloendothelial cells in the hepatic sinusoids is highly protective. Hepatic abscess formation can occur when this defense system is overwhelmed, by bacterial invasion from either the biliary tree (eg, acute cholangitis), the portal vein (pyelephlebitis), the hepatic artery, direct trauma, or adjacent bacterial infection. The incidence of pyogenic liver abscess is ~ 15 cases/100,000 hospital admissions, and over one-third of such cases are secondary to direct extension from a biliary tract infection. Bacteria less commonly invade the liver from the portal system (eg, with appendicitis or IBS), systemic circulation (eg, *Staphylococcus aureus* abscesses in children), or penetrating trauma (eg, complication of ventriculoperitoneal shunt placement). Over half of liver abscesses are polymicrobic (Box 21–2), but a single organism may be involved in abscesses from a systemic source (eg, *Candida* spp. in neutropenic hosts). Either hepatic lobe may be involved; however, the right lobe is more commonly involved given its size and propensity to receive most portal blood flow. Abscesses may be single or multiple, ranging from widely scattered microabscesses (eg, in *S aureus* sepsis) to single large polymicrobic abscesses. Of pyogenic liver abscesses, ~ 15% have no known cause and are classified as cryptogenic.

Clinical Findings

A. Signs and symptoms. The patient may present with high fever, rigors, and severe right-sided abdominal pain. A more acute and severe clinical picture (with fever, jaundice, abdominal pain, and shock) may be seen with multiple abscesses, usually associated with acute cholangitis. However, up to half of cases may have chronic symptoms of malaise, fatigue, weight loss, and poorly localized pain that worsens with movement. If the abscess is adjacent to the liver capsule, referred right shoulder pain may occur, which may worsen with coughing. Breath sounds may be reduced over the right lung base secondary to an associated pleural effusion. Physical exam often reveals tender hepatomegaly, which is often accentuated by percussion over the surface of the liver.

B. Laboratory findings. Hepatic biochemical abnormalities are nonspecific, including a slightly elevated total bilirubin, elevated aminotransferases (two- to threefold), and hypoalbuminemia. Alkaline phosphatase and γ-glutamyl transferase levels may be elevated up to fivefold of normal values, especially

BOX 21-2

Microbiology of Pyogenic Liver Abscess

	Adults	Children
Most Common	Escherichia coli Klebsiella pneumoniae Proteus mirabilis Pseudomonas aeruginosa Streptococcus species (e.g. S milleri) Bacteroides fragilis Fusobacterium necrophorum Clostridium perfringens Peptostreptococci and microaerophilic streptococci	Staphylococcus aureus Escherichia coli Klebsiella pneumoniae Proteus mirabilis Fusobacterium necrophorum Bacteroides fragilis
Less Common	Salmonella typhi Staphylococcal species Yersinia enterocolitica Burkholderia pseudomallei Pasteurella multocida Listeria monocytogenes Candida species Mycobacterium tuberculosis (eg, miliary)	Candida albicans Salmonella typhi

when associated with biliary tract obstruction. Leukocytosis with a left shift is common, and anemia is often noted. Blood cultures may be positive in ≤ 50% of cases.

C. Imaging. Abdominal CT with contrast is the procedure of choice. It allows for the precise localization and visualization of small abscesses (< 1 cm); detects gas within abscesses in ≤ 30% of cases (which suggests that gas-producing bacteria are present); distinguishes tumors, cysts, and hematomas; defines other intraabdominal abnormalities; and allows for CT-guided aspiration of the abscess if indicated. Abscesses appear as well-defined hypodense lesions that enhance on CT with contrast; rim enhancement is relatively uncommon. Right-upper-quadrant ultrasonography is a rapid alternative and has 70–90% sensitivity for differentiating cystic vs solid intrahepatic lesions. As seen sonographically, an abscess may be a hypodense or hyperdense ill-defined lesion. Note that both imaging tests may be negative in identifying intrahepatic abscesses in the neutropenic host (eg, hepatic candidiasis).

Differential Diagnosis

The major diagnostic challenge is to distinguish pyogenic from amebic abscess, because treatment differs depending on the etiology. Amebic abscess may be suggested by a hepatic abscess in an immigrant or traveler from an endemic area, a young or previously healthy adult, or a positive enzyme-linked immunosorbent assay for E histolytica. Pyogenic abscess is suggested by a positive blood culture and the presence of associated biliary tract infection, underlying liver disease, or IBS. Tender hepatomegaly and liver lesions on imaging may also be seen with liver cysts, metastatic carcinoma, lymphoma, and infarction.

Treatment

Drainage of the abscess and IV administration of antibiotics are the mainstays of treatment. Drainage is often done via percutaneous catheter drainage or percutaneous needle aspiration, usually under CT or ultrasound guidance. Recently, percutaneous needle aspiration has been deemed as safe and effective as continuous catheter drainage; however, repeated aspirations may be necessary in ≤ 30%. Percutaneous drainage may not be necessary in cases with relatively small abscesses (< 5-cm diameter), and successful treatment may be achieved with antibiotics alone, depending on the clinical stability of the patient. Open abdominal surgery is reserved for cases that fail to respond to percutaneous drainage.

Initial antibiotic regimens should include metronidazole until amebic abscess is ruled out by serologies (Box 21–3). The antibiotics should cover the most common bacterial pathogens, including gram-negative bacilli and anaerobes. Ampicillin, an amino-

BOX 21-3

Empiric Therapy of Pyogenic Liver Abscess in Patients with Normal Renal Function

	Children	Adults
First Choice	• Nafcillin (100–200 mg/kg/d in 4 equal doses per 6 h) and gentamicin (2–2.5 mg/kg every 8 h) and metronidazole (30–50 mg/kg/d IV in 3 equal doses, per 8 h) • Metronidazole (30–50 mg/kg/d IV in 3 equal doses per 8 h) and third-generation cephalosporin (eg, cefta-zidime), 25–50 mg/kg IV per 8 h)	• Ampicillin (2 g every 6 h) and gentamicin (2 mg/kg load, then 1.7 mg/kg IV every 8 h) and metronidazole (1 g IV load, then 500 mg IV every 8 h) • Metronidazole (1 g IV load, then 500 mg IV every 8 h) and third-generation cephalosporin (eg, cefta-zidime, 2 g IV every 8 h) OR ticarcillin/clavulanate (3.1 g IV every 6 h) OR pipercillin/tazobactam 3.375 g IV every 6 h) OR ampicillin/sulbactam (3 g IV every 6 h)
Alternative	• Imipenem (15–25 mg/kg IV every 6 h) and metronidazole	• Imipenem (500 mg IV every 6 h) and metronidazole • Ciprofloxacin (400 mg IV every 12 h) and metroni-damycin (600–900 mg IV every 8 h)

glycoside, and metronidazole have been effective, although an increase in the incidence of ampicillin-resistant *Enterobacteriaceae* has been noted, and aminoglycoside nephrotoxicity is a serious limitation of this regimen. An alternative regimen is a third-generation cephalosporin plus metronidazole (or clindamycin if amebic abscess has been ruled out) or a β-lactam/β-lactamase inhibitor combination plus metronidazole. In patients with a history of recent exposure to third-generation cephalosporins and prolonged hospitalization, certain gram-negative bacilli (ie, *Serratia* spp., *Pseudomonas* spp., indole-positive *Proteus* spp., *Citrobacter* spp., *Enterobacter* spp., and *Acinetobacter* spp.) may have developed resistance to all cephalosporins and β-lactam/β-lactamase inhibitor combinations. Pending susceptibility studies, alternative regimens for these patients include a carbapenem, or a fourth-generation cephalosporin or ciprofloxacin plus clindamycin or metronidazole. (Fluoroquinolones are the antibiotics of choice in patients allergic to penicillin, and a combination of ciprofloxacin plus either clindamycin or metronidazole is a reliable alternative.) Antibiotics should be continued for a minimum of 6 weeks, usually to 12 weeks (2–3 weeks IV, followed by oral regimen). Some authors recommend treatment for ≤ 6 months if the abscess is streptococcal.

Prognosis

Despite aggressive treatment, the mortality ranges from 10–25%. An increase in mortality is noted in patients with multiple abscesses, increased age, and associated comorbid conditions. Morbidity and mortality may be caused by formation of portal or splenic thromboses, pleural or pericardial effusions, rupture into the pericardium, fistula formation, empyema, or sepsis.

2. AMEBIC ABSCESS

Essentials of Diagnosis

- Fever and right-upper-quadrant abdominal pain.
- Cystic lesion on abdominal imaging.
- Positive serology for antibody to *Entamoeba histolytica*.

General Considerations

E histolytica is endemic worldwide, with an estimated 10% of the world's population being infected. It is more prevalent in India, Africa, the Far East, and Central and South America, especially in areas with poor hygiene. Amebic liver abscess is the most common extraintestinal complication of amebiasis (occurring in 8.5% of cases). Hepatic infection occurs when trophozoites in the colon ascend in the portal system and invade the parenchyma. Subsequent ischemia and lysis of neutrophils with release of toxic products contribute to parenchymal destruction. Trophozoites advance away from the necrosis and are located in the outer edge of the abscess. The term abscess is actually a misnomer because the central necrosis contains proteinaceous material without neutrophils.

Clinical Findings

A. Signs and symptoms. Amebic abscesses may be difficult to distinguish from pyogenic abscesses. Patients with an amebic abscess are usually more acutely ill, with fever and abdominal pain for < 10-days duration. An indolent course is uncommon. Patients are also younger, usually from high-prevalence areas, or are recent travelers. If the pericardium is involved, the patient may present with chest pain or congestive heart failure, and a pericardial friction rub may be present. Dyspnea, cough, and pleuritic chest pain may be present when rupture into the pleural space occurs. Diarrhea is relatively uncommon, occurring in < 30% (despite the colon being the organism's point of entry). Jaundice and tender hepatomegaly are uncommon.

B. Laboratory findings. Aminotransferase levels are variable; however, alkaline phosphatase is usually elevated and albumin decreased. Leukocytosis without eosinophilia is common. The erythrocyte sedimentation rate may be elevated, and anemia may be present. Serum antibodies to amoebae via enzyme-linked immunosorbent assay or indirect hemagglutination assay are present in > 90% of cases. However, serology may be negative in acute disease (but positive on repeated testing in 7–10 days) and may be positive if the patient had amebiasis in the past (as the antibody levels may persist for years after acute infection).

C. Imaging. Both CT and ultrasonography are sensitive imaging studies for diagnosis of amebic abscess, but it is difficult to distinguish amebic abscesses from pyogenic abscesses or complex cysts. On sonography, the abscess usually appears as a round hypoechoic lesion near the liver capsule, with a paucity of significant wall echoes. CT with contrast may demonstrate a well-defined low attenuation lesion with a thick enhancing wall and surrounding zone of edema. Either CT or ultrasonography allows for percutaneous aspiration if pyogenic abscess needs to be ruled out. Of note, viable trophozoites are seen only in the periphery of the abscess. Fluid from the center of the abscess yields no organisms and varies in appearance, from yellow to reddish-brown ("anchovy paste").

Treatment

Because amebicidal therapy is highly effective, percutaneous aspiration is not necessary. Catheter drainage should be considered only when amebic serologies are negative, bacterial superinfection of an amebic abscess is suspected, or a left-hepatic-lobe abscess threatens rupture into the pericardium. Metronidazole is the drug of choice (Box 21–4). This must be followed by a luminal agent, as *E histolytica* is present in the colon previous to hepatic invasion. Luminal agents include diloxanide furoate, paromomycin, or diiodohydroxyquin. Symptoms usually respond in 3 days. If no improvement occurs after 3 days of treatment, consider percutaneous aspiration of the abscess to rule out a bacterial process.

Prognosis

Mortality caused by uncomplicated amebic abscess is < 1%. Mortality is higher if the abscess ruptures into the peritoneum, pleural space, or pericardium. Cure of the amebic abscess apparently results in immunity, because recurrence in patients with positive amebic antibodies is extremely rare.

LIVER INFECTIONS IN PATIENTS WITH HIV

General Considerations

The majority of patients with AIDS have abnormalities on hepatic biochemical tests at some point in their illness. Opportunistic infections and neoplasms affect the liver in ≤ 80% of patients with AIDS in autopsy studies. The types of hepatic disease in HIV infection vary (Table 21–6). Acute hepatocellular damage is usually caused by viruses (eg, the hepatitis viruses, CMV, Epstein-Barr virus, herpes simplex virus, and HIV itself) or hepatotoxic drugs (eg, azidothymidine, dideoxyinosine, isoniazid, rifampin, ritonavir, or trimethoprim-sulfamethoxazole). The most common viral cause of hepatitis in HIV is HBV, and 20% of persons who are HIV-positive become chronic carriers (in contrast to 5% of HIV-negative adults). Granulomatous hepatitis is one of the most

BOX 21–4

Treatment of Amebic Liver Abscess		
	Children	Adults
Amebicidal Agent	Metronidazole, 35–50 mg/kg/d to max 2250 mg/d per mouth in three divided doses for 10 days	Metronidazole 750 mg by mouth three times daily OR 500 mg IV every 6 h for 10 days
Luminal Agent	Diloxanide furoate, 20 mg/kg/d in three divided doses for 10 days OR Paromomycin, 25–35 mg/kg/d in three divided doses for 10 days, OR Diiodohydroxyquin, 30–40 mg/kg/d to max 1950 mg in three divided doses for 20 days	Diloxanide furoate, 500 mg by mouth three times daily for 10 days, OR Paromomycin, 30 mg/kg/d by mouth in three divided doses for 10 days OR Diiodohydroxyquin, 650 mg by mouth three times daily for 20 days

Table 21–6. Opportunistic hepatic infections in AIDS.

Liver Pathology	Microorganisms
Granulomas	• Mycobacteria (eg, *M avium* complex and *M tuberculosis*) • Fungi (*Cryptococcus, Histoplasma, Pneumocystis carinii*)
Pyogenic abscess	• Enteric gram-negative bacilli, staphylococci, streptococci, *Listeria monocytogenes*
Vascular lesions	• Human herpesvirus 8 (Kaposi's sarcoma) • *Bartonella henselae* (peliosis hepatis)
Hepatitis	• Hepatitis viruses, cytomegalovirus, herpes simplex virus, HIV
Lymphomatous infiltrates	• Epstein Barr virus (associated B-cell lymphoma)

common presentations of hepatic infection in HIV patients, usually secondary to mycobacterial disease (eg, *Mycobacterium avium* complex), fungi (eg, disseminated histoplasmosis), or protozoa (eg, *Pneumocystis carinii* infection in patients receiving aerosolized pentamidine prophylaxis). Mass lesions are most commonly neoplastic. Vascular lesions may be caused by peliosis hepatis (*Bartonella henselae* infection) or Kaposi's sarcoma.

Clinical Findings

Liver disease in HIV patients has an extremely variable presentation depending on the cause. Patients may be asymptomatic or have a fever of unknown origin (eg, in granulomatous hepatitis). Fever and right-upper-quadrant abdominal pain are common in acute viral hepatitis from any cause. Liver infection may be heralded as weight loss and hepatomegaly (eg, in peliosis hepatis). Jaundice is relatively uncommon and, when present, is usually caused by drug-induced hepatotoxicity (eg, with isonicotinic acid hydrazide or trimethoprim-sulfamethoxazole). Extrahepatic findings on exam may give clues to the diagnosis, eg, the presence of concomitant cutaneous lesions (in Kaposi's sarcoma or bartonellosis) or pulmonary tuberculosis. Hepatic biochemical tests are almost always abnormal, however, in nonspecific patterns. CD4 cell counts may aid in the differential diagnosis. For example, tuberculosis, Kaposi's sarcoma, and acute viral hepatitis are possible at any time in the course of disease, even with a normal CD4 count. Patients with CD4 < 100/mm^3 are more susceptible to such infections as *M avium* complex and CMV.

Diagnostic Approach

A detailed history and physical are imperative and should focus on previous opportunistic infections, hepatotoxic medications, alcohol use, and recent travel. Hepatic biochemical testing is usually not helpful in diagnosis. Evidence for hepatocellular damage warrants further serologic testing, such as hepatitis viral

serologies, and a trial of cessation of potentially toxic medications. If workup remains negative, consider liver biopsy. If a cholestatic pattern predominates on biochemical testing, imaging can be used to search for focal lesions or dilated biliary ducts. Consider ERCP in patients who present with fevers, jaundice, and abdominal pain or who have dilated biliary ducts on imaging, for potential biliary drainage, cultures, and biopsy specimens for further testing. Patients with HIV usually have histopathologic abnormalities on liver biopsy. About one-third of biopsy specimens yield nonspecific findings, however liver biopsy remains the most specific diagnostic tool for effective diagnosis of liver infection in HIV.

INFECTIONS OF THE BILIARY TRACT

ACUTE CALCULOUS CHOLECYSTITIS

Essentials of Diagnosis
• Severe abdominal pain and tenderness localized to the right upper quadrant.
• Nausea and vomiting.
• Fever and leukocytosis.

General Considerations

Acute calculous cholecystitis, associated with cholelithiasis, accounts for > 90% of cases of cholecystitis. This severe inflammation of the gallbladder wall results from stasis of bile secondary to an obstructed gallbladder infundibulum or cystic duct by a stone. Obstructed bile and the associated increase in pressure lead to damage of the gallbladder mucosa and the release of inflammatory mediators. Bacteria may be present in the inflamed gallbladder in up to half of cases, but they likely play a secondary role in the inflammatory process. Distention and edema of the gallbladder wall may lead to ischemia, with resulting gangrene, empyema, or perforation. Cholecystitis in children usually results from pigment stones that develop in hemolytic disease.

Clinical Findings
A. Signs and symptoms. Patients may have had previous episodes of biliary colic associated with cholelithiasis, but acute cholecystitis is heralded by severe and sustained pain that is more localized to the right upper quadrant. Children may have periumbilical, back, or poorly localized abdominal pain. Nausea, emesis, and fever are common. On exam, right-upper-quadrant tenderness is invariably present and may be associated with guarding and rebound caused by peritoneal irritation. Murphy's sign may be present, characterized by sudden cessation of inspiration

secondary to severe tenderness during right upper quadrant palpation. Approximately 20% of cases have jaundice, and 20% have a palpable mass in the right upper quadrant secondary to irritated omentum overlying the inflamed gallbladder.

B. Laboratory findings. The leukocyte count is usually high, with an associated bandemia. The total bilirubin may be elevated; however, the level rarely rises above 4 mg/dL. Mild elevations in alkaline phosphatase and aminotransferase levels are also present.

C. Imaging. Abdominal ultrasound is the test of choice. It has 88–94% sensitivity and 78–80% specificity for detecting acute cholecystitis, suggested by a thickened gallbladder wall (> 5 mm), positive sonographic Murphy's sign, and the presence of pericholic fluid. Hepatobiliary imaging with ^{99m}Tc (eg, dimethyl iminodiacetic acid scan) may be useful in detecting an obstructed cystic duct, which is often the precipitating event in acute cholecystitis. The test is reliable when the total bilirubin is < 5 mg/dL, and is 98% sensitive and 81% specific for acute cholecystitis. However, biliary scintigraphy is more time consuming, involves injection of radiopharmaceuticals, and does not allow for imaging of the gall bladder and surrounding structures. Plain films of the abdomen may show radiopaque gallstones (≤ 15% of cases); however, they are not helpful in the diagnosis of acute cholecystitis.

Differential Diagnosis

Fever, nausea, vomiting, and right-upper-quadrant abdominal pain may be present in a number of other disorders, such as acute hepatitis, liver abscess, acute pancreatitis, perforated peptic ulcer, right-lower-lobe pneumonia with associated pleurisy, and appendicitis (especially in pregnancy). Definite localization of tenderness over a palpable gallbladder with radiation of pain to the right scapular area strongly supports the diagnosis of acute cholecystitis.

Complications

Perforation of the gallbladder may occur, especially if gangrene develops from progressive ischemia and gas-forming bacteria, including *Escherichia coli* in diabetic patients and *Clostridium perfringens* in emphysematons cholecystitis. This syndrome is more common in males and diabetics, and ~ 30% of cases are associated with acalculous cholecystitis. Empyema may result from bacterial invasion of the gallbladder wall, usually involving enteric gram-negative bacilli and anaerobes. Treatment is essentially the same as for acute cholecystitis; however, urgent surgical treatment is usually indicated in patients with empyema. Repeated episodes of acute calculous cholecystitis or chronic irritation of the gall bladder wall by stones may lead to chronic cholecystitis. Cholangitis and pancreatitis are potential complications if gallstones migrate and obstruct the common bile duct or pancreatic duct.

Treatment

In most cases, acute calculous cholecystitis will subside with conservative therapy alone. Bowel rest should be instituted and IV fluids administered. Antibiotics are most likely required in such clinical settings as sepsis, empyema, emphysematous cholecystitis, and cholangitis. In these patients, antibiotic options include a β-lactam/β-lactamase inhibitor, a carbapenem, ciprofloxacin plus metronidazole or clindamycin, or trovafloxacin. Ampicillin should be used with caution, given recent emergence of ampicillin-resistant *E coli* in community-acquired infections with this organism. If urgent cholecystectomy is considered, prophylactic antibiotics may be administered perioperatively; regimens include a second-generation cephalosporin with moderate anaerobic activity, such as cefoxitin or cefotetan.

Laparoscopic cholecystectomy is now considered the procedure of choice for removal of the gallbladder. Cholecystectomy is mandatory if there is evidence of emphysematous cholecystitis or perforation.

ACUTE ACALCULOUS CHOLECYSTITIS

General Considerations

Acute acalculous cholecystitis is infection of the gallbladder in the absence of gallstones. It is less common than gallstone-associated disease (2–12% of cases of acute cholecystitis); however it is much more serious. Gangrene of the gallbladder is 30-fold more common than in calculous cholecystitis, and perforation is ~ 5-fold more common, which leads to a higher mortality (≥ 67% mortality, in contrast to 3%). Patients with this syndrome are usually elderly or seriously ill and include patients with severe burns and trauma, patients who are recuperating from major surgery, or those receiving intensive care and parenteral nutrition. Comorbid conditions with higher risk of developing acalculous cholecystitis include cardiovascular disease, diabetes mellitus, systemic arteritis (eg, polyarteritis nodosa), and immunocompromise (eg, AIDS). The pathophysiology is poorly understood, but may be associated with bile stasis and gallbladder dysfunction. Bile stasis and paucity of gallbladder contractions may occur in critically ill patients and patients who receive parenteral nutrition. The retained bile may lead to gallbladder wall inflammation and ischemia, with subsequent microbial invasion of the gallbladder mucosa. In immunocompetent patients, the most common offending microorganisms include gram-negative bacilli and anaerobes. In immunocompromised patients including patients with AIDS (particularly in those who have not yet received benefit from highly active antiretroviral therapy), organisms include CMV, *Cryptosporidium* spp., microsporidia, *Isospora* spp., *Salmonella* spp., and *Campylobacter* spp.

Clinical Findings

A. Signs and symptoms. Acute acalculous cholecystitis is often clinically indistinguishable from calculous cholecystitis, with fever, right upper abdominal pain and tenderness, nausea, vomiting, and anorexia. This syndrome is extremely difficult to diagnose, because many patients are critically ill with vague, generalized complaints or are unable to provide a history given sedation or mechanical ventilation in an intensive care unit.

B. Laboratory findings. Leukocytosis, hyperbilirubinemia, and mild elevations in aminotransferase levels are common.

C. Imaging. As in acute calculous cholecystitis, abdominal ultrasound often reveals a thickened gallbladder wall, distention, subserosal edema, and pericholic fluid. The sensitivity and specificity of abdominal CT may approach 100% in detecting this disease.

Treatment

Removal of the infected gallbladder and administration of antibiotics are imperative. IV fluids and antibiotics should be started promptly. Antibiotics should cover gram-negative bacilli and anaerobes (see treatment of acute cholangitis).

ACUTE CHOLANGITIS

Essentials of Diagnosis
- Fever, jaundice, and leukocytosis.
- Severe right-upper-quadrant abdominal pain.
- Nausea and vomiting.
- Possible progression to hypothermia, hypotension, and altered mental status.

General Considerations

First described by Charcot in 1877, acute cholangitis is acute biliary infection superimposed on an obstructed biliary tree. Bile is normally sterile, because of constant bile flow into the duodenum and the presence of secretory IgA in the biliary tract. However, in the presence of obstruction, bile under pressure may be infected by ascending bacteria in the common bile duct from the gut or from the portal or systemic circulation (Box 21–5). Obstruction of the common bile duct is primarily from stones ($\leq$ 80% of cases), which usually arise from the gallbladder but may spontaneously form in the bile duct (eg, postcholecystectomy). Obstruction may also be secondary to carcinoma of the common bile duct or adjacent pancreas, biliary stricture, or sclerosing cholangitis. In children, acute cholangitis occurs in the presence of ductal abnormalities or immunocompromise. It is most often a complication of the Kasai procedure for biliary atresia, which establishes biliary drainage via a Roux-en-Y connection to the porta hepatis. Cholangitis results from the removal of the protective sphincter of Oddi during the procedure and ascension of bacteria from the jejunal limb.

This syndrome may range from an acute ascending cholangitis, associated with incomplete common bile duct obstruction and ascending bacteria from the duodenum, to acute obstructive suppurative cholangitis, which features complete bile duct obstruction,

BOX 21–5

Microbiology of Cholangitis

	Children	Adults
More Common	Escherichia coli Klebsiella pneumoniae Proteus mirabilis Enterococcus faecalis Pseudomonas aeruginosa Enterobacteriaceae Bacteroides fragilis Clostridium perfringens	Escherichia coli Klebsiella pneumoniae Pseudomonas aeruginosa Proteus mirabilis Enterococcus faecalis Viridans streptococci Bacteroides fragilis Clostridium perfringens
Less Common	Viridans streptococci Serratia spp. Haemophilus influenzae Candida albicans Cryptococcus neoformans Clonorchis sinensis Echinococcus granulosus	Enterobacteriaceae Serratia spp. Morganella morgani Aeromonas spp. Pseudomonas maltophila Citrobacter freundii Peptostreptococci Fusobacterium spp.

pus in the biliary tree, and potential for progression to sepsis and intrahepatic abscess formation.

Clinical Findings

A. Signs and symptoms. A previous history of biliary colic with jaundice may be present. The classic triad of fever, jaundice, and right-upper-quadrant pain, known as Charcot's triad, is present in only 20–70% of cases. Patients with acute obstructive suppurative cholangitis may present with septic shock, including altered mental status and hypotension (which, along with the classic triad, make up Reynolds pentad). Children infrequently present in septic shock, and fever may be their only symptom. Hepatomegaly is variably palpable in association with biliary obstruction; however, right-upper-quadrant and epigastric pain is usually present on exam.

B. Laboratory findings. Most patients have elevated leukocyte counts, hyperbilirubinemia, and elevated alkaline phosphatase levels. Serum aminotransferase levels are often elevated, although to a lesser degree (only severalfold). Up to one-third of cases have elevated serum amylase caused by concomitant obstruction of the pancreatic duct; 10% of cases have clinical evidence of gallstone pancreatitis.

C. Imaging. Both abdominal ultrasonography and CT may demonstrate dilated biliary ducts, but CT scan is more effective in demonstrating both the cause (70% vs 38%) and the level (88% vs 60%) of the obstruction. Cholangiography via PTC or ERCP provides the most accurate means of determining the cause and location of the obstruction. If choledocholithiasis is suspected, ERCP is the procedure of choice because it allows for papillotomy or papillary dilation with stone extraction or stent placement.

Differential Diagnosis

Fever, jaundice, right-upper-quadrant pain, and abnormal liver tests can also be seen in acute viral hepatitis (often with higher aminotransferase levels and lower total bilirubin), acute common bile duct obstruction, sepsis-associated cholestasis, liver abscess (jaundice less common), and sclerosis cholangitis (fever is uncommon). Biliary tract imaging or liver biopsy may be required to distinguish between an obstructive process and hepatocellular damage.

Complications

Prolonged, untreated obstructive jaundice may lead to hepatocellular damage and possible cirrhosis. Hypoprothrombinemia may predispose the patient to excessive bleeding. In contrast to hypoprothrombinemia in hepatocellular disease, prolonged prothrombin times associated with obstructive jaundice may be corrected with daily intake of vitamin K.

Treatment

Antibiotics and biliary drainage are the mainstays of treatment, because acute cholangitis is invariably fatal without urgent decompression of the biliary tree. Before drainage, IV fluid resuscitation and IV vitamin K (if elevated prothrombin time) should be administered. The empiric antibiotic regimen of choice should have broad-spectrum coverage of enteric gram-negative bacilli, however it is controversial whether gram-positive cocci and anaerobes should be covered in the empiric regimen (Box 21–6). No studies have shown a particular antibiotic regimen superior over others. Combinations of antibiotics include a 7- to 10-day course of a β-lactam/β-lactamase inhibitor, an amino penicillin with an aminoglycoside and metronidazole, a second-generation cephalosporin with antianaerobic activity, a third-generation cephalosporin plus metronidazole or clindamycin, or a ureidopenicillin plus either metronidazole or clindamycin. Ciprofloxacin plus metronidazole, or clindamycin, or imipenem, appear to be promising alternatives. Aminoglycosides must be used with caution (especially after the fifth day of use), given their potential for nephrotoxicity. Ampicillin should be used with caution given the recent emergence of ampicillin-resistant *E coli* in community acquired infections caused by this organism. Prolonged therapy with ceftriaxone should be avoided given its propensity to form biliary sludge.

Of cases of acute cholangitis, ≤ 75% initially respond to IV fluids and antibiotics, allowing for a small delay in biliary drainage. However, biliary decompression with drainage of the obstructed biliary tree is crucial in the management of this syndrome in severely ill patients. Classically, common bile duct exploration and placement of a T-tube were the procedures of choice. Now drainage can be accomplished with either PTC or ERCP during the diagnostic workup of these patients. They are both associated with less morbidity (34% vs 66%) and mortality (10% vs 33%) than open abdominal surgery, although PTC is associated with significant bleeding in the context of liver dysfunction. ERCP is usually more appropriate, as it allows for stone extraction or placement of a biliary stent during the procedure. After decompression of the biliary tree, antibiotics should be continued until there is full resolution of symptoms or for 7–10 days of therapy. Longer courses are advocated for refractory or recurrent disease. In children with post-Kasai procedure cholangitis, many support the use of long-term prophylaxis with trimethoprim-sulfamethoxazole (20 mg/kg/d of trimethoprim).

Prognosis

With appropriate treatment, mortality from acute cholangitis is < 10%. Mortality rates are higher in those with acute obstructive suppurative cholangitis, sepsis, and severe underlying disease. Clinical factors associated with poorer prognosis include old age, female sex, evidence of acute renal failure, concomitant liver abscess or cirrhosis, and malignant biliary

BOX 21-6

Empiric Therapy of Acute Cholangitis in Patients with Normal Renal Function

	Children	Adults
First Choice	• Ampicillin/sulbactam (300 mg/kg/d IV divided every 6 h) or ticarcillin/clavulanate (300 mg of ticarcillin/kg/d IV divided every 4 h) • Ampicillin (50–100 mg/kg/d IV divided every 6 h), gentamicin (2–2.5 mg/kg IV every 8 h), and metronidazole (30–50 mg/kg/d IV divided every 8h)	• Pipercillin/tazobactam (3.375 g IV every 6 h) OR ampicillin/sulbactam (3 g IV every 6 h), OR ticarcillin/clavulanate (3.1 g IV every 6 h) • Pipercillin or ticarcillin (4 g IV every 6 h) and metronidazole (1 g IV load, then 500 mg IV every 6 h) • Ampicillin (2 g IV every 6 h), gentamicin (2 mg/kg, load then 1.7 mg/kg IV every 8 h) and metronidazole (1 g IV load, then 500 mg IV every 8 h)
Alternative	• Third-generation cephalosporin (eg, cefoperazone, 100–150 mg/kg/d IV divided per 12 h, OR ceftazidime, 25–50 mg/kg IV every 8 h) and metronidazole (30–50 mg/kg/d IV divided every 8 h) • Imipenem (15–25 mg/kg IV every 6 h)	• Third-generation cephalosporin (eg, cefoperazone 2–4 g IV every 12 h OR ceftazidime, 2 g IV every 8 h) and metronidazole (1 g IV load, then 500 mg IV every 8 h) • Imipenem (500 mg IV every 6 h)
Penicillin Allergic	• Aztreonam (30 mg/kg IV every 8 h) and metronidazole	• Aztreonam (2 g IV every 8 h) and metronidazole • Clindamycin (400 mg IV every 12 h) and metronidazole (above doses) or clindamycin (600–900 mg IV every 8 h)

tract obstruction. Acidosis (pH < 7.4), hyperbilirubinemia (total bilirubin > 90 mmol/L), hypoalbuminemia (albumin < 30 g/L), and thrombocytopenia (platelet count < 150) also predicted poorer outcome.

In children, the incidence of cholangitis after the Kasai procedure is highest in the first postoperative year (43–78%). This incidence is significantly lower if an intussusception valve is designed at the site of the jejunostomy. Each episode of postoperative cholangitis carries a 1% mortality rate in these patients.

RECURRENT PYOGENIC CHOLANGITIS

Also known as oriental cholangiohepatitis, recurrent pyogenic cholangitis is characterized by recurrent attacks of suppurative cholangitis. It is endemic in Southeast Asia and may be seen in Asian immigrants. The bile duct infections are caused by gram-negative bacilli and less commonly anaerobes (Box 21–5) via transient portal bacteremia, in the context of bile stasis and ductal epithelium damage. The recurrent infections lead to the formation of large, muddy-brown pigment stones within the ducts. The initial damage to bile duct epithelium may be secondary to parasitic infection (eg, *Clonorchis sinensis, Opisthorchis* spp., or *Ascaris lumbricoides*) or a low-protein diet (leading to pigment stone formation), both common in Southeast Asia. The biliary damage is usually localized to the left hepatic lobe.

This syndrome peaks in 30- to 40-year-olds. Patients may have a history of recurrent attacks of acute cholangitis. Clinically, recurrent pyogenic cholangitis is indistinguishable from acute cholangitis. Abdominal CT is the imaging test of choice, which identifies the characteristic dilated central intrahepatic ducts that taper peripherally, often localized to the left hepatic lobe. As in acute cholangitis, ERCP can be used to visualize the biliary tree and allow for drainage. Treatment includes prompt administration of broad-spectrum antibiotics and IV fluids. Drainage may be needed in the 15% of cases that fail antibiotic therapy. Removal of pigment stones and relieving biliary strictures may help prevent future attacks.

SCLEROSING CHOLANGITIS

Primary sclerosing cholangitis is a cholestatic disease of unknown etiology, featuring chronic inflammation and scarring of the intra- and extrahepatic bile ducts. Although the cause is unknown, recurrent damage of the bile ducts has been a proposed mechanism, possibly from chronic portal bacteremia (eg, in IBS), toxins from enteric flora, chronic viral infections, or ischemic damage. It is more common in men aged 20–40 years and often occurs in patients with IBS. Cholangiography reveals a characteristic beaded appearance to the biliary tree, secondary to focal areas of ductal dilatation proximal to strictures. There is no effective treatment to date. Survival is improved with liver transplantation.

In contrast, secondary sclerosing cholangitis occurs as a known complication of obstructive cholangitis (eg, choledocholithiasis), toxic damage to the biliary tract (eg, intraductal formaldehyde during echinococcal cyst extirpation), ischemia (eg, vasculitis), or a neoplastic process (eg, cholangiocarcinoma). Obstructive cholangitis may be seen with a number of different infections, including *A lumbricoides,* recurrent pyogenic cholangitis, or *Cryptococcus neoformans.* Clinical presentation is similar to that of primary sclerosing cholangitis, including jaundice, pruritus, and right-upper-quadrant abdominal pain. Fever and weight loss are less common. A history of recurrent bouts of ascending cholangitis may be elicited. Cholangiography often shows focal strictures and dilated ducts, in contrast to the more uniform involvement of the biliary tree in primary sclerosing cholangitis. Treatment of recurrent episodes of cholangitis is similar to that of acute cholangitis, namely IV fluids, antibiotics directed against the specific pathogen, and biliary drainage. Pruritus is treated symptomatically, usually with topical emollients, antihistamines, or cholestyramine. Focal biliary strictures can be treated with endoscopic dilation or stent placement.

AIDS-RELATED CHOLANGITIS

AIDS-related cholangitis is a form of secondary cholangitis caused by opportunistic infections in late-stage AIDS. It was first discovered to be caused by *Cryptosporidium* spp. and CMV in the mid 1980s, and later found to be also associated with microsporidia, *Isospora* spp., *M avium* complex, and human herpes virus 8. Portal tract invasion by these pathogens leads to bile duct injury and ischemia, with subsequent scarring of the biliary tract. Such organisms may also contribute to sphincter of Oddi dysfunction and development of papillary stenosis, which is seen in $\leq 70\%$ of cases.

Clinically, patients present with right-upper-quadrant pain and fever; however, jaundice is distinctly less common than in acute cholangitis (10% of cases). Nausea, vomiting, weight loss, and diarrhea are common. Patients typically have elevated alkaline phosphatase, mildly elevated aminotransferases, and CD4 cell count $< 100/mm^3$. Stool cultures may be positive for *Cryptosporidium,* and bile culture obtained during ERCP may grow microsporidia. Definitive diagnosis is via biopsy of the involved tissue. ERCP is the procedure of choice for cholangiography, biopsies, and possible sphincterotomy if papillary stenosis is present.

There is no effective treatment for this condition. The course of cholangitis is not significantly influenced by therapy directed at specific pathogens, including ganciclovir, foscarnet, paromomycin, or azithromycin. Pain management is imperative, and ursodeoxycholic acid may improve pain and cholestasis in some patients. Prognosis is poor with a median survival of 7 months after diagnosis. Death is usually secondary to another opportunistic process in late-stage AIDS.

REFERENCES

Infections Of The Liver

Cheney CP, Chopra S, Graham C: Hepatitis C. Infect Dis Clinics NA 2000;14:633 (Excellent comprehensive review of HCV.)

Chu KM et al: Pyogenic liver abscess. An audit of experience over the past decade. Arch Surgery 1996;131:148 (Retrospective study of 83 patients hospitalized in Hong Kong with pyogenic liver abscesses, showing the in-hospital mortality rate is distressingly high [18%] despite aggressive drainage and antibiotic therapy.)

Fauci AS, Hoffman GS: Granulomatous hepatitis. In Mandell GL et al: *Mandell, Douglas, and Bennett's Principles and Practice of Infectious Diseases,* 4th ed. Churchill Livingstone, 1995 (Reviews the pathogenesis and diagnostic approach to both infectious and noninfectious causes of granulomatous hepatitis.)

Herlong HF: Approach to the patient with infection of the liver. In Gorbach SL et al: *Infectious Diseases,* 1st ed. Saunders, 1992 (Discusses the differential diagnosis of liver infection in patients with either abnormal liver tests or focal hepatic lesions.)

Hoofnagle JH, DiBisceglie AM: The treatment of chronic viral hepatitis. N Engl J Med 1997;336:347 (Focuses on the role of IFN in chronic hepatitis B and hepatitis C.)

Kamath PS: Clinical approach to the patient with abnormal liver test results. Mayo Clin Proc 1996;71:1089 (Describes each serum liver test and differentiates hepatocellular vs cholestatic diseases on liver testing.)

Lee WM: Hepatitis B virus infection. N Engl J Med 1997;337:1733 (Detailed review of the epidemiology, virology, clinical course, and management of HBV.)

Lemon SM: Type A viral hepatitis. In Gorbach SL et al: *Infectious Diseases,* 1st ed. Saunders, 1992 (Overview of the virology, epidemiology, pathogenesis, and clinical manifestations of HAV.)

Lemon SM, Thomas DL: Vaccines to prevent viral hepatitis. N Engl J Med 1997;336:196 (Reviews the efficacy of and indications for the hepatitis A and B vaccines.)

Nevens F et al: Lamivudine therapy for chronic hepatitis B: a six-month randomized dose-ranging study. Gastroenterology 1997;113:1258 (51 patients with chronic hepatitis B were randomized to 3 different doses of lamivudine for 6 months treatment. Lamivudine [maximal effect at 100 mg/d] was well tolerated and induced sustained viral replication for 24 weeks.)

Poles MA, Lew EA, Dieterich DT: Diagnosis and treatment of hepatic disease in patients with HIV. Gastroenterol Clin North Am 1997;26:291 (Reviews the wide spectrum of hepatic disease in AIDS including infections and neoplasms, stressing the diagnostic approach.)

Ralls PW: Focal inflammatory disease of the liver. Radiol Clin North Am 1998;36:377 (Reviews hepatic imaging and image-guided intervention and their role in amebic, pyogenic, and echinococcal liver infections.)

Ravdin JI: Amebiasis. Clin Infect Dis 1995;20:1453 (Excellent review of the epidemiology, pathogenesis, and treatment of amebiasis and amebic liver abscess.)

Reichard O et al: Randomised, double-blind, placebo-controlled trial of interferon α-2b with and without ribavirin for chronic hepatitis C. The Swedish study group. Lancet 1998;351:83 (Ribavirin plus IFN combination therapy resulted in significantly more sustained virologic responses than IFN alone [36% vs 18% at 24 weeks follow-up] in patients with high baseline HCV RNA levels.)

Saini S: Imaging of the hepatobiliary tract. N Engl J Med 1997;336:1889 (Reviews imaging studies of choice for various hepatic disease processes.)

Schalm SW et al: Ribavirin enhances the efficacy but not the adverse effects of interferon in chronic hepatitis C. Meta-analysis of individual patient data from European centers. J Hepatol 1997;26:961 (This meta-analysis of 186 patients showed that sustained normalization of alanine aminotransferase and HCV RNA negativity was significantly higher in IFN plus ribavirin combination therapy than either monotherapy, without an increase in toxicity.)

Yu SC et al: Pyogenic liver abscess: treatment with needle aspiration. Clin Radiol 1997;52:912 (Authors report their experience in the aspiration of 101 liver abscesses and suggest this method may be as safe and effective as continuous catheter drainage.)

Infections Of The Biliary Tract

Bass NM: Sclerosing cholangitis and recurrent pyogenic cholangitis. In Feldman M et al: *Sleisenger and Fordtran's Gastrointestinal and Liver Disease,* 6th ed. Saunders, 1998 (Detailed overview of both primary and secondary sclerosing cholangitis.)

Lai FCS et al: Endoscopic biliary drainage for severe acute cholangitis. N Engl J Med 1992;362:1582 (Eighty-two patients with acute cholangitis associated with choledocholithiasis were randomized to surgical or endoscopic biliary drainage. The latter was as effective and associated with lower mortality [10 vs 32%] than surgery.)

Lee DWH, Chung SCS: Biliary infection. Baillieres Clin Gastroenterol 1997;11:707 (Reviews the pathophysiology and clinical features of cholangitis, stressing the importance of collaboration between surgeons, endoscopists, and radiologists in its management.)

Nash JA, Cohen SA: Gallbladder and biliary tract disease in AIDS. Gastroenterol Clin North Am 1997;26:323 (A comprehensive review stressing that 75% of patients with this syndrome can be diagnosed with a causative opportunistic infection.)

Scheimann AO, Ferry GD, Aach RD: Cholangitis and cholecystitis. In Feigin RD, Cherry JD: *Textbook of Pediatric Infectious Diseases,* 4th ed. Saunders, 1998 (Overview of biliary tract infections in children.)

Strasberg SM: Cholelithiasis and acute cholecystitis. Baillieres Clin Gastroenterol 1997;11:643 (Comprehensive review focusing on pathogenesis and management of cholelithiasis and acute calculous cholecystitis.)

Van den Hazel SJ et al: Role of antibiotics in the treatment and prevention of acute and recurrent cholangitis. *Clin Infect Dis* 1994;19:279 (This review stresses the importance of antibiotics in acute and recurrent cholangitis, including preferred regimens for treatment, prevention, and maintenance therapy.)

Obstetric & Gynecologic Infections   **22**

Yenjean S. Hwang, MD & Merle A. Sande, MD

GYNECOLOGIC INFECTIONS

VULVOVAGINITIS

Essentials of Diagnosis

- Risk factors: use of antibiotics, elevated levels of estrogen, sexually active lifestyle, history of sexually transmitted diseases.
- Vulvar irritation, dysuria, vaginal discharge with or without odor, labial erythema.
- Change in vaginal pH.
- Microscopic examination of vaginal secretions may show characteristic yeast forms, clue cells, or trichomonads.

General Considerations

Vulvovaginitis is an extremely common syndrome; one study found that vulvovaginitis was diagnosed in more than 25% of the women attending sexually transmitted diseases clinics. It is estimated that 75% of all women experience at least one episode of vulvovaginal candidiasis in their lifetime. The organisms that cause vulvovaginitis cause very similar symptoms, so that a specific diagnosis cannot be made on symptoms alone (Table 22–1).

The most common infectious agents that cause vulvovaginitis are *Candida albicans* and other *Candida* species, *Trichomonas vaginalis* (which is discussed in Chapter 15), and agents involved in bacterial vaginosis (BV) (Box 22–1). Other etiologic agents include *Staphylococcus aureus,* herpes simplex virus (HSV), and papillomavirus. Much rarer agents, seen mainly in immunocompromised patients, include *M tuberculosis, Salmonellae, Enterobacteriaceae,* actinomycetes, and schistosomes. Noninfectious vaginitis can be caused by a foreign body, a genital neoplasm, estrogen deficiency in postmenopausal women leading to atrophic vaginitis, chemical vaginitis, and allergic reactions. Lichen planus can cause desquamative vaginitis, and fixed-drug eruptions can cause lesions in the genital area. This section will focus on candidal vaginitis, trichomonal vaginitis, and BV.

Vulvovaginal candidiasis accounts for approximately one-third of all cases of vulvovaginitis. *Candida albicans* probably accounts for 80–90% of cases of vulvovaginal candidiasis. *Candida tropicalis* accounts for 5% and is associated with a higher rate of recurrence after treatment. *Torulopsis glabrata* accounts for 10%, and this type of vulvovaginal candidiasis may be more difficult to eradicate with standard therapies. The relative incidence of vaginitis caused by fungi other than *C albicans* appears to be increasing in some populations, which is attributed in part to the common use of topical antifungal agents in short courses. Factors favoring overgrowth of yeasts include the use of antibiotics, presence of high estrogen levels as in pregnancy and during oral-contraceptive use, wearing of tight clothing, and impairment of cell-mediated immunity or phagocytic cell function (as often occurs in women with AIDS or during post-transplant or post-chemotherapy periods).

BV is a polymicrobial infection associated with *Gardnerella vaginalis,* a gram-variable pleomorphic rod. This condition is more frequent in sexually active women and in populations with a higher prevalence of sexually transmitted diseases. The pathophysiology of BV is unclear, but a loss of the normal predominance of *Lactobacillus* species and increases in vaginal pH and numbers of anaerobic and aerobic bacteria are suspected. The characteristic fishy odor of BV may be caused by increased numbers of such anaerobes as *Bacteroides, Prevotella, Peptostreptococcus,* and *Mobiluncus* species and genital mycoplasmas. There is evidence to support the idea that BV is a sexually transmitted disease, in that *G vaginalis* can be isolated from the urethras of more than 80% of the male sexual partners of women with BV. However, *G vaginalis* can also be isolated from prepubescent girls who are not sexually active and from sexually inactive women. BV can be seen in women or girls who have never been sexually active, and the disease can recur even without sexual reexposure. BV tends to occur in women older than those who are at risk for gonorrhea and chlamydia. Women who are diagnosed as having BV should be screened for other sexually transmitted diseases, but it is not currently recommended that their sexual partners be routinely treated as well.

Table 22–1. Typical features of common vaginitides.[1]

	Candida	Trichomonas	Bacterial Vaginosis
Vulvar irritation	++	++	– to +
Dysuria	+	20%	–
Labial erythema	– to +	– to +	–
Satellite lesions	+	–	–
Consistency of discharge	Curdy	Frothy 25%	Homogenous, frothy sometimes
Color of discharge	White	Yellow-green, 25%	Gray, white
Vaginal pH	≤4.5	≥4.7	≥4.7
Epithelial cells	Normal	Normal	Clue cells
PMNs per epithelial cells	Variable	>1	<1
Bacteria	Endogenous flora	Endogenous flora	Gram-variable coccobacilli
Pathogens on microscopy	Yeasts and pseudohyphae, 50%	Trichomonads 70%	Gram-variable coccobacilli

[1]*Source:* Adapted from Rein MF: Vulvovaginitis and cervicitis. In *Mandell, Douglas, and Bennett's Principles and Practice of Infectious Diseases,* Churchill Livingstone, 1995.

BOX 22–1

Microbiology of Vulvovaginitis

	Children	Aduts
More Frequent	• *Gardnerella vaginialis* • Group A streptococci • *Candida albicans*	• *Candida* • *Trichomonas vaginalis* • Bacterial vaginosis (*Gardnerella vaginalis*)
Less Frequent	• *Haemophilus influenzae* • *Enterobius vermicularis*	• *Staphylococcus aureus* • Herpes simplex virus • Human papillomavirus • *Mycobacterium tuberculosis* • *Salmonellae* • *Enterobacteriaceae* • *Actinomyces* • Schistosomes

Clinical Findings (see Table 22–1, "Typical Features of Common Vaginitides")

A. Signs and Symptoms. Perivaginal pruritis is frequent with all three types of common infectious vaginitides, ie, candidal, trichomonal, and bacterial agents. Dysuria may be present. In candidal vulvovaginitis, there is often little or no vaginal discharge, but if present, it is usually thick and curdy. The labia may be pale or erythematous; there may also be small satellite papules or papulopustules at the margin of the erythematous area. Trichomonal vaginitis is also associated with vaginal irritation and sometimes dysuria and labial erythema. There may be a frothy greenish discharge. BV can present in the same manner but with a characteristically strong odor to the vaginal discharge, which is also usually gray-white in color. Physical examination may reveal very few abnormal findings, as there is rarely uterine or adnexal tenderness.

B. Laboratory Findings. The vaginal pH in candidal vaginitis is normal (4.5), whereas in trichomonal vaginitis and BV it is usually elevated. Adding 10% potassium hydroxide to vaginal discharge fails to elicit a fishy odor in candidiasis, whereas trichomonal vaginitis and BV have characteristically fishy odors (positive "whiff" test). Yeast forms may be visible under microscopy on a KOH preparation, although they are not visible in 30–50% of women who have candidal vulvovaginitis. With trichomonal vaginitis, microscopy should reveal trichomonads in 70% of cases. Epithelial cells appear normal, and there may be an increased number of polymorphonuclear cells. On wet mount examination of vaginal discharge in BV, clue cells, which are vaginal epithelial cells studded with tiny coccobacilli, can be seen. Culturing for *G vaginalis* can be performed, but the appearance of clue cells on the wet mount appears to be the most specific criterion for the diagnosis of BV.

Differential Diagnosis

As discussed above, other types of vaginal infections and processes can mimic vulvovaginitis caused by *Candida, Trichomonas,* and *Gardnerella* species.

Complications

Trichomonal infection can be complicated by vaginitis emphysematosa, in which gas-filled pockets of tissue fill the vaginal wall. This condition will resolve upon treatment of the trichomonal infection. Women with trichomonal vaginitis are more likely to have vaginal-cuff cellulitis after hysterectomy and, if they are pregnant, are more likely to have premature or prolonged rupture of membranes, premature labor, low-birth-weight babies, and postabortion infection. Women with BV are at increased risk for salpingitis, vaginal-cuff and wound infections after surgery, postpartum fever, chorioamnionitis, premature labor, and premature delivery. The treatment of both candidal and trichomonal vaginitis may be complicated by frequent recurrences.

Treatment

Vulvovaginal candidiasis is usually treated with topical antifungal agents (Box 22–2). There are a wide variety of treatments, all of which appear to be equally effective. Commercially available preparations, usually imidazoles or triazoles, are safe in pregnancy and tolerated well by patients. Treatment with an imidazole for 7 days yields a cure rate of approximately 80–94%. Shorter (3-day) regimens have approximately the same cure rate with improved patient compliance. Single-dose regimens do not appear to be as effective as the 3- or 7-day treatments. Pregnant women may require longer treatment. Oral therapy with fluconazole, ketoconazole, and itraconazole is available as well, but the potential toxicities are greater, and most patients do not require systemic therapy. Recurrent infection can be a problem with vulvovaginal candidiasis and probably results from endogenous relapse caused by small numbers of yeasts that have survived treatment. The rate of recurrence may be decreased by administering short courses of topical or oral antifungal agents during days 5–11 of the menstrual cycle, switching to a lower-estrogen-dose formulation of an oral contraceptive, and treating the male partner if he has candidal balanitis.

Trichomonal vaginitis should be treated with metronidazole (see Chapter 15 for more detailed discussion). The sexual partner should be treated simultaneously. Metronidazole is contraindicated in early pregnancy and in lactating women.

BV can be treated with metronidazole. Clindamycin and oral cephalosporins are also acceptable therapy. Vaginal regimens are also available, and cure rates are reported to be similar to those achieved with oral metronidazole.

Prognosis

Topical treatment of candidal vulvovaginitis has a cure rate range of 80–94%. However, 3–6 weeks after completion of treatment, *Candida* can be cultured from quite a few women (9–33%) who have undergone this treatment. Subspeciation of *Candida* suggests that approximately 40% of these women are infected with new strains of *Candida* species. Our current understanding of the mechanism of recurrence is extremely limited. Therapy to decrease the number of recurrences is aimed at eliminating or minimizing the aforementioned risk factors.

In *Trichomonas vaginalis* infection, a single dose of metronidazole reportedly provides a cure rate of 90%. For BV, cure rates associated with treatment with metronidazole are reported to be 80–90%.

CERVICITIS

Essentials of Diagnosis

- Risk factors: young (under age 24), unmarried, sexually active women; lower socioeconomic status, a new sexual partner within the past 2 months, a history of gonococcal infection, and a history of *T vaginalis* infection; women who use an intrauterine device (IUD) are prone to infection with actinomycetes.
- Erythema around the cervical os, mucopurulent cervical discharge, fever, chills, and uterine tenderness may be present, or patients may be asymptomatic.
- Ten to thirty polymorphonuclear leukocytes per oil immersion field on Gram stain of cervical discharge.
- Ligase chain reaction (LCR) and polymerase chain reaction (PCR) tests for rapid diagnosis of cervicitis caused by *Chlamydia trachomatis* and *Neisseria gonorrhoeae.*

General Considerations

Cervicitis is also covered in Chapter 15. The most common causes of cervicitis are *N gonorrhoeae* and *C trachomatis* (Box 22–3). Populations at higher risk

BOX 22-2

Empiric Therapy of Vulvovaginitis

	Candida spp.	*Trichomonas* spp.	Bacterial vaginosis
First Choice	• Fluconazole, 150 mg orally × 1 • Miconazole, 1200 mg supp × 1; 200 mg supp qhs × 3 days; or 2% cream qhs × 7 days • Clotrimazole, 500 mg supp × 1; 200 mg supp qhs × 3 days; 100 mg supp qhs × 7 days; 1% cream qhs × 7 days • Butoconazole, 2% cream qhs × 3 days • Terconazole, 0.4% cream qhs × 7 days	• Metronidazole, 2.0 g orally × 1	• Metronidazole, 500 mg orally twice a day × 7 days • Metronidazole vaginal gel, 1 applicator intravaginally twice a day × 5 days
Second Choice	• Nystatin, 100,000 U supp qhs × 14 days • Ketoconazole, 200 mg orally twice a day × 3–5 days • Itraconazole, 200 mg orally twice a day × 1 day or 200 mg orally daily × 3 days • Fluconazole, 100 mg orally daily × 1–3 days	• Metronidazole, 500 mg orally bid × 7 days	• Clindamycin, 300 mg orally twice a day × 7 days • Clindamycin 2% vaginal cream 5 g intravaginally qhs × 7 days
Pregnancy	• Any topical treatment listed above	• Clotrimazole, 100 mg supp qhs × 14 days • Metronidazole, 2.0 g orally × 1 (only in 2nd or 3rd trimester)	• Clindamycin, orally or cream as above

for cervicitis include young (under age 24), unmarried, sexually active women of lower socioeconomic status. Their risk increases if they have had a new sexual partner in the past 2 months, a history of gonorrhea, or a history of infection with *T vaginalis.* Asymptomatic or latent infection appears to be common with both organisms, leading to such complications as salpingitis, tubo-ovarian abscess, pelvic inflammatory disease (PID), and potential infertility. Concomitant infection with more than one organism can occur.

Rates of chlamydial infection have been estimated to be 5–30% (of women attending prenatal clinics). Pregnant women need prompt treatment because chlamydial infection can be transmitted to the infant; also, chlamydial genital infection has been associated with complications during labor such as an increased risk of premature rupture of membranes, preterm labor, and infants who are small for their gestational age.

Rates of asymptomatic infection with *N gonorrhoeae* have been estimated to be approximately 5% in women attending family planning clinics. Reported rates of infection during pregnancy are 2–7.3%. Asymptomatic infection at nongenital sites is important with *N gonorrhoeae,* because up to 40% of infected women have positive rectal cultures, and 22% have positive pharyngeal cultures. As with chlamydial infection, infection with *N gonorrhoeae* can be complicated by salpingitis, tubo-ovarian abscess, and PID. Disseminated gonococcemia can occur. In pregnancy, gonococcal infection has been associated with a higher rate of maternal and fetal morbidity.

Other causes of cervicitis include HSV, human papillomavirus, and other agents.

BOX 22-3

Microbiology of Cervicitis

More Frequent	• *C trachomatis* • *N gonorrhoeae* • Herpes simplex virus • Human papillomavirus
Less Frequent	• Adenovirus • Measles virus • Cytomegalovirus • *Enterobius vermicularis* • Amoebae • *M tuberculosis* • Group B streptococci • *N meningitidis*

Clinical Findings

A. Signs and Symptoms. The diagnosis of cervicitis is suggested by the presence of a mucopurulent cervical discharge. Fever and pelvic pain may occur, particularly when the infectious process is complicated by salpingitis. On physical examination, erythema around the cervical os may be present; the os may also be raised and very friable. The clinical presentation cannot reliably distinguish among etiologic agents of cervicitis.

B. Laboratory Findings. Gram stain of cervical discharge may show numerous (10–30) polymorphonuclear leukocytes per oil immersion field. The presence of gram-negative diplococci on the Gram stain confirms the diagnosis of *N gonorrhoeae,* but their absence does not rule out the possibility. Chlamydial infection is suggested by the presence of intracytoplasmic inclusions on Giemsa stain of cervical discharge. Fluorescent antibody staining and enzyme-linked immunosorbent assays (ELISA) to identify chlamydial antigens are also available, but positive results need to be confirmed by culture. LCR or PCR tests of cervical discharge or LCR tests of urine can help make a rapid diagnosis of chlamydia or gonorrhea infection. For both chlamydia and gonorrhea, culturing is also useful.

Differential Diagnosis

A diagnosis such as vaginitis is suggested by the vaginal discharge. Vaginal candidiasis, however, results in a typical whitish, curdy discharge; bacterial vaginosis (BV) and trichomonas vaginosis can result in a foul-smelling discharge, without the striking number of white cells found in cervicitis caused by chlamydial or gonorrheal infection.

Complications

Cervicitis caused by chlamydia or gonorrhea infection will progress to PID in 10–40% of women with cervicitis. Other complications include Fitz-Hugh-Curtis syndrome, or perihepatitis, which is characterized by fever and right upper quadrant pain. Chlamydial cervicitis in a pregnant woman can result in postpartum endometritis or, if she undergoes an abortion, postabortion infection. Premature rupture of membranes, preterm labor, and small-for-gestational-age infants can result from untreated chlamydial infection in pregnant women. Infection acquired by the infant during delivery leads to such complications as pneumonia in 40–50%, as well as nasopharyngeal infection and ophthalmia neonatorum.

Gonococcal infection can be complicated by bacteremia, leading to polyarthritis; endocarditis, myopericarditis, meningitis, and hepatitis can also occur. Infection in pregnant women has been associated with a higher incidence of prematurity, prolonged rupture of membranes, maternal peripartum fever, chorioamnionitis, and intrauterine growth retardation. In the newborn, gonococcal infection acquired at birth can result in pneumonia, nasopharyngeal infections, and ophthalmia neonatorum. Ophthalmia neonatorum prophylaxis consists of the instillation of 1% silver nitrate or erythromycin ointment in each eye.

Treatment

Penicillinase-producing *N gonorrhoeae* species are becoming more prevalent, making penicillin an ineffective choice for empiric therapy of cervicitis. Current recommendations are in Box 22–4. The recommendations recognize that simultaneous infection with *C trachomatis* and *N gonorrhoeae* is common, so that both organisms should be treated. Pregnant women should not receive tetracyclines. In addition, the newer macrolides have not been approved for use in pregnant women.

Prognosis

As stated previously, 10–40% of cervicitis cases caused by gonococcal or chlamydial infection in women will progress to PID, with the potential for infertility.

Prevention & Control

Both *C. trachomatis* and *N. gonorrhoeae* are reportable diseases. All sexual partners of the patient should be notified and treated promptly. The effects of untreated cervicitis in pregnant women and neonates can be minimized by the screening and prompt treatment of high-risk pregnant women when they are seen for prenatal care. Administration of erythromycin ointment or silver nitrate drops to neonates is an important step in prophylaxis against ophthalmia neonatorum.

BOX 22-4

Empiric Therapy of Cervicitis

	Adults & Adolescents	Pregnant Women
First Choice	• Ceftriaxone, 125 mg IM once, or cefixime, 400 mg orally once, **PLUS** doxycycline, 100 mg orally bid × 7 days	• Ceftriaxone, 125 mg IM once, or cefixime 400 mg, orally once, **PLUS** erythromycin 500 mg orally four times a day × 14 days

Second Choice	• Ceftriaxone, 125 mg IM once, or cefixime, 400 mg orally once, **PLUS**
	  • Erythromycin, 500 mg orally × 7 days
	  • Ofloxacin, 300 mg orally twice a day × 7 days
	  • Azithromycin, 1.0 mg orally once	

Penicillin Allergic	• Spectinomycin, 2.0 g IM once **PLUS**
	  • Doxycycline 100 mg orally twice a day × 7 days
	  • Erythromycin, 500 mg orally four times a day for 7 days
	  • Azithromycin, 1.0 g orally once
		• Spectinomycin, 2.0 g IM once, **PLUS** erythromycin, 500 mg orally four times a day for 14 days

PELVIC INFLAMMATORY DISEASE

Essentials of Diagnosis

- Risk factors: young sexually active women with multiple sexual partners, frequent sexual intercourse, and new sexual partners within the previous 30 days.
- Signs: a pelvic mass may be discovered by examination or ultrasonography.
- CDC minimum criteria: lower abdominal tenderness, cervical motion tenderness, and adnexal tenderness. Women who present with these symptoms should be treated empirically for PID in the absence of other diagnoses to explain their signs and symptoms.
- CDC routine criteria: temperature of greater than 38.3 °C, abnormal cervical or vaginal discharge, elevated erythrocyte sedimentation rate or C-reactive protein, and laboratory documentation of chlamydial or gonorrheal infection. The presence of these findings provides further support for the diagnosis of PID.
- CDC elaborate criteria: histopathologic evidence of endometritis on biopsy, tubo-ovarian abscess on sonography or other radiologic tests, and laproscopic abnormalities consistent with PID. The presence of these findings provides the strongest support for the diagnosis of PID.

General Considerations

The vague term "pelvic inflammatory disease" is used to refer to acute, subacute, chronic, or recurrent infection caused by the ascent of cervical microorganisms to the endometrium, fallopian tubes, and other pelvic structures (Box 22–5). Therefore, salpingitis, tubo-ovarian abscess, pelvic peritonitis, and endometritis will be included in the term pelvic inflammatory disease or PID.

Women at risk for PID are those who have untreated cervicitis due to *N gonorrhoeae* or *C trachomatis*. It is estimated that 10–40% of women with these infections do not receive adequate treatment and, in these women, symptomatic PID subsequently develops. *N gonorrhoeae* accounts for 40–60% of women with acute salpingitis, whereas *C trachomatis* accounts for 20–25%. Other risk factors for PID include sexual activity among teenagers, a new partner in the previous 30 days, frequent intercourse, bacterial vaginosis, frequent douching, and tobacco and substance abuse. Use of an IUD slightly increases the risk of PID—it is thought that this increased risk is due to introduction of organisms into the upper reproductive tract at the time of insertion.

PID is an ascending, polymicrobial infection. Organisms most frequently implicated in PID are *N gonorrhoeae*, *C trachomatis*, and genital *Myco-*

BOX 22–5

Microbiology of PID

More Frequent	• *Neisseria gonorrhoeae* • *Chlamydia trachomatis* • *Bacteroides* spp. • *Peptostreptococcus* • *Enterobacteriaceae* • Streptococci • *Mycoplasma hominis* and *Ureaplasma urealyticum* • *Garneralla vaginalis*
Less Frequent	• *Actinomyces* (in IUD users) • *Mycobacterium tuberculosis*

plasma spp. Anaerobes such as *Peptococcus, Peptostreptococcus,* and *Bacteroides* are often involved. *E coli, Gardnerella vaginalis, H influenzae,* and group B streptococcus are the most frequent aerobes involved.

Clinical Findings

A. Signs and Symptoms. Lower abdominal, adnexal, and cervical motion tenderness are present in most patients with PID. (These are the CDC's minimum criteria for the diagnosis of PID.) The pain and tenderness are often associated with the onset of menses and may radiate to the back and down both lower extremities. A temperature of greater than 38.3 °C and abnormal cervical or vaginal discharge provide further support for the diagnosis (see CDC routine criteria listed under "Essentials for Diagnosis" above).

B. Laboratory Findings. Findings on laboratory studies, unfortunately, can be within normal limits. Abnormalities such as a leukocytosis, elevated sedimentation rate, or C-reactive protein can support the diagnosis, but their absence or presence does not confirm the diagnosis. Gram stain of cervical secretions may reveal the presence of gram-negative diplococci, suggesting *N gonorrhoeae* as the causative organism. Culdocentesis may also be performed, and the fluid obtained should be examined for white cells; the presence of numerous white cells suggests PID, but appendicitis can also present in the same manner.

C. Imaging. Ultrasonography of the pelvis may reveal an inflammatory mass consistent with tubo-ovarian abscess. Laproscopy remains the most accurate method for diagnosing PID and should be performed in cases in which the diagnosis remains uncertain. Hyperemia of the tubal surface, edema of the tubal walls, and an exudate on the tubal surface are consistent with PID. Cultures can be obtained at the time of laproscopic examination and may help guide therapy.

Differential Diagnosis

Appendicitis can present in a fashion similar to PID. A good history and physical examination may help differentiate between the two, although the diagnosis may not be established with certainty until the appendix is visualized at surgery. Ectopic pregnancy is suspected based on an elevated β-hcG level and ultrasound. Ultrasound may also be helpful in excluding entities such as ovarian cysts or ovarian torsion. Endometriosis can mimic chronic PID in that patients may present with complaints of chronic abdominal pain. However, they may also complain of irregular or heavy menstrual bleeding, which is more typical of endometriosis than of PID.

Nongynecologic problems such as irritable bowel syndrome or gastroenteritis should be suspected in patients who present with diarrhea and other bowel complaints. History and physical examination will also help differentiate cholecystitis from PID. Nephrolithiasis and pyelonephritis can also be differentiated from PID by location of abdominal pain, history, and urinalysis.

Complications

At least 25% of women with PID have serious sequelae, such as infertility, ectopic pregnancy, and chronic pelvic pain. Acute complications include pelvic peritonitis if there is rupture of an abscess or extension of the infectious process into the peritoneal space. Pelvic cellulitis with thrombophlebitis may result. Abscess, bacteremia, and septic shock may develop.

Treatment

Treatment should begin with empiric antibiotics as soon as the diagnosis is suspected. The CDC has published recommendations for the treatment of PID (Box 22–6). PID may be treated on an outpatient basis, with oral antibiotics. Ambulatory patients should, however, be reevaluated within 72 hours of beginning treatment. Under certain circumstances, hospitalization is recommended. The patient should be hospitalized when the diagnosis is uncertain and a surgical emergency such as acute appendicitis cannot be excluded; a pelvic or tubo-ovarian abscess is suspected; the patient is pregnant, an adolescent, or noncompliant; or the patient has failed or not tolerated outpatient therapy.

Regimen A (see Box 22–6) provides recommenda-

BOX 22-6

Empiric Therapy of PID

	Adults & Adolescents	Pregnant Women
Regimen A	• Outpatient treatment: Doxycycline, 100 mg orally twice a day × 14 days **PLUS** metronidazole, 500 mg orally twice a day × 14 days • Inpatient treatment: Doxycycline, 100 mg IV or orally every 12 h **PLUS** one of the following: • Cefoxitin, 2.0 g IV every 8 h • Cefotetan, 2.0 g IV every 12 h	• Inpatient treatment only recommended Substitute erythromycin for doxycycline
Regimen B	• Outpatient treatment; Doxycycline, 100 mg orally twice a day × 14 days **PLUS** one of the following: • Ceftriaxone, 250 mg IM once • Cefoxitin 2.0 g IM **PLUS** probenicid, 1 g orally once • Other parenteral third-generation cephalosporin (ceftizoxime or cefotaxime) • Inpatient treatment: Clindamycin, 900 mg IV every 8 hours, **PLUS** gentamicin, 2 mg/kg loading dose IV or IM, then maintenance dose 1.5 mg/kg IV every 8 hours. Single daily dosing may be substituted. This regimen is preferred if tubo-ovarian abscess is suspected.	• Inpatient treatment only recommended. Substitute erythromycin for doxycycline.
Penicillin Allergic	• Clindamycin and gentamicin as above; do not use fluoroquinolones in adolescents younger than 16. • Other alternatives: Ofloxacin, 400 mg IV every 12 h, **PLUS** metronidazole, 500 mg IV every 8 h; ciprofloxacin, 200 mg IV every 12 h plus doxycycline, 100 mg IV or orally every 12 h, plus metronidazole, 500 mg IV every 8 h.	• Clindamycin and gentamicin for adults

tions for treating gonorrhea and chlamydia. Regimen B provides recommendations for treating gonorrhea and chlamydia, as well as anaerobes. All sexual partners should be notified, treated empirically for chlamydia and gonorrhea, and tested for other sexually transmitted diseases.

In the case of a tubo-ovarian abscess, the patient should be hospitalized and begun on broad-spectrum antibiotics that provide anaerobic coverage. Surgical intervention is indicated when there is failure to defervesce within 72 hours or when there is an increase in the size of the abscess. Most tuboovarian abscesses 4–6 cm in diameter resolve in response to medical therapy alone, but only 40% of abscesses larger than 10 cm respond to medical therapy alone.

Prognosis

A recent meta-analysis of 34 treatment regimens from 1966 to 1992 found cure rates to be above 90% for the commonly used treatment regimens, which form the basis for the current CDC treatment guidelines.

The incidence of infertility after the first bout of PID is approximately 12%. This rises to 25–35% after the second episode, and to 50–75% after three or more episodes. The risk of ectopic pregnancy increases to sevenfold that of a woman who has never had PID. Infertility rates are higher after tubo-ovarian abscess, with only 7–14% of women able to conceive.

Prevention & Control

Prevention consists of treating women and their sexual partners for cervicitis and aggressively screening women at high risk.

INFECTIONS AFTER GYNECOLOGIC SURGERY

Essentials of Diagnosis

- Risk factors: more common in women who are premenopausal, undergoing abdominal versus vaginal hysterectomy, or of lower socioeconomic status and in women who undergo surgeries of longer duration or have bacterial vaginosis (BV) at the time of surgery.
- Lower abdominal and pelvic pain and fever lasting from 2 days to several weeks after operation.
- Variable tenderness on abdominal and pelvic examinations; palpable abdominal mass may be present with pelvic abscess.
- Leukocytosis and elevated sedimentation rate; blood cultures and cultures of purulent cervical or wound drainage may be helpful.
- Computed tomography and ultrasonography can help confirm the presence of an abscess.

General Considerations

The usual pathogens in gynecologic, postoperative infections are endogenous pelvic flora (Box 22–7). These are *Lactobacillus* spp., streptococci, *Gardnerella vaginalis, Enterobacteriaceae,* and anaerobes. Although *Fusobacterium* spp. and *B fragilis* are not usually present in the vaginal flora, they are often found in pelvic infections postoperatively. Factors such as hospitalization can cause a dramatic

---

BOX 22–7

Microbiology of Gynecologic Postoperative Infections

More Frequent	• Streptococci • *Bacterioides* • *Prevotella* • *Gardnerella* • *Enterobacteriaceae*

---

shift in the vaginal flora and predispose a patient to a postoperative pelvic infection. Use of spermicidal vaginal preparations, use of the female condom, douching, and the phase of the menstrual cycle can also affect the vaginal flora. Risk factors for the development of a postoperative infection include abdominal (versus vaginal) hysterectomy, lower socioeconomic status, premenopausal status, duration of surgery, and BV.

Clinical Findings

Pelvic Cellulitis. Pelvic cellulitis is the most common infection after hysterectomy. Patients present on the second or third postoperative day with lower abdominal and pelvic pain, usually more severe on one side. The temperature is usually above 38.5 °C. On abdominal and pelvic examination there is tenderness over the parametrial area. Cultures may be obtained from the vaginal cuff, although some believe that such cultures can be misleading because of contamination by vaginal flora.

Cuff Cellulitis and Abscess. Cuff cellulitis after hysterectomy usually manifests within 10 days of discharge from the hospital, with central lower abdominal and pelvic pain, vaginal discharge, and low-grade fever. Examination of the abdomen reveals slight suprapubic tenderness, and pelvic examination reveals no masses and only vaginal surgical margin tenderness. An inflammatory reaction at the surgical margin of the vaginal cuff is normal and does not require treatment.

Cuff abscess occurs when a well-localized collection develops above the vaginal cuff. These patients usually present on the second or third postoperative day with fever and a sense of fullness in the lower abdomen. Purulent material obtained from the surgical margin should be cultured aerobically and anaerobically.

Pelvic Abscess. Patients with pelvic abscesses are usually premenopausal women. They may present weeks after the original procedure. Typically patients may have received a course of antibiotics in the hospital for presumed pelvic cellulitis, but they relapse after discharge. Patients present with high spiking fevers, especially in the late afternoon or early evening, and may complain of pelvic or lower abdominal pain. There may be notable leukocytosis and considerable elevation in the erythrocyte sedimentation rate. Ultrasonography or computed tomography can confirm the presence of an abscess.

Treatment

Patients with pelvic cellulitis can be treated with single-agent antibiotic therapy. Cefotetan, cefoxitin, ampicillin/sulbactam, and ticarcillin/clavulanic acid are all reasonable choices (Box 22–8). In patients with β-lactam allergies, clindamycin and gentamicin can be used. Therapy should be continued until the

---

BOX 22-8

Empiric Therapy of Gynecologic Postoperative Infections

	Pelvic Cellulitis	Cuff Cellulitis and Abscess	Pelvic Abscess
First Choice	• Cefotetan, 2.0 g IV every 12 h • Cefoxitin, 2.0 g IV every 8 h • Ampicillin/sulbactam, 3.0 g IV every 6 h • Ticarcillin/clavulanic acid, 3.1 g IV every 6 h	• For cuff cellulitis: amoxicillin/clavulanic acid, 500 mg orally three times per day; need reevaluation in 72 h • For cuff abscess, as for pelvic cellulitis	• Penicillin G 5 million units IV every 6 h or ampicillin 2.0 g IV every 6 h, **PLUS** gentamicin, 2.0 mg/kg IV load, then 1.7 mg/kg IV every 8 h • Follow with amoxicillin/clavulanic acid, 500 mg orally three times per day, or metronidazole, 500 mg orally three times per day, for 7 days
Second Choice	• Imipenem, 500 mg IV every 6 h		• Imipenem, 500 mg IV, every 6 h
Penicillin Allergic	• Clindamycin, 900 mg IV every 8 h, **PLUS** gentamicin, 2.0 mg/kg IV load, then 1.7 mg/kg IV every 8 h	• Clindamycin and gentamicin as for pelvic cellulitis	• Clindamycin and gentamicin as for pelvic cellulitis

---

patient is afebrile for at least 24 hours, and administration of oral antibiotics after parenteral treatment is generally thought to be unnecessary.

Patients with cuff cellulitis can be treated with oral antibiotics, such as amoxicillin, clavulanic acid, or both, as outpatients, as long as they monitor their temperature at home and are reevaluated within 72 hours (Box 22–8). For cuff abscess, parenteral antibiotic therapy is needed and should be continued until the patient has been afebrile for at least 24 hours (Box 22–8).

Treatment of pelvic abscesses requires parenteral antibiotic therapy (Box 22–8). Surgical drainage is not always necessary, because antibiotic therapy alone may be successful. Clindamycin and gentamicin are often used, because *B fragilis* and other gram-negative anaerobes are often isolated from pelvic abscesses. Parenteral antibiotics should be administered until the patient has been afebrile for 48–72 hours. Other parameters to monitor are the white blood cell count, amount of drainage, and abdominal pain and tenderness. Often recommended is treatment with oral antibiotics for 7 days after completion of a course of parenteral antibiotics. The patient should be reevaluated in 2 weeks to ensure that reaccummulation of the fluid has not occurred. Surgical drainage is necessary in patients who fail to respond to antibiotic therapy alone. Catheter drainage of the abscess should continue until the drainage ceases. Laporotomy is required in patients for whom all of the above measures fail.

Prevention & Control

The risk of these gynecologic postoperative infections can be reduced by treatment of BV in women who will be undergoing gynecologic procedures. Minimizing operative time and using the vaginal approach to hysterectomy can also help prevent these infections.

INTRAPARTUM & POSTPARTUM INFECTIONS

This section discusses major infections that occur during the intrapartum period (chorioamnionitis) and the postpartum period (postpartum endometritis, puerperal ovarian vein thrombophlebitis, and episiotomy infection), as well as during or after abortion.

CHORIOAMNIONITIS

Essentials of Diagnosis

• Risk factors: preterm labor, prolonged rupture of membranes, multiple vaginal examinations, and preexisting bacterial vaginosis (BV); also, a hematogenous spread of organisms due to a bacteremic episode can occur.

- Gram stain and culturing of amniotic fluid may be useful.
- Characteristic leukocyte esterase and glucose concentrations in amniotic fluid.
- Fever, tachycardia, and uterine tenderness in pregnant women.
- Fetal tachycardia and heart rate abnormalities; evidence of fetal distress.

General Considerations

Chorioamnionitis refers to infection of the uterus and its structures during pregnancy. This syndrome is also referred to as intra-amniotic infection syndrome or IAIS. This infection is more common in women with preterm labor, occurring in up to 25% of such women; in women at term, the incidence is only 1 to 2%. It tends to occur in a setting of prolonged rupture of membranes or after multiple vaginal examinations, which allow the ascent of the causative organisms into the uterus and its contents (Box 22–9). Preexisting bacterial vaginosis is also a predisposing factor. Some cases are caused by the hematogenous spread of organisms into the uterus during a bacteremic episode. Organisms that have been cultured from amniotic fluid include vaginal flora such as *Gardnerella vaginalis, Mycoplasma hominis,* streptococci, and anaerobes. Gram-negative rods, especially *E coli,* and enterococci, are also commonly isolated. Infections with group B streptococci or *E coli* are particularly associated with the complication of bacteremia and are the most frequent isolates in neonates born to mothers with chorioamnionitis.

Clinical Findings

A. Signs and Symptoms. The diagnosis of chorioamnionitis is made on clinical grounds. Asymptomatic cases make the diagnosis more difficult; 5–10% of women with preterm labor and intact membranes have symptomatic infection, whereas another 10% have subclinical infection. In patients with preterm premature rupture of membranes, up to 25%

may have subclinical infection. Signs and symptoms usually seen in women with chorioamnionitis include fever, tachycardia, and uterine tenderness. The fetus may show signs of distress, including tachycardia and decreased variability in heart rate. Amniotic fluid is rarely foul smelling or purulent. Term pregnant women may experience dysfunctional labor, requiring induction or cesarean delivery for arrested progress of labor.

B. Laboratory Findings. Amniotic fluid can be aspirated and analyzed to support the clinical diagnosis of chorioamnionitis. A Gram stain and culture of the fluid may be helpful. Increased leukocyte esterase activity and glucose concentration (< 10–15 mg%) may also be diagnostic.

Complications

One complication of chorioamnionitis is dysfunctional labor, necessitating induction or cesarean delivery. Approximately three-quarters of women with chorioamnionitis require augmentation of labor with oxytocin. Cesarean delivery is required in approximately 40%. Left untreated, chorioamnionitis can result in bacteremia in the mother and pneumonia and bacteremia in the neonate.

Treatment

Antibiotics should be administered as soon as the diagnosis is made (Box 22–10). Prompt delivery, usually within 12 hours, is an essential part of treatment.

Prognosis

No maternal deaths from chorioamnionitis were reported in states in which such statistics were tracked from the 1980s to early 1992. However, postpartum infection in the mother is very common. Perinatal mortality is increased, with premature infants at higher risk than term infants.

Prevention & Control

Chorioamnionitis can be prevented or its incidence decreased by the treatment of bacterial vaginosis in pregnant women. Minimizing vaginal examinations and manipulations, especially in women with preterm labor or prolonged rupture of membranes will also decrease the risk.

POSTPARTUM ENDOMETRITIS

Essentials of Diagnosis

- Risk factors: lower socioeconomic status, cesarean delivery, prolonged rupture of membranes and duration of labor, preexisting bacterial vaginosis (multiple vaginal examinations and use of internal fetal monitors).

BOX 22–9		
Microbiology of Chorioamnionitis		
More Frequent	• *Enterobacteriaceae* • Enterococci • Anaerobes • Streptococci	
Less Frequent	• *Gardnerella vaginalis* • *Mycoplasma hominis* • Herpes simplex virus	

BOX 22-10

Empiric Therapy of Chorioamnionitis

	Adults & Adolescents
First Choice	• Ampicillin, 2.0 g IV every 6 hours, or penicillin G, 5 million units every 6 hours **PLUS:** • Gentamicin, 2.0 mg/kg IV load, then 1.7 mg/kg IV every 8 h[1]
Second Choice	• Cefotetan, 2.0 g IV every 12 h • Cefotaxime, 2 g IV every 8 h • Cefoxitin, 2.0 g IV every 6 h • Ampicillin/sulbactam, 3.0 g IV every 6 h • Piperacillin/tazobactam, 3.375 g IV every 6 h • Ticarcillin/clavulanic acid, 3.1 g IV every 6 h • Imipenem, 500 mg IV every 6 h

Penicillin Allergic	• Gentamicin, 2.0 mg/kg IV load, then 1.7 mg/kg IV every 8 h[1] **PLUS** one of the following:
	  • Vancomycin, 1.0 g IV every 12 h
	  • Erythromycin, 1.0 g IV, every 6 h
	  • Clindamycin, 900 mg IV every 8 h

[1]Single daily dosing may be substituted.

• Fever on first or second postpartum day; lower abdominal pain and uterine tenderness.
• Leukocytosis and bacteremia possible.

General Considerations

Postpartum infection of the uterus is more common after cesarean delivery, with an incidence ranging from less than 10% on private services to 50% in indigent patients in large teaching hospitals. In comparison, the incidence of endometritis is only 0.9–3.9% after vaginal delivery. Other risk factors for postcesarean endometritis include longer duration of labor or of ruptured membranes, bacterial vaginosis, multiple vaginal examinations, and use of an internal fetal monitor.

Endometritis is a polymicrobial infection. Group B streptococci, *Gardnerella vaginalis, E coli,* anaerobes, and enterococci are common culprits (Box 22–11). Endometritis after vaginal delivery typically occurs 2 days to 6 weeks after delivery and has been associated with *Chlamydia trachomatis*. Group A β-hemolytic streptococci can cause endometritis as

well, sometimes in association with toxic shock. Nosocomial transmission and outbreaks occur and require special isolation procedures. *Ureaplasma urealyticum* and *Mycoplasma hominis* have also been isolated from the endometrium and blood of affected patients.

Clinical Findings

A. Signs and Symptoms. Generally fever develops on the first or second postpartum day. Lower abdominal pain is also usually present. On pelvic examination there may be uterine tenderness.

B. Laboratory Findings. Leukocytosis is usually present. Transvaginal uterine cultures can be obtained, but results are often difficult to interpret because of the presence of contaminants. Blood cultures will yield growth in 10–20% of patients.

Differential Diagnosis

Other conditions such as puerperal ovarian vein thrombophlebitis (see next section), wound infection, or pelvic infection should be considered. Puerperal ovarian thrombophlebitis is rare but is usually associated with postcesarean endometritis. Half to two-

BOX 22-11

Microbiology of Postpartum Fever

	Postpartum Endometritis, POVT	Episiotomy Infection
More Frequent	• Group B streptococci • Enterococci • Aerobic streptococci • *Gardnerella vaginalis* • *E coli* • *Prevoltella bivia* • *Bacteroides* • *Peptostreptococci*	• Streptococci • Staphylococci • *Enterobacteriaceae* • Anaerobes
Less Frequent	• *Ureaplasma urealyticum* • *Mycoplasma hominis* • *Chlamydia trachomatis* (in late endometritis) • Group A β-hemolytic streptococci	• *Clostridium perfringens* (myonecrosis)

thirds of patients will have a characteristic palpable abdominal mass. Wound infections or other pelvic infections should be considered when the patient fails to respond to antimicrobial therapy appropriate for the treatment of postpartum endometritis. Noninfectious causes of postpartum fever, such as breast engorgement and drug fever, should also be considered.

Complications

Bacteremia can occur with postpartum endometritis and does occur in 10–20% of patients. However, it does not correlate with severity of illness or with prolonged recovery.

Treatment

Mild to moderately severe postpartum endometritis is treated with an extended-spectrum penicillin (ticarcillin/clavulanic acid or ampicillin/sulbactam) or second-generation cephalosporin (cefotetan or cefoxitin) (Box 22–12). Severe posparttum endometritis can be treated with clindamycin and gentamicin, especially after cesarean delivery. Therapy should be continued until the patient is afebrile for 24 hours, is free of abdominal pain, and no longer has a leukocytosis. There is no need to continue oral antibiotics after the patient is discharged from the hospital. However, women known to have chlamydial endometritis should receive oral erythromycin or doxy-

---

BOX 22-12

Empiric Therapy of Postpartum Fever

	Postpartum Endometritis	Puerperal Ovarian Vein Thrombophlebitis	Episiotomy Infection
First Choice	• Cefoxitin, 2.0 g IV every 6–8 h • Ticarcillin/clavulanic acid, 3.1 g IV every 6 h • Imipenem, 0.5 g IV every 6 h • Ampicillin/sulbactam, 3.0 g IV every 6 h • Piperacillin/tazobactam, 3.375 g IV every 6 h • One of the above **PLUS** doxycycline, 100 mg IV, every 12 h, if chlamydial endometritis	• Cefoxitin, 2.0 g IV every 6–8 h • Ticarcillin/clavulanic acid, 3.1 g IV every 6 h • Piperacillin/tazobactam, 3.375 g IV every 6 h • Ampicillin/sulbactam, 3.0 g every 6 h • One of the above **PLUS** heparin IV	• Clindamycin, 450–900 mg IV every 8 h, and ampicillin, 2.0 g IV every 6 h, and gentamicin, 2.0 mg/kg IV load, then 1.7 mg/kg IV every 8 h **PLUS** surgical debridement • Clindamycin, 900 mg IV every 8 h and penicillin G, 24 million units IV in 4–6 divided doses, per day **PLUS** surgical debridement, hyperbaric oxygen, or both if clostridial nfection

Second Choice	• Clindamycin, 450–900 mg IV every 8 h **PLUS** one of the following:
	  • Gentamicin, 2.0 mg/kg IV load, then 1.7 mg/kg every 8 h[1]
	  • Cefotaxime, 2.0 g IV every 8 h
	  • Ceftriaxone, 2.0 g IV every 24 h
		• Imipenem, 500 mg IV every 6 h	• Ceftriaxone, 2.0 g IV every 12 h if clostridial infection

Penicillin Allergic	• Clindamycin, 450–900 mg IV every 8 h, and gentamicin, 2.0 mg/kg IV load, then 1.7 mg/kg every 8 h	• Clindamycin and gentamicin as for postpartum endometritis	• Erythromycin, 1.0 g IV every 6 h if clostridial infection

[1]Single daily dosing may be substituted.

cycline for a full course even when they have responded well to parenteral therapy as above.

Several possibilities should be considered when a patient fails to respond to antimicrobial therapy. First, the diagnosis should be questioned and other diagnoses should be considered. Second, the treatment regimen may not cover drug-resistant pathogens. Multi-drug-resistant anaerobes are emerging and do account for some treatment failures. Third, an undrained abscess may be present. Finally, enterococcal species superinfection may exist. Enterococcal superinfection should be considered when enterococci are isolated in pure culture or in heavy growth from an endometrial specimen. In the past, ampicillin plus gentamicin were effective for enterococcal infection. However, the prevalence of β-lactam resistance, high-level aminoglycoside resistance, and, more recently, even vancomycin resistance complicates empiric treatment of enterococcal infection. Depending on the incidence of multiple-drug-resistant enterococci at a given locale, vancomycin plus gentamicin may be the best choice for suspected enterococcal infection until susceptibility test results are available. In cases in which the isolate is also resistant to vancomycin, infectious disease experts should be consulted. Cephalosporins have no role in the treatment of enterococcal infection but may be needed to treat other suspected pathogens.

Prognosis

The prognosis is usually good, because intravenous antibiotic therapy is quite effective.

Prevention & Control

Prophylactic antibiotics should be administered to any patient who is undergoing a cesarean section after labor or rupture of membranes, regardless of duration. Cefazolin, 1–2 g IV after the umbilical cord is clamped, with a second dose given 4 hours later in high-risk patients, is adequate prophylaxis. Alternatively, metronidazole or clindamycin and gentamicin can be given to patients with a β-lactam allergy. Even with prophylactic antibiotics, postpartum endometritis will develop in 15% of women.

PUERPERAL OVARIAN VEIN THROMBOPHLEBITIS (POVT)

Essentials of Diagnosis

- Acute onset of fever, chills, and lower abdominal pain.
- Sausage-shaped or ropelike abdominal mass on physical examination.
- Computed tomography (CT), Doppler ultrasonography, and magnetic resonance imaging (MRI) can help confirm the diagnosis.

General Considerations

Puerperal ovarian vein thrombophlebitis (POVT) occurs in the postpartum period and is a result of thrombosis of the ovarian veins (Box 22–11). It is usually associated with postcesarean endometritis, but it can occur in the absence of endometritis. Its incidence is 1 per 2000 deliveries or 1–2 per 100 patients with postpartum infection. In many patients, POVT is diagnosed after failure to respond to a therapeutic trial of antibiotics for presumed postpartum endometritis.

Clinical Findings

A. Signs and Symptoms. The onset of symptoms usually occurs 2–4 days postpartum and is usually acute. Patients experience pain in the lower abdomen, often on the right side. Fever and chills also occur. The degree of tachycardia that occurs is often disproportionate to the degree of temperature elevation. An abdominal mass can be palpated in half to two-thirds of patients and is sausage shaped or ropelike. The mass usually extends from the right uterine cornua to the upper abdomen. Signs of respiratory distress may be present if pulmonary embolization has occurred.

B. Laboratory Findings. Laboratory studies are not helpful in diagnosis. Leukocytosis may be present, and coagulation studies are sometimes abnormal. Results of blood cultures are usually sterile.

C. Imaging. Computed tomography, duplex Doppler ultrasonography, and magnetic resonance imaging can be used to confirm the diagnosis.

Differential Diagnosis

Puerperal ovarian vein thrombophlebitis must be differentiated from postpartum endometritis. Indeed, many women with POVT are first diagnosed with postpartum endometritis. When appropriate therapy fails, the correct diagnosis of POVT often is made. Other diagnoses to be considered include postpartum episiotomy infection (see next section), PID, pelvic abscess, or other nongynecological sources of fever.

Complications

The complication of pulmonary embolization should always be considered, especially if tachypnea, hypoxia, chest pain, or other signs of respiratory distress develop.

Treatment

Continuous intravenous anticoagulation with heparin is important. The optimal duration of anticoagulation is not known, but many clinicians treat for 7–10 days (if pulmonary embolization has not occurred). Administration of broad-spectrum antibiotics against common pelvic pathogens is also helpful (Box 22–12).

Prognosis, Prevention, & Control

The prognosis with POVT is good when pulmonary embolization has not occurred. Early mobilization after delivery and prophylactic anticoagulation for high-risk patients can help reduce the risk of POVT.

EPISIOTOMY INFECTIONS

Essentials of Diagnosis

- Edema and erythema along the site of episiotomy.
- More serious infections involving deeper layers of tissue may not manifest with edema and erythema of the overlying skin.
- Local pain; if there is more serious infection, fever and chills along with other systemic complaints.

General Considerations

Infections of episiotomies are rare, with an incidence of 0.1%. There is a higher risk of infection, up to 1–2%, with episiotomies that involve third- or fourth-degree extensions. A classification scheme for episiotomy-related infections separates such infections based on their depth of infection. A simple episiotomy infection is a localized infection that involves only the skin and superficial fascia along the incision. Edema and erythema may be present along the incision site. Causative organisms include streptococci, staphylococci, *Enterobacteriaceae,* and anaerobes (Box 22–11). A superficial fascia infection without necrosis can present without very striking clinical signs or symptoms except that the skin is edematous and erythematous along the incision. Superficial fascia infection with necrosis (or necrotizing fasciitis) involves infection of the superficial fascia that spreads into the fascial clefts overlying the deep fascia. The skin overlying the wound may not appear eyrthematous or edematous, but the patient will have considerable systemic manifestations of infection. Skin involvement occurs after vessels supplying the overlying skin are thrombosed. Myonecrosis is extremely rare and refers to infection beneath the deep fascia, involving muscle. *Clostridium perfringens* is the usual etiologic agent. Myonecrosis can occur as a complication of an inadequately treated or untreated necrotizing fasciitis. It can also occur in the subgluteal muscles surrounding the hip joint or psoas muscle after introduction of organisms by a paracervical or pudendal needle.

Clinical Findings

A. Signs and Symptoms. As noted previously, the patient will usually have localized edema and erythema along the incision site if the infection is a simple infection. When necrotizing fasciitis occurs, the skin may not appear erythematous or edematous at all. However, the patient may experience extreme systemic manifestations such as high fever and chills. Pain is often more severe than clinical signs of infection. Definitive diagnosis of necrotizing fasciitis is made at surgery when the surgeon finds extensive undermining of surrounding tissues and lack of resistance in the superficial fascial plane to probing with a blunt instrument. Necrotizing fasciitis is a medical emergency and requires immediate surgical intervention.

B. Laboratory Findings. Laboratory findings will vary with the extent of infection; a patient with a simple episiotomy infection may have very few laboratory abnormalities, whereas a patient with myonecrosis can present with severe hypotensive shock.

C. Imaging. Imaging is not necessary except in unusual cases. The diagnosis is made by inspection of the episiotomy site in cases of simple and superficial infections and by surgical exploration in more serious infections.

Complications

Sepsis as well as pelvic abscess and extensive necrosis of pelvic structures may occur if early infections are not diagnosed and treated promptly.

Treatment

Simple infections may be treated with an oral antibiotic such as amoxicillin/clavulanic acid. Optimal therapy for more serious infections involves both systemic antibiotics and surgical débridement (Box 22–12).

Prognosis

For simple episiotomy infections, the prognosis is quite good, with few complications seen. More serious infection such as myonecrosis can have a graver prognosis.

SEPTIC ABORTION

Essentials of Diagnosis

- Occurs in the presence of retained products of conception or operative trauma; more likely when pregnancy is advanced, technical difficulties during the procedure occur, and a sexually transmitted pathogen is present.
- Fever, chills, abdominal pain, or vaginal bleeding within 4 days of abortion.
- Tachycardia, tachypnea, or abdominal tenderness on physical examination. The patient may be in frank hypotensive shock.
- Sanguinopurulent discharge and uterine tenderness on pelvic examination.
- Leukocytosis, anemia, or positive cervical or blood cultures.
- Pelvic ultrasound can confirm the presence of retained products of conception.

General Considerations

Postabortion infection can occur in the presence of retained products of conception or operative trauma. It is an ascending process, and risk factors include more advanced pregnancies, technical difficulties, and the presence of a sexually transmitted pathogen. The most common causative organisms are endogenous pelvic flora (Box 22–13). However, *Clostridium perfringens* can be the causative agent of postabortion infection and can cause a characteristic presentation of massive intravascular hemolysis.

Clinical Findings

A. Signs and Symptoms. Patients commonly present within 4 days of the procedure with fever, chills, abdominal pain, and vaginal bleeding. Often there has been passage of placental tissue.

Patients with mild infection or simple endometritis may appear mildly ill with low-grade fever and mild uterine tenderness. Patients with more serious infection will present with severe systemic manifestations, sometimes in hypotensive shock.

On physical examination, there will be elevated temperature, tachycardia, tachypnea, and uterine tenderness. Sanguinopurulent discharge may be evident on pelvic examination. The patient with bacteremia and resultant hypotensive shock may be agitated and disoriented. The patient with *C perfringens* infection may display jaundice, mahogany-colored urine, and striking anemia caused by intravascular hemolysis.

B. Laboratory Findings. A complete blood count will reveal leukocytosis and sometimes hemolytic anemia, which is severe with *C perfringens*. Gram stain and culturing of cervical material may reveal the causative organism. Blood cultures should be obtained and may reveal the causative organism in the patient with bacteremia.

C. Imaging. Pelvic ultrasound can be performed to confirm the presence of retained products of conception.

Differential Diagnosis

Other diagnoses to be considered in this setting include appendicitis, pyelonephritis, pelvic abscess, and noninfectious causes of fever.

BOX 22–13

Microbiology of Septic Abortion	
More Frequent	• *Bacteroides* • Group A and B streptococci • *Enterobacteriaceae* • *Chlamydia trachomatis*
Less Frequent	• *Clostridium perfringens*

Complications

Postabortion infection can progress to bacteremia and frank shock. Perforation of the uterus may occur both during abortion and during curettage. Pelvic or adnexal abscesses may result from untreated infection. Necrotizing myometritis with *Clostridium* spp. can also occur.

Treatment

Simple postabortion endometritis requires only oral doxycycline (Box 22–14). More serious infections require curettage and parenteral antibiotic therapy. Laproscopy or laporotomy and hysterectomy may be necessary when the condition fails to respond to curettage and appropriate antibiotics.

Prognosis

The prognosis is generally good for simple postabortion endometritis. Patients in whom therapy fails have a high risk of infertility owing to the necessity of hysterectomy, whereas patients with *C perfringens* infection may have a grave prognosis.

Prevention & Control

Screening for sexually transmitted diseases before abortion may decrease the risk of acquiring this infection. Performing abortion procedures in medical facilities with proper infection control has resulted in a dramatic decline in the number of these infections in the past decade.

INFECTIONS OF SPECIAL CONCERN DURING PREGNANCY

GROUP B STREPTOCOCCUS (GBS)

Essentials of Diagnosis

• High fever after delivery or uterine and adnexal tenderness.
• Early neonatal infection presents as fever, lethargy, respiratory distress, jaundice, and hypotension. Late-onset neonatal infection presents as meningitis and, less commonly, as bacteremia.
• Isolation of group B streptococcus (GBS) from neonatal or maternal blood cultures or a history of maternal colonization with GBS.

General Considerations

GBS is estimated to cause approximately 15,000 infant and 48,000 maternal infections in the United States each year. GBS causes postpartum endometritis in the mother and early-onset disease (bacteremia) or late-onset disease (meningitis) in the neonate. It is

BOX 22–14

Empiric Therapy of Septic Abortion

	Adults & Adolescents

First Choice	• Doxycycline, 100 mg every 12 h IV or orally **PLUS** one of the following:
	   • Cefoxitin, 2.0 g every 6–8 h IV
	   • Ticarcillin/clavulanic acid, 3.1 g every 6 h
	   • Imipenem, 0.5 g every 6 h IV
	   • Meropenem, 1.0 g every 8 h IV
	   • Ampicillin/sulbactam, 3.0 g every 6 h IV
	   • Piperacillin/tazobactam, 3.375 g every 6 h IV
	• Doxycycline, 100 mg orally every 12 h for mild symptoms

Second Choice	• Clindamycin, 450–900 mg IV every 8 h **PLUS** one of the following:
	   • Gentamicin, 2.0 mg/kg IV load then 1.7 mg/kg IV every 8 h[1]
	   • Cefotaxime, 2.0 g IV every 8 h

Penicillin Allergic	• Clindamycin, 450–900 mg IV every 8 h, and gentamicin, 2.0 mg/kg IV load, then 1.7 mg/kg every 8 h[1]

[1]Single daily dosing may be substituted.

also the cause of intrapartum chorioamnionitis, urinary tract infections, and postpartum wound infections. GBS can be part of the normal fecal and vaginal flora, and asymptomatic carriage rates vary from 5–40%, depending on the culture technique used and the population studied.

Risk factors for carriage of GBS include use of an intrauterine device and age younger than 20 years. Although vaginal colonization can be transient, approximately one-third of pregnant women are colonized throughout their pregnancy. Transmission to the neonate is estimated to occur 60% of the time when the mother is colonized. Early-onset disease is probably acquired by the neonate in utero or as the neonate passes through an infected birth canal. The number of cases of early-onset disease is estimated to be 1.3–3.7/1000 live births. Early-onset disease tends to occur in premature and low-birth-weight babies in the first 6–12 hours of life. Additional risk factors for early-onset disease include premature rupture of membranes, multiple births, maternal chorioamnionitis, maternal GBS bacteremia, and low levels of maternal type-specific capsular antibodies. The overall mortality is now approximately 15%.

Late-onset disease occurs in 0.5–1.8/1000 live births, and the mortality is approximately 10%. It usually presents 1 or more weeks after birth. The mode of transmission is by contact with hospital nursery personnel. Typically the maternal history and the birth are not complicated, and most affected infants are full term.

Clinical Findings

The neonate will display nonspecific signs such as fever, lethargy, respiratory distress, jaundice, and hypotension. There may be seizure activity if the onset is late. Isolation of the organism from blood or other sites (cervical cultures) is diagnostic. A history of maternal colonization may be obtained.

Treatment

Treatment of GBS infection in the mother and neonate includes empiric broad-spectrum antibiotics until culture results are known. Penicillin is the antibiotic of choice, once cultures are confirmed.

Prevention & Control

Several groups have shown that treatment of GBS in the mother with intrapartum antibiotics helps reduce the incidence of neonatal GBS disease by about 33–50%. Several groups have published guidelines for prophylaxis (Box 22–15). The American Academy of Pediatrics in 1992 recommended universal screening of all women for GBS by obtaining cultures from the distal vagina and anorectum at 26–28 weeks' gestation. Intrapartum prophylaxis should then be given to GBS carriers who are

BOX 22–15

Prophylaxis of Group B Streptococcal Infection

First Choice	• Ampicillin, 2.0 g once IV • Penicillin G, 5 million units IV, then 2.5 million units every 4 h IV • Penicillin potassium, 500 mg every 6 h orally if delivery not imminent
Second Choice	• Erythromycin, 1.0–2.0 g IV every 6 h • Vancomycin, 1.0 g IV every 12 h • Clindamycin, 600 mg IV every 6 h
Penicillin Allergic	• Erythromycin, 1.0–2.0 g IV every 6 h

at risk for neonatal sepsis. Risk factors include preterm labor, preterm premature rupture of membranes, multiple gestation, intrapartum fever, and real or anticipated membrane rupture for a period of 18 or more hours.

The American College of Obstetricians and Gynecologists (ACOG) 1992 guidelines did not advocate routine screening but rather the administration of intrapartum antibiotics (penicillin G, ampicillin, or erythromycin) based on the presence of certain risk factors: preterm labor, preterm premature rupture of membranes, prolonged membrane rupture, a sibling affected by GBS disease, and intrapartum maternal fever. Currently, ACOG advocates following their 1992 guidelines or obtaining routine cultures in women beginning at 32 weeks' gestation and treating with penicillin G those women with positive cultures at the time of labor.

The CDC advocates either the 1992 ACOG guidelines or screening all women at 35–37 weeks' gestation and administering intrapartum penicillin G for all culture-positive women. Several studies have shown, however, that despite the many guidelines, there is significant variability in screening and treatment among practitioners.

TERATOGENIC INFECTIONS & OTHER INFECTIONS OF CONCERN IN PREGNANCY

Certain infections, whether primarily acquired or reactivated during pregnancy, are of special concern.

These infections are important either because of their teratogenic effects or the morbidity and mortality with which they are associated in neonates. The teratogenic infections covered in this section are syphilis, toxoplasmosis, cytomegalovirus, rubella, and varicella. Measles, mumps, and parvovirus are discussed as well, as they can cause significant morbidity in the neonate. Herpesvirus and papillomavirus are also discussed, as they can be very common problems during pregnancy. Tables 22–2 and 22–3 describe these infections and summarize their treatment, prevention, and control during pregnancy and afterward.

SYPHILIS IN PREGNANCY

Esentials of Diagnosis

- Presentation similar to nonpregnant women.
- Late abortion after fourth month of pregnancy, stillbirth, or congenital syphilis in the neonate.

General Considerations

Congenital syphilis has become more of a problem in recent years, owing to the dramatic increase in the number of cases of syphilis. Pregnancy in a woman with syphilis may have any of the following outcomes: late abortion after the fourth month of pregnancy, stillbirth, a congenitally infected infant, or a healthy uninfected infant. There is no difference in presentation or diagnosis of syphilis in pregnant women. Any suspicious lesion in a pregnant woman should be examined, and serologic testing over a 6–8 week period should be performed. A positive nontreponemal (rapid plasma reagin [RPR] or Venereal Disease Research Laboratory [VDRL]) test result should be followed up with a fluorescent treponemal antibody absorption (FTA-ABS) test for confirma-

Table 22–2. Infections of special concern during pregnancy.

	Maternal Diagnosis	Fetal Diagnosis	Risk of Transmission	Congenital/Fetal Effects
Syphilis	Positive RPR or VDRL confirmed by FTA-ABS	Positive IgM, positive PCR on amniotic fluid	Almost 100% if mother has primary or secondary syphilis; 80% in early latent syphilis	Stillbirth, late abortion; hepatospleno-megaly, deafness, jaudice, interstital keratitis, congenital stigmata
Toxoplasmosis	Serology (IgG, IgM)	Elevated IgM, consistent clinical presentation, positive PCR on amniotic fluid	17% in first trimester; 65% in third trimester; 40% overall	Microcephaly, hydrocephalus, chorioretinitis, blindness
Cytomegalovirus (CMV) infection	Serology or isolation of CMV in urine or blood. PCR on blood	CMV in urine or blood; PCR on amniotic fluid, blood, CSF	Difficult to estimate due to large number of subclinical infections; incidence of congenital infection during pregnancy is about 1%. 40–60% of breastfed infants become seropositive	Hepatosplenomegaly, jaundice, chorioretinitis, hearing loss, microcephaly. Most often results from primary maternal infection; majority of congenital infections result from maternal reactivation of infection and are not associated with sequelae
Rubella	Serology (IgM and IgG); viral isolation can take up to 6 weeks	Serology; persistence of IgG after 1 month of life	80% in first trimester, 25% second trimester; risk of congenital anomalies greatest with infection in the first trimester	Hepatosplenomegaly, jaundice, pneumonitis, microcephaly, cataracts, heart abnormalities, glaucoma, mental retardation
Varicella-zoster virus (VZV) infection	Serology, DFA of preparation of lesions	Culture of lesions; DFA of infected cells, if any; serology	5–7% of pregnant women with VZV	Growth retardation, limb aplasia, cutaneous scarring, hearing loss, chorioretinitis, cataracts; neonatal chickenpox—benign course or disseminated infection
Herpes simplex virus	Isolation of virus, DFA preparation of lesions, PCR	Same as for maternal diagnosis	Difficult to estimate owing to high number of women who are asymptomatic shedders of virus. Incidence of congenital infection is < 0.1%.	Localized skin disease, encephalitis, keratoconjunctivitis, chorioretinitis, disseminated disease

tion. A nonreactive or borderline FTA-ABS test result in light of a positive nontreponemal test result should prompt a search for the cause of a biologic false-positive test, such as malaria, leishmaniasis, hepatitis, leprosy, antiphospholipid syndrome, or lupus anticoagulant.

If the mother has primary or secondary syphilis, it is very likely that the infant will be infected, as the spirochetemia that accompanies primary or secondary syphilis is usually quite intense. If the mother has early latent syphilis, there is an 80% chance of fetal infection. Once spirochetes enter the fetal circulation, dissemination to the tissues rapidly follows. The most severe cases of fetal infection follow maternal infection early in pregnancy, and fetal death may occur if the burden of spirochetemia is high. If spirochetemia occurs later in pregnancy, the child may be stillborn or die of congenital syphilis in the neonatal period. When intrauterine infection occurs relatively late in pregnancy, the child may be born with mild or no symptoms of infection. Signs and symptoms of infection may develop 2–4 weeks after birth. Occasionally congenital infection does not become apparent until several months have passed. It is also possible for the infant to acquire infection upon passage through the birth canal, by contact with a syphilitic lesion. Infants who acquire infection in this manner often have a presentation similar to sexually acquired syphilis.

Clinical Findings

A. Signs and Symptoms. Pregnancy does not affect the presentation of syphilis. Please see Chapters 15 and 65 for a more detailed discussion of syphilis.

Table 22–3. Treatment, prevention, and control of infections of special concern in pregnancy.

	Treatment of Mother	Treatment of Neonate	Prevention & Control
Syphilis	As for nonpregnant women. Follow with monthly VDRL or RPR titers and retreat if four-fold or higher increase in titers.	Aqueous crystalline penicillin G 100,000–150,000 U/kg/d in 3 divided doses for 14 days	Screening and treatment of high risk women
Toxoplasmosis	Spiramycin, 1.5 twice a day orally throughout pregnancy; or pyrimethamine, 25 mg once daily orally, plus sulfa-diazine, 1.0 g 4 times per day orally plus folinic acid, 6 mg 3 times/week orally, thoroughout pregnancy	If overt infection: pyrimethamine, 2 mg/kg orally every 2–3 d, and sulfadiazine, 100–200 mg/kg/d orally, and folinic acid, 5 mg orally every 3 days for 6 months, then 6 months of alternating monthly herapy with spiramycin. If the diagnosis is in question, administer pyrimethamine for 21 days, then spiramycin until a definitive diagnosis is made	Cook meat thoroughly; wash fruits and vegetables thoroughly; avoid contact with cat litter
CMV	None	None	Vaccine under investigation
Rubella	None	None	Vaccination of all women of child-bearing age
VZV	Acyclovir, 10 mg/kg every 8 h IV or 800 orally 5 times per day; VZIg, if given, should be given within 96 h of exposure	Acyclovir, 10 mg/kg every 8 h	Avoid exposure of nonimmune pregnant women to chickenpox or zoster
HSV	Acyclovir, 200 mg orally 5 times per day for 7–10 days for primary infection; 200 mg orally 5 times per day for 5 days for recurrences	Acyclovir, 10 mg/kg IV every 8 h	Cesarean delivery if active lesions

B. Laboratory Findings. Darkfield examination of a chancre may show *T pallidum*. Nontreponemal serology, VDRL or RPR, will be positive. Such tests should be followed up with an FTA-ABS for confirmation. If the findings on FTA-ABS are negative, the clinician should search for a cause of a biologic false-positive treponemal test. Polymerase chain reaction (PCR) on amniotic fluid has been shown to be very sensitive and specific. Spirochetes may be recoverable from fetal blood or from amniotic fluid. Maternal immunoglobulin G (IgG) that has crossed the placenta will cause positive results on nontreponemal and treponemal tests of cord and fetal blood. Serial quantitative serologic testing of the infant may show a rising titer—this is consistent with congenital infection.

Differential Diagnosis

Cutaneous lesions in the newborn are not always caused by syphilis. Erythroblastosis fetalis, congenital toxoplasmosis, rubella, and cytomegalovirus (CMV) infection can also cause cutaneous lesions and fetal abnormalities.

Treatment

The treatment of a pregnant woman with syphilis is the same as that in the general population. Some clinicians recommend that penicillin-allergic pregnant patients be desensitized to penicillin, as penicillin is thought to be the only antibiotic that reliably treats the fetus as well as the mother. Some practitioners recommend a second dose of benzathine penicillin G 1 week after the initial dose, especially in the third trimester. After treatment, the woman should be monitored with quantitative serologic titers and retreated if there is a fourfold or higher increase in the titer.

The neonate should receive aqueous crystalline penicillin G (100,000–150,000 U/kg/d in 3 divided doses) for 14 days or aqueous procaine penicillin G intramuscularly (IM) for 14 days.

Prognosis, Prevention, & Control

In a series of 403 pregnancies in women with positive serology for syphilis, 18% resulted in congenital syphilis (half of the babies were stillborn neonates). Of the mothers who gave birth to babies with congenital syphilis, 81% had not received any treatment for syphilis. Prevention of congenital syphilis requires prompt treatment of mothers who have syphilis as well as aggressive screening for syphilis in high-risk populations.

TOXOPLASMOSIS IN PREGNANCY

Essentials of Diagnosis

- Maternal infection as mild or subclinical flulike illness; sometimes cervical lymphadenopathy, fatigue, malaise, or atypical lymphocytosis.
- Infants can be asymptomatic or have chorioretinitis, blindness, deafness, seizures, microcephaly, hydrocephalus, fever, jaundice, hepatosplenomegaly, pneumonitis, or coagulopathy.
- Serologic diagnosis of mother and newborn; fetal ultrasound can be performed after maternal infection is confirmed. PCR testing on amniotic fluid can also be performed.

General Considerations

Toxoplasmosis is caused by the intracellular parasite *Toxoplasma gondii.* The prevalence of disease varies by geographic location. Congenital infection is relatively uncommon in the United States, where screening is not routinely done, but is very common in France, where universal screening is mandatory. Please see Chapter 81 for more discussion of toxoplasmosis in the general population.

In pregnancy, infection is often subclinical or mild and self-limited. A mononucleosis-like syndrome can occur, with fatigue, malaise, cervical lymphadenopathy, and atypical lymphocytosis. Pregnancy does not appear to predispose to more severe illness, but there may be an increased incidence of pregnancy-related complications in women who acquire primary infection while pregnant. The overall risk of fetal infection is 40%, and the later in pregnancy the woman acquires infection, the higher the risk of transmission to the fetus. The earlier in pregnancy the woman acquires infection, however, the higher the risk of severe manifestations of infection in the fetus. Transmission rates have been reported as 17% in the first trimester and 65% in the third trimester.

Clinical Findings

A. Signs and Symptoms. As stated, maternal infection may be very mild. In the infected infant, however, disease can be severe. There may be chorioretinitis, blindness, deafness, seizures, microcephaly, hydrocephalus, fever, jaundice, hepatosplenomegaly, pneumonitis, and coagulopathy. In many asymptomatic infants, chorioretinitis can develop, which may lead to blindness in adolescence or adulthood.

B. Laboratory Findings and Imaging. Diagnosis depends on serology, both in the mother and

infant. The mother's IgG and IgM titers should be measured. If titers are elevated and consistent with maternal infection, fetal ultrasound should be performed, looking for intracerebral calcifications, microcephaly, aqueductal stenosis, and hydrocephalus. After birth, infants suspected of having congenital toxoplasmosis should have serial serologies. The presence of IgM antibody indicates acute infection, whereas declining IgG titers in the absence of IgM antibodies indicate passive transfer of maternal antibodies. PCR tests on amniotic fluid appear to be as accurate as conventional diagnostic tests.

Differential Diagnosis

Congenital toxoplasmosis should be differentiated from congenital syphilis, erythroblastosis fetalis, congenital rubella, and cytomegalovirus infection (CMV).

Treatment

Many practitioners consider documentation of first-trimester fetal infection a reason for termination of pregnancy. Maternal infection between conception and the 24th week of gestation may also justify termination of the pregnancy.

When maternal infection is confirmed, treatment with spiramycin (1.5 g twice a day orally) should be started and continued throughout the pregnancy. Such treatment has been reported to reduce the incidence of fetal infection by 60%. Toxicity is minimal, and although generally available in Europe, spiramycin can be obtained in the United States only by application to the U.S. Food and Drug Administration (FDA). Pyrimethamine and sulfadiazine also can reduce the rate of transmission to the fetus and prevent progressive fetopathy but are associated with more toxicity. Folinic acid, 6 mg orally 3 times a week, should be given with this regimen. Because of the potential for teratogenicity, some clinicians recommend that pyrimethamine be begun only after the 14th week of gestation.

In the neonate, treatment of overt toxoplasmosis involves 6 months of therapy with pyrimethamine plus sulfadiazine and folinic acid and an additional 6 months of alternating monthly therapy with spiramycin. Healthy infants suspected of having congenital infection can be treated with pyrimethamine and sulfadiazine for 21 days followed by spiramycin until a definitive diagnosis is established.

Prognosis

The prognosis is good for the mother; 15% of infants born to infected mothers will be severely affected.

Prevention & Control

Prevention of toxoplasmosis can be achieved by thoroughly cooking meat, thoroughly washing fruits and vegetables, and avoiding contact with cat litter and soil or other materials contaminated with cat feces.

CYTOMEGALOVIRUS IN PREGNANCY

Essentials of Diagnosis

- The mother may be asymptomatic or have a mononucleosis-like illness.
- The infant may demonstrate cytomegalic inclusion disease, characterized by hepatosplenomegaly, jaundice, thrombocytopenia, chorioretinitis, cerebral calcifications, and microcephaly. Interstitial pneumonitis may develop.
- Maternal infection may be suggested by characteristic atypical lymphocytes and abnormal hepatic transaminases; the diagnosis can be made by isolation of cytomegalovirus (CMV) in urine or peripheral blood leukocytes, by serology, or by PCR on blood.
- Neonatal infection may be diagnosed by demonstration of CMV in urine; PCR testing of amniotic fluid is not yet standardized.

General Considerations

CMV is thought to be the most common congenital infection in humans. Rates of seropositivity in the adult population range from 35% to close to 100%, depending on the population studied. Approximately 1% of all live-birth infants in the United States are infected by CMV. 90% of infants with infection will be asymptomatic at birth, but manifestations of infection such as sensorineural hearing loss, chorioretinitis, mental retardation, and neurologic deficits will develop later in 10–20% of infants. More severe symptoms will occur in infants who are symptomatic at birth.

CMV differs from other causes of congenital infection in that mothers with both primary infection and a history of infection can transmit the virus to the fetus. Children born to mothers with a history of infection prior to conception are less likely to be symptomatic at birth, and the presence of maternal antibody may help prevent the serious sequelae of congenital infection. Transmission occurs by the passage of virus across the placenta or by ascending infection from the cervix. It can also occur during the neonate's passage through the birth canal, but this will not cause congenital infection.

Clinical Findings

A. Signs and Symptoms. Maternal infection may be asymptomatic, subclinical, or similar to mononucleosis. Congenital infection can be asymptomatic initially, although in 10–20% of asymptomatic infants neurologic deficits such as sensorineural hearing loss will develop later, usually within the first 2 years of life. Symptomatic cytomegalic inclusion dis-

ease develops in 6–19% of infants infected in utero. This is characterized by hepatosplenomegaly, jaundice, thrombocytopenia, chorioretinitis, cerebral calcifications, and microcephaly. Interstitial pneumonitis may also develop. The mortality rate of infants who are symptomatic at birth is approximately 29%. Perinatal infection can occur, in which the neonate acquires the virus from the mother who is seropositive, during passage through the birth canal. Most infections occurring in this manner are subclinical, although there have been some cases of interstitial pneumonitis developing in these infants, especially in premature infants.

B. Laboratory Findings. The mother may demonstrate seroconversion on serologic testing. Hepatic transaminase levels may be abnormal, and atypical leukocytes may be present. Virus can be isolated from the urine and peripheral blood leukocytes, but urine positivity may persist for months to years and does not establish acute infection. CMV-specific immunoglobulin M (IgM) can be detected in cord blood in approximately 60% of infected infants, but false-positive reactions also occur. Polymerase chain reaction (PCR) testing may be used to detect virus in amniotic fluid, but the technique has not yet been standardized.

Treatment

There is no approved treatment available for congenital infection. Viruria can be suppressed with adenine arabinoside, but rebounds as soon as therapy is stopped. Ganciclovir therapy is being studied in research protocols.

Prognosis

As stated earlier, neurologic deficits will develop in 10–20% of asymptomatic infants within the first 2 years of life. Of infants infected in utero, cytomegalic inclusion disease will develop in between 6% and 19%, with a mortality rate approaching 30%.

Prevention & Control

Prevention is difficult owing to the number of subclinical infections. There are experimental live attenuated vaccines under investigation in immunocompromised adults. Routine screening of pregnant women is not recommended at this time.

RUBELLA IN PREGNANCY

Essentials of Diagnosis

- Mild maculopapular rash, generalized lymphadenopathy, and transient arthritis in mothers.
- Cataracts, heart abnormalities, deafness, microcephaly, mental retardation, hepatosplenomegaly, hemolytic anemia, pneumonia, and striate radiolucencies in the bones. Extensive permanent sequelae in infants.

- Serologic diagnosis in mother and infant; virus isolation can be accomplished, but may take several weeks.`

General Considerations

There are a notable number of women of childbearing age who are susceptible to rubella, and thus their infants are at risk for congenital rubella, a disease with many serious and permanent sequelae. Rubella in pregnant women is similar to that in nonpregnant women; the likelihood of subclinical infection is similar as well. Spontaneous abortion occurs in 4–9% and stillbirths in 2–3% of pregnancies complicated by rubella infection.

The sequelae of fetal infection are thought to be caused by the effect of rubella virus on fetal cells, that is, prevention of cells from multiplying properly, resulting in fewer cells and smaller organs.

Transmission of infection is greatest in the first trimester, with rates up to 80% for the first 12 weeks of pregnancy, 54% during the 13th and 14th weeks, and 25% during the second trimester. Fetal infection occurs with both symptomatic and asymptomatic maternal infection, although the risk of fetal anomalies is greatest when infection occurs during the first trimester.

Clinical Findings

A. Signs and Symptoms. As already stated, maternal infection is characterized by a mild maculopapular rash, generalized lymphadenopathy, and transient arthritis. Maternal infection may also be subclinical.

Congenital rubella infection is characterized by hepatosplenomegaly, jaundice, hemolytic anemia, pneumonia, and striated radiolucencies in the bones. More permanent sequelae include microcephaly, sensorineural hearing loss, congenital heart abnormalities such as patent ductus arteriosus, cataracts, glaucoma, microophthalmia, and mental retardation. Delayed manifestations include endocrinopathies, such vascular abnormalities as arteriosclerosis and hypertension, and panencephalitis.

B. Laboratory Findings. Viral isolation may take up to 6 weeks, so serologies are often relied upon to make the diagnosis. Neutralization and hemagglutination (HI) antibodies appear soon after onset of the rash and persist indefinitely. Seroconversion of the HI antibodies is diagnostic. Complement fixation (CF) antibodies appear several days after onset of the rash and disappear after 10–20 years in 50% of individuals. CF antibody titers may be helpful in individuals in whom the HI antibody titer remains stable. A rubella immunoglobulin M (IgM) assay may also help to define recent infection. In infants, diagnosis is made by isolation of the virus from various body fluids (positive in approximately 90% of infected infants) or by serology. Persistence of immunoglobulin G (IgG) antibody over time supports the diagnosis of congenital rubella, as titers of passively transmitted maternal antibody begin to disappear after about 1 month.

Treatment

There is no treatment for infected infants or mothers, other than supportive care.

Prognosis

The overall mortality for infants is 5–35%.

Prevention & Control

Currently a live attenuated vaccine is available, which induces immunity in approximately 95% of recipients. Although the risk of transmission of vaccine virus to the fetus is small, vaccination is contraindicated in known pregnancy. If a woman receives vaccine and then discovers that she is pregnant, she should be counseled with respect to the risks of vaccine to the fetus, and termination of the pregnancy may be considered.

All unvaccinated women of childbearing age should have their rubella antibody titers evaluated, because clinical history of previous rubella infection is unreliable. If a woman is seronegative and not pregnant, she should receive the vaccine.

VARICELLA INFECTION DURING PREGNANCY

Essentials of Diagnosis

- Typical vesicular rash in the mother.
- Infants may have characteristic vesicular rash, disseminated disease, or congenital anomalies or might be asymptomatic at birth but have an episode of zoster many years later.
- Maternal varicella infection diagnosed clinically by examination of direct fluorescent antibody (DFA) preparations of infected cells from lesions or by serology.
- Neonatal infection diagnosed serologically.

General Considerations

The incidence of varicella infection as a complication in pregnancy is estimated to be about 0.01–0.7 cases/1000 pregnancies. Varicella infection in adults is more severe than in children. Pregnant women may have a more severe form of the disease than nonpregnant women, with a 41% mortality among infected women in the former group. Varicella-zoster virus (VZV) infection can have several effects on a pregnant woman and her fetus. Intrauterine infection with VZV can occur, rarely leading to congenital anomalies. Postnatal disease can also occur in newborns, ranging from a benign course characterized by typical lesions to a fatal disseminated form of disease. Zoster can also appear in the infant or child years after birth, even when the newborn subject was asymptomatic at birth. Such congenital anomalies as hypoplastic limbs and cutaneous scarring seen with VZV are thought to be caused by viral damage to developing tissues in a dermatomal distribution.

Clinical Findings

A. Signs and Symptoms. Maternal disease is relatively easy to diagnose, as the mother will have the characteristic rash. Maternal infection at any stage of pregnancy can result in fetal growth retardation, aplasia of a single limb, cutaneous lesions, neurologic damage such as hearing loss, psychomotor retardation, microophthalmia, chorioretinitis, and cataracts. Neonatal disease ranges from benign cutaneous rash to disseminated disease with pneumonitis.

B. Laboratory Findings. Maternal infection can be diagnosed clinically, with confirmation by immunofluorescence of scrapings from a lesion. Seroconversion is also diagnostic. In the newborn, immunofluorescence or culturing of a lesion provides the diagnosis, as does persistence of antibody long after maternal antibodies are expected to disappear.

Prognosis

Although the actual rate of fetal transmission is unknown, 5–7% of pregnancies complicated by VZV infection in the first trimester result in a newborn with congenital malformations. In pregnancies complicated by infection within 3 weeks of delivery, 17–24% of babies are infected at birth or shortly thereafter. Infants born to mothers with current varicella infection are at greatest risk of the development of disseminated disease, which is associated with a mortality rate of 30%.

Treatment & Prevention

Pregnant, nonimmune women who have been exposed to the virus can be given varicella immune globulin within 96 hours of the exposure. However, there is no evidence that this practice will prevent viremia and, thus, fetal infection. Acyclovir should be given to the infected mother. Infants should receive varicella immune globulin if the mother develops disease 5 days before delivery or 2 days after delivery. Infants with disseminated disease should receive antiviral therapy.

HERPES SIMPLEX VIRUS INFECTIONS IN PREGNANCY

Essentials of Diagnosis

- Characteristic lesions in mothers.
- Vesicular rash, keratoconjunctivitis, encephalitis, and disseminated disease in neonates.
- History of herpes infection in mothers or their partners and positive results on viral cultures, im-

munofluorescence, or polymerase chain reaction (PCR) tests of cerebrospinal fluid (CSF).

General Considerations

Neonatal herpes simplex virus (HSV) infection is estimated to occur in 2–7 infants/10,000 live births. Most cases are acquired during labor and delivery and are caused by HSV-2. Risk factors for neonatal HSV infection include active genital lesions at delivery, primary infection (greater risk than with recurrence), a history of genital herpes in mothers or their partners, delivery through an infected birth canal, delivery by cesarean section 6 or more hours after rupture of membranes, and instrument-assisted delivery. Premature infants are more likely than term infants to be infected. It is estimated that 0.1–0.39% of all pregnant women shed HSV at delivery. Cultures of the mother's genital tract collected days or weeks before delivery do not predict an infant's chances of exposure at the time of delivery.

Clinical Findings

A. Signs and Symptoms. The mother may have active genital lesions or be asymptomatic. Of infants affected by HSV infection, 40% have mothers do not recall a history of HSV infection. An infant will commonly show signs of infection at 1–3 weeks of age. HSV infection can result in skin disease with the characteristic vesicular lesions, keratoconjunctivitis and chorioretinitis, encephalitis, and disseminated disease.

B. Laboratory Findings. Most useful for diagnosis is isolation of the virus from skin lesions from the mother or infant. Immunofluorescent smears of cells from lesions are more rapid than culturing. DFA preparations of infected cells from lesions may provide a diagnosis relatively quickly. Serology is generally not useful, as it is often difficult to differentiate acute from past infection with the virus as well as whether the infection is due to HSV-1 or -2. Polymerase chain reaction (PCR) tests on cervical fluid may be more sensitive in detecting asymptomatic viral shedding in women.

Treatment & Prevention

The mother may be treated with oral acyclovir if she has active lesions. The neonate needs treatment with acyclovir intravenously. Predicting shedding of virus at the time of delivery is difficult. The American College of Obstetricians and Gynecologists (ACOG) recommends that cultures be taken to confirm the diagnosis of HSV when a pregnant woman has typical lesions. If there are no visible lesions at the time of delivery, vaginal delivery is acceptable. Weekly surveillance cultures of a woman with a history of HSV are not necessary. Amniocentesis in an attempt to confirm fetal infection is not recommended. Cesarean delivery should be performed when there are active lesions near the time of labor, when membranes are ruptured for less than 6 hours, or when there are prodromal symptoms of a recurrence.

Prognosis

It has been estimated that for a woman experiencing a primary episode of genital herpes at the time of delivery, there is a 50% risk of her neonate acquiring neonatal herpes, whereas for a woman who has a recurrence of genital herpes at the time of delivery, the risk is 3%.

HUMAN PAPILLOMAVIRUS IN PREGNANCY

Essentials of Diagnosis

- Condylomata acuminata in mothers.
- Laryngeal papillomas in children born to infected mothers.
- Polymerase chain reaction (PCR) analysis of lesions in mother and child to make rapid diagnosis.

General Considerations

Human papillomavirus (HPV) is the causative agent of genital warts, or condylomata acuminata. Various subtypes are more likely to cause malignant transformation of cervical cells, leading to cervical intraepithelial neoplasia and cervical cancer. In children, the virus can cause laryngeal papillomas, with exposure to the virus presumably occurring during passage through the birth canal. However, the virus can be transmitted to the child even when the mother has subclinical infection and no apparent lesions; as well, infants delivered by cesarean section have virus DNA in their nasopharynx, suggesting that there may be transplacental transmission of virus. The number of children who are born to infected mothers and later develop laryngeal papillomas is not known.

Clinical Findings

A. Signs and Symptoms. Infection in the pregnant woman may be notable for the great increase in size and number of genital lesions. The lesions may grow so large that vaginal delivery is impossible, necessitating cesarean delivery. The infant may be asymptomatic at birth, but laryngeal papillomas may develop within the first 2–5 years of life. These papillomas are located on the vocal cords and epiglottis but can involve the whole larynx and tracheobronchial tree.

B. Laboratory Findings. In the mother, cervical scrapings, biopsies of lesions, or scrapings from the lesions will display typical HPV-induced histologic or cytologic changes. PCR can detect viral DNA rapidly. Biopsies or scrapings from the child's lesions can also be tested by PCR.

Treatment

Lesions are treated if they cause discomfort or when it is anticipated that they will interfere with delivery. Trichloroacetic acid (50% or 80%) in 70% ethanol applied to the lesions three times a week or once a week is inexpensive and safe for the mother and fetus. Cryotherapy and laser ablation are also safe and well-tolerated in pregnant women. Podophyllin, 5-fluorouracil cream, and interferon therapy should not be administered to pregnant women.

Currently, the American College of Obstetricians and Gynecologists does not recommend routine cesarean delivery in women who have HPV infection.

Prognosis, Prevention, & Control

In the mother, genital warts usually diminish in size after delivery. In the child, surgery may be required to remove laryngeal papillomas. One study found that 32% of children born to mothers with genital papillomavirus had positive oral scrapings for papillomavirus DNA. Prevention consists of screening high-risk women aggressively for HPV.

MEASLES, MUMPS, & PARVOVIRUS INFECTION IN PREGNANCY

Measles infection complicates 6–40/100,000 pregnancies. There appears to be an increased risk of stillbirth, abortion, prematurity, and low birth weight in infants born to mothers who had infection while pregnant. There is no recognizable pattern of congenital anomalies with measles infection. Pregnant, nonimmune women who are exposed to the virus should be given immune serum globulin (0.25 mg/kg) within 6 days of the exposure. Such prophylaxis may modify maternal infection, but effects on fetal infection are unknown. Vaccination against measles is contraindicated within 3 months of conception because of the possibility of transmitting vaccine virus to the fetus.

Mumps infection occurs less frequently than measles during pregnancy, with an incidence of 0.8–10 cases/100,000 pregnancies. Mumps in pregnant women is similar to mumps in nonpregnant women. Transplacental infection does occur, but it is very rare. Virus has been isolated from breast milk, so transmission of virus from lactating women to their infants is possible. Virus can also be isolated from placental and fetal tissues, and there is a possible association between mumps during pregnancy and fetal endocardial fibroelastosis. Perinatal mumps can occur as well and may be complicated by pneumonia. Maternal infection may increase the risk of fetal loss. There is no effective treatment for an infected mother or child, other than supportive care. Prevention is best accomplished by ensuring that all women of childbearing age have been vaccinated against mumps.

Parvovirus (see Chapter 42) causes erythema infectiosum in childhood and aplastic crises in patients with hemolytic anemia. It is an uncommon infection during pregnancy (< 1% of all pregnancies), and an uncommon cause of stillbirths in women who have been exposed to the virus. Fetal hydrops and fetal death have been linked to some cases of parvovirus B19 infection during pregnancy. A large prospective study found that 17% of pregnant women who became immunoglobulin M (IgM)–positive in the first trimester suffered fetal losses, whereas 6% of women who became IgM-positive during the third trimester suffered fetal losses. If a pregnant woman has an illness compatible with parvovirus B19 infection, parvovirus antigen or DNA may be detectable in serum as may specific IgM antibodies. The fetus should be monitored by ultrasonography and maternal serum alpha-fetoprotein (AFP) levels. Elevated AFP levels have been detected 6 weeks before fetal death and 4 weeks before anomalies are noted on ultrasonography.

REFERENCES

Vulvovaginitis

Hiller SL et al: Role of bacterial vaginosis-associated microorganisms in endometritis. Am J Obstet Gynecol 1996;175:435.

Fleury FJ: Adult vaginitis. Clin Obstet Gynecol 1981;24:407.

Spiegel CA: Bacterial vaginosis. Clin Microbiol Rev 1991;4:485.

Cervicitis

Centers for Disease Control and Prevention: Guidelines for treatment of sexually transmitted diseases. MMWR 1998;47(No. RR-1).

Lee RV: Sexually transmitted diseases. In Burrow GN, Ferris TF (editors): *Medical Complications during Pregnancy*. Saunders, 1995.

Rein MF: Vulvovaginitis and cervicitis. In Mandell GL, Bennett JE, Dolin R (editors): *Mandell, Douglas and Bennett's Principles and Practice of Infectious Diseases*. Churchill Livingstone, 1995.

Sanford JP et al (editors): *The Sanford Guide to Antimicrobial Therapy 1997*. Antimicrobial Therapy, Inc., 1997.

Pelvic Inflammatory Disease

Centers for Disease Control and Prevention: Guidelines for treatment of sexually transmitted diseases. MMWR 1998;47(No. RR-1).

Hager WD et al: Criteria for the diagnosis and grading of salpingitis. Obstet Gynecol 1983;61:113.

Mead PB: Infections of the female pelvis. In Mandell GL, Bennett JE, Dolin R (editors): *Mandell, Douglas and Bennett's Principles and Practice of Infectious Diseases*. Churchill Livingstone, 1995.

Newkirk GR: Pelvic inflammatory disease: A contemporary approach. Am Fam Phys 1996;53(4):1127.

Walker CK et al: Pelvic inflammatory disease: Meta-analysis of antimicrobial regimen efficacy. J Infect Dis 1993;168:969.

Infections After Gynecologic Surgery

Larsson PG et al: Clue cells in predicting infections after abdominal hysterectomy. Obstet Gynecol 1991;77:450.

Mead PB: Infections of the female pelvis. In Mandell GL, Bennett JE, Dolin R (editors): *Mandell, Douglas and Bennett's Principles and Practice of Infectious Diseases*. Churchill Livingstone, 1995.

Soper DE et al: Bacterial vaginosis and trichomoniasis are risk factors for cuff cellulitis after abdominal hysterectomy. Am J Obstet Gynecol 1990;163:1016.

Chorioamnionitis

Gibbs RS, Duff P: Progress in pathogenesis and management of clinical intra-amniotic infection. Am J Obstet Gynecol 1991;164:1317.

Postpartum Endometritis

Hemsell D: Prophylactic antibiotics in gynecologic and obstetric surgery. Rev Infect Dis 1991;13(10):S821.

Hiller SL et al: Role of bacterial vaginosis-associated microorganisms in endometritis. Am J Obstet Gynecol 1996;175:435–51.

Hoyme UB et al: The microbiology and treatment of late postpartum endometritis. Obstet Gynecol 1986; 68:226.

Mead PB: Infections of the female pelvis. In Mandell GL, Bennett JE, Dolin R (editors): *Mandell, Douglas and Bennett's Principles and Practice of Infectious Diseases*. Churchill Livingstone, 1995.

Newton ER et al: A clinical and microbiologic analysis of risk factors for puerperal endometritis. Obstet Gynecol 1990;75:402.

Puerperal Ovarian Vein Thrombophlebitis (POVT)

Mead PB: Infections of the female pelvis. In Mandell GL, Bennett JE, Dolin R (editors): *Mandell, Douglas and Bennett's Principles and Practice of Infectious Diseases*. Churchill Livingstone, 1995.

Duff P, Gibbs RS: Pelvic vein thrombophlebitis: diagnostic dilemma and therapeutic challenge. Obstet Gynecol Surv 1983;38:365.

Episiotomy Infections

Mead PB: Infections of the female pelvis. In Mandell GL, Bennett JE, Dolin R (editors): *Mandell, Douglas and Bennett's Principles and Practice of Infectious Diseases*. Churchill Livingstone, 1995.

Septic Abortion

Stubblefield PG, Grimes DA: Septic abortion. N Engl J Med 1994;331:310.

Group B Streptococcus (GBS)

American College of Obstetricians and Gynecologists: Prevention of early-onset group B streptococcus in newborns. Committee on Obstetric Practice 1996; No. 173.

Boyer KW, Gotoff SP: Prevention of early onset neonatal group B streptococcal disease with selective intrapartum chemoprophylaxis. N Engl J Med 1986;314: 1995.

Centers for Disease Control: Prevention of neonatal group B streptococcal disease: A public health perspective. MMWR 1996;45:RR-7:1.

Clark P et al: Effectiveness of the ACOG guidelines in reducing the incidence of neonatal group B streptococcal sepsis. Am J Obstet Gynecol 1996;174:405.

Gibbs RS et al: Neonatal group B streptococcal sepsis during 2 years of a universal screening program. Obstet Gynecol 1994;84:496.

Mercer BM et al: Prenatal screening for group B streptococcus I: Impact of antepartum screening on antenatal prophylaxis and intrapartum care. Am J Obstet Gynecol 1995;173:837.

Noya FJ, Baker CJ: Prevention of group B streptococcal infection. Infect Dis Clin North Am 1992;6:41.

Pylipow M et al: Selective intrapartum prophylaxis for group B streptococcus colonization: Management and outcome of newborns. Pediatrics 1994;93:631.

Rouse DJ et al: Strategies for the prevention of early-onset neonatal group B streptococcal sepsis: A decision analysis. Obstet Gynecol 1994;83:483.

Towers C et al: Are the ACOG risk factors for GBS prophylaxis practical? Am J Obstet Gynecol 1996;174: 406.

Syphilis in Pregnancy

Coles FB et al: Congenital syphilis surveillance in upstate New York, 1989–1992: Implications for prevention and clinical management. J Infect Dis 1995; 171:732.

Greenwood AM et al: Treponemal infection and the outcome of pregnancy in a rural area of the Gambia, West Africa. J Infect Dis 1992;166:842.

McFarlin BL et al: Epidemic syphilis: Maternal factors associated with congenital infection. Am J Obstet Gynecol 1994;170:535.

Rawstron SA et al: Maternal and congenital syphilis in Brooklyn, NY: Epidemiology, transmission, and diagnosis. Am J Dis Child 1993;147:727.

Toxoplasmosis in Pregnancy

Couvreur J, Desmonts G: Toxoplasmosis, pp 112–142. In MacLeod C (editor): *Parasitic Infections in Pregnancy and the Newborn*. Oxford University Press, 1988.

Hohlfield P et al: Prenatal diagnosis of congenital toxoplasmosis with a polymerase-chain-reaction test on amniotic fluid. N Engl J Med 1994;331:695.

Hunter K et al: Prenatal screening of pregnant women for infections caused by cytomegalovirus, Epstein-Barr virus, herpes virus, rubella, and *Toxoplasma gondii*. Am J Obstet Gynecol 1983;145:269.

Sever J et al: Toxoplasmosis: Maternal and pediatric findings in 23,000 pregnancies. Pediatrics 1988;82: 181.

Shay-Pederson B, Lorentzen-Styr A: Uterine toxoplasma infections and repeated abortion. Am J Obstet Gynecol 1977;138:357.

Cytomegalovirus in Pregnancy

Alford C, Bvritt W: Cytomegalovirus, pp 1981–2010. In Fields BN, et al (editors): *Virology,* 2nd ed. Raven Press, 1990.

Fowler KB et al: The outcome of congenital cytomegalovirus in relation to maternal antibody status. N Engl J Med 1992;326:663.

Varicella Infection During Pregnancy

Brunell PA: Varicella in pregnancy, the fetus, and the newborn: Problems in management. J Infect Dis 1992;166(Suppl 1):S42.

Enderes G et al: Consequences of varicella and herpes zoster in pregnancy: Prospective study of 1739 cases. Lancet 1994;343:1547.

Katz VIL et al: Varicella during pregnancy—maternal and fetal effects. West J Med 1995;163:446.

Rouse DJ et al: Management of the presumed susceptible varicella (chickenpox)-exposed gravia: A cost-effectiveness/cost-benefit analysis. Obstet Gynecol 1996;87:932.

Herpes Simplex Virus Infections In Pregnancy

American College of Obstetricians and Gynecologists: Perinatal herpes simplex virus infections. Technical Bulletin No. 122, 1988.

Arvin AM et al: Failure of antepartum maternal cultures to predict the infant's risk of exposure to herpes simplex virus at delivery. N Engl J Med 1986;315:796.

Boggess KA et al: Herpes simplex type 2 detection by culture and polymerase chain reaction and relationship to genital symptoms and cervical antibody status during the third trimester of pregnancy. Am J Obstet Gynecol 1997;176:443.

Brown ZA et al: Neonatal herpes simplex virus infection in relation to asymptomatic maternal infection at the time of labor. N Engl J Med 1991;324:1247.

Human Papillomavirus In Pregnancy

American College of Obstetricians and Gynecologists: Genital human papillomavirus infections. Technical Bulletin No. 193, June 1994.

Fife KH et al: Cancer-associated human papillomavirus types are selectively increased in the cervix of women in the first trimester of pregnancy. Am J Obstet Gynecol 1996;174:1487.

Puranen M et al: Vertical transmission of human papillomavirus from infected mothers to their newborn babies and persistence of the virus in childhood. Am J Obstet Gynecol 1996;174:694.

Puranen M et al: Exposure of an infant to cervical human papillomavirus infection of the mother is common. Am J Obstet Gynecol 1997;176:1039.

Measles, Mumps, & Parvovirus Infection In Pregnancy

Eberhart-Philips et al: Measles in pregnancy: A descriptive study of 58 cases. Obstet Gynecol 1993;82:797.

Public Health Laboratory Service Working Party on Fifth Disease: Prospective study of human parvovirus (B19) infection during pregnancy. Br Med J 1990; 300:1166.

General

Burrow GN et al (editors): *Medical Complications during Pregnancy.* Saunders, 1995.

Centers for Disease Control and Prevention: Guidelines for treatment of sexually transmitted diseases. MMWR 1998;47(No. RR-1).

Cunningham FG et al (editors): *Williams' Obstetrics.* Appleton & Lange, 1997.

Mandell GL et al (editors): *Mandell, Douglas and Bennett's Principles and Practice of Infectious Diseases.* Churchill Livingstone, 1995.

Sanford JP, et al (editors): *The Sanford Guide to Antimicrobial Therapy 1997.* Antimicrobial Therapy, Inc. 1997.

Section III.
Special Patient Populations

Patients With Aids

23

Dani-Margot Zavasky, MD, Julie L. Gerberding, MD, MPH & Merle A. Sande, MD,

Essentials of Diagnosis

- Predisposing factors include sexual activity with an infected person, injection drug use, blood product transfusion, especially between 1978 and 1985, perinatal exposure to an infected mother, and percutaneous occupational exposure.
- Key signs and symptoms include systemic illness with fevers, night sweats, weight loss, diarrhea, lymphadenopathy, depressed immunity as evidenced by opportunistic infections, and unusual malignancies such as Kaposi's sarcoma and lymphomas.
- Laboratory findings of antibody to human immunodeficiency virus (HIV)-1, 23–1 confirmed with Western blot, viral genome by polymerase chain reaction or branched DNA assay, HIV p24 antigen, and lymphopenia, especially depressed CD4 cell count. (See tables 23–1, 23–2)

General Considerations

When the first clusters of cases of *Pneumocystis carinii* pneumonia and Kaposi's sarcoma were identified in 1981, it was not known that this was just a prologue to one of the most significant pandemics in the history of mankind and that, < 20 years later, 50 million people would be affected. Our knowledge of the disease started with the dramatic growth in the number of cases of unusual opportunistic infections in patients without prior inherited immunodeficiency disorders. Acquired immunodeficiency syndrome (AIDS) entered the medical and colloquial vocabulary. Not until 1983 was the offending agent identified as a virus. Known initially as lymphadenopathy-associated virus, then human T-cell lymphotropic virus type III, and AIDS-associated retrovirus, the microorganism acquired its current name, human immunodeficiency virus (HIV), in 1986. See Chapter 40 for a discussion of the virology of HIV and other retroviruses.

A. Epidemiology. Retrospective examination of sera collected for studies of the genetics of hematologic diseases indicate that HIV was already present in sub-Saharan Africa in the 1950s and in the United States by the late 1970s. In 1985, a related but distinct virus, HIV-2, was also found to be endemic in parts of West Africa and to cause AIDS. To date, this virus has been relatively restricted geographically, although it has been imported into the Western Hemisphere.

AIDS has been now reported in more than 150 countries. The United Nations estimates that as of December 2000, 58 million people have been infected with HIV. 22 million people have already died, of which 3 million died in 2000. As we are entering the third decade of AIDS history, the epidemic continues to spread rapidly through several continents. A total of 16,000 persons are infected per day worldwide, including 1600 children < 15 years of age. Women constitute over 40% of the adult cases. About 7000 people die from complications of HIV infection every day. Most infected persons live in either sub-Saharan Africa (> 70%) or South/Southeast Asia (> 20%).

In recent years, the epidemic has been particularly explosive in South/Southeast Asia and Central and Eastern Europe. The predominant mode of transmission appears to be heterosexual contact in Asia and injection drug use in Europe. Increasing syphilis incidence in Central/Eastern Europe signifies an increase in sexually transmitted diseases (STDs) of all kinds, including HIV, in this part of the world. There were 700,000 HIV infected patients by the end of 2000 compared with just 420,000 at the end of 1999.

In the United States, 920,000 AIDS cases and 460,000 deaths from AIDS were reported through December 2000. The total number of infected individuals in the United States probably exceeds 1 million; 45,000 of which became infected in 2000. The epidemiology of HIV infection is changing in the United States as the pandemic evolves. In 1992, 50% of all cases occurred in gay men and 25% in intravenous drug users , whereas 15% were derived from heterosexual contacts. Currently, the greatest increase in viral spread is occurring in the heterosexual population, similar to that observed in sub-Saharan Africa. The trends also confirm increase of infection in blacks and Hispanics, with blacks constituting ~ 41% of all adult cases. Also, women now account for 23% of all adult cases in the United States. The epidemic appears to affect predominantly women of color, particularly black women of African descent living in the southeastern part of the United States, in small rural communities (as opposed to the large cities, where HIV transmission in this same population occurred in the 1980s). Cases of AIDS in Hispanic women of Puerto Rican ancestry also predominate in the Northeast, especially in the states of Connecticut, New York, and New Jersey. However, in the Southwest and the West, Hispanic women of mostly Mexican and Central American descent have the same infection rate as white women. The facilitators of transmission in this heterosexual population again appear to be multiple sexual partners and the exchange of sex for money and drugs, especially crack cocaine.

In 1997, HIV/AIDS dropped from the first to the second leading cause of death in young adults in the United States. In 2000 it wasn't even one of the top 10 causes of death in young adults. The death rate in black men is fourfold that in white men and is also higher in black women than white men. Improved medical management of HIV disease resulted in an overall 23% decrease in AIDS deaths, especially among homosexual men, beginning in 1996. Also, between 1992 and 1995, perinatal AIDS cases decreased by 27% as a result of the widespread use of maternal and infant antiretroviral prophylaxis with zidovudine (AZT).

B. Pathogenesis. HIV is transmitted between humans in at least three ways: sexually, perinatally, and by exposure to contaminated body fluids, especially blood. The virus has been demonstrated in particularly high titers in semen and cervical secretions, and a majority of infections result from sexual contact. Infection is facilitated by breaks in epithelial surfaces, which provide direct access to the underlying tissues or bloodstream. The relative fragility of the rectal mucosa together with a large number of sexual contacts probably contributed to the predominance of the disease among male homosexuals in the initial stages of the epidemic. Heterosexual transmission accounts for an increasing proportion of new cases in the western world but has always been the dominant mode of transmission in the developing countries. Sexual transmission appears to be more efficient from men to women. The risk of perinatal transmission from an infected mother to her child has been estimated at 20–30%.

Testing of donor blood and the use of recombinant or specially treated coagulation factors have now virtually eliminated blood products transfusion as a source of infection in developed countries. Transmission of infection by blood is now largely associated with the sharing of needles and syringes by injection drug users. In some areas of the world, the seroprevalence of HIV infection among injection drug users has been as high as 70%. Transmission of infection to health care workers is rare but occurs after 0.3% of exposures to blood during needle punctures.

Transmission of HIV does not occur through a casual (nonsexual) contact with infected individuals or through insect vectors. The virus has been detected in saliva, tears, urine, and breast milk, but with the exception of breast milk, these fluids are not sources of infection.

PREDICTORS OF DISEASE PROGRESSION

The course of HIV disease is dictated by the severity of the individual's immune deficiency and the resulting complications. The recent impact of highly active antiretroviral therapy (HAART) on the slowing progression of HIV infection has been dramatic; however, therapy is complicated and expensive, thus not available to the vast majority of patients worldwide that would benefit.

The determinants of progression of the HIV disease have been under intense scrutiny by the research community. Results of prior studies emphasized the role of high viral load, presence of particularly virulent strains (eg, those that produce syncytium formation in culture) and low T-lymphocyte function as predictors of rapid disease progression. Recently, several coreceptors for HIV have been identified. The two most important of these are CCR5 and CXCR4. Individuals homozygous for a deletion in the CCR5 gene are resistant to infection regardless of multiple exposures to the virus. Some infected persons who are heterozygous for this deletion have been noted to have a prolonged AIDS-free survival. In current clinical practice, however, two main markers are used to monitor disease progression and to evaluate the need for and response to treatment: CD4 lymphocyte count and viral load.

CD4 Lymphocyte Count (Immunologic Monitor)

CD4 lymphocytes are the major cellular target for HIV. Both absolute CD4 counts and the rate of decline have prognostic predictive value and are used to determine the need for antiretroviral therapy and for opportunistic infection prophylaxis. CD4 counts do not accurately indicate viral load per se, but they predict the short-term risks for progression to AIDS-related illness.

Quantitative HIV RNA (See table 23–2) (Virologic Monitor)

The quantitative titer of circulating HIV RNA (viral load) is the single best predictor of long-term progression and response to treatment. Viral load is used to assess the steady-state concentration of HIV, the response to treatment, and, most likely, tissue HIV RNA production.

Two main methods are generally used to measure viral load: reverse transcriptase-polymerase chain reaction (RT-PCR) and branched-chain DNA (bDNA) amplification. (See table 23–2) By 2001, three commercial assays based on these methods or modifications of these methods were used to measure viral load: Amplicor HIV Monitor (RT-PCR, lower limit of detection = 400 viral copies/mL), Quantiplex HIV assay (bDNA, lower limit of detection = 500 copies/mL), and Nuclisens (lower limit of detection = 40 copies/mL). Assays with even more sensitivity such as Amplicor Ultrasensitive (lower limit of detection = 20 copies/mL) and Quantiplex HIV 3.0 (lower limit of detection = 50 copies/mL) are currently undergoing clinical evaluation. To optimize interpretation, two measurements of viral load should be obtained on two separate occasions in the same laboratory using the same assay. When possible, viral load testing should be delayed until 4 weeks after intercurrent infections are treated, acute illnesses have resolved, and following an immunization.

Current guidelines for viral load testing suggest that the pretreatment measurement be obtained to evaluate the patient's prognosis and that tests be repeated every 3–4 months until treatment is started. Once treatment is initiated, a measurement should be obtained 4–8 weeks later to determine whether the expected initial therapeutic response (0.5–0.75 log reduction in titer) has been achieved. Another measurement should be made 3–4 months later to determine whether HIV replication is fully suppressed (below the level of detection). If not, then adherence should be assessed and treatment modifications considered. Once the patient is on a stable antiviral regimen, viral load tests should be obtained every 3–4 months to monitor ongoing virologic response.

CLINICAL SYNDROMES

HIV infection can produce a huge array of clinical syndromes. In general, these syndromes correlate with the duration of illness and severity of immunosuppression. The major clinical syndromes and their treatment are described in Box 23–1. The following sections describe the most common symptoms associated with HIV infection at various stages of infection.

1. CONSTITUTIONAL SYMPTOMS

Fever (with or without night sweats) is common in patients infected with HIV, especially in the setting of advanced disease. The absolute CD4 cell count can help to guide the evaluation and differential diagnosis.

A. Early Disease (CD4 > 500). Etiology similar to that in immunocompetent patients except for more common bacterial pneumonia and tuberculosis . Acute HIV infection is also associated with fever.

B. Midstage Disease (CD4 200–500). Particular attention should be given to the possibility of disseminated tuberculosis. In sexually active adults, STDs and anorectal infections often go unrecognized as sources of fever.

C. Late Disease (CD4 75–200). When fever accompanies an accelerated catabolic state with weight loss and anorexia, the presence of an opportunistic infection or malignancy (mainly lymphoma), signifying the onset of AIDS should be suspected. Systemic symptoms with fever also predominate over pulmonary complaints in early PCP. Common etiologies of fever at this stage of HIV disease are also disseminated tuberculosis, nonthyphoid *Salmonella* bacteremia, bartonellosis, and fungal diseases including histoplasmosis, coccidioidomycosis, and cryptococcosis.

D. Advanced Disease (CD4 < 75). Even though diseases as outlined in late-stage disease can also occur at this stage, disseminated mycobacterium avium complex and systemic cytomegalovirus (CMV) infections are common.

2. CENTRAL NERVOUS SYSTEM (CNS)

Altered Mental Status

Changes in mentation involve cognitive dysfunction, decreased level of consciousness, and delirium and psychosis. Altered mental status can be caused by both infectious and noninfectious disorders. Differential diagnosis, again, is influenced by the known degree of immunosuppression, that is, the stage of HIV disease. Most infections occur in patients with CD4 counts < 200.

The mainstay of evaluation includes history (especially of substance abuse), neurological examination, neuroimaging (computer tomography or MRI), cerebrospinal fluid examination, and thorough review of medications. Altered mental status at any CD4 count can be caused by bacterial meningitis, neurosyphilis, as well as by noninfectious etiologies such as metabolic disorders, seizures, or trauma. Recreational drug use and prescription medication toxicity are other possibilities.

A. Late Disease (CD4 75–200). At this stage of the HIV disease, patients can be afflicted with cryptococcal meningitis, herpes virus family (CMV, HSV, and VZV) encephalitis, and *Toxoplasma* encephalitis. Patients are also vulnerable to HIV-associated dementia (AIDS dementia complex) and primary CNS lymphoma, which can be the result of Epstein-Barr virus-associated transformation of infected cells.

B. Advanced Disease (CD4 < 75). Disorders typical for late disease as well as progressive multifo-

BOX 23-1

Clinical Syndromes, Opportunistic Infections, and Neoplasms Caused by HIV

Syndrome & Cause	Clinical Presentation	Laboratory Correlates	Treatment and Prophylaxis
Early Disease (CD4 > 500) Acute Retroviral Syndrome (HIV)	• Fever • Adenophathy • Pharyngitis • Rash • Myalgia/arthralgia • Diarrhea • Headache • Nausea/emesis • Hepatosplenomegaly • Neuropathy • Encephalopathy	• Thrombocytopenia • Lymphopenia, then atypical lymphocytosis • Transaminitis • High-level HIV viremia	Usually resolves in 1–2 weeks; may benefit from antiretroviral therapy
Aseptic meningitis (HIV)	• Headache • Photophobia • Fever	• CSF: lymphocytic pleocytosis; mild, modest increase in protein	
Immune Thrombocytopenic Purpura (ITP)	• Easy bruising • Epistaxis • Splenomegely	• Thrombocytopenia; no evidence of production defect on bone marrow aspiration	Have benefitted from antiretrovirals, especially AZT +/– prednisone. Options for refractory cases: IVIG, Danazol, alpha-interferon, splenectomy
Midstage Disease (CD4 200–500) Mycobacterium tuberculosis (TB)	Classic reactivation pulmonary disease with higher CD4 counts; cough, fever, weight loss, upper lobes infiltrate, pulmonary cavities. Atypical presentation with lower CD4 with hilar adenopathy, diffuse pulmonary infiltrates without cavitation, pleural effusions, or extrapulmonary disease (blood, lymph nodes, CNS, genitourinary tract,pleura).	CXR; sputum: AFB smear and culture; bronchoscopy if sputum is negative; blood cultures for AFB positive in 40%; pleural or lymph node biopsy	• Four-drug regimen: isoniazid, rifampin, pyrazinemide, ethanbutol. • Same treatment principles as in HIV-negative population. • MDR–TB treatment individualized. • Purified protein derivative (PPD) of 5 mm or greater should be prophylaxed with isoniazid.

BOX 23–1

Clinical Syndromes, Opportunistic Infections, and Neoplasms Caused by HIV (continued)

Syndrome & Cause	Clinical Presentation	Laboratory Correlates	Treatment and Prophylaxis
Kaposi's Sarcoma (HHV-S)	• Mucocutaneous palpable, firm, nontender nodules or ecchymosis–like lesions; violaceous, brown or black. • Oral lesions common. • Visceral disease: GI with bleeding, perforation, and obstruction; pulmonary with dyspnea cough, bronchospasm. • Lesions may become painful. • Edema formation.	Biopsy recommended; visceral disease visualized during bronchoscopy or endoscopy.	• Local therapy for cosmetic reasons: radiotherapy, cryotherapy, retinoic acid, intralesonal vinblastine. • Systemic chemotherapy with, most commonly, doxorubicin, bleomycin, vincristine (ABV), or liposomal doxorubicin, or daunorubicin as a single agent. • Marked reduction incidence with HAART.
Pneumococcal Disease (Streptococcus pneumoniae)	• Sinusitis or pneumonia with productive cough, fever, pleuritic chest pain; evidence of consolidation or effusion on physical exam. • Meningitis bacteremia common.	CXR with lobar; positive sputum; or BAL; positive blood culture, pleural fluid or CSF.	• Ceftriaxone 2 g IV daily consolidation (each 12 h for meningitis), or cefotaxime, or others, depending on susceptibility. • Pneumococcal vaccine recommended for all HIV-positive patients.
Thrush (oral Candidiasis)	• Pseudomembranous form with white plaques that can be wiped off leaving erythematous or bleeding base. • Erythematous form with smooth, red patches.	KOH prep of the scraping and culture.	• Fluconazole, 200 mg first dose, then 100 mg PO per day for 14 d. Clotrimazole troches 10 mg PO 5×/day or Nystatin sol. or tab 3–5 ×/day for 5 days.

cal leukoencephalopathy are caused by a human polyomavirus known as JC virus. Primary CNS lymphoma and advanced AIDS dementia complex are more common at this stage.

Headache

Headache may pose a challenging diagnostic dilemma. Besides a vast array of opportunistic CNS infections and malignancies, it can result from muscle tension, or a systemic illness without a direct affliction of intracranial structures. Headache can be induced by a medication frequently used for treatment of HIV disease, for example, AZT, or by migraine not related to HIV infection. At any stage of the HIV disease, patients are more susceptible to bacterial meningitis or sinusitis as well as to neurosyphilis. Other opportunistic infections tend to occur at specific levels of immunosuppression.

A. Early Disease (CD4 > 500). Aseptic meningitis probably caused by HIV itself can accompany acute seroconversion in the early stage of HIV disease.

B. Midstage Disease (CD4 200–500). Aseptic meningitis syndrome is even more common than in earlier stages and can assume a form of chronic meningitis.

C. Late Disease (CD4 75–200). Many disorders mentioned above that can alter mental status also cause headache. These include cryptococcal meningitis and *Toxoplasma* encephalitis.

D. Advanced Disease (CD4 < 75). Both progressive multifocal leukoencephalopathy and primary CNS lymphoma are more frequent.

3. GASTROINTESTINAL SYMPTOMS

Dysphagia

Swallowing difficulty (dysphagia) is frequently accompanied by pain (odynophagia). Patients complain about the sensation of food sticking. Appropriate diagnosis and treatment are important not only to alleviate the discomfort but also to prevent weight loss and malnutrition. At any stage of HIV disease, patients can develop reflux esophagitis. However, esophageal complaints and disorders are more typical for late to advanced disease.

A. Midstage Disease (CD4 200–500). Early thrush (oral mucosal candidiasis) can occur with some esophageal discomfort. In that setting, PCP prophylaxis is indicated irrespective of the CD4 count.

B. Late Disease (CD4 75–200). Most common cause is *Candida* esophageal mucosal infection with frequent concomitant oral lesions. HSV type 1 or 2 can induce mucosal ulceration.

C. Advanced Disease (CD4 < 75). Same as

late disease, but CMV and aphthous ulcers are more frequently encountered.

Diarrhea

Diarrhea is a commonly encountered clinical problem in HIV-infected patients and may be caused by HIV itself. Symptoms range from frequent loose stools to fulminant diarrhea, producing profound weight loss, malabsorption, and intravascular fluid depletion. A thorough evaluation is warranted because virtually any gastrointestinal pathogen may be found.

Both small bowel and colon can be affected, causing enteritis or colitis, respectively. Symptoms of enteritis include profuse, watery diarrhea often with symptoms of bloating, nausea, and periumbilical cramping. Volume depletion and malabsorption may be marked. Colitis presents with fever, lower abdominal pain, tenesmus, and passage of frequent, small volume stools with mucus and sometimes blood. Characteristics of symptoms can guide the choice of initial diagnostic procedure but are unreliable to predict the most likely pathogen. CD4 cell count can, again, be useful in outlining differential diagnosis.

At any CD4 cell count, the following agents should be considered: *Clostridium difficile; Salmonella, Campylobacter, Shigella,* and *Cyclospora* spp.; *Entamoeba histolytica; Giardia lamblia; Isospora belli;* enteroviruses; and *Strongyloides stercoralis.* Most of the antiretroviral drugs also cause diarrhea.

A. Late Disease (CD4 75–200). *Cryptosporidium parvum* and *Microsporidium* spp. should also be considered in addition to those listed above.

B. Advanced Disease (CD4 < 75). *Mycobacterium avium* complex and CMV should be included in the differential diagnosis.

4. RESPIRATORY SYMPTOMS (DYSPNEA/COUGH)

The differential diagnosis of lower respiratory symptoms is extensive and largely depends on the stage of HIV disease with consideration to current PCP prophylaxis, history of travel, or area of residence. Tuberculosis can occur with various clinical signs, depending on the degree of immunosuppression and should be considered in every HIV patient regardless of CD4 count. Appropriate isolation precautions should be undertaken according to clinical suspicion. Irrespective of CD4 counts, typical bacterial causes of pneumonia should also be considered, especially *Streptococcus pneumoniae, Haemophilus influenzae, Legionella pneumophila, Mycoplasma pneumoniae,* and *Chlamydia pneumoniae.*

A. Late Disease (CD4 75–200). PCP should always be considered, particularly in the setting of a lack of appropriate prophylaxis. Fungal pneumonias with

Coccidioides immitis, Cryptococcus neoformans, or *Histoplasma capsulatum* are also possible. Kaposi's sarcoma is also known to cause pulmonary lesions, especially with worsening immunodeficiency.

B. Advanced Disease (CD4 < 75). Besides the above etiologies, *Pseudomonas aeruginosa* and *Aspergillus* species can be encountered, especially with neutropenia or repeated hospital exposure. Non-Hodgkin's lymphoma can also affect lungs. Isolation of CMV and *Mycobacterium avium* complex is common, but they rarely cause symptomatic pulmonary disease.

5. CUTANEOUS LESIONS

Various dermatologic diseases are extremely common in HIV infection, affecting ~90% of patients. Some of the conditions occur in immunocompetent individuals but are more severe and resistant to therapy in HIV-infected persons. Other skin conditions are unique to HIV disease and tend to follow the degree of immunosuppression. Patients with HIV disease tend also to have a preponderance for drug sensitivity reactions compared with an HIV-negative population.

A. Early Disease (CD4 > 500). Primary HIV infection may be associated with rash. Lesions associated with STDs (eg, genital HSV or genital warts) can be seen. Staphylococcal folliculitis, impetigo, ecthyma, hidradenitis, and cellulitis are the most common bacterial skin infections. Kaposi's sarcoma lesions can also occur at this stage.

B. Midstage Disease (CD4 200–500). Mucocutaneous candidiasis, oral hairy leukoplekia, herpes zoster, psoriasis, seborrheic dermatitis, and atopic dermatitis become evident.

C. Late Disease (CD4 75–200). Skin infections occurring earlier in the HIV course become more chronic (HSV, for instance) and refractory to therapy. Opportunistic fungal infections (eg, cryptococcosis or histoplasmosis) can present as skin lesions. Eosinophilic folliculitis associated with pruritus tends to affect patients with worsening immunosuppression.

D. Advanced Disease (CD4 < 75). Very unusual skin lesions can occur that warrant biopsy to establish a diagnosis. Bacillary angiomatosis and *Molluscum contagiosum* can develop, signifying a profound immunosuppression.

Treatment

In the past 2 years, tremendous progress has been made in treatment of HIV infection. New combination treatment regimens can suppress virus replication below the level of detection in many individuals. However, cure is still not possible.

Antiretroviral treatment guidelines are undergoing rapid evolution, but some consensus about general principles has been achieved. First, the major goal of treatment is to suppress viremia and prevent immunosuppression. To reduce the risk that drug-resistant isolates will emerge, therapy should be implemented only when the patient is ready to adhere to a treatment regimen. Treatment is recommended for all patients with symptomatic HIV infection (eg, AIDS, thrush, and fever of unknown origin). For asymptomatic patients, the decision is more complex. Potential benefits of starting therapy in these patients include the following:

- Earlier control of HIV replication.
- Decreased opportunity for mutations to occur.
- Decreased total body viral burden.
- Prevention of immunosuppression.
- Delay in progression to AIDS.

However, these potential benefits must be weighted against treatment risks:

- Reduced quality of life due to drug toxicity and the inconvenience of treatment.
- Earlier development of drug resistance.
- Limitations in future drug options.
- Unknown long-term treatment toxicity.

Most experts believe that treatment should be offered to asymptomatic patients when immunosuppression has developed (ie, CD4 < 350) or when viral load is high (ie, > 30,000 copies/mL with bDNA assay or 55,000 copies/mL with RT-PCR), especially if the patient desires treatment and is likely to adhere to it. (See table 23–3)

Monotherapy is no longer recommended for HIV treatment. A combination of three antiviral drugs, to fully suppress plasma HIV below the level of detection, is now recommended. Antiviral drugs are grouped into three categories: (See table 23–4)

- Nucleoside reverse transcriptase inhibitors (NRTI): nucleoside analogs that inhibit HIV reverse transcriptase (RT), interfering with formation of DNA.
- Nonnucleoside reverse transcriptase inhibitors (NNRTI): inhibit RT by a different mechanism than NRTI.
- Protease inhibitors (PI): prevent cleavage of viral proteins precursors interfering in viral maturation and assembly.

Table 23–4 lists the drugs that were approved for HIV treatment by 1998. Adherence, side effects, and drug-drug interaction should be considered when choosing a regimen. All medications are started at the same time at the full dose (although dose escalations are needed for ritonavir, nevirapine, and ritonavir in combination with saquinavir).

Table 23–1. Laboratory tests commonly used in the diagnosis of infection with HIV-1.

Test	Primary Purpose(s)	Sensitivity %	Specificity %

HIV-1 antibody tests
A. Detection of antibody in serum or plasma
  1. Enzyme-linked Immunosorbent Assay (ELISA) followed by
    Western blot for confirmation. Current ELISA assay detects antibodies
    to both HIV-1 and HIV-2.			

	For all high-risk groups *(Table 1)*; antibody becomes positive approx. 3 wks. post-disease acquisition in majority; 6 mos. after infection, 95% pts antibody-positive.	99.9	99.9

Western blot: 1. No antibodies (bands) detected = **negative**
       2. Antibody (bands) to Gp41 and Gp 120/160 or
         either of latter plus p24= **positive**
       3. Any other pattern of positive = **indeterminate.**
         Proceed to plasma viral load testing.			

2. Rapid detection method: Examples: Single use diagnostic system (SUDS)	Results available in 30 minutes or less When quick answer needed, e.g., test blood of source pt in occupational exposure. Pts who may not comply with return visit: ER, STD clinics	99.9	99.6
3. Home test kits, e.g., Home Access Express. **NOTE: Other kits sold on internet unreliable.**	Encourage individuals at risk to determine their antibody status. Convenient. Anonymity maintained.	100	99.95

B. Detection of HIV-1 antibody in other body fluids
  1. Antibody in oral mucosal
    transudate (OraSure)
	Major advantage is avoidance of need for a needlestick. Easy to use; collected by health care worker	99.9	99.9

2. Antibody in urine (Sentinel or Calypte): HIV-1 Urine ELISA	Rapid—results in 2.5 hrs. Like rapid tests, could be used on source blood if occupational exposure or in ERs, STD clinics	99.7	94

Table 23–2. Detection and measurement of HIV-1.

Test	Current Use	% Positive
Detection/measurement of HIV **A. HIV-1 p24 antigen** (Assumes acid pretreatment to dissociate immune complexes)	• Diagnosis of acute HIV syndrome (antibody not detectable for ≥2 months) • Used to screen all donated blood	% positive depends on method/stage of disease, eg, in acute retroviral syn.: 100%; if CD4 200–500, 45–70%; if CD4 <200, 75–100%

B. Measurement of plasma "viral burdens"
Due to assay differences, use same assay repeatedly for a given patient. REsults with RT-PCR consistently 2-fold or more greater than bDNA
  For given assay, need change of ≥0.5 $\log_{10}$ for significant change
	• Current methods:
	  (1) Couples reverse transcription (RT) to a **DNA PCR amplification** (RT-PCR) (Roche)
	NOTE: Ideally collect with EDTA & separate plasma within 6 hrs.
	  (2) Amplification of RNA of HIV; a **nucleic acid sequence-based amplification** (NASBA) (Organon Teknika)
	  (3) Identification of HIV RNA then **signal amplification by DNA branched-chain technique** (referred to as bDNA) (Chiron-Bayer)
		>98
		
		>98
		
		>98

Table 23–3. Timing of antiretroviral treatment.

When should antiretroviral treatment be started? The most important factor in answering this question is to determine if the patient is ready to comply with the difficult regimens since lack of compliance guarantees failure of the treatment and facilitates the emergence of resistant subpopulations of virus, making it more difficult to treat the patient later. It also creates the potential for spread of resistant viruses to others. Studies indicate that about 1/3 of patients are totally adherent, 1/3 partially adherent and 1/3 almost totally nonadherent to prescribed treatment. Two important factors affect adherence: (1) the number of pills and (2) ease of administration of the regimen (qd better than bid, which is better than tid). Mixing medications with different frequency and food restrictions makes total adherence nearly impossible. In one study of 88 pts, virologic failure occurred in 22% of pts who were adherent for >95% of doses and in 61% of those with 80% to 94.5% adherence. Every effort should be made to come to an agreement or contract with the patients as to what he/she is capable of or willing to comply with prior to initiating treatment. Frequent follow-up with advice and encouragement to the patient is important to help maintain compliance and to detect noncompliance. In 2001, a shift to a more conservative (later initiation of treatment was supported, based on saving drugs as long as possible from developing resistance and on minimizing long-term drug toxicity without sacrificing efficacy.

An exception to late therapy is the acute retroviral (HIV) syndrome: Most authorities would treat immediately with HAART in an attempt to rapidly control viral proliferation, establish a lower viral set-point, and preserve the immunologic response (virus-specific cytotoxic T-cells and CD4 helper cells) against HIV.

Ranges of CD4 Cell Count and Viral Load Levels for Therapy Initiation

CD4 + Cells, x10⁶/L	<5,000	Plasma HIV RNA Level, copies/mL 5,000–30,000 βDNA (55,000 PCR)	>30,000 βDNA (>55,000 PCR)
<350	Consider therapy	Recommend therapy	Recommend therapy
>350	Defer therapy	Defer therapy	Recommend therapy

Note: Therapy is recommended in symptomatic patients.

Table 23-4. Quick reference guide to antiretrovirals

Inhibitor type	Generic	Brand	Dose	Comments and Common Side Effects
Nucleoside Analogs (NRTIs)	Zidovudine (AZT or ZDV)	Retrovir	300 mg twice daily	Initial nausea, headache, fatigue, anemia, neutropenia, neuropathy, myopathy
	Lamivudine (3TC)	Epivir	150 mg twice daily	Generally well tolerated; active against HBV
	AZT + 3TC	Combivir	1 tablet twice daily	Combination tablet containing 300 mg of AZT and 150 mg of 3TC
	Didanosine (ddI)	Videx	200 mg twice daily or 400 mg once daily on empty stomach (>60 kg body weight) or 250 mg (orally, each day) (<60 kg body weight)	Clinical data supports twice-daily dosing as more effective. Peripheral neuropathy in 15%, pancreatitis; avoid alcohol. Contains antacid: ok to give tablets at same time as all NRTIs, nevirapine and efavirenz; delavirdine and indinavir must be taken at least 1 h prior to ddI: nelfinavir can be taken 1 h after ddI
	Zalcitabine (ddC)	Hivid	0.375–0.75 mg 3 times daily	Peripheral neuropathy in 17–31% of trial participants; oral ulcers
	Stavudine (d4T)	Zerit	40 mg twice daily (>60 kg body weight) 30 mg bid (for <60 kg)	Peripheral neuropathy (1–4% in early studies; 24% in expanded access patients with CD4+ counts <50)
	Abacavir (ABC)	Ziagen	300 mg twice daily	About 3%–5% hypersensitivity reaction: fever, malaise, possible rash, GI. Resolves within 2 days after discontinuation. DO NOT RECHALLENGE. Also: rash alone without hypersensitivity.
Protease Inhibitors (PIs)	Amprenavir	Agenerase	1200 mg (8 cap) twice daily	Rash (20%), diarrhea, nausea
	Indinavir	Crixivan	800 mg (2 cap) every 8 h on empty stomach or with snack containing <2 g of fat.	Kidney stones in 6–8%: good hydration essential. Occasional nausea and GI upset. Store in original container which contains dessicant; without this, IDV is stable for only about 3 days
	Lopinavir	Kaletra	Coformulated lopinavir 400 mg + ritonavir, 100 mg *3 capsules twice daily with food*	GI side effects common but mild. No significant food effect. Available in limited expanded access;
	Nelfinavir	Viracept	1,250 mg (5 tab) twice daily with food	Diarrhea common; occasional nausea
	Ritonavir	Norvir	600 mg (6 cap) twice daily; start with 300 mg twice daily and increase to full dose over 14 days	Nausea, diarrhea, numb lips for ≥ 5 weeks; occasional hepatitis. Store capsules in refrigerator. Stable at room temperature for ≤ 1 month. Used at lower dosages as pharmacokinetic enhancer of other protease inhibitors
	Saquinavir soft gel cap	Fortovase	1,600 mg (8 cap) twice daily or 1,200 mg (6 cap) 3 times daily with fat-containing food (>28 g)	Soft gel formulation with improved absorption, essentially replacing previous hard gel formulation (Invirase). Long-term storage in refrigerator. Stable at room temperature for 3 months.
	Amprenaviir	Agenerase	1200 mg twice daily avoid high-fat meal	Skin rash in 28%; rarely severe in 1%; nausea, vomiting, and diarrhea common in 1/3; paresthesias and depression not uncommon.
Non-Nucleoside Reverse Transcriptase Inhibitors (NNRTIs)	Delavirdine	Rescriptor	400 mg (2 tab) 3 times daily	Transient rash. P450 3A4 inhibitor. 600-mg-twice-daily dosing being studied
	Efavirenz	Sustiva	600 mg (3 cap) once daily at bedtime	Initial dizziness, insomnia, transient rash, P450 3A4 inducer; avoid clarithromycin
	Nevirapine	Viramune	200 mg (1 tab) once daily for 2 weeks, then 200 mg twice daily or 400 mg once daily	Transient rash, hepatitis. P450 3A4 inducer. Once daily dosing recommendation based on limited clinical data

Table 23–5. Summary of suggested initial treatment of HIV infection.[1]

Preferred		Alternative	
Column A	Column B	Column A	Column B
Efavirenz	Stavudine + lamivudine	Abacavir	Didanosine + lamivudine
Indinavir ± ritonavir[1]	Stavudine + didanosine	Amprenavir	
Ritonavir[2] + saquinavir	Zidovudine + lamivudine	Delavirdine	
Nevirapine	Zidovudine + didanosine	Lopinavir/ritonavir (Kaletra)	
		Nelfinavir + saquinavir	
		Ritonavir	
		Saquinavir SGC[3]	

[1]Antiretroviral drug regimens are comprised of of one choice from column A and one from column B. Drugs are listed in alphabetical, not priority order.
[2]Increasingly, ritonavir is used in combination with other protease inhibitors because it lowers their metabolism (via P450 inhibition) and maintains high trough antiviral activity. This allows bid dosing while still preventing viral escape.
[3]Use of saquinavir hard-gel capsule is not recommended, except in combinatino with ritonavir.

Numerous clinical trials confirmed that antiretroviral combination therapy results in greater reductions of viral RNA copies, less frequent emergence of resistance, and a more sustained therapeutic response. Available data and clinical experience support using a combination of two NRTIs along with a PI as the most potent combination available (HAART). However, the choice of drugs has to be individualized based not only on the patient's virologic and immunologic response but also on the patient's tolerance of side effects, ease of use, potential drug-drug interactions, and cost. With growing numbers of new antiretrovirals, the recommendations about the best combination therapy continue to be modified. Alternatives to the two NRTI-one PI combination are indicated in Table 23–5).

For suggestions when initial treatment fails, See Table 23–6. Responses to failure.

Medical care should focus on providing comfort, preventing the opportunistic infections, and managing the new complexities of antiretroviral therapy. In the terminal stage of HIV disease, treatment of the virus itself along with opportunistic infections and especially the malignancies is often palliative and should be instituted after careful consideration of the potential complications of therapy. A thorough discussion of these facts with the patients will facilitate realistic treatment expectations. The use of life-support measures, including cardiopulmonary resuscitation and mechanical ventilation, should also be addressed as early as possible. The survival rate for AIDS patients with respiratory failure has actually improved in the past few years, and intensive care is certainly not contraindicated. However, the expected benefit from aggressive measures must be balanced against the overall quality of life in the face of progressive disease.

Prognosis

Throughout the course of HIV disease, there is an active viral replication and concomitant stimulation and destruction of the immune system, even during the clinically asymptomatic period. The rate of progression of the infection that eventually culminates in complete destruction of the CD4 lymphocytes is determined by a balance between the pathogen virulence factors and the host genetic make-up and immune defenses against HIV.

Prevention & Control

Vaccine against HIV is not yet available, and prevention of infection relies on controlling transmission of the virus. Control encompasses both prevention counseling and postexposure prophylaxis.

Assessment of risk factors as well as specific risk reduction information should be a part of routine primary care and a component of evaluation at the specific HIV testing centers and STD clinics. A supportive, nonjudgmental atmosphere, along with repeated,

Table 23–6. Responses to failure of treatment.

What is the appropriate treatment when the antiretroviral regimen fails? Failure may be due to many different reasons, and it is important to identify the cause. Most treatment failures are due to a patient's lack of compliance with the complicated triple-drug therapies. Patients may not recognize that they are being noncompliant or may be too embarrassed to admit it. The following actions and/or recommendations should be considered in the event of failure of the treatment:

- When the increase in viral RNA is likely due to a aptient's **noncompliance** to treatment, **one may initially reinstitute the original regimen**, especially if the patient stopped all drugs at once (it has been shown that after a year on treatment, when drugs are stopped simultaneously, the viral isolates will still be sensitive to all three drugs, and patients will again respond to reinitiation of the original treatment).
- When the increase in vrial RNA is likely due to the patient's **erratic compliance** with the treatment, or **if the patient was compliant and still showed a rise in viral RNA,** the virus may well be resistant to all drugs. **In that event, a change in treatment is warranted, and, if possible, all drugs should be changed.**
- When treatment failure cannot be shown to be due to either noncompliance or erratic compliance, **drug malabsorption** or a **drug-drug interaction,** both of which can decrease the effective plasma drug concentrations, should be considered. The use of plasma drug levels in cases where the cause of failure is not apparent may also be of value.
- **Tests for detection of mutations that confer resistance (genotyping) and phenotypic tests for detection of resistance to antiretroviral drugs are now commercially available and are recommended for supporting the above clinical decisions regarding which drugs should be used next.**

specific information targeting specific identified risk factors, is most effective.

Injection drug users should be encouraged to join a drug rehabilitation program and offered evaluation for entry into methadone maintenance programs if available in the community. Short of discontinuation of drug injection, some behavioral modifications can reduce the risk of a potential HIV transmission; for example, using sterile equipment or cleaning drug paraphernalia, especially needles and syringes, with water and then bleach (for at least 30 seconds). Some communities also offer needle/syringe exchange programs. Eliminating needle sharing or reducing the number of sharing partners could further reduce the risk of transmission.

Promotion of safer sexual practices should be an essential part of prevention counseling. Such practices focus on implementation of consistent condom use and the reduction of the number of partners. Screening and treatment of STDs further contribute to reducing the risk of sexual transmission of HIV.

Counseling should also incorporate issues of contraception and a possibility of virus transmission from an infected mother to her baby. All pregnant HIV-infected individuals should receive antiviral treatment to prevent viral transmission to the baby.

Even though only AZT monotherapy was studied and proved to reduce the risk of HIV transmission to the neonate, a single drug antiviral regimen is no longer acceptable for treatment of the mother. Thus combination therapy should be used. Mothers should also be counseled about the potential risk of HIV transmission via breast milk, and alternative infant feeding should be initiated.

Prevention of occupational exposures should involve education and reinforcement of universal precautions and implementation of devices and safe disposal of contaminated materials that would minimize a possibility of exposure to infected body fluids. Postexposure prophylaxis with antiviral medications after an occupational high-risk exposure to contaminated body fluids has become widely accepted, and specific treatment protocols have been implemented by various health-care institutions. In general, postexposure prophylaxis should be initiated as soon as possible after a known or a potential exposure and should consist of a combination either of zidovudine and lamivudine or stavudine and didanosine. With either regimen, consideration should be given to the addition of a protease inhibitor (nelfinavir or indinavir) if exposure is especially risky (large volume/high titer) or if the source patient has a high viral load (> 50,000 copies/mL), has advanced AIDS, or has been previously treated with one or both nucleoside analogues in the recommended two-drug regimens. Triple therapy is the regimen preferred by most health-care providers.

Experience with occupational postexposure prophylaxis has led recently to considerations for expansion of prophylactic treatment of individuals with recent sexual exposure to HIV. The current proposed regimen is the same as for occupational exposure. Postexposure prophylaxis should only constitute a backup for failure of primary prevention measures. Counseling and implementation of risk reduction programs should always be the mainstay of prevention of HIV transmission.

REFERENCES

Carpenter CJ et al: Antiretroviral therapy for HIV infection in 1997. JAMA 1997;277:1962.

Centers for Disease Control: Update: trends in AIDS incidence–United States, 1996. MMWR 1997;46:861.

De Roda Husman AM et al: Association between CCR5 genotype and the clinical course of HIV-1 infection. Ann Intern Med 1997;127:882.

Karon JM et al: Prevalence of HIV infection in the United States, 1984–1992. JAMA 1996;276:126.

Saag MS et al: HIV viral load markers in clinical practice. Nature Med 1996;2:625.

Sande MA, Volberding PA: The Medical Management of AIDS, 5th ed. WB Saunders, 1999.

Sande MA et al: The Stanford Guide to HIV/AIDS Therapy. 2001.

Vlahov D et al: Prognostic indicators for AIDS and infectious disease death in HIV-infected injection drug users. JAMA 1998;279:35.

World Health Organization: HIV/AIDS. The global epidemic. Wkly Epidemiol Rec 1997;72:17.

Essentials of Diagnosis

- Signs and symptoms include fever, chills, pulmonary infiltrates, skin rash, allograft dysfunction in transplant recipients.
- Distinguishing features include the following:

  1. Type of transplant [liver, lung, heart, pancreas, kidney, small bowel, peripheral blood stem cell (PBSC), bone marrow].

  2. Immunosuppression history (type, dose, duration).

  3. Cytomegalovirus (CMV) serology of donor and recipient (pretransplant).

  4. History of infectious diseases.

  5. Exposures (travel, tuberculosis, animals, occupation, etc).

General Considerations

Solid-organ, PBSC and bone marrow transplantation have become therapeutic options for many human diseases. PBSC, bone marrow, liver, kidney, heart, and lung transplantation have become standard therapy for selected end-stage diseases. Pancreas (including islet cell) and small bowel transplantation are also being evaluated in this regard. PBSC involves using stem cells mobilized by the administration of recombinant human granulocyte macrophage colony-stimulating factor. There are several types of PBSC or bone marrow transplants:

- Allogeneic transplantation involves transplantation from a human leukocyte antigen identical or non-identical relative or an unrelated donor who is fully or partially matched for human leukocyte antigens.
- Syngeneic transplantation involves transplantation from an identical twin who is completely identical for all genetic loci.
- Autologous transplantation involves harvesting PBSC or bone marrow from a patient, treating the same patient with high doses of intensive chemotherapy and subsequently reconstituting the same patient with his/her own PBSC or bone marrow.

Infection remains a major complication of all types of transplantation. The optimal approach to infection in transplant recipients is prevention; failing this, its prompt and aggressive diagnosis and therapy are essential. The sources of infectious agents post-transplantation include endogenous organisms, the transplant allograft itself, and the environment. An important principle to consider when evaluating transplant recipients for infection is that the usual inflammatory response to an infectious organism may be attenuated as a result of immunosuppressive therapy and therefore that the signs and symptoms of infections may be blunted and diagnostic techniques may be compromised. Because of this, aggressive and often invasive investigations of seemingly minor findings may be warranted.

Pretransplantation Infectious Diseases Evaluation

Before transplantation, all potential candidates should be evaluated for active infection that may require therapy or preclude transplantation, risk factors for infection, including latent infections that might be reactivated post-transplantation, and the use of immunosuppressive agents. A complete history should be obtained, focusing on any history of infection and any unusual exposures (Table 24–1). A complete physical examination should also be performed. Table 24–1 outlines infectious disease tests that should be performed pretransplantation.

Further investigations are pursued depending on elicited risks. For example, serologic testing for *Coccidioides immitis* may be performed on a patient with a history of travel to or residence in the southwestern United States or Mexico. Patients who have traveled to or resided in an area where *Strongyloides stercoralis* is endemic should be examined for evidence of infection with this parasite. Lung transplant candidates should be evaluated for colonization of the respiratory tract with such agents as *Aspergillus* spp.

Timing of Post-Transplantation Infection

A. Solid-Organ Transplantation. There are three time frames, influenced by surgical factors, the level of immunosuppression, and environmental exposures, during which infections of specific types

Table 24–1. Clues to the diagnosis of infections in transplant recipients.

History
- Immunosuppressive therapy: type and duration (current or past)
- Antibiotic allergies
- Past medical history: infectious diseases
  Oral: dental caries, sinusitis, pharyngitis, herpes
  Respiratory: pneumonia, tuberculosis
  Cardiovascular: valvular heart disease, heart murmur (need for endocarditis prophylaxis)
  Gastrointestinal: diverticulitis, diarrheal disease, hepatitis A, B, and C, intestinal parasitic infection
  Genitourinary: urinary tract infections, prostatitis, vaginitis, genital herpes, genital warts, syphilis, gonorrhea, pelvic inflammatory disease, chlamydial infection
  Cutaneous: skin and nail infections, varicella zoster virus infection
  Osteoarticular: osteomyelitis; prosthetic joint(s)
  Childhood illnesses: chickenpox, measles, rubella
  Other: mononucleosis
- Vaccinations

Exposure History
- Travel history: prior residence, travel, or both associated with the geographically restricted endemic mycoses, and/or parasitic disease, especially *Strongyloides stercoralis,* malaria, etc.
- Tuberculosis: exposure, prior tuberculous skin testing, chest x-ray abnormality
- Risk factors for bloodborne pathogen infection [including human immunodeficiency virus (HIV)]
- Animal and pet exposure (including vaccination status of pets)
- *Brucella* exposure
- Occupational exposure: farming, animal husbandry, gardening
- Drinking water source
- Exposure to young children
- Dietary habits: consumption of raw meat and seafood and unpasteurized milk products

Complete Review of Systems

Complete Physical Examination

Laboratory Testing
- Pretransplantation:
  Tuberculin skin test
  Chest and sinus x-ray
  Urinalysis and urine culture for bacteria
  Serologic tests: cytomegalovirus, varicella zoster virus, Epstein-Barr virus, herpes simplex virus,* *Toxoplasma gondii,*** syphilis, hepatitis A virus, hepatitis B virus, hepatitis C virus, HIV, (*coccidioides immitis* if history of exposure present—see text)
- Post-transplantation:
  Cultures and stains for bacteria, viruses, fungi, mycobacteria, etc, as indicated
  Serologic testing as indicated

**Heart transplant candidate
*Optional

most frequently occur after solid-organ transplantation (Box 24–1). These include the first month; the second through the sixth months; and the late post-transplant period (beyond 6 mo).

Most infections during the first month post-transplantation are related to surgical complications and are similar to infections occurring in general surgical patients. These include bacterial and candidal wound infections, pneumonia, urinary tract infections, line sepsis, and infections of biliary, chest, and other drainage catheters. In general, any episode of unexplained fever or bacteremia occurring in the early post-transplantation period should be suspected as being caused by technical or anatomical problems related to the allograft. In the first month post-transplantation, renal and pancreas transplant recipients are at risk for perigraft abscesses, infected or uninfected hematomas, lymphoceles, and urinary leaks. Liver transplant recipients are at risk for portal vein thrombosis, hepatic vein occlusion, hepatic artery thrombosis, biliary stricture formation and leaks, infected and uninfected hematomas and hepatic and perihepatic abscesses. Heart transplant recipients are at risk for mediastinitis and infection at the aortic suture line, with resultant mycotic aneurysm, and lung transplant recipients at risk for disruption of the bronchial anastomosis and pneumonia. The only common viral infection seen during the first month post-transplantation is reactivated herpes simplex virus (HSV) infection in individuals seropositive for this virus pretransplantation. The prophylactic use of acyclovir during this period, however, has significantly reduced the incidence of reactivated HSV infection.

The period from the second to sixth month post-solid-organ transplantation is the time during which infections "classically" associated with solid-organ transplantation manifest. Opportunistic pathogens such as CMV, *Pneumocystis carinii, Aspergillus* spp., *Nocardia* spp., *Toxoplasma gondii,* and *Listeria*

BOX 24-1

Microbiology of Infection in Solid-Organ Transplant Recipients

Solid–Organ Transplant Recipients	First post-transplant month	• Bacteria • *Candida* spp. • Herpes simplex virus
	Months 2–6 post-transplant	• Cytomegalovirus • *Pneumocystis carinii* • *Aspergillus* spp. • *Nocardia* spp. • *Toxoplasma gondii* • *Listeria monocytogenes* • *Mycobacterium tuberculosis* • *Histoplasma capsulatum* • *Coccidioides immitis*
	From 6 months onward post-transplant	• Respiratory viruses • Urinary tract infection • *Streptococcus pneumoniae* • Varicella zoster virus (reactivation) • Cytomegalovirus (retinitis) • Nontuberculous mycobacteria
	Anytime post-transplant	• *Cryptococcus neoformans* • Hepatitis B or C • Human immunodeficiency virus
PBSC and Bone Marrow Transplant Recipients	First post-transplant month (neutropenia)	• Herpes simplex virus • *Candida* spp. • *Aspergillus* spp. • Bacteria
	Second and third post-transplant months (acute graft-versus-host disease)	• Cytomegalovirus • *Aspergillus* spp. • Bacteria • Adenovirus • RSV • Parainfluenza virus • BK virus
	From 3 months onward post-translant	• Varicella zoster virus (reactivation) • *S pneumoniae* • *Haemophilus influenzae* • Respiratory viruses

monocytogenes manifest during this period. In addition, during the early and middle periods, reactivation disease syndromes are occasionally encountered because of organisms present in the recipient pretransplantation. The introduction of high-dose immunosuppression may result in clinical illness owing to reactivation of *Mycobacterium tuberculosis,* an occult focus of bacterial infection, viral hepatitis, *Histoplasma capsulatum,* or *C immitis.* Chronic or latent infection of the donor that involves the allograft, such as HIV, hepatitis B virus (HBV), hepatitis C virus (HCV), or fungal or mycobacterial infection, may be transmitted to the immunosuppressed recipient and become clinically apparent during the early and middle periods.

From 6 months post-transplant onward, most solid-organ transplant recipients do relatively well, suffering from the same infections seen in the general community. These include influenza virus infection, urinary tract infection, and pneumococcal pneumonia. The only opportunistic viral infection commonly seen during this period is reactivated varicella zoster virus (VZV) infection manifesting as shingles. Rarely, CMV retinitis occurs.

Two situations, however, predispose patients to other infections in this late post-transplant period. First, patients who have had frequent episodes of acute rejection requiring augmented immunosuppressive therapy or those with chronic rejection who are maintained at a high baseline level of immunosuppression remain at increased risk for the opportunistic agents more classically seen in the second to the sixth months post-transplant (CMV, *P carinii, L monocytogenes, T gondii, Aspergillus* spp., and *Nocardia* spp.). Second, patients with chronic infections such as HIV, HBV, and HCV infections, may suffer from morbidity associated with these agents.

B. PBSC and Bone Marrow Transplantation. There are three time frames within which the majority of infections develop after PBSC and bone marrow transplantation (Box 24–1). These include the first month after transplant (before engraftment); the second through the third month after transplant (engraftment); and the late post-transplant period, 3 months or later after transplant. During the first month after transplantation, before engraftment, granulocytopenia and damaged mucosal surfaces caused by pretransplant chemotherapy and radiotherapy are the predominant defects in host defenses. At this time, patients are most susceptible to infections caused by gram-negative and gram-positive aerobic bacteria and fungi. Reactivated HSV infections in patients previously seropositive for HSV are also common, similar to the situation in solid-organ transplant patients. And, similar to the situation in solid-organ transplant patients, the prophylactic use of acyclovir during this period has significantly reduced the incidence of reactivated HSV infection.

During the second to third month after PBSC and bone marrow transplant when engraftment has occurred, patients have profound impairment of both cellular and humoral immunity. These abnormalities are more severe and persist longer in patients with acute graft-versus-host disease (which is the major risk factor for infection during the second to third month after transplantation). Autologous and syngeneic transplant recipients who are not usually at risk for graft-versus-host disease experience significantly fewer and less severe infections after engraftment than allogeneic transplant recipients. Interstitial pneumonia related to CMV and pulmonary aspergillosis are the major infectious complications seen in patients with graft-versus-host disease, especially when high doses of immunosuppressive therapy are given for treatment. Gram-positive bacterial infections related to indwelling intravenous catheters, gram-negative bacteremia in patients with graft-versus-host disease of the gastrointestinal tract, pulmonary infection caused by adenovirus, respiratory syncytial virus, or parainfluenza

virus, hemorrhagic cystitis caused by BK virus or adenovirus, as well as viral gastroenteritis, may be seen during this time period.

The period from 3 months onward after PBSC and bone marrow transplantation is characterized by gradual recovery over several months of both cellular and humoral immunity. The process of donor-derived immune reconstitution is generally complete by 1–2 years after transplantation. Except for reactivation of VZV infections (shingles) and infections of the respiratory tract caused by *Streptococcus pneumoniae* and *Haemophilus influenzae* or common respiratory viruses, PBSC and bone marrow transplant recipients without graft-versus-host disease experience relatively few late infections. Immune recovery, however, is seriously delayed by chronic graft-versus-host disease, which causes persistent and profound defects in both cellular and humoral immune responses. Decreased secretory IgG production, impaired splenic function, inadequate opsonizing antibody, and the bronchopulmonary sicca syndrome characteristic of chronic graft-versus-host disease contribute to respiratory tract infections. Late onset interstitial pneumonia that is caused by CMV or *P carinii* may occur in patients with ongoing graft-versus-host disease. The destructive effects of chronic graft-versus-host disease on mucocutaneous surfaces also provide a source for infection by staphylococci and other bacteria.

BACTERIAL INFECTIONS

COMMON BACTERIAL INFECTIONS

Clinical findings and treatment of common bacterial infections in transplant recipients are discussed in the relevant syndrome and organism chapters (see chapter cross references below).

A. Liver Transplant Recipients. Bacterial infections of the liver, biliary tract, peritoneal cavity, bloodstream, and surgical wound are the most commonly seen bacterial infections in liver transplant recipients (see Chapter 21). Most such infections occur within the first month (or two) after transplantation. Many of these infections are related to technical problems with the liver graft such as bile leaks or biliary obstruction. Bacterial liver abscesses are sometimes associated with biliary strictures but more often are related to ischemia of the allograft from thrombosis of the hepatic artery. Computed tomography, ultrasonography, cholangiography, and/or angiography are required to evaluate anatomic abnormalities. The flora of these infections typically involves enterococci, anaerobes, gram-negative enteric rods, and staphylococci. Risk factors for bacterial infections in liver transplant recipients include CMV infection, acute rejection, prolonged hospitalization, increased operative transfusion requirements, prolonged duration of surgery, rejection, reoperation, retransplantation, and elevated bilirubin or creatinine levels. In liver transplant recipients, the presence of a Roux-en-Y choledocho-jejunostomy increases the risk of sepsis overall, infectious complications related to liver biopsy, and enterococcal and *Pseudomonas* bacteremia by facilitating reflux of enteric organisms into the biliary system and hence into the hepatic allograft.

Prevention

Selective bowel decontamination reduces gram-negative infections in liver transplant recipients.

B. Lung Transplant Recipients. The most common type of bacterial infection in the lung transplant recipient is pulmonary (see Chapters 9 and 10). This is a result of denervation of the lungs and airways abolishing the cough reflex distal to the tracheal or bronchial anastomosis, impaired mucociliary clearance, and airway inflammation secondary to rejection. The anastomosis is particularly vulnerable to local pathogen colonization as suture material present may initiate a local immune response. Lung transplant recipients are also at risk for mediastinitis because of leaks from the airway anastomosis. Risk factors for bacterial pneumonia after single lung transplantation include underlying primary or secondary pulmonary hypertension in the presence of airway complications of stenosis or dehiscence.

Prevention

The incidence of bacterial pneumonia in lung transplant recipients may be dramatically reduced by the use of antimicrobial agents tailored to the results of cultures and stains for bacteria and fungi from the airways of the donor and recipient at the time of transplantation.

C. Heart Transplant Recipients. Pulmonary infections are the predominant bacterial infections seen in heart transplant recipients (see Chapter 11). Other types of bacterial infections seen in heart transplant recipients include wound infections (of which midline sternotomy infection can be particularly devastating); bacteremia, which most commonly results from vascular catheter infection; and urinary tract infection (see Chapter 16).

D. Renal Transplant Recipients. Renal transplant recipients are at risk for urinary tract infections (see Chapter 16). Multiple factors, including renal insufficiency, nutritional inadequacies, decreased amounts of urine flowing across the uroepithelium, opportunities for sepsis from dialysis accesses, underlying diabetes mellitus, and/or polycystic kidney disease, contribute to this increased incidence. Patients who receive a simultaneous pancreas transplant with bladder drainage have the added risk of enzymatic digestion of the protective glycosaminoglycan layer overlying the uroepithelium. In addition, the change in urinary pH caused by urinary, pancreatic, and endocrine secretions and underlying glycosuria favor bacterial urinary tract infection in combined kidney and pancreas transplant recipients. Pathogens causing urinary tract infections in renal transplant recipients include enterococci, staphylococci, and *Pseudomonas aeruginosa*, in addition to the usual enteric gram-negative bacteria. Wound infections may also be seen.

Prevention

Prophylaxis with trimethoprim-sulfamethoxazole reduces the incidence of bacterial infection of the urinary tract and bacteremia after renal transplantation. However, controversy exists regarding the exact dosing, timing, and duration of trimethoprim-sulfamethoxazole for urinary tract infection prophylaxis in renal transplant recipients.

E. Pancreas and Small Bowel Transplant Recipients. The most common bacterial infections in pancreas transplant recipients are wound and intra-abdominal infections (see Chapters 12 and 13). Human small bowel transplant recipients are likewise at risk for intra-abdominal and wound infections.

F. PBSC and Bone Marrow Transplant Recipients. Since the early 1980s, the bacterial causes of infection in patients undergoing PBSC and bone marrow transplantation during the initial 3 mo after transplant have changed from predominantly gram-negative bacillary organisms to mostly gram-positive organisms. The extensive use of indwelling central intravenous catheters, more severe cases of oral mucositis from chemotherapeutic agents, the administration of oral quinolones for prophylaxis, and the empiric treatment of febrile episodes with antibiotics directed primarily against gram-negative bacilli have likely contributed to this rise in gram-positive bacterial infections. Coagulase-negative staphylococci, viridans streptococci, *Staphylococcus aureus*, and *Corynebacterium* spp. are the most common gram-positive bacterial pathogens seen in this group of patients.

An increased risk of both colonization and bacteremia caused by viridans streptococci has been associated with quinolone prophylaxis in PBSC and bone marrow transplant recipients. Septic shock and the adult respiratory distress syndrome are occasionally seen in association with viridans streptococcal bacteremia. Despite the apparent decline in gram-negative bacterial infections, the possibility of infection caused by *Escherichia coli* and other *Enterobacteriaceae*, as well as *P aeruginosa* and other nonfermenting gram-negative bacilli, must still be considered when decisions about empiric antibiotic therapy are being made.

Bacteremia and soft tissue infections are the most common presentations of bacterial infections during the initial months after PBSC and bone marrow transplant (see Chapter 13). Exit site infections of intravenous catheters, infections involving the perirectal area, and oral mucositis are common local types of bacterial infection. Bacterial infections of the respiratory tract may occur at anytime, including 4 or more months after transplantation. At this later time period, encapsulated bacteria (eg, *S pneumoniae* and *H influenzae*) are frequent pathogens that may cause pneumonia, bronchitis, sinusitis, and, less commonly, meningitis.

Prevention

Bacterial infections in PBSC and bone marrow transplant patients with graft-versus-host disease after engraftment may be prevented by prophylaxis with trimethoprim-sulfamethoxazole. Oral chemophylaxis with quinolones in granulocytic patients is widely used. Oral quinolones are well tolerated and eliminate most gram-negative bacterial infections. The use of quinolones for prophylaxis is, however, controversial.

LEGIONELLA SPECIES

General Considerations

Legionella infection can occur in any type of transplant recipient, can be nosocomial or community acquired, and can be seen at any time post-transplant. *Legionella pneumophila* is the most common species involved but *Legionella micdadei, Legionella bozemanii, Legionella dumoffii,* and other *Legionella* spp., may be pathogens in transplant recipients. More details are found in Chapter 58.

Clinical Findings

A. Signs and Symptoms. *Legionella* infection typically causes pneumonia with symptoms of fever, chills, headache, diarrhea, chest pain, malaise, dyspnea, and cough.

B. Laboratory Findings. Prompt request for diagnostic tests for *Legionella* spp. including direct fluorescent antibody testing and culture of sputum or bronchoalveolar lavage specimens as well as urinary antigen testing in any patient with suspected legionellosis is recommended. Serologic testing is of limited usefulness because of the need to obtain acute and convalescent phase titers and because seroconversion is not specific for *Legionella* infection. Furthermore, the humoral response may be compromised in transplant recipients. Molecular diagnostic assays are under development.

C. Imaging. Pulmonary infiltrates are typically seen on chest X-ray.

Treatment

Treatment is classically with a quinolone or macrolide with or without rifampin (Box 24–2). If legionellal pneumonia is nosocomial, a search should be made for sources of legionella in the environment, especially in the hot water supply and ventilation systems.

NOCARDIA SPECIES

General Considerations

Nocardial infections have been reported to occur in all types of transplant recipients. Nocardial infection is most commonly caused by *Nocardia asteroides,* but other species of *Nocardia* may also cause infections in transplant recipients. More details are found in Chapter 63.

Clinical Findings

A. Signs and Symptoms. The most common presentation is pulmonary and includes fever and cough. Central nervous system and cutaneous infections may be present.

B. Laboratory Findings. Gram and modified acid fast stains and cultures of sputum or bronchoalveolar lavage fluid are useful in the diagnosis of pulmonary nocardial infection. All transplant patients with nocardiosis should be evaluated for central nervous system disease.

C. Imaging. Pulmonary infiltrates, pleural effusions, cavitating lesions, or nodules may be visualized on chest x-ray. Nocardial brain abscess, inflamed meninges, and ventriculitis may also be seen.

Treatment

Sulfonamides, either alone or in combination with trimethoprim, are the treatment of choice for nocardiosis (Box 24–2). Alternatives include minocycline, chloramphenicol, erythromycin, amikacin, ampicillin, amoxicillin-clavulanate, ciprofloxacin, imipenem, meropenem, ceftriaxone, cefuroxime, and cefotaxime, but antibiotic susceptibility testing should be performed because resistance may be present. Antimicrobial therapy should be continued for a prolonged period after cure because of the tendency for relapse, although the optimal duration of therapy is unknown.

Prevention

Trimethoprim-sulfamethoxazole used for *P carinii* prophylaxis may prevent nocardiosis (Box 24–3).

SALMONELLA SPP.

There is an increased incidence of salmonellal infection in renal transplant recipients. The most common presentation is a febrile illness with bacteremia. *Salmonella* infections are discussed further in Chapter 53.

LISTERIA MONOCYTOGENES

General Considerations

Transplant recipients are at greatest risk for infection caused by *L monocytogenes* during the first 2–3 mo after transplant, but listerial infection may occur

BOX 24-2

Empiric Therapy of Infections in Transplant Recipients

Common bacteria	• Multiple regimens (see specific chapters cited in text)
Legionella spp.	• Quinolone or • Erythromycin (1 g IV or orally 4 times daily) +/- rifampin (600 mg IV or orally once or twice daily) • Another macrolide
Nocardia spp.	• Sulfonamides [eg sulfadiazine (1.5–2.0 g four times daily) or trimethoprim-sulfamethoxazole (15 mg/kg/d IV or orally, in three divided doses)]
Listeria monocytogenes	• Ampicillin (200 mg/kg/day IV in six divided doses) plus gentamicin (6 mg/kg/d IV in four divided doses); trimethoprim-sulfamethoxazole is an alternative
Cytomegalovirus	• Ganciclovir (5 mg/kg IV twice daily)
Herpes simplex virus mucocutaneous disease	• Acyclovir (200 mg orally 5 times daily or 400 mg orally 3 times daily or 5 mg/kg IV every 8 h); alternatives include famciclovir, valacyclovir, and foscarnet
Varicella zoster virus	• Localized dermatomal VZV: acyclovir (10 mg/kg IV every 8 h or 800 mg orally 5 times daily for 7–10 d); alternatives include famciclovir (500 mg orally three times daily) or valacyclovir (1000 mg orally 3 times daily) • Primary VZV infection: acyclovir (10 mg/kg IV every 8 h) plus VZ immune globulin.
Epstein-Barr virus	(see Table 24-2)
Fungi	• Amphotericin B* (0.3–1.5 mg/kg IV daily) or • Fluconazole (100–800 mg IV or orally daily) +/− flucytosine (100–150 mg/kg/d orally in four divided doses) or • Itraconazole (200–800 mg orally, once or twice daily)
Pneumocystis carinii	• Trimethoprim–sulfamethoxazole (15–20 mg/kg/d IV or orally in divided doses) or • Pentamidine (4 mg/kg/d IV for 14–21 days.)
Strongyloides stercoralis	• Thiabendazole (50 mg/kg/d in two divided doses) or ivermectin (200 µg/kg/d)
Toxoplasma gondii	• Clindamycin (400–600 mg orally or 600–1200 mg IV, 4 times daily) and pyrimethamine (50–100 mg orally daily) or • Sulfadiazine (1–1.5 g orally, 4 times daily) and pyrimethamine (50–100 mg orally daily)

*A lipid preparation of amphotericin B may be appropriate (varicol close)

at any time after transplant. Listeriosis occurs in all types of transplant patients and may be transmitted via contaminated food. It is most commonly seen from the months of July through October. More details are found in Chapter 51.

Clinical Findings

A. Signs and Symptoms. Two-thirds of infected transplant patients have infections involving the central nervous system including meningitis, meningoencephalitis, and encephalitis, and one-third have primary bacteremia. Patients with meningitis present with headache, fever, signs of meningeal irritation, depressed level of consciousness, seizures, and/or focal neurological defects. The portal of entry for *L monocytogenes* is the gastrointestinal tract, and patients may report cramps and diarrhea as the initial manifestations of their infection.

B. Laboratory Findings. In patients with central nervous system infection, cerebrospinal fluid examination often, but not always, reveals a predominance of polymorphonuclear leukocytes, a low concentration of glucose, and a negative Gram stain. Importantly, *L. monocytogenes* may be confused

BOX 24-3

Control of Infections in Transplant Recipients

Prophylactic Measures	Pretransplant infectious disease evaluation	See Table 24-1
	Vaccinations (administered following PBSC and bone marrow transplantations)	• Tetanus-diphtheria (12, 14 and 24 months post-transplant) • Influenza (annual, lifelong, before and ≥6 months post-transplant • Pneumococcus (23-valent, 12 and 24 months post-transplant) • Hepatitis B (12, 14 and 24 months post-transplant) • *Haemophilus influenzae* type B (12, 14 and 24 months post-transplant) • Polio (inactivated) (12, 14 and 24 months post-transplant) • MMR (live-attenuated, ≥24 months post-transplant and 2nd dose 6–12 months after)
	Vaccinations (administered prior to solid-organ transplantation)	• Varicella zoster virus for non-immune solid organ transplant candidates (see text for cautions) • Tetanus-diphtheria (booster, or primary series as appropriate) • Pneumococcus (23-valent) • Hepatitis A virus (series, if non-immune) • Hepatitis B virus (series, if non-immune) • Influenza (annual, lifelong)
	Cytomegalovirus prophylaxis	• Ganciclovir (1 g orally 3 times daily or 5 mg/kg IV daily to twice daily) • Valacyclovir (2 g orally 4 times daily) • Immune globulin (various regimens) • Acyclovir (800 mg orally 4–5 times daily or 5 mg/kg IV 3 times daily) • Protective matching • CMV seronegative, filtered, or leukocyte-poor blood products
	Herpes simplex virus stomatitis prophylaxis	• Acyclovir (200 mg orally 3 times daily or 400 mg orally 2 times daily) • Valacyclovir (500 mg orally daily)
	Varicella zoster virus prophylaxis	• Immune globulin and/or acyclovir on exposure • Vaccination (see above)
	Pneumocystis carinii prophylaxis	• Trimethoprim-sulfamethoxazole (either 1 single strength or 1 double strength tablet every day or 1 double strength tablet 2 or 3 times daily on 2 days of the week)[1] • Pentamidine (300 mg nebulized monthly) • Atovaquone (1500 mg orally daily) • Dapsone (50 mg orally twice daily or 100 mg daily)
	Toxoplasma gondii prophylaxis	• Trimethoprim-sulfamethoxazole (see above for *P carini* dosages) • Pyrimethamine (25 mg orally daily)

BOX 24–3 (continued)

Control of Infections in Transplant Recipients

	Bacterial infection prophylaxis (PBSC and bone marrow transplant recipients)	• Quinolone (various regimens)
	Fungal infection prophylaxis (PBSC and bone marrow and select solid organ transplant recipients)	• Fluconazole (400 mg orally or IV daily)
	Mycobacterium tuberculosis infection prophylaxis	• Isoniazid (300 mg orally daily)
Isolation Precautions	Avoidance of epidemiologic exposures post-transplantation	• See text
	Mycobacterium tuberculosis	• Airborne isolation
	Varicella zoster virus infection	• Avoid contact if VZV nonimmune
	Cytomegalovirus infection	• Universal precautions

[1]May also prevent nocardiosis, toxoplasmosis, and some bacterial infections.

with diphtheroids in Gram-stained smears of pus or sputum.

Treatment

Intravenous ampicillin and gentamicin are recommended for treatment (Box 24–2). Trimethoprim-sulfamethoxazole is also effective.

Prevention

Trimethoprim-sulfamethoxazole, used for *P carinii* prophylaxis, may additionally prevent listeriosis (Box 24–3).

VIRAL INFECTIONS

CYTOMEGALOVIRUS

General Considerations

CMV is extensively discussed in Chapter 33. CMV infection occurs in the majority of solid-organ and allogeneic PBSC and bone marrow transplant recipients, primarily in the first 3 mo post-transplant. CMV infection also occurs in 40–45% of recipients of syngeneic or autologous PBSC and bone marrow transplant recipients, but symptomatic infections are infrequent in these groups. CMV may be transmitted to transplant recipients via infected donor material or transfused cellular products.

Three major patterns of CMV transmission are observed in transplant recipients. **Primary infection** develops when a CMV seronegative individual receives cells latently infected with the virus from a seropositive donor followed by viral reactivation. **Secondary** infection or reactivation infection develops when endogenous latent virus is reactivated in a CMV seropositive individual post-transplantation. **Superinfection** or **reinfection** occurs when a seropositive recipient receives latently infected cells from a seropositive donor and the virus that reactivates post-transplantation is of donor origin.

After primary infection with CMV, long-term cellular and humoral immunity usually develop, but CMV remains latent or persistent within the host. Viral persistence is controlled in the immunocompetent host by an intact cellular immune system. Immunosuppression administered after transplantation may lead to uncontrolled viral replication and consequently symptomatic CMV infection. A solid-organ transplant recipient without prior immunity to CMV pretransplantation who receives an organ containing latent or persistent virus (primary infection) is at higher risk of uncontrolled viral replication than a patient who has prior immunity to CMV pretransplantation (secondary infection or reinfection). In PBSC and bone marrow transplant recipients the CMV seropositive recipient with a CMV seronegative donor is at higher risk of uncontrolled viral replication than patients in other serologic groups. Likewise, the higher the degree of immunosuppression, the higher the risk of uncontrolled viral replication. In solid-organ transplant recipients, the use of antilymphocyte preparations (eg. OKT3 monoclonal antibodies) and fulminant hepatitis at the time of transplantation (in liver transplant recipients) are risk factors for symptomatic CMV infection. Graft-versus-host disease is a risk factor for CMV infection in PBSC and bone marrow transplant recipients.

In the immunosuppressed transplant recipient, CMV has four major effects:

1. It causes infectious diseases syndromes (see below).

2. It has been implicated in causing increased immunosuppression, which may explain the frequent association of CMV with other opportunistic infections such as fungal and *Pneumocystis* infections.

3. It has been associated with allograft rejection in the form of early onset allograft rejection in renal transplant recipients and chronic allograft rejection (allograft atherosclerosis) in cardiac transplant recipients (in some, but not all, studies) as well as possibly the vanishing bile duct syndrome in liver transplant recipients (controversial).

4. It has been implicated in exerting a negative effect on survival after solid-organ transplantation.

CMV infection therefore has a potential impact on both patient and graft outcome.

Clinical Findings

A. Signs and Symptoms. CMV infection exhibits a wide range of clinical manifestations from asymptomatic infection to severe lethal CMV disease. Most cases of CMV disease after transplantation are of mild to moderate severity and are rarely fatal in the current decade. Manifestations of mild to moderate disease include fever and malaise without additional signs or symptoms. Myalgias, arthralgias, and, at times, arthritis may occur.

Organ involvement by CMV correlates with the organ transplanted as follows: Hepatitis occurs most frequently in liver transplant recipients; pancreatitis occurs most frequently in pancreas transplant recipients; and pneumonitis occurs most frequently in lung, heart and lung, and PBSC and bone marrow transplant recipients. Gastroenteritis is also frequently seen in PBSC and bone marrow transplant recipients. In addition, myocarditis, although rare, typically presents in heart transplant recipients. Other sites of involvement of CMV include the gallbladder, pancreas, epididymis, biliary tract, retina, skin, endometrium, and central nervous system. CMV retinitis is distinctive in that it usually presents > 6 mo post–solid-organ transplantation.

B. Laboratory Findings. CMV may be associated with leukopenia or thrombocytopenia. The diagnosis of CMV infection in tissue has traditionally been based on the recognition of cytomegalic inclusion bodies. CMV may also be detected in tissue specimens by immunohistochemistry or DNA hybridization techniques. Tube cell culture and shell vial culture techniques can be used to detect replicating CMV in body fluids and tissue with the former having the disadvantage of taking 7–14 days of incubation for CMV to exhibit cytopathic effect. The rapid shell vial culture technique, however, can detect the presence of CMV after 16 hours of incubation. Importantly, akin to bacterial blood cultures, multiple viral blood cultures may be necessary to detect CMV by the shell vial assay. Detection of CMV antigenemia in blood leukocytes of transplant recipients is at least as sensitive as and more rapid than the shell vial technique and provides an earlier marker of CMV infection.

Molecular techniques can detect CMV DNA in peripheral blood leukocytes, whole blood, serum, plasma, and other clinical specimens and can detect CMV RNA in peripheral blood leukocytes and whole blood.

The serologic diagnosis of CMV infection is suboptimal compared to the above techniques; many patients with positive CMV cultures do not show concomitant evidence of seroconversion. Serologic testing, however, is recommended for the pretransplantation evaluation of the CMV serostatus of transplant donors and recipients.

Treatment

Effective currently available antiviral agents for the treatment of CMV include ganciclovir, foscarnet, cidofovir, and intravenous immune globulin (Box 24–2). In solid-organ transplant recipients, intravenous ganciclovir is the mainstay of therapy. Ganciclovir alone is generally of little benefit for treatment of either CMV pneumonia or gastroenteritis in PBSC and bone marrow transplant recipients, although the combination of intravenous ganciclovir plus intravenous immune globulin appears to have some efficacy. The absorption of ganciclovir after oral administration is low, and its use cannot be recommended for the treatment of CMV infection and disease after transplantation.

Side effects of ganciclovir include leukopenia, thrombocytopenia, anemia, nausea, infusion site reactions, diarrhea, renal toxicity, seizures, mental status changes, fever, rash, and abnormal liver function tests. Hematologic and renal function should be monitored while patients are receiving ganciclovir. Renal toxicity may occur when ganciclovir is used in conjunction with other nephrotoxic agents such as amphotericin B, azathioprine, aminoglycosides, and cyclosporine.

The possibility of viral resistance should be considered in patients with poor clinical response or persistent viral excretion during ganciclovir therapy. Mutations in viral thymidine kinase and/or DNA polymerase genes mediate resistance.

Prevention

A. Selection of Organs from CMV Seronegative Donors for CMV Seronegative Recipients. Knowledge of the CMV serostatus of the donor and recipient pretransplant will predict which patients will develop CMV disease. Although the solid-organ transplant patient at highest risk for development of CMV infection is the seronegative recipient of a seropositive allograft, protective matching of seronegative donors and recipients is not currently advocated (Box 24–3).

B. Use of CMV Seronegative, Filtered, or Leukocyte-Poor Blood Products. The use of CMV seronegative, filtered, or leukocyte poor blood products reduces CMV transmission, and these should be used at least in seronegative recipients.

C. Active Immunization with a Vaccine. In theory, one of the simplest interventions for the prevention of CMV disease after transplantation would be immunization of seronegative recipients with a vaccine given once in anticipation of future viral challenge. A live attenuated CMV vaccine, which uses the Towne strain of virus, is both safe and immunogenic; however, there is no significant decrease. in the incidence of CMV disease in renal transplant recipients receiving this vaccine. New interest in developing a vaccine subunit product has emerged over the last few years. A subunit vaccine containing recombinant glycoprotein B, which is being developed by several biotechnology companies, is undergoing clinical trials.

D. Passive Immunization with Immune Globulins. Immune globulin preparations (including unscreened or unselected and hyperimmune globulin preparations) have been studied as agents for CMV prophylaxis. In solid-organ transplant recipients, intravenous immune globulins have been shown to be effective in preventing CMV disease in renal and non-high-risk (CMV-seropositive donor/CMV-seronegative recipient) liver transplant recipients. It appears that, at least in solid-organ transplant recipients, hyperimmune globulin is more effective in this role than standard immune globulin. Notably, immune globulin prophylaxis typically costs several thousand dollars per patient.

E. Prophylaxis with Antiviral Agents. Oral acyclovir has little role in preventing CMV after transplantation with the exception of possible efficacy in renal transplant recipients. Oral valacyclovir has been shown to be effective in preventing CMV infection and disease in renal transplant recipients. Prophylactic intravenous ganciclovir can prevent CMV disease in PBSC and bone marrow transplant recipients but is associated with neutropenia.

On the basis of published randomized trials, a 2-week course of intravenous ganciclovir may be considered for CMV prophylaxis in certain solid-organ transplant recipients; a 4-week course is recommended for CMV seropositive recipients of heart allografts. Intravenous ganciclovir alone is not effective, however, in solid-organ transplant populations at highest risk for CMV disease, including lung transplant recipients and donor CMV seropositive recipients CMV seronegative individuals, unless it is ad-

ministered for a prolonged period (90 days). The studies to date have used intravenous ganciclovir, which is not ideal because of the ongoing need for intravenous access and the costs engendered. In this regard, oral ganciclovir has been shown as effective in preventing CMV infection and disease in liver and kidney transplant recipients and has been widely adapted for CMV prophylas, replacing intravenous ganciclovir in most instances.

Limitations associated with oral ganciclovir use include the need to take multiple tablets each day, cost, potential emergence of ganciclovir-resistant CMV stains, and the emergence of late onset CMV disease (following discontinuation of prophylacis). New agents, such as valganciclovir as well as other promising compounds that are being developed, may provide improved CMV prophylacis for solid-organ and PBSC and bone marrow transplant recipients.

F. Adoptive Transfer of CMV Specific T-Cell Clones Generated from the Donor. The development of CMV specific cytotoxic T-lymphocyte responses enhances survival from serious CMV infections. Thus, adoptive transfer of CMV specific T-cell clones generated from the PBSC or bone marrow donor is being studied as an approach to restoring immunity to CMV in the PBSC or marrow recipient.

G. Preemptive Therapy. Preemptive therapy of CMV involves the administration of antiviral agents to a subgroup of patients before the appearance of disease. This is dependent on a laboratory marker or patient characteristic that identifies a subgroup of individuals at high risk of disease at a time when antimicrobial intervention would be maximally effective in aborting the disease process. Compared with a prophylactic approach of administering antiviral agents to all patients, only patients at risk of developing symptomatic CMV infection receive specific antiviral therapy. Therefore fewer patients receive an antiviral agent and probably for a shorter period, leading to advantages in terms of cost, emergence of resistant viral strains, and medication side effects.

Candidate laboratory tests for this therapeutic mode include molecular and antigenemia tests. Many transplantation programs are using molecular or antigenemia tests to monitor their transplant recipients after transplantation and intervening with preemptive therapy based on a positive result.

Identifying patient characteristics that place the transplant recipient at risk for CMV infection is another facet of preemptive therapy. Such risk factors include the use of OKT3 monoclonal antibodies in solid-organ transplant recipients and the presence of fulminant hepatitis at the time of transplantation in liver transplant recipients. Many transplantation programs are intervening with preemptive ganciclovir when antilymphocyte therapy is used in solid-organ transplant recipients. A similar approach based on other risk factors requires further study but may also be beneficial.

HERPES SIMPLEX VIRUS

General Considerations

Herpes simplex virus most commonly causes reactivation infection but may cause primary infection transmitted by person to person contact or via the transplant donor. Herpes simplex virus antibodies are found in three-quarters of adult transplant recipients. After primary infection, the virus remains latent in sensory nerve ganglia. Herpes simplex virus infection occurs in all types of transplant recipients. More information is found in Chapter 33.

Clinical Findings

A. Signs and Symptoms. Herpes simplex virus reactivation results in oral or genital mucocutaneous lesions usually during the first month after transplant. Herpes simplex virus occasionally causes pneumonitis, tracheobronchitis, esophagitis, hepatitis, or disseminated infection.

Most orolabial infections are mild, although severe ulceration and discomfort, which may be complicated by bacterial superinfection or esophageal involvement, are noted in some patients. Anogenital infection usually presents as large areas of ulceration and may or may not have the typical vesicular appearance of HSV infection in the nonimmunocompromised host.

Herpes simplex virus can cause pneumonia and may be associated with a high mortality rate. This usually occurs as a secondary pneumonia in intubated patients with severe pneumonia caused by other agents. The virus is reactivated in the oropharynx. The mucosa is traumatized by the endotracheal tube, and the virus is presumably spread via the endotracheal tube to the lower respiratory tract. Certain caveats must be noted. Herpes simplex virus isolated from sputum or other respiratory secretions does not definitively imply HSV pneumonitis. Also, even if HSV is believed to be causing pneumonitis, another pathogen should be sought as HSV is often a secondary pathogen.

Herpes simplex virus esophagitis causes dysphagia and mimics candidal esophagitis. Esophagitis may complicate orolabial infection, particularly if the mucosa has been traumatized by endotracheal intubation or nasogastric tubes. Herpes simplex virus is also a cause of diffuse or focal hepatitis in solid-organ transplant recipients, usually during the first 2 months after transplantation. Diffuse or focal hepatitis secondary to herpes simplex virus is characterized by a rapidly progressive course accompanied by hypotension, disseminated intravascular coagulation, metabolic acidosis, gastrointestinal bleeding, and associated bacteremia. Disseminated HSV disease may rarely occur. Uncommonly, disseminated cutaneous infection with HSV may occur at sites of previous skin injury such as burns or eczema (eczema herpeticum).

B. Laboratory Findings. The diagnosis is made by performing a direct immunofluorescence test, Tzanck test, molecular diagnostic assay or culture of tissue and body fluids or both. Typing of isolates may be performed by a variety of techniques. Serologic techniques are helpful in the determination of the pretransplantation serologic status of transplant recipients.

Treatment

Treatment of HSV infection is with acyclovir (Box 24–2). Side effects of acyclovir include local inflammation or phlebitis after intravenous infusion, renal toxicity caused by precipitation and crystallization of the drug in the renal tubules, confusion, delirium, lethargy, tremors, seizures, nausea, light-headedness, diaphoresis, and rash. Mucocutaneous infection in transplant recipients should be treated with oral acyclovir if the infection has a benign course or with intravenous acyclovir in more serious cases. Disseminated or deep HSV infection should always be treated with intravenous acyclovir.

Newer agents, such as famciclovir and valacyclovir, may be used instead of acyclovir. Although more toxic than acyclovir, ganciclovir and foscarnet are also effective against HSV. A concern with respect to chronic acyclovir use is the development of acyclovir resistant mutants of HSV. Acyclovir resistance may arise from mutations in the genes for thymidine kinase or DNA polymerase. Acyclovir resistance has been associated with progressive and severe disease in immunocompromised patients, particularly in those with HIV, and it is possible that resistance will become a problem for transplant recipients in years ahead.

Prevention

Low-dose acyclovir prevents HSV stomatitis in transplant recipients (Box 24–3).

VARICELLA ZOSTER VIRUS

General Considerations

Varicella zoster virus causes two distinct clinical diseases after transplant. Ninety percent of adult transplant recipients are VZV seropositive pretransplant; VZV reactivation in this group will cause herpes zoster (shingles). The remaining 10% are VZV seronegative and thus are at risk for primary infection. More information is found in Chapter 33.

Clinical Findings

A. Signs and Symptoms. Localized dermatomal reactivation results in herpes zoster and may involve two or more adjoining dermatomes. There may be a few sites of cutaneous dissemination at distant sites. Additionally, a syndrome of unilateral pain without skin eruption associated with rises in specific antibody to VZV has been described in transplant patients. Primary VZV infection occurs after exposure of a VZV seronegative transplant recipient to VZV. The virus is transmitted by contact with an infected individual (usually via the respiratory route). This can occur at any time after transplantation and, although rare, can cause a life-threatening disseminated infection characterized by hemorrhagic pneumonia, skin lesions, encephalitis, pancreatitis, disseminated intravascular coagulation, and hepatitis. Primary VZV can also cause a chickenpox syndrome or hepatitis alone.

B. Laboratory Findings. Unilateral vesicular lesions in a dermatomal pattern are usually sufficiently characteristic of herpes zoster to enable a clinical diagnosis; however, culture of VZV on susceptible cell lines, demonstration of multinucleated giant cells on Tzanck smear, and/or direct immunofluorescence or identification of VZV using molecular techniques is recommended for confirmation. These techniques can also be used for diagnosis of primary infection.

Treatment

For localized dermatomal zoster, the recommended treatment is intravenous acyclovir (Box 24–2). Oral famciclovir, valacyclovir, or acyclovir may be used as an alternative. For primary VZV infection, treatment consists of intravenous acyclovir in addition to varicella zoster immune globulin.

Prevention

Because of the high mortality rate associated with primary VZV infection in transplant recipients, all candidates should be screened for antibody to VZV pretransplantation (see Box 24–3). Seronegative individuals should be urged to report promptly all exposures to VZV and varicella zoster immune globulin should be administered within 96 hours of exposure. Intravenous acyclovir should be administered within 24 hours of eruption of a skin rash if one occurs. Unfortunately, progression to severe disease and death can still occur. The use of low-dose acyclovir as HSV prophylaxis probably prevents VZV reactivation and

possibly primary infection, although this has not been formally studied. Despite concerns regarding the use of live vaccines in transplant recipients, a recent study has demonstrated the safety of the VZV vaccine in pediatric renal transplant recipients. This vaccine should preferably be administered several months prior to solid-organ transplant, should reduce morbidity in seronegative solid-organ transplant recipients, and should provide considerable cost savings.

It is important to keep in mind that although most infections in transplant recipients are not communicable to health care workers, contact with a patient who has VZV infection, be it shingles or chickenpox, is a risk for all seronegative contacts including healthy staff working in transplant centers.

EPSTEIN BARR VIRUS

General Considerations

Epstein Barr virus (EBV) infection in transplant recipients may be associated with post-transplantation lymphoproliferative disease (PTLD), which is a significant cause of morbidity and mortality (Table 24–2). Post-transplantation lymphoproliferative disease occurs in solid-organ transplant recipients as well as in PBSC and bone marrow transplant recipients. The term PTLD acknowledges the fact that these lesions are heterogeneous and may not meet the diagnostic criteria for lymphoma. The spectrum of PTLD ranges from polyclonal to monoclonal. Monoclonal lesions may or may not contain detectable chromosomal abnormalities. PTLD is often multicentric and may involve the central nervous system, eyes, gastrointestinal tract, liver, spleen, lymph nodes, lungs, allograft, oropharynx, and other organs.

The pathogenesis of PTLD involves EBV replication often stimulated by antilymphocyte therapy, followed by cyclosporin-induced inhibition of virus specific cytotoxic T lymphocytes that normally control the expression of EBV infected, transformed B cells.

Table 24–2. Treatment of EBV-related conditions in the solid-organ recipient.[1]

Conditions	Clinical Findings	Treatment	Outcome
Uncomplicated post-transplantation infectious mononucleosis	Fever, pharyngitis, cervical adenopathy, {+/−} splenomegaly	• Acyclovir	Good
Benign polyclonal polymorphic	Fever, pharyngitis, cervical adenopathy,	• Acyclovir, ganciclovir,{+/−} ↓ immunosuppression	Good
B-cell hyperplasia	Fever, {+/−} pharyngitis, adeno-therapy	• Acyclovir, ganciclovir, ↓ immunosuppression, IFN-α,[2] gamma globulin, anti-B-cell monoclonal antibodies	Intermediate
Early malignant transformation in polyclonal polymorphic B-cell lymphoma			
Monoclonal polymorphic B-cell	Solid tumor masses in allograft, soft tissue, brain, gastrointestinal tract, lung, liver	• ↓ Immunosuppression, chemotherapy, radiation therapy, resection	Poor

[1]Adapted, with permission, from Hanto DW: Classification of Epstein-Barr virus-associated post-transplant lymphoproliferative diseases: implications for understanding their pathogenesis and developing rational treatment strategies. Annu Rev Med 1995; 46: 381.
[2]IFN, interferon.

Risk factors for PTLD include EBV seronegativity pretransplantation, antilymphocyte therapy for rejection or graft-versus-host disease, and CMV seromismatch. Increased levels of circulating EBV-infected lymphocytes and decreased EBV nuclear antigen antibody responses have been associated with the development of PTLD in solid-organ transplant recipients in some, but not all, studies. More information is provided in Chapter 33.

Clinical Findings

Epstein Barr virus infection (without PTLD) may manifest as malaise, fever, headache, and sore throat. Clinical presentations of PTLD are varied and include a mononucleosis-like syndrome with fever, adenopathy, tonsillitis, and sore throat, fever, abdominal pain, anorexia, jaundice, bowel perforation, gastrointestinal bleeding, renal dysfunction, hepatic allograft dysfunction, pneumothorax, pulmonary infiltrates, and weight loss.

Treatment

Treatment of EBV-related PTLD is outlined in Table 24–2. High-level EBV oropharyngeal shedding found in primary infection is inhibited by acyclovir and ganciclovir, suggesting that antiviral therapy may be useful early when levels of viral replication are low. Unfortunately, once PTLD is established, treatment has been disappointing with the exception of drastically reducing the level of immunosuppression, which appears to have a beneficial effect in localized or polyclonal as well as multifocal or monoclonal PTLD. Disease localized to the transplanted organ or lymph nodes can be reversed with reduced immunosuppression and antiviral therapy; extranodal, multifocal, and brain disease typically require chemotherapy, radiation therapy, or both and are associated with a high mortality rate.

OTHER VIRUSES

General Considerations

Other viruses occasionally cause infection in transplant recipients. Adenovirus (Chapter 32), parainfluenza virus (Chapter 30), respiratory syncytial virus (Chapter 31), and influenza virus (Chapter 29) may cause upper respiratory tract infections and pneumonia (see also Chapter 9). Sporadic outbreaks of gastroenteritis caused by coxsackievirus (Chapter 27) or rotavirus occur (Chapter 37). BK virus (Chapter 45) and adenovirus viruria (Chapter 32) have been associated with hemorrhagic cystitis. BK virus has been associated with allograft nephropathy in renal transplant recipients. Both HBV and HCV may cause liver dysfunction after transplantation (Chapter 39). Transplant recipients are also at risk for human papilloma virus-associated malignancies (Chapter 45).

FUNGAL INFECTIONS

PNEUMOCYSTIS CARINII

General Considerations

P carinii pneumonia has been virtually eliminated in transplant recipients by the use of prophylactic trimethoprim-sulfamethoxazole. Clusters of cases of *P carinii* pneumonia have been reported, and a question of person-to-person transmission has been raised. More details are found in Chapter 79.

Clinical Findings

A. Signs and Symptoms. *P carinii* pneumonia typically presents with fever, dyspnea, nonproductive cough, and hypoxemia out of proportion to the physical and radiographic findings present. There is an increased incidence of pneumothorax.

B. Laboratory Findings. The diagnosis is made by examining bronchoalveolar lavage fluid or lung biopsy specimens by one of several techniques including calcifluor white, methenamine silver, and Wright Geimsa staining as well as monoclonal antibody or molecular techniques. In the case of lung biopsy specimens, histopathologic examination is also helpful.

C. Imaging. Typical radiographic findings include diffuse interstitial or interstitial and alveolar infiltrates, but atypical findings may be noted.

Treatment

P carinii pneumonia is treated with high doses of trimethoprim-sulfamethoxazole or intravenous pentamidine (Box 24–2). The former regimen is preferable.

Prevention

Trimethoprim-sulfamethoxazole provides excellent prophylaxis for *P carinii* pneumonia and should be given to all transplant recipients following transplantation (Box 24–3). Prolonged prophylaxis is indicated for heart-lung and lung transplant recipients and for patients with ongoing risk factors for *P carinii* pneumonia such as multiple episodes of rejection, ongoing graft-versus-host disease, treatment with antilymphocyte therapy, or persistent allograft dysfunction. Importantly, prophylaxis should be reinstituted if it has been discontinued, in patients receiving augmented immunosuppression. Alternatives to trimethoprim-sulfamethoxazole for prophylaxis include intravenous or aerosolized pentamidine, dapsone, and atovaquone. For single lung allograft recipients who cannot tolerate trimethoprim-sulfamethoxazole, there is some controversy about the use of aerosolized pentamidine that may be inadequately delivered to the remaining diseased and therefore poorly ventilated lung.

CANDIDA SPECIES

General Considerations

Among the *Candida* species, *C albicans* is most frequently implicated in causing infections in transplant recipients, however, *C krusei, C glabrata, C zeylanoides,* and *C tropicalis* have also been reported as pathogens and may infect any type of transplant recipient. More details are found in Chapter 73.

Clinical Findings

A. Signs and Symptoms. Most fungal infections caused by *Candida* spp. occur in the first 2 months after transplantation. Localized infection of the oral cavity, gastrointestinal tract, or skin may occur. Serious candidal infections after transplant can present in myriad ways including intra-abdominal abscesses (most commonly in patients having undergone abdominal surgery such as liver and pancreas transplantation), hepatosplenic candidiasis (in PBSC and bone marrow transplant recipients), pulmonary infection, urinary tract infections (including cystitis, pyelonephritis, ureteral obstruction, and parenchymal fungal balls), esophagitis, arthritis, endocarditis, aortitis, brain abscess, and mediastinitis. Catheter-related sepsis from infection by *Candida* spp. (and rarely other fungi) is a common presentation of fungal infection in transplant recipients and, as in other populations, is associated with prolonged hospitalization, especially in intensive care units, with central venous catheters in place.

B. Laboratory Findings. The diagnosis of candidal infections in transplant recipients is made by obtaining fungal stains and cultures of appropriate specimens. Fine needle aspiration cytology may be useful in the diagnosis of the hepatosplenic candidiasis syndrome in PBSC and bone marrow transplant recipients as well as fungal pyelonephritis in renal transplant recipients.

Treatment

Agents used for the treatment of serious candidal infections in transplant recipients include amphotericin B, fluconazole, ketoconazole, itraconazole and caspofungin (Box 24–2). The choice of the agent depends on the clinical presentation and typical fungal susceptibility pattern of the organism. Importantly, azole antifungal drugs may increase blood levels of cyclosporin.

Prevention

The use of a selective bowel decontamination regimen may reduce the incidence of candidal infections in liver transplant recipients. Fluconazole has been shown to prevent both deep and superficial candidial infections, excluding those caused by *C krusei,* in liver and PBSC and bone marrow transplant recipients (Box 24–3).

CRYPTOCOCCUS NEOFORMANS

General Considerations

Infections caused by *C neoformans* can occur at any time after transplantation in any type of transplant recipient. More details are found in Chapter 74.

Clinical Findings

A. Signs and Symptoms. Cryptococcal infection may present with a subacute or occasionally more acute meningitis, pneumonia, pleural infection, cutaneous lesions, fever alone, and rarely other unusual forms of infection such as retinitis, arthritis, pyelonephritis, or fever of unknown origin (see Chapter 18). Cutaneous involvement has been described. In men, foci of cryptococcal infection within the prostate gland may be a source of hematogenous dissemination.

B. Laboratory Findings. The cryptococcal antigen test, performed on serum and cerebrospinal fluid (and occasionally pleural fluid), provides a sensitive and rapid means of diagnosis. In *neoformans* meningitis, cerebrospinal fluid may show a lymphocytic pleocytosis, hypoglycorrhachia, and an elevated protein level. Culture and fungal stains (including calcifluor white, India ink, and methenamine silver stains) are helpful in the diagnosis. The cryptococcal antigen test may also be used to monitor response to therapy. Importantly, cryptococcuria, when demonstrated, is almost always indicative of systemic infection; *C neoformans* is rarely a contaminant or nonpathogenic colonizer of the urinary tract. A cerebrospinal fluid examination should be performed in any transplant recipient with unexplained fever as well as in any such patient with *C neoformans* isolated from any site.

MYCELIAL FUNGI

General Considerations

The *Aspergillus* spp. most frequently implicated in causing disease in transplant recipients include *A fumigatus, A flavus, A niger,* and *A terreus.* In addition, an expanding list of unusual organisms including *Pseudalleschia boydii, Scopulariopsis brumptii, Trichosporon beigelii, Fusarium* spp., zygomycetes, and others, have been reported as causes of serious fungal infections in transplant recipients. Most fungal infections caused by *Aspergillus* spp. occur in the first 3 months after solid-organ transplantation and are associated with a high mortality rate. In PBSC and bone marrow transplant recipients, the onset of aspergillal infections is bimodal, peaking 16 and 96 days after transplant. The portal of entry of *Aspergillus* spp. is usually the respiratory tract (lungs and sinuses). Rarely, dissemination from a primary skin lesion or contiguous spread from a previously sustained skin lesion to bone may occur. *Aspergillus* spp. may also invade the gastrointestinal tract or rarely gain entry through an intravenous catheter. More details are found in Chapters 75 and 77.

Zygomycetes, including *Rhizopus* spp., *Mucor* spp., *Absidia* spp., and *Cunninghamella bertholletiae* have been reported as pathogens in transplant recipients. Underlying metabolic disturbances resulting in an acidotic state such as that associated with diabetic ketoacidosis or that found in pancreatic transplant recipients with a bicarbonate leak and deferoxamine therapy are risk factors for zygomycosis. Zygomycetes are associated with rhinocerebral, pulmonary, gastrointestinal, cutaneous, and disseminated infections.

Endemic dimorphic fungal infections with geographically restricted endemic mycoses (*H capsulatum, C immitis, B dermatitidis,* and *Paracoccidioides brasiliensis*) can occur at any time after transplantation. In many cases, and especially with histoplasmosis, disseminated infection is seen. For more details, see Chapter 70.

Clinical Findings

A. Signs and Symptoms. In patients with aspergillosis, pulmonary symptoms including nonproductive cough, pleuritic chest pain, dyspnea, and low-grade fever predominate. From the lungs, *Aspergillus* spp. may disseminate to almost any organ including the brain, liver, spleen, kidneys, heart, pericardium, blood vessels, thyroid, gastrointestinal tract, bones, and joints. Clinical manifestations of central nervous system aspergillosis include alteration of mental status, diffuse central nervous system depression, seizures, evolving cerebrovascular accidents, and headache. *Aspergillus* spp. may cause peritonitis in renal transplant recipients on continuous ambulatory peritoneal dialysis and may cause intra-abdominal abscesses in liver transplant recipients.

B. Laboratory Findings. One should consider all pulmonary infections in transplant recipients to be possibly caused by mycelial fungi. Positive cultures for *Aspergillus* spp. in transplant recipients should never be ignored even though the isolation of *Aspergillus* spp. from respiratory and wound specimens does not always imply disease because this fungus may be a colonizer or a laboratory contaminant. Repeated isolation of *Aspergillus* spp. from sputum is suggestive of invasive disease, and the combination of positive sputum cultures and cavitary lung disease is highly suggestive of invasive disease. Conversely, sputum cultures are not always positive for *Aspergillus* spp. in patients with invasive aspergillosis. Bronchoalveolar lavage may be more helpful in this regard. The diagnosis of extrapulmonary infection is more difficult. Any suspicious lesion (eg, skeletal or cutaneous) should be biopsied.

C. Imaging. Chest radiographic findings in cases of pulmonary aspergillosis include nodular opacities, interstitial infiltrates, cavitary lung disease, or a pulmonary embolus type pattern; the chest x-ray may also be normal. For more details see Chapter 70.

Treatment

Treatment of deep fungal infections in transplant recipients does not differ significantly from that in other types of immunocompromised hosts (Box 24–2). Immunosuppression should be reduced as tolerated. Surgical extirpation or debridement should be performed for diagnostic and therapeutic purposes, if appropriate. Intravenous amphotericin B has been the mainstay of treatment for deep fungal infections in transplant recipients. The combination of cyclosporin and amphotericin B has been associated with renal failure. Some organisms (eg *P boydii*) are resistant to amphotericin B, emphasizing the need for identification of all fungal isolates in transplant recipients. Lipid formulations of amphotericin B have fewer side effects, especially including nephrotoxicity, than the standard preparation, but are more costly. Because of the high frequency of toxicity seen with amphotericin B, the use of azole antifungal agents for treating select fungal infections in transplant recipients is attractive. This is discussed further in chapters dealing with specific fungal organisms.

Prevention

Laminar air flow isolation in PBSC and bone marrow transplant units prevents aspergillal infections. Intravenous amphotericin B should be given to PBSC and bone marrow transplant recipients with a well-documented history of invasive aspergillosis pretransplant.

MYCOBACTERIAL INFECTIONS

MYCOBACTERIUM TUBERCULOSIS

General Considerations

All types of transplant recipients are at increased risk for both primary and reactivation *M tuberculosis* infection and disseminated disease is more commonly seen in transplant recipients than in nonimmunocompromised populations. For more information, see Chapter 61.

Clinical Findings

A. Signs and Symptoms. Presentations of *M tuberculosis* infection after transplantation include typical cavitary pulmonary disease as well as noncavitary pulmonary, intestinal, skeletal, cutaneous, disseminated, and central nervous system disease. *M tuberculosis* infection in transplant recipients is usually accompanied by pyrexia. *M tuberculosis* is highly contagious, and all patients with pulmonary tuberculosis should be promptly isolated.

B. Laboratory Findings and Imaging. The diagnosis of tuberculosis differs little in the transplant population compared to other populations.

Treatment

See Chapter 61.

Prevention

A detailed history of tuberculosis exposure should be obtained on all transplant candidates and a tuberculin test should be performed on all solid-organ transplant candidates and on PBSC and bone marrow transplant candidates with a history of tuberculosis exposure. Isoniazid prophylaxis is recommended for patients with positive tuberculin tests or other risk factors for tuberculosis. If possible isoniazid prophylaxis should be administered for nine months pre-transplantation. If this is not feasible, isoniazid can be given following transplantation. In addition, tuberculin test positive transplant recipients who have not previously received treatment or prophylaxis might benefit from isoniazid prophylaxis when they receive antilymphocyte preparations.

NONTUBERCULOUS MYCOBACTERIA

General Considerations

Nontuberculous mycobacteria reported as pathogens in transplant recipients include *M kansasii, M avium-intracellulare, M fortuitum, M xenopi, M haemophilum, M marinum, M chelonai, M abscessus, M gastri, M scrofulaceum, M szulgai,* and *M thermoresistibile,* among others. These infections are rare, generally occur late in the post-transplant period and are most commonly chronic, manifesting as cutaneous lesions of the extremities, tenosynovitis, and/or joint infection. Less frequently, allograft, pulmonary, or intestinal involvement may occur. For more details, see Chapter 62.

PARASITIC INFECTIONS

Parasitic infections in transplant recipients are generally not associated with distinctive presentations with the exception of *Trypanosoma cruzi, Toxoplasma gondii,* and *S stercoralis.*

TRYPANOSOMA CRUZI

General Considerations

In patients with *T cruzi*-associated cardiomyopathy undergoing heart transplantation, a new acute phase of Chagas' disease may develop. This is characterized by fever, cutaneous lesions (with or without parasites), and myocarditis (with or without parasites) and is responsive to specific drug therapy. Parasites have been demonstrated in the transplanted hearts of such patients, (see also Chapter 85).

TOXOPLASMA GONDII

General Considerations

Toxoplasmosis after transplantation is usually the result of reactivation of latent donor-derived disease in *T gondii* seronegative heart transplant recipients. This typically occurs in the seropositive donor heart because of a predilection of the parasite to invade muscle tissues. Rarely, *T gondii* infection may be seen in other types of transplant recipients. Most cases occur within 2 months post-transplantation although cases have been reported between 1 day and 7 years after transplantation. For more details, see Chapter 81.

Clinical Findings

A. Signs and Symptoms. Clinical presentations include meningoencephalitis, brain abscess, pneumonia, myocarditis, pericarditis, hepatitis, and choreoretinitis.

B. Laboratory Findings. The diagnosis is made with certainty only by histopathologic demonstration of trophozoites with surrounding inflammation in tissue. Biopsy specimens may be stained with Wright-Geimsa or periodic acid-Schiff stains or with specific antibodies. Pulmonary organisms may be detected in bronchoalveolar lavage samples; the diagnosis of cardiac disease typically requires multiple cardiac biopsy specimens. Serologic testing is not very useful; however, a positive IgM titer or a fourfold rise in IgG titer supports the diagnosis of toxoplasmosis. Elevations of antibody levels in cerebrospinal fluid or vitreous fluid relative to those in peripheral blood are also indicative of infection in these sites. Antigen detection and molecular techniques are being developed and may be useful.

Treatment

Toxoplasmosis is treated with pyrimethamine with folinic acid and either sulfadiazine or clindamycin (Box 24–2).

Prevention

Toxoplasmosis is generally prevented by the same doses of trimethoprim-sulfamethoxazole used for *P carinii* prophylaxis (Box 24–3). An alternative is pyrimethamine.

STRONGYLOIDES STERCORALIS

General Considerations

S stercoralis is the one helminth that deserves special mention as concerns transplant recipients (see also Chapter 86).

Clinical Findings

A. Signs and Symptoms. There have been reports of hyperinfection syndromes with *S stercoralis* after transplantation. This may result in gastrointestinal and pulmonary symptoms including tachypnea, dyspnea, cough, and hemoptysis. Enterocolitis and widespread dissemination of larvae to extraintestinal organs (eg heart, lung, central nervous system, and skin) may occur and larvae may entrain gram-negative bacilli resulting in gram-negative bacteremia and occasionally meningitis.

B. Laboratory Findings. The diagnosis may be made by examining stool specimens for rhabditiform larvae; several stool specimens should be examined since the yield of a single stool examination is only ~27%. Other means of diagnosis include duodenal aspirate, urine, ascitic fluid, wound and sputum examination, jejunal biopsy, culture, and serologic testing. Eosinaphilia may be present.

C. Imaging. Alveolar or interstitial infiltrates may be seen on chest x-ray.

Treatment

Thiabendazole or ivermectin is used to treat strongyloidiasis (Box 24–2).

Prevention

As noted in the discussion on the pretransplantation evaluation, patients who have traveled to or resided in an area of endemic infection should be examined for evidence of infection with this parasite pretransplantation.

Differential Diagnosis in Transplant Recipients

The main differential diagnosis of infections in transplant recipients is rejection. Drug toxicity must also be considered.

Prevention of Infections in Transplant Recipients

A. Vaccinations. Vaccinations as outlined in Box 24–3 should be administered prior to solid-organ transplantation. Live vaccines should generally be avoided. However, for the nonimmune solid-organ transplant candidate with a high likelihood of exposure to measles, consideration may be given to the administration of the measles vaccine prior to transplant (studies are required to document the safety of this approach). Similarly, the MMR vaccine is recommended (Box 24–3) following PBSC and bone marrow transplantation. A recent study has demonstrated the safety of the varicella vaccine in pediatric renal transplant recipients and consideration may be given to immunization of solid-organ transplant candidates with no history of chickenpox. Immunization with live vaccines (eg measles vaccine, varicella vaccine), if performed, should be done as early as possible prior to solid-organ transplantation. All solid-organ transplant recipients should receive influenza vaccinations yearly and pneumococcal vaccine should be administered every 5–6 years, although the immune response to these vaccines may be impaired in transplant recipients.

For PBSC and bone marrow transplant recipients, vaccinations are administered following transplantation (Box 24–3).

B. Avoidance of Epidemiologic Exposures Post-transplantation. After transplantation, patients should be again counseled regarding measures aimed at reducing infections. Patients who are not immune to VZV should be counseled to avoid exposure to persons with chickenpox or shingles. If such an exposure does occur, a physician should be contacted immediately. All fresh fruits and vegetables should be washed. All meat and seafood should be cooked thoroughly. The source of the patient's drinking water should be reviewed. Patients with cats should avoid changing litter boxes if possible. (If changing the litter box is unavoidable, gloves should be worn and the litter box should be changed daily.) Gloves should be worn to clean fish aquaria. A mask should be worn when cleaning bird cages (if this activity is unavoidable). Patients should avoid contact with people who have colds, influenza, tuberculosis, and other contagious infections. Towels should not be shared with others unless they are washed between uses. Any plans for travel outside the United States, Canada, or western Europe should be discussed with the patient's physician before departure. All persons living in the same quarters as the patient should receive a yearly influenza vaccine, and inactivated (rather than oral) polio vaccine should be administered to those requiring polio vaccination.

C. Donor-Related Transmission of Infectious Agents. All potential organ and PBSC and bone marrow donors should be evaluated for any latent or active infection. Serologic studies of the donors should include tests for HIV-1, HIV-2, HBV, HCV, syphilis, CMV, and in many cases, *T gondii* and EBV.

REFERENCES

Basgoz N, Preiksaitis JK: Post-transplant lymphoproliferative disorder. Infect Dis Clin N Am 1995;9:901.

Guidelines for preventing opportunistic infections among hematopoietic stem cell transplant recipients. MMWR. Oct 20, 2000, Vol. 49, No. RR-10.

Hanto DW: Classification of Epstein-Barr virus-associated post-transplant lymphoproliferative diseases: implications for understanding their pathogenesis and developing rational treatment strategies. Annu Rev Med 1995;46:381.

Hibberd PL, Rubin RH: Clinical aspects of fungal infection in organ transplant recipients. Clin Infect Dis 1994;19: S33.

Maurer JR, et al: Infectious complications following isolated lung transplantation. Chest 1992;101:1056.

Patel R, Paya C: Infections in solid-organ transplant recipients. Clin Microbiol Rev 1997;10:86.

Paya CV: Prevention of cytomegalovirus disease in recipients of solid-organ transplants. Clin Infect Dis 2001; 32:596.

Rubin RH: Infection in the organ transplant recipient. In RH Rubin, LS Young: Clinical Approach to Infection in the Compromised Host, 3rded. Plenum, 1994.

Rubin RH, Tolkoff-Rubin NE: Antimicrobial strategies in the care of organ transplant recipients. Antimicrob Agents Chemother 1993;37:619.

Sia I, Patel R: New strategies for prevention and therapy of CMV in solid-organ transplant patients. Clin Microbiol Rev 2000;13:83.

Singh N, et al: Infections with cytomegalovirus and other herpesvirus in 121 liver transplant recipients: transmission by donated organ and the effect of OKT3 antibodies. J Infect Dis 1988;158:124.

Sweny P: Infection in solid-organ transplantation. Curr Opin Infect Dis 1992;51:437.

Walker RC, et al: Pretransplantation assessment of the risk of lymphoproliferative disorder. Clin Infect Dis 1995;20: 1346.

Waser M, et al: Infectious complications in 100 consecutive heart transplant recipients. Eur J Clin Microbiol Infect Dis 1994;13:12.

Patients With Neutropenia & Fever

25

David Dockrell, MD & Linda L. Lewis, MD

Essentials of Diagnosis

- Patients with a polymorphonuclear count of < 500/mm³ or between 500 and 1000/mm³, and is rapidly falling, are at greatest risk of infection.
- Underlying conditions, risk factors, and duration of neutropenia.
- Physical findings that suggest specific microbial etiology of fever with attention to possible foci of infection (eg, the mouth, lungs, perirectal area, etc).
- Cultures of blood or tissue that yield bacteria, fungus, or virus.

General Considerations

A. Epidemiology. The characteristics of patients who develop neutropenic fever have changed over the past 30 years. Neutropenic fever was reported initially in patients treated with chemotherapy for acute leukemia. Current chemotherapeutic regimens are more potent and induce greater myelosuppression. The increasing prevalence of bone marrow transplantation has also altered the host profile at risk of neutropenic fever. Patients with AIDS, aplastic anemia, congenital deficiencies, and Felty's syndrome are also at risk of developing neutropenia.

The extent and duration of neutropenia are critically important in determining the risk of infection in the patient with febrile neutropenia. For example, patients who undergo bone marrow transplantation are at particular risk because of the extent and duration of neutropenia. Similarly, chemotherapeutic agents such as cytosine arabinoside, which induce prolonged neutropenia, are associated with a greater risk of infection.

Alterations to other aspects of host immunity are also critical. Bone marrow transplantation induces neutropenia as well as defects in T-cell and B-cell function, altering the spectrum of pathogens causing febrile episodes. The administration of glucocorticoids modifies the existing immunodeficiency in patients with cancer or other diseases. The underlying diagnosis may modify the immunosuppression as may occur in patients with Hodgkin's disease who may have underlying T-cell dysfunction, and in patients with HIV-associated neutropenia.

Disruption of the host's normal mechanical barriers further facilitates infection. Indwelling intra-venous catheters are a common source of infectious complications. Mucositis induced by chemotherapy allows bacteremia with the normal flora of the mouth and gut. Patients treated with prolonged antibacterial therapy become colonized with fungi, and mucositis allows these organisms to cause invasive disease. This may explain the observation that patients who are neutropenic because of chemotherapy are at greater risk for invasive mycoses than patients with HIV-associated neutropenia. Some diseases may be associated with a lower incidence of infection or an increased susceptibility to particular infecting organisms while the patient is neutropenic. For example, patients with aplastic anemia may have a low risk of bacterial infection but are at particular risk of *Aspergillus* infections.

B. Microbiology. Over the last 25 years, changes have occurred in the pathogens that cause documented infection in febrile neutropenic patients. These reflect changes induced by altered host factors and changes in the manner in which antimicrobial therapy is administered to these patients. Box 25–1 lists characteristic pathogens currently encountered in cases of neutropenic fever. Traditionally, gram-negative bacteria were the predominant causes of neutropenic fever, and *Pseudomonas aeruginosa,* in particular, was a common pathogen. Over the years, the spectrum of infectious pathogens has changed and gram-positive infections have increased, accounting for 63% of isolated bacterial pathogens in a recent National Cancer Institute survey. Reasons for this increase include the use of indwelling intravenous catheters and empirical antimicrobial regimens, which are less effective at preventing gram-positive infections than gram-negative infections. The commonest organisms responsible for infections associated with indwelling intravenous catheter use are coagulase-negative staphylococci, *S aureus,* and viridans group streptococci. Other organisms, such as *P aeruginosa, Acinetobacter* spp., *Bacillus* spp., *Corynebacterium* spp., *Candida* spp., and *Malassezia furfur,* are also encountered.

Staphylococcal, streptococcal, and enterococcal infections are increasing in frequency. Management of these infections is complicated by increasing methicillin resistance among staphylococci and multidrug resistance among enterococci. Streptococcal

BOX 25-1

Microbiology of Neutropenia in Adults and Children

Type of Organism	More Frequent	Less Frequent
Gram-Positive Bacteria	• *S aureus* • Coagulase-negative staphylococci • Enterococci • Viridans streptococci	• *Corynebacterium jeikeium* • *Bacillus* spp. • *Clostridium* spp.
Gram-Negative Bacteria	• *E coli* • *K pneumoniae* • *P aeruginosa*	• *Enterobacter* spp. • *Acinetobacter* spp. • *Stenotrophomonas maltophilia* • *Citrobacter freundii* • *Serratia marcescens* • *Legionella* spp.
Mycobacteria		• *M fortuitum* • *M cheloneae*
Fungi	• *C albicans* • *C kruzei* • *C tropicalis* • *T glabrata* • *Aspergillus* spp.	• *Mucor* • *Rhizopus* • *Fusarium* • *Trichosporon* • *Pseudoallescheria boydii* • *Cryptococcus* • *Malassezia furfur*
Viruses	• *Herpes simplex virus* • *Varicella-zoster virus*	• Cytomegalovirus
Parasites		• *Pneumocystis carinii* • *Toxoplasma gondii* • *Strongyloides stercoralis*

infections, including infections with *S mitis* and viridans group streptococci, are associated with oral mucositis and with ciprofloxacin prophylaxis. Fungal infections are increasing at many centers and include *C albicans*, non-*albicans Candida* spp. such as *C tropicalis*, *C kruzei*, and *Torulopsis glabrata*, and filamentous fungi (*Aspergillus* spp., *Mucor*, *Fusarium*, and *Pseudoallescheria boydii*). Filamentous fungi are increasingly recognized in association with prolonged neutropenia resulting in respiratory tract or disseminated infection.

Gram-negative infections are still encountered, but the spectrum of pathogens has changed. *P aeruginosa*, once a frequent pathogen in patients with neutropenic fever, has dramatically decreased in incidence for unclear reasons and has been reported to occur in just 1% of cases enrolled in National Institutes of Health treatment protocols in neutropenic populations. It remains a significant pathogen in some subpopulations, such as children with HIV infection. *Escherichia coli* and *K pneumoniae* are the

most frequently isolated gram-negative bacteria, but the emergence of antibiotic-resistant *Enterobacter* spp., *Serratia marcescens*, *Stenotrophomonas maltophilia*, or *Acinetobacter* spp. has become an increasing problem. Other pathogens encountered include *Corynebacterium jeikeium* and *Bacillus* spp. that cause intravenous catheter-associated infections; rapidly growing mycobacteria that cause exit-site or tunnel infections associated with intravenous catheters; *Legionella* spp. that cause nosocomial pneumonia; infection with *Nocardia* spp.; *P carinii* pneumonia; *Clostridium septicum* septicemia; *C difficile* colitis; herpes virus infections, particularly cytomegalovirus in bone marrow transplant recipients; histoplasmosis, blastomycosis, or coccidioidomycosis that cause pneumonia or disseminated infection in endemic areas; cryptococcal infections; and, occasionally, parasitic infections such as *Strongyloides stercoralis* or *Toxoplasma gondii*.

An identifiable pathogen is documented in ~ 30%–50% of cases of neutropenic fever, which represents a decrease in the number of documented infections causing neutropenic fever as compared with the number documented 20–30 years ago.

Clinical Findings

The absence of neutrophils and, consequently, signs of inflammation creates a unique challenge for the clinician attempting to determine the cause of neutropenic fever. Although up to 90% of patients become febrile during neutropenia, in most cases, fever is the only sign of infection. This necessitates a thorough history with identification of risk factors for particular types of infection. The history of the underlying illness, its therapy, duration of neutropenia, prophylactic antibiotics administered, previous infections causing neutropenic fever and their treatment, travel and exposure history, thorough knowledge of the most frequent pathogens causing neutropenic fever at the institution and their antimicrobial susceptibilities, and inquiry about specific symptoms and review of systems should be carefully ascertained. A thorough history can help direct the physical examination and subsequent laboratory testing (see Table 25–1). In many cases, no specific clues are identified, and empirical treatment will be initiated without identification of a specific infectious syndrome to explain fever.

A. Signs and Symptoms. The physical examination of patients with neutropenic fever should be thorough and repeated at regular intervals because the clinical status of these patients can change rapidly. The head and neck should be carefully examined. Mucositis, gingivostomatitis, or dental disease should be documented and are clues to infection with viridans group streptococci or anaerobes; sinus tenderness and nasal eschar may suggest fungal sinusitis, especially *Mucor* or *Aspergillus.* The skin should be examined carefully for nodules, which may be found with *Candida* occasionally (Figure 25–1).

Evidence of ecthyma gangrenosum, which is classically associated with *P aeruginosa* infection but has also been associated with *E coli* bacteremia or candidemia, should be sought. These lesions are small, round, indurated nodules that appear initially as vesicles, become hemorrhagic, and then ulcerate. They are most often located in the perirectal or perivaginal area. Ecthyma gangrenosum must be distinguished from the black, necrotic lesions that may range in size from a centimeter or less to many centimeters and that are most often caused by *Mucor* spp. or dematiaceous fungi. These lesions may be located in any body area. Lesions around the face or within the mouth are often caused by members of the genus *Mucor,* whereas lesions on the extremities or trunk may be caused by dematiaceous fungi or *Mucor* spp. Areas of cellulitis should be searched for, especially in the perirectal area, and infection may be caused by *Pseudomonas* spp. or other gram-negative bacteria. The perianal area should be inspected but a rectal exam avoided because it may induce bacteremia. All sites of indwelling catheters should be inspected and subcutaneous tunnels examined for areas of fluctuance or tenderness. The lungs should be examined for evidence of pneumonitis, and the abdomen palpated for signs of typhlitis (inflammation involving the cecum, seen especially in children with acute lymphocytic leukemia).

Table 25–1. Assessment of patients with neutropenia.

Assessment	Comments
Physical Examination:	
Skin rashes	Lesions may suggest bacteremia or candidemia
Ecthyma gangrenosum	Consider *P aeruginosa* but rarely *E coli* or *Candida* spp.
Black eschar	Fungi, especially *Aspergillus* or *Mucor*
Inspection of all intravascular devices	Potential site of infection (inspect in particular for tunnel or exit-site infections); bacteria include coagulase-negative staphylococci, *S aureus,* occasional gram-negative bacteria, fungi (*Candida* spp., often non-*albicans*)
Mouth examination	Mucositis is a risk factor for infection with *viridans* streptococci and anaerobes
Sinus tenderness	Fungal infection
Right lower quadrant abdominal tenderness	Consider cecal inflammation (typhlitis)
Perirectal inflammation	*Pseudomonas* infection; rarely anaerobic infection
Chest Radiograph:	
Localized infiltrate	Bacterial or mycobacterial infection
Nodular infiltrate or nodular density with surrounding hyperlucency; cavitary lesions	Filamentous fungi or *Nocardia* spp.; *Aspergillus* spp.
Diffuse interstitial infiltrate	Viral or *Pneumocystis carinii*
Other Factors:	
Fever persists or recurs after 1 week of antibiotic therapy	Filamentous fungal infection likely
Fever and abdominal pain at time of resolution of neutropenia	Hepatosplenic candidiasis
Bone marrow transplant recipient	Wide range of potential pathogens (see Chapter 24)

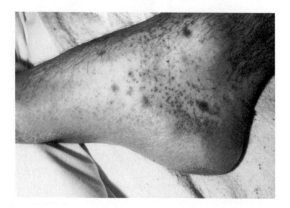

Figure 25–1. The foot of a patient who received high-dose chemotherapy for AML and developed neutropenic fever shows multiple nodules. Biopsy and culture of one of these lesions revealed *C albicans*.

B. Laboratory Findings. At least two blood cultures should be performed initially. If an indwelling venous catheter is in place, blood for cultures should be obtained through the catheter (all lumens) and peripherally. Only 10–20% of patients with neutropenic fever have documented bacteremia or fungemia.

Techniques such as shell vial for virus or polymerase chain reaction analyses have application in special settings, such as the detection of cytomegalovirus infections after bone marrow transplantation. In addition, an aspirate or biopsy should be obtained from any suspected focus of infection identified by exam and diagnostic imaging. For example, a bronchoalveolar lavage should be considered on any patient with respiratory symptoms or abnormal results from chest radiography. An open-lung biopsy may be necessary in patients who have progressive pulmonary disease without previous diagnosis and who have not responded to empiric therapy.

Specimens should be stained and cultured for bacteria, including anaerobes, and for fungi, mycobacteria, and, in selected patients, viruses. Cryptococcal antigen tests on serum or spinal fluid should be performed in selected patients. Fungal serologies for *Histoplasma* spp., *Coccidioides* spp., or *Blastomyces* spp. should be performed in patients who reside in or have traveled to endemic areas.

Stool samples should be sent for *C difficile* toxin assay for patients with unexplained diarrhea, as pseudomembranous colitis secondary to *C difficile* toxin often complicates the use of antimicrobial agents in patients with neutropenic fever. Other causes of diarrhea in febrile neutropenic patients include neutropenic colitis, enteric pathogens, cytomegalovirus, and parasitic infection. Disseminated strongyloidiasis should be suspected in patients who travel to or reside in endemic areas. If the cause of di-

arrhea is not established quickly by tests such as *C difficile* toxin assay, stool culture, and examination for parasites, colonoscopy may be necessary to detect cytomegalovirus or neutropenic colitis. Surveillance cultures of the stool are not useful.

C. Imaging. A chest radiograph should always be performed on every patient at regular intervals, although the absence of neutrophils often means there is no demonstrable abnormality. Patchy infiltrates may be detected and early in the course of neutropenia often correspond to bacterial infections. If such infiltrates occur in a patient with a longer history of neutropenia, fungal infection becomes an increasingly more likely cause. *Aspergillus* spp. are particularly likely in those with new infiltrates despite antibiotic therapy (Figure 25–2) and with pleural-based nodules, cavitary lesions, or masses with an area of hyperlucency referred to as a halo sign. In these patients, a bronchoalveolar lavage followed by open biopsy is recommended if bronchoalveolar lavage is nondiagnostic.

Other potential pathogens that present with patchy infiltrates include *Legionella pneumophila*, *Nocardia asteroides* (which is either localized or a diffuse miliary infiltrate), rarely mycobacteria, and in endemic areas *Histoplasma capsulatum*, *Coccidioides immitis*, or *Blastomyces dermatitidis*. Diffuse infiltrates can be seen in infections caused by *Legionella* spp., *Pneumocystis carinii*, viruses (especially cytomegalovirus), and parasitic infection.

Computed tomography or magnetic resonance scanning may be useful if head and neck or abdominal/perirectal infection is suspected. The diagnostic utility of nuclear imaging in the evaluation of neutropenic fever has not been established. Abdominal pain and fever associated with an elevation of hepatic enzymes coinciding with the recovery of the neutrophil count is suggestive of hepatosplenic candidiasis (Figure 25–3). Computed tomography or ultrasound of the liver and spleen reveals bull's eye lesions, and diagnosis is confirmed by finding pseudohyphae and granulomata upon computed tomography or ultrasound-guided needle biopsy.

Differential Diagnosis

Although only 30–50% of patients with neutropenic fever have documented infections, it is assumed that many of the remainder have occult infection. However, there may be other causes of a febrile episode or of a particular symptom or sign attributed to infection. Numerous tumors can give rise to fever. This has been noted in Hodgkin's lymphoma, non-Hodgkin's lymphoma, and other solid tumors characterized by necrosis. Drugs, including numerous antibiotics used in the management of neutropenic fever, have been reported to cause fever, but this occurs infrequently. Although chemotherapeutic agents like cytosine arabinoside, bleomycin, and 2-CDA are associated with fever, the fever is usually transient and occurs long before the

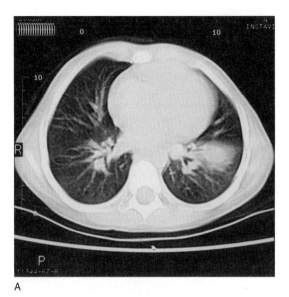 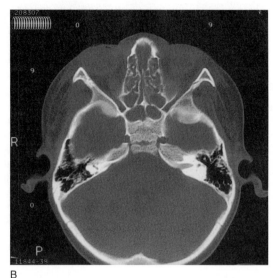

A   B

Figure 25–2. (A) Computed tomography of the chest of a child with neutropenia, persistent fever, and cough revealing a dense, nodular infiltrate in the left perihilar area. (B) Computed tomography of the head of a child with neutropenia, persistent fever, and bloody nasal discharge revealing completely opacified ethmoid and sphenoid sinuses. Surgical exploration revealed pansinusitis with multiple areas of black eschar. Cultured material in both cases grew *Aspergillus* species.

subsequent development of neutropenia. Use of G-CSF or GM-CSF may also cause fever. Drugs that may mask fever, such as corticosteroids, acetaminophen, and nonsteroidal anti-inflammatory drugs, may also be considered when evaluating neutropenic fever. The administration of blood products and, especially, amphotericin B is a common cause of transient increases in temperature associated with the infusion and should be considered in the differential diagnosis.

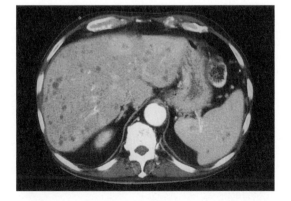

Figure 25–3. Abdominal computed tomography with contrast in a child with prolonged neutropenia, fever, and abdominal pain. Multiple lucent lesions scattered throughout the liver and spleen are typical of hepatosplenic candidiasis.

Finally, patients with cancer are at increased risk of deep venous thrombosis and subsequent pulmonary emboli, which are associated with hypoxia and fever.

The signs and symptoms associated with neutropenic fever may have alternative explanations. Chest radiograph abnormalities and hypoxemia may be caused by noninfectious conditions such as tumor, pulmonary complications of chemotherapeutic agents such as bleomycin or cyclophosphamide, pulmonary emboli, pulmonary edema, radiotherapy, transfusion-related acute lung injury, pulmonary hemorrhage, or transient hypoxemia associated with neutrophil recovery and migration into the lung associated with GM-CSF therapy. Diarrhea may be the result of chemotherapy or use of antibiotics. Skin rashes can be caused by drugs. A rare cause of fever with nodular skin rash, sometimes including vesicles, pustules, or bullae, is Sweet's syndrome (acute febrile neutrophilic dermatosis), which may be associated with acute myelogenous leukemia.

Complications

Superinfection is a recognized complication of febrile neutropenia in patients receiving antimicrobial agents. It is usually defined as the development of documented infection during or < 1 week after the discontinuation of antimicrobial therapy. Superinfection occurs in ≤ 20% of cancer patients with neutropenic fever. Fungi account for 25–67% of superinfections. Risk factors for superinfection include a longer duration of profound neutropenia (< 100 neutrophils/mm^3), persistence of fever after 3 days of therapy, and presence of a central venous catheter.

Treatment

The initiation of empirical antibiotic therapy for any febrile neutropenic patient with a single oral temperature elevation > 38.5°C or three or more oral temperatures recorded at > 38.0°C within 24 h has become the standard of care. Even though many patients have no demonstrable infection, it is assumed that most have occult infection. The rapidity with which these patients' clinical status can deteriorate during infectious episodes and the demonstration that empirical therapy decreases mortality have supported the use of empirical therapy for neutropenic fever.

The selection of empirical therapy should be influenced by the epidemiological and pathogenic concerns mentioned. Its design should consider the predominant microorganisms encountered at a given center, their expected susceptibility patterns, and the clinical features and laboratory test results.

The initial empiric regimen should include an antimicrobial agent or combination of drugs with a broad spectrum of coverage against gram-positive and gram-negative bacteria. This regimen should be modified if fever persists or recurs while on treatment. Initial anaerobic coverage is not usually required but should be included in cases with marked oral mucositis or documented bowel or perirectal involvement. Initial empiric antifungal therapy is not necessary but should be added for treatment failure or in cases with signs or symptoms suggestive of fungal infection in association with prolonged neutropenia.

The initial regimen is intended to treat the cause of fever, as well as to prevent subsequent episodes. The selection of an empiric regimen should consider its efficacy as well as its cost, toxicity, and potential to increase antibiotic resistance and superinfection. Because of the emergence of vancomycin-resistant enterococci, many clinicians no longer include vancomycin in initial empiric therapeutic regimens.

Box 25–2 outlines possible empirical regimens. A β-lactam, either alone or in combination with an aminoglycoside or a fluoroquinolone, is often used.

BOX 25–2

Empirical Therapy for Neutropenia

	Initial Regimen	Modification of Regimen After 3 Days of Persistent Fever	Modification of Regimen After 5–7 Days of Persistent Fever
First Line	• Ceftazidime, 2 g (50 mg/kg)[1] every 8 h IV, plus tobramycin/gentamicin, 2.0 mg/kg load then 1.7 mg/kg (2.0 mg/kg load then 1.7 mg/kg)[1] every 8 h IV • Cefepime, 2 g (50 mg/kg)[1] every 8–12 h or Amikacin, 7.5 mg/kg every 12 h IV (5 mg/kg every 8 h)[1] • Piperacillin, 3 g every 4 h (75 mg/kg every 6 h)[1] IV, plus tobramycin [or as above], doses as above • Piperacillin plus tazobactam, 4.5 g every 8 h +/− aminoglycosideas above[1] • Ceftazidime 100 mg/kg	Consider adding vancomycin 1 g (10 mg/kg every 6 h)[1] every 12 h IV	Amphotericin, 0.5–0.6 mg/kg (0.5–0.6 mg/kg)[1] daily IV
Second Line	• Imipenem-cilastin, 0.5 g (12.5 mg/kg)[1] every 6 h IV • Meropenem, 1 g (20–40 mg/kg)[1] every 8 h IV		
Penicillin Allergy	• Aztreonam, 2 g (30 mg/kg)[1] every 6 h plus clindamycin, 900 mg every 8 h (10 mg/kg every 6 h)[1]IV or vancomycin, 1 g every 12 h IV (10 mg/kg every 6 h IV)[1]		

[1]Pediatric dose in parentheses. Less experience with cefepime, meropenam, and oral regimens.

The β-lactam used most often is ceftazidime because of its activity against *P aeruginosa* and other such gram-negative bacteria as the *Enterobacteriaceae*. The new fourth-generation cephalosporin, cefepime, may be useful, because of its ability to remain bactericidal against *Enterobacteriaceae* that have developed resistance to ceftazidime as well as its improved gram-positive coverage compared with that of ceftazidime. The choice of an aminoglycoside (gentamicin, tobramycin, or amikacin) is dictated by local resistance patterns and cost. The administration of two β-lactam antibiotics concurrently should be avoided.

An acceptable alternative to combination therapy is monotherapy with ceftazidime, cefepime, piperacillin-tazobactam, or a carbapenem such as imipenem-cilastin or meropenem. The main concern with ceftazidime, but not cefepime, monotherapy is its poor gram-positive coverage and the emergence of resistance in some gram-negative organisms. For these reasons, centers with high rates of gram-positive infections or infections by *Serratia marcescens, Enterobacter* spp., or *Citrobacter freundii* should avoid ceftazidime monotherapy.

Clinical trials have shown imipenem-cilastin or meropenem to be equivalent to ceftazidime-containing regimens. Carbapenems are more active against gram-positive and most gram-negative microorganisms, compared with ceftazidime. Imipenem-cilastin therapy may cause seizures in some patients, whereas meropenem has a low risk of associated seizures. Piperacillin-tazobactam monotherapy is also effective empiric therapy for febrile neutropenia patients. Like cefepime and the carbapenems, piperacillin-tazobactam has a broad spectrum of activity against gram-positive and gram-negative microorganisms. Among these regimens, only the carbapenems and piperacillin-tazobactam have activity against anaerobes. If the clinical suspicion of anaerobic infection is high, metronidazole should be added to therapy with either ceftazidime or cefepime. In β-lactam–allergic patients, a combination of ciprofloxacin or aztreonam, together with either clindamycin or vancomycin is appropriate.

Apart from its use in some penicillin-allergic patients and in centers with high incidences of coagulase-negative staphylococci or methicillin-resistant *S aureus,* vancomycin is usually not included in the initial therapeutic regimen because of concerns about the emergence of vancomycin resistance. Studies conducted in the early 1980s suggested that empiric therapy with vancomycin-containing regimens was more effective than therapy that did not include vancomycin. More recent studies showed that patients are not adversely affected by a policy of withholding vancomycin use until there is clinical or microbiological evidence that it is required. Vancomycin therapy may be added in patients with an indwelling intravenous catheter who remain febrile after 3 days of empirical treatment with no other obvious source of infection.

Some patients with febrile neutropenia have a low mortality risk (3%) from infection. Their profiles include the development of neutropenic fever while a clinically stable outpatient; the presence of a tumor responsive to chemotherapy; and the absence of any current comorbidity. These patients account for ~ 40% of patients with febrile neutropenia. Strategies being evaluated for the management of these patients include (a) 48 h of intravenous antibiotics followed by oral antibiotics, (b) parenteral antibiotics administered as an outpatient, or (c) oral antibiotics. A recent randomized clinical trial conducted in carefully selected low-risk patients confirmed that oral antibiotics are as effective as intravenous antibiotics in the hospital setting. Whether this conclusion is generalizable to the outpatient population remains to be determined.

Ciprofloxacin has a special place in the management of low-risk adult patients as described above. While it can be used parenterally, its special advantage is that it is an effective oral agent against *P aeruginosa* and other gram-negative bacteria. Because of its limited gram-positive coverage, however, it should be combined with either amoxicillin-clavulanate or clindamycin. Alternatively, the improved gram-positive spectrum of levofloxacin may make it useful in this setting.

Approximately 66% of patients can be maintained on their empirical regimen throughout the period of neutropenia. The remainder may require modification because of the results of cultures or other tests or because of recurrent or persistent fever.

If microbiological tests identify a specific organism, empiric therapy may be modified if necessary; however, patients should continue to receive broad-spectrum antibiotic coverage throughout the period of neutropenia. The isolation of a gram-positive organism before or during therapy may require the addition of vancomycin or anti-staphylococcal penicillin. If a gram-negative organism is isolated before the initiation of therapy in a patient who has subsequently defervesced, the initial regimen may not need to be modified. However, if a gram-negative organism is isolated from a sample collected after treatment has been initiated, antimicrobial resistance or superinfection should be suspected, and modification of the gram-negative coverage is warranted.

In patients who remain febrile after 5 days of empiric antimicrobial therapy, antifungal therapy should be added. Fungal infections are associated with prolonged periods of neutropenia. Fungi are difficult to recover ante mortem but are a frequent finding at post mortem in patients who died with neutropenic fever. Once fungal infections disseminate, there is a high associated mortality. Amphotericin B (0.5–0.6 mg/kg/d) is the empiric therapy of choice. Amphotericin-lipid complex formulations have lower nephrotoxicity than amphotericin but have not been shown to be more effective and are much more expensive.

Although fluconazole or itraconazole may be equivalent to amphotericin B in managing non-neutropenic patients with candidemia, the role of empiric imidazole therapy in febrile neutropenic patients is not established. Fluconazole resistance is increasing among *Candida* spp.; *C kruzei, C tropicalis, Torulopsis glabrata,* and non-*albicans* species are usually resistant. *Aspergillus* infections usually require higher daily doses of amphotericin B (1.0–1.5 mg/kg/d). Hepatosplenic candidiasis usually requires prolonged amphotericin B treatment with total doses of 3–5 g. Some patients receiving empirical amphotericin may develop breakthrough candidiasis. This may be owing to infection with resistant strains of *Candida* or, more commonly, by infection associated with intravascular catheters.

Broad-spectrum antimicrobial therapy should be continued until after recovery from neutropenia. Such therapy results in less relapse of fever than treatment for a 7- to 10-day period. If the period of neutropenia ends shortly after the initiation of antibiotics, therapy should continue for a 7- to 10-day course.

Intravascular catheter infections are usually treated with antibiotics rotated through each port or lumen. As many of the organisms causing these infections are indolent, initial attempts are made to treat without removing the catheter. A catheter should be removed if (a) blood cultures remain positive 48 h after the commencement of antibiotics, (b) *Candida* or *Bacillus* infections are present, or (c) exit-site infections, caused by *A flavus* or mycobacteria, or tunnel infections are present (indicated by tenderness or induration along the subcutaneous track of the catheter).

The hematopoietic growth factors G-CSF and GM-CSF are emerging as important adjuvants to the management of neutropenic fever. By increasing the proliferation and differentiation of bone marrow progenitor cells, they help restore neutrophil and macrophage function. These agents have been demonstrated to reduce the period of neutropenia, shorten the period of hospitalization, and decrease the incidence of bacteremia. However, they have not been consistently demonstrated to decrease overall mortality. These agents should be considered in patients whose expected duration of neutropenia is > 1 week. Side effects of these agents include fever, rash, hypoxia, bone pain, and fluid retention. Various cytokines are being investigated as adjuvants to antimicrobial therapy in the management of neutropenic fever.

Prognosis

The outcome of neutropenic fever can be defined in terms of microbiologic response and clinical outcome and is related to recovery from neutropenia. Among patients with documented bacterial infections, treatment with ceftazidime or cefepime monotherapy, cephalosporin-aminoglycoside combinations, piperacillin-tazobactam, or carbapenem monotherapy have been associated with microbiologic cure rates > 90%. Fungal microbiological response rates are much lower.

Clinical response rates are often defined in terms of resolution of fever after 4 days of treatment, need to alter initial empirical antimicrobial agents, and survival. Overall β-lactam monotherapy has been associated with resolution of fever after 4 days of therapy in ~ 60%, need for subsequent antimicrobial-agent modification in ~ 60%, and overall survival of 90–98%. The mortality rate associated with documented bacterial causes of neutropenic fever has fallen from 90% in the 1950s to <10% in the 1990s.

Fungal and vancomycin-resistant enterococcal infections are associated with a higher mortality—> 50%. The incidence of superinfection is between 20% and 25%, and their mortality is > 50%. The ultimate prognosis for most patients is closely linked to their underlying malignancy. For example, in an analysis of hepatosplenic candidiasis, the prognosis of the underlying leukemia was the most important determinant of outcome.

Prevention & Control

Several strategies have been used to decrease the incidence of neutropenic fever. Trials of antibiotic prophylaxis have had mixed results. Initial trials using trimethoprim-sulfamethoxazole showed some promise, but the emergence of resistance limited its use. In trials, ciprofloxacin therapy reduced the risk of gram-negative infections but not gram-positive infections and did not decrease fever-related morbidity or infection-related mortality. Concerns about the emergence of resistance to this agent have led many authorities to recommend that ciprofloxacin prophylaxis be limited to groups whose length of neutropenia places them at a particularly high risk of infectious complication (eg, bone marrow transplant patients).

Antifungal prophylaxis with fluconazole decreases the incidence of infections by susceptible *Candida* spp. but is also associated with the emergence of resistant *Candida* spp. Oral bowel decontamination regimens have been studied, but they are not palatable and are minimally effective. *Pneumocystis carinii* prophylaxis with trimethoprim-sulfamethoxazole is effective and recommended for febrile-neutropenia patients receiving high doses of glucocorticoids.

Environmental measures should be taken to lessen the incidence of infection in patients who are neutropenic. Simple isolation with careful hand washing has been demonstrated to be as efficacious as and more practical than reverse isolation. The use of a total protective environment with constant positive airflow and vigorous surface decontamination does not merit the extra expense. Despite decreasing the number of infections, no clear survival benefit has been proven.

Some authorities recommend a cooked diet to avoid the acquisition of organisms in uncooked food. Spices such as freshly ground black pepper are best avoided because of potential contamination by fungal spores. Similarly, potted plants should not be part of the patient's environment because of associated fungal spores and bacteria found in the soil. Environmental sources contribute to fungal colonization. Construction work in or around a hospital will significantly increase the number of *Aspergillus* spores in the air. In centers where this is a problem, high-efficiency particulate air filters may be helpful. Similarly, water purification systems will decrease the risk of nosocomial *Legionella* infections.

REFERENCES

Freifeld A et al: A double-blind comparison of empirical oral and intravenous antibiotic therapy for low-risk febrile patients with neutropenia during cancer chemotherapy. N Engl J Med 1999;341:305.

Hathorn JW, Lyke K: Empirical treatment of febrile neutropenia: evolution of current therapeutic approaches. Clin Infect Dis 1997;24:(Suppl 2)S256.

Hughes WT, et al: 1997 guidelines for the use of antimicrobial agents in neutropenic patients with unexplained fever. Clin Infect Dis 1997;25:551.

Lee JW, Pizzo PA: Management of the cancer patient with fever and prolonged neutropenia. Hematol Oncol Clin North Am 1993;7:937.

Pizzo PA: Fever in immunocompromised patients. N Engl J Med 1999;341:893.

Ramphal R et al: Clinical experience with single agent and combination regimens in the management of infection in the febrile neutropenic patient. Am J Med 1996;100:(Suppl 6A)83S.

Rolston KVI, Rubenstein EB, Freifeld A: Early empiric antibiotic therapy for febrile neutropenia patients at low risk. Infect Dis Clin North Am 1996;10:223.

Patients with Recurrent Infections and Leukocyte Abnormalities

Timothy R. La Pine, MD, & Harry R. Hill, MD

A critical and delicate balance in both cellular and humoral function is essential for complete immunologic responsiveness to invasive microbial pathogens. Any alteration in immune regulation or responsiveness may render a host susceptible to recurrent or life-threatening infections. Understanding the specific functional mechanisms involved in leukocyte production, activation, migration, and immune regulation leading to cytoxic killing is of extreme clinical significance when evaluating patients with suspected immunodeficiency.

Leukocyte abnormalities should be suspected in the following patients: (1) those who have an increased frequency of infections compared to patients of similar age and exposure risks; (2) those whose infections with common, often nonpathogenic or usually inconsequential pathogens are more severe than would normally be expected; (3) those whose infections are of prolonged duration and require prolonged antimicrobial therapy often with incomplete clearing between episodes or requiring surgical intervention; (4) those with multiple complicated infections, involving different organ systems; and (5) those who have infections with unusual or opportunistic organisms.

The specific components of immune responsiveness are exceedingly complex and require the close cooperation of a variety of cellular elements (T lymphocytes, B lymphocytes, phagocytes, and natural killer cells) as well as humoral factors (immunoglobulins, lymphokines, monokines, interferons, acute-phase reactants, and the complement system). For clinical utility, defects in leukocyte immunoresponsiveness can be categorized into four functional systems: (1) defects in the T-lymphocyte system (including T cells and lymphokines); (2) defects in the B-lymphocyte system (including B cells and secretory immunoglobulins); (3) defects in the phagocyte system (including neutrophils, monocytes, and macrophages); (4) defects in the complement system. Box 26–1 summarizes the syndromes commonly found with each type of defect. The tests used to screen patients with suspected immunodeficiency are listed in Table 26–1, and further confirmatory tests are listed in Table 26–2.

T-LYMPHOCYTE DEFECTS

Essentials of Diagnosis

- Systemic illness after vaccinations with live virus or *Mycobacterium* Bacille Calmette-Guérin vaccine.
- Chronic oral candidiasis or mucocutaneous candidiasis persisting after 6 months of age with resistance to therapy.
- Graft-vs-host disease after blood transfusions.
- Persistently low absolute lymphocyte counts.
- Hypocalcemia/tetany with DiGeorge facies.
- Intracellular infections (caused by bacteria, protozoans, viruses, or fungi).

General Considerations

The T-lymphocyte system is composed of several subtypes of effector cells that include regulatory T cells, helper and suppressor T cells, cytotoxic T cells, and T cells involved in delayed hypersensitivity reactions. The major function of the T-lymphocyte system is in host defense against intracellular pathogens (viruses, fungi, protozoa, and intracellular bacteria such as mycobacteria and *Listeria* spp.). The T lymphocyte system also functions in tumor surveillance, delayed hypersensitivity reactions, and graft-versus-host disease.

Thymus-dependent T cells are derived from pluripotent hematopoietic stem cells residing in developing bone marrow stores. As early as the eighth gestational week, immature T cells infiltrate the thymus where they differentiate and mature before migrating to specific lymphoid tissues. During their intrathymic maturation, T cells develop specific outer membrane glycoproteins. Mature T cells express T-cell antigen receptors as well as the CD3 membrane glycoproteins. Nearly 70% of the T cells also express the CD4 membrane glycoproteins, the helper-inducer T-cell marker. The remaining 30% express the CD8 membrane glycoprotein, the cytotoxic-suppressor T-cell marker. The CD4 and CD8 membrane glycoproteins are typically

BOX 26-1

Defects in Immune Responsiveness

T- Lymphocyte–Mediated Defects	• Severe combined immunodeficiency • DiGeorge syndrome • Wiskott-Aldrich syndrome • Ataxia telangiectasia
B-Lymphocyte Abnormalities	• Bruton's agammaglobulinemia • Hyper IgM syndrome • Selective IgA deficiency • Common variable immunodeficiency
Phagocytic Cell Defects	• Leukocyte adhesion deficiency • Jobs syndrome • Chronic granulomatous disease • Chediak-Higashi syndrome
Complement Defects	• Deficiency of C1 and C4 • C2 deficiency • C3 deficiency • Deficiency of C5, 6, 7, 8, 9 • Properdin deficiency

not presented on the same mature T cell and serve as functional markers of helper and cytotoxic-suppressor T-cell populations in the peripheral blood or tissues.

The T-lymphocyte system orchestrates pathogen annihilation through antigen-dependent cellular interactions. Antigen-presenting cells, mainly the monocytes and macrophages (but also the Langerhans cells of the skin, the Kupffer cells of the liver, and specific endothelial cells) process soluble antigen and present it in combination with HLA class II antigens on their cellular surface. Thymus-dependent CD4 helper-inducer T cells recognize and bind to this altered antigen-HLA class II complex through helper T-cell receptors. During this process, interleukin-1 (IL-1) is released from the antigen-presenting cells. The binding of the free IL-1 to its receptor on the helper T-cell surface initiates T-cell activation. Once activated, the CD4 helper T cells produce IL-2, which functions as a T-cell promoter, causing the T cells to proliferate and release a number of factors, thus initiating a cascade of events that serves to amplify and regulate the immune response with the cooperation and recruitment of many other cell types. IL-2 also interacts directly with CD8 cytotoxic T-cells that bind viral anti-

Table 26–1. Laboratory tests used to screen for immunodeficiency.[1]

Antibody Deficiency	Serum IgM, IgG, and IgA levels IgG antibody response to protein (diphtheria, tetanus, and influenza) and polysaccharide (*S pneumoniae*) antigens Isohemagglutinin titers for IgM antibody response Serum IgG subclass levels
Cell-Mediated Immunodeficiency	Total lymphocyte count Delayed hypersensitivity skin tests (diphtheria, tetanus, Candida, PPD, and mumps) for T-cell function Tests for HIV antibodies and viral load if suspected
Complement Deficiency	Total hemolytic complement activity Alternative pathway hemolytic activity Serum C2, C3, C4, C5, and Factor B levels
Phagocyte Defect	Complete blood count with ANC NBT test for respiratory burst activity (defect in CGD) Serum IgE levels for HIE (Job) syndrome

[1]PPD, purified protein derivative; ANC, absolute neutrophil count; NBT, nitroblue tetrazolium test; CGD, chronic granulomatous disease; HIE, hyper IgE.

Table 26–2. Laboratory tests to confirm and define immunodeficiency.[1]

Antibody Deficiency	B-cell enumeration (total B cells, CD19, and CD20) and surface IgM-, IgG-, IgA-, and IgD-bearing B cells) In vitro Ig biosynthesis
Cell-Mediated Immunodeficiency	Enumerate total T-cell and T-cell subsets (CD3, CD4, CD8, etc) Measure T-cell proliferation with mitogens, antigens, and allogeneic cells (MLR) and lymphokine production Enzyme assays for ADA or PNP deficiency
Complement Deficiency	Specific component determinations
Phagocyte Defect	Leukocyte adhesive glycoprotein analysis (CD11a/CD18, CD11b/CD18, CD11c/CD18, and sialyl Lewis-X) Adherence and aggregation Chemotaxis and random motility Phagocytosis and killing of bacteria Assays for respiratory burst activity (chemiluminescence and oxygen radical production) Enzyme assay (MPO, G6PD) for phagocyte enzyme defects Cytochrome B or cytosolic protein measurements for CGD

[1]MLR, mixed lymphocyte reaction; MPO, myeloperoxidase; G6PD, glucose-6-phosphate dehydrogenase.

gens present on the surfaces of infected cells, resulting in cellular destruction.

T-cell immunodeficiency can result from defects in the (1) maturation, differentiation, and activation of hematopoietic stem cells; (2) specific thymic defects, including the thymic microenvironment and associated humoral factors; (3) specific T-cell defects; (4) defective production of cytokines; (5) defective expression of cytokine receptors; (6) defective production of regulatory proteins needed for T-cell activation; and (7) destruction of T cells. Any defect in T-cell immunity is also associated with variable degrees of B-cell deficiency because most of the maturation, differentiation, and activation processes of B cells requires T cell help. Box 26–2 summarizes treatment options for patients who have lekocyte deficiencies.

BOX 26–2

Treatment and Management Options for Patients with Leukocyte Deficiencies

T–Cell Deficiencies	• Bone marrow or stem cell transplantation • IL–2 replacement if deficient • Fetal thymic tissue transplants are of limited therapeutic value in DiGeorge patients • Future gene replacement therapies are being explored • Prophylactic TMP/SMX as indicated • IPV, no live vaccines
B–Cell Deficiencies	• Bone marrow or stem cell transplantation • Future gene replacement therapies are being explored • IVIG but not with selective IgA deficiency • IPV, no live vaccines
Phagocytic Cell Defects	• Leukocyte infusions • G–CSF • Future gene replacement therapies are being explored • Gamma interferon for CGD patients may be beneficial in Job patients • Prophylactic antibiotic therapy as indicated
Complement Defects	• Methyltestosterone derivatives in C1 esterase deficiency • Prophylactic antibiotic therapy as indicated • Meningococcal vaccine • Pneumoccal vaccine

SEVERE COMBINED IMMUNODEFICIENCY

Clinical Findings

The most severe forms of leukocyte immunodeficiency are the syndromes of severe combined immunodeficiency (SCID). This immunodeficiency category includes a spectrum of X-linked, autosomal recessive, and sporadic genetic defects characterized by the inability to mount normal T-lymphocyte (cell-mediated) and B-lymphocyte (humoral) immunity. These syndromes include X-linked SCID, adenosine deaminase deficiency, and ZAP-70 deficiency, which are characterized by the onset of viral, bacterial, fungal, or protozoal infections before 6 months of age.

Infants lacking both T- and B-cell immunity whose T lymphocytes are phenotypically normal but unable to respond appropriately should be evaluated for the following:

- Familial defects in the surface expression of the T-cell receptor CD3 glycoproteins.
- Primary abnormalities in the expression of the IL-1 receptor.
- IL-2 unresponsiveness.
- Failure to produce IL-2.
- IL-2 receptor β-chain mutation.
- T-cell signal transduction defects.
- Bare lymphocyte syndrome (aberrant gene regulation of major histocompatibility complex).
- Major histocompatibility complex class II deficiency.

Patients with SCID usually suffer from failure to thrive, persistent oral candidiasis, recurrent diarrhea, and pneumonia (usually interstitial, often caused by *Pneumocystis carinii*) in the first months of life. Several immunologic defects are associated with a similar clinical pattern. Seventy-five percent of the patients with SCID are male.

Diagnosis

Prenatal diagnosis of SCID may be made by fetal blood sampling of T-lymphocyte subsets and T-cell functional studies as early as 20 weeks gestation.

Treatment

The only curative therapy for SCID is allogeneic bone marrow transplantation, although the use of cytokines, particularly recombinant human IL-2, may be of value for SCID patients who fail to produce IL-2.

1. X-LINKED SCID

In X-linked SCID, the failure to express normal IL-2Rγ may result in impaired early intrathymic T-cell maturation and function, leading to this severe immunodeficiency syndrome. Maternal carriers can be identified by the pattern of T-cell X chromosome inactivation and by the localization of the gene defect to Xq-13 by linkage analysis.

Prenatal diagnosis can be made as early as the 10th gestational week by analysis of unbalanced patterns of X chromosome inactivation in maternal and fetal T cells with the use of somatic cell hybridization or methylation differences between the active and inactive X chromosome. The analysis of X chromosome inactivation has been useful in detecting carriers in the X-linked primary immunodeficiency diseases (X-linked SCID, X-linked agammaglobulinemia, and the Wiskott-Aldrich syndrome). Polymerase chain reaction can also be used to amplify specific DNA sequences used to detect X chromosome inactivation in patients with X-linked SCID and other primary immunodeficiencies.

2. ADENOSINE DEAMINASE DEFICIENCY

About 50% of the patients with autosomal recessive SCID have an associated adenosine deaminase (ADA) deficiency. The gene for ADA deficiency has been mapped to chromosome 20q-13. Absence of this enzyme in purine metabolism leads to the accumulation of toxic metabolites including deoxyadenosine triphosphate, which is capable of killing both dividing and resting T cells.

Clinical Findings

In addition to the classic symptoms of SCID, this disease is characterized by the presence of skeletal abnormalities including concavity and flaring of the anterior ribs, an abnormal contour and articulation of the posterior ribs and transverse processes, platyspondylisis and an abnormal bony pelvis.

Diagnosis

The diagnosis is made by measuring ADA levels in hemolyzed red blood cells. Heterozygotes are symptom-free but have half the normal enzyme concentration. Prenatal diagnosis is possible by measuring ADA levels in cultured amniotic cells during the second trimester.

Treatment

Bone marrow transplantation or enzyme replacement with bovine ADA has been used with some success in the management of this disease. Promising recent attempts to treat patients with ADA deficiency have used autologous lymphocytes or cord blood stem cells corrected in vitro with retroviral vector-inserted normal human ADA DNA.

3. ZAP-70 DEFICIENCY

Clinical Findings

Another autosomal recessive form of SCID includes the abnormality of the protein kinase ZAP-70.

Two families of protein kinases are involved with T-cell receptor signal transduction leading to T-cell maturation and differentiation: (1) the Src family of protein kinases, Fyn and LCK and (2) the ZAP-70 and Syk protein kinases. Patients with ZAP-70 deficiency have compromised T-cell receptor signal transduction, leading to impaired T-cell differentiation.

This disorder is characterized by the presence of normal numbers of peripheral T cells with a deficiency of the CD8, cytotoxic-suppressor, T cells and a T-cell receptor signal transduction defect present in the helper CD4 T cells. These patients have normal immunoglobulin concentrations and natural killer cell function. Some intrathymic CD4 maturation occurs in these patients, but their peripheral blood is deficient in CD8 cells.

Diagnosis

The diagnosis of this disease is suggested by family history, symptoms of SCID, and the characteristic peripheral T-cell phenotype and function.

Treatment

At present, bone marrow transplantation is the only curative therapy.

4. PURINE-NUCLEOSIDE PHOSPHORYLASE DEFICIENCY

Clinical Findings

Purine-nucleoside phosphorylase (PNP) deficiency is an extremely rare autosomal recessive disorder characterized by a deficiency in the enzyme PNP, which is associated with marked T-cell immunodeficiency with a relatively intact humoral immunity. The gene coding PNP is located on chromosome 14q. The accumulation of deoxyguanosine triphosphate destroys dividing T cells.

Patients usually have recurrent viral, bacterial, and fungal infections. Two-thirds of these patients have neurologic disorders ranging from mild developmental delay or muscle spasticity to severe mental retardation.

Diagnosis

The diagnosis can be made by measuring PNP in hemolyzed erythrocytes. Heterozygotes have half the normal level of this enzyme and associated serum uric acid levels are low in these patients. Prenatal diagnosis is possible by assaying PNP levels cultured in amniotic cells during the second trimester.

Treatment

Bone marrow or stem cell transplant is the only successful therapy. Enzyme replacement therapy, as well as viral gene transfer, are currently being investigated as promising future therapies.

DIGEORGE SYNDROME

Clinical Findings

DiGeorge syndrome is a polytropic developmental defect consisting of congenital aplasia or dysplasia of the thymus and parathyroid glands, leading to lymphopenia with decreased T-cell populations as a result of monosomy of chromosome 22q-11. DiGeorge syndrome mainly affects the structures derived from the 3rd, 4th, and 5th pharyngeal pouches, but the 1st, 2nd, 5th, and 6th pouches and all branchial arches may also be involved. This is due to the failure of a population of neural crest cells to migrate and interact with endodermally derived cells of the branchial pouches and arches.

A. Signs and Symptoms. The syndrome is characterized by neonatal tetany associated with hypocalcemia caused by hypoparathyroidism. Cardiac outflow tract malformations are also seen (interrupted aortic arch, truncus arteriosus, right-sided aortic arch, tetralogy of Fallot, patent ductus arteriosus, or a ventricular septal defect). Abnormal facial features include low-set ears, hypertelorism, short philtrum, and a fish-shaped mouth. The thymus of these infants may be absent, hypoplastic, or atopic, and the parathyroid glands may be absent or reduced in size.

B. Laboratory Findings. T-cell immunity in patients with DiGeorge syndrome is variable and ranges from diminished cell numbers to complete absence of T-cell immunity. Some DiGeorge syndrome patients have normal B-cell immunity as measured by normal concentrations of immunoglobulin and normal antibody responses after immunization. Other patients, however, have low immunoglobulin levels and fail to make specific antibody in response to immunizations. Natural killer cell activity is normal.

Diagnosis

Prenatal diagnosis of DiGeorge syndrome can be performed by fluorescence in situ hybridization of fetal tissue to look for the chromosomal monosomy at 22q-11.

Treatment

Treatment of patients with DiGeorge syndrome has included the implantation of fetal thymic tissue, fetal thymic epithelium, or fetal thymus in a diffusion chamber, all of which have demonstrated limited success. Bone marrow transplantation, which provides donor postthymic T cells to reconstitute the patient's immunity, has been successfully used to treat patients with DiGeorge syndrome.

WISKOTT-ALDRICH SYNDROME

Clinical Findings

The Wiskott-Aldrich syndrome gene has been mapped to the short arm of the X chromosome. Recently a novel gene has been isolated that is absent in Wiskott-Aldrich syndrome patients. This gene encodes a protein that appears to be an important immunoregulator of both T-lymphocytes and platelets.

A. Signs and Symptoms. Wiskott-Aldrich syndrome is an X-linked recessive disease characterized by recurrent pyogenic infections within the first years of life. Thrombocytopenia is characterized by both small-sized and poorly functioning platelets. Eczema is also present at some time in most patients.

B. Laboratory Findings. Wiskott-Aldrich syndrome patients have low serum concentrations of IgM. IgA and IgE concentrations are high, and the IgG level is normal, elevated, or only slightly depressed. These patients are unable to produce antibody in response to polysaccharide antigens. T-cell numbers and function progressively decrease in this disorder, leading to a profound leukopenia. Patients have increased susceptibility to autoimmunity and malignancy.

Diagnosis

Prenatal diagnosis is facilitated by fetal blood sampling and the analysis of thrombocyte numbers and size, as well as an analysis of the pattern of X chromosome inactivation to detect carriers.

Treatment

Bone marrow transplantation, or more recently stem cell transplantation, may correct the immunologic defects and platelet disorder observed in these patients.

ATAXIA-TELANGIECTASIA

Clinical Findings

Ataxia telangiectasia, an autosomal recessive disorder, is thought to be a specific gene defect affecting mitogenic signal transduction, miotic recombination, and cell cycle control. The defect can result in recombination errors that interfere with the rearrangement of T- and B-cell genes and the inability to repair damaged DNA. The defects observed in DNA repair in these patients after x-ray irradiation results in a high incidence of chromosomal translocation, specifically in chromosomes 7 and 14.

A. Signs and Symptoms. Ataxia telangiectasia is characterized by progressive cerebellar ataxia, oculocutaneous telangiectasia, chronic sinopulmonary disease, and a high incidence of malignancy. Clinically progressive ataxia becomes apparent when the child begins to walk, whereas telangiectasia develops between 2 and 8 years of age, predominantly on the bulbar conjunctiva as well as exposed flexor surfaces of the arms.

B. Laboratory Findings. Nearly 70% of these patients have a selective IgA deficiency and more than one-half of these patients have an associated IgG-2 subclass deficiency. Eighty percent of the patients have depressed or absent IgE levels. The most notable T-cell abnormalities include leukopenia and a decrease in helper T-cell/suppressor T-cell ratios, in addition to an overall decrease in the total number of cytotoxic T cells.

Diagnosis

Serum α-fetoprotein levels are persistently elevated in these patients, which may be a useful but nonspecific aid in the diagnosis.

Treatment

Therapy consists of intravenous immunoglobulin therapy using IgA-depleted preparations. Gene therapy for ataxia telangiectasia is currently under investigation.

B-LYMPHOCYTE DEFECTS

Essentials of Diagnosis

- Decreased humoral immunity with variable to absent antibody isotype production.
- Recurrent gastrointestinal and/or sinopulmonary infections.
- Recurrent bacterial pneumonia or meningitis and severe sepsis.
- Enteroviral or other viral infections.
- Nodular lymphoid hyperplasia and malignancies.

General Considerations

The B-lymphocyte system is derived from stem cells residing in bone marrow stores. These stem cells produce cytoplasmic IgM heavy chains, which become pre-B cells. These pre-B cells continue to differentiate to become mature surface IgM- or IgM- and IgD-bearing B cells, which seed peripheral lymphoid tissue via the circulation. Upon stimulation, IgM-bearing B cells undergo class switching to IgG, IgA, or IgE-bearing B cells. These B cells can then differentiate to immunoglobulin-secreting plasma cells with the help of T cells and T-cell-derived lymphokines. Some of the B cells further differentiate into small memory B cells, which are involved in secondary immune responses.

The major function of B cells and the plasma cells is to produce antibodies to protein and carbohydrate antigens present on microorganisms, toxins, or other antigenic substances potentially harmful to the host. These antibodies are classified into nine different immunoglobulin isotypes, including IgM, IgD, IgG1, IgG2, IgG3, IgG4, IgA1, IgA2, and IgE. IgM antibodies are made first and are the most efficient in activating the classical complement system, which facilitates the opsonization and subsequent ingestion of microorganisms.

IgG antibodies are the only maternal antibodies that are transplacentally passed to developing infants. These antibodies are responsible for much of the infant's defense against invading microorganisms and their toxic substances through their opsonization and neutralization effects. IgA antibodies are selectively transported across mucous membranes by a secretory moiety. These IgA antibodies prevent the attachment of microorganisms or absorption of harmful antigens through mucous membranes. IgE antibodies are mainly responsible for allergic reactions and protection against parasites. Any defect in the maturation and differentiation of B cells (from the hematopoietic stem cells to plasma cells and their secretory immunoglobulins) or T cells and their receptors or lymphokines may produce B-cell immunodeficiency syndromes.

Patients with B-cell deficiencies, usually have recurrent pyogenic infections, particularly of the sinopulmonary tract, and to a lesser extent the gastrointestinal tract. Enterovirus infections may also be problematic.

BRUTON'S AGAMMAGLOBULINEMIA

Clinical Findings

Bruton's agammaglobulinemia is an X-linked recessive disease that affects only males. The underlying defect is an arrest in the differentiation of pre-B cells caused by the absence of a Bruton's tyrosine kinase, which functions in B-cell differentiation.

A. Signs and Symptoms. This defect is characterized by recurrent pyogenic infections usually starting by 5–6 months of age. Affected individuals may not be symptomatic before 6 months of age because of transplacentally acquired maternal IgG antibodies. Infections are usually caused by encapsulated bacterial pathogens, including *Streptococcus pneumoniae, Neisseria meningitidis,* and *Haemophilus influenzae* type b. Sinopulmonary infections are predominant. There is an unusual susceptibility to persistent echovirus or coxsackievirus infection, including lethal meningoencephalitis as well as vaccine-associated poliomyelitis.

B. Laboratory Findings. Immunoglobulins of all classes are absent as are circulating immunoglobulin-bearing mature B cells. Absent plasma cells from lymphoid tissue and functional serum antibody are hallmarks of Bruton's agammaglobulinemia. T lymphocytes are normal in number and function. Approximately half of the patients have a family history of an affected male sibling or maternal male relative who is affected.

Diagnosis

Female carriers do not exhibit antibody deficiency and can be detected by analyzing the unbalanced pattern of X chromosome inactivation in peripheral blood mononuclear cells. Prenatal diagnosis of suspected patients is facilitated by sex determination of the fetus and direct sampling of fetal blood for mature B cells or by DNA markers.

Treatment

Therapy (Box 26–2) consists of the administration of intravenous immunoglobulin and clinical surveillance for infections and the development of lymphoreticular and other malignancies.

X-LINKED HYPOGAMMAGLOBULINEMIA WITH NORMAL TO INCREASED IgM CONCENTRATIONS

Clinical Findings

Patients with this immune deficiency have an increased IgM concentration, recurrent pyogenic infections, autoimmune disease, and lymphoproliferative disease, especially IgM surface-bearing B-cell lymphomas of the intestinal tract. The hyper-IgM syndrome can be inherited in an X-linked or an autosomal recessive fashion. The underlying cause of the X-linked hyper-IgM syndrome is a deficiency in the expression of the T-cell CD40 ligand, which specifically binds B cells and drives the immunoglobulin isotype switch. The gene for the CD40 ligand has been cloned and mapped to Xq-26.

A. Signs and Symptoms. Neutropenia is commonly associated with this disease, and nearly half of these patients have hepatosplenomegaly. Chronic liver disease and lymphomas are the long-term associated consequences of this disorder.

B. Laboratory Findings. These patients have normal or increased concentrations of serum IgM and, in some cases, IgD but decreased or absent IgG, IgA, and IgE. T-cell numbers and function, other than the absence of the CD40 ligand, appear to be normal. The interaction of CD40 with its ligand, however, may also be involved in early thymic T-cell maturation. This may explain an increased susceptibility to opportunistic infections such as *Pneumocystis carinii* pneumonia seen in some patients.

Diagnosis

Prenatal diagnosis can be performed by DNA analysis and from cytometry for the CD40 ligand on T cells.

Treatment

Bone marrow transplantation has recently been tried in the treatment of hyper-IgM syndrome. Stem cell transplantation has also been attempted. Replacement therapy with a recombinant, soluble form of the CD40 ligand or gene therapy may be developed for these patients in the future.

SELECTIVE IgA DEFICIENCY

Clinical Findings

The incidence of selective IgA deficiency is ~1/400–1/1000. Studies of the IgA heavy-chain constant-region genes, situated on chromosome 14, have revealed that there are no structural deletions in individuals with selective IgA deficiency. A gene located in the major histocompatibility complex class III region on chromosome 6 recently has been implicated for both selective IgA deficiency and common variable immunodeficiency, suggesting a relationship in these two disorders. The cause of selective IgA deficiency appears to be a terminal block in B-cell differentiation to plasma cells capable of secreting the IgA isotype.

Symptomatic patients usually have recurrent infections of the respiratory and gastrointestinal tracts, autoimmune disease, allergy, and malignancy. Approximately two-thirds of the patients do not have an increased susceptibility to infection, presumably because of the protective effects of IgG and IgM.

Diagnosis

Selective IgA deficiency has been defined as a serum IgA concentration of < 5 mg/dL in severe deficiency and less than two standard deviations below the mean of age-matched control in partial deficiency. In some IgA deficient patients, secretory IgA is low but present; the serum concentration of IgA may return to normal within 4 years of diagnosis. These patients have normal T-cell immunity.

Treatment

Therapy with IgA is not possible in patients with selective IgA deficiency because (1) the half-life of IgA is short (~7 days), (2) administered IgA is not transported to the mucosal surfaces, and (3) the presence of anti-IgA autoantibodies in IgA-deficient patients may cause anaphylactic reactions when blood components containing IgA are transfused. In ~20% of the IgA-deficient patients who have frequent infections, there is an associated IgG-2 subclass deficiency.

Some of these patients, including those with anti-IgA antibodies, can benefit from treatment with intravenously administered immune globulin containing low levels of IgA.

COMMON VARIABLE IMMUNODEFICIENCY

Clinical Findings

The underlying clinical defect in common variable immunodeficiency (CVID), or late-onset hypogammaglobulinemia, is that the B cells do not differentiate into plasma cells. This may be caused by a primary B-cell defect (failure to terminally glycosylate and secrete immunoglobulins), a failure of helper T-cell factor production, or an increase in specific suppressor T-cell effects. The immunologic defect seen in this disorder is not limited only to B cells but also includes macrophages and immunoregulatory T cells. The defects in T-cell immunity include abnormalities of activation and lymphokine production, which usually progresses with age.

Many patients (11%) with CVID have a first-degree relative with selective IgA deficiency or CVID. It appears that a susceptibility gene or group of genes for both CVID and selective IgA deficiency are located within the major histocompatibility complex class III region of the chromosome 6. It is likely that in both these disorders there are exogenous factors that act intrinsically or extrinsically on genetically susceptible individuals to determine the degree of expression of the immunoglobulin genes in these patients.

A. Signs and Symptoms. Patients with CVID commonly have chronic diarrhea and associated malabsorption. Autoimmune diseases, hepatitis, gastric carcinoma, and lymphoreticular malignancy have been observed in older patients. Nodular intestinal lymphoid hyperplasia and a sarcoidlike syndrome associated with hepatosplenomegaly are additional features of this disease.

B. Laboratory Findings. Common variable immunodeficiency is characterized by markedly decreased serum immunoglobulin levels, normal or nearly normal numbers of circulating immunoglobulin-bearing mature B cells, impaired antibody responses, and recurrent bacterial sinopulmonary infections associated with chronic progressive bronchiectasis.

Diagnosis

Assessing a male patient with recurrent infections and significant hypogammaglobulinemia, the absence of mature immunoglobulin B cells in the peripheral blood or X chromosome inactivation analysis of the patient's mother can be helpful in distinguishing sporadic cases of X-linked agammaglobulinemia from cases of CVID.

Treatment

Management of CVID includes immunoglobulin replacement therapy, antimicrobial therapy and pulmonary drainage, and immunomodulatory therapies including recombinant human IL-2 conjugated with polyethylene glycol and cimetidine.

DEFECTS IN THE PHAGOCYTIC SYSTEM & ITS RELATED IMMUNODEFICIENCY SYNDROMES

Essentials of Diagnosis

- Cutaneous bacterial abscesses, cellulitis, and mucocutaneous candidiasis.

- Frequent pneumonias, otitis media, and sinusitis.
- Osteomyelitis.
- Periodontitis and lymphadenitis.
- Granulomatous lesion.

General Considerations

The phagocytic system includes polymorphonuclear leukocytes (neutrophils and eosinophils) and mononuclear phagocytes (circulating monocytes, tissue macrophages, and fixed macrophages). Major phagocytic functions include adherence to endothelium, aggregation, diapedesis, chemotaxis, attachment, phagocytosis, and degranulation, leading to pathogen destruction. The phagocytic system is responsible for defense against extracellular bacterial or fungal invasion in association with opsonins, antibodies, complement, and some acute-phase proteins. Neutrophils are one of the first lines of defense against bacterial invasion and neutrophil disorders include leukocyte adhesion deficiency, Chediak-Higashi syndrome, chronic granulomatous disease, and Job's syndrome.

LEUKOCYTE ADHESION DEFICIENCY

Clinical Findings

Neutrophil adherence to and migration through capillary endothelium is a critical early event in the acute inflammatory response. The adhesive interactions between neutrophils and endothelial cell surfaces are regulated by two novel families of glycoproteins: the integrins and the selectins. The β-2 integrins are membrane-bound glycoprotein receptors found on the surface of neutrophils. The β-2 integrins CD11/CD18 are required for neutrophil adherence to endothelial cell surfaces. The selectins also are membrane-bound glycoproteins that mediate neutrophil adhesion to endothelial cells. These include L-selectin, which is found on the surface of neutrophils, and P-selectin and E-selectin, which are expressed on the surface of activated endothelial cells.

The interaction between the β-2 integrins and the selectins serves to regulate neutrophil responses during inflammation. In general, P-selectin and E-selectin on the activated endothelial cell surface and L-selectin on the neutrophil cell surface function to facilitate neutrophil rolling and tethering to activated capillary endothelium. Once this tethering has occurred and the neutrophil itself is activated, the β-2 integrin CD11/CD18 receptors on the neutrophil form a tight adhesion with the endothelial cell surface that facilitates neutrophil polarization, leading to migration.

Two types of leukocyte adhesion deficiency (LAD) have been described. The first is congenital β-2 integrin CD11/CD18 deficiency (LAD-I). A second type, LAD-II, has been described for a deficiency of Sialyl Lewis X, the neutrophil ligand for E-selectin on endothelial cells. Deficiency of the CD11/CD18 complex (LAD-I) is transmitted as an autosomal recessive trait. The gene encoding CD18 has been mapped to chromosome 21. The underlying defect results from heterogeneous mutations affecting the CD18 gene, which impair its synthesis.

This disorder is characterized by frequent infections, poor wound healing, leukocytosis, and a history of delayed umbilical cord separation. Patients usually suffer from recurrent bacterial skin abscesses, otitis media, periodontitis, omphalitis, perirectal abscesses, pneumonia, and sepsis.

The striking feature of these infections is the almost total absence of leukocytes in the lesions. The most prevalent invading microorganisms are *Staphylococcus aureus*, group A streptococci, *Proteus mirabilis, Pseudomonas aeruginosa,* and *Escherichia coli.* Based on the severity of the deficiency, two phenotypes (severe and moderate) have been defined.

The severe form is associated with complete absence of CD11/CD18 expression, whereas the moderate form demonstrates ~10–20% of normal expression. The degree of deficiency is closely related to the severity of the patient's clinical manifestations; patients with the severe form of leukocyte adhesion deficiency usually die within the first few years of life. In contrast, the patients with at least some expression of these adhesive glycoproteins usually have a milder disease course and can survive into adulthood.

Diagnosis

The diagnosis can be made by assessing the expression of CD11b or CD18 on the patient's neutrophils by flow cytometry. Further confirmation can be made by assessing expression of these glycoproteins after exposure to a degranulating stimuli. The expression of these glycoproteins is increased 5- to 20-fold after stimulation with degranulating agents. This method is also helpful for identification of symptom-free heterozygotes where the expression of these glycoproteins is about half that seen in normal carriers and for prenatal diagnosis.

Treatment

Therapy consists mainly of early, aggressive antibiotic therapy to reduce bacterial infections (see Box 26–2). During severe infections, granulocyte transfusions in addition to antibiotic therapy have had therapeutic benefit. Bone marrow transplantation has been successfully used to treat some patients. Gene therapy, replacing the defective CD18 gene in the patient's myeloid precursor cells, may become available in the future. In vitro correction of CD18-deficient lymphocytes by retrovirus-mediated gene transfer has been accomplished. A transfection efficiency of 5–10% may be sufficient to change the disease course from severe to moderate.

JOB'S SYNDROME

Clinical Findings

Job's syndrome of hyperimmunoglobulin E and recurrent infections is transmitted by autosomal dominant inheritance with incomplete penetrance. It is characterized by extremely high serum IgE values (often > 1000–2000 IU/mL), recurrent serious infections, and chronic eczematoid dermatitis usually beginning early in infancy. The infections primarily involve the skin and sinopulmonary tract and usually present as recurrent furunculosis, cutaneous abscess formation, bronchitis, pneumonia, and chronic otitis media and sinusitis. Some of the skin abscesses are cold without classical signs and symptoms of inflammation: redness, heat, and pain.

The most common infecting microorganisms are *S aureus*, and *C albicans*, but infections caused by *H influenzae* group A streptococci, gram-negative pathogens, and fungi are also observed. Pneumatoceles, bronchiectasis, and bronchopleural fistula formation are not uncommon after episodes of acute or chronic pneumonia. Chronic mucocutaneous candidiasis, primarily involving the mouth, nails, skin, and vagina, is also found in about half of the patients.

Associated features include coarse facial features with a broad nasal bridge and broad nasal alae, growth retardation, osteoporosis and bone fractures, keratoconjunctivitis, asymmetric sterile polyarthritis, and eosinophilia.

In addition to markedly elevated serum IgE concentrations, other immunologic abnormalities include elevated specific anti-*S aureus* and anti-*Candida* IgE antibodies, an intermittent defect in neutrophil chemotaxis, low antibody response to booster immunizations, and poor antibody and cell-mediated responses to newly encountered antigens. The underlying defect is most likely associated with a T-cell abnormality characterized by inadequate production of γ-interferon, which normally suppresses IgE production. The intermittent neutrophil chemotactic abnormality, which likely has a major role in the pathogenesis of the recurrent abscesses seen in these patients, most likely results from this γ-interferon deficiency.

Diagnosis

Differentiation of patients with the Job syndrome from those with atopic dermatitis is sometimes difficult and is dependent on the presence of recurrent deep abscesses along with the classic facial features.

Treatment

Management consists of controlling the pruritic eczematoid dermatitis with emollient creams, topical steroids, and antihistamines. Prophylactic oral dicloxacillin or trimethoprim-sulfamethoxazole for *S aureus* infections or oral fluconazole for preventing *C albicans* infections usually benefit patients. Intravenous immunoglobulin therapy should be reserved for patients with confirmed IgG subclass deficiency, a finding rarely observed in our experience. Plasmapheresis has been attempted for a few patients who do not respond to more conservative therapies. Reported experimental immunomodulatory therapies include the use of levamisole, ascorbic acid, cimetidine, and transfer factor. γ-Interferon therapy has been shown to increase these patient's neutrophil chemotactic response in vitro and decrease eczema and respiratory secretions in vivo.

CHRONIC GRANULOMATOUS DISEASE

Clinical Findings

Chronic granulomatous disease (CGD) is a group of genetic disorders characterized by recurrent infections with catalase-positive microorganisms of the respiratory tract, skin, and soft tissues. Symptoms usually occur by 2 years of age. CGD has X-linked (65%) or autosomal-recessive (35%) inheritance.

This defect is due to lesions in membrane-associated NADPH-oxidase necessary for the production of oxygen radicals, which are required in intracellular killing (Figure 26–1). This results in the inability of phagocytes to generate superoxide anion, hydrogen peroxide, and other oxygen radicals needed to kill catalase-positive bacteria. The catalase-negative species, including pneumococci, streptococci, and *H influenzae*, rarely cause serious infections in these patients. CGD should be suspected in any patient with subcutaneous abscesses or furunculosis associated with abscess formation in a lymph node, the liver, or lung, or in patients with infections with organisms normally of low virulence (*Staphylococcus epidermidis*, *Serratia marcescens*, and *Aspergillus* spp.), which are catalase positive.

The underlying defect in X-linked CGD is due to a defect in a gene encoded on the X chromosome that has been identified as the cytochrome b heavy-chain gene.

Diagnosis

The diagnosis of CGD is demonstrated by an absent or greatly diminished respiratory burst by stimulated phagocytes. Available assays include nitroblue tetrazolium dye reduction, chemiluminescence, measurement of oxygen consumption, and the products of oxidative metabolism, superoxide anion, and hydrogen peroxide. A documented inability of blood granulocytes to kill ingested catalase-positive bacteria confirms CGD. Symptom-free carriers of the X-linked form of CGD can be identified by determining the respiratory burst activity of their neutrophils, which is approximately half of normal, and by genetic analysis.

Prenatal diagnosis can be made during the second trimester by sampling of fetal blood and nitroblue tetrazolium testing, which serves as a screen for su-

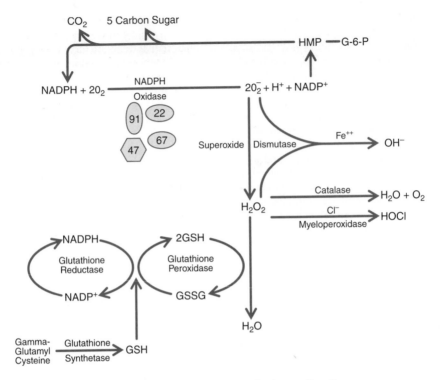

Figure 26–1. The respiratory burst in phagocytic cells.

peroxide production. Molecular reagents prepared from cloned DNA may also prove to be clinically useful for prenatal diagnosis in the future.

Treatment

Prophylaxis with trimethoprim-sulfamethoxazole may prolong infection-free intervals by preventing infections, especially with staphylococci. Therapy also includes treatment with γ-interferon, which has decreased infections by as much as 70%, and bone marrow transplantation, which to date has shown only limited success and should be reserved for those patients who cannot be optimally treated in other ways. Patients with CGD are excellent candidates for future gene therapy because the genetic lesions have been identified and the genes cloned.

CHEDIAK-HIGASHI SYNDROME

Clinical Findings

The Chediak-Higashi syndrome is an autosomal recessive disorder, which is characterized by recurrent pyogenic infections, a bleeding tendency caused by a platelet storage pool deficiency, partial oculocutaneous albinism, and giant granules in the cytoplasm of many cells, particularly peripheral leukocytes. The underlying defect results from abnormal cell membrane fluidity, which leads to abnormal granular fusion as

well as other defects, including the inability of neutrophils to move normally, concentrate serotonin into platelets, and express normal lytic functions.

Symptoms generally begin in early childhood with recurrent pyoderma, subcutaneous abscesses, otitis, sinusitis, severe periodontal disease, bronchitis, and pneumonia. The most common microorganisms are S aureus and β-hemolytic streptococci. Approximately 85% of patients have an associated organ infiltration by histiocytes and atypical lymphocytes. Hepatosplenomegaly, lymphadenopathy, neurologic abnormalities, pancytopenia, and a bleeding tendency are also commonly seen.

Diagnosis

The diagnosis is made by identification of the characteristic giant cytoplasmic granules in the patient's leukocytes or microscopic examination of hair shafts for abnormal giant melanosomes. Prenatal diagnosis is possible by measuring the large acid phosphatase-positive lysosomes in cultured amniotic fluid cells, chorionic villus cells, or fetal blood leukocytes.

Treatment

In addition to prophylaxis with antibiotics and the prompt treatment of acute infection with antimicrobial agents, high doses of ascorbate may be beneficial. Bone marrow transplantation may be curative.

Splenectomy has been used in the treatment of patients unresponsive to other forms of therapy and has resulted in clinical, hematologic, and immunologic improvement.

THE COMPLEMENT SYSTEM & ITS RELATED DEFECTS

Essentials of Diagnosis

- Recurrent infections with encapsulated bacteria.
- Recurrent sepsis with *Neisseria* species.

General Considerations

The complement system is composed of an interacting series of glycoproteins, which upon activation, interact in an orderly sequence to produce biologically active substances that enhance leukocyte reactions and that result in the lysis of cells or invading pathogens. The system can be activated through two major pathways: (1) the classical pathway, which is activated by binding of IgG1, IgG2, IgG3, or IgM to antigens; and (2) the alternative pathway, which is initiated by direct attachment of activated C3 to the surface of bacteria, viruses, fungi, and virus-infected cells (Figure 26–2).

Once the alternative pathway is triggered, an amplification loop is activated that induces more C3b formation. Surface-bound C3b in conjunction with C3 convertase, C4b2a (classical pathway), or C3bBb (al-

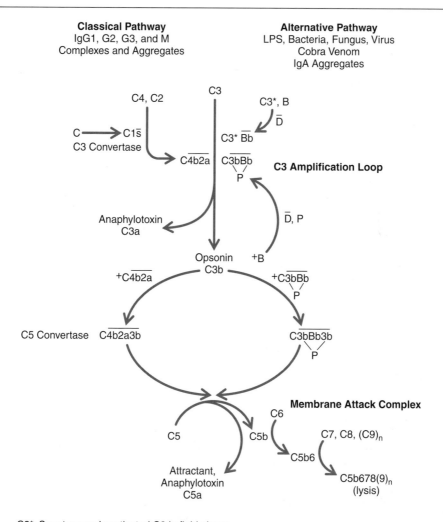

C3*: Spontaneously activated C3 in fluid phase

Figure 26–2. The classic and alternative complement pathways. (Modified with permission from PIDJ 1991).

ternative pathway) serves as a C5 convertase, which initiates the formation of the membrane attack complex (C5b678[9]n). All of the activated components of the complement system are tightly controlled by regulatory proteins including C1 esterase inhibitor, factor I, C4-binding protein, factor H, decay-accelerating factor, S protein, and C8-binding protein.

The major effects of active complement components include anaphylotoxic (C3a and C5a), opsonic (C3b, C3bi, and C4b), chemotactic (C5a), and cytolytic activity (membrane attack complex). Deficiency of early components of the classical pathway result in a high incidence of collagen vascularlike disease (C1q, C1r, C1s, C4, or C3 deficiency). Patients who lack these components often present with some combination of recurrent infections (usually pneumococcal), arthritis, skin rash, and glomerulonephritis. Box 26–2 summarizes treatment options for patients who have these deficiencies. This infection risk is most likely a result of suboptimal removal of circulating immune complexes from the circulation from failure to attach C3b and iC3b to the particles.

DEFICIENCY OF C1 COMPLEX & C4

These deficiencies are also transmitted by autosomal recessive inheritance. Because activation of the alternative pathway may be sufficient for host defense against many pathogens, deficient patients generally have few infectious complications. Lupuslike illness and other autoimmune disorders occur in a majority of the patients.

DEFICIENCY OF C2

C2 deficiency is transmitted as an autosomal recessive trait and is the most commonly reported complement deficiency. The incidence of homozygous C2 deficiency is ~1 in 28,000 to 40,000, whereas the heterozygous carrier rate is estimated at ~1.2% in the general population based on screening of normal blood donors. Patients can have recurrent pneumonia, bacteremia, or meningitis caused by *S pneumoniae* (present in about two-thirds of reported infections), *H influenzae,* and *N meningitidis.* Autoimmune or rheumatic complications are present in about half of the patients. The lupuslike disease in C2-deficient patients is characterized by early onset, marked photosensitivity, low-titered or absent antinuclear antibody, and a low incidence of renal involvement.

DEFICIENCY OF C3

C3 deficiency is transmitted by autosomal recessive inheritance. C3 is positioned at the junction of the classical and alternative complement pathways and is important for opsonization of most encapsulated bacteria; generation of C3a and C5a; and initiation of the membrane attack complex. Patients with total C3 deficiency usually have severe episodes of recurrent pneumonia, sepsis, meningitis, and peritonitis. The most common pathogens isolated are *S pneumoniae, H influenzae, N meningitidis,* and *S aureus.* Lupuslike illness and glomerulonephritis occur in 15–21% of patients.

DEFICIENCY OF C5-C9

Individuals with these deficiencies are completely asymptomatic, whereas others have unusual susceptibility to recurrent Neisseria infections (*N meningitidis* or *N gonorrhoeae*). Deficiency of the terminal complement components is also transmitted by autosomal recessive inheritance. Recurrent episodes of meningococcemia, meningococcal meningitis, and disseminated gonococcal infection have occurred in ~50% of reported patients. The rate of C5–C9 deficiency in patients with disseminated *Neisseria* infections may be as high as 10–15%. In contrast to early complement component deficiencies, autoimmune diseases are only occasionally diagnosed in these patients.

PROPERDIN DEFICIENCY

This is the only deficiency of complement that is transmitted by X-linked recessive inheritance. Properdin acts to stabilize the alternative pathway C3 convertase (C3bBb). Affected patients have recurrent pyogenic infections and fulminant meningococcemia.

REFERENCES

Ammann AJ et al: *Antibody (B-cell) Immunodeficiency Disorders in Medical Immunology,* 9th ed. Appleton & Lange, 1997.

Arrufo A et al: The CD-40 ligand, gp 39, is defective in activated T cells from patients with X-linked hyper IgM syndrome. Cell 1993;72:291.

Bordignon C et al: Gene therapy in peripheral blood lymphocytes and bone marrow for ADA immunodeficient patients. Science 1995;270:470.

Castigli E et al: Severe combined immunodeficiency with selective T-cell cytokine genes. Pediatr Res 1993;33:52.

Christenson JC et al: Infections complicating congenital immunodeficiency syndromes. In Rubin RH, Young LS: *Clinical Approach to Infection in the Compromised Host.* Plenum Medical Book, 1994.

Christenson JC et al: Primary immunodeficiency syndromes. In Armstrong D, Cohen J: *Infectious Diseases.* Mosby Year Book (In Press).

Conley ME: Molecular approaches to analysis of X-linked immunodeficiencies. Annu Rev Immunol 1992;322:1063.

Cunningham-Rundles C: Disorders of the IgA system. In Stiehm ER: *Immunologic Disorders in Infants and Children.* WB Saunders, 1996.

Davies KA et al: Complement deficiency: an immune complex disease. Springer Semin Immunopathol 1994;15:397.

Eisentein EM et al: Evidence for a generalized signaling abnormality in B cells from patients with common variable immunodeficiency. Adv Exp Med Biol 1995;371-B:699.

Figueroa JE et al: Infectious diseases associated with complement deficiencies. Clin Microbiol Rev 1991;4:359.

Fisher A et al: Bone marrow transplantation (BMT) in Europe for primary immunodeficiencies other than severe combined immunodeficiency: a report from the European Group for BMT and the European Group of Immunodeficiency. Blood 1994;83:1149.

Fleisher TA et al: Introduction to diagnostic laboratory immunology. J Am Med Assoc 1997;278:1823.

Frank MM: Complement in disease: inherited and acquired complement deficiencies. In Frank HH et al: *Immunologic Diseases,* 5th ed. Little Brown, 1995.

Frank MM: Complement deficiencies. In Stites DP et al: *Medical Immunology.* Appleton & Lange, 1997.

Hermaszewsk RA, Webster AD: Primary hypogammaglobulinemia: A survey of clinical manifestations and complications. Quart J Med 1993;86:31.

Hill HR: Modulation of host defenses with interferon-gamma in pediatrics. J Infect Dis 1993;167:S23.

Kavanaugh A: Evaluation of patients with suspected immunodeficiency. Am Fam Phy 1994;49:167.

Kurahashi H et al: Isolation and characterization of a novel gene deleted in Di George syndrome. Human Mol Genet 1995;4:541.

La Pine TR et al: Immunomodifiers applicable to the prevention and management of infectious diseases in children. In *Advances in Pediatric Infectious Diseases.* Mosby Year Book, 1994.

La Pine TR et al: Immunomodulatory agents. In Feigin RD, Cherry JD: *Textbook of Pediatric Infectious Diseases.* WB Saunders, 1998.

Marx J: Tyrosine kinase defect also causes immunodeficiency. Science 1993;259:897.

Oxelius VA et al: Linkage of IgA deficiency to Gm allotypes: the influence of Gm allotypes on IgA-IgG deficiency. Clin Exp Immunol 1995;99:211.

Parlsow TG: Immunoglobulin genes, B cells, and the humoral immune response. In Stites DP et al: *Basic & Clinical Immunology.* Appleton & Lange, 1994.

Pfeffer KD et al: Pulmonary infections in patients with primary immune defects. In Fishman JA: Pulmonary Diseases and Disorders. McGraw-Hill, 1998.

Puck JM: Primary immunodeficiency diseases. J Am Med Assoc 1997;278:1835.

Quie PG et al: Disorders of the polymorphonuclear phagocytic system. In Stiehm ER: *Immunologic Disorders in Infants and Children.* WB Saunders, 1996.

Roos D: The genetic basis of chronic granulomatous disease. Immunol Rev 1994;138:121.

Shyur SD et al: Recent advances in the genetics of primary immunodeficiency syndromes. J Pediatr 1996;129:8.

Smith S et al: The immunocompromised host. Pediatr Rev 1996;17:435.

Sneller MC: New insights into common variable immunodeficiency. Ann Int Med 1993;118:720.

Springer TA: Traffic signals for lymphocyte recirculation and leukocyte migration: the multistep paradigm. Cell 1994;76:301.

Stiehm ER: *Immunologic Disorders in Infants and Children,* 4th ed. WB Saunders, 1996.

Sullivan KE et al: A multi institutional survey of the Wiskott-Aldrich syndrome. J Pediatr 1994;125:876.

Taylor AMR et al: Fifth international workshop on ataxia-telangiectasia. Cancer Res 1993;53:138.

Winkelstein JA et al: Genetically determined deficiencies of complement. In Scriver CR, Beauclit AL, Sly WS: *Molecular Basis of Inherited Disease.* McGraw-Hill, 1995.

Yang KD et al: Neutrophil function disorders: pathophysiology, prevention and therapy. J Pediatr 1991;119:343.

Yang KD et al: Functional biology of the granulocyte/monocyte series. In Bick R: *Hematology: Clinical and Laboratory Practice.* Mosby Year Book, 1993.

Yang KD, et al: Disorders of leukocyte function. In Emery AEH et al: *Emery and Rimoin's Principles and Practice of Medical Genetics.* Churchill Livingstone, 1996.

Yang KD, et al: Phagocytic system in primary immune deficiency disease, a molecular genetic approach. In Ochs HD et al: *Primary Immunodeficiency Disorders: A Molecular and Genetic Approach.* Oxford University Press. (In Press)

Yel L, et al: Mutations in the μ heavy-chain gene in patients with agammaglobulinemia. N Engl J Med 1996;355:1486.

Section IV.
Viral Infections

Enteroviruses

27

W. Lawrence Drew, MD, PhD

Essentials of Diagnosis

- Isolation of enterovirus in tissue culture.
- Detection of antigen or antibody not practical for routine diagnosis.
- Detection of enterovirus in cerebrospinal fluid (CSF) by polymerase chain reaction.
- CSF usually has lymphocytic pleocytosis with normal glucose and protein.
- Typical illness is febrile rash, macular or vesicular (hand, foot, mouth syndromes).
- Most clinical illness occurs in patients < 20 years old.

General Considerations

Enteroviruses are one of three types of picornaviruses that cause disease in humans. As the name indicates, picornaviruses are small (pico) ribonucleic acid (RNA) viruses that have a naked capsid structure. The family includes > 230 members divided into five genera but only three—enteroviruses, rhinoviruses, and hepatoviruses (hepatitis A virus)—cause human disease. These genera can be distinguished by their stability at pH 3, optimum temperature for growth, mode of transmission, and the diseases they cause. Rhinoviruses are discussed in Chapter 28 and the hepatitis A virus is discussed in Chapter 39.

Nearly 70 serotypes of human enteroviruses exist, and they are divided into three subgroups: polio-, coxsackie-, and echoviruses. The capsids of these viruses are very stable in harsh environmental conditions (eg, sewage systems) and in the gastrointestinal tract, which facilitates their transmission by the fecal-oral route. Although they may initiate their infection in the gastrointestinal tract, the enteroviruses rarely cause enteric disease. Instead they cause myriad illnesses, especially diseases of the central nervous system and other systemic diseases. Several different disease syndromes may be caused by one enterovirus serotype, and several different serotypes may cause the same disease. The most well-known and well-studied picornavirus is poliovirus.

Coxsackieviruses are named after the town of Coxsackie, New York, where the viruses were first isolated. They are divided into two groups, A and B, on the basis of certain biologic and antigenic differences. These two groups are further subdivided into numeric serotypes by additional antigenic differences.

The name echovirus is derived from "Enteric Cytopathic Human Orphan," because these agents were not thought to be associated with clinical disease. Thirty-one serotypes are now recognized. These viruses have a greater tendency than polioviruses to affect the meninges and cause meningitis, but a lesser tendency to infect anterior horn cells.

A. Epidemiology. The incubation period for enterovirus disease is usually 2–10 days but may be longer depending on the virus, the target tissue, and the age of the individual. Enteroviruses are highly contagious; poor sanitation and crowded living conditions foster transmission of enteroviruses, and sewage contamination of water supplies can result in enterovirus epidemics.

Humans are the major natural hosts of enteroviruses, and there is no evidence of spread from animals to humans. The enteroviruses are primarily spread person to person by enteric routes but may also be spread in droplets and cause respiratory infections. The most frequently isolated enteroviruses are coxsackieviruses A9, A16, and B1 to B5; and echoviruses 6, 9, 11, 16, and 30. These viruses are found worldwide, and each year there is a tendency for one of these to be the dominant circulating virus. Disease is most frequent in persons < 20 years of age but, as with poliovirus infection, it is generally less severe in children. However, coxsackie B virus and some of the echoviruses can cause severe disease. Secondary infections occur in ≤ 70% of susceptible individuals living in households where the viruses have caused infection. Summer and fall are the major seasons for contracting enterovirus disease.

B. Microbiology. As with all picornavirus RNA, the RNA of the enteroviruses is surrounded by a very small icosahedral capsid ~ 30 nm in diameter. The genome of these viruses resembles messenger RNA (mRNA). It is a single strand of (+)-sense RNA of ~ 7.2–8.5 kilobases. It encodes a polyprotein that is proteolytically cleaved to produce the enzymatic and structural proteins of the virus. In addition to the capsid proteins, these viruses encode at least one protease and an RNA-dependent RNA polymerase.

The specificity of enterovirus interaction with cellular receptors is the major determinant of their tissue tropism and the diseases they cause. The VP_1 proteins at the vertices of the virion contain a canyon into which the receptor binds. The receptors for polioviruses have recently been identified as tissue-specific intercellular adhesion molecules (ICAMs), which are members of the immunoglobulin superfamily. Several serotypes of coxsackievirus recognize intercellular adhesion molecule 1 (ICAM-1). ICAM-1 is expressed on epithelial cells, fibroblasts, and endothelial cells. Poliovirus binds to a molecule of similar structure. The cells in which the poliovirus receptor is expressed correlate directly with the organs infected by poliovirus infection.

On binding to the receptor, the enteroviruses are internalized by receptor-mediated endocytosis, and the virions dissociate in the acidic environment of the endosome, releasing the genome into the cytoplasm. The genome then binds to ribosomes, and a polyprotein is synthesized within 10–15 min of infection. The polyprotein is initially cleaved by cellular proteases until a viral protease is generated to cleave the rest of the polyprotein.

The RNA-dependent RNA polymerase generates a negative-strand RNA template from which the new mRNA genome and templates can be synthesized. The amount of viral mRNA increases rapidly in the cell, with the number of viral RNA molecules reaching 400,000/cell.

Cellular RNA and protein synthesis are inhibited during infection by several enteroviruses; a viral protease blocks translation of cellular mRNA, and permeability changes induced by enteroviruses reduce the ability of cellular mRNA to bind to the ribosome. Viral mRNA also competes with cellular mRNA for the factors required in protein synthesis. These activities contribute to the cytopathic effect of the virus on the target cell.

As the viral genome is being replicated and translated, the structural proteins are cleaved from the polyproteins. After insertion of the viral genome, assembly of viral RNA into the viral capsid occurs in the cytoplasm, and the virion is released when lysis and destruction of the cell occur.

C. Pathogenesis. Differences in pathogenesis of the enteroviruses mainly result from differences in tissue tropism of the various subgroups. Poliovirus has been studied extensively and is the prototype for the pathogenesis of the enteroviruses.

The upper respiratory tract, the oropharynx, and the intestinal tract are the portals of entry for the enteroviruses. The virus initiates replication in the mucosa and lymphoid tissue of the tonsils and pharynx and later infects the gut. The virions are impervious to stomach acid, proteases, and bile and infect lymphoid cells of Peyer's patches and the intestinal mucosa. Primary viremia spreads the virus to receptor-bearing target tissues, where a second phase of viral replication may occur, resulting in symptoms and a secondary viremia. Virus shedding from the oropharynx can be detected for a short time before symptoms begin, whereas virus production and shedding into stool may last for ≤ 4 months, even in the presence of a humoral immune response.

The nature of the enterovirus disease is determined by the tissue tropism of the virus. Poliovirus has one of the narrowest tissue tropisms, recognizing a receptor expressed on anterior horn cells of the spinal cord, dorsal root ganglia, motor neurons, and few other cells. Coxsackieviruses and echoviruses recognize receptors expressed on more cell types and tissues and cause a broader repertoire of diseases. Coxsackievirus and echovirus receptors may be found in the central nervous system and on heart, lung, pancreatic, and other cells. Differences in the susceptibility to and severity of poliovirus and coxsackievirus infection with age may also be attributed to differences in distribution and amount of receptor expression. Adults are generally more susceptible to serious disease with poliovirus, whereas newborns experience the most serious symptoms from coxsackie B and echovirus infections.

Most enteroviruses are cytolytic, replicating rapidly and causing direct damage to the target cell. Histologic examination reveals cell necrosis and mononuclear cell infiltrates.

The production of antibody is the major protective immune response to enteroviruses. Secretory antibody can prevent the initial establishment of infection in the oropharynx and gut, and serum antibody prevents viremic spread to the target tissue. However, in the individual with poor immune response, antibody production may be too late to block infection of the target tissue, and patients with a deficiency of antibody production may have persistent enterovirus infections. Serum-neutralizing antibody generally develops 7–10 days after the initial onset of infection.

Cell-mediated immunity is not likely to be involved in protection but may play a role in pathogenesis. T cells appear to contribute to coxsackie B virus-induced myocarditis in mice. Indeed, certain late enterovirus syndromes (eg, myocarditis, myositis, and nephritis) may be immunologically mediated rather than resulting from direct viral invasion. Immune responses to the virus may cross-react with cellular antigens.

CLINICAL SYNDROMES

The clinical syndromes of the enteroviruses are determined by several factors, including the viral serotype, infecting dose, tissue tropism, portal of entry, age, sex, pregnancy status, and state of health (Box 27–1).

POLIOVIRUS INFECTION

Polio vaccines and global eradication efforts have eliminated poliomyelitis from the Western Hemisphere and are expected to eliminate "wild" polio infections from the world in the near future. However, vaccine-associated cases of polio do occur.

Clinical Findings
A. Signs and Symptoms. Poliovirus may cause one of four outcomes, depending on the progression of the infection:

- Asymptomatic illness results if the virus is limited to infection of the oropharynx and the gut. At least 90% of poliovirus infections are asymptomatic.
- Abortive poliomyelitis, the minor illness, is a nonspecific febrile illness occurring in ~5% of infected individuals. Symptoms of fever, headache, malaise, sore throat, and vomiting occur within 3–4 days of exposure.
- Nonparalytic poliomyelitis or aseptic meningitis occurs in 1–2% of patients with poliovirus infections. The virus progresses into the central nervous system and the meninges, causing stiff neck and back pain in addition to the symptoms of minor illness.
- Paralytic polio, the major illness, occurs in 0.1–2.0% of persons with poliovirus infections and is the most severe outcome. Major illness follows 3–4 days after minor illness has subsided, thereby producing a biphasic illness. In this disease the virus spreads from the blood to the anterior horn cells of the spinal cord and the motor cortex of the brain. The severity of the paralysis is determined by the extent of the neuronal

infection and the neurons affected. Spinal paralysis may involve one or more limbs, whereas bulbar (cranial) paralysis may involve a combination of cranial nerves and even the medullary respiratory center.

Paralytic poliomyelitis is characterized by an asymmetric flaccid paralysis with no sensory loss. The degree of paralysis may vary from involving only a few muscle groups (eg, one leg) to complete flaccid paralysis of all four extremities. The paralysis may progress over the first few days and may result in complete recovery, residual paralysis, or death. Most recovery occurs within 6 months.

Bulbar poliomyelitis can be more severe and may involve the muscles of the pharynx, vocal cords, and respiratory system, resulting in death in 75% of patients.

B. Laboratory Findings. The peripheral blood white blood cell (WBC) level is only moderately elevated with a relative lymphopenia. The CSF WBC count is elevated with a lymphocytosis, and the protein level is > 35 mg/100 mL.

C. Differential Diagnosis. With the disappearance of poliomyelitis from the Western Hemisphere, it is more likely that a patient presenting with febrile flaccid paralysis is suffering from the Guillain-Barré syndrome, whose etiology is unknown. The CSF examination shows elevation of protein but no pleocytosis. Alternatively there are rare instances of paralytic illness associated with entero-, echo-, or coxsackieviruses. Rheumatic fever, cytomegalovirus (CMV) polyradiculopathy, bacterial meningitis, and infectious mononucleosis are other illnesses that may be mistaken for poliomyelitis.

D. Complications. Pneumonia, urinary tract infections, and decubiti are early complications, whereas the post-polio syndrome is a late complication. This entity is characterized by a recrudescence of increased fatigue and impaired motor function many years after the acute poliomyelitis illness.

COXSACKIEVIRUS & ECHOVIRUS INFECTIONS

Several clinical syndromes may be caused by either coxsackievirus or echovirus (eg, aseptic meningitis) (see Box 27–1), but certain illnesses are especially associated with coxsackieviruses. For example, coxsackie A viruses are highly associated with herpangina, whereas myocarditis and pleurodynia are more frequently caused by coxsackie B serotypes.

1. HERPANGINA

Clinical Findings
A. Signs and Symptoms. This syndrome is inappropriately named because it has no relation to her-

BOX 27–1		
Enterovirus Infection		
	Pediatric	Adult
More Common	• Febrile rash • Meningitis	• Meningitis
Less Common	• Hand-foot-mouth • Herpangina syndrome • Neonatal "*sepsis*"	• Pleurodynia • Myoperi- carditis

pesvirus. Rather, it is caused by several types of coxsackie A virus. Fever, sore throat, pain on swallowing, anorexia, and vomiting characterize herpangina. The classic finding is vesicular, ulcerated lesions around the soft palate and uvula. Less typically the lesions may affect the hard palate.

B. Laboratory Findings. The coxsackie A virus can be recovered from throat, feces, or vesicular lesions. There are no consistent blood abnormalities.

C. Differential Diagnosis. Primary herpes simplex virus (HSV) stomatitis may resemble herpangina, but the latter is usually confined to the posterior pharynx, whereas HSV also affects the anterior mouth, gums, and lips.

D. Course. The disease is self-limited and requires only symptomatic management.

2. PLEURODYNIA (BORNHOLM DISEASE)

Clinical Findings

A. Signs and Symptoms. This syndrome, also known as the *devil's grip,* is an acute illness caused by coxsackie B virus. Patients have sudden onset of fever and unilateral low thoracic, pleuritic chest pain, which may be excruciating. Abdominal pain and even vomiting may also occur. Although a pleural friction rub may be heard, the physical findings of pneumonia are not present. Muscles on the involved side may be extremely tender. The pain tends to appear and disappear abruptly and repeatedly, for example, hourly, and can be very severe.

B. Laboratory Findings. Chest x-ray films are almost always normal, as are blood leukocyte counts. The virus can be recovered from throat samples, stool samples, or both.

C. Course. Pleurodynia lasts an average of 4 days and may relapse after the patient has been asymptomatic for several days. High fever and the waxing and waning of the pain help to distinguish pleurodynia from other pleuritic processes, for example, pulmonary embolism. The absence of lung abnormalities eliminates pneumonia as a diagnosis.

3. MENINGITIS

Clinical Findings

A. Signs and Symptoms. Viral, or aseptic, meningitis is an acute febrile illness accompanied by headache and signs of meningeal irritation, including nuchal rigidity, Kernig's or Brudzinski's sign, or both. Petechiae or skin rash may occur in patients with enteroviral meningitis. Both echo- and coxsackieviruses cause viral "aseptic" meningitis.

B. Laboratory Findings. Examination of the CSF reveals a predominantly lymphocytic pleocytosis, but very early in the disease, polymorphonuclear leukocytes (PMNs) may be more numerous. CSF glucose levels are usually normal but may be slightly low. CSF protein levels are normal to slightly elevated. Blood counts and chemistry examinations are normal. The causative virus can be recovered from throat, stool, and CSF, but culture of enteroviruses requires an average of 5 days. Polymerase chain reaction of CSF is becoming a most useful rapid diagnostic test.

C. Differential Diagnosis. The major differential diagnosis is bacterial meningitis, which is characterized by more severe illness and prostration. The CSF reveals elevated PMNs, low glucose, high protein, and a positive Gram stain. Other viruses, for example, mumps, Epstein-Barr (EB), and lymphocytic choriomeningitis (LCM) viruses, may cause an indistinguishable meningitis, but associated clinical features help to identify these etiologies.

D. Course. Unless associated encephalitis (meningoencephalitis) exists, recovery is uneventful. If encephalitis is present, permanent neurologic sequelae may ensue.

4. ENTEROVIRAL EXANTHEMS

Clinical Findings

A. Signs and Symptoms. This syndrome may occur in patients infected with either echo- or coxsackieviruses and is usually accompanied by fever. The rash is usually maculopapular but occasionally may appear as petechial or even vesicular.

B. Laboratory Findings. The virus can be recovered from throat samples, stool samples, or both.

C. Differential Diagnosis. The petechial type of eruption must be differentiated from that of meningococcemia. The child with enteroviral infection is not as ill and does not usually have a PMN leukocytosis in blood like the child with meningococcemia.

5. HAND-FOOT-AND-MOUTH DISEASE

Clinical Findings

A. Signs and Symptoms. This syndrome is a vesicular exanthem usually caused by coxsackievirus A16. The name is descriptive, since the main features of this infection are vesicular lesions of the hands, feet, mouth, and tongue. The oral lesions are identical to those of herpangina.

B. Laboratory Findings. There are no consistent laboratory abnormalities, but the virus can be recovered from throat and stool samples in an average of 5 days.

C. Course. The patient is mildly febrile, and the illness subsides in a few days.

6. ACUTE BENIGN PERICARDITIS

Clinical Findings

A. Signs and Symptoms. The chest pain, pericardial friction rub, and clinical illness often follow a preceding febrile illness, which may have been associated with a rash.

B. Laboratory Findings. EKG reveals changes characteristic of pericarditis, but there are no consistent blood abnormalities. Pericardial fluid cultures may be positive for virus, but throat and stool cultures are often negative due to the time lag between the viral illness and the development of this late complication.

C. Differential Diagnosis. Pericarditis is usually a disease of young adults but may be seen in older individuals, in whom the distinction from myocardial infarction may be difficult. Usually the symptoms are similar, but in pericarditis, fever may greater and more prolonged than in a patient with myocardial infarction. Other causes of pericarditis, for example, bacterial causes, must be considered, including complications of pneumonia and tuberculosis.

7. MYOCARDITIS

Clinical Findings

A. Signs and Symptoms. Myocarditis is caused by coxsackie B virus and occurs in older children and adults but is most threatening in newborns. Neonates with these infections have febrile illnesses and the sudden, unexplained onset of heart failure. Cyanosis, tachycardia, cardiomegaly, and hepatomegaly occur. In older children or adults the cardiac involvement is usually late, ie, days to weeks after initial symptoms.

B. Laboratory Findings. Electrocardiographic changes are those found in patients with myocarditis, but there are no characteristic blood abnormalities. Viral culture of pericardial fluid or myocardial biopsy may be positive but is often negative due to the late-onset nature of this complication.

C. Course. Myocarditis is usually self-limited but may be fatal due to arrhythmia or heart failure, especially in newborns.

D. Complications. Myocarditis may progress to chronic myocardiopathy.

8. OTHER SYNDROMES

Echoviruses may also produce severe disseminated infection in infants. Enterovirus 70 and a variant of coxsackie A24 have recently been associated with an extremely contagious ocular disease, acute hemorrhagic conjunctivitis. The infection causes subconjunctival hemorrhages and conjunctivitis. The disease has a 24-h incubation period and resolves within 1 or 2 weeks.

Respiratory disease, hepatitis, and diabetes are some additional syndromes attributed to enteroviruses. Coxsackieviruses A21 and A24 and echoviruses 11 and 20 can cause coldlike symptoms if the upper respiratory tract becomes infected. Enterovirus 72, or hepatitis A virus, causes hepatitis A (see Chapter 39). Coxsackie B infections of the pancreas have been suspected to cause insulin-dependent diabetes because of the destruction of the islets of Langerhans.

Diagnosis

Poliovirus. Poliovirus grows well in monkey kidney tissue culture, and the virus may be isolated from the pharynx during the first few days of illness and from the feces for ≤ 30 days. The CSF is rarely positive for the virus, although a pleocytosis of 25–300 leukocytes usually occurs. Neutrophils may predominate early, especially in aseptic meningitis. Protein and glucose levels in CSF are usually normal or only slightly abnormal. Serologic tests can document seroconversion to one of the three poliovirus serotypes.

Coxsackievirus and Echovirus. Coxsackievirus and echovirus can usually be isolated from the throat and stool during acute infection and often from CSF in patients with meningitis. Virus is rarely isolated in pericarditis or myocarditis, since the symptoms occur several weeks after the initial infection. The coxsackie B viruses can be grown on primary monkey or human embryo kidney cells. Many coxsackie A virus strains do not grow in tissue culture and must be grown in suckling mice.

Polymerase chain reaction analysis of CSF appears to be more sensitive than culturing and is becoming the diagnostic procedure of choice for documenting enteroviral meningitis.

Serologic confirmation of poliovirus infection can be made by detection of specific immunoglobulin M (IgM) or a fourfold increase in antibody titer between acute illness and convalescence; however, the many serotypes for echo- and coxsackieviruses make this approach impractical.

Treatment

No specific antiviral therapy is approved for enterovirus infections, but pleconaril, a drug active against picornaviruses in vitro, is being evaluated for the treatment of enteroviral meningitis and viremia. Immune globulin has been used in immunocompromised patients with chronic enteroviral infection of the central nervous system (Box 27–2) and can diminish viral titers in body fluids.

Prevention & Control

Poliovirus. The prevention of paralytic poliomyelitis is one of the triumphs of modern medicine. In the western world, complete control has been

---

BOX 27–2

Treatment of Enterovirus Infection

First Choice	Immune globulin for chronic infection of CNS in incubation period
Pediatric Considerations	• See above

BOX 27–3

Control of Enterovirus Infection

Prophylactic Measures	• Poliovirus vaccine, which induces a protective antibody response • No vaccines exist for coxsackieviruses or echoviruses. Transmission can presumably be reduced by improvements in hygiene and living conditions
Isolation Precautions	• Careful handwashing after patient contact • Stool precautions

achieved by the use of vaccines, and worldwide eradication of poliomyelitis is expected soon.

Two types of poliovirus vaccine exist: a formalin-inactivated product known as the inactivated, killed, or Salk vaccine, and an attenuated one known as the live, oral, or Sabin vaccine (Box 27–3). Both vaccines can induce a protective antibody response.

Oral vaccine is attenuated (ie, rendered less virulent) by passage in cell cultures. Attenuation yields a virus capable of replicating in the oropharynx and intestinal tract and of being shed in feces for weeks, but not of being invasive. The remote potential for reverting to virulence and causing paralytic disease is the major drawback of the live vaccine and is estimated to occur in 1 per 4 million doses administered (versus 1 in 100 of those infected with "wild" poliovirus).

The risk of vaccine-associated paralytic poliomyelitis is increased in immunocompromised individuals and is more likely to occur in susceptible adults than susceptible children. Since the live vaccine strain may spread to close, especially household, contacts (a virtue in achieving mass immunization), vaccine-associated poliomyelitis may occur in those contacted by the original recipient, rather than the actual vaccine recipient. Because of the above considerations, killed vaccine is now the recommended prophylaxis, and oral live polio vaccine is used only for those refusing injections or for those traveling to areas with endemic poliomyelitis.

Coxsackievirus and Echovirus. No vaccines exist for these viruses (see Box 27–3). Transmission can presumably be reduced by improvements in hygiene and living conditions.

REFERENCES

Expanded Program on Immunization, Pan American Health Organization: Certification of poliomyelitis eradication in the Americas. Morbid Mortal Weekly Rep 1994; 43:720.

Ramlow J et al: Epidemiology of the post-polio syndrome. Am J Epidemiol 1992;136:769.

Rotbart HA: Nucleic acid detection systems for enteroviruses. Clin Microbiol Rev 1991;4:156.

Rhinoviruses

28

W. Lawrence Drew, MD, PhD

Essentials of Diagnosis
- Leading cause of upper respiratory infection.
- Virus grows preferentially at 33 °C in diploid fibroblast cells.
- Typical illness includes rhinorrhea and low-grade fever but little evidence of lower respiratory illness.

General Considerations

Rhinoviruses are the most frequent cause of the common cold. One hundred two serotypes have been identified by neutralization with specific antisera, and additional strains have been isolated but are not yet typed.

A. Epidemiology. Rhinoviruses can be transmitted by two mechanisms: aerosols and direct contact (eg, with contaminated hands or inanimate objects). Surprisingly, aerosols may not be the major route, and hands appear to be an important vector. Rhinoviruses can be recovered from the hands of 40–90% of persons with colds and from 6–15% of inanimate objects around them. The virus can survive on these objects for many hours.

Rhinoviruses produce clinical illness in only half of those infected, and thus many asymptomatic individuals are capable of spreading the virus. Rhinovirus "colds" affect people in temperate climates most frequently in the early fall, which may reflect the return to school rather than any change in the virus itself. Rates of infection are highest in infants and children, who are also the primary vector introducing colds into family units. Secondary infections occur in ~50% of family members, especially other children.

Although many different rhinovirus serotypes may be found in a given community, only a few predominate during a specific cold season. They tend to be the newly categorized serotypes, suggesting that a gradual antigenic drift occurs.

B. Microbiology. Many microbiological features of rhinoviruses are similar to those of enteroviruses (see Chapter 27). As with all picornaviruses, the RNA of rhinoviruses is surrounded by a very small icosahedral capsid approximately 30 nm in diameter. The genome of these viruses resembles messenger RNA (mRNA). It is a single strand of (+)-sense RNA of ~7.2–8.5 kb. It encodes a polyprotein that is proteolytically cleaved to produce the enzymatic and structural proteins of the virus. In addition to the capsid proteins, these viruses encode at least one protease and an RNA-dependent RNA polymerase. A virus-encoded protease blocks translation of cellular mRNA.

C. Pathogenesis. In contrast to enteroviruses, rhinoviruses are unable to replicate in the gastrointestinal tract. This contrast probably reflects differences in surface receptors between the two groups of viruses rather than degradation of rhinovirus by gastric acid. Also rhinoviruses replicate optimally at 33 °C, which may explain their predilection for the anterior nares.

At least 80% of the rhinoviruses share a common receptor, ICAM-1, which is a member of the immunoglobulin family and is expressed on epithelial, fibroblast, and lymphoblastoid cells.

Secretory and serum antibodies are generated in response to the rhinovirus and can be detected within a week of infection. No antigen is common to all rhinoviruses. Although secretory immunoglobulin A (IgA) is probably more important than serum antibody in preventing and controlling infection, its half-life is brief. A better correlate of immunity is the level of serum antibody that begins to wane ~18 months after infection.

Interferon, generated in response to the infection, may both limit the progression of the infection and contribute to the symptoms. The release of cytokines during inflammation can promote the spread of the virus by enhancing the expression of viral receptors. Cell-mediated immunity does not appear to play an important role in controlling rhinovirus infections.

Infection can be initiated by as little as one infectious viral particle. During the peak of illness, titers of 500 to 1,000 infectious virions are reached in nasal secretions. Most viral replication occurs in the nose, and the severity of symptoms correlates with the quantity (titer) of virus in nasal secretions. Biopsies of nasal mucosa taken during a "cold" reveal severe edema of the subepithelial tissue but minimal inflammatory cell response. Infected ciliated epithelial cells may be sloughed from the nasal mucosa.

RHINOVIRUS INFECTION

Clinical Findings

A. Signs and Symptoms. Upper respiratory infections (URIs) caused by rhinoviruses usually

BOX 28-1

Rhinovirus Infection

	Children	Adults
More Common	Upper respiratory infection	Upper respiratory infection
Less Common		

begin with sneezing, soon followed by rhinorrhea (Box 28–1). The rhinorrhea increases and is then accompanied by nasal stuffiness. Mild sore throat also occurs, along with headache, malaise, and chills. The illness peaks in 3–4 days, but cough and nasal symptoms may persist for 7–10 days longer. High fever and shaking chills are not usual features of rhinovirus URIs.

B. Laboratory Findings. The clinical syndrome of the common cold is usually so characteristic that laboratory diagnosis is unnecessary. Rhinoviruses cause up to one half of URIs, but coronaviruses, parainfluenza viruses, and other agents also cause a sizable proportion of colds. Also at times it may be difficult to distinguish allergic rhinitis from an URI.

Nasal washings are the best type of clinical specimen for recovering the virus. Rhinoviruses grow in vitro only in cells of primate origin, with human diploid fibroblast cells (eg, WI-38) as the optimum system. As already stated, these viruses grow best at 33 °C, which is not the optimum temperature for any other clinically important viruses. Thus their isolation may require a separate incubator. Isolation in tissue culture occurs 4–5 days on average. The virus is identified by typical cytopathic effects and the demonstration of acid lability. Serotyping is rarely necessary but is done by using pools of specific neutralizing sera.

Serologic testing to document rhinovirus infection is not practical. No antigen is common to all rhinoviruses; thus it would be necessary to have the patient's viral isolate or a prototype of the specific rhinovirus prevalent in the community in order to perform this kind of testing.

C. Differential Diagnosis. Several other viruses can cause similar syndromes, especially coronaviruses, adenoviruses, and parainfluenza viruses. Allergic rhinitis is not associated with fever and often is accompanied by an itching conjunctivitis. Also the peripheral blood may show eosinophilia.

D. Complications. In otherwise healthy individuals, rhinovirus illnesses are uncomplicated, but in those with chronic lung disease, exacerbations of bronchitis may occur. In severely immunocompromised patients, lower respiratory disease may occur.

Treatment

There is no specific therapy for rhinovirus (Box 28–2). Nasal vasoconstrictors may provide relief, but their use may be followed by rebound congestion and worsening symptoms. Antibacterial agents are not beneficial unless a true bacterial infection (eg, sinusitis) occurs. Even when nasal secretions have become purulent, a carefully performed Gram's stain will usually show few if any bacteria. Rigorous studies of vitamin C therapy have not shown efficacy. Topical interferon provides antiviral activity but itself produces upper respiratory symptoms. Drugs that block viral attachment, penetration, or replication have been discovered and are being evaluated in clinical trials.

Prognosis

Because rhinovirus illnesses are usually uncomplicated, the prognosis for recovery is excellent, but as mentioned above in the complications section, exacerbations of chronic lung disease may occur, and fatal illnesses in immunocompromised patients have been reported.

Prevention & Control

There are three potential methods of prevention or control of rhinoviruses: vaccines, antiviral agents (especially interferon), and interruption of transmission (Box 28–3).

BOX 28-2

Treatment of Rhinovirus Infection

First Choice	No specific antiviral Rx
Second Choice	Symptomatic treatment with vasoconstrictors and antipyretics
Pediatric Considerations	Aspirin should be avoided

BOX 28-3

Control of Rhinovirus Infection

Prophylactic Measures	Avoid direct hand to hand and aerosol contact with symptomatic patients
Isolation Precautions	Vaccines not likely. Antiviral chemotherapy being evaluated

The multiple serotypes and apparent antigenic drift in rhinovirus antigens suggest that successful vaccines are unlikely. Formalin-inactivated, parenterally administered vaccines induce antibody in serum but not in nasal secretions and are not as useful as those given intranasally.

Prophylactic topical interferon is effective but associated with unacceptable side effects. Since transmission is person to person, infection may be reduced by minimizing finger to nose and hand to hand spread as well as by covering coughs and sneezes.

REFERENCES

Colonno RJ: Virus receptors: The Achilles' heel of human rhinovirus. Adv Exp Med Biol 1992;312:61.

Gwaltney JM Jr: Combined antiviral and antimediator treatment of rhinovirus colds. J Infect Dis 1992;166:776.

Smith TJ et al: Structure of human rhinovirus complexed with Fab fragments from a neutralizing antibody. J Virol 1993;67:1148.

Speller SA et al: The nature and spatial distribution of amino acid substitutions conferring resistance to neutralizing monoclonal antibodies in human rhinovirus type 2. J Gen Virol 1993;193.

29

Influenza

Lisa Danzig, MD & Keiji Fukuda, MD, MPH

Essentials of Diagnosis

- Acute onset of fever, chills, myalgia, headache, sore throat, nonproductive cough, and severe malaise
- Winter or epidemic setting
- Variable white blood cell counts
- Nasopharyngeal specimen ideally collected within 2–3 days of illness; placed into viral transport media; virus usually isolated within 2–6 days of inoculation into tissue culture
- Direct antigen assay positive on nasopharyngeal specimens for influenza A
- Increased school absenteeism or emergency room visits signal outbreak

General Considerations

Influenza is a highly contagious, acute, febrile respiratory illness caused by influenza A and B viruses. The hallmark of these viruses is their ability to undergo rapid ongoing antigenic change and to cause annual or near-annual epidemics of febrile respiratory disease affecting all age groups. In addition, the unpredictable emergence of new influenza A subtypes can lead to explosive global pandemics of disease. Although most cases are self-limited, influenza is a major source of mortality among those at increased risk for influenza-related complications. Annual vaccination of persons at high risk for serious complications is the most effective approach for reducing influenza-related morbidity and mortality.

Influenza viruses, which include influenza A virus, influenza B virus, influenza C virus, and thogotovirus, belong to the *Orthomyxoviridiae* family. Influenza A and B viruses cause epidemic disease in humans (influenza C viruses usually cause a mild, coldlike illness) and are designated by type, site, and year of isolation. Influenza A (but not B or C) viruses are further designated by subtype. For example, influenza A/Texas/36/91/(H1N1) refers to an influenza type A virus of the H1N1 subtype that was isolated in Texas in 1991 and has a strain designation of 36 to distinguish it from other 1991 Texas isolates of this subtype.

A. Epidemiology. In the United States, epidemic influenza activity often begins each year in the late fall or early winter months and may continue in different regions of the country through the spring. From year to year, the onset, duration, and geographic distribution of regional epidemics can vary greatly, and sporadic cases and outbreaks can occur anytime, including during the summer months. Within more circumscribed communities and institutions, epidemics or outbreaks usually last ~6–8 weeks.

Influenza A(H1N1), influenza A(H3N2), and influenza B viruses are in worldwide circulation. Any one or any combination of these three viruses may be the cause of a season's epidemic activity. During each influenza season, an estimated 10–20% of the U.S. population may develop influenza, but attack rates of 40–50% within institutions are not unusual. In communities, influenza cases often appear first among school-age children, and attack rates in this group are usually the highest (and lowest among the elderly).

By contrast, rates of serious complications are highest among the elderly, the very young, and those with underlying chronic cardiopulmonary conditions that place them at high risk for complications. Influenza-related mortality is usually tabulated in terms of "excess" deaths. This concept was developed by William Farr and refers to the idea that influenza-related mortality can be quantified during influenza epidemics by determining the increase in deaths beyond the expected number of deaths if there was no epidemic. In the United States, the average annual toll of excess deaths from influenza-related complications is ~20,000; > 40,000 deaths may occur during severe years. Although pandemics are often associated with dramatic increases in mortality, the cumulative death toll from seasonal epidemic influenza since the 1968 pandemic exceeds the total for the 1918 pandemic (see below).

Pandemics of influenza occur when a new subtype of influenza A virus emerges and leads to increased morbidity and mortality in all age groups. This is a dramatic event that occurs relatively infrequently and unpredictably. The most devastating pandemic of the twentieth century began in 1918 and was associated with the emergence of the influenza A(H1N1) virus. Between the spring of 1918 and the spring of 1919, three waves of "Spanish flu" swept around the world leading to > 550,000 deaths in the United States and > 20 million deaths worldwide. In contrast to the usual mortality pattern, influenza-related deaths in this pandemic occurred for unknown reasons predominantly among people 20–40 years of age.

Two subsequent pandemics, which began in 1957 (the "Asian flu") and in 1968 ("Hong Kong flu"), were associated with the emergence of the influenza

A (H2N2)virus and the influenza A (H3N2) virus, respectively. In contrast to these events, the reappearance of influenza A (H1N1) virus in 1977 was not considered a true pandemic because illness largely was confined to people younger than 20 years of age. Based on these events, evidence of earlier pandemics, and the continuing evolution of influenza A viruses, the occurrence of another pandemic is likely.

The ability of influenza viruses to cause recurrent epidemics and pandemics can be attributed in large part to their propensity for antigenic change. This occurs through two distinct processes known as antigenic "drift" and "shift." In antigenic drift, which both influenza A and B viruses exhibit, point mutations in the viral RNA result in immunologically significant alterations to HA and NA. Drift occurs more rapidly in influenza A subtypes than in influenza B viruses. Eventually, one of the newer influenza strains becomes the predominant strain because neutralizing antibody levels to older strains rise in the general population and exert a selective evolutionary pressure favoring the emergence of a new strain. Typically, a virus strain may predominate for a few years before a significantly different variant emerges to replace it.

Antigenic shift refers to the appearance of a virus bearing either a novel HA or a novel combination of HA and NA. Shift is exhibited only by influenza A viruses and may occur in one of two ways. Genes from influenza A viruses normally in circulation among pigs or birds may reassort (ie, mix) with genes from influenza A viruses circulating among humans, resulting in the appearance of a new influenza A virus subtype containing genes from both viruses. Pigs are thought to serve as a "mixing vessel" for genetic reassortment among influenza viruses because they are susceptible to avian, swine, and human influenza A viruses. Avian species are thought to serve as the ultimate reservoir of influenza A viruses. Alternatively, new influenza A virus subtypes may appear among humans as a result of direct transmission of animal viruses to humans. An example of this type of antigenic shift was seen recently in Hong Kong. During May through December 1997, a total of 18 people in Hong Kong were hospitalized because of disease related to influenza A (H5N1) infections. Previous to this outbreak, H5N1 viruses had been known to cause disease only in birds. The potential for this influenza A virus to cause a pandemic remains uncertain.

Antigenic shift results in a radical alteration in antigenicity. The emergence of a novel influenza A virus can lead to a pandemic but only if the new virus is sufficiently transmissible among humans to maintain epidemic activity and is capable of causing disease.

B. Microbiology. Influenza A and B viruses are single-stranded, negative-sense (complimentary to mRNA) RNA viruses, which contain eight segments of RNA, associated nucleoprotein, and three polymerases. Segmentation of the RNA is an important feature because it facilitates the exchange of genes (ie, genetic reassortment) among influenza viruses. The genome is surrounded by a lipid bilayer from which hemagglutinin (HA) and neuraminadase (NA) proteins protrude as "spikes." HA and NA are glycoproteins and contain the major antigenic determinants of influenza viruses. HA is responsible for the attachment of virus to oligosaccharide-containing terminal sialic acids and the penetration of virus into cells. HA is the major antigen against which the host's protective antibody response is directed. NA is less abundant on the viral surface, and its function is less well understood but is related, in part, to the release of virus from infected cells. Antibody to NA restricts the spread and severity of influenza infection. Currently, 15 HA and 9 NA subtypes are known. Among these, two HA subtypes (H1 and H3) and two NA subtypes (N1 and N2) are found on currently circulating human influenza viruses.

The viral envelope also contains two matrix proteins (M1 and M2), which form the basis for classifying influenza viruses into types A or B. M1 protein is thought to add rigidity to the lipid bilayer, whereas M2 protein functions as a pH-activated ion channel. The M2 protein is therapeutically important because it appears to contain the site of action for amantadine and rimantadine, two antiviral agents with specific activity against influenza A (but not influenza B) viruses.

C. Pathogenesis. Aerosol produced by the coughing or sneezing of infectious individuals is thought to be the primary way in which influenza viruses are spread. However, transmission of virus by direct contact with infected respiratory secretions may also occur. The incubation period for influenza is typically 1–4 days. Virus can be isolated from the nasopharynx of adults for ≤ 3–4 days after illness develops. Infection and viral replication occur primarily in the columnar epithelial cells of the respiratory tract and result in the loss of cilia, inflammation,, and the eventual necrosis and desquamation of the respiratory epithelium. Regeneration of the epithelial cells takes ~3–4 weeks during which pulmonary abnormalities may persist. Although constitutional manifestations are pronounced in influenza, viremia has been difficult to document.

Infection leads to the induction of both B- and T-cell responses. Neutralizing serum and mucosal antibodies to HA are the primary mediators of protection against infection and clinical illness. Serum antibodies to HA can persist for decades. Antibodies to NA are inefficient in neutralizing influenza viruses but help restrict the release of virus from infected cells, reduce the intensity of infection, and enhance recovery. The role of T-cell-mediated immunity is less well understood.

INFLUENZA INFECTION

Clinical Findings

The spectrum of influenza infection ranges from subclinical cases to fulminating viral pneumonia.

A. Signs and Symptoms (Box 29–1). There are no specific physical examination findings associated with influenza. The patient usually appears ill and has fever. A clear nasal discharge is common. A typical uncomplicated case of influenza illness begins abruptly and is manifested by sore throat, headache, fever, chills, myalgias, anorexia, and extreme fatigue. Fever is usually between 38 and 40 °C but may be higher and usually lasts for ~3 days (but ≤ 5 days). Other respiratory tract manifestations include cough, which is usually nonproductive, and a runny or stuffy nose. Substernal tenderness, photophobia, abdominal pain, and diarrhea occur less frequently. Despite severe sore throat, the mucous membranes of the pharynx may be unremarkable or hyperemic without exudates. Small tender cervical lymph nodes may be palpable, and the lungs are usually clear, although scattered rhonchi and crackles can be heard in as many as a quarter of patients.

In the elderly, fever may be absent and the presenting signs may be anorexia, lassitude, confusion, and rhinitis. In children, fevers are often higher and can lead to febrile seizures. Gastrointestinal manifestations, such as vomiting, abdominal pain, and diarrhea, and other complications such as myositis, croup (tracheobronchitis), and otitis media also occur more frequently in children. Unexplained fever may be the primary manifestation in neonates.

B. Laboratory Findings. Results of routine laboratory tests are not specific for influenza. Leukocyte counts are variable. Severe leukopenia has been described in overwhelming illness. Leukocytosis of > 15,000 cells/mL should raise the suspicion of a secondary bacterial process. Specific laboratory tests to confirm influenza include viral culture, rapid antigen detection, and serology.

Virus can be isolated from nasal washing and nasopharyngeal swab specimens obtained within 3–4 days of illness. Virus is grown either in embryonated hens' eggs or in primary tissue culture systems, such as Madin-Darby canine kidney cells. Viral culture offers specific information and the ability to further characterize the isolate, but the sensitivity of this technique is highly dependent on the timing of when the specimen is obtained. Results usually are not available for at least 3 days.

Rapid diagnostic techniques to identify viral antigens in clinical specimens include immunofluorescence, enzyme immunoassay, and time-resolved fluoroimmunoassay. Several rapid test kits are now commercially available that either can 1) detect influenza A but not influenza B virus; 2) detect influenza A or B virus but not distinguish between them; or 3) detect influenza A or B virus and distinguish between them. In general, these tests are more specific than sensitive but head-to-head comparison data are not available. These tests can yield results within 30 min. Reverse transcriptase polymerase chain reaction assays have also been used to detect influenza virus RNA in clinical specimens.

Serologic techniques for measuring antibody against influenza include hemagglutination inhibition, neutralization, enzyme immunoassay, and complement fixation. In general, serology is a sensitive technique for establishing influenza infections. However, serologic tests usually require acute and convalescent serum samples to demonstrate a significant increase in antibody level. The measurement of influenza antibody levels in a single-serum sample is rarely helpful. Ideally, acute and convalescent blood samples should be collected, respectively, within 2–3 days of illness and at 3 weeks after the start of illness. The most commonly used serologic test to document influenza virus infection is hemagglutination inhibition because it (and neutralization) is more sensitive than complement fixation and allows subtype and strain-specific antibody to be measured.

C. Imaging. A chest X-ray may show an infiltrate in those with primary viral pneumonia or a complicating bacterial pneumonia.

Differential Diagnosis

Other respiratory viruses, including respiratory syncytial virus, adenovirus, parainfluenza virus, and rhinovirus, as well as other organisms, such as *My-*

BOX 29–1

Influenza

	Children	Adults[a]
More Frequent	• High fever (>103 °F) (unexplained fever in neonates) • Gastrointestinal manifestations (vomiting, abdominal pain, diarrhea) • Myositis • Croup • Otitis media	• Abrupt onset fever (>100 °F) • Headache, myalgia • Malaise • Resolution within 1–2 weeks
Less Frequent		• Gastrointestinal • Persistent fatigue

[a]In the elderly, fever may be absent, and presenting signs may be anorexia, lassitude, confusion, and rhinitis.

coplasma pneumoniae, can produce illness similar to influenza. However, outbreaks of febrile respiratory illness cases during the winter through spring months are characteristic of influenza. Information on local influenza activity is usually available from the local health department.

Complications

The most common serious complications of influenza include exacerbation of underlying chronic pulmonary and cardiopulmonary diseases, such as worsening of chronic obstructive pulmonary disease, asthma, and congestive heart failure, as well the development of pneumonia. Secondary bacterial pneumonias occur much more frequently than primary viral pneumonia and usually are associated with *Streptococcus pneumoniae, Staphylococcus aureus,* and *Haemophilus influenzae.* With complicating bacterial pneumonia, the patient typically reports a period of improvement followed by the appearance of signs and symptoms suggestive of pneumonia, such as pleuritic chest pain, productive cough, and fever. On chest radiography, lobar consolidation can be seen and sputum smears show polymorphonuclear leukocytes with bacteria.

Primary viral pneumonia is an infrequent but often fatal complication in which influenza progresses within the first 24–48 h of illness and leads to increasing dyspnea, tachypnea, and cyanosis. On presentation, fever and cough are usually present and the patient appears uncomfortable and dyspneic. On chest auscultation, diffuse fine rales with wheezes or coarse breath sounds may be evident. Sputum may be scanty but can be blood streaked. Chest roentgenograms usually show bilateral interstitial infiltrates or a picture consistent with acute respiratory distress syndrome. The Gram stain of the sputum often shows few polymorphonuclear cells or bacteria. Virologic cultures of the respiratory secretions often yield virus. The value of antiviral medications in this setting is unknown. Cases of viral pneumonia described in the 1918 and 1957 pandemics were associated with underlying cardiac valvular disease (frequently mitral stenosis from rheumatic heart disease) and pregnancy.

In addition to these pneumonias, mixed viral and bacterial pneumonias with features of both etiologies have been described. Other respiratory tract complications include bacterial sinusitis, croup, and otitis media.

Reye's syndrome has been described primarily in children < 18 years of age. In almost all cases, Reye's syndrome appears to be a complication resulting from the use of salicylates, most commonly aspirin, to treat certain viral illnesses. Reye's syndrome usually presents several days after an unremarkable viral illness. The syndrome usually presents with nausea and vomiting followed by central nervous system (CNS) changes such as lethargy, delirium, seizures, or coma. Reye's syndrome has been primarily seen in children treated with aspirin for influenza B virus and varicella-zoster virus infections but also for infections by influenza A virus. Since the 1980s, the incidence of Reye's syndrome has decreased dramatically in the United States after warnings were issued regarding the link between the treatment of children with aspirin and this syndrome.

Myocarditis and pericarditis were reported in association with influenza during the 1918–1919 pandemic but have been documented infrequently since then. Minor electrocardiogram changes in the setting of influenza can often be seen in patients with underlying heart disease. Myositis with rhabdomyolysis and myoglobinuria has been reported but is uncommon. Toxic shock syndrome associated with secondary staphylococcal infection after acute influenza also has been reported. In addition, a number of CNS complications including encephalopathy, encephalitis, transverse myelitis, and Guillain-Barré syndrome have all been reported, but their association with influenza remains unclear.

Treatment

Uncomplicated cases of influenza are usually treated symptomatically. Salicylates should be avoided in children < 18 years of age because of the risk of Reye's syndrome. There are two classes of licensed antiviral agents, the adamantines and the neuraminadase inhibitors, with specific activity against influenza viruses. The adamantines, amantadine hydrochloride and rimantadine hydrochloride, have specific activity against influenza A virus but not B virus. The neuraminadase inhibitor drugs, zanamivir and oseltamivir, have activity against both influenza A and B viruses. Amantadine is licensed for use in children and adults, whereas rimantadine is licensed for use in adults. Both drugs can be given for treatment of or prophylaxis against influenza A virus but are ineffective against influenza B virus. These chemically related drugs are equally effective and appear to inhibit viral replication by blocking the ion channel function of the viral M2 protein. Viral resistance to both compounds is associated with changes in the M2 protein. Although the rapid emergence of resistant viruses has been demonstrated both in vitro and in vivo, the risk of transmission of these resistant viruses remains unclear. Resistant viruses have been most often isolated from individuals receiving treatment and less often from contacts.

When administered prophylactically, both agents are ~70–90% effective in preventing illness caused by influenza A viruses. Subclinical infections still can occur while taking these drugs. Although chemoprophylaxis can be used alone in persons for whom vaccination is contraindicated, it is preferable to administer these agents as an adjunct to vaccination in high-risk groups. Since these drugs do not interfere with antibody response to vaccination, they can be used to provide prophylaxis to persons who were vaccinated but who have not yet had adequate time (usually 2 weeks) to mount a vaccine antibody response. To control an institutional influenza outbreak, antiviral agents are most effective when administered to all residents.

When administered within 48 h of illness onset, these agents have also been shown to reduce the severity and duration of influenza in young and healthy adults and children. Similar controlled studies have not been conducted among persons at high risk for complications.

The major pharmacological differences between these agents are their pharmacokinetic and side-effect profiles. More than 90% of amantadine is excreted unchanged by the kidneys, whereas ~75% of rimantadine is metabolized by the liver (however, unmetabolized rimantadine and its metabolites are renally excreted).

Both medications can lead to CNS and gastrointestinal side effects. In one study, the incidence of CNS side effects in young and healthy adults using 200 mg/d was higher among those taking amantadine (14%) than rimantadine (6%) or placebo (4%). CNS side effects include nervousness, anxiety, difficulty concentrating, and light-headedness. More serious side effects (eg, marked behavioral changes, delirium, hallucinations, agitation, and seizures) have been associated with high plasma drug concentrations, particularly among persons with renal insufficiency, seizure disorders, or certain psychiatric disorders, or among elderly persons who were taking amantadine at doses of 200 mg/d. Approximately 3% of those taking either drug develop gastrointestinal side effects, such as nausea and anorexia. Side effects cease soon after stopping the drug, and lower doses appear to be associated with a lower incidence of side effects.

The usual therapeutic and prophylactic dosage of amantadine and rimantadine in adults < 65 years is 100 mg orally twice a day (Box 29–2). Doses should be reduced in children younger than 10 years, adults 65 years and older, especially those in nursing homes, and persons with renal insufficiency or severe hepatic dysfunction (for rimantadine).

The neuraminidase inhibitors were approved in 1999 for treatment of uncomplicated influenza. Zanamivir is orally inhaled and was approved for treatment of persons > 7 years. Oseltamivir is orally administered and was approved for treatment of persons > 1 year. Similar to the adamantines, both neuraminidase inhibitors can be effective in reducing illness by approximately one day when used within 2 days of illness. Although only oseltamivir has been approved for chemoprophylaxis, recent community studies suggest that both zanamivir and oseltamivir are approximately 80% effective in reducing febrile influenza illness when administered as chemopropylaxis. Oseltamivir was approved in 2000 for chemoprophylaxis of persons > 13 years.

In placebo controlled studies of persons with uncomplicated influenza, persons receiving zanamivir or placebo reported similar rates of adverse events including diarrhea, nausea, sinusitis, nasal signs and symptoms, bronchitis, cough, headache, dizziness, and ear, nose throat infections. In patients with asthma or chronic obstructive pulmonary disease, more patients taking zanamivir than placebo had a > 20% decrease in forced expiratory volume in 1 second (FEV1) or peak expiratory flow. In addition, persons with underlying asthma or chronic obstructive pulmonary disease have been reported to experience respiratory deterioration following use of zanamivir. Caution should be exercised when prescribing zanamivir to patients with asthma or chronic obstructive pulmonary disease. Such patients should have a fast acting bronchodilator available when inhaling zanamivir. Oseltamivir has been associated with higher levels of nausea or vomiting (approximately 9-10%) than in persons taking placebo.

Resistance to the neuraminidase inhibitors can be induced in influenza A and B viruses in-vitro but there is little information to indicate the clinical significance of these findings. Available information suggests that resistance to these compounds develops less frequently than with the adamantines.

The recommended dosage of zanamivir is two inhalations (a total of 10 mg) twice daily about 12 hours apart for five days. The manufacturer does not recommend changes in dosage based on age or renal function. Inhaled zanamivir has a half-life of about 2.5–5.1 hours and is excreted unchanged in urine. The recommended dosage of oseltamivir for treatment in persons > 13 years or for younger children who weigh > 40 is 75 mg twice daily. In children < 13 years and who weigh < 40 kg the recommended dosages vary by weight: 30 mg twice daily for children < 15 kg; 45 mg twice daily for children > 15 kg to 23 kg; and 60 mg twice daily for children > 23 to 40 kg. Oseltamivir is approved for chemoprophylaxis in children > 13 years and the dosage is 75 mg once a day. There is no recommended change in dosage for elderly persons. However, in patients with renal dysfunction and a creatinine clearance between 10 and < 30, the recommended treatment dosage is 75 mg once a day and the recommended chemoprophylaxis dosage is 75 mg every other day. No recommendations are available for patients undergoing renal dialysis.

Ribavirin has been reported to have efficacy against influenza A and B infections when administered as an aerosol for treatment.

Prognosis

In most cases, illness from influenza resolves within a week, but cough and malaise may persist for several days to a few weeks longer. In a minority of patients, fatigue may persist for months.

Prevention & Control

Annual administration of influenza vaccine is the most effective approach for preventing illness caused by influenza. In the United States, the currently licensed vaccine is an inactivated vaccine (either killed whole virus or subunit preparations) that contains three contemporary circulating strains of influenza A (H1N1), influenza A (H3N2), and influenza B virus. Because influenza viruses exhibit ongoing antigenic

BOX 29-2

Treatment and Prophylaxis for Influenza. *

Antiviral Agent	Age (years)				
	1–6 years	7–9 years	10–12 years	13–64 years	≥65 years
Amantadine[a] Treatment	5mg/kg/day up to 150 mg in two divided doses[b]	5mg/kg/day up to 150 mg in two divided doses[b]	100mg twice daily[c]	100mg twice daily[c]	≤100 mg/day
Prophylaxis	5mg/kg/day up to 150 mg in two divided doses[b]	5mg/kg/day up to 150 mg in two divided doses[b]	100mg twice daily[c]	100mg twice daily[c]	≤100 mg/day
Rimantadine[d] Treatment	NA	NA	NA	100mg twice daily[c]	100 or 200[f] mg/day
Prophylaxis	5mg/kg/day up to 150 mg in two divided doses[b]	5mg/kg/day up to 150 mg in two divided doses[b]	100mg twice daily[c]	100mg twice daily[c]	100 or 200[f] mg/day
Zanamivir[g] Treatment	NA	10mg twice daily	10mg twice daily	10mg twice daily	10mg twice daily
Prophylaxis[h]	NA	NA	NA	NA	NA
Oscltamivir					
Treatment	dose varies by child's weight[j]	dose varies by child's weight[j]	dose varies by child's weight[j]	75mg twice daily	75mg twice daily
Prophylaxis	NA	NA	NA	75mg/day	75mg/day

[a]The drug package insert should be consulted for dosage recommendations for administering amantadine to persons with creatinine clearance ≤50 ml/min/1.73m².
[b]5mg/kg of amantadine or rimantadine syrup = 1 tsp./22 lbs.
[c]Children ≥ 10 years of age who weigh <40 kg should be administered amantadine or rimantadine at a dosage of 5 mg/kg/day.
[d]A reduction in dosage to 100 mg/day of rimantadine is recommended for persons who have severe hepatic dysfunction or those with creatinine clearance ≥10 ml/min. Other persons with less severe hepatic or renal dysfunction taking 100 mg/day of rimantadine should be observed closely, and the dosage should be reduced or the drug discontinued, if necessary.
[e]Only approved for treatment in adults.
[f]Elderly nursing-home residents whould be administered only 100 mg/day of rimantadine. A reduction in dosage to 100 mg/day should be considered for all persons ≥ 65 years of age if they experience possible side effects when taking 200 mg/day.
[g]Zanamivir administered via inhalation using a plastic device included in the package with the medication. Patients will benefit from instruction and demonstration of proper use of the device.
[h]Zanamivir is not approved for prophylaxis.
[i]A reduction in the dose of oscltamivir is recommended for persons with creatinine clearance <30 ml/min.
[j]The dose recommendation for children who weigh <15 kg is 30 mg twice a day, for >15 to 23 kg children the dose is 45 mg twice a day, for >23 to 40 kg children the dose is 60 mg twice a day, and for children >40 kg, the dose is 75 mg twice a day.
NA=Not applicable.
*Adapted from CDC. Prevention and control of influenza: recommendations of the Advisory Committee on Immunization Practices (ACIP). MMWR Morbid Mortal Weekly Rep 2001 (In press).

changes, one or two of the vaccine viruses are updated almost every year.

The recommended timing for influenza vaccination is from September through mid-November. However, influenza activity frequently peaks after December and unvaccinated persons who are at high risk for complications should continue to be offered vaccine after November.

Live attenuated influenza virus (LAIV) vaccines have been under development since the 1960s. LAIVs have several potential advantages over inactivated influenza vaccine, including greater induction of mucosal IgA and intranasal administration as a spray or nose drops. Currently, studies on trivalent formulations of LAIV vaccines are under way.

The effectiveness of inactivated influenza vaccine depends in large part on the degree of match between circulating viral strains and vaccine strains as well as the age and health status of the recipient. In controlled trials among children and young adults, influenza vaccines are ~70–90% effective in reducing influenza when there is a good match between vaccine and circulating viruses. A meta-analysis of influenza vaccine studies among the elderly found the effectiveness of vaccines to be 56% in preventing illness, 50% in reducing hospitalization, and 68% for preventing death.

In elderly nursing home residents, vaccine effectiveness is ~30% for preventing illness, but ~47–95% for reducing hospitalization, pneumonia, and death.

Each year, comprehensive recommendations on the use of influenza vaccines are published by the Centers for Disease Control and Prevention in an April or May issue of *Morbidity and Mortality Weekly Report* (Table 29–1, adapted from Centers for Disease Control and Prevention, 2000). In general, influenza vaccination is recommended for the groups listed in Table 29–1.

Information on vaccinating people with human immunodeficiency virus (HIV) infection against influenza is limited. The main issues in question are whether persons with HIV are at elevated risk of influenza or serious complications from influenza, whether immunization poses a risk of accelerating HIV replication, and whether immunization is protective. Recent studies suggest that persons with HIV are at high-risk for developing complications from influenza. Because vaccine may result in protective antibody levels, it is felt that influenza vaccination will benefit many HIV-infected patients.

A. Side Effects of Vaccinations. The most common side effects of influenza virus vaccine consist of local effects, particularly soreness around the vaccination site, which occurs in as many as one-third of recipients. Fever, malaise, and myalgia are infrequent, and recent studies suggest that split-virus influenza vaccine does not lead to higher rates of systemic symptoms than placebo in young adults and the elderly.

B. Complications of Influenza Vaccination. The most serious potential neurologic complication

---

Table 29–1. Target population for influenza vaccination.*

I. Groups at increased risk for complications of influenza:

- Persons aged ≥65 years.
- Residents of nursing homes and other chronic-care facilities housing persons who have chronic medical disorders.
- Adults and children with chronic pulmonary and cardiac diseases, including children with asthma.
- Adults and children with chronic metabolic diseases (including diabetes mellitus), renal dysfunction, hemoglobinopathies, or immunosuppression.
- Children and teenagers (aged 6 months to 18 years) receiving continuous aspirin therapy and therefore may be at risk for developing Reye's syndrome following influenza.
- Women who will be in the second or third trimester of pregnancy during the influenza season.

II. Groups that can transmit influenza to persons at high risk:
Persons who are clinically or subclinically infected can transmit influenza virus to persons for whom they care or with whom they live. As some persons at high risk (eg, the elderly, transplant recipients, and persons with AIDS) can have a low antibody response to influenza vaccine, efforts to protect these members of high-risk groups against influenza might be improved by reducing the likelihood of influenza exposure from their care givers.

The following groups should be vaccinated:

- Physicians, nurses, and other personnel in both hospital and outpatient care settings.
- Employees of nursing homes and other chronic care facilities who have contact with residents.
- Providers of home care to persons at high risk (eg, visiting nurses and volunteer workers).
- Members (including children) of a household containing high-risk persons.

III. Other groups:
   A. Persons infected with HIV: Limited data are available regarding the frequency and severity of influenza illness in the setting of HIV infection. Decreased immunogenicity may occur with advanced disease, and booster immunization does not improve the immune response for these persons. In addition, the effect that influenza immunization has been shown to have on the replication of HIV type 1 has been inconsistent in studies. Because influenza can result in serious illness and complications and because influenza vaccination may result in protective antibody titers, vaccination will benefit many HIV-infected patients.

   B. Breastfeeding mothers: Influenza vaccine does not affect the safety of breastfeeding for mothers or infants. Breastfeeding does not adversely affect immune response and is not a contraindication for vaccination.

   C. Persons traveling to foreign countries: Exposure risk varies by season and destination. In the tropics, influenza can occur throughout the year; in the Southern Hemisphere, most activity occurs from April through September. Because of the short incubation period for influenza, exposure to the virus during travel can result in clinical illness that begins while traveling, which can be a potential danger, in particular for persons at increased risk for complications.

   Persons preparing to travel to the tropics at any time of year, or to the Southern Hemisphere from April through September should review their influenza vaccination histories and, if not vaccinated the previous fall or winter, should consider influenza vaccination before travel. Persons in high-risk groups should be especially encouraged to receive the most current vaccine. Persons at high risk who received the previous season's vaccine before travel should be revaccinated in the fall or winter with the current vaccine.
   D. Among the general population:
     - Anyone who wishes to avoid influenza.
     - Persons who provide essential community services (to minimize disruption of essential activities during influenza outbreaks).
     - Students or other persons in institutional settings (eg, those who reside in dormitories), in order to minimize the disruption of routine activities during epidemics.

IV. Persons who should NOT be vaccinated:
   - Persons with known anaphylactic hypersensitivity to eggs or to other components of the influenza vaccine (use of antiviral agent is optional at preventing influenza) without first consulting a physician.
   - Adults with acute febrile illness usually should not be vaccinated until their symptoms have abated; however, minor illness with or without fever should not contraindicate the use of influenza vaccine, particularly among children with mild upper respiratory tract infection or allergic rhinitis.

*Adapted from Centers for Disease Control, Morbid. Mortal. Weekly Rep. 2000; 49(R-3).

of influenza vaccine is Guillain-Barré syndrome (GBS), a demyelinating condition of the peripheral nerves. The association between this disorder and influenza vaccine remains unclear, in large part because the disorder is uncommon both among persons who receive and do not receive influenza vaccine. The baseline annual incidence of GBS is about one to two cases per 100,000 adults. In 1976, administration of "swine flu" vaccine was associated with an increase of slightly under one case of GBS per 100,000 adults administered the vaccine. In addition, most of the risk for developing swine flu vaccine-associated GBS occurred within the 6 weeks after vaccine administration and peaked at 3 weeks after vaccination. These vaccine-associated GBS cases were also less likely to be associated with antecedent illnesses and surgical procedures than other non-vaccine–associated GBS cases. Since then, four studies of influenza seasons between 1977 and 1991 did not find a statistically significant increase in the risk of GBS among vaccine recipients. However, a study of the 1992–93 and 1993--94 seasons found an increased risk of approximately one additional GBS case per million vaccinated persons. At this point, the association of GBS and influenza vaccines subsequent to the 1976 swine flu vaccine remains uncertain, but if these vaccines do pose a risk of GBS, the risk is quite small. Influenza vaccine is recommended for people at high risk for influenza-related complications because the risk of serious disease in these persons outweighs their risk of GBS.

C. Contraindications for Influenza Vaccination. Influenza vaccine is contraindicated in infants younger than 6 months because of the high risk of febrile reactions. Only split-virus preparations should be used in children ≤ 13 years of age. Inactivated influenza vaccine is also contraindicated in people with acute febrile disease and persons known to have anaphylactic hypersensitivity reactions to eggs or other components of influenza vaccine. A physician should be consulted when a person at high risk for serious complications has such an allergic history; desensitization therapy and antiviral agents are options for preventing influenza in such persons.

REFERENCES

Arruda E, Hayden FG: Update on therapy of influenza and rhinovirus infections. In Mill J et al: *Antiviral Chemotherapy,* Elsevier, 1996;175.

Betts RF: Influenza Virus. In Mandell: *Principles and Practices of Infectious Diseases,* 1995;1546.

Breese-Hall C, Dolin R, Gala CL, et al: Children with Influenza A infection: treatment with rimantidine. Pediatrics 1987;80:275.

Centers for Disease Control and Prevention: Prevention and control of influenza: recommendations of the Advisory Committee on Immunization Practices (ACIP). Morbid Mortal Weekly Rep 2000;49(RR-3).

Centers for Disease Control and Prevention: Update: influenza activity—United States and worldwide, 1996–1997 season, and composition of the 1997–98 influenza vaccine. Morbid Mortal Weekly Rep 1997; 46:15.

Cox NJ, Kawaoka Y: Orthomyxoviruses: influenza. In Collier L et al: *Topley & Wilson's Microbiology & Microbial Infections,* 9th ed. Virology 1998;1:385.

Douglas RG. Prophylaxis and treatment of influenza. N Engl J Med 1990;322:443.

Govaert TM, Thijs CT, Masurel N, Sprenger MJ, Dinant GJ, Knottnerus JA: The efficacy of influenza vaccination in elderly individuals: a randomized double-blind placebo-controlled trial. J Am Med Assoc 1994;272:1661.

Gross PA, Hermogenes AW, Sacks HS, Lau J, Levandowski RA. The efficacy of influenza vaccine in elderly persons: a meta-analysis and review of the literature. Ann Intern Med 1995;123:518.

Hayden FG, Belshe RB, Clover RD, Hay AJ, Oakes MG, Soo W: Emergence and apparent transmission of rimantidine-resistant influenza A virus in families. N Engl J Med 1989;321:1696.

Hayden FG, Treanor JJ, Betts RF, Lobo M, Esinhart JD, Hussey EK: Safety and efficacy of the neuraminadase inhibitor GG167 in experimental human influenza. J Am Med Assoc 1996;275:295.

Hayden FG et al: Efficacy and safety of the neuraminadase inhibitor Zanamivir in the treatment of influenzavirus infections. New Engl J Med 1997;337:874.

Kilbourne ED: *Influenza.* Plenum, 1987.

Kilbourne ED, Arden NH: Inactivated influenza vaccines. In Plotkin, M, *Vaccines,* 3rd ed. Saunders (In press).

Lasky T et al: The Guillain-Barré syndrome and the 1992–1993 and 1993–1994 influenza vaccines. N Engl J Med 1998;339:1797.

Murphy BR, Webster RG: Orthomyxoviruses. In Fields BN et al: *Virology ,* 2nd ed. Raven, 1990;1091.

Neuzil KM et al: Influenza-associated morbidity and mortality in young and middle-aged women. JAMA 1999;281:901.

Nichol KL, Margolis KL, Wuorenma J, Von Sternberg T: The efficacy and cost effectiveness of vaccination against influenza among elderly persons living in the community. N Engl J Med 1994;331:778.

Subbarao K et al: Characterization of an avian influenza A (H5N1) virus isolated from a child with fatal respiratory illness. Science 1998;279:393.

Waner JL, Todd SJ, Shalaby H, Murphy P, Wall LV. Comparison of Directogen Flu-A with viral isolation and direct immunofluorescence for the rapid detection and identification of influenza A virus. J Clin Microbiol 1991;29:479.

Yuen KY et al: Lancet 1998;351:467.

30

Parainfluenza Virus

Gregory Sonnen, MD, & Nancy Henry, MD, PhD

Essentials of Diagnosis

- Ubiquitous viral agent.
- Usually diagnosed on clinical findings.
- Can infect upper and lower respiratory tract in all ages.
- Most common etiology of acute laryngotracheobronchitis (croup) in infants and toddlers.
- Frequent cause of lower respiratory tract infection in children.
- Yearly reinfection is common.

General Considerations

A. Epidemiology. Parainfluenza is a ubiquitous virus. It is the primary cause of acute laryngotracheobronchitis (croup) in children aged 6 months to 3 years. It is capable of infecting the lower respiratory tract as well by manifesting as bronchiolitis or pneumonia (Box 30–1). Outbreaks can follow regular epidemic patterns or be sporadic. Certain antigenic types (described below) do follow epidemic patterns.

B. Microbiology. Parainfluenza virus is a spherical, enveloped RNA virus of the *Paramyxoviridae* family. It ranges in size from 100 to 300 nm. The virus has six structural proteins: HN (hemagglutinin-neuraminidase), F (fusion), M (matrix), NP (nucleoprotein), P (phosphoprotein), and L (large). Parainfluenza is not related to influenza virus. The virus has been divided into four types (1, 2, 3, and 4) and two subtypes (4A and 4B) based on antigenic composition. Antigenic shift does not occur as is common in the influenza virus. The virus is labile and sensitive to low pH, heat, and lipid solvents.

C. Pathogenesis. The virus is spread person to person commonly via respiratory droplet nuclei. Other routes include direct contact with respiratory secretions and fomites. The virus adheres to and invades the respiratory epithelium and is transferred from cell to cell. Viremia is uncommon. Pathologic epithelial changes have been noted from the nasal mucosa to the alveoli.

CLINICAL SYNDROMES

ACUTE LARYNGOTRACHEOBRONCHITIS (CROUP)

Clinical Findings

A. Signs and Symptoms. Acute laryngotracheobronchitis, often referred to as croup, is a respiratory illness commonly seen in children 6 months to 3 years of age (Table 30–1). Symptoms, usually nocturnal, include a harsh "seal bark" cough, inspiratory stridor, and, in severe cases, respiratory distress. Rarely the airway may be compromised. Low-grade fever and rhinorrhea may be present. Respiratory symptoms usually recur for 3–5 nights and lessen in severity as the illness progresses.

B. Laboratory Findings. Viral isolation is usually not necessary for appropriate clinical management. If an etiology is sought, culture may be taken from respiratory secretions. The preferred medium is monkey kidney cell medium. Viral antigen may be isolated from respiratory secretions by either enzyme immunoassay or immunofluorescence assay. Serologic evidence is of little clinical value.

C. Imaging. Radiography is usually not necessary for the diagnosis of croup. If the diagnosis is in question, an anterior-posterior radiograph of the neck will demonstrate subglottic narrowing. This finding is commonly called the "steeple sign." Lateral films should also be obtained to rule out other processes such as epiglottitis.

D. Differential Diagnosis. The differential diagnosis of croup includes any situation resulting in upper airway narrowing. Included in this category would be epiglottitis, bacterial tracheitis, foreign body aspiration, retropharyngeal abscess, diphtheria, allergic angioedema, and spasmodic croup.

E. Complications. Children with a medical history involving narrowing of the upper airway are at higher risk of airway compromise from croup. Diagnoses such as subglottic stenosis and tracheomalacia would fall into this category.

BOX 30–1

Parainfluenza Syndromes

	Children	Adults
More Common	• Acute laryngotra-cheobronchitis (croup) • Upper respiratory tract illness	• Upper respiratory tract illness
Less Common	• Bronchiolitis • Pneumonia	• Pneumonia (primarily the elderly)

Diagnosis

Croup is usually diagnosed based on history and physical examination alone. Radiography can help confirm the diagnosis but is often not needed.

Treatment

Treatment is aimed at reducing upper airway edema and inflammation to optimize the upper airway (Box 30–2). In the vast majority of cases, cool, humidified air is optimal. Home use of a humidifier in the child's room is an optimal home therapy. If the child is in distress or fails to respond to humidified air, nebulized racemic epinephrine is indicated. If racemic epinephrine is used, the patient should be closely observed for an appropriate amount of time (usually 4 h). Some patients will experience a "rebound" swelling of the laryngeal mucosa after epinephrine administration. Dexamethasone, adminis-

tered either orally or intramuscularly, will help reduce inflammation and prevent recurrence of symptoms. Dexamethasone is preferred for its long half-life. An inhaled helium-oxygen mixture can be helpful in refractory cases. Nebulized budesonide is very efficacious, but is not yet FDA approved for use in the United States. Intubation is indicated for severe distress or airway collapse.

BRONCHIOLITIS

Clinical Findings

A. Signs and Symptoms. Bronchiolitis is an acute respiratory illness in children aged 6 weeks to 2 years (see Table 30–1). Respiratory syncytial virus is the most common cause (see Chapter 31), with parainfluenza being a much less common cause. Patients present with clear rhinorrhea, fever, tachypnea, cough, and expiratory wheezing. Auscultation of the lungs will also reveal a prolonged expiratory phase. Severe cases will be hypoxemic. Some patients advance to respiratory failure.

B. Laboratory Findings. Laboratory findings are the same as for croup (above).

C. Imaging. Chest radiography will reveal hyperexpansion. Patchy infiltrates and atelectasis may be present.

D. Differential Diagnosis. The differential diagnosis of bronchiolitis includes pneumonia, asthma exacerbation, foreign body aspiration, pulmonary edema, and noxious chemical inhalation.

E. Complications. Children with underlying cardiac or pulmonary disease (eg, congenital heart disease, pulmonary hypertension, bronchopulmonary

Table 30–1. Parainfluenza clinical findings.

Syndrome	Age	Clinical Findings
Acute laryngotracheo-bronchitis (croup)	• Usually 6 months to 3 years	• Symptoms usually nocturnal • Initially harsh cough, "seal bark cough" • Inspiratory stridor • Respiratory distress • Neck radiograph will show subglottic narrowing, "steeple sign" • Symptoms repeat for 3–5 nights
Bronchiolitis	• Usually 6 weeks to 2 years	• Cough • Clear rhinorrhea • Tachypnea • Expiratory wheezing • Hypoxia in severe cases
Pneumonia	• Any age • Primarily infants and the elderly	• Dyspnea • Rales on exam • Febrile
Upper respiratory tract infection (URI)	• Any age • 2–5% of all adult URIs	• Cough • Rhinorrhea • Usually afebrile • Serous otitis media

BOX 30-2

Treatment of Parainfluenza Syndromes

Croup	• Cool, humidified oxygen • Racemic epinephrine, 2.25%, 0.05 cc/kg nebulized in 3 cc saline (max = 0.5 cc) • Dexamethasone, 0.6 mg/kg IM or 0.15 to 0.6 mg orally (max = 10 mg) • Helium-oxygen mixture can reduce the work of breathing in severe respiratory distress • Nebulized budesonide is useful, but is not yet FDA approved • Intubation if airway is severely compromised
Bronchiolitis	• Supportive care • Humidified oxygen, if needed • Bronchodilators remain controversial • Steroids provide no benefit in uncomplicated bronchiolitis • Mechanical ventilation for severe disease
Pneumonia	• Supportive care • Humidified oxygen, if needed • Parenteral antibiotics if bacterial etiology cannot be ruled out
URI	• Supportive care
Host with Severe Combined Immunodeficiency	• Aerosolized ribavirin may modify the infection

dysplasia, asthma, or cystic fibrosis) are at significant risk of serious morbidity from bronchiolitis.

Diagnosis

Bronchiolitis is usually diagnosed based on history and physical examination alone (see Table 30–1). Air trapping will result in hyperexpansion as revealed by chest radiography. Hypoxia and hypercarbia are poor prognostic indicators and warrant aggressive therapy.

Treatment

Therapy is aimed at maintaining oxygenation and adequate air exchange. Supportive care is effective in the vast majority of cases. Tachypneic infants will have increased insensible fluid losses. Intravenous fluids may be needed if dehydration is present. Nasal suctioning to maintain clear nasal passages is warranted in all infants. Oxygen should be provided immediately if hypoxia is present. Bronchodilators may provide some benefit. Mechanical ventilation is indicated if signs of respiratory failure are present. Corticosteroids will be of benefit if the patient has asthma.

PNEUMONIA

Clinical Findings

A. Signs and Symptoms. Pneumonia from parainfluenza may occur at any age (see Table 30–1). Typical presenting symptoms may include fever, dyspnea, tachypnea, purulent sputum, and hypoxemia. Diffuse or localized rales may be auscultated.

B. Laboratory Findings. Laboratory findings are the same as for croup (above).

C. Imaging. Chest radiography may demonstrate patchy or localized infiltrates.

D. Differential Diagnosis. A bacterial or mycoplasmal pneumonia often cannot be excluded.

E. Complications. Patients with underlying pulmonary, immunologic, and cardiac diseases are at risk for serious morbidity.

Diagnosis

Diagnosis is based on physical and radiographic evidence (see Table 30–1). The etiology of pneumonia may be difficult to differentiate, especially in children. A sputum sample is often difficult to obtain from infants and toddlers. If a bacterial source cannot be ruled out, antibiotics are warranted.

Treatment

Antibiotics should be used to cover all appropriate community acquired pneumonias unless a specific etiology can be isolated. Oxygen should be used for hypoxia. Mechanical ventilation should be utilized for respiratory failure.

Prevention & Control

Thorough hand washing will limit the spread of parainfluenza (Box 30–3). No vaccine is currently available. Droplet isolation of the hospitalized patient is indicated. Symptomatic children should be excluded from school or daycare.

BOX 30–3

Control of Parainfluenza Infection

Prophylactic Measures	• Handwashing • No vaccine currently available
Isolation Precautions	• Droplet isolation for hospitalized symptomatic patients • Children should be excluded from school and daycare until symptoms resolve

REFERENCES

American Academy of Pediatrics, Committee on Infectious Diseases: Parainfluenza viral infections. In Peter G (editor): *1997 Red Book: Report of the Committee on Infectious Diseases,* 24th ed. American Academy of Pediatrics, 1997.

Hall CB: Parainfluenza viruses. In Feigin RD, Cherry JD (editors): *Textbook of Pediatric Infectious Diseases,* 3rd ed. Saunders, 1992.

Klassen TB, Rowe PC: Outpatient management of croup. Curr Opin Pediatr 1996;8:449.

Wend CG, Hertz MI: Respiratory syncytial virus and parainfluenza virus infections in the immunocompromised host. Sem Resp Infect 1995;10:224.

Respiratory Syncytial Virus

Gregory Sonnen, MD, & Nancy Henry, MD, PhD

Essentials of Diagnosis

- Most important respiratory pathogen of infancy.
- Passively acquired maternal antibodies provide no protection.
- Can infect upper and lower respiratory tract.
- Symptomatic reinfection occurs throughout life.
- Children with pulmonary or cardiac disease can have serious morbidity from infection.
- Yearly reinfection is common throughout life.

General Considerations

A. Epidemiology. Respiratory syncytial virus (RSV) produces a yearly epidemic in temperate climates. Most commonly, it causes bronchiolitis but can also cause upper respiratory infections, tracheobronchitis, and pneumonia (Table 31–1). In the United States, RSV activity is greatest from December through April. Some variation occurs year to year. The epidemic lasts from 2 to 5 months. Essentially all children are infected during the first 3 years of life. Yearly reinfection is common throughout life. The virus is responsible for ~90,000 hospital admissions and 4,500 deaths/year in the United States.

B. Microbiology. RSV is a 120- to 300-nm enveloped RNA virus of the *Paramyxoviridae* family. It is in the genus *Pneumovirus*. The viral RNA encodes 10 proteins, 7 of which are structural (F, G, L, M, N, P, and SH). Two antigenic strains have been identified and are differentiated based on the G surface glycoprotein. The epidemiologic and clinical significance of the antigenic variation is unknown. The virus is very labile regarding temperature variation; however, the lability of this virus does not reflect on its high degree of communicability.

C. Pathogenesis. The virus is transferred via droplet nuclei, direct contact, and fomites. The virus has been shown to remain viable on fomites for hours and on the human hand for ≥ 30 min. Nosocomial infections are very frequent and warrant strict adherence to hospital isolation procedures.

RSV adheres to and invades the respiratory epithelium. It has an incubation period of 2–8 days. The virus spreads cell to cell via intracytoplasmic bridges. It has potential to cause pathologic changes along the entire respiratory tract. Pulmonary pathology commonly noted during autopsy of infants with RSV bronchiolitis includes peribronchiolar mononuclear infiltration, epithelial necrosis of bronchioles, luminal plugging, airway hyperinflation, and atelectasis. Patients with RSV pneumonia also show evidence of mononuclear interstitial infiltration.

CLINICAL SYNDROMES

BRONCHIOLITIS

Clinical Findings

A. Signs and Symptoms. Bronchiolitis is an acute respiratory illness affecting primarily infants (Box 31–1). RSV is the most common etiology. Patient ages range from 6 weeks to 2 years, with a peak incidence from 2 to 6 months of age. Presenting symptoms commonly include low-grade fever, clear rhinorrhea, tachypnea, cough, and expiratory wheezing. Hypoxemia and respiratory failure may occur in advanced or complicated cases. Dehydration may be present owing to increased insensible fluid losses and poor intake of fluids.

B. Laboratory Findings. Viral isolation and antigen testing are performed from nasopharyngeal washings. Instillation of 1–2 cc of sterile saline in a nasal passage followed by prompt suction with an in-line suction trap will obtain a good specimen. Culturing requires 3–5 days and is optimal on human heteroploid, monkey kidney, human kidney, and fibroblast cells. Viral antigen can be detected with an immunofluorescence assay or enzyme immunoassay.

C. Imaging. Chest radiographs commonly display hyperinflation. Occasionally atelectasis or diffuse infiltrates are seen.

D. Differential Diagnosis. The differential diagnosis of bronchiolitis includes pneumonia, asthma exacerbation, foreign-body aspiration, and noxious-chemical inhalation.

E. Complications. In healthy infants, the disease lasts 3–7 days. Children with an underlying pulmonary or cardiac disease can have prolonged courses lasting weeks. Recurrent episodes of wheezing

Table 31–1. RSV clinical findings.

Syndrome	Age Group	Clinical Findings
Upper respiratory tract illness	• More common in older children and adults	• Cough • Profuse rhinorrhea • Serous otitis media • Pharyngitis
Tracheobronchitis	• All ages	• Hoarseness • Cough
Bronchiolitis	• Range of 6 weeks to 2 years • Peak of 2–6 months	• Tachypnea • Cough • Expiratory wheezing • Clear rhinorrhea • Radiographic evidence of pulmonary hyperinflation • Low-grade fever
Pneumonia	• Infants, toddlers, & the elderly	• Respiratory distress • Diffuse, fine rales • Radiographic evidence of diffuse interstitial infiltrates • Fever

may occur in ≤ 50% of infants infected by RSV. The wheezing may last until 3 years of age.

PNEUMONIA

A. Signs and Symptoms. Pneumonia from RSV typically occurs in infants and the elderly. Typical presenting symptoms may include fever, dyspnea, tachypnea, and hypoxemia. Diffuse, fine rales may be auscultated.

B. Laboratory Findings. Same as laboratory findings for bronchiolitis (above).

C. Imaging. Chest radiography demonstrates diffuse interstitial infiltrates.

D. Differential Diagnosis. Exclusion of a bacterial etiology may be difficult.

E. Complications. Patients with underlying pulmonary, immunologic, and cardiac disease are at risk for serious morbidity.

Diagnosis

Diagnosis of most RSV infections is based on physical and radiographic findings (see Table 31–1). Rapid antigen detection is often helpful, especially in compromised infants. Evidence of hypoxemia at presentation warrants aggressive therapy.

Treatment

Therapy is aimed at maintaining oxygenation and adequate air exchange. Supportive care is effective in the vast majority of cases. Tachypneic infants will have increased insensible fluid losses. Intravenous fluids may be needed if dehydration is present. Nasal suctioning to maintain clear nasal passages is warranted in all infants. Oxygen should be provided im-

BOX 31–1

RSV Syndromes

More Common	• Bronchiolitis (primarily infants) • Pneumonia • Tracheobronchitis • Upper respiratory tract ilness • Asthma exacerbation	• Upper respiratory tract illness • Asthma exacerbation
Less Common	• Otitis media	• Tracheobronchitis • Pneumonia (primarily the elderly)

BOX 31-2

Treatment of RSV

Condition	Indications	Dosage
Supportive Care	• All uncomplicated cases of bronchiolitis and pneumonia	• Humidified oxygen • Antipyretics • Parenteral hydration, if needed
Mechanical Ventilation	• Respiratory failure	• Titrate to maintain oxygenation and adequate air exchange
Immunoprophylaxis with Palivizumab Intramuscular Monoclonal Antibody Injection	• Infants < 2 years old with broncho-pulmonary dysplasia who require oxygen or have needed oxygen in the 6 months before RSV season • Infant < 1 year old with bronchopul-monary dysplasia who are on any chronic respiratory treatment • Infants < 1 year old with a gesta-tional age of ≤ 28 weeks at birth • Infants < 6 months old with a gesta-tional age of 29–32 weeks at birth • Infants < 6 months old with a gesta-tional age of 32–35 weeks who have passive exposure to smoke, attend day care, or experience other pulmonary risk factors • Not FDA approved alone for congenital heart disease • Contraindicated in cyanotic congenital heart disease	• 15 mg/kg intramuscularly in the anterolateral thigh • Dose is given montly from November through April in most temperate climates. Consult local health offi-cials for RSV epidemiology in spe-cific regions
I-β-D-Ribofuranosyl-1,2,4-triazole-3-carboxamide (Ribavirin)	• Complex congenital heart disease • Pulmonary hypertension • Bronchopulmonary dysplasia • Chronic lung disease, including cystic fibrosis • Immunosuppressed state • Premature birth (less than 37 weeks gestation) • Healthy infants less than 6 weeks of age • Severely ill and recalcitrant to suppor-tive measures	• Administer 6 g, diluted to 20 mg/ml, aerosolized over 12 to 18 hours for 3 to 7 days. Administered via Viratek Small Particle Aerosol Gen-erator (SPAG 2) • For maximum efficacy, ribavirin should be administered as early as possible after onset of symptoms • Avoid use in pregnant women • Ribavirin may interfere with some mechanical ventilators
Corticosteroids	• Virus-induced asthma • No proven benefit in healthy infants with uncomplicated bronchiolitis	• Prednisone (or equivalent) 1 mg/kg divided twice a day for 5 d (max dose = 60 mg/d) • Higher doses are indicated in some cases and should be used with caution
Bronchodilators	• Asthma or clinical evidence of broncho-spasm • Benefit is controversial in healthy infants with uncomplicated bronchiolitis	• Albuterol 0.5%, 0.05 to 0.15 mg/kg dose nebulized every 4 h (max dose = 2.5 mg/dose) • Higher doses are indicated in some cases and should be used with caution

mediately if hypoxia is present. Bronchodilators may provide some benefit in bronchiolitis. Mechanical ventilation is indicated if signs of respiratory failure are present. Corticosteroids will benefit if the patient has asthma.

Immunoprophylaxis is highly effective if used appropriately (Box 31–2). Administration of ribavirin should be reserved for severe, refractory cases and infants compromised by cardiac, pulmonary, or immunologic disease. A history of prematurity also warrants consideration of ribavirin use. Ribavirin does interfere with some mechanical ventilators and small endotracheal tubes. Extreme caution should be observed with its use.

Prevention & Control

Thorough hand washing will limit the spread of RSV (Box 31–3). No vaccine is currently available. Immunoprophylaxis is effective in high-risk infants. Droplet isolation of the hospitalized patient is indicated. Strict isolation may be indicated in some hospital environments. Hospital isolation procedures should be strictly enforced. RSV is a common source of nosocomial infection. Symptomatic children should be excluded from school or daycare. Viral shedding usually lasts from 3 to 8 days after the onset of symptoms. Rare cases may shed virus for as long as 4 weeks.

BOX 31–3

Prevention & Control of RSV

Prophylactic Measures	• Hand washing, disinfection of fomites • RSV vaccine is in clinical trials • Immunoprophylaxis for high-risk infants (see Box 31–2)
Isolation Precautions	• Droplet isolation for hospitalized patients; strict isolation may be indicated in certain environments • Children should be excluded from school and daycare until symptoms resolve • Viral shedding can last as long as 4 weeks; usually 3 to 8 d

REFERENCES

American Academy of Pediatrics, Committee on Infectious Diseases: Prevention of RSV: Indications for the use of Palivizumab and update on the use of RSV-IGIV. Pediatrics 1998;102:1211.

American Academy of Pediatrics, Committee on Infectious Diseases: Reassessment of indications for ribavirin therapy. Pediatrics 1996;97:137.

American Academy of Pediatrics, Committee on Infectious Diseases: Respiratory syncytial virus. In Peter G, (editor): *1997 Red Book: Report of the Committee on Infectious Diseases,* 24th ed. American Academy of Pediatrics, 1997.

American Academy of Pediatrics, Committee on Infectious Diseases, Committee on Fetus and Newborn: Respiratory syncytial virus immune globulin intravenous: Indications for use. Pediatrics 1997;99:645.

Groothuis JR et al: Prophylactic administration of respiratory syncytial virus immune globulin to high-risk infants and young children. N Engl J Med 1993;329:1524.

Hall CB: Respiratory syncytial virus. In Feigin RD, Cherry JD (editors): *Textbook of Pediatric Infectious Diseases,* 3rd ed. Saunders, 1992.

32

Adenoviruses

W. Lawrence Drew, MD, PhD

Essentials of Diagnosis

- Respiratory symptoms (plus conjunctivitis).
- Disseminated infection in immunocompromised patients.
- Intranuclear inclusions in infected epithelial cells;
- Growth in tissue culture, especially in human embryonic epithelial cells (eg, kidney, lung).
- Antigen detection in clinical samples (eg, respiratory by immunofluorescence).
- Detection of antibody to the adenovirus group antigen by several different assays (eg, complement fixation, hemagglutination inhibition).

General Considerations

Adenoviruses were first isolated in 1953 in human adenoid cell culture. Since then approximately 100 serotypes, at least 47 of which infect humans, have been recognized. All human serotypes are included in a single genus within the family *Adenoviridae*. Based on homology studies and hemagglutination patterns, each of the 47 serotypes belongs to one of six subgroups. Disorders caused by the adenoviruses include respiratory tract infection, conjunctivitis, hemorrhagic cystitis, and gastroenteritis.

A. Epidemiology. From 5% to 10% of pediatric respiratory disease can be attributed to adenoviruses. Adenoviruses spread by either respiratory or fecal-oral contact but have been cultured from semen and may also be spread by sexual transmission. Adenoviruses may be shed intermittently from the pharynx and especially in the feces. Most infections are asymptomatic, which greatly facilitates their spread in the community.

Infections with serotypes 1, 2, and 5 are very common in children under 2 years of age and may occur as outbreaks especially in older children. Adenoviruses serotypes 4 and 7 seem especially able to spread and cause outbreaks among military recruits owing to very close, crowded living conditions. Outbreaks of swimming pool conjunctivitis have resulted from inadequate chlorination and the low antibody prevalence to these serotypes in children and young adults.

B. Microbiology. Adenoviruses are double-stranded DNA viruses with a genome molecular weight of 20×10^6 to 25×10^6 daltons. The core complex within the capsid includes viral DNA and at least two major proteins. In addition there are nine structural proteins.

The virions are nonenveloped icosahedrons with a diameter of 70–90 nm. Projections, or fibers, originate from each of the 12 vertices of the protein capsid. The capsid is composed of 240 capsomeres, which consist of hexons and pentons.

Replication of adenoviruses has been studied extensively in HeLa cell culture. One virus cycle takes ~ 32–36 h and produces 10,000 virions. The replicative cycle is divided into several stages: attachment, penetration, uncoating, and early and late events. Attachment is probably mediated by the viral fiber protein and a receptor on the host cell membrane. There are approximately 100,000 fiber receptors per cell. The virus enters the cell by endocytosis and is uncoated in the cytoplasm, with subsequent replication in the nucleus. This entire process requires 2 h. Early transcriptional events, after shutdown of host cell macromolecular synthesis, lead to gene products involved in viral DNA replication and cell transformation.

Viral DNA replication in the nucleus signals the beginning of the late phase. In addition, late transcripts encode viral structural proteins at a maximum rate 20 h after infection. Virion capsomeres are produced in the cytoplasm and then transported to the nucleus for viral assembly. DNA possibly enters the capsid through an opening at one of the vertices. The mature particle is stable and infectious. Infected host cells release the virus upon degeneration and cell disruption.

C. Pathogenesis. Adenoviruses infect epithelial cells lining respiratory and enteric organs. After local replication, viremia may occur with spread to visceral organs. This dissemination is more likely to occur in immunocompromised patients. Variations in target cell specificity among adenovirus serotypes result from differences in viral attachment proteins. The virus has a propensity to become latent in lymphoid tissue, such as adenoids, tonsils, or Peyer's patches, and can be reactivated by immunosuppression.

The histologic hallmark of adenovirus infection is a dense central intranuclear inclusion within an infected epithelial cell. Superficially, this inclusion may resemble those seen in cytomegalovirus infection, but one distinguishing feature is the absence of cellular enlargement (cytomegaly) in adenovirus-infected cells. These inclusions are concentrations of viral DNA and protein. In addition to inclusions, adenovirus infections are characterized by mononuclear cell infiltrates and epithelial cell necrosis. Type-specific neutralizing antibody is associated with protection from reinfection.

CLINICAL SYNDROMES

Adenoviruses cause primary infection in children and, less commonly, adults. Reactivation of virus occurs in immunocompromised children and adults. Several distinct clinical syndromes are associated with adenovirus infection (Box 32–1).

ACUTE RESPIRATORY DISEASE

A. Signs and Symptoms. Acute pharyngitis is usually nonexudative but is associated with fever. Acute respiratory disease is a syndrome of fever, cough, pharyngitis, and cervical adenitis seen primarily in outbreaks among military recruits usually with serotypes 4 and 7. Adenoviruses are definite but infrequent causes of true viral pneumonia in both children and adults including military recruits. Laryngitis, croup, and bronchiolitis may also occur. Pertussis-like illness with a prolonged clinical course has been associated with adenoviruses. Adenovirus conjunctivitis may occur concurrently with acute respiratory disease and may be the clue to an adenovirus etiology.

B. Laboratory Findings. The blood leukocyte count is normal as is the rest of the complete blood count and blood chemistry assays.

C. Imaging. In patients with clinical evidence of pneumonia, chest x-ray may reveal scattered interstitial infiltrates, usually in the lower lung fields.

D. Differential Diagnosis. Influenzal and other viral pneumonias, as well as nonbacterial pneumonias, eg, mycoplasma and chlamydial, are the major components of the differential diagnosis. Influenzal pneumonia has a pronounced seasonal epidemiology, but adenovirus does not.

CONJUNCTIVITIS

A. Signs and Symptoms. Adenoviruses cause a follicular conjunctivitis in which the mucosa of the palpebral conjunctiva becomes pebbled or nodular, while both conjunctivae (palpebral and bulbar) become inflamed. Conjunctivitis may occur sporadically or in outbreaks that can be traced to a common source, eg, swimming pools. Corneal involvement may occur with mechanical irritation of the eye and is most striking when it spreads in epidemic form, eg, shipyard conjunctivitis, also described as epidemic keratoconjunctivitis.

B. Differential Diagnosis. Adenovirus conjunctivitis is frequently bilateral and has a granular or follicular appearance. *C trachomatis* conjunctivitis is similar but is more severe in the bulbar conjunctiva than is adenovirus. Coexisting acute respiratory disease suggests adenovirus, as does preauricular adenopathy.

C. Complications. Keratitis may develop as the conjunctivitis subsides and may persist for months.

ACUTE GASTROENTERITIS

A. Signs and Symptoms. Adenovirus serotypes 40 and 41, which are very difficult to isolate in tissue culture, appear to be responsible for episodes of diarrhea in infants.

B. Laboratory Findings. Adenovirus does not cause an acute inflammatory response. Polymorphonuclear leukocytes are not present in stool smears and are not increased in peripheral blood counts.

C. Complications. Although mesenteric adenitis and intussusception may be complications of adenovirus infections, these associations remain unproven.

BOX 32–1

Adenovirus Infection		
	Children	Adults
More common	• Upper respiratory infection • Pharyngitis • Conjunctivitis	• Acute respiratory disease • Conjunctivitis
Less common	• Hemorrhagic cystitis • Pneumonia • Diarrhea • Pertussislike illness	• Systemic infection in immunocompromised patients • Pneumonia

Table 32–1. Clinical syndromes associated with adenoviruses.[1]

Clinical Syndrome	Virus Serotypes	Patient Group
Acute febrile pharyngitis	1, 2, 3, 4, 5, 7a	Young children
Pharyngo conjuntival fever	5a	Older children
Acute respiratory disease including fever, cough pharyngitis, cervical adenitis, and skin rash	2, 3, **4**, 5, **7**, 8, 11, 14, 21	Military recruits
Conjunctivitis	3, 7, 8, 9, 19	Children and adults
Acute gastroenteritis	**40, 41**	Infants
Acute hemorrhagic cystitis	**11, 21**	Young children
Systemic infection in immunocompromised patients	1, 2, 4, 5, 6, 7, 7a, 11, 31, 32, 34, 35	Children and adults

[1]Highlighted serotypes are especially associated with disease states.

ACUTE HEMORRHAGIC CYSTITIS

A. Signs and Symptoms. Acute hemorrhagic cystitis with dysuria and hematuria is associated with serotypes 11 and 21. This condition occurs predominantly in young boys with blood in urine persisting for an average of 3 days. The associated dysuria and frequency persist for an additional several days.

B. Laboratory Findings. Gross and, subsequently, microscopic hematuria is present for several days.

C. Imaging. No renal or bladder abnormalities are present in x-rays.

D. Differential Diagnosis. Other causes of hematuria include bacterial cystitis, stones, or tumors, but an acute self-limited illness suggestive of urinary tract infection is compatible with adenovirus infection, especially in young boys.

SYSTEMIC INFECTION IN IMMUNOCOMPROMISED PATIENTS

Immunocompromised patients (especially transplant recipients) are at risk of serious adenovirus infections, although not as often as from infections caused by the herpes viruses. Diseases include pneumonia and hepatitis as well as disseminated disease. These illnesses are severe and may be fatal. Infection appears to be from exogenous or endogenous (reactivation) sources. In AIDS patients, adenoviruses appear to be responsible for gastrointestinal disease, as revealed by biopsy. Adenoviruses are also recovered from urine or semen of AIDS patients, but their significance is unknown. There is no known effective treatment for adenovirus infections in patients.

Diagnosis of Adenovirus Infection

Direct detection of adenovirus antigens by fluorescent antibody immunoassays have been used with partial success to rapidly identify adenovirus in clinical samples, such as those from the respiratory tract. Enzyme immunoassay and electron microscopy are used to identify enteric adenovirus serotypes 40 and 41, which do not grow in heteroploid cell cultures but may be responsible for infant diarrhea (Table 32–1). Characteristic intranuclear inclusions can be seen in infected tissue during histologic examination. Inclusions, however, are rare and must be distinguished from those resulting from cytomegalovirus.

Isolation of the virus is best accomplished in cell cultures derived from epithelial cells, for example, primary human embryonic kidney (HEK) cells or continuous (transformed) lines such as HeLa or human epidermal carcinoma (Hep-2) cells. Recovery in cell culture requires an average of 6 days. Isolation of adenovirus in culture has variable significance. If the isolate is from a site not frequently colonized by adenovirus, isolation may be diagnostic of the etiology (eg, recovery from conjunctiva, bloody urine, or viscera such as the lung). However, recovery from stool but not the respiratory tract of a patient with pharyngitis provides little diagnostic help. Adenoviruses may be shed in feces for weeks to months after infection. Isolation of adenovirus from the throat of a patient with pharyngitis is usually diagnostic, if laboratory findings eliminate other common etiologies such as *Streptococcus pyogenes*.

Complement fixation, hemagglutination inhibition, enzyme immunoassay, and neutralization techniques have been used to detect specific antibodies after adenovirus infection. A seroconversion between acute and convalescent serum specimens is necessary before the result can be considered diagnostic of active infection, although a fourfold or greater rise in titer may also be of diagnostic significance. Serologic diagnosis is rarely used except occasionally to confirm the significance of a fecal or upper respiratory isolate.

BOX 32–2	
Control of Adenovirus Infection	
Prophylactic measures	• Vaccine (military recruits)
Isolation precautions	• Respiratory, enteric

Prevention & Control

Live, oral enteric-coated vaccines have been used to prevent adenovirus 4 and 7 infections in military recruits, but they are not used in the civilian population (Box 32–2). Because the virus may be oncogenic, it is unlikely that live virus vaccines will be widely used. However, genetically engineered subunit vaccines could be prepared and used in the future.

REFERENCES

Fox JP, Hall CE, Cooney M: The Seattle Virus Watch. VII. Observations of adenovirus infections. Am J Epidemiol 1977;105:362. (The definitive study of adenovirus respiratory infection in civilians.)

Hierholzer JC: Adenoviruses in the immunocompromised host. Clin Microbiol Rev 1992;5:262.

33

Herpesviruses

W. Lawrence Drew, MD, PhD

The herpesvirus group of the family *Herpesviridae* comprises large, enveloped, double-stranded DNA viruses found in both animals and humans. They are ubiquitous and produce infections ranging from painful skin ulcers to chickenpox to encephalitis. The major members of the group to infect humans are the two herpes simplex viruses (HSV-1 and -2), cytomegalovirus (CMV), varicella-zoster virus (VZV), Epstein-Barr virus (EBV), herpesvirus 6, and the recently discovered human herpesvirus types 7 and 8. Occasionally, the simian herpesvirus, herpes B virus, has caused human disease.

All herpesviruses are morphologically similar with an overall diameter of 180–200 nm. The nucleic acid core is ~ 30–45 nm in diameter, surrounded by an icosahedral capsid. The capsid is covered by a tegument and a lipoprotein envelope derived from the nuclear membrane of the infected host cell. The envelope contains at least nine glycoproteins that protrude beyond it as spikelike structures, while the tegument is a protein-filled area between the capsid and the envelope. Despite the morphologic similarity between these agents, substantial differences in the molecular composition of their genomes are reflected in their structural glycoproteins and polypeptides. Antigenic analysis is an important means for differentiation among herpesviruses despite some cross-reactions (eg, between HSV and VZV).

Susceptible tissue cultures vary significantly for the individual agents. HSV has the widest range; it replicates in numerous animal and human host cells. VZV is best grown in cells of human origin, although some laboratory-adapted strains can grow in primate cell lines. Human CMV replicates well only in human diploid fibroblast cell lines. EBV does not replicate in most commonly used cell culture systems but can be grown in continuous human or primate lymphoblastoid cell cultures. Human herpesvirus type 6 grows in lymphocyte cell cultures.

Characteristically, all of these agents produce an initial infection followed by a period of latent infection in which the genome of the virus is present in the cell, but infectious virus is not recovered. Reactivation of virus may then result in the first episode of clinically apparent disease or as recurrent disease. Complex host-virus interactions determine the expression of disease. With all of these agents, immunocompromised patients, especially those with altered cellular immunity, have more frequent and severe episodes, including clinically severe disease from reactivation of virus.

HERPES SIMPLEX VIRUS

Essentials of Diagnosis
- Intranuclear inclusions and multinucleated giant cells in tissue cytology.
- Grows rapidly in many types of tissue culture.
- HSV antigen can be detected in tissue by immunofluorescence.
- Polymerase Chain Reaction (PCR) analysis of cerebrospinal fluid (CSF) now considered best assay for HSV encephalitis.

General Considerations
A. Epidemiology. The term *herpes* (from the Greek herpein, to creep) and the clinical description of cold sores date back to Hippocrates. Two distinct epidemiologic and antigenic types of HSVs exist (HSV-1 and HSV-2). HSVs have worldwide distribution. There are no known animal vectors, and humans appear to be the only natural reservoir (Box 33–1 shows the syndromes caused by HSV). Direct contact with infected secretions is the principal mode of spread. Seroepidemiologic studies indicate that the prevalence of HSV antibody varies directly with the age and socioeconomic status of the population studied. In most underdeveloped countries, 90% of the population have HSV-1 antibody by the age of 30. In the United States, HSV-1 antibody is currently found in ~ 50–60% of the middle-class population. Among lower socioeconomic groups, however, the percentage approaches 90%.

Detection of HSV-2 antibody before puberty is unusual. The virus is associated with sexual activity, and direct sexual transmission is the major mode of spread. Approximately 15–30% of sexually active adults in western industrialized countries have HSV-2 antibody. The virus can be isolated from the cervix and urethra of ~ 5–12% of adults attending sexually transmitted disease clinics; many of these patients are asymptomatic or have small, unnoticed lesions on penile or vulvar skin. Genital herpes is not a reportable

BOX 33–1

Herpes Simplex Infection

	Children	Adults
More Common		• Mucocutaneous lesions, oral or genital
Less Common	• HSV stomatitis • HSV encephalitis • HSV disseminated	• HSV meningitis, encephalitis

disease in the United States, but it is estimated that 500,000 new cases occur per year.

B. Microbiology. The DNA genomes of both types of HSV are linear, double-stranded molecules with molecular weights of ~ 10^8 and are composed of ~ 160 kilobase pairs. Their nucleic acids demonstrate ~ 50% base sequence homology, which is considerably greater than that shown between these viruses and other herpesviruses. HSV-1 and HSV-2 share antigens in almost all their surface glycoproteins and other structural polypeptides. Numerous strains of both HSV-1 and HSV-2 exist. In fact, by restriction endonuclease analysis of the viral genome, most isolates of HSV-1 or HSV-2 are found to differ somewhat, except in epidemiologically related cases such as mother-infant and sexual partner transfer.

C. Pathogenesis. Herpes simplex virus produces both acute and latent infections.

1. Acute Infection. In acute infections, the initial stages entail envelope glycoprotein-mediated attachment of the virus to unidentified receptors and fusion with the host cell membrane. Viral DNA released in the cytoplasm is transported through nuclear pores to the nucleus. New viral DNA synthesis and transcription of mRNA occur in the nucleus. The virus buds through the nuclear membrane; this process adds the envelope material to the virus particles, which are then transported through the cytoplasm and out of the cell in a manner similar to the movement of other proteins.

The molecular events involving synthesis of virus-specific gene products are coordinated and regulated. Three classes of mRNA coding for three groups of virus polypeptides have been identified. The products, designated the alpha or immediate early (IE) polypeptides, are synthesized 2–4 h after infection. These IE polypeptides probably function as regulators of viral transcription. The beta or early (E) polypeptides include virus-specified thymidine kinase (TK) and DNA polymerase (Pol). These virus-specified enzymes differ from host cell enzymes and are therefore important targets of antiviral chemotherapy. The synthesis of early polypeptides shuts off the synthesis of immediate early polypep-

tides and induces the synthesis of a third group of gamma or late (L) polypeptides. The late polypeptides, synthesized 12–15 h after infection, are the major structural components of the viral particle.

Pathologic changes during acute infections consist of development of multinucleated giant cells, ballooning degeneration of epithelial cells, focal necrosis, eosinophilic intranuclear inclusion bodies, and an inflammatory response characterized by an initial polymorphonuclear neutrophil infiltrate and a subsequent mononuclear cell infiltrate. The virus can spread intra- or interneuronally or through the supporting cellular networks of an axon or nerve, resulting in latent infection of sensory and autonomic nerve ganglia. The spread of virus can occur by cell-to-cell transfer and can therefore be unaffected by circulating immune globulin.

2. Latent Infection. In humans, latent infection by HSV-1 has been demonstrated, by co-cultivation techniques, in trigeminal, superior cervical, and vagal nerve ganglia and occasionally in the S2-3 dorsal sensory nerve root ganglia. Latent HSV-2 infection has been demonstrated in the sacral (S2-3) ganglia. Latent infection of neural tissue by HSV does not result in the death of the cell; however, the exact mechanism of viral genome latency is incompletely understood. The HSV genome exists in a circular form in latently infected neuronal cells. Transcription of only a small portion of the viral genome is abortive and does not appear to be associated with detectable amounts of early eg, (Pol) or TK, or late polypeptides. Therefore, unfortunately, antiviral drugs directed at the viral DNA polymerase do not eradicate the virus in its latent state.

Reactivation of virus from latently infected ganglionic cells with subsequent release of infectious virions appears to account for most recurrences of both genital and oralabial infections. The mechanisms by which latent infection is reactivated are unknown. Precipitating factors that initiate reactivation of herpes simplex include fever, trauma (eg, oral intubation), and exposure to ultraviolet light.

D. Immunity. Host factors have a major effect on clinical manifestations of HSV infection. Many episodes of HSV infection are either asymptomatic or mildly symptomatic. If initial clinical episodes of the disease are symptomatic, they are more severe than recurrent episodes, probably because of the presence of anti-HSV antibodies and immune lymphocytes in persons with recurrent infections.

Neutralizing antibodies directed against HSV envelope glycoproteins appear to be important protective responses, particularly those that mediate antibody-dependent cellular cytotoxicity (ADCC) reactions. ADCC may be important in limiting early spread of HSV. By the second week of infection, cytotoxic T lymphocytes can be detected that are able to destroy HSV-infected cells before completion of the replication cycle. Prior infection with HSV-1 may protect against or shorten the duration of symptoms and lesions during subsequent infection with HSV-2. In immunosuppressed patients, especially those with depressed cell-mediated immunity, reactivation of HSV may be associated with prolonged viral excretion and persistence of lesions.

CLINICAL SYNDROMES

1. HERPES SIMPLEX TYPE 1 (HSV-1)

Clinical manifestations of infection with HSV-1 usually are found above the waist. They consist characteristically of grouped or single vesicular lesions that become pustular and coalesce to form single or multiple ulcers. On dry surfaces, these ulcers scab before healing; on mucosal surfaces, they re-epithelialize directly. HSV can be isolated from almost all ulcerative lesions, but the titer of virus decreases as the lesions progress. Infections generally involve ectoderm (skin, mouth, vagina, conjunctiva, and nervous system).

Primary infection with HSV-1 is often asymptomatic. When clinically evident, it appears most frequently as gingivostomatitis with fever, and vesicular or ulcerative lesions involving the buccal mucosa, tongue, gums, and pharynx. The lesions are quite painful, and the illness usually lasts 5–12 days. After this initial infection, HSV may become latent within sensory nerve root ganglia of the trigeminal nerve.

Recurrent lesions usually appear on an area of the lip and the immediately adjacent skin; these lesions are described as mucocutaneous and are commonly called cold sores or fever blisters. Because reactivation is usually from a single latent source, these lesions are typically unilateral. Their recurrence may be signaled by premonitory tingling or burning in the area. Systemic complaints are unusual, and the episode generally lasts approximately 7 days. HSV may be reactivated and excreted into the saliva with no apparent mucosal lesions present. HSV has been isolated from saliva in 5–8% of children and 1–2% of adults who were asymptomatic at the time.

HSV sometimes infects the finger or nail area. This infection, termed *herpetic Whitlow,* usually results from the inoculation of infected secretions through a small cut in the skin. Painful vesicular lesions of the finger develop and pustulate and are often mistaken for bacterial infection and mistreated accordingly. Health care workers, especially nurses and respiratory therapists, are at particular risk for this entity.

HSV infection of the eye is one of the most common causes of corneal damage and blindness in the developed world. Infections usually involve the conjunctiva and cornea, and characteristic dendritic ulcerations are produced. With recurrence of disease, there may be deeper involvement with corneal scarring. Occasionally there may be extension into deeper structures of the eye, egiritis, especially if topical steroids are used.

HSV encephalitis is a rare result of HSV-1 infection, occurring in ~ 1–10 humans/million/year. Although rare, herpes encephalitis accounts for ~ 10% of all cases of documented viral encephalitis in the United States. Most cases occur in adults with high levels of anti-HSV-1 antibody, suggesting reactivation of latent virus in the trigeminal nerve root ganglion and extension of productive (lytic) infection into the temporoparietal area of the brain.

Since the disease usually affects one temporal lobe, focal neurologic signs are frequent. Clinically, the disease can resemble brain abscess, tumor, or intracerebral hemorrhage.

2. HERPES SIMPLEX TYPE 2 (HSV-2)

Genital herpes is a common sexually transmitted disease. Both HSV-1 and HSV-2 can cause genital disease, and the symptoms and signs of acute infection are similar for both viruses. Of first episodes of genital HSV infection in the United States, 70% are caused by HSV-2. As with type 1 oral infection, the majority of genital infections are asymptomatic without lesions, and patients do not know they have been infected. Patients with asymptomatic genital HSV may be culture or PCR positive in genital secretions and are able to transmit the virus to sex partners.

A. Primary Genital Herpes Infection. The mean incubation period from sexual contact to onset of lesions is 5 days. Lesions begin as small erythematous papules that soon form vesicles and then pustules. Within 3 to 5 days the vesiculopustular lesions break to form painful coalesced ulcers that subsequently dry; some form crusts and heal without scarring. With primary disease the genital lesions are usually multiple, bilateral, and extensive. The urethra and cervix are also infected frequently, with discrete or coalesced ulcers on the exocervix. Bilateral enlarged tender inguinal lymph nodes are usually present and may persist for weeks to months. About one-third of patients show systemic symptoms such as fever, malaise, and myalgia, and 1–10% develop aseptic meningitis with neck rigidity and severe headache. First episodes of disease usually last 20–30 days.

B. Recurrent Genital Infection. In contrast to primary infection, recurrent genital herpes is a disease of shorter duration, usually localized in the genital region, without systemic symptoms. Prodromal paresthesias in the perineum, genitalia, or buttocks occur 12–24 h before the appearance of lesions. Recurrent genital herpes usually presents with grouped vesicular lesions in the external genital region. Local symptoms such as pain and itching are mild, lasting 4–5 days, and lesions usually last 10–14 days. Recurrent meningitis due to HSV-2 does occur.

3. NEONATAL HERPES

Neonatal herpes usually results from transmission of virus during delivery, as the neonate passes through infected genital secretions of the mother. True congenital in utero infection, although possible, is uncommon. The prevalence rate of neonatal herpes varies greatly among populations but is estimated at ~ 1/2500 live births in the United States. This estimate is based on the observation that ~ 0.5–1.0% of women excrete HSV from the cervix at the onset of labor and ~ 6% of babies born through infected birth canals develop neonatal HSV.

Manifestations of neonatal herpes vary. To a considerable degree, this is determined by the mother's antibody status. If she is experiencing primary HSV infection and has no antibody to pass to the baby, the consequences can be severe. If she is experiencing a reactivation, the baby can be completely protected by maternal antibody. Some infants show disseminated skin lesions only; others have widespread internal organ involvement; still others have involvement of the central nervous system only, with listlessness and seizures. Less commonly, HSV-1 causes neonatal herpes infection, usually resulting from genital HSV-1 lesions or colonization.

Diagnosis

Herpes simplex virus is easily isolated from lesions or tissue by using fibroblasts or a variety of other tissue culture cells. The cytopathic effects of HSV can usually be demonstrated 24–48 h after inoculation. Isolates of HSV-1 and HSV-2 (see below) can be differentiated by staining virus-infected cells with type-specific monoclonal antibodies to the two types or by analyzing restriction enzyme digests of purified viral DNA. Restriction endonuclease digests can also be used to define epidemiologic relationships, that is, identify strains acquired between sexual partners or through mother-infant transmission. A direct smear prepared from the base of a suspected lesion and stained by either the Giemsa or Papanicolaou method may show intranuclear inclusions or multinucleated giant cells typical of herpes (as demonstrated by the Tzanck test) but is less sensitive than a viral culture and doesn't distinguish HSV-1 from HSV-2. Enzyme immunoassays have been developed for direct detection of herpes antigen in lesions. Although early versions of these noncultural tests lacked sensitivity, more recent assessments show ~ 90% correlation with results from cultures. Rapid diagnosis of HSV mucocutaneous lesions can be accomplished with immunofluorescence or other antigen detection methods. Serology should not be used to diagnose active HSV infection, for example, genital or encephalitis; frequently there is no change in antibody titer when reactivation occurs. PCR on CSF is now the test of choice to diagnose HSV encephalitis. PCR positivity eliminates the need for brain biopsy, but the latter

BOX 33–2

Treatment of Herpes Simplex Infection		
	Children	Adults
First Choice	• Acyclovir	• Acyclovir
Second Choice		• Valacyclovir • Famciclovir

should still be performed if PCR is negative in a patient with highly suggestive clinical findings.

Treatment

Several antiviral drugs have been developed that inhibit HSV (Box 33–2). The most commonly used is the nucleoside analog acyclovir, which is converted by a viral enzyme (thymidine kinase) to a monophosphate and then by cellular enzymes to the triphosphate form, which is a potent inhibitor of the viral DNA polymerase. Acyclovir significantly decreases the duration of primary infection but has much less effect when used for treating recurrent infection. Valacyclovir is a prodrug of acyclovir that is better absorbed and can be used in lower and less frequent doses. Famciclovir is an oral drug that is converted to penciclovir, has good bioavailability, is equivalent to acyclovir but can also be given less frequently.

Prognosis

At least 80% of patients with clinically evident primary HSV infection develop recurrent episodes of herpes within 12 months. In patients whose lesions recur, the median number of recurrences is four or five per year. They are not evenly spaced, and some patients experience a succession of monthly attacks followed by a period of quiescence. Most recurrences result from reactivation of virus from dorsal root ganglia. Rarely, recurrent diseases may be caused by reinfection with a different strain of HSV. Ultimately recurrences of herpes diminish in frequency, especially with genital HSV-2 infection. Genital HSV-1 infection recurs to recur less frequently.

If untreated, HSV-1 encephalitis has a mortality of 70%, but intravenous acyclovir reduces mortality especially if given before coma occurs.

Because a normal immune response is absent in the neonate, neonatal HSV infection is an extremely severe disease with an overall mortality of ~ 60%, and neurologic sequelae are high in those who survive.

Prevention & Control

Avoiding contact with individuals with lesions reduces the risk of spread; however, virus may still be spread by individuals shedding virus asymptomatically from the saliva, urethra, and cervix. When lesions are present, sexual intercourse should be

BOX 33-3

Control of Herpes Simplex Infection

Prophylactic Measures	• Avoidance of contact with HSV positive lesions, secretions • Daily acyclovir (OR valaciclovir, famiciclovir) suppresses recurrences of HSV infections • Vaccine ineffective for treatment; under study for prophylaxis

BOX 33-4

Syndromes Caused by Varicella Infection

	Children	Adults
More Common	• Varicella	• Zoster (shingles)
Less Common	• Zoster (shingles) • VZ encephalitis	• Varicella • VZ encephalitis

avoided. Condoms should be used when individuals with a history of type 2 HSV or antibodies have sexual contact with susceptible people, even when lesions are absent. Daily acyclovir, valacyclovir, or famciclovir suppresses recurrences of HSV infections and is indicated for patients who have frequent attacks (Box 33-3). Because of the high morbidity and mortality of neonatal infection, special attention must be paid to preventing transmission during delivery. In some cases Cesarean section may be used to minimize contact of the infant with infected maternal genital lesions; however, Cesarean section may not be effective if rupture of the membranes precedes delivery by several hours. A recently completed trial of a recombinant HSV-2 vaccine in HSV-2–infected patients had no impact on the rate of recurrences. It is not known whether a vaccine would prevent primary infection, although an effective vaccine offers the best hope for controlling the spread of genital herpes infections. Several different vaccines are at various stages of development and testing. Subsequently a recombinant HSV vaccine was similarly ineffective in preventing primary genital HSV-2 infection.

VARICELLA-ZOSTER VIRUS

Essentials of Diagnosis

- Vesiculopustular, generalized rash in a febrile child (varicella or chicken pox)
- Dermatomal pustular eruption in elderly or immunocompromised patient (herpes zoster or shingles)
- Multinucleated, giant epithelial cells with intranuclear inclusions in skin scrapings, tissue biopsy
  Slow growth of virus (5–7 days) in diploid fibroblast cells if fresh vesicles are cultured
- Detection of VZV antigen by immunofluorescence of skin vesicles (best diagnostic test)

General Considerations

A. Epidemiology. VZV infection, the cause of both varicella (chickenpox) and herpes zoster, is ubiquitous (Box 33-4). Nearly all persons contract chickenpox before adulthood, and 90% of cases occur before the age of 10. The virus is highly contagious, with attack rates among susceptible contacts of 75%. Varicella occurs most frequently during the winter and spring months. The incubation period is 11–21 days. The major mode of transmission is respiratory, although direct contact with vesicular or pustular lesions may result in transmission. Infectivity is greatest 24–48 h before the onset of rash and lasts 3–4 days into the rash. Virus is rarely isolated from crusted lesions.

B. Microbiology. VZV has the same general structure as HSV but has its own DNA sequence and envelope glycoproteins. Cellular features of infected cells, such as multinucleated giant cells and intranuclear eosinophilic inclusion bodies, are similar to those of HSV-infected cells. VZV is more difficult to isolate in cell culture than HSV and grows best but slowly in human diploid fibroblast cells.

C. Pathogenesis. The viruses isolated from lesions of chickenpox and zoster (or shingles) are identical. Latency of VZV occurs in sensory ganglia, as shown by in situ hybridization detection of viral DNA in dorsal root ganglia of adults many years after varicella infection.

D. Immunity. Both humoral immunity and cell-mediated immunity are important factors in determining the frequency of reactivation and severity of varicella-zoster. Circulating antibody prevents reinfection, and cell-mediated immunity appears to control reactivation. In patients with depressed cell-mediated immune responses, especially those who have received bone marrow transplants or have Hodgkin's disease, AIDS, or lymphoproliferative disorders, reactivation can occur, and be severe.

Clinical Findings

VZV produces a primary infection in healthy children which is characterized by a generalized vesicular rash termed chickenpox. Chickenpox lesions generally appear on the head and ears, then spread centrifugally to the face, neck, trunk, and extremities. Lesions appear in different stages of evolution; this characteristic was one of the major features to differentiate varicella from smallpox, in which lesions were concentrated on the extremities and appeared at the same stage of disease. Varicella lesions are pruritic, and the number of vesicles may vary from 10 to several hundred. Involvement of mucous membranes is common, and fever may occur early in the course of disease.

Immunocompromised children may develop progressive varicella, which is associated with prolonged viremia, visceral dissemination, and the development of pneumonia, encephalitis, hepatitis, and nephritis. Progressive varicella has an estimated mortality of ~ 20%. In thrombocytopenic patients, the lesions may be hemorrhagic. Adult patients with varicella are more ill and may develop pneumonia.

Reactivation of VZV is associated with the disease herpes zoster. Although zoster is seen in patients of all ages, it increases in frequency with advancing age, when cell-mediated immunity is waning. Clinically, pain in a sensory nerve distribution may herald the onset of the eruption, which occurs several days to a week or two later. The vesicular eruption is usually unilateral, involving one to three dermatomes. New lesions may appear over the first 5–7 days. Multiple attacks of VZV infection are uncommon; if recurrent attacks of a vesicular eruption occur in one area of the body, HSV infection should be considered.

Complications

The complications of VZV infection are varied and depend on age and host immune factors. Postherpetic neuralgia is a common complication of herpes zoster in elderly adults. It involves persistence of severe pain in the dermatome after resolution of the skin lesions and appears to result from damage to the involved nerve root. Immunosuppressed patients may develop disseminated lesions with visceral infection, which resembles progressive varicella. Bacterial superinfection of varicella occurs and is usually caused by gram-positive cocci. Encephalitis may complicate varicella or zoster and may be associated with seizures and in some cases cerebellar signs.

Diagnosis

Varicella or herpes zoster lesions can usually be diagnosed clinically. Scrapings or swabs from the base of lesions may reveal characteristic cells with intranuclear inclusions or multinucleated giant cells identical to those produced by HSV. VZ virus can be isolated from aspirated vesicular fluid inoculated onto human diploid fibroblasts; however, the virus is difficult to grow from zoster (shingles) lesions older than 5 days, and cytopathic effects are usually not seen for 5–9 days. For rapid viral diagnosis, varicella zoster antigen may be demonstrated in cells from lesions by immunofluorescent antibody staining. PCR analysis of CSF may be useful to diagnose VZV encephalitis; cultures are rarely positive.

Treatment

Acyclovir has been shown to reduce fever and skin lesions in patients with varicella (Box 33–5), and its use is recommended in healthy patients over 18 years of age if treatment is begun within 24–48 h of onset of rash. There is insufficient data to justify universal treatment of all healthy children and teenagers with antiviral agents. In immunosuppressed patients, controlled trials of acyclovir have shown efficacy in reducing dissemination, and its use is definitely indicated. In addition, controlled trials of acyclovir have demonstrated effectiveness in the treatment of herpes zoster in immunocompromised patients. Acyclovir may be used to treat herpes zoster in immunocompetent adults, but it appears to have little or no impact on the development of post-herpetic neuralgia, the most important complication of zoster. Treatment should be started within 3 days of the onset of zoster. VZ virus is less susceptible than HSV to acyclovir, so the dosage for treatment is substantially higher. Famciclovir or valacyclovir are more convenient and may be more effective in preventing post-herpetic neuralgia. Some authorities recommend systemic corticosteroids for patients with zoster who are over 60 and have no contraindications. Although steroids do not prevent post-herpetic neuralgia, patients feel better and return to activity faster.

Prevention & Control

High-titer immune globulin administered within 72–96 h of exposure is useful in preventing infection or ameliorating disease in patients at risk for primary infection (ie, varicella) and serious complications (Box 33–6). Immunosuppressed children who are household or play contacts of patients with primary varicella are candidates for this immunoprophylaxis.

BOX 33–5

Treatment of Varicella Infection

	Children	Adults
First Choice	• Acyclovir for children > 12 years who have varicella but no definite consensus	• Varicella: acyclovir, 800 mg 5 times/day • Zoster: acyclovir, 800 mg 5 times/day; famciclovir, 500 mg/8 h; or valacyclovir, 1.0 g 3 times/day
Pediatric Considerations	• An antiviral agent is not recommended for children <12 years	

BOX 33-6

Control of Varicella Infection

Prophylactic Measures	An attenuated VZV vaccine is now recommended for healthy children >1 year of age VZ-specific immune globulin can diminish illness if given within 72 h of exposure. This is reserved for immunocompromised susceptible patients or other special circumstances
Isolation Precautions	If at all possible, patients with varicella or disseminated zoster should not be admitted to hospital; if unavoidable, these patients should be in strict isolation.

BOX 33-7

Cytomegalovirus Disease Syndromes

	Children	Adults
More Common	Perinatal infection, "Daycare" infection	
Less Common	Congenital infection	CMV retinitis (AIDS) • pneumonia (transplant recipients) • CMV enteritis, neurologic disease (all immunocompromised patients) • CMV mononucleosis

Once infection has occurred, high-titer immune globulin has not proved useful in ameliorating disease or preventing dissemination. Immune globulin is also not indicated for the treatment or prevention of reactivation (ie, zoster or shingles). In nonimmunosuppressed children, varicella is a relatively mild disease, and passive immunization is not indicated. Patients with varicella spread the virus by the respiratory route. In both syndromes virus is also present in the skin lesions. Varicella is a highly contagious disease, and rigid isolation precautions must be instituted in all hospitalized patients.

A live vaccine developed by a group of Japanese workers is effective and a single dose is now recommended for healthy children aged 12 months to 12 years and for selected healthy adults who are susceptible.

In immunocompromised children, chickenpox can be extremely serious, even fatal. For these children, the live vaccine is being evaluated and is not currently recommended.

CYTOMEGALOVIRUS

Essentials of Diagnosis
- "Owl eye" cells in tissue biopsy, cytology
- Cultured in diploid fibroblast cells
- Antibody detection of those patients seroconverting or at risk for reactivation
- CMV detection in blood or bodily fluids by antigenemia, PCR, or other DNA-based assays, eg hybrid capture, or by culture

General Considerations
A. Epidemiology. CMV is ubiquitous, and in developed countries ~50% of adults have developed antibody (Box 33–7). Age-specific prevalence rates show that ~ 10–15% of children are infected by CMV during the first 5 years of life, after which the rate of new infections levels off. The rate subsequently increases during young adulthood, probably through close personal contact or sexual transmission of the virus. CMV has been isolated from saliva, cervical secretions, semen, urine, and white blood cells.

Excretion of virus is prolonged after congenital and perinatal infections, probably because of immunologic tolerance, and high titers of virus may be shed for more than 5 years after birth. Transmission of infection in daycare centers has been shown to occur from asymptomatic excretors to other children and, in turn, to seronegative parents. Infected adults, especially immunocompromised adults, also excrete virus for prolonged periods after primary infection or reactivation of latent infection. Latent infection, which may reside in leukocytes and their precursors, can be transmitted by transfusion and organ transplantation.

B. Microbiology. Human CMV possesses the largest genome of the herpesviruses (~240 kilobase pairs), and its replication, although slow, is similar to that of HSV with the sequential appearance of immediate early, early, and late gene products. Strains of CMV demonstrate considerable genomic and phenotypic heterogeneity, and restriction endonuclease analysis of viral DNA has been useful for distinguishing strains epidemiologically. Antigenic variations have been observed but are not of clinical importance.

C. Pathogenesis and Immunity. Cytomegalovirus infects epithelial cells and leukocytes. In vitro, CMV DNA can be demonstrated in monocytes showing no cytopathology, indicating a restricted growth potential in these cells. In addition to nuclear inclusions ("owl eye cells"), CMV produces perinuclear cytoplasmic inclusions and enlargement of the cell (cytomegaly), a property which gives the virus its name.

After primary CMV infection, the virus becomes latent. The exact site(s) of latency and the mechanisms of persistence are not completely understood, but leukocytes, especially mononuclear leukocytes, are suspected to contain latent virus and account for transmission of the virus by blood and leukocyte transfusions. Also, organs such as the kidneys and heart harbor the virus, but the exact cell is not known. Latent CMV infection appears to be reactivated by immunosuppression (eg, by corticosteroids or HIV infection) and possibly by allogeneic stimulation (ie, the host response to transfused or transplanted cells). Cellular damage appears to be caused directly by the viral lytic infection or indirectly by the immune response of the host. An example of cellular damage resulting from a direct cytopathic effect is retinitis in severely immunocompromised AIDS patients, in which blindness occurs as a result of a necrotizing infection by the virus. The beneficial effects of ganciclovir therapy support this notion. In contrast, HCMV pneumonitis in transplant recipients frequently manifests subtle histologic alterations in the face of life-threatening clinical symptomatology and extensive inflammation accompanied by mild viral replication, suggesting that immune-mediated injury is the primary pathologic mechanism. In other instances, both direct and immunopathogenic mechanisms seem to be at work.

Clinical Findings

D. Congenital. Worldwide, 1% of infants excrete CMV in urine at delivery, as a result of infection in utero. On physical examination, 90% of these infants appear normal; however, long-term follow-up has indicated that up to 20% go on to develop sensory nerve hearing loss, psychomotor mental retardation, or both. The infants with symptomatic illness (~ 0.1% of all births) may have a variety of congenital defects or other disorders (such as hepatosplenomegaly, jaundice, anemia, thrombocytopenia, low birth weight, microcephaly, and chorioretinitis). Almost all babies with clinically evident congenital CMV infection are born of mothers who experience primary CMV infection during the pregnancy. Congenital infection frequently also results from reactivation in the mother with spread to the fetus, but such infection rarely leads to congenital abnormalities due to protection by passively transferred maternal antibody.

E. Perinatal. Most population-based studies have indicated that 10–15% of all mothers are excreting CMV from the cervix at delivery. Approximately one-third to one-half of all infants born to these mothers acquire infection. Almost all of these perinatally infected infants have no discernible illness unless the baby is premature or immunocompromised. CMV can also be efficiently transmitted from mother to child by breast milk, but these postpartum infections are also usually benign.

F. Post neonatal. As with intrapartum acquisition of infection, most CMV infections during childhood and adulthood are totally asymptomatic. In adults, CMV may cause a mononucleosis-like syndrome. In immunosuppressed patients, latent CMV may be reactivated and cause very serious disease. In patients receiving bone marrow transplants, interstitial pneumonia caused by CMV is the leading cause of death (90% mortality). In AIDS patients with low CD4 lymphocyte counts CMV often disseminates to visceral organs, causing chorioretinitis, gastroenteritis, neurologic disorders, and disease in other organs.

Diagnosis

Laboratory diagnosis of CMV infection depends on (1) detecting CMV cytopathology, antigen, or DNA in infected tissues or bodily fluids, (2) isolating the virus from tissue or bodily fluids, or (3) demonstrating seroconversion. CMV can be grown in serially propagated diploid fibroblast cell lines but generally requires 3–14 days, depending on the concentration of virus in the specimen. The time for detection can be shortened by centrifugation and immune staining, but culture of blood is less sensitive than antigenemia or DNA-based assays.

Because of the high prevalence of asymptomatic carriers and the known tendency of CMV to persist weeks or months in infected individuals, it may be difficult to attribute a specific disease to CMV by isolation of the virus from a peripheral site. Thus, the isolation of CMV from urine of immunosuppressed patients with interstitial pneumonia does not constitute evidence for CMV as the etiology of that illness. CMV pneumonia or gastrointestinal disease is best diagnosed by demonstrating CMV inclusions in biopsy tissue.

Treatment

Ganciclovir, a nucleoside analog of acyclovir, inhibits CMV replication and reduces the severity of CMV syndromes, such as retinitis and gastrointestinal disease (Box 33–8). When given with hyper immune globulin, ganciclovir is thought to reduce the mortality of CMV pneumonia in transplant recipients.

Foscarnet is an approved drug for therapy of CMV retinitis. Its toxic effects are primarily renal with electrolyte disturbances, whereas ganciclovir is most apt to inhibit bone marrow function. Ganciclovir inhibits CMV DNA polymerase as does foscarnet, but they act on different sites and cross-resistance is rare. Cidofovir is a third approved anti-CMV drug and is the first nucleotide analog to be used in clinical practice. It has a long half-life, which allows it to be given every 2 weeks during maintenance treatment of CMV retinitis, but it is significantly nephrotoxic.

Prevention & Control

The use of blood from CMV seronegative donors or blood that is treated to remove white cells decreases transfusion-associated CMV (Box 33–9).

BOX 33-8		
Treament of Cytomegalovirus Disease		
	Children	Adults
First Choice	Ganciclovir	Ganciclovir, 5 mg/kg/d IV or valgauciclovir 900–1800 mg orally
Second Choice		• Foscarnet, 90–120 mg/kg/d IV • Cidofovir, 5 mg/kg/q 2 weeks IV
Pediatric Considerations	No experience with treatments other than ganciclovir	

Similarly, the disease can be avoided in seronegative transplant recipients by using organs from CMV-seronegative donors. Hyperimmune human anti-CMV globulin has been used to ameliorate CMV disease associated with renal and hepatic transplants. Prophylactic or preemptive ganciclovir and valacyclovir reduce the frequency of CMV disease in both transplant and AIDS patients. There are experimental and clinical data indicating that the use of condoms decreases sexual transmission of CMV. CMV vaccines are being evaluated in clinical trials.

BOX 33-9	
Control of Cytomegalovirus Disease	
Prophylactic Measures	• Avoid organ transplantation or blood donation from CMV seropositive to CMV seronegative • Preemptive ganciclovir diminishes CMV disease in seropositive AIDS patients. Prophylactic ganciclovir or valacyclovir diminshes CMV disease in seropositive or mismatched transplant recipients. Preemptive ganciclovir disminshes CMV disease in seropositive or mismatched transplant recipients. • Vaccine trials are in progress

EPSTEIN-BARR VIRUS

Essentials of Diagnosis

• Atypical lymphocytes in peripheral blood smear
• Heterophile antibody present in high titer in serum
• Immunoglobulin G (IgG) seroconversion or development of antibody to EB nuclear antigen
• Adolescent, young adult with fever, lymphadenopathy, splenomegaly, pharyngitis, and prolonged fatigue
• Infectious mononucleosis may be complicated by laryngeal obstruction, CNS disease, splenic rupture

General Considerations

EBV is the etiologic agent of infectious mononucleosis and certain lymphoproliferative syndromes (Box 33–10).

A. Epidemiology. EBV can be cultured from the saliva of 10–20% of healthy adults. Excretion may persist weeks to months. Infection with EBV is by contact with infected secretions such as saliva. It is of low contagiousness, and most cases of infectious mononucleosis are contracted after repeated contact between susceptible persons and those asymptomatically shedding the virus. Secondary attack rates of infectious mononucleosis are low (< 10%), because most family or household contacts already have antibody to the agent. Antibodies to EBV are found in up to 90% of adults, although the percentage of susceptible adults is increasing in developed countries.

B. Microbiology. The complete 172-kilobase-pair nucleotide sequence of EBV has been mapped. At present there appear to be many fewer genomic strain variations among EBV isolates than among other herpesviruses. Although morphologically similar to the other herpesviruses, EBV can be cultured easily only in lymphoblastoid cell lines derived from B-lymphocytes of humans and higher primates. The virus generally does not produce cytopathic effects or the characteristic intranuclear inclusions of other herpesvirus infections. After infection with EBV, lymphoblastoid cells containing the viral genome can be cultivated continuously in vitro; they are thus transformed or immortalized.

Recent studies suggest that most of the viral DNA in transformed cells remains in circular, noninte-

BOX 33-10		
Epstein-Barr Virus Infection		
	Children	Adults
More Common	Infectious mononucleosis	
Less Common	EBV lymphoproliferaliferative disease	EBV lymphoproliferative disease

grated form as an episome, and a lesser amount is integrated into the host cell genome. Viral antigen expression has been studied by immunofluorescent staining of transformed cell lines under various conditions. One group of proteins called EBV nuclear antigens (EBNAs) appears in the nucleus before virus-directed protein synthesis. Viral capsid antigen (VCA) can be detected in cell lines that produce mature virions. Other cell lines, called nonproducers, contain no mature virions, but express certain virus-associated antigens called early antigens (EA). The latter may be seen as diffuse (D), and as restricted (R) aggregates of staining. Antibodies against these antigens can be detected by serological tests.

C. Pathogenesis. Although EBV initially infects epithelial cells, the hallmark of EBV disease is infection of B-lymphocytes. The virus enters B-lymphocytes by means of envelope glycoprotein binding to surface complement (C3d) receptor; 18 to 24 h later, EBV nuclear antigens are detectable within the nucleus of infected cells. Expression of the viral genome is associated with immortalization and proliferation of the cell. The EBV-infected B-lymphocytes are polyclonally activated to produce immunoglobulin and express a lymphocyte-determined membrane antigen that is the target of host cellular immune responses. During the acute phase of infectious mononucleosis, ~ 20% of circulating B-lymphocytes demonstrate EBV antigens. After infection subsides, EBV can be isolated from only ~ 1% of such cells.

EBV has been associated with several lymphoproliferative diseases including African Burkitt's lymphoma, nasopharyngeal carcinoma, and lymphomas in immunocompromised patients. The factors that render the EBV infections oncogenic in these cases are obscure. The distribution of EBV infections in Africa has suggested an infectious cofactor, such as malaria, which may cause immunosuppression and predispose to EBV-related malignancy. In the case of nasopharyngeal carcinoma, environmental carcinogens probably create the precancerous lesion, which then stimulates the EBV to reactivate. EBV-associated lymphomas have been shown to be of both monoclonal and polyclonal origin. Chromosomal translocations in B cells are characteristic of Burkitt's lymphoma and involve specific breaks in chromosomes at sites of genes encoding immunoglobulins. These translocations lead to expression of oncogenes that may contribute to clonal activation and ultimately to malignancy. Some breakdown in immune surveillance also appears to play a role in the development of malignancy because immunosuppressed patients are more prone to develop B-cell lymphomas. Transplant recipients may develop a lympho-proliferative syndrome with very high titers of EBV in blood.

D. Immunity. EBV-infectious mononucleosis results in the synthesis of circulating antibodies against viral antigens, as well as against unrelated antigens found in sheep, horse, and some beef red blood cells. These heterophile antibodies, a heterogeneous group of predominantly IgM antibodies, are commonly used as diagnostic tests for the disease. Some other immunologic functions are also affected by EBV infection. Cutaneous anergy and decreased cellular immune responses to mitogens and antigens are seen early in the course of mononucleosis.

Although EBV infects B-lymphocytes, the lymphocytosis associated with infectious mononucleosis is caused by an increase in the number of circulating T cells, which appear to be activated cells developed in response to the virus-infected B-lymphocytes. With recovery from illness, the atypical lymphocytosis gradually resolves, and cell-mediated immune functions return to preinfection levels.

Clinical Findings

As with most of the herpesviruses (except varicella), most primary EBV infections are asymptomatic. The clinical syndrome of infectious mononucleosis is characterized by fever, malaise, pharyngitis, tender lymphadenitis, and splenomegaly. These symptoms persist for days to one or more weeks but slowly resolve. Complication such as laryngeal obstruction, ruptured spleen, or a variety of CNS manifestations(aseptic meningitis, encephalitis, etc.) may occur in 1–5% of patients.

Patients with primary or secondary immunodeficiency are susceptible to EBV-induced lymphoproliferative disease. The risk is greatest in those experiencing primary EBV infection rather than reactivation. The most characteristic clinical findings are persistent fever, lymphadenopathy, and hepatosplenomegaly. In AIDS patients, several distinct additional EBV-associated syndromes occur, including hairy leukoplakia of the tongue interstitial lymphocytic pneumonia, especially in infants and lymphoma of the CNS and elsewhere.

Diagnosis

Laboratory confirmation of EBV infectious mononucleosis is usually documented by the demonstration of atypical lymphocytes, heterophile antibodies, or positive EBV-specific serologic findings. Hematologic examination reveals a markedly raised lymphocyte and monocyte count with > 10% atypical lymphocytes. Atypical lymphocytes, although not specific for EBV, are present with the onset of symptoms and disappear with resolution of disease. Alterations in liver function tests may also occur.

Although not specific for EBV, tests for heterophile antibodies are used most commonly for diagnosis of infectious mononucleosis. In commercial kits, animal erythrocytes are used in simple slide agglutination methods, which incorporate absorption to remove cross-reacting antibodies that may develop in other situations, such as serum sickness. The infectious mononucleosis heterophile antibody is absorbed by sheep erythrocytes but not by guinea pig kidney cells. Heterophile antibodies can usually be demonstrated by the end of the first week of illness but may occasionally be delayed until the third or fourth week. They may persist many months.

Approximately 5–15% of EBV-induced cases of infectious mononucleosis in adults and a much greater proportion in young children and infants fail to induce detectable levels of heterophile antibodies. In these cases EBV-specific serologic tests may be used to establish the diagnosis. Antibodies to VCA rise quickly and persist for life. The presence of IgM antibody to VCA is theoretically diagnostic of acute, primary EBV infection, but low levels may occur during reactivation of EBV, and cross-reactivation with antigens of other herpesviruses occur. Antibodies to EBNAs rise later in disease (after ~ 1 month) and also persist in low titers for life. Thus, a high titer to VCA and no titer to EBNAs suggest recent EBV infection, whereas antibody titers to both antigens are indicative of past infection. Persistent antibody to early antigens (anti-EA, -D, or -R) may be correlated with severe disease, nasopharyngeal carcinoma (anti-D), or African Burkitt's lymphoma (anti-R) but are not useful in diagnosing infectious mononucleosis. Isolation of EBV from clinical specimens is not practical because it requires fresh human B cells or fetal lymphocytes obtained from cord blood. PCR is being developed to assay EBV DNA in blood.

Treatment

Treatment of infectious mononucleosis is largely supportive. More than 95% of patients recover uneventfully. In a small percentage of patients, splenic rupture may occur; thus, restriction of contact sports or heavy lifting during the acute illness is recommended. The DNA polymerase enzyme of EBV has been shown to be sensitive to acyclovir, and acyclovir can decrease the amount of replication of EBV in tissue culture and in vivo (Box 33–11). Despite this antiviral activity, systemic acyclovir makes little impact on the clinical illness. Corticosteroids appear to be beneficial in reducing laryngeal edema and severe toxicity. They may also be indicated for CNS complications. Treatment of EBV lymphoproliferative disease includes diminution of immunosuppression as much as possible; acyclovir is also used.

Prevention & Control

Because EBV may be spread by direct person-to-person contact from even asymptomatic individuals, it is unavoidable. Isolation is not practiced owing to ubiquitous infection. The occurrence of Burkitt's lymphoma and nasopharyngeal carcinomas in restricted geographic areas offers the possibility of prevention by immunization with virus-specific antigen(s). This approach is under exploration at present. A subunit vaccine has proved effective in preventing the development of tumors in tamarind monkeys, which are highly susceptible to the oncogenic effects of the virus under experimental conditions.

HUMAN HERPESVIRUS TYPE 6

Essentials of Diagnosis

- Infant with high fever for several days; maculopapular rash after defervescence
- Can be isolated in cultures of monocytes but takes 10–30 days and may be false negative
- Detection of specific IgG and IgM by indirect immunofluorescence are diagnostic tests of choice
- Blood or saliva PCR for HHV-6 DNA may be positive, but diagnostic significance uncertain due to intermittent excretion in asymptomatic patients
- PCR positively in CSF diagnostic of encephalitis

General Considerations

In 1986 a human herpesvirus, now called human herpesvirus type 6 (HHV-6), was identified in cultures of peripheral blood lymphocytes from patients with lymphoproliferative diseases (Box 33–12). The virus, which is genetically distinct but morphologically similar to other herpesviruses, replicates in lymphoid tissue, especially CD4+ T lymphocytes, and has two distinct variants, A and B.

Initially it was thought that HHV-6 would grow only in freshly isolated B-lymphocytes, and the virus was referred to as the human B-lymphotropic virus

BOX 33–11

Treatment of Epstein-Barr Virus Infection	
First Choice	None
Second Choice	Corticosteroids if severe toxicity or airway obstruction
	Acyclovir and/or decrease immunosuppression for post transplant lymphoproliferative disease

BOX 33–12

Exanthem Subitum Syndromes	
More Common	Exanthem subitum
Less Common	Meningitis, encephalitis fever in transplant recipients

(HBLV); now it is clear that the virus is preferentially tropic for CD4+ T lymphocytes. HHV-6 establishes a latent infection in T cells but may be activated to a productive lytic infection by mitogenic stimulation. Resting lymphocytes and lymphocytes from healthy immune individuals are resistant to HHV-6 infection. In vivo, HHV6 replication is controlled by cell-mediated immune factors. It appears to be capable of reactivating in immunosuppressed patients, but its clinical significance in this situation is unknown.

Serologic studies indicate that almost all children are infected by age 2. This makes HHV-6 the most communicable of all human herpesviruses. Most adults shed HHV-6 in saliva, and close personal contact is the most likely route of spread; vertical transmission also occurs.

Clinical Findings

Exanthem subitum occurs in infants and is characterized by fever, eg, 39 °C for several days followed by defervescence and a light maculopapular rash spreading from the trunk to the extremities. CNS complications may occur with febrile seizures, meningitis and encephalitis. HHV-6 may also be a cause of febrile episodes in transplant recipients.

Diagnosis

Virus infection is best documented by seroconversion. Active virus infection can be documented by culture, antigenemia, or DNAemia, but since reactivation or is common, it is very difficult to use these tools to diagnose HHV-6 as the cause of disease. Also, culture takes 10–30 days.

Treatment

HHV-6 appears to be susceptible in vitro to ganciclovir and foscarnet and less susceptible to acyclovir, but no clinical data are available.

Prevention & Control

Because HHV-6 infection is ubiquitous and almost all infants excrete the virus by 2 years of age, no preventative measure is practical. No vaccine is in development, and isolation is not practical owing to ubiquitous infection.

OTHER HERPESVIRUSES

1. HERPESVIRUS TYPE 7

Isolation of human herpesvirus type 7 (HHV-7) was first reported in 1990. The virus was isolated from activated CD4+ T lymphocytes of a healthy individual. HHV-7 is distinct from all other known human herpesviruses but is most closely related to HHV-6. Seroepidemiologic studies indicate that this virus usually does not infect children until after infancy, and ~ 50% of infants are antibody positive by 2–4 years of age. As with HHV-6 this virus is frequently isolated from saliva, and close personal contact is the probable means of transmission. Also like HHV-6 this virus appears to be a cause of exanthem subitum. The diagnosis of acute infection can be made by the demonstration of seroconversion. No treatment has been identified.

2. HUMAN HERPESVIRUS TYPE 8 (Kaposi's sarcoma-associated herpes virus [KSHV])

KSHV was discovered in 1994 by identification of unique viral DNA sequences in an AIDS patient's Kaposi's sarcoma (KS) tissue. The method used was representational difference analysis. Specific HHV-8 DNA sequences are found in the great majority of KS tissues in the United States, including those from non-AIDS cases, and occasionally in other specimens including lymphomas. Recently the virus was isolated in culture and, when characterized, seemed most closely related to EBV. Serologic and virologic data suggest that this virus is at least a cofactor in the pathogenesis of KS.

REFERENCES

Benedetti J et al: Recurrence rates in genital herpes after symptomatic first episode infection. Ann Intern Med 1994;121:847. (Acyclovir treatment of first episodes does not decrease recurrence rates; higher recurrence rates are reported in men, which partly explains higher transmission rates from men to women.)

Caserta MT, Hall CB, Schnabel K et al: Neuroinvasion and persistence of human herpesvirus 6 in children. J Infect Dis 1994;170:1586.

Cone RW, Hackman RC, Huang MW et al: Human herpesvirus 6 in lung tissue form patients with pneumonitis after bone marrow transplantation. N Engl J Med 1993;329:156.

DeRodriguez W, Fuhrer J: Cytomegalovirus colitis in patients with acquired immunodeficiency syndrome. JR Soc Med 1994;87-203. (While diarrhea is common, bloody diarrhea is not.)

Einsele H, Steidle M et al: Early occurrence of human cytomegalovirus infection after bone marrow transplantation as demonstrated by the polymerase chain reaction technique. Blood 1991;77:1104.

Gershon AA et al: Varicella vaccine: the American experience. Infect Dis 1992;166(Suppl 11):S63-S68. (Live attenuated varicella vaccine is safe and effective in preventing chickenpox. The best immune responses occur in healthy children. Leukemic children have a 50% incidence of mild to moderate adverse effects but have a high degree of protection once immune responses to varicella-zoster virus have developed.)

Hall CB, Long CE, Schnabel KC et al: Human herpesvirus-6 infections in children: a prospective study of complications and reactivation. N Engl J Med 1994;331:432.

Jabs DA: Studies of ocular complication of AIDS: mortality in patients with the acquired immunodeficiency syndrome treated with either foscarnet or ganciclovir for cytomegalovirus retinitis. N Engl J Med 1992;326:213.

Jenkins M, Kohl S. New aspects of neonatal herpes. Infect Dis Clin North Am 1992;6:57.

Johnson RE, Nahmias AJ, Magder LS et al: A seroepidemiologic survey of the prevalence of herpes simplex virus type 2 infection in the United States. N Engl J Med 1989;321:7.

Kulhanjian JA, Soroush V, Au DS et al: Identification of women at unsuspected risk of primary infection with herpes simplex virus type 2 during pregnancy. N Engl J Med 1992;326:916.

Lakeman FD, Whitley RJ: Diagnosis of herpes simplex encephalitis: application of polymerase chain reaction to cerebrospinal fluid from brain biopsied patients and correlation with disease. Infect Dis 1995;171:857.

Rooney JF et al: Oral acyclovir to suppress frequently recurrent herpes labialis: a double-blind placebo-controlled trial. Ann Intern Med 1993;118:268.

Strauss SE: Shingles: sorrows, salves and solutions. JAMA 1993;269:1836 (Brief review of antiviral agents, steroids, topical treatment, and vaccines for VZV infection.)

Van Der Horst C et al: Lack of effect of peroral acyclovir for the treatment of acute infectious mononucleosis. Infect Dis 1991;164:788–92. (In this study, 120 patients received 600 mg of acyclovir or placebo five times daily for 10 days. Analysis of all end points in the two treatment groups revealed no significant differences. There was a trend toward suppression of EBV excretion in the oropharynx in acyclovir recipients. No toxicity was detected in patients treated with acyclovir.)

Wald A et al: Virologic characteristics of subclinical and symptomatic genital herpes infections. N Engl J Med 1995;333:770. (Subclinical shedding of HSV is common in women with frequent HSV recurrences.)

Wallace MR: Treatment of adult varicella with oral acyclovir: a randomized, placebo-controlled trial. Ann Intern Med 1993;117:358. (Therapy in the first 24 h decreases time to cutaneous healing, decreases duration of fever, and lessens symptoms.)

Wood MJ: A randomized trial of acyclovir for 7 days or 21 days with and without prednisolone for treatment of acute herpes zoster. N Engl J Med 1994;330:896. (Only a slight benefit in rash healing, pain reduction was conferred by adding corticosteroids or treating for 21 days with acyclovir.)

Measles

34

Gregory Sonnen, MD, & Nancy Henry, MD, PhD

Essentials of Diagnosis

- Epidemic systemic viral illness, primarily of children and young adults.
- Exanthematous disease with fever, cough, coryza, and conjunctivitis.
- Exanthem is a maculopapular, confluent rash that is centrifugally spread from the head to the extremities.
- Koplik's spots are a pathognomonic enanthem that occurs on the buccal mucosa.
- Incidence has drastically dropped in the postvaccination era.

General Considerations

A. Epidemiology. Rubeola, commonly known as measles, is a virus spread primarily in the winter and early spring. Like mumps and rubella, vaccination has drastically changed the epidemiology of measles. In the prevaccination era, rubeola followed a biannual epidemic cycle. It is prevalent throughout the world.

Measles vaccine was introduced for commercial use in 1963. From 1963 to 1967, ~900,000 children received the inactivated measles vaccine. The attenuated, live-virus vaccine was introduced in the late 1960s. By 1973, the inactivated vaccine was no longer available. Before 1963, between 200,000 and 600,000 cases were reported annually in the United States. However, even these reports represent only a fraction of the actual case rate. The number of reported cases dropped from 22,231 in 1968 to 1,497 in 1983.

In the mid-1980s a resurgence of reported cases occurred primarily in the preschool population. Nearly 19,000 cases were reported in 1989. The majority of these cases were in vaccine-eligible, unvaccinated preschool children living in urban areas. In the late 1980s and early 1990s several outbreaks occurred among adolescents and young adults, primarily on college campuses. Most of the cases were in patients with a history of receiving only a single dose of the vaccine. Since 1993, < 1,000 cases have been reported per year. This is likely owing to aggressive revaccination efforts. A second measles vaccination is now standard at ages 4–6 years.

B. Microbiology. Measles is caused by a pleomorphic 100- to 250-nm RNA virus of the *Paramyx-* *oviridae* family. It is a member of the genus *Morbillivirus*. The virus has three structural proteins complexed within its helical nucleocapsid. The lipoprotein envelope contains three proteins (F, H, and M). The F glycoprotein facilitates host cell adhesion and penetration. The H glycoprotein is a hemagglutinin. The M protein is a nonglycosylated protein that lines the inner lipid bilayer and facilitates viral maturation. The virus is labile and sensitive to heat, ultraviolet (UV) light, and extremes of pH.

C. Pathogenesis. Measles virus is spread primarily via respiratory droplet nuclei. Direct contact is also a mode of transmission. Humans are the only natural reservoir for the virus. The primary site of adhesion and invasion is the respiratory epithelium, with quick spread to lymphatic tissues and subsequent viremia.

Measles virus is communicable for 3–5 days before the outbreak of the rash. It remains communicable up to 4 days after the appearance of rash. Immunocompromised patients can shed virus for an extended period of time. Patients who develop subacute sclerosing panencephalitis do not continue to shed virus.

CLINICAL SYNDROMES

TYPICAL MEASLES

Clinical Findings

A. Signs and Symptoms. Typical measles, also referred to as "natural measles," can occur at any age (Table 34–1). Immunity is lifelong, so recurrence is extremely rare. A prodromal phase of 2–4 days is marked by fever, malaise, cough, coryza, conjunctivitis, and pharyngitis. A pathognomonic enanthem of measles (Koplik's spots) erupts on the buccal mucosa during this phase. These appear as small blue to white plaques.

The exanthem phase begins ~2 weeks after exposure. The maculopapular rash first appears on the brow and posterior auricular area. It progresses to

Table 34–1. Measles clinical findings.

	Typical Measles	Modified Measles	Atypical Measles
Cause	• Natural measles infection	• Rare • Incomplete live-virus vaccination series followed by natural measles infection	• Rare • Inactivated measles vaccination, followed by exposure to natural measles virus
Incubation	• 8–12 d	• Similar to typical measles	• 1–2 weeks
Prodromal phase	• 2–4 days duration • Symptoms progressive • Fever & malaise • Cough & coryza • Conjunctivitis • Pharyngitis • Koplik's spots (pathognomonic enanthem of measles) appear on days 9–11; blue to white spots on the lower buccal mucosa	• Similar prodromal symptoms, but less severe and shortened duration • Koplik's spots few to absent	• Sudden onset of high fever • Headache & myalgia • Abdominal pain • Koplik's spots rare
Exanthem phase	• Rash begins 2 weeks after exposure • Fever peaks on day 2 or 3 of rash • Erythematous maculopapular rash which progresses to confluence • Initially involves the forehead & posterior auricular area • Rash spreads from head to feet in 48 to 72 h • Rash begins to clear on day 3 to 4 • Clears from head to feet • Confluent areas desquamate, leaving brown, hyperpigmented areas	• Similar rash morphology and progression • No confluence	• Rash appears on second or third day of illness • Initially erythematous, maculopapular, and spreading from distal extremities to the head • Present on palms and soles • Can progress to vesiculation • Urticaria, purpura, & petechiae are common • Lobar pneumonia with effusion is common

cover the face and spreads to the distal extremities within 72 h. Large areas of the rash will progress to confluence, then desquamate leaving transient hyperpigmented areas. The rash usually begins to clear on the 3rd or 4th day. The fever peaks on the 2nd or 3rd day of the rash.

B. Laboratory Findings. The virus can be isolated from a nasopharyngeal swab, conjunctival swab, blood, and urine during the febrile course of the illness. Isolation of the virus can be technically difficult. A variety of tissue cultures can be used to grow the virus. Human and monkey kidney cell lines are typically used with clinical specimens. Acute and convalescent serologies can be helpful. Serologies should be drawn 2–4 weeks apart to monitor progression. Immunoglobulin M (IgM) is detectable from 3 to 30 days after the onset of rash. Measles antibody is detectable in the cerebrospinal fluid of patients with subacute sclerosing panencephalitis. These patients often have a high IgG titer in the serum as well.

C. Imaging. Chest radiographs may demonstrate diffuse infiltrates if pneumonia is present.

D. Differential Diagnosis. The differential diagnosis of measles includes Kawasaki disease, Stevens-Johnson syndrome, and other viral exanthems.

E. Complications. Acute complications can include meningoencephalitis, pneumonia, otitis media, and laryngotracheitis (Box 34–1). Measles meningoencephalitis occurs in 1 per 1000 cases. It has a high morbidity and mortality rate. "Black measles" is a severe, hemorrhagic variation of typical measles. It

BOX 34–1

Complications of Measles

More Common	• Meningoencephalitis • Pneumonia • Otitis media • Laryngotracheitis
Less Common	• Subacute sclerosing panencephalitis • Myocarditis/pericarditis • "Black measles" • Thrombocytopenia purpura • Stevens-Johnson syndrome • Mesenteric lymphadenitis • Appendicitis

is extremely rare in the postvaccination era. It has a high mortality rate. Patients present with a confluent hemorrhagic skin rash, encephalitis, and pneumonia. Bleeding often occurs via nose, mouth, and gastrointestinal tract.

Measles infection during pregnancy produces significant fetal morbidity and mortality, especially if infection occurs during the first trimester. Measles uncommonly produces severe abdominal pain during the acute febrile phase. Etiologies for this pain can be mesenteric lymphadenitis or appendicitis. Evidence of peritonitis warrants prompt surgical evaluation.

Subacute sclerosing panencephalitis (SSPE) is a rare, late-onset, lethal neurodegenerative sequela of measles infection. It occurs with an incidence of 0.6–2.2 cases/100,000 infections and 1 case/1 million vaccinations. SSPE results from a slowly progressive chronic infection with the virus. SSPE becomes clinically evident an average of 7 years after initial measles exposure. Symptoms include unusual behavior, developmental regression, ataxia, myoclonic jerks, visual impairment, and aphasia. All of these symptoms are progressive, leading ultimately to decorticate rigidity and death, which usually occurs 6–9 months after onset of symptoms. Confirmation of the diagnosis can be made by electroencephalogram, serology, and analysis of the cerebrospinal fluid. Cerebrospinal fluid shows high IgG as does serum. No current therapy is effective.

MODIFIED MEASLES

Modified measles occurs in individuals receiving an incomplete live virus vaccination series and subsequently being infected by the natural virus. It can also occur in infants under 9 months owing to the presence of maternally derived antibodies. It is similar to natural measles infection but less severe (see Table 34–1). The prodromal phase may be shorter and less severe. Koplik's spots may be scant or absent. The exanthem rash usually does not progress to confluence, but has a similar duration. Viral isolation is unaffected. All the complications and sequelae of typical measles can occur.

BOX 34–2

Treatment of Measles

	Indication	Dosage
Supportive Care	• Vast majority of cases	• Antipyretics/analgesics • Fluid
Vitamin A	• Patients 6 months to 2 years of age requiring hospitalization • Immunodeficiency • Ophthalmologic evidence of vitamin A deficiency • Impaired intestinal absorption • Malnutrition • Immigration from an area of high measles mortality	• Children >1 year: 200,000 IU orally • Children 6 months to 1 year: 100,000 IU orally • Repeat dose at 24 h and 4 weeks if clinical evidence of vitamin A deficiency
Immune Globulin	• Susceptible contacts of confirmed cases, especially infants, pregnant women, and immunocompromised • Infants under 5 months have passive immunity if mother has confirmed immunity	• Must be used within 6 days of exposure • 0.25 cc/kg IM • 0.5 cc/kg IM for immunocompromised • Max dose = 15 cc
Live-Virus Vaccine	• Indicated for susceptible contacts who are greater than 6 months of age, not pregnant, and immunocompetent	• Must be used within 72 h of exposure • 0.5 cc SQ • Clinical response variable when used postexposure
Ribavarin	• Severe cases • Immunocompromised	• Not FDA approved for measles treatment • No controlled clinical trials

BOX 34–3

Control of Measles

Vaccine	• Live attenuated measles vaccine is administered 0.5 cc SQ. Commonly given in combination with MMR (measles, mumps, rubella) vaccine • First dose is recommended at from 12 to 15 months of age • Second dose is recommended at school entry (age 4 to 6 years) • If no preschool dose is given, the second dose should be administered before age 12 • Improperly stored vaccine may result in failure • A dose may be given to infants age 6 to 11 months during epidemic conditions; these infants must still follow the two-dose guideline above
MMR Vaccine Contraindications	• Pregnancy • Febrile illness • Planned pregnancy within 3 months • Severe immunocompromised state • Blood product or immune globulin within 3 to 6 months (dose dependent) • Anaphylaxis to neomycin
MMR Vaccine Should Be Used with Caution in These Situations	• Seizure disorder • Thrombocytopenia • Egg allergy
Isolation Precautions	• Respiratory isolation required during the prodromal phase through 4 days from the onset of rash in healthy patients • Immunocompromised patients usually shed virus for an extended period

ATYPICAL MEASLES

Atypical measles occurs in some individuals who received the inactivated virus vaccine in the 1960s and were subsequently exposed to the natural virus. These patients have a prodromal phase noted by sudden onset of high fever, headache, myalgia, and abdominal pain (see Table 34–1). Lobar pneumonia with effusion is common. These patients rarely have Koplik's spots. The exanthem phase begins on the 2nd or 3rd day of illness. The maculopapular rash begins on the palms and soles and spreads centrally. It can progress to vesiculation. Urticaria, purpura, and petechiae are common.

Chest radiographs will commonly show lobar consolidation. Acute and convalescent titers and viral culture are useful. The differential diagnosis of this exanthem includes rickettsial disease, meningococcemia, and hemorrhagic fever.

Diagnosis

Diagnosis of measles is usually based on physical findings. Finding Koplik's spots and monitoring the usual progression of the exanthem are helpful clues. An attempt should be made to culture the virus during the febrile course of the illness. Culture can often be technically difficult. Serology should be obtained as well. Confirmation of a diagnosis should be promptly reported to a local government health agency for epidemiologic tracking.

Treatment

Treatment of measles is often supportive. Hospitalization is not warranted unless the patient is dehydrated, in respiratory distress, encephalopathic, or otherwise compromised. Young patients requiring hospitalization (Box 34–2) should receive vitamin A. Recent clinical studies have shown a decrease in morbidity and mortality in patients receiving vitamin A supplementation. Patients of any age may benefit from vitamin A supplementation if their cases are clinically severe. All patients in areas of known vitamin A deficiency (ie, Third World countries) should receive supplementation if measles is endemic to the area.

Immune globulin may be used to protect susceptible contacts of confirmed measles cases. Immune globulin must be used within 6 days of exposure for maximum efficacy. Contacts who received at least one dose of measles vaccine at age ≥ 12 months do not need immune globulin if they are immunocompetent. Candidates for immune globulin would include nonimmunized pregnant women, the immunocompromised, and infants < 1 year of age. Infants < 5 months of age do have passive maternal antibodies if their mother can be confirmed to be measles immune. If maternal immunity is confirmed, these infants do not need immune globulin. If children receive immune globulin, they should not receive measles vaccine for 5 months (if receiving 0.25 cc/kg immune globulin) or 6 months (if receiving 0.5 cc/kg immune globulin).

The live virus vaccine can modify the infection in a nonimmunized person, if given within 72 h of exposure. Clinical response varies. Usual vaccine contraindications apply to the vaccine if used in this modality (see Box 34–2).

Prevention & Control

Measles is highly communicable. Any hospitalized patient suspected of harboring the virus should be in droplet isolation. Good hand washing and appropriate handling of fomites should be observed as well. This isolation should be maintained during the prodromal phase and 4 days from the onset of the exanthem. Chil-

dren should also be excluded from school and daycare during this period. Isolation may need to be extended in complicated cases. Some immunocompromised patients can shed virus for an extended period.

School quarantine issues are often difficult. Virus is shed and communicable in the prodromal phase. The diagnosis of measles is often not suspect in this phase. The index case may have many contacts before diagnosis. Quarantine issues should be addressed individually and in conjunction with a local government health agency.

Live attenuated measles vaccine should be administered to healthy individuals at two intervals. The first dose is recommended at age 12–15 months. The second dose should be at age 4–6 years. Children who miss the second dose should receive it before age 12 years.

In epidemic conditions, a dose may be given from ages 6 to 11 months. These patients will still need a dose at age 12–15 months and at 4–6 years (Box 34–3).

REFERENCES

American Academy of Pediatrics, Committee on Infectious Diseases: Measles. In Peter G (editor): *1997 Red Book: Report of the Committee on Infectious Diseases,* 24th ed. American Academy of Pediatrics, 1997.

Centers for Disease Control and Prevention: Measles–United States, 1996, and the interruption of indigenous transmission. J Am Med Assoc 1997;277:1345.

Cherry JD: Measles. In Feigin RD, Cherry JD (editors):

Textbook of Pediatric Infectious Diseases, 3rd ed. Saunders, 1992.

Hussey GD, Klein M: A randomized, controlled trial of vitamin A in children with severe measles. N Engl J Med. 1990;323:160.

PeBenito R et al: Fulminating subacute sclerosing panencephalitis: Case report and literature review. Clin Pediatr 1997;36:149.

35

Mumps

Gregory Sonnen, MD & Nancy Henry, MD, PhD

Essentials of Diagnosis

- Epidemic parotitis, usually seen in childhood.
- Most common heralding symptom is painful parotid swelling.
- Headache and meningismus common.
- Orchitis is uncommon late complication seen in post-pubertal males; rarely leads to sterility.
- Other glandular tissue may be inflamed.

General Considerations

A. Epidemiology. Mumps, historically known as epidemic parotitis, was one of the most common early childhood infections before the routine use of mumps vaccination starting in 1968. Reported cases of mumps have dropped 98% when compared with the prevaccine era. It is spread primarily during the late winter and early spring. Before the vaccination era, mumps epidemics occurred in 3- to 4-year cycles.

B. Microbiology. Mumps virus is a 150-nm paramyxovirus. It is composed of single-stranded RNA contained in a helical nucleocapsid. The viral envelope contains hemolysin, hemagglutinin, and neuraminidase.

C. Pathogenesis. Mumps virus is spread via respiratory secretions, with humans being the only natural reservoir. The latent phase of the virus is from 12 to 25 days. The host is communicable from 2 days before to 9 days after the onset of parotid swelling. Mumps is often inappropriately thought to be "less communicable" than other pediatric viruses. This concept is probably owing to the high incidence (20–40%) of subclinical infections.

Clinical Findings

A. Signs and Symptoms. Mumps virus typically infects the parotid glands but has the ability to infect other glandular tissue (Box 35–1). Mumps parotitis rarely has prodromal symptoms. Children can have a prodrome of fever, myalgia, and headache. In two-thirds of infections, parotid pain and swelling are the heralding symptoms. Headache and meningismus are common. Fever and parotid swelling usually begin resolving within 1 week.

B. Laboratory Findings. Infection can be confirmed by viral culture or serology. Culture samples can be obtained by pharyngeal swab or from urine or cerebrospinal fluid during the febrile course of disease. The virus can be cultured on a variety of cell lines including embryonated chicken egg and chick embryo fibroblast. Serology can be confirmed via enzyme immunoassay, complement fixation, or hemagglutination inhibition. Acute and convalescent serologies are helpful to monitor the course of disease.

C. Differential Diagnosis. The differential diagnosis of mumps parotitis includes suppurative parotitis and salivary calculus. Anterior cervical lymphadenitis can often be confused with parotitis.

D. Complications. Orchitis is an uncommon complication of mumps in adults and adolescents, with the highest rate found in the 15- to 29-year age group.

BOX 35–1

Mumps Clinical Syndromes

More Common	• Parotitis (present in 2/3 of infections; usually the heralding symptom) • Mild fever • Meningismus, often with severe headache • Orchitis (rare in prepubescent boys)
Less Common	• Meningoencephalitis • Deafness • Arthritis • Pancreatitis • Thyroiditis • Mastitis • Oophoritis

---

BOX 35–2

Treatment of Mumps

- Maintain hydration
- Analgesics
- Opioids often needed for severe orchitis
- Lumbar puncture can be therapeutic for severe headache
- Mumps immune globulin is of little value, and no longer available in the United States

BOX 35-3

Control of Mumps

Vaccine	• Live-virus mumps vaccine is administered 0.5 cc SQ; commonly given in combination with MMR (measles, mumps, rubella) vaccine • First dose is recommended at from 12 to 15 months of age • Second dose is recommended at school entry (age 4 to 6 years) • If no preschool dose is given, the second dose should be administered before age 12
MMR Vaccine Contraindications	• Pregnancy • Febrile illness • Planned pregnancy within 3 months • Severe immunocompromised state • Blood product or immune globulin within 3 to 6 months (dose dependent) • Anaphylaxis to neomycin
MMR Vaccine Should Be Used with Caution in These Situations	• Seizure disorder • Thrombocytopenia • Egg allergy
Isolation Precautions	• Respiratory isolation should be maintained for 9 days after onset of parotitis • Infected children should be excluded from school and daycare during this period

It is rare in children. Orchitis is suspected when the patient has a high fever at the end of the first week of illness. This is soon accompanied by swelling, tenderness, and severe pain in the testis. Roughly 75% of mumps orchitis is unilateral. Rarely, testicular atrophy follows orchitis. Sterility is rare and is seen in cases of bilateral orchitis. Orchitis usually lasts 4–6 days.

Mumps infection during the first trimester of pregnancy confers an increased risk of spontaneous abortion but no increased risk of fetal malformation. Other uncommon complications include meningoencephalitis, deafness, arthritis, pancreatitis, thyroiditis, mastitis, and oophoritis.

Diagnosis

Diagnosis is based on physical findings and culture or serology. History of a mumps contact can be difficult to find owing to the significant number of subclinical cases. Cerebrospinal fluid will demonstrate a lymphocytic pleocytosis if meningitis is present.

Treatment

Therapy is aimed primarily at analgesia (Box 35–2). Opioids are often needed for the pain of orchitis, which can be quite severe. Local application of cool compresses may also help relieve some of the orchitis pain. Intravenous hydration may be needed for some patients. Lumbar puncture may be therapeutic for patients with severe headache. Mumps immune globulin has little clinical value. It is no longer available in the United States.

Prevention & Control

Virus is shed 1 day before onset of symptoms and continues to shed for 9 days after the onset of parotitis. Droplet isolation should be maintained on hospitalized patients during this period. Children should be excluded from school and daycare during this period.

The live virus vaccine is usually given in combination with the MMR vaccine (measles, mumps, and rubella). The first vaccine should be given between 12 and 15 months of age. The second dose is usually given between ages 4 and 6 years. If the second dose is missed, it should be given before age 12 years. Various contraindications exist for the vaccine (Box 35–3).

REFERENCES

American Academy of Pediatrics, Committee on Infectious Diseases: Mumps. In Peter G (editor): *1997 Red Book: Report of the Committee on Infectious Diseases,* 24th ed. American Academy of Pediatrics, 1997.

Brunell PA: Mumps. In Feigin RD, Cherry JD (editors): *Textbook of Pediatric Infectious Diseases,* 3rd ed. Saunders, 1992.

Rubella

36

Gregory Sonnen, MD, & Nancy Henry, MD, PhD

General Considerations

A. Epidemiology. The epidemiology of rubella, commonly referred to as German measles or 3-day measles, has changed dramatically in the past 30 years, owing exclusively to the widespread use of the rubella live attenuated virus vaccine. Before the use of this vaccination (1969), the virus had an epidemic cycle of 6–9 years. It is primarily a winter and early spring infection. The incidence of rubella infection in developed countries has declined by 99%, compared with pre-vaccine era data. In the vaccine era, current data suggest that 10% of young adults are still susceptible. The majority of these young adults lack vaccination.

A major concern of rubella is infection of nonimmune pregnant women. Polysystemic fetopathy is the hallmark of congenital rubella syndrome. Infection before 20 weeks of gestation confers a significant risk of congenital malformation with the highest risk before 12 weeks of gestation.

B. Microbiology. Rubella is a 70-nm single-stranded RNA virus of the *Togaviridae* family. It is the only virus in the genus *Rubivirus*. It has three polypeptide constituents (E1, E2, and C). E1 and E2 are glycosylated membrane peptides. The nucleocapsid is composed of polypeptide C and genomic RNA. The viral envelope is a lipoprotein complex. The virus is sensitive to heat, light, and pH extremes.

C. Pathogenesis. Humans are the only natural reservoir of the virus. Spread is chiefly via respiratory secretions and direct contact. The virus is communicable for 3–5 days before the rash and 7 days after the rash has appeared. The virus has a latent phase of 2–3 weeks before clinical disease appears.

POSTNATALLY ACQUIRED RUBELLA

Essentials of Diagnosis

- Exanthematous viral illness.
- A prodrome of cough, fever, myalgia, cervical lymphadenopathy, and pharyngitis is common in adults.
- Prodrome is rare in children.
- Exanthem is a fine maculopapular rash spreading from the face to the extremities within 24 h and lasting 3 days.

- Nonimmune pregnant women are at high risk for having a fetus with congenital rubella syndrome.

Clinical Findings

A. Signs and Symptoms. Postnatal infection is usually a mild illness accompanied by an exanthem rash (Box 36–1). Adults commonly have prodromal symptoms including pharyngitis, fever, headache, cough, lymphadenopathy, myalgia, and nausea for 1–5 days. Children rarely have a prodrome.

The exanthem is similar in adults and children. The erythematous, fine maculopapular rash first erupts on the face, then spreads to the distal extremities within 24 h and lasts 2–3 days. In children, the exanthem phase has little to no fever. Lymphadenopathy is common, as is mild, transient leukopenia. The exanthem phase in adults commonly involves arthritis, headache, and eye pain. Generalized pruritus may last 2 weeks.

B. Laboratory Findings. Culture may be obtained from nasopharyngeal secretions, blood, urine, cerebrospinal fluid, synovial fluid, and breast milk. The preferred medium is African green monkey kidney cells. No reliable clinical viral antigen test exists. Serology is performed via hemagglutination inhibition, latex agglutination, fluorescence immunoassay, passive hemagglutination, single radial hemolysis, and enzyme immunoassay. Serology should be performed on a suspected case. Absence of immunoglobulin G (IgG) indicates nonimmunity. Repeat serology at 4 and then 6 weeks. Seroconversion is indicative of infection.

C. Differential Diagnosis. The differential diagnosis includes measles, fifth disease, roseola, scarletina, and infectious mononucleosis.

D. Complications. Complications for children include encephalitis and thrombocytopenia. Adults can have myocarditis, orchitis, neuritis, erythema multiforme, and congenital rubella syndrome.

Diagnosis

Postnatally acquired rubella is diagnosed based on history and physical findings (see Box 36–1). All suspected cases that are nonimmune should have cultures and serology performed to confirm the diagnosis. If serology shows no rubella-specific IgG (eg, nonimmune), convalescent titers should be drawn at 4 and then 6 weeks postexposure. Seroconversion is

BOX 36–1

Postnatally Acquired Rubella

	Children	Adults
Prodromal Symptoms	• Prodromal symptoms are rare • Cough, coryza, lymphadenopathy, and diarrhea	• Prodromal symptoms are common • Eye pain, sore throat, headache, fever, cough, lymphadenopathy, myalgia, and nausea
Rash	• Initial presentation is exanthem rash • Rash is erythematous, maculopapular; found first on the face then spreading peripherally within 24 h • Usually lasts 2 to 3 days	• Rash occurs 1–5 days after prodromal symptoms appear • Rash is similar to children's rash
Exanthem Phase	• Fever is mild to none	• Arthritis and arthralgia are common
Clinical Signs	• Lymphadenopathy is common, typically posterior auricular and suboccipital • Mild, transient leukopenia	• Lymphadenopathy is common, typically posterior auricular and suboccipital • Persistent headache, eye pain, and pruritus may last for ≤ 2 weeks.
Rare Complications	• Encephalitis • Thrombocytopenia	• Myocarditis • Erythema multiforme • Congenital rubella syndrome

indicative of active infection. If active infection is identified in a nonimmune pregnant woman before 20 weeks' gestation, pregnancy termination should be discussed. The patient's religious, cultural, and personal values must be considered in this situation. Infection after 20 weeks gestation has a decreased risk of teratogenic effects on the fetus.

Treatment

Postnatally acquired rubella requires no specific treatment. Therapy should be symptomatic (Box 36–2). Use of immunoglobulin as postexposure prophylaxis in nonimmune patients is controversial. Routine administration of immunoglobulin for postexposure prophylaxis of rubella is not recommended. Symptoms in the mother may be reduced, but fetopathy may still occur. Immunoglobulin may be considered in cases where pregnancy termination was indicated but not possible.

CONGENITAL RUBELLA SYNDROME

Essentials of Diagnosis

- Polysystemic fetopathy.
- Infection before 20 weeks' gestation confers greatest risk to fetus.

- Common defects include cataracts, deafness, microcephaly, heart defects, hepatosplenomegaly.
- Late complications include mental retardation, developmental and behavioral disorders, endocrinopathies.
- Infant will shed virus up to 1 year.

Clinical Findings

Nonimmune pregnant women infected with rubella are at risk for having a fetus with congenital rubella syndrome (CRS). The risk and severity of the defects are higher earlier in the pregnancy. Roughly 85% of fetuses infected in the first trimester will have some anomalies.

Hallmarks of CRS include sensorineural deafness, intrauterine growth retardation, cataracts, retinopathy, and cardiac defects (Box 36–3). Some infections will result in spontaneous abortion. Uncommon findings also include dermal erythropoiesis, meningoencephalitis, glaucoma, microphthalmia, myocarditis, pneumonitis, hepatitis, thrombocytopenic purpura, and craniofacial deformities. Many of these infants will grow to have mental retardation, developmental delay, and behavioral disorders. Some will also have late-onset endocrinopathies such as insulin-dependent diabetes mellitus. The virus can be isolated as outlined above.

BOX 36-2

Treatment of Rubella Infection

Congenitally Infected Neonates	Children (Postnatal Infection)	Adults	Nonimmune Pregnant Women
• Specific IgM should be drawn • Cultures taken from nasal secretion, blood, urine, & cerebrospinal fluid • Auditory assessment • Early intervention for developmental and behavioral disorders • No medical therapy available	• Supportive care • Manage fever with acetaminophen (10–15 mg/kg every 4 h orally or rectally) or ibuprofen (6 to 8 mg/kg every 6 to 8 h orally)	• Supportive care • Analgesia with NSAIDs • Antihistamines for pruritus	• Draw blood for rubella-specific IgG immediately to identify immunity status • If no identifiable IgG, repeat serology should be drawn in 4 and 6 weeks; seroconversion indicates acute infection • Use of immunoglobulin for postexposure prophylaxis is controversial; 0.55 cc/kg may modify infection; this is not recommended • If confirmed infection before 20 weeks gestation, pregnancy termination should be considered

BOX 36-3

Congenital Rubella Syndrome

More Common Findings at Birth	• Intrauterine growth retardation • Cataracts • Retinopathy • Sensorineural deafness • Microcephaly • Long bone radiolucencies • Patent ductus arteriosus • Pulmonary artery stenosis • Hepatosplenomegaly • Dermal erythropoiesis (producing the "Blueberry Muffin" appearance)
Less Common Findings at Birth	• Active meningoencephalitis • Congenital glaucoma • Microphthalmia • Myocarditis • Interstitial pneumonitis • Hepatitis • Thrombocytopenia purpura • Craniofacial abnormalities
Late Complications	• Mental retardation • Developmental delay • Behavioral disorders • Endocrinopathies

BOX 36-4

Control of Rubella

Vaccine	• Live attenuated virus rubella vaccine (RA 27/3 strain) is administered 0.5 cc SQ. Commonly given in combination with MMR (measles, mumps, rubella) vaccine • First dose is recommended from 12 to 15 months of age • Second dose is recommended at school entry (age 4 to 6 years) • If no preschool dose is given, the second dose should be administered prior to age 12 • Susceptible persons should be screened for immunization status; these include prepubertal girls & boys, college students, military personnel, child care workers, health care workers, postpartum women
MMR Vaccine Contra-indications	• Pregnancy • Febrile illness • Planned pregnancy within 3 months • Severe immunocompromised state • Blood product or immune globulin within 3 to 6 months (dose dependent) • Anaphylaxis to neomycin
MMR Vaccine Should Be Used with Caution in These Situations	• Seizure disorder • Thrombocytopenia • Egg allergy
Isolation Precautions	• Postnatally acquired rubella requires respiratory isolation for 5 days before the rash through 1 week after appearance of the rash; this includes exlusion from school or daycare • Congenitally infected infants are considered contagious until 1 year of age unless nasal and urine cultures are negative at 3 months; parents must be made aware of the potential risk to nonimmunized pregnant mothers

Diagnosis

CRS is diagnosed based on history and physical findings (see Box 36–3). Some neonates, especially those affected later in pregnancy, may appear normal or have very mild findings at birth. Suspected CRS neonates should have a rubella-specific IgM drawn. Cultures should be obtained from nasal secretions, blood, urine, and cerebrospinal fluid.

Treatment

No medical therapy is available for CRS (but see Box 36–2). Cardiac defects warrant early intervention by a pediatric cardiologist. Early audiologic evaluation should be performed. A physician experienced with patients who have developmental disabilities should be involved. Early intervention for developmental delays and mental retardation is important. The primary care provider should be aware of potential endocrinopathies. Children with CRS often have very difficult behavioral disorders. Parents will benefit from behavioral management counseling.

Prevention & Control of Rubella

Rubella is communicable 3–5 days before the rash and ≤ 7 days after it appears in postnatally acquired cases. Hospitalized patients should be in droplet isolation. Pregnant hospital staff should avoid contact if their immunity status is in question. Infected children should be excluded from school and daycare during this period. CRS infants may shed the virus for ≤ 1 year. Parents should be aware of this factor and restrict the infant's exposure to pregnant women.

Universal vaccination has been key in reducing the occurrence of CRS. Prenatal screening of pregnant women's immunity status has also been important. Rubella immunization is usually given in combination with the MMR (measles, mumps, rubella) vaccine. The first vaccine should be given at 12–15 months of age. The second should be given at 4–6 years of age. If the second dose is missed, it should be given before 12 years of age. Various contraindications and precautions exist for the vaccine (Box 36–4).

REFERENCES

American Academy of Pediatrics, Committee on Infectious Diseases: Rubella. In Peter G (editor): *1997 Red Book: Report of the Committee on Infectious Diseases,* 24th ed. American Academy of Pediatrics, 1997.

Cherry JD: Rubella. In Feigin RD, Cherry JD (editors): *Textbook of Pediatric Infectious Diseases,* 3rd ed. Saunders, 1992.

Rubella and congenital rubella syndrome—United States, 1994–1997. Morbid Mortal Weekly Rep 1997;46:350.

37

Rotavirus

Gregory M. Sonnen, MD & Nancy Henry, MD, PhD

Essentials of Diagnosis

- Nonbloody diarrhea of 2–8 days' duration.
- Vomiting, fever, anorexia, and dehydration common.
- May infect any age group.
- Most common etiology of acute gastroenteritis in children < 2 years of age.
- Yearly reinfection common in infants and young children.

General Considerations

A. Epidemiology. Rotavirus is the most common etiology of acute diarrheal illness in children < 2 years old. It is responsible for > 1 million cases of reported diarrheal illness each year in children ages 1–4 years in the United States. Rotavirus is responsible for an average of 150 deaths per year in this same group. All of these deaths are secondary to severe dehydration. Worldwide, rotavirus is estimated to be responsible for 125 million cases of diarrhea in children < 5 years old. This effect results in mortality in 873,000 of these children. Mortality in developed counties has been reduced by aggressive rehydration therapy.

B. Microbiology. Rotavirus is a 70-nm icosahedral RNA reovirus that has five distinct antigenic groups (A, B, C, D, and E). Group A also has six serotypes. Group A is responsible for the majority of reported diarrheal illnesses in children in the United States. Groups B and C are responsible for adult diarrheal illnesses in Asia.

C. Pathogenesis. The virus is transmitted human to human via the fecal-oral route. The incubation time in humans is 1–3 days. Clinical disease is most prevalent in the winter. Rotavirus is also the most common cause of nosocomial diarrheal illness in children. Investigators have hypothesized a possible respiratory transmission route.

Clinical Findings (see Box 37–1)

A. Signs and Symptoms. Infants and children present with nonbloody diarrhea, which is often profuse. Emesis, anorexia, fever, and irritability are also common. In immunocompetent individuals, the disease is self-limited and lasts 2–8 days. The key to management is evaluation of the level of dehydration

at presentation. Children in the category of severe dehydration are usually acidotic and require immediate intervention. Clinically, children with severe dehydration can appear lethargic, obtunded, or in shock. Rarely, respiratory symptoms are present including rhinorrhea, cough, and wheeze. Some children with moderate dehydration also warrant prompt intervention.

B. Laboratory Findings. Group A rotavirus antigen may be detected from stool through either enzyme immunoassay (EIA) or latex agglutination (LA). Both are equally sensitive and specific for detection of rotavirus during the acute diarrheal phase of the disease. EIA has higher sensitivity when used late in the course of disease.

C. Imaging. Imaging has little value in rotavirus-induced gastroenteritis. Rare cases of paralytic ileus secondary to hypokalemia have been observed by abdominal radiography.

D. Differential Diagnosis. The differential diagnosis of acute winter childhood diarrheal illness should always include rotavirus, Norwalk virus, calcivirus, astrovirus, and coronavirus (see Chapter 38). In warm weather diarrhea, adenovirus is more common. If blood is present in the stool, bacterial agents should be considered, including, enteropathogenic *E coli*, *Shigella*, *Salmonella*, *Yersinia*, and *Campy-*

BOX 37–1	
Rotavirus Gastroenteritis Clinical Syndrome	
More Common	• Nonbloody diarrhea of 2- to 8-d duration • Vomiting, anorexia, and fever • Isotonic dehydration • Pharyngeal eyrthema
Less Common	• Hyper- or hyponatremic dehydration • Transient lactose intolerance • Rhinitis • Wheezing • Cervical lymphadenopathy • Serous otitis media

BOX 37–2

Treatment of Rotavirus Gastroenteritis

Primary Treatment	• Oral rehydration should be utilized for patients with mild (5%) to moderate (10%) isotonic dehydration • Parenteral rehydration should be reserved for moderate to severe dehydration, to correct electrolyte abnormalities, and for patients failing oral rehydration • Acetaminophen (10 to 15 mg/kg every 4 h orally or rectally) or ibuprofen (6 to 8 mg/kg every 6 to 8 h orally) for fever and irritability • Age appropriate oral feeding should resume slowly when vomiting subsides and rehydration is complete • Withholding lactose does not improve outcome in the majority of patients
Pediatric Considerations	• Correct sodium abnormalities slowly • Consider transient lactase deficiency if diarrhea persists more than 5 days • Antidiarrheal agents are contraindicated in children

lobacter species. If symptoms are prolonged or atypical, malabsorptive or maldigestive diarrhea, as well as intestinal parasites, should be considered.

E. Complications. Common complications are dehydration, uncommonly accompanied by electrolyte imbalances. Owing to mucosal damage of the small bowel lumen, transient lactose intolerance is uncommonly observed. Prolonged diarrhea or severe cramping, gas, or colic can be the result of lactase deficiency. If lactase deficiency is suspected, the patient should be placed on a lactose-free diet for 2–5 days.

Diagnosis

Diagnosis of rotavirus is based on history and physical findings. Since this virus produces a self-limiting disease in healthy individuals, identification of the virus is not needed in most cases. In immunocompromised patients, identification of an etiology is a higher priority, and stool should be sent promptly for analysis. Serum electrolytes and glucose should be evaluated in patients with moderate to severe dehydration.

Treatment

The primary therapy for rotavirus gastroenteritis is hydration (Box 37–2). If appropriate oral hydration can maintain fluid balance, no other intervention is needed. Small children and infants are prone to dehydration. Assessing the level of dehydration is key to deciding on therapy. Oral rehydration is appropriate for most children with mild to moderate dehydration. Parenteral rehydration is often needed if oral rehydration fails. Patients with severe dehydration warrant prompt parenteral rehydration. Careful attention should be paid to their hemodynamic status. Patients with either hypo- or hypernatremia should be slowly rehydrated to account for sodium or free-water deficits.

Orally administered immunoglobulin may modify the course of the illness in patients with immunodeficiencies who experience a prolonged rotaviral illness. Routine use is not recommended.

Prevention & Control

Rotavirus is spread by direct contact. Hand washing should limit spread of the virus (Box 37–3). Careful attention should be paid to potential fomites, especially in the hospital setting. Strict enteric isolation should be observed for all symptomatic hospitalized

BOX 37–3

Control of Rotavirus Gastroenteritis

Prophylactic Measures	• Hand washing • Disinfection or disposal of all potential fomites • Breast feeding decreases the severity of illness in young children • An oral, live-attenuated tetravalent vaccine will be commercially licensed in the very near future for use in infants and young children.
Isolation Precautions	• Strict enteric isolation of all hospitalized patients • If stool cannot be contained, infants and young children should be restricted from daycare, school settings, or both until diarrhea ceases

patients. Nosocomial infections with rotavirus are common. Infants and children should be excluded from school or daycare if their stool can not be contained. An oral, live-attenuated tetravalent vaccine was licensed by the FDA in 1998. In clinical trials, it significantly reduced morbidity. In 1999, the vaccine was taken off the market to investigate a possible relationship to intussusception. The results of this investigation are pending.

REFERENCES

American Academy of Pediatrics, Committee on Infectious Diseases: Rotavirus Infections. In Peter G (editor): *1997 Red Book: Report of the Committee on Infectious Diseases,* 24th ed. American Academy of Pediatrics, 1997.

American Academy of Pediatrics, Provisional Committee on Quality Improvement, Subcommittee on Acute Gastroenteritis: Practice parameter: The management of acute gastroenteritis in young children. Pediatrics 1996;97:424.

Kapikian AZ, Wyatt RG: Viral gastrointestinal infections. In Feigin RD, Cherry JD (editors): *Textbook of Pediatric Infectious Diseases,* 3rd ed. Saunders, 1992.

Midthun K, Kapikian AZ: Rotavirus vaccines: An overview. Clin Microbiol Rev 1996;9:423.

Other Gastrointestinal Viruses

38

W. Lawrence Drew, MD, PhD

HUMAN ENTERIC CALICIVIRUSES: NORWALK & RELATED VIRUSES

Essentials of Diagnosis

- Diarrhea, occurring in an outbreak especially in a closed environment.
- Tends to infect older children and adults rather than infants.
- Nausea and vomiting are common; bloody stools are rare.
- Incubation period 1–2 days; illness 1–4 days.
- Laboratory diagnosis by seroconversion; only performed in epidemiologic studies.

General Considerations

A. Epidemiology. Even in developed countries, antibodies to caliciviruses are nearly universal by age 5. Infections tend to occur in family or community outbreaks. In underdeveloped countries, infection by these viruses occurs presumably as a result of poor sanitation. In developed countries, outbreaks that occur year-round have been described in schools, resorts, hospitals, nursing homes, restaurants, and cruise ships. The primary method of spread is fecal-oral, but contaminated water or shellfish has accounted for common-source outbreaks. A measure of the importance of these agents is that ~ 10% of all gastroenteritis outbreaks and up to 90–95% of those that are nonbacterial are attributed to them. In contrast to infants, who are more often infected by rotaviruses, calicilike viruses cause disease primarily in older children and adults (Box 38–1). Immunity is probably short-lived at best, suggesting that humoral antibody is not adequately protective. The incubation period is 1–2 days, and shedding can persist for 1–2 weeks. The virus is not inactivated by chlorine, freezing, or heating to 60(C.

B. Microbiology. The Norwalk agent and related viruses are classified as caliciviruses, although they are also similar in appearance to parvoviruses and hepatitis A virus. Among the other human enteric caliciviruses are the Hawaii, Snow Mountain, and Sapporo viruses, which are named for where these strains were first de-

tected. The human enteric caliciviruses are now divided into two genera, provisionally named "Norwalk-like viruses" and "Sapporo-like viruses." None of these viruses can be isolated in tissue culture, but their viral nature was established by electron microscopic (EM) examination of feces, using antibodies to enhance detection (immune electron microscopy [IEM]).

Norwalk and human enteric caliciviruses are among the smallest of all viruses, only 27–38 nm in diameter. They are spherical, with 32 cup-shaped surface depressions. No envelope exists, and they exhibit icosahedral symmetry. The nucleoprotein of calicivirus is single-stranded RNA with a molecular weight of approximately 2.6×10^6 daltons. The details of attachment and penetration are uncertain. Replication occurs in the cytoplasm, with release of viral particles accomplished by cell destruction.

C. Pathogenesis. Jejunal biopsy in human volunteers infected with Norwalk viruses reveals blunting of villi, cytoplasmic vacuolation, and infiltration with mononuclear cells, but virus particles are not detected by EM of epithelial cells. The virus appears to cause a decrease in brush border enzymes and in turn malabsorption. Infection is not associated with a leukocyte response in stool samples.

Clinical Findings

A. Signs and Symptoms. Although calicilike viruses are typically associated with diarrheal illness, nausea and vomiting may occur frequently, especially in children. Bloody stools do not occur. Fever may be present in up to one-third of patients. The incubation period is 24–48 h, and the illness lasts 1–4 days.

BOX 38–1

Other Gastrointestinal Infections

	Children	Adults
More Common	• Norwalk virus and other enteric caliciviruses	
Less Common	• Astrovirus • Adenovirus	• Norwalk virus

BOX 38-2

Treatment of Other Gastrointestinal Infections

	Children	Adults
First Choice	• Symptomatic	• Symptomatic

BOX 38-3

Control of Other Gastrointestinal Infections

Prophylactic Measures	Good personal hygiene
Isolation Precautions	

B. Laboratory Findings. There are no characteristic blood or stool abnormalities; fecal leukocytes are absent.

C. Differential Diagnosis. The differential diagnosis includes gastroenteritis of any etiology, especially other viruses. Winter diarrhea in infants and children is more likely caused by rotavirus.

Diagnosis

A. Culture. None of the Norwalk or human enteric caliciviruses can be grown in tissue culture, although the development of a sensitive culture assay is a high priority.

B. Direct Detection. Standard EM of feces is usually negative for the Norwalk agent because they are present in low titer. Other caliciviruses may be present in sufficient concentration to permit detection. IEM is the main method of detection of Norwalk-type viruses but is rarely used except in research settings. IEM consists of examining the sample by EM after the addition of an antibody directed against the suspected agent. The antibody causes the virus to aggregate, facilitating recognition. Reverse transcription-polymerase chain reaction, enzyme immunoassay, and radioimmunoassay (RIA) detection of Norwalk antigen are alternative methods that are more sensitive than IEM, but are generally available only in research settings.

C. Serology. Seroconversion is the method used to identify most infections. Antibody to the Norwalk agent may be detected by RIA or immune adherence hemagglutination assay (IAHA). Antibodies to the other calicilike agents are more difficult to detect.

Treatment (Box 38-2)

No specific treatment is available. Bismuth subsalicylate may reduce gastrointestinal symptoms.

Prognosis

The prognosis is excellent for full recovery.

Prevention & Control (Box 38-3)

Outbreaks may be minimized by handling food carefully and maintaining the purity of the water supply.

ASTROVIRUSES

General Considerations

Astroviruses are small (28- to 38-nm) RNA viruses that exhibit five or six points on their surface. They have been seen in fecal specimens by EM, especially in infants and children with mild gastroenteritis. There are at least seven human serotypes. The route of spread is probably fecal-oral; > 70% of children acquire antibody by age 5 years. Infections occur sporadically rather than in outbreaks. Although detection by culture procedures or techniques is only partly successful, astroviruses have been isolated from humans, cows, cats, dogs, pigs, and sheep.

ADENOVIRUS

Adenoviruses, particularly the high numbered serotypes (38 and, especially, 40 and 41) are associated with gastroenteritis. (See Chapter 32 for an extensive consideration of adenoviruses.) The enteric adenoviruses are very difficult to grow in tissue culture but are detected by EM or EIA. They cause 5–15% of viral gastroenteritis in young children. The average incubation period is 10 days, much longer than the average of 1–2 days for the other viral causes of gastroenteritis. Most disease is in infants and young children and occurs sporadically rather than in outbreaks. The method of spread is fecal-oral.

REFERENCES

Blacklow NR, Greenberg HB: Viral gastroenteritis. N Engl J Med 1992;325:252. (A review of the biology and epidemiology of enteric viruses.)

Hedberg CW, Osterholm MT: Outbreaks of food-borne and water-borne viral gastroenteritis. Clin Microbiol Rev 1993;6:199. (A review including the Norwalk agent.)

Kapikian AZ: Viral gastroenteritis. J Am Med Assoc 1993;269:627. (Concise, well-referenced overview of the relative importance of these various agents.)

Hepatitis

39

W. Lawrence Drew, MD, PhD

The causes of hepatitis are varied and include viruses, bacteria, and protozoa, as well as drugs and toxins (eg, isoniazid, carbon tetrachloride, and ethanol). The clinical symptoms and course of acute viral hepatitis can be similar, regardless of etiology, and determination of a specific cause depends primarily on the use of laboratory tests (Box 39–1). Hepatitis may be caused by at least six different viruses whose major characteristics are summarized in Table 39–1. Non-A–non-B (NANB) hepatitis is a term previously used to identify cases of hepatitis not caused by hepatitis A or B. With the discovery of hepatitis viruses C, E, and G, most of the viral etiologies of NANB disease can be identified. Other viruses, such as Epstein-Barr virus and cytomegalovirus, can also cause inflammation of the liver, but hepatitis is not the primary disease they cause. Yellow fever is a form of hepatitis but is now rare. The relative contributions of the hepatitis viruses to acute and chronic viral hepatitis are shown in Table 39–1 and Table 39–2.

HEPATITIS A

Essentials of Diagnosis

- Increased risks in promiscuous homosexual men, travelers to underdeveloped areas, and institutionalized individuals.
- Malaise, anorexia, fever, dark urine, pale stools, jaundice, right upper quadrant pain, and tender hepatomegaly.
- Increased liver enzymes (ALT, AST), bilirubin, prothrombin time, and globulin.
- Serum positive for hepatitis A immunoglobulin M (IgM) antibody.
- May have history of recent (ie, 3–6 weeks previously) ingestion of undercooked shellfish or sewage-contaminated water.

General Considerations

A. Epidemiology. Hepatitis A virus is the cause of what was formerly termed infectious hepatitis or short-incubation hepatitis. It was first detected in the early 1970s in stools of patients incubating the disease. Humans appear to be the major natural hosts of hepatitis A virus. Several other primates (including chimpanzees and marmosets) are susceptible to ex-

perimental infection, and natural infections of these animals may occur.

The major mode of spread of hepatitis A is fecal-oral. Inoculation of infectious material intramuscularly can produce disease; transmission through blood transfusion rarely, if ever, occurs. Most cases of hepatitis A occur sporadically rather than being linked to a single contaminated source. The disease is common under conditions of crowding, and it occurs at high frequency in mental hospitals, schools for the developmentally disabled, and daycare centers. Because a chronic carrier state has not been observed with hepatitis A, perpetuation of the virus in nature presumably depends on sporadic subclinical infections and person-to-person transmission. Outbreaks of hepatitis A have been linked to the ingestion of undercooked shellfish from waters contaminated with human feces. Common-source outbreaks related to other foods, including vegetables, have also been reported.

The disease is widespread, but seroepidemiologic studies have shown marked variation in infection rates among different population groups. For example, rates are higher among those of lower socioeconomic status and among male homosexuals. Less than one-half of the general population of the United States now has serologic evidence of prior hepatitis A virus infection. Rates have been decreasing since 1970, apparently because of better sanitation and less crowding. In contrast, in many underdeveloped countries, > 90% of the adult population shows evidence of previous hepatitis A infection; in most cases, however, the evidence is of asymptomatic infection during childhood. The risk of overt disease is much higher in nonimmune infected adults than in children; travelers from developed countries who enter endemic areas are particularly susceptible.

B. Microbiology. Hepatitis A virus is an unenveloped, single-stranded small RNA (picorna)virus with cubic symmetry and a diameter of 27 nm (Figure 39–1). It is not inactivated by ether and is stable at −20 °C and low pH. These properties are similar to those of enteroviruses (see Chapter 27), but hepatitis A virus is distinct and now classified in a separate genus, *Hepatovirus*. The virus has been successfully cultivated in cell cultures but grows poorly.

C. Pathogenesis. The virus is believed to replicate initially in the enteric mucosa. It can be demon-

BOX 39-1

Hepatitis Infection

	Children	Adults
More Common	• Hepatitis A, B especially in underdeveloped countries and Far East	• Hepatitis A, B, C
Less Common	• Hepatitis C, G	• Hepatitis D, E, G

Table 39-2. Relative contribution of hepatitis viruses to chronic viral hepatitis—United States

Type	Cases/Year	Deaths/Year from Chronic Liver Disease
A	0	0
B	1×10^6	5,000
C	1×10^5	8–10,000
D	7×10^4	1,000
E	0	0

strated in feces by electron microscopy for 10–14 days before onset of disease. In most patients with symptoms of the disease, complete virus is no longer found in fecal specimens; however, viral antigen has been demonstrated in feces for ≤ 14 days thereafter. Multiplication in the intestines is followed by a period of viremia with spread to the liver. The response to replication in the liver consists of lymphoid cell infiltration, necrosis of liver parenchymal cells, and proliferation of Kupffer cells. The extent of necrosis often coincides with the severity of disease. A variable degree of biliary stasis may be present. Detectable levels of IgG antibody to hepatitis A virus persist indefinitely in serum, and patients with anti-hepatitis A virus antibodies are immune to reinfection.

Clinical Findings

A. Signs and Symptoms. In hepatitis A virus infection, an incubation period of 10–50 days (mean, 25 days) is usually followed by the onset of fever, poor appetite, nausea, pain in the right upper abdominal quadrant, and, within several days, jaundice. The patient may notice dark urine and clay-colored stools 1–5 days before the onset of clinical jaundice. The liver is enlarged and tender. Many persons who have serologic evidence of acute hepatitis A infection are asymptomatic or only mildly ill, without jaundice (anicteric hepatitis A). The infection-to-disease ratio is dependent on age; it may be as high as 20:1 in children and approximately 4:1 in adults. Most (99%) of cases of hepatitis A are self-limiting.

B. Laboratory Findings. Serum aminotransferase levels are elevated as a result of hepatic inflammation and damage. The serum bilirubin levels and

prothrombin time are also elevated, the latter being a sensitive marker of hepatocyte damage. The total leukocyte count is low because of neutropenia. Alkaline phosphatase is elevated especially in patients with a cholestatic picture, but it tends to subsequently decrease even when the bilirubin is still rising.

C. Imaging. Radiographic and radionucleotide studies may show hepatomegaly. Gall bladder and common bile duct examinations are usually normal.

D. Differential Diagnosis. All of the causes of acute hepatitis mentioned in the introduction to this chapter must be considered, but epidemiologic, age, and risk factors may help to predict a probable cause. See also Table 39–3.

E. Complications. In 0.1% of cases, fulminant fatal hepatitis associated with extensive liver necrosis may occur.

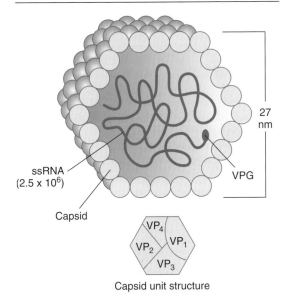

ssRNA (2.5×10^6)

Capsid

VPG

Capsid unit structure

VP₄ VP₂ VP₁ VP₃

Figure 39-1. Diagram of the proposed structure of the hepatitis A virus. The protein capsid is made up of four viral polypeptides (VP_1 to VP_4). Inside the capsid is a single-stranded (ss) molecule of RNA (molecular weight 2.5×10^6), which has a genomic viral protein (VPG) on the 5' end. (Reprinted from Ryan KJ et al: *Sherris Medical Microbiology*, 3rd ed. McGraw-Hill, 1994. McGraw-Hill, 1994; and by permission of Dr. J. A. Hoofnagle and of Abbott Laboratories, Diagnostic Division, North Chicago, Illinois.)

Table 39-1. Relative contribution of hepatitis viruses to acute viral hepatitis—United States.

Type	Portion (%) of All Hepatitis Infections
A	47%
B	33%
C	15%
D	2%
Other	3%

Table 39–3. Comparative features of viral hepatitis.

Feature	Hepatitis A	Hepatitis B	Hepatitis C	Hepatitis D	Hepatitis E	Hepatitis G
Incubation period	2–6 weeks (average 4 weeks)	6–23 weeks (average 10 weeks)	6–12 weeks	4–8 weeks		
Virus	27–nm RNA virus	42–nm DNA virus	RNA, flavivirus	Incomplete RNA virus	RNA similar to Calicivirus	RNA similar to Hepatitis C virus
Onset	Abrupt (variable)	Insidious (variable)	Insidious (variable)	Abrupt (variable)	Acute	?
Transmission	Fecal-oral	IDU, sexual	IDU, sexual (?)/ household	IDU, sexual	Fecal-oral	
Severity of acute infection	Self-limiting	Occasionally severe (up to 25% icteric)	Usually subclinical	Coinfection occasionally severe; superinfection often severe	Self-limiting, fulminant in pregnancy	?
Fulminant Hepatitis	Very rare (~0.1%)	Rare (<1% of icteric patients)	Very rare, if ever	Occurs with simultaneous hepatitis B	In pregnancy	
Symptoms	Fever, malaise, headache, anorexia, vomiting, dark urine, jaundice (often asymptomatic)	As with A but 10–20% with serum sickness-like reaction	As with A	As with A	As with A	
Carrier state % carriers in U.S.	None 0	Yes 0.1%	Yes 0.3–2%	Yes Very rare	?	Yes 1–2%
Chronicity	0%	5–10%	Up to 75%; cirrhosis (25–33%); hepatoma	Up to 30% of those with chronic hepatitis B	No	
Transmission by blood transfusion	Very rare	Rare with screening	Rare with screening	Rare with Hepatitis B screening	Probably not	Yes
Diagnosis	Anti-HAV, IgM/IgG	HbsAg; Anti-Hbc, IgM; Anti-Hbs, IgG	Anti-HCV, IgG; HCV RNA	Anti-HDV, IgM	Anti-HEV, IgM	HGV, RNA
Prevention	Immune globulin, killed vaccine	HBIG/Hepatitis B vaccine	Immune globulin(?)	Prevent B	Immune globulin	
Associated w/ cirrhosis	No	Yes	Yes, 20%	Yes, 40%	No	Rare
Associated w/ hepatocellular cancer	No	Yes	Yes	?	No	?
Treatment of chronic disease	None	Interferon alpha; ? 3TC	Interferon alpha & ribavirin	Interferon alpha	?	None indicated

Diagnosis

The best method for documentation of acute hepatitis A virus infection is the demonstration of high titers of virus-specific IgM antibody in serum drawn during the acute phase of illness. Because IgG antibody persists indefinitely, its demonstration in a single serum sample is not indicative of recent infection; a rise in titer between acute and convalescent sera must be documented. Immune electron microscopic identification of the viral antigen in fecal specimens and isolation of the virus in cell cultures remain research tools. Past infection is best demonstrated by anti-HAV IgG but absent IgM.

Treatment

There is no specific treatment for patients with acute episodes of hepatitis A infection (Box 39–2). Supportive measures include adequate nutrition and rest.

BOX 39–2

Treatment of Chronic Hepatitis Infection

	Children	Adults
First Choice		• Hepatitis B: interferon, 15–30 million U weekly • Hepatitis C: interferon, 9–10 million U weekly plus ribavirin • Hepatitis D: interferon, 5–10 million U daily • Hepatitis A, E: no known treatment • Hepatitis G: no treatment indicated
Second Choice		• Hepatitis B: possibly 3TC (Lamivudine), famciclovir
Penicillin Allergic		

Prognosis

The prognosis is excellent for > 99% of patients with hepatitis A infection. Only 0.1% of patients develop fatal acute hepatic necrosis.

Prevention & Control

A. Passive Immunization. Passive (ie, antibody) prophylaxis for hepatitis A has been available for many years. Immune serum globulin (ISG), manufactured from pools of plasma from large segments of the general population, is 80–90% protective if given before or during the incubation period of the disease. In some cases, infection occurs, but disease is ameliorated; that is, the patient develops anicteric, usually asymptomatic, hepatitis A.

At present, ISG should be administered to household contacts of hepatitis A patients and those known to have eaten uncooked foods prepared or handled by an infected individual. Once clinical symptoms have appeared, the host is already producing antibody, and administration of ISG is not indicated. Persons from areas of low endemicity who travel to areas with high infection rates may receive ISG before departure and at 3- to 4-month intervals as long as potential heavy exposure continues, but active immunization is preferable (see below).

B. Active Immunization. For hepatitis A, live attenuated vaccines have been evaluated but have demonstrated poor immunogenicity and have not been effective when given orally. Formalin-killed vaccines induce antibody titers similar to those of wild-virus infection and are almost 100% protective. Use of this vaccine is preferable to passive prophylaxis for those with prolonged or repeated exposure to hepatitis A.

HEPATITIS B

Essentials of Diagnosis

• Malaise, anorexia, fever, dark urine, pale stools, jaundice, right upper quadrant pain, and tender hepatomegaly.

• Increased risk in promiscuous homosexual men, injection drug users, transfusion recipients, hemophiliacs, hemodialysis patients, and patients with Down's syndrome.

• Increased liver enzymes (ALT, AST), bilirubin, prothrombin time, and globulin.

• Serum positive for hepatitis B core IgM antibody.

• Chronic hepatitis may be caused by hepatitis B and be diagnosed by the presence of hepatitis B surface antigen (HbsAg) in blood.

General Considerations

A. Epidemiology. Hepatitis B infection is found worldwide, with prevalence rates varying markedly among countries. Chronic carriers constitute the main reservoir of infection: in some countries, particularly in the Far East, ~ 5–15% of all persons carry the virus, though most are asymptomatic. Of patients with HIV infection, 10% are chronic carriers of hepatitis B.

In the United States, it is estimated that 1.5 million people are infected with hepatitis B, and it is estimated that 300,000 new cases occur annually. Approximately 300 of these individuals die with acute fulminant hepatitis, and 5–10% of infected patients become chronic hepatitis B virus carriers. As many as 4000 people die yearly of hepatitis B-related cirrhosis, and 1000 of hepatocellular carcinoma. Approximately 50% of infections in the United States are sexually transmitted, and the occurrence of hepatitis B surface antigen (HBsAg) is higher in certain populations, such as male homosexuals, patients on hemodialysis or immunosuppressive therapy, patients with Down's syndrome, and injection drug users.

Routine screening of blood donors for HBsAg has markedly decreased the incidence of post-transfusion hepatitis B; > 90% of cases developing after transfusion are now caused by other NANB hepatitis viruses. Multiple-pool blood products occasionally cause cases, and inadequately sterilized, blood-contaminated needles are still significant vehicles of transmission. Exposure by direct contact with blood or other bodily fluids, probably through small lesions, has resulted in hepatitis B infection of medical personnel. Attack rates are also high in spouses and sexual partners of infected patients.

Most hepatitis B infections of infants do not appear to be transplacentally transmitted to the fetus in utero, but are acquired during the birth process by the swallowing of infected blood or fluids or through abrasions. The rate of virus acquisition is high (~ 90%) in infants born to mothers who have acute hepatitis B infection or who carry HBsAg and hepatitis B e antigen (HBeAg). Most infants do not develop clinical disease; however, infection in the neonatal period is associated with failure to produce antibody to HBsAg and, thus, with chronic carriage in ~100% and perpetuation of infection by transmission in the family setting.

Hepatocellular carcinoma has been strongly associated with persistent carriage of hepatitis B virus, by serologic tests and detection of viral nucleic acid sequences integrated in tumor cell genomes. In many parts of Africa and Asia, primary liver cancer accounts for 20–30% of all types of malignancies, but only 1–2% in North and South America and Europe. The estimated risk of developing the malignancy for persons with chronic hepatitis B is increased between 10- and 300-fold in different populations. The mechanism of the association is unclear.

B. Microbiology. Hepatitis B virus is an enveloped DNA virus belonging to the family Hepadnaviridae. It is unrelated to any other human virus; however, related hepatotropic agents have been identified in woodchucks, ground squirrels, and kangaroos. A schematic of the hepatitis B virus is illustrated in Figure 39–2. The complete virion is a 42-nm, spherical particle that consists of an envelope around a 27-nm core. The core comprises a nucleocapsid that contains the DNA genome.

The viral genome consists of partially double-stranded DNA with a short, single-stranded piece. It comprises 3200 nucleotides, making it the smallest DNA virus known. Closely associated with the viral DNA is an RNA-dependent DNA polymerase, ie reverse transcriptase. Other components of the core are a hepatitis B core antigen (HBcAg) and HBeAg, which is a low-molecular-weight glycoprotein.

The envelope of the virus contains HBsAg, which is composed of one major and two other proteins. Antigenically there exist a group-specific determinant, termed *a,* and a number of subtypes that are important in epidemiologic typing, but not in immunity, because there is antigenic cross-reactivity and cross-protection between subtypes. Aggregates of HBsAg are often found in great abundance in serum during infection. They may assume spherical or filamentous shapes with a mean diameter of 22 nm and may con-

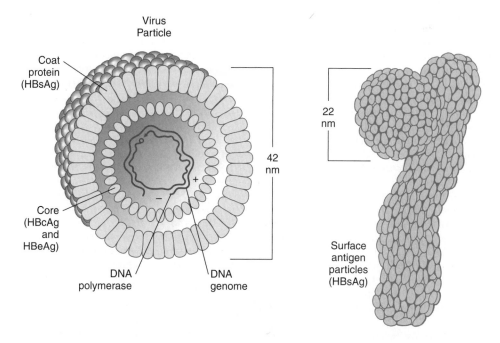

Figure 39–2. Schematic diagram of hepatitis B virion. The 42-nm particle is the "Dane Particle" or the hepatitis B virus. The 22-nm particles are the filamentous and circular forms of hepatitis B surface antigen or protein coat. (Reprinted from Ryan KJ et al: *Sherris Medical Microbiology,* 3rd ed. McGraw-Hill, 1994.)

tain portions of the nucleocapsid. Hepatitis B DNA can also be detected in serum and is an indication that infectious virions are present there. In infected liver tissue, evidence of HBcAg, HBeAg, and hepatitis B DNA is found in the nuclei of infected hepatocytes, whereas HBsAg is found in cytoplasm.

Despite extensive attempts, hepatitis B virus has not been propagated in the laboratory. Humans appear to be the major host; however, as with hepatitis A, infection of subhuman primates has been accomplished experimentally.

The replication of hepatitis B virus involves a reverse transcription step and, as such, is unique among DNA viruses. In viral replication, full-length positive viral RNA transcripts are inserted into maturing core particles late in the replicative cycle. These mRNA strands form a template for a reverse transcription step in which negatively stranded DNA is synthesized. The RNA template strands are then degraded by ribonuclease activity. A positive-stranded DNA is then synthesized, although this step is not completed before virus maturation and release. This results in the variable-length short positive DNA strands found in the virions together with complementary negative long strands. Release is by a secretory mechanism (**reverse endocytosis**) and does not cause cell lysis.

C. Pathogenesis. In the past, hepatitis B was known as post-transfusion hepatitis or as hepatitis associated with the use of illicit parenteral drugs (serum hepatitis). Over the past few years, however, it has become clear that the major mode of acquisition is through close personal contact with body fluids of infected individuals. HBsAg has been found in most body fluids, including saliva, semen, and cervical secretions. Transmission by person-to-person contact has been documented, as has vertical mother-to-child transmission, usually at the time of birth. Under experimental conditions, as little as 0.0001 mL of infectious blood has produced infection. Transmission is therefore also possible by vehicles such as inadequately sterilized hypodermic needles or instruments used in tattooing and ear piercing.

The factors determining the different clinical manifestations of acute hepatitis B are largely unknown; however, some appear to involve immunologic responses of the host. The serum sickness-like rash and arthritis that may precede the development of symptoms and jaundice appear related to circulating immune complexes that activate the complement system. Antibody to HBsAg is protective and associated with resolution of the disease. Cellular immunity also may be important in the host response, because patients with depressed T lymphocyte function have a high frequency of chronic infection with the hepatitis B virus. Antibody to HBcAg, is present in chronic carriers with persistent hepatitis B virion production and it does not appear to be protective.

The morphologic lesions of acute hepatitis B re-semble those of hepatitis A and NANB hepatitis. In chronic active hepatitis B, the continued presence of inflammatory foci of infection results in necrosis of hepatocytes, collapse of the reticular framework of the liver, and progressive fibrosis. The increasing fibrosis can result in the syndrome of postnecrotic hepatic cirrhosis.

Integrated hepatitis B viral DNA can be found in nearly all hepatocellular carcinomas. The virus has not been shown to possess a transforming gene but may well activate a cellular oncogene. It is also possible that the virus does not play such a direct molecular role in oncogenicity, because the natural history of chronic hepatitis B infection involves cycles of damage or death of liver cells interspersed with periods of intense regenerative hyperplasia. This significantly increases the opportunity for spontaneous mutational changes that may activate cellular oncogenes. Whatever the mechanism, the association between chronic viral infection and hepatocellular carcinoma is clear, and liver cancer is a major cause of disease and death in countries in which chronic hepatitis B infection is common. The proven success of immunization in aborting hepatitis B infection makes hepatocellular carcinoma of the liver a potentially preventable disease.

Clinical Findings

A. Signs and Symptoms. The clinical picture of hepatitis B is highly variable. The incubation period is from 45 days to as long as 160 days (mean, ~10 weeks). Acute hepatitis B is usually manifested by the gradual onset of fatigue, loss of appetite, nausea and pain, and fullness in the right upper abdominal quadrant. Early in the course of disease, pain and swelling of the joints and occasionally frank arthritis may occur. Some patients develop a rash. With increasing involvement of the liver, there is increasing cholestasis and, hence, clay-colored stools, darkening of the urine, and jaundice. Symptoms may persist for several months before finally resolving.

In general, the symptoms associated with acute hepatitis B are more severe and more prolonged than those of hepatitis A; however, anicteric disease and asymptomatic infection regularly occur. The infection-to-disease ratio, which varies according to age and method of acquisition, has been estimated to be approximately 6:1 or 7:1.

B. Laboratory Findings. In acute illness, the laboratory findings are as with hepatitis A; persistence of blood abnormalities beyond 6 months may indicate the development of chronic hepatitis B disease.

C. Imaging. As with hepatitis A

D. Differential Diagnosis. As with hepatitis A

E. Complications. Chronic hepatitis occurs in ~10% of all patients with hepatitis B infection The risk of chronic hepatitis B infection is much higher for newborns (100%), children (50%), and immuno-compromised patients. Chronic infection is associated with ongoing replication of virus in the liver and usually with the presence of HBsAg in serum. Chronic hepatitis may lead to cirrhosis, liver failure, hepatocellular carcinoma, or some combination of these. It is estimated that 10% of all chronic liver disease in the United States and Canada is caused by hepatitis B. Fulminant hepatitis, leading to extensive liver necrosis and death, develops in ~0.1% of cases.

Diagnosis

Nonspecific findings in blood are elevations of hepatic enzymes, globulin, and prothrombin time and decreases of albumin and blood leukocytes. The sequential appearance of hepatitis B antigens and antibodies is shown in Figure 39–3. During the acute episode of disease, when there is active viral replication, large amounts of HBsAg and hepatitis B virus DNA can be detected in the serum, as can fully developed virions and high levels of DNA polymerase and HBeAg. Although HBcAg is also present, antibody against it invariably occurs and prevents its detection. With resolution of acute hepatitis B, HBsAg and HBeAg disappear from serum with the development of antibodies (anti-HBs and anti-HBe) against them. The development of anti-HBs is associated with elimination of infection and protection against reinfection. Anti-HBc is detected early in the course of disease and persists in serum for years. It is an excellent epidemiologic marker of infection but is not protective.

In patients with chronic hepatitis B, evidence of viral persistence can be found in serum. HBsAg can be detected throughout the active disease process, and anti-HBs does not develop, which probably accounts for the chronicity of the disease. Anti-HBc is, however, detected. Two types of chronic hepatitis can be distinguished. In one, HBsAg is detected, but not HBeAg; these patients usually show minimal evidence of liver dysfunction. In the other, both antigens are found; the process is more active with continued hepatic damage that may result in cirrhosis. The presence of HBsAg and hepatitis B DNA (HB DNA) is indicative of active viral replication. The laboratory diagnosis of acute hepatitis B is best made by demonstrating the IgM antibody to HBcAg in serum. HBsAg may also be detected in serum. *Past* infection with hepatitis B is best determined by detecting anti-HBc IgG, anti-HBs IgG, or both. Chronic infection with hepatitis B is best detected by persistence of HBsAg in blood for >6–12 months. Vaccine recipients demonstrate an IgG antibody to HbsAg but not to HbcAg.

Treatment

There is no specific treatment for typical acute hepatitis B. A high-calorie diet is desirable. Corticosteroid therapy has no value in uncomplicated typical acute viral hepatitis, and recent studies suggest that it may increase the severity of chronic hepatitis caused by hepatitis B virus. Chronic hepatitis B is a treatable disease. Interferon alpha, 5–10 million U thrice weekly for 4–6 months, provides long-term benefit in a minority (~ 33%) of patients with chronic hepatitis B infection (see Box 39–2). Those who already demonstrate an acute immune response with low serum viral-DNA levels are the most likely to respond to treatment. Lamivudine (3Tc), a potent inhibitor of human immunodeficiency virus (HIV), is also active against hepatitis B virus, both in vitro and in initial clinical trials, but the virus can become resistant to this agent.

Prognosis

Ninety percent of acute hepatitis B cases resolve within 6 months; 0.1% are fatal due to acute hepatic

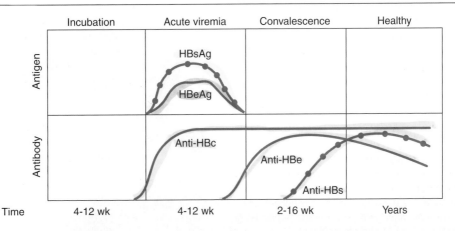

Figure 39–3. Sequence of appearance of viral antigens and antibodies in acute self-limiting cases of hepatitis B. HBsAg, hepatitis B surface antigen; HBeAg, hepatitis B e antigen; anti-HBc, antibody to hepatitis B core antigen; anti-HBe, antibody to HBeAg; anti-HBs, antibody to HBsAg. (Reprinted from Ryan KJ et al: *Sherris Medical Microbiology,* 3rd ed. McGraw-Hill, 1994.)

necrosis; and ~10% progress to chronic hepatitis. Of these, ≥ 10% will develop cirrhosis, hepatocellular carcinoma, or both.

Prevention & Control

Both active prophylaxis and passive prophylaxis of hepatitis B infection can be accomplished. Most preparations of ISG contain only moderate levels of anti-HBs; however, specific hepatitis B immune globulin (HBIG) with significant protective activity is now available. HBIG is prepared from sera of subjects who have high titers of antibody to HbsAg but are free of the antigen itself. Administration of HBIG soon after exposure to the virus greatly reduces the development of symptomatic disease. Postexposure prophylaxis with HBIG should be followed by active immunization with vaccine.

Inactivated hepatitis B vaccines have been available for several years. The first was developed by purification and inactivation of HbsAg from the blood of chronic carriers, but this vaccine is no longer in use. The current vaccine is a recombinant product derived from HBAg grown in yeast. Excellent protection has been shown in studies on homosexual men and medical personnel. These groups and others, such as laboratory workers and injection drug users, who come into contact with blood or other potentially infected materials, should receive hepatitis B vaccine as the preferred method of preexposure prophylaxis. Recently, immunization of all children has been recommended.

A combination of active and passive immunization is the most effective approach to prevent neonatal transmission and, thus, the development of chronic carriage in the neonate. Most hospitals recommend routine screening of pregnant women for the presence of HbsAg. Infants born to women who are positive should receive HBIG in the delivery room followed by three doses of hepatitis B vaccine beginning 24 h after birth.

A similar combination of passive and active immunization is used for nonimmunized persons who have been exposed by needle-stick or similar injuries from a hepatitis BsAg positive individual.

HEPATITIS D (DELTA HEPATITIS)

Essentials of Diagnosis

- Occurs only in patients with preexisting or concurrent hepatitis B.
- Occurs in the same groups at risk for hepatitis B.
- May be associated with fulminant hepatitis or rapid progression of chronic hepatitis B.
- Diagnosed by presence of IgM antibody to hepatitis D antigen or by IgG seroconversion to this antigen.

General Considerations

A. Epidemiology. Delta hepatitis is spread just as hepatitis B and is most prevalent in groups at high risk of hepatitis B infection. Injection drug users are those at greatest risk in the western world, and ~ 50% of such individuals may have IgG antibody to the delta virus antigen. Delta virus infection is rare in the U.S., northern Europe, and Japan but largely prevalent in southern Europe, Africa, and South America. Because blood is not yet routinely screened for the delta agent, blood products and dialysis transmission are possible sources for those who have prior hepatitis B. Nonparenteral and vertical transmission can also occur.

B. Microbiology. Delta hepatitis is caused by the hepatitis D virus. This small single-stranded RNA virus requires the presence of hepatitis B to provide its protein shell and is thus found only in persons with acute or chronic hepatitis B infection.

C. Pathogenesis. The method of replication of hepatitis D viral RNA is not clear. Associated with the RNA are proteins of 27 and 29 kDa that constitute the delta antigen. This protein-RNA complex is surrounded by HBsAg (Figure 39–4). Thus, although the delta virus produces its own antigens, it utilizes HBsAg in assembling its coat.

Clinical Findings

A. Signs and Symptoms. Two major types of delta infection have been noted.

- Simultaneous delta and hepatitis B infection: This infection is clinically identical to acute hepatitis A or B, except for a higher rate of fatal hepatic necrosis than is seen with hepatitis B alone.

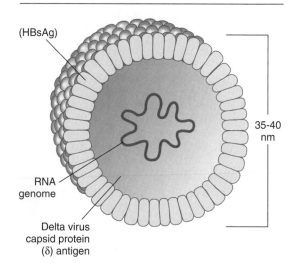

Figure 39–4. Schematic of delta hepatitis virus. Note outer layer derived from hepatitis B surface antigen. (Reprinted from Ryan KJ et al: *Sherris Medical Microbiology,* 3rd ed. McGraw-Hill, 1994.)

- Delta superinfection in those with chronic hepatitis B: This infection increases the severity and progression of chronic hepatitis B. Death due to liver disease may occur in 20% of superinfected patients.

B. Laboratory Findings. Similar to hepatitis A and B

C. Imaging. Similar to hepatitis A and B

D. Differential Diagnosis. Simultaneous infection with both delta and hepatitis B results in clinical hepatitis that is indistinguishable from acute hepatitis A or B; however, fulminant hepatitis is much more common than with hepatitis B virus alone.

E. Complications. Persons with chronic hepatitis B who acquire infection with hepatitis D suffer relapses of jaundice and have a high likelihood of developing chronic cirrhosis. Rapidly progressive liver disease and death may occur in ≤ 20% of doubly infected persons.

Diagnosis

Diagnosis of hepatitis D is made by demonstrating IgM or IgG antibodies, or both, to the delta antigen in serum. IgM antibodies appear within 3 weeks of infection and persist for several weeks. IgG antibodies persist for years.

Treatment

Response to interferon alpha treatment is less than in patients who have only hepatitis B. Recommended doses are higher (5–10 million U daily).

Prognosis

Superinfection with hepatitis D worsens the prognosis of preexisting hepatitis B, increasing the rate and rapidity of developing cirrhosis.

Prevention & Control

Because the capsid of delta hepatitis is HbsAg and hepatitis D depends on hepatitis B for its replication, measures aimed at limiting the transmission of hepatitis B, for example, through vaccination, prevent the transmission of delta hepatitis.

HEPATITIS C

Essentials of Diagnosis

- Acute hepatitis C usually is asymptomatic.
- First recognition of chronic hepatitis C is the presence of elevated liver enzymes in an asymptomatic patient.
- Unexplained chronic hepatitis is most commonly caused by hepatitis C.
- Diagnosis is by presence of hepatitis C IgG antibody.

General Considerations

Most NANB hepatitis is caused by an RNA virus termed hepatitis C virus. Its existence and role in the etiology of hepatitis was identified by preparing numerous complementary DNA clones from the presumed RNA virus in infectious serum. Peptides encoded by these clones were then tested for reaction with sera from cases of NANB hepatitis, and one was found to be highly specific.

A. Epidemiology. The transmission of hepatitis C by blood is well documented: indeed, it caused the great majority of post-transfusion NANB hepatitis. It is estimated that 2% of U.S. citizens have been infected with hepatitis C. Screening of donor blood for hepatitis C has markedly decreased transmission of the virus by blood products. Currently, the major mechanism of transmission is by intravenous drug abuse. Transmission of this virus in nontransfusion, community-acquired cases is less well understood. It may be sexually transmitted but to a much lesser degree than hepatitis B, and vertical transmission may occur. In the United States, 3.5 million people have antibody to hepatitis C, but the number of new cases of hepatitis C has decreased from 80,000 to ~30,000 yearly. Since the 1980s, outbreaks of what is now known as hepatitis C have been associated with intravenous immune globulin (IVIG). To reduce this risk, all U.S.-licensed IVIG products now have viral inactivation steps included in the manufacturing process. In addition all immunoglobulin products (including intramuscular immunoglobulin products that have not been associated with hepatitis C) that lack viral inactivation steps are now excluded if hepatitis C virus is detected by polymerase chain reaction (PCR) analysis.

B. Microbiology. Hepatitis C virus is an RNA virus in the flavivirus family (other members include the agents of yellow fever and dengue). It has a very simple genome consisting of just three structural and five nonstructural genes. There are at least six major genotypes, two of which have subtypes (1a and b, 2a and b). These genotypes have quite different geographic distributions and may be associated with differing severities of disease as well as response to therapy.

C. Pathogenesis. Hepatitis C does not cause acute hepatic cellular necrosis. Rather, there is an insidious infection with a progressive inflammatory response, leading to, in many cases, hepatic fibrosis and cirrhosis. The determinants of progression are not understood.

Clinical Findings

A. Signs and Symptoms. The incubation period of hepatitis C averages 6–12 weeks. The infection is usually asymptomatic or mild and anicteric but results in a chronic carrier state in 70–85% of adults. The average time from infection to the development of chronic hepatitis is 13–18 years. Cirrhosis is a late sequela of chronic hepatitis, which may occur in 15–33% of infected adults and is the leading reason for liver transplants. Chronic hepatitis tends to wax and wane and is often asymptomatic.

B. Laboratory Findings. Hepatitis C may be associated with elevated or normal ALT values in serum.

C. Complications. The risk of hepatocellular carcinoma is 1–5% after 30 years of chronic infection. Cirrhosis may occur in 15–33% of hepatitis C-infected adults.

Diagnosis

Antigens of hepatitis C are not detectable in blood, so diagnostic tests consist of attempts to demonstrate antibody. Unfortunately, the antibody responses in acute disease remain negative for 1–3 weeks after clinical onset and may never become positive in ≤ 20% of patients with acute, resolving disease. These antibody assays can be helpful in chronic hepatitis, especially when multiple antigens are sought. The first test developed to assist the diagnosis of hepatitis C measured antibody to the C-100 antigen of the virus. It is now acknowledged that this antibody is an inaccurate marker for the disease, and current second-generation tests measure antibodies to multiple hepatitis C antigens by either enzyme immunoassay or immunoblot testing. Even with these newer assays, IgG antibody to hepatitis C may not develop for ≤ 4 months, making the serodiagnosis of acute hepatitis C difficult. Assays of hepatitis C virus RNA by PCR or other methods may be used for diagnosis, estimating prognosis, predicting interferon responsiveness, and monitoring therapy.

Treatment

Interferon alpha is approved for the treatment of chronic hepatitis C, but it often provides only a transient benefit (see Box 39–2). The commonly used dose is 3 million U 3 times weekly for ≥ 6 months. Amino transferase levels decrease in only 40–70% of patients, but sustained improvement occurs in only 10–15% of patients. Responses are better in patients with genotypes other than 1 and those with low initial titers of viral RNA. Increasing dosage to 10 million U or extending treatment from 24 to 48 weeks may increase the number of sustained responses. Combination therapy with ribavirin appears to improve efficacy. Corticosteroids are not beneficial

Prognosis

Hepatitis C has a worse prognosis than, for example, hepatitis B, since such a high proportion of cases develop cirrhosis—≤ 33% of infected patients.

Prevention & Control

It is not clear whether prophylactic immune serum globulin protects against hepatitis C. Also, the development of a vaccine is complicated because of the antigenic variability of the virus and patients may be reinfected by different strains of wild-type virus. Reduction of needle sharing by intravenous drug users would greatly reduce the incidence of new cases. (Box 39–3.)

HEPATITIS E

General Considerations

Hepatitis E is the cause of another form of hepatitis, but this virus is spread by the fecal-oral route and therefore resembles hepatitis A. Hepatitis E virus is an RNA virus that appears similar to caliciviruses. The viral particles in stool are spherical, 20–32 nm in diameter, and unenveloped and exhibit spikes on their surface. Like hepatitis A, this virus causes only acute disease and may be fatal, especially in pregnant women. Most cases have been identified in India, Southeast Asia, the Middle East, and other areas with poor sanitation. Rarely have cases been identified in the United States, and these have been in visitors or immigrants from endemic areas.

BOX 39–3

Control of Hepatitis Infection

Prophylactic Measures	Hepatitis A	Hepatitis B	Hepatitis D
	Preexposure: • Vaccination with killed vaccine • Immune serum globulin Postexposure: • Immune serum globulin	Preexposure: • Vaccination with recombinant hepatitis B vaccine Postexposure: • Hepatitis B immune globulin followed by vaccine	• Vaccination with recombinant hepatitis B vaccine
Isolation Precautions	• Hepatitis A, E: enteric precautions • Hepatitis B, C, D: needle, blood precautions		

Diagnosis

Diagnosis of hepatitis E infection may be confirmed by demonstrating the presence of specific IgM antibody.

Treatment

No treatment is available for hepatitis E infection (see Box 39–2).

Prognosis

Hepatitis E does not appear to eventuate in chronic hepatitis, so the prognosis is good, except in the instance of fulminant hepatitis E of pregnancy, which may be fatal.

Prevention & Control

It is not known whether immune serum globulin provides protection.

HEPATITIS G

General Considerations

Although hepatitis C virus is the major cause of NANB hepatitis, additional etiologic agent(s) continue to be sought. In 1995 a newly discovered agent, hepatitis G, was identified in the sera of two patients. This agent is an RNA virus similar to hepatitis C and members of the flavivirus family. Up to 2% of volunteer blood donors are seropositive for hepatitis G antibody, and it is a transmissible blood-borne virus.

In addition to being closely related to hepatitis C, there are data to suggest that many patients infected by hepatitis C are also infected by hepatitis G. Given this close association, it has been difficult to ascertain the contribution of hepatitis G to clinical disease. Patients infected with both viruses do not appear to have worse disease than those infected by hepatitis C virus only.

Diagnosis

So far, it has not been possible to develop an antibody assay so that seroprevalence could be determined. Instead detection of infection with this virus requires a PCR assay for viral RNA in patients' sera.

Treatment

In very limited clinical studies, hepatitis G appears to be susceptible to interferon alpha treatment. Because it is not clear that hepatitis G virus causes disease, treatment is not currently indicated (see Box 39–2).

REFERENCES

de Franchis R et al: The natural history of asymptomatic hepatitis B. Ann Intern Med 1993;118:191–94. (A clinical and laboratory follow-up of HBsAg positive blood donors.)

Johnson Y, Lau N, Wright TL. Molecular virology and pathogenesis of hepatitis B. Lancet 1993;342:1335–39. (This short review covers details of molecular structure and replication of the virus.)

Sharara AI et al: Hepatitis C. Ann Intern Med 1996;125: 658–68.

40

HIV & Other Retroviruses

W. Lawrence Drew, MD, PhD

Essentials of Diagnosis

- Human immunodeficiency virus (HIV) RNA is detected and quantitated by polymerase chain reaction or branched DNA methods.
- Major diagnostic clues to HIV infection are a low CD4 lymphocyte count or an unexplained opportunistic infection.
- Human T-lymphotropic virus type 1 (HTVL-1) infection should be suspected in an adult patient with a T-cell malignancy or spastic paraparesis who is from Japan or the Caribbean basin.

General Considerations

A. Epidemiology. Two major groups of retroviruses are considered in this chapter: the oncoviruses ("onco-," related to a tumor) and the lentiviruses ("lenti-," slow). Oncoviruses have long been associated with a variety of cancers in animals, including leukemia, lymphoma, and sarcoma; however, until recent years, oncoviruses had not been found to infect humans. The first human retrovirus, human T-lymphotropic virus type 1 (HTLV-1), was discovered in the late 1970s. It was shown to cause adult T-cell leukemia, a rare malignancy found only in Japan, Africa, and the Caribbean (although serologic evidence shows that the virus also occurs in the United States and may be associated with some chronic neurologic conditions). A related virus, HTLV-2, has been associated with some cases of human leukemia, including hairy cell leukemia, however its precise role in these diseases remains unclear. The most important disease resulting from human retrovirus infection—the acquired immunodeficiency syndrome (AIDS)—is caused by lentiviruses termed HIV-1 and HIV-2. This chapter focuses on the virology of oncoviruses and lentiviruses and also describes the clinical presentations of the retroviruses other than HIV. See Chapter 23 for a discussion of the clinical presentation of HIV.

B. Microbiology. All retroviruses are remarkably similar in their basic composition. They are enveloped, single-stranded RNA viruses. They encode reverse transcriptase (an RNA-dependent DNA polymerase) that copies the genome into double-stranded DNA, which becomes integrated into the host cell genome. The structure of HIV-1 is depicted in Figure 40–1. In addition to the structural proteins shown in Figure 40–1, the virion contains three virus-specific proteins that are essential for viral replication: reverse transcriptase, protease, and an integrase. The *gag* (group-specific antigen) gene encodes the structural proteins of the virus. The *pol* (polymerase) gene encodes the reverse transcriptase. The *env* (envelope) gene encodes the two membrane glycoproteins found in the viral envelope. Not surprisingly, the surface protein (gp120 in HIV-1) is responsible for the host range of the virus and its antigenicity.

C. Pathogenesis. Like most enveloped viruses, all retroviruses are highly susceptible to inactivation and are thus not transmissible through air, dust, or fomites under normal conditions; that is, they require intimate, direct contact with tissue or bodily fluids from the infecting source. Oncoviruses do not kill the cell they infect but instead usually continue to produce new virus indefinitely. This property, combined with the fact that oncoviruses can transduce growth-promoting genes called oncogenes into the recipient cell, accounts in part for the ability of oncoviruses to cause malignancies.

With lentivirus infections, the cell-virus relationship is quite different. Some lentiviruses can persist for years in a latent state without causing much cell killing, only to become highly cytolytic when the infected cells are subjected to certain stimuli. The prototype lentivirus is the visna virus, which causes a slowly degenerative neurologic disease in sheep. Other lentiviruses, for example, HIV-1, can persistently replicate at high levels resulting in cell death. Although HIV-1 can infect a variety of human cell types, its most drastic effects appear to result from destruction of the CD4$^+$ subclass of T lymphocytes, which play a central role in the capacity of the host to mount effective immunologic responses to a wide range of infections.

VIROLOGY OF THE RETROVIRUSES

The genomes of transforming oncoviruses have a variety of structures, but one feature is common to nearly all of them. Some viral genes are replaced by genes derived from their hosts that render them oncogenic (see below).

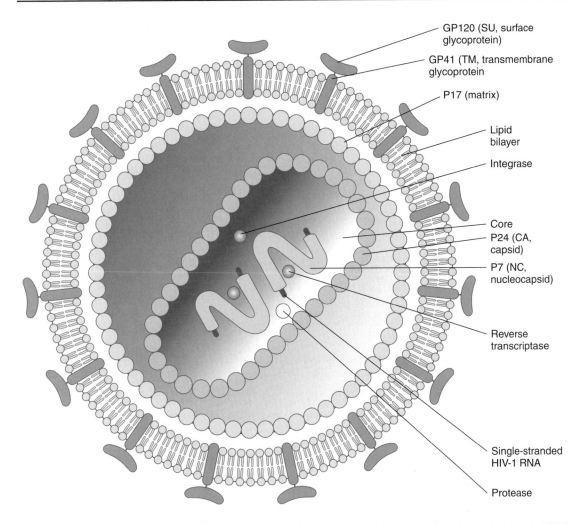

GP120 (SU, surface glycoprotein)

GP41 (TM, transmembrane glycoprotein

P17 (matrix)

Lipid bilayer

Integrase

Core
P24 (CA, capsid)

P7 (NC, nucleocapsid)

Reverse transcriptase

Single-stranded HIV-1 RNA

Protease

Figure 40–1. Structure of HIV-1. The virion is ~100 nm in diameter and contains two copies of a single-stranded RNA genome. The RNA genome is coated with the nucleocapsid protein (NC), and the RNA protein complexes are enclosed in a capsid (CA) composed of multiple subunits. Like all enveloped viruses, the membrane is acquired during budding from the host cell, but the surface (SU) and transmembrane (TM) glycoproteins found in the envelope are virally encoded. Between the capsid and the envelope is a matrix (MA) protein.

A comparison of the genetic makeup of HIV-1 with that of other retroviruses reveals a larger number of genes and a much more complex organization. HIV-1 contains, in addition to the usual ensemble of genes, an array of other genes (*tat, rev, nef, vif, vpr,* and *vpu*) (Figure 40–2). These additional genes apparently encode proteins that serve regulatory roles important in determining the long period of latency exhibited by the virus (see below). HTLV-1 encodes a similar array of regulatory proteins. To date, approximately nine subtypes of HIV-1 clads and five of HIV-2 have been discovered, based on their *env* and *gag* sequences.

Figure 40–3 depicts the life cycle of a typical retrovirus and illustrates the many unique steps in retroviral replication that could be potential targets of therapeutic intervention.

Viral Entry

The virions adsorb to cellular membrane receptors and enter the cell probably by direct fusion with the plasma membrane. For HIV-1, the virion attachment protein is the surface glycoprotein gp120, and the cell receptor is the CD4 molecule that occurs primarily on the plasma membrane of CD4+ T lymphocytes, cells of the monocyte macrophage series, and some other target cells. The HIV-1 transmembrane protein gp41 is responsible for fusion of viral and cell membranes, a process that is important for entry of the virus into the host cell.

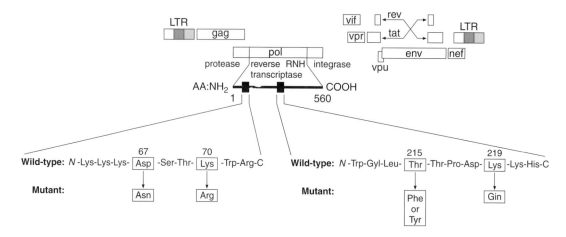

Figure 40–2. HIV mutation and resistance to zidovudine. HIV has a rapid mutation rate of approximately 1:10,000 replications. Certain mutations of the HIV-reverse transcriptase gene are capable of conferring resistance to the effects of the nucleoside analogs. Mutations at codons 67, 70, 215, and 219 have been shown to confer resistance to zidovudine in vitro. (Reprinted from Richman DD et al: Detection of mutations associated with zidovudine resistance in human immunodeficiency virus by use of the polymerase chain reaction. J Infect Dis 1991;164:1075–1081.)

HIV-1 can also infect cells such as fibroblasts and certain brain cells that lack the CD4 surface molecule, apparently because the fusion-inducing activity of the transmembrane protein is sufficient in these cases to promote entry. An additional aspect of fusion activity is that infected cells expressing viral glycoproteins in their membranes readily fuse with uninfected CD4$^+$ T lymphocytes to form large syncytia. This process appears to provide a means for cell-to-cell transmission of the virus that bypasses the usual extracellular phase and also damages the membrane of uninfected cells and affects their viability.

Viral RNA Replication

Among the RNA viruses, retroviral replication is unique. Soon after entry of the viral core into the cytoplasm of the infected cell, the RNA is copied into double-stranded DNA by reverse transcriptase, the virion-associated DNA polymerase. The process of reverse transcription results in a linear DNA molecule that enters the nucleus and integrates into the host cell chromosome. The viral integrase catalyzes the reaction required for the integration of the linear DNA into host DNA. Once the viral genetic information has been converted to DNA and integrated, it essentially becomes part of the cellular genome. The viral genes, called the provirus, replicate together with the host genome as long as the infected cell continues to divide.

Special sequences contained within the RNA are duplicated during the reverse transcription process so that the integrated provirus contains identical long terminal repeats at its ends. The long terminal repeat sequences contain the appropriate promoter and enhancer and other signals required for transcription of the viral genes by the host RNA polymerase II. Transcription produces both a full-length RNA genome and one or more spliced messenger RNAs (mRNAs). The predominant spliced mRNA is translated to produce the envelope glycoproteins, but, in HIV-1, a series of spliced mRNAs are produced that also encode a variety of viral regulatory proteins. With the exception of these regulatory proteins, all retroviral proteins are initially translated as polyproteins that are subsequently processed by proteolysis into the individual protein molecules. The enzyme responsible for most of these protein cleavages is the virus-specific protease that is encoded in either the *gag* gene or the *pol* gene of the virus. Of all the known retroviruses, HIV-1 possesses the most error-prone reverse transcriptase. This property accounts for the many nucleotide differences observed between isolates (even from the same infected individual) and for the variability of the gp120 antigen. It may explain in part the failure of the immune system to control the infection and the increases in viral virulence that appear to occur during the course of the infection.

Unique Feature of the Lentiviruses

A unique feature of HIV-1 and other members of the lentivirus subfamily is the ability to produce a complex array of regulatory proteins. Although much remains to be determined about the regulatory circuits that modulate HIV-1 gene expression, several features of the process have been established.

Regulation appears to occur at three levels: mRNA production, transport of unspliced versus spliced mRNAs from the nucleus to the cytoplasm, and maturation of viral proteins during budding. Regulation

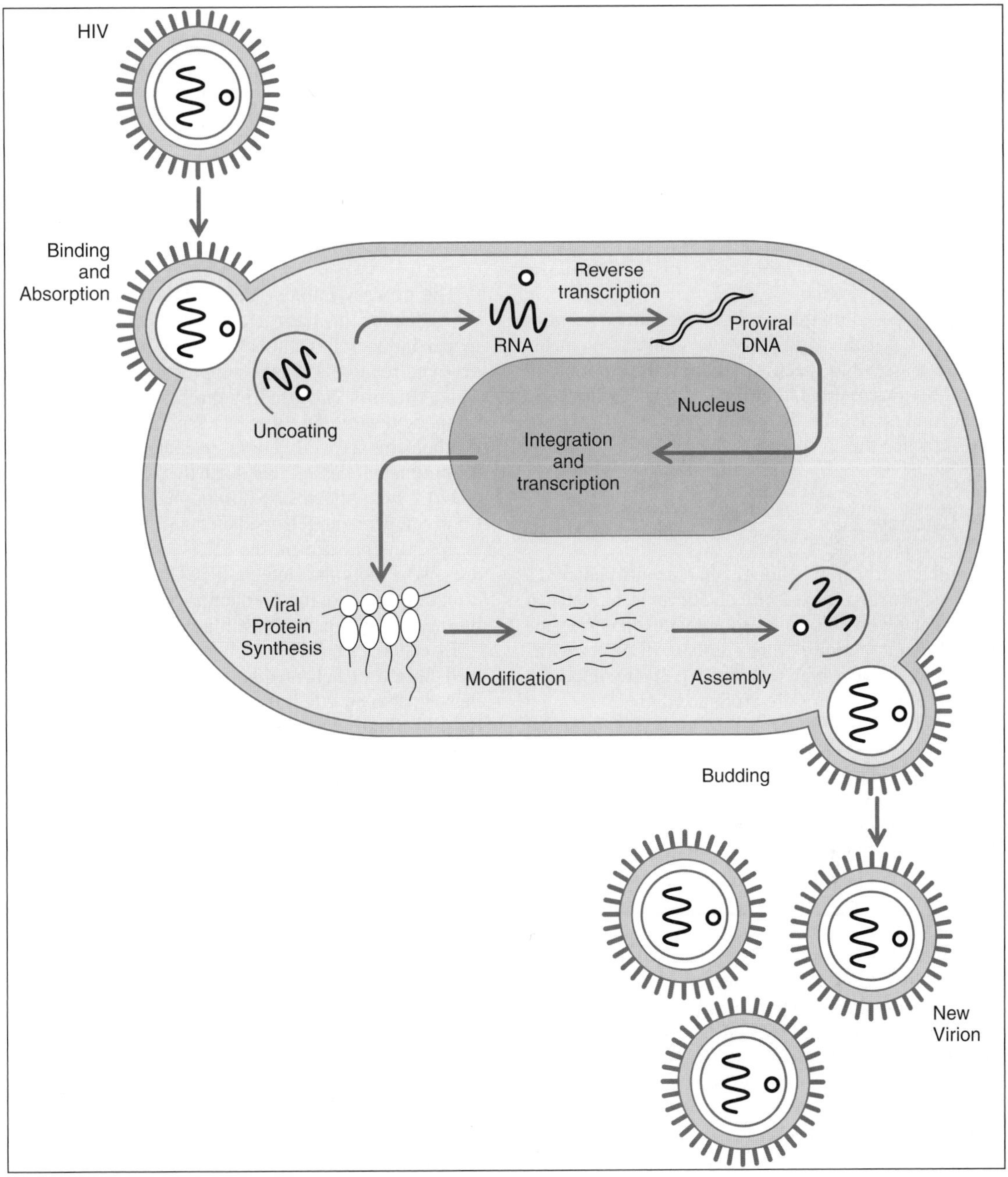

Figure 40–3. HIV life cycle and its inhibition. The nucleoside analogs exert their effect on HIV replication at the reverse transcription stage—that is, after the virus has entered the host cell genome. The affinity of HIV-reverse transcriptase for nucleoside analogs is greater than that for the endogenous substrates; the triphosphate form of the analogs preferentially attaches to a nucleotide-binding site of the enzyme, competitively inhibiting binding of the endogenous 5'-triphosphate molecule. The protease inhibitors block cleavage of polyproteins at a stage prior to assembly of immature viral proteins into particles.

may also occur at the level of mRNA translation. The HIV-1 regulatory proteins and their functions are listed in Table 40–1.

Two of the regulatory proteins, TAT and REV, play a positive role in promoting viral gene expression. The TAT protein increases the rate of viral mRNA synthesis, and REV promotes the transport of full-length mRNA to the cytoplasm before it can be spliced. The combined action of these two regulatory proteins is to promote the production of virus particles. The VIF protein promotes virus production at the level of maturation.

Superimposed on this complex regulatory network is the fact that the viral promoter contains elements that are sensitive to specific cellular transcription factors. This observation may help explain why virus production in CD4+ T lymphocytes is greatly increased when the cells are activated.

HIV Latency

Until recently, it was thought that the virus entered a latent stage in an infected host and became activated at a later date. Now it is understood that even during the asymptomatic period before clinical AIDS, the virus duplicates at a very high rate with a half-life of 2 days. Billions of HIV viruses are produced daily.

The long asymptomatic period after HIV infection (clinical latency) occurs despite active virus replication in the host. Several factors can terminate the long latent period of HIV-1. Mutations occur during viral replication that appear to increase cytopathic capacity and alter cell tropisms. In the same patient, the mutated forms of HIV-1 isolated from later stages of disease infect a broader range of cell types, grow more rapidly than those isolated in the asymptomatic period, and may induce syncytial formation (SI variants).

The virus replicates in macrophages, and these cells may serve as a reservoir for spread of the infection to other cell types by cell-to-cell fusion, which allows the virus to spread without being exposed to neutralizing antibodies. In addition to CD4$^+$ T lymphocytes and macrophages, the most prominent cell types infected are glial cells and astrocytes in the brain and cells of the bowel mucosa. Infected macrophages may participate in the breakdown of the blood-brain barrier, allowing exposure of the central nervous system. Although central nervous system and intestinal disturbances are a prominent part of full-blown AIDS, it is not clear whether they are a direct result of infection of these cells or mediated by cytokines from infected macrophages and T lymphocytes.

The primary immune defect in AIDS results from the reduction in number and effectiveness of CD4$^+$ helper-inducer T lymphocytes, both in absolute numbers and relative to CD8+ suppressor T lymphocytes. This reduction is caused by direct killing of CD4$^+$ T lymphocytes by the virus but may also involve other mechanisms as well. These mechanisms include autoimmune processes that lead to the elimination of CD4$^+$ T lymphocytes by opsonophagocytosis and antibody-dependent cell-mediated cytotoxicity directed at gp120 expressed on the CD4$^+$ cell surface. There are also functional defects in CD4$^+$ T lymphocytes affecting lymphokine production and leading to inhibition of some macrophage functions.

Effects on CD4$^+$ T lymphocytes lead to a generalized failure of cell-mediated immune responses, but there is also an effect on antibody production caused by polyclonal activation of B cells, possibly associated with other viral infections of these cells. This overwhelms the capacity of infected individuals to respond to specific antigens. The result of these processes is a disturbance of immune balance that can give rise to malignancies as well as to a range of opportunistic viral, fungal, and bacterial infections.

Transformation by Retroviruses

Oncogenic retroviruses appear to transform cells to an oncogenic state by three distinct mechanisms. First, the transforming viruses have acquired a cellular gene (called an "oncogene") that, when expressed in the infected cell, results in the loss of normal

Table 40–1. Human immunodeficiency virus (HIV) and human T-lymphotropic virus (HTLV) regulatory proteins.

Gene	Protein	Function
HIV *tat*	TAT	Increases rate of viral transcription.
HTLV *tax*	TAX	Same as for TAT.
HIV *rev*	REV	Increases transport of unspliced mRNAs.
HTLV *rex*	REX	Same as for REV.
HIV *nef*	NEF	Negative regulator of transcription.
HIV *vif*	VIF	Facilitates virus maturation during budding.

BOX 40–1

Oncovirus (HTLV) Infections

	Children	Adults
More Common	• Clinical syndromes not identified in children	• Adult T-cell leukemia
Less Common		• Tropical spastic paraparesis

BOX 40–2

Treatment of Oncovirus (HTLV) Infection

	Adults
First Choice	• Chemotherapy for malignancy
Second Choice	• Antiretroviral agents (investigational only)

BOX 40–3

Control of Oncovirus (HTLV) Infection

Prophylactic Measures	• As with HIV, prevention is best accomplished by eliminating exposure to bodily fluids, especially blood and semen.
Isolation Precautions	• Eliminate exposure to bodily fluids, especially blood.

growth control. On infection, the oncogene is expressed, resulting in the rapid onset of malignant disease. Persistent transformation by oncogene transduction is possible only for those retroviruses that are not cytocidal. More than 25 different oncogenes have been identified in a variety of animal retroviruses, but no human retroviruses are known that transform by this mechanism.

The second mechanism is called "insertional mutagenesis." Integration of a retrovirus near particular cellular genes can cause inappropriate expression of the gene, resulting in uncontrolled cell growth. These cellular genes are called "proto-oncogenes," and insertional activation by the virus is apparently caused by the close proximity of the integrated viral promoter or enhancer to the gene. Cancers that are caused by this mechanism have very long latent periods because integration is random and only rarely occurs near a cellular proto-oncogene. No human cancers are known to be caused by this mechanism.

The causative agent of adult T-cell leukemia, HTLV-1, exemplifies the third mechanism. In this case, the integrated provirus in the leukemic cells from any one patient is found at a unique location on a particular chromosome. Thus the tumors are probably monoclonal. However, the cancer is not the result of insertional mutagenesis because the chromosomal location of the provirus is never the same in any two patients. Instead, transformation results from the continual expression of the viral *tax* gene (the HTLV-1 homolog of the HIV-1 *tat* gene). Apparently, the TAX protein not only can activate viral transcription in the same manner as TAT but can also activate the expression of one or more cellular genes (possibly proto-oncogenes) resulting in malignant transformation. These leukemia viruses cause cancer after a long latency period.

ONCOVIRUSES (HTLV-1)

Clinical Findings

HTLV-1 infection is usually asymptomatic but can progress to adult T-cell leukemia in ~1 in 20 persons (Box 40–1). Adult T-cell leukemia caused by HTLV-1 is a neoplasia of CD4 helper T cells that can be acute or chronic. In addition to an elevated and abnormal lymphocyte count, lymphadenopathy, splenomegaly, and hepatomegaly also occur. The skin lesions vary from localized maculas, papule nodules, and plaques to generalized erythroderma. Adult T-cell leukemia is usually fatal within 1 year of diagnosis, regardless of treatment. A second syndrome associated with HTLV-1 infection is tropical spastic paraparesis. This is a slowly progressing neurologic disorder that usually begins as bilateral weakness of the lower extremities with hyper-reflexia. Numbness, back pain, and symptoms of bladder irritation also develop.

HTLV-1 infection is detected immunologically by the presence of HTLV-1 antibody in blood. A diagnosis of adult T-cell leukemia is supported by a high number of abnormal lymphocytes in blood and is confirmed by identification of HTLV-1 DNA in these cells.

Treatment & Control

Adult T-cell leukemia may respond briefly to chemotherapy, but no treatment has been proved effective against HTLV-1 infection. Zidovudine (azidothymidine [AZT]) and other inhibitors of reverse transcriptase are active against HTLV-1 in tissue culture, but controlled studies are needed. See Boxes 40–2 and 40–3 for additional comments.

REFERENCES

Levy JA: Pathogenesis of human immunodeficiency virus infection. Microbiol Rev 1993;57:183. (Detailed review of the mechanisms involved in the initiation and all stages of HIV infection.)

Rosenblatt JD: Human T-lymphotropic virus types I and II. West J Med 1993;158:379. (Molecular analogies to HIV explained.)

41

Poxviruses

W. Lawrence Drew, MD, PhD

Essentials of Diagnosis

- Multiple, large, eosinophilic cytoplasmic inclusions in epithelial cells (H & E stain).
- Vesicular or nodular skin lesions.
- Exposure by occupation or close personal contact.
- High index of suspicion in patients with skin lesions and exposure to sheep, goats, or cows.

General Considerations

Poxviruses are a large, complex family of viruses that cause disease in humans and other animals (Table 41–1). Of the many genera in this family, only species of Orthopoxvirus and Molluscipoxvirus are associated specifically with humans. The former contains variola virus (smallpox), which is currently of historical interest only, and the latter molluscum contagiosum virus. Poxviruses in other genera naturally infect animals (zoonoses) but cause incidental infection of humans.

A. Epidemiology. Molluscum contagiosum infection is spread through direct person-to-person contact or through sharing of common towels etc. The agents of the zoonotic poxvirus diseases spread by direct contact.

B. Microbiology. Poxviruses are the largest of all viruses, measuring 230 by 300 nm, and are ovoid to brick shaped. They have a capsid that is referred to as complex because it has neither helical nor icosahedral symmetry. An outer membrane and envelope enclose the core and core membrane. The viral genome is a single strand of large, linear, double-stranded DNA (molecular weight approximately 100×10^6–100×200^6).

Replication of poxviruses is unique among DNA-containing viruses, because the entire multiplication cycle takes place within the host cell cytoplasm. Viral penetration occurs within phagocytic vacuoles. Uncoating of the outer membrane occurs in the vacuole. Early gene transcription occurs within the viral core. Among the early proteins produced is an uncoating protein that removes the core membrane, liberating viral DNA into the cell cytoplasm. Replication of viral DNA follows in electron-dense cytoplasmic inclusions, referred to as factories. Late viral mRNA is translated into structural proteins, which are glycosylated, phosphorylated, and cleaved before assembly. Unlike other viruses, poxvirus membranes form de novo in the cytoplasm, rather than as part of

a host cell membrane that is picked up during a budding process. About 10,000 viral particles are produced per infected cell.

C. Pathogenesis. The pathologic hallmark of poxviruses is cell proliferation, manifested by the skin lesions that give this family of viruses its name. Most of the viruses of current human importance are primary pathogens in vertebrates other than humans (eg, cow, sheep, and goats) and infect humans only through accidental occupational exposure (zoonosis). As stated earlier, the exception to this is molluscum contagiosum.

CLINICAL SYNDROMES

MOLLUSCUM CONTAGIOSUM

Clinical Findings

A. Signs and Symptoms. The incubation period is 2–8 weeks. The lesions differ significantly from pox lesions in that they are nodular to wartlike. They begin as papules and progress to pearly, umbilicated nodules 2–10 mm in diameter, with a central caseous plug that can be readily expressed. They are most common on the trunk, genitalia, and proximal extremities and usually occur in a cluster of 5–20 nodules (Box 41–1). Lesions disappear in 2–12 months even without treatment. Often a history can be elicited of contact with an individual with skin lesions, eg, from wrestling or sexual contact.

B. Laboratory Findings. The lesions of molluscum contagiosum are caused by a poxvirus that is unclassified because it does not grow in cell cultures but can be confirmed histologically by finding large eosinophilic inclusions in the cytoplasm (molluscum bodies) of epithelial cells.

C. Differential Diagnosis. Molluscum contagiosum lesions may be mistaken for warts but can be distinguished by expression of cheesy material from the center of each lesion, by histologic examination, and by location.

Table 41–1. Diseases associated with poxvirus.

Virus	Disease	Source	Location
Variola	Smallpox (now extinct)	Humans	Extinct
Vaccinia	Vaccination complications	Vaccine	Research laboratories
Molluscum contagiosum	Many skin lesions	Humans	Worldwide
Orf	Localized lesion	Zoonosis: sheep, goats	Worldwide
Cowpox	Localized lesion	Zoonosis: cows	Europe
Pseudocowpox	Milker's nodule	Zoonosis: dairy cows	Worldwide
Monkeypox	Generalized disease	Zoonosis: monkeys, squirrels	Africa

ZOONOTIC POXVIRUSES

1. ORF & COWPOX

The poxviruses of animals such as sheep or goats (orf) and cows (cowpox) can infect humans, usually as a result of accidental direct contact.

Clinical Findings

A. Signs and Symptoms. Single or multiple nodular lesions are usually found on the fingers or face and are vesicular or pustular (cowpox) or granulomatous (orf). After progressing from a vesicular lesion to a nodular mass, the lesion usually regresses in 25–35 days.

B. Laboratory Findings. There are no characteristic abnormalities in blood counts or chemistries.

C. Differential Diagnosis. The lesion may be mistaken for anthrax. The anthrax lesion, however, is vesicular, then ulcerative, and finally, a black eschar and does not develop a nodular appearance.

D. Complications. Because orf and cowpox lesions resolve completely, there are no complications.

2. PSEUDOCOWPOX OR MILKER'S NODULES

Clinical Findings

A. Signs and Symptoms. Pseudocowpox or Milker's nodules is a cutaneous disease of cattle, distinct from cowpox, that can cause localized papular

lesions which progress to purplish nodules. Healing of the skin lesions may take 4–8 weeks.

B. Differential Diagnosis. The lesions can resemble the eschar of anthrax or the early lesion of orf or cowpox, but milker's nodules are nonulcerating.

3. MONKEYPOX

Over 100 cases of an illness resembling smallpox have been attributed to the monkeypox virus. Multiple vesiculopustular lesions occur, but the illness is not as severe. All have occurred in western and central Africa, especially Zaire. There has been concern that this agent might replace the smallpox virus and become epidemic in humans, but this has not materialized probably because animal poxviruses seem highly adapted to their particular host and require very close, usually direct, contact for transmission.

Treatment

Molluscum Contagiosum. Treatment of molluscum contagiosum, if lesions are extensive or cosmetically disfiguring, is curettage, forceps removal of central core, or application of liquid nitrogen or iodine solutions (Box 41–2).

BOX 41–1

Molluscum Contagiosum Infection

	Children	Adults
More Common	Lesions on exposed epithelial surfaces	Genital lesions, may be generalized in AIDS patients
Less Common		

BOX 41–2

Treatment of Molluscum Contagiosum Infection

	Children	Adults
First Choice	No systemic treatment	No systemic treatment
Second Choice		• Local Rx with liquid nitrogen or iodine solution • Laser, cryotherapy, curettage, especially in AIDS patients
Pediatric Considerations	Rx rarely necessary	

Zoonotic Poxviruses. Since the lesions of zoonotic poxviruses heal in 4–6 weeks, treatment is unnecessary.

Prevention & Control

Molluscum Contagiosum. Prevention of molluscum contagiosum consists of avoiding direct or indirect contact with individuals exhibiting characteristic skin lesions (Box 41–3).

Zoonotic Poxviruses. The zoonotic poxviruses can be avoided by avoiding contact with animals exhibiting skin lesions, especially when the human has potentially infected cuts or abrasions.

BOX 41–3

Control of Molluscum Contagiosum Infection

Prophylactic Measures	In adults, may be sexually transmitted and "safe sex" may decrease spread. Direct contact with lesions should be avoided.
Isolation Precautions	None required

REFERENCES

Baxby D, Bennett M, Getty B: Human cowpox 1969–93: a review based on 54 cases. Br J Dermatol 1994;131:598.

Buller RM, Palumbo GJ: Poxvirus pathogenesis. Microbiol Rev 1991;55:80.

Moss B: Vaccinia virus: a tool for research and vaccine development. Science 1991;252:1662.

Parvoviruses

42

W. Lawrence Drew, MD, PhD

Essentials of Diagnosis

- Erythema infectiosum: "slapped cheek" rash in a child.
- Aplastic crisis in patients with chronic hemolytic anemia or AIDS.
- Giant pronormoblasts seen in bone marrow.
- Specific antibody (immunoglobulin G [IgG] and IgM), although these may not develop in certain immunocompromised patients.
- Detection of specific nucleic acids (eg, by polymerase chain reaction [PCR] assay) or antigens in blood.

General Considerations

Parvoviruses are widespread bird and mammalian viruses. More than 50 types have been identified, but the most common identified human pathogen is parvovirus B19. It is the cause of erythema infectiosum (Fifth disease) and is responsible for episodes of aplastic crises in patients with chronic anemia, especially those with hemolytic anemia and AIDS (Box 42–1). B19 is also associated with arthritis and intrauterine infection.

A. Epidemiology. Up to 90% of the adult population have antibodies to B19. Most infections with this virus occur by 40 years of age. As many as 25% of these infections are asymptomatic and one half are unaccompanied by a rash. Erythema infectiosum is most common in children from ages 4 to 15 years, and it tends to occur in winter and spring. The route of natural transmission is presumably by respiratory droplets. Parenteral transmission of B19 has been described.

B. Microbiology. B19 virus is an extremely small (18- to 26-nm diameter), nonenveloped, icosahedral virion. The B19 virus genome contains one linear single-stranded DNA molecule with a molecular weight of $1.5–1.8 \times 10^6$ (5.5 kb in length). The viral genome codes for three structural and one nonstructural protein.

The replicative cycle includes infection of mitotically active cells such as erythroid precursor cells. The receptor molecule for B19 is a glycolipid antigen on the surface of erythrocytes. Transcription, replication, and assembly occur in the host cell nucleus. Steps in DNA replication most likely require host cell

functions present only in the late *"S"* phase, necessitating a mitotically active host cell.

C. Pathogenesis. Intranasal inoculation of volunteers with B19 virus suggests that the virus first replicates in the upper respiratory tract, followed by viremia and replication in erythroid precursor cells in the bone marrow. This replication inhibits proliferation of precursor erythrocytes. Infection of a normal host may result in mild nonspecific symptoms such as sore throat, malaise, and myalgia, and a slight drop in hemoglobin. Infection of hosts with chronic hemolytic anemia (eg, sickle cell anemia) may result in life-threatening reticulocytopenia, referred to as aplastic crisis.

The initial course of B19 virus infection in healthy children includes the symptoms just described, resulting from lytic virus infection, and a noninfectious, immunologic phase approximately 2–3 weeks after initial infection. The immunologic phase, which includes rash and arthralgia, is termed erythema infectiosum and appears to be immune mediated, since symptoms accompany the appearance of virus-specific IgM and circulating immune complexes. Antibody produced during infection presumably confers life-long immunity.

ERYTHEMA INFECTIOSUM

Clinical Findings

A. Signs and Symptoms. Erythema infectiosum (Fifth disease) begins with a distinctive rash on the face resembling a cheek that has been slapped. The rash then usually spreads, especially to exposed skin such as the arms and legs, and then subsides over a 1–2 week period. Relapse of the rash may occur often. In adults, arthritis of hands, wrists, knees, and ankles predominates, and the rash often does not occur or it may precede the arthritis.

B. Laboratory Findings. There are no distinctive blood abnormalities in patients with erythema infectiosum. In patients with aplastic crisis, there is profound anemia with no reticulocytosis.

C. Complications. The most serious complication of parvovirus infection is the aplastic crisis that occurs in patients with chronic anemia, including

BOX 42-1

Parvovirus Infection

	Children	Adults
More Common	Erythema infectiosum	Febrile arthritis
Less Common	Fetal infection Stillbirth	Aplastic crisis

BOX 42-2

Control of Parvovirus Infection

Prophylactic Measures	Presumed respiratory transmission but most contagious in the preclinical stage.
Isolation Precautions	Respiratory

those with human immunodeficiency viral infection who cannot control viral replication.

APLASTIC CRISIS

Clinical Findings

A. Signs and Symptoms. Aplastic crisis is accompanied by fever and nonspecific symptoms of malaise, myalgia, chills, and itching. Parvovirus infection in these patients may be associated with maculopapular rash with arthralgia and some joint swelling.

B. Laboratory Findings. The infection is characterized by transient reduction of erythropoiesis in the bone marrow and results in a transient reticulocytopenia (7–10 days) and a decrease in hemoglobin levels. In AIDS or immunocompromised patients, these abnormalities may persist, constantly or intermittently, for months to years.

Other Complications

In addition to chronic marrow suppression, mentioned above, B19 infection is also associated with fetal infection and stillbirth, although infection of pregnant women may occur without any adverse effect on the fetus. However, there is no evidence that B19 causes congenital abnormalities.

Diagnosis

B19 virus is not recovered in tissue culture but can be directly detected in serum or throat washes during the prodromal period or aplastic crisis by enzyme and radioimmunoassay, nucleic acid hybridization, and immune electron microscopy. PCR is a very sensitive method for detecting B19 but may remain positive for months after B19 infection. The presence of characteristic "giant" pronormoblasts in bone marrow may provide a clue to parvovirus as the cause of an aplastic crisis.

More readily available and applicable to patients with erythema infectiosum and aplastic crisis is the virus-specific IgM test, which indicates current or recent infection. This test is not useful in AIDS patients because they do not mount an IgM antibody response.

Treatment

No specific antiviral treatment is known, but chronic B19-induced anemia may be treatable with immune globulin.

Prognosis

B19 infection can be chronic in immunocompromised patients, with intermittent worsening of anemia for months to years.

Prevention & Control

Control of respiratory spread could decrease transmission of B19 virus; however, patients with clinically apparent erythema infectiosum are no longer infectious. Transmission therefore would occur before preventive measures (eg, isolation) are enacted (Box 42–2).

REFERENCES

Cassinotti P et al: Association between human parvovirus B19 infection and arthritis. Ann Rheumat Dis 1995;54: 498.

Frickhofen N, Abkowitz JL, Safford M et al: Persistent B19 parvovirus infection in patients infected with human immunodeficiency virus type 1 (HIV1): a treatable cause of anemia in AIDS. Ann Intern Med 1990;113:926.

Gratacos E et al: The incidence of human parvovirus B19 infection during pregnancy and its impact on perinatal outcome. J Infect Dis 1995;171:1360.

Heegaard ED, Hornsleth A: Parvovirus: the expanding spectrum of disease. Acta Paediatr 1995;84:109.

Viral Infection of the Central Nervous System

43

W. Lawrence Drew, MD, PhD

Many viruses causing infection of the central nervous system (CNS) are covered in chapters devoted to each type of virus. For example, enteroviruses, the agents most frequently causing meningitis and occasionally encephalitis, are covered in Chapter 27. The herpes viruses that cause meningitis, encephalitis, or both, especially herpes simplex virus (HSV), varicella-zoster virus (VZV), and Epstein-Barr virus (EBV), are discussed in Chapter 33. This chapter considers viruses that cause CNS diseases (Box 43–1) as their primary manifestations.

ARTHROPOD-BORNE VIRAL ENCEPHALITIS

Essentials of Diagnosis

- Summer and fall cases, especially if in a cluster or outbreak, suggest arboviruses or enteroviruses.
- History of exposure to mosquitoes suggests arbovirus infection, especially in geographic areas of high endemicity (eg, swamps of Florida).
- Maculopapular rash suggests enterovirus disease.
- Lymphocytic pleocytosis in cerebrospinal fluid (CSF) with normal glucose and protein concentrations suggests viral meningitis.

General Considerations

Arthropod-borne (arbo) viruses causing encephalitis are members of the toga-, flavi-, and bunyavirus families. The medically important togaviruses include rubella virus, which is discussed in Chapter 36, and the equine encephalitis viruses. The flavivirus family, which includes St. Louis encephalitis (SLE) and West Nile viruses, also includes dengue and yellow fever viruses; the latter described in detail in Chapter 44. The bunyaviruses causing CNS disease are members of the California encephalitis (CE) virus group, but other pathogenic bunyaviruses include the hantaviruses, which are discussed in Chapter 44. The older term, arbovirus, refers to those encephalitis-causing viruses that have an arthropod vector, eg, mosquitoes or ticks. These viruses have a very broad host range, including mammals, birds, amphibians, and reptiles.

A. Epidemiology. Togaviruses and flaviviruses are prototypical arboviruses. As arboviruses, they infect both vertebrates and invertebrates, and they initiate a viremia in a vertebrate host and a persistent, productive infection of the salivary gland of the invertebrate to provide virus for infection of other host animals. If the virus is not in the blood, the arthropod vector cannot pick it up. The infection cycle involves transmission of the virus by the arthropod vector and amplification in a susceptible, natural host to allow reinfection of other arthropods. Humans are usually dead-end hosts that cannot spread the virus back to the vector because a persistent viremia is not maintained. Table 43–1 lists vectors, natural hosts, and a geographic distribution for representative togaviruses and flaviviruses.

These viruses are usually restricted to a specific genus of arthropod vector and its vertebrate host. The most common vector is the mosquito, but some arboviruses are also spread by ticks and sand flies. Not all arthropods can act as good vectors for each virus. For example, *Culex quinquefasciatus* is resistant to infection by western equine encephalitis (WEE) virus (a togavirus) but is an excellent vector for SLE virus (a flavivirus). As with mosquito-borne viruses, the life cycle of the tick dictates the pattern of spread of tick-borne viruses.

In endemic regions, the risk of arbovirus infection increases during the rainy season. Pools of standing water, drainage ditches, and sumps in cities can provide breeding grounds for mosquitoes, such as *Culex* spp., the vector of SLE and West Nile virus. During the summer months the arboviruses are cycled between a host (eg, bird) and an arthropod (eg, mosquito). This cycle maintains and increases the amount of virus in the environment. In the winter neither the normal host nor the vector remains to maintain the virus. The virus may persist in arthropod larvae or eggs or in reptiles or amphibians that remain in the locale, or it may be blown by the winds or migrate with the birds and then return during the summer.

Birds and small mammals are the usual hosts for the togaviruses and flaviviruses, but reptiles, amphibians, and, rarely, humans can also act as hosts. Development of a large population of viremic animals can occur in these species to continue the infection cycle

BOX 43–1

Other Viral Infections of the CNS

	Children	Adults
More Frequent	WEE, EEE, CE	SLE
Less Frequent	SLE	WEE, EEE, VEE, West Nile Virus
Rare	Progressive multifocal leukoencephalopathy, rabies	Progressive multifocal leukoencephalopathy Creutzfeldt-Jakob disease, rabies

of the virus. Although some of these viruses are called equine encephalitis viruses, the horse sometimes is a dead-end host. However, as with humans, the horse may develop clinical disease.

CE viruses are arthropod-borne members of the bunyavirus family. Bunyaviruses were known as arboviruses until the discovery of hantaviruses, members of the family that are transmitted to humans without the aid of arthropod vectors. Despite its name, CE occurs almost exclusively in the eastern half of the United States and especially in the North Central States. The name derives from the fact that the first representative of this virus group was isolated in Kern County, Calif., but the most common type causing disease in the United States is the La Crosse virus, which was first isolated in Wisconsin. This virus causes the most prevalent arbovirus infection in children in the United States.

The age distribution of patients with arthropod-borne encephalitis is striking. SLE and West Nile virus cause clinical illness in older adults, CE in school-aged children, and western and eastern equine encephalitis (WEE and EEE) predominately in infants and young children.

B. Microbiology. The toga- and flaviviruses are enveloped, single-stranded ribonucleic acid (RNA) viruses. Until recently the flaviviruses were included in the *Togaviridae* family, but differences in size, morphology, gene sequence, and replication have made it necessary to classify them as an independent virus family.

The flaviviruses also have plus-strand RNA and an envelope. However, the virions are slightly smaller than those of the togaviruses (37–50 nm in diameter). All the flaviviruses are serologically related, and antibodies to one virus may cross-neutralize another virus.

CE viruses are intermediate-sized RNA viruses (90-120 nm in diameter) in the bunyavirus genus that are spherical in appearance. They are enveloped and contain three separate pieces of negative-strand RNA of differing lengths.

C. Pathogenesis. The togaviruses and flaviviruses can cause lytic or persistent infections of both vertebrate and invertebrate hosts. Infections of invertebrates are usually persistent, with continued virus production.

Female mosquitoes acquire the togaviruses and flaviviruses on taking a blood meal from a viremic vertebrate host. The virus infects the epithelial cells of the mid-gut of the mosquito, spreads through the basal lamina of the mid-gut to the circulation, and then infects the salivary glands. The virus sets up a persistent infection and replicates to high titers in these cells. The salivary glands can then release virus into the saliva; however, certain strains of WEE virus are limited to the mid-gut and cannot infect the salivary glands.

After biting a host, the female mosquito regurgitates virus-containing saliva into the victim's bloodstream. The virus circulates freely in the plasma and comes into contact with susceptible target cells such as the endothelial cells of the capillaries, macrophages, and monocytes.

Table 43–1. Arthropod-borne viruses causing CNS disease.

Virus Family and Type	Vector	Hosts	Distribution	Disease
TOGAVIRUSES				
Eastern equine encephalitis (EEE)	*Aedis culiseta*	Birds	North America (East and Gulf Coasts); South America	Mild systemic or severe encephalitis
Western equine encephalitis (WEE)	*Culex culiseta*	Birds	North and South America	Mild systemic encephalitis
Venezuelan equine encephalitis	*Aedes culex*	Small mammals; horses	North, South, and Central America	Mild systemic or severe encephalitis
FLAVIVIRUSES				
St. Louis encephalitis	*Culex* spp.	Birds	North America	Encephalitis
Powassan	*Ixodes* ticks	Small mammals	North America	Encephalitis
Japanese encephalitis	*Culex* spp.	Pigs; birds	Asia	Encephalitis
West Nile	*Culex* spp.	Birds	Africa, Europe, U.S.	Fever, encephalitis, hepatitis
Russian spring-summer encephalitis	*Ixodes* and *Dermacentor* ticks	Birds	Russia	Encephalitis
BUNYAVIRUSES				
California (La Crosse Virus)	*Aedes* spp.	Small mammals	Eastern one-half of North America	Mild systemic encephalitis

Following replication of the virus in these cells, the initial viremia produces systemic symptoms such as fever, chills, headaches, backaches, and flulike symptoms within 3–7 days of infection. Some of these symptoms can be attributed to the interferon produced after infection of these target cells. This is considered a mild systemic disease, and most virus infections do not progress beyond this point.

After replication in cells of the reticuloendothelial system, a secondary viremia may result. This can produce sufficient virus to infect target organs such as the brain, liver, skin, and vasculature, depending on the tissue tropism of the virus. Access to the brain is provided by infection of the endothelial cells lining the small vessels of the brain or choroid plexus.

The vertebrate-invertebrate cycle of CE viruses is very similar to that for toga- and flaviviruses and includes *Aedes triseriatus* as the vector mosquito and the squirrel or chipmunk as the usual host.

Clinical Findings

A. Signs and Symptoms. Infection by the togaviruses usually causes a low-grade disease characterized by flulike symptoms (ie, chills, fever, rash, and aches) that correlate with systemic infection during the initial viremia. EEE, WEE, and Venezuela equine encephalitis (VEE) virus infections can progress to encephalitis (as the names imply) in humans and horses, with EEE causing the most severe disease. These viruses are usually more of a problem to livestock than to humans.

Most infections with flaviviruses are relatively benign, although encephalitic or hemorrhagic disease can occur. The encephalitis viruses include St. Louis, Japanese, Murray Valley, and Russian spring-summer viruses. Infections with West Nile and other viruses usually are limited to a mild systemic disease, possibly with a hemorrhagic rash, but the 1999 outbreak on the East Coast of the United States with cases of fatal encephalitis underscores the potential severity of infection with West Nile virus.

Inapparent, mild illnesses or aseptic meningitis occur with CE virus infection, the latter after an incubation period of approximately 48 h. Encephalitis caused by CE occurs approximately 1 week after exposure and is manifested by seizures and generalized cerebral dysfunction mimicking herpes simplex encephalitis. It is most common in school-aged children.

B. Laboratory Findings. The togaviruses, flaviviruses, and CE viruses can be grown in both vertebrate and mosquito cell lines but are difficult and dangerous to isolate. When isolation of the virus is necessary, the best systems are suckling mice and mosquito cell lines. In addition to cytopathology, the viruses grown in culture can be detected by immunofluorescence or by hemadsorption of avian erythrocytes. After isolation, the viruses can be distinguished by analysis of the genomic RNA or by monoclonal antibodies.

A variety of serologic methods can be used to diagnose arbovirus infections. Seroconversion or a fourfold increase in titer between acute and convalescent sera is used to indicate a recent infection. The serologic cross-reactivity between viruses in a group or complex limits identification of the actual viral species in many cases.

C. Imaging. Magnetic resonance imaging (MRI) may help to distinguish HSV encephalitis from other types; HSV characteristically causes temporal lobe lesions, whereas arboviruses cause focal lesions in basal ganglia and thalami.

Differential Diagnosis

The arthropod-borne encephalitides are similar to each other, but the specific etiology may be suggested by geographic location and age of the patient as well as the severity of the illness. For example, WEE is more apt to occur in the far western United States, Colorado, and Texas; EEE is endemic along the entire East Coast; SLE in the eastern states, Texas, and Mississippi; and CE in the Midwest. The 1999 outbreak of West Nile virus infections in New York was originally thought to be due to SLE, but this virus is now endemic in the Eastern United States. West Nile attacked adults and had a fatality rate of 10%. WEE has its highest attack rate in infants < 1 year of age and is most severe in this age group. EEE is more severe than WEE, with a mortality rate of ≥ 20% in infants and children. SLE is similar in severity to WEE, with 5% mortality in those with encephalitis, but SLE tends to attack adults rather than infants or children. CE, in contrast, attacks patients aged 5–18 years.

Arbovirus encephalitis must be distinguished from that caused by herpes simplex viruses (HSV, VZV, and EBV), especially since the latter infections can be treated with antiviral agents. Herpesvirus encephalitis occurs sporadically without any seasonal pattern and occurs with or without mosquito exposure. HSV and VZV encephalitis may be preceded or accompanied by characteristic vesiculopustular skin lesions. HSV tends to be localized to the temporal lobe, causing EEG and imaging abnormalities in this location.

Complications

In infants < 1 year old with encephalitis, death may occur in up to 20% and neurologic sequelae in > 50% of survivors. The rates of these complications are less in older children and adults.

Treatment

No treatments exist for arbovirus diseases other than supportive care.

Prognosis

Attack rates for encephalitis are approximately 1 per 1000 infections. In older children and adults,

≥ 95% recover from encephalitis, and sequelae are uncommon, but in infants there is high mortality and frequent residua in survivors.

Prevention & Control

The easiest means to prevent the spread of any arbovirus is elimination or avoidance of its vector and breeding grounds (Box 43–2). Killed vaccines against Japanese encephalitis, EEE, WEE, and Russian spring-summer encephalitis viruses are available. These vaccines are for individuals working with the specific virus or at risk of contact. A live vaccine against VEE virus is available but only for use in domestic animals.

LYMPHOCYTIC CHORIOMENINGITIS (LCM)

Lymphocytic choriomeningitis (LCM) virus is an arenavirus, the same family as Lassa virus. All arenaviruses have a common reservoir in animals, especially small rodents. The infected animals may be asymptomatic or minimally diseased but excreting the virus in their secretions.

Epidemiology

LCM virus infects hamsters and mice; chronic infection is common in these animals and leads to chronic viremia and virus shedding in saliva, urine, and feces. Infection of humans may occur by way of aerosols, contamination of food, or fomites. Bites are not a usual mechanism of spread. Persistently infected rodents do not usually exhibit illness. The incubation period for LCM infections averages 10–14 days.

Microbiology

Arenaviruses are pleomorphic and enveloped with lipid; the virion has a mean diameter of 120 nm. They contain two-stranded RNA in a linear or circular configuration. The total molecular weight of this RNA is 3.2×10^6 daltons–4.8×10^6 daltons.

Pathogenesis

Arenaviruses are able to infect macrophages and possibly cause the release of mediators of cell and vascular damage. In certain laboratory animals the clinical severity of arenavirus disease appears to be directly related to the host's immunologic response. The greater the immune (especially T lymphocyte) response, the worse the disease. Whether these mechanisms are operative in human infection is not clear. LCM virus may actually produce an encephalitis as well as meningitis. Perivascular mononuclear infiltrates may be seen in neurons of all sections of brain as well as in the meninges.

Clinical Syndrome

LCM illness occurs in most infected individuals but is usually nonspecific or influenzalike. Current estimates show that ~35% of infected persons exhibit clinical evidence of CNS infection. The name of the virus suggests that meningitis is a typical clinical event, but actually a febrile illness, if it occurs, may be subacute and persist for several months. Encephalitis occurs in approximately one-third of patients with CNS manifestations.

Laboratory Diagnosis

The diagnosis of LCM virus infection is usually made through serologic tests, although the virus can be recovered by inoculation of blood (early) or CSF (late in illness) into suckling mice or Vero monkey cells.

Treatment & Prevention

Only supportive therapy for patients with LCM infection is currently available. Prevention of these rodent-borne infections rests on control of the vector's contact with humans. Most human cases of LCM in the United States have resulted from contact with pet hamsters or in rodent-breeding facilities. If hamsters must be kept as pets, scrupulous hand washing is recommended after contact.

RABIES

Essentials of Diagnosis

- Subacute onset of neurologic abnormalities including hallucinations, combativeness, muscle spasms, seizures, and focal paralysis.
- Detection of negri bodies or rabies antigen in animal or human brain tissue (70–90%).
- Rabies-neutralizing antibody in serum or CSF diagnostic in an unimmunized patient.

General Considerations

Rabies is an acute fatal viral illness of the CNS. It can affect all mammals and is transmitted between them by infected secretions, most often by bite. It was first recognized more than 3000 years ago and has been among the most feared of infectious diseases. It is said that Aristotle recognized that rabies could be spread by a rabid dog.

A. Epidemiology. Rabies exists in two epizooic forms: the urban form is associated with unimmu-

---

BOX 43–2	
Control of Arthropod-borne Viral Encephalitis	
Prophylactic Measures	• Avoid mosquito and tick bites • Vaccines for certain arboviruses
Isolation Precautions	• None

nized dogs or cats and is essentially nonexistent in the United States; the sylvatic form occurs in wild skunks, foxes, wolves, raccoons, bats, and mongooses. Throughout the world there are striking geographic differences in specific animals. For example, raccoons are a significant reservoir of rabies in the southwestern United States but not on the West Coast; the bat is a frequent vector in Latin America, and the wolf in Eastern Europe. Rodents are not important vectors of rabies. Human or cattle infection is incidental, and does not contribute to maintenance or transmission of the disease.

Human exposures may be from wild animals or from unimmunized dogs or cats. Domestic animal bites are the most frequent vectors in developing countries because of lack of enforcement of animal immunization. Infection in domestic animals usually represents a spillover from infection in wildlife reservoirs. Human infection tends to occur where animal rabies is common and where there is a large population of unimmunized domestic animals. Worldwide, the occurrence of human rabies is estimated to be about 15,000 cases per year, with the highest attack rates in Southeast Asia, the Philippines, and the Indian subcontinent. In the United States, fewer than five cases of human rabies are reported yearly.

B. Microbiology. The rabies virus is a bullet-shaped, enveloped, single-stranded RNA virus of the rhabdovirus group. The virion is large, with a diameter of ~180 nm. Knoblike glycoprotein excrescences or projections, which elicit neutralizing and hemagglutination-inhibiting antibodies, cover its surface.

In the past, a single antigenically homogeneous virus was believed responsible for all rabies; however, differences in cell culture growth characteristics of isolates from different animal sources, some differences in virulence for experimental animals, and antigenic differences in surface glycoproteins have indicated strain heterogeneity among rabies virus isolates. These studies may help to explain some of the biological differences noted, as well as the occasional case of vaccine failure.

C. Pathogenesis. The essential first event in human or animal rabies infection is the introduction of virus through the epidermis, usually as a result of an animal bite. Inhalation of heavily contaminated material, such as bat droppings, eg, by cave explorers, can also cause infection. Rabies virus first replicates in striated muscle tissue at the site of inoculation. It then enters the peripheral nervous system at the neuromuscular junctions and spreads up the nerves to the CNS, where it replicates exclusively within the gray matter. It then passes centrifugally along autonomic nerves to reach other tissues, including the salivary glands, adrenal medulla, kidneys, and lungs.

Passage into the salivary glands in animals explains transmission of the disease by infected saliva. The incubation period ranges from 10 days to a year, depending on the amount of virus introduced, the amount of tissue involved, the host immune mechanisms, and the distance the virus must travel from the site of inoculation to the CNS. Thus the incubation period is generally shorter with face wounds than with leg wounds. Immunization early in the incubation period frequently aborts the infection.

The neuropathology of rabies resembles that of other viral diseases of the CNS, with infiltration of lymphocytes and plasma cells into CNS tissue and nerve cell destruction. The pathognomonic lesion is the negri body, an eosinophilic cytoplasmic viral inclusion distributed throughout the brain, particularly in the hippocampus, cerebral cortex, cerebellum, and dorsal spinal ganglia.

Clinical Findings

A. Signs and Symptoms. Rabies in humans usually results from a bite by a rabid animal or contamination of a wound by an animal's saliva. It presents as an acute, fulminant, fatal encephalitis; human survivors have been reported only occasionally. The disease begins as a nonspecific illness marked by fever, headache, malaise, nausea, and vomiting. Abnormal sensations at or around the site of viral inoculation occur frequently and probably reflect local nerve involvement. The onset of encephalitis is marked by periods of excess motor activity and agitation. Hallucinations, combativeness, muscle spasms, signs of meningeal irritation, seizures, and focal paralysis occur. Periods of mental dysfunction are interspersed with completely lucid periods; as the disease progresses, however, the patient lapses into coma. Autonomic nervous system involvement often results in increased salivation.

Brain stem and cranial nerve dysfunction is characteristic, with double vision, facial palsies, and difficulty in swallowing. The combination of excess salivation and difficulty in swallowing produces the traditional picture of foaming at the mouth. Hydrophobia, the painful, violent involuntary contractions of the diaphragm and accessory respiratory, pharyngeal, and laryngeal muscles initiated by swallowing liquids, is seen in about 50% of cases. Involvement of the respiratory center produces respiratory paralysis, the major cause of death. The median survival after onset of symptoms is 4 days, with a maximum of 20 days unless artificial supportive measures are instituted. Recovery is rare and has been seen only in partially immunized individuals.

B. Laboratory Findings. Laboratory diagnosis of rabies in animals or deceased patients is accomplished by demonstration of virus in brain tissue. As negri bodies are not seen in at least 20% of rabies victims, their absence does not rule out the diagnosis. Viral antigen can be demonstrated rapidly by immunofluorescence procedures. Intracerebral inoculation of infected brain tissue or secretions into suckling mice results in death in 3–10 days. Histologic examination of their brain tissue shows negri bodies;

both negri bodies and rhabdovirus particles may be demonstrated by electron microscopy. Specific antibodies to rabies virus can be detected in serum, but generally only late in the disease.

Differential Diagnosis

Rabies may initially be mistaken for Guillain-Barré syndrome, an ascending peripheral polyneuritis, but encephalitic symptoms and signs do not develop in the latter illness.

Complications

Pneumonia and other infectious complications of intensive care are almost invariable. Respiratory paralysis results from infection of the respiratory center.

Treatment

In the late 1800s Pasteur, noting the long incubation period of rabies, suggested that a vaccine to induce an immune response before the development of disease might be useful in prevention. He apparently successfully vaccinated Joseph Meister, a boy severely bitten and exposed to rabies, with multiple injections of a crude vaccine made from dried spinal cords of rabies-infected rabbits. This treatment emerged as one of the most noteworthy accomplishments in the annals of medicine (Box 43–3 and Prevention & Control section below for more information).

Prognosis

Of patients with rabies, > 90% die owing to complications of the illness or progressive neurologic dysfunction, especially respiratory paralysis.

Prevention & Control

Prevention is the mainstay of controlling human rabies. Intensive supportive care has resulted in two or three long-term survivors; despite the best modern medical care, however, the mortality still exceeds 90%. In addition, because of the infrequency of the disease, many cases die without definitive diagnosis. Human hyperimmune antirabies globulin interferon and vaccine do not alter the disease once symptoms have developed. Currently, the prevention of rabies is divided into preexposure and postexposure prophylaxis.

A. Preexposure prophylaxis. This type of prophylaxis is recommended for individuals at high risk of contact with rabies virus, such as veterinarians, spelunkers, laboratory workers, and animal handlers. The vaccine currently used in the United States for preexposure prophylaxis uses an attenuated rabies virus grown in human diploid cell culture and inactivated with beta-propriolactone. Preexposure prophylaxis consists of two subcutaneous injections of vaccine given 1 month apart, followed by a booster dose several months later.

B. Postexposure prophylaxis. This type of prophylaxis requires careful evaluation and judgment. Every year more than 1 million Americans are bitten by animals, and in each instance a decision must be made whether to initiate postexposure rabies prophylaxis. In this decision the physician must consider (1) whether the individual came into physical contact with saliva or another substance likely to contain rabies virus; (2) whether there was significant wounding or abrasion; (3) whether rabies is known or suspected in the animal species and area associated with the exposure; (4) whether the bite was provoked or unprovoked (ie, the circumstances surrounding the exposure); and (5) whether the animal is available for laboratory examination. Any wild animal or ill, unvaccinated, or stray domestic animal involved in a possible rabies exposure, such as an unprovoked bite, should be captured and killed. The head should be sent immediately to an appropriate laboratory, usually at the state health department, for search for rabies antigen by immunofluorescence. If examination of the brain by this technique is negative for rabies virus, it can be assumed that the saliva contains no virus and that the exposed person requires no treatment. If the test is positive, the patient should be given postexposure prophylaxis.

Postexposure prophylaxis consists of immediate, thorough washing of the wound with soap and water; passive immunization with 20 IU per kg hyperimmune globulin, of which at least half the dose should be infiltrated around the wound site; and active immunization with antirabies vaccine (Box 43–4). With human diploid vaccine, five doses given on days 1, 3, 7, 14, and 28 are recommended. Physicians should always seek the advice of the local health department when the question of rabies prophylaxis arises.

NIPAH VIRUS

In 1998, a newly emergent paramyxovirus was identified as the cause of an outbreak of encephalitis, with the first death occurring in the village of Nipah, Malaysia. The cases occurred in farmers and abattoir workers who had close contact with diseased pigs that had a respiratory illness. Nipah virus is closely

---

BOX 43–3		
Treatment of Rabies		
	Children	Adults
First Choice	Treatment consists of immune enhancement: immune globulin and vaccine (see Box 43–5 for dosages)	Treatment consists of immune enhancement: immune globulin and vaccine (see Box 43–5 for dosages)

BOX 43–4

Control of Rabies

Prophylactic Measures	• Postexposure: immune globulin 20 IU per kg; infiltrate ½ into wound; vaccine 1.0 ml of human diploid cell vaccine (HDCV) or inactivated vaccine (RVA) on days 0, 3, 7, 14, and 28. • Pre-exposure: vaccine
Isolation Precautions	• Not necessary for infected patient

---

related to another recently emerged paramyxovirus known as Hendra virus. Thus, the potential for new viral pathogens to emerge continues unabated.

PROGRESSIVE MULTIFOCAL LEUKOENCEPHALOPATHY

Essentials of Diagnosis

- Progressive cerebral deterioration in an immunocompromised patient, leading to paralysis and death in < 1 year.
- Multiple lesions in white matter, as revealed by MRI.
- Virions visible on brain biopsy.
- Normal CSF findings (cell count, glucose, protein).
- JC virus (JCV) DNA detectable in CSF by PCR.

General Considerations

A. Epidemiology. Progressive multifocal leukoencephalopathy (PML) is a rare syndrome that occurs in immunocompromised patients, including those with AIDS, and is caused by a papovavirus known as JC virus (JCV). The virus was first recovered by coculturing of brain tissue from a patient with progressive multifocal leukoencephalopathy and Hodgkin's disease. Polyomavirus infections are ubiquitous, and most humans are infected with JCV by the age of 15 years.

B. Microbiology. The polyomaviruses are small (44 nm in diameter), icosahedral, and lack an envelope. The double-stranded DNA is a circular, supercoiled molecule.

C. Pathogenesis. Respiratory transmission is the probable mode of spread. Immune suppression after organ transplantation or during pregnancy is capable of reactivating latent infections.

Clinical Findings

A. Signs and Symptoms. Clinical symptoms develop insidiously but progress relentlessly. Patients may have multiple neurologic symptoms unattribut-

able to a single anatomic lesion. Impairment of speech, vision, coordination, mentation, or some combination of these occurs and is followed by paralysis of the arms and legs and finally death in approximately 1 year.

B. Laboratory Findings. CSF is normal and does not contain antibody to JCV but may be positive for JCV by PCR. Histologic examination of brain tissue from cases of progressive multifocal leukoencephalopathy reveals cytologic changes within the oligodendrocytes. These cells are adjacent to areas of demyelination. There is little if any inflammatory cell response. Electron microscopy can be used to visualize viral particles in brain tissue, and immunofluorescence can confirm the identity of viral antigen.

JCV grows best in primary human fetal glial cells, which are not readily available. Culture of JCV is therefore performed only in a few research laboratories.

C. Imaging. MRI is characteristic with multiple high signal-intense lesions predominantly in white matter.

Differential Diagnosis

Although the MRI is characteristic, similar clinical and radiologic findings can occur with VZV infections in AIDS patients.

Complications

There is progressive worsening of cerebral and neurologic function with death usually occurring 3–6 months from onset.

Treatment

No specific treatment is available, but some stabilization or improvement may occur if the immunosuppression can be reduced, eg, control of HIV infection.

Prognosis

Rarely there may be regression of symptoms especially if immunosuppression can be reduced. Otherwise the disease is fatal and may be especially rapid in AIDS patients.

Prevention & Control

The ubiquitous nature of polyomaviruses and the lack of understanding of their modes of transmission make preventing primary infection unlikely. Minimizing the duration and degree of immunosuppression can decrease reactivation of polyomavirus and the development of PML.

DISEASES CAUSED BY UNCONVENTIONAL AGENTS

Evidence has accumulated during the past 30 years that a variety of progressive neurologic diseases in both animals and humans are caused by viral or other filterable agents that share some of the properties of viruses. These illnesses have been termed slow viral diseases because of the protracted period between infection and the prolonged course of the illness, but a better term is persistent viral infection. Most persistent viral infections involve well-differentiated cells, such as lymphocytes and neuronal cells. These diseases are associated with unconventional viruses that are small, filterable infectious agents transmissible to certain experimental animals, but that do not appear to be associated with immune or inflammatory responses by the host and have not been cultivated in cell culture.

Viral persistence can result from integration of viral nucleic acid into the host genome, mutations that interfere with or severely limit viral replication or antigenicity, failure of host immune systems to recognize virus or infected cells, or some combination of these.

A group of progressive degenerative diseases of the central nervous system with similar pathology has been described. Two of the illnesses, Creutzfeldt-Jakob disease and kuru, occur in humans; two others, scrapie in sheep and goats and progressive encephalopathy in mink, occur in animals. Although the pathogenesis of these four illnesses is not well understood, there are various degrees of neuronal loss, spongiform neurologic changes, and astrocyte proliferation. The incubation periods are months to years, and the diseases have protracted and inevitably fatal courses.

The causes of these diseases are transmissible agents with unusual physical and chemical properties, but their nature is still obscure. They are small and filterable to diameters of 5 nm or less, multiply to high titers in the reticuloendothelial system and brain, produce characteristic infections, and can remain viable even in formalinized brain tissue for many years. They are resistant to ionizing radiation, boiling, and many common disinfectants. Recognizable virions have not been found in tissues, and the agents have not been grown in cell culture. Treatment of infectious material with proteases and nucleases does not decrease infectivity.

Brain extracts from scrapie-infected animals contain a glycoprotein called PrP that is not found in the brains of normal animals. PrP has been termed a prion (proteinaceous infectious particle), and purified proteinaceous extracts of brain tissue in very high dilutions have been shown to transmit disease to exper-imental animals. Repeated attempts to find associated nucleic acids have been generally unrewarding. PrP is encoded in a host gene, and specific prion mRNA has been found in both normal and infected tissue. Why the mRNA is translated in the disease and how prion production is apparently initiated by an external source of infectious PrP remain unanswered. During scrapie infection, prion protein may aggregate into birefringent rods and form filamentous structures termed scrapie-associated fibrils, which are found in membranes of scrapie-infected brain tissues.

CREUTZFELDT-JAKOB DISEASE

Essentials of Diagnosis

- Progressive mentation abnormalities leading to disorders of gait and myoclonus.
- Occurs in sixth and seventh decades in previously normal patients.
- May be history of corneal transplant, neurosurgical procedures, or use of human growth hormone.
- Characteristic brain biopsy abnormalities of spongiform degeneration, neuron loss, and astrogliosis.

General Considerations

Creutzfeldt-Jakob disease is a progressive, fatal illness of the central nervous system that is seen most frequently in the sixth and seventh decades of life. The disease is sporadic and found worldwide, with an incidence of disease of 1 case/million people per year. The mode of acquisition is unknown, but a higher incidence of the disease among Israelis of Libyan origin who eat sheep eyeballs has led to speculation that the disease may be transmitted by the ingestion of scrapie-infected tissue. Infection has been transmitted by corneal transplants, by contact with infected electrodes used in a neurosurgical procedure, and by pituitary-derived human growth hormone. In these cases, the incubation period of the disease was ~15–20 months.

Other evidence suggests that a longer latency may follow natural infection. It has been transmitted to chimpanzees, mice, and guinea pigs by inoculation of infected brain tissue, leukocytes, and certain organs. High levels of infectious agent have been found, especially in the brain, where they may reach 10^7 infectious doses per gram of brain. Nonpercutaneous transmission of disease has not been observed, and there is no evidence of transmission by direct contact or airborne spread.

Clinical Findings

A. Signs and Symptoms. The initial clinical manifestation is a change in cerebral function, usually diagnosed initially as a psychiatric disorder. Forgetfulness and disorientation progress to overt dementia, with the development of changes in gait, increased tone in the limbs, myoclonus, and seizures. The disorder runs a course of 12 months to 4–5 years, eventually leading to death.

B. Laboratory Findings. Brain biopsy provides definitive diagnosis and includes spongiform degeneration, neuron loss, and astrogliosis. There are also birefringent rods and fibrillar structures similar to those in scrapie. Identification of Creutzfeldt-Jakob prion protein (PrP CjD) by fluorescent antibody directed against it is a useful diagnostic adjunct to neuropathologic examination of brain tissue.

C. Imaging. EEG is abnormal and characteristic in more than 75% of patients with periodic, symmetric, biphasic or triphasic sharp wavers. Computed tomography (CT) scan or MRI reveals brain atrophy.

Differential Diagnosis

Cases of Creutzfeldt-Jakob disease may resemble PML, but the latter occurs in immunocompromised patients, including those with AIDS, whereas Creutzfeldt-Jakob disease occurs in older, nonimmunocompromised individuals.

Treatment

There is no effective therapy of Creutzfeldt-Jakob disease, and all cases have been fatal.

Prevention

The small risk of nosocomial infection is related only to direct contact with brain tissue. Stereotactic neurosurgical equipment, especially that used in patients with undiagnosed dementia, should not be reused. In addition, organs from patients with undiagnosed neurologic disease should not be used for transplants. Growth hormone from human tissue has now been replaced by a recombinant genetically engineered product. The agent of Creutzfeldt-Jakob disease has not been transmitted to animals by inoculation of body secretions, and no increased risk of disease has been noted in family members or medical personnel caring for patients. Disinfection of potentially infectious material can be accomplished by treatment for 1 h with 0.5% sodium hypochlorite solution or by autoclaving at 121 °C for 1 h.

KURU

Kuru was a subacute, progressive neurologic disease of the Fore people of the Eastern Highlands of New Guinea. In the local Fore dialect, *kuru* means to tremble with fear or to be afraid. The disease was brought to the attention of the western world by Gadjusek and Zigas in the mid-1950s. Although the illness was localized and decreasing in incidence, its study has thrown light on the infectious nature of similar transmissible encephalopathies. Epidemiologic studies indicated that kuru usually afflicted adult women or children of either sex. The disease was rarely observed outside of the Fore region, and outsiders in the region did not contract the disease. The symptoms and signs were ataxia, hyperreflexia, and spasticity, which led to progressive starvation and death. Mental alertness was unaffected until the late stages of illness.

Pathologic examination revealed changes only in the CNS, with diffuse neuronal degeneration and spongiform changes of the cerebral cortex and basal ganglia. No inflammatory response was noted. Inoculation of infectious brain tissue into primates produced a disease that caused similar neurologic symptoms and pathologic manifestations after an incubation period of approximately 40 months.

Epidemiologic studies indicated that transmission of the disease in humans was associated with ritual cannibalism, practiced mainly by women and young children and occasionally by men. This ritual involved the handling and ingestion of organs of deceased relatives. Inoculation through lesions in the skin and mucous membranes was shown to be the most likely mode of transmission, with clinical disease developing 4–20 years after exposure. Since the elimination of cannibalism from the Fore culture, kuru has disappeared.

REFERENCES

Adams DH. Does the infective agent of scrapie replicate without nucleic acid? An assessment. Med Hypoth 1991;35:253. (A review of the biology of prions, especially the scrapie agent.)

Calisher CH: Medically important arboviruses of the United States and Canada. Clin Microbiol Rev 1994;7:89.

Cantor SB et al: A decision-analytic approach to post exposure rabies prophylaxis. Am J Publ Health 1994;84:1144.

Centers for Disease Control and Prevention: Inactivated Japanese encephalitis virus vaccine: recommendations of the Advisory Committee on Immunization Practices (ACIP). Morbid Mortal Weekly Rep 1993;42:1.

Centers for Disease Control and Prevention: Human rabies: Alabama, Tennessee, and Texas, 1994. Morbid Mortal Weekly Rep 1995;44:269.

Centers for Disease Control and Prevention: Compendium of animal rabies control, 1995. Morbid Mortal Weekly Rep 1995;44:1.

Fishbein DB, Robinson LE: Rabies. N Engl J Med 1993;329:1632. (Epidemiology of rabies.)

Jahrling PB, Peters CJ: Lymphocytic choriomeningitis

virus: a neglected pathogen of man. Arch Pathol Lab Med 1992;116:486. (Editorial review.)

Krebs JW, Strine TW, Smith JS, Rupprecht CE, Childs JE: Rabies surveillance in the United States during 1993. J Am Vet Med Assoc 1994;205:1695.

Lantos PL: From slow virus to prion: a review of transmissible spongiform encephalopathies. *Histopathology* 1992; 20:1. (A review of spongiform encephalopathies, three of which occur in humans [Creutzfeldt-Jakob disease, Gerstmann-Straussler-Scheinker disease, and kuru].)

Major EO, Amemiya K, Tornatore CS, Houff SA, Berger JR: Pathogenesis and molecular biology of progressive multifocal leukoencephalopathy, the JC virus-induced demyelinating disease of the human brain. Clin Microbiol Rev 1992;5:49.

Prusiner SB. Transgenetic investigations of prion diseases of humans and animals. Bio Sci 1993;339(1288):239. (A review of the biology of prion disease.)

Rupprecht CE, Smith JS: Raccoon rabies: the re-emergence of an epizootic in a densely populated area. Semin Virol 1994;5:155.

Weber T, Turner RW, Frye S, et al: Progressive multifocal leukoencephalopathy diagnosed by amplification of JC virus-specific DNA from cerebrospinal fluid. AIDS 1994;8:49.

Miscellaneous Systemic Viral Syndromes

44

W. Lawrence Drew, MD, PhD

This chapter includes a variety of viral infections that produce severe systemic syndromes (Table 44–1). In some cases, these infections are transmitted by arthropod vectors; in others, they are acquired by direct contact with the reservoir animal or its excreta. The illnesses may be hemorrhagic fever (eg, dengue, Marburg, Ebola, or Lassa fevers), generalized fever (yellow fever or Colorado tick fever), or pneumonia (caused by hantavirus infection). Only two of these are endemic in the United States, hantavirus infection and Colorado tick fever. All of these viruses are RNA viruses, and vaccine has been developed for one (yellow fever).

DENGUE & YELLOW FEVER

General Considerations

Dengue and yellow fever are both caused by flaviviruses, and each is spread by an arthropod vector. The etiologic agents of dengue are the dengue virus types 1–4, whereas yellow fever is caused by the yellow fever virus. Flaviviruses produce a wide range of diseases including hemorrhagic fevers, arthritis, encephalitis, and hepatitis. Hepatitis C is caused by a flavivirus and is discussed in Chapter 40. Until recently the flaviviruses were included in the *Togaviridae* family, but differences in size, morphology, gene sequence, and replication strategy have made it necessary to classify them as an independent virus family.

A. Epidemiology. The flaviviruses are also classified as arboviruses (see Chapter 43) because they are usually spread by arthropod vectors and as zoonotic viruses because they are spread by animals. These viruses have a very broad host range, including vertebrates (eg, mammals, birds, amphibians, and reptiles) and invertebrates (eg, mosquitoes and ticks).

A cycle of infection occurs in which the virus is transmitted by the arthropod vector and amplified in a susceptible host to allow reinfection of other arthropods. Humans are usually *dead-end* hosts that cannot spread the virus back to the vector because a persistent viremia is not maintained.

These viruses are maintained by *Aedes* spp. mosquitoes in a sylvatic or jungle cycle, in which mon-

keys are the natural host, and also in an urban cycle, in which humans are the host. *A aegypti* is a vector for each of these viruses and is a household mosquito. It breeds in pools of water, open sewers, and other accumulations of water in cities.

Dengue occurs throughout the world, with long-known endemic areas in tropical Asia, Polynesia, Micronesia, and East and West Africa. In recent years there has been an upsurge of dengue in South and Central America, the Caribbean, and India, and the spread is predominantly human-mosquito-human, with persistent viremia in the human allowing infection of mosquitoes. Yellow fever is also found in the Caribbean and the tropics, including Africa but not Asia, and the spread is monkey to mosquito (*A aegypti*) to monkey or to human. In the past decade there has been a major increase in cases especially in Africa. Dengue is the most prevalent flavivirus and causes ≤ 100 million infections/year. In the past, dengue occurred in outbreaks within the United States, and the presence of *A aegypti* and *A albopictus,* another potential vector, in the coastal southern United States means that future outbreaks could occur.

B. Microbiology. The flaviviruses are spherical (40–60 nm) enveloped, positive, single-stranded ribonucleic acid (RNA) viruses. They attach to specific receptors expressed on many different cell types from many different species. Flaviviruses can also attach to the Fc receptors on macrophages, monocytes, and other cells when they are coated with antibody. The antibody actually enhances the infectivity of these viruses by providing new receptors for the virus and by promoting its uptake into these target cells.

The virus enters the cell by receptor-mediated endocytosis. The envelope fuses with the membrane of the endosome on acidification of the vesicle to deliver the capsid and genome into the cytoplasm.

Once released into the cytoplasm, the flavivirus genomes are translated via complementary RNA into several proteins. Assembly and budding of flaviviruses occur predominantly in the cytoplasm by using intracellular membranes or vesicles, rather than at the cell surface. Virus release occurs during lysis of the cell.

Table 44-1. Important viral fevers.

Family	Agent	Disease	Reservoir/Vector	Outbreak Locations	Route of Transmission	Mortality (%)
Arenaviridae	Machupo	Bolivian hemorrhagic fever	Vesper mouse (R)	Bolivia	Inhalation of dried rodent excreta	10–20
	Lassa	Lassa fever	*Mastomys* rodents (R)	West Africa including hospital workers	Inhalation of dried rodent excreta plus person-to-person (body fluids)	15–25
Flaviviridae	Yellow fever virus	Yellow fever	Humans, simians (R) *Aedes aegypti* (V)	Equatorial Africa, South America	Mosquito bite	10
	Dengue (1–4)	Dengue fever (DF) Dengue hemorrhagic fever (DHF)	Human (R), ?monkeys, *Aedes*, ticks (V)	Tropical worldwide	Arthropod bite	DF = 0; DHF = 15
Bunyaviridae	Phleboviruses: Rift Valley	Rift Valley fever	Cattle, sheep (R) *Aedes*, others (V)	South Africa—sheep Egypt-Aswan Dam Mauritania-Senegal R. Dam	Mosquito bite	1
	Hantaviruses: Sin Nombre	Hantavirus pulmonary syndrome	Deer mouse (R)	Southwestern United States	Inhalation of dried rodent excreta	10–50
	Nairoviruses: Congo	Congo-Crimean hemorrhagic fever	Hares, hedgehogs, ticks (V)	Western Russia, Balkans, East Africa	Tick bites plus person-to-person (blood)	20–50
Filoviridae	Marburg	Marburg virus disease	Unknown	Germany, Yugoslavia—lab workers: South Africa; Kenya	Person-to-person (body fluids)	20–25
	Ebola	Ebola hemorrhagic fever	Unknown	Sudan Zaire	Person-to-person (body fluids)	70–90
Reoviridae	Coltvirus	Colorado tick fever	Mammals (squirrels, chipmunks, rabbits, deer); tick (*D andersoni*)	Western United States and Canada	Tick bite	<1

C. Pathogenesis. The flavivirus can cause lytic or persistent infections of both vertebrate and invertebrate hosts. Infections of invertebrates are usually persistent, with continued virus production and no damage to the insect.

Female mosquitoes acquire the flaviviruses on taking a blood meal from a viremic, vertebrate host. The virus infects the epithelial cells of the mid-gut of the mosquito, spreads through the basal lamina of the mid-gut to the circulation, and then infects the salivary glands. The virus sets up a persistent infection and replicates to high titers in these cells. The salivary glands can then release virus into the saliva.

After biting a host, the female mosquito regurgitates virus-containing saliva into the victim's bloodstream. The virus circulates transiently in the plasma, and primary replication occurs in lymph nodes.

The initial viremia, after replication of the virus in these tissues, produces systemic symptoms such as fever, chills, headaches, backaches, and flulike symptoms within 3–7 days of infection. Some of these symptoms can be attributed to the interferon produced after infection of these target cells. Most yellow fever infections do not progress beyond this point, but secondary multiplication of virus occurs in liver, spleen, kidneys, heart, and bone marrow with severe toxicity.

D. Immune Response. Both humoral and cellular immunities are elicited and are important to the control of primary infection and prevention of future infections with the flaviviruses. Unlike viruses that initially replicate in the lung, intestine, or viscera, the primary infection by these viruses is in lymph nodes. This presents the virus immediately to macrophages, the reticuloendothelial system, and the immune response.

Replication of the flaviviruses in the macrophage and endothelial cells produces a double-stranded RNA replicative intermediate that is a good inducer of interferon. The interferon produced soon after infection is released into the bloodstream to limit further replication of virus and stimulate the immune response. The interferon also causes the rapid onset of flulike symptoms characteristic of mild systemic disease.

Circulating immunoglobulin M (IgM) is produced within 6 days of infection, followed by IgG. The antibody blocks the viremic spread of the virus and subsequent infection of other tissues. Immunity to one flavivirus can protect against other flaviviruses by recognition of the common antigens expressed on all members of the viral family. One example of this may be occurring in the Far East, where Japanese encephalitis but not yellow fever virus is endemic despite the presence of the *A aegypti* mosquito vector for yellow fever.

Cell-mediated immunity is also important in control of the primary infection. Natural killer cells, T-cells, and macrophages are activated by interferon and can respond to the cell surface antigens displayed on the infected cells.

Immunity to these viruses is a double-edged sword. Inflammation resulting from the cell-mediated immune response can destroy tissue. Prior immunity can promote hypersensitivity reactions such as delayed-type hypersensitivity, formation of immune complexes with virions and viral antigens, and activation of complement. A non-neutralizing antibody can also enhance uptake of the flaviviruses into macrophages and other cells that express Fc receptors. Such an antibody can be generated to a related strain of virus in which the neutralizing epitope is not expressed or different. The consequences of such partial immunity can be devastating. For example, prior infection by one strain of dengue virus will predispose an individual to dengue hemorrhagic fever (DHF) when infected by another strain of dengue. The weakening and rupture of the vasculature are believed to result from activation of complement and other hypersensitivity reactions. In 1981 an epidemic of dengue-2 virus in Cuba infected a population previously exposed to dengue-1 (between 1977 and 1980). More than 100,000 cases of DHF-dengue shock syndrome (DHF/DSS) resulted, with 168 deaths.

Clinical Findings

A. Signs and Symptoms

Dengue: After an incubation period of 5–6 days, dengue infection may be asymptomatic or associated with a nonspecific illness or with classical dengue. The latter consists of fever, erythematous rash, and severe myalgias involving the back, head, muscles, and joints. The severity of the myalgia is reflected in the alternative name "breakbone fever." After 1–2 days of fever and rash, the patient's high temperature returns to normal, only to recur 3–4 days later. The recurrence of fever is followed by a second rash that involves face, trunk and limbs but not palms or soles. The fever abates as the second rash develops.

Between the two febrile periods the patient remains symptomatic with gastrointestinal or respiratory symptoms or both. Generalized lymphadenopathy is often present. Resolution occurs in the second week, and fatalities are very rare. On rechallenge with a related strain, dengue can cause severe hemorrhagic disease and shock (DHF/DSS), which occur in tens to hundreds of thousands of cases per year. The hemorrhagic-shock symptoms are attributed to rupture of the vasculature, internal bleeding, and loss of plasma. In addition there is high fever, nausea or vomiting, ecchymosis, and edema of the hands and face.

Yellow fever: The incubation period of yellow fever is 3–6 days. Most infections with yellow fever virus are subclinical or anicteric. Icteric yellow fever infections are characterized by severe systemic disease, with failure of the liver, kidney, and heart and hemorrhage of blood vessels. Liver involvement leads to the jaundice from which the disease obtains its name, but massive gastrointestinal hemorrhages (so-called "black vomit") may also occur.

Diagnosis

The principal means of diagnosis is antibody assay, and a variety of serologic methods can be used to diagnose infections. A fourfold increase in titer or seroconversion between acute and convalescent sera is used to indicate a recent infection. The serologic cross-reactivity between viruses in a group or complex limits identification of the actual viral species in many cases. IgM and complement fixing (CF) antibodies are short-lived (1–2 months) and can be useful in documenting acute infection. Demonstrations of viral antigen or viral RNA (by polymerase chain reaction [PCR] assay) in blood or tissue can also prove the diagnosis.

Laboratory Findings

Leukopenia is typical; thrombocytopenia is especially prominent in DHF and yellow fever. Abnormal clotting parameters occur in both, as do increases in liver enzymes. Jaundice occurs in yellow fever, not dengue. Rising creatinine may occur in both diseases.

Flaviviruses can be grown in both vertebrate and mosquito cell lines but are difficult and dangerous to isolate. In addition to cytopathology, the viruses grown in culture can be detected by immunofluorescence or by hemadsorption of avian erythrocytes. After isolation the viruses can be distinguished by RNA analysis or immunoassays.

Treatment

No treatment exists for flavivirus diseases other than supportive care.

Prognosis

The fatality rate from DHF is up to 15% as a result of multiple organ failures. The mortality rate from yellow fever is approximately 10% and also results from multiple organ failures (liver, kidney, and heart).

Prevention & Control

The easiest means to prevent the spread of flaviviruses is elimination of its vector and breeding grounds. After the discovery by Walter Reed and colleagues that yellow fever was spread by *Aedes aegypti*, the number of cases was reduced by controlling the mosquito population.

Vaccination provides effective protection. A live vaccine (17D) is available against yellow fever virus, for individuals working with the virus or at risk for contact. International travelers to yellow fever-endemic zones should be immunized.

The yellow fever vaccine is attenuated from the 17D strain isolated from a patient in 1927 and passaged extensively in monkeys, mosquitoes, embryonic tissue culture, and embryonated eggs. The vaccine elicits lifelong immunity to yellow fever and possibly other cross-reacting flaviviruses. Vaccines against dengue virus are also being developed.

MARBURG & EBOLA VIRUS

General Considerations

Two unique RNA viruses, the Marburg and Ebola viruses, are members of a new family known as filoviruses. These agents can cause severe or fatal hemorrhagic fevers and are endemic in Africa. Laboratory workers have been exposed to the Marburg agent while working with tissue cultures from African green monkeys. Travelers in or residents of central Africa (eg, Zaire or the Sudan) may be infected by the Ebola virus.

A. Epidemiology. Marburg virus infection was first detected among laboratory workers in Marburg, Germany, who had been exposed to tissues from apparently healthy African green monkeys. However, it is not clear that these monkeys were, or are, the reservoir for this virus because inoculation of Marburg virus into these monkeys produces death rather than a carrier state. Rare cases of Marburg virus infection have been reported in Zimbabwe and Kenya.

Ebola virus has caused disease only in Zaire and the Sudan. In rural areas of central Africa, ≤ 18% of the population have antibody to this virus, suggesting that subclinical infections do occur. The source of the virus and means of transmission are unknown but are possibly simian viruses. Rarely, secondary cases of filovirus infections have occurred in healthcare workers, usually as a result of accidental needle-stick exposure.

B. Microbiology. Filoviruses are single-stranded RNA viruses with a filamentous or threadlike appearance. The filamentous forms have a diameter of 80 nm but may vary in length from 1,000 to ~14,000 nm. Their symmetry is helical, and they are enveloped. Virus is replicated in the cytoplasm and is released by budding from the cell membrane.

Clinical Findings

A. Signs and Symptoms. Illness usually begins with flulike symptoms such as headache and myalgia. Within a few days, nausea, vomiting, and diarrhea occur; a rash may often develop. Subsequently, there is hemorrhage from multiple sites and death.

B. Laboratory Findings. Lymphopenia followed by neutrophilia and severe thrombocytopenia.

Diagnosis

A. Direct Examination. Direct fluorescent-antibody (FA) assay can detect viral antigens in tissues; virions can be seen by electron microscopy in serum or liver tissue.

B. Culture. Isolation of the virus is the procedure of choice to diagnose filovirus infections. Marburg virus may grow rapidly in tissue cultures (Vero cells), although Ebola virus recovery may require animal (eg, guinea pig) inoculation. All specimens for filovirus diagnosis must be handled with extreme care to prevent accidental infection.

C. Serology. IgG and IgM antibodies to filovirus antigens can be detected by immunofluorescence assay (IFA), enzyme-linked immunosorbent assay (ELISA), or radioimmunoassay (RIA). Seroconversion or a fourfold rise of IgG antibody levels is diagnostic of active infection, as is the detection of specific IgM antibody.

Treatment

No treatment is known.

Prognosis

The mortality rate in patients with symptomatic Marburg or Ebola virus infection is ≤ 80%.

Prevention & Control

Since the source of filoviruses is unknown, no measures are available for preventing primary infection. Secondary cases in healthcare workers can be prevented by avoiding exposure to contaminated needles, blood, and so on.

HANTAVIRUSES

Essentials of Diagnosis

- Acute severe respiratory infection in a young adult.
- Exposure to deer mice, eg, in a remote cabin.
- Occurrence of disease in far western United States, especially Four Corners states.
- Diagnosis by serology.
- Can detect viral RNA by PCR of respiratory samples.

General Considerations

Hantaviruses are members of the bunyavirus group, which is the largest family of viruses and contains several human pathogens including California encephalitis virus (see Chapter 43). The hantavirus group was first recognized as causing hemorrhagic fevers with renal failure in Asia and Eastern Europe but became much more prominent in the United States when the hantavirus pulmonary syndrome was described in the United States.

A. Epidemiology. Unlike other bunyaviruses, which have an arthropod vector, hantaviruses spread from mammal to mammal, including humans, by exposure to aerosolized feces, infected urine, or other secretions.

Hantaviruses have been found throughout the world in a variety of rodents and other species. Most of these viruses are associated with hemorrhagic fever, with or without renal failure. In the United States, however, the most notable hantavirus is the Sin Nombre virus, which is associated with the severe pulmonary syndrome. This virus is found in 10–80% of deer mice in rural areas of North America. Spread of virus from rodents to humans is thought to result from intimate contact with the rodent habitat.

B. Microbiology. These viruses are spherical particles 80–120 nm in diameter. The envelope of the virus contains two glycoproteins and encloses three unique nucleocapsids. The nucleocapsids consist of three separate strands of RNA, the RNA-dependent RNA polymerase, and two nonstructural proteins.

C. Pathogenesis. In the hemorrhagic fever and hantavirus pulmonary syndromes, the primary lesion is leakage of plasma and erythrocytes through the vascular endothelium. In the former infection these changes are most prominent in the kidney and are accompanied by hemorrhagic necrosis of the kidney; in the latter the primary site of illness is the lung.

Clinical Findings

A. Signs and Symptoms. Hemorrhagic fevers are characterized by fever, petechial hemorrhages, ecchymoses, epistaxis, hematemesis, melena, and bleeding of gums. Death occurs in ≤ 50% of cases with hemorrhagic phenomena.

Hantavirus pulmonary syndrome (HPS) begins with a prodrome of fever, headache, myalgia, and, often, gastrointestinal symptoms lasting approximately 4–5 days. This is followed by the onset of cough and dyspnea. Tachycardia and tachypnea are present, and hypotension may supervene. The respiratory status may progress to acute respiratory distress syndrome (ARDS) and respiratory failure in several hours. HPS should be especially suspected in healthy young individuals who rapidly develop febrile ARDS and who may have been exposed to rodents.

B. Laboratory Findings. There are no specific laboratory abnormalities, but hemoconcentration (due to vascular leak) leukocytosis, possibly with left shift, abnormal or increased lymphocytes, thrombocytopenia, or prolonged PTT are seen in the more severe cases. In addition, there is evidence of progressively worsening lung function.

C. Imaging. Bilateral, diffuse, interstitial pulmonary infiltrates evolve rapidly in patients with HPS.

D. Differential Diagnosis. Acute, severe pneumonia of multiple causes must be distinguished from HPS. In particular, pneumonia caused by influenza A virus, *Legionella* spp., *Chlamydia pneumoniae,* or *Pneumocystis carinii* may be similar, but the epidemiology, age of the patient, and other factors provide clues to the etiology.

E. Complications. The principal complication of hantavirus infection is the severe impairment of lung function.

Diagnosis

A. Culture. Virus may be recovered by inoculation of animals or by cell culture.

B. Direct detection. Hantavirus RNA can be detected by PCR in clinical specimens from patients with high levels of viremia.

C. Serology. IgM-specific assays are the main method to rapidly document acute infection. Seroconversion or a fourfold increase in IgG antibody is useful to document recent infection, but cross-reactions within viral genera are common.

Treatment

Ribavirin has been used to treat hantavirus pulmonary syndrome, but its efficacy is not established. Supportive therapy of ARDS is critical to survival.

Prognosis

HPS is fatal in approximately 50% of those who develop clinical illness.

Prevention & Control

Human disease is prevented by interrupting the contact between humans and rodents. Rodent control also minimizes transmission.

COLORADO TICK FEVER

Colorado tick fever, an acute disease characterized by fever, headache, and severe myalgia, was originally described in the nineteenth century and is now believed to be one of the most common tick-borne viral diseases in the United States. Although hundreds of infections occur annually, the exact number is not known because it is not a reportable disease. It is caused by a coltvirus, a member of the reovirus family. This family also includes the rotaviruses, which are discussed in Chapter 37.

A. Epidemiology. Colorado tick fever has occurred in western and northwestern areas of the United States and western Canada, where the wood tick *Dermacentor andersoni* is distributed. Ticks acquire the virus by feeding on viremic hosts, and they subsequently transmit the virus in saliva when they feed on a new host. Many ticks have been shown to be infected; however, *D andersoni* is the predominant vector and the only proven source of human disease. Natural hosts can be one of many mammals, including squirrels, chipmunks, rabbits, and deer. Exposure to ticks is the major risk factor. Human disease is reported during the spring, summer, and fall months. Colorado tick fever is not contagious but has been transmitted by blood transfusion.

B. Microbiology. The coltvirus virion contains double-stranded RNA and is a spherical isohedron measuring 70–85 nm. There is no envelope, and the virus is resistant to lipid solvents.

C. Pathogenesis. The viral life cycle includes vertebrates, secondary hosts, and invertebrates (insects). Replication occurs in the cytoplasm of various cells of insect and mammalian origin. Colorado tick fever virus infects hematopoietic cells without severely damaging them. Viremia therefore can persist for weeks or months even after symptomatic recovery.

Clinical Findings

A. Signs and Symptoms. Acute disease occurs after an incubation period of 3–6 days. Although mild or subclinical infections can occur, most infections are symptomatic with fever, chills, headache, photophobia, myalgia, arthralgia, and lethargy. Neither respiratory nor gastrointestinal symptoms are prominent features. Hemorrhagic disease, confusion, and meningeal signs are unusual but, when they do occur, are more likely in children. Few physical signs are present on examination, but fever, conjunctivitis, lymphadenopathy, hepatosplenomegaly, and maculopapular or petechial rash may be present.

B. Laboratory Findings. A leukopenia involving both neutrophils and lymphocytes is an important hallmark of the disease. Leukocyte counts are generally less than 4,500/mm^3, with a relative lymphocytosis. Despite these findings, disease in children and adults is relatively mild, and uncomplicated recovery can be expected.

C. Imaging. None reported.

D. Differential Diagnosis. Colorado tick fever must be differentiated from Rocky Mountain spotted fever, a tick-borne bacterial infection characterized by extensive rash and severe systemic illness.

E. Complications. There are no serious complications.

Diagnosis

Specific diagnosis can be made by direct detection of viral antigens, viral isolation, or serologic tests. Because the disease is mild and geographically limited, laboratory tests are not broadly available.

A. Direct Detection. Detection of viral antigen in erythrocytes by immunofluorescence staining has been used as a rapid method of diagnosis.

B. Viral Isolation. Viral isolation can be performed with serum or plasma during the first few days of disease, before the appearance of neutralizing antibody, and later with the blood clot or washed erythrocytes. Viremia is long lasting and isolation is best accomplished by inoculating suckling mice. Infected mice appear ill in 4–5 days, and viral antigen can be detected by immunofluorescence. Colorado tick fever virus can also be adapted to cell culture, but primary isolation in cell culture is not sensitive.

C. Serology. A fourfold rise in antibody between the acute and convalescent specimen or the presence of Colorado tick fever virus-specific IgM in either specimen is presumptive evidence of acute or very recent infection. A sharp decline in IgM antibody occurs ~45 days after onset of illness.

Treatment

No specific treatment is available. The disease is generally self-limited, suggesting that supportive care is sufficient. As mentioned, viremia is long lasting, implying that infected patients should not donate blood soon after recovery.

Prognosis

Recovery occurs in > 99% of cases.

Prevention & Control

Prevention includes avoiding tick-infested areas, using protective clothing and tick repellents, and removing ticks before they bite. In contrast with tick-borne rickettsial disease, in which prolonged feeding is required for transmission, the virus from the tick's saliva can enter the bloodstream rapidly. A formalinized Colorado tick fever vaccine has been developed and evaluated but is not practical for use by the general public.

LASSA & OTHER HEMORRHAGIC FEVERS

Lassa fever, with its focus of endemicity in West Africa, is the best known of the arenavirus hemorrhagic fevers. Other agents, such as Junin and Machupo, cause similar syndromes in different geographic areas (Argentina and Bolivia, respectively). Lymphocytic choriomeningitis virus (LCM) is an arenavirus that causes viral meningitis (see Chapter 43).

A. Epidemiology. Each arenavirus infects specific rodents; for example, the natural host of Lassa fever virus is a small Nigerian rodent. Chronic infection is common in these animals and leads to chronic viremia and virus shedding in saliva, urine, and feces. Infection of humans is primarily from droppings and may occur by way of aerosols, contamination of food, or fomites. Bites are not a usual mechanism of spread. Persistently infected rodents do not usually exhibit illness. Human-to-human infection occurs with Lassa fever virus through contact with infected secretions or body fluids, but this mode of spread rarely if ever occurs with other arenaviruses. Arenaviruses do not require insects for spread. The incubation period for arenavirus infections averages 10–14 days.

B. Microbiology. Arenaviruses are pleomorphic, helical, and enveloped, with a size of 50–300 nm. They contain RNA in a linear configuration. Replication is in the cytoplasm, with budding from the host cell cytoplasm.

C. Pathogenesis. Arenaviruses are able to infect macrophages and possibly cause the release of mediators of cell and vascular damage. In certain laboratory animals the clinical severity of arenavirus disease appears to be directly related to the host's immunologic response. The greater the immune (especially T lymphocyte) response, the worse the disease. Whether these mechanisms are operative in human infection is not clear. In patients with the hemorrhagic fever, petechiae and visceral hemorrhage occur, as do liver and spleen necrosis, but not vasculitis.

Clinical Findings

Clinical illness is characterized by fever and coagulopathy. Hemorrhage and shock occur and occasionally cardiac and liver damage. Pharyngitis, diarrhea, and vomiting may be very prevalent, especially in patients with Lassa fever. The diagnosis is suggested by recent travel to endemic areas.

Diagnosis

The diagnosis of arenavirus infections is usually made through serologic tests, although the virus can be recovered by inoculation of blood or cerebrospinal fluid into suckling mice or Vero monkey cells. Throat specimens can yield arenaviruses, as can urine. Substantial risk is present for laboratory workers handling body fluids. Therefore, if the diagnosis is suspected, laboratory personnel should be warned and specimens processed only in facilities specialized for the isolation of contagious pathogens.

Treatment

Only supportive therapy for patients with arenavirus infection is currently available. Uncontrolled studies suggest that ribavirin may be useful for those with Lassa fever.

Prognosis. Death occurs in $\leq 50\%$ of those with Lassa fever and in a smaller percentage among those infected with the other arenaviruses.

Prevention & Control

Prevention of these rodent-borne infections rests on control of the vector's contact with humans. Laboratory-acquired cases can be reduced by processing samples for arenavirus isolation in at least P_3 biosafety facilities and not in the usual clinical virology laboratory.

REFERENCES

Cosgriff TM: Mechanisms of disease in Hantavirus infection: Pathophysiology of hemorrhagic fever with renal syndrome. Rev Infect Dis 1991;13:97.

Duchin JS et al: Hantavirus pulmonary syndrome: A clinical description of 17 patients with a newly recognized disease. N Engl J Med 1994;330:949.

Fisher-Hoch SP, McCormick JB: Arena viruses. In Warrell D: *The Oxford Textbook of Medicine,* 3rd ed. Oxford: Oxford University Press, 1996, p. 429.

Holmes GP et al: Lassa fever in the United States: Investigation of a case and new guidelines for management. N Engl J Med 1990;323:1120.

Ketai LH et al: Hantavirus pulmonary syndrome: Radiographic findings in 16 patients. Radiology 1994;191:665.

Monath TP: Yellow fever: Victor, Victoria? Conqueror, conquest? Epidemics and research in the last forty years and prospects for the future. Am J Trop Med Hyg 1991; 45:1–43.

Ramirez-Ronda CH: Dengue in the Western Hemisphere. Infect Dis Clin North Am 1994;8:107. (Describes disease and epidemiology.)

Robertson SE et al: Yellow fever: A decade of reemergence. J Am Med Assoc 1996;276:1157–62.

Simonsen L et al: Evaluation of the magnitude of the 1993 hantavirus outbreak in the southwestern United States. J Infect Dis 1995;172:729.

Zeitz PS et al: A case-control study of hantavirus pulmonary syndrome during an outbreak in the southwestern United States. J Infect Dis 1995;171:864. (The syndrome is associated with cleaning and agricultural activity in rodent-infested areas.)

Papovaviruses

45

W. Lawrence Drew, MD, PhD

PAPILLOMAVIRUSES

Essentials of Diagnosis
- Causes warts and genital lesions; latter may be premalignant or malignant.
- Hyperplasia of prickle cells and excess keratin in skin biopsy, vacuolated squamous epithelial cells.
- Human papillomavirus (HPV) antigen detected in clinical samples by immunofluorescence assay (IFA), immunoperoxidase.
- HPV DNA detected in biopsies, cervical smears.

General Considerations
A. Epidemiology. Papillomaviruses (HPVs) cause skin warts, most commonly in children and young adults, which may reflect acquired immunity in older age groups (Box 45–1). Laryngeal papillomas are found most commonly in young children and middle-aged adults. Genital warts (condylomas) are most common among sexually active patients and are sexually transmitted. Recent studies suggest that genital HPV infections may occur in 20% of females and are associated with cervical dysplasia, neoplasia, or both.

B. Microbiology. HPVs are nonenveloped, icosahedral virions measuring 50 nm in diameter. Their DNA is double-stranded and circular. The capsid consists of two structural proteins forming 72 capsomeres. Classification of HPV is based on DNA relatedness because these viruses cannot be grown in tissue culture. Based on DNA sequence homology, at least 77 HPV types have been identified. Viruses in similar groups frequently cause similar types of warts.

C. Pathogenesis. HPVs infect and replicate in cutaneous and mucosal epithelium, inducing epithelial proliferations (warts). These growths remain local and generally regress spontaneously. However, the HPV genome can persist in transformed cells and may be involved in maintaining tumor growth by increasing cell proliferation or prolonging the life of epithelial cells.

CLINICAL SYNDROMES

SKIN WARTS

There are two main types of skin warts: flat, or superficial, and plantar, or deep growths. Most persons are infected with the common HPV types (1 through 4), which infect keratinized surfaces, usually on the hands and feet, and occur frequently in childhood or early adolescence. They regress spontaneously if given time.

BENIGN HEAD & NECK TUMORS

Single oral papillomas are benign epithelial tumors of the oral cavity. They are pedunculated with a stalk and usually have a rough papillary appearance to their surface. They can occur in humans of any age group, are usually solitary, and rarely recur after surgical excision. Laryngeal papillomas are most often caused by HPV-11 and are the most common benign epithelial tumors of the larynx; however, laryngeal papillomatosis is usually considered a life-threatening condition in children because of the danger of airway obstruction. Occasionally, papillomas may extend down the trachea and into the bronchi.

ANOGENITAL WARTS

Genital warts (condyloma acuminata) occur almost exclusively on the squamous epithelium of the external genitalia and perianal areas, and ~90% are caused by HPV-6 and -11. Anogenital lesions infected with these HPV types rarely progress from benign to malignant conditions in otherwise healthy individuals.

CERVICAL DYSPLASIA & NEOPLASIA

Cytologic changes characteristic of infection (koilocytotic cells) in cervical smears that are Papanicolaou stained are detected in ~5% of women. Infection of the

BOX 45-1

Papillomavirus Infection

	Children	Adults
More Common	Skin warts	• Anogenital warts (condyloma accuminata) • Cervical infection, dysplasia
Less Common	Laryngeal pap-illomas	• Cervical carcinoma • Laryngeal papillomas

BOX 45-2

Treatment of Papillomavirus Infection

	Children	Adults
First Choice	Spontaneous regression	Spontaneous regression
Second Choice	Electrocautery, cryotherapy, or chemical means	Same
Pediatric Considerations	Podophylline	

female genital tract by HPV-16 and -18 and, in 30% by other types is associated with intraepithelial cervical dysplasia, neoplasia, and cancer. The first neoplastic changes noted by light microscopy are termed dysplasia and ~40–70% of these lesions undergo spontaneous regression. The development of cervical cancer is thought to proceed through a continuum of progressive cellular changes from mild (cervical intraepithelial neoplasia I [CIN I]) to moderate (CIN II), to severe (CIN III) dysplasia, carcinoma in situ, or both. This sequence of events has been documented to progress over a period of 1–4 years.

Diagnosis

A wart can be confirmed microscopically by its characteristic histologic appearance, consisting of hyperplasia of prickle cells and the production of excess keratin (hyperkeratosis). HPV infection is suggested by the presence of koilocytotic (vacuolated) squamous epithelial cells that are rounded and occur in clumps. HPV virions can be seen by electron microscopy in lesions as can HPV antigens by immunofluorescent and immunoperoxidase techniques. Use of molecular probes to detect HPV DNA is the method of choice for establishing the presence of HPV genomes in cervical swabs and in tissue. HPVs do not grow in cell cultures, and tests for HPV antibodies are rarely used except in epidemiologic surveys.

Treatment

Spontaneous disappearance of warts is the rule, but because this may take many months to years, intervention is sometimes warranted, especially for painful or bulky lesions (Box 45–2). Removal by surgical cryotherapy, electrocautery, or chemical means can be effective, although recurrences are common. Application of podophylline or salicylic acid with formalin or glutaraldehyde is effective. Injection of interferon is also beneficial. Surgery may be necessary for laryngeal papillomas.

Prevention & Control

Vaccination with formalin-inactivated HPV or autogenous preparations from the patient's own lesions has been at least partly effective, especially for anogenital warts (Box 45–3). Neither of these approaches is widely used, but vaccines may assume greater importance if an etiologic relationship between HPV and carcinoma is established. At present the best prevention is avoidance of direct contact with infected tissue.

POLYOMAVIRUSES

Essentials of Diagnosis

• These viruses are latent in humans and reactivate to cause disease in immunocompromised patients.
• JC virus is the cause of progressive multifocal leukoencephalopathy; BK virus causes urinary tract disease.
• Papovavirus disease is diagnosed by urinary cytology or detection of viral antigens or DNA in clinical specimens.

General Considerations

A. **Epidemiology.** There are two important hu-

BOX 45-3

Control of Papillomavirus Infection

Prophylactic Measures	Avoid direct contact with infected tissue
Isolation Precautions	Vaccines being evaluated

man papovaviruses: BK and JC viruses. SV40 is a simian polyomavirus that may be present in monkey kidney cultures and did contaminate certain lots of oral poliovirus vaccine (see below). The most important disease caused by a papovavirus is progressive multi-focal leukoencephalopathy (PML) (see Chapter 43).

Approximately 60–80% of adults have antibody to both BK and JC viruses (BKV and JCV, respectively). There is a major rise in antibody prevalence during childhood, with BKV infections occurring earlier than those caused by JCV. These viruses remain latent and are reactivated by immunosuppression.

B. Microbiology. Polyoma virions are nonenveloped icosahedrons ~45 nm in diameter. The genomes of BKV, JCV, and SV40 are closely related and are divided into early, late, and noncoding regions. The early region codes for nonstructural T (transformation) proteins, and the late region codes for three viral capsid proteins (VP1, VP2, and VP3), which are receptor-binding sites. The noncoding region is the site of DNA replication and transcription control. The replicative cycle includes penetration by endocytosis, followed by uncoating and viral multiplication in the nucleus. Infection may result in cell lysis or nonproductive infection. The viral replication cycle takes 48–72 h.

C. Pathogenesis. Polyomaviruses have a high specificity for certain hosts and particular cells within that host. In humans both JCV and BKV probably infect via the respiratory tract, spread by viremia, and infect the kidney. In immunocompromised patients, reactivation of virus in the kidney leads to urinary tract infection (BKV) or viremia and central nervous system infection (JCV). Suppressed T cell function appears most responsible for reactivation. Histopathology results from the cytolytic effects of the virus rather than local immunologic factors. BKV and JCV cause tumors when injected into hamsters; however, they are not consistently associated with any human tumors.

Early lots of poliomyelitis vaccine were contaminated with SV40, a simian polyomavirus, which was undetected in the cell cultures of monkey origin used to prepare the vaccine. Although many people were vaccinated with the contaminated lots, no SV40-related tumors have been reported during 25 years of follow-up.

CLINICAL SYNDROMES

Primary infection is virtually always asymptomatic, although mild respiratory symptoms might occur, and cystitis has been reported (Box 45–4). In

BOX 45–4

Polyomavirus Infection

	Children	Adults
More Common	Asymptomatic infection	Asymptomatic infection
Less Common	Cystitis	• PML (JC virus) • Ureteral stenosis or hemorrhagic cystitis (BK virus)

~40% of immunocompromised patients, urinary excretion of BKV and JCV is commonly observed. Reactivation also occurs in pregnancy, but no effect on the fetus has been established.

Ureteral stenosis in renal transplant patients appears to be associated with BKV, as does hemorrhagic cystitis in bone marrow transplant recipients. (See Chapter 43 for discussion of PML.)

Diagnosis

Cytologic examination of urine is the simplest method for documenting active polyomavirus infection. Virus may be demonstrated in tissue or cells by immunofluorescent, immunoperoxidase, or DNA hybridization techniques, and biopsy of brain has been the definitive method for diagnosing PML. Polymerase chain reaction analysis of cerebrospinal fluid is replacing biopsy as a noninvasive procedure for diagnosing JCV infection of the CNS. Culturing of polyomaviruses can be performed but requires specialized cells and may take weeks to months. Serology is not useful to diagnose PML because serum antibody is common in the general population.

Treatment

No treatment is established for BKV or JCV infection. PML has been treated with numerous different antiviral agents, and there have been conflicting results, especially with cytosine arabinoside. Spontaneous remission may occur, and diminishing immunosuppression may be beneficial.

Prevention & Control

No preventive or control measures have been established for BKV or JCV infection.

REFERENCES

Bauer HM et al: Genital human papillomavirus infection in female university students as determined by a PCR-based method. JAMA 1991;265:472.

Holman RC et al: Epidemiology of progressive multifocal leukoencephalopathy in the United States: Analysis of national mortality and AIDS surveillance data. Neurology 1991;41:1733.

Koutsky LA et al: A cohort study of the risk of cervical intraepithelial neoplasia grade 2 or 3 in relation to papillomavirus infection. N Engl J Med 1992;327:1272.

Markowitz RB et al: Incidence of BK virus and JC virus viruria in human immunodeficiency virus-infected and uninfected subjects. J Infect Dis 1993;167:13.

Staphylococci

46

Karen Bloch, MD, MPH

STAPHYLOCOCCUS AUREUS

Essentials of Diagnosis

- Large gram-positive cocci (0.7–1.5 μm in size).
- Colonies surrounded by zone of hemolysis on blood agar.
- Colonies pigmented pale yellow to deep orange macroscopically.
- Cluster in grapelike bunches microscopically.
- Biochemically differentiated from streptococci by presence of the enzyme catalase.
- Biochemically differentiated from other staphylococci by presence of the enzyme coagulase.
- Analysis of chromosomal DNA can identify clonal isolates (useful in epidemiologic studies).

General Considerations

A. Epidemiology. *Staphylococcus aureus* colonizes the human skin, vagina, nasopharynx, and gastrointestinal tract. Colonization occurs shortly after birth and may be either transient or persistent. Published studies differ widely in estimates of the prevalence of *S aureus* carriage. Between 10% and 35% of healthy adults have transient or persistent nasopharyngeal colonization. This percentage is increased among health care workers and individuals with repetitive needle exposure such as diabetics, patients on hemodialysis, and injection drug users. Vaginal carriage in premenopausal women approaches 10%, with the highest prevalence rates found at the start of the menstrual cycle.

Phage typing and molecular techniques have demonstrated that invasive disease is usually caused by the colonizing strain; therefore it is not surprising that groups with the highest prevalence of colonization are at the highest risk for *S aureus* infection. Fortunately, progression to infection is relatively unusual, occurring in only 2.5% of colonized nursing home patients and 37% of postoperative patients (compared with 11% of noncolonized postsurgical patients).

Acute infections in noncolonized patients are usually attributed to physical contact with a colonized individual. Studies have proven that health care workers can serve as vectors for transmission of staphylococci. The importance of person-to-person transmission underscores the need for strict hand washing in hospital settings. Other, less common, methods of acquisition include airborne transmission and spread from clothing and bed linens.

B. Microbiology. Staphylococci are aerobic, nonmotile, gram-positive cocci frequently cultured from environmental and clinical specimens. Although these organisms are generally considered commensal (ie, nonpathogenic normal flora) when cultured from the skin, nasopharynx, intestinal tract, and vagina, they may at times cause life-threatening disease. The clinical interpretation of a culture growing staphylococci depends on the bacterial species, host characteristics, and culture source.

Staphylococci share common characteristics that allow differentiation from other gram-positive cocci (Table 46–1). All species produce the enzyme catalase. Staphylococci are distinguished microscopically from other gram-positive cocci by a propensity to form clusters, as suggested by the genus name, which comes from the Greek *staphule,* meaning "bunch of grapes." Despite these common properties, individual staphylococcal species differ with respect to microbiologic properties, epidemiologic patterns, and clinical manifestations. Many of these differences relate to the production of the enzyme coagulase, and the genus has traditionally been subdivided into *S aureus* (which is coagulase-positive) and the relatively homogeneous coagulase-negative staphylococci (CoNS).

On blood agar media, *S aureus* can be distinguished macroscopically from CoNS by a ring of hemolysis surrounding the colonies. Colonies often have a golden-yellow hue (*aureus* meaning golden in Latin) as a result of the presence of carotenoids. While these morphologic characteristics may serve as general guides for differentiation of *S aureus* from the CoNS, definitive diagnosis is made by demonstrating the presence of coagulase through agglutination of rabbit plasma.

Table 46–1. Properties of staphylococci associated with virulence and disease.

Factor	Action or Associated Syndrome	*S aureus* (%)[1]	CoNS (%)[1]
Cell Capsule	• Impairs opsonization and phagocytosis	++−+++	+
Catalase	• Degrades H_2O_2 to $H_2O + O_2$ • Prevents PMN[3] respiratory burst	++++	++++
Coagulase	• Catalyzes conversion of fibrinogen to fibrin • Fibrin matrix inhibits phagocyte migration • Promotes abscess formation	++++	0
Inducible Beta-Lactamase	• Cleaves beta-lactam ring • Transmissible by plasmid • Confers resistance to penicillin	+++	+++
Intrinsic Beta-Lactam Resistance	• Production of low-affinity penicillin-binding proteins • Confers resistance to all beta-lactams (including methicillin)	++	+++
Exotoxins	• Hemolysis • Skin necrosis • Phagocyte inhibition	+	0
Epidermolytic Toxins	• Exfoliation	+	0
TSST-1	• Toxic shock syndrome	+	0
Enterotoxins	• Nausea/vomiting	+	0
Biofilm Production	• Adhesion to prosthetic material	+[2]	+++

[1]Symbols: 0, none; +, variable; ++, some (<50%); +++, common (>50%); ++++, uniform (>95%)
[2]Mucoid strains
[3]PMN: Polymorphonuclear cell

S aureus possesses a number of properties that contribute to organism virulence and host disease (Table 46–1): the presence of an extracellular capsule (sometimes called a slime layer), the enzymes catalase and coagulase, and membrane exotoxins that inhibit host immune defenses. More than 70% of strains harbor transmissible plasmids that produce beta-lactamase under certain conditions. These inducible beta-lactamases inactivate penicillin and some first-generation cephalosporins. In addition, an increasing proportion of isolates have intrinsic (as opposed to inducible) resistance to all beta-lactam–containing antibiotics. These strains, known collectively as methicillin-resistant *S aureus* (MRSA), produce penicillin-binding proteins with low affinity for penicillin, nafcillin, and other beta-lactam drugs. Because antibiotics cannot attach to their target site, the bacteria are not inhibited or killed in the presence of these drugs. Finally, some bacteria produce toxins that damage specific host organ systems such as the gastrointestinal tract (enterotoxins) and dermis (epidermolytic toxins).

C. Pathogenesis. Much is now known about the process of *S aureus* infection, which proceeds in a series of steps. Adherence, a necessary condition for colonization, occurs when a bacterium attaches to the teichoic acid component of the host cell wall. Adherence and colonization do not activate the host immune system. Invasion occurs when the epidermis is disrupted through an injury or an iatrogenic procedure, and bacteria gain access to the tissues or bloodstream, activating immune defenses. The interplay between bacterial virulence factors (Table 46–1) and host susceptibility factors (Table 46–2) determines

Table 46–2. Host susceptibility factors for infection with staphylococci.

Factor	Example	Impairment
Repetitive needle exposure	• Insulin-dependent diabetics • Injection drug users • Hemodialysis patients	• Increased colonization • Breaks in skin integrity
Qualitative PMN[1] impairment	• Chronic granulomatous disease • Leukocyte adhesion disorder	• Decreased phagocytosis
Quantitative PMN impairment	• Post-chemotherapy neutropenia • Congenital neutropenia	• Decreased phagocytosis
Impaired PMN chemotaxis	• Job's syndrome	• Decreased migration to site of infection
Exfoliative skin condition	• Thermal burns • Bullous skin diseases	• Break in skin integrity
Foreign body	• Prosthetic joints • Vascular access devices • Ventriculo-peritoneal shunts	• Break in skin integrity (at time of insertion) • Local alteration in immunity

[1]PMN, polymorphonuclear cell.

whether bacterial proliferation occurs. The final step in the pathogenesis of clinically apparent infection is tissue injury, either localized, as with an abscess, or systemic, as in toxic shock syndrome.

CLINICAL SYNDROMES

S aureus causes a wide spectrum of clinical disease, ranking among the most common bacterial causes of skin and soft tissue infection, gastroenteritis, wound infection, septic arthritis, bacteremia, endocarditis, and osteomyelitis. This section focuses on syndromes unique to *S aureus* and on syndromes for which *S aureus* is the most common bacterial agent.

PYOGENIC CUTANEOUS INFECTIONS

Clinical Findings
A. Signs and Symptoms. *S aureus* is the leading bacterial cause of pyogenic skin lesions (Box 46–1). Folliculitis, infection of the hair follicles, is a local suppurative process causing indurated papules or pustules, often with a hair exiting from the center of the lesion. There is local erythema and tenderness, but the patient is not systemically ill.

A furuncle ("boil") begins as a hair follicle infection and extends locally to form an abscess, characterized by liquefaction of necrotic tissue. Clinically, this presents as a well-circumscribed, fluctuant, ten-

der, erythematous collection. Infection on occasion spreads to the surrounding epidermis, causing cellulitis. Common sites for furuncles include the face, neck, axilla, back and groin.

Carbuncles differ from furuncles in that they extend to the deeper subcutaneous tissues. They are most commonly found on the posterior neck and upper back. These infections are less circumscribed than furuncles and may be associated with draining fistulae. Patients with carbuncles are often systemically ill, exhibiting fevers, chills, and malaise.

B. Laboratory Findings. Folliculitis and furunculosis are usually localized processes, and the peripheral WBC count is normal. Carbunculosis is associated with a systemic immune response, manifested by leukocytosis and a predominance of immature WBC. Blood cultures are frequently positive in patients with carbuncles.

C. Differential Diagnosis. The differential diagnosis of folliculitis includes pseudofolliculitis barbae, insect bites, acne vulgaris, foreign body reactions, and milia. Alternative diagnoses for furunculosis include pilonidal cysts, cystic acne, and hidradenitis suppurativa. A carbuncle may be confused with a furuncle, a deep-seated skin infection such as necrotizing fasciitis, or a kerion.

D. Complications. These infections are generally self-limited and do not disseminate beyond the skin. Local complications include cellulitis and osteomyelitis of adjacent bone. There have been anecdotal reports of facial lesions ascending intracranially to cause septic cavernous vein thrombosis. Bacteremia, a relatively common complication of carbunculosis, may result in secondary infections including endocarditis, hematogenous osteomyelitis, and pneumonia.

BOX 46–1

Cutaneous Syndromes Caused by *S aureus*

	Pyogenic	Impetigo	SSSS[1]

More Common	• Folliculitis
	  Papules
	  Pustules
	• Furuncles
	  Abscesses
		• Scarlatiniform eruption
		• Blisters eroding to honey-colored crust
		• Local tenderness
		• Regional lymphadenopathy
			• Bullous impetigo
			  Local erythroderma
			  Flaccid bullae rupturing to brown crust
			  Involvement of face, trunk, perineum

Less Common	• Carbuncles
	  Coalescent abscesses with draining fistulae
	• Fever
	• Systemically ill
	• Elevated WBC count
		• Fever
		• Bacteremia
			• Generalized SSS
			  Diffuse dermal desquamation
			  Nikolsky's sign
			  Fever
			  Leukocytosis
			  Bacteremia

[1]Staphylococcal scalded skin syndrome

Diagnosis

Pyogenic skin infections are diagnosed by clinical exam, with culture of purulent material obtained by incision and drainage to confirm staphylococcal infection and determine antibiotic susceptibility patterns. Blood cultures may also guide antibiotic therapy in patients with signs of systemic illness.

Treatment

Treatment for folliculitis and furunculosis is primarily supportive (Box 46–2). Stringent attention to hygiene is key; the affected areas should be washed at least twice daily with a mild antibacterial soap, and overlying clothing should be loose fitting. Furuncles either spontaneously drain or require incision and drainage once they have matured (come to a head). Antibiotic therapy is rarely necessary for these conditions. Carbuncles require both local surgical débridement and parenteral antibiotic therapy.

Recurrent pyogenic skin infections are common in patients with nasopharyngeal colonization. Eradication of staphylococcal carriage with mupiricin may be indicated after repeated episodes of furunculosis. This regimen has good short-term efficacy; however, recolonization frequently occurs, and emergence of mupiricin resistance has been reported.

NONPYOGENIC SKIN INFECTIONS

Clinical Findings

A. Signs and Symptoms. Impetigo and staphylococcal scalded skin syndrome (SSSS) are primarily childhood diseases. More than 70% of cases of impetigo are caused by *S aureus*, with the remainder attributed to pyogenic streptococci or mixed infection. Impetigo begins as a scarlatiniform eruption in a previously traumatized area that blisters then

BOX 46–2

Empiric Treatment of *S aureus* Skin Infections

	Pyogenic	Impetigo	SSSS[1]

First Choice	• Folliculitis and furuncles
	  Local hygiene
	  I & D of mature furuncles
	• Carbuncles
	  Surgical débridement
	  PRSP[2] 1–2 g IV every 4 h for 10–14 days
		• Pediatric:
		  Dicloxacillin, 12.5–50 mg/kg/d orally, divided into 4 daily doses **OR** mupiricin 2% ointment topically 3 times daily[3]
		• Adult:
		  Dicloxacillin 500 mg orally every 6 h for 7 days
			• Aggressive hydration
			• Close monitoring of fluid status
			• Pediatric:
			  PRSP,[2] 150 mg/kg/d IV, every 6 h for 10–14 days
			• Adult:
			  PRSP,[2] 1–2 gm IV every 4 h for 10–14 days

Second Choice	• Carbuncles
	  Surgical débridement
	  Cefazolin, 1–2 g IV every 8 h for 10–14 days
		• Pediatric:
		  Cephalexin, 25–50 mg/kg/d orally, divided into 4 daily doses for 7 days
		• Adult:
		  Cephalexin, 500 mg orally every 6 h for 7 days
			• Pediatric:
			  Cefazolin, 20 mg/kg/d IV every 8 h for 10–14 days
			• Adult:
			  Cefazolin, 1–2 g IV every 8 h for 10–14 days

Penicillin Allergic	• Carbuncles
	  Surgical débridement
	  Vancomycin, 15 mg/kg/ twice daily for 10–14 days
		• Pediatric:
		  Erythromycin, 40 mg/kg/d orally, divided into 4 doses for 7 days
		• Adult:
		  Erythromycin, 500 mg orally every 6 h for 7 days
			• Pediatric:
			  Vancomycin, 40 mg/kg/d IV divided into 6-h doses
			• Adult:
			  Vancomycin, 15 mg/kg/d IV every 12 h for 10–14 days

[1]Staphylococcal scalded skin syndrome
[2]Penicillinase-resistant, semisynthetic penicillin–nafcillin or oxacillin
[3]Topical therapy only indicated for mild, self-limited disease

ruptures to form a wet, honey-colored crust (Figure 46–1). Common sites for infection are the face and trunk. The primary symptom in impetigo is localized pain; fever and constitutional symptoms are rarely seen (Box 46–1). Physical exam often reveals regional lymphadenopathy.

Staphylococcal scalded skin syndrome encompasses three distinct clinical scenarios: bullous impetigo, staphylococcal scarlet fever, and generalized scalded skin syndrome. The histologic finding common to all these conditions is cleavage of the epidermis at the level of the stratum granulosum caused by an exfoliative toxin. Bullous impetigo, the most common of the three types of SSSS, is almost exclusively seen in children < 5 years old. The disease begins as localized erythroderma progressing rapidly to form multiple vesicles, which coalesce into flaccid bullae. Constitutional symptoms are minimal during the early phases, and the bullae spontaneously rupture after 1–2 days to form nontender, brown, varnishlike crusts (Figure 46–2). Commonly involved areas include the face, trunk, and perineum. A variant of this condition, staphylococcal scarlet fever, causes a scarlatiniform rash with late, limited desquamation, without an intermediate bullae stage.

Generalized scalded skin syndrome (known as Ritter's syndrome in neonates) differs from the more benign bullous impetigo in that there is diffuse dermal involvement, causing extensive desquamation. Nikolsky's sign, the sloughing of intact skin on light touch, is frequently seen. Following spontaneous bullae rupture, the skin is denuded and painful (Figure 46–3), and fever is common.

B.   Laboratory Findings. Patients with generalized SSSS may have leukocytosis with a predominance of immature white cells. Blood cultures, particularly in adults, may be positive.

C.   Differential Diagnosis. The differential diagnosis of impetigo includes herpes simplex and varicella zoster infections, contact dermatitis, sca-

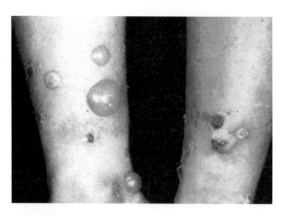

Figure 46–2. Discrete, superficial, crusted lesions seen after bullae rupture in bullous impetigo. (Reprinted with permission from Pediatr Ann 1993;22:236.)

bies, and tinea corporis. SSSS may be confused with other bullous skin diseases (pemphigus vulgaris and bullous pemphigoid), Stevens-Johnson syndrome, thermal burn, and dermatitis herpetiformis.

D.   Complications. Suppurative lymphadenitis, cellulitis, and staphylococcal sepsis are uncommon complications of impetigo. Complications of generalized SSSS include dehydration, bacteremia, and secondary infections. Mortality in children with generalized SSSS is 1–10%, whereas the mortality rate among adults is > 50%.

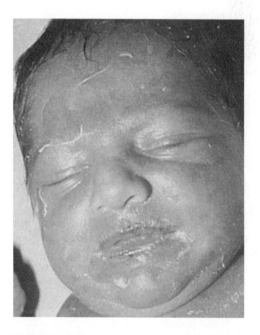

Figure 46–3. Diffuse epidermal desquamation characteristic of the generalized staphylococcal scaled skin syndrome (SSSS). (Reproduced by permission of Pediatr Rev 1996;17:18.)

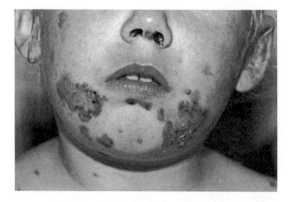

Figure 46–1. Perioral impetigo with honey-colored crusting of denuded cutaneous lesions. (Reprinted with permission from Pediatr Ann 1993;22:236.)

Diagnosis

Impetigo is diagnosed by the presence of the classic golden crusts on physical examination; a microbiologic diagnosis is rarely necessary. SSSS can be diagnosed by rupturing an intact bulla and culturing the extravasated fluid for *S aureus*. Latex agglutination or ELISA confirms the presence of the staphylococcal exfoliative toxin.

Treatment

Mild cases of (nonbullous) impetigo may be treated with topical mupiricin; however, more serious infections need oral antibiotics (Box 46–2). Bullous impetigo requires treatment with an oral antistaphylococcal agent. The high rates of morbidity and mortality in generalized SSSS mandate hospitalization for aggressive hydration and parenteral antibiotics. Extensive desquamation predisposes patients to secondary infections, and they should receive aggressive topical care such as that given to burn victims.

Table 46–3. Major criteria for diagnosis of toxic shock syndrome.

1. Temperature >38.9° C
2. Systolic blood pressure < 90 mm Hg
3. Diffuse erythroderma followed in 1–2 weeks by desquamation
4. Involvement of at least three of the following organ systems:
   - Gastrointestinal: vomiting or diarrhea
   - Musculoskeletal: myalgia or creatinine phosphokinase >5 times normal level
   - Mucous membrane: conjunctival injection, vaginal or oropharyngeal hyperemia
   - Renal: BUN or creatinine >2 times normal level or pyuria without evidence of UTI
   - Hepatic: bilirubin or transaminases >2 times normal level
   - Blood: platelet count of <100,000/mm^3
   - Central nervous system: confusion without focal neurologic deficits
5. Serologic exclusion of Rocky Mountain spotted fever, measles, and leptospirosis

Probable diagnosis:
   Desquamation *plus* 3 other major criteria
   All five major criteria in the absence of desquamation

TOXIC SHOCK SYNDROME

The toxic shock syndrome (TSS) is a heterogeneous complex of symptoms attributed to TSST-1 toxin-producing *S aureus*. Two variants have been described: menstruation-associated and nonmenstrual disease. Cases of menstruation-associated disease are correlated with the use of superabsorbent tampons. Diaphragm contraception, parturition, indwelling foreign bodies, and recent surgery predispose to nonmenstrual disease.

Clinical Findings

A. Signs and Symptoms. Myalgias, headache, malaise, watery diarrhea, and confusion (in the face of a normal neurologic exam) are early symptoms of TSS, typically preceding the rash by 2–3 days. Erythroderma is initially seen on the palms and soles, progressing to a confluent generalized rash. Hypotension and fever are invariably present at this stage. Multisystem organ failure may be present early or late in the disease course. Dermal desquamation, particularly of the palms and soles is a late sequela of TSS, occurring 7–14 days after the onset of symptoms.

B. Laboratory Findings. The laboratory abnormalities in TSS reflect the diverse organ systems involved. Laboratory abnormalities included as criteria for case definition (see Table 46–3) include an elevation in creatine phosphokinase, acute renal insufficiency, sterile pyuria, elevated liver function tests, and thrombocytopenia. Disordered electrolytes (particularly hypocalcemia and hypophosphatemia), neutrophil predominance on white blood cell differential, and anemia, while not explicitly mentioned in the case definition, may also be found in patients with TSS.

C. Differential Diagnosis. Other entities causing rash, hypotension, or fever that may be confused with staphylococcal TSS include streptococcal TSS, Rocky Mountain spotted fever, viral infection with exanthem (such as measles or EBV), meningococcemia, leptospirosis, the septic shock syndrome, Kawasaki's disease, and drug-induced reactions (such as erythema multiforme or toxic epidermal necrolysis). A thorough history with particular attention to tick exposures, ill contacts, travel, pets, and medication use is essential in excluding the mimicking conditions.

D. Complications. Case fatality rates for TSS range from 3% to 6% and are higher for nonmenstrual disease. Digital gangrene may occur as a result of sustained hypotension and impaired extremity perfusion. Neuropsychiatric symptoms such as emotional lability, impaired memory, and decreased concentration are common sequelae in survivors.

Diagnosis

Formal criteria for the diagnosis of TSS have been developed to facilitate surveillance and standardize case definition (Table 46–3). Increased awareness of the association between menstruation, tampon use, and TSS has led to improved diagnosis of menstruation-associated disease. Nonmenstrual disease lacks unifying epidemiologic characteristics, which makes diagnosis more difficult. Postoperative TSS is particularly difficult to diagnose, as surgical wound inflammation may be minimal, and early signs are nonspecific.

The diagnosis of TSS is supported by a culture of TSST-1–producing *S aureus* from an infected focus, although this is not a criterion for case definition. TSST-1–producing staphylococci are isolated from the vagina in 85% of menstruation-associated disease but are isolated from infected foci in only 40–60% of cases of nonmenstrual disease. *S aureus* bacteremia rarely occurs with TSS.

Treatment

Treatment requires identification and removal of foreign bodies (such as tampons) and irrigation and débridement of infected wounds. Aggressive hydration and close hemodynamic monitoring are essential in the early stages of TSS. All patients should be treated with parenteral agents active against staphylococci (Box 46–3). In vitro, clindamycin inhibits TSST-1 protein synthesis, providing at least a theoretical basis for combination therapy with this agent and a penicillinase-resistant penicillin.

PRIMARY BACTEREMIA & ENDOCARDITIS

Staphylococci (both *S aureus* and CoNS) have emerged as the two most common organisms cultured from patients with primary bloodstream infections. The term "primary bacteremia" refers to positive blood cultures without an identifiable anatomic focus of infection. Differentiation of primary bacteremia from infective endocarditis (IE), in which infection of the cardiac valves leads to continuous bacterial seeding of the bloodstream, may challenge even the most experienced clinician. Primary *S aureus* bacteremia is associated with insulin-dependent diabetes, the presence of a vascular graft, and, most significantly, the presence of an indwelling intravascular catheter. Risk factors for IE include structurally ab-

normal valves, recent injection drug use, and the presence of a prosthetic cardiac valve.

Clinical Findings

A. Signs and Symptoms. Patients with primary *S aureus* bacteremia are systemically ill, with fever, chills, malaise, and hypotension. *S aureus* endocarditis is usually an acute disease, with a presentation indistinguishable from *S aureus* bacteremia. For the most part, patients lack the classic cutaneous stigmata associated with subacute bacterial endocarditis (Box 46–4). A new or changed cardiac murmur, or evidence of embolic disease, in the setting of *S aureus* bacteremia strongly supports the diagnosis of IE. Endocarditis in injection drug users involves the tricuspid valve in 75% of cases, and respiratory complaints, attributable to septic pulmonary embolization with infarction, predominate.

B. Laboratory Findings. Laboratory findings in primary bacteremia and IE are nonspecific; an elevated WBC count is the most common abnormality. The erythrocyte sedimentation rate, which is elevated in subacute IE, may be normal. Because endocarditis causes continuous seeding of the bloodstream, it is common to see "high-grade" bacteremia, with multiple positive blood cultures from different venous sites drawn at disparate time intervals.

C. Imaging. The classic radiographic finding in patients with right-sided endocarditis is the presence of multiple pleural-based densities (so-called "cannon-ball lesions") caused by septic pulmonary emboli. Radiologic signs with left-sided disease are manifestations of congestive heart failure, ranging

---

BOX 46–3

Treatment of Staphylococcal Toxic Shock Syndrome

	Agent/Dose/Route/Duration
Supportive Measures	• Removal of foreign bodies/tampons • Irrigation of the vaginal vault • Irrigation and débridement of infected wounds • Close hemodynamic monitoring • Vigorous fluid or vasopressor support • Consider IV gamma-globulin, 400 mg/kg as a single dose[1]
First Choice	• PRSP,[2] 2 g IV every 4 h for 10–14 days **PLUS** • Clindamycin, 900 mg IV every 8 h
Second Choice	• Cefazolin, 1–2 g IV every 8 h for 10–14 days **PLUS** • Clindamycin, 900 mg IV every 8 h
Penicillin Allergic **PLUS**	• Vancomycin, 15 mg/kg IV every 12 h for 10–14 days • Clindamycin, 900 mg IV every 8 h

[1]No controlled studies; reserve for life-threatening situations
[2]Penicillinase-resistant, semisynthetic penicillin—nafcillin or oxacillin

BOX 46-4

S aureus Native Valve Endocarditis

	Right-sided	Left-sided
Common	• Fever • Leukocytosis • Heart murmur (~50%) • Pleuritic chest pain • Cough • Hemoptysis • Dyspnea	• Fever • Leukocytosis • Heart murmur (~85%) • Systemic emboli • Hemodynamic compromise • Congestive heart failure
Uncommon	• Hemodynamic compromise • Congestive heart failure • Systemic emboli	• Osler's nodes • Janeway lesions • Splinter hemorrhages • Roth spots

from increased interstitial markings to parenchymal opacification from pulmonary edema.

D. Differential Diagnosis. Culture of *S aureus* from the blood should prompt a thorough search for an infected primary focus. Common local infections predisposing to secondary bacteremia include infections of indwelling intravenous catheters or other prosthetic material, postoperative wound infections, septic arthritis, osteomyelitis, and cellulitis. In the absence of an identifiable anatomic focus of infection, the clinician must differentiate primary bacteremia from infective endocarditis.

E. Complications. Complications of *S aureus* bacteremia are primarily from bacterial seeding of the viscera, with subsequent end-organ infections such as endocarditis (a sequela of uncomplicated bacteremia in 5–10% of cases), osteomyelitis, septic arthritis, cerebral abscess, and perinephric abscess. Mortality with primary bacteremia ranges from 25% to 40%. Factors associated with a fatal outcome include the absence of a removable source of infection (such as an intravenous line), age > 60 years, and underlying pulmonary disease.

Morbidity in left-sided IE is due to progressive valve destruction or embolic phenomena. Valve failure results in congestive heart failure, which may be insidious or may present as acute pulmonary edema following rupture of the chordae tendineae. New-onset heart block is the earliest sign of a myocardial ring abscess. Recurrent systemic emboli on appropriate therapy or persistent bacteremia are indications for surgical valve replacement. The mortality rate for left-sided IE ranges from 20% to 44%, as compared with < 5% for right-sided disease.

F. Differential Diagnosis. Differentiating primary bacteremia from IE causing continuous in-travascular seeding is often difficult: the probability that blood cultures growing *S aureus* represent IE varies from 10% to 40%, depending on the population studied. The distinction between these two syndromes is important as IE requires prolonged therapy and carries a worse prognosis.

Several sets of diagnostic criteria for IE have been proposed. The most sensitive is the Duke Criteria, which incorporates echocardiogram findings with clinical factors to stratify the risk of IE. Patients with community-acquired *S aureus* bacteremia or nosocomially acquired cases with known cardiac valvular disease or prosthetic valves have the highest probability of having IE and should be evaluated for cardiac involvement with a transthoracic echocardiogram.

Treatment

Optimal empiric treatment for primary bloodstream infection is based on the likelihood that an organism is resistant to methicillin (defined as an MIC ≥ 8 µg/ml). Penicillinase-resistant semisynthetic penicillins (PRSP) such as oxacillin or nafcillin are the recommended agents for community-acquired infections, or nosocomial infections in institutions with documented low prevalence rates for MRSA. In facilities with significant isolation rates for MRSA, empiric treatment with vancomycin is indicated. A PRSP should be substituted as soon as the bacteria is proven susceptible, as vancomycin is less active against *S aureus,* and patients treated with this agent have longer duration of fever and bacteremia. Regardless of which agent is used, treatment for uncomplicated bacteremia should be continued 10–14 days.

Bacteremia attributed to an infected indwelling central venous catheter is difficult to eradicate without removal of the foreign body. Subcutaneous infection along the catheter tunnel, hemodynamic instability, fever or rigors more than 48 hours after initiating antibiotic treatment, persistently positive blood cultures, or septic venous thrombophlebitis mandate prompt catheter removal.

Therapy for IE is guided by the clinical scenario (Box 46–5). Patients with uncomplicated, right-sided, methicillin-sensitive *S aureus* endocarditis respond to 2 weeks of treatment. Extrapulmonary embolic disease, persistent symptoms or bacteremia after more than 96 hours of therapy, high-level aminoglycoside resistance, or concurrent left-sided valvular involvement require a full course of therapy, lasting 4–6 weeks.

Aminoglycosides act synergistically with beta-lactams against staphylococci; their use reduces the time to clearing of the bacteria from the bloodstream, although they do not affect mortality rates in IE. Synergy occurs at relatively low doses of aminoglycosides, with optimal peak and trough levels for gentamicin 3.0 and 0.5 μm/mL, respectively.

The penicillin allergic patient with IE presents a treatment challenge. For patients without a history of immediate-type hypersensitivity, a first-generation cephalosporin is the preferred agent. Patients with a history of anaphylaxis or other severe penicillin allergy should receive vancomycin. The potential for antagonism between vancomycin and rifampin exists, and adjuvant therapy with rifampin should be reserved for patients failing monotherapy.

OSTEOMYELITIS

Clinical Findings

A. Signs and Symptoms. Osteomyelitis is divided into two subcategories based on the acuity of onset. Acute osteomyelitis, more commonly seen in children, is associated with sudden onset of bony pain, fever, and malaise. Acute disease is often the result of seeding of the bone during *S aureus* bacteremia, with the most common anatomic locations corresponding to highly vascularized osseous areas such as the metaphyses of long bones. Chronic osteomyelitis is a more indolent process, characterized by low-grade fevers and chronic nonhealing ulcers or draining sinus tracts in the skin overlying the infected bone. Bony necrosis is pathognomonic for chronic osteomyelitis. Chronic osteomyelitis commonly affects the feet and lower extremities and is often preceded by minor injury or surgery of tissues adjacent to the affected bone. Individuals with impaired vascular perfusion, such as diabetics, are at a particularly high risk for chronic bone infections.

B. Laboratory Findings. The laboratory findings are nonspecific and include an elevated WBC count and erythrocyte sedimentation rate. Blood cultures may be positive in acute osteomyelitis.

C. Imaging. Advances in imaging technology have improved the ability to diagnose osteomyelitis. Plain films are of limited use for acute osteomyelitis, as bony abnormalities are not detectable until at least 10 days after the onset of symptoms. Both the MRI scan and the technetium bone scan have increased sensitivity for detecting early osteomyelitis. The technetium scan uses a radiolabeled isotope, which localizes to areas of osseous regeneration. This tech-

---

BOX 46–5

Treatment of *S aureus* Endocarditis

Scenario	Agent/Dose/Route/Duration[1]
Left-sided Native Valve Endocarditis	• PRSP, 2 g IV every 4 h for 4–6 weeks **PLUS** • Gentamicin, 1 mg/kg IV every 8 h for 3–5 days
Right-sided Native Valve Endocarditis[2]	• PRSP, 2 g IV every 4 h for 2 weeks **PLUS** • Gentamicin, 1 mg/kg IV every 8 h for 2 weeks
Penicillin Allergy	• Cefazolin,[3] 2 g IV every 4 h for 4–6 weeks **PLUS** • Gentamicin, 1 mg/kg IV every 8 h for 3–5 days **OR** • Vancomycin, 15 mg/kg every 12 h for 4–6 weeks
MRSA (Native Valve)	• Vancomycin, 15 mg/kg every 12 h for 4–6 weeks
Prosthetic Valve (PVE)	• PRSP, 2 g IV every 4 h for ≥6 weeks **PLUS** • Rifampin, 300 mg every 8 h for ≥6 weeks **PLUS** • Gentamicin, 1 mg/kg IV every 8 h for 2 weeks
MRSA (Prosthetic Valve)	• Vancomycin, 15 mg/kg every 12 h for ≥6 weeks **PLUS** • Rifampin, 300 mg every 8 h for ≥6 weeks **PLUS** • Gentamicin, 1 mg/kg IV every 8 h for 2 weeks

[1] Penicillinase-resistant, semisynthetic penicillin—nafcillin or oxacillin
[2] 2-week course not indicated if patient unable to tolerate PRSP or if evidence of metastatic disease beside septic pulmonary emboli
[3] Cephalosporins contraindicated if penicillin allergy is immediate hypersensitivity reaction

nique is limited by the difficulty in differentiating bony regeneration due to injury from that due to infection. Another imaging modality, the indium scan, involves the venous injection of radiolabeled autologous WBC, which localize to sites of granulocyte aggregation in infected bone. The clinical utility of the indium scan is limited by poor discrimination of osteomyelitis from simple cellulitis and low sensitivity for diagnosing the chronic form of osteomyelitis.

D. Complications. Bacteremia caused by osteomyelitis may lead to secondary end-organ infections. More commonly osteomyelitis causes extensive local bony destruction. Patients with peripheral vascular disease, particularly diabetics, may require surgical revascularization to cure osteomyelitis of the lower extremities. In situations where surgical revascularization is not an option or has failed, localized amputation may be necessary.

Diagnosis

Because of the need for prolonged antibiotic therapy with osteomyelitis, a concerted effort to obtain a microbiologic diagnosis before initiating therapy should be made. Culture of cutaneous sinus tracts has an unacceptably low sensitivity and specificity and is not recommended for diagnostic purposes. All patients should have a surgical bone biopsy, as this is the only reliable way of obtaining adequate culture results to guide therapy.

Treatment

The treatment of osteomyelitis presents a particular challenge as antibiotics penetrate bone poorly; antibiotic concentrations in bone are only 5% that of serum. All successful treatment regimens require high dosing for prolonged durations (Box 46–6). Standard regimens require intravenous therapy for 4–6 weeks. The requirement of multiple daily doses is impractical for outpatient administration and has led to increasing interest in less complicated regimens. Treatment with parenteral antibiotics followed by oral therapy in children achieves cure rates equivalent to those of standard parenteral regimens but has not been studied sufficiently in adults to make recommendations regarding oral antibiotics for this age group.

Surgical débridement is required for chronic osteomyelitis, particularly in the presence of necrotic bone or sequestrum. Patients with chronic osteomyelitis should receive at least 6 weeks of parenteral therapy after surgical débridement. Infections in patients who are unable to tolerate surgery or who have refractory disease can be suppressed with

---

BOX 46–6

Treatment of Osteomyelitis

	Children	Adults
General Care	• Débridement of devitalized bone	
Methicillin Sensitive	• PRSP,[1] 150 mg/kg/day IV divided every 6 h **FOLLOWED BY**[2] • Dicloxacillin, 500–100 mg/kg/d orally divided into 4 daily doses • Treat for 4–6 weeks	• PRSP,[1] 2.0 gm IV every 4 h • Treat for 4–6 weeks
MRSA	• Vancomycin, 40 mg/kg/d IV divided every 6 h • Treat for 4–6 weeks	• Vancomycin, 15 mg/kg every 12 h • Treat for 4–6 weeks
Penicillin Allergic	• Cefazolin, 20 mg/kg IV every 8 h **FOLLOWED BY**[2,3] • Clindamycin, 30 mg/kg/d orally divided into 4 daily doses **OR** • Vancomycin, 40 mg/kg/d IV divided every 6 h • Treat for 4–6 weeks	• Cefazolin,[3] 2.0 g IV every 8 h **OR** • Vancomycin, 15 mg/kg every 12 h • Treat for 4–6 weeks

[1]Penicillinase-resistant, semisynthetic penicillin—nafcillin or oxacillin
[2]Consider change to oral regimen when WBC count has normalized and ESR is reduced by at least 20%
[3]Cephalosporins contraindicated if penicillin allergy is immediate hypersensitivity reaction

ciprofloxacin (750 mg orally twice daily) and rifampin (600 mg orally each day), given indefinitely.

COAGULASE-NEGATIVE STAPHYLOCOCCI

Essentials of Diagnosis
- Gram-positive cocci.
- No zone of hemolysis surrounding colonies on blood agar.
- Colonies gray or white macroscopically.
- Cluster in grapelike bunches microscopically.
- Biochemically differentiated from streptococci by production of the enzyme catalase.
- Biochemically differentiated from *S aureus* by absence of the enzyme coagulase.
- Analysis of chromosomal DNA can identify clonal isolates (useful in epidemiologic studies).

General Considerations
A. Epidemiology. Like *S aureus,* coagulase-negative staphylococci (CoNS) are normal human flora. *S epidermidis* is the most common bacteria cultured from intact skin, while *S saprophyticus* is commonly cultured from the vagina of asymptomatic women. With the exception of *S saprophyticus,* which causes cystitis in young, sexually active women, infections with CoNS occur almost exclusively in the presence of foreign bodies.

B. Microbiology. As with all Staphylococcus species, CoNS are aerobic, nonmotile, gram-positive cocci. This group is comprised of > 30 species, of which about half are known human pathogens. The most clinically important are *S epidermidis, S saprophyticus,* and *S haemolyticus.* Although species can be differentiated by biochemical tests, this is rarely clinically indicated, as the high prevalence of methicillin-resistance among CoNS mandates treatment with vancomycin. Molecular analysis can determine if organisms from the same species are clonally related, which may be useful for epidemiologic investigations.

C. Pathogenesis. Less is known about the mechanisms through which CoNS cause disease. As noted above, adherence, colonization, and invasion occur almost exclusively in the setting of indwelling foreign bodies, such as intravenous catheters or implanted prosthetic devices. CoNS attach to foreign material by the production of an exopolysaccharide slime layer and are able to alter the local immune response through a poorly understood mechanism, hindering host eradication. These organisms are much less virulent than *S aureus* and generally produce indolent infections with inflammation restricted to local tissues.

BACTEREMIA & ENDOCARDITIS

The rising incidence of CoNS bacteremia in the last decade may be attributed to the increasingly common use of prosthetic devices, especially intravascular catheters, among hospitalized patients. Positive peripheral blood cultures are indicative of infection rather than skin contamination in only 10% of cases, and the challenge lies in differentiating these two entities.

Clinical Findings
A. Signs and Symptoms. Clinical signs of CoNS bacteremia are often minimal; the finding of fever and leukocytosis support infection rather than colonization, particularly in a host with an indwelling vascular catheter or implanted prosthetic material. While erythema or purulence at a catheter site is compelling evidence supporting catheter-associated bacteremia, only 50% of patients with bacteremia from vascular lines develop local signs of infection.

Although CoNS rarely infect native cardiac valves, they are the most common cause of early (defined as occurring < 12 months postoperatively) prosthetic valve endocarditis (PVE). The majority of cases of early PVE are caused by intraoperative seeding. Infections are indolent, with fever the most common sign. Diagnosis may be delayed by the lack of physical findings specific for endocarditis; most patients do not develop audible murmurs until valve destruction is advanced.

B. Laboratory Findings. Laboratory abnormalities in CoNS bacteremia and endocarditis are variable. Prosthetic valve endocarditis due to CoNS is usually an indolent process, with nonspecific laboratory findings, including anemia and hematuria. Patients who have CoNS native valve endocarditis present with typical laboratory findings for subacute endocarditis, including elevated erythrocyte sedimentation rate (~90%), anemia (~75%), positive rheumatoid factor (~33%), and hematuria (~33%). Leukocytosis is present in only 40–45% of patients with either bacteremia or endocarditis.

C. Imaging. Transthoracic echocardiography may be useful in native valve endocarditis or in the later stages of PVE when there is significant valve dehiscence. Diagnosis of PVE may be difficult in the early stages when bacteremia may be intermittent. A diagnosis of PVE is supported by new conduction abnormalities on the electrocardiogram, suggestive of valve ring abscess. The most sensitive technique for diagnosing valvular infection is the transesophageal echocardiogram, which allows excellent visualization of the valve ring and prosthesis.

D. Differential Diagnosis. A positive blood

culture for CoNS represents one of two entities: contamination with skin flora (~90% of cases) or a true infection. The presence of prosthetic biomaterial, either in the form of a temporary indwelling venous catheter or an implanted device, increases the probability of infection as the majority of bloodstream infections are caused by seeding from infected foci. Patients with CoNS bacteremia should have all temporary indwelling catheters removed or replaced, and the tip sent for a semiquantitative culture.

E. Complications. Hemodynamic instability consistent with septic shock occurs in 10–20% of patients with CoNS bacteremia. Complications of CoNS native valve endocarditis are comparable to those seen with subacute bacterial endocarditis: systemic embolization, valve ring abscess with conduction system disturbance, or congestive heart failure occur in two-thirds of patients, and ~25–50% of patients require valve replacement. Of early PVE cases caused by CoNS, > 85% are complicated by congestive heart failure or prolonged fever despite appropriate antibiotic therapy.

Diagnosis

The diagnosis of CoNS bacteremia or endocarditis is supported by multiple positive cultures from separate venipunctures. Molecular techniques proving clonality of two or more species may argue for true infection (rather than contamination), but access to these tests is generally restricted to research laboratories. In health care settings where molecular testing is not available, the finding of multiple isolates with identical antibiotic susceptibility patterns supports infection rather than contamination. However, the finding of even a single positive culture may be clinically significant and should be interpreted in the context of the patient's clinical condition.

Treatment

The recommended regimens for CoNS bacteremia are given in Box 46–7. Although > 70% of CoNS are resistant to PRSPs, beta-lactam resistance is heterotypically expressed, and antibiograms may falsely suggest methicillin sensitivity.

Bacteremia from infected indwelling vascular lines may be cured in > 75% of cases with the catheter remaining intact. Indications for catheter removal include hemodynamic instability, cutaneous tunnel infections, and persistent fever or bacteremia after > 48 h of antibiotic treatment.

A diagnosis of PVE is usually an indication for surgical replacement of the infected valve. A trial of conservative therapy with antibiotics alone may be attempted in hemodynamically stable patients without evidence of congestive heart failure or ring abscess. Treatment requires at least 6 weeks of therapy, with synergistic dosing of gentamicin for the initial 2-week period (Box 46–7). The clinician should have a low threshold for surgical intervention in patients with persistent fever or bacteremia, or in patients who develop new signs of congestive heart failure. Patients who complete medical therapy should be followed closely after discontinuation of antibiotics, as relapse is also an indication for surgery.

URINARY TRACT INFECTIONS

S saprophyticus is a common cause of uncomplicated urinary tract infection (UTI) in young women, accounting for as many as 15% of all cases of cystitis in this group. There is a seasonal variation in incidence, with the majority of cases occurring in late summer and fall. Risk factors for *S saprophyticus* UTI include recent sexual intercourse, delayed postcoital urination, and contraception with diaphragm/spermicide combinations.

Clinical Findings

A. Signs and Symptoms. *S saprophyticus* causes typical symptoms of cystitis: fever, dysuria,

BOX 46–7		
Treatment of CoNS Bacteremia and Prosthetic Valve Endocarditis		
	Bacteremia	PV endocarditis
General Care	• Remove indwelling catheters if persistent fever or bacteremia, hypotension, or tunnel infection	• Surgical consult for congestive failure or valve ring abscess
Antibiotic Regimens	• Vancomycin, 15 mg/kg every 12 h • Treat for 10–14 days	• Vancomycin, 15 mg/kg every 12 h for ≥6 weeks **PLUS** • Rifampin, 300 mg every 8 h for ≥6 weeks **PLUS** • Gentamicin, 1 mg/kg IV every 8 h for 2 weeks

and suprapubic pain. Approximately 20% of women show signs of upper tract disease. It is likely that the number of cases of *S saprophyticus* pyelonephritis is significantly higher, as localization studies suggest that renal infections may occur in the absence of flank pain.

B. Laboratory Findings. In uncomplicated pyelonephritis and cystitis, the laboratory findings are restricted to hematuria and pyuria. A Gram stain of centrifuged urine sediment typically reveals gram-positive cocci.

C. Complications. Complications secondary to *S saprophyticus* are rare. There have been anecdotal case reports of bacteremia and endocarditis complicating *S saprophyticus* urinary tract infections. Infection in males, though unusual, is associated with anatomic abnormalities of the urinary tract or urethral catheterization, and ~40% require hospitalization.

Diagnosis

Definitive diagnosis of *S saprophyticus* UTI is by culture of organisms from a sterile midstream urine collection. A colony count of $> 10^2$ bacteria in an appropriate clinical setting (a young woman with symptoms of cystitis) is considered to be diagnostic. However, because cystitis in young women is usually uncomplicated and easily treated empirically, many authorities do not recommend urine cultures and proceed with therapy if microscopy reveals red or white cells in the sediment of a spun urine.

Treatment

S saprophyticus is sensitive to the antibiotics em-

pirically used to treat community-acquired, uncomplicated UTIs (see Chapter 16). Treatment failures of *S saprophyticus* UTIs have been reported with single-day therapy (particularly with the fluoroquinolones), leading to the current recommendation of 3 days of antibiotics, regardless of which agent is used. Of note, *S saprophyticus* is variably sensitive to vancomycin, and this agent should not be used for empiric therapy.

Prevention & Control

Prevention efforts for the ubiquitous methicillin-sensitive *S aureus* and CoNS have centered around strict aseptic technique for procedures and compulsive attention to hand washing. Intranasal mupiricin may be effective in eradicating *S aureus* carriage during a hospital outbreak or if epidemiologic investigation implicates a health care worker as a vector for nosocomial infections.

Staphylococcal infection control efforts have concentrated on limiting the nosocomial spread of MRSA (Box 46–8). Patients colonized or infected with MRSA should be isolated or cohorted, and health care workers should don protective gowns and gloves before patient contact. Hand washing after contact with colonized patients is particularly important as MRSA can survive > 3 h on cutaneous surfaces but is rapidly eradicated by washing with an antibacterial soap. Airborne transmission rarely occurs but is of concern if a patient with respiratory colonization produces copious secretions or requires frequent tracheal suctioning. Both patient isolation and use of masks by contacts is advisable in this setting.

BOX 46–8

Nosocomial Control of MRSA[1]	
Nasopharyngeal Colonization	• Single room or cohorting of colonized patients • Use of gloves for patient contact • Strict hand washing
Wound/Tracheostomy/Urinary Tract Colonization or Infection	• Single room or cohorting of colonized patients • Use of gloves for patient contact • Strict hand washing • Gown for direct contact • Dress wounds for hospital transport • Mask (if aerosolization or splashing likely)
Burns or Extensive Skin Involvement/Lower Respiratory Tract Involvement	• Single room or cohorting of colonized patients • Use of gloves for patient contact • Strict hand washing • Gown • Dress wounds for hospital transport • Mask (if aerosolization or splashing likely)

[1]Modified from Mulligan et al., Methicillin-resistant *S. aureus:* a consensus review of the microbiology, pathogenesis, and epidemiology with implications for prevention and management. Am J Med 1993;94:313.

REFERENCES

Archer GL, Climo MW: Antimicrobial susceptibility of co-agulase-negative staphylococci. Antimicrob Agents Chemother 1994;38:2231.

Chesney PJ: Toxic shock syndrome. In Crossley KB, Archer GL: *The Staphylococci in Human Disease,* 1st ed. Churchill Livingstone, 1997.

Dagan R: Impetigo in childhood: changing epidemiology and new treatment. Pediatr Ann 1993;22:235. (A thorough discussion of pediatric bullous and nonbullous impetigo.)

DiNubile MJ: Short-course antibiotic therapy for right-sided endocarditis caused by *Staphylococcus aureus* in injection drug users. Ann Intern Med 1994;121:873.

Gemmell CG: Staphylococcal scalded skin syndrome. J Med Microbiol 1995;43:318. (Emphasizes the role of toxins in the pathogenesis of SSSS and reviews the disease in adults.)

Gentry LO: Antibiotic therapy for osteomyelitis. Infect Dis Clin N Am 1990:4;485.

Jarvis WR: The epidemiology of colonization. Infect Control Hosp Epidemiol 1996;17:47. (A summary of the impact of colonization on nosocomial infection.)

Kloos WE, Bannerman TL: Update on clinical significance of coagulase-negative staphylococci. Clin Microbiol Rev 1994;7:117. (Thorough discussion of specimen collection, strain identification, and antibiotic susceptibilities.)

Kunin CM: Urinary tract infections in women. Clin Infect Dis 1994;18:1.

Lew DP, Waldvogel FA: Osteomyelitis. N Engl J Med 1997:336;999.

Low DE: Clinical microbiology: issues in identification and susceptibility testing. In Crossley KB, Archer GL: *The Staphylococci in Human Disease,* 1st ed. Churchill Livingstone, 1997.

Mortara LA, Bayer AS: *Staphylococcus aureus* bacteremia and endocarditis. Infect Dis Clin North Am 1993;7:53.

Mulligan ME, Murray-Leisure KA, et al: Methicillin-resistant *Staphylococcus aureus*: a consensus review of the microbiology, pathogenesis, and epidemiology with implications for prevention and management. Am J Med 1993;94:313.

Raad II, Bodey GP: Infectious complications of indwelling vascular catheters. Clin Infect Dis 1992;15:197.

Rupp ME, Archer GL: Coagulase-negative staphylococci: pathogens associated with medical progress. Clin Infect Dis 1994;19:231.

Stamm WE, Hooton TM: Management of UTI infections in adults. N Engl J Med 1993;329:1328.

Stevens DL: The toxic shock syndromes. Inf Dis Clin North Am 1996;10:727.

Wenzel RP et al: The significance of nasal carriage of *Staphylococcus aureus* and the incidence of postoperative wound infection. J Hosp Infect 1995;31:13. (Discusses the prevalence and significance of nasal carriage, and reviews methods of eradication.)

Whitener C, Capulo G, Weilekamp MR, Karchmer AW: Endocarditis due to coagulase-negative staphylococci. Infect Dis Clin North Am 1993;7:81.

Wilson WR, Karchmer AW, et al: Antibiotic treatment of adults with infective endocarditis due to streptococci, enterococci, staphylococci, and HACEK microorganisms. JAMA 1995;274:1706. (A consensus statement by authorities in the field for treatment of IE.)

Streptococcus pneumoniae

47

Jeffrey N. Martin, MD, MPH

Essentials of Diagnosis
- Most common infections include pneumonia, meningitis, sinusitis, and otitis media.
- Predisposing factors include extremes of age (ie, infants and elderly) and underlying host defects in antibody, complement, and splenic function.
- Transmission is human to human both in the community and nosocomially.
- Pneumonia: productive cough, fever, chills, sweats, and dyspnea; lobar or segmental consolidation on chest x-ray; lancet-shaped gram-positive diplococci on Gram stain of sputum or growth of *S pneumoniae* from sputum, blood, or pleural fluid.
- Meningitis: headache, stiff neck, fever, chill, and photophobia; nuchal rigidity, Kernig's or Brudzinski's sign; lancet-shaped gram-positive diplococci on Gram stain of cerebrospinal fluid (CSF), growth of *S pneumoniae* from CSF or blood, or positive counter immunoelectrophoresis or latex agglutination of CSF.

General Considerations

A. Epidemiology. *S pneumoniae* may exist in humans as either a nasopharyngeal colonist or as a pathogen in one of many clinical syndromes (Box 47–1). Although *S pneumoniae* has been found in other mammals, humans are thought to be the principal reservoir. As a colonist, *S pneumoniae* is found in up to 40% of children and 10% of adults. Infants typically acquire their first colonizing isolate at 6 months. Intermittent colonization then occurs throughout childhood and adult years. There is a seasonal pattern to colonization, with the highest prevalence occurring in winter. Pneumococci are transmitted from human to human by extensive direct contact with secretions harboring the organism. Persons residing in environments that promote such extensive close contact, such as day care centers, prisons, homeless shelters, and military barracks, have historically been at risk for pneumococcal infection.

In the United States, *S pneumoniae* is estimated to account for 500,000 cases of pneumonia, 50,000 cases of bacteremia, 3000 cases of meningitis, and 7 million cases of acute otitis media. Of these syndromes, bacteremia (with or without a site of primary infection such as pneumonia or meningitis) has the most clearly elucidated epidemiology because of its precise blood culture-based definition. The incidence of bacteremia is strongly age related. A surveillance study in South Carolina estimated the incidence of bacteremia among infants, young adults, and elderly (age ≥ 70) to be 160, 5, and 70 cases per 100,000 persons, respectively. African-Americans, American Indians, and Alaskan Natives are at highest risk for bacteremia. As is true for *S pneumoniae* colonization, there is a distinct seasonality to bacteremia with peaks coming at midwinter. Overall, pneumococcal disease accounts for ~ 40,000 annual deaths in the United States. The case fatality rate for bacteremia is 15–20%.

In addition to the numerical incidence of pneumococcal disease, it is instructive to look at the prominent role *S pneumoniae* plays in several common syndromes. In a variety of studies that prospectively identify causes of community-acquired pneumonia, *S pneumoniae* is routinely the most common detectable agent. For example, in patients who require hospitalization for pneumonia, *S pneumoniae* accounts for up to one-third of cases. Aside from areas of the world experiencing meningococcal epidemics, *S pneumoniae* is the most common organism of meningitis in adults and now, with the advent of *Haemophilus influenzae* type b immunization, is also most common in children. One-third to one-half of all cases of acute otitis media with an identifiable etiology is caused by *S pneumoniae*.

Any of the syndromes caused by *S pneumoniae* can occur in normal hosts, but frequently one or more predisposing conditions exist. The best characterized of these are underlying host immunologic defects in antibody, complement, and splenic function. Because of the importance of antibodies in the opsonization of the encapsulated pneumococcus, individuals with defective antibody function (eg, congenital agammaglobulinemia, common variable hypogammaglobulinemia, selective immunoglobulin-G subclass deficiency, multiple myeloma, chronic lymphocytic leukemia, or lymphoma) are at significant risk for invasive infections. Various early complement deficiencies as well as either congenital or acquired asplenia (eg, iatrogenic or sickle cell disease) also convey substantial risk. Asplenic patients deserve special note because of the rapidity at which they can clinically deteriorate from unchecked bacteremia. In contemporary urban settings, HIV infection is

BOX 47-1

Syndromes Caused by *Streptococcus pneumoniae*

More Common	• Pneumonia (with or without bacteremia) • Acute sinusitis • Otitis media[1] • Meningitis • Primary bacteremia[1]
Less Common	• Empyema • Septic arthritis • Peritonitis • Endocarditis • Pericarditis • Cellulitis • Endometritis • Osteomyelitis • Brain abscess

[1]More common in children than adults.

responsible for a large burden of pneumococcal disease. HIV disease, through a variety of host defense defects, places infected persons at ~ 200-fold-greater risk for invasive pneumococcal infection. HIV-infected patients who are African-American, who have a CD4 lymphocyte count < 200 × 10[6]/liter, or who have a history of pneumonia have particularly elevated risk. The presence of pneumococcal bacteremia in patients with no clinically apparent host immunodeficiency should prompt the clinician to obtain patient consent for HIV testing.

Various other chronic illnesses, such as alcoholism, cirrhosis, renal insufficiency, nephrotic syndrome, chronic pulmonary disease, congestive heart failure, and diabetes, place patients at significant risk for pneumococcal disease. Likewise, patients who have received organ or bone marrow transplants or who are being treated with alkylating agents, antimetabolites, or glucocorticoids are also at risk. Finally, a particular anatomic defect, basilar skull fracture, carries risk for pneumococcal meningitis.

B. Microbiology. *S pneumoniae* is a gram-positive coccus, but typically the organism grows as pairs in what is termed a lancet-shaped diplococcus. In truth, this shape represents two lancets joined on end, pointing away from each other. In liquid medium, pneumococci may also be found growing in chains. On blood agar plates, pneumococcal colonies are often umbilicated (ie, have central dimpling) and are sometimes grossly mucoid. They are surrounded by a greenish zone, known as α-hemolysis, which is the result of hemoglobin breakdown by pneumococcus-produced α-hemolysin. In the clinical microbiology

laboratory, α-hemolysis is the first clue in distinguishing *S pneumoniae* from a variety of other species in a mixed flora sample. In addition to α-hemolysis, the microbiology laboratory uses catalase negativity, solubility in bile salts, and susceptibility to optochin to identify *S pneumoniae* (Table 47–1).

S pneumoniae is easy to identify by the above criteria when it grows in normally sterile body sites (eg, blood or pleural fluid). Detection in a mixed-flora environment such as sputum, however, requires a skilled and persevering clinical microbiologist. Given the abundance of other α-hemolytic oral species, it is incumbent on the microbiologist to look carefully for the characteristic umbilicated or mucoid appearance of *S pneumoniae* and to subculture a number of α-hemolytic colonies. The clinician can be motivating in this endeavor by communicating the patient's clinical presentation to the microbiologist and by carefully reviewing the Gram stain of the original specimen for the presence of lancet-shaped diplococci.

Once called *Diplococcus pneumoniae, S pneumoniae* is now known to belong to the *Streptococcus* genus. Like most other members of this genus, *S pneumoniae* is non-spore forming and nonmotile. Unlike many streptococcal species, *S pneumoniae* does not have a Lancefield serogroup. Yet, within the *S pneumoniae* species, there are 90 identified serotypes. Two numbering schemes for serotyping exist. In the American system, serotypes are numbered starting from 1 to 90 in the order in which they were first described. In the more widely used Danish system, serotypes are grouped based on antigenic similarities and given both a number and a letter (eg, 19A, 19B, and 19C). The basis of the serotype is antigenic differences in the polysaccharides that constitute the pneumococcal external capsule. Almost all clinical strains, with the uncommon exception of some isolates from conjunctivitis, have a capsule. In the microbiology laboratory, the interaction of serotype-specific antibody with capsule results in the enhancement of the microscopic appearance of the capsule, which is known as the quellung reaction. Although serotyping is no longer an important clinical tool, it remains useful for epidemiologic studies; sur-

Table 47–1. Clues to diagnosis of *Streptococcus pneumoniae* infection

• Gram-positive coccus; grows as lancet-shaped diplococci or in chains
• Grows readily in conventional blood culture or solid media, but fastidious nature necessitates rapid transport of clinical material to microbiology laboratory for processing
• α-Hemolytic (greenish) on solid media; colonies are often umbilicated or mucoid
• Catalase-negative
• Bile salt soluble
• Susceptible to optochin
• Counter immunoelectrophoresis or latex agglutination may be useful in evaluation of cerebrospinal fluid that was obtained after antibiotics were administered

veys of the most prevalent serotypes found in invasive infections have informed the composition of the current polyvalent vaccine.

Whereas the external capsule is a distinguishing feature of *S pneumoniae,* its cell wall is similar to that of other streptococci. Multilayered peptidoglycan, a heteropolymer of repeating *N*-acetylglucosamine and *N*-acetyl muramic acid, is the principal component. Peptides, attached to *N*-acetyl muramic acid, are cross-linked by *trans-* and carboxypeptidases to provide structure to the cell wall. These peptidases are also known as penicillin-binding proteins because they are the binding sites for a variety of β-lactam antibiotics. The covalent binding of β-lactams inactivates these enzymes resulting in the eventual demise of the organism. Teichoic acid (ribotol- or glycerol-phosphate polymers) is the other principal component of the cell wall and is often covalently bound to peptidoglycan. Lipoteichoic acid exists as a component of both the cell membrane and cell wall. There are other minor components of the cell wall, some of which are common to all streptococci, and some of which, like C-substance (a polysaccharide), are unique to *S pneumoniae.* Various soluble products are produced by *S pneumoniae* and are discussed in the next section.

C. Pathogenesis. Diseases caused by *S pneumoniae* are principally the result of an exuberant inflammatory response that the host mounts to the organism. The critical factor in the success of the pneumococcus is its ability to evoke this response but simultaneously, at least until specific anticapsular antibody is produced, to evade nonspecific attempts at phagocytosis. Highly destructive toxins, analogous to those produced by *Streptococcus pyogenes* or gram-negative species, are not present although some toxins are produced and play a secondary role. Although details vary slightly depending on the organ system involved, the pathogenic progression consists of nasopharyngeal adherence and colonization, spread to adjacent organs with local replication, evasion of nonspecific clearance mechanisms, and finally activation of the host inflammatory reaction.

The initiating event in all cases is nasopharyngeal colonization, in which bacterial surface adhesins join to epithelial cell receptors that contain the disaccharide GlcNAcβ1-4Gal. After pneumococci are established in the nasopharynx, they may then gain entry into and replicate in contiguous structures such as the sinuses, eustachian tubes, or bronchi. They may also penetrate the nasopharyngeal mucosa, even without a clinically demonstrable focus of infection, and achieve access to the systemic circulation via the cervical lymphatics. Entry into the lungs is limited in normal hosts by a functioning glottis and larynx, but entry is enhanced when these mechanisms are disturbed, as seen with alcohol intoxication, convulsions, anesthesia, or stroke.

Even after pneumococci gain entry to the above structures, infection rarely occurs because they are typically cleared in the normal host by nonspecific mechanisms (eg, mucociliary motion or cough reflex). Replication can proceed, however, when normal clearance is impaired, as seen, for example, when eustachian tubes or sinus orifices are congested (eg, from viral infection or allergy) or bronchial clearance is altered (eg, from chronic effects of smoking or acute effects of viral infection). In the lung, various mechanisms are now being described that may enhance pneumococcal adherence and replication. These include the finding that pneumococci bind to immobilized fibronectin that is exposed during tissue injury and that cytokines may induce pneumocytes to express the receptor for platelet-activating factor—a receptor that also binds pneumococcal C-substance.

Once established in its target organs, *S pneumoniae* is able to replicate unimpeded because of its ability to evade nonspecific phagocytosis by polymorphonuclear cells. The external capsule provides this crucial protection. As such, the capsule is an essential factor in the virulence of the organism. The exact mechanism of this protective effect is not known; it is likely a combination of the lack of capsular receptors on phagocytes, repellent electrochemical forces on the capsule, and the ability of the capsule to mask opsonizers such as antibody and complement. Whatever the exact mechanism, *S pneumoniae* organisms that are genetically engineered to lack capsules are avirulent.

Once it begins replicating, *S pneumoniae* causes disease by evoking an intense inflammatory reaction. Both the peptidoglycan and teichoic acid components of the cell wall and capsular polysaccharide can activate the alternative pathway of complement. Nonspecific antibodies to cell wall polysaccharides (formed to ubiquitous streptococcal species) are able to activate complement by the classical pathway. Together, these means of activating complement result in the attraction of numerous leukocytes and abundance of exudative fluid. In the lungs, this accumulation of pneumococci and inflammatory material leads to consolidation of alveoli, radiolucency, and impaired gas exchange—the defining characteristics of pneumonia. Although abscess formation is rare, the expanding volume of infected material can spread to uninvolved areas via Kohn's pores. Extensive direct spread can result in empyema or pericardial infection. If the infection is not contained, pneumococci can spread via lymphatics to hilar lymph nodes, the thoracic duct, and finally into the systemic circulation where metastatic infection may occur in the meninges, peritoneum, joints, or endocardium.

As mentioned, *S pneumoniae* may gain access to the subarachnoid space via hematogenous spread and choroid seeding from either a nasopharyngeal or pulmonary focus. Less commonly, meninges may become infected via direct extension from an infected sinus or middle ear. As in the lungs, an intense inflammatory response is evoked by the presence of pneumococci in the subarachnoid space. Interleukin-1 and tumor necrosis factor, released by macrophages responding to the insult, play a prominent role and contribute to increased blood-brain barrier permeability. The end result is mounting intracranial pressure and ultimately diminished blood flow to the brain.

Before the advent of antibiotics, this pathogenic process could be arrested by the development of specific anticapsular antibody. This typically occurs at 5–8 days after the onset of infection. Hence, outcome depended on whether antibody production occurred before the patient succumbed to the severe manifestations of infection. In the contemporary era, it is now appreciated that the pathogenic process can also be arrested by the administration of antibiotics. However, the persistently high case fatality rate associated with pneumococcal disease (especially bacteremia) despite antibiotic administration bespeaks the continued contributory role of host defenses in successfully responding to infection.

S pneumoniae produces several toxins that are currently thought to play a secondary role in pathogenesis. Pneumolysin is a toxin with two functions. It can insert into cell membranes of polymorphonuclear cells and ciliated epithelium, thereby inhibiting their function, and it can activate the classical complement pathway. Other products such as pneumococcal surface protein, hemolysin, and autolysin are also con-

tributory because mutants lacking these typically are less virulent. Autolysin in particular is important because autolysis of organisms may enhance the release and expression of a variety of proinflammatory factors (eg, cell wall components) that were discussed above.

CLINICAL SYNDROMES

PNEUMONIA

This section focuses on the clinical findings, diagnosis, and treatment of pneumococcal pneumonia. Please see Chapters 9 and 10 for a general discussion of pneumonia and upper respiratory infection.

Clinical Findings

A. Signs and Symptoms. The so-called classic presentation of pneumococcal pneumonia consists of an abrupt onset of a shaking chill followed shortly after by fever and production of rusty sputum (Box 47–2). This classic presentation, however, is not the most common. Typically, patients present because of a change in preexisting symptoms. Many have had

BOX 47–2

Clinical Findings in Pneumococcal Pneumonia

	Symptoms	Signs	Laboratory Tests[1]
More Common	• Fever • Chills • Sweats • Cough • Rusty sputum production • Dyspnea	• Fever, tachycardia, tachypnea • Consolidative findings on chest exam	• Hypoxemia • Elevated leukocyte count
Less Common[2]	• Pleuritic chest pain • Nausea, vomiting, diarrhea • Confusion	• Hypothermia • Hypotension • Cyanosis • Oral herpes lesions • Nuchal rigidity • Abdominal distension and absent bowel sounds • Pleural rub • Murmur • Altered mental status	• Low serum bicarbonate, anion gap • Elevated total bilirubin and lactate dehydrogenase

[1]Radiographic and microbiologic findings are discussed in the text.
[2]Many of these findings represent the presence of concomitant pneumococcal disease in other organ systems.

several days of a viral upper respiratory infection marked by coryza, sore throat, and nonproductive cough, or they have chronic pulmonary disease with its attendant persistent productive cough. In these patients, the development of pneumonia is heralded by the onset of fever (which can be as high as 40 °C), chills, sweats, malaise, dyspnea, and a change in the nature of the cough. Cough may either turn productive in those without prior production or increase in volume and change color in those with prior production. Less common symptoms include pleuritic chest pain and—for reasons that are poorly understood— nausea, vomiting, and diarrhea. Some patients, particularly the elderly, will present with merely an alteration in mental status. Thus, the very common entity of pneumococcal pneumonia must be entertained for a wide variety of clinical presentations.

On physical examination, persons with pneumococcal pneumonia are usually markedly ill appearing and may be cyanotic. Altered vital signs such as elevated temperature, tachycardia, and tachypnea (> 22 breaths/min) are common but, as noted above, can be absent in the elderly. In fact, in the elderly, hypothermia may be present. With the exception of the appearance of oral herpes lesions, the majority of the physical findings relate to the lungs. Dullness to percussion, increased tactile fremitus, bronchophony, whispered pectoriloquy, and egophony are sometimes present as clues to underlying consolidation, but often only rales are heard. It must be remembered, however, that even the presence of rales in an otherwise normal individual must be considered an abnormal finding and prompt further radiographic consideration of pneumonia. Conditions associated with pneumonia, meningitis (eg, nuchal rigidity), and endocarditis (eg, murmur) should also be routinely evaluated.

B. Laboratory Findings. An elevated leukocyte count, often with early forms (left-shifted), is common. However, in certain patient populations (eg, alcohol abusers and persons with HIV infection), the absence of a high leukocyte count does not have sufficient negative predictive value to exclude pneumococcal disease. In acutely ill patients, a low serum bicarbonate concentration and an anion gap may be seen. This should prompt arterial blood gas determination to document the presence and extent of acidemia. Although determination is not necessarily indicated in all patients presenting with suspected pneumonia, an elevated bilirubin level and lactate dehydrogenase are prevalent. Pulse oximetry on room air should be performed in all patients. Individuals with low pulse oximetry readings and for whom acid-base status is unsettled should have arterial blood gas measurements.

Two sets of blood cultures should be performed on all patients with suspected pneumonia in that this may be the only way (aside from pleural fluid culture) to diagnose definitively the etiologic agent.

Nevertheless, the majority of patients with pneumococcal pneumonia are not bacteremic. Hence, particular attention must be paid to the adequate collection and processing of expectorated sputum. Although *S pneumoniae* can be a colonist, its growth in sputum culture in a patient with clinically diagnosed pneumonia is usually satisfactory proof of pneumococcal pneumonia. The sensitivity of culture, however, is often solely dependent on the rigor practiced by microbiology staff in the identification and subculturing of α-hemolytic colonies. Findings on Gram stain of the sputum can also be helpful but require careful interpretation. The presence of characteristic gram-positive lancet-shaped diplococci accompanied by an abundance of leukocytes (> 25 per low [100×]-power field) and a paucity of epithelial cells (< 10 per low-power field) on Gram stain suggests pneumococcal pneumonia, but the absence of this Gram stain pattern does not exclude pneumococcal disease. Although there are increasing regulations regarding clinician-prepared Gram stains, clinicians should routinely review stains that are prepared by microbiology staff.

C. Imaging. The sine qua non of pneumococcal pneumonia is the presence of an infiltrate on chest radiography. The clinical diagnosis of pneumonia has to be seriously questioned if, after 24 h of observation and volume repletion, a patient has not yet developed an infiltrate. A variety of radiographic findings can be observed. Lobar or segmental consolidation is classic but is less common than subsegmental involvement. Multiple subsegmental consolidation may be seen, and, occasionally, multilobar consolidation may be present. Pleural effusion is the other common finding, and the failure of a patient to improve necessitates prompt investigation of this fluid for the presence of empyema. Lung abscesses are rare, and their presence suggests serotype-3 infection. More commonly, the presence of an abscess suggests preexisting cavitary disease or coinfection with other abscess-producing organisms.

D. Differential Diagnosis. In patients presenting with community-acquired pneumonia (ie, acute pulmonary infection in a patient who has not been hospitalized nor has resided in a long-term-care facility in the 14 days prior to the onset of symptoms), a number of agents must be considered along with *S pneumoniae* in the differential diagnosis. *H influenzae, Branhamella (Moraxella) catarrhalis, Chlamydia pneumoniae,* and *Mycoplasma pneumoniae* are the most common agents, but, in certain populations, *Legionella* spp., *Klebsiella pneumoniae, Staphylococcus aureus, Escherichia coli, Chlamydia psittaci, Coxiella burnetti, Mycobacterium tuberculosis, Coccidioides immitis, Histoplasma capsulatum, Blastomyces dermatitidis, Cryptococcus neoformans,* and several respiratory viruses (eg, influenza virus, adenovirus, parainfluenza virus, and hantavirus) must also be considered. In immunocompromised hosts, the differential diagnosis expands to include a variety of other opportunistic pathogens.

A number of studies have attempted to develop algorithms that can distinguish the causative organism on clinical grounds, but none has provided sufficient predictive value upon which to base pathogen-directed empiric treatment decisions. Hence, a broad differential must be considered upon initial presentation, and definitive diagnosis can be made only with the appropriate microbiologic testing.

E. Complications. Bacteremia, progressive respiratory failure, and hemodynamic instability (ie, septic shock) are the most severe complications of pneumococcal pneumonia. As noted above, patients with either anatomic or functional asplenia are at particularly high risk for sepsis. Spread of infection via either contiguous extension or hematogenous routes constitutes the basis of extrapulmonary complications.

Empyema deserves special attention because it both is common and has severe manifestations if unrecognized. Empyema, which can occur either from hematogenous or contiguous spread, is defined by pleural fluid containing frank pus, a positive Gram stain or positive culture, or a pH of ≤ 7.1. Untreated, it can result in persistent fever and may be the focus for further spread of infection. Rarely, rupture through the chest wall (ie, empyema necessitatis) can occur. If empyema fluid is not properly drained, it may heal with residual fibrosis and result in long-term functional pulmonary defects.

Purulent pericarditis, arthritis, endocarditis, and meningitis are also possible complications.

Diagnosis

The diagnostic approach to pneumococcal pneumonia first involves correctly diagnosing the syndrome of pneumonia and second involves defining *S pneumoniae* as the causative agent. Whether the setting is community acquired or nosocomial, the diagnosis of pneumonia is made by chest radiography of patients with suggestive predisposing factors, symptoms, and physical-examination findings. This avoids the unnecessary costs and medication side effects that are associated with prescribing antibiotics to the large numbers of individuals who have viral upper-respiratory-tract infections and who do not have pneumonia. Although chest radiography has been dismissed by some as being cost ineffective in the outpatient setting, this ignores the incalculable costs of the subsequent development of antibiotic resistance that occurs when antibiotics are inappropriately prescribed. Thus, a chest radiograph is required for all patients in whom pneumonia is suspected.

No constellation of presenting signs or symptoms has proven to be adequately predictive of pneumonia caused by *S pneumoniae*. Hence, once the diagnosis of pneumonia has been established on clinical and radiographic grounds, definitive diagnosis of pneumo-

coccal pneumonia is based on the identification of the organism in normally sterile fluid (see above and Table 47–1 for microbiologic identification of *S pneumoniae*). With the rare exception of when transthoracic biopsies are performed, normally sterile fluid means either blood or pleural fluid. As stated above, detection of *S pneumoniae* in culture of expectorated sputum, although not entirely specific, is sufficient for a probable diagnosis of pneumococcal pneumonia and evidence enough for specific pathogen-directed therapy. The unambiguous sighting of gram-positive diplococci on sputum Gram stain without growth in culture is the least definitive evidence but may be sufficient if other pathogens are excluded and if the patient has an epidemiologic profile consistent with pneumococcal disease.

Obtaining both blood and sputum for culture is the only way to specifically diagnose pneumococcal pneumonia, but there is debate whether to perform these procedures at all, particularly in the outpatient setting. It has been argued that broad-spectrum empiric antibiotics are sufficiently effective in most patients and that specific identification of the pathogen is not required. Until a definitive trial addresses this issue and accounts, by modeling, for the far-reaching effects of broad-spectrum antibiotic use, it is the author's opinion that, when practical to perform, all patients should receive both blood and sputum cultures.

Obtaining cultures can benefit both the individual patient and society. For individuals, determining the specific causative agent allows for altering from empiric broad-spectrum therapy to definitive treatment with an antibiotic that is usually less toxic, expensive, and disruptive to normal flora. In patients who are not responding to initial empiric therapy, a pretreatment culture may be the only opportunity to identify the causative agent and assess its antibiotic resistance patterns. Likewise, the absence of *S aureus* or gram-negative species in well-collected pretreatment sputum specimens essentially excludes these as pathogens and obviates the need to cover them when reconsidering the antibiotic regimen. For society, in addition to the cost savings derived from cheaper and less toxic antibiotic choices, the benefits of specific pathogen detection include the diminution of antibiotic resistance (and its associated costs) and the epidemiologic surveillance for pathogens such as drug-resistant *S pneumoniae* and *Legionella* spp. Knowledge of the prevalence of these pathogens in the community is essential for health care providers as they make empiric treatment decisions for subsequent patients who present with pneumonia.

Treatment

The approach to treatment of any of the syndromes caused by *S pneumoniae* must be considered in two parts—empiric and definitive therapy. Empiric therapy is prescribed when a patient presents with a clinical syndrome (eg, pneumonia) and, as is often the case, the causative agent has not yet been identified. Empiric therapy must cover all the epidemiologically likely agents. Definitive treatment is used once *S pneumoniae* has been identified as the causative agent.

On presentation with a clinical syndrome compatible with pneumonia, most patients are treated empirically with broad-spectrum antibiotics (see Chapter 23). Assuming that a patient is responsive to an empiric regimen that covers *S pneumoniae,* a switch to definitive therapy depends on the confidence that the clinician and microbiology laboratory have that *S pneumoniae* is the sole causative agent. As noted above, growth of *S pneumoniae* in normally sterile body fluids like blood or pleural fluid is definitive proof of pneumococcal disease. In these instances, if other copathogens have been adequately excluded, a switch to definitive therapy is indicated. Growth of *S pneumoniae* in a culture of expectorated sputum offers suggestive but not definitive proof because some persons may have pneumococcal colonization without pneumococcal disease. The isolated appearance of gram-positive lancet-shaped diplococci on sputum Gram stain (without culture growth) is again suggestive but is also the least definitive. Switching to definitive therapy in these latter two patient groups is a matter of clinical judgment and depends on several factors, including the epidemiologic likelihood of *S pneumoniae* compared to other pathogens, microbiologic exclusion of other pathogens, patient tolerance of empiric therapy, and cost.

In the past, definitive therapy of pneumococcal pneumonia routinely consisted of penicillin because *S pneumoniae* was uniformly susceptible. In fact, antimicrobial susceptibility was not routinely tested. This has changed markedly in the past decade. Full susceptibility to penicillin is defined as a minimal inhibitory concentration (MIC) of ≤ 0.06 µg/mL. A recent 30-center survey in the United States found that 14% of isolates had intermediate-level susceptibility (MIC $\geq 0.1–1.0$ µg/mL), and 9.5% had high-level resistance (MIC ≥ 2.0 µg/mL). Furthermore, resistance to other antibiotics has also been increasing and is associated with penicillin resistance.

Because of the emergence of resistance, all pneumococcal isolates, including those from expectorated sputum, must undergo antimicrobial susceptibility testing. The choice of definitive therapy must be guided by these results (Box 47–3). Fully susceptible isolates may be treated with parenteral or oral penicillin, depending on the condition of the patient and gastrointestinal function. Fortunately, isolates demonstrating intermediate-level penicillin resistance can still be treated with parenteral penicillin. Because of its excellent bioavailability, amoxicillin is recommended for definitive oral therapy of intermediately resistant strains. Although some highly resistant isolates may also respond to parenteral penicillin or oral amoxicillin, clinical experience in this area is lacking. Hence, agents should be used for which in vitro susceptibility has been shown (eg, ceftriaxone disodium; cefotaxime sodium; a fluoroquinolone such as sparfloxacin or levofloxacin; or vancomycin).

When only a characteristic Gram stain serves as evidence of pneumococcal infection, such isolates should be considered at least intermediately resistant for purposes of definitive therapy unless no such resistance has been reported in the area. Whether these isolates should be considered highly resistant (thus necessitating choices other than parenteral penicillin or oral amoxicillin) again depends on the known prevalence of high-level resistance in the community and whether the empiric regimen to which the patient is responding would be expected to cover isolates with high-level penicillin resistance. If the regimen would not be expected to cover high-level penicillin-resistant isolates and if the patient is nonetheless responding, high-level resistance is unlikely.

Adequate duration of therapy for pneumococcal pneumonia is not known precisely, but patients should be treated for at least 5 days after they become afebrile.

MENINGITIS

This section focuses on the clinical findings, diagnosis, and treatment of pneumococcal meningitis. Please also see Chapter 52 for a general discussion of meningitis.

Clinical Findings

A. Signs and Symptoms. The clinical presentation of pneumococcal meningitis is similar to other bacterial causes of acute meningitis (Box 47–4). Severe headache, photophobia, neck stiffness, chills, and fever are common. Because of the rapid onset of severe symptoms, most patients present within a short time from the onset of symptoms. Depending on the initiating source of the infection, there may also be pulmonary complaints (see above) or symptoms referable to sinusitis or otitis (see Chapter 9).

Patients with meningitis usually appear extremely ill. Many seek quiet areas with low light because of headache and photophobia. Tachycardia and fever, except in those who have difficulty mounting an elevated temperature (eg, the elderly or those with end-stage renal disease), are almost always present. The hallmarks of meningitis are the presence of one or more of the following three findings: nuchal rigidity, Kernig's sign, or Brudzinski's sign. If patients present within the initial few hours of symptoms, mental status may be normal. If they present later or if treatment has for some reason been withheld, deterioration in mental status and ultimately obtundation may ensue. Papilledema and focal neurologic signs, including cranial

BOX 47-3

Definitive Treatment of *Streptococcus pneumoniae* Pneumonia Based on Penicillin Susceptibility[1]

	Susceptible (MIC <0.1 µg/mL)		Intermediate Resistance (MIC 0.1–1.0 µg/mL)		Highly Resistant (MIC ≥ 2.0 µg/mL)	
	Children	Adults	Children	Adults	Children	Adults
First Choice	Penicillin V (7 mg/kg orally every 6 h—maximum 500 mg/dose) OR Penicillin G (16,500 U/kg IV every 4 h—maximum 1 million U/dose)	Penicillin V (500 mg orally four times daily) OR Penicillin G (1 million U IV million every 4 h)	Amoxicillin (13.3 mg/kg orally three times daily—maximum 500 mg/dose) OR Penicillin G (33,000 U/kg IV every 4 h—maximum 2 million U/dose)	Amoxicillin (500 mg orally three times daily) OR Penicillin G (2 million U IV every 4 h)	Cefpodoxime[2] (5 mg/kg orally every 12 h—maximum 200 mg/dose) OR Ceftriaxone[2] (25 mg/kg IV every 12 h—maximum 1 g/dose)	Cefpodoxime[2] (200 mg orally twice daily) OR Ceftriaxone[2] (1 g IV every 12 h)
Second Choice	Amoxicillin (13.3 mg/kg orally three times daily—maximum 500 mg/dose) OR Cefazolin (20 mg/kg IV every 8 h—maximum 1 g/dose)	Amoxicillin (500 mg orally three times daily) OR Cefazolin (1 g IV every 8 h)	Cefuroxime axetil (15 mg/kg orally twice daily—maximum 500 mg/dose) OR Cefazolin (20 mg/kg IV every 8 h—maximum 1 g/dose)	Cefuroxime axetil (500 mg orally twice daily) OR Cefazolin (1 g IV every 8 h)	Cefotaxime[2] (25 mg/kg IV every 6 h—maximum 1 g/dose)	Cefotaxime[2] (1 g IV every 6 h)
Penicillin Allergic	Erythromycin (7.5 mg/kg orally every 6 h or 5 mg/kg IV every 6 h—maximum 500 mg/dose) OR Clindamycin 4 mg/kg orally four times daily—maximum 300 mg/dose or 8.3 mg/kg IV every 8 h—maximum 300 mg/dose)	Erythromycin (500 mg orally or IV every 6 h) OR Clindamycin (300 mg orally four times daily or 600 mg IV every 8 h)	Clindamycin (4 mg/kg orally four times daily—maximum 300 mg/dose or 8.3 mg/kg IV every 8 h—maximum 600 mg/dose)	Clindamycin (300 mg orally four times daily or 600 mg IV every 8 h)	Vancomycin (10 mg/kg IV every 6 h)	Vancomycin (1 g IV every 12 h)

[1]Choices for oral and parenteral therapy are given. The use of oral vs parenteral therapy depends on the patient's clinical course and gastrointestinal function. All dosages assume normal renal function.

[2]Assuming in vitro susceptibility. If not susceptible to cephalosporins, a suitable fluoroquinolone (such as sparfloxacin or levofloxacin) or vancomycin must be used.

BOX 47–4

Clinical Findings in Pneumococcal Meningitis

	Symptoms	Signs	Laboratory Tests[1]
More Common	• Headache • Stiff neck • Fever • Chills • Sweats • Photophobia	• Fever, tachycardia • Nuchal rigidity • Kernig's and Brudzinski's signs	• Elevated leukocyte count • Increased intracranial pressure (>180 mm H_2O) • CSF pleocytosis (500 to 10,000 cells/mm^3, with polymorphonuclear cell predominance) • Elevated CSF protein (100–500 mg/dL) • Depressed CSF glucose (<40 mg/dL)
Less Common[2]	• Cough • Earache or facial pressure/postnasal discharge • Confusion	• Hypotension • Papilledema • Focal neurologic deficits • Hyperesthesia • Altered mental status • Consolidative findings on chest exam • Purulent discharge from nose or ear; bulging tympanic membrane	• Hypoxemia

[1]Radiographic and microbiologic findings are discussed in the text.
[2]Many of these findings represent the presence of concomitant pneumococcal disease in other organ systems.

neuropathies, may be present especially later in the course of disease. Hyperesthesia (abnormal acuteness of sensitivity to touch) is common. The remainder of the physical examination may reveal evidence of the primary source of infection (eg, purulent discharge from nose or ear, bulging tympanic membrane, or consolidative findings on chest examination). Unlike meningococcal meningitis, a rash is not found.

B. Laboratory Findings. As with pneumococcal pneumonia, an elevated leukocyte count is common in pneumococcal meningitis. Other routine laboratory tests are typically normal. Lumbar puncture, which must be performed as rapidly as the diagnosis of meningitis is entertained, shows increased intracranial pressure (> 180 mm H_2O), CSF pleocytosis (from 500 to $> 10,000$ cells/mm^3, with polymorphonuclear-cell predominance), an elevated protein concentration (100–500 mg/dL), and depressed glucose (< 40 mg/dL). Gram stain is often positive for characteristic gram-positive organisms. In contrast to the evaluation of pneumonia, in which a positive Gram stain is not always definitive, the presence of gram-positive diplococci on CSF Gram stain is definitive for the diagnosis of pneumococcal meningitis. In untreated patients, the sensitivity of Gram stain has been estimated to be as high as 90%. CSF culture is positive in most cases, and blood cultures may also show growth. In situations in which antibiotics have been administered before lumbar puncture, both Gram stain and culture may be negative. Cell count, protein, and glucose levels, however, are usually abnormal in these situations and not substantially different from the untreated state. Because these abnormalities are not specific for pneumococcal infection, immunologic methods such as counter immunoelectrophoresis or latex agglutination may be helpful for definitive diagnosis. These techniques provide no additional information to routine Gram stain and culture in the evaluation of CSF samples obtained before therapy.

C. Imaging. Cranial radiography (computed tomography or magnetic resonance scans) is often not indicated in the evaluation of meningitis. In fact, it is contraindicated if it results in undue delays in performing lumbar punctures or initiating empiric therapy. Radiography is indicated when there is clinical evidence of increased intracranial pressure (eg, papilledema) or focal neurologic findings. In these instances, radiography is performed to evaluate whether it is safe to perform a lumbar puncture and to diagnose central nervous system mass lesions, which may require further diagnostic maneuvers. Radiography is rarely useful to confirm positively the presence of meningitis—this is the task of the clinician and the microbiology laboratory. Radiography can be useful in assessing concomitant sinusitis, mastoiditis, or subdural empyema.

D. Differential Diagnosis. The differential diagnosis of acute meningitis is broad and contains both nonbacterial infectious and noninfectious etiologies (see Chapter 52). Once lumbar puncture has been performed and the profile of CSF findings suggests bacterial infection, the differential can be narrowed significantly. The differential diagnosis of acute bacterial meningitis is dependent on age group. In neonates, *S agalactiae,* members of the family *Enterobacteriaceae,* and *Listeria monocytogenes* predominate. With the marked decrease in *H influenzae* type B infections caused by immunization, *S pneumoniae* and *N meningitidis* are now the most prevalent organisms seen in older infants and children. In adults, *S pneumoniae, N meningitidis,* and *L monocytogenes* (in older adults) are most common.

E. Complications. The principal immediate and life-threatening complication of meningitis is decreased blood flow to the brain. Rather than a complication, it is best thought of as part of the pathogenic process that occurs if meningitis is unsuccessfully treated. Decreased blood flow may result either from increased intracranial pressure and loss of cerebrovascular autoregulation or from direct vasculitic effects on blood vessels.

Diagnosis

In patients with compatible clinical findings of meningitis, a lumbar puncture is always indicated except when evidence on imaging suggests a risk of herniation. Although lumbar puncture is critical to diagnose meningitis in general and to detect *S pneumoniae* specifically, delays in performing it should not delay empiric administration of antibiotics. Blood cultures should also be performed, and it is usually possible to collect them before antibiotic treatment. In such cases in which antibiotics must be given before lumbar puncture, blood cultures may serve as the only definitive means of specific pathogen detection.

Treatment

As with pneumonia, patients presenting with acute meningitis receive broad-spectrum empiric regimens that should include coverage for *S pneumoniae* (see Chapter 52). Unlike pneumonia, ascertainment of the causal pathogen is more common in acute bacterial meningitis, thus giving the clinician more frequent opportunities to switch to definitive therapy. Either a characteristic CSF Gram stain or culture for *S pneumoniae* is definitive proof of pneumococcal meningitis.

Antimicrobial susceptibility testing of *S pneumoniae* is the most important factor in determining definitive therapy (Box 47–5). Unlike the situation in

---

BOX 47–5

Definitive Treatment of *Streptococcus pneumoniae* Meningitis Based on Penicillin Susceptibility[1]

	Susceptible (MIC < 0.1 µg/mL)		Intermediate or Highly Resistant (MIC ≥ 0.1 µg/mL)	
	Children	Adults	Children	Adults
First Choice	Penicillin G (50,000 U/kg IV every 4 h—maximum 4 million U/dose)	Penicillin G (4 million U IV every 4 h)	Ceftriaxone[2] (50 mg/kg IV every 12 h—maximum 2 g/dose)	Ceftriaxone[2] (2 g IV every 12 h)
Second Choice	Ceftriaxone (50 mg/kg IV every 12 h—maximum 2 g/dose) OR Cefotaxime (50 mg/kg IV every 6 h; maximum 2 g/dose)	Ceftriaxone (2 g IV every 12 hours OR Cefotaxime (2 g IV every 6 h)	Cefotaxime[2] (50 mg/kg IV every 6 h—maximum 2 g/dose)	Cefotaxime[2] (2 g IV every 6 h)
Penicillin Allergic	Vancomycin[3] (15 mg/kg IV every 6 h)	Vancomycin[3] (1 g IV every 12 h)	Vancomycin (15 mg/kg IV every 6 h)	Vancomycin (1 g IV every 12 h)

[1]All dosages assume normal renal function. Adjunctive dexamethasone should be given to children at least 15 min before the first dose of antibiotics. See text for discussion of steroid use in adults.
[2]Assuming in vitro susceptibility. If not susceptible to ceftriaxone or cefotaxime, vancomycin must be used. Even if isolates are resistant to ceftriaxone and cefotaxime, one of these agents should be considered for use in addition to vancomycin.
[3]Either cefotaxime or ceftriaxone may be considered if the penicillin allergy is known not to be anaphylactic immediate type. The penetration of these agents is more reliable than vancomycin.

pneumonia cases, in meningitis cases, isolates that are intermediately resistant to penicillin should not be treated with standard or even higher dosages of penicillin. Instead, susceptibility to ceftriaxone disodium or cefotaxime sodium must be determined. Most isolates that are intermediately resistant to penicillin and some that are highly resistant retain susceptibility to cefotaxime sodium and ceftriaxone disodium. In such cases, these third-generation cephalosporins are the drugs of choice. Vancomycin must be used when there is resistance to both cefotaxime sodium and ceftriaxone disodium. Even if there is resistance to both ceftriaxone and cefotaxime, using one of these agents in addition to vancomycin should be considered. If only a positive Gram stain serves as evidence of pneumococcal meningitis and susceptibility results are not available, it is prudent to consider these isolates as resistant and continue the empiric regimen (if the patient is responding) or change to vancomycin if this was not part of the empiric regimen and the patient is not responding. Antibiotic treatment should be given for 10–14 days.

The use of glucocorticoids, although accepted in children, is still controversial in adults. It may be considered for adults in whom the CSF Gram stain is positive, coma is present, or there is evidence of increased intracranial pressure. Glucocorticoids are best considered in the context of empiric therapy because the first dose should be given before antibiotics.

OTHER SYNDROMES

Primary pneumococcal bacteremia (ie, no identifiable anatomic focus) is common in children but infrequent in adults. *S pneumoniae* is the major pathogen of otitis media in children, being responsible for between 33% and 50% of all cases in which an etiologic agent can be identified. It is also one of the two most important (along with *H influenzae*) agents implicated in acute sinusitis. Empyema, typically a complication of pneumonia but rarely a primary diagnosis, has been discussed above. Less common syndromes include endocarditis and pericarditis (see Chapter 11), septic arthritis and osteomyelitis (see Chapter 14), peritonitis (see Chapter 12), endometritis (see Chapter 22), brain abscess (see Chapter 7), and cellulitis (see Chapter 13). Most of these can occur as either a primary infection or as a complication of an initiating clinical focus (eg, pneumonia). (Refer to other chapters in this text for a complete description of these syndromes, including a discussion of empiric and definitive treatments.)

The principles discussed above regarding the various levels of certainty in the attribution of a syndrome to *S pneumoniae,* knowledge of local prevalence of drug-resistant isolates, and the importance of the antimicrobial susceptibility pattern of the iso-late (if obtained) are similarly pertinent when determining empiric and definitive therapy for other syndromes.

Prevention & Control

A polyvalent vaccine against *S pneumoniae,* manufactured by both Merck (Pneumovax 23) and Lederle (Pnu-Immune 23), contains 25 μg of capsular polysaccaride from each of the 23 most common serotypes responsible for invasive pneumococcal infections in the United States. Vaccine serotypes represent ≥ 85–90% of the isolates responsible for invasive infections. It is important to note that the six serotypes that are the most frequent causes of penicillin-resistant infections are included. The vaccine has been shown to be effective for the prevention of invasive pneumococcal disease (eg, bacteremia with or without pneumonia) in immunocompetent adults aged ≥ 65 years and in persons aged ≥ 2 years with chronic illnesses such as diabetes mellitus, alcoholism, cirrhosis, chronic pulmonary disease, coronary artery disease, and congestive heart failure (Box 47–6). Although convincing data on vaccine effectiveness in other immunocompromised populations (eg, HIV infection in persons from developed countries [data from sub-Saharan Africa show no vaccine efficacy], leukemia, Hodgkin's disease, multiple myeloma, and chronic renal failure) have not been presented, methodologic constraints or frank absence of dedicated studies has precluded excluding a protective role. Therefore, vaccination is generally recommended for these populations.

For infants < 2 years old, for whom the 23-valent vaccine is ineffective, a heptavalent vaccine (Prevnar, Wyeth-Lederle) containing the capsular polysaccharides of serotypes 4, 6B, 9V, 14, 18C, 19F, and 23F conjugated to a nontoxic diphtheria protein has been found effective in the prevention of invasive pneumococcal disease (Box 47–6). A series of immunizations with this conjugate vaccine in infants 2, 4, and 6 months old followed by a fourth dose when these infants are 12–15 months old is now recommended for all newborns. The vaccine is also recommended for high-risk children (eg, those with sickle cell disease or asplenia) between 2 and 5 years of age.

The Advisory Committee on Immunization Practices of the US Public Health Service has recently published updated recommendations on revaccination. This committee does not recommend routine revaccination but suggests that individuals ≥ 2 years old who are at highest risk for serious pneumococcal infection and for whom rapid declines in antibody titers are known to occur should receive a second vaccination 5 years after the initial vaccine. These individuals include patients with HIV disease, functional or anatomic asplenia, leukemia, lymphoma, Hodgkin's disease, multiple myeloma, generalized malignancy, chronic renal failure, nephrotic syndrome, or transplants and those receiving immuno-

BOX 47-6

Control of Invasive *Streptococcus pneumoniae* Infections

Prophylactic Measures	23-valent polysaccharide vaccine is recommended for the following persons[1]: • Aged ≥ 65 y • Aged 2–64 y with chronic illnesses such as chronic cardiovascular disease (coronary artery disease, congestive heart failure, and cardiomyopathies), chronic pulmonary disease (chronic obstructive pulmonary disease but not isolated asthma), diabetes mellitus, alcoholism, chronic liver disease (including cirrhosis), cerebrospinal fluid leaks, and functional or anatomic asplenia (including sickle cell disease) • Aged 2–64 y living in special environment or social settings, such as Alaskan natives and certain American Indian populations as well as residents of nursing homes and other long-term-care facilities • Aged 2–64 y who are immunocompromised, including those with HIV infection, leukemia, lymphoma, Hodgkin's disease, multiple myeloma, generalized malignancy, chronic renal failure, or nephrotic syndrome; those receiving immunosuppressive chemotherapy (including corticosteroids); and those who have received an organ or bone marrow transplant Heptavalent conjugate vaccine is recommended for the following persons: • Aged <2 y and high-risk children between 2 and 5 years of age Daily oral penicillin V is recommended for children with functional (eg, sickle cell disease) or anatomic asplenia
Isolation Precautions	None required

[1]See text for recommendations for revaccination.

suppressive therapy. It is also recommended that individuals ≥ 65 years old receive a second vaccination 5 years after the initial vaccine, provided that the first vaccine was administered when they were < 65 years old.

In children with either functional (eg, sickle cell disease) or anatomic asplenia, chemoprophylaxis with daily oral penicillin V provides another means of prevention and is also recommended.

Although human-to-human transmission of *S pneumoniae* is common, illness among contacts is very infrequent in nonepidemic settings. Accordingly, isolation of hospitalized patients or immunization of contacts is not recommended.

REFERENCES

Advisory Committee on Immunization Practices: Prevention of pneumococcal disease: recommendations of the Advisory Committee on Immunization Practices (ACIP). Morbid Mortal Wkly Rep 1997;46(RR-8):1. (Evidence-based review of the epidemiology of pneumococcal disease and guidelines for the use of the polyvalent polysaccharide vaccine.)

Advisory Committee on Immunization Practices: Preventing pneumococcal disease among infants and young children: recommendations of the Advisory Committee on Immunization Practices (ACIP). Morbid Mortal Wkly Rep 2000;49(RR-9). (New recommendations on use of conjugate vaccine.)

Afessa B, Greaves WL, Frederick WR: Pneumococcal bacteremia in adults: a 14-year experience in an inner-city university hospital. Clin Infect Dis 1995;21(2):345. (Review of 304 cases of pneumococcal bacteremia from an inner-city hospital in Washington, DC. Case-fatality rates did not change significantly in the past six decades.)

Bartlett JG et al: Community-acquired pneumonia in adults: guidelines for management. Clin Infect Dis 1998;26:811. (Comprehensive guidelines on the diagnosis and management of community-acquired pneumonia from the Infectious Diseases Society of America. Much emphasis is provided on the prominent role of *S pneumoniae* in this disease.)

Bradley JS, Scheld WM: The challenge of penicillin-resistant *Streptococcus pneumoniae* meningitis: current antibiotic therapy in the 1990s. Clin Infect Dis 1997;24(Suppl 2):S213. (Thoughtful review of the current predicament faced by clinicians treating pneumococcal meningitis in areas where penicillin resistance is prevalent.)

Breiman RF et al: Pneumococcal bacteremia in Charleston County, South Carolina. A decade later. Arch Intern Med 1990;150(7):1401. (A contemporary reevaluation of the incidence of pneumococcal bacteremia in Charleston County, SC, one decade after the initial sentinel surveillance study was performed. This study is among the most valuable sources for population-based estimates of the incidence and risk factors for pneumococcal bacteremia.)

Doern GV et al: Antimicrobial resistance of *Streptococcus pneumoniae* recovered from outpatients in the United States during the winter months of 1994 to 1995: results of a 30-center national surveillance study. Antimicrob Agents Chemother 1996;40(5):1208. (A 30-center surveillance study of outpatient isolates from throughout the United States that found that 14.1% of pneumococcal strains exhibited intermediate-level penicillin resistance and 9.5% showed high-level resistance.)

Friedland IR: Comparison of the response to antimicrobial therapy of penicillin-resistant and penicillin-susceptible pneumococcal disease. Pediatr Infect Dis J 1995;14(10):885. (Prospective observational study of pneumococcal disease (pneumonia, sepsis, and peritonitis—excluding meningitis) in children found that intermediate-level penicillin resistance is of little significance in outcome and that standard β-lactam therapy is still highly effective.)

Henrichsen J: Six newly recognized types of *Streptococcus pneumoniae*. J Clin Microbiol 1995;33(10):2759. (Description of the six newest *S pneumoniae* serotypes and an interesting historical overview of the serotyping schemes.)

Jernigan DB, Cetron MS, Breiman RF: Minimizing the impact of drug-resistant *Streptococcus pneumoniae* (DRSP): a strategy from the DRSP Working Group. JAMA 1996;275(3):206. (Suggestions on how to curb the global emergence of drug-resistant *S pneumoniae* with emphasis on enhanced surveillance, increased vaccination, and more judicious antibiotic use.)

Tuomanen EI, Austrian R, Masure HR: Pathogenesis of pneumococcal infection. N Engl J Med 1995;332(19):1280. (Review of the pathogenesis of *S pneumoniae*-mediated disease with a special emphasis on how the inflammation evoked by the cell wall of *S pneumoniae* differs from that evoked by endotoxin.)

48

Streptococcus pyogenes

Dennis L. Stevens, PhD, MD

Essentials of Diagnosis

- Pharyngitis: presence of sore throat, submandibular adenopathy, fever, pharyngeal erythema, exudates.
- Rheumatic fever: migratory arthritis, carditis, Syndenham's chorea, pharyngitis.
- Cellulitis: pink skin, fever, tenderness, swelling.
- Scarlet fever: sandpaper-like erythema, strawberry tongue, streptococcal pharyngitis or skin infection, high fever.
- Post-streptococcal glomerulonephritis: acute glomerulonephritis (hematuria, proteinuria) following pharyngitis or impetigo.
- Impetigo: dry, crusted lesions of the skin, weeping golden-colored fluid.
- Erysipelas: salmon red rash of face or extremity, well-demarcated border, fever, occasionally bullous lesions.
- Streptococcal toxic shock syndrome: isolation of Group A streptococcus from a normally sterile site, sudden onset of shock and organ failure.
- Necrotizing fasciitis, myonecrosis: deep, severe pain, fever, purple bullae shock, tissue destruction of fascia or muscle, organ failure.

General Considerations

A. Epidemiology. *Streptococcus pyogenes* is a human pathogen without an animal reservoir. Group A streptococci (GAS) cause most streptococcal disease, but other groups are important pathogens in some settings (Box 48–1). Group A streptococcal infections have the highest incidence in children younger than age 10. The asymptomatic prevalence is also higher (15–20%) in children, compared with that in adults (<5%). Age is not the only factor; crowded conditions in temperate climates during the winter months are associated with epidemics of pharyngitis in school children as well as military recruits. Impetigo is most common in children from ages 2 to 5 and generally occurs in the summer in temperate climates and year-round in tropical areas .

Similarly, 90% of cases of scarlet fever occur in children 2 to 8 years old, and, like pharyngitis, it is most common in temperate regions during the winter months. An experiment of nature in the Faroe Islands suggested that susceptibility to scarlet fever is not dependent on young age per se. Scarlet fever had disappeared from that isolated island for several decades until it was reintroduced by a visitor with unsuspected scarlet fever. An epidemic of scarlet fever ensued, with significant attack rates in all age groups, suggesting that other factors (such as the lack of protective antibody against scarlatina toxin or the introduction of a new strain) rather than age, predisposed those individuals to clinical illness.

In contrast to pharyngitis, impetigo, and scarlet fever, bacteremia has had the highest age-specific attack rate in the elderly and in neonates. Between 1986 and 1988, the prevalence of bacteremia increased 800–1000% in adolescents and adults in Western countries. Although some of this increase is attributable to IV drug abuse and puerperal sepsis, most of the increase is owing to cases of streptococcal toxic shock syndrome (strepTSS).

Human mucus membranes and skin serve as the natural reservoirs of *Streptococcus pyogenes.* Pharyngeal and cutaneous acquisition is spread person to person via aerosolized microdroplets and direct contact, respectively. Epidemics of pharyngitis and scarlet fever have also resulted from ingestion of contaminated nonpasteurized milk or food. Epidemics of impetigo have been reported, in tropical areas, day care centers, and among underprivileged children. Group A streptococcal infections in hospitalized patients occur during child delivery (puerperal sepsis), times of war (epidemic gangrene), surgical convalescence (surgical wound infection, surgical scarlet fever), or as a result of burns (burn wound sepsis). Thus, in most clinical streptococcal infections, the mode of transmission and portal of entry are easily ascertained. In contrast, among patients with strepTSS, the portal of entry is obvious in only 50% of cases.

B. Microbiology. Streptococci are gram-positive coccoid bacteria that grow in chains. Streptococci colonize the mucus membranes of animals, produce catalase, and may be aerobic, anaerobic, or facultative. Streptococci require complex media containing blood products for optimal growth. On blood agar plates, streptococci may cause complete (B), incomplete (A), or no hemolysis (C). The exhaustive work of Rebecca Lancefield has allowed hemolytic streptococci to be classified into Groups A through O based on acid extractable antigens of cell wall material. The availability of rapid latex agglutination kits provides even small clinical laboratories the means to identify streptococci according to Lancefield's grouping. Bacitracin susceptibility, bile esculin hydrolysis, and the CAMP test

BOX 48-1

Streptococcal Infections

	Adults	Children
More Common	• Cellulitis • Erysipelas • Bacteremia • Necrotizing fasciitis • Streptococcal toxic shock syndrome	• Pharyngitis • Scarlet fever • Impetigo • Post-strepto-coccal glomer-ulonephritis • Rheumatic fever • Bacteremia (neonates)
Less Common	• Pharyngitis • Scarlet fever • Impetigo (homeless)	• Erysipelas • Streptococccal toxic shock syndrome • Necrotizing fasciitis, ex-cept after chickenpox

(flame-type synergistic hemolysis on a *Staphylococcus aureus* blood agar streak) are useful presumptive tests for classifying Groups A, D, or B streptococci, respectively. Modern schemes of classification of hemolytic and nonhemolytic streptococci use complex biochemical and genetic techniques.

C. Pathogenesis. Complex interactions between host epithelium and streptococcal factors such as M-protein, lipoteichoic acid components, and fimbriae are necessary for adherence. Fibronectin-binding protein (protein F) also contributes to adherence since protein F–deficient mutants are incapable of binding to epithelial cells.

Within the tissues, streptococci may evade opsonphagocytosis by destroying or inactivating complement-derived chemoattractants and opsonins (C5a peptidase) and by binding immunoglobulins. Expression of M-protein, in the absence of type-specific antibody, also protects the organism from phagocytosis by polymorphonuclear leukocytes and monocytes.

Bacterial Cell Structure & Extracellular Products

A. Capsule. Some strains of *S pyogenes* possess luxuriant capsules of hyaluronic acid, resulting in large mucoid colonies on blood agar. Luxuriant production of M-protein may also impart a mucoid colony morphology, and this trait has been associated with M-18.

B. Cell wall. The cell wall is composed of a peptidoglycan backbone with integral lipoteichoic acid components. The function of lipoteichoic acid components is not well known; however, both peptidoglycan and lipoteichoic acid components have important interactions with the host.

C. M-proteins. Over 80 different M-protein types of Group A streptococci are currently described. M-protein also protects the organism against phagocytosis by polymorphonuclear leukocytes, although this property can be overcome by type-specific antisera.

D. Streptolysin O. Streptolysin O belongs to a family of oxygen-labile, thiol-activated cytolysins and causes the broad zone of β hemolysis surrounding colonies of *S pyogenes* on blood agar plates. Thiol-activated cytolysin toxins bind to cholesterol on eukaryotic cell membranes, creating toxin-cholesterol aggregates that contribute to cell lysis via a colloid-osmotic mechanism. In situations in which serum cholesterol is high, ie, nephrotic syndrome, falsely elevated anti-streptolysin O antibody (ASO) titers may occur because both cholesterol and anti-ASO antibodies will "neutralize Streptolysin O." Striking amino acid homology exists between Streptolysin O and other thiol-activated cytolysin toxins.

E. Streptolysin S. Streptolysin S is a cell-associated hemolysin and does not diffuse into the agar media. Purification and characterization of this protein have been difficult, and its only role in pathogenesis may be in direct or contact cytotoxicity.

F. Deoxyribonucleases A, B, C, and D. Expression of deoxyribonucleases (DNases) in vivo elicits production of anti-DNase antibody following both pharyngeal and skin infection; this is most true for DNase B with Group A streptococci.

G. Hyaluronidase. This extracellular enzyme hydrolyses hyaluronic acid in deeper tissues, facilitating the spread of infection along fascial planes. Anti-hyaluronidase titers rise following *S pyogenes* infections, especially those involving the skin.

H. Pyrogenic exotoxins. Streptococcal pyrogenic exotoxins types A, B, and C, also called scarlatina or erythrogenic toxins, induce lymphocyte blastogenesis, potentiate endotoxin-induced shock, induce fever, suppress antibody synthesis, and act as superantigens. The identification of these three different types of pyrogenic exotoxins may in part explain why some individuals may have multiple attacks of scarlet fever.

Although all strains of Group A streptococci are endowed with genes for streptococcal pyrogenic exotoxin B, not all strains produce it, and even among producing strains, the quantity of toxin synthesized varies greatly from strain to strain.

Pyrogenic exotoxin C, like streptococcal pyrogenic exotoxin A, is bacteriophage-mediated, and expression is likewise highly variable. Recently, mild cases of scarlet fever in England and the United States have been associated with streptococcal pyrogenic exotoxin C positive strains.

I. Other superantigens. Two new superantigens, mitogenic factor and streptococcal superantigen, have recently been described; however, their roles in pathogenesis have not been fully investigated.

CLINICAL SYNDROMES

PHARYNGITIS & THE ASYMPTOMATIC CARRIER

Clinical Findings

Patients with streptococcal pharyngitis have abrupt onset of sore throat, submandibular adenopathy, fever, and chilliness but usually not frank rigors. Cough and hoarseness are rare, but pain on swallowing is characteristic. The uvula is edematous, the tonsils are hypertrophied, and the pharynx is erythematous with exudates, which may be punctate or confluent. Acute pharyngitis is sufficient to induce antibody against M-protein, Streptolysin O, DNase and hyaluronidase, and, if present, pyrogenic exotoxins. Depending on the infecting strain, pharyngitis may progress to scarlet fever, bacteremia, suppurative head and neck infections, rheumatic fever, post-streptococcal glomerulonephritis, or strepTSS. Pharyngitis is usually self-limited and pain, swelling, and fever resolve spontaneously in 3–4 days even without treatment (Boxes 48–2 and 48–3).

Diagnosis

Definitive diagnosis is difficult when based only on clinical parameters, especially in infants, among which rhinorrhea may be the dominant manifestation. Even in older children with all of the above physical findings, the correct clinical diagnosis is made in only 75% of patients. Absence of any one of the classic signs greatly reduces the specificity. Rapid antigen detection tests in the office setting have a sensitivity and specificity of 40–90%. A popular approach in clinical practice is to obtain two throat swab samples from the posterior pharynx or tonsillar surface. A rapid strep test is performed on the first, and, if positive, the patient is treated with antibiotics and the second swab discarded. If the rapid strep test is negative, the second is sent for culture, and treatment is withheld, pending a positive culture.

SCARLET FEVER

During the last 30–40 years, outbreaks of scarlet fever in the Western world have been infrequent and notably mild, and the illness has been referred to as pharyngitis with a rash or benign scarlet fever (Table 48–1). In contrast, in the latter half of the 19th century, mortalities of 25–35% were common in the

---

BOX 48–2

Treatment of Impetigo[1]

	Children	Adults
First Choice	<60 lbs: Benzathine penicillin, 600,000 U IM	>60 lbs: Benzathine penicillin, 1.2 million U IM
Second Choice	<60 lbs: Penicillin G or V, 200,000 units (125 mg) QID × 10 days	>60 lbs: Penicillin G or V, 400,000 U (250 mg) QID × 10 days
Options for Penicillin-Allergic Patients	Erythromycin ethylsuccinate, 40–50 mg/kg QID × 10 days PO[2]	Erythromycin ethylsuccinate, 40–50 mg/kg QID × 10 days PO[2]

[1]Topical agents such as bacitracin or mupirocin ointment may be useful in limiting the spread of impetigo to other children or family members.
[2]Oral cephalosporins, such as cefalexin, cephradine, cefadroxil, cefaclor, cefixime, cefuroxime, cefpodoxime, and cefdinir, given orally for 10 days, are also good alternatives to erythromycin in penicillin-allergic patients.

BOX 48–3

Treatment of Recurrent Streptococcal Pharyngitis and Tonsillitis

	Children	Adults
First Choice	<60 lbs: Benzathine penicillin, 600,000 U IM	>60 lbs: Benzathine penicillin, 1.2 million U IM
Second Choice	Ampicillin plus clavulinic acid, 20–40 mg/kg/day, PO (may require IV treatment)	Ampicillin plus clavulinic acid, 20–40 mg/kg/day, PO (may require IV treatment)
Options for Penicillin-Allergic Patients	Clindamycin, 10 mg/kg/day, PO	Clindamycin, 10 mg/kg/day, PO

United States, Western Europe, and Scandinavia. The fatal or malignant forms of scarlet fever have been described as either septic or toxic. Septic scarlet fever refers to patients who develop local invasion of the soft tissues of the neck and complications such as upper-airway obstruction, otitis media with perforation, meningitis, mastoiditis, invasion of the jugular vein or carotid artery, and bronchopneumonia.

Toxic scarlet fever is rare today, but, historically, patients initially developed severe sore throat, marked fever, delirium, skin rash, and painful cervical lymph nodes. In severe toxic cases, fevers of 107°F, pulses of 130–160 beats per minute, severe headache, delirium, convulsions, little if any skin rash, and death within 24 hours were common. These cases occurred before the advent of antibiotics, antipyretics, and anticonvulsants, and deaths were acutely the result of uncontrolled seizures and hyperpyrexia. In contrast, children with septic scarlet fever had prolonged courses and succumbed 2–3 weeks after the onset of pharyngitis. Complications of streptococcal pharyngitis and malignant forms of scarlet fever have been less common in the antibiotic era. Even before antibiotics became available, necrotizing fasciitis and myositis were not described in association with scarlet fever.

STREPTOCOCCAL PYODERMA (Impetigo contagiosa)

Impetigo is most common in patients with poor hygiene or malnutrition. Colonization of the unbroken skin occurs first, then intradermal inoculation is initiated by minor abrasions, insect bites, etc. Single or multiple thick-crusted, golden-yellow lesions develop within 10–14 days. Penicillin orally or parenterally, or bacitracin or mupiricin topically, are effective treatments for impetigo and also reduce transmission of streptococci to susceptible individuals (see Box 48–2). None of these treatments, including penicillin, prevents post-streptococcal glomerulonephritis.

ERYSIPELAS

Erysipelas is caused exclusively by *S pyogenes* and is characterized by an abrupt onset of fiery red swelling of the face or extremities. Distinctive features are well-defined margins, particularly along the nasolabial fold, scarlet or salmon red rash, rapid progression, and intense pain. Flaccid bullae may develop during the second to third day of illness, yet extension to deeper soft tissues is rare. Surgical débridement is not necessary, and treatment with penicillin is effective (Box 48–4). Swelling may progress despite treatment, although fever, pain, and the intense redness diminish. Desquamation of the involved skin occurs 5–10 days into the illness. Infants and elderly adults are most commonly afflicted, and, historically, erysipelas, like scarlet fever, was more severe before the turn of the century.

CELLULITIS

Group A streptococci are the most common cause of cellulitis; however, alternative diagnoses may be obvious when associated with a primary focus, such as an abscess or boil (*Staphylococcus aureus*), dog bite (*Capnocytophagia*), cat bite (*Pasteurella multocida*), freshwater injury (*Aeromonas hydrophila*), seawater injury (*Vibrio vulnifica*), animal carcasses, *Erysipelothrix rhusiopathia,* and so on. Clinical clues to the etiologic diagnosis are important because aspiration of the leading edge and punch biopsy yield a causative organism in only 15% and 40% of cases, respectively. Patients with lymphedema of any cause, such as lymphoma, filariasis, or postsurgical regional lymph node dissection (eg, mastectomy, carcinoma of the prostate), are predisposed to developing streptococcal cellulitis, as are patients with chronic venous stasis. Recently, recurrent saphenous vein donor site cellulitis has been attributed to Group A, C, or G streptococci.

Group A streptococci may invade the epidermis and subcutaneous tissues, resulting in local swelling, erythema, and pain. The skin becomes indurated and, unlike the brilliant redness of erysipelas, is a pinkish color. If fever, pain, or swelling increase, if bluish or violet bullae or discoloration appear, or if signs of systemic toxicity develop, a deeper infection, such as necrotizing fasciitis or myositis, should be considered (see below). An elevated serum creatinine phosphokinase suggests deeper infection, and prompt surgical inspection and débridement should be performed (see Box 48–4).

Table 48–1. Characteristics of Scarlet Fever.

	Benign	Septic	Toxic
Clinical Findings	• Red rash • Pharyngitis	• Red rash • Pharyngitis • Local invasion of vital structures of the neck	• Red rash • Pharyngitis • Profound fever (>108°F) • Dehydration • Convulsions
Outcome		Slow, lingering death due to bleeding, suffocation	High mortality rate; rapid death due to status epilepticus, dehydration, etc.

BOX 48-4

Treatment of Cellulitis and Erysipelas

	Children	Adults
First Choice	<60 lbs: Penicillin G or V, 200,000 U (125 mg) QID × 10 days	>60 lbs: Penicillin G or V, 400,000 U (250 mg) QID × 10 days
Second Choice	<60 lbs: Dicloxacillin, 125 mg QID × 10 days	>60 lbs: Dicloxacillin, 250–500 mg QID × 10 days
Options for Penicillin-Allergic Patients	Erythromycin ethylsuccinate, 40–50 mg/kg QID × 10 days PO[1]	Erythromycin ethylsuccinate, 40–50 mg/kg QID × 10 days PO[1]

[1]Oral cephalosporins, such as cefalexin, cephradine, cefadroxil, cefaclor, cefixime, cefuroxime, cefpodoxime, and cefdinir, given orally for 10 days, are good alternatives to erythromycin in penicillin-allergic patients.

LYMPHANGITIS

Cutaneous infection with bright red streaks ascending proximally is invariably caused by Group A streptococcus. Prompt parenteral antibiotic treatment is mandatory since bacteremia and systemic toxicity develop rapidly once streptococci reach the bloodstream via the thoracic duct.

NECROTIZING FASCIITIS

Necrotizing fasciitis, originally called streptococcal gangrene, is a deep-seated infection of the subcutaneous tissue that results in progressive destruction of fascia and fat but may spare the skin itself. Necrotizing fasciitis has become the preferred term since *Clostridium perfringens, Clostridium septicum,* and *S aureus* can produce a similar pathologic process. Infection may begin at the site of trivial or unapparent trauma. Within the first 24 hours, swelling, heat, erythema, and tenderness develop and rapidly spread proximally and distally from the original focus.

During the next 24–48 hours, the erythema darkens, changing from red to purple and then to blue, and blisters and bullae form that contain clear yellow fluid. On the fourth or fifth day, the purple areas become frankly gangrenous. From the seventh to the tenth day, the line of demarcation becomes sharply defined, and the dead skin begins to reveal extensive necrosis of the subcutaneous tissue. Patients become increasingly prostrated and emaciated and may become unresponsive, mentally cloudy, or even delirious. Historically, aggressive fasciotomy and débridement (bearclaw fasciotomy) and irrigations with Dakan's solution (hypochlorous acid) achieved mortalities as low as 20%, even before antibiotics were available (Box 48–5). The time course of progression of necrotizing fasciitis is more rapid, and mortalities have been higher in the 1980–1990s, suggesting increased virulence of streptococci.

MYOSITIS

Historically, streptococcal myositis has been an extremely uncommon infection, only 21 cases being documented from 1900 to 1985. Recently, the prevalence of streptococcal myositis has increased in the United States, Norway, and Sweden. Translocation of streptococci from the pharynx to the deep site of trauma (muscle) likely occurs hematogenously. Symptomatic pharyngitis or penetrating trauma is uncommon. Severe pain may be the only presenting symptom; swelling and erythema may be the only signs of infection. In most cases, a single muscle group is involved; however, because patients are frequently bacteremic, multiple sites of myositis or abscess can occur.

Distinguishing streptococcal myositis from spontaneous gas gangrene caused by *C perfringens* or *C septicum* may be difficult, although the presence of crepitus or gas in the tissue would favor clostridial infection. Myositis is easily distinguished from necrotizing fasciitis anatomically by surgical exploration

BOX 48-5

Treatment of Necrotizing Fasciitis/Myositis and Streptococcal TSS

	Children	Adults
First Choice	Penicillin G, 250,000 U/kg/d in 4–6 divided doses IV, **PLUS** clindamycin, 25–40 mg IV in 3–4 divided doses	Clindamycin, 1800–2100 mg q 24 hours, IV, in 3–4 divided doses, **PLUS** penicillin G, 2 million U q 4 hours, IV[1]
Options for Penicillin-Allergic Patients	Clindamycin, see above	Clindamycin, see above

[1]Good in vitro activity but not as effective as clindamycin in animal models of necrotizing fasciitis/myositis caused by Group A streptococcus.

or incisional biopsy, although clinical features of both conditions overlap and both necrotizing fasciitis and myonecrosis may occur together.

In published reports, the case-fatality rate of necrotizing fasciitis is between 20 and 50%, whereas that of streptococcal myositis is between 80 and 100%. Aggressive surgical débridement is extremely important because of the poor efficacy of penicillin described in human cases as well as in experimental models of streptococcal myositis (see Box 48–5).

PNEUMONIA

Pneumonia caused by Group A streptococcus is most common in women in the second and third decades of life and causes large pleural effusions and empyema. Several liters of pleural fluid may accumulate within hours. Chest tube drainage is mandatory, although management is complicated by multiple loculations and fibrinous effusions, resulting in restrictive lung disease.

STREPTOCOCCAL TOXIC SHOCK SYNDROME

In the late 1980s, invasive GAS infections occurred in North America and Europe in previously healthy individuals of all ages. This illness is associated with bacteremia, deep soft-tissue infection, shock, multi-organ failure, and death in 30% of cases. StrepTSS occurs sporadically, although minor epidemics have been reported. Most patients present with a viral-like prodrome, history of minor trauma, recent surgery, or varicella infection. The prodrome may be caused by a viral illness that predisposed to strepTSS, or these vague early symptoms may be related to the evolving infection. In cases associated with necrotizing fasciitis, the infection may begin deep in the soft tissue at a site of minor trauma that frequently does not result in a break in the skin. Although surgical procedures and viral infections such as varicella and influenza may provide portals of entry, no portal can be ascertained in 45% of cases. Preceding symptomatic pharyngitis is rare. Shock and organ failure are related to the production of cytokines by monocytes and lymphocytes stimulated with exotoxins, including pyrogenic exotoxins A, B, and C.

Clinical Findings

A. Signs and Symptoms. The abrupt onset of severe pain is a common initial symptom of strepTSS. The pain most commonly involves an extremity but may also mimic peritonitis, pelvic inflammatory disease, acute myocardial infarction, or pericarditis. Treatment with nonsteroidal anti-inflammatory agents may mask the presenting symptoms or

predispose to more severe complications, such as shock.

Fever is the most common presenting sign, although some patients present with profound hypothermia secondary to shock. Confusion is present in over half of the patients and may progress to coma or combativeness. On admission, 80% of patients have tachycardia, and over half will have systolic blood pressure of <110 mm Hg. Of those with normal blood pressure on admission, most become hypotensive within 4 hours. Soft-tissue infection evolves to necrotizing fasciitis or myositis in 50–70% of patients, and these require emergent surgical débridement, fasciotomy, or amputation. An ominous sign is progression of soft-tissue swelling to violaceous or bluish vesicles or bullae (see section on necrotizing fasciitis).

Many other clinical presentations may be associated with strepTSS, including endophthalmitis, myositis, perihepatitis, peritonitis, myocarditis, meningitis, septic arthritis, and overwhelming sepsis. Patients with shock and multiorgan failure without signs or symptoms of local infections have a worse prognosis since definitive diagnosis and surgical débridement may be delayed.

B. Laboratory Findings. Hemoglobinuria is present and serum creatinine is elevated in most patients at the time of admission. Serum albumin concentrations are moderately low (3.3 grams/dl) on admission and drop progressively over 48–72 hours. Hypocalcemia, including ionized hypocalcemia, is detectable early in the hospital course. The serum creatine kinase level is a useful test to detect deeper soft-tissue infections, such as necrotizing fasciitis or myositis.

The initial hematologic studies demonstrate only mild leukocytosis, but a dramatic left shift (43% of white blood cells may be band forms, metamyelocytes, and myelocytes). The mean platelet count is normal on admission but may drop rapidly by 48 hours, even in the absence of criteria for disseminated intravascular coagulopathy.

Group A streptococcus is isolated from blood in 60% of cases and from deep tissue specimens in 95% of cases. M types 1, 3, 12, and 28 are the most common strains isolated. Pyrogenic exotoxins A and/or B have been found in isolates from the majority of patients with severe infection. Infections in Norway, Sweden, and Great Britain have been primarily caused by M type 1 strains that produce pyrogenic exotoxin B. Other novel pyrogenic exotoxins are being described that may also explain the recent enhanced virulence of Group A streptococcus.

C. Course. Shock is apparent early in the course, and fluid management is complicated by profound capillary leak. Adult respiratory distress syndrome occurs frequently (55%), and renal dysfunction, which precedes hypotension in many patients, may progress despite treatment. In patients who survive, serum creatinine levels return to normal within 4–6 weeks, although many will require dialysis. The recommended antibiotic therapy for strepTSS is shown in Box 48–5. Overall, 30% of patients die despite aggressive treatment including IV fluids, colloid, pressors, mechanical ventilation, and surgical interventions, such as fasciotomy, débridement, exploratory laparotomy, intraocular aspiration, amputation, and hysterectomy.

Nonsuppurative Complications

The nonsuppurative complications of *S pyogenes* infection are acute rheumatic fever and acute glomerulonephritis.

A. Rheumatic Fever. The prevalence of acute rheumatic fever (ARF) in the Western world decreased dramatically after World War II (0.5–1.88 cases per 100,000 school age children per year). In contrast, in India and Sri Lanka, the prevalence of ARF has remained 140/100,000 for children between 5 and 19 years of age. Socioeconomic factors seem to be important because the highest rates in all countries have been among the impoverished in large cities. Although improved living conditions and the development of penicillin have had important roles in reducing the prevalence of ARF in the United States, the decreases had begun before antibiotics were available.

In addition, a resurgence of ARF has occurred predominantly among U.S. military recruits and white middle-class civilians. A particularly frightening aspect of these recent civilian cases was the low incidence of symptomatic pharyngitis (24–78%). Thus our modern primary prevention strategy (diagnosis of acute GAS pharyngitis with penicillin treatment within 10 days) would not have prevented ARF in these cases (Box 48–6).

The clinical manifestations of acute rheumatic fever are multiple, and because each is not specific for ARF, several criteria must be met to establish a definitive diagnosis. Simply put, two major manifestations or one major and two minor manifestations plus, in either case, evidence of an antecedent GAS infection are required for definitive diagnosis. The major manifestations and the frequency with which they occur during first attacks of ARF are as follows: arthritis (75%), carditis (40–50%), chorea (15%), and subcutaneous nodules (<10%). The minor manifestations are fever, arthralgia, heart block, presence of acute-phase reactants in the blood (C-reactive protein, leukocytosis, and elevated erythrocyte sedimentation rate), and prior history of ARF or rheumatic heart disease.

Carditis, when present, occurs during the first 3 weeks of illness and may involve pericardium, myocardium, and endocardium. Patients with pericarditis may have chest pain or pericardial effusion, whereas those with myocarditis may have intractable heart failure. Manifestations of acute endocarditis involve the development of new murmurs of mitral re-

BOX 48–6

Prophylaxis for Rheumatic Fever

	Children	Adults
First Choice	<60 lbs: Benzathine penicillin, 600,000 units IM, once per month	>60 lbs: Benzathine penicillin, 1.2 million units IM, once per month
Second Choice	Phenoxomethyl penicillin, 250 mg q day, PO	Phenoxomethyl penicillin, 250 mg q day, PO
Options for Penicillin-Allergic Patients	Erythromycin 250 mg/day, PO[1] OR <60 lbs: sulfadizine orally, 0.5 gm/day	Erythromycin 250 mg/day QID × 10 days PO[1] OR >60 lbs: sulfadizine, 1 gm/day

[1]Oral cephalosporins, such as cefalexin, cephradine, cefadroxil, cefaclor, cefixime, cefuroxime, cefpodoxime, and cefdinir, given orally for 10 days, are good alternatives to erythromycin in penicillin-allergic patients.

gurgitation, or aortic regurgitation, the latter being sometimes associated with a low-pitched apical mid-diastolic flow murmur (Carey Coombs murmur). Murmurs of mitral stenosis and aortic stenosis are not detected acutely during first attacks of ARF but are chronic manifestations of rheumatic heart disease. Migratory arthritis involves several joints, most frequently the knees, ankles, elbows, and wrists, in more than 50% of patients. Each involved joint has evidence of inflammation that characteristically resolves within 2–3 weeks with no progression to chronic arthritis or articular damage.

Subcutaneous nodules occur several weeks into the course of ARF and are found over bony surfaces or tendons. They last only 1–2 weeks and have in some cases been associated with severe carditis. Erythema marginatum is an evanescent, nonpainful erythematous eruption occurring on the trunk or proximal extremities. Individual lesions can develop and disappear within minutes, but the process may wax and wane over several weeks or months. Syndenham's chorea often occurs later in the course than other manifestations of ARF and is characterized by rapid nonpurposeful choreiform movements of the face, hands, and feet. Attacks usually disappear during sleep but may persist for 2–4 months.

B. Post-streptococcal Glomerulonephritis. Acute glomerulonephritis (AGN) can follow either pharyngeal or skin infection and is associated with GAS strains possessing M types 12 and 49, respectively. During epidemics of skin or pharyngeal infection produced by a nephritogenic strain, attack rates of 10–15% have been documented with latent periods of 10 days after pharyngitis and 3 weeks after pyoderma. Nonspecific symptoms include lethargy, malaise, headache, anorexia, and dull back pain. The classic signs of AGN are all related to fluid overload and are manifested initially by edema, both dependent and periorbital. Hypertension develops in most patients and is usually mild. Severe cases may be characterized by ascites, pleural effusion, encephalopathy, and pulmonary edema, although evidence of heart failure per se is lacking.

Evidence of glomerular damage by renal biopsy has been documented in nearly 50% of contacts of siblings with AGN, suggesting that, as in ARF, subclinical disease is not uncommon after infection with certain strains of GAS. Unlike rheumatic fever, but similar to scarlet fever, glomerulonephritis occurs most commonly in children between 2 and 6 years of age. Like ARF and scarlet fever, AGN may affect several members of the same family. Recurrences or secondary attacks occur only rarely, and there is little to suggest that AGN progresses to chronic renal failure.

The differential diagnosis of post-streptococcal AGN must include Henoch-Schönlein disease, polyarteritis nodosa, idiopathic nephrotic syndrome, leptospirosis, hemolytic uremic syndrome (*Escherichia coli* 0157:H7), and malignant hypertension. The diagnosis is simpler if there is a recent history of symptomatic GAS pharyngitis, impetigo, or scarlet fever. Elevated or rising antibody titers to streptococcal antigens such as ASO, anti-DNase A or B, and/or antihyaluronidase are helpful, although ASO concentration may be low in patients with pyoderma. A careful urinalysis to document proteinuria and hematuria should be performed, but it is mandatory to demonstrate red blood cell casts because the latter is the hallmark of glomerular injury. The blood urea nitrogen and creatinine values are elevated and if nephrotic syndrome is present the serum cholesterol level is elevated and serum albumin concentration is low. Twenty-four-hour excretion of protein is usually less than 3 g, and total hemolytic complement and C3 levels are markedly reduced.

Treatment of Group A Infections

During epidemics, particularly when rheumatic fever or a post-streptococcal glomerulonephritis are prevalent, treatment of asymptomatic carriers may be necessary. Studies by the U.S. military have shown that monthly injections of benzathine penicillin greatly reduce the incidence of streptococcal pharyngitis and rheumatic fever in young soldiers living in crowded conditions.

Erythromycin resistance of *S pyogenes* is currently 4% in Western countries; however, in Japan in 1974, the rate reached 72%. Sulfonamide resistance currently is reported in <1% of GAS isolates.

Resistance to penicillin has not been described, yet in some settings there is a lack of in vivo efficacy despite in vitro susceptibility to penicillin. Three mechanisms may explain this lack of efficacy.

Penicillin failure in pharyngitis, tonsillitis, or mixed infections may be caused by inactivation of penicillin in situ by beta lactamases produced by cocolonizing organisms such as *Bacteroides fragilis, Haemophilus influenzae,* or *S aureus.* For example, the failure rate of penicillin treatment of GAS pharyngitis may approach 25%, and, if such patients are treated with a second course of penicillin, the failure rate may approach 80%, perhaps owing to selection of beta-lactamase–producing bacteria. In contrast, cures of 90% have been achieved when treatment consisted of amoxicillin plus clavulanate, oral cephalosporin, or clindamycin.

Streptococcal cellulitis responds quickly to penicillin, although, in some cases in which staphylococcus is of concern, nafcillin or oxacillin may be a better choice. For treatment of streptococcal pneumonia, prolonged penicillin therapy, thoracoscopy, and decortication of the pleura may be necessary.

REFERENCES

Bisno AL: Group A streptococcal infections and acute rheumatic fever. N Engl J Med 1991;325:783. (An excellent review article about Group A streptococcus. The emphasis of this chapter is on rheumatic fever but there are excellent sections on virulence factors, epidemiology, and streptococcal infections in general.)

Cone LA, Woodard DR, Schlievert PM, et al: Clinical and bacteriologic observations of a toxic-shock like syndrome due to Streptococcus pyogenes. N Engl J Med 1987;317:146. (Case report of an early case of streptococcal toxic shock syndrome.)

Martin PR, Hoiby EA: Streptococcal serogroup A epidemic in Norway 1987–1988. Scand J Infect Dis 1990;22:421. (An excellent population-based study demonstrating a remarkable recent increase in Group A streptococcal bacteremia in age groups from 18 to 50 years of age.)

Schwartz B, Facklam RR, Breiman RF: Changing epidemiology of Group A streptococcal infection in the USA. Lancet 1990;336:1167. (A survey of Group A streptococcal isolates sent to the CDC over the last decade. A clear indication that invasive infections are currently associated with M types 1 and 3.)

Stevens DL: Invasive Group A streptococcus infections. Clin Infect Dis 1992;14:2. (A review article describing the changing epidemiology of scarlet fever, necrotizing fasciitis, myositis, bacteremia, and the streptococcal toxic shock syndrome.)

Stevens DL, Bryant-Gibbons AE, Bergstrom R, Winn V: The Eagle effect revisited: Efficacy of clindamycin, erythromycin, and penicillin in the treatment of streptococcal myositis. J Infect Dis 1988;158:23. (This article demonstrates the remarkable efficacy of clindamycin but failure of penicillin in an animal model of streptococcal necrotizing fasciitis and myonecrosis.)

Stevens DL, Bryant AE, Hackett SP: Sepsis syndromes and toxic shock syndromes: Concepts in pathogenesis and a perspective of future treatment strategies. Curr Opin Infect Dis 1993;6:374. (A comparative review of the cellular basis of cytokine and lymphokine mediated shock caused by gram-negative and gram-positive bacteria.)

Stevens DL, Tanner MH, Winship J, et al: Severe Group A streptococcal infections associated with a toxic shock-like syndrome and scarlet fever toxin A. N Engl J Med 1989;321:1. (A report of the clinical, laboratory, and systemic complications associated with 20 patients with streptococcal toxic shock syndrome. An analysis of strains reveals that most were M types 1 and 3 and most strains produced pyrogenic exotoxin type A.)

Enterococci

Robin Patel, MD

Essentials of Diagnosis

- Gram stain shows gram-positive cocci that occur in singles, pairs, and short chains; recovery of microorganism from culture of blood or other sterile source.
- Lancefield group D antigen.
- Clinical isolates: *Enterococcus faecalis,* 74%; *E faecium,* 16%; other species, 10%.
- Facultative anaerobes grow in 6.5% NaCl at pH 9.6 and at temperatures ranging from 10 °C to 45 °C, and grow in the presence of 40% bile salts and hydrolyze esculin and L-pyrrolidonyl-β-naphthylamide.
- Infections typically of a gastrointestinal or genitourinary origin.
- The most common infections are urinary tract infection, bacteremia, endocarditis, intra-abdominal and pelvic infection, and wound and soft tissue infection.

General Considerations

A. Epidemiology. Enterococci are able to grow and survive under harsh conditions and can be found in soil, food, water, and a wide variety of animals. The major habitat of these organisms is the gastrointestinal tract of humans and other animals, where they make up a significant portion of the normal gut flora. Most enterococci isolated from human stools are *E faecalis,* although *E faecium* are also commonly found in the human gastrointestinal tract. Small numbers of enterococci are occasionally found in oropharyngeal and vaginal secretions and on the skin, especially in the perineal area. Because enterococci are part of the normal gut flora of almost all humans, infections caused by these organisms may be endogenously acquired from the patient's own flora.

Enterococcal infections also occur in hospitalized patients or in patients undergoing peritoneal or hemodialysis, and the organisms causing such infections often appear to be exogenously acquired. There is clear-cut evidence for spread of strains of enterococci between patients and even for dissemination of such strains from one institution to another. Strains of enterococci causing nosocomial infections have been found on the hands of medical personnel and on environmental surfaces in hospitals and in nursing homes. Most likely, enterococci from patients or hospital personnel first colonize the gastrointestinal tract (or occasionally the skin and groin or other contiguous areas) before causing infections in other patients. Devices such as electronic rectal thermometers may also aid in the spread of enterococci, especially antibiotic-resistant enterococci.

Enterococci account for 12% of nosocomial bacterial infections. The most common nosocomial enterococcal infections involve the urinary tract (62% of cases) and are often associated with urinary tract instrumentation or structural abnormalities. Wound infections are the next most common presentation of nosocomial enterococcal infections, usually involving abdominal or pelvic sites (25% of cases). Bacteremia (10% of cases) is the third most commonly reported nosocomial enterococcal infection.

Risk factors for acquiring nosocomial enterococcal infection or colonization, especially those caused by vancomycin-resistant enterococci (VRE), include being critically ill; having severe underlying disease; being immunosuppressed (especially patients on oncology or transplant wards); having renal insufficiency; undergoing intra-abdominal or cardiothoracic surgical or other invasive procedures; having an indwelling urinary or central venous catheter; having a prolonged hospital or intensive care unit stay; intrahospital transfer between floors; multi-antimicrobial agent, third-generation cephalosporin, anti-anaerobic antimicrobial or vancomycin therapy; proximity to infected patients; care by colonized staff; and the receipt of selective bowel decontamination, sucralfate, or enteral feedings.

B. Microbiology. Enterococci are gram-positive cocci that occur in singles, pairs, and short chains. The genus *Enterococcus* contains over a dozen species. *E faecalis* isolates account for ~74% of organisms encountered in the clinical microbiology laboratory. *E faecium* accounts for 16% of such isolates. The other *Enterococcus* species, including *E durans, E avium, E casseliflavus, E gallinarum, E raffinosus,* and *E hirae* (among others), are encountered clinically in ~10% of cases. Enterococci are facultative anaerobes that are able to grow in 6.5% NaCl at pH 9.6 and at temperatures ranging from 10 to 45 °C. They carry the Lancefield group D antigen and will grow in the presence of 40% bile salts. They hydrolyze esculin and L-pyrrolidonyl-β-naphthylamide.

Enterococci are characterized by intrinsic resistance to many antibiotics (eg, oxacillin, clindamycin, cephalosporins, and aminoglycosides) and the capacity to acquire resistance to many others. The uniformly poor activity of β-lactams, particularly cephalosporins, against enterococci results from reduced affinity of the penicillin-binding proteins. Unlike most streptococci, enterococci are inhibited but not killed by apparently active penicillins (ampicillin, mezlocillin, penicillin, piperacillin), carbapenems (imipenem, meropenem), and glycopeptides (vancomycin or teicoplanin). Cephalosporins are not clinically useful against enterococci.

Enterococci are also naturally resistant to clinically achievable levels of aminoglycosides used alone. For treating serious enterococcal infections, combination therapy is recommended, generally penicillin, ampicillin, or vancomycin with an aminoglycoside, usually gentamicin or streptomycin. The rationale for this approach is to weaken the cell wall with the cell wall-active agent, thereby facilitating entry of the then bactericidal aminoglycoside. Such combinations have been shown to be synergistic, as long as the organism is susceptible to the cell wall-active agent and does not demonstrate high-level resistance to the aminoglycoside (gentamicin minimum inhibitory concentration $\leq$ 500 μg/mL, streptomycin minimum inhibitory concentration $\leq$ 2000 μg/mL).

Acquired resistance in enterococci can develop by genetic mutation or by acquiring altered DNA from a resistant organism. Enterococci have been reported to have acquired high-level resistance to aminoglycosides, cell wall-active agents (including penicillins and vancomycin), chloramphenicol, clindamycin, erythromycin, and the newer quinolones. *E faecium* isolates exhibit more antibiotic resistance than do other species.

Most enterococci with high-level resistance to aminoglycosides contain aminoglycoside-modifying enzymes. When high-level resistance to aminoglycosides is a concern, only gentamicin and streptomycin minimum inhibitory concentrations need to be tested in the clinical microbiology laboratory because the enzyme that neutralizes gentamicin also modifies tobramycin, amikacin, kanamycin, and netilmicin but not streptomycin. In addition to enzymatic resistance, ribosomal modification has been described as a second mechanism for high-level streptomycin resistance.

Acquired resistance to ampicillin and penicillin is generally caused by altered penicillin-binding proteins. This confers higher levels of resistance than the intrinsic resistance present in enterococci. This mechanism confers resistance to all β-lactams (including the carbapenems). β-lactamase production among enterococci is rare and has been reported in a few hospitals.

In the background of increasing resistance of enterococci to penicillins and aminoglycosides, vancomycin resistance emerged in the late 1980s. In vancomycin-resistant cells, an abnormal pentapeptide peptidoglycan precursor, with which vancomycin interacts minimally, is synthesized and incorporated into the cell wall of the organism. Resistance to the glycopeptide antibiotic vancomycin in enterococci, as understood to date, is phenotypically and genotypically heterogeneous. Three glycopeptide resistance phenotypes, VanA, VanB, and VanC, have been described in enterococci; they can be distinguished by the level and inducibility of resistance to vancomycin and teicoplanin. VanA-type glycopeptide resistance is characterized by acquired inducible resistance to both vancomycin and teicoplanin, and it is transferable. VanB-type glycopeptide resistance is characterized by acquired inducible resistance to various concentrations of vancomycin but not to teicoplanin, and it is also transferable. VanC-type glycopeptide resistance is characterized by low-level vancomycin resistance but teicoplanin susceptibility and has been described as an intrinsic property of most isolates of *E gallinarum, E casseliflavus,* and *E flavescens.* VanD-, VanE- and VanG- type glycopeptide resistance have been recently described and do not appear to be common.

C. Pathogenesis. Little is known about specific pathogenesis and virulence factors of enterococci. Enterococcal bacteremia has, however, been associated with high mortality rates (42–68%). In many cases, enterococci cause infections in severely debilitated hosts and are part of a polymicrobial infection. Thus their independent contribution to mortality and morbidity is difficult to assess. The intrinsic and acquired resistance of enterococci to many antimicrobial agents, as discussed previously, is an important factor that allows these organisms to survive and proliferate in patients receiving antimicrobial therapy. In addition, enterococci are able to adhere to heart valves and renal epithelial cells, properties that likely contribute to their ability to cause endocarditis and urinary tract infections, respectively.

Although enterococci are found in one-fifth of intra-abdominal infections, their exact role in polymicrobial infection is controversial. In cases of intra-abdominal infections, selective therapy against *Escherichia coli* and *Bacteroides fragilis,* which has minimal in vitro activity against enterococci, has been found to be sufficient to reduce enterococcal counts. Nevertheless, in animal models of experimental polymicrobial intra-abdominal infection, enterococci have been found to enhance abscess formation, weight loss, and mortality. Similarly, clinical reports have indicated the emergence of enterococcal abscesses and bacteremia after treatment of intra-abdominal sepsis with antimicrobial agents that lack significant in vitro enterococcal activity. A recent multicenter study of intra-abdominal infection has found that the presence of enterococci in the initial cultures, in addition to serious underlying disease, independently predicts treatment failure with broad-spectrum antimicrobial regimens that lack specific enterococcal activity.

CLINICAL SYNDROMES

URINARY TRACT INFECTION

Urinary tract infections, including uncomplicated cystitis, pyelonephritis, prostatitis, and perinephric abscess, are the most common type of clinical infections produced by enterococci (Box 49–1). Most enterococcal urinary tract infections are nosocomial and are associated with urinary catheterization or instrumentation.

BACTEREMIA & ENDOCARDITIS

Nosocomial enterococcal bacteremias are commonly polymicrobial. Portals of entry for enterococcal bacteremia include the urinary tract, intra-abdominal or pelvic sources, wounds (especially burns, decubitus ulcers, and diabetic foot infections), intravascular catheters, and the biliary tree. Metastatic infections other than endocarditis are rare in enterococcal bacteremia.

Enterococci account for ~5–10% of all cases of infective endocarditis (see Chapter 11). Most cases are caused by *E faecalis,* but *E faecium, E casseliflavus, E durans, E gallinarum,* and *E raffinosus* have also been isolated from patients with endocarditis. Only ~2% of cases of enterococcal bacteremia are associated with endocarditis, and this is much more common in patients whose bacteremia is community acquired versus those with nosocomial enterococcal bacteremia. Enterococcal endocarditis is a disease of older patients, with males outnumbering females in most series. Most cases occur in patients with underlying valvular heart disease or prosthetic valves, although enterococci are capable of causing infections of anatomically normal valves. An association between enterococcal endocarditis and urinary tract infection or urinary instrumentation in older men and abortion or childbirth in younger women has been suggested. Enterococci usually produce left-sided endocarditis with more frequent involvement of the mitral than the aortic valve. The typical clinical course of enterococcal endocarditis is that of subacute bacterial endocarditis. There is a suggestion that the relapse rate is higher in patients who have had symptoms of endocarditis for ≥ 3 months before treatment, which has implications for length of therapy (see below).

INTRA-ABDOMINAL & PELVIC INFECTION

Enterococci are frequently found as part of mixed aerobic and anaerobic flora in intra-abdominal and pelvic infections. As discussed above, the exact role of enterococci in these mixed aerobic and anaerobic intra-abdominal and pelvic infections is unclear. Enterococci can cause spontaneous peritonitis in patients with nephrotic syndrome or cirrhosis and can cause peritonitis in patients undergoing chronic ambulatory peritoneal dialysis. Monomicrobial enterococcal peritonitis is also occasionally seen as a complication of abdominal surgery or trauma. Enterococci can produce abscesses and bacteremia as a complication of endometritis, Cesarean section, and acute salpingitis.

WOUND & SOFT TISSUE INFECTION

Enterococci may be isolated from mixed cultures with gram-negative bacilli and anaerobes in surgical wound infections, decubitus ulcers, and diabetic foot infections; the significance of enterococci in these settings is difficult to assess. Enterococcal wound colonization and sepsis have been described in burn patients whose wounds have been covered with porcine xenografts presumably contaminated with enterococci. Enterococci occasionally cause chronic osteomyelitis.

MENINGITIS

Enterococci rarely cause meningitis. Most cases occur in patients who have anatomic defects of the central nervous system or who have had previous neurosurgery or head trauma. Rarely, however, meningitis may be a complication of high-grade bacteremia such as that seen in patients with enterococcal endocarditis. Meningitis may also be seen in association with enterococcal bacteremia in patients with human immunodeficiency virus infection and acute leukemia and in neonates and transplant recipients.

NEONATAL SEPSIS

Enterococci may cause neonatal sepsis characterized by fever, lethargy, and respiratory difficulty accompanied by bacteremia, meningitis, or both. Early

BOX 49–1	
Enterococcal Infections	
More Common	• Urinary tract infection • Bacteremia • Endocarditis • Wound and soft tissue infection • Intra-abdominal and pelvic infection
Less Common	• Meningitis • Neonatal sepsis

onset bacteremia in otherwise normal neonates may be seen, as well as nosocomial bacteremia, meningitis, or both, which has been described in premature or low-birth-weight neonates who have nasogastric tubes and intravascular devices.

Diagnosis

The diagnosis of enterococcal infection is made by isolating enterococci from typically sterile sites (eg, urine, blood, intra-abdominal or pelvic fluid, or spinal fluid). As discussed above, community acquisition of enterococcal bacteremia suggests the possible presence of endocarditis. The diagnosis of endocarditis, in the appropriate clinical context (see Chapter 11), may be further confirmed by the presence of clinical findings consistent with endocarditis as well as by the use of echocardiography. The diagnosis of intra-abdominal and pelvic infections, in the appropriate clinical context, can be assisted by the use of ultrasound or computed tomographic imaging with drainage, Gram stain, and culture of any fluid collection(s) present.

The diagnosis of enterococcal meningitis can be confirmed by the isolation of enterococci from the spinal fluid. Typically, enterococcal meningitis is associated with a low cerebrospinal fluid leukocyte count (< 200/mL), although this is not always the case.

The isolation of enterococci from respiratory secretions is of questionable significance, although there are very rare well-documented cases of enterococcal pneumonia and even lung abscesses in patients with severe and debilitating diseases.

Treatment

Penicillin or ampicillin remains the antibiotic of choice for treating enterococcal infections such as urinary tract infections, peritonitis, and wound infections (ie, infections that do not require bactericidal treatment) (Box 49–2). Vancomycin is the alternative agent for patients allergic to penicillin or for organisms with high-level penicillin resistance that are β-lactamase negative and vancomycin susceptible.

Combination therapy with a cell wall-active agent such as penicillin, ampicillin, or vancomycin, along with an aminoglycoside, is essential for the treatment of enterococcal endocarditis and probably for enterococcal meningitis as well. The situation is not as clear-cut for enterococcal bacteremia alone; there is no consensus as to whether combination therapy is required in this setting.

For the treatment of enterococcal endocarditis, combinations of cell wall-active agents such as penicillin, ampicillin, or vancomycin with aminoglycosides (usually streptomycin or gentamicin) are required (see Chapter 11 for specific treatment recommendations). In most cases, 4 weeks of combination therapy appear to be adequate, with a 6-week regimen reserved for patients who have had symptoms for > 3 months before starting treatment, for patients with prosthetic valves, or for patients who have relapsed after previous shorter courses of therapy.

Most strains of enterococci are susceptible to nitrofurantoin, and this agent has been successfully used to treat uncomplicated enterococcal infections limited to the urinary tract. The quinolones such as ciprofloxacin, ofloxacin, levofloxacin, gatifloxacin, enoxacin, and norfloxacin have in vitro activity against enterococci and may be useful for treating some enterococcal urinary tract infections, but their effectiveness for enterococcal infections in general has not been convincingly demonstrated, and increasing resistance has been demonstrated. Tetracyclines and chloramphenicol may exhibit in vitro activity against some strains of enterococci, but they are only bacteriostatic against enterococci, and clinical failures of chloramphenicol and tetracyclines have been reported.

The emergence of multiply resistant enterococci now greatly complicates therapeutic choices. For patients who have endocarditis caused by enterococci with high-level gentamicin resistance, it is useful to test for high-level streptomycin resistance because some highly gentamicin-resistant strains are synergistically killed by cell wall-active agents plus streptomycin. For endocarditis due to strains with both high-level streptomycin and gentamicin resistance, no combination will consistently produce synergism. These patients may be treated with prolonged courses (8–12 weeks) of intravenous ampicillin given by continuous infusion, although this approach should be considered experimental at this time. Surgical excision of infected valves may be required in such cases.

Infections caused by enterococci with high-level penicillin resistance and β-lactamase negativity should be treated with vancomycin. β-lactamase–producing, penicillin- and ampicillin-resistant enterococci remain susceptible to β-lactam–β-lactamase inhibitor combinations such as ampicillin-sulbactam and amoxicillin-clavulanate. VRE that remain susceptible to penicillin or ampicillin may be treated with penicillin or ampicillin. Infections caused by organisms with both high-level penicillin resistance and vancomycin resistance should be treated with either quinupristin-dalfopristin or linezolid. Notably, *E faecium* is more susceptible to quinupristin-dalfopristin than is *E faecalis*. Neither quinupristin-dalfopristin nor linezolid have bactericidal activity against VRE resulting in enormous challenges in the management of VRE endocarditis.

Prevention & Control

Prophylaxis for Infective Endocarditis. Antimicrobial prophylaxis for enterococcal endocarditis is recommended for patients with certain cardiac lesions predisposing to endocarditis who undergo invasive procedures with an increased risk of enterococcal

BOX 49-2

Treatment of Enterococcal Infections[1]

	Uncomplicated Urinary Tract Infection	Bacteremia, Intraabdominal or Pelvic Infection, Wound or Soft Tissue Infection, and Neonatal Sepsis
First Choice	• Amoxicillin, 250–500 mg orally every 8h OR • Ampicillin, 250–500 mg orally every 6 h	• Aqueous crystalline penicillin G, 18–30 million U/24 h IV either continuously or in 6 equally divided doses with or without gentamicin[2] (1 mg/kg IV/IM every 8h) OR • Amipicillin sodium 12 g/24 h IV in 6 equally divided doses with or without gentamicin[2] (1 mg/kg IM/IV every 8 h)
Second Choice	• Nitrofurantoin, 50–100 mg orally every 6 h OR • Ofloxacin, 200 mg orally every 12 h OR • Ciprofloxacin, 250–500 mg orally every 12 h OR • Levofloxacin, 250 mg orally every d OR • Norfloxacin, 400 mg orally every 12 h OR • Enoxacin, 200–400 mg orally every 12 h OR • Gatifloxacin, 200–400 mg orally every d	• Vancomycin, 30 mg/kg/24 h IV in 2 doses, not to exceed 2 g/24 h unless serum levels are monitored with or without gentamicin[2] (1 mg/kg IV/IM every 8 h)
Pediatric Considerations	• Amoxicillin, 25–50 mg/kg/d in divided doses every 8 h	• Penicillin G , 100,000–250,000 U/kg/24 h IV/IM in divided doses every 4 h with or without gentamicin[2] (1 mg/kg IM/IV every 6 h) OR • Ampicillin, 100–200 mg/kg/24 h IM/IV in 4–6 divided doses with or without gentamicin[2] (1 mg/kg IV/IM every 6 h)
Penicillin Allergic/ High-Level Penicillin Resistance, β-Lactamase-Negative	• Nitrofurantoin, 50–100 mg orally every 6 h OR • Ofloxacin, 200 mg orally every 12 h OR • Ciprofloxacin, 250–500 mg orally every 12 h OR • Levofloxacin, 250 mg orally every d OR • Norfloxacin, 400 mg orally every 12 h OR • Enoxacin, 200–400 mg orally every 12 h OR • Gatifloxacin, 200–400 mg orally every d	• Vancomycin, 30 mg/kg/24 h IV in 2 doses, not to exceed 2 g/24 h unless serum levels are monitored with or without gentamicin[2] (1 mg/kg IV/IM every 8 h)
Vancomycin and Penicillin Resistance	• Nitrofurantoin, 50–100 mg orally every 6 h	• Quinupristin/Dalfopristin, 7.5 mg/kg IV every 8 h • Linezolid, 600 mg IV orally every 12 h

[1]Doses provided are for patients with normal renal function (creatinine clearance >70 mL/min). Abbreviations: IV, intravenously; IM, intramuscularly.
[2]For isolates without high-level gentamicin resistance.

bacteremia. Details of patients, procedures, and regimens are outlined in Chapter 11.

Prevention of Vancomycin Resistance. From 1989 to 1993, the percentage of nosocomial enterococcal infections reported to the Centers for Disease Control and Prevention's National Nosocomial Infection Surveillance System that were caused by VRE increased from 0.3 to 7.9%. This overall increase primarily reflected the 34-fold increase in the percentage of VRE infections in patients in intensive care units (ie, from 0.4 to 13.6%), although a trend toward an increased percentage of VRE infections in non-intensive care patients was also noted.

Laboratory experiments have achieved the transfer of high-level vancomycin resistance from enterococci to *Staphylococcus aureus,* and reduced susceptibility of *S aureus* to vancomycin has recently been described in clinical *S aureus* isolates, although the mechanism of the latter resistance differs from that in enterococci. Vancomycin resistance has also been transferred by conjugation or transformation from enterococci to *Streptococcus sanguis, Lactococcus lactis, Streptococcus pyogenes,* and *Listeria monocyto-*

genes. The *vanA* gene has been found in vancomycin-resistant clinical isolates of *Oerskovia turbata* and *Arcanobacterium haemolyticum* (typically these organisms are vancomycin susceptible) isolated from the stools of two patients during an outbreak of VRE infection in London. The *vanA* gene has been identified in a *Bacillus circulans* clinical isolate. The *vanB* gene has recently been found in a vancomycin-resistant isolate of *Streptococcus bovis* isolated from a stool swab collected from a patient on admission as surveillance for VRE. The potential for emergence of vancomycin resistance in clinical isolates of *Staphylococcus epidermidis, Streptococcus pneumoniae,* viridans streptococci, and *Corynebacterium* spp. as a result of transfer of vancomycin resistance genes from enterococci is also a public health concern.

In November 1994, the Hospital Infection Control Practices Advisory Committee of the Centers for Disease Control and Prevention issued the following recommendations for preventing and controlling the spread of vancomycin resistance with a special focus on VRE. It was recommended that each hospital through collaboration of its quality improvement and

Table 49–1 Recommendations for preventing the spread of vancomycin resistance: prudent vancomycin use.

Situations in Which the Use of Vancomycin Is	
Acceptable	**Discouraged**
• For treatment of serious infections caused by β-lactam-resistant gram-positive microorganisms • For treatment of infections caused by gram-positive microorganisms in patients who have serious allergies to β-lactam antimicrobial agents • When antibiotic-associated colitis fails to respond to metronidazole therapy or is severe and potentially life-threatening • For prophylaxis as recommended by the American Heart Association for endocarditis following certain procedures in patients at high risk for endocarditis (see Chapter 11) • Prophylaxis for major surgical procedures involving implantation of prosthetic materials or devices (eg, cardiac and vascular procedures and total hip replacement) at institutions that have a high rate of infections caused by methicillin-resistant *Staphylococcus aureus* or methicillin-resistant *S epidermidis.* (A single dose of vancomycin administered immediately before surgery is sufficient unless the procedure lasts more than 6 h, in which case the dose should be repeated. Prophylaxis should be discontinued after a maximum of two doses)	• Routine prophylaxis other than in a patient who has a life-threatening allergy to β-lactam antibiotics • Empiric antimicrobial therapy for a febrile, neutropenic patient unless initial evidence indicates that the patient has an infection caused by gram-positive microorganisms (eg, an inflamed exit site of a Hickman catheter) and the prevalence of infections caused by methicillin-resistant *S. aureus* in the hospital is substantial • Treatment in response to a single blood culture positive for coagulase-negative *Staphylococcus* spp. if other blood cultures taken during the same time frame are negative (ie, if contamination of the blood culture is likely) (Because contamination of blood cultures with skin flora (eg, *S epidermidis*) could result in inappropriate administration of vancomycin, phlebotomists and other personnel who obtain blood cultures should be trained to minimize microbial contamination of specimens) • Continued empiric use for presumed infections in patients whose cultures are negative for β-lactam-resistant, gram-positive microorganisms • Systemic or local (eg, "antibiotic lock") prophylaxis for infection or colonization of indwelling central or peripheral intravascular catheters • Selective decontamination of the digestive tract • Eradication of methicillin-resistant *S aureus* colonization • Primary treatment of antibiotic-associated colitis • Routine prophylaxis of very-low-birth-weight infants (ie, infants who weigh less than 1,500 g) • Routine prophylaxis for patients on continuous ambulatory peritoneal dialysis • Treatment chosen for dosing convenience of infections caused by β-lactam sensitive, gram-positive microorganisms in patients who have renal failure • Use of vancomycin solution for topical application or irrigation

BOX 49-3

Prevention of VRE Transmission

- All patients harboring VRE should be placed in private rooms or the same room as other patients who have VRE.
- Clean, nonsterile gloves should be worn when entering the room of a VRE-infected or -colonized patient.
- When caring for such a patient, a change of gloves is necessary after contact with material that could contain high concentrations of VRE (eg, stool).
- A gown should be worn when entering the room of a VRE patient if (a) substantial contact with the patient or with environmental surfaces in the patient's room is anticipated; (b) the patient is incontinent; or (c) the patient has had an ileostomy or colostomy, has diarrhea, or has a wound drainage not contained by the dressing.
- Gloves and gowns should be removed before leaving the patient's room, and the health care worker's hands should be washed with antiseptic soap or waterless antiseptic agent.
- Dedicated noncritical items such as stethoscopes, sphygmomanometers, and rectal thermometers should be assigned to a single patient or cohort of patients infected or colonized with VRE.
- If such devices are to be used on other patients, they should be adequately cleaned and disinfected first.

infection control programs; pharmacy and therapeutics committee; microbiology laboratory; clinical departments; and nursing, administrative, and housekeeping services, develop a comprehensive institution-specific strategic plan to detect, prevent, and control infection and colonization with VRE. The first aspect of this plan incorporated prudent vancomycin use. (Vancomycin has been reported as a risk factor for infection and colonization with VRE.) (Table 49–1.)

In addition, education programs concerning the epidemiology of VRE and the potential impact of this pathogen on the cost and outcome of patient care were recommended for hospital staff including attending and consulting physicians; medical residents and students; pharmacy, nursing, and laboratory personnel; and other direct patient care providers. Specific recommendations were also issued for the microbiology laboratory regarding the detection, reporting, and control of VRE. In addition, recommendations were given regarding how to proceed when VRE are isolated from a clinical specimen, how to screen for detection of VRE, and how to prevent transmission of VRE once identified (Box 49–3). Recommendations for screening for roommates found to be infected or colonized with VRE were also issued.

REFERENCES

Centers for Disease Control and Infection: Nosocomial enterococci resistant to vancomycin—United States, 1989–1993. Morbid Mortal Weekly Rep 1993; 42: 597–99.

Hospital Infection Control Practices Committee. 1995 Recommendations for preventing the spread of vancomycin resistance. J Infect Control Hosp Epidemiol 1995;6: 105–13.

50

Other Gram-Positive Cocci

Robin Patel, MD

VIRIDANS GROUP STREPTOCOCCI, INCLUDING *ABIOTROPHIA DEFECTIVA* & *ABIOTROPHIA ADJACENS*

Essentials of Diagnosis

- Facultatively anaerobic gram-positive cocci, catalase negative, coagulase negative.
- α or γ hemolytic on blood agar.
- *Abiotrophia defectiva* and *Abiotrophia adjacens* require pyridoxal or thiol group supplementation.
- *Streptococcus milleri* group organisms often exhibit Lancefield antigens A, C, F, or G and often have a butterscotch odor.

General Considerations

A. Epidemiology. Viridans streptococci are part of the normal microbial flora of humans and animals and are indigenous to the upper respiratory tract, the female genital tract, all regions of the gastrointestinal tract, and, most significantly, the oral cavity. Clinically significant species that are currently recognized as belonging to the viridans group of streptococci include *Streptococcus anginosus S constellatus, S cristatus, S gordonii, S intermedius, S oralis, S mitis, S mutans, S cricettus, S rattis, S parasanguis, S salivarius, S thermophilus, S sanguinis, S sobrinus,* and *S vestibularis.*

Detailed studies of the ecology of strains in the oral cavity and oropharynx have been performed. The buccal mucosa and initial dental plaque are associated with *S sanguis* and *S mitis,* the dorsum of the tongue with *S mitis* and *S salivarius,* mature supragingival plaque with *S gordonii,* and subgingival plaque with *S anginosus.* In healthy individuals, adherence of viridans streptococci may provide "colonization resistance" within the oral cavity preventing the establishment of more pathogenic bacteria. Fibronectin, a complex glycoprotein found on the surface of oral epithelial cells, selectively promotes attachment of *S salivarius, S mutans,* and other gram-positive cocci to oral epithelial cells. If fibronectin is lost, as occurs in chronically ill or hospitalized patients, adherence of gram-negative bacilli to oral epithelial cells is increased, predisposing to the development of invasive gram-negative bacillary infections.

Viridans streptococci are strongly associated with bacterial endocarditis (see Chapter 11). Notably, endocarditis caused by *A defectiva* and *A adjacens* carries a higher mortality rate than that reported for viridans streptococci overall. Relapse is reported more frequently in endocarditis cases caused by *A defectiva* and *A adjacens.* In endocarditis cases caused by other viridans streptococci, members of the *S milleri* group are associated with deep-seated abscesses in visceral organs.

B. Microbiology. Viridans group streptococci are facultatively anaerobic gram-positive cocci that do not produce catalase or coagulase and, on blood agar, are typically α or γ hemolytic. Although some isolates react with Lancefield grouping antisera, the species do not conform to the specific serogroups, and many isolates are entirely nongroupable. Resistance to optochin and lack of bile solubility can distinguish viridans streptococci from *Streptococcus pneumoniae* (which also produces α hemolysis on blood agar) . Most viridans streptococci grow well on conventional blood culture media. On solid agar, viridans streptococci are usually facultatively anaerobic, but some strains may be capnophilic or microaerophilic. The colonies vary in size and appearance depending on the composition of the medium and the atmosphere of incubation. In broth cultures, viridans streptococci appear as spherical or ovoid cells that form chains or pairs. The organisms are nonmotile and non-spore forming, and they ferment carbohydrates with acid but not gas production.

Viridans streptococci can be distinguished by their biochemical characteristics. *S milleri, S constellatus,* and *S anginosus* constitute the *S milleri* group of viridans streptococci. Members of the *S milleri* group of viridans streptococci often require CO_2 for growth and typically grow as tiny colonies that may be α, β, or γ hemolytic on sheep blood agar. Members of the *S intermedius* group often exhibit Lancefield antigens A, C, F, or G and often have a butterscotchlike odor.

A defectiva and *A adjacens* are defined by their requirement for pyridoxal or thiol group supplementation for growth. These organisms form satellite colonies around *Staphylococcus aureus* and other microbes, and their colonies are typically small.

C. Pathogenesis. Viridans streptococci have been considered to be bacteria of low virulence. An exception is those members of the *S milleri* group that have a propensity for producing localized purulent collections. The reasons for this pathogenic characteristic are unknown. Infections with viridans streptococci usually result from spread of organisms outside of their normal habitat, especially in patients at risk for endocarditis or immunocompromised patients. Their most important virulence trait consists of an ability to adhere to and propagate on cardiac valves, leading to endocarditis; the presence of extracellular dextran likely plays a role in this regard. In addition to causing infective endocarditis, certain species of viridans streptococci, notably *S mutans,* have a strong association with the development of dental caries. The high cariogenic potential of *S mutans* is thought to be related to its ability to adhere in large masses to teeth and to produce high concentrations of acid from the fermentation of dietary sugars.

CLINICAL SYNDROMES

1. ENDOCARDITIS

Viridans streptococci have a strong association with bacterial endocarditis (see Chapter 11) (Box 50–1). *A defectiva* and *A adjacens* were once an important cause of culture-negative endocarditis. However, current laboratory media and techniques enable these "nutritionally variant streptococci" to be identified more readily.

2. BACTEREMIA

Viridans streptococci account for 2.6% of positive blood cultures reported from clinical laboratories; however, of these, only about one-fifth are thought to be clinically significant (the remainder are attributed to contamination or transient bacteremia). Viridans streptococci are, however, one of the leading causes of bacteremia in febrile neutropenic patients. Viridans streptococcal bacteremia in neutropenic patients usually occurs in association with aggressive cytoreductive therapy for acute leukemia or allogeneic bone marrow transplantation. The prophylactic administration of trimethoprim-sulfamethoxazole or the quinolones, the presence of mucositis, and the presence of indwelling central venous catheters are

BOX 50–1

Major Gram-Positive Cocci Infections

Organisms	Syndromes
Viridans group streptococci (including *Abiotropha* spp.)	• Endocarditis • Bacteremia, especially in febrile neutropenic patients • Meningitis • Other infections
Group B Streptococcus (*Streptococcus agalactiae*)	• Neonatal infection: bacteremia, pneumonia, meningitis, bone and joint infection • Postpartum infection: bacteremia, endometritis, endoperimetritis • Group B streptococcal infection in adults: pneumonia, endocarditis, arthritis, osteomyelitis, skin and soft tissue infections
S dysgalactiae subspp. *equisimilis* and *S zooepidemicus*	• Pharyngitis • Post-streptococcal glomerulonephritis • Cutaneous and subcutaneous infections • Arthritis/osteomyelitis • Endocarditis
S bovis	• Bacteremia • Endocarditis • Urinary tract infection • Meningitis • Neonatal sepsis

associated with viridans streptococcal bacteremia in these populations.

Patients may present with fever alone; however, neurologic, pulmonary, and cardiovascular manifestations may be seen, and a fulminant shock syndrome characterized by hypotension, rash, palmar desquamation, and the adult respiratory distress syndrome may be present. Notably, clinically apparent endocarditis is seldom present in neutropenic patients with viridans streptococcal bacteremia.

Bacteremia associated with *S milleri* group isolates is often associated with deep-seated abscesses in visceral organs.

3. MENINGITIS

When viridans streptococci are recovered from cerebrospinal fluid, they are most often contaminants. Viridans streptococci, however, are rare causes of meningitis, which may occur in patients of all ages, including neonates. Clinical manifestations are typical of acute pyogenic meningitis with evidence of meningeal irritation, neurologic deficits, seizures, and altered sensorium.

4. OTHER VIRIDANS STREPTOCOCCI INFECTIONS

Viridans streptococci may be associated with a variety of other infections, including pneumonia, pericarditis, peritonitis, acute bacterial sialadenitis, orofacial and odontogenic infections, endophthalmitis, otitis media, sinusitis, liver abscesses, pelvic abscesses, subphrenic abscesses, appendicitis, abdominal wound infections, cholangitis, mediastinitis, brain abscesses, subcutaneous abscesses, and cellulitis.

Diagnosis

The diagnosis of viridans streptococcal infection is made by isolating viridans streptococci from typically sterile sites. As mentioned above, communityacquired viridans streptococcal bacteremias are strongly associated with bacterial endocarditis. This diagnosis may be further confirmed by the presence of clinical findings consistent with endocarditis as well as by the use of echocardiography. *A defectiva* and *A adjacens* require pyridoxal or thiol group supplementation for growth. There is sufficient pyridoxal in human blood to support the growth of *A defectiva* and *A adjacens* in most blood culture media (with the notable exception of unsupplemented tryptic soy broth). For subculture, however, solid media must be supplemented with 0.001% pyridoxal or 0.01% L-cysteine to sustain growth. As an alternative, the culture plate may be cross-streaked with *Staphylococcus aureus* to provide these factors and permit the growth of the streptococci as satellite colonies. In addition, as noted above, members of the *S milleri* group are associated with deep-seated abscesses in visceral organs. Therefore infections caused by these organisms should alert the clinician to initiate an appropriate investigation for the detection of a possible subclinical focus of infection.

Treatment

Viridans streptococci with a minimum inhibitory concentration (MIC) of ≤ 0.12 μg/mL to penicillin are defined as penicillin susceptible. Those with a penicillin MIC of 0.25 to 2.0 μg/mL are intermediately susceptible to penicillin. Those with a penicillin MIC of > 2 μg/mL are resistant to penicillin. A high frequency of penicillin-resistant viridans streptococcal infections may be noted in febrile neutropenic patients. For serious infections, such as endocarditis, with these resistant or intermediately susceptible organisms, combination therapy consisting of a penicillin plus an aminoglycoside is recommended. Viridans streptococci are usually resistant to aminoglycosides when traditional breakpoint concentrations for these agents are applied. However, in vitro studies in experimental models of endocarditis have demonstrated synergistic bactericidal activity between combinations of penicillin and aminoglycosides.

Many other β-lactam antibiotics have in vitro activity similar to penicillin against streptococci. In particular, ceftriaxone is an alternative agent to penicillin for the outpatient treatment of viridans streptococcal endocarditis. Other agents with consistently good in vitro activity against viridans streptococci are cefazolin, vancomycin, and imipenem. *A defectiva* and *A adjacens* are less susceptible in vitro to penicillin than are most other streptococci. It is recommended that all patients with *A defectiva* and *A adjacens* endocarditis be treated with combination therapy consisting of a penicillin plus an aminoglycoside.

Prevention & Control

Endocarditis prophylaxis, as discussed in Chapter 11 on bacterial endocarditis, is used to prevent viridans group streptococcal endocarditis.

GROUP B STREPTOCOCCUS (*S AGALACTIAE*)

Essentials of Diagnosis

- Group B streptococcus (*S agalactiae*).
- Facultative gram-positive diplococci.
- Grayish white in color on sheep blood agar with a narrow zone of β hemolysis.
- Group B cell wall antigen positive.
- Resistant to bacitracin and trimethoprim-sulfamethoxazole.
- Hydrolyzes sodium hippurate.

General Considerations

A. Epidemiology. Group B streptococci are especially associated with neonatal and puerperal infections but cause infections in nonobstetric, nonneonatal populations as well. The incidence of early onset neonatal group B streptococcal infection (defined as the onset of symptoms during the first 5 days of life) is 1.3/1000 live births and appears to be declining. The attack rate for late onset neonatal infection (defined as onset of symptoms from 6 days to 3 months of age) is 0.5/1000 live births.

Group B streptococci colonize the mucous membrane of newborns via vertical transmission of the organism from the mother. This takes place either in utero via the ascending route or at the time of delivery. The rate of vertical transmission to neonates born to women colonized with group B streptococci at the time of delivery ranges from 20% to 72%. A high genital inoculum at the time of delivery is associated with a higher rate of vertical transmission. In addition, infants born to heavily colonized women are more likely to develop invasive early onset group B streptococcal disease. Heavily colonized infants have significantly increased rates of early and late onset group B streptococcal disease. Nosocomial transmission of group B streptococci may occur and may be influenced by poor hand washing by health care providers and by crowding.

Several factors have been identified that increase the incidence of invasive early onset infection among neonates born to colonized mothers. They include rupture of the membranes > 18 h before delivery; multiple births; premature rupture of the membranes (< 37-week gestation); maternal fever or amnionitis, or both; black race; age < 20 years; history of previous miscarriage; and preterm delivery.

Group B streptococci may be isolated from genital or lower gastrointestinal tract specimens or both of 5–40% of pregnant women. Lower socioeconomic status, having < three pregnancies, the presence of an intrauterine device, sexual activity, age of < 20 years, and the first half of the menstrual cycle are associated with an increased rate of detection of group B streptococcal colonization in the female genital tract, whereas being of Mexican-American heritage is associated with a decreased rate. Group B streptococci may be harbored in the urinary tract during pregnancy in association with asymptomatic bacteriuria; bacteriuria is a marker for high inoculum in the genital tract.

Group B streptococci are associated with postpartum febrile morbidity with or without bacteremia. In addition, adults with diabetes mellitus, chronic hepatic dysfunction, HIV infection, or malignancies requiring immunosuppressive therapy are also susceptible to group B streptococcal infections.

B. Microbiology. Group B streptococci are facultative gram-positive diplococci that are easily grown on a variety of bacteriologic media. On sheep blood agar, isolated colonies are 3–4 mm in diameter and grayish white in color. A narrow zone of β hemolysis surrounds the flat, somewhat mucoid colonies, although a small number of strains may be γ hemolytic. Group B-specific cell wall antigen may be detected by countercurrent immunoelectrophoresis, enzyme-linked immunosorbent assay, indirect immunofluorescence, staphylococcal coagglutination, or latex agglutination. Group B streptococci are resistant to bacitracin and trimethoprim-sulfamethoxazole, hydrolyze sodium hippurate, and produce an orange pigment during anaerobic growth on certain media. Group B streptococci produce CAMP (named for Christie, Atkins, and Munch-Petersen) factor, which is a thermostable extracellular protein that results in synergistic hemolysis on sheep blood agar in conjunction with the β hemolysin of *S aureus.*

C. Pathogenesis. Preterm labor may be associated with an increased rate of symptomatic group B streptococcal infection in the neonate because ascending infection caused by group B streptococci may be a primary pathogenic event initiating preterm rupture of the membranes. Low levels of antibody to the capsular antigen of group B streptococci may predispose to neonatal infection. In addition, complement and heat-stable opsonins may play a role in the pathogenesis of group B streptococcal infections.

In addition to host factors, bacterial virulence factors contribute to the host-parasite interaction that determines the outcome between exposure and the development of asymptomatic group B streptococcal colonization or symptomatic group B streptococcal infection. Specifically, a high quantity of cell-associated sialic acid, and its elaboration in supernatant fluid at high concentrations, is associated with virulence. The unique capsular structures of group B streptococci might also enhance the invasiveness of one serotype over another.

CLINICAL SYNDROMES

1. EARLY-ONSET GROUP B STREPTOCOCCAL NEONATAL INFECTION

Early-onset group B streptococcal neonatal infection has three major clinical expressions: bacteremia with no identifiable focus of infection, pneumonia, and meningitis (Box 50–1). Signs and symptoms of early-onset group B streptococcal neonatal infection include lethargy, poor feeding, jaundice, abnormal temperature, grunting respirations, pallor, and hypotension.

In most infants with pneumonia, symptoms of respiratory distress are present at or within a few hours after birth. Signs of respiratory distress associated with pneumonia include apnea, grunting, tachypnea, and cyanosis. The radiographic findings in infants with pneumonia may be indistinguishable from those of hyaline membrane disease.

Infants with meningitis have a clinical presentation that initially cannot be distinguished from that of infants without meningeal invasion. Lumbar puncture is required to identify neonates with meningitis.

The mortality of early-onset group B streptococcal infection is 10–15% but may be higher in infants with lower birth weights. One-half of patients with meningitis develop seizures within 24 hours of onset; if seizures persist, a poor outcome may follow.

2. LATE-ONSET GROUP B STREPTOCOCCAL NEONATAL INFECTION

The mean age of onset of late-onset group B streptococcal neonatal infection is 24 days. Bacteremia with concomitant meningitis is a frequent presentation. Signs and symptoms include poor feeding, irritability, and fever. Some infants present with fulminant infection characterized by progression within a few hours from the absence of symptoms to a morbid state with septic shock and seizures with cerebrospinal fluid Gram stains demonstrating sheets of organisms. This fulminant presentation is associated with an increased risk for mortality or permanent neurologic sequelae. Neutropenia on admission, prolonged seizures, and high concentrations of polysaccharide antigen in admission cerebrospinal fluid specimens are also associated with fatal outcomes or permanent neurologic sequelae.

Of all survivors of early- or late-onset group B streptococcal meningitis, 25% to 50% will have permanent neurologic sequelae. One-third of patients with these complications will have severe blindness, deafness, and/or global developmental delay. In the remainder of patients, the deficits are subtler and may be detectable only when language and cognitive function are adequately tested.

Bacteremia without an apparent focus and bone and joint infections are other clinical presentations of late onset group B streptococcal disease. Infants with bacteremia should be evaluated for foci of infection including cellulitis, adenitis, otitis media, conjunctivitis, peritonitis, endocarditis, or deep abscesses. Group B streptococcal osteomyelitis is characterized by an indolent onset in which diminished movement of the involved extremity is the most common symptom. Septic arthritis is associated with an acute onset of symptoms usually in the context of bacteremia. Fever is uncommon in both bone and joint infections. Lower extremity involvement is most commonly observed in patients with septic arthritis, whereas osteomyelitis has a predilection for involvement of the proximal humerus. However, involvement of the femur, tibia, and flat and small bones may be seen.

3. PERIPARTUM INFECTIONS

Group B streptococci cause symptoms of endometritis including fever, malaise, and moderate uterine tenderness. Pelvic abscesses, septic shock, and septic thrombophlebitis are rarely seen. Group B streptococci also cause peripartum bacteriuria that may be asymptomatic or may be diagnosed in association with cystitis or, less frequently, pyelonephritis.

4. GROUP B STREPTOCOCCAL PNEUMONIA

This may occur in patients with diabetes mellitus or neurologic disease. Chest radiographs may demonstrate bilateral or lobar infiltrates. Infection is frequently polymicrobial, although group B streptococci are usually the predominant organisms. Empyema may be present.

5. ENDOCARDITIS (ACUTE OR SUBACUTE ONSET)

Endocarditis caused by group B streptococci is rare. The mitral valve is more frequently involved than the aortic valve, and tricuspid valve involvement is found mainly in intravenous drug users. Underlying heart disease is present in more than one-half of cases, and rheumatic heart disease is the most common underlying condition. Valvular disease, atherosclerotic heart disease, and mitral valve prolapse have also been described as predisposing factors. Large friable vegetations are a frequent feature of group B streptococcal endocarditis. Embolization may occur early. Rapid valvular destruction may occur necessitating early valve replacement in some patients.

6. ARTHRITIS

This is typically monoarticular and most commonly affects the knee, hip, or shoulder joints (see Chapter 14). Diabetes mellitus is a predisposing factor, as are osteoarthritis and the presence of a prosthetic joint. The most common presenting signs are fever and joint pain in a patient with septicemia. Osteomyelitis may occur as a consequence of adjacent arthritis, peripheral vascular disease, orthopedic surgery, or concomitant infections such as frontal sinusitis. Hematogenously acquired osteomyelitis is most likely to involve the vertebrae. Osteomyelitis may complicate foot ulcers in adults with long-standing diabetes mellitus. In patients with prosthetic joints, group B streptococci typically cause acute onset septic arthritis with local pain, erythema, and swelling.

7. SKIN & SOFT TISSUE INFECTIONS

Group B streptococci may cause cellulitis, foot ulcers, abscesses, and infection of decubitus ulcers (see Chapter 13).

8. OTHER GROUP B STREPTOCOCCAL INFECTIONS

Meningitis, keratitis, endophthalmitis, urinary tract infections in nonobstetric populations, and other unusual presentations may also occur.

Diagnosis

The diagnosis of group B streptococcal infection is made by the isolation of the organism from typically sterile sites (eg, blood, cerebrospinal fluid, abscess material). Antigen detection methods may be used to permit a presumptive diagnosis, especially in neonates. Countercurrent immunoelectrophoresis, latex agglutination, staphylococcal coagglutination, and enzyme immunoassays may be used to detect group B streptococcal antigen in various body fluids. A number of selective media enhance the accurate detection by culture of low numbers of group B streptococci from sites such as the genital or gastrointestinal tract of pregnant women. These media usually contain Todd-Hewitt broth with or without sheep red blood cells and antimicrobial agents such as nalidixic acid and gentamicin or colistin. Molecular and antigen detection methods can also be used to detect group B streptococcal genital or gastrointestinal tract colonization in pregnant women.

Treatment

Group B streptococci are uniformly susceptible to penicillin, although less so than *S pyogenes*. Penicillin G is therefore the drug of choice; however, because of the increased penicillin MIC (as compared with *S pyogenes*), the combination of penicillin plus an aminoglycoside is recommended for the treatment of group B streptococcal endocarditis (Box 50–2). Penicillin plus an aminoglycoside exhibit in vitro and in vivo synergistic killing of the organism. Group B streptococci are also susceptible to ampicillin, imipenem, vancomycin, and first-, second- (excluding cefoxitin), and third-generation cephalosporins, although degrees of activity vary. Some isolates are resistant to clindamycin, erythromycin, and clarithromycin; tetracycline resistance is frequently seen. Group B streptococci are uniformly resistant to nalidixic acid, trimethoprim-sulfamethoxazole, and aminoglycosides.

Parenteral therapy of a 10-day duration is recommended for treatment of bacteremia, pneumonia, pyelonephritis, and soft tissue infections, whereas a 14-day minimum duration is recommended for treatment of meningitis and a 4-week minimum for treatment of endocarditis or ventriculitis. In adults with endocarditis, cardiac surgery early in the course may be necessary because of rapid left-sided valvular destruction. In practice, many neonates are empirically treated with ampicillin plus gentamicin.

Prevention & Control

Prevention of early onset neonatal sepsis and post-partum maternal febrile morbidity may be achieved by administration of intravenous ampicillin or penicillin during labor. Women colonized with group B streptococci may be identified by obtaining cultures using lower vaginal and anorectal swabs processed in selective broth media or by using rapid antigen or molecular detection methods when patients are admitted to the hospital. The American College of Obstetrics and Gynecology, the American Academy of Pediatrics, and the Centers for Disease Control and Prevention have developed two strategies (a screening approach and a nonscreening approach) for preventing perinatal group B streptococcal disease (Box 50–3).

To prevent early onset sepsis, maternal chemoprophylaxis should be initiated at least 4 h before delivery and at high doses (see Box 50–3). This allows time to achieve sufficient concentrations of ampicillin or penicillin in the fetal circulation and in the amniotic fluid. Management of neonates born to women receiving chemoprophylaxis should be based on clinical findings.

STREPTOCOCCUS DYSGALACTIAE SUBSPP. *EQUISILIMIS* & *STREPTOCOCCUS ZOOEPIDEMICUS*

Essentials of Diagnosis

- Associated with domestic animals.
- Formerly known as groups C and G streptococci.
- Pharyngitis, skin and soft tissue infections, and arthritis are common syndromes.

General Considerations

A. Epidemiology. *S dysgalactiae* subspp. *equisimilis* and *S zooepidemicus* have been isolated from the throat, nose, skin, and genital and intestinal tracts of asymptomatic carriers and from the umbilicus of as many as two-thirds of asymptomatic newborns. Domestic animals (eg, horses, cattle, pigs, and chickens) may be infected; epidemic infections have been noted in horses, cattle, sheep, and pigs. Many cases of human infection can be traced to an animal source. Human infection has also been associated with consumption of homemade cheese and unpasteurized cow's milk. Underlying conditions have been noted in most patients with *S dysgalactiae* subspp. *equisimilis* and *S zooepidemicus* infections. These include cardiopulmonary disease, diabetes mellitus, chronic dermatologic conditions, malignancy, immunosuppression, alcohol abuse, renal or hepatic insufficiency, and injection drug abuse. These streptococci also cause recurrent cellulitis at the saphenous vein donor site in patients who have undergone coronary artery bypass surgery.

B. Microbiology. *S dysgalactiae* subspp. *equi-*

BOX 50-2

Treatment of Other Gram-Positive Cocci Infections [1,2]

Viridans group streptococci (Penicillin MIC ≤0.12 µg/mL), group B streptococcus (*S agalactiae*), *S dysgalactiae* subspp. *equisimilis*, *S zooepidemicus*, and *S bovis*

First Choice	Penicillin G sodium 12–18 million U/24 h IV either continuously or in 6 divided doses **PLUS** gentamicin sulfate 1 mg/kg IV/IM every 8 h
Second Choice	Ampicillin 1–2 g IV/IM every 4–6 h Cefazolin 1 g IV/IM every 8 h Cefotaxime 1–2 g IV/IM every 8 h Ceftriaxone 1–2 g once daily IV/IM Imipenem 500 mg IV/IM every 6 h Vancomycin 30 mg/kg 24 h IV in 2 divided doses, not to exceed 2 g/24 h unless serum levels are monitored
Penicillin Allergic	Vancomycin 30 mg/kg 24 h IV in 2 divided doses not to exceed 2 g/24 h unless serum levels are monitored
Pediatric Considerations	Penicillin G IV/IM, 100,000–250,000 U/kg/24 h in divided doses every 4 h **PLUS** gentamicin 1 mg/kg IV/IM every 6 h Ampicillin 100–200 mg/kg/24 h IV/IM in 4–6 divided doses Vancomycin 10 mg/kg 6 h IV not to exceed 2 g/24 h unless serum levels are monitored Ceftriaxone 50–100 mg/kg 24 h IV/IM not to exceed 4 g/24 h Imipenem 12.5 mg/kg every 6 h IV/IM not to exceed 4 g/24 h Cefazolin 25–100 mg/kg 24 h IV/IM in 3–4 divided doses Cefotaxime 50–180 mg/kg 24 h IV/IM in 4–6 divided doses

[1]Doses provided assuming normal renal function.
[2]Oral alternatives may be appropriate for nonsevere infections with these organisms.

---

similis and *S zooepidemicus* include the organisms formerly known as groups C and G streptococci (*S equisimilis, S equi, S zooepidemicus, S dysgalactiae,* and *S canis*).

CLINICAL SYNDROMES

1. PHARYNGITIS

The symptoms of pharyngitis caused by these organisms mimic those of *S pyogenes* pharyngitis (Box 50–1; see also Chapter 48). Poststreptococcal glomerulonephritis has been described following *S dysgalactiae* subspp. *equisimilis* and *S zooepidemicus* pharyngitis. Notably, however, no antistreptolysin O antibody response will be detected as these organisms do not produce streptolysin O. *S dysgalactiae* subspp. *equisimilis* pharyngitis has been associated with sterile reactive arthritis. Acute rheumatic fever, however, has not been described in association with *S dysgalactiae* subspp. *equisimilis* and *S zooepidemicus* pharyngitis.

2. SKIN & SOFT TISSUE INFECTIONS

Cellulitis, wound infections, pyoderma, erysipelas, impetigo, and cutaneous ulcers can be caused by these organisms (see Chapter 13). Breaches in skin integrity may provide a portal of entry leading to bacteremia. *S dysgalactiae* subspp. *equisimilis* and *S zooepidemicus* have been isolated in patients with cellulitis after vein harvest for coronary artery bypass grafting and in patients with conditions associated with abnormal venous or lymphatic drainage. Lymphangitis may accompany cellulitis. Bacteremia often occurs as a complication of skin and soft tissue infections.

3. ARTHRITIS

The skin is the presumed portal of entry in many patients (see Chapter 14). Almost any joint may be involved and frequently the arthritis is polyarticular. Prosthetic joint infection may occur. There have been isolated case reports of *S dysgalactiae* subspp. *equisimilis* and *S zooepidemicus* osteomyelitis.

BOX 50–3

Prevention and Control of Perinatal Group B Streptococcal Disease

Screening Approach	• All pregnant women should be screened at 35- to 37-week gestation for group B streptococcal carriage. • All identified carriers and women who deliver preterm before a culture result is available should be offered intrapartum antimicrobial prophylaxis (see below).
Nonscreening Approach	Intrapartum antimicrobial agents should be offered to women with risk factors (eg, those with elevated intrapartum temperature, membrane rupture ≥ 18 h, premature onset of labor or rupture of membranes at < 37 wks): Ampicillin 2 g IV every 4–6 h (until delivery), or penicillin G 5 million U IV every 8 h (until delivery). In penicillin-allergic patients, use clindamycin IV or erythromycin IV until delivery.

4. OTHER INFECTIONS

S dysgalactiae subspp. *equisimilis* and *S zooepidemicus* may rarely cause pneumonia or sinusitis. Infective endocarditis caused by *S dysgalactiae* subspp. *equisimilis* and *S zooepidemicus* is uncommon. Patients may present acutely or subacutely. Destruction of valve leaflets, myocardial abscesses, conduction abnormalities, and severe congestive heart failure may be seen. Major systemic emboli to the spleen, kidneys, myocardium, and central nervous system may occur. Rare reports of *S dysgalactiae* subspp. *equisimilis* and *S zooepidemicus* meningitis exist. These organisms have been associated with puerperal sepsis and endometritis. Neonatal sepsis with *S dysgalactiae* subspp. *equisimilis* and *S zooepidemicus* occurs in premature or low birth weight infants and in the setting of premature rupture of the membranes. The onset of disease is typically within the first week of life.

Bacteremia may occur in *S dysgalactiae* subspp. *equisimilis* and *S zooepidemicus* infections. Other infections caused by *S dysgalactiae* subspp. *equisimilis* and *S zooepidemicus* include pericarditis, pyomyositis, brain abscess, epiglottitis, cervical lymphadenitis, intra-abdominal infection, subdural empyema, arterial-venous fistula infection, peritonitis in dialysis patients, panophthalmitis, and spinal epidural abscess. A toxic shocklike syndrome has also been reported.

Diagnosis

The diagnosis of *S dysgalactiae* subspp. *equisimilis* and *S zooepidemicus* infection is made by isolating these organisms from typically sterile sites.

Treatment

The antimicrobial agent of choice for *S dysgalactiae* subspp. *equisimilis* and *S zooepidemicus* is penicillin G. Other agents with good in vitro activity include cefazolin, vancomycin, the semisynthetic penicillins, and cefotaxime (Box 50–2). The addition of gentamicin to penicillin, cefotaxime, or vancomycin may result in a better outcome in cases of serious infection such as bacterial endocarditis caused by *S dysgalactiae* subspp. *equisimilis* and *S zooepidemicus.*

STREPTOCOCCUS BOVIS

Essentials of Diagnosis

• Grow in 40% bile, hydrolyze esculin.
• Do not grow in 6.5% sodium chloride.
• Pyrrolidonyl arylamidase reactivity negative.

General Considerations

A. Epidemiology. *S bovis* is a normal inhabitant of the gastrointestinal tract. *S bovis* bacteremia is highly associated with bacterial endocarditis as well as with underlying lesions of the colon, including malignancy. In some series, the prevalence of malignancy in patients with *S bovis* bacteremia exceeds 50%. As such, all patients with *S bovis* bacteremia should undergo a careful workup to exclude colonic neoplasms.

B. Microbiology. *S bovis* are group D streptococci and share properties in common with enterococci including the ability to grow in the presence of 40% bile and to hydrolyze esculin. A number of other tests, however, including growth in 6.5% sodium chloride and pyrrolidonyl arylamidase reactivity differentiate *S bovis* from enterococci.

CLINICAL SYNDROMES

S bovis causes bacteremia, endocarditis, urinary tract infection, meningitis, and neonatal sepsis (Box 50–1). The gastrointestinal tract is the usual portal of entry in cases of *S bovis* bacteremia although the hepatobiliary tree, urinary tract, and even dental procedures have been implicated as possible sources.

Diagnosis

Isolation of *S bovis* from typically sterile sites permits the clinical diagnosis of infection.

Treatment

S bovis is very susceptible to penicillin (MICs range from 0.01 to 0.12 μg/mL) (Box 50–2). Other effective agents include ampicillin, the antipseudomonal penicillins, ceftriaxone, erythromycin, clindamycin, and vancomycin. Penicillin alone given for 4 weeks is adequate to treat patients with *S bovis* endocarditis. Vancomycin is a reasonable alternative in penicillin-allergic patients. Bacterial endocarditis prophylaxis regimens are given in Chapter 11 and are relevant to *S bovis* endocarditis.

OTHER GRAM-POSITIVE COCCI

The following organisms are too rare to merit extensive discussion of clinical syndromes, diagnosis, and treatment (see Box 50–4).

STREPTOCOCCUS INIAE

S iniae has recently been described as a cause of cellulitis, bacteremia, endocarditis, meningitis, and septic arthritis associated with the preparation of the aquacultured fresh fish tilapia.

LEUCONOSTOC SPECIES

Leuconostoc spp. are gram-positive cocci or coccobacilli that grow in pairs and chains; *Leuconostoc* spp. may be morphologically mistaken for streptococci. They are vancomycin-resistant facultative anaerobes that are commonly found on plants and vegetables and less commonly in dairy products and wine. *Leuconostoc* spp. have been documented to cause bacteremias, intravenous line sepsis with localized exit site infection and/or bacteremia, meningitis, and dental abscess. Many patients with *Leuconostoc* spp. infection are severely ill, immunocompromised, or both.

Despite exhibiting resistance to vancomycin, *Leuconostoc* spp. are susceptible to most other agents with activity against streptococci, including penicillin, ampicillin, clindamycin, minocycline, erythromycin, tobramycin, and gentamicin. Some clinical data suggest that penicillin or ampicillin are the agents of choice for treating infections due to *Leuconostoc* spp.

BOX 50–4

Rare Gram-Positive Cocci Infections

Organisms	Syndromes
Streptococcus iniae	• Cellulitis • Bactermeia • Endocarditis • Meningitis • Septic arthritis
Leuconostoc spp.	• Bacteremia • Line sepsis • Meningitis • Dental abscess
Pediococcus spp.	• Bacteremia
Stomatococcus mucilaginosus	• Endocarditis • Bacteremia in febrile neutropenic patients • Line sepsis • Meningitis • Peritonitis
Aerococcus spp.	• Endocarditis • Bacteremia • Urinary tract infection
Gemella spp.	• Endocarditis • Meningitis • Arthritis • Bacteremia • Urinary tract infection • Wound infection
Alloiococcus otitis	• Otitis media (possible association)
Micrococcus spp.	• Endocarditis
Lactococcus spp.	• Endocarditis
Globicatella spp.	• Bacteremia • Urinary tract infection • Meningitis
Helcococcus kunzii	• Wound infection (possible association)

PEDIOCOCCUS SPECIES

Pediococcus spp. are also vancomycin-resistant gram-positive cocci. They may be isolated from blood cultures, typically in immunocompromised patients.

STOMATOCOCCUS MUCILAGINOSUS

Stomatococcus mucilaginosus is a gram-positive coccus that may cause endocarditis, bacteremia, intravascular catheter infection, meningitis, and peritonitis. Many patients infected with *S mucilaginosus* have underlying serious diseases, neutropenia, the presence of foreign bodies, cardiac valvular disease, and/or a history of intravenous drug use. Destruction of the oral mucous membranes because of chemotherapy or radiotherapy has been hypothesized to play a role in the dissemination of stomatococci from their normal habitat in the oral cavity. Resistance to penicillin has been documented among some *S mucilaginosus* strains, and susceptibility to other commonly used antimicrobials varies with the isolate. Stomatococci are uniformly susceptible to vancomycin.

AEROCOCCUS SPECIES

Although aerococci may appear as contaminants in clinical cultures, occasional reports of a clinically significant role of these organisms in cases of endocarditis, bacteremia, and urinary tract infection have been noted. Aerococci are susceptible to penicillin and vancomycin.

GEMELLA SPECIES

Gemella haemolysans has been isolated (as a pathogen) in cases of endocarditis, meningitis, and prosthetic joint infections. *G morbillorum* has been isolated from blood, respiratory, genitourinary, wound, and abscess cultures and from an infection of an arterial-venous shunt. *Gemella* spp. appear to be susceptible to penicillin and vancomycin.

ALLOIOCOCCUS OTITIS

Alloiococci have been isolated from the middle ear fluid of children with chronic otitis media and a role for these organisms in the pathogenesis of persistent otitis media has been suggested.

MICROCOCCUS SPECIES

Micrococci are frequently contaminants in clinical cultures but may occasionally cause infections such as infective endocarditis. A review of micrococcal endocarditis in cardiac surgery patients noted that MICs of penicillin ranged from 3.12 to 40.0 µg/mL and those of vancomycin spanned from 1.56 to 10.0 µg/mL. All of the isolates tested were susceptible to cephalothin.

LACTOCOCCUS SPECIES

Lactococcus spp. may be associated with bacterial endocarditis. Lactococci are susceptible to vancomycin and moderately susceptible to penicillin.

GLOBICATELLA SPECIES

Globicatella sanguis, the sole species in this genus, has been isolated from patients with bacteremia, urinary tract infection, and meningitis.

HELCOCOCCUS KUNZII

Helcococcus kunzii, the only member of this newly described genus, has been isolated from wound cultures, notably those from foot ulcers, characteristically as part of a mixture of bacteria. The clinical significance of this organism is not yet defined.

REFERENCES

Centers for Disease Control: Decreasing incidence of perinatal group B streptococcal disease—United States, 1993–1995. 1997; 46(21):473–477.
Centers for Disease Control: Prevention of perinatal group B streptococcal disease: a public health perspective. Morbid Mortal Wkly Rep 1996;45(RR-7):1–24.
Committee on Infectious Diseases/Committee on Fetus and Newborn: Revised guidelines for prevention of early-onset group B streptococcal (GBS) infection. Pediatrics 1997;99:489–496.
Committee on Obstetric Practice, American College of Obstetricians and Gynecologists: Prevention of early-onset group B streptococcal disease in newborns, Comm Opin 173, American College of Obstetricians and Gynecologists, 1996.

51

Gram-Positive Aerobic Bacilli

Jeffrey Loutit, MB, ChB, & David Relman, MD

LISTERIA MONOCYTOGENES

Essentials of Diagnosis

- Incriminated foods include unpasteurized milk, soft cheeses, undercooked poultry, and unwashed raw vegetables.
- Asymptomatic fecal and vaginal carriage can result in sporadic neonatal disease from transplacental and ascending routes of infection.
- Incubation period for foodborne transmission is 21 days.
- Organism causes disease especially in neonates, pregnant women, immunocompromised hosts, and elderly.
- Organism is grown from blood, cerebrospinal fluid (CSF), meconium, gastric washings, placenta, amniotic fluid, and other infected sites.

General Considerations

A. Epidemiology. *L monocytogenes* is found in soil, fertilizer, sewage, and stream water; on plants; and in the intestinal tracts of many mammals. It is a foodborne pathogen that causes bacteremic illness and meningoencephalitis, with few if any gastrointestinal manifestations. Contaminated food appears to be the most common source for both sporadic and outbreak-related cases. An estimated 2500 cases occur each year in the United States. The median incubation period for foodborne transmission is ~ 30 days. Foods that have been linked to outbreaks of listeriosis include Mexican style cheeses, unpasteurized milk, and undercooked chicken. The organisms can multiply at 4°C; therefore, foods refrigerated for prolonged periods are well-recognized sources for microbial transmission. Although the incidence of listeriosis is relatively low, there are several populations at increased risk for disease. These populations include persons older than 70 years, pregnant women, and patients with defects in cell-mediated immunity, including transplant hosts, those receiving high-dose corticosteroids, and patients with AIDS. The case fatality rate associated with listeriosis is ~ 23%; listeriosis is estimated to account for almost one-third of all food-related disease deaths. Asymptomatic vagi-

nal and fecal carriage in pregnant women can result in sporadic neonatal disease, either from transplacental infection or from exposure during delivery.

B. Microbiology. *L monocytogenes* is a facultative anaerobic, non–spore-forming, gram-positive bacillus that can grow in acidic conditions, high salt concentrations, and a wide temperature range, including the temperatures of household refrigerators. There are ≥ 13 serotypes of *L monocytogenes,* of which types 1B and 4B are the most commonly associated with disease.

C. Pathogenesis. *L monocytogenes* displays unusual capabilities in its interactions with host cells and its mechanisms of pathogenesis. After entering the small intestine, the organisms induce their uptake into epithelial cells and macrophages. E-cadherin serves as a host cell receptor. Once internalized, the bacteria rupture the phagolysosomal vacuolar membrane, using a pore-forming hemolysin, listeriolysin O, and escape into the host cell cytoplasm. *Listeria* multiplies readily within this environment; it also moves about the cytoplasm by nucleating host cell actin polymerization at one pole of the bacterial cell, using its protein ActA (Figure 51–1). An actin "comet tail" is formed as actin regulatory proteins are recruited, and the process extends. The actin tail itself is fixed, and the bacteria are propelled by polymerization at the proximal end of the tail at speeds of ~ 0.1 μm/s. Many of the bacteria migrate to the periphery of the cytoplasm, pushing against the host cell outer membrane to form elongated protrusions. These protrusions are then ingested by adjacent cells; *Listeria* bacteria then secrete phospholipases and listeriolysin O that rupture the double membrane that separates them from this second cell's cytoplasm. This mechanism allows *Listeria* spp. to spread from cell to cell without directly contacting the extracellular environment. Several other pathogens induce actin polymerization as a means of movement within the host cell cytoplasm, including *Shigella* spp., *Rickettsia* spp., and vaccinia virus.

Clinical Findings (Box 51–1)

A. Central Nervous System (CNS) Infection. Although most cases of listeriosis occur after ingestion of contaminated food, few patients complain of gastrointestinal symptoms or display gastrointestinal

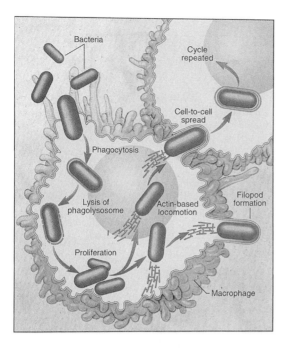

Figure 51–1. Intracellular life-cycle of *Listeria monocytogenes.* (Reproduced with permission from Southwick and Purich [1996].)

signs. The CNS is the site most commonly involved, where disease results in three different clinical presentations: meningitis, meningoencephalitis, and rhomboencephalitis. Meningitis is the most common manifestation of listeriosis in adults and children. *L monocytogenes,* after *Escherichia coli* and the group B streptococci, is the third most common cause of bacterial meningitis in adults and neonates, and it accounts for

5–15% of cases. The clinical manifestations of *Listeria* meningitis are similar to other forms of bacterial meningitis; however, the proportion of neutrophils among CSF leukocytes is often lower, and Gram stains of CSF are usually negative. In some cases, meningitis is accompanied by clinical signs of encephalitis. This organism, unlike other bacterial causes of meningitis, exhibits a tropism for brain parenchyma and, in particular, the brain stem, resulting in rhomboencephalitis. The latter is often preceded by 4–10 days of nonspecific flulike symptoms, followed by cranial nerve deficits, particularly of the sixth and seventh nerves. Brain stem involvement may lead to hemiparesis, ataxia, and even respiratory compromise. In most cases of meningoencephalitis, the CSF monocyte differential counts may reach 80–90%, but cases with no pleocytosis and normal CSF protein and glucose levels have been reported. Brain abscess is a rare manifestation of CNS listeriosis.

B. Bacteremia. Bacteremia or non-CNS focal infection occurs in 5–30% of adult cases. The diagnosis is based on positive blood cultures. *Listeria* causes focal infections in bone, native and prosthetic joints, eyes, spinal cord, pleura, peritoneum, and liver. Endocarditis, myocarditis, and mycotic aneurysms have also been described. Approximately one-third of women who contract *Listeria* infection are pregnant. Women in their third trimester are at greatest risk, but symptoms are usually mild, often mimicking a flulike illness. Blood cultures, if obtained, may be positive, but symptoms usually resolve spontaneously without therapy.

C. Neonatal Infection. Neonatal *Listeria* infection may present as an amnionitis, and infection is associated with premature labor. An uncommon clinical syndrome called granulomatosis infantiseptica has been described. This syndrome is caused by dissemination of *L monocytogenes* in utero. Abscesses and granulomata form within the fetal liver, lung, spleen, kidneys, brain, and skin. The mortality rate is high, ranging from 35% to 55%.

Diagnosis

L monocytogenes can be easily cultivated in the microbiology laboratory from blood, CSF, meconium, gastric washings, placenta, amniotic fluid, and other specimens. A CSF Gram stain with gram-positive or-variable rods should suggest *Listeria* infection, but this organism may be mistaken as a diphtheroid.

Treatment

There are no clinical trials comparing different antibiotic regimens for the treatment of listeriosis. Ampicillin or penicillin is generally recommended as the treatment of choice (Box 51–2). Gentamicin is added for severe infections, because the combination of ampicillin and an aminoglycoside is more effective than ampicillin alone in animal models. These agents should be given intravenously. The duration of therapy required to prevent relapse is not known;

BOX 51–1

Listeriosis in Children and Adults

	Children	Adults
More Common	• Neonatal disease Early onset: pneumonia, septicemia Late onset: meningitis	• Asymptomatic carriage • Influenzalike illness
Less Common	• Granulomatosis infantisepticam	• Amnionitis • Bacteremia and/or meningitis in patients with decreased cell-mediated immunity

BOX 51–2

Treatment of Listeriosis

	Children	Adults
First Choice	• Penicillin G, 300,000 U/kg/d in 6 divided doses	• Ampicillin, 200 mg/kg/d in 6 divided doses
Second Choice	• Trimethoprim, 20 mg/kg/d, plus sulfamethoxazole, 100 mg/kg/d in 4 divided doses	• Trimethoprim-sulfamethoxazole as per children
Penicillin Allergic	• Trimethoprim, 20 mg/kg/d, plus sulfamethoxazole, 100 mg/kg/d in 4 divided doses	• Trimethoprim-sulfamethoxazole as per children

however, 10–14 days is recommended in patients without meningitis, 2–3 weeks is recommended for those with meningitis, and 3–6 weeks is recommended for immunosuppressed patients. Another effective agent is trimethoprim-sulfamethoxazole, because high intracellular levels are achieved, and it is bactericidal for *Listeria* species.

Prognosis

Listeria infection of the CNS is associated with a high mortality rate. Of patients with meningoencephalitis, 36–51% die. Most of those who survive have persistent neurologic sequelae. Early recognition and rapid institution of antibiotics are critical for improving outcome.

Prevention

Patients at risk for listeriosis should be advised on how to minimize their exposure to this organism (Box 51–3). This advice should include cooking well all food from animal sources, washing raw vegetables thoroughly, and keeping uncooked meat separated from vegetables and cooked foods. Patients should also avoid consumption of unpasteurized milk, soft cheeses, or foods made with raw milk, and they should wash hands, knives, and cutting boards after handling uncooked food. An additional recommendation for

high-risk persons is to heat all leftovers or ready-to-eat foods until these foods are steaming hot.

ANTHRAX

Essentials of Diagnosis

- Contact with infected animals, carcasses, hair, wool, or hides from goats, sheep, cattle, swine, horses, buffalo, or deer.
- Incubation period lasting 1–7 days, usually 2–5 days, after exposure.
- Painless lesion progressing to papule, to vesicle, to necrosis, and to eschar.
- Rapid development of chest pain, dyspnea, and circulatory collapse after brief flulike syndrome.
- Direct gram-stained smear and/or cultures of lesions or discharges.
- Widened mediastinum on chest radiograph in inhalational disease.

General Considerations

Anthrax is primarily a disease of herbivores, but

BOX 51–3

Control of Listeriosis

Prophylactic Measures	• Therapy of infection diagnosed during pregnancy may prevent vertical transmission • Avoid contact between untreated manure from herds of cattle or sheep and foods for human consumption • Pregnant women and immunosuppressed patients should avoid unpasteurized dairy products, soft cheeses, undercooked meats, and raw unwashed vegetables
Isolation Precautions	• Standard precautions, but cases should be reported to the regional health department for recognition and control of common source outbreaks

humans acquire the disease through contact with infected animals or animal products.

A. Epidemiology. Historically, anthrax has been an occupational disease of persons who handle animal hair, skin, and other contaminated products. The incidence of this disease in the United States has fallen dramatically; only six cases of anthrax were reported to the Centers for Disease Control and Prevention from 1978 through 1998. The cutaneous form of the disease is most common. Continued concern about this disease stems from the unfortunate development of anthrax spores as biological weapons by a number of nations.

B. Microbiology. *Bacillus anthracis,* a sporulating gram-positive rod, is the causative agent of anthrax. *B anthracis* is distinguished from other *Bacillus* species in the laboratory based on its colony morphology and capsule.

C. Pathogenesis. *B anthracis* persists in soil as a nonreplicating spore. These spores are highly resistant to temperature extremes, drying, UV light, high pH, high salinity levels, and routine methods of disinfection. The virulence of *B anthracis* is due to the presence of a polysaccharide capsule that prevents phagocytosis and to the production of 2 two-component exotoxins. Each of these toxins is of an A-B structure. They share the same B component, known as protective antigen, which binds each of these binary toxins to host cells and mediates internalization. Lethal toxin causes rapid cell death by the action of its A subunit, a zinc metalloprotease that cleaves a critical intracellular signaling molecule. Edema toxin contains an A subunit that acts as a calmodulin-dependent adenylate cyclase and catalyzes production of cyclic AMP within host cells. This toxin is believed to be responsible for the dramatic tissue edema that characterizes cutaneous anthrax. The genes encoding the three toxin components are located on one plasmid, and the genes encoding the capsule are on a second plasmid. Strains missing either of these plasmids are avirulent. Expression of these toxins takes place upon germination of spores within macrophages and vegetative growth of the bacilli, after they have been inoculated into an animal host. Subcutaneous inoculation occurs via abrasions or breaks in the skin, and it leads to cutaneous disease with occasional systemic dissemination. Inhaled spores are deposited in the alveoli, phagocytosed by macrophages, and taken to regional lymph nodes where bacterial growth and disease first become manifest. Gastrointestinal anthrax results from ingestion of grossly contaminated or undercooked meat, and it is extremely rare. Only the spore is infectious for humans; hence, human-to-human transmission of disease does not occur.

Clinical Findings

There are three forms of the disease in humans: cutaneous, inhalational, and gastrointestinal (Box 51–4).

A. Cutaneous Anthrax. Cutaneous disease accounts for > 95% of all cases of anthrax. This disease

BOX 51–4

Anthrax Syndromes in Children and Adults	
More Common	• Cutaneous disease accounts for 95% of cases
Less Common	• Spectrum of disease includes inhalational, gastrointestinal, and meningeal

begins as a small, painless, but often pruritic papule. As the papule enlarges, it becomes vesicular and, within 2 days, ulcerates to form a distinctive black (hence the name of the disease) eschar, with surrounding edema. Gram stain of the vesicular fluid may reveal gram-positive rods and rare polymorphonuclear leukocytes.

B. Inhalational Anthrax. Inhalational anthrax is much less frequent and accounts for < 5% of cases; the incubation period is ~ 10 days, but it may be more prolonged in some cases. This form of the disease begins with an upper-respiratory flulike syndrome, and after a few days it takes a fulminant course, manifested by dyspnea, cough and chills, and a high-grade bacteremia. Inhalational anthrax is not a disease of the lung parenchyma, but is rather a hemorrhagic mediastinitis. Nearly all patients with this disease die within several days.

C. Gastrointestinal Anthrax. Gastrointestinal disease is accompanied by mucosal ulceration, mesenteric adenitis, and ascites; it is reported in Africa and Asia but has not been described in the United States.

Diagnosis

An appropriate epidemiologic history involving animal exposure is the cornerstone of the diagnosis of cutaneous anthrax. Other diagnostic features include edema out of proportion to the size of the skin lesion, the lack of pain during the initial phases of the infection, and the rarity of polymorphonuclear leukocytes on Gram stain. The organism can be readily cultivated and forms nonhemolytic gray-white colonies. A critical diagnostic feature of inhalational anthrax is a widened mediastinum on chest radiography. Patients with this disease usually die before organism growth in blood cultures is detected; however, organisms can sometimes be detected in blood with the Gram stain, owing to the high burden of bacteria in the endovascular compartment.

Treatment (Box 51–5)

Cutaneous anthrax responds well to penicillin G, which should be continued for 7–10 days. Doxycycline is also effective for cutaneous disease. Other antibiotics, such as ciprofloxacin and chloramphenicol, are alternative drugs for penicillin-allergic patients. The addition of streptomycin to penicillin may offer

BOX 51–5

Treatment of Anthrax

	Children	Adults
First Choice	• Penicillin G, 250,000–400,000 U/kg/d in 4–6 doses IV; consider addition of streptomycin	• Penicillin G, 16–24 million U/d IV divided every 4–6 h; consider addition of streptomycin
Second Choice	• Ciprofloxacin, 20–30 mg/kg/d IV in 2 doses OR • Doxycycline, 2–4 mg/kg/d IV in 2 doses OR • Chloramphenicol, 12–25 mg/kg/d IV in 4 doses	• Ciprofloxacin, 800 mg/d IV in 2 doses • Doxycycline, 200 mg/d IV in 2 doses OR • Chloramphenicol, 50 mg/kg/d IV in 4 doses
Pediatric Considerations	• Doxycycline should not be given to children < 8 y old, and ciprofloxacin should not be given to children in general, unless disease is life-threatening	
Penicillin Allergic	• Doxycycline (dosage as above)	• Ciprofloxacin (dosage as above)

additional benefit. Penicillin resistance has been reported among some naturally occurring isolates; these strains have remained sensitive to ciprofloxacin. Despite the early use of antibiotics, cutaneous lesions continue to progress through the eschar phase. Surgery or excision of lesions is contraindicated. With appropriate antibiotic therapy, fatalities are rare (< 1%).

Despite the use of antibiotics as described above, inhalational anthrax is almost always fatal, once it becomes clinically manifest. If anthrax is suspected, public health authorities should be notified immediately.

Prevention

Doxycycline or ciprofloxacin (Box 51–6) may prevent development of inhalational disease if given to exposed individuals before onset of disease. Either of these antibiotics should be given for at least 6 weeks before or 2 weeks after the third dose of anthrax vaccine. The currently licensed anthrax vaccine contains protective antigen, and it has been shown to be effective in limited studies against inhalational disease in monkeys and cutaneous disease in humans.

OTHER *BACILLUS* SPECIES

General Considerations

Bacillus species other than *B anthracis* are found in soil, decaying organic matter, and water, but they are rare causes of disease. Risk factors associated with *Bacillus* infection include the presence of intravascular catheters, intravenous drug use, sickle cell disease, and immunosuppression—particularly corticosteroid use, transplantation, AIDS, and neutropenia secondary to chemotherapy. The hardy growth characteristics of *Bacillus* spp. cause them to arise as common laboratory contaminants; however, they are also capable of causing severe invasive illness.

B cereus and *B subtilis* are the most frequent *Bacillus* spp. to cause invasive infection. Pneumonia, meningoencephalitis, endocarditis (native and prosthetic valves), and intravascular catheter infection have been well described. High-grade bacteremia with *B cereus* can be seen in the presence of indwelling intravascular catheters and always necessitates the removal of the catheter along with appropriate antimicrobial therapy. *B cereus* also causes soft-tissue and bone infections, including necrotizing fasciitis, particularly after contamination of wounds by soil. The characteristics of diseases associated with *Bacillus* spp. are indistinguishable from those associated with other pyogenic bacteria, and diagnosis depends on culture data.

Clinical Findings

B cereus accounts for 1–3% of all foodborne disease reported in the United States, although 10–14% of humans are colonized by this organism in their intestinal tract. There are two clinical syndromes associated with ingestion of this organism, an emetic and a diarrheal syndrome. The emetic syndrome is characterized by a short incubation period (1–6 h). Patients present with vomiting and abdominal cramp-

BOX 51-6	
Control of Anthrax	
Prophylactic Measures	• Doxycycline, 200 mg (2–4 mg/kg in children), **OR** ciprofloxacin, 1 g (20–30 mg/kg in children) orally per d in 2 divided doses may be used for exposed individuals (neither doxycycline nor ciprofloxacin should be given to children < 8 y old or < 18 y old, respectively, if the likelihood of exposure is high) • Surveillance and control of industrial and agricultural sources of *B anthracis* • Cell-free vaccine is available for those at risk but is not licensed for children or pregnant women
Isolation Precautions	• Standard precautions • Contaminated dressings or bedclothes should be burned or steam-sterilized to destroy the spores

ing. The emetic syndrome is usually associated with ingestion of contaminated cooked rice and is caused by a preformed, heat-resistant 5- to 10-kDa emetic toxin. The diarrheal syndrome has a longer incubation period (6–14 h), and it is characterized by watery diarrhea, abdominal cramping, and, less commonly, by vomiting. The diarrheal syndrome is associated with ingestion of contaminated vegetables, sauces, and puddings, and it is attributed to at least two heat-labile enterotoxins produced by *B cereus*. The durations of illness are 2–10 h for the emetic syndrome and 16–48 h for the diarrheal syndrome. The symptoms in both syndromes are self-limited, and supportive care only is necessary. Outbreaks of foodborne illness caused by *B subtilis, B licheniformis,* and *B pumilus* have also been reported.

B cereus is also a major cause of ocular infections such as endophthalmitis after eye trauma, and it is often associated with intraocular foreign bodies. The onset of infection is rapid, leading to destruction of the vitreous and retinal tissue with subsequent loss of vision within 12–48 h. Panophthalmitis and endophthalmitis with *B cereus* have also been described in injection drug abusers, without ocular trauma.

Treatment

B cereus is resistant to penicillin and other beta-lactam drugs, including cephalosporins. Active antimicrobial agents include vancomycin, clindamycin, aminoglycosides, carbapenems, and ciprofloxacin. Non-*B cereus* spp. are susceptible to penicillin and cephalosporins. Appropriate empiric therapy for suspected *Bacillus* spp. infections (other than anthrax) is vancomycin or clindamycin, with or without an aminoglycoside. Intraocular infections require aggressive therapy with systemic antibiotics plus intravitreous clindamycin or an aminoglycoside. Intravitreous dexamethasone and early vitrectomy are also recommended for sight-threatening *B cereus* ocular infection.

DIPHTHERIA

Essentials of Diagnosis

- Mildly painful tonsillitis/pharyngitis with associated membrane, cervical adenopathy, and signs of systemic toxicity; "bull neck" appearance.
- Hoarseness and stridor.
- Palatal paralysis.

General Considerations

A. Epidemiology. Humans are the only known natural hosts for *C diphtheriae,* the organism that causes diphtheria. This organism is usually spread via upper respiratory tract droplets, but it can also be spread by direct contact with skin lesions. Transmission appears to be more common when people are living indoors in crowded conditions. Disease is transmitted by those incubating the disease, those convalescing from infection, and also healthy carriers. The organism itself can survive for ≤ 6 months in dust, which may also serve as the vehicle for transmission. Immunization against diphtheria toxin prevents the serious complications of disease, by blocking the ability of the toxin to enter cells and also by reducing colonization of the nasopharynx by toxin-producing strains. Diphtheria is a rare disease in the United States; however, this disease can easily spread in populations that lack adequate levels of antitoxin immunity, as dramatically demonstrated in the former Soviet Union in the early 1990s.

B. Microbiology. *C diphtheriae* is a gram-positive rod with club-shaped swellings at each end. Most strains produce an exotoxin, diphtheria toxin, which is encoded by a gene carried by a lysogenic bacteriophage and is responsible for the disease.

C. Pathogenesis. *C diphtheriae* attaches to the

mucosal surfaces of the nasopharynx. There it remains in the superficial layers of the mucosa. When iron concentrations are low, lysogenic diphtheria bacilli produce high concentrations of diphtheria toxin. The conversion of nontoxigenic, nonlysogenic *C diphtheriae* to toxin-producing strains can occur within the nasopharynx after bacterial infection with the beta-corynephage. Diphtheria toxin is composed of A and B fragments. The B fragment is recognized by a specific host cell membrane receptor resulting in endocytosis of the entire molecule. Once the toxin is inside the endosome, acidification results in a conformational change of the B fragment. A membrane channel is formed, allowing passage of fragment A into the host cell cytoplasm. Fragment A blocks protein synthesis by cleaving NAD and covalently attaching ADP-ribose to the essential host protein, elongation factor-2. ADP-ribosylation interferes with the ability of elongation factor-2 to add amino acids to a peptide chain, blocking protein synthesis. Its effects are seen throughout the body but are most prominent in the heart and kidney and on nerves. Local cytotoxic effects lead to production of the characteristic "pseudomembrane." Anti-toxin antibody can neutralize toxin adsorbed to cells, but, once the toxin penetrates, its toxic affects are irreversible.

Clinical Findings (Box 51–7)

A. Respiratory Diphtheria. The incubation period for respiratory diphtheria is generally 2–4 days, but it can last ≤ 7 days. Initial symptoms include a low-grade fever. Sore throat and malaise are the most common manifestations of pharyngeal diphtheria. Unvaccinated patients tend to have more severe disease. The development of cell necrosis, secondary to the exotoxin, is commensurate with the presence of the characteristic membrane (Figure 51–2A). Initially the membrane is white and smooth, but later it becomes gray with patches of green and black necrosis. As the membrane spreads, it can interfere with airflow. Involvement of the posterior pharynx is often accompanied by cervical adenopathy and swelling, giving rise to a "bull neck" appearance (Figure 51–2B). With extensive disease there is increased release of exotoxin, resulting in myocardial and neurologic complications, thereby increasing the mortality associated with this disease.

B. Cutaneous Diphtheria. Cutaneous diphtheria usually begins with pustules that progress to ulcer formation with a gray-brown membrane at the base. Commonly, *C diphtheriae* will superinfect existing skin lesions such as insect bites, ecthyma, and impetigo. Cutaneous infections induce high levels of antitoxin antibody that prevent progression to systemic disease; therefore, the infections tend to be indolent and are not usually associated with signs of intoxication. Cutaneous infection poses a greater risk of environmental contamination and transmission to others than does pharyngeal infection.

C. Cardiac Disease. Myocarditis with clinically-significant cardiac dysfunction is observed in 10–20% of patients with pharyngeal disease. The likelihood and severity of myocarditis are correlated with the extent and severity of respiratory tract compromise. ST segment and T-wave changes and first-degree block are found by electrocardiography in less severe disease, whereas left bundle branch block and atrioventricular block are associated with high mortality. In severe cases, patients usually sustain permanent injury to the myocardium.

D. Neurologic Disease. Neurologic complications occur in ~ 10% of respiratory cases and are predicted by the severity of respiratory tract involvement. Symptoms and signs develop 10–28 days after the respiratory complaints and reflect both cranial nerve involvement and a peripheral neuropathy that can lead to complete paralysis. These complications are usually reversible.

Diagnosis

Prompt recognition and treatment of respiratory diphtheria are critical for preventing complications and mortality. A dark pharyngeal membrane that cannot be removed without bleeding, systemic toxicity, neurologic abnormalities such as 9th and 10th cranial nerve deficits, and/or electrocardiograph changes should alert the clinician to the possibility of diphtheria. The microbiology laboratory should be notified about the possibility of diphtheria, because special media, such as Loeffler's or tellurite selective media, must be used to prevent overgrowth of normal flora.

Treatment

All patients should be hospitalized and isolated. Rapid institution of antitoxin is critical because it is most effective if given within 4 days of the onset of illness (Box 51–8). Hyperimmune antiserum produced

BOX 51–7	
Diphtheria Syndromes in Children and Adults	
More Common	• Membranous nasopharyngitis • Obstructive laryngotracheitis • Abrupt onset low-grade fever, malaise
Less Common	• Cutanous • Vaginal • Conjunctival • Otic • Complications including cardiac and neurologic toxicity

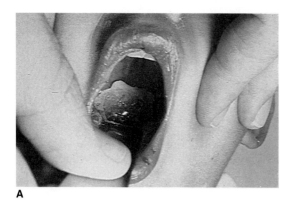

A

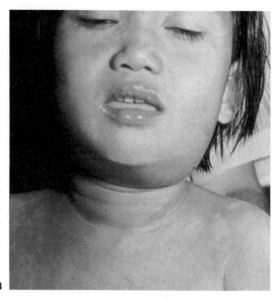

Figure 51–2. Nasopharyngeal diphtheria. A. Characteristic membrane and cell necrosis. B. Cervical adenopathy and swelling ("bull neck" appearance). (Reproduced with permission from Margileth AM: In Mandell G and Brook I: *Cervical Lymphadenopathy. Atlas of Infectious Diseases,* Vol IV. *Upper Respiratory and Head and Neck Infections.* Churchill Livingstone, 1995.)

B

in horses has been used for > 100 years. The dose of antitoxin is adjusted to the severity of disease. Sensitivity of the patient to horse protein must be assessed (see recommendations in Box 51–8). An initial scratch test may be performed on the volar forearm with a 1:100 dilution. If negative, this should be followed by an intracutaneous injection of 0.02 mL of a 1:1000 dilution of antitoxin in saline. No additional benefit is provided by repeated doses. Antibiotics should be initiated as soon as possible to kill organisms, stop toxin production, and eliminate the carrier state. Erythromycin for 2

weeks is the treatment of choice and should be given intravenously until the patient is able to handle oral medications. Procaine penicillin for 2 weeks is an alternative. Other measures include airway and cardiac support. If diphtheria is suspected, the patient should be isolated until two cultures from the affected site are negative. Cultures should be taken from all persons who have been in close contact with a diphtheria patient, to determine whether they are pharyngeal carriers. All carriers need to be treated with erythromycin or penicillin for 14 days.

BOX 51–8

Treatment of Diphtheria

	Children	Adults
First Choice	• Antitoxin (available from CDC [phone (404) 639-8200]) Pharyngeal/laryngeal disease (< 48 h), 20,000–40,000 U IV Nasopharynx disease, 40,000–60,000 U IV Extensive disease or > 3 d, 80,000–120,000 U IV **PLUS** Erythromycin, 40–50 mg/kg/d (max, 2 g/d)	• As for children (erythromycin, 2 g/d in 4 doses)
Second Choice	• Penicillin G, 100,000–150,000 U/kg/d divided every 6 h (max 1.2 million U) **OR** • Penicillin aqueous procaine, 25,000–50,000 U/kg/d divided every 12 h (max 1.2 million U)	• As for children (penicillin G, 12 million–20 million U/d divided every 4–6 h)
Penicillin Allergic	• Erythromycin	• Erythromycin

BOX 51-9

Control of Diphtheria

Prophylactic Measures	• Notify public health officials
	• Close contact tracing
	• Observe close contacts for 7 d
	• Culture close contacts
	• Antimicrobial prophylaxis for close contacts:
	  Oral erythromycin, 40–50 mg/kg/d (children); 2 g/d (adults) × 7 d
	  Single IM dose benzathine penicillin G, 600,000 U for those < 30 kg or 1.2 million U for those > 30 kg
	• Immunization with toxoid vaccine
	  Primary series
	    Children 6 wk–7 y, DTaP (3 IM injections at 4- to 8-wk intervals, then a 4th IM dose 6–12 mo after 3rd dose)
	    Children > 7 y and adults, dT (2 IM injections at 4- to 8-wk intervals, then a 3rd IM dose 6–12 mo after 2nd dose)
	  Booster
	    Children receiving primary series < 4 wk, DTaP at school entry, then every 10 y
	    Children/adults, dT every 10 y

Isolation Precautions	• Droplet precaution isolation until 2 negative nasopharyngeal cultures

Prevention

Children 6 weeks to 7 years of age should be immunized with three injections of vaccine containing formalin-inactivated diphtheria toxin (Box 51–9). Susceptibility to diphtheria correlates inversely with serum levels of anti-toxin antibody. Because these levels wane, adults should receive booster vaccinations every 10 years.

CORYNEBACTERIUM JEIKEIUM

Infection with *Corynebacterium jeikeium,* formerly known as *Corynebacterium* CDC group JK, almost invariably occurs in a hospital setting, because these bacteria commonly colonize the skin of hospitalized patients. Patients at highest risk for colonization include those receiving broad-spectrum antibiotics and those with neutropenia. The most common form of disease is bacteremia and is most often seen in neutropenic patients after breaks in the integument of their skin, such as with intravascular catheters. Endocarditis with this organism has been described, but it is rare, as are extravascular infections such as pneumonia, peritonitis, and prosthetic knee infections. The treatment of choice is vancomycin (1 g every 12 h); the length of therapy is dictated by the disease process. Prosthetic valve endocarditis with *C jeikeium* often requires removal of the valve for control of the infection.

OTHER CORYNEBACTERIUM SPECIES

Corynebacterium species colonize the skin and are therefore frequently recovered as contaminants in blood cultures; however, serious infections can occur. In particular, immunocompromised hosts and those with indwelling vascular catheters have an increased risk of infection with these organisms. *C ulcerans, C pseudotuberculosis, C bovis, C striatum,* and *C pseudodiphtheriticum* rarely cause human disease, but severe upper respiratory tract, cardiac, and CNS diseases have been reported. *Rhodococcus equi* (previously *C equi*) has recently been reported to cause pneumonia and cavitary pulmonary disease in patients with AIDS and renal transplantation. The treatment of choice for this organism is erythromycin or imipenem-cilastatin, plus rifampin.

ERYSIPELOTHRIX RHUSIOPATHIAE

General Considerations

Erysipelothrix rhusiopathiae is a gram-positive bacillus that causes occupationally related skin infections and, rarely, septicemia in humans.

A. Epidemiology. *E rhusiopathiae* is ubiquitous in nature and is an uncommon cause of human disease. It can infect mammals, birds, fish, shellfish, and insects, and it may reside in swine, which serve as a reservoir. Disease in humans is most commonly seen in persons with an appropriate exposure, usually including butchers, slaughterhouse workers, and especially fish handlers. Most cases of skin infection ("erysipeloid") occur in the summer and early fall. The organism is often traumatically inoculated and intense inflammation of the dermis follows.

B. Microbiology and Pathogenesis. The organism is non-spore forming and nonmotile and is a facultative anaerobe. The organism may appear as a beaded gram-positive rod owing to partial decolorization during the staining process. It grows well on sheep blood agar and exhibits alpha hemolysis. The organism tolerates a high-salt environment and can survive in saltwater. *E rhusiopathiae* is catalase negative, oxidase negative, and weakly fermentative.

Clinical Findings

Skin lesions are usually purplish-red with a sharply defined, raised, serpiginous border; they most commonly involve the proximal region of the hands and fingers. Lesions spread slowly, and, over time, the central portion heals leaving a pale center with a surrounding purplish-red border. Proximal lymphadenopathy and systemic symptoms are rare. Acute or subacute endocarditis secondary to *E rhusiopathiae* is uncommon, but is severe when it occurs. The aortic valve is most commonly involved, and 40% of patients will have or just had the characteristic skin lesion of erysipeloid.

Diagnosis

The diagnosis requires an appropriate epidemiologic history. The skin lesion may resemble erysipelas caused by *Streptococcus pyogenes,* but the rate of progression is slower, and there is a lack of lymphangitis, lymphadenopathy, and systemic symptoms. Full-thickness skin biopsy with appropriate culture will yield the organism in the majority of cases. Blood cultures should also be obtained.

Treatment

Treatment of choice for *E rhusiopathiae* infection is penicillin. Erysipeloid is usually self-limited and resolves over the course of 3 weeks, but therapy will hasten the resolution of symptoms. Endocarditis should be treated with intravenous penicillin at 12–20 million U/day, in 4–6 divided doses for 4–6 weeks. It is noteworthy that *E rhusiopathiae* is resistant to vancomycin. Despite appropriate therapy, the mortality rate for patients with *E rhusiopathiae* endocarditis is 30–40%.

REFERENCES

Bisgard KM, et al: Respiratory diphtheria in the United States, 1980 through 1995. Am J Publ Health 1998;88: 787.

Cossart P, Lecuit M: Interactions of *Listeria monocytogenes* with mammalian cells during entry and actin-based movement: bacterial factors, cellular ligands and signaling. EMBO J 1998;17:3797.

Dixon TC et al: Anthrax. N Engl J Med 1999;341:815.

Dobie RA, Tobey DN: Clinical features of diphtheria in the respiratory tract. JAMA 1979;242:2197.

Mead PS et al: Food-related illness and death in the United States. Emerg Infect Dis 1999;5:607.

Portnoy DA et al: Molecular determinants of *Listeria monocytogenes* pathogenesis. Infect Immun 1992;60:1263.

Shafazand S et al: Inhalational anthrax: epidemiology, diagnosis, and management. Chest 1999;116:1369.

Southwick FS, Purich DL: Intracellular pathogenesis of listeriosis. N Engl J Med 1996;334:770.

52

Neisseria Gonorrhoeae & Neisseria Meningitidis

D. Scott Smith, MD & David A. Relman, MD

Neisseria gonorrhoeae was first described by Albert Neisser in 1879, in the ocular discharge and exudate from newborn infants with conjunctivitis. Descriptions of a condition resembling the disease gonorrhea can be found in the written record as early as 130 AD, when Galen created a descriptor for the malady by using the Greek words *gonos* (seed) and *rhoea* (flow) to characterize what was believed to be the morbid loss of semen. *Neisseria meningitidis* is thought to be responsible for epidemics in the Napoleonic and Persian armies in the early 1800s. The pathogen was first described in 1886 by Weichselbaum, who observed gram-negative diplococci in the cerebrospinal fluid (CSF) of a young patient who died with purulent meningitis.

Within the family *Neisseriaceae,* there are five genera—*Neisseria, Branhamella, Moraxella, Kingella,* and *Acinetobacter. N meningitidis* and *N gonorrhoeae* are the organisms that are pathogenic for humans in the *Neisseria* genus (Table 52–1). Approximately 10 other *Neisseria* species have been isolated from humans, but these usually establish a commensal relationship with their host and usually do not cause disease. They lack virulence factors, such as pili and virulence-associated outer membrane proteins (OMPs).

NEISSERIA GONORRHOEAE

Essentials of Diagnosis

- Transmission associated with unprotected sex.
- Purulent urethral discharge, dysuria in men.
- Vaginal discharge, dysuria, intermenstrual bleeding in women.
- Dermatitis-arthritis syndrome with disseminated infection.
- Gram-negative diplococci inside neutrophils on stained smears of urethral, cervical, skin, or joint material.
- Fastidious organism requires special media and growth conditions.
- DNA amplification methods (PCR, LCR) offer improved sensitivity and specificity.

General Considerations

A. Epidemiology. *N gonorrhoeae* is found only in humans. It is primarily transmitted sexually by contact with infected secretions. It is the most common reportable infectious disease in the United States, with 300,000–400,000 cases occurring per year—a rate of ~ 130/100,000 persons per year. *Chlamydia* infections are more common but are not reportable in all states. The incidence of *N gonorrhoeae* rose during the late 1960s in the United States, peaked in the mid 1970s, and has since declined, but it now may be increasing in certain risk groups such as teenagers. The highest incidence is observed in those 20–24 y of age, in African-Americans, and in lower socioeconomic groups. Most cases are reported in men (male to female ratio, 4:3), which may reflect a greater frequency of symptoms in males. Incidence is higher in men, but prevalence is higher in women. The greatest decline in the prevalence of gonorrhea during the last 15 y has been noted in sexually active gay men, with > 10-fold decreases. This is attributable to safer sex practices in the early wake of the HIV epidemic.

The estimated risk of transmission from an infected female to a male by vaginal intercourse is 20% per exposure. The male-to-female transmission risk is less well studied, but is thought to be ~ 50% per contact. Transmission by rectal intercourse is relatively efficient, although it has not been quantified. Infection can also be transmitted perinatally. High rates of promiscuity are required to maintain a high prevalence of gonorrhea in a population. The so-called "core transmitters" of disease are those who frequently have unprotected intercourse with new partners.

B. Microbiology. *Neisseria* species are gram-negative cocci, 0.6–1.0 μm in their longest dimension, that usually form pairs (diplococci) with flattened adjacent edges. Their appearance has been likened to kidney beans. Motility is sometimes ob-

Table 52–1. Features of *Neisseria gonorrhoeae* and *Neisseria meningitidis*

	Neisseria gonorrhoeae	*Neisseria meningitidis*
Clinical	Men: purulent urethral discharge, dysuria. Women: usually asymptomatic, vaginal discharge, dysuria without frequency.	Petecchial rash (may involve palmar, plantar, and mucosal surfaces), fever, headache, stiff neck, vomiting, seizures, confusion.
Laboratory	Gram-stain of cervical or urethral swab shows gram-negative diplococci in association with PMNs. Culture of the affected site demonstrates the organism.	Gram stain: gram-negative intracellular diplococci. CSF: cloudy, purulent, high levkocyte count with PMN predominance, increased protein, decreased glucose. Culture of CSF, blood, or aspirated petecchial lesion demonstrates organism. Latex agglutination of CSF or urine may be indicated in treated patients but is similar to Gram stain of CSF for sensitivity.
Epidemiology	Sexual transmission.	Crowded or closed population settings (eg, boarding schools and military camps). Most cases in children and young adults.

served, although they are usually nonmotile. When grown on solid media, gonococci and meningococci form transparent or opaque, mucoid, nonpigmented, nonhemolytic colonies that are 1–5 mm in diameter.

Both *N gonorrheae* and *N meningitidis* require specially treated media such as chocolate agar to improve their growth. Chocolate agar is a heme-based growth medium enriched with glucose and other defined supplements; Thayer-Martin medium is chocolate agar with vancomycin, nystatin, and colistin, which inhibit other common commensals, as well as *Neisseria* species other than *gonorrhoeae* and *meningitidis*. Modified Thayer-Martin medium is now commonly used and also contains trimethoprim to inhibit *Proteus* spp. Growth is optimal at 35–37 °C and requires a carbon dioxide-enriched atmosphere. Fatty acids are toxic to *N gonorrhoeae;* hence, untreated cotton from some clinical swabs may prevent subsequent growth. *Neisseria* species are strictly aerobic, but, when nitrate is provided as an electron acceptor, these species can grow anaerobically. *Neisseria* colonies form within ~ 24–48 h on the solid media mentioned above. *Neisseria* species are usually identified by their carbohydrate utilization patterns. The principal distinguishing metabolic difference between *N meningitidis* and *N gonorrhoeae* is that the latter utilizes maltose. Both can generate acid from glucose. The *Neisseria* species are classified within the beta subdivision of the division *Proteobacteria.*

C. Pathogenesis. *N gonorrhoeae* has a complex set of molecular mechanisms for invasion and survival in humans. The activation of this complex armamentarium of cellular machinery begins when the pathogen arrives on a mucosal surface. The basic sequence of steps includes (a) long-range attachment by means of pili, (b) close attachment, (c) invasion of mucosal columnar cells, perhaps mediated by porin proteins, (d) transportation through the cell in phagosomes, and (e) occasional "transcytosis" into the submucosa and then, rarely, invasion into the blood

stream. Once established in the host, *N gonorrhoeae* is antigenically heterogeneous, changing its surface structures to avoid host defenses. Several important antigenic structures include pili, porin proteins, opacity (Opa) proteins, reduction-modifiable protein, and lipooligosaccharide (LOS). Pili are the hairlike structures that extend several micrometers from the cell surface and enhance attachment to host cells, as well as help resist phagocytosis. There is great variability in their antigenic structure, through expression of different pilin structural subunit types, as well as variability in expression of different Opa proteins. Gonococci can express several LOS chains simultaneously, but, unlike lipopolysaccharide from other gram-negative bacteria, the gonococcal LOS does not have long O-antigen side chains. The endotoxic effects of LOS are responsible for the systemic toxicity observed in patients with disseminated disease.

Iron acquisition by *N gonorrhoeae* at the mucosal surface is a critical requirement for survival and growth. This organism and *N meningitidis* express receptors on their surface for human lactoferrin and transferrin, to capture iron from the host.

Clinical Findings

Genital infection with *N gonorrhoeae* most often presents as urethritis in men and cervicitis in women.

A. Genital Infection in Men. In men dysuria usually precedes development of a urethral discharge, which is creamy, yellow, profuse, and sometimes blood tinged. The incubation period ranges from 1 to 10 d after exposure, but > 90% of men become symptomatic within 5 d. Most untreated cases resolve spontaneously within several weeks. The most common complication of urethral gonorrhea in men is epididymitis. However, *N gonorrhoeae* causes only 10% of all cases of infectious epididymitis. Other less common complications of genital infection include penile edema, penile lymphangitis, periurethral abscess, and infection of the Cowper's glands. Stricture of the urethra is now uncommon, but was a more frequent complication in the past.

The microbiological differential diagnosis for urethritis includes other infectious agents such as *Chlamydia trachomatis* and *Ureaplasma urealyticum.* Reiter's syndrome should be considered in patients with urethritis, conjunctivitis, and arthritis. Dysuria and an itching sensation characterize chlamydial urethritis and, in contrast to gonococcal urethritis, may not have profuse purulent discharge. Of men with chlamydial urethral infection, ~ 25% are asymptomatic.

B. Genital Infection in Women. In women, uncomplicated *N gonorrhoeae* genital infection is manifest as a purulent cervicitis. Although most women who are seen in acute care settings have symptoms with infection, population-based screening efforts identify many infected women who are asymptomatic. The incubation period in women is less well defined but is ~ 10 d. Symptoms include vaginal discharge, dyspareunia, dysuria without increased frequency, and intermenstrual bleeding. On physical exam, there may be mucopurulent cervical discharge, edema of the cervix, and mucosal friability.

Gonococcal infection in women may progress to involve the uterus and fallopian tubes, causing either acute or chronic salpingitis or pelvic inflammatory disease (PID). Bilateral lower abdominal pain is the most common symptom of PID. There are also signs and symptoms of accompanying lower genital tract infection, as well as cervical-motion tenderness. Fever, leukocytosis, and elevated erythrocyte sedimentation rate or C-reactive protein are common. In PID, anaerobes and chlamydiae may accompany the gonococcal infection. Tubal scarring and infertility are the dreaded sequelae. Perihepatitis (Fitz-Hugh-Curtis syndrome) is a rare complication that occurs by extension of the infection from the fallopian tubes to the peritoneum and the liver capsule. It is accompanied by right upper quadrant tenderness. Laparoscopy demonstrates adhesions between the liver and the parietal peritoneum.

The consequences of gonorrhea during pregnancy include an increased risk of spontaneous abortion, inappropriate rupture of membranes, preterm labor, and fetal mortality. The clinical presentation is essentially the same as that described with genital infection, except that, after the first trimester, PID is less commonly observed because the conceptus obstructs the opening of the uterine cavity. It is unclear whether pregnancy alters the risk for disseminated gonococcal infection.

C. Anorectal Gonorrhea. Anorectal gonorrhea is observed in ~ 40% of women with genital infection who have receptive anal intercourse and in the same percentage of gay men with genital infection. Only a minority of persons with positive rectal cultures are asymptomatic; in those who are symptomatic, complaints and findings include tenesmus, purulent discharge, pruritus, and rectal bleeding.

D. Ocular Infection. Gonococcal conjunctivitis occurs by direct inoculation of gonococci into the eye. In adults, this occurs primarily by self-inoculation in persons with active genital infection. In neonates, infection can occur during delivery or postpartum. In adults and neonates, the conjunctivitis is severe, with copious purulent exudate. Corneal ulceration and even blindness can result, especially in the newborn.

E. Disseminated Gonococcal Infection. Disseminated gonococcal infection results from hematogenous spread of gonococci. It occurs in ~ 3% of infected patients. Arthritis and skin lesions, including pustules and hemorrhagic papules, are the most common manifestations of dissemination ("arthritis-dermatitis syndrome") and are mediated in part by immune complexes, as well as other indirect immunologic mechanisms. The arthritis most commonly affects the knees, ankles, and wrists. Fever and leukocytosis with polymorphonuclear leukocyte (PMN) predominance are also observed. Cultures of blood or synovium are positive in only about half of all patients with disseminated gonococcal infection, but cultures of mucosal sites are positive in ~ 80% of cases.

Diagnosis

The cornerstone of diagnosis is the Gram stain or culture. One is looking for gram-negative diplococci associated with neutrophils. Gram stain of urethral exudate from men has a sensitivity of 90% and specificity of 98% when compared with culture. Staining of endocervical exudates is 50% sensitive and 95% specific in the hands of an experienced microscopist. Stained smears of the throat or rectum are not helpful because there are confounding flora that make specific diagnosis a challenge. Cultures need not be done for men in the setting of a positive Gram stain, but are indicated for samples from women or in any case in which there is a question of drug resistance. To cultivate the organism, a swab specimen is streaked on enriched selective medium, such as modified Thayer-Martin, and incubated in 5% carbon dioxide at 37 °C. If immediate inoculation with optimal growth conditions is not possible, a transport culture system (ie, JEMBEC) can be used.

In systemic disease, blood culture is necessary. An isolator tube system is preferred. *N gonorrhoeae* can be cultured from the blood in ~ 30% of cases of gonococcal arthritis. Skin pustule cultures are also useful in defining systemic disease, especially if antibiotic therapy has already been started, because blood cultures will be of lower yield.

Other diagnostic modalities may be used when laboratory culture is not practical or there are specimen transport problems. Assays based on the polymerase chain reaction or ligase chain reaction offer a rapid diagnosis and may offer better specificity and sensitivity than culture; they are becoming more widely available in the United States. Serologic detection of antibodies to gonococcal pili and OMPs by using immunoblotting, radioimmunoassay, or enzyme-linked immunosorbent assay are available for epidemiologic or research purposes but are not clinically useful because of antigenic heterogeneity, the delay in the development of antibody in the setting of acute infection, and the cost.

Treatment

Many antibiotics are safe and effective for the treatment of *N gonorrhoeae* (Box 52–1). In choosing a regimen, consideration must be given to the site of infection, other concurrent infections, and the possibility of resistance. The treatment of sex partners is also a crucial consideration in treating any patient with *N gonorrhoeae* (see Prevention & Control section below). Ceftriaxone in a single dose is the treatment of choice for uncomplicated gonorrhea at all sites. Ciprofloxacin has the advantages of a single oral dose, less expense than ceftriaxone, and effectiveness in patients who are intolerant of cephalosporins; however, resistance has been observed with ciprofloxacin, and it is not active against *Treponema pallidum.*

Complicated infections or disseminated gonococcal infections, such as arthritis, perihepatitis, or bacteremia resulting in petechial or pustular skin lesions, require a higher dose of antibiotics than uncomplicated gonorrhea infections and a longer duration of therapy. These regimens should be continued for 24–48 h after clinical improvement is noted (ie, they become afebrile, or joint erythema or skin lesions improve) and then switched to an oral regimen for a total of 7 d. Patients with gonococcal meningitis or endocarditis require higher doses and longer duration of therapy. Meningitis is treated with ceftriaxone for 14 d. Endocarditis should be treated for ≥ 4 wk.

Concurrent infection with *C trachomatis* is estimated to occur in 40% of those infected with *N gonorrhoeae.* Therefore doxycycline or azithromycin must be added to the antigonococcal regimen. In pregnant women, for whom doxycycline is contraindicated, an erythromycin base can be used. If erythromycin cannot be tolerated, amoxicillin for 7–10 d is indicated.

Antibiotic resistance has been a major concern, as penicillin resistance has spread and, more recently, fluoroquinolone resistance has been increasingly reported. Beta-lactams remain the drugs of choice in most instances. Antibiotic resistance occurs by one or more mechanisms, including chromosomal mutations leading to decreased penicillin-binding-protein affinity, decreased outer membrane permeability, or beta-lactamase production.

Prevention & Control

The primary measures for prevention of gonorrhea include sexual abstinence and barrier methods with sexual intercourse ("safer sex") (Box 52–2). Once a case of gonorrhea is identified, treatment of sex partners is an essential element of control of the disease. Epidemiologic treatment refers to the treatment of contacts of patients after a history of exposure to the disease, but without confirmation of infection. This is done in situations in which the risk of unnecessary treatment is outweighed by the risk of developing complications of the infection or the probability of transmission to other contacts. The prevention of gonorrhea must also be considered in sexual assault cases, and antigonococcal medications are included in the recommendations for treatment.

NEISSERIA MENINGITIDIS

Essentials of Diagnosis

- Transmission in crowded or closed populations.
- Meningitis most common, but bacteremia, pneumonia, and other syndromes can occur in absence of meningitis.
- Disease often associated with petechial or purpuric rash, which may involve palms and soles.
- Neutrophil-predominant cell profile in CSF, with low-glucose and high-protein concentrations.
- Gram-negative diplococci inside neutrophils on stained smears of CSF and aspirated skin lesions.
- Fastidious organism requires special media and growth conditions.
- Blood and CSF most useful specimens for recovery of organism.
- Improved sensitivity of detection with PCR in CSF, but not widely available.

General Considerations

A. Epidemiology. *N meningitidis* is found only in humans and is a member of the normal oropharyngeal flora in 5–15% of healthy adults and children. In crowded or closed populations such as in boarding schools or military camps, higher carriage rates are observed. Transmission is from person to person by the respiratory route through nasopharyngeal secretions. *N meningitidis* is communicable and spreads within families and communities; there is a 500- to 1200-fold increased risk of developing meningococcal disease among household contacts of an index case in the 30–60 d after exposure, compared with the risk of developing disease among the general population.

Meningococcal disease usually occurs as isolated cases, but sporadic small epidemics occasionally take place. Group A strains in particular tend to cause widespread epidemics in 8- to 12-y cycles, especially in sub-Saharan Africa (Figure 52–1). The case rates in endemic areas of Africa vary widely, but overall the rate is 10–25 cases per 100,000 population per year. In

BOX 52-1

Therapy for *Neisseria gonorrhoeae* Infection

	Adults	Children
First choice: Uncomplicated urethritis, cervicitis, pharyngitis, proctitis, prostatitis, ophthalmia neonatorum, conjunctivitis[1]	• Ceftriaxone, 125 mg IM, single dose **OR** • Cefixime, 400 mg PO in a single dose **OR** • Ciprofloxacin, 500 mg PO in a single dose **PLUS** • Doxycycline,[2] 100 mg PO twice per day × 7 d **OR** • Azithromycin, 1 g PO, single dose	• Ceftriaxone, 25–50 mg/kg IV or IM, single dose (not to exceed 125 mg) **OR** • Cefotaxime, 100 mg/kg IV or IM, single dose (not to exceed 1 g)
Alternatives[3]	• Spectinomycin, 2 g IM, single dose **OR** • Ofloxacin, 400 mg PO, single dose **PLUS** • Doxycycline, 100 mg PO twice per day × 7 d **OR** • Erythromycin base, 500 mg PO four times daily × 7 d **OR** • Amoxicillin, 500 mg PO 3 times daily	• Spectinomycin, 40 mg/kg (not to exceed 2 g) IM, single dose **PLUS** • Erythromycin (base or stearate), 20–40 mg/kg/d in 4 divided doses (not to exceed 2 g/d)
Complicated infections: Disseminated gonococcal infection (dermatitis-arthritis syndrome), meningitis,[4] endocarditis	• Ceftriaxone, 1–2 g IV or IM every 12–24 h for 1–2 d after improvement or 7 d **OR** • Cefotaxime, 1–2 g IV every 8 h for 1–2 d after improvement or 7 d **PLUS** • Doxycycline, 100 mg PO twice daily × 7 d	• Ceftriaxone, 50 mg/kg/d (not to exceed 1 g/d) IV or IM × 7 d **PLUS** • Erythromycin (base or stearate), 20–40 mg/kg/d in 4 divided doses (not to exceed 2 g/d)
Alternatives	• Spectinomycin, 2 g IM every 12 h **OR** • Chloramphenicol, 1 g every 6 h	• Spectinomycin, 40 mg/kg (not to exceed 2 g) IV or IM × 7 d **PLUS** • Erythromycin (base or stearate), 20–40 mg/kg/d in 4 divided doses (not to exceed 2 g/d)

[1] Irrigate eyes immediately and frequently with saline until discharge is eliminated.
[2] Doxycycline or tetracycline is given for possible chlamydial co-infection.
[3] In pregnancy, ceftriaxone and erythromycin should be used; see text.
[4] Longer duration and higher doses are indicated; see text.

BOX 52-2

Prevention and Control of *Neisseria gonorrhoeae* Infection

Prophylactic measures	Avoid sexual exposure: abstinence, barrier methods (ie, condoms).
Chemoprophylaxis (ie, post exposure for sexual assault[1])	• Ceftriaxone, 125 mg IM single dose PLUS • Metronidazole, 2 g orally in a single dose PLUS • Azithromycin, 1 g orally in a single dose OR • Doxycycline, 100 mg orally twice a day for 7 d • Postexposure hepatitis B vaccination (without HBIG)
Control	Case finding by active surveillance. Treat contacts of known cases ("epidemiologic treatment") if the risk of unnecessary therapy is less than the risk of developing complications of the infection or the probability of transmission to other contacts
Isolation Precautions	• None

[1]These antibiotics treat the likely infections in victims of sexual assault (see N Engl J Med 1990; 322:713).

---

the United States, the average annual incidence is 1–2 cases per 100,000 population per year. Most cases are seen in children and young adults (ages 5–19 y).

Microbiologic characterization of *N meningitidis* has been useful in understanding the epidemiology of this disease. The *N meningitidis* polysaccharide capsule provides the basis for a serogroup typing system. The most important serogroups causing invasive disease are A, B, C, W-135, and Y. These different polysaccharide capsular types are associated with characteristic epidemiological patterns. Group A strains are linked to worldwide epidemics, whereas B and C strains are considered endemic, causing sporadic cases and limited outbreaks. Currently ~ 50% of all cases in the United States are caused by serogroup B and another 20% by serogroup C. The remainder are primarily serogroups Y and W-135. The proportions of disease caused by serogroups C and Y have been rising in recent years. Each serogroup has been further subdivided into serotypes. For example, *N meningitidis* group B has 12 serotypes based on unique OMPs. These further subtypings of serogroups have been important both for epidemiologic studies and for vaccine development.

B. Microbiology. See discussion in *N gonorrhoeae* section.

C. Pathogenesis. Adherence, colonization, and invasion are the three essential properties of *N meningitidis* that enable infection in the human host. Before

attachment can occur, secretory immunoglobulin A (IgA) must be inactivated. This is accomplished by secretion of a protease that cleaves IgA_1. *N meningitidis* cells attach selectively to nonciliated pharyngeal mucosal cells, leading to colonization of the nasopharynx and upper respiratory tract. The PilC molecule and the OMPs Opa and Opc (opacity proteins) are important for adherence to the nasopharyngeal epithelial cells. The expression of Opa also mediates host cell invasion. The capsular polysaccharide facilitates invasion into the bloodstream and is antiphagocytic. The Opa and Opc groups of proteins have a high variability in their surface expression; this involves variation in promoter activity and frameshifts, which result in reversible on-off switching at the transcriptional and translational levels.

Host genetic factors, as well as other cofactors such as passive smoke and concurrent infection in the upper respiratory tract, appear to play a role in the development of meningococcal disease. Viral infection may increase the development of nasopharyngeal infection with *N meningitidis,* and thus lead to higher carriage rates in households or groups of exposed individuals. It should be noted however that exposure to pathogenic strains of *N meningitidis* most often leads to a carrier state, but not always to active infection.

The protection provided by the host complement system is demonstrated by the enhanced susceptibility to bacteremic *Neisseria* disease of those patients

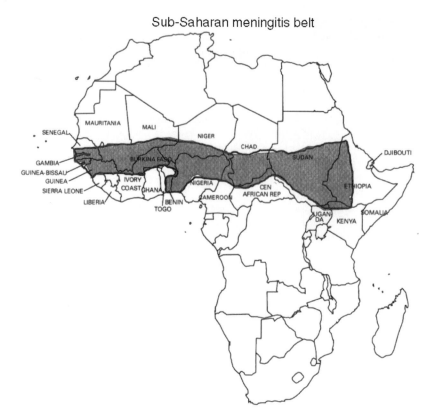

Figure 52–1. Sub-Saharan meningitis belt. Reprinted with permission from Centers for Disease Control. Control and prevention of meningococcal disease and control and prevention of serogroup C meningococcal disease: Evaluation and management of suspected outbreaks: Recommendations of the Advisory Committee on Immunization Practices (ACIP). Morbid Mortal Wkly Rep 1997;46(RR-5):4.

who are complement deficient. The importance of another protective factor, specific IgG antibody to *N meningitidis,* is demonstrated by the increased incidence of serious *N meningitidis* infection in children between the ages of 6 mo and 2 y. This time interval corresponds to the time between loss of maternal antibodies and the development of natural immunity. Infections in outbreak situations, eg, in young adults, generally represent new infection with a virulent strain in individuals without specific antibodies.

Meningococcal endotoxin, primarily LOS, induces meningococcal sepsis. LOS mediates production of cytokines such as tumor necrosis factor-alpha (TNF-alpha), interleukin (IL)-1, IL-6, and interferon-gamma. The expression of these host inflammatory mediators results in increased endothelial permeability and myocardial depression and hypotension. Damage to the vascular endothelium results in petechial or purpuric skin lesions. These lesions reflect a similar process that occurs in multiple organs, leading to shock. Other inflammatory mediators such as prostaglandins, leukotrienes, and platelet-activating factor enhance granulocytic function and intravascular clotting and thrombosis. This in turn leads to disseminated intravascular coagulation, adrenal hemorrhage, decreased vascular resistance, circulatory collapse, and finally death.

Clinical Findings

N meningitidis causes acute bacterial meningitis with or without meningococcemia. Its potential to progress rapidly mandates early recognition and use of empiric antimicrobial treatment. Pharyngitis precedes meningitis in most patients and is followed by fever with chills and malaise. The classic symptoms of meningitis are headache, nausea and vomiting, and stiff neck. A prominent feature is a petechial rash that starts distally on the extremities and progresses to the trunk. It often involves the palms and soles. Skin lesions evolve over hours and may continue to develop for a day or more despite appropriate antibiotic treatment (Figure 52–2). Fulminant meningococcemia (Waterhouse-Friderichsen syndrome) occurs in 5–15% of cases. Fulminant disease is associated with vascular collapse, often presaged by apprehension, restlessness, and mental status changes, all develop-

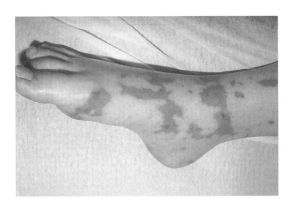

Figure 52–2. Purpuric rash showing subcutaneous ecchymosis and involving the plantar surface of a patient with meningococcemia. (Courtesy of D Scott Smith, Stanford Univ. Hosp., Stanford, CA).

ing within a few hours. Acute meningococcemia can occur in the absence of meningitis and presents as the sepsis syndrome.

High fever is usually observed; absence of fever is a poor prognostic sign. Pneumonia from *N meningitidis* is reported in as many as 15–20% of patients with meningococcemia or meningitis and may occur by itself. Case fatality rates vary according to the prevalence of the disease and socioeconomic conditions. The fatality rate in meningococcal meningitis may be as low as 7% in industrialized countries and as high as 70% for meningococcemia in some developing countries.

Chronic meningococcemia is less common than other bacteremic meningococcal syndromes and presents with fever, headache, rash (90%), and joint pains (66%) that occur intermittently or over a period of days or weeks. The skin lesions occur with the febrile episodes. These lesions are maculopapular (47%) or petecchial (12%) or erythematous and nodular with a pustular center (13%). Without diagnosis and treatment, localized infection such as meningitis, endocarditis, or arthritis develops. Chronic meningococcemia is very responsive to antibiotic therapy.

Diagnosis

The diagnosis of meningococcal infection is made by isolation of the organism or detection of its antigen from blood or cerebrospinal fluid (CSF). If possible, blood, CSF, throat swab, and petecchial lesions should be cultured prior to antibiotic use. Collection of these specimens, however, should never delay treatment. Leukocytosis is often as high as 20,000–30,000 cells/mm^3. Blood cultures are positive in 50% of cases of meningitis before antibiotics and in ~ 5% of cases after antibiotics are given. Gram stains of skin lesions are positive in ~ 70% of cases. This is a useful diagnostic test especially if antibiotics have been given before the culture specimens could be obtained.

The CSF pleocytosis of meningococcal meningitis is typical of most acute bacterial meningitides with a predominance of PMNs. The CSF glucose is low with a normal or high CSF protein. Gram stain of the CSF is positive in ~ 75% of cases. CSF should be inoculated onto chocolate agar as soon as possible (within minutes) because of the fastidious nature of this organism, like *N gonorrhoeae*. A latex agglutination test is available and may be indicated for diagnosis in patients treated with antibiotics. This test is expensive and may not improve diagnostic specificity compared with a Gram stain performed by an experienced microscopist. Positive throat and nasopharyngeal cultures in the setting of meningitis should be interpreted with caution, because there are many coincidental meningococcal carriers.

Differential Diagnosis

The differential diagnosis is broad, given the clinical presentation of infections caused by *N meningitidis*. The primary considerations in the setting of meningitis with a rash should include the rickettsial diseases such as Rocky Mountain spotted fever, epidemic typhus, and Brill-Zinsser disease. Toxic shock syndrome caused by *Staphylococcus aureus* may mimic meningococcemia, and therefore additional appropriate antimicrobial coverage is required. Other diseases to consider include viral exanthems such as infection with echovirus type 9, typhoid fever, and vasculitis syndromes such as polyarteritis nodosa, Churg-Strauss syndrome, and Henoch-Schonlein purpura.

Treatment

Treatment should be initiated as soon as the diagnosis is considered (Box 52–3). Intravenous penicillin G or ceftriaxone is the standard of therapy. The duration of therapy is dependent on the clinical response, but 7 d is considered adequate for both meningitis and chronic meningococcemia.

The clinical importance of isolates found to have altered penicillin-binding proteins with intermediate resistance to penicillin (MIC of 0.1–1.0 μg/ml) is unclear, as patients with these strains respond well to penicillin. For patients who do not respond adequately to therapy, the bacterial isolate should be tested for antibiotic resistance, and the therapy changed to ceftriaxone or cefotaxime if the isolate is resistant to penicillin.

N meningitidis has traditionally been exquisitely sensitive to penicillin, but recent reports from Spain, England, South Africa, Argentina, Canada, and the United States indicate an increasing percentage of penicillin-resistant strains. A third-generation cephalosporin such as ceftriaxone should be used if there is resistance in the area or if the microbiologic diagnosis might include *Haemophilus influenzae* or *Streptococcus pneumoniae*.

BOX 52-3

Therapy for *Neisseria meningitidis* Infection

	Adults	Children
First Choice	• Penicillin G, 24 million U IV per 24 h in divided doses every 2–4 h	• Penicillin G, 0.25 million U/kg/d IV (every 2–4 h for 4–10 d)
Alternatives	• Ceftriaxone, 2 g IV every 12 h OR • Chloramphenicol, 50–100 mg/kg/d PO or IV every 6 h	• Ceftriaxone, 80–100 mg/kg/d IV (every 12 h for 4–10 d) OR • Chloramphenicol, 50–100 mg/kg/d PO or IV (every 6 h)

Chloramphenicol is effective for meningococcal infection, although there are reports of resistance in parts of sub-Saharan Africa. Although it is usually considered bacteriostatic, chloramphenicol is bactericidal against the meningococcus and achieves high CSF levels. It remains an excellent alternative in beta-lactam–allergic patients and in situations in which multiple dosing of parenteral drug is not feasible. Data to support the use of corticosteroids as adjunctive therapy in meningococcal meningitis are limited.

BOX 52-4

Prevention and Control of *Neisseria meningitidis* Infection

Prophylactic Measures	• Quadrivalent vaccine[1] (A, C, Y, W–135) (Menomune) 0.5 ml SC × 1 (may need to be repeated if < 4 y old)
Control with chemoprophylaxis	• Rifampin, 10 mg/kg (≤ 600 mg) PO every 12 h × 4 doses • Ciprofloxacin, 500 or 750 mg PO per single dose • Ceftriaxone, 250 mg IM per single dose (adults); 125 mg IM per single dose (children < 12 y)
Isolation Precautions	• Should remain in respiratory isolation until appropriate antibiotic therapy has been given for 24 h

[1]This vaccine is suggested for high-risk groups (see text).

Prevention & Control

Antimicrobial chemoprophylaxis should be given to close contacts of patients with meningococcal disease, because this is a primary means of prevention of disease (Box 52–4). Close contacts are defined as household members, day care center contacts, and anyone directly exposed to the patient's oral secretions. Antimicrobial prophylaxis should be administered as soon as possible (ideally within 24 h) after case identification, because the secondary attack rate is highest within the first few days of onset of disease in the primary patient. Chemoprophylaxis given > 14 d after the onset of illness in the primary (index) case is of limited or no value. Nasal and oropharyngeal cultures are of no value in determining the need for chemoprophylaxis.

The three antibiotics used for chemoprophylaxis against meningococcal disease are rifampin, ciprofloxacin, and ceftriaxone. Rifampin is the best studied and may be the most efficacious, but it is not the most convenient. It requires multiple dosing, is not recommended in pregnancy, and may cause gastrointestinal side effects. Ciprofloxacin is given as a single dose and is generally well tolerated, but it is not recommended in pregnancy or for children < 18 y of age. Ceftriaxone is also given as a one-time dose but requires intramuscular injection.

A quadrivalent vaccine for meningococcal serogroups A, C, Y, and W-135 is available in the United States. Efficacy varies by age and serogroup. Protection against disease caused by serogroups A and C is 85–100% in older children and adults. The vaccine polysaccharides elicit bactericidal antibody that is serogroup specific. The serogroup B polysaccharide is poorly immunogenic in humans, and thus no useful vaccine against serogroup B is currently available; however, with the recent determination of the complete serogroup B meningococcus genome sequence, a set of immunogenic outer surface proteins from this organism has been revealed. A candidate vaccine has been created from some of these proteins. Serogroup B is the most common cause of meningococcal disease in Europe, North America, and several countries in Latin America.

Vaccine protection decreases over time and more rapidly in young children. In children older than 4 y, one study documented an efficacy of 67% at 3 y after vaccination. The current vaccine is useful in controlling serogroup C meningococcal outbreaks. It is also recommended in the following high-risk groups: (1) complement-deficient hosts (C3, C5–C9), (2) asplenic individuals, (3) travelers to endemic areas, (4) research or laboratory personnel, and (5) military recruits.

REFERENCES

Neisseria gonorrhoeae

Apicella MA, Detterer M, Lee FKN: The pathogenesis of gonococcal urethritis in men: confocal and immuno-electron microscopic analysis of urethral exudates from men infected with *Neisseria gonorrhoeae*. J Infect Dis 1996;173:636.

Centers for Disease Control and Prevention: 1998 Guidelines for treatment of sexually transmitted diseases. Morbid Mortal Wkly Rep 1998;47(RR-1):1 (http://aepo-xdv-www.epo.cdc.gov/wonder/prevguid/p0000480/entire.htm).

Deitsch KW, Moxon ER, Wellems TE: Shared themes of antigenic variation and virulence in bacterial, protozoal, and fungal infections. Microbiol Mol Biol Rev 1997;61:281.

Lind I: Antimicrobial resistance in *Neisseria gonorrhoeae*. Clin Infect Dis 1997;24 (Suppl 1):S93.

Neisseria meningitidis

Benoit FL: Chronic meningococcemia. Am J Med 1963; 35:103.

Kristiansen BE, Knapskog AB: Secondary prevention of meningococcal disease. Br Med J 1996;312:591.

Moore PS, Broome CV: Cerebrospinal meningitis epidemics. Sci Am 1994;271:38.

Pizza M et al: Identification of vaccine candidates against serogroup B meningococcus by whole-genome sequencing. Science 2000;287:1816.

Quagliarello VJ, Scheld WM: Treatment of bacterial meningitis. N Engl J Med 1997;336(10):708.

Riedo FX, Plikaytis BD, Broome CV: Epidemiology and prevention of meningococcal disease. Pediatr Infect Dis J 1995;14:643.

Salzman MB, Rubin LG. Meningococcemia. Inf Dis Clin N Am 1996;10(4):709.

53

Enteritis Caused by *Escherichia coli* & *Shigella* & *Salmonella* Species

Gary W. Procop, MD, & Franklin Cockerill III, MD

Essentials of Diagnosis

- Enteritis: diarrhea, which may be watery, bloody, or dysenteric; abdominal pain; and fever and/or;
- Systemic disease: highly variable presentations that may include enteric fever, hemolytic uremic syndrome, or bacteremia with infectious foci in distant sites.
- History of exposure, possibly in known endemic areas or associated with an outbreak, through the ingestion of unclean water, unpasteurized juice or milk, undercooked meats, or other possibly contaminated food.
- Microbiologic isolation and identification of enteric pathogens or molecular detection.

General Considerations

The *Enterobacteriaceae* are a diverse family of bacteria that, in nature, exist in soil, on plant material, and in the intestines of humans and other animals. Another ecological niche in which these organisms thrive is the hospital. Many of these organisms cause a wide variety of extraintestinal diseases that are often nosocomial and commonly present in debilitated or immunocompromised hosts. These manifestations have been examined previously in this volume and include urinary tract infections (chapter 16), skin and soft tissue infections (chapter 13), lower respiratory infections and pneumonia (chapter 10), and infective endocarditis and sepsis syndrome (chapters 11 and 17). The genera most frequently associated with extraintestinal disease are *Escherichia, Enterobacter, Klebsiella, Proteus, Citrobacter,* and *Serratia.*

Some members of the *Enterobacteriaceae,* however, cause primarily enteric disease or enteric-associated systemic disease (Box 53–1). These are *Shigella* and *Salmonella* species and particular strains of *E coli* and *Yersinia enterocolitica.* This chapter is devoted to enteritis and enteric-associated systemic disease caused by diarrheagenic strains of *E coli* and of *Shigella* and *Salmonella* species. Enteritis and associated mesenteric lymphadenitis caused by *Y enterocolitica* are covered separately (see chapter 60).

The family *Enterobacteriaceae* consists of at least 27 definitive genera and numerous enteric groups. The final classification of the enteric groups has yet

to be resolved. Although there is diversity within this group, members have several common, characteristic features. All *Enterobacteriaceae* are gram-negative, facultative anaerobic bacilli that have the ability to reduce nitrate to nitrite. They produce catalase, ferment D-glucose with or without gas production, and do not produce oxidase. This latter characteristic is useful in differentiating this group of organisms from other nosocomial gram-negative pathogens, such as *Pseudomonas aeruginosa,* which is oxidase positive.

Traditionally, phenotypic characterization has been the method of choice for differentiating the members of the *Enterobacteriaceae,* but, with increasing frequency, genotypic methods are being used to detect particular genera and pathogenic varieties. Phenotypic methods, however, remain the standard for routine identification of these organisms in the clinical microbiology laboratory. The characteristics that are most useful for identification include colony morphology (particularly distinctive for some *Proteus* strains), indole production from tryptophan, reactions of the methyl red and Voges-Proskauer tests, motility, the ability to produce hydrogen sulfide, and the ability to use various organic substances. Several pathogenic *Enterobacteriaceae,* particularly many of the diarrheagenic *E coli,* fail to demonstrate unique phenotypic characteristics and continue to pose a challenge for microbiologists.

ESCHERICHIA COLI

Essentials of Diagnosis

- Enteritis caused by *E coli* may be watery (any *E coli* subtype), mucoid [enteroaggregative *E coli* (EAggEC)], hemorrhagic [enterohemorrhagic *E coli* (EHEC)], or dysenteric [enteroinvasive *E coli* (EIEC)] and is associated with fever and abdominal pain.
- Hemolytic uremic syndrome, caused by EHEC,

BOX 53-1

Enterobacteriaceae Syndromes

	Children	Adults
More Common	• Enterocolitis	• Enterocolitis
Less Common	• Hemolytic uremic syndrome [with EHEC (more common in children than adults)] • Enteric fever (with *Salmonella*) • Dysentery (with *Shigella*)	• Hemolytic uremic syndrome (with EHEC) • Enteric fever (with *Salmonella*) • Dysentery (with *Shigella*)

consists of hemolytic anemia, uremia, and systemic symptomatology.

- Risks for *E coli*-induced enteritis include ingestion of fecally contaminated food (EHEC, EIEC) or water [enterotoxigenic *E coli* (ETEC), EIEC, EAggEC, enteropathogenic *E coli* (EPEC), and diffusely adherent *E coli* (DAEC)], especially in endemic areas, or close contact with infected individuals (EIEC, EHEC).
- *E coli*-induced enteritis is also indicated by microbiologic isolation and identification of enteric pathogens or molecular evidence of infection in the appropriate clinical setting.

General Considerations

A. Epidemiology. *E coli* is the most common member of the *Enterobacteriaceae* to be isolated in the clinical microbiology laboratory. Most *E coli* isolates are either opportunistic or nosocomial pathogens (ie, causes of urinary tract or wound infections) or normal flora (ie, enteric contaminants of urine cultures or normal stool flora in stool cultures). There are, however, at least six diarrheagenic varieties of *E coli*. Some of these produce enteritis alone, whereas others produce enteritis-associated systemic disease that may be fatal. The six types of diarrheagenic *E coli* are the ETEC, EHEC, EIEC, and three distinct subtypes of enteroadherent *E coli*—the EPEC, EAggEC, and DAEC.

1. ETEC. The ETEC are spread by the fecal-oral route and are most common in developing countries that lack appropriate sanitation and drinking-water treatment facilities. Disease may occur at any time of the year, but incidence peaks in the warm, wet seasons that favor environmental bacterial replication. The most important mode of transmission is contaminated, improperly treated drinking water. Fruits and vegetables that are washed with contaminated water and not cooked before they are eaten also serve as vehicles of transmission. Person-to-person spread is uncommon.

In a normal host, exposure to ETEC leads to the development of mucosal immunity, presumably secondary to secretory immunoglobulin A (IgA) antibodies directed toward the fimbriae-associated colonization factor antigens (CFAs). In endemic areas, natural resistance is usually well developed in adults. These individuals serve as carriers and shed large numbers of toxigenic *E coli* into the environment. Disease occurs in those lacking mucosal immunity, principally neonates and travelers from nonendemic areas.

2. EHEC. The EHEC are commensals and pathogens of live stock. Food, water, or unpasteurized beverages that are contaminated with animal feces are the principal modes of spread, but person-to-person transmission is also possible. EHEC commonly colonize cattle. Beef frequently becomes contaminated with bovine feces during the slaughter process. Ground beef that is contaminated is especially hazardous, because grinding distributes the bacteria through the meat. When hamburgers are made from contaminated beef and not cooked thoroughly, the bacteria are able to survive. The EHEC are more acid tolerant than many other bacterial enteric pathogens, with the possible exception of *Shigella* species, and relatively small inocula can survive gastric passage in humans and cause disease. Good cooking practices and food preparation hygiene can significantly reduce the likelihood of EHEC infections (see "Prevention" section).

3. EIEC. The EIEC are spread by the fecal/oral route. Contaminated food and water are the usual vehicles of spread and food-borne outbreaks have occurred. Person-to-person transmission is possible but is uncommon. Compared with *Shigella* species, a higher infective dose of EIEC is required to cause disease. Infections by EIEC are thought to be rare, but this is unclear, because EIEC may be mistaken for *Shigella* species.

4. Enteroadherent *E coli*. Contaminated food, water, and fomites serve as vehicles for the fecal/oral transmission of the enteroadherent *E coli*. Of the three types of enteroadherent *E coli*, the EPEC primarily cause disease in neonates and young children, with most cases occurring in children < 2 years old and particularly in those < 6 months old. Unlike ETEC, the EPEC are rarely a cause of traveler's diarrhea. Disease, however, may occur in adults if sufficiently high inocula are ingested. This organism has caused outbreaks in pediatric wards, nurseries, and day care centers and in adults that have consumed contaminated food from a buffet. The prevalence of disease in the United States is thought to be much lower than earlier in this century, but is still probably underestimated. In developing countries, the EPEC are highly prevalent and are an important cause of childhood diarrheal disease and dehydration-associated deaths. In some areas, the incidence of EPEC-associated enteritis surpasses the incidence of rotavirus infection and may represent 30%–40% of childhood diarrheal diseases.

The EAggEC are also a cause of diarrheal disease in both developing and developed countries and have caused serious outbreaks in nurseries. Infants are most commonly affected, and growth retardation may be caused by persistent diarrhea. In the United States, EAggEC have been shown to cause persistent diarrhea in patients infected by the human immunodeficiency virus (HIV).

Although not extensively studied, the DAEC seem to infect children > 1 year of age, rather than neonates.

B. Microbiology. All *E coli* isolates, regardless of subtype, demonstrate a typical morphology on sheep's blood agar and chocolate agar. Colonies are typically gray and flat to slightly raised. On sheep's blood agar, colonies produce a distinctive smell from the metabolism of tryptophan to indole and may be associated with β-hemolysis. Most *E coli* strains, with the notable exception of the EIEC, rapidly ferment lactose and produce typical colonies on Mac-Conkey and eosin methylene blue agars. Like other members of the *Enterobacteriaceae,* these organisms do not produce oxidase. Both the production of indole from tryptophan and the absence of oxidase activity may be detected in the laboratory through the use of rapid "spot" tests.

Many of the diarrheagenic *E coli,* namely the ETEC, EPEC, EAggEC, DAEC, and non-O157:H7 EHEC, demonstrate colony morphology and biochemical reactions in standard tests (biophysical profile) that are identical to normal-flora *E coli.* For this reason, the identification of these organisms is a problem for clinical microbiologists. If these diarrheagenic varieties are not suspected clinically and additional testing is not performed, they will be erroneously dismissed as normal flora. Fortunately, in most instances, enteritis caused by these agents is self-limited and resolves without antimicrobial therapy. The most commonly encountered EHEC strain, *E coli* O157:H7, and the EIEC have distinctive features that may be used to screen for these organisms.

1. ETEC. ETEC strains have been associated with a wide variety of somatic antigens, a few flagellar antigens, and certain CFAs. In the appropriate clinical setting and in the absence of other enteric pathogens, the presence of *E coli* with a particular somatic:flagellar (O:H) antigen profile in the stool is supportive evidence of an ETEC infection. However, the mere presence of a particular O:H profile is not proof that a strain is toxigenic, because these antigens may also be found on nontoxigenic *E coli.* Definitive proof that a strain is toxigenic requires the demonstration of either enterotoxins or the genes that encode them.

Animal models and cell culture assays have been used to detect the heat-labile (LT) and heat-stable (ST) enterotoxins, but those methods have largely been replaced by immunoassays. Commercial immunoassay kits are now available for both the LT and ST toxins. Molecular assays, designed for the detection of the genes that encode for these toxins, are another method of detection. Signal amplification assays with nucleic acid probes have been used directly on stool and on colony blots of suspect isolates. Polymerase chain reaction (PCR)-based assays have also been used to detect these genes. If PCR is attempted directly on stool specimens, a preamplification treatment may be necessary to remove PCR inhibitors that are inherently present in stool. Better results may be obtained if PCR is performed on isolated colonies, rather than stool.

2. EHEC. The most common EHEC, *E coli* O157:H7, has a few distinguishing characteristics that make screening for this organism possible. *Escherichia coli* O157:H7, unlike most *E coli,* does not rapidly ferment sorbitol and fails to produce β-glucuronidase. Microbiologic assays that detect these traits have been developed to detect *E coli* O157:H7. A modified MacConkey plate, which contains sorbitol rather than lactose (SMAC), is the screening method most commonly used. Nonfermenting colonies on a SMAC plate may be further tested for their ability to produce β-glucuronidase. β-Glucuronidase is an enzyme that cleaves 4-methylumbelliferyl-β-glucuronide and yields a UV light (366 nm)-excitable end product. Nonfermenting colonies on a SMAC plate and/or isolates that fail to produce β-glucuronidase are then tested for the presence of the O157 antigen, usually by agglutination with type-specific antiserum. Isolates that are O157-positive are then examined for the H7 flagellar antigen by motility inhibition. Specific H7 antiserum, present in a semisolid medium, will inhibit the motility of organisms with the H7 flagellar antigen, whereas the motility of non-H7 strains is unaffected.

In South America and Australia, the non-O157:H7 EHEC serotypes cause more hemorrhagic colitis (HC) and hemolytic-uremic syndrome (HUS) than the O157:H7 serotype. These serotypes are more difficult to detect, because they are able to ferment sorbitol and are therefore phenotypically similar to normal-flora *E coli* on the SMAC screening agar. The identification of these strains is more complicated and relies on methods to detect the shigalike toxin or verotoxin (VT), the *VT* gene, or other markers of pathogenicity.

Cultured Vero or HeLa cells may be used to detect the presence of VT, but this test is costly and labor intensive, and it has largely been replaced by immunoassays. A wide variety of molecular assays have been developed for the detection of EHEC. These methods include PCR-based assays and nucleic acid probes for the detection of the *VT* gene or other markers of pathogenicity, such as the pO157 plasmid and the *eae* gene encoding intimin, which is necessary for attachment to enterocytes.

Although these detection methods are not currently used in most clinical microbiology laboratories, they may be more widely used in the future. Many of these methods offer greater sensitivity than the SMAC agar, and they detect non-O157:H7 serotypes. However, problems with these technologies do exist. Substances present in stool may inhibit PCR. Some non-nucleic acid amplification methods, such as the measurement of free fecal cytotoxin or culture enhancement by using O157 immunomagnetic beads, may have sensitivities that are superior to PCR-based assays. Determining the significance of the detection of either VT or the *VT* gene is another problem. The presence of VT or the *VT* gene is supportive evidence, but not definitive proof, that the isolate is the cause of disease. There are > 200 serotypes of *E coli* that can express VT and only a fraction of these have been associated with HC. The serotypes O26:H11, O111:H-, O103:H2, and O113:H21 are other EHEC that have been associated with HC and/or HUS outbreaks. Therefore, when VT or the *VT* gene is detected in stool or stool isolates, the detection of other virulence factors or particular O:H serotypes would be necessary to further characterize the isolate.

The principal disadvantage of most molecular detection technologies is cost. In many instances, an expensive screening test is not cost effective, especially when the pathogen is infrequently encountered and less expensive screening methods exist. These technologies, however, are attractive in outbreak situations or when the incidence of disease is high.

3. EIEC. *E coli* and *Shigella* species are so closely related that they are currently classified in the same biogroup. The EIEC have several phenotypic characteristics that are more typical of *Shigella* spp. than *E coli*. Like *Shigella* spp. and unlike most *E coli*, the EIEC are nonmotile, do not ferment lactose or ferment it only slowly, and do not decarboxylate lysine. However, complete characterization of EIEC strains discloses the presence of some biochemical features that are typical of the genus *Escherichia*. Nevertheless, the phenotypic differentiation of EIEC from a *Shigella* species is difficult, and many isolates may be misidentified as *Shigella* species. The isolation of an enteritis-associated bacterium that has a mixture of *Shigella*-like and *Escherichia*-like biochemical characteristics is a clue to the presence of this organism. The subsequent detection of EIEC-associated O antigen groups/O:H subtypes is useful to confirm that the organism is an EIEC.

The stool from patients with EIEC enteritis is indistinguishable from the stool of patients with shigellosis and may be watery or dysenteric. *Shigella* antigen testing is of no use in differentiating these bacteria, because EIEC may cross-react with *Shigella* antiserum. In a similar manner, tests of invasiveness, in cell culture or animal model (Sereny test), are positive with both EIEC and *Shigella* spp. Molecular methods, such as enzyme-linked immunosorbent assays, nucleic acid probes, or PCR, have been used for the detection of *Shigella*/EIEC species, but they are less useful for differentiation.

4. Enteroadherent *E coli*. The biophysical profiles of the enteroadherent *E coli* subtypes are indistinguishable from normal-flora *E coli* in routine bacteriologic studies. These varieties, which do represent distinct pathogenic subtypes, adhere differently from one another to HEp-2 cells in cell culture. The EPEC adhere to the HEp-2 monolayer in a localized pattern, the EAggEC produce three-dimensional aggregates, and the DAEC adhere diffusely. Although these adherence patterns are reliably produced, the HEp-2 assay requires cell culture capability and interpretation experience.

The EPEC can also be identified by the production of an attaching and effacing lesion (A/E) and absence of verotoxin (VT) (EHEC produce the A/E lesion, but also produce VT). If the phenotype is used for identification, it is important to demonstrate the absence of VT, because EHEC also produces an A/E lesion. Like the other diarrheagenic *E coli*, the EPEC have been associated with particular somatic antigens. Many of the EPEC possess specific O:H profiles that may be used for organism identification. Antiserum directed against some of these O antigens is commercially available and may be used to screen suspect colonies. A positive screening test then requires confirmation, which may include titration, complete O:H typing, or molecular analysis (see below).

Both direct DNA probes and PCR-based assays may be used for the detection of genes that encode pathogenic factors of the enteroadherent *E coli*. The presence of the *eae* gene, which is associated with the A/E phenotype, and the EAF plasmid, which contains the *bfp* gene cluster, are important for pathogenesis of EPEC; detection of these genes and the absence of the *VT* gene are important for molecular identification of the EPEC. Molecular detection of EAggEC may be accomplished by identifying a 65-MDa plasmid by either DNA probe or PCR technology. The molecular detection of the DAEC has been accomplished through the detection of a particular fimbria (F1845)-associated gene, but false positive reactions may occur.

All of the ancillary tests, both phenotypic and genotypic, used to identify the enteroadherent *E coli* subtypes are impractical and cost prohibitive for most clinical microbiology laboratories. These tests are most efficiently and cost-effectively performed by reference or public health laboratories that have expertise in identifying these organisms. In most instances, however, the complete identification of the enteroadherent *E coli* subtype is unwarranted, because most patients have a self-limited course with appropriate supportive therapy. If diarrhea from an infectious etiology becomes persistent, antimicrobial therapy is warranted and should be based on the organism's particular antimicrobial susceptibility profile.

C. Pathogenesis. Regardless of the diarrheagenic *E coli* subtype, successful gastric transit is a prerequisite to disease. Generally, the larger the inoculating dose, the greater the likelihood that viable bacteria will survive gastric passage. Foodstuffs contaminated with bacteria buffer gastric acid and thereby facilitate gastric passage. Individuals with achlorhydria or hypochlorhydria are at an increased risk for bacterial enteritis, because the diminished gastric acidity decreases bacterial killing. The bacteria that survive gastric passage enter the small intestine and colonize the epithelium of the small intestine, colon, or both, depending on the infecting diarrheagenic *E coli* subtype.

1. ETEC. The ETEC produce LT and/or ST toxins. The plasmid-encoded LT enterotoxin of the ETEC is highly homologous to a toxin of *Vibrio cholerae* and has the same mechanism of action. This toxin consists of two subunits, B and A. The B subunit, which binds to gangliosides on the surface of the enterocytes, facilitates entry of the enzymatic A subunit into the cytosol. The A subunit ribosylates the adenylate cyclase regulatory G protein, Gs, which results in a massive increase in cytosolic cyclic AMP (cAMP). This, in turn, results in alteration of the chloride ion channels and causes osmotic diarrhea.

One of the *E coli* ST toxins, ST_a, results in osmotic diarrhea, similar to the LT toxin, but through activation of guanylate cyclase and increased cytologic cyclic GMP (cGMP) levels. The other ST toxin, ST_b, does not cause alterations in cAMP or cGMP levels, but increases intracellular calcium, promotes the secretion of bicarbonate, and stimulates serotonin and prostaglandin E_2 release. In addition, unlike the other toxins, ST_b damages enterocytes and causes epithelial cell loss and partial villous atrophy. These changes also contribute to diminished absorption and osmotic diarrhea.

2. EHEC. The EHEC represent a variety of organisms possessing a set of virulence factors that cause HC and sometimes HUS. In the United States and Canada, the most common EHEC is *E coli* O157:H7. In some parts of the world, EHEC O:H serotypes other than O157:H7 are more commonly associated with HC/HUS.

The EHEC are a subset of *E coli* that produce disease through the combination of a variety of virulence factors. The most important virulence factor is a lysogenic bacteriophage-encoded toxin that is typical of *Shigella dysenteriae* type 1. This shiga toxin is also known as a VT because of its toxicity to Vero cells. VT binds to G3b, a glycolipid receptor. After binding, a portion of the VT enters the cell and disrupts protein synthesis by enzymatically altering the 28S ribosomal subunit. The high concentration of G3b on intestinal villous tip cells and renal endothelial cells may partially explain the damage to the intestine and kidneys in HC and HUS, respectively.

Although important, the presence of VT alone is probably insufficient for the production of disease, because there are VT-producing *E coli*, which do not produce HC/HUS. Another virulence factor of the EHEC is a chromosomal 35-kilobase locus of enterocyte effacement (LEE), as also found in the EPEC. This locus contains the *eae* gene, which codes for an outer membrane protein, an intimin, that mediates adherence between the EHEC and the enterocyte. This locus also confers the A/E phenotype that is typical of EHEC and EPEC. Finally, plasmid-encoded hemolysins are also probably virulence factors.

3. EIEC. The EIEC that reach the small intestine adhere to the cell surface of mucosal enterocytes. The watery-diarrhea phase, which begins next, may be secondary to the elaboration of an enterotoxin. This enterotoxin may be encoded for by the plasmid-based gene *sen*. The adherent bacteria then penetrate into the cell. Cell entry is facilitated by both chromosomal and plasmid-encoded invasive factors. Within the cell, the bacterium moves through the cytoplasm by alterations in cellular actin. The EIEC then infects adjacent enterocytes. Eventually, cell death and mucosal sloughing occur, which evoke the intense inflammatory response and the dysenteric phase of the disease.

4. Enteroadherent *E coli*. The enteroadherent *E coli* subtypes, like all other diarrheagenic *E coli*, initiate pathogenesis by colonization of the intestinal mucosa. An intimate attachment occurs between bacterium and enterocyte that is distinctly different from the mucosal colonization seen with the ETEC. The enteroadherent *E coli* cause diarrhea without the production of better described virulence factors such as LT and ST of the ETEC or VT of the EHEC. However, some strains have been shown to produce an enterotoxin. Microbial colonization appears limited to the mucosal surface, and deep-tissue invasion is not seen, but a chromosomally encoded, cell entry gene product has been identified in some strains. Although some of the pathogenic mechanisms of these organisms have been described, to a large extent they have yet to be elucidated.

The EPEC, like the EHEC, contain a chromosomal LEE gene cluster. This locus includes the *eae* gene, which encodes for an intimin outer membrane protein (OMP). This OMP mediates adherence between the bacterium and the enterocyte. The LEE locus also contains the genes responsible for the attaching and effacing lesion (A/E lesion). After attaching, the bacterium causes changes that result in the effacement of the microvilli of the cell membrane, which can only be fully appreciated when viewed by electron microscopy. However, a portion of the A/E lesion, the aggregated intracytoplasmic, filamentous actin, may be detected in cell culture or intestinal biopsy by using immunohistochemical stains. Some strains may produce an enterotoxin and may contain a cell entry gene product. The precise relationship, however, between these products and the production of disease remains to be determined.

The EAggEC adhere to enterocytes via a fimbria designated aggregative adherence fimbria I or AAF/I, a 38-kDa OMP. Another fimbria (AAF/II) has also been implicated in cytoadherence. It is currently thought that, after colonization, the EAggEC promote enhanced mucus secretion. This mucus forms a protective biofilm, which contains the EAggEC and may diminish nutrient absorption. Finally, the production of enterotoxin may cause enterocyte damage and diarrhea.

Enterocyte surface adherence by the DAEC probably also occurs through the fimbriae (F1845) and/or outer membrane proteins. The precise mechanism of disease, however, remains to be determined.

CLINICAL SYNDROMES

The diarrhea produced by these organisms is variable and may be watery, mucoid, dysenteric, or bloody, and it may be associated with serious and even fatal systemic sequelae. The presentation and course of disease are largely dependent on the infecting *E coli* subtype, as well as the age and nutritional status of the patient. Infants and children, especially if malnourished, are particularly susceptible to dehydration and may succumb rapidly. The mechanism of disease production also varies with the *E coli* subtype. The enteritis caused by these organisms results from toxin production, enterocyte invasion, intimate bacterial/enterocyte adherence, or a combination of these mechanisms.

1. ETEC

Clinical Findings

Patients with ETEC enteritis usually have an abrupt onset of watery diarrhea that does not contain blood, pus, or mucus (ie, is nondysenteric). The diarrhea is usually mild to moderate in severity, but some patients may have severe fluid loss, like that seen in patients with cholera. A low-grade fever, nausea, and abdominal pain may also be present. Dehydration may become severe and life threatening in neonates and children, necessitating aggressive fluid and electrolyte replacement. A self-limited course, with resolution in 2–5 days, is most common in adult travelers who acquire the disease.

2. EHEC

Clinical Findings

Disease caused by the EHEC usually follows the ingestion of contaminated food or beverage. The incubation phase averages 3–4 days, with a range from 1 to 8 days. Individuals remain asymptomatic during the incubation phase. Early in the course of disease, patients develop watery diarrhea that is usually not bloody. Accompanying symptoms may include nausea and vomiting, abdominal cramping, and a low-grade fever. The diarrhea may then become noticeably bloody within a few days. It is interesting that fecal leukocytes are characteristically few and are detected in only ~ 50% of patient's stools. In most patients, the disease is self-limited. However, ≤ 10% of children and a lesser number of adults may develop HUS.

HUS is a severe systemic disease with a significant mortality. It consists of the triad of microangiopathic hemolytic anemia, renal failure, and a thrombocytopenia that may be part of a consumptive coagulopathy. The kidneys are particularly susceptible to damage (see below). In general, the kidneys may have a "flea-bitten" appearance secondary to punctate cortical hemorrhages that result from multifocal occlusion of afferent arterioles. Biopsies demonstrate microvascular deposition of immunoglobulins, complement components, and fibrin by immunofluorescence. Arteriolar and intimal hyperplasia and subintimal fibrin deposits may be seen in histologic sections. Additional findings may include microinfarcts, acute tubular necrosis, and interstitial edema. Renal failure commonly develops, with resultant oliguria, azotemia, and hematuria. Patients who survive HUS suffer morbidity caused by central nervous system and renal sequelae.

3. EIEC

Clinical Findings

Volunteer studies and occasional, well-documented outbreaks have helped to establish the EIEC as a cause of enteritis. Patients infected by EIEC have moderate-to-severe diarrhea that begins watery, but may become dysenteric with sheets of leukocytes, blood, and mucus. The watery diarrhea is similar to that produced by ETEC infection, and the dysentery is indistinguishable from that produced by *Shigella* species infection. Fever and abdominal cramping are also frequently present.

4. ENTEROADHERENT *E COLI*

Clinical Findings

The presentation and course of disease caused by the enteroadherent *E coli* (EPEC, EAggEC, and DAEC) are variable and depend to some degree on the infecting *E coli* subtype. The EPEC primarily cause acute, profuse, watery diarrhea, which rarely may become persistent. Stools are typically not bloody, mucoid, or dysenteric. Low-grade fever with nausea and vomiting may be present. Microscopic examination of the stool may disclose rare fecal leukocytes.

The EAggEC produce an acute, secretory diarrhea that is usually watery to mucoid and may also become prolonged. In some instances, gross blood may be present. A low-grade fever is common, but vomiting is infrequent.

The DAEC seem to produce a watery diarrhea, usually without blood or fecal leukocytes, but too few studies have been performed to adequately characterize this disease.

Differential Diagnosis

The differential diagnosis of diarrheal diseases is extensive and includes infectious etiologies, inflammatory-bowel disease, irritable-bowel syndrome, postsurgical dumping syndromes, and even some neoplasms, such as hypersecretory villous adenomas or vasointestinal peptide-producing neuroendocrine tumors. This extensive differential is successfully narrowed through the examination of the patient (history and physical exam), laboratory studies, and often endoscopy with biopsy

The physical examination of the patient, as well as exposure/travel history, past medical history, and the duration and presentation of current disease, yields clues to the cause of the diarrhea.

Laboratory tests, radiologic studies, and special procedures, such as endoscopy with biopsy are useful in delineating the cause of disease. A colonoscopy with biopsy is often necessary to determine the cause of persistent diarrhea, particularly when microbiologic studies are negative. Inflammatory bowel disease, ischemic colitis, lymphocytic/collagenous colitis, and neoplasia are often suspected clinically and confirmed with histopathologic studies.

The stool of patients with fever and new-onset diarrhea should be cultured for common bacterial enteric pathogens. Fecal leukocyte testing is not useful, because fecal leukocytes may be present in the stool of patients who have enteritis caused by a wide variety of pathogens, as well as in the stool of patients who have noninfectious enteritis. Clinical microbiologists use selective and differential agar media to screen the stool for *Salmonella, Shigella,* and *Campylobacter* species and for *E coli* O157:H7. In most laboratories, cost-effective screening for *E coli* O157:H7 is performed only when patients have bloody stools or a history of bloody stools. In a similar manner, the culture for even rarer bacterial enteric pathogens, such as *Y enterocolitica* and *Vibrio* species, is most often performed upon request and usually after exclusion of more typical pathogens. If bacterial agents that resemble normal flora on routine bacterial media are suspected (ETEC, EPEC, EAggEC, DAEC, or EHEC other than O157:H7), the laboratory should be notified so that confirmatory testing may be performed.

Other methods used to detect infectious agents in the stool include the direct examination, immunofluorescence enzyme-linked immunosorbent assays and cell culture-based assays. The microscopic examination of stool, often by using special stains (ie, trichrome or modified acid-fast stain), is used to detect ova and parasites. Immunoassays and ELISAs are available for the detection of *Giardia lamblia, Cryptosporidium parvum,* rotavirus, and *Clostridium difficile* toxins. Some laboratories use cell culture-based assays to detect *C difficile* toxin. Similar assays may be used to detect the VT of EHEC and shiga toxin of *Shigella dysenteriae* 1.

Individually, these microbiologic assays may be relatively inexpensive, but when numerous tests are ordered nonjudiciously, costs rapidly accrue. Microbiologic assays, like any laboratory assay, should be used to answer specific clinical questions. In patients with enteritis, the most likely causes of disease should be explored first. Patients who develop diarrhea after 3 d of hospitalization and who have been treated with antimicrobial agents probably do not warrant bacterial stool cultures or a stool examination for ova and parasites. These patients should be tested for *C difficile* toxin, because they are more likely to have pseudomembranous colitis.

Complications

All of the diarrheagenic *E coli* may produce dehydration and electrolyte abnormalities. The EAggEC may cause chronic disease and EIEC, like *Shigella* species, may cause a protein-losing enteropathy if dysentery is produced. Disease secondary to these agents is usually most pronounced in children, who may become dehydrated rapidly.

The most severe complication of EHEC infection is the development of HUS. This devastating disease most commonly occurs in children and has a significant mortality rate (3%–10%). Patients develop microangiopathic hemolytic anemia, thrombocytopenia, and renal failure. Patients that do not succumb may suffer significant morbidity secondary to renal and central nervous system dysfunction.

Diagnosis

Enteritis caused by the ETEC, EPEC, EIEC, DAEC, and EAggEC is usually self-limited and may be associated with travel or a particular outbreak. In most instances, the presence of one of these organisms is assumed, and the diagnosis is based on history, physical examination, and the exclusion of other enteric pathogens. A definitive diagnosis cannot be made, unless specific assays are performed. These confirmatory assays are costly and usually clinically unnecessary. In outbreak situations, however, complete microbiologic characterization of clinical isolates, with strain analysis, may be warranted for public health purposes.

The severe sequelae that may occur secondary to EHEC infections necessitate the identification of suspicious isolates on SMAC screening agar. The diagnosis of EHEC is strongly associated with bloody diarrhea or a history of bloody diarrhea and is often associated with the ingestion of undercooked beef. The presence of *E coli* O157:H7 is determined by culture and serotyping.

Treatment

Treatment of fluid and electrolyte loss is usually achieved through oral rehydration. The use of the World Health Organization Oral Rehydration Salts (ORS) solution is recommended. Intravenous rehydration may be necessary for infants, individuals with excessive vomiting, or those with severe dehydration.

Bismuth subsalicylate, 1 oz of liquid or two (262.5-mg) tablets taken every 30 min for 4 h, may decrease the amount of diarrhea and the duration of disease. Antimicrobial therapy is generally not indicated, because of the self-limited nature of most of these diseases. Some contend that empiric therapy may decrease symptomatology and shorten the clinical course. It is a concern, however, that the overuse of antimicrobial agents will promote resistant strains. If chronic or persistent diarrhea develops in patients infected by one of the enteroadherent *E coli* strains, specific antimicrobial therapy should be used. If available, the antimicrobial susceptibility profile should be used to guide therapy. If unavailable, a trial of empiric therapy for *E coli* is warranted (Box 53–2). Antimicrobial therapy has not been shown to decrease the morbidity/mortality of patients with HC/HUS. Antimicrobial therapy may worsen the clinical course, possibly by decreasing competitive enteric flora. A synthetic analog of G3b and diatomaceous earth, SYNSORB-Pk (Synsorb Biotech, Inc.), holds promise as a treatment of HC/HUS. Taken orally, this agent should absorb the VT and, it is hoped, prevent HUS.

As previously noted, disease caused by the EIEC is very much like shigellosis. It is unclear, however, if duration of disease and shedding of viable organisms by patients infected with EIEC are diminished by antimicrobial therapy, as occurs in patients with shigellosis. The diagnosis of EIEC infection requires the isolation of the organism; therefore, an antimicrobial susceptibility profile should be available to guide therapy.

Infections by the EHEC are severe and sometimes fatal. Antimicrobial therapy and antimotility agents may worsen the clinical course. Fluid and electrolyte replacement should be used as needed to treat dehydration. Transfusion, dialysis, and other supportive measures may be required for patients with HUS. Antimotility agents should not used by patients with severe infectious enteritis regardless of the etiology, but should be especially avoided by patients infected by EHEC. These drugs increase the duration and severity of disease by inhibiting the passage of the pathogenic bacteria and their toxins.

Prevention & Control

The diarrheagenic *E coli,* with the notable exception of EHEC, are transmitted in a human fecal-oral cycle. Most of these organisms thrive in underdeveloped countries secondarily to poor living conditions, ineffective sanitation, and unsafe drinking water. Improvements in sanitation and the quality of drinking water, as well as raising the standards of living, would greatly diminish the prevalence of these diseases (Box 53–3). In endemic areas, political instability, war, and a weak socioeconomic infrastructure contribute to the persistence of these organisms. Prophylactic antibiotics are not recommended for most travelers, but individuals at high risk for severe disease may benefit from antimicrobial prophylaxis. Travelers should drink bottled water and avoid eating raw, locally washed vegetables. Bismuth subsalicylate, 2 oz or two tablets four times daily, provides some prophylactic benefit, but should not be used as a substitute for other preventive measures. There are currently no vaccines approved for human use against the diarrheagenic *E coli.*

The EHEC inhabit the intestinal tracts of cattle and other animals. Control of this organism in its natural reservoir is currently impractical. Antimicrobial agents should not be used for its suppression in animals, because these practices provide selective pressures that promote antimicrobial resistance. Infections by the EHEC can be diminished by thoroughly cooking food, consuming only clean water and pasteurized juices, using good food preparation techniques, and maintaining good personal hygiene.

A wide variety of foods have served as vehicles for the transmission of EHEC. These include beef and beef products, dried salami, yogurt, and fresh-pressed apple cider. Of these, ground beef is especially prone to contamination and should never be eaten unless thoroughly cooked. When cooking or reheating meats, all parts of the meat should reach at least 70 °C. Children, who are at higher risk for HUS, should never be given undercooked hamburger.

Only pure, clean water should be consumed and used in food preparation. Wells, especially if they are

---

BOX 53–2

Empiric Therapy for Diarrheagenic, Non-EHEC, *E coli* Infection[1]

	Children	Adults
First Choice	Trimethoprim-sulfamethoxazole (TMP/SMX) > 1 month: TMP, 10 mg/kg/d, + SMX, 50 mg/kg/d orally twice daily for 3–5 d	Ciprofloxacin, 500 mg orally twice daily (or another quinolone)

[1]In most instances, disease secondary to diarrheagenic *E coli* infection resolves without therapy. If disease becomes chronic, a trial of antimicrobial therapy is warranted, but other etiologies of chronic diarrhea should also be considered.

BOX 53-3

Prevention & Control of Bacterial Gastroenteritis/Enteric Fever

Prophylactic Measures	• Appropriate sewage disposal and waste treatment
	• Treatment of drinking water (ie, chlorination)
	• Good personal hygiene
	• Thorough cooking of food, especially eggs and hamburger
	• Good food preparation skills (ie, avoid cross-contamination)
	• Bismuth subsalicylate for travelers may aid other prophylactic measures
Isolation Precautions	• Good handwashing necessary, especially if the infecting organism is *Salmonella typhi, Salmonella paratyphi, Shigella* spp., or *E coli* O157:H7.
	• Patients recovering from enteric fever (*S typhi* or *S paratyphi*) should not work as food preparers until stool cultures are negative.

---

near farms, should be periodically checked for enteric pathogens. Only pasteurized milk and juices should be consumed. Pasteurization is an effective means of eliminating EHEC, but care must be taken to avoid inadvertent postpasteurization contamination.

Good food preparation practices can also diminish the likelihood of EHEC infection. Hands should be washed thoroughly before food preparation and whenever raw meats have been touched. In addition, great care must be taken to avoid cross-contamination of foods that may not be thoroughly cooked before ingestion. Vegetables and fruits should be rinsed thoroughly under clean, free-flowing water. Cutting boards, knives, and other cooking utensils should be washed after they have been in contact with raw meat.

The infectious dose of *E coli* O157:H7 is so low that person-to-person transmission may occur. Anyone with EHEC HC must thoroughly wash their hands to avoid transmitting the bacteria. Children with a diarrheal disease should be carefully monitored for good hand washing. Finally, children with a diarrheal disease or history of recent diarrheal disease, especially bloody diarrhea, should avoid contact with other children, particularly contact during swimming.

SHIGELLA SPECIES

Essentials of Diagnosis

• Enteritis caused by *Shigella* species may be watery (*Shigella sonnei, Shigella boydii*) or dysenteric (*Shigella dysenteriae, Shigella flexneri*).
• Risks include ingestion of fecally contaminated food or water and contact with infected individuals.
• Definitive diagnosis requires microbiologic isolation and identification of *Shigella* species or molecular evidence of infection.

General Considerations

A. Epidemiology. Dysentery is a disease of antiquity and has been described throughout the ages. It was not until the 19th century that dysentery was recognized to be caused by either parasitic amoebae or certain bacteria. In 1898, Shiga recognized and isolated bacteria from patients with dysentery that would agglutinate when exposed to the patient's serum. Today, the most commonly recognized agents of bacterial dysentery are *Shigella* species and the EIEC (see above).

Shigella species are unique among bacterial enteric pathogens in that < 200 and possibly ≥ 10 organisms may transverse the gastric acid barrier and cause disease. For this reason, person-to-person transmission is common. Person-to-person transmission results in increased frequencies of shigellosis in day care centers, schools, and custodial-care facilities. Disease is most common in infants and young children and frequently occurs in family members of patients. Peak incidence occurs in the summertime, and common houseflies are thought to contribute to the spread of disease. Outbreaks have also occurred from fecally contaminated food. Transmission through contaminated water is most common in developing countries that lack adequate sewage and water treatment facilities.

In the United States, *S sonnei* is the most commonly encountered *Shigella* species, whereas *S boydii* has a worldwide distribution. The prevalence of shigellae appears to be cyclic, with replacement of the predominant strain approximately every 20 years. This cycling of prevalence is presumably secondary to slowly acquired herd immunity in a given host population. Epidemic shigellosis, caused by *S dysenteriae* and *S flexneri,* is prevalent in underdeveloped countries, but may develop anywhere that poverty, overcrowding, or conditions of war exist.

B. Microbiology. Shigella are nonmotile, facultative anaerobic, gram-negative bacilli that are closely related to the genus *Escherichia.* At least 40 serotypes compose four groups or species. These are *S dysente-*

riae (serogroup A), *S flexneri* (serogroup B), *S boydii* (serogroup C), and *S sonnei* (serogroup D).

The numbers of shigellae present in the stool vary with the course of disease. Early in the watery-diarrhea phase, shigellae are abundant and number 10^3–10^9 shigellae/g of feces. During this phase of disease, shigellae are easily recovered on MacConkey or eosin methylene blue (EMB) agar, where they appear as lactose nonfermenting colonies. Later in the course of disease, in the dysentery and post-convalescent phases, bacterial stool counts decline to 10^2–10^3 shigellae/g of feces. Furthermore, the recovery of shigellae is inversely proportional to specimen transport time, especially in stool specimens with a low number of shigellae. During the latter phase of disease, culture is best accomplished by rapid specimen transport or bedside medium inoculation, combined with the use of enrichment broth and moderately to highly selective media, such as xylose-lysine-desoxycholate medium and *Shigella-Salmonella* medium.

In many laboratories, suspect colonies, lactose nonfermenters, are screened by using a three-tube set: (i) one tube containing triple sugar iron (TSI) or Kligler iron agar (KIA), (ii) the second containing lysine iron agar (LIA), and (iii) the third containing Christensen's urea agar (CU) (also see the *Salmonella* Microbiology section below). On the TSI and KIA, shigellae characteristically produce an alkaline slant and acid butt without the production of gas. Rare isolates may produce gas. Negative reactions are produced on the LIA and CU, because shigellae do not decarboxylate lysine or hydrolyze urea. In addition, shigellae do not produce hydrogen sulfide, which is detected by the TSI, KIA, and LIA systems. An attempt to agglutinate organisms that are thought to represent *Shigella* species may be performed by using group antisera. Isolates with a suggestive screen profile are further characterized by additional biochemical reactions in either traditional or automated systems.

Useful clues in the identification of shigellae include the following: the majority of shigellae cannot ferment mucate, cannot use acetate, and are negative for indole and *ortho*-nitrophenyl-β-galactopyranoside.

C. Pathogenesis. Shigellosis may produce either predominantly watery diarrhea or watery diarrhea that progresses to dysentery. The severity of disease is largely determined by the invading organism. *S dysenteriae* and *S flexneri* are the agents most commonly associated with bacillary dysentery, whereas the other *Shigella* species more often produce watery diarrhea.

The pathogenesis of the watery-diarrhea phase of bacillary dysentery is caused by a combination of lumenal bacterial replication and superficial mucosal invasion in the small intestine. During this phase of disease, large numbers of shigellae are present in the lumen of the small intestine. This phase of the dis-

ease is correlated with the onset of cramping abdominal pain, fever, and toxemia.

Within days, the lumenal contents of the small intestine do not contain shigellae, and the site of infection is the colon. The shigellae invade colonic mucosa and occasionally invade to the level of the submucosa. Factors that are important for invasion are present on the bacterial chromosome, as well as on a 140-MDa plasmid. Eventually, epithelial cell death occurs, and the mucosa sloughs, possibly secondarily to shigatoxin production. The loss of mucosa evokes an intense inflammatory response and allows for the introduction of coliform bacteria. Microabscesses, epithelial ulcerations, and pseudomembranes that consist of sloughed epithelial cells, bacteria, fibrin, and inflammatory cells may be seen. This phase of the disease correlates with tenesmus and fractionated stools that contain blood, mucus, and inflammatory debris.

Clinical Findings

A. Signs and Symptoms. Early in the course of disease, when bacteria are present in the small intestine, patients develop acute, watery diarrhea; fever; and abdominal pain. Patients may become toxemic and fever may reach as high as 104 °F. Later in the course of disease, the primary site of infection is the colon. In this phase, fever continues, but is usually less pronounced. The pain that is present is usually in the lower abdominal quadrants. Stools become dysenteric, consisting of a mixture of neutrophils, blood, mucus, and debris. Frequent, small-volume or fractionated stools may occur, and tenesmus is often present. Patients experience pain upon rectal examination. Colonoscopy discloses hyperemic and friable-to-ulcerated colonic mucosa.

B. Differential Diagnosis. When watery diarrhea predominates, other bacterial, parasitic, and viral enteric pathogens must be considered. *Entamoeba histolytica* and EIEC must also be considered in patients with dysentery. Infection with *E histolytica* is most commonly associated with travel to or living in endemic locales. These organisms are readily recognized on a microscopic examination of the stool for ova and parasites. Dysentery caused by the EIEC, however, may pose a diagnostic challenge for the clinical microbiologist. The EIEC, unlike other *E coli,* are often nonmotile, may not ferment lactose or may ferment it slowly, are lysine decarboxylase negative, and may cross-react with *Shigella* antisera. Laboratory personnel must recognize this potential pitfall and exclude this organism through additional testing (see above).

Noninfectious causes of diarrhea must also be considered. The differential diagnosis of noninfectious colitis is extensive and includes inflammatory-bowel disease, lymphocytic/collagenous colitis, neoplasia, and numerous other disorders. Patients with inflammatory-bowel disease may also have fecal leukocytes, limiting the usefulness of this test. An accurate diagnosis may be achieved through a thorough history and physical examination, excluding enteric pathogens through appropriate microbiologic studies, and by obtaining and reviewing gastrointestinal biopsies via endoscopy and histopathologic studies.

C. Complications. The most common complications of bacillary dysentery include dehydration and a protein-losing enteropathy. In rare instances, a toxic megacolon may occur and may result in perforation, intra-abdominal hemorrhage, peritonitis, and possibly death. Some patients, particularly those with HLA-B27 phenotypes, may develop a postinfectious arthritis or Reiter's syndrome.

Diagnosis

Patients with acute diarrhea, which may be watery to dysenteric; fever; abdominal pain; and systemic symptomatology/toxemia may have shigellosis. A history of exposure to individuals with shigellosis, travel to endemic areas, and exposure to a high-risk population, such as persons in a custodial-care facility, should raise the index of suspicion. The presence of leukocytes in the stool, although supportive, is by no means definitive for shigellosis. Fecal leukocytes may be present in the stools of patients with other bacterial enteritides, amoebic dysentery, pseudomembranous colitis, and noninfectious disease, such as inflammatory-bowel disease. The definitive diagnosis requires the microbiologic identification of a *Shigella* species.

Shigellae are particularly susceptible to some environmental changes, and they die rapidly in transport. Therefore, it is imperative to rapidly transport the stool of patients suspected of having shigellosis to the laboratory. This is especially important for patients in the latter stages of disease, in whom the number of shigellae in the stool are relatively few.

Treatment

Fluid and electrolyte replacements are necessary for patients with dehydration. In most instances, this is readily accomplished by oral rehydration. Unlike in many other bacterial enteritides, antibiotic therapy is important in the treatment of shigellosis (Box 53-4). Antibiotic therapy limits the clinical course of the disease, may decrease the likelihood of intestinal complications, and decreases the fecal excretion of viable pathogenic organisms, which in turn diminishes transmission. Fluoroquinolones are the treatment of choice for adults. TMP/SMX is the treatment of choice for children. Alternatives are ampicillin, chloramphenicol, and nalidixic acid. In areas of known resistance to TMP/SMX, such as parts of Southeast Asia, Africa, and South America, quinolones should be used for adults, and one of the above mentioned alternatives for children with shigellosis. When available, the antimicrobial-susceptibility profile should guide therapy.

Antimotility agents, such as diphenoxylate, should not be used. The inhibition of diarrhea increases the contact between the intestinal mucosa and the pathogenic organisms and their toxins and may cause more fulminant disease.

Prognosis

The prognosis is generally good for patients with endemic or sporadic shigellosis. Infants and the elderly, especially if malnourished, suffer the highest mortality. Epidemic shigellosis caused by *S dysenteriae*, however, is a severe and often life-threatening disease with mortality rates from 5% to 20%. This disease must be treated aggressively with antimicrobial and rehydration therapies.

Prevention & Control

The development and refinement of sewage dis-

BOX 53-4

Treatment of Shigella Gastroenteritis[1]

	Children	Adults
First Choice	Trimethoprim-sulfamethoxazole (TMP/SMX) • > 1 month: TMP, 10 mg/kg/d, + SMX 50 mg/kg/d orally, divided every 12 h	Ciprofloxacin: 500 mg orally every 12 h (or another quinolone)
Second Choice	Ampicillin: • > 1 month: 25 mg/kg every 6 h • 1–4 wk: 25 mg/kg every 8 h • < 1 wk: 25 mg/kg every 12 h	Ampicillin: 0.5–1 g orally every 6 h or 1–2 g IV every 4–6 h
Penicillin Allergic	• TMP/SMX (as above) OR Nalidixic acid, 55 mg/kg/day, orally, divided every 4 h	Trimethoprim-sulfamethoxazole: 160/800 mg orally every 12 h or 3–5 mg/kg IV every 6–8 h

[1]The recommended duration of therapy for all treatment regimens is 3–5 d

posal and drinking water treatment systems are important in developing countries. In both developed and developing countries, personal hygiene, good hand washing practices, and clean living conditions are important preventive measures, particularly in custodial-care facilities (see Box 53–3). Fly control and hygienic food preparation practices should also diminish the incidence of disease.

SALMONELLA SPECIES

Essentials of Diagnosis

I. Enteric fever.

- Enteric fever is a systemic disease that may or may not be preceded by a diarrheal illness.
- Key signs and symptoms include possible diarrhea or constipation that precedes constitutional symptoms and possible hepatosplenomegaly; other signs and symptoms may include "rose spots," paroxysmal bradycardia, and mental status changes (so called "typhoid psychosis").
- Enteric fever is usually associated with the ingestion of water that has been contaminated by human feces.
- "*S typhi*," "*S paratyphi*," or rarely other *Salmonella* "species" (see General Considerations section below for clarification of current *Salmonella* taxonomy) from blood or bone marrow are isolated early in the course of disease and/or from the stool later in the course of disease, or there is molecular evidence of infection.

II. *Salmonella* enteritis.

- Enteritis caused by *Salmonella* species usually results in watery diarrhea that in some instances may become hemorrhagic or dysenteric.
- *Salmonella* enteritis is usually associated with the ingestion of contaminated, undercooked foods, particularly undercooked eggs.
- There is microbiologic isolation and identification of *Salmonella* species or molecular evidence of infection.

General Considerations

For decades, phenotypic studies have been used to identify and categorize the *Salmonella* species. These organisms have been categorized by antisera directed against particular bacterial somatic (O) and flagellar (H) antigens. Serologic stratification has resulted in the identification of > 2000 *Salmonella* serotypes. These serotypes have traditionally been treated as individual species. More recently, molecular analysis has revealed significantly less variability among the salmonellae than serologic studies have implied. Newer taxonomy recognizes two *Salmonella* species,

S enterica and *S bongori,* and six subspecies of *S enterica.* Although this taxonomy is more precise, many healthcare providers have a greater familiarity with the previous nomenclature. For this reason, reference to previous nomenclature is appropriate and should avoid confusion, facilitate communication, and ensure optimal patient care. Therefore, for the remainder of this chapter, the *Salmonella* serotypes will be treated traditionally as species.

A.   Epidemiology. *Salmonella* species cause various clinical manifestations, depending on the infecting serotype, but all commonly begin with oral intake of fecally contaminated food or water. Salmonellosis is usually characterized as enteric fever or enteritis.

1.   Enteric fever. The agents of enteric fever are maintained in a human fecal-oral cycle. Enteric fever, therefore, is most commonly seen in areas of developing countries that lack adequate waste disposal and drinking water treatment facilities. In endemic areas, children and young adults are most commonly affected, but any age and either sex may contract enteric fever. The Indian subcontinent and parts of Africa, Asia, and Central and South America are endemic for enteric fever. In developed countries, clean drinking water and adequate waste disposal have dramatically diminished the prevalence of enteric fever, and most cases of enteric fever are imported from endemic areas.

Enteric fever is distinguished from enteritis if systemic manifestations predominate and there is bacterial dissemination throughout the body and extensive involvement of the reticuloendothelial system. Classically, the enteric fevers are typhoid fever or paratyphoid fever, caused by *S typhi* or *S paratyphi,* respectively. Infrequently, other strains may cause enteric fever. *S typhi* is found exclusively in humans, and *S paratyphi* is found predominantly in humans. Contraction of disease, therefore, requires the presence of individuals either recovering from enteric fever or harboring the organism. Enteric fever remains a major public health problem in much of the world, and in some areas it ranks among the top five causes of death.

Enteric fever is a severe, life-threatening disease that, despite antimicrobial therapy, still causes significant mortality. Some individuals who have had enteric fever become chronic carriers. These individuals are usually asymptomatic and most frequently harbor the bacteria in the gallbladder, which contains calculi. In areas where *Schistosoma haematobium* is endemic, the bacteria may also be harbored in the bladder, associated with schistosome eggs. Chronic carriers are public health threats, because they continue to shed pathogenic bacteria into the environment over long periods of time and may substantially contaminate local water supplies, particularly in areas lacking appropriate treatment facilities. If carriers are food handlers and poor hand washers, epidemics may occur through contaminated food.

2. *Salmonella* **enteritis.** *Salmonella* enteritis is characterized as enteritis if gastrointestinal disease predominates, without extensive involvement of the systemic reticuloendothelial system. *Salmonella* serotypes, other than *S typhi* or *S paratyphi,* are usually responsible for this disorder. Occasionally bacteremia occurs and there may be extraintestinal manifestations caused by seeding of distant organs. In some instances, the intestinal symptomatology may be minimal, and extraintestinal symptomatology may be the primary manifestation.

Although the number of cases of typhoid fever has diminished dramatically over the past 100 years in the United States, the number of cases of nontyphoid salmonellosis continues to increase. These organisms colonize the intestinal tracts of a wide variety of animals and are also transmitted by the fecal-oral route, through the ingestion of contaminated meats and animal products. Some *Salmonella* serotypes occur in many different animals, whereas others tend to occur in particular animals. For example, *S typhimurium* and *S enteritidis* are often associated with chickens, whereas *Salmonella arizonae* is associated with reptiles.

Person-to-person transmission of *Salmonella* species among food handlers and healthcare workers is possible but is not a common mode of transmission. Infants and neonates, however, are at an increased risk for infection if exposed to an infected mother or other family members.

B. Microbiology. Salmonellae are nonfastidious members of the *Enterobacteriaceae* that will grow on most routine media, including broth-based blood culture systems. Most *Enterobacteriaceae* ferment lactose, but the vast majority of *Salmonella* species (99%) do not. This feature has permitted the use of selective and differential agar media to separate these enteric pathogens from the legions of other bacteria present in the stool. MacConkey and EMB agars are the most common media used for this purpose. These agars contain bile salts and/or dyes that suppress the growth of gram-positive bacteria and lactose and pH indicators for the determination of an organism's ability to ferment lactose. On MacConkey agar, lactose fermenters appear as pink to red colonies, whereas nonlactose fermenters appear clear. On EMB agar, the lactose fermenters appear as blue to violet colonies and may incorporate dyes that are present in the media into the colony, which gives them a green metallic sheen. Bacterial colonies that do not ferment lactose appear light purple to clear.

When plating stool for the detection of *Salmonella* and/or *Shigella* species, a moderately or highly selective agar is often used in conjunction with the MacConkey or EMB plates. Moderately selective agars for the isolation of *Salmonella* and *Shigella* species include Hektoen-enteric and xylose-lysine-desoxycholate agars. Highly selective media, such as *Salmonella-Shigella* agar, brilliant green agar, and bismuth-sulfate agar, are most effectively used in outbreak situations. If used appropriately, an enrichment broth, such as selinite broth, may also be used to increase the recovery of *Salmonella* species from stool.

Bacteria that are suspected to be *Salmonella* or *Shigella* species are often then tested in the three-tube set as described above. In the TSI/KIA system, the majority of salmonellae produce an alkaline slant over an acid butt and produce gas. However, strains of *S paratyphi* A can ferment lactose, which produces an acid over acid reaction. Although most salmonellae produce hydrogen sulfide from sodium thiosulfate metabolism, ~ 90% of *S paratyphi* A and 50% of *S cholerasuis* isolates do not. Hydrogen sulfide production is detected by the TSI, KIA, and LIA systems and, when present, reacts with ferric ammonium citrate to form a black precipitate. It is significant that *S paratyphi* A, which produce an A/A TSI reaction and do not produce hydrogen sulfide, may be discarded as non-*Salmonella Enterobacteriaceae.*

The LIA system detects lysine decarboxylation, deamination, and the production of hydrogen sulfide. The hydrogen sulfide-producing bacteria genera *Morganella, Proteus,* and *Providencia* may be differentiated from *Salmonella* by their ability to deaminate phenylalanine. Except for *S paratyphi* A, the salmonellae generate a positive reaction for the decarboxylation of lysine. *Salmonella* species, like *Shigella* species, do not produce urease and generate no reaction on CU agar. This medium is included in the three-tube set to help differentiate *Salmonella* species from some of the other hydrogen sulfide producers and to detect *Y enterocolitica.*

Isolates with an appropriate biochemical profile in the three-tube set are often serotyped and definitively identified by traditional or automated biochemical testing.

For patients with enteric fever, the percent yield from blood or bone marrow culture vs stool culture varies during the course of disease (see Clinical Findings). Clinicians must be aware of which sites render the highest yield during each phase of the disease and submit appropriate specimens for culture.

C. Pathogenesis.
1.   Enteric fever. The clinical course of enteric fever may be separated into three phases: an early phase that includes incubation and the onset of symptoms; the middle phase, which is the time of maximal symptomatology; and a late phase that includes diminishing symptoms, recovery, and possible carriage.

The incubation phase begins after ingestion of *S typhi* and usually lasts between 10 and 14 days. The incubation time, however, is variable and to a certain extent is inversely proportional to the size of the inoculum. Normal stomach acid functions as a physiologic barrier to infection, and ~ 10^5 organisms are required to survive gastric passage. A smaller inoculum may cause disease in patients with achlorhydria or decreased gastric acid production.

The next phase of the disease is characterized by bacterial invasion of the mucosa. The salmonellae adhere to the lumenal surface of the enterocytes, particularly specialized enterocytes, termed M cells, which overlie the Peyer's patches. The low number of organisms present in the stool at this stage of disease explains the common occurrence of negative stool cultures.

After adhesion, the enterocyte cell membrane becomes ruffled, and there are cytoskeletal alterations. The bacteria are then internalized by endocytosis and transmigrate through the enterocyte. They exit the basilar aspect of the cell through the basement membrane and are free in the lamina propria. The organisms are phagocytosed by mononuclear phagocytes in Peyer's patches and/or are drained by terminal lacteals to regional lymph nodes. This is followed by lymphatic and hematogenous dissemination of the bacteria to organs with fixed tissue histiocytes, such as the liver, spleen, and bone marrow. The salmonellae are able to alter the environment within macrophages and survive phagocytosis. This intracellular location also protects the bacteria from phagocytosis by polymorphonuclear leukocytes, to which they are susceptible, and to aminoglycoside antibiotics, which have poor intracellular penetration. Another virulence factor that these organisms possess is a capsule that has antiphagocytic properties and protects them from complement and antibody-mediated killing.

Bacteria, which involve the liver, may be subsequently passed into the bile. These organisms thrive in bile and may colonize the gallbladder, especially if gallstones are present. A bacterial enterohepatic circulation occurs wherein bacteria that have been shed into the bile pass into the small bowel and again adhere to and invade the small intestinal mucosa.

2. *Salmonella* gastroenteritis. Although the pathogenic mechanisms by which *S typhi* causes enteric fever have been well documented, the precise pathophysiology of *Salmonella* gastroenteritis has yet to be ascertained. The salmonellae that survive food processing and gastric acidity probably adhere to the apical portion of enterocytes by specific pili. *Salmonella* species may release an enterotoxin similar to the LT enterotoxin of the ETEC or the enterotoxin of *V cholerae*. Alternatively, these organisms may cause changes in arachidonic acid metabolites and subsequent alterations in cytosolic second messengers other than cyclic AMP. It is known that the invasion of enterocytes by salmonellae causes the production of interleukin-8, a potent neutrophil chemotactic factor. Diarrhea may in part result from disruption of the epithelium through the influx of neutrophils and release of their toxic contents.

Salmonella species survive poorly at low pHs and are killed rapidly by stomach acid. Unlike *Shigella* species, a substantial number of salmonellae are required to successfully cross the gastric acid barrier and cause disease. Any decrease in gastric acidity increases the likelihood of *Salmonella* survival. Anyone, such as persons that have had gastric surgery, with hypo- or achlorhydria are at increased risk for salmonellosis. Undercooked foods that are contaminated with salmonellae buffer gastric acid and thereby facilitate the passage of bacteria into the small intestine. Neonates and infants that may be relatively hypochlorhydric are at increased risk for infection. Persons with an impaired immune response are also at risk for nontyphoidal salmonellosis.

ENTERIC FEVER

Clinical Findings

A. Signs and Symptoms. Patients are asymptomatic during the incubation phase. Early in the course of disease, patients may experience diarrhea or constipation. Patients then develop a variety of nonspecific symptoms, such as fever, chills, weakness, malaise, myalgia, and cough. Signs, that are not always present, such as rose spots, paroxysmal bradycardia in sharp contrast to the clinical presentation and elevated temperature, and hepatosplenomegaly are clues to the diagnosis. Profound mental status changes and picking at bed clothing, termed typhoid psychosis, may develop in some patients with enteric fever. The middle phase of disease is the time of maximal symptomatology. If complications do not intervene (see below), patients begin to feel progressively better through the latter half of the disease course.

B. Laboratory Findings. Blood culture is superior to stool culture during the early to mid stages of disease. During the first half of the disease course, bone marrow cultures have the greatest yield but are more difficult to obtain. Peripheral blood findings are variable, and pancytopenia may be seen. During the latter half of the disease course, stool cultures and occasionally urine cultures become positive and provide greater yields than blood cultures.

C. Differential Diagnosis. Typhoid fever was so named because of its clinical resemblance to typhus, the louse-borne rickettsial disease. The causative organisms are not closely related and are transmitted by very different mechanisms, but both may cause nonspecific signs, such as fever and rash. In addition, both of these diseases occur in impoverished areas and cause epidemics during war. Because of a better understanding of the microbiology, pathophysiology, and histopathology of these diseases, distinguishing between these diseases today is no longer a problem. An accurate diagnosis is usually made through the combined use of serology, culture, and immunohistochemistry. Other infectious diseases, such as visceral leishmaniasis and malaria, may produce fever and hepatosplenomegaly similar to that seen in typhoid fever. These as well as other infectious and noninfectious causes of hepatosplenomegaly are excluded by history, physical examination, laboratory studies, and, in some instances, liver biopsy.

D. Complications. A characteristic of the enteric fevers is extensive Peyer's patch and mesenteric lymphoid hyperplasia. The mucosa overlying the Peyer's patches becomes thinned and often necrotic, which creates a breach in the mucosal barrier and a conduit through which coliform bacteria may invade the bowel wall. Extensive shedding of the necrotic mucosa and underlying lymphoid tissue results in ulceration. Perforation and peritonitis may occur. Massive intraluminal or intra-abdominal hemorrhage may result if ulceration or perforation involves mesenteric blood vessels. These severe complications manifest in ~ 10%–15% of untreated patients with typhoid fever.

Intestinal perforation usually occurs during the latter portion of the middle stage or the early portion of the late stage, when symptoms are beginning to wane. Perforation may present as worsening abdominal pain or rapidly progressive hypotension if hemorrhage occurs. In the absence of rapidly progressing hypotension, abdominal imaging is useful in advanced typhoid fever if perforation is suspected. Emergency surgery is necessary for survival.

The development of a chronic carrier state is a complication of enteric fever and is of more importance to the public health system than to the patient. Chronic carriers shed viable, pathogenic organisms into the environment and serve as sources for subsequent outbreaks. *S typhi* is the serotype that is most often associated with the chronic carrier state. Much more rarely, patients infected with other serotypes may develop a chronic carrier state. Most often, chronic carriers harbor *S typhi* in the gallbladder in association with calculi. Urinary tract carriage is associated with *Schistosoma haematobium* infection or urinary tract calculi. Chronic carriers require long-term therapy, follow-up cultures, and occasionally surgery for the eradication of these organisms.

Diagnosis

In the appropriate clinical setting, the definitive diagnosis of enteric fever requires isolation and biochemical characterization of the etiologic agent. Febrile patients who have visited endemic areas may have enteric fever. Some patients with enteric fever may have an insidious onset, but eventually become severely ill. The Widal antigen/antibody agglutination is a presumptive test that is still used for the diagnosis of typhoid fever. This test, however, lacks both sensitivity and specificity. Blood and/or bone marrow culture, followed by empiric therapy, is a more reliable method of diagnosing enteric fever. Early in the course of disease, blood and bone marrow cultures yield the highest recovery of organisms, while later in the course of disease, stool and sometimes urine cultures are more likely to become positive. The submission of appropriate specimens for culture is important, so that rapid isolation of the causative agent and susceptibility testing can be performed. Antimicrobial susceptibility testing is necessary to optimally direct therapy, because of possible antimicrobial resistance.

Treatment

Chloramphenicol, TMP/SMX, ampicillin, third-generation cephalosporins, and quinolones have been used successfully for the treatment of enteric fever (Box 53–5). Unfortunately, antimicrobial resistance has emerged to each of these agents. Some *Salmonella* isolates are multidrug resistant. For this reason, whenever possible, antimicrobial therapy should be based on an individual isolate's susceptibility profile, obtained by standard methods. Until such data are available, empiric therapy should be used, based on known antimicrobial-resistance profiles.

Chloramphenicol was the first drug used for the treatment of typhoid fever. However, increasing resistance, high relapse rates, bone marrow toxicity, and the promotion of a chronic carrier state have limited its usefulness. If isolates are susceptible to chloramphenicol, advantages include its high efficacy, low cost, and oral administration.

Ampicillin and TMP/SMX were used to treat enteric fever after chloramphenicol resistance emerged. For susceptible isolates, these drugs are effective, easily administered, and do not have the high rate of relapse associated with chloramphenicol.

The third-generation cephalosporin, ceftriaxone, is highly effective for the treatment of typhoid fever in adults and children. Third-generation cephalosporins are especially useful as empiric therapy in areas in which multiple-drug resistance has been reported. When the susceptibility profile of a particular isolate is known, the antimicrobial agent may be changed to a drug with a narrower spectrum of activity. Hopefully, this will also diminish the selection of organisms with resistance to third-generation cephalosporins.

Currently, ciprofloxacin is the drug of choice for adults from India, Asia, or the Middle East. In these areas, *S typhi* strains that are resistant to chloramphenicol, ampicillin, and/or TMP/SMX have been reported. Chromosomally mediated quinolone resistance has emerged, however, but it is hoped that it will not spread as rapidly as the plasmid-mediated resistance to chloramphenicol, ampicillin, and TMP/SMX. First- and second-generation cephalosporins and aminoglycosides should not be used to treat *S typhi* infections, regardless of the in vitro susceptibility profile. Patients with typhoid fever who develop mental status changes may benefit from a short course of dexamethasone.

SALMONELLA ENTERITIS

Clinical Findings

A. Signs and Symptoms. *Salmonella* enteritis, frequently caused by *S enteritidis, S cholerasuis,* or *S*

BOX 53–5

Treatment of Enteric Fever[1]

	Children	Adults
First Choice	Ceftriaxone: • > 4 wk: 50–100 mg/kg/d IV every 12–24 h • 1–4 wk: 50–75 mg/kg d IV every 24 h • < 1 wk: 50 mg/kg/d IV every 24 h	Ceftriaxone, 1–2 g IV every 12 h
Second Choice	Ampicillin: • > 1 month: 25 mg/kg IV or orally every 6 h • 1–4 wk: 25 mg/kg IV every 8 h • < 1 wk: 25 mg/kg IV every 12 h	Ciprofloxacin, 500–750 mg orally every 12 h or 200–400 mg IV every 8–12 h (or another quinolone) **OR** Ampicillin, 0.5–1 g orally every 6 h or 1–2 g IV every 4–6 h
Penicillin Allergic	Trimethoprim-sulfamethoxazole (TMP/SMX) • > 1 month: TMP, 10 mg/kg/d + SMX, 50 mg/kg/d orally divided every 12 h	Trimethoprim-sulfamethoxazole, 160/800 mg orally every 6 h or 8–10 mg/kg IV trimethoprim equivalent every 6 h Chloramphenicol: 0.25–0.75 g orally every 6 h or ≤ 1 g IV every 6 h for severe infections

[1]Empiric therapy should be based on known antimicrobial susceptibility profiles and should be modified, based on the antimicrobial susceptibility profile of the infecting isolate. In areas of known multidrug resistance, children should be treated with ceftriaxone, and adults should be treated with ceftriaxone or a quinolone. In areas without known resistance, ampicillin, trimethoprim-sulfamethoxazole, or chloramphenicol may be used. Two weeks of antimicrobial therapy are usually required.

typhimurium, occurs between 12 and 48 h after the consumption of contaminated food. Patients experience fever, abdominal cramping, and diarrhea that may be accompanied by nausea and vomiting. The diarrhea varies in consistency from watery to dysenteric.

B. Laboratory Findings. Microscopic examination of the stool usually discloses nonspecific neutrophils.

C. Differential Diagnosis. The differential diagnosis of infectious diarrhea includes parasitic, viral, and bacterial etiologies. Noninfectious causes of diarrhea, such as inflammatory-bowel disease, lymphocytic/collagenous colitis, neoplasia, and numerous other disorders, must be considered. Patients with inflammatory-bowel disease may also have fecal leukocytes, further limiting the usefulness of this test. An accurate diagnosis can be achieved with a thorough history and physical examination, excluding enteric pathogens by appropriate microbiologic studies, and obtaining and reviewing gastrointestinal biopsies by using endoscopy and histopathologic studies.

D. Complications. In immunocompetent individuals, the disease usually lasts ≤ 1 week and resolves without specific antimicrobial therapy. Neonates and young children, the elderly, and pregnant women are at increased risk for severe disease. In addition, immunocompromised individuals and patients with sickle cell disease or other hemoglobinopathies are at increased risk for bacteremia and the establishment of metastatic foci of infection. The complications of *Salmonella* infections may be separated into four categories: (i) dehydration and electrolyte abnormalities, (ii) local inflammatory response, (iii) bacteremia with the spread of organisms to distant sites, and (iv) postinfectious arthritis.

1. Extensive diarrhea. Regardless of the cause, extensive diarrhea may lead to fluid and electrolyte abnormalities. Dehydration and electrolyte imbalance may cause tissue ischemia, central nervous system changes, and fatal dysrhythmias. Young children and the elderly, especially if malnourished, often suffer the greatest morbidity and mortality.

2. Mesenteric lymphoid hypertrophy. Mesenteric lymphoid hypertrophy is associated with enteric fever, but patients with *Salmonella* enteritis may develop mesenteric lymphadenitis. These patients develop severe abdominal pain that may mimic acute appendicitis. Although mesenteric lymphadenitis is most commonly associated with *Y enterocolitica,* it may also occur in patients with bacterial enteritis of other etiologies.

3. Bacteremia. By definition, bacteremia is a part of the disease process in enteric fever, but patients with *Salmonella* enteritis also occasionally develop bacteremia. *Salmonella* bacteremia may result in dissemination of bacteria and foci of infection into virtually any organ. The spread of bacteria to distant sites has resulted in a wide variety of diseases, including abscesses of the liver and spleen, acute and chronic cholecystitis, soft-tissue infections, urogenital infections, pneumonia and empyema, meningoencephalitis, and osteomyelitis. Osteomyelitis may be associated with areas of prior trauma or underlying bony abnormalities or, classically, has been associated with sickle cell anemia or other hemoglobinopathies.

Atherosclerotic plaques may also become infected during *Salmonella* bacteremia. These are serious infections, because infected plaque material is almost impossible to sterilize with antibiotics alone. These plaques become an intravascular focus of infection and continually seed the bloodstream. In the laboratory, intravascular infections, including plaque infections, are detected as high-grade bacteremia, wherein > 50% of three or more blood cultures are positive. The abdominal aorta is a common site for atherosclerotic disease and is the vessel most commonly infected. Abdominal aortic plaque infections may result in a life-threatening aortoduodenal fistula or in mycotic aneurysms. Intravascular infections usually require combined medical and surgical therapy. If the patients are not surgical candidates, they may require long-term, suppressive antimicrobial therapy.

Endocarditis is not common in either *Salmonella* enteritis-associated bacteremia or typhoid fever. Patients with structural cardiac anomalies, such as previous rheumatic heart disease or ventricular aneurysm, are at higher risk for developing endocarditis, regardless of the etiologic agent.

4. Post-infectious arthritis. As with other bacterial etiologies, patients with salmonellosis may develop a post-infectious arthritis. The joint pain usually begins about 2 weeks after the diarrheal illness, and multiple joints are affected. This reactive, immune-mediated arthritis may last for months. Like patients with Reiter's syndrome, individuals with an HLA-B27 phenotype are at increased risk for developing this complication.

Diagnosis

Patients with *Salmonella* enteritis have positive stool cultures and occasionally positive blood cultures. Apart from the agents of enteric fever, *Salmonella cholerasuis* is more likely to result in bacteremia than other *Salmonella* species. After isolation, *Salmonella* species are rapidly grouped by using antisera and are differentiated by various biochemical reactions.

Over the past decade, several molecular methods have been explored for the rapid detection of *Salmonella* species, including enzyme-linked immunosorbent assays, indirect immunofluorescence, and polymerase chain reactions. Advances in molecular diagnostics should permit the rapid detection of antigens or nucleic acids that are unique to these organisms. Many of these tests, however, are not commercially available and may be cost prohibitive compared with culture.

Treatment

Uncomplicated enteritis caused by *Salmonella* species should not be treated with antimicrobial agents. Antimicrobial agents may prolong bacteria shedding and promote antimicrobial resistance. Fluid and electrolyte replacement should be used to treat dehydration. In most instances, oral rehydration is sufficient, but, if severe electrolyte anomalies exist, intravenous rehydration may be necessary. Antimotility agents should not be used, because these agents inhibit the clearance of pathogenic bacteria and their toxins. Patients at risk for or with systemic disease/complications should be treated. A third-generation cephalosporin, such as ceftriaxone, may be used for patients with severe disease, until antimicrobial susceptibility data are available (see Box 53–5). Prophylactic therapy is appropriate for individuals at increased risk for severe disease (Box 53–6). In the absence of an antimicrobial-susceptibility profile, empiric therapy should be used.

Systemic infections should be treated with antimicrobial agents based on the particular isolate's susceptibility profile. Intravascular infections and osteomyelitis may require long-term antimicrobial therapy, possibly combined with surgery to effect a cure.

Prevention & Control

The prevention of all *Salmonella* infections requires an interruption of the fecal-oral cycle (see Box 53–3). Developed countries with adequate sewage disposal, clean drinking water, and an effective public health service have dramatically lowered the prevalence and incidence of enteric fever. Infections by *S typhi* have been particularly affected, because humans are the only known reservoir for this organism. Diminishing infections caused by other *Salmonella* strains are more difficult, because these organisms are commensals in the intestinal tracts of a wide variety of animals. Infections by these organisms are usually associated with contaminated or incompletely cooked foods. The control of these infections may be effected through education and efforts that stress the importance of rinsing meats when appropriate, avoiding cross-contamination of food preparation utensils, avoiding raw-egg–containing products, and thoroughly cooking meats.

Of particular public health interest is the association of *S enteritidis* with chicken eggs. Ovarian infections in chickens may result in the transovarial passage of *Salmonella* species. Therefore, even thoroughly washed eggs with intact shells may transmit *S enteritidis*. Foods that require uncooked egg whites and/or yolks should be prepared by using pas-

BOX 53-6

Prophylaxis for *Salmonella* Enteritis[1]

	Children	Adults
First Choice	Trimethoprim-sulfamethoxazole (TMP/SMX) • > 1 month: TMP, 8 mg/kg/d + SMX, 40 mg/kg/d orally every 8 h	• Ciprofloxacin: 500 mg orally every 12 h (or an other quinolone)
Second Choice	• Amoxicillin: 6.7–13.3 mg/kg orally every 8 h	• Amoxicillin: 250–500 mg orally every 8 h **OR** • Trimethoprim-sulfamethoxazole, 160/800 mg orally every 12–24 h or 3–5 mg/kg IV every 6–8h

[1]For groups at high risk for bacteremia or metastatic spread. Uncomplicated enteritis caused by *Salmonella* spp. should *not* be treated with antimicrobial agents.

teurized egg products. For this reason, raw eggs and foods or beverages that contain raw eggs should not be ingested. Additionally, cracked eggs should never be consumed, because these are even more likely to be contaminated with *Salmonella* species. The thorough cooking of eggs renders them safe for consumption.

Beef and poultry may become contaminated with feces during the slaughter process. If possible, these products should be washed with free-flowing water and cooked thoroughly before consumption. Knives, cutting boards, and other utensils become contaminated during contact with uncooked foods. These fomites may cross-contaminate other foods and thereby transmit *Salmonella* species. Utensils and food preparation surfaces that have been used to process uncooked food should be washed thoroughly before they are used to process other foods. The thorough cooking of food and pasteurization of milk and other liquids substantially reduce the risk of *Salmonella* enteritis.

Vaccinations are available for individuals at risk for typhoid fever; prophylactic antimicrobial agents are not recommended. Current recommended candidates for vaccination include travelers to endemic areas and people who are household contacts of infected persons. In the United States, the traditional vaccine consists of heat-killed, phenol-treated organisms. This vaccine offers 55%–77% protection, but its usefulness is limited by side effects. The minor side effects include fever, headache, and local pain at the site of injection and may last from hours to several days, but more severe reactions may occur. This vaccine requires two injections 4 weeks apart. The minimum age for vaccination is 6 months, and a booster is required every 3 years.

A newer, capsular polysaccharide vaccine, ViCPS, appears to offer similar protection after a single injec-

tion and has fewer side effects. This vaccine has a minimum age requirement of 2 years and requires a booster every 2 years.

An attenuated, live-bacteria, oral vaccine has been licensed in the United States and may rapidly become the vaccine of choice for many individuals. This vaccine, Ty21a, appears to be safe and effective, with no serious side effects. It relies on the development of natural immunity by using an attenuated *S typhi* strain. Therefore, patients on antimicrobial therapy should not be given this vaccine concomitantly. As with other "live" vaccines, this vaccine should not be given to persons that are immunocompromised. It is not recommended for children < 6 years old. Because of these limitations, the oral vaccine will not completely replace the injectable vaccines. A booster dose is needed every 5 years.

None of the typhoid vaccines offer long lasting protection, and booster doses are required to maintain protective antibody levels. In addition, none of the vaccines are 100% effective and should be used in conjunction with other preventive measures. Information regarding typhoid fever prevention and the prevention of other travel-associated diseases is available from the Centers for Disease Control and Prevention toll free at 1-888-232-3228 or on the internet at http://www.cdc.gov/travel.

Future directions for vaccine development include vaccines that elicit longer lasting immunity and confer immunity to more than one enteric pathogen. Such vaccines have been created, using molecular techniques. The insertion into *Salmonella* strains of genetic material that encodes for the somatic antigens of *S sonnei* and *V cholera* has allowed for the genetic construction of bacteria with multiple somatic antigens. It is hoped that vaccination with these genetically engineered bacteria will confer protection to several enteric pathogens.

REFERENCES

Dupont HL: Shigella species (bacillary dysentery). In Mandell GL et al: *Principles and Practice of Infectious Diseases,* 4th ed. Churchill Livingstone, 1995.

Ericsson CD: Travelers' diarrhea: epidemiology, prevention, and self-treatment. Infect Dis Clin North Am 1998; 12:285.

Miller SI, Hohmann EL, Pegues DA: Salmonella (including *Salmonella typhi*). In Mandell GL et al: *Principles and Practice of Infectious Diseases,* 4th ed. Churchill Livingstone, 1995.

Nataro JP, Kaper JB: Diarrheagenic *Escherichia coli.* Clin Microbiol Rev 1998;11:142.

Ryan ET, Kain KC: Health advice and immunizations for travelers. N Engl J Med 2000;342:1716.

Spangler BD: Structure and function of cholera toxin and the related *Escherichia coli* heat-labile enterotoxin. Microbiol Rev 1992;56:622.

Wolf MK: Occurrence, distribution, and associations of O and H serogroups, colonization factor antigens, and toxins of enterotoxigenic *Escherichia coli.* Clin Microbiol Rev 1997;10:569.

Pseudomonas aeruginosa

54

David Dockrell, MD, & Walter Wilson, MD

Essentials of Diagnosis

- Nosocomial acquisition.
- Predisposing factors include immunosuppression (neutropenia, cystic fibrosis [CF], AIDS, corticosteroid use, diabetes mellitus); presence of a foreign body, prosthesis, or instrumentation; prolonged hospitalization and antibiotic use; intravenous drug use.
- Most common infections include pneumonia, bacteremia, urinary tract infection, otitis media, skin and skin structure infections, including ecthyma gangrenosa.
- Gram stain shows gram-negative bacilli; recovery of microorganism from culture of blood or other tissue.

General Considerations

A. Epidemiology. The genus *Pseudomonas* consists of a number of human pathogens, the most important of which is *Pseudomonas aeruginosa. P aeruginosa* is an opportunistic pathogen found widely in soil, water, and organic material, reflecting its limited nutritional requirements. A moist environment is favored. Human colonization in the community is rare, and, when it occurs, the skin, gut, and upper or lower airway are colonized. Carriage of *P aeruginosa* in the community is associated with predisposing medical conditions, which allow the organism to bridge normal host defenses such as loss of the normal mechanical barrier provided by skin encountered in burn patients or abnormalities in pulmonary physiology encountered in patients with bronchiectasis or CF. In addition, prolonged antibiotic use by eliminating the normal host flora predisposes to *P aeruginosa* colonization.

Nosocomial colonization is much more frequent and most often occurs in patients with predisposing conditions leading to impaired immunity, especially neutropenia, the presence of instrumentation disrupting host defenses, the prolonged use of extended spectrum antibiotics, and the existence of hospital reservoirs of infection. Hospital epidemics have been investigated by a variety of epidemiologic tools including serotyping, antibiogram patterns, and phage typing, but increasingly DNA fingerprinting is used. Potential sources of infection in the hospital environment include infected respiratory equipment, endo-scopes, infusion solutions, intravascular catheters, whirlpools, sinks, drains, and indoor plants.

B. Microbiology. On the basis of ribosomal RNA and DNA sequence homology, the *Pseudomonas* genus is divided into five groups. Group I contains *P aeruginosa* in addition to *P fluorescens* and *P alcaligenes;* Group II contains *P mallei, P pseudomallei,* and *Burkholderia cepacia;* Group III contains the *Comamonas* species; Group IV contains *P diminuta;* and Group V contains *Stenotrophomonas maltophilia* (formerly *Xanthomonas maltophilia*). *Pseudomonas* spp. are gram-negative, straight or slightly curved rods that are motile by means of flagella. They are nonsporing and facultative aerobes. Table 54–1 outlines the essential microbiological features of *P aeruginosa* by which it can be distinguished from other non-*Pseudomonas* gram-negative bacteria. Differentiation from other *Pseudomonas* spp. is more difficult and uses differences in sugar oxidation, growth characteristics at 42 °C, and flagella stains. The production of the pigment pyocyanin by approximately half of *P aeruginosa* strains is specific, and a sweet grapelike odor is often said to be characteristic of *P aeruginosa.*

C. Pathogenesis. The pathogenicity of *P aeruginosa* is a function of host and microbial factors. *P aeruginosa* is an opportunistic pathogen. Host defects may result from alterations in the normal physical barriers to infection. These may be breached by physical alterations such as occur to the skin in burn patients or by prosthetic materials such as catheters that bypass these mechanical barriers. The presence of an effective immune response to *P aeruginosa* requires functional neutrophils in adequate number, the presence of specific immunoglobulin G (IgG) antibodies, and complement activation by both classical and alternative pathways. The production of high titers of antibody to exoenzyme A early on in *P aeruginosa* septicemia results in an improved outcome as compared with a less favorable outcome in those patients with low titers of antibody to exoenzyme A. Immunological defects contribute to infection and may consist of neutropenia, hypogammaglobulinemia, complement defects, or more subtly, age, prolonged hospitalization, or diabetes. Bronchiectasis and CF are lung diseases associated with pathological

Table 54–1 Clues to the diagnosis of *P aeruginosa*.

Morphology and staining properties	• Gram-negative rod, straight or slightly curved, nonsporulating • Motile with single polar flagellum • Occurs singly, in pairs or short chains
Cultivation	• Grows readily on most common media • Obligate aerobe • Optimal culture at 37 °C • Nutritionally versatile and organic growth factors not required
Distinguishing microbiological characteristics	• Carbohydrate fermentation; negative • Sugar oxidation; positive (glucose xylose); negative (maltose) • Indophenol oxidase; positive • Simmons citrate; positive • L-Argenine dehydrolase; positive • L-Lysine decarboxylase; negative • L-Ornithine decarboxylase; negative • Gas production from nitrate • Positive hydrogen sulfide production in Kliger iron agar • Positive growth at 42 °C in brain heart infusion
Other microbiological tests	• Serology not routinely used in diagnosis (used in the diagnosis of *P pseudomallei* and *P mallei*) • Serotyping and nucleic acid techniques have epidemiologic applications (eg, the investigation of nosocomial epidemics)

changes that predispose to colonization and often infection with *P aeruginosa*.

Bacterial factors also contribute. Colonization often precedes infection. Colonization is aided by the bacterial pili and production of mucoid exopolysaccharide. Pili or fimbriae are of particular importance in pulmonary colonization. The alginate capsule is a feature of mucoid strains and has an important role in CF pathogenesis (see below). It protects the organism from antibodies, complement, and phagocytosis. In addition, mucoid strains are associated with decreased susceptibility to antibiotics, especially aminoglycosides. Enzymes that contribute to invasiveness are produced, including alkaline protease, hemolysins, and elastase. Alkaline protease induces necrosis in tissues, possesses strong anticoagulant activity, and inactivates a variety of cytokines including tumor necrosis factor (TNF). Elastase has a variety of pathogenic effects including the degradation of IgG and IgA, complement cleavage, inactivation of TNF, and interferon gamma, and is linked to the pathogenesis of the characteristic skin lesions of *Pseudomonas* septicemia referred to as ecthyma gangrenosum.

Hemolysins aid tissue invasion by degrading lipids and lecithin. One hemolysin, phospholipase c, degrades phosphatidylcholine, a component of lung surfactant, resulting in atelectasis. Cytotoxin, formerly called leukocidin, inhibits neutrophil function and is linked to the pathogenesis of *Pseudomonas*-induced

acute lung injury in adult respiratory distress syndrome. Pyocyanin alters the function of ciliated respiratory epithelium and enhances tissue damage by means of the generation of toxic free radicals.

As with other gram-negative bacteria, lipopolysaccharide plays a key role in the manifestations of septic shock. It stimulates the production of TNF and other cytokines, prostaglandins, leukotrienes, β-endorphins, kinins, complement activation, and the activation of the coagulation and fibrinolytic cascades. Exotoxin A acts by a method similar to diphtheria toxin to inhibit protein synthesis. This toxin plays a significant role in the necrosis observed in animal models of *Pseudomonas* corneal or lung injury. Mutant strains of bacteria that do not produce exotoxin A produce less severe injury than strains expressing exotoxin. Exotoxin A may also be immunosuppressive to both T and B lymphocytes. Exoenzyme S ribosylates proteins of the *ras* gene superfamily and alters local host defense mechanisms.

Clinical Syndromes

Box 54–1 summarizes the principal clinical symptoms associated with *P aeruginosa* infection.

PULMONARY INFECTIONS

Pseudomonas lung infections occur in patients with chronic lung disease or impaired immunity, usually in association with nosocomial factors such as endotracheal intubation, respiratory therapy, prolonged hospitalization, antibiotic use, and neutropenia. Pneumonia takes two forms: primary and bacteremic. Primary pneumonia arises in predisposed patients following nosocomial colonization and aspiration of *P aeruginosa*. Pneumonia is characterized by fever, tachypnea, cough with purulent sputum, shortness of breath, cyanosis, and often signs of sepsis.

The diagnosis of pneumonia caused by *P aeruginosa* is established by the chest x-ray findings of bilateral bronchopneumonia often with radiolucencies resembling *Staphylococcus aureus* pneumonia (Figure 54–1) and recovery of *P aeruginosa* from pulmonary secretions or blood culture. *P aeruginosa* frequently colonizes hospitalized patients, especially those with chronic pulmonary disease or those with endotracheal intubation and mechanical ventilation. Colonization, especially in ventilated patients, is often difficult to differentiate from infection, and the diagnosis of infection requires the presence of signs and symptoms of infection together with recovery of *P aeruginosa* from expectorated sputum, blood cultures, bronchoalveolar lavage, or a protected brushing sample obtained at bronchoscopy. *P aeruginosa* is particularly common in patients with ventilator-associated pneumonia. One study found it caused 27% of cases of ventilator-associated pneumonia and identified risk factors such as chronic obstructive pul-

BOX 54–1

P aeruginosa Clinical Syndromes

Syndrome	Major Clinical Syndromes	Other Clinical Syndromes
Pulmonary Infections	• Primary pneumonia • Ventilator-associated pneumonia	• Bacteremic pneumonia
Infections in Patients with Cystic Fibrosis	• Pneumonia • Bronchitis	
Bacteremia	• Bacteremia in association with neutropenia or AIDS	• Nosocomial bacteremia
Soft-Tissue Infections	• Ecthyma gangrenosum • Burn wound sepsis	• Hot tub folliculitis • Web space infection of the toe • Green nail syndrome
Urinary-Tract Infection	• Catheter-associated UTI	• Complicated UTI
Ear Infections	• Otitis externa (swimmer's ear) • Malignant otitis externa	• Chronic suppurative otitis media • Auricular perichondritis associated with ear piercing
Orthopedic Infections	• Prosthetic joint infection • Post-traumatic open fracture osteomyelitis • Puncture wound osteomyelitis of the foot • Vertebral osteomyelitis • Diabetic foot infection	• Chronic osteomyelitis • Sternoarticular osteomyelitis • Symphysis pubis osteomyelitis
Endocarditis	• Endocarditis in intravenous drug addicts	• Prosthetic valve endocarditis
Ophthalmologic Infection	• Keratitis	• Endophthalmitis
Central Nervous System Infections	• Meningitis/brain abscess associated with post-traumatic open skull fracture or postoperative neurosurgical procedure	• Meningitis in neonates or neutropenic patients • Brain abscess associated with endocarditis • Meningitis/brain abscess associated with contiguous suppurative focus
Gastrointestinal Infections		• Rectal abscess, typhlitis in neutropenic patients • Necrotizing enterocolitis in infants
AIDS	• Pneumonia, bacteremia, and sinusitis	• Meningitis, osteomyelitis, malignant otitis externa

monary disease, mechanical ventilation for more than 8 days, and prior antibiotic use. In the rare instances in which community acquired pneumonia is found, it occurs primarily in patients with chronic obstructive airways disease and history of prior antibiotic use.

Bacteremic pneumonia is caused by septic embolization of the lung. Neutropenia complicating chemotherapy, underlying hematologic malignancy, or AIDS are the usual settings for this type of pneumonia. This is usually a rapidly fatal disease. Pathologically, two characteristic pulmonary lesions are encountered. One type is hemorrhagic nodules, which

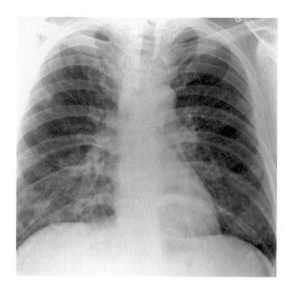

Figure 54–1. *Pseudomonas aeruginosa* pneumonia in an immunocompromised host. Note the bilateral pneumonia on chest x-ray with radiolucencies resembling the appearance of *S aureus* pneumonia.

are primarily subpleural and surround pulmonary vessels without inflammatory infiltrates. The second type is umbilicated nodules with liquifactive necrosis and leukocyte infiltration or more frequently with coagulative necrosis. These lesions are the pulmonary form of cutaneous ecthyma gangrenosum. The radiologic appearance of bacteremic pneumonia evolves over 1 to 3 days and is initially manifested by pulmonary congestion and edema with subsequent alveolar infiltrates, pulmonary hemorrhage, and finally cavitation.

INFECTIONS IN PATIENTS WITH CYSTIC FIBROSIS

Patients with CF demonstrate particularly complex host-parasite interactions involving *P aeruginosa*. CF is characterized by mutations in the CF transmembrane conductance regulator resulting in abnormal chloride ion secretion and cellular dehydration. A continuous cycle of cellular inflammation with increased numbers of neutrophils in bronchoalveolar lavage fluid, increased interleukin 8 secretion, viscous mucus, mucus plugging of airways, and infection results. Whether *P aeruginosa* infections play a role in the pathogenesis of the disease is still a matter of debate, but research has established a complex interaction.

Colonization rates for *P aeruginosa* increase with age and reach 60–80% for adult CF patients. One of the effects of the genetic mutation causing CF is an increase in levels of the receptor, α-sialo GM_1, on

respiratory epithelium. *P aeruginosa* isolates from CF patients who are colonized demonstrate the mucoid phenotype discussed above and form a biofilm that protects the bacteria from antibiotics, immunoglobulin, complement, and oxygen-free radicals. Conversely, strains lose the polysaccharide O side chains of lipopolysaccharide and become susceptible to complement, which prevents invasive infection and bacteremia. Motility is lost, and loss of flagella correlates with decreased nonopsonic phagocytosis. Immunoevasion is accomplished with the aid of a variety of bacterial products, especially elastase (which proteolyses immunoglobulin, complement, and cytokines) and cytotoxin (which induces T-lymphocyte, macrophage, and neutrophil cytotoxicity).

Colonization is facilitated by prior antimicrobial treatment of respiratory infections, which eradicates existing respiratory flora. Acute exacerbations with productive cough caused by bronchitis or pneumonia occur and are associated with further reduction of respiratory reserve. Fever is usually absent. Antimicrobial treatment of acute exacerbations is necessary, although eradication of the carrier state does not usually occur. Prophylactic or suppressive antimicrobial therapy has not been demonstrated to be efficacious; however, intermittent antipseudomonal therapy, including the use of nebulized antimicrobial agents, in particular, tobramycin, improves pulmonary function and decreases exacerbation of infection. Chest physiotherapy is essential in limiting infections. Ultimately, respiratory failure may lead to heart-lung or double lung transplantation, and *P aeruginosa* infection contributes to the high morbidity and mortality associated with transplantation in this population.

BACTEREMIA

P aeruginosa is a common cause of nosocomial bacteremia, which may be either primary (no identifiable source) or secondary (recognizable extravascular source). Community-acquired *P aeruginosa* bacteremia is very rare. Host factors contributing to nosocomially acquired *P aeruginosa* bacteremia include neutropenia caused by hematological malignancy or chemotherapy, hypogammaglobulinemia, AIDS, organ transplantation, insulin-dependent diabetes mellitus, burns, premature births or advanced age, instrumentation or catheterization, high-dose corticosteroid use, and prolonged antibiotic therapy. *P aeruginosa* bacteremia is associated with higher mortality than bacteremia caused by other gram-negative microorganisms, although this observation may reflect the host's underlying immunosuppression.

A poor prognosis is associated with an absolute neutrophil count of < 100 cells/mL^3, septic shock, renal failure, or a serious underlying illness. Primary bacteremia or bacteremia-complicating pneumonia or skin infections are also associated with a poor prognosis. Clinical signs of *P aeruginosa* bacteremia are those of gram-negative sepsis and include fever, tachycardia, respiratory distress, hypotension, obtundation, and renal failure. *P aeruginosa* bacteremia has a particular propensity to cause jaundice. Disseminated intravascular coagulation is less frequently encountered with *P aeruginosa* bacteremia than other gram-negative bacteremias.

The classic skin lesion of *P aeruginosa* bacteremia is ecthyma gangrenosum, which is characterized by the presence of a small vesicle with a rim of surrounding erythema that undergoes necrosis and ulcerates with localized gangrene and black discoloration (Figure 54–2). Histopathology reveals the invasion of small arteries and veins by bacteria and is characterized by the absence of a significant inflammatory infiltrate. Lesions occur most frequently on the extremities, buttocks, perineum, or axilla, although they may occur anywhere including within the oral cavity. Although occasionally reported in infections with other organisms including *Escherichia coli* and *Candida* spp., these lesions are highly suggestive of *Pseudomonas* infection. However, only a minority of bacteremic infections develop this lesion. Other skin lesions encountered include vesiculopustular or maculopapular lesions and cellulitis. The diagnosis is made by the characteristic appearance of gram-nega-

tive microorganisms on Gram stain and recovery of *P aeruginosa* from blood or tissue cultures.

SKIN & SOFT TISSUE INFECTIONS

Infections caused by *P aeruginosa* involving the skin may be primary or secondary. Secondary infections have been described above and include ecthyma gangrenosum, subcutaneous nodules, vesicles, bullae, cellulitis, deep abscesses, and necrotizing fasciitis. Primary skin lesions are noted as complications of neutropenia, burns, decubitus ulcers, prematurity, exposure to a moist environment, and hydrotherapy. Burn wound sepsis is a serious complication that may be caused by *P aeruginosa*. Colonization of the burn may lead to invasive disease. The signs are black, brown, or violet discoloration of the burn eschar; destruction of granulation tissue leading to rapid eschar separation and subcutaneous hemorrhage; erythematous nodules; edema or hemorrhage of adjacent uninfected tissue; black neoeschar formation; or signs of septicemia. This complication of burns has a high associated mortality. Diagnosis is by skin biopsy of both burn tissue and adjacent viable tissue. The presence of > 10^5 organisms per gram of tissue cultured, the presence of *P aeruginosa* in adjacent healthy tissue, vasculitis, or inflammation at the burn margin are diagnostic.

Other skin and soft tissue infections caused by *P aeruginosa* include the following: hot tub- or hydrotherapy-associated folliculitis, which is usually self-limited (Figure 54–3); web space infection of the toe associated with humid climates or tinea pedis infection and characterized by maceration and scaling with purulent discharge, which may be green in color; green nail syndrome, which is characterized by paronychia occurring in association with a history of frequent submersion of the hands in water and nail discoloration caused by incorporation of pigment in the nail; green foot syndrome resulting from *P aeruginosa* colonization of rubber-soled shoes producing pigment that stains the feet, but in which *P aerugi-*

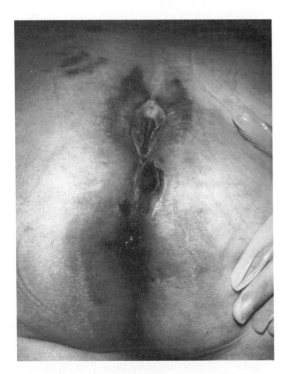

Figure 54–2. Ecthyma gangrenosum in the perirectal region of a neutropenic patient receiving chemotherapy for hemolytic malignancy. Note the necrotic center of the lesions with surrounding erythema.

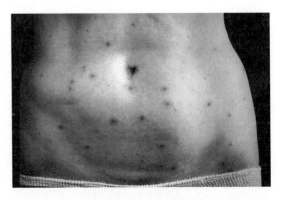

Figure 54–3. *Pseudomonas aeruginosa* hot tub folliculitis.

nosa does not cause direct infection; diving suit dermatitis; necrotizing fasciitis after Cesarean section, and noma neonatorum, a complication of premature infants in developing countries where necrotizing hemorrhagic lesions of mucosal surfaces or the groin result in fulminant infection and often death.

URINARY TRACT INFECTION

Urinary tract infection (UTI) with *P aeruginosa* occurs primarily in two settings: nosocomial infection or complicated urinary tract infection. Nosocomial infections involve patients with urinary catheterization, instrumentation, or surgery. Renal transplant recipients have a high risk of *P aeruginosa* urinary tract infection. Complicated urinary tract infections are often nosocomially acquired and occur in association with renal stones, chronic prostatitis, or urinary tract malformations. Rarely community-acquired *P aeruginosa* cystitis occurs in young patients as the result of transient colonization.

The clinical presentation of *P aeruginosa* UTI includes dysuria, increased frequency of micturition, and hematuria. Fever and flank pain occur in cases of pyelonephritis. Diagnosis is made by the recovery of *P aeruginosa* from cultures of a midstream or catheterized urine sample in association with pyuria or hematuria. Urinary tract infections contribute significantly to the total number of patients with *P aeruginosa* bacteremia and are associated with a better outcome than bacteremia associated with other sources.

Rare complications of *Pseudomonas* UTI include the sloughing of bladder mucosa associated with ulceration of the urinary bladder or renal infarcts caused by invasion of small blood vessels representing a form of ecthyma gangrenosum in the kidney. Treatment of UTI infection is complicated by the tenacity with which *P aeruginosa* adheres to urinary epithelium predisposing to chronic infection and relapse.

EAR, NOSE & THROAT INFECTIONS

P aeruginosa infection of the external auditory canal may be acute or may be a chronic serious infection called malignant otitis externa. Acute diffuse otitis externa is often referred to as swimmer's ear. *P aeruginosa* may be part of the normal flora of the external auditory canal or may colonize the canal as a result of exposure to water. Swimming, a humid climate, and local trauma result in inflammation, desquamation, and bacterial proliferation. The clinical signs and symptoms are erythema, discharge, pain, and pruritus. An aggressive hemorrhagic form has been associated with hot tub use. Topical antibiotics, topical corticosteroids, and drying agents are usually effective therapy, although relapse is frequent.

Malignant otitis externa is the contiguous spread of necrotizing *P aeruginosa* infection from beyond the external auditory canal to the adjacent soft tissue and bone and is a serious infection usually occurring in elderly diabetics with microvascular disease but may also occur in elderly nondiabetics, or in association with systemic corticosteroid treatment, AIDS, or rarely in infants. Irrigation of the ear with water in these patients may represent a risk factor. Infection spreads from the external auditory canal through adjacent cartilage and soft tissue to the parotid space, the temporal bone, and mastoid air cells and then to the base of the skull.

Symptoms include severe pain and discharge sometimes associated with decreased hearing, but systemic symptoms are rare. On examination the external auditory canal is erythematous and edematous, and granulation tissue may be observed. The middle ear is usually spared. Ipsilateral fascial nerve palsy is a common early finding. Potential complications include parotid swelling and trismus, palsies of the 9th through 12th cranial nerves, cavernous venous thrombosis, and rarely, brain abscess or meningitis. An elevated erythrocyte sedimentation rate (ESR) in the absence of significant elevation of white blood cell count is common. For the radiologic diagnosis, magnetic resonance imaging may be more sensitive than computed tomography scans, and radionucleotide scans, such as indium-labeled white blood cell scans, are useful to detect early bone involvement.

P aeruginosa is usually recovered from cultures of the external auditory canal or from débrided tissue. Antimicrobial therapy should be combined with local débridement, and in more severe cases, extensive débridement is warranted. Cure is also dependent on successful management of underlying conditions such as diabetes mellitus or reduction of corticosteroid therapy. Early diagnosis improves the outcome, and an adequate response to therapy may be assessed by documenting decreased otalgia, a decrease in erythrocyte sedimentation rate, and improved radiologic appearance.

P aeruginosa is the most frequent pathogen identified in chronic suppurative otitis externa infections in all ages and is also a recognized pathogen in mastoiditis in diabetics, sinusitis in patients with AIDS, and perichondritis of the auricle following ear piercing or other traumatic procedures performed on the pinna.

ORTHOPEDIC INFECTIONS

Bone and joint infections caused by *P aeruginosa* may result as complications of surgery, in particular the implantation of joint prostheses, or pelvic or genitourinary surgery, in association with intravenous (IV) drug abuse, trauma resulting in open fractures such as motor vehicle or farm related accidents, complicated UTIs, diabetic foot ulcers, or puncture wounds of the foot. *P aeruginosa* has a predilection to infect fibrocartilaginous structures. *P aeruginosa* prosthetic joint infections may occur as a result of contamination during implantation, aspiration, or injection of the joint with corticosteroids.

In addition, *P aeruginosa* prosthetic joint infections may occur as a result of repeated surgical manipulation of the joint, joint revision, or reimplantation of the prosthesis. Polymicrobial osteomyelitis with *P aeruginosa* and other microorganisms is commonly associated with farm or motor vehicle accidents when open fractures become contaminated with water, soil, or vegetative materials. Vertebral osteomyelitis occurs in IV drug abusers or as a complication of UTI or genitourinary surgery. The lumbosacral spine is principally involved, although cervical involvement occurs in IV drug abusers. Sternoarticular pyarthrosis may occur in IV drug abusers or occasionally as a complication of infective endocarditis. Infection of the symphysis pubis may occur after pelvic or genitourinary surgery and must be differentiated from nonpyogenic osteitis pubis.

Puncture wound infections of the foot occur at all ages and have a particular association with punctures through rubber-soled sneakers. These infections occur as a result of the growth of *P aeruginosa* in the moist inner sole layer of the shoes, and puncture wounds through the shoe inoculate *P aeruginosa* directly into the bones of the foot and surrounding soft tissue.

Chronic osteomyelitis may occur as a result of contiguous infection following trauma, surgery, or as a complication of diabetic foot ulcers due to direct inoculation or local expansion of the organism. These infections tend to be indolent with pain and decreased range of movement in the absence of fever or leukocytosis. An elevated erythrocyte sedimentation rate, abnormalities on CT scanning or MRI or a positive radionuclide scan suggest the diagnosis, but confirmation requires demonstration of the organism on a Gram stain and recovery of *P aeruginosa* from cultures. Puncture wounds of the foot may be more acute in presentation, and typically the initial pain after the injury resolves and recurs a few days later with pain and swelling over the site of inoculation. Osteomyelitis of any of the bones of the foot may result (Figure 54–4).

Effective treatment requires antimicrobial therapy combined with surgical débridement. Successful treatment of *P aeruginosa* prosthetic joint infection requires resection of the prosthesis and other foreign material together with débridement and antimicrobial therapy.

ENDOCARDITIS

P aeruginosa endocarditis occurs predominantly in two settings: in association with IV drug use (IVDU) or with prosthetic valve endocarditis (PVE). The majority of cases of native valve endocarditis caused by *P*

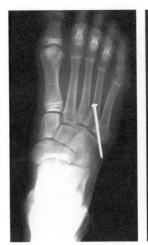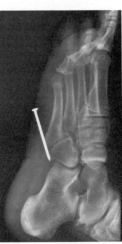

Figure 54–4. Puncture wound osteomyelitis of the calcaneus due to *Pseudomonas aeruginosa*. Note the loss of the border of the calcaneus adjacent to the tip of the nail.

aeruginosa occur in association with IVDU. Risk factors for endocarditis associated with IVDU include the use of substances that are not boiled after mixing before injection, the injection of drugs at shooting galleries, and the use of pentazocine and tripelennamine. Intravenous drug users often have a combination of these factors. Despite the strong association of IVDU with *P aeruginosa* endocarditis, *S aureus* and streptococci more frequently cause endocarditis in IVDU.

The tricuspid valve is most frequently infected in intravenous drug users, occurring in over two-thirds of cases. Infection of the mitral, aortic, or pulmonic valves may also occur, and infection of multiple valves is common. Evidence of prior valvular pathology is usually absent, although foreign materials in injected substances may predispose by causing endothelial damage and fibrosis. The infection is usually subacute with fever and cardiac murmur occurring in the absence of other classic stigmata of infective endocarditis, such as Osler nodes, Janeway lesions, or Roth spots.

Presentation may be due to complications arising from septic pulmonary embolization characterized by cough, sputum production, pleuritic chest pain, or new infiltrates on chest x-ray. Left-sided valvular disease is less frequently encountered, and embolic complications and cardiogenic shock are frequent sequelae. Ecthyma gangrenosum is rarely encountered in patients with endocarditis.

PVE caused by *P aeruginosa* is often highly aggressive. Diagnosis is based upon clinical illness compatible with infective endocarditis and blood cultures positive for *P aeruginosa*. Definitive diagnosis is made by recovery of *P aeruginosa* from blood cultures or tissue obtained at surgery or autopsy.

In addition to antibiotic therapy, surgical intervention is often necessary especially in left-sided valvular infections. Successful treatment of *P aeruginosa* PVE requires surgical intervention together with antimicrobial therapy. Infection of the tricuspid valve may also require surgery if bacteremia persists after 2 weeks of effective antimicrobial therapy or recurs after a 6-week course of antibiotics. The procedure of choice is tricuspid valvulectomy. In cases without a history of IVDU, a tricuspid valve replacement can be performed ~6–8 weeks after valvulectomy. Poor prognostic factors in *P aeruginosa* endocarditis are an age > 30 years, fever lasting > 2 weeks on appropriate antimicrobial-agent therapy, embolization, mural vegetation, left-sided infection, PVE, and mixed infection, particularly with *S aureus* as the copathogen.

OPHTHALMOLOGIC INFECTION

P aeruginosa infections involving the eye take two predominant forms: keratitis and endophthalmitis. Keratitis often results from corneal ulceration induced by trauma. Risk factors include the use of contact lenses, especially extended wear soft contact lenses; topical ophthalmic steroid use; contaminated ophthalmic solutions; burn patients; prolonged coma; tracheostomy; ocular irradiation; or AIDS. In intensive care units, tracheal colonization, corneal drying, corneal abrasion, and a decrease in the bactericidal effect of lacrimal secretions contribute to the increased risk of infection.

Symptoms include pain, erythema, photophobia, purulent discharge, and blurred vision. On exam, a necrotic pale corneal ulcer is observed with adherent mucopurulent discharge and hypopyon formation (pus in the anterior chamber). Loss of vision may be rapid, and this condition is an ophthalmologic emergency necessitating prompt diagnosis and treatment. Diagnosis is made by ophthalmologic examination, scrapings from the ulcer, demonstration of organism presence on Gram stain, and organism recovery from culture. Treatment requires the application of antibiotic-containing ophthalmic solution combined with subconjunctival injection of antibiotics.

Endophthalmitis may result from keratitis, hematogenous spread, direct trauma, or surgery. The clinical signs and symptoms include a painful red eye with chemosis, hypopyon, anterior uveitis, decreased visual acuity, and in severe cases panophthalmitis. Therapy consists of combined topical, subconjunctival, intraocular and systemic treatment often combined with vitrectomy.

CENTRAL NERVOUS SYSTEM INFECTION

Infection of the central nervous system (CNS) with *P aeruginosa* occurs as a result of immunosuppression and altered local defenses. Spread to the CNS may be from a local source, such as malignant otitis externa or sinusitis, direct inoculation at the time of head trauma, or surgery (including the placement of external or internal shunts or dural grafts), or by hematogenous spread from a remote focus such as endocarditis. Infection may result in either meningitis or brain abscess.

Signs and symptoms of infection depend on whether bacteremia is associated with the infection. Bacteremic cases are usually acute with fever and signs of sepsis in addition to headache, nuchal rigidity, and photophobia characteristic of meningitis. Spinal fluid analysis demonstrates elevated protein and gram-negative bacteria on Gram stain, and in nonneutropenic patients an elevation in neutrophils is usual. Cases linked to direct inoculation resulting from head trauma, surgery, or neurosurgical procedure may occur with a more indolent course of fever, headache, and nonspecific signs of CNS infection. Spinal fluid analysis may establish the diagnosis. Cases complicated by abscess formation require aspiration or biopsy to confirm the diagnosis. Successful treatment requires correction of structural defects, removal of foreign materials, and drainage of abscesses when possible, in addition to antimicrobial treatment.

GASTROINTESTINAL INFECTIONS

The gastrointestinal tract is the principal portal of entry for *Pseudomonas* bacteremia in neutropenic patients receiving chemotherapy. In addition, these patients may develop localized gastrointestinal infection. Although infection may involve any part of the gastrointestinal tract, it particularly involves the cecum and rectum. Localized areas of necrosis and gangrene in the cecum are termed typhlitis. *Pseudomonas* infection of the cecum is characterized by hemorrhagic, necrotic ulcers with bacterial invasion of the submucosal blood vessels and an absence of inflammatory cells. Patients present with abdominal pain, and peritonitis may occur. The abdominal radiograph may reveal signs of perforation of a viscus. The rectum is also a source of bacterial abscesses in neutropenic patients, and *P aeruginosa* is most frequently the cause. Rectal abscesses may be the source of bacteremia or may result in localized spread causing gangrene. These lesions must be carefully searched for because the absence of inflammation in neutropenic patients may delay diagnosis. Rectal abscesses require prompt surgical drainage.

The second group of patients with ulcerative intestinal lesions due to *P aeruginosa* is young infants who develop necrotizing enterocolitis. Risk factors include prematurity, comorbid illness, and admission to the neonatal intensive care unit. Clinical signs are fever, irritability, vomiting, bloody diarrhea, dehydration, and abdominal distension. An abdominal radiograph may demonstrate pneumatosis intestinalis, portal air, or free peritoneal air.

INFECTION IN PATIENTS WITH AIDS

P aeruginosa infections may occur in patients with AIDS. Risk factors for infection include a CD4 count of < 100 cells/mL^3, neutropenia or functional neutrophil defects, intravascular catheterization, hospitalization, and prior use of antibiotics including ciprofloxacin or trimethoprim-sulfamethoxazole. Many cases are community acquired. Bacteremia is common, and the lung or an intravenous catheter is the most frequent portal of entry. An impaired ability to mount immunotype-specific antibodies to *Pseudomonas* lipopolysaccharide antigen has been noted in HIV-positive individuals with bacteremia. Relapse is frequent, and mortality is high, 40%. Pneumonia is usually associated with cavitation and a high relapse rate. Bacterial sinusitis is an important and frequently undetected illness in HIV-positive individuals, and *P aeruginosa* is a frequent cause. Fluoroquinolone resistance may result from its use for the treatment of *Mycobacterium avium* complex.

Other infections caused by *P aeruginosa* described in patients with AIDS include malignant otitis externa, corneoscleritis, corneal ulceration and orbital cellulitis, meningitis, peritonitis, soft tissue infections, and osteomyelitis including osteitis pubis.

Diagnosis

The diagnosis of a *P aeruginosa* infection requires the identification of the clinical syndrome by history, physical examination, and laboratory testing. The specific syndrome influences the duration of antimicrobial therapy and the need for surgical intervention. In patients with positive blood cultures, it is critical to determine the source of bacteremia. Microbiological diagnosis requires the recovery of *P aeruginosa* from culture. Gram-negative bacilli in culture should be screened for the presence of oxidase. Oxidase production excludes most gram-negative bacilli other than *Pseudomonas* spp. Definitive diagnosis requires the use of specific microbiological tests to distinguish *P aeruginosa* from other *Pseudomonas* spp.

Treatment

Antimicrobial therapy of *P aeruginosa* infections is outlined in Box 54–2. Resistance of *P aeruginosa* in vitro to many antimicrobial agents is widespread and is increasing in frequency. Susceptibility testing should be performed on all clinically significant isolates to guide the selection of appropriate antimicrobial therapy. In addition, the following principles should be considered:

• Antibiotics active in vitro against *P aeruginosa* often include extended spectrum penicillins with or without the combination of a β-lactamase inhibitor; some third-generation cephalosporins (ceftazidime, cefoperazone); fourth-generation cephalosporins (cefepime); carbapenems (imipenem, meropenem); monobactam (aztreonam); aminoglycosides (gentamicin, tobramycin, amikacin, netilmicin); and fluoroquinolones (for example ciprofloxacin).

• In general, therapy with a β-lactam antibiotic should not be used as monotherapy. In severe infections a β-lactam should be combined with an aminoglycoside or a fluoroquinolone. Successfully used in the treatment of other gram-negative infections, once-daily dosing of aminoglycosides can be considered in *P aeruginosa* infections.

• A fluoroquinolone is the only effective antimicrobial that may be administered orally.

• Patients with a history of major β-lactam allergy may be treated with a fluoroquinolone, aztreonam, or, cautiously, a carbapenem often combined with an aminoglycoside in severe infections.

• Optimal therapy often requires surgical intervention. Examples include left-sided endocarditis, PVE, necrotizing enterocolitis, malignant otitis externa, osteomyelitis, and prosthetic joint infection.

• Modifications of antimicrobial therapy may be necessary when antimicrobial susceptibility data are available.

CF patients represent a particular challenge to therapy. Altered pharmokinetics frequently necessitate higher doses of antimicrobial agents than in other patients. Colonization with resistant strains is common in patients with CF. The administration of intermittent antimicrobial therapy to CF patients with chronic pseudomonal infections and the use of nebulized antimicrobial agents may reduce the frequency of *Pseudomonas* infection in CF patients. Despite theoretical concerns about fluoroquinolone incorporation into developing cartilage in pediatric patients, ciprofloxacin has been used successfully and safely in these patients.

Antimicrobial resistance is increasing worldwide among strains of *P aeruginosa.* β-Lactam resistance may be due to mutational derepression of the *ampC* chromosomal β-lactamase, the acquisition of plasmid- or transposon-mediated β-lactamases, reduced permeability of *P aeruginosa* to antimicrobial agents, multidrug efflux pump systems, and, in the case of carbapenems, loss of the D2 porin. Zinc-containing β-lactamases confer resistance to carbapenems. Many strains produce inducible cephalosporinases that account for the rapid emergence of resistance during therapy. Aminoglycoside resistance may be caused by decreased uptake owing to overproduction of the major outer membrane protein H1, aminoglycoside modifying enzymes, or modification of ribosomal targets. Mutations in the *gyrA* gene may cause resistance to ciprofloxacin and other fluoroquinolones.

BOX 54–2

Treatment of *P aeruginosa* Clinical Syndromes[1]

Syndrome	First Choice	Alternative Choice	Comments (Including Choice for Penicillin-Allergic Patients)
Pneumonia	EITHER • Ceftazidime, 1–2 g (50 mg/kg) every 8 h OR • Cefepime, 1–2 g (50 mg/kg) every 12 h IV OR • Piperacillin, ticarcillin, or mezlocillin, 3 g (75 mg/kg) every 4 h IV OR • Ciprofloxacin, 400 mg (5–10 mg/kg) every 12 h IV or 500–750 mg (7.5–15 mg/kg every 12 h orally OR • Imipenem-cilastatin, 0.5 g (12.5 mg/kg) every 6 h IV, or meropenem, 1 g (40 mg/kg) every 8 h IV OR • Aztreonam, 2 g (30 mg/kg) every 6 h IV PLUS • Gentamicin or tobramycin, 2 mg/kg load, then 1.7 mg/kg every 8 h IV, or amikacin, 10 mg/kg load and 7.5 mg/kg every 12 h IV • Treat for 14–21 days	In selected patients, monotherapy with ceftazidime, cefepime, ciprofloxacin, imipenem-cilastatin, meropenem, or aztreonam Treatment for at least 14–21 days	Penicillin allergic: aztreonam, ciprofloxacin, imipenem-cilastatin, or meropenem plus aminoglycoside Antibiotic dose adjustment for patients with cystic fibrosis Treatment for at least 14–21 days
Bacteremia	Same treatment as for pneumonia; treat for at least 2 weeks	Same treament with monotherapy as for pneumonia; treat for at least 2 weeks	Same as per pneumonia
Burn Wound Sepsis	Same treatment as for pneumonia; duration of treatment individualized	Same treatment as for pneumonia; duration of therapy individualized	Beta-lactam allergic: see above Avoid treating burn wound sepsis with monotherapy

Urinary Tract Infections	Upper tract infections: treat as per pneumonia with two agents for 2 weeks; may complete course with oral ciprofloxacin Lower tract infection: ciprofloxacin, 500 mg (7.5 mg/kg) twice a day orally for 3–7 days	Upper tract disease: treat with monotherapy as per pneumonia for 2 weeks	Aztreonam, carbapenem, ciprofloxacin (same doses) IV for beta-lactam–allergic patient Monotherapy usually suffices; if bacteremic, complicated upper tract disease, renal abscess formation, or neutropenic, treat as for bacteremia
Malignant Otitis Externa	Ceftazidime, cefepime, or ciprofloxacin (same doses as for pneumonia) for 4–8 weeks	Imipenem–cilastatin or –meropenem IV at same doses used for pneumonia for 4–8 weeks	Ciprofloxacin for beta-lactam–allergic patients
Orthopedic Infections	Same treatment as for pneumonia for 6 weeks	Single-agent therapy with ceftazidime, imipenem–cilastatin, or ciprofloxacin is less studied but may be a valid choice; doses as for pneumonia; treatment duration ≥ 6 weeks	For penicillin-allergic patient, see above Puncture wound osteomyelitis, ciprofloxacin, 500 mg (7.5 mg/kg) every 12 h orally for 4–6 weeks
Endocarditis	Ticarcillin, mezlocillin, piperacillin, ceftazidime, or cefepime PLUS Tobramycin or gentamicin, 8–12 mg/kg/d. Peak tobramycin or gentamicin conc in serum, 12–20 µg/ml; treatment for at least 6 weeks	Carbapenem, aztreonam, or ciprofloxacin, combined with aminoglycosides, is the alternative, but limited experience and optimal dosage require clarification	Aztreonam, carbapenem, or ciprofloxacin, and aminoglycoside combination for beta-lactam–allergic patient Ciprofloxacin, 500 mg (7.5 mg/kg) every 12 orally, may be useful for long-term suppression of prosthetic valve endocarditis
Ophthalmic Infections	Keratitis: Gentamicin ophthalmic solution, 8 mg/ml every 30–60 min, plus subconjunctival gentamicin, 20 mg for first 3 days; total duration of therapy, ≥ 1 week. Same doses for pediatric patients	Ophthalmic solution of enoxacin	Endophthalmitis: Combine parenteral and subconjunctival antipseudomonal penicillin and aminoglycoside with ophthalmic gentamicin and intraophthalmic gentamicin Alternative: Ceftazidime or cefepime by parenteral, subconjunctival, and intraoccular routes Duration: Intraoccular antibiotics for 7 days, other antibiotics till signs of infection resolve exact duration undetermined.

BOX 54-2 (continued)

Treatment of *P aeruginosa* Clinical Syndromes[1]

Syndrome	First Choice	Alternative Choice	Comments (Including Choice for Penicillin-Allergic Patients)
Central Nervous System Infections	Ceftazidime or cefepime, 50–100 mg/kg (same doses for pediatric patients) up to 2 g every 6 h or antipseudomonal penicillin (see above), meropenem, aztreonam, or ciprofloxacin plus aminoglycoside or ciprofloxacin parenterally ± intrathecally; treatment duration at least 2 weeks		Beta-lactam–allergic patient; see above. Imipenem-cilastatin should not be used because of risk of seizures
Gastrointestinal Infections	Same antibiotics and doses as for pneumonia	Same antibiotics and doses as for pneumonia	Same antibiotics for penicillin-allergic patient as for pneumonia Necrotizing enterocolitis (ticarcillin, piperacillin, or mezlocillin, 75 mg/kg every 6–8 h **PLUS** Tobramycin or gentamicin, 5–7 mg/kg/d) Consult specialist text for dosages in low-birth-weight infants

[1]Pediatric doses are given in parentheses.

Prevention & Control

P aeruginosa is primarily a nosocomial pathogen, and control measures should be focused on hospital infection control. Appropriate sterilization of all equipment and prompt recognition of hospital outbreaks are essential. Hand washing after patient examination and additional measures such as wound and contact isolation for multiply resistant *P aeruginosa* should be performed. In particular, measures to decrease the spread of *P aeruginosa* between patients at CF clinics are necessary.

OTHER *PSEUDOMONAS* SPECIES OF MEDICAL IMPORTANCE

P PSEUDOMALLEI MELIOIDOSIS

This organism is endemic in Southeast Asia with the highest prevalence in Thailand. The organism is a saprophyte living in the soil. Infection may be subclinical, acute, subacute, or chronic. Pulmonary infection is most common. Histologically, the acute illness is represented by lung abscesses and the subacute form by caseation necrosis. Upper lobe cavities must be distinguished from those caused by tuberculosis. Debilitated patients may develop hematogenous spread of the organism to other organs. Skin lesions from direct inoculation cause suppurative lesions often in association with nodular lymphangitis and regional lymphadenopathy.

Diagnosis is made in a patient from an endemic area with a compatible clinical illness who has a positive *P pseudomallei* culture or a fourfold increase or decrease in antibody titer. Appropriate therapy requires a combination of antimicrobial agents and surgical drainage. Ceftazidime alone or in combination with either trimethoprim-sulfamethoxazole or amoxicillin clavulanate is the therapy of choice. The duration of therapy ranges from 3 to 12 months with the longest duration of treatment necessary in chronic extrapulmonary disease. Imipenem, piperacillin-tazobactam, chloramphenicol, and tetracycline are alternative agents; the microorganism is resistant to ciprofloxacin and aztreonam.

P MALLEI (GLANDERS)

Infection with *P mallei* (glanders) is the result of contact with an infected equine source such as horses, donkeys, or mules. The disease is confined to Africa, Asia, and South America. Human disease takes the following forms: acute suppurative infection with localized nodules and lymphangitis, mucocutaneous granuloma and ulcer, acute pulmonary infection with nodules and lymphadenopathy, acute septicemia, or a chronic suppurative form. Seroconversion or recovery of *P mallei* from culture confirms the diagnosis. Antimicrobial therapy is usually with the same agents effective for melioidosis administered for a period of 1–2 months often combined with surgical drainage.

STENOTROPHOMONAS MALTOPHILIA

This organism is a free-living microorganism that causes nosocomial infection in debilitated patients particularly in the intensive care or chronic ventilatory units. Infections encountered include pneumonia, UTI, wound infection, bacteremia, and, rarely, peritonitis, cholangitis, or endovascular infections. The emergence of this bacterium as a serious pathogen is caused by its antibiotic resistance pattern. It produces inducible β-lactamases and has low outer membrane permeability but is often susceptible to trimethoprim-sulfamethoxazole or ticarcillin-clavulanate. Alternative agents include ciprofloxacin, minocycline, doxycycline, and occasionally third-generation cephalosporins, but the microorganism is usually resistant to carbapenem or aminoglycosides.

BURKHOLDERIA CEPACIA

This microorganism is a cause of nosocomial infections similar to those caused by *Stenotrophomonas maltophilia*. It is also an important pathogen in patients with CF, and infection is associated with progressive lung disease and high mortality. CF patients who are colonized with *B cepacia* preoperatively and undergo lung transplantation have higher post-transplantation mortality than those who are not colonized. In CF clinics, colonization rates are high. *B cepacia* is resistant to aminoglycosides and most β-lactam agents. Some strains are variably susceptible to third-generation cephalosporins, ciprofloxacin, trimethoprim-sulfamethoxazole, ampicillin-sulbactam, chloramphenicol, or meropenem.

REFERENCES

Arbulu A, Holmes RJ, Asfaw I: Surgical treatment of intractable right-sided infective endocarditis in drug addicts: 25 years experience. J Heart Valve Dis 1993; 2:129.

Brewer SC, Wunderink RJ, Jones CB, Leeper KV: Ventilator associated pneumonia due to *Pseudomonas aeruginosa.* Chest 1996;109:1019.

Buret A, Cripps AW: The immunoevasive activities of *Pseudomonas aeruginosa.* Relevance for cystic fibrosis. Am Rev Respir Dis 1993;148:793.

Chen HY, Yuan M, Livermore DM: Mechanisms of resistance to β-lactam antibiotics amongst *Pseudomonas aeruginosa* isolates collected in the UK in 1993. J Med Microbiol 1995;43:300.

Mendelson MH et al: *Pseudomonas aeruginosa* bacteremia in patients with AIDS. Clin Infect Dis 1994;18:886.

Pollack M: *Pseudomonas aeruginosa.* In GL Mandell, JE Bennett, R Dolin: *Mandell, Douglas and Bennett's Principles and Practice of Infectious Diseases.* Churchill Livingstone 1995.

Helicobacter pylori

55

Jay V. Solnick, MD, PhD, & Javeed Siddiqui, MD, MPH

Essentials of Diagnosis
- Positive serum immunoglobulin G usually indicates active infection.
- Serology is generally not helpful for documentation of cure.
- Urea breath test and stool antigen test are useful to document cure.
- Acid suppression therapy decreases the sensitivity of the urea breath test.
- Culture and susceptibility testing may be useful in refractory cases.

General Considerations

Pathologists have noted spiral bacteria in biopsies and autopsy specimens of gastric mucosa for over 100 years. Their significance was alternately debated and ignored until 1982, when Barry Marshall and Robin Warren cultivated the organism for the first time and suggested that it might be a cause of chronic gastritis and peptic ulcer disease. Although initially called *Campylobacter pylori,* subsequent taxonomic studies showed that the bacterium was not a true *Campylobacter* species, and it was renamed *Helicobacter pylori.* Despite initial skepticism, Marshall and Warren's early proposal that *H pylori* caused gastritis and peptic ulcer disease proved correct. Furthermore, there is now overwhelming evidence that *H pylori* is linked to adenocarcinoma and non-Hodgkin's lymphoma of the stomach. The clinical significance of this organism has been emphasized by a National Institutes of Health consensus panel that recommended antibiotic therapy for the large majority of peptic ulcer patients who are infected with *H pylori* and by the classification of *H pylori* as a carcinogen by the World Health Organization.

A. Epidemiology.
1. Prevalence of infection. *H pylori* is one of the most prevalent bacterial disease agents of humans and has been isolated from human stomachs in all parts of the world. In developing countries the prevalence is 70–90%, and most persons acquire *H pylori* infection before the age of 10 years. In the United States and other developed countries, approximately one-third of the population is infected. The prevalence of infection is greater among African-Americans and Hispanics than non-Hispanic whites, which seems to be explained only partially by socioeconomic factors. Prevalence also increases with age, from ~ 10% in children to ~ 50% by 50 years of age. In part, this is because, with each year of life, there is an incremental increase in chances of acquiring *H pylori* infection. However, probably more important is the "cohort effect"; because infection is typically acquired in childhood and the overall prevalence of *H pylori* in developed countries is declining, individuals born 50 years ago (when *H pylori* was more common) are found more often to be infected than persons born more recently. Once acquired, infection is persistent, usually for the lifetime of the patient.

2. Transmission. There are no well-documented environmental reservoirs of *H pylori.* Only humans and some nonhuman primates are infected. While it is known that infection is transmitted from person to person, the exact mechanism is unclear. *H pylori* cannot generally be cultivated from stools of infected patients, although some evidence suggests that cultures may be positive if patients have diarrhea. Recent cultivation of *H pylori* from vomitus raises the intriguing possibility that transmission occurs during episodes of gastroenteritis by the gastro-oral route.

3. Prevalence of disease. Although all persons infected with *H pylori* will have histologic evidence of gastritis, only ~ 15–20% will have clinical disease at some point in their lifetime that is associated with *H pylori* infection (Table 55–1). Thus, although it clearly is a pathogen (recall that only ~ 20% of patients infected with *Mycobacterium tuberculosis* will have disease at some point in their lives), most people infected with *H pylori* will never have clinical sequelae of infection.

B. Microbiology.
H pylori is a microaerophilic gram-negative rod that has a gently curved or S-shaped morphology that resembles *Campylobacter* spp. The organism displays a unique "corkscrew" motility produced by its four to eight unipolar flagella. Optimal growth occurs at 37 °C under microaerobic conditions on brucella agar or other rich medium supplemented with blood or serum. Since cultivation of *H pylori* from gastric biopsy requires 4–7 days, agar plates are typically supplemented with antibiotics (trimethoprim, vancomycin, polymyxin-B, and amphotericin B) to suppress overgrowth by fungi

Table 55–1. Association of *Helicobacter pylori* with upper gastrointestinal tract conditions.

Condition	Strength of Association
Chronic histologic gastritis	Causal relationship established
Peptic ulcer disease	Causal relationship established for ulcers not related to NSAIDs[1] or to Zollinger-Ellison syndromes
Gastric adenocarcinoma	Causal relationship established; cofactors are likely to be important
Gastric lymphoma	Causal relationship established
Nonulcer dyspepsia	Poor
Gastroesophageal reflux (GERD)	*H pylori* may be protective
Gastroesophageal junction tumors	*H pylori* may be protective
Cardiovascular disease	Poor

[1]NSAIDs, Nonsteroidal anti-inflammatory drugs.

and other bacteria. *H pylori* is identified by the formation of pinpoint translucent colonies, its gram-negative staining characteristics, and positive tests for oxidase, catalase, and urease. Urease is produced in abundance by *H pylori* and is the basis for two tests commonly used to diagnose *H pylori* infection. Analysis of the complete *H pylori* genome reveals a large number of genes that are predicted to encode ion pumps, but few genes that encode regulatory factors; these findings are consistent with the notion of an organism that has adapted to a highly acidic environment. *"Helicobacter heilmannii"* is a related uncultivated bacterium that is uncommon but appears also to be associated with gastritis, peptic ulcer disease, and gastric malignancy. Several other species of *Helicobacter* can occasionally infect the large intestines and perhaps the hepatobiliary system, and they are sometimes associated with diarrheal disease.

C. Pathogenesis.
1. Histopathology. All persons infected with *H pylori* have a chronic gastritis characterized by mononuclear inflammatory cells as well as an associated neutrophilic infiltration. Both the organism and the gastritis tend to be located preferentially in the gastric antrum. The role of *H pylori* in causing this chronic gastritis, previously thought to be a natural result of aging, has been clearly demonstrated by the finding that eradication of *H pylori* eliminates the gastritis and by two experimental self-inoculation studies in which physicians have voluntarily ingested *H pylori*. The organism can be found predominantly in the mucus gel layer, although a minority of bacteria will be adherent to the gastric epithelium. *H pylori* exhibits a profound tissue tropism, and it attaches only to gastric epithelium in the stomach or to epithelium in the proximal duodenum that has undergone gastric metaplasia.

2. Mechanisms of tissue injury. Polar flagella and a spiral morphology permit *H pylori* to move within gastric mucus and, on occasion, attach to gastric epithelium. Because the majority of bacterial cells are not attached to the epithelium, soluble factors are thought to play a role in generating the inflammatory response. About 60% of strains isolated from patients in the United States produce a vacuolating cytotoxin called VacA, which induces acidic vacuoles in the cytoplasm of eukaryotic cells. Although the exact role of VacA in disease is unknown, patients infected with strains that produce VacA are more likely to develop peptic ulcer disease and gastric adenocarcinoma than patients infected with strains that do not produce VacA. Interestingly, all *H pylori* strains have the gene for VacA, but cytotoxin activity is, for the most part, found only in those strains that also contain a 40-kilobase pathogenicity island called CagA. These strains also have the ability to induce interleukin-8, which serves to recruit and activate neutrophils. Like all gram-negative bacteria, *H pylori* produces lipopolysaccharide, which can disrupt gastric mucus. Interestingly, the *H pylori* lipopolysaccharide has a relatively low proinflammatory activity compared with that from enteric gram-negative bacteria such as *Escherichia coli*. This probably reflects its ability to coexist with the host over decades, usually causing little overt disease. The histologic gastritis may also reflect autoimmune mechanisms, because portions of the *H pylori* lipopolysaccharide side chains mimic host Lewis antigens expressed on gastric epithelium. *H pylori* also induces gastric mucosal injury by provoking apoptosis.

H pylori urease hydrolyzes urea into ammonia and carbon dioxide, which is then converted to bicarbonate. Urease is essential for *H pylori* colonization probably in part because the bicarbonate protects the bacterium from the effects of gastric acid. Urease also has toxic effects on gastric epithelial cells, so it functions both as colonization and virulence factor.

3. Altered gastric homeostasis. *H pylori* infection induces the expression of gastrin, an acid-stimulating peptide, and suppresses expression of the acid-inhibiting somatostatin. However, gastric acid production is not always increased in patients infected with *H pylori*. During the first few weeks to months of infection, there is thought to be a transient hypochlorhydria. After this stage, there may be increased or eventually decreased gastric acid, depending on a variety of factors. In general, gastric acid is increased in patients who develop duodenal ulcers but decreased in patients who develop gastric cancer.

Clinical Findings
A. Acute Infection. Limited human inoculation studies suggest that acute *H pylori* infection may be associated with nausea, vomiting, upper abdominal pain, and bloating. It seems likely that some patients diagnosed with "gastroenteritis" have acute *H pylori*

infection, particularly children, in whom most infections occur. Symptoms last several days and resolve spontaneously. There are no currently available methods for detection of acute *H pylori* infection, so the diagnosis is virtually never made. Because the acute illness is transient and most patients will not develop clinical sequelae of infection, there is little reason to look for *H pylori* infection in patients with a syndrome of gastroenteritis. Like many infectious diseases, *H pylori* acquisition may be asymptomatic.

B. Chronic Active Gastritis. Most if not all patients who acquire *H pylori* infection will remain persistently colonized and will develop chronic active gastritis. This is a pathologic and not a clinical diagnosis, which should not be confused with erosive or other forms of gastritis that can be diagnosed by gross visual examination with an endoscope.

C. Peptic Ulcer Disease. Approximately 15–20% of *H pylori*-infected persons will develop peptic ulcer disease at some point in their lifetimes. If one excludes ulcers due to nonsteroidal anti-inflammatory drugs (NSAIDs), > 80% of peptic ulcers can be attributed to *H pylori* infection. This conclusion is based on the observation that *H pylori*-associated ulcers treated with acid suppression alone will commonly recur when therapy is stopped after initial healing, while those treated with antibiotics that eradicate *H pylori* recur much less often. Since ulcers related to NSAIDs are more often gastric than duodenal, the association between *H pylori* infection and duodenal ulcer is stronger than that with gastric ulcer. In the absence of NSAIDs or other conditions such as Zollinger-Ellison syndrome or Crohn's disease, physicians should presume that ulcers in patients infected with *H pylori* are caused by the infection.

D. Gastric Malignancy. Although uncommon in the United States and other developed countries, gastric adenocarcinoma is the second leading cause of cancer worldwide and the second leading cause of cancer death. Persons infected with *H pylori* have approximately a sixfold increased risk of developing gastric cancer compared with those that are uninfected. Although the incidence of gastric cancer in the United States is declining, it remains relatively common among Hispanics, African-Americans, and Asians. These populations, like those in developing countries, have a higher prevalence of *H pylori* infection and are typically infected at a younger age than non-Hispanic whites. Overall, < 1% of infected persons in developed countries will develop gastric cancer, but, in developing countries, particularly in Asia, the risk may be as high as 10%.

Gastric cancer and duodenal ulcer disease are almost mutually exclusive outcomes of *H pylori* infection. Persons in developed countries are more likely to develop duodenal ulcer, while those in developing countries more commonly develop gastric cancer. It is thought that the difference lies in whether infection produces high gastric acid, which may lead to duodenal ulcer, or low gastric acid with atrophic gastritis, which is the histologic precursor to gastric adenocarcinoma. The factors that determine whether one progresses down one path or the other are largely unknown.

Gastric mucosa-associated lymphoid tissue (MALT) lymphoma is a rare disease that is strongly associated with *H pylori* infection. If identified early, the tumor can be cured with effective *H pylori* therapy in > 75% of patients. Therefore, antibiotic therapy is considered the standard of care for treatment of patients with *H pylori* infection and gastric MALT lymphoma.

E. Nonulcer Dyspepsia. Nonulcer dyspepsia is a poorly defined entity whose etiology is not well understood. Several large randomized clinical trials have now evaluated the effects of antibiotics for *H pylori* on nonulcer dyspepsia. In general, antibiotic therapy produces symptomatic improvement in 20–25% of patients; however, these results are similar in placebo-treated controls.

F. Other Diseases and Syndromes. There are multiple reports of associations between *H pylori* infection and cardiovascular disease, as well as several rheumatologic diseases. Since *H pylori* infection is so common, a causal relationship is difficult to demonstrate, and none has yet been established.

Diagnosis

Several methods for diagnosis of *H pylori* are available, both noninvasive and endoscopic (Table 55–2).

A. Serology. Serum enzyme-linked immunosorbent assay for immunoglobulin G is sensitive and specific for detection of *H pylori* infection. Presuming that the patient has not been recently treated for *H pylori*, in which case an antibody test may be falsely positive because seroreversion has not yet occurred, a positive serum immunoglobulin G for *H pylori* indicates that there is active infection in the gastric mucosa. *H pylori* serum immunoglobulin M measurements are reported by some commercial laboratories, but the methods have not been well standardized and they are currently of no clinical value. Assays based on whole blood are generally less accurate and offer no significant advantages over those based on serum.

B. Urea Breath Test. Two urea breath tests have been approved by the U.S. Food and Drug Administration. The patient ingests either $[^{14}C]$-urea or $[^{13}C]$-urea. If *H pylori* is present in the stomach, these substrates are hydrolyzed and either $[^{14}C]$- or $[^{13}C]$-labeled CO_2 can be measured in a sample of expired air. Both tests are highly sensitive and specific for active *H pylori* infection. ^{13}C is a naturally occurring radioisotope of carbon and involves no ionizing radiation exposure to the patient. The radiation exposure from a $[^{14}C]$-urea breath test is negligible, amounting to approximately the excess radiation dose accumulated by a transcontinental airline flight. Patients should avoid taking H2 receptor antagonists or

Table 55–2. Diagnostic tests for *Helicobacter pylori*.

	Advantages	Disadvantages[1]
Non invasive		
Serum ELISA	Inexpensive	Not useful for follow-up
Urea breath test	Useful for follow-up	Expensive; may be falsely negative in patients on acid suppression therapy
Stool antigen test	Inexpensive; useful for follow-up	Inconvenient
Whole blood assay	Inexpensive; rapid	Less accurate than serum ELISA
Invasive (endoscopic)		
Histology	Visualization of pathology	May miss low-grade infection
Rapid urease	Rapid	May be falsely positive in bacterial overgrowth
Culture	Antibiotic susceptibility	Not maximally sensitive; not available routinely; requires 4–7 d

[1]ELISA, Enzyme-linked immunosorbent assay.

proton pump inhibitors for 1–2 weeks before a urea breath test, because these agents increase the likelihood of a false-negative test.

C. Endoscopy. Histologic examination of an endoscopic biopsy is a sensitive test for *H pylori* when performed by an experienced pathologist, and the specificity is nearly 100%. Organisms are most easily seen with silver stains such as Warthin-Starry or Genta, but routine hematoxylin and eosin or Giemsa stains are usually sufficient. Multiple biopsies should be obtained because the infection is not uniformly distributed. A rapid urease test may also be performed on gastric biopsies by placing the sample in a vial containing urea and a pH-sensitive dye, which will change color in the presence of bacterial urease activity. This test is inexpensive and accurate, and the results may be available in as soon as a few hours. Cultivation of *H pylori* from gastric biopsies is not commonly performed because it requires special media, and laboratories are often not experienced with growing this fastidious organism. However, cultivation offers the unique advantage over other techniques that the isolate is available for antibiotic susceptibility testing. This may be particularly important in patients who have failed initial attempts at therapy. If a local laboratory cannot cultivate *H pylori,* samples can be placed directly in a sterile tube, frozen (preferably at −70 °C, but −20 °C will usually suffice), and shipped on dry ice to a reference laboratory.

D. Stool Antigen Test. A recently developed stool antigen test is approved by the U.S. Food and Drug Administration for evaluation of *H pylori* infection. It is > 90% sensitive and specific for detection of chronic infection, as well as for confirming eradication of *H pylori* when performed 4 weeks after completion of antibiotic therapy.

Treatment

A. Indications for Antibiotic Therapy. All patients with peptic ulcer disease and *H pylori* infection should be treated with antibiotics, unless an alterna-

tive cause such as NSAIDs can be clearly demonstrated. This includes patients newly presenting with ulcer disease as well as those with a well-documented history of ulcer. Often these latter patients will be intermittently taking H2 blockers or proton pump inhibitors, which can be stopped after effective antibiotic therapy. Patients with MALT lymphoma should also receive antibiotic treatment for *H pylori*. Cost-benefit analyses have suggested that it may be economical to treat empirically patients who have dyspepsia and *H pylori* infection. However, the now documented failure of *H pylori* therapy to ameliorate the symptoms of nonulcer dyspepsia, together with growing problems with antibiotic resistance, renders this strategy less attractive. Furthermore, controversial data suggest that eradication of *H pylori* may be associated with an increased incidence of gastroesophageal reflux disease (GERD) and carcinoma of the gastroesophageal junction. Preventive antibiotic therapy may also be considered in a patient with *H pylori* infection and a family history of gastric adenocarcinoma. Because long-term therapy with acid suppression in *H pylori*-infected patients with GERD has sometimes been associated with increased risk of atrophic gastritis, some have suggested that these patients receive therapy for *H pylori* to prevent gastric cancer. This remains controversial, particularly in light of the evidence that *H pylori* eradication may exacerbate symptoms of GERD. *H pylori* screening and treatment in patients with no symptoms and no risk factors for gastric cancer are not indicated based on current data.

B. Antibiotic Regimens. Several general guidelines are helpful to identify a proper treatment regimen. First, results for all proton pump inhibitors studied to date are essentially equivalent, so the choice should be guided primarily by cost. Second, related antibiotics in a class should not be substituted for those that are recommended. For example, amoxicillin and tetracycline should not be replaced with ampicillin and doxycycline, respectively, nor should any macrolide be used other than clarithromycin, until further studies are done. Third, all effective regimens include at least two antibiotics in addition to acid suppression. Finally, antibiotic therapy should be continued for a minimum of 1 week, although 2 weeks is preferable. In ulcer disease the acid suppression therapy should be administered for 2 additional weeks.

Many treatment regimens are available that yield cure rates of ≥ 80–90% and differ primarily in cost, convenience, and side effects rather than in efficacy (Box 55–1). The initial regimen developed for *H pylori* treatment was a combination of an H2 blocker twice daily, tetracycline four times daily, bismuth subsalicylate four times daily, and metronidazole three times daily. Amoxicillin can be substituted for tetracycline, although there may be some marginal loss of efficacy. A proton pump inhibitor is now commonly substituted for the H2 blocker. An effective alternative is a proton pump inhibitor or ranitidine bismuth citrate (a combination of ranitidine and bismuth) each given twice daily together with two of the following: amoxicillin, clarithromycin, or metronidazole, each given twice daily. The latter approach is significantly more expensive than the bismuth-containing regimen, but twice-daily dosing may promote adherence.

C. Follow-up Testing. In the past, follow-up testing has not been routinely recommended, in part because noninvasive methods were not available. Serology is generally not useful for follow-up because a prolonged period is required for seroreversion after effective therapy. Currently, both the urea breath test and the stool antigen test are noninvasive methods that accurately detect *H pylori* eradication when performed ≥ 4 weeks after completion of antibiotic therapy. Patients with gastric ulcer, particularly those in whom the clinical history raises concern about gastric cancer, and patients with MALT lymphoma, should undergo follow-up endoscopy after completion of therapy. Patients who are still infected with *H pylori* after therapy are likely never to have cleared the organism or are likely to have recrudescent infection rather than reinfection. The reinfection rate in adults after successful therapy documented ≥ 4 weeks after treatment is < 1% per year.

D. Antibiotic Resistance. Antibiotic resistance to metronidazole is present in ~ 30% of *H pylori* strains in the United States, but can be as high as 90% in some populations, depending on the frequency of metronidazole use. A clear relationship between in vitro resistance and clinical efficacy has not been consistently demonstrated; this probably reflects heterogenous mechanisms of resistance. Clarithromycin resistance occurs in 5–15% of strains. It is associated with mutations in the 23S rRNA gene and results in marked loss of efficacy. Because clarithromycin and metronidazole are the two agents for which resistance most commonly develops, it may be prudent not to use them together as initial therapy, to avoid development of resistance to both agents. Resistance to amoxicillin, bismuth, and tetracycline in *H pylori* strains is rare.

E. Therapy in Treatment Failures. The patient in whom the initial regimen fails to eradicate adherent *H pylori* should be treated with an alternative combination (Table 55–3). If metronidazole or clarithromycin was part of the original treatment, it is reasonable to presume that resistance has developed and to substitute clarithromycin or metronidazole, respectively, or to use amoxicillin. Resistance to metronidazole may sometimes be overcome by increasing the dose to 500 mg three times daily or even four times daily if tolerated. One may also consider sending a gastric biopsy for culture and susceptibility testing to a research lab if such testing is not locally available. Susceptibility testing should be performed against clarithromycin, metronidazole, amoxicillin, and tetracycline by the agar dilution method. This method has replaced the epsilometer agar diffusion gradient (E-Test, AB Biodisk) for *H pylori* antibiotic resistance testing.

F. Treatment of *H pylori* Infection in Children. *H pylori* infection is uncommon among children

---

BOX 55–1

Preferred Treatment Regimens for *Helicobacter pylori*

Drug	Dose	Frequency
H2 blocker or proton pump inhibitor	As directed	2 Times daily
Bismuth subsalicylate	2 tablets	4 Times daily
Tetracycline	500 mg orally	3 Times daily
Metronidazole	500 mg orally	3 Times daily
Proton pump inhibitor plus two of the following[1]:	As directed	2 Times daily
• Amoxicillin	1 g orally	2 Times daily
• Clarithromycin	500 mg orally	2 Times daily
• Metronidazole	500 mg orally	2 Times daily

[1]Ranitidine bismuth subsalicylate, 400 mg orally 2 times daily, may be substituted.

Table 55–3. Approaches to treatment failure.

Ensure adherence to regimen
Avoid clarithromycin if used previously
Avoid metronidazole if used previously, or consider increased dose
Consider culture of gastric biopsy with antibiotic susceptibility testing

in the United States and other developed countries, as are peptic ulcer disease and gastric malignancy. Although the same agents that are used to treat *H pylori* in adults appear to be effective in children, there are no standard guidelines on when or how children should be treated. *H pylori* therapy in children with gastrointesti-nal symptoms should not be undertaken without consultation from a pediatric gastroenterologist.

Prevention & Control

There are no available guidelines regarding prevention of infection. However, persons infected with *H pylori* who have diarrhea or vomiting should probably be considered contagious. Oral and parenteral vaccines, primarily based on *H pylori* urease, have been studied extensively in animal models, although none has proven effective at providing sterilizing immunity. Therapeutic-vaccination studies in animals and preliminary studies in humans are also ongoing.

REFERENCES

Blaser MJ: Hypothesis: the changing relationships of *Helicobacter pylori* and humans; implications for health and disease. J Infect Dis 1999;179:1523.

Dunn BE, Cohen H, Blaser MJ: *Helicobacter pylori*. Clin Microbiol Rev 1997;10:720.

Graham DY: Therapy of *Helicobacter pylori*: current status and issues. Gastroenterology 2000;118:S2.

Mitchell HM: The epidemiology of *Helicobacter pylori*. Curr Top Microbiol Immunol 1999;241:11.

Proceedings of the American Digestive Health Foundation's (ADHF) International Update Conference on *Helicobacter pylori*. Gastroenterology 1997;113(Supplement):S1.

Haemophilus, Bordetella, & Branhamella Species

56

Joseph W. St. Geme III, MD

HAEMOPHILUS INFLUENZAE & OTHER HAEMOPHILUS SPECIES

Essentials of Diagnosis

- *Haemophilus influenzae* is generally acquired via the aerosol route or by direct contact with respiratory secretions.
- The most common associated syndromes include otitis media, sinusitis, conjunctivitis, bronchitis, pneumonia, and, to a lesser extent, meningitis, epiglottitis, arthritis, and cellulitis.
- Gram stain shows pleomorphic gram-negative coccobacilli.
- In cases of meningitis, epiglottitis, arthritis, and cellulitis, organisms are typically recovered from blood, and type-b polysaccharide capsular material may be detected in the urine.
- Organisms and type-b polysaccharide capsule may also be present in other appropriate sterile body fluids, such as cerebrospinal fluid (CSF) in meningitis and joint fluid in arthritis.

General Considerations

A. Epidemiology. Before 1990, strains of *Haemophilus influenzae* type b were found in the upper respiratory tract of 3–5% of children and a small percentage of adults. Colonization rates with type-b strains are even lower now, reflecting routine immunization of infants against *H influenzae* type b. Non–type-b encapsulated *H influenzae* are present in the nasopharynx of < 2% of individuals, whereas nonencapsulated (nontypable [see below]) strains colonize the respiratory tract of 40–80% of children and adults.

Historically, *H influenzae* type b was the leading cause of bacterial meningitis and epiglottitis in children < 5 years old and a major cause of septic arthritis, pneumonia, pericarditis, and facial cellulitis in this same age group. In the United States, ~ 1 in 200 children experienced invasive (bacteremic) disease with this organism before the age of 5 years, with a peak incidence of disease at 6–7 months of age. Invasive disease was more frequent in boys, children of African descent, Alaskan Eskimos, Apache and Navajo Indians, child care center attendees, and children living in overcrowded conditions. Other factors predisposing to invasive disease included sickle cell disease, asplenia, human immunodeficiency virus (HIV) infection, certain immunodeficiency syndromes, and malignancies. The introduction of efficacious vaccines and their routine use in infants, beginning in 1991, resulted in a marked decrease in the incidence of *H influenzae* type-b infections, which now are quite rare. The Immunization Practices Advisory Committee of the Centers for Disease Control and Prevention and the Committee on Infectious Diseases of the American Academy of Pediatrics currently recommend administration of a licensed conjugate vaccine to all children starting at 2 months of age. Invasive disease in this country now occurs primarily in undervaccinated children.

Nonencapsulated strains of *H influenzae* are a common cause of localized respiratory tract disease in both children and adults. In children, these organisms are the most common cause of purulent conjunctivitis, the second most common cause of otitis media (after *Streptococcus pneumoniae*), and a frequent cause of sinusitis. Among children in developing countries, they are a frequent cause of pneumonia and an important source of mortality. In adults they are especially common as a cause of community-acquired pneumonia and exacerbations of underlying lung disease and also account for ~ 30% of cases of otitis media and sinusitis. Beyond producing localized disease, nontypable *H influenzae* is an occasional cause of serious systemic disease, such as sepsis, meningitis, and pyogenic arthritis, particularly in neonates and individuals with compromised immunity.

In the mid-1980s, *H influenzae* biogroup *aegyptius* was recognized as the etiology of Brazilian purpuric fever (BPF), a septicemic illness occurring in young children and associated with a case fatality rate of ~ 60%. In most cases, disease is preceded by purulent conjunctivitis. Both epidemics and sporadic cases have been reported, primarily in the neighboring Brazilian states of Sao Paulo and Parana and in the more distant state of Mato Grosso. Almost all cases of BPF occurring in Brazil have been caused by the same bacterial clone, referred to as the BPF clone.

Disease resulting from non–type-b encapsulated *H influenzae* occurs on occasion and is most common in patients living in underdeveloped countries. For example, among children in Papua, New Guinea, ~ 25% of *H influenzae* isolates associated with acute lower respiratory tract infection and roughly 15% of *H influenzae* isolates recovered from CSF are non–type-b encapsulated strains. In the United States, as the incidence of invasive disease from *H influenzae* type b has declined, serotype f strains have grown in importance as an etiology of *H influenzae* sepsis, meningitis, and pneumonia.

H ducreyi is the causative agent of chancroid, a sexually transmitted disease characterized by genital ulceration and inguinal lymphadenitis. Chancroid is a common cause of genital ulcers in developing countries. In contrast, it is relatively uncommon in the United States. Nevertheless, a number of large outbreaks have been identified in the United States since 1981. After a peak of 5000 cases in 1988 and a gradual decline since then, 243 cases of chancroid were reported in 1997 in the United States. These outbreaks have generally resulted from prostitution and its relationship to illicit drug use. Most cases have involved heterosexual transmission, and affected individuals have been primarily black or Hispanic. There is recent evidence that chancroid, like other forms of genital ulcer disease, is an important cofactor in the transmission of HIV. In addition, as many as 10% of patients with chancroid may be coinfected with *Treponema pallidum* or herpes simplex virus.

Haemophilus spp. other than *H influenzae* and *H ducreyi* are members of the normal flora in the upper respiratory tract and occasionally the genital area. These organisms have been reported in association with a number of local and systemic infections. Together, *H parainfluenzae, H aphrophilus,* and *H paraphrophilus* account for ~ 5% of cases of infective endocarditis.

B. Microbiology. *H influenzae* is a nonmotile, non–spore-forming, gram-negative bacterium. Microscopic examination reveals pleomorphic coccobacilli with an average size of 1×0.3 μm. *H influenzae* is capable of growing both aerobically and anaerobically. It requires supplements known as factors X and V under aerobic conditions and factor X alone in an anaerobic environment. These factors have not been precisely identified. Factor X can be supplied by heat-stable, iron-containing pigments, including hemin and hemoglobin, whereas factor V can be supplied by nicotinamide adenine dinucleotide (NAD), nicotinamide adenine dinucleotide phosphate (NADP), or nicotinamide nucleoside. Factor V is present in red blood cells but must be released to support growth. Consequently, growth media such as Fildes, which contains erythrocytes that have been disrupted by peptic digestion, and chocolate agar, which contains 1% hemoglobin, are required for optimal growth. Incubation in the presence of 5–10% carbon dioxide facilitates primary isolation of some strains.

Isolates of *H influenzae* are classified by their polysaccharide capsule, with six known capsular types (serotypes a–f). In addition, strains can be nonencapsulated; these strains are defined by their failure to react with typing antisera against capsular serotypes a–f and are referred to as nontypable. Based on the results of biochemical reactions that determine the production of indole and the presence of ornithine decarboxylase and urease, isolates can be separated into eight different subgroups called biotypes. Most type-b isolates are biotype I, whereas nontypable strains are usually biotype II or III. Clinical isolates that are biotypes IV through VIII are relatively uncommon and are almost always nontypable. In recent years, the use of multilocus enzyme electrophoresis has demonstrated that the population structure of *H influenzae* is clonal and that most nontypable strains are not recent capsule-deficient variants of extant encapsulated clones. Nontypable strains are genetically distinct and are more heterogeneous than encapsulated *H influenzae*.

H influenzae biogroup *aegyptius* represents a distinct subgroup of *H influenzae* biotype III with a predilection for causing purulent conjunctivitis. Historically, this organism was referred to as *H aegyptius* and was considered distinct from *H influenzae*. However, no single phenotypic characteristic consistently distinguishes one organism from the other. Moreover, DNA hybridization studies indicate that these two organisms belong to the same species. To account for the fact that these organisms cannot be phylogenetically separated but appear to differ clinically, the name *H influenzae* biogroup *aegyptius* has been used instead of *H aegyptius*.

H ducreyi also has fastidious growth requirements, including a need for factor X, thus resulting in placement in the genus *Haemophilus*. However, recent studies of DNA homology and ribosomal RNA gene sequences indicate major differences between *H ducreyi* and other *Haemophilus* species.

A variety of other *Haemophilus* species have occasionally been implicated in human disease, including *H parainfluenzae, H aphrophilus, H paraphrophilus, H haemolyticus, H parahaemolyticus,* and *H segnis*. Like *H influenzae* and *H ducreyi*, these species are small, pleomorphic, gram-negative coccobacilli. Growth requirements include factor X, factor V, or both (Table 56–1). For some species, growth requires incubation in the presence of carbon dioxide.

C. Pathogenesis. *H influenzae* is transmitted by airborne droplets or by direct contact with respiratory tract secretions. Colonization with a particular strain can persist for weeks to months, and most individuals remain asymptomatic throughout this period. A variety of bacterial factors appear to influence the process of respiratory tract colonization. The lipid A

Table 56–1. Differential characteristics of *Haemophilus* species
associated with human disease.

Organism	Growth Factor Requirement		Hemolysis	Catalase	CO₂ Dependence
	X	V			
H influenzae	+	+	−	+	−
H parainfluenzae[1]	−	+	−	±	−
H aphrophilus	+	−	−	−	+
H paraphrophilus[1]	−	+	−	±	+
H haemolyticus	+	+	+	+	−
H parahaemolyticus	−	+	+	+	−
H segnis[1]	−	+	−	±	−
H ducreyi	+	−	+	−	+

[1]Differentiation of *H parainfluenzae*, *H paraphrophilus*, and *H segnis* is facilitated by assessment of lactose and mannose fermentation. *H paraphrophilus* ferments both lactose and mannose, *H parainfluenzae* ferments mannose alone, and *H segnis* ferments neither.

component of *H influenzae* lipopolysaccharide (also called lipo-oligosaccharide) and possibly low-molecular-weight glycopeptides cause ciliostasis and thereby interfere with mucociliary clearance. In addition, both pilus and nonpilus adherence factors facilitate direct bacterial binding to respiratory epithelium. Like several other mucosal pathogens, *H influenzae* produces an immunoglobulin A1 (IgA1) protease, an enzyme that cleaves human IgA1 and likely facilitates evasion of the local immune response. Bacterial antigenic variation may also promote evasion of local immunity.

In certain circumstances, colonization is followed by contiguous spread within the respiratory tract, resulting in local disease in the middle ear, sinuses, conjunctiva, or lungs. Anatomic factors, deficiencies in local immune function, viral respiratory infection, exposure to cigarette smoke, and allergies predispose to localized respiratory tract disease. On occasion, bacteria penetrate the nasopharyngeal epithelial barrier and enter the bloodstream. The determinants of this event remain poorly defined but may include bacterial lipo-oligosaccharide. In most cases, bacteremia probably is transient. However, in nonimmune hosts, intravascular bacteria, especially those that express the type-b capsule, are sometimes able to survive, replicate, and disseminate to distant sites. In the absence of specific antibody, the type-b polysaccharide capsule promotes resistance to serum bactericidal activity and to phagocytosis.

The pathogenesis of disease caused by *H ducreyi* begins with intradermal inoculation, generally during sexual intercourse. Although the mechanisms of virulence remain poorly defined, several putative virulence factors have recently been identified and characterized. Most isolates express fine flexible pili, which by analogy with other pathogens may be important in initiating infection. More recent data indi-

cate that *H ducreyi* lipo-oligosaccharide is important for adherence to keratinocytes and is capable of causing ulcers in rabbits and mice. In addition, *H ducreyi* elaborates at least two toxins, including a cell-associated cytotoxin that kills cultured human foreskin fibroblasts and a secreted toxin that kills epithelial cells (cytolethal distending toxin). Both toxins presumably contribute to the pathology associated with chancroid. *H ducreyi* also expresses a protein that confers resistance to serum killing.

CLINICAL SYNDROMES

H influenzae was first isolated during the 1892 influenza pandemic and was originally believed to be the causative agent of influenza. Although subsequent studies revealed the fallacy of this idea, *H influenzae* has proved to be a common cause of localized respiratory tract and systemic disease, including meningitis, epiglottitis, pneumonia, pyogenic arthritis, cellulitis, otitis media, and sinusitis, among others (Box 56–1).

1. MENINGITIS

Meningitis is the most common and serious form of invasive *H influenzae* type-b disease. In the mid-1980s, before the introduction of effective vaccines, ~ 10,000–12,000 cases of *H influenzae* type-b meningitis occurred in the United States each year, and 95% of cases involved children < 5 years old. Nowadays, there are < 200 cases/year, with most episodes occurring after 5 years of age.

Clinical Findings
A. Signs and Symptoms. Symptoms usually

BOX 56–1

Clinical Manifestations of *H influenzae* Disease[1]

Disease	Signs and Symptoms
Meningitis	• Irritability • Lethargy • Photophobia • Stiff neck
Epiglottitis	• Sore throat • Dysphagia • Dyspnea • Drooling
Pyogenic Arthritis	• Joint pain • Swelling • Decreased range of motion
Cellulitis	• Skin erythema (sometimes with violaceous hue) • Warmth • Tenderness
Otitis Media	• Ear pain • Bulging tympanic membrane with distorted landmarks and decreased mobility
Sinusitis	• Nasal discharge • Fever • Cough • Headache • Facial tenderness
Pneumonia	• Cough • Tachypnea • Crackles on auscultation
Exacerbation of Lung Disease	• Increased dyspnea • Sputum production • Sputum purulence

[1]For all *H influenzae* diseases, fever is a prominent sign.

include fever, irritability, lethargy, and vomiting. Antecedent symptoms of an upper respiratory infection are common. Occasionally, the course is fulminant, with rapid neurologic deterioration leading to respiratory arrest. Shock is present in 20% of cases of meningitis and can be associated with coagulopathy and purpura.

B. Laboratory Findings. Bacteria can almost always be recovered from CSF. In roughly 70% of patients with *H influenzae* meningitis, Gram stain of the CSF is positive for gram-negative coccobacilli. In cases of culture-proven meningitis, capsular antigen can be detected ~ 90% of the time in CSF and even more frequently in concentrated urine. False-positive reactions are uncommon, but occasionally occur owing to cross-reactivity with *E coli, S pneumoniae, Staphylococcus* spp., or *Neisseria meningitidis*.

C. Complications. Complications of *H influenzae* type-b meningitis include subdural effusion or empyema, ischemic or hemorrhagic cortical infarction, cerebritis, ventriculitis, intracerebral abscess, and hydrocephalus. The overall mortality rate is ~ 5%. Among survivors, between 5% and 10% have permanent sensorineural hearing loss, and ~ 30% have some other significant handicap. Tests for more subtle neurologic deficits reveal sequelae in up to one-half of survivors. Meningitis caused by nontypable *H influenzae* is usually associated with sinusitis, otitis media, or an anatomic communication between the upper respiratory tract and the central nervous system, and results from direct extension from the contiguous focus of infection.

2. EPIGLOTTITIS

Epiglottitis is a life-threatening infection involving cellulitis of the epiglottis and the aryepiglottic folds. Complete obliteration of the vallecular and pyriform sinuses is typical, and acute airway obstruction can occur.

Clinical Findings

A. Signs and Symptoms. Symptoms are often sudden in onset and usually include high fever, sore throat, and dyspnea, with rapid progression to dysphagia, pooling of secretions, and drooling. In children < 2 years old, fever may be low grade, dysphagia and drooling may be minimal, and a croup-like cough may be present. Regardless of age, the patient is usually restless and anxious and adopts a sitting position with the neck extended and the chin protruding to reduce airway obstruction. Abrupt deterioration can occur within a few hours, resulting in death unless an artificial airway is established.

B. Laboratory Findings. Cultures of the epiglottis usually are positive but should be obtained only after establishment of an artificial airway.

C. Imaging. Direct laryngoscopy at the time of controlled placement of an endotracheal tube reveals a red and swollen epiglottis and swollen aryepiglottic folds. On lateral neck radiograph, the swollen epiglottis produces the "thumb sign."

3. PNEUMONIA

Clinical Findings

A. Signs and Symptoms. Generally, *H in-*

fluenzae pneumonia is more insidious in onset than is pneumonia caused by *Staphylococcus aureus* or *Streptococcus pneumoniae.* Productive cough, fever, pleuritic chest pain, and dyspnea dominate the clinical presentation.

B. Imaging. Pneumonia caused by *H influenzae* is usually associated with a consolidative pulmonary infiltrate. In 50% of cases caused by *H influenzae* type b, there is evidence of pleural involvement on initial chest radiograph, and up to 90% of these patients have pleural fluid recoverable by thoracentesis.

C. Complications. An important complication is contiguous spread to the pericardium, resulting in purulent pericarditis, which is manifest by severe dyspnea (grunting in infants), tachycardia, and cardiac failure. Although patients with *H influenzae* type-b pneumonia often have persistent pleural reaction with secondary restrictive lung function at the time of hospital discharge, long-term abnormalities are rare.

4. PYOGENIC ARTHRITIS

In the pre-*Haemophilus* vaccine era, *H influenzae* type b was the most common cause of pyogenic arthritis in children < 2 years of age.

Clinical Findings

In most cases a single large, weight-bearing joint (hip, knee, or ankle) is involved, and in 10–20% of patients, contiguous osteomyelitis develops. Response to systemic antibiotics in combination with prompt drainage of the joint is dramatic, but long-term follow-up is important because residual joint dysfunction can occur. On occasion, culture-negative arthritis develops during treatment of *H influenzae* type-b meningitis, presumably as a result of immune complex deposition in the joint. In 75% of patients with reactive arthritis, signs of joint inflammation begin after a week or more of therapy.

5. CELLULITIS

Cellulitis is the result of metastatic spread of blood-borne *H influenzae* type b.

Clinical Findings

A. Signs and Symptoms. Typically, the patient presents with fever and a warm, tender area of erythema or violaceous discoloration on the cheek or in the periorbital area. Cheek (buccal) cellulitis invariably occurs in children < 1 year of age. The age of the child, the location of the cellulitis, and the occasional distinctive violaceous color should suggest the etiology.

B. Laboratory Findings. Aspirate cultures, ei-

ther from the center of the lesion or the leading edge, usually yield the organism.

C. Complications. Related to the fact that bacteremia is generally present, ~ 10% of children develop another focus of infection, for example, meningitis. *H influenzae* is not associated with cellulitis that occurs as a complication of trauma to the skin.

6. OTITIS MEDIA

Among *H influenzae* isolates from patients with acute otitis media, > 90% are nontypable. Based on studies reported from the United States and Scandinavia, the peak age-specific incidence of *H influenzae* acute otitis media is between 6 and 15 months.

Clinical Findings

Characteristic manifestations include ear pain, fever, irritability, sleep disturbance, and otorrhea. On examination, the tympanic membrane is usually red or yellow and bulging with distorted landmarks. Pneumatic otoscopy reveals decreased mobility, indicative of middle ear fluid.

In addition to producing acute otitis media, nontypable *H influenzae* is the most common bacterial etiology of otitis media with effusion, which is typically asymptomatic and is characterized by a minimally discolored and often retracted tympanic membrane. Nontypable *H influenzae* is also associated with dual infection of the conjunctiva and the middle ear, referred to as the "conjunctivitis-otitis syndrome."

7. SINUSITIS

H influenzae accounts for ~ 30% of all cases of acute sinusitis. The majority of patients with sinusitis have nasal discharge or cough that persists without improvement for > 10 days. Other patients present acutely with high fever and purulent nasal discharge. Physical examination often reveals tenderness over the involved paranasal sinuses.

8. EXACERBATIONS OF UNDERLYING LUNG DISEASE

Because sputum frequently is contaminated by pharyngeal bacterial flora, the interpretation of *H influenzae* growth from sputum cultures is difficult. Nevertheless, there is reasonable evidence that *H influenzae* plays a role in exacerbations of chronic bronchitis, bronchiectasis, and cystic fibrosis. Most isolates in these patients are nontypable. The clinical presentation is characterized by increases in dyspnea, sputum production, and sputum purulence, sometimes associated with fever.

9. NEONATAL SEPSIS

During the past 2 decades, nontypable *H influenzae* has become recognized as a cause of early onset neonatal sepsis similar to that caused by group B streptococcus. Disease occurs primarily in premature neonates and is associated with a mortality rate of nearly 50%.

Clinical Findings
A. Signs and Symptoms. Most infants develop symptoms within the first few hours of life, with pneumonia and respiratory distress dominating the clinical presentation. Meningitis occurs infrequently.

B. Laboratory Findings. *H influenzae* usually can be cultured from the genitourinary tract of mothers of infected infants, often in association with maternal postpartum endometritis. At least one study indicates that a large percentage of these isolates are biotype IV, a subgroup of nontypable *H influenzae* found uncommonly at other sites of infection. Genotypic analysis of these biotype IV strains suggests that they represent a distinct *Haemophilus* species.

10. BRAZILIAN PURPURIC FEVER

Clinical Findings
A. Signs and Symptoms. Brazilian purpuric fever is characterized by high fever, abdominal pain, and vomiting. In most patients, purpura and vascular collapse develop within 12 h of fever onset. Patients range in age between 3 months and 10 years, and ~ 90% have a recent history of conjunctivitis, which in most cases begins 1–2 weeks before the onset of fever.

B. Laboratory Findings. Aside from blood cultures, laboratory studies are nonspecific. Leukocyte counts are often elevated, with a preponderance of neutrophils and band forms, and thrombocytopenia and prolonged coagulation times are also seen.

11. CHANCROID

Clinical Findings
A. Signs and Symptoms. Chancroid usually begins with a papule on the genitalia that develops after an incubation period of 4–7 days. The papule is typically surrounded by erythema and evolves over 2–3 days to a pustule, which spontaneously ruptures to form a sharply circumscribed ulcer. The ulcer is characterized by tenderness and a tendency to bleed. The surrounding skin generally lacks evidence of inflammation. Roughly 50% of patients develop inflamed inguinal lymph nodes, which often become fluctuant and rupture spontaneously. On occasion, chancroid presents with multiple ulcers that coalesce. In addition, ulcers can appear and then resolve spontaneously, with the development of suppurative inguinal adenitis 1–3 weeks later.

B. Laboratory Findings. Gram stain of material obtained by swabbing a lesion can show gram-negative bacteria in a "school of fish" configuration.

Diagnosis
Consideration of the diagnosis of meningitis, epiglottitis, pneumonia, pyogenic arthritis, or cellulitis is usually prompted by the history and physical examination (Table 56–2). In most cases of invasive *H influenzae* type-b disease, blood cultures are positive. *H influenzae* is often cultivated from samples of pleural fluid, joint fluid, or pericardial fluid in affected patients.

The type-b capsular polysaccharide is secreted during bacterial growth, and detection of capsular antigen in serum, CSF, urine, and other normally sterile body fluids can help establish the diagnosis. Antigen detection techniques are most valuable in patients who have received prior antibiotic therapy and have sterile cultures. In addition, they may be useful in confirming a diagnosis before bacterial growth is appreciated in the clinical laboratory, thus allowing for earlier chemoprophylaxis of contacts (see below). Of note, *H influenzae* type-b conjugate vaccines can produce positive reactions in urine and CSF for days to weeks after vaccination.

Because *H influenzae* is a common commensal organism in the upper respiratory tract, establishing *H influenzae* as an etiology of localized respiratory tract disease is challenging. Procedures such as tympanocentesis, sinus aspiration, tracheal or lung aspiration, bronchoscopy, and bronchoalveolar lavage can provide a definitive diagnosis, but generally are re-

Table 56–2. Clues to the laboratory diagnosis of *H influenzae*, *B pertussis*, and *B catarrhalis* disease.

	H influenzae	*B pertussis*	*B catarrhalis*
Morphology	Pleomorphic, gram-negative coccobacilli	Small, gram-negative coccobacilli or rods	Kidney-shaped, gram-negative diplococci
Cultivation	Fildes or chocolate agar	Regan-Lowe, Bordet-Gengou, or others	Blood or chocolate agar
Other diagnostics	Assay for type-b antigen in sterile body fluids	Direct immunofluorescence or polymerase chain reaction assay	None
Serology	Available, generally not useful	Moderately useful	Not available

served for patients with persistent or recurrent infection or an underlying immunodeficiency. Several studies have examined the predictive value of surface cultures of the nose, throat, or nasopharynx in patients with acute or chronic sinusitis. Although the organisms isolated from direct aspiration of infected sinuses are generally recovered from surface cultures, they are not consistently the predominant organisms. As a result, surface cultures are of minimal value in establishing an etiologic diagnosis; nevertheless, they may be useful to exclude a particular cause.

In patients with chancroid, an accurate diagnosis relies on cultivation of *H ducreyi* from the lesion. Selective and supplemental media are necessary for isolation. Although a variety of media have been used, the highest rates of recovery from clinical samples have been obtained with chocolate agar containing Isovitale X and 3 μg/mL of vancomycin; GC agar base containing 1–2% hemoglobin, 5% fetal bovine serum, and 3 μg/mL of vancomycin; and Mueller-Hinton agar supplemented with horse blood, Isovitale X, and vancomycin. For optimal recovery, cultures are incubated at 33 °C in a humid CO_2-enriched environment. Colonies are of pinpoint size at 24 h and increase to 1–2 mm in diameter at 48 h.

In blood culture, *Haemophilus* species other than *H influenzae* and *H ducreyi* have a tendency to grow in small colonies along the sides of the bottle or in the red blood cell mass, leaving the broth clear. As a result, recovery of these organisms from the blood of patients with endocarditis is enhanced by routine subculture of blood cultures to chocolate agar, use of a biphasic system, or use of a system that detects growth radiometrically.

Treatment

Empiric therapy for invasive disease caused by *H influenzae* generally includes either a third-generation cephalosporin, such as cefotaxime or ceftriaxone, or the combination of ampicillin and chloramphenicol (Box 56–2). In the United States, ~ 30% of *H influenzae* isolates are resistant to ampicillin, and thus ampicillin should never be used alone as empiric therapy. Ampicillin resistance usually is related to plasmid-mediated production of β-lactamase, but occasionally is caused by decreased affinity of certain penicillin-binding proteins. To distinguish one form of resistance from the other, both disk susceptibility testing and a β-lactamase assay should be performed. Chloramphenicol is bactericidal for *H influenzae* and reliably penetrates into the CSF. Although resistance to chloramphenicol has been reported, it remains rare in the United States, especially among invasive isolates.

In recent years, the third-generation cephalosporins have become the treatment of choice for *H influenzae* meningitis. Both cefotaxime and ceftriaxone have potent activity against *H influenzae* (including ampicillin-resistant isolates) and achieve high levels in the CSF. For patients with uncomplicated meningitis, therapy for 7–10 days is adequate. For patients who fail to respond promptly or develop complications, therapy for > 10 days may be necessary. Based on empiric experience, most experts recommend that other invasive infections caused by *H influenzae* also be treated with an appropriate parenteral antibiotic for 7–10 days.

Among patients with invasive *H influenzae* disease, antibiotic therapy represents only one component of management. In patients with meningitis, optimal ven-

BOX 56–2

Treatment of *H influenzae* Systemic Disease

	Medication	Children	Adults
First Choice	• Cefotaxime or • Ceftriaxone	• 150–200 mg/kg/d divided every 8 h • 50–100 mg/kg/d divided every 12 h	• 1–2 g every 4–8 h • 2 g every 12 h
Second Choice	• Ampicillin, if susceptible, or • Chloramphenicol if susceptible	• 200–400 mg/kg/d divided every 6 h • 75–100 mg/kg/d divided every 6 h (adjusted according to serum levels)	• 200–400 mg/kg/d divided every 6 h • 50–100 mg/kg/d divided every 6 h (ad-justed according to serum levels)
Adjunctive Therapy (for Meningitis)	• Dexamethasone	• 0.6 mg/kg/d divided every 6 h for 4 d or • 0.8 mg/kg/d divided every 12 h for 2 d	• 0.6 mg/kg/d divided every 6 h for 4 d or • 0.8 mg/kg/d divided every 12 h for 2 d

tilation and judicious fluid administration are important. In addition, dexamethasone should be administered with the first dose or before initiation of antibiotic therapy, whenever possible (without delaying institution of treatment). Dexamethasone serves to diminish production of tumor necrosis factor and other cytokines that contribute to development of cerebral edema and neurologic sequelae. Patients with epiglottitis require placement of an artificial airway, and children with pneumonia often require treatment with supplemental oxygen. When pleural empyema, purulent pericarditis, or pyogenic arthritis is present, prompt drainage is essential to good outcome.

Otitis media, sinusitis, pneumonia, and exacerbations of underlying lung disease are often treated effectively with oral amoxicillin, but amoxicillin-clavulanate, trimethoprim-sulfamethoxazole, an oral second- or third-generation cephalosporin, erythromycin-sulfisoxazole, azithromycin, and clarithromycin are acceptable alternatives (Box 56–3). Historically, treatment of otitis media and sinusitis was continued for 7–14 days, but recent evidence suggests that shorter courses of therapy are equally efficacious. Treatment for 7–10 days is usually adequate for pneumonia and bronchitis.

Several antibiotic regimens are effective in the treatment of chancroid. These include ceftriaxone, 250 mg IM as a single dose, azithromycin, 1 g orally as a single dose, and erythromycin, 500 mg orally four times daily for 7 days. Alternative regimens that have not been evaluated as thoroughly include ciprofloxacin, 500 mg orally twice daily for 3 days, and amoxicillin-clavulanate, 500 mg-125 mg, orally three times daily for 7 days. If therapy is successful, ulcers begin to improve within 3 days and usually resolve after 7 days of treatment. Clinical isolates often have plasmid-mediated resistance to ampicillin, chloramphenicol, tetracyclines, and sulfonamide and may be resistant to other antibiotics as well. Thus, when patients do not respond to treatment promptly, susceptibility testing should be performed. Short courses of therapy may be ineffective in patients with HIV infection.

Traditionally, uncomplicated infections from other *Haemophilus* species have been treated with ampicillin. *Haemophilus* endocarditis has been treated with high-dose ampicillin, often in combination with an aminoglycoside. However, resistance to ampicillin, usually related to β-lactamase production, is being recognized with increasing frequency. Consequently, a second- or third-generation cephalosporin (eg, ceftriaxone) should be used until antibiotic susceptibility results are available (see Box 56–2).

Prevention & Control

Antibody to the *H influenzae* type-b capsule is bactericidal for type-b organisms and confers protection against invasive disease (Box 56–4). Accord-

---

BOX 56–3

Treatment of *H influenzae* Localized Respiratory Tract Disease

	Medication	Children	Adults
First Choice	• Amoxicillin, if susceptible	• 40 mg/kg/d divided into 3 equal doses	• 500 mg three times daily
Second Choice	• Amoxicillin plus clavulanate (Augmentin)	• 40 mg/kg/d divided into 2 or 3 equal doses (amoxicillin component)	• 500 mg three times daily[1] (amoxicillin component)
	• Trimethoprim-sulfamethoxazole (TMP-SMX)	• 8–12 mg TMP/40–60 mg SMX/kg/d divided into 2 equal doses	• 160 mg TMP/800 mg SMX twice daily
	• Oral second- and third-generation cephalosporins	• Depends on particular agent	• Depends on particular agent
	• Erythromycin-sulfisoxazole	• 40 mg/kg/d divided into 3–4 equal doses (erythromycin component)	• 500 mg four times daily (erythromycin component)
	• Azithromycin	• 10 mg/kg loading dose, then 5 mg/kg per day	• 500 mg loading dose, then 250 mg per day
	• Clarithromycin	• 15 mg/kg/d divided into 2 equal doses	• 500 mg twice daily

[1]Both twice daily and three times daily formulations are available.

BOX 56–4

Control of *H influenzae* Infection

Prophylactic Measures	Vaccines are available and effective for type b disease. Chemoprophylaxis: • Rifampin, 20 mg/kg/d once per day for 4 d; maximum dose 600 mg/d for type b disease • Amoxicillin, 20 mg/kg/d, **OR** • Sulfisoxazole, 50 mg/kg/d for selected patients with recurrent otitis media
Isolation Precautions	• Droplet precautions for first 24 h of treatment for type-b disease • None for nontypable disease

ingly, the existing vaccines against *H influenzae* type b contain some derivative of type-b polysaccharide, also called polyribosylribitol phosphate (PRP). To enhance the immunogenicity of these vaccines in young infants, the polysaccharide is conjugated to an immunogenic carrier protein. There are currently four licensed conjugate vaccines, all differing to some extent in the size of the polysaccharide, the chemical linkage between the polysaccharide and the carrier, or the type of protein (see Table 56–3). In addition, these vaccines differ in immunologic characteristics. As a result of differences in immunogenicity, three of the four (HbOC, PRP-T, and PRP-OMP) are licensed for use in infants, and the fourth (PRP-D) is approved only for children ≥ 12 months of age. For HbOC and PRP-T, the primary series of infancy consists of three doses (at 2, 4, and 6 months of age), whereas for PRP-OMP the primary series includes two doses (at 2 and 4 months). In all cases, a booster dose is required between 12 and 15 months of age.

All four of the conjugate vaccines are well tolerated, with the most common adverse effect being transient redness and swelling at the site of injection. Conjugate vaccines can be administered at the same time as other vaccines, including diphtheria-tetanus–whole-cell pertussis (DTP) or diphtheria-tetanus-acellular pertussis (DTaP), polio, hepatitis B, mumps-measles-rubella (MMR), varicella, pneumococcal vaccines, and meningococcal vaccine, and in some cases have been combined during production with DTP, DTaP, or hepatitis B. Postlicensing studies indicate that the available conjugate vaccines are highly effective against *H influenzae* type b and have decreased the incidence of invasive *H influenzae* type-b disease by > 95%; however, these vaccines provide no protection against non–type-b strains.

There are currently no vaccines available for prevention of disease caused by nontypable *H influenzae* or other *Haemophilus* species. However, work is underway to identify nontypable *H influenzae* and *H ducreyi* antigens that are surface exposed and elicit protective antibody, and several promising candidates exist.

Chemoprophylaxis is another important intervention for preventing invasive disease caused by *H influenzae* type b. The intent is to eradicate nasopharyngeal colonization and thereby prevent subsequent invasion of the bloodstream in individuals at increased risk for invasive disease. Eradication of colonization will also interrupt transmission to other susceptible hosts. In households with a child < 12 months old, the index case and all members of the household should receive rifampin

Table 56–3. *Haemophilus influenzae* type b conjugate vaccines licensed for use in children.

Vaccine	Trade Name	Polysaccharide	Linkage	Protein carrier
HbOC	HibTITER	Small	None	CRM$_{197}$ mutant *Corynebacterium diphtheriae* toxin
PRP-T	ActHIB OmniHIB	Large	6-Carbon	Tetanus toxoid
PRP-OMP	PedvaxHIB	Medium	Thioether	*N meningitidis* outer membrane protein complex
PRP-D[1]	ProHIbiT	Medium	6-Carbon	Diphtheria toxoid

[1]PRP-D is licensed for children ≥ 12 months old. The other three vaccines are licensed for use in infants.

prophylaxis. The same is true in households with at least one contact < 48 months old who is incompletely immunized against *H influenzae* type b and in families with a fully immunized but immunocompromised child, regardless of age. When two or more cases of invasive disease occur within a 60-day period among attendees of a child care center and incompletely vaccinated children attend the facility, rifampin is recommended for all attendees and supervisors. Management of a single case at a child care center is controversial and depends on the age and immunization status of attendees and the duration of daily contact between attendees and the index patient. Because most secondary cases in households occur during the first week after hospitalization of the index case, chemoprophylaxis should be initiated as soon as possible.

Chemoprophylaxis is also a consideration in children who have recurrent otitis media caused by nontypable *H influenzae* (or other typical pathogens). In this situation, chronic prophylaxis with either amoxicillin or sulfisoxazole may be effective in reducing infectious episodes, an effect that must be balanced against the possibility of selecting for resistant organisms. According to a recent report, among patients who develop conjunctivitis caused by the BPF clone of *H influenzae* biogroup *aegyptius,* oral rifampin may be effective in preventing BPF.

BORDETELLA SPECIES

Essentials of Diagnosis

- Key signs and symptoms of whooping cough include sudden attacks of severe, repetitive coughing, the presence of an inspiratory whoop at the end of an episode of coughing, and post-tussive vomiting.
- Predisposing factors include the lack of adequate immunization with a pertussis vaccine and exposure to an adult with a coughing illness of > 14 days.
- *Bordetella pertussis* is acquired by the respiratory route via exposure to aerosol droplets.
- Definitive diagnosis is established by recovery of organisms from nasopharyngeal mucus or detection of *B pertussis* antigens by direct immunofluorescent assay of nasopharyngeal secretions.

General Considerations

A. Epidemiology. *Bordetella pertussis* is a respiratory pathogen with a tropism for ciliated respiratory epithelial cells and is the usual cause of an acute respiratory infection called pertussis or whooping cough, which was described as far back as 1500. *B parapertussis* accounts for ~ 5% of cases of pertussis in the United States and typically produces more mild

disease. The term pertussis means "intense cough," reflecting the most striking feature of the illness.

Pertussis is a common disease worldwide, with ~60 million cases and > 500,000 deaths each year. During the prevaccine era in the United States, pertussis was the leading cause of death from a communicable disease among children < 14 years, and in 1945, pertussis caused more deaths in infants in the United States than did diphtheria, polio, measles, and scarlet fever combined. The introduction of a pertussis vaccine in the late 1940s resulted in a more than 100-fold decrease in the incidence of pertussis by 1970. However, in recent years there has been a steady increase in the incidence of disease, with epidemics in a number of states. In 1996, 7796 cases were reported to the Centers for Disease Control and Prevention, representing the highest number since 1967. Of note, it is estimated that only 10% of actual cases are reported.

Pertussis is transmitted person-to-person by the respiratory route and is highly contagious, with attack rates of > 90% in unimmunized populations exposed to aerosol droplets at close range (eg, nonimmune household contacts). Asymptomatic infection has been demonstrated but is considered unlikely to be a major factor in transmission. Adolescents and adults have been recently recognized as a major reservoir for *B pertussis* and account for nearly 25% of reported cases, usually with mild or atypical symptoms. They are the usual source for infection in infants and children. Patients are most contagious during the first stage of illness, before the onset of paroxysms (see Clinical Findings, below); communicability then diminishes rapidly but may persist for 3 weeks or more after the onset of cough.

Pertussis is endemic, with superimposed periodic outbreaks that usually occur every 3–4 years. The majority of cases are diagnosed between July and October. Approximately 35% of reported cases occur in infants < 6 months, and ~ 60% occur in children < 5 years. Infants born prematurely are at increased risk for severe pertussis, with higher frequencies of hospitalization and death. The incubation period ranges between 6 and 20 days and is usually 7–10 days.

B. Microbiology. *B pertussis* is a small, gram-negative organism that grows as coccobacilli or short rods ranging in size from 0.2×0.5 µm to 0.5×2.0 µm. It is a fastidious obligate aerobe with an optimum growth temperature of 35–37 °C. Some evidence suggests that growth is impaired in an environment containing 5 to 10% CO_2. A number of substances, including fatty acids, heavy metal ions, sulfides, and peroxides, inhibit growth. Media for primary isolation include Bordet-Gengou, modified Stainer-Scholte, Jones-Kendrick charcoal, and Regan-Lowe charcoal-horse blood agar, which contain substances such as starch, charcoal, ion-exchange resins, or a high percentage of blood to inactivate the inhibitory substances.

Other *Bordetella* species associated with human disease include *B parapertussis, B bronchiseptica, B hinzii,* and *B holmesii* (Table 56–4). *B pertussis* and *B parapertussis* are obligate human pathogens, whereas *B bronchiseptica* causes disease predominantly in animals. *B hinzii* and *B holmesii* have been recently recognized as rare causes of bacteremia in immunocompromised patients and infect avian or canine hosts as well. All *Bordetella* species possess DNA with a high mole percent of guanine plus cytosine (66 to 70%). Interestingly, based on DNA hybridization and multilocus enzyme electrophoresis studies, *B pertussis, B parapertussis,* and *B bronchiseptica* are not sufficiently diverse to be classified as separate species. Nevertheless, they are associated with distinct clinical syndromes and continue to be considered individual species.

C. Pathogenesis. *B pertussis* produces a number of molecules that have been implicated in the pathogenesis of disease, including filamentous hemagglutinin (FHA), fimbriae (types 2 and 3), pertactin, pertussis toxin, adenylate cyclase toxin, dermonecrotic toxin, tracheal cytotoxin, and lipo-oligosaccharide. Among these factors, all but tracheal cytotoxin and lipo-oligosaccharide are activated by a regulatory locus referred to as the *Bordetella* virulence gene (Bvg) system. The roles for these factors can be considered in the context of the sequence of events involved in the pathogenesis of disease, namely entry into the host and attachment to a target tissue, persistence in the respiratory tract, and production of local damage. *B pertussis* does not invade beyond the respiratory mucosa. Thus systemic manifestations presumably result from dissemination of bacterial components, such as pertussis toxin.

FHA, types 2 and 3 fimbriae, pertactin, and pertussis toxin facilitate attachment to respiratory epithelium. Tracheal cytotoxin is derived from the bacterial cell wall and causes ciliostasis and sloughing of ciliated cells, thus allowing the organism to overcome mucociliary clearance. Adenylate cyclase toxin, a pore-forming cytotoxin that belongs to the RTX family, inhibits phagocyte functions, including chemotaxis, phagocytosis, oxidative burst, and bactericidal activity, and presumably enables the organism to evade local immunity. Pertussis toxin also impairs phagocyte functions, including neutrophil chemotaxis

and phagocytosis. Tracheal cytotoxin, adenylate cyclase toxin, dermonecrotic toxin, and lipo-oligosaccharide may contribute to local damage to the respiratory mucosa.

CLINICAL SYNDROME

Classical pertussis occurs in three clinical stages: catarrhal, paroxysmal, and convalescent (Box 56–5).

Clinical Findings
A. Signs and Symptoms. The catarrhal stage is characterized by nonspecific upper respiratory symptoms, including rhinorrhea, mild cough, and low-grade fever. During this stage, which typically lasts 1–2 weeks, the disease is highly communicable. The paroxysmal stage is marked by sudden attacks or paroxysms of severe, repetitive coughing, often culminating with the characteristic whoop and frequently followed by vomiting. A marked lymphocytosis usually accompanies this stage of the disease, with lymphocyte counts sometimes exceeding 50,000/mm³ and usually representing 70% or more of total circulating leukocytes. The paroxysmal stage typically lasts 1–4 weeks and can be associated with a variety of complications, including secondary bacterial infections such as pneumonia and otitis media, toxic central nervous system manifestations such as seizures and encephalopathy, and effects of increased intrathoracic and intra-abdominal pressure such as pneumothorax, hernia, and rectal prolapse. The beginning of the convalescent (recovery) stage is marked by a reduction in frequency and intensity of coughing spells. After clinical pertussis, immunity to disease is lifelong.

Although most cases of pertussis follow a characteristic course, exceptions exist. In infants < 3 months, the catarrhal stage is usually no longer than a few days, and the paroxysmal and convalescent stages are extremely protracted, with coughing spells that continue throughout the first year of life. In infants < 6 months, apnea is a common manifestation, and the whoop is often absent. Paradoxically, in infants, cough and whoop may become louder and more classic during convalescence, reflecting growth in body mass and increased strength. In immunized children, all three

Table 56–4. Differential characteristics of *Bordetella* species associated with human disease.

Organism	Motility	Oxidase	Urease	Utilizes Citrate	Reduces Nitrate
B pertussis	–	+	–	–	–
B parapertussis	–	–	+	+	–
B bronchiseptica	+	+	+	+	+
B hinzii[1]	+	+	–	+	–
B holmesii[1]	–	–	–	–	–

[1] *B hinzii* and *B holmesii* have been identified as causes of disease only infrequently.

BOX 56-5

Clinical Manifestations of *B pertussis* Disease (Whooping Cough)

Catarrhal Stage	• Low-grade fever • Rhinorrhea • Mild cough
Paroxysmal Stage	• Paroxysms of severe, repetitive coughing, often with whoop and vomiting
Convalescent Stage	• Decreasing intensity and frequency of cough

stages are shortened, and in adults, only a protracted cough may be present. Post-tussive vomiting is common in pertussis at all ages and is a major clue to the diagnosis in adolescents and adults. With subsequent respiratory illnesses over the next several months, paroxysmal coughing may recur, though not because of recurrence of active *Bordetella* infection.

B. Laboratory Findings. During the catarrhal stage, organisms are most readily isolated from cultures of the posterior nasopharynx. During the paroxysmal stage, it is increasingly difficult to recover the organism from the respiratory tract.

C. Imaging. The chest radiograph is mildly abnormal in the majority of hospitalized infants, showing perihilar infiltrates or interstitial edema and patchy atelectasis. Pneumothorax, pneumomediastinum, and soft tissue air are sometimes seen.

D. Complications. Surveillance data on pertussis in the United States from 1980 to 1989 demonstrated that the clinical course in infants was complicated by pneumonia in 21.7% of cases, by seizures in 3.0% of cases, and by encephalopathy in 0.9% of cases. The mortality rate was 1.3% in infants < 1 month and 0.3% in infants 2–11 months of age. Considering all individuals with pertussis, pneumonia develops in ~ 10%, seizures in ~ 2%, and encephalopathy in 0.5% to 1%.

Diagnosis

The traditional approach for diagnosing pertussis involves culturing *B pertussis* or *B parapertussis* from nasopharyngeal mucus (see Table 56–2). Mucus should be collected by aspiration or by swabbing the nasopharynx with a dacron or calcium alginate swab. After plating on an appropriate medium, *B pertussis* is usually detected in 3–5 days, and *B parapertussis* is visible in 2–4 days. Regan-Lowe agar or a related charcoal-horse blood agar containing 40 µg/mL cephalexin is the preferred medium for primary isolation.

The organism is rarely found after the fourth week of illness, and culture is less likely to be positive in immunized individuals and in those who have received antibiotics. Examination of nasopharyngeal secretions by direct immunofluorescent assay is considered an alternative approach to diagnosis. However, direct immunofluorescent assay has low sensitivity and variable specificity and requires experienced personnel for interpretation. Polymerase chain reaction has been used on an investigational basis and is more rapid than culture but is variably sensitive.

B pertussis infections stimulate a heterogeneous antibody response that differs among individuals, depending on age, previous exposure to the organism, and immunization status, and thus no single serologic test is diagnostic. Nevertheless, in experienced research laboratories, the serologic diagnosis of pertussis has excellent sensitivity and specificity when acute serum is collected early in the illness and paired acute and convalescent sera are tested for antibodies to a number of antigens.

Absolute lymphocytosis is often present in patients with classic pertussis but represents a nonspecific finding, especially in infants. The degree of lymphocytosis usually parallels the severity of the patient's cough. The lymphocytes include both T cells and B cells and are normal small cells rather than large atypical lymphocytes. Adults and partially immunized children have less marked increases in lymphocyte count.

Because laboratory confirmation of pertussis can be difficult, clinicians often need to make the diagnosis on the basis of characteristic manifestations, including a prolonged paroxysmal cough, an inspiratory whoop, post-tussive emesis, and lymphocytosis. For sporadic cases, cough of > 14 days duration in combination with either paroxysms, whoop, or post-tussive vomiting has a sensitivity of 81% and a specificity of 58% for culture confirmation. In a study of university students, 25% of subjects with a coughing illness for 7 or more days had pertussis.

Treatment

Infants < 6 months and other patients with potentially severe disease often require hospitalization for supportive care to manage coughing paroxysms, apnea, cyanosis, feeding difficulties, and other complications. Antibiotic therapy initiated during the catarrhal stage promotes more rapid clinical improvement (Box 56–6). However, after the onset of paroxysms, antimicrobial agents usually have little discernible effect on the course of illness. Nevertheless, they are recommended to limit the spread of the organism to others. The drug of choice is erythromycin. Currently, the recommended duration of therapy is 14 days, although recent evidence suggests that a 7-day course is also efficacious. Azithromycin and clarithromycin are alternatives based on clinical studies demonstrating the ability of these drugs to eradicate the organism.

Trimethoprim/sulfamethoxazole is another possi-

BOX 56–6

Treatment of *B pertussis* Disease	
First Choice	• Erythromycin, 40–50 mg/kg/d orally divided into four equal doses for 14 d (but see text); maximum dose: 2 g/d
Second Choice	• Azithromycin, 10 mg/kg/d once per day for 5 days; maximum dose 500 mg/d; or clarithromycin, 10 mg/kg/d divided into 2 equal doses for 7 d; maximum dose, 1 g/d • Trimethoprim-sulfamethoxazole (TMP-SMX), 8 mg TMP, 40 mg SMX/kg/d orally divided into two doses

ble alternative, but its efficacy is unproven. In in vitro studies, *B pertussis* is also susceptible to fluoroquinolones and to a lesser extent ampicillin and rifampin. *B parapertussis* is less susceptible in vitro to all agents except erythromycin.

Among patients with pertussis who are treated with erythromycin, nasopharyngeal cultures almost always become negative within 5 days after initiating therapy. In order to prevent secondary transmission effectively, antibiotic treatment also should be prescribed for all household and other close contacts, including those who have been immunized against *B pertussis,* since vaccine-induced immunity is not absolute and may not prevent infection. Individuals exposed to a patient with pertussis should be closely monitored for respiratory symptoms over the ensuing 2–3 weeks.

Corticosteroids, albuterol, and pertussis-specific immunoglobulin may be effective in reducing paroxysms of coughing but require further evaluation before they can be recommended.

Prevention & Control

Universal immunization with pertussis vaccine is critical for control of pertussis (Box 56–7). Whole-cell and acellular pertussis vaccines in combination with diphtheria and tetanus toxoids (DTP and DTaP, respectively) are available in the United States and should be administered to all children < 7 years. The primary series includes doses at 2, 4, 6, and 15–18 months of age, followed by a booster at 4–6 years of age. Whole-cell vaccines are prepared from a suspension of inactivated *B pertussis* cells, whereas acellular vaccines contain one or more antigens derived from *B pertussis* and lack endotoxin. These antigens include pertussis toxin, filamentous hemagglutinin, fimbriae type 2, fimbriae type 3, and pertactin. All acellular vaccines contain pertussis toxin, in an inactivated form.

Based on household studies of children in the United States exposed to pertussis, the efficacy of whole-cell vaccines for children who received at least three doses is estimated to be 50 to 90%, depending on the case definition. Protection is greatest against

culture-confirmed, more severe cases. Vaccine-induced immunity persists for at least 3 years and then diminishes. Although whole-cell vaccines have been highly effective in reducing the burden of disease and deaths due to *B pertussis,* they are associated with a number of troublesome adverse effects, including redness, induration, and tenderness at the injection site, low-grade fever, drowsiness, irritability, and anorexia. Less common serious adverse reactions include seizures, hypotonic-hyporesponsive episodes, fever > 40 °C, and persistent, severe, inconsolable crying lasting 3 or more hours. Encephalopathy, other neurologic conditions, and sudden infant death syndrome have been attributed to vaccination with whole-cell pertussis vaccines, but evidence for a causal association is lacking.

Acellular pertussis vaccines were first demonstrated to be efficacious in studies in Japan involving children 2 years of age and older, and in 1991, two different formulations were licensed in the United States for use as the fourth and fifth (booster) doses in the routine series. More recent studies in Europe compared acellular and whole-cell vaccines in infants and found them to be associated with similar levels of protective efficacy. Concentrations of serum antibody to PT, FHA, fimbriae, and pertactin were at least as high after immunization with the acellular vaccines as they were after vaccination with a whole-cell vaccine. Furthermore, adverse reactions were

BOX 56–7

Control of *B pertussis* Infection	
Prophylactic Measures	• Vaccines are available and effective • Chemoprophylaxis for contacts: erythromycin or alternative (same as treatment dose)
Isolation Precautions	Droplet precautions for first 5 d of treatment

significantly less frequent among recipients of the acellular vaccines. With this information in mind, five acellular vaccines are now approved in the United States for use during infancy, and licensure of additional products is anticipated. Given their efficacy and safety profile, acellular vaccines are preferred over whole cell vaccines in the United States.

Once a case of pertussis has been diagnosed, all contacts should be identified. Close contacts < 7 years who have received fewer than four doses of pertussis vaccine (DTP or DTaP) should have pertussis immunization initiated or continued. As mentioned above, contacts should also receive chemoprophylaxis with erythromycin or a suitable alternative.

For the hospitalized patient, droplet precautions are recommended for 5 days after initiation of effective therapy. Similarly, outpatients should be excluded from day care or school until 5 days of treatment are completed. If antibiotic therapy is not administered, precautions should be continued until 3 weeks after the onset of paroxysms.

BRANHAMELLA CATARRHALIS

Essentials of Diagnosis

- *Branhamella catarrhalis* is presumed to be acquired by direct contact with contaminated respiratory tract secretions or by droplet spread.
- The most common infections include otitis media, sinusitis, and, to a lesser extent, exacerbations of underlying lung disease.
- Gram stain of infected fluid shows gram-negative diplococci. Culture of infected fluids when indicated is also useful.

General Considerations

A. Epidemiology. *B catarrhalis* was previously thought to be a harmless commensal organism, but it is now clear that this organism is an important cause of human disease. *B catarrhalis* colonizes the nasopharynx of 5 to 10% of adults and ~ 30% of children. Colonization rates may be even higher during the winter months. *B catarrhalis* accounts for ~ 15% of all cases of otitis media. Evidence that *B catarrhalis* is a true middle ear pathogen comes from the observation that antibodies specific for this organism develop after otitis media in which a pure culture of *B catarrhalis* is obtained from middle ear fluid. *B catarrhalis* also causes sinusitis and can be recovered alone or in combination with other bacteria from direct sinus aspirates of patients with clinical and radiographic evidence of acute bacterial sinusitis.

B. Microbiology. The taxonomic position of *B catarrhalis* remains controversial. There are conflict-

ing proposals to classify this organism as a member of the genus *Moraxella,* subgenus *Branhamella,* or to leave it as the only species in the genus *Branhamella.* The genera *Branhamella* and *Moraxella* are classified along with the genera *Neisseria, Kingella,* and *Acinetobacter* in the family *Neisseriaceae.* In contrast to *Moraxella* spp., which are rod-shaped, *B catarrhalis* appears as gram-negative diplococci with kidney-shaped cells and thus is morphologically indistinguishable from *Neisseria.* It grows well on blood agar and chocolate agar, forming small, opaque, gray-white colonies, 1–3 mm in diameter, which are circular and firm. Nevertheless, recovery from mucosal surfaces is facilitated by the use of selective media such as Thayer-Martin or TV broth (Mueller-Hinton broth supplemented with trimethoprim and vancomycin). Isolates typically produce cytochrome oxidase, catalase, and DNase. They are unable to ferment maltose, glucose, lactose, or sucrose, thus distinguishing them from *N gonorrhoeae* and *N meningitidis.* *B catarrhalis* lipopolysaccharide molecules lack long O-polysaccharide side chains and are referred to as lipo-oligosaccharide. These organisms are nonencapsulated.

C. Pathogenesis. The pathogenesis of localized respiratory tract disease due to *B catarrhalis* begins with colonization of the upper respiratory tract mucosa. Subsequently, the organism spreads contiguously to produce disease in the middle ear, the sinuses, or the lower respiratory tract. Factors that increase the likelihood of spread to the tracheobronchial tree include smoking, intercurrent viral infection, corticosteroid use, and other forms of immunosuppression. The determinants of colonization remain poorly defined but may include pili, which are present on most isolates, and a nonpilus protein called UspA1. Persistence on the respiratory mucosa may relate to the ability of the organism to resist complement-dependent bactericidal activity, which is mediated by a high-molecular-weight protein referred to as UspA2 (antigenically related to UspA1 and also called HMW-OMP). In animal models of *B catarrhalis* lower respiratory infection, the organism appears to release a potent chemotactic factor and elicits a striking neutrophil response in the lung.

CLINICAL SYNDROMES

B catarrhalis causes bronchitis and pneumonia in patients with underlying lung disease, especially chronic obstructive pulmonary disease. It is also a rare cause of invasive disease, including meningitis, endocarditis, bacteremia without a focus, septic arthritis, and cellulitis. In addition, it is a recognized cause of acute conjunctivitis and is periodically mistaken as *Neisseria gonorrhoeae* in newborn infants with conjunctivitis. *B catarrhalis* occasionally colonizes the genital mucosa and has been reported as a cause of urethritis.

BOX 56–8

Clinical Manifestations of *B catarrhalis* Disease

Otitis Media	• Ear pain • Fever • Bulging tympanic membrane with distorted landmarks and decreased mobility
Sinusitis	• Nasal discharge • Fever • Cough • Headache • Facial tenderness
Exacerbation of Lung Disease	• Increased dyspnea • Fever • Sputum production • Sputum purulence

Clinical Findings

A. Signs and Symptoms. The signs and symptoms of *B catarrhalis* acute otitis media and sinusitis are indistinguishable from those present when acute otitis media and sinusitis are caused by other pathogens (Box 56–8). However, episodes of *B catarrhalis* otitis media are more likely to resolve spontaneously than are those caused by *Streptococcus pneumoniae* or *H influenzae*. The clinical manifestations of lower respiratory tract infection caused by *B catarrhalis* also are similar to those caused by other bacteria. Episodes of bronchitis in patients with chronic obstructive pulmonary disease are characterized by increased cough, purulent sputum, shortness of breath, and sometimes low-grade fever. Pneumonia due to *B catarrhalis* occurs almost exclusively in elderly persons and in patients with chronic obstructive pulmonary disease and is characterized by fever as high as 39.4 °C, cough, purulent sputum, and shortness of breath.

B. Laboratory Findings. Nasopharyngeal and throat cultures are not helpful in establishing a microbiological diagnosis but can be useful in excluding certain organisms.

Diagnosis

Tympanocentesis is necessary to establish the etiology of otitis media, and sinus aspiration is required

BOX 56–9

Treatment of *B catarrhalis* Disease

Medication	Children	Adults
• Amoxicillin plus clavulanate (Augmentin)	• 40 mg/kg/d divided into 3 equal doses[1] (amoxicillin component)	• 500 mg three times daily (amoxicillin component)
• Trimethoprim-sulfamethoxazole (TMP-SMX)	• 8–12 mg TMP/40–60 mg SMX/kg/d divided into 2 equal doses	• 160 mg TMP/800 mg SMX twice daily
• Oral second- and third-generation cephalosporins	• Depends on particular agent	• Depends on particular agent
• Erythromycin-sulfisoxazole	• 40 mg/kg/d divided into 3–4 equal doses (erythromycin component)	• 500 mg four times daily (erythromycin component)
• Azithromycin	• 10 mg/kg loading dose, then 5 mg/kg/d	• 500 mg loading dose, then 250 mg/d
• Clarithromycin	• 15 mg/kg/d divided into 2 equal doses	• 500 mg twice daily

[1]Both twice daily and three times dialy formulations are available.

to confirm the cause of sinusitis (see Table 56–2). However, these procedures are rarely performed. In patients with pneumonia, auscultation sometimes reveals evidence of consolidation, and chest radiograph sometimes shows patchy or lobar infiltrates. Pleural effusion and empyema are uncommon. The most practical approach to establish the diagnosis of *B catarrhalis* pneumonia or bronchitis is to examine a gram-stained sputum sample, which will show a predominance of intracellular and extracellular gram-negative diplococci.

Treatment

Approximately 80% of isolates produce β-lactamase, and at least three different *B catarrhalis* β-lactamases have been identified, including BRO-1, BRO-2, and BRO-3. The activity of these β-lactamases can be inhibited by β-lactamase inhibitors such as clavulanate and sulbactam. Most *B catarrhalis* infections can be treated with oral agents, including Augmentin (amoxicillin plus clavulanate), erythromycin, trimethoprim-sulfamethoxazole, and tetracycline (Box 56–9). *B ca-*

tarrhalis is also uniformly susceptible to ticarcillin, piperacillin, mezlocillin, azlocillin, most second- and third-generation cephalosporins, chloramphenicol, newer macrolides, and aminoglycosides. *B catarrhalis* is resistant to penicillin, ampicillin, vancomycin, clindamycin, and methicillin. Approximately 1–2% of isolates are resistant in vitro to tetracycline or erythromycin. Isolates producing β-lactamase may be reported by the clinical laboratory as susceptible to penicillin and ampicillin, because of the low activity of the BRO-β-lactamases. However, clinical treatment failures with such organisms suggest they should be considered resistant to these antibiotics. Similarly, cefaclor and possibly other cephalosporins may be inactivated by the BRO-β-lactamases.

Prevention & Control

Currently, there are no measures for prevention and control of *B catarrhalis* infection. However, a number of laboratories are characterizing *B catarrhalis* surface antigens, hoping to develop a vaccine effective against this organism.

REFERENCES

Catlin BW: *Branhamella catarrhalis*: an organism gaining respect as a pathogen. Clin Microbiol Rev 1990; 3:293.

Centers for Disease Control and Prevention: 1998 Guidelines for Treatment of Sexually Transmitted Diseases. MMWR 1998;47:18.

Centers for Disease Control and Prevention: Pertussis vaccination: use of acellular pertussis vaccines among infants and young children. MMWR 1997;46:1.

Centers for Disease Control and Prevention: Progress toward elimination of *Haemophilus influenzae* type b disease among infants and children—United States, 1987–1995. MMWR 1996;45:901.

Centers for Disease Control and Prevention: Recommendations for use of *Haemophilus* b conjugate vaccines and a combined diphtheria, tetanus, pertussis, and *Haemophilus* b vaccine. MMWR 1993;42:1.

Farizo KM et al: Epidemiologic features of pertussis in the United States, 1980–1989. Clin Infect Dis 1992; 14:708.

Hewlett EL: Pertussis: current concepts of pathogenesis. Ped Infect Dis J 1997;16:578.

Klingman KL, Murphy TF: Purification and characterization of a high-molecular-weight outer membrane protein of *Moraxella (Branhamella) catarrhalis*. Infect Immun 1994;62:1150.

Mink CM et al: A search for *Bordetella pertussis* infection in university students. Clin Infect Dis 1992; 14:464.

Morse SA: Chancroid and *Haemophilus ducreyi*. Clin Microbiol Rev 1989;2:137.

Murphy TF: *Branhamella catarrhalis*: epidemiology, surface antigenic structure, and immune response. Microbiol Rev 1996;60:267.

Paradise JL. Managing otitis media: a time for change. Pediatrics 1995;96:712.

St. Geme JW III: Nontypeable *Haemophilus influenzae* disease: epidemiology, pathogenesis, and prospects for prevention. Infect Agents Dis 1993;2:1.

St. Geme JW III: Early events in the pathogenesis of *Haemophilus influenzae* disease. In Miller VL, et al: *Molecular Genetics of Bacterial Pathogenesis,* American Society for Microbiology, 1994:157.

St. Geme JW III: Progress towards a vaccine for nontypable *Haemophilus influenzae*. Ann Med 1996;28:31.

Strebel PM et al. Pertussis in Missouri: evaluation of nasopharyngeal culture, direct fluorescent antibody testing, and clinical case definitions in the diagnosis of pertussis. Clin Infect Dis 1993;16:276.

Wright SW, Edwards KM, Decker MD, Zeldin MH: Pertussis infection in adults with persistent cough. JAMA 1995;273:1044.

Vibrio & Campylobacter

57

Gary W. Procop, MD, & Frank R. Cockerill III, MD

VIBRIO INFECTIONS

VIBRIO CHOLERAE INFECTIONS

Essentials of Diagnosis

- History of exposure, particularly travel to endemic or epidemic locales.
- Acute onset of voluminous, watery diarrhea, with low-grade fever and mild abdominal pain, which are disproportionate to the amount of diarrhea.
- During outbreaks, the presence of straight-to-curved gram-negative bacilli, with a single polar flagellum, in the stool of infected patients.
- In wet preparations, these organisms demonstrate a characteristic darting or "shooting star" motility. The identification may be confirmed by motility inhibition with specific antisera.
- Cultures of *V cholerae* from stool with differential media, such as thiosulfate-citrate-bile salts-sucrose (TCBS) medium.
- Bacterial growth in nutrient broth, without 1% NaCl supplementation. This characteristic is useful for separating *V cholerae* from most other *Vibrio* species.
- Detection of *V cholerae* toxin by latex agglutination or enzyme-linked immunosorbent assay (ELISA) or the detection of *V cholerae*-specific nucleic acid sequences by polymerase chain reaction (PCR)-based methods.

General Considerations

A. Epidemiology. Cholera is a disease of antiquity and probably represents some of the diarrheal illnesses described by Hippocrates and other early physicians. Robert Koch discovered *V cholerae* in 1884. Since the 17th century, at least eight epidemics of cholera have swept the globe. At least seven of the eight pandemics originated from the Ganges River delta, where cholera is endemic. *V cholerae* is transmitted by the fecal-oral route, often by way of contaminated water supplies.

The areas where cholera remains endemic lack adequate sewage disposal systems and water treatment facilities. Cholera epidemics often occur during war, when basic human needs are not met. Throughout the past 30 years, cholera epidemics have repeatedly occurred in overcrowded refugee camps. In the 1994 Rwandan refugee camps, a significant proportion of the deaths were caused by cholera. During this time, 600,000 people are believed to have been infected with *V cholerae* 01, which resulted in ~ 45,000 deaths.

B. Microbiology. The *Vibrionaceae* share many characteristics with the *Pseudomonadaceae* and the *Enterobacteriaceae*. Genera in this family that cause human disease include *Vibrio, Aeromonas,* and *Plesiomonas.* The genus *Vibrio* consists of gram-negative bacilli that are straight or curved and are motile usually by means of a single polar flagellum. Most species are oxidase producers, have the ability to ferment glucose, and can grow in the presence or absence of oxygen.

During cholera outbreaks, the clinical diagnosis may be supported by examination of the stool. In cholera, a preponderance of straight-to-curved gram-negative bacilli with a single polar flagellum may be seen. In wet preparations, these exhibit a characteristic darting or "shooting star" motility. Motility inhibition, after exposure to type-specific antiserum, confirms the identity of these organisms.

The culturing of *V cholerae* from stool is most effectively achieved with TCBS agar. The colonies of *V cholerae* are able to ferment the sucrose in TCBS and appear yellow. Suspicious colonies should be subcultured to a nonselective agar, such as blood or chocolate agar, and after sufficient growth is present, oxidase testing and agglutination testing with polyvalent *V cholerae* antiserum can be performed.

V cholerae and a closely related species, *V mimicus,* unlike other *Vibrio* species, are able to grow in nutrient broth without 1% NaCl supplementation. Additional biochemical features, such as the ability to decarboxylate lysine and ornithine and the inability to hydrolyze arginine, are characteristics that may help to separate *V cholerae* and *V mimicus* from other vibrios. *V cholerae* and *V mimicus* may be easily separated, since *V cholerae* ferments sucrose, while *V mimicus* does not.

CLINICAL SYNDROMES

Cholera is a fulminant diarrheal disease caused by *V cholerae* (Box 57–1). Patients with cholera develop frequent, watery stools, which may reach volumes ≤1 L/h. If these patients are untreated, they will develop rapid dehydration and electrolyte abnormalities, which may result in death within hours from the onset of disease. Therefore cholera is a medical emergency.

V cholerae is noninvasive and produces diarrhea by the elaboration of a potent enterotoxin. This enterotoxin consists of two subunits that have been well characterized. The circular, pentameric B-subunit binds monosialosyl ganglioside residues on the surface of the intestinal epithelial cell and introduces the enzymatic A-subunit into the cytoplasm. The A-subunit functions as an adenosine diphosphate (ADP) ribosylase and transfers an ADP-ribose moiety from cytoplasmic nicotinamide adenine dinucleotide (NAD) to the cell-membrane–associated adenylate cyclase. ADP-ribosylation renders adenylate cyclase unresponsive to feedback inhibition. The result is dramatically increased intracellular cyclic adenosine monophosphate (cAMP) levels. Elevated cytoplasmic cAMP levels cause massive fluid and electrolyte transit into the bowel lumen, resulting in the characteristic "rice water" stool of cholera.

Clinical Findings

A. Signs and Symptoms. Patients with cholera initially develop increased peristalsis, a feeling of fullness, and occasionally vomiting. Diarrhea develops rapidly and soon becomes watery. Abdominal pain and high fever are usually minimal or absent and distinctly disproportionate to the amount of diarrhea. Fever, when present, is usually caused by dehydration. Electrolyte abnormalities, from voluminous diarrhea, may manifest as muscle weakness, intestinal ileus, or even cardiac dysrhythmia. The clinical manifestations of infection and the possibility of severe complications correlate with the patient's hydration and electrolyte abnormalities. Mental status changes secondary to hypoglycemia may also occur. Without urgent fluid and electrolyte replacement therapy, hypovolemic shock and death may occur rapidly.

B. Laboratory Findings. The stool from patients with cholera tends to lose its fecal odor as the disease progresses and may develop a sweet odor. Also, as the disease progresses and normal fecal material is passed, the stool becomes watery, turbid, and gray. Small flecks of mucus in this gray water give these stools their "rice water" appearance. Blood and neutrophils are generally not present in choleric stools. In the appropriate clinical and epidemiological context (eg, during outbreaks of cholera), a direct examination of stool can be useful for the presumptive identification of *V cholerae*. A microscopic examination of stool that discloses straight or curved bacilli with rapid, darting, or "shooting star" motility is suggestive of *V cholerae*. Inhibition of the motility of the organism by *V cholerae* O1 antiserum further supports the diagnosis of cholera.

Stool from patients with diarrheal disease suspected to be caused by *V cholerae* should be cultured on a selective and differential media, such as TCBS. Latex agglutination and ELISA-based methods to detect the presence of cholera toxin have been developed. These methods are rapid and may be useful in rapidly detecting patients with cholera in the early phases of disease. Polymerase chain reaction based methods of organism detection have been used successfully to detect *V cholerae* nucleic acids from choleric stools.

C. Imaging. Rarely, patients with cholera may develop an ileus as an early manifestation of disease. Abdominal imaging techniques are especially important in such patients since excessive fluid accumulation and visceral rupture may occur.

D. Differential Diagnosis. *Salmonella* species, *Shigella* species, *Yersinia enterocolitica, Campylobacter* species, and the enteric pathogenic *E coli;* viruses such as rotavirus and Norwalk agent; and parasites, such as *Giardia lamblia* and species of *Cyclospora* and *Cryptosporidium* are common pathogens that should be considered in the differential diagnosis of diarrheal disease. The diagnosis of these pathogens is achieved by a careful history combined with laboratory testing.

E. Complications. Profound dehydration and hypoglycemia may result in altered mental status, unconsciousness, seizures, and renal failure. Electrolyte abnormalities may manifest as muscle weakness, intestinal ileus, or sudden death caused by cardiac arrhythmia. Vomiting exacerbates the dehydration, makes oral rehydration difficult, and may lead to aspiration pneumonia. During pregnancy the fluid and electrolyte imbalances may result in fetal death.

BOX 57–1

Clinical Syndromes of Cholera	
More Common	• Exposure to unsafe drinking water, particularly in areas where cholera is endemic or epidemic • Acute onset of watery diarrhea • Low-grade fever and minimal abdominal pain distinctly out of proportion to the degree of diarrhea
Less Common	• Ileus

Rarely, patients with cholera may develop an intestinal ileus. These patients may accumulate large amounts of fluid in the lumen of the intestine. When this occurs at the onset of disease, the patient may be suspected to have an acute abdomen and cholera may not be suspected. If an ileus develops later in the course of disease and stool volume is used as a basis of fluid replacement, these patients may be inadequately rehydrated and viscus rupture could occur.

Treatment

A. Primary Therapy. Primary therapy of cholera consists of fluid and electrolyte replacement. Published guidelines for fluid and electrolyte replacement in cholera are available. Either a citrate (10 mmol/L)- or bicarbonate (30 mmol/L)-based solution may be used for oral rehydration. These should contain sodium (90 mmol/L), potassium (20 mmol/L), chloride (80 mmol/L), and glucose (111 mmol/L). The glucose is actively transported into enterocytes. This osmotically drives water from the lumen and into the body. In developing countries, the water residua from boiled rice may be used for rehydration. This is an inexpensive and excellent source of oligosaccharides, which like glucose, aid in the osmotic shifting of water from the lumen to the body.

Intravenous fluid replacement therapy is necessary for patients with severe dehydration (≥10% of their body weight) and acidosis (pH <7.2). These patients should be rehydrated with 50% normal saline with 44 mmol/L of bicarbonate. Potassium replacement may be given as needed.

If vomiting is not prominent, oral replacement is usually adequate. If mental status changes are present, hypoglycemia should be treated with intravenous glucose infusion (bolus 3–4 mL/kg of a 25% glucose solution, followed by continuous infusion of 10 mg/kg/h).

B. Antimicrobial Therapy. Treatment with tetracycline will shorten the duration of cholera (Box 57–2). Pregnant women and children who develop cholera should be treated with ampicillin. If allergies to penicillin exist, trimethoprim-sulfamethoxazole and furazolidone are also effective.

Prognosis

The prognosis for patients infected during cholera epidemics is often poor. This directly parallels the lack of basic medical care, such as fluid and electrolyte replacement, which exists in the situations that foster epidemic cholera. If patients with cholera are given appropriate fluid, electrolyte, and glucose replacements, the prognosis is good. In many instances, the fluid replacement is roughly based on the volume lost. Patients who are not recognized to have an intestinal ileus may fare poorly. These patients may initially be misdiagnosed or if recognized to have cholera may not receive adequate fluid and electrolyte replacement.

Prevention & Control

A clean water supply and effective sanitation are essential for preventing epidemic cholera. The economic means for effective waste disposal and preventive healthcare are not available to the impoverished; therefore cholera persists. In sporadic cases, patient isolation with appropriate waste disposal and hand washing are important means of preventing the spread of disease.

Two vaccines are currently being studied for high-risk individuals to use. These are a B-subunit, killed whole-cell vaccine (BC-WC) and a live, recombinant attenuated, orally administered vaccine (CVD 103-HgR). These vaccines may offer some protection, but they are not an alternative for clean water. In refugee-type settings, in conjunction with preventive measures, these vaccines may help to diminish the spread and mortality of cholera.

OTHER *VIBRIO* INFECTIONS

Essentials of Diagnosis

- History of ingestion of raw or possibly undercooked shellfish and/or exposure to seawater.
- Enteritis: acute onset of predominantly watery diarrhea, which may contain blood and/or neutrophils.
- Extraintestinal: cellulitis, wound infections, or septicemia, which may be associated with multiple bullous to ulcerative skin lesions, especially in patients with liver cirrhosis.
- Culture of etiologic agent, with enhanced growth of most species after NaCl supplementation.

General Considerations

A. Epidemiology. In the United States and other developed countries, *Vibrio*-associated disease is caused almost exclusively by species other than *V cholerae*. These vibrios are normal inhabitants of marine environments and are transmitted to humans through the ingestion of raw or undercooked shellfish, through the contamination of foods by seawater, or through exposure to seawater. These organisms may cause gastroenteritis, soft tissue infections, or both. Diseases caused by these organisms usually occur during summer or early fall. The warmer summer waters may enhance the growth of vibrios and water-associated recreational activities increase the risk of exposure.

B. Microbiology. As may be expected, the vast majority of these marine vibrios require NaCl for optimal growth. In many instances, these organisms may grow suboptimally on general agar media, unless they are supplemented with NaCl. They grow better on media that contain salt, such as MacConkey and TCBS agar. On MacConkey agar, most of these organisms do not ferment lactose and would be considered possible enteric pathogens. Notable excep-

BOX 57-2

Treatment of Cholera

Principal Consideration	Fluid and Electrolyte Replacement, Acid–Base, and Glucose Management	
	Children[1]	Adults
First Choice	• Ampicillin, 250 mg orally or IV every 6 h for 5 d	• Tetracycline, 250 mg orally or IV every 6 h for 5 d • During pregnancy, ampicillin is the drug of choice (dosage as below)
Second Choice	• TMP/SMX[2] orally or IV (>2 months old); TMP, 3–6 mg, + SMX, 15–30 mg/kg every 12 h for 5 d	• Ampicillin, 250 mg orally or IV every 6 h for 5 d
Penicillin Allergic	• TMP/SMX[2] (dosage as above) OR • Furazolidone (liquid = 3.33 mg/ml): >5 years old, 7.5–15 ml; 1–4 years old, 5.0–7.5 ml; 1 month–1 year old, 2.5–5.0 ml orally every 6 h for 5 d	• Tetracycline (dosage as above) OR • TMP/SMX[2] orally or IV: TMP, 160 mg, + SMX, 800 mg orally or IV every 12 h for 5 d OR • Furazolidone, 100 mg orally every 6 h for 5 d

[1]Tetracycline and the quinolones are generally not given to children because of potential toxicity; however, in cases in which strains of *V cholerae* are resistant to other drugs and severe disease is present, tetracycline or quinolones may be considered.
[2]TMP/SMX, Trimethoprim sulfamethoxazole; treatment may be changed based on susceptibility studies.

tions are *Vibrio mimicus* and *Vibrio vulnificus,* which are lactose positive and may be overlooked as normal enteric flora. *V mimicus* has many biochemical characteristics similar to *V cholerae* and also grows readily without additional NaCl. *V mimicus* is readily differentiated from *V cholerae* on TCBS agar, by its inability to ferment sucrose. The most common vibrio enteric pathogen in the United States, *V parahaemolyticus,* also is sucrose negative.

If a vibrio infection is suspected, TCBS agar should be used for the detection of possible pathogens. This selective and differential medium inhibits growth of many commensal organisms by the presence of bile (oxygall), sodium cholate, and sodium citrate, while the presence of sucrose and the indicator bromthymol blue allow for the differentiation of sucrose fermenters and nonfermenters. *V cholerae, V alginolyticus,* and a few other less commonly encountered vibrios are sucrose positive, whereas *V parahaemolyticus, V vulnificus,* and most of the remaining clinically significant isolates are sucrose negative.

Vibrios are facultative anaerobic gram-negative bacilli, which may appear pleomorphic in Gram stains. The clinically relevant *Vibrio* species may be subcategorized into six groups based on their growth requirements and ability to perform certain biochemical tests. The key biochemical reactions necessary to separate the vibrios into these six groups include the following: (1) the requirement of NaCl for growth in nutrient broth; (2) oxidase production; (3) nitrate re-

ductive capacity; (4) *myo*-inositol fermentation; and (5) the presence or absence of arginine dehydrolase, lysine decarboxylase, and ornithine decarboxylase. Additional biochemical reactions may be used for complete speciation.

These tests are used in the microbiology laboratory to exclude certain diagnostic possibilities. Most vibrios are oxidase positive, with the exception of *V metschnikovii.* With the exception of *V cholerae* and *V mimicus,* isolates require 1% NaCl supplementation to adequately perform biochemical tests. The six groups are as follows:

• Group 1 consists of *V cholerae* and *V mimicus.* These are readily distinguished from the other vibrios by their ability to grow in nutrient broth, without NaCl supplementation.
• Group 2 consists of *V metschnikovii,* which is differentiated from other vibrios by its inability to produce oxidase and reduce nitrate to nitrite.
• Group 3 consists of *V cincinnatiensis,* which is differentiated from other vibrios by its ability to ferment *myo*-inositol.
• Group 4 consists of *V hollisae,* which is differentiated from other vibrios by its inability to hydrolyze arginine and to decarboxylate lysine and ornithine.
• Group 5 consists of *V damsela, V fluvialis,* and *V furnissii.* Unlike some of the other vibrios, this group produces arginine dihydrolase.
• Group 6 consists of *V alginolyticus, V para-*

haemolyticus, V vulnificus, and *V carchariae.* These organisms are differentiated from other vibrios by a combination of their ability to produce lysine decarboxylase and their inability to hydrolyze arginine.

CLINICAL SYNDROMES

Noncholera vibrios cause both enteritis and extraintestinal disease (Box 57–3). In the United States, *Vibrio* species other than *V cholerae* are far more common causes of *Vibrio*-associated gastroenteritis. These agents include *V parahaemolyticus, V mimicus, V hollisae,* and others. The enteritis caused by these organisms is characterized by fever, mild-to-moderate abdominal pain and cramping, and diarrhea, which may be either watery or bloody. Many of the pathogenic, noncholera vibrios are also halophilic (NaCl enhances growth) and have been associated with the consumption of raw or undercooked shellfish. *V parahaemolyticus* is the most common cause of shellfish-associated gastroenteritis in the United States. In most instances, the enteritis is self-limited,

BOX 57–3	
Clinical Syndromes of Other *Vibrio* Species	
Enteric Disease	• Recent ingestion of raw or undercooked shellfish • Acute onset of diarrhea, which is usually watery, but may be bloody and dysenteric • Low-grade fever, chills, and mild-to-moderate abdominal cramping
Extraintestinal Disease	• Exposure of a wound to seawater or recent ingestion of raw or undercooked shellfish • Poor wound healing with suppuration, cellulitis, and possibly subcutaneous abscess formation • A sepsislike syndrome associated with hemorrhagic vesicular or bullous skin lesions, especially in individuals with liver cirrhosis or another immunocompromising condition

but complications may occur. Septicemia with severe morbidity and death has occurred following noncholera *Vibrio* gastroenteritis.

Extraintestinal disease may be caused by *V vulnificus* or *V alginolyticus.* These organisms are also halophilic and are associated with shellfish ingestion and saltwater exposure. Manifestations of extraintestinal disease may include wound infections, cellulitis, bullous skin lesions, or septicemia. Patients with cellulitis and wound infections caused by these organisms often report exposure to saltwater. In immunocompromised patients, such as those with cirrhosis or diabetes mellitus, fatal septicemia may occur. If these organisms are suspected clinically, the clinician should notify the laboratory, since NaCl supplementation is required for optimal growth.

NONCHOLERA GASTROENTERITIS

Clinical Findings

A. Signs and Symptoms. Noncholera gastroenteritis is often associated with recent ingestion of raw or undercooked shellfish and often occurs in the summer or early fall in the United States. A typical presentation includes explosive diarrhea, low-grade fever and chills, and mild-to-moderate abdominal pain with cramping. The diarrhea is usually watery but may contain blood and neutrophils.

Dehydration is not as severe as that seen with *Vibrio cholerae* infections, but deaths may occur in children and the elderly. The incubation period is ~ 1 day but ranges from 5 h to 4 days. The diarrhea produced is probably secondary to a combination of exotoxin production and superficial invasion. The patients in which exotoxin production predominates may demonstrate a more watery stool. When mucosal invasion occurs, a dysenteric stool similar to that present in shigellosis may be seen. Secondary spread of these organisms is rare.

B. Laboratory Findings. Dehydration and electrolyte abnormalities are usually less severe than those present in cholera but may become profound in children and the elderly. Culture and biochemical identification of the isolate is the standard method of establishing the etiologic agent of disease. The key biochemical reactions for rapidly subcategorizing *Vibrio* species are listed in the Microbiology section. Many of the group characteristics are based on an organism's ability to perform particular biochemical tests. Therefore it is important to remember that 1% NaCl supplementation is required for some organisms to adequately perform biochemical reactions. NaCl enrichment broths or tellurite-taurocholate-peptone broth may be used for enhanced recovery of these organisms.

C. Differential Diagnosis. See differential diagnosis for *V cholerae* infection.

EXTRAINTESTINAL DISEASE

Clinical Findings

A. Signs and Symptoms. Patients with septicemia, wound infections, or ear infections caused by a *Vibrio* species frequently have a history of shellfish ingestion or saltwater exposure. Clinical manifestations vary depending on the site of infection. Healing wounds, in appropriately exposed individuals, may become secondarily infected by marine vibrios. Suppuration may occur, and subcutaneous abscesses may form. A spreading, violaceous appearance around the wound, which is warm to the touch is indicative of cellulitis. The clinical findings of *V alginolyticus*-associated otitis media are nonspecific. Findings in *V alginolyticus*-associated otitis externa include a reddened, often painful external auditory canal.

In immunocompromised and debilitated patients, especially those with liver cirrhosis, a septicemia syndrome, with multiple bullous skin lesions may occur. This is usually caused by *V vulnificus* and is often fatal. *V vulnificus,* which may be introduced by the ingestion of raw or undercooked shellfish, may transmigrate the intestinal mucosa and invade the bloodstream with little or no gastrointestinal symptomatology. Infected patients often develop signs and symptoms of septic shock, such as fever, chills, and hypotension. Shortly thereafter, erythematous skin lesions occur, which develop into hemorrhagic vesicles-bullae and finally ulcerate. Although this syndrome is rare, it is important to recognize it, since its mortality rate is ~ 50%.

B. Laboratory Findings. Hematopoietic findings are variable and may demonstrate either leukocytosis or leukopenia with left-shifted hematopoiesis. The isolation of vibrios from patients with extraintestinal disease is usually not difficult. The selective and differential agars are not required since the sites of culture are normally sterile. Vibrios causing extraintestinal disease are usually isolated on routine 5% sheep's blood agar. If an extraintestinal *Vibrio* infection is suspected, the microbiology laboratory should be notified. The supplementation of media with 1% NaCl may aid in the more rapid identification of the *Vibrio* species.

C. Imaging. Ultrasound or computerized tomography guidance may be useful for identifying and assisting in drainage of deep abscesses.

D. Differential Diagnosis. Improperly cared for wounds may be colonized and infected by a variety of bacteria. When these wounds have been exposed to salt water or the patient has recently eaten raw or undercooked shellfish, a vibrio infection should be considered.

Although immunocompromised patients may be infected by a variety of microbes, an extraintestinal vibrio infection should be considered when skin lesions and a sepsislike syndrome are present in association with the recent ingestion of raw or undercooked shellfish.

E. Complications. The diarrhea that results from noncholera vibrio infections rarely results in significant dehydration, except in children and the elderly. The hydration status of pregnant women should be carefully monitored to prevent severe dehydration and possible fetal loss.

Extraintestinal vibrio infections may result from septicemia following ingestion of raw shellfish or from direct inoculation of marine vibrios. If septicemia occurs, metastatic foci of infection may be present in virtually any organ. The consequences of extraintestinal vibrio infections during pregnancy are unclear because of the paucity of cases.

Treatment

A. Primary Therapy. Enteritis caused by *V parahaemolyticus* is usually self-limited and requires no therapy. In severe cases of noncholera *Vibrio* gastroenteritis, the principles of cholera therapy should be followed. Patients with extraintestinal disease due to *V vulnificus,* and *V alginolyticus* should undergo appropriate wound débridement and abscess drainage as indicated and should be treated with antimicrobial agents (Box 57–4). Patients with systemic symptomatology may also require extensive supportive measures for survival.

B. Antimicrobial Therapy. Antimicrobial therapy does not shorten the duration of noncholera enteritis and is not recommended in uncomplicated cases. If enteritis is complicated by septicemia, specific antimicrobial therapy should be determined based on the antimicrobial susceptibility profile.

Extraintestinal vibrio infections may be treated with tetracycline, cefotaxime, or possibly ciprofloxacin until the antimicrobial susceptibility profile becomes available.

Prognosis

The prognosis for noncholera gastroenteritis is usually excellent. The prognosis may become guarded in children, the elderly, and pregnant women with severe dehydration.

If appropriate surgical and medical therapy is given, the prognosis for extraintestinal *Vibrio* infections is usually good in the immunocompetent host. In immunocompromised patients, especially those with cirrhosis or diabetes mellitus, the prognosis is guarded to poor.

Prevention & Control

Noncholera vibrio enteritis and many cases of extraintestinal vibrio infections may easily be avoided by abstinence from raw shellfish (Box 57–5). The thorough cooking of shellfish renders it safe for consumption. Regardless of the hazards, raw oysters and clams remain popular in many parts of the world. Warnings concerning the possible health hazards

---

BOX 57–4

Treatment of *V vulnificus* and *V alginolyticus* Infections

Principal Consideration	Surgical Débridement and Abscess Drainage Combined with Antimicrobial Therapy	
	Children[1]	Adults
First Choice	• Cefotaxime IV: newborn to 1 wk, 50 mg/kg/dose every 12 h; 1–4 wk, 50 mg/kg/dose every 8 h; 1 month–12 years & <50 kg, 50–180 mg/kg/d divided every 4–6 h; 1 month–12 years & >50 kg, adult dose until symptoms have subsided	• Tetracycline, 250 mg IV every 6 h until symptoms have subsided • During pregnancy, cefotaxime is the drug of choice (dosage as below)
Second Choice	• Tetracycline IV: 25–50 mg/kg/d divided every 8–12 h	• Cefotaxime, 2 g IV every 4–8 h until symptoms have subsided OR • Ciprofloxacin, 400 mg IV every 12 h until symptoms have subsided
Penicillin Allergic	• Tetracycline (dosage as above)	• Tetracycline (dosage as above)

[1]Tetracycline may discolor the teeth of young patients. Treatment may be changed based on susceptibility studies.

---

should be posted in plain view in restaurants that serve these dishes, and additional caution should be directed specifically to individuals with liver disease or other immunocompromising conditions. Individuals with healing wounds should avoid exposing the wounds to seawater.

Large-scale commercial oyster and clam farming is becoming more established. In the future, this may present additional hazards. The colonization of an entire mollusk bed by pathogenic vibrios could occur if abundant shellfish are present in close proximity. Additionally, the spread of pathogenic vibrios among mollusk beds could result if numerous beds are located in close proximity. This could result in large numbers of contaminated shellfish being present in the same harvest and could result in epidemics. Therefore, in the future, adequate monitoring systems may be needed more than ever before to prevent possible outbreak situations.

CAMPYLOBACTER INFECTIONS

Essentials of Diagnosis
- History of ingestion of appropriate foodstuffs.
- Causes enteritis, characterized by rapid onset of watery to bloody diarrhea with low-grade to moderate fever and moderate-to-severe abdominal cramping.
- Extraintestinal infections include sepsis, thrombophlebitis, endocarditis, and infection of aortic aneurysm.
- Laboratory isolation of a gram-negative "seagull" shaped bacteria, which becomes coccoid as the culture ages.
- These bacteria grow optimally in a microaerophilic, 5–10% oxygen environment; the growth of some species is enhanced by culture at 42 °C.

BOX 57–5

Control of *Vibrio* Infections

Prophylactic Measures	• Clean water and effective sanitation • Avoidance of raw or undercooked shellfish • Avoidance of seawater
Isolation Precautions	• Avoidance of stool from infected patients

General Considerations

A. Epidemiology. *Campylobacter* species are intestinal commensals in many animals, including cattle, pigs, sheep, chickens, and turkeys. Contamination of foodstuffs during meat and dairy processing is thought to significantly contribute to the spread of disease. Unpasteurized dairy products, undercooked meats, and contaminated water serve as the vehicles for *Campylobacter* and other bacterial pathogens. Human-to-human transmission by way of a fecal-oral route or through contaminated blood is also possible.

In developing countries where overcrowding and poor sanitation conditions exist, the carriage rate of *Campylobacter jejuni* from healthy individuals is much higher and human-to-human transmission may be greater. *Campylobacter* is one of the etiologic agents of the infantile and childhood diarrhea diseases in developing countries. Although carrier rates are elevated in adults, symptomatic disease is less common; this is presumably because of enhanced immunity. In tropical climates, the incidence is higher during the rainy season and may be related to the corresponding overcrowding and contamination of local water supplies.

In developed countries, the carriage rate is very low (< 1%). This may result from more effective treatment of human waste, requisite pasteurization of dairy products, and educational efforts regarding the thorough cooking of meat products. In developed countries, campylobacteriosis tends to occur sporadically and year round, with peak incidence in months of the spring or fall. In many instances, infections can be linked to the ingestion of undercooked meats, contaminated milk, or contaminated water supplies.

B. Microbiology. *Campylobacter* are weakly gram-negative, curved or "seagull" shaped bacteria, with single polar flagella (Figure 57–1). Although usually bacillary, many *Campylobacter* species become coccoid as the culture ages. Special culture conditions, including selective media, a microaerophilic environment (5–10% oxygen), and for some species, culture at 42 °C (vs 35–37 °C), are required for optimal recovery of *Campylobacter* species.

Several *Campylobacter* species cause human disease (Box 57–6). *C jejuni* and *C fetus* are the prototypic etiologic agents for enteric and extraintestinal disease, respectively. Table 57–1 shows the principal biochemical reactions used to separate these and other *Campylobacter* species.

C. Pathogenesis. Establishment of infection in the small bowel and colon requires that an adequate inoculum is ingested and sufficient organisms survive after passage through the stomach and that the organisms attach and possibly invade enterocytes. Studies with volunteers have shown that as few as 500–1000 organisms may cause disease. Approximately 9000 organisms reportedly provide the highest illness-to-infection ratio; however, strain variation occurs.

Like *Salmonella, Campylobacter* organisms are susceptible to hydrochloric acid. Entry with foods that buffer stomach acid is important for gastric passage of viable organisms. *C jejuni* thrives in the small intestine and colon and is able to replicate in human bile. Infection is initiated by adhesion and colonization. Bacterial proteins that are important for this phase of infection include the superficial bacterial antigen PEB1, and possibly the newly characterized periplasmic binding protein P29. Peritrichous, pilus-like structures that are present only when the organism is grown in the presence of bile, may also aid in adhesion.

Motility and the adhesion properties of the flagellar protein flagellin are additional virulence factors important for bacterial infection. The pathologic changes in the bowel wall and the occasional detection of *C jejuni* bacteremia are highly suggestive of bacterial invasion. Mild infections may show only an increased cellularity of the lamina propria due to neutrophils, lymphocytes, plasma cells, and histiocytes. Severe cases may disclose exudative enteritis with ulceration and crypt abscesses.

Extracellular toxins that cause cytopathic changes have been demonstrated. Additionally, a choleralike exotoxin has been suggested as a mechanism of diarrhea. The importance of these toxins remains to be elucidated, since non–toxin-producing strains have also been shown to cause disease.

C fetus is the *Campylobacter* species most frequently isolated from blood and is an important agent of extraintestinal disease. Enhanced invasion in a mouse model has been associated with the presence of a surface S protein. The S protein serves as a capsule and imparts an antiphagocytic property to the bacterium. This antiphagocytic property is due in part to the inhibition of the opsonizing complement component C3b. The S protein is antigenically variable as a result of rearrangements between highly homologous protein-encoding genes.

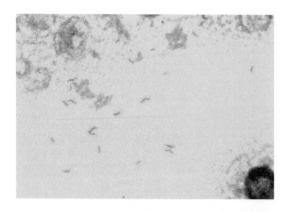

Figure 57–1. Curved, "seagull"-shaped, *Campylobacter fetus* in a blood culture. (Gram stain, 1000 ×)

BOX 57-6

Clinical Syndromes of Campylobacteriosis

	Intestinal (*C jejuni*)	Extraintestinal (*C fetus*)
More Common	• Acute onset of diarrhea, which may be watery or bloody • Associated low-grade-to-moderate fever, nausea, vomiting, malaise, and moderate-to-severe abdominal pain	• Septicemia, fever, chills, and myalgias, without definitive localization • Endocarditis • Thrombophlebitis with vessel necrosis • Fetal loss
Less Common	• Electrolyte abnormalities caused by volume depletion • Guillain-Barré syndrome	• Pericarditis • Cellulitis • Salpingitis • Reiter's syndrome • Meningoencephalitis • Septic arthritis • Spontaneous bacterial peritonitis • Guillain-Barré syndrome • Osteomyelitis • Empyema

CAMPYLOBACTER ENTERITIS

Clinical Findings

A. Signs and Symptoms. The incubation period for *Campylobacter* enteritis is between 1 and 7 days. The rapidity of onset and the severity of disease appear to be related to the inoculating dose. Prodromal fever, headache, malaise, and myalgias are often present 1–2 days before the onset of diarrhea. *Campylobacter*-induced diarrhea is variable in consistency and ranges from watery to bloody. The diarrhea is often accompanied by a low-grade to moderate fever and moderate-to-severe abdominal cramping, which is relieved by defecation. The disease is usually self-limited over several days; however, relapses can occur in 5–10% of untreated patients.

B. Laboratory Findings. Direct examination of stool specimens often demonstrate curved, vibriolike rods with a characteristic darting motility. Leuko-cytes are present in 75% of patients with *Campylobacter* enteritis. Culture on selective media with incubation at 42 °C, in a microaerophilic environment, is used for the enhanced detection of most of the enteropathic *Campylobacter* species (Figure 57–2). The most common causes of *Campylobacter* enteritis, *C jejuni* and *C coli,* both grow well at 42 °C in a microaerophilic environment and are resistant to cephalothin. Therefore a selective antibiotic media containing cephalothin is often used. Under these conditions, colonies appear gray and spreading and are oxidase positive. Gram stain reveals gram-negative, curved organisms. The differentiation of *C jejuni* from *C coli* depends principally on the ability of the isolate to hydrolyze hippurate (*C jejuni* subspecies *jejuni* hydrolyzes hippurate and *C coli* do not). These techniques, however, will not identify the far rarer cases of enteritis caused by *C fetus* and some other *Campylobacter* species, which do not grow well at 42 °C and are inhibited by cephalothin.

Table 57–1. Important reactions for *Campylobacter* species.

	Species	Hippurate Hydrolysis	Growth at 25°C	Growth at 42°C	Susceptibility to Nalidixic Acid	Susceptibility to Cephalothin
More Common	• *C jejuni* • *C coli* • *C fetus*	+ − −	− − +	+ + −	Variable Susceptible Variable	Resistant Resistant Susceptible
Less Common	• *C upsaliensis* • *C hyointestinalis*	− −	− +	+ +	Susceptible Resistant	Susceptible Susceptible

Figure 57–2. Stool culture of patient with campylobacteriosis due to *Campylobacter jejuni*. The extensive watery diarrhea has flushed the bowel of normal enteric flora; note the absence of growth on both the MacConkey and the Hektoen-Enteric agar.

EXTRAINTESTINAL CAMPYLOBACTERIOSIS

Clinical Findings

A. Signs and Symptoms. *Campylobacter fetus,* a less frequent cause of enteritis, is the most common cause of extraintestinal disease; other *Campylobacter* species that may also cause extraintestinal disease include *C jejuni, C coli, C laridis, C sputorum,* and *C hyointestinalis.*

C fetus infection may manifest as fever, chills, and myalgias, without definitive localization; additionally, this organism displays a propensity to infect vascular structures. Endocarditis, intravascular infection of abdominal aortic aneurysms, and septic thrombophlebitis with vessel necrosis have been reported. Fetal death, even with appropriate antibiotic therapy, may occur. Fetal complications most commonly occur during the second trimester of pregnancy. Additional manifestations may include pericarditis, meningoencepalitis, septic arthritis and osteomyelitis, spontaneous bacterial peritonitis, salpingitis, empyema, and cellulitis.

B. Laboratory Findings. In cases of suspected extraintestinal campylobacteriosis, cultures should be plated on nonselective 5% sheep's blood agar and incubated at 37 °C in a microaerophilic environment. Subcultures from blood culture broth systems should be handled in a similar fashion. Identification of *C fetus* may be accomplished by testing susceptibility to cephalothin (susceptible), growth inhibition at 42 °C, positive catalase reaction, and characteristic Gram stain morphology.

Differential Diagnosis

The differential diagnosis for *Campylobacter* enteritis includes all enteric bacterial, viral, and parasitic pathogens. This differential is usually resolved by clinical history, stool culture, ova and parasite examination, and, if necessary, viral testing (ELISA, culture, or electron microscopy).

The differential diagnosis for extraintestinal campylobacteriosis varies according to the site involved. Although *C fetus* may be identified by routine blood culture methods, the incubation conditions used are not optimal for isolation. A high index of suspicion must be maintained since special bacterial culturing techniques may be necessary for optimal recovery of the organism.

Complications

Like other bacterial enteritides, complications of *Campylobacter* enteritis include volume depletion and electrolyte imbalances. Patients with an HLA-B27 phenotype may develop postinfectious arthropathies (Reiter's syndrome) similar to that produced by other bacterial enteric pathogens. Guillain-Barré syndrome rarely occurs following *Campylobacter* enteritis. Guillain-Barré syndrome has been associated with autoantibodies directed to *N*-acetylgalactosaminyl GD1a, GD1b or similar epitopes. Similar epitopes have been shown to occur in the lipopolysaccharides of *C jejuni* and may represent the immunogenic stimulus.

Extraintestinal disease may occur as the result of septicemia and include septic thrombophlebitis, abscess formation, and endocarditis.

Treatment

Fluid and electrolyte replacement therapy is of principal importance (Box 57–7). The benefit of antibiotic therapy for enteric campylobacteriosis remains to be determined. Antibiotic treatment is indicated in patients with high fever, bloody stools, worsening clinical symptoms, or greater than eight stools per day. Erythromycin is the drug of choice for children. Ciprofloxacin is an alternative therapy for adults. Point mutations in the DNA gyrase gene, *gyrA,* have been

BOX 57-7		
Treatment of Campylobacteriosis		
	Children	Adults
First Choice	• Erythromycin, 30–50 mg/kg/d in divided doses for 5–7 d	• Erythromycin, 250 mg orally every 6 h for 5–7 d
Second Choice		• Ciprofloxacin, 500 mg orally every 12 h for 5–7d

shown to confer quinolone resistance. This may occur during therapy; therefore both antimicrobial susceptibility data and close clinical follow-up are required.

Parenteral antibiotics should be administered for extraintestinal disease based on the results of antimicrobial susceptibility testing. Endocarditis requires at least 4 weeks of therapy. Depending on susceptibility, central nervous system infections should be treated with ampicillin, a third-generation cephalosporin, or chloramphenicol.

Prognosis

Severe dehydration and electrolyte imbalances may cause death. This most frequently occurs in children, particularly in underdeveloped and impoverished areas that lack adequate healthcare. Long-term sequelae such as Reiter's syndrome or Guillain-Barré syndrome, although infrequent, may be disabling.

Extraintestinal disease caused by *C fetus* may contribute significantly to morbidity and mortality in immunocompromised patients. These patients may be at increased risk for bacterial enteric infections and associated extraintestinal disease. Infections may be persistent and more severe than in normal hosts. In these patients, the time to initiation of appropriate antibiotic therapy is an important prognostic indicator.

Prevention

Pasteurization, washing foods when feasible, thorough cooking, and hand washing are useful preventive measures (Box 57–8).

BOX 57–8

Control of Campylobacteriosis

Prophylactic Measures	• Avoidance of under-cooked food • Adequate handwashing

---

REFERENCES

Blaser MJ: *Campylobacter* and related species. In Mandell GL et al: *Principles and Practice of Infectious Diseases,* 4th ed. Churchill Livingstone, 1995, pp. 1948.

Carpenter CCJ: Other pathogenic vibrios. In Mandell GL et al: *Principles and Practice of Infectious Diseases,* 4th ed. Churchill Livingstone, 1995.

Greenough WB III: *Vibrio cholerae* and cholera. In Mandell GL et al: *Principles and Practice of Infectious Diseases,* 4th ed. Churchill Livingstone, 1995.

Kaper JB et al: Cholera. Clin Microbiol Rev 1995;8:48.

Keusch GT: Cholera. In JD Wilson et al: *Harrison's Principles of Internal Medicine,* 12th ed. McGraw-Hill, 1991.

Kuzniec S et al: Abdominal aortic aneurysm infected with *Campylobacter fetus* spp. *fetus.* Report of a case and review of the literature. Rev Hosp Clin Fac Med Sao Paulo 1995;50:284.

McLaughlin JC: Vibrio. In Murray PR et al: *Manual of Clinical Microbiology,* 6th ed. American Society for Microbiology Press, 1995, 465.

Nachamkin I: *Campylobacter* and Arcobacter. In Murray PR et al: *Manual of Clinical Microbiology,* 6th ed. American Society for Microbiology Press, 1995.

Wallis MR: The pathogenesis of *Campylobacter jejuni.* Br J Biomed Sci 1994;51:57.

58

Legionella

Michael Bell, MD

Essentials of Diagnosis

- Key signs and symptoms may include minimally productive cough, low-grade fever, headache, and altered mental status.
- Risk factors include smoking, advanced age, history of cardiac or pulmonary disease, male gender, and cell-mediated immune suppression.
- Common infections include pneumonia with multisystem involvement (Legionnaires' disease) and nonspecific febrile illness without pulmonary involvement (Pontiac fever).
- Gram stain of respiratory secretions may reveal numerous neutrophils without evident organisms.
- Aerobic, pleomorphic, faintly staining gram-negative rods are non-spore forming and unencapsulated.

General Considerations

A. Epidemiology. More than 25 species and 48 serogroups of *Legionella* have been identified. *Legionella pneumophila* (especially serogroup 1) causes ~ 70–80% of cases of legionellosis, but *L micdadei, L bozemanii, L dumoffi, L feelei, L longbeacheii,* and other species are also pathogenic. The true incidence of legionellosis, which includes Legionnaires' disease and Pontiac fever, is difficult to establish. Although most developed countries conduct surveillance for infection, underdetection is common, in part because laboratory tests are often not performed or, when performed, lack sensitivity. Between 500 and 1500 cases in the United States are reported annually to the Centers for Disease Control and Prevention (CDC), but the true incidence is believed to be between 13,000 and 20,000 cases a year. Few population-based incidence studies have been conducted. Among members of a prepaid health plan in Seattle, Washington, the annual incidence was 12 cases per 100,000 between 1963 and 1975. In Nottingham, England, 1.4 cases per 100,000 population occurred annually between 1977 and 1991.

Legionella species have been detected in virtually all sources of fresh water, including lakes, ponds, rivers, and soil runoff, especially in areas where there is thermal pollution. However these natural water supplies are rarely identified as sources of human infection. Aerosols from artificial reservoirs of water,

including cooling towers, evaporative condensers, air conditioners, humidifiers, fountains, and whirlpool spas, are most often implicated in outbreaks. Cooling towers and evaporation condensers are especially prone to *Legionella* colonization because they recycle warm, unfiltered water and accumulate organic debris and biofilm over time. This milieu supports the growth of other microflora, including amoebae. Amoebae may be essential to the life cycle of *Legionella* species; the organism appears to multiply intracellularly in these protozoa in the same way it multiplies in human monocytes. Removal of amoebae by filtration will also eliminate viable *Legionella* species from water reservoirs.

Potable-water (especially hot-water) distribution systems are also important reservoirs supporting growth of *Legionella* species. Environmental sampling in hospitals, hotels, and homes has demonstrated colonization in 10–50% of hot-water faucets or water heaters, even at sites where no cases of legionellosis have occurred. Electric water heaters are especially prone to colonization because, unlike gas systems that apply heat to the bottom of the tank, electrical heating elements are in the sides of the tank. The temperature of the sediment deposited in the bottom of the tank is thus cool enough to support growth of the organism. Temperature appears to influence the risk of *Legionella* colonization in all water systems. Growth is promoted between 35 °C and 45 °C, and organisms may remain viable at temperatures ≤ 66 °C.

Legionella species are transmitted to humans through aspiration, inhalation, or instillation of infected water. There is no evidence to support person-to-person transmission. Cooling-tower exhausts proximate to air conditioning intake vents are an important cause of large outbreaks among occupants of hospitals, hotels, and other buildings. Transmission to persons residing as far as 1–2 miles from the cooling towers has also been suggested. Residential air conditioners that do not use water for cooling do not promote *Legionella* transmission, but home air humidifiers probably do. Showers, faucets, and respiratory therapy equipment have also been sources of outbreaks. One major outbreak of Legionnaires' disease on a cruise ship, involving at least nine separate week-long cruises, was associated with contamination of a whirlpool spa. The water taken aboard the ship probably contained *L pneumophila,* but the potable water supply was properly disinfected (chlorinated) before consumption. However, the water reserved for the spa was not adequately decontaminated by the brominator. *L pneumophila* colonized the organic debris trapped in the sand filter of the spa, creating the potential for infectious aerosols that caused exposure and infection among passengers. In another important outbreak, the humidification mist used to preserve vegetables in a grocery store was linked to transmission of legionellosis to several shoppers.

The sources of sporadic cases of *Legionella* infection are not clear, although > 65% of known cases are not associated with outbreaks. Given the enormous number of potential water sources, it is not surprising that establishing a source of exposure is difficult in the absence of an obvious outbreak. As mentioned above, persons residing near cooling towers may be at increased risk. Tobacco use, alcohol abuse, and conditions that affect pulmonary defense mechanisms are risk factors for legionellosis. Some experts believe that aspiration of infected potable water may be an important source of sporadic and also epidemic legionellosis.

Nosocomially acquired Legionnaires' disease accounts for ~ 23% of all cases reported to CDC. After one case of nosocomial infection is identified, subsequent cases are usually detected. Hence, the CDC recommends that identification of one definite or two possible cases of nosocomial Legionnaires' disease within 6 months should prompt an epidemiologic investigation and intensified surveillance. The capacity of *Legionella* species to colonize hospital plumbing systems for prolonged periods provides an ongoing source for transmission to patients. In older facilities or in those in which renovation results in areas of water stagnation and build-up of organic and inorganic sediments, *Legionella* colonization is not uncommon. In one recent investigation, the hospital water distribution system was associated with cases of Legionnaires' disease among immunosuppressed patients over a period of 17 years. Mortality from nosocomially acquired Legionnaires' disease in the United States is ~ 40%, compared with 20% for community-acquired cases.

B. Microbiology. *Legionella* species are slender, aerobic gram-negative bacilli that may appear as coccobacilli measuring 1–2 μm in clinical specimens. *Legionella* species are fastidious; visible colonies appear on agar only after 2–7 days of culturing at 35 °C. Buffered charcoal yeast extract agar is the preferred culture medium. *Legionella* species are not encapsulated and do not form spores. They are catalase positive and oxidase negative.

C. Pathogenesis. *Legionella* species reach the lower respiratory tract via aspiration, inhalation, or instillation of infected water. They are facultative intracellular bacteria that infect host alveolar macrophages and reside within ribosome-lined phagocytic vacuoles. Much as the organism evades the lysosomal defenses of host amoebae, it interferes with macrophage lysosomal fusion and multiplies within that cell's phagosome. New bacilli are released when the infected macrophage ruptures. This process initiates the inflammatory response and pulmonary infiltrates that are the hallmark of Legionnaires' disease. Humoral antibodies develop in infected persons as well as those with subclinical exposures, but they do not appear to be protective. However, cell-mediated responses may confer resistance to subsequent infections. Cytokine production, which activates macrophages and enhances intracellular killing of *Legionella* species, may also be an important host defense.

CLINICAL SYNDROMES

Legionella species are associated with outbreaks of either Pontiac fever, a self-limited influenzalike condition in otherwise healthy people, or Legionnaires' disease, a severe pneumonic disease more common among elderly and immunocompromised individuals (Box 58–1). The spectrum of illness is much broader than these two clinical entities suggest, ranging from completely asymptomatic infection to fulminant respiratory failure and death.

1. PONTIAC FEVER

In 1968, the first documented outbreak of Pontiac fever syndrome affected people in a health department building in Pontiac, Michigan. Epidemiologic investigation demonstrated that the infection was airborne and implicated water aerosols that were produced by a faulty air conditioning system as the source of exposure. Sentinel guinea pigs exposed to air in the building developed bronchopneumonia, and lung tissue cultures grew *L pneumophila* (serogroup 1). Paired acute and convalescent serum specimens from 37 patients were tested by the indirect fluorescent antibody technique, using *L pneumophila* serogroup 1 antigen, and 31 (84%) had rises in titer from < 32 to ≥ 64. Since that time, numerous outbreaks of Pontiac fever, almost always attributable to an obvious source of contaminated water, have been detected in communities across the country.

Pontiac fever is a self-limited infection characterized by fever, chills, headache, myalgia, fatigue, and upper respiratory tract symptoms. It is not associated with a pneumonia or pulmonary infiltrates, although some patients do have a mild nonproductive cough. The incubation period is short, usually 36 h, and the attack rate is high (≤ 95%), even among individuals

---

BOX 58–1

Legionella Syndromes

	Legionnaires' Disease[1]	Pontiac Fever
More Common	• Pneumonia	• Self limited, acute flulike illness characterized by malaise, myalgia, fever, chills, and headache
Less Common	• Diarrhea, nausea, vomiting, abdominal pain • Lethargy, encephalopathy • Hypotension, adult respiratory distress syndrome	• Nonproductive cough, nausea

[1]Among immunosuppressed patients, extrapulmonary disease has included sinusitis, cellulitis, pericarditis, endocarditis, pyelonephritis, pancreatitis, and perirectal abscess.

---

with no underlying illness. Patients recover spontaneously, usually within 1 week of symptom onset.

2. LEGIONNAIRES' DISEASE

Legionella species cause both community-acquired and nosocomial pneumonia among normal individuals, as well among those with depressed cell-mediated immunity (transplant recipients, patients treated with corticosteroids, and those with AIDS). Immunosuppressed patients, those who smoke tobacco, elderly persons, and patients with underlying cardiovascular and pulmonary illnesses are at increased risk. Men are two- to threefold more likely than women to acquire this infection.

Unlike Pontiac fever, for which the incubation period is short (1–2 days), the onset of Legionnaires' disease may occur ≤ 14 days after exposure, although onset usually occurs within 2–10 days. The attack rate is also relatively low (< 8%), when compared with Pontiac fever.

A. Signs and Symptoms. The clinical severity of Legionnaires' disease is highly variable. In mild cases, dry cough and low-grade fever are predominant symptoms. Severe cases, especially among immunosuppressed patients, are complicated by multisystem organ failure and adult respiratory distress syndrome.

Early symptoms are nonspecific and do not distinguish Legionnaires' disease from other causes of pneumonia. Common symptoms include fever, headache, malaise, myalgia, nausea, anorexia, and a minimally productive cough. Neurologic symptoms in addition to headache include changes in mental status that range from lethargy to encephalopathy. Chest pain, which may be pleuritic, and modest hemoptysis are sometimes associated with this infection. Nausea, vomiting, and abdominal pain occur in a minority of patients.

B. Laboratory Findings. Laboratory abnormalities are nonspecific, although hyponatremia (Na < 130 mEq/L) is more likely in legionellosis than in other causes of pneumonia.

C. Imaging. Chest x-ray findings are almost always present by the third day of illness and tend to begin as a unilateral lower-lobe infiltrate. The infiltrate may progress despite antibiotic treatment, but the degree of radiographic abnormality does not correlate with severity of clinical illness. In one recent report, cardiac disease, diabetes mellitus, creatinine (≥ 1.8 mg/dL), septic shock, progressive infiltrates, mechanical ventilation, hyponatremia, and blood urea levels (≥ 30 mg/dL) were factors related to poor outcome, but appropriate antibiotic treatment and improvement in chest radiographic appearance were favorable prognostic factors. Multivariate analysis showed that an Acute Physiology and Chronic Health Evaluation (APACHE II [see Rutledge et al, 1991]) score of ≥ 15 at admission and severe hyponatremia were independent predictors of mortality.

D. Differential Diagnosis. The differential diagnosis includes pulmonary embolus as well as the usual bacterial and viral causes of pneumonia. A prospective study designed to identify factors that distinguished Legionnaires' disease from other causes of community-acquired pneumonia in the emergency department of a university hospital was recently published. Epidemiologic and demographic data and clinical, laboratory, and radiologic features of patients with Legionnaires' disease were compared with those of patients with community-acquired pneumonia caused by other bacterial pathogens. Legionnaires' disease was more frequent in middle-aged, healthy alcohol-drinking male patients than other causes of pneumonia. Lack of response to initial treatment with β-lactam antibiotic and headache, diarrhea, severe hyponatremia, and elevation in serum creatine kinase levels on presentation were also more common among patients with Legionnaires' disease. In contrast, cough, sputum production, and thoracic pain were less common in Legionnaires' patients than in other pneumonia patients. Multivariate analysis demonstrated that underlying disease, diarrhea, and elevation in the creatine kinase were independent predictors of Legionnaire's disease.

E. Complications. In the increasingly large population of immunocompromised individuals, *Legionella* species have been documented to cause extrapulmonary disease that can include cellulitis, wound infection, perirectal abscess, pancreatitis, pyelonephritis, peritonitis, hemodialysis fistula infection, pericarditis, myocarditis, and prosthetic valve endocarditis.

Diagnosis

Diagnosis of *Legionella* infection depends on a high index of suspicion and special laboratory tests. Definitive diagnosis of legionellosis is based on recovery of the organism from respiratory secretions or tissues. Cultures of sputum, transtracheal aspirates, and blood are each 100% specific, although the sensitivities are 80%, 90%, and 20%, respectively. Pretreating respiratory specimens with acid and use of selective media can improve culture sensitivity. In special cases, coculture with amoebae or intraperitoneal inoculation of guinea pigs will increase the diagnostic yield.

Serologic comparison of acute and convalescent serum specimens demonstrating a fourfold rise in titer (≥ 128) of immunoglobulin G antibody (indirect fluorescent antibody assay) is > 95% specific when the *L pneumophila* serogroup 1 antigen is used (but less specific with other *Legionella* antigens) and demonstrates a sensitivity of ~ 50%. Clinical utility of serologic diagnosis is limited, however, because 4–12 weeks are required for the human body to mount a full antibody response. This test is therefore mainly useful as an epidemiologic tool.

Direct fluorescent antibody tests can identify *Legionella* antigens in respiratory specimens and tissue with a high degree of specificity, but, as with other tests, the direct fluorescent antibody test is not sensitive (< 60%). Commercially available tests for excreted urinary antigen detect only infections caused by *L pneumophila* serogroup 1, but because this serogroup accounts for > 70% of *Legionella* infections, they are useful rapid tests in many clinical settings.

Finally, tests using polymerase chain reaction amplification of ribosomal RNA and DNA sequences specific to *L pneumophila* are now available and have been demonstrated to be sensitive and specific for confirming the presence of the organism in cultures. However, the sensitivity of these tests when performed on respiratory tract samples may not be better than that of direct fluorescent antibody tests, and their specificity is worse.

Treatment

Erythromycin is the recommended treatment for Legionnaires' disease and other serious *Legionella* infections; however, failures have occurred, and adverse effects are common (Box 58–2). Erythromycins, intravenous azithromycin, and levofloxacin are currently approved by the US Food and Drug Administration for treatment of Legionnaires' disease. Although prospective controlled comparisons have not been performed, clarithromycin and quinolone antibiotics are also effective. Other agents with activity against *Legionellaceae* include doxycycline, minocycline, rifampin, and trimethoprim-sulfamethoxazole. For severe illness and for treatment of immunosuppressed patients, combination treatment either with rifampin plus a macrolide or quinolone or with a quinolone plus a macrolide (eg, levofloxacin plus azithromycin) is recommended.

Prevention & Control

Isolation of patients with known or suspected *Legionella* infection is not required, because direct person-to-person transmission has not been observed (Box 58–3). Epidemiologic investigation of sporadic community-acquired cases of *Legionella* infection is not usually productive because of the large number of exposures to potential water sources. When a community outbreak is suspected, conventional epidemiologic methods (ie, case definition, hypothesis generation, and case control study) should be used to confirm the presence of an outbreak and identify the source of exposure. Samples from suspicious water reservoirs should be cultured, and in some cases the potential for these sources to produce aerosol particles in the respirable size range should be evaluated with an air particle-size sampler. Smoke or other tracer materials can be used to evaluate the movement of aerosols and routes of access to ventilation systems, air intake passages, or other modes of dispersion.

In cases of known or suspected nosocomial infection, a detailed environmental investigation of all sources of water exposure is often indicated, especially when two or more unexplained cases have occurred. In addition to evaluating water reservoirs in the facility (eg, cooling towers and evaporative condensers), respiratory-therapy equipment should be checked and procedures should be reviewed to identify occult sources of exposure to potable water. In addition, samples from the water distribution system (eg, showers, faucets, and taps) should be cultured for *Legionella* species.

It is very difficult if not impossible to decontaminate water supplies. Cooling towers and evaporative condensers must be drained, scoured to remove organic debris and sediment, and then disinfected with chlorine. Follow-up maintenance must include periodic chlorination or treatment with alternate disinfec-

BOX 58-2

Treatment of Legionnaires' Disease

	Adults	Children
First Choice	• Erythromycin, 2 g orally daily in divided doses or 4 g IV daily in divided doses (latter dosage is associated with reversible ototoxicity) OR • Azithromycin, 500 mg IV daily • Clarithromycin, 500 mg orally twice daily • Levofloxacin, 250–500 mg orally or IV daily • Ciprofloxacin, 500–700 mg orally twice daily; 200–400 mg IV every 12 h • Ofloxacin, 200–400 mg orally or IV every 12 h	• Erythromycin, 30–60 mg/kg orally daily in divided doses OR • Azithromycin (age > 2 y), 12 mg/kg orally daily (not to exceed 500 mg/d) • Clarithromycin (age > 6 mo), 7.5 mg/kg orally twice daily (not to exceed 500 mg/dose)
Second Choice	• Doxycycline, 100 mg orally or IV every 12 h	• Doxycycline, (age > 8 y), 2–4 mg/kg orally daily in two doses
Considerations for Immunosuppressed Patients[1]	• Combination treatment with macrolide/azolide plus quinolone or macrolide/azolide plus rifampin	

[1]When treating transplant recipients, consider the influences of macrolides and rifampin on cyclosporine metabolism; a quinolone alone may be preferable.

BOX 58-3

Prevention and Control of *Legionella* Infection

Isolation Requirements	None indicated. No evidence of person-to-person transmission
Environmental Control	• In hospitals with a significant immunocompromised population, superheating and flushing of water supplies identified as reservoirs of *L pneumophila* has been attempted with variable success. • Adjunctive use of copper-silver ionization and ultraviolet systems has been reported effective. Hyperchlorination is no longer recommended. • Drain, scrub, and disinfect water reservoirs; periodic maintenance treatment required.

tants. Similarly, contaminated water heaters should be drained, cleaned, and then disinfected. Superheating (> 60 °C) is also recommended for water heaters and distal water distribution systems. However, this procedure can result in severe scalding and must be used with caution. Hyperchlorination has also been used, but can result in high levels of trihalomethanes, which are putative carcinogens. Over time, hyperchlorination corrodes the plumbing system, leading to enhanced opportunities for sediments that promote the growth of *Legionella* species.

Metal ionization procedures are advocated by some, but are not known to work better than conventional methods. One copper-silver ionization system was sequentially installed onto the hot-water recirculation lines of two hospital buildings colonized with *L pneumophila* serogroup 1. A third building with the same water supply, also colonized with *L pneumophila*, served as a control. Within 4–12 weeks of application, the levels of detectable *L pneumophila* in the two treated systems dropped to zero, but remained positive in the untreated system. However, concentrations of copper and silver in excess of Environmental Protection Agency standards can accumulate at the bottoms of hot-water tanks subjected to this type of treatment. Its long-term effectiveness has not been determined.

In cases in which water treatments fail, the entire current and past water distribution system engineering and structural design should be reviewed to identify old pipes that may bypass the part of the system undergoing disinfection. These pipes may introduce contaminated water downstream if they are not disinfected.

Detailed guidelines for preventing nosocomial legionellosis and for decontaminating water reservoirs and distribution systems are available from CDC at http://www.cdc.gov.ncidod/diseases/hip/pneumonia/pneu_mmw.htm.

REFERENCES

Bhopal RS, Barr G: Maintenance of cooling towers following two outbreaks of Legionnaires' disease in a city. Epidemiol Infect 1990;34:189.

Centers for Disease Control and Prevention: Sustained transmission of nosocomial Legionnaires' disease. Morbid Mortal Wkly Rep 1997;46:416.

Edelstein P: Antimicrobial chemotherapy for Legionnaires' disease: a review. Clin Infect Dis 1995;21:S265.

el-Ebiary M, et al: Prognostic factors of severe *Legionella* pneumonia requiring admission to ICU. Am J Respir Crit Care Med 1997;156:1467.

Fields BS et al: Virulence of a *Legionella anisa* strain associated with Pontiac fever: an evaluation using protozoan, cell culture, and guinea pig models. Infect Immun 1990;(9):3139.

Foy HM et al: Legionnaires' disease in a prepaid medical-care group in Seattle 1963–75. Lancet 1979;i:767.

Friedman H et al: Immunologic response and pathophysiology of *Legionella* infection. Semin Respir Infect 1998;13:100.

Goetz A, Yu VL: Copper-silver ionization: cautious optimism for *Legionella* disinfection and implications for environmental culturing. Am J Infect Control 1997;25(6):449.

Hoge CW, Breirman RF: Advances in the epidemiology and control of *Legionella* infections. Epidemiol Rev 1991;13:329.

Jernigan DB et al: Outbreak of Legionnaires' disease among cruise ship passengers exposed to a contaminated spa. Lancet 1996;347:494.

Kaufmann AF et al: Pontiac fever: isolation of the etiologic agent (*Legionella pneumophila*) and demonstration of its mode of transmission. Am J Epidemiol 1981;114:337.

Keller DW et al: Community outbreak of Legionnaires' disease: an investigation confirming the potential for cooling towers to transmit *Legionella* species. Clin Infect Dis 1996;22:257.

Klein NC, Cunha BA: Treatment of Legionnaires' disease. Semin Respir Infect 1998;13:140.

Koide M et al: Relation between the polymerase chain reaction and the indirect fluorescent antibody method in the diagnosis of *Legionella* infection. Clin Infect Dis 1996;23:656

Lin YS et al: Disinfection of water distribution systems for *Legionella*. Semin Respir Infect 1998;13:147.

Liu Z et al: Intermittent use of copper-silver ionization for *Legionella* control in water distribution systems: a potential option in buildings housing individuals at low risk of infection. Clin Infect Dis 1998;26:138.

Rutledge R et al: Acute Physiology and Chronic Health Evaluation (APACHE II) score and outcome in the surgical intensive care unit: an analysis of multiple intervention and outcome variables in 1,238 patients. Crit Care Med 1991;19(8):1048.

Sopena N et al: Comparative study of the clinical presentation of *Legionella* pneumonia and other community-acquired pneumonias. Chest 1998;113:1195.

Jorge Villacian, MD, & James Steckelberg, MD

Essentials of Diagnosis

- Foul odor of draining purulence.
- Presence of gas in tissues.
- No organism growth on aerobic culture media.
- Infection localized in the proximity of mucosal surface.
- Presence of septic thrombophlebitis.
- Tissue necrosis and abscess formation.
- Association with malignancies (especially intestinal).
- Mixed organism morphologies on Gram stain.

General Considerations

A. Epidemiology and Ecology. Anaerobic bacteria are the predominant component of the normal microbial flora of the human body. The following sites harbor the vast majority of them:

- Skin: Mostly gram-positive bacilli such as *Propionibacterium acnes*
- Gastrointestinal tract: In the oral cavity *Prevotella* spp., *Porphyromonas* spp., *Peptostreptococcus* spp., microaerophillic streptococci, and *Fusobacterium* spp. are the most important anaerobes found; they significantly outnumber aerobic bacteria (1000:1 ratio). On the colonic lumen, *Bacteroides fragilis*, other *Bacteroides* spp., clostridia, and the previously mentioned oral flora are by far the predominant colonizing organisms (1000:1 ratio to aerobes) and play a crucial role in maintaining the delicate balance of local microflora as well as in metabolizing bile acids and cholesterol and absorbing vitamin K.
- Respiratory tract: *Fusobacterium nucleatum, B fragilis, Prevotella melaninogenica,* and *Peptostreptococcus* spp. are the most common anaerobic organisms in this site.
- Female genital tract: *Lactobacillus* spp., the predominant species in this location, protect against bacterial vaginosis.
- Exogenous infectious sources: In nature, species of the *Clostridium* genus are found in decaying vegetation, soil, ocean sediment, and in human and animal gastrointestinal tracts. Tetanus and botulism (caused by the toxins of *C tetani* and *C botulinum*) are examples of exogenously acquired anaerobic

infections. The facultative gram-negative anaerobic bacillus *Capnocytophaga canimorsus* is part of the normal oral flora of canine species, but in susceptible hosts such as immunocompromised individuals, it may cause septic shock and disseminated intravascular coagulation, an example of an animal-to-human transmission of infection.

B. Microbiology. Anaerobes are defined as bacteria that cannot grow on the surface of solid media in an atmosphere containing $\geq 18\%$–20% of oxygen even when this atmosphere is enriched with $\leq 10\%$ of CO_2. The degree of oxygen tolerance differs among these microorganisms; a facultative anaerobe is a bacterium that can grow in either the presence or absence of oxygen, and a strict anaerobe is one that requires $< 0.5\%$ oxygen to grow on an agar surface. Microaerophilic is a term used for bacteria that grow poorly aerobically but distinctly better under 10% CO_2.

Anaerobic bacterial species are numerous; taxonomic data are sometimes confusing and have undergone recent changes. For the purpose of this chapter, we have focused on the most representative pathogens (Table 59–1).

C. Pathogenesis. The pathogenic role of anaerobic bacteria was well established at the beginning of the 1900s. Most infections that involve anaerobes arise from the host's normal indigenous flora, as these bacteria are widely distributed among humans and other animal species. Organisms that are most important are those present in significant numbers at the sites of infection as well as those with high virulence or greater antimicrobial resistance.

The characteristic pathologic features of anaerobic infections are suppuration, abscess formation, and tissue destruction. Several factors contribute to the survival and spread of these organisms:

Microbial Factors:

- Anaerobic environment causes defective neutrophil killing and microbial growth is slower; therefore antibiotic susceptibility decreases.
- Bacterial enzymes such as collagenase and hyaluronidase promote tissue destruction.
- Organisms such as *B fragilis* have a polysaccharide capsule that impairs phagocytosis.
- Toxin-mediated effects are important in the patho-

Table 59–1. Important anaerobic bacteria.

Gram-Positive Bacilli	Gram-Positive Cocci	Gram-Negative Bacilli	Gram-Negative Cocci
Spore forming: • *Clostridium botulinum* • *C tetani* • *C difficile* • *C septicum* • *C ramosum* **Nonspore forming:** • *Propionibacterium* spp. • *Lactobacillus* spp. • *Bifidobacterium* spp. • *Actinomyces* spp.	• Microaerophilic streptococci • *Peptococcus niger* • *Prevotella melaninogenica* • *Peptostreptococcus* spp	• *B fragilis* • *Porphyromona* spp • *Prevotella melaninogenica* • *Fusobacterium nucleatum* • *F necrophorum*	• *Veillonella* spp.

genicity of most of the genus *Clostridium.* This occurs in the form of absorption of preformed toxin such as in cases of botulism or as a result of bacterial overgrowth and toxin production, which is the mechanism of antibiotic-associated *C difficile* colitis.

• Synergism plays a crucial role in anaerobic pathogenesis, especially in the context of mixed infections because the presence of other aerobic bacteria helps create the optimal environmental conditions for the proliferation and virulence of anaerobes.

Host Factors: Normal anaerobic flora become pathogenic under circumstances in which natural barriers that prevent it from gaining access to sterile sites are disrupted. This might happen by a variety of different mechanisms and depends on the site in which the florae occur.

• In pleuropulmonary infections, the usual precipitating factor is an alteration of the level of alertness that may impair the gag and cough reflexes. General anesthesia, cerebrovascular accidents, a variety of drug overdoses, and alcohol intoxication are examples of situations in which normal oropharyngeal flora gains access to the "sterile" lower respiratory tract; dysphagia, and esophageal or gastric outlet obstruction may also lead to aspiration of large amounts of anaerobes.

• Trauma and tissue ischemia are two important mechanisms that predispose to anaerobic infection: seriously contaminated wounds are an example in which poor blood flow and tissue necrosis provide an ideal environment for *C perfringens* to grow and produce significant amounts of toxin eventually leading to gas gangrene.

• Systemic diseases, such as diabetes mellitus in which the immune response is impaired and vascular compromise might be present, predispose to soft tissue infections of the lower extremities in which anaerobic organisms are commonly found. The presence of foreign devices in different sites may be associated with certain anaerobic infections. Classically, women with intrauterine devices may develop actinomycosis. Central nervous system shunts can become infected with skin colonizing *Propionibacterium* spp.

Iatrogenic Factors:

• In postsurgical abdominal infections, manipulation of bowel causes translocation of bacteria into the peritoneal cavity: anaerobes are universally present as copathogens in a polymicrobial flora.

• Administration of broad-spectrum antimicrobial agents alters the normal colonic flora and allows *C difficile* to proliferate uninhibited; toxin production by this organism leads to the development of antibiotic-associated pseudomembranous colitis.

CLINICAL SYNDROMES

Box 59–1 summarizes different clinical syndromes associated with anaerobic bacteria. The sections that follow describe the various syndromes, including clinical findings. For some syndromes, specific diagnosis and treatment information is included as well. For other syndromes, see summary diagnosis and treatment sections at the end of the chapter.

HEAD & NECK

1. EAR & PARANASAL SINUSES

The flora in as many as two-thirds of chronic sinusitis and otitis cases includes *B fragilis, Prevotella* spp., *Peptostreptococcus* spp., and *Porphyromonas* spp. It is not surprising that ~50% of patients with chronic otitis media are infected with anaerobic bacteria, *B fragilis* being the most common. Mastoiditis may arise as a complication in some of these cases.

BOX 59-1

Infections Frequently Associated with Anaerobic Bacteria

Site	Clinical Syndrome	Anaerobe Involved
Head & Neck	• Chronic sinusitis • Chronic otitis media/mastoiditis • Odontogenic infections • Periodontal infections • Peritonsillar abscess • Neck space infections	• *Bacteroides fragilis* group • *Porphyromonas* spp. • *Prevotella* spp. • *Peptostreptococcus* spp. • *Fusobacterium* spp. • *Necrophorum* spp.
Central Nervous System	• Brain abscess • Subdural empyema • Epidural abscess	• *B fragilis* group • *Peptostreptococcus* spp. • *Fusobacterium* spp. • *Prevotella* spp. • *Actinomyces* spp. • Microaerophilic streptococcus
Respiratory Tract	• Aspiration pneumonitis • Empyema	• *B fragilis* group • *Prevotella melaninogenica* • *Bacteroides* spp. • *Peptostreptococcus* spp. • *Fusobacterium* spp. • Clostridia • *Veillonella* spp.
Intra-abdominal	• Peritonitis • Intra-abdominal abscess • Appendicitis • Pyogenic liver abscess • Postsurgical wound infections • Enteritis necroticans • Neutropenic enterocolitis	• *Bacteroides* spp. • *Peptostreptococcus* spp. • *Fusobacterium* spp. • *Lactobacillus* spp. • *Eubacterium* spp. • Clostridia
Female Genital Tract	• Endometritis • Amnionitis • Septic abortion • Postsurgical wound infections • Pelvic inflammatory disease • IUD-related bacterial vaginosis	• *Peptostreptococcus* spp. • *Prevotella* spp. • *Porphyromonas* spp. • Clostridia • *Actinomyces* spp. • *Eubacterum nodatum*
Skin, Soft Tissue, and Bone Infections	• Bite wound infections • Diabetic foot infections • Infected decubitus ulcers • Burn wound infections • Paronychia • Breast abscess • Infected sebaceous and pilonidal cysts • Anaerobic cellulitis • Necrotizing fasciitis • Myonecrosis (gas gangrene) • Chronic osteomyelitis	• *B fragilis* group • *Fusobacterium* spp. • *Prevotella* spp. • *Porphyromonas* spp. • Clostridia • *Peptostreptococcus* spp.
Toxin-Mediated Clostridial Diseases	• Botulism • Tetanus • Antibiotic-associated pseudomembranous colitis	• *Clostridium botulinium* • *C tetani* • *C difficile*

Clinical findings related to these infections are found in Chapter 9.

2. ORAL CAVITY

This site is heavily colonized with anaerobes. Consequently, many infections involving oral cavity structures as well as the pharyngeal spaces involve anaerobic bacteria.

Clinical Findings

Odontogenic infections including endodontal processes and periapical and dental abscesses may become more serious by spreading to the perimandibular space; here they present with pain and swelling and require surgical intervention. Gingivitis, pyorrhea, and periodontitis involve anaerobes as well; an extreme of this type of process is necrotizing ulcerative gingivitis (Vincent's angina or trench mouth), which manifests as severe tissue destruction, pain, and malodorous discharge. AIDS and Down's syndrome are conditions that predispose to periodontal disease and subsequently to odontogenic infections.

3. PHARYNGEAL SPACES

Clinical Findings

Ludwig's angina is a bilateral infection of the sublingual and submandibular spaces that commonly involves anaerobic bacteria and causes swelling of the oral tissues, especially at the base of the tongue, where it may lead to respiratory compromise. It manifests as indurated cellulitis and begins on the mouth. A dental source of infection can be found in 50–90% of cases. Lemiere's syndrome is a life-threatening complication of *Fusobacterium necrophorum* infection in the posterior compartment of the lateral pharyngeal space, which consists of suppurative thrombophlebitis of the internal jugular vein often accompanied by bacteremia and metastatic abscesses to the lungs and liver. Surgical intervention is almost always necessary in conjunction with intravenous antibiotics.

A. Signs and Symptoms. Clinical features of infection of the pharyngeal spaces are dysphagia, hoarseness, nuchal rigidity, fever, and trismus. In Ludwig's angina, a brawny, boardlike swelling of the submandibular spaces, which does not pit on pressure, is present when the mouth is held open and the tongue is pushed up to the roof of the mouth.

B. Imaging. Once the diagnosis is made (see below), imaging studies help delineate the extent of the process. Soft tissue x-ray of the neck may show widening of the different pharyngeal spaces involved. Ultrasonography, radionuclide scanning, and computerized tomography (CT) are useful for localizing infections of the head and neck.

CENTRAL NERVOUS SYSTEM

Oral anaerobes are commonly involved in brain abscesses, occasionally in epidural and subdural empyemas, and very rarely in meningitis. These infections usually arise in the setting of chronic otitis media, sinusitis, or odontogenic processes. Less frequently, brain abscesses can be secondary to hematogenous spread from distant sites in which case they tend to be multiple. Anaerobic infections can also be found as a complication of neurosurgical procedures.

Clinical Findings

A. Signs and Symptoms. Clinical features are those of a space-occupying lesion, including headache, vomiting, altered mental status, focal neurologic symptoms, and seizures. Fever is present in only half of cases; depending on the location of the lesion, corresponding neurologic deficits can be seen. Funduscopic examination may reveal papilledema.

B. Laboratory Findings. Microbiology findings may include *B fragilis, Peptostreptococcus, Fusobacterium, Prevotella* spp., *Actinomyces, Propionibacterium,* or microaerophilic streptococci in conjunction with aerobic organisms such as staphylococci, streptococci, and gram-negative bacilli.

Invasive procedures such as lumbar puncture should only be performed after careful physical exam to evaluate for increased intracranial pressure or impending herniation. Cerebrospinal fluid examination may show a moderate pleocytosis, high protein concentration, and normal glucose level suggestive of parameningeal inflammatory foci.

C. Imaging. The diagnosis is confirmed by contrast-enhanced CT or magnetic resonance imaging.

RESPIRATORY TRACT

Aspiration of oral and dental flora results in anaerobic pleuropulmonary infections. Predisposing conditions are alterations in mental status, gingivitis, and periodontal disease.

Clinical Findings

A. Signs and Symptoms. Pulmonary abscesses of anaerobic origin usually have an indolent subacute or chronic presentation with symptoms such as malaise, weight loss, pleuritic chest pain, and cough that may be accompanied by foul smelling sputum and can be mistaken for malignancy; a febrile response depends on the patient's age and immune status.

Pathologically, early in the course, pneumonitis is present and then may evolve to form an abscess causing significant tissue destruction. The pleural cavity is frequently involved, and this results in empyema. Commonly affected anatomical sites are dependent regions such as the posterior segments of the upper lobes and the superior segments of the lower lobes (see Imaging section below).

B. Laboratory Findings. Organisms of the *B fragilis* group, other *Bacteroides* spp., *Prevotella melaninogenica, Fusobacterium* spp., peptostrepto-cocci, *Peptococcus* spp., gram-negative bacilli such as *Clostridium* spp., or occasionally gram-positive cocci of the *Veillonella* spp. are found. In most cases, aerobic organisms are also present, and successful treatment needs to cover such pathogens as well.

For microbiologic diagnosis, expectorated sputum is not useful as a result of the presence of abundant normal anaerobic flora of the upper airways and oropharyngeal cavities; therefore, invasive proce-dures including bronchoscopy with bronchoalveolar lavage is important in identifying the causative or-ganisms. Empyema fluid should always be inoculated into appropriate anaerobic vials and sent for anaero-bic culture.

C. Imaging. Initial findings on chest x-ray are those of a pneumonic infiltrate. This may evolve to form abscesses in which air-fluid levels can be de-tected. For optimal delineation of extent of involve-ment, CT of the chest should be performed.

INTRA-ABDOMINAL

The gastrointestinal tract harbors a rich microbial flora, and any process that involves perforation or manipulation of a hollow viscus could potentially re-sult in the translocation of bacteria into normally ster-ile sites. In the oral cavity, there are 10^7–10^8 an-aerobes/mL of oral contents; the proportion is 10–1000/mL in the stomach, 10^4–10^6 anaerobes/mL in the terminal ileum, and 10^{11}/g of stool in the colon.

1. BOWEL

Upper-gastrointestinal-tract processes such as per-forated peptic ulcer tend to involve gram-positive anaerobic and aerobic bacteria, whereas lower-tract diseases like appendicitis and colonic perforations are associated with coliforms and anaerobic gram-nega-tive species including *B fragilis, Bacteroides* spp., and *Fusobacterium* spp. Therefore, peritonitis (sec-ondary to perforated viscus) and intra-abdominal ab-scesses always involve anaerobes as a component of a mixed flora. Postsurgical infections may have an anaerobic component as well. See Chapter 12 for clinical findings related to these infections.

Colonic malignancies are commonly associated with members of the *Clostridium* species—*septicum, tertium,* and *perfringens,* all of which may cause bac-teremia and gas gangrene of the bowel. Enteritis necroticans (caused by *C perfringens*) and neu-tropenic enterocolitis or typhlitis (caused by *C sep-ticum*) are two representative severe clostridial bowel infections.

2. LIVER & BILIARY TREE

Biliary tract infections in nonobstructed biliary systems seldom involve anaerobes, but in patients with obstruction caused by tumors, *B fragilis* or *C perfringens* can be present. Bacterial liver abscesses are usually polymicrobial, and anaerobes constitute part of the flora.

The diagnosis of hepatic or intra-abdominal anaer-obic abscesses is made with imaging studies such as CT. If large abscesses are present, drainage is a com-ponent of successful therapy and can be achieved ei-ther surgically or in some cases by percutaneous CT or ultrasound-guided techniques. See Chapter 12 for clinical findings related to these infections.

FEMALE GENITAL TRACT

Alteration of the normal microbial flora of the fe-male genital tract causes bacterial vaginosis, which predisposes to different infections in which anaerobes are frequently encountered. These are usually mixed and include endometritis, pelvic inflammatory dis-ease, and tubo-ovarian abscesses, as well as obstetric infections such as amnionitis, septic abortions, septic pelvic thrombophlebitis, and postsurgical wound in-fections.

Pelvic inflammatory disease is associated in 30–40% of cases with anaerobes; these infections and their sequelae result in high rates of infertility, ec-topic pregnancy, and premature delivery.

Anaerobic pathogens encountered are *Peptostrep-tococcus* spp., *Prevotella* spp., *Porphyromonas* spp., and members of the clostridia family. *B fragilis* is not usually involved in gyneco-obstetric infections but, when present, carries a poor prognosis. *Actinomyces* spp. and *Eubacterium nodatum* are associated with infections in women with intra-uterine contraceptive devices. In addition to targeting anaerobes, antimi-crobial treatment should cover aerobic bacteria as well as atypical organisms such as chlamydia.

Clinical Findings
A. Signs and Symptoms. Clues to anaerobic pelvic infection are foul smelling discharge, presence of gas in tissues, and septic thrombophlebitis.

B. Laboratory Findings. The diagnosis of bac-terial vaginosis is suggested by secretions with a pH of > 4.5, a "fishy" odor when treated with 10% hydrogen peroxide, and visualization of "clue" cells.

SKIN, SOFT TISSUE, & BONE INFECTIONS

A wide variety of infections at these sites involve anaerobic bacteria. Specific pathogens depend on the mechanism of injury disrupting normal skin barrier defenses as well as on the state of the host's immune system. Infections can be localized or widespread and life threatening and may invade deep structures such as bone.

Bite wounds and clenched fist injuries often involve anaerobes, but antibiotic coverage must also include oral aerobic organisms, in particular, *Eikinella corrodens* in human bites and *Pasteurella multocida* in animal bites. Infected decubitus ulcers, pilonidal and sebaceous cysts, diabetic foot and burn wound infections, breast abscesses, and paronychia (mainly in children who suck their thumbs) have a polymicrobial flora in which anaerobes are present.

Involvement of the fascia leads to serious infections including necrotizing fasciitis and soft tissue gas gangrene (associated with *C perfringens*). When the perineal and scrotal regions are affected, this syndrome is known as Fournier's gangrene.

Clinical Findings

A. Signs and Symptoms. Signs and symptoms in general range from pain, erythema, swelling, and suppuration at the site of infection to bacteremia, sepsis syndrome, and tissue crepitance in the most serious cases. The absence of fever may reflect overwhelming infection.

B. Laboratory Findings. Microbiologic diagnosis is difficult and superficial swabs are usually not helpful. Deep tissue specimens obtained surgically are preferred in severe cases or when prolonged therapy is anticipated. The organisms that are most frequently encountered in diabetic foot and decubitus ulcer infections include *B fragilis, Fusobacterium* spp., *Prevotella melaninogenica, Porphyromonas, Peptostreptococcus,* and members of the *Clostridium* genus. Gas gangrene is associated with *C perfringens* and *C septicum*. Necrotizing fasciitis involves *Bacteroides* spp. as well as clostridia.

BACTEREMIA

Anaerobes cause from 5 to 10% of all bacteremias. *B fragilis* and related species account for 60–80% of all cases, followed by clostridia and peptostreptococci. Organisms such as *Propionibacterium* usually represent contamination of blood cultures by skin organisms. For true bacteremias, the common portals of entry are the gastrointestinal tract, female genital tract, lower respiratory tract, head and neck, and skin. Fewer than 5% of neutropenic bacteremias are secondary to anaerobes.

Clinical Findings

A. Signs and Symptoms. Clinical presentation will depend on the site of primary infection and can include fever, chills, and malaise. As previously mentioned, clostridial bacteremias should prompt the search for colonic malignancies.

OSTEOMYELITIS

It is not uncommon to find anaerobes in cases in which the predisposing factor is vascular insufficiency as in diabetic foot ulcers. Other examples are skull or facial bone infections arising from chronic otitis media, sinusitis, or mastoiditis. Clinically, these infections tend to run indolent courses and may occasionally present with foul smelling drainage through sinus tracts. Gram-negative bacilli and peptostreptococci are frequently involved.

TOXIN-MEDIATED INFECTIONS

1. TETANUS

Tetanus is a disease of global incidence produced by the toxin of *Clostridium tetani*. The risk of acquiring it increases in people > 60 years of age and in neonates, especially in Third World countries where poor sanitary conditions predispose to umbilical stump contamination. Immunization campaigns have played a crucial role in bringing about the observed decreasing incidence in the United States.

The pathogenesis of tetanus involves the absorption of preformed toxin, or, less commonly, invasion of toxin-producing organisms from contaminated wounds; it may complicate surgical wounds colonized with *C tetani*. Incubation periods vary depending on the portal of entry. The toxin tetanospasmin blocks the transmission of inhibitory neurons, which results in flexor and extensor muscle spasms that are triggered by sensory stimuli.

Most cases progress over 2 weeks. With adequate supportive therapy (Box 59–2), complete recovery may be seen in 1 month. Autonomic dysfunction and respiratory compromise are potential complications. Mortality rates are 1:100,000 in North America and 28:100,000 in Third World countries.

Clinical Findings

A. Signs and Symptoms. Muscle spasms are accompanied by pain and manifest as decorticate posturing with intact sensorium. "Risus sardonicus"

BOX 59-2

Treatment of Infections Caused by Anaerobes[1]

Group	First Choice	Alternatives	Comments
Anaerobic Gram-Negative Bacilli	Metronidazole, 500 mg IV every 6 h	Clindamycin, 900 mg IV every 8 h	*Fusobacterium* spp. sensitive to penicillin G; carbapenems[2] or β-lactam–β-lactamase inhibitor combinations[3] also effective
Anaerobic Gram-Negative Cocci (*Veillonella* spp.)	Penicillin G, 10–24 million U IV, continuous infusion or every 4–6 h interval dosing	Clindamycin, 900 mg IV every 8 h	Metronidazole activity unpredictable; not recommended for treatment
Anaerobic Gram-Positive Nonspore-Forming Bacilli	Penicillin G, 10–24 million U IV, continuous infusion or every 4–6 h interval dosing	Clindamycin, 900 mg IV every 8 h	Widespread resistance to metronidazole
Anaerobic Gram-Positive Spore-Forming Bacilli (*Clostridium* spp.)	Penicillin G, 10–24 million U IV, continuous infusion or every 4–6 h interval dosing	Metronidazole, 500 mg IV every 6 h	In resistant organisms, carbapenems[2] or β-lactam–β-lactamase inhibitors[3] effective
Anaerobic Gram-Positive Cocci	Penicillin G, 10–24 million U IV, continuous infusion or every 4–6 h interval dosing	Clindamycin, 900 mg IV every 8 h	
Antibiotic-Associated Colitis	Metronidazole, 250 mg orally three times a day (7–14 days)	Vancomycin, 125 mg orally four times a day (7–10 days)	Stop other antibiotics if possible

[1]Combination therapy directed against concomitant aerobic pathogens is of paramount importance in successful treatment of anaerobic infections; other agents used will depend on specific infection sites and resistance patterns of other organisms. All dosing information is for adult patients with normal renal and hepatic functions. Pediatric dosing: penicillin G, 25,000 U/kg/d; metronidazole, 30 mg/kg/d; clindamycin, 25 mg/kg/d (in patients with normal renal and hepatic functions).
[2]Imipenem, 500 mg IV every 6 h, or meropenem, 1 g IV every 8 h if resistance to other first-line agents is encountered.
[3]Ticarcillin-clavulanic acid, 3.1 g IV every 6 h; piperacillin-tazobactam, 3.375 g IV every 6 h; ampicillin-sulbactam, 1.5–3.0 g IV every 6 h; amoxicillin-clavulanic acid, 500 mg orally every 8 h.

is the term used to describe the facial expression produced by increased tone of the orbicularis oris. Trismus (or "lockjaw") is often present as a heralding manifestation of generalized disease.

Diagnosis

Diagnosis of tetanus is made clinically; conditions that might have similar features are strychnine poisoning and dystonic reactions.

Treatment

Treatment should be supportive. Sedation is important: benzodiazepines, propofol, and in severe cases, paralyzing agents can be used; the role of antibiotics is controversial (see Box 59–2). When autonomic dysfunction is present, alpha and beta adrenergic blocking agents are recommended.

2. BOTULISM

This clinical syndrome is caused by the neurotoxin of *C botulinum*. There are seven types (A–G) of neurotoxin, all of which inhibit the release of acetylcholine at the level of peripheral neuromuscular junctions. In the majority of cases, the disease is acquired by ingestion of preformed toxin in home-canned vegetables, fruits, and fish. In Japan, the former Soviet

Union, Scandinavia, and the Great Lakes region of the United States, type E toxin causes disease in people who consume raw or lightly smoked fish. There are four categories of botulism:

- Food borne (most common)
- Wound botulism caused by the absorption of toxin from a wound contaminated by *C botulinum* (the rarest form)
- Infant botulism resulting from in vivo elaboration of toxin by colonizing organisms in the bowel
- Undetermined, which refers to cases that occur in individuals > 1 year old in whom no food or wound source is identified

Clinical Findings

Signs and Symptoms. Symptoms and signs arise 12–36 h after food ingestion and consist of acute onset and progressive flaccid paralysis involving the facial musculature and the cranial nerves bilaterally, then descending symmetrically to the pharynx, thoracic region, and the upper and lower extremities. This evolves into respiratory failure without impairment of consciousness. Fever is classically absent.

In cases of infant botulism, which is found in children 6 days to 11 months old, constipation is the initial symptom, followed by lethargy, feeding difficulties, altered cry, floppiness, ophthalmoplegia, and respiratory failure.

B. Laboratory Findings. Besides clinical findings and careful history, stool and serum toxin assays help establish the diagnosis.

C. Differential Diagnosis. Differential diagnosis of botulism includes myasthenia gravis, Lambert-Eaton paraneoplastic syndrome, and Guillain-Barré syndrome.

Treatment

Treatment is mainly supportive; antitoxin made from equine serum can be used. In the United States, it is obtained through state health departments or the Centers for Disease Control. The standard dose is one vial intravenously and one vial intermittently. It may be repeated every 4 h in severe progressive cases. Clinical trials evaluating its efficacy are lacking. Full recovery takes from 3 months to 1 year. Risk of death ranges from 4 to 25%, depending on the promptness with which the diagnosis is made.

3. ANTIBIOTIC-ASSOCIATED COLITIS

Clostridium difficile is the principal causative agent of antibiotic-associated colitis. Two types of toxin are produced by *C difficile*: (1) an enterotoxin (the most important in its pathogenesis) and (2) an enterotoxin that is cytophatic. This organism is present in the bowel flora of ≤ 50% of neonates. This rate declines to 4% by age 2 years. However, antibiotic

treatment and hospitalization have been proven to increase the carriage rate ≤ 46%. Chemotherapeutic agents (for malignancies) and antibiotics (most commonly ampicillin, clindamycin, and the cephalosporins) are associated with *C difficile* pseudomembranous colitis. Bowel stasis and surgery predispose to this disease as well, although, in some cases, no identifiable risk factor is found.

Clinical Findings

A. Signs and Symptoms. Clinical presentation ranges from mild diarrhea to toxic megacolon. Fever is present frequently, and pseudomembrane formation is characteristic.

B. Laboratory Findings. The diagnosis is confirmed by toxin assays and cell culture cytotoxicity assays that neutralize with antisera to toxin B. Colonoscopy may provide helpful information by enabling direct observation of the classical pseudomembranes in the colonic mucosal surface. Stool cultures are not diagnostic because of the considerable rates of asymptomatic carrier states.

Treatment

In treating patients who have *C difficile*-associated pseudomembranous colitis, if possible, an attempt to stop or narrow broad-spectrum antibiotic therapy (if the patient is receiving it for other reasons) should be made. Oral metronidazole is the first choice for treatment (Box 59–2). Oral vancomycin should be avoided to prevent further selection of vancomycin-resistant enterococci but can be used in cases of relapse or as a second choice in patients unable to tolerate metronidazole.

Diagnosis of Anaerobic Bacterial Infections

The likelihood of anaerobes being part of the infecting flora should be carefully considered when obtaining cultures. In general, anaerobic cultures are needed in complicated infections, in debilitated hosts (those with underlying chronic illnesses or malignancies as well as elderly individuals), in cases where prolonged therapy is anticipated, and in infections where empiric therapy is failing.

Specimens from the oral cavity, upper respiratory tract, or vagina are rich in indigenous anaerobic flora and therefore not useful for diagnostic purposes. Fluid obtained from normally sterile sites, as well as pus or tissue samples are preferred. Fluid or pus from these sites should be inoculated into special anaerobic vials for transport to the microbiology laboratory, and in the case of tissues, an airtight bag might be used.

Cultures are grown in both selective (directed at specific pathogens) and nonselective media; this approach increases the diagnostic yield. An anaerobic environment must be maintained.

Newer diagnostic techniques include detecting the

metabolic end products of carbohydrate fermentation by gas-liquid chromatography. Toxin assays are available for the diagnosis of botulism and *C difficile*-associated colitis.

Treatment of Anaerobic Bacterial Infections

The first principle of treatment for anaerobic bacterial infections is to keep in mind that in most cases, other pathogens coexist as part of a polymicrobial flora; therefore, adequate antibiotic coverage for those should be provided as well (Box 59–2). Drainage of abscesses and surgical débridement of wounds to remove devitalized tissue are of great importance to achieve therapeutic success.

Historically, penicillin has been one of the most useful antibiotics against anaerobic bacteria, but the increasing frequency of β-lactamase–producing strains of *B fragilis, Prevotella melaninogenica,* and *Porphyromonas* spp. has limited its value. Penicillin G is still the drug of choice for clostridia, but *C perfringens, C ramosum, C clostridiforme,* and *C butyricum* exhibit some degree of resistance.

Cephalosporins in general should not be considered drugs of choice for gram-negative anaerobic coverage, but cefoxitin and ceftizoxime exhibit some activity against these bacteria. Cefoxitin has been used as monotherapy in uncomplicated intra-abdominal infections. First-generation cephalosporins (eg, cefazolin) are active against gram-positive anaerobic cocci.

Tetracycline and its derivatives, frequently administered in the past, are now mostly inactive. Quinolones such as ciprofloxacin and ofloxacin have very poor coverage, but newer compounds with increased anaerobic activity are being developed.

Chloramphenicol has good anaerobic coverage, although occasional resistance may be seen with *B fragilis* and certain clostridia. Penetration to the central nervous system is adequate. The main limiting factor preventing widespread use of chloramphenicol is toxicity (risk of bone marrow suppression, mainly with oral formulations).

Clindamycin is one of the drugs of choice when anaerobes are suspected, however, its spectrum against aerobic gram-negative bacilli is limited; in the setting of polymicrobial infections, the addition of an aminoglycoside, second- or third-generation cephalosporin, or aztreonam is recommended. The central nervous system penetration of clindamycin is very poor. About 30% of *Bacteroides gracilis* and some organisms in the *B fragilis* group can be resistant to clindamycin.

Metronidazole is another potent antianaerobic drug with even less activity against aerobes than clindamycin. It should not be used as monotherapy if aerobes are suspected. Central nervous system penetration is good.

BOX 59–3

Prevention and Control of Anaerobic Infections

- Thorough cleansing and débridement of wounds
- Avoid contamination of sterile sites with "normal" flora from adjacent structures
- Ensuring good vascular supply to tissues
- Minimize use of broad-spectrum antibiotics
- Prevent aspiration of oropharyngeal contents into lower airways
- Attempt to reduce duration of labor (in the case of obstetrical infections)
- Immunization (see Table 59-1) and, when appropriate, toxin neutralization

---

The combination of β-lactams with β-lactamase inhibitors is active against most anaerobes as well as against many aerobes. These agents include amoxicillin-clavulanic acid (oral) the intravenous ampicillin-sulbactam, ticarcillin-clavulanic acid, and piperacillin-tazobactam.

The carbapenems (imipenem and meropenem) have excellent anaerobic activity as well as broad gram-positive and gram-negative aerobic coverage. Both the β-lactam and β-lactamase inhibitor combinations and the carbapenems are typically more expensive than combination regimens using older agents.

Prevention

Preventive measures are aimed at minimizing contamination of sterile sites with fluids that contain high amounts of normal microbial flora (as is the case with intra-abdominal postsurgical infections) (Box 59–3). Preventing aspiration of oropharyngeal con-

---

Table 59–2. Tetanus immunization.

Active Immunization

- DTP (diphtheria, pertussis, tetanus): Recommended doses (IM) should be given at 2, 4, 6, and 15–18 mo, and at 4–6 years of age.

- DT (diphtheria, tetanus): Recommended for patients above 7 years old; 2 doses (IM) 4–8 weeks apart and a third dose 6–12 mo later confer immunity for at least 5 years; boosters should be given to *all* patients every 10 years and more frequently if high-risk activities have occurred

Passive Immunization

Human tetanus immunoglobulin (500 IU IM) may shorten the duration and lessen the severity of tetanus cases; should be administered prophylactically to patients not immunized during the previous 5 years who have a tetanus-prone wound or if immunodeficiency is suspected; active immunization should also be initiated at the time the immunoglobulin is given

tents into the lower airways is important to control anaerobic pneumonitis and empyemas. For obstetrical infections, reducing the duration of labor (if possible) can help. Good cleansing and débridement of wounds decreases the risk of soft tissue infections. Ensuring adequate vascular supply is also important in these situations.

In *C tetani* infections, active, and in some cases passive, immunization are important (Table 59–2). Avoiding the unnecessary use of broad-spectrum antibiotics for prolonged periods of time is one of the cornerstones for preventing *C difficile*-associated colitis.

REFERENCES

Aldridge KE: The occurrence, virulence and antimicrobial resistance of anaerobes in polymicrobial infections. Am J Surg 1995;169(Suppl 5A):2S.

Bokkenheuser V: The friendly anaerobes. CID 1993;16 (Suppl 4):S427.

Bonten M: Diagnosis and treatment of nosocomial pneumonia. Br Jr Hosp Med 1995;57(7):335.

Connor DH et al (editors): *Pathology of Infectious Diseases,* Appleton & Lange, 1997.

Eschenbach DA: Bacterial vaginosis and anaerobes in obstetric-gynecologic infection. Curr Inf Dis 1993;16 (Suppl 4):S282.

Finegold SM: Overview of clinically important anaerobes. Curr Inf Dis 1995;20(Suppl 2):S205.

Finegold SM et al: Current perspectives on anaerobic infections: Diagnostic approaches. Inf Dis Clin North Am 1993;7(2):257.

Goldstein EJC: Selected nonsurgical anaerobic infections: Therapeutic choices and the effective armamentarium. Curr Inf Dis 1994;18(Suppl 4):S273.

Gorbach SL: Antibiotic treatment of anaerobic infections. Curr Inf Dis 1994;18(Suppl 4):S305.

Gorbach SL et al (editors): *Infectious Diseases.* WB Saunders, 1992.

Mandell G et al (editors): *Mandell, Douglas, and Bennett's Principles and Practice of Infectious Diseases,* 4th ed. Churchill Livingstone, 1995.

Murray PR et al: *Manual of Clinical Microbiology,* 6th ed. ASM Press, 1995.

Rosenblatt JE: Clinical relevance of susceptibility testing of anaerobic bacteria. Curr Inf Dis 1993;16(Suppl 4):S446.

Sanders CV, Aldridge KE: Current antimicrobial therapy of anaerobic infections. Eur J Clin Microbiol Infect Dis 1992;11(11):999.

60

Brucella, Francisella, Pasteurella, Yersinia, & HACEK

Elie F. Berbari, MD, & Walter R. Wilson, MD

BRUCELLOSIS

Essentials of Diagnosis
- Suspected in patients with chronic fever of unknown etiology who have a history of occupational exposure or come from a high prevalence area.
- Leukopenia.
- Blood culture or bone marrow cultures on appropriate media.
- Serum antibody titer ≥ 1:160.
- Polymerase chain reaction.

General Considerations
Brucellosis (also called undulant fever, Mediterranean fever, Malta fever) is an infection that causes abortion in domestic animals. It is caused by one of six species of *Brucella* coccobacilli. It may occasionally be transmitted to humans, in whom the disease could be acute or chronic with ongoing fever and constitutional symptoms without localized findings.

A. Epidemiology. Brucellosis is transmitted to humans by either direct contact with infected cattle, goat, or sheep (eg, through milk, urine, and products of pregnancy) or indirectly by ingesting contaminated animal products (eg, unpasteurized dairy products). Human-to-human transmission does not occur. The natural reservoir of brucellosis in the United States is domestic animals, especially cattle, bison, sheep, goats, and swine.

The disease exists worldwide, mainly in the Mediterranean basin, the Arabian peninsula, the Indian subcontinent, Mexico, and Central and South America. In the United States, the incidence of brucellosis fell from 4.5 cases/100,000 population annually in the late 1940s to < 0.5 cases/100,000 by the 1990s. Most reported cases in the United States are due to ingestion of unpasteurized goat milk product imported from Mexico or to occupational exposure involving meat-packing plant employees, veterinarians, laboratory personnel, farmers, and ranchers. Recently, bison herds in the Rocky Mountain plains of the United States have become infected with brucellae and could potentially infect domestic cattle in the United States.

B. Microbiology. Sir David Bruce, a British microbiologist, isolated the microorganisms responsible for brucellosis in 1886. Brucellae are nonspore-forming, noncapsulated, small gram-negative coccobacilli. They grow best aerobically in high-peptone media at 37 °C and at pH 6.7. Incubation time could take ≤ 30 days for visible growth on solid media. Colonies are small, smooth, translucent, and amber colored. Of the six known *Brucella* species, only four are reported to cause human disease: *B abortus* (cattle), *B melitensis* (goats), *B suis* (pigs), and *B canis* (dogs). Brucellae may be distinguished from each other by their requirements for carbon monoxide atmosphere for growth, growth in the presence of dyes, production of hydrogen sulfide and urease, and specific agglutination in antisera.

C. Pathogenesis. Routes of infection include ingestion of the contaminated food or dairy products by way of the gastrointestinal tract, direct inoculation through skin cuts or mucus membrane contact, or inhalation of the organisms via the respiratory tract. Subsequently, the microorganisms enter the lymphatics and replicate intracellularly in the regional lymph nodes and from there disseminate hematogenously and localize in the reticuloendothelial system (ie, spleen, liver, other lymph nodes, and bone marrow). The bacilli multiply intracellularly within the phagocytic cell where they may be killed rapidly, or the organisms may replicate and destroy the phagocytic cell. This results in proliferation within the reticuloendothelial system and the formation of noncaseating granulomas in affected tissue. In most instances, the granulomas undergo a process of healing, with fibrosis, death of the organisms, and frequently calcification.

Clinical Findings
A. Signs and Symptoms. After a 2- to 8-week incubation period, affected patients present with a spectrum of disease that varies from an asymptomatic form to a severe illness with bacteremia (Box 60–1). Affected patients typically present with fever, sweats, headaches, malaise, and weight loss. If undiagnosed, these symptoms may persist for months to a year. When symptoms last for more than 12 months with-

BOX 60-1

Brucellosis in Adults and Children

	Acute	Localized	Chronic[1]	Relapsing Brucellosis
More Common	• Malaise, fever, chills, lethargy, weakness, weight loss, anorexia • Headaches, myalgias, back pain • Lymphadenopathy, splenomegaly, hepatomegaly	• Bone and joint (spondylitis, arthralgias) • Gastrointestinal (spleen abscess, splenic calcifications) • Infective endocarditis • Respiratory (hilar adenopathy, perihilar infiltrates) • Genitourinary (perinephric abscess, epididymitis)	• Weakness, fatigue, mental depression, vague pains, intermittent fever • Splenomegaly • Calcification in liver and spleen, including "bulls-eye" calcification	Long periods of no symptoms with intermittent fever and chills
Less Common	Monoarticular arthralgias	Fever, chills, malaise, weight loss		

[1]Defined as chronic when duration of symptoms is > 12 m.

out any localization, the disease is classified as chronic. Physical examination, though normal in most cases, may reveal bilateral diffuse lymphadenopathy, splenomegaly, and hepatomegaly in 20%–30% of patients.

In the localized form, the infection may affect virtually any organ system. The osteoarticular, gastrointestinal, genitourinary, and cardiovascular are among the more common affected systems. These forms have signs and symptoms related to the affected organ system. An infectious discitis with adjacent vertebral bony osteomyelitis typically in the lumbar area, is the most common manifestation of localized osteoarticular disease. Sacroilitis is also characteristic of the musculoskeletal form of the infection. Infective endocarditis occurs in < 2% of brucellosis cases.

Patients with chronic brucellosis may have long periods of no symptoms followed by the intermittent recurrence of fever, chills, myalgias, and nonspecific symptoms. This form of relapsing brucellosis may persist for decades and is often refractory to antimicrobial therapy and is frequently associated with multiple or large calcific lesions in the liver and spleen. Many other common illnesses can mimic the most common clinical presentation of brucellosis.

B. Laboratory Findings. Patients typically have a mild anemia, neutropenia, and rarely thrombocytopenia. The diagnosis of brucellosis is made with certainty when *Brucella* spp. are recovered from cultures of the blood, bone marrow, or other site. Bone marrow cultures are more often positive than are blood cultures. Blood cultures are often negative in

chronic or localized forms. The standard *Brucella* serum agglutination test is the most widely used serologic test for the diagnosis of *Brucella*. The antibodies measured are directed against the lipopolysaccharide. A titer of at least 1:160 is representative of a past or present infection. A fourfold increase or decrease over a 2- to 4-week period represents acute infection.

The current serum agglutination test does not detect antibodies directed against *Brucella canis*, and diagnosis requires a special serologic test or a positive culture. After successful therapy, the antibody titer may become negative in approximately a year but may remain positive in low titer throughout the patient's life. Persistence of an elevated titer indicates ongoing infection. The prozone phenomena could lead to a false negative test.

Polymerase chain reaction may be used for diagnosis. Primers are directed at different sites of the genomic bacterial DNA. The specificity and sensitivity of this technique may provide a valuable tool for the diagnosis of brucellosis; however, the test is not widely available.

Differential Diagnosis

The differential diagnosis is one of a fever of unknown origin and includes typhoid fever, infectious mononucleosis, Q-fever, hepatitis, and a host of noninfectious syndromes including lymphoma and systemic lupus erythematosus. Infection with *Vibrio cholerae, Francisella tularensis,* or *Yersinia enterocolitica* may give a falsely elevated serum agglutination test since antigen of these microorganisms can cross-react with antigen of *Brucella* spp.

Treatment

Several antimicrobial agents are active against *Brucella* spp. (Box 60–2). Combination therapy of two or more active antimicrobial agents is superior to monotherapy as evidenced by a reduction in relapse rates. Antimicrobial therapy shortens the duration of symptoms and reduces the incidence of complications. Tetracyclines are considered the cornerstone of therapy. Several possible combinations have been used: The World Health Organization recommends a 6-week combination regimen of doxycycline and rifampin. Doxycycline and streptomycin are considered equally efficacious.

The optimum therapy for endocarditis is unclear. Most patients will require a prolonged period (6 months) of combination antimicrobial therapy, and valvular replacement surgery is often necessary. Although rare, infective endocarditis represents 80% of human brucellosis-related deaths.

Prognosis

With appropriate antimicrobial therapy, the mortality rate of brucellosis is < 1%, although the mortality rate is 3%–5% in untreated cases. It appears that the humoral antibodies play a role in the protection against subsequent infection. Thus patients with brucellosis might be less susceptible to acquire a new infection.

Prevention & Control

The prevention of brucellosis requires the eradication or the control of the infection in animals (Box 60–3). The use of *Brucella* vaccines (*B abortus* strain 19, *B melitensis* strain Rev-1) has resulted in the elimination of the disease in some animals. The use of effective barriers such as gloves, masks, and goggles can protect individuals at risk from potentially infected animals. Pasteurization of milk will effectively kill *Brucella* spp. in dairy products.

TULAREMIA

Essentials of Diagnosis

- Suspected in patients with fever, lymphadenopathy, and skin lesions who have a history of animal exposure (including to wild animals, ticks, or deerflies) or are coming from a high prevalence area or in laboratory personnel who work with *Francisella* spp.

BOX 60–2

Treatment of Brucellosis

	Acute Brucellosis		Endocarditis-Meningitis-Spondylitis-Localized Forms[1]	
	Adults	Children	Adults	Children
First Choice	Doxycycline, 100 mg orally twice daily, **PLUS** rifampin, 600–900 mg orally daily for 4–6 weeks	Doxycycline,[2] 2 mg/kg orally twice daily, **PLUS** rifampin, 15 mg/kg orally daily for 4–6 weeks	Doxycycline, 100 mg orally twice daily, **PLUS** rifampin, 600–900 mg orally daily for 6 mo, **PLUS** streptomycin, 1 g IM daily for the first 2–3 weeks	Doxycycline,[2] 2 mg/kg orally twice daily, **PLUS** rifampin, 15 mg/kg orally daily for 6 mo, **PLUS** streptomycin, 10 mg/kg IM twice daily for the first 7–14 days
Second Choice	Doxycycline, 100 mg orally twice daily for 4–6 weeks, **PLUS** streptomycin, 1 g IM daily for the first 15 days[4]	TMP/SMX,[3] 2.5 mg/kg orally of TMP component 4 times daily, **PLUS** rifampin, 15 mg/kg orally daily for 4–6 weeks		TMP/SMX,[3] 2.5 mg/kg orally of TMP component 4 times daily, **PLUS** rifampin, 15 mg/kg orally daily for 6 mo, **PLUS** gentamicin, 1.5–2 mg/kg (IV or IM) in three daily doses for the first 7–14 days

[1]May require splenectomy or drainage of abscess.
[2]Should not be used in children under the age of 8 or in pregnant women after 6 months of gestation.
[3]Trimethoprim-sulfamethoxazole.
[4]Should be the regimen of choice in spondylitis.

BOX 60–3

Control of Brucellosis

Prophylactic Measures	• *Brucella* vaccines (*B abortus* strain 19, *B melitensis* strain Rev-1) have eliminated the disease in some animals • Gloves, masks, and goggles can protect individuals at risk from potentially infected animals • Pasteurization of milk kills *Brucella* in dairy products
Isolation Precautions	• Standard precautions only

- Blood culture or other biologic specimen cultures on appropriate culture media.
- Serum antibody titer ≥ 1:160 or a fourfold increase or decrease in titer.

General Considerations

Francisella tularensis is the causative agent of tularemia (also called rabbit fever or deerfly fever), an infectious disease that occurs primarily in animals. It may occasionally cause human disease, which most often manifests itself by one or more skin lesions, regional lymphadenopathy, fever, and constitutional symptoms.

A. Epidemiology. Tularemia is widely distributed, with a higher prevalence in the northern hemisphere. Once common before World War II in the United States, the incidence of tularemia has declined steadily since the 1950s. Currently, the incidence is 0.05–0.15 cases/100,000 population. More than one-half of the cases in the United States occur in Missouri, Arkansas, Oklahoma, Texas, and Illinois. The incidence is higher during the summer months because of the increase in tick-acquired disease.

Transmission of *F tularensis* to humans occurs through dermal or mucosal contact with infected animals, mainly wild mammals, amphibians, fish, birds, or as the result of an insect bite (eg, ticks, deerflies, and mosquitoes). In the United States, the most common reservoirs are rabbits and ticks. Occasionally, the infection is acquired through inhalation of aerosolized organisms. The organism is highly infectious for laboratory personnel.

B. Microbiology. *F tularensis* is a small aerobic, nonmotile, catalase-positive pleomorphic gram-negative coccobacilli. The cell wall of *F tularensis* is high in fatty acids. Some strains contain a lipid-rich capsule that increases virulence. *F tularensis* requires a sulphudryl-containing medium for growth and, therefore, does not grow on most routine commercially available media. Growth requires 2–4 days and

produces small, smooth, opaque colonies. The organism may be identified on the basis of its morphology, growth requirements, fluorescent staining, and agglutinins with specific antisera. Most strains are β-lactamase producers.

C. Pathogenesis. After contact with the microorganisms, penetration occurs through sites of inapparent skin disruption. Subsequently, *F tularensis* multiplies locally and in the skin produces papules that ulcerate, become encrusted, and form an eschar. The microorganisms then reach regional lymph nodes where they replicate and disseminate to the blood. The organisms are engulfed by cells of the reticuloendothelial system in which they may survive intracellularly for prolonged periods. Occasionally, the microorganisms are inhaled, and a pneumonic form of the disease occurs. Rarely, ingestion of the microorganisms can cause pharyngitis, cervical, and mesenteric lymphadenopathy. Early lesions are characterized histopathologically by focal necrosis occurring in organs of the reticuloendothelial system that subsequently undergo granulomatous reaction. Healing is associated with fibrosis and calcification of the granulomata.

Clinical Findings

A. Signs and Symptoms. The clinical manifestations of tularemia are protean and depend on the portal of entry of the microorganism, virulence of the microorganism, and the immune status of the human host. It can vary from a subclinical illness to a fulminant disease with sepsis and death. Five different clinical syndromes have been described (Box 60–4). The incubation period is 3–5 days.

In the most common form of infection, the ulceroglandular type, a red, tender cutaneous papule is noted at the site of an insect bite or dermal penetration with ulceration on the affected limb and concomitant tender regional adenopathy. The ulcer becomes crusted and black-colored, forming an eschar, which is a characteristic feature of the cutaneous site of entry. Symptoms include fever (39–40.6 °C), chills, headaches, and generalized malaise. Patients often are acutely ill with severe prostration and occasionally hypotension, septicemia, and death. If untreated, fever may persist for a month or longer. On physical examination, the temperature elevation is often associated with a paradoxically relative bradycardia. Hepatosplenomegaly is common, especially in untreated cases.

Tularemia should be suspected in febrile patients with skin lesions and lymphadenopathy especially when a history of contact with wild animals, ticks, or deerflies is present.

B. Laboratory Findings. Organisms are rarely seen on Gram stain of affected tissue. Blood cultures or other biologic specimens need special culture media for growth. Serologic studies using the microagglutination test, or the enzyme immunoassay

BOX 60–4

Tularemia Infections

	Ulceroglandular (75–85%)	Typhoidal (5–15%)	Pulmonary (7–10%)	Oculoglandular (0–5%)	Oropharyngeal (1%)
More Common	• Macular skin lesion that later becomes a pruritic papule, followed by ulceration and eschar formation • Regional tender, warm, erythematous, fluctuant, lymphadenopathy • Fever, chills • Hepatosplenomegaly	• Fever, chills, weight loss • Hepatosplenomegaly, abdominal pain • Pulmonary infiltrates	• Nonproductive cough • Bilateral patchy infiltrates	• Unilateral painful purulent conjunctivitis • Preauricular or cervical lymphadenopathy	• Acute exudative or membranous pharyngitis • Cervical lymphadenopathy
Less Common	• Generalized maculopapular rash • Generalized adenopathy • No skin lesions • Pulmonary infiltrates	• Skin lesion • Lymphadenopathy	• Lobar pneumonia • Pleural effusion	• Nodular lesions or ulceration of the conjunctiva	

test, are reliable and widely available. A fourfold increase or decrease in the titers is diagnostic of infection. A titer of $\geq 1{:}160$ may represent recent or acute infection. As many as 50% of cases will have positive titers by the second week of the illness. Titers may remain elevated for months to years after an acute infection.

C. Imaging. In 30% of cases, a chest roentgenogram will show infiltrates, despite normal clinical findings. Typical chest roentgenogram findings in the pneumonic form would include lobar or subsegmental infiltrates, hilar adenopathy, or diffuse infiltrates.

Differential Diagnosis

The differential diagnosis of the ulceroglandular form is one of other diseases that are associated with skin ulcer and lymphadenopathy, such as pyoderma caused by streptococci or staphylococcus, sporotrichosis (*Sporothrix schenckii*), cat-scratch disease, rat-bite fever, plague, anthrax, brucellosis, typhoid fever, infectious mononucleosis, and hematologic malignancies.

Complications

The most common complication is suppuration of an involved lymph node. Other complications such as meningitis, osteomyelitis, endocarditis, and peritonitis occur rarely.

Treatment

Aminoglycosides, mainly streptomycin or gentamicin, are considered the drugs of choice for all forms of tularemia (Box 60–5). Other antimicrobial agents such as tetracyclines and chloramphenicol have been used in patients who cannot tolerate aminoglycosides. Their bacteriostatic effect against *F tularensis* may account for the high relapse rates. Relapse is not caused by resistant microorganisms and may be treated with another course of the same antimicrobial regimen.

BOX 60–5

Treatment of Tularemia

	Adults	Children
First Choice	• Streptomycin, 7.5–15 mg/kg IM twice daily for 10 days OR • Gentamicin, 1.5–2 mg/kg IM or IV three times daily for 10 days	• Streptomycin 15–20 mg/kg IM twice daily for 10 days OR • Gentamicin, 2 mg/kg IM or IV three times daily for 10 days
Second Choice	• Chloramphenicol, 7.5–12.5 mg/kg orally four times daily for 14 days OR • Tetracycline, 500 mg orally four times daily for 14 days	• Chloramphenicol, 7.5 mg/kg orally four times daily for 14 days

---

Prognosis

Immunity after infection with *F tularensis* is life-long. The mortality rate is 5–15% in untreated cases and 1% in treated cases. The typhoidal form is associated with a high mortality rate.

Prevention & Control

Avoidance of exposure to contact with potential sources of infection is the best means of prevention (Box 60–6). Gloves, masks, and goggles should be worn when handling potentially infected animals. A live attenuated vaccine is available for individuals at high risk such as veterinarians and meatpacking plant employees.

PLAGUE

Essentials of Diagnosis

- Suspected in patients living in or traveling from an endemic area who have acute onset of fever, prostration, and tender adenopathy.
- *Yersinia pestis* may be recovered from blood cultures or cultures of an aspirate from buboes or sputum in the pneumonic form in 80%–100% of cases.
- Gram stains of bubo aspirate or sputum demonstrate the characteristic bipolar "safety pin" gram-negative microorganisms.
- *Y pestis* grows aerobically on most culture media after 48–72 h of incubation.

General Considerations

The genus *Yersinia*, named after Alexander Yersin (1863–1943), includes *Y pestis, Y enterocolitica,* and *Y pseudotuberculosis. Y pestis* is the cause of plague, a disease that has left its mark on human history since the medieval time. *Y enterocolitica* and *Y pseudotuberculosis* also cause mesenteric lymphadenitis.

A. Epidemiology. Plague occurs worldwide. The most important reservoir for this enzootic disease is rodents: *Rattus rattus* and *Rattus sylvaticus.* The ectoparasite *Xenopsylla cheopsis* (oriental rat flea) represents the most important and efficient vector of transmission to humans. Humans acquire the disease by a fleabite.

Most cases currently occur in developing countries in Africa and Asia. In the United States, most cases occur in the southwestern states during the months of May to October when individuals are outdoors and in contact with rodents and fleas.

B. Microbiology. *Y Pestis,* a member of the *Enterobacteriaceae* family, is a nonmotile gram-negative bacilli with bipolar Gram staining. This microorganism grows aerobically on most culture media after 48–72 h of incubation. It produces V and W antigens that play a role in the virulence of the organism.

C. Pathogenesis. After inoculation by an in-

BOX 60–6

Control of Tularemia

Prophylactic Measures	• Avoidance of exposure to potential sources of infection • Gloves, masks, and eye covers should be worn when handling potentially infected animals • Live attenuated vaccine is available for individuals at high risk
Isolation Precautions	• Standard precautions only

fested flea, *Y pestis* cells are phagocytized quickly by leukocytes and macrophages, where they replicate rapidly and produce the virulence antigens. The microorganisms are resistant to intracellular killing and they multiply in the regional lymph nodes and disseminate to the blood and other viscera causing profound toxemia. A severe bleeding diathesis may occur as a result of the effect of plague toxin on blood vessel walls or as a consequence of disseminated intravascular coagulation.

Clinical Findings

A. Signs and Symptoms. After an incubation period of 2–8 days following the bite of an infected flea, patients present with sudden onset of fever, chills, weakness, and headaches (Box 60–7). The bubonic form of plague is characterized by the appearance of buboes, which are swollen, painful regional lymphadenopathy (typically inguinal or axillary), appearing after a few hours or on the next day. On physical examination, patients are toxic, lethargic, and agitated. The temperature is usually elevated to 41 °C. Buboes are matted, extremely tender and are 2–10 cm in diameter. Rarely, a vesiculopapular lesion from the fleabite is present. Bleeding from the gastrointestinal tract, respiratory tract, or the genitourinary tract is common (so-called red death). Petechiae and large ecchymoses occur along with gangrene of the distal extremities, nose, or penis (so-called Black Death).

The septicemic form of plague is characterized by high-grade bacteremia without palpable lymphadenopathy. Signs and symptoms are otherwise similar to the bubonic form. In this form of the disease, death occurs in 3–5 days in ~ 50% of cases. *Y pestis* reaches the lungs by way of the hematogenous route or less commonly via the airborne route and causes pneumonia. The pneumonic form is highly contagious and is spread by inhalation of droplet nuclei from a patient with pneumonic plague.

B. Laboratory Findings. *Y pestis* may be recovered from blood cultures or cultures of an aspirate from buboes or sputum in the pneumonic form in 80–100% of cases. Gram stains of bubo aspirate or sputum demonstrate the characteristic bipolar "safety pin" gram-negative microorganisms.

Differential Diagnosis

The differential diagnosis includes tularemia, lymphogranuloma venereum, cat-scratch disease, or severe staphylococcal and streptococcal infections.

Complications

See Signs and Symptoms.

Treatment

Streptomycin, the drug of choice for the treatment of plague, reduces the case fatality rate from > 50% in untreated cases to 10% in treated cases (Box 60–8). For patients who are allergic to or unable to tolerate streptomycin, tetracycline is a satisfactory alternative agent. In meningitis, the use of an antimicrobial agent with good penetration into the cerebrospinal fluid is essential. Chloramphenicol is administered at a loading dose of 25 mg/kg followed by 15 mg/kg intravenously every 6 h for a 10-day course.

Prevention & Control

A. Primary prevention. Patients with suspected pulmonic plague should be placed in strict respiratory isolation until the sputum culture is negative (Box

BOX 60–7

Plague

	Bubonic (90–95%)	Pneumonic (5%)	Septicemic (5%)
More Common	• Abrupt fever (39–41°C), chills • Nausea-vomiting • Prostration • Headaches and delirium • Tender regional lymphadenopathy (buboes) • Vasculitis, bleeding, gangrene	• Blood streaked sputum • Cough, dyspnea, chest pain, cyanosis • Prostration • Cavitation or consolidation on chest radiogram • Vasculitis, bleeding, gangrene	• Abrupt fever (39–41°C) • Shaking chills • Nausea/vomiting • Prostration • Headaches and delirium • Vasculitis, bleeding, gangrene
Less Common	• Vesicopapular lesion (flea bite site) • Generalized lymphadenopathy • Distal extremity gangrene		• No detectable lymphadenopathy

BOX 60–8

Treatment of Plague

	Adults	Children
First Choice	• Streptomycin, 15–22.5 mg/kg IM twice daily for 10 days OR • Gentamicin, 2 mg/kg IV three times daily for 10 days	• Streptomycin, 15 mg/kg IM twice daily for 10 days OR • Gentamicin, 1–2.5 mg/kg IM or IV three times daily for 10 days
Second Choice	• Tetracycline, 500–1000 mg orally four times daily for 10 days	• Tetracycline,[1] 7–12.5 mg/kg IV four times daily for 10 days OR • Chloramphenicol, 25 mg/kg loading dose followed by 12.5 mg/kg IM four times daily for 10 days

[1]Should not be used in children under the age of 8 or in pregnant women after 6 months of gestation.

60–9). Chemoprophylaxis with tetracyclines or sulfonamides should be administered to individuals who have had close contact with patients with plague pneumonia and for household contacts of flea-borne plague cases.

B. Secondary Prevention. For persons at high risk of exposure, two forms of vaccines are available: a live attenuated and a formalin-killed plague vaccine.

YERSINIOSIS

Essentials of Diagnosis
• Suspected in a child living in or traveling from a high-prevalence area who has fever, abdominal pain, and diarrhea followed by a reactive polyarthritis.
• *Yersinia* spp. are recovered from cultures of specimens of stool, mesenteric lymph nodes, blood, or abscess material.
• Inoculation of duplicate sets of cultures for incubation at 37 and 25 °C, respectively, enhances recovery of the microorganisms.

General Considerations
A. Epidemiology. Conditions that are associated with increased risk for *Yersinia* spp. infections (yersiniosis) include iron overload states (such as in patients who receive chronic blood transfusions or those with hemochromatosis) and the use of desferrioxamine, a bacterial siderophore. Infections caused by *Y enterocolitica* are more common in children than adults. The disease is more prevalent in northern Europe than in the United States. It is acquired by in-

gestion of contaminated food or water or by direct contact with an infected animal. The organism has been recovered from a variety of wild and domestic animals including pigs, rodents, rabbits, dogs, and horses, as well as from water and dairy products. The ability of the microorganism to grow at 4 °C allows it to survive in refrigerated food and dairy products.

Y pseudotuberculosis infection occurs rarely. The microorganism has been recovered from many species of wild and domestic animals and from food,

BOX 60–9

Control of Plague

Prophylactic Measures	Chemoprophylaxis should be administered as follows to individuals who have had close contact with patients with plague pneumonia and for household contacts of flea-borne plague cases: • Tetracycline, 7.5 mg/kg orally 4 times daily for 7 days (should not be used in children under the age of 8 or in pregnant women after 6 months of gestation) • Sulfonamides, 7.5–15 mg/kg orally 4 times daily for 7 days
Isolation Precautions	• Patients with suspected pneumonic plague should be placed in strict respiratory isolation until the sputum culture is negative

water, and other environmental sources. The disease is thought to be acquired by contact with infected animals or by ingestion of contaminated food. The disease is more common in Europe and typically affects children and adults during the winter months.

B. Microbiology. *Y enterocolitica* or *Y pseudotuberculosis* are the pathogens of the nonplague yersiniosis. They cause a gastrointestinal infection that may manifest itself by diarrhea or fever and abdominal pain that mimics acute appendicitis. These microorganisms are gram-negative bipolar stained bacilli, nonlactose fermenting and urease positive. They are motile at 25 °C but not at 37 °C. They are iron dependent and grow well on conventional culture media at 37 °C and in normal saline at 4 °C. *Y enterocolitica* produces a heat-stable enterotoxin and lipopolysaccharide endotoxin similar to that produced by other enteric gram-negative bacilli. The virulence of *Y pseudotuberculosis* appears to be related to the production of a lipopolysaccharide endotoxin and to the ability to survive intracellularly. *Yersinia* spp. lack siderophores and are dependent on siderophores produced by other bacteria for growth.

C. Pathogenesis. The portal of entry of *Y enterocolitica* and *Y pseudotuberculosis* is the gastrointestinal tract. These microorganisms cause terminal ileitis and adenitis. Pathogenic strains of *Y enterocolitica* cause mucosal ulceration and necrosis of Peyer's patches and therefore diarrhea. Bacteremia occurs rarely and is associated with suppurative lesions in the liver, spleen, and other organs. Reiter's syndrome is a reactive polyarthritis and occurs in 20%–30% of patients following infection with *Y enterocolitica*. Cross-reactions between the HLA-B27 antigen and the *Yersinia* antigen are postulated to be the underlying mechanism of arthritis.

Clinical Findings

The spectrum of disease caused by *Y enterocolitica* and *Y pseudotuberculosis* is wide and may be divided into two categories: infectious (intestinal and extraintestinal) and postinfectious (Box 60–10).

A. Signs and Symptoms. An intestinal infection is the most common manifestation. Typically, patients present with fever, abdominal pain, and diarrhea that is occasionally bloody for a 1- to 3-week duration. A clinical syndrome indistinguishable from acute appendicitis may occur in older children and adolescents. On laparotomy, thickening of the terminal ileum and cecal wall is present. The appendix is normal. Perforation of the intestine or dilatation of the colon with marked systemic toxicity (toxic megacolon) occurs rarely.

Extraintestinal infections are rare. A septicemic syndrome preceding enterocolitis or associated with transfusions of contaminated blood has a mortality rate of 50%. The iron present in blood and storage at 4 °C are favorable conditions for the growth of *Yersinia* spp. Other extraintestinal manifestations include cutaneous lesions such as cellulitis, vesicobullous lesions, and other manifestations including diffuse lymphadenopathy, splenomegaly, and acute pharyngitis.

Hepatic involvement is common in adults and can be present in two different forms. The acute form mostly occurring in patients with iron overload states is the result of involvement of the liver and sometimes the spleen with abscesses. The chronic form is characterized by a granulomatous inflammation in the liver and can be associated with a positive rheumatoid factor or a positive antinuclear antibody in the serum. The chronic form is thought to be secondary to an immunological phenomenon.

Postinfectious manifestations include polyarthritis involving the weight-bearing joints and occurs in 10%–30% of Scandinavian adults with *Y enterocolitica* infection. Of patients with arthritis, 70% have the histocompatibility antigen HLA-B27. Arthritis begins a few days to a month following the onset of diarrhea and can persist ≤ 4 months. Erythema nodosum occurs

BOX 60–10

Yersiniosis

	Intestinal	Extraintestinal	Post–infective
More Common	• Enteritis: abdominal pain, diarrhea • Mesenteric adenitis • Pseudoappendicitis syndrome	• Septicemia • Pharyngitis • Hepatic involvement • Skin manifestations • Lymphadenopathy syndrome	• Polyarthritis: knees, ankles, wrist, fingers, toes • Erythema nodosum
Less Common	• Perforation of the bowel • Toxic megacolon	• Transfusion-related sepsis • Endocarditis	• Uveitis • Glomerulonephritis • Guillain-Barré syndrome • Hemolytic uremic syndrome

BOX 60-11

Treatment of Yersiniosis

	Adults	Children
First Choice	• Gentamicin, 1.5 mg/kg IV three times daily for 10 days	• Gentamicin, 1–2.5 mg/kg IV three times daily for 10 days
Second Choice	• Tetracycline, 500–1000 mg orally four times daily for 10 days OR • Chloramphenicol, 7.5–12.5 mg/kg orally or IV four times daily for 10 days	• Tetracycline,[1] 7–12.5 mg/kg IV four times daily for 10 days OR • Chloramphenicol, 25 mg/kg loading dose followed by 12.5 mg/kg IM four times daily for 10 days

[1]Should not be used in children under the age of 8 or in pregnant women after 6 months of gestation.

in 20%–30% of cases with arthritis. Other postinfectious manifestations include uveitis, glomerulonephritis, Guillain-Barré syndrome and the hemolytic-uremic syndrome.

B. Laboratory Findings. Laboratory findings are nonspecific and might include leukocytosis, anemia, and elevated erythrocyte sedimentation rates.

Differential Diagnosis

The differential diagnosis of polyarthritis is wide and includes acute rheumatic fever, juvenile rheumatoid arthritis, Kawasaki disease, and other postinfectious arthritides.

Complications

See Signs and Symptoms.

Treatment

Diarrhea and mesenteric adenitis are usually self-limited, and antimicrobial therapy has not been demonstrated to affect the course of the infection. Immunocompromised hosts and patients with extraintestinal infections should be treated with antimicrobial therapy (Box 60–11). The optimal therapy is unclear. *Yersinia* spp. are susceptible in vitro to gentamicin, fluoroquinolones, trimethoprim-sulfamethoxazole, third-generation cephalosporins, tetracycline, and chloramphenicol. Empirical therapy with an aminoglycoside alone or in combination with trimethoprim-sulfamethoxazole, or a third-generation cephalosporin, or chloramphenicol is recommended.

Prognosis

Mortality is rare, except in the septicemic form, where yersiniosis is associated with 50% mortality.

Prevention & Control

Hospitalized patients with *Yersinia* spp. infections should be placed in enteric isolation (Box 60–12).

Pasteurization of dairy products and proper cooking of meat or boiling water kills the microorganism in contaminated food. Contact with potentially infected animals in endemic areas should be minimized.

PASTEURELLA

Essentials of Diagnosis

• History of a cat or dog bite or other exposure.
• Pain, erythema, swelling, and drainage at the bite site.
• Gram-negative bipolar bacilli on Gram stain of the drainage.
• Culture of the organism confirms the diagnosis.

General Considerations

Pasteurella multocida infection, a disease that primarily affects animals, may occasionally affect humans, causing a wide variety of infections ranging from soft tissue infection to bacteremia and endocarditis.

BOX 60-12

Control of Yersiniosis

Prophylactic Measures	• Pasteurization of dairy products and proper cooking of meat or boiling water kills the microorganisms in contaminated food • Contact with potentially infected animals in endemic areas should be minimized
Isolation Precautions	• Hospitalized patients with *Yersinia* spp. infections should be placed in enteric isolation

BOX 60-13

Pasteurella Infection

	Soft Tissue/Bone	Respiratory System
More Common	• Erythema, pain, and swelling • Serosanguineous drainage • Regional lymphadenopathy • Low-grade fever	• Pharyngitis • Pneumonia
Less Common	• Abscess • Tenosynovitis • Arthritis	• Sinusitis • Otitis • Mastoiditis • Empyema

A. Epidemiology. *Pasteurella multocida* has been recovered from cultures of specimens from the nasopharynx and the gastrointestinal tract of a large number of asymptomatic wild and domestic animals. The highest carriage rates occur in cats (50%–90%), dogs or swine (50%), and rats (15%). Infections are usually preceded by a cat or dog bite or scratch on an extremity. Occasionally, infection may occur without a bite or scratch in persons who have frequent contact with animals. Fifteen percent of cases have no history of animal exposure.

B. Microbiology. *Pasteurella* spp. are small, nonmotile, non-spore-forming, bipolar staining gram-negative coccobacilli. Growth occurs aerobically at 37 °C in ordinary culture media and is enhanced by using blood- or serum-enriched agar under increased carbon dioxide tension. Among the *Pasteurella* spp. that can cause disease in humans, *P multocida* is the most common. Different species of *Pasteurella* may be distinguished by their biochemical reactions and their requirements for V factor.

C. Pathogenesis. A localized infection occurs after inoculation of the microorganism in soft tissue or a joint space. It is characterized by polymorphonuclear leukocyte infiltrates followed by necrosis and, in some cases, by abscess formation. When bacteremia occurs, microabscesses may develop in multiple organs.

Clinical Findings

A. Signs and Symptoms. Hours to days after direct contact with an animal (usually by way of a dog or cat bite), a soft tissue infection develops (Box 60–13). Patients complain of an acute onset of pain, erythema, and swelling at the site of inoculation, usually on the hand, leg, arm, or head and neck. Serosanguineous drainage occurs 1–2 days later. A low-grade fever and regional lymphadenopathy are commonly seen. Abscess formation and septic arthritis or osteomyelitis rarely complicate local infection of the extremity.

B. Laboratory Findings. Gram-negative bipolar bacilli appear on Gram stain of the drainage. Cultures of the organism confirm the diagnosis.

Differential Diagnosis

After an animal bite, the differential diagnosis should include infection caused by anaerobes, staphylococci, streptococci, tularemia, and cat-scratch disease.

Complications

Occasionally, *P multocida* may affect the respiratory system. These infections occur in persons who have frequent contact with animals. *P multocida* has been recovered from the sputum cultures of asymptomatic patients with chronic obstructive pulmonary disease and in these patients may cause pneumonia.

BOX 60-14

Treatment of Pasteurella Infection

	Adults	Children
First Choice	Amoxicillin–clavulanic acid, 250–500 mg orally three times daily for 10 days	Amoxicillin–clavulanic acid 13.3 mg/kg orally three times daily for 10 days
β–Lactam Allergy	Ciprofloxacin, 500–750 mg orally twice daily	TMP/SMX, 4–6 mg/kg TMP orally twice daily

BOX 60–15

Control of *Pasteurella* Infection	
Prophylactic Measures	• Avoidance of contact with wild or domestic animals

Occasionally, pharyngitis occurs in patients with close contact with infected animals, especially cats. Rarely, *P multocida* may cause meningitis, sinusitis, pharyngeal abscess, otitis, empyema, peritonitis, pyelonephritis, surgical wound infection, and endocarditis. Associated bacteremia can occur with any organ infection.

Treatment

Animal bites need to be carefully assessed. Examination of the joints, tendons, and neurovascular axis of a limb is mandatory. Bite wounds should be cleaned with normal saline, and devitalized tissue should be débrided. If necessary, the tetanus toxoid vaccine should be administered, and potential exposure to rabies should be assessed.

The microbiology of animal bites is polymicrobial and includes *Pasteurella* spp., staphylococci, streptococci, and anaerobes. Antimicrobial therapy should be active against these microorganisms (Box 60–14). Amoxicillin-clavulanic acid, cefuroxime, or doxycycline are effective therapy. Ciprofloxacin is effective against *P multocida;* however, it lacks activity against anaerobes, streptococci, and staphylococci. In patients unable to tolerate β-lactams, doxycycline or combination therapy with ciprofloxacin and clindamycin is an effective alternative therapy for animal bites. In monomicrobial infection with *P multocida,* penicillin is the treatment of choice.

Prevention & Control

Avoidance of contact with wild or domestic animals is probably the only means of preventing human *P multocida* infections (Box 60–15).

HACEK INFECTION

Essentials of Diagnosis

• Suspected in patients with periodontal disease with signs and symptoms suggestive of infective endocarditis.
• Large valvular heart vegetation on echocardiography.
• Small, pleomorphic gram-negative coccobacilli that grow best in enriched media and increased CO_2 tension.

General Considerations

The fastidious bacteria of the HACEK group include *Haemophilus aphrophilus* and *H paraphrophilus, Actinobacillus actinomycetemcomitans, Cardiobacterium hominis, Eikenella corrodens,* and *Kingella kingae.* These organisms may be considered part of the normal flora of the upper respiratory tract. Because they share common clinical and microbiological properties, they will be reviewed together.

All HACEK microorganisms produce a similar clinical syndrome including infective endocarditis, periodontal disease, and bacteremia (Box 60–16). Rarely, these microorganisms may cause brain abscess, meningitis, pneumonia, intra-abdominal infections, gynecologic infections, arthritis, osteomyelitis, and human bite wound infection (*E corrodens*).

A. Epidemiology. The most common infectious disease caused by these microorganisms is infective endocarditis. These microorganisms account for 3% of infective endocarditis cases. The incidence of HACEK endocarditis is ~ 0.32/100,000 person years of life. HACEK microorganisms are part of the usual microflora of the oral cavity, and this serves as the portal of entry for bacteremia, which may result in infective endocarditis or, very rarely, infections in other organ systems.

B. Microbiology. Microorganisms of the HACEK group are small, pleomorphic gram-negative coccobacilli that grow best in enriched media (such as sheep blood agar or chocolate agar) and increased CO_2 tension. Cultures often require prolonged incubation times (average 5–7 days) for growth. They are

BOX 60–16

HACEK Infections		
	Infective	Other Sites
More Common	• Fever • Periodontal disease • New or changing cardiac murmur • Splenomegaly • Embolic phenomena	• Brain abscess: fever, confusion, focal findings • Meningitis • Arthritis: swelling, pain, and effusion of the affected joint
Less Common		

BOX 60–17

Treatment of HACEK Endocarditis

	Adults	Children
First Choice	• Ceftriaxone, 2 g IV daily for 4–6 weeks OR • Cefotaxime, 2 g IV three times daily for 4–6 weeks	• Ceftriaxone, 100 mg/kg IV daily for 4–6 weeks OR • Cefotaxime, 50 mg/kg IV three times daily for 4–6 weeks
Second Choice	• Ampicillin, 2 g IV 6 times daily **PLUS** gentamicin, 1 mg/kg IM or IV every 8 h for 4–6 weeks	• Ampicillin, 50–75 mg/kg IV every 6 h **PLUS** gentamicin, 1 mg/kg IM or IV every 8 h for 4–6 weeks

distinguished among each other by their biochemical reactions.

Clinical Findings

A. Signs and Symptoms. The presentation of endocarditis is often insidious in onset and includes fever, splenomegaly, embolic phenomena, and a new or changing cardiac murmur. More than half of patients with endocarditis will have had a dental procedure within the 6 months before onset of symptoms or poor dentition at the time of diagnosis. Valvular or congenital structural heart disease or the presence of a prosthetic heart valve was present in 60% and 27% of cases, respectively. Cardiac valvular vegetation observed by echocardiography is characteristically large. This finding probably reflects the chronicity of infection before diagnosis. Signs and symptoms of other HACEK infections are related to the affected site of infection.

B. Laboratory Findings. The diagnosis of HACEK infections requires the cultivation of the bacteria from sterile sites. Biological specimens need to be incubated in enriched media under increased CO_2 tension for 5–7 days.

C. Imaging. Echocardiography can reveal large endocardial or valvular vegetation.

Differential Diagnosis

The differential diagnosis includes infective endo-carditis caused by other microorganisms, such as staphylococci, enterococci, and fungi.

Treatment

With the emergence of β-lactamase-producing HACEK organisms, third-generation cephalosporins (eg, cefotaxime or ceftriaxone) are now considered the treatment of choice (see Box 60–17). The treatment of infections other than infective endocarditis caused by HACEK organisms requires the same antimicrobial therapy used in infective endocarditis; however, the length of therapy might be shorter, depending on the site of infection. With susceptible microorganisms, combination therapy using penicillin or ampicillin and aminoglycoside is satisfactory. The American Heart Association recommends that native valve and prosthetic valve endocarditis be treated for 4 and 6 weeks, respectively.

Prognosis

Native or prosthetic valve endocarditis caused by HACEK organisms may be cured in 82%–87% of the cases by medical or medical and surgical therapies.

Prevention & Control

Follow American Heart Association guidelines for prevention of infective endocarditis, after dental and other procedures in patients at high risk. See Chapter 11 for cardiovascular-intravascular infection guidelines for subacute bacterial endocarditis prophylaxis.

REFERENCES

Brucellosis

Akova M et al: Quinolones in treatment of human brucellosis: comparative trial of ofloxacin-rifampin versus doxycycline-rifampin. Antimicrob Agents Chemother 1993;37:1831.

Ariza J et al: Treatment of human brucellosis with doxycycline plus rifampin or doxycycline plus streptomycin. a randomized, double-blind study. Ann Intern Med 1992;117:25.

Trujillo IZ et al: Brucellosis. Infect Dis Clin North Am 1994;8:225.

Young EJ: An overview of human brucellosis. Clin Infect Dis 1995;21(2):283.

Tularemia

Jacobs RF: Tularemia. Adv Ped Infect Dis 1996;12:55.

Stewart SJ: Tularemia: association with hunting and farming. FEMS Immunol Med Microbiol 1996;13:197.

Plague & Yersiniosis

Baert F et al: The clinical spectrum. Acta Clin Belgica 1994;49:76.

Butler T: Yersinia infections: centennial of the discovery of the plague bacillus. Clin Infect Dis 1994;19:655.

Perry RD, Fetherston JD: *Yersinia pestis*: etiologic agent of plague. Clin Microbiol Rev 1997;10:35.

Smith MD et al: In vitro antimicrobial susceptibilities of strains of *Yersinia pestis*. Antimicrob Agents Chemother 1995;39:2153.

***Pasteurella* Infection**

Goldstein EJ: Bite wounds and infection. Clin Infect Dis 1992;14:633.

HACEK Infection

Das M et al: Infective endocarditis caused by HACEK microorganisms. Annu Rev Med 1997;48:25.

61

Tuberculosis

Julie Brahmer, MD, & Merle A. Sande, MD

Essentials of Diagnosis

- The cardinal symptoms of tuberculosis (TB) are fatigue, weight loss, fever, and night sweats.
- The most commonly infected populations include the homeless, institutionalized patients, and HIV-positive patients.
- In most cases, a TB skin test (PPD) is positive.
- To establish presence of infection, an acid-fast bacilli (AFB) smear demonstrates the acid-fast bacillus.
- In primary pulmonary TB, an infiltrate in the lower lobes of the lung is usually seen on chest x-ray. In contrast, apical lung infiltrates are commonly seen in the reactivation of pulmonary TB.

General Considerations

Mycobacterium tuberculosis is still an important pathogen. Approximately one-third of the world's population is infected with *M tuberculosis,* according to World Health Organization estimates, resulting in 2.9 million annual deaths. In the United States, tuberculosis is on the rise, after several decades of steady decline.

The disease develops in a subset of those who are infected. In most patients, the reason disease develops is unclear unless they are immunosuppressed by either HIV infection or other immunocompromising diseases. HIV has played a major role in the resurgence of tuberculosis in the United States and in the emergence of multidrug-resistant disease. Prompt diagnosis and treatment of active disease is important in all patients to prevent severe disease and infection of the surrounding population. In those infected with the tuberculosis bacillus, the prevention of active tuberculosis disease is also important.

A. Epidemiology. In the United States, tuberculosis had been on the decline until 1985, when the number of cases began to increase. This increase was undoubtedly a result of the HIV epidemic. Cases continued to increase until 1995, when the 22,813 new cases documented in the United States constituted a 6.4% drop from 1994. This drop resulted from a decreased incidence in the U.S.-born population. The overall incidence of tuberculosis in the United States is quite low, but case rates are high among specific groups such as HIV-infected patients, the homeless, recent immigrants from countries that have a high prevalence of tuberculosis, intravenous drug users, inner-city dwellers, and minorities.

In the late 1980s, tuberculosis caused by organisms resistant to antimicrobial agents increased sharply, especially in New York City, where, in 1991, one-third of all cases were resistant to at least one agent. The rates of resistance in the United States began to decrease in 1995. Of cases reported, the isoniazid (INH) resistance rate was 7.6%, and the INH-rifampin resistance rate was 1.4%. The decrease in resistance rates was most likely caused by the introduction of directly observed therapy and intensive case management.

One lesson learned from the resurgence of tuberculosis and multidrug-resistant tuberculosis is the importance of tuberculosis control strategies and the importance of making sure patients adhere to the medication regimens. The Centers for Disease Control recommends that all tuberculosis patients be observed taking their medications by health care providers ("directly observed therapy," [DOT]). The decrease in U.S. case rates has been attributed to the institution of DOT. Other factors thought to have decreased the case and resistance rates are improved laboratory methods for identifying tuberculosis, broader use of drug-susceptibility testing, expanded use of preventive therapy in high-risk groups, decreased transmission of tuberculosis in congregative settings, improved follow-up of persons with TB, and increased federal resources for state and local TB control efforts.

M tuberculosis is transmitted in the air. The bacillus is packaged in a droplet nucleus and coughed out into the surrounding air by one person and inhaled by another. Patients with bronchopulmonary TB with a productive cough are particularly infectious. Other factors that increase the infectivity of a person are the extent of cavitary disease of the lung, presence of AFB on the sputum smear, unprotected coughing, and crowding in a household. Generally, patients with extrapulmonary TB are not infectious.

B. Microbiology. *M tuberculosis* is an AFB that is curved or straight and nonmotile. It is slow growing, taking $\leq$ 18 h for one replication. Typically, it may take 2–6 weeks to grow a significant colony. The bacillus is non-pigment producing, which can be used to differentiate it from some other atypical mycobacteria.

C. Pathogenesis. A person is infected with *M tuberculosis* by inhaling bacilli in droplet nuclei. The particles must be retained in the lung. Thus the inhaled particles, which are < 5 μm in size, travel to the alveolus during inspiration and are retained in the lung. Larger particles are filtered out before they reach the alveoli. In the alveolus, the bacillus activates the immune system. The first line of defense is the alveolar macrophage. These macrophages engulf the bacilli. Some macrophages are capable of killing the bacillus, whereas others cannot. The bacilli multiply within the cells. The factors controlling the macrophages' ability to kill *M tuberculosis* are not all known and may be genetic. At any rate, T cells are then attracted to these macrophages and recognize the *M tuberculosis* protein presented by the macrophage. The T cell lyses the infected macrophage. Memory T cells then develop which are thought to contribute to the delayed hypersensitivity reaction relied on by the purified protein derivative (PPD) skin test. These memory T cells also enable patients previously infected with TB to resist reinfection. Other factors that influence the progression of infection to disease include the intensity of exposure, interval since infection, age, and other coexisting or comorbid diseases. Extrapulmonary disease develops when the bacillus is not contained in the lungs and travels to other organs by way of the bloodstream.

Infection by *M tuberculosis* is reflected by a positive skin test reaction, although, in some immunocompromised patients, a PPD test result may be negative even though these patients are infected. Those who are immunosuppressed have an increased chance of developing illness, which may be caused by an ineffective cell-mediated response (Box 61–1). Cell-mediated immunity is thought to be the mechanism by which a contained TB infection is kept quiescent. Patients who are HIV positive (who have ineffective cell-mediated immunity) and are infected with TB have a 7% chance per year of developing active tuberculosis.

Active tuberculosis disease is defined as tissue involvement by the *M tuberculosis* bacillus that progresses to produce clinical symptoms and signs. On average, illness develops in 3–5% of infected patients. Of the other 95–97% of infected patients, 5% develop active tuberculosis in their lifetime. *M tuberculosis* infection can cause several clinical syndromes.

CLINICAL SYNDROMES

PULMONARY TUBERCULOSIS

The most common syndrome in adults is pulmonary TB, which accounts for ~ 80% of cases of active disease.

Clinical Findings

A. Signs and Symptoms. Symptoms of infection consist of fatigue, weight loss, fever, night sweats, and a productive cough. Most children who are infected with TB usually have no symptoms. Early symptoms can also include hemoptysis, which also occurs later in the disease when there is significant necrosis of lung parenchyma or if previous cavitations erode into arterioles. Patients with subpleural parenchymal inflammation with pleural membrane involvement or with TB pleuritis without parenchymal disease can experience pleuritic chest pain. Severe shortness of breath is not common. However, extensive pulmonary tuberculosis can cause respiratory failure.

B. Laboratory Findings. Routine laboratory test abnormalities are not common. Hyponatremia due to the syndrome of inappropriate secretion of antidiuretic hormone can be seen in some patients with pulmonary TB. However, adrenal involvement with TB can cause adrenal insufficiency, which may also be present with hyponatremia. Anemia secondary to this chronic disease is common.

C. Imaging. Pulmonary TB usually produces infiltrates observable on chest x-rays, but occasionally, chest x-rays are normal. Primary TB is the disease that develops before the development of an immune response to the bacillus. Primary TB has different characteristics than secondary reactivation of a pulmonary TB disease. Primary TB usually involves the lower lobes. Five percent of cases show a lobar or segmental infiltrate associated with ipsilateral hilar adenopathy. Fifteen percent of cases may have bilateral hilar adenopathy, but this is more commonly unilateral. A pleural effusion may also be present.

Children with primary pulmonary TB often have hilar adenopathy and occasionally a lower-lobe infiltrate that can be seen on chest x-ray. Secondary or reactivation TB, which is by far the most common presentation, characteristically involves the lung apices (posterior apical segments) or, rarely, the superior

BOX 61–1

Mycobacterium tuberculosis

	Children	Adults
More Common	• Lymphatic • Other extrapulmonary sites	• Pulmonary
Less Common	• Pulmonary	• Extrapulmonary

segments of the lower lobes. This is seen in 95% of patients with localized pulmonary TB. The typical parenchymal pattern is cavitary lesions with associated air space consolidation of a patchy or confluent nature.

Old, healed pulmonary TB lesions can produce fibrosis or calcific lesions on chest x-ray. These lesions can cause volume loss or contraction of the involved lobe. Cavities also may persist. New infiltrates or masses in areas of old tuberculosis infections may represent carcinoma, bacterial infection, hemorrhage, mycetoma, or recurrence of TB.

D. Differential Diagnosis. Differential diagnosis of pulmonary TB includes other atypical mycobacterium infections (*Mycobacterium avium* complex or *M kansasii*) and viral infections (see Chapter 62).

E. Complications. Complications of pulmonary TB include lung bulla formation, poor lung function, overwhelming infection, and death.

EXTRAPULMONARY TUBERCULOSIS

Extrapulmonary TB accounts for ~ 20% of cases of active tuberculosis. Extrapulmonary TB is more common in immunocompromised patients and in infants and young children. Of these extrapulmonary sites, meningeal and lymphatic locations for disease are more common in infants and young children. In adolescents, the extrapulmonary sites tend to be the pleura, genitourinary tract, or peritoneum. Overall, the most common extrapulmonary site of TB in children is in the lymphatic system.

Other sites of infection in adults can include pleura, genitourinary tract, gastrointestinal tract, bone, meninges, peritoneum, and adrenals. When the *M tuberculosis* bacillus infects the lung, it often disseminates and involves multiple organs, including the bone marrow. This is called disseminated or miliary tuberculosis, but it may be asymptomatic. Extrapulmonary TB develops when the bacillus overwhelms the immune system and disseminates by way of the lymphatics, the bloodstream, or both. In these cases, disease is documented by biopsy, positive blood cultures, or both.

Signs and symptoms of extrapulmonary TB depend on the organ system involved. Weight loss, night sweats, and fever are the classic but nonspecific signs of tuberculosis. Clinicians should do blood cultures as well as biopsy and culture of the suspected tissue.

TUBERCULOSIS IN PATIENTS WITH HIV INFECTION

HIV patients can have a wide variety of organ system involvement. In early HIV infection, pulmonary TB can be a presenting infection and an AIDS-defin-

ing illness. In advanced HIV infection, dissemination is common. A variety of unusual sites of infection have been documented, including brain, pericardium, and other more common extrapulmonary sites such as those for peritoneal and gastric TB. Overall, the most common site of TB disease in an HIV-positive patient is pulmonary; however, these patients are at increased risk for developing disseminated disease (Box 61–2).

Diagnosis

Diagnoses of extrapulmonary and pulmonary TB are the same. A skin test (PPD) is used to prove infection: 0.1 mL of PPD is placed intradermally on the volar surface of the forearm by means of a 26-gauge needle. At 48–72 h after injection, the diameter of induration, not erythema, is measured. A positive skin test reaction is caused by a delayed-type hypersensitivity response, which is directed at the TB protein antigens. Other tests include demonstration of the bacillus by means of culture or AFB smear of affected organs or blood culture in disseminated disease.

A. Interpreting Tuberculin Skin Tests. The criteria vary for interpreting a PPD test as positive. An induration ≥ 5 mm is considered positive in patients who are at high risk of infection and developing disease; these include patients with known or suspected HIV infection, which includes all injection drug users. This group also includes close contacts of patients with active disease and patients with a chest x-ray suggestive of previously inactive tuberculosis. An induration of ≥ 10 mm is considered positive in patients who are at intermediate risk of infection and developing TB. This group includes known HIV-negative injection drug users, immigrants from high-prevalence countries (such as Asia and Mexico), residents of long-term care or correctional facilities, locally identified high-prevalence groups (migrant workers, the homeless, and high-risk racial or ethnic groups), and children ≤ 4 years old. Patients also at intermediate risk of TB include those with an immunosuppressive illness other than HIV or those receiving immunosuppressive therapy. These include patients with diabetes, renal failure, or hematologic malignancies or those receiving steroids on a long-

BOX 61–2

Mycobacterium TB in AIDS Patients (CD4 < 100)

	Children	Adults
More Common	• Disseminated • Pulmonary	• Pulmonary • Disseminated
Less Common	• Other extrapulmonary sites	• Other extrapulmonary sites

term basis (> 15 mg of prednisone/d). Finally, an induration of ≥ 15 mm is considered positive in patients with no known risk of developing TB or being infected with TB.

B. False-positive PPDs. False-positive results can occur in two situations. Patients who are infected with atypical mycobacteria such as *M avium* or *M kansasii* may have false-positive PPD results. Bacillus Calmette-Guérin (BCG) vaccination can also cause a positive result. However, a history of prior BCG vaccination should be ignored when one is interpreting skin test results in individuals with a high likelihood of being infected with *M tuberculosis*.

C. False-negative PPDs. False-negative results are much more common. In patients with distant infection, reactivity to a PPD test can decrease over time. These patients may require a "boost" PPD given 2 weeks after the first injection. There are multiple other factors to consider that cause a false-negative reaction (Table 61–1). Patients with coexisting diseases can also have false-negative reactions. In these patients, administration of other antigens such as those for *Candida* infection and mumps may be used to rule out anergy. However, some patients can have selective PPD nonreactivity.

D. Bacteriologic Evaluation. Smears and cultures of sputum are the most reliable ways to diagnose active pulmonary tuberculosis. Three separate early-morning sputum samples should be collected for AFB staining. Cultures should be performed on all specimens of patients suspected of having tuberculosis. Because *M tuberculosis* grows so slowly, it may take ≤ 6 weeks to identify the organism by culture. Drug susceptibility testing should be done on all positive cultures. In extrapulmonary TB, AFB stains and cultures are done on the infected tissue.

E. Polymerase Chain Reaction (PCR) Technique. Rapid diagnosis by the PCR technique is another option for the diagnosis of TB. It is commercially available and recently received approval by the U.S. Food and Drug Administration. PCR is approved only for testing AFB-positive sputum smears. In a research setting, PCR's specificity and sensitivity are > 95%. It does not take the place of acid-fast smears or mycobacterial cultures. Many more studies must be performed to better define the utility of PCR in the clinical setting.

Treatment

Treatments of active extrapulmonary and pulmonary TB are the same. Treatment should be started presumptively before diagnosis in patients with severe disease thought to be TB. Treatment usually does not reduce the isolation rate of AFB in the first several days. In patients with less severe disease or those who present diagnostic dilemmas, therapy can be withheld until a diagnosis is made or until several specimens have been collected.

Patients should be started initially on a four-drug regimen until drug susceptibility tests are finalized, unless the patient is from an area where drug resistance is very low. Most communities in the United States have a > 4% incidence of cases resistant to at least one drug. However, if a community has a < 4% resistance rate, an initial three-drug regimen is acceptable.

A. Choice of Treatment Regimen. There are several available regimens for treatment (Box 61–3). Several considerations should be made when deciding on a particular regimen. These include the probability of primary resistance, previous treatment for tuberculosis, patient compliance, other coexisting illnesses, drug susceptibility of the organism, and history of hypersensitivity to or side effects of antituberculosis drugs. The risk factors for drug resistance include > 4% of INH resistance in the community, prior treatment with INH, exposure to a known drug-resistant case, immigration from countries with a high incidence of drug resistance (countries in Asia, Africa, or Central or South America), HIV coinfection, and intravenous drug use. These patients should be placed on an initial four-drug regimen (Table 61–2).

Tuberculosis treatment is based on three basic principles. Regimens for treatment of the disease must contain multiple drugs to which the organism is susceptible. The medications must be taken regularly. Finally, drug therapy must continue for an extended period because of the slow growing nature of the *M tuberculosis* bacillus.

If patients do not take their medications regularly, many adverse consequences can result. *M tuberculo-*

Table 61–1. Factors causing a false-negative PPD test.[1]

Technical errors
- Improper administration
- Inaccurate reading
- Loss of potency of antigen

Patient-related factors
- Age
- Nutritional status
- Medications—corticosteroids, immunosuppressives, antineoplastic agents
- Severe tuberculosis
- Coexisting diseases such as renal failure
- HIV infection
- Viral illness or vaccination
- Lymphoreticular malignancies
- Sarcoidosis
- Solid tumors
- Lepromatous leprosy
- Sjögren's syndrome
- Ataxia telangiectasia
- Uremia
- Primary biliary cirrhosis
- Systemic lupus erythematosus
- Severe systemic disease of any etiology

[1]Adapted from Brahmer, JR, Small PM: Tuberculosis and nontuberculous mycobacterial infections. In Stein JH (ed): *Textbook of Internal Medicine*, 5th ed. Mosby Yearbook, 1998.

BOX 61-3

Treatment of *Mycobacterium* TB

	Children	Adults

First-Line Drugs	• Isoniazid
	  • Daily dose 10–15 mg/kg/d (300 mg/d max)
	  • 2× weekly dose 20–40 mg/kg/dose (900 mg/dose max)
	• Rifampin
	  • Daily dose and 2× weekly 10–20 mg/kg/d (600 mg/d per dose max)
	• Pyrazinamide
	  • Daily dose 15–30 mg/kg/d
	  • 2× weekly 50–70 mg/kg/dose
	  • Max dose 2 g
	• Streptomycin
	  • Daily dose 20–40 mg/kg/d IM (max dose 1 g)
	  • 2× weekly dose 25–30 mg/kg/dose IM
	• Ethambutol
	  • Daily dose 15–25 mg/kg/d
	  • 2× weekly dose 50 mg/kg/dose
	  • Max dose 2.5 g
		• Ethambutol (bacteriostatic)
		  • Daily dose 25 mg/kg/d for 2 mo, then 15 mg/kg/d
		  • 2× weekly dose 50 mg/kg/dose
		• Isoniazid (bactericidal)
		  • Daily dose 5–10 mg/kg/d (300 mg/d max)
		  • 2× weekly dose 15 mg/kg (900 mg max)
		• Pyrazinamide (bactericidal)
		  • Daily dose 25 mg/kg/d (2.5 g/d max)
		  • 2× weekly dose 50–70 mg/kg/dose
		• Rifampin (bactericidal)
		  • Daily and 2× weekly dose 10 mg/kg/d (600 mg/d max)
		• Streptomycin
		  • 15 mg/kg IM daily for initial 2 mo
		  • Rest of Rx if needed 1.0 g IM 2–3×/week (25–30 mg/kg/dose)

Second-Line Drugs	• Ethionamide
	  • 10–20 mg/kg/d (max dose 1 g)
	• Kanamycin
	  • Daily dose 15 mg/kg/d IM
	  • 2× weekly dose 15–25 mg/kg/dose IM or IV
	  • Max dose 1 g
	• Cycloserine
	  • Daily dose 10–20 mg/kg/d (max dose 1 g)
		• Amikacin (bactericidal)
		  • 7.5–10 mg/kg IV or IM daily
		• Capreomycin sulfate
		  • 1 g/d (15 mg/kg/d) IM
		• Ciprofloxacin
		  • 750 mg orally or IV twice a day
		• Clofazimine
		  • 50 mg/d + 300 mg 1×/mo supervised or 100 mg/d orally
		• Cycloserine (bacteriostatic)
		  • 750–1000 mg/d (15 mg/kg/d) in 2–4 doses/d orally
		• Ethionamide (bacteriostatic)
		  • 500–1000 mg/d (10–15 mg/kg/d) orally in 1–3 doses/d
		• Ofloxacin
		  • 400 mg orally or IV twice a day
		• Para-aminosalicylic acid (bacteriostatic)
		  • 4–6 g orally twice a day (200 mg/kg/d)
		• Rifabutin
		  • 300 mg/d orally

Special Considerations	• Other drugs used in children but rarely are listed in second line under adults; optimal doses for children have not been established. • Ethambutol is not recommended in children < 13 years of age	• In patients older than 60 years, the daily dose of streptomycin should be only 10 mg/kg/d (max dose of 750 mg)

Table 61–2. Treatment options per risk of antimicrobial resistance.[1,2]

Risk Group	First Option	Second Option	Third Option
U.S. born & not living in an area of increased resistance (<4%) & no risk factors for MDR TB	• 1st 2 mo, INH + RIF + PZA • Followed by 16 weeks of INH + RIF daily or 2× per week	• INH + RIF + PZA+ SM or ETB daily for 2 weeks • Then 2×/week for 6 weeks by DOT • Then INH + RIF 2x/week for 16 weeks by DOT	• INH + RIF + PZA + ETB or SM for 6 mo 3×/week by DOT
Recent immigrant from Latin America or Asia or living in an area of increased resistance or previous treatment without RIF	• INH + RIF + PZA + ETB or SM for 2 mo • If INH + RIF sensitive, then DC PZA + ETB or SM after 2 mo of four-drug treatment • Then INH + RIF daily or 2×/ week for 4 mo	• DOT preferred unless compliance is quite certain	
Proven, high-risk, or known exposure to MDR TB	Injectable drug (amikacin or capreomycin or kanamycin) + fluoroquinolone (cipro or oflox) + ETB + PZA + INH + RIF + cycloserine or ethionamide or aminosalicylic acid	Daily treatment recommended, not intermittent	
HIV+ or AIDS, pulmonary or extrapulmonary	Same as row 2 above: stop protease inhibitor	If INH or RIF can't be used, treatment should be for 18 and 12 mo after cultures are negative	Maintenance treatment is not required

[1]Adapted with permission from *The Sanford Guide to Antimicrobial Therapy,* Antimicrobial Therapy, Inc., 1997.
[2]Abbreviations: MDR, multidrug resistant; INH, isoniazid; RIF, rifampin; PZA, pyrazinamide; SM, streptomycin; ETB, ethambutol; DC, discontinue.

sis can develop resistance. It can take a long time for the patient to become noninfective or for the disease to be contained. These factors are why DOT was introduced. Some experts advocate that DOT should be used in all patients. However, this would be an expensive burden on the public health system. Most physicians use DOT for patients who have a history of noncompliance, risk factors for noncompliance such as substance abuse, and multidrug-resistant TB.

B. Monitoring During Treatment. While treating patients for tuberculosis, clinicians should monitor for clearing of the organism and for side effects of the medication. Before treatment is begun, laboratory tests of liver and renal functions should be performed and a baseline blood count obtained. If a patient is starting on pyrazinamide, a baseline uric acid level should be established. If a patient is to be treated with ethambutol, visual acuity and red-green color perception should be checked because this drug is known to produce optic neuritis. Ethambutol should not be used in children who are too young to report vision changes (Table 61–3).

C. Follow-up. Monthly follow-up should be done to check for symptoms of toxicity or disease progression. The patient with TB (pulmonary or extrapulmonary) should have a follow-up sputum monthly until the *M tuberculosis* culture is negative. Successful drug therapy using a combination regimen should eradicate the TB bacillus from the sputum of

Table 61–3. Side effects of anti-TB drugs.[1]

Anti-TB Drug	Major Side Effects	Major Drug Interactions
Ethambutol	• Optic neuritis	None noted in the PDR
Isoniazid	• Hepatitis • Peripheral neuropathy (prevent by co-administering pyridoxime)	• Inhibits some cytochrome P-450 enzymes • Warfarin (potentiation) • Benzodiazepines (potentiation) • Theophylline (potentiation)
Pyrazinamide	• Arthralgia • Hyperuricemia	None noted by the PDR
Rifampin	• Elevated liver function tests • Flulike syndrome • Discoloration of secretions which stain	• Induces cytochrome P-450 system • Inhibits effects of oral contraceptives, quinidine, corticosteroids, warfarin, methadone, digoxin, and oral hypoglycemics
Streptomycin	• Ototoxicity	• Potentiates the action of neuromuscular blocking agents

[1]Adapted with permission from *Physicians Desk Reference,* Medical Economics Co., Inc., 1997, and *The Sanford Guide to Antimicrobial Therapy,* Antimicrobial Therapy, Inc., 1997.

BOX 61–4

Control of *Mycobacterium* TB

Prophylactic Measures	• Preventative therapy for PPD-positive patients and known household contacts • See Table 61–5 for preventative therapy
Isolation Precautions	• Negative pressure room for patient with pulmonary TB until AFB sputum smear quantifications are significantly decreased • Masks for health care workers are of unproven efficacy

~ 85% of patients in 2 months and ~ 100% of patients within 6 months. It is therefore important to obtain a sputum TB culture after the first 2–3 months of treatment and again after 6 months of treatment to document the negative cultures. If organisms are still present in the sputum after 3 months of treatment, patients should be evaluated for noncompliance, poor absorption of medications, or resistance of organisms. These patients should be referred to a tuberculosis specialist, as should patients for whom therapy has failed, patients with known drug-resistant organisms, and patients with complicated drug toxicities secondary to the treatment regimen.

Prevention & Control

The key to prevention and control of TB centers on preventing exposure and, if infection occurs, preventing disease progression (Box 61–4). It is important to prevent exposure of the surrounding population to a patient with active tuberculosis. Thus isolation of patients with suspected TB is critical. Isolation can be achieved at home, if the patient lives alone, or in a special room in the hospital. Isolation rooms should have negative pressure and have six exchanges of air per hour with no recirculation of that air within the hospital. These rooms also should have ultraviolet lights to kill the bacilli in that room. Any patient with a cough and an infiltrate consistent with TB on a chest x-ray should always be isolated. Before a patient can be removed from isolation, three negative sputum AFB smears should be obtained. If the patient's disease is TB, the patient can be removed from isolation when the sputum AFB smear quantification decreases significantly (ie, 4+ to 1+). Masks have been a mainstay in preventing infection in health care workers, but efficacy remains unproven. The bacillus is spread from an infected patient by way of airborne droplets with active pulmonary disease only. Extrapulmonary TB is not contagious except when health care workers directly handle infected specimens (see below).

Prevention of disease in patients exposed to tuberculosis is important. It is accomplished by preventive therapy with INH. Patients who are at risk of infection have either a positive PPD, a history of exposure such as household contacts with a patient who has active TB, or both. A patient with a positive PPD test should

Table 61–4. Preventive therapy for tuberculosis infection.[1]

Tuberculin Reaction Classification	Persons Recommended for Preventive Therapy

≥5 mm is positive if high risk
  • Known or suspected HIV infection including injection drug users
  • Close contacts of active cases
  • Chest radiograph suggests previous inactive tuberculosis
	All persons regardless of age

≥10 mm is positive if intermediate risk
  • HIV-negative injection drug users
  • Immunosuppressive illness or therapy (diabetic, renal failure, hematologic malignancy, rapid weight loss illness, prolonged prednisone use >15 mg/d)
  • Immigrants from high-prevalence countries
  • Residents of long-term care or correctional facilities
  • Locally identified high-prevalence groups (migrant workers, homeless, high-risk racial or ethnic groups)
  • Children ≤4 years old
	All persons regardless of age
	All persons regardless of age
	
	Only if <35 years old
	Only if <35 years old
	
	Only if <35 years old

≥15 mm is positive if no known risk	Only if <35 years old

New converters on serial testing
  • ≥10 mm increase if <35 years old
  • ≥15 mm increase if ≥35 years old
	
	All persons
	All persons

PPD negative but high risk
  • Anergic HIV-infected persons
  • High-risk contacts of active cases
	
	All persons
	Treat until repeat PPD is negative 12 weeks later

[1]Adapted with permission from *Medical Knowledge Self Assessment Plan 11,* American College of Physicians, 1997.

Table 61–5. Prophylaxis for drug-resistant *M tuberculosis.*[1,2]

Resistance	Prophylaxis Therapy	
	First Option	**Other Options**
INH-Resistant Organisms	• RIF, 600 mg/d orally for 6–12 months • Children (<4 years), RIF + INH for 9 mo	• ETB + RIF daily × 6–12 mo • PZA + RIF daily × 2 mo; then INH + RIF daily until sensitivities are known (if index case is INH resistant, DC INH & continue RIF × 9 mo)
INH + RIF-Resistant Organisms	• PZA (25–30 mg/kg/d orally) + ETB (15–25 mg/kg/d orally) for 6 mo (if HIV positive, treat for 12 mo)	• PZA + ciprofloxacin (750 mg orally twice a day) or ofloxacin (400 mg orally twice a day) for 6–12 mo

[1]Adapted with permission from JP Sanford, ed., *The Sanford Guide to Antimicrobial Therapy,* Antimicrobial Therapy, Inc., 1997.
[2]Abbreviations: INH, isoniazid; RIF, rifampin; PZA, pyrazinamide; SM, streptomycin; ETB, ethambutol; DC, discontinue.

have a screening chest x-ray. If signs of active disease are present, a screening sputum evaluation should be done. The risk of having infection is extremely high in children who are the household contacts. Known exposed children < 6 years of age should have a chest x-ray done even if the PPD is negative, since these children can have a severe course if active TB is left untreated. If a household contact's first PPD is negative, another PPD should be placed in 8–12 weeks (which, if the patient has been truly exposed, should be positive at this time). If the second PPD is negative, preventative therapy can be stopped if the patient is no longer in danger of being exposed.

Prevention Among Health Care Workers

Health care workers should have regular PPD checks unless they have a history of PPD positivity. Most centers recommend yearly PPDs. PPDs should be placed on anyone who is a household contact of a patient with active TB or anyone who has had close contact with an active case of TB. Also, patients who are in extended-care facilities or correctional facilities should have a PPD at the time of initial placement because of the high risk of infecting a large group of people.

Patients who qualify for preventative therapy should receive INH, 300 mg by mouth daily for a minimum of 6 months (Table 61–4). If the patient has radiographic evidence of previous tuberculosis, he or she should be treated with INH for 12 months. Children should be given a dose of INH of 10 mg/kg/d to a maximal dose of ≤ 300 mg/d. People receiving INH for prevention should be monitored monthly for signs of INH toxicity. Patients with symptoms of hepatitis,

such as gastrointestinal complaints, jaundice, anorexia, or some combination of these symptoms, should have liver function tests performed. If those tests are abnormal, INH should be stopped. Patients with an increased risk of INH hepatitis should have their liver function checked regularly. These patients include those > 35 years of age, alcohol users, and those with preexisting liver disease. INH therapy should not be given to patients with active liver disease or to pregnant women. It is important to remember that patients with radiographic evidence of tuberculosis must be first evaluated for active disease before beginning preventative treatment.

If a person has a high risk of exposure to INH- or rifampin-resistant organisms, the data for the efficacy of preventative therapy are limited. If the risk of infection with INH-resistant organisms is high and the patient would be unable to tolerate the disease, rifampin should be used. If the patient was exposed to INH- and rifampin-resistant organisms, a multidrug preventive therapy should be used. Each case must be assessed individually (Table 61–5).

BCG vaccination has been used in some countries to improve the ability of a person who is acutely infected with *Mycobacterium* TB to contain the infection. The reported effectiveness of BCG vaccination varies, and the indications for use are limited. In the United States, the only people who might benefit from a BCG vaccination could be people who are repeatedly exposed to TB. Because BCG will cause a PPD test to be positive, it can complicate the diagnosis of a TB infection. However, the history of a BCG vaccination should be ignored when a PPD is placed, and the patient should be treated based on the guidelines in Table 61–4 or the patient's symptoms of active disease.

REFERENCES

American College of Physicians: Medical Knowledge Self Assessment Plan 11, 1997.

Arky R: *Physicians Desk Reference.* Medical Economics Co, 1997.

Barnes PF: Rapid diagnostic tests for tuberculosis. Am J Resp Crit Care Med 1997;155:1497.

Brahmer JR, Small PM: Tuberculosis and nontuberculous mycobacterial infections. In Stein JH: *Textbook of Internal Medicine,* 5th ed. Mosby Yearbook, 1998.

Department of Health and Human Services: Tuberculosis morbidity—United States, 1994. Morbid Mortal Weekly Rep 1995;44:387.

Hopewell PC: Tuberculosis in persons with human immunodeficiency virus infection. In MA Sande, PA Volberding: *The Medical Management of AIDS,* 5th ed. Saunders, 1997.

Long SS (editor): *Mycobacterium tuberculosis.* In *Principles and Practice of Pediatric Infectious Diseases,* Churchill Livingstone, 1997, p. 881.

Sanford JP (editor): *The Sanford Guide to Antimicrobial Therapy,* Antimicrobial Therapy, Inc., 1997.

Other Mycobacteria

62

Julie Brahmer, MD, Yenjean Hwang, MD & Merle A. Sande, MD

Essentials of Diagnosis

- Demonstration of the acid-fast bacillus.
- Infections more common in immunocompromised hosts.
- Infections mainly pulmonary or soft tissue.

General Considerations

The increasingly relative importance of the atypical mycobacteria, many of which are ubiquitous in the environment, was recognized with the decline in tuberculous disease. Generally, atypical mycobacteria are unusual causes of disease in patients who are immunocompetent but can in immunocompromised hosts such as AIDS and cancer patients. Most infections caused by atypical mycobacteria are skin and soft tissue abscesses, sometimes following pulmonary infection or implantation of prosthetic devices. There have been a few reports of epidemics of iatrogenic infection with atypical mycobacteria, associated with injection of contaminated materials.

A. Epidemiology. Atypical mycobacteria may account for 35% of isolations of potentially pathogenic mycobacteria in the United States; the rate of infection from atypical mycobacteria, however, ranges from 0.5% to 30% of all infections caused by mycobacteria. An estimated 3 million of the 6 million cases of leprosy worldwide remain untreated.

B. Microbiology. The atypical mycobacteria are classified into four groups according to their growth characteristics, as well as pigment production in culture. Runyon class I includes organisms such as *Mycobacterium kansasii,* which are characterized by pigment production upon exposure to light (photochromogens). Runyon class II, including *Mycobacterium scrofulaceum,* are scotochromogens, which produce pigment in the light or in the dark. Runyon class III includes nonpigment producers (nonchromogens) such as *Mycobacterium avium* complex (MAC). Runyon class IV organisms, such as *Mycobacterium abscessus,* are characterized by rapid growth in culture, on the order of 2–30 days, as compared with the other mycobacteria, which often take 6–8 weeks to cultivate.

C. Pathogenesis. Sources of the atypical mycobacteria include soil, water, and domestic and wild animals (see Table 62–1 for habitats of common medically important mycobacteria). Most infections are acquired through aspiration or inoculation of atypical mycobacteria from the environment. Incubation periods are very long, averaging 5 years. Affected patients are of all age groups, but the peak age of onset is in young adults; children are rarely affected.

Pulmonary disease often results from inhalation of organisms, whereas direct inoculation of the organism or a foreign body contaminated with the organism results in soft-tissue disease. Ingestion of organisms can result in gastrointestinal involvement. Person-to-person transmission does not usually occur, with the exception of *Mycobacterium leprae,* which is transmitted by nasal droplets, although there is some evidence that transmission may occur by soil. Disseminated disease does not usually occur except in immunocompromised hosts.

CLINICAL SYNDROMES

MYCOBACTERIUM AVIUM COMPLEX (DISSEMINATED & PULMONARY DISEASE)

M avium is the most common atypical mycobacterium to cause disease in humans. In immunocompetent patients, *M avium* can cause pulmonary disease (Box 62–1). It is the most common pulmonary pathogen of all the atypical mycobacteria. There are several risk factors for pulmonary *M avium* infection besides AIDS. Patients with underlying pulmonary disease, those who have had a gastrectomy, and those with cystic fibrosis can develop pulmonary infection. Pulmonary disease can also develop in a subgroup of women without pulmonary disease but with mitral valve prolapse, pectus excavatum, and thoracic scoliosis.

In immunocompromised patients such as those with AIDS who have a CD4 lymphocyte count of < 100, *M avium* can cause osteomyelitis, peritonitis, oral lesions, and disseminated disease (Box 62–2). It may also cause colonization without disease in these patients. In children with AIDS, MAC is also common, occurring in 24% of children with a CD4 count

Table 62–1. Mycobacterium species, their habitats, and the diseases they cause.[1]

Mycobacterium species	Habitat	Common Diseases in Humans
Tuberculosis complex		
M tuberculosis	• Humans	• Bronchopulmonary
M bovis	• Humans, cattle	• Soft tissue & gastrointestinal tract
Photochromogens		
M kansasii	• Water, cattle	• Skeletal
M marinum	• Fish, water	• Skin and soft tissue
M simiae	• Primates	• Bronchopulmonary
M asiaticum	• Primates	• Pulmonary (rare)
Scotochromogens		
M scrofulaceum	• Soil, water, foodstuffs	• Lymphadenitis
M szulgai	• Unknown	• Bronchopulmonary
M gordonae	• Water	• Pulmonary (rare)
M flavescens	• Soil, water	• Pulmonary (rare)
M xenopi	• Water	• Bronchopulmonary
Nonchromogens		
M avium-intracellulare	• Soil, water, swine, cattle, birds	• Pulmonary, lymphadenitis, disseminated
M ulcerans	• Unknown	• Skin and soft tissue
M gastri	• Soil, water	• Pulmonary (rare)
M terrae	• Soil, water	• Pulmonary (rare)
Rapid growers		
M fortuitum	• Soil, water, animals, marine life	• Skin, soft tissue, disseminated
M abscessus	• Soil, water, animals, marine life	• Skin, soft tissue, disseminated, skeletal
M chelonae	• Soil, water, animals, marine life	• Skin, soft tissue, disseminated, skeletal
M smegmatis	• Moist surfaces, urogenital flora	• Pulmonary (rare)
M leprae	• Humans, nine-branded armadillos	• Skin, soft tissue, disseminated (rare)

[1]Adapted from Long SS (editor): *Principles and Practice of Pediatric Infectious Diseases,* Churchill Livingstone, 1997.

of < 100. Patients with underlying malignancies and defects of cell-mediated immunity and those on chronic steroids or cytotoxic chemotherapy are also susceptible.

M avium can cause other disease syndromes, including skeletal infections, lymphadenitis, deep subcutaneous nodules, fasciitis, panniculitis, and synovitis. In children, it can cause superficial lymphadenitis and cutaneous disease such as ulcers, abscesses, or plaques, and intracerebral infection has been reported.

Clinical Findings

A. Signs and Symptoms. Patients with pulmonary disease caused by *M avium* infection can present with a productive cough, fever, weight loss, and,

less commonly, hemoptysis (Table 62–2). Symptoms of disseminated disease are constitutional, such as fever, weight loss, and malaise. MAC very rarely causes pneumonia in AIDS patients. Hepatosplenomegaly and adenopathy can be noted by physical exam. Gastrointestinal involvement in AIDS patients can present with three different syndromes, including chronic diarrhea and abdominal pain, chronic malabsorption, and extrabiliary obstructive jaundice secondary to periportal lymphadenopathy. MAC should be suspected in AIDS patients who exhibit all of the following signs or symptoms: CD4 counts of < 100, fever lasting for > 30 days, a hematocrit of < 30%, and an albumin concentration of < 3.0 mg/dL.

B. Imaging. MAC involving the lung can classi-

BOX 62–1

MAC in Immunocompetent Patients

	Children	Adults
More Common	• Superficial lymphadenitis • Cutaneous ulcers, abscesses and plaques	• Colonization • Pulmonary infection—productive cough hemoptysis in < 25%, fever and weight loss in 33%
Less Common	• Pulmonary • Disseminated disease	• Cutaneous lesions • Lymphadenitis • Disseminated disease

BOX 62-2

MAC in AIDS Patients (CD4 < 100)

	Children	Adults
More Common	• Disseminated disease • Pulmonary disease	• Colonization-gastrointestinal and respiratory tracts • Fever, drenching night sweats, weight loss, diarrhea, abdominal pain, anorexia, hepatosplenomegaly, adenopathy, and anemia
Less Common	• Isolated lymphadenitis • Isolated cutaneous lesions	• Pulmonary infection • Osteomyelitis, peritonitis, oral lesions, appendicitis

cally cause pulmonary infiltrates seen on chest x-ray in the upper lobes or disseminated. Chest x-ray findings in these patients can vary from small thin-walled cavities to lobar infiltrates and isolated nodules. In older women, x-ray abnormalities include fibronodular and interstitial abnormalities with upper-lobe predominance. Chest x-rays can mimic reactivation tuberculosis with cavitation.

MYCOBACTERIUM LEPRAE (LEPROSY)

M leprae is the etiologic agent of Hansen's Disease or leprosy. Although not a common problem in the United States, it is in other parts of the world. With the advent of effective antimicrobial agents, the number of cases of leprosy worldwide has fallen from 12 million in 1982 to 6 million in 1991. It remains a significant problem, however, because the incidence of new cases has not yet declined, and much of the affected population lives in areas where effective medical treatment is difficult to obtain. Leprosy is endemic in Asia, Africa, Latin America, and the Pacific.

In the United States, Canada, and Europe, there are

Table 62–2. Clinical findings in *Mycobacterium avium* complex infection.[1]

Acid-fast bacillus, nonphotochromogen
Slow grower (10–21 days) at 36 ° C
CXR findings vary from small thin-walled cavities to lobar in filtrates and isolated nodules.
Diagnosis clinically:
• Presence of pulmonary cavities not attributable to another disease and 2 or more positive sputum or bronchial wash specimens with moderate to heavy growth of MAC
• Infiltrate present but no cavities present, with failure of sputum cultures to convert to negative with either pulmonary toilet or 2 weeks of specific antimicrobial therapy
• Lung biopsy with histological confirmation and positive culture
• One positive blood culture
• Isolation of MAC from any other sterile body site
• Positive bone marrow, lymph node, or liver biopsy

[1]For clinical findings in AIDS patients, see Box 62–7.

virtually no cases of leprosy except those that are imported from areas where leprosy is endemic. Risk factors for acquisition of leprosy in endemic areas include poverty and rural residence. However, even in endemic areas, the distribution of leprosy can vary greatly, sometimes with significant differences in incidence of leprosy in adjacent villages. In North America, armadillo contact has been reported as a risk factor for acquisition. Other risk factors that have been reported in certain populations are the human leukocyte antigens HLA-DR3 (with the tuberculoid or paucibacillary form of disease) and HLA-MTI (with the lepromatous or multibacillary form of disease). Interestingly, the proportions of the lepromatous and tuberculoid types of leprosy (Box 62–3) vary geographically; in Mexico, 90% are lepromatous, whereas, in India and Africa, 90% are tuberculoid.

Clinical Findings

A. Signs and Symptoms. The manifestations of leprosy involve the skin, upper respiratory system, peripheral nerves, and, in men, testes (Table 62–3). The peripheral neuropathy that is seen in leprosy results in impaired sensation of fine touch, temperature, and pain, whereas proprioception and vibratory sensation are intact. Such loss of sensation leads to recurrent trauma and ulceration in the extremities. For example, loss of sensation in the feet can lead to chronic nonhealing ulcers, especially at the metatarsal heads. Large nerve trunks may also be affected. A common nerve trunk that is affected in leprosy is the ulnar nerve at the elbow, which results in clawing of the fourth and fifth digits of the hand, dorsal interosseus muscle atrophy, and loss of sensation in the hand along the ulnar nerve distribution.

The lepromatous or multibacillary form of leprosy is characterized by symmetric skin nodules, plaques, and thickened dermis. Usually, the ear lobes and extremities are affected. Diffuse lepromatosis is seen usually in patients from Mexico, who show areas of diffuse dermal infiltration and no focal lesions. Untreated, lepromatous leprosy results in a high level of continuous bacteremia. Peripheral neuropathy is

BOX 62-3

Mycobacterium leprae Syndromes

Lepromatous Forms	Tuberculoid Forms
• Symmetrical skin plaques, nodules, or thickened dermis, usually on cooler parts of the body • Infiltration of upper respiratory system and nasal cartilage, resulting in "saddle nose" deformity • Symmetric and generalized peripheral neuropathy • Diffuse lepromatosis seen in Mexican patients, diffuse dermal infiltration without focal lesions • Normal-looking skin will show organisms in clumps, foam cells in deep dermis, and granulomas in liver, spleen, and lymph nodes	• Few hypopigmented anesthetic macules with distinct elevated and erythematous borders • Large and asymmetric peripheral nerve involvement • Neural leprosy causes large functionally impaired nerve trunks without skin lesions • Lesions and rims should be biopsied (normal-looking skin will not have abnormalities); granulomas with invasion and destruction of dermal nerves

symmetric and generalized. There is a characteristic deformity associated with this type of leprosy, "saddle-nose deformity," which occurs because of infiltration of the upper respiratory system and nasal cartilage. Other upper respiratory system effects include chronic nasal congestion and epistaxis.

The tuberculoid, or paucibacillary, form of leprosy is characterized by one or few hypopigmented macules, which are anesthetic and variable in size. These macules have distinct and elevated borders. Peripheral neuropathy in this form of leprosy is usually asymmetric and affects large nerves. Neural leprosy is characterized by functional impairment of large nerve trunks without skin lesions. The upper respiratory system is not involved.

B. Laboratory Findings. *M leprae* is an acid-fast, Gram-stain-variable bacillus. Its size varies from 1 to 8 μm long by 0.3 to 0.5 μm wide. It cannot be distinguished morphologically from other mycobacteria. *M leprae*'s distinguishing characteristics include loss of acid fastness by pyridine extraction, presence of dopa-oxidase activity, and a doubling time of 12 days in the mouse footpad. It is an obligate intracellular parasite but can remain viable outside its natural hosts, i.e. humans and the nine-banded armadillo, for several days. Doubling time of the bacillus is very slow, but, by the time of diagnosis in a lepromatous patient, the number of bacilli present, 10^{15}, is enormous, greater than any human bacterial infectious agent. *M leprae* has a predilection

for cooler areas of the body because it grows best at temperatures under 37 °C, hence its characteristic effects on extremities, the nose, and the pinna of the ears.

C. Complications. Leprosy patients may develop Lepra type 1 reaction (downgrading and reversal reactions), Lepra type 2 reaction (erythema nodosum leprosum), or a reaction called Lucio's reaction. Lepra type 1 reactions usually occur in borderline leprosy patients, before therapy (downgrading reaction) or after initiation of therapy (reversal reaction). The reaction consists of inflammation within previous skin lesions, new multiple-satellite maculopapular skin lesions, neuritis, and low-grade fever. Irreversible nerve damage can occur unless therapy with corticosteroids is started promptly. The recommended treatment is prednisone, 40–60 mg daily, tapered over 2–3 months. Lepra type 2 reactions affect nearly half of lepromatous patients, usually within 2 years of instituting antimicrobial therapy. Painful papules on the extensor surface of extremities, neuritis, fever, uveitis, lymphadenitis, orchitis, and glomerulonephritis can occur. Treatment of erythema nodosum leprosum requires a short course of corticosteroids. Lucio's reaction is seen in patients with diffuse lepromatosis and consists of shallow recurrent ulcerations on the lower extremities. Occasionally, the lesions can be generalized, and, in that case, Lucio's reaction can be fatal.

Table 62–3. Clinical findings in *Mycobacterium leprae* infection.

- Acid-fast bacillus, Gram stain variable
- Presence of dopa-oxidase activity, loss of acid fastness by pyridine extraction
- Multiplies in mouse foot with doubling time of 12 d
- Hematoxylin and eosin stain of skin biopsy shows organisms; sometimes silver stain positive

MYCOBACTERIUM KANSASII (CHRONIC PULMONARY INFECTION)

M kansasii is the most common nontuberculous mycobacterium after MAC to be isolated in tertiary care centers. *M kansasii* is a pathogen worldwide, and in the United States the incidence is highest in the Midwest and Southwest. It commonly affects individuals in certain occupations, such as miners, welders, and sandblasters. Patients with underlying pulmonary pathology can be infected also. However, *M kansasii* rarely causes disease in children. Children who are affected tend to be immunocompetent and without an underlying pulmonary disease.

Clinical Findings

The most common clinical syndrome caused by *M kansasii* is a chronic pulmonary infection that resembles pulmonary tuberculosis.

A. Signs and Symptoms. Symptoms of infection are nonspecific and can include cough, fatigue, and shortness of breath. Uncommonly, *M kansasii* can cause local lymphadenitis, a skin infection that resembles sporotrichosis. With disseminated infections, skin lesions can be present, such as erythema nodosum, erythema multiforme, and induration.

In AIDS patients, *M kansasii* is the second most common infection caused by atypical mycobacterium. It tends to produce a disseminated disease similar to MAC. *M kansasii*-disseminated disease was present at the time of the index AIDS diagnosis in 0.2% of patients. *M kansasii* can also produce isolated oral ulcers, osteomyelitis, soft tissue infections, tenosynovitis, and arthritis. It may also produce necrotizing pulmonary nodules.

B. Laboratory Findings. Nonspecific.

C. Imaging. On chest x-ray, *M kansasii* is difficult to distinguish from *M tuberculosis*. In children, mediastinal and hilar lymph nodes are commonly enlarged.

D. Differential Diagnosis. Atypical mycobacterium should be suspected if a patient does not respond to conventional therapy for *M tuberculosis*.

MYCOBACTERIUM SCROFULACEUM (LYMPHADENITIS)

M scrofulaceum is a ubiquitous scotochromogenic mycobacterium that commonly exists in soil and water and contaminates reagents and foodstuffs. It readily colonizes respiratory secretions of healthy children and adults. The most common clinically evident disease in humans is lymphadenitis, which is commonly seen in children < 12 years old.

Clinical Findings

A. Signs and Symptoms. The clinical presentation is a single node or cluster of nodes in the submandibular area. The nodes slowly enlarge over weeks. The patient experiences very few local or systemic symptoms except for mild lymph node tenderness on palpation. Over weeks to months, if left untreated, the infection comes to the surface, ruptures, and forms a draining sinus, which then calcifies.

B. Laboratory Findings. Nonspecific.

MYCOBACTERIUM BOVIS (TUBERCULOSIS IN ANIMALS)

M bovis is considered to be part of the *M tuberculosis* complex. It is a nonchromogen and generally takes 21–40 days to isolate in culture. Its natural reservoir is humans and cattle, and it generally causes tuberculosis in cattle, goats, cats, dogs, primates, and other wildlife. It is rarely a cause of tuberculosis in humans, although there are reports of it causing 3% of the tuberculosis cases in certain places such as San Diego, California. An attenuated strain of *M bovis* is used for bacille Calmette-Guérin (BCG) vaccine. Transmission of the organism occurs by inhalation of aerosol or by direct inoculation. Transmission by ingestion of contaminated milk from infected cows did occur prior to routine pasteurization. Clinical syndromes associated with *M bovis* include soft tissue infection. Soft tissue infection has been reported after accidental self-inoculation with BCG by a health care worker.

Clinical Findings

M bovis will cause pulmonary infection indistinguishable from that caused by *M tuberculosis*. Bacteremia, mycotic aortic aneurysm, vertebral osteomyelitis, and granulomatous hepatitis have been reported as complications of bladder instillation of BCG for the treatment of bladder cancer.

A. Laboratory Findings. Nonspecific.

MYCOBACTERIUM MARINUM (CLASSIC FISH TANK GRANULOMA)

M marinum is an acid-fast bacillus that is in Runyon class I, the photochromogens. It grows optimally at 32 °C and inhabits water and marine organisms. Infection of humans generally occurs after a trauma that takes place in water (eg, fish spines, nips by crustaceans); it can be acquired through open skin that comes into contact with swimming pools, aquariums, domestic fish tanks, or stagnant bodies of water.

Clinical Findings

A. Signs and Symptoms. The typical lesions of *M marinum* infection, which can resemble cutaneous sporotrichosis, are small papules on the extremities that enlarge, turn blue-purple, and then suppurate and ulcerate. Dissemination is rare, although it can occur in immunocompromised hosts.

B. Laboratory Findings. A skin biopsy should be taken for culture. Pathology shows granulomatous inflammation, but it is rare to find acid-fast bacilli on stain.

C. Differential Diagnosis. *M marinum* can resemble sporotrichosis.

Diagnosis

The diagnosis of atypical mycobacterial infections

may be difficult to make with certainty. It is often unclear whether the presence of an atypical mycobacterium in a clinical specimen indicates infection or colonization. The diagnosis of an infection with mycobacteria should be made only in the presence of an illness associated with mycobacteria and when other causes of disease have been excluded. Another clue that helps distinguish colonization from infection is the quantity of growth in culture. Heavy growth of one organism in culture is more suggestive of infection than of colonization; light growth is suggestive of colonization, unless the organism was isolated from a normally sterile body fluid. It is often helpful to notify the microbiology laboratory when infection with an atypical mycobacterium is suspected, because the nontuberculous mycobacteria often have very specialized culture requirements.

Experience is needed for accurate interpretation of the appearance of mycobacteria in stained specimens. Typically, fluorochrome, Kinyoun, and Ziehl-Neelsen stains are used. Cultures are incubated at 37 °C in 10% carbon dioxide and 90% air, usually for ≥ 6–8 weeks. (More detailed information regarding laboratory diagnosis can be found in a standard microbiology text.) Typically, detection of growth in culture can be made within 2 weeks, but identification and speciation may take ≤ 2–4 weeks. Susceptibility testing has not been standardized, and all significant isolates need to be tested for antibiotic susceptibility. However, susceptibility to an antibiotic in vitro has not been directly correlated to clinical efficacy.

Diagnosis of MAC, *M bovis,* and *M marinum* infections is determined by acid-fast bacillus smear and culturing from the infected tissue. Diagnosis of *M scrofulaceum* infection is made by identification of granulomatous inflammation in skin biopsy and isolation of the organism from culture. Diagnosis of *M kansasii* infection is difficult, especially since there can be a concurrent infection with *M tuberculosis.*

Diagnosis of leprosy depends on clinical information as well as biopsy of affected dermis; viable organisms stain brightly and uniformly (see Table 62–3). Nonviable organisms stain in an irregular manner. A skin biopsy taken from a patient with suspected leprosy should be stained with hematoxylin and eosin, as well as with Fite stain for acid fastness.

The two polar forms of leprosy are the lepromatous, or multibacillary, and the tuberculoid, or paucibacillary (see Box 62–3 for features of both). Most patients will have intermediate forms. In lepromatous patients, skin biopsies should be taken at sites of skin lesions, but normal looking skin will also have pathologic changes. Lesions will show many bacilli in clumps and foam cells loaded with bacilli in the dermis. Granulomatous changes may be seen in the liver, spleen, and lymph nodes. In tuberculoid patients, biopsies should be done only at sites of lesions because biopsies of normal appearing skin will be nondiagnostic. Skin biopsies from tuberculoid patients will show few or no organisms but will show granulomas of epithelial cells, lymphocytes, and foreign-body giant cells near dermal appendages, especially dermal nerves. The pathognomic lesion for tuberculoid leprosy is acute granulomatous invasion and destruction of dermal nerves. Most patients, however, have intermediate, or borderline, forms of leprosy, and their biopsies will show a mixture of findings.

An intradermal skin test is available that uses heat-killed *M leprae.* However, use of the skin test to make the diagnosis of leprosy is unreliable. Although the skin test will be positive in tuberculoid patients, treated lepromatous patients and unaffected individuals in endemic areas will show positive results as well. Lepromatous patients will be anergic specifically to *M leprae* but will have a normal response to intradermal recall antigens, such as purified protein derivative. Various *M leprae* lipid and carbohydrate constituents are believed to impair macrophage and T-lymphocyte function specifically against *M leprae.* There also seems to be an increase in the number of T-suppressor cells. Cytokines such as interleukin 2 (IL-2), interferon γ (IFN-γ), IL-4, IL-5, and IL-10 are also thought to play a role in expression of disease.

Treatment of Atypical Mycobacterial Infections

MAC Infection. Treatment of pulmonary disease, disseminated disease, subcutaneous infections, and bone infections in immunocompetent patients consists of a regimen of three drugs (Box 62–4). Clarithromycin at a dose of 500 mg by mouth two times a day is given with ethambutol at a dose of 15–25 mg per kg by mouth every day. These two drugs are also then given with rifabutin, 300 mg by mouth every day for ≤ 24 months. If there is an isolated lung lesion, surgical removal of the nodule is a treatment option. Other second-line drugs include azithromycin, clofazimine, ciprofloxacin, and amikacin. The regimen used should be tailored to in vitro susceptibility tests. Patients with pulmonary disease should have sputum samples tested every month during the course of treatment. In 80–90% of patients, the sputum should convert to negative in 1–2 months. The therapy should be extended for 12 months after the sputum conversion.

HIV-positive patients with disease can be treated with a three-drug regimen that includes clarithromycin or azithromycin, ethambutol, and/or rifabutin (Box 62–5). An alternative regimen includes clarithromycin or azithromycin, ethambutol, plus/minus rifabutin and one of the following: ciprofloxacin, ofloxacin, or amikacin. A recent study of treatment regimens showed that therapy with rifabutin, ethambutol, and clarithromycin resulted in a longer mean survival than did therapy with rifampin, ethambutol, clofazimine, and ciprofloxacin. The efficacy of these regimens in children with HIV infection has not been well established.

BOX 62-4

Treatment of MAC in Immunocompetent Patients

	Adults	Children
First Choice	Clarithromycin 500 mg PO twice daily + ethambutol 15–25 mg/kg PO + rifabutin 300 mg PO once daily for as many as 24 months, treat for at least 12 months after sputum conversion; surgical excision if one isolated pulmonary nodule	Clarithromycin, 7.5 mg/kg PO twice daily (max. dose 500 mg/dose) in children > 6 months old + ethambutol, 15 mg/kg/d as a single dose in children > 13 years old + rifabutin
Second Choice	Rifampin + ethambutol + clofazamine + ciprofloxacin, 750 mg PO twice daily	

Once immunosuppressed patients with AIDS are treated, they must be placed on lifelong suppressive therapy that includes clarithromycin or azithromycin plus ethambutol. Alternative drugs include clarithromycin or azithromycin alone or rifabutin.

AIDS patients who do not have documented active MAC disease and whose CD4 count is < 100 may be placed on primary prophylactic therapy, which consists of a single drug (Box 62–6). Those drugs used in primary prophylaxis are clarithromycin, azithromycin, or rifabutin. Clarithromycin reduces the MAC infection rate by 68% and was associated with a 38% mortality rate as compared with 47% with placebo.

M leprae Infection. Leprosy generally requires a long duration of treatment, and compliance is a major problem. Lepromatous leprosy requires a longer treatment time course than tuberculoid leprosy because of the greater number of organisms involved. Currently, the recommended treatment is dapsone and rifampin for 6 months for tuberculoid leprosy (Box 62–7). Dapsone alone is not recommended because of reports of emerging resistance. For lepromatous leprosy, dapsone with rifampin or clofazimine for 24 months is recommended. Nonetheless, there have been reports of relapses even after such long courses of treatment. Other agents such as ethionamide, prothionamide, the aminoglycosides, minocycline, clarithromycin, and the fluoroquinolones may also prove to be beneficial.

M kansasii Infection. Response to antimycobacterial therapy tends to be poor, but there have been reports of clinical responses. Treatment must be tailored to each individual patient depending on the in vitro sensitivities of *M kansasii* and whether immunosuppression is present. Treatment should consist of a three- to five-drug regimen depending on sensitivities. A common regimen for *M kansasii* includes rifampin (10 mg/kg/d for a maximum of 400

BOX 62-5

Treatment of MAC in AIDS patients

First Choice	Same regimen as adult treatment of MAC in immunocompetent patients. May substitue azithromycin (500 mg once daily) for clarithromycin
Second Choice	Clarithromycin or azithromycin + ethambutol + rifabutin + 1 or more of the following • Ciprofloxacin, 750 mg PO twice daily • Ofloxacin, 400 mg PO twice daily • Amikacin, (7.5–15 mg/kg) IV or IM
Pediatric Considerations	Treatment regimens for pediatric AIDS patients are not well established.

BOX 62-6

Control of MAC Infection in AIDS Patients

Prophylactic Measures	• Lifelong prophylaxis in AIDS patients with CD4 < 100: clarithromycin, 500 mg PO twice daily or azithromycin, 1200 mg PO weekly, or rifabutin, 300 mg PO once daily. • Secondary prophylaxis in AIDs patients after treatment of MAC disease: clarithromycin OR azithromycin PLUS ethambutol (15 mg/kg/d)
Isolation Precautions	• None

BOX 62-7

Treatment of *Mycobacterium leprae*

	Adults	Children
First Choice: Tuberculoid	Dapsone, 100 mg once daily unsupervised + rifampin, 600 mg once per month supervised for 6 months	Correspondingly lower dose
First Choice: Lepromatous	Dapsone, 100 mg once daily + clofazamine, 50 mg once daily unsupervised **OR** rifampin, 600 mg once daily + clofazamine, 300 mg every month supervised for 24 months	Correspondingly lower doses
Alternative Choice	Ethionamide, 250 mg once daily or prothionamide, 375 mg once daily in place of clofazamine; minocycline, clarithromycin, or fluoroquinolone reportedly bactericidal	

mg/d), isoniazid (5 mg/kg/d for a maximum of 300 mg/d), and ethambutol (15–25 mg/kg/d). Treatment should be continued for ~ 18 months and has been shown to have about a 90% response rate.

M kansasii has been shown to be sensitive in vitro to clarithromycin, erythromycin, amikacin, and the fluoroquinolones. These medications, along with sulfamethoxazole or bactrim, are second-line drugs. If lymphadenitis is present, the lymph node should be totally excised. There is no rationale for incision and drainage. In AIDS patients with disseminated disease, treatment should be extended for 15 months after cultures are negative. Treatment regimens in children have not been well established.

M scrofulaceum Infection. Antituberculosis drugs are not helpful. The treatment of choice is surgical excision of involved nodes. Clarithromycin may be useful in patients not responsive to excision.

M bovis Infection. Treatment of *M bovis* is the same as for *M tuberculosis,* although *M bovis* is uniformly resistant to pyrazinamide.

M marinum Infection. Treatment of *M marinum* infection consists of rifampin and ethambutol.

Prevention & Control of Atypical Mycobacterium Infection

No isolation measures are needed since the organisms are found in the environment. Prophylaxis is needed only in AIDS patients with MAC (see Box 62–6).

REFERENCES

Adal KA, Wispelwey B: *Mycobacterium avium* complex peritonitis in a patient with alcoholic liver disease. J Clin Gastroenterol 1996;22(3):245.

Atiyeh BS et al: Bacille Calmette-Guérin (BCG)-itis of the hand: a potential health hazard for health workers. Ann Plast Surg 1996;36(3):325.

Baron E, Peterson L, Finegold S: Mycobacteria, p 590. In Baron EJ, Peterson LR, Finegold SM: *Diagnostic Microbiology,* CV Mosby, 1993.

Beehek PW et al: Granulomatous hepatitis caused by bacillus Calmette-Guérin (BCG) infection after bladder instillation. Gut 1996;38(4)616.

Choudhri S et al: Clinical significance of nontuberculous mycobacteria isolates in a Canadian tertiary care center. Clin Infect Dis 1995;21:128.

Dankner WM et al: *Mycobacterium bovis* infections in San Diego: a clinicoepidemiologic study of 73 patients and a historical review of a forgotten pathogen. Medicine 1993;72:11.

Domingo P et al: Appendicitis due to *Mycobacterium avium* complex in a patient with AIDS. Arch Intern Med 1996;127(10):1114.

Garcia-Vivar ML et al: *Mycobacterium kansasii* septic arthritis in a patient with acquired immunodeficiency syndrome. Arthritis Rheum 1996;39(5):881.

Hellinger WC, Odenburg WA, Alvarez S: Vascular and other serious infections with *Mycobacterium bovis* after bacillus of Calmette-Guérin therapy for bladder cancer. South Med J 1995;88(12):1212.

Long SS (editor): *Principles and Practice of Pediatric Infectious Diseases,* Churchill Livingstone, 1997, p 904.

Mandell Gerald L (editor): *Mandell, Douglas and Bennett's Principles and Practice of Infectious Diseases,* 4th ed, Churchill Livingstone, 1995, p. 2264.

Morb Mortal Weekly Rep: Infection with *Mycobacterium abscessus* associated with intramuscular injection of adrenal cortex extract—Colorado and Wyoming, 1995–1996. 1996;45(33):713.

Nandwani R et al: *Mycobacterium kansasii* scalp abscesses in an AIDS patient. J Infect 1995;31(1):79.

Neusch R et al: Oral manifestation of disseminated *Mycobacterium kansasii* infection in a patient with AIDS. Dermatology 1996;192(2):183.

Noordeen SK: A look at world leprosy. Lepr Rev 1991;62:72.

Parent LJ et al: Disseminated *Mycobacterium marinum* infection and bacteremia in a child with severe combined immunodeficiency. Clin Infect Dis 1995;21(5):1325.

Patel S: Septic arthritis due to *Mycobacterium marinum.* J Rheum 1995;22(8):1607.

Pierce M et al: A randomized trial of clarithromycin as prophylaxis against disseminated *Mycobacterium avium* complex infection in patients with advanced acquired deficiency syndrome. N Engl J Med 1996;335(6):384.

Robinson P et al: Oral *Mycobacterium avium* complex infection in a patient with HIV-related disease, a case report. Oral Surg Oral Med Oral Pathol Oral Radiol Endod 1996;81(2):177.

Rozenblit A et al: Infected aortic aneurysm and vertebral osteomyelitis after intravesical bacillus Calmette-Guérin therapy. Am J Roentgenol 1996;167(3):711.

Sanford JP (editor): *The Sanford Guide to Antimicrobial Therapy,* Antimicrobial Therapy, Inc., 1997.

Shafran SD et al: A comparison of two regimens for the treatment of *Mycobacterium avium* complex bacteremia in AIDS: rifabutin, ethambutol, and clarithromycin versus rifampin, ethambutol, clofazimine, and ciprofloxacin. Canadian HIV Trials Network Protocol 010 Study Group. N Engl J Med 1996;335(6):377.

Thomas A et al. Relapses during long-term follow-up with drug-susceptible *M. leprae* among multibacillary leprosy patients treated with multidrug therapy regimens: case reports. Int J Lepr Other Mycobact Dis 1995;62(3):391.

Weingardt JP et al: Disseminated *Mycobacterium avium* complex presenting with osteomyelitis of the distal femur and proximal tibia. Skeletal Radiol 1996; 25 (2):193.

Yamamura M et al: Defining protective responses to pathogens: cytokine profiles in leprosy lesions. Science 1991;169:1565.

63

Actinomycetes

Phyllis C. Tien, SM, MD & David A. Relman, MD

Actinomycetes are variably acid-fast, gram-positive bacilli that are sometimes filamentous and branched. Originally thought to be fungi due to their hyphae-like appearance, they are now recognized as bacteria based on their cell wall components, reproduction by fission without sporulation or budding, inhibition by antibacterial agents, and molecular phylogenetic analysis. The actinomycete chromosomes contain a high content of guanosine and cytosine. The actinomycetes include the genera *Mycobacterium* and *Corynebacterium,* which are discussed in Chapter 61 and Chapter 62, respectively. The actinomycetes also include the genera *Nocardia, Actinomyces, Rhodococcus, Tsukumurella, Gordona, Actinomadura,* and *Streptomyces,* as well as the Whipple's disease bacillus *Tropheryma whippelii.* Of these, members of the genus *Nocardia* are the most significant from a clinical standpoint, followed by organisms from the genus *Actinomyces.* The other actinomycetes discussed in this chapter are less common causes of disease in humans.

NOCARDIA

Essentials of Diagnosis
- Gram-positive, variably acid-fast, branching filaments with aerial hyphae.
- Colonies have characteristic chalky-white or cotton ball appearance.
- Suspect when chronic pulmonary disease is accompanied by CNS or skin lesions.
- No specific antibody or antigen detection tests.

General Considerations
A. Epidemiology. *Nocardia* spp. are strictly aerobic, ubiquitous soil-dwelling organisms that are largely responsible for the decomposition of organic plant material. Infection usually occurs via inhalation of these organisms in airborne dust particles, leading to pulmonary disease. However, infection can also be acquired via direct percutaneous inoculation by thorns, animal scratches, bites, surgical wounds, and intravenous catheters. Dissemination commonly occurs to the central nervous system (CNS), skin, and subcutaneous tissues.

Nocardiosis is chiefly an opportunistic infection and occurs especially in patients with lymphoma and leukemia and to a lesser extent in patients with solid tumors. It is becoming more frequently recognized in patients with AIDS (~ 10% of all nocardial infections since 1980), those receiving organ transplants (especially renal and heart), and those receiving therapy with cytotoxic agents. Underlying pulmonary conditions, such as chronic obstructive pulmonary disease and bronchiectasis, also predispose individuals to pulmonary nocardiosis. Children with chronic granulomatous disease are at elevated risk of developing this infection. One-third of patients with nocardiosis, however, have no apparent predisposing factor. The disease affects men approximately threefold as often as it affects women and most often affects men and women between the ages of 30 and 50 years.

Approximately 90% of nocardial infections in the United States are due to *Nocardia asteroides* (and the related species *Nocardia farcinica* and *Nocardia nova,* which together form the *N asteroides* complex). Other pathogenic species implicated in disease include *Nocardia brasiliensis, Nocardia otitidiscaviarum,* and *Nocardia transvalensis.* While infection with *N asteroides* is geographically widespread, most cases of *N brasiliensis* infection in the United States have originated in the southern regions of the United States, especially Texas, southern California, Oklahoma, and Florida. Cases have also been reported from North Carolina.

B. Microbiology. See earlier introductory comments.

C. Pathogenesis. Disease occurs after virulent strains of *Nocardia* successfully evade the bactericidal defenses of the host's immune response. *Nocardia* virulence is to a large extent determined by the dynamically changing and complex structure of the bacterial cell envelope. Structural changes result in alterations of cell surface characteristics, of cell-cell interactions, and of specific growth patterns, and all have important effects on *Nocardia* virulence and host-parasite interactions.

Neutrophils predominate in the early lesions, inhibiting nocardial cell growth, but not killing the organism. *N asteroides* has the ability to resist intracellular killing by inhibiting phagosome-lysosome fusion, decreasing lysosomal enzyme activity in macrophages, and neutralizing phagosomal acidification. It also resists the oxidative killing mechanism of phagocytes by producing a unique surface-associated and secreted superoxide dismutase.

As a result of this evasive bactericidal response, cell-mediated responses are required for eventual control of this disease. The host mounts a lymphocyte response and releases antibodies and/or lymphocyte signals enabling activated macrophages to kill *Nocardia* spp. When there is an inadequate cell-mediated immune response, a more indolent infection may ensue, because neutrophils alone are not sufficient to resolve infection.

Clinical Findings (See Box 63–1.)

A. Pulmonary Disease. Pulmonary disease is the most common manifestation of nocardiosis. *N asteroides* is estimated to cause 80% of pulmonary cases. It may present as a necrotizing pneumonia with or without cavitation, a slowly enlarging pulmonary nodule, or pneumonia with associated empyema. The course of disease ranges from acute to chronic with a tendency to wax and wane.

Pulmonary nocardiosis comprises a constellation of protean and nonspecific findings. Symptoms and signs include fever, night sweats, anorexia, weight loss, productive cough with hemoptysis, and pleural pain. Initial pulmonary parenchymal disease may spread to adjacent lung tissue, progress to form one or more pulmonary abscesses, and spread to pleural surfaces or to distant sites, such as the skin and the brain. Nocardiosis must be suspected when soft-tissue and/or CNS disease develops in conjunction with chronic or subacute pulmonary disease.

Radiographic findings are also variable but most frequently include localized infiltrates, irregular nodules, pleural effusions, and hilar adenopathy. Less common findings include masses, miliary lesions, diffuse alveolar and interstitial infiltrates, and calcified granulomatous lesions suggestive of fungal infection or tuberculosis.

Other respiratory tract manifestations include tracheitis, bronchitis, and pleuropulmonary fistula. Mediastinitis with superior vena cava syndrome and sinusitis have also been reported.

B. Disseminated Disease. Approximately 50% of all *Nocardia* infections disseminate, usually from a primary pulmonary infection. Disseminated nocardiosis is defined as disease involving two or more organs of the body. It often occurs late in the course of disease and may be life threatening, especially in severely immunocompromised patients. The CNS is the most frequently affected site, but cutaneous and subcutaneous tissues, eyes (especially the retina), kidneys, joints, bone, and heart tissue can also be involved.

C. CNS Disease. CNS infections are seen in about one-third of all cases of nocardiosis, usually as part of disseminated disease. Patients with pulmonary or disseminated nocardiosis should have a magnetic resonance imaging (MRI) examination of the head to rule out occult CNS *Nocardia* infection. A single *Nocardia* colony isolated from the cerebrospinal fluid or another normally sterile site with a suggestive clinical picture should not be ignored, because these organisms are rarely laboratory contaminants and are not common members of the normal flora. Of patients with systemic nocardiosis, 45% have CNS infections, with the lung being the most common source of infection. Brain abscess is the most common clinical manifestation. Rarely, meningitis can also occur. Presentations may vary from an acute, rapidly evolving infection to a more common, insidious onset with infection persisting for months or even years without fever or leukocytosis. Hemiparesis, body tremors, Parkinsonian features, seizures, coma, and ataxia can occur. Bizarre (even psychotic) personality and behavioral presentations dominate certain chronic cases.

Lesions can be found in any anatomic site of the CNS and are often loculated with satellite extensions. CNS nocardiosis is associated with high morbidity and mortality if prompt antimicrobial therapy is not initiated. In compromised hosts, infection is more rapidly progressive and associated with increased mortality.

D. Cutaneous Disease. Cutaneous nocardiosis, in contrast to invasive pulmonary and disseminated nocardiosis, usually occurs in immunocompetent individuals. Primary disease is often precipitated by local trauma or surgical wound. Secondary cutaneous disease is the result of hematogenous dissemination. *N brasiliensis* is the predominant agent in primary cutaneous disease.

Localized cutaneous nocardiosis presents as pustules, abscesses, or cellulitis, all of which are usually self-limited. These lesions mimic those of cutaneous *Streptococcus* or *Staphylococcus* infection. *Nocardia* infections tend to be more indolent, however. Frequently, infection spreads to regional lymph nodes, which then suppurate. The resulting lymphocutaneous syndrome is referred to as the sporotrichoid form of cutaneous nocardiosis because it is difficult to distinguish from infection with the fungus *Sporothrix schenckii*. Thus, an appropriate laboratory diagnostic workup is required for a definitive diagnosis.

BOX 63–1	
Nocardiosis in Adults and Children	
Nocardiosis	• Invasive pulmonary disease and dissemination, especially to CNS, but also to kidney, skin, bone, and retina, more common in immunosuppressed patients • Cutaneous infections, ie, cellulitis, abscess, pyoderma, mycetomas

Mycetoma is a separate, distinct manifestation of cutaneous and subcutaneous nocardial infection. Other organisms can cause mycetomas, but *Nocardia* species appear to be the most common cause in the United States. Mycetoma is a chronic, localized, slowly progressive subcutaneous infection that can eventually invade the fascia, muscle, and bone if left untreated. It usually starts as a painless nodule after traumatic inoculation. It may become purulent and necrotic, and suppurate with formation of draining sinus tracts containing granules. Granules are conglomerations of the causal organism whose size, color, and degree of hardness vary by microbial species. Mycetoma is the only clinical form of nocardiosis regularly associated with the presence of such granules. The granules tend to be white, unlike the granules of *Actinomyces* spp., which are yellow and hence named "sulfur granules."

Mycetomas can be caused by a number of actinomycetes, in which case they are properly termed actinomycetomas as a group, or they can be caused by fungi, in which case they are referred to as eumycetomas. Microorganisms known to cause actinomycetomas include *N brasiliensis, Actinomadura madurae, Actinomadura pelletieri, Streptomyces somaliensis,* and, less commonly, *N asteroides, N otitidiscaviarum, Nocardiopsis dassonvillei,* and *N transvalensis.* In North America, South America, Mexico, and Australia, *N brasiliensis* is the chief cause of actinomycetomas, whereas in Africa, it is *S somaliensis.* Mycetomas tend to be well-delineated infections. Actinomycetomas most often affect persons who live in warm, rural environments. The most common site of infection is the foot, but infections in the leg, arm, hand, face, and neck are also seen.

E. Ocular Disease. Ocular infections such as keratitis and endophthalmitis with *Nocardia* spp. have been reported in both immunocompetent and immunocompromised patients. Though rare, these occur after traumatic corneal injury. *Nocardia* keratitis may mimic noninfectious inflammatory eye conditions and precipitate steroid therapy, which may worsen this (and other) ocular infection(s). Corneal scrapings should be performed on all patients with keratitis for the purpose of diagnosis.

Diagnosis

A Gram stain that shows thin, delicate, variably gram-positive, irregularly stained or beaded branching filaments is suggestive of nocardiosis. The diagnosis must be confirmed by culture. Currently, there is no reliable serodiagnostic test.

This normally elusive organism can usually be detected in pus or abscess drainage from a fistula, which should be submitted in a sterile tube or syringe. Fibers from sterile cotton swabs can interfere with the interpretation of smears, so the use of swabs should be discouraged. Surgical tissues and biopsy material from lung, skin, or brain should be kept moist during transport. When examining sputum specimens, early-morning expectorated samples should be collected on 3 separate days. Single smears and cultures are positive in only one-third of cases, so multiple specimens are encouraged.

Nocardia spp. grow readily on most of the media used for bacterial, fungal, and mycobacterial growth. Their growth can be enhanced if they are incubated at between 32 and 35 °C in the presence of 5–10% carbon dioxide. They are slow growing, so the laboratory should be alerted when *Nocardia* infection is suspected. Colonies from pure cultures form within 48–72 h, but, with complex specimens such as respiratory samples, other more rapidly growing bacteria can easily obscure small *Nocardia* colonies. To enhance recovery and inhibit bacterial and fungal overgrowth, a variety of selective media have been used including paraffin agar and buffered charcoal-yeast extract medium (originally designed to isolate *Legionella* species).

After recovery of a *Nocardia* isolate, biochemical tests to determine the ability of the isolate to decompose casein, xanthine, hypoxanthine, and tyrosine are performed to distinguish the different *Nocardia* species. Additional biochemical tests are often necessary for further speciation. Gas chromatography and high-performance liquid chromatography (HPLC) analyses of the mycolic acid composition of nocardiae provide a more rapid technique to distinguish the different species. However, the results must be interpreted cautiously, because the type of culture medium, incubation temperature, and other factors can alter mycolic acid composition. A more rapid and accurate approach to identify different species may be polymerase chain reaction-restriction fragment length polymorphism (PCR-RFLP) analysis.

Differential Diagnosis

Clinically, pulmonary nocardiosis must be distinguished from other bacterial infections such as mycoplasma infections, actinomycosis, tuberculosis, and fungal infections and carcinomas.

Treatment

Sulfonamides have been the mainstay of therapy for *Nocardia* infections since the first report of a cure in 1944. Prior to the 1940s, infections with *Nocardia* spp. were almost always fatal. Today the combination of trimethoprim and sulfamethoxazole (TMP-SMX) is generally the drug of choice despite inadequate in vitro data regarding synergy with this drug combination (Box 63–2). Between 90 and 95% of pulmonary infections with susceptible strains of *N asteroides* respond favorably to treatment. Oral or intravenous TMP-SMX is recommended for adults with normal renal function. Sulfonamide levels should be followed initially to ensure that a serum level of between 100 and 150 mg/dL is achieved. Levels should be drawn 2 h after oral ingestion of the drug.

BOX 63-2

Treatment of Nocardiosis

First Choice	• TMP (160 mg)-SMX (800 mg) IV or PO every 6 h for 6–12 m[1]
Second Choice	• Oral agents: minocycline (at 100–200 mg twice a day), amoxicillin-clavulanate, or fluoroquinolones such as ciprofloxacin or ofloxacin • Parenteral agents: imipenem, amikacin, or third-generation cephalosporins

[1]CNS disease and immunosuppressed patients should receive ≥ 12 mo of therapy. TMP-SMX should be used in combination with imipenem, amikacin, or third-generation cephalosporins for CNS disease and in immunosuppressed patients who do not respond to single-agent therapy.

Intolerance of sulfonamides, especially in AIDS patients and in transplant patients, is reported frequently. Rash is a common adverse effect in these patients. TMP-SMX may enhance the nephrotoxicity of cyclosporin A in transplant recipients. Treatment failure has been reported in individuals with CNS infection and/or in immunocompromised individuals. Issues of patient compliance, microbial susceptibility, sequestered pus, and superinfection may have contributed to the poor outcome in these patients.

Other antimicrobial agents have shown in vitro activity against *Nocardia* spp. There are three oral agents other than sulfonamides which are useful in treating nocardiosis. Minocycline is the only tetracycline with excellent in vitro activity against the majority of pathogenic strains. Amoxicillin-clavulanate is effective, but certain species such as *N nova, N otitidiscaviarum,* and *N transvalensis* are resistant to this antibiotic. The fluoroquinolones such as ciprofloxacin and ofloxacin are less consistent in their activity against *Nocardia* spp., but penetrate most tissues well. Susceptibility studies should guide the choice of therapy.

Useful parenteral agents include imipenem, amikacin, and the third-generation cephalosporins. These drugs can be used alone or in combination with sulfonamides. Although good clinical responses have been achieved with imipenem, drug-induced seizures may deter use in individuals with brain abscesses. Amikacin has variable penetration of the CNS, but has been successfully used to treat CNS infection when the minimum inhibitory concentration (MIC) of the isolate was < 0.12 µg/mL. Third-generation cephalosporins have excellent CNS penetration and low toxicity.

The optimal duration of therapy and the indications for combination therapy remain uncertain, but long-term therapy is the rule, because relapse is common. In the nonimmunosuppressed individual, therapy for pulmonary and systemic nocardiosis should be continued for a minimum of 6–12 months. Complete resolution of primary cutaneous nocardiosis without bone involvement can be achieved with 2–4 months of therapy.

Immunosuppressed patients, regardless of their presentation, should receive a minimum of 12 months of therapy. Parenteral therapy may be necessary for only 3–6 weeks, depending on patient response. The use of immunosuppressive agents should be minimized, especially early in treatment of nocardiosis. Because high failure rates occur in patients with CNS disease and patients who are immunosuppressed, combination parenteral therapy with TMP-SMX and amikacin, imipenem, or a third-generation cephalosporin might be considered. Once a clinical response is achieved, the patient can be switched to single-agent therapy. Individuals with HIV coinfection should probably receive continuous suppressive therapy.

Prevention & Control

Because *Nocardia* spp. are ubiquitous and nocardiosis is sporadic and dependent on host factors, there are no effective prevention and control measures.

ACTINOMYCES

Essentials of Diagnosis

- "Sulfur granules" in specimens and sinus tract drainage: hard, irregularly shaped, yellow particles measuring from 1 to 5 mm in size
- Gram-positive branching filaments arranged in ray-like projections under the microscope
- Colonies with characteristic "molar tooth" appearance
- Production of extensive fibrosis with "woody" induration
- No specific antibody or antigen detection tests

General Considerations

A. Epidemiology. The *Actinomyces* species are facultative anaerobes that commonly inhabit the oral cavity, the gastrointestinal tract, and the female genital tract, where they exist as commensals. Diversity within this genus is broad, which has led to taxonomic revision and reclassification of some species as members of the *Arcanobacterium* genus, eg, *Actinomyces pyogenes*. Disease occurs when mechanical insult disrupts the mucosal barrier or organisms gain access to privileged sites. For example, actinomycosis commonly occurs after dental procedures, trauma, surgery, or aspiration. *Actinomyces israelii* causes the majority of human disease owing to this genus, but other species, including *Actinomyces naeslundii, Actinomyces viscosus, Actinomyces enksonii, Actinomyces odontolyticus,* and *Actinomyces meyeri* have also been implicated. Actinomycosis is threefold more common in men than women.

B. Microbiology: See earlier introductory comments.

C. Pathogenesis. After inoculation into submucosal tissues, infection spreads slowly across anatomic boundaries, forming chronic, destructive abscesses and sinus tracts surrounded by thick fibrotic tissue, creating what is often described as "woody" induration. Lesions enlarge, become soft and fluctuant, and then suppurate, discharging purulent material containing granules. The neutrophil is the dominant responding leukocyte cell type; however, granulomata form over time. As the disease progresses, fistulas may extend from the abscess to either the skin or, less commonly, bone.

Actinomyces infections are usually polymicrobial. Multiple other organisms, including *Actinobacillus, Eikenella, Fusobacterium, Bacteroides,* and *Capnocytophaga* spp., members of the *Enterobacteriaceae,* staphylococci, and streptococci, are usually present in various combinations. These organisms may exert a synergistic effect on the disease process by secreting collagenase and hyaluronidase and thus facilitating extension of the lesion. *Actinomyces* virulence factors are not well understood. *Actinomyces* fimbriae may play an important role in bacterial self- or coaggregation with other oral bacterial species.

Clinical Findings (See Box 63–3.)

There are three major clinical presentations and types of disease: cervicofacial (~ 50% of all cases), abdominal (~ 20%), and thoracic (~ 15%).

A. Cervicofacial Disease. Cervicofacial actinomycosis usually follows dental or gingival manipulations or intraoral trauma. The most common site of involvement is the perimandibular region, where soft tissue swelling, abscess, or mass lesions can occur. Pain and fever are variably present. Actinomycosis can also cause periapical dental infections and sinusitis, especially of the maxillary sinus, as well as soft tissue infections of the head, neck, salivary glands, thyroid, external ear, and temporal bone.

B. Abdominal Disease. Abdominal disease usually follows gastrointestinal surgery, particularly emergency gall bladder and colonic surgery, appen-

dicitis, or foreign-body penetration. Ileocecal involvement, which often follows appendicitis, is seen most frequently. Infection is indolent with symptoms reported from 1 month to 2 years before a definitive diagnosis. Associated findings include weight loss, fever, palpable tender mass, visible sinus tracts with drainage, or fistulas. Fistulas invading the abdominal wall or perineum form in approximately one-third of abdominal actinomycotic abscesses. Unless draining sinus tracts are present, surgery is required for diagnosis.

C. Thoracic Disease. Thoracic disease usually follows aspiration of infected oral material. However, direct extension from cervicofacial or abdominal disease can occur. The usual presentation is either a mass or pneumonia. Occasionally there is pleural involvement. The disease has an insidious onset and a subacute course. Typical symptoms include cough, hemoptysis, chest wall discomfort, fever, and weight loss. Radiographic findings are variable, including patchy infiltrates, mass lesions, or cavitary lesions. Empyema, osteomyelitis, and draining fistulous tracts can occur when there is extension directly into the pleural space, ribs, and chest wall. In the presence of pleural or chest wall involvement, diagnosis should not be difficult. However, because *Actinomyces* spp. are members of the normal oral flora, organisms cultured from sputum or bronchoscopic washings are not diagnostic. Diagnosis requires percutaneous needle aspiration, bronchoscopic biopsy, or open-lung biopsy.

D. Other Manifestations. Other less frequent presentations include pelvic actinomycosis, which has been recognized with greater frequency since its association with the use of intrauterine contraceptive devices. Clinical disease may take the form of endometritis, salpingo-oophoritis, or tubo-ovarian abscess. Liver, bone, pericardial, endocardial, CNS, and perianal involvement has also been reported.

Diagnosis

"Sulfur granules" are hard, irregularly shaped yellow particles that range in size from 0.1 to 5 mm. Microscopically, they appear as masses of bacterial filaments that may be arranged in ray-like projections. Their presence is typical, but not unique to this disease. Other organisms such as *Nocardia* spp., *Streptomyces* spp., and staphylococci in botryomycosis may form similar granules. A definitive diagnosis is made by growing the organism from an appropriate specimen in anaerobic culture media.

Timely procurement of specimens before initiation of antimicrobial therapy and submission to the laboratory using anaerobic transport kits optimize recovery of the organism by culture. Tissue, pus, or sulfur granules are the specimens of choice, and swabs should be avoided because the cotton filaments may be confused on microscopy with the organism. Multi-

---

BOX 63–3	
Actinomycosis in Adults and Children	
More Common	• Cervicofacial, especially perimandibular region (~ 50% of cases) • Draining sinus fistulas common
Less Common	• Thoracic (~ 15%) • Abdominal disease (~ 20%) • Pelvic disease associated with intrauterine device use

ple specimens should be obtained because organisms may be scarce in pathology specimens.

Growth usually appears within 5–7 days but can take as long as 2–4 weeks, so the lab should be alerted if actinomycosis is suspected. Growth plate media containing 5% sheep blood or rabbit blood supplemented with hemin and vitamin K should be used. However, other types of media including anaerobic blood culture medium, enriched thioglycolate medium, and chopped meat-glucose medium will support the growth of these organisms. Plates should be incubated at 35 to 37 °C in an anaerobic chamber. Often colonies are viewed first as "spiderlike" in appearance and mature to resemble a "molar tooth." Biochemical tests are performed to distinguish the various species. There are no specific antibody or antigen detection tests.

Differential Diagnosis

Cervicofacial actinomycosis is often clinically misdiagnosed as a tumor, tuberculosis, or fungal infection. Actinomycosis often imitates a carcinoma, sarcoma, diverticular abscess, inflammatory bowel disease, or tuberculosis. Thoracic actinomycosis must be differentiated from other bacterial disease (tuberculosis and nocardiosis), systemic mycoses, and neoplastic disease.

Treatment

Penicillin is the drug of choice for actinomycosis (Box 63–4). Prolonged therapy is necessary to achieve a cure and minimize relapse. Intravenous penicillin G for 2–6 weeks followed by oral penicillin for 6–12 months is a reasonable regimen. Treatment should extend beyond the resolution of measurable disease. Long-term therapy is necessary because of the amount of reactive fibrosis formed by infection. Relapse is common especially after a short course of empiric antibiotic therapy. For patients with penicillin allergies, tetracycline is the preferred agent. Minocycline erythromycin and clindamycin are also reasonable alternatives. In vitro susceptibility data suggest that oxacillin, dicloxacillin, cephalexin,

metronidazole, and the aminoglycosides should be avoided.

Prevention & Control

Currently, there are no recommended prevention and control measures. However, because of the association between intrauterine device (IUD) use and pelvic actinomycosis, women should consider alternative forms of contraception.

OTHER ACTINOMYCETES

Species of the *Rhodococcus* genus have occasionally been implicated in human disease. *Rhodococcus* spp. differ from *Nocardia* spp. in that they do not produce aerial hyphae. *Gordona* and *Tsukumurella,* formerly classified in the *Rhodococcus* genus, are also rare causes of human disease. *Rhodococcus equi,* the species that is most commonly implicated in human disease, is found in soil and in the intestinal contents of grazing herbivore animals. Because most infections have been associated with immune system dysfunction, there has been an increase in reported cases of *R equi* infection since the onset of the HIV epidemic in the 1980s.

Pulmonary disease is the most common clinical manifestation of *R equi* infection, and occurs after inhalation of the organisms. Cutaneous infections, bacteremia, and catheter-associated sepsis have also been reported. Prolonged combination therapy with erythromycin or imipenem plus rifampin is currently the treatment of choice. Intestinal *R equi* disease may mimic Whipple's disease.

The disease that bears George Whipple's name affects primarily white, middle-aged males and causes arthralgias, abdominal pain, diarrhea, weight loss, fever, and lymphadenopathy. The causative agent, *T whippelii,* is an actinomycete that is difficult to cultivate in vitro. The gastrointestinal tract and its lymphatic drainage, the heart, and the CNS are the sites most commonly involved by this chronic, systemic disease. The diagnosis can be made by detection of numerous periodic acid-Schiff reagent (PAS)-positive macrophages within the intestinal lamina propria or by detection of the characteristic bacilli or their DNA within affected tissues or fluids, using electron microscopy or the polymerase chain reaction, respectively. Most patients respond to antibiotics; the recommended regimen consists of a combination of parenteral penicillin and streptomycin for 2 weeks, followed by ≥ 1 year of TMP-SMX. If untreated, the disease is fatal. Relapse within the CNS occurs in approximately one-third of patients, despite treatment.

The genus *Streptomyces* consists of a plethora of species of which most are considered saprophytes; they are found throughout the environment. *Streptomyces* spp. are primarily soil inhabitants. Three species, *S somaliensis, Streptomyces paraguayensis,*

BOX 63–4

Treatment of Actinomycosis	
First Choice	Penicillin G, 18–24 million U IV every day in 6 divided doses for 2–6 w, followed by penicillin VK, 250–500 mg PO 4 times a day for at least 6–12 m
Second Choice/ Penicillin-Allergic	Tetracycline, minocycline, erythromycin, or clindamycin (standard doses not available)

and *Streptomyces anulatus,* have been implicated in human disease, primarily in the formation of actinomycetomas. *S somaliensis* and *S paraguayensis* are rarely, if ever, found in the United States. They primarily inhabit Latin America, although *S somaliensis* is also known to cause disease in the arid regions of Africa and Arabia. *S anulatus,* on the other hand, has been associated with lung disease and sepsis, brain abscess, and panniculitis, as well as cervical lymphadenitis in an immunocompromised patient in the United States. Isolation of the streptomycetes should follow procedures used for the isolation of nocardiae. Colonies are usually glabrous or waxy and heaped. Definitive identification usually is extremely difficult. Streptomycin in combination with either dapsone or TMP-SMX has been suggested as treatment for infection with *Streptomyces* spp.

REFERENCES

Nocardia

Beaman B, Beaman L: *Nocardia* species: host-parasite relationship. Clin Microbiol Rev 1994;7:213.

Lerner P: Nocardiosis. Clin Infect Dis 1996;22:891.

McNeil M, Brown J: The medically important aerobic actinomycetes: epidemiology and microbiology. Clin Microbiol Rev 1994;7:357.

Threlkeld S, Hooper D: Update on management of patients with *Nocardia* infection. Curr Clin Top Infect Dis 1997;17:1.

Warren N. Actinomycosis, nocardiosis, and actinomycetoma. Dermatol Clin 1996;14:85.

Actinomyces

Fiorino AS: Intrauterine contraceptive device-associated actinomycotic abscess and *Actinomyces* detection on cervical smear. Obstet Gynecol 1996;87:142.

Smego RA Jr, Foglia G: Actinomycosis. Clin Infect Dis 1998;26:1255.

Warren N: Actinomycosis, nocardiosis, and actinomycetoma. Dermatol Clin 1996;14:85.

Other Actinomycetes

Linder R: *Rhodococcus equi* and *Arcanobacterium haemolyticum*: two "coryneform" bacteria increasingly recognized as agents of human infection. Emerg Infect Dis 1997;3:145.

McNeil M, Brown J: The medically important aerobic actinomycetes: epidemiology and microbiology. Clin Microbiol Rev. 1994;7:357

Relman DA: Whipple's disease. In Blaser MJ et al: *Infections of the Gastrointestinal Tract.* Raven Press, 1995.

Verville T et al: *Rhodococcus equi* infections of humans: 12 cases and review of the literature. Medicine 1994;73:119.

Treponema pallidum

64

Fred A. Lopez, MD & David A. Relman, MD

Essentials of Diagnosis

- Spiral, motile, coil-shaped, elongated (0.10 µm × 5–20 µm) spirochete.
- No reliable method for sustained in vitro cultivation.
- Direct detection with darkfield microscopy or immunofluorescent antibody in early syphilis.
- Nontreponemal antibody tests (rapid plasma reagin, Venereal Disease Research Laboratory [VDRL]) for screening, treatment follow-up.
- *Treponema*-specific antibody tests (fluorescent treponemal antibody test, microhemagglutination-*T pallidum* test) for confirmation.
- Cerebrospinal fluid (CSF) lymphocytosis, elevated CSF protein, or reactive CSF VDRL test suggests neurosyphilis.
- PCR, DNA probes, and immunoblotting techniques promising in congenital syphilis, early syphilis, or neurosyphilis.
- All patients with *T pallidum* infection should be tested for HIV coinfection and vice versa.

General Considerations

The term syphilis was first used in 1530 by the Italian physician Girolamo Fracastoro in his epic poem *Syphilis Sive Morbus Gallicus*. Much has been learned since then about this sexually transmitted disease caused by *T pallidum*. Public health screening programs and the introduction of antibiotics led to a marked decline in the number of new cases of syphilis in the United States after World War II. However, the advent of AIDS was associated with an increase in new cases of syphilis, necessitating the reeducation of health care personnel in the evaluation and management of this disease.

A. Epidemiology. Genital herpes and syphilis are the most common causes of genital ulcerations in patients presenting to sexually transmitted disease clinics in the United States. Syphilis is usually transmitted by sexual contact with the infectious lesions of primary and secondary syphilis. Syphilis develops in ~ 30–60% of sexual contacts of individuals with infectious syphilis. Syphilis is less commonly transmitted in utero or by means of blood transfusion, nongenital body contact, and accidental direct inoculation.

The incidence of primary and secondary syphilis (called early syphilis) reached a nadir in 1956 and then increased slowly. Two "epidemics" of early syphilis in the past 20 years have highlighted the role of human behavior in syphilis epidemiology: one peaked in 1982 and primarily involved bisexual and homosexual men; the second peaked in 1990 when 50,223 new cases of primary and secondary syphilis were reported. This epidemic was associated with crack cocaine use and its effects on sexual behavior and disproportionately involved African Americans. The incidence of this outbreak was highest in the southern United States and in the nation's large metropolitan areas. The incidence of congenital syphilis also rose from 4.3 cases/100,000 live births in 1983 to 107 cases/100,000 births in 1991, a change attributed to the increase in primary and secondary syphilis among women, more active surveillance, and the adoption of a more sensitive case definition for congenital syphilis in 1988–1989.

The incidence of all stages of syphilis including congenital syphilis has decreased since 1991. The number of new cases of primary and secondary syphilis in the United States in 1997 was 8,500, an incidence of 3.2 cases/100,000 persons, the lowest rate since 1941. In 1997, the incidence of congenital syphilis was 27 cases/100,000 live births, the lowest rate since the change in the surveillance case definition.

B. Microbiology. The order *Spirochaetales* and family *Spirochaetaceae* include human pathogens within the three genera, *Treponema, Leptospira*, and *Borrelia*. *T pallidum* subspecies *pallidum* is the causative agent of syphilis and is transmitted primarily through sexual contact. Nonvenereally transmitted treponemal infections include those caused by *T carateum* (pinta), *T pallidum* subspecies *pertenue* (yaws), and *T pallidum* subspecies *endemicum* (bejel or endemic syphilis). Clinical and epidemiological characteristics are used to distinguish among these treponemal infections because of the similarities in serologic host responses, microbial morphology, and antigenic composition. No currently available nucleic acid-based test reliably differentiates between the subspecies of *T pallidum*.

T pallidum is a microaerophilic spirochete that is tightly wound into a spiral shape, measuring 5–20 µm in length and 0.1–0.2 µm in width. With the ability to bend along its long axis, active motility is achieved with "corkscrewlike" motions. These organisms, too slender to be seen with light microscopy, can be readily visualized by darkfield microscopy, by direct immunofluorescent staining, or by silver staining.

This agent has resisted characterization because it cannot be sustained by in vitro culture methods. Instead, it requires rabbit or guinea pig inoculation for laboratory propagation. The organism is surrounded by an outer membrane consisting primarily of phospholipids and a low concentration of membrane proteins, a characteristic that when coupled with the organism's slow multiplication time may explain its ability to persist in the infected host. Examination of the full 1.14-Mbp genome sequence of *T pallidum* reveals a large family of duplicated genes that are predicted to encode outer membrane porins and adhesins. These genes may reflect a mechanism for antigenic variation as well as targets for vaccine-induced immunity.

Axial filaments, or endoflagella, are attached to each end of the organism in the periplasmic space and mediate host cell adherence and motility. Recent investigations suggest that a sensory transducing chemotaxis protein may modulate this flagella-associated motility. The organism also contains a peptidoglycan layer and is susceptible to β-lactam agents such as penicillin. Replication of this organism occurs by transverse fission.

C. Pathogenesis. *T pallidum* gains access to subepithelial tissues through microperforations in the skin or intact mucous membranes. A visible localized reaction occurs at the site of inoculation after 10–90 days, a reflection of the slow dividing time of this organism. This reaction takes the form of a papule before ulcerating to form the classic lesion of primary syphilis, the chancre (Figure 64–1).

Histopathologic examination reveals perivascular inflammation consisting of lymphocytes and plasma cells. Spirochetes also disseminate to regional lymph nodes and enter the bloodstream during this stage. The chancre usually heals spontaneously within 1–8 weeks, likely because of the phagocytosis of treponemes by macrophages. The secondary stage of infection begins ~ 6–10 weeks after the disappearance of the chancre. Spirochetemia is at its greatest level during this stage, despite a vigorous humoral immune response, and patients often present with constitutional complaints of malaise, fever, weight loss, and generalized lymphadenopathy.

Most patients develop skin and mucous membrane lesions. The lesions of both primary and secondary syphilis are highly infectious. The resolution of the signs and symptoms of untreated secondary syphilis heralds the beginning of the latent stage of infection, a clinically asymptomatic stage belied only by a positive treponemal serology. This phase is divided into an early latent stage, that is, the first year after infection, and the late latent stage. Approximately one-third of untreated patients with latent infection will go on to develop manifestations of late (or tertiary) disease after an indeterminate period of time.

Destructive tissue lesions of the tertiary stage of infection involve the skin and bone (leading to a gumma), the aorta, and the central nervous system (CNS). Histopathologic examination of these lesions reveals the characteristic obliterative endarteritis seen in other stages of syphilis. The lesions of late syphilis contain few visible spirochetes, suggesting a role for a delayed-type hypersensitivity reaction to *T pallidum*.

Much of the information regarding the natural course of untreated syphilis was obtained from two reports including the Oslo Study of untreated Norwegian patients diagnosed with early syphilis (1890–1951), and the Tuskegee Study, initiated by the United States Public Health Service (U.S. PHS) in 1932. This prospective study of ~ 400 black men with untreated latent syphilis in Macon County, Alabama, was terminated in 1972.

PRIMARY SYPHILIS

Clinical Findings

A. Signs and Symptoms. The lesions of primary syphilis appear at the site of inoculation after an incubation period that is inversely proportional to the number of infecting organisms, usually 3 weeks (Box 64–1). The chancre is an ulcerative lesion that varies in size from several millimeters to 2 cm. Although classically described as a solitary lesion, multiple lesions may be present (Figure 64–2). They are generally located on the genitalia and anorectal areas, but any area on the body can be affected including the oropharynx and the extremities. This superficial ulcer is usually painless with well-defined, indurated borders surrounding a firm, clean base. Local and regional lymphadenopathy is bilateral, nonsuppurative, painless, and often described as "rubbery."

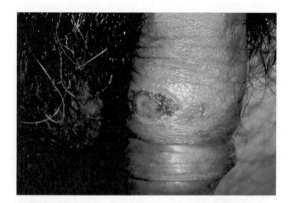

Figure 64–1. Primary syphilis. Classic chancre on the penis. (Courtesy of Dr Joseph Engelman and Dr Jennifer M. Flood).

BOX 64–1

Acquired Syphilis in Adults

	Primary Syphilis	Secondary Syphilis	Latent[1]	Late	Neurosyphilis
More Common	• Genital ulcer (chancre) • Inguinal lymph-adenopathy	• Skin and mucous membranes: disseminated macular and papular rash; condylomata lata; mucous patch • Constitutional, flu-like syndrome with generalized lymphadenopathy	• Asymptomatic by definition	• Benign (gummatous): skin, bone, and soft tissue granulomatous lesions • Cardiovascular: aortic insufficiency, saccular aortic aneurysm, coronary ostial stenosis	• Asymptomatic • Meningovascular (strokelike syndrome) • General paresis: neuropsychiatric abnormalities of dementia • Tabes dorsalis: ataxia, areflexia, lower extremity pain, incontinence, impaired proprioception
Less Common		• Musculoskeletal: osteitis, arthritis, periostitis, osteomyelitis • Gastrointestinal: gastritis, hepatitis • Nephropathy • Neurosyphilis: aseptic meningitis			• Ocular: optic atrophy, blindness, ptosis • Otic: deafness, tinnitus

[1]Early, <1 year after infection; late, ≥1 year after infection.

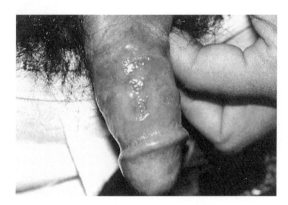

Figure 64–2. Primary syphilis. Multiple chancres on the penis. (Courtesy of Dr Joseph Engelman).

B. Laboratory Findings. Definitive diagnosis can be made by visualization of spirochetes in exudates from these lesions with darkfield or immunofluorescent antibody microscopy. Nontreponemal serologic testing is reactive in 70–80% of patients with primary syphilis but is less sensitive at the time that the chancre first appears. Treponemal antibody tests, specifically the fluorescent treponemal antibody test, are more sensitive during this stage of infection.

C. Differential Diagnosis. Primary syphilitic genital lesions can be mistaken for lesions associated with trauma, herpes simplex virus, malignancy, chancroid, lichen planus, granuloma inguinale, or lymphogranuloma inguinale. Darkfield examination is helpful in diagnosis. The painful vesicular lesions of herpes are distinguished by multinucleated giant cells when unroofed and examined with a microscope. The ulcerated and nonindurated lesions of chancroid are associated with painful lymphadenopathy. Lymphogranuloma venereum and granuloma inguinale infections are seen primarily in tropical countries.

SECONDARY SYPHILIS

Clinical Findings

A. Signs and Symptoms. The secondary stage of syphilis occasionally overlaps with the primary phase but usually begins ~ 6 weeks after resolution of the chancre; however, it can develop as late as 6 months after infection (see Box 64–1). Most patients have some degree of skin or mucocutaneous involvement. A faint and evanescent macular rash of the trunk and abdomen known as *roseola syphilitica* is sometimes seen initially. A generalized, symmetric, nonpruritic rash consists of some combination of erythematous or copper-colored macular, papular, papulosquamous, or pustular lesions. These lesions can be found on the palms, soles, genitalia, and oral mucous

membranes (Figure 64–3). The rash of syphilis often provides a diagnostic challenge, deserving of its moniker "the great imitator."

Condylomata lata refer to eroded papules that can fuse together to create flat, highly infectious lesions in moist, intertriginous areas such as the anogenital region (Figure 64–4). They occur in 10–25% of secondary infections. Mucous patches refer to the slightly raised, grayish, painless ulcerations seen on mucous membranes in ~ 15–30% of patients with secondary syphilis. A patchy, "moth-eaten" appearance of hair on the scalp, eyebrows, and beard is well described.

The CNS and gastrointestinal, renal, and musculoskeletal systems may also be affected during the secondary stage of syphilis. Patients with syphilitic meningitis typically present with headache, nausea and emesis, stiff neck, and cranial neuropathies involving the third, sixth, seventh, and eighth cranial nerves. CSF analysis reveals a mononuclear pleocytosis, an elevated protein, and, in half of patients, hypoglycorrhachia. Optic neuritis, iritis, and uveitis can be seen during this stage as well. Although only 1–2% of patients with secondary syphilis have documented acute aseptic meningitis, CSF findings may be abnormal in ~ 25–50% of patients.

Syphilitic gastritis causes emesis and epigastric pain. Endoscopic examination usually reveals ulcerations or pronounced gastric folds that contain spirochetes. Of patients with primary or secondary syphilis, ~ 10% will have elevated liver function tests (characteristically alkaline phosphatase) and hepatomegaly, the results of hepatic necrosis and granulomatous inflammation. Renal disease is caused by immune complex-mediated mechanisms and presents as nephrotic syndrome or glomerulonephritis. Synovitis, osteitis, or periostitis can be seen in ≤ one-fifth of patients.

B. Laboratory Findings. *T pallidum* can be detected directly with darkfield and immunofluorescent microscopy in condylomata lata and mucous patches.

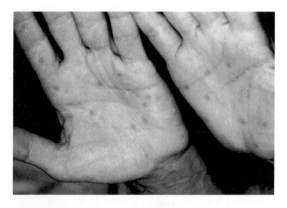

Figure 64–3. Secondary syphilis. Classic maculopapular lesions on the palms. (Courtesy of Dr Joseph Engelman).

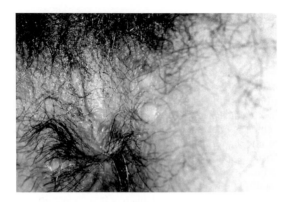

Figure 64–4. Secondary syphilis. Condylomata lata in the perianal area. (Courtesy of Dr Joseph Engelman).

Nontreponemal and treponemal serologic tests are usually reactive during this stage of disease (see Diagnosis below).

C. Differential Diagnosis. The differential diagnosis of the dermatologic manifestations of secondary syphilis is quite extensive and should include pityriasis rosea, tinea versicolor, erythema multiforme, drug eruption, viral exanthems, psoriasis, ringworm, and scabies. The pale, pinkish condylomata lata lesions tend not to be as raised as the venereal warts of condyloma accuminata. Mucous patches can be confused with herpes simplex lesions, aphthous ulcerations, candidiasis, and Stevens-Johnson syndrome. Both mucous patches and condylomata lata contain spirochetes, which can be visualized by darkfield examination.

LATENT SYPHILIS

Clinical Findings

The manifestations of primary and secondary syphilis resolve without therapy, and the ensuing clinically silent phase of infection known as the latent stage is characterized by positive serologies and normal CSF (see Box 64–1). Patients can relapse with manifestations of secondary syphilis during this stage, usually during the early latent period. Asymptomatic infection lasting greater than one year, late latent syphilis, persists for the remainder of life in approximately two-thirds of untreated patients. The other one-third of patients develops symptomatic disease, ie, late syphilis.

LATE SYPHILIS

Clinical Findings

Tertiary disease, usually seen 5–20 years after initial infection, traditionally includes cardiovascular syphilis, late benign (or gummatous) syphilis, and neurosyphilis (see Box 64–1). Fewer organisms are found in lesions during this stage.

A. Cardiovascular Syphilis. The incidence of cardiovascular involvement is probably underestimated, although clinically significant disease eventually develops in ~ 10% of all untreated patients. Lesions include coronary ostial stenosis and coronary artery insufficiency, aortic valvular regurgitation with left ventricular hypertrophy and congestive heart failure, and saccular aortic aneurysms of the ascending and transverse portions of the thoracic aorta. These aneurysms usually do not dissect and rupture but can present as pulsating supraclavicular chest wall masses with associated hoarseness, dysphagia, dyspnea, and cough due to impingement on adjacent vital structures. Syphilis should always be considered in patients whose chest radiograph reveals ascending aortic calcifications or those with isolated aortic valvular disease and positive treponemal serologies, particularly if other manifestations of late disease are present.

B. Late Benign Syphilis. The classic lesion of late benign syphilis seen in ~ 15% of untreated patients is the gumma, a granulomatous inflammatory process that usually affects the skin, subcutaneous tissues, and bone but may involve the liver, respiratory tract, stomach, heart, and almost any other organ of the body. Usually nodular before ulcerating, gummas are noninfectious, indurated, violaceous, and painless. Gummas may heal or become chronic, resulting in destructive local disease. The differential diagnosis includes causes of other granulomatous processes such as mycobacterial and fungal infections, sarcoidosis, and malignancies.

C. Neurosyphilis. Clinically apparent CNS involvement is estimated to occur in ~ 5–10% of all syphilis patients and can be seen at any stage of infection; however, early silent dissemination of *T pallidum* to the CNS is almost the rule. Asymptomatic neurosyphilis is usually accompanied by CSF cellular or protein abnormalities, the presence of *T pallidum* in the CSF, or a positive CSF VDRL test. These CSF abnormalities resolve spontaneously in many patients; the likelihood of developing symptomatic CNS infection is proportional to the degree of these abnormalities.

Symptomatic neurosyphilis classically takes the forms of aseptic meningitis (see Secondary Syphilis), meningovascular syphilis, and parenchymatous neurosyphilis (general paresis and tabes dorsalis), in ascending order of frequency. Meningovascular syphilis usually occurs 4–10 years after infection and presents with stroke-like symptoms in younger patients, a consequence of endarteritis obliterans of the cerebral arteries. CSF abnormalities characteristically include a lymphocytic pleocytosis, an elevated protein, and a reactive VDRL.

Parenchymatous neurosyphilis, a consequence of neuronal destruction by *T pallidum*, is divided into two discrete syndromes, tabes dorsalis (more common) and general paresis. It is not uncommon, however, to see patients exhibiting neurologic features of both syndromes. Tabes dorsalis results from progressive demyelination of the posterior columns and dorsal roots. It is manifested by sharp pains of the lower extremities, dysuria, and ataxia; physical findings may include areflexia and loss of pain, temperature, and position sense. Patients with general paresis present with a slowly progressive dementia. Neuropsychiatric manifestations include tremors, dysarthria, ataxia, delusions, and personality changes. The irregular Argyll-Robertson pupil of parenchymatous syphilis results from pupillary constriction to accommodation but not to light. The clinical diagnosis is supported by CSF abnormalities in patients with positive treponemal serologies. Unlike the other forms of late syphilis, the lesions of general paresis contain a significant number of spirochetes.

The effect of concomitant HIV infection on the clinical course of syphilis, including neurosyphilis, is discussed in a later section (see Syphilis and HIV, below).

CONGENITAL SYPHILIS

Clinical Findings

A. Signs and Symptoms. Most infants acquire congenital syphilis from the transplacental dissemi-

nation of maternal *T pallidum* after the 16th week of gestation and less commonly from contact with an infectious lesion during the time of delivery (Box 64–2). The likelihood of fetal infection is inversely related to the duration of time that the mother has been infected; the risk of fetal transmission declines from 70–100% during early syphilis to 10–30% during latent disease. Congenital infections can be prevented by the appropriate identification and treatment of infected pregnant women. In 1988, the Centers for Disease Control increased the sensitivity of the congenital syphilis case definition by including all infants, symptomatic and asymptomatic, born to mothers with untreated or inadequately treated syphilis.

Congenital syphilis is divided into an early stage and a late stage. The early stage, seen primarily in infants 2–25 weeks of age, may be asymptomatic or may be associated with long bone skeletal abnormalities including osteochondritis and periostitis, hepatosplenomegaly and abnormal liver function studies, low birth weight, serous nasal discharge (*snuffles*), maculopapular rash, anemia, nephrotic syndrome, and CNS abnormalities. If untreated, these lesions may result in late congenital syphilis, which classically appears after 2 years and is manifest by frontal bossing, saddle nose, interstitial keratitis, notched and peg-shaped upper Hutchinson's incisors (Figure 64–5), poorly developed mulberry molars, anterior bowing of the lower extremities, perioral and

---

BOX 64–2

Syphilis in Children

	Early Congenital	Late Congenital[1]	Acquired
More Common	• Osteochondritis and periostitis • Snuffles/rhinitis • Maculopapular rash, condylomata lata • Anemia • Low birth weight • Hepatosplenomegaly • Fever	• Dental abnormalities (Hutchinson's incisors, mulberry molars) • Poorly developed maxilla • High palatal arch • Saddle nose • Frontal bossing • Interstitial keratitis	See Box 64–1 (Acquired Syphilis in Adults)
Less Common	• Lymphadenopathy • Aseptic meningitis • Meningovascular syphilis • Pseudoparalysis • Nephropathy • Pneumonitis • Ascites • Mucous patch	• Saber shins • Clutton's joints • Rhagades • Eighth nerve deafness • Flaring scapulae • Mental retardation • Hydrocephalus	See Box 64–1 (Acquired Syphilis in Adults)

[1]Older than 2 years

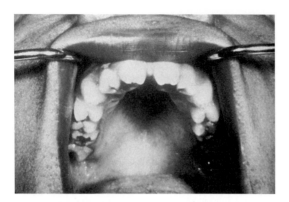

Figure 64–5. Congenital syphilis. Classic Hutchinson's teeth. (Courtesy of U.S. PHS).

perinasal fissures, bilateral effusions of the knee (Clutton's joints), and deafness.

B. Laboratory Findings. See Diagnosis below.

C. Differential Diagnosis. The differential diagnosis of congenital syphilis includes other congenitally acquired infections such as toxoplasmosis, rubella, cytomegalovirus, herpes simplex, and hepatitis B.

D. Complications. Infants with untreated early syphilis may develop manifestations of late congenital syphilis, as previously described.

Diagnosis

A. Direct Microscopic Examination. Darkfield microscopy reveals *T pallidum* in the transudative fluid of a chancre in which the density of organisms approaches 10,000–100,000/mL (Figure 64–6). These spirochetes exhibit "corkscrew" motility and central flexion. Highly suspicious lesions should be examined on three successive days before excluding syphilis. Alternative diagnostic methods such as fluo-

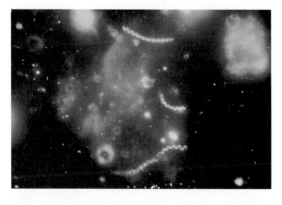

Figure 64–6. Darkfield examination of lesion containing *T pallidum*. (Courtesy of U.S. PHS).

rescent antibody staining should be considered for the evaluation of oral lesions because saprophytic spirochetes in the oral cavity morphologically mimic *T pallidum.* Silver or specific immunofluorescent antibody stains may be useful in detecting pathogenic spirochetes in tissue biopsy specimens.

B. Serologic Tests. The majority of syphilis cases are diagnosed with serologic testing. These tests are categorized according to the type of antibody produced by the host: nonspecific and specific. Nonspecific, or nontreponemal, antibody tests use reaginic lipoidal antigens to demonstrate the presence of cross-reacting antibodies (immunoglobulin G [IgG] and IgM) elicited by *T pallidum* infection. Specific, or treponemal, antibody tests use *T pallidum* antigens for the detection of antibodies.

The nontreponemal antibody tests include the rapid plasma reagin and the VDRL flocculation assays. These screening tests may be reactive in the setting of other infectious and noninfectious conditions such as intravenous drug use, tuberculosis, vaccinations, pregnancy, infectious mononucleosis, HIV infection, rickettsial diseases, other spirochetal diseases, connective tissue diseases, and bacterial endocarditis. False-negative nontreponemal tests can be seen early in the course of disease when antibody levels are low and later in the disease in the face of overwhelming antibody levels, for example, during secondary syphilis, necessitating dilution of the serum sample to overcome this "prozone" effect. Approximately 75%, 100%, and 75% of patients with untreated primary, secondary, and late syphilis, respectively, will have reactive nontreponemal tests. Positive test results are usually quantitated in order to monitor therapy. The nontreponemal tests are not interchangeable (rapid plasma reagin titers usually higher at any given time), and the optimal approach for patient management should include the use of the same laboratory and test. Conversion to nonreactivity (seroreversion) or a sustained decline in titer of at least fourfold is expected in patients with early syphilis 2 years after effective therapy.

The more sensitive and specific treponemal antibody tests are used primarily for confirmation of results from nontreponemal antibody testing. The *T pallidum* hemagglutination and the microhemagglutination-*T pallidum* tests are dependent on the agglutination of antitreponemal antibodies from the patient's serum with red blood cells that have surface-associated *T pallidum.* In the fluorescent treponemal antibody test, a killed strain of *T pallidum* serves as the antigen for the patient's absorbed serum. Labeled antihuman immunoglobulin is then visualized with fluorescent microscopy. The fluorescent treponemal antibody test is more sensitive in detecting early syphilis than the other specific tests.

Seropositivity with the specific treponemal tests usually persists for the lifetime of the individual, a quality that does not allow monitoring response to therapy. However, seroreversion can be seen in promptly treated primary syphilis and in advanced HIV infection. In addition, treponeme-specific antibody tests are reactive in diseases caused by other pathogenic treponemes including yaws, pinta, and bejel, as well as Lyme disease, relapsing fever, and leptospirosis; false positives have also been reported in individuals with malaria and leprosy.

Molecular techniques, including polymerase chain reaction, are not routinely available, but may have use in resolving selected diagnostic conundrums involving early primary syphilis, congenital syphilis and neurosyphilis.

C. Neurosyphilis. The diagnosis of neurosyphilis is based on both clinical and laboratory findings. Although some experts evaluate the CSF of all patients with late latent syphilis, the U.S. PHS recommends a lumbar puncture when any of the following are present: clinical manifestations of neurologic involvement, evidence of nonneurologic late active syphilis, treatment failure, or late latent disease (including syphilis of unknown duration) in the HIV coinfected host. VDRL reactivity in the CSF is specific for the diagnosis of neurosyphilis, although caution should be exercised when interpreting a positive result from a traumatic lumbar puncture. In addition, the modest sensitivity of this test (~ 50%) does not rule out neurosyphilis when negative. Patients with systemic serologic evidence of syphilis and a CSF lymphocytic pleocytosis or an elevated CSF protein level should be treated for presumptive neurosyphilis.

D. Congenital Syphilis. U.S. PHS recommendations for the evaluation of an infant with suspected congenital syphilis include radiographs of the long bones, routine examination of the CSF including VDRL reactivity, nontreponemal serologies of the infant's blood, and immunofluorescent antibody staining of the placenta or amniotic fluid/cord. If this initial evaluation is negative, specific antitreponemal IgM antibody testing is indicated. The definitive diagnosis of congenital syphilis requires identification of *T pallidum* in neonatal tissue.

Treatment

The drug of choice for all stages of syphilis is penicillin. Specific treatment recommendations are dictated by the stage of disease. Because of the organism's slow replication, prolonged treponemicidal antimicrobial therapeutic levels are necessary. Although alternatives to penicillin are available, nonpenicillin-based therapy is not recommended for patients who are pregnant or have congenital syphilis, neurosyphilis, or HIV coinfection.

Patients with spirochetal diseases may develop an acute systemic reaction consisting of fever, chills, headache, and myalgias within the first day after effective therapy. This Jarisch-Herxheimer reaction is usually seen during treatment of the earlier stages of syphilis, especially the secondary stage, and resolves

spontaneously after 12–24 h. This reaction is probably caused by the lysis of spirochetes with subsequent release of antigen and toxic by-products. Symptomatic relief with anti-inflammatory agents may be helpful.

The recommendations given in Boxes 64–3, 64–4, and 64–5 for therapy and follow-up are based primarily on U.S. PHS recommendations.

A. Incubating Syphilis. Treatment of presumed incubating syphilis with the same regimen prescribed for early syphilis is recommended for all sexual contacts of patients with primary, secondary, or early latent syphilis, within the prior 90 days. Although the use of multiple-dose azithromycin and ceftriaxone appear promising in the treatment of early syphilis, single-dose therapy with either agent for incubating syphilis requires further evaluation.

B. Primary and Secondary Syphilis. The recommended therapy for adults with acquired primary and secondary syphilis is indicated in Box 64–3. Erythromycin therapy is less effective than penicillin, doxycycline, or tetracycline. Single-dose ceftriaxone or azithromycin therapy should not be used as alternative therapy. Follow-up in non-HIV infected patients should include nontreponemal titers at 3, 6, and 12 months after treatment.

Clinical manifestations of infection that recur or do not resolve or fourfold increases in nontreponemal titers suggest treatment failure or reinfection and should dictate further evaluation for neurosyphilis and HIV infection. Effective therapy usually results in a fourfold decrease in titer by 3–6 months after treatment, and a sustained fourfold or greater decline is considered an appropriate therapeutic response. Seroreversion fails to occur by 24 months after appropriate treatment in ~ 25% of patients with primary and secondary infection. Patients who are considered treatment failures and have no evidence of neurosyphilis should be treated with the benzathine penicillin G regimen recommended for late latent syphilis.

C. Early Latent Syphilis. Adults and children with early latent infection are treated in the same manner as those with primary and secondary syphilis.

D. Late Latent Syphilis or Syphilis of Unknown Duration. Nontreponemal serologic followup is recommended at 6, 12, and 24 months. Assessment for neurosyphilis and possible retreatment should be considered for patients in whom titers increase fourfold, in those in whom a fourfold decline is not seen in 1–2 years, or in whom clinical manifestations develop.

Late Syphilis. Patients with late benign syphilis or cardiovascular syphilis and no evidence of neurosyphilis are treated in the same manner as those with late latent disease. In addition to antitreponemal agents, therapy for cardiovascular syphilis consists of appropriate medical and surgical management of heart failure and aneurysm. Reversal of the complications of aortitis is unlikely, although progression of disease

BOX 64-3

Treatment of Acquired Syphilis in Adults[1]

	Primary, Secondary, Early Latent	Late Latent, Latent of Unknown Duration, Late[2]	Neurosyphilis
First Choice	• Benzathine penicillin G, 2.4 million U IM once	• Benzathine penicillin G, 2.4 million U IM weekly for 3 weeks	• Aqueous crystalline penicillin G, 3–4 million Units IV every 4 h for 10–14 d (consider following with benzathine penicillin G, 2.4 million U IM)
Second Choice	• Doxycycline, 100 mg PO twice daily for 14 d OR • Tetracycline, 500 mg PO four times daily for 14 d OR • Erythromycin, 500 mg PO four times daily for 14 d (less effective)	• Doxycycline, 100 mg PO twice daily for 28 d OR • Tetracycline, 500 mg PO four times daily for 28 d	• Procaine penicillin, 2.4 million Units IM once daily for 10–14 d PLUS probenecid, 500 mg PO four times daily for 10–14 d (consider following with benzathine penicillin G, 2.4 million U IM)
Penicillin Allergic	• Doxycycline, tetracycline, or erythromycin as above	• Doxycycline or tetracycline as above	• No alternative to penicillin; desensitize and treat with penicillin

[1]All patients who are pregnant or have HIV infection, congenital syphilis, or neurosyphilis should be treated with penicillin-based regimens.
[2]Except neurosyphilis.

may be halted with antibiotics. The lesions of late benign syphilis are responsive to penicillin therapy.

Neurosyphilis. All patients with ocular and auditory involvement secondary to syphilis should be treated for presumed neurosyphilis. Follow-up examination of the CSF should be performed every 6 months. Effective therapy should result in a decrease of the CSF cell count by 6 months. CSF protein and VDRL titers do not respond as quickly as the cell count, but repeat therapy may be warranted if these two parameters are still abnormal 2 years after treatment. Treatment of the late stages of neurosyphilis is most effective at hindering further CNS damage but is unlikely to result in resolution of symptoms.

Congenital Syphilis. The appropriate therapy and follow-up of early congenital syphilis should prevent the development of late congenital syphilis (see Box 64–5). Benzathine penicillin G, 50,000 U/kg administered once intramuscularly, is recommended for neonates without clinical or laboratory evidence of syphilis when the mother's syphilis serologies indicate treatment failure; neonates whose mothers have received prenatal erythromycin therapy for syphilis or have received therapy for syphilis in the month before parturition should also be treated with this regimen.

Treponemicidal CSF concentrations of penicillin may not be attained with the procaine penicillin regimen recommended for early congenital syphilis. Nontreponemal antibody test results should be nega-

tive by 6 months after therapy. Rising or persistent titers should prompt appropriate reevaluation and management including CSF examination and retreatment. Infants with abnormal CSF examinations should have follow-up lumbar punctures performed every 6 months with an expected serial decline in the cell count to normal levels by 2 years after therapy and a negative CSF-VDRL by 6 months. Retreatment is indicated if these parameters are not met.

Syphilis & Pregnancy

Therapy for all pregnant women known to be infected for <1 year should include benzathine penicillin G, 2.4 million U given intramuscularly 1 week apart for a total of two doses. Other stages of disease are treated in the same manner outlined for nonpregnant adults, except there is no alternative to penicillin-based therapy. Nontreponemal antibody titers should be performed monthly with principles of retreatment guided by the disease stage. Treatment of all sexual partners is imperative.

Syphilis & HIV

HIV antibody testing is recommended for all patients with *T pallidum* infection because of the increased incidence of HIV coinfection in these patients. Transmission of HIV may be facilitated by genital ulcer disease. A weakened cellular immune system may explain why HIV-infected individuals

BOX 64–4

Treatment of Acquired Syphilis in Children[1]

	Primay, Secondary, Early Latent	Late Latent, Latent of Unknown Duration, Late[2]	Neurosyphilis
First Choice	• Benzathine penicillin G, 50,000 U/kg IM, not to exceed the adult dose of 2.4 million U administered in one dose	• Benzathine penicillin G, 50,000 U/kg IM, not to exceed the adult dose of 2.4 million Units, weekly for a total of three doses	• Aqueous crystalline penicillin G, 50,000 U/kg IV every 4–6 h for 10–14 d (not to exceed recommended adult dose); consider following with benzathine penicillin G, 50,000 U/kg IM (not to exceed 2.4 million Units)
Second Choice	• Tetracycline, 500 mg PO four times daily for 14 d OR • Doxycycline, 100 mg PO twice daily for 14 d (in non-pregnant children ≥ 8 years of age) • Erythromycin, 500 mg PO four times daily for 14 d in children < 8 years of age	• Tetracycline, 500 mg PO four times daily for 4 weeks, OR • Doxycycline, 100 mg PO twice daily for 4 weeks (in nonpregnant children ≥ 8 years of age) • Consider penicillin desensitization for children < 8 years of age	As above
Pencillin Allergic	See second choice	See second choice	Desensitize and treat with penicillin

[1]All patients who are pregnant or have HIV infection, congenital syphilis, or neurosyphilis should be treated with penicillin-based regimens.
[2]Except neurosyphilis.

develop atypical laboratory and clinical features of syphilis. Persistent chancres and initial presentations with secondary syphilis are reported more frequently in HIV-infected individuals. False-positive and false-negative serologies are more common in this patient population. Diminished serologic responses to therapy have also been observed in patients with early syphilis and HIV coinfection. The earlier appearance of neurosyphilis and other later stages of disease in HIV-infected patients has been ascribed to a decrease in the efficacy of standard therapy for early syphilis, although at least one recent randomized, double-blind study does not confirm this observation.

Confounding the evaluation and management of neurosyphilis in these patients are the elevated CSF protein and cell counts that can be seen in HIV infec-

BOX 64–5

Treatment of Congenital Syphilis is Children[1]

	Newborn	Older Infants & Children
First Choice	• Aqueous crystalline penicillin G, 50,000 U/kg IV every 12 h for the first week of life and every 8 h afterwards for a total of 10 days	• Aqueous crystalline penicillin G, 50,000 U/kg IV every 4–6 h for a total of 10 days
Second Choice: Penicillin Allergic	Procaine penicillin G, 50,000 U/kg IM in a single daily dose for 10 days; penicillin after desensitization	Pencillin after desensitization

[1]All patients who are pregnant or have HIV infection, congenital syphilis, or neurosyphilis should be treated with penicillin-based regimens.

BOX 64–6

Control of Syphilis

Prophylactic Measures	• Prompt notification of public health department for contact followup and treatment • Recommend safe sexual practices including condom use • Screening of patients with HIV-infection, and those who are pregnant or have another STD • Consider screening individuals who are sexually active and live in endemic areas • Education and behavior modification of high-risk individuals • Effective, expedient, accessible, and affordable diagnostic and therapeutic interventions for infected individuals • Appropriate clinical and laboratory followup of treated individuals
Isolation Precautions	• Contact isolation for moist mucocutaneous lesions of congenital syphilis, primary, and secondary syphilis

tion alone. Despite these observations, standard serologic tests for syphilis are still recommended for diagnosis. However, some experts recommend more aggressive treatment of syphilis and more thorough evaluation of CNS infection in the HIV-infected host regardless of the stage of *T pallidum* infection. Penicillin-based therapies are recommended; close follow-up of response to therapy is essential.

Prevention & Control

No vaccine is currently available for the prevention of syphilis (Box 64–6). Primary prevention measures include behavior modification of patients engaged in high-risk practices such as sexual promiscuity and health programs designed to educate the public about sexually transmitted diseases, including the benefits of condom use. Secondary prevention measures include effective, affordable, prompt, and more accessible diagnostic and therapeutic interventions with appropriate follow-up for infected patients. Screening of all HIV-infected individuals and pregnant women is part of any effective public health prevention program. Reliable and thorough case reporting with partner notification and epidemiologic treatment is also essential.

REFERENCES

Abramowicz M, ed: Drugs for sexually transmitted diseases. Med Lett Drugs Ther 1995;37:117–22.

Berry MC, Dajani AS: Resurgence of congenital syphilis. Infect Dis Clin North Am 1992;6:19–29.

Centers for Disease Control and Prevention: 1998 guidelines for treatment of sexually transmitted diseases. Morb Mortal Wkly Rep 1998;47:28–49.

Centers for Disease Control and Prevention: Summary of notifiable diseases, United States 1997. Morbid Mortal Weekly Rep 1997;46:1–87.

Centers for Disease Control and Prevention: Primary and Secondary Syphilis—United States, 1997. Morbid Mortal Weekly Rep 1998;47:493–497.

Fiumara NJ, Lessel S: Manifestations of late congenital syphilis: an analysis of 271 patients. Arch Dermatol 1970;102:78–83.

Fraser CM et al: Complete genome sequence of *Treponema pallidum,* the syphilis spirochete. Science 1998;281:375–388.

Gordon SM et al: The response of symptomatic neurosyphilis to high-dose intravenous penicillin G in patients with human immunodeficiency virus infection. N Engl J Med 1994;331:1469–73.

Hook EW III, Marra CM: Acquired syphilis in adults. N Engl J Med 1992;326:1060–69.

Hutchinson CM et al: Altered clinical presentation of early syphilis in patients with human immunodeficiency virus infection. Ann Intern Med 1994;121:94–99.

Larsen SA, Steiner BM, Rudolph AH: Laboratory diagnosis and interpretation of tests for syphilis. Clin Microbiol Rev 1995;8:1–21.

Marra CM et al: Resolution of serum and cerebrospinal fluid abnormalities after treatment of neurosyphilis: influence of concomitant human immunodeficiency virus infection. Sex Transm Dis 1996;23:184–89.

Nakashima AK et al: Epidemiology of syphilis in the United States, 1941–1993. Sex Transm Dis 1996; 23: 16–23.

Peter G, ed: *1997 Redbook: Report of the Committee on Infectious Diseases,* 24th ed. American Academy of Pediatrics, 1997, pp. 504–514.

Peterman TA et al: Incubating syphilis in patients treated for gonorrhea: a comparison of treatment regimens. J Infect Dis 1994;170:680–92.

Rolfs RT et al: A randomized trial of enhanced therapy for early syphilis in patients with and without human immunodeficiency virus infection. N Engl J Med 1997; 337:307–14.

St. Louis ME. Strategies for syphilis prevention in the 1990's. Sex Transm Dis 1996;23:58–67.

Stoll BJ: Congenital syphilis: evaluation and management of neonates born to mothers with reactive serologic tests for syphilis. Pediatr Infect Dis J 1994;13:845–53.

Tramont EC: Syphilis in adults: from Christopher Columbus to Sir Alexander Fleming to AIDS. Clin Infect Dis 1995;21:1361–69.

Borrelia & *Leptospira* Species

Sandra Chaparro, MD & Jose G. Montoya, MD

BORRELIA SPECIES

RELAPSING FEVER

Essentials of Diagnosis

- The most common presentation is fever with rash, headache, shaking chills, myalgias, arthralgias, and—during the acute phase—hepatosplenomegaly.
- Louse-borne relapsing fever (LBRF) is epidemic, caused by *B. recurrentis,* and characterized by one or two relapses.
- Tick-borne relapsing fever (TBRF) is endemic, caused by several *Borrelia* species, and characterized by multiple clinical relapses.
- Organisms can be visualized in blood smears of febrile patients, unlike other spirochetal pathogens, using dark-field microscopy or Giemsa or Wright stains.
- Helical (3–10 spirals) spirochetes, 8–30 μm × 0.3 μm, motile (flagella).
- Weil-Felix reaction: Proteus OX-K agglutinin titers are elevated (this is more common in LBRF).

General Considerations

The syndrome of relapsing fever consists of two clinical entities: epidemic relapsing fever caused by *Borrelia recurrentis* (LBRF) and transmitted by the human body louse and endemic relapsing fever caused by *Borrelia* spp. (TBRF) and transmitted by arthropods (Table 65–1).

A. Epidemiology.

1. Louse-borne epidemic relapsing fever (LBRF). This form of relapsing fever is transmitted person to person. Human body lice (*Pediculus humanus corporis*) ingest human blood infected with *B recurrentis.* The spirochetes multiply in the hemolymph of the lice. Humans become infected with *B recurrentis* when the fluids from a crushed louse contaminate mucous membranes or abrasions or other breaks in the skin. Humans are the only host for *B recurrentis*—its occurrence reflects socioeconomic

and ecologic factors. Endemic foci are still observed in parts of Africa, South America, and the Far East.

2. Tick-borne endemic relapsing fever (TBRF). TBRF is caused by ≥ 15 different types of *Borrelia* spp. and is transmitted to humans by ticks (*Ornithodoros* spp.). The spirochete is capable of invading all tissues of the tick. Infections in humans occur when saliva or excrement is released while the tick is feeding. The ticks are nocturnal feeders and are rarely noticed. The tick's bite does not cause pain, and feeding is completed after 5–20 min. Many rodents and small animals are reservoirs for *Borrelia* spp. The spirochete's geographic distribution and occurrence is determined by the biology of the tick. Ticks carrying *Ornithodoros* spp. are mostly found at altitudes of 1500–6000 feet and in humid, warm climates. TBRF has been reported in Africa, Asia, South America, and the western United States during the summer.

B. Microbiology. *Borrelia* spp. belong to the family *Treponemataceae.* They are motile helical bacteria, 8–30 μm long, 0.2–0.5 μm wide, and with 3–10 loose spirals. Desiccation and UV light kill *Borrelia* spp. The generation time of these organisms is 18–26 h. They are not cultured in routine clinical laboratories but can be grown in chick embryos.

C. Pathogenesis. After inoculation in humans from the tick or louse vector, an acute febrile illness ensues, accompanied by a spirochetemia. The bacteria are present in the bloodstream only during the febrile illness. During the afebrile period the bacteria are sequestered in internal organs such as the central nervous system (CNS), bone marrow, liver, and spleen. There is a cycle of antigenic variation with specific antibody responses that explains the relapses of the disease. Each remission is the result of mobilization, opsonization by antibodies produced against the variant strain, agglutination, and phagocytosis of the organism by antibodies produced against the variant strain. Borreliae can cross the placenta and produce abortion or severe infection in neonates.

Clinical Findings

A. Signs and symptoms. LBRF and TBRF have similar signs and symptoms. The mean incubation period is 7 days (range, 2–18 days). Symptoms include sudden onset of fever, headache, photophobia,

Table 65–1. Summary of relapsing fever syndromes[1]

	TBRF	LBRF
Agent	Borrelia spp.	Borrelia recurrentis
Vector	Ornithodoros spp.	Pediculus humanus corporis
Reservoir	Rodents, small animals	Humans
Epidemiologic	Endemic	Epidemic
Distribution	Africa, Asia, South America, and western U.S. (during the summer)	Ethiopia, South America, Far East

[1]TBRF; tick-borne relapsing fever; LBRF; louse-borne relapsing fever

BOX 65–1

Relapsing Fever in Children and Adults[1]

	Acute	Relapse
More Common	• Fever • Rash • Headache • Shaking chills • Nausea, vomiting • Myalgias • Arthralgias • Cough • Conjunctival injection • Petechia (more in LBRF) • Hepatospleno-megaly	• Single relapse with LBRF • Multiples re-lapses with TBRF
Less Common	• Nuchal rigidity (meningitis) • Pulmonary rales, ronchi, pleuritic pain • Lymphadenopathy • Jaundice • Gastrointestinal and CNS hemor-rhage • Myocarditis • Rupture of the spleen	

[1]LBRF, louse-borne relapsing fever; TBRF, tick-borne relapsing fever; CNS, central nervous system.

sweats, shaking chills, cough, nausea, vomiting, myalgias, and arthralgias (Box 65–1). Common findings include conjunctival suffusion, petechia, upper-quadrant abdominal tenderness, and hepatosplenomegaly. Other complications include gastrointestinal or CNS hemorrhage or both and myocarditis. A truncal rash at the end of the primary febrile episode with tachycardia is common. The fever may be accompanied by hypotension and shock. Fever can reappear with less intensity after 10 days. LBRF has usually a single or few relapses; TBRF has multiple relapses. Each successive relapse of TBRF is milder and of shorter duration. Each intervening afebrile period is longer than the previous one.

B. Laboratory findings. LBRF and TBRF are established by the detection of the spirochetes in blood from febrile patients. *Borrelia* spp. can be detected in 70% of cases with dark-field microscopy, Giemsa-, Wright-, or acridine orange-stained preparations of blood smears or thick and thin smears. Serologies have limited value and are not standardized because of antigenic variation. Cross-reaction may occur with other spirochetes (5–10%). Welix-Felix agglutination of Proteus OX-K in convalescent-phase serum supports the diagnosis. Leukocytosis, mild normocytic anemia, and thrombocytopenia are common. There may also be an elevated sedimentation rate, increased prothrombin and partial thromboplastin times, and an increase in aspartate aminotransferase and bilirubin.

Differential Diagnoses

LBRF and TBRF may be confused with malaria, typhoid fever, hepatitis, leptospirosis, salmonellosis, infectious mononucleosis, viral respiratory infections, rat bite fever, Colorado tick fever, Rocky Mountain spotted fever, and dengue fever. Epidemiologic features and detection of spirochetemia can help to exclude these diagnoses.

Treatment

Relapsing fever responds to doxycycline, tetracy-

cline, erythromycin, penicillin, and chloramphenicol (Box 65–2). One single dose of 500 mg of tetracycline (or erythromycin in children, pregnant patients, or patients with penicillin allergies) for LBRF and a 10-day course for TBRF are usually satisfactory. Antibiotic treatment can induce a Jarisch-Herxheimer reaction within 2 h; this reaction coincides with clearing of the spirochetes. This reaction is not prevented with corticosteroids.

Prognosis

With appropriate therapy, mortality rates from relapsing fever are < 5%. In untreated patients the fatality rate for LBRF may reach 40%, and in TBRF is ≤ 5%.

Prevention

LBRF can be prevented with good personal hy-

BOX 65-2

Treatment of Relapsing Fever in Children and Adults[1,2]		
	LBRF (single dose)	TBRF (7 day course)
First Choice	• Doxycycline 100 mg	• 100 mg at 12-h intervals
Second Choice	• Tetracycline 500 mg • Erythromycin 500 mg • Chloramphenicol 500 mg • Penicillin G (procaine) 600,000 IU	• 500 mg at 6-h intervals • 500 mg at 6-h intervals • 500 mg at 6-h intervals • 600,000 IU daily
Pediatric Considerations[3]	• Erythromycin 40 mg/kg/day • Penicilin G (procaine) 10,000 IU/kg/day	• 40 mg/kg/day • 10,000 IU/kg/day
Penicillin Allergic	• Tetracycline 500 mg • Erythromycin 500 mg	• 500 mg at 6-h intervals • 500 mg at 6-h intervals

[1]Antibiotic treatment can induce a Jarish-Herxheimer reaction within 2 h and coincides with clearing of the spirochetes.
[2]LBRF, louse-borne relapsing fever: TBRF, tick-borne relapsing fever
[3]Tetracycline should be avoided in children < 9 years of age.

giene, delousing procedures, and secondary prevention with case detection and treatment (Box 65–3). TBRF requires avoidance or elimination of the tick, using acaricides.

LYME DISEASE

Essentials of Diagnosis
- Most common in the northeastern, upper midwestern, and western parts of the United States.
- *Borrelia burgdorferi* is the longest (20–30 μm) and narrowest (0.2–0.3 μm) spirochete member of the *Borrelia* genus and has the fewest flagella (7–11).
- Erythema migrans (EM) is a red expanding lesion with central clearing that is commonly seen during the early stage of Lyme disease.
- The most common systems affected are the skin (EM), the joints (arthritis), the CNS (facial palsy), and the heart (conduction defects).

- Serology is not standardized; it is insensitive in early infection and does not distinguish active from inactive infection.
- Grows in Barbour-Stoenner-Kelly medium from skin biopsy and other specimens.
- Polymerase chain reaction (PCR) can be useful in synovial-fluid analysis. It has limited value with blood, cerebrospinal fluid (CSF), and urine.

General Considerations
Lyme disease is a tick-borne illness caused by the spirochete *B burgdorferi*. Lyme disease can be divided into early disease (stage 1, EM), disseminated infection (stage 2), and late disease (stage 3, persistent infection). The first stage involves the skin, followed by stages 2 and 3, which often affect the skin, joints, CNS, and heart. However, any of the stages may fail to appear or may overlap with one another (Table 65–2).

A. Epidemiology. Lyme disease is the most

BOX 65-3

Control of relapsing fever[1]		
	LBRF	TBRF
Prophylactic Measures	• Good personal hygiene • Delousing procedures • Improving socioeconomic conditions (crowding, poverty, homelessness)	• Wear cloth to protect skin • Avoid rodent- and tick-infested dwellings • Pest control, repellents, acaricide

[1]LBRF, louse-borne relapsing fever; TBRF, tick-borne relapsing fever.

Table 65–2. Clinical stages of Lyme disease in children and adults

Stage	Timing
Localized erythema chronicum migrans	Early infection
Disseminated infection	Within days or years
Persistent infection	Months to years

common vector-borne infection in the United States. In 1997, there were 12,801 cases reported in the United States. It is transmitted by ticks from the genus *Ixodes*. The *Ixodes* tick goes through a 2-year life cycle that is composed of three stages: larva, nymph, and adult. Tick larvae acquire the spirochete via a blood meal from an infected host. Both the nymph and female adult infect humans. A tick must be attached for at least 24 h to transmit the spirochete. Tick engorgement and attachment for ≥ 72 h are predictors of subsequent human infection. *Ixodes* ticks in the northeastern and midwestern United States belong to the *Ixodes dammini (scapularis)* species, in the western United States to *Ixodes pacificus*, in Europe to *Ixodes ricinus*, and in Asia to *Ixodes persulcatus*. Rodents and small mammals are the natural hosts of the larval and nymphal stages. The incidence of Lyme disease reflects a changing dynamic between the principal reservoir, the white-footed mouse, its food supply, and the suitability of its local habitat. Deer, horses, dogs, and other larger mammals and birds may be occasional hosts to the adult ticks. Most cases have their onset during summer and occur in association with hiking, camping, and residence in wooded, rural, or coastal areas.

B. Microbiology. Of spirochetes in the *Borrelia* genus, *B burgdorferi* is the longest (20–30 μm) and narrowest (0.2–0.3 μm), and has the fewest flagella (7–11). This organism can be grown from skin biopsy and other specimens on an artificial medium called Barbour-Stoenner-Kelly at 33°C. The *B burgdorferi* surface membrane is studded with lipoproteins called outer-surface proteins (OSPs) A, B, C, D, E, and F; other prominent flagellar antigens include flagellar protein, heat shock protein, and protoplasmic cylinder antigen. *B burgdorferi* is capable of altering its surface lipoproteins by recombining gene cassettes in a manner that resembles the mechanism of antigenic variation among the relapsing fever borreliae. The antigenic variability seen among different isolates has important implications for serologic tests and vaccine development. In the United States, most strains belong to the genomic group *B burgdorferi sensu stricto,* and in Europe most strains belong to the groups known as *B garinii* and *B afzelii*.

C. Pathogenesis. After inoculation in the skin, *B burgdorferi* replicates within the dermis producing EM and spreads hematogenously to other organs. The organism has tropism for the skin, joints, heart and CNS. A rise in immunoglobulin M (IgM) is detected within 2–3 weeks after the onset of infection; an increase in IgG and IgA is established after 2–3 months of infection. Host genetic factors may determine the likelihood of tissue damage; for example, patients with human leukocyte antigens DR4 and DR2 may be more susceptible to chronic arthritis.

Clinical Findings

A. Signs and symptoms. *B burgdorferi* infection can involve the skin, musculoskeletal system, CNS, and cardiac tissues (Box 65–4).

1. Skin. EM appears at the site of the tick bite 3–30 days after the bite and begins as a red macule or papule with areas of redness that expand with partial central clearing. The lesion often feels warm to hot; it may burn, prickle, or itch, and it is more common in the thigh, groin, and axilla. The lesion usually fades within 3–4 weeks (range, 1 day–14 months). The migratory nature of skin lesions most likely represents spirochetemia with secondary seeding of the skin

---

BOX 65–4

Systems Affected in Lyme Disease (in Children and Adults)[1]

More Common	• **Skin:** Erythema chronicum migrans and acrodermititis chronica atrophicans • **Joints:** Asymmetric monoarticular or oligoarticular arthritis • **CNS:** Facial palsy, peripheral neuritis, encephalitis, cerebral vasculitis, and chronic encephalopathy • **Cardiac:** AV blocks of various degrees
Less Common	• **Eye:** Conjuctivitis, keratitis, uveitis, retinitis, and optic neuritis • **Liver:** Hepatitis • **Lung:** Adult respiratory distress syndrome • **Congenital:** Intrauterine fetal death, prematurity, cortical blindness, or no adverse outcome

[1]CNS, central nervous systems; AV, atreoventricular.

rather than multiple tick bites. EM may be accompanied by fatigue, fever, chills, achiness, headache, and lymphadenopathy. It can also present with CNS and liver involvement. Multiple annular secondary lesions tend to be smaller and less migratory and to lack indurated centers. Acrodermatitis chronica atrophicans lesions follow years after EM. There is usually bluish-red discoloration, and then the lesion becomes sclerotic or atrophic. This condition has been associated with elevated antibodies to *B burgdorferi* and usually responds to antibiotic therapy; it is seen primarily in elderly women in Europe.

2. Musculoskeletal system. Joint symptoms are the second most common clinical manifestation after EM. These symptoms may begin 5–6 weeks (range, 1 week to 2 years) after the bite, and they include, at one end of the spectrum, subjective joint pain, and at the other, arthritis or chronic erosive synovitis. The arthritis is usually of sudden onset, monoarticular or oligoarticular, and migratory. The knee is the most frequently involved joint, followed by the shoulder, elbow, temporomandibular joint, ankle, wrist, and hip. Initially, recurrent attacks of arthritis are common, but their frequency decreases by 10–20% each year. During recurrences, usually more joints are involved than in the initial episode. These attacks last ~ 1 week, with intervals of 1 week to 2 years between attacks. Joint fluid leukocyte counts range from 500 to 110,000 cells/mm^3. Of all patients with Lyme disease, ~ 10% develop a severe chronic erosive arthritis often associated with IgG antibody response to OSPs A and B of the organism and with human leukocyte antigen DR4.

3. CNS. Neurologic abnormalities begin within 4 weeks (range, 2–11 weeks) after the tick bite. The most common symptoms are headache, stiff neck, photophobia, facial palsy, and peripheral nerve paresthesias. CSF findings are similar to those seen in viral meningitis with lymphocytic pleocytosis of ~ 100 cells/mm^3 and elevated protein levels. Cranial nerve VII is the most frequently involved; unilateral or bilateral facial palsies occur in 11% of patients, and these findings can be seen in 50% of patients with meningitis. Other cranial nerves, particularly III, IV, V, and VIII, are less often involved. Months to years after the initial infection, patients may have chronic encephalopathy (manifested by memory impairment, mood changes, sleep disturbances, and difficulty with concentration), polyneuropathy, or, less commonly, leukoencephalitis. These patients may present with neuropsychiatric symptoms, focal CNS disease, or severe fatigue. However, it is often difficult to establish *B burgdorferi* as the etiologic agent in patients who present with fatigue or psychiatric manifestations.

4. Cardiac tissue. Cardiac involvement begins within 5 weeks (range, 3–21 weeks) after the bite, in ~ 5–10% of patients. Such abnormalities usually consist of atrioventricular block (first degree, Wenckebach, or complete heart block) and can last for 3 days–6 weeks. Some patients can present with myopericarditis, pericardial effusion, and chronic cardiomyopathy.

5. Other clinical findings. Other unusual manifestations include ophthalmologic involvement (conjunctivitis, keratitis, uveitis, choroiditis, retinal detachments, and optic neuritis), hepatitis, myositis, dermatomyositis, eosinophilic lymphadenitis, and adult respiratory distress syndrome.

6. Congenital infection. Maternal-fetal transmission of *B burgdorferi* has been reported with adverse fetal and neonatal outcome in a few cases (congenital heart disease, encephalitis, cortical blindness, intrauterine fetal death, and premature birth). Of note, a prospective study found no association between congenital malformation and infection by *B burgdorferi*. Despite the fact that there is no definitive proof that *B burgdorferi* causes fetal damage or an adverse outcome in the offspring, prompt diagnosis in the mother and treatment should be emphasized.

B. Laboratory findings. The diagnosis of Lyme disease is made on clinical findings, epidemiologic features, and an elevated antibody response to *B burgdorferi*. The available laboratory tests (with the exception of a positive culture from an EM lesion) can be unreliable. Serologic testing only should be undertaken when clinical and epidemiologic features suggest Lyme disease as the diagnosis. Most patients with *B burgdorferi* are found to have detectable antibodies when tested with enzyme-linked immunosorbent assay (60–70% within 2–4 weeks of infection and 90% by the disseminated and persistent stages). However, serologic tests lack standardization, their accuracy is often unsubstantiated, and false-positive results are common. IgM antibody appears 2–4 weeks after the EM lesion, peaks at 6–8 weeks, and declines after 4–6 months. IgG antibody appears 6–8 weeks after the EM lesion, peaks at 4–6 months, and remains at low levels despite antibiotic therapy. A fourfold rise in antibody titer would be suggestive of recent infection. Western blot analysis is used to confirm results obtained by enzyme-linked immunosorbent assay. The finding that a patient has significant amounts of anti-*B burgdorferi*–specific antibodies can be interpreted only in the context of the clinical setting. Demonstrating that a patient has an immune response against this organism does not mean that the patient is actively infected or that any symptoms are necessarily related to *B burgdorferi* infection. Detection of spirochetal DNA by PCR is useful in synovial fluid (75–85% of sensitivity). However, the sensitivity of PCR in CSF, blood, or urine samples has not been well established.

Differential Diagnosis

Lyme disease mimics many different diseases (Table 65–3). The EM lesion may be confused with streptococcal cellulitis, erythema multiforme (the latter lesions tend to be smaller, urticarial, or vesicular

Table 65–3. Differential diagnosis of Lyme disease[1]

Stage	Clinical manifestation	Other diagnoses
Localized Infection	• Erythema chronicum migrans	• Streptococcal cellulitis • Erythema multiforme • Erythema marginatum • Tinea corporis (ringworm) • Nummular eczema • Granuloma annulare
Disseminated Infection	• 7th nerve palsy	• Idiopathic Bell palsy • CNS tumor • Myocarditis (viral and other etiologies) • Acute rheumatic fever
	• Carditis	• Endocarditis
	• Meningitis	• Viral meningitis • Parameningeal infections • Postinfectious meningoencephalitis • Leptospiral meningitis • Tuberculous meningitis • Listeria partially treated • Bacterial (pyogenic) meningitis • Subacute (to chronic) meningitis
	• Arthritis	• Acute rheumatic fever • Malignant effusion • Post-traumatic effusion • Hemophilia • Pyogenic arthritis
Persistent Infection	• Arthritis	• Juvenile rheumatoid arthritis • Henoch-Schönlein purpura • Serum sickness • Collagen vascular disease • Psoriatic arthritis • Postinfectious arthritis • Behçet's disease • Chronic fatigue syndrome

[1]CNS, Central nervous system.

and may occur on mucosal surfaces), and erythema marginatum (these lesions are smaller and migrate rapidly in minutes to hours). Lyme arthritis can be distinguished from other rheumatoid diseases, such as acute rheumatic fever, based on the EM lesion and the brief episode of synovitis. The chronic form of Lyme arthritis may resemble pauciarticular juvenile rheumatoid arthritis, psoriatic arthritis, Reiter's syndrome, and reactive arthritis caused by members of the *Salmonella, Shigella, Campylobacter,* and *Yersinia* genera. This form of arthritis may also be associated with rubella, hepatitis B, or echoviruses. The aseptic meningitis in Lyme disease may resemble enteroviral, leptospiral, or early tuberculous meningitis. It is important to consider sarcoidosis, Behçet's disease, and multiple sclerosis when the disease becomes chronic.

Treatment

Early disease responds readily to several oral agents (such as doxycycline, amoxicillin, or cefuroxime), which are usually prescribed for 2–3 weeks (Box 65–5). There are few published, controlled trials that compare different regimens for late Lyme disease. In-

travenous therapy, usually ceftriaxone or penicillin, is used for 2–3 weeks for late Lyme disease.

A. Erythema migrans. In EM, oral antibiotic therapy with doxycycline shortens the duration of the rash and prevents the development of late sequelae. Amoxicillin is also effective and preferred for children under 9 years of age and in pregnant or lactating women.

B. Musculoskeletal disease. Treatment for one month with oral doxycycline or amoxicillin is usually effective. For refractory cases, intravenous therapy with ceftriaxone or penicillin G, and arthroscopic synovectomy may lead to clinical improvement. Analgesics such as acetaminophen or nonsteroidal anti-inflammatory agents should be used in patients with symptomatic arthritis.

C. Neurologic disease. Patients with facial nerve palsy alone can be treated with oral doxycycline or amoxicillin. Intravenous penicillin G, ceftriaxone, or cefotaxime is effective for meningitis, cranial or peripheral neuropathies, encephalitis, or other late neurologic complications.

D. Cardiac disease. Patients with cardiac atrioventricular block can be treated with doxycycline or

BOX 65–5

Treatment of Lyme Disease in Children and Adults

	Oral Therapy	Intravenous therapy
First Choice	• Doxycycline, 100 mg twice per day • Amoxicillin, 500 mg three times per day	• Ceftriaxone, 2000 mg daily
Second Choice	• Clarithromycin, 500 mg twice per day • Azithromycin, 500 mg daily • Cefuroxime, 500 mg twice per day	• Cefotaxime, 2000 mg at 8-h intervals • Penicillin G, 5 million IU at 6-h intervals
Pediatric Considerations[1]	• Amoxicillin, 50 mg/kg/day	• Ceftriaxone, 75 mg/kg/day • Penicillin G, 300,000 IU/kg/day
Penicillin Allergic	• Clarithromycin, 500 mg twice per day • Azithromycin, 500 mg daily	• Doxycycline, 100 mg twice per day • Azithromycin, 500 mg daily

[1]Tetracycline should be avoided in children < 9 years of age.

amoxicillin if the PR interval is < 0.3 s. For those patients with more severe cardiac involvement, intravenous ceftriaxone or penicillin should be considered. High-degree atrioventricular block may require temporary pacing.

Prognosis

Most patients treated promptly with an appropriate antibiotic have an uncomplicated course. True failures are rare, and in most cases re-treatment or prolonged treatment is the result of misdiagnosis and misinterpretation of serologic results rather than inadequate therapy.

Prophylaxis

Routine use of antimicrobial prophylaxis after a tick bite is not recommended. However, some experts recommend amoxicillin for pregnant women who remove an engorged deer tick after exposure in an endemic area. Persons who develop a rash or illness within a month after a tick bite should seek prompt medical attention. Strategies to prevent Lyme disease include avoiding tick habitats, wearing protective clothing, using repellents to avoid tick attachment, promptly removing attached ticks, and using community measures to reduce tick abundance (Box 65–6). The Lyme vaccine is made from recombinant OSP-A of *B burgdorferi*. Antibodies produced in response to the vaccine destroy spirochetes in the gut of the engorged tick before they can be transmitted. It is indicated for use in adults, in three doses intramuscularly at 0, 1, and 12 months. Ideally the third dose should be given in March because the tick season in the Northeast and upper Midwest usually begins in April. The efficacy of the vaccine has been reported to be 76% after the third dose; however, the long-term safety, timing of booster doses, and cost effectiveness are unknown. Use of this vaccine should be limited to persons with frequent or prolonged exposure to tick habitats in endemic areas.

LEPTOSPIRA SPECIES

Essentials of Diagnosis

- The most severe forms of leptospirosis commonly present with liver and renal involvement.
- Transmission occurs by indirect contact with an infected animal.
- Predisposing factors include occupational exposure (veterinarians and farmers) and recreational exposure (campers and swimmers).

BOX 65–6

Control of Lyme disease

Prophylactic Measures	• Doxycycline, 100 mg twice per day by mouth • Amoxicillin, 500 mg at 8-h intervals per 10 days by mouth • Vaccine in high-risk workers and persons living or visiting endemic areas
Isolation Precautions	• Wear cloth to protect skin • Repellents, insecticides • Check for ticks every 24 h

BOX 65–7

Leptospirosis in Children and Adults

More Common	**Anicteric** • Septic phase: (3–7 d) Fever, headache, myalgias, abdominal pain, nausea, vomiting • Immune phase: (0 d–1 mo) Lower fever, intense headache, aseptic meningitis, conjuctival injection, uveitis, hepatosplenomegaly, pulmonary involvement, skin rashes
Less Common	**Icteric** • Septic phase: (3–7 d) • Imune phase: (10–30 d) Jaundice, renal dysfunction, vasculitis, pulmonary hemorrhage, myocarditis

- These organisms can be detected by dark-field examination, silver or fluorescent antibody stains, or PCR. Tween 80-albumin is the best medium for culture.
- Motile spirochete, 0.1 x 6–20 μm, with hooked end.
- Isolation from any clinical specimen or seroconversion or fourfold increase in antibody titers is diagnostic.

General Considerations

Leptospirosis is caused by multiple species of *Lep-tospira* and is characterized by two different forms of disease. There is a mild form (anicteric) and a severe form (icteric, also known as Weil's syndrome) of leptospirosis.

A. Epidemiology. Leptospirosis is a zoonosis of worldwide distribution and is especially common in tropical regions. Rodents, dogs, cats, other wild mammals, fish, and birds are important reservoirs. The bacteria can live in the renal tubules of dogs for long periods of time. Transmission to humans occurs by indirect contact with urine, blood, or tissue of an infected animal (eg, by veterinarians or farmers); human-to-human transmission is rare. It can be contracted during recreational activities involving water. Leptospirosis has been reported during the summer and autumn months in the southern and western United States and especially in Hawaii.

B. Microbiology. Leptospires are spirochetes belonging to the genus *Leptospira,* which is composed of two species: *L interrogans* and *L biflexa.* The pathogenic leptospires belong to the first species and are divided into 200 serotypes that have major antigens in common and are combined into 23 serogroups. Leptospires are motile spirochetes, 0.1 μm wide, 6–20 μm long, and with hooked ends.

C. Pathogenesis. The bacteria enter the abraded skin or mucous membranes and spread by blood to multiple organs including liver (liver disease occurs in severe cases due to hepatocellular dysfunction including decreased production of clotting factors and albumin, and reduced esterification of cholesterol), kidneys (renal failure due to tubular damage by immune complexes, hypoxemia, or direct toxic effect of the leptospires), CNS (in the first week, the leptospira can

BOX 65–8

Treatment of Leptospirosis in Children and Adults

	Anicteric	Icteric
First Choice	• Ampicillin, 500 mg four times daily by mouth • Amoxicillin, 500 mg four times daily by mouth • Doxycycline, 100 mg four times daily by mouth	• Penicillin G, 1.5 million IU four times daily intravenously • Ampicillin, 1000 mg four times daily intravenously • Amoxicillin, 1000 mg four times daily intravenously
Second Choice	• Tetracycline, 2000 mg/day by mouth	• Erythromycin,[2] 500 mg four times daily intravenously
Pediatric Considerations[1]	• Ampicillin, 50 mg/kg/day by mouth • Amoxicillin, 50 mg/kg/day by mouth	• Penicillin G, 6–8 million IU/m[2] day intravenously • Erythromycin,[2] 50 mg/kg/day intravenously
Penicillin Allergic	• Doxycycline, 100 mg four times daily by mouth	• Erythromycin,[2] 500 mg four times daily intravenously

[1]Tetracycline should be avoided in children < 9 years of age.
[2]Erythromycin is active in in-vitro and animal models but no human clinical data is available.

be found in the CSF, but no meningitis is seen until the serum antibody appears), eye (can produce chronic or recurrent uveitis), muscle (changes include cytoplasmic vacuoles and polymorphonuclear leukocyte infiltration), and blood vessels (vasculitis, capillary injury, and hemolysis are characteristic features).

Clinical Findings

A. Signs and symptoms. Leptospirosis has an incubation period of 1–2 weeks. Among infected patients who develop leptospirosis, 90% have the anicteric form, and 10% have the icteric form. There are two phases—septic and immune. The septic phase lasts 4–7 days and consists of a flulike syndrome; during this phase leptospiras can be found in the bloodstream. The immune phase lasts 4–30 days and consists of aseptic meningitis, uveitis, iritis, rash, and hepatic and renal involvement. During this phase, leptospiras can be found in urine and aqueous humor (Box 65–7).

1. Anicteric leptospirosis. The septic phase is characterized by fever, headache, myalgias, abdominal pain, nausea, and vomiting. The immune phase consists of less prominent fever, intense headache, aseptic meningitis, conjunctival suffusion, uveitis, hepatosplenomegaly, pulmonary involvement, and skin rashes.

2. Icteric leptospirosis. The septic phase resembles that of the anicteric leptospirosis. The most prominent manifestation during the immune phase is hepatorenal dysfunction with hemorrhagic diathesis.

B. Laboratory findings. Laboratory findings in anicteric leptospirosis include normal leukocyte counts with neutrophilia and elevated ESR and CSF protein. Pulmonary and myocardial involvement; high bilirubin levels; increases in alkaline phosphatase, aspartate aminotransferase, alanine aminotransferase, creatine phosphokinase, creatinine, and blood urea nitrogen; and thrombocytopenia are commonly found in icteric leptospirosis. The diagnosis is made by isolation of the organism from any clinical specimen or seroconversion or fourfold increase in antibody titer. The bacteria can be isolated from blood or CSF during the first 10 days. Tween 80-albumin medium is preferred, and multiple cultures should be performed. The organisms can also be detected by dark-field examination, PCR, silver stains of body fluids or fluorescent antibody stains of tissue. *Leptospira*-specific antibodies can be detected by macroscopic agglutination with killed antigen, microscopic agglutination with live

---

BOX 65–9

Control of leptospirosis

Prophylactic Measures	• Doxycycline 200 mg once a week
Isolation Precautions	• Effective rat control • Avoidance of infected urine and tissues from animals • Vaccination of animals

---

antigen (more specific) and enzyme-linked immunosorbent assay. Agglutinins appear after 6–12 days, and peak titers are reached in 3–4 weeks. Cross-reaction is common with other spirochetal diseases.

Differential Diagnoses

Differential diagnoses include dengue, dengue fever, hemorrhagic fever, LBRF, TBRF, and other diseases caused by arthropod-borne and rodent-borne pathogens.

Complications

Aseptic meningitis is the most common complication in the anicteric cases. Renal failure, liver damage, pulmonary hemorrhage, vasculitis, and myocarditis are less common but are the usual causes of death.

Treatment

Penicillin G or doxycycline are effective even when treatment is delayed (Box 65–8). Penicillin G or ampicillin should be used in severely ill patients. In less severely ill patients, an oral dose of ampicillin, doxycycline, or amoxicillin can be used.

Prognosis

In the absence of jaundice, the disease is rarely fatal. The mortality rate in icteric patients under 30 years of age is 5%; in the elderly the rate is 30–40%.

Prevention

Doxycycline can prevent infection (Box 65–9). However, prevention is problematic because exposure is difficult to predict. Effective rat control and avoidance of infected urine and known contaminated water sources are important preventive measures.

REFERENCES

Cadavid D, Barbour AG: Neuroborreliosis during relapsing fever: Review of the clinical manifestations, pathology and treatment of infections in humans and experimental animals. Clin Infect Dis 1998;26:151.

Farr RW: Leptospirosis. Clin Infect Dis 1995;21:1.

Fraser CM, Casjens S, Huang WM, et al: Genomic sequence of a Lyme disease spirochaete, *Borrelia burgdorferi.* Nature 1997; 390:580.

Medical Letter on Drugs and Therapeutics: Lyme disease vaccine. Med Lett Drugs Ther 1999;41:29.

Medical Letter on Drugs and Therapeutics. Treatment of Lyme disease. Med Lett Drugs Ther 1997;39:47.

Trevejo RT et al: Evaluation of two-test serodiagnostic method for early Lyme disease in clinical practice. J Infect Dis 1999;179:931.

Zhang J-R, Hardham JM, Barbour AG, Norris SJ: Antigenic variation in Lyme disease borreliae by promiscuous recombination of VMP-like sequence cassettes. Cell 1997; 89:275.

Mycoplasma & Ureaplasma

Jose G. Montoya, MD

Mycoplasma and *Ureaplasma* species (mycoplasmas) are ubiquitous in nature and are commonly found in plants, animals, and humans. These bacteria contain the smallest amount of double-stranded DNA that is capable of producing a free-living microorganism; they measure between 0.15 and 0.3 μm in diameter and ≤ 2 μm in length. They are believed to have evolved from a putative common ancestor of the gram-positive bacteria by a process of genome reduction and adoption of a dependent, parasitic life style. *Mycoplasma* and *Ureaplasma* spp. lack a cell wall. Therefore, they cannot be visualized with the Gram stain and are not susceptible to antibiotics that act on cell wall synthesis (eg, penicillins and cephalosporins). They are capable of growing in cell-free media, but require many exogenous nutrients for growth, including sterols. In addition to *Ureaplasma urealyticum,* 13 species of *Mycoplasma* have been isolated from humans; however, most of them are not regarded as pathogens.

Mycoplasmas are the etiologic agents and cofactors of several clinical syndromes in humans. *Mycoplasma pneumoniae* is a common cause of community-acquired pneumonia. *U urealyticum* and *Mycoplasma genitalium* most often cause genitourinary tract infections; *U urealyticum* has also been associated with perinatal morbidity and mortality, as well as with disease outside the genitourinary tract, especially in children. *Mycoplasma hominis* is an infrequent cause of bone, joint, and upper urinary tract disease.

M PNEUMONIAE INFECTION & DISEASE

M pneumoniae is an important cause of upper and lower respiratory infections in both adults and children. Extrapulmonary involvement, including dermatological, neurological, cardiac, musculoskeletal, and vasculitic involvement, has also been associated with *M pneumoniae* infection in humans.

Essentials of Diagnosis

- Community acquired pneumonia.
- Extrapulmonary involvement is not infrequent.
- Inflammatory cells on sputum Gram stain but no predominant bacterial type.
- Coombs-positive hemolytic anemia.
- Cold agglutinin titer of ≥ 1:32.
- Fourfold change in specific immunoglobulin G (IgG) or IgM titers.

General Considerations

A. Epidemiology. Infected humans are the only source of *M pneumoniae* organisms for transmission to new susceptible hosts. *M pneumoniae* is spread from one individual to another by respiratory droplets produced by coughing. Individuals at any age can be infected and develop disease, but those between the ages of 5 and 20 years are most often affected. *M pneumoniae* is a leading cause of pneumonia in school-aged children and young adults—especially those in military and college populations. Infections occur throughout the world and without regard for time of year. Immunity after infection is not long lasting.

B. Microbiology. *M pneumoniae* cannot be visualized with any routine stain because of its small size and lack of cell wall. It is difficult to cultivate in the laboratory due to its fastidious growth requirements; however, it does grow slowly in enriched liquid culture media and on special mycoplasma agar, such as SP 4, under aerobic conditions. *M pneumoniae* may require ≥ 21 days before growth can be easily detected in a culture; *M hominis* and *U urealyticum* require 2–5 days.

C. Pathogenesis. The initial step in disease causation by *Mycoplasma* spp. is attachment to the cilia and microvilli of epithelial cells lining the respiratory tract. Respiratory epithelial cells express complex oligosaccharides containing sialic acid in their apical regions that bind a *Mycoplasma* surface protein known as P1, located on a polar attachment structure. *Mycoplasma* attachment to these cells precipitates a cascade of events characterized by ciliostasis, desquamation of the involved cells, and an inflammatory reaction. Mechanisms of cytotoxicity may include direct damage to respiratory epithelial cells by substances elaborated by mycoplasmas such as hydrogen peroxide and free-oxygen radicals or damage resulting from the host inflammatory response. The plasma membrane surfaces of *Mycoplasma* spp. are covered with variable lipoproteins that display antigenic and immunomodulatory properties.

Clinical Findings (Box 66–1.)

A. Respiratory Involvement.

1. Signs and Symptoms. *M pneumoniae* is associated with pharyngitis, nonpurulent otitis media, tracheobronchitis, and community-acquired pneumonia in humans. The latter two syndromes are by far the most common among those caused by *M pneumoniae*. Despite earlier descriptions of an association with bullous myringitis, this finding does not appear to be a common feature of *M pneumoniae* infection. The pneumonia is usually self-limited and does not require hospitalization. However, in patients with sickle cell disease and other hemoglobinopathies, respiratory involvement by *M pneumoniae* can be severe and life-threatening.

Patients develop respiratory symptoms 2–3 weeks after exposure to the respiratory secretions of another infected individual. *M pneumoniae* respiratory tract disease usually presents with gradual onset of fever, malaise, headache, and cough. The cough is usually minimally productive or nonproductive and is "hacking" in most patients; it can become debilitating or incapacitating and may produce sternal discomfort. Most of these symptoms resolve spontaneously in the vast majority of patients. However, in a minority, these upper respiratory symptoms progress to tracheobronchitis or pneumonia. On occasion, *M pneumoniae* pneumonia begins abruptly. Pleuritic chest pain is rare and must be distinguished from the chest soreness due to muscle strain in cases of severe cough. Body temperature usually fluctuates between 101 and 102 °F; however, occasional temperature spikes > 102 °F can be seen. On physical examination, most patients do not appear acutely ill. The pharynx may appear erythematous, but cervical lymphadenopathy is rare or absent. *M pneumoniae* is a rare cause of isolated pharyngitis in children and adults. Lung auscultation may be entirely normal or may disclose only a few crackles.

2. Laboratory findings. Examination of sputum with the Gram stain usually reveals inflammatory cells in the absence of large numbers of bacteria or a predominant type. The peripheral leukocyte count is either within normal range or moderately elevated.

3. Imaging. Chest radiographic abnormalities are usually out of proportion to the physical examination findings. *M pneumoniae* has a predilection for the lower lobes and usually causes patchy alveolar or reticular infiltrates; however, lobar infiltrates have been described. Pleural effusions, if present, are small. Unusual radiological findings described in association with *M pneumoniae* pneumonia include diffuse interstitial infiltrates, mediastinal mass, hilar adenopathy, and pneumatocoeles.

B. Dermatologic Involvement.

M pneumoniae infection has been associated with erythema multiforme major, or the Stevens-Johnson syndrome. Erythema multiforme major is an acute and often recurrent inflammatory disease of skin and mucous membranes. Erythema multiforme has been reported in as many as 7% of patients with *M pneumoniae* pneumonia, but has been associated, albeit less often, with other infectious agents including herpes simplex virus. Skin lesions of erythema multiforme include urticarial papules, macules with a "target" appearance, vesicles, and bullae. They occur on the backs of hands, palms, soles, and extensor surfaces of limbs, and they may become generalized. Stevens-Johnson syndrome is a vesiculobullous disease of the skin, mouth, eyes, and genitals. Most bullae affect the trunk, mouth, and genitals. The conjunctiva are usually injected. Drugs such as phenytoin, phenobarbital, sulfonamides, and penicillins can also be implicated as causative agents of erythema multiforme and Stevens-Johnson syndrome.

C. Cardiac and Vascular Involvement.

Raynaud's phenomenon has been described particularly in women with *M pneumoniae* infections. It may be related to the development in these patients of cold-sensitive IgM antibodies directed against the I antigen on circulating erythrocytes (cold agglutinins). These autoantibodies are responsible for a subclinical hemolytic anemia in ~ 50% of patients and a clinically significant anemia in a smaller percentage of patients. Cardiac arrhythmias including conduction defects, hemopericardium, myopericarditis, and congestive heart failure have also been associated with *M pneumoniae* infection. Other reported vascular complications include internal carotid artery occlusion, cerebral infarction, and infection of aneurysms and vascular grafts.

BOX 66–1

Mycoplasma pneumoniae Disease

More Common	• Tracheobronchitis • Pneumonia
Less Common	• Erythema multiforme • Stevens-Johnson syndrome • Raynaud's phenomenon • Congestive heart failure, myopericarditis, hemopericardium • Aseptic meningitis, meningoencephalitis • Transverse myelitis • Guillain-Barré syndrome, peripheral neuropathy

D. Neurologic Involvement. A number of neurologic syndromes have been ascribed to *M pneumoniae,* although a causal relationship is not well established. These syndromes include aseptic meningitis, meningoencephalitis, transverse myelitis, brain stem dysfunction, Guillain-Barré syndrome, and peripheral neuropathy. Cerebrospinal fluid (CSF) examination usually reveals < 500 leukocytes/mm^3, a slightly elevated protein concentration, and normal to slightly decreased glucose concentration. In most cases a microbiological diagnosis has been established by serology. *M pneumoniae* rarely has been cultivated from CSF and has never been cultivated from brain tissue. A case of fatal encephalitis has been described in which *M pneumoniae* DNA was detected in CSF by polymerase chain reaction. It is important to emphasize that efforts should be made to rule out other causes of CNS disease before *M pneumoniae* is established as the etiologic agent.

E. Other Clinical Manifestations. Polyarthralgia, arthritis, and immune complex-associated renal disease have been associated with *M pneumoniae* infection.

Diagnosis

Methods for diagnosing *M pneumoniae* infection include cultivation, antigen and nucleic acid detection, and serology. Cultivation of *M pneumoniae* from tracheal aspirates, nasopharyngeal swabbings, sputum, or any body fluid should be attempted if the methods are available but they have a low yield and are cumbersome to perform due to the complex growth requirements of the organism. Specimens for culture should be transported in special media.

Detection of *M pneumoniae* antigens directly in sputum specimens is feasible by using a direct fluorescent antibody method or antigen-capture enzyme immunoassay, but the role of these antigens in the diagnosis of *M pneumoniae* disease has not been well established. Methods for detecting *M pneumoniae* DNA are also commercially available for use with throat swabs but are not available in most laboratories.

Serological testing is the most widely available and widely used approach for diagnosing *M pneumoniae* infections. Serological tests are rarely helpful during the acute illness. Paired measurements are most helpful; a fourfold titer difference between the acute and the convalescent serum antibody titer is considered diagnostic. Single measurements are of value for epidemiological purposes. IgG- and IgM-specific antibodies can be detected with indirect immunofluorescent antibody or enzyme immunoassay methods. Because of ease of use and reliability, enzyme immunoassay has become the preferred method. A complement fixation assay is less sensitive and is reserved for epidemiological purposes.

Demonstration of cold agglutinins can help to support the diagnosis of *M pneumoniae* pneumonia, although the finding is nonspecific. Cold agglutinins have been observed in adenovirus infections, infectious mononucleosis, cytomegalovirus infection, lymphoma, and other diseases. Nonetheless, a titer of ≥ 1:32 is highly suggestive of infection with *M pneumoniae.* Cold agglutinins can also be detected at the bedside by drawing 1 mL of the patient's blood into a blue top tube (containing citrate as the anticoagulant) and cooling the tube at 4 °C for 3–4 min. The reversible appearance of macroagglutination indicates the presence of cold agglutinins at a titer of approximately ≥ 1:64.

Differential Diagnosis

Legionella spp., *Chlamydia pneumoniae, Chlamydia psittaci, Streptococcus pneumoniae, Haemophilus influenzae,* and *Moraxella catarrhalis* can cause a pneumonia with clinical features that are indistinguishable from those associated with *M pneumoniae.*

Treatment

The efficacy of antimicrobial agents in patients with *M pneumoniae* pneumonia is difficult to evaluate because this is often a self-limited disease. Antibiotics most likely shorten the duration of symptoms and may have an important role when infected patients are immunocompromised or are severely affected by the disease.

The most effective antimicrobial agents are macrolides, fluoroquinolones, and tetracyclines (Box 66–2). Macrolides are the first-line agents for treatment of *M pneumoniae*-associated disease. Azithromycin and clarithromycin are better tolerated and easier to administer than erythromycin, but are more expensive. Fluoroquinolones should not be used in patients younger than 18 years, and tetracyclines should not be used in children younger than 9. The newer fluoroquinolones (levofloxacin, moxifloxacin, and gatifloxacin) with enhanced activity against *S pneumoniae* have reliable activity in vitro against *M pneumoniae.* Most patients with pneumonia do not require hospitalization and are treated on an empirical basis. The recommended duration of therapy is not clear. Clinical relapse occurs in ~ 10% of patients and may warrant a longer course of antibiotic therapy, eg, 3 weeks.

Radiological improvement may lag behind clinical improvement for weeks.

Prevention

There are currently no recommended specific control measures for *M pneumoniae* outbreaks in closed communities. However, some studies have suggested the usefulness of prophylactic antibiotics administered to close contacts of case patients. One study demonstrated that the administration of azithromycin, 500 mg on day 1 and 250 mg on days 2–5, to individuals at risk was beneficial in reducing the disease attack rate during an institutional outbreak of *M pneumoniae* pneumonia. There is no available vaccine.

BOX 66-2

Treatment of *Mycoplasma pneumoniae* Infections[1]

First Choice	• Azithromycin, orally, 500 mg on day 1 followed by 250 mg daily on days 2–5 **OR** • Azithromycin, IV, 500 mg daily **OR** • Clarithromycin,[2] orally, 500 mg daily **OR** • Erythromycin, orally, 250–500 mg four times daily **OR** • Erythromycin, IV, 500 mg four times daily
Second Choice	• Levofloxacin, orally or IV, 500 mg daily **OR** • Doxycycline, orally or IV, 100 mg twice daily
Pediatric Considerations	• Use macrolide only • Erythromycin 40 mg/kg/day • Tetracyclines are contraindicated in children < 9 years of age • Fluoroquinolones are not recommended in persons < 18 years of age

[1]Cell wall antibiotics have no role in the treatment of mycoplasma infections.
[2]IV clarithromycin is not available.

INFECTIONS CAUSED BY *U UREALYTICUM* & OTHER MYCOPLASMAS

U urealyticum, M hominis, and *M genitalium* are commensals of the genitourinary tract of both women and men and in newborns. *U urealyticum* is an infrequent cause of urethritis in males, urinary calculi, chorioamnionitis, spontaneous abortion, and premature birth. *M genitalium* is also associated with male urethritis. *M hominis* is a rare cause of pyelonephritis, pelvic inflammatory disease, and postabortal and postpartum fevers.

U urealyticum and *M hominis* can cause disease outside the genitourinary tract in immunosuppressed patients or in otherwise immunocompetent patients after manipulation or trauma of the genitourinary tract. *M hominis* can cause sternal wound infections and osteomyelitis, arthritis (especially in hypogammaglobulinemic patients), brain abscess, pneumonia, and peritonitis. It has been associated with neonatal pneumonia and sepsis. In immunosuppressed patients, *U urealyticum* can cause arthritis, osteomyelitis, sinusitis, and pneumonia. It can also cause neonatal pneumonia and sepsis.

A thorough search for other causes should be completed before *U urealyticum* or *M hominis* can be considered the etiologic agent of any of the above syndromes.

Mycoplasma penetrans, Mycoplasma pirum, and *Mycoplasma fermentans* have been associated with HIV infection and with the progression to AIDS; however, there is little evidence for a causal role of these organisms in this disease process. The associations more likely reflect the enhanced susceptibility of the HIV-infected host to secondary mycoplasma infection.

M hominis can be treated with tetracyclines or with clindamycin. *U urealyticum* infections can be treated with tetracyclines, erythromycin, or azithromycin. Both *U urealyticum* and *M hominis* can be resistant to the tetracyclines. *M hominis* is resistant to the macrolides.

REFERENCES

Fenollar F et al: *Mycoplasma* infections of aneurysms or vascular grafts. Clin Infect Dis 1999;28:694.

Hutchison CA et al: Global transposon mutagenesis and a minimal *Mycoplasma* genome. Science 1999;286:2165.

Klausner JD et al: Enhanced control of an outbreak of *Mycoplasma pneumoniae* pneumonia with azithromycin prophylaxis. J Infect Dis 1998;177:161.

Razin S, Yogev D, Naot Y: Molecular biology and pathogenicity of mycoplasmas. Microbiol Mol Biol Rev 1998;62:1094.

Rottem S, Naot Y: Subversion and exploitation of host cells by mycoplasmas. Trends Microbiol 1998;6:436.

67

Chlamydia

Jose G. Montoya, MD

General Considerations

Chlamydia trachomatis, Chlamydia psittaci, and *Chlamydia pneumoniae* are among the most prevalent microbial pathogens in humans worldwide. *C trachomatis* is responsible for a variety of sexually transmitted disease (STD) syndromes in both sexes. In addition, certain serotypes of *C trachomatis* are responsible for trachoma, the most common infectious cause of blindness in humans. *C psittaci* is a zoonotic pathogen associated with atypical pneumonia. *C pneumoniae* infects approximately one-half of the world's human population and is a cause of upper and lower respiratory tract disease. It has also been associated with atherosclerotic cardiovascular disease.

A. Epidemiology. In the United States, genital infections by *C trachomatis* serovars D through K occur frequently among sexually active adolescents and young adults. These serovars are also important perinatal pathogens. In 1998, > 600,000 cases were reported in the United States (237 per 100,000 population), making it the most common notifiable infectious disease in this country. Asymptomatic infection is rather common in both women and men. Prevalence rates vary according to the geographic locale and the specific populations. The prevalence of urethral infection among young men is < 10% for those seen in general medical settings, between 10% and 15% for asymptomatic soldiers undergoing routine medical care, and > 10% for heterosexual men seen in STD clinics. The prevalence of *C trachomatis* genital infection among women is 5% for asymptomatic college students, > 10% for women monitored in family-planning clinics, and > 20% for women seen in STD clinics. Chlamydial genital infections are found at a higher rate among women who use oral contraceptives or have cervical ectopy. It is estimated that 5–25% of pregnant women in the United States carry *C trachomatis* in their cervix. Of the neonates who get infected during birth, ~ 25% develop inclusion conjunctivitis, and 10% develop pneumonia.

Lymphogranuloma venereum (caused by serovars L1, L2, and L3) is a rare disease in the United States. The vast majority of cases are transmitted sexually, but transmission by nonsexual routes has been documented.

C trachomatis serovars A, B, Ba, and C cause trachoma, one the most common causes of preventable blindness in the world. These serovars are usually transmitted from person to person (most often involving a child) via hands and fomites. Endemic areas include Asia, the Middle East, sub-Saharan Africa, and northern Africa.

C psittaci is usually transmitted to humans by contact with birds or from occupational exposure in avian-processing plants or poultry farms. Essentially all common birds and several wild species are capable of carrying the organism and shedding it while remaining healthy. Only brief exposure to an area where an infected bird has been present is necessary for transmission of *C psittaci*. Rarely, the bite of a bird transmits the disease.

C pneumoniae was established as a human respiratory pathogen in 1983, and it is now associated with 6–12% of cases of community-acquired pneumonia. Approximately 50% of persons worldwide have been infected by early adulthood. Outbreaks of *C pneumoniae* respiratory disease have been described especially in military recruits but also in the general population; the highest rates of *C pneumoniae* pneumonia are found among the elderly. There is no seasonal predominance. Exchange of respiratory secretions by aerosol route or by hand appears to be the primary mode of transmission of *C pneumoniae*. In more recent years, this organism has been associated with atherosclerosis and coronary artery disease.

B. Microbiology. Members of the genus *Chlamydia* are small, obligate intracellular prokaryotic organisms. They contain DNA, RNA, ribosomes, and a discrete cell envelope. The envelope lacks peptidoglycan between the inner and outer membranes, which explains why cell wall-active antibiotics have no role in the treatment of chlamydial infections. During their unique life cycle, *Chlamydia* species are observed in two distinct forms: the extracellular elementary body and the intracellular reticulate body. The elementary body is responsible for person-to-person transmission. It attaches to, and is engulfed by mammalian target cells. Within the phagosome, the elementary bodies reorganize and develop into reticulate bodies, which are adapted for intracellular survival and multiplication. After multiple rounds of replication by binary fission, the reticulate bodies condense and form elementary bodies. The elementary bodies eventually rupture the host cell to continue the cycle by infecting other contiguous cells. The complete genome sequences of *C trachomatis* and *C pneumoniae* reveal a large number of genes that are most similar to versions found in eukaryotes, emphasizing the coevolution of pathogen and host. Despite their distant relationship with the gram-negative bacilli, both *Chlamydia* species contain genes that appear to encode a "type III" secretion system typically associated with invasiveness and other virulence attributes.

Members of the genus *Chlamydia* share a common heat-stable lipopolysaccharide antigen and specific cell envelope protein antigens which facilitate their classification into a number of serotypes. Protein antigenic and gene sequence variability of the major outer-membrane protein have led to the identification of at least 20 sero- and sequence types of *C trachomatis*. The vast majority of the serotypes can be assigned to one of three major groups: (1) serovar group A, B, Ba, and C, which is associated with trachoma; (2) serovar group D, E, F, G, H, I, J, and K, which is associated with sexually transmitted and perinatally acquired infections; and (3) serovar group L1, L2, and L3, which is associated with lymphogranuloma venereum and hemorrhagic proctocolitis.

C. Pathogenesis. *Chlamydia* species rupture mammalian cells after unregulated replication of elementary bodies; pathology results from this cell lysis, as well as damage caused by recruited inflammatory cells and cytokine mediators. Repeated or persistent exposure is believed to elicit more intense host inflammatory responses, some of which may be directed at chlamydial heat shock proteins. A crucial and common pathologic endpoint of chlamydial infection is scarring of mucous membranes, especially of the conjunctiva (trachoma) and female upper genital tract (resulting in infertility).

The elementary body of *C trachomatis* attaches to host epithelial cells by using heparan sulfate as a bridging ligand and later infects mononuclear leukocytes in lymph nodes via the local lymphatic draining system. Immunity against *C trachomatis* appears to protect only partially against reinfection.

C psittaci is acquired through inhalation of respiratory secretions or aerosolized droppings of infected birds; it spreads via the bloodstream and eventually reaches reticuloendothelial cells of the spleen and liver. Pneumonitis is characterized by edema, necrosis, erythrocytes, and a chronic inflammatory cellular infiltrate.

Little is known regarding the pathogenesis of *C pneumoniae*. It appears that *C pneumoniae* has a less rigid cell wall than that in other chlamydial species.

Diagnosis

Chlamydial infections require laboratory studies for a definitive diagnosis. Available laboratory techniques include cytology, culture, serology, and demonstration of chlamydial antigens or nucleic acid sequences.

Treatment

Antimicrobial agents such as the tetracyclines, certain macrolides, and some fluoroquinolones are highly active against *Chlamydia* infections. Clinically relevant resistance to these antibiotics has not been observed. All sex partners of patients with sexually transmitted chlamydial infections should be referred for evaluation and treatment.

C TRACHOMATIS INFECTIONS

Essentials of Diagnosis

- Typical intracytoplasmic inclusions in Giemsa-stained cell scrapings from the conjunctiva.
- Ligase chain reaction (LCR) or polymerase chain reaction (PCR) in first-void urine.
- Positive culture in McCoy or HeLa cells of body fluids or secretions.
- Positive microimmunofluorescence serology for suspected cases of lymphogranuloma venereum and infants with pneumonia.
- Complement fixation titer of 1:64 or greater in patients with presumed lymphogranuloma venereum.

Clinical Syndromes

C trachomatis is associated with urethritis, proctitis, conjunctivitis, and arthritis in women and men; epididymitis in men; and mucopurulent cervicitis (MPC), acute salpingitis, bartholinitis, and the Fitz-Hugh and Curtis syndrome in women (Box 67–1). *C trachomatis* and *Neisseria gonorrhoeae* (see Chapter 52) coinfections are common in women with MPC and men with urethritis. In men, *C trachomatis* is the most common etiologic agent of the nongonococcal (NGU) and postgonococcal urethritis (PGU) syndromes. In college-age women, in the absence of infection with *Escherichia coli* or *Staphylococcus saprophyticus, C trachomatis* is the most common etiologic agent of urethritis.

A. Urethritis. Urethritis is characterized in women by the presence of dysuria and frequency without urgency or hematuria and in men by discharge, frequency, and dysuria. Urethritis should be documented by the presence of mucopurulent or purulent discharge, by a Gram stain of urethral secretions demonstrating ≥ 5 leukocytes per oil immersion field, or by demonstrating a positive leukocyte esterase test or ≥ 10 leukocytes per high-power field on first-void urine. NGU is diagnosed in men with urethritis in whom gram-negative intracellular diplococci (*N gonorrhoeae*) cannot be detected in a gram-stained urethral discharge or swab specimen. PGU is diagnosed in men with persistent urethritis 2–3 weeks after treatment of gonococcal urethritis with beta-lactam antibiotics, which are ineffective against *C trachomatis.* Although the discharge from chlamydial urethritis is more watery, less purulent, and less abundant than the discharge from gonococcal urethritis, attempts to

BOX 67–1

C trachomatis Infections

	Women	Men	Children
More Common	• Mucopurulent cervicitis • Acute salpingitis[1] • Endometritis[1] • Bartholinitis • Acute urethral syndrome	• Nongonococcal urethritis • Postgonococcal urethritis • Epididymitis	• Inclusion conjunctivitis in infants • Pneumonia in infants
Less Common	• Perihepatitis • Proctitis • Conjunctivitis • Reiter's syndrome	• Proctitis • Conjunctivitis • Reiter's syndrome	• Otitis media • C trachomatis in genital secretions should raise the suspicion of sexual abuse

[1]These syndromes are also categorized under the syndrome PID.

distinguish between the two on clinical grounds alone can be problematic. Physical examination in cases of chlamydial urethritis can be entirely normal or reveal meatal erythema and tenderness, urethral discharge, or both. It should be emphasized that asymptomatic *C trachomatis* infections can lead to long-term sequelae in the genitourinary tract.

B. Mucopurulent Cervicitis. MPC is defined by the presence of mucopurulent or purulent endocervical discharge in the endocervical canal or in an endocervical swab specimen. It has been suggested that the diagnosis can also be made on the basis of easily induced cervical bleeding. The most common complaints are vaginal discharge, vaginal bleeding, abdominal pain, and dysuria, although most infected women are asymptomatic. Physical examination reveals cervical edema, ectopy, and a propensity of the endocervical mucosa to bleed when rubbed with a swab.

C. Proctitis. Proctitis can be caused by *C trachomatis* serovars D through K and serovars L1, L2, and L3. It occurs primarily in men who have sex with men and practice receptive anorectal intercourse. It can occur also in heterosexual women. Patients usually present with rectal pain, tenesmus, and rectal exudate; hematochezia may be present. Gram stain of the rectal discharge reveals neutrophils. Anoscopic examination reveals mucopurulent discharge with a patchy mucosal friability of the distal third segment of the rectum. The L1, L2, and L3 strains rarely cause disease in the United States and produce a more severe syndrome of ulcerative proctitis or even proctocolitis; this presentation can be confused with herpes simplex virus (HSV) proctitis or Crohn's disease. Proctocolitis can lead to perianal fistulas and rectal strictures.

D. Lymphogranuloma Venereum. *C trachomatis* serovars L1, L2, and L3 are also responsible for the syndrome of lymphogranuloma venereum (LGV).

The most frequent manifestation of LGV among heterosexual men is tender unilateral inguinal or femoral lymphadenopathy or both. The lymphadenopathy becomes associated with perinodal inflammation and formation of a bubo. Men who have sex with men and women may present with the proctocolitis syndrome (see above). Most patients present at the time of lymphadenopathy and no longer have the primary painless self-limited nodular or ulcerative lesion at the inoculation site.

E. Epididymitis. Epididymitis should be suspected in patients with unilateral testicular pain, with or without fever, and unilateral epididymal tenderness or swelling on physical examination. In men younger than 35 years, *C trachomatis* is by far the most common etiologic agent, followed by *N gonorrhoeae*. In men older than 35, *E coli* and *Pseudomonas aeruginosa* are the most common etiologic agents; these infections usually occur in the setting of urologic manipulation. In each case of suspected epididymitis, torsion of the ipsilateral testicle should be ruled out. Clinically available tests to rule out testicular torsion include Doppler ultrasound and nuclear medicine studies. In patients in whom the clinical suspicion for testicular torsion is high (eg, a young person who presents with acute unilateral testicular pain without urethritis), surgical exploration may be indicated. In patients with chronic unilateral testicular pain who do not respond to appropriate antibacterial therapy, other etiologies such as carcinoma or tuberculosis should be considered.

F. Pelvic Inflammatory Disease. Pelvic inflammatory disease (PID) comprises a spectrum of inflammatory disorders of the female upper genital tract, including any combination of endometritis, salpingitis, tubo-ovarian abscess, and pelvic peritonitis. *C trachomatis* and *N gonorrhoeae* are the two most common etiologic agents. Other organisms such as anaerobes, *Streptococcus agalactiae, Gardnerella vaginalis,* enteric gram-negative bacilli, *Ureaplasma urealyticum,* and *Mycoplasma hominis* have also been implicated as etiologic agents of PID. PID can present with subtle or mild symptoms and may also be asymptomatic. Initially, symptoms may not necessarily indicate involvement of the genital tract. PID should be suspected in sexually active women who present with lower abdominal pain or tenderness, adnexal tenderness, and/or cervical motion tenderness and in whom no other cause for these symptoms can be identified. Other causes of abdominal pain in this setting include ectopic pregnancy and acute appendicitis. In addition, PID can present with fever (>101 °F), abnormal vaginal or cervical discharge, vaginal bleeding, dyspareunia, or some combination of these symptoms. Erythrocyte sedimentation rate or C-reactive protein may be elevated.

G. Reiter's Syndrome. Reiter's syndrome consists of conjunctivitis or uveitis, urethritis, arthritis, and mucocutaneous lesions that usually occur in human leukocyte antigen (HLA)-B27-positive individuals ~ 1–6 weeks after acquisition of a sexually transmitted or dysenteric agent. The first three features constitute the classic triad. Reiter's syndrome can present with all of the features mentioned above or in any combination of those symptoms. NGU may in fact be the first sign of this syndrome. In women, cervicitis can be part of the syndrome. The knees are the most commonly affected joints. Reiter's has been described after infection with enteric pathogens such as *Salmonella, Shigella,* or *Campylobacter* species, as well as *C trachomatis* genital-tract infection.

H. Perinatal Infections. Perinatal infections with *C trachomatis* result from exposure of the neonate to the organism present in the mother's cervix. Initial infection results in colonization of the mucous membranes of the eye, oropharynx, urogenital tract, and rectum. Infection of the newborn with *C trachomatis* is first manifested by the presence of conjunctivitis, which usually develops between 5 and 14 days after birth. Other infectious agents capable of causing conjunctivitis in neonates include *N gonorrhoeae, Haemophilus influenzae, S pneumoniae,* and HSV. Typically, *N gonorrhoeae* has an incubation period of only 1–3 days. However, laboratory tests are required for a microbiologic diagnosis. Pneumonia can develop in neonates as a subacute, afebrile respiratory syndrome with onset at between 1 and 3 months of age. Infants usually develop cough, tachypnea, and bilateral diffuse interstitial infiltrates. Neonatal infections of the oropharynx, genital tract, and rectum are usually asymptomatic.

I. Eye Infections. *C trachomatis* causes eye disease in children and adults, and this disease takes two distinct clinical and epidemiological forms: trachoma and adult inclusion conjunctivitis. Trachoma is a chronic inflammatory condition of the ocular and palpebral conjunctiva and cornea caused by *C tra-*chomatis* serovars A, B, Ba, and C. It occurs in the setting of poor hygiene and crowded conditions. A follicular conjunctivitis is usually followed by superficial neovascularization of the cornea (pannus formation). Subsequent scarring of the conjunctiva and cornea eventually leads to blindness. Adult inclusion conjunctivitis results from sexual transmission of *C trachomatis* serovars D through K. It usually presents as an acute unilateral follicular conjunctivitis and periauricular lymphadenopathy; this presentation is clinically similar to that of adenovirus or HSV conjunctivitis. If left untreated, it can evolve into a syndrome of chronic conjunctivitis but rarely results in conjunctival or corneal scarring.

Diagnosis

A. Urethritis. In men with suspected nongonococcal or postgonococcal urethritis, the diagnosis of urethritis should be confirmed based on the results of urinalysis with ≥ 10 leukocytes per high-power field or on Gram stain examination of the urethral discharge revealing > 4 neutrophils per oil immersion field. The absence of *N gonorrhoeae* should be documented with a properly performed Gram stain examination of the urethral material. Nucleic acid amplification methods for use with either urine or urethral/cervical swab specimens are the most sensitive and specific tests for the definitive diagnosis of *C trachomatis* genital-tract infection. The two most commonly used amplification methods are LCR and PCR. Since these methods can be used with first-void urine, an uncomfortable swab procedure is not necessary, thereby facilitating widespread diagnostic testing and screening of populations at risk.

B. Epididymitis, Proctitis, and Mucopurulent Cervicitis. In young men with epididymitis, urethritis needs to be ruled out (see preceding section). In a similar fashion, *N gonorrhoeae* should be excluded in patients who have both testicular pain and urethral discharge. Amplification of *C trachomatis* DNA from urine based on PCR or LCR is the diagnostic approach of choice. This sensitive and specific approach has also replaced cervical-swab specimen culture for assessing the possibility of *C trachomatis* cervicitis. For the diagnostic workup of proctitis, a rectal culture or direct immunofluorescence test for *C trachomatis* is indicated.

C. PID. The diagnosis of PID is difficult. Symptoms, signs, and laboratory tests are not specific. Women with symptomatic PID can present with any combination of the following: pelvic pain including adnexal and/or cervical-motion tenderness, palpable adnexal mass, and/or elevated erythrocyte sedimentation rate, C-reactive protein, or peripheral leukocyte count.

D. Reiter's Syndrome. In those with clinical features of Reiter's syndrome, evidence of *C trachomatis* should be sought. A stool examination should also be performed for the gastrointestinal-tract pathogens associated with Reiter's syndrome, and the possibility of the HLA-B27 haplotype should be assessed.

E. Lymphogranuloma Venereum. The diagnosis of LGV is confirmed by isolation of an LGV serovar from the lymph node or rectum and occasionally from the urethra or cervix. An LGV complement fixation titer of ≥ 1:64 or a microimmunofluorescence titer of ≥ 1:512 is considered diagnostic.

F. Perinatal Infections. Purulent conjunctival discharge in a neonate should be evaluated with Gram stain and bacterial cultures to rule out *N gonorrhoeae, Haemophilus* spp., *S pneumoniae,* and *Staphylococcus aureus. C trachomatis* antigen can be detected directly, and the organism can be cultivated from conjunctival discharge. A Giemsa-stained scraping of the conjunctiva is less sensitive for detecting *Chlamydia* cells but is the most rapid method for diagnosis. Chlamydial culture of sputum, pharynx, eye, and rectum should be obtained in infants with pneumonia. Serological tests may help if a fourfold change is observed in immunoglobulin (Ig) G or IgM titers, but a single IgG measurement may be misleading because of passive transfer of maternal antibody. The two samples should be obtained ≥ 4 weeks apart and analyzed in parallel.

G. Eye Infections. Trachoma can be diagnosed on clinical grounds and in the proper epidemiological setting. Confirmation of the diagnosis can be achieved by Giemsa-stained cell scrapings from the conjunctiva and detection of typical intracytoplasmic inclusions.

Treatment

A. Urethritis. Adults with NGU or PGU should be treated as soon as possible after diagnosis. A single-dose regimen based on azithromycin for example has the important advantage of improved adherence (Box 67–2). Doxycycline, erythromycin, or ofloxacin can also be used. Ofloxacin is also often effective against *N gonorrhoeae.* Other drugs used against *N gonorrhoeae* such as the cephalosporins and ciprofloxacin are not effective against *C trachomatis.* Patients with recurrent or persistent urethritis should be evaluated for the possibility of nonadherence, reinfection, or an alternative diagnosis. In this setting, patients should be re-treated if they do not comply fully or have been re-exposed to an untreated sex partner. A combination regimen consisting of metronidazole plus erythromycin has been suggested for patients with a history of recurrent urethritis, who have adhered to the initial regimen and have not been re-exposed. In the absence of reliable negative data for *N gonorrhoeae,* empiric antibiotic coverage for this organism should be provided as well.

B. Mucopurulent Cervicitis, Proctitis, Epididymitis, and PID. Patients with mucopurulent cervicitis, proctitis, and epididymitis should be tested for *C trachomatis* and *N gonorrhoeae,* as above, and

BOX 67–2

Treatment of *C trachomatis* Genital Infections (Serovars D–K)[1,2]

First Choice	• Azithromycin, 1 g orally in a single dose OR • Doxycycline, 100 mg orally twice a day for 7 d
Second Choice	• Erythromycin base, 500 mg orally four times a day for 7 d OR • Erythromycin ethylsuccinate, 800 mg orally three times a day for 7 d OR • Ofloxacin, 300 mg orally twice a day for 7 d
Pediatric Considerations[3]	• Erythromycin, 40 mg/kg/d orally, divided into 4 doses/day, for 14 days OR • Doxycycline (children ≥ 8 years old), 4 mg/kg/d orally in 2 divided doses for 14 days

[1]Sex partners should be evaluated, tested, and treated if they had sexual contact with the patient during the 60 days preceding onset of symptoms. The most recent partner should be treated even if time of the last sexual contact was >60 days preceding onset of symptoms.
[2]Coinfection with *C trachomatis* often occurs among patients who have gonococcal infection.
[3]Children with genital *C trachomatis* infection should raise the possibility of sexual abuse.

treated with drugs effective against both (Box 67–2). PID is managed similarly, except that antimicrobial coverage against anaerobes is often included. In addition, treatment is often begun via an intravenous route. Erythromycin is the drug of choice for pregnant women with *C trachomatis* infection; amoxicillin has also been successful in this setting. Single-dose azithromycin is another alternative during pregnancy. Tetracyclines and fluoroquinolones are contraindicated in pregnant women.

C. Lymphogranuloma Venereum. LGV is treated with doxycycline (Box 67–3). Alternative drugs include macrolides such as erythromycin. The activity of azithromycin against *C trachomatis* suggests that it may be effective in treating LGV given in multiple doses over 2–3 weeks, but clinical data regarding its use for this disease are lacking.

Patients with suspected or proven *C trachomatis* infection should be instructed to refer their sex partners (sexual contacts during the 60 days preceding

BOX 67–3

Treatment of Lymphogranuloma Venereum (Serovars L1, L2, and L3)[1]

First Choice	• Doxycycline, 100 mg orally twice a day for 21 days
Second Choice	• Erythromycin base, 500 mg orally four times a day for 21 days

[1]Sex partners should be evaluated, tested, and treated if they had sexual contact with the patient during the 30 days preceding onset of symptoms

onset of symptoms or diagnosis of chlamydial infection) for diagnostic testing, treatment, or both. However, the last sexual contact should be treated even if the time of the last sexual contact was > 60 days before onset of symptoms or diagnosis. Patients and their sex partners should abstain from sexual activity until treatment courses are completed.

Unless symptoms persist or reinfection is suspected, patients treated with doxycycline or azithromycin do not need to be retested for chlamydial infection because these drugs are highly effective. A test of cure may be considered 3 weeks after completion of a course of erythromycin.

D. Perinatal Infection. Erythromycin is the drug of choice for infants with *C trachomatis* ocular infection, as well as with *C trachomatis* pneumonia (Box 67–4). Mothers of infants with chlamydial infection and the sex partners of these women should be assessed and treated for *C trachomatis* infection. Newborns of mothers who have untreated chlamydial infections should be monitored closely for symptoms of conjunctivitis or pneumonia. Prophylactic antibiotics are not indicated in this setting.

BOX 67–4

Treatment of Other *C trachomatis* Infections

Infant Pneumonia and Ocular Infections	• Erythromycin, 50 mg/kg/d in four divided doses for 10–14 d
Adult Inclusion Conjunctivitis[1]	• Doxycycline, 100 mg orally twice a day for 1–3 weeks OR • Erythromycin, 250 mg four times a day orally for 1–3 weeks

[1]Topical treatment is not recommended.

E. Infections in Young Children. Chlamydial infections in preadolescent children should raise the possibility of sexual abuse. Because of the potential for a criminal investigation, the diagnosis of *C trachomatis* in this situation requires isolation in cell culture.

In children who weigh < 45 kg, erythromycin is the drug of choice. In children who weigh ≥ 45 kg but who are < 8 years of age, azithromycin is the drug of choice. In children, ≥ 8 years of age, doxycycline can be used as an alternative to azithromycin. (See Box 67–2.)

F. Eye Infections. Patients with trachoma conjunctivitis respond well to a tetracycline, azithromycin, or erythromycin (Box 67–4). Public health programs for management of endemic trachoma consist of mass application of tetracycline or erythromycin ophthalmic ointment to all children in affected communities for 21–60 days or on an intermittent basis. Surgical correction of eyelids is also undertaken.

Adult inclusion conjunctivitis is usually treated with an oral tetracycline or erythromycin. All sexual contacts should be evaluated, treated for *C trachomatis* infection, or both.

Prevention

Programs aimed at the detection of asymptomatic chlamydial infection and treatment of both symptomatic and asymptomatic cases have proven to be effective in decreasing the prevalence of *Chlamydia* infections in the United States. In addition, behavioral interventions designed for primary prevention of STDs are of paramount importance. A sexual history should be obtained from all patients who are sexually active as a first step in identifying patients at risk and in delivering prevention messages. A professional, compassionate, and nonjudgmental attitude is essential. The most effective strategy for prevention of STDs is avoidance of infected sex partners; however, this is difficult given the prevalence of asymptomatic infection. Information should be provided regarding abstinence especially to those who are being treated for an STD or whose partners are undergoing treatment. The direct relationship between the number of sex partners and the likelihood of STDs must be discussed. A vaccine against chlamydial disease has not yet been developed. Institution of basic hygienic practices such as hand washing is beneficial in reducing the prevalence of trachoma. In addition, mass treatment with azithromycin appears to result in markedly decreased levels of disease.

C PSITTACI INFECTIONS

Essentials of Diagnosis

- History of contact with birds.
- Positive *C psittaci*-specific microimmunofluorescence serologies.
- Positive complement fixation titers (not species specific).

Clinical Findings

A. Signs and Symptoms. Pneumonia, pericarditis, myocarditis, and endocarditis have been attributed to *C psittaci* infection (psittacosis or ornithosis) (Box 67–5). The incubation period for the pneumonia is usually 1–2 weeks. Its onset is gradual with body temperature increasing over a period of 5–7 days; however, there are cases in which the onset is sudden with rigors and temperatures as high as 104 °F. Headache is a salient and important symptom; it can be severe and incapacitating. Cough is usually nonproductive and hacking; however, on occasion a mucoid sputum or hemoptysis may develop. Epistaxis, photophobia, myalgias, and back and neck muscle stiffness are also common accompanying symptoms. Pleurisy, friction rub, and pleural effusion are rare, as are mental status changes, which can eventually progress to coma. Other unusual manifestations include gastrointestinal symptoms, such as abdominal pain, nausea, vomiting, or diarrhea.

On physical exam, the pulse rate may be slow relative to the degree of fever (pulse-temperature dissociation). However, this relative bradycardia may be influenced by the physical conditioning and resting heart rate of the individual. Lung auscultation may be entirely normal even in patients who are severely ill or have extensive radiological changes. Splenomegaly has been described in ≤ 70% of patients with *C psittaci* pneumonia. Abdominal distension, constipation, or pulmonary infarction can occur as late complications.

B. Laboratory Findings. The peripheral leukocyte count and erythrocyte sedimentation rate are usually normal or can be only slightly elevated.

C. Imaging. Chest radiographic changes are protean and nonspecific. Radiological abnormalities include infiltrates, which can be patchy, diffuse, lobar, atelectatic, wedge shaped, nodular, or miliary.

Diagnosis

The diagnosis of psittacosis can be confirmed by isolation of *C psittaci* or by serological tests. However, owing to its fastidious growth requirements and the associated hazards of its growth to laboratory personnel, most clinical laboratories do not attempt cultivation of this organism. Serological testing is best performed using acute and convalescent serum samples.

Treatment

Patients with *C psittaci* infection should be treated with a tetracycline (Box 67–6). Patients usually respond with amelioration of their symptoms within 24–48 h after institution of therapy. In patients allergic to or intolerant of tetracyclines, erythromycin can be used as an alternative.

The recommended treatment of psittacosis in children ≥ 8 years of age is 500 mg of tetracycline every 6 h, orally, for 7–10 days. Erythromycin also can be used (50 mg/kg/d up to 2 g/d for 7–10 days). Tetracycline may be more effective than erythromycin.

Prevention

Imported birds should be quarantined and treated with a tetracycline for 30 days. An additional course of tetracycline for 15 days should be given by the importers or owners. Some birds will still shed the organism if treatment courses of < 45 days are used.

C PNEUMONIAE INFECTIONS

Essentials of Diagnosis

- Hoarseness may accompany atypical pneumonia.
- Positive *C pneumoniae*-specific microimmunofluorescence serologies.
- Positive complement fixation titers (not species specific).

BOX 67–5

C psittaci Infections in Adults and Children

More Common	• Community-acquired pneumonia with nonproductive cough, fever, and headache (exposure to birds)
Less Common	• Mononucleosis-like syndrome with pharyngitis, hepatosplenomegaly, and lymphadenopathy • Typhoidal form with fever, bradycardia, malaise, and splenomegaly • Endocarditis, myocarditis, and pericarditis

---

BOX 67–6

Treatment of *C psittaci* Infections

First Choice	• Tetracycline, 500 mg four times a day for 10–21 days OR • Doxycycline 100 mg orally twice a day for 10–21 days
Second Choice	• Erythromycin base, 500 mg orally four times a day for 7 d (erythromycin may be less efficacious in severe cases)
Pediatric Considerations	• Erythromycin, 50 mg/kg/d orally up to 2 g/d for 7–10 days OR • Tetracycline (children ≥ 8 years old), 500 mg every 6 h for 7–10 days

BOX 67-7

C pneumoniae Infections in Adults and Children

More Common	• Community-acquired pneumonia • Possible association with atherosclerotic cardiovascular disease • Possible association with adult-onset asthma and acute exacerbations among adults with asthma
Less Common	• Bronchitis • Pharyngitis • Sinusitis • Endocarditis • Lumbosacral meningoradiculitis • Erythema nodosum • Encephalitis

BOX 67-8

Treatment of *C pneumoniae* Infections

First Choice	• Azithromycin, 500 mg/d for 10 d OR • Clarithromycin, 500 mg twice a day for 10–14 days OR • Levofloxacin, 500 mg every day for 10–14 days
Second Choice	• Tetracycline, 500 mg four times a day for 10–14 days OR • Doxycycline, 100 mg orally twice a day for 10 to 14 days
Pediatric Considerations	• Erythromycin, 50 mg/kg/d orally for 10–14 days OR • Clarithromycin, 15 mg/kg/d orally for 10 days

• Isolation and PCR techniques available in research laboratories only.

Clinical Findings

Upper- and lower-respiratory-tract infections including sinusitis, pharyngitis, bronchitis, and pneumonia have been associated with *C pneumoniae* infection (Box 67–7). Bronchitis and pneumonia are the most common syndromes seen in clinical practice. The incubation period for *C pneumoniae* pneumonia has been estimated at ~ 21 days. Patients usually present with a history of fever and prominent upper respiratory symptoms followed by sore throat and nonproductive cough. Physical exam can be entirely normal or can reveal mild to moderate respiratory distress, usually with minimal auscultatory changes. The leukocyte count is usually normal or slightly elevated. Chest radiography may reveal minimal segmental infiltrates. Despite this more common picture, *C pneumoniae* pneumonia can be life threatening in patients older than 65 years. More recent serologic and anatomic data suggest that chronic *C pneumoniae* infections may play a role in atherosclerosis and in the progression of coronary artery disease. The clinical relevance of this information is not clear at this time.

Diagnosis

Serological methods are commonly used for the diagnosis of *C pneumoniae* infections. They are rarely helpful in the acute setting, and they are mostly used for surveillance purposes. Complement fixation methods do not differentiate among infections caused by *C trachomatis, C psittaci,* and *C pneumoniae*. Microimmunofluorescence methods detect *C pneumoniae*-specific antibodies and are the approaches most commonly used in clinical practice. Acute and convalescent sera samples obtained ≥ 3–4 weeks apart should be analyzed in parallel. Isolation of this organism and PCR-based methods are not routinely performed outside research laboratories.

Treatment

C pneumoniae infection should be treated with a tetracycline, a macrolide, or a fluoroquinolone (Box 67–8).

The recommended treatment regimens for *C pneumoniae* infections in children include erythromycin (50 mg/kg/d for 10–14 days) or clarithromycin (15 mg/kg/d for 10 days). Some patients may require retreatment.

REFERENCES

Campbell LA, Kuo CC, Grayston JT: *Chlamydia pneumoniae* and cardiovascular disease. Emerg Infect Dis 1998; 4(4):571.

Centers for Disease Control and Prevention: Compendium of measures to control *Chlamydia psittaci* infection among humans (psittacosis) and pet birds (avian chlamydiosis), 1998. Morb Mortal Wkly Rep 1998;47(RR-10):1.

Centers for Disease Control and Prevention: 1998 Guidelines for treatment of sexually transmitted diseases. Morb Mortal Wkly Rep 1998;47(RR-1):1.

Gaydos CA et al: Molecular amplification assays to detect chlamydial infections in urine specimens from high school female students and to monitor the persistence of chlamydial DNA after therapy. J Infect Dis 1998;177: 417.

Gregory DW, Schaffner W: Psittacosis. Sem Resp Infect 1997;12(1):7.

Kalman S et al: Comparative genomes of *Chlamydia pneumoniae* and *C trachomatis*. Nat Genet 1999;21:385.

Meier CR et al: Antibiotics and risk of subsequent first-time acute myocardial infarction. J Am Med Assoc 1999; 281:427.

Jeffery Loutit, MB, ChB

Coxiella, Ehrlichia, and *Rickettsia* spp. are small, obligate intracellular bacteria that usually cause disease when they accidentally encounter a human host. Once inside a host cell, *Coxiella* and *Ehrlichia* spp. remain within a vacuole where they progress through distinct developmental stages; in contrast, the *Rickettsia* spp. escape the endocytic vacuole and replicate within the host cell cytoplasm. *Ehrlichia* and *Rickettsia* spp. are transmitted by arthropod vectors.

COXIELLA BURNETII INFECTION (Q FEVER)

Essentials of Diagnosis
Acute Infection
- Key symptoms and signs: fever, severe headache, myalgias, arthralgias, retrobulbar pain, cough; possible pneumonitis and hepatitis on examination.
- Predisposing factors: occupation as a dairy farmer, abattoir worker, or veterinarian; exposure to parturient or newborn animals, particularly cattle, sheep, and goats.
- Commonest environment for infection: a rural setting, but urban cases of Q fever also reported.
- Commonest infections: acute febrile illness, pneumonitis, and hepatitis.
- Key laboratory feature: positive antibodies to the phase-II antigens.
Chronic Infection
- Key symptoms and signs: fever and heart murmur.
- Predisposing factors: same as those for acute disease, plus prosthetic or abnormal heart valves.
- Commonest features: fever and endocarditis; echocardiogram rarely positive.
- Key laboratory features: levels of antibodies to phase-I antigens in excess of phase-II antigens.

General Considerations
Coxiella burnetii is the causative agent of Query or Q fever. This disease name originated with the description of a 1935 outbreak of a febrile illness of unknown etiology in nine abattoir workers in Brisbane, Australia. The disease agent, based on its morphology and obligate intracellular lifestyle, was originally classified as a member of the family *Rickettsiaceae*. However, molecular analysis and in particular ribosomal-DNA sequencing have revealed the relationships between *C burnetii* and the *Legionella* spp. within the gamma subdivision of the *Proteobacteria*, and its more distant relationships to the rickettsia and the alpha subdivision of *Proteobacteria*.

A. Epidemiology. Cattle, sheep, and goats are the primary reservoirs for *C burnetii*, although the organism is found in a wide variety of domesticated animals. Inhalation of aerosolized organisms and ingestion of unpasteurized milk or cheese are common mechanisms of transmission to humans. Infection of domestic livestock usually occurs via the aerosol route and fails to cause clinically apparent or significant disease. Persistence of *C burnetii* in a latent phase in a host may be followed years later by reactivation and disease, especially during the late stages of pregnancy, because the organism exhibits tropism for the placenta. Many cases of human Q fever occur as a result of close association with animals at the time of parturition or soon thereafter, particularly sheep, cattle, cats, rabbits, and dogs. Ticks can also serve as transmission vehicles for *C burnetii*, but this mechanism is primarily involved in transmission of the organism to animals rather than humans.

Humans at risk for disease include dairy farmers and slaughterhouse and laboratory workers. Q fever is endemic throughout the world, except in New Zealand, but it is particularly common in the Middle East and Mediterranean regions. Although seemingly uncommon in the United States, Q fever is believed to be grossly underdiagnosed owing to its protean manifestations and to low clinical suspicion of Q fever as a probable disease; 70% of cases are reported from California and the western mountain states. Urban transmission has been described and is thought to result from close association with parturient animals.

B. Microbiology. *C burnetii* is a short, pleomorphic gram-negative rod and an obligate intracellular pathogen.

C. Pathogenesis. *C burnetii* enters cells, allows the endocytic vacuole to fuse with lysosomes, multiplies within the acidic environment of the resulting phagolysosome, and ultimately destroys the host cell

(Figure 68–1). Although the exact mechanisms by which *C burnetii* survives within the phagolysosome are unclear, it does require an acid environment at that point in its life cycle; in fact, pharmacologic strategies to block acidification of intracellular vacuoles, for example using chloroquine, are therapeutic (see Treatment section below). *C burnetii* also has the ability to form sporelike structures, enabling it to survive diverse environmental conditions. The organism exists in either of two antigenic phases (I or II), owing to variation in the expression of different membrane lipopolysaccharides and proteins. Fresh isolates exhibiting phase-I antigens are highly infectious. Conversion to phase II occurs after serial passage in the laboratory, although reversion to phase-I antigen occurs with passage through laboratory animals. The immune response to these phase-associated antigens is useful in the diagnosis of *C burnetii* infections. Antibodies to phase-II antigen are found in the blood of patients with acute disease, whereas antibodies to phase-I antigen are more often detected in patients with chronic disease, such as endocarditis. The virulence-associated mechanisms of this organism are poorly understood.

Tissues affected by Q fever reveal vascular injury and granulomatous inflammation along with hemorrhage and necrosis. Q fever is one of many causes of granulomatous hepatitis.

Clinical Findings

A. Acute infection. Seroepidemiologic studies indicate that ~ 50% of "cases" of Q fever in humans are asymptomatic. Symptomatic cases usually present with an acute febrile illness. Disease manifestations include a flulike illness, isolated fever, pneumonitis, hepatitis, exanthema with fever, pericarditis, myocarditis, and meningoencephalitis (Box 68–1). Most important in the diagnosis of acute Q fever is a history of contact with a newborn or parturient animal, which is found in two-thirds of all cases. There is marked geographic variation with respect to the clinical features of disease presentation; eg, hepatitis is seen more commonly in France than in Nova Scotia, and pneumonitis is more common in Nova Scotia than in France. The route of transmission does not seem to be a major factor in determining disease presentation.

The incubation period of Q fever ranges from 4 to 39 days, with an average of 14 days. Patients frequently present with an acute onset of fever >38.5°C, rigors, and a severe headache. Other symptoms may include retrobulbar pain, malaise, myalgias, arthralgias, neck stiffness, nausea, vomiting, cough, pleuritic chest pain, diarrhea, and jaundice. Hepatosplenomegaly may be found on examination, and a maculopapular rash is present in 20% of cases. Hepatic involvement may range from mild subclinical elevations of hepatic transaminase levels to marked enzyme and bilirubin elevations accompanied by typical clinical features of hepatitis. A patchy interstitial infiltrate, as seen with other causes of "atypical" pneumonia such as *Mycoplasma pneumoniae,* is often found on chest radiograph. The leukocyte count is usually normal, but thrombocytopenia may be seen on 25% of cases. The illness is usually self-limited and lasts 2–4 weeks.

B. Chronic Infection. Approximately 2% to 11% of patients with Q fever progress to a chronic infection, of which endocarditis accounts for 60–70% of cases. Q fever endocarditis develops almost exclusively in patients with previous valvular heart disease, in transplant recipients, and in patients with underlying immunosuppression. Aortic and prosthetic valves are most commonly involved. Vegetation is rarely seen on echocardiogram, and routine blood cultures are negative. A clue to the diagnosis of Q fever endocarditis is the finding of a systemic inflammatory syndrome or unexplained accelerated valve failure in a patient with a history of valvular heart disease. Manifestations of

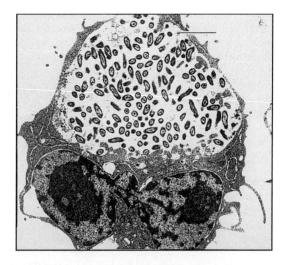

Figure 68–1. Transmission electron micrograph of *Coxiella burnetii* within a phagocyte. (From Baca OC et al: Possible biochemical adaptations of *Coxiella burnetii* for survival within phagocytes: effect of antibody. In Schlessinger D: *Microbiology 1984.* American Society for Microbiology, 1984.)

BOX 68–1	
Q fever in Children and Adults	
More Common	• Flulike illness • Pneumonitis • Hepatitis
Less Common	• Chronic disease (ie, endocarditis or granulomatous hepatitis)

this disease may include hepatosplenomegaly, a purpuric rash, renal insufficiency, and embolic phenomena. Laboratory findings include leukocytosis (25% of patients), leukopenia (15%), increased hepatic transaminase levels (40–60%), thrombocytopenia (25–50%), anemia (40%), increased creatinine levels (65%), antinuclear antibodies (35%), and rheumatoid factor (60%). Another common presentation of chronic Q fever is fever of unknown origin. Bone and joint involvement due to Q fever are uncommon, but they have been reported in both children and adults. Chronic hepatitis is another uncommon manifestation of Q fever.

Diagnosis

The diagnosis of Q fever is based on an appropriate clinical history, along with a clear or possible history of animal exposure. The bacteria can be cultured from the blood, urine, and sputum by inoculation into chicken embryos or cultured human fibroblasts, but this procedure requires a specialized laboratory. In addition, the risk of transmission to laboratory workers is high; therefore, it should only be attempted in laboratories with considerable experience in handling this organism. The routine approach for the diagnosis of Q fever is a serological one, with detection of antibody to phase-I and -II antigens. Complement fixation, indirect fluorescent antibody (IFA), and enzyme-linked immunosorbent assays are available. Acute Q fever is diagnosed by a fourfold or greater increase in levels of antibodies directed against the *C burnetii* phase-II antigens. Titers become positive by 8–14 days after onset of the illness and peak at 4–8 weeks using IFA testing or at 12–13 weeks using complement fixation testing. Chronic disease, eg, endocarditis, is diagnosed by detecting levels of antibodies to *C burnetii* phase-I antigens in excess of levels of antibodies directed against the phase-II antigens. A complement fixation antibody titer against the phase-I antigens of >1:200 is considered also diagnostic.

Treatment

Acute Q fever is usually self-limited. However, antimicrobial agents are recommended to prevent the development of chronic infection and possibly to decrease the duration of symptoms (Box 68–2). Doxycycline is effective, provided that it is started early in the disease. Quinolones, because of their cerebrospinal fluid penetration, should be considered for the treatment of meningoencephalitis. Treatment of chronic Q fever has never been studied in a controlled setting. Recommended regimens include rifampicin or ciprofloxacin plus doxycycline (Box 68–3). The duration of therapy necessary for a cure is also unknown, but ≥12 months is required, and some experts recommend a minimum of 3 years. In many cases, lifelong treatment may be necessary. Current studies are assessing the use of hydroxychloroquine in conjunction with doxycycline and/or ciprofloxacin, since blockade of intracellular acidification with the former improves the bactericidal activity of the latter for *C burnetii* in vitro.

Prevention & Control

There is no currently available vaccine for the prevention of Q fever. Procedures should be in place to protect laboratory workers from being exposed to the organism and patients with the disease should be placed in standard-precaution isolation.

EHRLICHIA INFECTION (EHRLICHIOSIS)

Essentials of Diagnosis

- Key symptoms and signs: abrupt onset of high fever, headache, myalgias, chills 8–9 days after tick bite; rash (36% of human monocytic ehrli-

BOX 68–2

Treatment of Acute Q Fever

	Children	Adults
First Choice	• Doxycycline, 100 mg twice daily for 15–21 days	• Doxycycline 100 mg twice daily for 15–21 days
Second Choice	• Chloramphenicol, 50–100 mg in 4 doses/day	• Chloramphenicol, 2–4 g/day
Pediatric Considerations	• Avoid tetracyclines unless disease is severe	
Penicillin Allergic	• As above	• As above

BOX 68-3

Treatment of Chronic Q Fever

	Children	Adults
First Choice	• Doxycycline, 100 mg twice daily for 3 years, perhaps for life OR Doxycycline as above PLUS TMP/SMX OR Rifampicin OR Chloroquine	• Doxycycline, 100 mg twice daily for 3 years, perhaps for life OR Doxycycline as above PLUS TMP/SMX OR Rifampicin OR Chloroquine
Pediatric Considerations	• Tetracycline should not be used in children < 8 years old • Fluoroquinolones should not be used in children and adolescents < 18 years old	

chiosis [HME] patients; only 2% of human granulocytic ehrlichiosis [HGE] patients); central nervous system involvement (20–25% of patients).
- Predisposing factors: tick and rural exposure (April through September).
- Presentation: most present as flu-like illness.
- Key laboratory features: thrombocytopenia, leukopenia, and elevated liver transaminases.
- Diagnosis: confirmed by a fourfold or greater rise in titers with an IFA.

General Considerations

Human ehrlichiosis was first recognized in the United States in 1986 as a life threatening tick-borne illness similar to Rocky Mountain spotted fever (RMSF), but with a much lower incidence of rash.

A. Epidemiology. Ehrlichiosis is not a reportable disease, so its true incidence is unknown. The majority of cases of HME have been reported from the south, central, and southeastern United States. Cases have also been reported from Western Europe, Scandinavia, and Africa. In contrast, most cases of HGE have been reported from the upper midwestern and northeastern United States. This difference in disease geography reflects the distinct habitats of the respective tick vectors. *Amblyoma americanum* transmits HME and is found throughout the southeastern and south central United States. The white-tailed deer serves as a reservoir for the etiologic agent, *E chaffeensis.* The *Ixodes* species are the tick vectors of HGE (as well as Lyme disease and babesiosis), and they are found in the Northeast, upper Midwest, and Pacific Coast regions of the United States. The white-tailed deer is the primary host for adult *Ixodes* ticks, but small rodents—especially the white-footed

mouse—play an important role in the deer-tick-rodent cycle and transmission of the agent of HGE to humans. Of infected humans, 80–100% report tick exposure within the 10 days preceding the onset of illness.

The median age of patients reported with HME is 44 years; 75% are male. The median age of HGE cases is 60 years, with a similar sex ratio. Cases of HME occur from April through December, but HGE cases are seen throughout the year, owing to the seasonal feeding patterns of the different tick vectors in different regions of the United States.

B. Microbiology. There are two forms of human ehrlichiosis in North America, HME and HGE; their clinical features are indistinguishable. The causative agent of HME, *Ehrlichia chaffeensis,* was the first member of this genus to be detected in humans in the United States; HGE was first recognized in 1994, and it is caused by an organism closely related to *Ehrlichia equi* and *Ehrlichia phagocytophila. Ehrlichia sennetsu* is the only other known pathogen for humans in this genus, but it has been reported only in Western Japan. Canine ehrlichiosis is caused by *Ehrlichia canis* and *Ehrlichia ewingii,* which infect macrophages and granulocytes, respectively. *E phagocytophila* is a pathogen of ruminants in Europe and exhibits tropism for neutrophils. *E equi* causes both equine and canine disease.

C. Pathogenesis. *Ehrlichia* species are small, obligate intracellular organisms whose life cycle includes the formation of intraleukocytic inclusions, termed morulae. Replication and development of organisms within morulae lead to rupture and release of elementary bodies into the circulatory system and subsequent infection of other leukocytes. Recent data indicate that the granulocytic *Ehrlichia* species may enhance their survival within neutrophils by down-regulating expression of one component of the host NADPH oxidase enzyme complex, a critical feature of the oxidative burst machinery.

Clinical Findings

A. Signs and Symptoms. The symptoms and signs of human ehrlichiosis are nondescript, thereby making the diagnosis difficult. The median incubation period is 8–9 days after tick bite, with a range of 0–34 days. The clinical presentation characteristically includes an abrupt onset of high fever (>39°C), headache, myalgias, and shaking chills (Box 68–4). Other symptoms include malaise, confusion, rigors, sweats, nausea, vomiting, and abdominal pain. Rash is reported in 36% of patients with HME but only 2% of those with HGE.

B. Laboratory Findings. The laboratory findings of human ehrlichiosis are relatively consistent and include thrombocytopenia in 72–92% of patients, elevated liver transaminase levels in the serum in 85–90% of patients, and leukopenia in 50–75% of patients. These laboratory findings are most pronounced at the end of the first week of illness. Morulae are rarely seen on acute-phase peripheral blood smears of patients with HME but are seen more commonly in the peripheral blood smears of patients with HGE. Detection of morulae in peripheral blood smears remains an insensitive and time-consuming task, and, when found, morulae have been reported most often by clinical hematology laboratory technicians (Figure 68–2).

C. Differential Diagnosis. Diseases in the differential diagnosis include ehrlichiosis (see Diagnosis section), typhus, Q fever, tularemia, early Lyme disease, viral hepatitis, leptospirosis, influenza, and Colorado tick fever. Coinfection with other tick-borne agents must always be considered.

D. Complications. Central nervous system involvement is reported in 20–25% of patients, with symptoms ranging from confusion through coma. Other severe complications may occur, such as disseminated intravascular coagulation, respiratory fail-

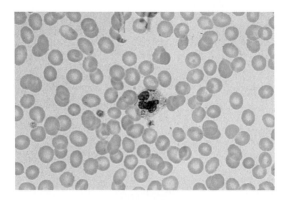

Figure 68–2. Granulocyte containing a morula from a patient with HGE. (Courtesy of Jesse Goodman.)

ure, renal insufficiency, and opportunistic infections secondary to neutropenia. Most elderly patients with HME who have been reported have also been hospitalized. Case fatality rates are 2–5% for HME and 7–10% for HGE. However, it is also now clear from seroprevalence studies that many patients have mild or asymptomatic infection.

Diagnosis

It is necessary and important to consider the diagnosis of ehrlichiosis based only on epidemiological and clinical features, to facilitate administration of empiric therapy, because there is no widely available rapid diagnostic test other than detection of visible morulae. Ehrlichiosis should be considered in any febrile patient in an endemic region with exposure to ticks within the preceding 3 weeks. The diagnosis becomes more likely if thrombocytopenia, elevated hepatic transaminases, or leukopenia is present. There are no absolute clinical criteria that distinguish ehrlichiosis from RMSF, although patients with ehrlichiosis are less likely to have a rash and more likely to have leukopenia and elevated hepatic transaminases. In addition to finding intraleukocytic morulae, serology offers a reliable but retrospective method for diagnosing *Ehrlichia* infection. Acute and convalescent titers are required. IFA detection assays are available for both HME and HGE. Although *E chaffeensis* and the agent of HGE can be cultured, this method of detection and PCR-based assays are not widely available.

Treatment

Doxycycline is the agent of choice for both HGE and HME (Box 68–5). The clinical response is rapid, usually within 24–48 h. Chloramphenicol has been used in younger children to prevent teeth discoloration secondary to tetracyclines; however, in vitro and in vivo failures have been described. Enhanced mortality and morbidity from ehrlichiosis are associated with delayed administration of appropriate therapy, advanced age, and a higher percentage of in-

---

BOX 68–4

Ehrlichiosis in Children and Adults

More Common	• Flulike illness • High fever, headache, chills, myalgias, arthralgias
Less Common	• Rash, diarrhea, abdominal pain, pulmonary infiltrates, respiratory failure, disseminated intravascular coagulation

BOX 68-5

Treatment of Ehrlichiosis

	Children	Adults
First Choice	• Doxycycline, 3 mg/kg/day in 2 divided doses for a minimum of 5–7 days	• Doxycycline, 100 mg twice daily for 14 days (to treat possible concomitant Lyme disease)
Second Choice	• Chloramphenicol for HME, but it is ineffective against the human ehrlichiosis agent in vitro	• Chloramphenicol for HME, but it is ineffective against the human ehrlichiosis agent in vitro
Pediatric Considerations	• Benefit of short-course doxycycline outweighs the potential risk of tooth staining	

fected leukocytes. Although most patients respond to therapy within several days, most experts advocate a 14-day course of therapy, in part to treat more adequately for possible concomitant *Borrelia burgdorferi* infection.

Prevention & Control

Preventive measures against tick exposure should be used to prevent transmission of ehrlichiosis. If tick exposure occurs, thorough whole-body examination for and prompt removal of attached ticks are important for prevention of transmission.

RICKETTSIAL INFECTIONS

The *Rickettsia* species are small, pleomorphic coccobacilli and obligate intracellular pathogens that depend on the host as a source of energy. Humans are only accidental hosts for these organisms and are usually infected by means of an arthropod vector. Rickettsia multiply at the bite site, invade the bloodstream, and establish infection by infecting endothelial cells throughout the microvasculature. Subsequent vascular lesions caused by damage to endothelial cells accounts for the pathologic changes that occur throughout the body. This damage is most marked in RMSF.

ROCKY MOUNTAIN SPOTTED FEVER

Essentials of Diagnosis

• Key symptoms and signs: abrupt onset of high fevers, headaches, myalgias, malaise, and a flu-like illness 3–12 days after tick bite; rash (80–90% of patients, initially maculopapular, then petechial, classically involving the palms and soles).
• Predisposing factors: tick exposure (April through September), pet owners, animal handlers, and outdoor activities.
• Commonest geographic location of infection: rural.
• Confirmatory serology via IFA.
• PCR with blood or skin biopsy: sensitive and specific but not widely available.

General Considerations

RMSF is caused by *Rickettsia rickettsii* and is an acute tick-borne illness occurring during seasonal tick activity. The disease is characterized by acute onset of fever, headache, and a rash of the extremities spreading to the trunk.

A. Epidemiology. Transmission of *R rickettsii* to humans by the *Dermacentor* tick occurs only if there is prolonged contact of at least several hours between the tick and the human host. RMSF is found only in the Western Hemisphere, with ~600 reported cases per year in the United States. Of those cases, ~50% occur in the mid-Atlantic states, but all states except Hawaii and Vermont have reported cases. Most (90%) of cases occur from April through September. Children in the 5- to 9-year age group have the highest incidence of infection. Another peak of disease incidence is observed among males >60 years of age.

Clinical Findings

A. Signs and Symptoms. Only 3% of cases present with the classic triad of fever, rash, and history of a tick bite. The incubation period is 3–12 days (average 7 days), which is then followed by abrupt onset of high fevers, headaches, malaise, and myalgias, followed by 1 to 2 days of a nonspecific flulike illness (Box 68–6). Early in the course of illness, chills, rigors, neck stiffness, anorexia, nausea, vomit-

BOX 68-6

Rocky Mountain Spotted Fever in Children and Adults

More Common	• High fever, headaches, malaise • Chills, rigors, neck stiffness • Anorexia, nausea, vomiting, abdominal pain • Maculopapular rash of ankles, wrists, spreading to arms, legs, trunk, face, palms and soles • Rash becomes petechial
Less Common	• Conjunctival suffusion • Photophobia • Cough • Mental confusion, obtundation

ing, and abdominal pain occur frequently. Conjunctival suffusion, photophobia, cough, and neurologic symptoms may also be present. In severe cases, mental confusion and obtundation may develop. Only 14% of patients with RMSF will have a rash on day 1, but, by day 3, 49% will have the characteristic rash. In 20% of cases, the rash occurs only after day 6, while 9–16% of patients will never develop a rash even though their illness is equally severe.

The initial rash of RMSF is erythematous and macular, involving the ankles and wrists. It then spreads to involve the palms, soles, trunk, and face. The rash becomes papular as local edema and perivascular inflammatory cell infiltrates accrue (Figure 68–3). The lesions are petechial in 41–59% of patients after day 6 of the illness if antibiotics are not

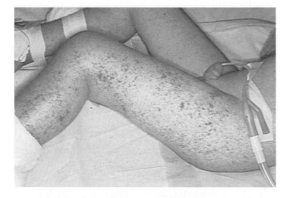

Figure 68–3. Petechial and hemorrhagic lesions on a boy with Rocky Mountain spotted fever. (From Woodward TE et al: Cutaneous manifestations of rickettsial infections. In Mandell GL, Stevens DL: *Atlas of Infectious Diseases,* Vol. II: Skin, soft tissue, bone and joint infections. Churchill Livingstone, 1995.)

administered early. The centripetal progression and the involvement of the palms and soles are the important diagnostic features. However, it is important to realize that, at day 3, at which time most people will present for care, the features considered most critical for rendering a diagnosis of RMSF are absent.

Gastrointestinal manifestations such as nausea, vomiting, diarrhea, and abdominal pain occur in 39–63% of patients. Liver involvement is frequently manifested by mild to moderate elevations of hepatic enzymes. Pulmonary findings in RMSF are the most worrisome. The pathology of lung biopsy specimens from infected patients is characterized by widespread endothelial damage. Neurological involvement is the most significant cause of morbidity and mortality in RMSF. Clinically evident encephalitis is seen in ≤28% of cases. Symptoms vary from confusion, lethargy, stupor, delirium, and ataxia to coma and convulsions. Of all patients, 30% will have lymphohistiocytic meningitis. The course of untreated RMSF is marked by slowly advancing severity of illness, with high temperatures plus hemorrhagic and neurologic signs.

B. Laboratory Findings. The leukocyte count is usually slightly decreased or normal, but an elevated band count of >10% is seen in 69% of patients. Thrombocytopenia occurs in 52% of patients, and 32% will have platelet counts of <100,000/ml³. Other abnormalities include hyponatremia and elevated serum aminotransferase and bilirubin levels.

C. Imaging. Pneumonitis and capillary endothelial injury can result in life-threatening noncardiac pulmonary edema which may be seen on chest x-ray.

D. Differential Diagnosis. The differential diagnosis of RMSF includes influenza, enteroviral infection, typhoid fever, leptospirosis, infectious mononucleosis, viral hepatitis, and bacterial sepsis—especially meningococcemia, HME, and HGE.

E. Complications. Fulminant RMSF (>5 days from onset to death) is seen more commonly in black male patients with glucose-6-phosphate dehydrogenase deficiency and in the elderly. For those patients with RMSF who are hospitalized for >2 weeks, ~50% will have long-term neurologic complications.

Diagnosis

Confirmatory serology is retrospective in nature; therefore, the physician must have a high index of suspicion based on clinical findings to start therapy. There are no diagnostic laboratory tests other than specific serologic and PCR-based tests. The leukocyte count is usually slightly decreased or normal, but an elevated band count of >10% is seen in 69% of patients. Thrombocytopenia occurs in 52% of patients, and 32% will have platelet counts of <100,000/ml³. Other abnormalities include hyponatremia and elevated serum aminotransferase and bilirubin levels. A PCR assay for RMSF using whole blood is now available through state health departments or the Centers for Disease Control and Prevention. None of the currently available serologic tests are useful for diagnosis in the acute phase of illness. The most sensitive and specific serologic assay is an IFA test. A diagnostic titer of >64 is usually detectable between 7 and 10 days after the onset of symptoms. The less sensitive latex agglutination test is more widely available and will demonstrate a rise in titer to >128, 7–9 days after the onset of symptoms. Immunohistologic examination by immunofluorescence or immunoenzyme staining for *R rickettsii* in skin biopsy specimens can demonstrate the presence of the organism as early as days 3–8 of the illness and has a reported sensitivity and specificity of 70% and 100%, respectively.

Treatment

Doxycycline is the drug of choice for the treatment of RMSF, except in cases of pregnancy and drug allergy or in children <9 years of age (Box 68–7). Although chloramphenicol has been recommended in these groups, many experts feel that it is safe to give a short course of doxycycline for the treatment of a potentially life-threatening infection in children <9 years old. The likelihood of permanent tooth staining from a short course of doxycycline is very low. Although there are in vitro data indicating that fluoroquinolones may be efficacious, these agents have not been widely used in the treatment of RMSF and cannot be recommended at this time. Treatment is continued for ≥2 days after defervescence to reduce the risk of relapse. If therapy is started early, most patients defervesce within 48 to 72 h. Severely ill patients treated late in the course of disease may take considerably longer to recover.

Prevention

Avoidance of tick bites is the best method of prevention. Protective clothing, tick repellents, and careful total body inspection can reduce the risk of inoculation. Prompt removal of ticks with forceps by firm traction is the preferred method. It is essential not to crush the tick so as to prevent release of rickettsiae.

RICKETTSIALPOX

Essentials of Diagnosis
- Eschar at site of mite bite.
- Regional lymphadenopathy.
- Generalized erythematous papulovesicular eruption on the trunk, extremities, and mucous membranes 9–14 days after exposure.
- Systemic symptoms including chills, fever, myalgias, anorexia, and photophobia.
- Predisposing factors include urban dwelling in close proximity to house mice.
- Serology for *R rickettsii* will cross-react with antibodies to *Rickettsia akari*.

General Considerations

Rickettsialpox has been reported infrequently in the United States. This disease is a mild, self-limited illness caused by *R akari* and is transmitted to humans by a house mite. Both the house mouse and house mite are reservoirs for the organism.

Clinical Findings

A painless papule develops 7–14 days after the mite bite. The papule then becomes vesicular, dries, crusts over, and evolves into a black eschar. The onset of clinical illness, characterized by abrupt onset of high fever, sweats, headache, myalgias, and malaise, occurs 4–7 days after the appearance of the initial papule. The systemic symptoms are usually mild, but, if untreated, the patient will have daily temperature elevations up to 39–39.5°C for 7–10 days. A maculopapular rash appears at the onset of fever and quickly becomes vesicular. The vesicles are small and nonpruritic, and they may be numerous or few. Within a week, the vesicles

BOX 68–7

Treatment of Rocky Mountain Spotted Fever

	Children	Adults
First Choice	• Doxycycline, 100 mg twice daily for children over 100 lb.; 2 mg/lb., divided twice daily in children < 100 lb.	• Doxycycline, 100 mg twice daily for 7–10 days
Second Choice	• Chloramphenicol, 50–75 mg/kg/day divided into four daily doses • Tetracycline, 25–50 mg/kg/day divided into four daily doses	• Chloramphenicol, 50–75 mg/kg/day divided four times a day • Tetracycline 2g/day divided four times a day
Pediatric Considerations	• In children <9 years of age, the risk of tooth staining with tetracycline and doxycycline must be considered	

crust over and disappear with no sequelae. The diagnosis is best established by the epidemiologic history, the presence of a primary eschar, and a serum IFA test. Therapy with doxycycline or chloramphenicol is effective (see Treatment section for Rocky Mountain spotted fever). Preventive steps involve eliminating house mice and their mites.

OTHER SPOTTED FEVERS

Other spotted fevers include Mediterranean spotted fever, South African tick bite fever, Siberian tick typhus, Queensland tick typhus, and Oriental spotted fever. All of these rickettsioses are associated with an eschar and regional adenopathy. A generalized maculopapular rash involving the palms and soles usually appears about 5 days into the illness. Fever lasts ~5 to 10 days if untreated. Diagnosis is based on epidemiology, clinical features including the presence of an eschar, and serology. Treatment with doxycycline is effective.

ENDEMIC (MURINE) TYPHUS

The organism principally responsible for endemic or murine typhus is *Rickettsia typhi*. More recently, *Rickettsia felis* has been characterized as a cause of endemic typhus in southern California and Texas. Transmission of these organisms to humans occurs via the flea. Clinical features include fever, headache, myalgias, and a maculopapular rash. Infected rats and opossums are the reservoirs for *R typhi* and *R felis*. The disease is endemic in the Southeast and Gulf states of the United States, especially Texas, and in southern California. During feeding on humans, when normal hosts are not available, the fleas deposit feces containing rickettsias. Humans become infected when the organisms are rubbed into the bite wound.

The incubation period for endemic typhus is 6–14 days. Initial symptoms include headache, malaise, backache, and chills. Severe shaking chills, fever, and a more severe headache soon follow. Symptoms last for 10–14 days if untreated. The rash appears at about the fifth day and comprises pink macules starting on the extremities, which then spread to the trunk but do not involve the palms and soles. The rash may become maculopapular but is not hemorrhagic, and in fact it is not seen at all in 20–46% of cases. Pulmonary manifestations are common, particularly a nonproductive cough. Although many patients will have a severe headache, analysis of cerebrospinal fluid is usually normal. Complement-fixing antibodies are important in making the diagnosis. Treatment with tetracycline, doxycycline, or chloramphenicol usually resolves symptoms within 24–48 h. Prevention of endemic typhus involves reduction of the rodent reservoir and control of the flea vector.

EPIDEMIC (LOUSE-BORNE) TYPHUS

The etiologic agent of epidemic typhus is *Rickettsia prowazekii*. Epidemic typhus is a severe acute disease characterized by high fever, intense headache, a macular skin rash, and diffuse vascular lesions. Although this organism was responsible for the deaths of millions of people during World Wars I and II, the disease is now most commonly reported from northeastern and central Africa. A large proportion of the population is usually louse infested before epidemic typhus occurs. An infected louse deposits infected feces at the feeding site. Scratching then distributes the organism into the broken skin. Typhus is spread from human to human only via the body louse. In the eastern United States, cases of *R prowazekii* infection have been reported in patients with no history of lice infestation. These patients all described contact with flying squirrels or their nests.

Epidemic typhus is far more severe than endemic typhus. After 7 days of incubation, patients develop sudden onset of severe headache, prostration, and high fever. A rash, appearing on the fifth day, consists of pink macules and is most common in the axillae. It occurs in 50–90% of patients. The rash coalesces, becomes petechial, and spreads to the trunk but usually does not involve the palms or soles. Conjunctival involvement is common. The disease is similar to RMSF, but the character and evolution of the rash, as well as the epidemiologic setting, distinguish the two diseases. An IFA test is the most sensitive and practical approach for diagnosing epidemic typhus. Chloramphenicol and tetracycline are effective therapies; patients usually become afebrile within 48 h. Relapse is rare if treatment is started early. A single 100-mg dose of doxycycline has also resulted in successful resolution of symptoms. Prevention requires mass delousing of the population at risk with permethrin or lindane.

SCRUB TYPHUS

Orientia tsutsugamushi causes scrub typhus; it is transmitted by the bite of an infected mite. The disease is found in Southeast Asia, India, and northeastern Australia. Symptoms and signs of disease consist of an eschar at the bite site, regional and then generalized adenopathy, high fever, and a macular rash on the trunk, which appears after 5 days. The rash becomes maculopapular as it spreads to the extremities. Serology is the most practical diagnostic approach. Chloramphenicol and doxycycline are the therapeutic agents of choice, with rapid resolution of symptoms after the onset of therapy. A recent report of doxycycline-resistant scrub typhus in northern Thailand was the first to describe drug resistance in a rickettsial organism.

REFERENCES

Coxiella burnetii Infection (Q Fever)

Heinzen RA, Hackstadt T, Samuel JE: Developmental biology of *Coxiella burnetii.* Trends Microbiol 1999; 7(4):149.

Maurin M, Raoult D: Q fever. Clin Microbiol Rev 1999; 12(4):518.

Raoult D et al: Treatment of Q fever endocarditis: comparison of 2 regimens containing doxycycline and ofloxacin or hydroxychloroquine. Arch Intern Med 1999;159(2):167.

Ehrlichia Infection (Ehrlichiosis)

Anderson BE et al: *Ehrlichia chaffeensis,* a new species associated with human ehrlichiosis. J Clin Microbiol 1991;29:2838.

Chen SM et al: Identification of a granulocytotropic *Ehrlichia* species as the etiologic agent of human disease. J Clin Microbiol 1994;32:589.

McQuiston JH et al: The human ehrlichioses in the United States. Emerg Infect Dis 1999;5(5):635.

Rocky Mountain Spotted Fever

Azad AF, Beard CB: Rickettsial pathogens and their arthropod vectors. Emerg Infect Dis 1998;4(2):179.

Thorner AR et al: Rocky Mountain spotted fever. Clin Infect Dis 1998;27(6):1353.

Rickettsialpox

Comer JA et al: Serologic evidence of rickettsialpox (*Rickettsia akari*) infection among intravenous drug users in inner-city Baltimore, Maryland. Am J Trop Med Hyg 1999;60(6):894.

Kass EM et al: Rickettsialpox in a New York City hospital, 1960–1989. N Engl J Med 1994;331:1612.

Endemic (Murine) Typhus

Higgins JA et al: *Rickettsia felis:* a new species of pathogenic rickettsia isolated from cat fleas. J Clin Microbiol 1996;34(3):671.

Epidemic (Louse-Borne) Typhus

Raoult D, Roux V: The body louse as a vector of reemerging human diseases. Clin Infect Dis 1999; 29(4):888.

Bartonella

69

Phyllis C. Tien, SM, MD & Jeffery S. Loutit, MB ChB

Essentials of Diagnosis

- Key signs and symptoms include dermal lesion (bacillary angiomatosis and chronic phase of *Bartonella bacilliformis* infection); papule at inoculation site followed by proximal lymphadenopathy (cat scratch disease); fever, bacteremia, acute hemolytic anemia (acute phase of *B bacilliformis* infection); persistent or relapsing fever (fever and bacteremia/endocarditis).
- Predisposing factors include louse exposure, low income, and homelessness (*Bartonella quintana*-associated bacillary angiomatosis, fever, and bacteremia/endocarditis); cat exposure (cat scratch disease and *Bartonella henselae*-associated bacillary angiomatosis, fever and bacteremia/endocarditis); sandfly exposure in endemic areas of South American Andes (*B bacilliformis* infection).
- History of HIV or immunocompromise (bacillary angiomatosis).
- Key laboratory findings include small, curved, pleomorphic weakly gram-negative bacilli, best visualized with Warthin-Starry silver stain of tissue.

General Considerations

There are currently 11 known species of *Bartonella*, four of which are considered to be pathogenic in humans, namely *B bacilliformis*, *B quintana*, *B henselae*, and *Bartonella elizabethae*. *B henselae* and *B elizabethae* have only recently been isolated and identified, but *B quintana* and *B bacilliformis* have long been known as the causes of trench fever (*B quintana*) and Oroya fever and verruga peruana (*B bacilliformis*). The bartonellae establish intimate relationships with animal hosts, often within the vascular compartment but without causing disease.

The relationship between *B bacilliformis* and the other three *Bartonella* species that are pathogenic in humans was established in the early 1990s. This followed the recognition of a new clinical syndrome, bacillary angiomatosis in HIV-infected individuals, in 1983. *B henselae* was first identified with molecular methods as a cause of this syndrome in 1990, and both *B henselae* and *B quintana* were cultured from tissue samples of patients with bacillary angiomatosis in 1992. *B henselae* was also associated with cat scratch disease in 1992.

B bacilliformis is closely related to *B henselae*, *B quintana*, and *B elizabethae*, as indicated by 16S ribosomal RNA gene sequence analysis. Therefore, these last three organisms, formerly designated as *Rochalimaea* species, have been reclassified as members of the genus *Bartonella*.

The spectrum of human disease associated with the bartonellae includes regional and disseminated granulomatous disease in immunocompetent hosts (cat scratch disease), persistent bacteremia or endocarditis, and vascular proliferative disease (verruga peruana or bacillary angiomatosis) in immunocompromised hosts (Box 69–1). *B henselae* and *B quintana* are the recognized causes of bacillary angiomatosis, while only *B henselae* has been implicated as a cause of cat scratch disease. Finally, these two species along with *B elizabethae* have all been identified in patients with endocarditis and bacteremia.

A. Epidemiology. *B quintana* is globally endemic. However, epidemics do occur. These epidemics are associated with conditions of poor sanitation and personal hygiene as seen in battlefield troops in World War I. Recent reports have shown a reemergence of trench fever among chronic alcoholics and the homeless in urban areas of the United States and western Europe. Urban trench fever is sporadic, both geographically and temporally, for unclear reasons. The human body louse, *Pediculus humanus*, is the only known vector of *B quintana*.

B henselae is also globally endemic. Cat contact appears to be the single most important factor in the development of cat scratch disease and *B henselae*-associated bacillary angiomatosis, which reflects the fact that cats are the most important reservoir for *B henselae*.

There are ~ 22,000 cases of cat scratch disease reported per year in the United States, making this the most common *Bartonella*-associated disease. Over 80% of cases occur in individuals < 21 years of age. The number of cases peaks in the fall and winter months. This seasonality may reflect differences in human behavior that place persons at risk of exposure to *Bartonella* species, or it may reflect breeding patterns of cats and fleas. Approximately 18% of household members with cats are seropositive for *B henselae* antibodies. Risk factors for the development of cat scratch disease include ownership of a kitten (es-

BOX 69-1

Bartonella Infection Syndromes

	Children	Adults
More Common	Cat scratch disease	• Bacillary angiomatosis • Persistent bacteremia and/or endocarditis
Less Common	• Bacillary angiomatosis • Persistent bacteremia and/or endocarditis • *B bacilliformis*-associated disease	• *B bacilliformis*-associated disease • Cat scratch disease

pecially one with fleas) and being scratched or bitten by a kitten.

Cats in the southeastern United States, coastal California, the Pacific Northwest, and the south central plains have the highest prevalence of *B henselae* antibodies (36–81%). These areas of high prevalence are regions of greater warmth and humidity and closely correlate with the distribution in the United States of the cat flea, *Ctenocephalides felis.* The lack of *B henselae* antibody in cats is highly predictive of the absence of bacteremia. Approximately 40% of cats are bacteremic with *B henselae;* kittens are more likely to be bacteremic than adult cats, as are cats that spend most of their time outdoors. *B henselae* has also been isolated from fleas of bacteremic cats. The cat flea has been shown to be a competent vector in the transmission of *B henselae* among cats. In the absence of the cat flea, direct cat-to-cat transmission among kittens has not been demonstrated. The role of the flea in transmission of *B henselae* to humans has not been elucidated.

Recently, an association between another *Bartonella* species, *Bartonella clarridgeiae,* and cat scratch disease was reported after isolation of this organism from the blood of a flea-infested kitten that induced cat scratch disease in a human. However, the role of *B clarridgeiae* as a cause of human infection is unclear.

Although > 90% of patients with cat scratch disease report recent cat contact, only two-thirds of patients with bacillary angiomatosis report recent cat exposure, suggesting that there are other risk factors for developing bacillary angiomatosis. Both *B henselae* and *B quintana* are known causes of bacillary angiomatosis, and yet the risk factors and reservoirs for infection with these organisms are quite different. For *B quintana*-associated disease, risk factors include low income, homelessness, and exposure to lice. Risk factors for *B henselae*-associated bacillary angiomatosis are similar to those for cat scratch disease, including cat ownership and being scratched or bitten by a cat. *B henselae* has also been found in fleas from cats owned by patients with bacillary angiomatosis.

Despite the advent of serologic testing for *Bar-*

tonella species, the incidence of bacillary angiomatosis remains unknown. Of all reported cases of bacillary angiomatosis, ~ 90% are men that are coinfected with HIV. Cases have been reported from all areas of the United States, with greater numbers in New York City, San Francisco, and some parts of Florida and Texas. Bacillary angiomatosis is uncommon in immunocompetent individuals; conversely, it can occur in patients who are immunosuppressed from causes other than HIV. *Bartonella* bacteremia with fever occurs in both immunosuppressed and immunocompetent individuals. Because special, nonroutine techniques are required for its isolation, bacteremia with *Bartonella* spp. is likely to be underreported.

B bacilliformis is geographically confined to intermediate altitudes (between 1000 and 3000 m) of the South American Andes. This coincides with the limited distribution of its sandfly vector, *Lutzomyia vernicarum.*

B. Microbiology. *Bartonella* species are small, slightly curved gram-negative rods measuring 2μm by 0.6 μm. They are classified within the alpha subdivision of the division *Proteobacteria,* as are the *Rickettsia, Ehrlichia,* and *Brucella.* They are oxidase-negative, aerobic, and fastidious in their laboratory growth requirements. *B henselae* and, to a lesser extent, *B quintana,* display twitching motility when mounted in saline, due to the presence of pili. *B bacilliformis* has polar flagella.

Bartonella species can be cultivated when plated on freshly prepared, enriched (blood-containing) solid media and placed in a humidified atmosphere containing 5% CO_2. Optimum temperature for growth is 35–37 °C, except for *B bacilliformis,* which grows best at 25–30 °C. Colonies are detected in 5–21 days. The colonies of *Bartonella* species from primary isolation are either white, raised, rough, and autoadherent or small, tan, moist appearing, and imbedded in the agar. Both types of colonies are usually seen in the same culture, but *B henselae* is usually more heterogeneous with a larger proportion of the rough morphology than *B quintana,* which has predominantly smooth colonies. *B henselae* and *B quintana* are difficult to distinguish because they are closely related at both the phenotypic and genotypic levels.

C. Pathogenesis. Pili are believed to be key factors in host cell attachment as well as important virulence factors for *B henselae* and *B quintana*. The pathologic features of cat scratch disease and bacillary angiomatosis are quite different. The hallmark of cat scratch disease is granuloma formation, with progression from lymphoid hyperplasia through granuloma formation to suppuration. Involved lymph nodes demonstrate a mixture of nonspecific inflammatory reactions including granulomata and stellate necrosis with lymphocytic infiltrates and multinucleated giant cells.

Bacillary angiomatosis is a result of lobular proliferation of blood vessels. Small capillaries are arranged around ectatic ones with edema, mucin, or fibrotic stroma surrounding the lobules. The endothelial cells that make up the vascular lobules occur either singly, in small groups, or in areas of solid proliferation. Endothelial cell necrosis may also be seen along with neutrophils and sometimes macrophages. In most cases, clusters of neutrophils and neutrophilic debris are seen adjacent to the capillaries scattered throughout the lesion. It is believed that *B henselae* and *B quintana* directly stimulate the vascular proliferation seen in the lesions of bacillary angiomatosis. Angioproliferative lesions, however, have not been reported in patients with other forms of *B henselae* and *B quintana* infection such as trench fever and cat scratch disease.

The flagella of *B bacilliformis* allow invasion of human erythrocytes, and the resulting cell lysis leads to the severe hemolytic anemia seen in the early stages of South American bartonellosis (Oroya fever). The nodular skin lesions that develop in the late stages of this disease reveal a characteristic vascular proliferation of endothelial cells that resembles bacillary angiomatosis.

CLINICAL SYNDROMES

BACILLARY ANGIOMATOSIS

A. Signs and Symptoms. The most common manifestation of bacillary angiomatosis is a dermal lesion (Table 69–1). Three types of lesions are seen: cutaneous papules, subcutaneous nodules, and hyperpigmented plaques, in decreasing order of frequency. Papules are usually red-purple in color and range in size from a few millimeters to several centimeters, often surrounded by a collarette of scale (Figure 69–1). They vary in number, are often friable and bleed easily, are occasionally tender, and may resolve spontaneously even in immunosuppressed patients.

Table 69–1. Clinical Manifestations of Bartonella Infections

Bacillary Angiomatosis	• Neovascular proliferative lesion, primarily of skin • Liver and spleen involvement leads to bacillary peliosis • May affect mucous membranes, lung, bone, and CNS
***B bacilliformis* Infection**	• Acute phase: febrile bacteremic illness (Oroya fever) associated with acute hemolytic anemia • Chronic phase: subcutaneous nodules (verruga peruana) resemble bacillary angiomatosis
Cat Scratch Disease	• Erythematous papule 3–5 days after cat contact at inoculation site • Proximal lymphadenopathy usually of head, neck, or upper extremity • Lymph nodes may suppurate
Fever and Bacteremia	• Often relapsing or persistent • Endocarditis is sometimes associated • Trench fever associated with *B. quintana* bacteremia

These lesions are easily removed by curettage. Slight hyperpigmentation and induration may persist.

Subcutaneous nodules or lobules are the second most common presentation and may vary markedly in size and number. Underlying cortical bone erosion may be associated with these nodules. There is often minimal epidermal change or hyperpigmentation, but, infrequently, the overlying skin changes may resemble cellulitis. While cutaneous disease is associated with both *Bartonella* species, subcutaneous and bony disease is associated almost exclusively with *B quintana*. Regional lymph node enlargement may be present; these nodules may be tender but rarely ulcerate or bleed.

Less common are indurated hyperpigmented plaques, which are often oval in shape and several cen-

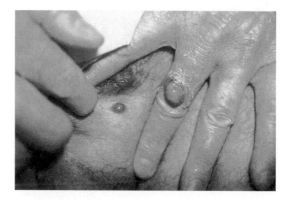

Figure 69–1. Typical papular and nodular lesions of bacillary angiomatosis in the same patient. At the macroscopic level, these lesions are easily confused with those of Kaposi's sarcoma. (Reprinted with permission from Ann Intern Med 109:451, Figure 2, 1988.)

timeters in diameter. These hyperkeratotic plaques are typically found on the extremities.

Liver and spleen involvement by *Bartonella* spp. with or without cutaneous disease is frequently associated with *B henselae* in the immunocompromised host. The spectrum of liver and spleen pathology varies from a nonspecific necrotizing inflammatory reaction to bacillary peliosis. Bacillary peliosis is characterized by cystic blood-filled spaces throughout the tissue parenchyma. Since the advent of AIDS, peliosis, a previously rare entity associated with chronic debilitating illnesses (such as tuberculosis and malignancy) and anabolic steroid use, has increased. Bacillary peliosis is fatal in rare cases.

Bacillary angiomatosis may also involve the mucus membranes of the mouth, nose, larynx, bronchi, conjunctiva, and anus; the lung and pleura; bone; and the central nervous system. Bacillary angiomatosis should strongly be considered in any HIV-infected patient with skin and lytic bone lesions.

B. Laboratory Findings. Patients with bacillary peliosis may have elevated serum alkaline phosphatase levels, as well as thrombocytopenia or pancytopenia.

C. Imaging. Computed tomographic scans of patients with bacillary peliosis often show multiple hypodense areas that are enhanced following the use of contrast agents, scattered throughout an enlarged liver, and ascites.

D. Differential Diagnosis. The differential diagnosis of a bacillary angiomatosis skin lesion includes Kaposi's sarcoma, pyogenic granuloma, simple hemangioma, angiokeratoma, and verruga peruana (in the appropriate geographic region). Lesions of bacillary angiomatosis and Kaposi's sarcoma cannot be distinguished by gross appearance.

CAT SCRATCH DISEASE

Clinical Findings
A. Signs and Symptoms. Cat scratch disease typically begins with an erythematous ("inoculation") papule 3–5 days after cat contact or scratch (Table 69–1). The papule may appear on the skin, conjunctiva, or other mucous membrane. Lymphadenopathy follows 1–7 weeks later in a proximal distribution with the lymph nodes of the axilla, cervical, and submandibular areas most commonly involved. The lymph node is often tender, markedly swollen, and may ultimately suppurate. In 75% of all cases, the illness is mild, with myalgias, malaise, anorexia, and, rarely, nausea and abdominal pain. Fever is present in about one-third of patients; temperatures above 39 °C occur in < 10%. Cat scratch disease is typically a benign and self-limited illness that lasts 6–12 weeks. Most cases of cat scratch disease occur in individuals with normal immune systems, but several cases have been described in immunocompromised patients.

B. Differential Diagnosis. The differential diagnosis of cat scratch disease includes many infections known to cause lymphadenopathy: atypical mycobacterial infection, tuberculosis, streptococcal and staphylococcal adenitis, toxoplasmosis, infectious mononucleosis, tularemia, histoplasmosis, and brucellosis.

C. Complications. In as many as 14% of patients, dissemination or other complications occur. Parinaud's oculoglandular syndrome is the result of conjunctival inoculation and is characterized by granulomatous conjunctivitis and preauricular adenopathy. It occurs in ~ 2% of all patients with cat scratch disease and usually resolves without sequelae. Hepatosplenic granulomata, lytic bone lesions, pneumonitis, and central nervous system involvement with encephalopathy and neuroretinitis can also occur. Symptoms of encephalopathy usually occur 1–6 weeks after the initial symptoms of cat scratch disease. Patients may become acutely confused and disoriented, rapidly progressing to coma, but they usually recover completely within 4 weeks. Neuroretinitis may be associated with a decrease in visual acuity, but marked improvement has been noted both with and without antibiotic treatment.

B BACILLIFORMIS-ASSOCIATED DISEASE

About 3 weeks after the bite of an infected sandfly, acute *B bacilliformis* infection becomes manifest as a febrile bacteremic illness (Oroya fever). It is accompanied by an acute hemolytic anemia that is caused by bacterial attachment and invasion of erythrocytes (Table 69–1). Patients exhibit malaise, fever, chills, diaphoresis, headache, and mental status changes. Lymphadenopathy, hepatosplenomegaly, and thrombocytopenia are also seen. At the end of the acute bacteremic phase, there is a transient immunosuppression that renders the patient susceptible to a wide range of opportunistic bacterial, viral, and parasitic secondary infections. Mortality during this acute phase is higher among persons without previous exposure to this agent. Overall, mortality is estimated to be ~ 8%.

After the acute phase of infection, 15% of patients develop a chronic form of disease manifested by painless superficial or subcutaneous nodules (verruga peruana). These nodules are histologically similar to those of bacillary angiomatosis.

FEVER & BACTEREMIA/TRENCH FEVER/ENDOCARDITIS

The four *Bartonella* species that are pathogenic for humans are capable of causing sustained or relapsing bacteremia accompanied by only fever (Table 69–1). All except *B bacilliformis* also cause endocarditis. After *B quintana* enters the body through broken skin from the excreta of the infected human body louse (*Pediculus humanus*), there is an incubation period of between 5 and 20 days before the onset of trench fever. Patients complain of fever, myalgias, malaise, headache, bone pain—particularly of the legs, and a transient macular rash. Usually the illness continues for 4–6 weeks. Sustained or recurrent bacteremia is common, with or without symptoms.

The form of trench fever described in the United States and Europe in the 1990s (urban trench fever) has no distinguishing features other than fever, malaise, and weight loss. Endocarditis has been reported in conjunction with *B quintana* bacteremia.

In HIV-infected patients, *B henselae* bacteremia usually presents insidiously with malaise, fatigue, weight loss, and fevers. Endocarditis may occur in immunocompetent hosts with patients presenting with fever and malaise.

Diagnosis

Difficulty in the identification and isolation of *Bartonella* species from blood and tissue has made a diagnosis of infection with these organisms a challenge. Direct examination of tissue (not blood) with special stains is required, and special conditions for cultivation from tissue and blood are necessary.

The detection of these small, curved gram-negative bacilli in pathology specimens is best made by using the Warthin-Starry silver stain, electron microscopy, immunofluorescence, or the polymerase chain reaction. Conventional stains such as acid-fast, Giemsa, periodic acid-Schiff, and the Brown-Brenn modification of Gram's stain fail to demonstrate the bacilli. The Warthin-Starry stain results are not pathognomonic since it also stains other bacteria, including spirochetes and species of *Nocardia, Legionella,* and *Campylobacter.* Polymerase chain reaction-based assays offer high sensitivity and specificity but are not widely available.

Isolation of *B henselae* and *B quintana* after homogenization of tissue such as liver, spleen, lymph node, and skin can be performed by direct plating or by cocultivation with an endothelial cell line. The cocultivation method, while useful in recovering organisms, may not be practical for most microbiology laboratories. Growth of strains on freshly prepared heart infusion agar containing 5% or 10% defibrinated rabbit or horse blood has been more successful than growth on other cell-free media such as chocolate or 5% sheep blood agar.

The lysis-centrifugation blood culture system is currently the best method to isolate *Bartonella* species from the blood. If bacteremia with a *Bartonella* species is suspected, the laboratory must be informed in order that lysis centrifugation-processed blood can be placed on the appropriate media and incubated for at least 7–14 days. Because of the fastidious nature of these organisms, the interval from collection to processing should be minimized. Other alternatives to the lysis centrifugation method include screening suspected blood culture bottle contents with an acridine orange staining procedure and subculturing positive bottles.

Differentiation of the *Bartonella* species can be accomplished with biochemical and molecular methods. Cellular fatty acid analysis by gas liquid chromatography can be helpful, but many laboratories do not have the necessary capabilities to perform this test. The Microscan rapid anaerobic panel has been used with some success to distinguish between *B henselae* and *B quintana.* Other methods have included polymerase chain reaction–restriction fragment length polymorphism analysis of the citrate synthase gene and 16S rDNA sequence analysis.

Serologic testing is easier and more rapid than cultivation of the organism and has become the mainstay for confirming the diagnosis of cat scratch disease. Both immunofluorescence assays and enzyme immunoassays are available to detect cerebrospinal fluid and serum immunoglobulin G (IgG) and IgM directed against *Bartonella* spp. A titer of > 1:64 or a fourfold rise in titer is considered positive. Because of the cross-reactivity of antibodies against *B quintana* and *B henselae,* definitive species identification is difficult with these methods.

Treatment

Treatment of *Bartonella*-associated disease varies according to the clinical syndrome (Box 69–2). All recommendations are based on anecdotal evidence of treatment response since controlled trials have not been performed.

Bacillary angiomatosis should always be treated. Spontaneous resolution of superficial skin papules has been reported, but relapse and bacterial dissemination are common. Nevertheless, therapeutic endpoints remain undefined.

Anecdotal evidence strongly favors the use of oral erythromycin for treatment of bacillary angiomatosis at a dose of 500 mg four times per day for 8–12 weeks. Intravenous erythromycin should be administered to patients with severe disease or patients who are unable to take oral medications. Longer courses may be necessary in patients with bacteremia/endocarditis or bacillary peliosis and those with disease recurrence. The newer macrolides, azithromycin and clarithromycin, may also be effective, but experience with these drugs is more limited. Oral doxycycline (100 mg twice daily) has been consistently successful in the treatment of bacillary angiomatosis. Jarisch-Herxheimer–like reactions after the first several doses of doxycycline or erythromycin can occur, however. Use of an antipyretic before treatment may attenuate this response.

Limited data support the use of ciprofloxacin in the treatment of bacillary angiomatosis. Inhibitors of cell wall synthesis, such as the penicillins and cephalosporins, uniformly fail to cure the disease, despite the fact that in vitro testing indicates that both *B quintana* and *B henselae* are sensitive to these antibi-

BOX 69-2

Treatment of *Bartonella* Infections

	First Choice	Second Choice
Cat Scratch Disease	Symptomatic therapy (resolves spontaneously)	Azithromycin, 500 mg PO once on the first day, and 250 mg once daily for four subsequent days
Bacillary Angiomatosis	Erythromycin, 500 mg PO 4 times a day for at least 8 wks[a]	Doxycycline, 100 mg PO twice daily for at least 8 wks[1]
B bacilliformis Infection	Chloramphenicol (recommended in endemic regions)	
Fever and Bacteremia	Erythromycin, 500 mg PO 4 times a day for at least 4 wks[1]	

[1]Longer courses required if patient has bacillary peliosis, endocarditis, or relapses.

otics. Susceptibility testing is not standardized for *B henselae* or *B quintana* and is difficult to perform. In vitro data should not be used to guide therapy at this time.

Cat scratch disease usually resolves spontaneously over a 2- to 8-week period. Aspiration of a suppurative node may provide symptomatic relief. Antibiotic therapy is not consistently successful, nor is it routinely indicated, unless the disease occurs in an immunocompromised host. Despite the success of macrolides and tetracyclines in the treatment of bacillary angiomatosis, they have not been used as widely in the treatment of cat scratch disease. A prospective, randomized, double-blind trial has suggested that azithromycin treatment for 5 days reduces lymph node size more rapidly than placebo. Rifampin, ciprofloxacin, trimethoprim-sulfamethoxazole, and gentamicin have been proposed as effective agents, based only on a retrospective review of the literature. Mild or moderate disease should receive only symptomatic therapy, since antimicrobial agents do not change the clinical outcome of cat scratch disease in the majority of cases.

Urban trench fever has been suppressed and sometimes cured with erythromycin or azithromycin given for at least 4 weeks; however, as with *B henselae* bacteremia, response to antimicrobial agents is variable, and some patients experience a relapse of symptoms after cessation of antibiotics. Some cases of endocarditis require valve replacement and most require prolonged antibiotic therapy.

The response of Oroya fever and verruga peruana to therapy is variable. Chloramphenicol has been recommended in endemic regions due to the possibility of intercurrent *Salmonella* infection and the high case fatality rate.

Prevention & Control

Cat owners can, and immunocompromised indi-

viduals should, reduce their risk of cat scratch disease or bacillary angiomatosis (Box 69–3). Cat owners who are immunocompromised should (1) wash hands after animal contact and keep all wounds and abrasions as clean as possible; (2) avoid cats < 1 year of age or avoid rough play with them since they are more prone to "carry" the organism; and (3) keep cats as free from fleas as possible. Declawing of cats is not recommended. Antibiotic treatment of infected cats is not useful.

B quintana infection may be prevented or controlled by delousing procedures. These include regular changing or washing of clothes and bedding. Insecticides such as permethrin should also be used to control louse infestation. Oroya fever and verruga peruana can be prevented by avoiding the bite of the sandfly vector. These insects tend to be nocturnal feeders.

BOX 69-3

Control of *Bartonella* Infections

Prophylactic Measures	• Wash hands after animal contact; keep wounds and abrasions clean • Avoid cats less than one year of age or minimize rough play • Keep cats as free from fleas as possible • Regular changing and washing of clothes and bedding • Insecticides such as permethrin to control louse infestation • Avoid the bite of the sandfly
Isolation Precautions	• None

REFERENCES

Anderson BE, Neuman MA: *Bartonella* spp. as emerging human pathogens. Clin Microbiol Rev 1997;10(2):203.

Loutit JS. *Bartonella* infections. Curr Clin Topics Infect Dis 1997;17:269.

Maurin M, Raoult D: *Bartonella quintana* infections. Clin Microbiol Rev 1996;9(3):273.

Koehler JE, et al. Molecular epidemiology of *Bartonella* infections in patients with bacillary angiomatosis-peliosis. N Engl J Med 1997;337(26):1876.

Koehler JE, et al: *Rochlimaea henselae* infection: a new zoonosis with the domestic cat as reservoir. JAMA 1994;271(7):531.

Koehler JE, et al: Isolation of *Rochalimaea* species from cutaneous and osseous lesions of bacillary angiomatosis. N Engl J Med 1992;327(23):1625.

Zangwill KM, et al: Cat scratch disease in Connecticut: epidemiology, risk factors and evaluation of a new diagnostic test. N Engl J Med 1993;329(1):8.

Section VI.
Fungal Infections

Histoplasma capsulatum

70

Zelalem Temesgen, MD

Essentials of Diagnosis

- Thin-walled oval yeast measuring 2–4 mm in diameter.
- Dimorphic: mycelial in nature, yeast in tissue.
- Endemic within Ohio and Mississippi River Valleys.
- Associated with activities that disturb dust or soil enriched with bird, chicken, and bat excrement.
- Complement fixation antibody titer 1:32 or greater.
- Simultaneous appearance of anti-H and anti-M antibodies.
- Infection most often is asymptomatic or may cause chronic pulmonary infection; less commonly, disseminated infection involving the adrenals, ulcerative gastroenteritis lesions, or central nervous system.
- Recovery of organism from culture of tissue, blood, sputum, or other source.

General Considerations

A. Epidemiology. *Histoplasma capsulatum,* the etiologic agent of histoplasmosis, is an endemic, dimorphic fungus that causes a wide spectrum of disease in both immunocompetent and immunocompromised individuals. It is found in temperate zones around the world. In the United States, it is endemic within the Ohio and Mississippi River Valleys. Its natural habitat is soil, especially soil with high organic content such as soil enriched with bird, chicken, and bat excrement. Many types of both occupational and recreational activities (eg, cave exploring, excavation) have resulted in outbreaks of histoplasmosis.

B. Microbiology. *H capsulatum* is dimorphic; it grows as a mycelial form outside the human host but converts into its pathogenic yeast form at the body temperature of mammals. The yeast forms seen in tissue are small, thin-walled, oval structures measuring 2–4 mm in diameter.

C. Pathogenesis. The vast majority of infections caused by *H capsulatum* are acquired by inhalation and deposition of mycelial fragments into the alveoli. The organism converts into its pathogenic yeast form and is phagocytosed by alveolar macrophages. The yeast forms multiply within the macrophages, eventually causing the destruction of these macrophages. The released yeasts spread to the regional lymph nodes and other organs via the lymphatics and blood. Specific T cell-mediated immunity develops in 2–4 weeks and inhibits the growth of the organisms. Resolution occurs with production of a granulomatous inflammatory response and leads to the formation of granulomas, which may be caseating but usually become calcified. The yeasts persist for prolonged periods within caseating granulomas.

CLINICAL SYNDROMES

A variety of clinical syndromes have been described in association with histoplasmosis (Box 70–1).

PULMONARY INFECTIONS

1. ACUTE PRIMARY HISTOPLASMOSIS

Clinical Findings

A. Signs and Symptoms. Among persons with normal cell-mediated immunity, only ~ 1% will develop a mild symptomatic but usually self-limited infection after a low-inoculum exposure to *H capsulatum*. Fever, malaise, nonproductive cough, chest pain, and fatigue are the most common symptoms.

B. Imaging. In symptomatic persons, chest roentgenograms show focal infiltrates, hilar or mediastinal lymphadenopathy, or a combination.

C. Differential Diagnosis. The differential diagnosis of pulmonary histoplasmosis includes tuberculosis, pneumonia caused by other fungi, and bacterial pneumonia.

D. Complications. Most patients recover fully

BOX 70-1

Clinical Syndromes in Histoplasmosis	
More Common	Acute primary pulmonary histoplasmosis
Less Common	• Disseminated histoplasmosis (in adults with defective cell-mediated immunity) • Chronic pulmonary histoplasmosis • Mediastinal granulomatosis • Fibrosing mediastinitis

without treatment but some may experience fatigue and weakness for months. Persons with defects in cell-mediated immunity or persons who have been exposed to a high inoculum of the organisms may develop severe symptomatic infection characterized by severe dyspnea and hypoxemia. Diffuse infiltrates or multiple poorly defined pulmonary nodules are noted on chest roentgenograms. Some may present with disseminated disease.

About 10% of patients develop acute pericarditis. Another 10% experience arthritis with erythema nodosum. These responses are thought to represent immunologic reactions and as such respond to anti-inflammatory therapy and do not usually require antifungal treatment.

2. CHRONIC PULMONARY HISTOPLASMOSIS

Clinical Findings

A. Signs and Symptoms. Chronic pulmonary histoplasmosis consists of progressive focal consolidation and cavitation and is most often seen in those with preexisting lung disease such as chronic obstructive pulmonary disease. The main symptoms are productive cough, malaise, fatigue, and weight loss. The lesions are localized in the apical or subapical regions of the lung. The early form of the disease usually presents as interstitial infiltrates but later undergoes necrosis, cavitation, and fibrosis that extend to involve adjacent areas of the lung.

B. Laboratory Diagnosis. Though anemia and leukocytosis may occasionally be present, routine laboratory studies are usually not helpful to suggest or establish diagnosis.

C. Differential Diagnosis. Differential diagnosis of chronic histoplasmosis includes tuberculosis and pneumonia caused by other endemic fungi.

D. Complications. Cavities may extend into adjacent lung tissue. This may undergo fibrosis and contribute to progressive restrictive and obstructive lung disease, which may in turn result in respiratory failure and death.

3. MEDIASTINAL GRANULOMATOSIS

A. Signs and Symptoms. After exposure to *H capsulatum,* the healing process in the lungs is characterized by a granulomatous inflammatory response resulting in the formation of caseated lymph nodes surrounded by fibrosis. Occasionally, these nodes coalesce to form a large lesion in the mediastinum and may attach to adjacent structures such as the bronchi, trachea, and esophagus. Fibrosis of the attached nodes can result in compression of these structures, causing various symptoms such as cough, dysphagia, odynophagia, formation of esophagopulmonary fistula, and development of post-obstructive pneumonia or bronchiectasis.

B. Laboratory Findings. Thoracoscopy or thoracotomy is required for definitive diagnosis. Necrotizing granulomata are usually found in histological specimens, but the microorganisms themselves may be difficult to stain or recover from cultures.

C. Complications. Approximately 40% of mediastinal granulomas are asymptomatic, but as many as a third of cases may progress to fibrosing mediastinitis within a 2-year period.

4. FIBROSING MEDIASTINITIS

In rare instances, the healing process may be complicated by a hyperintense fibrotic reaction culminating in a relentless progressive invasion of mediastinal structures including the esophagus and respiratory and vascular structures. Fibrosing mediastinitis due to histoplasmosis is the most common cause other than malignancy of the superior vena cava syndrome. The intense fibrotic reaction is thought to be caused by continuous antigenic stimulation by the yeast forms that persist within the granuloma.

DISSEMINATED HISTOPLASMOSIS

A. Signs and Symptoms. Although occasionally seen in normal adults, disseminated histoplasmosis is mainly a disease of infants and adults with defective cell-mediated immunity. It presents as a systemic febrile illness with malaise and weight loss as the main and consistent symptoms. Extrapulmonary involvement is common and may be manifested by hepatosplenomegaly, meningitis or focal central nervous system parenchymal lesions, oral and mucocutaneous lesions, adrenal insufficiency, and endocarditis.

B. Laboratory Findings. Anemia, leukopenia, thrombocytopenia, and elevation of serum alanine aminotransferase and alkaline phosphatase values are often noted on laboratory evaluation.

C. Imaging. The most common findings on chest roentgenograms are diffuse infiltrates, but as many as a third of affected individuals may have normal chest x-ray findings.

HISTOPLASMOSIS IN AIDS

Clinical Findings

A. Signs and Symptoms. Histoplasmosis has been recognized as an opportunistic infection in patients with AIDS since the early days of the HIV epidemic and has been an AIDS-defining illness since 1987. It occurs in ~ 5% of patients residing in areas known to be endemic for *H capsulatum.* Sporadic cases have also been reported in nonendemic areas, but many of these patients have resided for variable periods of time in or near endemic areas, and their disease likely represents reactivation of infection acquired elsewhere. In the vast majority of cases, infection with *H capsulatum* in AIDS patients presents as disseminated disease with fever, weight loss, and malaise.

B. Laboratory Findings. Associated laboratory abnormalities may include a decrease in peripheral blood counts (leukopenia, anemia, thrombocytopenia), hyponatremia, and elevated liver enzymes. Lymphadenopathy and hepatosplenomegaly may be present.

C. Imaging. Diffuse reticulonodular infiltrates are typically noted on chest roentgenograms. However, as many as one third of patients have normal findings on the initial chest roentgenograms.

D. Complications. Central nervous system involvement in the form of meningitis, focal brain lesion, or diffuse encephalitis may complicate the course in 10–20% of cases. In 10–20% of cases, histoplasmosis in AIDS patients presents as septic shock, with fever, disseminated intravascular coagulopathy, and multiorgan failure.

Diagnosis

Histoplasmosis can be diagnosed on the basis of serologic testing, antigen detection, histopathological examination, or culture.

A. Serology. Serologic tests provide important supplemental information in cases where proof of infection cannot be obtained through culture or histopathological examination. Currently, the complement fixation and immunodiffusion tests are the serologic tests that are most commonly employed.

Complement Fixation Test. Complement fixation antibodies may be detected at ~ 3 weeks after acquiring infection and wane over several months. In chronic or disseminated infection, they might remain elevated for years. Titers of 1:32 or greater may be indicative of active infection. Titers of 1:8 or 1:16 should raise suspicion for infection. Cross-reaction may occur with blastomycosis and coccidiomycosis, but in these instances, titers are usually lower.

Immunodiffusion. Immunodiffusion assays detect antibodies to two glycoprotein antigens, designated M and H antigens. Antibodies to M and H antigens appear later in infection than complement fixation antibodies. Anti-M antibodies may persist for years after acute infection. Anti-H antibodies are detected later than antibodies to M antigen and also disappear earlier. Thus they are more specific indicators of active infection. The simultaneous appearance of anti-M and anti-H antibodies occurs in < 20% of patients and is indicative of active infection.

B. Antigen Detection. A radioimmunoassay that detects a heat-stable *H. capsulatum* polysaccharide antigen has recently been developed. This assay may be applied to serum, urine, or cerebrospinal fluid and is particularly useful in cases of disseminated infection, where it has a sensitivity of > 90%. The sensitivity of this assay to detect *H capsulatum* polysac-

BOX 70–2

Treatment of Histoplasmosis[1]

	Immunocompromised Patients	Central Nervous System Disease	Nonmeningeal, Non-Life-Threatening Disease	AIDS Patients
First Choice	• Amphotericin B, 0.7–1.0 mg/kg daily for a total of ≥ 35 mg/kg	• Amphotericin B, 0.7–1.0 mg/kg daily for a total of ≥ 35 mg/kg	• Itraconazole, 200–400 mg/daily for 6–12 m	• Amphotericin B, 0.7–1.0mg/kg for 14 d • Maintenance: itraconazole, 200 mg orally twice per d[2]
Second Choice	• Itraconazole, 200–400 mg daily PO	• Itraconazole, 200–400 mg daily PO	• Amphotericin B, 0.7 mg–1.0 mg/kg	• Itraconazole, 200–400 mg/daily

[1]Although data to make firm recommendations are not yet available. in situations in which neither amphotericin B nor itraconazole can be used, high-dose fluconazole (eg, 800 mg daily) may be an option. The efficacy and safety of itraconazole preparations have not been established in children. A few pediatric patients 3–16 years old have been treated with oral itraconazole (100 mg/d) for systemic fungal infections with no serious unexpected adverse effects.
[2]After 12 weeks of treatment, the dose of itraconazole can be decreased to 200 mg daily.

charide antigen in localized or chronic infection is considerably lower. Recent studies suggest that this test may also have a role in monitoring response to treatment. At present, this test is performed at only one laboratory in the United States.

C. Histopathological Examination. Histopathological evaluation of tissues can establish the diagnosis of histoplasmosis earlier than can culture. The site most commonly utilized for this purpose is the bone marrow, but other tissues such as lungs, skin, lymph nodes, liver, or respiratory tract secretions or washings can be evaluated. Organisms are identified through the use of special stains such as the Grocott silver methenamine and Wright-Giemsa methods.

D. Culture. A positive culture from samples of body fluids or tissue specimens is diagnostic. Newly available blood-culturing techniques, such as the lysis-centrifugation blood-culturing method, have greatly enhanced the yield of blood cultures in disseminated histoplasmosis. In AIDS patients with disseminated histoplasmosis, blood cultures are positive in ≤ 90% of cases. The yield is much lower in chronic and localized infection. It may take 2–4 weeks or more of incubation for colonies of *H capsulatum* to appear on culture media. After initial growth, rapid (within a few hours) identification of the organism may be performed with the aid of nucleic acid probe testing. Another method, the exoantigen test, which utilizes antigen-antibody reaction to identify the mold forms of dimorphic fungi, may be used for this purpose but usually requires a longer period (~ 2 weeks).

Treatment

Amphotericin B is the drug of choice for immunocompromised patients and for patients with life-threatening disease or central nervous system disease (Box 70–2). For nonmeningeal, non-life-threatening histoplasmosis, the triazole antifungal agent itraconazole has become the preferred agent. It has supplanted the previous azole mainstay of therapy, ketoconazole, because of its lower incidence of side effects and increased efficacy.

Histoplasmosis in AIDS should be treated with an intensive primary or induction therapy followed by lifelong suppressive or maintenance therapy since complete eradication of the organism is impossible. Amphotericin B is the antifungal agent of choice for

---

BOX 70–3	
Control of Histoplasmosis	
Precautions	Individuals who are at risk (eg, immunocompromised, HIV-infected) should avoid activities associated with acquiring infection, such as cleaning chicken coops and exploring caves
Prophylaxis	• Prophylaxis with itraconazole may be conisdered for AIDS patients living in endemic areas • AIDS patients with histoplasmosis who have completed intitial therapy should receive lifelong suppressive treatment with itraconazole.

---

induction treatment. Itraconazole is preferred for the maintenance phase of therapy. Nonmeningeal and nonseptic cases may be treated with itraconazole in both the initial and chronic phases of treatment. In situations where neither amphotericin B nor itraconazole may be used (because of intolerance, reactions, or allergy), fluconazole is an alternative option.

Prognosis

Prognosis is variable and hard to generalize. Disseminated histoplasmosis, if untreated, especially in immunocompromised patients, will lead invariably to death.

Prevention & Control

Individuals, such as HIV infected persons, who are at increased risk for acquiring serious infection, should be educated to avoid leisure and work activities that may lead to disturbance of potentially histoplasma-contaminated dust or soil (Box 70–3). At present, the routine use of azoles (eg, itraconazole) for primary prophylaxis of histoplasmosis in HIV-infected persons is not recommended but remains an option in highly endemic areas. HIV-infected persons diagnosed with histoplasmosis should remain on lifelong suppressive therapy with itraconazole to prevent relapse.

REFERENCES

Ajello L: Distribution of *Histoplasma capsulatum* in the United States. In Ajello L, Chick W, Fursolow MF: *Histoplasmosis.*Charles C. Thomas, 1971.

Bullock WE: *Histoplasma capsulatum.* In Mandel GL, Bennett JE, Dolin R: *Principles and Practice of Infectious Diseases,* 4th ed. Churchill Livingstone, 1995.

Dismukes WE et al: Itraconazole therapy for blastomycosis and histoplasmosis. Am J Med 1992;93:489.

Hajjeh RA: Disseminated histoplasmosis in patients infected with the human immunodeficiency virus. Clin Infect Dis 1995;21(Suppl 1):S108.

Kauffman CA: Newer developments in therapy for endemic mycoses. Clin Infect Dis 1992;19(Suppl 1):S28.

Sarosi GA, Johnson PC: Disseminated histoplasmosis in patients infected with the human immunodeficiency virus. Clin Infect Dis 1992;14(Suppl 1):S60.

Sharkey-Mathis PK et al: Histoplasmosis in the acquired immunodeficiency syndrome (AIDS): Treatment with itraconazole and fluconazole. J Acquir Immune Defic Syndr 1993;6:809.

Stockman L et al: Evaluation of commercially available acridinium ester-labeled chemiluminescent DNA probes for culture identification of *Blastomyces dermatitidis, Coccidioides immitis, Cryptococcus neoformans,* and *Histoplasma capsulatum.* J Clin Microbiol 1993;31:845.

Wheat LJ et al: *Histoplasma capsulatum* polysaccharide antigen detection in diagnosis and management of disseminated histoplasmosis in patients with the acquired immunodeficiency syndrome. Am J Med 1989;87:396.

Wheat LJ: Histoplasmosis in Indianapolis. Clin Infect Dis 1992;14(Suppl 1):s91.

Wheat LJ et al: Prevention of relapse of histoplasmosis with itraconazole in patients with the acquired immunodeficiency syndrome. Ann Intern Med 1993;118:610.

Wheat LJ: Histoplasmosis: Recognition and treatment. Clin Infect Dis 1994;19(Suppl 1):S19.

Wheat LJ: Endemic mycoses in AIDS: A clinical review. Clin Microbiol Rev 1995;8:146.

Wheat LJ et al: Itraconazole treatment of disseminated histoplasmosis in patients with the acquired immunodeficiency syndrome. Am J Med 1995;98:336.

71

Blastomyces dermatitidis

Zelalem Temesgen, MD

Essentials of Diagnosis

- Round thick-walled yeast with broad-based budding.
- Dimorphic: mycelial in nature, yeast in tissue.
- Associated with activities in proximity to waterways.
- Associated with exposure to dust, eg excavation.
- Endemic in states surrounding the Mississippi and Ohio Rivers.
- Pyogranulomas on histopathological examination.
- Acute or chronic infection of lung, skin, bone, or genitourinary tract.
- Recovery of microorganism from culture of tissue.

General Considerations

A. Epidemiology. *Blastomyces dermatitidis* is an endemic fungus that causes acute and chronic infections in humans and other animals. It is found primarily in the south central, southeastern, and midwestern United States, especially in the states surrounding the Mississippi and Ohio Rivers. Outside the United States, cases have been reported from Canadian provinces bordering the Great Lakes, Africa, India, the Middle East, and Central and South America.

Both clusters and sporadic cases of blastomycosis have been reported. Outdoor activities in proximity to waterways as well as exposure to dust from construction and excavation have been noted as possible risk factors for acquiring infection.

B. Microbiology. *B dermatitidis* is a dimorphic fungus, which means that it occurs as a mold in nature and in a yeast form in tissue (and at a temperature of 37 °C). The yeast cells are round and thick walled with daughter cells forming from a broad-based bud.

C. Pathogenesis. The lungs are the initial portal of entry for blastomycosis in humans, although primary cutaneous blastomycosis as a result of accidental skin inoculation in the laboratory or after dog bites has been reported.

Infection begins with inhalation of conidia of the mycelial phase of the organism. In the lungs, the fungus converts to its yeast phase. Inflammatory response occurs in the form of polymorphonuclear leukocyte infiltration followed by macrophage infiltration and granuloma formation. The infection can spread via the bloodstream and lymphatic system to distant sites. Cellular immunity is the major protecting factor in preventing progression of disease in blastomycosis.

CLINICAL SYNDROMES

B dermatitidis may cause disease in virtually every organ of the body. The most common clinical syndromes associated with blastomycosis are described in the following sections (Box 71–1).

PULMONARY INFECTION

Pulmonary blastomycosis characteristically presents as an acute or chronic pneumonitis.

1. ACUTE PULMONARY INFECTION

Clinical Findings

A. Signs and Symptoms. After exposure to *B dermatitidis,* a significant proportion of individuals have asymptomatic disease. The true frequency of asymptomatic or subclinical disease is unknown. In one large outbreak, 46% of infected individuals were asymptomatic.

Symptomatic acute pulmonary infection presents similarly to an acute bacterial pneumonia with fever, chills, and productive cough, with or without hemoptysis or pleuritic chest pain.

B. Imaging. The appearance of the chest radiograph is variable and nonspecific. The most common radiological appearance of pulmonary blastomycosis is airspace consolidation. Other radiographic features include nodular masses, interstitial disease, and cavitation. Pleural effusions are occasionally noted, but they are usually small. Hilar and mediastinal adenopathy or calcification of parenchymal lesions is uncommon.

C. Differential Diagnosis. Differential diagnosis of pulmonary blastomycosis includes other types

Clinical Syndromes in Blastomycosis in Adults and Children	
More Common	• Pulmonary
Less Common	• Cutaneous • Skeletal • Genitourinary
Uncommon	• Central nervous system • Disseminated

of pneumonia (eg, bacterial and fungal) and tuberculosis, as well as lymphoma and malignant neoplasms.

D. Complications. The course of pulmonary infection is variable. The disease may clear with or without treatment or progress to chronic pulmonary disease. Occasionally, overwhelming pulmonary infection with *B dermatitidis* results in the adult respiratory distress syndrome (ARDS) and respiratory failure, indistinguishable from ARDS caused by bacterial sepsis and characterized by severe impairment of gas exchange and hemodynamic instability.

This syndrome is also associated with significant mortality. In one report, only 13 of 29 patients survived. Although also seen in immunocompetent individuals, it is much more often encountered in immunocompromised individuals, including those with AIDS. Large amounts of *B dermatitidis* are easily recovered from respiratory cultures, and examination of lung tissue will show histopathological changes characteristic of ARDS, as well as the presence of a large number of the causative organisms. Aggressive therapy with large doses of amphotericin B (0.7–1.0 mg/kg) should be initiated promptly, and many patients require mechanical ventilatory assistance. Survivors may regain good pulmonary function.

2. CHRONIC PULMONARY INFECTION

Clinical Findings

A. Signs and Symptoms. The symptoms usually noted in chronic pneumonia caused by blastomycosis include weight loss, fever, night sweats, productive cough, and pleuritic chest pain. These symptoms are usually present for 2–6 months before diagnosis. Chronic pulmonary blastomycosis may be accompanied by extrapulmonary disease.

B. Imaging. The radiological presentation of chronic disease is variable and nonspecific and includes alveolar infiltrates, masses, nodules, and cavities. There is no specific pattern or distribution that corresponds with disease stage.

C. Differential Diagnosis. Same as for acute pulmonary infection.

D. Complications. Complications of chronic pulmonary blastomycosis include acute deterioration and respiratory failure, as well as hematogenous dissemination to extrapulmonary sites.

EXTRAPULMONARY INFECTION

Extrapulmonary disease is usually seen in conjunction with pulmonary infection and is the result of hematogenous dissemination of *B dermatitidis*. The exception is primary cutaneous blastomycosis, which occurs as a result of accidental inoculation in the laboratory, during autopsy, or after dog bites.

1. CUTANEOUS BLASTOMYCOSIS

Cutaneous blastomycosis is the most commo manifestation of extrapulmonary blastomycosis (40%–80% of reported cases). Areas of the body not covered by clothing are sites of predilection, but lesions can occasionally be found on mucocutaneous surfaces. The skin lesions start as papules or pustules but later advance to form either verrucous (ie, fungating, heaped up) or ulcerative lesions. The verrucous lesions, both by their gross and microscopic (hyperplasia, acanthosis) appearance, may be mistaken for cancer. Other differential diagnosis includes skin lesions caused by other fungi (eg, *Histoplasma capsulatum, Coccidioides immitis,* and *Sporothrix schenckii*), as well as lesions caused by nocardiosis and atypical mycobacteria (eg, *Mycobacterium marinum*). Both types of skin lesions may be present in the same patient.

2. SKELETAL BLASTOMYCOSIS

Bone involvement represents the second most frequent manifestation of extrapulmonary disease, having been reported in ≤ 25% of extrapulmonary cases. The most commonly affected bones are the vertebrae, pelvis, sacrum, ribs, and long bones, but any bone can be involved. The usual presenting symptoms consist of soft tissue abscesses or chronic draining sinuses adjacent to areas of osteomyelitis. Vertebral disease, with involvement of the vertebral body and development of large paraspinal abscesses, may be indistinguishable from tuberculosis. The typical radiographic appearance is a well-circumscribed osteolytic lesion.

Vertebral disease may be indistinguishable from tuberculosis. In addition, differential diagnosis includes bacterial osteomyelitis, osteomyelitis caused by other fungi, and a Brodie abscess.

3. GENITOURINARY BLASTOMYCOSIS

Blastomycosis of the genitourinary tract follows skin and bone infection in the frequency of its extrapulmonary involvement. Men are more prone to be infected than women. Prostatic involvement is the most common presentation, followed by epididymoorchitis. Symptoms include urinary obstruction with an enlarged and tender prostate and pyuria.

Yield of cultures may be improved by collection of urine after prostatic massage. In women, both endometrial infection as a result of sexual contact with a man with blastomycosis on the penis and tuboovarian abscess after hematogenous dissemination have been reported.

4. BLASTOMYCOSIS OF THE CENTRAL NERVOUS SYSTEM

Central nervous system blastomycosis is an uncommon complication of disseminated disease. It presents either as an abscess or meningitis. Abscesses present as mass lesions, either intracranially or in an epidural location. Meningitis is difficult to diagnose. Cerebrospinal fluid evaluation is usually not diagnostic. Culture of ventricular fluid may on occasion yield the organism. Cultures of large volumes of spinal fluid increase the likelihood of a positive culture.

BLASTOMYCOSIS & AIDS

Blastomycosis is an uncommon infection among patients with AIDS and is not recognized as an AIDS-defining opportunistic infection according to present Centers for Disease Control guidelines. When it occurs, it is a late manifestation of HIV infection, usually affecting individuals with prior diagnosis of an AIDS-defining illness and CD4 lymphocyte counts of < 200 cells/mm^3. It can present either with disease limited to the lungs and pleura or with disseminated infection involving multiple visceral organs. There is also more frequent involvement of the central nervous system. Cutaneous lesions appear to be less common.

A higher frequency of diffuse interstitial or miliary pattern is noted on chest radiograms. Relapse is common, necessitating chronic maintenance treatment to prevent recurrent disease.

BLASTOMYCOSIS IN OTHER IMMUNOCOMPROMISED HOSTS

Blastomycosis has been reported to cause infection in other immunocompromised patients including patients on long-term glucocorticoid treatment, solid-organ transplant recipients, patients with hematologi-

cal malignancies, patients with disorders of neutropenia, patients demonstrating humoral immune dysfunction, and patients with combined immunologic dysfunction. Infection in these individuals differs from that of normal hosts in several ways. The pulmonary involvement is more extensive; a greater frequency of progression to respiratory failure and ARDS is observed.

Diffuse interstitial alveolar changes and pleural effusions are much more common than in normal hosts. Multiple visceral organ disease, with or without central nervous system involvement, is also more common.

Diagnosis

Blastomycosis is diagnosed by identification and isolation of the organism in tissue, exudate, or histopathologic sections.

A. Direct Examination. Sputum, pus, and body fluids such as urine, pleural fluid, or cerebrospinal fluid can be evaluated by direct microscopic examination. Wet preparation, potassium hydroxide preparation, or calcofluor white stain can be used for this purpose. *B dermatitidis* is recognized and identified on the basis of its size and characteristic morphologic features (broad-based buds, refractile cell wall).

B. Histopathologic Examination. Histopathologic sections should be screened for presence of the fungus by using the Gomori methenamine silver stain or the periodic acid-Schiff stain. Fluorescent stains may be helpful when the fungal elements are sparse. Pyogranulomas, if noted, suggest the possibility of blastomycosis.

C. Culture. *B dermatitidis* usually requires 5 days to 4 weeks for growth to be detected but may be detected in as little as 2–3 days. Conversion of the mycelial form to the yeast form is required for confirmation of the diagnosis. *B dermatitidis* may also be identified by nucleic acid probe testing or by the presence of a specific A band in the exoantigen test.

D. Serology. Several serologic methods, including serum complement fixation tests, immunodiffusion tests, radio immunoassays, and enzyme-linked immunosorbent assays, have been developed. None has been useful because of low sensitivity and specificity rates.

Treatment

Acute pulmonary infection caused by *B dermatitidis* sometimes resolves spontaneously without specific therapy. However, it is not possible to determine which patients will progress to serious infection or develop extrapulmonary disease. For this reason, many authorities recommend treating all cases of active blastomycosis. If withholding treatment is considered, extrapulmonary disease should be excluded. If treatment is withheld, patients must be carefully monitored for a prolonged period for evidence of relapse, progression, or extrapulmonary infection.

Amphotericin B is the drug of choice for immuno-

BOX 71-2

Treatment of Blastomycosis in Adults and Children

	Life-Threatening Infection, Central Nervous System Infection, AIDS[1]	All others
First Choice	• Amphotericin B; daily dose: 0.3–0.6 mg/kg (total dose: 1.5–2.5 mg/kg)	• Itraconazole, 200–400 mg PO daily for a minimum of 6 mo
Second Choice	• Itraconazole, 200–400 mg PO daily for a minimum of 6 mo[2] • Ketoconazole, 400–800 mg daily for a minimum of 6 mo • Fluconazole, 200–400 mg daily for a minimum of 6 mo[3]	• Amphotericin; daily dose: 0.3–0.6 mg/kg (total dose: 1.5–2.5 mg/kg) • Ketoconazole; 400–800 mg daily for a minimum of 6 mo • Fluconazole; 200–400 mg daily for a minimum of 6 mo

[1]Patients with AIDS require lifelong suppressive treatment with daily itraconazole at a dose of 200 mg orally after completing initial treatment with amphotericin B. The efficacy and safety of itraconazole preparations have not been established in children. A few pediatric patients 3–16 years old have been treated with oral itraconazole (100 mg/d) for systemic fungal infections with no serious unexpected adverse effects.
[2]Itraconazole may not be an effective agent for central nervous system infection. See footnote 1 for pediatric patients.
[3]Fluconazole should probably not be used, if possible, in treatment of life-threatening blastomycosis.

compromised patients, including those with AIDS, patients with life-threatening infections, and patients with central nervous system disease (Box 71–2). Because relapse of blastomycosis after amphotericin therapy is dose related and rarely occurs in patients who had received > 1.5 g of the drug, a total cumulative dose of amphotericin between 1.5 and 2.5 g is recommended.

Itraconazole, a triazole antifungal agent, is the drug of choice for those patients who do not require amphotericin B (see above). It should be used at a dose of 200 mg/d orally. The dose can be increased to 400 mg/d for persistent or progressive disease. A minimum of 6 months of therapy is recommended by most authorities.

Ketoconazole, another oral antifungal agent with a similar mechanism of action to itraconazole, may be used at a dose of 400 mg/d by mouth. Doses of ≤ 800 mg/d may be required for persistent and unresponsive disease. Treatment should be continued for ≥ 6 months.

Both itraconazole and ketoconazole require gastric acid for absorption. There are significant drug-drug interactions with drugs such as terfenadine, rifampin, phenytoin, and carbamazepine. In addition, neither itraconazole nor ketoconazole is excreted in the urine as an active drug. Therefore treatment of genitourinary blastomycosis with these agents may be inadequate.

Fluconazole, another triazole antifungal agent, has been shown to be moderately effective in the treatment of non–life-threatening blastomycosis at a dose of 200–400 mg/d.

Patients with AIDS and immunocompromised patients with ongoing immunosuppression require chronic oral maintenance treatment (eg, itraconazole, 200 mg/d) to prevent recurrence.

Surgery may be indicated for evacuation of large abscesses, diagnostic biopsy, or removal of central nervous system mass lesions, or débridement of devitalized and necrotic bone in patients with osteomyelitis refractory to pharmacotherapy.

Prognosis

The mortality rate for blastomycosis in HIV-infected patients is much higher than the mortality rate from blastomycosis in the general population. In one report, of 24 patients with HIV and blastomycosis, 15 (63%) had disseminated disease, and 13 (54%) died

BOX 71-3

Control of Blastomycosis

Precautions	At-risk individuals residing in endemic areas should avoid activities such as exposure to dust, construction, or excavation
Prophylaxis	AIDS patients with blastomycosis should receive lifelong suppressive treatment with 200 mg of itraconazole[1] daily by mouth after completion of initial therapy

[1]The efficacy and safety of itraconazole preparations have not been established in children. A few pediatric patients 3–16 years old have been treated with oral itraconazole (100 mg/d) for systemic fungal infections with no serious unexpected adverse effects.

as a result of their infection. Previous reports have suggested a mortality rate of ~ 10% in those with disseminated blastomycosis but without concomitant HIV infection.

Prevention & Control

Individuals residing in endemic areas who are at increased risk (eg, immunocompromised or HIV-in-fected individuals) should avoid activities associated with acquiring infection, such as exposure to dust, construction, or excavation. AIDS patients with blastomycosis who have completed initial therapy should receive lifelong suppressive treatment with itraconazole (Box 71–3).

REFERENCES

Baumgardner DJ et al: Epidemiology of blastomycosis in a region of high endemicity in north central Wisconsin. Clin Inf Dis 1992;15:629–35.

Bradsher RW: Blastomycosis. Clin Inf Dis 1992;14(Suppl 1):S82–S90.

Bradsher RW: A clinician's view of blastomycosis. Curr Top Med Mycol 1993;5:181–200.

Brown LR et al: Roentgenologic features of pulmonary blastomycosis. Mayo Clin Proc 1991;66:29–38.

Chapman SW: Blastomyces dermatitidis. In Mandel GL et al: Principles and Practice of Infectious Diseases, 4th ed. Churchill Livingstone, 1995.

Craft PP: A case report of disseminated blastomycosis and the adult respiratory distress syndrome. J Fam Pract 1995;40:597–60.

Johnson P, Sarosi G: Current therapy of major fungal diseases of the lung. Infect Dis Clin North Am 1991; 5: 635–45.

Meyer KC et al: Overwhelming pulmonary blastomycosis associated with the adult respiratory distress syndrome. N Engl J Med 1993;329:1231–36.

Pappas PG et al: Blastomycosis in patients with the acquired immunodeficiency syndrome. Ann Int Med 1992: 116:847–53.

Pappas PG et al: Blastomycosis in immunocompromised patients. Medicine 1993;72:311–25.

Serody JS et al: Blastomycosis in transplant recipients: report of a case and review. Clin Inf Dis 1993;16:54–58.

Wheat LJ: Endemic mycosis in AIDS: a clinical review. Clin Microbiol Rev 1995;8:146–59.

Winer-Muram HT, Rubin SA: Pulmonary blastomycosis. J Thorac Imag 1992;7:23–28.

Witzig RS et al: Blastomycosis and human immune deficiency virus: Three new cases and review. South Med J 1994;87:715–19.

Coccidioides

72

Caroline Milne, MD, & Merle Sande, MD

Essentials of Diagnosis

- Predisposing factors include travel to the dry desert climates found in the southwestern United States and exposure to dust.
- The commonest source of infection is dust inhalation in the southwestern United States.
- The commonest infection is pneumonia.
- Key laboratory findings include growth of the fungus and complement fixing (CF) antigen detection by immunodiffusion.

General Considerations

Coccidioidomycosis was first described as a disease a little more than a century ago in Buenos Aires, Argentina. It was in San Francisco that the organism causing the clinical disease was given its name, *Coccidioides immitis*. Many diseases were later found to be caused by this organism, including San Joaquin Valley Fever.

A. Epidemiology. Coccidioidomycosis is not a new disease. Recently, however, there has been an increase in the number of cases reported in the United States. *C immitis* is endemic to the southwestern United States, found primarily in southern California, southern Nevada, southern New Mexico, and Arizona. Other endemic areas have similar dry desert climates such as Mexico and South and Central America. This disease is no longer limited to residents of these areas. As travel increases, coccidioidomycosis must always be considered when the clinical picture fits. This fact emphasizes the importance of obtaining a good travel history.

Exposure to dust affects the incidence of coccidioidomycosis. Incidence is highest in the summer and fall when the soil is dry and dusty. Earthquakes and dust storms also increase incidence. In the United States an estimated 100,000 infections occur annually.

Infection doesn't necessarily mean clinical manifestation of disease. Infection has been studied among soldiers stationed in the San Joaquin Valley during WWII. The soldiers were skin tested and questioned about illnesses. Of all reported infections, 60% were found to be asymptomatic, another 35% were self-limited, and 5% resulted in disseminated disease.

B. Microbiology and Pathogenesis. *C immitis* is a fungus that lives in the soil. As the fungus matures it forms alternate cells along a hypha, called arthroconidia. This stage of the fungus can become airborne and be inhaled by a human host, which causes infection. A very small number of arthroconidia are needed to cause infection. Once the host is infected, multiple divisions of the inhaled arthroconidia occur in the lung, forming spherules and then thousands of endospores. Each endospore can repeat the development of a spherule. Thus, a cyclic process occurs, and multiplication is rapid. The immunologic response to *C immitis* is primarily cellular. Functioning T lymphocytes are essential to control infection.

Clinical Findings

A. Signs and Symptoms. In symptomatic disease, first manifestations occur 1–3 weeks after initial exposure. The symptoms are clinically nonspecific and include cough with scant sputum production, fever, headache, and pleuritic chest pain in the majority of cases (Table 72–1).

A skin rash is common with primary infection. Both erythema nodosum and erythema multiforme are referred to as "specific erythemas" of coccidioidomycosis. These erythemas are associated with an intense immunologic response and with a good prognosis. People who exhibit these erythemas will likely not progress to disseminated disease.

The most common clinical manifestation of disease is pneumonia (Box 72–1). Most are self-resolved and likely go undiagnosed. Pulmonary complications occur infrequently and include asymptomatic nodules or thin-walled cavities, slow resolving pneumonia, or chronic lung infection.

Nodules occur in 5–7% of patients and are usually solitary and asymptomatic. The morbidity associated

Table 72–1. Clinical features of primary coccidioidal infection.[1]

Symptom	Frequency (%)
Cough	89
Fever	82
Chest pain	70
Headache	74
Shortness of breath	63
Malaise	59
Myalgias	52
Rash	52

[1]Source: Werner 1972.

BOX 72-1

Coccidioidal Infection

	Children	Adults
More Common	• Mild upper respiratory infection • Subacute, self-limited pneumonia	• Mild upper respiratory infection • Self-limited pneumonia
Less Common	• Complicated pulmonary infection • Extrapulmonary disease	• Complicated pulmonary infection • Extrapulmonary disease

with these lesions occurs during surgical resection of the nodules to exclude cancer. More recently percutaneous fine-needle biopsy has been used for diagnosis.

Cavities occur in younger patients, are most frequently asymptomatic, and are usually self-resolved, disappearing within 2 years of appearance. Complications, however, can occur and are usually associated with air fluid levels or infiltrates surrounding the cavity. Infection rarely spreads to other areas of the lung. If rupture of the cavity occurs, surgical repair is required.

Disseminated disease is unusual. Fewer than 5% of infected persons experience disseminated disease. Extrapulmonary disease includes granulomatous skin lesions or subcutaneous abscess, septic arthritis, osteomyelitis, and meningitis. Risk factors for extrapulmonary disease have been found to be male sex, pregnant women, immunosuppression, nonwhites (especially Filipinos and blacks), and possibly age (the very old or young).

Meningitis occurs in one-third to one-half of all patients with coccidioidal dissemination. The clinical symptoms are not specific to *C immitis* infection and include headache, vomiting, nuchal rigidity, confusion, and diplopia. Lumbar puncture is essential to diagnosis. The cerebrospinal fluid reveals a pleocytosis with a predominance of mononuclear cells. Most have an eosinophilia as well. Usually the glucose is low, and the protein elevated. The cerebrospinal fluid should be sent both for culture and serologic tests (complement-fixing antigen).

Coccidioidal meningitis should be suspected in patients with the clinical syndrome and a recent coccidioidal infection. Meningitis usually occurs within 6 months of initial infection; however, meningitis can occur late if immunosuppressed. Early diagnosis is important, and, if left untreated, coccidioidal meningitis is fatal. Even with diagnosis, treatment is difficult.

B. Laboratory Findings. Coccidioidal infections should be considered in patients with a pulmonary syndrome and who live in or have a history of travel to endemic areas. As stated earlier, most of these infections are self-limited, and physicians living outside endemic areas will likely see only complicated cases.

The vast majority of cases are asymptomatic and will be identified by a positive skin test only. Positive skin tests are neither definitive nor helpful in establishing the diagnosis of coccidioidomycosis, because of the high number of asymptomatic infections. Definitive diagnosis is established via culture of the organism or antibody or antigen detection. Antigen detection kits are not currently commercially available.

C immitis readily grows in the laboratory and is detectable as early as 2–5 days after inoculation. The fungal growth is further evaluated via a species-specific DNA probe. Results are available the day growth is detected. It is important to notify the laboratory of your suspicions, because laboratory identification may be dangerous to the lab technician. Arthrospores readily become airborne and may be inhaled.

There are two coccidioidal antigens that are targeted for antibody detection, the tube precipitin reading (TP) antigen and the CF antigen. Antibody detection kits are not available, and instead laboratories use immunodiffusion tests. Both tests are reported qualitatively; if immunodiffusion CF is positive, a follow-up quantitative test is necessary. The concentration of CF antibodies is proportional to the extent of the disease. Ordering physicians must be aware of false-negative results in detecting anticoccidioidal

BOX 72-2

Treatment of Coccidioidal Infection in Adults

Site	Primary	Alternative
Pulmonary and Extrapulmonary	Fluconazole, 400–800 mg orally daily (duration 12–18 months)	Itraconazole 200 mg orally twice a day (duration 12–18 months) **OR** Amphotericin B 0.6–1.0 mg/kg/d IV × 7 d then 0.8 mg/kg/day total dose 2.5 gms or more)
Meningitis	Fluconazole 400–600 mg orally daily indefinitely.	Amphotericin B IV as above and intrathecal 0.1–0.3 md daily

BOX 72–3

Indications for Treatment of Coccidioidal Infection

Site/Indications	Treatment
Fever lasting longer than 1 month Extensive or progressive pulmonary disease Immunosuppressed patients HIV-infected patients Pregnant patients	Amphotericin B is used as initial drug of choice because of rapid improvement in symptoms, followed by oral azoles. Amphotericin B: 0.6–1.0 mg/kg/day for 7 days, then 0.8 mg/kg/ every other day. Total dose 2.5 g. Oral azoles: Itraconazole 200 mg twice a day **OR** fluconazole 400 mg/day for 3–12 months.
Disseminated disease	Amphotericin B, 0.5–0.7 mg/kg/day. Total dose, usually 15–45 mg/kg. Total dose not clearly defined.

antibodies; these results are most prevalent in early primary infection or in immunosuppressed patients.

Differential Diagnosis

Coccidioidal infections are suspected in patients with pulmonary symptoms and the appropriate travel or residence in an endemic area. Bacterial or other fungal pneumonias should be included in the differential.

Complications

Most coccidioidal infections are self-resolved. Pulmonary complications can occur and include asymptomatic nodules, slowly resolving pneumonia, or chronic lung infection. The most serious complication includes disseminated disease and can affect any organ system.

Treatment

In most cases the decision to treat is the real question. Recall that even for patients who develop symptoms of initial infection, the disease is usually self-limited. In patients in whom treatment is indicated, coccidioidomycosis is very difficult to cure. Treatment for initial infection is indicated only for patients with deficiencies in T-cell immunity. A physician may decide to treat a severe pulmonary infection, but there is no expert consensus. Treatment is indicated for chronic pulmonary infection and extrapulmonary dissemination. Accepted-standard-of-care therapies include amphotericin B and oral azole antifungal agents (Boxes 72–2 and 72–3). Fluconazole and itraconazole have been shown to have similar success rates. Length of treatment is controversial, because relapse is common. Treatment may be lifelong. Most physicians will treat pulmonary and disseminated disease for 12–18 months. It has been found that negative serial coccidioidin skin tests and very high CF antibody titers are independently associated with increased risk of relapse. Rising CF titers after completion of therapy are an indication of relapse and warrant retreatment. Patients with meningitis are likely never cured and require indefinite treatment. Only fluconazole and amphotericin B have been shown to be effective therapies. If amphotericin B is used, both parenteral and intrathecal therapy is indicated.

Prevention

There is no vaccine available against *C immitis* infection. General prevention includes avoiding exposure to the fungus in its natural setting and decreasing the amount of airborne dust. Environmental measures including paving dirt roads and planting grass may be implemented (see Kirkland and Fierer, 1996).

REFERENCES

Deresinski SC: History of coccidioidomycosis: "dust to dust." In Stevens DA, ed: *Coccidioidomycosis.* Plenum, 1980.

Diaz M A: Pan-American 5 year study of fluconazole therapy for deep mycoses in the immunocompetent host. Pan-American Study Group. Clin Infect Dis 1992;14(Suppl 1):S68.

Drutz DJ: Coccidioidomycosis, Part II. Am Rev Resp Dis 1978;117:727.

Feigin R, Cherry J (editors): *Textbook of Pediatric Infectious Diseases,* 4th ed. Saunders, 1998.

Galgiani JN: Coccidioidomycosis. West J Med 1993; 159:153.

Kirkland TN, Fierer J: Coccidioidomycosis: a reemerging infectious disease. Emerg Infect Dis 1996;2(3):192.

Oldfield EC: Prediction of relapse after treatment of coccidioidomycosis. Clin Infect Dis 1997;25:1205.

Stevens DA: Coccidioidomycosis. N Engl J Med 1995; 332(16):1077.

Stevens DA: Editorial response: adequacy of therapy for coccidioidomycosis. Clin Infect Dis 1997;25:1211.

Werner SB: An epidemic of coccidioidomycosis among archeology students in Northern California. N Engl J Med 1972;286:507.

73 *Candida* species

Christopher R. Fox, MD & Merle A. Sande, MD

Essentials of Diagnosis

- Characteristic appearance of yeast and hyphae on KOH preparations.
- Formation of germ tubes in serum is presumptive diagnosis for *Candida albicans.*
- Cultures must be interpreted with caution because positive culture may represent colonization rather than infection.
- Serology not useful.

General Considerations

A. Epidemiology. *Candida* organisms are commensal with humans and, in the absence of alterations in host defense mechanisms, usually do not cause disease. *Candida* exists as normal flora within the oral cavity, throughout the gastrointestinal (GI) tract, in expectorated sputum, in the vagina, and in the bladder of patients with indwelling catheters. There are >150 species within the genus *Candida,* although the majority are not known to cause disease in humans. *C albicans, C krusei, C glabrata, C tropicalis, C pseudotropicalis, C guilliermondii, C parapsilosis, C lusitaniae,* and *C rugosa* are known human pathogens.

Candida species cause a wide spectrum of clinical diseases that range from mild, superficial infection of the skin and mucous membranes to life-threatening, invasive, multisystem disease. Infection with *Candida* requires an alteration in the normal milieu that allows the fungus to proliferate and evade host responses.

Under correct conditions, *Candida* is able to infect any of the body's mucosal surfaces, as well as the skin. Three-quarters of women report vaginal candidiasis within their lifetime, and the incidence appears to have increased over the last 20 years. Risk factors include recent antibiotic use, pregnancy, oral contraceptive use, diabetes, and human immunodeficiency virus (HIV) infection.

Oral thrush is another frequent manifestation of mucosal candidiasis with similar risk factors to vaginal candidiasis. These risks include systemic disease such as HIV infection or diabetes, inhaled or oral corticosteroid use, and neutropenia induced by chemotherapy.

In addition to the local forms of disease described above, *Candida* species may cause invasive disease with systemic manifestations and multiple infected organs. Although once limited to the oncology ward and bone marrow transplant unit, candidemia is now more frequent in all areas of the hospital, with *Candida* the fourth most common organism reported from hospital blood cultures. Specific risk factors for invasive disease include previous isolation of *Candida* from another site, the use of antimicrobial agents, prolonged neutropenia, indwelling central catheters, and the use of parenteral nutrition.

Although the majority of *Candida* infections are caused by *C albicans,* several non-*albicans* species are emerging as important pathogens and deserve mention. *C krusei* appears to be less virulent than *C albicans* and rarely causes disease in the normal host. However, in those with depressed immune function, *C krusei* is able to cause significant infection. Candidemia, ocular infection, endocarditis, and renal disease all occur with some frequency. *C krusei* infection has important therapeutic implications as the organism is generally resistant to fluconazole. *C glabrata,* another *Candida* species with increasing recovery rates, usually has intermediate resistance to fluconazole.

B. Microbiology. *Candida* is a fungus that exists primarily in the yeast state, although it may be found in tissue in both yeast and mold forms. The yeast cells are 4–6 μm in diameter and reproduce primarily by budding but also by sexual reproduction. In culture, *Candida* forms smooth white colonies, and a presumptive diagnosis of *C albicans* can be made by observing the formation of germ tubes within 90 min of placing the organism in serum. *Candida* will grow on agar plates and in routine blood culture bottles, although the lysis-centrifugation and the BACTEC systems have increased recovery of the organism.

C. Pathogenesis. As previously mentioned, *Candida* is part of the normal flora in many areas of the body and, without alteration in host defense, does not cause disease. Factors particularly important to preventing infection are normal bacterial flora, intact skin and mucous membranes within the GI tract, and normal cell-mediated immunity. Alterations of any of the above mechanisms predispose to infection. This is seen clinically as the use of antibiotics (which alter the normal bacterial flora), maceration of the skin, GI surgery, HIV infection, and chemotherapy-induced neutropenia, all of which increase rates of *Candida* infection.

Candida produces proteins expressed within the cell wall that promote binding and adherence to epithelial cells, endothelium, platelet and fibrin clots, and plastics. These proteins likely help the organism attach to and invade damaged mucosa and may play a role in *Candida* infection in hosts with indwelling bladder and central venous catheters. *Candida* species also produce proteases and phospholipases, which may aid the organism in evading host defenses and invading mucosal surfaces.

CLINICAL SYNDROMES

CANDIDA DERMATITIS

Clinical Findings

A. Signs and Symptoms. Skin infections with *Candida* are common and may manifest in a variety of forms. Intertrigo occurs in warm, moist areas of skin, such as under the breast, in the groin, and in the axilla. Initially pustular or vesicular, lesions eventually become confluent to form an erythematous, macerated area of skin with a scalloped border and satellite lesions (Box 73–1). Erosio interdigitalis blastomycetica is similar to intertrigo but involves the areas between the fingers and toes. Paronychia is infection of the nail bed, seen more commonly in diabetics and people who frequently immerse their hands in water. *Candida* spp. may cause onychomycosis, particularly in HIV-infected patients. *Candida* spp. cause a rash in neonates in the region of diaper contact. Other common skin manifestations include folliculitis, balanitis, perianal candidiasis, and a generalized cutaneous eruption with widespread lesions resembling intertrigo that spread to involve the abdomen, chest, back, and extremities.

Chronic mucocutaneous candidiasis (CMC) is an abnormality of cell-mediated immunity that presents with recurrent infections of the skin and mucus membranes that may progress to disfiguring lesions (*Candida* granulomas) despite antifungal therapy. Symptoms usually begin in the first several years of life. CMC is associated with autoimmune endocrine failure, particularly hypoparathyroidism and adrenal insufficiency (polyglandular autoimmune syndrome type I), and endocrine disease often presents years to decades after the onset of CMC.

Cutaneous lesions may be superficial evidence of disseminated candidiasis and candidemia. Lesions are typically red or pink nodules 5–10 mm in diameter and may be single or widespread. Lesions resembling ecthyma gangrenosum or purpura fulminans have also been described.

B. Laboratory Findings. *Candida* organisms, seen as budding yeast and hyphae, may be present on wet mount or KOH preparations of skin scrapings. Biopsy specimens may reveal characteristic fungal elements on histology.

C. Differential Diagnosis. *Candida* infection of the skin and nails may be confused with other infections, both fungal and nonfungal, as well as noninfectious conditions such as contact or allergic dermatitis.

D. Complications. *Candida* infection of the skin and nails may cause discomfort and disturb cosmetic appearance of the skin but does not usually cause long-term sequelae. CMC may progress to cause large disfiguring lesions.

Diagnosis

Diagnosis of *Candida* infection involving the skin or nails is generally made by recognition of the clinical pattern followed by demonstration of fungal elements on a KOH preparation of skin scrapings. *Candida* infection may also be diagnosed by microscopic examination of biopsy specimens. Culture of the skin should be interpreted with caution, as the presence of *Candida* spp. may represent colonization rather than infection.

Treatment

Treatment of *Candida* skin infections is generally straightforward. Intertrigo is managed by decreasing moisture in infected areas and by application of topical antifungal therapy. Nystatin cream, topical azoles (miconazole, clotrimazole), and amphotericin B cream are all effective when applied 2–3 times daily. Paronychia may be treated by keeping the area dry and with topical antifungal therapy. Onychomycosis requires several months of treatment with oral azoles, such as itraconazole, or terbenifine. Relapses may occur. Griseofulvin is not active against *Candida*.

CMC is treated with oral ketoconazole or fluconazole. Transfer factor, an immunomodulating factor composed of a cell-free leukocyte extract, was used in the past but has fallen out of favor because of lack of efficacy. Months to years of treatment are generally required.

ORAL CANDIDIASIS

Clinical Findings

A. Signs and Symptoms. *Candida* infections of the oral cavity are relatively common and may present in several forms. Any of the forms may be asymptomatic or may cause soreness and burning. The most common, acute pseudomembranous candidiasis, or oral thrush, presents with multiple white patches on the tongue, palate, and other areas of oral mucosa. These lesions may be easily removed by scraping with a tongue blade to reveal an erythematous, irritated mucosa (Box 73–1).

Dermatologic and Mucosal Candidiasis

	Dermatitis	Oral	Esophageal	GI (Nonesophageal)	Vulvovaginal
More Common	• Erythematous, macerated skin with scalloped border and satellite lesions • Typically in warm, moist areas (groin, under breasts) • Paronychia • Onychomycosis	• Multiple white patches on tongue, palate, and pharnx that are easily removed with tongue blade, leaving erythematous mucosa	• Asymptomatic • Dysphagia • Odynophagia • Epigastric pain • Nausea and vomiting • Hematemesis • Concurrent oral thrush	• Infection in benign ulcers • Ulceration and pseudomembrane formation within small and large intestine	• Vulvar pruritus • Vaginal discharge (may range from thin and white to thick and curdlike) • Odorless or mild odor • Vulvar burning • Dyspareunia • Exam revealing white plaques on erythematous mucosa
Less Common	• Generalized cutaneous eruption • Single or multiple 5–10-mm papules[1] • *Candida* granulomas[2]	• Erythematous mucosa on palate and tongue without white plaques • Erythema and edema of mucosa of denture wearers • Adherent white plaques (not removable with tongue blade) on erythematous base	• Stricture • Perforation	• Diffuse involvement of stomach similar to thrush • Deep ulceration • Hemorrhage • Perforation	

[1]Part of disseminated candidiasis
[2]Typically seen as part of chronic mucocutaneous candidiasis

In addition to oral thrush, oral *Candida* infection occurs in several distinct forms. Acute atrophic candidiasis causes erythematous mucosa found typically on the palate and tongue, chronic atrophic candidiasis results in erythema and edema of the mucosa of denture wearers who do not practice adequate hygiene, and angular cheilitis causes erythema and fissuring of the corners of the mouth. Finally, *Candida* leukoplakia is described as adherent white nodules on an erythematous base and often does not respond to topical therapy. This condition also carries an increased risk of malignant transformation.

B. Laboratory Findings. Budding yeast and hyphae may be seen on a KOH preparation or on preparations made with para-aminosalicyclic acid (PAS) stain, Giemsa stain, or Gram stain. Culture of oral scrapings may grow *Candida* species, although this is not a specific test.

C. Differential Diagnosis. Oral candidiasis must be differentiated from bacterial and viral infection as well as malignancy.

D. Complications. While uncomfortable for those affected, it is unclear if oral candidiasis predisposes to *Candida* infection at other sites. There are reports that *Candida* esophagitis may follow oral thrush, although esophagitis was not excluded at the initial presentation in these reports. In those with oral infection and infection at a second site, it is likely that immune system deficits allow for multiple infections rather than spreading from the oral cavity.

Diagnosis

The diagnosis of oral *Candida* infection may be suspected when the characteristic appearance of the mucosa is present and, in the case of oral thrush, when scraping of the mucosa removes the white plaque and leaves an inflamed mucosa. Demonstration of dimorphic fungi on KOH-, Giemsa-, Gram-, or PAS-stained oral scrapings strongly supports the diagnosis. Culture of *Candida* species from oral scrapings is not generally required, and as *Candida* may be part of the normal flora of the oral cavity, positive cultures may not represent true infection.

Treatment

Generally, oral *Candida* infection should initially be treated with topical agents (Box 73–3). Nystatin suspension or clotrimazole troches are generally effective therapy. If infection occurs in a denture wearer, the dentures must be removed. Once the infection is cured, proper dental hygiene is important to prevent recurrence. Topical antifungal creams will treat angular cheilitis.

If topical therapy fails, or in those with severe infection, systemic therapy may be used. In patients with advanced HIV infection, itraconazole doses may require adjustment because of achlorhydria and impaired absorption. Treatment failure should prompt a search for other causes, such as bacterial infection or malignancy.

In those infected with HIV or with other immune deficits, frequent recurrences are common, and maintenance therapy may be necessary. Daily treatment with topical antifungal agents or fluconazole, 50–100 mg daily, every other day, or once weekly may prevent recurrence. Maintenance therapy with fluconazole should be avoided if possible because of concerns for the emergence of resistant fungal strains.

BOX 73–2

Deep-Tissue *Candida* Infection

	Urinary Tract	Candidemia and Disseminated Candidiasis	Endocarditis
More Common	• Asymptomatic • Patient with risk factors[1]	• Patient with risk factors[2] • Presentation ranges from asymptomatic to septic shock • Positive blood cultures • Microabscesses involving multiple organs	• Patient with risk factors[3] • Fever, malaise, weight loss • Embolic phenomena
Less Common	• Dysuria, frequency, urgency • Pyuria • Involvement of ureters or renal parenchyma	• Negative blood cultures (does not exclude disseminated disease)	• Valve perforation • Congestive heart failure (CHF) • Myocarditis

[1]Indwelling bladder catheter, diabetes mellitus, systemic antibiotic use.
[2]Malignancy, neutropenia, organ transplantation, GI surgery, burns, intravascular catheters, broadspectrum antibiotics.
[3]Valvular surgery, IV drug use, bacterial endocarditis, IV catheters, chemotherapy.

BOX 73-3

Treatment of Oral Candidiasis

Topical	• Nystatin suspension (100,000 U/mL), 4–6 mL four times per day × 7–10 d OR • Clotrimazole troches (10 mg), 4–5 times/d × 7–10 d • Dentures must be removed and properly cleaned daily
Systemic	• Fluconazole, 100 mg PO every day × 10–14 d OR • Itraconazole, 200 mg PO every day × 10–14 d[1]

[1]Dose of itraconazole may need to be increased in patients with HIV infection secondary to achlorhydria and decreased absorption.

ESOPHAGEAL CANDIDIASIS

Clinical Findings

A. Signs and Symptoms. *Candida* infection of the esophagus can present with a range of clinical findings (Box 73–1). Between 20 and 50% of patients may be asymptomatic. Others will note dysphagia, odynophagia, epigastric pain, nausea and vomiting, or hematemesis. Fever may be present. Frequently, patients will have concurrent symptoms of oral thrush. Physical exam of patients with esophagitis yields few clues to its diagnosis. Oral thrush is seen in the majority.

B. Imaging. Barium studies and endoscopy are both useful for diagnosis of *Candida* esophagitis. The findings found with these methods are described in the diagnosis section.

C. Differential Diagnosis. *Candida* esophagitis may be confused with other causes of esophagitis, including bacterial, viral, and reflux esophagitis. Host factors (such as the status of the immune system), clinical findings, and endoscopic appearance of the esophagus are helpful in making this distinction, although frequently more than one cause of esophagitis are present concurrently.

D. Complications. Complications of esophagitis relate to deep invasion and inflammation of the mucosa. Although uncommon, perforation and strictures do occur. In some cases, long and complex strictures are not amenable to endoscopic dilatation and require surgical intervention. Dissemination of the fungus from the lower esophagus and stomach may occur, especially in neutropenic patients.

Diagnosis

Radiographic techniques using barium contrast (barium swallow) and endoscopy are useful for diagnosis of *Candida* esophagitis. The barium swallow has a characteristic appearance, with a shaggy-appearing mucosa and sometimes nodules and cobble stoning. This technique does not allow firm diagnosis, which requires histology or culture.

Endoscopy is the preferred method of diagnosis, as it allows direct visualization of the mucosa and biopsy of affected areas. The mucosa typically has adherent white plaques that may be removed with the endoscope to reveal an erythematous mucosa. Brushings of the mucosa may be prepared as for oral disease. Histologic specimens reveal fungal elements, which are more apparent on PAS-stained and silver-stained material than with hematoxylin-eosin staining.

Treatment

A subset of patients may be treated empirically. In those with HIV infection, oral thrush, and mild to moderate symptoms of esophagitis, treatment with topical agents or an azole may be warranted. If no oral thrush is present, or if treatment fails, endoscopy should be performed to exclude other causes of disease.

As with oral thrush, topical agents may be successful in treating esophagitis (Box 73–4). If patients fail topical treatment, have severe disease, or are considered to be at high risk for disseminated disease, systemic therapy should be used. Therapy for 10 days is generally adequate.

CANDIDA VULVOVAGINITIS

Clinical Findings

A. Signs and Symptoms. Risk factors for *Candida* infection of the vagina include pregnancy, oral contraceptive use, diabetes mellitus, HIV infection, and antimicrobial therapy, although the majority of infections occur in the absence of these risks. Typical complaints are vulvar pruritus and vaginal discharge (Box 73–1), although a wide range of symptoms exists. Pruritus, the most common complaint, is often in-

---

BOX 73-4

Treatment of *Candida* Esophagitis

Topical	• Nystatin suspension (100,000 units/mL) 10–30 mL 4–5 times daily • Clotrimazole troches (10 mg) 5 times daily
Systemic	• Fluconazole 50–200 mg PO every day × 10 days • Itraconazole[1] 50–200 mg PO every day × 10 days • Amphotericin B 0.3–0.6 mg/kg/day IV × 10 days

[1]Patients with HIV or an acid suppresive therapy may have poor absorption due to high gastric pH.

tense, and the discharge, classically described as cottage cheese–like, may range from a thin, white, scant discharge to homogeneously thick. Odor, if present, is mild. Other symptoms may include vulvar burning, external dysuria, vaginal irritation and soreness, and dyspareunia. Symptoms may peak the week prior to menses and wane with the onset of menstrual flow.

Examination may reveal discrete papular or pustular lesions of the vulva, with erythema and swelling of the vulva and labia. The discharge is present within the vaginal vault, and the vaginal mucosa is inflamed and may have adherent white plaques similar to oral thrush. The cervix appears normal.

B. Laboratory Findings. The vaginal pH is normal (<4.5). Examination of a saline or wet mount preparation of the vaginal discharge may show fungal elements and should not reveal abundant white cells. A KOH preparation is more sensitive in detecting the fungus, as other cellular debris is lysed. Both budding yeast and hyphae are typically present. Culture of the vagina will usually isolate *Candida*, although this must be interpreted cautiously, as *Candida* can be part of the vaginal flora without causing disease.

C. Differential Diagnosis. The signs and symptoms of *Candida* vulvovaginitis are relatively nonspecific, and therefore the presentation may be confused with bacterial vaginosis, trichomoniasis, and other sexually transmitted diseases. Two or more of these conditions may coexist.

D. Complications. Some women may develop severe, recurrent infections despite removal of identified risk factors and antifungal therapy. Infection of the vagina is not associated with risk of deep tissue or bloodstream invasion.

Diagnosis

The diagnosis of vulvovaginitis is typically made by history, physical examination, and light microscopy. In women with appropriate symptoms and fungal elements on wet mount or KOH preparation, therapy is indicated without further testing. As up to 50% of symptomatic women with culture-proven infection have negative microscopy, vaginal culture is indicated in those patients with symptoms and no microscopic findings. A vaginal pH >4.5 or a large number of white cells on wet mount should prompt a search for a different or possibly coexistent process.

Treatment

Numerous agents are available for treatment of *Candida* vulvovaginitis in both topical and oral preparations (Box 73–5). Among topical agents, cure rates range from 75 to 90%, with the azole preparations (clotrimazole, miconazole, terconazole) having slightly better efficacy than nystatin. The formulation (cream versus suppository versus vaginal tablet) does not alter the success rate; therefore the choice of formulation is a matter of patient preference. Currently there is a trend toward higher doses of topical agents with shorter durations of therapy, with success re-

BOX 73–5	
Treatment of *Candida* Vulvovaginitis[1]	
Topical	• Butoconazole, 2% cream, 5 g every day × 3 d
	• Clotrimazole, 1% cream, 5 g every day × 7–14 d
	• Clotrimazole, vaginal tablet, 100 mg every day × 7 d
	• Clotrimazole, vaginal tablet, 200 mg every day × 3 d
	• Clotrimazole, vaginal tablet, 500 mg every day × 1 d
	• Econazole, vaginal tablet, 150 mg every day × 3 d
	• Fenticonazole, 2% cream, 5 g every day × 7 d
	• Miconazole, 2% cream, 5 g every day × 7 d
	• Miconazole, vaginal suppository, 100 mg every day × 7 d
	• Miconazole, vaginal suppository, 200 mg every day × 3 d
	• Miconazole, vaginal suppository, 1200 mg every day × 1 d
	• Nystatin suppository, 100,000 U every day × 14 d
	• Terconazole, 0.4% cream, 5 g every day × 7 d
	• Terconazole, 0.8% cream, 5 g every day × 3 d
	• Terconazole, vaginal suppository, 80 mg every day × 3 d
	• Tioconazole, 2% cream, 5 g every day × 3 d
	• Tioconazole, 6.5% cream, 5 g every day × 1 d
Systemic	• Fluconazole, 150 mg PO once
	• Itraconazole, 400 mg PO once

[1]Women with recurrent infection and no reversible risk factors may require suppressive therapy.

ported with even high-dose, one-time therapy. Anecdotal failure rates are fairly high with one-dose therapy; thus this is best reserved for women with infrequent infections and mild or moderate symptoms.

Oral azole agents are quite effective for vaginal infection and are more convenient than topical therapy but are more expensive. Fluconazole and itraconazole single-dose therapy are at least as effective as topical therapy.

Cure of *Candida* vulvovaginitis during pregnancy can be difficult, with relapses frequently occurring. If therapy is extended to 1–2 weeks, topical antifungal therapy is effective. Oral azoles should be avoided during pregnancy.

In women with frequent recurrent infections, therapy is often disappointing, with symptoms recurring within weeks of withdrawal of antifungal agents. In these women, predisposing factors such as diabetes or HIV infection should be considered. HIV testing is appropriate in women with risk factors for HIV infection. If fasting blood glucose values are normal, further testing for diabetes is not required. Oral contraceptives should be discontinued if possible, although continuation of low-dose estrogen preparations, as long as long-term antifungal therapy is used, may be considered. Vaginal douching and treatment of the sexual partner are not recommended. Frequently, no risk factors are identified, and prophylactic therapy is required. The best-studied regimen with proven efficacy for prophylaxis is ketoconazole, 100 mg daily. Toxicity, such as hepatitis, is infrequent but may occur. Other regimens with anecdotal support include fluconazole, 100–200 mg once weekly, and clotrimazole vaginal tablets, 500 mg once weekly.

CANDIDURIA, *CANDIDA* CYSTITIS & URINARY TRACT CANDIDIASIS

The presence of *Candida* spp. in the urine is common and does not necessarily represent infection. Candiduria is commonly associated with antibiotic use, indwelling urinary catheters, and diabetes mellitus and frequently resolves if predisposing factors can be corrected. Patients are generally asymptomatic, although some will have symptoms similar to bacterial cystitis, with dysuria, frequency, and urgency (Box 73–2). Urinalysis shows fungal elements and may reveal pyuria. At cystoscopy, the mucosa of the bladder typically has an inflamed appearance with adherent white plaques that may be removed with the scope.

Candida spp. may also cause urethritis, typically in male sexual partners of women with vaginal *Candida* infection, as well as higher urinary tract infection. The upper urinary tract and renal parenchyma may be infected from ascending infection or, more commonly, from hematogenous spread as part of a syndrome of disseminated candidiasis. With ascending infection, perinephric abscesses, papillary necrosis, fungus balls, and calyceal involvement have all been described. Risk factors are generally present and include diabetes mellitus, urinary tract obstruction, and renal stones. With hematogenous spread, the renal parenchyma becomes studded with multiple microabscesses.

Diagnosis

Candiduria is usually discovered when a urine culture reveals the presence of *Candida* spp. The presence of pyuria generally indicates true infection if other etiologies, such as bacterial infection, have been excluded. Infection may also be diagnosed by demonstrating the presence of a typical appearing fungus in biopsy specimens obtained during cystoscopy.

Of particular importance for treatment is whether candiduria represents colonization or true infection, and whether the upper urinary tract is involved, a distinction that can be troublesome. Those with risk factors for ascending infection (diabetes, stones) and those at risk for disseminated disease are more likely to have upper urinary tract infection. Computerized tomographic scans or ultrasound may reveal microabscesses or fungus balls.

Treatment

When treating *Candida* infection of the urinary tract, careful consideration must be given to whether candiduria represents colonization or true infection, and whether the upper urinary tract is involved. Asymptomatic candiduria usually does not require antifungal treatment, but indwelling catheters should be removed as soon as possible. (Treatment is summarized in Box 73–6.) In the presence of pyuria, diabetes mellitus, or renal transplantation, treatment is indicated. Oral fluconazole is recommended as the initial agent. Bladder irrigation with amphotericin B is also effective. Patients with candiduria should be treated prior to instrumentation of the urinary tract.

In patients with evidence of systemic toxicity, *Candida* infection at other sites, risk factors for ascending infection (structural or metabolic abnormality of the urinary tract such as stones or diabetes), or risk factors for disseminated candidiasis (burns, neutropenia, or GI surgery), consideration must be given to the possibility of upper urinary tract infection or disseminated candidiasis. Upper urinary tract involvement usually will respond to oral fluconazole, although intravenous amphotericin B is required for infections resistant to fluconazole or unresponsive to initial fluconazole treatment. Fungus balls and large perinephric abscesses may require surgical intervention. Treatment of disseminated candidiasis is discussed next.

CANDIDEMIA & DISSEMINATED CANDIDIASIS

Candidemia may present in a variety of fashions, ranging from asymptomatic to fulminant sepsis. The candidemic patient generally has risk factors for infection, such as malignancy, chemotherapy-induced neutropenia, organ transplantation, GI surgery, burns, indwelling catheters, or exposure to broad-spectrum antibiotics.

Disseminated candidiasis must be assumed to be present in those with positive blood cultures, although negative cultures do not preclude the possibil-

BOX 73-6

Treatment of Urinary Tract Candidiasis

Asymptomatic Candiduria	• Remove prosthetic material (e.g., urinary catheters) • No antibiotic therapy required unless patient is diabetic, nuetropenic, transplant recipient, has anatomic abnormality of GU tract, or is undergoing GU procedure • Fluconazole 200 mg PO on first day, then 100 mg PO every day × 4 days • Amphotericin bladder irrigation[1]
Upper Urinary Tract Infection	• Fluconazole 400–800 mg PO/IV every day[2] • Amphotericin B 0.8–1.0 mg/kg/day IV[2] • Remove bladder catheters if possible • Fungus balls or large perinephric abscesses may require surgery • Rule out disseminated Candidiasis

[1]Amphotericin 50 mg in 1 liter sterile water infused at 40 mL/hour through continuous infusion/drainage system.
[2]Treatment continued until clinical improvement, definite resolution of parenchymal involvement, and for 14 days after any positive blood cultures.

ity of disseminated disease. Dissemination usually manifests with many microabscesses involving multiple organs, especially the liver, spleen, and eye, but almost any organ may be involved (Box 73–2).

Diagnosis

Candidemia is diagnosed by recovering *Candida* species in blood culture. Candidemia may be isolated or may occur in the setting of disseminated candidiasis. The possibility of disseminated candidiasis should be considered in any patient with deep *Candida* infection, multiple sites of infection, or positive blood cultures. Disseminated candidiasis is diagnosed by tissue culture of biopsy material or demonstration of *Candida* in histologic specimens. At present, serology is available but has false-negative and false-positive rates too high to be of use clinically.

Treatment

The treatment of candidemia is the subject of much debate and controversy. Because isolation of *Candida* from the blood carries a high morbidity and because there is currently no method to predict which patients will not require treatment, there is agreement that all patients with candidemia should be treated. The standard treatment in the past has been amphotericin B, with or without 5-FC. Currently, fluconazole appears to be a reasonable alternative, although there are limited data comparing mortality of fluconazole-treated patients versus those treated with amphotericin. One randomized study of candidemic patients demonstrated fluconazole to be equally efficacious but associated with less toxicity when compared with amphotericin.

Fluconazole may be used as initial treatment of candidemia in a stable patient (Box 73–7). If patients had been treated with fluconazole for 2 days or greater at the time of candidemia, deteriorate on fluconazole therapy, or are unstable (hypotension, need

BOX 73-7

Treatment of Candidemia and Disseminated Candidiasis[1]

	Adults	Children
First Choice	• Fluconazole, 400–800 mg PO/IV every day[2] • Remove intravascular catheters if possible • Monitor for evidence of end-organ infection	• Fluconazole, 6 mg/kg twice per day • Remove intravascular catheters if possible • Monitor for evidence of end-organ infection
Alternative[3]	• Amphotericin B, 0.8–1.0 mg/kg/d[4] IV with or without 5-FC, 100 mg/kg/d IV	• Amphotericin B, 0.8–1.0 mg/kg/d IV with or without 5-FC (5-FC adjusted to achieve peak level of 40–60 µg/mL)

[1]Treatment is continued until clinical improvement, definite resolution of parenchymal involvement, and for 14 days after the last positive blood culture.
[2]Fluconazole, 400 mg daily, is preferred as initial dosage in stable patients.
[3]Preferred in patient on fluconazole for > 2 days at time of positive blood culture, worsening on fluconazole therapy, unstable (eg, hypotension, mechanical ventilation, etc.), or infection with *C. krusei*.
[4]Amphotericin, 0.5–0.7 mg/kg/d IV, may be used as initial dose in stable patient.

for mechanical ventilation, multiple comorbid factors, etc.) at the time their candidemia is diagnosed, then treatment with amphotericin is warranted. Smaller doses may be used if amphotericin if chosen as the initial regimen for stable patients. Because of the potential bone marrow toxicity of 5-FC, particularly when combined with amphotericin, the dose of 5-FC is generally reduced when part of the treatment regimen. Treatment is generally continued until clinical improvement is seen and for 2 weeks after the last positive blood culture.

For all patients with candidemia, the possibility of disseminated infection must be considered. If infection with *C krusei* is suspected or documented, fluconazole should not be used as initial therapy because this species has a high level of resistance to fluconazole. *C glabrata* has an intermediate level of resistance, and fluconazole therapy may be used with caution. Clinical deterioration should prompt an early change of therapy to amphotericin. Treatment for disseminated disease should continue until there is definite resolution of parenchymal involvement and for 2 weeks after the last positive blood culture.

Intravenous catheters should be removed from candidemic patients if possible. In addition, all patients with candidemia should be followed clinically for at least 3 months, as deep infection caused by hematogenous spread may not manifest initially. Patients should be instructed to report any symptoms, which may represent late complications, such as fever, fatigue, jaundice, visual disturbances, abdominal pain, or bone pain.

CANDIDA ENDOCARDITIS

Endocarditis caused by *Candida* species has been reported with increasing frequency, particularly after valvular surgery. Other predisposing factors include underlying valvular disease, concomitant bacterial endocarditis, intravenous drug use, intravenous catheters, and chemotherapy. Aortic and mitral valves are commonly infected. The symptoms are similar to that of bacterial endocarditis with fever, malaise, weight loss, and signs and symptoms of embolic phenomena. Splinter hemorrhages, Osler's nodes, Janeway lesions, hepatosplenomegaly, hematuria, proteinuria, and pyuria may all occur. *Candida* has the ability to cause large vegetations and large emboli, which may be catastrophic, and valvular lesions may progress to cause perforation, congestive heart failure, and myocarditis (Box 73–2).

Diagnosis

Blood cultures are generally positive in *Candida* endocarditis, although negative cultures may occur in up to 25% of patients. Echocardiography reveals vegetations, which may become quite large. Transesophageal echocardiography is more sensitive for detection of vegetations than transthoracic echocardiography. The role of serologic tests (*Candida* antibodies) is uncertain, as both false positive and false negative results occur with some frequency.

Treatment

Treatment of *Candida* endocarditis generally requires combined surgical and medical therapy. Once the diagnosis is established, therapy with amphotericin B should be initiated and the valve replaced as soon as possible (Box 73–8). Antifungal therapy is generally required for a total of 6–10 weeks, and patients should be monitored for a minimum of 2 years after completion of therapy because of the high risk of relapse. For those in whom surgical treatment is not possible, such as those too ill to survive an operation, there exist case reports of treatment success with medical therapy alone (amphotericin B followed by fluconazole).

GI CANDIDIASIS (NONESOPHAGEAL)

Candida species may infect any mucosal surface of the GI tract. After esophageal candidiasis, infection of the stomach is most common. Typically, the organism is seen infecting benign ulcers, although a diffuse mucosal form of infection resembling thrush has been described. In the small and large bowel, ulceration and pseudomembrane formation are common. Mucosal GI involvement may cause deep ulcerations with resulting hemorrhage or perforation (Box 73–1).

Candida may also infect the peritoneum, liver, spleen, gallbladder, or pancreas. Peritoneal infection is associated with peritoneal dialysis, GI surgery, and GI perforation. Dissemination beyond the abdomen is uncommon. Involvement of the liver, spleen, and pancreas occurs most commonly in immunocompromised hosts, particularly with chemotherapy-induced neutropenia. Often, other manifestations of disseminated candidiasis are present. Fungus balls may form in the gallbladder and biliary tree and cause obstruction. Abscesses may involve the liver and spleen.

Diagnosis

Involvement of nonesophageal mucosal involvement of the GI tract is generally diagnosed by characteristic appearance during endoscopy and by demonstration of *Candida* by histology or culture of biopsy

---

BOX 73–8

Treatment of *Candida* Endocarditis

- Surgical replacement of valve
- Amphotericin B 0.8–1.0 mg/kg/day IV every day, continued for 6–10 weeks after operation

specimens. Involvement of the peritoneum, liver, spleen, gallbladder, and pancreas may be difficult to diagnose. Fluid returned after peritoneal dialysis may grow *Candida* in culture. Computer tomography or magnetic resonance imaging may reveal splenic or hepatic abscesses. Laparoscopy may be required for definitive diagnosis.

Treatment

Fluconazole is recommended for initial therapy of mucosal involvement in the stomach, small intestine, or colon (Box 73–9). Amphotericin B may also be used. *Candida* peritonitis may also be treated with fluconazole alone or amphotericin B followed by fluconazole. Peritoneal dialysis catheters should be removed if possible. For patients with a perforated viscus, prophylactic therapy is not indicated and should be reserved for those patients with intraoperative findings consistent with *Candida* infection and positive peritoneal cultures.

Involvement of the liver, spleen, gallbladder, or pancreas should be treated with fluconazole or amphotericin followed by fluconazole. Dosages and duration of therapy are the same as for candidemia and disseminated disease. Large abscesses and fungus balls may require drainage or surgical removal.

OTHER *CANDIDA* SYNDROMES

Candida species are capable of causing many other infectious syndromes, which will be mentioned briefly. Infection of the respiratory tract may result in bronchopneumonia or diffuse nodular infiltrates. Within the central nervous system (CNS), *Candida* spp. may cause meningitis and parenchymal abscesses, usually as part of a disseminated infection. *Candida* spp. have been described as the etiologic agents for osteomyelitis, septic arthritis, myositis, and chostochondritis. Ocular infection may involve any structure within the eye and is common following hematogenous dissemination.

Diagnosis

The diagnosis of *Candida* infection of the lung, CNS, musculoskeletal system, or eye generally requires demonstration of the organism by tissue culture or on histologic examination. However, visualization of the typical well-demarcated white retinal or vitreal lesion by funduscopic examination in the setting of positive blood cultures is adequate for the diagnosis of *Candida* endophthalmitis. It should be noted that sputum culture is generally not sufficient for diagnosis of respiratory involvement, particularly in an intubated patient, as the organism may only be colonizing the respiratory tract.

Treatment

Amphotericin B has been the standard treatment for *Candida* infection in the CNS, eye, lung, and musculoskeletal system. Prosthetic material or other foreign bodies should be removed, if possible. The role of 5-FC is not clear, but it may be added to amphotericin. There is growing support for the use of the azole class, particularly fluconazole, as treatment for deep *Candida* infection. While case reports of success with fluconazole exist, there are very limited data regarding fluconazole in these settings and virtually no data comparing fluconazole with amphotericin.

Prevention & Control of *Candida* Infections

Candida species are ubiquitous; thus prevention of disease is best accomplished by elimination of risk factors as opposed to elimination of the organism

---

BOX 73–9

Treatment of Non-esophageal GI Candidiasis

Mucosal[1]	• Fluconazole 50–200 mg PO/IV every day × 10 days • Amphotericin B 0.3–0.6 mg/kg/day IV × 10 days
Liver, Spleen, Gallbladder, Peritoneum	• Fluconazole 400–800 mg PO/IV every day[2] • Amphotericin B 0.8–1.0 mg/kg/day IV[3]

[1]Stomach, small intestine, large intestine.
[2]Treatment continued until clinical improvement, definite resolution of parenchymal involvement, and for 14 days after any positive blood cultures.
[3]Treatment continued as for fluconazole; may change to fluconazole after initial therapy with amphotericin if clinically improved.

BOX 73–10

Prevention & Control of Candidiasis

Prophylactic Measures	• *Candida* ubiquitous, therefore cannot eliminate organism • Eliminate risk factors if possible (indwelling catheters, Total parenteral nutrition [TPN], etc.) • Good hygiene among health care workers to eliminate spread to those at risk • Prophylactic therapy generally not indicated; concern for creation of resistant organisms
Isolation Precautions	• Generally not required

(Box 73–10). Antibiotic therapy should be focused to treat specific organisms whenever possible. Indwelling vascular and bladder catheters should be removed as early as possible. In the hospital environment, health care professionals should practice good hand washing to minimize introduction of *Candida* infection to patients at risk.

The role of prophylactic therapy is unclear but generally not supported. Prophylactic therapy has been shown to reduce mortality in bone marrow transplant patients but not in any other setting. Prophylactic therapy for candidemia may be warranted in patients' with negative blood cultures who have multiple risk factors for infection and have isolation of *Candida* from multiple sites but is generally discouraged because of concern for creating resistant organisms. Empiric therapy may also be employed in certain settings, such as neutropenic patients who remain persistently febrile for 7–14 days despite broad spectrum antibiotics and exclusion of other possible causes of infection or in patients with two or more risk factors for invasive *Candida* infection and isolation of *Candida* from sputum or urine. Fluconazole is the preferred agent in these settings.

REFERENCES

Cormican MG, Pfaller MA: Epidemiology of candidiasis. Comp Ther 1995;21:653.

Edwards JE Jr: *Candida* species. In Mandell GL, Bennett JE, Dolin R: Principals and Practice of Infectious Diseases, 4th ed. Churchill Livingstone, 1995.

Edwards JE Jr et al: International conference for the development of a consensus on the management and prevention of severe candidal infections. Clin Infect Dis 1997;25:43.

Haulk AA, Sugar AM: *Candida* esophagitis. Adv Intern Med 1991;36:307.

Mooney MA, Thomas I, Sirois D: Oral candidosis. Int J Dermatol 1995;34:760.

Nguyen MH et al: Candida prosthetic valve endocarditis: Prospective study of six cases and review of the literature. Clin Infect Dis 1996;22:262.

Rex JH et al: A randomized trial comparing fluconazole with amphotericin B for the treatment of candidemia in patients without neutropenia. New Engl J Med 1994; 331:1325.

Samaranayake YH, Samaranayake LP: Candida krusei: Biology, epidemiology, pathogenicity and clinical manifestations of an emerging pathogen. J Med Microbiol 1994; 41:295.

Sobel JD: Candida vulvovaginitis. Sem Dermatol 1996; 15:17.

Cryptococcus neoformans

74

James J. Chamberlain, MD & Donald L. Granger, MD

Essentials of Diagnosis

- Routine laboratory tests often normal.
- One-third of patients are afebrile.
- Definitive diagnosis made by fungal culture maintained at 37°C for 6 weeks.
- Cryptococcal antigen 95% sensitive in CNS infection in centrifuged CSF.
- India ink examination positive in only 50% of meningoencephalitis cases.
- CSF lymphocytes often low in CNS infection, especially in AIDS patients.
- Cryptococcal antigen most sensitive detection method in serum.
- Chest radiograph variable—multiple areas of infiltration in lower lobes most common in pulmonary disease.
- Molecular detection by PCR might soon become laboratory standard.

General Considerations

A. Epidemiology and Ecology. *Cryptococcus neoformans* exists as two distinct varieties known as variety *neoformans* and variety *gattii* (Table 74–1). *Cryptococcus neoformans* variety *neoformans* exists throughout the world and is found frequently in pigeon droppings that have accumulated over time. The concentrations of these organisms are often quite high in old pigeon droppings found in barns, on window ledges, and around the upper floors of old buildings. Pigeons carrying the organism do not seem to be clinically affected, and wet or fresh droppings rarely contain *C neoformans*. *C neoformans* variety *neoformans* has been isolated from the droppings of other birds as well, including parakeets and canaries.

The variant *gattii* has been isolated most frequently from tropical and subtropical climates, most commonly in Australia, Southeast Asia, Brazil, Venezuela, Zaire, and southern California. This finding appears to be related to the distribution of the river red gum tree *(Eucalyptus camaldulensis),* which harbors the organism. Infectivity correlates with flowering of eucalyptus trees. The organism does not cause outbreaks or clusters of infection, and a lack of history of exposure to bird droppings or flowering Eucalyptus trees should not exclude the diagnosis of *Cryptococcus* infection—or "cryptococcosis."

AIDS and the use of immunosuppressive drug therapy have produced a dramatic rise in the number of infections due to *C neoformans* over the past 25 years (see Chapter 40). In fact, more cases of cryptococcosis were described in the United States in 1976 (338 cases) than had been described worldwide by 1955 (~ 300 cases). Prior to the AIDS epidemic, nearly half of the cases of *Cryptococcus* infection were described in patients with altered cellular immunity, including leukemias, lymphomas, sarcoidosis, and chronic corticosteroid use, and in immunosuppressed patients who had undergone organ transplantation. It is interesting that nearly every case of cryptococcosis in patients with AIDS has been caused by the variety *neoformans.* This phenomenon has led to a dramatic increase in the incidence of cryptococcosis caused by variety *neoformans,* especially in central Africa, where the majority of infections were caused by variety *gattii* before the AIDS epidemic. The reason for this skewed epidemiologic finding remains speculative at this time.

Cryptococcosis remains the most common life-threatening fungal infection seen in patients with AIDS and usually is seen in patients with CD4 counts of < 100 cells/mm^3. Estimates of the prevalence of cryptococcosis in patients with AIDS range from 6% to 10%. *C neoformans* is also the third most common organism affecting the central nervous system (CNS) in AIDS cases. Considerable variation seems to exist in the frequency of cryptococcosis among AIDS patients in different regions of the world, with as few as 3% of patients being infected in parts of Europe but possibly ≤ 30% of sub-Saharan Africans being affected. Males are affected approximately threefold as often as females, regardless of the presence of AIDS.

B. Microbiology. *Cryptococcus neoformans* is an encapsulated, yeastlike fungus that reproduces by budding. During budding, one or two daughter cells are often seen being released but are still connected to the mother cell by a thin pole of extracellular polysaccharide material.

Encapsulated yeast cells generally appear round or oval shaped in tissue samples and are usually 4 to 8 μm in size. *Cryptococcus* cells may be as large as 15 μm as they begin to bud. The size of the polysaccharide capsule encircling the organism varies greatly

Table 74–1. Characteristics of *C neoformans* varieties.

Characteristic	Variety neoformans	Variety *gattii*
Geographic distribution	• Worldwide	• Tropical and subtropical regions
Reservoir	• Pigeon feces	• Eucalyptus trees
Host predisposition	• AIDS • Sarcoid • Lymphoma • Corticosteroids • CLL, ALL • Organ transplantation	• Mostly normal hosts
Infection in AIDS	Yes	Rare

and depends mainly on surrounding growth conditions. The size of the capsule in vitro does not correlate with virulence of a particular strain.

C neoformans grows at 37 °C on Sabouraud's or malt extract agar, a characteristic that distinguishes this species from other nonpathogenic *Cryptococcus* species. The organisms are usually visible within 72 h as white or tan-colored, mucoid, smooth colonies.

The variety *neoformans* comprises capsular serotypes A and D, and variety *gattii* capsular serotypes B and C. The two varieties of *C neoformans* may be distinguished on canavanine-glycol-bromthymol blue agar. Variety *gattii* grows to produce a color change to cobalt blue; variety *neoformans* does not grow, and the indicator remains yellow. In addition, *Cryptococcus* spp. hydrolyze urea and assimilate maltose, sucrose, glucose, and galactose, but not lactose. Carbohydrates are not fermented by species in this genus. *C neoformans* produces melanin from catecholamines by phenoloxidase. This enzyme has recently been cloned and characterized. It is a type of laccase. Melanin production has been shown to be a virulence factor.

C. Pathogenesis. *C neoformans* is thought to be acquired by humans through inhalation of infected particles from bird droppings (var. *neoformans*) or from flowering *Eucalyptus camaldulensis* trees (var. *gattii*). Some infections caused by *C neoformans* may be the result of reactivation of latent infection, although this point is controversial. There is no evidence that acquisition occurs directly from other humans or animals. Soil that is contaminated with the organism, when disturbed by wind, allows the organism to become airborne. Inhaled *C neoformans* particles, often < 2 μm in size, are usually deposited in the lungs and quickly phagocytized by alveolar macrophages. This cellular response in normal hosts usually results in inapparent infection. Whether the organism is usually eradicated at this stage is not known, but anecdotal reports suggest that a dormant state may occur in some individuals. It is during the primary exposure that a defect in cellular immunity or a particularly large inoculum may lead to the proliferation and dissemination of the organism, most commonly to the CNS.

The main factors responsible for virulence include (a) the surrounding polysaccharide capsule, (b) the enzyme phenoloxidase, (c) ability to grow at 37°C, and (d) alpha mating type. The polysaccharide capsule has been shown to impair host phagocytosis and may impede migration of leukocytes. Phagocytic cells may be unable to engulf heavily encapsulated organisms due to the size of the pathogen. Capsular elements also activate the complement system, which probably has a significant effect on host defense, depending on the amount of capsular material surrounding the organism. In addition, the alternative complement pathway could be activated by cell wall components that might deplete host humoral factors locally. Oxidative killing mechanisms of macrophages and neutrophils are important elements of host defense and may be impeded by *Cryptococcus* spp. *C neoformans* produces the enzyme phenoloxidase, which converts hydroxybenzoic substrates to melanin. This activity may protect against oxidative host defenses. The organism has never been shown to produce toxins.

Before the advent of highly active antiretroviral therapy (HAART), cryptococcosis carried a high mortality. During diagnosis and initial treatment with antifungal therapy, ≤ 25% of patients with AIDS died. At 1 year after diagnosis of *C neoformans*, 30–60% of patients with AIDS died from the disease. Cancer patients diagnosed with cryptococcal meningitis have a median overall survival of only 2 months. These findings serve to emphasize the importance of immunocompetence in susceptibility to cryptococcosis and its correlation with severity of either AIDS or lymphoreticular malignancy.

Clinical Findings

A. Signs and Symptoms.

CNS Infection. The most common clinical manifestation of *C neoformans* infection is chronic infection of the brain and meninges, termed meningoencephalitis. The use of this term has become customary because cryptococcal organisms truly invade the cerebral, cerebellar, and brain stem parenchyma as well as the meninges.

The most common symptom of meningoencephalitis is headache. Signs of meningeal inflammation including stiff neck and photophobia are present in ~ 50% of patients but are usually mild. Malaise, dizziness, and nausea may be present as well. As the disease progresses over several weeks, patients may develop altered mental status, visual loss, cranial nerve palsies, ataxia, seizures, coma, and brain stem herniation. Signs and symptoms of increased intracranial pressure may predominate, including severe headache, neck stiffness, projectile vomiting, altered consciousness, and papilledema. Many patients with cryptococcosis never have fever.

Pulmonary Infection. Pulmonary disease is another potentially fatal manifestation of infection with *C neoformans*. However, the majority of patients probably experience subclinical disease, with half experiencing no symptoms. Still, the scope of disease may range from acute, self-limited pneumonia in otherwise healthy individuals or chronic, stable colonization in patients with underlying lung disease to a severe, progressive pneumonia in AIDS patients, with mortality approaching 50%. The most common symptoms seen in pulmonary infection include dry cough, low-grade fever, sputum production, and pleuritic chest pain. Pleural effusions are rarely seen on chest radiograph. Dissemination to the CNS should probably be regarded as the most serious complication of pulmonary cryptococcosis and may occur during any stage of pulmonary infection, even as the pulmonary disease seems to be resolving.

Other Infections. *C neoformans* may affect other organ systems as well. Skin lesions may be observed in ≤ 10% of patients and signify disseminated disease with a high risk of CNS involvement. Up to 5–10% of patients have skeletal involvement with cryptococcosis. The vertebrae and long bones are most often affected. Cryptococcosis may affect the eyes, adrenal cortex, genitourinary system, gastrointestinal system, and most any other organ system in rare instances.

D. Infections in AIDS or Immunocompromised Patients. In patients who are infected with the human immunodeficiency virus (HIV), cryptococcosis is considered an AIDS-defining illness. The clinical course of CNS infection in AIDS patients seems to be more acute, with fever and headache being prominent early in the course. Findings are similar to those seen in non-AIDS patients as the disease progresses but may develop more rapidly. The vast majority of AIDS patients have meningoencephalitis at the time of diagnosis with cryptococcosis. Pulmonary disease seems to produce symptoms more commonly in patients with AIDS, with a greater proportion experiencing fever, cough, dyspnea, and weight loss. *Cryptococcal* organisms may be cultured from areas outside the CNS in < 20% of AIDS patients. Skin lesions are seen more commonly in AIDS patients and often resemble the papules seen in molluscum contagiosum infection. Liver and spleen involvement is probably more common in AIDS patients but is nonetheless rare.

B. Laboratory Findings. Routine laboratory tests including leukocyte counts, hematocrit, and blood chemistries are often normal in cryptococcosis, even in severe infections. Molecular identification of *C neoformans* in serum and other fluids and tissues by polymerase chain reaction may soon become standard practice in many laboratories.

CNS Infection. The diagnosis of *C neoformans* infection of the CNS is made definitively by fungal culture of the pellet of centrifuged CSF. Culture media should be maintained aerobically at 37°C for 6 weeks before a culture is deemed negative. Cryptococcal antigen is positive by latex agglutination nearly 95% of the time in the supernate of centrifuged CSF. Serial dilutions of CSF run by latex agglutination allow titers to be reported, which may be useful in assessing prognosis or monitoring response to therapy in patients who are not immunocompromised. Antigen titers do not seem to correlate with severity of infection or response to treatment in patients with AIDS. The presence of cryptococcal antigen in serum is suggestive but not diagnostic of CNS disease in non-AIDS patients. However, ≤ 95% of AIDS patients with documented CNS infection will have positive cryptococcal antigen in serum. Positive identification of cryptococcal organisms in CSF by India ink preparation occurs in ≤ 50% of cases of meningoencephalitis. Lymphocytes in the CSF are present in low numbers, especially in AIDS patients. One study of cryptococcal meningitis in patients with AIDS showed an average of four lymphocytes/mm^3 in the CSF. CSF glucose is generally low but may be normal. Protein in the CSF is usually elevated, as is the opening pressure. Computed tomography and magnetic resonance imaging may detect the presence of nodules (cryptococcomas), hydrocephalus, or gyral enhancement. Nearly 50% of patients may have an abnormal computed tomography scan. Cryptococcomas may be seen in ≤ 25% of patients with meningoencephalitis.

Pulmonary Infection. Diagnosing the presence of *C neoformans* in the lung is less satisfying and more difficult to interpret. Colonization with cryptococcal organisms has often been noted on repeated cultures of sputum from patients with chronic pulmonary disease. Culture of sputum or bronchoalveolar lavage should be considered the gold standard for diagnosis of pulmonary cryptococcosis. Patients with symptoms of pulmonary disease and cryptococcal antigen titers ≥ 8 on bronchoalveolar lavage specimens should be considered to have pulmonary cryptococcosis. The chest radiograph may not necessarily be helpful in the diagnosis of suspected pulmonary disease. Most commonly, chest radiographs are normal or show a nonspecific pattern of interstitial infiltrates and lymphadenopathy. Occasionally, patients have multiple large, dense nodules that are subsequently found to be caused by cryptococcosis. Pleural effusions are rarely noted on chest radiographs.

The diagnosis of disseminated infection in the bloodstream—or "cryptococcemia"—is best made based on the presence of cryptococcal antigen, as detected by latex agglutination or by cultivating the organisms using "isolator" blood cultures. The capsular polysaccharide becomes soluble in the serum of infected patients and may be detected with rabbit anti-*C neoformans* antiserum with ~ 95% sensitivity. Antigen titers ≥ 8 are thought to signal active disease. This method of detecting *C neoformans* infection is more sensitive than culture or India ink stain, which are roughly 75% and 50% sensitive, respectively. False-positive antigen detection may occur in patients with rheumatoid factor in their blood or by cross-reaction with the polysaccharide antigen of *Trichosporon beigelii.*

Other Infections. Skin and mucosal lesions, which may be secondary to disseminated cryptococcosis, should be biopsied for both histologic diagnosis and culture. Skeletal lesions should be biopsied as well if the diagnosis is in doubt.

Treatment

The treatment of patients with cryptococcosis is determined by whether they are HIV positive or negative and whether they have localized pulmonary or disseminated (usually meningitis) involvement.

A. HIV-negative patients. For mild to moderate pulmonary infection without evidence of dissemination, oral fluconazole for 6–12 months is adequate (Box 74–1). In meningitis, cryptococcemia, or severe pulmonary infection, preferred treatment includes a combination of amphotericin B plus 5-flucytosine for 2 weeks followed by oral fluconazole daily for a minimum of 10 weeks (Box 74–1). 5-Flucytosine is given every 6 h. Serum levels should be monitored and the dose adjusted to give 20–40 µg/ml peak concentrations. Complete blood counts are required to detect toxicity and should be done twice per week.

Amphotericin B is limited by significant adverse effects and complications including infusion-related toxicity, nephrotoxicity, and hypokalemia. 5-Flucytosine causes myelosuppression, most notably thrombocytopenia and neutropenia, as well as gastrointestinal complaints.

B. HIV-positive patients. For mild to moderate pulmonary infection, lifelong daily fluconazole is recommended (Box 74–2). Alternatively, a combination of fluconazole plus 5-flucytosine may be given for 10 weeks.

Treatment of CNS with severe pulmonary or disseminated involvement of other body sites consists of two phases. First, induction/consolidation therapy is given to control the infection and reduce viable cryptococci in CSF and tissues to an undetectable level. This is followed by maintenance therapy, which prevents relapse. It is currently unclear whether maintenance therapy may be discontinued in patients with prolonged successful HAART. Induction/consolidation therapy is with amphotericin B plus 5-flucytosine for 2 weeks followed by fluconazole for 10 weeks. Maintenance therapy consists of daily fluconazole for life (Box 74–2).

Drug interactions are an important consideration when azole antifungal drugs are used. In one case, a coadministered drug (eg, omeprazole) may decrease gastrointestinal absorption (eg, of itraconazole) or increase metabolism (eg, of fluconazole by rifampin), rendering antifungal therapy less active. Conversely, azoles may lead to unexpected toxicity of the coadministered drug (eg, warfarin) by altering hepatic metabolism via a cytochrome P-450 system. Drug interactions in HIV-infected patients taking complex therapeutic regimens require careful review when therapy with an antifungal drug, especially an azole, is initiated.

Another important consideration in the treatment of cryptococcal meningitis is that of increased intracranial pressure. A large proportion of deaths, especially early in the course of disease, are attributable to elevated intracranial pressure. Patients who present with or develop coma or other signs of increased intracranial pressure should undergo daily lumbar puncture with removal of 30 cc of CSF until symptoms resolve. Treatment with acetazolamide and ventriculoperitoneal shunting has been tried as well. The effect of these interventions on mortality is not known.

BOX 74–1

Treatment of Cryptococcal Disease in HIV-Negative Patients		
	Mild to Moderate Pulmonary Disease	CNS or Severe Pulmonary Disease
First Choice	• Fluconazole, 200–400 mg/d for 6–12 months	• Amphotericin B, 0.7–1.0 mg/kg/d for 2 weeks; then fluconazole, 400 mg/d for a minimum of 10 weeks
Second Choice	• Amphotericin B, 0.5–1.0 mg/kg/d (total, – 1000–2000 mg0	• Amphotericin B, 0.7–1.0 mg/kg/d plus 5 flucytosine, 100 mg/kg/d for 6–10 weeks

Treatment of Cryptococcal Disease in HIV-Positive Patients

	Mild to Moderate Pulmonary Disease	CNS, Severe Pulmonary, or Disseminated Involvement of Other Body Sites
First Choice	• Fluconazole, 200–400 mg/d (for life)	• Induction/consolidation: Amphotericin B, 0.7–1.0 mg/kg/d plus 5-flucytosine, 100 mg/kg/d for 2 weeks; then fluconazole, 400 mg/d for minimum of 10 weeks • Maintenance: Fluconazole, 200–400 mg PO daily for life
Second Choice	• Fluconazole, 400 mg/d plus flucytosine, 100 mg/kg/d for 10 weeks	• Induction/consolidation: Amphotericin B, 0.7–1.0 mg/kg/d for 6–10 weeks • Maintenance: Itraconazole, 200 mg PO twice daily for life

Prognosis

Cure of CNS cryptococcosis in AIDS patients is rare. Consequently, management is aimed at long-term suppression therapy. The effect of HAART on ability to cure cryptococcosis is unknown. Close follow-up throughout the course of initial therapy and maintenance therapy is imperative in AIDS-associated CNS cryptococcosis to monitor for relapse. Immunosuppressed patients with neoplastic disease may also be difficult to cure and require long-term suppressive therapy. In others the mortality rate of treated CNS infection may be 25–30%, although this varies in different series. Often prognosis is largely influenced by the underlying immunosuppressive condition, for example, in lymphoreticular malignancies.

Factors signaling a poor prognosis include abnormal mental status, advanced age (> 60 years), crypto-coccemia, high titers of cryptococcal antigen in CSF or blood, and CSF measurements of high opening pressure, low white blood cell count (< 20 cells/mm^3), low glucose, and a positive India ink preparation. Serious morbid complications include chronic brain syndrome with dementia and acute and chronic hydrocephalus.

Prevention & Control

Prophylaxis for cryptococcosis is not currently recommended. However, in AIDS patients with CD4 counts of < 200 cells/mm^3, the incidence of cryptococcosis has been reduced from 7% to 1% in patients taking fluconazole (200 mg PO daily). Having AIDS patients or other immunocompromised patients avoid areas that are heavily populated with pigeons may be appropriate. The use of active immunization with capsular polysaccharide has not been successful.

REFERENCES

Baughman RP et al: Detection of cryptococcal antigen in bronchoalveolar lavage fluid: a prospective study of diagnostic utility. Am Rev Respir Dis 1992;145:1226.

Cameron ML et al: Manifestations of pulmonary cryptococcosis in patients with acquired immunodeficiency syndrome. Rev Infect Dis 1991;13:64.

Chuck SL, Sande MA. Infections with *Cryptococcus neoformans* in the acquired immunodeficiency syndrome. N Engl J Med 1989;321:794.

Clumeck N et al: The African AIDS experience in contrast with the rest of the world. In Leoung G, Mills J: *Opportunistic Infections in Patients with the Acquired Immune Deficiency Syndrome*. Marcel Dekker, 1989.

Ellis DH, Pfeiffer TJ: Natural habitat of *Cryptococcus neoformans* var. *gattii*. J Clin Microbiol 1990;28:1642.

Kwon-Chung KJ, Bennett JE: Epidemiologic differences between the two varieties of *Cryptococcus neoformans*. Am J Epidemiol 1984;120:123.

Larsen RA et al: Fluconazole combined with flucytosine for treatment of cryptococcal meningitis in patients with AIDS. Clin Infect Dis 1994;16:741.

Swinne-Desgain D: Clinical isolates of *Cryptococcus neoformans* from Zaire. Eur J Clin Microbiol 1986;5:50.

Larsen RA et al: Fluconazole compared with amphotericin B plus flucytosine for cryptococcal meningitis in AIDS: a randomized trial. Ann Intern Med 1990;113:183.

Powderly WG: Cryptococcal meningitis and AIDS. Clin Infect Dis 1993;17:837.

Mitchell TG, Perfect JR: *Cryptococcus* in the era of AIDS—100 years after the discovery of *Cryptococcus neoformans*. Clin Microbiol. Rev. 1995;8:515.

Nelson MR et al: The value of serum cryptococcal antigen

in the diagnosis of cryptococcal infection in patients infected with the human immunodeficiency virus. J Infect 1990;21:175.

Saag MS et al: Comparison of amphotericin B with fluconazole in the treatment of acute AIDS-associated cryptococcal meningitis. N Engl J Med 1992;326:83.

Sobel JD et al: Practice guidelines for the treatment of fungal infections. Clin Infect Dis 2000;30:652.

Van der Horst CM et al: Treatment of cryptococcal meningitis associated with the acquired immunodeficiency syndrome. N Engl J Med 1997;337:15.

Aspergillus, Pseudallescheria, & Agents of Mucormycosis

75

Michael R. Keating, MD

ASPERGILLUS INFECTION

Essentials of Diagnosis
- Filamentous fungus with septate hyphae 3–6 μm in diameter.
- Branching of hyphal elements typically at 45° angle.
- Specific IgG antibodies generally of no use diagnostically since most patients are immunosuppressed and will not generate antibody response.
- Pulmonary lesions, localized or cavitary in susceptible host.

General Considerations

A. Epidemiology. *Aspergillus* spp. are found worldwide and grow in a variety of conditions. They commonly grow in soil and moist locations and are among the most common molds encountered on spoiled food and decaying vegetation, in compost piles, and in stored hay and grain. *Aspergillus* spp. often grow in houseplant soil, and such soil may be a source of *Aspergillus conidia* or spores in the home, office, or hospital setting. The airborne conidia are extremely heat resistant and can withstand extreme environmental conditions.

Most human disease with *Aspergillus* spp. is acquired via inhalation of conidia. Conidia are 2.5–3 μm in size and can easily reach the alveoli with inhalation. Other routes of transmission are by direct inoculation of skin, inhalation into the nose and sinuses, or injection into the bloodstream among drug abusers. Person-to-person transmission does not occur.

Nosocomial acquisition is an important problem among severely immunosuppressed, hospitalized patients. Hospital air and air ducts are known sources of *A conidia.* Unfiltered air is more likely to contain spores. Construction, building remodeling, and other forms of environmental disruption have been associated with nosocomial outbreaks of aspergillosis. Potted plants are frequently excluded from patient care areas where high-risk patients may be present.

The most critical determinant for inhalation of *A conidia* progressing to invasive disease is the status of the host defenses. The pulmonary macrophage is the first line of defense against inhaled conidia. Macro-phage function may be rendered ineffective by high-dose corticosteroid therapy or other immunomodulating chemotherapy. The tissue neutrophil is also pivotal. Altered phagocytosis or cellular killing by the neutrophil may lead to invasive disease. Neutropenia caused by leukemia, chemotherapy, bone marrow transplantation, or aplastic anemia is a well-known risk factor for invasive aspergillosis. Patients with late stages of HIV infection also are prone to invasive disease. Increased risk is also associated in children with chronic granulomatous disease and in patients with poorly controlled diabetes mellitus.

B. Microbiology. *Aspergillus* spp. are rapidly growing filamentous fungi or molds that are ubiquitous in the environment and found worldwide. The septate hyphae are characteristically 3–6 μm in diameter and usually branch at 45° angles. Growth usually occurs in the laboratory within 2–3 days. Of the > 500 species of *Aspergillus,* only a few cause human infection. *A fumigatus* is the most common human pathogen. Others, such as *A niger, A flavus,* and *A terreus,* can also cause human infection but are encountered less frequently. Isolated cases have been caused by a number of other *Aspergillus* spp. The species of *Aspergillus* are differentiated by the structure of the asexual conidiaphore or spore-forming structure on growth in the laboratory.

C. Pathogenesis. *Aspergillus* spp. may invade tissue in patients with altered host defenses or may colonize ectatic segments or cavities in the lung. Following inhalation of conidia, in the absence of appropriate host response, hyphal elements invade bronchial tissue with a particular propensity for angioinvasion. Angioinvasion may lead to disseminated invasive aspergillosis involving multiple organs in profoundly immunosuppressed patients. Furthermore, angioinvasion causes hemorrhagic infarction and necrosis of involved tissue. This may result in hemoptysis when there is pulmonary involvement or stroke when the brain is infected. The enlarging site of *Aspergillus* infection with central necrosis has a tendency to cavitate, yielding characteristic findings on imaging studies.

Colonization of preexisting cavitary lesions may lead to the formation of a fungus ball or aspergilloma composed of exuberant filamentous growth of *Aspergillus* spp. The cavity of an aspergilloma is lined by vascular granulation tissue, while the cavity itself contains hyphal elements, inflammatory cells, amorphous debris, and mucus. Superficial invasion of the cavity wall may occur, but dissemination is rare unless the patient also has other risk factors for invasive disease. Erosion into adjacent pulmonary vessels may occur and result in hemoptysis, which on occasion may be massive and result in death.

CLINICAL SYNDROMES

Most individuals who are exposed to *Aspergillus* spores are asymptomatic. In fact, inhalation of spores is probably a common event; however, in an at-risk patient, the spectrum of disease caused by *Aspergillus* spp. can range from hypersensitivity phenomenon to colonization to overwhelming and rapidly progressing disseminated life-threatening disease (see Box 75–1).

1. INVASIVE PULMONARY ASPERGILLOSIS

Invasive pulmonary aspergillosis in the immunocompromised host is among the most serious manifestations of disease caused by *Aspergillus* spp. Key risk factors for invasive aspergillosis include neutropenia, especially profound neutropenia (< 100 neutrophils/mL) and prolonged neutropenia (> 12 days); prolonged high-dose corticosteroid therapy, graft-versus-host disease after bone marrow transplantation, acute rejection after solid-organ transplantation, cytomegalovirus disease after transplantation, advanced AIDS, and poorly controlled diabetes mellitus. On very rare occasions, invasive pulmonary aspergillosis may occur in previously healthy adults or in patients with alcoholic liver disease. Chronic necrotizing aspergillosis is an indolent form of invasive pulmonary aspergillosis that occurs in patients who are less profoundly immunosuppressed than those with the risk factors cited above.

Clinical Findings

A. Signs and Symptoms. Severely immunosuppressed patients with invasive aspergillosis may be completely asymptomatic when the disease is first suspected. The initial clue may only be a positive sputum culture or an abnormal chest x-ray. Nonproductive cough, dyspnea, and chest pain are common among patients with symptoms. Pleuritic chest pain is occasionally seen. Fever is usually present but may be suppressed by corticosteroid therapy. Hemoptysis may develop as a consequence of angioinvasion and, in the appropriate host, should raise the suspicion of invasive pulmonary aspergillosis.

B. Laboratory Findings. Hypoxemia is often present in patients with extensive pulmonary involvement. Other laboratory abnormalities are nonspecific. Because of the immunodeficient state, serum antibodies to *Aspergillus* spp. are usually negative. The detection of circulating *Aspergillus* antigen is a promising investigational test but is not yet available commercially. Cultures of the sputum or respiratory secretions are often positive. Unfortunately, recovery of *Aspergillus* isolates from the sputum of otherwise healthy

---

BOX 75–1

Aspergillus Infection

	Children	Adults
More Common	• Allergic bronchopulmonary aspergillosis • Aspergilloma • Invasive pulmonary aspergillosis • Disseminated aspergillosis	• Farmer's lung • Allergic bronchopulmonary aspergillosis • Aspergilloma • Invasive pulmonary aspergillosis • Disseminated aspergillosis • *Aspergillus* sinusitis
Less Common	• Osteomyelitis • Endocarditis • Endophthalmitis	• Endophthalmitis • Osteomyelitis • Disk space infection • Endocarditis • Otomycosis • *Aspergillus* tracheobronchitis

people is occasionally seen so it may be difficult and a challenge to distinguish airway colonization from positive cultures caused by invasive disease. Furthermore, 20–30%of patients with invasive pulmonary aspergillosis will have negative sputum cultures unless serial sampling is done. Positive blood cultures for *Aspergillus* spp. are exceedingly rare.

C. Imaging. The chest x-ray findings in patients with invasive pulmonary aspergillosis vary considerably. Focal pneumonitis, diffuse patchy disease, mononodular and multinodular densities, and pleural-based infiltrates may be seen. Rounded nodular infiltrates are the most common finding. Serial chest x-rays may show rapid progression of pulmonary involvement, and cavitation in this setting is common. Computed-tomography (CT) imaging of the chest may show a characteristic halo sign around nodular infiltrates that are highly suggestive of angioinvasive *Aspergillus* infection.

D. Differential Diagnosis. The differential diagnosis of a new infiltrative lung process in an immunosuppressed patient is very broad. Other fungi including *Pseudallescheria boydii* and the order Mucorales can cause an identical syndrome. *Nocardia* lung infection can be similar in presentation. Mycobacterial infection is less likely but must be considered. Bacterial infection including that caused by *Staphylococcus aureus* and *Pseudomonas aeruginosa* is possible. *Rhodococcus equi* is a rare but emerging pathogen that presents this way, especially if cavitation is present.

E. Complications. The propensity for angioinvasion leads to hematogenous dissemination in undiagnosed or untreated cases. Virtually any organ may be involved (see disseminated aspergillosis).

Diagnosis

The diagnosis of invasive pulmonary aspergillosis in the immunosuppressed patient is a significant challenge. A definitive diagnosis is established when tissue specimens demonstrate invasive fungal elements (see Figure 75–1); however, a positive sputum specimen in a high-risk patient and imaging evidence consistent with *Aspergillus* infection should be regarded as presumptive invasive pulmonary aspergillosis and justification for empiric antifungal therapy. In patients with negative cultures or in whom sputum cultures cannot be obtained, bronchoscopy and bronchoalveolar lavage may help establish a microbiologic diagnosis. Bronchoscopic transbronchial biopsy may yield a false negative result due to the patchy nature of pulmonary aspergillosis and to a sampling error of the biopsy. In patients with pleural-based nodular disease, percutaneous lung biopsy may be considered. Pneumothorax and bleeding are potential complications of this approach. Thorascopic or open lung biopsy is the most effective method to establish the diagnosis.

Treatment

Invasive pulmonary aspergillosis may be a rapidly

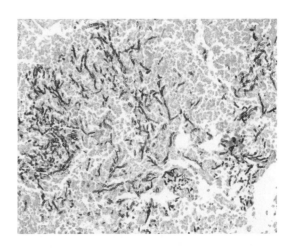

Figure 75–1. Invasive fungal elements of *Aspergillus fumigatus* in a lung biopsy specimen from a patient with invasive pulmonary aspergillosis. Note the septate hyphae and branching ($\times$ 200, methenamine silver stain).

progressive infection and prompt institution of antifungal therapy is critical once the diagnosis is suspected or confirmed (see Box 75–2). Amphotericin B remains the drug of choice. Treatment failures are common. Alternatives to amphotericin B include lipid amphotericin B preparations. These preparations are considerably less nephrotoxic than standard amphotericin B and appear to be equally efficacious. Unfortunately, these new lipid preparations are currently exceedingly expensive. Itraconazole is an oral azole with activity against *Aspergillus* spp. Its use should be reserved for patients who are not severely immunosuppressed, who have an indolent or chronic infection, or who are intolerant of amphotericin B therapy. The optimal duration of antifungal therapy is not known, but the cumulative total dose is $\leq$ 2 g of amphotericin B. In patients with a single focus of pulmonary infection, resection should be considered.

Prognosis

The prognosis for invasive pulmonary aspergillosis is generally poor. Cure or improvement on therapy is seen in $\sim$ 50% of cases. Response is more likely if neutropenia recovers and immunosuppression is reduced or reversed.

Prevention & Control

Because invasive aspergillosis in the immunosuppressed or neutropenic patient is difficult to diagnosis and treat, much attention has been focused on prevention as a way of reducing the frequency of infection (Box 75–3). Two general approaches have been used: reduction of environmental exposure and prophylactic antifungal therapy. *Aspergillus* spp. are an ubiquitous component of dust, building material, and organic debris.

BOX 75-2

Treatment of *Aspergillus* Infection in Children and Adults

Treatment Option	Farmer's Lung	Allergic Bronchopulmonary Aspergillosis	Aspergilloma	Invasive Pulmonary Aspergillosis and Disseminated Asperillosis	Aspergillus Sinusitis
Corticosteroids	Prolonged subacute or chronic symptoms may require prednisone therapy at 1 mg/kg for 1–2 wks followed by a tapering regimen	Prednisone, 0.5 mg/kg/d prolonged with slow taper	No	Stop or reduce if possible	No
Amphotericin B	No	No	No	1.0–1.5 mg/kg/d IV (2–3 g total target dose) in adults; 30–35 mg/kg total dose in children	1–1.5 mg/kg, if needed (2–3 g total target dose) in adults; 30–35 mg/kg total dose in children
Intraconazole	No	Investigational	No	400 mg PO once daily as second-line option for indolent case or after IV amphotericin B induction therapy; itraconazole dose for children, 5–6 mg/kg/d	No
Surgery	No	No	In selected cases	An option for localized disease	Surgical débridement; surgical excision and drainage may be adequate

Reducing exposure to at-risk hospitalized patients can be achieved in several ways. Potted plants should be removed from the environment adjacent to at-risk patients. Certain foods, such as cereal and spices, have been found to be contaminated with *Aspergillus* spores and should not be offered to hospitalized patients that are at risk for aspergillosis. Construction in and adjacent to hospitals has been associated with outbreaks of nosocomial aspergillosis. Patients should not be treated in areas of the hospital where construction or remodeling is occurring. If a patient must be transported through areas of construction within the hospital, an efficient mask should be worn by the patient. Efforts should be made to seal areas undergoing construction or remodeling to prevent contamination of the air in patient areas.

HEPA filtration of air has been shown to significantly reduce or eliminate *Aspergillus* spores. Patient rooms with laminar airflow and HEPA filtration appear to be effective in reducing the risk of exposure in the hospital. Unfortunately, the construction and maintenance of HEPA-filtered facilities are very expensive and not available to all patients. Other strategies that have been used include high air exchange rates, surveillance air sampling, positive pressure in the patient's room and immediate environment, and regular filter changing of point-of-use air filtration systems.

BOX 75-3

Control and Prevention of Nosocomial Invasive *Aspergillus* spp.
in Immunosuppressed Patients

	Strategy	Goal or Limitations
Reduction of environmental exposure	• Remove potted plants from patient care areas • Avoid dried spices (eg, pepper) and cereals • Seal off hospital remodeling projects • HEPA filtration and laminar air flow patient room and care areas • Wear high filtration masks during transportation in hospital	• Eliminate source of spores • Reduce air contamination • Remove spores from air in key domiciliary areas; reduce exposure risk in non-domiciliary areas
Prophylactic antifungal therapy	• Amphotericin B, 1 mg/kg/d IV • Amphotericin B, 0.1–0.15 mg/kg/d • Lipid preparations of amphotericin B • Oral itraconazole, 200–400 mg/d; for children 3–6 mg/kg/d • Intranasal or aerosolized amphotericin B	• Too toxic to be used prophylactically • Usually can be tolerated but dose may be too low to be effective • No clinical data; prohibitive cost • Limited clinical data; unpredictable absorption • Promising approach; more data needed

The use of intravenous amphotericin B for prophylaxis against *Aspergillus* spp. has been investigated. When given prophylactically at a dose of 1 mg/kg/d, the toxicity is prohibitively high. When used prophylactically at lower doses of 0.1–0.25 mg/kg/d, the toxicity is less, but in most studies, this dosage was insufficient to prevent aspergillosis. The lipid formulations of amphotericin B are attractive for prophylaxis alternatives; however, the high cost of these preparations limit their widespread use.

Among the oral azoles, only itraconazole has sufficient activity against *Aspergillus* to be considered as a viable prophylactic agent. There are limited data confirming its efficacy in preventing aspergillosis in high-risk patients. Moreover, the absorption of itraconazole from the gastrointestinal tract may be inadequate in these patients.

Use of intranasal installation of amphotericin B or aerosolization of amphotericin B was an effective prophylaxis in several small pilot studies. More data are necessary regarding optimal dose, frequency, and duration before this approach can be widely recommended for prophylaxis.

2. ASPERGILLOMA

An aspergilloma of the lung may develop in individuals who have preexisting cavitary lung disease caused by conditions such as tuberculosis, sarcoidosis, silicosis, or bronchiectasis. Also known as a fungus ball or mycetoma, aspergillomas can be regarded as heavy *Aspergillus* colonization of the preexisting cavity.

Clinical Findings

A. Signs and Symptoms. The most common symptom is hemoptysis, and, on rare occasions, severe or fatal hemoptysis can develop. Other symptoms are usually related to the underlying lung disease.

B. Laboratory Findings. Patients with an aspergilloma of the lung typically have elevated IgG levels specific for *Aspergillus* spp. Sputum smear may show the presence of filamentous fungi, and culture is intermittently positive for *Aspergillus* spp.

C. Imaging. The chest x-ray will show typical findings of a fungus ball with an air crescent sign. Both CT and magnetic resonance imaging (MRI) of the chest reveal the fungus ball (see Figure 75–2).

D. Differential Diagnosis. In a patient with a history of prior lung disease, hemoptysis should lead to the suspicion of a fungus ball. Other fungi including *Pseudallescheria boydii* can cause a similar syndrome. Other causes of hemoptysis including tuberculosis, pulmonary embolism, lung cancer, and bronchiectasis need to be considered.

E. Complications. Death due to overwhelming hemoptysis is a rare complication of aspergilloma.

Diagnosis

The diagnosis is established by demonstrating the typical findings on imaging studies and the presence of *Aspergillus* organisms from sputum culture. The other common causes of hemoptysis need to be excluded with the appropriate investigations.

Treatment

Treatment for aspergilloma must be individualized

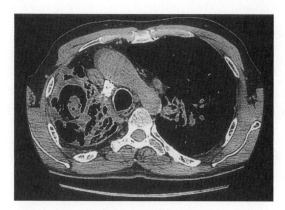

Figure 75–2. Nonenhanced high-resolution chest CT showing a large aspergilloma in a patient with bronchiectasis of the right lung.

(see Box 75–2). For patients with mild hemoptysis, observation alone is warranted. Patients with more significant hemoptysis may benefit from lobectomy, but preexisting lung disease may place the patient at increased risk for surgical complications. There is no role for systemic antifungal therapy. No consistent benefit has been derived from intracavitary installation of amphotericin B.

Prognosis

Most patients with mild stable hemoptysis do very well. In some patients, the fungus ball may gradually enlarge, and close observation of these patients is warranted.

3. DISSEMINATED ASPERGILLOSIS

Disseminated aspergillosis is a life-threatening, usually fatal form of aspergillosis that occurs in immunosuppressed patients. By definition, two or more noncontiguous sites are involved. Most patients with disseminated disease have invasive pulmonary aspergillosis as the primary site of infection. Common sites of dissemination include central nervous system, skin, liver, kidney, skin, and gastrointestinal tract.

Clinical Findings

A. Signs and Symptoms. Patients with disseminated aspergillosis are usually critically ill. There are no typical signs or symptoms of disseminated disease, and findings will depend on the sites of dissemination. Pulmonary symptoms may predominate if invasive pulmonary aspergillosis is present. Altered mental status, particularly when associated with focal neurological findings, is suggestive of central nervous system involvement. Renal and hepatic involvement may be completely asymptomatic. Invasion of the renal artery or vein may cause thrombosis

or infarction. Cutaneous involvement may appear as small erythematous papules and microabscesses or as large black necrotic lesions.

B. Laboratory Findings. Despite hematogenous route of dissemination, blood cultures are rarely positive. Urine cultures may be positive for *Aspergillus* cells when the kidney is involved. Elevated hepatic enzymes or serum creatinine may reflect involvement of the liver or kidney.

C. Imaging. CT imaging or MRI of the brain may show a single lesion or multiple mass lesions. CT imaging of the abdomen may reveal nodules in affected organs. Cavitation is common.

D. Complications. The complications of disseminated disease are related to the sites of specific organ involvement. For example, brain abscesses may be associated with mental status changes or seizure, splenic abscesses may be suspected if there is left upper quadrant pain, or complete heart block may be present if there is cardiac involvement. Multiorgan dysfunction often develops.

Diagnosis

The diagnosis can be suspected in severely immunosuppressed hosts with multiorgan dysfunction. Often the diagnosis is presumptive, but the diagnosis may be confirmed by biopsy of suspected sites of dissemination. Unfortunately, in ≤ 30% of cases of disseminated aspergillosis, the diagnosis is established at autopsy.

Treatment, Prevention, & Control

The treatment, prevention, and control of disseminated aspergillosis are identical to that of invasive pulmonary aspergillosis.

4. ALLERGIC BRONCHOPULMONARY ASPERGILLOSIS

Allergic bronchopulmonary aspergillosis is an eosinophilic pneumonia or hypersensitivity reaction, which generally occurs in adults with a prior history of allergic asthma. It is also seen in patients with cystic fibrosis.

Clinical Findings

A. Signs and Symptoms. The presenting symptoms are usually worsening asthma that is difficult to control and cough productive of thick brownish plugs of sputum. Low-grade fever may be present, and some patients may exhibit nonspecific constitutional symptoms such as malaise and fatigue.

B. Laboratory Findings. Peripheral eosinophilia is a hallmark of allergic bronchopulmonary aspergillosis and is usually > 1000 cells/mL. Other findings include elevated serum IgE levels, serum precipitans to *Aspergillus fumigatus,* and immediate wheal and flare response to *Aspergillus* skin testing.

Culture of the sputum reveals large numbers of *A fumigatus* colonies. Antibodies in both the IgG and the IgE class that are specific for *A fumigatus* are elevated.

C. Imaging. Pulmonary infiltrates are commonly seen on chest x-ray and usually involve the upper lobes. Transient recurrent infiltrates may also be seen. CT imaging of the chest is helpful in identifying the presence of central bronchiectasis that may develop in untreated patients.

D. Differential Diagnosis. Other common causes of eosinophilic pneumonia include parasitic infestation and drug-induced lung disease. Allergic bronchopulmonary aspergillosis must also be distinguished from a number of idiopathic eosinophilic pneumonias including Löffler's syndrome, chronic eosinophilic pneumonia, Churg-Strauss syndrome, and hypereosinophilic syndrome.

E. Complications. Undiagnosed disease may develop into a chronic state typically with involvement in the upper lobes of the lungs. Bronchiectasis, usually involving the central airways, and fibrosis may develop. Hemoptysis with chronic disease is common.

Diagnosis

The main criteria for establishing the diagnosis of allergic bronchopulmonary aspergillosis are a history of bronchial asthma, presence of peripheral eosinophilia, immediate reaction to *Aspergillus fumigatus* antigen, pulmonary infiltrates on chest x-ray, serum precipitants to *A fumigatus,* elevated serum IgE level, and central bronchiectasis on CT imaging of the chest (see Table 75–1). Supportive diagnostic criteria include a history of brownish sputum production, sputum culture positive for *A fumigatus,* and elevated antibodies specific for *A fumigatus* of the IgG and IgE class. Microscopic examination of sputum may reveal brown, lancet-shaped crystals originating from the Charcot-Leyden crystal proteins found in the cytoplasm of eosinophils.

Treatment

Treatment of allergic bronchopulmonary aspergillosis requires corticosteroids therapy (Box 75–2).

Table 75–1. Diagnostic criteria for allergic bronchopulmonary aspergillosis.

Key diagnostic criteria
1. Bronchial asthma
2. Peripheral eosinophilia
3. Immediate wheal and flare response to *Aspergillus fumigatus* antigen
4. Pulmonary infiltrates on chest x-ray
5. Serum precipitans to *A fumigatus*
6. Elevated serum IgE level
7. Central bronchiectasis

Specific supportive criteria
1. Brownish sputum production
2. Sputum cultures positive for *A fumigatus*
3. Elevated specific IgG and IgE

After initial control of symptoms, the corticosteroid therapy should be slowly tapered. Itraconazole has been used in some patients who have difficulty controlling allergic bronchopulmonary aspergillosis, but its role is still under investigation. Inhaled corticosteroid therapy does not appear to be effective.

Prognosis

Recurrent disease is common, and prolonged maintenance of low-dose corticosteroid therapy is required in many patients.

5. FARMER'S LUNG

Farmer's lung, also known as extrinsic allergic alveolitis or hypersensitivity pneumonitis, is an allergic inflammatory reaction induced by inhalation of *Aspergillus* spores, often in exposure to mold and hay. It usually occurs after inhalation during an overwhelming exposure to spores. A multitude of other antigenic stimuli can induce a similar syndrome. Other examples of hypersensitivity pneumonitis induced by *Aspergillus* include compost lung, tobacco worker's disease (from mold on tobacco leaves), and malt worker's lung (from moldy barley).

Clinical Findings

A. Signs and Symptoms. Symptoms include cough and shortness of breath, which generally develop 6–8 h after exposure. On occasion, fever and chills may be present. The presentation tends to be acute, but subacute and chronic forms of the disease may be present when there is chronic low-level exposure.

B. Laboratory Findings. Neutrophilia may be seen, but eosinophilia is typically not present. *Aspergillus* serum precipitans will be elevated in most cases, but their presence is not diagnostic. Skin testing with *Aspergillus* antigen may be positive but is not diagnostic and is most helpful for epidemiological purposes.

C. Imaging. Chest x-ray findings may be normal even in patients with significant symptoms. Conversely, the chest x-ray may show diffuse bilateral pulmonary infiltrates or discrete nodular infiltrates. With more chronic symptoms, pulmonary function testing may show a restrictive pattern.

D. Differential Diagnosis. Acute and subacute Farmer's lung will occasionally resemble an infectious pneumonitis. Farmer's lung must be distinguished from other conditions that cause respiratory symptoms and pulmonary infiltrates, including collagen vascular diseases, eosinophilic pneumonitis, and drug-induced lung disease. In its more chronic form, it may resemble idiopathic pulmonary fibrosis and other interstitial lung disorders.

E. Complications. Recovery from acute Farmer's lung is the most common outcome. Individuals with chronic exposure and ongoing allergic reaction may develop pulmonary fibrosis with a restrictive pattern seen on pulmonary function testing.

Diagnosis

The diagnosis should be suspected from the history of exposure and the symptom complex. Laboratory testing can help distinguish *Aspergillus*-induced Farmer's lung from other causes of Farmer's lung.

Treatment

The optimal treatment for Farmer's lung is removal or avoidance of exposure. In most individuals, the syndrome is self-limited; however, patients with prolonged subacute or chronic symptoms may require prednisone therapy (see Box 75–2).

Prognosis

In most individuals, symptoms are self-limited, especially when the source of exposure can be avoided or removed. In patients with more chronic symptoms, with exposure avoidance and short-course prednisone therapy, the prognosis is excellent.

Prevention & Control

The cornerstone of prevention of Farmer's lung involves identification and avoidance of exposure to *Aspergillus* spores. Since the majority of individuals will not develop a hypersensitivity reaction after exposure, prevention and control measures only need to be instituted after the initial diagnosis.

6. *ASPERGILLUS* SINUSITIS

Aspergillus spp. are capable of causing a variety of infections involving the paranasal sinuses (Table 75–2). Although uncommon, *Aspergillus* sinusitis is related to the immune status and immunologic response of the host.

A. Signs and Symptoms. In the severely immunosuppressed or neutropenic patient, *Aspergillus* sinusitis or rhinosinusitis may occur. Symptoms include headache, toothache, nasal congestion, purulent nasal discharge, and sinus or eye pain. Fever is commonly encountered. The nasal mucosa may exhibit hyperemia or necrosis that may extend into the mouth. Ptosis and loss of extraocular eye movement are prominent signs, indicating extensive invasion into the orbit. Sudden onset of blindness may occur.

In patients with normal immune status and a history of chronic sinusitis, a fungus ball or aspergilloma can form in the sinus. Persistent pain and discharge are common symptoms. An allergic fungal sinusitis may develop in patients with a history of allergic rhinitis and recurrent sinusitis. Facial pain and nasal discharge are predominant symptoms of this syndrome.

B. Laboratory Findings. Cultures of nasal secretions are usually positive for *Aspergillus* spp. in patients with invasive and noninvasive forms of sinus infection.

C. Imaging. High-resolution CT imaging of the sinuses is essential for assessing the extent of invasive disease. Destruction of bone is common in advanced cases with erosions into the orbit, the brain, or the roof of the mouth. No bony destruction occurs in noninvasive disease.

D. Differential Diagnosis. The differential diagnosis of fungal sinusitis varies according to the extent of invasion. Noninvasive sinusitis must be distinguished from neoplasia, inflammatory conditions, and bacterial causes. Other noninvasive fungal pathogens include *Fusarium* spp., *Curvularia* spp., *Bipolaris* spp., and *Pseudallescheria boydii*. Other fungal pathogens capable of causing invasive disease include the order Mucorales, *Fusarium* spp., and *P boydii*.

E. Complications. Untreated invasive fungal sinusitis can rapidly develop into the rhinocerebral form with direct invasion into the central nervous system. Angioinvasion may lead to widespread dissemination and death.

Diagnosis

Aspiration of sinus contents should be cultured and stained for fungal elements. Endoscopic examination of the nose should be considered. High-resolution CT imaging can detect invasion and extent of involvement.

Treatment

Treatment of invasive sinusitis in the immunosuppressed patient requires a combination of surgical débridement and antifungal therapy. Proper presurgical assessment of the extent of disease is vital to ensure that operative débridement and drainage are adequate.

Table 75–2. Clinical aspects of *Aspergillus* sinusitis.

	Noninvasive	Invasive
Host	Immunocompetent	Immunosuppressed and usually profoundly
Tempo of Infection	Chronic and indolent	Acute and progressive
Pathologic features	Fungus ball and chronic local infeciton	Bony destruction with invasion of adjacent structures
Clinical features	Pain, congestion, and discharge	Pain, congestion, and discharge
Fever	Rare	Usually present
Treatment	Excision and drainage	Wide surgical débridement and amphotericin B, 1.0 mg/kg/d

Antifungal therapy with amphotericin B is illustrated in Box 75–2. For noninvasive disease, including chronic sinusitis and sinus aspergilloma, surgical excision and drainage alone are adequate, and systemic antifungal therapy is usually not needed.

Prognosis

The prognosis of noninvasive fungal sinusitis is excellent after adequate débridement and drainage. For locally invasive disease, the prognosis is fair with débridement and antifungal therapy. The prognosis with extensive invasive disease is poor.

Prevention & Control

Prevention and control of invasive sinusitis is identical to that for invasive pulmonary aspergillosis.

7. OTHER FORMS OF *ASPERGILLUS* INFECTION

A variety of less commonly encountered infections may occur in both immunocompetent and immunosuppressed patients. Endophthalmitis may occur following surgery or trauma to the globe or as a rare manifestation of invasive disseminated aspergillosis. Osteomyelitis may occur in children with chronic granulomatous disease and in adults who are immunosuppressed. Disk space infection with adjacent vertebral osteomyelitis has been described in both normal hosts and in injection drug abusers. Endocarditis may occur in patients with a prosthetic valve or native valve endocarditis may occur in injection drug abusers. Otomycosis can occur in the setting of chronic external otitis.

In immunosuppressed patients, an invasive form of the disease with extensive bony destruction can occur. *Aspergillus* tracheobronchitis is seen most commonly in lung transplant recipients but can also occur in other immunosuppressed patients (Figure 75–3). Invasive aspergillosis may begin in the skin and disseminate to other sites. For example, focal infection may develop at intravenous catheter sites in neutropenic patients and cause progressive local infection before there is evidence of systemic dissemination.

PSEUDALLESCHERIA BOYDII INFECTION

Essentials of Diagnosis

- Filamentous fungus that is morphologically similar to *Aspergillus* spp.
- Most serious infections occur in immunosuppressed patients.
- Recovery from culture must be distinguished from colonization or contamination.

General Considerations

P boydii is a mold that is capable of causing infec-

Figure 75–3. Direct stain of a tracheal aspiration specimen in a patient with *Aspergillus* tracheobronchitis. Note the fruiting body of *Aspergillus fumigatus.* It is unusual to see this in direct patient specimens (× 800, KDH stain).

tion in immunosuppressed patients and less frequently in immunocompetent patients. Overall, infection with *P boydii* is rare.

A. Epidemiology. Although a relatively common environmental mold, *P boydii* is a rare cause of human disease. It can be easily recovered from soil, water, and manure. Both community and nosocomial acquisition have been documented. In most instances, its recovery from culture specimens will reflect colonization or contamination; however, it is capable of causing serious infection in selected patients. When recovered from clinical specimens, it cannot be dismissed as a nonpathogen without careful consideration of its pathogenic potential in the clinical setting from which it was recovered.

B. Microbiology. *P boydii* is a common environmental mold sometimes referred to as *Petrolidium boydii.* It is the sexual spore-producing form of *Scedosporium apiospermum.* In tissue, *P boydii* produces thin septate hyphae that are similar in appearance to *Aspergillus* hyphae. Hence it is not possible to distinguish *P boydii* infection from *Aspergillus* infection based on histopathology, and culture confirmation is necessary to establish the diagnoses and guide therapy.

C. Pathogenesis. The portal of entry of *P boydii* is inhalation for lung and sinus infection or by direct inoculation of the skin at the site of trauma. Little is known about specific host defense mechanisms that permit opportunistic infection. Abscess formation and tissue necrosis are the typical findings of infection.

Clinical Findings

Infection caused by *P boydii* is similar to that caused by *Aspergillus* spp. but considerably rarer. Among normal hosts, *P boydii* may cause fungus balls in the sinuses or in the lungs in patients with preexisting cavitary lung disease or chronic sinusitis. Penetrating trauma may result in soft tissue infection. It is the most common cause of maduromycosis in the United States. Infection involving the globe after penetrating trauma has been reported relatively frequently. A unique syndrome of *P boydii* in normal hosts is an overwhelming pneumonia after near drowning and aspiration of fresh or brackish water. Dissemination to the brain and other tissues has been reported in this setting.

Among immunosuppressed patients, infection occurs in those with prolonged and profound immunodeficiency. Susceptible hosts include those with severe neutropenia, those with prolonged high-dose corticosteroid therapy, children with chronic granulomatous disease, and patients with HIV infection. Clinically and histologically, *P boydii* opportunistic infection in the immunosuppressed patient resembles invasive aspergillosis. This includes the propensity for hematogenous dissemination. Pulmonary infection is the most commonly encountered site of infection, but soft tissue infection, central nervous system infection, and other sites may be seen.

Diagnosis

Diagnosis of infection with *P boydii* is based on the recovery from biopsy specimens taken from the site of infection. Its recovery from sputum in a susceptible host with an appropriate syndrome is presumptive evidence of infection. Blood cultures are rarely positive.

Treatment

The microbiologic differentiation of *P boydii* infection from that of aspergillosis is important because *P boydii* is resistant to amphotericin B. The preferred therapy in adults is intravenous miconazole (see Box 75–4). Miconazole is rarely used to treat other fungal infections because of its substantial toxicity, which includes nausea, vomiting, anemia, and a variety of central nervous system effects. Cardiac arrest while receiving miconazole therapy has been reported. Nevertheless, for life-threatening infections, miconazole remains the drug of choice. Preliminary data

BOX 75–4

Treatment of Pseudallescheriosis	
First Choice	Miconazole, 800 g IV every 8°; for children: 20–40 mg/k in 3 divided doses
Second Choice	Itraconazole, 400 mg PO once daily; for children; 5–6 mg/kg/d
Role of Surgery	In selected cases
Comments	Amphotericin B resistant

suggest that other azoles, such as itraconazole and ketoconazole, are effective. Their use should be reserved for indolent cases or in patients who are intolerant of miconazole. The duration of therapy is not well established and should be based on response to treatment and improvement of underlying predisposing factors.

MUCORMYCOSIS

Essentials of Diagnosis

- Filamentous fungus with hyphae of uneven, often very large diameter (5–50 µm).
- No or rare septation of the hyphal elements, which branch at irregular angles.
- No availability of antibody or antigen testing to assist diagnosis.
- Often abundant in biopsy or clinical specimens on fungal stain but no growth from fungal cultures.

General Considerations

Mucormycosis refers to a spectrum of infections caused by fungi of the phylogenetic order Mucorales. These infections are generally quite rare and usually occur in patients with either severe immunodeficiency, uncontrolled diabetes, or trauma.

A. Epidemiology. The agents of mucormycosis are ubiquitous in nature and commonly recovered from decaying organic manner. *Rhizopus* spp. are especially common on moldy bread. Nevertheless, in contrast to *Aspergillus* species, the agents of mucormycosis are rarely recovered in the hospital setting.

B. Microbiology. Although there are numerous fungi capable of causing mucormycosis, the four most common genera in order of frequency are *Rhizopus, Rhizomucor, Absidia,* and *Cunninghamella.* These fungi are relatively rapid growing and will grow on most media in the mycology laboratory in 2–5 days. They grow only as mold, and the hyphae tend to be uneven in diameter and often quite large, ranging in size from 5 to 50 µm (Figure 75–4). Branching occurs at irregular angles, in contrast to the 45° angles of branching by *Aspergillus* spp. Septation of the hyphae is usually absent. Environmental specimens often grow rapidly and abundantly, but it is common for no growth to occur from specimens obtained from infected tissue in patients with mucormycosis. The reason for this is unknown.

C. Pathogenesis. Although inhalation of spores produced by these fungi is probably a daily occurrence, infection rarely occurs, even among susceptible hosts. Therefore the presumed portal of entry is respiratory with deposition of spores on the nasal mucosa for rhinocerebral mucormycosis and in the alveoli for pulmonary mucormycosis. Gastrointestinal mucormycosis is thought to occur following ingestion of spores, and cutaneous mucormycosis is a consequence of direct inoculation of traumatized

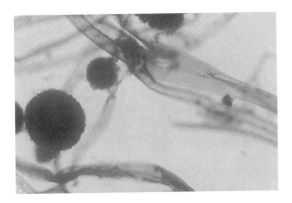

Figure 75–4. Culture specimen of *Mucor* sp., showing irregular hyphae without septation. The fruiting body of *Mucor* sp. is also present (× 800, lactophenol cotton blue mount).

skin. Alteration of macrophage and neutrophil function secondary to diabetic ketoacidosis and corticosteroids allows the initial sporulation and filamentous growth. Once tissue invasion is achieved in a susceptible host, the disease can progress at an alarming rate or be quite indolent. Angioinvasion by hyphal elements is common and results in ischemic and hemorrhagic necrosis.

CLINICAL SYNDROMES

1. RHINOCEREBRAL MUCORMYCOSIS

Rhinocerebral mucormycosis occurs most commonly in patients with uncontrolled diabetes, especially after an episode of diabetic ketoacidosis. It may also occur in leukemic patients who have had prolonged neutropenia and therapy with broad-spectrum antibiotics and occasionally in organ transplant recipients.

Clinical Findings
A. Signs and Symptoms. The earliest symptoms in rhinocerebral mucormycosis are facial pain, headache, and nasal stuffiness. As the disease progresses, orbital pain and facial anesthesia may be noted. Double vision or loss of vision may develop after invasion of the orbit by the rapidly spreading infection. Mental status changes herald the penetration into the brain with ensuing cavernous sinus thrombosis, carotid artery thrombosis, and cerebral abscess formation. Serial cranial nerve abnormalities, especially of nerves 5 and 7, can occur.

Physical findings include proptosis of the globe and loss of extraocular movement as orbital involvement progresses. Inspection of the nares may reveal black necrotic tissue indicative of angioinvasion and

necrosis. A black eschar on the hard palate is a hallmark of mucormycosis.

B. Laboratory Findings. There are no typical laboratory abnormalities associated with the condition except as noted above. The onset of symptoms may occur during the recovery phase of diabetic ketoacidosis. Most leukemic patients that develop this syndrome do so while still profoundly neutropenic. Cultures of nasal secretions or biopsy specimens are commonly negative even when hyphal elements are present.

C. Imaging. X-rays of the sinuses are generally insensitive but will demonstrate opacification of one or more sinuses. CT imaging or MRI is an essential part of the evaluation. Bony destruction can be found where disease has extended into the orbit, the mouth, or the central nervous system.

D. Differential Diagnosis. Few other conditions are able to produce the syndrome of rhinocerebral mucormycosis in the appropriate patient population. Invasive *Aspergillus* or *Fusarium* sinusitis may cause a similar syndrome, particularly in the neutropenic leukemic patient.

2. PULMONARY MUCORMYCOSIS

Pulmonary mucormycosis occurs most commonly in patients with prolonged neutropenia due to chemotherapy for the treatment of leukemia or malignancy. Most of the patients have had antecedent prolonged courses of broad-spectrum antibiotics. It occurs less commonly in diabetic patients and tends to be less fulminant in this setting.

A. Signs and Symptoms. The onset of symptoms may be subacute to acute to fulminant. Most patients are critically ill and toxic appearing. Respiratory localization is evident based on the common occurrence of cough and shortness of breath. Pleuritic pain and hemoptysis are common. Fever is usually present and may have an abrupt spiking onset. Physical findings may be absent or reflect focal pulmonary infection.

B. Laboratory Findings. Hypoxemia may be present depending on the extent of pulmonary involvement. Sputum cultures may grow an agent of mucormycosis or may be negative.

C. Imaging. Chest x-ray may reveal unifocal or multifocal infiltrates or nodules. As the disease progresses, cavitation is very common.

D. Differential Diagnosis. Mucormycosis may simulate other opportunistic fungal infections involving the lung such as invasive pulmonary aspergillosis. At the onset of symptoms, pulmonary mucormycosis can resemble pulmonary embolization caused by the presence of dyspnea, hemoptysis, and pleuritic chest pain.

E. Complications. Hematogenous dissemination of infection, particularly in the fulminant form of disease is common. Frequent sites of dissemination include the central nervous system, gastrointestinal tract, spleen, kidneys, heart, and liver. Fulminant disease is almost uniformly fatal, and patients rarely survive > 2 weeks.

3. OTHER FORMS OF MUCORMYCOSIS

Mucormycosis endocarditis is a rare infection that occurs in patients with prosthetic valves. Most of the symptoms are caused by embolization from the large valvular vegetations that form. Valve replacement surgery can be curative. Gastrointestinal mucormycosis develops in patients with profound malnutrition. Involvement of multiple sites in the gastrointestinal tract is seen. Abdominal pain and fever are the usual symptoms. Cutaneous mucormycosis can occur by direct inoculation of the skin in patients with burns, diabetes mellitus, or trauma (Figure 75–5). The skin may also be a sight of hematogenous dissemination. Hemodialysis patients receiving desferoxamine therapy for aluminum overload are at increased risk for any form of mucormycosis caused by *Rhizopus* spp.

Diagnosis

The diagnosis of mucormycosis usually requires demonstration of the organism in biopsy specimens (Figure 75–6). In the rhinocerebral form of mucormycosis, nasal specimens are usually satisfactory for establishing the diagnosis. The tendency to angioinvasion and tissue necrosis often produces a black eschar that should suggest a diagnosis from physical findings. Open lung biopsy may be necessary to establish the premortem diagnosis of pulmonary mucormycosis in the absence of sites of hematogenous dissemination that may be sampled. In general, the full-blown clinical syndrome in the appropriate host should suggest the diagnosis. It requires a high index of suspicion in the early stages of infection. Culture of infected material

Figure 75–6. Sinus biopsy specimen in a patient with rhinocerebral mucormycosis. Note the large, aseptate hyphae with irregular branching (× 400, methenamine silver stain).

may be negative, but staining of biopsy specimens can show abundant angioinvasive hyphal elements, suggesting the diagnosis.

Treatment

Once the diagnosis of mucormycosis has been established, the initial approach to therapy should be to correct aggressively any predisposing factors (see Box 75–5). In patients with diabetic ketoacidosis or hyperglycemia, metabolic abnormalities need to be corrected and controlled. Patients receiving immunosuppressive therapy, especially corticosteroids, should have this reduced as much as possible. Antifungal therapy should be instituted with amphotericin B. The duration of therapy should be based on clinical response. The available azoles do not appear to be effective against the agents of mucormycosis. The newer liposomal preparations of amphotericin B are attractive alternatives to standard amphotericin B because of their reduced nephrotoxicity, although they

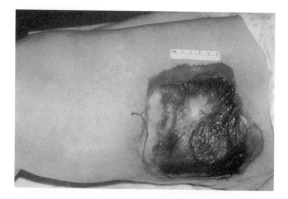

Figure 75–5. Large black necrotic ulceration on the thigh of a patient with poorly controlled diabetes mellitus. This fatal infection began as a papule and enlarged over 4 weeks.

BOX 75–5	
Treatment of Mucormycosis in Children and Adults	
First Choice	Amphotericin B, 1–1.5 mg/kg/d IV
Second Choice	Lipid formulation of amphotericin B
Role of Surgery	Débridement required for rhinocerebral form
Comments	Azoles appear to be ineffective

are no more effective than the standard preparation. Amphotericin B toxicity is high in patients with mucormycosis because of the high dose required and underlying patient conditions.

In the rhinocerebral form of mucormycosis, aggressive débridement of the involved sinuses, enucleation, and extensive orbital débridement may be necessary. Some patients will require serial débridements that can be quite disfiguring but may improve their chances for survival. Cutaneous mucormycosis should also be aggressively débrided.

Prognosis

Patients with pulmonary mucormycosis, gastrointestinal mucormycosis, or disseminated disease rarely survive. Rhinocerebral infection also has a poor prognosis but with early diagnosis and aggressive surgical and antifungal therapy, survivors have been reported.

Prevention & Control

Fortunately, mucormycosis is rare. There are no proven preventative or prophylactic strategies. Because it is a relatively ubiquitous spore-transmitted fungal infection, many of the strategies used to prevent transmission of *Aspergillus* spp. may be effective in reducing the transmission of the agents of mucormycosis. It is unknown whether antifungal prophylaxis has any impact on the incidence of mucormycosis.

REFERENCES

Andriole V: Infections with Aspergillus species. Clin Infect Dis 1993;17(Suppl 2):S481. (Authoritative overview of the diagnosis and management of aspergillosis.)

Bohme A, et al: Itraconazole for prophylaxis of systemic mycoses in neutropenic patients with haematological malignancies. J Antimicrob Chemother 1996;38(6):953. (Nonrandomized trial of itraconazole prophylaxis, showing no definite benefit in the reduction of *Aspergillus* infection.)

Denning D: Therapeutic outcome in invasive aspergillosis. Clin Infect Dis 1996;23(3):608. (Comprehensive literature review of the therapeutic response and mortality of invasive aspergillosis.)

Denning D: Treatment of invasive aspergillosis. J Infect 1994;28(Suppl 1):25. (Review of the therapeutic options available for the treatment of aspergillosis.)

DeShazo RD, Chapin K, Swain RE: Fungal sinusitis. N Engl J Med 1997;337(4):254. (State-of-the-art discussion of the spectrum of infection associated with fungal sinusitis.)

Walsh T, et al: Recent progress and current problems in management of invasive fungal infections in patients with neoplastic diseases. Curr Opin Oncol 1992; 4(4):647. (Summary of the progress and challenges in the management of invasive fungal infection in cancer patients.)

Walsh T, et al: Recent advances in the epidemiology, prevention and treatment of invasive fungal infections in neutropenic patients. J Med Vet Mycol 1994;32(Suppl 1):33. (Summary of recent advances in the understanding of the epidemiology of invasive fungal infections in neutropenic patients.)

Warnock D: Fungal complications of transplantation: diagnosis, treatment, and prevention. J Antimicrob Chemother 1995;36(Suppl B):73.

76

Sporothrix schenckii

Zelalem Temesgen, MD

Essentials of Diagnosis

- Cigar-shaped yeast.
- Dimorphic: mycelial in nature, yeast in tissue.
- Associated with activities that involve contact with soil, sphagnum moss, decaying wood, or vegetation.
- Gardeners, forestry workers, miners, animal health care providers most at risk.
- Raised skin lesions with proximal spread along lymphatic channels.
- Recovery of microorganism from culture.

General Considerations

A. Epidemiology. *Sporothrix schenckii,* the causative agent of sporotrichosis, is a ubiquitous fungus commonly found in the soil, on sphagnum moss, on decaying wood, and on a variety of other vegetation. It is found worldwide but prefers a temperate or tropical climate with high humidity. Most cases of sporotrichosis are sporadic, but large human epidemics have been reported. Sporotrichosis has been reported in a variety of animal species including dogs, cats, horses, cows, camels, dolphins, goats, mules, birds, pigs, rats, and armadillo. Most human cases are secondary to vocational exposure. Gardeners, forestry workers, miners, laboratory workers, veterinarians, animal health technicians, and veterinary students are considered most at risk. Cases of zoonotic transmission as well as person-to-person transmission have been reported.

B. Microbiology. *S schenckii* is a dimorphic fungus. It forms mycelia (hyphal form) in vitro in temperatures <37 °C. It converts to its characteristic cigar-shaped yeast form in vivo and in cultures incubated at 37 °C. Colonies appear rapidly within 3–5 days of incubation. Moist and white at first, they develop a brown to black pigmentation with prolonged incubation.

C. Pathogenesis. Most cases of sporotrichosis result from direct inoculation of the fungus into the skin. Less frequently, access occurs through inhalation of spores leading to development of primary pulmonary infection.

CLINICAL SYNDROMES

S schenckii causes three distinct clinical syndromes: cutaneous, extracutaneous, and disseminated sporotrichosis (Box 76–1).

CUTANEOUS SPOROTRICHOSIS

Cutaneous sporotrichosis, the most common form of sporotrichosis, can present in one of two ways. In lymphangitic cutaneous sporotrichosis, lesions appear at the site of direct inoculation of the fungus into the skin. These initial lesions are often raised, erythematous, and warm. The organisms replicate locally, then advance proximally through the lymphatic channels, leading to the development of secondary lesions along these lymphatic channels. In the fixed form of cutaneous sporotrichosis, the organisms replicate locally but do not spread through the lymphatic channels.

Differential diagnosis includes skin infection caused by other fungi, skin infection caused by tuberculosis and atypical mycobacteria, bacterial skin infection, and foreign body granuloma.

EXTRACUTANEOUS SPOROTRICHOSIS

The main extracutaneous sites affected by sporotrichosis are the joints, lungs, and central nervous system. Other less commonly affected sites include the genitourinary tract, ocular adnexa, sinuses, larynx, and vocal cords.

1. OSTEOARTICULAR SPOROTRICHOSIS

The joints commonly affected are the joints of the hand, elbow, ankle, and knee. Onset is insidious, presenting with pain and swelling of a single joint with minimal fever or systemic toxicity. Over time, a sinus

BOX 76–1

Syndromes in Sporothricosis

More Common	• Cutaneous sporothricosis: lymphangitic form and fixed form
Less Common	• Extracutaneous sporothricosis: osteoarticular, pulmonary, and central nervous system • Disseminated

tract may develop and, if left untreated, other joints may be involved. Differential diagnosis includes rheumatoid arthritis, gout, and tuberculosis. Joint aspirations and synovial biopsies, often multiple, are required to establish the diagnosis.

2. PULMONARY SPOROTRICHOSIS

Pulmonary sporotrichosis can occur either as a primary lung infection subsequent to direct inhalation of *S schenckii* spores or in the setting of disseminated disease. Onset is insidious and associated symptoms include productive cough, fever, weight loss, fatigue, and malaise. Cavitary or nodular lesions involving the upper lobes, bilateral in about one third of the cases, are noted on chest roentgenograms. Conditions

associated with pulmonary sporotrichosis include alcoholism, tuberculosis, chronic obstructive pulmonary disease, diabetes, sarcoidosis, steroid use, and malignancies.

3. CENTRAL NERVOUS SYSTEM SPOROTRICHOSIS

Central nervous system involvement is an uncommon complication of sporotrichosis and has been reported in the setting of alcoholism, AIDS, and Hodgkin's disease. It presents as a chronic meningitis process with headache as the most common feature. Fever and neurologic deficits are unusual. Lymphocytic pleocytosis, a low glucose, and an elevated protein value are noted on cerebrospinal fluid analysis. Repeated lumbar punctures and cultures of large volume of cerebrospinal fluid are usually required to make a diagnosis.

DISSEMINATED SPOROTRICHOSIS

Immunosuppressed individuals, especially those with the acquired immunodeficiency syndrome and those with hematological malignancies, may present with widespread cutaneous disease as well as involvement of multiple organs, including the lungs,

BOX 76–2

Treatment of Sporothricosis

	Cutaneous	Osteoarticular	Pulmonary	Central Nervous System	Disseminated
First Choice	• Itraconazole (100–200 mg once daily)	• Itraconzaole (200 mg twice daily)	• Itraconazole (200 mg twice daily)	• Amphotericin B (1–2 g) total	• Amphotericin B (1–2 g) total
Second Choice or Adjunct	• SSKI, 5–10 drops orally 3 times/d; advance gradually to 40–50 drops 3 times/d (for adults) • Terbinafine (250 mg twice daily) • Hyperthermia	• Amphotericin B (1–2 g) total[2]	• Amphotericin B (1–2 g) total • Surgical resection	• Itraconazole (200 mg twice daily)[3]	• Itraconazole (200 mg twice daily)

[1] The addition of 5-fluorocytosine may be necessary.
[2] Intra-articular amphotericin B is used occasionally. Total doses of amphotericin B are required at a minimum.
[3] No data are available on the use of itraconazole for central nervous system infections.

joints, and central nervous system. Blood cultures may occasionally be positive. Elevation of the erythrocyte sedimentation rate, anemia, and leukocytosis are noted on routine laboratory evaluation. Culture of skin lesions and joints is usually diagnostic.

Diagnosis

In patients with typical cutaneous syndrome of ascending lymphangitis, demonstration of the characteristic appearance of the microorganism on stains performed on tissue biopsy is highly suggestive of diagnosis. Definitive diagnosis requires recovery of microorganisms from culture. Multiple attempts to isolate the organisms may be necessary.

Several serologic testing procedures such as agglutination tests, ELISA, complement fixation, precipitation, and immunodiffusion tests have been developed to aid in the diagnosis of sporotrichosis. While these may prove to be useful, especially in the diagnosis of meningitis, methodologies have not been standardized, and they have not yet found wide clinical application.

Skin tests are useful only as an epidemiological tool.

Treatment

Several therapeutic modalities such as local treatment, systemic therapy, and surgery have been used for the treatment of sporotrichosis (Box 76–2).

A saturated solution of potassium iodide (SSKI) is an effective regimen for cutaneous disease. Its mechanism of action is not well understood. SSKI drops are taken orally, and the dose is progressively increased to a maximum tolerated dose. Treatment is continued until the resolution of the skin lesions.

More recently, itraconazole, a triazole antifungal agent, has become the drug of choice for treatment of lymphocutaneous sporotrichosis. As stated above, treatment should be continued until resolution of infection, which usually takes 3–6 months. Itraconazole has been shown to be effective therapy for cutaneous as well as visceral sporotrichosis, with the exception of meningitis.

Osteoarticular sporotrichosis requires treatment with itraconazole or amphotericin B, but relapses can occur. There have been reports of successful treatment of osteoarticular sporotrichosis with intra-articular instillation of amphotericin B. Patients with pulmonary sporotrichosis should be treated with either itraconazole or amphotericin B, depending on the severity of their infection. Surgical resection may be necessary. Patients with disseminated disease should be treated

---

BOX 76–3

Sporotrichosis: Prevention

Precautions	Avoid direct skin contact with and wear gloves and long sleeves when handling known sources of *schenckii*, eg decayed wood or vegetation.
Prophylaxis	AIDS patients with sporotrichosis who have completed initial therapy should receive life-long suppressive treatment with itraconazole.

---

with intravenous amphotericin B. Itraconazole may be an acceptable alternative if they are not acutely ill.

Terbinafine, an allylamine antifungal agent, has successfully been used to treat both the fixed and lymphatic forms of cutaneous sporotrichosis. Treatment of meningitis caused by *S schenckii* requires the use of intravenous amphotericin B. The addition of 5-fluorocytosine may be necessary. There are no data on the role of azoles in this setting.

Sporotrichosis in the setting of AIDS responds poorly to all therapeutic modalities. Amphotericin B is the drug of choice; itraconazole can be used in less severe cases. After induction therapy with amphotericin B, treatment needs to be continued with itraconazole, indefinitely, to prevent relapse.

Local heat therapy (ie, application of heat, for example, in the form of a warm pack) directly on the affected skin lesion, can be useful either as an adjunct therapy to other forms of therapy or as an alternative treatment in pregnant women, in whom the use of SSKI and azoles is contraindicated.

Prognosis

Prognosis is variable and difficult to generalize. Disseminated sporotrichosis, if untreated, causes death.

Prevention & Control

Avoiding direct skin contact with known sources of *S schenckii* (eg, sphagnum moss) and wearing protective gloves and long sleeves in occupational or recreational activities, such as handling of rose bushes, wires, decayed wood, and vegetation, may help prevent sporotrichosis (Box 76–3).

REFERENCES

Coles BF et al: A multistate outbreak of sporotrichosis associated with sphagnum moss. Am J Epidemiol 1992;136:475.

Heller HM, Fuhrer J: Disseminated sporotrichosis in patients with AIDS: case report and review of the literature. AIDS 1991;5:1243.

Kauffman CA: Old and new therapies for sporotrichosis. Clin Infect Dis 1995;21:981.

Reed KD et al: Zoonotic transmission of sporotrichosis: case report and review. Clin Infect Dis 1993;16:384.

Rex JH: *Sporothrix schenckii.* In Mandel GL, Bennett JE, Dolin R: *Principles and Practice of Infectious Diseases,* 4th ed. Churchill Livingstone, 1995.

Werner AH, Werner BE: Sporotrichosis in man and animal. Int J Dermatol 1994;33:692.

Winn RE: A contemporary view of sporotrichosis. Curr Top Med Mycol 1995;6:73.

Fusarium, Penicillium, Paracoccidioides, & Agents of Chromomycosis

Michael R. Keating, MD

FUSARIUM INFECTION

Essentials of Diagnosis
- Worldwide geographic distribution.
- Mold, septate hyphae 3–8 μm in diameter.
- A rare infection in severely immunocompromised patients.
- Blood cultures often but not always positive.
- No serologic tests available.
- Cutaneous involvement is common feature.

General Considerations
A. Epidemiology. *Fusarium* spp. is an emerging fungal pathogen. Although long recognized as a cause of local infection involving nails, traumatized skin, or the cornea (eg, in contact lens wearers), deep or disseminated infection was not described until the mid 1970s. Despite its worldwide distribution and its frequent recovery from soil and vegetative material, infection is quite rare. Only ~ 100 cases involving invasive disease in immunosuppressed patients have been described in the medical literature.

Most cases of serious disease occur in patients with hematologic malignancy and chemotherapy-induced neutropenia. Profound neutropenia and prolonged neutropenia increase the risk for infection. The respiratory tract is the most common portal of entry leading to infection, but other sites of acquisition include a disrupted skin barrier, the digestive tract, and a central venous catheter. *Fusarium* onychomycosis also appears to be a potential source of disseminated infection in at-risk patients.

B. Microbiology. *Fusarium* spp. are filamentous fungi that are soil saprophytes and plant pathogens. The hyphae range in size from 3 to 8 μm and are generally septate. Growth from clinical specimens usually occurs after 4–5 days of incubation in the laboratory (Figure 77–1). Dichotomous branching is common, and branches usually occur at an angle of 45°. Consequently, *Fusarium* spp. are indistinguishable from *Aspergillus* spp. (see Chapter 75) when seen in tissue. Although there are many different species, human disease appears to be limited to *F oxysporum, F solani, F moniliformie,* and *F proliferatum.* Like other filamentous fungi, the different *Fusarium* spp. may be identi-

fied by the distinguishing characteristics of their fruiting bodies and microconidia.

C. Pathogenesis. The clinical pathogenic pattern of infection caused by *Fusarium* spp. is very similar to that of *Aspergillus* infection. Although much rarer than invasive aspergillosis, the same pathogenic mechanisms that allow *A conidia* to invade tissue contribute to the development of *Fusarium* infection. Alteration in macrophage function by steroid therapy and neutropenia allow the *Fusarium* microconidia to replicate unimpaired in host tissue. Angioinvasion leads to early dissemination particularly to skin structures. The reason for the marked propensity to disseminate to skin is unknown. Colonization with *Fusarium* spp. without infection is common, particularly among burn patients.

Clinical Findings
A. Signs and Symptoms. Invasive fusariosis usually develops with the abrupt onset of high spiking fevers (Box 77–1). Although myalgias are a common feature, infection of muscle is uncommon but has been reported. Focal symptoms may depend on the site of infection. Shortness of breath, cough, and hemoptysis are present in patients with pulmonary involvement. Central venous catheter infection may be associated with tunnel tract tenderness or exudation.

Physical findings are also dependent on the extent of invasive disease and sites of dissemination. Almost 80% of patients will have cutaneous involvement. Typically, this will begin as a erythematous indurated maculopapular lesion, which will enlarge and eventually ulcerate, leaving a nodular lesion with a necrotic, often black center (Figure 77–2). Multiple lesions are commonly seen and may resemble ecthyma gangrenosum. Localization to the extremities is most common. Primary cutaneous fusariosis may present with a single necrotic skin lesion. Multiple skin lesions suggest disseminated disease. A rhinocerebral form of infection has been described that is indistinguishable from rhinocerebral mucormycosis or aspergillosis.

B. Laboratory Findings. Neutropenia is usually present at the onset of the signs and symptoms of infection, but there are no other commonly associated hematologic or chemistry abnormalities. Blood cul-

Figure 77–1. Laboratory specimen of *Fusarium* spp. showing characteristic hyphae elements and typical spindle-shaped fruiting bodies (× 800).

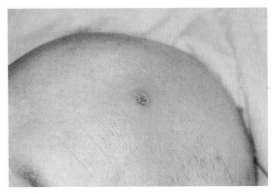

Figure 77–2. Photograph of a typical cutaneous lesion of *Fusarium* infection on the scalp of a neutropenic patient after allogeneic bone marrow transplantation.

tures are positive in 60% of patients with invasive fusariosis, which is in marked distinction to invasive aspergillosis, where blood cultures are negative. The reason for this difference is unknown. There are no serological tests available for diagnosing *Fusarium* infection.

C. Imaging. The chest roentgenogram in a patient with pulmonary involvement may show nonspecific infiltrates, nodular lesions, or cavitary lesions. With rhinocerebral infection, opacification of one or all the sinus cavities and destruction of bony structures can best be imaged with computed tomography. A bone scan may be helpful to determine if there is bone involvement underlying extensive cutaneous involvement.

D. Differential Diagnosis. In addition to invasive fusariosis, the differential diagnosis of persistent neutropenic fever includes invasive aspergillosis and other infection with opportunistic filamentous fungi. Although *Candida*, *Aspergillus*, and *Rhizopus* spp. are all capable of causing similar skin lesions in disseminated invasive disease, *Fusarium* spp. are the most likely of these organisms to do this. Histologically and clinically, fusariosis resembles invasive as-

pergillosis and infection due to *Pseudoallescheria boydii* (see Chapter 75).

E. Complications. Widespread or metastatic cutaneous involvement can develop from a single primary focus of infection. Disseminated disease may involve the heart, liver, kidneys, spleen, brain, and other vital organs.

Diagnosis

The diagnosis is confirmed by the recovery of *Fusarium* isolates from blood or biopsy specimens. Skin lesions developing in the setting of new fever in a neutropenic patient should be biopsied for histopathology and culture. The recovery of *Fusarium* spp. from sputum can suggest the diagnosis in the appropriate host with a syndrome compatible with invasive fusariosis; however, colonization of the respiratory tract can occur with this organism.

Treatment

Amphotericin B is the treatment of choice (Box 77–2). Response to therapy is usually poor, and in vitro susceptibility testing suggests that more than half of the strains tested are resistant to amphotericin B. It is unknown if the lipid preparations of amphotericin B offer any therapeutic advantage, but patients have been successfully treated with lipid preparations of amphotericin B. The use of granulocyte colony stimulating factors and granulocyte transfusions has been reported to be effective in some patients. *Fusarium* spp. are uniformly resistant to 5-flucytosine. The role of treatment with azoles is unknown. The most important factor contributing to successful treatment is recovery of neutropenia.

Prognosis

Invasive fusariosis is a lethal disease. The overall mortality rate according to the medical literature is > 70%.

BOX 77–1	
Fusariosis in Adults and Children	
More Common	• High fever, acute onset • Myalgias • Shortness of breath, hemoptysis, cough • Cutaneous involvement • Positive blood culture
Less Common	• Rhinocerebral infection • Central nervous system involvement • Intra-abdominal organ involvement

BOX 77-2

Treatment of Fusariosis in Adults and Children

First Choice	Amphotericin B, 1–1.5 mg/kg/d until neutropenia resolved and full response
Second Choice	Lipid preparation of amphotericin B (dose dependent on specific preparation)
Comment	• Treatment with granulocyte colony stimulating factor and granulocyte transfusion should be considered • Many strains are amphotericin B resistant • Recovery of neutropenia is critical

Prevention & Control

Because the skin and nails are potential portals of entry, before chemotherapy-induced neutropenia, patients with significant onychomycosis should be evaluated by a dermatologist for *Fusarium* infection (Box 77–3). Futhermore, high-risk neutropenic patients with skin trauma and contamination should be carefully examined for potential inoculation with *Fusarium* spp. This may need to include biopsy and culture.

PENICILLIUM INFECTIONS

Essentials of Diagnosis

- *Penicillium marneffei* infection found in both immunocompetent and immunosuppressed patients.
- *P marneffei* found in Southeast Asia and southern China.
- Mold, septate hyphae 1.5–5 μm in diameter.
- May be cultured from a variety of specimens including blood.
- *Penicillium* spp. other than *P marneffei* occur worldwide.

BOX 77-3

Control of Fusariosis

Prophylactic Measures	• Evaluate patients with significant onychomycosis for fusarium infection prior to chemotherapy • High-risk patients with skin trauma and contamination should be examined for inoculation with Fusarium spp.
Isolation Precautions	None

- Infection with *Penicillium* spp. is rare; occurs in immunosuppressed patients.

General Considerations

A. Epidemiology. *Penicillium* spp. are ubiquitous in nature and may be recovered with ease from a variety of sources within the hospital environment. These molds commonly contaminate clinical specimens and cause contamination in the laboratory. Colonization of nonsterile anatomical sites in humans is common. In most cases where *Penicillium* spp. are recovered from clinical specimens, they represent colonization. Nevertheless, colonization must be distinguished from the possibility of invasive disease.

Unique among the *Penicillium* spp., *P marneffei* is an endemic mycosis that is found in Southeast Asia and southern China. Most of the cases in the world literature have been reported from these areas; however, an increasing number of cases have been reported among individuals, particularly those with AIDS, who have traveled to or resided in the endemic parts of Southeast Asia and southern China. In Thailand, penicilliosis is the third most common opportunistic infection in patients with AIDS. Little is known about the environmental reservoir of *P marneffei*. Infection is acquired via inhalation, inoculation of the skin, and possibly ingestion. Person-to-person transmission does not occur. There is a marked predominance of male cases (~ 90%).

B. Microbiology. *Penicillium* spp. are among the most common filamentous fungi found in nature. These blue-green molds grow rapidly in the mycology laboratory and produce fine septate hyphae with 1.5–5 μm wide elements. In tissue specimens, the mycelial elements are somewhat larger at 15–20 μm in width and exhibit branching at ~ 45° angles. One of the *Penicillium* spp., *P marneffei*, is unique because of its dimorphic characteristic. In tissue specimens, it grows as a small yeast cell that resembles *Histoplasma capsulatum*. In the laboratory, *P marneffei* will grow as a mold with hyphal characteristics similar to the other *Penicillium* spp. The species may be distinguished by their characteristic conidia forms. Except for *P marneffei*, the *Penicillium* spp. are rarely speciated by mycology laboratories.

C. Pathogenesis. Infection caused by *Penicillium* spp. other than *P marneffei* occurs almost exclusively among profoundly immunosuppressed patients and is exceedingly rare. *Penicillium* spp. lack the necessary virulence factors to commonly cause human infection, and only in the setting of extreme immunodeficient states can invasive infection occur.

In contrast, *P marneffei* is capable of causing infection in both immunocompetent and immunocompromised patients. In immunocompetent patients, *P marneffei* infection may resemble histoplasmosis with a granulomatous reaction involving the reticuloendothelial system. The organism is capable of surviving within macrophages. On occasion, a more suppurative reaction can occur in immunocompetent patients, resulting in abscess formation in various organs, especially the lung, skin, liver, and subcutaneous tissues. *P marneffei* infection in immunosuppressed patients can be granulomatous or necrotizing and is likely to disseminate.

Clinical Findings

A. Signs and Symptoms. Infections caused by *Penicillium* spp. other than *P marneffei* are very rare, and recovery of *Penicillium* spp. from clinical specimens will almost always represent colonization; however, in the severely immunocompromised host, repeated recovery may represent opportunistic infection. Isolated case reports of invasive penicilliosis, including prosthetic valve endocarditis, peritonitis, endophthalmitis, and infections at other sites, have been reported in the literature.

The most common presentation of *P marneffei* infection is chronic illness with fever and weight loss (Box 77–4). A nonproductive cough is frequently present. Other specific symptoms may be present depending on the extent of infection. Because skin involvement occurs in nearly two-thirds of patients, skin lesions are usually present and are most commonly found on the face, upper trunk, and arms. They are papular in appearance and resemble molluscum contagiosum. Generalized lymphadenopathy is also often present. Hepatosplenomegaly may be detected on abdominal examination and is more common in children.

B. Laboratory Findings. Anemia is the most common laboratory abnormality present and is found in approximately three-quarters of patients. Blood cultures are positive in over half of patients. There are currently no serological tests to diagnose *P marneffei* infection.

C. Imaging. In patients with pulmonary involvement, the chest x-ray may show multiple infiltrates,

abscesses, and cavitation. Hilar involvement may be present, but there is usually no hilar calcification.

D. Differential Diagnosis. *P marneffei* may closely resemble tuberculosis, particularly in patients with HIV infection. The disease also closely resembles histoplasmosis and cryptococcosis as it occurs in HIV-infected patients.

Diagnosis

The diagnosis of invasive disease by *Penicillium* spp. other than *P marneffei* must be based on histologic evidence of tissue invasion and recovery of the organism from tissue culture. In addition, recovery from a sterile body fluid such as blood or synovial fluid is suggestive of infection but must be interpreted with caution in view of the frequency with which *Penicillium* spp. contaminate laboratory specimens.

Infection with *P marneffei* occurs only in people who have lived or traveled in the endemic areas of Southeast Asia and southern China. An exposure history is critical in considering the diagnosis. Blood cultures will establish the diagnosis, but other specimens including bone marrow, skin, abscess fluid, lymph nodes, sputum, and others may yield the organism. *P marneffei* must be distinguished from *Histoplasma capsulatum*, which it closely resembles in the laboratory.

Treatment

The drug of choice for treatment of *P marneffei* infection is amphotericin B, although in vitro resistance has been described (Box 77–5). The addition of 5-flucytocine appears to enhance the efficacy of am-

---

BOX 77–4

Penicillium marneffei Infection in Adults and Children

More Common	• Chronic illness • Fever • Weight loss • Cutaneous involvement • Generalized lymphadenopathy • Anemia • Positive blood culture
Less Common	• Diarrhea • Pericarditis • Bone and joint involvement • Central nervous system involvement

---

BOX 77–5

Treatment of *Penicillium marneffei* Infection in Adults and Children

First Choice	• Amphotericin B, 0.5–1.0 mg/kg/d for 2 wk, followed by 6 wk of itraconazole, 200 mg daily in adults or 3–5 mg/kg daily in children
Second Choice	• Itraconazole, 200 mg daily in adults or 3–5 mg/kg daily in children for 2 months
Comment	• 5-flucytosine, 100–150 mg/kg in 4 divided doses daily, may be given in addition to amphotericin • More severe cases may need a more prolonged course of amphotericin ± 5-flucytosine • Chronic maintenance therapy is indicated in patients with AIDS

photericin B therapy especially in more severe cases. Itraconazole also appears to be highly active against the organism; however, it should be reserved for indolent cases or for use following an initial response to amphotericin B. A standard course of therapy is 2 weeks of amphotericin followed by 6 weeks of itraconazole. Relapse rarely occurs in immunocompetent patients but is common among AIDS patients. Chronic maintenance therapy with itraconazole is indicated in patients with AIDS.

Prognosis

With early diagnosis and initiation of appropriate fungal therapy, the prognosis is very good; however, among patients in whom the diagnosis is delayed, the mortality rate is high.

Prevention & Control

Because very little is known about the environmental niche of *P marneffei*, there are no recommendations or guidelines for prevention and control of this infection.

PARACOCCIDIOIDOMYCOSIS

Essentials of Diagnosis

• Patients usually immunocompetent.
• Patients in endemic areas with chronic pulmonary and mucotaneous lesions involving the mouth, nose, larynx, and face; regional or diffuse lymphadenopathy.
• Found in Latin America, from Mexico to Argentina.
• Dimorphic fungus: yeast form in tissue specimens and at 37 °C; mold form when grown at room temperature in the laboratory.
• Thick-walled yeast, 4–40 μm, with multiple buds when seen in tissue specimens.
• Complement fixation or immunodiffusion.

General Considerations

Paracoccidioidomycosis is caused by *Paracoccidioides brasiliensis*. Also known as South American blastomycosis, it is the most prevalent systemic mycosis found in Central and South America and is the most common endemic mycosis in this area.

A. Epidemiology. Paracoccidioidomycosis is acquired only in Central and South America and ranges from Mexico to Argentina. Most cases occur in Brazil, and fewer cases are seen in Colombia, Venezuela, Ecuador, and Argentina. In other Latin American countries, it is considered rare. It has never been reported in Belize, Nicaragua, Suriname, French Guiana, Guyana, Chile, or any of the Caribbean islands. Cases reported in nonendemic areas such as North America and Europe have occurred in patients who have traveled to or lived in the endemic areas. Within the geographic range for *P brasiliensis*, there

is considerable variability in endemicity. It is commonly found in tropical or subtropical forests, where there are mild temperatures with little seasonal variation and very high humidity. The precise ecological niche in the environment has not been established. Soil has been postulated to be the reservoir.

Nearly 95% of the cases of paracoccidioidomycosis occur in males. It is also unusual in adolescents and children. There is evidence that estrogen has an inhibitory effect on conidia of *P brasiliensis*, and this may explain the difference in incidence among the sexes. Inoculation of the skin was once thought to be the portal of entry; however, the evidence now suggests respiratory acquisition. There is no evidence of person-to-person transmission.

B. Microbiology. *P brasiliensis* is a dimorphic fungus. In clinical specimens, it appears as a thick-walled yeast that ranges in size from 4 to 40 μm. Multiply budding yeast cells (the so-called "pilot wheel" or "mariner's wheel" cells) may be seen from tissue specimens and are a characteristic feature (Figure 77–3). In the laboratory, when this yeast is grown on enriched media at 37°C, colonies will appear in 5–10 days. In contrast, when grown at room temperatures (19°–28°C), the mycelial form or mold will grow in 20–30 days. The thin septate hyphae can develop a variety of conidia, but induction of conidial growth can be difficult and unequivocal identification of *P brasiliensis* requires documentation of dimorphic growth in the laboratory.

C. Pathogenesis. After the conidia of *P brasiliensis* are inhaled, fungal growth begins within the alveoli and small airways of the lungs. The yeast stimulates a vigorous neutrophilic and then macrocytic response. Spread to regional lymph nodes usually occurs early in infection. At the same time, more widespread dissemination may occur, particularly to the reticuloendothelial system. Depending on the host response, the infection may be controlled, may become clinically

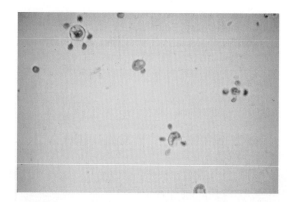

Figure 77–3. Laboratory specimen demonstrating the multiply budding yeast cells characteristic of *P brasiliensis*. The same morphology may also be seen in tissue specimens (× 400).

apparent, or may become dormant. The inflammatory response seen is a mix of granulomatous, suppurative, and necrotizing. Host response and the status of the immune system are critical determinants in the expression of disease. Both humoral and cellular immune responses are required to control the infection. Although serious infection has been reported with increasing frequency in recent years in patients with AIDS or other forms of severe immunosuppression, it is not a common opportunistic infection in these patients despite its endemic nature. The widespread use of prophylactic trimethoprim-sulfamethoxazole in AIDS and transplant patients may explain the relatively infrequent occurrence in these patients.

Clinical Findings

A. Signs and Symptoms. The manifestations of infection with *P brasiliensis* range from asymptomatic or subacute to chronic and focal to disseminated. Although all patients are presumed to have a pulmonary portal of entry, and 80% will have evidence of pulmonary infection, not all will have symptoms that suggest respiratory disease. The majority of patients present with symptoms involving mucosal surfaces of the mouth, nose, or larynx; a variety of cutaneous lesions; or general or localized lymphadenopathy. Symptoms will vary by the extent of involvement, and sites may include the liver, spleen, central nervous system, gastrointestinal tract, and bones. Of note, like *H capsulatum, P brasiliensis* has a particular propensity to involve the adrenal glands. Most patients with any evidence of disseminated disease will have some degree of adrenal involvement; however, overt Addison's disease is very uncommon.

Patients with respiratory symptoms will present with cough, purulent sputum production, and dyspnea (Box 77–6). Fever may or may not be present. Many patients will have nonspecific constitutional symptoms such as weight loss, weakness, and malaise. Mucocutaneous involvement is characterized by ulcerations in the mouth, cheilosis, and dysphagia.

On physical examination, the pulmonary findings are often less prominent than would be expected based on the radiographic findings. Examination of the mouth may reveal polymorphic ulcerations. The lips may be indurated and painful. Lymphadenopathy is often present, and spontaneous drainage commonly occurs. A variety of cutaneous lesions may be seen including abscesses, nodules, papules, ulcers, and verrucous lesions. It is very common for pulmonary, mucocutaneous, and lymph node involvement to co-exist in the same patient.

B. Laboratory Findings. Direct examination of sputum or lymph node drainage with a potassium hydroxide smear may reveal the yeast forms. Culture of sputum or drainage will also be positive. Blood cultures may be positive in disseminated disease, particularly among children and young adults. Serologic tests will be positive in most patients with infection.

C. Imaging. The chest x-ray will generally show diffuse bilateral interstitial and alveolar infiltrates. Less frequently encountered findings include multiple nodules, cavitation, and hilar lymphadenopathy. Calcification occasionally occurs but not as frequently as in histoplasmosis or tuberculosis.

D. Differential Diagnosis. Tuberculosis may coexist with paracoccidioidomycosis in as many as one-quarter of the cases, and care must be taken to distinguish two diseases that can resemble each other. The differential diagnosis also includes histoplasmosis, blastomycosis, lymphoma, leishmaniasis, leprosy, and malignancies.

E. Complications. Chronic untreated pulmonary disease may lead to fibrosis, pulmonary hypertension, and cor pulmonale. Chronic symptomatic adrenal insufficiency is a rare complication of disseminated disease, but adrenal function may recover after long-term antifungal therapy.

Diagnosis

The diagnosis of paracoccidioidomycosis can be suspected when an appropriate clinical syndrome occurs in a patient who has lived or traveled in Latin America. Given the syndrome's strong propensity to become dormant and remain so for years, even a remote history of exposure in the endemic area can be considered significant. The presence of multiply budding yeast cells on direct examination of sputum or pus is presumptive evidence of paracoccidioidomycosis. These cells may also be seen on histologic examination of a lymph node or other tissue. Definitive diagnosis requires culture from sputum, pus, blood, or a biopsy specimen. Serologic tests will be positive in 95% of cases by the immunodiffusion test and 80–95% by complement fixation. The skin test for paracoccidioides is of no help diagnostically and is suitable only for epidemiological investigation.

BOX 77–6	
Paracoccidioidomycosis in Adults and Children	
More Common	• Chronic illness • Fever • Mucocutaneous involvement (mouth, nose, larynx) • Cutaneous involvement • Lymphadenopathy • Pulmonary involvement
Less Common	• Hepatosplenic disease • CNS involvement • Bone and joint involvement • Arteritis

Treatment

The azoles are now considered the treatment of choice for paracoccidioidomycosis (Box 77–7). In clinical trials, 95% of patients responded to a standard ketoconazole regimen, and 8% of patients relapsed. Itraconazole may be superior to ketoconazole, but there is less experience with this agent. A similar response rate has been observed but with a lower relapse rate. Similar findings have been noted with fluconazole.

Paracoccidioidomycosis can also be treated with sulfonamides. Although the response rate is excellent, there is a relapse rate of ~ 15%. Therapy with sulfadiazine can be instituted and continued for 4 weeks until a clear clinical response is detected. The maintenance dose is continued for 3–5 years. Amphotericin B can be used in life-threatening infections or in patients who are intolerant of or have failed sulfonamide therapy. Azole therapy should follow amphotericin therapy for several months. Trimethoprim-sulfamethoxazole can be substituted for sulfadiazine in both the initial and maintenance phases of therapy and should be given lifelong in AIDS patients with a history of paracoccidioidomycosis.

Prognosis

The prognosis for paracoccidioidomycosis is excellent when the diagnosis is established early in the course of the disease and therapy is promptly instituted. In patients with advanced disease and a wasting syndrome characterized by weight loss, fatigue, and malnutrition, the prognosis is less favorable but is enhanced by aggressive supportive care, including nutritional repletion, correction of anemia, and bed rest.

Prevention & Control

Prophylactic trimethoprim-sulfamethoxazole will prevent primary or relapse paracoccidioidomycosis (Box 77–8)

CHROMOMYCOSIS

Essentials of Diagnosis

- Patients are usually immunocompetent.
- Found worldwide but usually in tropical or subtropical areas.
- Mold in culture; forms sclerotic body or muriform cell in tissue.
- Infection results from direct inoculation from contaminated soil or vegetative substances.
- Chronic indolent cutaneous verrucous lesions, most often on the feet.

General Considerations

Chromomycosis, also known as chromoblastomycosis, is a chronic subcutaneous infection caused by several different fungi. Although rarely seen in the United States, it is common worldwide.

A. Epidemiology. Chromomycosis occurs worldwide but is most frequently encountered in tropical and subtropical regions. The most common occurrence is in barefoot individuals, particularly among agricultural workers. The organisms causing chromomycosis are found commonly in soil, rotting wood, and decaying vegetation. Infection follows only after traumatic exposure to soil or other material, and person-to-person transmission does not occur.

B. Microbiology. A variety of different agents is capable of producing the clinical syndrome chromomycosis. The most common is *Fonsecaea pedrosoi*. Others that may be encountered include *Fonsecaea compactum*, *Cladosporium carrionii*, *Phialophora verrucosa*, *Botryomyces caespitosus*,

---

BOX 77–7

Treatment of Paracoccidioidomycosis in Adults and Children

First Choice	• Ketoconazole, 400 mg/d for adults or 5–10 mg/kg daily for children, for 6–18 months or itraconazole, 100 mg/d for adults or 3–5 mg/kg daily in children, for 6 months
Second Choice	• Amphotericin B, 0.5–1.0 mg/kg/d, total cumulative dose of 1–3 g in adults or 25–30 mg/kg in children • Sulfadiazine, 2–6 g/d in adults or 120–150 mg/kg in children, for 4 wk followed by 500 mg/d in adults or 25–50 mg/kg/d in children, for 3–5 y
Comment	• If amphotericin B is used as initial therapy, itraconazole or sulfadiazine should be given as maintenance therapy, as above • Trimethoprim-sulfamethoxazole may be substituted for sulfadiazine and should be given as lifelong maintenance therapy in patients with AIDS • Fluconazole may be as effective as itraconazole

---

BOX 77–8

Control of Paracoccidioidomycosis

Prophylactic Measures	Trimethoprim-sulfamethoxazole
Isolation Precautions	None

Rhinocladiella aquaspersa, Exophiala spinifera, and *E jeanselmei.* These fungi share a number of characteristics. Most are exceedingly slow growing and require 4–6 weeks in the mycology laboratory before growth may be encountered on culture plates. The colonies tend to be dark green to brown or black in color, and the hyphae are septate. Speciation can be difficult and requires an experienced mycologist.

C. Pathogenesis. After an incubation period of several weeks following traumatic subcutaneous inoculation, clinical infection begins. Histologically, there is a pyogranulomatous reaction and significant pseudoepithelial hyperplasia yielding the characteristic verrucoid appearance. Sclerotic bodies, also known as muriform cells, are the characteristic histologic finding. These are actually brown, round, fungal elements that are thick-walled and septated. Their presence on histologic examination is pathonomonic. Occasionally, there may be associated branched septated hyphae adjacent to the muriform cells.

Figure 77–4. Annular crusted-type chromomycosis involving the hand of a patient.

Clinical Findings

A. Signs and Symptoms. Chromomycosis is a chronic skin and soft tissue infection that may develop over months, years, or decades (Box 77–9). Frequently, patients seek medical attention for cosmetic reasons after years of infection. The feet are the most common location after inoculation from being barefoot. The hands, arms, and legs may also be involved. Typically, a lesion will start as a papule and slowly enlarge to develop into a nodule or plaque (Figure 77–4).

Different morphologic forms of infection have been described. The verrucous form has a bulky, wartlike appearance and can be very disfiguring. It is often described as cauliflowerlike in appearance. Ulceration, crusting, and bacterial superinfection are common. The annular form tends to be more flattened with a slowly advancing edge of infection with central healing and scarring. This form is more likely to lead to lymphedema, which in its extreme manifestation may resemble elephantiasis. Infection remains localized with satellite lesions and only rarely disseminates.

B. Laboratory Findings. Blood chemistries

and cell counts are usually normal in patients with chromomycosis.

C. Imaging. Plain film roentgenograms of affected sites will show only soft tissue changes. Bony involvement is rarely seen.

D. Differential Diagnosis. A wide variety of infections can cause a syndrome similar to that of chromomycosis. Blastomycosis, sporotrichosis, and mycetoma are other fungal infections that may present as chronic skin and subcutaneous infection. Yaws, tertiary syphilis, leishmaniasis, tuberculosis, and infection with atypical mycobacterium are other possibilities. Carcinoma, on rare occasion, may resemble chromomycosis.

Diagnosis

The diagnosis of chromomycosis requires scraping or biopsy. The presence of the characteristic sclerotic body is diagnostic. These are easily seen with a KOH stain, particularly when collected from verrucous form of infection. Annular infections tend to have a lower number of organisms and may require biopsy. Scrapings and biopsy specimens submitted to culture should be held in the mycology laboratory for ≥ 4–6 weeks to allow sufficient time for growth to occur. There are no serological tests to assist in the diagnosis of mucormycosis.

Treatment

Treatment of chromomycosis is difficult, and failure to achieve a cure is common (Box 77–10). Early, localized infection can be treated with wide surgical excision. Cryotherapy with liquid nitrogen has also been successful in eradicating early infection.

More established infection will require antifungal therapy; 5-flucytosine has been extensively used.

BOX 77–9		
Chromomycosis in Adults and Children		
More Common	• Chronic infection • Foot involvement • Cauliflowerlike appearance	
Less Common	• Hand, arm, leg involvement • Marked lymphedema • Dissemination (very rare)	

BOX 77-10

Treatment of Chromomycosis in Adults and Children

First Choice	• Wide surgical excision or cryotherapy with liquid nitrogen
Second Choice	• Itraconazole, 100 mg/d x 18 mo; for children, 5–6 mg/kg/d • 5-Flucytosine, 100–150 mg in 4 divided doses/d x ≥ 18 mo; for children, 50–150 mg/kg/d
Comment	• Terbinafine may be an option; more data needed • Results with fluconazole have been disappointing but 400 mg/d is an option; for children, 3–6 mg/kg/d • Failure to respond to antifungal therapy is often seen

BOX 77-11

Control of Chromomycosis

Prophylactic Measures	• Foot infection can be prevented by wearing shoes. • At-risk individuals (eg, agricultural workers) should minimize trauma to hands and extremities.
Isolation Precautions	None

Many cases will have partial response, but relapse is common, and resistance develops frequently. Retreatment with 5-flucytosine is usually unsuccessful because resistance develops. The role of the azoles in the treatment of chromomycosis continues to evolve. Ketoconazole is ineffective. Both itraconazole and fluconazole have been used with some success. The optimal duration of therapy has not been established, and failures and relapses are common. Amphotericin B has been tried in resistant cases but is generally not recommended. Terbinafine has been used in a very small number of patients with promising results. More experience with this agent is needed before it can be recommended. The optimal therapeutic approach to chromomycosis remains to be determined.

Prognosis

Untreated chromomycosis leads to a disfiguring, slowly enlarging lesion. Elephantiasis can develop as a result of the disruption and obstruction of lymphatics.

Prevention & Control

Chromomycosis of the feet can be prevented by wearing shoes (Box 77–11). Agricultural workers and other at-risk individuals should attempt to limit trauma to their hands and extremities. Because the organisms causing this infection are ubiquitous in soil and vegetative material, control efforts directed at reducing or eradicating the organisms are impractical.

REFERENCES

Duong TA: Infection due to *Penicillium marneffei,* an emerging pathogen: review of 155 reported cases. Clin Infect Dis 1996;23:125. (Authoritative review of the history, epidemiology, mycology, clinical manifestations, diagnosis, and treatment of Penicillium marneffei.)

Goldani LZ, Sugar AM: Paracoccidioidomycosis and AIDS: an overview. Clin Infect Dis 1995;21:1275. (Discussion of the clinical manifestation and treatment of Paracoccidioidomycosis in patients with AIDS.)

Manns BJ et al: Paracoccidioidomycosis: case report and review. Clin Infect Dis 1996;23:1026. (Report of a fatal case of paracoccidioidomycosis that occurred > 15 years after the patient left the endemic area, with a succinct review of key features of paracoccidioidomycosis.)

Martino P et al: Clinical patterns of *Fusarium* infections in immunocompromised patients. J Infect 1994;28(Suppl 1):7. (Large series of patients with Fusarium infection and comprehensive literature review focusing on clinical aspects.)

Patterson TF et al: The epidemiology of pseudallescheriasis complicating transplantation: nosocomial and community-acquired infection. Mycoses 1990;33(6):297. (Discussion of the epidemiological aspects of both nosocomial and community-acquired Pseudallescheriasis.)

Perfect JR, Schell WA: The new fungal opportunists are coming. Clin Infect Dis 1996;22(Suppl 2):S112. (Nice summary of emerging fungal pathogens including Penicillium marneffei, Fusarium spp., and Pseudallescheria boydii.)

Vartivarian SE et al: Emerging fungal pathogens in immunocompromised patients: classification, diagnosis, and management. Clin Infect Dis 1993;17(Suppl 2): S487. (Overview of several new and frequently encountered emerging pathogens including Fusarium, with concise description of clinical features.)

Dermatophytes

78

D. Scott Smith, MS, MD & David A. Relman, MD

Essentials of Diagnosis

- Characteristic pattern of inflammation on glabrous skin surfaces. The active border of infection is scaly, red, and slightly elevated.
- Wet mount preparation with potassium hydroxide (10–20%). Skin scraping of the active border shows branching, translucent, rod-shaped filaments (hyphae) in keratinized material under low-power microscopy (10–40×). Hyphae are uniformly wide and regularly septated.
- Wood's light examination (UV light at 365 nm) shows blue-green fluorescence for *Microsporum canis* and *Microsporum audouinii*. *Trichophyton schoenleinii* is pale green, and tinea versicolor shows white-yellow fluorescence.
- Culture should be performed with hair, nail, and skin specimens from particularly inflammatory lesions, to make a definitive mycologic diagnosis.

General Considerations

Dermatophytes are molds that infect keratinized tissues including skin, hair, and nails. Whereas 40 dermatophyte species are known to infect humans, only about 15 of these are common causes of disease. These organisms belong to three genera, *Microsporum, Trichophyton,* and *Epidermophyton.* Because these fungi have such similar infectivity, morphology, and pathogenicity, they are often categorized according to the clinical syndrome and the preferred anatomic site with which they are associated, such as tinea capitis, tinea pedis, etc. "Tinea" comes from the Latin word meaning worm or moth. These superficial mycoses often create serpiginous skin markings.

Although tinea versicolor (caused by *Malassezia furfur* or *Pityrosporum* spp.) is not formally considered a dermatophytosis, it is also discussed in this chapter, as it also affects superficial skin layers.

A. Epidemiology. Dermatophytes are found in three distinct environmental niches and display specific adaptation to these sites: animals, humans, and soil. Therefore, they are classified as anthropophilic, zoophilic, or geophilic organisms. As these names imply, infection occurs following exposure to either infected humans, animals (such as cats, dogs, or cattle), or soil.

Dermatophytoses occur worldwide, and vary in their presentation according to the site of infection.

Improved living standards in the United States since the end of World War II have decreased the incidence of tinea capitis. On the other hand, dramatic increases in the incidence of tinea pedis and tinea cruris due to *Trichophyton rubrum,* an anthropophilic dermatophyte, have been observed in recent years in developed nations. *T rubrum* is the most common dermatophyte pathogen worldwide, affecting up to one-third of the population of industrialized countries. Tinea pedis occurs almost exclusively among people who wear shoes, because the latter provide warmth and moisture, conditions that are preferred by the causative organisms.

Transmission of zoophilic dermatophytes occurs through direct contact with infected animals or fomites, such as via troughs and stalls used by infected animals. Geophilic dermatophyte infections occur from direct contact with soil and are seen in greenhouse workers, but infections with these organisms are relatively less common than those caused by anthropophilic dermatophytes.

B. Microbiology. The dermatophytes belong to three anamorphic (asexual or imperfect) genera, *Epidermophyton, Microsporum,* and *Trichophyton* of the Deuteromycota (Fungi Imperfecti). Members of the *Epidermophyton* genus have macroconidia that are smooth-walled and either single or in clusters, but these fungi have no microconidia. Members of the *Microsporum* genus have macroconidia with fusiform or cylindrical and roughened walls. There are fewer microconidia, and they are found alone along the hyphae as pear-shaped structures. *Trichophyton* species have macroconidia with smooth cylindrical walls. Their microconidia are numerous, and spherical or pear shaped; they appear in clusters along the hyphae.

Conidia are used as the basis for dermatophyte speciation. Because dermatophytes form only hyphae and arthrospores in the nonviable keratinized tissue of infected humans, they must be cultivated in the laboratory to develop conidia for purposes of identification. Colonies form at room temperature on Sabouraud's agar, and their color, texture and morphology are also useful in species identification.

C. Pathogenesis. Host factors that enhance the development of dermatophytoses include genetic-susceptibility markers; abraded skin; occlusive clothing, footwear, or dressings; and the presence of other cutaneous diseases like atopic dermatitis. The dermatophytes invade the keratinized layers of skin by producing keratinases, enzymes that digest keratin. While adhering to and invading host skin, the dermatophytes elicit a diverse set of clinical responses. Most lesions are contained within a certain anatomic boundary and may even be self-limited, but widespread dermatophyte infection has been observed in patients with AIDS, patients on immunosuppressive drug regimens, and those who have endocrinopathies such as Cushing's disease. The pathogenic features of superficial dermatophyte infections of the skin are illustrated in Figure 78–1.

Trichophyton is also the name of a crude extract from certain dermatophytes that produces a tuberculin-like response in most adults. There are two moieties of the galactomannan peptide responsible for antigenic response. The carbohydrate portion is responsible for an immediate response, and the peptide portion is associated with a delayed response and probably immunity as well. Resistance to infection is T cell mediated and may be acquired after infection, but it varies in duration and degree, depending on host factors, species of the fungus, and site of infection.

Clinical Findings

The superficial mycoses are named according to the site of infection, which usually corresponds to the site of local inoculation. The degree of inflammation is often dictated by the nature of the environment from which the fungus originates. For example, anthropophilic dermatophytes elicit a milder immune response in humans than do the zoophilic fungi. The anthropophilic *M audouinii* causes minimal inflammation as compared with the zoophilic *M canis*. Table 78–1 lists the microbiological differential diagnosis for each clinical syndrome discussed below.

A. Tinea Capitis. Tinea capitis or scalp ringworm mainly affects prepubertal children ages 4–14 (Figure 78–2). It is most commonly observed in crowded living conditions and in areas of poverty. Infection of the hair shaft distinguishes this disease from other dermatophytoses that involve the glabrous skin. Tinea capitis is often classified according to one of three patterns of fungal invasion noted microscopically: endothrix, ectothrix, or favus. Endothrix infections invade the inside of the hair shaft, and the cuticle is not destroyed; thus, clinically it appears as simple scaling of the scalp. It may resemble seborrheic dermatitis or dandruff. There may be gray patches of

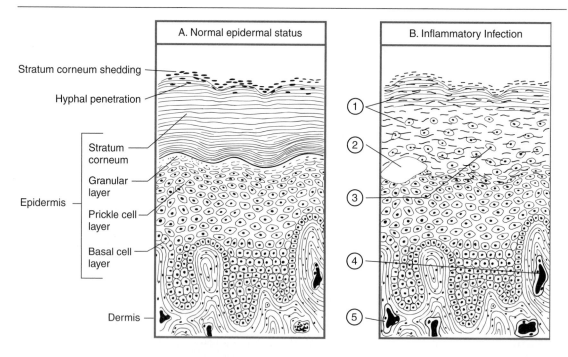

Figure 78–1. Pathogenic features of dermatophyte infection of the stratum corneum (from Hernandez AD: Dermatophytoses. Hosp Med 1985:227). A. The normal epidermis undergoes continual shedding of the stratum corneum, protecting it from dermatophytes. B. Inflammatory reaction that accompanies dermatophytoses. (1) Penetration of the stratum corneum by dermatophytes induces a cell-mediated reaction against the fungus; (2) vesiculation occurs in severe cases; (3) the stratum corneum contains nucleated cells; the inflammatory reaction increases epidermal cell division rates, and these cells pass more rapidly through the epidermis, so full differentiation does not occur; (4) loss of normal translucency causes the stratum corneum to appear white and dermal vessels to dilate; (5) mononuclear inflammatory cells infiltrate the dermis.

Table 78–1. Differential diagnosis for dermatophytoses.

Tinea Type	Dermatophytes	Clinical Presentation	Differential Diagnosis	Diagnosis
Tinea capitis (ringworm of the scalp)	T tonsurans[1] T mentagrophytes[2] T violacium[1] M canis[2] M audouinii[1] M gypsum[3]	Circular bald patches, short hair stubs, pruritic, advancing red border	Alopecia areata, psoriasis, seborrheic dermatitis, bacterial infections	UV light for M canis and M audouinii KOH mount of hair follicles and scrapings Cultures
Tinea barbae (ringworm of the facial hair)	T verrucosum[2] T mentagrophytes[2]	Inflammatory lesions, follicular pustules, pruritic	Folliculitis, pyoderma	KOH mounts of exfoliated skin Cultures
Tinea corporis (ringworm of the smooth nonhairy skin)	T rubrum[1] T mentagrophytes[2] M canis[2]	Circular scaly patches, advancing red borders, pruritic	Eczema, psoriasis, pityriasis rosea, erythema annulare centrifigum, and subacute cutaneus lupus, drug allergy	KOH mount of skin scraping from leading edge Culture if indicated
Tinea cruris (ringworm of the groin)	T rubrum[1] T mentagrophytes[2] E floccosum[1]	Well-demarcated, scaling circinate lesions with erythematous raised borders; scrotum is rarely involved	Cutaneous Candida, erythrasma, eczematous dermatitis, psoriasis	Vesicle from eczematous lesion: KOH and culture if indicated
Tinea pedis (ringworm of the feet)	T rubrum[1] T mentagrophytes[2] E floccosum[1]	Interdigital: erythema, maceration and scale Moccasin foot: erythema, thick hyperkeratotic scales Inflammatory: vesicles on medial foot Ulcerative: especially in web spaces and secondary bacterial infection	Other fungi: Scytalidium hyalinum or S cytalidium dimidiatum, erythrasma, candidiasis, psoriasis, and dyshidrosis	KOH mount of skin scraping from leading edge and culture if indicated
Tinea unguium (onycho- mycosis)	T rubrum[1] T mentagrophytes[2]	Small yellow spot begins at nail base; nail becomes brittle, friable, thickened	Nail bed tumors, yellow-nail syndrome, pachyonychia congenita, traumatic onychodystrophy	KOH mount of nail shaving or nail bed detritus and culture if indicated
Other nondermatophytes				
Tinea versicolor	Pityrosporum ovale P orbiculare (also called Malassezia furfur) Not formally a dermatophyte	Begins as multiple small circular macules (white, pink or brown) that enlarge radially Usually asymptomatic May itch	Vitiligo, pityriasis alba, seborrheic dermatitis, secondary syphilis, and pityriasis rosea	KOH mount of skin scraping Wood's light = irregular pale yellow-white fluorescence; fades with treatment (some lesions do not fluoresce)
Fungal "id" reaction	Not a dermatophyte at the local site but associated with certain tinea infestations	Adults: vesicular eruption of the palms Children: erythematous lichenoid papules	Adults: associated with tinea pedis Children: associated with kerions of the scalp	Look for and diagnose the primary offending dermatophyte

[1] Anthropophilic.
[2] Zoophilic.
[3] Geophilic.

779

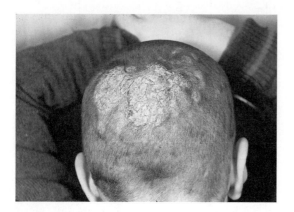

Figure 78–2. Inflammatory tinea capitis with kerion and patchy alopecia (From the Department of Dermatology, Stanford University Hospital).

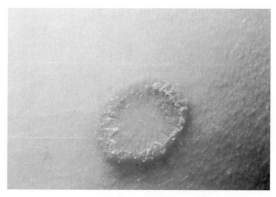

Figure 78–3. Tinea corporis lesion with raised inflammatory edges (Department of Dermatology, Stanford University Hospital).

alopecia with minimal or no inflammation or "black dot" alopecia, in which hairs break off at the roots.

The ectothrix infections present with gray or scaling patches of alopecia with minimal or no inflammation. The "black dot" appearance is also seen. Kerions and prominent inflammatory lesions may be observed, as the dermatophytes that cause ectothrix infections invade both the inside and the outside of the hair shaft and follicles. Kerions are boggy, suppurative, and usually painful. Kerions are most commonly seen with *M canis* and rarely with *Trichophyton mentagrophytes* or *Trichophyton verrucosum*.

Favus infection leads to crusting and matted hair on the scalp with such severe invasion that permanent alopecia often results. It is primarily seen in Eastern Europe and Africa.

B. Tinea Barbae. Tinea barbae, like tinea capitis, affects the hair follicles and shafts but in the facial area, and it is often diagnosed only after it fails to respond to several courses of antibacterial agents. Affected hairs are easily removed, unlike those in bacterial folliculitis, which resist removal. The zoophilic dermatophytes *T mentagrophytes* and *T verrucosum* are the most common causes of tinea barbae. The condition often begins with a small clump of follicular pustules, then develops into a boggy, erythematous tumorlike abscess.

C. Tinea Corporis. Tinea corporis or ringworm refers primarily to lesions affecting the nonhairy or glabrous skin, but this condition may also result from extensions of scalp or groin infections. Lesions are usually sharply demarcated and ringlike with a raised border (Figure 78–3). The infections can range from mildly to highly inflammatory with pustules, vesicles, and marked erythema. The central area may become brown or hypopigmented and less scaly as the active border progresses.

D. Tinea Cruris. Tinea cruris or jock itch is more common in men and may involve the perineum

and the perianal and thigh areas, but it rarely affects the scrotum. (*Candida* infections, in contrast, typically involve the scrotum.) Tinea cruris typically presents with bilateral asymmetric erythematous plaques that spread distally from the groin. There is often central clearing and an active erythematous border, which may have vesicles or papules. Pruritis and burning are common complaints.

This infection is usually transmitted from the patient's foot to the groin. Tinea cruris often occurs in the summer months after sweating or wearing wet clothing or in the winter months after wearing many layers of clothing, leading to the predisposing warm moist conditions conducive to fungal growth.

E. Tinea Pedis. Tinea pedis, also known as athlete's foot, is the most common dermatophyte infection diagnosed overall, and it is usually caused by the anthropophilic organism *T rubrum*. Occlusive footwear promotes warmth and sweating which provide an ideal environment for fungal growth. Tinea pedis presents in four general fashions (a) interdigital infection with erythema, maceration, and scale formation; (b) "moccasin foot" with erythema and thick hyperkeratotic scales; (c) inflammatory infection with vesicles usually on the medial foot; and (d) a less common ulcerative infection affecting the web spaces of the toes, sometimes superinfected with bacteria, and often seen in immunocompromised patients. If tinea unguium is present, tinea pedis may persist because of constant reinfection from the nails.

F. Tinea Unguium. Tinea unguium or onychomycosis is an infection of the fingernails or toenails. Infections typically begin along the leading edge of the nail or the lateral border and involve the nail plate; the result is opaque, chalky or yellow nail discoloration. The nail may also become thickened and brittle. Inflammatory changes of the skin around the nail including paronychia are not seen with tinea unguium. Toenails are more frequently involved than fingernails, and the incidence of this infection increases with age.

The nondermatophytic molds such as *Scopulariopsis* and *Scytalidium* spp., *Acremonium fusarium,* and *Candida* spp. cause ~ 5% of fungal nail diseases. This prevalence varies by geography, and these molds may account for ≤ 50% of fungal nail infections in Southeast Asia. These fungi are important to distinguish, because not all respond to the same therapy.

G. Tinea Incognito. Tinea incognito refers to dermatophyte infections that are disguised, often because they are treated with topical steroids and then lose some of their characteristic clinical features. Steroids may temporarily reduce inflammation, but the fungus is able to grow unchecked by the impaired immune response. The rash changes such that scaling margins disappear, borders become irregular, and a once localized process may expand. The diagnosis is easily made once steroids are stopped for a few days and scaling reappears and hyphae can be seen on microscopy. Tinea incognito is most often observed in the groin, face, and hands.

H. Dermatophytid. Dermatophytid or the "id" reaction is an allergic response to tinea processes that causes sterile dermatitis at distant sites. The most common presentation is a patient with tinea pedis who develops itching and burning on the hands, usually on the sides of the fingers near the crease. Vesicles may appear that enlarge to bullae. Desquamation of the palms and soles occurs less commonly, without inflammation. The lesions persist until the primary process resolves.

I. Tinea Versicolor. Tinea versicolor is a common fungal infection of the superficial layer of skin caused by members of the *Malassezia* genus, especially *Malassezia furfur,* formerly known as both *Pityrosporum orbiculare* and *Pityrosporum ovale.* These organisms are lipophilic and make use of medium-chain-length fatty acids. They are members of the normal skin flora, but certain conditions promote proliferation, such as excess heat, humidity, pregnancy, oral contraceptives, malnutrition, burns, Cushing's disease, corticosteroid therapy, or other forms of immunosuppression.

Clinically, tinea versicolor has a characteristic distribution and lesions; it begins as small circular macules of various colors (thus the name "versicolor"), such as white, pink, or brown, that expand radially. The varied color with this rash stems from the pathologic response of the host. For example, reddish macules or patches are related to a hyperemic inflammatory response; the hypopigmented lesions are caused by alterations in melanosome formation and transfer of pigment to keratinocytes; the tan or dark macules or patches are also related to alterations in melanosome formation. The color of the lesions is uniform in each individual. The upper trunk is the area that is most commonly affected, because the organism is found in highest numbers in areas of increased sebaceous activity. The lesions often become more obvious in summer, when the hypopigmented areas contrast more sharply with the unaffected tanned skin. The lesions are usually asymptomatic, but they may itch if there is inflammation.

Diagnosis

In addition to clinical recognition and diagnosis on clinical grounds, there are three specific techniques that are useful in the work-up and more definitive diagnosis of superficial mycoses: UV light examination, direct microscopy, and culture. Direct examination of the patient's skin in a darkened room by using UV light (a Wood's lamp) is useful only for infections—primarily tinea capitis or corporis—caused by certain species, including *M. audouinii, M canis,* and *T schoenleinii.* These infections give off a blue-green color.

Specimens for diagnosis by microscope or culture can be collected using a razor or scalpel to scrape keratinized or flaking material from the leading edge of the newest lesion. Nail scrapings are ideal if the nail is scraped underneath the nail plate, initially to clean it and then to collect a specimen onto a microscope slide or to inoculate culture. A few drops of 10–20% KOH solution is placed on the slide to dissolve keratin. Heating accelerates the process. This enables visualization of hyphae seen with dermatophytes or of hyphae and spores seen in candidal and tinea versicolor infections.

Because KOH wet mounts cannot differentiate among dermatophyte species, the organisms should be cultivated to reveal the distinguishing forms of conidia. From a clinical perspective, it is usually not necessary to identify the dermatophyte species, because topical and oral agents are active against all of them. Species identification is important for scalp infections, severe or inflammatory skin infections, and certain nail infections, because systemic treatment is

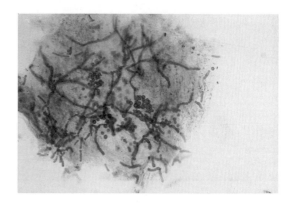

Figure 78–4. Skin scraping from a patient with tinea versicolor illustrating characteristic "spaghetti and meatball" appearance of the round *M furfur* yeast and short hyphae (PAS stain, 160× magnification) (Department of Dermatology, Stanford University Hospital).

BOX 78-1

Treatment of Dermatophytoses

	First Choice	Second Choice	Adjunctive measures
Tinea Capitis	• Terbinafine 250 mg orally per d (× 2–3 weeks for *T tonsurans*; × 4–8 weeks for M canis) • Pediatric considerations: safe	• Griseofulvin, 500 mg orally per d (adults × 4–6 weeks; children, 10–20 mg/kg/d × 6–8 weeks)	• Selenium sulfate shampoo may hasten eradication of the organism • For highly inflamed kerions, a short course of prednisone should be considered • Antibiotics as indicated
Tinea Barbae	• Same as for tinea capitis	• Same as for tinea capitis	• Antibiotics, eg, dicloxacillin for bacterial superinfection; avoid shaving
Tinea Corporis	• The following drugs in cream preparation are efficacious: terbinafine, miconazole, clotrimazole, and ciclopiroxolamine **NOTE:** Each cream is applied twice daily to the affected area for 2–3 weeks (use for 1 week beyond resolution) • Pediatric considerations: these are safe in children dosed twice daily	• Terbinafine, 250 mg orally once per d × 2–3 weeks NOTE: If highly inflammatory zoophilic infection, extended oral therapy may be indicated	• For highly inflamed kerions, a short course of prednisone should be considered
Tinea Cruris or Pedis	• Same as tine corporis	• Undecylenic acid or tolnaftate or haloprogin topical cream twice per d for 2–3 weeks	• Avoid tight clothing • Avoid occlusive shoes • Dry feet thoroughly
Tinea Versicolor	• Selenium sulfide lotion 2.5% (Selsun or Exsel) applied from base of scalp to knees for 10 min each day for 7 d (topical treatment used only for limited disease, but with high recurrence rates) • Pediatric considerations: selenium sulfide lotion safe with same schedule of application • Itraconazole, 200 mg orally once daily for 5–7 d	• Ketoconazole, 400 mg oral single dose or 200 mg orally for 7 d • Fluconazole, 400 mg oral single dose (repeat in 1 week)	• Hot laundering of clothing may reduce recurrence rate

BOX 78-1 (CONTINUED)

Treatment of Dermatophytoses

	First Choice	Second Choice	Adjunctive measures
Tinea Unguium (Onycho-mycosis)	• Terbinafine, 250 mg orally daily ×6 weeks for fingers and ×12 weeks for toes OR • Pulse dosing: 500 mg daily ×1 week/month for 4 months for toes and 2 months for fingers • Pediatric considerations: safe in children	• Fluconazole, 150–300 mg orally each week ×3–6 months for fingers or ×6–12 months for toes • Itraconazole, 200 orally four times per d ×3 months for toes • Pulse dosing: 200 mg orally twice daily ×1 week per month ×2 months for fingers	• Keep nails short and clean, clipped straight • Use cotton gloves for dry manual work and vinyl gloves for wet work • Change instruments between care of normal and infected nails • Use antifungal foot and shoe powder

necessary for scalp infections, treatment may be prolonged and expensive, and species identification may enable prevention of zoophilic infections. Some nail infections may be caused by a mold (eg, *Scopulariopsis* spp.), which, despite being indistinguishable from dermatophytoses on a gross visual basis, will not respond to the same therapy. Culture is usually performed using Sabouraud's agar slants, which are incubated at room temperature for 1–3 weeks. The specific dermatophyte is then identified by colony color and texture, as well as by light microscopy, which reveals the specific morphologic patterns.

Diagnosis of tinea versicolor is made by Wood's light examination, which shows irregular whitish-yellow areas of fluorescence, although some lesions do not fluoresce. Potassium hydroxide wet mount preparations show short, broad hyphae and clusters of budding cells, which are often described as having the appearance of "spaghetti and meatballs" (Figure 78–4). Cultivation is possible but rarely indicated and requires the addition of oil to the fungal culture media because the organism is lipophilic.

Treatment

The principles of treatment are outlined in Box 78–1, according to the specific clinical presentation. Most tinea infections involving the skin can be treated with topical agents such as an imidazole twice a day for 2 or 3 weeks. Terbinafine is also available both in topical and oral formulations and appears to be a more potent drug, requiring shorter dosing with longer lasting clinical responses. Terbinafine and newer related drugs block ergosterol synthesis at an earlier step than do the azole drugs.

If the infection is widespread, involving a large surface area, or if it is particularly inflammatory, systemic drugs are indicated. For infections of the hair and nails, débridement is important prior to systemic treatment. Several oral medications including itraconazole, fluconazole, and terbinafine can be dosed on a daily basis or in so-called "pulsed" regimens for effective treatment of infections of the keratinized tissues. The concept underlying pulse dosing takes advantage of drug deposition in the nail so that the total dose can be reduced; elevated amounts of drug are given repeatedly for short intervals corresponding to the length of time for a finger or toenail to grow. For example, a slightly higher daily dose is given for 1 week each month for the length of time estimated for the infected nail to grow again.

Treatment of tinea versicolor is with a 2.5% selenium sulfide suspension applied to the entire skin surface from the lower posterior scalp area down to the thighs for 10 min every day for 7 days. Another common regimen is to apply the lotion and wash it off after 24 h, repeating once a week for a month. Antifungal creams are useful. Single dose oral treatment with ketoconazole, itraconazole, or fluconazole has also been shown to be effective. Other important

BOX 78-2

Prevention & Control of Dermatophytoses

Prophylactic Measures	• Identify and avoid exposures to animals or fomites suspected of harboring dermatophytes • Boil or wash clothing using a commercial facility • Disinfect public shower and bathing areas
Isolation Precautions	• None

adjunctive measures to minimize reinfection include discarding or boiling frequently worn garments that are in contact with the skin. The lesions may take months to clear as they result from depigmentation, which persists despite eradication of the fungus.

Prevention & Control

Several interventions have been shown useful in the prevention and control of dermatophytes, depending on their type and anatomic location (Box 78–2).

In general, ensuring a clean and dry body surface; avoiding occlusive gloves or shoes that may promote tinea unguium, manus, or pedis; and avoiding sweat-dampened clothing that enables tinea versicolor to thrive all control this infection. Regular cleaning of showers and changing areas at public pools with bleach is thought to control some infection, as is the use of chemicals on an individual basis, such as foot powders.

REFERENCES

Aly R, Berger T: Common superficial fungal infections in patients with AIDS. Clin Infect Dis 1996;22(Suppl 2):S128.

Assaf RR, Weil ML: The superficial mycoses. Dermatol Clin 1996;14(1):57.

Brautigam M: Randomised double blind comparison of terbinafine and itraconazole for treatment of toenail tinea infection. Br Med J 1995;311:919.

Elewski BE: Onychomycosis: pathogenesis, diagnosis, and management. Clin Microbiol Rev 1998;11(3):415.

McClellan KJ, Wiseman LR, Markham A: Terbinafine: an update of its use in superficial mycoses. Drugs 1999; 58(1):179.

Schmidt A: *Malassezia furfur:* a fungus belonging to the physiological skin flora and its relevance in skin disorders. Cutis 1997;59:21.

Silva-Lizama E: Tinea versicolor. Int J Dermatol. 1995; 34:(9)611.

Pneumocystis carinii

79

James J. Chamberlain, MD & Kristen Ries, MD

Essentials of Diagnosis

- *Pneumocystis carinii,* when examined using molecular techniques, most closely resembles a fungus.
- Stains of either bronchoalveolar-lavage (BAL) or transbronchial-biopsy samples yield a diagnosis in > 90% of patients and should be considered the gold standard in diagnosis.
- BAL with transbronchial biopsy increases diagnostic yield to ~ 100%.
- *P carinii* has not yet been cultured in vitro.
- Polymerase chain reaction (PCR) (especially on sputum) increases sensitivity but reduces specificity.
- The prophylactic use of aerosolized pentamidine reduces the sensitivity of sputum and bronchoscopic samples.

General Considerations

A. Epidemiology. In 1983, *P carinii* pneumonia (PCP) was described as the AIDS-defining illness in ≤ 60% of the first 1000 patients diagnosed with AIDS in the United States. Subsequently, the advent of prophylactic measures has reduced the incidence of PCP presenting as the initial diagnosis for AIDS to < 50% of cases. In addition, the hospitalization rate is also declining for patients with AIDS who also have PCP. This decline has presumably been caused by successful use of prophylaxis against the organism. An analysis from Ontario, Canada, demonstrated that hospital admissions caused by PCP decreased from 48% to 29% over a 2-year period with the initiation of prophylaxis with aerosolized pentamidine. Another Canadian study tracked PCP cases over the decade from 1981 to 1991 and showed that PCP episodes peaked in 1989 and subsequently began to decline.

Of AIDS patients who do not receive prophylaxis against *P carinii,* ≤ 80% will develop at least one episode of PCP and ~ 25% of AIDS patients not receiving prophylaxis will die from PCP. Of patients who have experienced PCP as their AIDS-defining illness, ≤ 70% will develop recurrent disease in the ensuing 2 years without the use of prophylactic medication, and 50% of these cases will occur in the 9 months after the initial episode.

CD4 lymphocyte levels in immunocompromised patients have become the most useful factor in predicting risk for developing *P carinii* infections. Retrospective data have demonstrated that PCP rarely occurs in patients with CD4+ counts of > 200 cells/mm³ and that > 90% of AIDS patients will have a CD4 count of < 200 cells/mm³ in the 2 months before becoming infected with *P carinii.* The percentage of lymphocytes that are CD4 also seems an important prognostic factor because > 95% of patients had a CD4+ percentage of < 20% in the 2 months before infection.

Although *P carinii* infection in children is clinically similar to that seen in adults, the numbers of CD4 lymphocytes in pediatric patients differ from those of adults and vary by the age of the patient. The relationship of the CD4 count and the age of a child must be understood to ascertain the degree of immunosuppression. Severe immunosuppression in children < 12 months old is seen with a total CD4 count of < 750 cells/mm³ or a CD4 percentage of < 15%. For HIV-infected children between 1 and 5 years old, a CD4 T-lymphocyte count of < 500 cells/mm³ or a CD4 percentage of < 15% is indicative of immunosuppression and increased risk for PCP.

New information suggests that PCP occurs as a result of transmission from human hosts and not from reactivation of latent infection as once thought. The organism is probably not maintained in the lungs of immunocompetent humans for any significant period, and it has been difficult to detect in normal individuals at autopsy. Further support for the theory of person-to-person spread is that PCP infections seem to peak ~ 4 months after winter viruses. The organism may be spread via aerosolized secretions by persons in the community with viral infections. Clustered outbreaks of PCP also suggest person-to-person spread.

Mortality in cases of mild to moderate PCP (partial arterial oxygen pressure [PaO₂] ≥ 70 mm Hg and alveolar-arterial oxygen gradient [A-a] ≤ 35 mm Hg) has substantially decreased as physicians treating the disease have gained experience. The early to mid 1980s saw mortality rates of ≤ 25% in mild to moderate disease. More recent large, multicenter trials have demonstrated mortality rates of < 1%. However, patients with PCP who develop respiratory failure still suffer profound mortality rates (≤ 45–72%).

B. Microbiology. *P carinii* is an obligate extracellular organism that characteristically evolves from a trophozoite of a single cell into a 5- to 10-mm-diameter cyst that contains up to eight sporozoites, each 1 to 2 mm in size. The developed cysts release sporozoites, which evolve into trophozoites. The majority of organisms in pulmonary tissue exist in the trophozoite form.

The molecular biology of *P carinii* is interesting, and new discoveries have led to significant modification in the understanding and classification of this organism. *P carinii* has long been considered a member of the protozoan kingdom. However, in 1988, *P carinii* ribosomal RNA sequences were found to more closely parallel certain fungal ribosomal RNA sequences. More recent inspection of *P carinii* gene sequences and fungal sequences from each of the seven fungal phyla seems to suggest that *P carinii* is a fungal organism. In particular, there appears a noticeable morphologic similarity between *P carinii* and the ustomycetous red yeast fungi, which is evidenced by a striking resemblance in mitochondrial RNA segments by PCR analysis.

It is interesting that the strain of *P carinii* that infects organisms may not be clonal. Within humans, the organism appears to be genetically diverse; isolates from four distinctly different geographic regions of the world show DNA diversity. Different mammalian hosts appear to harbor genetically diverse strains of *P carinii* as well. *P carinii* has been proven unable to grow when organisms from one species are deposited in the lungs of a differing species.

C. Pathogenesis. Recent data continue to suggest that *P carinii* infections are acquired via inhalation between hosts. Thus, infectious episodes are thought to occur as a result of reinfection and are not caused by reactivation of latent organisms. Once acquired, the organisms seem to adhere to alveolar cells of the lung. Replication of the organism is slow, and the resultant host immune response is relatively deliberate as well.

Impaired gas exchange at the alveolar level, a hallmark of PCP infection, appears to be caused by both the extensive proliferation of *P carinii* organisms and the subsequent host response. The presence of a foamy alveolar exudate, alveolar macrophages, interstitial edema, and type I alveolar cell destruction has been demonstrated by electron and light microscopy during the course of infection. The efficacy of corticosteroids in moderate to severe PCP infection is presumably caused by blunting of the host immune response. The importance of the correlation between the degree of immune response and the severity of disease is supported by the association between the number of neutrophils seen on BAL specimens and increased mortality.

CLINICAL SYNDROMES

P CARINII PNEUMONIA

Clinical Findings

A. Signs and Symptoms. The triad of shortness of breath with exertion, nonproductive cough, and fever describes the typical case of PCP (Box 79–1). Symptoms are usually slow to progress and typically worsen over several weeks to months. Cough may be productive of purulent sputum, especially if the patient is concomitantly infected with a bacterial pathogen. Shortness of breath at rest occurs late in the course of disease and signals moderate to severe hypoxia.

The physical exam is relatively nonspecific in diagnosing PCP because ≤ 50% of patients may have normal pulmonary examinations. Fine rales may be auscultated in ≤ 40% of patients, most with severe PCP. Patients may have restriction of their inspiratory ability, which is usually not mentioned unless the patient is questioned specifically.

B. Laboratory Findings. The serum lactate dehydrogenase (LDH) level has long been considered a useful laboratory value in the diagnosis of PCP. However, although LDH sensitivity may be > 80%, the test lacks specificity. The serum LDH level does appear to be of prognostic value. Serum LDH levels have been shown to portend a poor prognosis and increased mortality if they are elevated at diagnosis or if they persistently rise despite treatment.

C. Imaging. The chest radiograph is an important tool in the assessment of patients thought to be infected with PCP. Although nearly any pattern may be seen on chest radiograph, the typical appearance seen in ~ 80% of cases is one of diffuse bilateral interstitial infiltrates. Chest radiographs that show consolidation, nodularity, or cavitations may be seen in < 5% of cases. The finding of pneumothoraces, cysts, or pneumatoceles is not uncommon in patients with advanced disease. Of patients with PCP, ≤ 10% may have cysts (as seen on chest radiographs) and ≤ 6% may have pneumothoraces. The vast majority of AIDS patients with a pneumothorax have active *P carinii* infections.

EXTRAPULMONARY *P CARINII* INFECTIONS

Extrapulmonary *P carinii* infections occur in < 3% of patients and must be diagnosed with histopathologic samples. Primary prophylaxis for PCP with pentamidine may confer a higher risk for extrapulmonary infection. Symptoms of extrapulmonary involvement are nonspecific, usually consisting of fevers, chills, and sweats. Although any area of the

---

BOX 79-1

Signs and Symptoms of *Pneumocystis carinii* Pneumonia

More Common	Less Common
• Fever • Cough (usually nonproductive) • Dyspnea (especially with exertion) • Elevated lactate dehydrogenase • Diffuse interstitial infiltrates on chest radiograph	• Pneumothorax (especially if prophylactic treatment with pentamidine) • Pleural effusions rare

---

body may be involved, splenomegaly with cysts and thyroiditis are most common.

Diagnosis

The practice of diagnosing PCP morphologically by traditional staining methods (silver methenamine and toluidine blue) of induced sputum samples in HIV-infected individuals has fallen out of favor. Although relatively simple and inexpensive, staining of sputum samples induced by hypertonic saline inhalation is clearly dependent on operator and laboratory experience, and sensitivity varies tremendously between centers. These classic staining techniques yield a diagnosis in only 30–90% of patients suspected of being infected with PCP. Subsequently, a large number of patients may continue to be treated with potentially toxic drug regimens without a definitive diagnosis. The practice of indirect immunofluorescent stain with monoclonal antibodies has increased the sensitivity of induced sputum samples to ~ 70% or to > 90% in some reports.

Bronchoscopy with BAL with or without transbronchial biopsy has become the gold standard in the diagnosis of PCP. Several studies have demonstrated a sensitivity of > 90% for both BAL and transbronchial biopsy. The combination of BAL and transbronchial biopsy leads to a sensitivity of ~ 100%. The complications of transbronchial biopsy, including bleeding and pneumothorax, have led most clinicians to use BAL as the initial diagnostic method during bronchoscopy if diagnosis is not obtained by induced sputum.

PCR technology on induced sputum samples has improved sensitivity to ~ 100% but appears to result in diminished specificity. PCR may become a reasonable diagnostic tool as PCR technique improves, resulting in less contamination and fewer false-positive results.

Chemoprophylaxis for PCP with aerosolized pentamidine has led to a considerable reduction in the rate of recovery of PCP in sputum and bronchoscopy samples. Performing BAL bilaterally or on multiple lobes seems to maintain sensitivity at > 90%.

Treatment

The primary treatment of moderate to severe pulmonary or extrapulmonary infection caused by *P carinii* remains the combination of trimethoprim (TMP) and sulfamethoxazole (SMX), either orally or intravenously (IV).

Several medications (atovaquone, trimetrexate, and pentamidine) and combination regimens (dapsone + TMP and clindamycin + primaquine) probably afford nearly equal efficacy to TMP-SMX in mild to moderate PCP and may be better tolerated in specific populations of patients (Boxes 79–2 and 79–3).

A. TMP-SMX. TMP-SMX was the first regimen approved for use in the treatment of PCP, and this regimen is still considered the best initial treatment choice for PCP infection. If tolerated, this combination should be regarded as the initial treatment choice for all PCP infections.

In moderate to severe pulmonary infection with *P carinii*, TMP-SMX has been shown to significantly improve survival when compared with IV pentamidine (86% vs 61%) in randomized trials. Several drug regimens subsequently discussed appear to have similar efficacy compared with TMP-SMX in mild to moderate PCP and may be better tolerated. However, the fact that TMP-SMX also has excellent antimicrobial activity against organisms causing community-acquired bacterial pneumonia and *Toxoplasma* infections should be considered when choosing an agent for treating *P carinii* infections.

Treatment with TMP-SMX is often limited by adverse effects, which occur in the majority of patients to some degree (65–100%). A morbilliform rash is the most commonly observed adverse reaction among patients treated with TMP-SMX; the rash occurs ~ 20–45% of the time and limits treatment in ≤ 20% of patients. Antihistamines may be used to reduce the severity of the rash. Additional side effects of TMP-SMX include fever, nausea and vomiting, neutropenia, anemia, thrombocytopenia, and elevated serum aminotransferase levels.

B. Pentamidine isethionate. IV pentamidine isethionate is a suitable alternative treatment for PCP if TMP-SMX is not tolerated. Pentamidine appears to be comparable to TMP-SMX in effectiveness in mild to moderate disease. However, a randomized trial

BOX 79-2

Treatment of *Pneumocystis carinii* Pneumonia in Adults

	Treatment	Comments
First Choice	• For mild to moderate infections: Trimethoprim, 15 mg/kg/d, and sulfamethoxazole, 100 mg/kg/d PO or IV, three times daily or four times daily, for 14–21 d (21 d in AIDS) • For moderate to severe infections (see comments): Trimethoprim as above with or without prednisone, 40 mg PO twice , daily for 5 d then 20 mg PO daily for 11 d	• Corticosteroids (prednisone) are currently recommended in patients with PO <70 mm Hg or an alveolar-arterial oxygen gradient (P(A–a)O) >35 mm Hg.
Second Choice	• Pentamidine, 3–4 mg/kg IV daily for 14–21 d (21 d in AIDS) • Trimetrexate, 45 mg/m IV daily (over 60–90 min) + folinic acid (leucovorin), 20 mg/m/d PO or IV divided every 6 h for 21 d • Atovaquone suspension, 750 mg PO twice daily for 21 d • Clindamycin, 600 mg IV four times daily or 300–450 mg PO four times daily, + primaquine, 15 mg PO daily for 21 d • Dapsone, 100 mg PO daily + trimethoprim 5 mg/kg PO three times daily for 21 d	• Patients with severe disease should probably receive 4 mg of petamidine. • Folinic acid must be administered at the initiation of trimetrexate therapy and continued for 3 d after cessation of therapy. • Atovaquone should be taken with food; failure to do so may result in threefold reduction in absorption.
Penicillin Allergic	• No change; treat as above	

comparing IV pentamidine isethionate with TMP-SMX in moderate to severe disease resulted in a significant mortality advantage for patients treated with TMP-SMX (86% vs 61%).

Aerosolized pentamidine isethionate has been used in the treatment of mild to moderate PCP. Unfortunately, although it results in fewer systemic adverse effects, the aerosolized form of pentamidine isethionate has resulted in lower response rates and a higher frequency of relapse. The use of aerosolized pentamidine isethionate is expensive and requires compressed air to be delivered effectively.

The most common adverse effects associated with the use of pentamidine isethionate include nephrotoxicity, hyperkalemia, hypocalcemia, hypomagnesemia, hypoglycemia, and hypotension. The hypotension seems to be related to the rate at which the drug is administered and usually responds to IV fluids. Hyperglycemia and insulin dependence can also occur. Acute pancreatitis has also been reported.

C. Trimetrexate. Trimetrexate is relatively new in the spectrum of drugs used to treat PCP. The U.S. Food and Drug Administration approved trimetrexate for use in moderate to severe PCP in late 1993. Trimetrexate is related structurally to methotrexate and is thought to possess a similar mechanism of action. Trimetrexate presumably inhibits dihydrofolate reductase, which diminishes the production of nucleic acid precursors, resulting in cell death. Thus, a reduced form of folic acid, folinic acid (leucovorin), must be administered with trimetrexate to reduce toxicity to host cells.

Trimetrexate has been compared with TMP-SMX in a randomized, double-blind, multicenter trial in a group of patients with moderate to severe PCP. Trimetrexate was relatively well tolerated; only 8% of patients terminated treatment before 21 days because of adverse effects. By comparison, 28% of patients who received TMP-SMX had discontinued therapy by 21 days ($P < 0.001$). However, by 21 days

BOX 79-3

Treatment of *Pneumocystis carinii* Pneumonia in Children

	Treatment	Comments
First Choice	• Trimethoprim-sulfamethoxazole, 15–20 mg TMP—75–100 mg SMX/ kg/d IV, PO[1] divided into four doses, administered one dose per 6 h	• Steroids appear to be beneficial in moderate to severe disease • There are no controlled trials of steroids in young children • Suggested dosage 2 mg/kg/d for 7–10 days followed by a tapering dose during the next 10–14 d
Second Choice	• Pentamidine isethionate, 4 mg base/ kg/d IV for 10–14 d • Alternatives: trimethoprim and dapsone; primaquine and clinda-mycin; trimetrexate and folinic acid; atovaquone; for nonsevere disease	

[1]Oral therapy should be reserved for those with mild disease and no evidence of malaborption or diarrhea.

after initiation of treatment, a significantly larger number of patients receiving trimetrexate had been considered treatment failures as measured either by lack of efficacy or death (38%) vs those receiving TMP-SMX (20%). Thus, trimetrexate should be considered a relatively safe treatment option in patients with moderate to severe PCP who do not respond to or are intolerant of TMP-SMX or in patients in whom TMP-SMX is contraindicated.

Trimetrexate, as mentioned, has been well tolerated, with ≤ 10% of patients discontinuing therapy at 21 days. The principal dose-limiting side effect has been myelosuppression, especially neutropenia and thrombocytopenia, occurring in 10–15% of patients. Elevated serum aminotransferase, alkaline phosphatase, and creatinine levels have been reported as well. Rash and anemia may also occur in patients receiving trimetrexate.

D. Atovaquone. Atovaquone is a hydroxynapthoquinone drug that has proven to be an effective alternative in the treatment of mild to moderate PCP. Several multicenter prospective trials have shown atovaquone to be much better tolerated than either TMP-SMX or pentamidine isethionate. Although atovaquone is somewhat more likely to result in treatment failure, the favorable side effect profile of atovaquone compared with TMP-SMX and pentamidine isethionate has led to equivalent overall clinical success rates of ~ 60–80%. Mortality rates appear similar between atovaquone and pentamidine isethionate ≤ 8 weeks after completion of treatment. However, mortality appeared significantly higher with atovaquone (7%) as compared with TMP-SMX (0.6%) in a randomized multicenter trial ($P = 0.003$).

The adverse effects of atovaquone that lead to termination of treatment seem to occur in < 10% of patients over a typical 21-day course of treatment. Gastrointestinal complications arise most frequently and include nausea, vomiting, diarrhea, hepatitis, and constipation. In addition, an erythematous rash has occurred in ≤ 25% of patients who take atovaquone. Fever and cough are also common side effects.

E. Clindamycin and Primaquine. The use of the combination of clindamycin and primaquine has been proven quite effective in the treatment of mild to moderate PCP.

Several prospective trials have proven that clindamycin and primaquine are ≥ 90% effective in treating mild to moderate PCP. No significant difference has been demonstrated between clindamycin and primaquine when compared with either TMP-SMX or dapsone-TMP, in mild to moderate disease.

Adverse effects have occurred in up to one-third of patients receiving clindamycin and primaquine, and they may be related to the dose of primaquine used. When primaquine has been dosed at 30 mg/d instead of the more frequently used dose of 15 mg/d, the incidence of dose-limiting side effects has nearly doubled. The most significant dose-limiting adverse effect observed in patients taking clindamycin and primaquine is a vesicular, desquamating, or ulcerating rash. Anemia is a frequent problem as well, which is likely related to the strong oxidative effects of primaquine that lead to its contraindication in patients with glucose-6-phosphate dehydrogenase deficiency. The primaquine component of this treatment combination may lead to methemoglobinemia as well. Less common side effects include nausea and vomiting, neutropenia, and gastrointestinal complaints.

F. Dapsone and TMP. The combination of dapsone and TMP has been shown to possess similar efficacy to TMP-SMX in the treatment of mild to moderate PCP, with significantly fewer treatment-limiting unfavorable effects. Of patients with mild to moderate PCP, > 90% may be expected to respond to treatment with dapsone and TMP.

Adverse reactions to this combination regimen seem to occur at a much lower rate than to either pentamidine or TMP-SMX. Side effects requiring termination of treatment have occurred in < 10% of patients receiving dapsone and TMP. In clinical trials, the major side effects most commonly include rash (occasionally requiring discontinuation of therapy), elevated hepatic transaminases, neutropenia and thrombocytopenia, hemolytic anemia, and methemoglobinemia with serum levels that can exceed 20%. Of note, dapsone is a potent oxidant, an effect that can cause severe hemolysis in patients with glucose-6-phosphate dehydrogenase deficiency, and it should be used with caution in this population of patients.

G. Corticosteroids. The use of corticosteroids has unquestionably been shown to reduce mortality by ~ 50% in patients with moderate to severe PCP. In addition, the need for mechanical ventilation is dramatically reduced in this group of patients. Patients with mild to moderate PCP have not demonstrated benefit from the use of adjuvant corticosteroid use. The suppression of the host inflammatory response to the presence of *P carinii* infection is thought to be the mechanism of the beneficial effect of corticosteroids. Corticosteroid use may exacerbate mucocutaneous herpes simplex, cytomegalovirus infections, and the lesions of Kaposi's sarcoma.

Prognosis

Many clinical markers or scoring systems have been suggested to diagnose and predict outcome in PCP. Most if not all of these factors have been shown to have little value in the management of disease. The degree of hypoxia is an important prognostic factor that affects recommended treatment. The adjuvant use of corticosteroids and choice of treatment regimen should be based on whether the disease is classified as mild to moderate ($PaO_2 > 70$ mm Hg and $P[A-a]O \leq 35$ mm Hg) or moderate to severe ($PaO_2 < 70$ mm Hg or $P[A-a]O \geq 35$ mm Hg). However, it is probably better to err on the side of using corticosteroids.

Prevention & Control

Prophylaxis for PCP has clearly been shown to be effective in reducing the incidence of disease and improving survival in patients at risk for developing the disease (Box 79–4). No chemoprophylactic treatment regimen has been shown to be more effective than TMP-SMX. In addition, TMP-SMX provides protection against the bacteria that cause community-acquired pneumonia, as well as against toxoplasmosis. Aerosolized pentamidine isethionate and dapsone with or without pyrimethamine or TMP should continue to be regarded as second-line agents in the prevention of PCP.

A. TMP-SMX. No drug regimen has been shown to be more effective for preventing PCP in immunocompromised patients than TMP-SMX. Several primary and secondary prevention trials have proven that TMP-SMX is superior to aerosolized pentamidine isethionate and dapsone in patients who tolerate the drug. Patients who have experienced an initial episode of PCP have a more than threefold greater

BOX 79–4

Prophylaxis for *Pneumocystis carinii* Pneumonia		
	Adults	Children
First Choice	• TMP-SMX, 1 DS tablet PO daily or PO 3 times per week, usually on Monday, Wednesday, and Friday	• TMP-SMX, 5 mg TMP–25 mg SMX/kg/d half given every 12 h or as single dose daily for 3 consecutive d/wk or 7 d/wk
Second Choice	• Pentamidine, 300 mg aerosolized via nebulizer once per month • Dapsone, 50–100 mg PO daily or 100 mg PO two times per week with or without pyrimethamine, 50 mg PO 2 times per week, with folinic acid, 10 mg PO (to reduce toxicity) with each dose of pyrimethamine • Altovaquone, 1500 mg (10 ml) PO daily	• Pentamidine, 300 mg nebulized monthly or dapsone 2 mg/kg (not to exceed 100 mg) PO daily

risk of developing a subsequent recurrence at 18 months while receiving aerosolized pentamidine isethionate than while receiving TMP-SMX. The use of TMP-SMX three times weekly seems to afford protection against *P carinii* infection that is equal to that from daily treatment.

Of patients receiving prophylaxis against PCP with TMP-SMX, ≤ 75% may not tolerate the drug. Because TMP-SMX is cheaper and more effective than other treatment options, desensitization protocols have been used to allow some patients who were previously intolerant to TMP-SMX to continue taking the drug. Several published reports indicate that the majority of patients with previous mild to moderate adverse reactions and some with severe anaphylactic responses to TMP-SMX may be safely and successfully desensitized with oral protocols. Thus, most patients who were previously thought to be unable to tolerate TMP-SMX for prophylaxis against PCP may be safely and effectively desensitized with oral desensitization protocols and continue to take TMP-SMX. Some physicians have recommended that all patients who started treatment with SMX should use a desensitization protocol, thus preventing many allergic reactions.

B. Dapsone. Dapsone with or without pyrimethamine or TMP is as potent as inhaled pentamidine isethionate but less effective than TMP-SMX in the primary prevention of PCP in HIV-infected individuals. Dapsone is also poorly tolerated, with only 25% of patients in one randomized trial who were able to complete the daily treatment regimen. Dapsone does have the advantage over pentamidine isethionate in efficacy against *Toxoplasma* infections.

Twice weekly dapsone and pyrimethamine appears to be an effective and perhaps better tolerated alternative to daily dosing regimens. Toxicities associated with prophylactic dapsone are the same as those listed in the treatment section.

C. Aerosolized Pentamidine Isethionate. Pentamidine isethionate delivered once monthly via an ultrasonic nebulizer is a reasonable but less effective alternative to oral systemic therapy in PCP prophylaxis. Aerosolized pentamidine isethionate is very well tolerated, with < 15% of patients being unable to tolerate treatment. Unfortunately, aerosolized pentamidine isethionate is more likely to result in extrapulmonary *P carinii* infection because very little inhaled drug is absorbed systemically. Aerosolized pentamidine isethionate has been shown to reduce the sensitivity of diagnostic procedures used in the diagnosis of PCP as well.

When adverse effects are encountered with inhaled pentamidine isethionate, they are mainly limited to a dry cough and bad taste in the mouth. Spontaneous pneumothorax is a potentially dangerous effect of aerosolized pentamidine isethionate. The small amount of systemic absorption may occasionally result in rash, renal impairment, and pancreatitis. Use of an albuterol inhaler before the nebulized pentamidine isethionate is recommended as routine by some to prevent bronchospasm and to promote better penetration of the drug.

REFERENCES

American Academy of Pediatrics, Committee on Infectious Diseases: Pneumocystis. In Peter G: 1997 Red Book: Report of the Committee on Infectious Diseases, 24th ed. American Academy of Pediatrics, 1997.

Bozzette SA, et al: A randomized trial of three antipneumocystis agents in patients with advance human immunodeficiency virus infection. NIAID AIDS Clinical Trials Group. N Engl J Med 1995;332:693.

Chien SM, et al: Changes in hospital admissions patterns in patients with human immunodeficiency virus infection in the era of *Pneumocystis carinii* prophylaxis. Chest 1992;102:1035.

Dohn MN, et al: Oral atovaquone compared with intravenous pentamidine for *Pneumocystis carinii* pneumonia in patients with AIDS. Ann Intern Med 1994;121:174.

Fulton B, Wagstaff AJ, McTavish D: Trimetrexate: a review of its pharmacodynamic and pharmacokinetic properties and therapeutic potential in the treatment of *Pneumocystis carinii* pneumonia. Drugs 1995;49(4):563.

Girard P-M, et al: Dapsone-pyrimethamine compared with aerosolized pentamidine as primary prophylaxis against *Pneumocystis carinii* pneumonia and toxoplasmosis in HIV infection. N Engl J Med 1993;328:1514.

Hughes W, et al: Comparison of atovaquone (566C80) with trimethoprim-sulfamethoxazole for the treatment of *Pneumocystis carinii* pneumonia in patients with the acquired immunodeficiency syndrome (AIDS). N Engl J Med 1993;328:1521.

Kennedy CA, Goetz MB: Atypical roentgenographic manifestations of *Pneumocystis carinii* pneumonia. Arch Intern Med 1992;152:1390.

Kovacs JA, et al: Diagnosis of *Pneumocystis carinii* pneumonia: improved detection in sputum with use of monoclonal antibodies. N Engl J Med 1988;318:589.

Lipschik GY, et al: Improved diagnosis of *Pneumocystis carinii* infection by polymerase chain reaction on induced sputum and blood. Lancet 1992;340:203.

Mason GR, et al: Prognostic implications of bronchoalveolar lavage neutrophilia in patients with *Pneumocystis carinii* pneumonia and AIDS. Am Rev Respir Dis 1989;139:1336.

Masur H, et al: Consensus statement on the use of corticosteroids as adjunctive therapy for *Pneumocystis carinii* pneumonia in the acquired immunodeficiency syndrome. N Engl J Med 1990;323:1500.

Miller RF, et al: Pneumocystis carinii infection: current treatment and prevention. J Antimicrob Chemother 1996;37(Suppl B):33.

Nelson JD: Pocket Book of Pediatric Antimicrobial Therapy. Williams & Wilkins, 1998.

Safrin S: New developments in the management of *Pneumocystis carinii* disease. AIDS Clin Rev 1993/1994:95.

Safrin S, et al: Comparison of three regimens for treatment of mild to moderate *Pneumocystis carinii* pneumonia in patients with AIDS. Ann Intern Med 1996;124:792.

Sattler FR, et al: Trimethoprim-sulfamethoxazole with pentamidine for treatment of *Pneumocystis carinii* pneumonia in the acquired immunodeficiency syndrome. Ann Intern Med 1988;109:280.

Sattler FR, et al: Trimetrexate with leucovorin versus trimethoprim-sulfamethoxazole for moderate to severe episodes of *Pneumocystis carinii* pneumonia in patients with AIDS: a prospective, controlled multicenter investigation of the AIDS Clinical Trials Group Protocol 029/031. J Infect Dis 1994;170:165.

Sistek CJ, Wordell CJ, Hauptman SP: Adjuvant corticosteroid therapy for *Pneumocystis carinii* pneumonia in AIDS patients. Ann Pharmacother 1992;26:1127.

Stringer JR, Walzer PD: Molecular biology and epidemiology of *Pneumocystis carinii* infection in AIDS [editorial]. AIDS 1996;10:561.

Toma E, et al: Clindamycin/primaquine versus trimethoprim-sulfamethoxazole as primary therapy for *Pneumocystis carinii* pneumonia in AIDS: a randomized, double-blind trial. Clin Infect Dis 1993;17:178.

Wakefield AE, et al: *Pneumocystis carinii* shows DNA homology with the ustomycetous red yeast fungi. Mol Microbiol 1992;6:1903.

Yung RC, et al: Upper and middle lobe bronchoalveolar lavage to diagnose *Pneumocystis carinii* pneumonia. Am Rev Respir Dis 1993;148:1563.

Section VII.
Parasitic Infections
Part A. Protozoa

Malaria and Babesia

80

Gary W. Procop, MD & David H. Persing, MD, PhD

PLASMODIUM SPP.

- Exposure history, such as travel, recent transfusion, or living in close proximity to an international airport.
- Nonfalciparum malaria: chills and fever spikes, followed by defervescence and fatigue; symptoms may be cyclic every 48–72 h.
- Falciparum malaria: fever spikes and chills, often noncyclic and associated with rapidly progressive systemic symptoms.
- Detection and identification of a *Plasmodium* species in a thick and thin blood smear, respectively.
- Molecular detection of *P falciparum*'s histidine-rich protein by enzyme-linked immunosorbent assay (ELISA) or *Plasmodium* DNA by polymerase chain reaction (PCR) followed speciation by probe hybridization or DNA sequencing.

General Considerations

A. Epidemiology. Malaria, a disease of antiquity, was recognized by Hippocrates and described possibly as early as 1700 BC in ancient Chinese texts. Malaria is a global disease that occurs most commonly in the tropics; however, transmission may also occur in temperate zones. In the 19th and early 20th centuries, *Plasmodium* species were widely distributed in the United States. This distribution included the southern United States, the Mississippi River Valley, and extensions as far north as Minnesota and Michigan.

Today, primarily in tropical areas, *Plasmodium* parasites continue to cause > 100 million cases of malaria per year. This results in an estimated 1–2 million deaths annually, many of whom are children. In fact, greater than 90% of severe, life-threatening malaria occurs in children. The distribution of the mosquito vector and the prevalence of disease in indigenous populations are the major factors that determine the distribution of the *Plasmodium* parasite.

Mosquito-infested areas, such as swamps, have long been associated with high attack rates of malaria. Environments that support long-standing, stagnant water promote mosquito breeding. Currently, endemic areas include parts of the Caribbean, northern South America, Central America, parts of Africa, India, parts of Australia, Southeast Asia, and many of the Asian Pacific Islands.

Malaria also occurs sporadically in nonendemic areas. In many instances, this represents imported, latent disease. Malarial relapses may present months after travelers have returned from endemic areas. These patients have usually been incompletely treated or have taken insufficient chemoprophylaxis.

Relapsing malaria is caused by reactivation of the latent hypnozoite phase of *P vivax* or *P ovale*. Patients who develop malaria may be treated with a wide variety of agents. The most commonly used antimalarial drugs, chloroquine and mefloquine, are effective against the symptomatic, erythrocytic phase of *P vivax* and *P ovale* and may result in apparent cures. These drugs, however, are ineffective against the hepatic hypnozoites. Patients treated in such a manner are incompletely treated and are at risk for malarial relapse.

Some patients may report never having had a previous episode of malaria. Specific questioning, however, often reveals a brief lapse in chemoprophylaxis. A lapse in chemoprophylaxis may result in a window period of subprophylactic drug levels. During this window period, sporozoites injected by an infected mosquito during a blood meal may reach and infect the liver. Any parasites (merozoites) that emerge from the liver while the patient is taking chemoprophylaxis are rapidly killed and the patient remains asymptomatic. Hypnozoites, however, may become active months after return from an endemic area, long after the cessation of chemoprophylaxis. The proper identification of *P vivax* and *P ovale* is important because only these species form hepatic hypnozoites and may result in malarial relapse.

In nonendemic areas, the cases of so-called "airport malaria" may occur. It is thought that mosquito vectors from endemic areas may be transported with airline cargo. An individual in a nonendemic area who lives in close proximity to an airport may become infected if bitten by these mosquitos. The propagation of the parasite is usually not sustained in the environment. This is either because of a lack of a suitable mosquito host or because of the low number of parasites in the community. When the prevalence of malaria is low, the probability of a mosquito ingesting gametocytes is very low. Additionally, if infected mosquitos are rare, they may take a nonhuman blood meal and thereby disrupt the parasitic cycle.

Mosquito transmission is the most common route of infection, but other modes of transmission exist. Transmission may result from intravenous drug abuse (shared needles) or blood transfusion. In these instances, only the erythrocytic cycle is established, because hepatocytes can be infected only by the sporozoite form of the parasite.

B. Microbiology. Numerous *Plasmodium* species exist; however, only four species are known to infect humans. These species are *P falciparum, P vivax, P ovale,* and *P malariae.* Worldwide, *P vivax* causes the vast majority of disease (~ 80%), followed by *P falciparum* (~ 15%).

Depending on the infecting plasmodial organism, malaria differs in severity, complications, prognosis, and treatment. Therefore, with the exception of differentiating *P vivax* from *P ovale,* it is important to promptly and properly speciate the organism. Malaria is typically separated into two disease types: falciparum and nonfalciparum. This distinction emphasizes the severity of *P falciparum* malaria, which is a medical emergency in the nonimmune individual. Among the nonfalciparum species, it is important to distinguish *P vivax* and *P ovale* from *P malariae.* The former two species have a dormant hepatic stage, which requires separate treatment to avoid malarial relapse.

The identification of *Plasmodium* organisms and the differentiation of the various species remain primarily based on parasite morphology in Giemsa-stained blood preparations. Organism detection is the initial task in the laboratory diagnosis of malaria. This is accomplished by the examination of a thick blood preparation. The examination of a thick preparation is an important part of the examination of blood for parasites and should not be bypassed, unless plasmodia have already been detected in a routine peripheral blood smear. The thick preparation increases the diagnostic yield compared with the examination of the thin blood smears. In the thick preparation, a larger volume of blood may be screened more rapidly. This becomes critical in detecting low-grade parasitemia, such as that associated with long-term *P malariae* infections or early in the course of malaria.

Thick preparations are made by placing 1–2 drops of the patient's blood together on a glass slide. The blood is not smeared and allowed to air dry. This slide is then stained by the Giemsa method, without methanol fixation. The unfixed erythrocytes (RBCs) lyse in the hypotonic stain solution. The stained preparation is first examined under 10× magnification, then under 100× oil immersion.

Filariasis is endemic to many of the same regions that harbor the malaria parasites and may cause cyclic fevers. The microfilariae are easily detected in thick blood preparations at 10× magnification. The purpose of the 100× oil immersion examination is to detect *Plasmodium* species.

In Giemsa-stained preparations, the *Plasmodium* parasites have red chromatin and light-blue cytoplasm (Figure 80–1). The ring forms of any *Plasmodium* species and the gametocytes of *P falciparum* are the structures most easily identified in thick preparations. Practice is required to differentiate *Plasmodium* amoeboid and schizont forms from platelets and debris. Thin blood smears must be examined if the thick preparations demonstrate the presence of a *Plasmodium* species.

The methanol-fixed, Giemsa-stained thin blood smear is used for *Plasmodium* speciation. Useful criteria for the differentiation of *Plasmodium* species are listed in Table 80–1. However, only rarely are all of these morphologic features present in a blood smear. Differentiation must be made on all information available. The morphologic criteria useful in differentiating the *Plasmodium* species are briefly discussed.

The crescent-shaped gametocyte is pathognomonic of *P falciparum* (Figure 80–2), but, unfortunately, this structure is not always present. Features in the

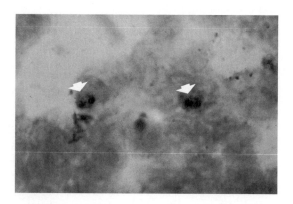

Figure 80–1. Thick preparation demonstrating two ring forms of *P vivax.* (Giemsa stain; 1000× magnification.)

Table 80–1. Useful differentiating characteristics of *Plasmodium* species.[a]

Morphologic Feature	P falciparum	P malariae	P vivax/P ovale
RBCs			
• Infected RBC size	• Normocellular	• Normocellular	• Increased
• RBC stippling	• Coarse dots, commalike, occasionally present (Maurer's dots)	• None present	• Fine stippling (Schuffner's dots— P vivax); (Jame's stippling— P ovale)
Rings			
• Parasite load	• Often high	• Often low	• Intermediate
• > 1 organism/cell	• Common	• Low	• Occasional
• Appliqué forms	• Present	• Usually absent	• Usually absent
Advanced forms			
• Advanced forms	• Usually absent, except in severe disease	• Present	• Present
• Ameboid forms	• N/A	• Basket, band, and indistinct amoeboid forms	• Indistinct forms
• Number of merozoites/cell	• N/A	• 6–12 (average 8)	• P vivax: 12–24 (average 16) • P ovale: 8–12 (average 8)
• Amount of RBC occupied by schizont	• N/A	• Entire cell	• P vivax: entire cell • P ovale: fills 2/3 of cell
• Distinctive "banana-shaped" gametocyte	• Present	• Absent	• Absent
Other Features			
• Cycle of fever	• Usually without established cycle	• 72 h	• 48 h
• Hypnozoites[b]	• Absent	• Absent	• Present

[a]Knowledge of species endemic to the area wherein the patient contracted malaria is also useful in limiting the diagnostic possibilities.
[b]In nonendemic areas, this is often demonstrated by reactivation several months after leaving an endemic area.

peripheral smear, that in combination may be used to identify *P falciparum,* include the presence of small, delicate-appearing ring trophozoites, infected erythrocytes that remain normocytic, and the presence of predominantly ring trophozoites, with a conspicuous absence or relative rarity of more advanced forms. A high parasitemia and erythrocytes infected with multiple organisms are more commonly seen in patients with falciparum malaria. Appliqué forms and two chromatin centers per ring trophozoite are also suggestive of *P falciparum,* but may be present in other *Plasmodium* species.

Unlike *P falciparum, P vivax* and *P ovale* produce thicker and larger ring trophozoites, the infected RBCs become macrocytic, and advanced forms, such as amoeboid trophozoites, schizonts, or both are usually present in the peripheral smear (Figures 80–3 and 80–4). In an appropriately pH-balanced Giemsa stain (pH 6.8–7.0), RBCs infected by *P vivax* or *P ovale* may demonstrate fine eosinophilic stippling. This fine stippling should not be confused with larger, coarse, comma-shaped dots (Maurer's dots) that may be present in *P falciparum*-infected erythrocytes. Appliqué forms are typically not present in *P vivax*- or *P ovale*-

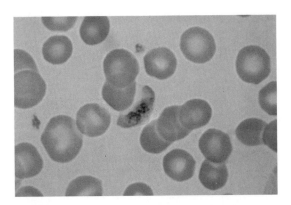

Figure 80–2. Pathognomonic, crescent-shaped gametocyte of *P falciparum.* (Giemsa stain; 1000× magnification.)

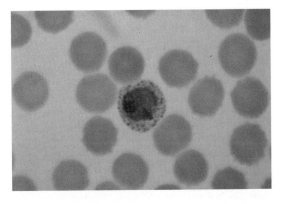

Figure 80–3. *Plasmodium vivax* late trophozoite/early schizont stage. Schuffner's dots are prominent. (Giemsa stain; 1000× magnification.)

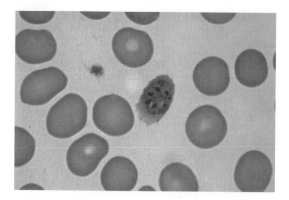

Figure 80–4. *P malariae* developing schizont; at least five merozoites are present. (Giemsa stain; 1000× magnification.)

infected erythrocytes, and ring trophozoites usually have only a single chromatin dot. Occasionally, more than one trophozoite may be present per erythrocyte. Although *P vivax* and *P ovale* can be differentiated from one another, this is difficult and requires parasitology expertise. Differentiation of *P vivax* and *P ovale* is usually not indicated or performed, because the disease produced by these organisms is similar and the treatment is identical.

P malariae-infected RBCs invariably contain some advanced plasmodial forms and, like *P vivax* and *P ovale,* the ring forms produced are thick. Stippling, however, is not observed. Specialized advanced forms, such as the band form and the basket form, are highly suggestive of *P malariae*. Like *P falciparum,* the ring trophozoites may occasionally contain two chromatin dots and the infected RBCs remain normocytic.

It should be noted that there may be coinfections with more than one *Plasmodium* species. Coinfections, especially in individuals who live in areas endemic for more than one *Plasmodium* species, are relatively common. These mixed infections are important to detect because of differences in disease prognosis and therapy.

C. Pathogenesis. The definitive host and vector for the *Plasmodium* parasite is the female *Anopheles* mosquito. Asexual reproduction and gametogenesis occur in the human intermediate host. The parasitic life cycle is similar for all *Plasmodium* species. However, important differences do exist.

Infecting sporozoites originate from the salivary gland of the female *Anopheles* mosquito. These are transmitted into the human during a blood meal. The sporozoites then migrate via the bloodstream to the liver where hepatocytes become infected. In the liver, tissue schizonts are formed. These contain numerous, asexually derived merozoites. From a single sporozoite, this phase of asexual reproduction results in a

10,000- to 30,000-fold organism amplification. This portion of the asexual reproduction cycle is common to all *Plasmodium* species.

Unique to the life cycle of *P vivax* and *P ovale* is the production of dormant hepatic hypnozoites. The hepatic hypnozoites may represent a form of parasite adaptation to climate. In temperate zones, this would enable the malarial parasite to "over-winter" in the human host. This strategy would prove advantageous when climatic conditions limit the activity of the mosquito vector. The hypnozoites, after a dormancy period between 6 and 12 months, become active and produce tissue schizonts.

Upon maturation, the tissue schizonts rupture, and the merozoites are released into the bloodstream. The merozoites then infect RBCs wherein occurs the second phase of asexual reproduction. Intra-erythrocytic asexual replication is also common to all *Plasmodium* species. *P falciparum* and *P malariae* may invade erythrocytes of any age, whereas *P vivax* and *P ovale* selectively parasitize only young RBCs. Younger RBCs still maintain their full complement of cytoplasmic membrane and expand with the growth of the organism. Older RBCs, infected with either *P falciparum* or *P malariae,* fail to expand with the growth of the parasite and remain normocytic with respect to uninfected RBCs. These features are useful in the laboratory differentiation of *Plasmodium* species.

After RBC infection, there is another cycle of asexual replication. Initially, a ring form develops (Figure 80–5), followed by differentiation into an amoeboid trophozoite form (Figure 80–3). This is followed by the development of an intra-erythrocytic schizont, which contains many merozoites (Figure 80–4). This phase results in a 6- to 32-fold asexual amplification of the organism for each infected RBC. The number of merozoites produced in the intra-erythrocytic schizont varies between species. Schizonts present in the blood smear are useful for speciation.

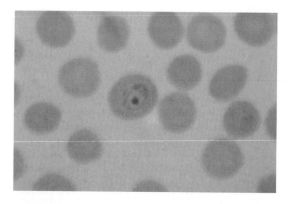

Figure 80–5. Ring form of *P vivax*. The infected cell is slightly macrocytic. (Giemsa stain; 1000× magnification.)

The developing parasites metabolize glucose and use RBC hemoglobin. The parasitic use of hemoglobin produces the characteristic hemozoin pigment as a waste product.

The erythrocyte-based, asexual reproduction cycle culminates with RBC rupture. The merozoites are released into the bloodstream where erythrocytes are again infected. This cycle of erythrocyte infection, merozoite replication, and RBC rupture is repetitive and may become highly synchronized. This synchronization is most classically seen in benign tertian malaria caused by *P vivax*. The rupture of the RBCs and release of the merozoites correlate with the clinical symptoms of malaria. The RBC-based reproduction cycle of *P vivax* and *P ovale* occurs every 48 h, whereas the erythrocytic cycle of *P falciparum* occurs between 36 and 48 h. The erythrocytic cycle of *P malariae* occurs approximately every 72 h.

The RBC-infecting merozoite may alternatively undergo differentiation into either a micro- or macrogametocyte. These gametocytes may be ingested by the female *Anopheles* mosquito during a blood meal. Fusion of the gametocytes takes place within the gut of the mosquito. The diploid zygote matures and invades the gut wall. Meiotic division ensues, which results in haploid sporozoites. The sporozoites migrate to the mosquito's salivary gland to complete the parasitic cycle.

FALCIPARUM MALARIA

Clinical Findings

A. Signs and Symptoms. Fevers are often continual, with irregular spikes and associated chills and paroxysms. Patients with severe falciparum malaria may disclose central nervous system changes (prostration, convulsions, and impaired consciousness) and develop respiratory distress, abnormal bleeding, and circulatory collapse. Fatigue and malaise are nonspecific symptoms of malaria. These are in part caused by hypoglycemia and anemia. Hypoglycemia results from both decreased oral intake during illness and plasmodial use of blood glucose by the Embden-Meyerhof pathway. Anemia results from parasite-associated hemolysis and in some instances disseminated intravascular coagulation. *Plasmodium* infections cause elevated tumor necrosis factor alpha (TNF-α) levels, particularly in individuals with severe disease. This may also contribute to hypoglycemia and anemia.

In situations of hyperparasitemia, intra- and extravascular hemolysis may be severe. Excessive hemolysis and hepatic involvement cause hyperbilirubinemia and jaundice. Free hemoglobin, bilirubin, and malarial pigment are excreted and turn the urine brown to black. This manifestation, although not limited to *P falciparum* malaria, is termed "blackwater fever."

Falciparum malaria, particularly in the nonimmune, constitutes a medical emergency. Although patients with hyperparasitemia have high mortality rates, even those with parasitemias < 5% may suffer severe morbidity and death. Fatalities result from the immediate effects and sequelae of microvascular obstruction and extensive hemolysis. The microvascular obstruction is caused by specific cytoadherence between *P falciparum*-parasitized RBCs and endothelial cells. Obstruction of the cerebral vasculature is the most serious manifestation and may cause mental status changes that range from mild confusion to coma. Similar microvascular compromise in various organ systems may result in renal failure, noncardiogenic pulmonary edema, or gastroenteritis.

B. Laboratory Findings. Three thick blood smears (see above), spaced ~ 12 h apart, should detect any of the *Plasmodium* species. High levels of parasitemia in patients infected by *P falciparum* may be obvious in peripheral blood smears examined secondary to an abnormal hematopoietic profile. In such instances, a microbiologist or pathologist with expertise in infectious disease pathology should examine the peripheral smear and determine which of the *Plasmodium* species is present. It should be remembered that the routine Wright stain, which is used in many institutions for the peripheral blood smear exam, is not pH balanced and may not disclose the eosinophilic stippling in *P vivax*- or *P ovale*-infected RBCs. Harbingers of a poor prognosis present in the thin smear include hyperparasitemia, the presence of mature plasmodial forms (indicative of a larger sequestered biomass of parasites), and a high proportion (> 5%) of polymorphonuclear leukocytes which contain phagocytosed malarial pigment (indicative of recent schizogony). Other laboratory findings are nonspecific and reflect the specific organ involvement.

Blood smears may disclose RBC fragmentation, reflecting the hemolytic process. Similarly, the urine may be dark in color, and hemoglobin and bilirubin may be detected. Other abnormal indices may be present in the urinalysis, depending on the severity of renal involvement. Hyperbilirubinemia may be present depending on hepatic involvement and the duration and severity of disease. Abnormal coagulation studies, including decreased fibrinogen levels, elevated D-dimers, and thrombocytopenia, may be present in patients with disseminated intravascular coagulation. Blood gas analysis may reveal hypoxemia, depending on the severity of pulmonary edema and the presence of hyaline membrane disease.

C. Imaging. Computed tomography or magnetic resonance imaging may be performed if mental status changes are present. These may reveal evidence of ischemic injury or edema and nonspecific changes.

D. Complications. The microvascular congestion, secondary to adhesion between parasitized RBCs and endothelial cells, results in protean clinical manifestations. Complications generally occur in the tissues most sensitive to hypoxia and ischemia. Alterations in cerebral blood flow cause mental status changes, including disorientation, headache, coma, and death. Hepatic and gastrointestinal involvement may result in jaundice and enterocolitis, respectively. Involvement of the alveolar capillaries causes noncardiogenic pulmonary edema, which may be exacerbated by fluid retention secondary to renal failure. Oxygen exchange may be further compromised with the development of adult respiratory distress syndrome. Acute renal failure is multifactorial and results from the renal overload of free hemoglobin and malarial pigment, as well as the microvascular compromise and associated hypoxia. Microvascular damage may result in activation of the coagulation and thrombolytic cascades. Disseminated intravascular coagulation exacerbates the hemolytic anemia and further compromises an already insufficient microvascular circulation.

Hypoglycemia, common in *Plasmodium* infections, worsens tissue injury. The causes of hypoglycemia are nutritional, immune mediated, parasitic, and iatrogenic. Inadequate oral intake and parasite use of glucose contribute to hypoglycemia. Immune-mediated mechanisms, such as elevations of TNF-α, may also contribute to hypoglycemia. Therapy-induced elevations in blood insulin, secondary to quinine and quinidine, cause hypoglycemia.

In pregnancy, *P falciparum* becomes sequestered in the maternal sinuses of the placenta (Figure 80–6). This and the aforementioned complications increase the probability of adverse outcomes for the fetus. Obstetric complications include spontaneous abortion, premature labor and delivery, and maternal death. Transplacental infection of the neonate or "congenital malaria" is rare, but may occur. Primaparas (women pregnant with their first child) are at increased risk for adult respiratory distress syndrome. Pulmonary edema and adult respiratory distress syndrome in pregnancy may be due to the physiologic hypervolemia of pregnancy and an increase in the peripheral vascular resistance after delivery. Pregnancy-associated and quinine-associated hypoglycemia may exacerbate that caused by the parasitosis.

NONFALCIPARUM MALARIA (*P VIVAX, P OVALE, P MALARIAE*)

Clinical Findings

A. Signs and Symptoms. Patients with nonfalciparum malaria invariably develop fever and chills that may become cyclic. Initially, patients experience chills, which are followed by fever (Box 80–1). Patients with malaria often manifest many nonspecific symptoms such as weakness, malaise, headache, and myalgias. As the disease progresses, signs of anemia, such as pale conjunctiva, may be seen. Splenomegaly and mild hepatomegaly may also be present. After hours of fever, defervescence occurs with marked diaphoresis. Patients are weakened and exhausted from the severity of the disease. In established infections caused by *P vivax* and *P ovale,* a periodicity may occur approximately every 48 h. *P vivax* and *P ovale* infections are clinically indistinguishable. Although similar, disease caused by *P ovale* is usually less severe, relapses less frequently, and more often sponta-

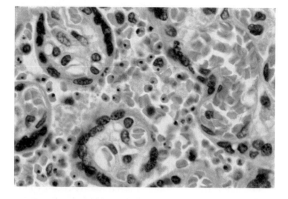

Figure 80–6. Sequestration of *P falciparum*-infected RBCs in the maternal sinuses of the placenta. This photomicrograph was taken after quinidine therapy. The corresponding peripheral blood smear was almost devoid of parasites. (Hematoxylin and eosin stain; 600× magnification.)

BOX 80–1

Plasmodium-Associated Syndromes	
P vivax/ P ovale	Cyclic episodes that consist of chills followed by fever, which is followed by defervescence and diaphoresis; cyclic every 48 h
P malariae	Cyclic episodes that consist of chills, followed by fever, which is followed by defervescence and diaphoresis; cyclic every 72 h; possible immune-complex–mediated glomerulonephritis
P falciparum	Continuous fevers with irregular spikes, possible hyperparasitemia with microvascular damage and compromise. This is a medical emergency in the nonimmune. Microvascular compromise may lead to central nervous system damage, renal and pulmonary failure, and death.

neously resolves. Both of these *Plasmodium* species produce latent disease and may produce relapses months after the initial infection.

Malaria from *P malariae* has a longer incubation period and possibly more severe paroxysms than are seen with *P vivax* and *P ovale*. The clinical periodicity of *P malariae* may become regular and occur in 72-h intervals. This is termed benign quartian malaria. Some infections with *P malariae* may be subclinical and persist for years, but *P malariae* does not produce latent disease.

B. Laboratory Findings. Three thick blood smears, spaced ~ 12 h apart, should detect any of the *Plasmodium* species. In instances of subclinical *P malariae* infection, parasitemia is extremely low and may be difficult to identify even in thick preparations.

Blood smears and urinalysis reveal evidence of hemolysis, but usually to a lesser degree than with infections caused by *P falciparum*. Elevated albumin levels are present in the urine of patients with *P malariae*-associated nephrotic syndrome.

C. Imaging. Hepatosplenomegaly and splenic complications, such as rupture, may be visualized by computed tomography scans or magnetic resonance imaging.

D. Complicatons. Complications with *P vivax* are rare, although coma and sudden death have been reported. Individuals with splenomegaly are at higher risk for splenic rupture. Infections with *P malariae* may be indolent and mild, but immune complex-associated glomerulonephritis and nephrotic syndrome may occur.

Differential Diagnosis

Nonfalciparum malaria. Many of the signs and symptoms of nonfalciparum malaria are nonspecific. There are many causes of anemia and hepatosplenomegaly. Malaria is endemic in many underdeveloped areas; indigenous people in these countries may suffer from protein-calorie malnutrition and are exposed to a wide variety of infectious agents. Impoverished children with dietary deficiencies may be anemic, and those with protein deficiencies may have protuberant abdomens. Numerous infectious diseases may present with hepatomegaly, splenomegaly, or both. Liver enlargement, spleen enlargement, or both may be seen in patients with amebic liver abscesses, Chaga's disease, visceral leishmaniasis, schistosomiasis, echinococcosis, clonorchiasis, and typhoid fever. Noninfectious causes of hepatosplenomegaly, anemia, or both include thalassemias and other hemoglobinopathies, myelofibrosis, and hematopoietic malignancies.

The symptoms of nonfalciparum malaria may also be nonspecific and may be present in a wide variety of diseases. This is especially true early in the course of malaria, before any synchronization of the erythrocytic cycle. Many tropical diseases, such as visceral leishmaniasis, filariasis, and dengue fever, may present with nonspecific symptoms similar to those present in malaria. If cyclic symptoms occur, filariasis should be considered. Pneumonia, urinary tract infections, and other less exotic causes of fever and chills must also be considered. Fever, chills, and night sweats are constitutional symptoms that may be seen with hematopoietic malignancies. *P malariae* has been associated with nephrotic syndrome, but other etiologies, such as post-infectious immune-complex glomerulonephritis and systemic lupus erythematosis, must be also be considered. The differential diagnosis of nonfalciparum malaria is extensive and may only be successfully narrowed by history, careful physical examination, and laboratory studies.

Falciparum Malaria. The differential diagnosis of falciparum malaria is also extensive. The focus of the differential diagnosis is usually based on the most severely affected organ system. If only generalized fever and chills are present, the differential is broad. These symptoms may be seen in a wide variety of infections (see above) or may represent the constitutional symptoms that may accompany some lymphoproliferative disorders. The mental status changes present in cerebral malaria may also be seen in patients with brain abscesses, meningitis, tumor, or cerebral or subdural hemorrhage. Gastrointestinal symptoms, such as abdominal pain and diarrhea, may be present in patients with bacterial or viral gastroenteritis, chronic colitis, or ischemic colitis. Similarly, involvement of the liver may suggest viral hepatitis, typhoid fever, or other hepatic disorders. The pulmonary edema and adult respiratory distress syndrome that may occur in falciparum malaria are clinically indistinguishable from those caused by many other etiologies. The astute cytologist, however, may detect the presence of a *Plasmodium* species in RBCs present in respiratory tract samplings (sputa or bronchoalveolar lavage) and may thereby identify the etiology of the respiratory pathology. The hemolytic anemia present in malaria may be clinically indistinguishable from other causes of hemolytic anemia but is usually readily distinguished by an examination of a peripheral blood smear.

When ring forms are present, the possibility of babesiosis must also be considered. Recent travel to *Plasmodium*- or *Babesia*-endemic areas is important supportive information. *Babesia* species may be excluded by the presence of advanced amoeboid or schizont forms and by the presence of malarial pigment. *Babesia* species do not produce amoeboid forms or schizonts, and they do not metabolize hemoglobin to form pigment. These criteria usually readily differentiate *Babesia* species from *P vivax, P ovale,* and *P malariae.* The differentiation of *Babesia* species and *P falciparum* is more difficult, because RBCs infected with either *Babesia* species or *P falciparum* usually contain only small, delicate ring forms. Furthermore, infections with both these organisms may show more than one ring form per RBC and high degrees of parasitemia.

A useful approach to the differentiation of *Babesia* and *P falciparum* is to search for pathognomonic forms, to perform an exhaustive search for advanced plasmodial forms and malarial pigment, and to obtain a detailed clinical and travel history. The pathognomonic forms of *Babesia* spp. and *P falciparum* are the tetrad of merozoites (Maltese cross) and the crescent-shaped gametocyte, respectively. Unfortunately, these forms are not always present in the blood smear. An exhaustive search may demonstrate a rare amoeboid or schizont form in *P falciparum* infections, especially in patients with severe disease, but this is not guaranteed. The presence of malarial pigment also differentiates *Plasmodium* species from *Babesia* species. In morphologically indeterminate instances, historical information may be the most helpful information available. Alternatively, molecular methods may be used to differentiate these organisms. These, however, are not routinely available in many areas.

Diagnosis

The first clue to clinicians of the possibility of malaria is often from a history of travel to a malaria-endemic area. Patients should be asked about their travel history, and the clinician should probe for any information about travel to malaria-endemic areas in either the recent or distant past. If patients have traveled to malaria-endemic areas, they should be asked if they received chemoprophylaxis and if they ever contracted malaria. Specific questioning concerning any travel to endemic areas in the past may reveal the possibility of infections with nonfalciparum *Plasmodium* species, which may cause disease months to years after the initial infection and return from endemic areas.

Mosquito-based transmission in naturally endemic areas is the most frequent mode of transmission, but less common modes of transmission may also occur. Plasmodial organisms in the erythrocytic phase may also be parenterally transmitted, through intravenous drug abuse (shared needles) or blood transfusion. This mode of transmission is infrequent in the United States and other nonendemic locales and is directly related to the frequency of infected donors. Historical information regarding having contracted malaria and recent travel to malaria-endemic areas is useful for screening potential blood donors. As mentioned earlier in this chapter, another group of individuals who may contract malaria are those who live in close proximity to an international airport.

The signs and symptoms of malaria depend somewhat on the infecting *Plasmodium* species. Early in the course of disease, nonsynchronized fever and chills may be present with other nonspecific symptoms such as fatigue, malaise, myalgia, and headache. The classic, nonfalciparum malarial cycle consists of shaking chills, followed by high, spiking fever, and finally defervescence with exhaustion. This cycle is most commonly seen with infections by *P vivax* but is also common with infections caused by *P ovale* and *P malariae*. The cyclic nature of the symptoms reflects the synchronization of the erythrocytic malarial cycle and is a clinical clue to malaria. When highly synchronized, this cycle occurs approximately every 48 h for infections caused by *P vivax* and *P ovale* and every 72 h for infections caused by *P malariae*.

The erythrocytic cycle of *P falciparum* becomes synchronized less frequently than malaria caused by other *Plasmodium* species. Patients with *P falciparum* infections more commonly demonstrate daily chills and fever spikes. The signs and symptoms of falciparum malaria are highly variable. The ischemic changes produced by the microvascular congestion may manifest in any organ system (see above). Therefore the clinical presentation usually depends on the organ system most severely affected. For this reason, malaria must remain in the differential diagnosis for a wide variety of disorders, especially if patients have recently visited malaria-endemic locales. Most patients demonstrate some degree of anemia and hypoglycemia. Headache, seizures, mental status changes, and coma may be seen in patients with cerebral malaria. Blackwater fever from the excretion of blood, hemoglobin, and malarial pigment is common in patients with renal involvement. The involvement of the gastrointestinal tract may produce nausea, vomiting, diarrhea, and abdominal pain. Hepatic involvement may result in jaundice, with elevations in serum levels of bilirubin and liver enzymes. Not surprisingly, primary gastrointestinal and hepatic manifestations of *P falciparum* malaria are commonly mistaken for self-limited bacterial or viral enteritis and viral hepatitis, respectively.

Although clinical history and physical examination findings may suggest malaria, the definitive diagnosis is made in the laboratory. Although ELISA and PCR-based assays for the detection of the malarial parasite are available, the examination of thick blood smears remains the most cost-effective method in the United States. Thick blood smears should be performed on the peripheral blood of patients suspected to have malaria. If the first blood smear is negative, two more should be performed at 12-h intervals. When a *Plasmodium* species is detected in a thick blood smear, thin blood smears should be made for plasmodial speciation.

If available, highly sensitive and specific molecular methods may be used for the detection of *Plasmodium* species. Molecular assays used for *Plasmodium* identification include the detection of *P falciparum*'s histidine-rich protein 2 by ELISA and the detection of *Plasmodium* nucleic acid by PCR. Dipstick technology has been applied to the detection of histidine-rich protein 2. This allows for a sensitive and specific molecular detection system to be available in the field. The detection of *Plasmodium* nucleic acids by the PCR may soon become the gold standard. PCR-based detection systems offer excellent sensitivity and specificity. This system is extremely useful for patients with low-grade parasitemia. The use of preamplification immunomagnetic separation of *Plasmodium* species and specific colorimetric detection of PCR products may enhance sensitivity and make this technology more user friendly. The PCR-based assay may use either species-specific DNA primers or broad-range *Plasmodium*-specific primers. When broad-range primers are used, speciation is accomplished by either DNA sequencing or Southern-blotting/microtiter plate hybridization with species-specific nucleic acid probes. In nonendemic areas, the molecular detection of plasmodia may be impractical, because costly reagents and kits may expire with only minimal use.

Treatment

In the treatment of malaria, specific antiplasmodial therapy and supportive care are essential to reduce morbidity and mortality. The basic principles of antiplasmodial therapy are defined below. Therapeutics and dosages for the most commonly used antimalarial agents are listed in Box 80–2. It should be noted that antimalarial drugs exist in both salt and base formulations, and potentially dangerous dosing errors may occur unless care is taken. Updated information regarding the treatment and prophylaxis of malaria are available through the Centers for Disease Control and Prevention and the World Health Organization.

P vivax, P ovale, P malariae, **and chloroquine-sensitive** *P falciparum.* Chloroquine phosphate is given to eradicate the RBC phase. Oral therapy is usually sufficient for infections with *P vivax, P ovale,* and *P malariae* and for *P falciparum* infections that are not severe. Intravenous administration of antiplasmodial agents should be used for patients with severe falciparum malaria. Side effects of chloroquine may include gastrointestinal disturbances, pruritis, dizziness, and headache. Chloroquine resistance is widespread among *P falciparum* and rarely has been reported for *P vivax.* Alternative regimens include mefloquine and quinine. Patients infected with either *P vivax* or *P ovale* must also be given primaquine phosphate to eradicate hepatic hypnozoites. The failure to use primaquine may result in malarial relapse at a later date. Primaquine phosphate may cause hemolytic anemia in patients with glucose-6-phosphatase deficiency; additional side effects include gastrointestinal and central nervous system disturbances. In infections caused by these organisms during pregnancy, chloroquine is the drug of choice, and quinine is an alternative. Although not yet approved by the Food and Drug Administration, mefloquine is also probably safe during pregnancy; mefloquine should not be used for severe falciparum malaria, since intravenous therapy is required and there is no parenteral formulation for mefloquine. Although quinine may be used in pregnancy, it may cause uterine contractions and contributes to hypoglycemia. Primaquine and halofantrine are contraindicated in pregnancy.

Chloroquine-resistant *P falciparum.* Oral regimens for patients that do not have severe disease or have severe disease and access to only minimal healthcare facilities consist of quinine given with pyrimethamine-sulfadoxine or followed by either tetracycline or clindamycin. Other oral therapies include mefloquine and quinidine gluconate. Injections of artesunate or artemether or suppositories of artemisinin or artesunate may be useful in instances of limited healthcare. If oral therapy is not possible or if severe disease is present, parenteral therapy with quinine hydrochloride or quinidine gluconate may be given. Pregnant women with chloroquine-resistant malaria who do not have severe disease may be treated with intravenous quinine, sulfonamide/ pyrimethamine (in areas such as India and some regions of Africa, where *P falciparum* is likely to be sensitive) and mefloquine. Mefloquine should not be used for severe falciparum malaria, since intravenous therapy is required, and there is no parenteral formulation for mefloquine. Exchange transfusion may be lifesaving for patients with hyperparasitemia and should be considered if this option exists. The indications for exchange transfusion are a parasitemia of > 10% combined with severe disease, therapeutic failure, or poor prognostic factors or a parasitemia of > 30%, even in the absence of clinical complications.

Prognosis

The prognosis of nonfalciparum malaria is generally good. These organisms are usually responsive to therapy. Relapses of *P vivax* or *P ovale* malaria can be avoided with appropriate therapy. *P malariae* responds well to therapy; however, rare renal involvement may contribute to morbidity and mortality.

The prognosis in falciparum malaria, especially for the nonimmune, is guarded. Malaria caused by *P falciparum* constitutes a medical emergency until proven otherwise. Multisystem organ damage may occur with extreme morbidity and high mortality. Death may occur rapidly from microvascular compromise and subsequent hypoxemia. Involvement of the central nervous system, lungs, and kidneys is especially devastating. Prompt administration of appropriate antimalarial agents, possible exchange transfusion and supportive care significantly reduce morbidity and mortality.

Prevention & Control

Vector Control. An understanding of the habit and behavior of the female *Anopheles* mosquito is useful in disease prevention. Marshlike areas and even microenvironments with standing water serve as breeding areas for the *Anopheles* mosquitos. Avoidance of mosquito-infested areas and elimination of

BOX 80-2

Treatment of Malaria

	Children	Adults
P falciparum malaria from areas with chloroquine resistance[1,2]		
First Choice	• Mefloquine, 25 mg/kg, not to exceed the adult dosage, PO, taken with ≥ 8 oz of water (single dose)	• Mefloquine, five 250-mg tablets (1250 mg) PO, with ≥ 8 oz of water (single dose)
Second Choice	Quinine sulfate, 25 mg/kg/d PO with one of the following: • Doxycycline,[3] 2 mg/kg/d for 7 d, given with the quinine OR • Followed by pyrimethamine-sulfadoxine (0.25 tablet: age <1 yr; 0.5 tablet, age 1–3 yr; 1.0 tablet, age 4–8 yr; 2 tablets, age 9–14 yr OR • Followed by clindamycin, 20–40 mg/kg/d in 3 divided doses	• Quinine sulfate, 650 mg PO every 8 h for 3–7 d, with one of the following: • Doxycycline, 100 mg twice daily for 7 d OR • Followed by 3 pyrimethamine-sulfadoxine tablets. OR • Followed by clindamycin, 900 mg three times a day for 5 d
Parenteral Therapy	• Quinine dihydrochloride, 20 mg of salt/kg IV loading dose in 5% dextrose given over 4 h, followed by 10 mg of salt/kg given over 2–4 h, every 8 h (maximum dose, 1800 mg/d) OR • Quinidine gluconate, 10 mg salt/kg loading dose in normal saline, with slow infusion lasting 1–2 h, (maximum dose, 600 mg), followed by continuous infusion at 0.02 mg/kg/min	• Quinine dihydrochloride, 20 mg of salt/kg IV loading dose in 5% dextrose given over 4 h, followed by 10 mg of salt/kg given over 2–4 h, every 8 h (maximum dose, 1800 mg/d) OR • Quinidine gluconate, 10 mg salt/kg loading dose in normal saline, with slow infusion lasting 1–2 h, (maximum dose, 600 mg), followed by continuous infusion at 0.02 mg/kg/min
Malaria caused by _P vivax_, _P ovale_, _P malariae_, and chloroquine-sensitive _P falciparum_		
First Choice	• Chloroquine, 10 mg base/kg PO loading dose (not to exceed 600 mg base), followed by 5 mg base/kg (not to exceed 300 mg base) given 6 h after the first dose and again on days 2 and 3	• Chloroquine, 600 mg base (1000 mg chloroquine phosphate) PO loading dose, followed by 300 mg base given 6 h after the first dose and again on days 2 and 3
Latent disease caused by _P vivax/P ovale_		
First Choice	• Primaquine phosphate, 0.3 mg base (0.5 mg salt) /kg/d × 14 d	• Primaquine phosphate, 15.3 mg base (26.5 mg salt) qd PO × 14 d OR • 45 mg base (79 mg salt) per wk × 8 wk

[1]Severe falciparum malaria should be treated with parenteral therapy; mefloquine should not be used for the treatment of severe falciparum malaria, since there is no parenteral formulation. Options include quinine (as above), quinidine, artesunate and artemether.

[2]Exchange transfusion may be life saving in nonimmune patients with severe falciparum malaria and is indicated if parasitemia is > 30% or if parasitemia is > 10% and poor prognostic factors are present (i.e. elderly, schizonts in peripheral blood), there are severe systemic manifestations (i.e. cerebral malaria, pulmonary or renal failure) or therapeutic failure.

[3]Do not use doxycycline in pregnant women or in children < 8 years of age.

standing water decrease the likelihood of being bitten. If these areas cannot be avoided, insect repellent should be used. *Anopheles* mosquitoes are evening and nighttime feeders; therefore a combination of mosquito netting and insect repellent at bedtime is encouraged. Mosquito netting impregnated with insecticides is optimal for nighttime barrier protection. The large-scale use of insecticides for vector control usually provides only a short-term solution; insecticide-resistant mosquito strains develop rapidly.

Chemoprophylaxis. Chloroquine is still a useful chemoprophylactic agent in areas without a high prevalence of chloroquine-resistant strains (Box 80–3). The emergence of chloroquine resistance in *P falciparum* and more recently in *P vivax* has limited the usefulness of this drug as a chemoprophylactic agent. In areas where chloroquine resistance is found, mefloquine, doxycycline, or chloroquine plus proguanil may be used for prophylaxis.

Months before departure, travelers to endemic areas should consult physicians experienced in tropical disease prevention. Chemoprophylaxis must begin weeks before departure to ensure an absence of drug hypersensitivity and adequate serum levels. Records should be kept during travel of any failure to maintain the dosing schedule. Chemoprophylaxis should continue for 4 weeks after leaving endemic areas. If episodes of noncompliance have occurred and the patient has not become ill, they are still at risk for malaria if they visited *P vivax*- or *P ovale*-endemic areas.

Information regarding various aspects of malaria, including treatment and prophylaxis, is regularly updated by the World Health Organization and Centers for Disease Control and Prevention. Respective World Wide Web sites are http://www.who.ch/ and http://www.cdc.gov/cdc.htm. Information on various aspects of malaria and other diseases is available from the Centers for Disease Control and Prevention via fax, toll free, at 1-888-232-3228.

Vaccine Development. A highly effective malaria vaccine is yet to be developed. This will likely remain a difficult task, particularly because of the antigenic variability characteristic of *Plasmodium* species. Vaccine targets currently being studied include the sporozoite, the merozoite, and the gametocyte. The respective goals of these vaccine targets are to prevent infection, to decrease the severity and complications of disease, and to arrest development in the mosquito and prevent the production of infective sporozoites.

BABESIA SPP.

Essentials of Diagnosis
- Nonspecific clinical manifestations.
- Exposure: tick exposure, blood transfusion, or both.
- Morphologic, serologic, or molecular evidence of infection.

BOX 80–3

Control of Malaria

Vector Control	• Avoid mosquito-infested areas. • Wear protective clothing during evening and nighttime hours. • Use mosquito repellant (containing 30–35% DEET for adults or 6–10% DEET for children). • Spray bedclothes and mosquito netting with the insect repellent permethrin. • Unless absolutely necessary, pregnant women should not travel to *P falciparum*-endemic areas.
Prophylactic Measures	• Chloroquine remains the drug of choice in areas without known chloroquine resistance. • Mefloquine is used in areas with known chloroquine-resistant strains. • Doxycycline should be used when mefloquine cannot be taken, except by pregnant women, children < 8 y old, or those who are hypersensitive to doxycycline. • Chloroquine & proguanil should be used only for patients who cannot take mefloquine or doxycycline
Emergency Self Treatment of Possible Malaria	• Individuals using chloroquine prophylaxis in areas where chloroquine-resistant strains may reside must have one or more treatment doses of Fansidar (25 mg pyrimethamine + 500 mg sulfadoxine/tablet) (adult dosage: 3 tablets PO as a single dose; pediatric dosage: 5–10 kg, ½ tablet; 11–20 kg, 1 tablet; 21–30 kg, 1 ½ tablets; 31–45 kg, 2 tablets; > 45 kg, adult dose

General Considerations

The members of the genera *Babesia* and *Theileria* are protozoan parasites. These organisms are of medical, veterinary, and economic importance. *Babesia* species cause disease in humans and animals. The genus *Theileria* is the etiologic agent of cattle fever in Eurasia and Africa; it has also been implicated in human disease.

Common to both genera is an intra-erythrocytic phase. These organisms develop pear-shaped intra-erythrocytic ring forms and are therefore referred to as piroplasms. An exo-erythrocytic schizont stage has been demonstrated only for *Theileria* species.

Babesia species were first discovered in cattle in 1888, and they were subsequently found to be the etiologic agent of Texas cattle fever. Human babesiosis was first definitively demonstrated in a splenectomized Yugoslavian cattle farmer in 1957. *Babesia divergens,* a cattle parasite, was the species implicated in this infection. This particular organism causes severe and fatal infections in Europe, in splenectomized individuals. This is in contrast to babesiosis in the United States.

Babesia species are highly endemic in the northeastern portion of North America, but infections have been reported from the southern, midwestern, and western United States. Unlike babesiosis in Europe, infections usually occur in normosplenic individuals and are usually caused by the smaller parasite *B microti*. This parasite is predomininately maintained in a white-footed mouse (*Peromyscus leucopus*) reservoir, but other small rodents may also be infected. *B microti* is transmitted from mouse to mouse and from mouse to human by the hard-bodied tick (*Ixodes scapularis,* previously known as *I dammini*). Transstadial (stage-to-stage) transmission occurs within the tick, but transovarial passage has not been demonstrated. The larval and nymph stages of *I scapularis* typically feed on small rodents and thereby acquire the *Babesia* parasite. The predominant host for the adult *Ixodes* tick is the white-tailed deer. Deer are not infected by *B microti,* but the expanding deer population may contribute to the distribution of both the tick and parasite. This tick vector and the mouse reservoir also harbor the etiologic agent of Lyme disease, *Borrelia burgdorferi* (Chapter 65), and the agent of human granulocytic ehrlichiosis (Chapter 68).

A new species of piroplasm, WA-1, has more recently been associated with human infection in the western United States. This organism is antigenically and genotypically distinct from *B microti*. Genotypic data suggest that this species may be more closely related to *B gibsoni,* a dog parasite, or the *Theileria* species. Presumably, a tick vector is also necessary for natural transmission, but this has yet to be established.

Clinical Findings

A. Signs and Symptoms. In North America, the majority of *Babesia* infections are asymptomatic, but severe and life-threatening infections are documented (Box 80–4). The symptoms in most mild infections are nonspecific and include myalgia, malaise, low-grade fever with chills, fatigue, nausea with or without vomiting, and headache. Severe manifestations probably reflect host susceptibility rather than parasite virulence. The manifestations of severe infection include exacerbations of the symptoms noted above, as well as hemolytic anemia. These patients may be jaundiced and develop dark urine secondary to intravascular hemolytic anemia. Severe manifestations occur more frequently in splenectomized, elderly, or immunocompromised individuals.

Coinfection with *B burgdorferi* should be considered in patients with babesiosis. *Borrelia* species, which cause relapsing fever and Lyme disease, are also transmitted by the *Ixodes* tick. There is also extensive geographic overlap in the distribution of *Borrelia* species and *B microti*. Krause et al studied patients infected with either *B microti* or *B burgdorferi* and compared them with patients coinfected by these organisms. They found that patients coinfected with *B microti* and *B burgdorferi* have longer and more severe disease than patients infected with *B burgdorferi* alone. In animal models, *Babesia* species are known to cause immunosuppression. Similarly, coinfected subjects have evidence of elevated spirochetemia. The exacerbation of symptoms found by Krause et al could conceivably result from transient immunosuppression by *Babesia* species and a subsequent increased spirochetemia.

The cattle-associated parasites *B divergens* and *B bovis* cause human babesiosis in Europe. In this region, splenectomized individuals are at increased risk for infection by these organisms. These patients develop a severe hemolytic disease and have a high fatality rate.

B. Laboratory Findings. Wright- or Giemsa-stained, thick blood preparations may be used to de-

---

BOX 80–4

Babesia-Associated Syndrome

More Common	• Asymptomatic
Less Common	• Mild infection: myalgia, low-grade fever with chills, fatigue, nausea, headache • Severe infection (more common in splenectomized, elderly, or immuno-compromised patients): hemolytic anemia (with jaundice and dark urine), exacerbation of the above symptoms

tect the presence of parasites. Thin blood smears are then used for morphologic studies. Most commonly, nonspecific ring forms are present (Figure 80–7), which must be differentiated from a *Plasmodium* species (see *Plasmodium* section above). Rarely, the parasites may appear as the characteristic "Maltese cross." This consists of a tetrad of merozoites and is pathognomonic for *Babesia* species.

C. Imaging. Magnetic resonance imaging or computed tomography scan of the abdomen may identify nonspecific changes in the spleen.

D. Differential Diagnosis. The nonspecific symptomatology seen in patients with babesiosis may also be seen in a wide variety of infectious diseases. Important etiologic agents in the differential diagnosis of tick-borne disease include *Rickettsia rickettsii* and other spotted fever group rickettsiae, *B burgdorferi* and other *Borrelia* species, *Ehrlichia chaffeensis* and *Ehrlichia canis,* and the coltivirus responsible for Colorado tick fever. Infections by these organisms often lack characteristic physical examination findings, and the definitive diagnosis may rely solely on laboratory findings. If the tick is retained, identification may be useful in limiting the differential diagnosis.

E. Complications. Most infections are asymptomatic, and complications are rare. Complications are more likely in immunocompromised hosts, the very young, and the elderly. Complications include an exacerbation of an already weakened state, severe hemolytic anemia and the sequelae thereof, or, rarely, adult respiratory distress syndrome. As previously mentioned, coinfecting pathogens transmitted by the same tick bite must be considered. Coinfections may produce more severe clinical manifestations and may contribute to higher mortality rates.

Diagnosis

Many *Babesia* infections are subclinical and are dis-

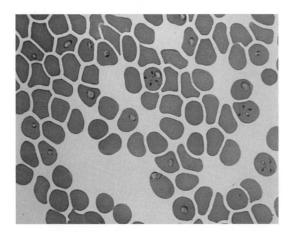

Figure 80–7. Small ring forms of the WA-1 strain of babesia. (Giemsa stain; 1000× magnification.)

covered incidentally. Babesiosis should be suspected in patients with mild, nonspecific symptoms who have recently visited endemic wooded areas and report a tick bite. Babesiosis should be considered in patients who have recently received an RBC transfusion. *Babesia* species, like *Plasmodium* species, may also be transmitted by this blood product. The symptoms of babesiosis are nonspecific. Therefore the definitive diagnosis of babesiosis is made in the laboratory.

As for the detection of *Plasmodium* species, thick and thin blood smears are used for the detection and speciation of *Babesia* species. The thick smear allows for the more rapid screening of greater quantities of blood. This is important because low-grade parasitemia may be present in *Babesia* infections. Species determination is often suggested by the species endemic to the geographic area of exposure. Organism morphology, particularly size, is important for speciation. These should be examined in thin blood smear preparations.

In some instances, the differentiation of *Babesia* species from *P falciparum* may be difficult. When only small ring forms are present in a blood smear, a *Babesia* species must be differentiated from a *Plasmodium* species, particularly *P falciparum.* The absence of hemozoin pigment and appliqué forms supports the identification of a *Babesia* species. Unfortunately, hemozoin pigment may also be absent in erythrocytes containing young plasmodial (ie, ring) trophozoites. *Babesia* species may also be excluded if the characteristic crescent-shaped gametocytes of *P falciparum* are identified. Similarly, malaria is excluded if the tetrad of merozoites, pathognomonic of *Babesia* species, is identified. Probably most important is historical information, such as a history of travel to an endemic area and exposure to the appropriate tick or mosquito vector.

In most instances, the combination of history, clinical presentation, and morphologic features is sufficient to establish the appropriate diagnosis. In difficult cases, molecular methods may be used to differentiate these organisms. The histidine-rich protein 2 of *P falciparum* may be detected in whole blood by ELISA, and species-specific nucleic acid may be detected for either organism by PCR.

Treatment

Mild *Babesia* infections in immunocompetent individuals usually resolve without antimicrobial therapy. In cases of severe disease or in immunocompromised patients, the combination of clindamycin and quinine is the treatment of choice (Box 80–5). The clindamycin may be given orally, intravenously, or intramuscularly. Intravenous quinidine may also be used.

Prognosis

The vast majority of patients infected by *B microti* have subclinical infections that usually resolve without incident. The prognosis for immunocompromised

BOX 80–5

Treatment of Babesiosis

	Children	Adults
First Choice	• Clindamycin (20 mg/kg/d) for 7–10 d, **PLUS** quinine (25 mg/kg/d PO) taken for 7–10 d	• Clindamycin (300–600 mg every 6 h) **PLUS** quinine (650 mg PO every 6–8 h) taken for 7–10 d

BOX 80–6

Control of Babesiosis

Prophylactic Measure	• Avoid tick-infected areas • Use appropriate clothing and tick repellants if avoidance is impractical • Perform a body and scalp search for ticks on leaving infested areas

individuals and the elderly is guarded, because these patients may have a more severe course. Patients who are coinfected with *B burgdorferi* carry a worse prognosis than do patients infected by either organism alone. Prognostic information is not available for infections caused by the WA-1 agent because so few cases have been reported. Splenectomized patients who may be infected by *B divergens* in Europe have a grave prognosis.

Prevention & Control

The avoidance of outdoor activities in tick-infested, *Babesia*-endemic areas is the most effective means of prevention (Box 80–6). If avoidance of these areas is impractical, tick repellents should be used, and appropriate clothing should be worn. After leaving tick-infested areas, one should perform a thorough body and scalp search for ticks.

REFERENCES

Breman JG, Campbell CC: Combatting severe malaria in African children. Bull WHO 1988;66:611.

Gelfand JA: Babesia. In Mandell GL, Bennett JE, and Dolin R, *Principles and Practice of Infectious Diseases,* 4th ed. Churchill Livingstone, 1995.

Krause PJ et al: Concurrent Lyme disease and babesiosis: evidence for increased severity and duration of illness. JAMA 1996;275:1657.

Krogstad DJ: Plasmodium species (malaria). In Mandell GL, Bennett JE, and Dolin R, *Principles and Practice of Infectious Diseases,* 4th ed. Churchill Livingstone, 1995.

Parra ME, Evans CB, Taylor DW: Identification of *Plasmodium falciparum* histidine-rich protein 2 in the plasma of humans with malaria. J Clin Microbiol 1991;29:1629.

Persing DH et al: Detection of *Babesia microti* by polymerase chain reaction. J Clin Microbiol. 1992;30:2097.

Pruthi RK et al: Human babesiosis. Mayo Clin Proc 1995;70:853.

Quick RE et al: Babesiosis in Washington State—a new species of *Babesia.* Ann Intern Med 1993;119:284.

Ryan ET, Kain KC: Health Advice and Immunizations for Travelers. NEJM 2000;342:1716.

Seesod N et al: An integrated system using immunomagnetic separation, polymerase chain reaction, and colorimetric detection for diagnosis of *Plasmodium falciparum.* Am J Trop Med Hyg 1997;56:322.

World Health Organization: Severe falciparum malaria. Trans R Soc Trop Med Hyg 2000;94(Suppl 1):1.

Toxoplasma gondii

81

Jose G. Montoya, MD

General Considerations

A. Epidemiology. *Toxoplasma gondii* infection, or toxoplasmosis, is a zoonosis (the definitive hosts are members of the cat family). The two most common routes of infection in humans are by oral ingestion of the parasite and by transplacental (congenital) transmission to the fetus. Ingestion of undercooked or raw meat that contains cysts or of water or food contaminated with oocysts results in acute infection.

In humans, the prevalence of toxoplasmosis increases with age. There are also considerable geographic differences in prevalence rates (eg, 10% in Palo Alto, CA; 15% in Boston, MA; 30% in Birmingham, AL; 70% in France; ≤ 90% in El Salvador). Differences in the epidemiology of *T gondii* infection in various geographic locales and between population groups within the same locale may be explained by differences in exposure to the organism. Occasionally, outbreaks occur within families or certain populations. The possibility of an outbreak should always be suspected with every case of recently acquired acute infection.

The incidence of congenital toxoplasmosis is directly correlated with three factors: (1) the prevalence of primary infection among women during pregnancy, (2) the gestational age at which a pregnant woman acquires the infection, and (3) the types of public health programs available for prevention, detection, and treatment of the infection during pregnancy. Although screening for *Toxoplasma* infection is compulsory during pregnancy in some countries such as Austria and France, routine serological screening is not performed in the United States. Without any therapeutic intervention, the incidence of congenital toxoplasmosis is ~ 15% for a fetus whose mother becomes infected during the first trimester, 30% during the second trimester, and 60% during the third trimester. Spiramycin decreases the incidence of fetal infection by ~ 60%. It has been reported that, if maternal infection is acquired during the first 2 weeks of gestation and spiramycin is administered for the entire pregnancy, the incidence of fetal infection is negligible.

As an opportunistic pathogen in HIV-infected persons, *T gondii* has had a major impact on public health. The incidence of toxoplasmosis in an HIV-infected population is directly correlated with four factors: (1) the prevalence of anti-*Toxoplasma* antibodies, (2) the degree of immunosuppression as estimated by the CD4 cell count, (3) the frequency with which effective prophylactic regimens against *Toxoplasma* reactivation are used, and (4) the frequency with which highly active antiretroviral therapy is used. Of individuals seropositive for both HIV and *Toxoplasma* with CD4 counts of < 100 cells/mm^3, 30%–50% will develop toxoplasmic encephalitis (TE) if prophylaxis is not used. Genetic factors may also play a role in predisposition of AIDS patients for this disease, based on findings from a murine model of TE and the observation that not all HIV-infected patients with positive *T gondii* serology develop TE. Human lymphocyte antigen DQ3 appears to be a genetic marker of susceptibility to development of TE in AIDS patients, and DQ1 may be a marker of resistance.

Even before the emergence of AIDS, TE had been recognized as a major cause of morbidity and mortality among non–HIV-immunosuppressed patients, especially in those whose underlying disease or therapy caused a deficiency in T-cell–mediated immunity (eg, Hodgkin's disease and heart, lung, kidney, and bone marrow transplantation).

B. Microbiology. *T gondii* is an obligate intracellular coccidian protozoan that exists in three forms: the oocyst (which releases sporozoites), the tachyzoite, and the tissue cyst (which contains and may release bradyzoites). The parasite undergoes two cycles, an enteroepithelial sexual cycle in the small bowel of members of the cat family and an extraintestinal asexual cycle in cats as well as in all other infected animals, including humans. Cats shed oocysts after they ingest any of the three forms of the parasite. Humans usually become infected by ingestion of tissue cysts (in meat) or oocysts (in cat feces); the outer walls of both are disrupted by enzymatic degradation, and the parasites are liberated into the intestinal lumen. They become tachyzoites and spread to virtually all cells and tissues of the body.

1. Oocyst. Oocysts are formed in the small bowel of members of the cat family and are excreted in their feces for 7–20 days. They are highly resistant to conditions found within the external environment. As many as 10 million oocysts may be shed in a single day and will become infectious (by sporulation) in 1–21 days, depending on temperature and availability of oxygen.

2. Tachyzoite. Tachyzoites are crescent or oval shaped and measure 2–4 μm wide by 4–8 μm long. They require an intracellular habitat to survive and multiply despite having their own Golgi apparatus, ribosomes, and mitochondria. Tachyzoites penetrate host cells by an active process involving the components of an "apical complex" (hence the term apicomplexan). They reside and multiply within an intracellular parasitophorous vacuole whose composition (eg, acidity) is dictated in large part by the parasite. In the laboratory, tachyzoites are propagated in the peritoneum of mice and in tissue-cultured mammalian cells. The presence of tachyzoites in human fluids or tissues is the hallmark of acute infection.

3. Tissue cyst. After cell entry and replication of the tachyzoite form, encystation and formation of tissue cysts may occur. The precise conditions that promote cyst formation are not known. The tissue cyst is formed within a host cell and may vary in size from those containing only a few organisms (bradyzoites) to those ≥ 200 μm in diameter containing several thousand bradyzoites. Tissue cysts stain well with periodic acid-Schiff reagent, Wright-Giemsa, Gomori-methenamine silver, and immunoperoxidase stains. The cysts are spherical when found in the brain and conform to the shape of muscle fibers when in heart and skeletal muscle tissue. The most common sites of latent infection are the central nervous system (CNS); eye; and skeletal, smooth, and heart muscles. Because of this persistence in tissues, demonstration of cysts in histologic sections does not necessarily mean that the infection was recently acquired or that it is clinically relevant.

4. Stage conversion. Tachyzoites and bradyzoites differ phenotypically. Tachyzoites multiply rapidly and synchronously, forming rosettes, thereby lysing the cell, whereas the more slowly replicating bradyzoites form tissue cysts. Major differences in energy metabolism and in antigenic structure of tachyzoites and bradyzoites reflect the expression of stage-specific pathways and molecules that promote parasite survival in diverse environments and under diverse conditions within the host.

C. Pathogenesis. *T gondii* multiplies inside cells at the site of invasion (the gastrointestinal tract appears to be the major route for and the initial site of infection in nature). After host cell disruption, parasites invade adjacent cells from which they spread throughout the body via lymphatics and the bloodstream. Humoral immunity and cellular immunity appear to curtail successfully the parasitemic phase; only those parasites protected by an intracellular habitat or within tissue cysts survive. An effective immune response is also responsible for a significant early reduction in the number of *T gondii* in all tissues. Thereafter, tachyzoites are rarely demonstrated in tissues.

The tissue cyst form is responsible for residual infection and persists primarily in brain, skeletal, and heart muscle, and in the eye. Whereas toxoplasmosis in severely immunodeficient individuals may be caused by primary infection, it most often is the result of recrudescence of a latent infection.

The histopathologic changes of toxoplasmic lymphadenitis are frequently diagnostic in immunocompetent individuals. There is a characteristic triad of findings: a reactive follicular hyperplasia, irregular clusters of epithelioid histiocytes encroaching on and blurring the margins of the germinal centers, and focal distension of sinuses with monocytoid cells.

Ocular involvement in immunocompetent patients produces acute retinochoroiditis characterized by necrosis and severe inflammation. Granulomatous inflammation of the choroid is secondary to the necrotizing retinitis.

Involvement of the CNS is characterized by multiple enlarging foci of necrosis and microglial nodules. Necrosis is the most salient feature of the disease because of vascular involvement. The presence of multiple brain abscesses is the most typical feature of TE in severely immunodeficient patients and is particularly characteristic in patients with AIDS. At autopsy in most AIDS patients with TE, cerebral hemispheres are involved, with a peculiar predilection for the basal ganglia. Pulmonary toxoplasmosis in the immunodeficient patient may present as interstitial pneumonitis, necrotizing pneumonitis, consolidation, and/or pleural effusion. Chorioretinitis in AIDS patients is characterized by segmental panophthalmitis and areas of coagulative necrosis associated with tissue cysts and tachyzoites.

D. Immunity to *T gondii*. After disease in the immunocompetent host, immunity against *T gondii* is lifelong. Cellular immunity appears to be more important than humoral immunity in defense of the brain. A well-orchestrated interaction between CD4 and CD8 T lymphocytes; lymphokine-activated killer, natural killer, and γδ T cells; and cytokines such as interferon-γ, tumor necrosis factor-α, interleukin-1 (IL-1), IL-2, IL-4, IL-6, IL-7, IL-10, IL-12, and IL-15 appears to determine the outcome of the parasite-human host interaction. Nitric oxide may have a tissue-specific protective role.

Clinical Findings

Primary infection in any host often goes unrecognized. In ~ 10% of immunocompetent individuals, it causes a self-limited and nonspecific illness that rarely requires treatment. The most frequently observed clinical manifestation in this setting is lymphadenopathy and fatigue without fever; other manifestations include chorioretinitis, myocarditis, and polymyositis (Box 81–1). Reinfection occurs but

BOX 81–1

Clinical Syndromes Associated with Toxoplasmosis[1]

Patient	Syndromes
Immunocompetent	
• Asymptomatic	• 90% of acute infection goes unrecognized
• Lymphadenitis	• Regional or generalized lymphadenopathy
• Chorioretinitis	• Intensely white focal retinal lesions with overlying vitritis, with or without associated scars; may result from reactivation of congenital or postnatally acquired disease or from recently acquired acute disease
• Myocarditis	• Arrythmias, pericarditis, heart failure
• Polymyositis	• Patients with acute toxoplasmosis have developed polymyositis/dermatomyositis-like syndromes
• Systemic	• Low-grade fever, general malaise, headache, sore throat, myalgia
	• Disseminated disease is extremely rare; may present with fever, pneumonitis, hepatitis, or, possibly, encephalitis
Immunocompromised	
• Encephalitis	• Focal or nonfocal neurological symptoms and/or mental status changes; usually occurs in the setting of advanced T-cell–mediated immunity impairment
• Chorioretinitis	• Can present atypically and/or with significant retinal necrosis
• Myelopathy	• Cervical, thoracic, or lumbar
• Pneumonitis	• Interstitial infiltrates
• Systemic	• Fever, multiorgan involvement, acute respiratory failure, and septic shocklike syndrome
Pregnant	
• Asymptomatic	• 90% of acute infection goes unrecognized
• Lymphadenitis	• Regional or generalized lymphadenopathy
Fetus	
• Neurologic disease	• Ultrasound may be normal or reveal ventricular dilatation, intracranial calcifications
• Generalized disease	• Ultrasound may be normal or reveal increased placental thickness, hepatomegaly, ascites
Newborn	
• Asymptomatic	• 85% of newborns with congenital disease appear normal at birth
• Neurologic disease	• Seizures, chorioretinitis, abnormal neurological exam, hydrocephalus, cerebral calcifications
• Generalized disease	• Fever, hepatosplenomegaly, lymphadenopathy, jaundice, thrombocytopenia, anemia

[1]Syndromes are not mutually exclusive. Patients may present simultaneously or sequentially with two or more syndromes (ie, an otherwise immunocompetent patient may have lymphadenitis and chorioretinitis, or a newborn may present with hydrocephalus, cerebral calcifications, and thrombocytopenia).

does not appear to result in clinically apparent disease. In contrast to the usually benign course of the initial infection in immunologically intact hosts, the congenitally infected fetus and newborn and immunocompromised patients are at high risk for severe or life-threatening disease caused by this parasite. Congenital toxoplasmosis is the result of maternal infection acquired during gestation. Among immunologically impaired individuals, toxoplasmosis most often occurs in those with defects in T-cell–mediated immunity such as those with hematological malig-

nancies, bone marrow and solid-organ transplants, or AIDS.

A. Signs and symptoms.

1. Infection in immunocompetent adults and children. Primary infection with *T gondii* in children and adults is asymptomatic in the vast majority of cases. Lymphadenopathy and fatigue, without fever, are the most common manifestations in the minority that become symptomatic. The lymph nodes most commonly involved are cervical, suboccipital, supraclavicular, axillary, and inguinal. Lymphadenopathy is usually regional; often a single posterior cervical node is enlarged. On palpation, the nodes are discrete, nontender, and nonfluctuant. Occasionally, lymph nodes may become matted. Fever, sore throat, maculopapular rash, malaise, night sweats, myalgias, hepatosplenomegaly, or atypical lymphocytes are variably present. The clinical picture may resemble infectious mononucleosis or cytomegalovirus (CMV) infection; however, toxoplasmosis probably causes < 1% of mononucleosis-like syndromes. In rare cases, lymphadenopathy may persist for months.

Toxoplasmic chorioretinitis can occur either in the setting of acute acquired infection (sporadic and epidemic) or as a reactivation of intrauterine or postnatally acquired infection. Patients who present with chorioretinitis as a late sequela of intrauterine infection are more frequently in the second and third decades of life (it is rare after age 40); bilateral disease, retinal scars, and involvement of the macula are hallmarks of the retinal disease in these cases. In contrast, patients who present with toxoplasmic chorioretinitis in the setting of acute toxoplasmosis are more often in the fourth to sixth decades of life and most often have unilateral involvement. The eye lesions usually spare the macula and are not associated with old scars.

2. Infection in pregnant women. Recognition of toxoplasmosis in pregnancy is important only because of the risk of transmission to the fetus. This risk is limited almost exclusively to those fetuses whose mothers acquire the infection for the first time during gestation. Acquisition of *Toxoplasma* infection before pregnancy in an otherwise healthy female does not pose a significant risk of transplacental transmission. On rare occasions, transmission to the fetus has occurred in immunocompetent women infected with *T gondii* within 3 months of conception. In immunocompromised women, such as those with HIV infection, acquisition of *T gondii* before conception (chronic infection) has then led to transmission to the fetus as a consequence of reactivation.

3. Congenital toxoplasmosis. Of newborns with congenital toxoplasmosis, ~ 85% appear normal at birth. Thus, one cannot rely on clinical examination alone to raise the possibility of this disease. However, if untreated, congenital toxoplasmosis will inevitably lead to disease in most infected children.

The earlier in gestation a mother is infected with *T gondii,* the more severe is the disease in the fetus and newborn, despite the lower frequency with which transmission occurs with shorter periods of gestation. Findings include chorioretinitis with blindness, epilepsy, psychomotor disorders and developmental delay, hearing loss, jaundice, rash, hematologic abnormalities, and pneumonitis. The classic triad of hydrocephalus, chorioretinitis, and cerebral calcifications is seen only rarely.

4. Infection in immunocompromised patients. In immunocompromised patients, toxoplas-

mosis almost always occurs as a result of reactivation of previously acquired infection. Toxoplasmosis may also result when a seronegative recipient receives a heart from a seropositive donor. In contrast to the relatively favorable course of toxoplasmosis in almost all immunocompetent individuals, it is a dreadful and often life-threatening disease in immunodeficient patients.

In this population, the brain is the most common affected organ. The clinical presentation of TE varies from a subacute, gradual process that evolves over weeks to an acute state of confusion, with or without focal neurologic deficits evolving over days. Clinical manifestations include alteration in mental status, seizures, motor weakness, cranial-nerve disturbances, sensory abnormalities, cerebellar signs, movement disorders, and neuropsychiatric findings. Constitutional symptoms and signs such as fever and malaise are variable.

The most common focal neurologic findings are hemiparesis and abnormalities of speech. Because *T gondii* causes predominantly encephalitis with little or no meningeal involvement, signs of meningeal irritation are rare. Cranial-nerve lesions develop secondary to brainstem involvement. Seizures, cerebral hemorrhage, and diffuse TE may present acutely and progress rapidly to death. Spinal-cord toxoplasmosis in AIDS patients can present with motor or sensory disturbances of single or multiple extremities, bladder dysfunction, and/or bowel dysfunction. Cervical and thoracic myelopathy and conus medullaris syndromes have also been reported.

Clinical manifestations of toxoplasmosis in immunocompromised patients also include pneumonitis, chorioretinitis, and multiorgan involvement that presents with acute respiratory failure and hemodynamic abnormalities similar to septic shock.

B. Laboratory findings. Laboratory approaches for the diagnosis of toxoplasmosis include serology, histology with various stains (hematoxylin and eosin, immunoperoxidase, Wright-Giemsa, and periodic acid-Schiff), isolation of the parasite by mouse or tissue culture inoculation, polymerase chain reaction (PCR), and radiological studies (Table 81–1). Histologic examination may reveal the characteristic morphology of the parasite in tissues; the presence of tachyzoites or multiple cysts is diagnostic of active infection. The presence of a solitary cyst may reflect chronic infection unless it is associated with inflammation. Almost any tissue can be inoculated into the peritoneal cavity of mice for isolation studies. Several body fluids can be examined by PCR for the detection of *T gondii* DNA, including cerebrospinal fluid (CSF), bronchoalveolar lavage fluid, vitreal fluid, aqueous humor, amniotic fluid, urine, and peripheral blood. PCR examination of brain tissue is discouraged because a positive result does not distinguish active from chronic infection.

For any individual in whom toxoplasmosis is con-

Table 81–1. Laboratory tests for the diagnosis of toxoplasmosis.

- Serology (IgG) is useful to establish whether the patient has been exposed to *T gondii*.[1] It can also indicate whether the infection is acute or chronic.[2,3]
- Histology (hematoxylin and eosin, immunoperoxidase, Wright-Giemsa and periodic acid-Schiff stains). The presence of tachyzoites is diagnostic of acute infection. Solitary cysts do not necessarily indicate acute or reactivated disease.
- Isolation of the parasite from any tissue by mouse or tissue culture inoculation is diagonostic.[2]
- PCR-based detection of DNA in amniotic fluid, CSF, ocular fluids, bronchoalveolar lavage, peripheral blood, and urine is diagnostic.[2]
- Radiographic studies are helpful when suspecting CNS toxoplasmosis in the fetus or newborn (ultrasound or CT) and immunocompromised patients (CT or MRI).
- In most cases, ocular toxoplasmosis is a clinical diagnosis.

[1]Confirmatory serological tests include the Sabin-Feldman dye test for IgG, IgM ELISA, IgA ELISA, differential agglutination test, and IgE ELISA.
[2]Consultation with a reference laboratory is strongly recommended.
[3]Serological diagnosis may not be useful in immunocompromised individuals.

sidered in the differential diagnosis, the most important initial step is to determine whether the patient has been exposed to the parasite. In virtually all situations, a negative serum immunoglobulin G (IgG) test essentially rules out earlier or recent exposure to the parasite. Rarely, cases of documented toxoplasmic chorioretinitis and TE have been reported in seronegative patients. If IgG antibodies are present and clinical suspicion is high, it is important to establish whether the patient's condition is caused by a recently acquired infection or by reactivation of chronic infection. A true negative IgM antibody test essentially rules out acquisition of the infection within the previous 6 months; however, it does not rule out reactivation of chronic infection. A positive *T gondii*-specific IgM antibody test can be interpreted in three ways: (1) as a true positive result consistent with recently acquired infection, (2) as a true positive result in the setting of a chronic infection (IgM antibodies have been shown to persist for as long as 5 years after the acute infection), or (3) as a false positive result. To establish which of these is most likely in a given case, confirmatory testing in a reference laboratory should be performed whenever feasible. Confirmatory tests include the Sabin-Feldman dye test, IgM enzyme-linked immunosorbent assay (ELISA), IgA ELISA, IgE ELISA, and differential agglutination test. These tests are available at the Toxoplasma Serology Laboratory at the Palo Alto Medical Foundation (650-853-4828). If the patient has received a blood transfusion, serologic tests may measure antibody acquired exogenously rather than endogenously. The use of serological tests to evaluate the response to therapy should be discouraged.

Despite the crucial role played by members of the feline family in the life cycle of *T gondii*, a history of cat exposure is not particularly helpful in assessing the likelihood of toxoplasmosis in a given patient. Transmission of *T gondii* almost always occurs without the awareness of the patient and may be unrelated to direct exposure to cat feces (eg, transmission of oocysts by contaminated vegetables or water). On the other hand, cats that remain indoors at all times and that are fed only cooked food do not pose a risk to humans. Serologic examination of cats should be discouraged; seropositivity does not predict shedding of oocysts.

1. Infection in immunocompetent adults and children. The diagnosis of toxoplasmosis in the vast majority of immunocompetent adults and children relies on serological tests. Recently acquired toxoplasmic lymphadenopathy is easily diagnosed serologically, but, unfortunately, it is not often suspected until after lymph node biopsy. Acute infection is supported by the documented appearance of IgG or IgM antibodies or by a greater than fourfold rise in antibody titer. Histology of appropriate specimens (lymph node or myocardium) may be helpful.

In most cases, toxoplasmic chorioretinitis is diagnosed by and treatment initiated on the basis of ophthalmologic examination and serology test results. PCR analysis of vitreous fluid or the measurement of intraocular production of *T gondii*-specific IgG antibodies may be useful in patients with presumed toxoplasmic chorioretinitis in whom response to appropriate anti-*Toxoplasma* therapy is considered inadequate or suboptimal and in patients with atypical eye findings.

2. Infection in pregnant women. The first step in addressing the possibility of toxoplasmosis in pregnancy is to establish whether acute infection has occurred. In the vast majority of cases, the diagnosis of acute infection during pregnancy is only possible with serological testing (Table 81–2). A serological diagnosis should be confirmed by a reference laboratory because the reliability of commercial IgM test kits varies considerably and because the presence of IgM antibody does not necessarily establish the diagnosis of the acute infection (see above).

3. Congenital toxoplasmosis. Prenatal assessment of fetal infection should be performed when a diagnosis of acute infection is established or highly suspected in a pregnant woman. Amplification of T *gondii* DNA by PCR and/or isolation of *T gondii* from amniotic fluid establishes the diagnosis of fetal infection and has entirely replaced the testing of blood samples obtained by periumbilical fetal blood sampling. Examination of amniotic fluid should be performed at 18 weeks. The reliability of the PCR test before 18 weeks of gestational age is unknown. The sensitivity of amniotic fluid PCR is ~70%. The sensitivity of inoculation of amniotic fluid into mice for isolation of *T gondii* is ~ 60%. The specificity of

Table 81–2. Interpretation of *Toxoplasma* serology in pregnant women.[1]

IgG result	IgM result	Interpretation and Recommendation
Negative	Negative	No serologic evidence of infection with *T gondii*
Negative	Equivocal or positive	Possible acute infection or false positive IgM. Send sample to reference laboratory
Equivocal	Negative	Indeterminate; obtain a new specimen for testing or retest for IgG in a different assay
Equivocal	Equivocal	Indeterminate; obtain a new specimen for both IgG and IgM testing
Equivocal	Positive	Possible acute infection. Send sample to reference laboratory
Positive	Negative	Infected with *T gondii* for > 6 months
Positive	Equivocal or positive	Possible acute infection. Send sample to reference laboratory

[1]Modified from US Food and Drug Administration Public Health Advisory: *Limitations of Toxoplasma IgM Commercial Test Kits.*

the PCR test is close to 100%. Ultrasonography is a useful test to establish the severity of the infection; however, it should not be used to confirm or rule out congenital toxoplasmosis. Abnormalities frequently reported with this method in cases of in utero infection include ventricular dilatation, intracranial calcifications, increased placental thickness, hepatic enlargement, and ascites.

The diagnosis of congenital toxoplasmosis in the newborn can be made by detecting specific IgA and IgM antibodies. Serum samples from the newborn should be obtained from peripheral blood and not from the umbilical cord, because it is essential that maternal contamination of blood obtained at birth be excluded. The presence of IgG antibodies in the newborn may reflect passive transplacental transfer of maternal antibodies. Other laboratory tests available for the diagnosis of congenital disease in infants include isolation of the parasite in mice or cell culture (eg, from placental tissue or body fluids) and PCR with body fluids, such as CSF, blood, and urine. Clinical evaluation of infants with presumed *T gondii* infection should always include ophthalmologic examination, radiologic studies (particularly to detect the presence of cerebral calcifications), and examination of CSF.

4. Infection in immunocompromised patients. It is important to maintain a high index of suspicion for toxoplasmosis in immunodeficient patients because its clinical manifestations are protean and nonspecific and, if left untreated, toxoplasmosis is a source of major morbidity and mortality.

Because reactivation of chronic infection is the most common cause of toxoplasmosis in AIDS- and non–AIDS-immunocompromised patients, the initial routine assessment of these patients, even in the absence of signs of toxoplasmosis, should include a serum *T gondii* IgG antibody test. Those with a positive result are at risk of reactivation of the infection; those with a negative result should be instructed on how to prevent infection.

The anti-*Toxoplasma* serologic status of heart transplant recipients should be routinely assessed before transplantation, and an appropriate prophylactic regimen should be instituted for all seronegative hosts if they receive a heart from a seropositive donor.

A definitive diagnosis of toxoplasmosis in the immunodeficient patient relies on histologic demonstration or isolation of the parasite or PCR-based detection of its DNA. In AIDS patients, CSF examination by PCR has been found to have a sensitivity of ~ 80% for the diagnosis of TE. CSF PCR for other organisms has also been found to be helpful in patients with AIDS, including amplification of Epstein-Barr virus, CMV, and JC virus DNA for the diagnosis of primary CNS lymphoma, CMV ventriculitis, and progressive multifocal leukoencephalopathy, respectively.

Computed tomography (CT) or magnetic resonance imaging (MRI) should be obtained when clinical manifestations suggest involvement of the CNS or spinal cord. These studies should be performed even if the neurological examination does not reveal focal deficits. MRI is the radiological test of choice and is more sensitive than CT.

A presumptive diagnosis of CNS toxoplasmosis can be made for patients with multiple ring-enhancing brain lesions (usually established by MRI), positive *T gondii*-specific IgG antibody titers, and advanced immunodeficiency (eg, CD4 count < 200 or patients who receive intensive immunosuppressive therapy) and justifies anti-*Toxoplasma* therapy. A clinical and radiologic response to specific therapy within 7–10 days supports the diagnosis.

Brain biopsy should be considered in immunodeficient patients with suspected TE if there is a negative IgG antibody test, a single lesion on MRI, inadequate clinical response to an optimal anti-*Toxoplasma* treatment regimen, or development of disease in the face of an effective prophylactic regimen against *T gondii*.

In heart transplant patients who present with a clinical syndrome that suggests toxoplasmosis, serologic test results may be misleading. Results consistent with chronic infection may be seen in the presence of acute toxoplasmosis. On the other hand, results that suggest apparent reactivation (rising IgG and IgM titers) may be found in the absence of clinically apparent infection. In these patients endomyocardial biopsy is useful.

Differential Diagnosis

The differential diagnosis of toxoplasmic lymphadenitis includes lymphoma, Epstein-Barr virus-associated infectious mononucleosis, CMV "mononucleosis," cat scratch disease, sarcoidosis, tuberculosis, tularemia, and metastatic carcinoma. For toxoplasmic encephalitis, the differential diagnosis includes primary CNS lymphoma, JC virus-associated progressive multifocal leukoencephalopathy, CMV ventriculitis, tuberculoma, cryptococoma, and bacterial or nocardial brain abscess. None of the signs described in newborns with congenital disease are pathognomonic for toxoplasmosis, and all of them may be mimicked by congenital infection with other pathogens, including CMV, *Treponema pallidum,* herpes simplex virus, and rubella virus.

Complications

In rare instances, toxoplasmosis causes myocarditis, polymyositis, pneumonitis, hepatitis, or encephalitis in healthy individuals. Early maternal infections sometimes result in death of the fetus in utero and spontaneous abortion.

Treatment

A. Infection in Immunocompetent Adults and Children. Immunocompetent adults and children with toxoplasmic lymphadenitis do not require treatment unless symptoms are severe or persistent. Infections acquired by laboratory accident or transfusion of blood products are potentially more severe, and these patients should always be treated. The combination of pyrimethamine, sulfadiazine, and folinic acid for 4–6 weeks is the most commonly used and recommended drug regimen (Box 81–2). Treatment should be administered for 2–4 weeks, followed by reassessment of the patient's condition.

The decision to treat active toxoplasmic chorioretinitis should be based on the results of an examination performed by an ophthalmologist. Pyrimethamine and sulfadiazine plus folinic acid are commonly used for this syndrome. Clindamycin has also been used with favorable clinical results. Systemic corticosteroids may be required in addition to the anti-*Toxoplasma* drugs.

B. Infection in Pregnant Women. Spiramycin is the drug of choice for pregnant women who have acquired primary *T gondii* infection during gestation (Box 81–3). It does not eliminate but does appear to decrease the incidence of fetal infection. Because there is usually a delay between acquisition of acute maternal infection, infection of the placenta, and subsequent infection of the fetus, identification of acute maternal infection warrants immediate institution of spiramycin [available from the U.S. Food and Drug Administration (301-827-2335)]. Maternal adverse effects associated with spiramycin include nausea, vomiting, anorexia, diarrhea, vertigo, dizziness, flushing of the face, feeling of coolness, and numbness. There is no evidence that spiramycin is teratogenic. Spiramycin should be continued throughout the pregnancy even if the amniotic-fluid PCR result is negative for fetal infection. If the amniotic-fluid PCR result is positive at ≥ 18 weeks, the institution of

---

BOX 81-2

Treatment of Toxoplasmosis in Immunocompetent Patients

Syndrome	Drug	Children	Adults
Lymphadenitis	None	No therapy[1]	No therapy[1]
Chorioretinitis (active), myocarditis, polymyositis, systemic[2]	• Pyrimethamine **PLUS**	• Loading dose: 2 mg/kg/d (maximum, 50 mg) for 2 days, then maintenance, 1 mg/kg/d (maximum 25 mg)	• Loading dose: 75–100 mg over 24 h, followed by 25 to 50 mg/d
	• Sulfadiazine[3] **PLUS**	• Loading dose: 75 mg/kg, then maintenance, 50 mg/kg every 12 h (maximum 4 g/d)	• Loading dose: 2–4 g initially, followed by 1 g four times per day
	• Folinic acid	• 5–20 mg, 3 times weekly	• 5–10 mg/d
	• Corticosteroids (if indicated)	• 1 mg/kg/d in 2 divided doses	• Dosing varies with clinical setting

[1]Treatment may be indicated if accompanying symptoms are severe or persistent.
[2]The role of other regimens, including drugs such as atovaquone, clarithromycin, azithromycin, trimethoprim/sulfamethoxazole, or dapsone, has not been well established.
[3]Clindamycin (300 mg by mouth every 6 h for a minimum of 3 weeks) is an alternative in patients allergic to sulfonamides.

BOX 81–3

Treatment of Toxoplasmosis in Pregnant Women

Syndrome	Drug	Dosages
Acute infection acquired during gestation	• Spiramycin (should be continued for the entire pregnancy even if amniotic fluid PCR is negative)	3 g/d
Amniotic fluid PCR-positive result at 18 weeks of gestation or later	• Pyrimethamine **PLUS** sulfadiazine **PLUS** folinic acid starting after 18th wk of gestation	Same doses as for immunocompetent patient

pyrimethamine, sulfadiazine, and folinic acid is recommended to treat fetal infection in utero.

Pregnant women with toxoplasmic chorioretinitis from reactivation of infection do not experience a higher risk of parasite transmission to the fetus than do pregnant women with prior infection and no ocular disease. However, when toxoplasmic chorioretinitis is thought to be a manifestation of primary infection acquired during gestation, it should be treated, because of the risks to both the mother and the fetus. The advice of an ophthalmologist should be sought.

C. Congenital Toxoplasmosis. The combination of sulfadiazine, pyrimethamine, and folinic acid for ≥ 12 months is a commonly advocated regimen for infants born to mothers with positive results in the amniotic fluid or in whom the disease is highly suspected or proven (Box 81–4).

D. Infection in Immunocompromised Patients. The regimens used to treat toxoplasmosis in immunocompromised patients are basically the same as those used in other clinical settings; however, the doses recommended for immunocompromised patients are usually higher. The standard regimen is the combination of pyrimethamine, sulfadiazine, and folinic (not folic) acid (Box 81–5). Clindamycin can be used instead of sulfadiazine in adult patients intolerant to sulfonamides. The recommended duration of treatment is 4–6 weeks after resolution of all signs and symptoms (often for a total of at least several months). The role of other drugs (eg, atovaquone, clarithromycin, azithromycin, trimethoprim-sulfamethoxazole, and dapsone) in the treatment of toxoplasmosis in immunocompromised patients has not been well established. If these drugs are used, they should be given preferably in combination with pyrimethamine. At the present time, monotherapy does not have a role in the treatment of toxoplasmosis.

In patients with AIDS, after treatment of the acute phase (primary or induction treatment), maintenance therapy (secondary prophylaxis) should be instituted. The maintenance regimen is the same as that used in the acute phase but with each drug at one-half the dose. Current recommendations suggest that maintenance therapy be continued for the life of the patient. It is not known at this time whether the immune reconstitution observed as a result of combination antiretroviral therapy in AIDS patients might allow the successful discontinuation of maintenance treatment. Some non-AIDS-immunocompromised patients may also require maintenance treatment as long as their immunosuppressive regimens continue to exert a significant impact on cell-mediated immunity.

Prevention & Control

Prevention of the primary infection is of paramount importance in pregnant women and immunodeficient patients who are seronegative (Box 81–6). Tissue cysts in meat are rendered noninfectious by heating the meat to 66 °C (meat should be cooked to

BOX 81–4

Treatment of Toxoplasmosis in Newborns

Drug	Dosages
Pyrimethamine **PLUS**	• Loading dose: 2 mg/kg/d (maximum, 50 mg) or 2 d, then 1 mg/kg/d for 2 or 6 mo. After 2 or 6 mo, 1 mg/kg/d every Monday, Wednesday, and Friday
Sulfadiazine[1] **PLUS** Folinic acid	• 50 mg/kg every 12 h • 5–20 mg 3 times weekly
Corticosteroids (if indicated)	1 mg/kg/d in 2 divided doses

[1]Clindamycin is an alternative in patients allergic to sulfonamides.

BOX 81-5

Treatment of Toxoplasmosis in Immunocompromised Patients

Drug	Children	Adults
Pyrimethamine **PLUS**	• Loading dose: 2 mg/kg/d (maximum, 50 mg) for 2 days, then maintenance, 1 mg/kg/d (maximum 25 mg)	• Loading dose: 200 mg over 24 h, followed by 50–75 mg/d
Sulfadiazine[1] **PLUS**	• Loading dose: 75 mg/kg, then maintenance, 50 mg/kg every 12 h (maximum 4 g/d)	• Loading dose: 2–4 g initially, followed by 1–1.5 g four times per day
Folinic acid	• 5–20 mg 3 times weekly	• 5–10 mg/d (≤ 50 mg/d)

[1]Clindamycin (300 mg by mouth every 6 h for a minimum of 3 weeks) is an alternative in patients allergic to sulfonamides.

BOX 81-6

Prevention of Primary *T gondii* Infection[1]

Infectious Form	Preventive Measure
Tissue cyst (meat)	• Wash hands thoroughly after contact with raw meat • Avoid mucous membrane contact when handling raw meat • Wash kitchen surfaces and utensils that have come in contact with raw meat • Cook meat well done (meat that is cured in brine may be infectious) • Avoid ingestion of dried meat • Refrain from skinning animals
Oocyst (cat feces)	• Wash fruits and vegetables before consumption • Avoid contact with materials potentially contaminated with cat feces • Wear gloves when gardening or handling cat litter • Disinfect cat litter with near boiling water for 5 min before handling

[1]Adapted from Liesenfeld O, Remington JS: Toxoplasmosis. In: Faro S, Soper D (editors) *Infectious Diseases in Women:* Saunders, Philadelphia, 2001, pp 57–79.

"well done" with no pink meat visible in the center), by smoking or curing it, or by freezing it to –20 °C (which is not achieved in most home freezers). Hands should be washed meticulously after handling raw meat or vegetables; eggs should not be eaten raw, and unpasteurized milk (particularly milk from goats) should be avoided. Flies and cockroaches should be controlled. Areas contaminated with cat feces should be avoided entirely. Disposable gloves should be worn while disposing of cat litter (if this task cannot be avoided altogether), working in the garden, or cleaning a child's sandbox. Oocysts are killed if the

BOX 81-7

Primary Prophylaxis in Immunodeficient Patients

Patient	Regimen
AIDS patients at high risk of developing TE	• Trimethoprim/sulfamethoxazole (either 160 mg/800 mg or 80 mg/400 mg/d) or dapsone (50 mg/d) plus pyrimethamine (50 mg/week)
Heart transplant patients whose donors are seropositive	• Pyrimethamine (25 mg by mouth once daily for 6 weeks, post-transplant)

cat litter container is soaked in nearly boiling water for 5 min. If the litter container is cleaned every day, oocysts will not have a chance to sporulate.

There is no vaccine currently available for prevention of toxoplasmosis in humans; primary prophylaxis against toxoplasmosis in patients with AIDS who are at high risk of developing TE has been shown to be effective. Primary prophylaxis is recommended for seropositive patients whose CD4 count has been < 100 cells/mm^3 (some experts use a cutoff of < 200 cells/mm^3), regardless of the HIV RNA viral load. Trimethoprim-sulfamethoxazole and dapsone plus pyrimethamine have been reported to be effective regimens in preventing the first episode of TE (Box 81–7). Pyrimethamine has been used post-transplantation for primary prophylaxis in seronegative heart transplant recipients whose donors are seropositive (Box 81–7).

REFERENCES

Dubey JP, Lindsay DS, Speer CA: Structures of *Toxoplasma gondii* tachyzoites, bradyzoites, and sporozoites and biology and development of tissue cysts. Clin Microbiol Rev 1998;11(2):267.

Liesenfeld O et al: False-positive results in immunoglobulin M (IgM) *Toxoplasma* antibody tests and importance of confirmatory testing: the Platelia Toxo IgM test. J Clin Microbiol 1997;35:174.

Montoya JG, Remington JS: *Toxoplasmic* chorioretinitis in the setting of acute acquired toxoplasmosis. Clin Infect Dis 1996;23:277.

Remington JS, McLeod R, Desmont G: Toxoplasmosis. In Remington JS, Klein J (eds): *Infectious Diseases of the Fetus and Newborn Infant,* 5th ed. Saunders, 1995.

Sinai AP, Joiner KA: Safe haven: the cell biology of nonfusogenic pathogen vacuoles. Annu Rev Microbiol 1997;51:415.

Wong S-Y, Remington JS: Toxoplasmosis in pregnancy. Clin Infect Dis 1994;18:853.

Pathogenic Amebas

82

Christopher R. Fox, MD & Merle A. Sande, MD

ENTAMOEBA HISTOLYTICA & ENTAMOEBA DISPAR

Essentials of Diagnosis
- Patient living in or having traveled to endemic area increases risk.
- Frequent loose stools with blood and mucus.
- Demonstration of cyst or trophozoite on stool wet mount or in biopsy specimen.
- Serology positive within 7–10 days of infection, may remain positive for years after infection resolved.
- Monoclonal antibodies and polymerase chain reaction emerging; may help differentiate *E histolytica* and *E dispar.*

General Considerations

A. Epidemiology. There are numerous distinct species of ameba within the genus *Entamoeba,* and the majority of these do not cause disease in humans. *E histolytica* is a pathogenic species that is capable of causing disease, such as colitis or liver abscess, in humans. *E dispar* is prevalent and is indistinguishable from *E histolytica* by conventional laboratory methods. *E dispar* exists in humans in only an asymptomatic carrier state and does not cause colitis.

It has been estimated that 10% of the world's population is infected with either *E histolytica* or *E dispar.* Of those infected, < 10% will manifest symptomatic disease. Infection is prevalent in Central and South America, southern and western Africa, the Far East, and India. Pregnant women, children, those of lower socioeconomic status, and those who live in crowded conditions or areas with poor sanitation are more likely to be infected.

In the United States, the prevalence of *E histolytica* and *E dispar* is much lower, approximately 4%. The risk factors for infection are the same as those above. In addition, those who travel to an endemic area, homosexual males, and institutionalized persons are at increased risk of infection.

B. Microbiology. *E histolytica* exists in one of two forms, a cyst or a trophozoite. Infection is generally through fecal-oral spread with ingestion of the cyst form, which is resistant to killing by the low pH of the stomach. Within the small bowel, the cyst divides into trophozoites, which then colonize the large intestine. The trophozoites may subsequently encyst and be shed into the stool. Once shed, they may remain viable for weeks to months.

During acute colitis, trophozoites may be shed into the stool. Unlike the cyst, the trophozoite cannot live outside the host because it is rapidly killed by poor environmental conditions and, if ingested, is degraded in the acid stomach environment.

C. Pathogenesis. *E histolytica* infection is enhanced by the production of several virulence factors. Production of proteolytic enzymes allows the trophozoite to disrupt tissue planes and invade the colonic epithelium. The trophozoite may ascend the portal venous structures to produce hepatic infection, and obstruction of the portal vessels by the trophozoites may produce hepatic necrosis. The trophozoites are able to lyse neutrophils through a contact-dependent mechanism that protects the trophozoite from ingestion and causes local tissue damage by release of the neutrophil's enzymes. Trophozoites are also resistant to complement-mediated lysis and produce adherence lectins that aid in the binding of the trophozoite to colonic epithelium, thereby facilitating invasion of the epithelium. These adherence proteins also aid in the contact-dependent lysis of tissue and white cells.

CLINICAL SYNDROMES

Infection with *E histolytica* causes multiple syndromes, which range from asymptomatic intestinal infection to fulminant colitis. In addition, *E histolytica* may cause disease at several nonintestinal sites, including the liver, lung, brain, and genitourinary tract. The clinical syndromes caused by *E histolytica* are outlined in Box 82–1.

BOX 82-1

Clinical Features of Amebiasis

	Intestinal	Hepatic	Extrahepatic
More Common	• Asymptomatic > (90%) • Frequent loose stools with blood and mucus • Abdominal pain	• Right-upper-quadrant pain, right shoulder pain, or both • Fever in first 2 weeks • Weight loss • Cough, even in absence of pulmonary disease	• Pleuropulmonary (cough, pleuritic chest pain, "anchovy paste" effusion) • Peritoneal (abdominal pain—ranges from mild to acute)
Less Common	• Fever • Volume depletion • Ameboma • Megacolon • Perforation	• Diarrhea • Hepatomegaly	• Pericardial (fever, chest pain, congestive heart failure, tamponade) • Cerebral (change in mental status, focal neurologic deficits) • Genitourinary (painful ulcers with profuse discharge)

INTESTINAL DISEASE

Clinical Findings

A. Signs and Symptoms. Of patients infected with *E histolytica,* > 90% are asymptomatic carriers who are colonized with the organism and pass cysts in the stool. This carrier state often resolves without treatment, although relapses and reinfection are common.

Acute amebic colitis usually presents with several weeks of lower abdominal pain and diarrhea with frequent loose to watery stools containing blood and mucus. Most patients are afebrile. Significant volume depletion is uncommon.

Chronic amebic colitis is characterized by low-grade inflammation resulting in intermittent bloody diarrhea and abdominal pain over a period of months to years. It is often difficult to distinguish chronic disease from inflammatory bowel disease, and this distinction must be made before corticosteroid or surgical therapy for inflammatory bowel disease, to avoid worsening amebic infection or to perform surgical therapy for a treatable infection.

Patients with fulminant amebic colitis present with fever, diffuse abdominal pain, and bloody diarrhea. This form of the disease is rare and presents most commonly in children. Colonic perforations frequently develop, and the patient may progress to toxic megacolon, particularly in the setting of corticosteroid treatment. Liver abscess is common in patients with fulminant colitis. Mortality in patients with fulminant colitis is high, approaching 50%.

Of patients with intestinal disease, ~ 1% will develop an ameboma. Most common in the cecum or ascending colon, ameboma is a chronic, localized amebic infection. The mass may be entirely asymptomatic or may be painful and tender. It is often confused with malignant lesions on imaging studies, and correct diagnosis can be made by biopsy.

B. Laboratory Findings. Laboratory findings in intestinal amebiasis are nonspecific, and there are no characteristic laboratory findings that should prompt a search for the organism. The stool is usually positive for erythrocytes. Fecal leukocytes are often not present, secondary to lysis by the parasite, despite invasion of the intestinal mucosa.

C. Imaging. The most useful imaging study for amebiasis is endoscopy. Colonoscopy or flexible sigmoidoscopy allows for direct visualization of the intestinal mucosa and provides an opportunity for mucosal biopsy. Endoscopy typically reveals inflamed mucosa with punctate, hemorrhagic ulcers interspersed with normal-appearing mucosa.

D. Differential Diagnosis. Acute intestinal amebiasis must be distinguished from bacterial dysentery caused by *Salmonella, Shigella, Campylobacter,* enteroinvasive *E coli,* and *Yersinia* spp. Amebiasis, particularly chronic infection, may be confused with inflammatory bowel disease.

E. Complications. Complications from amebic intestinal disease are rare, because the majority of patients are asymptomatic. Those complications that do occur include peritonitis, colonic perforation, stricture formation, and hemorrhage. Toxic megacolon, a serious complication of amebic colitis, occurs rarely, but its incidence is increased in persons treated with steroids during the course of their infection.

AMEBIC LIVER ABSCESS

Clinical Findings

A. Signs and Symptoms. Amebic liver abscess is the most common extraintestinal manifestation of amebiasis. Patients may note right-upper-quadrant pain that is either dull or pleuritic in nature. Often pain is referred to the right shoulder. Less than 50% of patients have an enlarged liver. In the acute setting, patients typically manifest fever. If symptoms have been present for > 2 weeks, fever is present in less than half of patients. Respiratory symptoms, such as cough, can occur even in the absence of pulmonary disease and may be the only complaint. In the subacute setting, weight loss is common. Diarrhea is found in less than one-third of patients with amebic liver abscess.

Exam may reveal abdominal tenderness, tender hepatomegaly, and crackles at the right lung base. Jaundice is uncommon.

B. Laboratory Findings. Patients with amebic liver abscess may have leukocytosis without eosinophilia, elevated alkaline phosphatase, and mild anemia. The transaminases are elevated in severe disease. Other findings include a high erythrocyte sedimentation rate and proteinuria.

C. Imaging. Ultrasound of the liver may show a round or an oval hypoechoic area contiguous with the liver capsule and without significant wall echoes. This is often a single lesion in the right hepatic lobe. Computer tomographic scanning and magnetic resonance imaging are sensitive studies for hepatic involvement, but the finding of a mass is not specific for amebic abscess. Each of these studies allows definition of the number of lesions as well as their size, and this information may be used to monitor a patient's course.

D. Differential Diagnosis. An amebic liver abscess needs to be differentiated from other mass lesions of the liver, which include bacterial abscess, echinococcal cyst, hepatoma, and metastatic cancer.

E. Complications. Amebic liver abscesses may rupture and thereby extend into surrounding tissues, including the pleural space, lung parenchyma, and pericardium. Pleural effusion may be present without frank rupture of the abscess.

Pleuropulmonary amebiasis. Pleuropulmonary disease is the most common complication of amebic liver abscess and usually presents with cough and pleuritic chest pain. Findings may reveal serous effusion, which does not imply disseminated disease. Amebic empyema, with "anchovy paste" material present upon drainage, occurs with rupture of the abscess into the pleural space and has an increased mortality. Consolidation of the lung parenchyma may occur with contiguous spread from a liver abscess. A patient who develops a hepatobronchial fistula will have a cough productive of large amounts of sputum and necrotic material, with the sputum possibly containing detectable amebas.

Peritoneal amebiasis. Peritoneal amebiasis occurs in 2–7% of patients with amebic liver abscess and represents the second most common complication of amebic liver abscess. Presentation may be dramatic enough to simulate a perforated viscus or may be more indolent with a slow leak of organisms into the peritoneal space.

Pericardial amebiasis. Pericardial disease is a rare but serious complication of amebic liver abscess. It usually results from the rupture of an abscess in the left lobe of the liver and presents with fever and chest pain and progresses to congestive heart failure, tamponade, and shock.

Cerebral amebiasis. Cerebral amebiasis is rare, with reports from clinical series of < 0.1% of patients. Autopsy series of patients with known amebiasis show central nervous system involvement of 1–2%. Cerebral abscess should be suspected in a person with known amebiasis who presents with mental status changes or focal neurologic signs.

Genitourinary amebiasis. Renal infection may occur either from direct extension of hepatic disease or by hematogenous or lymphatic spread. Genital lesions typically arise from fistulae from hepatic or colonic disease and present with painful ulcers with profuse discharge.

Diagnosis

The diagnosis of intestinal infection with *E histolytica* or *E dispar* is made by demonstration of cysts or trophozoites in the stool or by examination of biopsy specimens of mucosal tissue. Amebic trophozoites are destroyed by many agents, including antibiotics, antidiarrheal agents, barium, and tap water. Therefore, stool specimens should be examined by preparing wet mounts of specimens within 20 min of collection and examining immediately. Staining with iodine and trichrome maximizes the yield of positive specimens. Pathogenic trophozoites of *E histolytica* may be distinguished from nonpathogenic species by the presence of ingested erythrocytes within the organism.

Serology is useful in diagnosis of *E histolytica* infection. Antibodies to ameba develop only with infection by *E histolytica* and do not develop with *E dispar* infection. With invasive colitis or hepatic abscess, antibodies may be negative initially but become positive by 7–10 days in > 85–95% of patients. Antibodies cannot distinguish current infection from remote infection, as the antibodies may remain positive for years.

Monoclonal antibodies and polymerase chain reaction technology are newer technologies being used for diagnosis of amebic infection and appear to allow differentiation of *E histolytica* from *E dispar*. An enzyme-linked immunoabsorbent assay with monoclonal antibodies to a region that contains epitopes unique to *E histolytica* has been used to make this distinction in preliminary studies.

Amebic liver abscess should be suspected in any patient with an abnormal abdominal exam and appropriate risk factors, such as recent travel to an endemic area. Once a hepatic fluid collection is demonstrated radiographically, it is important to distinguish amebic abscess from pyogenic abscess. Serology once again is useful but may be negative for the first week of the infection. Often, percutaneous sampling of the fluid is required to look for cysts and trophozoites. Amebas may not be found in the liquefaction center of an abscess, but the results of Gram stain, culture, and serology will usually distinguish amebic abscess from other causes.

Diagnosis of other extraintestinal sites of infection requires clinical suspicion in the appropriate setting, such as a patient with known amebic abscess. Demonstration of amebas in these extrahepatic sites is not universally required but is often obtained, because drainage is required for empyema, peritoneal involvement, and, usually, pericardial involvement.

Treatment

Treatment of amebic disease requires both the elimination of the trophozoite form from the intestine or extraintestinal sites and the elimination of cysts from the intestine. If a luminal agent is not used to eradicate cysts, disease may recur.

Metronidazole is the agent of choice for treatment of amebic colitis. Doses of 750 mg three times daily for 5–10 days are extremely effective, and the drug can be given orally or intravenously. Side effects are generally gastrointestinal: nausea, vomiting, and abdominal discomfort. If ingested with alcohol, metronidazole produces a disulfiram-like reaction. The drug carries a potential risk of teratogenicity if used in pregnant women; however, because amebic disease is often more serious in pregnant women, treatment is generally recommended. No teratogenic effects were seen in > 2500 women inadvertently given metronidazole during pregnancy. In Europe, two additional nitroimidazole antibiotics (tinidazole and ornidazole) are available, are effective therapy, and are associated with fewer adverse effects than metronidazole. These drugs are not available in the United States.

Tetracycline or erythromycin is effective therapy for milder cases of colitis. Because these drugs will not eradicate ameba in the liver, their use should probably be restricted to patient who cannot tolerate metronidazole. Emetine and dehydroemetine have relatively high toxicity and must be given in a monitored environment. They offer no benefit over standard metronidazole therapy.

Three luminal agents are available for eradication of cysts after treatment with metronidazole or other agents. Diloxanide furoate has a > 90% efficacy but must be obtained from the Centers for Disease Control and Prevention in the United States. Iodoquinol (diiodohydroxyquin) requires 20 days of therapy and is in limited supply in the United States. Because of its high iodine content, it may interfere with thyroid function tests and should be avoided in those allergic to iodine. Other side effects include gastrointestinal discomfort, fever, and headache. Paromomycin is a nonabsorbable aminoglycoside that may cause loose stools. It is often preferred for circumstances in which systemic absorption is undesirable, such as in pregnancy.

Amebic liver abscess is responsive to medical therapy, and, as with intestinal disease, metronidazole is the preferred agent. Given as a 5- to 10-day treatment, metronidazole has a cure rate of > 95%. The role of aspiration or drainage is unclear but usually is not necessary. Because of the high response rate to medical therapy, aspiration is probably best used only in a few defined circumstances. In the patient who is not clinically improved within 3 days of initiation of therapy, aspiration is used to confirm the diagnosis and to exclude other causes of abscess, such as bacterial infection. Aspiration is also indicated for a ruptured abscess and in an abscess that is in danger of rupture, as characterized by a large fluid collection surrounded by a thin rim of hepatic tissue. If a left-lobe abscess is in danger of involving the pericardium, aspiration should be performed.

Medical therapy is generally sufficient for amebiasis involving the genitourinary tract, central nervous system, and lung parenchyma. Involvement of the pericardium and pleural space may require drainage because of the development of loculations. Treatment of amebiasis is outlined in Boxes 82–2 and 82–3.

Prognosis

Although infection with *E histolytica* can be debilitating, it is generally not life threatening. Once infection is identified, effective treatment exists. Relapse or reinfection is not unusual. Only a small minority of patients develops severe complications, such as colonic perforation, toxic megacolon, ruptured hepatic abscess, or cerebral amebiasis.

Prevention & Control

Prevention of amebic infection is greatly enhanced by effective sanitation and a clean water supply. Cysts are resistant to destruction by chlorine, but iodine or boiling is sufficient to kill the organism. Health education and public health efforts to identify and treat carriers may limit disease spread (Box 82–4). Travelers to endemic areas should avoid unpeeled fruits and vegetables and should avoid drinking water unless it has been properly treated. Several vaccines to *E histolytica* are under development and may provide the most effective means of disease control once released.

BOX 82–2

Treatment of Amebiasis in Adults

	Asymptomatic Cyst Passage	Intestinal Disease	Hepatic	Extrahepatic
First Choice	• Luminal agent— diloxanide furoate, 500 mg PO three times daily × 10 d OR • Paromomycin, 500 mg PO three times daily × 10 d OR • Iodoquinol, 650 mg PO three times daily × 20 d	• Metronidazole, 750 mg PO three times daily × 10 d • Followed by luminal agent	• Metroindazole, 750 mg PO three times daily or 500 mg IV every 6 h × 10 d • Followed by luminal agent	• Drug therapy is the same as for hepatic disease • Consider drainage
Alternative		• Tetracycline, 250 mg three times daily × 10 d • Erythromycin, 500 mg PO four times daily × 10 d • Tinidazole, 50 mg/kg per day × 3 d (not available in the United States • Followed by luminal agent	• Tinidazole or ornidazole, 2 g PO once (not available in the United States) • Followed by luminal agent	

BOX 82–3

Treatment of Amebiasis in Children

	Asymptomatic Cyst Passage	Intestinal Disease	Hepatic	Extrahepatic
First Choice	• Luminal agent— diloxanide furoate, 20 mg/kg/d in 3 divided doses × 10 d OR • Paromomycin, 30 mg/kg/d in 3 divided doses × 10 d OR • Iodoquinol, 20–40 mg/kg/d in 3 divided doses × 20 d	• Metronidazole, 30–50 mg/kg/d in 3 divided doses × 5–10 d • Followed by luminal agent	• Metronidazole, 30–50 mg/kg/d in 3 divided doses PO or IV × 5–10 d • Followed by luminal agent	• Drug therapy is the same as for hepatic disease • Consider drainage
Alternative	• Alternative drugs and dosages not established			

PATHOGENIC FREE-LIVING AMEBAS

ACANTHAMOEBA INFECTION

Amebas of the genus *Acanthamoeba* live as cysts and trophozoites in soil and in water. They can cause several disease syndromes in human hosts, including encephalitis, keratitis, and infections of the skin that resemble deep fungal infections. In addition, they can infect other human tissues and cause a granulomatous reaction. These amebas may be carried in an asymptomatic nasal carrier state. Immunocompromised patients, such as transplant recipients and HIV-infected persons, are at increased risk of contracting disease. Diving in warm water may increase infection rates.

The encephalitis caused by *Acanthamoeba* is a chronic, focal, necrotizing infection characterized by granuloma formation (granulomatous encephalitis). Patients usually present with the insidious onset of focal neurological deficits, fevers, headache, meningismus, seizures, and mental status changes. Common focal deficits include visual disturbances and ataxia. Diagnosis is difficult and is often made only at autopsy. Tissue biopsy specimens may provide diagnosis. Cerebrospinal fluid lymphocytosis may be present, but the organism has not been isolated from cerebrospinal fluid. Granulomatous encephalitis leads to death, with an average survival from the onset of symptoms of 40 days. No treatment is effective. Imidazole antifungal agents, amphotericin B, neomycin, flucytosine, sulfonamides, pentamidine, and propamidine have been used without success.

Acanthamoeba species cause keratitis, and > 200 cases have been described in the United States since the early 1970s. Risk factors include use of contact lenses, exposure to contaminated water, and trauma to the cornea. After exposure, patients typically note a foreign body sensation that is followed by eye pain, visual change, tearing, and conjunctivitis. Progression of disease may lead to blindness. The disease is frequently misdiagnosed initially as herpes simplex virus or bacterial keratitis. Correct diagnosis is made by demonstration of the organism on corneal scrapings or biopsy material. Treatment requires surgical débridement followed by a minimum of 3–4 weeks of medical therapy, which consists of topical treatment with propamidine, Neosporin, and miconazole. Other therapies are topical polyhexmethylene biguanide or the combination of topical miconazole and oral itraconazole.

NAEGLERIA FOWLERI INFECTION

Naegleria fowleri is a free-living ameba that causes a primary meningoencephalitis. It may live in warm water areas, including lakes, hot springs, mud puddles, and swimming pools. Most infections are in children or young adults and manifest 5–15 days after exposure to an infected water source. The organism invades the meninges through the cribiform plate, a process facilitated by diving in deep water. Those infected may have a viral prodrome with nausea, vomiting, headache, and malaise and rapidly progress to coma and death within 2–3 days. Most patients have meningeal signs.

Diagnosis must be suspected early, because, even with prompt treatment, there are only four documented survivors of this infection. Primary amebic meningoencephalitis should be considered in those with a viral prodrome rapidly progressing to coma. Patients typically have leukocytosis. Lumbar puncture should be performed with caution, as increased intracranial pressure raises the risk of herniation. Cerebrospinal fluid will show many erythrocytes and typical leukocyte counts of 400–25,000/μL, with 50–100% neutrophils. Protein may be mildly elevated, and glucose is normal to slightly low. If no bacteria are seen on Gram stain of a purulent cerebrospinal fluid, a wet mount should be examined for amebic trophozoites. The specimen should not be refrigerated or centrifuged, because this reduces the ameba's motility and makes trophozoites difficult to distinguish from the many leukocytes.

Treatment of primary amebic meningoencephalitis is generally unsuccessful. The documented survivors received intravenous and intrathecal amphotericin B. One patient also received miconazole, rifampin, and sulfisoxazole. Laboratory studies with a rabbit model have shown synergy between amphotericin B and rifampin or tetracycline. Intrathecal administration of antinaegleria antibody has also improved survival in animal models.

REFERENCES

Marciano-Cabral F, Petri WA Jr: Free-living amebae. In Mandell GL, Bennett JE, Dolin R: *Principles and Practice of Infectious Diseases,* 4th ed. Churchill Livingstone, 1995.

Ravdin JI: Amebiasis. Clin Infect Dis 1995;20:1453.

Reed SL: Amebiasis: an update. Clin Infect Dis 1992;14:385.

Reed SL, Wessel DW, Davis CE: *Entamoeba histolytica* infection and AIDS. Am J Med 1991;90:269.

Seidel J: Primary amebic meningoencephalitis. Pediatr Clin North Am 1985;32:881.

Warhurst DC: Diagnosis of amebic infection. In Rickwood D, Hames BD: *Medical Parasitology, A Practical Approach.* Oxford University Press, 1995.

83 Cryptosporidium, Cyclospora, & Isospora Species & Microsporidia

Stephanie Boade Silas, MD, & DeVon Hale, MD

Within the last decade, the AIDS epidemic has heightened awareness of several gastrointestinal spore-forming protozoan pathogens. The genera *Cryptosporidium, Isospora,* and *Cyclospora* are members of the subclass Coccidia and phylum Apicomplexa; the microsporidia are a group of organisms belonging to the phylum Microspora. The spectrum of disease caused by these protozoans goes beyond gastrointestinal manifestations, and the significance of these protozoan infections is becoming increasingly appreciated in both immunocompromised and immunocompetent hosts.

CRYPTOSPORIDIUM

Essentials of Diagnosis

- Key signs and symptoms include dehydration with watery diarrhea of variable quantity.
- Waterborne transmission is the most common mode of oocyst transmission.
- Patients at risk for person-to-person transmission include household contacts, sexual contacts, health care workers, and children in day care.
- Symptoms are prolonged and more severe in immunocompromised patients.
- Acid-fast staining of fixed stool specimens allows identification of oocysts; immunofluorescence and enzyme-linked immunosorbent assay techniques are also available.

General Considerations

A. Epidemiology. *Cryptosporidium* spp. were first described at the beginning of this century but were not reported as human pathogens until 1976. *Cryptosporidium* infection is present worldwide with 250 million–500 million annual cases. Increased infection rates occur during warm, humid months. In industrialized nations, oocyst passage is prevalent in 1–3% of the population, compared with 5–10% oocyst passage in less-developed nations. This difference has been attributed to existence in the developing countries of conditions such as poor sanitation, crowded households, and nearby animal reservoirs. Industrialized nations report an increased prevalence in rural areas, whereas less-developed nations have a higher urban prevalence. The significance of cryptosporidiosis may be underestimated because the seroprevalence in industrialized nations has been reported to be ≤ 35%. In developing nations, seroprevalence has been reported to be ≤ 100%. Patients with AIDS with diarrhea have an 11–21% oocyst passage prevalence in developed nations compared with a rate of ≤ 50% in Africa and Haiti. Chronic intestinal cryptosporidiosis that lasts > 1 month has been classified as an AIDS-defining opportunistic infection.

Transmission of oocysts occurs by person-to-person, animal-to-person, and environmental contacts. Those at risk for person-to-person transmission include household members, sexual partners, health workers, and children in day care. Nineteen percent of household contacts of infected patients have been diagnosed with secondary infection. Household pets, laboratory animals, and farm animals have all been associated with transmission to humans. Nosocomial infection has also been reported.

Waterborne oocyst transmission is considered the most important mode of transmission and is associated with the largest outbreaks. The initial cases of waterborne transmission were described in 1983, in Finnish individuals with diarrhea who had traveled to St. Petersburg (then Leningrad), Russia. Subsequently, other cases of traveler's diarrhea have been attributed to cryptosporidiosis. Many common source outbreaks have been described in Great Britain and the United States, the largest of which occurred in Milwaukee in 1993, affecting 403,000 people. Surface runoff from cow pastures was identified as the contaminating source of oocysts. Unboiled well water has also been implicated in transmission. Cryptosporidiosis related to apple cider has been associated with use of fallen apples in contaminated cow pastures. Oocysts, which survive well in cold, moist environments, are found in 65–87% of surface water. In one study, oocysts were found in 27% of drinking water samples from 66 inspected treatment plants, confirming the resistance of oocysts to current water treatment methods.

B. Microbiology. *Cryptosporidium parvum* is the species of this intracellular coccidian protozoan parasite that is responsible for illness in humans. Its life cycle occurs within a single host, beginning as an ingested thick-walled, round oocyst measuring 2–6 μm in diameter. Excystation, induced by enzymes and bile salts found in the small intestine, releases four motile sporozoites that infect the small intestine. Further differentiation and division occur within an intracellular but extracytoplasmic vacuole of the enterocyte. Each sporozoite matures and divides asexually, releasing four to eight merozoites. The merozoite reinfects the small intestine or begins sexual maturation to a zygote and ultimately a fully sporulated oocyst. Approximately one of five oocysts is thin walled and reinfects the host; the remaining thick-walled oocysts are passed in stool to the environment. *C parvum* is unique in its ability to complete its life cycle within a single host. In particular, the autoinfectivity of the merozoites and thin-walled oocysts allows *C parvum* to perpetuate infection without subsequent environmental exposures.

C. Pathogenesis. The mechanism of disease associated with *C parvum* infection is unknown. As few as 30 oocysts have been found to cause infection in healthy volunteers, with a mean infective dose of 132 oocysts. The organism is limited to the intestine and appendix in the immunocompetent host, but it may be found throughout the gastrointestinal tract, in the hepatobiliary system, and in the respiratory tract of immunocompromised patients.

The resulting diarrhea is postulated to be either secretory (ie, caused by an unidentified toxin) or osmotic (ie, caused by malabsorption from intestinal villi injury). Histologic findings include atrophy, blunting, fusion, or loss of villi. Crypt hyperplasia is seen, and the lamina propria of the intestine has an inflammatory infiltrate.

The immune response in cryptosporidiosis is also poorly understood. Patients with a variety of immune deficiencies, including both T-cell abnormalities and γ-globulin deficiencies, have prolonged and more severe infections. Acquired immunity can prevent reinfection and limit primary infection, but the mechanism of protection is not entirely understood. Selective antibodies may inhibit an important attachment step. Bovine colostrum containing anti-*C parvum* antibodies limited infection in immunodeficient patients, but similar colostrum without antibodies did the same in experimental mouse infections. Further, patients with AIDS have been shown to mount an antibody response yet still be unable to clear the infection. This response lends support to other evidence suggesting the importance of adequate CD4 cells in addition to immunoglobulin A antibodies for protection. The presence of particular cytokines may be important in this interaction. Human breast milk does not confer protection from infection.

CLINICAL SYNDROMES

Enteric cryptosporidiosis is the most common clinical presentation in patient populations. In addition, immunocompromised patients may present with cholecystitis or respiratory infections attributed to *C parvum* (Box 83–1). Asymptomatic infection has also been reported.

1. ENTERIC CRYPTOSPORIDIOSIS

Clinical Findings

A. Signs and Symptoms. An average of 5–7 days passes from oocyst ingestion to symptom onset. Symptoms are similar in both immunocompetent and immunocompromised patients but are prolonged and

BOX 83–1

Cryptosporidiosis Syndromes

	Enteric	Cholecystitis	Respiratory
More Common	• Watery diarrhea • Abdominal pain • Nausea • Vomiting • Fever	• AIDS patient • Right upper-quadrant pain • Fever • Nausea/vomiting • High alkaline phosphatase	• Immunocompromised • Cough • Dyspnea • Hoarseness
Less Common	• Malaise • Weight loss • Myalgia • Headache • Malabsorption	• Diarrhea • High bilirubin	• Sinusitis • Laryngotracheitis

considerably more severe in compromised patients. Patients complain of watery diarrhea in variable quantities of ≤ 25 L/day leading to significant dehydration. Abdominal cramps, malaise, low-grade fever, and anorexia are frequently reported. Nausea, vomiting, myalgia, headache, and weight loss may also occur. Symptoms are usually self-limited in immunocompetent hosts, lasting 5–14 days, although cases lasting several months have been reported in normal hosts. Oocysts can still be found in stool 2 weeks after symptom resolution.

B. Laboratory Findings. Stool samples are generally negative for erythrocytes and leukocytes but can be streaked with mucous. Leukocytosis and eosinophilia are rare. After prolonged illness, malabsorption of fat, D-xylose, and B_{12} can be measured.

C. Imaging. Abdominal films are nonspecific, revealing mucosal thickening and disordered motility. Endoscopy shows only focal nonspecific atrophy.

D. Differential Diagnosis. In the immunocompetent host, *C parvum* infection may present similarly to *Shigella, Salmonella,* and *Campylobacter* spp., as well as *Clostridium difficile* and *Giardia* spp., in patients with an appropriate history. Similar presentations occur with *Entamoeba histolytica* and other coccidia, and in immunodeficient patients, diagnoses of cytomegalovirus, *Mycobacterium avium,* and microsporidia should be entertained.

E. Complications. Toxic megacolon and reactive arthritis involving the wrists, hands, knees, ankles, or feet have been reported in association with cryptosporidiosis. Pancreatitis has also been reported in both immunocompetent and immunocompromised hosts presenting with cryptosporidiosis.

2. CHOLECYSTITIS

Up to 10% of AIDS patients with cryptosporidiosis present with cholecystitis. Cryptosporidial cholecystitis has thus far been diagnosed only in AIDS patients.

Clinical Findings

A. Signs and Symptoms. Patients present with fever, right upper quadrant pain, nausea, and vomiting with or without associated diarrhea.

B. Laboratory Findings. Laboratory studies reveal elevated alkaline phosphatase and bilirubin levels.

C. Imaging. Imaging with ultrasound or computed tomography usually shows an enlarged gallbladder with thickened walls and dilated ducts but may be normal in 25% of infected patients. Endoscopic retrograde cholangiopancreatography can reveal common bile duct beading or papillary stenosis.

D. Differential Diagnosis. Microsporidial and cytomegalovirus infections may have similar presentations in patients with AIDS.

E. Complications. Cryptosporidial cholecystitis has been complicated by pancreatitis, cholangitis, hepatitis, and chronic gallbladder carriage.

3. RESPIRATORY INFECTION

C parvum has rarely been identified in biopsy and lavage specimens of immunodeficient patients who present with dyspnea, hoarseness, wheezing, or cough as well as symptoms of laryngotracheitis and sinusitis. Chest films are generally normal or show modest infiltrates and increased bronchial markings. The respiratory syndrome has not yet been directly associated with *C parvum* diarrheal illness.

Diagnosis

The majority of diagnoses of *C parvum* infection are made by identification of the organism in stool specimens (Table 83–1). Stool should be examined while it is fresh or fixed in 10% formalin or polyvinyl alcohol. Oocysts can be identified by light microscopy without specific staining but are more readily seen with modified acid-fast staining. Phase-contrast microscopy reveals birefringent oocysts. Oocysts in duodenal aspirates or respiratory secretions can be similarly identified. Submitting three to four separate stool samples has been recommended for increased diagnostic yield. However, in a study of AIDS inpatients, one stool specimen resulted in 96% sensitivity, increasing to 100% with only two specimens. Orders should specify suspected *C parvum* because most laboratories do not routinely use acid-fast staining.

Immunofluorescence and enzyme-linked immunosorbent assay techniques are more sensitive and specific methods of diagnosis (Figure 83–1). Sensitivities of 93–100% and specificities of 99–100% have been reported for various direct immunofluorescent-antibody assays. The available enzyme-linked immunosorbent assay techniques have 72–100% sensitivity and 98–100% specificity. The clinical utility of polymerase chain reaction analysis is still developing.

Table 83–1. Laboratory diagnosis of cryptosporidiosis.

- Oocysts are < 4–6 μm in diameter, round, and thick-walled, containing four sporozoites
- Oocysts are identified in stool, duodenal aspirates, bile, or respiratory secretions
- Stool should be fresh or fixed in 10% formalin or PVA and may be stained with modified acid-fast stain.
- Intestinal biopsy shows intracellular but extracytoplasmic sporozoites on the brush border staining basophilic with H & E staining
- Phase contrast microscopy shows birefringent oocysts
- ELISA and immunofluorescent assays are more sensitive and specific methods of diagnosis
- PCR and serology studies are not clinically useful at this time

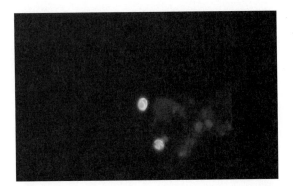

Figure 83–1. *Cryptosporidium* spp. oocysts are more difficult to detect on a routine ova and parasite exam. They are acid-fast positive but are most easily detected with a direct fluorescent antibody stain. This picture compares the size of the *C parvum* oocyst (4–6 µm) with that of a *Giardia* cyst (9–12 µm), using a combined-fluorescent-antibody stain (Meriflour stain reproduced with permission from Meridian, Inc.).

BOX 83–2

Treatment of Cryptosporidiosis[1]

	Adults	Children
First Choice	• Paromomycin, 500–750 mg orally four times daily	• Paromomycin, 25–35 mg/kg/d divided in 3 doses
Second Choice	• Azithromycin, 900 or 1200 mg orally once daily × 2 weeks	• None
Palliation	• Bovine transfer factor • Hyperimmune bovine colostrum • Octreotide	

[1]All treatments are investigational, without Food and Drug Administration approval.

Hematoxylin and eosin staining of intestinal biopsy specimens reveals basophilic organisms on the brush border that appear to project into the lumen because of the intracellular but extracytoplasmic location of the organism. Direct immunofluorescence can also be used on these biopsy specimens, and electron microscopy provides greater detail. However, the invasiveness of biopsy is rarely warranted and is not 100% sensitive.

Serologic antibody identification is available for *C parvum* infection but is still investigational and not clinically useful for diagnosis due to the persistence of antibody after infection. It is valuable as an epidemiologic tool, however.

Treatment

No reliable treatment is available at this time for cryptosporidiosis (Box 83–2). Supportive care with fluids and antidiarrheal agents can be offered while awaiting resolution in immunocompetent hosts or while addressing the underlying etiology of immunosuppression in compromised hosts. Paromomycin sulfate is currently the drug of choice for *C parvum,* surpassing spiramycin, for which there are no controlled studies. Paromomycin treatment is well tolerated by patients, but relapse is common even on therapy. For those patients relapsing off of therapy, however, 80% will again have a good response when they are back on paromomycin sulfate. Initial reports on the efficacy of a special lactose-free preparation of azithromycin have been promising. Hyperimmune bovine colostrum has been helpful in decreasing symptoms despite the persistence of oocyst shedding. Bovine transfer factor isolated from infected calf lymph node suspensions has been shown to attenuate symptoms, and octreotide has been similarly helpful. For all of the above therapeutic modalities, large randomized studies are needed for better understanding and documentation of effect.

Prognosis

Although cryptosporidiosis is self-limited in immunocompetent patients, patients with AIDS with enteric cryptosporidiosis present with disease, the severity of which is related to the degree of immunosuppression. In one series of patients with AIDS, 29% of cases were transient, 60% chronic, 8% fulminant, and 4% asymptomatic. Mean survival in these patients was 25 weeks.

Prevention & Control

C parvum oocysts are 30-fold more resistant to chlorine than are *Giardia* cysts. Oocysts are killed in water kept above 65°C for 30 min as well as water boiled for 1 min at any altitude. Oocyst death is also reported in water kept at < 20°C for 30 min, although more recent information suggests greater resistance to freezing than previously thought (Box 83–3).

Enteric precautions and good hygiene should reduce most person-to-person transmission as well as animal-to-human exposures because family contacts account for ≤ 50% of secondary cases. Also, apple juice and cider should be pasteurized or boiled before consumption. No prophylactic regimen for patients with AIDS is yet available, although paromomycin sulfate and azithromycin are being studied. Immunocompromised patients should be instructed to drink bottled or boiled water if water supplies are suspect.

BOX 83–3

Prevention & Control of Cryptosporidiosis

Prophylactic Measures	• Avoid contacts—sick animals and humans • Enteric precautions • Immunocompromised patients should drink boiled or bottled water if water supply is suspect • Halogenation is not effective • Water should be boiled for 1 min
Isolation Precautions	• No specific measures • Good hygiene

CYCLOSPORA

Essentials of Diagnosis

* Patients present with watery diarrhea, which is usually self-limited in immunocompetent patients but may be prolonged in the immunocompromised patient.
* A history of travel to areas such as Nepal, Haiti, and Peru, a history of berry consumption, or community outbreak of diarrhea may increase suspicion of diagnosis.
* Acid-fast stain of stool specimens reveals abundant oocysts.

General Considerations

Cyclospora is a coccidian that had been described as a "large cryptosporidium" or "cyanobacterium-like body" before being confirmed as a member of the phylum Apicomplexa in 1993. The life cycle in humans has not been fully detailed. The organism has been shown to infect jejunal enterocytes. Similar to *Isospora,* the oocysts are excreted unsporulated, requiring 7–13 days of optimal conditions outside of the host to mature. Each spherical oocyst has a diameter of 8–10 μm and contains two sporocysts, each of which contains two sporozoites. The oocyst is twice the size of *C parvum* (Figure 83–2).

Cyclospora catayensis infection in humans has been reported worldwide and was first described in Papua New Guinea in 1979. It is endemic in Haiti, Peru, and Nepal, where rainy-season outbreaks of *C catayensis* infection occur. Outside these areas, infection is usually travel related when not associated with an outbreak. Protective immunity is suggested because infection is more common in children and in non-natives. Infection has been reported in HIV-in-

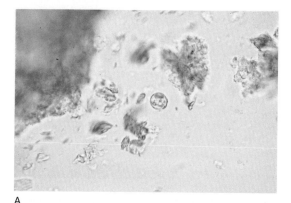

A

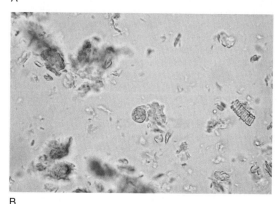

B

Figure 83–2. *C catayensis* oocysts have an 8- to 10-μm diameter and can be identified on a wet mount of the routine ova and parasite exam. They tend to have autofluorescent inclusions and will stain acid-fast positive with a Ziehl-Neelsen stain.

fected patients, but cyclosporiasis is primarily found in immunocompetent patients. In the United States, *Cyclospora* oocysts were identified in only 3 of 1042 submitted stools. The low prevalence in patients with AIDS in the United States is attributed to possible misdiagnoses as *C parvum*, nonuniform use of the acid-fast stain, trimethoprim-sulfamethoxazole (TMP-SMX) prophylaxis in these patients, and the coincident low prevalence in immunocompetent patients in the United States.

Transmission of *Cyclospora* has been linked to contaminated water and food sources. The organism is believed to be host specific to humans. In 1990, a Chicago outbreak was related to stagnant water in a storage tank, and in 1994, in Nepal, a British military unit experienced an outbreak related to water from a chlorinated and filtered tank. More recently, cyclosporiasis related to berry consumption has been in the news. In 1995, unwashed strawberries were related to outbreaks in New York and Florida. In 1996,

1465 cyclosporiasis cases in two Canadian provinces and 20 states in the United States were traced to consumption of Guatemalan raspberries. Lettuce and uncooked meat have been reported culprits as well.

The pathogenesis of cyclosporiasis is not well understood. The parasite is found in the upper small bowel and is associated with villous atrophy, crypt hyperplasia, and inflammatory changes similar to those seen in tropical sprue.

Clinical Findings

After an incubation of 2–11 days, immunocompetent patients experience a self-limited, but prolonged, relapsing watery diarrhea lasting an average of 19–43 days, although organism shedding may last ≤ 70 days (Box 83–4). In patients with AIDS, symptoms have been reported for ≤ 4 months. A median of six stools/day is reported. Fatigue, fever, indigestion, abdominal cramps, nausea, and vomiting may occur, as well as weight loss. A prodrome of both myalgia and arthralgia has been reported. Diarrhea may not be the primary complaint, and alternation with constipation is not infrequent. Asymptomatic infection has been reported in a study of immunocompetent Peruvians with documented infection in whom only 11–28% had diarrhea. No specific laboratory findings assist in diagnosis although abnormal D-xylose absorption has been reported.

A. Differential Diagnosis. A similar presentation may be found in cryptosporidiosis, isosporiasis, microsporidiosis, and sarcocystosis.

B. Complications. Biliary disease has been reported.

Diagnosis

Diagnosis is made by identification of the *Cyclospora* oocyst in fresh or iodine-preserved stool, duodenal aspirates, or small-bowel biopsies. With acid-fast or safranin O staining, oocysts can be seen as 10 μm spheres with clusters of refractile globules.

Table 83–2. Laboratory diagnosis of *Cyclospora* infection.

- Oocysts are 10-μm-diameter nonrefractile spheres that contain clusters of refractile globules
- Oocysts can be identified in fresh or iodine-preserved stool, duodenal aspirates, or small-bowel biopsies by modified acid-fast staining or safranin staining
- Oocysts autofluoresce blue under UV light, using a 365-nm excitation filter
- Antibody titers to *Cyclospora* infection rise during convalescence but are not clinically useful

The oocysts autofluoresce blue under UV light with a 365-nm excitation filter (Table 83–2).

Treatment

TMP-SMX is the first-line treatment for cyclosporiasis, with symptom resolution noted 2–3 days into therapy (Box 83–5). Immunosuppressed patients may require long-term suppressive therapy owing to an increased relapse rate. In addition to TMP-SMX, metronidazole, tinidazole, and ciprofloxacin hydrochloride have also been reported to stop oocyst excretion.

Prognosis

Infection is generally self-limited in immunocompetent hosts, but prolonged diarrhea with possible symptoms of malabsorption may occur in immunocompromised patients.

Prevention & Control

Reliable means of prevention of *Cyclospora* spp. infection are not yet known (Box 83–6). Efforts to decrease berry contamination have been directed toward using potable water in all aspects of berry

BOX 83–4

Cyclosporiasis Syndromes	
More Common	• Cyclical diarrhea • Fatigue • Anorexia
Less Common	• Dyspepsia • Nausea • Abdominal cramps • Weight loss • Vomiting • Myalgia/arthralgia

BOX 83–5

Treatment of Cyclosporiasis		
	Adults	Children
First Choice	• TMP/SMX 160/800 mg orally four times daily × 10 d for initial infection • TMP/SMX 160–800 mg—one tablet orally 3×/wk for prophylaxis	• TMP, 5 mg/kg; SMX, 25 mg/kg orally twice daily × 7 d
Second Choice	See text for possible alternatives	

BOX 83-6

Prevention & Control of *Cyclospora* and *Isospora* spp. and Microsporidia

Prophylaxis Measures	• No proven established methods • Enteric precautions • Immunocompromised patients should drink boiled or bottled water if water supply is suspect • TMP/SMX usage may be beneficial in patients with AIDS for prophylaxis of *Cyclospora* and *Isospora* infection • Bodily fluid precautions may be important in microsporidial infection • Agricultural measures to decrease water-borne contamination of raspberries are ongoing
Isolation Precautions	• No specific measures • Good hygiene

preparation, including water used for insecticide spray and for hand washing by workers. Gamma radiation used on berries is also being studied.

ISOSPORA

Essentials of Diagnosis

• Patients are usually either travelers to tropical areas with self-limited diarrhea or immunocompromised patients with a protracted diarrheal illness.
• Unsporulated oocysts are detected on wet mounts of stool samples by acid-fast staining.

General Considerations

A. Epidemiology. *Isospora* infection is endemic in several tropical and subtropical climates in areas of South America, Africa, and southwest Asia. In the United States, *Isospora belli* infection occurs primarily in patients with AIDS but is still quite rare in this population, accounting for ≤ 0.2% of AIDS-defining illnesses. Isospora infection is more common in patients with AIDS from developing countries in which the prevalence of spore passage is 15% compared with 5% in industrialized nations.

In immunocompetent patients, *I belli* has been identified in cases of chronic traveler's diarrhea and is present in outbreaks of diarrhea in institutional settings such as day care and mental facilities.

Because sporulation can occur only outside the host, transmission may occur through environmental sources such as food and water. A latency state has been postulated based on increased prevalence of infection in Latin American immigrants. In Los Angeles, Latin Americans account for ≤ 20% of AIDS cases but have 80% of *I belli* infections.

B. Microbiology. *I belli,* first described by Virchow in 1860, is a coccidian parasite that is host specific to humans. A 30 µm × 12 µm oval oocyst is ingested, releasing two sporocysts, each of which contains four sporozoites, which then infect enterocytes. An asexual cycle produces merozoites, which further infect epithelial cells; a sexual cycle produces immature, unsporulated oocysts that are passed in the feces. Sporulation occurs in a few days resulting in a mature oocyst.

C. Pathogenesis. The pathogenesis of *I belli* infection is not fully understood. Small-bowel histology reveals shortened villi, hypertrophic crypts, and inflammatory infiltration of the lamina propria with eosinophils. Symptoms of disease based on these histologic findings are likely caused by malabsorption.

Clinical Findings

A. Signs and Symptoms. After an incubation of < 1 week, immunocompetent patients present with an acute, self-limited diarrheal illness of varying severity resolving in 2 weeks (Box 83–7). Patients may pass 6–10 stools daily; the stools are foul smelling, watery, and soft. Malaise, anorexia, and abdominal cramps are common. Weight loss, headache, vomiting, and increased flatulence may occur, and occasionally fever may be documented. Oocyst shedding persists for 2–3 weeks beyond resolution of symptoms. Persistence of symptoms for months to years has been reported in some immunocompetent

BOX 83-7

Isosporiasis Syndromes

More Common	• Diarrhea • Malaise • Anorexia
Less Common	• Abdominal cramps • Weight loss • Headache • Vomiting • Flatulence • Chronic diarrhea • Eosinophilia • Malabsorption

patients. Immunocompromised patients present with the same symptom complex but with increased severity and a protracted course.

B. Laboratory Findings. Stool specimens contain no leukocytes or erythrocytes but may contain Charcot–Leyden crystals, which are eosinophilic granules indicative of the peripheral eosinophilia specific to *I belli* infection. Laboratory evidence of malabsorption may be present.

C. Imaging. Nonspecific mucosal thickening is seen on abdominal films.

D. Differential Diagnosis. Cryptosporidiosis and microsporidiosis can have similar presentations. Also, coinfection with *C parvum, Giardia* spp., and *Trichuris* spp. has been reported in AIDS patients.

E. Complications. Disseminated isosporiasis in a patient with AIDS has been reported with invasion of the bowel wall, lymph nodes, liver, and spleen. Acalculous cholecystitis and reactive arthritis have also been reported to complicate infection.

Diagnosis

Diagnosis of isosporiasis depends on identification of the oocyst in stool by wet mount with subsequent confirmation using modified acid-fast or trichrome staining. Colonoscopy aspiration or the duodenal string test may be helpful to obtain the necessary sample. Oocysts autofluoresce in UV light when viewed through a 450- to 490-nm excitation filter (Table 83–3).

Treatment

TMP-SMX has been shown to be effective treatment (Box 83–8). Patients with AIDS have a 50% chance of relapse, and low-dose suppressive treatment with TMP-SMX, pyrimethamine-sulfadoxine, or pyrimethamine alone is recommended. Alternative treatments include metronidazole, ciprofloxacin hydrochloride, roxithromycin, and diclazuril.

Prognosis

Untreated isosporiasis in the immunocompromised patient can lead to severe malnutrition and dehydration and may be fatal.

Table 83–3. Laboratory diagnosis of isosporiasis.

- Unsporulated oocysts are 20–33 µm × 10–19 µm and contain one or two immature sporonts
- When mature, the oocyst has two sporocysts, each with four sporozoites
- The thin, transparent oocyst wall can be detected on wet mount or by modified acid-fast or trichrome staining
- Oocysts autofluoresce under UV light by using a 450- to 490-nm excitation filter
- Duodenal string test or colonoscopy aspiration may be helpful

Prevention & Control

No proven means of prophylaxis for isosporiasis has yet been established due to unknown details of transmission and the possibility of a latency state (see Box 83–6). The common usage of TMP-SMX for *Pneumocystis carinii* prophylaxis may indeed also play a role in *I belli* prophylaxis. Because *I belli* infection appears to be mediated through water and environmental sources, good fecal-oral hygiene and adequate water treatment are recommended.

MICROSPORIDIA

Essentials of Diagnosis

- Most cases of microsporidiosis occur in male patients with HIV infection and CD4 counts of < 100.
- In HIV-infected patients, microsporidiosis most commonly presents as chronic diarrhea, although cholecystitis, respiratory infection, keratoconjunctivitis, and myositis have also been reported.
- Infections in non-HIV–infected patients are rare but include central nervous system infection, corneal infection, and myositis.
- Diagnosis is difficult and depends on identification of 1- to 2-µm spores.

General Considerations

A. Epidemiology. Microsporidia were first discovered in 1857, but it was not until 1973 that a human case of microsporidiosis was confirmed from a case described in 1959. Awareness of the diversity of microsporidial infections has heightened, especially in light of the AIDS epidemic. Central nervous system, respiratory, corneal, muscular, and gastrointestinal microsporidial infections have all been identified.

Microsporidiosis has been found worldwide. Before the AIDS epidemic, only 10 cases had been reported. Subsequently, hundreds of cases have been recognized, mostly in the United States. Between 23% and 33% of patients with AIDS with chronic diarrhea have been diagnosed with microsporidiosis, with *Enterocytozoon bieneusi* being the most common culprit. Most cases of microsporidiosis occur in male patients with HIV with severe immunosuppression and CD4 counts of < 100. Of 11 cases reported in non-HIV–infected patients, 4 had other forms of immunosuppression such as earlier liver and bone marrow transplants, and 4 had infections of the cornea, a site that is considered to be immunoprivileged. Infection in immunocompetent patients may be under-recognized because of transient infection or milder disease. Self-limited diarrhea has been docu-

BOX 83–8

Treatment of Isosporiasis

	Adults	Children
First Choice	TMP-SMX 160/800 orally four times daily × 10 d	TMP, 5 mg/kg; SMX, 25 mg/kg orally twice daily × 7 d
Second Choice	Pyrimethamine, 75 mg orally once daily × 10 d	
Prophylaxis in AIDS	• TMP-SMX, 160/800 orally once daily 3×/wk • Pyrimethamine/sulfadoxine, 25/500 orally once daily 3×/wk • Pyrimethamine, 25 mg orally daily	

mented in an immunocompetent traveler, and an asymptomatic carrier state has been identified.

Little is known about transmission of microsporidiosis, and there have been no reports of common-source outbreaks. However, microsporidium spores have been identified in respiratory secretions, urine, stool, and duodenal aspirates, suggesting that person-to-person transmission may occur by fecal-oral contacts, aerosolized secretions, sexual transmission, or direct corneal inoculation. Microsporidia infect insects, fish, snails, and mammals and are also present in surface water, which suggests the zoonotic and environmental transmission of these resistant spores. The spores have been shown to survive > 1 year in water kept at 4 °C.

B. Microbiology. Microsporidia are obligate intracellular, spore-forming protozoa of the order Microsporidia and the phylum Microspora. Primitive eukaryotes that lack mitochondria, microsporidia undergo a life cycle with three phases. In the first phase, infection, spores are ingested or inhaled. The host environment stimulates eversion of the spore coat, at which time a coiled tubular apparatus anchors the spore to the host cell. After the spore is attached, it allows the injection of sporoplasm into the cell, which begins the second phase, merogony. Within the cell, the parasite proliferates by fission, creating multiple multinucleated plasmodial meronts. Sporogony, the third phase, occurs when the meront cell matures and its membrane thickens to form a mature thick-walled spore with a diameter of 1–2 μm. Cell rupture releases ovoid spores that either reinfect the host or are passed into the environment by urine, stool, or respiratory secretions. These resistant spores can be viable for ≤ 4 months.

Five genera from the protozoan phylum Microspora have been implicated in human disease: *Encephalitozoon* (*Encephalitozoon hellem* and *Encephalitozoon cuniculi*), *Pleistophora, Enterocytozoon* (*Enterocytozoon bieneusi*), *Septata* (*Septata intestinalis*), and *Nosema*, which was recently reclas-

sified as *Vittaforma.* Unclassified species are placed under a sixth taxon, Microsporidium. The genera and species are separated primarily based on the location of the parasite in relation to the host, that is, whether the parasite is in direct contact with host cytoplasm, separated into a vesicle made by the host, or located in a parasitophorous vacuole.

C. Pathogenesis. Little is known of the etiology of microsporidia. Spores infect epithelia, mesenchymal cells, endothelia, and macrophages. Spores are found in enterocytes with associated intestinal villi shortening, fusion, and crypt elongation, as well as a lymphocytic infiltrate. *S intestinalis* spreads by lymphatics and blood vessels whereas *E bieneusi* spreads to the lungs by aspiration. Corneal infection is associated with ulceration, infected epithelium, and an infiltrate of macrophages and neutrophils.

CLINICAL SYNDROMES IN NON-HIV–INFECTED PATIENTS

Microsporidial infection in non-HIV–infected patients is rare, with < 20 cases reported. Central nervous system, corneal, muscular, enteric, and respiratory infections have all been identified (Box 83–9).

Central nervous system infections have been reported in two immunocompetent children presenting with fever, loss of consciousness, headache, and convulsions, as well as hepatomegaly. *E cuniculi* was isolated from the cerebrospinal fluid and the urine. Computed tomography of the brain and electroencephalography were normal. Corneal infection has been caused by *Nosema* spp., *Microsporidium ceylonensis,* and *Microsporidium africanum.* Patients have presented with decreased visual acuity, conjunctivitis, and corneal ulcers. Corneal biopsy reveals the organism.

Patients presenting with generalized muscle weakness have been diagnosed with myositis caused by *Pleistophora* spp. Laboratory tests revealed normal

BOX 83-9

Microsporidiosis in Non-HIV Patients

	E cuniculi	Nosema spp.	Pleistophora spp.	E bieneusi
Signs & Symptoms	• Fever • Loss of consciousness • Headaches • Convulsions • Hepatomegaly	• Decreased visual acuity • Conjunctivitis • Corneal ulcer	• Generalized muscle weakness	• Self-limited diarrhea

creatine kinase levels, and electromyograms showed myopathy. Muscle biopsies revealed scarring, fibrosis, inflammation, and *Pleistophora* infiltrate. Self-limited diarrhea caused by *E bieneusi* has been reported in an immunocompetent host. A patient with chronic myelogenous leukemia who had undergone allogenic bone marrow transplant was recently shown on autopsy to have microsporidial infection along with *Candida tropicalis* infection within lung sections.

CLINICAL SYNDROMES IN HIV-INFECTED PATIENTS

The most common manifestation of microsporidial infection in HIV-infected patients is enteric disease, but other recognized syndromes include biliary infection, pulmonary infection, keratoconjunctivitis, and myositis (Box 83–10).

4. GASTROINTESTINAL INFECTION

E bieneusi and *S intestinalis* are the most common etiologic agents identified in patients presenting with chronic diarrhea due to microsporidia. However, there is one case report of *E cuniculi* identified in intestinal infection.

Clinical Findings

A. Signs and Symptoms. Symptoms can persist over months and are associated with anorexia and a 10–20% weight loss. The diarrhea is usually loose and watery, with patients reporting 1–20 stools/day. The diarrhea is worse in the mornings and exacerbated by eating. A crampy abdominal pain can precede defecation. Nausea and vomiting are rarely present, and patients are afebrile.

B. Laboratory Findings. Stool specimens are negative for leukocytes or erythrocytes. Serum electrolytes can reveal low potassium, magnesium, and

BOX 83-10

Microsporidiosis Syndromes in HIV Patients (Syndrome and Organism)

	Enteric	Biliary	Pulmonary	Keratitis/Conjunctivitis	Myositis
	E bieneusi S intestinalis	E bienusi S intestinalis	E bienusi	E cuniculi E hellem	Pleistophora spp.
Signs & Symptoms	• Chronic diarrhea • Weight loss of 10–20% • Abdominal cramps • Absence of fever • Nausea • Vomiting	• Right upper quadrant pain • Diarrhea • Jaundice	• Cough • Dyspnea • Wheezing • Sinusitis	• Dry eyes • Foreign body sensation • Ocular pain • Tearing • Photophobia • Blurry vision	• Diffuse muscle weakness

zinc. Malabsorption is indicated by abnormal D-xylose absorption, low B_{12} levels, and increased fecal fat.

C. Differential Diagnosis. Differential diagnosis includes *C parvum* and other coccidial protozoa. Coinfection with *Mycobacterium avium* complex, *Giardia* spp., and *C parvum* in the small bowel and cytomegalovirus and *C parvum* in the large bowel has been reported.

D. Complications. Complications of gastrointestinal infection include biliary disease by direct extension and respiratory infection from aspiration. Nephritis by hematogenous spread of *S intestinalis* has been documented, and *S intestinalis* has also been identified in a rectal ulcer. Mortality of enteric microsporidiosis has been reported at 56%.

5. BILIARY INFECTION

E bieneusi and *S intestinalis,* often associated with cryptosporidial coinfection, have been identified in patients presenting with symptoms of cholecystitis.

Clinical Findings

A. Signs and Symptoms. Symptoms include right upper quadrant pain, concomitant diarrhea, and rarely jaundice.

B. Laboratory Findings. Laboratory studies reveal elevated alkaline phosphatase and transaminase levels that are twice to three times normal. Bilirubin levels are usually normal. CD4 counts are < 50.

C. Imaging. Imaging studies using computed tomography, ultrasound, or endoscopic retrograde cholangiopancreatography reveal dilated ducts and gallbladder thickening with sludge.

6. PULMONARY INFECTION

E bieneusi has been found in bronchial lavage specimens of patients presenting with cough, dyspnea, wheezing, or sinusitis. Chest x-rays show interstitial infiltrates.

7. KERATOCONJUNCTIVITIS

E cuniculi and *E hellem* as well as *S intestinalis* have caused corneal infections in HIV-infected patients. Patients present with dry eyes, foreign-body sensation, or ocular pain. Blurred vision, excessive tearing, and photophobia have also been reported. Conjunctival hyperemia may be present, and slit-lamp exam reveals a diffuse, superficial punctate keratopathy. Microsporidial corneal infections have been associated with systemic disease with concomitant bronchiolitis, sinusitis, nephritis, cystitis and ureteritis, hepatitis, and peritonitis.

8. MYOSITIS

Pleistophora infection in immunocompromised patients presents similarly to that in immunocompetent patients as already described.

Diagnosis

The small size of the *Microsporidium* spore makes diagnosis difficult (Table 83–4). The sensitivity and specificity of different identification techniques are not known. Microsporidial spores are gram positive and birefringent, and they have a positive periodic acid-Schiff–staining polar body. Spores can be found in stool, duodenal aspirates, urine, respiratory secretions, and conjunctival scrapings. Diagnostic yield may be enhanced by collecting three stools daily over 3 subsequent days. Spore concentration and sedimentation techniques can increase yield. Weber's modified trichrome, Gram, Giemsa, and chitin-binding fluorochrome stains have all been used successfully to identify spores. Diagnostic yield can be increased by preserving stool in formalin, pretreating in 10% potassium hydroxide, and centrifuging for 5 min before staining with the Weber's modified trichrome stain. Biopsy specimens can be similarly stained, but sensitivity may be decreased due to normal-appearing mucosa. If < 25 spores are identified from a stool specimen per coverslip, the likelihood of identifying organisms by electron microscopy of a biopsy specimen is low. *E bieneusi* usually involves the distal duodenum and proximal jejunum, and *S intestinalis* can also involve the colon.

Electron microscopy can more readily identify the small spores and is useful in speciation. Immunofluorescence and polymerase chain reaction techniques are also valuable for speciation.

Treatment

Microsporidial treatment efficacy is anecdotal at this time (Box 83–11). Albendazole has had the best success thus far in alleviating gastrointestinal and biliary symptoms. However, eradication of spores is rare, and relapse occurs 1–2 months after completion of 4 weeks of albendazole. Metronidazole was reported to have a transient clinical response only, and atovaquone has had mixed results. Fumagillin, itraconazole, and fluconazole are currently being studied. Palliative treatment with octreotide and nutrition

---

Table 83–4. Laboratory diagnosis of microsporidiosis.

- 1- to 2-μm, gram-positive, birefringent, PAS-positive ovoid spore
- By spore concentration and sedimentation techniques, spores can be identified with Weber's modified trichrome, Gram, giemsa, or chitin-binding fluorochrome stains
- Electron microscopy, immunofluorescence, and PCR techniques are valuable for speciation

BOX 83-11

Treatment of Microsporidiosis

	Adults	Children
Intestinal and Biliary	Albendazole, 400 mg twice orally daily x 3–4 weeks	No data available for albendazole use for a prolonged period in children
Keratopathy	Topical fumagillin and propamidine isethionate 0.1%	

adjustments such as prescribing low-fat and simple carbohydrate diets may be beneficial.

Topical fumagillin and propamidine isethionate (0.1%) have been effective in treating microsporidial keratopathy. One case report suggests that itraconazole may be beneficial in this realm as well.

Prevention & Control

Control of microsporidial infection will be difficult to address until transmission is better understood (see Box 83–6). Bodily fluid precautions seem warranted to prevent fecal-oral and urinary-oral transmission. Disinfecting, boiling, and autoclaving may also be of benefit. The necessity of respiratory precautions and isolation is uncertain.

REFERENCES

Abramowitz M (editor): Drugs for parasitic infections. Med Lett Drugs Ther 1995;37:961.

Blackman E et al: Cryptosporidiosis in HIV-infected patients: diagnostic sensitivity of stool examination, based on number of specimens submitted. Am J Gastroenterol 1997;92(3):451.

Bryan RT: Microsporidia. In Mandell GL, Bennett JE, Dolin R: *Principles and Practice of Infectious Diseases,* 3rd ed. Wiley, 1995.

Bryan RT: Microsporidiosis as an AIDS-related opportunistic infection. Clin Infect Dis 1995;21(suppl 1):S62.

Carter PL et al: Modified technique to recover microsporidia spores in sodium acetate-acetic acid–formalin-fixed fecal samples by light microscopy and correlation with transmission electron microscopy. J Clin Microbiol 1996;34(11):2670.

Dupont HL et al: The infectivity of *Cryptosporidium parvum* in healthy volunteers. N Engl J Med 1995; 332:855.

Fayer R, Nerad T: Effects of low temperatures on viability of *Cryptosporidium parvum* oocysts. Appl Environ Microbiol 1996;62:1431.

Goodgame RW: Understanding intestinal spore-forming protozoa: *Cryptosporidia, Microsporidia, Isospora,* and *Cyclospora.* Ann Intern Med 1996;124:429.

Gunnarsson G et al: Multiorgan microsporidiosis: report of 5 cases and review. Clin Infect Dis 1995;1:37.

Herwaldt BL et al: An outbreak in 1996 of cyclosporiasis associated with imported raspberries. N Engl J Med 1997;336:1548.

Heyworth MF: Parasitic diseases in immunocompromised hosts cryptosporidiosis, isosporiasis, and strongyloidiasis. Gastroenterol Clin North Am 1996;25:691.

Hoepelman AIM: Current therapeutic approaches to cryptosporidiosis in immunocompromised patients. J Antimicrob Chemother 1996;37:871.

Kelkar R et al: Pulmonary microsporidial infection in a patient with CML undergoing allogeneic marrow transplant. Bone Marrow Transplant 1997;19:178.

Mannheimer AB, Soave R: Protozoal infections in patients with AIDS cryptosporidiosis, isosporiasis, cyclosporiasis, and microsporidiosis. Infect Dis Clin North Am 1994;8:483.

Orenstein JM: Isosporiasis. In Connor DH, Chandler FW: *Pathology of Infectious Diseases.* Appleton & Lange, 1997.

Orenstein JM: Microsporidiosis. In Connor DH, Chandler FW: *Pathology of Infectious Diseases.* Appleton & Lange, 1997.

Orenstein JM: Cryptosporidiosis. In Connor DH, Chandler FW: *Pathology of Infectious Diseases.* Appleton & Lange, 1997.

Sears CL: *Isospora belli, Sarcocystis* species, *Balantidium coli, Blastocystis hominis,* and *Cyclospora.* In Mandell GL, Bennett JE, Dolin R: *Principles and Practice of Infectious Diseases,* 3rd ed. Wiley, 1995.

Soave R: *Cyclospora*: an overview. Clin Infect Dis 1996;23:429.

Sun T *Cyclospora* infection. In Connor DH, Chandler FW: *Pathology of Infectious Diseases.* Appleton & Lange, 1997.

Ungar BLP: *Cryptosporidium.* In Mandell GL, Bennett JE, Dolin R: *Principles and Practice of Infectious Diseases,* 3rd ed. Wiley, 1995.

84

Giardia

Stephanie Boade Silas, MD, & DeVon Hale, MD

Essentials of Diagnosis

- Key symptoms include initially profuse and watery diarrhea progressing to foul-smelling and often greasy stools that float.
- It is the most common pathogen in waterborne diarrheal illness.
- Patients at highest risk include infants, young children, travelers, and immunocompromised patients.
- In North America, the Rocky Mountains and mountainous regions of the northwest, northeast, and British Columbia are notorious *Giardia* reservoirs.
- Giardiasis is diagnosed either by identification of cysts or trophozoites on wet mounts of fresh stool or duodenal specimens or by antigen detection using enzyme-linked immunosorbent assay or immunofluorescence techniques.

General Considerations

Giardia, a genus of primitive eukaryotes, is a flagellated enteric protozoan of the class Zoomastigophorea. *Giardia lamblia,* also known as *Giardia intestinalis* or *Giardia duodenalis,* is the species known to infect humans. Its name comes from Vilem Lambl, who first reported the organism in 1859. However, the first description of *G lamblia* came from Anton von Leeuwenhoek in 1681, while examining his own stool during an episode of diarrhea.

A. Epidemiology. *G lamblia* is a global enteric pathogen. It is the most prevalent enteric parasite in the United States and Canada, and populations at highest risk include infants, young children, travelers, and immunocompromised patients. Between 1965 and 1984, the Centers for Disease Control and Prevention documented 90 outbreaks, making *G lamblia* the most common pathogen in waterborne diarrheal illness. Giardiasis plays a role in malnutrition and growth retardation in the developing world.

In some areas of the developing world, the overall prevalence of *Giardia* infection is as high as 20–30%, whereas prevalence in industrialized nations is 2–5%. Age-specific prevalence increases from infancy through childhood before falling in adolescence, and children < 10 years old in developing nations have a 15–20% prevalence of *G lamblia* infection. The highest giardiasis prevalence is seen in the subtropics and tropics. *G lamblia* accounts for < 5% of traveler's diarrhea, with increased risk after travel to southeast and south Asia, tropical Africa, Mexico, South America, and areas of the former Soviet Union, particularly St. Petersburg. In North America, the Rocky Mountains and the mountainous regions of the Northwest, Northeast, and British Columbia are notorious *G lamblia* reservoirs.

G lamblia is ingested orally, and transmission has been associated with contaminated water, person-to-person spread, and, less often, food-borne transmission. Most outbreaks are related either to untreated water or to inadequately purified water. The *G lamblia* cyst is particularly well suited to survive in cold water and is relatively resistant to chlorine.

Person-to-person transmission is related to poor fecal–oral hygiene. Children in day care facilities have an infection prevalence of ≤ 50%, and sexually active male homosexuals, regardless of HIV status, have a prevalence of 20%. Increased numbers of infections are also found in individuals in custodial situations. Food-borne cases related to infected food handlers have been increasingly reported.

Studies have confirmed the presence of a vast animal reservoir. The first associations involved the beaver as a source of water contamination. Subsequently, DNA similarities have been found in *Giardia* isolates from humans and both domestic and wild animals, including beavers, cattle, cats, coyotes, dogs, gerbils, and sheep.

B. Microbiology. The *G lamblia* life cycle has two stages, the trophozoite and the cyst. The pear-shaped trophozoite lives freely in the small bowel lumen and is 9–21 μm long × 5–15 μm wide (Figure 84–1). It has a convex dorsal surface, a flat ventral surface with a sucking disk, and four pairs of posterior flagella. Absorption of nutrients occurs through the dorsal surface. The sucking disk is composed of an array of microtubules containing tubulin, microribbons containing the protein giardin, and other contractile proteins. Within the trophozoite is a posteriorly placed median body and two anterior nuclei each with a prominent karyosome, giving *G lamblia* its characteristic facelike appearance. The trophozoite divides by binary fission, doubling in 9–12 h in culture. An aerotolerant anaerobe lacking mitochondria, the trophozoite scavenges phospholipids, fatty

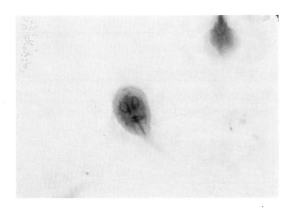

Figure 84–1. The *G lamblia* trophozoite is distinctive with its pear-shaped body (10–20 μm long and 7–10 μm wide). The location of the two nuclei with central karyosomes and the small curved parabasal body give it a facelike appearance.

acids, cholesterol, and pyrimidine. It metabolizes glucose to ethanol, acetate, and carbon dioxide. In vitro growth is optimized by conditions comparable with those found in the small intestine, including the presence of biliary lipids, intestinal mucus, epithelial cells, and low oxygen tension.

Encystation occurs in the small bowel, possibly because of high concentrations of bile salts and elevated pH. The highly resistant cyst is passed out of the host into the environment where trophozoite division occurs within the cyst. The mature *G lamblia* cyst is an oval structure (8–12 μm long × 7–10 μm wide) with four nuclei and an acid phosphatase-positive periphery encased in a thin wall that is composed primarily of *N*-acetylgalactosamine (Figure 84–2). Hundreds to thousands of cysts may be excreted per

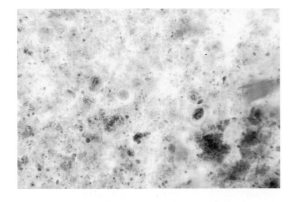

Figure 84–2. The *Giardia* cyst is an oval structure (8–12 μm long × 7–10 μm wide) with four nuclei and an acid phosphatase-positive periphery encased in a thin wall of *N*-acetylgalactosamine.

gram of stool. After ingestion and exposure to gastric acid and pancreatic enzymes, excystation releases two trophozoites to resume the cycle.

C. Pathogenesis. *G lamblia* infection requires the oral ingestion of as few as 10 cysts. Excystation, promoted by gastric acid, releases trophozoites, which then multiply and colonize the upper small bowel. Trophozoites attach to the brush border enterocytes by two proposed mechanisms. First, the ventral disk may be involved in attachment by either contractile proteins or flagellum-mediated hydrodynamic forces. Second, a receptor-ligand interaction mediated by lectin has been suggested. The attachment process enables the trophozoite to avoid peristalsis.

The exact mechanism of injury causing disease is uncertain, but several observations have been made. First, the brush border is disrupted by microvilli injury and villous atrophy, which cause a disaccharidase deficiency. It has been postulated that this injury may be caused by a proteinase or mannose-binding lectin. Second, increased epithelial turnover in the crypts has led to altered absorption, which may be caused by immature enterocytes. T lymphocytes may contribute to this crypt hyperplasia, which is also observed in graft vs host disease. Third, decreased bile salt concentrations with consequent diminished pancreatic lipase activity and impaired solubilization of fat has been reported in giardiasis patients. The trophozoite, although unable to deconjugate bile salts, does have an uptake mechanism for bile salts that, in low concentrations, stimulate growth. Low-bile-salt concentrations in giardiasis patients may also result from deconjugation by simultaneous colonization with *Enterobacteriaceae* or yeasts. This increased colonization of anaerobic and aerobic bacteria in giardiasis has not been uniformly reported, however, with all confirmatory studies coming only from India. Fourth, *G lamblia* infection inhibits trypsin. Thus, disaccharidase deficiency, immature enterocytes, and both lipase and trypsin inhibition suggest that the diarrhea in giardiasis is primarily malabsorptive. Evidence supports neither mucosal invasion nor the presence of an enterotoxin in the pathogenesis of giardiasis.

The immune response to *G lamblia* infection is initiated by antigen uptake into macrophages in Peyer's patches. This action generates both an antibody and a cellular response. Although serum immunoglobulins M and G are lethal to *G lamblia* by the classical complement pathway, secretory immunoglobulin A (IgA) appears to be more important in clearing and preventing infection. Intraluminal IgA can prevent adherence, and chronic giardiasis is associated with the failure to make IgA. *G lamblia* has been found to make an IgA protease that is protective to trophozoites.

A cellular immune response is also generated and shown in mice to be necessary for both cytotoxicity and coordination of IgA secretion. As already mentioned, the T-cell response may also contribute to the pathogenesis of *G lamblia* because the mononuclear cell submucosal infiltrate is associated with flattened villi and crypt hypertrophy.

Protective immunity does not develop after a single infection, possibly because of genomic plasticity and significant antigenic diversity described in *G lamblia* isolates. However, increased prevalence in the young and decreased symptoms in long-term residents of endemic areas suggest at least partial immune protection. Infection in infants < 6 months old is rare, and human milk is protective because of the presence of antibodies and cytotoxicity from free fatty acids generated from milk triglycerides.

Although occurring in immunocompetent hosts, a predisposition to chronic giardiasis is reported in patients with X chromosome-linked agammaglobulinemia, lymphoid nodular hyperplasia, and common variable immunodeficiency with variable levels of hypogammaglobulinemia. Patients with earlier gastric surgery and decreased gastric acidity also have an increased susceptibility to infection. Of interest, patients with AIDS have no more severe illness than patients without AIDS, in contrast to the disparity seen in intracellular protozoal infections such as *Cryptosporidium parvum*.

CLINICAL SYNDROMES

After ingestion of *G lamblia* cysts, 5–15% of patients will have asymptomatic cyst passage, and 25–50% of patients will have diarrhea. From 35% to 70% of these patients will have no evidence of infection. The three manifestations of infection include asymptomatic cyst passage, self-limited diarrhea, and chronic diarrhea with associated malabsorption and weight loss. Factors related to each of these manifestations are unknown but are believed to be related to specific host factors, parasite load, and virulence variation among *G lamblia* isolates.

1. ACUTE GIARDIASIS

Clinical Findings

A. Signs and Symptoms. After ingestion of cysts, an incubation period of 3–20 days exists before symptom onset. At the time of presentation, patients have generally had symptoms for 7–10 days. The predominant symptom in acute giardiasis is diarrhea, occurring in 90% of patients, accompanied by generalized malaise (Box 84–1). Patients describe initially profuse and watery stools progressing to foul-smelling and often greasy stools that float. Flatulence, bloating, and abdominal cramps are frequent concerns as are belching, nausea, and anorexia. Weight loss and vomiting are less frequent, and fever

BOX 84–1

Giardiasis

	Acute	Chronic
More Common	• Diarrhea • Malaise • Flatulence • Abdominal cramps	• Diarrhea • Alternating diarrhea with constipation • Abdominal pain worsening by eating • Malaise
Less Common	• Nausea • Weight loss • Vomiting • Urticaria	• Malabsorption • Macrocytic anemia • Lactose intolerance • Weight loss • Headache

is rare. Symptoms are usually self-limited to 2–4 weeks.

B. Laboratory Findings. Laboratory studies are notable for a normal peripheral leukocyte count without eosinophilia. Stool studies are negative for the presence of mucus, leukocytes, and blood.

C. Differential Diagnosis. *C parvum*, rotavirus, and toxigenic *Escherichia coli* may all have similar presentations.

D. Complications. Rare associations with urticaria and reactive arthritis have been reported in giardiasis. Biliary tract disease and pancreatitis have been reported, as have retinal arteritis and iridocyclitis. Gastric infections have been seen in *G lamblia* patients with achlorhydria.

2. CHRONIC GIARDIASIS

From 30% to 50% of individuals with acute giardiasis will progress to have chronic giardiasis.

Clinical Findings

A. Signs and Symptoms. Profound malaise and lassitude are frequently reported. Patients experience diarrhea alternating with constipation, frequent stools, and abdominal pain associated with eating. Weight loss of 10–20% of body weight is common, with a 10-lb weight loss reported in 50% of patients. Headache has also been associated with the syndrome.

B. Laboratory Findings. Laboratory studies are significant for biochemical evidence of malabsorption. D-Xylose, fat, protein, vitamin A, and vitamin B_{12} malabsorption have all been reported. Disaccharidase deficiency, particularly lactase, occurs in 20–40% of patients and may persist for several weeks beyond infection. Macrocytic anemia from folate deficiency and hypoalbuminemia has been reported.

C. Differential Diagnosis. Similar presentations can be seen in infections caused by coccidians such as *C parvum, I belli,* and *Cyclospora* spp., as well as infections caused by *Strongyloides* spp. and *Entamoeba histolytica.* Also, diagnoses of inflammatory bowel disease and irritable bowel syndrome should be considered.

D. Complications. Chronic giardiasis may play an important role in growth impairment and nutritional deficiency in the developing world.

Diagnosis

The key to diagnosis of *G lamblia* infection is the identification of trophozoites or cysts, both of which can be seen in stools by standard ova and parasite exam (Table 84–1). Trophozoites have a short survival time outside the small bowel when not contained within cysts and are more likely to be seen in fresh wet mounts of liquid stool. Semiformed stool may be preserved in formalin or polyvinyl alcohol. Staining with trichrome or iron hematoxylin reveals cysts. Formalin or zinc flotation concentration techniques may increase the yield of diagnosis. Generally, one stool exam has a 50–70% diagnostic yield, which improves to 85–90% after 3 stools collected over 2–3 days because of cyclic shedding. Purged samples have no effect on diagnostic yield.

Enzyme immunoassay and direct fluorescent-antibody assay kits are commercially available for testing for *G lamblia* infection. Both methods have reported sensitivities of 87–100% and specificities of 99–100% when compared with microscopic stool examination. Advantages of these techniques include a decrease in both examination time and required techni-

Table 84–1. Laboratory diagnosis of giardiasis.[1]

- The trophozoite is 10 μm × 15 μm with a convex dorsal surface, flat ventral surface, and 2 facelike nuclei
- The cyst is 10 μm × 10 μm, thin-walled, and with an eccentric nucleus
- Motile trophozoites are seen on microscopy of fresh stool specimens or on specimens obtained by duodenal aspirate, biopsy, or the string test
- Cysts and trophozoites are observed on wet mounts of fresh stools with or without prior formalin concentration. Cysts can also be found in specimens preserved in formalin or PVA, using trichrome or iron hematoxylin staining
- Antigen detection by ELISA is highly sensitive and specific and comparable in cost to standard stool O & P. It is best used when the sole diagnosis or exclusion of giardiasis is needed
- Antigen detection by IFA has the same sensitivity and specificity as standard O & P, but is advantageous in small labs with less-trained technicians
- DNA probes and PCR techniques are available but not yet useful clinically

[1]O & P, Ova and parasite examination; PVA, polyvinyl alcohol; IFA, immunofluorescent antibody assay

cian training. Both direct fluorescent-antibody assay and enzyme immunoassay are particularly valuable when the sole diagnosis or exclusion of *G lamblia* is needed, as may occur during an epidemic or for screening purposes. Although cost of antigen detection techniques is similar to ova and parasite microscopic exams, microscopy allows for diagnosis of other possible pathogens. One commercially available direct fluorescent antibody assay kit does detect both *G lamblia* and *C parvum,* however.

Other, more invasive techniques are rarely used but may contribute to diagnosis. The string test involves swallowing a capsule attached to a nylon string. The capsule sits in the jejunum for 4–6 h while the patient is fasting. The string is subsequently removed and examined for trophozoites by microscopy. A duodenal aspirate can be similarly examined. Also, a duodenal biopsy or endoscopic brushing can be examined for trophozoites, by using Giemsa stain.

Upper gastrointestinal aspirates can be cultured, but this test is generally not available clinically. Serology, too, has little clinical utility but may be helpful epidemiologically. Serum immunoglobulin M or IgA titers are indicative of recent infection as compared with IgG titers. Polymerase chain reaction and gene probe studies are still in experimental stages, with their most practical limitation being extraction of DNA from the stool sample.

Treatment

Historically, quinacrine hydrochloride has been the drug of choice for the treatment of giardiasis, with 90% efficacy. However, this drug is no longer produced in the United States. Despite having never received a Food and Drug Administration indication for giardiasis, metronidazole is the first-line treatment, with 80–95% efficacy after a 7-day course (Box 84–2). Its efficacy is considered to be related to inhibition of attachment. Because of the disulfiram effect of metronidazole, patients should be warned that concurrent use of ethanol could cause flushing, tachycardia, and nausea. Tinidazole is also considered a first-line agent with 90% efficacy, but it is also not available in the United States.

Second-line agents include furazolidone and paromomycin sulfate. Furazolidone, a nitrosourea with 80% efficacy, may be particularly useful in children because it comes in a liquid form. Paramomycin sulfate is an aminoglycoside with 60–70% efficacy. Because of its poor oral absorption, it may be beneficial for use in pregnant patients. Ideally, treatment for giardiasis in pregnancy should be delayed until after delivery. Metronidazole may be safe after the first trimester, however. Variable sensitivities of isolates to drug regimens occur, and resistance to metronidazole and furazolidone has been reported.

Other drugs with reported benefit against *G lamblia* infection include some antidepressants, fusidate

BOX 84-2

Treatment of Giardiasis

Adults	First Choice	• Metronidazole, 250 mg three times daily × 5–7 d OR • Tinidazole[1] 2 g × 1 OR • Quinacrine (Mepacrine)[1] 100 mg three times daily × 5 d
	Second Choice	• Furazolidone, 100 mg four times daily × 7–10 d OR • Paromomycin, 25–30 mg/kg/d divided three times daily × 5–10 d
Children		• Metronidazole, 5 mg/kg three times daily × 7 d OR • Furazolidone liquid, 6 mg/kg divided 4×/day for 10 d
Pregnancy		• Delay until after delivery if possible • Metronidazole may be used after first trimester—see above • Paromomycin, see above for dosing

[1]Not available in the United States.

BOX 84-3

Prevention & Control of Giardiasis

Prophylactic Measures	• Proper treatment of public water supplies including chlorination, flocculation, sedimentation, and filtration • In the wilderness, bring water to a rolling boil • Halogenation with chlorine or iodine tablets may be effective with warm water • Filters with < 1-μm pores can be used as well
Isolation Precautions	• No specific need for isolation • Good hygiene practices

sodium, D- and DL-propranolol, mefloquine, doxycycline, and rifampin. Albendazole, an anthelmintic benzimidazole derivative, may prove to be effective in treating giardiasis and may be especially useful in developing countries for dual coverage.

Prognosis

The natural history of untreated giardiasis is unknown. Chronic persistent diarrhea may develop in a small number of patients, some of whom, particularly children, may develop malnutrition and growth impairment. The prognosis of treated giardiasis, however, is excellent.

Prevention & Control

Because of the worldwide presence of *Giardia* spp., vast human and animal reservoirs, and environmental resilience, total elimination of giardiasis is not expected. Instead, prevention depends on focusing on the primary sources of infection, including water contamination and person-to-person contacts (Box 84–3). Chlorine kills cysts in warm water, and public water supplies should undergo chlorination, flocculation, sedimentation, and filtration. DNA techniques may be valuable in screening filtered water for cysts.

In the wilderness or in the developing world, water should be boiled before consumption. Inactivation is immediate at 100 °C, and water need only be brought to a rolling boil. At altitudes of ≥ 10,000 ft, where the boiling point is 90 °C, water can still be safely disinfected by simply bringing it to a boil. The margin of safety is further ensured by the time taken for the water to heat to this level and subsequently cool because keeping water at 70 °C for 10 min also results in 100% inactivation. Halogenation with iodine or chlorine tablets has proven useful but may not be effective in cold water. The questionable efficacy of halogenation is best exemplified by reported cases of giardiasis associated with chlorinated swimming pools. Water filters with pores < 1–2 μm may also be effective in preventing giardiasis.

Person-to-person spread of giardiasis could be lessened by improved hygiene, especially in those at high risk. However, evidence is not yet available to support the treatment of asymptomatic patients. Further, no vaccines for giardiasis are available. Vaccine development is limited because the initial infection itself does not confer protective immunity to the patient.

REFERENCES

Abramowitz MD: Drugs for parasitic infections. Med Lett Drugs Ther 1995;37:971.

Backer HD: Effect of heat on the sterilization of artificially contaminated water. J Travel Med 1996;3:1.

Farthing MJG: Giardiasis. Gastroenterol Clin North Am 1996;25:493.

Hill DR: *Giardia lamblia.* In Mandell GL, Bennett JE,

Dolin R: *Principles and Practice of Infectious Diseases,* 3rd ed. Wiley, 1995.

Marshall MM et al: Waterborne protozoan pathogens. Clin Microbiol Rev 1997;10:67.

Schwartz DA, Mixon JP, Owen RL: Giardiasis. In Connor DH, Chandler FW: *Pathology of Infectious Diseases.* Appleton & Lange, 1997.

85

Leishmania & Trypanosoma

D. Scott Smith, MD & David A. Relman, MD

The genera *Leishmania* and *Trypanosoma* are members of the family Trypanosomatidae. These protozoans cause diseases with widely varied clinical presentations as well as geographic distributions, including leishmaniasis, American trypanosomiasis (Chagas' disease), and African trypanosomiasis (sleeping sickness). For example, the endemic zones for African and American trypanosomiasis do not overlap, the diseases are transmitted by different vectors, they involve distinct mechanisms of pathogenesis, and they follow different clinical courses. Nonetheless, the causative agents share important biological features. Each is a hemoflagellate with a kinetoplast containing its own chromosomal DNA with highly conserved and repeated elements, each forms a single flagellum at some point during its life cycle, and each is highly adapted to life within an insect.

LEISHMANIA

Essentials of Diagnosis
- Epidemiologic factors: time spent in an endemic zone and exposure to sandfly vector.
- Physical exam: nonhealing ulcer (cutaneous infection); nonhealing mucosal membrane lesion, nasal obstruction, epistaxis, nasal septum perforation (mucocutaneous infection); fever, hepatosplenomegaly, emaciation (visceral infection).
- Laboratory examination of affected tissue:
  1. Giemsa stain shows phagosomal cells contain amatigotes at leading edge of biopsied ulcer.
  2. Histological analysis of bone, liver, or spleen tissue shows amastigotes.
  3. Culture of biopsied tissue, ie, skin, spleen, liver, or bone, reveals promastigotes.
  4. Serologic analysis using immunofluorescence assay (available through the Centers for Disease Control and Prevention [CDC]).
  5. Xenodiagnostic analyses of macerated tissue samples injected into animals for specific identification via growth in vivo.

  6. Polymerase chain reaction (PCR) (helpful but not widely available).

General Considerations
Infections with *Leishmania* spp. occur worldwide, in environments as varied as the semiarid deserts of the Middle East and the tropical rain forests of Central and South America. There are three major clinical forms of disease: visceral (kala-azar), mucocutaneous, and cutaneous. Even though each form tends to be associated with particular *Leishmania* species, some species can cause multiple forms of the disease, and some forms can be caused by multiple species. Leishmaniasis is a zoonosis with sandfly vectors and mammalian reservoirs. *Lutzomyia* sandflies are the primary vectors in the Americas, whereas *Phlebotomine* sandflies transmit the disease in the rest of the world.

A. Epidemiology. Leishmaniasis is endemic in ≥ 82 countries, with an at-risk population of 350 million people worldwide. The World Health Organization (WHO) estimates 12 million current cases, with an annual incidence of 600,000 new cases and 75,000 deaths. Reliable estimates are scarce owing to lack of surveillance or active reporting and the large number of asymptomatic or subclinical cases, as well as the challenge of diagnostic confirmation.

Leishmaniasis is endemic to all countries in the Americas except Canada, Uruguay, and Chile. Southern Texas is the only endemic area in the United States. There are often small geographic foci of transmission within endemic areas. Leishmaniasis is seen in the countries surrounding the Mediterranean Sea, as well as in central Africa and across the Middle East to India and China. Of visceral leishmaniasis cases worldwide, 90% occur in India, Bangladesh, southern Sudan, and northern Brazil; and 90% of cutaneous leishmaniasis cases occur in Afghanistan, Brazil, Iran, Saudi Arabia, and Syria. The vast majority of mucocutaneous leishmaniasis cases are found in Brazil and the geographic areas after which the subspecies and complexes are named (eg, *amazonensis* [Amazon region], *panamensis* [Panama], and *guyanensis* [Guyana]).

Leishmaniasis is most commonly observed in humans who live or work at the forest edge, where insect vectors are most abundant. These include rural settlers, farmers clearing forests, and road construction workers, as well as military personnel. Most cases of leishmaniasis in the United States are imported by those who have been exposed in rural areas of endemic regions, including Peace Corp workers, ornithologists, and field workers. Leishmaniasis is more common in adult males, probably in part because of occupational risks. Transmission of leishmaniasis has been associated with blood transfusions and intravenous drug abuse.

Although there are > 600 species of sandflies, only about one-tenth of these transmit leishmaniasis. Among these disease transmitters, both the *Phlebotomine* (found in the Mediterranean and Middle East regions) and the *Lutzomyia* (found in the Americas) sandflies are small and hairy and have a V-shaped wing configuration. They are inactive during daylight hours, and they stay in dark moist places that are rich in organic matter. The animal reservoirs in the Americas are primarily sylvatic and include sloths, opossums, and small forest rodents. Canines also serve as reservoirs for organisms that cause the visceral forms, especially as part of a peridomestic transmission cycle (Figure 85–1A). With the notable exception of dogs and humans, the mammalian hosts that serve as reservoirs generally do not show signs of disease.

B. Microbiology and Pathogenesis. Species of the genus *Leishmania* display a dimorphic life cycle; in the insect vector they assume a flagellated form (the promastigote), and, in human and mammalian hosts, the parasite takes on the amastigote form (devoid of flagellum) (Figure 85–1B). Amastigotes survive inside phagosomal cells, such as the histio-

cytes of the skin and other cells of reticuloendothelial origin. Amastigotes are 2–3 μm in length and can be round or oval. The species are morphologically indistinguishable from each other and from *Trypanosoma cruzi*, but *Leishmania* spp. can easily be differentiated from *T cruzi* in clinical specimens based on tissue tropism. The amastigotes transform into promastigotes once inside the sandfly gut. They then migrate forward to the proboscis to infect another host. Besides the insect vector, the life cycle usually includes a nonhuman animal reservoir. Humans are incidental hosts for *Leishmania* spp. Promastigotes are passed from the female sandfly to the skin of a vertebrate host during a blood meal. These promastigotes invade the reticuloendothelial cells of the vertebrate host, change into amastigote forms, multiply further, and invade other reticuloendothelial cells. Mammalian blood is essential to the sandfly's life cycle and promotes egg maturation within the female; only female sandflies seek blood meals. Once *Leishmania* amastigotes infect a sandfly, disease transmission to a new mammalian host is delayed for at least 7–10 days while the parasite undergoes differentiation.

The visceral form of leishmaniasis (kala-azar) provides an exception to this cycle from insects to animal reservoirs to humans, because there are no known animal reservoirs but only direct insect-to-human transmission. In India, for example, the organism and disease persist in the human population (anthroponoses) and are maintained by patients with persistent subclinical post-kala-azar dermal leishmaniasis, from whom parasites have been isolated from normal appearing skin.

Interferon gamma and other components of the

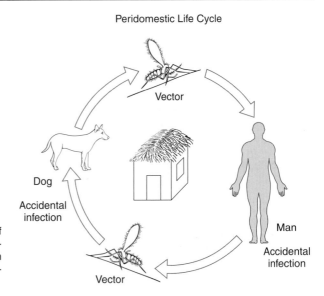

Peridomestic Life Cycle

Figure 85–1. Life cycle of *L donovani,* the agent of visceral leishmaniasis. A. Passage of promastigotes by an infected sandfly from a reservoir, such as a dog, to humans in the peridomestic setting. Illustration by Andres Patricio Reyes.

Vector

Dog
Accidental infection

Man
Accidental infection

Vector

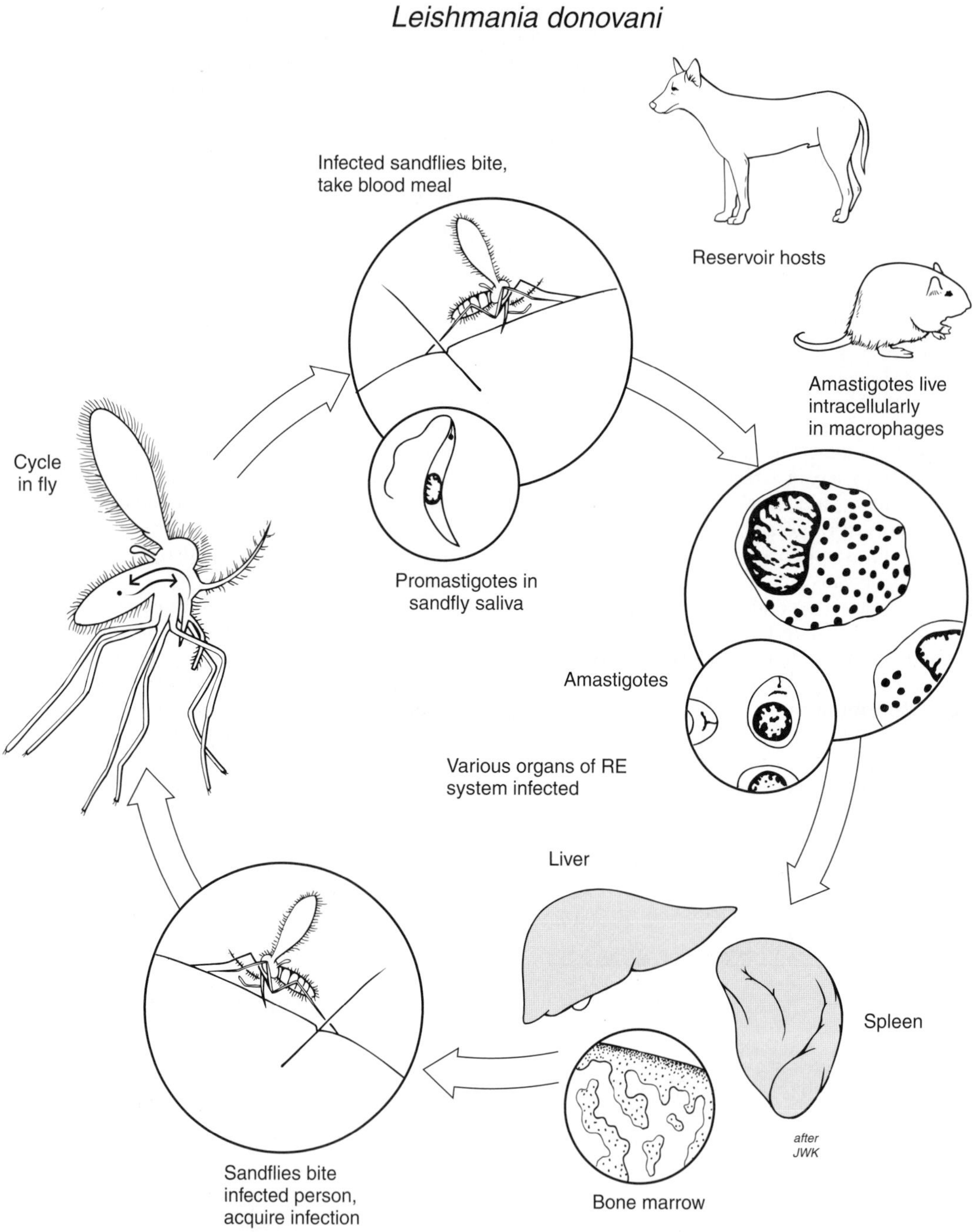

Leishmania donovani

Figure 85–1. B. Morphogenesis of infection. Republished by permission from Despommier DD, Karapelou JW: *Parasite Life Cycles.* Springer-Verlag, 1987.

Th1 cytokine response appear to be critical for host defense against disease. In an apparent attempt to subvert these defenses, *Leishmania mexicana* expresses several cysteine proteinases that down-regulate the Th1 cytokine response and induce the Th2 cytokines such as interleukin-4, thereby enhancing susceptibility of the host to disease progression.

Clinical Findings

A. Cutaneous Leishmaniasis. Cutaneous leishmaniasis begins as papules and, less commonly, as nodules at the site of the vector bite; it then progresses to ulcer formation (Figure 85–2). It is most commonly caused by *Leishmania major* and *Leishmania tropica* in the Old World and by *Leishmania mexicana, Leishmania braziliensis,* and *L panamensis* in the New World, and the infection exhibits an incubation period of 2–8 weeks. Satellite lesions appear in some cases. Most forms of the disease (> 80%) heal spontaneously within 3 months, although, on occasion, the cutaneous form can be disfiguring. In a more recently described form of cutaneous disease associated with *L braziliensis,* lymphadenopathy was found in three-fourths of patients and preceded the development of skin lesions; the latter healed spontaneously in only 20% of patients by 3 months after initial infection.

B. Mucocutaneous Leishmaniasis. Mucocutaneous leishmaniasis involves the mucosal membranes of the nose and mouth but may also involve the oropharynx and the larynx. *L braziliensis* is the cause of most mucocutaneous disease. An estimated 3% of patients with infection by this species develop mucosal disease. The disease begins as a primary cutaneous ulcer at the site of inoculation. During early stages it cannot be distinguished clinically from the more benign cutaneous forms of disease. The time delay from cutaneous disease to development of mu-

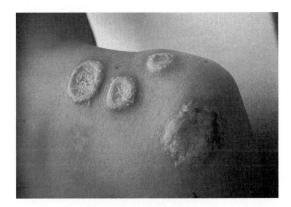

Figure 85–2. Cutaneous leishmaniasis on the shoulder of a patient with multiple sandfly bites. Courtesy of Fernando Martinez, Centro Internacional de Investigaciones Medicas, Cali, Colombia.

cosal involvement can vary from 1 month to 24 years. Mucosal disease may present as nasal obstruction or epistaxis. A slight reddening and swelling in the septum can be seen, which may progress to perforation. Although the disease is termed mucocutaneous, tracheal and genital mucosal involvement is rare.

C. Visceral Leishmaniasis. Visceral leishmaniasis or kala-azar is primarily caused by *Leishmania donovani* in the Indian subcontinent and Africa, *Leishmania infantum* in the Mediterranean region, and *Leishmania chagasi* in Latin America. The incubation period is generally 2–6 months. The disease begins with fever, hepatosplenomegaly, and pancytopenia. The onset of fever can be sudden or gradual, and there may be intervals when the patient has low-grade or no fever. Clinically evident disease is usually characterized by progressive weakness, emaciation, and, if untreated, death. Case fatality rates, even with treatment, are ≤ 11%. The ratio of inapparent infection to overt clinical disease varies depending on the age group and the endemic area but ranges from 6.5:1 to 18:1. This feature enables ongoing inapparent transmission of infection. A young age (infants and children) and malnutrition predispose to development of the disease. Viscerotropic (*L tropica*) disease in US troops who returned from the Persian Gulf was reported among a small number of individuals and resulted in a temporary ban on blood donations from this group.

The combination of visceral leishmaniasis and HIV infection is an increasingly important problem, especially in southern Europe. In general, the clinical presentation of visceral leishmaniasis in HIV-infected patients is similar to that in uninfected persons, but the gastrointestinal tract may be more frequently involved, and sometimes the hepatosplenomegaly is less pronounced or absent.

Diagnosis

The first step in diagnosis should be to establish an exposure history. It is important to distinguish the more innocuous cutaneous forms of leishmaniasis from the mucocutaneous forms, which are not usually self-limited. Therapy for leishmaniasis is not benign, and, therefore, diagnostic certainty is crucial. The differential diagnosis for each form of leishmaniasis is listed in Table 85–1.

The most common diagnostic approach is demonstration of the presence of parasites by microscopy in Giemsa-stained tissues or by culturing the organisms in specialized media. Aspiration and punch biopsy of the leading edge of a cutaneous or mucocutaneous lesion are the best techniques to obtain specimens for both culture and histology. The tissues of choice for diagnosis of visceral disease are liver, spleen, and bone marrow. Sternal bone biopsy is often the most easily accessible and safest procedure to obtain tissue for culture and smear. Giemsa-stained smears from either the culture (promastigotes) or the tissue biopsy

Table 85–1. Differential Diagnosis of leishmaniasis.

Infections	Cutaneous	Mucocutaneous	Visceral
Bacterial	• Tularemia • Furuncle/carbuncle • Cellulitis • Yaws • Syphilis • Atypical tuberculosis • Tuberculosis • Leprosy	• Tertiary yaws • Syphilis	• Brucellosis • Typhoid fever • Tuberculosis
Fungal	• Histoplasmosis • Sporotrichosis • Lobomycosis • Coccidioidomycosis • Blastomycosis • Chromomycosis	• Histoplasmosis • Paracoccidiodomycosis • Rhinosporidiosis	• Histoplasmosis
Viral	• Orf		• Infectious mononucleosis
Protozoan	• Drucunculiasis		• Acute Chagas' disease • Schistosomiasis • Amebic liver abscess • Malaria
Other (non-infectious)	• Basal or squamous cell carcinoma • Lymphoma or metastatic cancer • Discoid lupus • Sarcoidosis • Insect bite • Ecthyma • Kerion • Pyogenic granuloma • Foreign-body granuloma	• Basal cell carcinoma • Wegener's granulomatosis • Mid-line granuloma • Sarcoidosis	• Lymphoma

specimens (amastigotes) show the distinctive rod-shaped kinetoplasts of *Leishmania* spp. in the cytoplasm of the parasite. The cytoplasm stains blue with Wright-Giemsa with a large eccentric red nucleus. Small red kinetoplasts are features of *Leishmania* spp. that distinguish them from other intracellular pathogens with somewhat similar appearance, such as *Toxoplasma* and *Histoplasma* spp.

Many diagnostic techniques, including DNA hybridization, PCR, and monoclonal antibody tests, have been developed. These tests are not widely available or standardized. Xenodiagnostic techniques are also used. Consultation with physicians experienced in the diagnosis of leishmaniasis is available through the CDC by calling (770) 488-7760.

Treatment

The drugs of choice for leishmaniasis include the organic antimonial compound stibogluconate sodium and meglumine antimoniate (Box 85–1). Anti-*Leishmania* drugs can be obtained from the CDC by calling (404) 639-3670.

Several alternative regimens and therapies are used, because of increasing resistance and treatment failures including higher dosing and, in some instances, combination therapy to decrease the duration of treatment. The newer drugs include liposomal am-photericin B, pentamidine, as well as paromomicin, and cytokines (eg, interferon gamma), which are used in combination with the antimonials.

A. Cutaneous Leishmaniasis. Cutaneous leishmaniasis is usually self-limited, but, if it persists > 6 months or is disfiguring or disabling, then treatment is indicated. The challenge for local therapy is that the disease characteristically involves the dermis and may disseminate to the lymph nodes or mucous membranes. Antimonials are injected with or without steroids initially, on a twice-daily schedule. Infiltration of the lesions in a standardized way is difficult to achieve. Localized controlled heat has also been shown, in a placebo-controlled clinical trial, to be effective for treatment of cutaneous disease.

B. Mucocutaneous Leishmaniasis. Mucocutaneous forms of leishmaniasis are treated with stibogluconate. The electrocardiogram (ECG) should be monitored. For resistant cases, stibogluconate plus interferon gamma can be used, or amphotericin B or pentamidine is effective.

C. Visceral Leishmaniasis. Visceral leishmaniasis (kala-azar) has successfully been treated with stibogluconate. In immunocompromised patients, such as those with HIV infection, it is necessary to devise a suppressive regimen to minimize recurrence after adequate treatment has been completed. Re-

BOX 85–1

Treatment of Leishmaniasis

	First Choice	Comments and Alternatives
Cutaneous	• Meglumine antimonate (glucantime), 20 mg/kg/d IM or IV for 10 d • Stiboguconate, 20mg/kg/d IV or IM, preferably in two divided doses for 10 d • Pentamadine, 2–4 mg/kg IM every other day × 7–15 injections	• Local treatment with intralesional injection of stibogluconate, every other day x 8–24 injections for nondisseminated infections with *L major* and *L mexicana mexicana*
Mucocutaneous	• Stibogluconate, 20 mg/kg/d IV or IM, preferably in two divided doses, × 30 d	
Visceral	• Stibogluconate, 20 mg/kg/d IV or IM, preferably in two divided doses, × 30 d • If resistance: pentamidine, 4 mg/kg 3 times week for 5 weeks OR • Amphotericin B, 1 mg/kg IV every other day × 20 d	• May reduce the course from 28 to 15 d by adding aminosidine (paromomycin), 15 mg/kg/d IM

lapses of clinical disease typically occur after appropriate therapy with either antimony or amphotericin B (which has a higher initial cure rate in this population); therefore, a suppressive regimen has been suggested. Either pentamidine or paromomycin can be used alone as an acceptable choice for suppression, or either one can be combined with one of the following: interferon, ketoconazole, or fluconazole.

Prevention & Control

Because leishmaniasis is so widely endemic, control of both its reservoirs and its vectors remains a challenge (Box 85–2). Therefore, primary prevention efforts should focus on limiting vector contact, by using insect repellents and fine-mesh nets. No vaccine for humans is available. A strategy for preventing transmission of visceral leishmaniasis to humans in Latin America has been suggested, based on vaccination of dogs.

BOX 85–2

Control of Leishmaniasis

Prophylactic Measures	• Avoid exposure to sandfly vectors • Chemoprophylaxis not recommended • Immunoprophylaxis not available
Isolation Precautions	• None

TRYPANOSOMA

Three human pathogens are members of the genus *Trypanosoma.* These are *T cruzi,* the agent of American trypanosomiasis (also known as Chagas' disease), and *T brucei* subspecies *rhodesiense* and *gambiense,* both of which cause African sleeping sickness. Both of these diseases involve persistent circulation of parasites in the blood during some part of the disease course; these organisms are therefore referred to as hemoflagellates.

Trypanosomes have morphologically and physiologically different developmental stages in their insect and mammalian hosts. Like *Leishmania* spp., each stage contains a kinetoplast with highly conserved and repeating DNA sequences. Aside from morphology, the agents of African and American trypanosomiasis have little in common. The endemic zones of disease do not overlap, the organisms use different vectors, and their patterns of transmission are distinct. Furthermore, the clinical courses and response to therapy of these diseases are different.

AMERICAN TRYPANOSOMIASIS (CHAGAS' DISEASE)

Essentials of Diagnosis

• Epidemiologic factors: time spent in an endemic

zone; poor housing conditions, eg, mud or thatched housing; exposure to reduviid insect vector

- History and physical exam: Romaña's sign (swollen periorbital mucosal tissues after ocular inoculation); chagoma (skin nodule at the site of acute inoculation); in the chronic phase, congestive heart failure, dysphagia or regurgitation, and constipation
- Laboratory exam:
  1. Acute Chagas': trypomastigotes revealed by Giemsa smear of blood or buffy coat; culture of affected tissues, ie, the inoculation site; serologic enzyme immunoassay and enzyme-linked immunosorbent assay (ELISA); xenodiagnosis if available
  2. Chronic Chagas': radiological studies show congestive heart failure, megacolon, or megaesophagus; ECG shows right bundle branch block, arrhythmias

General Considerations

A. Epidemiology. *T cruzi* is found only in the Western Hemisphere, where it ranges from the southern United States to Argentina. An estimated 16 million–18 million people in Latin America have chronic *T cruzi* infections and ~ 50,000 die of Chagas' disease each year. In the United States, there has been concern about transmission of the organism via blood transfusion from unsuspected infected donors who are immigrants from endemic zones. Similar concerns arise for organ transplant recipients.

B. Microbiology. The life cycle of *T cruzi* involves an insect vector, the reduviid bug, and a mammalian reservoir. The insect vector, of which there are multiple species, is commonly known as an assassin bug because it preys on other insects; it is also called the kissing bug because it tends to bite the face. After taking a blood meal from an infected reservoir, *T cruzi* organisms multiply in the insect mid gut as epimastigotes and then develop into the infective form, the trypomastigote, in the insect hindgut. There are several nonhuman mammalian reservoirs that enable *T cruzi* to persist in nature, including peridomestic animals such as cats, dogs, and rats, as well as sylvatic animals such as opossums, raccoons, and armadillos.

C. Pathogenesis. When an infected reduviid bug takes a blood meal from a human, it defecates, leaving feces on the surface of the skin that is contaminated with the infective metacyclic stage of the trypanosomes. Trypanosomes proliferate at the site of inoculation and then pruritus at the bite wound causes *T cruzi* organisms to be rubbed into the wound or surrounding mucous membranes, introducing the organism to the bloodstream. In the bloodstream, they preferentially infect myocytes and neurons of the peripheral and central nervous system (CNS). After the amastigotes proliferate in the cytoplasm, they differentiate into trypanomastigotes. The cell subsequently ruptures, and the newly released trypanomastigotes invade local tissues and spread hematogenously. A mononuclear inflammatory response occurs. This intense inflammation leads to destruction of autonomic ganglia in the heart and gastrointestinal tract, and diffuse fibrosis and scarring occur in these organs.

Clinical Findings

In the acute phase of American trypanosomiasis, an indurated erythematous lesion occurs a few days after inoculation of *T cruzi* into the skin. This is called a chagoma. Periorbital swelling results when trypanosomes are inoculated into the conjunctival mucous membranes, and it is a classic sign of acute infection known as Romaña's sign. The patient experiences fever, hepatosplenomegaly, lymphadenopathy, transient skin rash, tender subcutaneous nodules (known as hematogenous chagomas), and nonpitting edema on the face or extremities. The acute phase is more commonly observed in children and is usually self-limited, lasting several weeks to months. Dissemination of organisms is common, regardless of whether chronic disease ultimately develops.

Chronic American trypanosomiasis is usually insidious. There may not be a history of documented acute disease. About 10–30% of infected patients develop chronic disease. These patients progress to have cardiac or gastrointestinal damage that results in clinical disease. Chronic infection may evolve over decades and most often involves the heart. Cardiac disease is manifested by biventricular hypertrophy and electrical disturbances, including premature ventricular contractions, partial or complete atrioventricular block, and right bundle branch block. Death can result from arrhythmia or congestive heart failure. Sudden death occurs in 40% of congestive heart failure patients with Chagas' disease. The second most commonly affected organ system is the gastrointestinal tract. The autonomic ganglia are destroyed, resulting in functional denervation, impaired motility, and thus dilation, leading to megaesophagus and megacolon.

Congenital Chagas' disease is characterized by hepatosplenomegaly, sepsis, myocarditis, and hepatitis; however, two-thirds of cases of congenital Chagas' disease are asymptomatic. Thus, routine testing for disease in the infants of infected mothers is warranted.

Acute infection and reactivation of infection in immunosuppressed transplant recipients and in HIV-infected patients can result in more severe clinical signs, sometimes involving the CNS. In HIV patients, reactivation has led to cerebral abscesses.

Diagnosis

The diagnosis of acute Chagas' disease is made by detecting parasites in the blood, by using a wet preparation of anticoagulated blood or buffy coat or by using a Giemsa-stained smear of the blood.

Both enzyme immunoassay and ELISA tests are available commercially and are approved by the US Food and Drug Administration for the diagnosis of Chagas' disease. False-positive results using these tests are an ongoing challenge, because there is cross-reactivity among patients with syphilis, malaria, leishmaniasis, and other parasitic diseases. PCR tests are also actively being studied and evaluated, although they are not yet available for routine clinical use. Serum samples can be sent to the CDC for indirect immunofluorescence and complement fixation testing (phone: [770] 488-4414).

Treatment

Acute American trypanosomiasis should be treated with nifurtimox (Box 85–3). In the United States, this drug is available through the CDC (phone: [404] 639-3670). A parasitologic cure using nifurtimox has been noted in 70–95% of parasitemic patients, but clinical cures are less well defined. Side effects with this drug occur in ~ 40–70% of adult patients and primarily include CNS problems such as disorientation, insomnia, paresthesias, seizures, and polyneuritis, as well as gastrointestinal symptoms including nausea, vomiting, and abdominal pain. Additionally, skin rash has been commonly noted.

Treatment of chronic infections and patients with end-organ damage includes supportive care. For example, pacemakers for cardiac conduction defects are sometimes indicated in this setting. Antiparasitic treatment is not indicated in chronic disease.

Prevention & Control

Disease control is directly related to the control of vectors (Box 85–4). Because of the potential chronic and insidious nature of this disease, some authorities recommend serologic screening of all persons at high risk who come from endemic areas. Such screening may have two benefits: (1) cardiac disturbances can often be treated with pacemakers, and (2) congenital disease can be prevented or treated.

The safety of the blood supply is a concern in en-demic areas and in other regions with immigrants from endemic areas, such as southern California. Two approaches include screening and rejection of donors based on risk factors such as prolonged residence in an endemic area and based on serology. Some endemic countries such as Brazil now use routine serologic screening and reject blood based on positive results.

Travelers to endemic areas are advised to avoid sleeping in structures that may harbor the insect vector and to use appropriate barriers to avoid contact with the insects.

BOX 85–4
Control of American Trypanosomiasis (Chagas' Disease)

Prophylactic Measures	• Avoid exposure to reduviid insect vectors
	• Chemoprophylaxis not recommended
	• Immunoprophylaxis not available
Isolation Precautions	• None

AFRICAN TRYPANOSOMIASIS

In Africa, a wide variety of trypanosomes infect wild animals but only two cause significant disease in humans: *T brucei gambiense* and *T brucei rhodesiense.*

Essentials of Diagnosis

- Epidemiologic factors: living or traveling in an endemic zone; exposure to tsetse fly.
- History and physical exam:
  1. General: periodic fevers, wasting, nutritional deficiencies.
  2. Skin: chancre at the site of inoculation, fleeting truncal rash, posterior cervical lymphadenopathy.
  3. Neurologic: disturbed sleep patterns (diurnal somnolence, nocturnal insomnia), mental status changes, cerebellar signs.
- Laboratory:
  1. Blood smear with Giemsa stain shows hemoflagellates.
  2. Aspiration and stain of chancre (may be positive for visible organisms before parasitemia occurs).
  3. Serology: indirect immunofluorescence, ELISA.
  4. Card agglutination test against common variant antigens.
  5. Cerebrospinal fluid (CSF): lymphocytic pleocytosis, elevated protein, motile trypanosomes.

BOX 85–3

Treatment of American Trypanosomiasis		
	Adult	Pediatric
First Choice	• Nifurtimox, 8–10 mg/kg/d PO in 4 divided doses for 120 d	• Nifurtimox, 15 mg/kg/d PO in 4 divided doses for 120 d
Alternative	• Benznidazole, 5 mg/kg/d PO for 60 d	• Benznidazole, 5 mg/kg/d PO for 60 d

General Considerations

A. Epidemiology. An estimated 50 million people are at risk for acquiring African trypanosomiasis worldwide, and there are 20,000 reported new cases annually. This is likely an underestimate because reporting in endemic countries is incomplete. There are no natural life cycles of *T brucei* outside Africa; thus, the only cases seen outside Africa are imported. Both *T brucei rhodesiense* and *T brucei gambiense* are carried by the tsetse fly vector of the genus *Glossina*, but by different species inhabiting distinct habitats (Figure 85–3). Therefore, because of vector habitat, *T brucei rhodesiense* (the agent of eastern African sleeping sickness) is seen in savanna and drier zones, whereas *T brucei gambiense* (the agent of western African sleeping sickness) is found near rivers and in forested areas. *T brucei gambiense* has primarily a human reservoir, while *T brucei rhodesiense* is an anthropozoonosis involving ungulates, such as cattle and antelope.

Transmission of *T brucei gambiense* was originally thought to be exclusively person to person, via insect vectors, but several animal hosts have been shown to harbor identical strains of the parasite, including pigs, cattle, dogs, sheep, and wild ungulates such as kob and hartebeest. The importance of these animal reservoirs remains uncertain. West African trypanosomiasis affects primarily rural populations, and the duration of the illness is months to years, which increases ongoing transmission. East African trypanosomiasis, in contrast, has a shorter clinical course, lasting < 9 months, and it primarily affects rural populations in proximity to the animal source and tourists visiting game parks. The animal reservoirs for *T brucei rhodesiense* include several domesticated animals, most importantly cattle, but a large number of wild animals including bushbuck, waterbuck, hartebeest, and lions. Many different domesticated animals become infected, but they succumb to the disease rapidly and are therefore unlikely to be important reservoirs for ongoing transmission. The number of infections in humans fluctuates tremendously depending on migration, land development programs, human conflict, and proximity of animal reservoirs to human populations. In addition to vector-borne transmission, congenital and blood transfusion transmission have been documented.

B. Microbiology. Blood-sucking tsetse flies of the genus *Glossina* become infective 18–35 days after

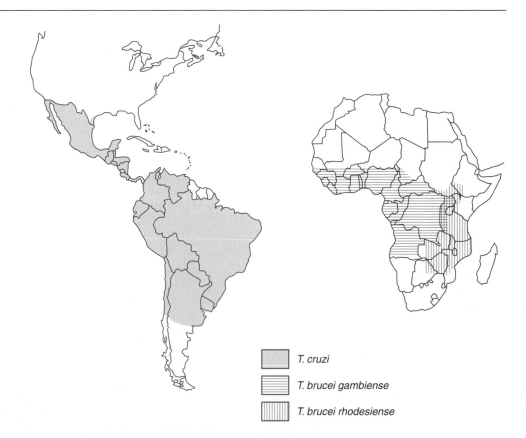

  T. cruzi

  T. brucei gambiense

  T. brucei rhodesiense

Figure 85–3. Distribution of human trypanosomiasis, according to *Trypanosoma* species (form of the disease). Republished from Mandell et al (editors): *Principles and Practice of Infectious Diseases,* 5th ed. Churchill Livingstone, 2000.

taking a blood meal from an infected mammalian host. Trypomastigotes are ingested and multiply in the midgut of the fly. These migrate to the salivary glands and become epimastigotes, which then turn into short, stumpy infective metacyclic trypanosomes. The fly remains infective for life and transmits by subsequent bites. Both *Glossina* males and females feed on mammalian blood, causing infection if enough organisms are injected. In endemic areas, usually < 1% of flies are infected, whereas during epidemic periods as many as 5% of flies carry parasites.

   C.   Pathogenesis. During the course of the infection with trypanosomes, the number of parasites in the blood and lymph tissues fluctuates according to the host's immune response. An increase in parasite number or parasitemia is related to the proliferation of parasite subpopulations that express an antigenically new or variant glycoprotein coat. A similar phenomenon is observed with *Neisseria* and *Borrelia* species. The declines in parasite number correspond with antibody-mediated destruction of trypanosomes. Each parasite carries genes encoding multiple, variant surface glycoproteins (VSG). Only one VSG is expressed at a single time, except during the switching from one VSG to another. This antigenic switching not only allows evasion of the host's immune system but also poses a major challenge to the development of a vaccine. Acquired immunity does develop, but it is specific for a limited number of VSGs.

   Resistance to African trypanosome infections depends on the presence of host interferon gamma and a strong Th1 cytokine response, as is the case for host resistance to *Leishmania* infections. Humoral and cellular immune responses are directed against the VSGs, among other trypanosomal components.

Clinical Findings

   There are three stages of African trypanosomiasis: (1) an initial phase characterized by a skin chancre at the site of inoculation, (2) a blood-borne and lymphatic dissemination phase, and (3) invasion of the choroid plexus and the subarachnoid space, causing

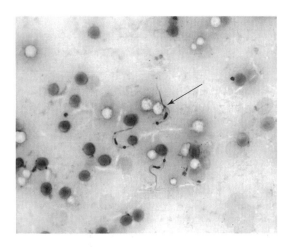

Figure 85–4. *T brucei rhodesiense* trypomastigotes in the blood of a patient with African sleeping sickness. Giemsa stain.

meningoencephalitis—hence the term "sleeping sickness." Chancres are reported in about one-third of infections and generally appear on the exposed surface of the skin where the flies have bitten. A chancre lasts ~ 3 weeks. Initially chancres are warm and tender but then scar or infrequently ulcerate. Lymphadenopathy develops in the area draining the ulcer.

   Once the ulcer subsides, the hemolymphatic stage appears, with characteristic periodic fevers coinciding with high parasitemia every day or two. Fatigue, arthralgia and headache, and often a fleeting truncal rash are observed with parasitemia. Patients are relatively asymptomatic between febrile periods. Myocarditis is common, and jaundice may occur from either hemolysis or hepatic damage.

   In the meningoencephalitic stage, persistent headache, disturbed sleep patterns including nocturnal insomnia and diurnal somnolence, extrapyramidal and cerebellar signs, and behavioral changes are common features of disease. Wasting and nutritional deficien-

---

BOX 85–5

Treatment of African Trypanosomiasis		
	Adult	Pediatric
First Choice	• Eflornithine, 400 mg/kg/d IM or IV in 4 divided doses for 14 d, then 300 mg/kg/d PO to complete 30 d **OR** • Suramin, 1 g IV on days 1, 3, 7, 14, 21; start with 200-mg test dose	• Suramin, 20 mg/kg IV on days 1, 3, 7, 14, 21; start with test dose
Alternative	• Pentamadine, 4 mg/kg/d IM × 10 d	• Pentamadine, 4 mg/kg/d IM × 10 d

cies are common and may lead to secondary infection due to immunosuppression. The leukocyte count is normal or modestly elevated with a lymphocytosis. Polyclonal hypergammaglobulinemia, especially involving immunoglobulin M, is a striking and constant feature as might be expected from prolonged antigenic stimulation. Anemia and hypoalbuminemia are also observed.

Diagnosis

A Giemsa or Wright-stained smear of peripheral blood during the acute febrile period is the best means of obtaining a diagnosis (Figure 85–4). *T brucei rhodesiense* tends to have higher parasite loads and may be easier to detect than *T brucei gambiense,* which may require more frequent repeated blood smears or use of concentration techniques, eg, microhematocrit centrifugation with examination of the buffy coat. If a chancre is present, aspiration and staining may yield a diagnosis before parasitemia is present. Organisms may be demonstrated from aspirates of lymph nodes and bone marrow. The CSF should be examined even if parasitemia is confirmed. This should be done after clearance of the parasites from the blood so that parasites are not introduced into the CSF. In CNS trypanosomal infection, the CSF reveals a lymphocytic pleocytosis, elevated protein, and sometimes motile trypanosomes. Often morular or so-called Mott cells are seen, which are plasma cells with large eosinophilic inclusions containing immunoglobulin G. Several immunodiagnostic tests are available including indirect immunofluorescence, ELISA, and a card agglutination test that uses a commonly occurring variant antigen.

Treatment

The two forms of African sleeping sickness can be treated in a similar fashion. Eflornithine (difluoromethyl-ornithine) inhibits ornithine decarboxylase, an essential parasite enzyme, and is an effective drug in both the early and later CNS stages of disease (Box 85–5). The side effects include vomiting, abdominal pain, and diarrhea. Seizures occur in < 5% of cases. Unfortunately, there is a current shortfall in drug supply, with no signs of immediate improvement. Suramin has also been shown to be effective. It

BOX 85–6

Control of African Trypanosomiasis

Prophylactic Measures	• Avoid exposure to tsetse fly vectors • Chemoprophylaxis not recommended • Immunoprophylaxis not available
Isolation Precautions	• None

is available in the United States only through the CDC. The urine should be checked prior to each dose for protein, and the dose or interval between doses should be altered if the specimen is positive. Pentamidine has been used as an alternative agent, but it is not US Food and Drug Adminstration-approved for this indication. Drug information is available through the CDC (daytime phone: [404] 639-3670; nighttime, phone [404] 639-2888).

African sleeping sickness tends to relapse, even after appropriate therapy; in this event, treatment should be repeated. Because parasitic confirmation of relapse may not be possible, increasing CSF protein or pleocytosis may be used as a marker of relapse. Infection does not confer immunity, and reinfection presents as new infection, often with chancres. Despite treatment, this disease is fatal in ~ 7% of patients.

Prevention & Control

One of the most effective public health measures for control of *T brucei gambiense*-associated disease may be recognition and treatment of humans, because they serve as the reservoir for this organism (Box 85–6). Control efforts that focus on clearance of tsetse fly habitat and destruction of wild game, as well as human population relocation, have not been terribly effective.

Individuals should avoid known foci of disease, wear protective clothing, and use insect repellents and mosquito nets to reduce the risk of infection. Chemoprophylaxis is not generally recommended for travelers to endemic areas. No vaccine is currently available.

REFERENCES

Berman JD: Human leishmaniasis: clinical, diagnostic, and chemotherapeutic developments in the last 10 years. Clin Infect Dis 1997;24:684.

Berman JD: Treatment of New World cutaneous and mucosal leishmaniases. Clin Dermatol 1996;14:519.

Freilij H, Altcheh J: Congenital Chagas' disease: Diagnostic and clinical aspects. Clin Infect Dis 1995;21:551.

Galel SA, Kirchhoff LV: Risk factors for Trypanosoma cruzi infection in California blood donors. Transfusion 1996;36:227.

Hyams KC, et al: The impact of infectious diseases on the health of U.S. troops deployed to the Persian Gulf during Operations Desert Shield and Desert Storm. Clin Infect Dis 1995;20:1497.

Kirchhoff LV: American trypanosomiasis (Chagas' disease)—a tropical disease now in the United States. N Engl J Med 1993;329:639.

Kirchhoff LV: American trypanosomiasis (Chagas' disease). Gastroenterol Clin N Am 1996;25:517.

Magell AJ: Epidemiology of leishmaniasis. Clin Dermatol 1995;13:505.

Reed SG: Diagnosis of leishmaniasis. Clin Dermatol 1996;14:471.

Tesh RB: Control of zoonotic visceral leishmaniasis: is it time to change strategies? Am J Trop Med Hyg 1995;52:287.

Wang CC: Molecular mechanisms and therapeutic approaches to the treatment of African trypanosomiasis. Annu Rev Pharmacol Toxicol 1995;35:93.

Weigle KA, et al: Epidemiology of cutaneous leishmaniasis in Colombia: a longitudinal study of the natural history, prevalence and incidence of infection and clinical manifestations. J Infect Dis 1993;168:699.

Weiss JB: DNA probes and PCR for diagnosis of parasitic infections. Clin Microbiol Rev 1995;8:113.

Nematodes

86

James M. Steckelberg, MD & Walter R. Wilson, MD

Essentials of Diagnosis

- Intestinal nematodes: demonstration of characteristic eggs or parasites in stool.
- Bloodstream nematodes (filariasis): clinical diagnosis can be made; fresh blood smear may be confirmatory.
- Tissue nematodes: clinical diagnosis can be made; skin snip or other tissue examination may show organism.

General Considerations

Nematodes (roundworms) are nonsegmented, tapered, bilaterally symmetrical, cylindrical organisms that have complete digestive tracts and reproduce sexually. Although > 500,000 species of nematodes have been described, only a small number are commonly encountered as human parasites. Most nematodes have complex life cycles, sometimes involving several larval forms and intermediate hosts or free-living stages. The pathogenic nematodes may be categorized as primarily intestinal or extraintestinal tissue parasites (Box 86–1).

INTESTINAL NEMATODE INFECTIONS

ASCARIASIS

Worldwide, more than 1 billion people are infested with *Ascaris lumbricoides,* the causative agent of ascariasis or roundworm. More than 4 million people are estimated to be infected in the United States. Infection occurs predominately in the southeastern states and more commonly in younger children, and it is associated with lower socioeconomic status. The organism is acquired through ingestion of embryonic forms of the worm, which are found in fecally contaminated soil.

After ingestion, the embryonic eggs hatch in the small intestine, and the larvae undergo a tissue migration phase. During the migration, the larvae penetrate the intestinal wall and travel intravenously to the pulmonary alveoli. In the lungs, the organisms provoke a cough, are swallowed by the host, and subsequently mature into the adult worm in the small intestine. A single adult female ascarid may produce 200,000 ova daily, which are shed in the feces.

Clinical Findings

The majority of ascarid infections are asymptomatic. During larval migration, eosinophilic pneumonia with mild fever, cough, wheezing, pulmonary infiltrates, and peripheral eosinophilia may be seen. Heavier worm loads may result in intestinal obstruction or symptoms caused by migration of the adult worm outside of the small intestine, most commonly into the common bile duct, causing biliary obstruction and associated complications. Rarely, adult worms may be expelled from the anus, nose, or mouth.

Differential Diagnosis

During tissue and pulmonary larval migration, other causes of pulmonary infiltrates with eosinophilia, including hookworm and strongyloides infection, as well as Löffler's syndrome, asthma, and allergic bronchopulmonary aspergillosis, should be considered. Heavy intestinal infection may cause obstruction that mimics other mechanical causes of bowel obstruction. Migration into the biliary system or appendix may be confused with acute cholecystitis, appendicitis, acute abdomen, or biliary obstruction caused by other more common causes.

Treatment

All patients with ascariasis should be treated, even if asymptomatic, to prevent biliary migration and obstruction (Box 86–2). Ascarids should be treated first in mixed parasitic infections, and they should be treated before general anesthesia because of the risk of inducing migration of hypermotile worms. In some cases, endoscopic removal of worms may be indicated. Stools should be reexamined 2 weeks after therapy and treatment repeated as necessary.

Prognosis

Prognosis is generally excellent, although reinfection is possible. In rare cases, obstruction of the small intestine by a mass of worms may cause an acute abdominal syndrome. In addition, obstruction of the common bile duct may cause acute biliary colic.

Prevention

Roundworm infection can be prevented by avoiding ingestion of fecally contaminated soil. Measures to accomplish this include hygienic disposal of fecal waste, avoidance of the use of night soil and proper washing of foods contaminated by soil, hand washing, and avoidance of pica.

ENTEROBIASIS

Also known as pinworm, infection by *Enterobius vermicularis* is the most common helminth infection in the United States. Enterobiasis is typically found in clusters of individuals living in close proximity, such as families or institutionalized groups. It is particularly common in school-age children. Adult females migrate nocturnally to the perianal areas, where eggs are deposited and subsequently distributed to fingers, fingernails, bedding, nightclothes, and other areas. Ingestion of the embryonated eggs results in development of intestinal adult worms in 1–2 months.

Clinical & Laboratory Findings

Many infections are asymptomatic. In symptomatic patients, nocturnal anal pruritus and interrupted sleep are typical. Laboratory tests are normal; eosinophilia is not seen with enterobiasis. Although adult worms that resemble small threads may be seen with the naked eye, diagnosis is usually made by documenting eggs in the perianal area in the early morning, before bathing or defecation. This can be done by pressing cellophane tape in the perianal area and examining the tape under the microscope or by using a commercial collection system such as the Swube (Becton Dickinson). Stool examination for eggs is usually not helpful.

Differential Diagnosis

Enterobiasis should be distinguished from other causes of perirectal irritation, including pruritis ani, rectal fissures, moniliasis, hemorrhoids, and strongyloidiasis, among other conditions.

Treatment

Treatment suggestions are given in Box 86–2.

Prognosis

Prognosis is excellent, although reinfection is common in the setting of continued exposure.

Prevention

Reinfection is common in households with an infected person; examination for asymptomatic carriers and simultaneous treatment of all infected household members may be required. Household members should practice hand washing before meals and after defecation and should launder bedding and bedclothes to eliminate environmental eggs.

ANCYLOSTOMIASIS & NECATORIASIS

Hookworm infestation is caused by *Ancylostoma duodenale* or *Necator americanus.* After hookworm eggs are passed in stool, the larvae hatch and mature in soil, where they become infective after 1 wk. Human infection occurs after direct penetration by larvae of the host's skin, usually through the feet. The

BOX 86–2

Treatment of Selected Intestinal Nematode Infections

	First Choice	Second Choice
Ascariasis	• Pyrantel pamoate, 10–11 mg/kg once • Mebendazole, 200–500 mg once (light infection) up to 100 mg twice daily for 3 d • Albendazole, 400 mg once (light infection) up to 400 mg once daily for 3 d	• Ivermectin, 100–200 µg/kg once daily for 32 d • Piperazine, 75 mg/kg once daily for 2 d • Levamisole, 150 mg once
Enterobiasis	• Pyrantel pamoate, 10–11 mg/kg once • Mebendazole, 100 mg once, repeat in 2 wk • Albendazole, 400 mg once, repeat in 2 weeks	• Pyvinium pamoate, 5 mg/kg once, repeat in 2 weeks
Hookworm	• Pyrantel pamoate, 10–11 mg/kg once daily for 3 d • Mebendazole, 100 mg twice daily for 3 d • Albendazole, 400 mg once (Ancylostoma[1]) or once daily for 3 d (Necator[1])	
Strongyloidiasis	• Albendazole, 400 mg/d once or twice daily for 3–7 d, may repeat in 1 wk • Ivermectin, 200 µg/kg once daily for 2 d	• Thiabendazole, 25 mg/kg twice daily for 3 d; continue for 5–7 d in disseminated infection
Trichuriasis	• Albendazole, 600 mg once • Mebendazole, 100 mg twice daily for 3 d	• Oxantel pamoate, 15 mg/kg once

[1]*Ancylostoma*, "Old World" hookworm: *Necator*, "New World" hookworm.

hookworm larvae then enter venules and are carried to the lungs, where they penetrate into alveoli. From the alveoli, the larvae migrate to the trachea. They induce cough and are swallowed by the host. The larvae mature into adult worms in the small intestine. Hookworms attach to intestinal mucosa by means of teeth and a well-developed mouth, and they feed on blood and nutrients sucked from the host. Humans are the only known hosts.

Clinical & Laboratory Findings

The initial allergic reaction to larval skin penetration and migration is known as "ground itch," and is manifested by intense pruritus and vesicular or maculopapular dermatitis. Patients may experience cough, wheezing, fever, and pulmonary infiltrates during pulmonary migration. Peripheral eosinophilia may be marked. During the intestinal phase, which may last several years, heavy worm burdens may result in protein malnutrition and iron deficiency anemia.

Differential Diagnosis

Early in infection, strongyloidiasis, cutaneous larva migrans, contact dermatitis, scabies, and other causes of pruritic dermatitis, especially of the extremities, should be considered. Later, other causes of eosinophilic pneumonia should be considered, in-

cluding *A lumbricoides* and *Strongyloides stercoralis* infections, as well as Löffler's syndrome. Chronic intestinal infestation, with nonspecific gastrointestinal symptoms, may mimic a multitude of gastrointestinal conditions and other causes of iron deficiency.

Treatment

Re-treatment at 2-wk intervals may be necessary to reduce the worm burden to low levels (see Box 86–2). Because light infections are usually asymptomatic, complete eradication may not be therapeutically necessary. In patients with iron deficiency, supplemental iron therapy (eg, ferrous sulfate, 200 mg 3 times daily for several months, followed by 200 mg daily until iron stores are repleted) may be necessary.

Prognosis

Prognosis with treatment is excellent.

STRONGYLOIDIASIS

Infection by *S stercoralis* (threadworm) is especially notable because the worm is parthenogenetic and larvae mature to an infective stage within the intestinal lumen. As a consequence, sequential generations of worms may persist in a single host over many years. Immunocompromise caused by organ transplantation, corticosteroid therapy, hematologic malignancies, or other conditions may result in massive autoinfection, termed the hyperinfection syndrome. Surprisingly, human immunodeficiency virus infection does not appear to increase susceptibility for hyperinfection.

Like other intestinal nematodes, the life cycle *of S stercoralis* is complex. The initial infection occurs through penetration of the skin by soil-borne free-living infectious larvae. The larvae ultimately reach the proximal intestine via blood-lung migration. Eggs from adult worms hatch in the intestine, producing larvae that may (i) reinfect the same host, (ii) pass to a new host directly via skin penetration, or (iii) give rise to soil-borne free-living adults that may, in turn, produce infectious larvae.

Clinical & Laboratory Findings

Many patients with chronic but low worm burden infections are asymptomatic or have irregular intestinal symptoms. During initial skin penetration, local skin irritation, pruritic dermatitis, urticaria, and serpiginous tracts ("larva currens") may be seen. During pulmonary migration, symptoms and signs of infection are similar to those of other nematodes that travel through the lung; that is, dry cough, wheezing, low-grade fever, dyspnea, and hemoptysis. Symptoms of chronic intestinal infestation are varied and nonspecific, and they may include bloating, abdominal distension, dyspepsia, epigastric pain, pruritus ani, diarrhea, and flatulence. In immunocompromised patients, hyperinfection syndrome may be manifested by gastrointestinal ulceration, peritonitis, ileus, biliary obstruction, cholecystitis, or hepatic granulomas. Invasion of extraintestinal organs, including meningitis, central nervous system invasion, pericarditis or myocarditis, or pleuritis, may also occur. Gram-negative or polymicrobial bacteremia with sepsis may complicate hyperinfection syndrome.

Diagnosis of strongyloidiasis is made by examination of stool or duodenal aspirate for *S stercoralis* larvae. Larvae may be present in stool only intermittently. Eggs *of S stercoralis* are rarely seen in stool specimens.

Differential Diagnosis

The myriad of presentations and potential tissue sites of *S stercoralis* requires a high index of suspicion for diagnosis. Chronic intestinal symptoms may mimic dyspepsia, irritable-bowel syndrome, inflammatory-bowel disease, malabsorption, sprue, giardial infection, or other causes of chronic or recurring diarrhea. Epigastric pain may resemble peptic ulcer disease. During tissue migration, eosinophilia, pulmonary infiltrates, wheezing, and cough may suggest nematode or ascarid infections as well as asthma, hypersensitivity pneumonitis, allergic bronchopulmonary aspergillosis, or Löffler's syndrome. Hyperinfection syndrome may

mimic sepsis or bacteremia caused by enteric organisms from other causes, such as aortoenteric fistula.

Treatment

Eradication is the goal of therapy (see Box 86–2). When immunosuppression can be anticipated, such as in patients being evaluated for organ transplantation, screening for *S stercoralis* and eradication should occur before immunosuppression.

Prognosis

In immunocompetent hosts, prognosis is good. Severe infection with multiple complications may occur in immunocompromised hosts with hyperinfection syndrome.

TRICHURIASIS

Trichuriasis or whipworm is caused by Trichuris trichiura. These small (30- to 50-mm–length) whip-like nematodes attach to the mucosa of the large intestine, especially the cecum; there is no extraintestinal phase. Infection occurs by ingestion of infective eggs from soil contaminated with feces; 2–4 wk of maturation in soil are required for the larvae within the eggs to become infective; thus, direct person-to-person transmission does not occur.

Clinical & Laboratory Findings

Mild to moderate worm burdens are usually asymptomatic. Heavy infections (> 30,000 eggs/g of feces) may be asymptomatic or cause nonspecific abdominal complaints, including abdominal cramping, bloating, distension, nausea, vomiting, flatulence, diarrhea, or tenesmus. Rectal prolapse and appendiceal obstruction with appendicitis are rare complications of strongyloidiasis. Eosinophilia is common; iron deficiency anemia may be seen with heavy infections that result in chronic occult blood loss.

Treatment

Treatment of symptomatic trichuriasis is outlined in Box 86–2.

Prognosis

Prognosis is excellent.

TISSUE NEMATODE INFECTIONS

LYMPHATIC FILARIASIS

Lymphatic filariasis is a bloodstream and lymphatic infection caused by the filarial nematodes

Wuchereria bancrofti, Brugia malayi, and *Brugia timori.* The disease is endemic in the tropics and subtropics of both hemispheres. A mosquito serves as an intermediate host and vector; the peak blood parasitemia and optimum time of the day or night for obtaining blood smears differ in various parts of the world, corresponding to the feeding pattern of the local mosquito vectors. After deposition by mosquitoes of infectious microfilariae into humans during a blood meal, 6–12 mo are required before adult worms mature and begin producing numerous circulating microfilariae to continue the life cycle. Symptoms of acute disease generally occur 8–16 mo after infection in nonindigenous peoples, but the incubation period may be longer in indigenous peoples.

Clinical & Laboratory Findings

Indigenous persons with filariasis are often asymptomatic. In the first few years after infection, variably present clinical manifestations include recurrent episodes of lymphangitis, notable for progression proximally to distally, unlike typical bacterial lymphangitis. These episodes may be accompanied by high fever and resolve within 7–10 d. Epididymitis or orchitis may occur intermittently. Other patients, especially travelers, may have allergic symptoms including urticaria, rashes, and eosinophilia. Chronic infection may result in lymphatic insufficiency, with lymphedema involving the extremities or external genitalia. Hydroceles may also occur. The term elephantiasis refers to advanced changes of chronic lymphedema, including subcutaneous thickening, skin hyperkeratosis, and fissuring.

Tropical pulmonary eosinophilia refers to a syndrome of nocturnal cough and wheezing with diffuse miliary chest x-ray infiltrates, eosinophilia, elevated immunoglobulin E concentrations, and high antifilarial antibody titers. The syndrome is caused by sequestration of *W bancrofti or B malayi* microfilariae in the lungs and responds to treatment with diethylcarbamazine citrate (DEC).

Diagnosis of filariasis is usually clinical in endemic areas. Confirmation requires demonstration of microfilaria in filtered blood samples, the timing of which should be adjusted to match the nocturnal or diurnal periodicity of the peak parasitemia in the region in which the infection was acquired. The organisms adapt their periodicity to local time zones, but this requires 10–14 d.

Microfilariae are more commonly seen in the bloodstream during the early stages of disease (1–2 years after infection) and are rare in the bloodstream during the lymphatic obstructive stage of disease. Administration of 50 mg of DEC may result in positive blood smears immediately (within 1 h) after administration in otherwise smear-negative individuals. Serologic testing may also be helpful, but both false positive and false negative test results occur.

Treatment

Symptomatic treatment of acute filarial lymphangitis (eg, antihistamines and aspirin) may be helpful in reducing the intensity of symptoms. DEC is an effective microfilaricidal drug, but the adult worms require a longer course of therapy and sometimes multiple courses of therapy to be eradicated. DEC (2 mg/kg) is administered 3 times daily for 2–3 wk. Allergic reactions (eg, fever, urticaria, or lymphangitis) to injured parasites may occur early in therapy; some authorities suggest smaller doses of DEC (50 mg on the first day, increasing to full dosage over 3–4 d) to minimize these reactions. Antihistamines may also be of benefit. Nonspecific side effects include headache, vertigo or dizziness, malaise, fever, or myalgias. Onchocerciasis should be excluded before DEC treatment. DEC is available in the United States from Lederle Laboratories (800-934-5556).

Prevention

Because transmission depends on mosquito vectors, control measures are directed at reducing mosquito populations and reducing the number of bites by mosquitoes.

OTHER FILARIAL INFECTIONS

1. LOIASIS

Loiasis (African eye worm infection) occurs in rainy areas of central and West Africa. The filarial parasites are transmitted by the bite of an infected *Chrysops* spp. horsefly. Organisms mature in the subcutaneous tissues, where adult worms may live for more than a decade and release microfilariae into the circulation.

Clinical Findings

Adult worms migrate through subcutaneous tissues at rates ≤ 1 cm/min. This may be asymptomatic, or, especially when migration occurs around or across the eye, noted as conjunctivitis or eyelid edema. Calabar swellings are subcutaneous edematous areas of 3–10 cm that are nonerythematous and do not pit; local pain, pruritus, and mild fever may be present. Calabar swellings are transient, resolving after 2–3 d or 1 wk, only to reappear at irregular intervals in different locations. Calabar swellings do not necessarily contain worms at the time that they appear.

Symptoms of loiasis vary depending on the host. Indigenous populations typically have relatively mild symptoms or are asymptomatic even though they are microfilaremic. Travelers typically have a more symptomatic course, with an increased number and severity of Calabar swellings, marked eosinophilia, leukocytosis, hypergammaglobulinemia, and elevated immunoglobulin E antibodies.

Treatment

Treatment is with DEC, 3 mg/kg 3 times daily for 21 d. Localized inflammatory reactions to dying adult worms in tissues are common. In patients with microfilaremia, reactions may be more severe including severe neurologic complications and death. Gradually escalating doses of DEC and in some patients systemic corticosteroids may be used. Ivermectin and albendazole have been investigated as alternative therapies to DEC.

2. ONCHOCERCIASIS

Infection with *Onchocerca volvulus* causes African river blindness, which is the second leading cause of blindness worldwide. Onchocerciasis is transmitted by the *Simulium* spp. blackfly and is found in equatorial West, central, and East Africa and portions of Central and South America. Larval forms penetrate the skin after the bite of the blackfly, where they mature into adults in the subcutaneous tissues. Microfilariae from mature females migrate back to the dermis where they are ingested by blackflies to continue the life cycle.

Clinical Findings

Cutaneous and connective tissue manifestations of onchocerciasis include the formation, usually within a year, of mobile nodules encapsulating the adult worms in a fibrous tissue mass. Multiple nodules may be present in subcutaneous or connective tissues, especially over bony prominences. Depigmentation, wrinkling, and thickening of skin may be seen with chronic infection. Visual loss is the most serious complication. The earliest eye lesions are punctate keratitis associated with microfilariae within the cornea and anterior chamber. Iridocyclitis and posterior synechiae may develop, which may result in a fixed and distorted pupil. Lesions of the posterior chamber of the eye are less common, including optic atrophy and choroiditis.

Diagnosis is suspected clinically and confirmed by examination of a skin snip obtained without anesthesia from the shoulder or buttock areas, demonstrating microfilariae. Adult worms may be found in biopsied or excised nodules. Slit-lamp examination of the cornea or anterior chamber of the eye may demonstrate microfilariae. Microfilariae are identifiable in urine in 17%–30% of patients > 10 years old.

Treatment

The treatment of choice is ivermectin, 150 5g/kg orally as a single dose, which kills microfilariae but is less effective against adult worms. Treatment is repeated at 3-mo intervals for 2–3 years. Diethylcarbamazine has been used historically but is less effective and more toxic than ivermectin, and it is no longer recommended by the World Health Organization.

Cutaneous nodules, especially on the scalp, may be surgically excised.

OTHER TISSUE NEMATODE INFECTIONS

1. TRICHINOSIS

Trichinella species are unique among the tissue-dwelling nematodes in that there is no intermediate arthropod vector stage. *Trichinella* nematodes parasitize carnivores. Adult worms parasitize the small intestine; infective larvae are released and migrate from the intestine to muscle tissues in the host, where the larvae encyst and remain viable and infectious for several years. When the host tissues are eaten, the cyst walls are digested and the larvae again mature within several days in the intestine of the new host, perpetuating the life cycle. Normal hosts of *Trichinella* spp. include swine, rats, bears, foxes, walrus, and other carnivorous mammals. Humans are an incidental host. Cooking meat to 55 °C core temperatures or freezing (−15 °C) for 3 wk kills *Trichinella* spp. larvae.

Clinical & Laboratory Findings

Mild infection is usually asymptomatic. Early (1 wk) after infection, gastrointestinal symptoms predominate, including diarrhea, nausea or vomiting. After the second week, during the muscle invasion stage, systemic symptoms predominate including fever, myalgias, and malaise in most patients. Periorbital edema with conjunctival chemosis and edema of the eyelids is characteristic and common. Symptoms last between 4 and 8 weeks. Rarely, myocarditis or encephalitis may complicate the clinical course. In the laboratory, eosinophilia after the 10th day, sometimes marked, is characteristic, as is elevated immunoglobulin E. Serum creatine phosphokinase and lactic dehydrogenase concentrations reflect myositis. *Trichinella* serology becomes positive at ≥ 3 wk after infection.

Treatment

Treatment for trichinosis remains controversial and is primarily supportive. If ingestion is known to occur within 24 h, albendazole (400 mg twice daily, (60 days), mebendazole (200–400 mg 3 times daily for 3 days, then 400–500 mg 3 times daily for 10 days), or thiabendazole (25 mg/kg/day for 1 wk) has been proposed to prevent infection. The drug is not beneficial for established infection or muscle larvae. No specific therapy has been unequivocally demonstrated to be of benefit during the muscle invasion stage.

Prognosis

Spontaneous recovery is the rule, although full recovery may require weeks to months. Death, typically from myocarditis, encephalitis, or pneumonitis, is rare.

Prevention

The incidence of human trichinosis has declined in developed countries with measures designed to reduce the prevalence of trichinosis in hogs. Trichina in wild game (or pork) can be killed by thorough cooking (internal temperature > 62 °C) throughout all parts of the meat or to > 56 °C for > 15 min, freezing < −15 °C for ≥ 20 d, or gamma radiation.

3. TOXOCARIASIS (VISCERAL LARVA MIGRANS)

Toxocariasis, or visceral larva migrans, is a syndrome caused by invasion of human extraintestinal tissues by larvae of *Ascaris* spp. for which humans are not the usual host of the adult worms. *Toxocara canis,* commonly found in dogs, is the most commonly implicated species; *Toxocara catis* (cats) and *Belascaris procyonis* (raccoons) have also been implicated. Puppies can be infected transplacentally or transmammarily. Pregnancy in dogs reactivates latent infections in the bitch. Animals harboring adult ascarids in the intestine shed copious numbers of eggs into the environment. The eggs become infectious after 3–4 wk and are highly resistant to harsh environmental conditions. Toxocara eggs may remain infectious for months to years. Human infection results from ingestion of eggs from fecally contaminated soil, as may occur for example in children with pica. Direct transmission from pets to humans does not occur, because the eggs require maturation in soil before they become infective.

In young animals, ingested eggs hatch in the intestine and the larvae migrate through extraintestinal tissues, including liver and lung. Larvae induce coughing and are swallowed and then mature into adults in the small intestine to complete the life cycle, which resembles that of *A lumbricoides* in humans. In older animals, humans, and other hosts such as mice or rats, larvae also hatch from ingested eggs and invade extraintestinal tissues, but the larvae are unable to fully mature and may continue to persist and migrate in tissues as "second-stage" larvae for ≤ 6 months. If these second-stage larvae are ingested by a dog or cat, the larvae may complete their life cycle and develop into adult intestinal worms. Eosinophilic granulomas caused by toxocariasis most often involve the liver or lungs; brain, eye, muscle, and skin involvement has also been reported.

Clinical & Laboratory Findings

Visceral larva migrans is predominately seen in children < 7 years old, and it may be associated with pica. Most cases appear to be asymptomatic. When present, symptoms are variable and depend on the organ systems involved but may include fever, cough or wheezing, and urticarial rash or skin nodules. Hepatomegaly is relatively common. Splenomegaly, lymphadenopathy, and evidence of myocarditis are less common.

Marked leukocytosis, sometimes exceeding 100,000 leukocytes/μl, and hypereosinophilia are common in visceral larva migrans. Polyclonal hypergammaglobulinemia and anti-A or anti-B antibodies to isohemagglutinin antigens (cross-reacting to *T canis* larval antigens) may occur. An eosinophilic spinal fluid pleocytosis may occur with central nervous system involvement. Chest x-ray abnormalities may be seen in one-third of patients. *Toxocara* serology may be helpful in confirming the diagnosis, but it should be remembered that in some populations the background prevalence of seropositivity in patients without clinically apparent visceral larva migrans may be high. Identification of larvae in tissue biopsy samples is diagnostic, but not sensitive. Stool examination is not usually helpful.

Ocular visceral larva migrans deserves special consideration. Infection of the eye with *Toxocara* larvae usually presents as a solitary finding in patients with no known history of visceral larva migrans and without concurrent multifocal, systemic symptoms or signs. The ocular findings are typically a unilateral posterior or peripheral eosinophilic inflammatory mass. Serologies may be negative. The ocular lesion may be mistaken for a retinoblastoma.

Treatment

No specific therapy has been proven effective. In many cases, symptoms are self-limited and supportive, symptomatic treatment is all that is required. Treatment with a variety of antihelminthic agents has been tried with limited success. These agents include albendazole, thiabendazole, mebendazole, diethylcarbamazine, or ivermectin. Corticosteroids may be of benefit in some patients, especially subconjunctival applications in ocular visceral larva migrans.

Prevention & Prognosis

Puppies, kittens, and household dogs and cats, especially when pregnant or nursing, should be screened and treated as necessary to prevent transmission to humans. Pica should be prevented. Most cases are self-limited although symptoms may persist for months to several years.

4. DRACUNCULIASIS

Dracunculiasis, or guinea worm infection, is caused by infection by the tissue nematode *Dracunculus medinensis*. The parasite has been widely distributed in the Indian subcontinent, the Arabian Peninsula, and certain areas of West and central Africa north of the equator. Human infection is acquired by drinking water that contains tiny copepods (*Cyclops* spp.; "water fleas") that carry the infectious third-stage larvae. The larvae migrate to subcutaneous connective tissue, usually in the lower extremities, where they develop into adult worms over an extended incubation period that can last up to a year. The adult female may reach 60–80 cm in length. When the extremities are exposed to water, the head of the gravid female protrudes through an ulceration in the host's extremity, a loop of uterus prolapses and discharges large numbers of first-stage larvae into the water. These are ingested by copepods to complete the life cycle.

An active eradication program by the World Health Organization has led to a dramatic reduction in the incidence of dracunculiasis world-wide. Because no nonhuman reservoir is recognized, the disease may be eradicable in the near future.

Clinical Findings

A peripheral chronic cutaneous ulceration, from which the worm may protrude, is the hallmark of dracunculiasis. A local painful, stinging or burning papule may be the first indication of impending ulceration. Generalized symptoms including fever, nausea, vomiting, dyspnea, urticaria or pruritus, or periorbital edema may be associated with development of ulceration. Ulcers on the foot frequently prevent ambulation and may result in long-lasting deformity and secondary infection (including ankle or knee joint in-

fection). Tetanus may also complicate dracunculiasis. Dead or dying worms may result in intense inflammatory reactions. Diagnosis in endemic areas is based on the typical clinical findings.

Treatment

No specific antihelminthic therapy is available to kill adult worms. Mechanical removal of worms has been practiced for centuries. General treatment is focused on controlling complications, including bed rest, elevation of the affected extremity, wound care, and antibacterial therapy for secondary bacterial wound infections. Metronidazole, 250 mg orally 3 times daily, mebendazole, 400–800 mg orally daily, or thiabendazole 25 mg/kg twice daily may be helpful in promoting the expulsion of the worm, as is immersion of the affected limb in water several times daily.

Prevention

Noncontaminated drinking water is the key to prevention of dracunculiasis. The World Health Organization prevention program has focused on provision of clean drinking water by using tube wells, hand pumps, or cisterns, by treating drinking water supplies with temephos (to eliminate the copepods), or by boiling water. Water can also by filtered to remove particles > 100 5m.

REFERENCES

Markell EK et al: *Medical Parasitology,* 7th ed. W.B. Saunders, 1992.

Strickland GT (editor): *Hunters Tropical Medicine,* 7th ed. W.B. Saunders, 1991.

Cestodes

87

Andrew D. Badley, MD, James M. Steckelberg, MD & Walter R. Wilson, MD

Human infections caused by cestodes, or tapeworms, may occur within the lumen of the bowel, where adult cestodes attach themselves to the host intestine (Box 87–1). Alternatively, human infection may be the result of dissemination of cestodes from the bowel to involve extraintestinal sites, often by larval forms of the parasite. The life cycle of cestodes is determined by definitive hosts, in whom the mature adult worm lives, and intermediate hosts, which harbor the larval forms of the parasite. Humans are a definitive host for six cestodes: *Diphyllobothrium latum, Taenia solium, Taenia saginata, Hymenolepis diminuta, Hymenolepis nana,* and *Dipylidium caninum.* In addition, humans may be intermediate hosts for *Echinococcus granulosis* and *Echinococcus multilocularis.* All forms of disease associated with infections caused by cestodes are treatable; therefore, a careful history and physical examination to identify potential patients is warranted.

Cestodes attach themselves to the intestinal mucosa by means of a specialized organ called the scolex, which has a distinctive morphology for each species of cestode. Attached to the scolex are one to several hundred segments called proglottids. Proglottids each contain both male and female reproductive organs and may be classified as immature, mature, or gravid, based on the state of maturation of their sex organs. A gravid proglottid contains a fully developed uterus, full of eggs. The uterine structure of a gravid proglottid helps to differentiate species of cestode.

DIPHYLLOBOTHRIUM LATUM INFECTION

Essentials of Diagnosis

- Stool examination reveals ovoid, yellow-brown eggs (60–75 μm by 40–50 μm).
- Chains of proglottids (up to 50 cm long) may be passed in stool.
- Proglottids are wider than long (3 by 11 mm).
- Scolex has no hooklets and two grooves (bothria).
- Gravid proglottid contains rosette-shaped central uterus.

General Considerations

D latum is found worldwide, and infection is acquired by ingestion of contaminated raw or improperly cooked freshwater fish. Because of enthusiasm for raw or undercooked fish, Siberia, Europe, Canada, Alaska, and Japan are endemic regions for *D latum* infection. Once the *D latum* cyst has been ingested, the worm matures within the human intestine and begins to produce eggs after 5 weeks. A mature *D latum* may reach lengths of several meters and contain ≤ 30,000 proglottids. Eggs and proglottids that are passed in stool hatch after 14 days in fresh water into ciliated coracidium larvae, which are ingested by the intermediate host, the aquatic copepod. Inside the copepod, the larvae develop into a second larval form, the procercoid. Once the copepod is ingested by a freshwater fish, the procercoid larva matures into the plerocercoid larva, which may encyst within fish tissues. Human ingestion of improperly prepared fish initiates infection by the plerocercoid larva cyst. Bears, seals, cats, mink, foxes, and wolves are alternate definitive hosts for *D latum.*

Clinical Findings

A. Signs and Symptoms. Infection with *D latum* is most often asymptomatic, but symptoms such as bloating, abdominal pain, or diarrhea may be present. More rarely, intestinal obstruction may occur. A rare complication of chronic, small-intestinal involvement with *D latum* is the development of Vitamin B_{12} deficiency, characterized by anemia with or without neurologic sequelae. This syndrome occurs most often in patients with a genetic predisposition to the development of pernicious anemia, commonly people of Scandinavia.

B. Laboratory Findings. Frequently the only abnormal finding in a patient infected with *D latum* is the presence of eggs or proglottids on examination of stool for ova and parasites. Blood examination may reveal a slight leukocytosis with eosinophilia and occasionally a megaloblastic anemia associated with B_{12} deficiency.

C. Imaging. Contrast studies of the gastrointestinal tract may reveal ribbonlike filling defects corresponding to the adult worm.

Differential Diagnosis

The most usual manifestation of *D latum* infection is asymptomatic carriage, which is incidentally discovered. If patients present with abdominal pain and diarrhea, the differential diagnosis includes a variety

BOX 87-1

Syndrome	More Common	Less Common
Diphyllobothrium latum infection	Bloating, abdominal pain, diarrhea	Intestinal obstruction, vitamin B$_{12}$ deficiency
Taenia solium infection	Asymptomatic	Indigestion, nausea
Cysticercosis (extraintestinal *T solium* infection)	Headache, seizures, neurologic deficits	Myositis, liver or heart failure
Taenia saginata infection	Asymptomatic	Abdominal cramps, malaise
Hymenolepis nana infection	Abdominal pain	Dizziness, anorexia; children—behavioral disturbance
Hymenolepis diminuata infection	Asymptomatic	
Dypylidium caninum infection	Asymptomatic	Indigestion, anorexia, anal pruritis
Echinococcal infection	Abdominal pain, mass	Seizures, headache, neurologic deficits, bone pain

of infectious and noninfectious causes. Diarrhea from *D latum* infection will not be associated with stool leukocytes; this aids in formulating a differential diagnosis. Noninfectious etiologies to consider include osmotic (eg, lactose intolerance) and secretory (eg, villous adenoma) etiologies, malabsorption syndromes (eg, celiac sprue), and motility disorders (eg, irritable bowel syndrome). Infectious etiologies causing diarrhea without stool leukocytes include rotavirus, Norwalk virus, *Giardia lamblia*, *Entamoeba histolytica*, *Cryptosporidium* spp., and toxigenic diarrhea caused by *Staphylococcus aureus*, *Bacillus cereus*, *Clostridium perfringens*, and enterotoxigenic *Escherichia coli*.

Complications

The complications vary with the clinical syndrome associated with infection. Chronic diarrhea may lead to malnutrition. Megaloblastic anemia secondary to B$_{12}$ deficiency results when the parasite disrupts the B$_{12}$-intrinsic factor complex, resulting in B$_{12}$ becoming unavailable for absorption by the host. B$_{12}$ deficiency may lead to neurologic sequelae including peripheral neuropathy, dementia, and possible severe combined degeneration of the posterior columns. Also, infection with *D latum* may rarely result in intestinal obstruction caused by a mass of entangled worms.

Treatment

Therapy for infection with *D latum* consists of either praziquantel or niclosamide (Box 87–2). Follow-up examinations of stool should be performed 1 and 3 months after treatment.

Prognosis

Since the disease is not commonly associated with severe symptoms, the prognosis of infected individuals is excellent. One exception is with patients who manifest B$_{12}$ deficiency, in whom the neurologic complications are reversible only if recognized and treated early.

Prevention & Control

Prevention of infection from *D latum* is achieved through adequate cooking of all freshwater fish or freezing of fish for 24–48 h at −18 °C (Box 87–3). Isolation of infected persons is not required.

TAENIA SOLIUM INFECTION

Essentials of Diagnosis

- Spheroidal yellow-brown eggs (31–43 μm).
- Scolex has hooklets and four suckers.
- Proglottids usually appear as short chains.
- Mature proglottids are square and nonmotile.
- Gravid proglottid has 7–13 lateral branches on each side of uterus.

General Considerations

T solium infection occurs worldwide; endemic areas include Mexico, South and Central America, Africa, Southeast Asia, India, and the Philippines. *T*

BOX 87–2

Syndrome	Adult treatment	Pediatric treatment
Diphyllobothrium latum infection	• Praziquantel, 10–20 mg/kg once OR • Niclosamide 2 g once	• Praziquantel, 10–20 mg/kg once OR • Niclosamide (11–34 kg), 1 g once; (>34 kg), 1.5 g once
Taenia solium infection	• Praziquantel, 10–20 mg/kg once OR • Niclosamide, 2 g once	• Praziquantel, 10–20 mg/kg once OR • Niclosamide (11–34 kg), 1 g once; (>34 kg), 1.5 g once
Cysticercosis (extraintestinal *T solium* infection)	• Surgery and either Praziquantel, 20 mg/kg three times daily × 15–30 d OR • Albendazole, 7.5 mg/kg three times daily × 8 d	Surgery and either Praziquantel, 20 mg/kg three times daily × 15–30 d OR • Albendazole, 7.5 mg/kg three times daily × 8 d
Taenia saginata infection	• Praziquantel, 10–20 mg/kg once OR • Niclosamide, 2 g once	• Praziquantel, 10–20 mg/kg once OR • Niclosamide (11–34 kg), 1 gm once; (>34 kg), 1.5 g once
Hymenolepis nana infection	• Praziquantel, 10–20 mg/kg once OR • Niclosamide, 2 g once	• Praziquantel, 10–20 mg/kg once OR • Niclosamide (11–34 kg), 1 gm once; (>34 kg), 1.5 g once
Hymenolepis diminuta infection	• Niclosamide, 2 g once	• Niclosamide (11–34 kg), 1 g once; (>34 kg), 1.5 g once
Dypylidium caninum infection	• Niclosamide, 2 g once	• Niclosamide (11–34 kg), 1 g once; (>34 kg), 1.5 g once
Echinococal infection	• Surgery and albendazole, 400 mg divided into 2 daily doses × 3 mo OR • Mebendazole, 50 mg/kg/d divided into 3 daily doses × 3 mo	• Surgery and albendazole, 15 mg/kg/d divided into 2 daily doses × 3 mo OR • Mebendazole, 50 mg/kg/d divided into 3 daily doses × 3 mo

solium infection is commonly linked to the ingestion of undercooked pork, although other animals may harbor the larval form of the parasite. Infection may be intestinal, which is typically asymptomatic, or extraintestinal (called cysticercosis, see below), which is caused by larval forms of *T solium* within the tissues of the human host. Ingestion of encysted *T solium* larvae is followed by the parasite scolex attaching to the intestinal mucosa, which allows the worm to grow into an adult within 12 weeks. There may be one or more adult worms present for ≤ 25 years, and these may reach lengths of 2 to 7 m. Each worm contains < 1000 proglottids. Identification of species is by the number of lateral branches on the side of the uterus within a gravid uterus.

Clinical Findings

A. Signs and Symptoms. Infection with the adult worm of *T solium* is usually asymptomatic, but

BOX 87-3

Syndrome	Preventative Measures
Diphyllobothrium latum infection	Adequate cooking of fish or freezing fish for 48 h
Taenia solium infection	Adequate cooking of pork or pork products
Cysticercosis (extraintestinal *T solium* infection)	As for *T solium*
Taenia saginata infection	Adequate cooking of beef and beef products; inspection of beef and destruction of infected carcasses
Hymenolepis nana infection	Adherence to good fecal-oral hygiene
Hymenolepis diminuta infection	Arthropod control measures (such as rat control)
Dypylidium caninum infection	Screening of dogs and cats; treatment of infected animals
Echinococcal infection	• Screening of household pets; treatment of infected animals • Destruction of infected carcasses • Education on routes of transmission (in endemic areas)

nonspecific abdominal symptoms including indigestion and nausea may be present.

B. Laboratory Findings. Patients with intestinal *T solium* infection will frequently have abnormal results of stool examinations for ova and parasites and occasionally will have a mild leukocytosis with eosinophilia.

Differential Diagnosis

Since infection with the adult worm of *T solium* is asymptomatic, the main diagnostic concern in a patient with intestinal *T solium* is whether the patient has cysticercosis. If the results of evaluation suggest that there is extraintestinal infection, then specific therapy for cysticercosis is required.

Complications

T solium infection of the intestine is not commonly associated with symptoms; however, in patients with high parasite loads, obstruction may occur.

Treatment

Therapy for *T solium* infection of the intestine consists of either praziquantel or niclosamide (see Box 87–2). Follow-up examinations of stool should be performed 1 month after treatment.

Prognosis

The prognosis for patients with intestinal *T solium* infection is excellent.

Prevention & Control

Prevention from infection with *T solium* involves adequate cooking of pork and pork products to a > 65 °C core temperature (Box 87–3). Freezing, pickling, and salting do not prevent infection. Immunization of swine and provision of animal feed that is free of eggs and proglottids are other preventative measures that have been reported to be effective in controlling infection. Since infected humans are capable of transmitting cysticercus to others, enteric precautions should be used, and stool specimens should be handled with attention to decontamination. In addition, adequate facilities for disposal of human sewage should be available.

CYSTICERCOSIS (*CYSTICERCUS CELLULOSEA* INFECTION)

Essentials of Diagnosis

- Surgical excision of involved tissue, with microscopic identification of parasite.
- Frequently calcified cysts present on x-ray or computed tomography (CT) scans.
- Positive serology indicating previous exposure to *T solium.*
- Fine-needle aspiration of cysts (characteristic cytomorphology).

General Considerations

Cysticercosis is caused by invasion of tissue by the larval forms of *T solium,* which have been referred to as *Cysticercus cellulosea,* although the name is not taxonomically correct and introduces confusion. Within a host infected by the adult *T solium,* eggs or proglottids are passed in the stool. Once eggs or proglottids are ingested by either pigs (intermediate hosts) or humans (definitive and intermediate hosts), eggs hatch in the gastric juice, allowing the cysticercus to migrate from the intestine to disseminated sites, via efferent mesenteric venules. Autoinfection may also occur in humans, wherein eggs produced by the adult intestinal worm hatch and invade the intestinal epithelium.

Clinical Findings

A. Signs and Symptoms. The symptoms associated with cysticercosis relate to the organ that is invaded by cysticerci and to the inflammatory reaction that occurs in response to the larva. Within the brain, cysticercosis may cause arachnoiditis or chronic meningitis, with associated headache, vertigo, vomiting, and cranial neuropathies. Alternate presentations include obstructive hydrocephalus with ataxia and dementia, intracranial vasculitis with focal neurologic signs and neuropsychiatric changes, or mass effect with seizures, headache, or focal neurologic deficits. In addition, cord compression with lower limb weakness and loss of bowel and bladder continence may occur. Cysts outside the central nervous system tend to occur within muscle, are most often asymptomatic, and eventually die, calcify, and may be incidentally detected on radiographs. Occasionally, muscle cysts will cause pseudohypertrophy that may be associated with myositis, high fever, and eosinophilia. Cysts may also occur within critical organs (commonly heart and liver) where they present as mass lesions with pain or obstructive symptoms.

B. Laboratory Findings. Patients with cysticercosis may have a mild elevation on leukocyte count, possibly with eosinophilia. In patients with meningitis associated with neurocysticercosis, cerebrospinal fluid examination may show either lymphocytic or eosinophilic pleocytosis, hypoglycorrhachia, and elevated protein. Recently a serologic test for *T solium* has been developed, but its performance characteristics remain to be validated. False positive results have been associated with infections caused by other cestodes. A negative serologic test does not exclude the diagnosis of cysticercosis.

C. Imaging. Living cysts associated with cysticercosis are often multiple and have a characteristic appearance on CT scans or magnetic resonance images, both enhancing and nonenhancing unilocular cysts. Patients with extraneurologic cysticercosis may have painless subcutaneous nodules, often on the shins, which are calcified and have a characteristic appearance on plain radiographs.

Differential Diagnosis

Patients who seek care for symptoms of infection with *T solium* most commonly do so because of the neurologic symptoms associated with neurocysticercosis. The most common neurologic symptoms are mass effect and seizures (related to intraparenchymal lesions), hydrocephalus (related to intraventricular cysts), chronic meningitis (related to subarachnoid cysts), and cord compression (owing to spinal cord cysts). The differential diagnosis of each of these symptoms is beyond the scope of this discussion, but malignancy may present in identical ways, and so it must be ruled out.

Complications

Visceral cysticercosis is also commonly asymptomatic, but may obstruct local structures (eg, biliary obstruction in hepatic cysticercosis). Neurocysticer-

cosis may lead to permanent neurologic impairment, coma, or even death.

Treatment

Therapy for cysticercosis includes surgery when feasible and necessary, in combination with praziquantel or albendazole (see Box 87–2). Therapy of cysticercosis commonly increases the local inflammation, thereby transiently causing a paradoxical worsening of the patient's symptoms. Whether corticosteroids should be used as adjunctive therapy for patients being treated for neurocysticercosis remains in debate.

Prognosis

The mortality rate for untreated neurocysticercosis approaches 50%, but treatment decreases this rate to 5–15%.

Prevention & Control

Guidelines for the prevention of cysticercosis are the same as for the prevention of *T solium* infection (Box 87–3).

TAENIA SAGINATA INFECTION

Essentials of Diagnosis

- Stool examination reveals spheroidal yellow-brown eggs (31–43 mm).
- Motile proglottids that appear singly in stool.
- Mature proglottids are square.
- Scolex has no hooklets and four suckers.
- Gravid proglottid has 15–20 lateral branches.

General Considerations

T saginata infection is commonly associated with the ingestion of undercooked beef. This is distinguished from infection with *T solium* because human infection with the larval form (as in cysticercosis) is extremely rare with *T saginata* infection. *T saginata* infection is common in areas of the world with intensive cattle breeding, such as central Asia and central and eastern Africa. Alternative intermediate hosts for *T saginata* include llamas, buffalo, and giraffes. The life cycle for *T saginata* is similar to that of *T solium;* larvae are ingested in infected meat, and the tapeworm attaches to the intestinal epithelium and matures in 12 weeks. Mature tapeworms produce gravid proglottids with characteristic 15–20 lateral branches, which contain numerous eggs. Ingestion of eggs or proglottids by cows leads to hatching of eggs, and larvae that migrate into striated muscle. Case reports exist about *T saginata* cysticercosis in humans, although the incidence is exceedingly uncommon.

Clinical Findings

A. Signs and Symptoms. Infection with *T sag-*

inata is most often asymptomatic, although a minority of patients may report nonspecific abdominal cramps or malaise. The proglottids of *T saginata* are motile, and patients may report seeing moving segments in the stool.

B. Laboratory Findings. Examination of the blood in patients with *T saginata* infection typically reveals no abnormalities, although a mild leukocytosis with eosinophilia may be present. Otherwise all laboratory tests except the microscopic stool examination will be normal. The stool examination will frequently reveal eggs and proglottids. The main basis for differentiating *T saginata* from *T solium* is the gravid proglottid, which for *T solium* has 7–13 lateral branches on each side of the uterus, whereas *T saginata* has 15–20 lateral branches.

Differential Diagnosis

Infection with *T saginata* is usually not associated with clinical symptoms. Patients most often seek medical attention after finding *T saginata* proglottids in stools or on clothing. The main differential diagnosis is to differentiate *T saginata* proglottids from *T solium* proglottids. If no gravid proglottids are present, then differentiation may not be possible, in which case patients should be treated as though they have infection with *T solium.*

Complications

Usually no complications are associated with *T saginata;* however, regurgitation and aspiration of proglottids may occur.

Treatment

Therapy for infection with *T saginata* is similar to treatment of intestinal *T solium,* a single dose of either praziquantel or niclosamide (see Box 87–2). Follow-up examinations of stool should be performed 1 month after treatment.

Prognosis

The prognosis for patients with intestinal *T saginata* infection is excellent.

Prevention & Control

Prevention of infection with *T saginata* involves thorough cooking of beef and beef products to > 65 °C core temperature (Box 87–3). Beef should also be inspected for the presence of cysts, and infected carcasses destroyed.

HYMENOLEPIS NANA INFECTION

Essentials of Diagnosis

- Adult worms and proglottids are rare.
- Spheroidal and thin-walled eggs (30–47 mm).
- Eggs contain two polar elements from which 4–8 filaments project (diagnostic).
- Scolex has hooklets and four suckers.

General Considerations

H nana is distributed worldwide and is called the dwarf tapeworm because of its small size (2–4 cm). Endemic areas include Asia, Africa, South and Central America, and southern and eastern Europe. Infection with *H nana* is acquired by the ingestion of eggs, commonly from human stool. The eggs hatch within the stomach or small intestine, and the resultant larvae attach to the bowel wall, where adult worms develop in several weeks. Eggs are released directly from the gravid proglottids while these proglottids are still attached to the adult worm; therefore proglottids are rarely seen on stool examination. Various arthropods such as fleas can serve as alternate intermediate hosts for *H nana*. Eggs produced within infected humans can lead to internal autoinfection, and poor fecal-oral hygiene can cause infection to be passed from one person to another.

Clinical Findings

A. Signs and Symptoms. Infection with *H nana* is most often asymptomatic, yet some patients may complain of headache, dizziness, anorexia, or abdominal pain. Whether these symptoms are related to the infection is uncertain. Children may have headache or sleep and behavioral disturbances, which resolve after successful treatment of the infection.

B. Laboratory Findings. As for patients with other cestode infections, examination of blood from patients with *H nana* infection is typically normal, although a mild leukocytosis with eosinophilia may be present. Microscopic stool examination will frequently reveal eggs, but finding proglottids is uncommon with *H nana* infection.

Differential Diagnosis

Since infection with *H nana* is usually asymptomatic, patients most often discover *H nana* infection as an incidental finding on stool examination done for another reason. In patients with nonspecific gastrointestinal complaints, peptic ulcer disease and malignancy need to be ruled out. Similarly, in children with behavioral symptoms, a variety of neurologic disorders of organic and psychologic origins need to be considered.

Complications

Through a mechanism that is still unclear, seizures have been reported with *H nana* infections.

Treatment

Cysts of *H nana* are more resistant to therapy than adult worms. Therefore higher doses or longer courses of therapy are required to eradicate cysts than with other cestode infections. Therapy for infection by *H nana* consists of a single dose of either praziquantel or niclosamide (see Box 87–2). Follow-up examinations of stool should be performed at 2 weeks and 3 months after therapy.

Prognosis

Since infection with *H nana* is usually asymptomatic and infection responds to therapy, the prognosis is excellent.

Prevention & Control

Infection with *H nana* can be prevented with good fecal-oral hygiene and adherence to the principles of sanitation (eg, appropriate disposal of human sewage) (Box 87–3). Incidental ingestion of arthropod hosts may also produce infection, although this mechanism of infection is uncommon.

HYMENOLEPIS DIMINUTA

Essentials of Diagnosis

- Proglottids are rare in stool, but adult worms may be present.
- Ovoid and thick-walled eggs (70–85 μm by 60–80μm).
- Eggs contain no polar elements.
- Scolex has no hooklets and four suckers.

General Considerations

H diminuta is also distributed worldwide, but the incidence of infection is much less common than with *H nana*. Infection with *H diminuta* is acquired by the ingestion of eggs, produced from an obligatory arthropod intermediate host. The eggs hatch within the stomach or small intestine, and the adult worms develop in several weeks. Eggs are similar in size to the eggs of *H nana* but may be distinguished by their lack of polar filaments and ovoid shape. In contrast to *H nana*, the life cycle of *H diminuta* requires an intermediate arthropod host, and adult worms may be passed in the stool of humans.

Clinical Findings

A. Signs and Symptoms. Infection with *H diminuta* is not associated with clinical symptoms.

B. Laboratory Findings. Microscopic stool examination will frequently reveal eggs and adult worms. Blood examination may demonstrate mild leukocytosis with eosinophilia.

Differential Diagnosis

The finding of *H diminuta* in human infection is commonly an incidental finding that is asymptomatic.

Complications

No complications have been reported.

Treatment

Therapy for infection for *H diminuta* consists of niclosamide in a one-time dose (see Box 87–2).

Prognosis

H diminuta responds promptly to therapy, so the prognosis is excellent.

Prevention & Control

Infection with *H diminuta* can be reduced by decreasing exposure to arthropod vectors, such as by rat control measures (Box 87–3).

DIPYLIDIUM CANINUM INFECTION

Essentials of Diagnosis

- Motile proglottids 23 by 8 mm.
- Proglottids have genital pores at either end and contain egg clusters.
- Eggs occur in compartmented clusters (diagnostic).
- Scolex has 4–7 rows of hooklets and 4 suckers.

General Considerations

D caninum is distributed worldwide and is associated with wild and domesticated cats and dogs. The life cycle is similar to that of *H diminuta*, with an obligatory arthropod intermediate host. The adult worm lives in dogs, cats, or humans, and gravid proglottids are released from the adult worm either singly or in short chains. Eggs are passed in the stool, and ingestion of eggs by the intermediate host results in the development of the larval form within the arthropod host. Ingestion of the arthropod that contains larvae results in the development of an adult worm in dogs, cats, or humans. Adult worms may reach 10–80 cm in length.

Clinical Findings

A. Signs and Symptoms. Infection with *D caninum* is not commonly associated with clinical symptoms, although indigestion or anorexia may be present. Also anal pruritus has been reported.

B. Laboratory Findings. Microscopic stool examination will frequently reveal characteristic egg clusters and proglottids. As with other cestode infections, blood examination may demonstrate mild leukocytosis with eosinophilia.

Differential Diagnosis

Since *D caninum* infection in humans is often asymptomatic, most patients do not seek medical care. Once eggs are found in the stool, the appearance of egg clusters is so characteristic that no other parasite could be confused with *D caninum*. When a patient does seek the care of a physician for indigestion or anorexia, a variety of gastric pathologies need to be ruled out (eg, peptic ulcer disease and gastric outlet obstruction).

Complications

No complications are associated with *D caninum* infection.

Treatment

Therapy for *D caninum* infection is niclosamide in a one-time dose (see Box 87–2).

Prognosis

The prognosis for *D caninum* infections is excellent.

Prevention & Control

Infection with *D caninum* can be reduced by screening domestic dog and cat stools and treating pets found to be infected (Box 87–3).

ECHINOCOCCAL INFECTION

Essentials of Diagnosis

- Radiographic finding of cyst
- Positive echinococcal serology
- Aspiration of cyst revealing echinococcal sand or hooks
- Typical histologic appearance of cyst wall

General Considerations

The normal life cycle of *Echinococcus* species does not involve humans. Human disease occurs when humans become an accidental intermediate host for the parasite, and tissue invasion is followed by the formation of cysts (hydatid cysts). The definitive hosts for echinococcal species are canines (usually dogs), in whom the adult worms live. There may be several hundred worms within a host, and the worms are small, usually 3–6 mm long.

The scolex is attached to the dog intestine, and to each scolex is attached a single proglottid. As the proglottids mature and become gravid proglottids containing several eggs, they detach and are passed in the stool. The eggs are resistant to desiccation and may remain viable for weeks. Eggs are ingested by intermediate hosts, commonly sheep and cattle but occasionally humans. The eggs hatch in the duodenum, and the larval forms penetrate the intestinal mucosa and disseminate through the blood stream to distant sites, most commonly the liver. Within tissues, the larva develops an encasing cyst composed of an outer layer and an inner fluid-filled layer. Within 1 year, cysts may reach 5–10 cm in diameter.

Inside the inner layer, daughter cysts form which may detach and float within the fluid, and daughter scolices may form. Ingestion of meat containing hydatid cysts leads to infection of definitive hosts, and adult worms develop. Infections with *Echinococcus granulosus* cause the formation of unilocular cysts. In contrast, infections with *Echinococcus multilocularis* are associated with multilocular cysts. *E multilocularis* also differs from *E granulosus* in that definitive hosts include foxes, wolves, cats, and dogs, and intermediate hosts include small rodents. Endemic areas for *E granulosus* include Africa, the Middle East, southern Europe, Latin America, and the southwestern United States. For *E multilocularis,* forested areas of Europe, Asia, and North America are endemic.

Clinical Findings

A. Signs and Symptoms. In humans, the presentation of infection depends on where the hydatid cyst forms. The principle locations for cysts in humans include liver (60%), lung (20%), muscle (4%), kidney (4%), spleen (3%), soft tissues (3%), brain (3%), bone (2%), and other (1%). Within the liver, cysts may be incidentally diagnosed or may present as pain or a visible mass. Pulmonary cysts are usually asymptomatic, but if sufficiently large, may cause cough, dyspnea, or pleuritic pain.

Although rare, hydatid cysts in the brain are potentially the most serious and may cause obstructive hydrocephalus with ataxia and dementia or mass effect with seizures, headache, or focal neurologic deficits. Bony hydatid cysts most commonly involve vertebrae and present with bone pain. Other presentations include soft tissue swelling and bone pain or pathologic fractures secondary to cysts weakening cortical bone. In ≤ 20% of infected patients, cysts will be multiple, so a thorough evaluation is required of all patients in whom the diagnosis is suspected.

B. Laboratory Findings. Eosinophilia may be present in ≤ 25% of patients, but it is a nonspecific marker. Serologic testing is available, by a variety of techniques, and, if positive, the results provide supportive evidence of echinococcal infection. However, a negative result of serologic testing does not rule out hydatid cyst disease. More recent serologic techniques may help to differentiate *E granulosus* infection from *E multilocularis* infection. Cross-reaction between cysticercosis and hydatid cyst disease has been noted with some serologic assays. Another potential diagnostic procedure is cyst aspiration, although it poses some risk for anaphylaxis (see complications). This test is potentially useful to diagnose *E granulosus* hydatid cysts. A small volume of fluid is removed and examined microscopically for the presence of hydatid sand (daughter cysts and scolices). If a cyst is old, sand may not be present, in which case a centrifuged specimen should be examined for the presence of hooks.

C. Imaging. Radiographically, cysts appear as either unilocular cysts with an air fluid level (*E granulosus*) or as multiloculated cysts with little or no fluid (*E multilocularis*).

Differential Diagnosis

Since the usual presentation of hydatid cysts is either liver pain or mass, lung mass with irritative symptoms of obstruction, or seizures with focal neurologic symptoms, the primary differential diagnosis is to rule out primary or metastatic malignancy of each of these organs. In a unilocular hydatid cyst, the radiographic appearance is often sufficient to exclude malignancy. In contrast, multilocular cysts caused by *E multilocularis* are slow growing, often with little or no fluid, and frequently have central necrosis, all suggestive of malignancy. Therefore biopsy and histologic examination are necessary for definite differentiation from malignancy.

Complications

On occasion, hydatid cysts may leak fluid into the systemic circulation of the host, causing sensitization of the host. Subsequent fluid leaks may then be responsible for the induction of an allergic response or even anaphylaxis. In addition, release of cyst tissue may be associated with embolization and the development of additional cysts at distant alternate sites. Cysts also may become secondarily infected, producing abscesses. Mechanical complications of the cyst are also possible, most commonly leading to portal hypertension, ascites, and portosystemic shunting.

Treatment

Therapy for hydatid cysts caused by infection with *E granulosus* combines surgical and pharmacological interventions (see Box 87–2). Solitary unilocular cysts at operable sites are generally treated with surgical excision, percutaneous drainage, or both. Extreme care must be taken to avoid spillage of cyst contents and subsequent seeding of other sites. One approach has been to remove a portion of the cyst fluid and instill a cystocidal agent such as 95% ethanol before removing the entire cyst. Some authorities also recommend pre- and postoperative therapy with either albendazole or mebendazole.

Recent experience with albendazole is a promising alternative. Mebendazole is an alternate therapy but may be less effective that albendazole. Complicated or multiloculated cysts (caused by *E multilocularis*)

require surgery, often in association with albendazole as above. An experimental approach to inoperable cysts involves oral therapy with albendazole or mebendazole, combined with percutaneous aspiration and instillation of 95% ethanol. Although promising, this approach has not been validated in large trials.

Prognosis

The prognosis of hydatid disease is variable. With early diagnosis and treatment of simple unilocular cysts, the outlook is excellent; in contrast, advanced multilocular disease at multiple sites with advanced portal hypertension is a potentially lethal condition. Medical therapy of inoperable *E granulosus* cysts is associated with cure in 30% of cases and improvement in 50%. Inoperable *E multilocularis* is associated with a 10-year mortality rate in 90% of cases. In such cases, indefinite treatment with albendazole or mebendazole is recommended by some authorities.

Prevention & Control

In areas endemic for hydatid disease, the disease is commonly transmitted incidentally during activities such as camping and picking berries. Education is the best prevention for transmission in these settings (Box 87–3). Routine screening of household pets and appropriate treatment of animals found to carry *Echinococcus* spp. is another important control measure. Pet owners should be educated as to techniques of good hygiene to prevent accidental inoculation of eggs from dog stools. Lastly, carcasses of infected hosts must be disposed of in ways that prevent transmission to canines.

REFERENCES

Garcia LS, Bruckner DA (editors): *Diagnostic Medical Parasitology,* 3rd ed. ASM Press, 1997.

Strickland GT (editor): *Hunters Tropical Medicine,* 7th ed. WB Saunders, 1991.

88

Trematodes

Walter R. Wilson, MD & James M. Steckelberg, MD

Essentials of Diagnosis

- Blood flukes: demonstration of eggs in feces, urine, or rectal biopsy
- Liver flukes: demonstration of eggs in feces
- Intestinal flukes: demonstration of adult worms or eggs in feces
- Lung flukes: demonstration of eggs in sputum or feces

All trematode species that are parasitic for humans are digenetic. Sexual reproduction in the adult fluke is followed by asexual multiplication in the larval stage. Most species of adult trematodes have an oral and ventral sucker. The life cycles of trematodes that are important human pathogens are similar among all five major species. Eggs are excreted in the feces of the host, hatch in fresh water, and require a primary host in snails before infection occurs in humans. Trematode infection may be classified into four general groups based on the final habitat of the adult flukes in humans as follows: blood flukes, liver flukes, intestinal flukes, and lung flukes (Table 88–1).

CLINICAL SYNDROMES

BLOOD FLUKE INFECTION (SCHISTOSOMIASIS)

General Considerations

The final habitat for blood flukes is the venous system of the bowel mesentery or the urinary bladder.

A. Epidemiology. It is estimated that schistosomiasis occurs in > 200 million people worldwide and is endemic in Asia, Africa, South America, and other parts of the world where the population is engaged in freshwater agriculture. The total number of infected individuals in the United States is estimated to exceed 500,000, and these cases are most often in immigrants from South America, Asia, and the Caribbean. The disease cannot spread in the United States because the specific snail that serves as an in-

termediate host does not yet exist in the United States. Unlike most other trematodes that are pathogenic for humans, adult schistosomes have separate sexes. The female fluke resides within a groove created by the fold of the lateral edges of the male fluke.

Each of the five blood fluke species that are pathogenic for humans has a specific geographic distribution as follows: *Schistosoma mansoni*, Arabian peninsula, Africa, Caribbean, and South America; *Schistosoma haematobium*, Middle East and Africa; *Schistosoma japonicum*, Japan, China, and The Philippines; *Schistosoma mekongi*, Southeast Asia; and *Schistosoma intercalatum*, west and central Africa. The specific geographic distribution depends on the presence of the specific snail intermediate host.

B. Microbiology and Pathogenesis. The life cycle of the five major species of blood flukes is as follows: adult flukes (1–2 cm in length) inhabit the venous system of the mesentery or urinary bladder; sexual reproduction results in the characteristically shaped eggs that are excreted in the feces; the eggs hatch in fresh water, releasing ciliated motile miracidia, which penetrate the body of the snail that serves as the intermediate host (a specific snail and geographic distribution exist for each species of blood fluke); within the snail, the miracidia multiply asexually and, 4–6 weeks later, hundreds of fork-tailed cercariae emerge; the cercariae penetrate human skin, lose their tails, and become schistosomes that migrate to the lungs and liver where maturation occurs; and ~ 6 weeks later, the mature adult fluke migrates to its final habitat in the venous systems. The mean life span of adult flukes in humans is estimated to be 5–10 years.

Clinical Findings

The three different stages (cercariae, mature flukes, and eggs) of the blood fluke in humans result in three major disease syndromes in chronologic order: dermatitis (swimmers' itch), fever and constitutional complaints (Katayama fever), and finally chronic fibro-obstructive disease (Box 88–1).

A. Signs and Symptoms. Dermatitis (swimmers' itch) is the acute form of schistosomiasis and is characterized by a pruritic and papular rash that usually occurs within 1–3 days after penetration of the cercariae. Swimmers' itch rarely occurs after primary

Table 88–1. Important trematodes parasitic for humans.

Type	Infection	Species	Intermediate Host		Site Parasitic in Humans
			Primary	**Secondary**	
Blood	Schistosomiasis	S mansoni	Snails	None	Inferior mesenteric veins
		S japonicum	Snails	None	Superior mesenteric veins
		S haematobium	Snails	None	Urinary bladder, venous plexus
		S mekongi	Snails	None	Mesenteric veins
		S intercalatum	Snails	None	Mesenteric veins
Liver	Clonorchiasis	C sinensis	Snails	Fish	Bile ducts
	Opisthorchiasis	O felineus	Snails	Fish	Bile ducts
	Fascioliasis	F hepatica	Snails	Watercress	Bile ducts
Intestinal	Fasciolopsiasis	F buski	Snails	Fresh water plants	Small bowel
Lung	Paragonimiasis	P westermani	Snails	Crabs and crayfish	Lungs

exposure and is more common in individuals who have been sensitized by earlier exposure.

Katayama fever occurs 4–8 weeks after penetration of the skin in humans and coincides with the production of eggs by the flukes. Katayama fever is most severe after *S japonicum* infection, but occasionally occurs in patients infected with *S mansoni* and rarely *S haematobium*. Patients experience an acute onset of fever, chills, headache, and cough. Physical findings often include lymphadenopathy and hepatosple-

nomegaly. Eosinophilia is common. Symptoms usually disappear within a few weeks after onset, but, rarely, death may occur, usually in association with *S japonicum* infection. Katayama fever may be the result of immune complex formation from massive antigenic challenge from exposure to fluke eggs.

In chronic fibro-obstructive schistosomiasis, tissue damage occurs from chronic inflammatory response to the deposition of eggs. This results in chronic granulomatous disease and eventual fibrosis. Liver

---

BOX 88–1

Signs and Symptoms of Trematode Infection

Trematode	More Common	Less Common
Blood flukes S mansoni S japonicum S makongi S intercalatum S haematobium	• Dermatitis (swimmers itch), Katayama fever; • Chronic granulomatous disease of liver, hepatobiliary system, hepatosplenomegaly • Portal hypertension, esophageal bleeding from varices • Dermatitis (swimmers itch), Katayama fever, hematuria, chronic granulomatous disease of bladder with ureteral obstruction, chronic renal failure	• Pulmonary schistosomiasis, central nervous system involvement with seizures • Transverse myelitis
Liver flukes C sinensis D felineus F hepatica	• Most patients have no symptoms • Early stage—Right upper quadrant pain, hepatomegaly, eosinophilia	• Biliary obstruction, cholangitis
Intestinal flukes F buski	• Most patients have no symptoms	• Abdominal pain, diarrhea, malabsorption
Lung flukes P westermani	• Many patients have not symptoms • Cough productive brown sputum, hemoptysis, eosinophilia	• Chronic bronchitis, bronshiectasis, lung abscess

and bowel are the sites most commonly affected in patients with infection caused by *S mansoni, S japonicum, S mekongi,* or *S intercalatum.* Patients often experience chronic abdominal pain and diarrhea. In the liver, fibrosis may result in portal hypertension, hepatosplenomegaly, esophageal varices, and variceal bleeding. Liver function tests usually remain normal for an extended period of time after infection. In chronic untreated cases, hepatic dysfunction, jaundice, ascites, and liver failure may occur.

In patients with *S haematobium* infection, the flukes are located in the vesicular plexus, and granulomatous formation occurs in the bladder and ureters. Hematuria is the most common complaint. With prolonged infection, fibrosis, ureteral obstruction, and chronic renal failure may occur. The frequency of bladder cancer may be higher in patients with chronic *S haematobium* infection.

Pulmonary schistosomiasis may occur in patients with advanced liver cirrhosis and portal hypertension. The development of portosystemic shunts enables fluke eggs to bypass the liver and enter the pulmonary circulation. Patients with *S haematobium* may also develop pulmonary schistosomiasis; the eggs may enter the inferior vena cava from the vesicular plexus and enter the pulmonary venous system.

Of patients with *S japonicum,* ~ 3% develop central nervous system schistosomiasis manifested by space-occupying lesions that may cause focal seizures. Rarely, granulomatous lesions resulting from ectopic eggs in the vasculature of the spinal cord may cause transverse myelitis.

B. Laboratory Findings. The most common laboratory findings seen in patients with schistosomiasis include eosinophilia, hematuria, anemia, and—in chronic end-stage infection—abnormal liver function tests, elevated serum creatinine, and uremia. The diagnosis is established by identifying the characteristic schistosomal eggs in the feces, urine, or a rectal biopsy specimen. Skin tests or serologic tests are helpful for epidemiologic studies but are not diagnostic of active infection.

Differential Diagnosis

Hepatic schistosomiasis may resemble any process that causes chronic hepatosplenomegaly and portal hypertension including alcoholic cirrhosis, Wilson's disease, chronic hepatitis C infection, and many other conditions. *S haematobium* must be differentiated from bladder or ureteral cancer, reflux disease, and other syndromes that cause hematuria or chronic renal failure.

BOX 88-2

Treatment of Trematode Infections

Species	First Choice	Second Choice
S mansoni	• Praziquantel, 20 mg/kg twice daily × 1 day	Oxamniquine, 15 mg/kg single dose. African-acquired infection, 20 mg/kg daily × 3 days
S haematobium	• Praziquantel, 20 mg/kg twice daily × 1 day	Metrifonate, 7.5 mg/kg single dose, weekly × 2 weeks
S intercalatum	• Praziquantel, 20 mg/kg twice daily × 1 day	No satisfactory alternative therapy
S japonicum *S mekongi*	• Praziquantel, 20 mg/kg three times daily × 1 day	No satisfactory alternative therapy
C sinensis *O felineus*	• Praziquantel, 25 mg/kg three times daily × 1 day	No satisfactory alternative therapy
F hepatica	• Bithionol 30–50 mg/kg on alternate days, × 10–15 doses (maximum dose, 2 g day)	No satisfactory alternative therapy
F buski *P westermani*	• Praziquantel, 25 mg/kg three times daily × 1 day • Praziquantel, 25 mg/kg three times daily × 2 days	No satisfactory alternative therapy

Treatment

The treatment for patients with schistosomiasis is shown in Box 88–2. Praziquantel is safe and effective therapy for all five species of schistosoma that infect humans. Eggs may be shed for some time after treatment, and follow-up stool or urine examination should be obtained several months after therapy to ensure eradication.

Prognosis

The prognosis of schistosomiasis is excellent among patients who are treated before end-stage hepatic or renal disease develops. In these patients, prognosis depends on the magnitude of end-organ disease.

Prevention

The only effective means of prevention is to avoid contact with fresh water in areas where schistosomiasis is endemic.

LIVER FLUKE INFECTIONS (CLONORCHIASIS, OPISTHORCHIASIS, & FASCIOLIASIS)

General Considerations

The final common habitat for the liver flukes is the bile ducts. The liver flukes that are the most common cause of human infections are *Clonorchis sinensis* (clonorchiasis), *Opisthorchis* spp. (opisthorchiasis), and *Fasciola hepatica* (fascioliasis).

C sinensis (Chinese or oriental liver fluke) is a flat, elongated fluke (~ 15 mm (3 mm) that inhabits the distal biliary capillaries. Humans are incidental hosts, and the infection is endemic in China, Hong Kong, Korea, and Southeast Asia. Eggs eliminated in the feces are then ingested by the specific snail intermediate host. After ingestion, the eggs hatch into miracidia. The organisms multiply and produce extremely high numbers of cercariae that exit the snail and penetrate the skin of freshwater fish. Once the cercariae are on the fish skin, they encyst as metacercariae, which are infective for humans. Humans and fish-eating mammals acquire infection by ingestion of raw or undercooked fish that contain metacercariae. After ingestion, metacercariae excyst in the duodenum of humans and pass through the ampulla of Vater, where the flukes mature into adults in the bile ducts.

O felineus and other species are endemic in Southeast Asia, Eastern Europe, and Russia and are common liver flukes of dogs and cats that may be transmitted to humans. The life cycle is similar to that of *C sinensis*.

F hepatica is a common liver fluke in sheep and cattle and is endemic in South America, Europe, Africa, Australia, and China. Humans are incidental hosts. Eggs are deposited in the biliary system and excreted in the feces. In fresh water, the eggs hatch, and the miracidia must reach and penetrate their specific snail host within 8 h. The cercariae emerge from snails and encyst on aquatic plants and sometimes in soil. The plants are consumed by humans, sheep, or cattle. The organisms excyst in the duodenum. The larvae penetrate through the intestinal wall into the peritoneum, enter through the capsule of the liver, and migrate to the bile ducts.

Clinical Findings

The majority of patients with *C sinensis* and *O felineus* infections are asymptomatic (Box 88–1). With heavy infection, biliary obstruction and cholangitis may occur. The frequency of cholangiocarcinoma may be increased in patients with chronic *C sinensis* infection. Diagnosis depends on demonstration of the characteristic eggs in the feces.

Unlike clonorchiasis or opisthorchiasis, patients parasitized by *F hepatica* are usually symptomatic, and there are two distinct clinical stages of infection. In the early stage, symptoms correspond to the hepatic migration of the larvae, and patients experience fever, right upper quadrant pain, hepatomegaly, and eosinophilia. Acute symptoms subside as the larvae enter the bile ducts, and most patients become asymptomatic in this later stage of infestation. Biliary obstruction, cholangitis, or biliary cirrhosis may occur rarely with heavy infestation. The definitive diagnosis is made by identifying the characteristic eggs in the feces or bile. A positive serologic test suggests infection. Computed tomography of the liver may show small nodules and tortuous tracts made by the migrating larvae.

Differential Diagnosis

In the acute phase of *F hepatica* infection, patients may resemble those with acute cholangitis, cholecystitis, liver abscess, or *Neisseria gonorrhoeae* infection (Fitz-Hugh and Curtis syndrome). However, the presence of eosinophilia suggests *F hepatica* infection.

Treatment

Praziquantel is effective therapy for symptomatic patients with *C sinensis* or *O felineus* infection. Bithionol is the drug of choice for *F hepatica* infection (Box 88–2).

Prognosis

The prognosis for treated patients with liver fluke infection is excellent.

Prevention

Avoiding consumption of raw or undercooked freshwater fish is the only effective means of prevention of *C sinensis* or *O felineus* infection. Individuals should avoid consumption of undercooked aquatic plants and grasses in areas where *F hepatica* is endemic.

INTESTINAL FLUKE INFECTION (FASCIOLOPSIASIS)

General Considerations

The final habitat of intestinal flukes is the small bowel. *Fasciolopsis buski* is endemic in the Far East and southeast Asia. Eggs are excreted in the feces, develop into cercariae in fresh water, and encyst on freshwater plants. After human consumption, the organisms excyst in the bowel and mature into adult flukes that measure 2–8 cm (1–2 mm. They reside in the upper portion of the small intestine where they attach to the mucosa.

Clinical & Laboratory Findings

Most patients are asymptomatic, but, with heavy infection, abdominal pain, diarrhea, and occasionally malabsorption may occur (Box 88–1). Diagnosis may be made by the demonstration of the characteristic eggs or adult flukes in the stool.

Differential Diagnosis

Most patients are asymptomatic, and the differential diagnosis is that of patients with diarrhea and abdominal pain caused by bacteria and other parasites.

Treatment

Praziquantel is effective therapy for intestinal flukes (Box 88–2).

Prognosis

The Prognosis is excellent.

Prevention

Individuals residing in endemic areas should avoid consumption of undercooked aquatic plants and grasses.

LUNG FLUKE INFECTION (PARAGONIMIASIS)

General Considerations

Paragonimus westermani is endemic in the Far East Indian subcontinent, Central and South America, and West Africa. Human lung flukes produce eggs in sputum that are swallowed, excreted in the feces, and mature in fresh water into miracidia, which penetrate snails. The mature cercariae exit the snail, penetrate into freshwater crayfish and crabs, and encyst. Infection in humans occurs after ingestion of raw, undercooked, or pickled freshwater crustacea. After ingestion, the organisms excyst in the duodenum, penetrate through the bowel wall, enter the peritoneal cavity, pass through the diaphragm into the pleural space, and enter the lungs where they mature into flukes that measure 7–15 mm (5–8 mm. Ectopic eggs in the brain may result in space-occupying lesions and focal seizures.

Clinical Findings

Many patients with minimal to moderate infection are asymptomatic (Box 88–1). With acute infections, symptomatic patients experience cough productive of brown sputum or hemoptysis and eosinophilia. Heavy untreated infection may progress to chronic bronchitis or bronchiectasis with large-volume sputum production, pleuritic chest pain, pleural effusion, and lung abscess. Diagnosis is made by identifying the characteristic eggs in the sputum or feces. A positive serology may be helpful in the diagnosis of ectopic infection. The diagnosis should also be suspected in individuals who do not reside in endemic areas but have a history of consumption of undercooked crustacea imported from endemic areas.

Differential Diagnosis

Pulmonary paragonimiasis resembles chronic bacterial infection, mycobacterial infection, or carcinoma of the lung. The presence of eosinophilia in these patients who reside in or have traveled to an endemic area should suggest the diagnosis of paragonimiasis.

Treatment

Praziquantel is effective therapy (Box 88–2).

Prognosis

The prognosis is excellent in patients who are treated before the development of chronic bronchitis or bronchiectasis.

Prevention

Individuals should avoid the consumption of raw or undercooked freshwater crustacea from areas where *P westermani* is endemic.

REFERENCES

Mahmoud AAF: Trematodes (schistosomiasis) and other flukes. In Mandel GL et al: *Principles and Practices of Infectious Diseases,* 4th ed. Churchill Livingstone, 1995.

Mahmoud AAF, Abdel Wahab MF: *Tropical and Geographic Medicine,* 2nd ed. McGraw-Hill, 1990.

Infections in Travelers

89

DeVon C. Hale, MD & Caroline Milne, MD

Essentials of Diagnosis
- Fever
- Weight loss
- Diarrhea
- Myalgia
- Headache
- Skin rash

General Considerations

International travel has become a normal part of life. Physicians who are knowledgeable regarding common infections encountered in international travel and ways to prevent infection can provide a great service to their patients.

Most travelers will not encounter "tropical disease"; a study of > 10,000 Swiss travelers to developing countries in the early 1980s revealed that the most commonly encountered illness was diarrhea. No persons were infected with cholera or typhoid. The risk of acquisition of disease depends on where one is traveling and the travel conditions. Standards of sanitation and native immunization rates vary, especially in developing countries. In most developed countries, risk of disease is no greater than in the United States. This chapter focuses on pretravel evaluation of the international traveler, including vaccination recommendations and advice to help in prevention of disease. We also discuss post-travel evaluation, with special attention paid to travelers' diarrhea, typhoid fever, and malaria.

PRETRAVEL EVALUATION

It is essential that physicians evaluating international travelers have accurate and current advice. Information for the practitioner can be found in *Health Information for the International Traveler* from the Centers for Disease Control and Prevention (CDC) and *International Travel and Health Vaccination Requirements and Health Advice* from the World Health Organization (WHO). Both titles are available, or on the CDC (http://www.cdc.gov/) or WHO (http://www.who.int/) web site, respectively. Information

about current outbreaks of disease (only yellow fever and cholera) can be found in the CDC's *Summary of Health Information for International Travel*, which is published biweekly.

The patient's initial pretravel visit should occur at least 6 weeks before departure. At that time, a pertinent medical history should be taken and physical examination performed. The patient's itinerary and travel conditions should also be elicited.

Travel advice should begin with general-safety advice; an estimated 0.5% of travelers will suffer some sort of accident. Motor vehicle accidents are responsible for 25% of all mortality abroad. The traveler should also be aware of where to obtain medical attention. If medical attention is needed abroad, the traveler can contact the American Embassy for names of physicians and hospitals. The primary physician's name and phone number should be carried on the traveler.

Preparation is the key to disease prevention. Travelers should carry a medical kit with necessary supplies and medications for self-treatment when able. Travelers on medications for chronic illnesses need a sufficient supply. Other important medications include commonly used pain relievers such as acetaminophen and aspirin, antihistamines for allergies, decongestants and cough suppressants, antacids, antidiarrheal agents, and laxatives. Topical antibiotics and anti-itch lotions could also be carried. Antibiotics to be used for treatment of specific illness, especially if the traveler will be in remote areas away from medical attention, may be considered. First-aid supplies such as bandages, gauze, tape, syringes, needles, scissors, and tweezers should be included in the medical kit. Other materials such as antimalarial agents, insect repellent, and water purification tablets should be carried when applicable (Table 89–1).

Travelers' diarrhea is the most common illness suffered abroad. This illness is most often acquired through contaminated food or water. Because of varying sanitation practices abroad, it is important that the traveler be aware of risk of diseases spread through food and water (Table 89–2). In general, tap water in developing countries is considered unsafe to drink. This includes ice cubes and other nonbottled drinks

Table 89–1. Traveler's medical supply kit.

First aid supplies	Medications
Bandages	Pain relievers (acetaminophen,
Gauze	ibuprofen)
Tape	Cough suppressants
Syringes	Decongestants
Needles	Antihistimines
Scissors	Antacids
Tweezers	Antidiarrheal agents
	Topical antibiotics
	Anti-itch lotions (calamine)
	Sunscreen

Table 89–3. Insect precautions.

Clothing should be worn to cover as much skin as possible
Screens should be placed on open windows
Mosquito bed nets should be used when windows will be open
DEET-containing insect sprays should be used
Clothing and bed nets can be rinsed in permethrin solutions

that may have been prepared by using nonpurified tap water. Boiling is the most effective method of making local water safe from biological hazards. For short trips many travelers rely on carbonated water and reputable brands of bottled water. Water purification pumps are available at most outdoor supply stores. Chemical methods of water purification are listed in Table 89–2. Both were found to be equally effective. Very cold water (< 4 °C) may need to be warmed to room temperature or have prolonged exposure to the purification agent for improved effectiveness. Food should be selected by using common sense. In general, raw and undercooked foods are more likely to be contaminated. Salads and raw fruits and vegetables are more likely to carry diarrhea-producing organisms. It is safest to choose well-cooked, hot foods. Food available from street vendors in developing countries has been associated with an increased risk of disease.

Incidences of diseases carried by mosquitoes and other arthropod vectors can also be decreased by taking preventive measures. (Table 89–3). *Anopheles* mosquitoes (the vector for malaria) bite between dusk and dawn. Avoidance of outdoor activities during this time is best if possible. Clothing should cover as much skin as possible, and sandals should be avoided. DEET (*N,N,*-dimethyl-*meta*-toluamide)-containing insect repellents are recommended. The CDC recommends solutions containing < 35% DEET for adults and 6–10% DEET-containing solutions for children. Bed nets should be used when windows will be open. For extra protection, clothing and bed nets can be treated with permethrin solutions.

Routine Immunization Recommendations

The CDC Advisory Committee on Immunization

Table 89–2. Safe water and water purification techniques.

Boil water—bring water to a boil
Use carbonated or bottled water
Use purchased water filters
Drink alcohol-containing beverages
Use chemical water purification methods
 Iodine, 2% tincture (10 drops/liter of water for 30 min)
 Chlorine bleach (4 drops/liter of water for 30 min)

Practices meets periodically to make vaccine recommendations based on scientific evidence of benefit versus risk to achieve protection against communicable disease. Routine vaccinations against diphtheria, tetanus, pertussis, measles, mumps, rubella, poliomyelitis, and *Haemophilus influenzae* infections are commonly administered during childhood in the United States. All international travelers should be current on these routine vaccinations. Immunization rates may be much lower in developing countries, and these diseases, which have low incidences in the United States, are more prevalent in these areas. Table 89–4 gives childhood dosing schedules, and Table 89–5 gives the pregnancy dosing schedules.

A. Diphtheria, Tetanus, and Pertussis. Diphtheria and tetanus remain health problems throughout the world. The diseases occur almost exclusively in unimmunized or inadequately immunized populations. The primary vaccination series consists of three doses of tetanus-diphtheria toxoid. Doses 1 and 2 are given 4–8 weeks apart. The third dose is given 6–12 months after the second. Although most adult travelers will have received their primary immunizations against these diseases as children, a booster is recommended every 10 years after completion of the primary series. See Chapter 56 for a detailed description of the clinical presentation of these diseases.

Pertussis is quite common in inadequately immunized countries, especially in western areas of the former Soviet Union. Vaccination against this disease is recommended for all travelers under age 7 years who have not received primary immunization against pertussis. Pertussis vaccination is not recommended for people over age 7 owing to greater perceived risk than benefit. See Chapter 56 for a detailed description of the clinical presentation of pertussis.

B. Measles. Measles is often a serious disease, especially in adults, because it can be complicated with bronchopneumonia. Vaccination is recommended for all persons born after 1957. Those born before 1957 are considered naturally immune because measles was endemic throughout the world. A 2-dose subcutaneous vaccine is expected to induce immunity. A single adult booster is recommended. See Chapter 34 for a detailed description of the clinical presentation of measles.

C. Mumps. Mumps vaccination is commonly completed with combination measles and rubella vaccines (MMR). The combined vaccination is a 2-dose schedule. Vaccination is recommended for all per-

Table 89–4. Recommended childhood immunization schedule United States, January-December, 2001.
Vaccines[1] are listed under routinely recommended ages. Bars indicate range of recommended ages for immunization. Any dose not given at the recommended age should be given as a "catch-up" immunization at any subsequent visit when indicated and feasible. Ovals indicate vaccines to be given if previously recommended doses were missed or given earlier than the recommended minimum age.

Age / Vaccine	Birth	1 mo	2 mos	4 mos	6 mos	12 mos	15 mos	18 mos	24 mos	4–6 yrs	11–12 yrs	14–16 yrs
Hepatitis B[2]		Hep B #1		Hep B #2		Hep B #3					HepB[2]	
Diphtheria Tetanus Pertussis[3]			DTaP	DTaP	DTaP		DTaP[3]			DTaP	Td	
H influenzae type b[4]			Hib	Hib	Hib	Hib						
Inactivated Polio[5]			IPV	IPV	IPV[5]					IPV[5]		
Pneumococcal Conjugate[6]			PCV	PCV	PCV	PCV						
Measles, Mumps, Rubella[7]						MMR				MMR[7]	MMR[7]	
Varicella[8]						Var					Var[8]	
Hepatitis A[9]										Hep A in selected areas[9]		

Approved by the Advisory Committee on Immunization Practices (ACIP), the American Academy of Pediatrics (AAP), and the American Academy of Family Physicians (AAFP).

[1]This schedule indicates the recommended ages for routine administration of currently licensed childhood vaccines, as of 11/1/00, for children through 18 years of age. Additional vaccines may be licensed and recommended during the year. Licensed combination vaccines may be used whenever any components of the combination are indicated and its other components are not contraindicated. Providers should consult the manufacturers' package inserts for detailed recommendations.

[2]**Infants born to HBsAG-negative mothers** should receive the 1st dose of hepatitis B (Hep B) vaccine by age 2 months. The 2nd dose should be at least one month after the 1st dose. The 3rd dose should be administered at least 4 months after the 1st dose and at least 2 months after the 2nd dose, but not before 6 months of age for infants.

Infants born to HBsAg-positive mothers should receive hepatitis B vaccine and 0.5 mL hepatitis B immune globulin (HBIG) within 12 hours of birth at separate sites. The 2nd dose is recommended at 1–2 months of age and the 3rd dose at 6 months of age.

Infants born to mothers whose HBsAg status is unknown should receive hepatitis B vaccine within 12 hours of birth. Maternal blood should be drawn at the time of delivery to determine the mother's HBsAg status; if the HBsAg test is positive, the infant should receive HBIG as soon as possible (no later than 1 week of age).

All children and adolescents who have not been immunized against hepatitis B should begin the series during any visit. Special efforts should be made to immunize children who were born in or whose parents were born in areas of the world with moderate or high endemicity of hepatitis B virus infection.

[3]The 4th dose of DTaP (diphtheria and tetanus toxoids and acellular pertussis vaccine) may be administered as early as 12 months of age, provided 6 months have elapsed since the 3rd dose and the child is unlikely to return at age 15–18 months. Td (tetanus and diphtheria toxoids) is recommended at age 11–12 years of age if at least 5 years have elapsed since the last dose of DTP, DTaP or DT. Subsequent routine Td boosters are recommended every 10 years.

[4]Three *Haemophilus influenzae* type b (Hib) conjugate vaccines are licensed for infant use. If PRP-OMP (PedvaxHIB® or ComVax® [Merck]) is administered at 2 and 4 months of age, a dose at 6 months is not required. Because clinical studies in infants have demonstrated that using some combination products may induce a lower immune response to the Hib vaccine component, DTaP/Hib combination products should not be used for primary vaccination in infants at 2, 4, or 6 months of age unless FDA-approved for these ages.

[5]An all-IPV schedule is recommended for routine childhood polio vaccination in the United States. All children should receive four doses of IPV at 2 months, 4 months, 6–18 months, and 4–6 years of age. Oral polio vaccine (OPV) should be used only in selected circumstances. (See MMWR *Morb Mortal Wkly Rep* May 19, 2000/49(RR-5);1–22).

[6]The heptavalent conjugate pneumococcal vaccine (PCV) is recommended for all children 2–23 months of age. It also is recommended for certain children 24–59 months of age. (See MMWR *Morb Mortal Wkly Rep* Oct. 6, 2000/49(RR-9);1–35).

[7]The 2nd dose of measles, mumps, and rubella (MMR)vaccine is recommended routinely at 4–6 years of age but may be administered during any visit, provided at least 4 weeks have elapsed since receipt of the1st dose and that both doses are administered beginning at or after 12 months of age. Those who have not previously received the second dose should complete the schedule by the 11–12 year old visit.

[8]Varicella (Var) vaccine is recommended at any visit on or after the first birthday for susceptible children, ie, those who lack a reliable history of chickenpox (as judged by a healthcare provider) and who have not been immunized. Susceptible persons 13 years of age should receive 2 doses, given at least 4 weeks apart.

[9]Hepatitis A (Hep A) is shaded to indicate its recommended use in selected states and/or regions, and for certain high risk groups; consult your local pulic health authority.(See MMWR *Morb Mortal Wkly Rep* Oct. 1, 1999/49(RR-12); 1–37).

For additional information about the vaccines listed above, please visit the National Immunization Program Home Page at www.cdc.gov/nip or call the National Immunization Hotline at 800-232-2522 (English) or 800-232-0233 (Spanish).

Table 89–5. Vaccination during pregnancy.

Disease Vaccination	Vaccine Type	Indications for Vaccination During Pregnancy
Live virus vaccine Measles Mumps Rubella	Live-attenuated	Contraindicated
Yellow fever	Live-attenuated	Contraindicated except if exposure to yellow fever virus is unavoidable
Poliomyelitis	Trivalent live-attenuated (oral polio vaccine)	Persons at substantial risk of exposure to polio
Inactivated virus vaccines Hepatitis A	Killed Virus	Data on safety in pregnancy are not available. Should weigh the theoretical risk of vaccination against the risk of disease
Hepatitis B	Recominant produced, purified hepatitis B surface antigen	Pregnancy is not a contraindication
Influenza	Inactivated type A and type B virus vaccines	Usually recommended only for patients with serious underlying disease. Consult health authorities for current recommendations
Japanese Encephalitis	Killed virus	Should reflect actual risks of disease and probable benefits of vaccine
Poliomyelitis	Killed virus (inactivated poilio vaccine)	Oral polio vaccine preferred when immediate protection of pregnant females is needed; however, inactivated polio vaccine is alternative if complete vaccination series can be administered before exposure
Rabies	Killed virus Rabies immunoglobulin	Substantial risk of exposure
Live bacterial vaccines Typhoid (Ty21a)	Live bacterial	Should reflect actual risks of disease and probable benefits of vaccine
Inactivated bacterial vaccines Cholera Typhoid	Killed bacterial	Should reflect actual risks of disease and probable benefits of vaccine
Plague	Killed bacterial	Selective vaccinatin of exposed persons
Meningococcal	Polysaccharide	Only in unusual outbreak situations
Pneumococcal	Polysaccharide	Only for high-risk persons
Haemophilus b conjugate	Polysaccharide-protein	Only for high-risk persons
Toxoids Tetanus-diphtheria	Combined tetanus-diphtheria toxoids, adult formulation	Lack of primary series, or no booster within past 10 years
Immune globulins, pooled or hyper-immune	Immune globulin or specific globulin preparations	Exposure or anticipated unavoidable exposure to measles, hepatitis A, hepatitis B, rabies, or tetanus

sons born after 1957, because adults born before 1957 are considered naturally immune. See Chapter 35 for a detailed description of the clinical presentation of mumps.

D. Rubella. The rubella virus is associated with some morbidity in adults. In pregnant women, there is a high rate of fetal death and deformation. A single dose of rubella virus vaccine is recommended for all people. This vaccination is commonly given in the two-dose MMR combination series. See Chapter 36 for a detailed description of the clinical presentation of rubella.

E. Poliomyelitis. Poliomyelitis remains endemic and epidemic in some parts of the world. The WHO has made a goal for complete eradication. A primary series of oral polio virus vaccine, which includes three doses, or enhanced-potency inactivated polio virus vaccine should be completed before

travel. For travelers to developing countries, who have completed a primary series, a single adult booster dose of oral polio vaccine OR inactivated polio vaccine is recommended. Inactivated polio vaccine is recommended to previously unvaccinated adults and immunocompromised hosts owing to the higher risk of vaccine-associated disease in these groups. See Tables 89–6 and 89–7 for dosing information. See Chapter 27 for a detailed description of the clinical presentation of this disease.

F. *Haemophilus influenzae* type b. *H influenzae* type b causes severe childhood disease including meningitis and pneumonia. Vaccination is recommended for all children under age 5 years, regardless of travel plans. An unvaccinated child 15–59 months old needs only a single dose. The vaccine is not recommended for children over age 5. See Table 89–8 for complete dosing schedules. See Chapter 56 for a

Table 89–6. Oral poliovirus vaccine.

Doses	Number of Doses	Comments
Primary series	3	Give doses 1, 2 and 3 6–8 wk apart, customarily at 2, 4, and 6 mo of age (For adults see text)
Supplementary	1	Give dose 4 to children 4–6 years of age
Additional	1	Give a dose, **once**, to persons traveling to developing countries

detailed description of the clinical presentation of this disease.

Other Recommended Vaccinations

A. Hepatitis B. Hepatitis B infection is associated with a high degree of morbidity and mortality (see also Chapter 39). It is most often spread via contact with bodily secretions such as blood or by intimate sexual contact. It can cause a fulminant acute hepatitis, a chronic hepatitis, or both, which may lead to increased risk of cirrhosis, hepatocellular carcinoma, and death. In most of the developed world, hepatitis B surface antigen prevalence is low—< 1% of the general population. In Africa, Southeast Asia, the Middle East (except Israel), the Pacific Islands, and certain parts of the Caribbean (Haiti and the Dominican Republic), the prevalence of disease carrier status is as high as 8%, regardless of socioeconomic status. Universal precautions are usually not taken in developing countries, and sterilization techniques may not be adequate; therefore, patient risk of acquisition of disease from medical care is much higher than in the United States. Although a hepatitis B viral vaccination series is now recommended for all health care providers and infants in the United States, many travelers may not be immunized before travel.

Previously unvaccinated persons who will provide health care, who are at risk of having to receive health care, or who might have any exposure to blood or other body secretions abroad are encouraged to receive the vaccination series. Travelers who plan on residing in a given endemic area for > 6 months should also receive the vaccine.

Primary vaccination consists of three intramuscular (i.m.) doses of recombinant DNA vaccine. After the initial vaccination, doses are scheduled at 1 month and 6 months. Table 89–9 gives the dosing schedule. Protection is increased with each dose of the vaccine; thus travelers who cannot complete the 6-month series before travel may still receive benefit from initiating the series. An alternative accelerated schedule is also available, with dose scheduling at 0, 1, and 2 months, followed by a booster at 12 months.

B. Hepatitis A. Hepatitis A virus is transmitted via ingestion of contaminated food or water. It is highly endemic in most of the developing world and in some areas of the developed world (see also Chapter 39). Risk of acquisition can be decreased by following the recommended food and water practices discussed earlier in this chapter. Hepatitis A vaccine or immunoglobulin protection is recommended for all travelers to areas with intermediate or high endemic rates. This includes all developing countries, eastern Europe, and Russia. For some travelers, screening for hepatitis A virus antibodies may be beneficial before primary immunization. This is indicated in travelers > 40 years old or those born in endemic areas.

Protection from disease can be obtained via two methods, inactivated vaccine or immunoglobulin. Two inactivated hepatitis A vaccines, HAVRIX and VAQTA, are currently approved for use in the United States. The vaccine is administered i.m. in a two- to three-dose series. See Tables 89–10 and 89–11 for recommended dose and schedules.

An alternative protection against hepatitis A virus is immunoglobulin. A single intramuscular dose (0.02 mL/kg) offers protection against hepatitis A virus for ≤ 3 months. Protection can be provided for ≤ 5 months with a larger dose (0.06 mL/kg) but must be repeated if protection is required for longer than that time. At present, hepatitis A vaccine is not approved for use in pregnancy or children < 2 years old; therefore, immunoglobulin is currently the prevention of choice in these groups. See Table 89–12 for dosing recommendations.

Rarely Indicated Vaccinations

A. Rabies. Rabies virus causes disease of the central nervous system (CNS), manifested as encephalitis (see also Chapter 43). It is transmitted by infected secretions of mammal hosts. Almost all ex-

Table 89–7. Inactivated poliovirus vaccine.

Doses	Number of Doses	Dose Volume	Comments
Primary series	3	As indicated by manufacturer	Give doses 1 and 2 4–8 wk apart; give dose 3 6–12 mo after dose 2
Booster	1		Give dose 4 to children 4–6 years of age
Additional	1		Give a dose, **once,** to persons traveling to developing countries

Table 89–8. Recommended *Haemophilus influenzae* type b routine vaccination schedule by age.

Vaccine	2 months	4 months	6 months	12 months	15 months
HbOC	Dose 1	Dose 2	Dose 3	—	Booster
PRP-OMP	Dose 1	Dose 2	—	Booster	—
PRP-D[1]	—	—	—	—	Single dose

[1]PRP-D is recommended only for children ≥ 15 months of age.

posures are secondary to animal bites; however, there are rare reported cases of nonbite infection. Rabies infection is a significant cause of morbidity and mortality throughout the world. It is estimated to cause ≤ 50,000 deaths each year. Endemic areas of the world include Mexico, parts of South America, India, Nepal, Sri Lanka, Thailand, and Vietnam.

Travelers to rabies-endemic regions, especially those who will have known exposure to animals, should consider preexposure prophylaxis. Preexposure vaccine does not eliminate the need for postexposure treatment; however, it does eliminate the need for immune serum globulin and decreases the number of vaccine booster doses needed.

There are three preexposure vaccinations available: human diploid cell rabies vaccine, rabies vaccine adsorbed, and chicken embryo rabies vaccine. They are given in 1.0-mL doses, i.m., on days 0, 7, and 28. Human diploid cell rabies vaccine can be given via the intradermal route, but this route is not recommended if any drugs interfering with immune response are used simultaneously. Rabies vaccines being used in other countries may contain neural-tissue–derived Semple vaccines or suckling mouse-brain products, which are considered less effective and have more associated side effects.

Postexposure vaccine should be given immediately after exposure. All wounds should be thoroughly cleaned with soap and water. For those not previously immunized, postexposure vaccination consists of five doses of human diploid cell rabies vaccine, rabies vaccine adsorbed, or chicken embryo rabies vaccine, each 1.0 mL i.m., on days 0, 3, 7, 14, and 28. In addition, rabies immune globulin, 20 IU/kg of body weight, is given one-half i.m. and one-half infiltrated into the wound site, on day 0. It can be given ≤

7 days after exposure if unavoidable. For those previously immunized, two doses of human diploid cell rabies vaccine or rabies vaccine adsorbed (1.0 mL i.m. on days 0 and 3) are administered. Immune serum globulin should not be used.

B. Japanese Encephalitis. Japanese encephalitis virus infection affects the CNS (see also Chapter 7). The illness may present as a febrile headache, meningitis, or encephalitis. Transmission occurs from the bite of the mosquito *Culex tritaeniorhynchus*, which is the major vector species. Risk of acquiring Japanese encephalitis virus is low and of exhibiting clinical manifestations of disease is lower; only 1:300 seroconverters develop encephalitis.

Risk increases with outdoor exposure to mosquitoes during transmission season and with travel to rural areas of endemic countries. Endemic countries include Malaysia, Myanmar, Cambodia, Laos, Nepal, Philippines, Sri Lanka, Taiwan, northern Thailand, and Vietnam.

Vaccination is rarely recommended for short-term tourists. Travelers who plan to live in endemic areas during transmission season should be considered for the vaccine.

The inactivated viral vaccine, JEVax, has an efficacy rate of > 90%. It is given in three separate 1.0-mL doses on days 0, 7, and 28. There is a significant occurrence of systemic side effects including hypersensitivity reactions. Reactions may be delayed up to 72 h; it is therefore recommended that the last dose of the series be administered at least 10 days before departure.

C. Plague. Plague is a bacterial illness caused by infection with *Yersinia pestis* (see also Chapter 60). The disease is spread to humans from the bite of the rodent flea. Human bubonic plague disease is

Table 89–9. Recomended doses of currently licensed hepatitis B vaccines.

Group[1]	Dose (µg)	
	Recombivax HB[2]	EngerixB[2]
Infants of HBsAG-negative mothers and children < 11 y old	2.5	10
Infants of HBsAG-positive mothers; prevention of perinatal infection	5.0	10
Children and adolescents 11–19 y old	5.0	10
Adults ≥ 20 y old	10.0	20
Dialysis patients and other immunocompromised persons	40.0[3]	40[4]

[1]HBsAG, Hepatitis B surface antigen.
[2]Both vaccines are routinely administered in a three-dose series. Engerix-B also has been licensed for a four-dose series administered at 0, 1, 2, and 12 months.
[3]Special formulation (40 µg in 1.0 mL).
[4]Two 1.0-mL doses given at one site, in a four-dose schedule at 0, 1, 2, 6 months.

Table 89–10. Recommended doses of HAVRIX[1]

Group	Age (Years)	Dose (EL.U.)[2]	Volume (mL)	No. Doses	Schedule (Months)[3]
Children and adolescents[4]	2–18	720	0.5	2	0, 6–12
Adults	>18	1400	1.0	2	0, 6–12

[1]Hepatitis A vaccine, inactivated, SmithKline Beecham Biologicals.
[2]EL.U = ELISA units.
[3]0 months represents timing of the initial dose; subsequent numbers represent months after the initial dose.
[4]An alternate formulation and schedule (three doses) are available for children and adolescents and consist of 360 EL.U./0.5-mL dose at 0, 1, and 6–12 months of age.

manifested by adenopathy (bubo), sepsis, multiorgan failure, and death. Plague pneumonia can be transmitted via infected cough aerosols. In recent years human plague has been reported in Angola, India, Kenya, Lesotho, Madagascar, Mozambique, Namibia, South Africa, Botswana, Tanzania, Uganda, Zimbabwe, Zaire, Myanmar, China, Mongolia, Vietnam, the United States, the former Soviet Union, Brazil, Bolivia, Ecuador, and Peru. .

Risk to travelers, even those traveling to areas where disease has been reported, is low. Because of this low risk, plague vaccination is recommended only for persons having direct contact with diseased rodents or infected animals. See Table 89–13 for plague vaccine doses and intervals.

D. Typhoid Fever. Typhoid fever is a systemic febrile infection caused by *Salmonella enterica* serovar Typhi (see also Chapter 53). Infection is caused when water or food is contaminated by an infected human carrier. Risk of acquisition of disease depends on sanitation standards; thus risk is greater for travelers to developing countries. Vaccination should be considered for travelers anticipating prolonged exposure to potentially contaminated food and water. The approved vaccinations may not offer complete protection, and, as always, preventive steps against food and water contamination should be taken.

Three typhoid vaccines are available in the United States, an oral live-attenuated vaccine, a parenteral heat-phenol–inactivated vaccine, and a capsular polysaccharide vaccine. The parenteral heat-phenol–inactivated vaccine is an older vaccine, has more associated side effects, and is no longer commonly used. The vaccines have comparable efficacy rates. See Table 89–14 for doses and schedules.

E. Yellow Fever. Yellow fever is caused by a flavivirus that is transmitted via *Aedes aegypti* and *Aedes sylvatic* mosquito vectors (see also Chapter 43). Clinical manifestations of disease vary from fever and headache to the classic triad of diseases found in severe infections: jaundice, hemorrhages, and severe albuminuria. Risk of transmission is low; however, this is a vaccine-preventable disease that is associated with high mortality and for which there is no treatment.

Yellow fever vaccination is the only required immunization for admission to certain countries including endemic areas of Africa and Central and South America. It is also required in areas where human infection may induce epidemics or cause transmission. Yellow fever vaccine must be administered at an approved yellow fever vaccination center, because International Certificates of Vaccinations are required for country admission. To be valid, the vaccination must occur ≥ 10 days before desired admission to the country.

Yellow fever vaccine is an attenuated live-virus vaccine. It is given to travelers > 9 months of age as a single dose. A booster dose is required every 10 years. Vaccination should not be given to pregnant women, and special consideration should be taken before immunization of immunocompromised hosts.

F. Dengue Fever. Dengue fever is caused by the Dengue virus, a member of the family *Flaviviridae,* and it is usually transmitted by *Aedes* mosquitoes. It is a disease most commonly seen in urban areas of the Indian subcontinent, Southern China, Southeast Asia, and South and Central America.

Dengue virus causes a sudden onset of high fever, severe headaches, myalgia, and arthralgia. It is associated with a rash that occurs 3–4 days after the onset of symptoms.

Currently, no vaccine is available. There is, however, a vaccine in development. Because the disease is acquired via mosquito transmission, preventive

Table 89–11. Recommended doses of VAQTA[1]

Group	Age (Years)	Dose (U)[2]	Volume (mL)	No. doses	Schedule (months)[3]
Children and adolescents	2–17	25	0.5	2	0, 6–18
Adults	> 17	50	1.0	2	56

[1]Hepatitis A vaccine, inactivated, Merck & Company, Inc.
[2]Units
[3]0 months represents timing of the initial dose; subsequent numbers represent months after the initial dose.

Table 89–12. Immune globulin for protection against viral hepatitis A.

Length of Stay	Body Weight		Dose Volume[2] (ml)	Comments
	lb	kg[1]		
Short-term travel (< 3 mos)	<50	<23	0.5	Dose volume depends on body weight and length of stay
	50–100	23–45	1.0	
	>100	>45	2.0	
Long-term travel (3–5 mo)	<22	<10	0.5	
	<50	<23	1.0	
	50–100	23–45	2.5	
	>100	>45	5.0	

[1]Kg = ~ 2.2 lbs.
[2]For intramuscular injection.

measures should be taken (see Pretravel Evaluation above). Treatment is primarily supportive. Medication to reduce fever should be avoided.

G. Cholera. Cholera is a bacterial diarrheal illness caused by *Vibrio cholera* (see also Chapters 20 and 57). Disease is spread via contaminated food and water. Clinical manifestation of disease ranges from mild, self-limited diarrhea to the voluminous watery diarrhea that quickly leads to dehydration and death.

The risk of cholera to the traveler is very low. The licensed vaccine in the United States offers only 50% effectiveness. Because of the low risk and the low benefit, cholera vaccine is indicated only for high-risk people working and living in endemic areas and in poor sanitary conditions. Endemic areas are present in South and Central America, Africa, and Asia. The vaccine is given as two subcutaneous, intradermal, or intramuscular doses at least 1 week apart. An additional booster dose is required every 6 months. See Table 89–15 for dosing recommendations.

H. Meningococcal Meningitis. *Neisseria meningitidis* causes a bacterial meningitis that is responsible for multiple epidemics of disease (see also Chapters 7 and 52). Epidemic areas include sub-Saharan Africa during the dry season (December–June). This area is know as the "meningitis belt." Recent epidemics have also occurred in Kenya, Tanzania,

Table 89–13. Plague vaccine.

Dose	Dose volume[1] (mL) ≥ 18–61 Years of Age[2]	Comments
Primary series 1 2 & 3	1.0 0.2	Give doses 1 and 2, 1–3 mo apart; dose 3 is given 5–6 mo after dose 2
Booster	0.2	Give booster doses 1–3 at 6-mo intervals for persons with ongoing exposure risks; give booster doses 4 and above at 1–2 year intervals after the preceding booster dose

[1]For intramuscular injection.
[2]No recommendations are given for other age groups because of insufficient data.

Burundi, and Mongolia. All travelers planning to visit countries in the meningitis belt during the dry season or any of the above-mentioned countries should receive the meningitis vaccine. The vaccination is required for pilgrims to Mecca, Saudi Arabia, for the annual Hajj.

The formulation of meningococcal polysaccharide vaccine available in the United States offers activity against serotypes A, C, Y, and W135. Serotype A is responsible for most of the disease outside the United States and Europe. Serotype C is now the most common cause of *Neisseria* meningitis and is part of the vaccine. Quadrivalent A/C/Y/W135 vaccine can be given in a single subcutaneous dose, in the volume indicated by the manufacturer.

DISEASES REQUIRING SPECIAL ATTENTION

1. TRAVELERS' DIARRHEA

General Considerations

Diarrhea is the most common illness affecting international travelers today (see also Chapter 20). Disease prevalence varies by destination, from a 5% incidence during travel to the United States and Canada to a 20%–50% incidence upon visiting tropic/subtropic developing countries. Although travelers' diarrhea tends to be a self-limited illness with very few people requiring medical attention (4%), even fewer requiring hospitalization (< 1%), and almost no one dying, the high incidence of the disease makes it exceedingly important. Frequently, travel time is limited, and there is no time for postponement or rescheduling because of illness.

Bacterial agents are most commonly responsible for travelers' diarrhea. The pathogen frequencies change depending on destination and season. Multiple studies conducted in the 1970s found that enterotoxigenic *Escherichia coli* is the major cause of the illness. Viral and protozoan causes of traveler's diarrhea are less frequent. See Table 89–16 for pathogens associated with traveler's diarrhea.

Table 89–14. Dosage and schedules for typhoid fever vaccination.

Vaccination	Age	Dosage			
		Dose/Mode of administration	Number of Doses	Interval Between Doses	Boosting Interval
Oral live-attenuated Ty21a vaccine					
Primary series	≥ 6 y	1 Capsule[1]	4	48 h	—[5]
Booster	≥ 6 y	1 Capsule[1]	4	48 h	Every 5 y
Vi capsular Polysaccharide vaccine					
Primary series	≥ 2 y	0.50 mL[2]	1	—	—
Booster	≥ 2 y	0.50 mL[2]	1	—	Every 2 y
Heat-pheno–inactivated par-enteral vaccine					
Primary series	6 mo–10 y	0.25 mL[3]	2	≥ 4 wk	—
	≥ 10 y	0.50 mL[3]	2	≥ 4 wk	—
Booster	6 mo–10 y	0.25 mL[3]	1	—	Every 3 y
	≥ 10 y	0.50 mL[3]	1	—	Every 3 y
	≥ 6 mo	0.10 mL[4]	1	—	Every 3 y

[1]Administer with cool liquid no warmer than 37 °C (98.6 °F).
[2]Intramuscularly.
[3]Subcutaneously.
[4]Intradermally.
[5]—, Not applicable.

Clinical Findings

Clinical symptoms of loose bowel movements, urgency, abdominal pain and cramping, low-grade fever, and nausea usually start soon after arrival at the travel destination. One study found the highest onset of symptoms on travel day 3. The mean duration of symptoms without treatment is 4.1 days. This can be shortened to 24 h when antidiarrheal medication is used.

Diagnosis

The diagnosis of traveler's diarrhea is a clinical one. Traveler's diarrhea is caused by a variety of bacteria, viruses, and parasites. The majority of cases are secondary to bacterial agents. Because cultures are time consuming and the natural course of the illness is relatively short, a clinical diagnosis and antibiotic treatment are an appropriate approach to treating this disease.

Treatment

A. Oral Rehydration. Oral rehydration is the cornerstone of therapy for uncomplicated traveler's diarrhea. Parents should be warned that infants and young children who are unable to communicate their thirst and fluid needs are at risk of dehydration. Most often, increased water intake is all that is necessary for otherwise healthy adults. For children or persons with severe dehydration, several oral rehydration formulations are currently marketed, or a rehydration solution can be made with simple ingredients: a half-teaspoon of salt can be mixed with 8 teaspoons of sugar in 1 liter of water.

B. Antimotility Drugs. Antimotility drugs such as loperamide (Immodium) are safe to use for relief of symptoms in typical cases of traveler's diarrhea. Loperamide has been shown to decrease intensity of symptoms and shorten the course of the illness. Should the traveler experience prolonged diarrhea, high fevers, or blood or mucoid stools, antimotility agents should be discontinued and medical attention sought.

C. Antimicrobial Agents. Antimicrobial agents as presumptive treatment for acute traveler's diarrhea may be beneficial and should be initiated at the onset of abdominal cramps and loose stools. Multiple placebo-controlled trials have shown faster recovery rates in patients who received fluoroquinolones than those

Table 89–15. Cholera vaccine.

Doses	Intradermal Route[1]	Subcutaneous or Intramuscular Route			Comments
	5 y of age and over	6 mo–4 y of Age	5–10 y of Age	>10 years of Age	
Primary series 1 & 2	0.2 mL	0.2 mL	0.3 mL	0.5 mL	Give 1 wk to 1 mo or more apart
Booster	0.2 mL	0.2mL	0.3 mL	0.5 mL	1 dose every 6 mo

[1]Higher levels of protection (antibody) may be achieved in children < 5 years of age by the subcutaneous or intramuscular routes.

Table 89–16. Etiologic agents associated with traverlers' diarrhea.[1]

Agent	Latin America	Asia
ETEC[2]	28–72%	20–39%
Shigella spp.	0–30%	4–17%
Salmonella spp.	0–16%	4–15%
Rotavirus	0–36%	*[3]
Protozoa (Giardia spp. Entamoeba histolytica)	0–9%	*
Campylobacter spp.	*	*
Vibrio parahemolyticus	*	1–16%

[1]Adapted from Black 1986 and Taylor & Echeverria 1986.
[2]ETEC, Enterotoxigenic E coli.
[3]*, Not studied.

who did not. Trimethoprim-sulfa has also been shown to decrease symptoms and duration of diarrhea. Fluoroquinolones are not approved for use in children or pregnant women. Trimethoprim-sulfa is safe to use in children. See Table 89–17 for antimicrobial agents and dosages used in treatment of travelers' diarrhea.

Although most travelers' diarrhea is self limited, travelers should be warned to seek medical attention if diarrhea is severe or does not resolve within several days, diarrhea is bloody or mucoid, diarrhea is associated with high fevers or shaking chills, or the patient is unable to maintain oral fluids, and dehydration becomes an issue.

Prevention

Because of the large number of agents responsible for this disease, vaccination is not an ideal form of prevention. Although investigation is underway directed at enterotoxigenic E coli, the most common pathogen, travelers will remain at risk of infections by the other etiologic agents.

Current forms of prevention can be directed at two routes—careful selection of food and water or chemoprophylaxis. As discussed earlier, it is extremely important for advising physicians to educate their patient regarding selection of food and water (see discussion of general travel advice above). Treatment of water or consumption of bottled carbonated drinks along with careful selection of fully cooked, peeled, or steamed hot foods is essential. Despite good advice, several studies have found that travelers are unable to strictly adhere to recommended water and food choices. In a study of Swiss travelers, 98% consumed food or beverages that they were warned to avoid.

Chemoprophylaxis has been well studied in travelers' diarrhea. It is well accepted that antimicrobial prophylaxis is highly effective. DuPont and Ericcson (1993) found that fluoroquinolone prophylaxis pre-

vents ≤ 90% of disease. If trimethoprim-sulfa is used, prevention is still provided, although to a lesser extent. Despite the effectiveness of antimicrobial agents, most clinicians agree that these should not be routinely provided for prophylaxis. There are numerous problems with routine chemoprophylaxis: (1) adverse drug reactions, such as skin rash, photosensitivity, Steven-Johnson syndrome, or bone marrow suppression; (2) colonic bacterial overgrowth; (3) interference with other medications; and (4), perhaps most importantly, the promotion of resistance to antimicrobial agents.

The decision to provide antimicrobial prophylaxis for travelers' diarrhea should be based on a risk-benefit analysis and recommended only in rare and unusual circumstances. For most travelers, the illness is self-limiting and non-life threatening. A patient who is chronically ill or immunosuppressed may benefit more from prevention, because the risk of acquisition of travelers' diarrhea could be life threatening.

Bismuth subsalicylate (eg, Pepto Bismol) is another consideration in chemoprophylaxis. As with antimicrobial agents, prophylaxis with bismuth subsalicylate has reduced the incidence of travelers' diarrhea. An analysis in the late 1970s of students studying abroad in Mexico revealed that prophylactic use of bismuth subsalicylate reduced the incidence of traveler's diarrhea by 62%. Despite the evidence in this single trial, the CDC does not recommend the use of bismuth subsalicylate as prophalaxis for travelers' diarrhea, based on risk of salicylate toxicity and other uncertain risks.

No antiperistaltic agents are effective in prevention of travelers' diarrhea. In fact, prophylactic use of antiperistaltic drugs may actually increase the incidence of disease.

2. TYPHOID FEVER

General Considerations

Typhoid fever is an enteric fever syndrome caused by S enterica serovar Typhi (see also Chapter 53). At one time, typhoid fever was one of the most common bacterial infections in the United States. With improved sanitation, the incidence of typhoid fever has declined. There is still some risk involved with international travel to developing countries and exposure to contaminated food and water. Acquisition of disease associated with all international travel is estimated to be 1:30,000. Travel to India, Peru, or North and West Africa can greatly increase risk of acquisition.

S enterica serovar Typhi infection is caused by contaminated food and water. It is strictly a human pathogen. The bacteria attach and penetrate intestinal mucosa and cause damage to the mucosa directly or via bacterial toxins. The bacteria then invade and multiply within macrophages and therefore reach systemic circulation and cause systemic disease.

Clinical Findings

Clinical manifestations vary from asymptomatic

Table 89–17. Antimicrobial treatment of traverlers' diarrhea.

Agent	Dose
TMP-SMX	160 mg TMP/800 SMX twice daily for 1–3 d
Ciprofloxacin	500 mg twice daily for 1–3 d
Ofloxacin	400 mg twice daily for 1–3 d

carriage (eg, as occurred with "Typhoid Mary") to gastroenteritis to enteric fever and bacteremia. Symptoms of enteric fever usually occur 1–2 weeks after exposure. Cough, sore throat, myalgia, and abdominal pain are early symptoms. With time, fever becomes prominent with changes in mental status. The patient may experience diarrhea or constipation. Significant physical findings include bradycardia associated with fever and hepatosplenomegaly.

Diagnosis

Diagnosis is made by isolation of the bacteria in a blood culture. Stool cultures may be negative both early and late in the illness.

Treatment

Treatment is different depending on disease manifestations. The treatment of chronic carriers is important because they are the likely source of disease spread. Eradication of the pathogen is difficult. Current therapeutic options are outlined in Table 89–18. If antibacterial therapy is not successful, cholecystectomy may become necessary because the bacteria tend to live in the scarred biliary tree or in the presence of gallstones.

The treatment of choice for enteric fever is a fluoroquinolone. If antimicrobial-agent resistance is a problem, trimethoprim-sulfa can be used.

Prevention

Prevention of typhoid fever via vaccination (Table 89–14) is recommended for travelers to developing countries who will have prolonged exposure to contaminated food and water. As always, careful selection of food and drink is strongly encouraged (see Pretravel Evaluation above and Table 89–2).

3. MALARIA

General Considerations

Malaria is a febrile illness caused by four different species of the genus *Plasmodium: P falciparum, P ovale, P vivax, and P malariae* (see also Chapter 80). These plasmodia infect humans via the bite of the female *Anopheles* mosquito. Rarely, malaria has been linked to blood transfusions and congenital transmission.

The risk of acquisition of these plasmodia depends on the country visited, the type of area visited (ie,

Table 89–18. Antimicrobial treatment of typhoid fever.

Agent	Dose
Ciprofloxacin	500 mg twice daily for 10 d
Ceftriaxone	2.0 gm i.v. daily for 5 d
Chloramphenicol	500 mg four times dialy for 14 d
Ofloxacin	15 mg/kg i.v. daily for 2–3 d

rural or urban), the time of year (ie, dry or rainy season), and the duration of the visit. There are 300–500 million cases of acute symptomatic malaria annually and 1.5–2.7 million deaths. The majority of the cases occur in sub-Saharan Africa, with Southeast Asia and Central and South America coming in a very distant second and third, respectively.

The high rate of disease and the continuing emergence of antimicrobial-agent resistance are concerns with malaria treatment. Chloroquine-resistant *P falciparum* is now reported in all countries except the Dominican Republic, Haiti, Central America west of the Panama Canal Zone, Egypt, and most of the Middle East (Figure 89–1). Pyrimethamine-sulfadoxine (Fansidar) resistance has been reported in Thailand, Myanmar, Cambodia, the Amazon area of South America, and sporadically in sub-Saharan Africa.

Clinical Findings

Cyclic fevers are the hallmark of plasmodium infection. The fevers occur as the red blood cells lyse, releasing new plasmodium into the bloodstream. Typically, the victim experiences a cold or chilling stage, followed by a febrile stage lasting several hours, followed by a third sweating stage. The timing of the fevers differs depending on the infecting species—48 h for *P vivax and P ovale* and 72 h for *P malariae*. *P falciparum* usually causes a continuous fever with intermittent spikes. Most victims also experience shaking chills, hypotension, cough, headache, and back ache. Complications of the illness vary but can include CNS involvement with delirium, seizures, coma, and renal failure. Clinical manifestations vary somewhat depending on species.

P falciparum causes the most severe manifestations. The complications are thought to result from diffuse microvascular disease secondary to adherent, parasitized red blood cells that aggregate and obstruct blood flow. Infection with *P falciparum* can lead to severe anemia, renal failure, pulmonary edema, and CNS complications, referred to as "cerebral malaria," which has a range of manifestations from impaired consciousness to seizures.

P vivax and *P ovale* typically cause less severe illness. The red blood cells do not aggregate with these infections; thus the microvascular manifestations are not seen. There is a dormant stage in the life cycle of these plasmodia; therefore, a late secondary illness can manifest as late as 12 months or longer after initial infection.

P malariae causes a low parasitemic infection, and associated symptoms are typically mild. Parasitized red blood cells do not aggregate; thus, with this infection, as well as with *P vivax* and *P ovale,* no microvascular damage is seen later in the infection. An immune complex glomerulonephritis is sometimes seen. The actual infection may persist for years.

The typical laboratory findings seen with malaria are related to the parasitized red blood cells and cell lysis. Anemia and increased lactate dehydrogenase,

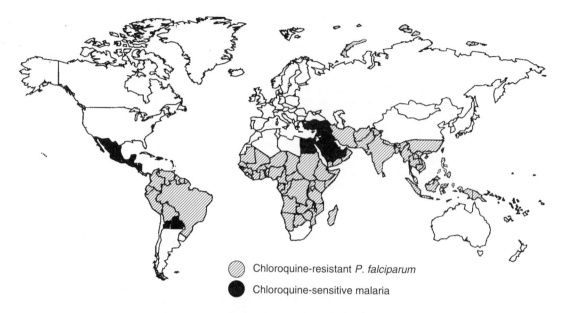

Chloroquine-resistant *P. falciparum*

Chloroquine-sensitive malaria

Figure 89–1. Distribution of malaria and chloroquine-resistant *Plasmodium falciparum,* 1997. Republished from Centers for Disease Control and Prevention: *Health Information for International Travelers 1999–2000.* CDC, 2000.

bilirubin, and reticulocyte counts are typically seen. Depending on the extent of the disease, increased blood urea nitrogen and creatinine associated with acute renal failure and thrombocytopenia can also be seen.

Diagnosis

The standard diagnosis of plasmodium infection is by Giesma-stained blood smears to visualize the parasite. The infected red blood cells can usually be seen on a Wright's stain as well. If the clinical suspicion is strong, and the initial blood smear is negative, the blood smear should be repeated in 6–12 h.

Treatment

Successful treatment of malaria requires rapid diagnosis and initiation of treatment. The species responsible should be confirmed via a peripheral blood smear before initiation of treatment. The selection of the antimalarial agent will depend on the infecting species and whether the patient is able to take oral medications.

Patients with *P falciparum* infection should be hospitalized until the physician is certain that serious complications such as cerebral malaria, adult respiratory distress syndrome, and renal failure will not occur. The obvious supportive treatments such as fluid resuscitation and management of complications should be done. Exchange transfusions may be helpful with severe parasitemia. The appropriate drug therapy depends on the *Plasmodium* species involved. Treatment therapies and doses are outlined in Table 89–19.

A.   Treatment of *P vivax* and *P ovale* Infec-

tions. Effective treatment of *P vivax* and *P ovale* infections can be obtained with chloroquine and primaquine. Chloroquine phosphate along with primaquine phosphate is recommended. Chloroquine is the only antimalarial agent approved for use during pregnancy. Primaquine is unsafe for use in pregnant women.

B.   Treatment of Chloroquine-Sensitive *P falciparum* and *P malariae* Infection. Infection with chloroquine-sensitive plasmodia can be treated with chloroquine. Side effects are minimal.

C.   Treatment of Chloroquine-Resistant *P falciparum* Infection. Multiple drugs are available for treatment of resistant *P falciparum* malaria. The treatment drug chosen should be different from the drug used for prophylaxis.

Quinine was one of the first drugs used for treatment of malaria. Its use became less frequent with the development of new synthetic antimalarial agents, but, as resistance continues to increase, quinine has again become popular. Lower cure rates have been reported in Southeast Asia, including Thailand, Myanmar, Vietnam, and Cambodia. Quinine is currently a first-line drug for use in chloroquine-resistant *P falciparum* infections.

If the infection was acquired in Southeast Asia, quinine should be extended to 10 days, and doxycycline should be added. Tetracyclines are not safe to use during pregnancy. If a patient in the United States is unable to use oral medications, a continuous intravenous infusion of quinidine gluconate is used.

Malarone (Atovaquone 250 mg plus proguanil 100 mg) has been approved for the treatment of mild to

Table 89–19. Drugs used in treatment of malaria.[1]

Species	Drug and Dosages	Side Effects and Contraindications
P vivax, P ovale	Chloroquine phosphate, 1.0 g initially, then 500 mg at 6 h, then 500 mg daily for 2 d (Pediatric dose, 10 mg base/kg orally, then 5 mg/kg BASE at 12, 24, and 36 h **PLUS** Primiquine phosphate, 26.3 mg daily for 14 d (Pediatric dose, 0.25 mg BASE/kg/d orally for 14 d	Side effects include nausea, anorexia, and pruritis; safe for use in pregnancy Contraindicated for use in G6PD-deficient patients secondary to hemolysis risk; Contrainidicated in pregnancy
Chloroquine-sensitive P falciparium or P malariae	Chloroquine phosphate, 1 g orally, then 500 mg in 6 h, then 500 mg daily for 2 d (Pediatric dosing as above)	As above
Chloroquine-resistant P falciparum	Quinine sulfate, 600 mg (500 mg base), three times daily for 7 d **PLUS** Doxycycline 100 mg, two times dialy for 7 d	Not recommended for patients using cardiac beta blockers or those with epilepsy or psychiatric disorders Contraindicated in pregnancy and children under 8 y old
Malarone	Atovaquone 250 mg **PLUS** Proguanil 100 mg, 4 tablets daily for 3 d	Side effects include nausea, vomiting, abdominal pain, and headache Contraindicated in pregnancy, in infants, while breast feeding and severe renal insufficiency

[1]Adapted from Sanford et al 2000. G6PD, Glucose-6-Phosphatase deficiency.

moderate malaria where the patient can take oral medication. It is given as four tablets as a single dose daily for 3 d. It is contraindicated in infants, pregnancy, and while breast feeding. Side effects are rare and include nausea, vomiting, abdominal pain, and headache. It should not be used in patients with severe renal impairment.

Prevention

Prevention against *Plasmodium* infection is twofold, consisting of personal-protection measures and chemoprophylaxis. Despite complete compliance with both medication and personal-protection measures, infection with *Plasmodium* spp. is still possible. This information should be stressed to the traveler, because a febrile illness after exposure should be taken seriously.

Personal-protection measures include the general arthropod protection steps discussed above. Most importantly, travelers should avoid the outdoors during

Table 89–20. Malaria chemoprophalactic regimens.[1]

Regimen	Drug and Dose	Side Effects and Contraindications
Travel to areas where chloroquine resistance has not been reported	Chloroquine, 500 mg/wk. Start 2 wk before travel and continue 4 wk after leaving malarious area [Pediatric dose 8.3 mg/kg/wk (maximum 500 mg)]	Mild; nausea, vomiting, puritis reported; safe for use in pregnancy
Travel to areas where chloroquine resistance has been reported	Mefloquine, 250 mg/wk; start 1 wk before travel and continue for 4 wk after leaving malarious area (Pediatric doses: 15–19 kg = 1/4 tablet/wk; 20–30 kg = 1/2 tablet/wk; 31–45 kg = 3/4 tablet/wk; > 45 kg = 1 tablet/wk **OR** Doxycycline,[2] 100 mg/d: start 1–2 d before travel and continue daily for 4 wk after leaving malarious area [Pediatric dose (after age 8 only): 1 mg/kg/d; maximum 100 mg/d] **OR** Malarone (atovaquone 250 mg **PLUS** proguanil 100 mg), start one day before travel and continue daily for 7 d after leaving the malaria area (Pediatric dosing: 11–20 kg 62.5/25, 21–30 kg 125/50, 31–40 kg 187.5/75, >40 kg adult dose)	Contraindicated in 1st trimester of pregnancy and in travelerswith history of neuro-psychiatric disorders or seizures; side effects include seizures and psychosis reported in 1/13,000 users, nausea, dizziness, and insomnia Contraindicated in pregnancy and children < 8 y old Contraindicated in pregnancy, infants, nursing mothers, and renal insufficiency Side effects nausea, vomiting, abdominal pain, and headaches

[1]Adapted from Sanford et al 2000.
[2]Only effective drug currently in Thailand.
[3]Only available in Canada, Africa, and Europe

the feeding time of the *Anopheles* mosquito, which is dusk to dawn. DEET-containing repellent and pyrethroid-containing flying-insect spray should be used in living and sleeping areas during evening and nighttime hours (see Table 89–3). Additional protection can be provided by treating clothing with permethrin spray.

Chemoprophylaxis is provided to travelers based on information regarding their risk of acquisition, risk of encountering drug-resistant *P falciparum,* and accessibility to medical care. Chemoprophylaxis should be started 1–2 weeks before travel and continued for 4 weeks after leaving the malaria-risk area. There are three chemoprophylaxis regimens. These regimens are outlined in Table 89–20 and described below:

1. For travel to areas where chloroquine resistance has not been reported, chloroquine alone is recommended. Use of chloroquine may be associated with side effects such as mild nausea and skin rash reported in some users.

2. For travel to areas where chloroquine resistance has been reported, if the traveler has no history of mefloquine sensitivity, neuropsychiatric problems, or seizures, mefloquine is recommended. This is a very effective means of malaria prophylaxis. It does have significant side effects that may limit its use. Evidence of CNS toxicity, such as seizures and psychotic behavior, has been reported in 1 European traveler per 13,000. Mefloquine is not recommended for use in combination with beta blockers.

Mefloquine is safe to use in the second and third trimester of pregnancy. Limited data suggest that it may also be safe in the first trimester. Studies are still underway on the use of mefloquine in the first trimester, and women who choose to use the drug are asked to report the use to the CDC for registry in pregnancy outcomes research.

3. Other options include doxycycline, starting on the day of arrival at risk destination and continuing for 4 weeks after leaving the area.

Doxycycline is unsafe for use in pregnancy or in children. Common side effects include photosensitivity and gastrointestinal toxicity.

4. Malarone (Atovaquone 250 mg plus proguanil 100 mg) is approved for the prophylaxis of chloroquine-resistant malaria and is given as one tablet daily starting 1 d before arriving in a malaria area and continuing for 7 d after leaving the area. Side effects are rare and include nausea, vomiting, abdominal pain, and headache.

REFERENCES

Avery ME, Snyder JD: Oral therapy for acute diarrhea. The underused simple solution. N Engl J Med 1990; 323:891.

Black RE: Pathogens that cause travelers' diarrhea in Latin America and Africa. Rev Infect Dis 1986;8(Suppl 2): S131.

Centers for Disease Control and Prevention. Dengue Fever. CDC Document no. 221030. CDC, 1994.

Centers for Disease Control and Prevention. *Health Information for International Travel 1996–97.* CDC,1996.

Dupont HL, Ericsson CD: Prevention and treatment of travelers diarrhea. N Engl J Med 1993;328:1821.

Dupont HL, et al: Antimicrobial agents in the prevention of travelers' diarrhea. Rev Infect Dis 1986;8(Suppl 2): S167.

Dupont HL, et al: Prevention of travelers' diarrhea by the tablet formulation of bismuth subsalicylate. J Am Med Assoc 1987;257:1347.

Dupont HL, et al: Antimicrobial therapy for travelers' diarrhea. Rev Infect Dis 1986;8(Suppl 2):S217.

Gilbert DN, et al: *The Sanford Guide to Antimicrobial Therapy 1998.* Antimicrobial Therapy, Inc., 1998.

Hargarten SW, Baker TD, Guptill K: Overseas fatalities of United States citizen travelers: an analysis of deaths related to international travel. Ann Emerg Med 1991; 20:622.

Hoke CH, et al: Protection against Japanese encephalitis by inactivated vaccines. N Engl J Med 1988;219:608.

Jarroll EJ, Bingham AK, Meyer EA: Giardia cyst destruction: effectiveness of six small-quantity water disinfection methods. Am J Trop Med Hyg 1980;29:8.

Johnson PC, et al: Comparison of loperamide with bismuth subsalicylate for the treatment of acute travelers' diarrhea. J Am Med Assoc 1986;255:757.

Steffen R. Epidemiologic studies of travelers diarrhea, severe gastrointestinal infections, and cholera. Rev Infect Dis 1986;8(Suppl 2):S122.

Steffen R, et al: Mefloquine compared with other malaria chemoprophylactic regimens in tourists visiting East Africa. Lancet 1993;341:848.

Steffen R, Gsell O: Prophalaxis of travellers' diarrhoea. J Trop Med Hyg 1981;84:239.

Steffen R, et al: Health problems after travel to developing countries. J Infect Dis 1987;156:84.

Taylor DN, Echeverria P: Etiology and epidemiology of travelers' diarrhea in Asia. Rev Infect Dis 1986;8(Suppl 2):S136.

Taylor DN, Polland RA, Blake PA: Typhoid in the United States and the risk to international travelers. J Infect Dis 1983;148:615.

World Health Organization. *WHO World Survey of Rabies.* WHO, 1993.

World Health Organization: Wkly Epidemiol Rec 1997; 72:269.

Zoonotic Infections

90

D. Scott Smith, MD & David A. Relman, MD

Essentials of Diagnosis

- Occupations such as abattoir worker and hobbies such as hunting, outdoor activities, and fishing.
- History of exposure to animals, birds, fish, and insect vectors such as mosquitoes, ticks, fleas, and lice; history of ingesting uncooked foods.
- Clinical syndromes such as atypical pneumonia, encephalitis, and granulomatous lymphadenopathy.
- Blood smear with visible microorganisms.
- Radiographic evidence of calcified lesions in brain or muscle.

General Considerations

Zoonoses are infectious diseases of vertebrate animals that are capable of spreading to and affecting humans. This traditional definition is often broadened to include other nonhuman hosts as reservoirs or sources of the infectious agent. Many zoonoses have only historical significance in the developed world; however, they continue to exact a major toll on human health in less-well-developed regions. Of equal or greater concern is that zoonoses are over-represented among diseases that are currently defined as "emerging." Emerging infectious diseases are those that are associated with newly recognized infectious agents or with agents that appear to be spreading and causing more cases of disease or more serious cases than they did previously. One survey has found that 114 of 156 emerging infectious diseases can be classified as zoonoses. The reasons for this important phenomenon are discussed later in this chapter.

A. Epidemiology. Zoonoses tend to occur under special circumstances of geography, climate, or human activity that create new opportunities for encounters between humans and zoonotic agents (see Pathogenesis below). As a result, zoonoses are often geographically focal, transient over months or years, and restricted to specific subpopulations. In the case of hantavirus pulmonary syndrome, the disease arises only when humans live or sleep near infected rodents, which in turn are found only in small geographic microenvironments. In general, humans at special risk for acquiring zoonoses are farmers, hunters, and those that handle and work with animals, birds, and fish. In addition, persons with unusual exposure to insect vectors and those that work in and near water are at increased risk for zoonoses. Most

often, humans act as "dead-end" hosts for zoonotic disease agents; ie, they do not contribute to overall, long-term persistence or spread of the agent in nature.

B. Microbiology. There are numerous diverse pathogenic microorganisms associated with zoonotic disease including viruses, bacteria, fungi, and parasites (Box 90–1). A reservoir is a host in which a microorganism lives and multiplies. A primary reservoir is a host on which a zoonotic agent depends for its continued survival in nature. This host does not usually develop disease. As an example, the white-footed mouse is a primary reservoir for *Borrelia burgdorferi,* the agent of Lyme disease, in the northeastern United States. Although an infected mouse does not exhibit signs of disease, it permits prodigious replication of this spirochete and circulation of the organism in the murine bloodstream. As a result, ixodid ticks often acquire the spirochete during a blood meal. A secondary reservoir in contrast, is not necessary for the survival of the microbe in nature but may be important for the transmission of disease to humans. Plague and its causative agent, *Yersinia pestis,* illustrate this concept (Figure 90–1). Wild rodents serve as primary reservoirs; commensal rodents such as urban rats may serve as secondary reservoirs and as such may play disproportionately important roles in transmission of disease to humans in a peridomestic setting, via their fleas, as was so acutely illustrated during the Middle Ages. Many of the most common reservoirs for human zoonotic diseases are domestic animals or animals adapted to urban and suburban environments. As humans build their homes and move into the habitats of the primary reservoirs, their chances for contact with zoonotic pathogens increase (see below). Table 90–1 lists some of the more common associations of animals with zoonotic agents.

A vector is an organism, usually an arthropod, that carries a zoonotic agent from one host to another. Common vectors include mosquitoes, ticks, and fleas. Vectors can be categorized as mechanical or biological, depending on the degree of intimacy with the microorganism they transmit. A mechanical vector transmits disease agents by means of contamination of its legs, proboscis, or even its gastrointestinal tract. Mechanical transmission requires no multiplication or specific interaction between vector and pathogen to enable disease spread. The common housefly is an ex-

BOX 90-1

Microbiology of Zoonoses

	Central Nervous System	Pulmonary	Abdominal Pain± Diarrhea	Rash	Cutaneous Lesion	Lymphadenopathy
More Frequent[1]	• Listeria monocytogenes • Toxoplasma gondii (in immunocompromised hosts)	• Coxiella burnetii • Histoplasma capsulatum	• Giardia lamblia • Cryptosporidium parvum • Salmonella spp. • Campylobacter jejuni	• Rickettsia rickettsii, R. typhi, R. conorii • Dengue fever virus • Salmonella typhi	• Borrelia burgdorferi • Pasteurella multocida • Trypanosoma cruzi	• Toxoplasma gondii • Bartonella henselae
Less Frequent[1]	• Leptospira spp. (interrogans) • Arboviruses: Japanese B encephalitis, Yellow fever, Dengue fever • Borrelia spp. • Rickettsia spp. • Trypanosoma gambiense or rhodiense	• Bacillus anthracis • Chlamydia psittaci • Francisella tularensis • Toxocara canis • Yersinia pestis • Sin Nombre hantavirus • Echinococcus granulosus	• Brucella spp. • Trichinella spiralis • Anisakis spp. • Echinococcus granulosus • Taenia solium (pig) or saginata (cow) • Listeria monocytogenes • Yersinia enterocolitica and Y. pseudotuberculosis • Campylobacter jejuni • Isospora belli	• Babesia microti and related spp. • Ehrlichia spp. • Brucella abortus • Pseudomonas mallei • Spirillum minor • Borrelia recurrentis • Trichinella spiralis • Histoplasma capsulatum • Acute infection: African Trypanosoma • Francisella tularensis	• Bacillus anthracis • Cowpox virus • Orf virus • Erysipelothrix rhusiopathiae • Rickettsia conorii • Orientia tsutsugamushi • Mycobacterium marinum • Spirillum minor • Streptobacillus moniliformis • Seal finger agent	• Yersinia pestis • Francisella tularensis • Dengue virus • Brucella spp. • Histoplasma capsulatum • Leishmania spp. • Acute Trypanosoma infection: African and American • Francisella tularensis • Trichinella spiralis

[1]In the United States

892

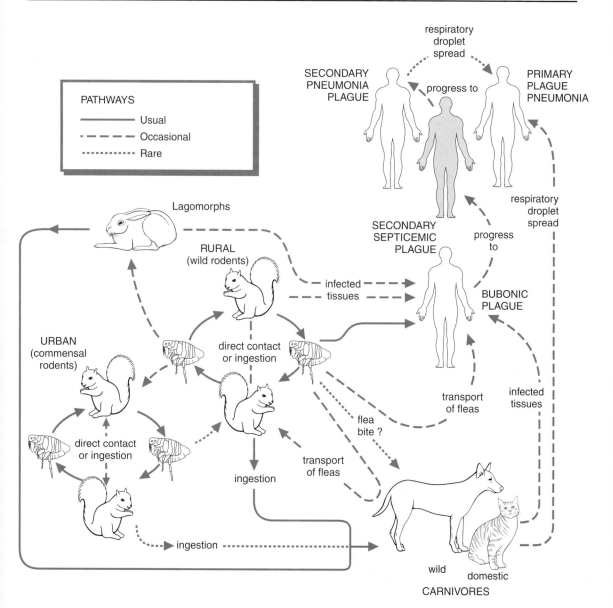

Figure 90–1. Transmission and maintenance of *Yersinia pestis,* the agent of plague, in nature. (Reprinted, with permission, from Plague. In Hoeprich PD et al: *Infectious Diseases,* 5th ed. Lippincott, 1994.)

ample. Biological vectors on the other hand may have a sophisticated and accommodating relationship with the infectious organism, enabling multiplication and cyclic development within vector gut or salivary glands. It is common for pathogens to recognize the distinct environments of a vector and to respond to the relevant cues by expressing a unique set of genes and gene products accordingly. These products facilitate adaptations to the vector. For example, *B burgdorferi* preferentially expresses the surface protein OspA in the tick gut. OspA may play a role in colonization of *B burgdorferi* and its translocation through the tick gut

wall. Nocturnal biting patterns of the mosquito vectors that transmit *Wucheria bancrofti,* one of the agents of human filariasis, match the nocturnal periodicity of parasitemia of the microfilariae. Other features of the feeding pattern of the vector may also enhance transmission efficiency or competence; for example, the *Simulium* black fly feeds on subcutaneous pools of blood, enabling it to ingest skin-dwelling microfilaria of *Onchocerca volvulus.*

C. Pathogenesis. There are three primary routes of transmission of zoonoses to humans: (1) through the skin, by the bite of a vector or animal (eg, *Pasteurella*

Table 90–1. Animals, birds, and fish and associated zoonotic disease agents.[1]

Animal	Dog	Cat	Ferret	Rabbit	Rats and Mice	Hamster and Guinea Pig	Turtle
Virus	Rabies	Rabies	Rabies		Hanta virus		
			Influenza		Lymphocytic choriomenin-gitis virus		
Bacterium	Pasteurella multocida	Pasteurella multocida	Campylobacter jejuni	Pasteurella multocida	Pasteurella multocida	Salmonella spp.	Salmonella spp.
	Brucella canis	Campylobacter jejuni	Salmonella spp.	Francisella tularensis	Salmonella spp.	Yersinia enterocolitica	Yersinia enterocolitica
	Campylobacter jejuni	Capnocytophaga canimorsus	Listeria monocytogenes	Yersinia pestis and Y enterocolitica	Yersinia pestis and Y enterocolitica	Campylobacter jejuni	Campylobacter jejuni
	Borrelia burgdorferi	Yersinia pestis	Leptospira spp.		Streptobacillus moniliformis or Spirillium minus	Pasteurella spp.	Aeromonas spp.
	Leptospira interrogans	Coxiella burnetti			Leptospira spp.	Leptospira spp.	
	Salmonella spp.	Salmonella spp.					
	Francisella tularensis	Francisella tularensis					
	Yersinia enterocolitica						
	Rickettsia rickettsiae						
Parasite	Giardia lamblia	Giardia lamblia	Giardia lamblia	Cheyletiella parasitovorax (rabbit fur mite)	Babesia microti	Hymenolepis nana	
	Toxocara canis	Toxocara cati	Toxocara spp.				
	Cryptosporidium parvum	Cryptosporidium parvum					
	Ancylostoma spp.	Toxoplasma gondii					
Fungus			Dermatophytes	Dermatophytosis (Trycophyton mentagrophytes)	Dermatophytosis (T. mentagrophytes)		

[1]These lists are not all-inclusive, but rather are meant to highlight diseases that are life-threatening or most comonly encountered.

Fish	Avian Species	Lizard/ Snake	Cattle	Sheep/ Goat	Horse	Pig	Fox, skunk bat, raccoon
							Rabies virus
				Viral encephalitis	Viral encephalitis		
Salmonella spp.	Salmonella spp.	Salmonella spp.	Bacillus anthracis	Bacillus anthracis	Bacillus anthracis	Bacillus anthracis	
Streptococcus iniae	Campylobacter jejuni	Yersinia enterocolitica	Brucella spp.	Brucella spp.	Brucella spp.	Brucella spp.	
Mycobacterium marinum	Listeria monocytogenes	Edwardsiella tarda	Babesia spp.		Leptospira spp.	Leptospira spp.	
Erysepelotrix rhusiopathiae	Pasteurella spp.	Plesiomonas spp.	Campylobacter spp.	Campylobacter spp.	Borrelia spp.		
Vibrio cholerae	Chlamydia psittaci		Leptospira spp.	Erysipelothrix rhusiopathiae	Francisella tularensis	Francisella tularensis	
	Yersinia enterocolitica		Listeria monocytogenes	Listeria monocytogenes	Salmonella spp.	Listeria monocytogenes	
			Borrelia spp.	Leptospira spp.		Campylobacter jejuni	
			Coxiella burnettii	Coxiella burnettii			
			Francisella tularensis	Francisella tularensis			
			Salmonella spp.	Salmonella spp.		Salmonella spp.	
			Pasteurella multocida				
			Yersinia enterocolitica	Yersinia enterocolitica		Yersinia enterocolitica	
				Rickettsia rickettsiae			
Diphyllobothrium latum	Cryptosporidium spp.		Cryptosporidium spp.	Cryptosporidium spp.	Cryptosporidium spp.	Cryptosporidium spp.	
			Toxoplasma gondii	Toxoplasma gondii			
			Taenia saginata	Giardia lamblia			
	Cryptococcus neoformans			Taenia solium		Taenia solium	
	Histoplasma capsulatum						

multocida from animal bites) or by direct inoculation (eg, cutaneous anthrax from animal skin handling), (2) through inhalation (eg, *Coxiella burnetii* or *Chlamydia psittaci*), and (3) by ingestion (eg, *Giardia lamblia* or *Brucella* or *Salmonella* species). The route of transmission usually determines the nature of the ensuing clinical syndrome in the human host, especially with regard to the sites of disease involvement. Some zoonotic agents are transmitted to humans by more than one route; for example, *C burnetii* is occasionally tickborne, and *Francisella tularensis,* the agent of tularemia, can be acquired from a tick as well as through direct inoculation of the skin from an abrasion while handling an infected animal. Furthermore, the route of disease transmission to humans may differ from the route between reservoir hosts.

The expression of zoonotic disease reflects an intimate interplay between nonhuman reservoirs, vectors, a human host, and a pathogen. This complex ecosystem is easily disrupted, and when disease emerges in one sector, it often spills over into or has consequences for another sector (Figure 90–2). A classification of factors responsible for the emergence of zoonotic disease can be organized according to host, vector, and pathogen. Host and vector factors include physical translocation and encroachment by one host into the territory of another, travel, crowding, human conflict, globalization of food supply, and environmental changes such as deforestation, global warming, and El Nino Southern Oscillation events. Pathogen factors include acquisition or expression of genes encoding toxins, adherence factors, or outer surface antigenic structures (antigenic variation) and other genetic events that confer upon the microorganism an improved growth rate or transmissibility, broadened host range, and drug resistance. The spread of Lyme disease in the northeastern United States over the past two decades is attributed to the reforestation of New England, human encroachment on deer and mouse habitats, uncontrolled deer population growth, and climate effects on tick population size.

Clinical Findings

Zoonotic disease should be suspected in the setting of fever and either an unusual history of exposure to a

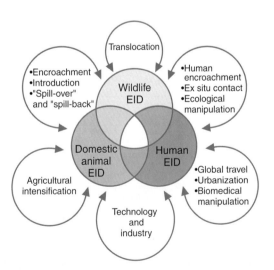

Figure 90–2. The overlap and interplay between emerging infectious diseases (EID) in wildlife, domestic animals, and humans. (Reprinted, with permission, from Daszak P et al: Emerging infectious diseases of wildlife. Science 2000;287:443.)

potential reservoir or vector or a more specific clinical syndrome suggestive of zoonotic disease. "Unusual" exposure histories include frequent, prolonged, or intimate contacts with animals, birds, fish, or disease vectors, especially those contacts that involve bites or scratches, or to sick nonhuman hosts. In general, clinical syndromes associated with zoonotic disease reflect the route of transmission. For example, agents that are transmitted by percutaneous inoculation tend to cause local cutaneous disease such as ulcers, cellulitis, or regional lymphadenopathy; airborne agents tend to cause pneumonia or other lower respiratory tract syndromes; and agents that are transmitted by ingestion usually lead to abdominal or intestinal syndromes. Therefore, the differential diagnosis can be limited to the subset of zoonotic agents that use that route of transmission. More specific syndromes that suggest zoonotic disease are fever and cutaneous eschar (eg, Mediterranean and other spotted fevers and scrub typhus); cough, respiratory distress, and widened mediastinum (inhalational anthrax); and fever, preauricular lymphadenopathy, and conjunctivitis or Parinaud's syndrome (tularemia, cat scratch disease, and others).

Diagnosis

The diagnosis of zoonotic diseases depends heavily on a high index of suspicion and a thorough clinical history. A careful series of questions often reveals travel, contacts, or activities that raise the probabilities of zoonosis substantially. Any potential clue should be pursued by acquiring further information about the intensity of the exposure and duration of stay in a particular location and background data on the prevalence of various zoonotic agents in relevant circumstances. In contrast, there are few clues from physical examination that are likely to be helpful. Bite wounds and lesions are certainly important findings. Cutaneous eschars or certain syndromes such as Parinaud's syndrome (conjunctivitis, preauricular lymphadenopathy, and fever) should suggest zoonoses as part of the differential diagnosis. The laboratory diagnosis of zoonoses relies on serologic testing and thus clinical suspicion of specific disease agents. The finding of microorganisms or poorly explained intracellular inclusions and structures on microscopic examination of a blood smear is a common initial indication of a zoonosis such as malaria, babesiosis, ehrlichiosis, or relapsing fever. Some zoonotic agents require special stains to be visualized under the microscope; for example, *Bartonella* species can be seen reliably only by using the Warthin-Starry silver stain. Agents that enter the body via an oral route may require stool examination and culture for a diagnosis.

Treatment

The diversity of zoonotic agents precludes any simple protocol for empiric therapy. However, certain clinical syndromes and exposures may be amenable to empiric therapy because of a restricted

BOX 90-2

Empiric Therapy of Zoonoses[1, 2]

	Children	Adults
Fever ± Rash and Animal/Vector Exposure[3]		
First Choice Second Choice	• Chloramphenicol, 50–100 mg/kg/d • Doxycycline, 2.2 mg/kg every 12–24 h[4]	• Doxycycline, 100 mg twice daily • Ciprofloxacin, 500 mg twice daily
Fever, Lymphadenopathy, and Animal/Vector Exposure[5]		
First Choice	• Trimethoprim-sulfamethoxazole, 6–12 mg/kg daily • Streptomycin, 20–40 mg/kg daily (if plague is suspected)	• Ciprofloxacin, 500 mg twice daily PO or IV • Streptomycin, 1 g IM or IV every 12 h if plague is suspected
Second Choice	• Doxycycline, 2.2 mg/kg every 12–24 h[4]	• Doxycycline, 100 mg twice daily
Fever, Local Cutaneous Lesion, and Animal/Vector Exposure[6]		
First Choice	• Amoxicillin, 6.7–13.3 mg/kg every 8 h	• Doxycycline, 100 mg twice daily • Penicillin G, 6–12 mU daily if anthrax or pasteurellosis is suspected
Second Choice	• Erythromycin, 30–50 mg/kg daily, or other macrolide	• Ciprofloxacin, 500 mg twice daily
Penicillin Allergic	• Erythromycin, 30–50 mg/kg daily, or other macrolide	• Ciprofloxacin, 500 mg twice daily, **OR** • Erythromycin, 500 mg four times daily, or other macrolide, especially if anthrax or pasteurellosis is suspected, respectively.
Respiratory Disease and Animal/Vector Exposure[7]		
First Choice	• Erythromycin, 30–50 mg/kg daily, or other macrolide	• Doxycycline, 100 mg twice daily
Second Choice	• Doxycycline, 2.2 mg/kg every 12–24 h[4]	• Erythromycin, 500 mg four times daily, or other macrolide
Diarrhea, Fever, and Animal/Vector Exposure[8]		
First Choice	• Ceftriaxone, 50–100 mg/kg every 12–24 h	• Ciprofloxacin, 500 mg twice daily
Second Choice	• Trimethoprim-sulfamethoxazole, 6–12 mg/kg/d	• Trimethoprim-sulfamethoxazole, 160 mg/800 mg twice daily

[1]Begin empiric therapy immediately for potentially life-threatening diseases, eg, Rocky Mountain spotted fever and malaria. Pursue diagnosis vigorously in potentially life-threatening cases.

[2]The route of administration for any of these antibiotics depends on the severity of the clinical illness, as well as, in some cases, the formulation of the specific drug (eg, streptomycin, intramuscularly).

[3]Must make diagnosis immediately if malaria is suspected.

[4]Tetracyclines may cause teeth discoloration in children younger than 9 years.

[5]Must make diagnosis immediately if plague is suspected; otherwise, most patients do not require empiric antimicrobial therapy.

[6]Must make diagnosis immediately if anthrax is suspected.

[7]Must make diagnosis immediately if pneumonic plague, tularemia, or anthrax is suspected.

[8]Most patients do not require empiric antimicrobial therapy.

BOX 90–3

Control of Zoonoses

	Fever ± Rash, and Animal/Vector Exposure	Fever, Lympha-denopathy, and Animal/Vector Exposure	Fever, Local Cutaneous Lesion, and Animal/Vec-tor Exposure	Respiratory Di-sease, and Ani-mal/Vector Exposure	Diarrhea, Fever, and Animal/Vec-tor/Exposure
Prophylactic Measures	• Avoid tick, mosquito bites	• Avoid cat bites or changing cat litter box	• Avoid tick, animal bites	• Avoid parturi-ent animals	• Avoid inges-tion of sus-pect food and water
Isolation Precautions	• Blood/universal if hemorrhagic fever is suspec-ted	• None	• Contact (??) for cutaneous anthrax	• Respiratory if pneumonic plague, or tularemia are suspected	• Enteric

list of possible zoonotic pathogens that share susceptibility to a few common antimicrobial agents (Box 90–2). For example, febrile illness in the United States in a person with a recent tick bite can be treated empirically with doxycycline until a specific diagnosis is achieved. Doxycycline provides reasonably good treatment for the following tick-borne diseases: Lyme disease, ehrlichiosis, Rocky Mountain spotted fever, tularemia, and relapsing fever. Some zoonoses such as Rocky Mountain spotted fever and anthrax are medical emergencies and, when suspected, require immediate empiric therapy.

Control

The complexity that governs the origin and spread of zoonoses also provides an equally diverse and interwoven set of opportunities for disease intervention and interruption (Box 90–3). Lyme disease is a useful example, in which strategies for disease reduction include tick avoidance, early detection and removal of attached ticks, tick reduction, by making acaricide-impregnated cotton balls available to white-footed mice in their burrows, and vaccination of humans. OspA is a potent immunogen and is the basis of the current Lyme disease vaccine (see Microbiology above). Vaccine programs can be expanded in some cases to other hosts: the spread of rabies in the eastern United States has been limited through vaccination of wild animals (oral vaccine-laden bait) and peridomestic animals that have close contact with potentially infected wild animals.

REFERENCES

Chomel BB: Zoonoses of house pets other than dogs, cats and birds. Ped Infect Dis J 1992;11:479.

Daszak P, Cunningham AA, Hyatt AD: Emerging infectious diseases of wildlife-threats to biodiversity and human health. Science 2000;287:443.

Hart CA, Trees AJ, Duerden BI: Zoonoses. J Med Microbiol 1997;46:4.

Talan DA et al: Bacteriologic analysis of infected dog and cat bites. N Engl J Med 1999;340:85.

Tan JS. Human zoonotic infections transmitted by dogs and cats. Arch Intern Med 1997;157:1933.

Walker DH et al: Emerging bacterial zoonotic and vector-borne diseases. J Am Med Assoc 1996;275:463.

Ectoparasitic Infestations & Arthropod Stings & Bites

91

Walter R. Wilson, MD & James M. Steckelberg, MD

Ectoparasitic infestation is extremely common worldwide and virtually every human who resides in nonpolar climates is bitten repeatedly by arthropods. Specific infectious diseases transmitted by arthropod bite are reviewed elsewhere in this book. This chapter describes ectoparasitic infestations and toxic reactions to arthropod stings and bites. There is considerable overlap between infestations and bites because ectoparasites either bite or burrow under the skin of their human host.

ECTOPARASITIC INFESTATION

Essentials of Diagnosis

- Ticks: capture of organism
- Mites (scabies): demonstration of organism in pruritic skin lesions, scrapings of burrow, or skin biopsy
- Lice: demonstration of organism or nits (eggs) on hair, skin, or clothing
- Fleas: history of exposure or capture of organism
- Myiasis: demonstration of maggots in tissue
- Leeches: history of exposure, capture of organism

General Considerations

Ectoparasites are arthropods or helminths that infest the skin or hair of humans or mammals and feed on blood, serum, or tissue. Ectoparasites attach to skin by mouth parts or burrow beneath skin where they may inflict local tissue injury or necrosis, cause hypersensitivity reactions, or inject pathogens or toxins into the host. Table 91–1 lists common ectoparasitic infestation in humans. Box 91–1 summarizes the signs and symptoms associated with the most common types of infestation.

A. Tick infestation. In the United States, the principal ticks that parasitize humans are deer ticks (*Ixodes* spp.), which transmit Lyme disease, babesiosis, and human granulocytic ehrlichiosis; wood ticks (*Dermacentor* spp.) and *Amblyomma americanum*,

which transmit tularemia, Rocky Mountain spotted fever, Colorado tick fever, and human monocytic ehrlichiosis; and soft ticks (*Ornithodoros* spp.), which transmit tick-borne relapsing fever.

Because ticks attach and feed on their blood meal painlessly, their presence is often not readily detected by their host. Tick secretions produce local reactions, fever, or paralysis. The local reactions include small pruritic, papulonodular lesions that may vary in size from a few millimeters to several centimeters, and an eschar may develop. Tick-induced fever and constitutional symptoms disappear within 24–48 h after removal of the tick.

Tick paralysis is an uncommon illness, which is thought to result from toxins found in tick saliva, most often in dog or wood ticks. Children, especially those with long hair where the tick may reside undetected, are most often those affected by tick paralysis. Ascending flaccid paralysis begins 5–6 d after attachment and progresses over several days, resulting in diminished deep-tendon reflexes and cranial-nerve palsies. Sensation remains intact and spinal fluid analysis is normal. Untreated, respiratory paralysis that requires endotracheal intubation may occur. Removal of the tick results in rapid improvement and complete recovery usually within hours to several days. Ticks should be removed by gentle retraction with tweezers or forceps.

B. Scabies and other mite infestation. Scabies, caused by *Sarcoptes scabiei,* the human itch mite, is prevalent worldwide and infests 300–500 million people annually. It is one of the most frequent causes of pruritic dermatitis and patient visits to a dermatologist. Female gravid mites 0.3–0.4 mm in length burrow beneath the stratum corneum.

Itching and rash occur as a result of hypersensitivity to the mite excreta deposited in its burrow. Scratching kills the burrowing mite, but symptoms persist as a result of infestation elsewhere. Patients complain of intense pruritus, often worse at night or after a hot shower or bath. A lymphocytic, eosinophilic infiltrate develops around the burrow resulting in a dark wavy line 5–15 mm in length that ends in a small bleb that contains the female mite. Lesions are most commonly located on the wrists, el-

Table 91–1. Common ectoparasitic infestation in humans.

Species	Site Infested

Ticks
  Ixodes spp.
  Dermacentor spp.
  Amblyomma americanum
	Attached to skin and scalp

Mites (*Sarcoptes scabiei*)	Skin beneath stratum corneum in skinfolds, navel, axilliae, buttocks, upper thighs, scrotum, belt line

Lice
  P humanus var. *capititis*
  P humanus var. *corporis*
  Pthirus pubis
	Head, neck, shoulders, hair, clothing, bed clothing, pubic, axillary hair, eyelashes

Fleas
  Ctenocephalides spp.
  Xenopsylla cheopis
	Dogs, cats, humans, carpets, floor mats, rats

Leeches
  H medicinalis
  Haemadipsa spp.
	Medicinal leech
	Aquatic and land leeches attach to exposed human skin

Myiasis (maggots)
  Dermatobia hominis
  Gasterophilus intestinalis
  Phoenicia spp.
	Larvae in furuncles of skin
	Larvae in skin
	Larvae in wounds or body cavities

bows, scrotum, and skin folds and along belt and clothing lines. The face, neck, arms, and soles are usually spared. Papulovesicular eczematous plaques and pustules may develop in untreated patients.

Crusted or Norwegian scabies results from hyperinfestation with thousands or millions of mites and usually occurs in patients with AIDS or other immunocompromised diseases. Crusted scabies is characterized by the presence of thick keratotic crusts, diffuse erythema, scaling, and dystrophic rashes—a condition resembling psoriasis. The characteristic burrow may not be visible in crusted scabies, and pruritus is often minimal or absent. Patients with AIDS and encrusted scabies are at risk of cellulitis and bacteremia resulting from skin fissures.

Transmission of scabies results from close person-to-person contact and is facilitated by crowded unsanitary conditions and sexual promiscuity. Outbreaks of scabies occur in households, hospitals, nursing homes, daycare centers, prisons, mental institutions, and chronic-care facilities. Medical-care personnel are at risk of acquisition. Patients with crusted scabies are highly contagious for others, including health care personnel, and should be placed in strict isolation until treated. Transmission of scabies via sharing of contaminated clothing or bedding is unlikely, because the mite does not survive > 18–24 h without its host.

BOX 91–1

Signs and Symptoms of Ectoparasitic Infestation

Ectoparasite (infestation)	More Common	Less Common
Ticks	• Pruritic papulonodule, erythema • Eschar	• Fever, malaise, myalgias, paralysis
Mites (scabies)	• Erythematous, pruritic maculo-papular rash • Pruritic erythematous burrows	• Crusted thick keratotic lesions, scaling, dystrophic nails
Lice	• Head: crusted, pruritic oozing lesions, matted hair • Body: pruritic, erythematous maculopapular rash • Pubic: pruritic maculopapular bluish lesions	• Blepharitis
Fleas	• Pruritic, erythematous papules, urticaria	• Vesicles, anaphylaxis
Flies (myiasis)	• Maggots in furuncles, wounds, or body cavities • Creeping dermal myiasis • Secondary bacterial infection	
Leeches	• Shallow bleeding ulcers	• Sepsis secondary bacterial infection from *Aeromonas hydrophila*

The diagnosis of scabies should be considered in individuals who have pruritus and rash in the characteristic distribution. Burrows should be unroofed and the scrapings examined microscopically for the characteristic mite or its eggs and fecal pellets. Biopsy or scraping of skin lesions in patients with crusted scabies should be examined microscopically.

Chiggers or other mites commonly infest humans and human habitats. The mouse mite is the vector of rickettsial pox in urban areas of the United States; trombiculid mites transmit scrub typhus in Southeast Asia. The larvae of trombiculid mites reside on grass and other plants and attach to human hosts by contact. The mites penetrate and burrow beneath the skin producing an intense pruritic papule ≤ 2 cm in diameter, which vesiculates, pustulates, and ulcerates. Scratching kills the mite.

House mites (*Dermatophagoides* spp.) are extremely common worldwide. They reside in furniture, carpets, curtains, and elsewhere in the house and feed on shed human dander. Their allergens cause asthma, rhinitis, eczema, and other hypersensitivity conditions in sensitized adults with known house dust allergies. A positive skin test may suggest the diagnosis.

Three species of lice infest humans and feed daily on blood. Their bite results in an intensely pruritic local lesion. In sensitized individuals, a generalized maculopapular, urticarial rash is common and may be associated with fever and constitutional symptoms.

Head lice (*Pediculus humanus* var. *capitis*) are transmitted by human-to-human contact or by shared headgear, brushes, or combs. The prevalence is highest among school children or institutionalized individuals.

Body lice (*P. humanus* var. *corporis*) transmit epidemic typhus, relapsing fever, and trench fever. Body lice inhabit bed or body clothing and emerge to feed on humans. The body louse cannot survive more than a few hours without a human host. Transmission of body lice is the result of human-to-human contact or sharing a bed or body clothing and is facilitated by overcrowding and poor sanitation such as may occur among homeless individuals or during war or natural disasters.

The pubic louse (*Phthirus pubis*) primarily infests the hair in the pubis but may also infest the eyelashes, axillary hair, or other hair. This louse is most often transmitted by sexual contact. Blepharitis occurs with eyelash infestation.

The diagnosis of pediculosis is confirmed by the identification of lice or their eggs (nits) attached to the hair or clothing.

C. Flea infestation. Fleas are insects 2–5 mm in body length that feed on blood from humans and other mammals. Body fleas may transmit plague [rat flea (*Xenopsylla cheopis*)], murine typhus, and possibly *Bartonella henselae*. Fleas infest dogs, cats, and other mammals, their nesting areas, carpets, floor mats, bedding, furniture, and other household areas.

They possess astonishing leaping ability, and the adult fleas attack humans who enter their proximity. During the blood meal, fleas excrete ingested blood and fecal materials that are often scratched into the bite wound. Erythematous, intensely pruritic papules and vesicles develop at the bite site. Secondary bacterial superinfection is common. The diagnosis is based on an index of suspicion and a history of contact with fleas, and it is confirmed by the capture of the characteristic creatures.

D. Myiasis (maggot) infestation. Maggots are the larvae of screw worm flies or bot flies. The larvae invade healthy or necrotic tissue or body cavities and produce different syndromes depending on the species of fly.

Furuncular myiasis results from human bot fly (*Dermatobia hominis*) larvae. In Central and South America, the adult female bot fly captures a mosquito or other blood-sucking insect and deposits eggs on the abdomen of the insect. When the carrier insect ingests a blood meal, the eggs are deposited on the skin surface and hatch, and the larvae penetrate the skin. The African tumva fly (*Cordylobia anthropophaga*) deposits eggs on wounds or clothing, which hatch on contact with skin and penetrate the skin. Furuncular myiasis results in a characteristic pustular lesion with a central breathing pore that emits bubbles under water. The larvae may be expressed, or surgical excision may be required.

1. Creeping dermal myiasis. Eggs of the horse bot fly (*Gasterophilus intestinalis*) are deposited on horses. Riders become infested when the eggs come in contact with bare skin and hatch and the larvae penetrate humans but do not mature. For weeks they migrate in the epidermis, resulting in a serpiginous pruritic lesion. Larvae may be plucked from beneath the skin by a needle.

2. Wound and cavity myiasis. Many species of flies are attracted to wounds draining blood, serum, or pus and deposit their eggs in such wounds. The larvae enter wounds or skin, where they penetrate deeply and produce large suppurative cavities. Larvae may also infest normal body cavities, such as the mouth, nares, ears, sinuses, vagina, and eyes. Larvae usually require surgical removal and debridement of tissue.

3. Leech infestation. Medicinal leeches (*Hirudo medicinalis*) have been used for centuries for phlebotomy and to reduce edema and venous congestion of surgical flaps or reattached body parts. These leeches may be procured commercially in the United States or elsewhere. Their use has been associated with wound infection and sepsis caused by *Aeromonas hydrophila,* which colonizes gullets of medicinal leeches. Aquatic and land leeches commonly attach to humans and other animals on exposure. Land leeches secrete a potent anticoagulant and bleeding may occur after the leech is removed. Secondary bacterial infection is more common after land leech than aquatic leech infestation. Attached leeches may be removed by gentle traction. Application of heat, alcohol, salt, or vinegar hastens removal.

Differential Diagnosis

Ectoparasitic infestation must be discriminated from other conditions that cause pruritic, maculopapular, pustulovesicular, or ulcerative dermatitis such as chronic contact dermatitis or neurodermatitis. Tick paralysis must be differentiated from Guillain-Barré syndrome, botulism, or polio. Crusted or Norwegian scabies resembles chronic eczema or psoriasis. Creeping dermal myiasis resembles cutaneous larva migrans caused by *Ancylostoma braziliense.*

Treatment

The treatment for ectoparasitic infestation is shown in Box 91–2. Secondary bacterial infections should be treated with appropriate antimicrobial therapy. Tetanus toxoid should be administered as needed in patients with significant cutaneous wounds, such as those caused by myiasis, leeches, or other infestation.

Prognosis

The prognosis in treated individuals is excellent and is influenced by the transmission of ectoparasite-specific infections, such as plague, typhus, and other serious bacterial infections.

Prevention

Prevention of tick infestation is facilitated by avoiding brushy vegetation, wearing protective clothing, tucking the trouser cuffs inside socks, and spraying clothing with 0.5 permethrin or an application of repellents containing *N,N*-diethyl-m-toluamide (DEET). Health care workers who treat patients with crusted scabies should wear protective gowns and gloves. Close contacts with patients with scabies should be treated even if they are asymptomatic. Bedding and clothing should be washed with hot soapy water. Combs and brushes belonging to patients infested with lice should be disinfected in hot water (65°C) for 5–15 min or soaked in insecticide for at least one hour. Clothing and bedding may be deloused by washing in hot water and drying in a clothing dryer at 65°C for 30–45 min or by fumigation with insecticide. Thorough cleaning of carpets, furniture, curtains, and other fabrics may reduce house mites. Fleas may be killed by spraying or dusting their nesting sites with insecticide. Myiasis risk may be reduced by good hygiene, including washing with soap and water after horseback riding or fly exposure. Openly draining wounds should be cleaned and dressed regularly. Wearing protective clothing reduces the risk of infestation by land or aquatic leeches.

BOX 91–2

Treatment of Ectoparasitic Infestation

Ectoparasite (infestation) and patient group	First Choice	Alternative[1]
Ticks (tick paralysis)	See text for treatment of local reactions; remove tick	
Scabies (mites) Immunocompetent patients Immunosuppressed patients (AIDS)	5% Permethrin cream from chin to toes; remove 8 h later with soap and water; repeat in 1 week. Safe for children > 2 mo old. Do not use during pregnancy. Permethrin as above, on day 1; then 6% salicyclic acid on days 2–7; then repeat cycles for 3 weeks	Ivermectin, 200 µg/kg, single oral dose
Lice	1% Permethrin to hair, body, or pubic areas kills lice and eggs; comb hair with nit comb after rinsing hair. See text for clothing treatment	0.5% Malathion is less effective. 1% Lindane is less effective and more toxic
Fleas Myiasis Leeches	See text for symptomatic therapy	

[1]Blank fields, No suitable alternative available.

ARTHROPOD STINGS & BITES

Essentials of Diagnosis

- Bees and hornets: painful wheal, flare, edema, history of exposure
- Ants: vesiculopustule, history of exposure
- Brown recluse spider: slowly healing necrotic ulcer, history of exposure
- Black widow spider: fang marks, severe painful muscle cramps, history of exposure
- Scorpions: most species—painful wheal, flare, edema, history of exposure; *Centruoides sculpturatus*—painful wheal, flare, salivation, lacrimation, severe painful muscle cramps, cranial nerve palsy, history of exposure

General Considerations

Arthropods are ubiquitous pests. The most common arthropod bite of humans is by mosquitoes. Mosquitoes are the vectors for many life-threatening infectious diseases, such as malaria, yellow fever, and viral encephalitis. These infections are discussed elsewhere in this book (see Chapters 80 and 89). This chapter reviews arthropod stings and bites that envenomate or produce local trauma. Table 91–2 lists the common arthropods that sting or bite humans. Box 91–3 summarizes the signs and symptoms associated with arthropod stings and bites.

A. Hymenoptera sting. The order *Hymenoptera* includes aphids (bees and bumblebees), vespids (wasps, hornets, and yellow jackets), and ants. Their venoms contain numerous peptides and enzymes that cause localized and systemic reactions. Although the stings are painful and death may occur as a result of multiple stings, most fatalities are the result of hypersensitive anaphylactic reactions. Honeybees and bumblebees attack when their colony is disturbed, lose their stinger during envenomation, and then die. African honeybees (killer bees) were introduced into Brazil in the 1950s, have migrated progressively northward, and now inhabit the southern United States. These bees are highly aggressive, swarm, and may attack without provocation, often inflicting a large number of stings before the victim can escape. Rarely, human death has resulted from killer bee attacks.

Common vespids include yellow jackets, which are distinguished by bright yellow and black abdominal bands, and hornets, which are usually black, brown, or grayish color. Vespids feed on decaying vegetative material, garbage, and especially foods and liquids containing sugar. Vespids become aggressive in late summer and fall when most stings occur. Vespids do not lose their stingers during attack.

The compositions of venom from aphids and vespids vary among species. Toxins include histamine, acetylcholine, kinens, and numerous enzymes such as hylauronidase phospholipases. Uncomplicated stings cause immediate pain, wheal, and flare reaction and local edema, which subside over a few hours. Multiple stings (100–500) may cause constitutional symptoms, hypotension, generalized edema, rhabdomyolysis, hemolysis, and death. Approximately 0.5%–5% of individuals in the United States have immediate type hypersensitivity and are at risk for mild to life-threatening anaphylaxis.

Ant bites are extremely common in the United States and worldwide. Fire ants are aggressive, red-colored ants that inhabit the southern United States. They excavate areas in fields and urban areas and, when disturbed, mobilize huge numbers of attacking ants that may inflict thousands of stings on a single person. Many other species of ants inhabit the United States, and all that are large enough and capable of biting humans when provoked. Ant venom contains proteins, enzymes, and cytotoxic hemolytic piperidines. The bite is followed by immediate pain, wheal, and flare and then by the formation of a pustule, which ulcerates and may become secondarily infected. Anaphylactic reactions to ant stings occur in ~ 0.5%–2% of sensitized individuals.

B. Spider bites. There are > 30,000 species of spiders but < 100 of these have fangs large enough to bite and envenomate humans. Spider venom is intended to immobilize and digest its prey and, when injected into humans, may cause local pain, tissue necrosis, or systemic toxicity. Two species of spiders in the United States are dangerous to humans—the brown or fiddle spider (*Loxosceles* spp.) and the widow spider (*Latrodectus* spp.).

The brown recluse spider (*L reclusa*) and at least four other species of *Loxosceles* are distributed throughout the United States and abroad. The brown recluse spider is a species that most commonly bites humans in the United States. This shy spider is 7–20 mm in body length and 2–4 cm in leg span. It has a characteristic dark violin-shaped spot on its dorsal surface. The spider emerges at night to hunt. Usually, it inhabits dark areas, such as basements, closets, attics, clothing, bed clothing, and other similar areas. Bites occur when the spiders are threatened or are involun-

Table 91–2. Common arthropods that sting or bite humans.

Species	Common Name
Apis mellifera	Honey bee
Apis spp.	Wasps, hornets, yellow jackets
Bombus spp.	Bumble bee
Solenopsis spp.	Ants
Loxosceles reclusa	Brown recluse spider
Latrodectus mactans	Black widow spider
Centruroides spp.	Scorpions

BOX 91-3

Signs and Symptoms of Arthropod Stings and Bites

Arthropod	More Common	Less Common
Hymenoptera (bee, wasp, hornet, yellow jacket, ant)	• Immediate pain, wheel, flair	• Anaphylaxis
Ant	• Immediate pain, erythema, edema, vesicle, pustule	
Spider Brown recluse (*Loxosceleus reclsa*)	• Minimal initial pain • Later pain, pruritic lesion central induration surrounded by zones of ischemia, erythema • Hemorrhagic neurosis, eschar necrosis	• Extensive necrosis • Myalgias, nausea, vomiting, hemolytic, anemia, death
Black widow (*Latrodectus mactans*)	• Minimal initial pain, two erythematous fang bites, painful muscle cramps	• Extreme rigidity, rhabdomyolysis, respiratory arrest, death
Scorpion Most scorpions	• Immediate pain, wheal flair erythema, edema	• Anaphylaxis
C sculpturatus	• Pain, paresthesia, muscle cramps, twitching, profuse salivation	• Cranial nerve or muscle paralysis, rhabdomyolysis, respiratory arrest, death

tarily pressed against the skin such as may occur during sleep or while dressing. Initially, the bite is usually painless or may cause mild stinging. Complex toxins include proteolytic enzymes that cause necrosis. Of these, sphingomyelinase B is the most potent and results in vascular thrombosis and extensive local necrosis. Within hours after the bite, the area becomes painful and pruritic with induration surrounded by a zone of pale ischemia surrounded by erythema. Most lesions resolve spontaneously within a few days. In severe cases, the central area becomes hemorrhagic and necrotic with the formation of a bulla. The bulla ulcerates to form an eschar that leaves a large area of necrosis. Healing may take months to years and may require skin grafting. Rarely, severe systemic reactions including hemolytic anemia and renal failure may occur.

The female widow spider bite envenomates a potent neurotoxin. The black widow (*L mactans*) is widely distributed throughout the United States (except Alaska) and is most prevalent in the southeast. The spider measures ~ 1 cm in body length and 5 cm in leg span, is shiny black, and has a red-orange hourglass on the ventral abdomen. The black widow webs are most often located in dark places, such as garages, barns, and outdoor privies. The spider bites when the web is disturbed or the spider is provoked. The initial bite may be painless or feel like a pinprick. Two small erythematous red fang marks are visible. The venom does not produce local necrosis. Alpha-latro toxin is the most active toxin, and it binds irreversibly to nerves and causes release and depletion of acetylcholine, norepinephrine, and other neurotransmitters. Painful muscle cramps develop in the area ~ 30–60 min after the bite. Severe pain, muscle cramps, and rigidity may become generalized and may be accompanied by tachycardia, hypertension, muscle weakness, urinary retention, and, in extreme cases, paralysis, respiratory arrest, and rhabdomyolysis. Pain and muscle rigidity usually begin to subside within 12–24 h but may recur over the next days to weeks before resolving.

Tarantulas are large, hairy, nonaggressive spiders that have become popular pets. When threatened, they may bite their owners. Their bite is similar to that of a bee sting, causing localized pain and swelling.

C. Scorpion stings. Scorpions are crablike creatures that are widely distributed throughout the United States. They are nocturnal, emerge at night to hunt, and sting with their mobile tail stinger when provoked. Among the > 40 species of scorpions in the United States, only the bark scorpion (*Centruroides sculpturatus*) is potentially lethal. Stings by other species cause symptoms similar to those of bee stings. Anaphylaxis may occur in previously sensitized individuals.

C sculpturatus inhabits the southwestern United

States and northern Mexico. Scorpions are ~ 7 cm in length and are yellow-brown. Envenomation is with a neurotoxin that affects sodium channels, resulting in nerve excitation. Symptoms include pain and hyperesthesia at the bite, which may progress to cranial and skeletal nerve hyperexcitability, muscle cramps and twitching, increased lacrimation, salivation, and hypertension. In severe cases, respiratory paralysis, rhabdomyolysis, and death may occur. Symptoms maximize within 6 h and usually subside within 1–2 d, but pain and paresthesias may persist for weeks.

Differential Diagnosis

The pustular ulcerative lesions resulting from ant bites resemble impetigo in children. Severe abdominal pain and abdominal muscle rigidity caused by a black widow spider bite must be differentiated from acute abdominal syndromes such as pancreatitis or peritonitis. However, in black widow spider bites, the abdomen is nontender to palpation. The muscle twitching and cramping from black widow spider and *C sculpturatus* scorpion bites may be confused initially with early tetanus. The increased salivation and hyperexcitability after *C sculpturatus* envenomation may resemble rabies.

Treatment

Treatment of arthropod stings and bites is outlined in Box 91–4. Administration of antihistamines, topical corticosteroids, and antimicrobial agents for secondary bacterial infection are general therapeutic measures for symptomatic arthropod stings. Anaphylaxis is treated by the administration of subcutaneous or, in severe cases, intravenous epinephrine, fluid resuscitation, bronchodilators, and, if necessary, endotracheal intubation and vasopressors. Patients with a history of severe allergy or anaphylaxis associated with insect stings should carry commercially available kits to treat anaphylaxis and other serious reactions when engaging in activities that place them at risk of arthropod exposure. Desensitization injections reduce the risk of recurrent anaphylaxis in hypersensitized individuals for bee and hornet stings.

BOX 91–4

Treatment of Arthropod Stings or Bites

Arthropod	Treatment
Hymenoptera	See text for symptomatic therapy
Spiders Brown recluse (*Loxosceles reclusa*)	See text. In adults, Dapsone, 50–100 mg twice daily within first 48–72 h may reduce necrosis. Antivenin not approved for use in United States
Black widow (*Latrodectus mactans*)	See text. Apply ice to bite, equine antivenin for severe cases only because of risk of anaphylaxis horse serum

Scorpions
  Most species
  Centruroides sculpturatus
	See text for symptomatic therapy Apply ice to bite. Caprine antivenin investigational and available in Arizona. Use for severe cases only because of risk of anaphylaxis to goat serum

---

Prognosis

The prognosis for most individuals after arthropod stings is excellent. Most deaths result from anaphylaxis. Deaths are rare in treated patients envenomated by brown recluse spiders, black widow spiders, or *C sculpturatus* scorpions.

Prevention

Spraying insecticides in dark areas inhabited by spiders reduces the risk of exposure. When camping outdoors, individuals should check their shoes, backpacks, and sleeping bags for scorpions.

REFERENCES

Goddard J: *Physicians Guide to Arthropods of Medical Importance.* CRC Press, 1993

Maguire JH, Spielman A: Ectoparasite infestations and arthropod bites and stings. In Fauci AS et al: *Harrison's Principles of Internal Medicine,* 14th ed. 1998

Subject Index

NOTE: Page numbers in **boldface** type indicate a major discussion. A *t* following a page number indicates tabular material, an *f* following a page number indicates a figure, and a *b* following a page number indicates a boxed feature. Drugs are listed under their generic names. When a drug trade name is listed, the reader is referred to the generic name.

NOTES

NOTES

NOTES

NOTES

NOTES

NOTES

NOTES

NOTES

NOTES

NOTES

NOTES

NOTES

NOTES

ISBN 0-07-118285-3

9 780071 182850

WILSON/CURR DIAG TREAT
INFECTIOUS DIS IE

ISBN 0-8385-1494-4

9 780838 514948

WILSON/CURR DIAG TREAT
INFECTIOUS DIS